Volume 1

Compact Edition

The Bedford Anthology of
World Literature

The Ancient, Medieval, and Early Modern World, Beginnings–1650

EDITED BY

Paul Davis
Gary Harrison
David M. Johnson
John F. Crawford

THE UNIVERSITY OF NEW MEXICO

BEDFORD / ST. MARTIN'S

Boston ◆ New York

For Bedford/St. Martin's

Developmental Editor: Caroline Thompson
Production Editor: Karen Stocz
Senior Production Supervisor: Nancy Myers
Marketing Manager: Adrienne Petsick
Editorial Assistant: Marisa Feinstein
Text Design: Anna Palchik and Jean Hammond
Cover Design: Donna Lee Dennison
Cover Art: Return of Ulysses to Penelope, from *The Odyssey.* Fresco, c. 1509 by Pintoricchio
   (Italian, c. 1454–1513). The National Gallery, London, England. © SuperStock,
   Inc./SuperStock
Composition: TexTech International
Printing and Binding: Quebecor World Taunton

President: Joan E. Feinberg
Editorial Director: Denise B. Wydra
Editor in Chief: Karen S. Henry
Director of Marketing: Karen R. Soeltz
Director of Editing, Design, and Production: Marcia Cohen
Assistant Director of Editing, Design, and Production: Elise S. Kaiser
Managing Editor: Elizabeth M. Schaaf

Library of Congress Control Number: 2008925872

For information, write: Bedford/St. Martin's, 75 Arlington Street, Boston, MA 02116
(617-399-4000)

ISBN-10: 0–312–44153–3
ISBN-13: 978-0–312–44153–1

Acknowledgments

Aeschylus, *Agamemnon* from *The Oresteia* translated by Robert Fagles. Copyright © 1994 by Robert Fagles.
   Reprinted with the permission of Viking Penguin, a division of Penguin Group (USA) Inc.

*Acknowledgments and copyrights are continued at the back of the book on pages 1953–56, which constitute an
extension of the copyright page. It is a violation of the law to reproduce these selections by any means whatsoever
without the written permission of the copyright holder.*

PREFACE

Our thinking about teaching world literature goes back to 1985, when we received a grant from the National Endowment of the Humanities to develop and team teach a new kind of course—one that integrated the rich literary traditions of Asia, India, the Arabic world, the Americas, and Europe. As year-long courses in world literature became more widely taught in the United States, and as the number and range of texts taught in these courses greatly increased, we developed *The Bedford Anthology of World Literature*, a six-volume collection designed to meet the challenges of taking—and teaching—the world literature course.

Now we have streamlined *The Bedford Anthology of World Literature* to address the need for a two-volume edition that can be used in both one- and two-semester courses. Basing our choices on reviews, expert advice, and our ongoing classroom experience, we provide a substantial and carefully balanced selection of Western and non-Western texts chronologically arranged in a compact, teachable format. We give special emphasis to the works most commonly taught in the survey course. By linking them to clusters of texts that represent themes that recur and resonate across cultures, we provide options for drawing connections among works and across traditions. A distinctive variety of pedagogical features gives students the help they need to understand individual works of literature, while extensive historical and background materials help them place the works in context. Throughout, a uniquely extensive illustration program brings the pedagogy into focus, and the literature and contextual materials to life.

AN ENTIRE WORLD OF LITERATURE

The Compact Edition offers **twenty-seven complete longer works with additional fiction, drama, poetry, letters, and essays** in the best available editions and translations. Complete works include Homer's *The Odyssey*, Sophocles's *Antigone*, *Beowulf*, Dante's *The Inferno*, and Shakespeare's *The Tempest* in Volume One; Molière's *Tartuffe*, Voltaire's *Candide*, Conrad's *Heart of Darkness*, Kafka's *The Metamorphosis*, and Achebe's *Things Fall Apart* in Volume Two. Even as we have reduced the number of texts for the two-volume format, we have nonetheless added some new works in order to respond to the ongoing revaluation and expansion of the canon as well as to better meet the pedagogical ends of world literature courses as they are being taught today. Among the additions to Volume One are new poems from Sappho and new excerpts from *The Aeneid*, Plato's *Republic*, Boethius's *The Consolation of Philosophy*, and Sir Thomas More's *Utopia*. In Volume Two we have added works including Immanuel Kant's "What is Enlightenment," selections from Frederick Douglass's *Narrative of the Life of Frederick Douglass, Written by Himself*, and new poems by Friedrich Hölderlin, Alphonse Lamartine, and Rosalía de Castro; also, Guy du Maupassant's "Regret," Henrik Ibsen's *A Doll's House*, Jawaharlal Nehru's "Speech on the Granting of Indian Independence," and excerpts from André Breton's *The Surrealist Manifesto*.

In addition to a broad selection of literature, we provide **a variety of help for understanding the readings**. Our thorough, informative, and readable introductions and headnotes provide biographical and literary background for each author and text. Generous footnotes, marginal notes, critical quotations, and cross-references help students navigate this wealth of information. Phonetic pronunciation guides help with unfamiliar author, character, and place names. For help with literary and historical vocabulary, key terms throughout the text refer students to a comprehensive glossary at the end of each volume. Further Research bibliographies following headnotes and introductions list sources for students who want to read more critical, biographical, or historical information about an author or work.

Each volume is divided into two parts to avoid organizing literary history within a European period frame.

Osmand Hamdy Bay, Excavation at Nippur, 1903
Mesopotamian cities were among the earliest urban centers in antiquity. With the invention of writing in Egypt and Mesopotamia sometime around 3000 B.C.E., rulers were able to oversee larger and larger administrative areas. One of the earliest uses of writing was in keeping track of the practical and myriad details of government, from taxes and birth and death records to business transactions. This extremely realistic painting shows the early twentieth-century excavation at Nippur, a major Mesopotamian city. (University of Pennsylvania Museum [Negative #S8-68o7])

The Ancient World

Beginnings - 100 C.E.

CHRONOLOGICAL STRUCTURE AND TEACHABLE ORGANIZATION

When we take into account the literary histories of Japan, China, India, the Arabic and Muslim world, Africa, and the Americas, a structure based upon traditional European periods, such as medieval and Renaissance, Enlightenment and Romanticism, becomes highly problematic. The literatures within the world's traditions developed within their own unique historical and cultural trajectories, and it is not really until the twentieth century—and even then not without caution—that we can speak of a modernism or postmodernism that reaches across the world's many borders. In light of these issues, we have arranged our texts chronologically throughout both volumes, while providing historical and cultural contexts in our general introductions and headnotes. We use a four-period model, dividing each volume into two parts, as follows.

The first part of Volume One focuses upon the ancient world, from the beginnings of literature to about 100 C.E., the second upon the medieval and Early Modern World through about 1650. Two **general introductions**, one for each part, provide historical and cultural contexts for the various literatures and traditions represented in the volume. We chose to end Volume One with the mid seventeenth-century because it marks that crucial moment when the histories of various regions

Comparative timelines in each general introduction list what happened, where, and when in three overarching categories: history and politics; literature; and science, culture, and technology.

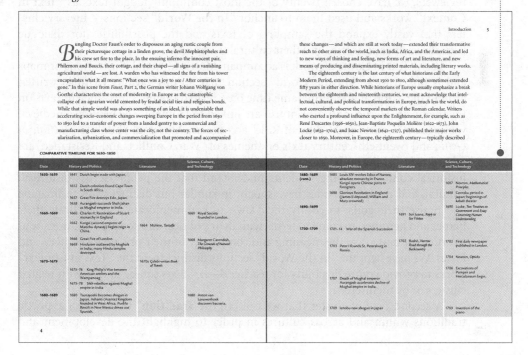

and empires became the history of the world. While considerable contact among civilizations took place in the ancient world and medieval period, the oceanic voyages of developing European nation states in the fifteenth through the seventeenth centuries vastly expanded the networks of intercultural contact, commerce, and confrontation. We believe that Shakespeare's *The Tempest* serves as the best hinge upon which to hang the change of volumes, because the play thematizes the shift to a global history, announcing the end of an era even as it inaugurates an inquiry into the vexing contradictions of the brave new world of increasing globalization that will resound through the works we find throughout the second volume.

Volume Two similarly divides into two parts with their own general introductions, the first focusing upon the period from about 1650 to 1850, the second from 1850 to the present. Volume Two begins with Molière's *Tartuffe*, Pu Song-Ling's "The Mural," and Bashō's *Narrow Road through the Backcountry*. These late seventeenth-century works point in their distinctive ways and in their particular contexts to the early modernity of France, China, and Japan, and arise in periods of social, economic, and cultural transformation that will accelerate through the eighteenth, nineteenth, and twentieth centuries.

TEXTS IN CONTEXT

Within the overall chronological framework of this anthology, we have grouped certain selections to give teachers a flexible means of helping students make connections with unfamiliar and diverse texts. Based on our research and the advice of our reviewers, we have chosen twenty of the most commonly taught texts as **"Text in Context"** works and used them to anchor **"In the World"** sections—literary clusters that vastly expand the sampling of texts and the possibilities for dialogue between various countries and their cultural traditions.

Each "Text in Context" work is accompanied by additional illustrations or maps and is linked to an "In the World" section that groups various writings written around the world at about the same time on a related theme. Thus, ancient texts on the theme of "Heroes and Adventure" are linked to Homer's *The Odyssey*; medieval writings on "Courts and Codes of Rule" accompany Murasaki Shikibu's *The Tale of Genji*; and twentieth-century texts on themes of "War, Conflict, and Resistance" are related to T. S. Eliot's *The Waste Land*. "In the World" clusters emphasize social and historical contexts, helping students understand that the people across historical, cultural, and national divides have sought in similar but distinct ways to imagine and praise their gods, to codify their laws, to commemorate and celebrate their heroes and heroines, to come to terms with their political and social revolutions, and to articulate and grasp the meaning and complexity of their private loves, lives, and losses. We have kept the "In the World" sections distinct from the "Text in Context" works to provide more flexibility for teachers—key texts can be taught with related clusters or by themselves.

A second type of cluster that we call **"In the Tradition"** traces specific poetic traditions within and across cultures in order to highlight the development and

Each Text in Context *work is linked to an* In the World *section, a cluster of writings on a related theme that were written around the world near the time of the* Text in Context *work.*

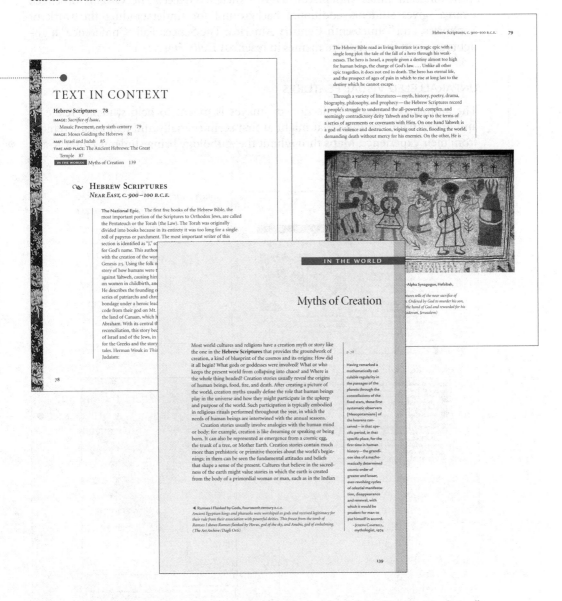

TEXT IN CONTEXT

Hebrew Scriptures   78
IMAGE: *Sacrifice of Isaac,*
   Mosaic Pavement, early sixth century   79
IMAGE: *Moses Guiding the Hebrews*   81
MAP: Israel and Judah   85
TIME AND PLACE: The Ancient Hebrews: The Great
   Temple   87
IN THE WORLD: Myths of Creation   139

❧ HEBREW SCRIPTURES
NEAR EAST, C. 900–100 B.C.E.

The National Epic. The first five books of the Hebrew Bible, the most important portion of the Scriptures to Orthodox Jews, are called the Pentateuch or the Torah (the Law). The Torah was originally divided into books because in its entirety it was too long for a single roll of papyrus or parchment. The most important writer of this section is identified as "J," …

78

Hebrew Scriptures, C. 900–100 B.C.E.   79

The Hebrew Bible read as living literature is a tragic epic with a single long plot: the tale of the fall of a hero through his weaknesses. The hero is Israel, a people given a destiny almost too high for human beings, the charge of God's law. . . . Unlike all other epic tragedies, it does not end in death. The hero has eternal life, and the prospect of ages of pain in which to rise at long last to the destiny which he cannot escape.

Through a variety of literatures — myth, history, poetry, drama, biography, philosophy, and prophecy — the Hebrew Scriptures record a people's struggle to understand the all-powerful, complex, and seemingly contradictory deity Yahweh and to live up to the terms of a series of agreements or covenants with Him. On one hand Yahweh is a god of violence and destruction, wiping out cities, flooding the world, demanding death without mercy for his enemies. On the other, He is

---

IN THE WORLD

Myths of Creation

Most world cultures and religions have a creation myth or story like the one in the **Hebrew Scriptures** that provides the groundwork of creation, a kind of blueprint of the cosmos and its origins: How did it all begin? What gods or goddesses were involved? What or who keeps the present world from collapsing into chaos? and Where is the whole thing headed? Creation stories usually reveal the origins of human beings, food, fire, and death. After creating a picture of the world, creation myths usually define the role that human beings play in the universe and how they might participate in the upkeep and purpose of the world. Such participation is typically embodied in religious rituals performed throughout the year, in which the needs of human beings are intertwined with the annual seasons.

Creation stories usually involve analogies with the human mind or body: for example, creation is like dreaming or speaking or being born. It can also be represented as emergence from a cosmic egg, the trunk of a tree, or Mother Earth. Creation stories contain much more than prehistoric or primitive theories about the world's beginnings; in them can be seen the fundamental attitudes and beliefs that shape a sense of the present. Cultures that believe in the sacredness of the earth might value stories in which the earth is created from the body of a primordial woman or man, such as in the Indian

◀ Ramses I Flanked by Gods, fourteenth century B.C.E.
Ancient Egyptian kings and pharaohs were worshipped as gods and received legitimacy for their rule from their association with powerful deities. This fresco from the tomb of Ramses I shows Ramses flanked by Horus, god of the sky, and Anubis, god of embalming. (The Art Archive/Dagli Orti)

p. 78

Having remarked a mathematically calculable regularity in the passages of the planets through the constellations of the fixed stars, these first systematic observers [Mesopotamians] of the heavens conceived — in that specific period, in that specific place, for the first time in human history — the grandiose idea of a mathematically determined cosmic order of greater and lesser, ever-revolving cycles of celestial manifestation, disappearance and renewal, with which it would be prudent for man to put himself in accord.
— JOSEPH CAMPBELL,
mythologist, 1974

139

---

diversity of certain genres and forms. We include three of these "In the Tradition" sections in this edition: "Poets of the Tang Dynasty," "Andalusian and European Love Lyrics," and "The Romantic Lyric." These clusters help students imagine a conversation among a variety of writers around similar ideas and forms.

"Time and Place" boxes further orient students in the era and culture connected with the literature they're reading or help make thematic connections among events from different times and places. Thus, "Ancient Greece: The Origins of Greek Drama" gives students additional background for understanding the work of Sophocles, and "Nineteenth-Century America: The Seneca Falls Conference" highlights an event that relates to themes in Ibsen's *A Doll's House*.

UNPARALLELED VISUAL FEATURES

The anthology's superb collection of images is meant to help students relate to and understand literature that might at first seem spatially and temporally remote from their experience. **Maps** throughout the anthology bring students closer to the

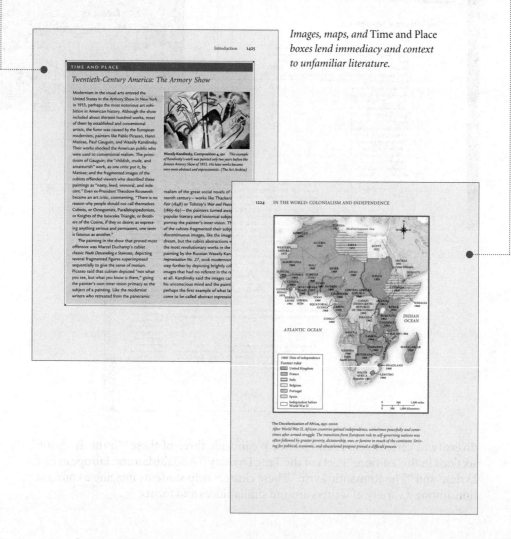

Images, maps, and Time and Place *boxes lend immediacy and context to unfamiliar literature.*

regions various literatures have come from, illustrating shifting national boundaries, industrial growth, the effects of conquest and colonialism, and the travels of Odysseus, Candide, Bashō, and Olaudah Equiano. **Illustrations** — art, photographs, cartoons, and cultural artifacts — offer perspectives on the context of literary works and their present-day relevance. Medieval images of Roland in the architecture of the Chartres Cathedral, twentieth-century performances of Shakespeare's *The Tempest* and Ibsen's *A Doll's House*, the ad Harriet Jacobs's owner ran for her capture and return, and a nineteenth-century Nigerian sculpture of a European missionary are just a few examples.

PRINT AND ONLINE ANCILLARIES

The instructor's manual, *Resources for Teaching* THE BEDFORD ANTHOLOGY OF WORLD LITERATURE, Compact Edition, provides additional information about the anthology's texts and authors; suggestions for discussion, research, and writing, both in the classroom and beyond; and suggestions for drawing additional connections among the various texts in the anthology. Lists of related print and media resources for each selection are also included. The manual concludes with advice for developing a world literature syllabus and sample syllabi.

Students using the free companion site at **bedfordstmartins.com/worldlit compact** will find additional historical background, quizzes, annotated research links, additional information about particular authors, and discussions of the enduring twenty-first century relevance of particular works. Web links throughout the anthology direct students to additional content on the free companion site.

Award-winning trade titles are available for packaging at significant savings. Add more value and choice to your students' learning experiences by packaging *The Bedford Anthology of World Literature*, Compact Edition, with any of a thousand titles from Farrar, Straus and Giroux; Picador; St. Martin's Press; and other Macmillan trade publishers — at discounts of up to 50 percent off the regular price. To learn more, contact your local Bedford/St. Martin's sales representative. To see a complete list of titles available for packaging, go to bedfordstmartins.com/tradeup.

The broad spectrum of literary texts, practical and accessible editorial apparatus, and teachable organization of the anthology offer teachers and students choices for navigating the familiar and unfamiliar territories of world literature. For some students, the excitement of discovery will lie in the exotic details of a foreign setting or in the music of a declaration of love, while others will delight in the broad panorama of history they construct when reading a variety of works from different traditions written around the same time. Others may find the contrast between cultures or historical eras to be the defining moment of discovery. Any number of possibilities exist for our students as they come into imaginative and critical contact with the people, places, and worlds that exist between the covers of *The Bedford Anthology of World Literature*, Compact Edition.

ACKNOWLEDGMENTS

This anthology and its predecessors began in a team-taught, multicultural "great books" course at the University of New Mexico, initially developed with a grant from the National Endowment for the Humanities. The grant gave us ample time to generate the curriculum for the course, and it also supported the luxury and challenge of team teaching. This anthology reflects the discussions of texts and teaching strategies that took place over many years among ourselves and colleagues who have participated with us in teaching the course—Cheryl Fresch, Virginia Hampton, Mary Rooks, Claire Waters, Richard K. Waters, Mary Bess Whidden, and most recently Feroza Jussawalla, Ron Shumaker, Birgit Schmidt-Rosemann, and Robin Runia. We especially want to thank our cherished colleague, co-teacher, and co-editor Patricia Clark Smith, whose creativity, camaraderie, and command of the world's literatures and languages are felt throughout these pages. Without her generous spirit and laughter, her insight and vision, her dedication to our students, and her love of life and teaching this anthology would not be what it is today. We also acknowledge Joseph B. Zavadil, who began our first anthology with us but died in the early stages of its development. Joe's wit, scholarship, and humanity also endures with us. Above all, we must thank the hundreds of students in our world literature classes over the last twenty years at the University of New Mexico. From their questions, challenges, suggestions, and ideas—and from their patience and curiosity—we have fashioned not only an anthology but a way of teaching world literature as a conversation in context—a way of teaching that we share here with our readers.

Reviewers from many colleges and universities helped shape the six books of *The Bedford Anthology of World Literature* (2004) with their advice and suggestions. We thank in particular a special group of reviewers who looked in depth at the manuscript for each of the six books, offering us targeted advice about the anthology's strengths and weaknesses:

Cora Agatucci, Central Oregon Community College; Michael Austin, Shepherd College; Maryam Barrie, Washtenaw Community College; John Bartle, Hamilton College; Jeffry Berry, Adrian College; Lois Bragg, Gallaudet University; Ron Carter, Rappahannock Community College; Robin Clouser, Ursinus College; Eugene R. Cunnar, New Mexico State University; Karen Dahr, Ellsworth Community College; Kristine Daines, Arizona State University; Sarah Dangelantonio, Franklin Pierce College; Jim Doan, Nova SE University; Melora Giardetti, Simpson College; Audley Hall, North West Arkansas Community College; Dean Hall, Kansas State University; Joris Heise, Sinclair Community College; Diane Long Hoeveler, Marquette University; Glenn Hopp, Howard Payne University; Mickey Jackson, Golden West College; Feroza Jussawalla, University of New Mexico; Linda Karch, Norwich University; David Karnos, Montana State University; William Laskowski, Jamestown College; Pat Lonchar, University of the Incarnate Word; Donald Mager, The Mott University; Judy B. McInnis, University of Delaware; Becky McLaughlin, University of South Alabama; Tony J. Morris, University of Indianapolis; Deborah Schlacks, University of Wisconsin; James Snowden, Cedarville University; David T. Stout,

Luzerne County Community College; Arline Thorn, West Virginia State College; Ann Volin, University of Kansas; Mary Wack, Washington State University; Jayne A. Widmayer, Boise State University; and William Woods, Wichita State University.

We are grateful to the perceptive instructors—more than two hundred of them—who responded to our questionnaire in the early stages of planning the Compact Edition. These teachers shared valuable information with us about their courses, their students, and what they wanted in a world literature anthology:

Allison Adair, Boston University; Kristelle Aherne, Masconomet High School; Donald Alban, Liberty University; William Allegrezza, Indiana University Northwest; Maurice Amen, Holy Cross College; Dustin Anderson, Florida State University; Janet Anderson, Clackamas Community College; Robert Anderson, Oakland University; Helen Andretta, York College–CUNY; Kit Andrews, Western Oregon University; Lauryn Angel-Cann, University of North Texas; Gabriel Arquilevich, Ventura College; Melvin Arrington, University of Mississippi; Clinton Atchley, Henderson State University; Carolyn Ayers, St. Mary's University of Minnesota; Alison Baker, California Polytechnic State University–Pomona; Anne Baker, North Carolina State University; Christopher Baker, Armstrong Atlantic State University; Kimberly Baker, Illinois Institute of Art; Robert Baker, Fairmont State College; David Barney, Palm Beach Community College South; Terry Barr, Presbyterian College; Bette-B Bauer, College of Saint Mary; Evelyn Beck, Piedmont Technical College; Daniel Bender, Pace University–Pleasantville; Lysbeth Benkert, Northern State University; Kate Benzel, University of Nebraska at Kearney; Eric Berlatsky, University of Maryland; Mark Bernheim, Miami University; Debra Berry, Community College of Southern Nevada; Stephan Bertman, Lawrence Technological University; Linda Best, Kean University; Michael Bibby, Shippensburg University of Pennsylvania; Suzanne Black, Southwest State University; Marlin Blaine, California State University–Fullerton; Laurel Bollinger, University of Alabama–Huntsville; Scott Boltwood, Emory and Henry College; Ashley Bonds, Copiah-Lincoln Community College; Shelly Borgstrom, Rogers State University; Lucia Bortoli, Ohio State University; Paul Brandt, Kent State University; Christopher Brooks, Wichita State University; Jennifer Browdy de Hernandez, State University of New York at Albany; Kevin Brown, Lee University; Jeb Butler, Boston College; Jeff Butler, University of Iowa; Pamela Butsch, Jefferson Community College Southwest; William Cain, Wellesley College; Juan Calle, Broward Community College North; Lynne Callender, Legacy High School; Mike Campbell, Yakima Valley Community College; Erskine Carter, Black Hawk Col-Quad Cities; Cindy Catherwood, Metropolitan Community College–South; Patricia Cearley, South Plains College; Iclal Cetin, State University of New York at Buffalo; Julie Chappell, Tarleton State University; Amy Chesbro, Washtenaw Community College; Barbara Christian, University of Alaska–Anchorage Kenai Peni; Holly Ciotti, Glendale High School; William Clemente, Peru State College; Jeff Cofer, Bellevue Community College; Barbara Cole, Sandhills Community College; Ernest Cole, University of Connecticut; Christine Colon, Wheaton College; Michael Colson, Allan Hancock College; Susan Comfort, Indiana University of Pennsylvania; Helen Connell, Barry University;

Randy Connor, Los Medanos College; Linda Conway, Howard College; Stephen Cooper, Troy State University; Deborah Core, Eastern Kentucky University; Judith Cortelloni, Lincoln College; Peter Cortland, Quinnipac University; Timothy Costello, Moorhead Area Schools; James Cotter, Mount St. Mary College; Robert Cox, Southeast Kentucky Community and Technical College–Middlesboro; James Crawford, Walters State Community College; Merilee Cunningham, University of Houston–Downtown; Rita Dandridge, Norfolk State University; Craig Davos, Smith College; Anne Dayton, Slippery Rock University of Pennsylvania; Laura Dearing, Jefferson Community College Southwest; Paula Del Fiore, Cranston High School West; Anna Dewart, Coastal Georgia Community College; Emily Dial-Driver, Rogers State University; Sheila Diecidue, University of South Florida; Martha Diede, Northwest College; S. Dobranski, Georgia State University; Mary Dockray-Miller, Lesley University; Brian Doherty, University of Texas; Virginia Doland, Biola University; Cecilia Donohue, Madonna University; Stephen Donohue, Rock Valley College; Maria Doyle, State University of West Georgia; Kendall Dunkelberg, Mississippi University for Women; Emily Dziuban, University of Tennessee–Knoxville; Mark Eaton, Azusa Pacific University; Marie Eckstrom, Rio Hondo College; George William Eggers, University of Connecticut; Sarah Eichelman, Walters State Community College; Juliene Empric, Eckerd College; Bruce Engle, Morehead State University; Carol Fadda-Conrey, Purdue University–Main Campus; Scott Failla, Barnard College; Carol-Ann Farkas, Massachusetts College of Pharmacy and Allied Health; Pamela Faulkner, Concord College; Donald Fay, Kennesaw State University; Maryanne Felter, Cayuga Community College; Jill Ferguson, Notra Dame de Namur University; Suzanne Ferriss, Nova Southeastern University; Lois Feuer, California State University–Dominguez Hills; Matthew Fike, Winthrop University; Hannah Fischthal, Saint John's University; Johanna Fisher, SUNY College at Buffalo; Christine Flanagan, University of the Sciences in Phildelphia; Agnes Fleck, College of Saint Scholastica; Erwin Ford, Albany State University; Robert Forman, Saint John's University; Michael Fournier, Georgia State University; Stephen Fox, Gallaudet University; Christina Francis, Arizona State University; Wanda Fries, Somerset Community College; Joanne Gabel, Reading Area Community College; Maria Galindo, Ocean County College; Paul Gallipeo, Adirondack Community College; Susan Gardner, La Sierra University; David Garlock, Baruch College CUNY; Margaret Geiger, Cuyahoga Community College–Eastern; Erin Geller, Halls High School; Nate Gordon, Kishwaukee College; Kevin Grauke, University of North Texas; Karen Gray, University of Louisville; David Greene, Adelphi University; Nicole Greene, Xavier University of Louisiana; Loren Gruber, Missouri Valley College; Rachel Habermehl, University of Minnesota–Crookston; Keith Hale, South Texas Community College; Dewey Hall, Mt. San Antonio College; Randolph Handel, Santa Fe Community College; Leigh Harbin, Angelo State University; Vasantha Harinath, North Central State College; William Harris, University of Texas at Brownsville; Betty Hart, University of Southern Indiana; Joetta Harty, George Washington University; Janis Haswell, Texas A&M University at Corpus Christi; Roberta Hawkins, Shorewood High School; Wilda Head, Central Baptist College; Kathy Heininge, University of California–Davis; Ed Higgins, George Fox University; Barbara Hiles-Mesle, Graceland College; James

Hirsh, Georgia State University; Nika Hoffman, Crossroads School for Arts and Sciences; Randall Holt, Columbia Gorge Community College; Rebecca Hooker, University of New Mexico; Brooke Hopkins, University of Utah; Elizabeth Huergo, Montgomery College–Rockville; Laurie Hughes, Richland Community College; Byan Hull, Portland Community College–Sylvania; Elizabeth Huston, Eastfield College; Richard Iadonisi, Grand Valley State University; Candice Jackson, Tougaloo College; Robert Jakubovic, Raymond Walters College; Elaine Kauvar, Baruch College CUNY; Anita Kerr, North Carolina State University; John Lux, Baruch College CUNY; Jamie Marchant, Auburn University; J. Eric Miller, Kennesaw State University; Deborah Preston, Georgia Perimeter College; Wylene Rholetter, Auburn University; Charles Riley, Baruch College CUNY; Mark Trevor Smith, Southwest Missouri State University; and Tami Whitney, Creighton University.

For help in shaping the Compact Edition, we thank the many reviewers who provided in-depth feedback on the table of contents, choice of translations, organization, and editorial apparatus:

Christine Abbott, Como Coso Community College; Oty Agbajoh-Laoye, Monmouth University; Heidi E. Ajrami, Victoria College; Allison E. Alison, Southeastern Community College; Lemiya Almaas, University of Minnesota–Twin Cities; Donald F. Andrews, Chattanooga State Technical Community College; Frances B. Auld, University of South Florida; Diane S. Baird, Palm Beach Community College; J. T. Barbarese, Rutgers University–Camden; Mojgan Behmand, George Mason University; Marilyn Booth, University of Illinois–Urbana-Champaign; Arnold J. Bradford, Northern Virginia Community College; Julie Brannon, Jacksonville University; Caridad Caballero, University of Georgia; Farida (Farrah) M. Cato, University of Central Florida; Barbara Mather Cobb, Murray State University; Ruth M. Cook, Milligan College; Carole Creekmore, Georgia Perimeter College–South; Robert W. Croft, Gainesville College; Jason DePolo, North Carolina A&T State University; Dwonna Goldstone, Austin Peay State University; David R. Greene, Long Island University–C.W. Post; Michael Grimwood, North Carolina State University; Anna R. Holloway, Fort Valley State University; Melissa Jackson, Midland College; Lars R. Jones, Florida Institute of Technology; Rodney D. Keller, Brigham Young University–Idaho; Pam Kingsbury, University of North Alabama; Roger Lathbury, George Mason University; Dianna Laurent, Southeastern Louisiana University; Michael Mackey, Community College of Denver; J. Hunter Morgan, Glenville State College; John H. Morgan, Eastern Kentucky University; James Norton, Marian College; Keith R. Prendergast, Pensacola Junior College; Peter Quinn, Salem State College; Wylene Rholetter, Auburn University; Jennifer O. Rosti, Roanoke College; Mimosa Stephenson, University of Texas at Brownsville; Matthew Stewart, Boston University; Charles F. Warren, Salem State College; Sally Padgett Wheeler, Georgia Perimeter College–Rockdale.

Finally, we thank the fourteen members of our Editorial Advisory Board, who reviewed the table of contents and sections of the manuscript at multiple stages, providing valuable advice throughout this book's development.

Editorial Advisory Board

No anthology of this size comes into being without critical and supportive friends and advisors. Our thanks go to the Department of English at the University of New Mexico (UNM) and its chair, David Jones, who supported our work. Among our colleagues and associates, we particularly want to thank Helen Damico, Feroza Jussawalla, Mary Power, Carmen Nocentelli-Truett, and Ron Shumaker, as well as Paul Lauter, Manjeet Tangri, and Fidel Fajardo-Acosta. Robin Runia provided research and editorial assistance and drafted the "Time and Place" box on the Encyclopedia Project.

An anthology of this scope is an undertaking that calls for a courageous, imaginitive, and supportive publisher. Joan Feinberg, Denise Wydra, Karen Henry, Steve Scipione, and Alanya Harter at Bedford/St. Martin's possess these qualities; we especially appreciate their confidence in our ability to carry out this task. Kaitlin Hannon guided the project in its early stages, and Carrie Thompson stepped in to develop the manuscript and see it through to completion. Abby Bielagus and Marisa Feinstein assisted with numerous tasks, large and small. Martha Friedman and Connie Gardner served as photo researchers, and Jean Hammond and Anna Palchik fine-tuned the design. Adrienne Petsick enthusiastically developed and coordinated the marketing plan. We also owe special thanks to Karen Stocz for skillfully copyediting and guiding the manuscript through production, Elizabeth Schaaf for overseeing the production process, and Rebecca Merrill for producing the Web site.

Most of all, we thank our families, especially Mary Davis, Patricia Clark Smith, Marlys Harrison, and Mona Johnson, for their patience and encouragement.

Paul Davis
Gary Harrison
David M. Johnson
John F. Crawford

A NOTE ON TRANSLATION

As anthologies of world literature have included an increasing number of texts from around the world, the use of quality translations of these texts has become not only necessary, but a mark of excellence for a particular anthology. The necessity for reading texts in translation has brought a recognition that different versions of the same text vary in quality and accessibility—not just any rendition will do. Teachers now *request* certain translations of favorite literary works, such as the Christian Bible, Homer's *The Odyssey* or Dante's *Divine Comedy*. A translation might adequately communicate the literal meaning of the original work, but miss entirely its cultural background or the artistry of a passage—both of which support and enhance that meaning. At the other extreme is the impressionistic version that recreates the spirit of the original work, but deviates from its meaning, thereby misleading the reader. Every translator faces the dilemma of what Benedetto Croce has stated as the extremes—either "Faithful ugliness or faithless beauty."

Among the most important and most popular texts from the ancient world are Homer's epics and the Greek dramas; Robert Fitzgerald's translation of Homer's *The Odyssey* and Robert Fagles's excellent versions of Homer's *The Iliad*, Aeschylus' *Agamemnon*, and Sophocles' *Antigone* are faithful to the original Greek and uniquely accessible to the modern reader. In a similar fashion, Horace Gregory's translations of Catullus and Rolfe Humphries' translations of Ovid span the distance between ancient Rome and today. Despite the fact that the scholarship of the King James Version of the Bible needs to be updated, we use this version because it is considered the most literary translation in English. Not only do many readers of English grow up with the King James, its antiquated syntax and vocabulary resonate with a sense of the sacred, and are echoed throughout later literature in English. R. M. Liuzza has provided us with what is possibly the most accurate modern poetic translation of *Beowulf*.

The best translations do not merely duplicate a work but re-create it in a new idiom. Because of poetic elements such as rhyme, meter, stanzas, and figures of speech, translating poetry presents unique challenges. Stephen Spender and J. L. Gili's translations of Federico García Lorca are excellent, as are the translations by several hands of the poets of the Tang dynasty in China. We use several different translators for Ghalib's and Pablo Neruda's poems, providing the reader with different perspectives on one of the major poets of the nineteenth century and one of the most important poets of the twentieth century.

Translating from one culture to another adds an additional layer of complexity, be it philosophical or symbolic. For example, as one of the most important religious documents of ancient India, the Bhagavad Gita alludes continuously to the complexities of classical Hinduism; Barbara Stoler Miller offers a unique, interpretive bridge from this ancient text to a modern reader. She also provides us with a multi-voiced version of the Indian classic by Kalidasa, *Shakuntala and the Ring of Recollection*, which also invokes Hindu themes—particularly that of *dharma* or duty. In terms of symbolism, while "cherry blossom" in a line of poetry to American readers may suggest a particular spring bloom or flower of the fruit tree, to Japanese readers "cherry blossom" invokes a cultural tradition that, depending on context, may suggest ideas of purity, transience, delicacy, and even of self-sacrifice. Richard Bodner's translation of Bashō's *Narrow Road through the Backcountry* and Edward Seidensticker's translation of *The Tale of Genji* are both sensitive to such cultural nuance, and both translations do justice to the poetic and prose passages of each work.

Some translations are so excellent they become classics in their own right. This is true of David Magarshack's translation of Tolstoy's *The Death of Ivan Ilych*, his rendering of Chekhov's *The Cherry Orchard*, and Richard Wilbur's *Tartuffe*. Edith Grossman's subtle and sophisticated version of *Don Quixote* is one of the best modern translations of a world classic. J. A. Underwood's refreshingly updated version of *The Metamorphosis* demonstrates why Kafka remains one of the most influential and timely writers of the past century.

No translation can substitute for reading the world's classics in their original languages. Nonetheless, the art of translation in the modern age has reached such a high level of both accuracy and artistry that we now have access to a full range of translations of world literature in its variety and significance. *The Bedford Anthology of World Literature*, Compact Edition, offers what we believe are the most reliable and readable translations of the major works included here.

About the Editors

Paul Davis (Ph.D., University of Wisconsin), professor emeritus of English at the University of New Mexico, has been the recipient of several teaching awards and academic honors, including that of Master Teacher. He has taught courses since 1962 in composition, rhetoric, and nineteenth-century literature and has written and edited many scholarly books, including *The Penguin Dickens Companion* (1999), *Dickens A to Z* (1998), and *The Lives and Times of Ebenezer Scrooge* (1990). He has also written numerous scholarly and popular articles on solar energy and Victorian book illustration. His most recent book is *Critical Companion to Charles Dickens* (2007).

Gary Harrison (Ph.D., Stanford University), professor and director of graduate studies at the University of New Mexico, has won numerous fellowships and awards for scholarship and teaching. He has taught courses in world literature, British Romanticism, and literary theory at the University of New Mexico since 1987. Harrison's publications include a critical study on William Wordsworth, *Wordsworth's Vagrant Muse: Poetry, Poverty, and Power* (1994); as well as several articles on topics such as John Clare's poetry, Romanticism and ecology, nineteenth-century culture, and teaching world literature.

David M. Johnson (Ph.D., University of Connecticut), professor emeritus of English at the University of New Mexico, has taught courses in world literature, mythology, the Bible as literature, philosophy and literature, and creative writing since 1965. He has written, edited, and contributed to numerous scholarly books and collections of poetry, including *Fire in the Fields* (1996) and *Lord of the Dawn: The Legend of Quetzalcoatl* (1987). He has also published scholarly articles, poetry, and translations of Nahuatl myths. His most recent book of poetry is *Rebirth of Wonder: Poems of the Common Life* (University of New Mexico Press, 2007).

John F. Crawford (Ph.D., Columbia University; postdoctoral studies, Yale University), associate professor of English at the University of New Mexico, has taught medieval, world, and other literature courses since 1965 at a number of institutions, including California Institute of Technology and Hunter College and Herbert Lehmann College of CUNY. The publisher of West End Press, an independent literary press with 120 titles, Crawford has also edited *This Is About Vision: Interviews with Southwestern Writers* (1990) and written articles on multicultural literature of the Southwest.

Pronunciation Key

This key applies to the pronunciation guides that appear in the margins and before most selections in *The Bedford Anthology of World Literature*, Compact Edition. The syllable receiving the main stress is CAPITALIZED.

a	mat, alabaster, laugh	MAT, AL-uh-bas-tur, LAF
ah	mama, Americana, Congo	MAH-mah, uh-meh-rih-KAH-nuh, KAHNG-goh
ar	cartoon, Harvard	kar-TOON, HAR-vurd
aw	saw, raucous	SAW, RAW-kus
ay (or a)	may, Abraham, shake	MAY, AY-bruh-ham, SHAKE
b	bet	BET
ch	church, matchstick	CHURCH, MACH-stik
d	desk	DESK
e	Edward, melted	ED-wurd, MEL-tid
ee	meet, ream, petite	MEET, REEM, puh-TEET
eh	cherub, derriere	CHEH-rub, DEH-ree-ehr
f	final	FIGH-nul
g	got, giddy	GAHT, GIH-dee
h	happenstance	HAP-un-stans
i	mit, Ipswich, impression	MIT, IP-swich, im-PRESH-un
igh (or i)	eyesore, right, Anglophile	IGH-sore, RITE, ANG-gloh-file
ih	Philippines	FIH-luh-peenz
j	judgment	JUJ-mint
k	kitten	KIT-tun
l	light, allocate	LITE, AL-oh-kate
m	ramrod	RAM-rahd
n	ran	RAN
ng	rang, thinker	RANG, THING-ker
oh (or o)	open, owned, lonesome	OH-pun, OHND, LONE-sum
ong	wrong, bonkers	RONG, BONG-kurz
oo	moot, mute, super	MOOT, MYOOT, SOO-pur
ow	loud, dowager, how	LOWD, DOW-uh-jur, HOW
oy	boy, boil, oiler	BOY, BOYL, OY-lur
p	pet	PET
r	right, wretched	RITE, RECH-id
s	see, citizen	SEE, SIH-tuh-zun
sh	shingle	SHING-gul
t	test	TEST
th	thin	THIN
th	this, whether	*TH*IS, WEH-*th*ur
u	until, sumptuous, lovely	un-TIL, SUMP-choo-us, LUV-lee
uh	about, vacation, suddenly	uh-BOWT, vuh-KAY-shun, SUH-dun-lee
ur	fur, bird, term, beggar	FUR, BURD, TURM, BEG-ur
v	vacuum	VAK-yoo-um
w	western	WES-turn
y	yesterday	YES-tur-day
z	zero, loser	ZEE-roh, LOO-zur
zh	treasure	TREH-zhur

When a name is given two pronunciations, usually the first is the most familiar pronunciation in English and the second is a more exact rendering of the native pronunciation.

In the pronunciations of French names, nasalized vowels are indicated by adding "ng" after the vowel.

Japanese words have no strong stress accent, so the syllables marked as stressed are so given only for the convenience of English speakers.

CONTENTS

TEXT IN CONTEXT   *173*

HOMER [Greece, eighth century B.C.E.]   *173*

TEXT IN CONTEXT   *802*

∾ The Medieval and Early Modern World, 100 C.E.–1650   973

TEXT IN CONTEXT

IN THE WORLD: Varieties of Humanism   *1726*

The Ancient World

Beginnings – 100 C.E.

*P*rior to the development of urban civilizations about five thousand years ago, much of the world's population lived on farms or in small villages. Many anthropologists believe that women were central figures in this life, and that the people of this time widely worshipped goddesses. Village life was often organized around the health and fertility of crops, herds, and people, and women were the childbearers, the nurturers, and the principal tenders of crops. Men tended to herd domestic animals and hunt wild game. Eventually, as farming populations increased in the rich alluvial plains along major rivers, like the Nile in Egypt, the Indus in Pakistan, and the Tigris and Euphrates in Mesopotamia, people began to produce a surplus of food. Small trading centers gradually grew into cities. As labor became more specialized and efficient, more workers were drawn away from cyclical, seasonal, agricultural communities, where women were important, to these newer, more urban centers; power became more centralized and the organization of larger public projects gained in importance. The creation of a military marked the increasing importance of men in urban society.

COMPARATIVE TIMELINE FOR THE ANCIENT WORLD

Date	History and Politics	Literature	Science, Culture, and Technology
B.C.E. 7000–3000	7000–1500 Neolithic, agricultural communities 3500–3000 Beginning of cities along rivers in Mesopotamia and Egypt; development of bureaucracies, patriarchal institutions.	c. 3200 Development of cuneiform writing in Mesopotamia, hieroglyphic writing in Egypt.	7000–1500 Mother goddesses; weaving, metallurgy 3500–3000 Development of irrigation, mathematics, and calendars in Mesopotamia and Egypt. c. 3400 First walled towns along the Nile in Egypt
B.C.E. 3000–2000	c. 3000 Beginning of the Minoan civilization on Crete. c. 2700 Gilgamesh, legendary king of Uruk in Mesopotamia 2600–1500 Harappan civilization along the Indus River. c. 2340–c. 2305 The Akkadian Sargon I establishes the first empire in history.	c. 3000 Earliest surviving Egyptian papyri 2600–1500 Development of writing in India	c. 2700–2500 Pyramids built in Egypt c. 2060 Ziggurat at Ur in Mesopotamia

The new urban dwellers developed systems of mathematics and bookkeeping. Political organizations and bureaucracies evolved that coordinated the building of palaces, temples, pyramids, and statues. Priests created yearly calendars to mark the passage of seasons and to regulate annual ceremonies. The invention of writing was the glue that held these urban complexities together. Writing was first used to keep business accounts and tax records. It was later used to record and thus preserve an extensive religious literature that had previously been transmitted orally: myths about the origins of the world, hymns to the presiding deities, and stories about the creation of human culture. With the written word, epics were composed to honor famous warriors and their exploits; histories of kings who had created empires or dynasties and then lost them were chronicled; and an extensive history of warfare was set down. New, increased attention was paid to this world and to individuals' needs, which led to a new consciousness of the self. Poems dealt with love, sadness, and loss. Midway through the first millennium B.C.E., new religions emerged that spoke of virtue and suffering, and philosophical treatises expounded the secular ingredients of a good life.

Date	History and Politics	Literature	Science, Culture, and Technology
B.C.E. **2000–1500**	c. 2000 Greek-speaking Achaeans enter Greece.	c. 2000 *The Descent of Inanna*	
	2000–1400 Age of the Patriarchs in Hebrew history: Abraham, Isaac, Jacob, Joseph; sojourn in Egypt.	c. 2000–c. 1200 *The Epic of Gilgamesh*	
	c. 1800 First Dynasty of Babylon	c. 1800 *The Epic of Creation*	18th century Code of Hammurabi
	c. 1700 Height of Minoan sea-empire	c. 1700 Development of writing called Linear A in Crete	
	c. 1600–c. 1028 Shang dynasty in China		c. 1600 Chariots used in China.
B.C.E. **1500–1000**	c. 1500–1100 Mycenaean Age (Heroic Age) on the Greek mainland		1500–1000 Spread of the Vedic religion; creation of the caste system in India.
	c. 1500–c. 700 Invasion of Aryan tribes in India; the Vedic Age		1353–1336 Amenhotep IV (Akhenaten) of Egypt promotes monotheism.
	c. 1450 Downfall of Minoans on Crete		
	13th century Hebrews' Exodus from Egypt	c. 1320 "Hymn to Aten"	13th century Moses and the Ten Commandments
	c. 1250 Hebrew conquest of Canaan		
	c. 1200 Trojan War and the fall of Troy	c. 1200 Development of a writing system in China; Phoenician alphabet of 22 letters	
	1200–1030 Period of Judges in Israel		

COMMON THEMES IN ANCIENT LITERATURE

Urban civilization would not have been possible without the invention of writing. About 3200 B.C.E., both the Mesopotamians and the Egyptians began to develop a writing system—commonly defined as a system of human communication by means of conventional visible marks linked to spoken language. It is not known which culture was actually first. After a PICTOGRAPHIC stage, which tends to be an early stage in all writing systems, the Mesopotamians developed CUNEIFORM, a series of wedge-shaped marks that designated syllables and were capable of expressing a full range of meaning. The ancient Egyptian priesthood produced a picture-based system that the Greeks called "sacred carvings," or HIEROGLYPHICS. Other major writing systems followed in the Indus Valley in India (2600–1900 B.C.E.), in China (1200 B.C.E. to the present), and in Phoenicia and Greece in the Levant (1050 B.C.E. to the present). In the Americas, a writing system was invented by the Maya (250 C.E. to 900).

The Idea of Cosmogony.   COSMOGONY is a picture or model of the cosmos that demonstrates how life on earth with its rulers and systems of government is

Date	History and Politics	Literature	Science, Culture, and Technology
B.C.E. 1200–1000 (cont.)	1200–1000 Iron Age invasions; further conquest of India by Aryans, who spread the Vedic religion. 1100 Dorian invasion of Greece; destruction of Mycenaean fortresses; migration of Greeks to Asia Minor. c. 1027–221 Zhou (Chou) dynasty in China		
B.C.E. 1000–500	1000–922 Reigns of Kings David and Solomon in Israel c. 1000–600 Brahmanic Age in India 922 Israel divided into two kingdoms	c. 1000 The Rig Veda 900–500 Book of Genesis, Book of Exodus (Hebrew Scriptures) 9th century The Upanishads	
	826 Founding of Carthage 753 Legendary founding of Rome by Romulus 721 Northern Kingdom of Israel is conquered by Assyria (Shalmaneser V) and disappears. 721–705 Assyrian dynasty founded by Sargon II	c. 800 Greece adopts an alphabet. 8th century Hesiod, *Theogony* Homer, *The Iliad* and *The Odyssey*	c. 800 Lycurgus, the legendary lawgiver of Sparta 776 First Olympic Games

coordinated with the powers and patterns of the heavens. The discovery by Meso-potamian mathematicians and astronomers of the movement of planets through constellations of fixed stars led to what was probably the earliest systematic cos-mogony, one that mapped out basic celestial relationships and cyclical patterns of movement. A hierarchy of deities reflecting heavenly patterns became the model and justification for an earthly hierarchical system of kings, priests, and under-lings. The organization of gods into various roles was the glorified example of the specialization of earthly culture into religion, politics, education, and agriculture and the division of society into social classes. The temple, or ZIGGURAT, the earthly residence of the god or gods, took its place in the center of the city-state, where rulers (often deified) and nobility mirrored the divine pantheon of deities by ordering the course of civic and social life and participating in the fertility cycles of nature. About the third millennium B.C.E. the ancient Egyptians developed a similar cosmogony, an orderly and eternal system that they believed had been cre-ated by the gods even though chaos and the forces of disorder periodically threat-ened it.

Date	History and Politics	Literature	Science, Culture, and Technology
B.C.E. **1000–500** **(cont.)**		7th century *The Epic of Gilgamesh* (standard version)	7th–6th centuries Zoroastrianism in Persia; Hebrew prophets in Israel
			669–633 Assurbanipal, king of Assyria, creates extensive library.
		6th century *Ramayana* Development of Latin alphabet	6th century Rise of Doric and Ionic architecture in Greece.
	605–562 Nebuchadnezzar's reign in Babylonia	6th–3rd centuries Laozi (Lao Tzu)	6th–3rd centuries Period of the "Hundred Philosophers" in China
	594 Solon's reforms in Athens	c. 600 Sappho, poems	
	587–586 Jerusalem destroyed by Nebuchadnezzar; Babylonian captivity of the Jews.		563–483 Siddhartha Gautama, founder of Buddhism
	c. 550 Cyrus the Great establishes Persian empire.	551–479 Confucius (Kongfuzi), *The Analects*	
	546 Fall of Ionia (western Turkey) to Persia	c. 544 Beginnings of Attic tragedy in Greece	c. 550 Zoroastrianism becomes official religion of Persia.
	539 Fall of Babylon to Cyrus (Persia)		c. 539–468 Mahavira, founder of Jainism
	509 Brutus establishes Roman Republic		c. 520–515 Second Temple is built in Palestine.
	507 Cleisthenes' democratic reforms in Athens		

Behind both the Mesopotamian and Egyptian models of heaven and earth was the idea of immutability, or permanence, an abstract force thought to hold the cosmic hierarchy in place, ensuring its functioning, its rightness in the midst of change or flux. This idea was at the core of all civilizations that were sustained for any length of time. Sumerians, who created the first Mesopotamian civilization in the fourth millennium B.C.E., called the collective rules and regulations governing the universe the ME's, and first entrusted them to the goddess Inanna. The Egyptians referred to cosmic order as MA'AT, which was the responsibility of the sun-god Re and eventually became the goddess Maat, who accompanied Re in his sun-boat. The priests of India called the principle of justice DHARMA, while the ancient Chinese invoked the principle of the DAO. The principle of justice in ancient Greece was named MOIRA; it eventually evolved into LOGOS. In Israel, a just universe was guaranteed by the Jewish god YAHWEH, who, the Jews believed, personally intervened in history to uphold righteousness.

Creation myths, often the earliest literature of ancient civilizations, were written to express a cosmogony: how the world came into being, who runs it,

Date	History and Politics		Literature		Science, Culture, and Technology	
B.C.E. 500–300	490	Athenians defeat Persians at the Battle of Marathon.	5th century	Book of Job (Hebrew Scriptures)	5th century	Phidias sculpts Athena Parthenos and Zeus in Athens.
					486	Contests for best comedy in Athens
	461–429	Age of Pericles (Golden Age) in Athens	458	Aeschylus, *The Oresteia* (*Agamemnon, The Libation Bearers, The Eumenides*)	c. 450	Invention of the crossbow in China
			c. 441	Sophocles, *Antigone*		
	431–404	Peloponnesian War	c. 430	Herodotus, *History of the Persian Wars*	432	Completion of Parthenon in Athens
			c. 420	Thucydides, *History of the Peloponnesian War*		
	c. 403–221	Warring States period in China	c. 400	Brahmi syllabic script in India	c. 400	Rise of Daoism (Taoism) in China
			4th century–1st century	*Majjhima Nikaya, Samyutta Nikaya, Mahaparinibbana Sutta* (Buddhist texts)	399	Execution of Socrates in Athens
			4th century	*Dao De Jing* (Tao Te Ching)		

and how humans participate in it. A religious interpretation of the sky and the cosmos in early stories is usually balanced by a concern with the earth, the cycle of seasons that becomes the basis of religious ritual. The transformation of a seed into a plant is compared to the phases in the life of a spiritual being, a god or a goddess. Out of this natural process came the complex rituals or ceremonies in which the birth, growth, and death of the god of nature were dramatized and acted out. Often these dramas contain the secrets of immortality and life after death. In ancient Sumer, the story of the descent of the goddess Inanna into the underworld reflects the vegetation cycle; in Egypt the same cycle is dramatized in the story of Isis and the death and resurrection of Osiris. In Greece, the yearly agricultural cycles are invoked by the story of Demeter and Persephone; and in Syria, in the story of Attis. The Christian Easter services and rituals seem a successor to these ceremonies. The celebrated correlation between gods and humankind, between the heavens and the earth was institutionalized in an astronomically based religious calendar that marked the major annual festivals. Since then, priests and rulers throughout the ancient Near East and the Mediterranean have validated

Date	History and Politics	Literature	Science, Culture, and Technology
B.C.E. 500–300 (cont.)		c. 369–286 Writings of Zhuangzi (Chuang Tzu)	c. 386 Plato founds the Academy in Athens.
		4th century Plato, *Apology* and *The Republic*	c. 370 Death of Hippocrates, the Greek Father of Medicine
		c. 371–c. 288 Writings of Mencius (Mengzi)	
		4th century Aristotle, *Poetics*	c. 336 Aristotle founds the Lyceum.
	331 Founding of Alexandria in Egypt	c. 341–270 Epicurus "Letter to a Friend"	c. 330 Founding of the library at Alexandria
	323 Death of Alexander the Great		
	c. 322–c. 185 Maurya empire in India	4th century B.C.E.–4th century C.E. *Mahabharata*	
	305 Ptolemy becomes the ruler of Egypt.		
B.C.E. 300–1		c. 350–250 *Song of Songs* (Hebrew Scriptures)	3rd century First Great Wall of China is completed during Qin dynasty.
	c. 273–c. 232 Reign of Ashoka, the first Buddhist emperor in history, in India.	3rd century B.C.E.–1st century C.E. *Uttaradhyayana Sutra* (Jain text)	250–100 Hebrew Scriptures translated into Greek (Septuagint)
	270 Rome rules all of Italy.		

their agendas and creeds with celestial authority, as if to say, "This is the way that the gods intended it!"

Empires and Heroes.   The negative side of civilization has always been its organized warfare, slavery, rape, theft, and destruction. The spread of a patriarchal warrior culture characterized the third millennium B.C.E. in both Mesopotamia and Egypt. Both peoples in those regions devoted their resources to waging war with neighboring city-states and empire-building. Ruling bureaucracies became more and more complex, while religion and law became increasingly codified. In the third millennium B.C.E., migrant tribes from the north called Aryans invaded India and imposed patriarchal institutions, such as the caste system, on settlements along the Indus River—an indigenous culture now called Harappan. These Aryan tribes, which gradually moved across India, were part of a larger nomadic group from Central Asia called Indo-Europeans that swept in a series of waves into Greece and Italy, overwhelming the agricultural communities in their path. A similar pattern of conquest occurred in China during the Shang dynasty (c. 1600–c. 1028 B.C.E.), when a

Date	History and Politics	Literature	Science, Culture, and Technology
B.C.E. **300–1** (cont.)	264–146 Punic Wars: Rome versus Carthage		
	221–206 Qin (Ch'in) dynasty, the first Chinese empire		
	206 B.C.E.–220 C.E. Han dynasty in China		
	200 Roman conquest of Greece begins	2nd century Apollodorus, *Bibliotheca*	c. 170 First paved roads in Rome
			165 Invention of parchment (vellum) in Asia Minor
			136 Confucianism becomes official doctrine in China.
	63 Rome seizes control of Palestine.	1st century Catullus, poems	
	60 First Triumvirate of Rome (Julius Caesar, Pompey, Crassus)	1st century B.C.E.– 1st century C.E. *Bhagavad Gita*	

nomadic Eurasian people brought a militaristic culture to the mainland, introducing horses, the chariot, metallurgy, and a class-based society to the region.

Later literature romanticizes these early periods of empire-building and immortalizes warrior-kings and other heroes in magnificent epic poems about what historians refer to as the Heroic Ages. The most famous of such eras are the Greek Heroic Age, which occurred near the end of the second millennium B.C.E.; the Heroic Age of India, which followed a few centuries later; and the Heroic Age of northern Europe, which is dated from the fourth to the sixth centuries C.E. There was, however, the much earlier Heroic Age that flourished some fifteen hundred years before Greece—the Sumerian Heroic Age of Mesopotamia. It inspired several cycles of epic poems, only one of which has survived, *The Epic of Gilgamesh*. The most famous epics of ancient times—*The Iliad* and *The Odyssey* from Greece, the *Ramayana* and *Mahabharata* from India, and the Old English *Beowulf*—share characteristics. They celebrate the unusual and sometimes miraculous exploits of individual heroes, men assisted or thwarted by divine beings. They abound in epithets, formulas, catalogs, and speeches, features that testify to their stories' origins

Date	History and Politics		Literature		Science, Culture, and Technology	
B.C.E. 300–1 (cont.)	44	Assassination of Caesar				
	43	Second Triumvirate of Rome (Antony, Octavian, Lepidus)				
	27	Establishment of empire by Augustus Caesar				
C.E. 1–300	27 B.C.E.–180 C.E.	*Pax Romana* (more than 200 years of peace)	c. 19	Virgil, *The Aeneid*		
			c. 8	Ovid, *Metamorphoses*	c. 5 B.C.E.–c. 30 C.E.	Jesus of Nazareth (founder of Christianity)
	25–220	Later Han dynasty in China				
					70	Colossus begun at Rome
			c. 100	Ashvaghosha, *The Life of Buddha*	c. 100	Buddhism enters China
			2nd century	Suetonius, *The Lives of the Twelve Caesars* Marcus Aurelius, *Meditations*	c. 105	Invention of paper in China
			3rd century	Diogenes Laertius, *Lives of Eminent Philosophers*	118–126	Construction of the Pantheon at Rome

in an earlier oral tradition. The Greek Heroic tradition is the one that is most known in the West; in addition to the warrior's code of honor and courage, the Greek epic values the intelligence and beauty of individuals, including women. The heroes of the *Ramayana*—Rama, the incarnation of the god Vishnu, and Sita, his wife—became models of love, heroism, and friendship for millions of Hindus. The central action of *Mahabharata,* a war among cousins and bands of brothers, is complemented with moral digressions, elaborate rituals, and romantic episodes that have been a source of education, art, and literature in India to the present day.

Religion and Philosophy.   A profound change of a religious and moral nature took place in Europe and Asia in the period 700–400 B.C.E. evidenced by a decrease of interest in the mythic stories about the cosmic realm and the emergence of a literature concerned with the philosophical challenges of this world. ZOROASTRIAN-ISM, which had been founded by Zoroaster perhaps as early as 1200 B.C.E. and saw the world in terms of a struggle between good and evil, became the religion of the Persian state during this time. In India, some teachers rejected the ritual life pre-scribed by the VEDAS and the dominance of the BRAHMINS, or the caste of priests, and turned to the program of personal development described in the UPANISHADS. BUDDHISM, one of the earliest world religions, was founded at this time. In China this was the age of Confucius, Laozi (Lao Tzu), and the great Chinese schools of philosophy. The transformation in Greece began with such sixth century B.C.E. philosophers as Heraclitus and Pythagoras and continued in Periclean Athens with Socrates, Plato, and Aristotle. In the seventh and sixth centuries B.C.E., the great Hebrew prophets of Israel—Isaiah, Jeremiah, and Ezekiel—transformed Judaism. These revolutionary thinkers as well as others focused attention on "historical reality"; that is, a shift of focus from a preoccupation with the transcendent reality of the heavens and issues of faith to a concern with the phenomenal, physical world of the present that can be discovered by rational thought.

During this period, moral and religious philosophers struggled to discover a basic principle that governed life. Some proposed that humans were primarily moti-vated by desire or pleasure. Others saw humans as essentially rational creatures capable of creating a just society. The concept of sin was developed to explain the existence of evil in the world. The doctrine of karma articulated the relationship between action and consequences, extending even into previous lifetimes. In poetry, parables, sermons, maxims, and proverbs, the great prophets and teachers of this period created ethical systems that described the nature of the good life and its possible fruits. Some individual belief systems pointed to a variety of rewards available in this lifetime: prosperity, enlightenment, peace of mind, nirvana. Others emphasized punishment, depicting the physical and mental pain one would suffer—usually after death—if one failed to follow a particular path.

The Legacy of Literature.   It is difficult to overestimate the role of writing and literacy in the history of the world. However ancient texts are interpreted or even misunderstood, their very longevity offers a potential link between the peoples of ancient civilizations and the present day. A Sanskrit text from the first century C.E. may be the inspiration for a Chinese novel of a thousand years later. The power of writing and the almost magical possibility of immortality that it holds were understood by the Egyptian scribe who wrote:

> Man dies, his body is dust,
>> his family all brought low to the earth;
> But writing shall make him remembered,
>> alive in the mouths of any who read.
> Better a book than a builded mansion,
>> better than body's home in the West,
> Splendid above a fine house in the country
>> or stone-carved deeds in the precinct of God.
>> —(from *Papyrus Chester Beatty IV,* c. 1300–1100 B.C.E.)

A comparison of writing with nonwriting cultures shows the profound impact of the written word. The first use of writing appears to have been record keeping. It is thought that Mesopotamian scribes were associated with temples and palaces and considered so important that special schools were established to train them. They kept business records and transcribed sacred knowledge that in part validated the importance of priests. As written documentation accumulated, it provided a means of attending to the evolution of a society's political, social, and religious institutions.

Ownership of written texts was sometimes exploited for power. Rulers and priests often guarded written records thought to be magical and powerful. Writing made it possible to manipulate the letters of god's name for purposes of divination, for example the use of runes by the Scandinavians and the practices of the Jewish cabalists. Ceremonial texts of Egypt, Mesopotamia, and India were not shared with ordinary mortals since they were seen as privileged communications from the gods. The BRAHMINS, the priest caste of India, took another tack. They preserved an oral tradition for passing down their teachings as a means of restricting access to sacred lore. The guru tradition in Hinduism and Buddhism, by contrast to all of the above, combines literate and oral modes of communication in order to better *share* wisdom; a guru's talks or information addresses are an essential addition to what has been recorded in books.

Literacy altered oral literatures by "fixing" their stories. Once they were written down, these literatures could be analyzed, canonized, and re-created in art and philosophy. Written texts became the basis for schools of religion and philosophy. Theologians, philosophers, and critics have argued about the meaning of the particular words and literal and allegorical interpretations of religious writings ever since they were published. Lengthy commentaries have been written on minute particulars of religious doctrine, sometimes causing schisms or even wars.

Literacy constitutes the very core of modern society. The teachings of Confucius, passed down for more than two thousand years, continue to shape Chinese society today. The poetry of Laozi is probably more popular today than ever, with new translations appearing regularly. Following the dictates of the Vedas and the Upanishads for almost three thousand years, Hinduism is practiced by almost a billion people today. The Hebrew Scriptures, with their ideals of law and righteousness, spawned Judaism and two additional world religions: Christianity, with more than a billion and a half followers, and Islam, whose followers approach one billion. And the various literatures of Greece, which greatly expanded the boundaries of human potential and creativity, are ever present in almost every aspect of Western politics, art, literature, and philosophy.

A note on dating ancient literatures: The designations B.C. and A.D., proposed by a Scythian monk, Dionysius Exiguus, in 525 C.E. in response to a request by Pope John I to prepare a chronology, stand for "before Christ" and "anno Domini," or "in the year of the Lord." Revising Diocletian's calendar from the third century, Dionysius Exiguus fixed December 25 as the date of Jesus' birth and made the following January 1 the start of 1 A.D. He called the previous year 1 B.C. and numbered preceding years accordingly, back to the date of creation. Dionysius' calendar was adopted in Europe by the eighth century, with other parts of the world following in later years. Today, however, as a way of recognizing the diversity of religions and cultures around the globe, publishing houses, scholars, and writers are increasingly substituting B.C.E. ("before the common era") and C.E. ("common era") for B.C. and A.D., which refer to the same periods of time, respectively.

MESOPOTAMIA

The various peoples who created the city-states and empires along the Tigris and Euphrates Rivers in what is today Iraq are referred to collectively as Mesopotamians—from the Greek "between the rivers." Sometime before 3500 B.C.E., a

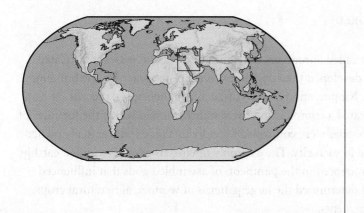

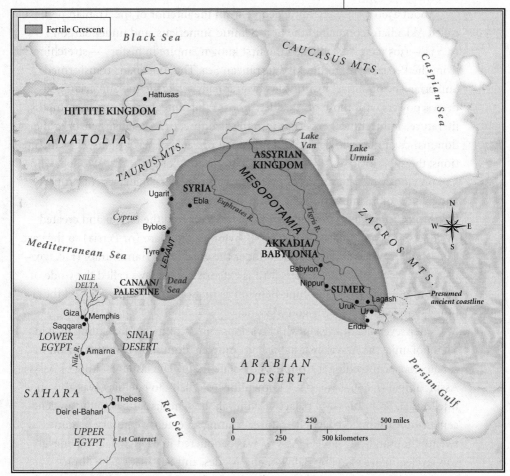

The Ancient Near East, Second Millennium B.C.E.

The region of the Near East between the Tigris and Euphrates Rivers, called Mesopotamia (meaning "between the rivers"), is thought to be the birthplace of civilization—non-nomadic societies characterized by agriculture and cities. The inhabitants of Mesopotamia raised crops on this rich but dry land by developing and using complex irrigation systems so successful they resulted in a surplus of food. This in turn led to population growth and the emergence of cities.

remarkable people called Sumerians settled in this area and with sophisticated irrigation systems developed the agricultural surplus necessary for the building of cities like Uruk, Nippur, and Eridu. Written and archeological records indicate that Sumerians created a complex, interwoven theocracy, in which the fortunes of the individual city-states were controlled by individual gods who actually owned religious real estate in each city. The assembly of citizens who determined earthly, urban affairs was mirrored in the pantheon of assembled gods that influenced human events and determined the large patterns of weather, agricultural crops, and military engagements.

About 2300 B.C.E., a Semitic people from the interior of the Arabian peninsula called Akkadians conquered the non-Semitic Sumerians, and under Sargon I (c. 2340–2305 B.C.E.) established the first known empire in history—stretching from the Persian Gulf to the Mediterranean Sea. The Akkadians transformed Sumerian sociopolitical institutions by gradually replacing the Sumerian goddesses' powers with those of Akkadian gods. While integrating Sumerian myths, literature, and technical expertise into their culture, the Akkadians ensured the dominance of males in their society through private property rights, class distinctions, the superiority of sky-gods, and centralization of authority. Women, who had previously held positions as priestesses and diviners, managers of property and owners of businesses, slowly lost power.

Around 2000 B.C.E., other Semitic peoples entered the region and created three separate kingdoms: the Assyria, Babylonia, and Elam (or Persia) to the east. The whole region was again united under the great King Hammurabi (r. c. 1792–1750 B.C.E.), who became famous for his extensive set of laws called the Code of Hammurabi and for establishing Babylon as the seat of his authority and the home temple for the storm-god Marduk.

After several centuries in which various tribes competed for dominance in Mesopotamia, the Assyrians established complete dominion over the region in c. 800 B.C.E., controlling it from the city-state Assur. The last great king of Assyria, Assurbanipal (r. 669–633 B.C.E.), known for his cruelty to enemies, was also an intellectual. From his royal palace at Ninevah, he sent his scribes to the ancient centers of learning to collect literature, creating an extensive library of some twenty thousand clay tablets. Assyria was conquered in 626 B.C.E. and Ninevah was leveled in 612 B.C.E. by Babylonians, Medes, and Scythians. The library was buried under sand for two thousand years. In the mid-nineteenth century, archeologists discovered clay tablets at Ninevah and at other Mesopotamian sites along the Tigris and Euphrates Rivers; ancient history was rewritten as a result. Assurbanipal's library is the primary source of most information about Akkad and Babylon before 1000 B.C.E. In addition to administrative records, the library contained vast literature of Sumer and Babylon.

Mesopotamian Literature.   Unearthed at various sites in Iraq, many toward the close of the nineteenth century, Mesopotamian literary texts display a rich variety similar to that found in early Egyptian writing and in the Hebrew Scriptures. They include myths, hymns of praise to deities, epic histories, lamentations, and wisdom literature. *The Epic of Creation* (p. 144), also known as the *Enuma Elish,* is the most famous creation story to come out of the Babylonian Empire, the political successor to the Sumerians of the third millennium. This extended account describes how order was first created out of primordial chaos when the god Marduk defeated Tiamat, a serpentine female. The oldest extant goddess stories in the Western world come from Sumer and center around Inanna (p. 897), who was the Queen of Heaven and Earth, the morning and evening star, and the goddess of love, agriculture, and warfare. Her stories date from 3500 to 1900 B.C.E.—and perhaps even earlier. *The Epic of Gilgamesh* (p. 48) is essentially the maturation journey of a young king, whose name has been found in Sumerian king-lists and is associated with the kingship of Uruk on the Euphrates River around 2500 B.C.E. In the epic, after battling a giant and grieving the death of his friend Enkidu, Gilgamesh goes on an extended personal journey, searching for the answers to human mortality and the ultimate meaning of life. As part of his journey, he is told a flood story similar to the one in the Hebrew Scriptures.

www   For more information about the culture and context of Mesopotamia in the ancient world, see bedfordstmartins.com/worldlitcompact.

THE ANCIENT HEBREWS

The history of the ancient Hebrews is the story of the Hebrews' search for God's blessings and their transformation from a nomadic, tribal people into a settled kingdom in Palestine. For hundreds of years, Israel was caught between Egypt's and Mesopotamia's struggles for control of Palestine (a narrow strip of land, 150 miles long and 70 miles wide, between the eastern end of the Mediterranean Sea and the inland deserts), enduring a mixture of victories and defeats. Eventually, they were exiled. Throughout this time, Israel's poets, priests, and prophets assembled the Hebrew Scriptures—what Christians refer to as the Old Testament—a remarkable collection of history, religion, and literature. The great poets and prophets of Israel continually recast the material world in terms of its spiritual destiny, its relationship to a transcendent authority, and the human capacity for righteousness and blessings. From the nation of Israel

Samuel Anoints David, **Wall Painting from Dura Europos, early fourth century**
King David united the tribes of Israel, founding a dynasty and creating the first successful Jewish kingdom. (Z. Radovan, Jerusalem)

came a consciousness of personal morality, a code of ethics based on allegiance to a single deity and an awareness of divine purpose in history.

The Exodus and the Ten Commandments.[1]   Early in the second millennium B.C.E., nomadic tribes of Hebrews followed the Fertile Crescent southward through Palestine to Egypt, where they were enslaved by the Egyptians sometime between c. 1500–1300 B.C.E. According to Hebrew Scripture, God (referred to by the letters YHWH and known as Yahweh) reveals himself to Moses telling Moses to free his people from slavery. Under Moses' guidance, the Hebrews escape from Egypt about 1250 B.C.E. and cross the Sinai Desert to Mt. Sinai, where they receive the spiritual and legal foundation of their religion in the form of the Ten Commandments. Prepared for conquest, they journey to the land of Canaan (also known as Palestine), invade towns and villages, and eventually settle down. Yahweh proved to be a fierce partisan; he was wrathful whether dealing with Hebrew backsliders at Mt. Sinai, Sodom and Gomorrah, or the Canaanite enemy. For the next five hundred years

---

[1]See **Authorship and Archeology** on page 19 for the recent controversy about dating the history of ancient Israel.

or so—until the time of military defeat and exile in 586 B.C.E.—the religion of Mt. Sinai and the polytheistic practices of the indigenous religion, the Canaanite religion of Baal and Ashtorath, struggled for supremacy within the Israelite community. Hebrew scriptures record a number of times when Canaanite elements had to be purged from the religion of Yahweh.

David, Solomon, and a Kingdom Divided.   The twelfth and eleventh centuries B.C.E. were a time of warfare when Hebrew military leaders, called judges, arose. These leaders defended various groups against invasion and then played a unifying, political role in the region. Substantial progress toward national unity was made by Saul, the first king of Israel (c. 1020 B.C.E.), when the people banded together in the face of their common enemy, the Philistines. Credit for finally creating a united kingdom, however, is given to David, who reigned from c. 1000 to 960 B.C.E. King David consolidated his rule through military victories and by establishing Jerusalem as Israel's national capital, but like Saul's, David's life was tragically marred by rebellion and personal conflicts—a pattern that harkens back to the Book of Genesis. Solomon's reign, from 960 to 922 B.C.E., the Golden Age of Israel, was a time of peace and prosperity. At this time the Israelites fortified their cities and built a magnificent temple in Jerusalem, where the worship of Yahweh was centered.

When Solomon died, the kingdom was divided into a large northern state of Israel, with a capital at Shechem, and a small southern state of Judah. Caught in the middle of the rivalry between Egypt and Assyria, the northern kingdom—Israel—disappeared in 722 B.C.E., its former inhabitants becoming the "Ten Lost Tribes" of Israel. In 621 B.C.E. Josiah became king of Judah and, discovering the Book of Deuteronomy during a temple renovation, instituted broad religious reforms, such as the destruction of pagan shrines and the reinstitution of Passover, in accordance with its instructions. Nebuchadnezzar of Babylon established control over the region by defeating Egypt in 605 B.C.E. Unwise successors to Josiah rebelled against Babylonian rule, and Nebuchadnezzar defeated Jerusalem in 587 B.C.E., burning buildings and leveling the Temple. Jewish survivors were deported to Babylon, the start of a long succession of Jewish settlements outside of Palestine known by the Greek term *DIASPORA*, meaning dispersion.

Foreign Occupation.   After the Persian king Cyrus captured Babylon in 539 B.C.E., he allowed the Hebrews in captivity, now referred to as Jews, to return to Jerusalem in 538 B.C.E.; meanwhile a number of outsiders, like the Persians, the Greeks, and the Ptolemies, ruled the region. When the Syrian king Antiochus IV (175–163 B.C.E.) attempted to force the Jews to accept **HELLENISTIC** culture—Greek language, art, and religion — the Jews answered with the Maccabeean Revolt (167–160 B.C.E.) and, victorious, enjoyed some independence during the next hundred years, until 64 B.C.E. when Pompey annexed Syria, and Palestine came under the control of the Romans. Herod the Great, a builder who renovated the Temple in Jerusalem, was made king of Judea (the Greco-Roman name for Judah) in 37 B.C.E. by Octavius Caesar. When Herod died in 4 B.C.E., Judea was split up into three portions, provinces governed by procurators who answered directly to the emperor. Pontius Pilate, the procurator of Judea from 26–36 C.E., condemned the Jewish teacher, Jesus of Nazareth, to death.

The Jews and their council of elders, the Sanhedrin, were granted a great degree of self-governance until the ascension of the Roman emperor Caligula in 37 C.E. Sanctioning persecution of the Jews, Caligula had his own image hung in the Temple in Jerusalem. Unrest eventually led to a Jewish revolt in 66 C.E., to which Rome responded under Emperor Vespasian and his son General Titus by destroying Jerusalem in 70 C.E., ending that city's role as a religious center for 1900 years. After the Council at Jamnia in 90 C.E., when Jewish rabbis decided on the contents of the Hebrew Scriptures, one further revolt against Rome took place under the leadership of Simon bar Kochba in 135 C.E. The Jews, who were defeated, were forbidden to set foot in Jerusalem, and the province of Judea was renamed Palestine.

Biblical Literature.   Outside of Judaism, the Hebrew Scriptures (p. 78) are usually included in the Bible under the title of "Old Testament." The Bible, from the Greek *biblia,* meaning "little books," is indeed a collection of little books: thirty-nine in the Old Testament and twenty-seven in the New Testament. The classification "Old Testament" is a Christian one that divides the Bible into the "old" covenant between God and his people and the "new" covenant (New Testament) established by Jesus with his followers. For religious Jews, there is still only one covenant. What Christians call the Old Testament, Jews call Tanach (*TANAK*) a word whose consonants stand for the three major groups of books in the Hebrew Bible: the Torah (the Law), the Nebi'im (the Prophets), and the Ketubim (the Writings).

As the all-time best-seller and the most translated book in the world — translated into most of the written languages on earth — the Bible is probably the single most influential book in Western history. As a history of ancient Judaism and early Christianity the Bible covers a period of about two thousand years, and for approximately two millennia the Bible, with its belief in a Father-God, its code of ethics, its attitude toward women, its view of history, and its prophecies for the future, has had an impact on all aspects of Western society. Although science has challenged the truth of certain portions of the Bible, it remains the basic religious document for about fifteen million Jews and for some two billion Christians throughout the world today. The Hebrew Scriptures are also a foundation document for Islam, which has approximately 1.2 billion followers. In addition to its influence on religion, the Bible as a literary document has had a pervasive influence on Western writing: from Dante's *Divine Comedy* and Chaucer's *Canterbury Tales* in the Middle Ages to the twentieth-century poetry of T. S. Eliot and W. H. Auden and the novels of William Faulkner and Toni Morrison.

Authorship and Archeology.   The authorship of the Hebrew Scriptures was once thought a simple matter. Some scholars, even into the twentieth century, thought that Moses wrote the Torah and the Book of Job, Joshua wrote the Book of Joshua, and Samuel wrote Samuel, Judges, and Ruth—in other words, that the names of the biblical books roughly indicated their authorship. But over the years textual scholars have noted stylistic differences, inconsistencies, and chronological oddities in the writings. A basic inconsistency, for example, is found in the first two creation stories in Genesis, in which the Hebrew names for God differ: His name in the first creation story (Genesis 1:1–2:3) is *Elohim;* His names, plural, in the second creation story, beginning with Genesis 2:4, are *Yahweh* and *Yahweh Elohim.* In the nineteenth century a document theory arose that stated that four major historical narrations were combined by editors to constitute the Torah, or Pentateuch (meaning "first five books"), as well as the Books of Joshua, Samuel, and Kings: the "J" document originating around 900 B.C.E.; the "E" document, from around 700 B.C.E.; the "D" document, from around 650 B.C.E.; and the "P" document, from around 500 B.C.E. These various strands were joined together and officially recognized around 400 B.C.E. by Ezra, a postexilic Jewish priest, or the school of Ezra. The entire Hebrew Bible was finally canonized at the Council of Jamnia, 90 C.E., when an official list of books was selected by religious leaders to be the official Jewish Scripture or Bible.

Several archeologists in recent decades have questioned the traditional account of Israel's history, maintaining that archeological evidence does not support the common dating of the exodus, the settlement of Canaan, and the Golden Age of a united kingdom under David and Solomon, with Jerusalem as its capital and Solomon's Temple on Temple Mount. At one extreme are literalists who believe that the events in the early books of the Hebrew Scriptures acutally happened as recorded. At the other extreme are biblical minimalists who assert that the Old Testament is a literary work created by writers and editors between the fifth and second centuries B.C.E., whose intent was to impose an ideological framework on Israel's history; they doubt that Moses, Joshua, David, and Solomon ever existed. A third group occupies a middle ground, maintaining that the Old Testament is largely the result of folk memory and is therefore a mixture of fact, fiction, and myth.

A number of biblical stories have become part of the cultural heritage of the West: Adam and Eve in the Garden of Eden, Noah and his ark, Joseph and his brothers. Stories about King David deal with his courage against Goliath, his friendship for Jonathan, and his indiscretions with Bathsheba. Whereas works of Western literature are almost always attributed to an individual author, the literature of the Hebrew Bible often seems the work of a collective voice, a community's songs and stories that tell about its sufferings, dreams, and joys. It is not a single hero who escapes the clutches of Egyptian slave masters but a whole people who assume heroic stature on their journey to the Promised Land. And even when an individual such as Job is speaking, the forceful debate of an entire intellectual community that has wrestled with the issues of God's justice and the meaning of suffering can be heard. Lyric poetry, which appears throughout the Bible, celebrates victories and laments sorrows. The Psalms remain the primary collection of biblical lyric poetry, but the Song of Songs is a masterpiece of image and metaphor that evokes the passion of love. The Book of Job is the one biblical work that resembles Greek drama. Both the Greeks and the Hebrews saw a world made up of conflict, adventure, and war, but focusing on obedience to God, the Hebrews participated in a spiritual odyssey with religious earnestness and conscience.

ANCIENT GREECE

While not as old as the civilizations of Mesopotamia and Egypt, Greece and Israel are still thought of as the "cradle of Western civilization." It is possible to trace a line of development from their ancient cultures on the Mediterranean Sea to Europe and present-day America. In the hands of the Greek poets, Greece's early gods and goddesses became not so much objects of worship as idealized models of human behavior, extending the boundaries of human possibilities; their epic heroes exemplified the strength, courage, and honor of the warrior. The Greeks invented philosophy and drama, and they were among the first peoples to write history. While other ancient cultures were deeply involved in organizing and controlling the general populace through military might and religious doctrine, Greek art celebrated the intelligence and beauty of the individual. As the Hebrews debated what it meant to be the "chosen people of God," the Greeks conceived of their cities as places where individuals might grow into their full potential as human beings. The Greek counterpart to Moses receiving God's laws on Mt. Sinai is Socrates in the marketplace discussing self-knowledge with his students.

The Early Greeks.   The Greeks, like other heroic societies, displayed an ongoing disposition for war; warfare was a continuous theme in their society, dating back to the invasion of the Greek peninsula in the second millennium B.C.E. when nomadic warriors called Achaeans brought with them male gods of war and a culture of domination. A different kind of influence on Greek culture came from the island of Crete, where, protected by the sea from the early invasions of the Indo-Europeans (or **ARYANS**), a prosperous goddess culture with labyrinthine palaces, bull rituals, and powerful priestesses developed from c. 3000–1500 B.C.E. The demise of that society, which has been called the Minoan civilization, around 1400 B.C.E. was probably caused by a combination of natural disasters—volcanic eruptions, earthquakes, and floods—and invasions from the mainland by a feudal, warrior people called the Myceneans. They took their name from the citadel at Mycenae, which was ruled by the legendary King Agamemnon sometime during the Mycenean Age (c. 1500–1100 B.C.E.).

These warriors were a blend of non-Hellenic, black-haired Cretans and Hellenic peoples from the north, Homer's "brown-haired Achaeans (Akhaians)." Their written language, labeled by scholars as Linear B, was an early form of Greek, and their religion integrated deities from Crete and northern Indo-European figures, resulting in a fusion of myths. The Myceneans lived in a series of fortress-cities, largely in the Peloponnesus, the southern portion of Greece. The Mycenean Age, also called the Heroic Age in Greek history, produced several warrior heroes of legendary stature. One of their most famous expeditions resulted in the destruction of Troy in northwestern Asia Minor about 1200 B.C.E.—the narrative material of Homer's great epics.

Shortly after the destruction of Troy, another group of Indo-Europeans, the Dorians, apparently conquered the Mycenean fortresses with their iron implements c. 1100 B.C.E., ending the Mycenean Age. A number of uprooted Greeks settled on the coast of Asia Minor, into regions that came to be known as Ionia and Aeolia, the legendary homeland of Homer.

The Athenian Polis.　　Just as major rivers determined the location of the earliest civilizations, geography played an important role in the culture of the Greek city-state, or POLIS. Greece comprises a mountainous peninsula and 1,600 islands, 169 of which are inhabited. The relative independence of the Greek city-states, isolated by mountains or water, fostered the growth of individualism, self-sufficiency, and freedom, ideals consistent with the heroic outlook. The ancient Greeks used water routes for trade as well as adventure. During the eighth and seventh centuries B.C.E., Greeks colonized numerous parts of the Mediterranean. When the production of wine and olive oil stimulated the growth of shipping and trade among the colonies, a merchant class came into being. To allay the threat of strife between nobles and peasants over the ownership of land, the institution of the "tyrant" arose in city-states like Athens and Corinth. Originally *tyrant* simply meant an individual who seized and held power without constitutional authority. Some tyrants, however, like Peisistratus in Athens, were good rulers who resolved civil conflict and economic problems; others were tyrants in the modern sense, seizing power and brutally maintaining it.

Athens was fortunate with its rulers. Towards the end of the seventh century B.C.E., Draco reformed the criminal justice system by replacing blood feuds or extended vendettas between families or clans with public trials. In 594 B.C.E., threatened by a worsening economy and a possible rebellion, Athens elected an extraordinary leader, or ARCHON, the philosopher-poet Solon. With the goals of allowing all citizens to participate in government and legally protecting the weak majority from the wealthy and stronger minority, Solon moved Athens in the direction of a community of free men. He promoted the growth of olives by banning the export of all other agricultural produce and by making the cutting down of an olive tree punishable by death. He then withdrew to Cyprus and Egypt to test whether his reforms would better Athenian life in his absence. When order broke down, Peisistratus, who traced his ancestry to Nestor—the Homeric king of Pylos—seized power and used force to protect Solon's reforms. He built temples and founded the great DIONYSIAC FESTIVALS, which probably led to the invention of drama. After a popular uprising brought Cleisthenes to power in 510 B.C.E., the Athenian city-state became a democracy. It was every citizen's duty to participate in the *polis;* citizenship, however, was limited to men and those born from citizen stock. Every citizen by definition was thought to be qualified for public office, and the use of slaves allowed wealthy citizens the time for public service. Under this model of democracy, which promoted a balance between communal commitment and personal freedom for male citizens, Athens prospered materially and artistically like no other Greek state.

The Golden Age.   After repulsing invasions by the Persians (490–479 B.C.E.), the Athenians grew confident in their military might and, dreaming of an empire, organized the Delian League, a naval confederacy. Supported by imperialism and tribute money from allies, the Golden Age of Athens dawned, an age characterized by an ingenious flowering of thought and culture. This Classical Age, with its sense of excellence and form, set standards in art and literature for generations to come. Pericles, who came to power in 461 B.C.E., began a building program to make Athens worthy of its international renown. A new Parthenon—or temple—with a towering statue of the goddess Athena crowned the Acropolis, the central citadel. Other buildings and works of art enhanced the beauty of schools and marketplaces. In his funeral oration (431 B.C.E.), Pericles described the qualities of judgment, harmony, and industry that characterized the Athenian ideal.

The rivalry between Athens and the city-state of Sparta in the southern Peloponnesus, stemming from a desire for economic and political control over the

A View of the Parthenon, 447–438 B.C.E.

Situated above Athens on the Acropolis, or "Sacred Rock," the Parthenon is an international symbol of the Golden Age of Greece and a reflection of its classical ideals. Dedicated to the goddess Athena, the Parthenon was built under the urging of Pericles and played important religious and civic roles in Greek society. (© Wolfgang Kaehler / CORBIS)

region, finally led to war. In the sixth century B.C.E., under the direction of its legendary lawgiver Lycurgus, Sparta had developed into a military state with a highly disciplined mercenary army supported by a serf class and became increasingly isolated from other city-states. By 500 B.C.E. Sparta dominated the Peloponnesus through a confederacy of allies called the Peloponnesian League. Although Sparta supported Athens in the wars against Persia, the competition with Athens heated up after the Persian navy was defeated at Plataea in 479 B.C.E. and Athens grew more powerful, finally resulting in the Peloponnesian War that lasted for some twenty-seven years, from 431–404 B.C.E. For the Athenians, Pericles' death, bad judgments, a disastrous invasion of Sicily, internal rebellions, and the desertion of allies all led to defeat in 404 B.C.E. Continuous warfare waged by thousands of Greek mercenaries led to the decline of the ideals of the *polis*. Despite its victory, Sparta eventually faded, defeated by Thebes in 371 B.C.E.

In 359 B.C.E. Philip II seized the royal reins of Macedonia, a region in the northern part of Greece. After defeating Athens at the battle of Chaeronea in 338 B.C.E.,

Philip controlled Greece through the Hellenic League until he was murdered in 336 B.C.E. Philip's plans were adopted by his twenty-year-old son Alexander, who led an army of four thousand men eastward, liberating the Greek cities of Asia Minor. He defeated the Persian army at the eastern Anatolian city of Issus in 333 B.C.E. and sent the King of Persia, Darius III, into a hasty retreat eastward across Persia. His brilliant military skills and heroic ambition led to the conquest of both Persia and Egypt. Although Alexander, whose favorite literary work was Homer's *Iliad*, died of a fever at the early age of thirty-two in Babylon, he did far more than simply reincarnate the mythical Achilles (Akhilleus) through his military triumphs in the ancient Near East. He opened wealthy Persia to Western trade and spread the Greek language and the ideals of Greek education and culture to the eastern Mediterranean world. He also founded the city of Alexandria in Egypt, whose libraries became extraordinarily important to philosophical and scientific learning.

Greek Literature.   The heroes of the Trojan War and all that they symbolized provided important themes for the whole of the classical age in Greece and Rome—be it for military, intellectual, or artistic endeavors. Homer's *The Iliad* (eighth century B.C.E.), the most well-known account of the war and the literary standard for epics ever since, focuses on the exploits of Achilles. With some nostalgia Homer depicts a heroic age four to five hundred years in the past and celebrates the patriarchal, feudal lifestyles of the Achaean warlords. Although savage at times, Achilles is nevertheless the epitome of the Greek hero and the heroic view of life: someone with superior mental and physical abilities who uses conquest and adventure to achieve honor and glory—the ultimate goals of his life. Throughout *The Iliad* (p. 537) the reader is made aware that while groups of men or whole armies are fighting over Helen and Troy, the real measure of heroism rests with individual warriors and their achievements.

In *The Odyssey* (p. 185), Homer expands the heroic model to include Odysseus's wily intelligence and imagination. Homer weaves Odysseus's return to Ithaca into a series of adventures and near-fatal encounters that test him both physically and mentally. Odysseus's affairs with Circe (Kirké) and Calypso (Kalypso) reveal both his strengths and frailties, a man whose desires sometimes conflict with his ideals. Odysseus never falters, however, when it comes to survival. Homer's Ionian audience from the west coast of Asia Minor was a FEUDAL ARISTOCRACY who likely identified with Odysseus, Achilles, and the warrior culture of the Myceneans. The subjects of fertility, sexuality, agriculture, and life after death, traditionally associated with goddesses and CHTHONIC, or underworld, rituals, were largely neglected by Homer; absent in his work also are most of the goddesses who had been prominent on Crete.

Centuries after Homer's heroic models first appeared they continued to inspire Greeks who strove for excellence and fame in the *polis* as well as on the battlefield.

Initially linked to war, the heroic code of honor came to stand for seeing life as a series of challenges that one must courageously face and overcome, for meeting each day forthrightly, whether one's challenges were intellectual, material, or political. Such an approach is reflected in this statement from Pericles' funeral oration: "[. . . we] place the real disgrace of poverty not in owning to the fact but in declining the struggle against it."

In addition to the epic, Greek poets also achieved excellence in the LYRIC, poems that were accompanied by a lyre, employed a variety of meters, and expressed personal feelings about topics like love and death. The lyric, sung by a single performer, was distinguished from choral poetry, which was sung by a chorus and danced. The earliest Greek lyric poets, Sappho (p. 560), Terpander, and Alcaeus, lived on the island of Lesbos in the seventh century B.C.E. Sappho's genius was recognized by her contemporaries and those who followed, who regarded her as the "Tenth Muse," after the nine muses of Greek mythology; unfortunately, like the work of other lyric poets, most of her poems have been lost. By the time Roman poets inherited the genre of the lyric, the lyre was no longer used for accompaniment; there is a large sampling of extant lyrics by Roman poets like Catullus (p. 793), Horace, and Propertius.

An Age of Unusual Creativity.   The world's first generally literate society developed in the city-states of Greece and Ionia during the sixth and fifth centuries B.C.E. As a result, citizens involved in public life were increasingly expected to be able to read and write. Artists, thinkers, and writers were drawn in particular to the intellectual and creative ferment of Athens. Although the ancient Greeks undoubtedly borrowed habits of mind and systems of knowledge from earlier civilizations, such as the priestly wisdom of Egypt, theirs was a unique passion for thinking and philosophy, matched only perhaps by the "hundred philosophers" in China, c. fourth century B.C.E. Departing somewhat from the popular Greek stories of gods and goddesses and the folk festivals of the time, intellectuals began to examine the social and physical world, speculate about its composition, and arrive at theories independent of religious tradition or institutions. Greek writers largely invented new literary forms and executed them brilliantly. Herodotus (p. 957) and Thucydides (p. 700), for example, invented the writing of history. Herodotus is considered the "Father of History" in the Western tradition, and Thucydides one of its earliest practitioners. Plato (p. 715) and Aristotle (p. 747) in the fourth century B.C.E. broadened the Greek tradition of philosophical and scientific writing begun by earlier thinkers of the sixth and fifth centuries like Heraclitus, Empedocles, and Pythagorus—the first man to call himself a *philosopher*, meaning a "lover of wisdom."

In the fifth century B.C.E., Attic tragedy, with its roots in religious ritual, became central to the festival life of the city. Although the exact origins of Greek drama are still debated, Aristotle maintained it began with the DITHYRAMB, or choral ode, used in religious ceremonies focusing on the figure of Dionysus. Greek comedy (from *komos,* "revel") probably originated in phallic ceremonies and fertility rites, while tragedy (from *tragoidia,* meaning "goat-song") first had to do with the Dionysian themes of death and resurrection enacted by a chorus dressed as goats or satyrs—figures sacred to Dionysus. Drama evolved from a dialogue between a leader and a chorus that gradually introduced additional speakers and eliminated the chorus. Tradition holds that the Greek playwright Aeschylus (525–456 B.C.E.) added a second actor for genuine dialogue; he also brought in costumes, masks, and thick-soled boots to "elevate" the action.

On the stages of Athens, the heroic legacy of Homer was questioned, revised, and adjusted to fit urban responsibilities. The great themes of the Trojan War were the subjects of Greek plays that were performed at the two major Athenian festivals in honor of Dionysus: the Lenaea in January and February, and the Great Dionysia in March and April, at which dramatists were awarded prizes by a jury. Most Greek cities, even some small ones, had outdoor theaters and valued the psychological and social roles that drama could play in civic life.

Aeschylus (p. 575), the first great tragedian, explored human suffering and the complexities of human relationships through the legends of the House of Atreus and its curse—the underlying family saga for the Trojan War. In *The Oresteia,* Aeschylus prepares his audience for civic duty by submitting Orestes' murder of his mother to a newly created court system, thus interrupting the cyclical pattern of blood revenge. The *Oresteia* ends with a hymn to the newly constituted political and judicial system, a patriarchal system that muffles the powerful feminine Furies by transforming them into the Eumenides—the "gracious ones." Sophocles (496–406 B.C.E.) uses a different cycle of stories to create a tragic hero in *Oedipus Rex* and a new kind of strong, proud heroine in *Antigone* (p. 645), a play that explores the conflicting demands of loyalty to family and civic obedience. Ever since Homer, who depicted the glory as well as the suffering of combat, there had been an ambivalence about the personal and social consequences of war among Greece's artists and thinkers. With the character of Antigone, Sophocles showed how militarism could lead to personal tragedy.

The Peloponnesian War brought about important changes in Athenian society. Disillusionment with the social upheaval resulting from the war upset the balance between the individual and the state by questioning whether democracy and the ideal city-state were indeed workable. Methods of argumentation taught by professional teachers, known as SOPHISTS, were seen as undermining traditional, civic values and promoting individual cleverness and skepticism. The most renowned teacher of the time, Socrates (c. 470–399 B.C.E.), was seen as further weakening the appeal of civic responsibility through his teachings on personal knowledge and the inner voice, even though he himself had served in the army as a HOPLITE and had been elected to the Council, a body that prepared the political agenda for the general Assembly to which all citizens were welcome. In the unstable atmosphere of the war's aftermath and the decline of Athens, charges were brought against Socrates, who in Plato's work, *Apology* (p. 720), questions whether personal honesty is compatible with public service. He was convicted and sentenced to death in 399 B.C.E. Socrates's most famous pupil, Plato (c. 427–347 B.C.E.), founded a school, Academy, in 387 B.C.E. His own star pupil was Aristotle (384–322 B.C.E.), the philosopher who conceived of logic and then used it to codify human knowledge.

ANCIENT CHINA

The richness of China's cultural heritage results from a vast country with numerous tribes, languages, and dialects. Nevertheless, early in its history it began to develop a national identity centered around the Chinese language, which is one of the world's oldest surviving languages. Because the written language was separated from the phonetic or spoken value of the Chinese characters, people from various regions of the country who might speak different dialects could share a common written language, a common heritage, and identity. Supplementing the common language is a body of literature. Early on the Chinese established an identity through the continuous reworking of a literary tradition that over the centuries created and preserved a cultural coherence. This has presented a problem for historians; although there are written records for history prior to Confucius in the sixth century B.C.E., there was such doctoring of texts that it has been difficult to reconstruct with accuracy ancient Chinese history.

Chinese civilization is thought to have developed in the Yellow River basin and along the river's tributaries, completely separate from other riverine civilizations along the Tigris and Euphrates, Nile and Indus Rivers. Because of mountains, deserts, and sea, China was relatively isolated from the rest of Asia. Millet, a hardy grain, was the basis of an agricultural surplus that provided for the growth of cities and the rudiments of political organization. Unlike the civilizations of Mesopotamia, Egypt, Israel, Greece, and India, China did not assemble creation myths about the origins of the cosmos or stories about deities who informed the primordial origins of Chinese civilization. Mythic creators like P'an Ku are a product of a much later period, the Han dynasty (third century C.E.). Instead, the cultural histories are accounts of legendary men, fabled emperors and culture heroes from a

www For more information about the culture and context of Greece in the ancient world, see bedfordstmartins.com/worldlitcompact.

**Ritual Vessel,
500–450 B.C.E.**
*The ding, a three-
legged vessel, held
food offered to
ancestral spirits.
Symbols and written
characters were
usually cast onto
its surface. This
particular example
shows highly abstract
and stylized animal-
like and geometric
elements. (Los
Angeles County
Museum of Art, Gift
of Mr. and Mrs.
Lidow. Photograph
© 2003 Museum
Associates/LACMA)*

golden age of China—figures who became the cultural models or paradigms for
succeeding generations. An early sage Fu Xi (Fu His) is believed to have invented
fishing nets and the basic symbols for the *I Jing (I Ching),* the *Book of Changes,* the
central collection of oracles which connect the basic principles of the cosmos to
individual decisions. The great Yu, founder of the Xia (Hsia) dynasty (early second
millennium B.C.E.) is credited in the *Shu Jing (Book of History)* with solving the
problem of flooding by devising an elaborate irrigation system during the Shang
dynasty (c. 1600–c. 1028 B.C.E.), the first historical dynasty. The Shang people were
a complex agricultural society that developed a bureaucracy, a writing system, and
the rudiments of ancestor worship—the core religion of the Chinese household.
The Chinese incorporated ancestral worship into the concept of filial piety—the
reverence of children for their parents—by making the male head of the family or
clan responsible for periodic ceremonies and offerings of food before the ancestral
tablets, such as on the anniversaries of the passing of the deceased. Later, the philosopher Confucius (Kongfuzi, 551–479 B.C.E.) defined filial piety as the worship of
parents (alive or dead) and made it the foundation of both family and civic life.

Chinese Dynasties.   The Chinese conceived of their history in terms of a series of
dynasties, each of which began with a powerful family that established a powerful
government supported by the Mandate of Heaven. Heaven or *t'ien* appears to be a

universal moral order that actively shapes history; when a particular dynasty disintegrated into evil practices and immorality, it was overthrown. The Zhou rulers
of the eleventh century B.C.E., for example, explained the overthrowing of the previous Shang dynasty in these terms: when the dynasty ruled with an absence of
virtue, it became the will of heaven to change rulers—despite the relative power
of the two factions. Dynastic stability was also punctuated by peasant revolts and
nomadic invasions from the Asia steppes. The Zhou people came from western
China, and guided by the founders of the Zhou dynasty (c. 1027–221 B.C.E.), King
Qu and King Ch'eng, took control of the Yellow River basin and consolidated the
region into a central state. Duke Zhou, Wu's younger brother and regent to King
Ch'eng, instituted feudalism by appointing "lords" to rule over large plots of land,
in return for service to the emperor. For the next few centuries a strong central
government prevailed in the region. To avoid conflict, very strict rules about the
succession of rulers were drawn up; only the first son of a legal wife could succeed
the father. The emperor was the "father" of the Chinese people, who had a divine
"Mandate of Heaven" to govern as long as he was a virtuous ruler; the Zhou had
been able to overthrow the previous Shang rule because of their corruption. Laws
that later inspired Confucian thinkers accumulated under the Zhou ruler.

Chinese historians refer to the years c. 403–221 B.C.E. as the Warring States
Period, an extended period of political and social upheaval as well as philosophical
controversy; it was also a time of great productivity and intellectual ferment, the
time of the "hundred philosophers." China's philosophical systems were divided
over the methods of effective government, whether political systems could be
repaired or not. On the one hand there was Confucius and Confucian teachers like
Mencius (Mengzi, c. 371–c. 288 B.C.E.) (p. 706) who developed an ideal social
theory consisting of a hierarchical structure held together by duty and authority.
In Confucius' collected sayings, *The Analects* (p. 570), he explains the fundamental
structure of harmonious, respectful family relationships, the model of which can
then be extended into the realm of rulers and subjects. Mencius further believed
that the innate goodness of human beings could provide the basis for a caring
society if government provided a moral context for this possibility.

On the other hand, the philosopher Mozi (Mo Tzu) from the fifth century
B.C.E. preached universal love, proposing that love for one's family could be the
glue that held society together. But the real radical alternative philosophy to
Confucian public service was Daoism. The basic texts of Daoism are the five-
thousand-character *Dao de Jing* (*Tao Te Ching*, p. 699) by Laozi (Lao Tzu, c. sixth
to third century B.C.E.), called the "Bible" of Daoism, and the writings of Zhuangzi
(Chuang Tzu, p. 783). By the time of Zhuangzi (fourth century B.C.E.), the Daoist
disdain for political power and public office was overtly competitive with

Confucianism. The Daoist reaction to the endless wars and political intrigue was to declare war as futile and wasteful.

By the second century B.C.E., Confucianism had become official doctrine in China, and it remains so today, having survived attempts to discredit it or to reduce it to rigid, unworkable dogma. Despite the inherent conservatism of Confucianism, which emphasizes filial piety (respect and loyalty on the part of children for their parents and ancestors), dutiful respect for authority, and deference to tradition, it has influenced various democratic movements in the East as well as the West. In terms of sheer numbers, no social philosophy focusing on standards of conduct for individuals, families, and governments has influenced more people in the history of the world than Confucianism.

ANCIENT INDIA

Developing in the Indus Valley around 2600 B.C.E., somewhat later than the birth of Mesopotamia and Egypt, Indian civilization became home to a complex and influential culture, including three major religions. India's largest body of artistic and literary material is associated with **HINDUISM**, both a religion and a total way of life with an extended history of some 3,000 years that is still part of a living culture today — probably the longest continuous religious tradition in the world. Hinduism, which originated with the Vedas — a sacred collection of hymns and rituals — is not a single religion, but a large, loose confederation of beliefs and practices ranging from simple fertility rites to a highly sophisticated philosophical **MONISM**, a belief that tries to explain things in terms of a single principle.

Great diversity in India resulted from an unusual mix of Aryan invaders and indigenous cultures in the second millennium B.C.E. A large **PANTHEON** of deities and an elaborate **COSMOLOGY** were coordinated with a unique, highly structured society that has largely remained the same throughout millennia. When doctrines and practices during the **BRAHMANIC PERIOD** (c. 1000–600 B.C.E.) became too rigid, two additional world religions were spawned, **BUDDHISM** and **JAINISM**, founded by Gautama Buddha (563–483 B.C.E.) and Mahavira (died c. 468 B.C.E.), respectively. A substantial body of religious literature has sustained the people of the Indian subcontinent; magnificent hymns and epics, which, like the Greek epics of Homer, have been continuing sources of plot and characters as retold and reinvented in plays, poems, film, fiction, and comic books even to the present day.

The Indus Valley.   The earliest civilization in India took hold along the Indus River in northwestern India in an area that today is mostly part of Pakistan. The Indus Valley civilization occupied a territory about the size of Texas, stretching almost a thousand miles from the Arabian Sea north to the Himalayan foothills

and east to today's city of New Delhi. Only archeological remains are left of this civilization's highly structured and deeply spiritual people, who developed a standardized system of weights and measures, brick architecture, elaborate granaries, drainage systems, a pictographic script, and a number of thriving villages. Its two most famous cities, some three hundred fifty miles apart, are Mohenjo-Daro in the south and Harappa in the north—a name borrowed from a modern town. Both of these cities are thought to have flourished about the same time, from 2600 to 1500 B.C.E., and had approximately thirty-five thousand inhabitants each, although some recent archaeology now dates the founding of Harappa around 3300 B.C.E.

The people of ancient India used sea trade, especially with Mesopotamia, to supplement their living from the land and their agricultural surplus. Like Mesopotamia a few centuries earlier, the Indus cities developed a writing system, of which thousands of samples have been unearthed but so far undeciphered— a fact that accounts for the scarcity of information about Harappan culture. The absence of great temples and tombs in the civilization's remains such as were found in Mesopotamia and Egypt suggest a corresponding absence of a powerful kingship. Moreover, few weapons and no representations of warfare have been found, indicating the sense of security felt by this civilization, which lasted more than a thousand years. Based on the similarity of its men's and women's graves, scholars

Terracotta Vase with Goat, 2000 B.C.E. *Although not much is known about the Indus Valley civilization, this beautifully crafted and painted vase from the ancient city of Mohenjo-Daro suggests a highly advanced culture. (The Art Archive)*

have speculated that Harappa was an egalitarian, middle-class society made up of traders, merchants, craftsmen, and artists. As in other agricultural societies, Harappa's religion appears to have focused on fertility. Seals found at Harappa show a god wearing bull's horns seated in a yogic position with an erect phallus, a prototype for the later god Shiva, the lord of yoga in Hinduism. Images of fertility goddesses depict plants growing out of the wombs of the female deities.

The Aryan Invasion and the Vedic Age (c. 1500–c. 700 B.C.E.).   Early in the second millennium B.C.E. Aryans, nomadic tribes from the steppes of southern Russia and the grasslands of central Asia, swept in waves across ancient settlements. One group descended southeast into the Indus Valley. Historians originally called these tribes "Aryans" because the people who spoke Sanskrit were known as "Aryas"; Sanskrit was thought to be the parent language of all languages in the West. Later it was decided that there had to be an older language, called Indo-European or Indo-Germanic, from which Sanskrit had been derived. Other Indo-European groups, called Achaeans and Dorians, migrated northwest and invaded Greece in the second millennium B.C.E. They later moved into Italy and, finally, England.

The Aryans were light-skinned, hard-drinking warriors who used bows and arrows, bronze axes, and chariots drawn by pairs of horses to overrun the Harappan civilization and conquer a people who spoke a non–Indo-European language known as Dravidian, which includes the Tamil and Malayalam tongues. The Aryans called these indigenous people by the derogatory name *Dashyus,* which at first meant "enemies" but thereafter consistently meant "dark skinned." Aryans borrowed and assimilated parts of the Dravidian culture. Large numbers of the dark-skinned Dravidians were driven south into the Indian peninsula and Sri Lanka, where their descendants live today.

Ancient scriptures called the Vedas, which means "sacred knowledge," are the only known source of information about the next thousand years. Composed in Sanskrit, the Aryans' language, the Vedas describe a pantheon of warrior deities led by the god Indra, the wielder of the thunderbolt, whose roots were in nature but who were models for warrior chieftains. The Aryans had brought with them their language, a strongly patriarchal culture, and a sense of superiority; embodied in Vedic mythology is the imperative of racial separation and the "caste" system, which eventually became fixed in the social fabric of India. Initially, the Kshatriyas, or warriors, who occupied the top rung of the social ladder, were the governing caste. Next were the Brahmins, or the priestly caste; the Vaishya, the financial caste of merchants, farmers, and producers; and the Shudras, the laboring caste—the hands and feet for all those above them. Caste determined (and determines) not only one's occupation but one's dietary laws and one's circle of friends as well; it determines how and whom one may marry. Over centuries, the number of societal groups multiplied with the creation of several thousand subgroups.

The Brahmins and Literacy.   The warriors eventually relinquished control of the Vedas to the priestly class, the Brahmins, who took charge of religious ritual by singing the appropriate hymns contained in the Rig Veda (p. 159)—the oldest Veda dating from c. 1000 B.C.E. The **BRAHMANIC PERIOD** (c. 1000–600 B.C.E.) refers to the latter part of the Vedic Age when the Brahmins grew more powerful and gradually rose to the top of the caste system. Brahmins became the official guardians of the Vedas, and for a time they forbade the writing down of the texts. The hymns themselves were passed down orally from father to son for a thousand years. The Brahmins adapted the Aramaic alphabet, a branch of Phoenician, to Sanskrit, and produced what is called the Brahmi script. They then violently kept other castes from having contact with written texts. A Shudra convicted of reciting the Vedas would have his tongue split; if he possessed a written text, he was cut in two.

Shiva, 800–1000 c.e.
Shiva the Destroyer is here represented as Lord of the Dance. The ring of fire that surrounds him represents the cosmos, and the dwarf that he's stepping on represents ignorance. (The Art Archive/ Musée Guimet, Paris/ Dagli Orti)

The Brahmins also became the official interpreters of the Vedas by writing the *Brahmanas,* or *Works of the Brahmins,* the earliest of which is dated about 800 b.c.e. In the *Brahmanas,* the Vedas are elevated to eternal truths that can be understood only by the Brahmins themselves. Earlier nature deities were redefined and arranged into a new hierarchy. At the same time there was a search for the supreme deity and a questioning of whether the new deity, Brahma, was one of the old gods or a truly new one. Eventually a trinity took over: Brahman, the universal spirit, comprises Brahma, the creator; Vishnu, the preserver; and Shiva, the destroyer.

During attempts to systematize the divine pantheon, the numbers of deities actually increased; it seems as if no deity was ever really discarded. The Brahmins became the medium through which the bounty of the gods flowed. The core of their religion, Hinduism, involved the recitation of the Vedas and the performance of fire-sacrifices involving the sacred drug soma. Later, milk and curds were added. During the Brahmanic Period sacrifices changed from acts of reverence to essential acts ensuring the continuance of the cosmos.

The Heroic Age (c. 550 B.C.E.–100 C.E.).   The Heroic Age gave rise to two great literary epics that paint a vivid picture of Indian life from 1000 to 500 B.C.E., when the Aryans ceased to live as nomads and created villages. Written in Sanskrit, the *Rāmāyana* (p. 549) and the *Mahabharata* were edited and revised for a period of some nine hundred years, from c. 550 B.C.E. to 400 C.E. Called *itihasa* (historical narrative), these works deal with the period when settlements eastward, along the Ganges River, slowly expanded into numerous small kingdoms and the foundations of rule in Indian royal houses were laid. The *Rāmāyana* of Valmiki, an epic of twenty-four thousand verses, is the story of prince Rama of Kosala, his exile and adventures. The *Mahabharata (War of the Descendants of Bharata)* by Vyasa, in about one hundred thousand verses (ten times longer than *The Iliad* and *The Odyssey* combined), tells the story of a civil war between clans while interweaving extensive legends, royal histories, and caste law. The *Mahabharata* includes the very popular Bhagavad Gita (p. 928), or *Song of the Gods*. Like Homer's epics, the *Rāmāyana* and the *Mahabharata* have conveyed values as well as themes for art and literature—most recently, for television and film. Unlike the Homeric epics, however, the *Rāmāyana* and *Mahabharata* are considered sacred texts, providing religious and moral guidance for Hindus even today.

Buddhism and Jainism.   At about the same time that the Brahmin class gained exclusive control of the social machinery of Hinduism in the sixth and fifth centuries B.C.E., a group of sages instigated a reform movement to challenge the dominance of Hinduism. Coming to the fore during a time of great ferment and change in the northeastern provinces of Bihar and Uttar Pradesh, these men criticized the Brahmin priests and their preoccupation with ceremony and sacrifice, teaching instead that knowledge and austerities could lead directly to identification with the universal spirit or world soul. Two great religions were born in India during this period, Buddhism and Jainism. Buddhism was founded by Siddhartha Gautama, or the Buddha (563–483 B.C.E.), and Jainism by Mahavira (c. 539–468 B.C.E.).

The Maurya Empire (c. 322–c. 185 B.C.E.).   After his death, the Buddha's
teachings spread throughout India. One of Buddhism's high points occurred
during the reign of the emperor Ashoka (c. 273–c. 232 B.C.E.). India was first
unified by Chandragupta Maurya (r. 322–297 B.C.E.), whose movement
originated in the state of Magadha, in the Ganges basin. Ashoka, the third ruler
of the Maurya empire, converted to Buddhism, erected monasteries, and sent
missionaries to Syria, Egypt, and Greece. With its abundant prosperity and a
flourishing of art, Ashoka's reign was considered a golden age in ancient India.
In 185 B.C.E. the Maurya empire fell and fragmented into small states; India
would not be united again until the Gupta dynasty (320–c. 550 B.C.E.). The third
Gupta king, Chandragupta II, brought about India's second golden age.

ANCIENT ROME

According to legend, Romulus, the mythic son of Mars and Rhea Silvia, founded
Rome in 753 B.C.E., but the Romans ultimately traced their ancestry to a survivor
of the Trojan War, Aeneas, who wandered the Mediterranean Sea and eventually
arrived on Italy's shores, a journey recounted in Virgil's classic epic, *The Aeneid*.
From the eighth to the third centuries B.C.E., Rome's history was characterized by
rivalries among various factions and the conquest of neighboring armies. By using
alliances and military might, Rome gained control of the entire Italian peninsula
by 270 B.C.E. Beyond its borders, Rome became involved in a protracted hundred-
year war (264–146 B.C.E.) with the nearby North African city of Carthage, known as
the PUNIC WARS. The term *punic* comes from the Greek for Phoenicians, who were
the original settlers at Carthage under the leadership of Hamilcar Barca and his
two sons, Hannibal and Hasdrubal.

Victory over Carthage, which had dominated the central Mediterranean
since the seventh century B.C.E., made Rome the undisputed ruler of the western
Mediterranean. Rome then began to look further beyond its shores and became an
empire by conquering Sicily, Sardinia, Corsica, Spain, and North Africa as well as a
section of Macedonia. Unlike Athens, Rome had a rather enlightened foreign
policy; it encouraged the residents of conquered tribes and cities to become
Roman citizens with all the privileges and protections that that entailed.

The Republic.   According to legend, Rome was ruled by a succession of seven
kings from 753 to 509 B.C.E. Although details of this period are lacking, it is
known that the kings created an advisory body, the Senate, which survived for

WWW   For more information about the culture and context of India and Rome in the
ancient world, see bedfordstmartins.com/worldlit compact.

two thousand years—through monarchy, a republic, and imperial rule. A legend
of rape and revolt is told in connection with the creation of a Roman republic
in 509 B.C.E.: the son of King Tarquin is said to have raped a socialite named
Lucretia, who then committed suicide. Led by Lucius Junius Brutus, the
Liberator, Lucretia's family and friends drove out King Tarquin and established
a republic to prevent further abuse of power. Rome was then a republic ruled
by twin consuls, a Senate and a popular Assembly. The two consuls served for
one year and took turns ruling, alternating monthly. A fasces, a bundle of rods
enclosing an ax, was used in consul processions, symbolizing the consuls' power
to scourge and execute. (Fasces later became the symbol of the twentieth-century
Italian Fascists.) Ancient Roman society was divided into two classes. The elite
PATRICIANS (from *patres,* meaning "fathers") were the heads of the oldest families
who occupied the Senate. The PLEBEIANS, the general populace and lower class,
made up the Assembly. The next two hundred years saw a power struggle
between these two classes. With the patricians numbering only about one
hundred thirty families in the early republic, the plebeians sometimes exploited
their majority status to gain power by refusing services, such as serving their
time in the army. It wasn't until 287 B.C.E. that the Assembly gained the power
to make laws. The uneven distribution of wealth and power led to civil wars
and slave revolts that threatened the growing empire from within.

Finally, in the first century B.C.E., a civil war resulted in a division of power
between Pompey, whose power lay in the east, and Julius Caesar, who had spread
Roman rule to the west with his Gallic wars. These two leaders were temporarily
joined by Crassus to make up the First Triumvirate in 60 B.C.E. A war between
Pompey, favored by the senatorial party, and Caesar, leader of the popular party,
ended with Caesar's victory at Pharsala in 48 B.C.E. The Roman historian Suetonius
(75–160 C.E.) credited Julius Caesar with correcting the calendar—the Julian calendar—and with numerous public projects, but praised him above all for his
brilliance as a military commander: "He was perfect in the use of arms, an accomplished rider, and able to endure fatigue beyond all belief."

Shortsighted conspirators, upset by Caesar's aggregation of power and dreaming of the return of the old republic, arranged for Caesar's assassination in 44 B.C.E.,
plunging Rome into another thirteen years of civil war. Caesar's nephew and
adopted son, Gaius Julius Caesar Octavianus, joined forces with Mark Antony and
Lepidus to form the Second Triumvirate in 43 B.C.E. Together they ventured into
Greece to defeat Caesar's murderers, Brutus and Cassius, at Philippi in 42 B.C.E.,
resulting in a division of the Roman world between the east and the west. Mixing
love and politics, Antony joined forces with Cleopatra, queen of Egypt, while
Octavian eliminated his rivals and consolidated his forces in the west. The

Pont du Gard, 19 B.C.E.

A happy result of the Roman love of water and building, the Pont du Gard straddles the river Gard, and is an outstanding example of Roman engineering. Water was brought into Nimes (a Roman city in what is now southern France) via an aqueduct, of which the Pont du Gard is only a small part, through a series of aboveground and underground channels. (© Adam Woolfitt / CORBIS)

seemingly inevitable battle between Antony and Cleopatra and Octavian occurred at Actium in 31 B.C.E.; defeated, Antony and Cleopatra fled to Egypt, where they committed suicide. Uniting an empire that stretched from the Straits of Gibraltar to Palestine, Octavian took the name Augustus, established a constitutional monarchy, and inaugurated the Augustan Age, a golden age of art and literature.

Pax Romana **and Roman Society.**   The term *PAX ROMANA* refers to the unprecedented two hundred years of relative peace that began with Augustus and ended with the emperor Marcus Aurelius (161–180 C.E.), a time when resources could be devoted to peaceful projects rather than to armaments and war. Throughout their vast empire, the Romans built roads, bridges, aqueducts, baths, sewers, and public buildings. Undergirding their bureaucratic system was a concept of universal law rooted in Nature, which declared the equality of all men and protected the individual against the state. This ideal of law lifted justice from the prerogative of local or tribal powers to an impersonal, universal legal structure that included all inhabitants of an expanding empire. This law, which embraced the ideal of a free society, was Rome's greatest contribution to Western civilization. The Romans systematized education, inculcating the Latin virtues of *PIETAS* (duty), *GRAVITAS* (seriousness), and *AMOR IMPERII* (love of empire). Symbolizing this state religion was the emperor Augustus, who was given the title *pater patriae*, Father of the Country, in 2 B.C.E. This Roman religion of patriotism produced the man of letters, the man of politics, the man of the world embodied in such figures as the great statesman and philosopher Cicero (106–43 B.C.E.), the poet Horace (65–8 B.C.E.), and the writer and statesman Pliny the Younger (c. 62–c. 113 C.E.).

Romans appeared to be as organized in the home as they were in the public arena. They valued family life highly and made the eldest male in every

Female Artist, 50–79 B.C.E.
Women had many freedoms in Roman society. Here, a female artist paints a portrait under the watchful gaze of two friends. (The Art Archive/Archaeological Museum Naples/Dagli Orti)

household — the *pater familias* — the authority over all important matters, including marriage, religion, fidelity, dowries — even life and death. As in Greece, it was a civic duty in the empire to have children. Although upper-class women played subordinate roles to men, they were not sequestered in their homes as Athenian women seem to have been. Through birth control and abortion, they freed themselves from bearing children continuously and developed lives outside the home. They shopped in markets and attended festivals and dinner parties with their husbands. Women were allowed to attend elementary school; some were educated by private tutors to become musicians, poets, and artists. Although they were given no true political positions and only honorary titles, they were some- times highly influential behind the scenes. By the second century C.E., women were involved in business, sports, and the arts; they also chose their own marriage partners.

Under Rome's later rulers, Tiberius, Caligula, and Claudius I (first century C.E.), the empire stretched from Britain to Mesopotamia, the largest empire in the history of the West up to that time. Nevertheless, the period between 14 C.E. and 96 C.E. was filled with the insanity of Emperors Nero and Caligula, the burning of Rome, the defeat of a Jewish uprising, the destruction of Jerusalem, and the ongoing persecution of a new religious sect calling themselves Christians. The period from 96 to 180 C.E. — under the reigns of Nerva, Trajan, Hadrian, Antoninus Pius, and Marcus Aurelius — was a peaceful period. Something, however, seems to have been missing in the personal lives of the people, many of whom increasingly turned to imported mystery religions for spiritual purpose and direction. These religions promised communion with a messiah and a future paradise as compensa- tion for suffering and despair.

In the third century, the empire was weakened by an internal east-west divi- sion. Constantine, who granted official tolerance to the new Christian sect in 313 and later converted to Christianity himself, moved his capital to Constantinople in the east. Invaders from the north increasingly penetrated the frontiers of the empire, until finally Rome was sacked by Alaric and his Visigoths in 410. The Roman Empire in the west formally came to an end when the barbarian Odoacer replaced the last emperor, Romulus Augustulus, in 476 C.E.

Roman Literature.   The Latin alphabet, which was to become the script for English and other Western European languages, was developed from the Greek language by way of the Etruscans around the sixth century B.C.E. The Etruscans adjusted a number of Greek vowels and consonants in order to spell the many names and words borrowed from the Greek during the imperial Roman period.

Latin became the dominant language in Europe for some two millennia. As the official liturgical language of Christianity until the Reformation in the sixteenth century and the language of scholars, Latin was spread throughout medieval Europe through the agency of the Roman Catholic Church.

In literature as well as in their PANTHEON of deities, Rome was indebted to ancient Greece and to the many cultures it encountered throughout its empire. Lucretius (c. 99–c. 55 B.C.E.), for example, wrote his lengthy poem, *On the Nature of Things,* using the theories of the Greek philosopher Epicurus (c. 341–270 B.C.E.). From the time of his *Eclogues* (37 B.C.E.), Virgil, the most famous poet of the Roman Empire, was well known at Augustus's court and was probably beginning to plan the epic poem that would do for Rome what Homer's epics had done for Greece — namely, the creation of mythic-historic roots. In *The Aeneid* (p. 809), Virgil seeks to create a founding myth of Rome's origins that will celebrate Augustus's accomplishments and support a vision of Rome's world mission. Though modeled after Homer's *The Odyssey,* the travails of Aeneas's own journey through the Mediterranean reflect in miniature the labors undertaken by Roman Senators, legions, and slaves to create the empire. Understanding the anxiety that Roman intellectuals felt about the impending end of an age, Virgil attempts to allay the fears of his Roman audience through Jupiter, who says: "I set no limits to their fortunes and / no time; I give them empire without end." Later, in Book 4, Virgil creates a new hero by portraying Aeneas with psychological depth and complexity in his relationship with Dido, the queen of Carthage. After the publication of *The Aeneid,* Augustus was designated the second founder of Rome, a realm that for a time was called the *urbs aeterna* (the eternal city). The Greek *POLIS* had been expanded by Rome into a grand COSMOPOLIS.

Both Catullus (c. 84–c. 54 B.C.E.) and Ovid (43 B.C.E.–17 C.E.) wrote personal poems as well as poems on mythical subjects. Catullus (p. 793), in particular, is remembered for his love poems, with their expression of sensitive feeling and their portrayal of the pangs of rejection and despair. Ovid, the first century poet laureate of love under Augustus, is best known for his *Metamorphoses* (p. 168), a compendium of Greek and Roman myths. The ancient stories of gods and goddesses that had once been used to illustrate the spiritual mysteries of life became, in Ovid's skillful hands, the marvelously entertaining materials of literature. He concluded the *Metamorphoses* with the prediction, "My fame shall live to all eternity"; and so far he has not been proven wrong, influencing a long line of poets, including Dante, Petrarch, Chaucer, Shakespeare, Alexander Pope, and T. S. Eliot.

Unlike the arts of sculpture and ceramics in ancient Rome, which owed a distinct and direct debt to Hellenistic models, Latin writers achieved a unique excellence because of the Latin language, which was suited to the musicality and concision of Latin poetry and prose. While we envision the Romans as grounded in reality and concerned with the promotion and protection of empire, Latin writers, in addition to political themes, explored human relationships, especially those between men and women, with great honesty and sensitivity. It is certainly appropriate to call the epoch which included Virgil, Cicero, Ovid, and Catullus the Golden Age of Latin Literature.

❧ THE EPIC OF GILGAMESH
MESOPOTAMIA, C. 2000–C. 1200 B.C.E.

www   For a quiz on *The Epic of Gilgamesh,* see bedfordstmartins .com/worldlit compact.

The Epic of Gilgamesh is the most influential literary epic to come out of ancient Mesopotamia. It narrates the journey of Gilgamesh, a young king of Uruk, whose search for solace from despair and human mortality leads to the threshold of life itself. Although the story is more than four millennia old and from a culture long past, Gilgamesh is familiar; he is an individual, a person with deep feelings who treats life as an adventure, makes mistakes, battles giants, grieves for the death of a friend, and embarks on a long quest into the unknown in search of a way out of the pain of loss and the meaning of life. Gilgamesh is someone with whom a modern reader can sympathize, even identify. It is the kind of story that resonated throughout Mesopotamia and continued to influence regional literature long after the conquest of Babylonia by the Persians in 539 B.C.E.

This narration is called an EPIC because it contains the basic features of the form later established as standard by Homer:[1] a hero of national stature performing extraordinary deeds in a world setting, whose mortal challenges and triumphs are associated with the immortal arena of gods and goddesses. Unlike Homer's epics, however, which were performed or recited at religious and literary festivals, it is not clear that the Gilgamesh narration was ever used for the purpose of ritual or entertainment. Lines from the beginning of *The Epic of Gilgamesh* suggest a didactic role for the story, that Gilgamesh's adventures were intended to instruct: "He went on a distant journey, pushing himself to exhaustion, / but then was brought to peace. / He carved on a stone stela all of his toils, / and built the wall of Uruk-Haven." It seems that *Gilgamesh* is not simply a series of

---

[1] **Homer** (c. 700 B.C.E.): Author of two epics about the Trojan War (c. 1200 B.C.E.), *The Iliad,* a war among the Greeks, and *The Odyssey,* the story of Odysseus' arduous return home to the Greek island of Ithaca after the Trojan War.

Gilgamesh,
722–705 B.C.E.
In this relief from the
palace of Sargon II,
the Sumerian hero
Gilgamesh holds a
tamed lion cub.
(Giraudon / Art
Resource, NY)

adventures written to glorify a king, but a story that points to the wisdom of acceptance.

The Epic of Gilgamesh is apparently based on a historical figure. The name Gilgamesh has been found in lists of Sumerian kings, and it is believed that Gilgamesh reigned in the city of Uruk—the modern Warka—on the Euphrates River sometime between 2800 and 2500 B.C.E. Uruk had been a major religious center in the fourth millennium B.C.E. Since Mesopotamian gods and goddesses were thought to actually reside in their temples, religious cities were treated as reflections or models of the cosmos. Uruk, for example, was balanced between two deities: One half of the city was devoted to the sky-god An or Anu; the other half was devoted to the earth-goddess Inanna. Her temple was named Eanna, meaning the house of An. In the narration, Gilgamesh's father is a mortal; in the translation used here, Gilgamesh's spirit guardian is called **Lugalbanda**; the name Lugulbanda is also found on the king-lists of Uruk, two kings before Gilgamesh. It is probable that Lugalbanda was Gilgamesh's father, though another king reigned between them. In the narration, Gilgamesh's mother is Ninsun, a goddess who provides his partial divinity. Tablets from this period indicate that after his reign Gilgamesh was considered a god—a deification not unlike that of the Greek Heracles or Orpheus that occurred when an extraordinary mortal warranted eternal elevation.

loo-gahl-BAHN-dah

The Transmission of *The Epic of Gilgamesh*.

In the mid-nineteenth century, a young English archeologist, Austen Henry Layard, and a Turkish archeologist, Hormuzd Rassam, made a discovery which eventually revolutionized the history of Western literature. In their excavations along the Tigris River in Mesopotamia, they found at Ninevah the ancient library of the last great Assyrian king, Assurbanipal (seventh century B.C.E.). As the clay tablets were slowly translated, scholars learned that most of them were business records, but they also discovered fragments of two great literary works, the Babylonian *The Epic of Creation* and *The Epic of Gilgamesh*. These two works of literature antedated both Homer's epics and the Bible by over one thousand years.

Individual Sumerian stories about Gilgamesh, such as "Gilgamesh and the giant Humbaba" or "Gilgamesh and the Bull of Heaven," were passed down orally until poets around 2100 B.C.E. began to record some of his adventures. These stories were written down in cuneiform on clay tablets and shaped into the longest and finest composition in Akkadian during the Old Babylonian period between 1900 and 1600 B.C.E. Unfortunately, a complete text from this period does not exist. Other fragments of versions have been found in the Hittite and Hurrian languages from late second millennium B.C.E. The most complete version comes from Assurbanipal's library and is called the Standard Version. The author of this version is traditionally given as Sin-leqe-unnini, a scribe and priest from the Kassite period (c. 1600–1150 B.C.E.). It is impossible to determine, however, his exact role in the transformation of an oral narrative into a text consisting of eleven tablets, whether he contributed to the composition of the text or merely transcribed the story in clay.

Just as Faust's story was the medieval legend which became the myth of modern scientific man and was given such different artistic renderings by Marlowe, Goethe, and Mann, so Gilgamesh is the central legend of ancient civilized humanity that becomes *the* myth of humanity and civilization.

– WILLIAM IRWIN THOMPSON, historian, 1981

After scholars translated Mesopotamian tablets it became possible to conclude that the myths and epics written in Akkadian, the dialects of Babylonia and Assyria, were widely known throughout the ancient Near East. In 1872 George Smith announced to the newly founded Society of Biblical Archeology that in *The Epic of Gilgamesh* he had found a flood story that was very similar to the flood in Genesis. Either the writer of the biblical version was acquainted with the Babylonian account in some form or another, or the two accounts drew upon a common source. Because of the questions about meaning and chronology raised by Middle Eastern archeology and the comparison of literary text from the Bible with other literatures from the region, biblical scholarship was permanently transformed. Similarities between Gilgamesh and the Greek heroes Achilles and Odysseus suggest a line of transmission from *The Epic of Gilgamesh* to the Homeric epics: both Gilgamesh and Achilles are partly of divine origin and both are fated to die; and the relationship between Achilles and Patroclus resembles that of Gilgamesh and Enkidu. Gilgamesh and Odysseus each go on arduous quests and are aided by mysterious women—Siduri and Circe, respectively—and both must cross the water to the edge of the world. The fact that the character of Gilgamesh is so approachable is the strongest argument for believing that there was a line of transmission from *The Epic of Gilgamesh* to the Homeric epics.

The Story of Gilgamesh.   Gilgamesh's tale begins with a celebration of the feats that made him famous and secured for him a place in history. He was a wise king known for his building projects, especially for the great wall circling the city. The stories that follow cluster around two major events: Gilgamesh's friendship with Enkidu and his grand journey to the edge of the world in search of immortality.

Characteristic of most great heroes down through the ages, Gilgamesh is of mixed parentage, divine and human, which sets him apart from ordinary men and raises his destiny to a cosmic level. As a young untested king, Gilgamesh's youthful energy creates problems: He indulges in an antiquated custom of claiming first sexual rights to brides and other women in Uruk. He also alienates sons from their fathers. The people are fed up and cry out to the father of the gods, Anu, for assistance. Anu provides for the creation of **Enkidu**, a young man capable of challenging Gilgamesh and diverting him from his present lifestyle.

ENG-kee-doo

Because Enkidu initially lives with animals and frees them from traps, he comes to the attention of trappers, who complain about him. The translated text says that a temple prostitute is used to domesticate Enkidu, but *prostitute* has perhaps an inappropriate connotation for a woman who was probably a temple priestess familiar with the arts of sexuality and well suited to initiate Enkidu into carnal mysteries. After six days and seven nights of lovemaking, Enkidu finds himself estranged from the animals and ready to enter civilized society in order to confront Gilgamesh, who knows of Enkidu from his dreams, an important source of visionary knowledge for the Sumerians.

p. 537

Gilgamesh and Enkidu. After they test each other's strength in a wrestling match, Enkidu and Gilgamesh become close friends and soul mates, reminiscent of other friendships from antiquity, such as Achilles and Patroclus in *The Iliad* and David and Jonathan in the Bible, male friendships said by Plato to be deeper than those between men and women. In some ways, however, the two men appear to be opposites: Gilgamesh is a civilized ruler, while Enkidu is a hairy man of nature; Gilgamesh is at home in the court, Enkidu lives in the wild with animals. If Gilgamesh represents the urban male, then Enkidu complements him by being the natural man, the man of instinct and intuition. The pair might in fact represent wholeness or health, as if Enkidu were a psychological extension or alter ego of Gilgamesh.

Together they are well prepared to face their first challenge — a rite of passage for young warriors coming of age. They confront the giant Humbaba, who dwells in cedar forests on the other side of the mountains. The defeat of this giant symbolizes the extension of civilization, and it gives the two men the confidence to return to Uruk as independent, self-reliant warriors. The first part of the epic reaches a climax when Gilgamesh encounters the goddess Ishtar, who asks him to be her lover. This is not a simple request for sexual pleasure; she represents the earth's fertility and is proposing that Gilgamesh become the year-king. As such, he would symbolize the annual vegetative cycle and would be sacrificed to the Great Mother in order to guarantee the harvest at the end of the season. Gilgamesh's negative response includes a litany of Ishtar's former lovers,[2] all of whom were sacrificed in some manner. Gilgamesh's rejection of this role amounts to a major turning point in masculine consciousness. Free from the annual agricultural cycle of the Mother Goddess, Gilgamesh is charting a new destiny for the patriarchal hero as a solitary individual meeting challenges on his own and searching for personal answers.

Rejected and angry, Ishtar tries to punish the young warriors with the Bull of Heaven, which they kill in what amounts to the first bullfight in literature. As a final insult, Enkidu tears out the bull's right thigh (symbolic of genitals?) and flings it in Ishtar's face.

A price must be paid, however, for the destruction of Humbaba and the Bull of Heaven, and for the humiliation of Ishtar and the old religion. The two heroes, after all, have defied the gods and created a new independence for humans. In some sense they have gone too far, which is always the initial appearance of extending psychological boundaries and developing a new consciousness. The Greek story of Prometheus explores a similar transition from an old to a new order with tragic consequences,

> If a superman and demigod like Gilgamesh failed to attain everlasting life, or at least ever recurrent youth, how utterly futile it is for a mere mortal to aspire to such a blessed estate and to hope to escape death! It is true, Utnapishtim and his wife obtained eternal life, but that was an exceptional case; and, furthermore, it was by divine favor, not through their own efforts. The rule still holds good that all men must die.
>
> – ALEXANDER HEIDEL, historian and linguist, 1949

---

[2] **Ishtar's . . . lovers:** Refers to the king-lovers who become replacements for the goddess in the underworld. The lovers then are part of the annual agricultural cycles, the growth of grains, in the ancient Near East. It is not known whether the king-lovers were actually sacrificed in an imitation of harvesting or whether they were part of a religious ceremony. Gilgamesh's rejection of Ishtar seems to point to a change in Sumerian culture whereby the role of the goddess was deemphasized and the status of warriors, kings, and sky-gods was elevated.

as does the Renaissance tale of Faustus.[3] Enkidu must die, not a glorious death in battle, but a withering away in illness. Enkidu dreams of the Sumerian land of the dead, where the deceased resemble bats residing in dust and darkness. The real price therefore of individual consciousness is not death, but dread of death, which drives Gilgamesh to question his mortality and to seek answers in a faraway land.

The Journey to the Edge of the World.   Following the path of the sun, Gilgamesh embarks on his great journey to find **Utnapishtim**, the one mortal who has been granted immortality by the gods. Although it is impossible to determine the exact influence that *Gilgamesh* had on later works of literature in Greece and Israel, a number of patterns or motifs in *Gilgamesh* later appear as standard fare in epic works. On the other side of the mountains, Gilgamesh confronts guardians who are part human and part animal,[4] signifying their allegiance to two worlds. He meets a mysterious woman, Siduri, in a paradisal garden. She assists him in dealing with **Urshanabi** the ferryman.[5] To reach Utnapishtim they must cross the waters of death or chaos. Finally, Gilgamesh accomplishes his goal by questioning Utnapishtim about mortality.

There are two parts to Utnapishtim's answer. First, he explains that the essence of life is change. Then he tells Gilgamesh his life story, which largely is the story of a great flood, complete with ark, rain, and birds as emissaries. Gilgamesh does not, however, learn how to obtain immortality from the gods. Gilgamesh then begs Utnapishtim and is granted a chance to obtain eternal life magically through passing a test — but Gilgamesh fails. He is then told where to find the plant of eternal youth, which he says he will call "The Old Men Are Young Again," but once he has retrieved it, it is stolen and eaten by a snake[6] — another failure. An all-too-human picture of mortality emerges at the close of Gilgamesh's journey.

It is impossible to conclude with certainty about the lessons learned by Gilgamesh from Siduri and Utnapishtim, but it appears that the advice he receives recommends a gentle kind of hedonism, of the sort found in Ecclesiastes: Although one cannot completely understand the mysteries of life, the essence of life is change, and death is the end result; one should accept this and live life to its fullest. Gilgamesh returns to Uruk and becomes a great king about whom stories are told for generations. It is remarkable that his story should seem so contemporary, so relevant to the experience of life today.

oot-nah-PISH-tim

oor-shah-NAH-bee

If Gilgamesh is not the first human hero, he is the first tragic hero of whom anything is known. The narrative is incomplete and may remain so; nevertheless it is today the finest surviving epic poem from any period until the appearance of Homer's *Iliad:* and it is immeasurably older.

– N. K. SANDARS, archeologist, 1964

---

[3] **Prometheus . . . Faustus:** The Greek Prometheus was imprisoned for his rebellion against Zeus; the medieval and Renaissance figure of Faustus was willing to trade his soul for knowledge and understanding. Marlowe's play about Faustus ends with the hero's descent into hell.

[4] **part human . . . animal:** Deities who are a combination of animal and human forms are called theriomorphic figures; power or wisdom results from their connection to two different realms. An angel is powerful, for example, because it is linked to both the earth and the sky.

[5] **Urshanabi the ferryman:** The traditional ferryman in myth and religious tales transports souls into the realm of the dead. The Greek ferryman is called Charon. The ferryman in Buddhist tradition carries individuals across a river to the shore of enlightenment.

[6] **eaten by a snake:** Possibly a tale that explains a snake's capacity for "rebirth" through its shedding of skin.

■ **FURTHER RESEARCH**

Translations

Dalley, Stephanie. *Myths from Mesopotamia*. 1991.

Ferry, David. *Gilgamesh: A New Rendering in English Verse*. 1992.

Mason, Herbert. *Gilgamesh: A Verse Narrative*. 1970.

Sandars, N. K. *The Epic of Gilgamesh*. 1960. A detailed, informative introduction.

Background and Criticism

Heidel, Alexander. *The Gilgamesh Epic and Old Testament Parallels*. 1963.

Jacobsen, Thorkild. *The Treasure of Darkness: A History of Mesopotamian Religion*. 1976.

Kramer, Samuel Noah. *Sumerian Mythology*. 1944.

Thompson, William Irwin. *The Time Falling Bodies Take to Light: Mythology, Sexuality & The Origins of Culture*. 1981. An insightful discussion of *Gilgamesh* and the transition from neolithic to Sumerian civilization.

■ **PRONUNCIATION**

Enkidu: ENG-kee-doo

Lugulbanda: loo-gool-BAHN-dah (more commonly written Lugalbanda: loo-gahl-BAHN-dah)

Urshanabi: oor-shah-NAH-bee

Utnapishtim: oot-nah-PISH-tim

❧ The Epic of Gilgamesh

Translated by N. K. Sandars

PROLOGUE

GILGAMESH KING IN URUK

I will proclaim to the world the deeds of Gilgamesh. This was the man to whom all things were known; this was the king who knew the countries of the world. He was wise, he saw mysteries and knew secret things, he brought us a tale of the days before the flood. He went on a long journey, was weary, worn-out with labour, returning he rested, he engraved on a stone the whole story.

When the gods created Gilgamesh they gave him a perfect body. Shamash[1] the glorious sun endowed him with beauty, Adad the god of the storm endowed him with courage, the great gods made his beauty perfect, surpassing all others, terrifying like a great wild bull. Two thirds they made him god and one third man.

A note on the translation: In order to provide what the translator terms a "straightforward narrative," she does not indicate gaps or omissions in the poetry of the original Akkadian version; she has also chosen to render the text in prose. All notes are the editors'.

---

[1] **Shamash:** Also the god of law and the husband of Ishtar, Queen of Heaven and goddess of love and fertility.

In Uruk[2] he built walls, a great rampart, and the temple of blessed Eanna[3] for the god of the firmament Anu,[4] and for Ishtar the goddess of love. Look at it still today: the outer wall where the cornice runs, it shines with the brilliance of copper; and the inner wall, it has no equal. Touch the threshold, it is ancient. Approach Eanna the dwelling of Ishtar, our lady of love and war, the like of which no latter-day king, no man alive can equal. Climb upon the wall of Uruk; walk along it, I say; regard the foundation terrace and examine the masonry: is it not burnt brick and good? The seven sages[5] laid the foundations.

1

THE COMING OF ENKIDU

Gilgamesh went abroad in the world, but he met with none who could withstand his arms till he came to Uruk. But the men of Uruk muttered in their houses "Gilgamesh sounds the tocsin for his amusement, his arrogance has no bounds by day or night. No son is left with his father, for Gilgamesh takes them all, even the children; yet the king should be a shepherd to his people. His lust leaves no virgin to her lover, neither the warrior's daughter nor the wife of the noble; yet this is the shepherd of the city, wise, comely, and resolute."

The gods heard their lament, the gods of heaven cried to the Lord of Uruk, to Anu the god of Uruk: "A goddess made him strong as a savage bull, none can withstand his arms. No son is left with his father for Gilgamesh takes them all; and is this the king, the shepherd of his people? His lust leaves no virgin to her lover, neither the warrior's daughter nor the wife of the noble." When Anu had heard their lamentation the gods cried to Aruru, the goddess of creation, "You made him, O Aruru, now create his equal; let it be as like him as his own reflection, his second self, stormy heart for stormy heart. Let them contend together and leave Uruk in quiet."

So the goddess conceived an image in her mind, and it was of the stuff of Anu of the firmament. She dipped her hands in water and pinched off clay, she let it fall in the wilderness, and noble Enkidu was created. There was virtue in him of the god of war, of Ninurta himself. His body was rough, he had long hair like a woman's; it waved like the hair of Nisaba, the goddess of corn. His body was covered with matted hair like Samuqan's, the god of cattle. He was innocent of mankind; he knew nothing of the cultivated land.

Enkidu ate grass in the hills with the gazelle and lurked with wild beasts at the water-holes; he had joy of the water with the herds of wild game. But there was a trapper who met him one day face to face at the drinking-hole, for the wild game had entered his territory. On three days he met him face to face, and the trapper was

---

[2] **Uruk:** An important city in southern Babylonia; after the flood it was the seat of a dynasty of kings. Gilgamesh was the fifth and most famous king of this dynasty.

[3] **walls . . . Eanna:** A temple precinct sacred to Anu and Ishtar.

[4] **Anu:** Father of the gods and god of the firmament or "Great Above."

[5] **seven sages:** Wise men who brought civilization to the seven oldest cities of Mesopotamia.

frozen with fear. He went back to his house with the game that he had caught, and he was dumb, benumbed with terror. His face was altered like that of one who has made a long journey. With awe in his heart he spoke to his father: "Father, there is a man, unlike any other, who comes down from the hills. He is the strongest in the world, he is like an immortal from heaven. He ranges over the hills with wild beasts and eats grass; he ranges through your land and comes down to the wells. I am afraid and dare not go near him. He fills in the pits which I dig and tears up my traps set for the game; he helps the beasts to escape and now they slip through my fingers."

His father opened his mouth and said to the trapper, "My son, in Uruk lives Gilgamesh; no one has ever prevailed against him, he is strong as a star from heaven. Go to Uruk, find Gilgamesh, extol the strength of this wild man. Ask him to give you a harlot, a wanton[6] from the temple of love; return with her, and let her woman's power overpower this man. When next he comes down to drink at the wells she will be there, stripped naked; and when he sees her beckoning he will embrace her, and then the wild beasts will reject him."

So the trapper set out on his journey to Uruk and addressed himself to Gilgamesh saying, "A man unlike any other is roaming now in the pastures; he is as strong as a star from heaven and I am afraid to approach him. He helps the wild game to escape; he fills in my pits and pulls up my traps." Gilgamesh said, "Trapper, go back, take with you a harlot, a child of pleasure. At the drinking-hole she will strip, and when he sees her beckoning he will embrace her and the game of the wilderness will surely reject him."

Now the trapper returned, taking the harlot with him. After a three days' journey they came to the drinking-hole, and there they sat down; the harlot and the trapper sat facing one another and waited for the game to come. For the first day and for the second day the two sat waiting, but on the third day the herds came; they came down to drink and Enkidu was with them. The small wild creatures of the plains were glad of the water, and Enkidu with them, who ate grass with the gazelle and was born in the hills; and she saw him, the savage man, come from far-off in the hills. The trapper spoke to her: "There he is. Now, woman, make your breasts bare, have no shame, do not delay but welcome his love. Let him see you naked, let him possess your body. When he comes near uncover yourself and lie with him; teach him, the savage man, your woman's art, for when he murmurs love to you the wild beasts that shared his life in the hills will reject him."

She was not ashamed to take him, she made herself naked and welcomed his eagerness; as he lay on her murmuring love she taught him the woman's art. For six days and seven nights they lay together, for Enkidu had forgotten his home in the hills; but when he was satisfied he went back to the wild beasts. Then, when the gazelle saw him, they bolted away; when the wild creatures saw him they fled. Enkidu would have followed, but his body was bound as though with a cord, his knees gave way when he started to run, his swiftness was gone. And now the wild creatures had all fled away; Enkidu was grown weak, for wisdom was in him, and the

---

[6] **harlot . . . wanton:** "Harlot" or "wanton" has perhaps an inappropriate connotation for someone who is probably a temple priestess of Ishtar.

thoughts of a man were in his heart. So he returned and sat down at the woman's feet, and listened intently to what she said. "You are wise, Enkidu, and now you have become like a god. Why do you want to run wild with the beasts in the hills? Come with me. I will take you to strong-walled Uruk, to the blessed temple of Ishtar and of Anu, of love and of heaven: There Gilgamesh lives, who is very strong, and like a wild bull he lords it over men."

When she had spoken Enkidu was pleased; he longed for a comrade, for one who would understand his heart. "Come, woman, and take me to that holy temple, to the house of Anu and of Ishtar, and to the place where Gilgamesh lords it over the people. I will challenge him boldly, I will cry out aloud in Uruk, 'I am the strongest here, I have come to change the old order, I am he who was born in the hills, I am he who is strongest of all.'"

She said, "Let us go, and let him see your face. I know very well where Gilgamesh is in great Uruk. O Enkidu, there all the people are dressed in their gorgeous robes, every day is holiday, the young men and the girls are wonderful to see. How sweet they smell! All the great ones are roused from their beds. O Enkidu, you who love life, I will show you Gilgamesh, a man of many moods; you shall look at him well in his radiant manhood. His body is perfect in strength and maturity; he never rests by night or day. He is stronger than you, so leave your boasting. Shamash the glorious sun has given favours to Gilgamesh, and Anu of the heavens, and Enlil, and Ea the wise has given him deep understanding. I tell you, even before you have left the wilderness, Gilgamesh will know in his dreams that you are coming."

Now Gilgamesh got up to tell his dream to his mother, Ninsun, one of the wise gods. "Mother, last night I had a dream. I was full of joy, the young heroes were round me and I walked through the night under the stars of the firmament, and one, a meteor of the stuff of Anu, fell down from heaven. I tried to lift it but it proved too heavy. All the people of Uruk came round to see it, the common people jostled and the nobles thronged to kiss its feet; and to me its attraction was like the love of woman. They helped me, I braced my forehead and I raised it with thongs and brought it to you, and you yourself pronounced it my brother."

Then Ninsun, who is well-beloved and wise, said to Gilgamesh, "This star of heaven which descended like a meteor from the sky; which you tried to lift, but found too heavy, when you tried to move it it would not budge, and so you brought it to my feet; I made it for you, a goad and spur, and you were drawn as though to a woman. This is the strong comrade, the one who brings help to his friend in his need. He is the strongest of wild creatures, the stuff of Anu; born in the grass-lands and the wild hills reared him; when you see him you will be glad; you will love him as a woman and he will never forsake you. This is the meaning of the dream."

Gilgamesh said, "Mother, I dreamed a second dream. In the streets of strong-walled Uruk there lay an axe; the shape of it was strange and the people thronged round. I saw it and was glad. I bent down, deeply drawn towards it; I loved it like a woman and wore it at my side." Ninsun answered, "That axe, which you saw, which drew you so powerfully like love of a woman, that is the comrade whom I give you, and he will come in his strength like one of the host of heaven. He is the brave companion who rescues his friend in necessity." Gilgamesh said to his mother, "A friend,

a counsellor has come to me from Enlil, and now I shall befriend and counsel him."
So Gilgamesh told his dreams; and the harlot retold them to Enkidu.

And now she said to Enkidu, "When I look at you you have become like a god.
Why do you yearn to run wild again with the beasts in the hills? Get up from the
ground, the bed of a shepherd." He listened to her words with care. It was good
advice that she gave. She divided her clothing in two and with the one half she
clothed him and with the other herself; and holding his hand she led him like a child
to the sheepfolds, into the shepherds' tents. There all the shepherds crowded round
to see him, they put down bread in front of him, but Enkidu could only suck the
milk of wild animals. He fumbled and gaped, at a loss what to do or how he should
eat the bread and drink the strong wine. Then the woman said, "Enkidu, eat bread, it
is the staff of life; drink the wine, it is the custom of the land." So he ate till he was full
and drank strong wine, seven goblets. He became merry, his heart exulted and his
face shone. He rubbed down the matted hair of his body and anointed himself with
oil. Enkidu had become a man; but when he had put on man's clothing he appeared
like a bridegroom. He took arms to hunt the lion so that the shepherds could rest at
night. He caught wolves and lions and the herdsmen lay down in peace; for Enkidu
was their watchman, that strong man who had no rival.

He was merry living with the shepherds, till one day lifting his eyes he saw a man
approaching. He said to the harlot, "Woman, fetch that man here. Why has he come?
I wish to know his name." She went and called the man saying, "Sir, where are you
going on this weary journey?" The man answered, saying to Enkidu, "Gilgamesh has
gone into the marriage-house and shut out the people. He does strange things in
Uruk, the city of great streets. At the roll of the drum work begins for the men, and
work for the women. Gilgamesh the king is about to celebrate marriage with the
Queen of Love, and he still demands to be first with the bride, the king to be first and
the husband to follow, for that was ordained by the gods from his birth, from the
time the umbilical cord was cut. But now the drums roll for the choice of the bride
and the city groans." At these words Enkidu turned white in the face. "I will go to the
place where Gilgamesh lords it over the people, I will challenge him boldly, and I will
cry aloud in Uruk, 'I have come to change the old order, for I am the strongest here.'"

Now Enkidu strode in front and the woman followed behind. He entered Uruk,
that great market, and all the folk thronged round him where he stood in the street
in strong-walled Uruk. The people jostled; speaking of him they said, "He is the spit
of Gilgamesh." "He is shorter." "He is bigger of bone." "This is the one who was
reared on the milk of wild beasts. His is the greatest strength." The men rejoiced:
"Now Gilgamesh has met his match. This great one, this hero whose beauty is like a
god, he is a match even for Gilgamesh."

In Uruk the bridal bed was made, fit for the goddess of love. The bride waited
for the bridegroom, but in the night Gilgamesh got up and came to the house. Then
Enkidu stepped out, he stood in the street and blocked the way. Mighty Gilgamesh
came on and Enkidu met him at the gate. He put out his foot and prevented Gilgamesh from entering the house, so they grappled, holding each other like bulls.
They broke the doorposts and the walls shook, they snorted like bulls locked
together. They shattered the doorposts and the walls shook. Gilgamesh bent his knee

with his foot planted on the ground and with a turn Enkidu was thrown. Then immediately his fury died. When Enkidu was thrown he said to Gilgamesh, "There is not another like you in the world. Ninsun, who is as strong as a wild ox in the byre, she was the mother who bore you, and now you are raised above all men, and Enlil has given you the kingship, for your strength surpasses the strength of men." So Enkidu and Gilgamesh embraced and their friendship was sealed.

2

The Forest Journey

Enlil[7] of the mountain, the father of the gods, had decreed the destiny of Gilgamesh. So Gilgamesh dreamed and Enkidu said, "The meaning of the dream is this. The father of the gods has given you kingship, such is your destiny, everlasting life is not your destiny. Because of this do not be sad at heart, do not be grieved or oppressed. He has given you power to bind and to loose, to be the darkness and the light of mankind. He has given you unexampled supremacy over the people, victory in battle from which no fugitive returns, in forays and assaults from which there is no going back. But do not abuse this power, deal justly with your servants in the palace, deal justly before Shamash."

The eyes of Enkidu were full of tears and his heart was sick. He sighed bitterly and Gilgamesh met his eye and said, "My friend, why do you sigh so bitterly?" But Enkidu opened his mouth and said, "I am weak, my arms have lost their strength, the cry of sorrow sticks in my throat, I am oppressed by idleness." It was then that the lord Gilgamesh turned his thoughts to the Country of the Living; on the Land of Cedars the lord Gilgamesh reflected. He said to his servant Enkidu, "I have not established my name stamped on bricks as my destiny decreed; therefore I will go to the country where the cedar is felled. I will set up my name in the place where the names of famous men are written, and where no man's name is written yet I will raise a monument to the gods. Because of the evil that is in the land, we will go to the forest and destroy the evil; for in the forest lives Humbaba[8] whose name is 'Hugeness,' a ferocious giant." But Enkidu sighed bitterly and said, "When I went with the wild beasts ranging through the wilderness I discovered the forest; its length is ten thousand leagues in every direction. Enlil has appointed Humbaba to guard it and armed him in sevenfold terrors, terrible to all flesh is Humbaba. When he roars it is like the torrent of the storm, his breath is like fire, and his jaws are death itself. He guards the cedars so well that when the wild heifer stirs in the forest, though she is sixty leagues distant, he hears her. What man would willingly walk into that country and explore its depths? I tell you, weakness overpowers whoever goes near it: it is not an equal struggle when one fights with Humbaba; he is a great warrior, a battering-ram. Gilgamesh, the watchman of the forest never sleeps."

---

[7] **Enlil:** As god of earth, wind, and spirit, Enlil is the active manifestation of Anu.

[8] **Humbaba:** A nature divinity, guardian spirit of the forest.

Gilgamesh replied: "Where is the man who can clamber to heaven? Only the gods live for ever with glorious Shamash, but as for us men, our days are numbered, our occupations are a breath of wind. How is this, already you are afraid! I will go first although I am your lord, and you may safely call out, 'Forward, there is nothing to fear!' Then if I fall I leave behind me a name that endures; men will say of me, 'Gilgamesh has fallen in fight with ferocious Humbaba.' Long after the child has been born in my house, they will say it, and remember." Enkidu spoke again to Gilgamesh, "O my lord, if you will enter that country, go first to the hero Shamash, tell the Sun God, for the land is his. The country where the cedar is cut belongs to Shamash."

Gilgamesh took up a kid, white without spot, and a brown one with it; he held them against his breast, and he carried them into the presence of the sun. He took in his hand his silver sceptre and he said to glorious Shamash, "I am going to that country, O Shamash, I am going; my hands supplicate, so let it be well with my soul and bring me back to the quay of Uruk. Grant, I beseech, your protection, and let the omen be good." Glorious Shamash answered, "Gilgamesh, you are strong, but what is the Country of the Living to you?"

"O Shamash, hear me, hear me, Shamash, let my voice be heard. Here in the city man dies oppressed at heart, man perishes with despair in his heart. I have looked over the wall and I see the bodies floating on the river, and that will be my lot also. Indeed I know it is so, for whoever is tallest among men cannot reach the heavens, and the greatest cannot encompass the earth. Therefore I would enter that country: because I have not established my name stamped on brick as my destiny decreed, I will go to the country where the cedar is cut. I will set up my name where the names of famous men are written; and where no man's name is written I will raise a monument to the gods." The tears ran down his face and he said, "Alas, it is a long journey that I must take to the Land of Humbaba. If this enterprise is not to be accomplished, why did you move me, Shamash, with the restless desire to perform it? How can I succeed if you will not succour me? If I die in that country I will die without rancour, but if I return I will make a glorious offering of gifts and of praise to Shamash."

So Shamash accepted the sacrifice of his tears; like the compassionate man he showed him mercy. He appointed strong allies for Gilgamesh, sons of one mother, and stationed them in the mountain caves. The great winds he appointed: the north wind, the whirlwind, the storm and the icy wind, the tempest and the scorching wind. Like vipers, like dragons, like a scorching fire, like a serpent that freezes the heart, a destroying flood and the lightning's fork, such were they and Gilgamesh rejoiced.

He went to the forge and said, "I will give orders to the armourers; they shall cast us our weapons while we watch them." So they gave orders to the armourers and the craftsmen sat down in conference. They went into the groves of the plain and cut willow and boxwood; they cast for them axes of nine score pounds, and great swords they cast with blades of six score pounds each one, with pommels and hilts of thirty pounds. They cast for Gilgamesh the axe "Might of Heroes" and the bow of Anshan;[9]

---

[9] **Anshan:** A district in southwest Persia, probably the source of wood for making bows.

and Gilgamesh was armed and Enkidu; and the weight of the arms they carried was thirty score pounds.

The people collected and the counsellors in the streets and in the market-place of Uruk; they came through the gate of seven bolts and Gilgamesh spoke to them in the market-place: "I, Gilgamesh, go to see that creature of whom such things are spoken, the rumour of whose name fills the world. I will conquer him in his cedar wood and show the strength of the sons of Uruk, all the world shall know of it. I am committed to this enterprise: to climb the mountain, to cut down the cedar, and leave behind me an enduring name." The counsellors of Uruk, the great market, answered him, "Gilgamesh, you are young, your courage carries you too far, you cannot know what this enterprise means which you plan. We have heard that Humbaba is not like who die, his weapons are such that none can stand against them; the forest stretches for ten thousand leagues in every direction; who would willingly go down to explore its depths? As for Humbaba, when he roars it is like the torrent of the storm, his breath is like fire and his jaws are death itself. Why do you crave to do this thing, Gilgamesh? It is no equal struggle when one fights with Humbaba, that battering-ram."

When he heard these words of the counsellors Gilgamesh looked at his friend and laughed, "How shall I answer them; shall I say I am afraid of Humbaba, I will sit at home all the rest of my days?" Then Gilgamesh opened his mouth again and said to Enkidu, "My friend, let us go to the Great Palace, to Egalmah,[10] and stand before Ninsun the queen. Ninsun is wise with deep knowledge, she will give us counsel for the road we must go." They took each other by the hand as they went to Egalmah, and they went to Ninsun the great queen. Gilgamesh approached, he entered the palace and spoke to Ninsun. "Ninsun, will you listen to me; I have a long journey to go, to the Land of Humbaba, I must travel an unknown road and fight a strange battle. From the day I go until I return, till I reach the cedar forest and destroy the evil which Shamash abhors, pray for me to Shamash."

Ninsun went into her room, she put on a dress becoming to her body, she put on jewels to make her breast beautiful, she placed a tiara on her head and her skirts swept the ground. Then she went up to the altar of the Sun, standing upon the roof of the palace; she burnt incense and lifted her arms to Shamash as the smoke ascended: "O Shamash, why did you give this restless heart to Gilgamesh, my son; why did you give it? You have moved him and now he sets out on a long journey to the Land of Humbaba, to travel an unknown road and fight a strange battle. Therefore from the day that he goes till the day he returns, until he reaches the cedar forest, until he kills Humbaba and destroys the evil thing which you, Shamash, abhor, do not forget him; but let the dawn, Aya, your dear bride, remind you always, and when day is done give him to the watchman of the night to keep him from harm." Then Ninsun the mother of Gilgamesh extinguished the incense, and she called to Enkidu with this exhortation: "Strong Enkidu, you are not the child of my body, but I will receive you as my adopted son; you are my other child like the foundlings they bring

---

[10] **Egalmah:** The palace home of the goddess Ninsun.

to the temple. Serve Gilgamesh as a foundling serves the temple and the priestess who reared him. In the presence of my women, my votaries and hierophants, I declare it." Then she placed the amulet for a pledge round his neck, and she said to him, "I entrust my son to you; bring him back to me safely."

And now they brought to them the weapons, they put in their hands the great swords in their golden scabbards, and the bow and the quiver. Gilgamesh took the axe, he slung the quiver from his shoulder, and the bow of Anshan, and buckled the sword to his belt; and so they were armed and ready for the journey. Now all the people came and pressed on them and said, "When will you return to the city?" The counsellors blessed Gilgamesh and warned him, "Do not trust too much in your own strength, be watchful, restrain your blows at first. The one who goes in front protects his companion; the good guide who knows the way guards his friend. Let Enkidu lead the way, he knows the road to the forest, he has seen Humbaba and is experienced in battles; let him press first into the passes, let him be watchful and look to himself. Let Enkidu protect his friend, and guard his companion, and bring him safe through the pitfalls of the road. We, the counsellors of Uruk entrust our king to you, O Enkidu; bring him back safely to us." Again to Gilgamesh they said, "May Shamash give you your heart's desire, may he let you see with your eyes the thing accomplished which your lips have spoken; may he open a path for you where it is blocked, and a road for your feet to tread. May he open the mountains for your crossing, and may the nighttime bring you the blessings of night, and Lugulbanda,[11] your guardian god, stand beside you for victory. May you have victory in the battle as though you fought with a child. Wash your feet in the river of Humbaba to which you are journeying; in the evening dig a well, and let there always be pure water in your water-skin. Offer cold water to Shamash and do not forget Lugulbanda."

Then Enkidu opened his mouth and said, "Forward, there is nothing to fear. Follow me, for I know the place where Humbaba lives and the paths where he walks. Let the counsellors go back. Here is no cause for fear." When the counsellors heard this they sped the hero on his way. "Go, Gilgamesh, may your guardian god protect you on the road and bring you safely back to the quay of Uruk."

After twenty leagues they broke their fast; after another thirty leagues they stopped for the night. Fifty leagues they walked in one day; in three days they had walked as much as a journey of a month and two weeks. They crossed seven mountains before they came to the gate of the forest. Then Enkidu called out to Gilgamesh, "Do not go down into the forest; when I opened the gate my hand lost its strength." Gilgamesh answered him, "Dear friend, do not speak like a coward. Have we got the better of so many dangers and travelled so far, to turn back at last? You, who are tried in wars and battles, hold close to me now and you will feel no fear of death; keep beside me and your weakness will pass, the trembling will leave your hand. Would my friend rather stay behind? No, we will go down together into the heart of the forest. Let your courage be roused by the battle to come; forget death and follow me, a man resolute in action, but one who is not foolhardy. When two

---

[11] **Lugulbanda:** The third king in the king-list, the hero of several poems, and the spirit guardian of Gilgamesh.

go together each will protect himself and shield his companion, and if they fall they leave an enduring name."

Together they went down into the forest and they came to the green mountain. There they stood still, they were struck dumb; they stood still and gazed at the forest. They saw the height of the cedar, they saw the way into the forest and the track where Humbaba was used to walk. The way was broad and the going was good. They gazed at the mountain of cedars, the dwelling-place of the gods and the throne of Ishtar. The hugeness of the cedar rose in front of the mountain, its shade was beautiful, full of comfort; mountain and glade were green with brushwood.

There Gilgamesh dug a well before the setting sun. He went up the mountain and poured out fine meal on the ground and said, "O mountain, dwelling of the gods, bring me a favourable dream." Then they took each other by the hand and lay down to sleep; and sleep that flows from the night lapped over them. Gilgamesh dreamed, and at midnight sleep left him, and he told his dream to his friend. "Enkidu, what was it that woke me if you did not? My friend, I have dreamed a dream. Get up, look at the mountain precipice. The sleep that the gods sent me is broken. Ah, my friend, what a dream I have had! Terror and confusion; I seized hold of a wild bull in the wilderness. It bellowed and beat up the dust till the whole sky was dark, my arm was seized and my tongue bitten. I fell back on my knee; then someone refreshed me with water from his water-skin."

Enkidu said, "Dear friend, the god to whom we are travelling is no wild bull, though his form is mysterious. That wild bull which you saw is Shamash the Protector; in our moment of peril he will take our hands. The one who gave water from his water-skin, that is your own god who cares for your good name, your Lugulbanda. United with him, together we will accomplish a work the fame of which will never die."

Gilgamesh said, "I dreamed again. We stood in a deep gorge of the mountain, and beside it we two were like the smallest of swamp flies; and suddenly the mountain fell, it struck me and caught my feet from under me. Then came an intolerable light blazing out, and in it was one whose grace and whose beauty were greater than the beauty of this world. He pulled me out from under the mountain, he gave me water to drink and my heart was comforted, and he set my feet on the ground."

Then Enkidu the child of the plains said, "Let us go down from the mountain and talk this thing over together." He said to Gilgamesh the young god, "Your dream is good, your dream is excellent, the mountain which you saw is Humbaba. Now, surely, we will seize and kill him, and throw his body down as the mountain fell on the plain."

The next day after twenty leagues they broke their fast, and after another thirty they stopped for the night. They dug a well before the sun had set and Gilgamesh ascended the mountain. He poured out fine meal on the ground and said, "O mountain, dwelling of the gods, send a dream for Enkidu, make him a favourable dream." The mountain fashioned a dream for Enkidu; it came, an ominous dream; a cold shower passed over him, it caused him to cower like the mountain barley under a storm of rain. But Gilgamesh sat with his chin on his knees till the sleep which flows over all mankind lapped over him. Then, at midnight, sleep left him; he got up and said to his friend, "Did you call me, or why did I wake? Did you touch me, or why am I terrified? Did not some god pass by, for my limbs are numb with fear? My friend,

I saw a third dream and this dream was altogether frightful. The heavens roared and the earth roared again, daylight failed and darkness fell, lightning flashed, fire blazed out, the clouds lowered, they rained down death. Then the brightness departed, the fire went out, and all was turned to ashes fallen about us. Let us go down from the mountain and talk this over, and consider what we should do."

When they had come down from the mountain Gilgamesh seized the axe in his hand: he felled the cedar. When Humbaba heard the noise far off he was enraged; he cried out, "Who is this that has violated my woods and cut down my cedar?" But glorious Shamash called to them out of heaven, "Go forward, do not be afraid." But now Gilgamesh was overcome by weakness, for sleep had seized him suddenly, a profound sleep held him; he lay on the ground, stretched out speechless, as though in a dream. When Enkidu touched him he did not rise, when he spoke to him he did not reply. "O Gilgamesh, Lord of the plain of Kullab,[12] the world grows dark, the shadows have spread over it, now is the glimmer of dusk. Shamash has departed, his bright head is quenched in the bosom of his mother Ningal. O Gilgamesh, how long will you lie like this, asleep? Never let the mother who gave you birth be forced in mourning into the city square."

At length Gilgamesh heard him; he put on his breastplate, "The Voice of Heroes," of thirty shekels' weight; he put it on as though it had been a light garment that he carried, and it covered him altogether. He straddled the earth like a bull that snuffs the ground and his teeth were clenched. "By the life of my mother Ninsun who gave me birth, and by the life of my father, divine Lugulbanda, let me live to be the wonder of my mother, as when she nursed me on her lap." A second time he said to him, "By the life of Ninsun my mother who gave me birth, and by the life of my father, divine Lugulbanda, until we have fought this man, if man he is, this god, if god he is, the way that I took to the Country of the Living will not turn back to the city."

Then Enkidu, the faithful companion, pleaded, answering him, "O my lord, you do not know this monster and that is the reason you are not afraid. I who know him, I am terrified. His teeth are dragon's fangs, his countenance is like a lion, his charge is the rushing of the flood, with his look he crushes alike the trees of the forest and reeds in the swamp. O my Lord, you may go on if you choose into this land, but I will go back to the city. I will tell the lady your mother all your glorious deeds till she shouts for joy: and then I will tell the death that followed till she weeps for bitterness." But Gilgamesh said, "Immolation and sacrifice are not yet for me, the boat of the dead shall not go down, nor the three-ply cloth be cut for my shrouding. Not yet will my people be desolate, nor the pyre be lit in my house and my dwelling burnt on the fire. Today, give me your aid and you shall have mine: what then can go amiss with us two? All living creatures born of the flesh shall sit at last in the boat of the West, and when it sinks, when the boat of Magilum[13] sinks, they are gone; but we shall go forward and fix our eyes on this monster. If your heart is fearful throw away fear; if there is terror in it throw away terror. Take your axe in your hand and attack. He who leaves the fight unfinished is not at peace."

---

[12] **Kullab:** Part of Uruk.   [13] **boat of Magilum:** Possibly the "boat of the dead."

Humbaba came out from his strong house of cedar. Then Enkidu called out, "O Gilgamesh, remember now your boasts in Uruk. Forward, attack, son of Uruk, there is nothing to fear." When he heard these words his courage rallied; he answered, "Make haste, close in, if the watchman is there do not let him escape to the woods where he will vanish. He has put on the first of his seven splendours[14] but not yet the other six, let us trap him before he is armed." Like a raging wild bull he snuffed the ground; the watchman of the woods turned full of threatenings, he cried out. Humbaba came from his strong house of cedar. He nodded his head and shook it, menacing Gilgamesh; and on him he fastened his eye, the eye of death. Then Gilgamesh called to Shamash and his tears were flowing, "O glorious Shamash, I have followed the road you commanded but now if you send no succour how shall I escape?" Glorious Shamash heard his prayer and he summoned the great wind, the north wind, the whirlwind, the storm and the icy wind, the tempest and the scorching wind; they came like dragons, like a scorching fire, like a serpent that freezes the heart, a destroying flood and the lightning's fork. The eight winds rose up against Humbaba, they beat against his eyes; he was gripped, unable to go forward or back. Gilgamesh shouted, "By the life of Ninsun my mother and divine Lugulbanda my father, in the Country of the Living, in this Land I have discovered your dwelling; my weak arms and my small weapons I have brought to this Land against you, and now I will enter your house."

So he felled the first cedar and they cut the branches and laid them at the foot of the mountain. At the first stroke Humbaba blazed out, but still they advanced. They felled seven cedars and cut and bound the branches and laid them at the foot of the mountain, and seven times Humbaba loosed his glory on them. As the seventh blaze died out they reached his lair. He slapped his thigh in scorn. He approached like a noble wild bull roped on the mountain, a warrior whose elbows are bound together. The tears started to his eyes and he was pale, "Gilgamesh, let me speak. I have never known a mother, no, nor a father who reared me. I was born of the mountain, he reared me, and Enlil made me the keeper of this forest. Let me go free, Gilgamesh, and I will be your servant, you shall be my lord; all the trees of the forest that I tended on the mountain shall be yours. I will cut them down and build you a palace." He took him by the hand and led him to his house, so that the heart of Gilgamesh was moved with compassion. He swore by the heavenly life, by the earthly life, by the underworld itself: "O Enkidu, should not the snared bird return to its nest and the captive man return to his mother's arms?" Enkidu answered, "The strongest of men will fall to fate if he has no judgement. Namtar, the evil fate that knows no distinction between men, will devour him. If the snared bird returns to its nest, if the captive man returns to his mother's arms, then you my friend will never return to the city where the mother is waiting who gave you birth. He will bar the mountain road against you, and make the pathways impassable."

Humbaba said, "Enkidu, what you have spoken is evil: you, a hireling, dependent for your bread! In envy and for fear of a rival you have spoken evil words."

---

[14] **seven splendours:** Unclear, but probably natural armaments like winds.

Enkidu said, "Do not listen, Gilgamesh: this Humbaba must die. Kill Humbaba first and his servants after." But Gilgamesh said, "If we touch him the blaze and the glory of light will be put out in confusion, the glory and glamour will vanish, its rays will be quenched." Enkidu said to Gilgamesh, "Not so, my friend. First entrap the bird, and where shall the chicks run then? Afterwards we can search out the glory and the glamour, when the chicks run distracted through the grass."

Gilgamesh listened to the word of his companion, he took the axe in his hand, he drew the sword from his belt, and he struck Humbaba with a thrust of the sword to the neck, and Enkidu his comrade struck the second blow. At the third blow Humbaba fell. Then there followed confusion for this was the guardian of the forest whom they had felled to the ground. For as far as two leagues the cedars shivered when Enkidu felled the watcher of the forest, he at whose voice Hermon and Lebanon used to tremble. Now the mountains were moved and all the hills, for the guardian of the forest was killed. They attacked the cedars, the seven splendours of Humbaba were extinguished. So they pressed on into the forest bearing the sword of eight talents. They uncovered the sacred dwellings of the Anunnaki[15] and while Gilgamesh felled the first of the trees of the forest Enkidu cleared their roots as far as the banks of Euphrates. They set Humbaba before the gods, before Enlil; they kissed the ground and dropped the shroud and set the head before him. When he saw the head of Humbaba, Enlil raged at them. "Why did you do this thing? From henceforth may the fire be on your faces, may it eat the bread that you eat, may it drink where you drink." Then Enlil took again the blaze and the seven splendours that had been Humbaba's: he gave the first to the river, and he gave to the lion, to the stone of execration, to the mountain and to the dreaded daughter of the Queen of Hell.

O Gilgamesh, king and conqueror of the dreadful blaze; wild bull who plunders the mountain, who crosses the sea, glory to him, and from the brave the greater glory is Enki's![16]

3

ISHTAR AND GILGAMESH, AND
THE DEATH OF ENKIDU

Gilgamesh washed out his long locks and cleaned his weapons; he flung back his hair from his shoulders; he threw off his stained clothes and changed them for new. He put on his royal robes and made them fast. When Gilgamesh had put on the crown, glorious Ishtar lifted her eyes, seeing the beauty of Gilgamesh. She said, "Come to me Gilgamesh, and be my bridegroom; grant me seed of your body, let me be your bride and you shall be my husband. I will harness for you a chariot of lapis lazuli and of gold, with wheels of gold and horns of copper; and you shall have mighty demons of the storm for draftmules. When you enter our house in the fragrance of cedarwood, threshold and throne will kiss your feet. Kings, rulers, and princes will bow down before you; they shall bring you tribute from the mountains and the plain.

---

[15] **Anunnaki:** Gods of the underworld and judges of the dead.   [16] **Enki:** God of sweet water and wisdom.

Your ewes shall drop twins and your goats triplets; your pack-ass shall outrun mules; your oxen shall have no rivals, and your chariot horses shall be famous far-off for their swiftness."

Gilgamesh opened his mouth and answered glorious Ishtar, "If I take you in marriage, what gifts can I give in return? What ointments and clothing for your body? I would gladly give you bread and all sorts of food fit for a god. I would give you wine to drink fit for a queen. I would pour out barley to stuff your granary; but as for making you my wife—that I will not. How would it go with me? Your lovers have found you like a brazier which smoulders in the cold, a backdoor which keeps out neither squall of wind nor storm, a castle which crushes the garrison, pitch that blackens the bearer, a water-skin that chafes the carrier, a stone which falls from the parapet, a battering-ram turned back from the enemy, a sandal that trips the wearer. Which of your lovers did you ever love for ever? What shepherd of yours has pleased you for all time? Listen to me while I tell the tale of your lovers. There was Tammuz,[17] the lover of your youth, for him you decreed wailing, year after year. You loved the many-coloured roller, but still you struck and broke his wing; now in the grove he sits and cries, "kappi, kappi, my wing, my wing." You have loved the lion tremendous in strength: seven pits you dug for him, and seven. You have loved the stallion magnificent in battle, and for him you decreed whip and spur and a thong, to gallop seven leagues by force and to muddy the water before he drinks; and for his mother Silili[18] lamentations. You have loved the shepherd of the flock; he made meal-cake for you day after day, he killed kids for your sake. You struck and turned him into a wolf, now his own herd-boys chase him away, his own hounds worry his flanks. And did you not love Ishullanu,[19] the gardener of your father's palm-grove? He brought you baskets filled with dates without end; every day he loaded your table. Then you turned your eyes on him and said, 'Dearest Ishullanu, come here to me, let us enjoy your manhood, come forward and take me, I am yours.' Ishullanu answered, 'What are you asking from me? My mother has baked and I have eaten; why should I come to such as you for food that is tainted and rotten? For when was a screen of rushes sufficient protection from frosts?' But when you had heard his answer you struck him. He was changed to a blind mole deep in the earth, one whose desire is always beyond his reach. And if you and I should be lovers, should not I be served in the same fashion as all these others whom you loved once?"

When Ishtar heard this she fell into a bitter rage, she went up to high heaven. Her tears poured down in front of her father Anu, and Antum her mother. She said, "My father, Gilgamesh has heaped insults on me, he has told over all my abominable behaviour, my foul and hideous acts." Anu opened his mouth and said, "Are you a father of gods? Did not you quarrel with Gilgamesh the king, so now he has related your abominable behaviour, your foul and hideous acts."

Ishtar opened her mouth and said again, "My father, give me the Bull of Heaven to destroy Gilgamesh. Fill Gilgamesh, I say, with arrogance to his destruction; but if you refuse to give me the Bull of Heaven I will break in the doors of hell and smash

---

[17] **Tammuz:** God of vegetation who is born in the spring and dies in the fall.   [18] **Silili:** Perhaps a divine mare.
[19] **Ishullanu:** The gardener of Anu.

the bolts; there will be confusion of people, those above with those from the lower depths. I shall bring up the dead to eat food like the living; and the hosts of dead will outnumber the living." Anu said to great Ishtar, "If I do what you desire there will be seven years of drought throughout Uruk when corn will be seedless husks. Have you saved grain enough for the people and grass for the cattle?" Ishtar replied. "I have saved grain for the people, grass for the cattle; for seven years of seedless husks there is grain and there is grass enough."

When Anu heard what Ishtar had said he gave her the Bull of Heaven to lead by the halter down to Uruk. When they reached the gates of Uruk the Bull went to the river; with his first snort cracks opened in the earth and a hundred young men fell down to death. With his second snort cracks opened and two hundred fell down to death. With his third snort cracks opened, Enkidu doubled over but instantly recovered, he dodged aside and leapt on the Bull and seized it by the horns. The Bull of Heaven foamed in his face, it brushed him with the thick of its tail. Enkidu cried to Gilgamesh, "My friend, we boasted that we would leave enduring names behind us. Now thrust in your sword between the nape and the horns." So Gilgamesh followed the Bull, he seized the thick of its tail, he thrust the sword between the nape and the horns and slew the Bull. When they had killed the Bull of Heaven they cut out its heart and gave it to Shamash, and the brothers rested.

But Ishtar rose up and mounted the great wall of Uruk; she sprang on to the tower and uttered a curse: "Woe to Gilgamesh, for he has scorned me in killing the Bull of Heaven." When Enkidu heard these words he tore out the Bull's right thigh and tossed it in her face saying, "If I could lay my hands on you, it is this I should do to you, and lash the entrails to your side." Then Ishtar called together her people, the dancing and singing girls, the prostitutes of the temple, the courtesans. Over the thigh of the Bull of Heaven she set up lamentation.

But Gilgamesh called the smiths and the armourers, all of them together. They admired the immensity of the horns. They were plated with lapis lazuli two fingers thick. They were thirty pounds each in weight, and their capacity in oil was six measures, which he gave to his guardian god, Lugulbanda. But he carried the horns into the palace and hung them on the wall. Then they washed their hands in Euphrates, they embraced each other and went away. They drove through the streets of Uruk where the heroes were gathered to see them, and Gilgamesh called to the singing girls, "Who is most glorious of the heroes, who is most eminent among men?" "Gilgamesh is the most glorious of heroes, Gilgamesh is most eminent among men." And now there was feasting, and celebrations and joy in the palace, till the heroes lay down saying, "Now we will rest for the night."

When the daylight came Enkidu got up and cried to Gilgamesh, "O my brother, such a dream I had last night. Anu, Enlil, Ea, and heavenly Shamash took counsel together, and Anu said to Enlil, 'Because they have killed the Bull of Heaven, and because they have killed Humbaba who guarded the Cedar Mountain one of the two must die.' Then glorious Shamash answered the hero Enlil, 'It was by your command they killed the Bull of Heaven, and killed Humbaba, and must Enkidu die although innocent?' Enlil flung round in rage at glorious Shamash, 'You dare to say this, you who went about with them every day like one of themselves!'"

So Enkidu lay stretched out before Gilgamesh; his tears ran down in streams and he said to Gilgamesh, "O my brother, so dear as you are to me, brother, yet they will take me from you." Again he said, "I must sit down on the threshold of the dead and never again will I see my dear brother with my eyes."

While Enkidu lay alone in his sickness he cursed the gate as though it was living flesh, "You there, wood of the gate, dull and insensible, witless, I searched for you over twenty leagues until I saw the towering cedar. There is no wood like you in our land. Seventy-two cubits high and twenty-four wide, the pivot and the ferrule and the jambs are perfect. A master craftsman from Nippur has made you; but O, if I had known the conclusion! If I had known that this was all the good that would come of it, I would have raised the axe and split you into little pieces and set up here a gate of wattle instead. Ah, if only some future king had brought you here, or some god had fashioned you. Let him obliterate my name and write his own, and the curse fall on him instead of on Enkidu."

With the first brightening of dawn Enkidu raised his head and wept before the Sun God, in the brilliance of the sunlight his tears streamed down. "Sun God, I beseech you, about that vile Trapper, that Trapper of nothing because of whom I was to catch less than my comrade; let him catch least, make his game scarce, make him feeble, taking the smaller of every share, let his quarry escape from his nets."

When he had cursed the Trapper to his heart's content he turned on the harlot. He was roused to curse her also. "As for you, woman, with a great curse I curse you! I will promise you a destiny to all eternity. My curse shall come on you soon and sudden. You shall be without a roof for your commerce, for you shall not keep house with other girls in the tavern, but do your business in places fouled by the vomit of the drunkard. Your hire will be potter's earth, your thievings will be flung into the hovel, you will sit at the cross-roads in the dust of the potter's quarter, you will make your bed on the dunghill at night, and by day take your stand in the wall's shadow. Brambles and thorns will tear your feet, the drunk and the dry will strike your cheek and your mouth will ache. Let you be stripped of your purple dyes, for I too once in the wilderness with my wife had all the treasure I wished."

When Shamash heard the words of Enkidu he called to him from heaven: "Enkidu, why are you cursing the woman, the mistress who taught you to eat bread fit for gods and drink wine of kings? She who put upon you a magnificent garment, did she not give you glorious Gilgamesh for your companion, and has not Gilgamesh, your own brother, made you rest on a royal bed and recline on a couch at his left hand? He has made the princes of the earth kiss your feet, and now all the people of Uruk lament and wail over you. When you are dead he will let his hair grow long for your sake, he will wear a lion's pelt and wander through the desert."

When Enkidu heard glorious Shamash his angry heart grew quiet, he called back the curse and said, "Woman, I promise you another destiny. The mouth which cursed you shall bless you! Kings, princes and nobles shall adore you. On your account a man though twelve miles off will clap his hand to his thigh and his hair will twitch. For you he will undo his belt and open his treasure and you shall have your desire; lapis lazuli, gold and carnelian from the heap in the treasury. A ring for your hand and a robe shall be yours. The priest will lead you into the presence of the gods. On your account a wife, a mother of seven, was forsaken."

As Enkidu slept alone in his sickness, in bitterness of spirit he poured out his heart to his friend. "It was I who cut down the cedar, I who levelled the forest, I who slew Humbaba and now see what has become of me. Listen, my friend, this is the dream I dreamed last night. The heavens roared, and earth rumbled back an answer; between them stood I before an awful being, the sombre-faced man-bird; he had directed on me his purpose. His was a vampire face, his foot was a lion's foot, his hand was an eagle's talon. He fell on me and his claws were in my hair, he held me fast and I smothered; then he transformed me so that my arms became wings covered with feathers. He turned his stare towards me, and he led me away to the palace of Irkalla, the Queen of Darkness,[20] to the house from which none who enters ever returns, down the road from which there is no coming back.

"There is the house whose people sit in darkness; dust is their food and clay their meat. They are clothed like birds with wings for covering, they see no light, they sit in darkness. I entered the house of dust and I saw the kings of the earth, their crowns put away for ever; rulers and princes, all those who once wore kingly crowns and ruled the world in the days of old. They who had stood in the place of the gods like Anu and Enlil, stood now like servants to fetch baked meats in the house of dust, to carry cooked meat and cold water from the water-skin. In the house of dust which I entered were high priests and acolytes, priests of the incantation and of ecstasy; there were servers of the temple, and there was Etana, that king of Kish whom the eagle carried to heaven in the days of old. I saw also Samuqan, god of cattle, and there was Ereshki-gal the Queen of the Underworld; and Belit-Sheri squatted in front of her, she who is recorder of the gods and keeps the book of death. She held a tablet from which she read. She raised her head, she saw me and spoke: 'Who has brought this one here?' Then I awoke like a man drained of blood who wanders alone in a waste of rushes; like one whom the bailiff has seized and his heart pounds with terror."

Gilgamesh had peeled off his clothes, he listened to his words and wept quick tears, Gilgamesh listened and his tears flowed. He opened his mouth and spoke to Enkidu: "Who is there in strong-walled Uruk who has wisdom like this? Strange things have been spoken, why does your heart speak strangely? The dream was marvellous but the terror was great; we must treasure the dream whatever the terror; for the dream has shown that misery comes at last to the healthy man, the end of life is sorrow." And Gilgamesh lamented, "Now I will pray to the great gods, for my friend had an ominous dream."

This day on which Enkidu dreamed came to an end and he lay stricken with sickness. One whole day he lay on his bed and his suffering increased. He said to Gilgamesh, the friend on whose account he had left the wilderness, "Once I ran for you, for the water of life, and I now have nothing." A second day he lay on his bed and Gilgamesh watched over him but the sickness increased. A third day he lay on his bed, he called out to Gilgamesh, rousing him up. Now he was weak and his eyes were

---

[20] **Irkalla . . . Darkness:** She is also called Ereshkigal.

blind with weeping. Ten days he lay and his suffering increased, eleven and twelve days he lay on his bed of pain. Then he called to Gilgamesh, "My friend, the great goddess cursed me and I must die in shame. I shall not die like a man fallen in battle; I feared to fall, but happy is the man who falls in the battle, for I must die in shame." And Gilgamesh wept over Enkidu. With the first light of dawn he raised his voice and said to the counsellors of Uruk:

> "Hear me, great ones of Uruk,
> I weep for Enkidu, my friend,
> Bitterly moaning like a woman mourning
> I weep for my brother.
> O Enkidu, my brother,
> You were the axe at my side,
> My hand's strength, the sword in my belt,
> The shield before me,
> A glorious robe, my fairest ornament;
> An evil Fate has robbed me.
> The wild ass and the gazelle
> That were father and mother,
> All long-tailed creatures that nourished you
> Weep for you,
> All the wild things of the plain and pastures;
> The paths that you loved in the forest of cedars
> Night and day murmur.
> Let the great ones of strong-walled Uruk
> Weep for you;
> Let the finger of blessing
> Be stretched out in mourning;
> Enkidu, young brother. Hark,
> There is an echo through all the country
> Like a mother mourning.
> Weep all the paths where we walked together;
> And the beasts we hunted, the bear and hyena,
> Tiger and panther, leopard and lion,
> The stag and the ibex, the bull and the doe.
> The river along whose banks we used to walk,
> Weeps for you,
> Ula of Elam and dear Euphrates
> Where once we drew water for the water-skins.
> The mountain we climbed where we slew the Watchman,
> Weeps for you.
> The warriors of strong-walled Uruk
> Where the Bull of Heaven was killed,
> Weep for you.
> All the people of Eridu
> Weep for you Enkidu.
> Those who brought grain for your eating
> Mourn for you now;
> Who rubbed oil on your back

> Mourn for you now;
> Who poured beer for your drinking
> Mourn for you now.
> The harlot who anointed you with fragrant ointment
> Laments for you now;
> The women of the palace, who brought you a wife,
> A chosen ring of good advice,
> Lament for you now.
> And the young men your brothers
> As though they were women
> Go long-haired in mourning.
> What is this sleep which holds you now?
> You are lost in the dark and cannot hear me."

He touched his heart but it did not beat, nor did he lift his eyes again. When Gilgamesh touched his heart it did not beat. So Gilgamesh laid a veil, as one veils the bride, over his friend. He began to rage like a lion, like a lioness robbed of her whelps. This way and that he paced round the bed, he tore out his hair and strewed it around. He dragged off his splendid robes and flung them down as though they were abominations.

In the first light of dawn Gilgamesh cried out, "I made you rest on a royal bed, you reclined on a couch at my left hand, the princes of the earth kissed your feet. I will cause all the people of Uruk to weep over you and raise the dirge of the dead. The joyful people will stoop with sorrow; and when you have gone to the earth I will let my hair grow long for your sake, I will wander through the wilderness in the skin of a lion." The next day also, in the first light, Gilgamesh lamented; seven days and seven nights he wept for Enkidu, until the worm fastened on him. Only then he gave him up to the earth, for the Anunnaki, the judges, had seized him.

Then Gilgamesh issued a proclamation through the land, he summoned them all, the coppersmiths, the goldsmiths, the stone-workers, and commanded them, "Make a statue of my friend." The statue was fashioned with a great weight of lapis lazuli for the breast and of gold for the body. A table of hardwood was set out, and on it a bowl of carnelian filled with honey, and a bowl of lapis lazuli filled with butter. These he exposed and offered to the Sun; and weeping he went away.

4

THE SEARCH FOR EVERLASTING LIFE

Bitterly Gilgamesh wept for his friend Enkidu; he wandered over the wilderness as a hunter, he roamed over the plains; in his bitterness he cried, "How can I rest, how can I be at peace? Despair is in my heart. What my brother is now, that shall I be when I am dead. Because I am afraid of death I will go as best I can to find Utnapishtim[21] whom they call the Faraway, for he has entered the assembly of the gods." So

---

[21] **Utnapishtim:** A wise king and priest of Shurrupak who survived the primordial flood and was taken by the gods to live in Dilmun, the Sumerian garden paradise. He is similar to the biblical Noah.

Gilgamesh travelled over the wilderness, he wandered over the grasslands, a long journey, in search of Utnapishtim, whom the gods took after the deluge; and they set him to live in the land of Dilmun, in the garden of the sun; and to him alone of men they gave everlasting life.

At night when he came to the mountain passes Gilgamesh prayed: "In these mountain passes long ago I saw lions, I was afraid and I lifted my eyes to the moon; I prayed and my prayers went up to the gods, so now, O moon god Sin, protect me." When he had prayed he lay down to sleep, until he was woken from out of a dream. He saw the lions round him glorying in life; then he took his axe in his hand, he drew his sword from his belt, and he fell upon them like an arrow from the string, and struck and destroyed and scattered them.

So at length Gilgamesh came to Mashu, the great mountains about which he had heard many things, which guard the rising and the setting sun. Its twin peaks are as high as the wall of heaven and its paps reach down to the underworld. At its gate the Scorpions stand guard, half man and half dragon; their glory is terrifying, their stare strikes death into men, their shimmering halo sweeps the mountains that guard the rising sun. When Gilgamesh saw them he shielded his eyes for the length of a moment only; then he took courage and approached. When they saw him so undismayed the Man-Scorpion called to his mate, "This one who comes to us now is flesh of the gods." The mate of the Man-Scorpion answered, "Two thirds is god but one third is man."

Then he called to the man Gilgamesh, he called to the child of the gods: "Why have you come so great a journey; for what have you travelled so far, crossing the dangerous waters; tell me the reason for your coming?" Gilgamesh answered, "For Enkidu; I loved him dearly, together we endured all kinds of hardships; on his account I have come, for the common lot of man has taken him. I have wept for him day and night, I would not give up his body for burial, I thought my friend would come back because of my weeping. Since he went, my life is nothing; that is why I have travelled here in search of Utnapishtim my father; for men say he has entered the assembly of the gods, and has found everlasting life. I have a desire to question him concerning the living and the dead." The Man-Scorpion opened his mouth and said, speaking to Gilgamesh, "No man born of woman has done what you have asked, no mortal man has gone into the mountain; the length of it is twelve leagues of darkness; in it there is no light, but the heart is oppressed with darkness. From the rising of the sun to the setting of the sun there is no light." Gilgamesh said, "Although I should go in sorrow and in pain, with sighing and with weeping, still I must go. Open the gate of the mountain." And the Man-Scorpion said, "Go, Gilgamesh, I permit you to pass through the mountain of Mashu and through the high ranges; may your feet carry you safely home. The gate of the mountain is open."

When Gilgamesh heard this he did as the Man-Scorpion had said, he followed the sun's road to his rising, through the mountain. When he had gone one league the darkness became thick around him, for there was no light, he could see nothing ahead and nothing behind him. After two leagues the darkness was thick and there was no light, he could see nothing ahead and nothing behind him. After three leagues the darkness was thick, and there was no light, he could see nothing ahead and nothing behind him. After four leagues the darkness was thick and there was no light, he could see nothing ahead and nothing behind him. At the end of five leagues the darkness was thick and there was no light, he could see nothing ahead and nothing behind him. At the end of six leagues the darkness was thick and there was no light, he could see nothing ahead and nothing behind him. When he had gone seven leagues the darkness was thick and there was no light, he could see nothing ahead and nothing behind him. When he had gone eight leagues Gilgamesh gave a great cry, for the darkness was thick and he could see nothing ahead and nothing behind him. After nine leagues he felt the north wind on his face, but the darkness was thick and there was no light, he could see nothing ahead and nothing behind him. After ten leagues the end was near. After eleven leagues the dawn light appeared. At the end of twelve leagues the sun streamed out.

There was the garden of the gods; all round him stood bushes bearing gems. Seeing it he went down at once, for there was fruit of carnelian with the vine hanging from it, beautiful to look at; lapis lazuli leaves hung thick with fruit, sweet to see. For thorns and thistles there were haematite and rare stones, agate, and pearls from out of the sea. While Gilgamesh walked in the garden by the edge of the sea Shamash saw him, and he saw that he was dressed in the skins of animals and ate their flesh. He was distressed, and he spoke and said, "No mortal man has gone this way before, nor will, as long as the winds drive over the sea." And to Gilgamesh he said, "You will never find the life for which you are searching." Gilgamesh said to glorious Shamash, "Now that I have toiled and strayed so far over the wilderness, am I to sleep, and let the earth cover my head for ever? Let my eyes see the sun until they are dazzled with looking. Although I am no better than a dead man, still let me see the light of the sun."

Beside the sea she lives, the woman of the vine, the maker of wine; Siduri[22] sits in the garden at the edge of the sea, with the golden bowl and the golden vats that the gods gave her. She is covered with a veil; and where she sits she sees Gilgamesh coming towards her, wearing skins, the flesh of the gods in his body, but despair in his heart, and his face like the face of one who has made a long journey. She looked, and as she scanned the distance she said in her own heart, "Surely this is some felon; where is he going now?" And she barred her gate against him with the cross-bar and shot home the bolt. But Gilgamesh, hearing the sound of the bolt, threw up his head and lodged his foot in the gate; he called to her, "Young woman, maker of wine, why do you bolt your door; what did you see that made you bar your gate? I will break in your door and burst in your gate, for I am Gilgamesh who seized and killed the Bull of Heaven, I killed the watchman of the cedar forest, I overthrew Humbaba who lived in the forest, and I killed the lions in the passes of the mountain."

Then Siduri said to him, "If you are that Gilgamesh who seized and killed the Bull of Heaven, who killed the watchman of the cedar forest, who overthrew Humbaba that lived in the forest, and killed the lions in the passes of the mountain, why are your cheeks so starved and why is your face so drawn? Why is despair in your

---

[22] **Siduri:** A divine wine-maker who has advice for Gilgamesh.

heart and your face like the face of one who has made a long journey? Yes, why is your face burned from heat and cold, and why do you come here wandering over the pastures in search of the wind?"

Gilgamesh answered her, "And why should not my cheeks be starved and my face drawn? Despair is in my heart and my face is the face of one who has made a long journey, it was burned with heat and with cold. Why should I not wander over the pastures in search of the wind? My friend, my younger brother, he who hunted the wild ass of the wilderness and the panther of the plains, my friend, my younger brother who seized and killed the Bull of Heaven and overthrew Humbaba in the cedar forest, my friend who was very dear to me and who endured dangers beside me, Enkidu my brother, whom I loved, the end of mortality has overtaken him. I wept for him seven days and nights till the worm fastened on him. Because of my brother I am afraid of death, because of my brother I stray through the wilderness and cannot rest. But now, young woman, maker of wine, since I have seen your face do not let me see the face of death which I dread so much."

She answered, "Gilgamesh, where are you hurrying to? You will never find that life for which you are looking. When the gods created man they allotted to him death, but life they retained in their own keeping. As for you, Gilgamesh, fill your belly with good things; day and night, night and day, dance and be merry, feast and rejoice. Let your clothes be fresh, bathe yourself in water, cherish the little child that holds your hand, and make your wife happy in your embrace; for this too is the lot of man."

But Gilgamesh said to Siduri, the young woman, "How can I be silent, how can I rest, when Enkidu whom I love is dust, and I too shall die and be laid in the earth. You live by the seashore and look into the heart of it; young woman, tell me now, which is the way to Utnapishtim, the son of Ubara-Tutu? What directions are there for the passage; give me, oh, give me directions. I will cross the Ocean if it is possible; if it is not I will wander still farther in the wilderness." The wine-maker said to him, "Gilgamesh, there is no crossing the Ocean; whoever has come, since the days of old, has not been able to pass that sea. The Sun in his glory crosses the Ocean, but who beside Shamash has ever crossed it? The place and the passage are difficult, and the waters of death are deep which flow between. Gilgamesh, how will you cross the Ocean? When you come to the waters of death what will you do? But Gilgamesh, down in the woods you will find Urshanabi,[23] the ferryman of Utnapishtim; with him are the holy things, the things of stone. He is fashioning the serpent prow of the boat. Look at him well, and if it is possible, perhaps you will cross the waters with him; but if it is not possible, then you must go back."

When Gilgamesh heard this he was seized with anger. He took his axe in his hand, and his dagger from his belt. He crept forward and he fell on them like a javelin. Then he went into the forest and sat down. Urshanabi saw the dagger flash and heard the axe, and he beat his head, for Gilgamesh had shattered the tackle of the boat in his rage. Urshanabi said to him, "Tell me, what is your name? I am Urshanabi, the

---

[23] **Urshanabi:** A boatman comparable to the Greek Charon.

ferryman of Utnapishtim the Faraway." He replied to him, "Gilgamesh is my name, I am from Uruk, from the house of Anu." Then Urshanabi said to him, "Why are your cheeks so starved and your face drawn? Why is despair in your heart and your face like the face of one who has made a long journey; yes, why is your face burned with heat and with cold, and why do you come here wandering over the pastures in search of the wind?"

Gilgamesh said to him, "Why should not my cheeks be starved and my face drawn? Despair is in my heart, and my face is the face of one who has made a long journey. I was burned with heat and with cold. Why should I not wander over the pastures? My friend, my younger brother who seized and killed the Bull of Heaven, and overthrew Humbaba in the cedar forest, my friend who was very dear to me, and who endured dangers beside me, Enkidu my brother whom I loved, the end of mortality has overtaken him. I wept for him seven days and nights till the worm fastened on him. Because of my brother I am afraid of death, because of my brother I stray through the wilderness. His fate lies heavy upon me. How can I be silent, how can I rest? He is dust and I too shall die and be laid in the earth for ever. I am afraid of death, therefore, Urshanabi, tell me which is the road to Utnapishtim? If it is possible I will cross the waters of death; if not I will wander still farther through the wilderness."

Urshanabi said to him, "Gilgamesh, your own hands have prevented you from crossing the Ocean; when you destroyed the tackle of the boat you destroyed its safety." Then the two of them talked it over and Gilgamesh said, "Why are you so angry with me, Urshanabi, for you yourself cross the sea by day and night, at all seasons you cross it." "Gilgamesh, those things you destroyed, their property is to carry me over the water, to prevent the waters of death from touching me. It was for this reason that I preserved them, but you have destroyed them, and the *urnu* snakes with them. But now, go into the forest, Gilgamesh; with your axe cut poles, one hundred and twenty, cut them sixty cubits long, paint them with bitumen, set on them ferrules and bring them back."

When Gilgamesh heard this he went into the forest, he cut poles one hundred and twenty; he cut them sixty cubits long, he painted them with bitumen, he set on them ferrules, and he brought them to Urshanabi. Then they boarded the boat, Gilgamesh and Urshanabi together, launching it out on the waves of Ocean. For three days they ran on as it were a journey of a month and fifteen days, and at last Urshanabi brought the boat to the waters of death. Then Urshanabi said to Gilgamesh, "Press on, take a pole and thrust it in, but do not let your hands touch the waters. Gilgamesh, take a second pole, take a third, take a fourth pole. Now, Gilgamesh, take a fifth, take a sixth and seventh pole. Gilgamesh, take an eighth, and ninth, a tenth pole. Gilgamesh, take an eleventh, take a twelfth pole." After one hundred and twenty thrusts Gilgamesh had used the last pole. Then he stripped himself, he held up his arms for a mast and his covering for a sail. So Urshanabi the ferryman brought Gilgamesh to Utnapishtim, whom they call the Faraway, who lives in Dilmun at the place of the sun's transit, eastward of the mountain. To him alone of men the gods had given everlasting life.

Now Utnapishtim, where he lay at ease, looked into the distance and he said in his heart, musing to himself, "Why does the boat sail here without tackle and mast; why are the sacred stones destroyed, and why does the master not sail the boat? That man who comes is none of mine; where I look I see a man whose body is covered with skins of beasts. Who is this who walks up the shore behind Urshanabi, for surely he is no man of mine?" So Utnapishtim looked at him and said, "What is your name, you who come here wearing the skins of beasts, with your cheeks starved and your face drawn? Where are you hurrying to now? For what reason have you made this great journey, crossing the seas whose passage is difficult? Tell me the reason for your coming."

He replied, "Gilgamesh is my name. I am from Uruk, from the house of Anu." Then Utnapishtim said to him, "If you are Gilgamesh, why are your cheeks so starved and your face drawn? Why is despair in your heart and your face like the face of one who has made a long journey? Yes, why is your face burned with heat and cold, and why do you come here, wandering over the wilderness in search of the wind?"

Gilgamesh said to him, "Why should not my cheeks be starved and my face drawn? Despair is in my heart and my face is the face of one who has made a long journey. It was burned with heat and with cold. Why should I not wander over the pastures? My friend, my younger brother who seized and killed the Bull of Heaven and overthrew Humbaba in the cedar forest, my friend who was very dear to me and endured dangers beside me, Enkidu, my brother whom I loved, the end of mortality has overtaken him. I wept for him seven days and nights till the worm fastened on him. Because of my brother I am afraid of death; because of my brother I stray through the wilderness. His fate lies heavy upon me. How can I be silent, how can I rest? He is dust and I shall die also and be laid in the earth for ever." Again Gilgamesh said, speaking to Utnapishtim, "It is to see Utnapishtim whom we call the Faraway that I have come this journey. For this I have wandered over the world, I have crossed many difficult ranges, I have crossed the seas, I have wearied myself with travelling; my joints are aching, and I have lost acquaintance with sleep which is sweet. My clothes were worn out before I came to the house of Siduri. I have killed the bear and hyena, the lion and panther, the tiger, the stag and the ibex, all sorts of wild game and the small creatures of the pastures. I ate their flesh and I wore their skins; and that was how I came to the gate of the young woman, the maker of wine, who barred her gate of pitch and bitumen against me. But from her I had news of the journey; so then I came to Urshanabi the ferryman, and with him I crossed over the waters of death. Oh, father Utnapishtim, you who have entered the assembly of the gods, I wish to question you concerning the living and the dead, how shall I find the life for which I am searching?"

Utnapishtim said, "There is no permanence. Do we build a house to stand for ever, do we seal a contract to hold for all time? Do brothers divide an inheritance to keep for ever, does the flood-time of rivers endure? It is only the nymph of the dragon-fly who sheds her larva and sees the sun in his glory. From the days of old there is no permanence. The sleeping and the dead, how alike they are, they are like a painted death. What is there between the master and the servant when both have fulfilled their doom? When the Anunnaki, the judges, come together, and Mammetun the mother of destinies, together they decree the fates of men. Life and death they allot but the day of death they do not disclose."

Then Gilgamesh said to Utnapishtim the Faraway, "I look at you now, Utnapishtim, and your appearance is no different from mine; there is nothing strange in your features. I thought I should find you like a hero prepared for battle, but you lie here taking your ease on your back. Tell me truly, how was it that you came to enter the company of the gods and to possess everlasting life?" Utnapishtim said to Gilgamesh; "I will reveal to you a mystery, I will tell you a secret of the gods."

5

THE STORY OF THE FLOOD

"You know the city Shurrupak, it stands on the banks of Euphrates? That city grew old and the gods that were in it were old. There was Anu, lord of the firmament, their father, and warrior Enlil their counsellor, Ninurta the helper, and Ennugi watcher over canals; and with them also was Ea. In those days the world teemed, the people multiplied, the world bellowed like a wild bull, and the great god was aroused by the clamour. Enlil heard the clamour and he said to the gods in council, 'The uproar of mankind is intolerable and sleep is no longer possible by reason of the babel.' So the gods agreed to exterminate mankind. Enlil did this, but Ea because of his oath warned me in a dream. He whispered their words to my house of reeds, 'Reed-house, reed-house! Wall, O wall, hearken reed-house, wall reflect; O man of Shurrupak, son of Ubara-Tutu; tear down your house and build a boat, abandon possessions and look for life, despise worldly goods and save your soul alive. Tear down your house, I say, and build a boat. These are the measurements of the barque as you shall build her: let her beam equal her length, let her deck be roofed like the vault that covers the abyss; then take up into the boat the seed of all living creatures.'

"When I had understood I said to my lord, 'Behold, what you have commanded I will honour and perform, but how shall I answer the people, the city, the elders?' Then Ea opened his mouth and said to me, his servant, 'Tell them this: I have learnt that Enlil is wrathful against me, I dare no longer walk in his land nor live in his city; I will go down to the Gulf to dwell with Ea my lord. But on you he will rain down abundance, rare fish and shy wild-fowl, a rich harvest-tide. In the evening the rider of the storm will bring you wheat in torrents.'

"In the first light of dawn all my household gathered round me, the children brought pitch and the men whatever was necessary. On the fifth day I laid the keel and the ribs, then I made fast the planking. The ground-space was one acre, each side of the deck measured one hundred and twenty cubits, making a square. I built six decks below, seven in all, I divided them into nine sections with bulk-heads between. I drove in wedges where needed, I saw to the punt-poles, and laid in supplies. The carriers brought oil in baskets, I poured pitch into the furnace and asphalt and oil; more oil was consumed in caulking, and more again the master of the boat took into his stores. I slaughtered bullocks for the people and every day I killed sheep. I gave the shipwrights wine to drink as though it were river water, raw wine and red wine and oil and white wine. There was feasting then as there is at the time of the New Year's festival; I myself anointed my head. On the seventh day the boat was complete.

"Then was the launching full of difficulty; there was shifting of ballast above and below till two thirds was submerged. I loaded into her all that I had of gold and of living things, my family, my kin, the beast of the field both wild and tame, and all the craftsmen. I sent them on board, for the time that Shamash had ordained was already fulfilled when he said, 'In the evening, when the rider of the storm sends down the destroying rain, enter the boat and batten her down.' The time was fulfilled, the evening came, the rider of the storm sent down the rain. I looked out at the weather and it was terrible, so I too boarded the boat and battened her down. All was now complete, the battening and the caulking; so I handed the tiller to Puzur-Amurri the steersman, with the navigation and the care of the whole boat.

"With the first light of dawn a black cloud came from the horizon; it thundered within where Adad, lord of the storm, was riding. In front over hill and plain Shullat and Hanish, heralds of the storm, led on. Then the gods of the abyss rose up; Nergal pulled out the dams of the nether waters, Ninurta the war-lord threw down the dykes, and the seven judges of hell, the Anunnaki, raised their torches, lighting the land with their livid flame. A stupor of despair went up to heaven when the god of the storm turned daylight to darkness, when he smashed the land like a cup. One whole day the tempest raged, gathering fury as it went, it poured over the people like the tides of battle; a man could not see his brother nor the people be seen from heaven. Even the gods were terrified at the flood, they fled to the highest heaven, the firmament of Anu; they crouched against the walls, cowering like curs. Then Ishtar the sweet-voiced Queen of Heaven cried out like a woman in travail: 'Alas the days of old are turned to dust because I commanded evil; why did I command this evil in the council of all the gods? I commanded wars to destroy the people, but are they not my people, for I brought them forth? Now like the spawn of fish they float in the ocean.' The great gods of heaven and of hell wept, they covered their mouths.

"For six days and six nights the winds blew, torrent and tempest and flood overwhelmed the world, tempest and flood raged together like warring hosts. When the seventh day dawned the storm from the south subsided, the sea grew calm, the flood was stilled; I looked at the face of the world and there was silence, all mankind was turned to clay. The surface of the sea stretched as flat as a roof-top; I opened a hatch and the light fell on my face. Then I bowed low, I sat down and I wept, the tears streamed down my face, for on every side was the waste of water. I looked for land in vain, but fourteen leagues distant there appeared a mountain, and there the boat grounded; on the mountain of Nisir the boat held fast, she held fast and did not budge. One day she held, and a second day on the mountain of Nisir she held fast and did not budge. A third day, and a fourth day she held fast on the mountain and did not budge; a fifth day and a sixth day she held fast on the mountain. When the seventh day dawned I loosed a dove and let her go. She flew away, but finding no resting-place she returned. Then I loosed a swallow, and she flew away but finding no resting-place she returned. I loosed a raven, she saw that the waters had retreated, she ate, she flew around, she cawed, and she did not come back. Then I threw everything open to the four winds, I made a sacrifice and poured out a libation on the mountain top. Seven and again seven cauldrons I set up on their stands, I heaped up wood and cane and cedar and myrtle. When the gods smelled the sweet savour, they gathered like flies over the sacrifice. Then, at last, Ishtar also came, she lifted her necklace with the jewels of heaven that once Anu had made to please her. 'O you gods here present, by the lapis lazuli round my neck I shall remember these days as I remember the jewels of my throat; these last days I shall not forget. Let all the gods gather round the sacrifice, except Enlil. He shall not approach this offering, for without reflection he brought the flood; he consigned my people to destruction.'

"When Enlil had come, when he saw the boat, he was wrath and swelled with anger at the gods, the host of heaven, 'Has any of these mortals escaped? Not one was to have survived the destruction.' Then the god of the wells and canals Ninurta opened his mouth and said to the warrior Enlil, 'Who is there of the gods that can devise without Ea? It is Ea alone who knows all things.' Then Ea opened his mouth and spoke to warrior Enlil, 'Wisest of gods, hero Enlil, how could you so senselessly bring down the flood?

> Lay upon the sinner his sin,
> Lay upon the transgressor his transgression,
> Punish him a little when he breaks loose,
> Do not drive him too hard or he perishes;
> Would that a lion had ravaged mankind
> Rather than the flood,
> Would that a wolf had ravaged mankind
> Rather than the flood,
> Would that famine had wasted the world
> Rather than the flood,
> Would that pestilence had wasted mankind
> Rather than the flood.

It was not I that revealed the secret of the gods; the wise man learned it in a dream. Now take your counsel what shall be done with him.'

"Then Enlil went up into the boat, he took me by the hand and my wife and made us enter the boat and kneel down on either side, he standing between us. He touched our foreheads to bless us saying, 'In time past Utnapishtim was a mortal man; henceforth he and his wife shall live in the distance at the mouth of the rivers.' Thus it was that the gods took me and placed me here to live in the distance, at the mouth of the rivers."

6

THE RETURN

Utnapishtim said, "As for you, Gilgamesh, who will assemble the gods for your sake, so that you may find that life for which you are searching? But if you wish, come and put it to the test: only prevail against sleep for six days and seven nights." But while Gilgamesh sat there resting on his haunches, a mist of sleep like soft wool teased from the fleece drifted over him, and Utnapishtim said to his wife, "Look at him now, the strong man who would have everlasting life, even now the mists of sleep are drifting over him." His wife replied, "Touch the man to wake him, so that he may return to his own land in peace, going back through the gate by which he came." Utnapishtim said to his wife, "All men are deceivers, even you he will attempt to deceive; therefore bake loaves of bread, each day one loaf, and put it beside his head; and make a mark on the wall to number the days he has slept."

So she baked loaves of bread, each day one loaf, and put it beside his head, and she marked on the wall the days that he slept; and there came a day when the first loaf was hard, the second loaf was like leather, the third was soggy, the crust of the fourth had mould, the fifth was mildewed, the sixth was fresh, and the seventh was still on the embers. Then Utnapishtim touched him and he woke. Gilgamesh said to Utnapishtim the Faraway, "I hardly slept when you touched and roused me." But Utnapishtim said, "Count these loaves and learn how many days you slept, for your first is hard, your second like leather, your third is soggy, the crust of your fourth has mould, your fifth is mildewed, your sixth is fresh and your seventh was still over the glowing embers when I touched and woke you." Gilgamesh said, "What shall I do, O Utnapishtim, where shall I go? Already the thief in the night has hold of my limbs, death inhabits my room; wherever my foot rests, there I find death."

Then Utnapishtim spoke to Urshanabi the ferryman: "Woe to you Urshanabi, now and for ever more you have become hateful to this harbourage; it is not for you, nor for you are the crossings of this sea. Go now, banished from the shore. But this man before whom you walked, bringing him here, whose body is covered with foulness and the grace of whose limbs has been spoiled by wild skins, take him to the washing-place. There he shall wash his long hair clean as snow in the water, he shall throw off his skins and let the sea carry them away, and the beauty of his body shall be shown, the fillet on his forehead shall be renewed, and he shall be given clothes to cover his nakedness. Till he reaches his own city and his journey is accomplished, these clothes will show no sign of age, they will wear like a new garment." So Urshanabi took Gilgamesh and led him to the washing-place, he washed his long hair as clean as snow in the water, he threw off his skins, which the sea carried away, and showed the beauty of his body. He renewed the fillet on his forehead, and to cover his nakedness gave him clothes which would show no sign of age, but would wear like a new garment till he reached his own city, and his journey was accomplished.

Then Gilgamesh and Urshanabi launched the boat on to the water and boarded it, and they made ready to sail away; but the wife of Utnapishtim the Faraway said to him, "Gilgamesh came here wearied out, he is worn out; what will you give him to carry him back to his own country?" So Utnapishtim spoke, and Gilgamesh took a pole and brought the boat in to the bank. "Gilgamesh, you came here a man wearied out, you have worn yourself out; what shall I give you to carry you back to your own country? Gilgamesh, I shall reveal a secret thing, it is a mystery of the gods that I am telling you. There is a plant that grows under the water, it has a prickle like a thorn, like a rose; it will wound your hands, but if you succeed in taking it, then your hands will hold that which restores his lost youth to a man."

When Gilgamesh heard this he opened the sluices so that a sweet-water current might carry him out to the deepest channel; he tied heavy stones to his feet and they dragged him down to the water-bed. There he saw the plant growing; although it pricked him he took it in his hands; then he cut the heavy stones from his feet, and the sea carried him and threw him on to the shore. Gilgamesh said to Urshanabi the ferryman, "Come here, and see this marvellous plant. By its virtue a man may win back all his former strength. I will take it to Uruk of the strong walls; there I will give it to the old men to eat. Its name shall be 'The Old Men Are Young Again'; and at last I shall eat it myself and have back all my lost youth." So Gilgamesh returned by the gate through which he had come, Gilgamesh and Urshanabi went together. They travelled their twenty leagues and then they broke their fast; after thirty leagues they stopped for the night.

Gilgamesh saw a well of cool water and he went down and bathed; but deep in the pool there was lying a serpent, and the serpent sensed the sweetness of the flower. It rose out of the water and snatched it away, and immediately it sloughed its skin and returned to the well. Then Gilgamesh sat down and wept, the tears ran down his face, and he took the hand of Urshanabi; "O Urshanabi, was it for this that I toiled with my hands, is it for this I have wrung out my heart's blood? For myself I have gained nothing; not I, but the beast of the earth has joy of it now. Already the stream has carried it twenty leagues back to the channels where I found it. I found a sign and now I have lost it. Let us leave the boat on the bank and go."

After twenty leagues they broke their fast, after thirty leagues they stopped for the night; in three days they had walked as much as a journey of a month and fifteen days. When the journey was accomplished they arrived at Uruk, the strong-walled city. Gilgamesh spoke to him, to Urshanabi the ferryman, "Urshanabi, climb up on to the wall of Uruk, inspect its foundation terrace, and examine well the brickwork; see if it is not of burnt bricks; and did not the seven wise men lay these foundations? One third of the whole is city, one third is garden, and one third is field, with the precinct of the goddess Ishtar. These parts and the precinct are all Uruk."

This too was the work of Gilgamesh, the king, who knew the countries of the world. He was wise, he saw mysteries and knew secret things, he brought us a tale of the days before the flood. He went a long journey, was weary, worn out with labour, and returning engraved on a stone the whole story.

7

THE DEATH OF GILGAMESH

The destiny was fulfilled which the father of the gods, Enlil of the mountain, had decreed for Gilgamesh: "In nether-earth the darkness will show him a light: Of mankind, all that are known, none will leave a monument for generations to come to compare with his. The heroes, the wise men, like the new moon have their waxing and waning. Men will say, 'Who has ever ruled with might and with power like him?' As in the dark month, the month of shadows, so without him there is no light. O Gil-gamesh, this was the meaning of your dream. You were given the kingship, such was your destiny, everlasting life was not your destiny. Because of this do not be sad at heart, do not be grieved or oppressed; he has given you power to bind and to loose, to be the darkness and the light of mankind. He has given unexampled supremacy over the people, victory in battle from which no fugitive returns, in forays and assaults from which there is no going back. But do not abuse this power, deal justly with your servants in the palace, deal justly before the face of the Sun."

> The king has laid himself down and will not rise again,
> The Lord of Kullab will not rise again;
> He overcame evil, he will not come again;
> Though he was strong of arm he will not rise again;
>
> He had wisdom and a comely face, he will not come again;
> He is gone into the mountain, he will not come again;
> On the bed of fate he lies, he will not rise again,
> From the couch of many colours he will not come again.

The people of the city, great and small, are not silent; they lift up the lament, all men of flesh and blood lift up the lament. Fate has spoken; like a hooked fish he lies stretched on the bed, like a gazelle that is caught in a noose. Inhuman Namtar is heavy upon him, Namtar that has neither hand nor foot, that drinks no water and eats no meat.

For Gilgamesh, son of Ninsun, they weighed out their offerings; his dear wife, his son, his concubine, his musicians, his jester, and all his household; his servants, his stewards, all who lived in the palace weighed out their offerings for Gilgamesh the son of Ninsun, the heart of Uruk. They weighed out their offerings to Ereshkigal, the Queen of Death, and to all the gods of the dead. To Namtar, who is fate, they weighed out the offering. Bread for Neti the Keeper of the Gate, bread for Ningizzida the god of the serpent, the lord of the Tree of Life; for Dumuzi[24] also, the young shepherd, for Enki and Ninki, for Endukugga and Nindukugga,[25] for Enmul and Ninmul, all the ancestral gods, forbears of Enlil. A feast for Shulpae the god of feasting. For Samuqan, god of the herds, for the mother Ninhursag, and the gods of creation in the place of creation, for the host of heaven, priest and priestess weighed out the offering of the dead.

Gilgamesh, the son of Ninsun, lies in the tomb. At the place of offerings he weighed the bread-offering, at the place of libation he poured out the wine. In those days the lord Gilgamesh departed, the son of Ninsun, the king, peerless, without an equal among men, who did not neglect Enlil his master. O Gilgamesh, lord of Kullab, great is thy praise.

---

[24] **Dumuzi:** The Sumerian version of Tammuz.   [25] **Enki . . . Nindukugga:** Gods of the underworld.

TEXT IN CONTEXT

✌ HEBREW SCRIPTURES
NEAR EAST, C. 900 – 100 B.C.E.

The National Epic.   The first five books of the Hebrew Bible, the
most important portion of the Scriptures to Orthodox Jews, are called
the Pentateuch or the Torah (the Law). The Torah was originally
divided into books because in its entirety it was too long for a single
roll of papyrus or parchment. The most important writer of this
section is identified as "J," so named because he uses Jahweh (Yahweh)
for God's name. This author constructed a national epic that begins
with the creation of the world and the lives of the first humans in
Genesis 2:5. Using the folk materials of his day, the "J"author tells the
story of how humans were tempted by a talking snake and rebelled
against Yahweh, causing him to curse the natural world, inflict pain
on women in childbirth, and drive these first ancestors out of Eden.
He describes the founding of the Hebrews' tribal identity under a
series of patriarchs and chronicles this people's escape from Egyptian
bondage under a heroic leader called Moses. After receiving an ethical
code from their god on Mt. Sinai, the Hebrews triumphantly enter
the land of Canaan, which had been promised to their first patriarch,
Abraham. With its central themes of obedience, rebellion, and
reconciliation, this story became the founding story of the nation
of Israel and of the Jews, in the same way that the Trojan War story
for the Greeks and the story of Aeneas for the Romans were founding
tales. Herman Wouk in *This Is My God* summarizes this theme for
Judaism:

The Hebrew Bible read as living literature is a tragic epic with a single long plot: the tale of the fall of a hero through his weaknesses. The hero is Israel, a people given a destiny almost too high for human beings, the charge of God's law. . . . Unlike all other epic tragedies, it does not end in death. The hero has eternal life, and the prospect of ages of pain in which to rise at long last to the destiny which he cannot escape.

Through a variety of literatures—myth, history, poetry, drama, biography, philosophy, and prophecy—the Hebrew Scriptures record a people's struggle to understand the all-powerful, complex, and seemingly contradictory deity Yahweh and to live up to the terms of a series of agreements or covenants with Him. On one hand Yahweh is a god of violence and destruction, wiping out cities, flooding the world, demanding death without mercy for his enemies. On the other, He is

Sacrifice of Isaac, **Mosaic Pavement from the Beth-Alpha Synagogue, Hefzibah, early sixth century**
One of the most important stories in Hebrew Scriptures tells of the near sacrifice of Isaac by his father, the Hebrew patriarch Abraham. Ordered by God to murder his son, Abraham prepares to do so before he is stopped by the hand of God and rewarded for his willingness to perform the ultimate sacrifice. (Z. Radovan, Jerusalem)

a giving deity, as revealed in the terms of the covenant: In return for His peoples' obedience, faithfulness, and loyalty, He will bestow blessings on the chosen ones of Israel. Yahweh is very much like a stern but loving father who both reprimands and rewards his children.

The Jewish focus on Yahweh, on monotheism, and on a comprehensive code of ethics was shaped by Hebrew poets and prophets and formulated into basic concepts that influenced Western civilization.

Genesis.   The first book of the Hebrew Scriptures divides into two parts: primeval history (chapters 1–11) and patriarchal tales (chapters 12–50). According to modern scholarship the stories in Genesis were written and edited between 900 and 500 B.C.E. What has been called the Mythological Cycle (chapters 1–11) includes two accounts of creation, the Fall of man, the first murder, the deluge, and the Tower of Babel. The materials in this portion of Genesis are called myth or folklore by some scholars, not because they are considered false but because they deal with God and human relationships in a timeless, prehistorical manner and share similarities with the creation stories of other cultures in the ancient Near East. The Babylonian flood story from the second millennium B.C.E., in particular, helped shape the biblical version. These stories are studied for their effects on modern ideas about gender roles, the origins of sin or evil, the relationship of God to humans and to nature, the idea of estrangement from Eden, and the yearning for paradise.

The legends of the four patriarchs in the second part of Genesis explore family relationships and the role of Yahweh in setting a direction for the nation of Israel.

Patriarchs.   The second part of Genesis begins in chapter 12, with stories of tribal fathers, rivalry between brothers, and conflict between fathers and sons. Scholars tend to interpret these legendary stories of the patriarchs Abraham, Isaac, Jacob, and Joseph as histories of whole clans or tribes over a period of some six hundred years, c. 2000–1400 B.C.E. They believe the patriarchal patterns of conflict within these biblical tribal families parallel the rivalries among the Semitic tribes of nomads who were migrating from the Arabian peninsula into the Fertile Crescent and formulating their religion and culture during this time period. The writer of those biblical stories stresses the unique identity of the Hebrews, their having been chosen by a personal deity who entered into a series of covenants with the founding fathers and promised them a prosperous future.

Moses Guiding the Hebrews
Detail from a late Roman sarcophagus. (The Art Archive/Archaeological Museum Naples/Dagli Orti)

According to Hebrew Scriptures, Abraham, the first patriarch, came from Ur of the Chaldees, an ancient Sumerian city in Mesopotamia, sometime around 2000 b.c.e. His journey apparently represents the movement of Amorites into the southern portion of Canaan (the land of Palestine). The stories about Abraham and his descendants are full of twists and unexpected ironies: Concubines assist their own sons in the competition for the patriarchal inheritance, Jacob wins a wrestling match with an angel, and Joseph shows his brilliance interpreting dreams and managing an empire.

In 1700 b.c.e. a number of Canaanite and Amorite tribes moved farther on, to Egypt, where they were known as Hyksos (foreign chiefs). The migration of Joseph and his brothers southward into Egypt mirrors this historical event. Egyptians eventually enslaved the Hyksos interlopers, a fact to which the story of the Hebrew slaves at the beginning of the Book of Exodus may allude.

Exodus.   The Book of Exodus has the same dates of composition as Genesis: between 900 and 500 b.c.e. Exodus describes the emergence of the extraordinary leader Moses, the historical founder of Judaism and

The Bible, once thought of as a source of secular literature yet somehow apart from it, now bids fair to become part of the literary canon . . . Indeed, it seems we have reached a turning point in the history of criticism, for the Bible, under a new aspect, has reoccupied the literary culture.

– ROBERT ALTER and
FRANK KERMODE,
critics, 1987

the person primarily responsible for the transition of the Hebrew people
from a tribal to a national culture. Moses is believed to have led his
people out of slavery in Egypt sometime in the thirteenth century B.C.E.,
during the Nineteenth Dynasty ruled by the famous pharaohs Seti
(1308–1290 B.C.E.) and Ramses II (1292–1225 B.C.E.). The song of Miriam,
dating from the thirteenth century B.C.E., celebrates a victory over the
Egyptian chariots and is probably the oldest piece of literature in the
Bible.

> I will sing unto the Lord, for he hath triumphed gloriously:
> The horse and his rider hath he thrown into the sea.

During the forty years of crossing the Sinai Desert (the exact
route is uncertain), Moses prepared his people for settling down in
Canaan — the Promised Land — by transforming tribal groups with
various deities into a more or less unified group under the worship of
a single God, Yahweh. Moses provided the Israelites with a fundamental
religious code, as symbolized by the receiving of the Ten Commandments at Mt. Sinai and detailed in the books of Leviticus and
Deuteronomy. This code, influenced by the Code of Hammurabi[1]
and the Hittite legal system, circumscribed the Hebrews' sacred
calling as the chosen people of Yahweh and provided them with a
legal foundation for communal life and, eventually, nationhood.

The Book of Joshua, named after the successor to Moses, concludes
the "J" epic with the migration of the Hebrews into Canaan and an
idealized description of absolute victories over Canaanite towns.
Yahweh's origin as a tribal deity is revealed in Deuteronomy (chapters
6, 7, and 20), in which Yahweh prescribes ruthless treatment for
defeated populations. Overall, the Hebrews' Exodus story — from
slavery to migration to arrival in the Promised Land — served as an
inspirational model and narrative pattern for later Christians and Jews
as well as a symbol of hope for numerous groups throughout history
who were living in bondage.

Job.   The Book of Job is considered one of the great masterpieces of
Western literature, although its literary form is difficult to classify.
Dating probably from the sixth century B.C.E., Job is a series of
dialogues on the nature of God and divine justice. Even though, in
general, the book belongs to the wisdom tradition of the ancient Near

---

[1] **Code of Hammurabi:** An elaborate body of laws that King Hammurabi (r. 1792–1750 B.C.E.) used to sustain
his Babylonian empire.

East, it is unusual in that it calls into question the validity of the conventional wisdom that a good, pious person will ultimately be rewarded in this lifetime (with a large family and material prosperity) while an evil person will be punished. The problem with the conventional wisdom is simply that experience provides contradictory evidence: Some good or innocent people suffer; some evil people prosper.

It is around this basic issue of cosmic justice that the author of Job creates his debate, which is framed by prose folk material from an earlier age. The book begins with a description of Job, a righteous man, and a discussion in a fictional land between God and Satan—the "accuser"—who wonders whether Job's piety depends on his wealth. Job is then put to a test. When he is finally deprived of all the good things of his life, including his health, Job complains to God about his treatment, and three friends respond in the first cycle of speeches. His friends, in effect, reaffirm conventional wisdom, which argues that God is just and that Job must have sinned in order to have deserved his suffering.

As Job reaffirms his innocence and becomes increasingly isolated in his position, he demands that he be allowed to make his case in person and hear God's response. The climax arrives when God breaks his silence and responds in a whirlwind to Job's request with a discourse on power. The meaning and appropriateness of God's response have been subjects of discussion ever since. Because God does not answer Job's questions directly, it appears as if the author of the Book of Job understands faith to involve a transcendent deity whose connection to this world cannot be readily understood or experienced by human beings, even exemplary ones.

Psalms.   The word *psalm* means a song sung to a harp, indicating that the Book of Psalms, made up of 150 poems, was originally a hymnbook for temple services and for private prayers and meditations. Martin Luther[2] used psalms to create his hymnbook and Johann Sebastian Bach[3] set a number of psalms to music. The verses in the Book of Psalms are known for their concrete imagery and emotional sincerity.

Although as many as seventy-three psalms have been ascribed to David, the authorship of most, probably written after the Babylonian

> [The purpose of the Old Testament] is to record the Hebrews' continuous quest for God — his nature, his will, and his plans — as a basis for the teaching of divine law and morality. Every mood and every condition of human life — sorrow, joy, loneliness, companionship, love, hate, conspiracy, falsehood, truth, loyalty, heroism, cowardice, war, peace, kindness, brutality, hunger, luxury — all are depicted in simple, direct terms as part of the divine stream of history, teaching the lessons of the past as admonitions, sermons, and guides for all who will listen.
> – Buckner B. Trawick, critic, 1970

---

[2] **Martin Luther** (1483–1546 c.e.): The father of the Lutheran Reformation in the fifteenth century; he also translated the Bible into German and composed hymns in German that brought religious literature to ordinary people.

[3] **Johann Sebastian Bach** (1685–1750): German organist and composer.

captivity, between 400 and 100 B.C.E., is unknown. There are various types of psalms: royal psalms, associated with enthronement and the kingship of God; psalms of praise and thanksgiving; psalms of lament and confession.

Psalm 23, "The Lord is my shepherd," with its lyric beauty and comforting message, may be the most well known psalm of all. Psalm 104, "Bless the Lord, my soul," a creation hymn, has often been compared with the Egyptian "Hymn to Aten" and the Mesopotamian "Epic of Creation." Psalm 137, "By the rivers of Babylon we sat down and wept," is a lament the people of Israel sang in exile in Babylon after the destruction of Jerusalem by the Babylonians in 587 B.C.E.

The Song of Songs.   Because of its rather explicit sexual imagery, The Song of Songs is an unusual book to include in a collection of religious writings. In some translations this work is called the Song of Solomon since the first line ascribes the authorship to Solomon (r. c. 961–922 B.C.E.), who was considered a great poet like his father David. Despite the fact that Solomon lends prestige to the work, modern scholars believe that it was written down between 350 and 250 B.C.E., although it may have existed orally for several centuries prior to this. The book is also called Canticles or Canticle of Canticles; a canticle is a hymn using words from the Bible. It appears to have been integrated in Jewish Scripture at the end of the first century C.E. as an allegory of the love of God for the Israelites: King Solomon represented God, the Shulamite represented the Hebrews, and the love was spiritual rather than carnal. Early Christians interpreted the courtship songs as poetic expressions of the love of Christ for his Church, called the bride of Christ in the New Testament. Anthropologists have suggested that the songs are adaptations of pagan fertility ceremonies, like the annual wedding of the Babylonian Tammuz to the goddess Ishtar in the spring, the Egyptian ceremonies involving Osiris and Isis, and the Syrian rites between Adonis and Astarte. In a related interpretation, sociologists see the Song of Songs as a description of an ancient Far Eastern wedding celebration involving a week-long pageant of song and dance.

Not knowing exactly how to classify this piece of writing, some commentators have called it a "Wedding Idyll." An idyll or idyl is a lyric poem that uses picturesque, pastoral images that stress the romantic rather than the heroic. The images of doves, flowers, pomegranates, gardens, gazelles, goats, fawns, honey, raisins, apricots, and wheat not only reflect a natural setting for the songs, but have a long history of associations with sexuality, the human body, and bliss.

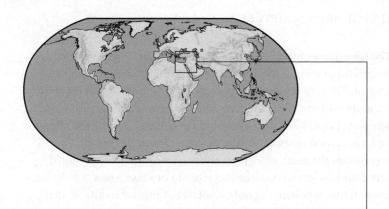

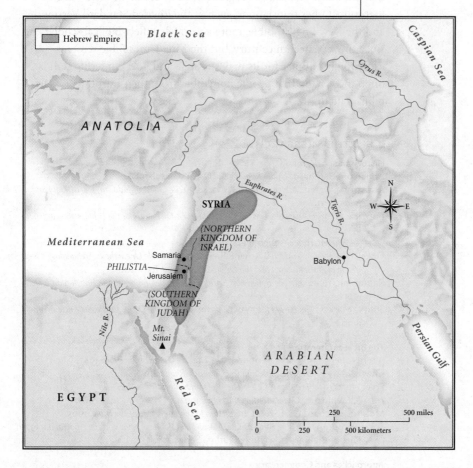

Israel and Judah

King Solomon ruled Israel from 960 to 922 B.C.E. This "Golden Age of Israel" was prosperous and peaceful. After Solomon's death, however, the kingdom was divided into two states, Israel in the north and Judah in the south. Israel vanished as a political entity in 722 B.C.E., and its peoples were dispersed throughout the Near East. In 597 B.C.E. Judah was conquered by King Nebuchadnezzar of Babylon, and in 586 B.C.E. most of the Jewish survivors were deported to Babylon, becoming the first diaspora community.

The King James Bible.   The King James, or Authorized Version, completed in 1611, has been chosen for the Bible selections in this volume. For English-speaking readers, it is the most significant literary translation of the Bible, and has influenced numerous English writers. The King James Bible was brought to the United States by the pilgrims, and was carried westward by the pioneers. Strangely enough, this version was the result of a group effort: in 1604, James I appointed fifty-four scholars who worked together to produce a new translation. These translators were not only scholars but literary stylists, so that they produced not only a religious document but a classic work of literature. Other translations, such as the Revised Standard Version and the New English Bible, more accurately reflect biblical scholarship since the seventeenth century, but the King James Bible remains exceedingly popular for its majestic style and poetic interludes. It is often the version that people remember from their introductions to biblical literature.

■ **FURTHER RESEARCH**

History and Background

Anderson, Bernhard. *Understanding the Old Testament.* 1986.

Armstrong, Karen. *A History of God: The 4000-Year Quest of Judaism, Christianity and Islam.* 1993.

Buttrick, George A. et al., eds., *The Interpreter's Dictionary of the Bible.* 1962, 1976. (5 vols.)

————. *The Interpreter's Bible.* 1952. (12 vols.)

Finkelstein, Israel, and Neil Asher Silberman. *The Bible Unearthed: Archaeology's New Vision of Ancient Israel and the Origin of Its Sacred Texts.* 2001.

Kaufmann, Yehezkel. *The Religion of Israel: From Its Beginnings to the Babylonian Exile.* 1961.

Smith, Mark S. *The Early History of God: Yahweh and the Other Deities in Ancient Israel.* 1990.

The Bible as Literature

Alter, Robert, and Frank Kermode. *The Literary Guide to the Bible.* 1987.

Chase, Mary Ellen. *The Bible and the Common Reader.* 1952.

Frye, Northrop. *The Great Code: The Bible and Literature.* 1982.

Harris, Stephen L. *Understanding the Bible.* 1992.

Moulton, Richard G. *A Short Introduction to the Literature of the Bible.* 1903.

Trawick, Buckner B. *The Bible as Literature: The Old Testament and the Apocrapha.* 1970. Part of the Barnes & Noble Outline Series.

Approaches and Commentary

Fromm, Erich. *You Shall Be As Gods: A Radical Interpretation of the Old Testament and Its Tradition.* 1966.

Kushner, Harold S. *When Bad Things Happen to Good People.* 1981.

Terrien, Samuel. *The Psalms and Their Meaning Today.* 1952.

The Ancient Hebrews: The Great Temple

The great Temple in Jerusalem was King Solomon's (r. c. 961 to 922 b.c.e.) crowning achievement and the Hebrews' premier religious monument. Its construction marked a period of unprecedented growth and prosperity. Decorated with gold leaf—a striking symbol of Israel's wealth and political power—the Temple was the house of the Hebrew god, Yahweh, and the home of the Ark of the Covenant, the revered chest that reputedly contained the stones on which were inscribed the Ten Commandments.

Bronze Calf, twelfth century b.c.e.   When Moses descended from Mt. Sinai, where he had received the Ten Commandments, he found the Hebrews venerating a golden calf. He destroyed the calf and banned the worship of foreign idols forever. (Z. Radovan, Jerusalem)

The Hebrews, as chronicled in their scriptures, had endured a long history of hardship and slavery and had never had the opportunity to rule themselves. That history came to an end in 1020 b.c.e. with the rise of King Saul and King David. David united the disparate Hebrew tribes, creating the first Hebrew nation in 1000 b.c.e. David's unification of the Hebrew peoples—accomplished by unifying Israel and Judah—created the first nation the Hebrews could call their own. It was in this nation that the Temple was built. The building of the Temple by David's son, Solomon, solidified and symbolized the new, united nation of Israel.

The Temple was destroyed by Babylonians four hundred years later, in 587 b.c.e. For a time, Judaism (the religion of the Jews) became centered more around the Hebrew Scriptures than temple rituals and the calendar for prescribed sacrifices. A second temple was built on the site of the first seventy years later. It was to survive for more than five hundred years. Jerusalem was eventually taken over by Rome, and Herod the Great, king of Judea (40–4 b.c.e.) even reconstructed and built an elaborate third temple. Under Roman rule, however, the Jews were more and more distrusted. One complaint had to do with the Temple itself, which was criticized for its bald display of wealth. Even Jesus disapproved of the proliferation of gold and the materialism that had enveloped the Temple.

The Third Temple was destroyed in 70 c.e., coinciding with the expulsion of the Hebrews from Jerusalem. The ruins of the Temple came to symbolize the dispersion of the Hebrew people all over the world, the Jewish Diaspora. The Temple is still invoked today as a symbol of lost nationhood. On the site where it once was now stands one of the most sacred sites in the Muslim world, the Dome of the Rock.

✺ Genesis

ORIGIN STORIES

1[1]

In the beginning God created the heaven and the earth.[2] And the earth was without form, and void, and darkness was upon the face of the deep,[3] and the spirit of God moved upon the face of the waters. And God said, "Let there be light": and there was light. And God saw the light, that it was good: and God divided the light from the darkness. And God called the light Day, and the darkness he called Night: and the evening and the morning were the first day.

And God said, "Let there be a firmament[4] in the midst of the waters: and let it divide the waters from the waters." And God made the firmament, and divided the waters which were under the firmament from the waters which were above the firmament: and it was so. And God called the firmament Heaven: and the evening and the morning were the second day.

And God said, "Let the waters under the heaven be gathered together unto one place, and let the dry land appear": and it was so. And God called the dry land Earth, and the gathering together of the waters called he Seas: and God saw that it was good. And God said, "Let the earth bring forth grass, the herb yielding seed, and the fruit tree yielding fruit after his kind, whose seed is in itself, upon the earth": and it was so. And the earth brought forth grass, and herb yielding seed after his kind, and the tree yielding fruit, whose seed was in itself, after his kind: and God saw that it was good. And the evening and the morning were the third day.

And God said, "Let there be lights in the firmament of the heaven, to divide the day from the night: and let them be for signs and for seasons, and for days and years. And let them be for lights in the firmament of the heaven, to give light upon the earth": and it was so. And God made two great lights: the greater light to rule the day, and the lesser light to rule the night: he made the stars also. And God set them in the firmament of the heaven, to give light upon the earth: and to rule over the day, and over the night, and to divide the light from the darkness: and God saw that it was good. And the evening and the morning were the fourth day.

And God said, "Let the waters bring forth abundantly the moving creature that hath life, and fowl that may fly above the earth in the open firmament of heaven." And God created great whales, and every living creature that moveth, which the waters brought forth abundantly after their kind, and every winged fowl after his

---

[1] Verse numbers have been specified only for chapters where verses have been omitted.

[2] **In . . . the earth:** Chapter 1 and the first paragraph of Chapter 2 tell the Priestly story of creation; God is designated in Hebrew as *Elohim.*

[3] **deep:** The Hebrew word for "deep" is *Tehom,* which is related linguistically to *Tiamat,* the feminine monster of chaos in Mesopotamian myth.

[4] **firmament:** The firmament is the solid dome of the sky.

kind: and God saw that it was good. And God blessed them, saying, "Be fruitful, and multiply, and fill the waters in the seas, and let fowl multiply in the earth." And the evening and the morning were the fifth day.

And God said, "Let the earth bring forth the living creature after his kind, cattle, and creeping thing, and beast of the earth after his kind": and it was so. And God made the beast of the earth after his kind, and cattle after their kind, and every thing that creepeth upon the earth after his kind: and God saw that it was good.

And God said, "Let us[5] make man[6] in our image, after our likeness: and let them have dominion over the fish of the sea, and over the fowl of the air, and over the cattle, and over all the earth, and over every creeping thing that creepeth upon the earth." So God created man in his own image, in the image of God created he him; male and female created he them. And God blessed them, and God said unto them, "Be fruitful, and multiply, and replenish the earth, and subdue[7] it, and have dominion over the fish of the sea, and over the fowl of the air, and over every living thing that moveth upon the earth."

And God said, "Behold, I have given you every herb bearing seed which is upon the face of all the earth, and every tree, in the which is the fruit of a tree yielding seed; to you it shall be for meat: and to every beast of the earth, and to every fowl of the air, and to every thing that creepeth upon the earth, wherein there is life, I have given every green herb for meat": and it was so. And God saw every thing that he had made: and behold, it was very good. And the evening and the morning were the sixth day.

2

Thus the heavens and the earth were finished, and all the host of them. And on the seventh day God ended his work which he had made. And he rested on the seventh day from all his work which he had made. And God blessed the seventh day, and sanctified it: because that in it he had rested from all his work which God created and made.

These[8] are the generations of the heavens and of the earth when they were created, in the day that the Lord God[9] made the earth and the heavens, and every plant of the field before it was in the earth, and every herb of the field before it grew: for the Lord God had not caused it to rain upon the earth, and there was not a man to till the ground. But there went up a mist from the earth, and watered the whole face

---

[5] **us:** The "us" and "our" either refer to what is called the "royal we," as in when a king refers to himself in the plural, or actually refer to members of God's heavenly court.

[6] **man:** The Hebrew for *man* is *adam,* referring to mankind.

[7] **subdue:** The meaning of *subdue* has troubled ecologists, especially if *subdue* means willful dominance and exploitation.

[8] This begins the second creation account and is from the "J" account; God is designated as *Jehovah* (Hebrew *Yahweh*). The order of events in this version differ from the first version.

[9] **Lord God:** In Hebrew, *Yahweh Elohim.* This version of creation is thought to be older than 1:1–2:4.

of the ground. And the Lord God formed man of the dust of the ground,[10] and breathed into his nostrils the breath of life; and man became a living soul.

And the Lord God planted a garden eastward in Eden; and there he put the man whom he had formed. And out of the ground made the Lord God to grow every tree that is pleasant to the sight and good for food: the tree of life also in the midst of the garden, and the tree of knowledge of good and evil. And a river went out of Eden to water the garden, and from thence it was parted, and became into four heads. The name of the first is Pison: that is it which compasseth the whole land of Havilah, where there is gold. And the gold of that land is good: there is bdellium and the onyx stone. And the name of the second river is Gihon: the same is it that compasseth the whole land of Ethiopia. And the name of the third river is Hiddekel: that is it which goeth toward the east of Assyria: and the fourth river is Euphrates. And the Lord God took the man, and put him into the garden of Eden, to dress it and to keep it. And the Lord God commanded the man, saying, "Of every tree of the garden thou mayest freely eat. But of the tree of the knowledge of good and evil, thou shalt not eat of it: for in the day that thou eatest thereof thou shalt surely die."

And the Lord God said, "It is not good that the man should be alone: I will make him an help meet for him." And out of the ground the Lord God formed every beast of the field, and every fowl of the air, and brought them unto Adam, to see what he would call them: and whatsoever Adam called every living creature, that was the name thereof. And Adam gave names to all cattle, and to the fowl of the air, and to every beast of the field: but for Adam there was not found an help meet for him. And the Lord God caused a deep sleep to fall upon Adam, and he slept: and he took one of his ribs, and closed up the flesh instead thereof. And the rib which the Lord God had taken from man, made he a woman, and brought her unto the man. And Adam said, "This is now bone of my bones, and flesh of my flesh: she shall be called woman,[11] because she was taken out of man."[12] Therefore shall a man leave his father and his mother, and shall cleave unto his wife: and they shall be one flesh. And they were both naked, the man and his wife, and were not ashamed.

3

Now the serpent was more subtle than any beast of the field which the Lord God had made, and he said unto the woman, "Yea, hath God said, 'Ye shall not eat of every tree of the garden'?" And the woman said unto the serpent, "We may eat of the fruit of the trees of the garden: but of the fruit of the tree which is in the midst of the garden, God hath said, 'Ye shall not eat of it, neither shall ye touch it, lest ye die.'" And the serpent said unto the woman, "Ye shall not surely die. For God doth know that in the day ye eat thereof, then your eyes shall be opened: and ye shall be as gods, knowing good and evil." And when the woman saw that the tree was good for food, and that it was

---

[10] **And . . . the ground:** A pun is intended linking *man* (Hebrew *adam*) to *ground* (Hebrew *adamah*).

[11] **woman:** Another Hebrew word for "man" is *ish* (compare note 6) and is used to distinguish him from "woman," *ishshah*.

[12] **man:** *Ish* in Hebrew.

pleasant to the eyes, and a tree to be desired to make one wise, she took of the fruit thereof, and did eat, and gave also unto her husband with her, and he did eat. And the eyes of them both were opened, and they knew that they were naked, and they sewed fig leaves together, and made themselves aprons. And they heard the voice of the Lord God walking in the garden in the cool of the day: and Adam and his wife hid themselves from the presence of the Lord God, amongst the trees of the garden.

And the Lord God called unto Adam, and said unto him, "Where art thou?" And he said, "I heard thy voice in the garden: and I was afraid, because I was naked, and I hid myself." And he said, "Who told thee that thou wast naked? Hast thou eaten of the tree whereof I commanded thee that thou shouldst not eat?" And the man said, "The woman whom thou gavest to be with me, she gave me of the tree, and I did eat." And the Lord God said unto the woman, "What is this that thou hast done?" And the woman said, "The serpent beguiled me, and I did eat." And the Lord God said unto the serpent, "Because thou hast done this, thou art cursed above all cattle, and above every beast of the field: upon thy belly shalt thou go, and dust shalt thou eat, all the days of thy life. And I will put enmity between thee and the woman, and between thy seed and her seed: it shall bruise thy head, and thou shalt bruise his heel." Unto the woman he said, "I will greatly multiply thy sorrow and thy conception. In sorrow thou shalt bring forth children: and thy desire shall be to thy husband, and he shall rule over thee." And unto Adam he said, "Because thou hast hearkened unto the voice of thy wife, and hast eaten of the tree, of which I commanded thee, saying, 'Thou shalt not eat of it': cursed is the ground for thy sake: in sorrow shalt thou eat of it all the days of thy life. Thorns also and thistles shall it bring forth to thee: and thou shalt eat the herb of the field. In the sweat of thy face shalt thou eat bread, till thou return unto the ground: for out of it wast thou taken, for dust thou art, and unto dust shalt thou return." And Adam called his wife's name Eve,[13] because she was the mother of all living. Unto Adam also, and to his wife, did the Lord God make coats of skins, and clothed them.

And the Lord God said, "Behold, the man is become as one of us, to know good and evil. And now, lest he put forth his hand, and take also of the tree of life, and eat and live for ever—": therefore the Lord God sent him forth from the garden of Eden, to till the ground from whence he was taken. So he drove out the man: and he placed at the east of the garden of Eden cherubim, and a flaming sword which turned every way, to keep the way of the tree of life.

CAIN AND ABEL: THE FIRST MURDER

4:1–17, 25–26

And Adam[14] knew[15] Eve his wife, and she conceived, and bare Cain, and said, "I have gotten a man from the Lord." And she again bare his brother Abel, and Abel was a keeper of sheep, but Cain was a tiller of the ground. And in process of time it came to

---

[13] **Eve:** That is, *Life.*

[14] **Adam:** used for the first time as a name.

[15] **knew:** as in sexual intercourse.

pass, that Cain brought of the fruit of the ground an offering unto the Lord. And Abel, he also brought of the firstlings of his flock, and of the fat thereof: and the Lord had respect unto Abel and to his offering. But unto Cain and to his offering he had not respect: and Cain was very wroth, and his countenance fell. And the Lord said unto Cain, "Why art thou wroth? And why is thy countenance fallen? If thou doest well, shalt thou not be accepted? and if thou doest not well, sin lieth at the door: and unto thee shall be his desire, and thou shalt rule over him." And Cain talked with Abel his brother: and it came to pass when they were in the field, that Cain rose up against Abel his brother, and slew him.

And the Lord said unto Cain, "Where is Abel thy brother?" And he said, "I know not: am I my brother's keeper?" And he said "What hast thou done? the voice of thy brother's blood crieth unto me from the ground. And now art thou cursed from the earth, which hath opened her mouth to receive thy brother's blood from thy hand. When thou tillest the ground, it shall not henceforth yield unto thee her strength: a fugitive and a vagabond shalt thou be in the earth." And Cain said unto the Lord, "My punishment is greater than I can bear. Behold, thou hast driven me out this day from the face of the earth, and from thy face shall I be hid, and I shall be a fugitive, and a vagabond in the earth: and it shall come to pass, that every one that findeth me shall slay me." And the Lord said unto him, "Therefore whosoever slayeth Cain, vengeance shall be taken on him sevenfold." And the Lord set a mark upon Cain, lest any finding him should kill him.

And Cain went out from the presence of the Lord, and dwelt in the land of Nod,[16] on the east of Eden. And Cain knew his wife, and she conceived and bare Enoch, and he builded a city, and called the name of the city after the name of his son, Enoch. . . . And Adam knew his wife again, and she bare a son, and called his name Seth: "For God," said she, "hath appointed me another seed instead of Abel, whom Cain slew." And to Seth, to him also there was born a son, and he called his name Enos: then began men to call upon the name of the Lord.

THE FLOOD

6

And it came to pass, when men began to multiply on the face of the earth, and daughters were born unto them, that the sons of God saw the daughters of men, that they were fair, and they took them wives of all which they chose. And the Lord said, "My spirit shall not always strive with men, for that he also is flesh: yet his days shall be an hundred and twenty years." There were giants in the earth in those days: and also after that, when the sons of God came in unto the daughters of men, and they bare children to them, the same became mighty men, which were of old, men of renown.[17]

And God saw that the wickedness of men was great in the earth, and that every imagination of the thoughts of his heart was only evil continually. And it repented

---

[16] **Nod:** The land of wandering.

[17] **There were . . . renown:** A folk explanation for a race of giants.

the Lord that he had made man on the earth, and it grieved him at his heart. And the Lord said, "I will destroy man, whom I have created, from the face of the earth: both man and beast, and the creeping thing, and the fowls of the air: for it repenteth me that I have made them."[18] But Noah found grace in the eyes of the Lord.

These are the generations of Noah: Noah was a just man, and perfect in his generations, and Noah walked with God. And Noah begat three sons: Shem, Ham, and Japheth. The earth also was corrupt before God; and the earth was filled with violence. And God looked upon the earth, and behold, it was corrupt: for all flesh had corrupted his way upon the earth. And God said unto Noah, "The end of all flesh is come before me; for the earth is filled with violence through them; and behold, I will destroy them with the earth."

"Make thee an ark of gopher wood:[19] rooms shalt thou make in the ark, and shalt pitch it within and without with pitch. And this is the fashion which thou shalt make it of: the length of the ark shall be three hundred cubits,[20] the breadth of it fifty cubits, and the height of it thirty cubits. A window shalt thou make to the ark, and in a cubit shalt thou finish it above; and the door of the ark shalt thou set in the side thereof: with lower, second, and third stories shalt thou make it. And behold, I, even I do bring a flood of waters upon the earth, to destroy all flesh wherein is the breath of life from under heaven, and every thing that is in the earth shall die. But with thee will I establish my covenant:[21] and thou shalt come into the ark, thou, and thy sons, and thy wife, and thy sons' wives with thee. And of every living thing of all flesh, two of every sort shalt thou bring into the ark, to keep them alive with thee: they shall be male and female. Of fowls after their kind, and of cattle after their kind, of every creeping thing of the earth after his kind, two of every sort shall come unto thee, to keep them alive. And take thou unto thee of all food that is eaten, and thou shalt gather it to thee; and it shall be for food, for thee, and for them." Thus did Noah; according to all that God commanded him, so did he.

7

And the Lord said unto Noah, "Come thou and all thy house into the ark: for thee have I seen righteous before me in this generation. Of every clean beast thou shalt take to thee by sevens, the male and his female: and of beasts that are not clean, by two, the male and his female. Of fowls also of the air, by sevens, the male and the female; to keep seed alive upon the face of all the earth. For yet seven days, and I will cause it to rain upon the earth forty days and forty nights: and every living substance that I have made will I destroy from off the face of the earth." And Noah did according unto all that the Lord commanded him. And Noah was six hundred years old when the flood of waters was upon the earth.

---

[18] **"I will . . . made them":** The story of the flood in Genesis is similar to the earlier flood story in *The Epic of Gilgamesh.*

[19] **gopher wood:** cypress.

[20] **cubit:** The exact modern equivalent is unknown and ranges from 12 to 25.2 inches.

[21] **covenant:** This is the first of several agreements between God and humankind; after the flood this covenant is sealed with a rainbow.

And Noah went in, and his sons, and his wife, and his sons' wives with him, into the ark, because of the waters of the flood. Of clean beasts, and of beasts that are not clean, and of fowls, and of every thing that creepeth upon the earth, there went in two and two unto Noah into the ark, the male and the female, as God had commanded Noah. And it came to pass after seven days, that the waters of the flood were upon the earth.

In the six hundredth year of Noah's life, in the second month, the seventeenth day of the month, the same day were all the fountains of the great deep broken up, and the windows of heaven were opened. And the rain was upon the earth forty days and forty nights. In the selfsame day entered Noah, and Shem, and Ham, and Japheth, the sons of Noah, and Noah's wife, and the three wives of his sons with them, into the ark, they, and every beast after his kind, and all the cattle after their kind, and every creeping thing that creepeth upon the earth after his kind, and every fowl after his kind, every bird of every sort. And they went in unto Noah into the ark, two and two of all flesh wherein is the breath of life. And they that went in, went in male and female of all flesh, as God had commanded him: and the Lord shut him in.

And the flood was forty days upon the earth, and the waters increased, and bare up the ark, and it was lifted up above the earth. And the waters prevailed, and were increased greatly upon the earth: and the ark went upon the face of the waters. And the waters prevailed exceedingly upon the earth, and all the high hills that were under the whole heaven were covered. Fifteen cubits upward did the waters prevail; and the mountains were covered. And all flesh died that moved upon the earth, both of fowl, and of cattle, and of beast, and of every creeping thing that creepeth upon the earth, and every man. All in whose nostrils was the breath of life, of all that was in the dry land, died. And every living substance was destroyed which was upon the face of the ground, both man and cattle, and the creeping things, and the fowl of the heaven; and they were destroyed from the earth: and Noah only remained alive, and they that were with him in the ark. And the waters prevailed upon the earth an hundred and fifty days.

8

And God remembered Noah, and every living thing, and all the cattle that was with him in the ark: and God made a wind to pass over the earth, and the waters assuaged. The fountains also of the deep and the windows of heaven were stopped, and the rain from heaven was restrained. And the waters returned from off the earth continually: and after the end of the hundred and fifty days the waters were abated. And the ark rested in the seventh month, on the seventeenth day of the month, upon the mountains of Ararat.[22] And the waters decreased continually until the tenth month: in the tenth month, on the first day of the month, were the tops of the mountains seen.

And it came to pass at the end of forty days, that Noah opened the window of the ark which he had made. And he sent forth a raven, which went forth to and fro,

---

[22] **Ararat:** A region in Armenia in eastern Turkey.

until the waters were dried up from off the earth. Also he sent forth a dove from him, to see if the waters were abated from off the face of the ground. But the dove found no rest for the sole of her foot, and she returned unto him into the ark: for the waters were on the face of the whole earth. Then he put forth his hand, and took her, and pulled her in unto him, into the ark. And he stayed yet other seven days; and again he sent forth the dove out of the ark. And the dove came in to him in the evening, and lo, in her mouth was an olive leaf plucked off: so Noah knew that the waters were abated from off the earth. And he stayed yet other seven days, and sent forth the dove, which returned not again unto him any more.

And it came to pass in the six hundredth and one year, in the first month, the first day of the month, the waters were dried up from off the earth: and Noah removed the covering of the ark, and looked, and behold, the face of the ground was dry. And in the second month, on the seven and twentieth day of the month, was the earth dried.

And God spake unto Noah, saying, "Go forth of the ark, thou, and thy wife, and thy sons and thy sons' wives with thee: bring forth with thee every living thing that is with thee, of all flesh, both of fowl, and of cattle, and of every creeping thing that creepeth upon the earth, that they may breed abundantly in the earth, and be fruitful, and multiply upon the earth." And Noah went forth, and his sons, and his wife, and his sons' wives with him: every beast, every creeping thing, and every fowl, and whatsoever creepeth upon the earth, after their kinds, went forth out of the ark.

And Noah builded an altar unto the Lord, and took of every clean beast, and of every clean fowl, and offered burnt offerings on the altar. And the Lord smelled a sweet savour, and the Lord said in his heart, "I will not again curse the ground any more for man's sake; for the imagination of man's heart is evil from his youth: neither will I again smite any more every thing living, as I have done. While the earth remaineth, seedtime and harvest, and cold and heat, and summer and winter, and day and night shall not cease."

9:1–15

And God blessed Noah, and his sons, and said unto them, "Be fruitful and multiply, and replenish the earth. And the fear of you and the dread of you shall be upon every beast of the earth, and upon every fowl of the air, upon all that moveth upon the earth, and upon all the fishes of the sea; into your hand are they delivered. Every moving thing that liveth shall be meat for you; even as the green herb have I given you all things. But flesh with the life thereof, which is the blood thereof, shall you not eat. And surely your blood of your lives will I require: at the hand of every beast will I require it, and at the hand of man, at the hand of every man's brother will I require the life of man. Whoso sheddeth man's blood, by man shall his blood be shed: for in the image of God made he man. And you, be ye fruitful and multiply, bring forth abundantly in the earth, and multiply therein."

And God spake unto Noah, and to his sons with him, saying, "And I, behold, I establish my covenant with you and with your seed after you: and with every living creature that is with you, of the fowl, of the cattle, and of every beast of the earth with you, from all that go out of the ark, to every beast of the earth. And I will establish my covenant with you, neither shall all flesh be cut off any more by the waters of a flood, neither shall there any more be a flood to destroy the earth." And God said, "This is the token of the covenant which I make between me and you, and every living creature that is with you, for perpetual generations. I do set my bow in the cloud, and it shall be for a token of a covenant between me and the earth.[23] And it shall come to pass, when I bring a cloud over the earth, that the bow shall be seen in the cloud. And I will remember my covenant, which is between me and you, and every living creature of all flesh: and the waters shall no more become a flood to destroy all flesh."

THE TOWER OF BABEL

11:1–9, 31–32

And the whole earth was of one language, and of one speech.[24] And it came to pass, as they journeyed from the east, that they found a plain in the land of Shinar, and they dwelt there. And they said one to another, "Go to, let us make brick, and burn them thoroughly." And they had brick for stone, and slime had they for mortar. And they said, "Go to, let us build us a city and a tower, whose top may reach unto heaven, and let us make us a name, lest we be scattered abroad upon the face of the whole earth." And the Lord came down to see the city and the tower, which the children of men builded. And the Lord said, "Behold, the people is one, and they have all one language: and this they begin to do: and now nothing will be restrained from them, which they have imagined to do. Go to, let us go down, and there confound their language, that they may not understand one another's speech." So the Lord scattered them abroad from thence upon the face of all the earth: and they left off to build the city. Therefore is the name of it called Babel, because the Lord did there confound the language of all the earth: and from thence did the Lord scatter them abroad upon the face of all the earth. . . .

And Terah took Abram his son, and Lot the son of Haran his son's son, and Sarai his daughter in law, his son Abram's wife, and they went forth with them from Ur of the Chaldees, to go into the land of Canaan: and they came unto Haran, and dwelt there. And the days of Terah were two hundred and five years: and Terah died in Haran.

ABRAHAM AND ISAAC

21:1–21

And the Lord visited Sarah as he had said, and the Lord did unto Sarah as he had spoken. For Sarah conceived, and bare Abraham a son in his old age, at the set time of which God had spoken to him. And Abraham called the name of his son that was

---

[23] **I do set . . . the earth:** Among ancient peoples, the rainbow was used by God to shoot lightning; here it is a sign of the covenant.

[24] **And the . . . speech:** The Tower of Babel explains the existence of diverse languages; the tower itself alludes to the *ziggurats,* or stepped pyramids, of Babylon.

born unto him, whom Sarah bare to him, Isaac.[25] And Abraham circumcised his son Isaac, being eight days old, as God had commanded him. And Abraham was an hundred years old when his son Isaac was born unto him. And Sarah said, "God hath made me to laugh, so that all that hear will laugh with me." And she said, "Who would have said unto Abraham that Sarah should have given children suck? for I have borne him a son in his old age." And the child grew, and was weaned: and Abraham made a great feast the same day that Isaac was weaned.

And Sarah saw the son of Hagar the Egyptian, which she had borne unto Abraham, mocking. Wherefore she said unto Abraham, "Cast out this bondwoman and her son: for the son of this bondwoman shall not be heir with my son, even with Isaac." And the thing was very grievous in Abraham's sight, because of his son.

And God said unto Abraham, "Let it not be grievous in thy sight because of the lad, and because of thy bondwoman. In all that Sarah hath said unto thee, hearken unto her voice: for in Isaac shall thy seed be called. And also of the son of the bondwoman will I make a nation, because he is thy seed."[26] And Abraham rose up early in the morning, and took bread, and a bottle of water, and gave it unto Hagar (putting it on her shoulder), and the child, and sent her away: and she departed, and wandered in the wilderness of Beer-sheba. And the water was spent in the bottle, and she cast the child under one of the shrubs. And she went, and sat her down over against him, a good way off, as it were a bowshot: for she said, "Let me not see the death of the child." And she sat over against him, and lifted up her voice, and wept. And God heard the voice of the lad, and the angel of God called to Hagar out of heaven, and said unto her, "What aileth thee, Hagar? fear not: for God hath heard the voice of the lad, where he is. Arise, lift up the lad, and hold him in thine hand: for I will make him a great nation." And God opened her eyes, and she saw a well of water, and she went, and filled the bottle with water, and gave the lad drink. And God was with the lad, and he grew, and dwelt in the wilderness, and became an archer. And he dwelt in the wilderness of Paran: and his mother took him a wife out of the land of Egypt. [. . .]

22:1–19

And it came to pass after these things, that God did tempt Abraham, and said unto him, "Abraham": and he said, "Behold, here I am." And he said, "Take now thy son, thine only son Isaac, whom thou lovest, and get thee into the land of Moriah; and offer him there for a burnt offering upon one of the mountains which I will tell thee of." And Abraham rose up early in the morning, and saddled his ass, and took two of his young men with him, and Isaac his son, and clave the wood for the burnt offering, and rose up, and went unto the place of which God had told him. Then on the third day Abraham lifted up his eyes, and saw the place afar off. And Abraham said unto his young men, "Abide you here with the ass, and I and the lad will go yonder and worship, and come again to you." And Abraham took the wood of the burnt offering, and laid it upon Isaac his son: and he took the fire in his hand, and a knife: and they went

---

[25] **Isaac:** Which means "He laughed."

[26] **seed:** The progenitor of the Arab nations.

both of them together. And Isaac spake unto Abraham his father, and said, "My father": and he said, "Here am I, my son." And he said, "Behold the fire and the wood: but where is the lamb for a burnt offering?" And Abraham said, "My son, God will provide himself a lamb for a burnt offering": so they went both of them together. And they came to the place which God had told him of, and Abraham built an altar there, and laid the wood in order, and bound Isaac his son, and laid him on the altar upon the wood. And Abraham stretched forth his hand, and took the knife to slay his son. And the angel of the Lord called unto him out of heaven, and said, "Abraham, Abraham." And he said, "Here am I." And he said, "Lay not thine hand upon the lad, neither do thou any thing unto him: for now I know that thou fearest God, seeing thou hast not withheld thy son, thine only son from me." And Abraham lifted up his eyes, and looked, and behold, behind him a ram caught in a thicket by his horns: and Abraham went and took the ram, and offered him up for a burnt offering in the stead of his son. And Abraham called the name of that place Jehovah-jireh, as it is said to this day, "In the mount of the Lord it shall be seen."

And the angel of the Lord called unto Abraham out of heaven the second time, and said, "By myself have I sworn, saith the Lord, for because thou hast done this thing, and hast not withheld thy son, thine only son, that in blessing I will bless thee, and in multiplying I will multiply thy seed as the stars of the heaven, and as the sand which is upon the sea shore, and thy seed shall possess the gate of his enemies. And in thy seed shall all the nations of the earth be blessed, because thou hast obeyed my voice." So Abraham returned unto his young men, and they rose up, and went together to Beer-sheba, and Abraham dwelt at Beer-sheba.

❧ Exodus

MOSES AND THE EXODUS

1^1

Now these are the names of the children of Israel, which came into Egypt, every man and his household came with Jacob. Reuben, Simeon, Levi, and Judah, Issachar, Zebulun, and Benjamin, Dan, and Naphtali, Gad, and Asher. And all the souls that came out of the loins of Jacob were seventy souls: for Joseph was in Egypt already. And Joseph died, and all his brethren, and all that generation.

And the children of Israel were fruitful, and increased abundantly, and multiplied, and waxed exceeding mighty, and the land was filled with them. Now there arose up a new king over Egypt, which knew not Joseph. And he said unto his people, "Behold, the people of the children of Israel are more and mightier than we. Come on, let us deal wisely with them, lest they multiply, and it come to pass that, when there falleth out any war, they join also unto our enemies, and fight against us,

---

[1] The story of the exodus begins c. 1300 B.C.E., several hundred years after the Joseph story in *Genesis*. The "new king" might belong to the Nineteenth Dynasty in Egypt.

and so get them up out of the land." Therefore they did set over them taskmasters to afflict them with their burdens: and they built for Pharaoh treasure cities, Pithom and Raamses. But the more they afflicted them, the more they multiplied and grew: and they were grieved because of the children of Israel. And the Egyptians made the children of Israel to serve with rigour. And they made their lives bitter with hard bondage, in mortar, and in brick, and in all manner of service in the field: all their service wherein they made them serve was with rigour.

And the king of Egypt spake to the Hebrew midwives (of which the name of the one was Shiphrah, and the name of the other Puah), and he said, "When ye do the office of a midwife to the Hebrew women, and see them upon the stools,[2] if it be a son, then ye shall kill him: but if it be a daughter, then she shall live." But the midwives feared God, and did not as the king of Egypt commanded them, but saved the men children alive. And the king of Egypt called for the midwives, and said unto them, "Why have ye done this thing, and have saved the men children alive?" And the midwives said unto Pharaoh, "Because the Hebrew women are not as the Egyptian women: for they are lively, and are delivered ere the midwives come in unto them." Therefore God dealt well with the midwives: and the people multiplied and waxed very mighty. And it came to pass, because the midwives feared God, that he made them houses. And Pharaoh charged all his people, saying, "Every son that is born, ye shall cast into the river, and every daughter ye shall save alive."

2

And there went a man of the house of Levi, and took to wife a daughter of Levi. And the woman conceived, and bare a son: and when she saw him that he was a goodly child, she hid him three months. And when she could not longer hide him, she took for him an ark of bulrushes, and daubed it with slime, and with pitch, and put the child therein, and she laid it in the flags by the river's brink.[3] And his sister stood afar off, to wit what would be done to him.

And the daughter of Pharaoh came down to wash herself at the river, and her maidens walked along by the river side: and when she saw the ark among the flags, she sent her maid to fetch it. And when she had opened it, she saw the child: and behold, the babe wept. And she had compassion on him, and said, "This is one of the Hebrews' children." Then said his sister to Pharaoh's daughter, "Shall I go and call to thee a nurse of the Hebrew women, that she may nurse the child for thee?" And Pharaoh's daughter said to her, "Go." And the maid went and called the child's mother. And Pharaoh's daughter said unto her, "Take this child away, and nurse it for me, and I will give thee thy wages." And the woman took the child, and nursed it. And the child grew, and she brought him unto Pharaoh's daughter, and he became her son. And she called his name Moses: and she said, "Because I drew him out of the water."[4]

---

[2] **stools:** Birth stools.

[3] Moses' birth resembles the birth story of Sargon of Akkad (c. 2300 B.C.E.); "Flag" means iris.

[4] **"Because . . . water":** A folk explanation is given for Moses' name; actually, *Moses* is Egyptian for "has begotten a child."

And it came to pass in those days, when Moses was grown, that he went out unto his brethren, and looked on their burdens, and he spied an Egyptian smiting an Hebrew, one of his brethren. And he looked this way and that way, and when he saw that there was no man, he slew the Egyptian, and hid him in the sand. And when he went out the second day, behold, two men of the Hebrews strove together: and he said to him that did the wrong, "Wherefore smitest thou thy fellow?" And he said, "Who made thee a prince and a judge over us? intendest thou to kill me, as thou killedst the Egyptian?" And Moses feared, and said, "Surely this thing is known." Now when Pharaoh heard this thing, he sought to slay Moses. But Moses fled from the face of Pharaoh, and dwelt in the land of Midian: and he sat down by a well. Now the priest of Midian had seven daughters, and they came and drew water, and filled the troughs to water their father's flock. And the shepherds came and drove them away: but Moses stood up and helped them, and watered their flock. And when they came to Reuel[5] their father, he said, "How is it that you are come so soon today?" And they said, "An Egyptian delivered us out of the hand of the shepherds, and also drew water enough for us, and watered the flock." And he said unto his daughters, "And where is he? why is it that ye have left the man? Call him, that he may eat bread." And Moses was content to dwell with the man, and he gave Moses Zipporah his daughter. And she bare him a son, and he called his name Gershom: for he said, "I have been a stranger in a strange land."

And it came to pass in process of time, that the king of Egypt died[6] and the children of Israel sighed by reason of the bondage, and they cried, and their cry came up unto God, by reason of the bondage. And God heard their groaning, and God remembered his covenant with Abraham, with Isaac, and with Jacob. And God looked upon the children of Israel, and God had respect unto them.

3

Now Moses kept the flock of Jethro his father in law, the priest of Midian: and he led the flock to the backside of the desert, and came to the mountain of God, even to Horeb. And the angel of the Lord appeared unto him, in a flame of fire out of the midst of a bush, and he looked, and behold, the bush burned with fire, and the bush was not consumed. And Moses said "I will now turn aside, and see this great sight, why the bush is not burnt." And when the Lord saw that he turned aside to see, God called unto him out of the midst of the bush, and said, "Moses, Moses." And he said, "Here am I." And he said, "Draw not nigh hither: put off thy shoes from off thy feet, for the place whereon thou standest is holy ground." Moreover he said, "I am the God of thy father, the God of Abraham, the God of Isaac, and the God of Jacob." And Moses hid his face: for he was afraid to look upon God.

And the Lord said, "I have surely seen the affliction of my people which are in Egypt, and have heard their cry, by reason of their taskmasters: for I know their sorrows, and I am come down to deliver them out of the hand of the Egyptians, and to

---

[5] **Reuel:** Called Jethro in Exodus 3:1, Reuel probably introduces Moses to Yahweh; see footnote 7.

[6] **King of Egypt died:** The *king* was probably Seti I; the oppressive building program was continued by Ramses II.

bring them up out of that land, unto a good land and a large, unto a land flowing with milk and honey, unto the place of the Canaanites, and the Hittites, and the Amorites, and the Perizzites, and the Hivites, and the Jebusites. Now therefore behold, the cry of the children of Israel is come unto me: and I have also seen the oppression wherewith the Egyptians oppress them. Come now therefore, and I will send thee unto Pharaoh, that thou mayest bring forth my people the children of Israel out of Egypt."

And Moses said unto God, "Who am I, that I should go unto Pharaoh, and that I should bring forth the children of Israel out of Egypt?" And he said, "Certainly I will be with thee, and this shall be a token unto thee, that I have sent thee: when thou hast brought forth the people out of Egypt, ye shall serve God upon this mountain." And Moses said unto God, "Behold, when I come unto the children of Israel, and shall say unto them, 'The God of your fathers hath sent me unto you'; and they shall say to me, 'What is his name?' what shall I say unto them?" And God said unto Moses, "I AM THAT I AM":[7] and he said, "Thus shalt thou say unto the children of Israel, 'I AM hath sent me unto you.'" And God said moreover unto Moses, "Thus shalt thou say unto the children of Israel, 'The Lord God of your fathers, the God of Abraham, the God of Isaac, and the God of Jacob, hath sent me unto you: this is my name for ever, and this is my memorial unto all generations.' Go and gather the elders of Israel together, and say unto them, 'The Lord God of your fathers, the God of Abraham, of Isaac, and of Jacob, appeared unto me, saying, "I have surely visited you, and seen that which is done to you in Egypt. And I have said, I will bring you up out of the affliction of Egypt, unto the land of the Canaanites, and the Hittites, and the Amorites, and the Perizzites, and the Hivites, and the Jebusites, unto a land flowing with milk and honey." ' And they shall hearken to thy voice: and thou shalt come, thou and the elders of Israel, unto the king of Egypt, and you shall say unto him, 'The Lord God of the Hebrews hath met with us: and now let us go (we beseech thee) three days' journey into the wilderness, that we may sacrifice to the Lord our God.'

"And I am sure that the king of Egypt will not let you go, no, not by a mighty hand. And I will stretch out my hand, and smite Egypt with all my wonders which I will do in the midst thereof: and after that he will let you go. And I will give this people favour in the sight of the Egyptians, and it shall come to pass that when ye go, ye shall not go empty: but every woman shall borrow of her neighbour, and of her that sojourneth in her house, jewels of silver, and jewels of gold, and raiment: and ye shall put them upon your sons, and upon your daughters, and ye shall spoil the Egyptians."

4

And Moses answered, and said, "But behold, they will not believe me, nor hearken unto my voice: for they will say, 'The Lord hath not appeared unto thee.'" And the Lord said unto him, "What is that in thine hand?" And he said, "A rod." And he said,

---

[7] **"I AM THAT I AM":** A translation of the Hebrew, *Ehyeh asher eheh;* the verb root *hayeh* is the infinitive "to be." The divine name *Yahweh* is the third person singular of *hayeh,* or "He is." In some translations, Yahweh is written Jehovah and is rendered as "I cause to happen what I cause to happen," indicating a God active in human history.

"Cast it on the ground." And he cast it on the ground, and it became a serpent: and Moses fled from before it. And the Lord said unto Moses, "Put forth thine hand, and take it by the tail": and he put forth his hand, and caught it, and it became a rod in his hand: "That they may believe that the Lord God of their fathers, the God of Abraham, the God of Isaac, and the God of Jacob, hath appeared unto thee."

And the Lord said furthermore unto him, "Put now thine hand into thy bosom." And he put his hand into his bosom: and when he took it out, behold, his hand was leprous as snow. And he said, "Put thine hand into thy bosom again." And he put his hand into his bosom again, and plucked it out of his bosom, and behold, it was turned again as his other flesh. "And it shall come to pass, if they will not believe thee, neither hearken to the voice of the first sign, that they will believe the voice of the latter sign. And it shall come to pass, if they will not believe also these two signs, neither hearken unto thy voice, that thou shalt take of the water of the river, and pour it upon the dry land: and the water which thou takest out of the river shall become blood upon the dry land."

And Moses said unto the Lord, "O my Lord, I am not eloquent, neither heretofore, nor since thou hast spoken unto thy servant: but I am slow of speech, and of a slow tongue." And the Lord said unto him, "Who hath made man's mouth? or who maketh the dumb or deaf, or the seeing, or the blind? have not I the Lord? Now therefore go, and I will be with thy mouth, and teach thee what thou shalt say." And he said, "O my Lord, send, I pray thee, by the hand of him whom thou wilt send." And the anger of the Lord was kindled against Moses, and he said, "Is not Aaron the Levite thy brother? I know that he can speak well. And also behold, he cometh forth to meet thee: and when he seeth thee, he will be glad in his heart. And thou shalt speak unto him, and put words in his mouth, and I will be with thy mouth, and with his mouth, and will teach you what ye shall do. And he shall be thy spokesman unto the people: and he shall be, even he shall be to thee instead of a mouth, and thou shalt be to him instead of God. And thou shalt take this rod in thine hand, wherewith thou shalt do signs."

And Moses went and returned to Jethro his father in law, and said unto him, "Let me go, I pray thee, and return unto my brethren, which are in Egypt, and see whether they be yet alive." And Jethro said to Moses, "Go in peace." And the Lord said unto Moses in Midian, "Go, return into Egypt: for all the men are dead which sought thy life." And Moses took his wife, and his sons, and set them upon an ass, and he returned to the land of Egypt. And Moses took the rod of God in his hand. And the Lord said unto Moses, "When thou goest to return into Egypt, see that thou do all those wonders before Pharaoh, which I have put in thine hand: but I will harden his heart, that he shall not let the people go. And thou shalt say unto Pharaoh, 'Thus saith the Lord, "Israel is my son, even my firstborn. And I say unto thee, Let my son go, that he may serve me: and if thou refuse to let him go, behold, I will slay thy son, even thy firstborn."'"

And it came to pass by the way in the inn, that the Lord met him, and sought to kill him. Then Zipporah took a sharp stone, and cut off the foreskin of her son,[8] and

---

[8] **cut off . . . son:** The implication of this story is that the practice of circumcision had been abandoned for a time.

cast it at his feet, and said, "Surely a bloody husband art thou to me." So he let him go: then she said, "A bloody husband thou art, because of the circumcision."

And the Lord said to Aaron, "Go into the wilderness to meet Moses." And he went, and met him in the mount of God, and kissed him. And Moses told Aaron all the words of the Lord, who had sent him, and all the signs which he had commanded him.

And Moses and Aaron went, and gathered together all the elders of the children of Israel. And Aaron spake all the words which the Lord had spoken unto Moses, and did the signs in the sight of the people. And the people believed: and when they heard that the Lord had visited the children of Israel, and that he had looked upon their affliction, then they bowed their heads and worshipped.

5

And afterward Moses and Aaron went in, and told Pharaoh, "Thus saith the Lord God of Israel, 'Let my people go, that they may hold a feast unto me in the wilderness.'" And Pharaoh said, "Who is the Lord, that I should obey his voice to let Israel go? I know not the Lord, neither will I let Israel go." And they said, "The God of the Hebrews hath met with us: let us go, we pray thee, three days' journey into the desert, and sacrifice unto the Lord our God, lest he fall upon us with pestilence, or with the sword." And the king of Egypt said unto them, "Wherefore do ye, Moses and Aaron, let[9] the people from their works? get you unto your burdens." And Pharaoh said, "Behold, the people of the land now are many, and you make them rest from their burdens." And Pharaoh commanded the same day the taskmasters of the people, and their officers, saying, "Ye shall no more give the people straw to make brick, as heretofore: let them go and gather straw for themselves. And the tale[10] of the bricks, which they did make heretofore, you shall lay upon them: you shall not diminish aught thereof: for they be idle; therefore they cry, saying, 'Let us go and sacrifice to our God.' Let there more work be laid upon the men, that they may labour therein, and let them not regard vain words."

And the taskmasters of the people went out, and their officers, and they spake to the people, saying, "Thus saith Pharaoh, 'I will not give you straw. Go ye, get you straw where you can find it: yet not aught of your work shall be diminished.'" So the people were scattered abroad throughout all the land of Egypt, to gather stubble instead of straw. And the taskmasters hasted them, saying, "Fulfill your works, your daily tasks, as when there was straw." And the officers of the children of Israel, which Pharaoh's taskmasters had set over them, were beaten, and demanded,[11] "Wherefore have ye not fulfilled your task, in making brick both yesterday and today, as heretofore?"

Then the officers of the children of Israel came and cried unto Pharaoh, saying, "Wherefore dealest thou thus with thy servants? There is no straw given unto thy servants, and they say to us, 'Make brick': and behold, thy servants are beaten: but the fault is in thine own people." But he said, "Ye are idle, ye are idle: therefore ye say,

---

[9] **let:** Hinder.

[10] **tale:** Number.

[11] **demanded:** Asked.

'Let us go and do sacrifice to the Lord.' Go therefore now and work: for there shall no straw be given you, yet shall ye deliver the tale of bricks." And the officers of the children of Israel did see that they were in evil case, after it was said, "Ye shall not minish[12] aught from your bricks of your daily task."

And they met Moses and Aaron, who stood in the way, as they came forth from Pharaoh. And they said unto them, "The Lord look upon you, and judge, because ye have made our savour to be abhorred in the eyes of Pharaoh, and in the eyes of his servants, to put a sword in their hand to slay us." And Moses returned unto the Lord, and said, "Lord, wherefore hast thou so evil entreated this people? why is it that thou hast sent me? For since I came to Pharaoh to speak in thy name, he hath done evil to this people, neither hast thou delivered thy people at all."

6:1–13

Then the Lord said unto Moses, "Now shalt thou see what I will do to Pharaoh: for with a strong hand shall he let them go, and with a strong hand shall he drive them out of his land." And God spake unto Moses, and said unto him, "I am the Lord. And I appeared unto Abraham, unto Isaac, and unto Jacob, by the name of God Almighty, but by my name JEHOVAH was I not known to them. And I have also established my covenant with them, to give them the land of Canaan, the land of their pilgrimage, wherein they were strangers. And I have also heard the groaning of the children of Israel, whom the Egyptians keep in bondage: and I have remembered my covenant. Wherefore say unto the children of Israel, 'I am the Lord, and I will bring you out from under the burdens of the Egyptians, and I will rid you out of their bondage: and I will redeem you with a stretched out arm, and with great judgments. And I will take you to me for a people, and I will be to you a God: and ye shall know that I am the Lord your God, which bringeth you out from under the burdens of the Egyptians. And I will bring you in unto the land concerning the which I did swear to give it, to Abraham, to Isaac, and to Jacob, and I will give it you for an heritage: I am the Lord.'"

And Moses spake so unto the children of Israel: but they hearkened not unto Moses, for anguish of spirit, and for cruel bondage. And the Lord spake unto Moses, saying, "Go in, speak unto Pharaoh king of Egypt, that he let the children of Israel go out of his land." And Moses spake before the Lord, saying, "Behold, the children of Israel have not hearkened unto me: how then shall Pharaoh hear me, who am of uncircumcised lips?" And the Lord spake unto Moses and unto Aaron, and gave them a charge unto the children of Israel, and unto Pharaoh king of Egypt, to bring the children of Israel out of the land of Egypt.

[Moses seeks to convince the Pharaoh to release the children of Israel with a series of contests or plagues: Aaron's rod turns into a snake, rivers are turned into blood, plagues of frogs, lice, and flies invade the land. Disease attacks the cattle. Boils and pestilence inflict humans. Hail and locusts destroy crops. In each case Pharaoh's heart hardens and he denies freedom to the Hebrews. Chapter 11 describes the ultimate catastrophe, the death of the firstborn of Egypt.]

---

[12] **minish**: Diminish.

11

And the Lord said unto Moses, "Yet will I bring one plague more upon Pharaoh, and upon Egypt; afterwards he will let you go hence: when he shall let you go, he shall surely thrust you out hence altogether. Speak now in the ears of the people, and let every man borrow of his neighbour, and every woman of her neighbour, jewels of silver, and jewels of gold." And the Lord gave the people favour in the sight of the Egyptians. Moreover the man Moses was very great in the land of Egypt, in the sight of Pharaoh's servants, and in the sight of the people. And Moses said, "Thus saith the Lord, 'About midnight will I go out into the midst of Egypt. And all the firstborn in the land of Egypt shall die, from the firstborn of Pharaoh that sitteth upon his throne, even unto the firstborn of the maidservant that is behind the mill, and all the firstborn of beasts. And there shall be a great cry throughout all the land of Egypt, such as there was none like it, nor shall be like it any more. But against any of the children of Israel shall not a dog move his tongue, against man or beast: that ye may know how that the Lord doth put a difference between the Egyptians and Israel. And all these thy servants shall come down unto me, and bow down themselves unto me, saying, "Get thee out, and all the people that follow thee": and after that I will go out.'" And he went out from Pharaoh in a great anger. And the Lord said unto Moses, "Pharaoh shall not hearken unto you, that my wonders may be multiplied in the land of Egypt." And Moses and Aaron did all these wonders before Pharaoh: and the Lord hardened Pharaoh's heart, so that he would not let the children of Israel go out of his land.

12:1–42[13]

And the Lord spake unto Moses and Aaron in the land of Egypt, saying, "This month shall be unto you the beginning of months: it shall be the first month of the year to you.

"Speak ye unto all the congregation of Israel, saying, 'In the tenth day of this month they shall take to them every man a lamb, according to the house of their fathers, a lamb for an house. And if the household be too little for the lamb, let him and his neighbour next unto his house take it according to the number of the souls: every man according to his eating shall make your count for the lamb. Your lamb shall be without blemish, a male of the first year: ye shall take it out from the sheep or from the goats. And ye shall keep it up until the fourteenth day of the same month: and the whole assembly of the congregation of Israel shall kill it in the evening. And they shall take of the blood and strike it on the two side posts and on the upper door post of the houses wherein they shall eat it. And they shall eat the flesh in that night roast with fire, and unleavened bread, and with bitter herbs they shall eat it. Eat not of it raw, nor sodden at all with water, but roast with fire: his head, with his legs, and with the purtenance thereof. And ye shall let nothing of it remain until the morning: and that which remaineth of it until the morning ye shall burn with fire.

---

[13] This section describes one of the most important Jewish religious festivals, Passover. Passover initiates the exodus, which provided a pattern of liberation from slavery for numerous peoples, Jews and non-Jews.

"'And thus shall ye eat it: with your loins girded, your shoes on your feet, and your staff in your hand: and ye shall eat it in haste: it is the Lord's Passover. For I will pass through the land of Egypt this night, and will smite all the firstborn in the land of Egypt, both man and beast, and against all the gods of Egypt I will execute judgment: I am the Lord. And the blood shall be to you for a token upon the houses where you are: and when I see the blood, I will pass over you, and the plague shall not be upon you to destroy you, when I smite the land of Egypt. And this day shall be unto you for a memorial: and you shall keep it a feast to the Lord, throughout your generations: you shall keep it a feast by an ordinance for ever. Seven days shall ye eat unleavened bread, even the first day ye shall put away leaven out of your houses: for whosoever eateth leavened bread, from the first day until the seventh day, that soul shall be cut off from Israel. And in the first day there shall be an holy convocation, and in the seventh day there shall be an holy convocation to you: no manner of work shall be done in them, save that which every man must eat, that only may be done of you. And ye shall observe the feast of unleavened bread: for in this selfsame day have I brought your armies out of the land of Egypt; therefore shall ye observe this day in your generations by an ordinance for ever.

"'In the first month, on the fourteenth day of the month at even, ye shall eat unleavened bread until the one and twentieth day of the month at even. Seven days shall there be no leaven found in your houses: for whosoever eateth that which is leavened, even that soul shall be cut off from the congregation of Israel, whether he be a stranger, or born in the land. Ye shall eat nothing leavened: in all your habitations shall ye eat unleavened bread.'"

Then Moses called for all the elders of Israel, and said unto them, "Draw out and take you a lamb, according to your families, and kill the Passover.[14] And ye shall take a bunch of hyssop, and dip it in the blood that is in the basin, and strike the lintel and the two side posts with the blood that is in the basin: and none of you shall go out at the door of his house until the morning. For the Lord will pass through to smite the Egyptians: and when he seeth the blood upon the lintel, and on the two side posts, the Lord will pass over the door, and will not suffer the destroyer to come in unto your houses to smite you. And ye shall observe this thing for an ordinance to thee and to thy sons for ever. And it shall come to pass when ye be come to the land, which the Lord will give you, according as he hath promised, that ye shall keep this service. And it shall come to pass, when your children shall say unto you, 'What mean ye by this service?' that ye shall say, 'It is the sacrifice of the Lord's Passover, who passed over the houses of the children of Israel in Egypt, when he smote the Egyptians, and delivered our houses.'" And the people bowed the head, and worshipped. And the children of Israel went away, and did as the Lord had commanded Moses and Aaron, so did they.

And it came to pass that at midnight the Lord smote all the firstborn in the land of Egypt, from the firstborn of Pharaoh that sat on his throne, unto the firstborn of the captive that was in the dungeon, and all the firstborn of cattle. And Pharaoh rose up in the night, he and all his servants, and all the Egyptians; and there was a great cry in Egypt: for there was not a house where there was not one dead.

---

[14] **the Passover:** Passover lamb.

And he called for Moses and Aaron by night, and said, "Rise up, and get you forth from amongst my people, both you and the children of Israel: and go, serve the Lord, as ye have said. Also take your flocks and your herds, as ye have said: and be gone, and bless me also." And the Egyptians were urgent upon the people that they might send them out of the land in haste: for they said, "We be all dead men." And the people took their dough before it was leavened, their kneading troughs being bound up in their clothes upon their shoulders. And the children of Israel did according to the word of Moses: and they borrowed of the Egyptians jewels of silver, and jewels of gold, and raiment. And the Lord gave the people favour in the sight of the Egyptians, so that they lent unto them such things as they required: and they spoiled the Egyptians.

And the children of Israel journeyed from Rameses to Succoth,[15] about six hundred thousand on foot that were men, besides children. And a mixed multitude went up also with them, and flocks and herds, even very much cattle. And they baked unleavened cakes of the dough, which they brought forth out of Egypt; for it was not leavened: because they were thrust out of Egypt, and could not tarry, neither had they prepared for themselves any victual.

Now the sojourning of the children of Israel, who dwelt in Egypt, was four hundred and thirty years. And it came to pass at the end of the four hundred and thirty years, even the selfsame day it came to pass, that all the hosts of the Lord went out from the land of Egypt. It is a night to be much observed unto the Lord, for bringing them out from the land of Egypt: this is that night of the Lord to be observed of all the children of Israel, in their generations. . . .

13:17–22

And it came to pass when Pharaoh had let the people go, that God led them not through the way of the land of the Philistines, although that was near: for God said, "Lest peradventure the people repent when they see war, and they return to Egypt": but God led the people about through the way of the wilderness of the Red Sea:[16] and the children of Israel went up harnessed[17] out of the land of Egypt. And Moses took the bones of Joseph with him: for he had straitly[18] sworn the children of Israel, saying, "God will surely visit you, and ye shall carry up my bones away hence with you."

And they took their journey from Succoth, and encamped in Etham, in the edge of the wilderness. And the Lord went before them by day in a pillar of cloud to lead them the way; and by night in a pillar of fire, to give them light; to go by day and night. He took not away the pillar of the cloud by day, nor the pillar of fire by night, from before the people.

---

[15] **Rameses to Succoth:** Rameses, a royal city, was in the north of Egypt; Succoth was thirty-two miles to the southeast. The shortest route to Canaan was along the coast, but it was heavily guarded by Egyptian forts.

[16] **Red Sea:** Probably the "Sea of Reeds," a papyrus marsh on the border of Egypt.

[17] **harnessed:** Possibly "the fifth generation of Israelites" or "equipped for battle."

[18] **straitly:** Strictly.

14

And the Lord spake unto Moses, saying, "Speak unto the children of Israel, that they turn and encamp before Pi-hahiroth, between Migdol and the sea, over against Baal-zephon: before it shall ye encamp by the sea. For Pharaoh will say of the children of Israel, 'They are entangled in the land, the wilderness hath shut them in.' And I will harden Pharaoh's heart, that he shall follow after them, and I will be honoured upon Pharaoh, and upon all his host, that the Egyptians may know that I am the Lord." And they did so.

And it was told the king of Egypt, that the people fled: and the heart of Pharaoh and of his servants was turned against the people, and they said, "Why have we done this, that we have let Israel go from serving us?" And he made ready his chariot, and took his people with him. And he took six hundred chosen chariots, and all the chariots of Egypt, and captains over every one of them. And the Lord hardened the heart of Pharaoh king of Egypt, and he pursued after the children of Israel: and the children of Israel went out with an high hand. But the Egyptians pursued after them (all the horses and chariots of Pharaoh, and his horsemen, and his army) and overtook them encamping by the sea, beside Pi-hahiroth, before Baal-zephon.

And when Pharaoh drew nigh, the children of Israel lifted up their eyes, and behold, the Egyptians marched after them, and they were sore afraid: and the children of Israel cried out unto the Lord. And they said unto Moses, "Because there were no graves in Egypt, hast thou taken us away to die in the wilderness? Wherefore hast thou dealt thus with us, to carry us forth out of Egypt? Is not this the word that we did tell thee in Egypt, saying, 'Let us alone, that we may serve the Egyptians?' For it had been better for us to serve the Egyptians, than that we should die in the wilderness."

And Moses said unto the people, "Fear ye not, stand still, and see the salvation of the Lord, which he will show to you today: for the Egyptians whom ye have seen today, ye shall see them again no more for ever. The Lord shall fight for you, and ye shall hold your peace."

And the Lord said unto Moses, "Wherefore criest thou unto me? Speak unto the children of Israel, that they go forward: but lift thou up thy rod, and stretch out thine hand over the sea, and divide it: and the children of Israel shall go on dry ground through the midst of the sea. And I, behold, I will harden the hearts of the Egyptians, and they shall follow them: and I will get me honour upon Pharaoh, and upon all his host, upon his chariots, and upon his horsemen. And the Egyptians shall know that I am the Lord, when I have gotten me honour upon Pharaoh, upon his chariots, and upon his horsemen."

And the angel of God, which went before the camp of Israel, removed and went behind them, and the pillar of the cloud went from before their face, and stood behind them. And it came between the camp of the Egyptians and the camp of Israel, and it was a cloud and darkness to them, but it gave light by night to these: so that the one came not near the other all the night. And Moses stretched out his hand over the sea, and the Lord caused the sea to go back by a strong east wind all that night, and made the sea dry land, and the waters were divided. And the children of Israel went into the midst of the sea upon the dry ground, and the waters were a wall unto them on their right hand, and on their left.

And the Egyptians pursued, and went in after them, to the midst of the sea, even all Pharaoh's horses, his chariots, and his horsemen. And it came to pass, that in the morning watch the Lord looked unto the host of the Egyptians, through the pillar of fire and of the cloud, and troubled the host of the Egyptians, and took off their chariot wheels, that they drave them heavily: so that the Egyptians said, "Let us flee from the face of Israel: for the Lord fighteth for them against the Egyptians."

And the Lord said unto Moses, "Stretch out thine hand over the sea, that the waters may come again upon the Egyptians, upon their chariots, and upon their horsemen." And Moses stretched forth his hand over the sea, and the sea returned to his strength when the morning appeared: and the Egyptians fled against it: and the Lord overthrew the Egyptians in the midst of the sea. And the waters returned, and covered the chariots, and the horsemen, and all the host of Pharaoh that came into the sea after them: there remained not so much as one of them. But the children of Israel walked upon dry land, in the midst of the sea, and the waters were a wall unto them on their right hand, and on their left. Thus the Lord saved Israel that day out of the hand of the Egyptians: and Israel saw the Egyptians dead upon the sea shore. And Israel saw that great work which the Lord did upon the Egyptians: and the people feared the Lord, and believed the Lord, and his servant Moses.

THE TEN COMMANDMENTS

19:1–24

In the third month when the children of Israel were gone forth out of the land of Egypt, the same day came they into the wilderness of Sinai. For they were departed from Rephidim, and were come to the desert of Sinai, and had pitched in the wilderness, and there Israel camped before the mount. And Moses went up unto God: and the Lord called unto him out of the mountain, saying, "Thus shalt thou say to the house of Jacob, and tell the children of Israel: 'Ye have seen what I did unto the Egyptians, and how I bare you on eagles' wings, and brought you unto myself. Now therefore, if ye will obey my voice indeed, and keep my covenant, then ye shall be a peculiar treasure unto me above all people: for all the earth is mine. And ye shall be unto me a kingdom of priests, and an holy nation.' These are the words which thou shalt speak unto the children of Israel."

And Moses came and called for the elders of the people, and laid before their faces all these words which the Lord commanded him. And all the people answered together, and said, "All that the Lord hath spoken we will do." And Moses returned the words of the people unto the Lord. And the Lord said unto Moses, "Lo, I come unto thee in a thick cloud, that the people may hear when I speak with thee, and believe thee for ever": and Moses told the words of the people unto the Lord.

And the Lord said unto Moses, "Go unto the people, and sanctify them today and tomorrow, and let them wash their clothes. And be ready against the third day: for the third day the Lord will come down in the sight of all the people, upon mount Sinai. And thou shalt set bounds unto the people round about, saying, 'Take heed to yourselves, that ye go not up into the mount, or touch the border of it: whosoever toucheth the mount shall be surely put to death. There shall not a hand touch it, but he shall surely be stoned, or shot through; whether it be beast or man, it shall not live': when the trumpet soundeth long, they shall come up to the mount."

And Moses went down from the mount unto the people, and sanctified the people; and they washed their clothes. And he said unto the people, "Be ready against the third day: come not at your wives."

And it came to pass on the third day in the morning, that there were thunders and lightnings, and a thick cloud upon the mount, and the voice of the trumpet exceeding loud, so that all the people that was in the camp trembled. And Moses brought forth the people out of the camp to meet with God, and they stood at the nether part of the mount. And mount Sinai was altogether on a smoke, because the Lord descended upon it in fire: and the smoke thereof ascended as the smoke of a furnace, and the whole mount quaked greatly. And when the voice of the trumpet sounded long, and waxed louder and louder, Moses spake, and God answered him by a voice. And the Lord came down upon mount Sinai, on the top of the mount: and the Lord called Moses up to the top of the mount, and Moses went up. And the Lord said unto Moses, "Go down, charge the people, lest they break through unto the Lord to gaze, and many of them perish. And let the priests also, which come near to the Lord, sanctify themselves, lest the Lord break forth upon them." And Moses said unto the Lord, "The people cannot come up to mount Sinai: for thou chargedst us, saying, 'Set bounds about the mount, and sanctify it.'" And the Lord said unto him, "Away, get thee down, and thou shalt come up, thou, and Aaron with thee: but let not the priests and the people break through, to come up unto the Lord, lest he break forth upon them." So Moses went down unto the people, and spake unto them.

20

And God spake all these words, saying, "I am the Lord thy God, which have brought thee out of the land of Egypt, out of the house of bondage:[19]

Thou shalt have no other gods before me.

Thou shalt not make unto thee any graven image, or any likeness of any thing that is in heaven above, or that is in the earth beneath, or that is in the water under the earth. Thou shalt not bow down to them, nor serve them: for I the Lord thy God am a jealous God, visiting the iniquity of the fathers upon the children, unto the third and fourth generation of them that hate me: and showing mercy unto thousands of them that love me, and keep my commandments.

Thou shalt not take the name of the Lord thy God in vain: for the Lord will not hold him guiltless that taketh his name in vain.

Remember the sabbath day, to keep it holy. Six days shalt thou labour, and do all thy work: but the seventh day is the sabbath of the Lord thy God: in it thou shalt not do any work, thou, nor thy son, nor thy daughter, thy manservant, nor thy maidservant, nor thy cattle, nor thy stranger that is within thy gates: for in six days

---

[19] **house of bondage:** Obeying the Ten Commandments becomes the necessary condition for entering into a covenant with God and receiving his blessings.

the Lord made heaven and earth, the sea, and all that in them is, and rested the seventh day: wherefore the Lord blessed the sabbath day, and hallowed it.

Honour thy father and thy mother: that thy days may be long upon the land, which the Lord thy God giveth thee.

Thou shalt not kill.

Thou shalt not commit adultery.

Thou shalt not steal.

Thou shalt not bear false witness against thy neighbour.

Thou shalt not covet thy neighbour's house, thou shalt not covet thy neighbour's wife, nor his manservant, nor his maidservant, nor his ox, nor his ass, nor any thing that is thy neighbour's."

And all the people saw the thunderings, and the lightnings, and the noise of the trumpet, and the mountain smoking: and when the people saw it, they removed, and stood afar off. And they said unto Moses, "Speak thou with us, and we will hear: but let not God speak with us, lest we die." And Moses said unto the people, "Fear not: for God is come to prove you, and that his fear may be before your faces, that ye sin not." And the people stood afar off, and Moses drew near unto the thick darkness where God was.

And the Lord said unto Moses, "Thus thou shalt say unto the children of Israel, 'Ye have seen that I have talked with you from heaven. Ye shall not make with me gods of silver, neither shall ye make unto you gods of gold. An altar of earth thou shalt make unto me, and shalt sacrifice thereon thy burnt offerings, and thy peace offerings, thy sheep, and thine oxen: in all places where I record my name I will come unto thee, and I will bless thee.'"

The Golden Calf

32

And when the people saw that Moses delayed to come down out of the mount, the people gathered themselves together unto Aaron, and said unto him, "Up, make us gods which shall go before us: for as for this Moses, the man that brought us up out of the land of Egypt, we wot not what is become of him." And Aaron said unto them, "Break off the golden earrings which are in the ears of your wives, of your sons, and of your daughters, and bring them unto me." And all the people brake off the golden earrings which were in their ears, and brought them unto Aaron. And he received them at their hand, and fashioned it with a graving tool, after he had made it a molten calf:[20] and they said, "These be thy gods, O Israel, which brought thee up out of the land of Egypt." And when Aaron saw it, he built an altar before it, and Aaron made proclamation, and said, "Tomorrow is the feast of the Lord." And they rose up early on the morrow, and offered burnt offerings, and brought peace offerings: and the people sat down to eat and to drink, and rose up to play.

---

[20] **molten calf:** The worship of the golden calf reflects both Egyptian and Canaanite practices.

And the Lord said unto Moses, "Go, get thee down: for thy people which thou broughtest out of the land of Egypt have corrupted themselves. They have turned aside quickly out of the way which I commanded them: they have made them a molten calf, and have worshipped it, and have sacrificed thereunto, and said, 'These be thy gods, O Israel, which have brought thee up out of the land of Egypt.'" And the Lord said unto Moses, "I have seen this people, and behold, it is a stiffnecked people. Now therefore let me alone, that my wrath may wax hot against them, and that I may consume them: and I will make of thee a great nation." And Moses besought the Lord his God, and said, "Lord, why doth thy wrath wax hot against thy people, which thou hast brought forth out of the land of Egypt, with great power, and with a mighty hand? Wherefore should the Egyptians speak and say, 'For mischief did he bring them out, to slay them in the mountains, and to consume them from the face of the earth'? Turn from thy fierce wrath, and repent of this evil against thy people. Remember Abraham, Isaac, and Israel thy servants, to whom thou swarest by thine own self, and saidst unto them, 'I will multiply your seed as the stars of heaven: and all this land that I have spoken of will I give unto your seed, and they shall inherit it for ever.'" And the Lord repented of the evil which he thought to do unto his people.

And Moses turned, and went down from the mount, and the two tables of the testimony were in his hand: the tables were written on both their sides; on the one side, and on the other they were written. And the tables were the work of God; and the writing was the writing of God, graven upon the tables. And when Joshua heard the noise of the people as they shouted, he said unto Moses, "There is a noise of war in the camp." And he said, "It is not the voice of them that shout for mastery, neither is it the voice of them that cry for being overcome: but the noise of them that sing do I hear."

And it came to pass, as soon as he came nigh unto the camp, that he saw the calf, and the dancing: and Moses' anger waxed hot, and he cast the tables out of his hands, and brake them beneath the mount. And he took the calf which they had made, and burnt it in the fire, and ground it to powder, and strewed it upon the water, and made the children of Israel drink of it. And Moses said unto Aaron, "What did this people unto thee, that thou hast brought so great a sin upon them?" And Aaron said, "Let not the anger of my lord wax hot: thou knowest the people, that they are set on mischief. For they said unto me, 'Make us gods which shall go before us: for as for this Moses, the man that brought us up out of the land of Egypt, we wot not what is become of him.' And I said unto them, 'Whosoever hath any gold, let them break it off': so they gave it me: then I cast it into the fire, and there came out this calf."

And when Moses saw that the people were naked (for Aaron had made them naked unto their shame amongst their enemies), then Moses stood in the gate of the camp, and said, "Who is on the Lord's side? let him come unto me." And all the sons of Levi gathered themselves together unto him. And he said unto them, "Thus saith the Lord God of Israel, 'Put every man his sword by his side, and go in and out from gate to gate throughout the camp, and slay every man his brother, and every man his companion, and every man his neighbour.'" And the children of Levi did according to the word of Moses; and there fell of the people that day about three thousand men. For Moses had said, "Consecrate yourselves today to the Lord, even every man upon his son, and upon his brother, that he may bestow upon you a blessing this day."

And it came to pass on the morrow, that Moses said unto the people, "Ye have sinned a great sin: and now I will go up unto the Lord; peradventure I shall make an atonement for your sin." And Moses returned unto the Lord, and said, "Oh, this people have sinned a great sin, and have made them gods of gold. Yet now, if thou wilt forgive their sin; and if not, blot me, I pray thee, out of thy book, which thou hast written." And the Lord said unto Moses, "Whosoever hath sinned against me, him will I blot out of my book. Therefore now go, lead the people unto the place of which I have spoken unto thee: behold, mine angel shall go before thee; nevertheless in the day when I visit, I will visit their sin upon them." And the Lord plagued the people, because they made the calf, which Aaron made.[21]

---

[21] The covenant is renewed when the commandments are again written on two tablets of stone. The final chapters of Exodus detail further laws and describe the construction of the Tabernacle.

Job

THE TRIALS OF JOB[1]

1

There was a man in the land of Uz,[2] whose name was Job,[3] and that man was perfect[4] and upright, and one that feared God, and eschewed evil. And there were born unto him seven sons and three daughters. His substance also was seven thousand sheep, and three thousand camels, and five hundred yoke of oxen, and five hundred she-asses, and a very great household; so that this man was the greatest of all the men of the east.[5] And his sons went and feasted in their houses, every one his day, and sent and called for their three sisters to eat and to drink with them. And it was so, when the days of their feasting were gone about, that Job sent and sanctified them, and rose up early in the morning, and offered burnt offerings according to the number of them all: for Job said, "It may be that my sons have sinned, and cursed God in their hearts." Thus did Job continually.

Now there was a day when the sons of God came to present themselves before the Lord, and Satan[6] came also among them. And the Lord said unto Satan, "Whence

---

[1] **The Trials of Job:** Job, a devout and prosperous man, is tested for his integrity by calamity and disaster.

[2] **Uz:** Probably Edom, a region south of the Dead Sea.

[3] **Job:** The etymology suggests either "inveterate foe" or the "penitent one."

[4] **perfect:** The import is not sinless perfection, but a whole person.

[5] **east:** The wealth described is that of a seminomadic sheikh; seven sons and three daughters was considered ideal.

[6] **Satan:** For the ancients, human events were decided in divine councils. The literal meaning of *satan* is "adversary" or "accuser," and is apparently a legal term, not yet the proper name for an evil being it later became.

comest thou?" Then Satan answered the Lord, and said, "From going to and fro in the earth, and from walking up and down in it." And the Lord said unto Satan, "Hast thou considered my servant Job, that there is none like him in the earth, a perfect and an upright man, one that feareth God, and escheweth evil?" Then Satan answered the Lord, and said, "Doth Job fear God for nought? Hast not thou made an hedge about him, and about his house, and about all that he hath on every side? thou hast blessed the work of his hands, and his substance is increased in the land. But put forth thine hand now, and touch all that he hath, and he will curse thee to thy face." And the Lord said unto Satan, "Behold, all that he hath is in thy power, only upon himself put not forth thine hand." So Satan went forth from the presence of the Lord.

And there was a day when his sons and his daughters were eating and drinking wine in their eldest brother's house: and there came a messenger unto Job, and said, "The oxen were plowing, and the asses feeding beside them, and the Sabeans[7] fell upon them, and took them away: yea, they have slain the servants with the edge of the sword, and I only am escaped alone to tell thee." While he was yet speaking, there came also another, and said, "The fire of God is fallen from heaven, and hath burnt up the sheep, and the servants, and consumed them, and I only am escaped alone to tell thee." While he was yet speaking, there came also another, and said, "The Chaldeans[8] made out three bands, and fell upon the camels, and have carried them away, yea, and slain the servants with the edge of the sword, and I only am escaped alone to tell thee." While he was yet speaking, there came also another; and said, "Thy sons and thy daughters were eating and drinking wine in their eldest brother's house. And behold, there came a great wind from the wilderness, and smote the four corners of the house, and it fell upon the young men, and they are dead, and I only am escaped alone to tell thee." Then Job arose, and rent his mantle, and shaved his head, and fell down upon the ground, and worshipped, and said, "Naked came I out of my mother's womb, and naked shall I return thither: the Lord gave, and the Lord hath taken away, blessed be the name of the Lord." In all this Job sinned not, nor charged God foolishly.

2

Again there was a day when the sons of God came to present themselves before the Lord, and Satan came also among them to present himself before the Lord. And the Lord said unto Satan, "From whence comest thou?" And Satan answered the Lord, and said, "From going to and fro in the earth, and from walking up and down in it." And the Lord said unto Satan, "Hast thou considered my servant Job, that there is none like him in the earth, a perfect and an upright man, one that feareth God, and escheweth evil? and still he holdeth fast his integrity, although thou movedst me against him, to destroy him without cause." And Satan answered the Lord, and said, "Skin for skin,[9] yea all that a man hath, will he give for his life. But put forth thine

---

[7] **Sabeans:** Nomads from Arabia.

[8] **Chaldeans:** The biblical name for Babylonians.

[9] **Skin for skin:** Value for value.

hand now, and touch his bone and his flesh, and he will curse thee to thy face." And the Lord said unto Satan, "Behold, he is in thine hand, but save his life."

So went Satan forth from the presence of the Lord, and smote Job with sore boils, from the sole of his foot unto his crown. And he took him a potsherd to scrape himself withal; and he sat down among the ashes.

Then said his wife unto him, "Dost thou still retain thine integrity? curse God, and die." But he said unto her, "Thou speakest as one of the foolish women speaketh; what? shall we receive good at the hand of God, and shall we not receive evil?" In all this did not Job sin with his lips.

Now when Job's three friends heard of all this evil that was come upon him, they came every one from his own place: Eliphaz the Temanite, and Bildad the Shuhite, and Zophar the Naamathite;[10] for they had made an appointment together to come to mourn with him, and to comfort him. And when they lifted up their eyes afar off, and knew him not, they lifted up their voice, and wept; and they rent every one his mantle, and sprinkled dust upon their heads toward heaven. So they sat down with him upon the ground seven days and seven nights, and none spake a word unto him; for they saw that his grief was very great.

3

After this, opened Job his mouth, and cursed his day. And Job spake, and said,

"Let the day perish wherein I was born, and the night in which it was said, 'There is a man-child conceived.'

Let that day be darkness, let not God regard it from above, neither let the light shine upon it.

Let darkness and the shadow of death stain it, let a cloud dwell upon it, let the blackness of the day terrify it.

As for that night, let darkness seize upon it, let it not be joined unto the days of the year, let it not come into the number of the months.

Lo, let that night be solitary, let no joyful voice come therein.

Let them curse it that curse the day, who are ready to raise up their mourning.

Let the stars of the twilight thereof be dark, let it look for light but have none, neither let it see the dawning of the day:

Because it shut not up the doors of my mother's womb, nor hid sorrow from mine eyes.

Why died I not from the womb? why did I not give up the ghost when I came out of the belly?

Why did the knees prevent me? or why the breasts, that I should suck?

For now should I have lain still and been quiet, I should have slept; then had I been at rest,

With kings and counsellors of the earth, which built desolate places for themselves,

Or with princes that had gold, who filled their houses with silver:

Or as an hidden untimely birth, I had not been; as infants which never saw light.

---

[10] **friends . . . Naamathite:** Job's friends probably come from northwest Arabia.

There the wicked cease from troubling: and there the weary be at rest.

There the prisoners rest together, they hear not the voice of the oppressor.

The small and great are there, and the servant is free from his master.

Wherefore is light given to him that is in misery, and life unto the bitter in soul?

Which long for death, but it cometh not, and dig for it more than for hid treasures:

Which rejoice exceedingly, and are glad when they can find the grave?

Why is light given to a man, whose way is hid, and whom God hath hedged in?

For my sighing cometh before I eat, and my roarings are poured out like the waters.

For the thing which I greatly feared is come upon me, and that which I was afraid of is come unto me.

I was not in safety, neither had I rest, neither was I quiet: yet trouble came."

First Cycle of Speeches[11]

4

Then Eliphaz the Temanite answered, and said.

"If we assay to commune with thee, wilt thou be grieved? But who can withhold himself from speaking?

Behold, thou hast instructed many, and thou hast strengthened the weak hands.

Thy words have upholden him that was falling, and thou hast strengthened the feeble knees.

But now it is come upon thee, and thou faintest; it toucheth thee, and thou art troubled.

Is not this thy fear, thy confidence, thy hope, and the uprightness of thy ways?

Remember, I pray thee, who ever perished, being innocent? or where were the righteous cut off?

Even as I have seen, they that plow iniquity, and sow wickedness, reap the same.

By the blast of God they perish, and by the breath of his nostrils are they consumed.

The roaring of the lion, and the voice of the fierce lion, and the teeth of the young lions, are broken.

The old lion perisheth for lack of prey, and the stout lion's whelps are scattered abroad.

Now a thing was secretly brought to me, and mine ear received a little thereof.

In thoughts from the visions of the night, when deep sleep falleth on men:

Fear came upon me, and trembling, which made all my bones to shake.

Then a spirit passed before my face: the hair of my flesh stood up.

It stood still, but I could not discern the form thereof: an image was before mine eyes, there was silence, and I heard a voice saying,

---

[11] **First Cycle of Speeches:** Gently Eliphaz broaches the central ideas that will recur throughout the friends' speeches: Man cannot be more righteous than God, and even celestial beings have no claim to purity in God's sight.

'Shall mortal man be more just than God? shall a man be more pure than his maker?

'Behold, he put no trust in his servants; and his angels he charged with folly:

'How much less on them that dwell in houses[12] of clay, whose foundation is in the dust, which are crushed before the moth.

'They are destroyed from morning to evening: they perish for ever, without any regarding it.

'Doth not their excellency which is in them go away? they die, even without wisdom.'"

5

"Call now, if there be any that will answer thee, and to which of the saints[13] wilt thou turn?

For wrath killeth the foolish man, and envy slayeth the silly one. I have seen the foolish taking root: but suddenly I cursed his habitation.

His children are far from safety, and they are crushed in the gate, neither is there any to deliver them.

Whose harvest the hungry eateth up, and taketh it even out of the thorns, and the robber swalloweth up their substance.

Although affliction cometh not forth of the dust, neither doth trouble spring out of the ground:

Yet man is born unto trouble, as the sparks fly upward.

I would seek unto God, and unto God would I commit my cause:

Which doeth great things and unsearchable: marvelous things without number.

Who giveth rain upon the earth, and sendeth waters upon the fields:

To set up on high those that be low; that those which mourn may be exalted to safety.

He disappointeth the devices of the crafty, so that their hands cannot perform their enterprise.

He taketh the wise in their own craftiness: and the counsel of the froward is carried headlong.

They meet with darkness in the daytime, and grope in the noonday as in the night.

But he saveth the poor from the sword, from their mouth, and from the hand of the mighty.

So the poor hath hope, and iniquity stoppeth her mouth.

Behold, happy is the man whom God correcteth: therefore despise not thou the chastening of the Almighty.

For he maketh sore, and bindeth up: he woundeth, and his hands make whole.

He shall deliver thee in six troubles, yea in seven[14] there shall no evil touch thee.

---

[12] **houses:** The human body.

[13] **saints:** Members of the heavenly court.

[14] **seven:** A frequent numerical device meaning "totality."

In famine he shall redeem thee from death: and in war from the power of the sword.

Thou shall be hid from the scourge of the tongue: neither shalt thou be afraid of destruction when it cometh.

At destruction and famine thou shalt laugh: neither shalt thou be afraid of the beasts of the earth.

For thou shalt be in league with the stones of the field: and the beasts of the field shall be at peace with thee.

And thou shalt know that thy tabernacle shall be in peace; and thou shalt visit thy habitation, and shalt not sin.

Thou shalt know also that thy seed shall be great, and thine offspring as the grass of the earth.

Thou shalt come to thy grave in a full age, like as a shock of corn cometh in, in his season.

Lo this, we have searched it, so it is; hear it, and know thou it for thy good."

6

But Job answered,[15] and said,

"Oh that my grief were thoroughly weighed, and my calamity laid in the balances together.

For now it would be heavier than the sand of the sea, therefore my words are swallowed up.

For the arrows of the Almighty are within me, the poison[16] whereof drinketh up my spirit: the terrors of God do set themselves in array against me.

Doth the wild ass bray when he hath grass? or loweth the ox over his fodder?

Can that which is unsavoury be eaten without salt? or is there any taste in the white of an egg?

The things that my soul refused to touch are as my sorrowful meat.

O that I might have my request! and that God would grant me the thing that I long for!

Even that it would please God to destroy me, that he would let loose his hand, and cut me off.

Then should I yet have comfort, yea I would harden myself in sorrow; let him not spare, for I have not concealed the words of the holy One.

What is my strength, that I should hope? and what is mine end, that I should prolong my life?

Is my strength the strength of stones? or is my flesh of brass?

Is not my help in me? and is wisdom driven quite from me?

To him that is afflicted pity should be showed from his friend; but he forsaketh the fear of the Almighty.

---

[15] **Job answered:** His distress has come from God, unjustly. He will not abstain from expressing his bitterness.

[16] **poison:** While fire arrows were used in the ancient Near East, there is no evidence of them in the Hebrew Scriptures outside this verse.

My brethren have dealt deceitfully as a brook, and as the stream of brooks they pass away,

Which are blackish by reason of the ice, and wherein the snow is hid:

What time they wax warm, they vanish: when it is hot, they are consumed out of their place.

The paths of their way are turned aside; they go to nothing, and perish.

The troops of Tema looked, the companies of Sheba waited for them.

They were confounded because they had hoped; they came thither, and were ashamed.

For now ye are nothing; ye see my casting down, and are afraid.

Did I say, 'Bring unto me'? or 'Give a reward for me of your substance'?

Or 'Deliver me from the enemy's hand,' or 'Redeem me from the hand of the mighty'?

Teach me, and I will hold my tongue: and cause me to understand wherein I have erred.

How forcible are right words? but what doth your arguing reprove?

Do ye imagine to reprove words, and the speeches of one that is desperate, which are as wind?

Yea, ye overwhelm the fatherless, and you dig a pit for your friend.

Now therefore be content, look upon me, for it is evident unto you if I lie.

Return, I pray you, let it not be iniquity; yea return again: my righteousness is in it.

Is there iniquity in my tongue? cannot my taste discern perverse things?

7

"Is there not an appointed time to man upon earth? are not his days also like the days of an hireling?

As a servant earnestly desireth the shadow, and as an hireling looketh for the reward of his work:

So am I made to possess months of vanity, and wearisome nights are appointed to me.

When I lie down, I say, 'When shall I arise, and the night be gone?' and I am full of tossings to and fro, unto the dawning of the day.

My flesh is clothed with worms and clods of dust, my skin is broken, and become loathsome.

My days are swifter than a weaver's shuttle, and are spent without hope.

O remember that my life is wind: mine eye shall no more see good.

The eye of him that hath seen me shall see me no more: thine eyes are upon me, and I am not.

As the cloud is consumed and vanisheth away: so he that goeth down to the grave shall come up no more.

He shall return no more to his house: neither shall his place know him any more.

Therefore I will not refrain my mouth, I will speak in the anguish of my spirit, I will complain in the bitterness of my soul.

Am I a sea, or a whale, that thou settest a watch over me?

When I say, 'My bed shall comfort me, my couch shall ease my complaint':

Then thou scarest me with dreams, and terrifiest me through visions:

So that my soul chooseth strangling, and death rather than my life.

I loathe it, I would not live alway: let me alone, for my days are vanity.

What is man, that thou shouldest magnify him? and that thou shouldest set thine heart upon him?

And that thou shouldest visit him every morning, and try him every moment?

How long wilt thou not depart from me? nor let me alone till I swallow down my spittle?

I have sinned: what shall I do unto thee, O thou preserver of men? why hast thou set me as a mark against thee, so that I am a burden to myself?

And why dost thou not pardon my transgression, and take away mine iniquity? for now shall I sleep in the dust, and thou shalt seek me in the morning, but I shall not be."

[In the intervening chapters Job dialogues with his friends: they question Job's innocence, while Job maintains his righteousness and requests an audience with God.]

GOD'S ANSWER AND JOB'S SUBMISSION[17]

38

Then the Lord answered Job out of the whirlwind, and said, "Who is this that darkeneth counsel by words without knowledge?

Gird up now thy loins like a man;[18] for I will demand of thee, and answer thou me.

Where wast thou when I laid the foundations of the earth? declare, if thou hast understanding.

Who hath laid the measures thereof, if thou knowest? or who hath stretched the line upon it?

Whereupon are the foundations thereof fastened? or who laid the cornerstone thereof;

When the morning stars sang together, and all the sons of God shouted for joy?

Or who shut up the sea with doors, when it brake forth as if it had issued out of the womb?

When I made the cloud the garment thereof, and thick darkness a swaddling band for it,

And brake up for it my decreed place, and set bars and doors,

And said, 'Hitherto shalt thou come, but no further: and here shall thy proud waves be stayed'?

Hast thou commanded the morning since thy days? and caused the day-spring to know his place,

---

[17] **God's . . . Submission:** Beginning with chapter 38, Job finally has a hearing before God.

[18] **Gird up . . . man:** Prepare for warfare.

That it might take hold of the ends of the earth, that the wicked might be shaken out of it?

It is turned as clay to the seal, and they stand as a garment.

And from the wicked their light is withholden, and the high arm shall be broken.

Hast thou entered into the springs of the sea? or hast thou walked in the search of the depth?

Have the gates of death been opened unto thee? or hast thou seen the doors of the shadow of death?

Hast thou perceived the breadth of the earth? Declare if thou knowest it all.

Where is the way where light dwelleth? and as for darkness, where is the place thereof,

That thou shouldest take it to the bound thereof, and that thou shouldest know the paths to the house thereof?

Knowest thou it, because thou wast then born? or because the number of thy days is great?

Hast thou entered into the treasures of the snow? or hast thou seen the treasures of the hail,

Which I have reserved against the time of trouble, against the day of battle and war?

By what way is the light parted, which scattereth the east wind upon the earth?

Who hath divided a watercourse for the overflowing of waters? or a way for the lightning of thunder,

To cause it to rain on the earth, where no man is: on the wilderness wherein there is no man;

To satisfy the desolate and waste ground, and to cause the bud of the tender herb to spring forth?

Hath the rain a father? or who hath begotten the drops of dew?

Out of whose womb came the ice? and the hoary frost of heaven, who hath gendered it?

The waters are hid as with a stone, and the face of the deep is frozen.

Canst thou bind the sweet influences of Pleiades? or loose the bands of Orion?

Canst thou bring forth Mazzaroth in his season, or canst thou guide Arcturus with his sons?

Knowest thou the ordinances of heaven? canst thou set the dominion thereof in the earth?

Canst thou lift up thy voice to the clouds, that abundance of waters may cover thee?

Canst thou send lightnings, that they may go, and say unto thee, 'Here we are'?

Who hath put wisdom in the inward parts? or who hath given understanding to the heart?

Who can number the clouds in wisdom? or who can stay the bottles of heaven,

When the dust groweth into hardness, and the clods cleave fast together?

Wilt thou hunt the prey for the lion? or fill the appetite of the young lions,

When they couch in their dens, and abide in the covert to lie in wait?

Who provideth for the raven his food? when his young ones cry unto God, they wander for lack of meat."

39

"Knowest thou the time when the wild goats of the rock bring forth? or canst thou mark when the hinds do calve?

Canst thou number the months that they fufill? or knowest thou the time when they bring forth?

They bow themselves, they bring forth their young ones, they cast out their sorrows.

Their young ones are in good liking, they grow up with corn: they go forth, and return not unto them.

Who hath sent out the wild ass free? or who hath loosed the bands of the wild ass?

Whose house I have made the wilderness, and the barren land his dwellings.

He scorneth the multitude of the city, neither regardeth he the crying of the driver.

The range of the mountains is his pasture, and he searcheth after every green thing.

Will the unicorn be willing to serve thee? or abide by thy crib?

Canst thou bind the unicorn with his band in the furrow? or will he harrow the valleys after thee?

Wilt thou trust him because his strength is great? or wilt thou leave thy labour to him?

Wilt thou believe him that he will bring home thy seed? and gather it into thy barn?

Gavest thou the goodly wings unto the peacocks, or wings and feathers unto the ostrich?

Which leaveth her eggs in the earth, and warmeth them in the dust,

And forgetteth that the foot may crush them, or that the wild beast may break them.

She is hardened against her young ones, as though they were not hers: her labour is in vain without fear:

Because God hath deprived her of wisdom, neither hath he imparted to her understanding.

What time she lifteth up herself on high, she scorneth the horse and his rider.

Hast thou given the horse strength? hast thou clothed his neck with thunder?

Canst thou make him afraid as a grasshopper? the glory of his nostrils is terrible.

He paweth in the valley, and rejoiceth in his strength: he goeth on to meet the armed men.

He mocketh at fear, and is not affrighted: neither turneth he back from the sword.

The quiver rattleth against him, the glittering spear and the shield.

He swalloweth the ground with fierceness and rage: neither believeth he that it is the sound of the trumpet.

He saith among the trumpets, 'Ha, ha': and he smelleth the battle afar off, the thunder of the captains, and the shouting.

Doth the hawk fly by thy wisdom, and stretch her wings toward the south?

Doth the eagle mount up at thy command? and make her nest on high?

She dwelleth and abideth on the rock, upon the crag of the rock, and the strong place.

From thence she seeketh the prey, and her eyes behold afar off.

Her young ones also suck up blood: and where the slain are, there is she."

40

Moreover the Lord answered Job, and said,

"Shall he that contendeth with the Almighty instruct him? he that reproveth God, let him answer it."

Then Job answered the Lord, and said,

"Behold, I am vile, what shall I answer thee? I will lay my hand upon my mouth.

Once have I spoken, but I will not answer: yea twice, but I will proceed no further."

Then answered the Lord unto Job out of the whirlwind, and said,

"Gird up thy loins now like a man: I will demand of thee, and declare thou unto me.

Wilt thou also disannul my judgment? wilt thou condemn me, that thou mayest be righteous?

Hast thou an arm like God? or canst thou thunder with a voice like him?

Deck thyself now with majesty and excellency, and array thyself with glory and beauty.

Cast abroad the rage of thy wrath: and behold every one that is proud, and abase him.

Look on every one that is proud, and bring him low: and tread down the wicked in their place.

Hide them in the dust together, and bind their faces in secret.

Then will I also confess unto thee, that thine own right hand can save thee.

Behold now behemoth,[19] which I made with thee, he eateth grass as an ox.

Lo now, his strength is in his loins, and his force is in the navel of his belly.

He moveth his tail like a cedar: the sinews of his stones are wrapped together.

His bones are as strong pieces of brass: his bones are like bars of iron.

He is the chief of the ways of God: he that made him can make his sword to approach unto him.

Surely the mountains bring him forth food, where all the beasts of the field play.

He lieth under the shady trees, in the covert of the reed, and fens.

The shady trees cover him with their shadow: the willows of the brook compass him about.

Behold, he drinketh up a river, and hasteth not: he trusteth that he can draw up Jordan into his mouth.

He taketh it with his eyes: his nose pierceth through snares."

41

"Canst thou draw out leviathan with an hook? or his tongue with a cord which thou lettest down?

Canst thou put an hook into his nose? or bore his jaw through with a thorn?

Will he make many supplications unto thee? will he speak soft words unto thee?

Will he make a covenant with thee? wilt thou take him for a servant for ever?

---

[19] **behemoth:** Other translations use "hippopotamus" or "crocodile" here; behemoth suggests a primeval monster of chaos.

Wilt thou play with him as with a bird? or wilt thou bind him for thy maidens?

Shall the companions make a banquet of him? shall they part him among the merchants?

Canst thou fill his skin with barbed irons? or his head with fish spears?

Lay thine hand upon him, remember the battle: do no more.

Behold, the hope of him is in vain: shall not one be cast down even at the sight of him?

None is so fierce that dare stir him up: who then is able to stand before me?

Who hath prevented me that I should repay him? whatsoever is under the whole heaven is mine.

I will not conceal his parts, nor his power, nor his comely proportion.

Who can discover the face of his garment? or who can come to him with his double bridle?

Who can open the doors of his face? his teeth are terrible round about.

His scales are his pride, shut up together as with a close seal.

One is so near to another that no air can come between them.

They are joined one to another, they stick together, that they cannot be sundered.

By his neesings a light doth shine, and his eyes are like the eyelids of the morning.

Out of his mouth go burning lamps, and sparks of fire leap out.

Out of his nostrils goeth smoke, as out of a seething pot or caldron.

His breath kindleth coals, and a flame goeth out of his mouth.

In his neck remaineth strength, and sorrow is turned into joy before him.

The flakes of his flesh are joined together: they are firm in themselves, they cannot be moved.

His heart is as firm as a stone, yea as hard as a piece of the nether millstone.

When he raiseth up himself, the mighty are afraid: by reason of breakings they purify themselves.

The sword of him that layeth at him cannot hold: the spear, the dart, nor the habergeon.

He esteemeth iron as straw, and brass as rotten wood.

The arrow cannot make him flee: slingstones are turned with him into stubble.

Darts are counted as stubble: he laugheth at the shaking of a spear.

Sharp stones are under him: he spreadeth sharp pointed things upon the mire.

He maketh the deep to boil like a pot: he maketh the sea like a pot of ointment.

He maketh a path to shine after him; one would think the deep to be hoary.

Upon earth there is not his like, who is made without fear.

He beholdeth all high things: he is a king over all the children of pride."

42

Then Job answered the Lord, and said,

"I know that thou canst do every thing, and that no thought can be withholden from thee.

Who is he that hideth counsel without knowledge? therefore have I uttered that I understood not, things too wonderful for me, which I knew not.

Hear, I beseech thee, and I will speak: I will demand of thee, and declare thou unto me.

I have heard of thee by the hearing of the ear: but now mine eye seeth thee.

Wherefore I abhor myself, and repent in dust and ashes."

And it was so, that after the Lord had spoken these words unto Job, the Lord said to Eliphaz the Temanite, "My wrath is kindled against thee, and against thy two friends: for ye have not spoken of me the thing that is right, as my servant Job hath. Therefore take unto you now seven bullocks, and seven rams, and go to my servant Job, and offer up for yourselves a burnt offering, and my servant Job shall pray for you, for him will I accept: lest I deal with you after your folly, in that ye have not spoken of me the thing which is right, like my servant Job." So Eliphaz the Temanite, and Bildad the Shuhite, and Zophar the Naamathite went, and did according as the Lord commanded them: the Lord also accepted Job. And the Lord turned the captivity of Job, when he prayed for his friends: also the Lord gave Job twice as much as he had before.

Then came there unto him all his brethren, and all his sisters, and all they that had been of his acquaintance before, and did eat bread with him in his house: and they bemoaned him, and comforted him over all the evil that the Lord had brought upon him: every man also gave him a piece of money, and every one an earring of gold. So the Lord blessed the latter end of Job more than his beginning: for he had fourteen thousand sheep, and six thousand camels, and a thousand yoke of oxen, and a thousand she-asses. He had also seven sons, and three daughters. And he called the name of the first Jemima, and the name of the second Kezia, and the name of the third Keren-happuch.[20] And in all the land were no women found so fair as the daughters of Job: and their father gave them inheritance among their brethren. After this lived Job an hundred and forty years, and saw his sons, and his sons' sons, even four generations. So Job died, being old, and full of days.[21]

---

[20] **Jemima . . . Keren-happuch:** Jemima means "dove"; Kezia means "cinnamon"; Keren-happuch means "horn of eye-shadow." The specific mention of daughters receiving an inheritance is unique in Hebrew Scriptures.

[21] **full of days:** Job's lifespan becomes double the usual expectation. The language here is reminiscent of descriptions of the patriarchs in the Book of Genesis.

❧ Psalm 23

1 The Lord is my shepherd, I shall not want.
2 He maketh me to lie down in green pastures: he leadeth me beside the still waters.
3 He restoreth my soul: he leadeth me in the paths of righteousness, for his name's sake.
4 Yea though I walk through the valley of the shadow of death, I will fear no evil: for
    thou art with me, thy rod and thy staff they comfort me.

5   Thou preparest a table before me, in the presence of mine enemies: thou anointest
    my head with oil, my cup runneth over.

6   Surely goodness and mercy shall follow me all the days of my life: and I will dwell in
    the house of the Lord for ever.

❧ Psalm 104[1]

1   Bless the Lord, O my soul, O Lord my God, thou art very great; thou art clothed
    with honour and majesty.

2   Who coverest thyself with light as with a garment: who stretchest out the heavens
    like a curtain:

3   Who layeth the beams of his chambers in the waters: who maketh the clouds his
    chariot: who walketh upon the wings of the wind:

4   Who maketh his angels spirits; his ministers a flaming fire:

5   Who laid the foundations of the earth, that it should not be removed for ever.

6   Thou coveredst it with the deep as with a garment: the waters stood above the
    mountains.

7   At thy rebuke they fled; at the voice of thy thunder they hasted away.

8   They go up by the mountains; they go down by the valleys unto the place which
    thou hast founded for them.

9   Thou hast set a bound that they may not pass over; that they turn not again to cover
    the earth.

10 He sendeth the springs into the valleys, which run among the hills.

11 They give drink to every beast of the field: the wild asses quench their thirst.

12 By them shall the fowls of the heaven have their habitation, which sing among the
    branches.

13 He watereth the hills from his chambers: the earth is satisfied with the fruit of thy
    works.

14 He causeth the grass to grow for the cattle, and herb for the service of man: that he
    may bring forth food out of the earth;

15 And wine that maketh glad the heart of man, and oil to make his face to shine, and
    bread which strengtheneth man's heart.

16 The trees of the Lord are full of sap; the cedars of Lebanon, which he hath planted;

17 Where the birds make their nests: as for the stork, the fir trees are her house.

18 The high hills are a refuge for the wild goats; and the rocks for the conies.

19 He appointed the moon for seasons: the sun knoweth his going down.

20 Thou makest darkness, and it is night: wherein all the beasts of the forest do creep
    forth.

---

[1]**Psalm 104:** Because of the similarity in imagery and tone, this creation hymn has been compared to the
Egyptian "Hymn to Aten" (see p. 152).

21 The young lions roar after their prey, and seek their meat from God.

22 The sun ariseth, they gather themselves together, and lay them down in their dens.

23 Man goeth forth unto his work and to his labour until the evening.

24 O Lord, how manifold are thy works! in wisdom hast thou made them all: the earth is full of thy riches.

25 So is this great and wide sea, wherein are things creeping innumerable, both small and great beasts.

26 There go the ships: there is that leviathan, whom thou hast made to play therein.

27 These wait all upon thee; that thou mayest give them their meat in due season.

28 That thou givest them they gather: thou openest thine hand, they are filled with good.

29 Thou hidest thy face, they are troubled: thou takest away their breath, they die, and return to their dust.

30 Thou sendest forth thy spirit, they are created: and thou renewest the face of the earth.

31 The glory of the Lord shall endure for ever: the Lord shall rejoice in his works.

32 He looketh on the earth, and it trembleth: he toucheth the hills, and they smoke.

33 I will sing unto the Lord as long as I live: I will sing praise to my God while I have my being.

ೲ Psalm 137[1]

1 By the rivers of Babylon, there we sat down, yea we wept, when we remembered Zion.

2 We hanged our harps upon the willows, in the midst thereof.

3 For there they that carried us away captive required of us a song, and they that wasted us required of us mirth: saying, "Sing us one of the songs of Zion."

4 How shall we sing the Lord's song in a strange land?

5 If I forget thee, O Jerusalem, let my right hand forget her cunning.

6 If I do not remember thee, let my tongue cleave to the roof of my mouth; if I prefer not Jerusalem above my chief joy.

7 Remember, O Lord, the children of Edom, in the day of Jerusalem, who said, "Rase it, rase it: even to the foundation thereof."

8 O daughter of Babylon, who art to be destroyed: happy shall he be that rewardeth thee, as thou hast served us.

9 Happy shall he be that taketh and dasheth thy little ones against the stones.

---

[1] **Psalm 137:** A lament in recognition of the exile of the Jews in Babylon after the destruction of Jerusalem by the Babylonians in 587 B.C.E. —the beginning of the Diaspora.

∾ The Song of Songs[1]

1

BRIDE:

1   The song of songs, which is Solomon's.

2   Let him kiss me with the kisses of his mouth:
 for thy love is better than wine.

3   Because of the savour of thy good ointments,
 thy name is an ointment poured forth,
 therefore do the virgins love thee.

4   Draw me, we will run after thee:
 the king[2] hath brought me into his chambers:

COMPANIONS:

 we will be glad and rejoice in thee,
 we will remember thy love more than wine:
 the upright love thee.

BRIDE:

5   I am black, but comely,
 O ye daughters of Jerusalem,
 as the tents of Kedar,
 as the curtains of Solomon.

6   Look not upon me, because I am black,
 because the sun hath looked upon me:
 my mother's children were angry with me,
 they made me the keeper of the vineyards,
 but mine own vineyard have I not kept.

7   Tell me, O thou whom my soul loveth,
 where thou feedest, where thou makest
 thy flock to rest at noon:
 for why should I be as one that turneth
 aside by the flocks of thy companions?

BRIDEGROOM:

8   If thou know not,
 O thou fairest among women,
 go thy way forth by the footsteps of the flock,
 and feed thy kids beside the shepherds' tents.

9   I have compared thee,
 O my love, to a company of horses in Pharaoh's chariots.

10   Thy cheeks are comely with rows of jewels,
 thy neck with chains of gold.

---

[1] **The Song of Songs:** The language and use of pronouns suggest that the speakers are a bride, bridegroom, and chorus of companions. To aid the reader, we indicate these different voices.

[2] **king:** Bridegroom.

COMPANIONS:

11   We will make thee borders of gold with studs of silver.

BRIDE:

12   While the king sitteth at his table,
           my spikenard[3] sendeth forth the smell thereof.

13   A bundle of myrrh[4] is my wellbeloved unto me;
           he shall lie all night betwixt my breasts.

14   My beloved is unto me as a cluster of
           camphire[5] in the vineyards of Engedi.[6]

BRIDEGROOM:

15   Behold, thou art fair, my love:
           behold, thou art fair, thou hast doves' eyes.

BRIDE:

16   Behold, thou art fair, my beloved,
           yea pleasant: also our bed is green.

BRIDEGROOM:

17   The beams of our house are cedar, and our rafters of fir.

2

BRIDE:

1   I am the rose of Sharon[7] and the lily of the valleys.

BRIDEGROOM:

2   As the lily among thorns, so is my love among the daughters.

BRIDE:

3   As the apple tree among the trees of the wood,
           so is my beloved among the sons.
           I sat under his shadow with great delight,
           and his fruit was sweet to my taste.

4   He brought me to the banqueting house,
           and his banner over me was love.

5   Stay me with flagons, comfort me with apples,
           for I am sick of love.

6   His left hand is under my head,
           and his right hand doth embrace me.

7   I charge you, O ye daughters of Jerusalem,
           by the roes, and by the hinds of the field,
           that ye stir not up, nor awake my love, till he please.

---

[3] **spikenard:** A fragrant ointment popular in the ancient world.

[4] **myrrh:** A resin made from several plants in Arabia and used for incense and perfume.

[5] **camphire:** Same as henna-blossom, a plant used for dyeing hair auburn or reddish-brown.

[6] **Engedi:** An oasis by the Dead Sea.

[7] **Sharon:** The coastal plain in north central Israel.

BRIDE:

8   The voice of my beloved! behold!
        he cometh leaping upon the mountains,
        skipping upon the hills.

9   My beloved is like a roe or a young hart:
        behold, he standeth behind our wall,
        he looketh forth at the window,
        showing himself through the lattice.

10   My beloved spake, and said unto me,
        "Rise up, my love, my fair one, and come away.

11   "For lo, the winter is past, the rain is over, and gone.

12   "The flowers appear on the earth,
        the time of the singing of birds is come,
        and the voice of the turtle[8] is heard in our land.

13   "The fig tree putteth forth her green figs,
        and the vines with the tender grape give a good smell.
        Arise, my love, my fair one, and come away."

BRIDEGROOM:

14   O my dove, that art in the clefts of the rock,
        in the secret places of the stairs: let me see thy countenance,
        let me hear thy voice, for sweet is thy voice,
        and thy countenance is comely.

COMPANIONS:

15   Take us the foxes, the little foxes,
        that spoil the vines: for our vines have tender grapes.[9]

BRIDE:

16   My beloved is mine, and I am his: he feedeth among the lilies.

17   Until the day break, and the shadows flee away:
        turn, my beloved, and be thou like a roe,
        or a young hart, upon the mountains of Bether.[10]

3

1   By night on my bed I sought him whom my soul loveth.
        I sought him, but I found him not.

2   I will rise now, and go about the city in the streets,
        and in the broad ways I will seek him whom my soul loveth:
        I sought him, but I found him not.

3   The watchmen that go about the city found me:
        to whom I said, "Saw ye him whom my soul loveth?"

---

[8] **turtle:** turtledove.

[9] **Take us . . . tender grapes:** The meaning of this fragment is unclear.

[10] **Bether:** Meaning unclear; another translation uses "rugged mountains."

4   It was but a little that I passed from them,
          but I found him whom my soul loveth:
          I held him, and would not let him go,
          until I had brought him into my mother's house,
          and into the chamber of her that conceived me.

5   I charge you, O ye daughters of Jerusalem,
          by the roes and by the hinds of the field,
          that ye stir not up, nor awake my love, till he please.

COMPANIONS:

6   Who is this that cometh out of the wilderness like pillars of smoke,
          perfumed with myrrh and frankincense,
          with all powders of the merchant?

7   Behold his bed, which is Solomon's:[11]
          threescore valiant men are about it,
          of the valiant of Israel.

8   They all hold swords, being expert in war:
          every man hath his sword upon his thigh,
          because of fear in the night.

9   King Solomon made himself a chariot of the wood of Lebanon.

10   He made the pillars thereof of silver,
          the bottom thereof of gold, the covering of it of purple;
          the midst thereof being paved with love,
          for the daughters of Jerusalem.

11   Go forth, O ye daughters of Zion, and behold king Solomon
          with the crown wherewith his mother crowned him
          in the day of his espousals, and in the day of the gladness of his heart.

4

BRIDEGROOM:

1   Behold, thou art fair, my love, behold thou art fair,
          thou hast doves' eyes within thy locks:
          thy hair is as a flock of goats, that appear from mount Gilead.[12]

2   Thy teeth are like a flock of sheep that are even shorn,
          which came up from the washing:
          whereof every one bear twins, and none is barren among them.

3   Thy lips are like a thread of scarlet, and thy speech is comely:
          thy temples are like a piece of a pomegranate within thy locks.

4   Thy neck is like the tower of David builded for an armoury,
          whereon there hang a thousand bucklers,
          all shields of mighty men.

---

[11] **Solomon's:** In the legendary style of King Solomon.

[12] **Gilead:** A mountain east of the Jordan.

5   Thy two breasts are like two young roes that are twins,
  which feed among the lilies.
6   Until the day break, and the shadows flee away,
  I will get me to the mountain of myrrh, and to the hill of frankincense.[13]
7   Thou art all fair, my love, there is no spot in thee.
8   Come with me from Lebanon,
   my spouse, with me from Lebanon:
   look from the top of Amana,
   from the top of Shenir and Hermon,[14]
   from the lions' dens, from the mountains of the leopards.
9   Thou hast ravished my heart, my sister, my spouse;
  thou hast ravished my heart with one of thine eyes,
  with one chain of thy neck.
10   How fair is thy love, my sister, my spouse!
  how much better is thy love than wine!
  and the smell of thine ointments than all spices!
11   Thy lips, O my spouse, drop as the honeycomb:
  honey and milk are under thy tongue,
  and the smell of thy garments is like the smell of Lebanon.
12   A garden inclosed is my sister, my spouse:
  a spring shut up, a fountain sealed.
13   Thy plants are an orchard of pomegranates,
  with pleasant fruits, camphire, with spikenard,
14   Spikenard and saffron, calamus[15] and cinnamon,
  with all trees of frankincense, myrrh and aloes,
  with all the chief spices:

BRIDE:

15   A fountain of gardens, a well of living waters,
  and streams from Lebanon.
16   Awake, O north wind, and come thou south;
  blow upon my garden,
  that the spices thereof may flow out:
  let my beloved come into his garden,
  and eat his pleasant fruits.

5

BRIDEGROOM:

1   I am come into my garden, my sister, my spouse,
  I have gathered my myrrh with my spice,

---

[13] **frankincense:** A gum resin from Arabian and north African trees, used for incense.

[14] **Amana, Shenir, Hermon:** Lebanese mountaintops.

[15] **calamus:** A member of the arum family, which yields an aromatic oil.

I have eaten my honeycomb with my honey,
I have drunk my wine with my milk: eat,
O friends; drink, yea drink abundantly, O beloved!

BRIDE:

2   I sleep, but my heart waketh:
it is the voice of my beloved that knocketh, saying,
"Open to me, my sister, my love, my dove, my undefiled:
for my head is filled with dew,
and my locks with the drops of the night."

3   I have put off my coat, how shall I put it on?
I have washed my feet, how shall I defile them?

4   My beloved put in his hand by the hole of the door,
and my bowels[16] were moved for him.

5   I rose up to open to my beloved,
and my hands dropped with myrrh,
and my fingers with sweet smelling myrrh,
upon the handles of the lock.

6   I opened to my beloved,
but my beloved had withdrawn himself,
and was gone: my soul failed when he spake:
I sought him, but I could not find him:
I called him, but he gave me no answer.

7   The watchmen that went about the city found me,
they smote me, they wounded me;
the keepers of the walls took away my veil from me.

8   I charge you, O daughters of Jerusalem,
if ye find my beloved,
that ye tell him that I am sick of love.

COMPANIONS:

9   What is thy beloved more than another beloved,
O thou fairest among women?
what is thy beloved more than another beloved,
that thou dost so charge us?

BRIDE:

10   My beloved is white and ruddy,
the chiefest among ten thousand.

11   His head is as the most fine gold,
his locks are bushy, and black as a raven.

12   His eyes are as the eyes of doves by the rivers of waters,
washed with milk, and fitly set.

13   His cheeks are as a bed of spices,
as sweet flowers: his lips like lilies,
dropping sweet smelling myrrh.

---

[16] **bowels:** Another translation says, "my heart was thrilled within me."

14   His hands are as gold rings set with the beryl:
     his belly is as bright ivory,
     overlaid with sapphires.

15   His legs are as pillars of marble,
     set upon sockets of fine gold:
     his countenance is as Lebanon, excellent as the cedars.

16   His mouth is most sweet, yea he is altogether lovely.
     This is my beloved, and this is my friend,
     O daughters of Jerusalem.

6

COMPANIONS:

1   Whither is thy beloved gone?
     O thou fairest among women,
     whither is thy beloved turned aside?
     that we may seek him with thee.

BRIDE:

2   My beloved is gone down into his garden,
     to the beds of spices, to feed in the gardens,
     and to gather lilies.

3   I am my beloved's, and my beloved is mine:
     he feedeth among the lilies.

BRIDEGROOM:

4   Thou art beautiful, O my love, as Tirzah,[17]
     comely as Jerusalem,
     terrible as an army with banners.

5   Turn away thine eyes from me,
     for they have overcome me:
     thy hair is as a flock of goats that appear from Gilead.

6   Thy teeth are as a flock of sheep which
     go up from the washing, whereof every one beareth twins,
     and there is not one barren among them.

7   As a piece of a pomegranate[18] are thy temples within thy locks.

8   There are threescore queens, and fourscore concubines,
     and virgins without number.

9   My dove, my undefiled is but one;
     she is the only one of her mother,
     she is the choice one of her that bare her.
     The daughters saw her, and blessed her;
     yea the queens and the concubines, and they praised her.

---

[17] **Tirzah:** At one time, a residence for the kings of Israel.

[18] **pomegranate:** Generally known in the ancient Mediterranean world as a symbol of the womb.

10   Who is she that looketh forth as the morning,
        fair as the moon, clear as the sun,
        and terrible as an army with banners?

11   I went down into the garden of nuts to see the
        fruits of the valley, and to see whether the vine flourished,
        and the pomegranates budded.

12   Or ever I was aware, my soul made me like
        the chariots of Amminadib.[19]

COMPANIONS:

13   Return, return, O Shulamite:[20] return, return,
        that we may look upon thee:

BRIDEGROOM:

        what will ye see in the Shulamite?
        as it were the company of two armies.

7

1   How beautiful are thy feet with shoes, O prince's daughter!
        the joints of thy thighs are like jewels,
        the work of the hands of a cunning workman.

2   Thy navel is like a round goblet,
        which wanteth not liquor:
        thy belly is like an heap of wheat,
        set about with lilies.

3   Thy two breasts are like two young roes that are twins.

4   Thy neck is as a tower of ivory:
        thine eyes like the fish-pools in Heshbon[21] by
        the gate of Bathrabbim: thy nose is as the tower
        of Lebanon, which looketh toward Damascus.

5   Thine head upon thee is like Carmel[22] and the
        hair of thine head like purple;
        the king is held in the galleries.

6   How fair, and how pleasant art thou, O love,
        for delights!

7   This thy stature is like to a palm tree,
        and thy breasts to clusters of grapes.

8   I said, "I will go up to the palm tree,
        I will take hold of the boughs thereof":
        now also thy breasts shall be as clusters of the vine,
        and the smell of thy nose like apples;

---

[19] **Amminadib:** Meaning unclear; another translation says, "set me in a chariot beside my prince."

[20] **Shulamite:** Meaning uncertain; it might mean "bride of Solomon."

[21] **Heshbon:** A city east of the Jordan in Moab.

[22] **Carmel:** A famous mountain along the northern coast.

9   And the roof of thy mouth like the best wine for my beloved,
           that goeth down sweetly, causing the lips
           of those that are asleep to speak.

BRIDE:

10   I am my beloved's, and his desire is towards me.

11   Come, my beloved, let us go forth into the field:
           let us lodge in the villages.

12   Let us get up early to the vineyards,
           let us see if the vine flourish,
           whether the tender grape appear,
           and the pomegranates bud forth:
           there will I give thee my loves.

13   The mandrakes[23] give a smell, and at our gates are
           all manner of pleasant fruits, new and old,
           which I have laid up for thee, O my beloved.

8

1   O that thou wert as my brother that sucked
           the breasts of my mother!
           when I should find thee without,
           I would kiss thee, yea, I should not be despised.

2   I would lead thee, and bring thee into my mother's house,
           who would instruct me: I would cause thee to
           drink of spiced wine, of the juice of my pomegranate.

3   His left hand should be under my head,
           and his right hand should embrace me.

4   I charge you, O daughters of Jerusalem,
           that ye stir not up, nor awake my love,
           until he please.

COMPANIONS:

5   (Who is this that cometh up from the wilderness,
           leaning upon her beloved?)

BRIDEGROOM:

           I raised thee up under the apple tree:
           there thy mother brought thee forth,
           there she brought thee forth that bare thee.

6   Set me as a seal upon thine heart,
           as a seal upon thine arm: for love is strong as death,
           jealousy is cruel as the grave:
           the coals thereof are coals of fire,
           which hath a most vehement flame.

---

[23] **mandrakes:** A plant of the night-shade family. Because of its human shape, the root was thought to be an aphrodisiac.

7   Many waters cannot quench love,
    neither can the floods drown it:
    if a man would give all the substance of his house for love,
    it would utterly be contemned.

COMPANIONS:

8   We have a little sister, and she hath no breasts:
    what shall we do for our sister,
9   in the day when she shall be spoken for?
If she be a wall, we will build upon her a palace of silver:
    and if she be a door, we will inclose her with boards of cedar.

BRIDE:

10 I am a wall, and my breasts like towers:
    then was I in his eyes as one that found favour.
11 Solomon had a vineyard at Baal-hamon,[24]
    he let out the vineyard unto keepers:
    every one for the fruit thereof was to bring
    a thousand pieces of silver.
12 My vineyard, which is mine, is before me: thou,
    O Solomon, must have a thousand,
    and those that keep the fruit thereof two hundred.

BRIDEGROOM:

13 Thou that dwellest in the gardens,
    the companions hearken to thy voice:
    cause me to hear it.

BRIDE:

14 Make haste, my beloved, and be thou like to a roe,
    or to a young hart upon the mountains of spices.

---

[24] **Baal-hamon:** An unknown place.

Myths of Creation

Most world cultures and religions have a creation myth or story like the one in the **Hebrew Scriptures** that provides the groundwork of creation, a kind of blueprint of the cosmos and its origins: How did it all begin? What gods or goddesses were involved? What or who keeps the present world from collapsing into chaos? and Where is the whole thing headed? Creation stories usually reveal the origins of human beings, food, fire, and death. After creating a picture of the world, creation myths usually define the role that human beings play in the universe and how they might participate in the upkeep and purpose of the world. Such participation is typically embodied in religious rituals performed throughout the year, in which the needs of human beings are intertwined with the annual seasons.

Creation stories usually involve analogies with the human mind or body: for example, creation is like dreaming or speaking or being born. It can also be represented as emergence from a cosmic egg, the trunk of a tree, or Mother Earth. Creation stories contain much more than prehistoric or primitive theories about the world's beginnings; in them can be seen the fundamental attitudes and beliefs that shape a sense of the present. Cultures that believe in the sacredness of the earth might value stories in which the earth is created from the body of a primordial woman or man, such as in the Indian

p. 78

Having remarked a mathematically calculable regularity in the passages of the planets through the constellations of the fixed stars, these first systematic observers [Mesopotamians] of the heavens conceived — in that specific period, in that specific place, for the first time in human history — the grandiose idea of a mathematically determined cosmic order of greater and lesser, ever-revolving cycles of celestial manifestation, disappearance and renewal, with which it would be prudent for man to put himself in accord.

– JOSEPH CAMPBELL, mythologist, 1974

◀ **Ramses I Flanked by Gods, fourteenth century B.C.E.**

Ancient Egyptian kings and pharaohs were worshiped as gods and received legitimacy for their rule from their association with powerful deities. This fresco from the tomb of Ramses I shows Ramses flanked by Horus, god of the sky, and Anubis, god of embalming. (The Art Archive / Dagli Orti)

p. 159

p. 152

p. 88

"The Song of Purusha." When humans discovered the role of the male in conception, an analogy was made to the role of father-sky and rain. In the beautiful Egyptian **"Hymn to Aten,"** the sun god Aten is not only the creator of the cosmos, but he is a caring deity who nurtures life on earth. Like a potter, the Hebrew Yahweh in **Genesis** formed Adam from clay. Followers of the Orphic religion in ancient Greece envisioned a primordial silver egg floating in space; from it Love (or Eros) was finally hatched and was the basis for the rest of creation.

The process of creation provides a repository of images and actions that people use to shape their attitudes and guide their behavior—the question of *whence* influences questions of *how* and *why*. Sumerian creation myths before 2000 B.C.E. pitted a primordial dragon of chaos against a warrior-champion, like the storm god Ninurta, who is the predecessor to warrior-god Marduk in Babylonian myth, who defeats the mistress of chaos Tiamat. A pattern of warrior-kings defeating the forces of chaos in the guise of serpentine monsters of the sea—often female—is later found throughout the literature of the ancient Near East and the Mediterranean: in Greek myth, it is Zeus or Apollo defeating Python, Typhon, or Typhoeus; in India, Indra defeats the water serpent Vritra; in Egypt, the dragon-like serpent is called Apep or Apophis; in Hebrew Scriptures the battle is between Yahweh and Rahab or Leviathan.[1]

This recurring story of battle suggests that combat or conflict was an early view of how the world functioned. The myths that depict the creation of the world as a struggle may also reflect the essential nature of the world, its functional paradigm. Darwin's theory of "survival of the fittest"[2] is a modern expression of such a cosmogony. The fact that the forces of chaos are often female in these ancient stories indicates a cultural shift away from female, earth deities to male, sky deities, a pattern which was reflected in the early cities along the Tigris and Euphrates Rivers in Mesopotamia and along the Nile in Egypt.

> Primitive man was sustained by a sense of union with his world: stones, trees, animals, spirits, people, all spoke to him and responded to him; and he was in them and of them. Civilized man throve on struggle and opposition; he must master or be mastered, and the more formidable the struggle the greater his own sense of life.
>
> – LEWIS MUMFORD, critic and historian, 1956

---

[1] **Leviathan:** By the time the Hebrew Scriptures (Old Testament) were written and edited, only vestiges of the old combat myth remained, scattered in several different books: the dragon or sea monster is called by various names, such as Leviathan or Tannin (see Isaiah 51:9–10; Isaiah 27:1; Psalm 74:12–14; Psalm 89:10; and Job 26:12–13).

[2] **"survival of the fittest":** Charles Darwin (1809–1882) was an English biologist who popularized the theory of evolution; his *The Origin of Species* was published in 1859. The "survival of the fittest" means that nature intends for individuals to compete with one another; the strongest, the smartest, or the most adaptable will survive, and the rest will eventually perish.

CREATING COSMOGONY

The early city-states tied their vision and understanding of the cosmos to a system or pattern of rulership on earth; in other words, the kingdom was synchronized with the cosmos, the basis of a cosmogony. The core idea that the microcosm of the palace and temple should reflect or mirror the macrocosm of the celestial realm became the fundamental philosophy of urban civilizations throughout the world.

The first key ingredients to this relationship between cosmos and kingdom were the development of astronomy and the belief, based on astronomers' observations, that the heavens were orderly. From a careful and systematic study of the heavens, the Sumerians had ascertained that the five visible planets followed regular patterns among the fixed stars. The next ingredient was the idea that the sociopolitical realm should somehow imitate the cosmic paradigm. So, like the sun at the center of the heavens, the king and later the

Somehow, [the Sumerian] study of the heavens and their search for a meaningful ordering of human affairs in the new city-states interpenetrated each other, and from this union came a fundamental conviction that we shall call the *cosmological conviction*.

– CORNELIUS LOEW, historian, 1967

Babylonian Tablet Calculating Jupiter's Movements, 500 B.C.E.
A revolution in human consciousness occurred when ancient cultures began studying the heavens and creating a systematic cosmogony. (British Museum, London, UK / The Bridgeman Art Library)

pharaoh was the centerpiece of the realm, usually depicted as the representative of the gods, the founder of cities, and the symbol of the city's health. In ancient Egypt and later in Rome, the king or pharaoh actually became a god.

The palace temple, or ZIGGURAT, was at the ceremonial center of the walled city and was itself a symbol of the cosmos. The first architects were a combination of priest, astronomer, and astrologer, men who designed official buildings to reflect the religious dimensions of the universe. A religious calendar marking appropriate and regular ceremonies coordinated the life of the city with the seasons of the agricultural year, themselves related to the movement of the sun and moon among the heavenly constellations. The great family of deities and their roles were the model for the ritual dramas performed at the temple and court and the source of legal prescriptions for the commoners.

Full-time, professional temple priests oversaw this elaborate bilevel world. The priest might appoint or anoint the king; or he may have simply been his instrument in religious matters. The art of writing, developed at this time (c. 3200 B.C.E.), was usually under the control of the priesthood. Writing was necessary for documenting religious rituals and keeping records of taxes and the movement of food and goods from the royal depositories to outlying areas of the realm. Indeed, in addition to the technology necessary for construction and food production, the linchpin of social order in the earliest cities was writing.

The ancient Egyptians developed the concept of *maat,* meaning "right order" or "justice," which they saw as the ruling dynamic of the heavens, and made it the social responsibility of both king and commoner, framing a moral society through laws, rules, and customs. For the ancient Egyptians, the concept of *maat* was represented by the sun-god Re or Aten, the "lord of *maat*"; each sunrise was an assertion of order over chaos and the serpent Apophis or Apep. The earthly, but not less divine, representative of this daily victory was the king or pharaoh.

The first five books of the Hebrew Scriptures—also called the Torah—portray Yahweh, the god of Israel, as the supreme lawgiver. The law, or torah, forms the center of Judaism and radiates into all aspects of Jewish life. The ancient Hebrews used the idea of

By what inner change did immemorial custom become written law, did the old village rituals become drama, and magical practices turn into an organized and unified religious cult, built upon cosmic myths that open up vast perspectives of time, space, power?

– LEWIS MUMFORD, critic and historian, 1956

a contract or covenant between their deity Yahweh and themselves to validate an elaborate regimen of rules and a future filled with bounty as a reward for righteousness and being the "chosen people."

The first ritual laws described in the Indian "The Song of Purusha," indicate that we live in an orderly and just universe, which is sustained by what the Hindus call *dharma.* As the basis of human morality and cosmic lawfulness, dharma is reflected in the caste system and is the foundation of karmic law, whereby good acts—mental or physical—bear good fruit and evil acts produce evil fruit. Unlike manmade laws, which are administered by some kind of legal system, the universal law of karma plays itself out irrespective of human agency. Karmic cause and effect extend to previous lifetimes and have consequences for one's next reincarnation.

Hesiod's retelling of a creation myth in ***Theogony*** depicts the evolution from female to male dominance in the cosmos through several generations of gods, from Uranus to Zeus. A pattern of father-son conflict is repeated in each generation of the gods, becoming a divine model for the earthly patriarchal family, and later a theme in Greek dramas such as *Oedipus the King.* Similar to other ancient cultures, the gods in both Homer and Hesiod are subordinate to an older moral power, the unbending control of Destiny or Fate (Moira).

p. 162

The selections presented here from Ovid's ***Metamorphoses*** focus on creation, the formation of the world out of the raw stuff of chaos, and the separation of the created world into the four basic elements of earth, air, fire and water. **"The Four Ages"** selection is drawn from an earlier Greek version in Hesiod's *Works and Days,* which depicts the devolution of civilizations from a golden to an iron age.

p. 168

p. 170

■ **PRONUNCIATION**

Akhenaten: ah-kuh-NAH-tun
Amenhotep: ah-men-HOH-tep
Aten: AH-tun
Eurydice: yoo-RID-uh-see
Gaia: GIGH-yuh
Hecate: HEH-kuh-tee
Orpheus: ORE-fee-us
Ouranos: YOO-ruh-nus
Purusha: poo-ROO-shuh
Styx: STIKS

THE EPIC OF CREATION

BABYLONIA, C. 1800 B.C.E.

About 2000 B.C.E. the Sumerians of Mesopotamia were invaded by a succession of conquerors from the northern banks of the Euphrates River. Of these groups, the Babylonians gained control over the whole river valley, laying the foundation for their rule in a mythology dominated by patriarchal, sky-deities, who were represented on earth by monarchs and warriors. At the conclusion of the Babylonian *The Epic of Creation,* or *Enuma Elis* (c. 1800 B.C.E.), the supreme, cosmic deity Marduk, who has conquered the forces of chaos in the form of the serpentine water-goddess Tiamat, assigns lesser deities to the administration of the heavenly bodies. For the Babylonians, the heavenly hierarchy involving the sun, the moon, and various constellations was the primary model on earth for the organization of political power, from the king down to the peasants as well as of the social classes themselves. An elaborate system of divinely inspired laws bridged the orderly cosmos and a harmonious, smoothly functioning populace.

The Epic of Creation is the most famous creation story to come out of the Babylonian empire. The poem is not an epic in the traditional sense — the story of a mortal hero of national importance who undergoes trials and challenges, such as *The Epic of Gilgamesh. The Epic of Creation* might better be called the Babylonian Genesis, since it is a religious text that tells of the origins of the universe. In addition to providing a picture of the workings of the world with its appropriate deities, *The Epic of Creation* provides the background for a calendar of religious rituals. It was recited annually, for example, at the Babylonian New Year's celebration, in which the reciprocal relationship between human fertility and the agricultural cycle was dramatized. The primordial battles of the gods and goddesses against the forces of chaos became the hierarchical model for Babylonian kings, whose battles were thought to imitate divine warfare.

The seven tablets on which this epic is inscribed date from the first millennium B.C.E., but it seems likely that the poem was composed much earlier, probably during the Old Babylonian period (c. 1800–1500 B.C.E.), when Marduk, the epic's hero, was worshiped as the titular deity of Babylon. The epic is organized in three sections: the creation of the primordial deities, the combat between Marduk and Tiamat,[1] and the creation of the world and human beings.

The epic begins with Apsu and Tiamat, who symbolize the origins of life itself, the mingling of masculine fresh water and feminine salt water in the southern marshes of Mesopotamia. All life was thought to have emerged from the luxuriant growth produced from the meeting of the

[*The Epic of Creation*] is religiously of great profundity, leading in its picture of Marduk toward the aspects of awe and majesty. Moreover, it is intellectually admirable in providing a unifying concept of existence: political order pervades both nature and society. Finally it is humanly satisfying: ultimate power is not estranged from mankind, but resides in gods in human form who act understandably.

– THORKILD JACOBSEN, historian, 1971

---

[1] **Tiamat:** The Hebrew word for "deep" in Genesis 1:2 is *tehom,* a word linguistically connected to the Sumerian sea monster Tiamat. The New English Bible translates *tehom* as "abyss," a word suggestive of the ancient chaos often personified as a dragon, and notes that the "mighty wind that swept over the surface of the waters" is related to the mythical storm-gods said to have created the cosmos. In *The Epic of Creation,* Tiamat becomes Chaos.

Euphrates and Tigris Rivers with the sea in the delta region. This couple spawns the first generation of gods, individual deities who assume the roles of nature-gods—the gods of water, wind, sky, earth, and other elements—representing the basic powers of the universe.

The next generation of gods, however, are unruly, and the parents cannot tolerate the noisy children; Father Apsu complains to Mother Tiamat, threatening to exterminate them. In a preemptive strike, the children, sensing repression, murder Apsu. At first rather passive, Tiamat eventually angers and threatens revenge against her children. For assistance, she creates a formidable army of monsters, beings with a mixture of animal and human features. The children consult intensely in the face of Tiamat's threat. The process by which they choose a leader reflects the political structures of the time: After Anshar directs his son to meet the challenge and his son is intimidated by Tiamat's might, an assembly is called and new nominations for a leader are presented. The magnificent storm-god Marduk, after setting down terms for supreme rule, is elected the champion of the new order of gods. Marduk and Tiamat then meet in a primordial battle, a cosmic conflagration.

The final section of the poem begins with Tiamat's defeat and the imprisoning of her forces—imprisoned rather than destroyed since chaos has the potential to return. Marduk takes the Tablets of Destiny from Qingu, who is killed. The world is created out of Tiamat's carcass; she is split in two and transformed into heaven and earth—which suggests a feminine basis for nature. Marduk then puts order to the cosmos by assigning gods to various tasks; Marduk sanctifies the sun, moon, stars, and their pathways in the heavens—the discoveries of Mesopotamia's own astronomers. Humankind is created from Qingu's blood—perhaps a reference to the essential rebelliousness of man's nature. Humans, as in much world mythology, are also given work: Ea "imposed the toil of the gods (on man) and released the gods from it." Humans are created to serve the gods; that is their purpose. Marduk then assigns various tasks to the gods. Finally, the destinies are fixed for the next year, and all the gods gather at a banquet to celebrate creation.

Though Tiamat is defeated, she continues to exist as the embodiment of chaos, as the potential threat of the sea and the power of tidal waves, a continuing threat to the lowland cities of Mesopotamia. One version of the end of time says that Marduk will defeat Tiamat again when she arises from chaos. Another view claims that the Chaos Mother swallows the world and returns it to formlessness in order to begin anew.

The exact date of composition of this poem has not been determined. The most complete version of the epic was found on tablets from King Assurbanipal's library (seventh century b.c.e.) at Nineveh, the ancient capital of Assyria. The hero of this epic is Marduk, the principal deity of Babylon, the old Babylonian metropolis. And the great temple Esagila that is erected in Marduk's honor at the end of the epic has been located in Babylon. It seems probable, therefore, that this creation story was handed down over a period of years during which the names of the gods changed according to current rulers, capital cities, and patron deities. In an earlier Sumerian version of the poem, the storm-god was

> For the Mesopotamian, the entire world which surrounded him was filled with life. Every contact between man and nature was an encounter between two living entities facing each other and pitting their will power against each other.
>
> – Silvestro Fiore, medievalist, 1965

called Ninurta; another version centered around the storm-god Enlil of Nippur. Yet another, discovered at Ashur, the capital of Assyria, features the hero Ashur. *The Epic of Creation* was known in Akkadian as *Enuma Elish,* from the poem's opening words, meaning "when skies above." The story was recited each year by a high priest on the fourth day of the Babylonian New Year Festival, or Akitu, which reenacted the primordial events of creation in preparation for the coming year.

FROM

∾ The Epic of Creation

Translated by Stephanie Dalley

TABLET I

When skies above[1] were not yet named
Nor earth below pronounced by name,
Apsu,[2] the first one, their begetter
And maker Tiamat,[3] who bore them all,
Had mixed their waters together,
But had not formed pastures, nor discovered reed-beds;
When yet no gods were manifest,
Nor names pronounced, nor destinies decreed,
Then gods were born within them.
10 Lahmu (and) Lahamu emerged,[4] their names pronounced.
As soon as they matured, were fully formed,

A note on the translation: This translation by Stephanie Dalley contains a number of acknowledged lacunae, or gaps. Repetitious sections, appropriate for ritual purposes but unnecessary to advance the story, have been cut. All notes are the editors' unless otherwise indicated. The translator provides the following explanation for gaps in the text: "[ ] Square brackets indicate short gaps in text due to damage of tablet clay. Text inside brackets is restored, often from parallel versions. ( ) Round brackets indicate words inserted to give a better rendering in English, or explanatory insertions. [( )] Square brackets enclosing round brackets indicate uncertainty as to whether or not there is a gap in the text. . . . Omission dots indicate an unknown word or phrase."

---

[1] **When skies above:** The first words in Akkadian are *Enuma elish,* sometimes used as the epic's name.

[2] **Apsu:** The sweet, fresh waters.

[3] **Tiamat:** At this point, salt water or the sea; she becomes the mother of the first generation of the gods and later a monstrous sea creature.

[4] **Lahmu (and) Lahamu emerged:** Perhaps the silt forming in the waters, the first land emerging as mud.

Anshar (and) Kishar[5] were born, surpassing them.
They passed the days at length, they added to the years.
Anu[6] their first-born son rivalled his forefathers:
Anshar made his son Anu like himself,
And Anu begot Nudimmud[7] in his likeness.
He, Nudimmud, was superior to his forefathers:
Profound of understanding, he was wise, was very strong at arms.
Mightier by far than Anshar his father's begetter,
20 He had no rival among the gods his peers.
The gods of that generation would meet together
And disturb Tiamat, and their clamour reverberated.
They stirred up Tiamat's belly,
They were annoying her by playing inside Anduruna.[8]
Apsu could not quell their noise
And Tiamat became mute before them;
However grievous their behaviour to her,
However bad their ways, she would indulge them.

[After setting up the primordial order of deities, the poem describes the conflict between the old and new generations of gods. Apsu proposes to eliminate the noisy children, but Ea overhears the plan and kills Apsu. Ea creates the storm-god Marduk, who is in charge of the four winds, to defend the new regime. Tiamat is incited to revenge the slaying of Apsu and is provided with earth-goddess weapons: giant snakes, dragons, scorpions, and demons. She appoints Qingu leader of the army. The gods must decide how to deal with Tiamat's threat; the old father god Anshar sends his son Anu to fight Tiamat, but Anu turns back, as does Nudimmud (Ea). Anshar then announces that Marduk has been chosen to face Tiamat; he demands that he be made sovereign of the universe. Marduk then arms himself.]

TABLET IV

. . . He fashioned a bow, designated it as his weapon,
30 Feathered the arrow, set it in the string.
He lifted up a mace and carried it in his right hand,
Slung the bow and quiver at his side,
Put lightning in front of him,
His body was filled with an ever-blazing flame.
He made a net to encircle Tiamat within it,
Marshalled the four winds so that no part of her could escape:
South Wind, North Wind, East Wind, West Wind,
The gift of his father Anu, he kept them close to the net at his side.

---

[5] **Anshar (and) Kishar:** Akin to "Grandfather Sky or Horizon" and Mother Earth.   [6] **Anu:** The sky.   [7] **Nudimmud:** Same as the Sumerian Ea, god of fresh water, wisdom, and incantations.   [8] **Anduruna:** The gods' dwelling.

He created the *imhullu*-wind (evil wind), the tempest, the whirlwind,
40   The Four Winds, the Seven Winds, the tornado, the unfaceable facing wind.
He released the winds which he had created, seven of them.
They advanced behind him to make turmoil inside Tiamat.
The lord raised the flood-weapon,[9] his great weapon,
And mounted the frightful, unfaceable storm-chariot.
He had yoked to it a team of four and had harnessed to its side
'Slayer', 'Pitiless', 'Racer', and 'Flyer';
Their lips were drawn back, their teeth carried poison.
They know not exhaustion, they can only devastate.
He stationed on his right Fiercesome Fight and Conflict,
50   On the left Battle to knock down every contender (?).
Clothed in a cloak of awesome armour,
His head was crowned with a terrible radiance.
The Lord set out and took the road,
And set his face towards Tiamat who raged out of control.
In his lips he gripped a spell,
In his hand he grasped a herb to counter poison.
Then they thronged about him, the gods thronged about him;
The gods his fathers thronged about him, the gods thronged about him.
The Lord drew near and looked into the middle of Tiamat:
60   He was trying to find out the strategy of Qingu her lover.
As he looked, his mind[10] became confused,
His will crumbled and his actions were muddled.
As for the gods his helpers, who march(ed) at his side,
When they saw the warrior, the leader, their looks were strained.
Tiamat cast her spell. She did not even turn her neck.
In her lips she was holding falsehood, lies, (wheedling),
　　'[How powerful is] your attacking force, O lord of the gods!
　　The whole assembly of them has gathered to your place!'

　　　(But he ignored her blandishments)

The Lord lifted up the flood-weapon, his great weapon
70   And sent a message to Tiamat who feigned goodwill, saying:
　　'Why are you so friendly on the surface
　　When your depths conspire to muster a battle force?
　　Just because the sons were noisy (and) disrespectful to their fathers,
　　Should you, who gave them birth, reject compassion?

---

[9] **flood-weapon:** Marduk was originally a weather god, as were many gods in the ancient Near East. The Greek Zeus, for example, is often pictured with a thunderbolt; Yahweh led the Israelites with cloud and fire — possibly storm clouds and lightning or volcanic eruption. Marduk's *imhullu*-wind is possibly a tornado.

[10] **As he . . . mind:** Probably refers to Qingu rather than Marduk.

You named Qingu as your lover,
You appointed him to rites of Anu-power, wrongfully his.
You sought out evil for Anshar, king of the gods,
So you have compounded your wickedness against the gods my fathers!
Let your host prepare! Let them gird themselves with your weapons!
80   Stand forth, and you and I shall do single combat!'
When Tiamat heard this,
She went wild, she lost her temper.
Tiamat screamed aloud in a passion,
Her lower parts shook together from the depths.
She recited the incantation and kept casting her spell.
Meanwhile the gods of battle were sharpening their weapons.
Face to face they came, Tiamat and Marduk, sage of the gods.
They engaged in combat, they closed for battle.
The Lord spread his net and made it encircle her,
90   To her face he dispatched the *imhullu*-wind, which had been behind:
Tiamat opened her mouth to swallow it,
And he forced in the *imhullu*-wind so that she could not close her lips.
Fierce winds distended her belly;
Her insides were constipated and she stretched her mouth wide.
He shot an arrow which pierced her belly,
Split her down the middle and slit her heart,
Vanquished her and extinguished her life.
He threw down her corpse and stood on top of her.
When he had slain Tiamat, the leader,
100   He broke up her regiments; her assembly was scattered.
Then the gods her helpers, who had marched at her side,
Began to tremble, panicked, and turned tail.
Although he allowed them to come out and spared their lives,
They were surrounded, they could not flee.
Then he tied them up and smashed their weapons.
They were thrown into the net and sat there ensnared.
They cowered back, filled with woe.
They had to bear his punishment, confined to prison.
And as for the dozens of creatures, covered in fearsome rays,
110   The gang of demons who all marched on her right,
He fixed them with nose-ropes and tied their arms.
He trampled their battle-filth (?) beneath him.
As for Qingu, who had once been the greatest among them,
He defeated him and counted him among the dead gods,[11]

---

[11] **the dead gods:** The meaning here is unclear; usually gods cannot be killed, only imprisoned or contained. Although Tiamat is split in half to create earth and sky, she is a "living" universe.

Wrested from him the Tablet of Destinies, wrongfully his,
Sealed it with (his own) seal and pressed it to his breast.
When he had defeated and killed his enemies
And had proclaimed the submissive (?) foe his slave,
And had set up the triumphal cry of Anshar over all the enemy,
120 And had achieved the desire of Nudimmud, Marduk the warrior
Strengthened his hold over the captive gods,
And to Tiamat, whom he had ensnared, he turned back.
The Lord trampled the lower part of Tiamat,
With his unsparing mace smashed her skull,
Severed the arteries of her blood,
And made the North Wind carry it off as good news.
His fathers saw it and were jubilant: they rejoiced,
Arranged to greet him with presents, greetings, gifts.
The Lord rested, and inspected her corpse.
130 He divided the monstrous shape and created marvels (from it).
He sliced her in half like a fish for drying:
Half of her he put up to roof the sky,[12]
Drew a bolt across and made a guard hold it.
Her waters he arranged so that they could not escape.
He crossed the heavens and sought out a shrine;
He levelled Apsu, dwelling of Nudimmud.
The Lord measured the dimensions of Apsu
And the large temple (Eshgalla), which he built in its image, was Esharra:
In the great shrine Esharra, which he had created as the sky,
140 He founded cult centres for Anu, Ellil,[13] and Ea. [. . .]

TABLET V

He fashioned stands for the great gods.
As for the stars, he set up constellations corresponding to them.
He designated the year and marked out its divisions,
Apportioned three stars each to the twelve months.
When he had made plans of the days of the year,
He founded the stand of Neberu to mark out their courses,
So that none of them could go wrong or stray.
He fixed the stand of Ellil and Ea together with it,
Opened up gates in both ribs,
150 Made strong bolts to left and right.
With her liver he located the Zenith;

---

[12] **to roof the sky:** Ancient peoples thought that the sky was a dome, called a firmament in Genesis.

[13] **Anu, Ellil:** Perhaps gods of wind or air.

He made the crescent moon appear, entrusted night (to it)
And designated it the jewel of night to mark out the days.
    'Go forth every month without fail in a corona,
    At the beginning of the month, to glow over the land.
    You shine with horns to mark out six days;
    On the seventh day the crown is half.
    The fifteenth day[14] shall always be the mid-point, the half of each month.
    When Shamash[15] looks at you from the horizon,

160   Gradually shed your visibility and begin to wane.
    Always bring the day of disappearance close to the path of Shamash,
    And on the thirtieth day, the [year] is always equalized, for Shamash is
        (responsible for) the year.
    A sign [shall appear (?)]: sweep along its path.
    Then always approach the [   ] and judge the case.
    [   ] the Bowstar to kill and rob.
    [. . .]

      (15 lines broken)

[After the gods proclaim their allegiance to Marduk, he makes Babylon the center of his cult and creates the first humans from the blood of the rebel Qingu. The primary duty of humans is to serve the gods.]

Tablet VI

When Marduk heard the speech of the gods,
He made up his mind to perform miracles.
He spoke his utterance to Ea,
And communicated to him the plan that he was considering.

170   'Let me put blood together, and make bones too.
    Let me set up primeval man: Man shall be his name.
    Let me create a primeval man.
    The work of the gods shall be imposed (on him), and so they shall be at leisure.'

[The rest of the poem is devoted to assigning cosmic tasks to various deities and arranging the ritual calendar for the coming year.]

---

[14] **The fifteenth day:** The word for the fifteenth day of the month, *šabattu*, is cognate with the Sabbath. (Translator's note.)   [15] **Shamash:** Sun-god.

Songs of hymns written in honor of deities are a major type of literature in almost every ancient culture. Songs were written to celebrate and praise a particular god or goddess, but they were also written to request guidance and protection. Hymns ask for inspiration and for forgiveness. Egyptian hymns are directed toward their major gods, but in particular they portray the people's concerns with the sun, the Nile, and cycles of fertility. The "Hymn to Aten" was written in honor of a new sun-god and is attributed to the Pharaoh **Akhenaten,** who attempted to create a religious revolution soon after he inherited the throne from his father in 1353 B.C.E. by forcing his followers to worship the sun-god **Aten,** rather than the longstanding deity Amun-Re (Amon-Re).

When Akhenaten ascended the throne during the Eighteenth Dynasty (c. 1570–1290 B.C.E.) in Egypt, he was called **Amenhotep** IV, after his father Amenhotep III. Although most of the kings and conquerors of ancient Egypt are shrouded in mystery, Akhenaten emerges as a distinct personage, one of the earliest in the ancient Near East and Mediterranean region, though his exact beliefs and motivations remain unknown. What is known is that he created a religious revolution. In the fifth year of his reign, he changed his name to Akhenaten ("In the service of Aten"), abolished the polytheistic temples, rituals, and festivals involved with the worship of Amun-Re, the supreme deity in the Egyptian pantheon, and maintained that the sun-god Aten was the sole god—considered by scholars to be the first example of monotheism. He then moved his wife, the stunningly beautiful Nefertiti, his children, and his court to a brand new city in Middle Egypt, which was named Akhetaten ("The Glory of Aten"). Akhenaten is also known to have fostered a new direction in Egyptian art with an emphasis on themes from nature; artistic works from this period show realistic depictions of Akhenaten's rather deformed body and his delight in his wife and children.

Depriving his followers of their traditional religious activity probably proved to be Akhenaten's undoing. It is likely that the religious establishment of his day created ferment, since immediately after the succession of Tutankhamen (King Tut), the religion of Amen was restored. Just as Akhenaten attempted to eliminate Amen's presence by removing references to him in the temples, so efforts were made to obliterate traces of Akhenaten's reign. The city of Aten was destroyed and the name Akhenaten was incised from monuments.

The "Hymn to Aten" was found inscribed in a tomb of one of Akhenaten's successors, Ay (r. 1325–1321 B.C.E.), in the area called El-Amarna by archeologists, the site of Akhenaten's old capital. As an artist and poet himself, it is probably that Akhenaten was the hymn's author, or at least its sponsor, since he is mentioned as the earthly son of Aten. Several hymns to Aten were found in the tombs of nobility at Amarna, but the most beautiful tribute to the sun-god is included in this section,

---

ah-kuh-NAH-tun

AH-tun

ah-men-HOP-tep

Religion was the dominant factor in virtually every aspect of the life of ancient Egyptians. Food production and the economy prospered because of the gods' concern; in turn, men set aside a certain part of their produce, profits, or labor for the gods. The kings were worshiped as supreme because they were considered the gods' representatives on earth; meanwhile the king and his court were inextricably involved with the various priesthoods, their temples, and the many rituals.

– T. G. H. JAMES,
critic, 1971

Akhenaten Offering
Lotus Flowers to Aten,
1353–1336 B.C.E.
King Akhenaten
imposed monotheism,
worship of the sun-
god Aten, on the
Egyptians. (© Archivo
Iconografico, S.A. /
CORBIS)

where Aten is pictured as a benevolent, universal creator. Because of the similarities between the "Hymn to Aten" and Psalm 104 in the Hebrew Scriptures, scholars have speculated that Akhenaten's monotheism influenced the monotheistic faith of the Hebrews.[1] According to legend, the Hebrews resided in Egypt for several centuries prior to their exodus in the thirteenth century B.C.E. In any case, the "Hymn to Aten" stands on its own as a triumphant poem celebrating Aten as the "sole God, like whom there is no other."

---

[1] **scholars have speculated . . . Hebrews:** Sigmund Freud theorized about these matters in his book *Moses and Monotheism* (1939).

FROM

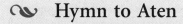 # Hymn to Aten

Translated by William Kelly Simpson

You rise in perfection on the horizon of the sky,
living Aten, who started life.
Whenever you are risen upon the eastern horizon
you fill every land with your perfection.

You are appealing, great, sparkling, high over every land;
your rays hold together the lands as far as everything you have made.
Since you are Re, you reach as far as they do,
and you curb them for your beloved son.
Although you are far away, your rays are upon the land;
10   you are in their faces, yet your departure is not observed.

Whenever you set on the western horizon,
the land is in darkness in the manner of death.
They sleep in a bedroom with heads under the covers,
and one eye does not see another.
If all their possessions which are under their heads were stolen,
they would not know it.
Every lion who comes out of his cave and all the serpents bite,
for darkness is a blanket.
The land is silent now, because he who made them
20   is at rest on his horizon.

But when day breaks you are risen upon the horizon,
and you shine as the Aten in the daytime.
When you dispel darkness and you give forth your rays
the two lands are in festival,
alert and standing on their feet,
now that you have raised them up.
Their bodies are clean, / and their clothes have been put on;
their arms are <lifted> in praise at your rising.

The entire land performs its work:
30   all the cattle are content with their fodder,
trees and plants grow,
birds fly up to their nests,
their wings <extended> in praise for your Ka.[1]

A note on the translation: The translator has used the following conventions to indicate problems with the text: "Brackets are employed for text which has been restored when there is a gap in the manuscript, and half brackets when the word or phrase is uncertain or imperfectly understood; three dots are used when the gap cannot be filled with any degree of certainty and represent an omission of indeterminate length. . . . Parentheses are used for phrases not in the original added as an aid to the reader; angle brackets are used for words which the copyist erroneously omitted. . . ." Unless otherwise indicated, the footnotes are the editors'.

---

[1] **Ka:** Life force, personality; sometimes translated as soul.

All the kine prance on their feet;
everything which flies up and alights,
they live when you have risen for them.
The barges sail upstream and downstream too,
for every way is open at your rising.
The fishes in the river leap before your face
40　when your rays are in the sea.

You who have placed seed in woman
and have made sperm into man,
who feeds the son in the womb of his mother,
who quiets him with something to stop his crying;
you are the nurse in the womb,
giving breath to nourish all that has been begotten.
When he comes down from the womb to breathe
on the day he is born,
you open up his mouth ⌜completely⌝, and supply his needs.
50　When the fledgling in the egg speaks in the shell,
you give him air inside it to sustain him.
When you grant him his allotted time to break out from the egg,
he comes out from the egg to cry out at his fulfillment,
and he goes upon his legs when he has come forth from it.

How plentiful it is, what you have made,
although they are hidden from view,
sole god, without another beside you;
you created the earth as you wished,
when you were by yourself, <before>
60　mankind, all cattle and kine,
all beings on land, who fare upon their feet,
and all beings in the air, who fly with their wings.

The lands of Khor and Kush[2]
and the land of Egypt:
you have set every man in his place,
you have allotted their needs,
every one of them according to his diet,
and his lifetime is counted out.
Tongues are separate in speech,
70　and their characters / as well;
their skins are different,

---

[2] **Khor and Kush:** Khor is Syro-Palestine in the northeast, and Kush is the Nubian region in the Sudan to the south. (Translator's note.)

for you have differentiated the foreigners.
In the underworld you have made a Nile
that you may bring it forth as you wish
to feed the populace,
since you made them for yourself, their utter master,
growing weary on their account, lord of every land.
For them the Aten of the daytime arises,
great in awesomeness.

80   All distant lands,
you have made them live,
for you have set a Nile in the sky[3]
that it may descend for them
and make waves upon the mountains like the sea
to irrigate the fields in their towns.
How efficient are your designs,
Lord of eternity:
a Nile in the sky for the foreigners
and all creatures that go upon their feet,
90   a Nile coming back from the underworld for Egypt.

Your rays give suck to every field:
when you rise they live,
and they grow for you.
You have made the seasons
to bring into being all you have made:
the Winter to cool them,
the Heat that you may be felt.
You have made a far-off heaven
in which to rise
100   in order to observe everything you have made.
Yet you are alone,
rising in your manifestations as the Living Aten:
appearing, glistening, being afar, coming close;
you make millions of transformations of yourself.
Towns, harbors, fields, roadways, waterways:
every eye beholds you upon them,
for you are the Aten of the daytime on the face of the earth.
When you go forth
every eye [is upon you].
110   You have created their sight
but not to see (only) the body . . .
which you have made. [. . .]

_____

[3] a Nile . . . sky: Egypt is watered by the Nile River, not by rain; "Nile in the sky" means rain.

VEDIC LITERATURE
INDIA, C. 1000–FIRST CENTURY B.C.E.

Only Mesopotamian and Egyptian literatures are dated earlier than the works that make up the Vedas, which are the foundation of Hinduism. The word VEDA means "knowledge," knowledge about how the world works, about superhuman powers and how to influence them. In the Hindu tradition there are four Vedas—Rig Veda, Yayur Veda, Sama Veda, and Atharva Veda—that feature a wide variety of literatures. The Rig Veda, which means the "knowledge" (*veda*) laid down in "verses" (*rig*), is the earliest known Indo-European document and the oldest Veda. It contains more than a thousand hymns arranged in ten sections or "song cycles": creation stories, sacrificial rites, and formulas for priests. The Yayur Veda includes priest chants, litanies, and the ritual sacrifices necessary to maintain the favor of the gods, who were dependent on sacrifices for their well-being. The Sama Veda is known for its songs of praise, and the Atharva Veda focuses on spells and magic. The Vedas and some of the Upanishads, which are commentaries or philosophical reflections on the Vedas, are thought to be divinely revealed works. Such texts are known as *SHRUTI* (*SRUTI*), revelation, in contrast to *SMIRTI* (*SMṚTI*), secondary revelation or tradition. Although they are difficult to date, it is believed that the Vedas were revealed in a series of visions to *RISHI* (*RṢI*) (poet-seers or sages), who began to recite them c. 1200 B.C.E., although they may have originated earlier. These revelations were passed down orally to succeeding generations by Brahmins, members of the priestly class, collected into a whole c. 1000 B.C.E., and written down c. 600 B.C.E.

Most of the deities in the Vedas, as with most deities in other ancient mythologies, were originally linked to natural forces. The hymns in the Vedas pay tribute to the beauty and power of the natural world—to fire and water, winds and storms, the rising and the setting sun. The Vedas, written in highly structured verse forms in Sanskrit, are memorized word for word by priests and storytellers. They are meant to be chanted and are thought to have a powerful psychological effect. Similar to the Hebrew account of creation in the first chapter of Genesis, in which the breath of God passes over the waters and is instrumental in the subsequent creation, the breath of the Supreme Being of Hinduism is synonymous with the creation and sustenance of the world, the transmission of the Vedas, the recitation of the Vedas, and yogic breathing.[1]

During the Brahmanic Age (c. 1000–600 B.C.E.), as the Indian culture became more settled and stable, the Brahmins, the priestly caste, began to assume the power of the superior caste once held by warriors. The Brahmins controlled the recitation of the Vedas and performed the sacrifices thought to sustain the life of the gods and the workings of the cosmos.

www For a quiz on "The Song of Purusha," see bedfordstmartins .com/worldlit compact.

In the songs of the *Vedas* we find the wonder of man before nature: fire and water, the winds and the storms, the sun and the rising of the sun are sung with adoration.

–JUAN MASCARÓ, translator and critic, 1965

---

[1] the breath of . . . yogic breathing: The English language makes these connections in the word *inspiration*, whose roots denote creativity, divinity, and breathing.

Vishnu Trivikrama, tenth century
The myth of Vishnu Trivikrama appears in the Rig Veda, one of the earliest Hindu texts. It tells the story of how Vishnu, in the guise of the dwarf Vamana, defeats the demon-king Bali by tricking Bali into granting him all he could encompass in three steps (trivikrama). *In this sculpted panel, Vishnu's foot is raised high, where it is worshiped by a small figure of Brahma. (Courtesy of The British Museum)*

The Indian archetypal model for the cosmic significance of sacrifice is the dismemberment of **Purusha** described in the hymn below.

The Sanskrit title of this poem is *Purusha-Sukta,* which literally means the "song of Purusha." In the following translation by Wendy Doniger O'Flaherty, Purusha is translated as "Man," meaning the primal man in a primordial setting, as Cosmic Man, whose body becomes the parts of the world. Others have suggested that the Universal Spirit took the form of a giant or Primal Person. In this context, the dismemberment of Purusha becomes an allegory of the soul's dispersion into the material world. The reference to the three Vedas in stanza nine and to the four social classes or *varnas* in stanza twelve indicate that this hymn comes rather late in the composition of the Rig Veda and is thought by some to form its conclusion.

poo-ROO-shuh

He [the village story-teller in India] has unquestioned faith in the validity of the *Vedas,* which he commenced learning when he was seven years old. It took him twelve years to master the intonation of the *Vedas.* He had also to acquire precise knowledge of Sanskrit's grammar, syllabification, meaning of words. . . . He has no doubt whatever that the *Vedas* were created out of the breath of God, and contain within them all that a man needs for his salvation at every level.

– R. K. NARAYAN, novelist, 1964

∾ The Rig Veda [c. 1000 B.C.E.]

Translated by Wendy Doniger O'Flaherty

THE SONG OF PURUSHA

1 The Man has a thousand heads, a thousand eyes, a thousand feet. He pervaded the earth on all sides and extended beyond it as far as ten fingers.

2 It is the Man who is all this, whatever has been and whatever is to be. He is the ruler of immortality, when he grows beyond everything through food.[1]

3 Such is his greatness, and the Man is yet more than this. All creatures are a quarter of him; three quarters are what is immortal in heaven.

A note on the translation: All selections from the Rig Veda are taken from Wendy Doniger O'Flaherty's translation. Translators treat Sanskrit names in different ways, as you'll see in the selections included here; some anglicize them more than others. We reprint the texts as the translator intended, but our editorial notes use the more accessible, anglicized spellings.

---

[1] **He is the ruler . . . food:** An obscure statement possibly meaning that Purusha transcends the world of eating and being eaten.

4   With three quarters the Man rose upwards, and one quarter of him still remains here.[2] From this he spread out in all directions, into that which eats and that which does not eat.

5   From him Virāj[3] was born, and from Virāj came the Man. When he was born, he ranged beyond the earth behind and before.

6   When the gods spread[4] the sacrifice with the Man as the offering, spring was the clarified butter, summer the fuel, autumn the oblation.

7   They anointed the Man, the sacrifice born at the beginning, upon the sacred grass.[5] With him the gods, Sādhyas,[6] and sages sacrificed.

8   From that sacrifice in which everything was offered, the melted fat[7] was collected, and he[8] made it into those beasts who live in the air, in the forest, and in villages.

9   From that sacrifice in which everything was offered, the verses and chants were born, the metres were born from it, and from it the formulas were born.[9]

10   Horses were born from it, and those other animals that have two rows of teeth;[10] cows were born from it, and from it goats and sheep were born.

11   When they divided the Man, into how many parts did they apportion him? What do they call his mouth, his two arms and thighs and feet?

12   His mouth became the Brahmin; his arms were made into the Warrior, his thighs the People, and from his feet the Servants were born.[11]

13   The moon was born from his mind; from his eye the sun was born. Indra and Agni[12] came from his mouth, and from his vital breath the Wind was born.

14   From his navel the middle realm of space arose; from his head the sky evolved. From his two feet came the earth, and the quarters of the sky from his ear. Thus they[13] set the worlds in order.

---

[2] The first four stanzas emphasize the fact that the Man is the whole universe.

[3] Virāj: The female or material creative principle.

[4] spread: This is the word used to indicate the performance of a Vedic sacrifice, "spread" or "stretched out" (like the earth spread upon the cosmic waters). [. . .] (Translator's note.)

[5] sacred grass: Special grasses upon which the gods sit.

[6] Sādhyas: Meaning "those who are yet to be fulfilled": a class of demigods.

[7] melted fat: Literally a mixture of butter and sour milk used in the sacrifice; figuratively, the fat that drained from the sacrificial victim. (Translator's note.)

[8] he: Purusha or the creator-god; later in Hinduism, the creator Brahma replaces Purusha.

[9] the verses . . . born: Verses, chants, metres, and formulas are ways of referencing the Vedas.

[10] two rows of teeth: Incisors above and below, like cats and dogs.

[11] His mouth . . . born: The four social classes of Indian society: Brahmin (priests); *Kshatriya* (warriors and administrators); *Vaishya* (merchants, farmers, producers); and *Shudra* (laborers or servants). The "Untouchables" are outside caste.

[12] Indra and Agni: The god of light and fertility and the god of fire.

[13] they: The gods.

15   There were seven enclosing-sticks[14] for him, and thrice seven fuel-sticks, when the gods, spreading the sacrifice, bound the Man as the sacrificial beast.

16   With the sacrifice the gods sacrificed to the sacrifice.[15] These were the first ritual laws.[16] These very powers reached the dome of the sky where dwell the Sādhyas, the ancient gods.

---

[14] **seven enclosing-sticks:** The enclosing-sticks are green twigs that keep the fire from spreading; the fuel sticks are seasoned wood used for kindling. (Translator's note.)

[15] **With the . . . sacrifice:** Purusha was both the victim of the sacrifice and the divinity to whom the sacrifice was directed.

[16] **the first ritual laws:** Literally, the *dharmas,* a protean word that here designates the archetypal patterns of behavior established during this first sacrifice to serve as a model for all future sacrifices. (Translator's note.)

✍ HESIOD

GREECE, EIGHTH CENTURY B.C.E.

Western culture owes a great debt to Hesiod, a Greek poet who lived in roughly the same era as Homer but who was interested in different kinds of myths and stories. Homer focused primarily on deities that became part of the Olympic PANTHEON,[1] a divine community gathered around Zeus and often resembling the heroic warrior culture of a past age with its patriarchal, feudal trappings; he avoided the types of stories Hesiod collected and preserved—stories about old, powerful goddesses like **Styx** and **Hecate;**[2] rebellions against Zeus and the creation of woman; about the chthonic, nocturnal worlds of sacrifice and spells; and sex, fertility, and death.

STIKS;
HEH-kuh-tee

In the first of his two major works, *Theogony,* Hesiod created a rather unusual mythic world—what has been called a philosophical myth of creation—through an extensive genealogy of abstract qualities and deities. His second work, *Works and Days,* is a picture of peasant life in the eighth century B.C.E. that dispenses advice about the appropriate attitudes and rituals needed to appease the gods. In addition to being a kind of ancient farmer's almanac, *Works and Days* is the oldest source of myths about Prometheus, the first woman, Pandora, and the Golden Age.

www For links to information about Hesiod, see bedfordstmartins .com/worldlit compact.

In *Theogony,* which means "the generations of the gods," Hesiod attempted to give coherence to a number of different creation stories and

---

[1] **Olympic pantheon:** From Mt. Olympus, the highest mountain in Greece; home of the gods and goddesses.

[2] **Styx and Hecate:** Styx is an ancient goddess of oaths after whom the river in Hades is named. Hecate is an ancient moon-goddess and the oldest member of the female trinity, or the triple goddess: Persephone (maid), Demeter (mother), and Hecate (crone).

GIGH-yuh
YOO-ruh-nus

short sketches of deities. Although there were several creation myths holding sway in ancient Greece at the time, Hesiod's version served as the perfect complement to Homer's writings, since it traced the history of divine patriarchal rule from Earth, Gaia, to Sky, Ouranos (Uranus), to Ouranos's son Kronos (Cronus), the head of the Titans,[3] to the reign of Zeus, son of Kronos and undisputed ruler of the Olympian deities. Like Indra, the creator-god of the Rig-Veda, Zeus was originally a storm-god, whose major weapon was the lightning bolt.

Reflecting most ancient mythology, Hesiod believed that creation occurred within an existent material world that was in a state of disorder or chaos. **Gaia**, or Earth, as the physical world, gave birth to the first sky-god, **Ouranos**. Ouranos and Gaia mated and produced the Titans and many other deities. Hesiod further believed, based on the family dynamics of the first generations of the gods, that life is difficult and that women are dangerous to men; these views have their roots in Ouranos's hate for his children, which leads him to hide them in Gaia's body. Groaning in pain, Gaia devises revenge: Kronos, one of her sons, will castrate his father with a flint knife. A pattern of father-son conflict is repeated in succeeding generations, becoming a divine model for the patriarchal family and later a theme in Greek drama.

The rebellion of the younger gods against the fathers in each generation is reminiscent of the scenes in the Babylonian *The Epic of Creation* that depict the younger generation of gods plotting a rebellion against the female dragon Tiamat and her husband Apsu. Family conflict also plays a central role in the stories about the patriarchs and their families in the Hebrew Scriptures.

> . . . it was Hesiod, in his . . . *Theogony* or *Descent of the Gods,* who first ventured to arrange all mythology into a comprehensive philosophical system.
>
> – WERNER JAEGER, historian, 1939

---

[3] Titans: An early race of giants who represent the primitive forces of nature.

FROM

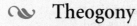

Theogony

Translated by Dorothea Wender

[THE CASTRATION OF URANUS]

Chaos was first of all, but next appeared
Broad-bosomed Earth,[1] sure standing-place for all
The gods who live on snowy Olympus' peak,
And misty Tartarus,[2] in a recess

---

[1] Earth: Called Gaea or Gaia (*Ge* in Greek); the Earth as a goddess.

[2] Tartarus: The lowest region of Hades where the most wicked were punished and the Titans confined.

Of broad-pathed earth, and Love,[3] most beautiful
Of all the deathless gods. He makes men weak,
He overpowers the clever mind, and tames
The spirit in the breasts of men and gods.
From Chaos came black Night and Erebos.[4]
10 And Night in turn gave birth to Day and Space[5]
Whom she conceived in love to Erebos.
And Earth bore starry Heaven,[6] first, to be
An equal to herself, to cover her
All over, and to be a resting-place,
Always secure, for all the blessed gods.
Then she brought forth long hills, the lovely homes
Of goddesses, the Nymphs who live among
The mountain clefts. Then, without pleasant love,
She bore the barren sea with its swollen waves,
20 Pontus. And then she lay with Heaven, and bore
Deep-whirling Oceanus and Koios; then
Kreius, Iapetos, Hyperion,
Theia, Rhea, Themis, Mnemosyne,
Lovely Tethys, and Phoebe, golden-crowned.
Last, after these, most terrible of sons,
The crooked-scheming Kronos[7] came to birth
Who was his vigorous father's enemy.
Again, she bore the Cyclopes, whose hearts
Were insolent, Brontes and Steropes
30 And proud-souled Arges,[8] those who found and gave
The thunder and the lightning-bolt to Zeus.
They were like other gods in all respects,
But that a single eye lay in the brow
Of each, and from this, they received the name,
Cyclopes, from the one round eye which lay
Set in the middle of each forehead.[9] Strength
And energy and craft were in their works.
Then Ouranos and Gaia bore three sons
Mighty and violent, unspeakable

---

[3] **Love:** The god Eros (Desire).

[4] **Erebos:** The mysterious darkness under the earth through which the dead pass en route to Hades.

[5] **Space:** Ether, the upper atmosphere.

[6] **Heaven:** Uranus (*Ouranos* in Greek); the Heaven or Sky as a god.

[7] **Kronos:** The offspring of Earth and Heaven are the original Titans, twelve in number, Oceanus through Phoebe; in general, they are deifications of various aspects of nature; a few gain individual importance later.

[8] **Cyclopes . . . Arges:** Here, the one-eyed giants are sons of Heaven and Earth. In *The Odyssey,* the Cyclops Polyphemus is the son of Poseidon.

[9] **one . . . forehead:** *Cyclopes* means "round-eyed."

40 Kottos and Gyes and Briareus,
Insolent children, each with a hundred arms
On his shoulders, darting about, untouchable,
And each had fifty heads, standing upon
His shoulders, over the crowded mass of arms,
And terrible strength was in their mighty forms.

And these most awful sons of Earth and Heaven
Were hated by their father from the first.
As soon as each was born, Ouranos hid
The child in a secret hiding-place in Earth
50 And would not let it come to see the light,
And he enjoyed this wickedness. But she,
Vast Earth, being strained and stretched inside her, groaned.
And then she thought of a clever, evil plan.
Quickly she made grey adamant,[10] and formed
A mighty sickle, and addressed her sons,
Urging them on, with sorrow in her heart,
'My sons, whose father is a reckless fool,
If you will do as I ask, we shall repay
Your father's wicked crime. For it was he
60 Who first began devising shameful acts.'

She spoke, but fear seized all of them, and none
Replied. Then crooked Kronos, growing bold,
Answered his well-loved mother with these words:
'Mother, I undertake to do the deed;
I do not care for my unspeakable
Father, for he first thought of shameful acts.'
He spoke, and giant Earth was glad at heart.
She set him in a hiding-place, and put
Into his hands the saw-toothed scimitar,
70 And told him all the plot she had devised.

Great Heaven came, and with him brought the night.
Longing for love, he lay around the Earth,
Spreading out fully. But the hidden boy
Stretched forth his left hand; in his right he took
The great long jagged sickle; eagerly
He harvested his father's genitals
And threw them off behind. They did not fall
From his hands in vain, for all the bloody drops
That leaped out were received by Earth; and when

---

[10] **grey adamant**: A mythical metal, like flint.

80 The year's time was accomplished, she gave birth
    To the Furies, and the Giants, strong and huge,
    Who fought in shining armour, with long spears,
    And the nymphs called Meliae[11] on the broad earth.

    The genitals, cut off with adamant
    And thrown from land into the stormy sea,
    Were carried for a long time on the waves.
    White foam surrounded the immortal flesh,
    And in it grew a girl. At first it touched
    On holy Cythera, from there it came
90 To Cyprus, circled by the waves. And there
    The goddess came forth, lovely, much revered,
    And grass grew up beneath her delicate feet.
    Her name is Aphrodite among men
    And gods, because she grew up in the foam,[12]
    And Cytherea, for she reached that land,
    And Cyprogenes from the stormy place
    Where she was born, and Philommedes[13] from
    The genitals, by which she was conceived.
    Eros is her companion; fair Desire[14]
100 Followed her from the first, both at her birth
    And when she joined the company of the gods.
    From the beginning, both among gods and men,
    She had this honour and received this power:
    Fond murmuring of girls, and smiles, and tricks,
    And sweet delight, and friendliness, and charm.

    But the great father Ouranos reproached
    His sons, and called them Titans,[15] for, he said
    They strained in insolence, and did a deed
    For which they would be punished afterwards.

---

[11] **Meliae:** Ash-tree nymphs.

[12] **foam:** The root of Aphrodite's name is linked to *aphros*, meaning "foam." Aphrodite is the goddess of love.

[13] **Philommedes:** Greek for "Genital loving."

[14] **fair Desire:** An abstraction elevated by Hesiod to a deity, similar to the other abstractions that follow.

[15] **Titans:** From *teino*, meaning "I strain"; probably a false etymology.

∾ OVID

ROME, 43 B.C.E.–17 C.E.

p. 793

Ovid was the last of a new wave of Roman poets who challenged the assumptions of previous writers whose works focused primarily on serious matters of the state and religion. Like **Catullus**, the greatest lyric poet of the earlier generation, Ovid turned to love and private feeling for his subject matter. Most important, however, Ovid was a great storyteller.

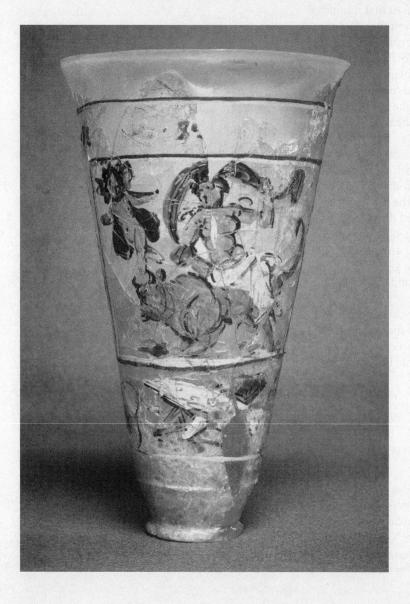

Europa and the Bull
Ovid's Metamorphoses *retells the classic stories of Greek mythology. Here, a Roman glass vase depicts a scene from the tale of Europa and the Bull in which Zeus, the King of the Gods, takes on the shape of a bull to woo the mortal Europa. (Musée Guimet, Paris, France / Peter Willi / Bridgeman Art Library)*

When he decided to retell the major Greek and Roman myths about transformation and love, he produced one of the most influential and readable works of all Latin literature, *Metamorphoses*, written sometime between 1 C.E. and 8 C.E. This encyclopedic collection of tales, loosely organized around the motif of changing form, has served readers from his time to the present day as a sourcebook of stories about figures such as Apollo and Daphne, Echo and Narcissus, **Orpheus** and **Eurydice**, Midas, and even the heroes of the Trojan War. Despite his somewhat cavalier attitude toward the "serious" poets of the earlier age, Ovid brilliantly managed to satisfy what Horace[1] claimed was the highest purpose of poetry: to please and to instruct.

Ovid's lovely account of the creation is notable for its attention to detail as the various elements of the created world are separated out from chaos. His account of "The Four Ages" of civilization is modeled after the much earlier Greek poet Hesiod as his extended poem *Works and Days* (eighth century B.C.E.). The ages are depicted as a succession of metals and a gradual devolution of behavior and living conditions: from the golden age, which resembles paradise, through the silver and bronze, to the greed and violence of the age of iron. Ovid recognizes that we continue to live in the Iron Age of warfare and family strife, in which "Piety lay vanquished, / And the maiden Justice, last of all immortals, / Fled from the bloody earth."

Hesiod's and Ovid's model of successive ages is roughly equivalent to the Hebrew fall of mankind in Eden, which resulted in expulsion from the garden. Traditionally, the golden age, as well as the Hebrew vision of Eden, was something in the distant past that was lost or abandoned. Writers looked back with a kind of nostalgia to an irreplaceable, paradisal condition. The Romans, however, took the past and projected into the future; they believed that they were entering the golden age with Caesar Augustus. Ovid's recreation of the golden age in Latin had a tremendous influence on the Middle Period. The myth of the golden age spread throughout the Mediterranean region, and served as an incentive for later explorers searching for paradise in the West.

ORE-fee-us;
yoo-RID-uh-see

My intention is to tell
of bodies changed /
To different forms
– OVID,
Metamorphoses

www For links
to more informa-
tion about Ovid,
see bedfordstmartins
.com/worldlit
compact.

---

[1] **Horace:** Quintus Horatius Flaccus (65–8 B.C.E.), Roman poet of the Augustan Age who wrote highly polished lyrics and odes; his *The Art of Poetry (Ars Poetica)* is an important document of literary criticism in verse.

Metamorphoses

Translated by Rolfe Humphries

FROM

BOOK 1

My intention is to tell of bodies changed
To different forms; the gods, who made the changes,
Will help me — or I hope so — with a poem
That runs from the world's beginning to our own days.[1]

The Creation

     Before the ocean was, or earth, or heaven,
Nature was all alike, a shapelessness,
Chaos, so-called, all rude and lumpy matter,
Nothing but bulk, inert, in whose confusion
Discordant atoms warred: there was no sun
10 To light the universe; there was no moon
With slender silver crescents filling slowly;
No earth hung balanced in surrounding air;
No sea reached far along the fringe of shore.
Land, to be sure, there was, and air, and ocean,
But land on which no man could stand, and water
No man could swim in, air no man could breathe,
Air without light, substance forever changing,
Forever at war: within a single body
Heat fought with cold, wet fought with dry, the hard
20 Fought with the soft, things having weight contended
With weightless things.
               Till God, or kindlier Nature,
Settled all argument, and separated
Heaven from earth, water from land, our air
From the high stratosphere, a liberation
So things evolved, and out of blind confusion
Found each its place, bound in eternal order.
The force of fire, that weightless element,
Leaped up and claimed the highest place in heaven;
Below it, air; and under them the earth
30 Sank with its grosser portions; and the water,
Lowest of all, held up, held in, the land.

---

[1] **to our own days:** In Book 15, Julius Caesar, assassinated in 44 B.C.E., is transformed into a star.

Whatever god it was, who out of chaos
Brought order to the universe, and gave it
Division, subdivision, he molded earth,
In the beginning, into a great globe,
Even on every side, and bade the waters
To spread and rise, under the rushing winds,
Surrounding earth; he added ponds and marshes,
He banked the river-channels, and the waters
40 Feed earth or run to sea, and that great flood
Washes on shores, not banks. He made the plains
Spread wide, the valleys settle, and the forest
Be dressed in leaves; he made the rocky mountains
Rise to full height, and as the vault of Heaven
Has two zones, left and right, and one between them
Hotter than these, the Lord of all Creation
Marked on the earth the same design and pattern.
The torrid zone too hot for men to live in,
The north and south too cold, but in the middle
50 Varying climate, temperature and season.
Above all things the air, lighter than earth,
Lighter than water, heavier than fire,
Towers and spreads; there mist and cloud assemble,
And fearful thunder and lightning and cold winds,
But these, by the Creator's order, held
No general dominion; even as it is,
These brothers brawl and quarrel; though each one
Has his own quarter, still, they come near tearing
The universe apart. Eurus[2] is monarch
60 Of the lands of dawn, the realms of Araby,
The Persian ridges under the rays of morning.
Zephyrus holds the west that glows at sunset,
Boreas, who makes men shiver, holds the north,
Warm Auster governs in the misty southland,
And over them all presides the weightless ether,
Pure without taint of earth.   These boundaries given,
Behold, the stars, long hidden under darkness,
Broke through and shone, all over the spangled heaven,
Their home forever, and the gods lived there,
70 And shining fish were given the waves for dwelling
And beasts the earth, and birds the moving air.

---

[2] **Eurus:** God of the East Wind, brother of Zephyrus (West Wind), Boreas (North Wind), and Auster (South Wind).

But something else was needed, a finer being,
More capable of mind, a sage, a ruler,
So Man was born, it may be, in God's image,
Or Earth, perhaps, so newly separated
From the old fire of Heaven, still retained
Some seed of the celestial force which fashioned
Gods out of living clay and running water.
All other animals look downward; Man,
80   Alone, erect, can raise his face toward Heaven.

The Four Ages

The Golden Age was first, a time that cherished
Of its own will, justice and right; no law.
No punishment, was called for; fearfulness
Was quite unknown, and the bronze tablets held
No legal threatening; no suppliant throng
Studied a judge's face; there were no judges,
There did not need to be. Trees had not yet
Been cut and hollowed, to visit other shores.
Men were content at home, and had no towns
90   With moats and walls around them; and no trumpets
Blared out alarums; things like swords and helmets
Had not been heard of. No one needed soldiers.
People were unaggressive, and unanxious;
The years went by in peace. And Earth, untroubled,
Unharried by hoe or plowshare, brought forth all
That men had need for, and those men were happy,
Gathering berries from the mountain sides,
Cherries, or blackcaps, and the edible acorns.
Spring was forever, with a west wind blowing
100   Softly across the flowers no man had planted,
And Earth, unplowed, brought forth rich grain; the field,
Unfallowed, whitened with wheat, and there were rivers
Of milk, and rivers of honey, and golden nectar
Dripped from the dark-green oak-trees.
                                        After Saturn[3]
Was driven to the shadowy land of death,
And the world was under Jove, the Age of Silver
Came in, lower than gold, better than bronze.
Jove made the springtime shorter, added winter,
Summer, and autumn, the seasons as we know them.

---

[3] **Saturn:** An ancient Roman fertility god, ruler of the Golden Age and father of Jove, who overthrew him.

110 That was the first time when the burnt air glowed
     White-hot, or icicles hung down in winter.
     And men built houses for themselves; the caverns,
     The woodland thickets, and the bark-bound shelters
     No longer served; and the seeds of grain were planted
     In the long furrows, and the oxen struggled
     Groaning and laboring under the heavy yoke.

     Then came the Age of Bronze, and dispositions
     Took on aggressive instincts, quick to arm,
     Yet not entirely evil. And last of all
120 The Iron Age succeeded, whose base vein
     Let loose all evil: modesty and truth
     And righteousness fled earth, and in their place
     Came trickery and slyness, plotting, swindling,
     Violence and the damned desire of having.
     Men spread their sails to winds unknown to sailors,
     The pines came down their mountain-sides, to revel
     And leap in the deep waters, and the ground,
     Free, once, to everyone, like air and sunshine,
     Was stepped off by surveyors. The rich earth,
130 Good giver of all the bounty of the harvest,
     Was asked for more; they dug into her vitals,
     Pried out the wealth a kinder lord had hidden
     In Stygian⁴ shadow, all that precious metal,
     The root of evil. They found the guilt of iron,
     And gold, more guilty still. And War came forth
     That uses both to fight with; bloody hands
     Brandished the clashing weapons. Men lived on plunder.
     Guest was not safe from host, nor brother from brother,
     A man would kill his wife, a wife her husband,
140 Stepmothers, dire and dreadful, stirred their brews
     With poisonous aconite, and sons would hustle
     Fathers to death, and Piety lay vanquished,
     And the maiden Justice, last of all immortals,
     Fled from the bloody earth.
                              Heaven was no safer.
     Giants attacked the very throne of Heaven,
     Piled Pelion on Ossa,⁵ mountain on mountain
     Up to the very stars. Jove struck them down
     With thunderbolts, and the bulk of those huge bodies

---

⁴ **Stygian:** In the underworld; associated with the Styx, the river that marks the threshold to Hades.

⁵ **Pelion . . . Ossa:** Mountains in Thessaly, in central Greece.

Lay on the earth, and bled, and Mother Earth,
150   Made pregnant by that blood, brought forth new bodies,
And gave them, to recall her older offspring,
The forms of men. And this new stock was also
Contemptuous of gods, and murder-hungry
And violent. You would know they were sons of blood.

TEXT IN CONTEXT

 # HOMER
GREECE, EIGHTH CENTURY B.C.E.

The two outstanding heroic epics of ancient Greece, *The Iliad* and *The Odyssey,* are attributed to Homer. These two great works, which set the standard for all subsequent epic poetry in the West, tell different parts of a single story about a Greek military expedition to the distant city of Troy,[1] the war with the Trojans, and the return of the heroes to their cities and kingdoms. The legend of the Trojan War is not a fixed history with an unchanging set of facts; stories about the engagement between the Trojans and the Greeks, which were passed down in oral form from the time of the war until the eighth century B.C.E., when Homer created his own versions of the events, vary according to the storyteller and his time and place. The heroic ideals universally associated with the battlefield at Troy constitute one of the most important legacies of the Greek Heroic Age (c. 1500–1100 B.C.E.), which was known for its sea voyages and military adventures. Later Greeks believed that the Trojan stories were a blend of history and legend, and that Homer was writing about a period some four to five hundred years older than himself. While very few heroes from either ancient Mesopotamia or Egypt are known, Homer, at the end of a long oral tradition, created a grand catalog of Greek heroes that bridged history and mythology and served as a source of traditional knowledge and morality for several hundred years.

www For links to more information about Homer, quizzes on *The Odyssey,* and information about the twenty-first-century relevance of Homer, see bedfordstmartins .com/worldlit compact.

---

[1]**Troy:** In ancient times Troy, or Ilium (Ilion), was a city on a hill in Asia Minor. The city, located today in the northwest corner of Turkey overlooking the Dardanelles (Hellespont), is now called Hissarlik.

The Iliad and
The Odyssey have
been called the Bible
of the Greeks. For
centuries these two
poems were the basis
of Greek education,
both of formal
school education
and of the cultural
life of the ordinary
citizen.

– H. D. F. KITTO,
classicist, 1951

Though a poet — not a priest or a prophet — Homer profoundly affected Greek religion, as Greek historian Herodotus (484–c. 424 B.C.E.) once commented: ". . . it was only — if I may so put it — the day before yesterday that the Greeks came to know the origin and form of the various gods, and whether or not all of them had always existed; for Homer and Hesiod are the poets who composed our theogonies[2] and described the gods for us, giving them all their appropriate titles, offices, and powers, and they lived, as I believe, not more than four hundred years ago." Hesiod's *Theogony* and Homer's *Iliad* and *Odyssey* collectively have been called the Bible of the ancient Greeks: the basis for religious ceremony as well as public education.

As the oldest surviving European poems, *The Iliad* and *The Odyssey* were the models for later epic works by such poets as the Roman Virgil (70–19 B.C.E.), the Italian Dante (1265–1321), the English Milton (1608–1674), and, in modern times, the West Indian poet Derek Walcott, winner of the Nobel Prize in Literature in 1992. Both *The Iliad* and *The Odyssey* are so filled with brilliant imagery that whole scenes come to life for the reader. This visualization of Greek deities made them accessible models for human behavior, unlike the mysterious and inscrutable Hebrew God, Yahweh,[3] a deity who was heard but not seen. Homer's images were later translated into the glories of Greek drama, sculpture, and vase paintings; scenes from and allusions to classical art and literature have been depicted again and again, from the European Renaissance up to the present day.

The Homeric Mystery.   Scholars have debated the Homeric questions — who Homer was, where he came from in Greece, and exactly when he wrote — for some two hundred years. And not all scholars are convinced, to further complicate matters, that the same poet wrote both *The Iliad* and *The Odyssey*. As many as seven cities in Ionia, the region of Asia Minor on the east coast of the Aegean, have claimed to be Homer's birthplace.

Because there are elements of the Ionian dialect in the poems thought to be his, it is probable that Homer, whom the Greeks called *theios Homeros*, meaning "divine Homer," was a descendant of the early

---

[2] theogonies: A theogony is an orderly description of the genealogies of the gods. Herodotus's dating puts both Hesiod and Homer in the eighth century B.C.E., roughly the same time period that modern scholars place them in. For an excerpt from Hesiod's *Theogony*, see page 162.

[3] Yahweh: The most common name given for God in the Hebrew Scriptures (Old Testament).

Greeks who migrated to Ionia after invaders from the north conquered the major city-states on mainland Greece, around 1100 B.C.E. Before the rise of Athens in the Classical Period, Ionia was the intellectual and cultural center of the Greek world. Ionian writer Hellanicus placed Homer in the twelfth century B.C.E., believing that Homer had to have been an eyewitness to the Trojan War to write such vivid descriptions of it. However, tradition suggests that Homer himself was blind. A blind bard, **Demodocus**, appears in *The Odyssey* (Book 8), and at the conclusion of the *Homeric Hymn to Delian Apollo,* a poem probably not written by Homer but dated in the seventh century B.C.E., the poet says to the maidens of Delos that a blind man from Chios[4] is the sweetest singer:

> "O maidens, what man to you is the sweetest of singers
> Who frequent this place, and whose songs give you greatest delight?"
> Then all of you answer in unison, choosing felicitous words:
> "A blind man who lives on the rugged island of Chios,
> All of whose songs in aftertime will be known as the best."

Even before epic stories were written down and widely circulated, oral versions were considered property. Fraternities of poets, or bards, held their epic materials in common for use at royal feasts or weddings.

In the sixth century, a professional group of poets on Chios who called themselves *Homeridai* (Sons of Homer) recited Homeric poetry. Homer might have been a single poet who composed the epics, or the name "Homer" might have been associated with a series of poets who recited and modified oral epics for several hundred years until *The Iliad* and *The Odyssey* reached their final form sometime in the sixth century. A combination of these two possibilities probably approaches the truth.

It was once believed that epic poems such as Homer's were too long to be memorized and must therefore have originated in written form, meaning that *The Iliad* and *The Odyssey* would have been composed and written down between 750 and 650 B.C.E., about the time when writing was revived in Greece with the adoption of the Phoenician alphabet. But studies in the 1930s by Milman Parry and his student Albert Lord in Yugoslavia, where an oral epic tradition still existed, substantiated that poems the length of *The Iliad,* about fifteen thousand verses, could indeed be memorized and recited. A number of

duh-MAH-duh-kus

[The Homeric age] did not erect any religious system but it remodelled its inheritance in accordance with two predominating lines of thought, anthropomorphism and rationalism. The latter played into the hands of the former by removing all the elements of the supernatural and the wonderful, and by refashioning the inherited myths in accordance with human standards.
— MARTIN P. NILSSON, *A History of Greek Religion,* classicist, 1949

---

[4] **Chios:** A small island just off the coast of Asia Minor (now Turkey).

Ancient Greece: The Trojan War

Many stories from Greek mythology have become part of the West's cultural consciousness; heroes such as Odysseus and Achilles are still referred to in literature today, 2,500 to 3,000 years after their stories were first told. One of the most compelling and enduring stories is that of the Trojan War. The mythic origins of the war are traced to Eris, the goddess of discord, who, at the wedding of the nymph Thetis to the mortal Peleus, rolled a golden apple across the floor inscribed with the words "For the Fairest." Shrewdly, Zeus chose Paris, a prince of Troy, to judge the beauty contest of Hera, who offered him power; Athena, who offered him wisdom; and Aphrodite, who promised Paris the most beautiful woman in the world. Paris chose Aphrodite, and the two losers became hostile towards Troy. While visiting King Menelaus of Sparta, Paris abducted Menelaus's beautiful wife, Helen, the daughter of Zeus and Leda and sister to Clytemnestra, and a portion of the Spartan treasury, then fled to Troy.

Angered by the betrayal, Menelaus called on his brother, King Agamemnon of Mycenae, to put together an army to take revenge on Troy. The brothers were joined by the armies of nearby city-states, Helen's former suitors, and heroes like Achilles, Odysseus, and Ajax.

Scene from the Trojan War, seventh century B.C.E. *One of the most famous mythological stories of all time, the climactic moment in the story of the Trojan War occurs when the Greeks, hidden inside a huge gift horse and wheeled into the besieged city of Troy, emerge at nightfall and destroy the city. (Erich Lessing / Art Resource, NY)*

The Greek ships congregated at Aulis on the east coast of Greece but were stalled there because of inadequate winds. Following an oracle, Agamemnon sacrificed his youngest daughter, Iphigenia, who had been lured to Aulis with the promise of marriage to Achilles. The winds were restored and the boats sailed for Troy, a fortress city in the northwest corner of Asia Minor.

For nine years this army attacked the outskirts of Troy—the final year of which is documented in Homer's *The Iliad*—failing to reach

factors made memorization possible. The verse was metered, and poets used a stringed instrument like a lyre to establish a rhythm. Most important, this kind of oral poetry featured poetic formulas, stock situations, and stock phrases used to set patterns. There is a set way, for example, of describing a feast or arrival at a palace. Stock epithets are used for describing nightfall, the sea, the sun, and major characters. Dawn comes with "her fingers of pink light," the sea is

Ancient Greece: The Trojan War continued

the city itself, which was protected by a wall. Achilles killed Hector, the most famous Trojan warrior, but Troy persisted. Odysseus and Diomedes sneaked into the city of Troy by night and stole the sacred statue of Athena, the Palladium, believed to be the source of Trojan strength. But even with its heroes dead and the Palladium stolen, Troy did not fall. Finally, guided by Odysseus, the Greeks resorted to deception. Epeius built a large wooden horse and the strongest warriors hid in its belly. When the rest of the Greeks sailed away leaving the horse behind them, the curious Trojans came out of the city and found Sinon, a lone Greek soldier, on the beach. Lying to the Trojans, he said he had been abandoned and that the horse was an atonement for the theft of the Palladium; however, it had been built too large to be pulled through the gates into Troy. Falling for the trick, the Trojans dragged the horse inside the walls. In the middle of the night, the Greek soldiers emerged from the horse, called their compatriots back from a nearby island, and then they sacked and burned Troy.

A number of Greek warriors reached their homes quickly and safely. Agamemnon arrived home with Cassandra only to be assassinated by his wife, Clytemnestra. Others took many years to return. Menelaus and Helen were detoured to Egypt, where they spent seven years before returning to Sparta. Most famous of the Greek wanderers, Odysseus of Homer's *The Odyssey* spent ten years filled with love and adventure making his way back to his wife, Penelope, and son, Telemachus, on the island of Ithaka. The most famous Trojan survivor was Aeneas, son of Aphrodite and Anchises, who set out from the ruins of Troy with his wife, Creusa, son, Iulus (also Ascanius), and his father, to fulfill his destiny by founding a new Troy in a distant land. After losing his wife and wandering the seas— much like Odysseus—he gained the Italian coast and founded a colony that later became Rome.

Although this story belongs to the realm of mythology and legend, it was probably influenced by a real war between the Greeks and the people of Troas around 1200 B.C.E. Histories of city-states and peoples and stories of conquest were crucial narratives in the ancient world, replete with mythological heroes and gods who intervened in the history of human beings. Greek myths provided the ancestry for Greek city-states, the stories for religious life, and the subjects of art and plays. In essence, mythology provided a cosmic context within which the drama of everyday life might be carried out.

"winedark." Athena is the "grey-eyed goddess" or the "grey-eyed daughter of Zeus" and Poseidon is the "Earthshaker." Zeus, the "lord of storm and lightning" uses Hermes, the "Wayfinder" with a "golden wand," as his messenger. Odysseus is the "canniest of men" and the "raider of cities."

It is possible that for several hundred years Homer's epics were recited orally and a written text also existed, and that by the fifth century, the commercial reproductions of the texts finally canonized them and prevented further interpolation.

p. 537

The Iliad.   The most famous account of the Trojan War is found in Homer's *Iliad,* which means the "Tale of Ilios," or "Tale of Troy." In its present version, it is a work divided into twenty-four books, one for each letter of the Greek alphabet. *The Iliad* is based on a body of mythic stories known collectively as The Judgment of Paris, which themselves begin with the story of the wedding between Pêleus and Thetis. At this wedding, Eris, goddess of discord, rolls a golden apple inscribed with the words "For the Fairest" across the floor. The goddesses Hera, Athena, and Aphrodite[5] all claim the apple. Zeus chooses Paris, the handsome prince of Troy, to decide which of the three goddesses deserves the title. After the goddesses bribe him, Paris picks Aphrodite, who has promised him the most beautiful woman in the world in return: Helen, wife of **Menelaus** (Meneláos). While on a mission to Sparta, Paris falls in love with Helen and takes her and other Spartan treasures back to Troy. Seeking revenge, Greek kings under the leadership of **Agamemnon** (Agamémnon), Menelaus' brother, band together in ships at Aulis, but an absence of wind prevents them from sailing to Troy. Agamemnon is persuaded by a seer to sacrifice his youngest daughter, Iphigenia, as a means of restoring the winds. (This becomes an important event in Aeschylus's dramatic trilogy, *The Oresteia* (458 B.C.E.).) When at Troy a Greek embassy fails to secure the return of Helen and the stolen treasures, and the war settles into a ten-year siege. Then in the tenth year, the point at which *The Iliad* begins, the action comes to a climax with a quarrel between Agamemnon and Achilles, the death of **Achilles**' close friend **Patroclus** (Patróklus) and the death of Hector (Hektor), the Trojans' greatest warrior. Achilles himself is then killed by Paris. The end of the war comes about when the Trojans are tricked into hauling a large wooden horse filled with **Achaeans**, or Greeks, into the city, precipitating Troy's destruction.

meh-nuh-LAY-us

ag-uh-MEM-nahn

uh-KIL-eez

puh-TROH-klus

uh-KEE-uns

The Odyssey.   The Greek title for Homer's *The Odyssey* is *Odysseia,* which means "poetry about Odysseus." Though somewhat shorter than *The Iliad* at twelve thousand verses, *The Odyssey* is also divided into twenty-four books, again corresponding to the twenty-four letters of the

---

[5] **Hera . . . Aphrodite:** The goddesses of marriage, wisdom, and love, respectively.

The Return of Odysseus, 460–450 B.C.E.

A Greek terracotta plaque depicting a scene from The Odyssey. *After many years away from home, Odysseus returns to Ithaka disguised as a beggar and confronts his faithful wife Penelope while his father, Laertes, his son Telemachus, and the swineherd Eumaios look on.*

Greek alphabet. It begins *IN MEDIAS RES,* or *in the middle of,* Odysseus's return to his home island of Ithaca at the close of the Trojan War. A number of important events have taken place, however, between the end of *The Iliad,* which concludes with the burning and burial of Hector, and Odysseus's heading home.

Achilles is killed by a poisoned arrow. When the seer Helenus, son of Priam, is captured by the Greeks, he tells them that Troy will fall only when Philoctetes reenters the war with Achilles' son, Neoptolemus. Using trickery, Odysseus and Neoptolemus lure the bowman Philoctetes from Lemnon to Troy, where he kills Paris with Herakles' bow. When the war still does not end, Odysseus and **Diomedes** sneak into the city of Troy by night and steal the sacred statue of Athena, the Palladium, believed to be the source of Trojan strength. But even with its heroes dead and the Palladium stolen, Troy does not fall. Finally, guided by Odysseus, the Greeks resort to deception. Epeios (Epeius) builds a large, hollow wooden horse and the Greeks' strongest warriors hide in its belly. When the rest of the Greeks sail away, leaving the horse

> Homer's anthropomorphism gave rise to the first criticism of religion. . . .
> – MARTIN P. NILSSON, classicist, 1949

digh-uh-MEE-deez

behind, the curious Trojans come out of the city and find Sinon, a lone Greek soldier, on the beach. Sinon tells the Trojans he has been abandoned and that the horse is an atonement for the theft of the Palladium. Falling for the trick, the Trojans drag the horse inside the city walls, and in the middle of the night, the Greek soldiers emerge from the horse and call their compatriots back from a nearby island. The Greeks then sack and burn Troy.

The victors divide the spoils. Menelaus retrieves Helen; Agamemnon claims Priam's daughter Cassandra; and Odysseus receives **Hecuba**. Hector's wife, Andromache, is the prize of Neoptolemus. The Greeks then set sail for home. Some, like Nestor, Diomedes, Idomeneus, Philoctetes, and Neoptolemus, reach their homes quickly and safely. Agamemnon arrives home with Cassandra only to be assassinated by his wife, Clytemnestra (Klytaimnéstra) and her lover, Aegisthus. Others take many years to reach their destinations. Menelaus and Helen are detoured to Egypt, where they spend seven years before returning to Sparta. Odysseus, the best known of the Greek wanderers, leaves Troy with twelve ships and about six hundred men and, because of the anger of three deities, spends ten years making his way back to his wife, Penelope (Penélopê), and his son **Telemachus** (Telémakhos).

During that decade about one hundred suitors gather at Odysseus's palace in Ithaca and press Penelope to choose a husband from among them, a new king. Penelope delays in making a choice by telling the suitors that she must first weave a funeral shroud for her father-in-law, Laertes; she then unravels the day's weaving each night. The suitors, meanwhile, live off the food and drink of the palace and make fun of the youthful, inexperienced Telemachus, who lacks the stature to replace his father on the throne.

The Odyssey begins during the tenth year of Odysseus's journey, meaning about twenty years after he originally left Ithaka for the Trojan War. Unlike *The Iliad, The Odyssey* is not held together by a unifying plot. It is a series of episodes of Odysseus's protracted homeward voyage, which divide rather neatly into three parts, or songs. The first introduces Telemachus, who is now old enough to become king but who must undergo rites of passage before assuming that role. The second comprises Odysseus's adventures on his return journey. And in the third, Odysseus and Penelope reunite and Odysseus disposes of the suitors. It was Homer who brought these three stories together and made them into a single epic.

HEH-kuh-bee

tuh-LEH-muh-kus

One way to read Odysseus's journey and his adventures is that Odysseus himself is gaining the necessary experience and self-knowledge to confront and finally defeat the hundred or so suitors who threaten his household and kingdom. The stories about the return of other chieftains to their kingdoms, especially Agamemnon's reception by his wife and her lover, serve as object lessons for Odysseus's own return. Quite another perspective on Odysseus is that he is the quintessential world traveler and that his adventures in various locales enable Homer to paint exotic pictures of the distant frontiers of the world while borrowing from the folklore of his day, including stories about lotus eating, the Cyclops (Kyklopês), island temptresses, rock-throwing giants, and water monsters. Seen in this light, Troy then symbolizes that exotic, seductive place on the threshold of consciousness that compels the wanderer in each of us to give up the security of the known and set out for uncharted territory. Although haunted by the *idea* of home, this Odysseus would have mixed feelings about actually returning home and having to admit to himself that the grand adventure of his life is over, that he now should be sensible and retire, leaving challenge and risk to the next generation, his son Telemachus. Telemachus's own journey for self-knowledge and experience contains echoes of his father's as the son moves towards maturity and the necessary preparations for inheriting the kingdom.

The Odyssey is unique for its fascinating, strong women. Penelope keeps her hand on Ithaca's throne while holding off a hoard of suitors for years. A brief glimpse of Helen confirms her reputation for beauty and power; she still exercises her charms over the opposite sex. Both Calypso and Circe are beautiful. Although some of Homer's best writing celebrates the attributes of warriors, his portrayal of the lovely princess Nausicaa, Odysseus's final temptation before home, is tender and sympathetic, as are his treatments of the soldier **Elpénor**, the nurse Eurycleia, and the loyal swineherd, Eumaios.

In *The Odyssey,* Homer's two epic heroes meet. When Odysseus visits Hades and meets the shade of Achilles, Odysseus speaks about the deified honor and fame associated with Achilles' deeds and his rank in the underworld; Achilles responds:

> Let me hear no smooth talk
> of death from you Odysseus, light of councils.
> Better, I say, to break sod as a farm hand
> for some poor country man, on iron rations,
> than lord it over all the exhausted dead.

. . . it was only — if I may so put it — the day before yesterday that the Greeks came to know the origin and form of the various gods, and whether or not all of them had always existed; for Homer and Hesiod are the poets who composed our theogonies and described the gods for us, giving them all their appropriate titles, offices, and powers, and they lived, as I believe, not more than four hundred years ago.

– HERODOTUS, historian, fifth century B.C.E.

el-PEE-nore

This speech somewhat undercuts the earlier image of a youthful Achilles who chooses glory regardless of the fatal consequences. Odysseus represents a more complicated, thoughtful warrior who will be honored by cultures that value mental as well as physical prowess. Although *The Iliad* was at one time considered by some scholars to be the superior poem, the complex character of Odysseus, his series of marvelous adventures, and the epic's strong, interesting women are likely to make *The Odyssey* the favorite with many modern readers.

The Transmission of *The Odyssey*.   It is unclear how *The Odyssey* originally ended. Two Alexandrian critics, Aristophanes (c. 257–180 B.C.E.) and Aristarchus (c. 217–c. 145 B.C.E.), responsible for the excellent editions of Homer in current use, maintained that the poem ended in Book 23 with the conjugal reunion of Odysseus and Penélopê. Book 24, lacking in artistic merit, seems to have been added at a later date by someone other than the work's original author. Whether it was part of the original text or not, Book 24, which contains scenes in Hades, Odysseus's reunion with his father, and a debate about revenging the deaths of the suitors, nevertheless contributes to the whole epic by resolving issues about the reprisals.

A comparison with the Mesopotamian *The Epic of Gilgamesh* (c. 1800 B.C.E.) suggests that the author of *The Odyssey* either knew about Gilgamesh or that there was some common source for both the Gilgamesh poet and Homer. The intimate friendship between Gilgamesh and Enkidu seem to be models for Akhilleus and Patróklos. The death of Enkidu sends the hero on an extended journey which ends in a visit to the netherworld, in much the same way that Patróklos's death and the death of numerous Greek heroes results in Odysseus's travels, which are intersected by a visit to Hades. Both Gilgamesh and Odysseus are assisted by prescient women — Siduri and Kirkê. Both journeys provide lessons about rulership.

The modern study of Homer's epics was transformed by a German archeologist, Heinrich Schliemann, who, in the 1870s–1890s discovered the remains of the legendary city of Troy — actually several Troys, one on top of the other — on the northwest coast of Turkey. He then uncovered Mycenae, the palace of the legendary King Agamemnon, on the Greek mainland. Schliemann uncovered a historical world to which one could attach Homer's texts. Modern readers can now better appreciate how the defeat of Troy provided Greece a legacy for hundreds of years. Important families traced their descent from Akhaian warriors. Greek cities claimed they had been founded by returning warriors from Troy. Other peoples found their ancestors in the Trojans. In the great Roman epic, *The Aeneid*, Virgil made use of the tradition that Trojan warrior Aeneas survived the defeat of Troy and eventually led a small band to the shores of Italy, where he established an ancestral line which led to Julius Caesar and the Roman Empire. The Trojan War thus provided the founding materials for several literary traditions, which highlight the importance of Schliemann's discoveries.

■ **FURTHER RESEARCH**

History and Background

Barr, Stringfellow. *The Will of Zeus: A History of Greece.* 1961.

Bowra, C. M. *Homer.* 1972.

Bury, J. B., and Russell Meiggs. *A History of Greece to the Death of Alexander the Great.* 1975.

Forsdyke, John. *Greece Before Homer: Ancient Chronology and Mythology.* 1964.

Nagy, Gregory. *The Best of the Achaeans: Concepts of the Hero in Archaic Greek Poetry.* 1999.

Nilsson, Martin P. *A History of Greek Religion.* 1964.

Rose, H. J. *A Handbook of Greek Literature: From Homer to the Age of Lucian.* 1996.

Homer and His Epics

Benardete, Seth. *The Bow and the Lyre: A Platonic Reading of the Odyssey.* 1997.

Clarke, Michael J. *Flesh and Spirit in the Songs of Homer: A Study of Words and Myths.* 1999.

Cohen, Beth. *The Distaff Side: Representing the Female in Homer's Odyssey.* 1995.

Graziosi, Barbara, and Johannes Haubold. *Homer: The Resonance of Epic.* 2005.

Griffin, Jasper. *The Odyssey.* 1987.

Hansen, William F. "The Homeric Epics and Oral Poetry," in Felix J. Oinas, ed., *Heroic Epic and Saga: An Introduction to the World's Great Folk Epics.* 1978.

Karydas, Helen Pournara. *Eurykleia and Her Successors: Female Figures of Authority in Greek Poetics.* 1998.

Kirk, G. S. *Homer and the Oral Tradition.* 1976.

Latacz, Joachim. *Homer, His Art and His World.* James P. Holoka. trans. 1996.

Mueller, Martin. *The Iliad.* 1984.

Steiner, George, and Robert Fagles, eds. *Homer: A Collection of Critical Essays.* 1962.

West, Martin L., ed. and trans. *The Homeric Hymns, Homeric Apocrypha, Lives of Homer.* 2003.

■ **PRONUNCIATION**

Achaeans (Akhaians): uh-KEE-unz

Achilles (Akhilleus): uh-KIL-eez

Aeneas (Aineías): uh-NEE-us

Aeolus (Aiolos): ee-YOH-lus

Agamemnon (Agamémnon): ag-uh-MEM-nahn

Aias (Aîas): IGH-yus

Alcinus (Alkínoös): al-KIN-oh-us

Alcmene (Alkmênê): alk-MEE-nee

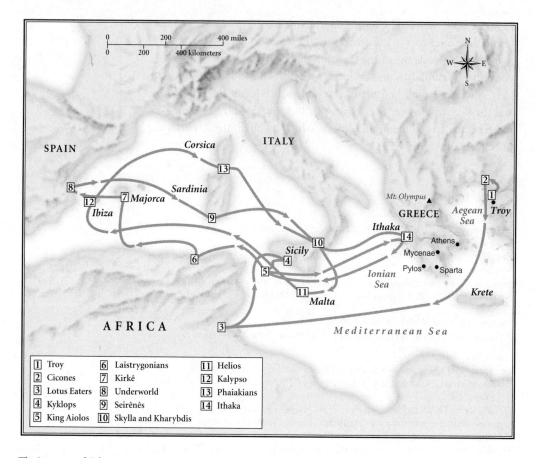

The Journeys of Odysseus

The journey of Odysseus is based on myth and legend; exact locations in The Odyssey *presented here are based on the best but by no means definitive attempts to reconstruct his travels.*

Alcyone (Alkýonê): al-SIGH-uh-nee
Arete (Arêtê): AH-ri-tay
Calydon (Kálydôn): KAL-i-dahn
Calypso (Kalypso): kuh-LIP-soh
Charybdis (Kharybdis): kuh-RIB-dis
Circe (Kirkê): SUR-see
Clytemnestra (Klytaimnéstra): kligh-tum-NES-truh
Couretes (Kourêtês): koo-REE-teez
Cyclops (Kyklopês): sigh-KLOH-peez
Demóducus (Demódokos): duh-MAH-duh-kus
Diomêdês: digh-uh-MEE-deez
Elpénor (Elpênor): el-PEE-nore
Eumaios: yoo-MAY-us, yoo-MIGH-yus

Eunus (Euênos): yoo-EE-nus
Euryclea (Eurýkleia): yoo-rih-KLIGH-uh
Hecabe (Hékabê): HEH-kuh-bee
Laertes (Laërtês): luh-UR-teez, lay-UR-teez
Laistrygonians: leh-strih-GOH-nee-unz
Marpessè: mar-PESS-uh
Meneláos: meh-nuh-LAY-us
Mycenae (Mykênai, Mykênê): migh-SEE-nee
Myrmidons: MUR-muh-donz
Nausikaa: naw-SIK-ay-uh
Patróklos (Patróklus): puh-TROH-klus
Phaiakians: fee-EE-shunz
Phémios: FEE-mee-us
Polyphemos (Polyphêmos): pah-luh-FEE-mus
Scylla (Skylla): SIL-ah
Sirens (Seirênês): sigh-REE-neez
Sisyphus (Sísyphos): SIZ-uh-fus
Tatar: TAH-tar
Teirêsias (Teirêsias): tigh-REE-seeus
Telemachus (Telémakhos): tuh-LEH-muh-kus

ꙮ The Odyssey

Translated by Robert Fitzgerald

BOOK 1
A GODDESS INTERVENES

Sing in me, Muse, and through me tell the story
of that man skilled in all ways of contending,
the wanderer, harried for years on end,
after he plundered the stronghold
on the proud height of Troy.
                              He saw the townlands
and learned the minds of many distant men,
and weathered many bitter nights and days
in his deep heart at sea, while he fought only
10 to save his life, to bring his shipmates home.
But not by will nor valor could he save them,
for their own recklessness destroyed them all—
children and fools, they killed and feasted on

A note on the translation: This translator does not use the more common Latinized spelling of names, such as Achilles and Achaeans, but versions closer to Greek spelling and pronunciation.

the cattle of Lord Hêlios,[1] the Sun,
and he who moves all day through heaven
took from their eyes the dawn of their return.

Of these adventures, Muse, daughter of Zeus,
tell us in our time, lift the great song again.
Begin when all the rest who left behind them
20   headlong death in battle or at sea
had long ago returned,[2] while he alone still hungered
for home and wife. Her ladyship Kalypso[3]
clung to him in her sea-hollowed caves—
a nymph, immortal and most beautiful,
who craved him for her own.
                                        And when long years and seasons
wheeling brought around that point of time
ordained for him to make his passage homeward,
trials and dangers, even so, attended him
30   even in Ithaka,[4] near those he loved.
Yet all the gods had pitied Lord Odysseus,
all but Poseidon,[5] raging cold and rough
against the brave king till he came ashore
at last on his own land.
                                    But now that god
had gone far off among the sunburnt races,
most remote of men, at earth's two verges,
in sunset lands and lands of the rising sun,
to be regaled by smoke of thighbones burning,
40   haunches of rams and bulls, a hundred fold.
He lingered delighted at the banquet side.

In the bright hall of Zeus upon Olympos
the other gods were all at home, and Zeus,
the father of gods and men, made conversation.
For he had meditated on Aigísthos, dead
by the hand of Agamémnon's son, Orestês[6]
and spoke his thought aloud before them all:
"My word, how mortals take the gods to task!
All their afflictions come from us, we hear.
50   And what of their own failings? Greed and folly

---

[1] **they killed . . . Hêlios:** This incident is found in Book 12.   [2] **when all . . . returned:** From Troy.   [3] **Kalypso:** Daughter of Atlas; a nymph is a lesser divinity, usually associated with nature, such as streams and springs. [4] **Ithaka:** Odysseus' island home off the western coast of Greece.   [5] **Poseidon:** God of the ocean; lines 86–89 provide the reason for his rage.   [6] **Orestês:** Aigísthos conspired with Klytaimnestra to kill Agamémnon when he returned from Troy; Orestês killed Aigísthos. See Book 11 of *The Odyssey*.

double the suffering in the lot of man.
See how Aigísthos, for his double portion,
stole Agamémnon's wife and killed the soldier
on his homecoming day. And yet Aigísthos
knew that his own doom lay in this. We gods
had warned him, sent down Hermês Argeiphontês,[7]
our most observant courier, to say:
'Don't kill the man, don't touch his wife,
or face a reckoning with Orestês
60 the day he comes of age and wants his patrimony.'
Friendly advice—but would Aigísthos take it?
Now he has paid the reckoning in full."

The grey-eyed goddess Athena replied to Zeus:
"O Majesty, O Father of us all,
that man is in the dust indeed, and justly.
So perish all who do what he had done.
But my own heart is broken for Odysseus,
the master mind of war, so long a castaway
upon an island in the running sea;
70 a wooded island, in the sea's middle,
and there's a goddess in the place, the daughter
of one whose baleful mind knows all the deeps
of the blue sea—Atlas,[8] who holds the columns
that bear from land the great thrust of the sky.
His daughter will not let Odysseus go,
poor mournful man; she keeps on coaxing him
with her beguiling talk, to turn his mind
from Ithaka. But such desire is in him
merely to see the hearthsmoke leaping upward
80 from his own island, that he longs to die.
Are you not moved by this, Lord of Olympos?
Had you no pleasure from Odysseus' offerings
beside the Argive[9] ships, on Troy's wide seaboard?
O Zeus, what do you hold against him now?"

To this the summoner of cloud replied:
"My child, what strange remarks you let escape you.
Could I forget that kingly man, Odysseus?
There is no mortal half so wise; no mortal
gave so much to the lords of open sky.

---

[7] **Hermês Argeiphontês:** Hermês is a messenger god; the meaning of *Argeiphontês* is uncertain, but it could signify "brightness."   [8] **Atlas:** A Titan who supports the world on his shoulders; father of Kalypso.   [9] **Argive:** A collective name for the Greeks fighting at Troy.

90   Only the god who laps the land in water,
      Poseidon, bears the fighter an old grudge
      since he poked out the eye of Polyphêmos,
      brawniest of the Kyklopês.[10] Who bore
      that giant lout? Thoösa, daughter of Phorkys,
      an offshore sea lord: for this nymph had lain
      with Lord Poseidon in her hollow caves.
      Naturally, the god, after the blinding—
      mind you, he does not kill the man;
      he only buffets him away from home.
100   But come now, we are all at leisure here,
      let us take up this matter of his return,
      that he may sail. Poseidon must relent
      for being quarrelsome will get him nowhere,
      one god, flouting the will of all the gods."

      The grey-eyed goddess Athena answered him:
      "O Majesty, O Father of us all,
      if it now please the blissful gods
      that wise Odysseus reach his home again,
      let the Wayfinder, Hermês, cross the sea
110   to the island of Ogýgia; let him tell
      our fixed intent to the nymph with pretty braids,
      and let the steadfast man depart for home.
      For my part, I shall visit Ithaka
      to put more courage in the son, and rouse him
      to call an assembly of the islanders,
      Akhaian[11] gentlemen with flowing hair.
      He must warn off that wolf pack of the suitors
      who prey upon his flocks and dusky cattle.
      I'll send him to the mainland then, to Sparta
120   by the sand beach of Pylos;[12] let him find
      news of his dear father where he may
      and win his own renown about the world."

      She bent to tie her beautiful sandals on,
      ambrosial, golden, that carry her over water
      or over endless land on the wings of the wind,
      and took the great haft of her spear in hand—

---

[10] **Kyklopês (Cyclops):** The encounter with Polyphêmos, a Kyklopês, is told in Book 9.   [11] **Akhaian:** Another name for the Greeks at Troy.   [12] **Pylos:** A city in southern Greece ruled by Nestor.

that bronzeshod spear this child of Power can use
to break in wrath long battle lines of fighters.

Flashing down from Olympos' height she went
130 to stand in Ithaka, before the Manor,
    just at the doorsill of the court. She seemed
    a family friend, the Taphian[13] captain, Mentês,
    waiting, with a light hand on her spear.
    Before her eyes she found the lusty suitors
    casting dice inside the gate, at ease
    on hides of oxen—oxen they had killed.
    Their own retainers made a busy sight
    with houseboys mixing bowls of water and wine,
    or sopping water up in sponges, wiping
140 tables to be placed about in hall,
    or butchering whole carcasses for roasting.

Long before anyone else, the prince Telémakhos
now caught sight of Athena—for he, too,
was sitting there unhappy among the suitors,
a boy, daydreaming. What if his great father
came from the unknown world and drove these men
like dead leaves through the place, recovering
honor and lordship in his own domains?
Then he who dreamed in the crowd gazed out at Athena.

150 Straight to the door he came, irked with himself
    to think a visitor had been kept there waiting,
    and took her right hand, grasping with his left
    her tall bronze-bladed spear. Then he said warmly:
    "Greetings, stranger! Welcome to our feast.
    There will be time to tell your errand later."

He led the way, and Pallas Athena followed
into the lofty hall. The boy reached up
and thrust her spear high in a polished rack
against a pillar where tough spear on spear
160 of the old soldier, his father, stood in order.
    Then, shaking out a splendid coverlet,
    he seated her on a throne with footrest—all
    finely carved—and drew his painted armchair

---

[13] **Taphian:** A neighboring, seafaring people.

near her, at a distance from the rest.
To be amid the din, the suitors' riot,
would ruin his guest's appetite, he thought,
and he wished privacy to ask for news
about his father, gone for years.

                   A maid
170 brought them a silver finger bowl and filled it
out of a beautiful spouting golden jug,
then drew a polished table to their side.
The larder mistress with her tray came by
and served them generously. A carver lifted
cuts of each roast meat to put on trenchers
before the two. He gave them cups of gold,
and these the steward as he went his rounds
filled and filled again.

              Now came the suitors,
180 young bloods trooping in to their own seats
on thrones or easy chairs. Attendants poured
water over their fingers, while the maids
piled baskets full of brown loaves near at hand,
and houseboys brimmed the bowls with wine.
Now they laid hands upon the ready feast
and thought of nothing more. Not till desire
for food and drink had left them were they mindful
of dance and song, that are the grace of feasting.
A herald gave a shapely cithern harp
190 to Phêmios,[14] whom they compelled to sing—
and what a storm he plucked upon the strings
for prelude! High and clear the song arose.

Telémakhos now spoke to grey-eyed Athena,
his head bent close, so no one else might hear:
"Dear guest, will this offend you, if I speak?
It is easy for these men to like these things,
harping and song; they have an easy life,
scot free, eating the livestock of another—
a man whose bones are rotting somewhere now,
200 white in the rain on dark earth where they lie,
or tumbling in the groundswell of the sea.
If he returned, if these men ever saw him,
faster legs they'd pray for, to a man,
and not more wealth in handsome robes or gold.

---

[14] **Phêmios:** The household bard.

But he is lost; he came to grief and perished,
and there's no help for us in someone's hoping
he still may come; that sun has long gone down.
But tell me now, and put it for me clearly—
who are you? Where do you come from? Where's your home
210 and family? What kind of ship is yours,
and what course brought you here? Who are your sailors?
I don't suppose you walked here on the sea.
Another thing—this too I ought to know—
is Ithaka new to you, or were you ever
a guest here in the old days? Far and near
friends knew this house; for he whose home it was
had much acquaintance in the world."

                              To this
the grey-eyed goddess answered:
220   "As you ask,
I can account most clearly for myself.
Mentês I'm called, son of the veteran
Ankhíalos; I rule seafaring Taphos.
I came by ship, with a ship's company,
sailing the winedark sea for ports of call
on alien shores—to Témesê, for copper,
bringing bright bars of iron in exchange.
My ship is moored on a wild strip of coast
in Reithron Bight, under the wooded mountain.
230 Years back, my family and yours were friends,
as Lord Laërtês[15] knows; ask when you see him.
I hear the old man comes to town no longer,
stays up country, ailing, with only one
old woman to prepare his meat and drink
when pain and stiffness take him in the legs
from working on his terraced plot, his vineyard.
As for my sailing here—
the tale was that your father had come home,
therefore I came. I see the gods delay him.
240 But never in this world is Odysseus dead—
only detained somewhere on the wide sea,
upon some island, with wild islanders;
savages, they must be, to hold him captive.
Well, I will forecast for you, as the gods
put the strong feeling in me—I see it all,

---

[15] **Laërtês:** Father of Odysseus.

and I'm no prophet, no adept in bird-signs.
He will not, now, be long away from Ithaka,
his father's dear land; though he be in chains
he'll scheme a way to come; he can do anything.

250   But tell me this now, make it clear to me:
You must be, by your looks, Odysseus' boy?
The way your head is shaped, the fine eyes — yes,
how like him! We took meals like this together
many a time, before he sailed for Troy
with all the lords of Argos in the ships.
I have not seen him since, nor has he seen me."

And thoughtfully Telémakhos replied:
"Friend, let me put it in the plainest way.
My mother says I am his son; I know not
260   surely. Who has known his own engendering?
I wish at least I had some happy man
as father, growing old in his own house —
but unknown death and silence are the fate
of him that, since you ask, they call my father."

Then grey-eyed Athena said:
                              "The gods decreed
no lack of honor in this generation:
such is the son Penélopê bore in you.
But tell me now, and make this clear to me:
270   what gathering, what feast is this? Why here?
A wedding? Revel? At the expense of all?
Not that, I think. How arrogant they seem,
these gluttons, making free here in your house!
A sensible man would blush to be among them."

To this Telémakhos answered:
"Friend, now that you ask about these matters,
our house was always princely, a great house,
as long as he of whom we speak remained here.
But evil days the gods have brought upon it,
280   making him vanish, as they have, so strangely.
Were his death known, I could not feel such pain —
if he had died of wounds in Trojan country
or in the arms of friends, after the war.
They would have made a tomb for him, the Akhaians,
and I should have all honor as his son.

Instead, the whirlwinds got him, and no glory.
He's gone, no sign, no word of him; and I inherit
trouble and tears—and not for him alone,
the gods have laid such other burdens on me.
290 For now the lords of the islands,
Doulíkhion and Samê, wooded Zakýnthos,
and rocky Ithaka's young lords as well,
are here courting my mother; and they use
our house as if it were a house to plunder.
Spurn them she dare not, though she hates that marriage,
nor can she bring herself to choose among them.
Meanwhile they eat their way through all we have,
and when they will, they can demolish me."

Pallas Athena was disturbed, and said:
300 "Ah, bitterly you need Odysseus, then!
High time he came back to engage these upstarts.
I wish we saw him standing helmeted
there in the doorway, holding shield and spear,
looking the way he did when I first knew him.
That was at our house, where he drank and feasted
after he left Ephyra, homeward bound
from a visit to the son of Mérmeris, Ilos.
He took his fast ship down the gulf that time
for a fatal drug to dip his arrows in
310 and poison the bronze points; but young Ilos
turned him away, fearing the gods' wrath.
My father gave it, for he loved him well.
I wish these men could meet the man of those days!
They'd know their fortune quickly: a cold bed.
Aye! but it lies upon the gods' great knees
whether he can return and force a reckoning
in his own house, or not.
                              If I were you,
I should take steps to make these men disperse.
320 Listen, now, and attend to what I say:
at daybreak call the islanders to assembly,
and speak your will, and call the gods to witness:
the suitors must go scattering to their homes.
Then here's a course for you, if you agree:
get a sound craft afloat with twenty oars
and go abroad for news of your lost father—
perhaps a traveller's tale, or rumored fame
issued from Zeus abroad in the world of men.

Talk to that noble sage at Pylos, Nestor,
330   then go to Meneláos,[16] the red-haired king
at Sparta, last man home of all the Akhaians.
If you should learn your father is alive
and coming home, you could hold out a year.
Or if you learn that he is dead and gone,
then you can come back to your own dear country
and raise a mound for him, and burn his gear,
with all the funeral honors due the man,
and give your mother to another husband.

When you have done all this, or seen it done,
340   it will be time to ponder
concerning these contenders in your house—
how you should kill them, outright or by guile.
You need not bear this insolence of theirs,
you are a child no longer. Have you heard
what glory young Orestês won
when he cut down that two-faced man, Aigísthos,
for killing his illustrious father?
Dear friend, you are tall and well set-up, I see;
be brave—you, too—and men in times to come
350   will speak of you respectfully.
                              Now I must join my ship;
my crew will grumble if I keep them waiting.
Look to yourself; remember what I told you."
Telémakhos replied:
                              "Friend, you have done me
kindness, like a father to his son,
and I shall not forget your counsel ever.
You must get back to sea, I know, but come
take a hot bath, and rest; accept a gift
360   to make your heart lift up when you embark—
some precious thing, and beautiful, from me,
a keepsake, such as dear friends give their friends."

But the grey-eyed goddess Athena answered him:
"Do not delay me, for I love the sea ways.
As for the gift your heart is set on giving,

---

[16] Meneláos (Menelaus): Brother of Agamémnon, husband of Helen of Troy.

let me accept it on my passage home,
and you shall have a choice gift in exchange."

With this Athena left him
as a bird rustles upward, off and gone.
370 But as she went she put new spirit in him,
a new dream of his father, clearer now,
so that he marvelled to himself
divining that a god had been his guest.
Then godlike in his turn he joined the suitors.

The famous minstrel still sang on before them,
and they sat still and listened, while he sang
that bitter song, the Homecoming of Akhaians—
how by Athena's will they fared from Troy;
and in her high room careful Penélopê,
380 Ikários' daughter, heeded the holy song.
She came, then, down the long stairs of her house,
this beautiful lady, with two maids in train
attending her as she approached the suitors;
and near a pillar of the roof she paused,
her shining veil drawn over across her cheeks,
the two girls close to her and still,
and through her tears spoke to the noble minstrel:
"Phêmios, other spells you know, high deeds
of gods and heroes, as the poets tell them;
390 let these men hear some other; let them sit
silent and drink their wine. But sing no more
this bitter tale that wears my heart away.
It opens in me again the wound of longing
for one incomparable, ever in my mind—
his fame all Hellas° knows, and midland Argos."   Greece

But Telémakhos intervened and said to her:
"Mother, why do you grudge our own dear minstrel
joy of song, wherever his thought may lead?
Poets are not to blame, but Zeus who gives
400 what fate he pleases to adventurous men.
Here is no reason for reproof: to sing
the news of the Danaans![17] Men like best

---

[17] **Danaans:** Another name for the Greeks at Troy.

a song that rings like morning on the ear.
But you must nerve yourself and try to listen.
Odysseus was not the only one at Troy
never to know the day of his homecoming.
Others, how many others, lost their lives!"

The lady gazed in wonder and withdrew,
her son's clear wisdom echoing in her mind.
410 But when she had mounted to her rooms again
with her two handmaids, then she fell to weeping
for Odysseus, her husband. Grey-eyed Athena
presently cast a sweet sleep on her eyes.

Meanwhile the din grew loud in the shadowy hall
as every suitor swore to lie beside her,
but Telémakhos turned now and spoke to them:
"You suitors of my mother! Insolent men,
now we have dined, let us have entertainment
and no more shouting. There can be no pleasure
420 so fair as giving heed to a great minstrel
like ours, whose voice itself is pure delight.
At daybreak we shall sit down in assembly
and I shall tell you—take it as you will—
you are to leave this hall. Go feasting elsewhere,
consume your own stores. Turn and turn about,
use one another's houses. If you choose
to slaughter one man's livestock and pay nothing,
this is rapine; and by the eternal gods
I beg Zeus you shall get what you deserve:
430 a slaughter here, and nothing paid for it!"

By now their teeth seemed fixed in their under-lips,
Telémakhos' bold speaking stunned them so.
Antínoös, Eupeithês' son, made answer:
"Telémakhos, no doubt the gods themselves
are teaching you this high and mighty manner.
Zeus forbid you should be king in Ithaka,
though you are eligible as your father's son."

Telémakhos kept his head and answered him:
"Antínoös, you may not like my answer,
440 but I would happily be king, if Zeus
conferred the prize. Or do you think it wretched?
I shouldn't call it bad at all. A king
will be respected, and his house will flourish.

But there are eligible men enough,
heaven knows, on the island, young and old,
and one of them perhaps may come to power
after the death of King Odysseus.
All I insist on is that I rule our house
and rule the slaves my father won for me."

450   Eurýmakhos, Pólybos' son, replied:
"Telémakhos, it is on the gods' great knees
who will be king in sea-girt Ithaka.
But keep your property, and rule your house,
and let no man, against your will, make havoc
of your possessions, while there's life on Ithaka.
But no, my brave young friend,
a question or two about the stranger.
Where did your guest come from? Of what country?
Where does he say his home is, and his family?
460   Has he some message of your father's coming,
or business of his own, asking a favor?
He left so quickly that one hadn't time
to meet him, but he seemed a gentleman."

Telémakhos made answer, cool enough:
"Eurýmakhos, there's no hope for my father.
I would not trust a message, if one came,
nor any forecaster my mother invites
to tell by divination of time to come.
My guest, however, was a family friend,
470   Mentês, son of Ankhíalos.
He rules the Taphian people of the sea."

So said Telémakhos, though in his heart
he knew his visitor had been immortal.
But now the suitors turned to play again
with dance and haunting song. They stayed till nightfall,
indeed black night came on them at their pleasure,
and half asleep they left, each for his home.

Telémakhos' bedroom was above the court,
a kind of tower, with a view all round;
480   here he retired to ponder in the silence,
while carrying brands of pine alight beside him
Eurýkleia went padding, sage and old.
Her father had been Ops, Peisênor's son,
and she had been a purchase of Laërtês

when she was still a blossoming girl. He gave
the price of twenty oxen for her, kept her
as kindly in his house as his own wife,
though, for the sake of peace, he never touched her.
No servant loved Telémakhos as she did,
490 she who had nursed him in his infancy.
So now she held the light, as he swung open
the door of his neat freshly painted chamber.
There he sat down, pulling his tunic off,
and tossed it into the wise old woman's hands.
She folded it and smoothed it, and then hung it
beside the inlaid bed upon a bar;
then, drawing the door shut by its silver handle
she slid the catch in place and went away.
And all night long, wrapped in the finest fleece,
500 he took in thought the course Athena gave him.

BOOK 2
A HERO'S SON AWAKENS

When primal Dawn spread on the eastern sky
her fingers of pink light, Odysseus' true son
stood up, drew on his tunic and his mantle,
slung on a sword-belt and a new-edged sword,
tied his smooth feet into good rawhide sandals,
and left his room, a god's brilliance upon him.
He found the criers with clarion voices and told them
to muster the unshorn Akhaians in full assembly.
The call sang out, and the men came streaming in;
10 and when they filled the assembly ground, he entered,
spear in hand, with two quick hounds at heel;
Athena lavished on him a sunlit grace
that held the eye of the multitude. Old men
made way for him as he took his father's chair.

Now Lord Aigýptios, bent down and sage with years,
opened the assembly. This man's son
had served under the great Odysseus, gone
in the decked ships with him to the wild horse country
of Troy—a spearman, Ántiphos by name.
20 The ravenous Kyklops in the cave destroyed him
last in his feast of men. Three other sons
the old man had, and one, Eurýnomos,
went with the suitors; two farmed for their father;

but even so the old man pined, remembering
the absent one, and a tear welled up as he spoke:
"Hear me, Ithakans! Hear what I have to say.
No meeting has been held here since our king,
Odysseus, left port in the decked ships.
Who finds occasion for assembly, now?
30 one of the young men? one of the older lot?
Has he had word our fighters are returning—
news to report if he got wind of it—
or is it something else, touching the realm?
The man has vigor, I should say; more power to him.
Whatever he desires, may Zeus fulfill it."

The old man's words delighted the son of Odysseus,
who kept his chair no longer but stood up,
eager to speak, in the midst of all the men.
The crier, Peisênor, master of debate,
40 brought him the staff and placed it in his hand;[18]
then the boy touched the old man's shoulder, and said:
"No need to wonder any more, Sir,
who called this session. The distress is mine.
As to our troops returning, I have no news—
news to report if I got wind of it—
nor have I public business to propose;
only my need, and the trouble of my house—
the troubles.

       My distinguished father is lost,
50 who ruled among you once, mild as a father,
and there is now this greater evil still:
my home and all I have are being ruined.
Mother wanted no suitors, but like a pack
they came—sons of the best men here among them—
lads with no stomach for an introduction
to Ikários, her father across the sea;
he would require a wedding gift, and give her
to someone who found favor in her eyes.
No; these men spend their days around our house
60 killing our beeves and sheep and fatted goats,
carousing, soaking up our good dark wine,
not caring what they do. They squander everything.
We have no strong Odysseus to defend us,

---

[18] **placed it . . . hand:** The person holding the staff has permission to speak.

and as to putting up a fight ourselves—
we'd only show our incompetence in arms.
Expel them, yes, if I only had the power;
the whole thing's out of hand, insufferable.
My house is being plundered: is this courtesy?
Where is your indignation? Where is your shame?
70 Think of the talk in the islands all around us,
and fear the wrath of the gods,
or they may turn, and send you some devilry.
Friends, by Olympian Zeus and holy Justice
that holds men in assembly and sets them free,
make an end of this! Let me lament in peace
my private loss. Or did my father, Odysseus,
ever do injury to the armed Akhaians?
Is this your way of taking it out on me,
giving free rein to these young men?
80 I might as well—might better—see my treasure
and livestock taken over by you all;
then, if you fed on them, I'd have some remedy,
and when we met, in public, in the town,
I'd press my claim; you might make restitution.
This way you hurt me when my hands are tied."

And in hot anger now he threw the staff to the ground,
his eyes grown bright with tears. A wave of sympathy
ran through the crowd, all hushed; and no one there
had the audacity to answer harshly
90 except Antínoös, who said:
                              "What high and mighty
talk, Telémakhos! No holding you!
You want to shame us, and humiliate us,
but you should know the suitors are not to blame—
it is your own dear, incomparably cunning mother.
For three years now—and it will soon be four—
she has been breaking the hearts of the Akhaians,
holding out hope to all, and sending promises
to each man privately—but thinking otherwise.

100 Here is an instance of her trickery:
she had her great loom standing in the hall
and the fine warp of some vast fabric on it;
we were attending her, and she said to us:
'Young men, my suitors, now my lord is dead,
let me finish my weaving before I marry,
or else my thread will have been spun in vain.

It is a shroud I weave for Lord Laërtês,
when cold death comes to lay him on his bier.
The country wives would hold me in dishonor
110 if he, with all his fortune, lay unshrouded.'
We have men's hearts; she touched them; we agreed.
So every day she wove on the great loom —
but every night by torchlight she unwove it;
and so for three years she deceived the Akhaians.
But when the seasons brought the fourth around,
one of her maids, who knew the secret, told us;
we found her unraveling the splendid shroud.
She had to finish then, although she hated it.

Now here is the suitors' answer —
120 you and all the Akhaians, mark it well:
dismiss your mother from the house, or make her marry
the man her father names and she prefers.
Does she intend to keep us dangling forever?
She may rely too long on Athena's gifts —
talent in handicraft and a clever mind;
so cunning — history cannot show the like
among the ringleted ladies of Akhaia,
Mykênê with her coronet, Alkmênê, Tyro.[19]
Wits like Penélopê's never were before,
130 but this time — well, she made poor use of them.
For here are suitors eating up your property
as long as she holds out — a plan some god
put in her mind. She makes a name for herself,
but you can feel the loss it means for you.
Our own affairs can wait; we'll never go anywhere else,
until she takes an Akhaian to her liking."

But clear-headed Telémakhos replied:
"Antínoös, can I banish against her will
the mother who bore me and took care of me?
140 My father is either dead or far away,
but dearly I should pay for this
at Ikários' hands, if ever I sent her back.
The powers of darkness would requite it, too,
my mother's parting curse would call hell's furies[20]
to punish me, along with the scorn of men.

---

[19] **Mykênê . . . Tyro:** Mykênê, Alkmênê, and Tyro were famous women; Alkmênê was the mother of Heraklês and Tyro was the grandmother of Jason.   [20] **furies:** Spirits who avenge crimes against women, especially mothers; their Greek name is Erinyes.

No: I can never give the word for this.
But if your hearts are capable of shame,
leave my great hall, and take your dinner elsewhere,
consume your own stores. Turn and turn about,
150   use one another's houses. If you choose
to slaughter one man's livestock and pay nothing,
this is rapine; and by the eternal gods
I beg Zeus you shall get what you deserve:
a slaughter here, and nothing paid for it!"

Now Zeus who views the wide world sent a sign to him,
launching a pair of eagles from a mountain crest
in gliding flight down the soft blowing wind,
wing-tip to wing-tip quivering taut, companions,
till high above the assembly of many voices
160   they wheeled, their dense wings beating, and in havoc
dropped on the heads of the crowd—a deathly omen—
wielding their talons, tearing cheeks and throats;
then veered away on the right hand through the city.
Astonished, gaping after the birds, the men
felt their hearts flood, foreboding things to come.
And now they heard the old lord Halithersês,
son of Mastor, keenest among the old
at reading birdflight into accurate speech;
in his anxiety for them, he rose and said:
170   "Hear me, Ithakans! Hear what I have to say,
and may I hope to open the suitors' eyes
to the black wave towering over them. Odysseus
will not be absent from his family long:
he is already near, carrying in him
a bloody doom for all these men, and sorrow
for many more on our high seamark, Ithaka.
Let us think how to stop it; let the suitors
drop their suit; they had better, without delay.
I am old enough to know a sign when I see one,
180   and I say all has come to pass for Odysseus
as I foretold when the Argives massed on Troy,
and he, the great tactician, joined the rest.
My forecast was that after nineteen years,
many blows weathered, all his shipmates lost,
himself unrecognized by anyone,
he would come home. I see this all fulfilled."

But Pólybos' son, Eurýmakhos, retorted:
"Old man, go tell the omens for your children

at home, and try to keep them out of trouble.
190 I am more fit to interpret this than you are.
Bird life aplenty is found in the sunny air,
not all of it significant. As for Odysseus,
he perished far from home. You should have perished with him—
then we'd be spared this nonsense in assembly,
as good as telling Telémakhos to rage on;
do you think you can gamble on a gift from him?
Here is what I foretell, and it's quite certain:
if you, with what you know of ancient lore,
encourage bitterness in this young man,
200 it means, for him, only the more frustration—
he can do nothing whatever with two eagles—
and as for you, old man, we'll fix a penalty
that you will groan to pay.
Before the whole assembly I advise Telémakhos
to send his mother to her father's house;
let them arrange her wedding there, and fix
a portion° suitable for a valued daughter.   a dowry
Until he does this, courtship is our business,
vexing though it may be; we fear no one,
210 certainly not Telémakhos, with his talk;
and we care nothing for your divining, uncle,
useless talk; you win more hatred by it.
We'll share his meat, no thanks or fee to him,
as long as she delays and maddens us.
It is a long, long time we have been waiting
in rivalry for this beauty. We could have gone
elsewhere and found ourselves very decent wives."

Clear-headed Telémakhos replied to this:
"Eurýmakhos, and noble suitors all,
220 I am finished with appeals and argument.
The gods know, and the Akhaians know, these things.
But give me a fast ship and a crew of twenty
who will see me through a voyage, out and back.
I'll go to sandy Pylos, then to Sparta,
for news of Father since he sailed from Troy—
some traveller's tale, perhaps, or rumored fame
issued from Zeus himself into the world.
If he's alive, and beating his way home,
I might hold out for another weary year;
230 but if they tell me that he's dead and gone,
then I can come back to my own dear country
and raise a mound for him, and burn his gear,

with all the funeral honors that befit him,
and give my mother to another husband."

The boy sat down in silence. Next to stand
was Mentor, comrade in arms of the prince Odysseus,
an old man now. Odysseus left him authority
over his house and slaves, to guard them well.
In his concern, he spoke to the assembly:
240   "Hear me, Ithakans! Hear what I have to say.
Let no man holding scepter as a king
be thoughtful, mild, kindly, or virtuous;
let him be cruel, and practice evil ways;
it is so clear that no one here remembers
how like a gentle father Odysseus ruled you.
I find it less revolting that the suitors
carry their malice into violent acts;
at least they stake their lives
when they go pillaging the house of Odysseus—
250   their lives upon it, he will not come again.
What sickens me is to see the whole community
sitting still, and never a voice or a hand raised
against them—a mere handful compared with you."

Leókritos, Euênor's son, replied to him:
"Mentor, what mischief are you raking up?
Will this crowd risk the sword's edge over a dinner?
Suppose Odysseus himself indeed
came in and found the suitors at his table:
he might be hot to drive them out. What then?
260   Never would he enjoy his wife again—
the wife who loves him well; he'd only bring down
abject death on himself against those odds.
Madness, to talk of fighting in either case.
Now let all present go about their business!
Halithersês and Mentor will speed the traveller;
they can help him: they were his father's friends.
I rather think he will be sitting here
a long time yet, waiting for news on Ithaka;
that seafaring he spoke of is beyond him."

270   On this note they were quick to end their parley.
The assembly broke up; everyone went home—
the suitors home to Odysseus' house again.
But Telémakhos walked down along the shore
and washed his hands in the foam of the grey sea,

then said this prayer:
            "O god of yesterday,
guest in our house, who told me to take ship
on the hazy sea for news of my lost father,
listen to me, be near me:
280 the Akhaians only wait, or hope to hinder me,
the damned insolent suitors most of all."

Athena was nearby and came to him,
putting on Mentor's figure and his tone,
the warm voice in a lucid flight of words:
"You'll never be fainthearted or a fool,
Telémakhos, if you have your father's spirit;
he finished what he cared to say,
and what he took in hand he brought to pass.
The sea routes will yield their distances
290 to his true son, Penélopê's true son,—
I doubt another's luck would hold so far.
The son is rare who measures with his father,
and one in a thousand is a better man,
but you will have the sap and wit
and prudence—for you get that from Odysseus—
to give you a fair chance of winning through.
So never mind the suitors and their ways,
there is no judgment in them, neither do they
know anything of death and the black terror
300 close upon them—doom's day on them all.
You need not linger over going to sea.
I sailed beside your father in the old days,
I'll find a ship for you, and help you sail her.
So go on home, as if to join the suitors,
but get provisions ready in containers—
wine in two-handled jugs and barley meal,
the staying power of oarsmen,
in skin bags, watertight. I'll go the rounds
and call a crew of volunteers together.
310 Hundreds of ships are beached on sea-girt Ithaka;
let me but choose the soundest, old or new,
we'll rig her and take her out on the broad sea."

This was the divine speech Telémakhos heard
from Athena, Zeus's daughter. He stayed no longer,
but took his heartache home,
and found the robust suitors there at work,
skinning goats and roasting pigs in the courtyard.

Antínoös came straight over, laughing at him,
and took him by the hand with a bold greeting:
320 "High-handed Telémakhos, control your temper!
Come on, get over it, no more grim thoughts,
but feast and drink with me, the way you used to.
The Akhaians will attend to all you ask for—
ship, crew, and crossing to the holy land
of Pylos, for the news about your father."

Telémakhos replied with no confusion:
"Antínoös, I cannot see myself again
taking a quiet dinner in this company.
Isn't it enough that you could strip my house
330 under my very nose when I was young?
Now that I know, being grown, what others say,
I understand it all, and my heart is full.
I'll bring black doom upon you if I can—
either in Pylos, if I go, or in this country.
And I will go, go all the way, if only
as someone's passenger. I have no ship,
no oarsmen: and it suits you that I have none."

Calmly he drew his hand from Antínoös' hand.
At this the suitors, while they dressed their meat,
340 began to exchange loud mocking talk about him.
One young toplofty gallant set the tone:
                              "Well, think of that!
Telémakhos has a mind to murder us.
He's going to lead avengers out of Pylos,
or Sparta, maybe; oh, he's wild to do it.
Or else he'll try the fat land of Ephyra—
he can get poison there, and bring it home,
doctor the wine jar and dispatch us all."

Another took the cue:
350   "Well now, who knows?
He might be lost at sea, just like Odysseus,
knocking around in a ship, far from his friends.
And what a lot of trouble that would give us,
making the right division of his things!
We'd keep his house as dowry for his mother—
his mother and the man who marries her."

That was the drift of it. Telémakhos
went on through to the storeroom of his father,
a great vault where gold and bronze lay piled

360 along with chests of clothes, and fragrant oil.
And there were jars of earthenware in rows
holding an old wine,
mellow, unmixed, and rare; cool stood the jars
against the wall, kept for whatever day
Odysseus, worn by hardships, might come home.
The double folding doors were tightly locked
and guarded, night and day, by the serving woman,
Eurýkleia, grand-daughter of Peisênor,
in all her duty vigilant and shrewd.

370 Telémakhos called her to the storeroom, saying:
"Nurse, get a few two-handled travelling jugs
filled up with wine—the second best, not that
you keep for your unlucky lord and king,
hoping he may have slipped away from death
and may yet come again—royal Odysseus.
Twelve amphorai will do; seal them up tight.
And pour out barley into leather bags—
twenty bushels of barley meal ground fine.
Now keep this to yourself! Collect these things,

380 and after dark, when mother has retired
and gone upstairs to bed, I'll come for them.
I sail to sandy Pylos, then to Sparta,
to see what news there is of Father's voyage."

His loving nurse Eurýkleia gave a cry,
and tears sprang to her eyes as she wailed softly:
"Dear child, whatever put this in your head?
Why do you want to go so far in the world—
and you our only darling? Lord Odysseus
died in some strange place, far from his homeland.

390 Think how, when you have turned your back, these men
will plot to kill you and share all your things!
Stay with your own, dear, do. Why should you suffer
hardship and homelessness on the wild sea?"

But seeing all clear, Telémakhos replied:
"Take heart, Nurse, there's a god behind this plan.
And you must swear to keep it from my mother,
until the eleventh day, or twelfth, or till
she misses me, or hears that I am gone.
She must not tear her lovely skin lamenting."

400 So the old woman vowed by all the gods,
and vowed again, to carry out his wishes;
then she filled up the amphorai with wine

and sifted barley meal into leather bags.
Telémakhos rejoined the suitors.
                                    Meanwhile
the goddess with grey eyes had other business:
disguised as Telémakhos, she roamed the town
taking each likely man aside and telling him:
"Meet us at nightfall at the ship!" Indeed,
410   she asked Noêmon, Phronios' wealthy son,
to lend her a fast ship, and he complied.
Now when at sundown shadows crossed the lanes
she dragged the cutter to the sea and launched it,
fitted out with tough seagoing gear,
and tied it up, away at the harbor's edge.
The crewmen gathered, sent there by the goddess.
Then it occurred to the grey-eyed goddess Athena
to pass inside the house of the hero Odysseus,
showering a sweet drowsiness on the suitors,
420   whom she had presently wandering in their wine;
and soon, as they could hold their cups no longer,
they straggled off to find their beds in town,
eyes heavy-lidded, laden down with sleep.
Then to Telémakhos the grey-eyed goddess
appeared again with Mentor's form and voice,
calling him out of the lofty emptied hall:
"Telémakhos, your crew of fighting men
is ready at the oars, and waiting for you;
come on, no point in holding up the sailing."

430   And Pallas Athena turned like the wind, running
ahead of him. He followed in her footsteps
down to the seaside, where they found the ship,
and oarsmen with flowing hair at the water's edge.
Telémakhos, now strong in the magic, cried:
"Come with me, friends, and get our rations down!
They are all packed at home, and my own mother
knows nothing! — only one maid was told."

He turned and led the way, and they came after,
carried and stowed all in the well-trimmed ship
440   as the dear son of Odysseus commanded.
Telémakhos then stepped aboard; Athena
took her position aft, and he sat by her.
The two stroke oars cast off the stern hawsers
and vaulted over the gunnels to their benches.
Grey-eyed Athena stirred them a following wind,

soughing from the north-west on the winedark sea,
and as he felt the wind, Telémakhos
called to all hands to break out mast and sail.
They pushed the fir mast high and stepped it firm
450 amidships in the box, made fast the forestays,
then hoisted up the white sail on its halyards
until the wind caught, booming in the sail;
and a flushing wave sang backward from the bow
on either side, as the ship got way upon her,
holding her steady course.
Now they made all secure in the fast black ship,
and, setting out the winebowls all a-brim,
they made libation to the gods,
                     the undying, the ever-new,
460 most of all to the grey-eyed daughter of Zeus.
And the prow sheared through the night into the dawn.

BOOK 3
THE LORD OF THE WESTERN APPROACHES

The sun rose on the flawless brimming sea
into a sky all brazen—all one brightening
for gods immortal and for mortal men
on plowlands kind with grain.
                        And facing sunrise
the voyagers now lay off Pylos town,
compact stronghold of Neleus.[21] On the shore
black bulls were being offered by the people
to the blue-maned god° who makes the islands tremble: Poseidon
10 nine congregations, each five hundred strong,
led out nine bulls apiece to sacrifice,
taking the tripes to eat, while on their altars
thighbones in fat lay burning for the god.
Here they put in, furled sail, and beached the ship;
but Telémakhos hung back in disembarking,
so that Athena turned and said:
"Not the least shyness, now, Telémakhos.
You came across the open sea for this—
to find out where the great earth hides your father
20 and what the doom was that he came upon.

---

[21] **Neleus:** Son of Poseidon and father of Nestor.

Go to old Nestor, master charioteer,
so we may broach the storehouse of his mind.
Ask him with courtesy, and in his wisdom
he will tell you history and no lies."

But clear-headed Telémakhos replied:
"Mentor, how can I do it, how approach him?
I have no practice in elaborate speeches, and
for a young man to interrogate an old man
seems disrespectful—"

30   But the grey-eyed goddess said:
"Reason and heart will give you words, Telémakhos;
and a spirit will counsel others. I should say
the gods were never indifferent to your life."

She went on quickly, and he followed her
to where the men of Pylos had their altars.
Nestor appeared enthroned among his sons,
while friends around them skewered the red beef
or held it scorching. When they saw the strangers
a hail went up, and all that crowd came forward
40   calling out invitations to the feast.
Peisístratos in the lead, the young prince,
caught up their hands in his and gave them places
on curly lambskins flat on the sea sand
near Thrasymêdês, his brother, and his father;
he passed them bits of the food of sacrifice,
and, pouring wine in a golden cup,
he said to Pallas Athena, daughter of Zeus:
"Friend, I must ask you to invoke Poseidon:
you find us at this feast, kept in his honor.
50   Make the appointed offering then, and pray,
and give the honeyed winecup to your friend
so he may do the same. He, too,
must pray to the gods on whom all men depend,
but he is just my age, you are the senior,
so here, I give the goblet first to you."

And he put the cup of sweet wine in her hand.
Athena liked his manners, and the equity
that gave her precedence with the cup of gold,
so she besought Poseidon at some length:
60   "Earthshaker, listen and be well disposed.
Grant your petitioners everything they ask:

above all, honor to Nestor and his sons;
second, to every man of Pylos town
a fair gift in exchange for this hekatomb;[22]
third, may Telémakhos and I perform
the errand on which last night we put to sea."

This was the prayer of Athena—
granted in every particular by herself.
She passed the beautiful wine cup to Telémakhos,
70 who tipped the wine and prayed as she had done.
Meanwhile the spits were taken off the fire,
portions of crisp meat for all. They feasted,
and when they had eaten and drunk their fill, at last
they heard from Nestor, prince of charioteers:
"Now is the time," he said, "for a few questions,
now that our young guests have enjoyed their dinner.
Who are you, strangers? Where are you sailing from,
and where to, down the highways of sea water?
Have you some business here? or are you, now,
80 reckless wanderers of the sea, like those corsairs
who risk their lives to prey on other men?"

Clear-headed Telémakhos responded cheerfully,
for Athena gave him heart. By her design
his quest for news about his father's wandering
would bring him fame in the world's eyes. So he said:
"Nestor, pride of Akhaians, Neleus' son,
you ask where we are from, and I can tell you:
our home port is under Mount Neion, Ithaka.
We are not here on Ithakan business, though,
90 but on my own. I want news of my father,
Odysseus, known for his great heart, and I
will comb the wide world for it. People say
he fought along with you when Troy was taken.
As to the other men who fought that war,
we know where each one died, and how he died;
but Zeus allotted my father death and mystery.
No one can say for sure where he was killed,
whether some hostile landsmen or the sea,
the stormwaves on the deep sea, got the best of him.
100 And this is why I come to you for help.

---

[22] **hekatomb:** Literally, *hekatomb* means a sacrifice to the gods of one hundred animals, but it may also indicate any large, public sacrifice.

Tell me of his death, sir, if perhaps
you witnessed it, or have heard some wanderer
tell the tale. The man was born for trouble.
Spare me no part of it for kindness' sake,
but put the scene before me as you saw it.
If ever Odysseus my noble father
served you by promise kept or work accomplished
in the land of Troy, where you Akhaians suffered,
recall those things for me the way they were."

110   Then Nestor, prince of charioteers, made answer:
"Dear friend, you take me back to all the trouble
we went through in that country, we Akhaians:
rough days aboard ship on the cloudy sea
cruising away for pillage after Akhilleus;
rough days of battle around Priam's town.
Our losses, then—so many good men gone:
Arês' great Aias lies there, Akhilleus lies there,
Patróklos, too, the wondrous counselor,
and my own strong and princely son, Antílokhos[23]—
120   fastest man of them all, and a born fighter.
Other miseries, and many, we endured there.
Could any mortal man tell the whole story?
Not if you stayed five years or six to hear
how hard it was for the flower of the Akhaians;
you'd go home weary, and the tale untold.
Think: we were there nine years, and we tried everything,
all stratagems against them,
up to the bitter end that Zeus begrudged us.
And as to stratagems, no man would claim
130   Odysseus' gift for those. He had no rivals,
your father, at the tricks of war.

        Your father?
Well, I must say I marvel at the sight of you:
your manner of speech couldn't be more like his;
one would say No; no boy could speak so well.
And all that time at Ilion,° he and I   Troy
were never at odds in council or assembly—
saw things the same way, had one mind between us
in all the good advice we gave the Argives.

---

[23] **Antílokhos:** Great heroes of the Trojan War at Priam's city of Troy are listed here: Aías (or Ajax); Akhilleus, the central hero of *The Iliad*, who withdrew from battle, then returned to avenge the death of his friend Patró-klos; and the clever Odysseus.

140　But when we plundered Priam's town and tower
　　and took to the ships, God scattered the Akhaians.
　　He had a mind to make homecoming hard for them,
　　seeing they would not think straight nor behave,
　　or some would not. So evil days came on them,
　　and she who had been angered,[24]
　　Zeus's dangerous grey-eyed daughter, did it,
　　starting a fight between the sons of Atreus.[25]
　　First they were fools enough to call assembly
　　at sundown, unheard of hour;
150　the Akhaian soldiers turned out, soaked with wine,
　　to hear talk, talk about it from their commanders:
　　Meneláos harangued them to get organized—
　　time to ride home on the sea's broad back, he said;
　　but Agamémnon wouldn't hear of it. He wanted
　　to hold the troops, make sacrifice, a hekatomb,
　　something to pacify Athena's rage.
　　Folly again, to think that he could move her.
　　Will you change the will of the everlasting gods
　　in a night or a day's time?
160　The two men stood there hammering at each other
　　until the army got to its feet with a roar,
　　and no decision, wanting it both ways.
　　That night no one slept well, everyone cursing
　　someone else. Here was the bane from Zeus.
　　At dawn we dragged our ships to the lordly water,
　　stowed aboard all our plunder
　　and the slave women in their low hip girdles.
　　But half the army elected to stay behind
　　with Agamémnon as their corps commander;
170　the other half embarked and pulled away.
　　We made good time, the huge sea smoothed before us,
　　and held our rites when we reached Ténedos,[26]
　　being wild for home. But Zeus, not willing yet,
　　now cruelly set us at odds a second time,
　　and one lot turned, put back in the rolling ships,
　　under command of the subtle captain, Odysseus;
　　their notion was to please Lord Agamémnon.

---

[24] **she . . . angered:** Athena was angry with the Greeks because her shrine had been violated when Cassandra tried to take refuge in it but was raped.　[25] **sons of Atreus:** Agamémnon and Meneláos.　[26] **But half the army . . . Ténedos:** Ténedos was an island off the Trojan coast. The question that troubled the various leaders was whether to hug the shoreline on the way home or take the more direct but dangerous route across the open water.

Not I. I fled, with every ship I had;
I knew fate had some devilment brewing there.
180 Diomêdês[27] roused his company and fled, too,
and later Meneláos, the red-haired captain,
caught up with us at Lesbos,
while we mulled over the long sea route, unsure
whether to lay our course northward of Khios,
keeping the Isle of Psyria off to port,
or inside Khios, coasting by windy Mimas.
We asked for a sign from heaven, and the sign came
to cut across the open sea to Euboia,
and lose no time putting our ills behind us.
190 The wind freshened astern, and the ships ran
before the wind on paths of the deep sea fish,
making Geraistos before dawn. We thanked Poseidon
with many a charred thighbone for that crossing.
On the fourth day, Diomêdês' company
under full sail put in at Argos port,
and I held on for Pylos. The fair wind,
once heaven set it blowing, never failed.

So this, dear child, was how I came from Troy,
and saw no more of the others, lost or saved.
200 But you are welcome to all I've heard since then
at home; I have no reason to keep it from you.
The Myrmidon[28] spearfighters returned, they say,
under the son of lionhearted Akhilleus;
and so did Poias' great son, Philoktêtês.[29]
Idómeneus brought his company back to Krete;
the sea took not a man from him, of all
who lived through the long war.
And even as far away as Ithaka
you've heard of Agamémnon—how he came
210 home, how Aigísthos waited to destroy him
but paid a bitter price for it in the end.
That is a good thing, now, for a man to leave
a son behind him, like the son who punished
Aigísthos for the murder of his great father.

---

[27] **Diomêdês:** One of the bravest chieftains in the Trojan War; his home was Argos. [28] **Myrmidon:** The Myrmidons were Akhilleus's warriors; his son, Neoptólemus, went to Troy to avenge his father's death. [29] **Philoktêtês:** Philoktêtês, who had been left behind on an island because of sickness, arrived at Troy for the conclusion of the war; Idómeneus was king of Krete.

You, too, are tall and well set-up, I see;
be brave, you too, so men in times to come
will speak well of you."

          Then Telémakhos said:
"Nestor, pride of Akhaians, Neleus' son,
220 that was revenge, and far and wide the Akhaians
will tell the tale in song for generations.
I wish the gods would buckle his arms on me!
I'd be revenged for outrage
on my insidious and brazen enemies.
But no such happy lot was given to me
or to my father. Still, I must hold fast."

To this Lord Nestor of Gerênia said:
"My dear young friend, now that you speak of it,
I hear a crowd of suitors for your mother
230 lives with you, uninvited, making trouble.
Now tell me how you take this. Do the people
side against you, hearkening to some oracle?
Who knows, your father might come home someday
alone or backed by troops, and have it out with them.
If grey-eyed Athena loved you
the way she did Odysseus in the old days,
in Troy country, where we all went through so much—
never have I seen the gods help any man
as openly as Athena did your father—
240 well, as I say, if she cared for you that way,
there would be those to quit this marriage game."

But prudently Telémakhos replied:
"I can't think what you say will ever happen, sir.
It is a dazzling hope. But not for me.
It could not be—even if the gods willed it."

At this grey-eyed Athena broke in, saying:
"What strange talk you permit yourself, Telémakhos.
A god could save the man by simply wishing it—
from the farthest shore in the world.
250 If I were he, I should prefer to suffer
years at sea, and then be safe at home;
better that than a knife at my hearthside
where Agamémnon found it—killed by adulterers.
Though as for death, of course all men must suffer it:

the gods may love a man, but they can't help him
when cold death comes to lay him on his bier."

Telémakhos replied:
"Mentor, grievously though we miss my father, why
go on as if that homecoming could happen?
260   You know the gods had settled it already,
years ago, when dark death came for him.
But there is something else I imagine Nestor
can tell us, knowing as he does the ways of men.
They say his rule goes back over three generations,
so long, so old, it seems death cannot touch him.
Nestor, Neleus' son, true sage, say how
did the Lord of the Great Plains, Agamémnon, die?
What was the trick Aigísthos used
to kill the better man? And Meneláos,
270   where was he? Not at Argos[30] in Akhaia,
but blown off course, held up in some far country,
is that what gave the killer nerve to strike?"

Lord Nestor of Gerênia made answer:
"Well, now, my son, I'll tell you the whole story.
You know, yourself, what would have come to pass
if red-haired Meneláos, back from Troy,
had caught Aigísthos in that house alive.
There would have been no burial mound for him,
but dogs and carrion birds to huddle on him
280   in the fields beyond the wall, and not a soul
bewailing him, for the great wrong he committed.
While we were hard-pressed in the war at Troy
he stayed safe inland in the grazing country,
making light talk to win Agamémnon's queen.
But the Lady Klytaimnéstra, in the first days,
rebuffed him, being faithful still;
then, too, she had at hand as her companion
a minstrel Agamémnon left attending her,
charged with her care, when he took ship for Troy.
290   Then came the fated hour when she gave in.
Her lover tricked the poet and marooned him
on a bare island for the seabirds' picking,
and took her home, as he and she desired.

---

[30] **Argos:** A region in the Peloponnese ruled by Agamémnon.

Many thighbones he burned on the gods' altars
and many a woven and golden ornament
hung to bedeck them, in his satisfaction;
he had not thought life held such glory for him.

Now Meneláos and I sailed home together
on friendly terms, from Troy,
but when we came off Sunion Point[31] in Attika,
the ships still running free, Onêtor's son
Phrontis, the steersman of Meneláos' ship,
fell over with a death grip on the tiller:
some unseen arrow from Apollo hit him.
No man handled a ship better than he did
in a high wind and sea, so Meneláos
put down his longing to get on, and landed
to give this man full honor in funeral.
His own luck turned then. Out on the winedark sea
in the murmuring hulls again, he made Cape Malea,[32]
but Zeus who views the wide world sent a gloom
over the ocean, and a howling gale
came on with seas increasing, mountainous,
parting the ships and driving half toward Krete
where the Kydonians live by Iardanos river.
Off Gortyn's coastline in the misty sea there
a reef, a razorback, cuts through the water,
and every westerly piles up a pounding
surf along the left side, going toward Phaistos—
big seas buffeted back by the narrow stone.
They were blown here, and fought in vain for sea room;
the ships kept going in to their destruction,
slammed on the reef. The crews were saved. But now
those five that weathered it got off to southward,
taken by wind and current on to Egypt;
and there Meneláos stayed. He made a fortune
in sea traffic among those distant races,
but while he did so, the foul crime was planned
and carried out in Argos by Aigísthos,
who ruled over golden Mykênai[33] seven years.
Seven long years, with Agamémnon dead,

300

310

320

330

---

[31] **Sunion Point:** The southern tip of Attica, near Athens; their route lies westward around this point toward the Peloponnese.   [32] **Cape Malea:** The southern cape of the Greek mainland; farther south is the island of Krete.
[33] **Mykênai:** Agamémnon's capital city, often used interchangeably by Homer with Argos.

he held the people down, before the vengeance.
But in the eighth year, back from exile in Attika,
Orestês killed the snake who killed his father.
He gave his hateful mother and her soft man
a tomb together, and proclaimed the funeral day
a festal day for all the Argive people.
That day Lord Meneláos of the great war cry
made port with all the gold his ships could carry.
340 And this should give you pause, my son:
don't stay too long away from home, leaving
your treasure there, and brazen suitors near;
they'll squander all you have or take it from you,
and then how will your journey serve?
I urge you, though, to call on Meneláos,
he being but lately home from distant parts
in the wide world. A man could well despair
of getting home at all, if the winds blew him
over the Great South Sea — that weary waste,
350 even the wintering birds delay
one winter more before the northward crossing.
Well, take your ship and crew and go by water,
or if you'd rather go by land, here are
horses, a car,° and my own sons for company   *chariot*
as far as the ancient land of Lakedaimon°   *Sparta*
and Meneláos, the red-haired captain there.
Ask him with courtesy, and in his wisdom
he will tell you history and no lies."

While Nestor talked, the sun went down the sky
360 and gloom came on the land,
and now the grey-eyed goddess Athena said:
"Sir, this is all most welcome and to the point,
but why not slice the bulls' tongues now, and mix
libations for Poseidon and the gods?
Then we can all retire; high time we did;
the light is going under the dark world's rim,
better not linger at the sacred feast."

When Zeus's daughter spoke, they turned to listen,
and soon the squires brought water for their hands,
370 while stewards filled the winebowls and poured out
a fresh cup full for every man. The company
stood up to fling the tongues and a shower of wine
over the flames, then drank their thirst away.
Now finally Telémakhos and Athena

bestirred themselves, turning away to the ship,
but Nestor put a hand on each, and said:
"Now Zeus forbid, and the other gods as well,
that you should spend the night on board, and leave me
as though I were some pauper without a stitch,
380 no blankets in his house, no piles of rugs,
no sleeping soft for host or guest! Far from it!
I have all these, blankets and deep-piled rugs,
and while I live the only son of Odysseus
will never make his bed on a ship's deck—
no, not while sons of mine are left at home
to welcome any guest who comes to us."

The grey-eyed goddess Athena answered him:
"You are very kind, sir, and Telémakhos
should do as you ask. That is the best thing.
390 He will go with you, and will spend the night
under your roof. But I must join our ship
and talk to the crew, to keep their spirits up,
since I'm the only senior in the company.
The rest are boys who shipped for friendship's sake,
no older than Telémakhos, any of them.
Let me sleep out, then, by the black hull's side,
this night at least. At daybreak I'll be off
to see the Kaukonians[34] about a debt they owe me,
an old one and no trifle. As for your guest,
400 send him off in a car, with one of your sons,
and give him thoroughbreds, a racing team."

Even as she spoke, Athena left them—seeming
a seahawk, in a clap of wings,—and all
the Akhaians of Pylos town looked up astounded.
Awed then by what his eyes had seen, the old man
took Telémakhos' hand and said warmly:
"My dear child, I can have no fears for you,
no doubt about your conduct or your heart,
if, at your age, the gods are your companions.
410 Here we had someone from Olympos—clearly
the glorious daughter of Zeus, his third child,
who held your father dear among the Argives.
O, Lady, hear me! Grant an illustrious name

---

[34] **the Kaukonians:** A tribe southwest of Pylos.

to me and to my children and my dear wife!
A noble heifer shall be yours in sacrifice,
one that no man has ever yoked or driven;
my gift to you—her horns all sheathed in gold."

So he ended, praying; and Athena heard him.
Then Nestor of Gerênia led them all,
420 his sons and sons-in-law, to his great house;
and in they went to the famous hall of Nestor,
taking their seats on thrones and easy chairs,
while the old man mixed water in a wine bowl
with sweet red wine, mellowed eleven years
before his housekeeper uncapped the jar.
He mixed and poured his offering, repeating
prayers to Athena, daughter of royal Zeus.
The others made libation, and drank deep,
then all the company went to their quarters,
430 and Nestor of Gerênia showed Telémakhos
under the echoing eastern entrance hall
to a fine bed near the bed of Peisístratos,
captain of spearmen, his unmarried son.
Then he lay down in his own inner chamber
where his dear faithful wife had smoothed his bed.

When Dawn spread out her finger tips of rose,
Lord Nestor of Gerênia, charioteer,
left his room for a throne of polished stone,
white and gleaming as though with oil, that stood
440 before the main gate of the palace; Neleus here
had sat before him—masterful in kingship,
Neleus, long ago a prey to death, gone down
to the night of the underworld.
So Nestor held his throne and scepter now,
lord of the western approaches to Akhaia.
And presently his sons came out to join him,
leaving the palace: Ekhéphron and Stratíos,
Perseus and Arêtós and Thrasymêdês,
and after them the prince Peisístratos,
450 bringing Telémakhos along with him.
Seeing all present, the old lord Nestor said:
"Dear sons, here is my wish, and do it briskly
to please the gods, Athena first of all,
my guest in daylight at our holy feast.
One of you must go for a young heifer

and have the cowherd lead her from the pasture.
Another call on Lord Telémakhos' ship
to invite his crewmen, leaving two behind;
and someone else again send for the goldsmith,
460 Laerkês, to gild the horns.
The rest stay here together. Tell the servants
a ritual feast will be prepared in hall.
Tell them to bring seats, firewood and fresh water."

Before he finished, they were about these errands.
The heifer came from pasture,
the crewmen of Telémakhos from the ship,
the smith arrived, bearing the tools of his trade—
hammer and anvil, and the precision tongs
he handled fiery gold with,—and Athena
470 came as a god comes, numinous, to the rites.

The smith now gloved each horn in a pure foil
beaten out of the gold that Nestor gave him—
a glory and delight for the goddess' eyes—
while Ekhéphron and Stratíos held the horns.
Arêtós brought clear lustral water
in a bowl quivering with fresh-cut flowers,
a basket of barley in his other hand.
Thrasymêdês who could stand his ground in war,
stood ready, with a sharp two-bladed axe,
480 for the stroke of sacrifice, and Perseus
held a bowl for the blood. And now Nestor,
strewing the barley grains, and water drops,
pronounced his invocation to Athena
and burned a pinch of bristles from the victim.
When prayers were said and all the grain was scattered
great-hearted Thrasymêdês in a flash
swung the axe, at one blow cutting through
the neck tendons. The heifer's spirit failed.
Then all the women gave a wail of joy—
490 daughters, daughters-in-law, and the Lady Eurydíkê,
Klyménos' eldest daughter. But the men
still held the heifer, shored her up
from the wide earth where the living go their ways,
until Peisístratos cut her throat across,
the black blood ran, and life ebbed from her marrow.
The carcass now sank down, and they disjointed
shoulder and thigh bone, wrapping them in fat,

two layers, folded, with raw strips of flesh.
These offerings Nestor burned on the split-wood fire
500   and moistened with red wine. His sons took up
five-tined forks in their hands, while the altar flame
ate through the bones, and bits of tripe went round.
Then came the carving of the quarters, and they spitted
morsels of lean meat on the long sharp tines
and broiled them at arm's length upon the fire.

Polykástê, a fair girl, Nestor's youngest,
had meanwhile given a bath to Telémakhos—
bathing him first, then rubbing him with oil.
She held fine clothes and a cloak to put around him
510   when he came godlike from the bathing place;
then out he went to take his place with Nestor.
When the best cuts were broiled and off the spits,
they all sat down to banquet. Gentle squires
kept every golden wine cup brimming full.
And so they feasted to their heart's content,
until the prince of charioteers commanded:
"Sons, harness the blood mares for Telémakhos;
hitch up the car, and let him take the road."

They swung out smartly to do the work, and hooked
520   the handsome horses to a chariot shaft.
The mistress of the stores brought up provisions
of bread and wine, with victuals fit for kings,
and Telémakhos stepped up on the painted car.
Just at his elbow stood Peisístratos,
captain of spearmen, reins in hand. He gave
a flick to the horses, and with streaming manes
they ran for the open country. The tall town
of Pylos sank behind them in the distance,
as all day long they kept the harness shaking.

530   The sun was low and shadows crossed the lanes
when they arrived at Phêrai.[35] There Dióklês,
son of Ortílokhos whom Alpheios fathered,
welcomed the young men, and they slept the night.
But up when the young Dawn's finger tips of rose

---

[35] **Phêrai:** Uncertain location; perhaps the modern Calamata.

opened in the east, they hitched the team
once more to the painted car,
and steered out eastward through the echoing gate,
whipping their fresh horses into a run.
That day they made the grainlands of Lakedaimon,
540 where, as the horses held to a fast clip,
they kept on to their journey's end. Behind them
the sun went down and all the roads grew dark.

BOOK 4
THE RED-HAIRED KING AND HIS LADY

By vales and sharp ravines in Lakedaimon
the travellers drove to Meneláos' mansion,
and found him at a double wedding feast
for son and daughter.

　　　　　　　　Long ago at Troy
he pledged her to the heir[36] of great Akhilleus,
breaker of men — a match the gods had ripened;
so he must send her with a chariot train
to the town and glory of the Myrmidons.
10 And that day, too, he brought Alektor's daughter
to marry his tall scion, Megapénthês,
born of a slave girl during the long war —
for the gods had never after granted Helen
a child to bring into the sunlit world
after the first, rose-lipped Hermionê,
a girl like the pale-gold goddess Aphroditê.

Down the great hall in happiness they feasted,
neighbors of Meneláos, and his kin,
for whom a holy minstrel harped and sang;
20 and two lithe tumblers moved out on the song
with spins and handsprings through the company.
Now when Telémakhos and Nestor's son
pulled up their horses at the main gate,
one of the king's companions in arms, Eteóneus,
going outside, caught sight of them. He turned
and passed through court and hall to tell the master,

---

[36] **the heir:** Neoptólemos, son of Akhilleus.

stepping up close to get his ear. Said he:
"Two men are here—two strangers, Meneláos,
but nobly born Akhaians, they appear.

30 What do you say, shall we unhitch their team,
or send them on to someone free to receive them?"

The red-haired captain answered him in anger:
"You were no idiot before, Eteóneus,
but here you are talking like a child of ten.
Could we have made it home again—and Zeus
give us no more hard roving!—if other men
had never fed us, given us lodging?
                              Bring
these men to be our guests: unhitch their team!"

40 Eteóneus left the long room like an arrow,
calling equerries after him, on the run.
Outside, they freed the sweating team from harness,
stabled the horses, tied them up, and showered
bushels of wheat and barley in the feed box;
then leaned the chariot pole
against the gleaming entry wall of stone
and took the guests in. What a brilliant place
that mansion of the great prince seemed to them!
A-glitter everywhere, as though with fiery

50 points of sunlight, lusters of the moon.
The young men gazed in joy before they entered
into a room of polished tubs to bathe.
Maidservants gave them baths, anointed them,
held out fresh tunics, cloaked them warm; and soon
they took tall thrones beside the son of Atreus.
Here a maid tipped out water for their hands
from a golden pitcher into a silver bowl,
and set a polished table near at hand;
the larder mistress with her tray of loaves

60 and savories came, dispensing all her best,
and then a carver heaped their platters high
with various meats, and put down cups of gold.
Now said the red-haired captain, Meneláos,
gesturing:
                "Welcome; and fall to; in time,
when you have supped, we hope to hear your names,
forbears and families—in your case, it seems,

no anonymities, but lordly men.
Lads like yourselves are not base born."

70   At this,
he lifted in his own hands the king's portion,
a chine of beef, and set it down before them.
Seeing all ready then, they took their dinner;
but when they had feasted well,
Telémakhos could not keep still, but whispered,
his head bent close, so the others might not hear:
"My dear friend, can you believe your eyes? —
the murmuring hall, how luminous it is
with bronze, gold, amber, silver, and ivory!
80 This is the way the court of Zeus must be,
inside, upon Olympos. What a wonder!"

But splendid Meneláos had overheard him
and spoke out on the instant to them both:
"Young friends, no mortal man can vie with Zeus.
His home and all his treasures are for ever.
But as for men, it may well be that few
have more than I. How painfully I wandered
before I brought it home! Seven years at sea,
Kypros, Phoinikia, Egypt, and still farther
90 among the sun-burnt races.
I saw the men of Sidon and Arabia
and Libya, too, where lambs are horned at birth.
In every year they have three lambing seasons,
so no man, chief or shepherd, ever goes
hungry for want of mutton, cheese, or milk —
all year at milking time there are fresh ewes.
But while I made my fortune on those travels
a stranger killed my brother, in cold blood, —
tricked blind, caught in the web of his deadly queen.
100 What pleasure can I take, then, being lord
over these costly things?
You must have heard your fathers tell my story,
whoever your fathers are; you must know of my life,
the anguish I once had, and the great house
full of my treasure, left in desolation.
How gladly I should live one third as rich
to have my friends back safe at home! — my friends
who died on Troy's wide seaboard, far

from the grazing lands of Argos.
110   But as things are, nothing but grief is left me
for those companions. While I sit at home
sometimes hot tears come, and I revel in them,
or stop before the surfeit makes me shiver.
And there is one I miss more than the other
dead I mourn for; sleep and food alike
grow hateful when I think of him. No soldier
took on so much, went through so much, as Odysseus.
That seems to have been his destiny, and this mine—
to feel each day the emptiness of his absence,
120   ignorant, even, whether he lived or died.
How his old father and his quiet wife,
Penélopê, must miss him still!
And Telémakhos, whom he left as a new-born child."

Now hearing these things said, the boy's heart rose
in a long pang for his father, and he wept,
holding his purple mantle with both hands
before his eyes. Meneláos knew him now,
and so fell silent with uncertainty
whether to let him speak and name his father
130   in his own time, or to inquire, and prompt him.
And while he pondered, Helen came
out of her scented chamber, a moving grace
like Artemis,[37] straight as a shaft of gold.
Beside her came Adrastê, to place her armchair,
Alkippê, with a rug of downy wool,
and Phylo, bringing a silver basket, once
given by Alkandrê, the wife of Pólybos,
in the treasure city, Thebes of distant Egypt.
He gave two silver bathtubs to Meneláos
140   and a pair of tripods, with ten pure gold bars,
and she, then, made these beautiful gifts to Helen:
a golden distaff, and the silver basket
rimmed in hammered gold, with wheels to run on.
So Phylo rolled it in to stand beside her,
heaped with fine spun stuff, and cradled on it
the distaff swathed in dusky violet wool.
Reclining in her light chair with its footrest,
Helen gazed at her husband and demanded:
"Meneláos, my lord, have we yet heard

---

[37] **Artemis:** Virgin goddess of the hunt and childbirth.

150 our new guests introduce themselves? Shall I
     dissemble what I feel? No, I must say it.
     Never, anywhere, have I seen so great a likeness
     in man or woman—but it is truly strange!
     This boy must be the son of Odysseus,
     Telémakhos, the child he left at home
     that year the Akhaian host made war on Troy—
     daring all for the wanton that I was."

     And the red-haired captain, Meneláos, answered:
     "My dear, I see the likeness as well as you do.
160 Odysseus' hands and feet were like this boy's;
     his head, and hair, and the glinting of his eyes.
     Not only that, but when I spoke, just now,
     of Odysseus' years of toil on my behalf
     and all he had to endure—the boy broke down
     and wept into his cloak."

                         Now Nestor's son,
     Peisístratos, spoke up in answer to him:
     "My lord marshal, Meneláos, son of Atreus,
     this is that hero's son as you surmise,
170 but he is gentle, and would be ashamed
     to clamor for attention before your grace
     whose words have been so moving to us both.
     Nestor, Lord of Gerênia, sent me with him
     as guide and escort; he had wished to see you,
     to be advised by you or assisted somehow.
     A father far from home means difficulty
     for an only son, with no one else to help him;
     so with Telémakhos:
     his father left the house without defenders."

180 The king with flaming hair now spoke again:
     "His son, in my house! How I loved the man,
     And how he fought through hardship for my sake!
     I swore I'd cherish him above all others
     if Zeus, who views the wide world, gave us passage
     homeward across the sea in the fast ships.
     I would have settled him in Argos, brought him
     over with herds and household out of Ithaka,
     his child and all his people. I could have cleaned out
     one of my towns to be his new domain.
190 And so we might have been together often
     in feasts and entertainments, never parted

till the dark mist of death lapped over one of us.
But God himself must have been envious,
to batter the bruised man so that he alone
should fail in his return."

A twinging ache of grief rose up in everyone,
and Helen of Argos wept, the daughter of Zeus,[38]
Telémakhos and Meneláos wept,
and tears came to the eyes of Nestor's son —
200   remembering, for his part, Antílokhos,
whom the son of shining Dawn had killed in battle.
But thinking of that brother, he broke out:
"O son of Atreus, when we spoke of you
at home, and asked about you, my old father
would say you have the clearest mind of all.
If it is not too much to ask, then, let us not
weep away these hours after supper;
I feel we should not: Dawn will soon be here!
You understand, I would not grudge a man
210   right mourning when he comes to death and doom:
what else can one bestow on the poor dead? —
a lock of hair sheared, and a tear let fall.
For that matter, I, too,
lost someone in the war at Troy — my brother,
and no mean soldier, whom you must have known,
although I never did, — Antílokhos.
He ranked high as a runner and fighting man."

The red-haired captain Meneláos answered:
"My lad, what you have said is only sensible,
220   and you did well to speak. Yes, that was worthy
a wise man and an older man than you are:
you speak for all the world like Nestor's son.
How easily one can tell the man whose father
had true felicity, marrying and begetting!
And that was true of Nestor, all his days,
down to his sleek old age in peace at home,
with clever sons, good spearmen into the bargain.
Come, we'll shake off this mourning mood of ours
and think of supper. Let the men at arms

---

[38] **Helen . . . daughter of Zeus:** Helen's mother was a mortal, Lêda, who was seduced by Zeus in the form of a swan.

230   rinse our hands again! There will be time
       for a long talk with Telémakhos in the morning."

The hero Meneláos' companion in arms,
Asphalion, poured water for their hands,
and once again they touched the food before them.
But now it entered Helen's mind
to drop into the wine that they were drinking
an anodyne, mild magic of forgetfulness.
Whoever drank this mixture in the wine bowl
would be incapable of tears that day—
240   though he should lose mother and father both,
       or see, with his own eyes, a son or brother
       mauled by weapons of bronze at his own gate.
       The opiate of Zeus's daughter bore
       this canny power. It had been supplied her
       by Polydamna, mistress of Lord Thôn,
       in Egypt, where the rich plantations grow
       herbs of all kinds, maleficent and healthful;
       and no one else knows medicine as they do,
       Egyptian heirs of Paian,[39] the healing god.
250   She drugged the wine, then, had it served, and said—
       taking again her part in the conversation—
       "O Meneláos, Atreus' royal son,
       and you that are great heroes' sons, you know
       how Zeus gives all of us in turn
       good luck and bad luck, being all powerful.
       So take refreshment, take your ease in hall,
       and cheer the time with stories. I'll begin.
       Not that I think of naming, far less telling,
       every feat of that rugged man, Odysseus,
260   but here is something that he dared to do
       at Troy, where you Akhaians endured the war.
       He had, first, given himself an outrageous beating
       and thrown some rags on—like a household slave—
       then slipped into that city of wide lanes
       among his enemies. So changed, he looked
       as never before upon the Akhaian beachhead,
       but like a beggar, merged in the townspeople;

---

[39] **Egyptian heirs of Paian:** *Paian* means "healer" and is another name for Apollo and Apollo's son Asclepius, god of healing. Egyptians were famous for their knowledge of herbs and drugs.

and no one there remarked him. But I knew him—
even as he was, I knew him,
270 and questioned him. How shrewdly he put me off!
But in the end I bathed him and anointed him,
put a fresh cloak around him, and swore an oath
not to give him away as Odysseus to the Trojans,
till he got back to camp where the long ships lay.
He spoke up then, and told me
all about the Akhaians, and their plans—
then sworded many Trojans through the body
on his way out with what he learned of theirs.
The Trojan women raised a cry—but my heart
280 sang—for I had come round, long before,
to dreams of sailing home, and I repented
the mad day Aphrodítê
drew me away from my dear fatherland,
forsaking all—child, bridal bed, and husband—
a man without defect in form or mind."

Replied the red-haired captain, Meneláos:
"An excellent tale, my dear, and most becoming.
In my life I have met, in many countries,
foresight and wit in many first rate men,
290 but never have I seen one like Odysseus
for steadiness and a stout heart. Here, for instance,
is what he did—had the cold nerve to do—
inside the hollow horse,[40] where we were waiting,
picked men all of us, for the Trojan slaughter,
when all of a sudden, you came by—I dare say
drawn by some superhuman
power that planned an exploit for the Trojans;
and Deïphobos,[41] that handsome man, came with you.
Three times you walked around it, patting it everywhere,
300 and called by name the flower of our fighters,
making your voice sound like their wives, calling.
Diomêdês and I crouched in the center
along with Odysseus; we could hear you plainly;
and listening, we two were swept
by waves of longing—to reply, or go.
Odysseus fought us down, despite our craving,

---

[40] **inside the hollow horse:** Appearing to have abandoned the fight against Troy, a group of warriors hid inside a wooden horse that the Trojans dragged inside the walls of their city, precipitating its downfall.   [41] **Deïphobos:** A Trojan prince married to Helen after Paris's death.

and all the Akhaians kept their lips shut tight,
all but Antiklos. Desire moved his throat
to hail you, but Odysseus' great hands clamped
310 over his jaws, and held. So he saved us all,
till Pallas Athena led you away at last."

Then clear-headed Telémakhos addressed him:
"My lord marshal, Meneláos, son of Atreus,
all the more pity, since these valors
could not defend him from annihilation—
not if his heart were iron in his breast.
But will you not dismiss us for the night now?
Sweet sleep will be a pleasure, drifting over us."

He said no more, but Helen called the maids
320 and sent them to make beds, with purple rugs
piled up, and sheets outspread, and fleecy
coverlets, in the porch inside the gate.
The girls went out with torches in their hands,
and presently a squire led the guests—
Telémakhos and Nestor's radiant son—
under the entrance colonnade, to bed.
Then deep in the great mansion, in his chamber,
Meneláos went to rest, and Helen,
queenly in her long gown, lay beside him.

330 When the young Dawn with finger tips of rose
made heaven bright, the deep-lunged man of battle
stood up, pulled on his tunic and his mantle,
slung on a swordbelt and a new edged sword,
tied his smooth feet into fine rawhide sandals
and left his room, a god's brilliance upon him.
He sat down by Telémakhos, asking gently:
"Telémakhos, why did you come, sir, riding
the sea's broad back to reach old Lakedaimon?
A public errand or private? Why, precisely?"

340 Telémakhos replied:
"My lord marshal Meneláos, son of Atreus,
I came to hear what news you had of Father.
My house, my good estates are being ruined.
Each day my mother's bullying suitors come
to slaughter flocks of mine and my black cattle;
enemies crowd our home. And this is why
I come to you for news of him who owned it.

Tell me of his death, sir, if perhaps
you witnessed it, or have heard some wanderer
350 tell the tale. The man was born for trouble.
Spare me no part for kindness' sake; be harsh;
but put the scene before me as you saw it.
If ever Odysseus my noble father
served you by promise kept or work accomplished
in the land of Troy, where you Akhaians suffered,
recall those things for me the way they were."

Stirred now to anger, Meneláos said:
"Intolerable—that soft men, as those are,
should think to lie in that great captain's bed.
360 Fawns in a lion's lair! As if a doe
put down her litter of sucklings there, while she
quested a glen or cropped some grassy hollow.
Ha! Then the lord returns to his own bed
and deals out wretched doom on both alike.
So will Odysseus deal out doom on these.
O Father Zeus, Athena, and Apollo!
I pray he comes as once he was, in Lesbos,
when he stood up to wrestle Philomeleidês—
champion and Island King—
370 and smashed him down. How the Akhaians cheered!
If only that Odysseus met the suitors,
they'd have their consummation, a cold bed!
Now for your questions, let me come to the point.
I would not misreport it for you; let me
tell you what the Ancient of the Sea,
who is infallible, said to me—every word.

During my first try at a passage homeward
the gods detained me, tied me down to Egypt—
for I had been too scant in hekatombs,
380 and gods will have the rules each time remembered.
There is an island washed by the open sea
lying off Nile mouth—seamen call it Pharos—
distant a day's sail in a clean hull
with a brisk land breeze behind. It has a harbor,
a sheltered bay, where shipmasters
take on dark water for the outward voyage.
Here the gods held me twenty days becalmed.
No winds came up, seaward escorting winds
for ships that ride the sea's broad back, and so
390 my stores and men were used up; we were failing

had not one goddess intervened in pity—
Eidothea, daughter of Proteus,
the Ancient of the Sea. How I distressed her!
I had been walking out alone that day—
my sailors, thin-bellied from the long fast,
were off with fish hooks, angling on the shore—
then she appeared to me, and her voice sang:
'What fool is here, what drooping dunce of dreams?
Or can it be, friend, that you love to suffer?

400 How can you linger on this island, aimless
and shiftless, while your people waste away?'

To this I quickly answered:
                            'Let me tell you,
goddess, whatever goddess you may be,
these doldrums are no will of mine. I take it
the gods who own broad heaven are offended.
Why don't you tell me—since the gods know everything—
who has me pinned down here?
How am I going to make my voyage home?'

410 Now she replied in her immortal beauty:
'I'll put it for you clearly as may be, friend.
The Ancient of the Salt Sea haunts this place,
immortal Proteus of Egypt; all the deeps
are known to him; he serves under Poseidon,
and is, they say, my father.
If you could take him by surprise and hold him,
he'd give you course and distance for your sailing
homeward across the cold fish-breeding sea.
And should you wish it, noble friend, he'd tell you

420 all that occurred at home, both good and evil,
while you were gone so long and hard a journey.'

To this I said:
                'But you, now—you must tell me
how I can trap this venerable sea-god.
He will elude me if he takes alarm;
no man—god knows—can quell a god with ease.'

That fairest of unearthly nymphs replied:
'I'll tell you this, too, clearly as may be.
When the sun hangs at high noon in heaven,

430 the Ancient glides ashore under the Westwind,
hidden by shivering glooms on the clear water,

and rests in caverns hollowed by the sea.
There flippered seals, brine children, shining come
from silvery foam in crowds to lie around him,
exhaling rankness from the deep sea floor.
Tomorrow dawn I'll take you to those caves
and bed you down there. Choose three officers
for company—brave men they had better be—
the old one has strange powers, I must tell you.
440   He goes amid the seals to check their number,
and when he sees them all, and counts them all,
he lies down like a shepherd with his flock.
Here is your opportunity: at this point
gather yourselves, with all your heart and strength,
and tackle him before he bursts away.
He'll make you fight—for he can take the forms
of all the beasts, and water, and blinding fire;
but you must hold on, even so, and crush him
until he breaks the silence. When he does,
450   he will be in that shape you saw asleep.
Relax your grip, then, set the Ancient free,
and put your questions, hero:
Who is the god so hostile to you,
and how will you go home on the fish-cold sea.'

At this she dove under a swell and left me.
Back to the ships in the sandy cove I went,
my heart within me like a high surf running;
but there I joined my men once more
at supper, as the sacred Night came on,
460   and slept at last beside the lapping water.
When Dawn spread out her finger tips of rose
I started, by the sea's wide level ways,
praying the gods for help, and took along
three lads I counted on in any fight.
Meanwhile the nereid° swam from the lap of Ocean   sea nymph
laden with four sealskins, new flayed
for the hoax she thought of playing on her father.
In the sand she scooped out hollows for our bodies
and sat down, waiting. We came close to touch her,
470   and, bedding us, she threw the sealskins over us—
a strong disguise; oh, yes, terribly strong
as I recall the stench of those damned seals.
Would any man lie snug with a sea monster?
But here the nymph, again, came to our rescue,
dabbing ambrosia under each man's nose—

a perfume drowning out the bestial odor.
So there we lay with beating hearts all morning
while seals came shoreward out of ripples, jostling
to take their places, flopping on the sand.
480   At noon the Ancient issued from the sea
and held inspection, counting off the sea-beasts.
We were the first he numbered; he went by,
detecting nothing. When at last he slept
we gave a battlecry and plunged for him,
locking our hands behind him. But the old one's
tricks were not knocked out of him; far from it.
First he took on a whiskered lion's shape,
a serpent then; a leopard; a great boar;
then sousing water; then a tall green tree.
490   Still we hung on, by hook or crook, through everything,
until the Ancient saw defeat, and grimly
opened his lips to ask me:
                              'Son of Atreus,
who counselled you to this? A god: what god?
Set a trap for me, overpower me—why?'

He bit it off, then, and I answered:
                              'Old one,
you know the reason—why feign not to know?
High and dry so long upon this island
500   I'm at my wits' end, and my heart is sore.
You gods know everything; now you can tell me:
which of the immortals chained me here?
And how will I get home on the fish-cold sea?'

He made reply at once:
                              'You should have paid
honor to Zeus and the other gods, performing
a proper sacrifice before embarking:
that was your short way home on the winedark sea.
You may not see your friends, your own fine house,
510   or enter your own land again,
unless you first remount the Nile in flood
and pay your hekatomb to the gods of heaven.
Then, and then only,
the gods will grant the passage you desire.'

Ah, how my heart sank, hearing this—
hearing him send me back on the cloudy sea
in my own track, the long hard way of Egypt.

Nevertheless, I answered him and said:
'Ancient, I shall do all as you command.
520 But tell me, now, the others—
had they a safe return, all those Akhaians
who stayed behind when Nestor and I left Troy?
Or were there any lost at sea—what bitterness!—
any who died in camp, after the war?'

To this he said:
                'For you to know these things
goes beyond all necessity, Meneláos.
Why must you ask?—you should not know my mind,
and you will grieve to learn it, I can tell you.
530 Many there were who died, many remain,
but two high officers alone were lost—
on the passage home, I mean; you saw the war.
One is alive, a castaway at sea;
the other, Aias,[42] perished with all hands—
though first Poseidon landed him on Gyrai
promontory, and saved him from the ocean.
Despite Athena's hate, he had lived on,
but the great sinner in his insolence
yelled that the gods' will and the sea were beaten,
540 and this loud brag came to Poseidon's ears.
He swung the trident in his massive hands
and in one shock from top to bottom split
that promontory, toppling into the sea
the fragment where the great fool sat.
So the vast ocean had its will with Aias,
drunk in the end on salt spume as he drowned.
Meanwhile your brother° left that doom astern   Agamémnon
in his decked ships—the Lady Hera[43] saved him;
but as he came round Malea
550 a fresh squall caught him, bearing him away
over the cold sea, groaning in disgust,
to the Land's End of Argos, where Thyestês
lived in the days of old, and then his son,
Aigísthos. Now, again, return seemed easy:
the high gods wound the wind into the east,
and back he sailed, this time to his own coast.

---

[42] **Aias:** The Lesser Aias who raped Kassandra in Athena's temple.   [43] **Lady Hêra:** Wife and sister of Zeus.

He went ashore and kissed the earth in joy,
hot tears blinding his eyes at sight of home.
But there were eyes that watched him from a height—
560 a lookout, paid two bars of gold to keep
vigil the year round for Aigísthos' sake,
that he should be forewarned, and Agamémnon's
furious valor sleep unroused.
Now this man with his news ran to the tyrant,
who made his crooked arrangements in a flash,
stationed picked men at arms, a score of men
in hiding; set a feast in the next room;
then he went out with chariots and horses
to hail the king and welcome him to evil.
570 He led him in to banquet, all serene,
and killed him, like an ox felled at the trough;
and not a man of either company
survived that ambush in Aigísthos' house.'

Before the end my heart was broken down.
I slumped on the trampled sand and cried aloud,
caring no more for life or the light of day,
and rolled there weeping, till my tears were spent.
Then the unerring Ancient said at last:
'No more, no more; how long must you persist?
580 Nothing is gained by grieving so. How soon
can you return to Argos? You may take him
alive there still—or else meanwhile Orestês
will have despatched him. You'll attend the feast.'

At this my heart revived, and I recovered
the self command to question him once more:
'Of two companions now I know. The third?
Tell me his name, the one marooned at sea;
living, you say, or dead? Even in pain
I wish to hear.'

590   And this is all he answered:
'Laërtês' son, whose home is Ithaka.
I saw him weeping, weeping on an island.
The nymph Kalypso has him, in her hall.
No means of faring home are left him now;
no ship with oars, and no ship's company
to pull him on the broad back of the sea.
As to your own destiny, prince Meneláos,

you shall not die in the bluegrass land of Argos;
rather the gods intend you for Elysion[44]
600 with golden Rhadamanthos at the world's end,
where all existence is a dream of ease.
Snowfall is never known there, neither long
frost of winter, nor torrential rain,
but only mild and lulling airs from Ocean
bearing refreshment for the souls of men—
the West Wind always blowing.
                                        For the gods
hold you, as Helen's lord, a son of Zeus.'

At this he dove under a swell and left me,
610 and I went back to the ship with my companions,
feeling my heart's blood in me running high;
but in the long hull's shadow, near the sea,
we supped again as sacred Night came on
and slept at last beside the lapping water.

When Dawn spread out her finger tips of rose,
in first light we launched on the courtly breakers,
setting up masts and yards in the well-found ships;
went all on board, and braced on planks athwart
oarsmen in line dipped oars in the grey sea.
620 Soon I drew in to the great stream[45] fed by heaven
and, laying by, slew bulls in the proper number,
until the immortal gods were thus appeased;
then heaped a death mound on that shore against
all-quenching time for Agamémnon's honor,
and put to sea once more. The gods sent down
a sternwind for a racing passage homeward.

So ends the story. Now you must stay with me
and be my guest eleven or twelve days more.
I'll send you on your way with gifts, and fine ones:
630 three chariot horses, and a polished car;
a hammered cup, too, so that all your days,

---

[44] **Elysion:** A portion of the afterworld located on the western edge of the world and reserved for heroes; ruled by Rhadamanthos, a son of Zeus.   [45] **the great stream:** The river Nile was believed to have its source in the heavens; it was therefore sacred and related to Zeus.

tipping the red wine for the deathless gods,
you will remember me."

Telémakhos answered:
"Lord, son of Atreus, no, you must not keep me.
Not that a year with you would be too long:
I never could be homesick here—I find
your tales and all you say so marvellous.
But time hangs heavy on my shipmates' hands
640   at holy Pylos, if you make me stay.
As for your gift, now, let it be some keepsake.
Horses I cannot take to Ithaka;
let me bestow them back on you, to serve
your glory here. My lord, you rule wide country,
rolling and rich with clover, galingale
and all the grains: red wheat and hoary barley.
At home we have no level runs or meadows,
but highland, goat land—prettier than plains, though.
Grasses, and pasture land, are hard to come by
650   upon the islands tilted in the sea,
and Ithaka is the island of them all."

At this the deep-lunged man of battle smiled.
Then he said kindly, patting the boy's hand:
"You come of good stock, lad. That was well spoken.
I'll change the gift, then—as indeed I can.
Let me see what is costliest and most beautiful
of all the precious things my house contains:
a wine bowl, mixing bowl, all wrought of silver,
but rimmed with hammered gold. Let this be yours.
660   It is Hephaistos'[46] work, given me by Phaidimos,
captain and king of Sidon. He received me
during my travels. Let it be yours, I say."

This was their discourse on that morning. Meanwhile
guests were arriving at the great lord's house,
bringing their sheep, and wine, the ease of men,
with loaves their comely kerchiefed women sent,
to make a feast in hall.
At that same hour,

---

[46] **Hephaistos:** The god of fire and metallurgy.

before the distant manor of Odysseus,
670 the suitors were competing at the discus throw
and javelin, on a measured field they used,
arrogant lords at play. The two best men,
Antínoös and Eurýmakhos, presided.
Now Phronios' son, Noêmon, came to see them
with a question for Antínoös. He said:
"Do any of us know, or not, Antínoös,
what day Telémakhos will be home from Pylos?
He took my ship, but now I need it back
to make a cruise to Elis, where the plains are.
680 I have a dozen mares at pasture there
with mule colts yet unweaned. My notion is
to bring one home and break him in for labor."

His first words made them stare—for they knew well
Telémakhos could not have gone to Pylos,
but inland with his flocks, or to the swineherd.
Eupeithês' son, Antínoös, quickly answered:
"Tell the story straight. He sailed? Who joined him—
a crew he picked up here in Ithaka,
or his own slaves? He might have done it that way.
690 And will you make it clear
whether he took the ship against your will?
Did he ask for it, did you lend it to him?"

Now said the son of Phronios in reply:
"Lent it to him, and freely. Who would not,
when a prince of that house asked for it, in trouble?
Hard to refuse the favor, it seems to me.
As for his crew, the best men on the island,
after ourselves, went with him. Mentor I noted
going aboard—or a god who looked like Mentor.
700 The strange thing is, I saw Lord Mentor here
in the first light yesterday—although he sailed
five days ago for Pylos."

                    Turning away,
Noêmon took the path to his father's house,
leaving the two men there, baffled and hostile.
They called the rest in from the playing field
and made them all sit down, so that Antínoös
could speak out from the stormcloud of his heart,
swollen with anger; and his eyes blazed:

710   "A bad business. Telémakhos had the gall
      to make that crossing, though we said he could not.
      So the young cub rounds up a first rate crew
      in spite of all our crowd, and puts to sea.
      What devilment will he be up to next time?—
      Zeus blast the life out of him before he's grown!
      Just give me a fast ship and twenty men;
      I'll intercept him, board him in the strait
      between the crags of Samê and this island.
      He'll find his sea adventure after his father
720   swamping work in the end!"

                        They all cried "Aye!"
      and "After him!" and trailed back to the manor.

      Now not much time went by before Penélopê
      learned what was afoot among the suitors.
      Medôn the crier told her. He had been
      outside the wall, and heard them in the court
      conspiring. Into the house and up the stairs
      he ran to her with his news upon his tongue—
      but at the door Penélopê met him, crying:
730   "Why have they sent you up here now? To tell
      the maids of King Odysseus—'Leave your spinning:
      Time to go down and slave to feed those men'?
      I wish this were the last time they came feasting,
      courting me or consorting here! The last!
      Each day you crowd this house like wolves
      to eat away my brave son's patrimony.
      When you were boys, did your own fathers tell you
      nothing of what Odysseus was for them?
      In word and act impeccable, disinterested
740   toward all the realm—though it is king's justice
      to hold one man abhorred and love another;
      no man alive could say Odysseus wronged him.
      But your own hearts—how different!—and your deeds!
      How soon are benefactions all forgotten!"

      Now Medôn, the alert and cool man, answered:
      "I wish that were the worst of it, my Lady,
      but they intend something more terrible—
      may Zeus forfend and spare us!
      They plan to drive the keen bronze through Telémakhos
750   when he comes home. He sailed away, you know,

to hallowed Pylos and old Lakedaimon
for news about his father."

                              Her knees failed,
and her heart failed as she listened to the words,
and all her power of speech went out of her.
Tears came; but the rich voice could not come.
Only after a long while she made answer:
"Why has my child left me? He had no need
of those long ships on which men shake out sail
760 to tug like horses, breasting miles of sea.
Why did he go? Must he, too, be forgotten?"

Then Medôn, the perceptive man, replied:
"A god moved him — who knows? — or his own heart
sent him to learn, at Pylos, if his father
roams the wide world still, or what befell him."

He left her then, and went down through the house.
And now the pain around her heart benumbed her;
chairs were a step away, but far beyond her;
she sank down on the door sill of the chamber,
770 wailing, and all her women young and old
made a low murmur of lament around her,
until at last she broke out through her tears:
"Dearest companions, what has Zeus given me?
Pain — more pain than any living woman.
My lord, my lion heart, gone, long ago —
the bravest man, and best, of the Danaans,
famous through Hellas and the Argive midlands —
and now the squalls have blown my son, my dear one,
an unknown boy, southward. No one told me.
780 O brute creatures, not one soul would dare
to wake me from my sleep; you knew
the hour he took the black ship out to sea!
If I had seen that sailing in his eyes
he should have stayed with me, for all his longing,
stayed — or left me dead in the great hall.
Go, someone, now, and call old Dólios,
the slave my father gave me before I came,
my orchard keeper — tell him to make haste
and put these things before Laërtês; he
790 may plan some kind of action; let him come

to cry shame on these ruffians who would murder
Odysseus' son and heir, and end his line!"

The dear old nurse, Eurýkleia, answered her:
"Sweet mistress, have my throat cut without mercy
or what you will; it's true, I won't conceal it,
I knew the whole thing; gave him his provisions;
grain and sweet wine I gave, and a great oath
to tell you nothing till twelve days went by,
or till you heard of it yourself, or missed him;
800   he hoped you would not tear your skin lamenting.
Come, bathe and dress your loveliness afresh,
and go to the upper rooms with all your maids
to ask help from Athena, Zeus's daughter.
She it will be who saves this boy from death.
Spare the old man this further suffering;
the blissful gods cannot so hate his line,
heirs of Arkêsios;[47] one will yet again
be lord of the tall house and the far fields."

She hushed her weeping in this way, and soothed her.
810   The Lady Penélopê arose and bathed,
dressing her body in her freshest linen,
filled a basket with barley, and led her maids
to the upper rooms, where she besought Athena:
"Tireless child of Zeus, graciously hear me!
If ever Odysseus burned at our altar fire
thighbones of beef or mutton in sacrifice,
remember it for my sake! Save my son!
Shield him, and make the killers go astray!"

She ended with a cry, and the goddess heard her.
820   Now voices rose from the shadowy hall below
where the suitors were assuring one another:
"Our so-long-courted Queen is even now
of a mind to marry one of us, and knows
nothing of what is destined for her son."

Of what was destined they in fact knew nothing,
but Antínoös addressed them in a whisper:

---

[47] **Arkêsios:** Father of Laërtês, grandfather of Odysseus.

"No boasting—are you mad?—and no loud talk:
someone might hear it and alarm the house.
Come along now, be quiet, this way; come,
830 we'll carry out the plan our hearts are set on."

Picking out twenty of the strongest seamen,
he led them to a ship at the sea's edge,
and down they dragged her into deeper water,
stepping a mast in her, with furled sails,
and oars a-trail from thongs looped over thole pins,
ready all; then tried the white sail, hoisting,
while men at arms carried their gear aboard.
They moored the ship some way off shore, and left her
to take their evening meal there, waiting for night to come.

840 Penélopê at that hour in her high chamber
lay silent, tasting neither food nor drink,
and thought of nothing but her princely son—
could he escape, or would they find and kill him?—
her mind turning at bay, like a cornered lion
in whom fear comes as hunters close the ring.
But in her sick thought sweet sleep overtook her,
and she dozed off, her body slack and still.

Now it occurred to the grey-eyed goddess Athena
to make a figure of dream in a woman's form—
850 Iphthimê, great Ikários' other daughter,
whom Eumêlos of Phêrai took as bride.
The goddess sent this dream to Odysseus' house
to quiet Penélopê and end her grieving.
So, passing by the strap-slit[48] through the door,
the image came a-gliding down the room
to stand at her bedside and murmur to her:
"Sleepest thou, sorrowing Penélopê?
The gods whose life is ease no longer suffer thee
to pine and weep, then; he returns unharmed,
860 thy little one; no way hath he offended."

Then pensive Penélopê made this reply,
slumbering sweetly in the gates of dream:

---

[48] **strap-slit:** By using a strap that passed through a slit in a door, a person on the outside could unbolt a door on the inside.

"Sister, hast thou come hither? Why? Aforetime
never wouldst come, so far away thy dwelling.
And am I bid be done with all my grieving?
But see what anguish hath my heart and soul!
My lord, my lion heart, gone, long ago —
the bravest man, and best, of the Danaans,
famous through Hellas and the Argive midlands —
870 and now my son, my dear one, gone seafaring,
a child, untrained in hardship or in council.
Aye, 'tis for him I weep, more than his father!
Aye, how I tremble for him, lest some blow
befall him at men's hands or on the sea!
Cruel are they and many who plot against him,
to take his life before he can return."

Now the dim phantom spoke to her once more:
"Lift up thy heart, and fear not overmuch.
For by his side one goes whom all men else
880 invoke as their defender, one so powerful —
Pallas Athena; in thy tears she pitied thee
and now hath sent me that I so assure thee."

Then said Penélopê the wise:
                    "If thou art
numinous and hast ears for divine speech,
O tell me, what of Odysseus, man of woe?
Is he alive still somewhere, seeth he day light still?
Or gone in death to the sunless underworld?"

The dim phantom said only this in answer:
890 "Of him I may not tell thee in this discourse,
alive or dead. And empty words are evil."

The wavering form withdrew along the doorbolt
into a draft of wind, and out of sleep
Penélopê awoke, in better heart
for that clear dream in the twilight of the night.

Meanwhile the suitors had got under way,
planning the death plunge for Telémakhos.
Between the Isles of Ithaka and Samê
the sea is broken by an islet, Asteris,
900 with access to both channels from a cove.
In ambush here that night the Akhaians lay.

BOOK 5
SWEET NYMPH AND OPEN SEA

Dawn came up from the couch of her reclining,
leaving her lord Tithonos'[49] brilliant side
with fresh light in her arms for gods and men.
And the master of heaven and high thunder, Zeus,
went to his place among the gods assembled
hearing Athena tell Odysseus' woe.
For she, being vexed that he was still sojourning
in the sea chambers of Kalypso, said:
"O Father Zeus and gods in bliss forever,
10   let no man holding scepter as a king
think to be mild, or kind, or virtuous;
let him be cruel, and practice evil ways,
for those Odysseus ruled cannot remember
the fatherhood and mercy of his reign.
Meanwhile he lives and grieves upon that island
in thralldom to the nymph; he cannot stir,
cannot fare homeward, for no ship is left him,
fitted with oars—no crewmen or companions
to pull him on the broad back of the sea.
20   And now murder is hatched on the high sea
against his son, who sought news of his father
in the holy lands of Pylos and Lakedaimon."

To this the summoner of cloud replied:
"My child, what odd complaints you let escape you.
Have you not, you yourself, arranged this matter—
as we all know—so that Odysseus
will bring these men to book, on his return?
And are you not the one to give Telémakhos
a safe route for sailing? Let his enemies
30   encounter no one and row home again."

He turned then to his favorite son and said:
"Hermês, you have much practice on our missions,
go make it known to the softly-braided nymph
that we, whose will is not subject to error,
order Odysseus home; let him depart.
But let him have no company, gods or men,
only a raft that he must lash together,

---

[49] Tithonos: The lover of Eos, the dawn goddess.

and after twenty days, worn out at sea,
he shall make land upon the garden isle,
40 Skhería,[50] of our kinsmen, the Phaiákians.
Let these men take him to their hearts in honor
and berth him in a ship, and send him home,
with gifts of garments, gold, and bronze—
so much he had not counted on from Troy
could he have carried home his share of plunder.
His destiny is to see his friends again
under his own roof, in his father's country."

No words were lost on Hermês the Wayfinder,
who bent to tie his beautiful sandals on,
50 ambrosial, golden, that carry him over water
or over endless land in a swish of the wind,
and took the wand with which he charms asleep—
or when he wills, awake—the eyes of men.
So wand in hand he paced into the air,
shot from Pieria[51] down, down to sea level,
and veered to skim the swell. A gull patrolling
between the wave crests of the desolate sea
will dip to catch a fish, and douse his wings;
no higher above the whitecaps Hermês flew
60 until the distant island lay ahead,
then rising shoreward from the violet ocean
he stepped up to the cave. Divine Kalypso,
the mistress of the isle, was now at home.
Upon her hearthstone a great fire blazing
scented the farthest shores with cedar smoke
and smoke of thyme, and singing high and low
in her sweet voice, before her loom a-weaving,
she passed her golden shuttle to and fro.
A deep wood grew outside, with summer leaves
70 of alder and black poplar, pungent cypress.
Ornate birds here rested their stretched wings—
horned owls, falcons, cormorants—long-tongued
beachcombing birds, and followers of the sea.
Around the smoothwalled cave a crooking vine
held purple clusters under ply of green;
and four springs, bubbling up near one another
shallow and clear, took channels here and there

---

[50] **Skhería:** Probably the island of Corcyra (Corfu), off the west coast of Greece.   [51] **Pieria:** Near Mt. Olympos (Olympus).

through beds of violets and tender parsley.
Even a god who found this place
80   would gaze, and feel his heart beat with delight:
so Hermês did; but when he had gazed his fill
he entered the wide cave. Now face to face
the magical Kalypso recognized him,
as all immortal gods know one another
on sight — though seeming strangers, far from home.
But he saw nothing of the great Odysseus,
who sat apart, as a thousand times before,
and racked his own heart groaning, with eyes wet
scanning the bare horizon of the sea.
90   Kalypso, lovely nymph, seated her guest
in a bright chair all shimmering, and asked:
"O Hermês, ever with your golden wand,
what brings you to my island?
Your awesome visits in the past were few.
Now tell me what request you have in mind;
for I desire to do it, if I can,
and if it is a proper thing to do.
But wait a while, and let me serve my friend."

She drew a table of ambrosia near him
100   and stirred a cup of ruby-colored nectar —
food and drink for the luminous Wayfinder,
who took both at his leisure, and replied:
"Goddess to god, you greet me, questioning me?
Well, here is truth for you in courtesy.
Zeus made me come, and not my inclination;
who cares to cross that tract of desolation,
the bitter sea, all mortal towns behind
where gods have beef and honors from mankind?
But it is not to be thought of — and no use —
110   for any god to elude the will of Zeus.

He notes your friend, most ill-starred by renown
of all the peers who fought for Priam's town —
nine years of war they had, before great Troy was down.
Homing, they wronged the goddess with grey eyes,
who made a black wind blow and the seas rise,
in which his troops were lost, and all his gear,
while easterlies and current washed him here.
Now the command is: send him back in haste.
His life may not in exile go to waste.

120　His destiny, his homecoming, is at hand,
　　　when he shall see his dearest, and walk on his own land."

　　　That goddess most divinely made
　　　shuddered before him, and her warm voice rose:
　　　"Oh you vile gods, in jealousy supernal!
　　　You hate it when we choose to lie with men—
　　　immortal flesh by some dear mortal side.
　　　So radiant Dawn once took to bed Orion
　　　until you easeful gods grew peevish at it,
　　　and holy Artemis, Artemis throned in gold,
130　hunted him down in Delos with her arrows.
　　　Then Dêmêtêr of the tasseled tresses yielded
　　　to Iasion, mingling and making love
　　　in a furrow three times plowed;[52] but Zeus found out
　　　and killed him with a white-hot thunderbolt.
　　　So now you grudge me, too, my mortal friend.
　　　But it was I who saved him—saw him straddle
　　　his own keel board, the one man left afloat
　　　when Zeus rent wide his ship with chain lightning
　　　and overturned him in the winedark sea.
140　Then all his troops were lost, his good companions,
　　　but wind and current washed him here to me.
　　　I fed him, loved him, sang that he should not die
　　　nor grow old, ever, in all the days to come.
　　　But now there's no eluding Zeus's will.
　　　If this thing be ordained by him, I say
　　　so be it, let the man strike out alone
　　　on the vast water. Surely I cannot 'send' him.
　　　I have no long-oared ships, no company
　　　to pull him on the broad back of the sea.
150　My counsel he shall have, and nothing hidden,
　　　to help him homeward without harm."

　　　To this the Wayfinder made answer briefly:
　　　"Thus you shall send him, then. And show more grace
　　　in your obedience, or be chastised by Zeus."

　　　The strong god glittering left her as he spoke,
　　　and now her ladyship, having given heed
　　　to Zeus's mandate, went to find Odysseus

---

[52] **Then Dêmêtêr . . . three times plowed:** Perhaps symbolic of an agricultural ritual; Dêmêtêr is goddess of cereals.

in his stone seat to seaward—tear on tear
brimming his eyes. The sweet days of his life time

160 were running out in anguish over his exile,
for long ago the nymph had ceased to please.
Though he fought shy of her and her desire,
he lay with her each night, for she compelled him.
But when day came he sat on the rocky shore
and broke his own heart groaning, with eyes wet
scanning the bare horizon of the sea.
Now she stood near him in her beauty, saying:
"O forlorn man, be still.
Here you need grieve no more; you need not feel

170 your life consumed here; I have pondered it,
and I shall help you go.
Come and cut down high timber for a raft
or flatboat; make her broad-beamed, and decked over,
so you can ride her on the misty sea.
Stores I shall put aboard for you—bread, water,
and ruby-colored wine, to stay your hunger—
give you a seacloak and a following wind
to help you homeward without harm—provided
the gods who rule wide heaven wish it so.

180 Stronger than I they are, in mind and power."

For all he had endured, Odysseus shuddered.
But when he spoke, his words went to the mark:
"After these years, a helping hand? O goddess,
what guile is hidden here?
A raft, you say, to cross the Western Ocean,
rough water, and unknown? Seaworthy ships
that glory in god's wind will never cross it.
I take no raft you grudge me out to sea.
Or yield me first a great oath, if I do,

190 to work no more enchantment to my harm."

At this the beautiful nymph Kalypso smiled
and answered sweetly, laying her hand upon him:
"What a dog you are! And not for nothing learned,
having the wit to ask this thing of me!
My witness then be earth and sky
and dripping Styx[53] that I swear by—
the gay gods cannot swear more seriously—

---

[53] **Styx:** A river in Hades as well as the name of an underworld goddess by whom oaths were sworn.

I have no further spells to work against you.
But what I shall devise, and what I tell you,
200 will be the same as if your need were mine.
Fairness is all I think of. There are hearts
made of cold iron—but my heart is kind."

Swiftly she turned and led him to her cave,
and they went in, the mortal and immortal.
He took the chair left empty now by Hermês,
where the divine Kalypso placed before him
victuals and drink of men; then she sat down
facing Odysseus, while her serving maids
brought nectar and ambrosia to her side.
210 Then each one's hands went out on each one's feast
until they had had their pleasure; and she said:
"Son of Laërtês, versatile Odysseus,
after these years with me, you still desire
your old home? Even so, I wish you well.
If you could see it all, before you go—
all the adversity you face at sea—
you would stay here, and guard this house, and be
immortal—though you wanted her forever,
that bride for whom you pine each day.
220 Can I be less desirable than she is?
Less interesting? Less beautiful? Can mortals
compare with goddesses in grace and form?"

To this the strategist Odysseus answered:
"My lady goddess, here is no cause for anger.
My quiet Penélopê—how well I know—
would seem a shade before your majesty,
death and old age being unknown to you,
while she must die. Yet, it is true, each day
I long for home, long for the sight of home.
230 If any god has marked me out again
for shipwreck, my tough heart can undergo it.
What hardship have I not long since endured
at sea, in battle! Let the trial come."

Now as he spoke the sun set, dusk drew on,
and they retired, this pair, to the inner cave
to revel and rest softly, side by side.

When Dawn spread out her finger tips of rose
Odysseus pulled his tunic and his cloak on,

while the sea nymph dressed in a silvery gown
240 of subtle tissue, drew about her waist
a golden belt, and veiled her head, and then
took thought for the great-hearted hero's voyage.
A brazen axehead first she had to give him,
two-bladed, and agreeable to the palm
with a smooth-fitting haft of olive wood;
next a well-polished adze; and then she led him
to the island's tip where bigger timber grew—
besides the alder and poplar, tall pine trees,
long dead and seasoned, that would float him high.
250 Showing him in that place her stand of timber
the loveliest of nymphs took her way home.
Now the man fell to chopping; when he paused
twenty tall trees were down. He lopped the branches,
split the trunks, and trimmed his puncheons true.
Meanwhile Kalypso brought him an auger tool
with which he drilled through all his planks, then drove
stout pins to bolt them, fitted side by side.
A master shipwright, building a cargo vessel,
lays down a broad and shallow hull; just so
260 Odysseus shaped the bottom of his craft.
He made his decking fast to close-set ribs
before he closed the side with longer planking,
then cut a mast pole, and a proper yard,
and shaped a steering oar to hold her steady.
He drove long strands of willow in all the seams
to keep out waves, and ballasted with logs.
As for a sail, the lovely nymph Kalypso
brought him a cloth so he could make that, too.
Then he ran up his rigging—halyards, braces—
270 and hauled the boat on rollers to the water.

This was the fourth day, when he had all ready;
on the fifth day, she sent him out to sea.
But first she bathed him, gave him a scented cloak,
and put on board a skin of dusky wine
with water in a bigger skin, and stores—
boiled meats and other victuals—in a bag.
Then she conjured a warm landbreeze to blowing—
joy for Odysseus when he shook out sail!
Now the great seaman, leaning on his oar,
280 steered all the night unsleeping, and his eyes

picked out the Pleiadês, the laggard Ploughman,[54]
and the Great Bear, that some have called the Wain,
pivoting in the sky before Orion;[55]
of all the night's pure figures, she alone
would never bathe or dip in the Ocean stream.
These stars the beautiful Kalypso bade him
hold on his left hand as he crossed the main.
Seventeen nights and days in the open water
he sailed, before a dark shoreline appeared;
290   Skhería then came slowly into view
like a rough shield of bull's hide on the sea.

But now the god of earthquake,° storming home   Poseidon
over the mountains of Asia from the Sunburned land,
sighted him far away. The god grew sullen
and tossed his great head, muttering to himself:
"Here is a pretty cruise! While I was gone
the gods have changed their minds about Odysseus.
Look at him now, just offshore of that island
that frees him from the bondage of his exile!
300   Still I can give him a rough ride in, and will."

Brewing high thunderheads, he churned the deep
with both hands on his trident—called up wind
from every quarter, and sent a wall of rain
to blot out land and sea in torrential night.
Hurricane winds now struck from the South and East
shifting North West in a great spume of seas,
on which Odysseus' knees grew slack, his heart
sickened, and he said within himself:
"Rag of man that I am, is this the end of me?
310   I fear the goddess told it all too well—
predicting great adversity at sea
and far from home. Now all things bear her out:
the whole rondure of heaven hooded so
by Zeus in woeful cloud, and the sea raging
under such winds. I am going down, that's sure.
How lucky those Danaans were who perished

---

[54] **Ploughman:** The name of the constellation Boötes means "ploughman."   [55] **the Wain . . . Orion:** The Great Bear, or Wain, refers to the Big Dipper, which in northern latitudes never sets. Orion, the Hunter, is another constellation.

on Troy's wide seaboard, serving the Atreidai!
Would God I, too, had died there—met my end
that time the Trojans made so many casts at me
320 when I stood by Akhilleus after death.
I should have had a soldier's burial
and praise from the Akhaians—not this choking
waiting for me at sea, unmarked and lonely."

A great wave drove at him with toppling crest
spinning him round, in one tremendous blow,
and he went plunging overboard, the oar-haft
wrenched from his grip. A gust that came on howling
at the same instant broke his mast in two,
hurling his yard and sail far out to leeward.
330 Now the big wave a long time kept him under,
helpless to surface, held by tons of water,
tangled, too, by the seacloak of Kalypso.
Long, long, until he came up spouting brine,
with streamlets gushing from his head and beard;
but still bethought him, half-drowned as he was,
to flounder for the boat and get a handhold
into the bilge—to crouch there, foiling death.
Across the foaming water, to and fro,
the boat careered like a ball of tumbleweed
340 blown on the autumn plains, but intact still.
So the winds drove this wreck over the deep,
East Wind and North Wind, then South Wind and West,
coursing each in turn to the brutal harry.

But Ino saw him—Ino, Kadmos' daughter,
slim-legged, lovely, once an earthling girl,
now in the seas a nereid, Leukothea.
Touched by Odysseus' painful buffeting
she broke the surface, like a diving bird,
to rest upon the tossing raft and say:
350 "O forlorn man, I wonder
why the Earthshaker, Lord Poseidon, holds
this fearful grudge—father of all your woes.
He will not drown you, though, despite his rage.
You seem clear-headed still; do what I tell you.
Shed that cloak, let the gale take your craft,
and swim for it—swim hard to get ashore
upon Skhería, yonder,
where it is fated that you find a shelter.
Here: make my veil your sash; it is not mortal;

360 you cannot, now, be drowned or suffer harm.
Only, the instant you lay hold of earth,
discard it, cast it far, far out from shore
in the winedark sea again, and turn away."

After she had bestowed her veil, the nereid
dove like a gull to windward
where a dark waveside closed over her whiteness.
But in perplexity Odysseus
said to himself, his great heart laboring:
"O damned confusion! Can this be a ruse
370 to trick me from the boat for some god's pleasure?
No I'll not swim; with my own eyes I saw
how far the land lies that she called my shelter.
Better to do the wise thing, as I see it.
While this poor planking holds, I stay aboard;
I may ride out the pounding of the storm,
or if she cracks up, take to the water then;
I cannot think it through a better way."

But even while he pondered and decided,
the god of earthquake heaved a wave against him
380 high as a rooftree and of awful gloom.
A gust of wind, hitting a pile of chaff,
will scatter all the parched stuff far and wide;
just so, when this gigantic billow struck
the boat's big timbers flew apart. Odysseus
clung to a single beam, like a jockey riding,
meanwhile stripping Kalypso's cloak away;
then he slung round his chest the veil of Ino
and plunged headfirst into the sea. His hands
went out to stroke, and he gave a swimmer's kick.
390 But the strong Earthshaker had him under his eye,
and nodded as he said:
                    "Go on, go on;
wander the high seas this way, take your blows,
before you join that race[56] the gods have nurtured.
Nor will you grumble, even then, I think,
for want of trouble."

                    Whipping his glossy team
he rode off to his glorious home at Aigai.[57]

---

[56] **that race:** The Phaiákians, who befriend Odysseus.   [57] **Aigai:** An island off the east coast of Greece.

But Zeus's daughter Athena countered him:
400 she checked the course of all the winds but one,
commanding them, "Be quiet and go to sleep."
Then sent a long swell running under a norther
to bear the prince Odysseus, back from danger,
to join the Phaiákians, people of the sea.

Two nights, two days, in the solid deep-sea swell
he drifted, many times awaiting death,
until with shining ringlets in the East
the dawn confirmed a third day, breaking clear
over a high and windless sea; and mounting
410 a rolling wave he caught a glimpse of land.
What a dear welcome thing life seems to children
whose father, in the extremity, recovers
after some weakening and malignant illness:
his pangs are gone, the gods have delivered him.
So dear and welcome to Odysseus
the sight of land, of woodland, on that morning.
It made him swim again, to get a foothold
on solid ground. But when he came in earshot
he heard the trampling roar of sea on rock,
420 where combers, rising shoreward, thudded down
on the sucking ebb — all sheeted with salt foam.
Here were no coves or harborage or shelter,
only steep headlands, rockfallen reefs and crags.
Odysseus' knees grew slack, his heart faint,
a heaviness came over him, and he said:
"A cruel turn, this. Never had I thought
to see this land, but Zeus has let me see it —
and let me, too, traverse the Western Ocean —
only to find no exit from these breakers.
430 Here are sharp rocks off shore, and the sea a smother
rushing around them; rock face rising sheer
from deep water; nowhere could I stand up
on my two feet and fight free of the welter.
No matter how I try it, the surf may throw me
against the cliffside; no good fighting there.
If I swim down the coast, outside the breakers,
I may find shelving shore and quiet water —
but what if another gale comes on to blow?
Then I go cursing out to sea once more.
440 Or then again, some shark of Amphitritê's°   sea nymph

may hunt me, sent by the genius of the deep.
I know how he who makes earth tremble hates me."

During this meditation a heavy surge
was taking him, in fact, straight on the rocks.
He had been flayed there, and his bones broken,
had not grey-eyed Athena instructed him:
he gripped a rock-ledge with both hands in passing
and held on, groaning, as the surge went by,
to keep clear of its breaking. Then the backwash
450   hit him, ripping him under and far out.
An octopus, when you drag one from his chamber,
comes up with suckers full of tiny stones:
Odysseus left the skin of his great hands
torn on that rock-ledge as the wave submerged him.
And now at last Odysseus would have perished,
battered inhumanly, but he had the gift
of self-possession from grey-eyed Athena.
So, when the backwash spewed him up again,
he swam out and along, and scanned the coast
460   for some landspit that made a breakwater.
Lo and behold, the mouth of a calm river
at length came into view, with level shores
unbroken, free from rock, shielded from wind—
by far the best place he had found.
But as he felt the current flowing seaward
he prayed in his heart:
                    "O hear me, lord of the stream:
how sorely I depend upon your mercy!
derelict as I am by the sea's anger.
470   Is he not sacred, even to the gods,
the wandering man who comes, as I have come,
in weariness before your knees, your waters?
Here is your servant; lord, have mercy on me."

Now even as he prayed the tide at ebb
had turned, and the river god made quiet water,
drawing him in to safety in the shallows.
His knees buckled, his arms gave way beneath him,
all vital force now conquered by the sea.
Swollen from head to foot he was, and seawater
480   gushed from his mouth and nostrils. There he lay,
scarce drawing breath, unstirring, deathly spent.

In time, as air came back into his lungs
and warmth around his heart, he loosed the veil,
letting it drift away on the estuary
downstream to where a white wave took it under
and Ino's hands received it. Then the man
crawled to the river bank among the reeds
where, face down, he could kiss the soil of earth,
in his exhaustion murmuring to himself:
490   "What more can this hulk suffer? What comes now?
In vigil through the night here by the river
how can I not succumb, being weak and sick,
to the night's damp and hoarfrost of the morning?
The air comes cold from rivers before dawn.
But if I climb the slope and fall asleep
in the dark forest's undergrowth — supposing
cold and fatigue will go, and sweet sleep come —
I fear I make the wild beasts easy prey."

But this seemed best to him, as he thought it over.
500   He made his way to a grove above the water
on open ground, and crept under twin bushes
grown from the same spot — olive and wild olive —
a thicket proof against the stinging wind
or Sun's blaze, fine soever the needling sunlight;
nor could a downpour wet it through, so dense
those plants were interwoven. Here Odysseus
tunnelled, and raked together with his hands
a wide bed — for a fall of leaves was there,
enough to save two men or maybe three
510   on a winter night, a night of bitter cold.
Odysseus' heart laughed when he saw his leaf-bed,
and down he lay, heaping more leaves above him.

A man in a distant field, no hearthfires near,
will hide a fresh brand in his bed of embers
to keep a spark alive for the next day;
so in the leaves Odysseus hid himself,
while over him Athena showered sleep
that his distress should end, and soon, soon.
In quiet sleep she sealed his cherished eyes.

Book 6
The Princess at the River

Far gone in weariness, in oblivion,
the noble and enduring man slept on;
but Athena in the night went down the land
of the Phaiákians, entering their city.
In days gone by, these men held Hypereia,[58]
a country of wide dancing grounds, but near them
were overbearing Kyklopês, whose power
could not be turned from pillage. So the Phaiákians
migrated thence under Nausíthoös

10 to settle a New World across the sea,
Skhería Island. That first captain walled
their promontory, built their homes and shrines,
and parcelled out the black land for the plow.
But he had gone down long ago to Death.
Alkínoös ruled, and Heaven gave him wisdom,
so on this night the goddess, grey-eyed Athena,
entered the palace of Alkínoös
to make sure of Odysseus' voyage home.
She took her way to a painted bedchamber

20 where a young girl lay fast asleep — so fine
in mould and feature that she seemed a goddess —
the daughter of Alkínoös, Nausikaa.
On either side, as Graces[59] might have slept,
her maids were sleeping. The bright doors were shut,
but like a sudden stir of wind, Athena
moved to the bedside of the girl, and grew
visible as the shipman Dymas' daughter,
a girl the princess' age, and her dear friend.
In this form grey-eyed Athena said to her:

30 "How so remiss, and yet thy mother's daughter?
leaving thy clothes uncared for, Nausikaa,
when soon thou must have store of marriage linen,
and put thy minstrelsy in wedding dress!
Beauty, in these, will make the folk admire,
and bring thy father and gentle mother joy.

---

[58] **Hypereia:** An unknown location.   [59] **Graces:** Attendants of Aphroditê, the Graces personify beauty, youth, and modesty.

Let us go washing in the shine of morning!
Beside thee will I drub, so wedding chests
will brim by evening. Maidenhood must end!
Have not the noblest born Phaiákians
40   paid court to thee, whose birth none can excel?
Go beg thy sovereign father, even at dawn,
to have the mule cart and the mules brought round
to take thy body-linen, gowns and mantles.
Thou shouldst ride, for it becomes thee more,
the washing pools are found so far from home."

On this word she departed, grey-eyed Athena,
to where the gods have their eternal dwelling—
as men say—in the fastness of Olympos.
Never a tremor of wind, or a splash of rain,
50   no errant snowflake comes to stain that heaven,
so calm, so vaporless, the world of light.
Here, where the gay gods live their days of pleasure,
the grey-eyed one withdrew, leaving the princess.

And now Dawn took her own fair throne, awaking
the girl in the sweet gown, still charmed by dream.
Down through the rooms she went to tell her parents,
whom she found still at home: her mother seated
near the great hearth among her maids—and twirling
out of her distaff yarn dyed like the sea—;
60   her father at the door, bound for a council
of princes on petition of the gentry.
She went up close to him and softly said:
"My dear Papà, could you not send the mule cart
around for me—the gig with pretty wheels?
I must take all our things and get them washed
at the river pools; our linen is all soiled.
And you should wear fresh clothing, going to council
with counselors and first men of the realm.
Remember your five sons at home: though two
70   are married, we have still three bachelor sprigs;
they will have none but laundered clothes each time
they go to the dancing. See what I must think of!"

She had no word to say of her own wedding,
though her keen father saw her blush. Said he:
"No mules would I deny you, child, nor anything.

Go along, now; the grooms will bring your gig
with pretty wheels and the cargo box upon it."

He spoke to the stableman, who soon brought round
the cart, low-wheeled and nimble;
80 harnessed the mules, and backed them in the traces.
Meanwhile the girl fetched all her soiled apparel
to bundle in the polished wagon box.
Her mother, for their luncheon, packed a hamper
with picnic fare, and filled a skin of wine,
and, when the princess had been handed up,
gave her a golden bottle of olive oil
for softening girls' bodies, after bathing.
Nausikaa took the reins and raised her whip,
lashing the mules. What jingling! What a clatter!
90 But off they went in a ground-covering trot,
with princess, maids, and laundry drawn behind.
By the lower river where the wagon came
were washing pools, with water all year flowing
in limpid spillways that no grime withstood.
The girls unhitched the mules, and sent them down
along the eddying stream to crop sweet grass.
Then sliding out the cart's tail board, they took
armloads of clothing to the dusky water,
and trod them in the pits, making a race of it.
100 All being drubbed, all blemish rinsed away,
they spread them, piece by piece, along the beach
whose pebbles had been laundered by the sea;
then took a dip themselves, and, all anointed
with golden oil, ate lunch beside the river
while the bright burning sun dried out their linen.
Princess and maids delighted in that feast;
then, putting off their veils,
they ran and passed a ball to a rhythmic beat,
Nausikaa flashing first with her white arms.

110 So Artemis goes flying after her arrows flown
down some tremendous valley-side —
                         Taÿgetos, Erymanthos[60] —

---

[60] **Taÿgetos, Erymanthos:** Erymanthos is a mountain in Arcadia sacred to Artemis; Taÿgetos is a mountain range in southern Greece.

chasing the mountain goats or ghosting deer,
with nymphs of the wild places flanking her;
and Lêto's[61] heart delights to see them running,
for, taller by a head than nymphs can be,
the goddess shows more stately, all being beautiful.
So one could tell the princess from the maids.

Soon it was time, she knew, for riding homeward —
120   mules to be harnessed, linen folded smooth —
but the grey-eyed goddess Athena made her tarry,
so that Odysseus might behold her beauty
and win her guidance to the town.
                                        It happened
when the king's daughter threw her ball off line
and missed, and put it in the whirling stream, —
at which they all gave such a shout, Odysseus
awoke and sat up, saying to himself:
"Now, by my life, mankind again! But who?
130   Savages, are they, strangers to courtesy?
Or gentle folk, who know and fear the gods?
That was a lusty cry of tall young girls —
most like the cry of nymphs, who haunt the peaks,
and springs of brooks, and inland grassy places.
Or am I amid people of human speech?
Up again, man; and let me see for myself."

He pushed aside the bushes, breaking off
with his great hand a single branch of olive,
whose leaves might shield him in his nakedness;
140   so came out rustling, like a mountain lion,
rain-drenched, wind-buffeted, but in his might at ease,
with burning eyes — who prowls among the herds
or flocks, or after game, his hungry belly
taking him near stout homesteads for his prey.
Odysseus had this look, in his rough skin
advancing on the girls with pretty braids;
and he was driven on by hunger, too.
Streaked with brine, and swollen, he terrified them,
so that they fled, this way and that. Only

---

[61] **Lêto:** Mother of Apollo and Artemis.

150 Alkínoös' daughter stood her ground, being given
     a bold heart by Athena, and steady knees.

     She faced him, waiting. And Odysseus came,
     debating inwardly what he should do:
     embrace this beauty's knees in supplication?
     or stand apart, and, using honeyed speech,
     inquire the way to town, and beg some clothing?
     In his swift reckoning, he thought it best
     to trust in words to please her — and keep away;
     he might anger the girl, touching her knees.
160 So he began, and let the soft words fall:
     "Mistress: please: are you divine, or mortal?
     If one of those who dwell in the wide heaven,
     you are most near to Artemis, I should say —
     great Zeus's daughter — in your grace and presence.
     If you are one of earth's inhabitants,
     how blest your father, and your gentle mother,
     blest all your kin. I know what happiness
     must send the warm tears to their eyes, each time
     they see their wondrous child go to the dancing!
170 But one man's destiny is more than blest —
     he who prevails, and takes you as his bride.
     Never have I laid eyes on equal beauty
     in man or woman. I am hushed indeed.
     So fair, one time, I thought a young palm tree
     at Delos[62] near the altar of Apollo —
     I had troops under me when I was there
     on the sea route that later brought me grief —
     but that slim palm tree filled my heart with wonder:
     never came shoot from earth so beautiful.
180 So now, my lady, I stand in awe so great
     I cannot take your knees. And yet my case is desperate:
     twenty days, yesterday, in the winedark sea,
     on the ever-lunging swell, under gale winds,
     getting away from the Island of Ogýgia.
     And now the terror of Storm has left me stranded
     upon this shore — with more blows yet to suffer,
     I must believe, before the gods relent.

---

[62] **Delos:** A small island in the Aegean Sea, south of the Greek mainland, and the birthplace of Apollo.

Mistress, do me a kindness!
After much weary toil, I come to you,
190 and you are the first soul I have seen—I know
no others here. Direct me to the town,
give me a rag that I can throw around me,
some cloth or wrapping that you brought along.
And may the gods accomplish your desire:
a home, a husband, and harmonious
converse with him—the best thing in the world
being a strong house held in serenity
where man and wife agree. Woe to their enemies,
joy to their friends! But all this they know best."

200 Then she of the white arms, Nausikaa, replied:
"Stranger, there is no quirk or evil in you
that I can see. You know Zeus metes out fortune
to good and bad men as it pleases him.
Hardship he sent to you, and you must bear it.
But now that you have taken refuge here
you shall not lack for clothing, or any other
comfort due to a poor man in distress.
The town lies this way, and the men are called
Phaiákians, who own the land and city.
210 I am daughter to the Prince Alkínoös,
by whom the power of our people stands."

Turning, she called out to her maids-in-waiting:
"Stay with me! Does the sight of a man scare you?
Or do you take this one for an enemy?
Why, there's no fool so brash, and never will be,
as to bring war or pillage to this coast,
for we are dear to the immortal gods,
living here, in the sea that rolls forever,
distant from other lands and other men.
220 No: this man is a castaway, poor fellow;
we must take care of him. Strangers and beggars
come from Zeus: a small gift, then, is friendly.
Give our new guest some food and drink, and take him
into the river, out of the wind, to bathe."

They stood up now, and called to one another
to go on back. Quite soon they led Odysseus
under the river bank, as they were bidden;
and there laid out a tunic, and a cloak,
and gave him olive oil in the golden flask.

230 "Here," they said, "go bathe in the flowing water."
But heard now from that kingly man, Odysseus:
"Maids," he said, "keep away a little; let me
wash the brine from my own back, and rub on
plenty of oil. It is long since my anointing.
I take no bath, however, where you can see me—
naked before young girls with pretty braids."

They left him, then, and went to tell the princess.
And now Odysseus, dousing in the river,
scrubbed the coat of brine from back and shoulders
240 and rinsed the clot of sea-spume from his hair;
got himself all rubbed down, from head to foot,
then he put on the clothes the princess gave him.
Athena lent a hand, making him seem
taller, and massive too, with crisping hair
in curls like petals of wild hyacinth,
but all red-golden. Think of gold infused
on silver by a craftsman, whose fine art
Hephaistos taught him, or Athena: one
whose work moves to delight: just so she lavished
250 beauty over Odysseus' head and shoulders.
Then he went down to sit on the sea beach
in his new splendor. There the girl regarded him,
and after a time she said to the maids beside her:
"My gentlewomen, I have a thing to tell you.
The Olympian gods cannot be all averse
to this man's coming here among our islanders.
Uncouth he seemed, I thought so, too, before;
but now he looks like one of heaven's people.
I wish my husband could be fine as he
260 and glad to stay forever on Skhería!

But have you given refreshment to our guest?"

At this the maids, all gravely listening, hastened
to set out bread and wine before Odysseus,
and ah! how ravenously that patient man
took food and drink, his long fast at an end.

The princess Nausikaa now turned aside
to fold her linens; in the pretty cart
she stowed them, put the mule team under harness,
mounted the driver's seat, and then looked down
270 to say with cheerful prompting to Odysseus:

"Up with you now, friend; back to town we go;
and I shall send you in before my father
who is wondrous wise; there in our house with him
you'll meet the noblest of the Phaiákians.
You have good sense, I think; here's how to do it:
while we go through the countryside and farmland
stay with my maids, behind the wagon, walking
briskly enough to follow where I lead.
But near the town—well, there's a wall with towers
280   around the Isle, and beautiful ship basins
right and left of the causeway of approach;
seagoing craft are beached beside the road
each on its launching ways. The agora,[63]
with fieldstone benches bedded in the earth,
lies either side Poseidon's shrine—for there
men are at work on pitch-black hulls and rigging,
cables and sails, and tapering of oars.
The archer's craft is not for the Phaiákians,
but ship designing, modes of oaring cutters
290   in which they love to cross the foaming sea.
From these fellows I will have no salty talk,
no gossip later. Plenty are insolent.
And some seadog might say, after we passed:
'Who is this handsome stranger trailing Nausikaa?
Where did she find him? Will he be her husband?
Or is she being hospitable to some rover
come off his ship from lands across the sea—
there being no lands nearer. A god, maybe?
a god from heaven, the answer to her prayer,
300   descending now—to make her his forever?
Better, if she's roamed and found a husband
somewhere else: none of our own will suit her,
though many come to court her, and those the best.'
This is the way they might make light of me.
And I myself should hold it shame
for any girl to flout her own dear parents,
taking up with a man, before her marriage.

Note well, now, what I say, friend, and your chances
are excellent for safe conduct from my father.
310   You'll find black poplars in a roadside park
around a meadow and fountain—all Athena's—

---

[63] **agora:** Greek for a place of assembly, especially a marketplace.

but Father has a garden in the place—
this within earshot of the city wall.
Go in there and sit down, giving us time
to pass through town and reach my father's house.
And when you can imagine we're at home,
then take the road into the city, asking
directions to the palace of Alkínoös.
You'll find it easily: any small boy
320 can take you there; no family has a mansion
half so grand as he does, being king.
As soon as you are safe inside, cross over
and go straight through into the mégaron[64]
to find my mother. She'll be there in firelight
before a column, with her maids in shadow,
spinning a wool dyed richly as the sea.
My father's great chair faces the fire, too;
there like a god he sits and takes his wine.
Go past him, cast yourself before my mother,
330 embrace her knees—and you may wake up soon
at home rejoicing, though your home be far.
On Mother's feeling much depends; if she
looks on you kindly, you shall see your friends
under your own roof in your father's country."

At this she raised her glistening whip, lashing
the team into a run; they left the river
cantering beautifully, then trotted smartly.
But then she reined them in, and spared the whip,
so that her maids could follow with Odysseus.
340 The sun was going down when they went by
Athena's grove. Here, then, Odysseus rested,
and lifted up his prayer to Zeus's daughter:
"Hear me, unwearied child of royal Zeus!
O listen to me now—thou so aloof
while the Earthshaker wrecked and battered me.
May I find love and mercy among these people."

He prayed for that, and Pallas Athena heard him—
although in deference to her father's brother
she would not show her true form to Odysseus,
350 at whom Poseidon smoldered on
until the kingly man came home to his own shore.

---

[64] **the mégaron:** The great hall.

BOOK 7
GARDENS AND FIRELIGHT

As Lord Odysseus prayed there in the grove
the girl rode on, behind her strapping team,
and came late to the mansion of her father,
where she reined in at the courtyard gate. Her brothers
awaited her like tall gods in the court,
circling to lead the mules away and carry
the laundered things inside. But she withdrew
to her own bedroom, where a fire soon shone,
kindled by her old nurse, Eurymedousa.
10   Years ago, from a raid on the continent,
the rolling ships had brought this woman over
to be Alkínoös' share—fit spoil for him
whose realm hung on his word as on a god's.
And she had schooled the princess, Nausikaa,
whose fire she tended now, making her supper.

Odysseus, when the time had passed, arose
and turned into the city. But Athena
poured a sea fog around him as he went—
her love's expedient, that no jeering sailor
20   should halt the man or challenge him for luck.
Instead, as he set foot in the pleasant city,
the grey-eyed goddess came to him, in figure
a small girl child, hugging a water jug.

Confronted by her, Lord Odysseus asked:
"Little one, could you take me to the house
of that Alkínoös, king among these people?
You see, I am a poor old stranger here;
my home is far away; here there is no one
known to me, in countryside or city."

30   The grey-eyed goddess Athena replied to him:
"Oh yes, good grandfer, sir, I know, I'll show you
the house you mean; it is quite near my father's.
But come now, hush, like this, and follow me.
You must not stare at people, or be inquisitive.
They do not care for strangers in this neighborhood;
a foreign man will get no welcome here.
The only things they trust are the racing ships

Poseidon gave, to sail the deep blue sea
like white wings in the sky, or a flashing thought."

40 Pallas Athena turned like the wind, running
ahead of him, and he followed in her footsteps.
And no seafaring men of Phaiákia
perceived Odysseus passing through their town:
the awesome one in pigtails barred their sight
with folds of sacred mist. And yet Odysseus
gazed out marvelling at the ships and harbors,
public squares, and ramparts towering up
with pointed palisades along the top.
When they were near the mansion of the king,
50 grey-eyed Athena in the child cried out:
"Here it is, grandfer, sir — that mansion house
you asked to see. You'll find our king and queen
at supper, but you must not be dismayed;
go in to them. A cheerful man does best
in every enterprise — even a stranger.
You'll see our lady just inside the hall —
her name is Arêtê; her grandfather
was our good king Alkínoös's father —
Nausíthoös by name, son of Poseidon
60 and Periboia. That was a great beauty,
the daughter of Eurymedon, commander
of the Gigantês[65] in the olden days,
who led those wild things to their doom and his.
Poseidon then made love to Periboia,
and she bore Nausíthoös, Phaiákia's lord,
whose sons in turn were Rhêxênor and Alkínoös.
Rhêxênor had no sons; even as a bridegroom
he fell before the silver bow of Apollo,
his only child a daughter, Arêtê.
70 When she grew up, Alkínoös married her
and holds her dear. No lady in the world,
no other mistress of a man's household,
is honored as our mistress is, and loved,
by her own children, by Alkínoös,
and by the people. When she walks the town

---

[65] **Gigantês:** Giants; as sons of Uranus and Gaia, they are similar if not identical to the Titans in Hesiod's *Theogony,* who battled unsuccessfully against the Olympians.

they murmur and gaze, as though she were a goddess.
No grace or wisdom fails in her; indeed
just men in quarrels come to her for equity.
Supposing, then, she looks upon you kindly,
80 the chances are that you shall see your friends
under your own roof, in your father's country."

At this the grey-eyed goddess Athena left him
and left that comely land, going over sea
to Marathon, to the wide roadways of Athens
and her retreat in the stronghold of Erekhtheus.[66]
Odysseus, now alone before the palace,
meditated a long time before crossing
the brazen threshold of the great courtyard.
High rooms he saw ahead, airy and luminous
90 as though with lusters of the sun and moon,
bronze-paneled walls, at several distances,
making a vista, with an azure molding
of lapis lazuli. The doors were golden
guardians of the great room. Shining bronze
plated the wide door sill; the posts and lintel
were silver upon silver; golden handles
curved on the doors, and golden, too, and silver
were sculptured hounds, flanking the entrance way,
cast by the skill and ardor of Hephaistos
100 to guard the prince Alkínoös's house —
undying dogs that never could grow old.
Through all the rooms, as far as he could see,
tall chairs were placed around the walls, and strewn
with fine embroidered stuff made by the women.
Here were enthroned the leaders of Phaiákia
drinking and dining, with abundant fare.
Here, too, were boys of gold on pedestals
holding aloft bright torches of pitch pine
to light the great rooms, and the night-time feasting.
110 And fifty maids-in-waiting of the household
sat by the round mill, grinding yellow corn,
or wove upon their looms, or twirled their distaffs,
flickering like the leaves of a poplar tree;
while drops of oil glistened on linen weft.

---

[66] **Marathon . . . Erekhtheus:** The tomb of Erekhtheus, the sixth king of Athens, was located in the Erekhtheum (or Erechtheum), a white marble temple sacred to Athena on the Acropolis. Marathon was the site of a famous battle at which the Athenians defeated the Persians in 490 B.C.E.

Skillful as were the men of Phaiákia
in ship handling at sea, so were these women
skilled at the loom, having this lovely craft
and artistry as talents from Athena.

To left and right, outside, he saw an orchard
120 closed by a pale—four spacious acres planted
with trees in bloom or weighted down for picking:
pear trees, pomegranates, brilliant apples,
luscious figs, and olives ripe and dark.
Fruit never failed upon these trees: winter
and summer time they bore, for through the year
the breathing Westwind ripened all in turn—
so one pear came to prime, and then another,
and so with apples, figs, and the vine's fruit
empurpled in the royal vineyard there.
130 Currants were dried at one end, on a platform
bare to the sun, beyond the vintage arbors
and vats the vintners trod; while near at hand
were new grapes barely formed as the green bloom fell,
or half-ripe clusters, faintly coloring.
After the vines came rows of vegetables
of all the kinds that flourish in every season,
and through the garden plots and orchard ran
channels from one clear fountain, while another
gushed through a pipe under the courtyard entrance
140 to serve the house and all who came for water.
These were the gifts of heaven to Alkínoös.

Odysseus, who had borne the barren sea,
stood in the gateway and surveyed this bounty.
He gazed his fill, then swiftly he went in.
The lords and nobles of Phaiákia
were tipping wine to the wakeful god, to Hermês—
a last libation before going to bed—
but down the hall Odysseus went unseen,
still in the cloud Athena cloaked him in,
150 until he reached Arêtê, and the king.
He threw his great hands round Arêtês knees,
whereon the sacred mist curled back;
they saw him; and the diners hushed amazed
to see an unknown man inside the palace.
Under their eyes Odysseus made his plea:
"Arêtê, admirable Rhêxênor's daughter,
here is a man bruised by adversity, thrown

upon your mercy and the king your husband's,
begging indulgence of this company—
160 may the gods' blessing rest on them! May life
be kind to all! Let each one leave his children
every good thing this realm confers upon him!
But grant me passage to my father land.
My home and friends lie far. My life is pain."

He moved, then, toward the fire, and sat him down
amid the ashes.[67] No one stirred or spoke
until Ekhenêos broke the spell—an old man,
eldest of the Phaiákians, an oracle,
versed in the laws and manners of old time.
170 He rose among them now and spoke out kindly:
"Alkínoös, this will not pass for courtesy:
a guest abased in ashes at our hearth?
Everyone here awaits your word; so come, then,
lift the man up; give him a seat of honor,
a silver-studded chair. Then tell the stewards
we'll have another wine bowl for libation
to Zeus, lord of the lightning—advocate
of honorable petitioners. And supper
may be supplied our friend by the larder mistress."

180 Alkínoös, calm in power, heard him out,
then took the great adventurer by the hand
and led him from the fire. Nearest his throne
the son whom he loved best, Laódamas,
had long held place; now the king bade him rise
and gave his shining chair to Lord Odysseus.
A serving maid poured water for his hands
from a gold pitcher into a silver bowl,
and spread a polished table at his side;
the mistress of provisions came with bread
190 and other victuals, generous with her store.
So Lord Odysseus drank, and tasted supper.
Seeing this done, the king in majesty
said to his squire:
                    "A fresh bowl, Pontónoös;

---

[67] **sat him down . . . ashes:** Since the hearth was the sacred center of the home, a guest who sits there has a safe refuge or sanctuary.

we make libation to the lord of lightning,
who seconds honorable petitioners."

Mixing the honey-hearted wine, Pontónoös
went on his rounds and poured fresh cups for all,
whereof when all had spilt they drank their fill.
200 Alkínoös then spoke to the company:
"My lords and leaders of Phaiákia:
hear now, all that my heart would have me say.
Our banquet's ended, so you may retire;
but let our seniors gather in the morning
to give this guest a festal day, and make
fair offerings to the gods. In due course we
shall put our minds upon the means at hand
to take him safely, comfortably, well
and happily, with speed, to his own country,
210 distant though it may lie. And may no trouble
come to him here or on the way; his fate
he shall pay out at home, even as the Spinners
spun for him on the day his mother bore him.
If, as may be, he is some god, come down
from heaven's height, the gods are working strangely:
until now, they have shown themselves in glory
only after great hekatombs — those figures
banqueting at our side, throned like ourselves.
Or if some traveller met them when alone
220 they bore no least disguise; we are their kin; Gigantês,
Kyklopês, rank no nearer gods than we."

Odysseus' wits were ready, and he replied:
"Alkínoös, you may set your mind at rest.
Body and birth, a most unlikely god
am I, being all of earth and mortal nature.
I should say, rather, I am like those men
who suffer the worst trials that you know,
and miseries greater yet, as I might tell you —
hundreds; indeed the gods could send no more.
230 You will indulge me if I finish dinner —?
grieved though I am to say it. There's no part
of man more like a dog than brazen Belly,
crying to be remembered — and it must be —
when we are mortal weary and sick at heart;
and that is my condition. Yet my hunger
drives me to take this food, and think no more

of my afflictions. Belly must be filled.
Be equally impelled, my lords, tomorrow
to berth me in a ship and send me home!
240 Rough years I've had; now may I see once more
my hall, my lands, my people before I die!"

Now all who heard cried out assent to this:
the guest had spoken well; he must have passage.
Then tipping wine they drank their thirst away,
and one by one went homeward for the night.
So Lord Odysseus kept his place alone
with Arêtê and the king Alkínoös
beside him, while the maids went to and fro
clearing away the wine cups and the tables.
250 Presently the ivory-skinned lady
turned to him—for she knew his cloak and tunic
to be her own fine work, done with her maids—
and arrowy came her words upon the air:
"Friend, I, for one, have certain questions for you.
Who are you, and who has given you this clothing?
Did you not say you wandered here by sea?"

The great tactician carefully replied:
"Ah, majesty, what labor it would be
to go through the whole story! All my years
260 of misadventures, given by those on high!
But this you ask about is quickly told:
in mid-ocean lies Ogýgia, the island
haunt of Kalypso, Atlas' guileful daughter,
a lovely goddess and a dangerous one.
No one, no god or man, consorts with her;
but supernatural power brought me there
to be her solitary guest: for Zeus
let fly with his bright bolt and split my ship,
rolling me over in the winedark sea.
270 There all my shipmates, friends were drowned, while I
hung on the keelboard of the wreck and drifted
nine full days. Then in the dead of night
the gods brought me ashore upon Ogýgia
into her hands. The enchantress in her beauty
fed and caressed me, promised me I should be
immortal, youthful, all the days to come;
but in my heart I never gave consent
though seven years detained. Immortal clothing

I had from her, and kept it wet with tears.
280 Then came the eighth year on the wheel of heaven
and word to her from Zeus, or a change of heart,
so that she now commanded me to sail,
sending me out to sea on a craft I made
with timber and tools of hers. She gave me stores,
victuals and wine, a cloak divinely woven,
and made a warm land breeze come up astern.
Seventeen days I sailed in the open water
before I saw your country's shore, a shadow
upon the sea rim. Then my heart rejoiced —
290 pitiable as I am! For blows aplenty
awaited me from the god who shakes the earth.
Cross gales he blew, making me lose my bearings,
and heaved up seas beyond imagination —
huge and foundering seas. All I could do
was hold hard, groaning under every shock,
until my craft broke up in the hurricane.
I kept afloat and swam your sea, or drifted,
taken by wind and current to this coast
where I went in on big swells running landward.
300 But cliffs and rock shoals made that place forbidding,
so I turned back, swimming off shore, and came
in the end to a river, to auspicious water,
with smooth beach and a rise that broke the wind.
I lay there where I fell till strength returned.
Then sacred night came on, and I went inland
to high ground and a leaf bed in a thicket.
Heaven sent slumber in an endless tide
submerging my sad heart among the leaves.
That night and next day's dawn and noon I slept;
310 the sun went west; and then sweet sleep unbound me,
when I became aware of maids — your daughter's —
playing along the beach; the princess, too,
most beautiful. I prayed her to assist me,
and her good sense was perfect; one could hope
for no behavior like it from the young,
thoughtless as they most often are. But she
gave me good provender and good red wine,
a river bath, and finally this clothing.
There is the bitter tale. These are the facts."

320 But in reply Alkínoös observed:
"Friend, my child's good judgment failed in this —

not to have brought you in her company home.
Once you approached her, you became her charge."

To this Odysseus tactfully replied:
"Sir, as to that, you should not blame the princess.
She did tell me to follow with her maids,
but I would not. I felt abashed, and feared
the sight would somehow ruffle or offend you.
All of us on this earth are plagued by jealousy."

330   Alkínoös' answer was a declaration:
"Friend, I am not a man for trivial anger:
better a sense of measure in everything.
No anger here. I say that if it should please
our father Zeus, Athena, and Apollo—
seeing the man you are, seeing your thoughts
are my own thoughts—my daughter should be yours
and you my son-in-law, if you remained.
A home, lands, riches you should have from me
if you could be contented here. If not,
340   by Father Zeus, let none of our men hold you!
On the contrary, I can assure you now
of passage late tomorrow: while you sleep
my men will row you through the tranquil night
to your own land and home or where you please.
It may be, even, far beyond Euboia—
called most remote by seamen of our isle
who landed there, conveying Rhadamanthos
when he sought Títyos,[68] the son of Gaia.
They put about, with neither pause nor rest,
350   and entered their home port the selfsame day.
But this you, too, will see: what ships I have,
how my young oarsmen send the foam a-scudding!"

Now joy welled up in the patient Lord Odysseus
who said devoutly in the warmest tones:
"O Father Zeus, let all this be fulfilled
as spoken by Alkínoös! Earth of harvests
remember him! Return me to my homeland!"

In this manner they conversed with one another;
but the great lady called her maids, and sent them

---

[68] **Títyos:** A giant who tried to rape Lêto and who was killed by Apollo and Artemis and placed in Tartarus, the lowest region of Hades.

360 to make a kingly bed, with purple rugs
     piled up, and sheets outspread, and fleecy
     coverlets in an eastern colonnade.
     The girls went out with torches in their hands,
     swift at their work of bedmaking; returning
     they whispered at the lord Odysseus' shoulder:
     "Sir, you may come; your bed has been prepared."

     How welcome the word "bed" came to his ears!
     Now, then, Odysseus laid him down and slept
     in luxury under the Porch of Morning,
370 while in his inner chamber Alkínoös
     retired to rest where his dear consort lay.

BOOK 8
THE SONGS OF THE HARPER

     Under the opening fingers of the dawn
     Alkínoös, the sacred prince, arose,
     and then arose Odysseus, raider of cities.
     As the king willed, they went down by the shipways
     to the assembly ground of the Phaiákians.
     Side by side the two men took their ease there
     on smooth stone benches. Meanwhile Pallas Athena
     roamed through the byways of the town, contriving
     Odysseus' voyage home — in voice and feature
10   the crier of the king Alkínoös
     who stopped and passed the word to every man:
     "Phaiákian lords and counselors, this way!
     Come to assembly: learn about the stranger,
     the new guest at the palace of Alkínoös —
     a man the sea drove, but a comely man;
     the gods' own light is on him."

                              She aroused them,
     and soon the assembly ground and seats were filled
     with curious men, a throng who peered and saw
20   the master mind of war, Laërtês' son.
     Athena now poured out her grace upon him,
     head and shoulders, height and mass — a splendor
     awesome to the eyes of the Phaiákians;
     she put him in a fettle to win the day,
     mastering every trial they set to test him.
     When all the crowd sat marshalled, quieted,

Alkínoös addressed the full assembly:
"Hear me, lords and captains of the Phaiákians!
Hear what my heart would have me say!
30 Our guest and new friend—nameless to me still—
comes to my house after long wandering
in Dawn lands, or among the Sunset races.
Now he appeals to me for conveyance home.
As in the past, therefore, let us provide
passage, and quickly, for no guest of mine
languishes here for lack of it. Look to it:
get a black ship afloat on the noble sea,
and pick our fastest sailer; draft a crew
of two and fifty from our younger townsmen—
40 men who have made their names at sea. Loop oars
well to your tholepins, lads, then leave the ship,
come to our house, fall to, and take your supper:
we'll furnish out a feast for every crewman.
These are your orders. As for my older peers
and princes of the realm, let them foregather
in festival for our friend in my great hall;
and let no man refuse. Call in our minstrel,
Demódokos, whom God made lord of song,
heart-easing, sing upon what theme he will."

50 He turned, led the procession, and those princes
followed, while his herald sought the minstrel.
Young oarsmen from the assembly chose a crew
of two and fifty, as the king commanded,
and these filed off along the waterside
to where the ship lay, poised above open water.
They hauled the black hull down to ride the sea,
rigging a mast and spar in the black ship,
with oars at trail from corded rawhide, all
seamanly; then tried the white sail, hoisting,
60 and moored her off the beach. Then going ashore
the crew went up to the great house of Alkínoös.
Here the enclosures, entrance ways, and rooms
were filled with men, young men and old, for whom
Alkínoös had put twelve sheep to sacrifice,
eight tuskers and a pair of shambling oxen.
These, now, they flayed and dressed to make their banquet.
The crier soon came, leading that man of song
whom the Muse cherished; by her gift he knew

the good of life, and evil—
70 for she who lent him sweetness made him blind.
Pontónoös fixed a studded chair for him
hard by a pillar amid the banqueters,
hanging the taut harp from a peg above him,
and guided up his hands upon the strings;
placed a bread basket at his side, and poured
wine in a cup, that he might drink his fill.
Now each man's hand went out upon the banquet.

In time, when hunger and thirst were turned away,
the Muse brought to the minstrel's mind a song
80 of heroes whose great fame rang under heaven:
the clash between Odysseus and Akhilleus,
how one time they contended at the godfeast
raging, and the marshal, Agamémnon,
felt inward joy over his captains' quarrel;
for such had been foretold him by Apollo
at Pytho[69]—hallowed height—when the Akhaian
crossed that portal of rock to ask a sign—
in the old days when grim war lay ahead
for Trojans and Danaans, by God's will.
90 So ran the tale the minstrel sang. Odysseus
with massive hand drew his rich mantle down
over his brow, cloaking his face with it,
to make the Phaiákians miss the secret tears
that started to his eyes. How skillfully
he dried them when the song came to a pause!
threw back his mantle, spilt his gout of wine!
But soon the minstrel plucked his note once more
to please the Phaiákian lords, who loved the song;
then in his cloak Odysseus wept again.
100 His tears flowed in the mantle unperceived;
only Alkínoös, at his elbow, saw them,
and caught the low groan in the man's breathing.
At once he spoke to all the seafolk round him:
"Hear me, lords and captains of the Phaiákians.
Our meat is shared, our hearts are full of pleasure
from the clear harp tone that accords with feasting;

---

[69] **at Pytho:** Apollo's shrine at Delphi, on the slopes of Mt. Parnassos.

now for the field and track; we shall have trials
in the pentathlon. Let our guest go home
and tell his friends what champions we are
110   at boxing, wrestling, broadjump and foot racing."

On this he led the way and all went after.
The crier unslung and pegged the shining harp
and, taking Demódokos's hand,
led him along with all the rest—Phaiákian
peers, gay amateurs of the great games.
They gained the common where a crowd was forming,
and many a young athlete now came forward
with seaside names like Tipmast, Tiderace, Sparwood,
Hullman, Sternman, Beacher and Pullerman,
120   Bluewater, Shearwater, Runningwake, Boardalee,
Seabelt, son of Grandfleet Shipwrightson;
Seareach stepped up, son of the Launching Master,
rugged as Arês,° bane of men: his build   god of war
excelled all but the Prince Laódamas;
and Laódamas made entry with his brothers,
Halios and Klytóneus, sons of the king.
The runners, first, must have their quarter mile.
All lined up tense; then Go! and down the track
they raised the dust in a flying bunch, strung out
130   longer and longer behind Prince Klytóneus.
By just so far as a mule team, breaking ground,
will distance oxen, he left all behind
and came up to the crowd, an easy winner.
Then they made room for wrestling—grinding bouts
that Seareach won, pinning the strongest men;
then the broadjump; first place went to Seabelt;
Sparwood gave the discus the mightiest fling,
and Prince Laódamas outboxed them all.
Now it was he, the son of Alkínoös,
140   who said when they had run through these diversions:
"Look here, friends, we ought to ask the stranger
if he competes in something. He's no cripple;
look at his leg muscles and his forearms.
Neck like a bollard;[70] strong as a bull, he seems;
and not old, though he may have gone stale under

---

[70] **bollard:** The posts on a dock used for mooring boats.

the rough times he had. Nothing like the sea
for wearing out the toughest man alive."

Then Seareach took him up at once, and said:
"Laódamas, you're right, by all the powers.
150   Go up to him, yourself, and put the question."

At this, Alkínoös' tall son advanced
to the center ground, and there addressed Odysseus:
"Friend, Excellency, come join our competition,
if you are practiced, as you seem to be.
While a man lives he wins no greater honor
than footwork and the skill of hands can bring him.
Enter our games, then; ease your heart of trouble.
Your journey home is not far off, remember;
the ship is launched, the crew all primed for sea."

160   Odysseus, canniest of men, replied:
"Laódamas, why do you young chaps challenge me?
I have more on my mind than track and field—
hard days, and many, have I seen, and suffered.
I sit here at your field meet, yes; but only
as one who begs your king to send him home."

Now Seareach put his word in, and contentiously:
"The reason being, as I see it, friend,
you never learned a sport, and have no skill
in any of the contests of fighting men.
170   You must have been the skipper of some tramp
that crawled from one port to the next, jam full
of chaffering hands: a tallier of cargoes,
itching for gold—not, by your looks, an athlete."

Odysseus frowned, and eyed him coldly, saying:
"That was uncalled for, friend, you talk like a fool.
The gods deal out no gift, this one or any—
birth, brains, or speech—to every man alike.
In looks a man may be a shade, a specter,
and yet be master of speech so crowned with beauty
180   that people gaze at him with pleasure. Courteous,
sure of himself, he can command assemblies,
and when he comes to town, the crowds gather.
A handsome man, contrariwise, may lack
grace and good sense in everything he says.

You now, for instance, with your fine physique—
a god's, indeed—you have an empty noddle.
I find my heart inside my ribs aroused
by your impertinence. I am no stranger
to contests, as you fancy. I rated well
190   when I could count on youth and my two hands.
Now pain has cramped me, and my years of combat
hacking through ranks in war, and the bitter sea.
Aye. Even so I'll give your games a trial.
You spoke heart-wounding words. You shall be answered."

He leapt out, cloaked as he was, and picked a discus,
a rounded stone, more ponderous than those
already used by the Phaiákian throwers,
and, whirling, let it fly from his great hand
with a low hum. The crowd went flat on the ground—
200   all those oar-pulling, seafaring Phaiákians—
under the rushing noise. The spinning disk
soared out, light as a bird, beyond all others.
Disguised now as a Phaiákian, Athena
staked it and called out:
                    "Even a blind man,
friend, could judge this, finding with his fingers
one discus, quite alone, beyond the cluster.
Congratulations; this event is yours;
not a man here can beat you or come near you."

210   That was a cheering hail, Odysseus thought,
seeing one friend there on the emulous field,
so, in relief, he turned among the Phaiákians
and said:
                    "Now come alongside that one, lads.
The next I'll send as far, I think, or farther.
Anyone else on edge for competition
try me now. By heaven, you angered me.
Racing, wrestling, boxing—I bar nothing
with any man except Laódamas,
220   for he's my host. Who quarrels with his host?
Only a madman—or no man at all—
would challenge his protector among strangers,
cutting the ground away under his feet.
Here are no others I will not engage,
none but I hope to know what he is made of.
Inept at combat, am I? Not entirely.
Give me a smooth bow; I can handle it,

and I might well be first to hit my man
amid a swarm of enemies, though archers
230 in company around me drew together.
Philoktêtês[71] alone, at Troy, when we
Akhaians took the bow, used to outshoot me.
Of men who now eat bread upon the earth
I hold myself the best hand with a bow—
conceding mastery to the men of old,
Heraklês, or Eurýtos[72] of Oikhalía,
heroes who vied with gods in bowmanship.
Eurýtos came to grief, it's true; old age
never crept over him in his long hall;
240 Apollo took his challenge ill, and killed him.
What then, the spear? I'll plant it like an arrow.
Only in sprinting, I'm afraid, I may
be passed by someone. Roll of the sea waves
wearied me, and the victuals in my ship
ran low; my legs are flabby."

                    When he finished,
the rest were silent, but Alkínoös answered:
"Friend, we take your challenge in good part,
for this man angered and affronted you
250 here at our peaceful games. You'd have us note
the prowess that is in you, and so clearly,
no man of sense would ever cry it down!
Come, turn your mind, now, on a thing to tell
among your peers when you are home again,
dining in hall, beside your wife and children:
I mean our prowess, as you may remember it,
for we, too, have our skills, given by Zeus,
and practiced from our father's time to this—
not in the boxing ring nor the palestra[73]
260 conspicuous, but in racing, land or sea;
and all our days we set great store by feasting,
harpers, and the grace of dancing choirs,
changes of dress, warm baths, and downy beds.
O master dancers of the Phaiákians!
Perform now: let our guest on his return
tell his companions we excel the world

---

[71] **Philoktêtês:** Inherited Heraklês' bow.   [72] **Eurýtos:** Eurýtos challenged Apollo to an archery contest and lost; his bow was given to Odysseus, who uses it at the end of the epic.   [73] **the palestra:** A public place for wrestling and other athletics.

in dance and song, as in our ships and running.
Someone go find the gittern[74] harp in hall
and bring it quickly to Demódokos!"

270   At the serene king's word, a squire ran
to bring the polished harp out of the palace,
and place was given to nine referees—
peers of the realm, masters of ceremony—
who cleared a space and smoothed a dancing floor.
The squire brought down, and gave Demódokos,
the clear-toned harp; and centering on the minstrel
magical young dancers formed a circle
with a light beat, and stamp of feet. Beholding,
Odysseus marvelled at the flashing ring.

280   Now to his harp the blinded minstrel sang
of Arês' dalliance with Aphroditê:
how hidden in Hephaistos' house they played
at love together, and the gifts of Arês,
dishonoring Hephaistos' bed—and how
the word that wounds the heart came to the master
from Hélios,° who had seen the two embrace;   the sun
and when he learned it, Lord Hephaistos went
with baleful calculation to his forge.
There mightily he armed his anvil block
290   and hammered out a chain whose tempered links
could not be sprung or bent; he meant that they should hold.
Those shackles fashioned hot in wrath Hephaistos
climbed to the bower and the bed of love,
pooled all his net of chain around the bed posts
and swung it from the rafters overhead—
light as a cobweb even gods in bliss
could not perceive, so wonderful his cunning.
Seeing his bed now made a snare, he feigned
a journey to the trim stronghold of Lemnos,
300   the dearest of earth's towns to him.[75] And Arês?
Ah, golden Arês' watch had its reward
when he beheld the great smith leaving home.
How promptly to the famous door he came,
intent on pleasure with sweet Kythereia![76]

---

[74] **the gittern:** An early ancestor of the guitar.   [75] **Lemnos . . . to him:** Hephaistos landed on the island of Lemnos when Zeus threw him off Olympos.   [76] **Kythereia:** A name for Aphroditê taken from the island Kythera (Cythera), to which Aphroditê floated after her birth from sea foam.

She, who had left her father's side but now,
sat in her chamber when her lover entered;
and tenderly he pressed her hand and said:
"Come and lie down, my darling, and be happy!
Hephaistos is no longer here, but gone
310 to see his grunting[77] Sintian friends on Lemnos."

As she, too, thought repose would be most welcome,
the pair went in to bed — into a shower
of clever chains, the netting of Hephaistos.
So trussed they could not move apart, nor rise,
at last they knew there could be no escape,
they were to see the glorious cripple now —
for Hêlios had spied for him, and told him;
so he turned back this side of Lemnos Isle
sick at heart, making his way homeward.
320 Now in the doorway of the room he stood
while deadly rage took hold of him; his voice,
hoarse and terrible, reached all the gods:
"O Father Zeus, O gods in bliss forever,
here is indecorous entertainment for you,
Aphroditê, Zeus's daughter,
caught in the act, cheating me, her cripple,
with Arês — devastating Arês.
Cleanlimbed beauty is her joy, not these
bandylegs I came into the world with:
330 no one to blame but the two gods[78] who bred me!
Come see this pair entwining here
in my own bed! How hot it makes me burn!
I think they may not care to lie much longer,
pressing on one another, passionate lovers;
they'll have enough of bed together soon.
And yet the chain that bagged them holds them down
till Father sends me back my wedding gifts —
all that I poured out for his damned pigeon,
so lovely, and so wanton."

340   All the others
were crowding in, now, to the brazen house —
Poseidon who embraces earth, and Hermês
the runner, and Apollo, lord of Distance.

---

[77] **grunting**: Non-Greek speaking.   [78] **the two gods**: Zeus and Hêra.

The goddesses stayed home for shame; but these
munificences ranged there in the doorway,
and irrepressible among them all
arose the laughter of the happy gods.
Gazing hard at Hephaistos' handiwork
the gods in turn remarked among themselves:

350   "No dash in adultery now."

                    "The tortoise tags the hare —
Hephaistos catches Arês — and Arês outran the wind."

"The lame god's craft has pinned him. Now shall he
pay what is due from gods taken in cuckoldry."

They made these improving remarks to one another,
but Apollo leaned aside to say to Hermês:
"Son of Zeus, beneficent Wayfinder,
would you accept a coverlet of chain, if only
you lay by Aphroditê's golden side?"

360   To this the Wayfinder replied, shining:
"Would I not, though, Apollo of distances!
Wrap me in chains three times the weight of these,
come goddesses and gods to see the fun;
only let me lie beside the pale-golden one!"

The gods gave way again to peals of laughter,
all but Poseidon, and he never smiled,
but urged Hephaistos to unpinion Arês,
saying emphatically, in a loud voice:
                        "Free him;

370   you will be paid, I swear; ask what you will;
he pays up every jot the gods decree."

To this the Great Gamelegs replied:
                        "Poseidon,
lord of the earth-surrounding sea, I should not
swear to a scoundrel's honor. What have I
as surety from you, if Arês leaves me
empty-handed, with my empty chain?"

The Earthshaker for answer urged again:
"Hephaistos, let us grant he goes, and leaves

380   the fine unpaid; I swear, then, I shall pay it."

Then said the Great Gamelegs at last:
"No more;
you offer terms I cannot well refuse."

And down the strong god bent to set them free,
till disencumbered of their bond, the chain,
the lovers leapt away—he into Thrace,[79]
while Aphroditê, laughter's darling, fled
to Kypros[80] Isle and Paphos, to her meadow
and altar dim with incense. There the Graces
390 bathed and anointed her with golden oil—
a bloom that clings upon immortal flesh alone—
and let her folds of mantle fall in glory.

So ran the song the minstrel sang.

Odysseus,
listening, found sweet pleasure in the tale,
among the Phaiákian mariners and oarsmen.
And next Alkínoös called upon his sons,
Halios and Laódamas, to show
the dance no one could do as well as they—
400 handling a purple ball carven by Pólybos.
One made it shoot up under the shadowing clouds
as he leaned backward; bounding high in air
the other cut its flight far off the ground—
and neither missed a step as the ball soared.
The next turn was to keep it low, and shuttling
hard between them, while the ring of boys
gave them a steady stamping beat.
Odysseus now addressed Alkínoös:
"O majesty, model of all your folk,
410 your promise was to show me peerless dancers;
here is the promise kept. I am all wonder."

At this Alkínoös in his might rejoicing
said to the seafarers of Phaiákia:
"Attend me now, Phaiákian lords and captains:
our guest appears a clear-eyed man and wise.
Come, let him feel our bounty as he should.
Here are twelve princes of the kingdom—lords

---

[79]**Thrace:** A country north and east of Greece; Thrace was the home of Arês and a warlike people.   [80]**Kypros:**
Aphroditê's shrine on Kypros (Cyprus) was at Paphos.

paramount, and I who make thirteen;
let each one bring a laundered cloak and tunic,
420 and add one bar of honorable gold.
Heap all our gifts together; load his arms;
let him go joyous to our evening feast!
As for Seareach — why, man to man
he'll make amends, and handsomely; he blundered."

Now all as one acclaimed the king's good pleasure,
and each one sent a squire to bring his gifts.
Meanwhile Seareach found speech again, saying:
"My lord and model of us all, Alkínoös,
as you require of me, in satisfaction,
430 this broadsword of clear bronze goes to our guest.
Its hilt is silver, and the ringed sheath
of new-sawn ivory — a costly weapon."

He turned to give the broadsword to Odysseus,
facing him, saying blithely:
                                    "Sir, my best
wishes, my respects; if I offended,
I hope the seawinds blow it out of mind.
God send you see your lady and your homeland
soon again, after the pain of exile."

440 Odysseus, the great tactician, answered:
"My hand, friend; may the gods award you fortune.
I hope no pressing need comes on you ever
for this fine blade you give me in amends."

He slung it, glinting silver, from his shoulder,
as the light shone from sundown. Messengers
were bearing gifts and treasure to the palace,
where the king's sons received them all, and made
a glittering pile at their grave mother's side;
then, as Alkínoös took his throne of power,
450 each went to his own high-backed chair in turn,
and said Alkínoös to Arêtê:
"Lady, bring here a chest, the finest one;
a clean cloak and tunic; stow these things;
and warm a cauldron for him. Let him bathe,
when he has seen the gifts of the Phaiákians,
and so dine happily to a running song.
My own wine-cup of gold intaglio
I'll give him, too; through all the days to come,

tipping his wine to Zeus or other gods
460　in his great hall, he shall remember me."

Then said Arêtê to her maids:
　　　　　　　　　"The tripod:
stand the great tripod legs about the fire."

They swung the cauldron on the fire's heart,
poured water in, and fed the blaze beneath
until the basin simmered, cupped in flame.
The queen set out a rich chest from her chamber
and folded in the gifts—clothing and gold
given Odysseus by the Phaiákians;
470　then she put in the royal cloak and tunic,
briskly saying to her guest:
　　　　　　　　　　　"Now here, sir,
look to the lid yourself, and tie it down
against light fingers, if there be any,
on the black ship tonight while you are sleeping."

Noble Odysseus, expert in adversity,
battened the lid down with a lightning knot
learned, once, long ago, from the Lady Kirkê.[81]
And soon a call came from the Bathing Mistress
480　who led him to a hip-bath, warm and clear—
a happy sight, and rare in his immersions
after he left Kalypso's home—where, surely,
the luxuries of a god were ever his.
When the bath maids had washed him, rubbed him down,
put a fresh tunic and a cloak around him,
he left the bathing place to join the men
at wine in hall.

　　　　　　The princess Nausikaa,
exquisite figure, as of heaven's shaping,
490　waited beside a pillar as he passed
and said swiftly, with wonder in her look:
"Fare well, stranger; in your land remember me
who met and saved you. It is worth your thought."

The man of all occasions now met this:
"Daughter of great Alkínoös, Nausikaa,

---

[81] **Lady Kirkê** (Circe): A sorceress; Odysseus encounters Kirkê on her island in Book 12.

may Zeus the lord of thunder, Hêra's consort,
grant me daybreak again in my own country!
But there and all my days until I die
may I invoke you as I would a goddess,
500 princess, to whom I owe my life."

He left her
and went to take his place beside the king.

Now when the roasts were cut, the winebowls full,
a herald led the minstrel down the room
amid the deference of the crowd, and paused
to seat him near a pillar in the center—
whereupon that resourceful man, Odysseus,
carved out a quarter from his chine of pork,
crisp with fat, and called the blind man's guide:
510 "Herald! here, take this to Demódokos:
let him feast and be merry, with my compliments.
All men owe honor to the poets—honor
and awe, for they are dearest to the Muse
who puts upon their lips the ways of life."

Gentle Demódokos took the proffered gift
and inwardly rejoiced. When all were served,
every man's hand went out upon the banquet,
repelling hunger and thirst, until at length
Odysseus spoke again to the blind minstrel:
520 "Demódokos, accept my utmost praise.
The Muse, daughter of Zeus in radiance,
or else Apollo gave you skill to shape
with such great style your songs of the Akhaians—
their hard lot, how they fought and suffered war.
You shared it, one would say, or heard it all.
Now shift your theme, and sing that wooden horse
Epeios built, inspired by Athena—
the ambuscade Odysseus filled with fighters
and sent to take the inner town of Troy.
530 Sing only this for me, sing me this well,
and I shall say at once before the world
the grace of heaven has given us a song."

The minstrel stirred, murmuring to the god, and soon
clear words and notes came one by one, a vision
of the Akhaians in their graceful ships
drawing away from shore: the torches flung

and shelters flaring: Argive soldiers crouched
in the close dark around Odysseus: and
the horse, tall on the assembly ground of Troy.
540 For when the Trojans pulled it in, themselves,
up to the citadel, they sat nearby
with long-drawn-out and hapless argument—
favoring, in the end, one course of three:
either to stave the vault with brazen axes,
or haul it to a cliff and pitch it down,
or else to save it for the gods, a votive glory—
the plan that could not but prevail.
For Troy must perish, as ordained, that day
she harbored the great horse of timber; hidden
550 the flower of Akhaia lay, and bore
slaughter and death upon the men of Troy.
He sang, then, of the town sacked by Akhaians
pouring down from the horse's hollow cave,
this way and that way raping the steep city,
and how Odysseus came like Arês to
the door of Deïphobos, with Meneláos,
and braved the desperate fight there—
conquering once more by Athena's power.

The splendid minstrel sang it.

560   And Odysseus
let the bright molten tears run down his cheeks,
weeping the way a wife mourns for her lord
on the lost field where he has gone down fighting
the day of wrath that came upon his children.
At sight of the man panting and dying there,
she slips down to enfold him, crying out;
then feels the spears, prodding her back and shoulders,
and goes bound into slavery and grief.
Piteous weeping wears away her cheeks:
570 but no more piteous than Odysseus' tears,
cloaked as they were, now, from the company.
Only Alkínoös, at his elbow, knew—
hearing the low sob in the man's breathing—
and when he knew, he spoke:
"Hear me, lords and captains of Phaiákia!
And let Demódokos touch his harp no more.
His theme has not been pleasing to all here.
During the feast, since our fine poet sang,
our guest has never left off weeping. Grief

580 seems fixed upon his heart. Break off the song!
Let everyone be easy, host and guest;
there's more decorum in a smiling banquet!
We had prepared here, on our friend's behalf,
safe conduct in a ship, and gifts to cheer him,
holding that any man with a grain of wit
will treat a decent suppliant like a brother.
Now by the same rule, friend, you must not be
secretive any longer! Come, in fairness,
tell me the name you bore in that far country;
590 how were you known to family, and neighbors?
No man is nameless—no man, good or bad,
but gets a name in his first infancy,
none being born, unless a mother bears him!
Tell me your native land, your coast and city—
sailing directions for the ships, you know—
for those Phaiákian ships of ours
that have no steersman, and no steering oar,
divining the crew's wishes, as they do,
and knowing, as they do, the ports of call
600 about the world. Hidden in mist or cloud
they scud the open sea, with never a thought
of being in distress or going down.
There is, however, something I once heard
Nausíthoös, my father, say: Poseidon
holds it against us that our deep sea ships
are sure conveyance for all passengers.
My father said, some day one of our cutters
homeward bound over the cloudy sea
would be wrecked by the god, and a range of hills
610 thrown round our city. So, in his age, he said,
and let it be, or not, as the god please.
But come, now, put it for me clearly, tell me
the sea ways that you wandered, and the shores
you touched; the cities, and the men therein,
uncivilized, if such there were, and hostile,
and those godfearing who had kindly manners.
Tell me why you should grieve so terribly
over the Argives and the fall of Troy.
That was all gods' work, weaving ruin there
620 so it should make a song for men to come!
Some kin of yours, then, died at Ilion,
some first rate man, by marriage near to you,
next your own blood most dear?
Or some companion of congenial mind

and valor? True it is, a wise friend
can take a brother's place in our affection."

BOOK 9
NEW COASTS AND POSEIDON'S SON

Now this was the reply Odysseus made:
"Alkínoös, king and admiration of men,
how beautiful this is, to hear a minstrel
gifted as yours: a god he might be, singing!
There is no boon in life more sweet, I say,
than when a summer joy holds all the realm,
and banqueters sit listening to a harper
in a great hall, by rows of tables heaped
with bread and roast meat, while a steward goes
10 to dip up wine and brim your cups again.
Here is the flower of life, it seems to me!
But now you wish to know my cause for sorrow—
and thereby give me cause for more.

What shall I

say first? What shall I keep until the end?
The gods have tried me in a thousand ways.
But first my name: let that be known to you,
and if I pull away from pitiless death,
friendship will bind us, though my land lies far.

20 I am Laërtês' son, Odysseus.

Men hold me

formidable for guile in peace and war:
this fame has gone abroad to the sky's rim.
My home is on the peaked sea-mark of Ithaka
under Mount Neion's wind-blown robe of leaves,
in sight of other islands—Doulíkhion,
Samê, wooded Zakynthos—Ithaka
being most lofty in that coastal sea,
and northwest, while the rest lie east and south.
30 A rocky isle, but good for a boy's training;
I shall not see on earth a place more dear,
though I have been detained long by Kalypso,
loveliest among goddesses, who held me
in her smooth caves, to be her heart's delight,
as Kirkê of Aiaia, the enchantress,
desired me, and detained me in her hall.
But in my heart I never gave consent.

Where shall a man find sweetness to surpass
his own home and his parents? In far lands
40 he shall not, though he find a house of gold.

What of my sailing, then, from Troy?
                                What of those years
of rough adventure, weathered under Zeus?
The wind that carried west from Ilion
brought me to Ísmaros, on the far shore,
a strongpoint on the coast of the Kikonês.[82]
I stormed that place and killed the men who fought.
Plunder we took, and we enslaved the women,
to make division, equal shares to all—
50 but on the spot I told them: 'Back, and quickly!
Out to sea again!' My men were mutinous,
fools, on stores of wine. Sheep after sheep
they butchered by the surf, and shambling cattle,
feasting—while fugitives went inland, running
to call to arms the main force of Kikonês.
This was an army, trained to fight on horseback
or, where the ground required, on foot. They came
with dawn over that terrain like the leaves
and blades of spring. So doom appeared to us,
60 dark word of Zeus for us, our evil days.
My men stood up and made a fight of it—
backed on the ships, with lances kept in play,
from bright morning through the blaze of noon
holding our beach, although so far outnumbered;
but when the sun passed toward unyoking time,
then the Akhaians, one by one, gave way.
Six benches were left empty in every ship
that evening when we pulled away from death.
And this new grief we bore with us to sea:
70 our precious lives we had, but not our friends.
No ship made sail next day until some shipmate
had raised a cry, three times, for each poor ghost
unfleshed by the Kikonês on that field.

Now Zeus the lord of cloud roused in the north
a storm against the ships, and driving veils
of squall moved down like night on land and sea.
The bows went plunging at the gust; sails

---

[82] **Kikonês:** Allies of Troy, the Kikonês lived on the northern coast of the Aegean Sea.

cracked and lashed out strips in the big wind.
We saw death in that fury, dropped the yards,
80 unshipped the oars, and pulled for the nearest lee:
then two long days and nights we lay offshore
worn out and sick at heart, tasting our grief,
until a third Dawn came with ringlets shining.
Then we put up our masts, hauled sail, and rested,
letting the steersmen and the breeze take over.

I might have made it safely home, that time,
but as I came round Malea the current
took me out to sea, and from the north
a fresh gale drove me on, past Kythera.[83]
90 Nine days I drifted on the teeming sea
before dangerous high winds. Upon the tenth
we came to the coastline of the Lotos Eaters,[84]
who live upon that flower. We landed there
to take on water. All ships' companies
mustered alongside for the mid-day meal.
Then I sent out two picked men and a runner
to learn what race of men that land sustained.
They fell in, soon enough, with Lotos Eaters,
who showed no will to do us harm, only
100 offering the sweet Lotos to our friends—
but those who ate this honeyed plant, the Lotos,
never cared to report, nor to return:
they longed to stay forever, browsing on
that native bloom, forgetful of their homeland.
I drove them, all three wailing, to the ships,
tied them down under their rowing benches,
and called the rest: 'All hands aboard;
come, clear the beach and no one taste
the Lotos, or you lose your hope of home.'
110 Filing in to their places by the rowlocks
my oarsmen dipped their long oars in the surf,
and we moved out again on our sea faring.

In the next land we found were Kyklopês,[85]
giants, louts, without a law to bless them.

---

[83] **Malea . . . Kythera:** Malea is at the southernmost tip of Greece; Kythera is an island farther south.
[84] **Lotos Eaters:** Usually identified with North Africans, perhaps near modern Libya; a wide range of interpretations exist for the lotus—from a mild narcotic or hallucinogen to an aphrodisiac.   [85] **Kyklopês:** According to ancient tradition, the Kyklopês (Cyclops) lived in Sicily.

In ignorance leaving the fruitage of the earth in mystery
to the immortal gods, they neither plow
nor sow by hand, nor till the ground, though grain—
wild wheat and barley—grows untended, and
wine-grapes, in clusters, ripen in heaven's rain.
120 Kyklopês have no muster and no meeting,
no consultation or old tribal ways,
but each one dwells in his own mountain cave
dealing out rough justice to wife and child,
indifferent to what the others do.

                                  Well, then:
across the wide bay from the mainland
there lies a desert island, not far out,
but still not close inshore. Wild goats in hundreds
breed there; and no human being comes
130 upon the isle to startle them—no hunter
of all who ever tracked with hounds through forests
or had rough going over mountain trails.
The isle, unplanted and untilled, a wilderness,
pastures goats alone. And this is why:
good ships like ours with cheekpaint at the bows
are far beyond the Kyklopês. No shipwright
toils among them, shaping and building up
symmetrical trim hulls to cross the sea
and visit all the seaboard towns, as men do
140 who go and come in commerce over water.
This isle—seagoing folk would have annexed it
and built their homesteads on it: all good land,
fertile for every crop in season: lush
well-watered meads along the shore, vines in profusion,
prairie, clear for the plow, where grain would grow
chin high by harvest time, and rich sub-soil.
The island cove is landlocked, so you need
no hawsers out astern, bow-stones[86] or mooring:
run in and ride there till the day your crews
150 chafe to be under sail, and a fair wind blows.
You'll find good water flowing from a cavern
through dusky poplars into the upper bay.
Here we made harbor. Some god guided us
that night, for we could barely see our bows
in the dense fog around us, and no moonlight

---

[86] **bow-stones:** An anchor made out of stones knotted in rope and hung over the bow of a boat.

filtered through the overcast. No look-out,
nobody saw the island dead ahead,
nor even the great landward rolling billow
that took us in: we found ourselves in shallows,
160 keels grazing shore: so furled our sails
and disembarked where the low ripples broke.
There on the beach we lay, and slept till morning.

When Dawn spread out her finger tips of rose
we turned out marvelling, to tour the isle,
while Zeus's shy nymph daughters flushed wild goats
down from the heights—a breakfast for my men.
We ran to fetch our hunting bows and long-shanked
lances from the ships, and in three companies
we took our shots. Heaven gave us game a-plenty:
170 for every one of twelve ships in my squadron
nine goats fell to be shared; my lot was ten.
So there all day, until the sun went down,
we made our feast on meat galore, and wine—
wine from the ship, for our supply held out,
so many jars were filled at Ísmaros
from stores of the Kikonês that we plundered.
We gazed, too, at Kyklopês Land, so near,
we saw their smoke, heard bleating from their flocks.
But after sundown, in the gathering dusk,
180 we slept again above the wash of ripples.

When the young Dawn with finger tips of rose
came in the east, I called my men together
and made a speech to them:
                                        'Old shipmates, friends,
the rest of you stand by; I'll make the crossing
in my own ship, with my own company,
and find out what the mainland natives are—
for they may be wild savages, and lawless,
or hospitable and god fearing men.'

190 At this I went aboard, and gave the word
to cast off by the stern. My oarsmen followed,
filing in to their benches by the rowlocks,
and all in line dipped oars in the grey sea.

As we rowed on, and nearer to the mainland,
at one end of the bay, we saw a cavern

yawning above the water, screened with laurel,
and many rams and goats about the place
inside a sheepfold—made from slabs of stone
earthfast between tall trunks of pine and rugged
200 towering oak trees.
          A prodigious man
slept in this cave alone, and took his flocks
to graze afield—remote from all companions,
knowing none but savage ways, a brute
so huge, he seemed no man at all of those
who eat good wheaten bread; but he seemed rather
a shaggy mountain reared in solitude.
We beached there, and I told the crew
to stand by and keep watch over the ship;
210 as for myself I took my twelve best fighters
and went ahead. I had a goatskin full
of that sweet liquor that Euanthês' son,
Maron, had given me. He kept Apollo's
holy grove at Ísmaros; for kindness
we showed him there, and showed his wife and child,
he gave me seven shining golden talents[87]
perfectly formed, a solid silver winebowl,
and then this liquor—twelve two-handled jars
of brandy, pure and fiery. Not a slave
220 in Maron's household knew this drink; only
he, his wife and the storeroom mistress knew;
and they would put one cupful—ruby-colored,
honey-smooth—in twenty more of water,
but still the sweet scent hovered like a fume
over the winebowl. No man turned away
when cups of this came round.
          A wineskin full
I brought along, and victuals in a bag,
for in my bones I knew some towering brute
230 would be upon us soon—all outward power,
a wild man, ignorant of civility.

We climbed, then, briskly to the cave. But Kyklops
had gone afield, to pasture his fat sheep,
so we looked round at everything inside:

---

[87] **talents:** Units of gold.

a drying rack that sagged with cheeses, pens
crowded with lambs and kids, each in its class:
firstlings apart from middlings, and the 'dewdrops,'
or newborn lambkins, penned apart from both.
And vessels full of whey were brimming there—
240 bowls of earthenware and pails for milking.
My men came pressing round me, pleading:
                                        'Why not
take these cheeses, get them stowed, come back,
throw open all the pens, and make a run for it?
We'll drive the kids and lambs aboard. We say
put out again on good salt water!'

                        Ah,
how sound that was! Yet I refused. I wished
to see the caveman, what he had to offer—
250 no pretty sight, it turned out, for my friends.
We lit a fire, burnt an offering,
and took some cheese to eat; then sat in silence
around the embers, waiting. When he came
he had a load of dry boughs on his shoulder
to stoke his fire at suppertime. He dumped it
with a great crash into that hollow cave,
and we all scattered fast to the far wall.
Then over the broad cavern floor he ushered
the ewes he meant to milk. He left his rams
260 and he-goats in the yard outside, and swung
high overhead a slab of solid rock
to close the cave. Two dozen four-wheeled wagons,
with heaving wagon teams, could not have stirred
the tonnage of that rock from where he wedged it
over the doorsill. Next he took his seat
and milked his bleating ewes. A practiced job
he made of it, giving each ewe her suckling;
thickened his milk, then, into curds and whey,
sieved out the curds to drip in withy baskets,
270 and poured the whey to stand in bowls
cooling until he drank it for his supper.
When all these chores were done, he poked the fire,
heaping on brushwood. In the glare he saw us.

'Strangers,' he said, 'who are you? And where from?
What brings you here by sea ways—a fair traffic?

Or are you wandering rogues, who cast your lives
like dice, and ravage other folk by sea?'

We felt a pressure on our hearts, in dread
of that deep rumble and that mighty man.
280   But all the same I spoke up in reply:
'We are from Troy, Akhaians, blown off course
by shifting gales on the Great South Sea;
homeward bound, but taking routes and ways
uncommon; so the will of Zeus would have it.
We served under Agamémnon, son of Atreus—
the whole world knows what city
he laid waste, what armies he destroyed.
It was our luck to come here; here we stand,
beholden for your help, or any gifts
290   you give—as custom is to honor strangers.[88]
We would entreat you, great Sir, have a care
for the gods' courtesy; Zeus will avenge
the unoffending guest.'

                    He answered this
from his brute chest, unmoved:
                              'You are a ninny
or else you come from the other end of nowhere,
telling me, mind the gods! We Kyklopês
care not a whistle for your thundering Zeus
300   or all the gods in bliss, we have more force by far.
I would not let you go for fear of Zeus—
you or your friends—unless I had a whim to.
Tell me, where was it, now, you left your ship—
around the point, or down the shore, I wonder?'

He thought he'd find out, but I saw through this,
and answered with a ready lie:
                              'My ship?
Poseidon Lord, who sets the earth a-tremble,
broke it up on the rocks at your land's end.
310   A wind from seaward served him, drove us there.
We are survivors, these good men and I.'

---

[88] **as custom . . . strangers:** The laws of hospitality, protected by Zeus, included the giving of gifts.

Neither reply nor pity came from him,
but in one stride he clutched at my companions
and caught two in his hands like squirming puppies
to beat their brains out, spattering the floor.
Then he dismembered them and made his meal,
gaping and crunching like a mountain lion—
everything: innards, flesh, and marrow bones.
We cried aloud, lifting our hands to Zeus,
320 powerless, looking on at this, appalled;
but Kyklops went on filling up his belly
with manflesh and great gulps of whey,
then lay down like a mast among his sheep.
My heart beat high now at the chance of action,
and drawing the sharp sword from my hip I went
along his flank to stab him where the midriff
holds the liver. I had touched the spot
when sudden fear stayed me: if I killed him
we perished there as well, for we could never
330 move his ponderous doorway slab aside.
So we were left to groan and wait for morning.

When the young Dawn with finger tips of rose
lit up the world, the Kyklops built a fire
and milked his handsome ewes, all in due order,
putting the sucklings to the mothers. Then,
his chores being all dispatched, he caught
another brace of men to make his breakfast,
and whisked away his great door slab
to let his sheep go through—but he, behind,
340 reset the stone as one would cap a quiver.
There was a din of whistling as the Kyklops
rounded his flock to higher ground, then stillness.
And now I pondered how to hurt him worst,
if but Athena granted what I prayed for.
Here are the means I thought would serve my turn:

a club, or staff, lay there along the fold—
an olive tree, felled green and left to season
for Kyklops' hand. And it was like a mast
a lugger of twenty oars, broad in the beam—
350 a deep-sea-going craft—might carry:
so long, so big around, it seemed. Now I
chopped out a six foot section of this pole
and set it down before my men, who scraped it;
and when they had it smooth, I hewed again

to make a stake with pointed end. I held this
in the fire's heart and turned it, toughening it,
then hid it, well back in the cavern, under
one of the dung piles in profusion there.
Now came the time to toss for it: who ventured
360 along with me? whose hand could bear to thrust
and grind that spike in Kyklops' eye, when mild
sleep had mastered him? As luck would have it,
the men I would have chosen won the toss—
four strong men, and I made five as captain.

At evening came the shepherd with his flock,
his woolly flock. The rams as well, this time,
entered the cave: by some sheep-herding whim—
or a god's bidding—none were left outside.
He hefted his great boulder into place
370 and sat him down to milk the bleating ewes
in proper order, put the lambs to suck,
and swiftly ran through all his evening chores.
Then he caught two more men and feasted on them.
My moment was at hand, and I went forward
holding an ivy bowl of my dark drink,
looking up, saying:
                    'Kyklops, try some wine.
Here's liquor to wash down your scraps of men.
Taste it, and see the kind of drink we carried
380 under our planks. I meant it for an offering
if you would help us home. But you are mad,
unbearable, a bloody monster! After this
will any other traveller come to see you?'

He seized and drained the bowl, and it went down
so fiery and smooth he called for more:
'Give me another, thank you kindly. Tell me,
how are you called? I'll make a gift will please you.
Even Kyklopês know the wine-grapes grow
out of grassland and loam in heaven's rain,
390 but here's a bit of nectar and ambrosia!'

Three bowls I brought him, and he poured them down.
I saw the fuddle and flush come over him,
then I sang out in cordial tones:
                              'Kyklops,
you ask my honorable name? Remember
the gift you promised me, and I shall tell you.

My name is Nohbdy: mother, father, and friends,
everyone calls me Nohbdy.'

And he said:

400 'Nohbdy's my meat, then, after I eat his friends.
Others come first. There's a noble gift, now.'

Even as he spoke, he reeled and tumbled backward,
his great head lolling to one side: and sleep
took him like any creature. Drunk, hiccuping,
he dribbled streams of liquor and bits of men.

Now, by the gods, I drove my big hand spike
deep in the embers, charring it again,
and cheered my men along with battle talk
to keep their courage up: no quitting now.
410 The pike of olive, green though it had been,
reddened and glowed as if about to catch.
I drew it from the coals and my four fellows
gave me a hand, lugging it near the Kyklops
as more than natural force nerved them; straight
forward they sprinted, lifted it, and rammed it
deep in his crater eye, and I leaned on it
turning it as a shipwright turns a drill
in planking, having men below to swing
the two-handled strap that spins it in the groove.
420 So with our brand we bored that great eye socket
while blood ran out around the red hot bar.
Eyelid and lash were seared; the pierced ball
hissed broiling, and the roots popped.

In a smithy
one sees a white-hot axehead or an adze
plunged and wrung in a cold tub, screeching steam —
the way they make soft iron hale and hard —:
just so that eyeball hissed around the spike.
The Kyklops bellowed and the rock roared round him,
430 and we fell back in fear. Clawing his face
he tugged the bloody spike out of his eye,
threw it away, and his wild hands went groping;
then he set up a howl for Kyklopês
who lived in caves on windy peaks nearby.
Some heard him; and they came by divers ways
to clump around outside and call:

'What ails you,

Polyphêmos? Why do you cry so sore
in the starry night? You will not let us sleep.
440 Sure no man's driving off your flock? No man
has tricked you, ruined you?'

                          Out of the cave
the mammoth Polyphêmos roared in answer:
'Nohbdy, Nohbdy's tricked me, Nohbdy's ruined me!'

To this rough shout they made a sage reply:
'Ah well, if nobody has played you foul
there in your lonely bed, we are no use in pain
given by great Zeus. Let it be your father,
Poseidon Lord, to whom you pray.'

450   So saying
they trailed away. And I was filled with laughter
to see how like a charm the name deceived them.
Now Kyklops, wheezing as the pain came on him,
fumbled to wrench away the great doorstone
and squatted in the breach with arms thrown wide
for any silly beast or man who bolted—
hoping somehow I might be such a fool.
But I kept thinking how to win the game:
death sat there huge; how could we slip away?
460 I drew on all my wits, and ran through tactics,
reasoning as a man will for dear life,
until a trick came—and it pleased me well.
The Kyklops' rams were handsome, fat, with heavy
fleeces, a dark violet.
                    Three abreast
I tied them silently together, twining
cords of willow from the ogre's bed;
then slung a man under each middle one
to ride there safely, shielded left and right.
470 So three sheep could convey each man. I took
the woolliest ram, the choicest of the flock,
and hung myself under his kinky belly,
pulled up tight, with fingers twisted deep
in sheepskin ringlets for an iron grip.
So, breathing hard, we waited until morning.

When Dawn spread out her finger tips of rose
the rams began to stir, moving for pasture,

and peals of bleating echoed round the pens
where dams with udders full called for a milking.
480 Blinded, and sick with pain from his head wound,
the master stroked each ram, then let it pass,
but my men riding on the pectoral fleece
the giant's blind hands blundering never found.
Last of them all my ram, the leader, came,
weighted by wool and me with my meditations.
The Kyklops patted him, and then he said:
'Sweet cousin ram, why lag behind the rest
in the night cave? You never linger so,
but graze before them all, and go afar
490 to crop sweet grass, and take your stately way
leading along the streams, until at evening
you run to be the first one in the fold.
Why, now, so far behind? Can you be grieving
over your Master's eye? That carrion rogue
and his accurst companions burnt it out
when he had conquered all my wits with wine.
Nohbdy will not get out alive, I swear.
Oh, had you brain and voice to tell
where he may be now, dodging all my fury!
500 Bashed by this hand and bashed on this rock wall
his brains would strew the floor, and I should have
rest from the outrage Nohbdy worked upon me.'

He sent us into the open, then. Close by,
I dropped and rolled clear of the ram's belly,
going this way and that to untie the men.
With many glances back, we rounded up
his fat, stiff-legged sheep to take aboard,
and drove them down to where the good ship lay.
We saw, as we came near, our fellows' faces
510 shining; then we saw them turn to grief
tallying those who had not fled from death.
I hushed them, jerking head and eyebrows up,
and in a low voice told them: 'Load this herd;
move fast, and put the ship's head toward the breakers.'
They all pitched in at loading, then embarked
and struck their oars into the sea. Far out,
as far off shore as shouted words would carry,
I sent a few back to the adversary:
'O Kyklops! Would you feast on my companions?
520 Puny, am I, in a Caveman's hands?

How do you like the beating that we gave you,
you damned cannibal? Eater of guests
under your roof! Zeus and the gods have paid you!'

The blind thing in his doubled fury broke
a hilltop in his hands and heaved it after us.
Ahead of our black prow it struck and sank
whelmed in a spuming geyser, a giant wave
that washed the ship stern foremost back to shore.
I got the longest boathook out and stood
530   fending us off, with furious nods to all
to put their backs into a racing stroke—
row, row, or perish. So the long oars bent
kicking the foam sternward, making head
until we drew away, and twice as far.
Now when I cupped my hands I heard the crew
in low voices protesting:
       'Godsake, Captain!
Why bait the beast again? Let him alone!'
'That tidal wave he made on the first throw
540   all but beached us.'

    'All but stove us in!'

'Give him our bearing with your trumpeting,
he'll get the range and lob a boulder.'

        'Aye

He'll smash our timbers and our heads together!'

I would not heed them in my glorying spirit,
but let my anger flare and yelled:
       'Kyklops,
if ever mortal man inquire
550   how you were put to shame and blinded, tell him
Odysseus, raider of cities, took your eye:
Laërtês' son, whose home's on Ithaka!'

At this he gave a mighty sob and rumbled:
'Now comes the weird° upon me, spoken of old.   *destiny*
A wizard, grand and wondrous, lived here—Télemos,
a son of Eurymos; great length of days
he had in wizardry among the Kyklopês,
and these things he foretold for time to come:

my great eye lost, and at Odysseus' hands.
560 Always I had in mind some giant, armed
in giant force, would come against me here.
But this, but you—small, pitiful and twiggy—
you put me down with wine, you blinded me.
Come back, Odysseus, and I'll treat you well,
praying the god of earthquake to befriend you—
his son I am, for he by his avowal
fathered me, and, if he will, he may
heal me of this black wound—he and no other
of all the happy gods or mortal men.'

570 Few words I shouted in reply to him:
'If I could take your life I would and take
your time away, and hurl you down to hell!
The god of earthquake could not heal you there!'

At this he stretched his hands out in his darkness
toward the sky of stars, and prayed Poseidon:
'O hear me, lord, blue girdler of the islands,
if I am thine indeed, and thou art father:
grant that Odysseus, raider of cities, never
see his home: Laërtês' son, I mean,
580 who kept his hall on Ithaka. Should destiny
intend that he shall see his roof again
among his family in his father land,
far be that day, and dark the years between.
Let him lose all companions, and return
under strange sail to bitter days at home.'

In these words he prayed, and the god heard him.
Now he laid hands upon a bigger stone
and wheeled around, titanic for the cast,
to let it fly in the black-prowed vessel's track.
590 But it fell short, just aft the steering oar,
and whelming seas rose giant above the stone
to bear us onward toward the island.
                             There
as we ran in we saw the squadron waiting,
the trim ships drawn up side by side, and all
our troubled friends who waited, looking seaward.
We beached her, grinding keel in the soft sand,
and waded in, ourselves, on the sandy beach.
Then we unloaded all the Kyklops' flock
600 to make division, share and share alike,

only my fighters voted that my ram,
the prize of all, should go to me. I slew him
by the sea side and burnt his long thighbones
to Zeus beyond the stormcloud, Kronos' son,
who rules the world. But Zeus disdained my offering;
destruction for my ships he had in store
and death for those who sailed them, my companions.
Now all day long until the sun went down
we made our feast on mutton and sweet wine,
610 till after sunset in the gathering dark
we went to sleep above the wash of ripples.

When the young Dawn with finger tips of rose
touched the world, I roused the men, gave orders
to man the ships, cast off the mooring lines;
and filing in to sit beside the rowlocks
oarsmen in line dipped oars in the grey sea.
So we moved out, sad in the vast offing,
having our precious lives, but not our friends.

BOOK 10
THE GRACE OF THE WITCH

We made our landfall on Aiolia Island,
domain of Aiolos Hippotadês,[89]
the wind king dear to the gods who never die—
an isle adrift upon the sea, ringed round
with brazen ramparts on a sheer cliffside.
Twelve children had old Aiolos at home—
six daughters and six lusty sons—and he
gave girls to boys to be their gentle brides;
now those lords, in their parents' company,
10 sup every day in hall—a royal feast
with fumes of sacrifice and winds that pipe
'round hollow courts; and all the night they sleep
on beds of filigree beside their ladies.
Here we put in, lodged in the town and palace,
while Aiolos played host to me. He kept me
one full month to hear the tale of Troy,
the ships and the return of the Akhaians,

---

[89] **Aiolos Hippotadês** (Aeolus): God of the winds; he inhabited a floating island off Sicily.

all which I told him point by point in order.
When in return I asked his leave to sail
20   and asked provisioning, he stinted nothing,
adding a bull's hide sewn from neck to tail
into a mighty bag, bottling storm winds;
for Zeus had long ago made Aiolos
warden of winds, to rouse or calm at will.
He wedged this bag under my afterdeck,
lashing the neck with shining silver wire
so not a breath got through; only the west wind
he lofted for me in a quartering breeze
to take my squadron spanking home.
30   No luck:
the fair wind failed us when our prudence failed.

Nine days and nights we sailed without event,
till on the tenth we raised our land. We neared it,
and saw men building fires along the shore;
but now, being weary to the bone, I fell
into deep slumber; I had worked the sheet
nine days alone, and given it to no one,
wishing to spill no wind on the homeward run.
But while I slept, the crew began to parley:
40   silver and gold, they guessed, were in that bag
bestowed on me by Aiolos' great heart;
and one would glance at his benchmate and say:
'It never fails. He's welcome everywhere:
hail to the captain when he goes ashore!
He brought along so many presents, plunder
out of Troy, that's it. How about ourselves—
his shipmates all the way? Nigh home we are
with empty hands. And who has gifts from Aiolos?
He has. I say we ought to crack that bag,
50   there's gold and silver, plenty, in that bag!'

Temptation had its way with my companions,
and they untied the bag.
                              Then every wind
roared into hurricane; the ships went pitching
west with many cries; our land was lost.
Roused up, despairing in that gloom, I thought:
'Should I go overside for a quick finish
or clench my teeth and stay among the living?'
Down in the bilge I lay, pulling my sea cloak

60 over my head, while the rough gale blew the ships
and rueful crews clear back to Aiolia.

We put ashore for water; then all hands
gathered alongside for a mid-day meal.
When we had taken bread and drink, I picked
one soldier, and one herald, to go with me
and called again on Aiolos. I found him
at meat with his young princes and his lady,
but there beside the pillars, in his portico,
we sat down silent at the open door.
70 The sight amazed them, and they all exclaimed:
'Why back again, Odysseus?'
                                    'What sea fiend
rose in your path?'
                              'Did we not launch you well
for home, or for whatever land you chose?'

Out of my melancholy I replied:
'Mischief aboard and nodding at the tiller—
a damned drowse—did for me. Make good my loss,
dear friends! You have the power!'

80   Gently I pleaded,
but they turned cold and still. Said Father Aiolos:
'Take yourself out of this island, creeping thing—
no law, no wisdom, lays it on me now
to help a man the blessed gods detest—
out! Your voyage here was cursed by heaven!'

He drove me from the place, groan as I would,
and comfortless we went again to sea,
days of it, till the men flagged at the oars—
no breeze, no help in sight, by our own folly—
90 six indistinguishable nights and days
before we raised the Laistrygonian height
and far stronghold of Lamos.[90] In that land
the daybreak follows dusk, and so the shepherd
homing calls to the cowherd setting out;
and he who never slept could earn two wages,
tending oxen, pasturing silvery flocks,

---

[90] **Lamos:** King of the Laistrygonians, whose location is uncertain. The next lines seem to refer to the long summer days of northern latitudes.

where the low night path of the sun is near
the sun's path by day. Here, then, we found
a curious bay with mountain walls of stone
100 to left and right, and reaching far inland,—
a narrow entrance opening from the sea
where cliffs converged as though to touch and close.
All of my squadron sheltered here, inside
the cavern of this bay.
                              Black prow by prow
those hulls were made fast in a limpid calm
without a ripple, stillness all around them.
My own black ship I chose to moor alone
on the sea side, using a rock for bollard;
110 and climbed a rocky point to get my bearings.
No farms, no cultivated land appeared,
but puffs of smoke rose in the wilderness;
so I sent out two picked men and a herald
to learn what race of men this land sustained.

My party found a track—a wagon road
for bringing wood down from the heights to town;
and near the settlement they met a daughter
of Antiphatês the Laistrygon—a stalwart
young girl taking her pail to Artakía,
120 the fountain where these people go for water.
My fellows hailed her, put their questions to her:
who might the king be? ruling over whom?
She waved her hand, showing her father's lodge,
so they approached it. In its gloom they saw
a woman like a mountain crag, the queen—
and loathed the sight of her. But she, for greeting,
called from the meeting ground her lord and master,
Antiphatês, who came to drink their blood.
He seized one man and tore him on the spot,
130 making a meal of him; the other two
leaped out of doors and ran to join the ships.
Behind, he raised the whole tribe howling, countless
Laistrygonês—and more than men they seemed,
gigantic when they gathered on the sky line
to shoot great boulders down from slings; and hell's own
crashing rose, and crying from the ships,
as planks and men were smashed to bits—poor gobbets
the wildmen speared like fish and bore away.
But long before it ended in the anchorage—
140 havoc and slaughter—I had drawn my sword

and cut my own ship's cable. 'Men,' I shouted,
'man the oars and pull till your hearts break
if you would put this butchery behind!'
The oarsmen rent the sea in mortal fear
and my ship spurted out of range, far out
from that deep canyon where the rest were lost.
So we fared onward and death fell behind,
and we took breath to grieve for our companions.

    Our next landfall was on Aiaia, island
150 of Kirkê,[91] dire beauty and divine,
sister of baleful Aiêtês, like him
fathered by Hêlios the light of mortals
on Persê, child of the Ocean stream.
                         We came
washed in our silent ship upon her shore,
and found a cove, a haven for the ship—
some god, invisible, conned us in. We landed,
to lie down in that place two days and nights,
worn out and sick at heart, tasting our grief.
160 But when Dawn set another day a-shining
I took my spear and broadsword and I climbed
a rocky point above the ship, for sight
or sound of human labor. Gazing out
from that high place over a land of thicket,
oaks and wide watercourses, I could see
a smoke wisp from the woodland hall of Kirkê.
So I took counsel with myself: should I
go inland scouting out that reddish smoke?
No: better not, I thought, but first return
170 to waterside and ship, and give the men
breakfast before I sent them to explore.
Now as I went down quite alone, and came
a bowshot from the ship, some god's compassion
set a big buck in motion to cross my path—
a stag with noble antlers, pacing down
from pasture in the woods to the riverside,
as long thirst and the power of sun constrained him.
He started from the bush and wheeled: I hit him
square in the spine midway along his back
180 and the bronze point broke through it. In the dust

---

[91] **Kirkê:** An enchantress who uses drugs and herbs to manipulate men.

he fell and whinnied as life bled away.
I set one foot against him, pulling hard
to wrench my weapon from the wound, then left it,
butt-end on the ground. I plucked some withies
and twined a double strand into a rope—
enough to tie the hocks of my huge trophy;
then pickaback I lugged him to the ship,
leaning on my long spearshaft; I could not
haul that mighty carcass on one shoulder.

190 Beside the ship I let him drop, and spoke
gently and low to each man standing near:
'Come, friends, though hard beset, we'll not go down
into the House of Death before our time.
As long as food and drink remain aboard
let us rely on it, not die of hunger.'

At this those faces, cloaked in desolation
upon the waste sea beach, were bared;
their eyes turned toward me and the mighty trophy,
lighting, foreseeing pleasure, one by one.

200 So hands were washed to take what heaven sent us.
And all that day until the sun went down
we had our fill of venison and wine,
till after sunset in the gathering dusk
we slept at last above the line of breakers.
When the young Dawn with finger tips of rose
made heaven bright, I called them round and said:
'Shipmates, companions in disastrous time,
O my dear friends, where Dawn lies, and the West,
and where the great Sun, light of men, may go

210 under the earth by night, and where he rises—
of these things we know nothing. Do we know
any least thing to serve us now? I wonder.
All that I saw, when I went up the rock
was one more island in the boundless main,
a low landscape, covered with woods and scrub,
and puffs of smoke ascending in mid-forest.'

They were all silent, but their hearts contracted,
remembering Antiphatês the Laistrygon
and that prodigious cannibal, the Kyklops.

220 They cried out, and the salt tears wet their eyes.
But seeing our time for action lost in weeping,
I mustered those Akhaians under arms,
counting them off in two platoons, myself

and my godlike Eurýlokhos commanding.
We shook lots in a soldier's dogskin cap
and his came bounding out—valiant Eurýlokhos!—
So off he went, with twenty-two companions
weeping, as mine wept, too, who stayed behind.

In the wild wood they found an open glade,
230   around a smooth stone house—the hall of Kirkê—
and wolves and mountain lions lay there, mild
in her soft spell, fed on her drug of evil.
None would attack—oh, it was strange, I tell you—
but switching their long tails they faced our men
like hounds, who look up when their master comes
with tidbits for them—as he will—from table.
Humbly those wolves and lions with mighty paws
fawned on our men—who met their yellow eyes
and feared them.
240   In the entrance way they stayed
to listen there: inside her quiet house
they heard the goddess Kirkê.
                                        Low she sang
in her beguiling voice, while on her loom
she wove ambrosial fabric sheer and bright,
by that craft known to the goddesses of heaven.
No one would speak, until Politês—most
faithful and likable of my officers, said:
'Dear friends, no need for stealth: here's a young weaver
250   singing a pretty song to set the air
a-tingle on these lawns and paven courts.
Goddess she is, or lady. Shall we greet her?'

So reassured, they all cried out together,
and she came swiftly to the shining doors
to call them in. All but Eurýlokhos—
who feared a snare—the innocents went after her.
On thrones she seated them, and lounging chairs,
while she prepared a meal of cheese and barley
and amber honey mixed with Pramnian wine,
260   adding her own vile pinch, to make them lose
desire or thought of our dear father land.
Scarce had they drunk when she flew after them
with her long stick and shut them in a pigsty—
bodies, voices, heads, and bristles, all
swinish now, though minds were still unchanged.

So, squealing, in they went. And Kirkê tossed them
acorns, mast, and cornel berries—fodder
for hogs who rut and slumber on the earth.

Down to the ship Eurýlokhos came running
270 to cry alarm, foul magic doomed his men!
But working with dry lips to speak a word
he could not, being so shaken; blinding tears
welled in his eyes; foreboding filled his heart.
When we were frantic questioning him, at last
we heard the tale: our friends were gone. Said he:
'We went up through the oak scrub where you sent us,
Odysseus, glory of commanders,
until we found a palace in a glade,
a marble house on open ground, and someone
280 singing before her loom a chill, sweet song—
goddess or girl, we could not tell. They hailed her,
and then she stepped through shining doors and said,
"Come, come in!" Like sheep they followed her,
but I saw cruel deceit, and stayed behind.
Then all our fellows vanished. Not a sound,
and nothing stirred, although I watched for hours.'

When I heard this I slung my silver-hilted
broadsword on, and shouldered my long bow,
and said, 'Come, take me back the way you came.'
290 But he put both his hands around my knees
in desperate woe, and said in supplication:
'Not back there, O my lord! Oh, leave me here!
You, even you, cannot return, I know it,
I know you cannot bring away our shipmates;
better make sail with these men, quickly too,
and save ourselves from horror while we may.'

But I replied:
                'By heaven, Eurýlokhos,
rest here then; take food and wine;
300 stay in the black hull's shelter. Let me go,
as I see nothing for it but to go.'

I turned and left him, left the shore and ship,
and went up through the woodland hushed and shady
to find the subtle witch in her long hall.
But Hermês met me, with his golden wand,

barring the way—a boy whose lip was downy
in the first bloom of manhood, so he seemed.
He took my hand and spoke as though he knew me:

'Why take the inland path alone,
310   poor seafarer, by hill and dale
upon this island all unknown?
Your friends are locked in Kirkê's pale;
all are become like swine to see;
and if you go to set them free
you go to stay, and never more make sail
for your old home upon Thaki.°   Ithaka

But I can tell you what to do
to come unchanged from Kirkê's power
and disenthrall your fighting crew:
320   take with you to her bower
as amulet, this plant I know—
it will defeat her horrid show,
so pure and potent is the flower;
no mortal herb was ever so.

Your cup with numbing drops of night
and evil, stilled of all remorse,
she will infuse to charm your sight;
but this great herb with holy force
will keep your mind and senses clear:
330   when she turns cruel, coming near
with her long stick to whip you out of doors,
then let your cutting blade appear,

Let instant death upon it shine,
and she will cower and yield her bed—
a pleasure you must not decline,
so may her lust and fear bestead
you and your friends, and break her spell;
but make her swear by heaven and hell
no witches' tricks, or else, your harness shed,
340   you'll be unmanned by her as well.'

He bent down glittering for the magic plant
and pulled it up, black root and milky flower—
a *molü*[92] in the language of the gods—

---

[92] **molü:** The exact nature of the magical *molü*, or moly, is unknown.

fatigue and pain for mortals to uproot;
but gods do this, and everything, with ease.

Then toward Olympos through the island trees
Hermês departed, and I sought out Kirkê,
my heart high with excitement, beating hard.
Before her mansion in the porch I stood
350 to call her, all being still. Quick as a cat
she opened her bright doors and sighed a welcome;
then I strode after her with heavy heart
down the long hall, and took the chair she gave me,
silver-studded, intricately carved,
made with a low footrest. The lady Kirkê
mixed me a golden cup of honeyed wine,
adding in mischief her unholy drug.
I drank, and the drink failed. But she came forward
aiming a stroke with her long stick, and whispered:
360 'Down in the sty and snore among the rest!'

Without a word, I drew my sharpened sword
and in one bound held it against her throat.
She cried out, then slid under to take my knees,
catching her breath to say, in her distress:
'What champion, of what country, can you be?
Where are your kinsmen and your city?
Are you not sluggish with my wine? Ah, wonder!
Never a mortal man that drank this cup
but when it passed his lips he had succumbed.
370 Hale must your heart be and your tempered will.
Odysseus then you are, O great contender,
of whom the glittering god with golden wand°   Hermês
spoke to me ever, and foretold
the black swift ship would carry you from Troy.
Put up your weapon in the sheath. We two
shall mingle and make love upon our bed.
So mutual trust may come of play and love.'

To this I said:
              'Kirkê, am I a boy,
380 that you should make me soft and doting now?
Here in this house you turned my men to swine;
now it is I myself you hold, enticing
into your chamber, to your dangerous bed,

to take my manhood when you have me stripped.
I mount no bed of love with you upon it.
Or swear me first a great oath, if I do,
you'll work no more enchantment to my harm.'

She swore at once, outright, as I demanded,
and after she had sworn, and bound herself,
390   I entered Kirkê's flawless bed of love.

Presently in the hall her maids were busy,
the nymphs who waited upon Kirkê: four,
whose cradles were in fountains, under boughs,
or in the glassy seaward-gliding streams.
One came with richly colored rugs to throw
on seat and chairback, over linen covers;
a second pulled the tables out, all silver,
and loaded them with baskets all of gold;
a third mixed wine as tawny-mild as honey
400   in a bright bowl, and set out golden cups.
The fourth came bearing water, and lit a blaze
under a cauldron. By and by it bubbled,
and when the dazzling brazen vessel seethed
she filled a bathtub to my waist, and bathed me,
pouring a soothing blend on head and shoulders,
warming the soreness of my joints away.
When she had done, and smoothed me with sweet oil,
she put a tunic and a cloak around me
and took me to a silver-studded chair
410   with footrest, all elaborately carven.
Now came a maid to tip a golden jug
of water into a silver finger bowl,
and draw a polished table to my side.
The larder mistress brought her tray of loaves
with many savory slices, and she gave
the best, to tempt me. But no pleasure came;
I huddled with my mind elsewhere, oppressed.

Kirkê regarded me, as there I sat
disconsolate, and never touched a crust.
420   Then she stood over me and chided me:
'Why sit at table mute, Odysseus?
Are you mistrustful of my bread and drink?

Can it be treachery that you fear again,
after the gods' great oath I swore for you?'

I turned to her at once, and said:
                                          'Kirkê,
where is the captain who could bear to touch
this banquet, in my place? A decent man
would see his company before him first.
430 Put heart in me to eat and drink—you may,
by freeing my companions. I must see them.'

But Kirkê had already turned away.
Her long staff in her hand, she left the hall
and opened up the sty. I saw her enter,
driving those men turned swine to stand before me.
She stroked them, each in turn, with some new chrism;
and then, behold! their bristles fell away,
the coarse pelt grown upon them by her drug
melted away, and they were men again,
440 younger, more handsome, taller than before.
Their eyes upon me, each one took my hands,
and wild regret and longing pierced them through,
so the room rang with sobs, and even Kirkê
pitied that transformation. Exquisite
the goddess looked as she stood near me, saying:
'Son of Laërtês and the gods of old,
Odysseus, master mariner and soldier,
go to the sea beach and sea-breasting ship;
drag it ashore, full length upon the land;
450 stow gear and stores in rock-holes under cover;
return; be quick; bring all your dear companions.'

Now, being a man, I could not help consenting.
So I went down to the sea beach and the ship,
where I found all my other men on board,
weeping, in despair along the benches.
Sometimes in farmyards when the cows return
well fed from pasture to the barn, one sees
the pens give way before the calves in tumult,
breaking through to cluster about their mothers,
460 bumping together, bawling. Just that way
my crew poured round me when they saw me come—

their faces wet with tears as if they saw
their homeland, and the crags of Ithaka,
even the very town where they were born.
And weeping still they all cried out in greeting:
'Prince, what joy this is, your safe return!
Now Ithaka seems here, and we in Ithaka!
But tell us now, what death befell our friends?'

And, speaking gently, I replied:
470 'First we must get the ship high on the shingle,
and stow our gear and stores in clefts of rock
for cover. Then come follow me, to see
your shipmates in the magic house of Kirkê
eating and drinking, endlessly regaled.'

They turned back, as commanded, to this work;
only one lagged, and tried to hold the others:
Eurýlokhos it was, who blurted out:
'Where now, poor remnants? is it devil's work
you long for? Will you go to Kirkê's hall?
480 Swine, wolves, and lions she will make us all,
beasts of her courtyard, bound by her enchantment.
Remember those the Kyklops held, remember
shipmates who made that visit with Odysseus!
The daring man! They died for his foolishness!'

When I heard this I had a mind to draw
the blade that swung against my side and chop him,
bowling his head upon the ground—kinsman[93]
or no kinsman, close to me though he was.
But others came between, saying, to stop me,
490 'Prince, we can leave him, if you say the word;
let him stay here on guard. As for ourselves,
show us the way to Kirkê's magic hall.'

So all turned inland, leaving shore and ship,
and Eurýlokhos—he, too, came on behind,
fearing the rough edge of my tongue. Meanwhile
at Kirkê's hands the rest were gently bathed,
anointed with sweet oil, and dressed afresh
in tunics and new cloaks with fleecy linings.
We found them all at supper when we came.

---

[93] **kinsman:** Related to Odysseus by marriage.

500 But greeting their old friends once more, the crew
could not hold back their tears, and now again
the rooms rang with sobs. Then Kirkê, loveliest
of all immortals, came to counsel me:
'Son of Laërtês and the gods of old,
Odysseus, master mariner and soldier,
enough of weeping fits. I know—I, too—
what you endured upon the inhuman sea,
what odds you met on land from hostile men.
Remain with me, and share my meat and wine;
510 restore behind your ribs those gallant hearts
that served you in the old days, when you sailed
from stony Ithaka. Now parched and spent,
your cruel wandering is all you think of,
never of joy, after so many blows.'

As we were men we could not help consenting.
So day by day we lingered, feasting long
on roasts and wine, until a year grew fat.
But when the passing months and wheeling seasons
brought the long summery days, the pause of summer,
520 my shipmates one day summoned me and said:
'Captain, shake off this trance, and think of home—
if home indeed awaits us,
                              if we shall ever see
your own well-timbered hall on Ithaka.'

They made me feel a pang, and I agreed.
That day, and all day long, from dawn to sundown,
we feasted on roast meat and ruddy wine,
and after sunset when the dusk came on
my men slept in the shadowy hall, but I
530 went through the dark to Kirkê's flawless bed
and took the goddess' knees in supplication,
urging, as she bent to hear:
                              'O Kirkê,
now you must keep your promise; it is time.
Help me make sail for home. Day after day
my longing quickens, and my company
give me no peace, but wear my heart away
pleading when you are not at hand to hear.'

The loveliest of goddesses replied:
540 'Son of Laërtês and the gods of old,
Odysseus, master mariner and soldier,

you shall not stay here longer against your will;
but home you may not go
unless you take a strange way round and come
to the cold homes of Death and pale Perséphonê.[94]
You shall hear prophecy from the rapt shade
of blind Teirêsias of Thebes,[95] forever
charged with reason even among the dead;
to him alone, of all the flitting ghosts,
550   Perséphonê has given a mind undarkened.'

At this I felt a weight like stone within me,
and, moaning, pressed my length against the bed,
with no desire to see the daylight more.
But when I had wept and tossed and had my fill
of this despair, at last I answered her:
'Kirkê, who pilots me upon this journey?
No man has ever sailed to the land of Death.'

That loveliest of goddesses replied:
'Son of Laërtês and the gods of old,
560   Odysseus, master of land ways and sea ways,
feel no dismay because you lack a pilot;
only set up your mast and haul your canvas
to the fresh blowing North; sit down and steer,
and hold that wind, even to the bourne of Ocean,
Perséphonê's deserted strand and grove,
dusky with poplars and the drooping willow.
Run through the tide-rip, bring your ship to shore,
land there, and find the crumbling homes of Death.[96]
Here, toward the Sorrowing Water, run the streams
570   of Wailing, out of Styx, and quenchless Burning[97] —
torrents that join in thunder at the Rock.
Here then, great soldier, setting foot obey me:
dig a well shaft a forearm square; pour out
libations round it to the unnumbered dead:
sweet milk and honey, then sweet wine, and last
clear water, scattering handfulls of white barley.
Pray now, with all your heart, to the faint dead;
swear you will sacrifice your finest heifer,

---

[94] **Perséphonê:** Queen of the Underworld.   [95] **Teirêsias of Thebes:** A famous blind soothsayer in the legends of Thebes who plays important roles in Sophocles' Oedipus plays.   [96] **homes of Death:** Homer locates Hades on the western and northern frontier of the Greek world; after Homer, Hades was ordinarily located beneath the earth, similar to the Christian Hell.   [97] **Sorrowing Water . . . Burning:** The rivers of Hades are Sorrowing Water (Acheron), Wailing (Cocytus), and Burning (Phlegethon).

at home in Ithaka, and burn for them
580 her tenderest parts in sacrifice; and vow
to the lord Teirêsias, apart from all,
a black lamb, handsomest of all your flock—
thus to appease the nations of the dead.
Then slash a black ewe's throat, and a black ram,
facing the gloom of Erebos;[98] but turn
your head away toward Ocean. You shall see, now
souls of the buried dead in shadowy hosts,
and now you must call out to your companions
to flay those sheep the bronze knife has cut down,
590 for offerings, burnt flesh to those below,
to sovereign Death and pale Perséphonê.
Meanwhile draw sword from hip, crouch down, ward off
the surging phantoms from the bloody pit
until you know the presence of Teirêsias.
He will come soon, great captain; be it he
who gives you course and distance for your sailing
homeward across the cold fish-breeding sea.'

As the goddess ended, Dawn came stitched in gold.
Now Kirkê dressed me in my shirt and cloak,
600 put on a gown of subtle tissue, silvery,
then wound a golden belt about her waist
and veiled her head in linen,
while I went through the hall to rouse my crew.

I bent above each one, and gently said:
'Wake from your sleep: no more sweet slumber. Come,
we sail: the Lady Kirkê so ordains it.'

They were soon up, and ready at that word;
but I was not to take my men unharmed
from this place, even from this. Among them all
610 the youngest was Elpênor—
no mainstay in a fight nor very clever—
and this one, having climbed on Kirkê's roof
to taste the cool night, fell asleep with wine.
Waked by our morning voices, and the tramp
of men below, he started up, but missed
his footing on the long steep backward ladder
and fell that height headlong. The blow smashed

---

[98] **Erebos:** The darkest region of Hades.

the nape cord, and his ghost fled to the dark.
But I was outside, walking with the rest,
620 saying:
> 'Homeward you think we must be sailing
to our own land; no, elsewhere is the voyage
Kirkê has laid upon me. We must go
to the cold homes of Death and pale Perséphonê
to hear Teirêsias tell of time to come.'

They felt so stricken, upon hearing this,
they sat down wailing loud, and tore their hair.
But nothing came of giving way to grief.
Down to the shore and ship at last we went,
630 bowed with anguish, cheeks all wet with tears,
to find that Kirkê had been there before us
and tied nearby a black ewe and a ram:
she had gone by like air.
For who could see the passage of a goddess
unless she wished his mortal eyes aware?

BOOK 11
A GATHERING OF SHADES

We bore down on the ship at the sea's edge
and launched her on the salt immortal sea,
stepping our mast and spar in the black ship;
embarked the ram and ewe and went aboard
in tears, with bitter and sore dread upon us.
But now a breeze came up for us astern —
a canvas-bellying landbreeze, hale shipmate
sent by the singing nymph with sun-bright hair;
so we made fast the braces, took our thwarts,
10 and let the wind and steersman work the ship
with full sail spread all day above our coursing,
till the sun dipped, and all the ways grew dark
upon the fathomless unresting sea.
>   By night
our ship ran onward toward the Ocean's bourne,
the realm and region of the Men of Winter,[99]
hidden in mist and cloud. Never the flaming

---

[99] **Men of Winter:** The fabled Cimmerians who live in perpetual darkness.

eye of Hêlios lights on those men
at morning, when he climbs the sky of stars,
20 nor in descending earthward out of heaven;
ruinous night being rove° over those wretches.   stretched
We made the land, put ram and ewe ashore,
and took our way along the Ocean stream
to find the place foretold for us by Kirkê.
There Perimêdês and Eurýlokhos
pinioned the sacred beasts. With my drawn blade
I spaded up the votive pit, and poured
libations round it to the unnumbered dead:
sweet milk and honey, then sweet wine, and last
30 clear water; and I scattered barley down.
Then I addressed the blurred and breathless dead,
vowing to slaughter my best heifer for them
before she calved, at home in Ithaka,
and burn the choice bits on the altar fire;
as for Teirêsias, I swore to sacrifice
a black lamb, handsomest of all our flock.
Thus to assuage the nations of the dead
I pledged these rites, then slashed the lamb and ewe,
letting their black blood stream into the wellpit.
40 Now the souls gathered, stirring out of Erebos,
brides and young men, and men grown old in pain,
and tender girls whose hearts were new to grief;
many were there, too, torn by brazen lanceheads,
battle-slain, bearing still their bloody gear.
From every side they came and sought the pit
with rustling cries; and I grew sick with fear.
But presently I gave command to my officers
to flay those sheep the bronze cut down, and make
burnt offerings of flesh to the gods below—
50 to sovereign Death, to pale Perséphonê.
Meanwhile I crouched with my drawn sword to keep
the surging phantoms from the bloody pit
till I should know the presence of Teirêsias.

One shade came first—Elpênor, of our company,
who lay unburied still on the wide earth
as we had left him—dead in Kirkê's hall,
untouched, unmourned, when other cares compelled us.
Now when I saw him there I wept for pity
and called out to him:
60   'How is this, Elpênor,

how could you journey to the western gloom
swifter afoot than I in the black lugger?'

He sighed, and answered:
                              'Son of great Laërtês,
Odysseus, master mariner and soldier,
bad luck shadowed me, and no kindly power;
ignoble death I drank with so much wine.
I slept on Kirkê's roof, then could not see
the long steep backward ladder, coming down,
70   and fell that height. My neck bone, buckled under,
snapped, and my spirit found this well of dark.
Now hear the grace I pray for, in the name
of those back in the world, not here — your wife
and father, he who gave you bread in childhood,
and your own child, your only son, Telémakhos,
long ago left at home.
                              When you make sail
and put these lodgings of dim Death behind,
you will moor ship, I know, upon Aiaia Island;
80   there, O my lord, remember me, I pray,
do not abandon me unwept, unburied,
to tempt the gods' wrath, while you sail for home;
but fire my corpse, and all the gear I had,
and build a cairn for me above the breakers —
an unknown sailor's mark for men to come.
Heap up the mound there, and implant upon it
the oar I pulled in life with my companions.'

He ceased, and I replied:
                              'Unhappy spirit,
90   I promise you the barrow and the burial.'

So we conversed, and grimly, at a distance,
with my long sword between, guarding the blood,
while the faint image of the lad spoke on.
Now came the soul of Antikleía, dead,
my mother, daughter of Autólykos,
dead now, though living still when I took ship
for holy Troy. Seeing this ghost I grieved,
but held her off, through pang on pang of tears,
till I should know the presence of Teirêsias.
100 Soon from the dark that prince of Thebes came forward
bearing a golden staff; and he addressed me:
'Son of Laërtês and the gods of old,

Odysseus, master of land ways and sea ways,
why leave the blazing sun, O man of woe,
to see the cold dead and the joyless region?
Stand clear, put up your sword;
let me but taste of blood, I shall speak true.'

At this I stepped aside, and in the scabbard
let my long sword ring home to the pommel silver,
110 as he bent down to the sombre blood. Then spoke
the prince of those with gift of speech:
                                   'Great captain,
a fair wind and the honey lights of home
are all you seek. But anguish lies ahead;
the god who thunders on the land prepares it,
not to be shaken from your track, implacable,
in rancor for the son whose eye you blinded.
One narrow strait may take you through his blows:
denial of yourself, restraint of shipmates.
120 When you make landfall on Thrinakia first
and quit the violet sea, dark on the land
you'll find the grazing herds of Hêlios
by whom all things are seen, all speech is known.
Avoid those kine, hold fast to your intent,
and hard seafaring brings you all to Ithaka.
But if you raid the beeves, I see destruction
for ship and crew. Though you survive alone,
bereft of all companions, lost for years,
under strange sail shall you come home, to find
130 your own house filled with trouble: insolent men
eating your livestock as they court your lady.
Aye, you shall make those men atone in blood!
But after you have dealt out death — in open
combat or by stealth — to all the suitors,
go overland on foot, and take an oar,
until one day you come where men have lived
with meat unsalted, never known the sea,
nor seen seagoing ships, with crimson bows
and oars that fledge light hulls for dipping flight.
140 The spot will soon be plain to you, and I
can tell you how: some passerby will say,
"What winnowing fan is that upon your shoulder?"
Halt, and implant your smooth oar in the turf
and make fair sacrifice to Lord Poseidon:
a ram, a bull, a great buck boar; turn back,
and carry out pure hekatombs at home

to all wide heaven's lords, the undying gods,
to each in order. Then a seaborne death
soft as this hand of mist will come upon you
150 when you are wearied out with rich old age,
your country folk in blessed peace around you.
And all this shall be just as I foretell.'

When he had done, I said at once,
                              'Teirêsias,
my life runs on then as the gods have spun it:
But come, now, tell me this; make this thing clear:
I see my mother's ghost among the dead
sitting in silence near the blood. Not once
has she glanced this way toward her son, nor spoken.
160 Tell me, my lord,
may she in some way come to know my presence?'

To this he answered:
                        'I shall make it clear
in a few words and simply. Any dead man
whom you allow to enter where the blood is
will speak to you, and speak the truth; but those
deprived will grow remote again and fade.'

When he had prophesied, Teirêsias' shade
retired lordly to the halls of Death;
170 but I stood fast until my mother stirred,
moving to sip the black blood; then she knew me
and called out sorrowfully to me:
                              'Child,
how could you cross alive into this gloom
at the world's end? — No sight for living eyes;
great currents run between, desolate waters,
the Ocean first, where no man goes a journey
without ship's timber under him.
                              Say, now,
180 is it from Troy, still wandering, after years,
that you come here with ship and company?
Have you not gone at all to Ithaka?
Have you not seen your lady in your hall?'

She put these questions, and I answered her:
'Mother, I came here, driven to the land of death
in want of prophecy from Teirêsias' shade;
nor have I yet coasted Akhaia's hills

nor touched my own land, but have had hard roving
since first I joined Lord Agamémnon's host
190 by sea for Ilion, the wild horse country,
to fight the men of Troy.
But come now, tell me this, and tell me clearly,
what was the bane that pinned you down in Death?
Some ravaging long illness, or mild arrows
a-flying down one day from Artemis?
Tell me of Father, tell me of the son
I left behind me; have they still my place,
my honors, or have other men assumed them?
Do they not say that I shall come no more?
200 And tell me of my wife: how runs her thought,
still with her child, still keeping our domains,
or bride again to the best of the Akhaians?'

To this my noble mother quickly answered:
'Still with her child indeed she is, poor heart,
still in your palace hall. Forlorn her nights
and days go by, her life used up in weeping.
But no man takes your honored place. Telémakhos
has care of all your garden plots and fields,
and holds the public honor of a magistrate,
210 feasting and being feasted. But your father
is country bound and comes to town no more.
He owns no bedding, rugs, or fleecy mantles,
but lies down, winter nights, among the slaves,
rolled in old cloaks for cover, near the embers.
Or when the heat comes at the end of summer,
the fallen leaves, all round his vineyard plot,
heaped into windrows, make his lowly bed.
He lies now even so, with aching heart,
and longs for your return, while age comes on him.
220 So I, too, pined away, so doom befell me,
not that the keen-eyed huntress° with her shafts   Artemis
had marked me down and shot to kill me, not
that illness overtook me — no true illness
wasting the body to undo the spirit;
only my loneliness for you, Odysseus,
for your kind heart and counsel, gentle Odysseus,
took my own life away.'

I bit my lip,
rising perplexed, with longing to embrace her,
230 and tried three times, putting my arms around her,

but she went sifting through my hands, impalpable
as shadows are, and wavering like a dream.
Now this embittered all the pain I bore,
and I cried in the darkness:
                              'O my mother,
will you not stay, be still, here in my arms,
may we not, in this place of Death, as well,
hold one another, touch with love, and taste
salt tears' relief, the twinge of welling tears?
240 Or is this all hallucination, sent
against me by the iron queen, Perséphonê,
to make me groan again?'

                    My noble mother
answered quickly:
                    'O my child — alas,
most sorely tried of men — great Zeus's daughter,
Perséphonê, knits no illusion for you.
All mortals meet this judgment when they die.
No flesh and bone are here, none bound by sinew,
250 since the bright-hearted pyre consumed them down —
the white bones long exanimate — to ash;
dreamlike the soul flies, insubstantial.

You must crave sunlight soon.
                              Note all things strange
seen here, to tell your lady in after days.'

So went our talk; then other shadows came,
ladies in company, sent by Perséphonê —
consorts or daughters of illustrious men —
crowding about the black blood.
260   I took thought
how best to separate and question them,
and saw no help for it, but drew once more
the long bright edge of broadsword from my hip,
that none should sip the blood in company
but one by one, in order; so it fell
that each declared her lineage and name.

Here was great loveliness of ghosts! I saw
before them all, that princess of great ladies,

Tyro,[100] Salmoneus' daughter, as she told me,
270   and queen to Krêtheus, a son of Aiolos.
She had gone daft for the river Enipeus,
most graceful of all running streams, and ranged
all day by Enipeus' limpid side,
whose form the foaming girdler of the islands,
the god who makes earth tremble, took and so
lay down with her where he went flooding seaward,
their bower a purple billow, arching round
to hide them in a sea-vale, god and lady.
Now when his pleasure was complete, the god
280   spoke to her softly, holding fast her hand:
'Dear mortal, go in joy! At the turn of seasons,
winter to summer, you shall bear me sons;
no lovemaking of gods can be in vain.
Nurse our sweet children tenderly, and rear them.
Home with you now, and hold your tongue, and tell
no one your lover's name—though I am yours,
Poseidon, lord of surf that makes earth tremble.'

He plunged away into the deep sea swell,
and she grew big with Pelias and Neleus,
290   powerful vassals, in their time, of Zeus.
Pelias lived on broad Iolkos seaboard
rich in flocks, and Neleus at Pylos.
As for the sons borne by that queen of women
to Krêtheus, their names were Aison, Pherês,
and Amytháon, expert charioteer.

Next after her I saw Antiopê,
daughter of Ásopos. She too could boast
a god for lover, having lain with Zeus
and borne two sons to him: Amphion and
300   Zêthos, who founded Thebes, the upper city,
and built the ancient citadel. They sheltered
no life upon that plain, for all their power,
without a fortress wall.

                    And next I saw
Amphitrion's true wife, Alkmênê, mother,

---

[100] **Tyro:** A queen of Thessaly who fell in love with a river god—Poseidon in disguise; she bore him two sons,
Pelias and Neleus, the father of Nestor.

as all men know, of lionish Heraklês,
conceived when she lay close in Zeus's arms;
and Megarê, high-hearted Kreon's daughter,
wife of Amphitrion's unwearying son.

310 I saw the mother of Oidipous, Epikastê,[101]
whose great unwitting deed it was
to marry her own son. He took that prize
from a slain father; presently the gods
brought all to light that made the famous story.
But by their fearsome wills he kept his throne
in dearest Thebes, all through his evil days,
while she descended to the place of Death,
god of the locked and iron door. Steep down
from a high rafter, throttled in her noose,
320 she swung, carried away by pain, and left him
endless agony from a mother's Furies.

And I saw Khloris, that most lovely lady,
whom for her beauty in the olden time
Neleus wooed with countless gifts, and married.
She was the youngest daughter of Amphion,
son of Iasos. In those days he held
power at Orkhómenos, over the Minyai.
At Pylos then as queen she bore her children—
Nestor, Khromios, Periklýmenos,
330 and Pêro, too, who turned the heads of men
with her magnificence. A host of princes
from nearby lands came courting her; but Neleus
would hear of no one, not unless the suitor
could drive the steers of giant Íphiklos
from Phylakê—longhorns, broad in the brow,
so fierce that one man only, a diviner,
offered to round them up. But bitter fate
saw him bound hand and foot by savage herdsmen.
Then days and months grew full and waned, the year
340 went wheeling round, the seasons came again,
before at last the power of Íphiklos,
relenting, freed the prisoner, who foretold
all things to him. So Zeus's will was done.

And I saw Lêda, wife of Tyndareus,
upon whom Tyndareus had sired twins

---

[101] **Epikastê:** Jocasta, mother and wife of Oidipous (Oedipus).

indomitable: Kastor, tamer of horses,
and Polydeukês, best in the boxing ring.[102]
Those two live still, though life-creating earth
embraces them: even in the underworld
350 honored as gods by Zeus, each day in turn[103]
one comes alive, the other dies again.
Then after Lêda to my vision came
the wife of Aloeus, Iphimedeia,
proud that she once had held the flowing sea
and borne him sons, thunderers for a day,
the world-renowned Otos and Ephialtês.
Never were men on such a scale
bred on the plowlands and the grainlands, never
so magnificent any, after Orion.
360 At nine years old they towered nine fathoms tall,
nine cubits in the shoulders, and they promised
furor upon Olympos, heaven broken by battle cries,
the day they met the gods in arms.

With Ossa's

mountain peak they meant to crown Olympos
and over Ossa Pelion's[104] forest pile
for footholds up the sky. As giants grown
they might have done it, but the bright son of Zeus°   Apollo
by Lêto of the smooth braid shot them down
370 while they were boys unbearded; no dark curls
clustered yet from temples to the chin.

Then I saw Phaidra, Prokris; and Ariadnê,
daughter of Minos,[105] the grim king. Theseus took her
aboard with him from Krete for the terraced land
of ancient Athens; but he had no joy of her.
Artemis killed her on the Isle of Dia
at a word from Dionysos.

Maira, then,

and Klymênê, and that detested queen,
380 Eríphylê,[106] who betrayed her lord for gold . . .

---

[102] **Lêda . . . boxing ring:** By Zeus, Lêda was the mother of Helen and Polydeukês (Pollux); by Tyndareus, Lêda was the mother of Kastor and Klytaimnéstra (Clytemnestra), Agamémnon's wife.   [103] **each day in turn:** Kastor and Polydeukês share one immortality between them.   [104] **Ossa Pelion:** Ossa and Pelion are mountains near Olympos.   [105] **Minos:** Minos, king of Krete, was the father of Phaidra (Phaedra) and Ariadnê. After Theseus, king of Athens, killed the Minotaur he took Ariadnê with him to Dia (Naxos). It is not clear why Dionysos wanted her killed.   [106] **Eríphylê:** Polynices, Oidipous's son, bribed Eríphylê with a golden necklace; she persuaded her husband, Amphiaraus, to join the attack on Thebes, where he was killed.

but how name all the women I beheld there,
daughters and wives of kings? The starry night
wanes long before I close.
                         Here, or aboard ship,
amid the crew, the hour for sleep has come.
Our sailing is the gods' affair and yours."

Then he fell silent. Down the shadowy hall
the enchanted banqueters were still. Only
the queen with ivory pale arms, Arêtê, spoke,
390   saying to all the silent men:
                         "Phaiákians,
how does he stand, now, in your eyes, this captain,
the look and bulk of him, the inward poise?
He is my guest, but each one shares that honor.
Be in no haste to send him on his way
or scant your bounty in his need. Remember
how rich, by heaven's will, your possessions are."

Then Ekhenêos, the old soldier, eldest
of all Phaiákians, added his word:
400   "Friends, here was nothing but our own thought spoken,
the mark hit square. Our duties to her majesty.
For what is to be said and done,
we wait upon Alkínoös' command."

At this the king's voice rang:
                         "I so command—
as sure as it is I who, while I live,
rule the sea rovers of Phaiákia. Our friend
longs to put out for home, but let him be
content to rest here one more day, until
410   I see all gifts bestowed. And every man
will take thought for his launching and his voyage,
I most of all, for I am master here."

Odysseus, the great tactician, answered:
"Alkínoös, king and admiration of men,
even a year's delay, if you should urge it,
in loading gifts and furnishing for sea—
I too could wish it; better far that I
return with some largesse of wealth about me—

I shall be thought more worthy of love and courtesy
420 by every man who greets me home in Ithaka."

The king said:
                    "As to that, one word, Odysseus:
from all we see, we take you for no swindler —
though the dark earth be patient of so many,
scattered everywhere, baiting their traps with lies
of old times and of places no one knows.
You speak with art, but your intent is honest.
The Argive troubles, and your own troubles,
you told as a poet would, a man who knows the world.
430 But now come tell me this: among the dead
did you meet any of your peers, companions
who sailed with you and met their doom at Troy?
Here's a long night — an endless night — before us,
and no time yet for sleep, not in this hall.
Recall the past deeds and the strange adventures.
I could stay up until the sacred Dawn
as long as you might wish to tell your story."

Odysseus the great tactician answered:
"Alkínoös, king and admiration of men,
440 there is a time for story telling; there is
also a time for sleep. But even so,
if, indeed, listening be still your pleasure,
I must not grudge my part. Other and sadder
tales there are to tell; of my companions,
of some who came through all the Trojan spears,
clangor and groan of war,
only to find a brutal death at home —
and a bad wife behind it.
                          After Perséphonê,
450 icy and pale, dispersed the shades of women,
the soul of Agamémnon, son of Atreus,
came before me, sombre in the gloom,
and others gathered round, all who were with him
when death and doom struck in Aegísthos' hall.
Sipping the black blood, the tall shade perceived me,
and cried out sharply, breaking into tears;
then tried to stretch his hands toward me, but could not,
being bereft of all the reach and power

he once felt in the great torque of his arms.
460   Gazing at him, and stirred, I wept for pity,
and spoke across to him:
                          'O son of Atreus,
illustrious Lord Marshal, Agamémnon,
what was the doom that brought you low in death?
Were you at sea, aboard ship, and Poseidon
blew up a wicked squall to send you under,
or were you cattle-raiding on the mainland
or in a fight for some strongpoint, or women,
when the foe hit you to your mortal hurt?'

470   But he replied at once:
                          'Son of Laërtês,
Odysseus, master of land ways and sea ways,
neither did I go down with some good ship
in any gale Poseidon blew, nor die
upon the mainland, hurt by foes in battle.
It was Aegísthos who designed my death,
he and my heartless wife, and killed me, after
feeding me, like an ox felled at the trough.
That was my miserable end—and with me
480   my fellows butchered, like so many swine
killed for some troop, or feast, or wedding banquet
in a great landholder's household. In your day
you have seen men, and hundreds, die in war,
in the bloody press, or downed in single combat,
but these were murders you would catch your breath at:
think of us fallen, all our throats cut, winebowl
brimming, tables laden on every side,
while blood ran smoking over the whole floor.
In my extremity I heard Kassandra,[107]
490   Priam's daughter, piteously crying
as the traitress Klytaimnéstra made to kill her
along with me. I heaved up from the ground
and got my hands around the blade, but she
eluded me, that whore. Nor would she close
my two eyes[108] as my soul swam to the underworld
or shut my lips. There is no being more fell,
more bestial than a wife in such an action,

---

[107] **Kassandra:** She was brought back from Troy by Agamémnon as a part of his booty.   [108] **close my two eyes:** That is, perform the proper burial rites.

and what an action that one planned!
The murder of her husband and her lord.
500 Great god, I thought my children and my slaves
at least would give me welcome. But that woman,
plotting a thing so low, defiled herself
and all her sex, all women yet to come,
even those few who may be virtuous.'

He paused then, and I answered:
                                    'Foul and dreadful.
That was the way that Zeus who views the wide world
vented his hatred on the sons of Atreus—
intrigues of women, even from the start.
510   Myriads
died by Helen's fault, and Klytaimnéstra
plotted against you half the world away.'

And he at once said:
                            'Let it be a warning
even to you. Indulge a woman never,
and never tell her all you know. Some things
a man may tell, some he should cover up.
Not that I see a risk for you, Odysseus,
of death at your wife's hands. She is too wise,
520 too clear-eyed, sees alternatives too well,
Penélopê, Ikários' daughter—
that young bride whom we left behind—think of it!—
when we sailed off to war. The baby boy
still cradled at her breast—now he must be
a grown man, and a lucky one. By heaven,
you'll see him yet, and he'll embrace his father
with old fashioned respect, and rightly.
                                    My own
lady never let me glut my eyes
530 on my own son, but bled me to death first.
One thing I will advise, on second thought;
stow it away and ponder it.
                                Land your ship
in secret on your island; give no warning.
The day of faithful wives is gone forever.

But tell me, have you any word at all
about my son's life? Gone to Orkhómenos
or sandy Pylos, can he be? Or waiting

with Meneláos in the plain of Sparta?
540 Death on earth has not yet taken Orestês.'

But I could only answer:
                                                'Son of Atreus,
why do you ask these questions of me? Neither
news of home have I, nor news of him,
alive or dead. And empty words are evil.'

So we exchanged our speech, in bitterness,
weighed down by grief, and tears welled in our eyes,
when there appeared the spirit of Akhilleus,
son of Peleus; then Patróklos' shade,
550 and then Antílokhos, and then Aias,
first among all the Danaans in strength
and bodily beauty, next to prince Akhilleus.
Now that great runner, grandson of Aíakhos,°   Akhilleus
recognized me and called across to me:
'Son of Laërtês and the gods of old,
Odysseus, master mariner and soldier,
old knife, what next? What greater feat remains
for you to put your mind on, after this?
How did you find your way down to the dark
560 where these dimwitted dead are camped forever,
the after images of used-up men?'

                                        I answered:
'Akhilleus, Peleus' son, strongest of all
among the Akhaians, I had need of foresight
such as Teirêsias alone could give
to help me, homeward bound for the crags of Ithaka.
I have not yet coasted Akhaia, not yet
touched my land; my life is all adversity.
But was there ever a man more blest by fortune
570 than you, Akhilleus? Can there ever be?
We ranked you with immortals in your lifetime,
we Argives did, and here your power is royal
among the dead men's shades. Think, then, Akhilleus:
you need not be so pained by death.'

                                        To this
he answered swiftly:
                                        'Let me hear no smooth talk
of death from you, Odysseus, light of councils.

Better, I say, to break sod as a farm hand
580 for some poor country man, on iron rations,
than lord it over all the exhausted dead.
Tell me, what news of the prince my son:° did he   Neoptólemos
come after me to make a name in battle
or could it be he did not? Do you know
if rank and honor still belong to Peleus
in the towns of the Myrmidons? Or now, may be,
Hellas and Phthia[109] spurn him, seeing old age
fetters him, hand and foot. I cannot help him
under the sun's rays, cannot be that man
590 I was on Troy's wide seaboard, in those days
when I made bastion for the Argives
and put an army's best men in the dust.
Were I but whole again, could I go now
to my father's house, one hour would do to make
my passion and my hands no man could hold
hateful to any who shoulder him aside.'

Now when he paused I answered:
                                   'Of all that —
of Peleus' life, that is — I know nothing;
600 but happily I can tell you the whole story
of Neoptólemos, as you require.
In my own ship I brought him out from Skyros
to join the Akhaians under arms.
                              And I can tell you,
in every council before Troy thereafter
your son spoke first and always to the point;
no one but Nestor and I could out-debate him.
And when we formed against the Trojan line
he never hung back in the mass, but ranged
610 far forward of his troops — no man could touch him
for gallantry. Aye, scores went down before him
in hard fights man to man. I shall not tell
all about each, or name them all — the long
roster of enemies he put out of action,
taking the shock of charges on the Argives.
But what a champion his lance ran through
in Eurýpulos[110] the son of Télephos! Keteians

---

[109] **Phthia:** Peleus's kingdom.   [110] **Eurýpulos:** Leader of the Keteians, a group of warriors who fought on the side of the Trojans.

in throngs around that captain also died —
all because Priam's gifts had won his mother
620   to send the lad to battle; and I thought
Memnon[111] alone in splendor ever outshone him.

But one fact more: while our picked Argive crew
still rode that hollow horse Epeios built,
and when the whole thing lay with me, to open
the trapdoor of the ambuscade or not,
at that point our Danaan lords and soldiers
wiped their eyes, and their knees began to quake,
all but Neoptólemos. I never saw
his tanned cheek change color or his hand
630   brush one tear away. Rather he prayed me,
hand on hilt, to sortie, and he gripped
his tough spear, bent on havoc for the Trojans.
And when we had pierced and sacked Priam's tall city
he loaded his choice plunder and embarked
with no scar on him; not a spear had grazed him
nor the sword's edge in close work — common wounds
one gets in war. Arês in his mad fits
knows no favorites.'

                     But I said no more,
640   for he had gone off striding the field of asphodel,
the ghost of our great runner, Akhilleus Aiákidês,
glorying in what I told him of his son.

Now other souls of mournful dead stood by,
each with his troubled questioning, but one
remained alone, apart: the son of Télamon,
Aîas, it was — the great shade burning still
because I had won favor on the beachhead
in rivalry over Akhilleus' arms.[112]
The Lady Thetis, mother of Akhilleus,
650   laid out for us the dead man's battle gear,
and Trojan children, with Athena,

---

[111] **Memnon:** King of the Ethiopians; he took ten thousand men to Troy to assist the Trojans.   [112] **in rivalry . . . arms:** After Akhilleus was killed, his armor was offered as a prize to Odysseus rather than to Aias, who then committed suicide.

named the Danaan fittest to own them. Would
god I had not borne the palm that day!
For earth took Aîas then to hold forever,
the handsomest and, in all feats of war,
noblest of the Danaans after Akhilleus.
Gently therefore I called across to him:
'Aîas, dear son of royal Télamon,
you would not then forget, even in death,
660   your fury with me over those accurst
calamitous arms?—and so they were, a bane
sent by the gods upon the Argive host.
For when you died by your own hand we lost
a tower, formidable in war. All we Akhaians
mourn you forever, as we do Akhilleus;
and no one bears the blame but Zeus.
He fixed that doom for you because he frowned
on the whole expedition of our spearmen.
My lord, come nearer, listen to our story!
670   Conquer your indignation and your pride.'

But he gave no reply, and turned away,
following other ghosts toward Erebos.
Who knows if in that darkness he might still
have spoken, and I answered?
                              But my heart
longed, after this, to see the dead elsewhere.
And now there came before my eyes Minos,
the son of Zeus, enthroned, holding a golden staff,
dealing out justice among ghostly pleaders
680   arrayed about the broad doorways of Death.

And then I glimpsed Orion, the huge hunter,
gripping his club, studded with bronze, unbreakable,
with wild beasts he had overpowered in life
on lonely mountainsides, now brought to bay
on fields of asphodel.
                         And I saw Títyos,
the son of Gaia, lying
abandoned over nine square rods of plain.
Vultures, hunched above him, left and right,
690   rifling his belly, stabbed into the liver,
and he could never push them off.
                                    This hulk
had once committed rape of Zeus's mistress,

Lêto, in her glory, when she crossed
the open grass of Panopeus toward Pytho.

Then I saw Tántalos[113] put to the torture:
in a cool pond he stood, lapped round by water
clear to the chin, and being athirst he burned
to slake his dry weasand with drink, though drink
700   he would not ever again. For when the old man
put his lips down to the sheet of water
it vanished round his feet, gulped underground,
and black mud baked there in a wind from hell.
Boughs, too, drooped low above him, big with fruit,
pear trees, pomegranates, brilliant apples,
luscious figs, and olives ripe and dark;
but if he stretched his hand for one, the wind
under the dark sky tossed the bough beyond him.

Then Sísyphos[114] in torment I beheld
710   being roustabout to a tremendous boulder.
Leaning with both arms braced and legs driving,
he heaved it toward a height, and almost over,
but then a Power spun him round and sent
the cruel boulder bounding again to the plain.
Whereon the man bent down again to toil,
dripping sweat, and the dust rose overhead.
Next I saw manifest the power of Heraklês—
a phantom, this, for he himself has gone
feasting amid the gods, reclining soft
720   with Hêbê of the ravishing pale ankles,
daughter of Zeus and Hêra, shod in gold.
But, in my vision, all the dead around him
cried like affrighted birds; like Night itself
he loomed with naked bow and nocked arrow
and glances terrible as continual archery.
My hackles rose at the gold swordbelt he wore
sweeping across him: gorgeous intaglio
of savage bears, boars, lions with wildfire eyes,
swordfights, battle, slaughter, and sudden death—
730   the smith who had that belt in him, I hope
he never made, and never will make, another.

---

[113]**Tántalos:** The nature of Tántalos's crime is uncertain. He might have revealed secrets of the gods, or he might have served his son's flesh to the gods.   [114]**Sísyphos:** A king of Corinth known for his teachery; it is not known what misdeed he is being punished for in this passage.

The eyes of the vast figure rested on me,
and of a sudden he said in kindly tones:
'Son of Laërtês and the gods of old,
Odysseus, master mariner and soldier,
under a cloud, you too? Destined to grinding
labors like my own in the sunny world?[115]
Son of Kroníon Zeus or not, how many
days I sweated out, being bound in servitude
740 to a man far worse than I, a rough master!
He made me hunt this place one time
to get the watchdog of the dead: no more
perilous task, he thought, could be; but I
brought back that beast, up from the underworld;
Hermês and grey-eyed Athena showed the way.'

And Heraklês, down the vistas of the dead,
faded from sight; but I stood fast, awaiting
other great souls who perished in times past.
I should have met, then, god-begotten Theseus
750 and Peirithoös,[116] whom both I longed to see,
but first came shades in thousands, rustling
in a pandemonium of whispers, blown together,
and the horror took me that Perséphonê
had brought from darker hell some saurian death's head.
I whirled then, made for the ship, shouted to crewmen
to get aboard and cast off the stern hawsers,
an order soon obeyed. They took their thwarts,
and the ship went leaping toward the stream of Ocean
first under oars, then with a following wind.

BOOK 12
SEA PERILS AND DEFEAT

The ship sailed on, out of the Ocean Stream,
riding a long swell on the open sea
for the Island of Aiaia.
                    Summering Dawn
has dancing grounds there, and the Sun his rising;
but still by night we beached on a sand shelf

---

[115] **grinding labors . . . world:** Under the "rough master" Eurýstheus, Heraklês was made to perform his famous twelve labors, one of which was to fetch the dog Cerberus from Hades.   [116] **Peirithoös:** A friend of Theseus; together they attempted to kidnap Perséphonê.

and waded in beyond the line of breakers
to fall asleep, awaiting the Day Star.

When the young Dawn with finger tips of rose
10   made heaven bright, I sent shipmates to bring
Elpênor's body from the house of Kirkê.
We others cut down timber on the foreland,
on a high point, and built his pyre of logs,
then stood by weeping while the flame burnt through
corse and equipment.
                     Then we heaped his barrow,
lifting a gravestone on the mound, and fixed
his light but unwarped oar against the sky.
These were our rites in memory of him. Soon, then,
20   knowing us back from the Dark Land, Kirkê came
freshly adorned for us, with handmaids bearing
loaves, roast meats, and ruby-colored wine.
She stood among us in immortal beauty
jesting:
          'Hearts of oak, did you go down
alive into the homes of Death? One visit
finishes all men but yourselves, twice mortal!
Come, here is meat and wine, enjoy your feasting
for one whole day; and in the dawn tomorrow
30   you shall put out to sea. Sailing directions,
landmarks, perils, I shall sketch for you, to keep you
from being caught by land or water
in some black sack of trouble.'

                     In high humor
and ready for carousal, we agreed;
so all that day until the sun went down
we feasted on roast meat and good red wine,
till after sunset, at the fall of night,
the men dropped off to sleep by the stern hawsers.
40   She took my hand then, silent in that hush,
drew me apart, made me sit down, and lay
beside me, softly questioning, as I told
all I had seen, from first to last.
                     Then said the Lady Kirkê:
'So: all those trials are over.
                     Listen with care
to this, now, and a god will arm your mind.
Square in your ship's path are Seirênês,° crying   Sirens
beauty to bewitch men coasting by;

50 woe to the innocent who hears that sound!
He will not see his lady nor his children
in joy, crowding about him, home from sea;
the Seirênês will sing his mind away
on their sweet meadow lolling. There are bones
of dead men rotting in a pile beside them
and flayed skins shrivel around the spot.

                                        Steer wide;
keep well to seaward; plug your oarsmen's ears
with beeswax kneaded soft; none of the rest
60 should hear that song.

                    But if you wish to listen,
let the men tie you in the lugger, hand
and foot, back to the mast, lashed to the mast,
so you may hear those harpies' thrilling voices;
shout as you will, begging to be untied,
your crew must only twist more line around you
and keep their stroke up, till the singers fade.
What then? One of two courses you may take,
and you yourself must weigh them. I shall not
70 plan the whole action for you now, but only
tell you of both.

                    Ahead are beetling rocks
and dark blue glancing Amphitritê,[117] surging,
roars around them. Prowling Rocks,[118] or Drifters,
the gods in bliss have named them—named them well.
Not even birds can pass them by, not even
the timorous doves that bear ambrosia
to Father Zeus; caught by downdrafts, they die
on rockwall smooth as ice.
80   Each time, the Father
wafts a new courier to make up his crew.

Still less can ships get searoom of these Drifters,
whose boiling surf, under high fiery winds,
carries tossing wreckage of ships and men.
Only one ocean-going craft, the far-famed
Argo, made it, sailing from Aiêta;
but she, too, would have crashed on the big rocks
if Hêra had not pulled her through, for love
of Iêson, her captain.

---

[117] **Amphitritê:** A sea nymph; wife of Poseidon.   [118] **Prowling Rocks:** Possibly the straits between Sicily and Italy.

90   A second course
lies between headlands. One is a sharp mountain
piercing the sky, with stormcloud round the peak
dissolving never, not in the brightest summer,
to show heaven's azure there, nor in the fall.
No mortal man could scale it, nor so much
as land there, not with twenty hands and feet,
so sheer the cliffs are — as of polished stone.
Midway that height, a cavern full of mist
opens toward Erebos and evening. Skirting
100 this in the lugger, great Odysseus,
your master bowman, shooting from the deck,
would come short of the cavemouth with his shaft;
but that is the den of Skylla, where she yaps
abominably, a newborn whelp's cry,
though she is huge and monstrous. God or man,
no one could look on her in joy. Her legs —
and there are twelve — are like great tentacles,
unjointed, and upon her serpent necks
are borne six heads like nightmares of ferocity,
110 with triple serried rows of fangs and deep
gullets of black death. Half her length, she sways
her heads in air, outside her horrid cleft,
hunting the sea around that promontory
for dolphins, dogfish, or what bigger game
thundering Amphitritê feeds in thousands.
And no ship's company can claim
to have passed her without loss and grief; she takes,
from every ship, one man for every gullet.

The opposite point seems more a tongue of land
120 you'd touch with a good bowshot, at the narrows.
A great wild fig, a shaggy mass of leaves,
grows on it, and Kharybdis lurks below
to swallow down the dark sea tide. Three times
from dawn to dusk she spews it up
and sucks it down again three times, a whirling
maelstrom; if you come upon her then
the god who makes earth tremble could not save you.
No, hug the cliff of Skylla, take your ship
through on a racing stroke. Better to mourn
130 six men than lose them all, and the ship, too.'

So her advice ran; but I faced her, saying:
'Only instruct me, goddess, if you will,

how, if possible, can I pass Kharybdis,
or fight off Skylla when she raids my crew?'

Swiftly that loveliest goddess answered me:
'Must you have battle in your heart forever?
The bloody toil of combat? Old contender,
will you not yield to the immortal gods?
That nightmare cannot die, being eternal
140 evil itself—horror, and pain, and chaos;
there is no fighting her, no power can fight her,
all that avails is flight.
                                    Lose headway there
along that rockface while you break out arms,
and she'll swoop over you, I fear, once more,
taking one man again for every gullet.
No, no, put all your backs into it, row on;
invoke Blind Force, that bore this scourge of men,
to keep her from a second strike against you.

150 Then you will coast Thrinákia,° the island   Sicily
where Hêlios' cattle graze, fine herds, and flocks
of goodly sheep. The herds and flocks are seven,
with fifty beasts in each.
                                    No lambs are dropped,
or calves, and these fat cattle never die.
Immortal, too, their cowherds are—their shepherds—
Phaëthousa and Lampetía, sweetly braided
nymphs that divine Neaira bore
to the overlord of high noon, Hêlios.
160 These nymphs their gentle mother bred and placed
upon Thrinákia, the distant land,
in care of flocks and cattle for their father.

Now give those kine a wide berth, keep your thoughts
intent upon your course for home,
and hard seafaring brings you all to Ithaka.
But if you raid the beeves, I see destruction
for ship and crew.
                                    Rough years then lie between
you and your homecoming, alone and old,
170 the one survivor, all companions lost.'

As Kirkê spoke, Dawn mounted her golden throne,
and on the first rays Kirkê left me, taking
her way like a great goddess up the island.

I made straight for the ship, roused up the men
to get aboard and cast off at the stern.
They scrambled to their places by the rowlocks
and all in line dipped oars in the grey sea.
But soon an off-shore breeze blew to our liking—
a canvas-bellying breeze, a lusty shipmate
180 sent by the singing nymph with sunbright hair.
So we made fast the braces, and we rested,
letting the wind and steersman work the ship.
The crew being now silent before me, I
addressed them, sore at heart:
                                          'Dear friends,
more than one man, or two, should know those things
Kirkê foresaw for us and shared with me,
so let me tell her forecast: then we die
with our eyes open, if we are going to die,
190 or know what death we baffle if we can. Seirênês
weaving a haunting song over the sea
we are to shun, she said, and their green shore
all sweet with clover; yet she urged that I
alone should listen to their song. Therefore
you are to tie me up, tight as a splint,
erect along the mast, lashed to the mast,
and if I shout and beg to be untied,
take more turns of the rope to muffle me.'

I rather dwelt on this part of the forecast,
200 while our good ship made time, bound outward down
the wind for the strange island of Seirênês.
Then all at once the wind fell, and a calm
came over all the sea, as though some power
lulled the swell.
                            The crew were on their feet
briskly, to furl the sail, and stow it; then,
each in place, they poised the smooth oar blades
and sent the white foam scudding by. I carved
a massive cake of beeswax into bits
210 and rolled them in my hands until they softened—
no long task, for a burning heat came down
from Hêlios, lord of high noon. Going forward
I carried wax along the line, and laid it
thick on their ears. They tied me up, then, plumb
amidships, back to the mast, lashed to the mast,
and took themselves again to rowing. Soon,
as we came smartly within hailing distance,

the two Seirênês, noting our fast ship
off their point, made ready, and they sang:

220   This way, oh turn your bows,
        Akhaia's glory,
    As all the world allows—
        Moor and be merry.

    Sweet coupled airs we sing.
        No lonely seafarer
    Holds clear of entering
        Our green mirror.

    Pleased by each purling note
        Like honey twining
230   From her throat and my throat,
        Who lies a-pining?

    Sea rovers here take joy
        Voyaging onward,
    As from our song of Troy
    Greybeard and rower-boy
        Goeth more learnèd.

    All feats on that great field
        In the long warfare,
    Dark days the bright gods willed,
240   Wounds you bore there,

    Argos' old soldiery
        On Troy beach teeming,
    Charmed out of time we see.
    No life on earth can be
        Hid from our dreaming.

The lovely voices in ardor appealing over the water
made me crave to listen, and I tried to say
'Untie me!' to the crew, jerking my brows;
but they bent steady to the oars. Then Perimêdês
250 got to his feet, he and Eurýlokhos,
and passed more line about, to hold me still.
So all rowed on, until the Seirênês
dropped under the sea rim, and their singing
dwindled away.
            My faithful company
rested on their oars now, peeling off
the wax that I had laid thick on their ears;
then set me free.
            But scarcely had that island

260   faded in blue air than I saw smoke
and white water, with sound of waves in tumult —
a sound the men heard, and it terrified them.
Oars flew from their hands; the blades went knocking
wild alongside till the ship lost way,
with no oarblades to drive her through the water.

Well, I walked up and down from bow to stern,
trying to put heart into them, standing over
every oarsman, saying gently,
                            'Friends,
270   have we never been in danger before this?
More fearsome, is it now, than when the Kyklops
penned us in his cave? What power he had!
Did I not keep my nerve, and use my wits
to find a way out for us?
                       Now I say
by hook or crook this peril too shall be
something that we remember.
                           Heads up, lads!
We must obey the orders as I give them.
280   Get the oarshafts in your hands, and lay back
hard on your benches; hit these breaking seas.
Zeus help us pull away before we founder.
You at the tiller, listen, and take in
all that I say — the rudders are your duty;
keep her out of the combers and the smoke;
steer for that headland; watch the drift, or we
fetch up in the smother, and you drown us.'

That was all, and it brought them round to action.
But as I sent them on toward Skylla, I
290   told them nothing, as they could do nothing.
They would have dropped their oars again, in panic,
to roll for cover under the decking. Kirkê's
bidding against arms had slipped my mind,
so I tied on my cuirass and took up
two heavy spears, then made my way along
to the foredeck — thinking to see her first from there,
the monster of the grey rock, harboring
torment for my friends. I strained my eyes
upon that cliffside veiled in cloud, but nowhere
300   could I catch sight of her.

And all this time,
in travail, sobbing, gaining on the current,
we rowed into the strait—Skylla to port
and on our starboard beam Kharybdis, dire
gorge of the salt sea tide. By heaven! when she
vomited, all the sea was like a cauldron
seething over intense fire, when the mixture
suddenly heaves and rises.
                              The shot spume
310 soared to the landside heights, and fell like rain.

But when she swallowed the sea water down
we saw the funnel of the maelstrom, heard
the rock bellowing all around, and dark
sand raged on the bottom far below.
My men all blanched against the gloom, our eyes
were fixed upon that yawning mouth in fear
of being devoured.
                        Then Skylla made her strike,
whisking six of my best men from the ship.
320 I happened to glance aft at ship and oarsmen
and caught sight of their arms and legs, dangling
high overhead. Voices came down to me
in anguish, calling my name for the last time.

A man surfcasting on a point of rock
for bass or mackerel, whipping his long rod
to drop the sinker and the bait far out,
will hook a fish and rip it from the surface
to dangle wriggling through the air:
                                        so these
330 were borne aloft in spasms toward the cliff.

She ate them as they shrieked there, in her den,
in the dire grapple, reaching still for me—
and deathly pity ran me through
at that sight—far the worst I ever suffered,
questing the passes of the strange sea.
                              We rowed on.
The Rocks were now behind; Kharybdis, too,
and Skylla dropped astern.
                              Then we were coasting
340 the noble island of the god, where grazed

those cattle with wide brows, and bounteous flocks
of Hêlios, lord of noon, who rides high heaven.

From the black ship, far still at sea, I heard
the lowing of the cattle winding home
and sheep bleating; and heard, too, in my heart
the words of blind Teirêsias of Thebes
and Kirkê of Aiaia: both forbade me
the island of the world's delight, the Sun.
So I spoke out in gloom to my companions:
350   'Shipmates, grieving and weary though you are,
listen: I had forewarning from Teirêsias
and Kirkê, too; both told me I must shun
this island of the Sun, the world's delight.
Nothing but fatal trouble shall we find here.
Pull away, then, and put the land astern.'

That strained them to the breaking point, and, cursing,
Eurýlokhos cried out in bitterness:
'Are you flesh and blood, Odysseus, to endure
more than a man can? Do you never tire?
360   God, look at you, iron is what you're made of.
Here we all are, half dead with weariness,
falling asleep over the oars, and you
say "No landing"—no firm island earth
where we could make a quiet supper. No:
pull out to sea, you say, with night upon us—
just as before, but wandering now, and lost.
Sudden storms can rise at night and swamp
ships without a trace.
                              Where is your shelter
370   if some stiff gale blows up from south or west—
the winds that break up shipping every time
when seamen flout the lord gods' will? I say
do as the hour demands and go ashore
before black night comes down.
                                    We'll make our supper
alongside, and at dawn put out to sea.'

Now when the rest said 'Aye' to this, I saw
the power of destiny devising ill.
Sharply I answered, without hesitation:
380   'Eurýlokhos, they are with you to a man.
I am alone, outmatched.

Let this whole company
swear me a great oath: Any herd of cattle
or flock of sheep here found shall go unharmed;
no one shall slaughter out of wantonness
ram or heifer; all shall be content
with what the goddess Kirkê put aboard.'

They fell at once to swearing as I ordered,
and when the round of oaths had ceased, we found
390 a halfmoon bay to beach and moor the ship in,
with a fresh spring nearby. All hands ashore
went about skillfully getting up a meal.
Then, after thirst and hunger, those besiegers,
were turned away, they mourned for their companions
plucked from the ship by Skylla and devoured,
and sleep came soft upon them as they mourned.

In the small hours of the third watch, when stars
that shone out in the first dusk of evening
had gone down to their setting, a giant wind
400 blew from heaven, and clouds driven by Zeus
shrouded land and sea in a night of storm;
so, just as Dawn with finger tips of rose
touched the windy world, we dragged our ship
to cover in a grotto, a sea cave
where nymphs had chairs of rock and sanded floors.
I mustered all the crew and said:
                   'Old shipmates,
our stores are in the ship's hold, food and drink;
the cattle here are not for our provision,
410 or we pay dearly for it.
                Fierce the god is
who cherishes these heifers and these sheep:
Hêlios; and no man avoids his eye.'

To this my fighters nodded. Yes. But now
we had a month of onshore gales, blowing
day in, day out — south winds, or south by east.
As long as bread and good red wine remained
to keep the men up, and appease their craving,
they would not touch the cattle. But in the end,
420 when all the barley in the ship was gone,
hunger drove them to scour the wild shore
with angling hooks, for fishes and sea fowl,

whatever fell into their hands; and lean days
wore their bellies thin.

                    The storms continued.
So one day I withdrew to the interior
to pray the gods in solitude, for hope
that one might show me some way of salvation.
Slipping away, I struck across the island
430 to a sheltered spot, out of the driving gale.
I washed my hands there, and made supplication
to the gods who own Olympos, all the gods—
but they, for answer, only closed my eyes
under slow drops of sleep.
                    Now on the shore Erýlokhos
made his insidious plea:
                    'Comrades,' he said,
'You've gone through everything; listen to what I say.
All deaths are hateful to us, mortal wretches,
440 but famine is the most pitiful, the worst
end that a man can come to.
                    Will you fight it?
Come, we'll cut out the noblest of these cattle
for sacrifice to the gods who own the sky;
and once at home, in the old country of Ithaka,
if ever that day comes—
we'll build a costly temple and adorn it
with every beauty for the Lord of Noon.
But if he flares up over his heifers lost,
450 wishing our ship destroyed, and if the gods
make cause with him, why, then I say: Better
open your lungs to a big sea once for all
than waste to skin and bones on a lonely island!'

Thus Erýlokhos; and they murmured 'Aye!'
trooping away at once to round up heifers.
Now, that day tranquil cattle with broad brows
were grazing near, and soon the men drew up
around their chosen beasts in ceremony.
They plucked the leaves that shone on a tall oak—
460 having no barley meal—to strew the victims,
performed the prayers and ritual, knifed the kine
and flayed each carcass, cutting thighbones free
to wrap in double folds of fat. These offerings,

with strips of meat, were laid upon the fire.
Then, as they had no wine, they made libation
with clear spring water, broiling the entrails first;
and when the bones were burnt and tripes shared,
they spitted the carved meat.
                                Just then my slumber
470   left me in a rush, my eyes opened,
and I went down the seaward path. No sooner
had I caught sight of our black hull, than savory
odors of burnt fat eddied around me;
grief took hold of me, and I cried aloud:
'O Father Zeus and gods in bliss forever,
you made me sleep away this day of mischief!
O cruel drowsing, in the evil hour!
Here they sat, and a great work they contrived.'

Lampetía in her long gown meanwhile
480   had borne swift word to the Overlord of Noon:
'They have killed your kine.'

                   And the Lord Hêlios
burst into angry speech amid the immortals:
'O Father Zeus and gods in bliss forever,
punish Odysseus' men! So overweening,
now they have killed my peaceful kine, my joy
at morning when I climbed the sky of stars,
and evening, when I bore westward from heaven.
Restitution or penalty they shall pay—
490   and pay in full—or I go down forever
to light the dead men in the underworld.'

Then Zeus who drives the stormcloud made reply:
'Peace, Hêlios: shine on among the gods,
shine over mortals in the fields of grain.
Let me throw down one white-hot bolt, and make
splinters of their ship in the winedark sea.'

—Kalypso later told me of this exchange,
as she declared that Hermês had told her.
Well, when I reached the sea cave and the ship,
500   I faced each man, and had it out; but where
could any remedy be found? There was none.
The silken beeves of Hêlios were dead.

The gods, moreover, made queer signs appear:
cowhides began to crawl, and beef, both raw
and roasted, lowed like kine upon the spits.

Now six full days my gallant crew could feast
upon the prime beef they had marked for slaughter
from Hêlios' herd; and Zeus, the son of Kronos,
added one fine morning.
510   All the gales
had ceased, blown out, and with an offshore breeze
we launched again, stepping the mast and sail,
to make for the open sea. Astern of us
the island coastline faded, and no land
showed anywhere, but only sea and heaven,
when Zeus Kroníon piled a thunderhead
above the ship, while gloom spread on the ocean.
We held our course, but briefly. Then the squall
struck whining from the west, with gale force, breaking
520 both forestays, and the mast came toppling aft
along the ship's length, so the running rigging
showered into the bilge.
                          On the after deck
the mast had hit the steersman a slant blow
bashing the skull in, knocking him overside,
as the brave soul fled the body, like a diver.
With crack on crack of thunder, Zeus let fly
a bolt against the ship, a direct hit,
so that she bucked, in reeking fumes of sulphur,
530 and all the men were flung into the sea.
They came up 'round the wreck, bobbing a while
like petrels on the waves.
                          No more seafaring
homeward for these, no sweet day of return;
the god had turned his face from them.
                                          I clambered
fore and aft my hulk until a comber
split her, keel from ribs, and the big timber
floated free; the mast, too, broke away.
540 A backstay floated dangling from it, stout
rawhide rope, and I used this for lashing
mast and keel together. These I straddled,
riding the frightful storm.
                          Nor had I yet
seen the worst of it: for now the west wind
dropped, and a southeast gale came on—one more

twist of the knife—taking me north again,
straight for Kharybdis. All that night I drifted,
and in the sunrise, sure enough, I lay
550 off Skylla mountain and Kharybdis deep.
There, as the whirlpool drank the tide, a billow
tossed me, and I sprang for the great fig tree,
catching on like a bat under a bough.
Nowhere had I to stand, no way of climbing,
the root and bole being far below, and far
above my head the branches and their leaves,
massed, overshadowing Kharybdis pool.
But I clung grimly, thinking my mast and keel
would come back to the surface when she spouted.
560 And ah! how long, with what desire, I waited!
till, at the twilight hour, when one who hears
and judges pleas in the marketplace all day
between contentious men, goes home to supper,
the long poles at last reared from the sea.

Now I let go with hands and feet, plunging
straight into the foam beside the timbers,
pulled astride, and rowed hard with my hands
to pass by Skylla. Never could I have passed her
had not the Father of gods and men, this time,
570 kept me from her eyes. Once through the straight,
nine days I drifted in the open sea
before I made shore, buoyed up by the gods,
upon Ogýgia Isle. The dangerous nymph
Kalypso lives and sings there, in her beauty,
and she received me, loved me.
                                        But why tell
the same tale that I told last night in hall
to you and to your lady? Those adventures
made a long evening, and I do not hold
580 with tiresome repetition of a story."

Book 13
One More Strange Island

He ended it, and no one stirred or sighed
in the shadowy hall, spellbound as they all were,
until Alkínoös answered:
                                "When you came
here to my strong home, Odysseus, under

my tall roof, headwinds were left behind you.
Clear sailing shall you have now, homeward now,
however painful all the past.
                              My lords,
10   ever my company, sharing the wine of Council,
the songs of the blind harper, hear me further:
garments are folded for our guest and friend
in the smooth chest, and gold
in various shaping of adornment lies
with other gifts, and many, brought by our peers;
let each man add his tripod and deep-bellied
cauldron: we'll make levy upon the realm
to pay us for the loss each bears in this."

Alkínoös had voiced their own hearts' wish.
20   All gave assent, then home they went to rest;
but young Dawn's finger tips of rose, touching
the world, roused them to make haste to the ship,
each with his gift of noble bronze. Alkínoös,
their ardent king, stepping aboard himself,
directed the stowing under the cross planks,
not to cramp the long pull of the oarsmen.
Going then to the great hall, lords and crew
prepared for feasting.
                        As the gods' anointed,
30   Alkínoös made offering on their behalf—an ox
to Zeus beyond the stormcloud, Kronos' son,
who rules the world. They burnt the great thighbones
and feasted at their ease on fresh roast meat,
as in their midst the godlike harper sang—
Demódokos, honored by all that realm.
                                        Only Odysseus
time and again turned craning toward the sun,
impatient for day's end, for the open sea.
Just as a farmer's hunger grows, behind
40   the bolted plow and share, all day afield,
drawn by his team of winedark oxen: sundown
is benison° for him, sending him homeward   blessing
stiff in the knees from weariness, to dine;
just so, the light on the sea rim gladdened Odysseus,
and as it dipped he stood among the Phaiákians,
turned to Alkínoös, and said:
"O king and admiration of your people,
give me fare well, and stain the ground with wine;
my blessings on you all! This hour brings

50 fulfillment to the longing of my heart:
   a ship for home, and gifts the gods of heaven
   make so precious and so bountiful.
                              After this voyage
   god grant I find my own wife in my hall
   with everyone I love best, safe and sound!
   And may you, settled in your land, give joy
   to wives and children; may the gods reward you
   every way, and your realm be free of woe."

   Then all the voices rang out, "Be it so!"
60 and "Well spoken!" and "Let our friend make sail!"

   Whereon Alkínoös gave command to his crier:
   "Fill the winebowl, Pontónoös: mix and serve:
   go the whole round, so may this company
   invoke our Father Zeus, and bless our friend,
   seaborne tonight and bound for his own country."

   Pontónoös mixed the honey-hearted wine
   and went from chair to chair, filling the cups;
   then each man where he sat poured out his offering
   to the gods in bliss who own the sweep of heaven.
70 With gentle bearing Odysseus rose, and placed
   his double goblet in Arêtê's hands,
   saying:
           "Great Queen, farewell;
   be blest through all your days till age comes on you,
   and death, last end for mortals, after age.
   Now I must go my way. Live in felicity,
   and make this palace lovely for your children,
   your countrymen, and your king, Alkínoös."

   Royal Odysseus turned and crossed the door sill,
80 a herald at his right hand, sent by Alkínoös
   to lead him to the sea beach and the ship.
   Arêtê, too, sent maids in waiting after him,
   one with a laundered great cloak and a tunic,
   a second balancing the crammed sea chest,
   a third one bearing loaves and good red wine.
   As soon as they arrived alongside, crewmen
   took these things for stowage under the planks,
   their victualling and drink; then spread a rug
   and linen cover on the after deck,
90 where Lord Odysseus might sleep in peace.

Now he himself embarked, lay down, lay still,
while oarsmen took their places at the rowlocks
all in order. They untied their hawser,
passing it through a drilled stone ring; then bent
forward at the oars and caught the sea
as one man, stroking.
                          Slumber, soft and deep
like the still sleep of death, weighed on his eyes
as the ship hove seaward.
100   How a four horse team
whipped into a run on a straightaway
consumes the road, surging and surging over it!
So ran that craft and showed her heels to the swell,
her bow wave riding after, and her wake
on the purple night-sea foaming.
                          Hour by hour
she held her pace; not even a falcon wheeling
downwind, swiftest bird, could stay abreast of her
in that most arrowy flight through open water,
110 with her great passenger — godlike in counsel,
he that in twenty years had borne such blows
in his deep heart, breaking through ranks in war
and waves on the bitter sea.
                          This night at last
he slept serene, his long-tried mind at rest.

When on the East the sheer bright star arose
that tells of coming Dawn, the ship made landfall
and came up islandward in the dim of night.
Phorkys, the old sea baron, has a cove
120 here in the realm of Ithaka; two points
of high rock, breaking sharply, hunch around it,
making a haven from the plunging surf
that gales at sea roll shoreward. Deep inside,
at mooring range, good ships can ride unmoored.
There, on the inmost shore, an olive tree
throws wide its boughs over the bay; nearby
a cave of dusky light is hidden
for those immortal girls, the Naiadês.[119]
Within are winebowls hollowed in the rock
130 and amphorai; bees bring their honey here;
and there are looms of stone, great looms, whereon

---

[119] **Naiadês:** Water nymphs who presided over rivers, lakes, springs, and fountains.

the weaving nymphs make tissues, richly dyed
as the deep sea is; and clear springs in the cavern
flow forever. Of two entrances,
one on the north allows descent of mortals,
but beings out of light alone, the undying,
can pass by the south slit; no men come there.

This cove the sailors knew. Here they drew in,
and the ship ran half her keel's length up the shore,
140 she had such way on her from those great oarsmen.
Then from their benches forward on dry ground
they disembarked. They hoisted up Odysseus
unruffled on his bed, under his cover,
handing him overside still fast asleep,
to lay him on the sand; and they unloaded
all those gifts the princes of Phaiákia
gave him, when by Athena's heart and will
he won his passage home. They bore this treasure
off the beach, and piled it close around
150 the roots of the olive tree, that no one passing
should steal Odysseus' gear before he woke.
That done, they pulled away on the homeward track.

But now the god that shakes the islands, brooding
over old threats of his against Odysseus,
approached Lord Zeus to learn his will. Said he:
"Father of gods, will the bright immortals ever
pay me respect again, if mortals do not?—
Phaiákians, too, my own blood kin?
                   I thought
160 Odysseus should in time regain his homeland;
I had no mind to rob him of that day—
no, no; you promised it, being so inclined;
only I thought he should be made to suffer
all the way.
        But now these islanders
have shipped him homeward, sleeping soft, and put him
on Ithaka, with gifts untold
bronze and gold, and fine cloth to his shoulder.
Never from Troy had he borne off such booty
170 if he had got home safe with all his share."

Then Zeus who drives the stormcloud answered, sighing:
"God of horizons, making earth's underbeam
tremble, why do you grumble so?

The immortal gods show you no less esteem,
and the rough consequence would make them slow
to let barbs fly at their eldest and most noble.
But if some mortal captain, overcome
by his own pride of strength, cuts or defies you,
are you not always free to take reprisal?
180 Act as your wrath requires and as you will."

Now said Poseidon, god of earthquake:
                                        "Aye,
god of the stormy sky, I should have taken
vengeance, as you say, and on my own;
but I respect, and would avoid, your anger.
The sleek Phaiákian cutter, even now,
has carried out her mission and glides home
over the misty sea. Let me impale her,
end her voyage, and end all ocean-crossing
190 with passengers, then heave a mass of mountain
in a ring around the city."

Now Zeus who drives the stormcloud said benignly:
"Here is how I should do it, little brother:
when all who watch upon the wall have caught
sight of the ship, let her be turned to stone—
an island like a ship, just off the bay.
Mortals may gape at that for generations!
But throw no mountain round the sea port city."

When he heard this, Poseidon, god of earthquake,
200 departed for Skhería, where the Phaiákians
are born and dwell. Their ocean-going ship
he saw already near, heading for harbor;
so up behind her swam the island-shaker
and struck her into stone, rooted in stone, at one
blow of his palm,
                        then took to the open sea.
Those famous ship handlers, the Phaiákians,
gazed at each other, murmuring in wonder;
you could have heard one say:
                                        "Now who in thunder
210 has anchored, moored that ship in the seaway,
when everyone could see her making harbor?"

The god had wrought a charm beyond their thought.
But soon Alkínoös made them hush, and told them:
"This present doom upon the ship—on me—

my father prophesied in the olden time.
If we gave safe conveyance to all passengers
we should incur Poseidon's wrath, he said,
whereby one day a fair ship, manned by Phaiákians,
220 would come to grief at the god's hands; and great
mountains would hide our city from the sea.
So my old father forecast.
                              Use your eyes:
these things are even now being brought to pass.
Let all here abide by my decree:
                                   We make
an end henceforth of taking, in our ships,
castaways who may land upon Skhería;
and twelve choice bulls we dedicate at once
230 to Lord Poseidon, praying him of his mercy
not to heave up a mountain round our city."

In fearful awe they led the bulls to sacrifice
and stood about the altar stone, those captains,
peers of Phaiákia, led by their king in prayer
to Lord Poseidon.

                    Meanwhile, on his island,
his father's shore, that kingly man, Odysseus,
awoke, but could not tell what land it was
after so many years away; moreover,
240 Pallas Athena, Zeus's daughter, poured
a grey mist all around him, hiding him
from common sight—for she had things to tell him
and wished no one to know him, wife or townsmen,
before the suitors paid up for their crimes.

The landscape then looked strange, unearthly strange
to the Lord Odysseus: paths by hill and shore,
glimpses of harbors, cliffs, and summer trees.
He stood up, rubbed his eyes, gazed at his homeland,
and swore, slapping his thighs with both his palms,
250 then cried aloud:
                       "What am I in for now?
Whose country have I come to this time? Rough
savages and outlaws, are they, or
godfearing people, friendly to castaways?
Where shall I take these things? Where take myself,
with no guide, no directions? These should be
still in Phaiákian hands, and I uncumbered,
free to find some other openhearted

prince who might be kind and give me passage.
260 I have no notion where to store this treasure;
first-comer's trove it is, if I leave it here.

My lords and captains of Phaiákia
were not those decent men they seemed, not honorable,
landing me in this unknown country — no,
by god, they swore to take me home to Ithaka
and did not! Zeus attend to their reward,
Zeus, patron of petitioners, who holds
all other mortals under his eye; he takes
payment from betrayers!
270   I'll be busy.
I can look through my gear. I shouldn't wonder
if they pulled out with part of it on board."

He made a tally of his shining pile —
tripods, cauldrons, cloaks, and gold — and found
he lacked nothing at all.
                              And then he wept,
despairing, for his own land, trudging down
beside the endless wash of the wide, wide sea,
weary and desolate as the sea. But soon
280 Athena came to him from the nearby air,
putting a young man's figure on — a shepherd,
like a king's son, all delicately made.
She wore a cloak, in two folds off her shoulders,
and sandals bound upon her shining feet.
A hunting lance lay in her hands.
                              At sight of her
Odysseus took heart, and he went forward
to greet the lad, speaking out fair and clear:
"Friend, you are the first man I've laid eyes on
290 here in this cove. Greetings. Do not feel
alarmed or hostile, coming across me; only
receive me into safety with my stores.
Touching your knees I ask it, as I might
ask grace of a god.
                              O sir, advise me,
what is this land and realm, who are the people?
Is it an island all distinct, or part
of the fertile mainland, sloping to the sea?"

To this grey-eyed Athena answered:
300   "Stranger,

you must come from the other end of nowhere,
else you are a great booby, having to ask
what place this is. It is no nameless country.
Why, everyone has heard of it, the nations
over on the dawn side, toward the sun,
and westerners in cloudy lands of evening.
No one would use this ground for training horses,
it is too broken, has no breadth of meadow;
but there is nothing meager about the soil,
310   the yield of grain is wondrous, and wine, too,
with drenching rains and dewfall.
                              There's good pasture
for oxen and for goats, all kinds of timber,
and water all year long in the cattle ponds.
For these blessings, friend, the name of Ithaka
has made its way even as far as Troy—
and they say Troy lies far beyond Akhaia."

Now Lord Odysseus, the long-enduring,
laughed in his heart, hearing his land described
320   by Pallas Athena, daughter of Zeus who rules
the veering stormwind; and he answered her
with ready speech—not that he told the truth,
but, just as she did, held back what he knew,
weighing within himself at every step
what he made up to serve his turn.

                         Said he:
"Far away in Krete I learned of Ithaka—
in that broad island over the great ocean.
And here I am now, come myself to Ithaka!
330   Here is my fortune with me. I left my sons
an equal part, when I shipped out. I killed
Orsílokhos, the courier, son of Idómeneus.
This man could beat the best cross country runners
in Krete, but he desired to take away
my Trojan plunder, all I had fought and bled for,
cutting through ranks in war and the cruel sea.
Confiscation is what he planned; he knew
I had not cared to win his father's favor
as a staff officer in the field at Troy,
340   but led my own command.
                         I acted: I
hit him with a spearcast from a roadside
as he came down from the open country. Murky

night shrouded all heaven and the stars.
I made that ambush with one man at arms.
We were unseen. I took his life in secret,
finished him off with my sharp sword. That night
I found asylum on a ship off shore
skippered by gentlemen of Phoinikia;° I gave   Phoenicia
350 all they could wish, out of my store of plunder,
for passage, and for landing me at Pylos
or Elis Town,[120] where the Epeioi are in power.
Contrary winds carried them willy-nilly
past that coast; they had no wish to cheat me,
but we were blown off course.
                                   Here, then, by night
we came, and made this haven by hard rowing.
All famished, but too tired to think of food,
each man dropped in his tracks after the landing,
360 and I slept hard, being wearied out. Before
I woke today, they put my things ashore
on the sand here beside me where I lay,
then reimbarked for Sidon, that great city.
Now they are far at sea, while I am left
forsaken here."

                         At this the grey-eyed goddess
Athena smiled, and gave him a caress,
her looks being changed now, so she seemed a woman,
tall and beautiful and no doubt skilled
370 at weaving splendid things. She answered briskly:
"Whoever gets around you must be sharp
and guileful as a snake; even a god
might bow to you in ways of dissimulation.
You! You chameleon!
Bottomless bag of tricks! Here in your own country
would you not give your stratagems a rest
or stop spellbinding for an instant?

You play a part as if it were your own tough skin.

No more of this, though. Two of a kind, we are,
380 contrivers, both. Of all men now alive
you are the best in plots and story telling.
My own fame is for wisdom among the gods—
deceptions, too.

---

[120] **Elis Town:** Elis was a famous city in the western Peloponnese.

Would even you have guessed
that I am Pallas Athena, daughter of Zeus,
I that am always with you in times of trial,
a shield to you in battle, I who made
the Phaiákians befriend you, to a man?
Now I am here again to counsel with you—
390 but first to put away those gifts the Phaiákians
gave you at departure—I planned it so.
Then I can tell you of the gall and wormwood
it is your lot to drink in your own hall.
Patience, iron patience, you must show;
so give it out to neither man nor woman
that you are back from wandering. Be silent
under all injuries, even blows from men.”

His mind ranging far, Odysseus answered:
“Can mortal man be sure of you on sight,
400 even a sage, O mistress of disguises?
Once you were fond of me—I am sure of that—
years ago, when we Akhaians made
war, in our generation, upon Troy.
But after we had sacked the shrines of Priam
and put to sea, God scattered the Akhaians;
I never saw you after that, never
knew you aboard with me, to act as shield
in grievous times—not till you gave me comfort
in the rich hinterland of the Phaiákians
410 and were yourself my guide into that city.

Hear me now in your father’s name, for I
cannot believe that I have come to Ithaka.
It is some other land. You made that speech
only to mock me, and to take me in.
Have I come back in truth to my home island?”

To this the grey-eyed goddess Athena answered:
“Always the same detachment! That is why
I cannot fail you, in your evil fortune,
coolheaded, quick, well-spoken as you are!
420 Would not another wandering man, in joy,
make haste home to his wife and children? Not
you, not yet. Before you hear their story
you will have proof about your wife.
                 I tell you,
she still sits where you left her, and her days

and nights go by forlorn, in lonely weeping.
For my part, never had I despaired; I felt
sure of your coming home, though all your men
should perish; but I never cared to fight
430   Poseidon, Father's brother, in his baleful
rage with you for taking his son's eye.

Now I shall make you see the shape of Ithaka.
Here is the cove the sea lord Phorkys owns,
there is the olive spreading out her leaves
over the inner bay, and there the cavern
dusky and lovely, hallowed by the feet
of those immortal girls, the Naiadês —
the same wide cave under whose vault you came
to honor them with hekatombs — and there
440   Mount Neion, with his forest on his back!"

She had dispelled the mist, so all the island
stood out clearly. Then indeed Odysseus'
heart stirred with joy. He kissed the earth,
and lifting up his hands prayed to the nymphs:
"O slim shy Naiadês, young maids of Zeus,
I had not thought to see you ever again!

                                    O listen smiling
to my gentle prayers, and we'll make offering
plentiful as in the old time, granted I
450   live, granted my son grows tall, by favor
of great Athena, Zeus's daughter,
who gives the winning fighter his reward!"

The grey-eyed goddess said directly:
                                    "Courage;
and let the future trouble you no more.
We go to make a cache now, in the cave,
to keep your treasure hid. Then we'll consider
how best the present action may unfold."

The goddess turned and entered the dim cave,
460   exploring it for crannies, while Odysseus
carried up all the gold, the fire-hard bronze,
and well-made clothing the Phaiákians gave him.
Pallas Athena, daughter of Zeus the storm king,
placed them, and shut the cave mouth with a stone,
and under the old grey olive tree those two
sat down to work the suitors death and woe.

Grey-eyed Athena was the first to speak, saying:
"Son of Laërtês and the gods of old,
Odysseus, master of land ways and sea ways,
470 put your mind on a way to reach and strike
a crowd of brazen upstarts.
                              Three long years
they have played master in your house: three years
trying to win your lovely lady, making
gifts as though betrothed. And she? Forever
grieving for you, missing your return,
she has allowed them all to hope, and sent
messengers with promises to each—
though her true thoughts are fixed elsewhere."

480   At this
the man of ranging mind, Odysseus, cried:
"So hard beset! An end like Agamémnon's
might very likely have been mine, a bad end,
bleeding to death in my own hall. You forestalled it,
goddess, by telling me how the land lies.
Weave me a way to pay them back! And you, too,
take your place with me, breathe valor in me
the way you did that night when we Akhaians
unbound the bright veil from the brow of Troy!
490 O grey-eyed one, fire my heart and brace me!
I'll take on fighting men three hundred strong
if you fight at my back, immortal lady!"

The grey-eyed goddess Athena answered him:
"No fear but I shall be there; you'll go forward
under my arm when the crux comes at last.
And I foresee your vast floor stained with blood,
spattered with brains of this or that tall suitor
who fed upon your cattle.
                              Now, for a while,
500 I shall transform you; not a soul will know you,
the clear skin of your arms and legs shriveled,
your chestnut hair all gone, your body dressed
in sacking that a man would gag to see,
and the two eyes, that were so brilliant, dirtied—
contemptible, you shall seem to your enemies,
as to the wife and son you left behind.

But join the swineherd first—the overseer
of all your swine, a good soul now as ever,

devoted to Penélopê and your son.
510   He will be found near Raven's Rock and the well
of Arethousa, where the swine are pastured,
rooting for acorns to their hearts' content,
drinking the dark still water. Boarflesh grows
pink and fat on that fresh diet. There
stay with him and question him, while I
am off to the great beauty's land of Sparta,
to call your son Telémakhos home again—
for you should know, he went to the wide land
of Lakedaimon, Meneláos' country,
520   to learn if there were news of you abroad."

Odysseus answered:
                    "Why not tell him, knowing
my whole history, as you do? Must he
traverse the barren sea, he too, and live
in pain, while others feed on what is his?"

At this the grey-eyed goddess Athena said:
"No need for anguish on that lad's account.
I sent him off myself, to make his name
in foreign parts—no hardship in the bargain,
530   taking his ease in Meneláos' mansion,
lapped in gold.
                    The young bucks here, I know,
lie in wait for him in a cutter, bent
on murdering him before he reaches home.
I rather doubt they will. Cold earth instead
will take in her embrace a man or two
of those who fed so long on what is his."

Speaking no more, she touched him with her wand,
shriveled the clear skin of his arms and legs,
540   made all his hair fall out, cast over him
the wrinkled hide of an old man, and bleared
both his eyes, that were so bright. Then she
clapped an old tunic, a foul cloak, upon him,
tattered, filthy, stained by greasy smoke,
and over that a mangy big buck skin.
A staff she gave him, and a leaky knapsack
with no strap but a loop of string.
                    Now then,

their colloquy at an end, they went their ways—
550　Athena toward illustrious Lakedaimon
far over sea, to join Odysseus' son.

BOOK 14
HOSPITALITY IN THE FOREST

He went up from the cove through wooded ground,
taking a stony trail into the high hills, where
the swineherd lived, according to Athena.
Of all Odysseus' field hands in the old days
this forester cared most for the estate;
and now Odysseus found him
in a remote clearing, sitting inside the gate
of a stockade he built to keep the swine
while his great lord was gone.
　　　　　　　　　　Working alone,
10　far from Penélopê and old Laërtês,
he had put up a fieldstone hut and timbered it
with wild pear wood. Dark hearts of oak he split
and trimmed for a high palisade around it,
and built twelve sties adjoining in this yard
to hold the livestock. Fifty sows with farrows
were penned in each, bedded upon the earth,
while the boars lay outside—fewer by far,
as those well-fatted were for the suitors' table,
20　fine pork, sent by the swineherd every day.
Three hundred sixty now lay there at night,
guarded by dogs—four dogs like wolves, one each
for the four lads the swineherd reared and kept
as under-herdsmen.
　　　　　　　When Odysseus came,
the good servant sat shaping to his feet
oxhide for sandals, cutting the well-cured leather.
Three of his young men were afield, pasturing
herds in other woods; one he had sent
30　with a fat boar for tribute into town,
the boy to serve while the suitors got their fill.

The watch dogs, when they caught sight of Odysseus,
faced him, a snarling troop, and pelted out
viciously after him. Like a tricky beggar

he sat down plump, and dropped his stick. No use.
They would have rolled him in the dust and torn him
there by his own steading if the swineherd
had not sprung up and flung his leather down,
making a beeline for the open. Shouting,
40   throwing stone after stone,
he made them scatter; then turned to his lord
and said:
                "You might have got a ripping, man!
Two shakes more and a pretty mess for me
you could have called it, if you had the breath.
As though I had not trouble enough already,
given me by the gods, my master gone,
true king hat he was. I hang on here,
still mourning for him, raising pigs of his
50   to feed foreigners, and who knows where the man is,
in some far country among strangers! Aye—
if he is living still, if he still sees the light of day.

Come to the cabin. You're a wanderer too.
You must eat something, drink some wine, and tell me
where you are from and the hard times you've seen."

The forester now led him to his hut
and made a couch for him, with tips of fir
piled for a mattress under a wild goat skin,
shaggy and thick, his own bed covering.
60
                                    Odysseus,
in pleasure at this courtesy, gently said:
"May Zeus and all the gods give you your heart's desire
for taking me in so kindly, friend."

                        Eumaios—
O my swineherd!¹²¹—answered him:
                            "Tush, friend,
rudeness to a stranger is not decency,
poor though he may be, poorer than you.
                            All wanderers
70   and beggars come from Zeus. What we can give
is slight but well-meant—all we dare. You know
that is the way of slaves, who live in dread

---

¹²¹ **O my swineherd!:** The poet addresses Eumaios directly here, something he does only with Eumaios in *The Odyssey.* It may indicate a special feeling for the old swineherd.

of masters—new ones like our own.
I told you
the gods, long ago, hindered our lord's return.
He had a fondness for me, would have pensioned me
with acres of my own, a house, a wife
that other men admired and courted; all
gifts good-hearted kings bestow for service,
80 for a life work the bounty of god has prospered—
for it does prosper here, this work I do.
Had he grown old in his own house, my master
would have rewarded me. But the man's gone.
God curse the race of Helen and cut it down,
that wrung the strength out of the knees of many!
And he went, too—for the honor of Agamémnon
he took ship overseas for the wild horse country
of Troy, to fight the Trojans."

This being told,
90 he tucked his long shirt up inside his belt
and strode into the pens for two young porkers.
He slaughtered them and singed them at the fire,
flayed and quartered them, and skewered the meat
to broil it all; then gave it to Odysseus
hot on the spits. He shook out barley meal,
took a winebowl of ivy wood and filled it,
and sat down facing him, with a gesture, saying:
"There is your dinner, friend, the pork of slaves.
Our fat shoats[122] are all eaten by the suitors,
100 cold-hearted men, who never spare a thought
for how they stand in the sight of Zeus. The gods
living in bliss are fond of no wrongdoing,
but honor discipline and right behavior.
Even the outcasts of the earth, who bring
piracy from the sea, and bear off plunder
given by Zeus in shiploads—even those men
deep in their hearts tremble for heaven's eye.
But the suitors, now, have heard some word, some oracle
of my lord's death, being so unconcerned
110 to pay court properly or to go about their business.
All they want is to prey on his estate,
proud dogs: they stop at nothing. Not a day
goes by, and not a night comes under Zeus,

---

[122] **shoats:** Young, weaned pigs.

but they make butchery of our beeves and swine—
not one or two beasts at a time, either.
As for swilling down wine, they drink us dry.
Only a great domain like his could stand it—
greater than any on the dusky mainland
or here in Ithaka. Not twenty heroes
120 in the whole world were as rich as he. I know:
I could count it all up: twelve herds in Elis,
as many flocks, as many herds of swine,
and twelve wide ranging herds of goats, as well,
attended by his own men or by others—
out at the end of the island, eleven herds
are scattered now, with good men looking after them,
and every herdsman, every day, picks out
a prize ram to hand over to those fellows.
I too as overseer, keeper of swine,
130 must go through all my boars and send the best."

While he ran on, Odysseus with zeal
applied himself to the meat and wine, but inwardly
his thought shaped woe and ruin for the suitors.
When he had eaten all that he desired
and the cup he drank from had been filled again
with wine—a welcome sight—,
he spoke, and the words came light upon the air:
"Who is this lord who once acquired you,
so rich, so powerful, as you describe him?
140 You think he died for Agamémnon's honor.
Tell me his name: I may have met someone
of that description in my time. Who knows?
Perhaps only the immortal gods could say
if I should claim to have seen him: I have roamed
about the world so long."

         The swineherd answered
as one who held a place of trust:
                "Well, man,
his lady and his son will put no stock
150 in any news of him brought by a rover.
Wandering men tell lies for a night's lodging,
for fresh clothing; truth doesn't interest them.
Every time some traveller comes ashore
he has to tell my mistress his pretty tale,
and she receives him kindly, questions him,
remembering her prince, while the tears run

down her cheeks — and that is as it should be
when a woman's husband has been lost abroad.
I suppose you, too, can work your story up
160 at a moment's notice, given a shirt or cloak.
No: long ago wild dogs and carrion
birds, most like, laid bare his ribs on land
where life had left him. Or it may be, quick fishes
picked him clean in the deep sea, and his bones
lie mounded over in sand upon some shore.
One way or another, far from home he died,
a bitter loss, and pain, for everyone,
certainly for me. Never again shall I
have for my lot a master mild as he was
170 anywhere — not even with my parents
at home, where I was born and bred. I miss them
less than I do him — though a longing comes
to set my eyes on them in the old country.
No, it is the lost man I ache to think of —
Odysseus. And I speak the name respectfully,
even if he is not here. He loved me, cared for me.
I call him dear my lord, far though he be."

Now royal Odysseus, who had borne the long war,
spoke again:
180   "Friend, as you are so dead sure
he will not come — and so mistrustful, too —
let me not merely talk, as others talk,
but swear to it: your lord is now at hand.
And I expect a gift for this good news
when he enters his own hall. Till then I would not
take a rag, no matter what my need.
I hate as I hate Hell's own gate that weakness
that makes a poor man into a flatterer.
Zeus be my witness, and the table garnished
190 for true friends, and Odysseus' own hearth —
by heaven, all I say will come to pass!
He will return, and he will be avenged
on any who dishonor his wife and son."

Eumaios — O my swineherd! — answered him:
"I take you at your word, then: you shall have
no good news gift from me. Nor will Odysseus
enter his hall. But peace! drink up your wine.
Let us talk now of other things. No more
imaginings. It makes me heavy-hearted

200 when someone brings my master back to mind—
my own true master.
                    No, by heaven,
let us have no oaths! But if Odysseus
can come again god send he may! My wish
is that of Penélopê and old Laërtês
and Prince Telémakhos.
                    Ah, he's another
to be distressed about—Odysseus' child,
Telémakhos! By the gods' grace he grew
210 like a tough sapling, and I thought he'd be
no less a man than his great father—strong
and admirably made; but then someone,
god or man, upset him, made him rash,
so that he sailed away to sandy Pylos
to hear news of his father. Now the suitors
lie in ambush on his homeward track,
ready to cut away the last shoot of Arkêsios'
line, the royal stock of Ithaka.
                    No good
220 dwelling on it. Either he'll be caught
or else Kroníon's[123] hand will take him through.

Tell me, now, of your own trials and troubles.
And tell me truly first, for I should know,
who are you, where do you hail from, where's your home
and family? What kind of ship was yours,
and what course brought you here? Who are your sailors?
I don't suppose you walked here on the sea."

To this the master of improvisation answered:
"I'll tell you all that, clearly as I may.
230 If we could sit here long enough, with meat
and good sweet wine, warm here, in peace and quiet
within doors, while the work of the world goes on—
I might take all this year to tell my story
and never end the tale of misadventures
that wore my heart out, by the gods' will.

My native land is the wide seaboard of Krete
where I grew up. I had a wealthy father,
and many other sons were born to him

---

[123] **Kroníon:** Zeus, son of Kronos.

of his true lady. My mother was a slave,
240 his concubine; but Kastor Hylákidês,
my father, treated me as a true born son.
High honor came to him in that part of Krete
for wealth and ease, and sons born for renown,
before the death-bearing Kêrês drew him down
to the underworld. His avid sons thereafter
dividing up the property by lot
gave me a wretched portion, a poor house.
But my ability won me a wife
of rich family. Fool I was never called,
250 nor turn-tail in a fight.

                My strength's all gone,
but from the husk you may divine the ear
that stood tall in the old days. Misery owns me
now, but then great Arês and Athena
gave me valor and man-breaking power,
whenever I made choice of men-at-arms
to set a trap with me for my enemies.
Never, as I am a man, did I fear Death
ahead, but went in foremost in the charge,
260 putting a spear through any man whose legs
were not as fast as mine. That was my element,
war and battle. Farming I never cared for,
nor life at home, nor fathering fair children.
I reveled in long ships with oars; I loved
polished lances, arrows in the skirmish,
the shapes of doom that others shake to see.
Carnage suited me; heaven put those things
in me somehow. Each to his own pleasure!
Before we young Akhaians shipped for Troy
270 I led men on nine cruises in corsairs
to raid strange coasts, and had great luck, taking
rich spoils on the spot, and even more
in the division. So my house grew prosperous,
my standing therefore high among the Kretans.
Then came the day when Zeus who views the wide world
drew men's eyes upon that way accurst
that wrung the manhood from the knees of many!
Everyone pressed me, pressed King Idómeneus
to take command of ships for Ilion.
280 No way out; the country rang with talk of it.
So we Akhaians had nine years of war.
In the tenth year we sacked the inner city,
Priam's town, and sailed for home; but heaven

dispersed the Akhaians. Evil days for me
were stored up in the hidden mind of Zeus.
One month, no more, I stayed at home in joy
with children, wife, and treasure. Lust for action
drove me to go to sea then, in command
of ships and gallant seamen bound for Egypt.
290   Nine ships I fitted out; my men signed on
and came to feast with me, as good shipmates,
for six full days. Many a beast I slaughtered
in the gods' honor, for my friends to eat.
Embarking on the seventh, we hauled sail
and filled away from Krete on a fresh north wind
effortlessly, as boats will glide down stream.
All rigging whole and all hands well, we rested,
letting the wind and steersmen work the ships,
for five days; on the fifth we made the delta.[124]
300   I brought my squadron in to the river bank
with one turn of the sweeps. There, heaven knows,
I told the men to wait and guard the ships
while I sent out patrols to rising ground.
But reckless greed carried them all away
to plunder the rich bottomlands; they bore off
wives and children, killed what men they found.

When this news reached the city, all who heard it
came at dawn. On foot they came, and horsemen,
filling the river plain with dazzle of bronze;
310   and Zeus lord of lightning
threw my men into blind panic: no one dared
stand against that host closing around us.
Their scything weapons left our dead in piles,
but some they took alive, into forced labor.
And I — ah, how I wish that I had died
in Egypt, on that field! So many blows
awaited me! — Well, Zeus himself inspired me;
I wrenched my dogskin helmet off my head,
dropped my spear, dodged out of my long shield,
320   ran for the king's chariot and swung on
to embrace and kiss his knees. He pulled me up,
took pity on me, placed me on the footboards,
and drove home with me crouching there in tears.

---

[124] **the delta:** Of the Nile River.

Aye—for the troops, in battle fury still,
made one pass at me after another, pricking me
with spears, hoping to kill me. But he saved me,
for fear of the great wrath of Zeus that comes
when men who ask asylum are given death.

Seven years, then, my sojourn lasted there,
330 and I amassed a fortune, going about
among the openhanded Egyptians.
But when the eighth came round, a certain
Phoinikian adventurer came too,
a plausible rat, who had already done
plenty of devilry in the world.

                        This fellow
took me in completely with his schemes,
and led me with him to Phoinikia,
where he had land and houses. One full year
340 I stayed there with him, to the month and day,
and when fair weather came around again
he took me in a deepsea ship for Libya,
pretending I could help in the cargo trade;
he meant, in fact, to trade me off, and get
a high price for me. I could guess the game
but had to follow him aboard. One day
on course due west, off central Krete, the ship
caught a fresh norther, and we ran southward
before the wind while Zeus piled ruin ahead.
350 When Krete was out of sight astern, no land
anywhere to be seen, but sky and ocean,
Kroníon put a dark cloud in the zenith
over the ship, and gloom spread on the sea.
With crack on crack of thunder, he let fly
a bolt against the ship, a direct hit,
so that she bucked, in sacred fumes of sulphur,
and all the men were flung into the water.
They came up round the wreck, bobbing a while
like petrels on the waves. No homecoming
360 for these, from whom the god had turned his face!
Stunned in the smother as I was, yet Zeus
put into my hands the great mast of the ship—
a way to keep from drowning. So I twined
my arms and legs around it in the gale
and stayed afloat nine days. On the tenth night,

a big surf cast me up in Thesprotia.[125]
Pheidon the king there gave me refuge, nobly,
with no talk of reward. His son discovered me
exhausted and half dead with cold, and gave me
370   a hand to bear me up till he reached home
where he could clothe me in a shirt and cloak.
In that king's house I heard news of Odysseus,
who lately was a guest there, passing by
on his way home, the king said; and he showed me
the treasure that Odysseus had brought:
bronze, gold, and iron wrought with heavy labor—
in that great room I saw enough to last
Odysseus' heirs for ten long generations.
The man himself had gone up to Dodona[126]
380   to ask the spelling leaves of the old oak
the will of God: how to return, that is,
to the rich realm of Ithaka, after so long
an absence—openly, or on the quiet.
And, tipping wine out, Pheidon swore to me
the ship was launched, the seamen standing by
to take Odysseus to his land at last.
But he had passage first for me: Thesprotians
were sailing, as luck had it, for Doulíkhion,[127]
the grain-growing island; there, he said,
390   they were to bring me to the king, Akastos.
Instead, that company saw fit to plot
foul play against me; in my wretched life
there was to be more suffering.

                         At sea, then,
when land lay far astern, they sprang their trap.
They'd make a slave of me that day, stripping
cloak and tunic off me, throwing around me
the dirty rags you see before you now.
At evening, off the fields of Ithaka,
400   they bound me, lashed me down under the decking
with stout ship's rope, while they all went ashore
in haste to make their supper on the beach.
The gods helped me to pry the lashing loose
until it fell away. I wound my rags
in a bundle round my head and eased myself

---

[125] **Thesprotia:** The west coast of the Greek mainland.   [126] **Dodona:** Site of the most famous oracle of Zeus; the rustlings of oak leaves were interpreted as messages from the god.   [127] **Doulíkhion:** An island off the west coast of Greece.

down the smooth lading plank into the water,
up to the chin, then swam an easy breast stroke
out and around, putting that crew behind,
and went ashore in underbrush, a thicket,
410 where I lay still, making myself small.
They raised a bitter yelling, and passed by
several times. When further groping seemed
useless to them, back to the ship they went
and out to sea again. The gods were with me,
keeping me hid; and with me when they brought me
here to the door of one who knows the world.
My destiny is yet to live awhile."

The swineherd bowed and said:
                                        "Ah well, poor drifter,
420 you've made me sad for you, going back over it,
all your hard life and wandering. That tale
about Odysseus, though, you might have spared me;
you will not make me believe that.
Why must you lie, being the man you are,
and all for nothing?
                            I can see so well
what happened to my master, sailing home!
Surely the gods turned on him, to refuse him
death in the field, or in his friends' arms
430 after he wound up the great war at Troy.
They would have made a tomb for him, the Akhaians,
and paid all honor to his son thereafter. No,
stormwinds made off with him. No glory came to him.

I moved here to the mountain with my swine.
Never, now, do I go down to town
unless I am sent for by Penélopê
when news of some sort comes. But those who sit
around her go on asking the old questions—
a few who miss their master still,
440 and those who eat his house up, and go free.
For my part, I have had no heart for inquiry
since one year an Aitolian[128] made a fool of me.
Exiled from land to land after some killing,
he turned up at my door; I took him in.

---

[128] **Aitolian:** Aitolia is a section of central Greece.

My master he had seen in Krete, he said,
lodged with Idómeneus, while the long ships,
leaky from gales, were laid up for repairs.
But they were all to sail, he said, that summer,
or the first days of fall — hulls laden deep
450   with treasure, manned by crews of heroes.
                                        This time
you are the derelict the Powers bring.
Well, give up trying to win me with false news
or flattery. If I receive and shelter you,
it is not for your tales but for your trouble,
and with an eye to Zeus, who guards a guest."

Then said that sly and guileful man, Odysseus:
"A black suspicious heart beats in you surely;
the man you are, not even an oath could change you.
460   Come then, we'll make a compact; let the gods
witness it from Olympos, where they dwell.
Upon your lord's homecoming, if he comes
here to this very hut, and soon —
then give me a new outfit, shirt and cloak,
and ship me to Doulíkhion — I thought it
a pleasant island. But if Odysseus
fails to appear as I predict, then Swish!
let the slaves pitch me down from some high rock,
so the next poor man who comes will watch his tongue."

470   The forester gave a snort and answered:
                                        "Friend,
if I agreed to that, a great name
I should acquire in the world for goodness —
at one stroke and forever: your kind host
who gave you shelter and the hand of friendship,
only to take your life next day!
How confidently, after that, should I
address my prayers to Zeus, the son of Kronos!

It is time now for supper. My young herdsmen
480   should be arriving soon to set about it.
We'll make a quiet feast here at our hearth."

At this point in their talk the swine had come
up to the clearing, and the drovers followed
to pen them for the night — the porkers squealing

to high heaven, milling around the yard.
The swineherd then gave orders to his men:
"Bring in our best pig for a stranger's dinner.
A feast will do our hearts good, too; we know
grief and pain, hard scrabbling with our swine,
490 while the outsiders live on our labor."

                              Bronze
axe in hand, he turned to split up kindling,
while they drove in a tall boar, prime and fat,
planting him square before the fire. The gods,
as ever, had their due in the swineherd's thought,
for he it was who tossed the forehead bristles
as a first offering on the flames, calling
upon the immortal gods to let Odysseus
reach his home once more.
500   Then he stood up
and brained the boar with split oak from the woodpile.
Life ebbed from the beast; they slaughtered him,
singed the carcass, and cut out the joints.
Eumaios, taking flesh from every quarter,
put lean strips on the fat of sacrifice,
floured each one with barley meal, and cast it
into the blaze. The rest they sliced and skewered,
roasted with care, then took it off the fire
and heaped it up on platters. Now their chief,
510 who knew best the amenities, rose to serve,
dividing all that meat in seven portions—
one to be set aside, with proper prayers,
for the wood nymphs and Hermês, Maia's[129] son;
the others for the company. Odysseus
he honored with long slices from the chine—
warming the master's heart. Odysseus looked at him
and said:
            "May you be dear to Zeus
as you are dear to me for this, Eumaios,
520 favoring with choice cuts a man like me."

And—O my swineherd!—you replied, Eumaios:
"Bless you, stranger, fall to and enjoy it
for what it is. Zeus grants us this or that,

---

[129] **Maia:** The goddess of spring is the oldest and loveliest of the Pleiades, the seven daughters of Atlas and Pleione.

or else refrains from granting, as he wills;
all things are in his power."

He cut and burnt

a morsel for the gods who are young forever,
tipped out some wine, then put it in the hands
of Odysseus, the old soldier, raider of cities,
530   who sat at ease now with his meat before him.
As for the loaves, Mesaúlios dealt them out,
a yard boy, bought by the swineherd on his own,
unaided by his mistress or Laërtês,
from Taphians, while Odysseus was away.
Now all hands reached for that array of supper,
until, when hunger and thirst were turned away
Mesaúlios removed the bread and, heavy
with food and drink, they settled back to rest.

Now night had come on, rough, with no moon,
540   but a nightlong downpour setting in, the rainwind
blowing hard from the west. Odysseus
began to talk, to test the swineherd, trying
to put it in his head to take his cloak off
and lend it, or else urge the others to.
He knew the man's compassion.

"Listen," he said,

"Eumaios, and you others, here's a wishful
tale that I shall tell. The wine's behind it,
vaporing wine, that makes a serious man
550   break down and sing, kick up his heels and clown,
or tell some story that were best untold.
But now I'm launched, I can't stop now.

Would god I felt

the hot blood in me that I had at Troy!
Laying an ambush near the walls one time,
Odysseus and Meneláos were commanders
and I ranked third. I went at their request.
We worked in toward the bluffs and battlements
and, circling the town, got into canebrakes,
560   thick and high, a marsh where we took cover,
hunched under arms.

The northwind dropped, and night

came black and wintry. A fine sleet descending
whitened the cane like hoarfrost, and clear ice
grew dense upon our shields. The other men,

all wrapt in blanket cloaks as well as tunics,
rested well, in shields up to their shoulders,
but I had left my cloak with friends in camp,
foolhardy as I was. No chance of freezing hard,
570 I thought, so I wore kilts and a shield only.
But in the small hours of the third watch, when stars
that rise at evening go down to their setting,
I nudged Odysseus, who lay close beside me;
he was alert then, listening, and I said:
'Son of Laërtês and the gods of old,
Odysseus, master mariner and soldier,
I cannot hold on long among the living.
The cold is making a corpse of me. Some god
inveigled me to come without a cloak.
580 No help for it now; too late.'

     Next thing I knew
he had a scheme all ready in his mind—
and what a man he was for schemes and battles!
Speaking under his breath to me, he murmured:
'Quiet; none of the rest should hear you.'

         Then,
propping his head on his forearm, he said:
'Listen, lads, I had an ominous dream,
the point being how far forward from our ships
590 and lines we've come. Someone should volunteer
to tell the corps commander, Agamémnon;
he may reinforce us from the base.'

     At this,
Thoas jumped up, the young son of Andraimon,
put down his crimson cloak and headed off,
running shoreward.
      Wrapped in that man's cloak
how gratefully I lay in the bitter dark
until the dawn came stitched in gold! I wish
600 I had that sap and fiber in me now!"

Then—O my swineherd!—you replied, Eumaios:
"That was a fine story, and well told,
not a word out of place, not a pointless word.
No, you'll not sleep cold for lack of cover,
or any other comfort one should give

to a needy guest. However, in the morning,
you must go flapping in the same old clothes.
Shirts and cloaks are few here; every man
has one change only. When our prince arrives,
610   the son of Odysseus, he will make you gifts—
cloak, tunic, everything—and grant you passage
wherever you care to go."

On this he rose
and placed the bed of balsam near the fire,
strewing sheepskins on top, and skins of goats.
Odysseus lay down. His host threw over him
a heavy blanket cloak, his own reserve
against the winter wind when it came wild.
So there Odysseus dropped off to sleep,
620   while herdsmen slept nearby. But not the swineherd:
not in the hut could he lie down in peace,
but now equipped himself for the night outside;
and this rejoiced Odysseus' heart, to see him
care for the herd so, while his lord was gone.
He hung a sharp sword from his shoulder, gathered
a great cloak round him, close, to break the wind,
and pulled a shaggy goatskin on his head.
Then, to keep at a distance dogs or men,
he took a sharpened lance, and went to rest
630   under a hollow rock where swine were sleeping
out of the wind and rain.

BOOK 15
HOW THEY CAME TO ITHAKA

South into Lakedaimon
into the land where greens are wide for dancing
Athena went, to put in mind of home
her great-hearted hero's honored son,
rousing him to return.

And there she found him
with Nestor's lad in the late night at rest
under the portico of Meneláos,
the famous king. Stilled by the power of slumber
10   the son of Testor lay, but honeyed sleep
had not yet taken in her arms Telémakhos.
All through the starlit night, with open eyes,
he pondered what he had heard about his father,

until at his bedside grey-eyed Athena
towered and said:
                    "The brave thing now, Telémakhos,
would be to end this journey far from home.
All that you own you left behind
with men so lost to honor in your house
20 they may devour it all, shared out among them.
How will your journey save you then?
                                        Go quickly
to the lord of the great war cry, Meneláos;
press him to send you back. You may yet find
the queen your mother in her rooms alone.
It seems her father and her kinsmen say
Eurýmakhos is the man for her to marry.
He has outdone the suitors, all the rest,
in gifts to her, and made his pledges double.
30 Check him, or he will have your lands and chattels
in spite of you.
                    You know a woman's pride
at bringing riches to the man she marries.
As to her girlhood husband, her first children,
he is forgotten, being dead — and they
no longer worry her.
                        So act alone.
Go back; entrust your riches to the servant
worthiest in your eyes, until the gods
40 make known what beauty you yourself shall marry.

This too I have to tell you: now take heed:
the suitors' ringleaders are hot for murder,
waiting in the channel between Ithaka
and Samê's rocky side; they mean to kill you
before you can set foot ashore. I doubt
they'll bring it off. Dark earth instead
may take to her cold bed a few brave suitors
who preyed upon your cattle.
                                Bear well out
50 in your good ship, to eastward of the islands,
and sail again by night. Someone immortal
who cares for you will make a fair wind blow.
Touch at the first beach, go ashore, and send
your ship and crew around to port by sea,
while you go inland to the forester,
your old friend, loyal keeper of the swine.
Remain that night with him; send him to town

to tell your watchful mother Penélopê
that you are back from Pylos safe and sound."

60 With this Athena left him for Olympos.
He swung his foot across and gave a kick
and said to the son of Nestor:
                              "Open your eyes,
Peisístratos. Get our team into harness.
We have a long day's journey."

                              Nestor's son
turned over and answered him:
                              "It is still night,
and no moon. Can we drive now? We can not,
70 itch as we may for the road home. Dawn is near.
Allow the captain of spearmen, Meneláos,
time to pack our car with gifts and time
to speak a gracious word, sending us off.
A guest remembers all his days
that host who makes provision for him kindly."

The Dawn soon took her throne of gold, and Lord
Meneláos, clarion in battle,
rose from where he lay beside the beauty
of Helen with her shining hair. He strode
80 into the hall nearby.
                              Hearing him come,
Odysseus' son pulled on his snowy tunic
over the skin, gathered his long cape
about his breadth of shoulder like a captain,
the heir of King Odysseus. At the door
he stood and said:
                              "Lord Marshal, Meneláos,
send me home now to my own dear country:
longing has come upon me to go home."

90 The lord of the great war cry said at once:
"If you are longing to go home, Telémakhos,
I would not keep you for the world, not I.
I'd think myself or any other host
as ill-mannered for over-friendliness
as for hostility.
                              Measure is best in everything.
To send a guest packing, or cling to him
when he's in haste—one sin equals the other.

'Good entertaining ends with no detaining.'
100 Only let me load your car with gifts
and fine ones, you shall see.
                                        I'll bid the women
set out breakfast from the larder stores;
honor and appetite—we'll attend to both
before a long day's journey overland.
Or would you care to try the Argive midlands
and Hellas, in my company? I'll harness
my own team, and take you through the towns.
Guests like ourselves no lord will turn away;
110 each one will make one gift, at least,
to carry home with us: tripod or cauldron
wrought in bronze, mule team, or golden cup."

Clearheaded Telémakhos replied:
                                        "Lord Marshal
Meneláos, royal son of Atreus,
I must return to my own hearth. I left
no one behind as guardian of my property.
This going abroad for news of a great father—
heaven forbid it be my own undoing,
120 or any precious thing be lost at home."

At this the tall king, clarion in battle,
called to his lady and her waiting women
to give them breakfast from the larder stores.
Eteóneus, the son of Boethoös, came
straight from bed, from where he lodged nearby,
and Meneláos ordered a fire lit
for broiling mutton. The king's man obeyed.
Then down to the cedar chamber Meneláos
walked with Helen and Prince Megapénthês.
130 Amid the gold he had in that place lying
the son of Atreus picked a wine cup, wrought
with handles left and right, and told his son
to take a silver winebowl.
                                        Helen lingered
near the deep coffers filled with gowns, her own
handiwork.
                                        Tall goddess among women,
she lifted out one robe of state so royal,
adorned and brilliant with embroidery,
140 deep in the chest it shimmered like a star.
Now all three turned back to the door to greet

Telémakhos. And red-haired Meneláos
cried out to him:
                "O prince Telémakhos,
may Hêra's Lord of Thunder see you home
and bring you to the welcome you desire!
Here are your gifts—perfect and precious things
I wish to make your own, out of my treasure."

And gently the great captain, son of Atreus,
150 handed him the goblet. Megapénthês
carried the winebowl glinting silvery
to set before him, and the Lady Helen
drew near, so that he saw her cheek's pure line.
She held the gown and murmured:
"I, too,
bring you a gift, dear child, and here it is;
remember Helen's hands by this; keep it
for your own bride, your joyful wedding day;
let your dear mother guard it in her chamber.
160 My blessing: may you come soon to your island,
home to your timbered hall."

                      So she bestowed it,
and happily he took it. These fine things
Peisístratos packed well in the wicker carrier,
admiring every one. Then Meneláos
led the two guests in to take their seats
on thrones and easy chairs in the great hall.
Now came a maid to tip a golden jug
of water over a silver finger bowl,
170 and draw the polished tables up beside them;
the larder mistress brought her tray of loaves,
with many savories to lavish on them;
viands were served by Eteóneus, and wine
by Meneláos' son. Then every hand
reached out upon good meat and drink to take them,
driving away hunger and thirst. At last,
Telémakhos and Nestor's son led out
their team to harness, mounted their bright car,
and drove down under the echoing entrance way,
180 while red-haired Meneláos, Atreus' son,
walked alongside with a golden cup—
wine for the wayfarers to spill at parting.
Then by the tugging team he stood, and spoke

over the horses' heads:
                              "Farewell, my lads.
Homage to Nestor, the benevolent king;
in my time he was fatherly to me,
when the flower of Akhaia warred on Troy."

Telémakhos made this reply:
190 "No fear
but we shall bear at least as far as Nestor
your messages, great king. How I could wish
to bring them home to Ithaka! If only
Odysseus were there, if he could hear me tell
of all the courtesy I have had from you,
returning with your finery and your treasure."

Even as he spoke, a beat of wings went skyward
off to the right — a mountain eagle, grappling
a white goose in his talons, heavy prey
200 hooked from a farmyard. Women and men-at-arms
made hubbub, running up, as he flew over,
but then he wheeled hard right before the horses —
a sight that made the whole crowd cheer, with hearts
lifting in joy. Peisístratos called out:
"Read us the sign, O Meneláos, Lord
Marshal of armies! Was the god revealing
something thus to you, or to ourselves?"

At this the old friend of the god of battle
groped in his mind for the right thing to say,
210 but regal Helen put in quickly:
"Listen:
I can tell you — tell what the omen means,
as light is given me, and as I see it
point by point fulfilled. The beaked eagle
flew from the wild mountain of his fathers
to take for prey the tame house bird. Just so,
Odysseus, back from his hard trials and wandering,
will soon come down in fury on his house.
He may be there today, and a black hour
220 he brings upon the suitors."

                    Telémakhos
gazed and said:
                    "May Zeus, the lord of Hêra,

make it so! In far-off Ithaka, all my life,
I shall invoke you as a goddess, lady."

He let the whip fall, and the restive mares
broke forward at a canter through the town
into the open country.
                          All that day
230 they kept their harness shaking, side by side,
until at sundown when the roads grew dim
they made a halt at Pherai. There Dióklês
son of Ortílokhos whom Alpheios fathered,
welcomed the young men, and they slept the night.
Up when the young Dawn's finger tips of rose
opened in the east, they hitched the team
once more to the painted car
and steered out westward through the echoing gate,
whipping their fresh horses into a run.
240 Approaching Pylos Height at that day's end,
Telémakhos appealed to the son of Nestor:
"Could you, I wonder, do a thing I'll tell you,
supposing you agree?
We take ourselves to be true friends—in age
alike, and bound by ties between our fathers,
and now by partnership in this adventure.
Prince, do not take me roundabout,
but leave me at the ship, else the old king
your father will detain me overnight
250 for love of guests, when I should be at sea."

The son of Nestor nodded, thinking swiftly
how best he could oblige his friend.
Here was his choice: to pull the team hard over
along the beach till he could rein them in
beside the ship. Unloading Meneláos'
royal keepsakes into the stern sheets,
he sang out:
                "Now for action! Get aboard,
and call your men, before I break the news
260 at home in hall to father. Who knows better
the old man's heart than I? If you delay,
he will not let you go, but he'll descend on you
in person and imperious; no turning

back with empty hands for him, believe me,
once his blood is up."

                    He shook the reins
to the lovely mares with long manes in the wind,
guiding them full tilt toward his father's hall.
Telémakhos called in the crew, and told them:
270 "Get everything shipshape aboard this craft;
we pull out now, and put sea miles behind us."

The listening men obeyed him, climbing in
to settle on their benches by the rowlocks,
while he stood watchful by the stern. He poured out
offerings there, and prayers to Athena.

Now a strange man came up to him, an easterner
fresh from spilling blood in distant Argos,
a hunted man. Gifted in prophecy,[130]
he had as forebear that Melampous, wizard
280 who lived of old in Pylos, mother city
of western flocks.
                    Melampous, a rich lord,
had owned a house unmatched among the Pylians,
until the day came when king Neleus, noblest
in that age, drove him from his native land.
And Neleus for a year's term sequestered
Melampous' fields and flocks, while he lay bound
hand and foot in the keep of Phylakos.
Beauty of Neleus' daughter put him there
290 and sombre folly the inbreaking Fury
thrust upon him. But he gave the slip
to death, and drove the bellowing herd of Iphiklos
from Phylakê to Pylos, there to claim
the bride that ordeal won him from the king.
He led her to his brother's house, and went on

---

[130] **a strange man . . . prophecy:** Melampous was a famous soothsayer; the purpose of the following complicated passage is to provide a genealogical connection between Melampous and Theoklýmenos, the young man
who approaches Telémakhos. Melampous was imprisoned when he tried to steal Phylakos's cattle so that his
brother could pay the bride-price for King Neleus's daughter. When Melampous prophesied the collapse of a
roof, Phylakos released him and gave him the cattle. The bride-price was paid, the brother received the bride,
and Melampous moved to Argos.

eastward into another land, the bluegrass
plain of Argos. Destiny held for him
rule over many Argives. Here he married,
built a great manor house, fathered Antíphatês
300   and Mantios, commanders both, of whom
Antíphatês begot Oikleiês
and Oikleiês the firebrand Amphiaraos.
This champion the lord of stormcloud, Zeus,
and strong Apollo loved; nor had he ever
to cross the doorsill into dim old age.
A woman, bought by trinkets, gave him over
to be cut down in the assault on Thebes.
His sons were Alkmáon and Amphílokhos.
In the meantime Lord Mantios begot
310   Polypheidês, the prophet, and
Kleitos — famous name! For Dawn in silks
of gold carried off Kleitos for his beauty
to live among the gods. But Polypheidês,
high-hearted and exalted by Apollo
above all men for prophecy, withdrew
to Hyperesia[131] when his father angered him.
He lived on there, foretelling to the world
the shape of things to come.

                       His son it was,
320   Theoklýmenos, who came upon Telémakhos
as he poured out the red wine in the sand
near his trim ship, with prayer to Athena:
and he called out, approaching:

                      "Friend, well met
here at libation before going to sea.
I pray you by the wine you spend, and by
your god, your own life, and your company;
enlighten me, and let the truth be known.
Who are you? Of what city and what parents?"

330   Telémakhos turned to him and replied:
"Stranger, as truly as may be, I'll tell you.
I am from Ithaka, where I was born;
my father is, or he once was, Odysseus.
But he's a long time gone, and dead, may be;

---

[131] **Hyperesia:** In the vicinity of Argos.

and that is what I took ship with my friends
to find out—for he left long years ago."

Said Theoklýmenos in reply:
"I too
have had to leave my home. I killed a cousin.
340   In the wide grazing lands of Argos live
many kinsmen of his and friends in power,
great among the Akhaians. These I fled.
Death and vengeance at my back, as Fate
has turned now, I came wandering overland.
Give me a plank aboard your ship, I beg,
or they will kill me. They are on my track."

Telémakhos made answer:
                              "No two ways
about it. Will I pry you from our gunnel
350   when you are desperate to get to sea?
Come aboard; share what we have, and welcome."

He took the bronze-shod lance from the man's hand
and laid it down full-length on deck; then swung
his own weight after it aboard the cutter,
taking position aft, making a place
for Theoklýmenos near him. The stern lines
were slacked off, and Telémakhos commanded:
"Rig the mast; make sail!" Nimbly they ran
to push the fir pole high and step it firm
360   amidships in the box, make fast the forestays,
and hoist aloft the white sail on its halyards.
A following wind came down from grey-eyed Athena,
blowing brisk through heaven, and so steady
the cutter lapped up miles of salt blue sea,
passing Krounoi abeam and Khalkis estuary
at sundown when the sea ways all grew dark.
Then, by Athena's wind borne on, the ship
rounded Pheai by night and coasted Elis,[132]
the green domain of the Epeioi; thence
370   he put her head north toward the running pack

---

[132] **passing Krounoi . . . Elis:** The exact location of Krounoi and Khalkis is not known; Elis is the site of the Olympics on the west coast of the Peloponnese.

of islets, wondering if by sailing wide
he sheered off Death, or would be caught.

                                                That night
Odysseus and the swineherd supped again
with herdsmen in their mountain hut. At ease
when appetite and thirst were turned away,
Odysseus, while he talked, observed the swineherd
to see if he were hospitable still—
if yet again the man would make him stay
380   under his roof, or send him off to town.

"Listen," he said, "Eumaios; listen, lads.
At daybreak I must go and try my luck
around the port. I burden you too long.
Direct me, put me on the road with someone.
Nothing else for it but to play the beggar
in populous parts. I'll get a cup or loaf,
maybe from some householder. If I go
as far as the great hall of King Odysseus
I might tell Queen Penélopê my news.
390   Or I can drift inside among the suitors
to see what alms they give, rich as they are.
If they have whims, I'm deft in ways of service—
that I can say, and you may know for sure.
By grace of Hermês the Wayfinder, patron
of mortal tasks, the god who honors toil,
no man can do a chore better than I can.
Set me to build a fire, or chop wood,
cook or carve, mix wine and serve—or anything
inferior men attend to for the gentry."

400   Now you were furious at this, Eumaios,
and answered—O my swineherd!—
                                        "Friend, friend,
how could this fantasy take hold of you?
You dally with your life, and nothing less,
if you feel drawn to mingle in that company—
reckless, violent, and famous for it
out to the rim of heaven. Slaves
they have, but not like you. No—theirs are boys
in fresh cloaks and tunics with pomade
410   ever on their sleek heads, and pretty faces.
These are their minions, while their tables gleam
and groan under big roasts, with loaves and wine.

Stay with us here. No one is burdened by you,
neither myself nor any of my hands.
Wait here until Odysseus' son returns.
You shall have clothing from him, cloak and tunic,
and passage where your heart desires to go."

The noble and enduring man replied:
"May you be dear to Zeus for this, Eumaios,
420 even as you are to me. Respite from pain
you give me—and from homelessness. In life
there's nothing worse than knocking about the world,
no bitterness we vagabonds are spared
when the curst belly rages! Well, you master it
and me, making me wait for the king's son.
But now, come, tell me:
what of Odysseus' mother, and his father
whom he took leave of on the sill of age?
Are they under the sun's rays, living still,
430 or gone down long ago to lodge with Death?"

To this the rugged herdsman answered:
"Aye,
that I can tell you; it is briefly told.
Laërtês lives, but daily in his hall
prays for the end of life and soul's delivery,
heartbroken as he is for a son long gone
and for his lady. Sorrow, when she died,
aged and enfeebled him like a green tree stricken;
but pining for her son, her brilliant son,
440 wore out her life.
                    Would god no death so sad
might come to benefactors dear as she!
I loved always to ask and hear about her
while she lived, although she lived in sorrow.
For she had brought me up with her own daughter,
Princess Ktimenê, her youngest child.
We were alike in age and nursed as equals
nearly, till in the flower of our years
they gave her, married her, to a Samian prince,
450 taking his many gifts. For my own portion
her mother gave new clothing, cloak and sandals,
and sent me to the woodland. Well she loved me.
Ah, how I miss that family! It is true
the blissful gods prosper my work; I have
meat and drink to spare for those I prize;

but so removed I am, I have no speech
with my sweet mistress, now that evil days
and overbearing men darken her house.
Tenants all hanker for good talk and gossip
460   around their lady, and a snack in hall,
a cup or two before they take the road
to their home acres, each one bearing home
some gift to cheer his heart."

      The great tactician
answered:
    "You were still a child, I see,
when exiled somehow from your parents' land.
Tell me, had it been sacked in war, the city
of spacious ways in which they made their home,
470   your father and your gentle mother? Or
were you kidnapped alone, brought here by sea
huddled with sheep in some foul pirate squadron,
to this landowner's hall? He paid your ransom?"

The master of the woodland answered:
        "Friend,
now that you show an interest in that matter,
attend me quietly, be at your ease,
and drink your wine. These autumn nights are long,
ample for story-telling and for sleep.
480   You need not go to bed before the hour;
sleeping from dusk to dawn's a dull affair.
Let any other here who wishes, though,
retire to rest. At daybreak let him breakfast
and take the king's own swine into the wilderness.
Here's a tight roof; we'll drink on, you and I,
and ease our hearts of hardships we remember,
sharing old times. In later days a man
can find a charm in old adversity,
exile and pain. As to your question, now:

490   A certain island, Syriê by name—
you may have heard the name—lies off Ortýgia[133]
due west, and holds the sunsets of the year.
Not very populous, but good for grazing

---

[133] **Ortýgia:** The name of a small island on the east coast of Sicily, but Ortýgia might be the island of Delos.

sheep and kine; rich too in wine and grain.
No dearth is ever known there, no disease
wars on the folk, of ills that plague mankind;
but when the townsmen reach old age, Apollo
with his longbow of silver comes, and Artemis,
showering arrows of mild death.

500   Two towns
divide the farmlands of that whole domain,
and both were ruled by Ktêsios, my father,
Orménos' heir, and a great godlike man.

Now one day some of those renowned seafaring
men, sea-dogs, Phoinikians, came ashore
with bags of gauds for trading. Father had
in our household a woman of Phoinikia,
a handsome one, and highly skilled. Well, she
gave in to the seductions of those rovers.

510   One of them found her washing near the mooring
and lay with her, making such love to her
as women in their frailty are confused by,
even the best of them.

                              In due course, then,
he asked her who she was and where she hailed from:
and nodding toward my father's roof, she said:
'I am of Sidon town, smithy of bronze
for all the East. Arubas Pasha's daughter.
Taphian pirates caught me in a byway
520   and sold me into slavery overseas
in this man's home. He could afford my ransom.'

The sailor who had lain with her replied:
'Why not ship out with us on the run homeward,
and see your father's high-roofed hall again,
your father and your mother? Still in Sidon
and still rich, they are said to be.'

                              She answered:
'It could be done, that, if you sailors take
oath I'll be given passage home unharmed.'

530   Well, soon she had them swearing it all pat
as she desired, repeating every syllable,
whereupon she warned them:
                              'Not a word
about our meeting here! Never call out to me

when any of you see me in the lane
or at the well. Some visitor might bear
tales to the old man. If he guessed the truth,
I'd be chained up, your lives would be in peril.
No: keep it secret. Hurry with your peddling,
540 and when your hold is filled with livestock, send
a message to me at the manor hall.
Gold I'll bring, whatever comes to hand,
and something else, too, as my passage fee—
the master's child, my charge: a boy so high,
bright for his age; he runs with me on errands.
I'd take him with me happily; his price
would be I know not what in sale abroad.'

Her bargain made, she went back to the manor.
But they were on the island all that year,
550 getting by trade a cargo of our cattle;
until, the ship at length being laden full,
ready for sea, they sent a messenger
to the Phoinikian woman. Shrewd he was,
this fellow who came round my father's hall,
showing a golden chain all strung with amber,
a necklace. Maids in waiting and my mother
passed it from hand to hand, admiring it,
engaging they would buy it. But that dodger,
as soon as he had caught the woman's eye
560 and nodded, slipped away to join the ship.
She took my hand and led me through the court
into the portico. There by luck she found
winecups and tables still in place—for Father's
attendant counselors had dined just now
before they went to the assembly. Quickly
she hid three goblets in her bellying dress
to carry with her while I tagged along
in my bewilderment. The sun went down
and all the lanes grew dark as we descended,
570 skirting the harbor in our haste to where
those traders of Phoinikia held their ship.
All went aboard at once and put to sea,
taking the two of us. A favoring wind
blew from the power of heaven. We sailed on
six nights and days without event. Then Zeus
the son of Kronos added one more noon—and sudden
arrows from Artemis pierced the woman's heart.

Stone-dead she dropped
into the sloshing bilge the way a tern
580　plummets; and the sailors heaved her over
as tender pickings for the seals and fish.
Now I was left in dread, alone, while wind
and current bore them on to Ithaka.
Laërtês purchased me. That was the way
I first laid eyes upon this land."

　　　　　　　　　　Odysseus,
the kingly man, replied:
　　　　　　　　　　　"You rouse my pity,
telling what you endured when you were young.
590　But surely Zeus put good alongside ill:
torn from your own far home, you had the luck
to come into a kind man's service, generous
with food and drink. And a good life you lead,
unlike my own, all spent in barren roaming
from one country to the next, till now."

So the two men talked on, into the night,
leaving few hours for sleep before the Dawn
stepped up to her bright chair.
　　　　　　　　　　　The ship now drifting
600　under the island lee, Telémakhos'
companions took in sail and mast, unshipped
the oars and rowed ashore. They moored her stern
by the stout hawser lines, tossed out the bow stones,
and waded in beyond the wash of ripples
to mix their wine and cook their morning meal.
When they had turned back hunger and thirst, Telémakhos
arose to give the order of the day.

"Pull for the town," he said, "and berth our ship,
while I go inland across country. Later,
610　this evening, after looking at my farms,
I'll join you in the city. When day comes
I hope to celebrate our crossing, feasting
everyone on good red meat and wine."

His noble passenger, Theoklýmenos,
now asked:
　　　　　　　"What as to me, my dear young fellow,
where shall I go? Will I find lodging here

with some one of the lords of stony Ithaka?
Or go straight to your mother's hall and yours?"

620 Telémakhos turned round to him and said:
"I should myself invite you to our hall
if things were otherwise; there'd be no lack
of entertainment for you. As it stands,
no place could be more wretched for a guest
while I'm away. Mother will never see you;
she almost never shows herself at home
to the suitors there, but stays in her high chamber
weaving upon her loom. No, let me name
another man for you to go to visit:
630 Eurýmakhos, the honored son of Pólybos.
In Ithaka they are dazzled by him now—
the strongest of their princes, bent on making
mother and all Odysseus' wealth his own.
Zeus on Olympos only knows
if some dark hour for them will intervene."

The words were barely spoken, when a hawk,
Apollo's courier, flew up on the right,
clutching a dove and plucking her—so feathers
floated down to the ground between Telémakhos
640 and the moored cutter. Theoklýmenos
called him apart and gripped his hand, whispering:
"A god spoke in this bird-sign on the right.
I knew it when I saw the hawk fly over us.
There is no kinglier house than yours, Telémakhos,
here in the realm of Ithaka. Your family
will be in power forever."

                    The young prince,
clear in spirit, answered:
                    "Be it so,
650 friend, as you say. And may you know as well
the friendship of my house, and many gifts
from me, so everyone may call you fortunate."

He called a trusted crewman named Peiraios,
and said to him:
                    "Peiraios, son of Klýtios,
can I rely on you again as ever, most
of all the friends who sailed with me to Pylos?

Take this man home with you, take care of him,
treat him with honor, till I come."

660   To this
Peiraios the good spearman answered:
"Aye,
stay in the wild country while you will,
I shall be looking after him, Telémakhos.
He will not lack good lodging."

                         Down to the ship
he turned, and boarded her, and called the others
to cast off the stern lines and come aboard.
So men climbed in to sit beside the rowlocks.
670 Telémakhos now tied his sandals on
and lifted his tough spear from the ship's deck;
hawsers were taken in, and they shoved off
to reach the town by way of the open sea
as he commanded them—royal Odysseus'
own dear son, Telémakhos.
                         On foot
and swiftly he went up toward the stockade
where swine were penned in hundreds, and at night
the guardian of the swine, the forester,
680 slept under arms on duty for his masters.

BOOK 16
FATHER AND SON

But there were two men in the mountain hut—
Odysseus and the swineherd. At first light
blowing their fire up, they cooked their breakfast
and sent their lads out, driving herds to root
in the tall timber.
                         When Telémakhos came,
the wolvish troop of watchdogs only fawned on him
as he advanced. Odysseus heard them go
and heard the light crunch of a man's footfall—
10 at which he turned quickly to say:
                         "Eumaios,
here is one of your crew come back, or maybe
another friend: the dogs are out there snuffling

belly down; not one has even growled.
I can hear footsteps—"

> But before he finished
his tall son stood at the door.
> The swineherd
rose in surprise, letting a bowl and jug
20 tumble from his fingers. Going forward,
he kissed the young man's head, his shining eyes
and both hands, while his own tears brimmed and fell.
Think of a man whose dear and only son,
born to him in exile, reared with labor,
has lived ten years abroad and now returns:
how would that man embrace his son! Just so
the herdsman clapped his arms around Telémakhos
and covered him with kisses—for he knew
the lad had got away from death. He said:
30 "Light of my days, Telémakhos,
you made it back! When you took ship for Pylos
I never thought to see you here again.
Come in, dear child, and let me feast my eyes;
here you are, home from the distant places!
How rarely anyway, you visit us,
your own men, and your own woods and pastures!
Always in the town, a man would think
you loved the suitors' company, those dogs!"

Telémakhos with his clear candor said:
40 "I am with you, Uncle. See now, I have come
because I wanted to see you first, to hear from you
if Mother stayed at home—or is she married
off to someone and Odysseus' bed
left empty for some gloomy spider's weaving?"

Gently the forester replied to this:
"At home indeed your mother is, poor lady,
still in the women's hall. Her nights and days
are wearied out with grieving."

> Stepping back
50 he took the bronze-shod lance, and the young prince
entered the cabin over the worn door stone.
Odysseus moved aside, yielding his couch,
but from across the room Telémakhos checked him:

"Friend, sit down; we'll find another chair
in our own hut. Here is the man to make one!"

The swineherd, when the quiet man sank down,
built a new pile of evergreens and fleeces—
a couch for the dear son of great Odysseus—
then gave them trenchers of good meat, left over
60 from the roast pork of yesterday, and heaped up
willow baskets full of bread, and mixed
an ivy bowl of honey-hearted wine.
Then he in turn sat down, facing Odysseus,
their hands went out upon the meat and drink
as they fell to, ridding themselves of hunger,
until Telémakhos paused and said:
                 "Oh, Uncle,
what's your friend's home port? How did he come?
Who ere the sailors brought him here to Ithaka?
70 I doubt if he came walking on the sea."

And you replied, Eumaios—O my swineherd—
"Son, the truth about him is soon told.
His home land, and a broad land, too, is Krete,
but he has knocked about the world, he says,
for years, as the Powers wove his life. Just now
he broke away from a shipload of Thesprotians
to reach my hut. I place him in your hands.
Act as you will. He wishes your protection."

The young man said:
80   "Eumaios, my protection!
The notion cuts me to the heart. How can I
receive your friend at home? I am not old enough
or trained in arms. Could I defend myself
if someone picked a fight with me?
                      Besides,
mother is in a quandary, whether to stay with me
as mistress of our household, honoring
her lord's bed, and opinion in the town,
or take the best Akhaian who comes her way—
90 the one who offers most.
                  I'll undertake,
at all events, to clothe your friend for winter,
now he is with you. Tunic and cloak of wool,
a good broadsword, and sandals—these are his.

I can arrange to send him where he likes
or you may keep him in your cabin here.
I shall have bread and wine sent up; you need not
feel any pinch on his behalf.
                                        Impossible
100 to let him stay in hall, among the suitors.
They are drunk, drunk on impudence, they might
injure my guest — and how could I bear that?
How could a single man take on those odds?
Not even a hero could.
                                The suitors are too strong."

At this the noble and enduring man, Odysseus,
addressed his son:
                        "Kind prince, it may be fitting
for me to speak a word. All that you say
110 gives me an inward wound as I sit listening.
I mean this wanton game they play, these fellows,
riding roughshod over you in your own house,
admirable as you are. But tell me,
are you resigned to being bled? The townsmen,
stirred up against you, are they, by some oracle?
Your brothers — can you say your brothers fail you?
A man should feel his kin, at least, behind him
in any clash, when a real fight is coming.
If my heart were as young as yours, if I were
120 son to Odysseus, or the man himself,
I'd rather have my head cut from my shoulders
by some slashing adversary, if I
brought no hurt upon that crew! Suppose
I went down, being alone, before the lot,
better, I say, to die at home in battle
than see these insupportable things, day after
day the stranger cuffed, the women slaves
dragged here and there, shame in the lovely rooms,
the wine drunk up in rivers, sheer waste
130 of pointless feasting, never at an end!"

Telémakhos replied:
                        "Friend, I'll explain to you.
There is no rancor in the town against me,
no fault of brothers, whom a man should feel
behind him when a fight is in the making;

no, no — in our family the First Born
of Heaven, Zeus, made single sons the rule.
Arkeísios had but one, Laërtês; he
in his turn fathered only one, Odysseus,
140   who left me in his hall alone, too young
to be of any use to him.
And so you see why enemies fill our house
in these days: all the princes of the islands,
Doulíkhion, Samê, wooded Zakýnthos,
Ithaka too — lords of our island rock —
eating our house up as they court my mother.
She cannot put an end to it; she dare not
bar the marriage that she hates; and they
devour all my substance and my cattle,
150   and who knows when they'll slaughter me as well?
It rests upon the gods' great knees.
                                        Uncle,
go down at once and tell the Lady Penélopê
that I am back from Pylos, safe and sound.
I stay here meanwhile. You will give your message
and then return. Let none of the Akhaians
hear it; they have a mind to do me harm."

To this, Eumaios, you replied:
                                        "I know.
160   But make this clear, now — should I not likewise
call on Laërtês with your news? Hard hit
by sorrow though he was, mourning Odysseus,
he used to keep an eye upon his farm.
He had what meals he pleased, with his own folk.
But now no more, not since you sailed for Pylos;
he has not taken food or drink, I hear,
sitting all day, blind to the work of harvest,
groaning, while the skin shrinks on his bones."

Telémakhos answered:
170   "One more misery,
but we had better leave it so.
If men could choose, and have their choice, in everything,
we'd have my father home.
                                        Turn back
when you have done your errand, as you must,
not to be caught alone in the countryside.

But wait—you may tell Mother
to send our old housekeeper on the quiet
and quickly; she can tell the news to Grandfather."

180 The swineherd, roused, reached out to get his sandals,
tied them on, and took the road.

        Who else
beheld this but Athena? From the air
she walked, taking the form of a tall woman,
handsome and clever at her craft, and stood
beyond the gate in plain sight of Odysseus,
unseen, though, by Telémakhos, unguessed,
for not to everyone will gods appear.
Odysseus noticed her; so did the dogs,
190 who cowered whimpering away from her. She only
nodded, signing to him with her brows,
a sign he recognized. Crossing the yard,
he passed out through the gate in the stockade
to face the goddess. There she said to him:
"Son of Laërtês and the gods of old,
Odysseus, master of land ways and sea ways,
dissemble to your son no longer now.
The time has come: tell him how you together
will bring doom on the suitors in the town.
200 I shall not be far distant then, for I
myself desire battle."

      Saying no more,
she tipped her golden wand upon the man,
making his cloak pure white and the knit tunic
fresh around him. Lithe and young she made him,
ruddy with sun, his jawline clean, the beard
no longer grew upon his chin. And she
withdrew when she had done.
        Then Lord Odysseus
210 reappeared—and his son was thunderstruck.
Fear in his eyes, he looked down and away
as though it were a god, and whispered:
          "Stranger,
you are no longer what you were just now!
Your cloak is new; even your skin! You are
one of the gods who rule the sweep of heaven!

Be kind to us, we'll make you fair oblation
and gifts of hammered gold. Have mercy on us!"

The noble and enduring man replied:
220 "No god. Why take me for a god? No, no.
I am that father whom your boyhood lacked
and suffered pain for lack of. I am he."

Held back too long, the tears ran down his cheeks
as he embraced his son.
                              Only Telémakhos,
uncomprehending, wild
with incredulity, cried out:
                              "You cannot
be my father Odysseus! Meddling spirits
230 conceived this trick to twist the knife in me!
No man of woman born could work these wonders
by his own craft, unless a god came into it
with ease to turn him young or old at will.
I swear you were in rags and old,
and here you stand like one of the immortals!"

Odysseus brought his ranging mind to bear
and said:
                "This is not princely, to be swept
away by wonder at your father's presence.
240 No other Odysseus will ever come,
for he and I are one, the same; his bitter
fortune and his wanderings are mine.
Twenty years gone, and I am back again
on my own island.
                          As for my change of skin,
that is a charm Athena, Hope of Soldiers,
uses as she will; she has the knack
to make me seem a beggar man sometimes
and sometimes young, with finer clothes about me.
250 It is no hard thing for the gods of heaven
to glorify a man or bring him low."

When he had spoken, down he sat.
                                      Then, throwing
his arms around this marvel of a father
Telémakhos began to weep. Salt tears

rose from the wells of longing in both men,
and cries burst from both as keen and fluttering
as those of the great taloned hawk,
whose nestlings farmers take before they fly.
260 So helplessly they cried, pouring out tears,
and might have gone on weeping so till sundown,
had not Telémakhos said:
                              "Dear father! Tell me
what kind of vessel put you here ashore
on Ithaka? Your sailors, who were they?
I doubt you made it, walking on the sea!"

Then said Odysseus, who had borne the barren sea:
"Only plain truth shall I tell you, child.
Great seafarers, the Phaiákians, gave me passage
270 as they give other wanderers. By night
over the open ocean, while I slept,
they brought me in their cutter, set me down
on Ithaka, with gifts of bronze and gold
and stores of woven things. By the gods' will
these lie all hidden in a cave. I came
to this wild place, directed by Athena,
so that we might lay plans to kill our enemies.
Count up the suitors for me, let me know
what men at arms are there, how many men.
280 I must put all my mind to it, to see
if we two by ourselves can take them on
or if we should look round for help."

                              Telémakhos
replied:
                  "O Father, all my life your fame
as a fighting man has echoed in my ears —
your skill with weapons and the tricks of war —
but what you speak of is a staggering thing,
beyond imagining, for me. How can two men
290 do battle with a houseful in their prime?
For I must tell you this is no affair
of ten or even twice ten men, but scores,
throngs of them. You shall see, here and now.
The number from Doulíkhion alone
is fifty-two picked men, with armorers,
a half dozen; twenty-four came from Samê,
twenty from Zakýnthos; our own island

accounts for twelve, high-ranked, and their retainers,
Medôn the crier, and the Master Harper,
besides a pair of handymen at feasts.
If we go in against all these
I fear we pay in salt blood for your vengeance.
You must think hard if you would conjure up
the fighting strength to take us through."

                      Odysseus
who had endured the long war and the sea
answered:
           "I'll tell you now.
Suppose Athena's arm is over us, and Zeus
her father's, must I rack my brains for more?"

Clearheaded Telémakhos looked hard and said:
"Those two are great defenders, no one doubts it,
but throned in the serene clouds overhead;
other affairs of men and gods they have
to rule over."

          And the hero answered:
"Before long they will stand to right and left of us
in combat, in the shouting, when the test comes —
our nerve against the suitors' in my hall.
Here is your part: at break of day tomorrow
home with you, go mingle with our princes.
The swineherd later on will take me down
the port-side trail — a beggar, by my looks,
hangdog and old. If they make fun of me
in my own courtyard, let your ribs cage up
your springing heart, no matter what I suffer,
no matter if they pull me by the heels
or practice shots at me, to drive me out.
Look on, hold down your anger. You may even
plead with them, by heaven! in gentle terms
to quit their horseplay — not that they will heed you,
rash as they are, facing their day of wrath.
Now fix the next step in your mind.
                      Athena,
counseling me, will give me word, and I
shall signal to you, nodding: at that point
round up all armor, lances, gear of war
left in our hall, and stow the lot away

back in the vaulted store room. When the suitors
340 miss those arms and question you, be soft
in what you say: answer:
                    'I thought I'd move them
out of the smoke. They seemed no longer those
bright arms Odysseus left us years ago
when he went off to Troy. Here where the fire's
hot breath came, they had grown black and drear.
One better reason, too, I had from Zeus:
suppose a brawl starts up when you are drunk,
you might be crazed and bloody one another,
350 and that would stain your feast, your courtship. Tempered
is iron can magnetize a man.'
                         Say that.
But put aside two broadswords and two spears
for our own use, two oxhide shields nearby
when we go into action. Pallas Athena
and Zeus All Provident will see you through,
bemusing our young friends.
                         Now one thing more.
If son of mine you are and blood of mine,
360 let no one hear Odysseus is about.
Neither Laërtês, nor the swineherd here,
nor any slave, nor even Penélopê.
But you and I alone must learn how far
the women are corrupted; we should know
how to locate good men among our hands,
the loyal and respectful, and the shirkers
who take you lightly, as alone and young."

His admirable son replied:
                         "Ah, Father,
370 even when danger comes I think you'll find
courage in me. I am not scatterbrained.
But as to checking on the field hands now,
I see no gain for us in that. Reflect,
you make a long toil, that way, if you care
to look men in the eye at every farm,
while these gay devils in our hall at ease
eat up our flocks and herds, leaving us nothing.

As for the maids I say, Yes: make distinction
between good girls and those who shame your house;

380 all that I shy away from is a scrutiny
     of cottagers just now. The time for that
     comes later — if in truth you have a sign
     from Zeus the Stormking."

                              So their talk ran on,
     while down the coast, and round toward Ithaka,
     hove the good ship that had gone out to Pylos
     bearing Telémakhos and his companions.
     Into the wide bay waters, on to the dark land,
     they drove her, hauled her up, took out the oars

390 and canvas for light-hearted squires to carry
     homeward — as they carried, too, the gifts
     of Meneláos round to Klýtios'[134] house.
     But first they sped a runner to Penélopê.
     They knew that quiet lady must be told
     the prince her son had come ashore, and sent
     his good ship round to port; not one soft tear
     should their sweet queen let fall.
                              Both messengers,
     crewman and swineherd — reached the outer gate

400 in the same instant, bearing the same news,
     and went in side by side to the king's hall.
     He of the ship burst out among the maids:
     "Your son's ashore this morning, O my Queen!"

     But the swineherd calmly stood near Penélopê
     whispering what her son had bade him tell
     and what he had enjoined on her. No more.
     When he had done, he left the place and turned
     back to his steading in the hills.

                              By now,
410 sullen confusion weighed upon the suitors.
     Out of the house, out of the court they went,
     beyond the wall and gate, to sit in council.
     Eurýmakhos, the son of Pólybos,
     opened discussion:
                         "Friends, face up to it;

---

[134] **Klýtios:** In Book 15 (l. 655), Telémakhos entrusts Theoklýmenos to Peiraios, son of Klýtios.

that young pup, Telémakhos, has done it;
he made the round trip, though we said he could not.
Well—now to get the best craft we can find
afloat, with oarsmen who can drench her bows,
420   and tell those on the island to come home."

He was yet speaking when Amphínomos,
craning seaward, spotted the picket ship
already in the roadstead under oars
with canvas brailed up; and this fresh arrival
made him chuckle. Then he told his friends:
"Too late for messages. Look, here they come
along the bay. Some god has brought them news,
or else they saw the cutter pass—and could not
overtake her."

430   On their feet at once,
the suitors took the road to the sea beach,
where, meeting the black ship, they hauled her in.
Oars and gear they left for their light-hearted
squires to carry, and all in company
made off for the assembly ground. All others,
young and old alike, they barred from sitting.
Eupeithês' son, Antínoös, made the speech:
"How the gods let our man escape a boarding,
that is the wonder.
440   We had lookouts posted
up on the heights all day in the sea wind,
and every hour a fresh pair of eyes;
at night we never slept ashore
but after sundown cruised the open water
to the southeast, patrolling until Dawn.
We were prepared to cut him off and catch him,
squelch him for good and all. The power of heaven
steered him the long way home.

Well, let this company plan his destruction,
450   and leave him no way out, this time. I see
our business here unfinished while he lives.
He knows, now, and he's no fool. Besides,
his people are all tired of playing up to us.
I say, act now, before he brings the whole
body of Akhaians to assembly—
and he would leave no word unsaid, in righteous

anger speaking out before them all
of how we plotted murder, and then missed him.
Will they commend us for that pretty work?
460　Take action now, or we are in for trouble;
we might be exiled, driven off our lands.
Let the first blow be ours.
If we move first, and get our hands on him
far from the city's eye, on path or field,
then stores and livestock will be ours to share;
the house we may confer upon his mother —
and on the man who marries her. Decide
otherwise you may — but if, my friends,
you want that boy to live and have his patrimony,
470　then we should eat no more of his good mutton,
come to this place no more.
　　　　　　　　　　Let each from his own hall
court her with dower gifts. And let her marry
the destined one, the one who offers most."

He ended, and no sound was heard among them,
sitting all hushed, until at last the son
of Nísos Aretíadês arose —
Amphínomos.
　　　　　　　He led the group of suitors
480　who came from grainlands on Doulíkhion,
and he had lightness in his talk that pleased
Penélopê, for he meant no ill.
Now, in concern for them, he spoke:
　　　　　　　　　　　"O Friends
I should not like to kill Telémakhos.
It is a shivery thing to kill a prince
of royal blood.
　　　　　　　We should consult the gods.
If Zeus hands down a ruling for that act,
490　then I shall say, 'Come one, come all,' and go
cut him down with my own hand —
but I say Halt, if gods are contrary."

Now this proposal won them, and it carried.
Breaking their session up, away they went
to take their smooth chairs in Odysseus' house.
Meanwhile Penélopê the Wise,
decided, for her part, to make appearance
before the valiant young men.

She knew now

500   they plotted her child's death in her own hall,
for once more Medôn, who had heard them, told her.
Into the hall that lovely lady came,
with maids attending, and approached the suitors,
till near a pillar of the well-wrought roof
she paused, her shining veil across her cheeks,
and spoke directly to Antínoös:

"Infatuate,

steeped in evil! Yet in Ithaka they say
you were the best one of your generation
510   in mind and speech. Not so, you never were.
Madman, why do you keep forever knitting
death for Telémakhos? Have you no pity
toward men dependent on another's mercy?
Before Lord Zeus, no sanction can be found
for one such man to plot against another!
Or are you not aware that your own father
fled to us when the realm was up in arms
against him? He had joined the Taphian pirates
in ravaging Thesprotian folk, our friends.
520   Our people would have raided *him,* then — breached
his heart, butchered his herds to feast upon —
only Odysseus took him in, and held
the furious townsmen off. It is Odysseus'
house you now consume, his wife you court,
his son you kill, or try to kill. And me
you ravage now, and grieve. I call upon you
to make an end of it! — and your friends too!"

The son of Pólybos it was, Eurýmakhos,
who answered her with ready speech:
530
"My lady

Penélopê, wise daughter of Ikários,
you must shake off these ugly thoughts. I say
that man does not exist, nor will, who dares
lay hands upon your son Telémakhos,
while I live, walk the earth, and use my eyes.
The man's life blood, I swear,
will spurt and run out black around my lancehead!
For it is true of me, too, that Odysseus,
raider of cities, took me on his knees
540   and fed me often — tidbits and red wine.

Should not Telémakhos, therefore, be dear to me
above the rest of men? I tell the lad
he must not tremble for his life, at least
alone in the suitors' company. Heaven
deals death no man avoids."

                Blasphemous lies
in earnest tones he told—the one who planned
the lad's destruction!
             Silently the lady
550 made her way to her glowing upper chamber,
there to weep for her dear lord, Odysseus,
until grey-eyed Athena
cast sweet sleep upon her eyes.

                At fall of dusk
Odysseus and his son heard the approach
of the good forester. They had been standing
over the fire with a spitted pig,
a yearling. And Athena coming near
with one rap of her wand made of Odysseus
560 an old old man again, with rags about him—
for if the swineherd knew his lord were there
he could not hold the news; Penélopê
would hear it from him.
            Now Telémakhos
greeted him first:
           "Eumaios, back again!
What was the talk in town? Are the tall suitors
home again, by this time, from their ambush,
or are they still on watch for my return?"

570 And you replied, Eumaios—O my swineherd:
"There was no time to ask or talk of that;
I hurried through the town. Even while I spoke
my message, I felt driven to return.
A runner from your friends turned up, a crier,
who gave the news first to your mother. Ah!
One thing I do know; with my own two eyes
I saw it. As I climbed above the town
to where the sky is cut by Hermês' ridge,
I saw a ship bound in for our own bay
580 with many oarsmen in it, laden down

with sea provisioning and two-edged spears,
and I surmised those were the men.

                               Who knows?"

Telémakhos, now strong with magic, smiled
across at his own father — but avoided
the swineherd's eye.

                So when the pig was done,
the spit no longer to be turned, the table
garnished, everyone sat down to feast
590 on all the savory flesh he craved. And when
they had put off desire for meat and drink,
they turned to bed and took the gift of sleep.

BOOK 17
THE BEGGAR AT THE MANOR

When the young Dawn came bright into the East
spreading her finger tips of rose, Telémakhos,
the king's son, tied on his rawhide sandals
and took the lance that bore his handgrip. Burning
to be away, and on the path to town,
he told the swineherd:

                  "Uncle, the truth is
I must go down myself into the city.
Mother must see me there, with her own eyes,
10 or she will weep and feel forsaken still,
and will not set her mind at rest. Your job
will be to lead this poor man down to beg.
Some householder may want to dole him out
a loaf and pint. I have my own troubles.
Am I to care for every last man who comes?
And if he takes it badly — well, so much
the worse for him. Plain truth is what I favor."

At once Odysseus the great tactician
spoke up briskly:

                "Neither would I myself
20 care to be kept here, lad. A beggar man
fares better in the town. Let it be said
I am not yet so old I must lay up
indoors and mumble, 'Aye, Aye' to a master.
Go on, then. As you say, my friend can lead me
as soon as I have had a bit of fire

and when the sun grows warmer. These old rags
could be my death, outside on a frosty morning,
and the town is distant, so they say."

30   Telémakhos
with no more words went out, and through the fence,
and down hill, going fast on the steep footing,
nursing woe for the suitors in his heart.

Before the manor hall, he leaned his lance
against a great porch pillar and stepped in
across the door stone.
                        Old Eurýkleia
saw him first, for that day she was covering
handsome chairs nearby with clean fleeces.
40 She ran to him at once, tears in her eyes;
and other maidservants of the old soldier
Odysseus gathered round to greet their prince,
kissing his head and shoulders.
                                Quickly, then,
Penélopê the Wise, tall in her beauty
as Artemis or pale-gold Aphroditê,
appeared from her high chamber and came down
to throw her arms around her son. In tears
she kissed his head, kissed both his shining eyes,
50 then cried out, and her words flew:
                                    "Back with me!
Telémakhos, more sweet to me than sunlight!
I thought I should not see you again, ever,
after you took the ship that night to Pylos—
against my will, with not a word! you went
for news of your dear father. Tell me now
of everything you saw!"

                        But he made answer:
"Mother, not now. You make me weep. My heart
60 already aches—I came near death at sea.
You must bathe, first of all, and change your dress,
and take your maids to the highest room to pray.
Pray, and burn offerings to the gods of heaven,
that Zeus may put his hand to our revenge.

I am off now to bring home from the square
a guest, a passenger I had. I sent him
yesterday with all my crew to town.

Peiraios was to care for him, I said,
and keep him well, with honor, till I came."

70 She caught back the swift words upon her tongue.
Then softly she withdrew
to bathe and dress her body in fresh linen,
and make her offerings to the gods of heaven,
praying Almighty Zeus
to put his hand to their revenge.

                        Telémakhos
had left the hall, taken his lance, and gone
with two quick hounds at heel into the town,
Athena's grace in his long stride
80 making the people gaze as he came near.
And suitors gathered, primed with friendly words,
despite the deadly plotting in their hearts—
but these, and all their crowd, he kept away from.
Next he saw sitting some way off, apart,
Mentor, with Antiphos and Halithersês,
friends of his father's house in years gone by.
Near these men he sat down, and told his tale
under their questioning.
              His crewman, young Peiraios,
90 guided through town, meanwhile, into the Square,
the Argive exile, Theoklýmenos.
Telémakhos lost no time in moving toward him;
but first Peiraios had his say:
            "Telémakhos,
you must send maids to me, at once, and let me
turn over to you those gifts from Meneláos!"

The prince had pondered it, and said:
                "Peiraios,
none of us knows how this affair will end.
100 Say one day our fine suitors, without warning,
draw upon me, kill me in our hall,
and parcel out my patrimony—I wish
you, and no one of them, to have those things.
But if my hour comes, if I can bring down
bloody death on all that crew,
you will rejoice to send my gifts to me—
and so will I rejoice!"

Then he departed,
leading his guest, the lonely stranger, home.

110 Over chair-backs in hall they dropped their mantles
and passed in to the polished tubs, where maids
poured out warm baths for them, anointed them,
and pulled fresh tunics, fleecy cloaks around them.
Soon they were seated at their ease in hall.
A maid came by to tip a golden jug
over their fingers into a silver bowl
and draw a gleaming table up beside them.
The larder mistress brought her tray of loaves
and savories, dispensing each.

120   In silence
across the hall, beside a pillar, propped
in a long chair, Telémakhos' mother
spun a fine wool yarn.

                    The young men's hands
went out upon the good things placed before them,
and only when their hunger and thirst were gone
did she look up and say:

                    "Telémakhos,
what am I to do now? Return alone
130 and lie again on my forsaken bed—
sodden how often with my weeping
since that day when Odysseus put to sea
to join the Atreidai[135] before Troy?

                    Could you not
tell me, before the suitors fill our house,
what news you have of his return?"

                    He answered:
"Now that you ask a second time, dear Mother,
here is the truth.

140   We went ashore at Pylos
to Nestor, lord and guardian of the West,
who gave me welcome in his towering hall.
So kind he was, he might have been my father
and I his long-lost son—so truly kind,

---

[135] **Atreidai:** As sons of Atreus, Agamémnon and Meneláos are known as Atreidai, or Atrides.

taking me in with his own honored sons.
But as to Odysseus' bitter fate,
living or dead, he had no news at all
from anyone on earth, he said. He sent me
overland in a strong chariot
150   to Atreus' son, the captain, Meneláos.
And I saw Helen there, for whom the Argives
fought, and the Trojans fought, as the gods willed.
Then Meneláos of the great war cry
asked me my errand in that ancient land
of Lakedaimon. So I told our story,
and in reply he burst out:
                'Intolerable!
That feeble men, unfit as those men are,
should think to lie in that great captain's bed,
160   fawns in the lion's lair! As if a doe
put down her litter of sucklings there, while she
sniffed at the glen or grazed a grassy hollow.
Ha! Then the lord returns to his own bed
and deals out wretched doom on both alike.

So will Odysseus deal out doom on these.
O Father Zeus, Athena, and Apollo!
I pray he comes as once he was, in Lesbos,
when he stood up to wrestle Philomeleidês —
champion and Island King —
170   and smashed him down. How the Akhaians cheered!
If that Odysseus could meet the suitors,
they'd have a quick reply, a stunning dowry!
Now for your questions, let me come to the point.
I would not misreport it for you; let me
tell you what the Ancient of the Sea,
that infallible seer, told me.
            On an island
your father lies and grieves. The Ancient saw him
held by a nymph, Kalypso, in her hall;
180   no means of sailing home remained to him,
no ship with oars, and no ship's company
to pull him on the broad back of the sea.'

I had this from the lord marshal, Meneláos,
and when my errand in that place was done
I left for home. A fair breeze from the gods
brought me swiftly back to our dear island."

The boy's tale made her heart stir in her breast,
but this was not all. Mother and son now heard
Theoklýmenos, the diviner, say:
190   "He does not see it clear—
                              O gentle lady,
wife of Odysseus Laërtiadês,
listen to me, I can reveal this thing.
Zeus be my witness, and the table set
for strangers and the hearth to which I've come—
the lord Odysseus, I tell you,
is present now, already, on this island!
Quartered somewhere, or going about, he knows
what evil is afoot. He has it in him
200   to bring a black hour on the suitors. Yesterday,
still at the ship, I saw this in a portent.
I read the sign aloud, I told Telémakhos!"

The prudent queen, for her part, said:
                              "Stranger,
if only this came true—
our love would go to you, with many gifts;
aye, every man who passed would call you happy!"

So ran the talk between these three.
                              Meanwhile,
210   swaggering before Odysseus' hall,
the suitors were competing at the discus throw
and javelin, on the level measured field.
But when the dinner hour drew on, and beasts
were being driven from the fields to slaughter—
as beasts were, every day—Medôn spoke out:
Medôn, the crier, whom the suitors liked;
he took his meat beside them.

                              "Men," he said,
"each one has had his work-out and his pleasure,
220   come in to Hall now; time to make our feast.
Are discus throws more admirable than a roast
when the proper hour comes?"

                              At this reminder
they all broke up their games, and trailed away
into the gracious, timbered hall. There, first,
they dropped their cloaks on chairs; then came their ritual:

putting great rams and fat goats to the knife—
pigs and a cow, too.
                    So they made their feast.

230 During these hours, Odysseus and the swineherd
were on their way out of the hills to town.
The forester had got them started, saying:
"Friend, you have hopes, I know, of your adventure
into the heart of town today. My lord
wishes it so, not I. No, I should rather
you stood by here as guardian of our steading.
But I owe reverence to my prince, and fear
he'll make my ears burn later if I fail.
A master's tongue has a rough edge. Off we go.
240 Part of the day is past; nightfall will be
early, and colder, too."

                    Odysseus,
who had it all timed in his head, replied:
"I know, as well as you do. Let's move on.
You lead the way—the whole way. Have you got
a staff, a lopped stick, you could let me use
to put my weight on when I slip? This path
is hard going, they said."

                    Over his shoulders
250 he slung his patched-up knapsack, an old bundle
tied with twine. Eumaios found a stick for him,
the kind he wanted, and the two set out,
leaving the boys and dogs to guard the place.
In this way good Eumaios led his lord
down to the city.
                    And it seemed to him
he led an old outcast, a beggar man,
leaning most painfully upon a stick,
his poor cloak, all in tatters, looped about him.

260 Down by the stony trail they made their way
as far as Clearwater, not far from town—
a spring house where the people filled their jars.
Ithakos, Nêritos, and Polýktor[136] built it,

---

[136] **Ithakos . . . Polýktor:** Early rulers of Ithaka.

and round it on the humid ground a grove,
a circular wood of poplars grew. Ice cold
in runnels from a high rock ran the spring,
and over it there stood an altar stone
to the cool nymphs, where all men going by
laid offerings.

270   Well, here the son of Dólios
crossed their path—Melánthios.

                                    He was driving
a string of choice goats for the evening meal,
with two goatherds beside him; and no sooner
had he laid eyes upon the wayfarers
than he began to growl and taunt them both
so grossly that Odysseus' heart grew hot:
"Here comes one scurvy type leading another!
God pairs them off together, every time.

280 Swineherd, where are you taking your new pig,
that stinking beggar there, licker of pots?
How many doorposts has he rubbed his back on
whining for garbage, where a noble guest
would rate a cauldron or a sword?

                                    Hand him
over to me, I'll make a farmhand of him,
a stall scraper, a fodder carrier! Whey
for drink will put good muscle on his shank!
No chance: he learned his dodges long ago—

290 no honest sweat. He'd rather tramp the country
begging, to keep his hoggish belly full.
Well, I can tell you this for sure:
in King Odysseus' hall, if he goes there,
footstools will fly around his head—good shots
from strong hands. Back and side, his ribs will catch it
on the way out!"

            And like a drunken fool
he kicked at Odysseus' hip as he passed by.
Not even jogged off stride, or off the trail,

300 the Lord Odysseus walked along, debating
inwardly whether to whirl and beat
the life out of this fellow with his stick,
or toss him, brain him on the stony ground.
Then he controlled himself, and bore it quietly.
Not so the swineherd.

                    Seeing the man before him,

he raised his arms and cried:
                                          "Nymphs of the spring,
daughters of Zeus, if ever Odysseus
310 burnt you a thighbone in rich fat—a ram's
or kid's thighbone, hear me, grant my prayer:
let our true lord come back, let heaven bring him
to rid the earth of these fine courtly ways
Melánthios picks up around the town—
all wine and wind! Bad shepherds ruin flocks!"

Melánthios the goatherd answered:
                                          "Bless me!
The dog can snap: how he goes on! Some day
I'll take him in a slave ship overseas
320 and trade him for a herd!
                                   Old Silverbow
Apollo, if he shot clean through Telémakhos
in hall today, what luck! Or let the suitors
cut him down!
                    Odysseus died at sea;
no coming home for him."

                              He flung this out
and left the two behind to come on slowly,
while he went hurrying to the king's hall.
330 There he slipped in, and sat among the suitors,
beside the one he doted on—Eurýmakhos.
Then working servants helped him to his meat
and the mistress of the larder gave him bread.

Reaching the gate, Odysseus and the forester
halted and stood outside, for harp notes came
around them rippling on the air
as Phêmios picked out a song. Odysseus
caught his companion's arm and said:
                                          "My friend,
340 here is the beautiful place—who could mistake it?
Here is Odysseus' hall: no hall like this!
See how one chamber grows out of another;
see how the court is tight with wall and coping;
no man at arms could break this gateway down!
Your banqueting young lords are here in force,
I gather, from the fumes of mutton roasting

and strum of harping—harping, which the gods
appoint sweet friend of feasts!"

                              And—O my swineherd!
350   you replied:
              "That was quick recognition;
but you are no numbskull—in this or anything.
Now we must plan this action. Will you take
leave of me here, and go ahead alone
to make your entrance now among the suitors?
Or do you choose to wait?—Let me go forward
and go in first.
                    Do not delay too long;
someone might find you skulking here outside
360   and take a club to you, or heave a lance.
Bear this in mind, I say."

                        The patient hero
Odysseus answered:
                "Just what I was thinking.
You go in first, and leave me here a little.
But as for blows and missiles,
I am no tyro at these things. I learned
to keep my head in hardship—years of war
and years at sea. Let this new trial come.
370   The cruel belly, can you hide its ache?
How many bitter days it brings! Long ships
with good stout planks athwart—would fighters rig them
to ride the barren sea, except for hunger?
Seawolves—woe to their enemies!"

                        While he spoke
an old hound, lying near, pricked up his ears
and lifted up his muzzle. This was Argos,
trained as a puppy by Odysseus,
but never taken on a hunt before
380   his master sailed for Troy. The young men, afterward,
hunted wild goats with him, and hare, and deer,
but he had grown old in his master's absence.
Treated as rubbish now, he lay at last
upon a mass of dung before the gates—
manure of mules and cows, piled there until
fieldhands could spread it on the king's estate.

Abandoned there, and half destroyed with flies,
old Argos lay.
                     But when he knew he heard
390 Odysseus' voice nearby, he did his best
to wag his tail, nose down, with flattened ears,
having no strength to move nearer his master.
And the man looked away,
wiping a salt tear from his cheek; but he
hid this from Eumaios. Then he said:
"I marvel that they leave this hound to lie
here on the dung pile;
he would have been a fine dog, from the look of him,
though I can't say as to his power and speed
400 when he was young. You find the same good build
in house dogs, table dogs landowners keep
all for style."

            And you replied, Eumaios:
"A hunter owned him—but the man is dead
in some far place. If this old hound could show
the form he had when Lord Odysseus left him,
going to Troy, you'd see him swift and strong.
He never shrank from any savage thing
he'd brought to bay in the deep woods; on the scent
410 no other dog kept up with him. Now misery
has him in leash. His owner died abroad,
and here the women slaves will take no care of him.
You know how servants are: without a master
they have no will to labor, or excel.
For Zeus who views the wide world takes away
half the manhood of a man, that day
he goes into captivity and slavery."

Eumaios crossed the court and went straight forward
into the mégaron among the suitors;
420 but death and darkness in that instant closed
the eyes of Argos, who had seen his master,
Odysseus, after twenty years.

            Long before anyone else
Telémakhos caught sight of the grey woodsman
coming from the door, and called him over
with a quick jerk of his head. Eumaios'

narrowed eyes made out an empty bench
beside the one the carver used—that servant
who had no respite, carving for the suitors.
430 This bench he took possession of, and placed it
across the table from Telémakhos
for his own use. Then the two men were served
cuts from a roast and bread from a bread basket.

At no long interval, Odysseus came
through his own doorway as a mendicant,
humped like a bundle of rags over his stick.
He settled on the inner ash wood sill,
leaning against the door jamb—cypress timber
the skilled carpenter planed years ago
440 and set up with a plumbline.

                    Now Telémakhos
took an entire loaf and a double handful
of roast meat; then he said to the forester:
"Give these to the stranger there. But tell him
to go among the suitors, on his own;
he may beg all he wants. This hanging back
is no asset to a hungry man."

The swineherd rose at once, crossed to the door,
and halted by Odysseus.

450   "Friend," he said,
"Telémakhos is pleased to give you these,
but he commands you to approach the suitors;
you may ask all you want from them. He adds,
your shyness is no asset to a beggar."

The great tactician, lifting up his eyes,
cried:
        "Zeus aloft! A blessing on Telémakhos!
Let all things come to pass as he desires!"

Palms held out, in the beggar's gesture, he
460 received the bread and meat and put it down
before him on his knapsack—lowly table!—
then he fell to, devouring it. Meanwhile
the harper in the great room sang a song.

Not till the man was fed did the sweet harper
end his singing—whereupon the company
made the walls ring again with talk.

                                        Unseen,
Athena took her place beside Odysseus
whispering in his ear:
470   "Yes, try the suitors.
You may collect a few more loaves, and learn
who are the decent lads, and who are vicious—
although not one can be excused from death!"

So he appealed to them, one after another,
going from left to right, with open palm,
as though his life time had been spent in beggary.
And they gave bread, for pity—wondering, though,
at the strange man. Who could this beggar be,
where did he come from? each would ask his neighbor;
480   till in their midst the goatherd, Melánthios,
raised his voice:
                        "Hear just a word from me,
my lords who court our illustrious queen!
                                        This man,
this foreigner, I saw him on the road;
the swineherd here was leading him this way;
who, what, or whence he claims to be, I could not
say for sure."

                        At this, Antínoös
490   turned on the swineherd brutally, saying:
                                        "You famous
breeder of pigs, why bring this fellow here?
Are we not plagued enough with beggars,
foragers and such rats?
                                        You find the company
too slow at eating up your lord's estate—
is that it? So you call this scarecrow in?"

The forester replied:
                        "Antínoös,
500   well born you are, but that was not well said.
Who would call in a foreigner?—unless
an artisan with skill to serve the realm,
a healer, or a prophet, or a builder,
or one whose harp and song might give us joy.

All these are sought for on the endless earth,
but when have beggars come by invitation?
Who puts a field mouse in his granary? My lord,
you are a hard man, and you always were—
more so than others of this company—hard
510 on all Odysseus' people and on me.
But this I can forget
as long as Penélopê lives on, the wise and tender
mistress of this hall; as long
as Prince Telémakhos—"

               But he broke off
at a look from Telémakhos, who said:
                     "Be still.
Spare me a long-drawn answer to this gentleman.
With his unpleasantness, he will forever make
520 strife where he can—and goad the others on."

He turned and spoke out clearly to Antínoös:
"What fatherly concern you show me! Frighten
this unknown fellow, would you, from my hall
with words that promise blows—may God forbid it!
Give him a loaf. Am I a niggard? No,
I call on you to give. And spare your qualms
as to my mother's loss, or anyone's—
not that in truth you have such care at heart:
your heart is all in feeding, not in giving."

530 Antínoös replied:
                  "What high and mighty
talk, Telémakhos! No holding you!
If every suitor gave what I may give him,
he could be kept for months—kept out of sight!"

He reached under the table for the footstool
his shining feet had rested on—and this
he held up so that all could see his gift.

But all the rest gave alms,
enough to fill the beggar's pack with bread
540 and roast meat.
           So it looked as though Odysseus
had had his taste of what these men were like
and could return scot free to his own doorway—
but halting now before Antínoös

he made a little speech to him. Said he:
"Give a mite, friend. I would not say, myself,
you are the worst man of the young Akhaians.
The noblest, rather; kingly, by your look;
therefore you'll give more bread than others do.

550 Let me speak well of you as I pass on
over the boundless earth!

                I, too, you know,
had fortune once, lived well, stood well with men,
and gave alms, often, to poor wanderers
like this one that you see — aye, to all sorts,
no matter in what dire want. I owned
servants — many, god knows — and all the rest
that goes with being prosperous, as they say.
But Zeus the son of Kronos brought me down.

560 No telling
why he would have it, but he made me go
to Egypt with a company of rovers —
a long sail to the south — for my undoing.
Up the broad Nile and in to the river bank
I brought my dipping squadron. There, indeed,
I told the men to stand guard at the ships;
I sent patrols out — out to rising ground;
but reckless greed carried my crews away
to plunder the Egyptian farms; they bore off

570 wives and children, killed what men they found.
The news ran on the wind to the city, a night cry,
and sunrise brought both infantry and horsemen,
filling the river plain with dazzle of bronze;
then Zeus lord of lightning
threw my men into a blind panic; no one dared
stand against that host closing around us.
Their scything weapons left our dead in piles,
but some they took alive, into forced labor,
myself among them. And they gave me, then,

580 to one Dmêtor, a traveller, son of Iasos,
who ruled at Kypros.° He conveyed me there.   Cyprus
From that place, working northward, miserably —"

But here Antínoös broke in, shouting:
                             "God!
What evil wind blew in this pest?
                   Get over,
stand in the passage! Nudge my table, will you?

Egyptian whips are sweet
to what you'll come to here, you nosing rat,
590 making your pitch to everyone!
These men have bread to throw away on you
because it is not theirs. Who cares? Who spares
another's food, when he has more than plenty?"

With guile Odysseus drew away, then said:
"A pity that you have more looks than heart.
You'd grudge a pinch of salt from your own larder
to your own handy man. You sit here, fat
on others' meat, and cannot bring yourself
to rummage out a crust of bread for me!"

600 Then anger made Antínoös' heart beat hard,
and, glowering under his brows, he answered:
　　　　　　　　　　　　　　　"Now!
You think you'll shuffle off and get away
after that impudence? Oh, no you don't!"

The stool he let fly hit the man's right shoulder
on the packed muscle under the shoulder blade—
like solid rock, for all the effect one saw.
Odysseus only shook his head, containing
thoughts of bloody work, as he walked on,
610 then sat, and dropped his loaded bag again
upon the door sill. Facing the whole crowd
he said, and eyed them all:
　　　　　　　　　　　　"One word only,
my lords, and suitors of the famous queen.
One thing I have to say.
There is no pain, no burden for the heart
when blows come to a man, and he defending
his own cattle—his own cows and lambs.
Here it was otherwise. Antínoös
620 hit me for being driven on by hunger—
how many bitter seas men cross for hunger!
If beggars interest the gods, if there are Furies
pent in the dark to avenge a poor man's wrong, then may
Antínoös meet his death before his wedding day!"

Then said Eupeithês' son, Antínoös:
　　　　　　　　　　　　　　"Enough.
Eat and be quiet where you are, or shamble elsewhere,
unless you want these lads to stop your mouth

pulling you by the heels, or hands and feet,
630   over the whole floor, till your back is peeled!"

But now the rest were mortified, and someone
spoke from the crowd of young bucks to rebuke him:
"A poor show, that — hitting this famished tramp —
bad business, if he happened to be a god.
You know they go in foreign guise, the gods do,
looking like strangers, turning up
in towns and settlements to keep an eye
on manners, good or bad."

But at this notion
640   Antínoös only shrugged.
                    Telémakhos,
after the blow his father bore, sat still
without a tear, though his heart felt the blow.
Slowly he shook his head from side to side,
containing murderous thoughts.
                    Penélopê
on the higher level of her room had heard
the blow, and knew who gave it. Now she murmured:
"Would god you could be hit yourself, Antínoös —
650   hit by Apollo's bowshot!"

                    And Eurýnomê
her housekeeper, put in:
                    "He and no other?
If all we pray for came to pass, not one
would live till dawn!"

                    Her gentle mistress said:
"Oh, Nan, they are a bad lot; they intend
ruin for all of us; but Antínoös
appears a blacker-hearted hound than any.
660   Here is a poor man come, a wanderer,
driven by want to beg his bread, and everyone
in hall gave bits, to cram his bag — only
Antínoös threw a stool, and banged his shoulder!"

So she described it, sitting in her chamber
among her maids — while her true lord was eating.
Then she called in the forester and said:
"Go to that man on my behalf, Eumaios,
and send him here, so I can greet and question him.

Abroad in the great world, he may have heard
670 rumors about Odysseus—may have known him!"

Then you replied—O swineherd!
       "Ah, my queen,
if these Akhaian sprigs would hush their babble
the man could tell you tales to charm your heart.
Three days and nights I kept him in my hut;
he came straight off a ship, you know, to me.
There was no end to what he made me hear
of his hard roving and I listened, eyes
upon him as a man drinks in a tale
680 a minstrel sings—a minstrel taught by heaven
to touch the hearts of men. At such a song
the listener becomes rapt and still. Just so
I found myself enchanted by this man.
He claims an old tie with Odysseus, too—
in his home country the Minoan land
of Krete. From Krete he came, a rolling stone
washed by the gales of life this way and that
to our own beach.
      If he can be believed
690 he has news of Odysseus near at hand
alive, in the rich country of Thesprotia,
bringing a mass of treasure home."

Then wise Penélopê said again:
"Go call him, let him come here, let him tell
that tale again for my own ears.
       Our friends
can drink their cups outside or stay in hall,
being so carefree. And why not? Their stores
lie intact in their homes, both food and drink,
700 with only servants left to take a little.
But these men spend their days around our house
killing our beeves, our fat goats and our sheep,
carousing, drinking up our good dark wine;
sparing nothing, squandering everything.
No champion like Odysseus takes our part.
Ah, if he comes again, no falcon ever
struck more suddenly than he will, with his son,
to avenge this outrage!"

      The great hall below
710 at this point rang with a tremendous sneeze—

"kchaou!" from Telémakhos—like an acclamation.
And laughter seized Penélopê.
                              Then quickly,
lucidly she went on:
                       "Go call the stranger
straight to me. Did you hear that, Eumaios?
My son's thundering sneeze at what I said!
May death come of a sudden so; may death
relieve us, clean as that, of all the suitors!
720 Let me add one thing—do not overlook it—
if I can see this man has told the truth,
I promise him a warm new cloak and tunic."

With all this in his head, the forester
went down the hall, and halted near the beggar,
saying aloud:
                  "Good father, you are called
by the wise mother of Telémakhos,
Penélopê. The queen, despite her troubles,
is moved by a desire to hear your tales
730 about her lord—and if she finds them true,
she'll see you clothed in what you need, a cloak
and a fresh tunic.
                       You may have your belly
full each day you go about this realm
begging. For all may give, and all they wish."

Now said Odysseus, the old soldier:
"Friend,
I wish this instant I could tell my facts
to the wise daughter of Ikários, Penélopê—
740 and I have much to tell about her husband;
we went through much together.
                                   But just now
this hard crowd worries me. They are, you said
infamous to the very rim of heaven
for violent acts: and here, just now, this fellow
gave me a bruise. What had I done to him?
But who would lift a hand for me? Telémakhos?
Anyone else?
                 No; bid the queen be patient.
750 Let her remain till sundown in her room,
and then—if she will seat me near the fire—
inquire tonight about her lord's return.

My rags are sorry cover; you know that;
I showed my sad condition first to you."

The woodsman heard him out, and then returned;
but the queen met him on her threshold, crying:
"Have you not brought him? Why? What is he thinking?
Has he some fear of overstepping? Shy
about these inner rooms? A hangdog beggar?"

760 To this you answered, friend Eumaios:
"No:
he reasons as another might, and well,
not to tempt any swordplay from these drunkards.
Be patient, wait—he says—till darkness falls.
And, O my queen, for you too that is better:
better to be alone with him, and question him,
and hear him out."

                    Penélopê replied:
"He is no fool; he sees how it could be.
770 Never were mortal men like these
for bullying and brainless arrogance!"

Thus she accepted what had been proposed,
so he went back into the crowd. He joined
Telémakhos, and said at once in whispers—
his head bent, so that no one else might hear:
"Dear prince, I must go home to keep good watch
on hut and swine, and look to my own affairs.
Everything here is in your hands. Consider
your own safety before the rest; take care
780 not to get hurt. Many are dangerous here.
May Zeus destroy them first, before we suffer!"

Telémakhos said:
                    "Your wish is mine, Uncle.
Go when your meal is finished. Then come back
at dawn, and bring good victims for a slaughter.
Everything here is in my hands indeed—
and in the disposition of the gods."

Taking his seat on the smooth bench again,
Eumaios ate and drank his fill, then rose
790 to climb the mountain trail back to his swine,

leaving the mégaron and court behind him
crowded with banqueters.

⠀⠀⠀⠀⠀⠀⠀⠀⠀⠀These had their joy
of dance and song, as day waned into evening.

BOOK 18
BLOWS AND A QUEEN'S BEAUTY

Now a true scavenger came in—a public tramp
who begged around the town of Ithaka,
a by-word for his insatiable swag-belly,
feeding and drinking, dawn to dark. No pith
was in him, and no nerve, huge as he looked.
Arnaios, as his gentle mother called him,
he had been nicknamed "Iros" by the young
for being ready to take messages.[137]

⠀⠀⠀⠀⠀⠀⠀⠀⠀⠀⠀⠀⠀⠀⠀This fellow
10⠀thought he would rout Odysseus from his doorway,
growling at him:

⠀⠀⠀⠀⠀⠀⠀⠀⠀"Clear out, grandfather,
or else be hauled out by the ankle bone.
See them all giving me the wink? That means,
'Go on and drag him out!' I hate to do it.
Up with you! Or would you like a fist fight?"

Odysseus only frowned and looked him over,
taking account of everything, then said:
"Master, I am no trouble to you here.
20⠀I offer no remarks. I grudge you nothing.
Take all you get, and welcome. Here is room
for two on this doorslab—or do you own it?
You are a tramp, I think, like me. Patience:
a windfall from the gods will come. But drop
that talk of using fists; it could annoy me.
Old as I am, I might just crack a rib
or split a lip for you. My life would go

---

[137] **Arnaios . . . take messages:** Arnaios got his nickname "Iros" from Iris, goddess of the rainbow and a messenger for the goddess Hêra.

even more peacefully, after tomorrow,
looking for no more visits here from you."

30 Iros the tramp grew red and hooted:
"Ho,
listen to him! The swine can talk your arm off,
like an old oven woman! With two punches
I'd knock him snoring, if I had a mind to—
and not a tooth left in his head, the same
as an old sow caught in the corn! Belt up!
And let this company see the way I do it
when we square off. Can you fight a fresher man?"

Under the lofty doorway, on the door sill
40 of wide smooth ash, they held this rough exchange.
And the tall full-blooded suitor, Antínoös,
overhearing, broke into happy laughter.
Then he said to the others:
                              "Oh, my friends,
no luck like this ever turned up before!
What a farce heaven has brought this house!
                                    The stranger
and Iros have had words, they brag of boxing!
Into the ring they go, and no more talk!"

50 All the young men got on their feet now, laughing,
to crowd around the ragged pair. Antínoös
called out:
            "Gentlemen, quiet! One more thing:
here are goat stomachs ready on the fire
to stuff with blood and fat, good supper pudding.
The man who wins this gallant bout
may step up here and take the one he likes.
And let him feast with us from this day on:
no other beggar will be admitted here
60 when we are at our wine."

                        This pleased them all.
But now that wily man, Odysseus, muttered:
"An old man, an old hulk, has no business
fighting a young man, but my belly nags me;
nothing will do but I must take a beating.
Well, then, let every man here swear an oath

not to step in for Iros. No one throw
a punch for luck. I could be whipped that way."

So much the suitors were content to swear,
70   but after they reeled off their oaths, Telémakhos
put in a word to clinch it, saying:
                    "Friend,
if you will stand and fight, as pride requires,
don't worry about a foul blow from behind.
Whoever hits you will take on the crowd.
You have my word as host; you have the word
of these two kings, Antínoös and Eurýmakhos—
a pair of thinking men."

                    All shouted, "Aye!"
80   So now Odysseus made his shirt a belt
and roped his rags around his loins, baring
his hurdler's thighs and boxer's breadth of shoulder,
the dense rib-sheath and upper arms. Athena
stood nearby to give him bulk and power,
while the young suitors watched with narrowed eyes—
and comments went around:
"By god, old Iros now retires."

                    "Aye,
he asked for it, he'll get it—bloody, too."

90   "The build this fellow had, under his rags!"

Panic made Iros' heart jump, but the yard-boys
hustled and got him belted by main force,
though all his blubber quivered now with dread.
Antínoös' angry voice rang in his ears:
"You sack of guts, you might as well be dead,
might as well never have seen the light of day,
if this man makes you tremble! Chicken-heart,
afraid of an old wreck, far gone in misery!
Well, here is what I say—and what I'll do.
100 If this ragpicker can outfight you, whip you,
I'll ship you out to that king in Epeíros,[138]
Ékhetos—he skins everyone alive.

---

[138] **Epeíros:** North of Ithaka.

Let him just cut your nose off and your ears
and pull your privy parts out by the roots
to feed raw to his hunting dogs!"

Poor Iros

felt a new fit of shaking take his knees.
But the yard-boys pushed him out. Now both contenders
put their hands up. Royal Odysseus
110 pondered if he should hit him with all he had
and drop the man dead on the spot, or only
spar, with force enough to knock him down.
Better that way, he thought — gentle blow,
else he might give himself away.

The two

were at close quarters now, and Iros lunged
hitting the shoulder. Then Odysseus hooked him
under the ear and shattered his jaw bone,
so bright red blood came bubbling from his mouth,
120 as down he pitched into the dust, bleating,
kicking against the ground, his teeth stove in.
The suitors whooped and swung their arms, half dead
with pangs of laughter.

Then, by the ankle bone,

Odysseus hauled the fallen one outside,
crossing the courtyard to the gate, and piled him
against the wall. In his right hand he stuck
his begging staff, and said:

"Here, take your post

130 Sit here to keep the dogs and pigs away.
You can give up your habit of command
over poor waifs and beggarmen — you swab.
Another time you may not know what hit you."

When he had slung his rucksack by the string
over his shoulder, like a wad of rags,
he sat down on the broad door sill again,
as laughing suitors came to flock inside;
and each young buck in passing gave him greeting,
saying, maybe,
140   "Zeus fill your pouch for this!
May the gods grant your heart's desire!"

"Well done

to put that walking famine out of business."

"We'll ship him out to that king in Epéiros,
Ékhetos—he skins everyone alive."

Odysseus found grim cheer in their good wishes—
his work had started well.
                          Now from the fire
his fat blood pudding came, deposited
150 before him by Antínoös—then, to boot,
two brown loaves from the basket, and some wine
in a fine cup of gold. These gifts Amphínomos
gave him. Then he said:
                          "Here's luck, grandfather;
a new day; may the worst be over now."

Odysseus answered, and his mind ranged far:
"Amphínomos, your head is clear, I'd say;
so was your father's—or at least I've heard
good things of Nísos the Doulíkhion,
160 whose son you are, they tell me—an easy man.
And you seem gently bred.
                          In view of that,
I have a word to say to you, so listen.

Of mortal creatures, all that breathe and move,
earth bears none frailer than mankind. What man
believes in woe to come, so long as valor
and tough knees are supplied him by the gods?
But when the gods in bliss bring miseries on,
then willy-nilly, blindly, he endures.
170 Our minds are as the days are, dark or bright,
blown over by the father of gods and men.

So I, too, in my time thought to be happy;
but far and rash I ventured, counting on
my own right arm, my father, and my kin;
behold me now.
                          No man should flout the law,
but keep in peace what gifts the gods may give.

I see you young blades living dangerously,
a household eaten up, a wife dishonored—
180 and yet the master will return, I tell you,
to his own place, and soon; for he is near.

So may some power take you out of this,
homeward, and softly, not to face that man
the hour he sets foot on his native ground.
Between him and the suitors I foretell
no quittance, no way out, unless by blood,
once he shall stand beneath his own roof-beam."

Gravely, when he had done, he made libation
and took a sip of honey-hearted wine,
190 giving the cup, then, back into the hands
of the young nobleman. Amphínomos, for his part,
shaking his head, with chill and burdened breast,
turned in the great hall.
                              Now his heart foreknew
the wrath to come, but he could not take flight,
being by Athena bound there.
                              Death would have him
broken by a spear thrown by Telémakhos.
So he sat down where he had sat before.

200 And now heart-prompting from the grey-eyed goddess
came to the quiet queen, Penélopê:
a wish to show herself before the suitors;
for thus by fanning their desire again
Athena meant to set her beauty high
before her husband's eyes, before her son.
Knowing no reason, laughing confusedly,
she said:
              "Eurýnomê, I have a craving
I never had at all—I would be seen
210 among those ruffians, hateful as they are.
I might well say a word, then, to my son,
for his own good—tell him to shun that crowd;
for all their gay talk, they are bent on evil."

Mistress Eurýnomê replied:
                              "Well said, child,
now is the time. Go down, and make it clear,
hold nothing back from him.
                              But you must bathe
and put a shine upon your cheeks—not this way,
220 streaked under your eyes and stained with tears.
You make it worse, being forever sad,

and now your boy's a bearded man! Remember
you prayed the gods to let you see him so."

Penélopê replied:
                    "Eurýnomê,
it is a kind thought, but I will not hear it—
to bathe and sleek with perfumed oil. No, no,
the gods forever took my sheen away
when my lord sailed for Troy in the decked ships.
230   Only tell my Autonoë to come,
and Hippodameía; they should be attending me
in hall, if I appear there. I could not
enter alone into that crowd of men."

At this the good old woman left the chamber
to tell the maids her bidding. But now too
the grey-eyed goddess had her own designs.
Upon the quiet daughter of Ikários
she let clear drops of slumber fall, until
the queen lay back asleep, her limbs unstrung,
240   in her long chair. And while she slept the goddess
endowed her with immortal grace to hold
the eyes of the Akhaians. With ambrosia
she bathed her cheeks and throat and smoothed her brow—
ambrosia, used by flower-crowned Kythereia°   Aphroditê
when she would join the rose-lipped Graces dancing.
Grandeur she gave her, too, in height and form,
and made her whiter than carved ivory.
Touching her so, the perfect one was gone.
Now came the maids, bare-armed and lovely, voices
250   breaking into the room. The queen awoke
and as she rubbed her cheek she sighed:
                                        "Ah, soft
that drowse I lay embraced in, pain forgot!
If only Artemis the Pure would give me
death as mild, and soon! No heart-ache more,
no wearing out my lifetime with desire
and sorrow, mindful of my lord, good man
in all ways that he was, best of the Akhaians!"

She rose and left her glowing upper room,
260   and down the stairs, with her two maids in train,
this beautiful lady went before the suitors.
Then by a pillar of the solid roof
she paused, her shining veil across her cheek,

the two girls close to her and still;
and in that instant weakness took those men
in the knee joints, their hearts grew faint with lust;
not one but swore to god to lie beside her.
But speaking for her dear son's ears alone
she said:

270   "Telémakhos, what has come over you?
Lightminded you were not, in all your boyhood.
Now you are full grown, come of age; a man
from foreign parts might take you for the son
of royalty, to go by your good looks;
and have you no more thoughtfulness or manners?
How could it happen in our hall that you
permit the stranger to be so abused?
Here, in our house, a guest, can any man
suffer indignity, come by such injury?

280   What can this be for you but public shame?"

Telémakhos looked in her eyes and answered,
with his clear head and his discretion:
"Mother,
I cannot take it ill that you are angry.
I know the meaning of these actions now,
both good and bad. I had been young and blind.
How can I always keep to what is fair
while these sit here to put fear in me? — princes
from near and far whose interest is my ruin;

290   are any on my side?

                      But you should know
the suitors did not have their way, matching
the stranger here and Iros — for the stranger
beat him to the ground.

                      O Father Zeus!
Athena and Apollo! could I see
the suitors whipped like that! Courtyard and hall
strewn with our friends, too weak-kneed to get up,
chapfallen to their collarbones, the way

300   old Iros rolls his head there by the gate
as though he were pig-drunk! No energy
to stagger on his homeward path; no fight
left in his numb legs!"

                      Thus Penélopê
reproached her son, and he replied. Now, interrupting,
Eurýmakhos called out to her:

"Penélopê,
deep-minded queen, daughter of Ikários,
if all Akhaians in the land of Argos
310   only saw you now! What hundreds more
would join your suitors here to feast tomorrow!
Beauty like yours no woman had before,
or majesty, or mastery."

She answered:
"Eurýmakhos, my qualities—I know—
my face, my figure, all were lost or blighted
when the Akhaians crossed the sea to Troy,
Odysseus my lord among the rest.
If he returned, if he were here to care for me,
320   I might be happily renowned!
But grief instead heaven sent me—years of pain.
Can I forget?—the day he left this island,
enfolding my right hand and wrist in his,
he said:
'My lady, the Akhaian troops
will not easily make it home again
full strength, unhurt, from Troy. They say the Trojans
are fighters too; good lances and good bowmen,
horsemen, charioteers—and those can be
330   decisive when a battle hangs in doubt.
So whether God will send me back, or whether
I'll be a captive there, I cannot tell.
Here, then, you must attend to everything.
My parents in our house will be a care for you
as they are now, or more, while I am gone.
Wait for the beard to darken our boy's cheek;
then marry whom you will, and move away.'

The years he spoke of are now past; the night
comes when a bitter marriage overtakes me,
340   desolate as I am, deprived by Zeus
of all the sweets of life.
How galling, too,
to see newfangled manners in my suitors!
Others who go to court a gentlewoman,
daughter of a rich house, if they are rivals,
bring their own beeves and sheep along; her friends

ought to be feasted, gifts are due to her;
would any dare to live at her expense?"

Odysseus' heart laughed when he heard all this—
350 her sweet tones charming gifts out of the suitors
with talk of marriage, though she intended none.
Eupeithês' son, Antínoös, now addressed her:
"Ikários' daughter, O deep-minded queen!
If someone cares to make you gifts, accept them!
It is no courtesy to turn gifts away.
But we go neither to our homes nor elsewhere
until of all Akhaians here you take
the best man for your lord."

Pleased at this answer,
360 every man sent a squire to fetch a gift—
Antínoös, a wide resplendent robe,
embroidered fine, and fastened with twelve brooches,
pins pressed into sheathing tubes of gold;
Eurýmakhos, a necklace, wrought in gold,
with sunray pieces of clear glinting amber.
Eurýdamas' men came back with pendants,
ear-drops in triple clusters of warm lights;
and from the hoard of Lord Polýktor's son,
Peisándros, came a band for her white throat,
370 jewelled adornment. Other wondrous things
were brought as gifts from the Akhaian princes.
Penélopê then mounted the stair again,
her maids behind, with treasure in their arms.

And now the suitors gave themselves to dancing,
to harp and haunting song, as night drew on;
black night indeed came on them at their pleasure.
But three torch fires were placed in the long hall
to give them light. On hand were stores of fuel,
dry seasoned chips of resinous wood, split up
380 by the bronze hatchet blade—these were mixed in
among the flames to keep them flaring bright;
each housemaid of Odysseus took her turn.

Now he himself, the shrewd and kingly man,
approached and told them:

"Housemaids of Odysseus,
your master so long absent in the world,
go to the women's chambers, to your queen.
Attend her, make the distaff whirl, divert her,
stay in her room, comb wool for her.
390   I stand here
ready to tend these flares and offer light
to everyone. They cannot tire me out,
even if they wish to drink till Dawn.
I am a patient man."

But the women giggled,
glancing back and forth — laughed in his face;
and one smooth girl, Melántho, spoke to him
most impudently. She was Dólios' daughter,
taken as ward in childhood by Penélopê
400 who gave her playthings to her heart's content
and raised her as her own. Yet the girl felt
nothing for her mistress, no compunction,
but slept and made love with Eurýmakhos.
Her bold voice rang now in Odysseus' ears:
"You must be crazy, punch drunk, you old goat.
Instead of going out to find a smithy
to sleep warm in — or a tavern bench — you stay
putting your oar in, amid all our men.
Numbskull, not to be scared! The wine you drank
410 has clogged your brain, or are you always this way,
boasting like a fool? Or have you lost
your mind because you beat that tramp, that Iros?
Look out, or someone better may get up
and give you a good knocking about the ears
to send you out all bloody."

But Odysseus
glared at her under his brows and said:
                              "One minute:
let me tell Telémakhos how you talk
420 in hall, you slut; he'll cut your arms and legs off!"

This hard shot took the women's breath away
and drove them quaking to their rooms, as though
knives were behind: they felt he spoke the truth.
So there he stood and kept the firelight high

and looked the suitors over, while his mind
roamed far ahead to what must be accomplished.

They, for their part, could not now be still
or drop their mockery—for Athena wished
Odysseus mortified still more.

430   Eurýmakhos,
the son of Pólybos, took up the baiting,
angling for a laugh among his friends.

"Suitors of our distinguished queen," he said,
"hear what my heart would have me say.
                                    This man
comes with a certain aura of divinity
into Odysseus' hall. He shines.
                                 He shines
around the noggin, like a flashing light,
440 having no hair at all to dim his lustre."

Then turning to Odysseus, raider of cities,
he went on:
                   "Friend, you have a mind to work,
do you? Could I hire you to clear stones
from wasteland for me—you'll be paid enough—
collecting boundary walls and planting trees?
I'd give you a bread ration every day,
a cloak to wrap in, sandals for your feet.
Oh no: you learned your dodges long ago—
450 no honest sweat. You'd rather tramp the country
begging, to keep your hoggish belly full."

The master of many crafts replied:
                          "Eurýmakhos,
we two might try our hands against each other
in early summer when the days are long,
in meadow grass, with one good scythe for me
and one as good for you: we'd cut our way
down a deep hayfield, fasting to late evening.
Or we could try our hands behind a plow,
460 driving the best of oxen—fat, well-fed,
well-matched for age and pulling power, and say
four strips apiece of loam the share could break:
you'd see then if I cleft you a straight furrow.

Competition in arms? If Zeus Kroníon
roused up a scuffle now, give me a shield,
two spears, a dogskin cap with plates of bronze
to fit my temples, and you'd see me go
where the first rank of fighters lock in battle.
There would be no more jeers about my belly.
You thick-skinned menace to all courtesy!
You think you are a great man and a champion,
but up against few men, poor stuff, at that.
Just let Odysseus return, those doors
wide open as they are, you'd find too narrow
to suit you on your sudden journey out."

Now fury mounted in Eurýmakhos,
who scowled and shot back:

                              "Bundle of rags and lice!
By god, I'll make you suffer for your gall,
your insolent gabble before all our men."

He had his foot-stool out: but now Odysseus
took to his haunches by Amphínomos' knees,
fearing Eurýmakhos' missile, as it flew.
It clipped a wine steward on the serving hand,
so that his pitcher dropped with a loud clang
while he fell backward, cursing, in the dust.
In the shadowy hall a low sound rose — of suitors
murmuring to one another.

                              "Ai!" they said,
"This vagabond would have done well to perish
somewhere else, and make us no such rumpus.
Here we are, quarreling over tramps; good meat
and wine forgotten; good sense gone by the board."

Telémakhos, his young heart high, put in:
"Bright souls, alight with wine, you can no longer
hide the cups you've taken. Aye, some god
is goading you. Why not go home to bed? —
I mean when you are moved to. No one jumps
at my command."

                    Struck by his blithe manner,
the young men's teeth grew fixed in their under lips,
but now the son of Nísos, Lord Amphínomos
of Aretíadês, addressed them all:

470

480

490

500

"O friends, no ruffling replies are called for;
that was fair counsel.
                    Hands off the stranger, now,
and hands off any other servant here
in the great house of King Odysseus. Come,
let my own herald wet our cups once more,
510 we'll make an offering, and then to bed.
The stranger can be left behind in hall;
Telémakhos may care for him; he came
to Telémakhos' door, not ours."

                    This won them over.
The soldier Moulios, Doulíkhion herald,
comrade in arms of Lord Amphínomos,
mixed the wine and served them all. They tipped out
drops for the blissful gods, and drank the rest,
and when they had drunk their thirst away
520 they trailed off homeward drowsily to bed.

BOOK 19
RECOGNITIONS AND A DREAM

Now by Athena's side in the quiet hall
studying the ground for slaughter, Lord Odysseus
turned to Telémakhos.

                    "The arms," he said.
"Harness and weapons must be out of sight
in the inner room. And if the suitors miss them,
be mild; just say 'I had a mind to move them
out of the smoke. They seemed no longer
the bright arms that Odysseus left at home
10   when he went off to Troy. Here where the fire's
hot breath came, they had grown black and drear.
One better reason struck me, too:
suppose a brawl starts up when you've been drinking—
you might in madness let each other's blood,
and that would stain your feast, your courtship.
                              Iron

itself can draw men's hands.' "

                    Then he fell silent,
and Telémakhos obeyed his father's word.
20   He called Eurýkleia, the nurse, and told her:

"Nurse, go shut the women in their quarters
while I shift Father's armor back
to the inner rooms — these beautiful arms unburnished.
caked with black soot in his years abroad.
I was a child then. Well, I am not now.
I want them shielded from the draught and smoke."

And the old woman answered:
                                    "It is time, child,
you took an interest in such things. I wish
30   you'd put your mind on all your house and chattels.
But who will go along to hold a light?
You said no maids, no torch-bearers."

                            Telémakhos
looked at her and replied:
                            "Our friend here.
A man who shares my meat can bear a hand,
no matter how far he is from home."

                            He spoke so soldierly
her own speech halted on her tongue. Straight back
40   she went to lock the doors of the women's hall.
And now the two men sprang to work — father
and princely son, loaded with round helms
and studded bucklers, lifting the long spears,
while in their path Pallas Athena
held up a golden lamp of purest light.
Telémakhos at last burst out:
                            "Oh, Father,
here is a marvel! All around I see
the walls and roof beams, pedestals and pillars,
50   lighted as though by white fire blazing near.
One of the gods of heaven is in this place!"

Then said Odysseus, the great tactician,
"Be still: keep still about it: just remember it.
The gods who rule Olympos make this light.
You may go off to bed now. Here I stay
to test your mother and her maids again.
Out of her long grief she will question me."

Telémakhos went across the hall and out
under the light of torches — crossed the court
60   to the tower chamber where he had always slept.

Here now again he lay, waiting for dawn,
while in the great hall by Athena's side
Odysseus waited with his mind on slaughter.

Presently Penélopê from her chamber
stepped in her thoughtful beauty.
                                        So might Artemis
or golden Aphroditê have descended;
and maids drew to the hearth her own smooth chair
inlaid with silver whorls and ivory. The artisan
70 Ikmálios had made it, long before,
with a footrest in a single piece, and soft
upon the seat a heavy fleece was thrown.
Here by the fire the queen sat down. Her maids,
leaving their quarters, came with white arms bare
to clear the wine cups and the bread, and move
the trestle boards where men had lingered drinking.
Fiery ashes out of the pine-chip flares
they tossed, and piled on fuel for light and heat.
And now a second time Melántho's voice
80 rang brazen in Odysseus' ears:
                                        "Ah, stranger,
are you still here, so creepy, late at night
hanging about, looking the women over?
You old goat, go outside, cuddle your supper;
get out, or a torch may kindle you behind!"

At this Odysseus glared under his brows
and said:
                "Little devil, why pitch into me again?
Because I go unwashed and wear these rags,
90 and make the rounds? But so I must, being needy;
that is the way a vagabond must live.
And do not overlook this: in my time
I too had luck, lived well, stood well with men,
and gave alms, often, to poor wanderers
like him you see before you—aye, to all sorts,
no matter in what dire want. I owned
servants—many, I say—and all the rest
that goes with what men call prosperity.
But Zeus the son of Kronos brought me down.
100 Mistress, mend your ways, or you may lose
all this vivacity of yours. What if her ladyship
were stirred to anger? What if Odysseus came?—
and I can tell you, there is hope of that—

or if the man is done for, still his son
lives to be reckoned with, by Apollo's will.
None of you can go wantoning on the sly
and fool him now. He is too old for that."

Penélopê, being near enough to hear him,
spoke out sharply to her maid:

110   "Oh, shameless,
through and through! And do you think me blind,
blind to your conquest? It will cost your life.[139]
You knew I waited—for you heard me say it—
waited to see this man in hall and question him
about my lord; I am so hard beset."

She turned away and said to the housekeeper:
"Eurýnomê, a bench, a spread of sheepskin,
to put my guest at ease. Now he shall talk
and listen, and be questioned."

120   Willing hands
brought a smooth bench, and dropped a fleece upon it.
Here the adventurer and king sat down;
then carefully Penélopê began:
"Friend, let me ask you first of all:
who are you, where do you come from, of what nation
and parents were you born?"

                              And he replied:
"My lady, never a man in the wide world
should have a fault to find with you. Your name

130 has gone out under heaven like the sweet
honor of some god-fearing king, who rules
in equity over the strong: his black lands bear
both wheat and barley, fruit trees laden bright,
new lambs at lambing time—and the deep sea
gives great hauls of fish by his good strategy,
so that his folk fare well.

                              O my dear lady,
this being so, let it suffice to ask me
of other matters—not my blood, my homeland.

140 Do not enforce me to recall my pain.
My heart is sore; but I must not be found

---

[139] **It will . . . life:** Melántho's affair with Eurýmakhos put her in league with the suitors.

sitting in tears here, in another's house:
it is not well forever to be grieving.
One of the maids might say — or you might think —
I had got maudlin over cups of wine."

And Penélopê replied:
                        "Stranger, my looks,
my face, my carriage, were soon lost or faded
when the Akhaians crossed the sea to Troy,
150 Odysseus my lord among the rest.
If he returned, if he were here to care for me,
I might be happily renowned!
But grief instead heaven sent me — years of pain.
Sons of the noblest families on the islands,
Doulíkhion, Samê, wooded Zakýnthos,
with native Ithakans, are here to court me,
against my wish; and they consume this house.
Can I give proper heed to guest or suppliant
or herald on the realm's affairs?
160   How could I?
wasted with longing for Odysseus, while here
they press for marriage.
                       Ruses served my turn
to draw the time out — first a close-grained web
I had the happy thought to set up weaving
on my big loom in hall. I said, that day:
'Young men — my suitors, now my lord is dead,
let me finish my weaving before I marry,
or else my thread will have been spun in vain.
170 It is a shroud I weave for Lord Laërtês
when cold Death comes to lay him on his bier.
The country wives would hold me in dishonor
if he, with all his fortune, lay unshrouded.'
I reached their hearts that way, and they agreed.
So every day I wove on the great loom,
but every night by torchlight I unwove it;
and so for three years I deceived the Akhaians.
But when the seasons brought a fourth year on,
as long months waned, and the long days were spent,
180 through impudent folly in the slinking maids
they caught me — clamored up to me at night;
I had no choice then but to finish it.
And now, as matters stand at last,
I have no strength left to evade a marriage,
cannot find any further way; my parents

urge it upon me, and my son
will not stand by while they eat up his property.
He comprehends it, being a man full grown,
able to oversee the kind of house

190   Zeus would endow with honor.
                                        But you too
confide in me, tell me your ancestry.
You were not born of mythic oak or stone."

And the great master of invention answered:
"O honorable wife of Lord Odysseus,
must you go on asking about my family?
Then I will tell you, though my pain
be doubled by it: and whose pain would not
if he had been away as long as I have

200   and had hard roving in the world of men?
But I will tell you even so, my lady.

One of the great islands of the world
in midsea, in the winedark sea, is Krete:
spacious and rich and populous, with ninety
cities and a mingling of tongues.
Akhaians there are found, along with Kretan
hillmen of the old stock, and Kydonians,
Dorians in three blood-lines, Pelasgians—[140]
and one among their ninety towns is Knossos.[141]

210   Here lived King Minos whom great Zeus received
every ninth year in private council—Minos,
the father of my father, Deukálion.
Two sons Deukálion had: Idómeneus,
who went to join the Atreidai before Troy
in the beaked ships of war; and then myself,
Aithôn by name—a stripling next my brother.
But I saw with my own eyes at Knossos once
Odysseus.
                Gales had caught him off Cape Malea,

220   driven him southward on the coast of Krete
when he was bound for Troy. At Ámnisos,
hard by the holy cave of Eileithuía,[142]

---

[140] **Kydonians . . . Pelasgians:** Kydonians, Dorians, and Pelasgians represent the migrations of various peoples into the Greek peninsula.   [141] **Knossos:** Knossos, the cultural center of the Minoan civilization on Krete (Crete), was also the name of the great palace of King Minos.   [142] **Eileithuía:** The goddess of childbirth who had a shrine at Ámnisos, on the coast near Knossos.

he lay to, and dropped anchor, in that open
and rough roadstead riding out the blow.
Meanwhile he came ashore, came inland, asking
after Idómeneus: dear friends he said they were;
but now ten mornings had already passed,
ten or eleven, since my brother sailed.
So I played host and took Odysseus home,
230 saw him well lodged and fed, for we had plenty;
then I made requisitions—barley, wine,
and beeves for sacrifice—to give his company
abundant fare along with him.

                     Twelve days
they stayed with us, the Akhaians, while that wind
out of the north shut everyone inside—
even on land you could not keep your feet,
such fury was abroad. On the thirteenth,
when the gale dropped, they put to sea."

240 Now all these lies he made appear so truthful
she wept as she sat listening. The skin
of her pale face grew moist the way pure snow
softens and glistens on the mountains, thawed
by Southwind after powdering from the West,
and, as the snow melts, mountain streams run full:
so her white cheeks were wetted by these tears
shed for her lord—and he close by her side.
Imagine how his heart ached for his lady,
250 his wife in tears; and yet he never blinked;
his eyes might have been made of horn or iron
for all that she could see. He had this trick—
wept, if he willed to, inwardly.

                     Well, then,
as soon as her relieving tears were shed
she spoke once more:

               "I think that I shall say, friend,
give me some proof, if it is really true
that you were host in that place to my husband
with his brave men, as you declare. Come, tell me
260 the quality of his clothing, how he looked,
and some particular of his company."

Odysseus answered, and his mind ranged far:
"Lady, so long a time now lies between,
it is hard to speak of it. Here is the twentieth year

since that man left the island of my father.
But I shall tell what memory calls to mind.
A purple cloak, and fleecy, he had on—
a double thick one. Then, he wore a brooch
made of pure gold with twin tubes for the prongs,
270   and on the face a work of art: a hunting dog
pinning a spotted fawn in agony
between his forepaws—wonderful to see
how being gold, and nothing more, he bit
the golden deer convulsed, with wild hooves flying.
Odysseus' shirt I noticed, too—a fine
closefitting tunic like dry onion skin,
so soft it was, and shiny.
                              Women there,
many of them, would cast their eyes on it.
280   But I might add, for your consideration,
whether he brought these things from home, or whether
a shipmate gave them to him, coming aboard,
I have no notion: some regardful host
in another port perhaps it was. Affection
followed him—there were few Akhaians like him.
And I too made him gifts: a good bronze blade,
a cloak with lining and a broidered shirt,
and sent him off in his trim ship with honor.
A herald, somewhat older than himself,
290   he kept beside him; I'll describe this man:
round-shouldered, dusky, woolly-headed;
Eurýbates, his name was—and Odysseus
gave him preferment over the officers.
He had a shrewd head, like the captain's own."

Now hearing these details—minutely true—
she felt more strangely moved, and tears flowed
until she had tasted her salt grief again.
Then she found words to answer:
                                  "Before this
300   you won my sympathy, but now indeed
you shall be our respected guest and friend.
With my own hands I put that cloak and tunic
upon him—took them folded from their place—
and the bright brooch for ornament.
                                  Gone now,
I will not meet the man again

returning to his own home fields. Unkind
the fate that sent him young in the long ship
to see that misery at Ilion, unspeakable!"

310 And the master improviser answered:
                                         "Honorable
wife of Odysseus Laërtiadês,
you need not stain your beauty with these tears,
nor wear yourself out grieving for your husband.
Not that I can blame you. Any wife
grieves for the man she married in her girlhood,
lay with in love, bore children to — though he
may be no prince like this Odysseus,
whom they compare even to the gods. But listen:
320 weep no more, and listen:
I have a thing to tell you, something true.
I heard but lately of your lord's return,
heard that he is alive, not far away,
among Thesprótians in their green land
amassing fortune to bring home. His company
went down in shipwreck in the winedark sea
off the coast of Thrinákia. Zeus and Hêlios
held it against him that his men had killed
the kine of Hêlios. The crew drowned for this.
330 He rode the ship's keel. Big seas cast him up
on the island of Phaiákians, godlike men
who took him to their hearts. They honored him
with many gifts and a safe passage home,
or so they wished. Long since he should have been here,
but he thought better to restore his fortune
playing the vagabond about the world;
and no adventurer could beat Odysseus
at living by his wits — no man alive.
I had this from King Phaidôn of Thesprótia;
340 and, tipping wine out, Phaidôn swore to me
the ship was launched, the seamen standing by
to bring Odysseus to his land at last,
but I got out to sea ahead of him
by the king's order — as it chanced a freighter
left port for the grain bins of Doulíkhion.
Phaidôn, however, showed me Odysseus' treasure.
Ten generations of his heirs or more
could live on what lay piled in that great room.

> The man himself had gone up to Dodona
> 350   to ask the spelling leaves of the old oak
> what Zeus would have him do—how to return to Ithaka
> after so many years—by stealth or openly.
> You see, then, he is alive and well, and headed
> homeward now, no more to be abroad
> far from his island, his dear wife and son.
> Here is my sworn word for it. Witness this,
> god of the zenith, noblest of the gods,
> and Lord Odysseus' hearthfire, now before me:
> I swear these things shall turn out as I say.
> 360   Between this present dark and one day's ebb,
> after the wane, before the crescent moon,
> Odysseus will come."

> Penélopê,
> the attentive queen, replied to him:
> "Ah, stranger,
> if what you say could ever happen!
> You would soon know our love! Our bounty, too:
> men would turn after you to call you blessed.
> But my heart tells me what must be.
> 370   Odysseus will not come to me; no ship
> will be prepared for you. We have no master
> quick to receive and furnish out a guest
> as Lord Odysseus was.
> Or did I dream him?

> Maids, maids: come wash him, make a bed for him,
> bedstead and colored rugs and coverlets
> to let him lie warm into the gold of Dawn.
> In morning light you'll bathe him and anoint him
> so that he'll take his place beside Telémakhos
> 380   feasting in hall. If there be one man there
> to bully or annoy him that man wins
> no further triumph here, burn though he may.
> How will you understand me, friend, how find in me,
> more than in common women, any courage
> or gentleness, if you are kept in rags
> and filthy at our feast? Men's lives are short.
> The hard man and his cruelties will be
> cursed behind his back, and mocked in death.
> But one whose heart and ways are kind—of him

390　strangers will bear report to the wide world,
　　and distant men will praise him."

　　　　　　　　　　　　　Warily
　　Odysseus answered:
　　　　　　　　　　"Honorable lady,
　　wife of Odysseus Laërtiadês,
　　a weight of rugs and cover? Not for me.
　　I've had none since the day I saw the mountains
　　of Krete, white with snow, low on the sea line
　　fading behind me as the long oars drove me north.
400　Let me lie down tonight as I've lain often,
　　many a night unsleeping, many a time
　　afield on hard ground waiting for pure Dawn.
　　No: and I have no longing for a footbath
　　either: none of these maids will touch my feet,
　　unless there is an old one, old and wise,
　　one who has lived through suffering as I have:
　　I would not mind letting my feet be touched
　　by that old servant."

　　　　　　　　And Penélopê said:
410　"Dear guest, no foreign man so sympathetic
　　ever came to my house, no guest more likeable,
　　so wry and humble are the things you say.
　　I have an old maidservant ripe with years,
　　one who in her time nursed my lord. She took him
　　into her arms the hour his mother bore him.
　　Let her, then, wash your feet though she is frail.
　　Come here, stand by me, faithful Eurýkleia,
　　and bathe, bathe your master. I almost said,
　　for they are of an age, and now Odysseus'
420　feet and hands would be enseamed like his.
　　Men grow old soon in hardship."

　　　　　　　　　　　Hearing this,
　　the old nurse hid her face between her hands
　　and wept hot tears, and murmured:
　　　　　　　　　　　　　"Oh, my child!
　　I can do nothing for you! How Zeus hated you,
　　no other man so much! No use, great heart;
　　O faithful heart, the rich thighbones you burnt
　　to Zeus who plays in lightning—and no man

430 ever gave more to Zeus—with all your prayers
for a green age, a tall son reared to manhood.
There is no day of homecoming for you.
Stranger, some women in some far off place
perhaps have mocked my lord when he'd be home
as now these strumpets mock you here. No wonder
you would keep clear of all their whorishness
and have no bath. But here am I. The queen
Penélopê, Ikários' daughter, bids me;
so let me bathe your feet to serve my lady—
440 to serve you, too.

                              My heart within me stirs,
mindful of something. Listen to what I say:
strangers have come here, many through the years,
but no one ever came, I swear, who seemed
so like Odysseus—body, voice and limbs—
as you do."

                   Ready for this, Odysseus answered:
"Old woman, that is what they say. All who have seen
the two of us remark how like we are,
450 as you yourself have said, and rightly, too."

Then he kept still, while the old nurse filled up
her basin glittering in firelight; she poured
cold water in, then hot.

                              But Lord Odysseus
whirled suddenly from the fire to face the dark.
The scar: he had forgotten that. She must not
handle his scarred thigh, or the game was up.
But when she bared her lord's leg, bending near,
she knew the groove at once.

460   An old wound
a boar's white tusk inflicted, on Parnassos[143]
years ago. He had gone hunting there
in company with his uncles and Autólykos,
his mother's father—a great thief and swindler
by Hermês'[144] favor, for Autólykos pleased him
with burnt offerings of sheep and kids. The god
acted as his accomplice. Well, Autólykos
on a trip to Ithaka

---

[143] **Parnassos:** The mountains rising above Apollo's famous shrine at Delphi.   [144] **Hermês:** In addition to his other tasks as messenger god, Hermês was patron of thieves and trickery.

arrived just after his daughter's boy was born.
470 In fact, he had no sooner finished supper
than Nurse Eurýkleia put the baby down
in his own lap and said:
                    "It is for you, now,
to choose a name for him, your child's dear baby;
the answer to her prayers."

                 Autólykos replied:
"My son-in-law, my daughter, call the boy
by the name I tell you. Well you know, my hand
has been against the world of men and women;
480 odium and distrust[145] I've won. Odysseus
should be his given name. When he grows up,
when he comes visiting his mother's home
under Parnassos, where my treasures are,
I'll make him gifts and send him back rejoicing."

Odysseus in due course went for the gifts,
and old Autólykos and his sons embraced him
with welcoming sweet words; and Amphithéa,
his mother's mother, held him tight and kissed him,
kissed his head and his fine eyes.
490   The father
called on his noble sons to make a feast,
and going about it briskly they led in
an ox of five years, whom they killed and flayed
and cut in bits for roasting on the skewers
with skilled hands, with care; then shared it out.
So all the day until the sun went down
they feasted to their hearts' content. At evening,
after the sun was down and dusk had come,
they turned to bed and took the gift of sleep.

500 When the young Dawn spread in the eastern sky
her finger tips of rose, the men and dogs
went hunting, taking Odysseus. They climbed
Parnassos' rugged flank mantled in forest,
entering amid high windy folds at noon
when Hêlios beat upon the valley floor
and on the winding Ocean whence he came.

---

[145] **odium and distrust:** By referring to himself as odious (*odyssamenos*), Autólykos is playing with the name Odysseus, meaning someone who is angry or wrathful.

With hounds questing ahead, in open order,
the sons of Autólykos went down a glen,
Odysseus in the lead, behind the dogs,
510   pointing his long-shadowing spear.
                                        Before them
a great boar lay hid in undergrowth,
in a green thicket proof against the wind
or sun's blaze, fine soever the needling sunlight,
impervious too to any rain, so dense
that cover was, heaped up with fallen leaves.
Patter of hounds' feet, men's feet, woke the boar
as they came up—and from his woody ambush
with razor back bristling and raging eyes
520   he trotted and stood at bay. Odysseus,
being on top of him, had the first shot,
lunging to stick him; but the boar
had already charged under the long spear.
He hooked aslant with one white tusk and ripped out
flesh above the knee, but missed the bone.
Odysseus' second thrust went home by luck,
his bright spear passing through the shoulder joint;
and the beast fell, moaning as life pulsed away.
Autólykos' tall sons took up the wounded,
530   working skillfully over the Prince Odysseus
to bind his gash, and with a rune° they stanched   magic spell
the dark flow of blood. Then downhill swiftly
they all repaired to the father's house, and there
tended him well—so well they soon could send him,
with Grandfather Autólykos' magnificent gifts,
rejoicing, over sea to Ithaka.
His father and the Lady Antikleía
welcomed him, and wanted all the news
of how he got his wound; so he spun out
540   his tale, recalling how the boar's white tusk
caught him when he was hunting on Parnassos.

This was the scar the old nurse[146] recognized;
she traced it under her spread hands, then let go,
and into the basin fell the lower leg
making the bronze clang, sloshing the water out.
Then joy and anguish seized her heart; her eyes

---

[146] **the old nurse:** Nurse Eurýkleia, daughter of Ops, was bought by Laërtês to be Odysseus's nurse, and later became Telémakhos's nurse.

filled up with tears; her throat closed, and she whispered,
with hand held out to touch his chin:

                              "Oh yes!

550 *You are Odysseus!* Ah, dear child! I could not
see you until now—not till I knew
my master's very body with my hands!"

Her eyes turned to Penélopê with desire
to make her lord, her husband, known—in vain,
because Athena had bemused the queen,
so that she took no notice, paid no heed.
At the same time Odysseus' right hand
gripped the old throat; his left hand pulled her near,
and in her ear he said:

560   "Will you destroy me,
nurse, who gave me milk at your own breast?
Now with a hard lifetime behind I've come
in the twentieth year home to my father's island.
You found me out, as the chance was given you.
Be quiet; keep it from the others, else
I warn you, and I mean it, too,
if by my hand god brings the suitors down
I'll kill you, nurse or not, when the time comes—
when the time comes to kill the other women."

570 Eurýkleia kept her wits and answered him:
"Oh, what mad words are these you let escape you!
Child, you know my blood, my bones are yours;
no one could whip this out of me. I'll be
a woman turned to stone, iron I'll be.
And let me tell you too—mind now—if god
cuts down the arrogant suitors by your hand,
I can report to you on all the maids,
those who dishonor you, and the innocent."

But in response the great tactician said:
580 "Nurse, no need to tell me tales of these.
I will have seen them, each one, for myself.
Trust in the gods, be quiet, hold your peace."

Silent, the old nurse went to fetch more water,
her basin being all spilt.

                       When she had washed
and rubbed his feet with golden oil, he turned,
dragging his bench again to the fire side

for warmth, and hid the scar under his rags.
Penélopê broke the silence, saying:
590   "Friend,
allow me one brief question more. You know,
the time for bed, sweet rest, is coming soon,
if only that warm luxury of slumber
would come to enfold us, in our trouble. But for me
my fate at night is anguish and no rest.
By day being busy, seeing to my work,
I find relief sometimes from loss and sorrow;
but when night comes and all the world's abed
I lie in mine alone, my heart thudding,
600   while bitter thoughts and fears crowd on my grief.
Think how Pandáreos' daughter, pale forever,
sings as the nightingale[147] in the new leaves
through those long quiet hours of night,
on some thick-flowering orchard bough in spring;
how she rills out and tilts her note, high now, now low,
mourning for Itylos whom she killed in madness—
her child, and her lord Zêthos' only child.
My forlorn thought flows variable as her song,
wondering: shall I stay beside my son
610   and guard my own things here, my maids, my hall,
to honor my lord's bed and the common talk?
Or had I best join fortunes with a suitor,
the noblest one, most lavish in his gifts?
Is it now time for that?
My son being still a callow boy forbade
marriage, or absence from my lord's domain;
but now the child is grown, grown up, a man,
he, too, begins to pray for my departure,
aghast at all the suitors gorge on.

620   Listen:
interpret me this dream: From a water's edge
twenty fat geese have come to feed on grain
beside my house. And I delight to see them.
But now a mountain eagle with great wings
and crooked beak storms in to break their necks

---

[147] **sings as the nightingale:** Aedon, the daughter of Pandáreos, was married to Zethos. Jealous of her sister-in-law Niobe's several sons, Aedon intended to kill Niobe's eldest son but by mistake killed her own son, Itylos. Turned into a nightingale by Zeus, Aedon mourns her terrible deed through the nightingale's song.

and strew their bodies here. Away he soars
into the bright sky; and I cry aloud —
all this in dream — I wail and round me gather
softly braided Akhaian women mourning
630 because the eagle killed my geese.
                                        Then down
out of the sky he drops to a cornice beam
with mortal voice telling me not to weep.
'Be glad,' says he, 'renowned Ikários' daughter:
here is no dream but something real as day,
something about to happen. All those geese
were suitors, and the bird was I. See now,
I am no eagle but your lord come back
to bring inglorious death upon them all!'
640 As he said this, my honeyed slumber left me.
Peering through half-shut eyes, I saw the geese
in hall, still feeding at the self-same trough."

The master of subtle ways and straight replied:
"My dear, how can you choose to read the dream
differently? Has not Odysseus himself
shown you what is to come? Death to the suitors,
sure death, too. Not one escapes his doom."

Penélopê shook her head and answered:
                                        "Friend,
650 many and many a dream is mere confusion,
a cobweb of no consequence at all.
Two gates for ghostly dreams there are: one gateway
of honest horn, and one of ivory.
Issuing by the ivory gate are dreams
of glimmering illusion, fantasies,
but those that come through solid polished horn
may be borne out, if mortals only know them.
I doubt it came by horn, my fearful dream —
too good to be true, that, for my son and me.
660 But one thing more I wish to tell you: listen
carefully. It is a black day, this that comes.
Odysseus' house and I are to be parted.
I shall decree a contest for the day.
We have twelve axe heads. In his time, my lord
could line them up, all twelve, at intervals
like a ship's ribbing; then he'd back away

a long way off and whip an arrow through.[148]
Now I'll impose this trial on the suitors.
The one who easily handles and strings the bow
670   and shoots through all twelve axes I shall marry,
whoever he may be—then look my last
on this my first love's beautiful brimming house.
But I'll remember, though I dream it only."

Odysseus said:
            "Dear honorable lady,
wife of Odysseus Laërtiadês,
let there be no postponement of the trial.
Odysseus, who knows the shifts of combat,
will be here: aye, he'll be here long before
680   one of these lads can stretch or string that bow
or shoot to thread the iron!"

                        Grave and wise,
Penélopê replied:
            "If you were willing
to sit with me and comfort me, my friend,
no tide of sleep would ever close my eyes.
But mortals cannot go forever sleepless.
This the undying gods decree for all
who live and die on earth, kind furrowed earth.
690   Upstairs I go, then, to my single bed,
my sighing bed, wet with so many tears
after my Lord Odysseus took ship
to see that misery at Ilion, unspeakable.
Let me rest there, you here. You can stretch out
on the bare floor, or else command a bed."

So she went up to her chamber softly lit,
accompanied by her maids. Once there, she wept
for Odysseus, her husband, till Athena
cast sweet sleep upon her eyes.

---

[148] **whip an arrow through:** A number of theories have arisen to explain how this archery contest was performed. This translation suggests that the wooden handles are missing and that it is the empty sockets of ax heads that are lined up.

BOOK 20
SIGNS AND A VISION

Outside in the entry way he made his bed—
raw oxhide spread on level ground, and heaped up
fleeces, left from sheep the Akhaians killed.
And when he had lain down, Eurýnomê
flung out a robe to cover him. Unsleeping
the Lord Odysseus lay, and roved in thought
to the undoing of his enemies.
                     Now came a covey of women
laughing as they slipped out, arm in arm,
10 as many a night before, to the suitors' beds;
and anger took him like a wave to leap
into their midst and kill them, every one—
or should he let them all go hot to bed
one final night? His heart cried out within him
the way a brach[149] with whelps between her legs
would howl and bristle at a stranger—so
the hackles of his heart rose at that laughter.
Knocking his breast he muttered to himself:
"Down; be steady. You've seen worse, that time
20 the Kyklops like a rockslide ate your men
while you looked on. Nobody, only guile,
got you out of that cave alive."
                     His rage
held hard in leash, submitted to his mind,
while he himself rocked, rolling from side to side,
as a cook turns a sausage, big with blood
and fat, at a scorching blaze, without a pause,
to broil it quick: so he rolled left and right,
casting about to see how he, alone,
30 against the false outrageous crowd of suitors
could press the fight.
                     And out of the night sky
Athena came to him; out of the nearby dark
in body like a woman; came and stood
over his head to chide him:

---

[149] **brach:** Female dog; bitch.

"Why so wakeful,
most forlorn of men? Here is your home,
there lies your lady; and your son is here,
as fine as one could wish a son to be."

40 Odysseus looked up and answered:
"Aye,
goddess, that much is true; but still
I have some cause to fret in this affair.
I am one man; how can I whip those dogs?
They are always here in force. Neither
is that the end of it, there's more to come.
If by the will of Zeus and by your will
I killed them all, where could I go for safety?
Tell me that!"

50   And the grey-eyed goddess said:
"Your touching faith! Another man would trust
some villainous mortal, with no brains — and what
am I? Your goddess-guardian to the end
in all your trials. Let it be plain as day:
if fifty bands of men surrounded us
and every sword sang for your blood,
you could make off still with their cows and sheep.
Now you, too, go to sleep. This all night vigil
wearies the flesh. You'll come out soon enough
60 on the other side of trouble."

            Raining soft
sleep on his eyes, the beautiful one was gone
back to Olympos. Now at peace, the man
slumbered and lay still, but not his lady:
Wakeful again with all her cares, reclining
in the soft bed, she wept and cried aloud
until she had had her fill of tears, then spoke
in prayer first to Artemis:
                    "O gracious
70 divine lady Artemis, daughter of Zeus,
if you could only make an end now quickly,
let the arrow fly, stop my heart,
or if some wind could take me by the hair
up into running cloud, to plunge in tides of Ocean,

as hurricane winds took Pandareos' daughters[150]
when they were left at home alone. The gods
had sapped their parents' lives. But Aphroditê
fed those children honey, cheese, and wine,
and Hêra gave them looks and wit, and Artemis,
80 pure Artemis, gave lovely height, and wise
Athena made them practised in her arts—
till Aphroditê in glory walked on Olympos,
begging for each a happy wedding day
from Zeus, the lightning's joyous king, who knows
all fate of mortals, fair and foul—
but even at that hour the cyclone winds
had ravished them away
to serve the loathsome Furies.

                        Let me be
90 blown out by the Olympians! Shot by Artemis,
I still might go and see amid the shades
Odysseus in the rot of underworld.
No coward's eye should light by my consenting!
Evil may be endured when our days pass
in mourning, heavy-hearted, hard beset,
if only sleep reign over nighttime, blanketing
the world's good and evil from our eyes.
But not for me: dreams too my demon sends me.
Tonight the image of my lord came by
100 as I remember him with troops. O strange
exultation! I thought him real, and not a dream."

Now as the Dawn appeared all stitched in gold,
the queen's cry reached Odysseus at his waking,
so that he wondered, half asleep: it seemed
she knew him, and stood near him! Then he woke
and picked his bedding up to stow away
on a chair in the mégaron. The oxhide pad
he took outdoors. There, spreading wide his arms,

---

[150] **Pandareos' daughters:** Pandareos stole a golden dog made by Hephaistos from a shrine of Zeus. After Pandareos and his wife were killed by the gods, Aphroditê, Hêra, and Artemis brought up their three daughters, until they were killed for their father's offense by winds directed by the Furies. This story represents a different tradition from the one in Book 19, in which Pandareos's daughter was changed into a nightingale.

he prayed:

110   "O Father Zeus, if over land and water,
after adversity, you willed to bring me home,
let someone in the waking house give me good augury,
and a sign be shown, too, in the outer world."

He prayed thus, and the mind of Zeus in heaven
heard him. He thundered out of bright Olympos
down from above the cloudlands in reply —
a rousing peal for Odysseus. Then a token
came to him from a woman grinding flour
in the court nearby. His own handmills were there,
120 and twelve maids had the job of grinding out
whole grain and barley meal, the pith of men.
Now all the rest, their bushels ground, were sleeping;
one only, frail and slow, kept at it still.
She stopped, stayed her hand, and her lord heard
the omen from her lips:
                    "Ah, Father Zeus
almighty over gods and men!
A great bang of thunder that was, surely,
out of the starry sky, and not a cloud in sight.
130 It is your nod to someone. Hear me, then,
make what I say come true:
let this day be the last the suitors feed
so dainty in Odysseus' hall!
They've made me work my heart out till I drop,
grinding barley. May they feast no more!"

The servant's prayer, after the cloudless thunder
of Zeus, Odysseus heard with lifting heart,
sure in his bones that vengeance was at hand.
Then other servants, wakening, came down
140 to build and light a fresh fire at the hearth.
Telémakhos, clear-eyed as a god, awoke,
put on his shirt and belted on his sword,
bound rawhide sandals under his smooth feet,
and took his bronze-shod lance. He came and stood
on the broad sill of the doorway, calling Eurýkleia:
"Nurse, dear Nurse, how did you treat our guest?
Had he a supper and a good bed? Has he lain
uncared for still? My mother is like that,

perverse for all her cleverness:
150 she'd entertain some riff-raff, and turn out
a solid man."

The old nurse answered him:
"I would not be so quick to accuse her, child.
He sat and drank here while he had a mind to;
food he no longer hungered for, he said—
for she did ask him. When he thought of sleeping,
she ordered them to make a bed. Poor soul!
Poor gentleman! So humble and so miserable,
he would accept no bed with rugs to lie on,
160 but slept on sheepskins and a raw oxhide
in the entry way. We covered him ourselves."

Telémakhos left the hall, hefting his lance,
with two swift flickering hounds for company,
to face the island Akhaians in the square;
and gently born Eurýkleia the daughter
of Ops Peisenóridês, called to the maids:
"Bestir yourselves! you have your brooms, go sprinkle
the rooms and sweep them, robe the chairs in red,
sponge off the tables till they shine.
170 Wash out the winebowls and two-handled cups.
You others go fetch water from the spring;
no loitering; come straight back. Our company
will be here soon, morning is sure to bring them;
everyone has a holiday today."

The women ran to obey her—twenty girls
off to the spring with jars for dusky water,
the rest at work inside. Then tall woodcutters
entered to split up logs for the hearth fire,
the water carriers returned; and on their heels
180 arrived the swineherd, driving three fat pigs,
chosen among his pens. In the wide court
he let them feed, and said to Odysseus kindly:
"Friend, are they more respectful of you now,
or still insulting you?"

Replied Odysseus:
"The young men, yes. And may the gods requite

those insolent puppies for the game they play
in a home not their own. They have no decency."

During this talk, Melánthios the goatherd
190 came in, driving goats for the suitors' feast,
with his two herdsmen. Under the portico
they tied the animals, and Melánthios
looked at Odysseus with a sneer. Said he:
                                "Stranger,
I see you mean to stay and turn our stomachs
begging in this hall. Clear out, why don't you?
Or will you have to taste a bloody beating
before you see the point? Your begging ways
nauseate everyone. There are feasts elsewhere."

200 Odysseus answered not a word, but grimly
shook his head over his murderous heart.
A third man came up now: Philoítios
the cattle foreman, with an ox behind him
and fat goats for the suitors. Ferrymen
had brought these from the mainland, as they bring
travellers, too — whoever comes along.
Philoítios tied the beasts under the portico
and joined the swineherd.

                         "Who is this," he said,
210 "Who is the new arrival at the manor?
Akhaian? or what else does he claim to be?
Where are his family and fields of home?
Down on his luck, all right: carries himself like a captain.
How the immortal gods can change and drag us down
once they begin to spin dark days for us! —
Kings and commanders, too."

                         Then he stepped over
and took Odysseus by the right hand, saying:
"Welcome, Sir. May good luck lie ahead
220 at the next turn. Hard times you're having, surely.
O Zeus! no god is more berserk in heaven
if gentle folk, whom you yourself begot,[151]
you plunge in grief and hardship without mercy!
Sir, I began to sweat when I first saw you,

---

[151] **you yourself begot:** Attributing fatherhood to Zeus was a way of paying a compliment.

and tears came to my eyes, remembering
Odysseus: rags like these he may be wearing
somewhere on his wanderings now—
I mean, if he's alive still under the sun.
But if he's dead and in the house of Death,
230 I mourn Odysseus. He entrusted cows to me
in Kephallênia,[152] when I was knee high,
and now his herds are numberless, no man else
ever had cattle multiply like grain.
But new men tell me I must bring my beeves
to feed them, who care nothing for our prince,
fear nothing from the watchful gods. They crave
partition of our lost king's land and wealth.
My own feelings keep going round and round
upon this tether: can I desert the boy
240 by moving, herds and all, to another country,
a new life among strangers? Yet it's worse
to stay here, in my old post, herding cattle
for upstarts.
           I'd have gone long since,
gone, taken service with another king; this shame
is no more to be borne; but I keep thinking
my own lord, poor devil, still might come
and make a rout of suitors in his hall."

Odysseus, with his mind on action, answered:
250 "Herdsman, I make you out to be no coward
and no fool: I can see that for myself.
So let me tell you this. I swear by Zeus
all highest, by the table set for friends,
and by your king's hearthstone to which I've come,
Odysseus will return. You'll be on hand
to see, if you care to see it,
how those who lord it here will be cut down."

The cowman said:
               "Would god it all came true!
260 You'd see the fight that's in me!"

                    Then Eumaios
echoed him, and invoked the gods, and prayed

---

[152] **Kephallênia:** An island near Ithaka, the modern Cephalonia.

that his great-minded master should return.
While these three talked, the suitors in the field
had come together plotting—what but death
for Telémakhos?—when from the left an eagle
crossed high with a rockdove in his claws.[153]

Amphínomos got up. Said he, cutting them short:
"Friends, no luck lies in that plan for us,
270   no luck, knifing the lad. Let's think of feasting."

A grateful thought, they felt, and walking on
entered the great hall of the hero Odysseus,
where they all dropped their cloaks on chairs or couches
and made a ritual slaughter, knifing sheep,
fat goats and pigs, knifing the grass-fed steer.
Then tripes were broiled and eaten. Mixing bowls
were filled with wine. The swineherd passed out cups,
Philoítios, chief cowherd, dealt the loaves
into the panniers, Melánthios poured wine,
280   and all their hands went out upon the feast.

Telémakhos placed his father to advantage
just at the door sill of the pillared hall,
setting a stool there and a sawed-off table,
gave him a share of tripes, poured out his wine
in a golden cup, and said:
                    "Stay here, sit down
to drink with our young friends. I stand between you
and any cutting word or cuffing hand
from any suitor. Here is no public house
290   but the old home of Odysseus, my inheritance.
Hold your tongues then, gentlemen, and your blows,
and let no wrangling start, no scuffle either."

The others, disconcerted, bit their lips
at the ring in the young man's voice. Antínoös,
Eupeithês' son, turned round to them and said:
"It goes against the grain, my lords, but still
I say we take this hectoring by Telémakhos.
You know Zeus balked at it, or else

---

[153] **an eagle crossed high . . . claws:** An ill omen.

we might have shut his mouth a long time past,
300   the silvery speaker."

                    But Telémakhos
paid no heed to what Antínoös said.

Now public heralds wound through Ithaka
leading a file of beasts for sacrifice, and islanders
gathered under the shade trees of Apollo,
in the precinct of the Archer°—while in hall   Apollo
the suitors roasted mutton and fat beef
on skewers, pulling off the fragrant cuts;
and those who did the roasting served Odysseus
310   a portion equal to their own, for so
Telémakhos commanded.
                         But Athena
had no desire now to let the suitors
restrain themselves from wounding words and acts.
Laërtês' son again must be offended.
There was a scapegrace[154] fellow in the crowd
named Ktésippos, a Samian, rich beyond
all measure, arrogant with riches, early
and late a bidder for Odysseus' queen.
320   Now this one called attention to himself:
"Hear me, my lords, I have a thing to say.
Our friend has had his fair share from the start
and that's polite; it would be most improper
if we were cold to guests of Telémakhos—
no matter what tramp turns up. Well then, look here,
let me throw in my own small contribution.
He must have prizes to confer, himself,
on some brave bathman or another slave
here in Odysseus' house."

330   His hand went backward
and, fishing out a cow's foot from the basket,
he let it fly.
             Odysseus rolled his head
to one side softly, ducking the blow, and smiled
a crooked smile with teeth clenched. On the wall

---

[154] **scapegrace:** Graceless; unprincipled.

the cow's foot struck and fell. Telémakhos
blazed up:
                    "Ktésippos, lucky for you, by heaven,
not to have hit him! He took care of himself,
340 else you'd have had my lance-head in your belly;
no marriage, but a grave instead on Ithaka
for your father's pains.
                              You others, let me see
no more contemptible conduct in my house!
I've been awake to it for a long time — by now
I know what is honorable and what is not.
Before, I was a child. I can endure it
while sheep are slaughtered, wine drunk up, and bread —
can one man check the greed of a hundred men? —
350 but I will suffer no more viciousness.
Granted you mean at last to cut me down:
I welcome that — better to die than have
humiliation always before my eyes,
the stranger buffeted, and the serving women
dragged about, abused in a noble house."

They quieted, grew still, under his lashing,
and after a long silence, Ageláos,
Damástor's son, spoke to them all:
                                      "Friends, friends,
360 I hope no one will answer like a fishwife.
What has been said is true. Hands off this stranger,
he is no target, neither is any servant
here in the hall of King Odysseus.
Let me say a word, though, to Telémakhos
and to his mother, if it please them both:
as long as hope remained in you to see
Odysseus, that great gifted man, again,
you could not be reproached for obstinacy,
tying the suitors down here; better so,
370 if still your father fared the great sea homeward.
How plain it is, though, now, he'll come no more!
Go sit then by your mother, reason with her,
tell her to take the best man, highest bidder,
and you can have and hold your patrimony,
feed on it, drink it all, while she
adorns another's house."

                    Keeping his head,
Telémakhos replied:

"By Zeus Almighty,
380 Ageláos, and by my father's sufferings,
far from Ithaka, whether he's dead or lost,
I make no impediment to Mother's marriage.
'Take whom you wish,' I say, 'I'll add my dowry.'
But can I pack her off against her will
from her own home? Heaven forbid!"

　　　　　　　　　　At this,
Pallas Athena touched off in the suitors
a fit of laughter, uncontrollable.
She drove them into nightmare, till they wheezed
390 and neighed as though with jaws no longer theirs,
while blood defiled their meat, and blurring tears
flooded their eyes, heart-sore with woe to come.
Then said the visionary, Theoklýmenos:
"O lost sad men, what terror is this you suffer?
Night shrouds you to the knees, your heads, your faces;
dry retch of death runs round like fire in sticks;
your cheeks are streaming; these fair walls and pedestals
are dripping crimson blood. And thick with shades
is the entry way, the courtyard thick with shades
400 passing athirst toward Érebos, into the dark,
the sun is quenched in heaven, foul mist hems us in . . ."

The young men greeted this with shouts of laughter,
and Eurýmakhos, the son of Pólybos, crowed:
"The mind of our new guest has gone astray.
Hustle him out of doors, lads, into the sunlight;
he finds it dark as night inside!"

The man of vision looked at him and said:
"When I need help, I'll ask for it, Eurýmakhos.
I have my eyes and ears, a pair of legs,
410 and a straight mind, still with me. These will do
to take me out. Damnation and black night
I see arriving for yourselves: no shelter,
no defence for any in this crowd—
fools and vipers in the king's own hall."

With this he left that handsome room and went
home to Peiraios, who received him kindly.
The suitors made wide eyes at one another
and set to work provoking Telémakhos
with jokes about his friends. One said, for instance:

420 "Telémakhos, no man is a luckier host
when it comes to what the cat dragged in. What burning
eyes your beggar had for bread and wine!
But not for labor, not for a single heave—
he'd be a deadweight on a field. Then comes
this other, with his mumbo-jumbo. Boy,
for your own good, I tell you, toss them both
into a slave ship for the Sikels.° That would pay you."   Sicilians

Telémakhos ignored the suitors' talk.
He kept his eyes in silence on his father,
430 awaiting the first blow. Meanwhile
the daughter of Ikários, Penélopê,
had placed her chair to look across and down
on father and son at bay; she heard the crowd,
and how they laughed as they resumed their dinner,
a fragrant feast, for many beasts were slain—
but as for supper, men supped never colder
than these, on what the goddess and the warrior
were even then preparing for the suitors,
whose treachery had filled that house with pain.

Book 21
The Test of the Bow

Upon Penélopê, most worn in love and thought,
Athena cast a glance like a grey sea
lifting her. Now to bring the tough bow out and bring
the iron blades. Now try those dogs at archery
to usher bloody slaughter in.
          So moving stairward
the queen took up a fine doorhook of bronze,
ivory-hafted, smooth in her clenched hand,
and led her maids down to a distant room,
10 a storeroom where the master's treasure lay:
bronze, bar gold, black iron forged and wrought.
In this place hung the double-torsion bow
and arrows in a quiver, a great sheaf—
quills of groaning.
          In the old time in Lakedaimon[155]

---

[155] **Lakedaimon:** The region of Sparta.

her lord had got these arms from Íphitos,
Eurýtos'[156] son. The two met in Messenia[157]
at Ortílokhos' table, on the day
Odysseus claimed a debt owed by that realm—
20 sheep stolen by Messenians out of Ithaka
in their long ships, three hundred head, and herdsmen.
Seniors of Ithaka and his father sent him
on that far embassy when he was young.
But Íphitos had come there tracking strays,
twelve shy mares, with mule colts yet unweaned.
And a fatal chase they led him over prairies
into the hands of Heraklês. That massive
son of toil and mortal son of Zeus
murdered his guest[158] at wine in his own house—
30 inhuman, shameless in the sight of heaven—
to keep the mares and colts in his own grange.
Now Íphitos, when he knew Odysseus, gave him
the master bowman's arm; for old Eurýtos
had left it on his deathbed to his son.
In fellowship Odysseus gave a lance
and a sharp sword. But Heraklês killed Íphitos
before one friend could play host to the other.
And Lord Odysseus would not take the bow
in the black ships to the great war at Troy.
40 As a keepsake he put it by:
it served him well at home in Ithaka.

Now the queen reached the storeroom door and halted.
Here was an oaken sill, cut long ago
and sanded clean and bedded true. Foursquare
the doorjambs and the shining doors were set
by the careful builder. Penélopê untied the strap
around the curving handle, pushed her hook
into the slit, aimed at the bolts inside
and shot them back. Then came a rasping sound
50 as those bright doors the key had sprung gave way—
a bellow like a bull's vaunt in a meadow—
followed by her light footfall entering
over the plank floor. Herb-scented robes

---

[156] **Eurýtos:** A famous archer; Íphitos provides the bow that Odysseus uses to slaughter the suitors.
[157] **Messenia:** A coastal region in southwestern Greece.   [158] **murdered his guest:** In a fit of madness and revenge Heraklês murdered Íphitos, angered because Eurýtos had refused to give him the prize, his daughter Iole, for an archery contest he had won.

lay there in chests, but the lady's milkwhite arms
went up to lift the bow down from a peg
in its own polished bowcase.

> Now Penélopê
sank down, holding the weapon on her knees,
and drew her husband's great bow out, and sobbed
60 and bit her lip and let the salt tears flow.
Then back she went to face the crowded hall,
tremendous bow in hand, and on her shoulder hung
the quiver spiked with coughing death. Behind her
maids bore a basket full of axeheads, bronze
and iron implements for the master's game.
Thus in her beauty she approached the suitors,
and near a pillar of the solid roof
she paused, her shining veil across her cheeks,
her maids on either hand and still,
70 then spoke to the banqueters:

> "My lords, hear me:
suitors indeed, you commandeered this house
to feast and drink in, day and night, my husband
being long gone, long out of mind. You found
no justification for yourselves — none
except your lust to marry me. Stand up, then:
we now declare a contest for that prize.
Here is my lord Odysseus' hunting bow.
Bend and string it if you can. Who sends an arrow
80 through iron axe-helve sockets, twelve in line?
I join my life with his, and leave this place, my home,
my rich and beautiful bridal house, forever
to be remembered, though I dream it only."

Then to Eumaios:
> "Carry the bow forward.

Carry the blades."

> Tears came to the swineherd's eyes
as he reached out for the big bow. He laid it
down at the suitors' feet. Across the room
90 the cowherd sobbed, knowing the master's weapon.
Antínoös growled, with a glance at both:

> "Clods.
They go to pieces over nothing.

> You two, there,
why are you sniveling? To upset the woman

even more? Has she not pain enough
over her lost husband? *Sit down.*
Get on with dinner quietly, or cry about it
outside, if you must. Leave us the bow.
100 A clean-cut game, it looks to me.
Nobody bends that bowstave easily
in this company. Is there a man here
made like Odysseus? I remember him
from childhood: I can see him even now."

That was the way he played it, hoping inwardly
to span the great horn bow with corded gut
and drill the iron with his shot — he, Antínoös,
destined to be the first of all to savor
blood from a biting arrow at his throat,
110 a shaft drawn by the fingers of Odysseus
whom he had mocked and plundered, leading on
the rest, his boon companions. Now they heard
a gay snort of laughter from Telémakhos,
who said then brilliantly:
                          "A queer thing, that!
Has Zeus almighty made me a half-wit?
For all her spirit, Mother has given in,
promised to go off with someone — and
is that amusing? What am I cackling for?
120 Step up, my lords, contend now for your prize.
There is no woman like her in Akhaia,
not in old Argos, Pylos, or Mykênê,
neither in Ithaka nor on the mainland,
and you all know it without praise of mine.
Come on, no hanging back, no more delay
in getting the bow bent. Who's the winner?
I myself should like to try that bow.
Suppose I bend it and bring off the shot,
my heart will be less heavy, seeing the queen my mother
130 go for the last time from this house and hall,
if I who stay can do my father's feat."

He moved out quickly, dropping his crimson cloak,
and lifted sword and sword belt from his shoulders.
His preparation was to dig a trench,
heaping the earth in a long ridge beside it
to hold the blades half-bedded. A taut cord
aligned the socket rings. And no one there
but looked on wondering at his workmanship,

for the boy had never seen it done.

140   He took his stand then
on the broad door sill to attempt the bow.
Three times he put his back into it and sprang it,
three times he had to slack off. Still he meant
to string that bow and pull for the needle shot.
A fourth try and he had it all but strung—
when a stiffening in Odysseus made him check.
Abruptly then he stopped and turned and said:
"Blast and damn it, must I be a milksop
all my life? Half-grown, all thumbs,
150 no strength or knack at arms, to defend myself
if someone picks a fight with me.
                                    Take over,
O my elders and betters, try the bow,
run off the contest."

                        And he stood the weapon
upright against the massy-timbered door
with one arrow across the horn aslant,
then went back to his chair. Antínoös
gave the word:
160   "Now one man at a time
rise and go forward. Round the room in order;
left to right from where they dip the wine."

As this seemed fair enough, up stood Leódês
the son of Oinops. This man used to find
visions for them in the smoke of sacrifice.
He kept his chair well back, retired by the winebowl,
for he alone could not abide their manners
but sat in shame for all the rest. Now it was he
who had first to confront the bow,
170 standing up on the broad door sill. He failed.
The bow unbending made his thin hands yield,
no muscle in them. He gave up and said:
"Friends, I cannot. Let the next man handle it.
Here is a bow to break the heart and spirit
of many strong men. Aye. And death is less
bitter than to live on and never have
the beauty that we came here laying siege to
so many days. Resolute, are you still,
to win Odysseus' lady Penélopê?
180 Pit yourselves against the bow, and look

among Akhaians for another's daughter.
Gifts will be enough to court and take her.
Let the best offer win."

         With this Leódês
thrust the bow away from him, and left it
upright against the massy-timbered door,
with one arrow aslant across the horn.
As he went down to his chair he heard Antínoös'
voice rising:

190   "What is that you say?
It makes me burn. You cannot string the weapon,
so 'Here is a bow to break the heart and spirit
of many strong men.' Crushing thought!
You were not born — you never had it in you —
to pull that bow or let an arrow fly.
But here are men who can and will."

He called out to the goatherd, Melánthios:
"Kindle a fire there, be quick about it,
draw up a big bench with a sheepskin on it,
200 and bring a cake of lard out of the stores.
Contenders from now on will heat and grease the bow.
We'll try it limber, and bring off the shot."

Melánthios darted out to light a blaze,
drew up a bench, threw a big sheepskin over it,
and brought a cake of lard. So one by one
the young men warmed and greased the bow for bending,
but not a man could string it. They were whipped.
Antínoös held off; so did Eurýmakhos,
suitors in chief, by far the ablest there.

210 Two men had meanwhile left the hall:
swineherd and cowherd, in companionship,
one downcast as the other. But Odysseus
followed them outdoors, outside the court,
and coming up said gently:
         "You, herdsman,
and you, too, swineherd, I could say a thing to you,
or should I keep it dark?
         No, no; speak,
my heart tells me. Would you be men enough
220 to stand by Odysseus if he came back?

Suppose he dropped out of a clear sky, as I did?
Suppose some god should bring him?
Would you bear arms for him, or for the suitors?"

The cowherd said:
                "Ah, let the master come!
Father Zeus, grant our old wish! Some courier
guide him back! Then judge what stuff is in me
and how I manage arms!"

               Likewise Eumaios
230 fell to praying all heaven for his return,
so that Odysseus, sure at least of these,
told them:
             "I am at home, for I am he.
I bore adversities, but in the twentieth year
I am ashore in my own land. I find
the two of you, alone among my people,
longed for my coming. Prayers I never heard
except your own that I might come again.
So now what is in store for you I'll tell you:
240 If Zeus brings down the suitors by my hand
I promise marriages to both, and cattle,
and houses built near mine. And you shall be
brothers-in-arms of my Telémakhos.
Here, let me show you something else, a sign
that I am he, that you can trust me, look:
this old scar from the tusk wound that I got
boar hunting on Parnassos—
Autólykos' sons and I."

              Shifting his rags
250 he bared the long gash. Both men looked, and knew,
and threw their arms around the old soldier, weeping,
kissing his head and shoulders. He as well
took each man's head and hands to kiss, then said—
to cut it short, else they might weep till dark—
"Break off, no more of this.
Anyone at the door could see and tell them.
Drift back in, but separately at intervals
after me.
         Now listen to your orders:
260 when the time comes, those gentlemen, to a man,
will be dead against giving me bow or quiver.

Defy them. Eumaios, bring the bow
and put it in my hands there at the door.
Tell the women to lock their own door tight.
Tell them if someone hears the shock of arms
or groans of men, in hall or court, not one
must show her face, but keep still at her weaving.
Philoítios, run to the outer gate and lock it.
Throw the cross bar and lash it."

270   He turned back
into the courtyard and the beautiful house
and took the stool he had before. They followed
one by one, the two hands loyal to him.

Eurýmakhos had now picked up the bow.
He turned it round, and turned it round
before the licking flame to warm it up,
but could not, even so, put stress upon it
to jam the loop over the tip
                         though his heart groaned to bursting.
280 Then he said grimly:
                         "Curse this day.
What gloom I feel, not for myself alone,
and not only because we lose that bride.
Women are not lacking in Akhaia,
in other towns, or on Ithaka. No, the worst
is humiliation—to be shown up for children
measured against Odysseus—we who cannot
even hitch the string over his bow.
What shame to be repeated of us, after us!"

290 Antínoös said:
                         "Come to yourself. You know
that is not the way this business ends.
Today the islanders held holiday, a holy day,
no day to sweat over a bowstring.
                                 Keep your head.
Postpone the bow. I say we leave the axes
planted where they are. No one will take them.
No one comes to Odysseus' hall tonight.
Break out good wine and brim our cups again,
300   we'll keep the crooked bow safe overnight,
order the fattest goats Melánthios has
brought down tomorrow noon, and offer thighbones burning

to Apollo, god of archers,
while we try out the bow and make the shot."

As this appealed to everyone, heralds came
pouring fresh water for their hands, and boys
filled up the winebowls. Joints of meat went round,
fresh cuts for all, while each man made his offering,
tilting the red wine to the gods, and drank his fill.
310   Then spoke Odysseus, all craft and gall:
"My lords, contenders for the queen, permit me:
a passion in me moves me to speak out.
I put it to Eurýmakhos above all
and to that brilliant prince, Antínoös. Just now
how wise his counsel was, to leave the trial
and turn your thoughts to the immortal gods! Apollo
will give power tomorrow to whom he wills.
But let me try my hand at the smooth bow!
Let me test my fingers and my pull
320   to see if any of the oldtime kick is there,
or if thin fare and roving took it out of me."

Now irritation beyond reason swept them all,
since they were nagged by fear that he could string it.
Antínoös answered, coldly and at length:
"You bleary vagabond, no rag of sense is left you.
Are you not coddled here enough, at table
taking meat with gentlemen, your betters,
denied nothing, and listening to our talk?
When have we let a tramp hear all our talk?
330   The sweet goad of wine has made you rave!
Here is the evil wine can do
to those who swig it down. Even the centaur[159]
Eurýtion, in Peiríthoös' hall
among the Lapíthai, came to a bloody end
because of wine; wine ruined him: it crazed him,
drove him wild for rape in that great house.
The princes cornered him in fury, leaping on him
to drag him out and crop his ears and nose.
Drink had destroyed his mind, and so he ended

---

[159] centaur: Half horse, half man, centaurs represent the uncivilized people of Thessaly. In this famous incident, centaurs were invited to the wedding of Peiríthoös; they got drunk and tried to rape the women. In this
version of the story, a single centaur, Eurýtion, attempts to carry off the bride.

340 in that mutilation—fool that he was.
Centaurs and men made war for this,
but the drunkard first brought hurt upon himself.

The tale applies to you: I promise you
great trouble if you touch that bow. You'll come by
no indulgence in our house; kicked down
into a ship's bilge, out to sea you go,
and nothing saves you. Drink, but hold your tongue.
Make no contention here with younger men."

At this the watchful queen Penélopê
350 interposed:
         "Antínoös, discourtesy
to a guest of Telémakhos—whatever guest—
that is not handsome. What are you afraid of?
Suppose this exile put his back into it
and drew the great bow of Odysseus—
could he then take me home to be his bride?
You know he does not imagine that! No one
need let that prospect weigh upon his dinner!
How very, very improbable it seems."

360 It was Eurýmakhos who answered her:
"Penélopê, O daughter of Ikários,
most subtle queen, we are not given to fantasy.
No, but our ears burn at what men might say
and women, too. We hear some jackal whispering:
'How far inferior to the great husband
her suitors are! Can't even budge his bow!
Think of it; and a beggar, out of nowhere,
strung it quick and made the needle shot!'
That kind of disrepute we would not care for."

370 Penélopê replied, steadfast and wary:
"Eurýmakhos, you have no good repute
in this realm, nor the faintest hope of it—
men who abused a prince's house for years,
consumed his wine and cattle. Shame enough.
Why hang your heads over a trifle now?
The stranger is a big man, well-compacted,
and claims to be of noble blood.
Ai!
Give him the bow, and let us have it out!

380 What I can promise him I will:
    if by the kindness of Apollo he prevails
    he shall be clothed well and equipped.
    A fine shirt and a cloak I promise him;
    a lance for keeping dogs at bay, or men;
    a broadsword; sandals to protect his feet;
    escort, and freedom to go where he will."

Telémakhos now faced her and said sharply:
"Mother, as to the bow and who may handle it
or not handle it, no man here
390 has more authority than I do — not one lord
    of our own stony Ithaka nor the islands lying
    east toward Elis: no one stops me if I choose
    to give these weapons outright to my guest.
    Return to your own hall. Tend your spindle.
    Tend your loom. Direct your maids at work.
    This question of the bow will be for men to settle,
    most of all for me. I am master here."

She gazed in wonder, turned, and so withdrew,
her son's clearheaded bravery in her heart.
400 But when she had mounted to her rooms again
    with all her women, then she fell to weeping
    for Odysseus, her husband. Grey-eyed Athena
    presently cast a sweet sleep on her eyes.

The swineherd had the horned bow in his hands
moving toward Odysseus, when the crowd
in the banquet hall broke into an ugly din,
shouts rising from the flushed young men:
                              "Ho! Where
do you think you are taking that, you smutty slave?"

410 "What is this dithering?"

                    "We'll toss you back alone
among the pigs, for your own dogs to eat,
if bright Apollo nods and the gods are kind!"

He faltered, all at once put down the bow, and stood
in panic, buffeted by waves of cries,
hearing Telémakhos from another quarter
shout:
"Go on, take him the bow!

                                Do you obey this pack?
420 You will be stoned back to your hills! Young as I am
     my power is over you! I wish to God
     I had as much the upper hand of these!
     There would be suitors pitched like dead rats
     through our gate, for the evil plotted here!"

     Telémakhos' frenzy struck someone as funny,
     and soon the whole room roared with laughter at him,
     so that all tension passed. Eumaios picked up
     bow and quiver, making for the door,
     and there he placed them in Odysseus' hands.
430 Calling Eurýkleia to his side he said:
                                "Telémakhos
     trusts you to take care of the women's doorway.
     Lock it tight. If anyone inside
     should hear the shock of arms or groans of men
     in hall or court, not one must show her face,
     but go on with her weaving."

                         The old woman
     nodded and kept still. She disappeared
     into the women's hall, bolting the door behind her.
440 Philoítios left the house now at one bound,
     catlike, running to bolt the courtyard gate.
     A coil of deck-rope of papyrus fiber
     lay in the gateway; this he used for lashing,
     and ran back to the same stool as before,
     fastening his eyes upon Odysseus.
                         And Odysseus took his time,
     turning the bow, tapping it, every inch,
     for borings that termites might have made
     while the master of the weapon was abroad.
450 The suitors were now watching him, and some
     jested among themselves:

                    "A bow lover!"

     "Dealer in old bows!"

                    "Maybe he has one like it
     at home!"

               "Or has an itch to make one for himself."

"See how he handles it, the sly old buzzard!"

And one disdainful suitor added this:
"May his fortune grow an inch for every inch he bends it!"

460 But the man skilled in all ways of contending,
satisfied by the great bow's look and heft,
like a musician, like a harper, when
with quiet hand upon his instrument
he draws between his thumb and forefinger
a sweet new string upon a peg: so effortlessly
Odysseus in one motion strung the bow.
Then slid his right hand down the cord and plucked it,
so the taut gut vibrating hummed and sang
a swallow's note.

470   In the hushed hall it smote the suitors
and all their faces changed. Then Zeus thundered
overhead, one loud crack for a sign.
And Odysseus laughed within him that the son
of crooked-minded Kronos had flung that omen down.
He picked one ready arrow from his table
where it lay bare: the rest were waiting still
in the quiver for the young men's turn to come.
He nocked it, let it rest across the handgrip,
and drew the string and grooved butt of the arrow,
480 aiming from where he sat upon the stool.

                              Now flashed
arrow from twanging bow clean as a whistle
through every socket ring, and grazed not one,
to thud with heavy brazen head beyond.

                              Then quietly
Odysseus said:
                "Telémakhos, the stranger
you welcomed in your hall has not disgraced you.
I did not miss, neither did I take all day
490 stringing the bow. My hand and eye are sound,
not so contemptible as the young men say.
The hour has come to cook their lordships' mutton—
supper by daylight. Other amusements later,
with song and harping that adorn a feast."

He dropped his eyes and nodded, and the prince
Telémakhos, true son of King Odysseus,
belted his sword on, clapped hand to his spear,

and with a clink and glitter of keen bronze
stood by his chair, in the forefront near his father.

BOOK 22
DEATH IN THE GREAT HALL

Now shrugging off his rags the wiliest fighter of the islands
leapt and stood on the broad door sill, his own bow in his hand.
He poured out at his feet a rain of arrows from the quiver
and spoke to the crowd:
                              "So much for that. Your clean-cut game is over.
Now watch me hit a target that no man has hit before,
if I can make this shot. Help me, Apollo."

He drew to his fist the cruel head of an arrow for Antínoös
just as the young man leaned to lift his beautiful drinking cup,
10   embossed, two-handled, golden: the cup was in his fingers:
the wine was even at his lips: and did he dream of death?
How could he? In that revelry amid his throng of friends
who would imagine a single foe—though a strong foe indeed—
could dare to bring death's pain on him and darkness on his eyes?
Odysseus' arrow hit him under the chin
and punched up to the feathers through his throat.

Backward and down he went, letting the winecup fall
from his shocked hand. Like pipes his nostrils jetted
crimson runnels, a river of mortal red,
20   and one last kick upset his table
knocking the bread and meat to soak in dusty blood.
Now as they craned to see their champion where he lay
the suitors jostled in uproar down the hall,
everyone on his feet. Wildly they turned and scanned
the walls in the long room for arms; but not a shield,
not a good ashen spear was there for a man to take and throw.
All they could do was yell in outrage at Odysseus:
"Foul! to shoot at a man! That was your last shot!"

"Your own throat will be slit for this!"

30   "Our finest lad is down!

You killed the best on Ithaka."

"Buzzards will tear your eyes out!"

For they imagined as they wished that it was a wild shot,
an unintended killing—fools, not to comprehend
they were already in the grip of death.
But glaring under his brows Odysseus answered:
"You yellow dogs, you thought I'd never make it
home from the land of Troy. You took my house to plunder,
twisted my maids to serve your beds. You dared
40   bid for my wife while I was still alive.
Contempt was all you had for the gods who rule wide heaven,
contempt for what men say of you hereafter.
Your last hour has come. You die in blood."

As they all took this in, sickly green fear
pulled at their entrails, and their eyes flickered
looking for some hatch or hideaway from death.
Eurýmakhos alone could speak. He said:
"If you are Odysseus of Ithaka come back,
all that you say these men have done is true.
50   Rash actions, many here, more in the countryside.
But here he lies, the man who caused them all.
Antínoös was the ringleader; he whipped us on
to do these things. He cared less for a marriage
than for the power Kronion has denied him
as king of Ithaka. For that
he tried to trap your son and would have killed him.
He is dead now and has his portion. Spare
your own people. As for ourselves, we'll make
restitution of wine and meat consumed,
60   and add, each one, a tithe of twenty oxen
with gifts of bronze and gold to warm your heart.
Meanwhile we cannot blame you for your anger."

Odysseus glowered under his black brows
and said:
            "Not for the whole treasure of your fathers,
all you enjoy, lands, flocks, or any gold
put up by others, would I hold my hand.
There will be killing till the score is paid.
You forced yourselves upon this house. Fight your way out,

70 or run for it, if you think you'll escape death.
    I doubt one man of you skins by."

    They felt their knees fail, and their hearts—but heard
    Eurýmakhos for the last time rallying them.

    "Friends," he said, "the man is implacable.
    Now that he's got his hands on bow and quiver
    he'll shoot from the big door stone there
    until he kills us to the last man.
                  Fight, I say,
    let's remember the joy of it. Swords out!
80 Hold up your tables to deflect his arrows.
    After me, everyone: rush him where he stands.
    If we can budge him from the door, if we can pass
    into the town, we'll call out men to chase him.
    This fellow with his bow will shoot no more."

    He drew his own sword as he spoke, a broadsword of fine bronze,
    honed like a razor on either edge. Then crying hoarse and loud
    he hurled himself at Odysseus. But the kingly man let fly
    an arrow at that instant, and the quivering feathered butt
    sprang to the nipple of his breast as the barb stuck in his liver.
90 The bright broadsword clanged down. He lurched and fell aside,
    pitching across his table. His cup, his bread and meat,
    were spilt and scattered far and wide, and his head slammed on the ground.
    Revulsion, anguish in his heart, with both feet kicking out,
    he downed his chair, while the shrouding wave of mist closed on his eyes.

    Amphínomos now came running at Odysseus,
    broadsword naked in his hand. He thought to make
    the great soldier give way at the door.
    But with a spear throw from behind Telémakhos hit him
    between the shoulders, and the lancehead drove
100 clear through his chest. He left his feet and fell
    forward, thudding, forehead against the ground.
    Telémakhos swerved around him, leaving the long dark spear
    planted in Amphínomos. If he paused to yank it out
    someone might jump him from behind or cut him down with a sword
    at the moment he bent over. So he ran—ran from the tables
    to his father's side and halted, panting, saying:

"Father let me bring you a shield and spear,
a pair of spears, a helmet.
I can arm on the run myself; I'll give
110   outfits to Eumaios and this cowherd.
Better to have equipment."

                    Said Odysseus:
"Run then, while I hold them off with arrows
as long as the arrows last. When all are gone
if I'm alone they can dislodge me."

                              Quick
upon his father's word Telémakhos
ran to the room where spears and armor lay.
He caught up four light shields, four pairs of spears,
120   four helms of war high-plumed with flowing manes,
and ran back, loaded down, to his father's side.
He was the first to pull a helmet on
and slide his bare arm in a buckler strap.
The servants armed themselves, and all three took their stand
beside the master of battle.
                         While he had arrows
he aimed and shot, and every shot brought down
one of his huddling enemies.
But when all barbs had flown from the bowman's fist,
130   he leaned his bow in the bright entry way
beside the door, and armed: a four-ply shield
hard on his shoulder, and a crested helm,
horsetailed, nodding stormy upon his head,
then took his tough and bronze-shod spears.
                                   The suitors
who held their feet, no longer under bowshot,
could see a window high in a recess of the wall,
a vent, lighting the passage to the storeroom.
This passage had one entry, with a door,
140   at the edge of the great hall's threshold, just outside.

Odysseus told the swineherd to stand over
and guard this door and passage. As he did so,
a suitor named Ageláos asked the others:
"Who will get a leg up on that window
and run to alarm the town? One sharp attack
and this fellow will never shoot again."

His answer
came from the goatherd, Melánthios:

"No chance, my lord.

150 The exit into the courtyard is too near them,
too narrow. One good man could hold that portal
against a crowd. No: let me scale the wall
and bring your arms out of the storage chamber.
Odysseus and his son put them indoors,
I'm sure of it; not outside."

The goatish goatherd
clambered up the wall, toes in the chinks,
and slipped through to the storeroom. Twelve light shields,
twelve spears he took, and twelve thick-crested helms,
160 and handed all down quickly to the suitors.
Odysseus, when he saw his adversaries
girded and capped and long spears in their hands
shaken at him, felt his knees go slack,
his heart sink, for the fight was turning grim.
He spoke rapidly to his son:
"Telémakhos, one of the serving women
is tipping the scales against us in this fight,
or maybe Melánthios."

But sharp and clear
170 Telémakhos said:

"It is my own fault, Father,
mine alone. The storeroom door—I left it
wide open. They were more alert than I.
Eumaios, go and lock that door,
and bring back word if a woman is doing this
or Mélanthios, Dólios' son. More likely he."

Even as they conferred, Melánthios
entered the storeroom for a second load,
and the swineherd at the passage entry saw him.
180 He cried out to his lord:

"Son of Laërtês,
Odysseus, master mariner and soldier,
there he goes, the monkey, as we thought,
there he goes into the storeroom.
Let me hear your will:
put a spear through him—I hope I am the stronger—

or drag him here to pay for his foul tricks
against your house?"

Odysseus said:

190   "Telémakhos and I
will keep these gentlemen in hall, for all their urge to leave.
You two go throw him into the storeroom, wrench his arms
and legs behind him, lash his hands and feet
to a plank, and hoist him up to the roof beams.
Let him live on there suffering at his leisure."

The two men heard him with appreciation
and ducked into the passage. Melánthios,
rummaging in the chamber, could not hear them
as they came up; nor could he see them freeze
200 like posts on either side the door.
He turned back with a handsome crested helmet
in one hand, in the other an old shield
coated with dust — a shield Laërtês bore
soldiering in his youth. It had lain there for years,
and the seams on strap and grip had rotted away.
As Melánthios came out the two men sprang,
jerked him backward by the hair, and threw him.
Hands and feet they tied with a cutting cord
behind him, so his bones ground in their sockets,
210 just as Laërtês' royal son commanded.
Then with a whip of rope they hoisted him
in agony up a pillar to the beams,
and — O my swineherd — you were the one to say:
"Watch through the night up there, Melánthios.
An airy bed is what you need.
You'll be awake to see the primrose Dawn
when she goes glowing from the streams of Ocean
to mount her golden throne.
                              No oversleeping
220 the hour for driving goats to feed the suitors."

They stooped for helm and shield and left him there
contorted, in his brutal sling,
and shut the doors, and went to join Odysseus
whose mind moved through the combat now to come.
Breathing deep, and snorting hard, they stood
four at the entry, facing two score men.
But now into the gracious doorway stepped
Zeus's daughter Athena. She wore the guise of Mentor,

and Odysseus appealed to her in joy:
230 "O Mentor, join me in this fight! Remember
how all my life I've been devoted to you,
friend of my youth!"

                For he guessed it was Athena,
Hope of Soldiers. Cries came from the suitors,
and Ageláos, Damástor's son, called out:
"Mentor, don't let Odysseus lead you astray
to fight against us on his side.
Think twice: we are resolved—and we will do it—
after we kill them, father and son,
240 you too will have your throat slit for your pains
if you make trouble for us here. It means your life.
Your life—and cutting throats will not be all.
Whatever wealth you have, at home, or elsewhere,
we'll mingle with Odysseus' wealth. Your sons
will be turned out, your wife and daughters
banished from the town of Ithaka."

Athena's anger grew like a storm wind as he spoke
until she flashed out at Odysseus:
                    "Ah, what a falling off!
250 Where is your valor, where is the iron hand
that fought at Troy for Helen, pearl of kings,
no respite and nine years of war? How many foes
your hand brought down in bloody play of spears?
What stratagem but yours took Priam's town?
How is it now that on your own door sill,
before the harriers of your wife, you curse your luck
not to be stronger?
                Come here, cousin, stand by me,
and you'll see action! In the enemies' teeth
260 learn how Mentor, son of Álkimos,
repays fair dealing!"

                For all her fighting words
she gave no overpowering aid—not yet;
father and son must prove their mettle still.
Into the smoky air under the roof
the goddess merely darted to perch on a blackened beam—
no figure to be seen now but a swallow.

Command of the suitors had fallen to Ageláos.
With him were Eurýnomos, Amphímedon,

270 Demoptólemos, Peisándros, Pólybos,
the best of the lot who stood to fight for their lives
after the streaking arrows downed the rest.
Ageláos rallied them with his plan of battle:
"Friends, our killer has come to the end of his rope,
and much good Mentor did him, that blowhard, dropping in.
Look, only four are left to fight, in the light there at the door.
No scattering of shots, men, no throwing away good spears;
we six will aim a volley at Odysseus alone,
and may Zeus grant us the glory of a hit.
280 If he goes down, the others are no problem."

At his command, then, "Ho!" they all let fly
as one man. But Athena spoiled their shots.
One hit the doorpost of the hall, another
stuck in the door's thick timbering, still others
rang on the stone wall, shivering hafts of ash.
Seeing his men unscathed, royal Odysseus
gave the word for action.

        "Now I say, friends,
the time is overdue to let them have it.
290 Battlespoil they want from our dead bodies
to add to all they plundered here before."

Taking aim over the steadied lanceheads
they all let fly together. Odysseus killed
Demoptólemos; Telémakhos
killed Eurýadês; the swineherd, Élatos;
and Peisándros went down before the cowherd.
As these lay dying, biting the central floor,
their friends gave way and broke for the inner wall.
The four attackers followed up with a rush
300 to take spears from the fallen men.

        Re-forming,
the suitors threw again with all their strength,
but Athena turned their shots, or all but two.
One hit a doorpost in the hall, another
stuck in the door's thick timbering, still others
rang on the stone wall, shivering hafts of ash.
Amphímedon's point bloodied Telémakhos'
wrist, a superficial wound, and Ktésippos'
long spear passing over Eumaios' shield
310 grazed his shoulder, hurtled on and fell.

No matter: with Odysseus the great soldier
the wounded threw again. And Odysseus raider of cities
struck Eurýdamas down. Telémakhos
hit Amphímedon, and the swineherd's shot
killed Pólybos. But Ktésippos, who had last evening thrown
a cow's hoof at Odysseus, got the cowherd's heavy cast
full in the chest—and dying heard him say:
"You arrogant joking bastard!
Clown, will you, like a fool, and parade your wit?
320 Leave jesting to the gods who do it better.
This will repay your cow's-foot courtesy
to a great wanderer come home."

                           The master
of the black herds had answered Ktésippos.
Odysseus, lunging at close quarters, put a spear
through Ageláos, Damastor's son. Telémakhos
hit Leókritos from behind and pierced him,
kidney to diaphragm. Speared off his feet,
he fell face downward on the ground.

330 At this moment that unmanning thunder cloud,
the aegis,[160] Athena's shield,
took form aloft in the great hall.

                          And the suitors mad with fear
at her great sign stampeded like stung cattle by a river
when the dread shimmering gadfly strikes in summer,
in the flowering season, in the long-drawn days.
After them the attackers wheeled, as terrible as falcons
from eyries in the mountains veering over and diving down
with talons wide unsheathed on flights of birds,
340 who cower down the sky in chutes and bursts along the valley—
but the pouncing falcons grip their prey, no frantic wing avails,
and farmers love to watch those beaked hunters.
So these now fell upon the suitors in that hall,
turning, turning to strike and strike again,
while torn men moaned at death, and blood ran smoking
over the whole floor.
                    Now there was one
who turned and threw himself at Odysseus' knees—
Leódês, begging for his life:

---

[160] **aegis:** The breastplate or shield with Medusa's head on it, used by Athena and Zeus; it caused panic among their enemies.

350   "Mercy,
mercy on a suppliant, Odysseus!
Never by word or act of mine, I swear,
was any woman troubled here. I told the rest
to put an end to it. They would not listen,
would not keep their hands from brutishness,
and now they are all dying like dogs for it.
I had no part in what they did: my part
was visionary—reading the smoke of sacrifice.
Scruples go unrewarded if I die."

360 The shrewd fighter frowned over him and said:
"You were diviner to this crowd? How often
you must have prayed my sweet day of return
would never come, or not for years!—and prayed
to have my dear wife, and beget children on her.
No plea like yours could save you
from this hard bed of death. Death it shall be!"

He picked up Ageláos' broadsword
from where it lay, flung by the slain man,
and gave Leódês' neck a lopping blow
370 so that his head went down to mouth in dust.

One more who had avoided furious death
was the son of Terpis, Phêmios, the minstrel,
singer by compulsion to the suitors.
He stood now with his harp, holy and clear,
in the wall's recess, under the window, wondering
if he should flee that way to the courtyard altar,
sanctuary of Zeus, the Enclosure God.
Thighbones in hundreds had been offered there
by Laërtês and Odysseus. No, he thought;
380 the more direct way would be best—to go
humbly to his lord. But first to save
his murmuring instrument he laid it down
carefully between the winebowl and a chair,
then he betook himself to Lord Odysseus,
clung hard to his knees, and said:
                        "Mercy,
mercy on a suppliant, Odysseus!
My gift is song for men and for the gods undying.
My death will be remorse for you hereafter.
390 No one taught me: deep in my mind a god

shaped all the various ways of life in song.
And I am fit to make verse in your company
as in the god's. Put aside lust for blood.
Your own dear son Telémakhos can tell you,
never by my own will or for love
did I feast here or sing amid the suitors.
They were too strong, too many; they compelled me."

Telémakhos in the elation of battle
heard him. He at once called to his father:
400   "Wait: that one is innocent: don't hurt him.
And we should let our herald live—Medôn;
he cared for me from boyhood. Where is *he?*
Has he been killed already by Philoítios
or by the swineherd? Else he got an arrow
in that first gale of bowshots down the room."

Now this came to the ears of prudent Medôn
under the chair where he had gone to earth,
pulling a new-flayed bull's hide over him.
Quiet he lay while blinding death passed by.
410   Now heaving out from under
he scrambled for Telémakhos' knees and said:
"Here I am, dear prince; but rest your spear!
Tell your great father not to see in me
a suitor for the sword's edge—one of those
who laughed at you and ruined his property!"

The lord of all the tricks of war surveyed
this fugitive and smiled. He said:
"Courage: my son has dug you out and saved you.
Take it to heart, and pass the word along:
420   fair dealing brings more profit in the end.
Now leave this room. Go and sit down outdoors
where there's no carnage, in the court,
you and the poet with his many voices,
while I attend to certain chores inside."

At this the two men stirred and picked their way
to the door and out, and sat down at the altar,
looking around with wincing eyes
as though the sword's edge hovered still.
And Odysseus looked around him, narrow-eyed,
430   for any others who had lain hidden

while death's black fury passed.
                                    In blood and dust
he saw that crowd all fallen, many and many slain.

Think of a catch that fishermen haul in to a halfmoon bay
in a fine-meshed net from the white-caps of the sea:
how all are poured out on the sand, in throes for the salt sea,
twitching their cold lives away in Hêlios' fiery air:
so lay the suitors heaped on one another.

Odysseus at length said to his son:
440 "Go tell old Nurse I'll have a word with her.
What's to be done now weighs on my mind."

Telémakhos knocked at the women's door and called:
"Eurýkleia, come out here! Move, old woman.
You kept your eye on all our servant girls.
Jump, my father is here and wants to see you."

His call brought no reply, only the doors
were opened, and she came. Telémakhos
led her forward. In the shadowy hall
full of dead men she found his father
450 spattered and caked with blood like a mountain lion
when he has gorged upon an ox, his kill—
with hot blood glistening over his whole chest,
smeared on his jaws, baleful and terrifying—
even so encrimsoned was Odysseus
up to his thighs and armpits. As she gazed
from all the corpses to the bloody man
she raised her head to cry over his triumph,
but felt his grip upon her, checking her.
Said the great soldier then:
460   "Rejoice
inwardly. No crowing aloud, old woman.
To glory over slain men is no piety.
Destiny and the gods' will vanquished these,
and their own hardness. They respected no one,
good or bad, who came their way.
For this, and folly, a bad end befell them.
Your part is now to tell me of the women,
those who dishonored me, and the innocent."

His own old nurse Eurýkleia said:
470   "I will, then.

Child, you know you'll have the truth from me.
Fifty all told they are, your female slaves,
trained by your lady and myself in service,
wool carding and the rest of it, and taught
to be submissive. Twelve went bad,
flouting me, flouting Penélopê, too.
Telémakhos being barely grown, his mother
would never let him rule the serving women—
but you must let me go to her lighted rooms
480 and tell her. Some god sent her a drift of sleep."

But in reply the great tactician said:
"Not yet. Do not awake her. Tell those women
who were the suitors' harlots to come here."

She went back on this mission through his hall.
Then he called Telémakhos to his side
and the two herdsmen. Sharply Odysseus said:
"These dead must be disposed of first of all.
Direct the women. Tables and chairs will be
scrubbed with sponges, rinsed and rinsed again.
490 When our great room is fresh and put in order,
take them outside, these women,
between the roundhouse and the palisade,
and hack them with your swordblades till you cut
the life out of them, and every thought of sweet
Aphroditê under the rutting suitors,
when they lay down in secret."

         As he spoke
here came the women in a bunch, all wailing,
soft tears on their cheeks. They fell to work
500 to lug the corpses out into the courtyard
under the gateway, propping one
against another as Odysseus ordered,
for he himself stood over them. In fear
these women bore the cold weight of the dead.
The next thing was to scrub off chairs and tables
and rinse them down. Telémakhos and the herdsman
scraped the packed earth floor with hoes, but made
the women carry out all blood and mire.
When the great room was cleaned up once again,
510 at swordpoint they forced them out, between
the roundhouse and the palisade, pell-mell
to huddle in that dead end without exit.

Telémakhos, who knew his mind, said curtly:
"I would not give the clean death of a beast
to trulls[161] who made a mockery of my mother
and of me too—you sluts, who lay with suitors."

He tied one end of a hawser to a pillar
and passed the other about the roundhouse top,
taking the slack up, so that no one's toes
520 could touch the ground. They would be hung like doves
or larks in springès triggered in a thicket,
where the birds think to rest—a cruel nesting.
So now in turn each woman thrust her head
into a noose and swung, yanked high in air,
to perish there most piteously.
Their feet danced for a little, but not long.

From storeroom to the court they brought Melánthios,
chopped with swords to cut his nose and ears off,
pulled off his genitals to feed the dogs
530 and raging hacked his hands and feet away.

As their own hands and feet called for a washing,
they went indoors to Odysseus again.
Their work was done. He told Eurýkleia:
                              "Bring me
brimstone and a brazier—medicinal
fumes to purify my hall. Then tell
Penélopê to come, and bring her maids.
All servants round the house must be called in."

His own old nurse Eurýkleia replied:
540 "Aye, surely that is well said, child. But let me
find you a good clean shirt and cloak and dress you.
You must not wrap your shoulders' breadth again
in rags in your own hall. That would be shameful."

Odysseus answered:
                      "Let me have the fire.
The first thing is to purify this place."

With no more chat Eurýkleia obeyed
and fetched out fire and brimstone. Cleansing fumes

---

[161] **trulls:** Calling the trulls harlots, Telémakhos refuses to use a sword to kill them, choosing instead the dishonorable method of hanging.

he sent through court and hall and storage chamber.
550 Then the old woman hurried off again
to the women's quarters to announce her news,
and all the servants came now, bearing torches
in twilight, crowding to embrace Odysseus,
taking his hands to kiss, his head and shoulders,
while he stood there, nodding to every one,
and overcome by longing and by tears.

BOOK 23
THE TRUNK OF THE OLIVE TREE

The old nurse went upstairs exulting,
with knees toiling, and patter of slapping feet,
to tell the mistress of her lord's return,
and cried out by the lady's pillow:
                                             "Wake,
wake up, dear child! Penélopê, come down,
see with your own eyes what all these years you longed for!
Odysseus is here! Oh, in the end, he came!
And he has killed your suitors, killed them all
10 who made his house a bordel[162] and ate his cattle
and raised their hands against his son!"

                              Penélopê said:
"Dear nurse . . . the gods have touched you.
They can put chaos into the clearest head
or bring a lunatic down to earth. Good sense
you always had. They've touched you. What is this
mockery you wake me up to tell me,
breaking in on my sweet spell of sleep?
I had not dozed away so tranquilly
20 since my lord went to war, on that ill wind
to Ilion.
                    Oh, leave me! Back down stairs!
If any other of my women came in babbling
things like these to startle me, I'd see her
flogged out of the house! Your old age spares you that."

Eurýkleia said:
"Would I play such a trick on you, dear child?

---

[162] **bordel:** Bordello, or brothel.

It is true, true, as I tell you, he has come!
That stranger they were baiting was Odysseus.
Telémakhos knew it days ago —
cool head, never to give his father away,
till he paid off those swollen dogs!"

The lady in her heart's joy now sprang up
with sudden dazzling tears, and hugged the old one,
crying out:
         "But try to make it clear!
If he came home in secret, as you say,
could he engage them singlehanded? How?
They were all down there, still in the same crowd."

To this Eurýkleia said:
         "I did not see it,
I knew nothing; only I heard the groans
of men dying. We sat still in the inner rooms
holding our breath, and marvelling, shut in,
until Telémakhos came to the door and called me —
your own dear son, sent this time by his father!
So I went out, and found Odysseus
erect, with dead men littering the floor
this way and that. If you had only seen him!
It would have made your heart glow hot! — a lion
splashed with mire and blood.
            But now the cold
corpses are all gathered at the gate,
and he has cleansed his hall with fire and brimstone,
a great blaze. Then he sent me here to you.
Come with me: you may both embark this time
for happiness together, after pain,
after long years. Here is your prayer, your passion,
granted: your own lord lives, he is at home,
he found you safe, he found his son. The suitors
abused his house, but he has brought them down."

The attentive lady said:
         "Do not lose yourself
in this rejoicing: wait: you know
how splendid that return would be for us,
how dear to me, dear to his son and mine;
but no, it is not possible, your notion
must be wrong.

Some god has killed the suitors,
70 a god, sick of their arrogance and brutal
malice—for they honored no one living,
good or bad, who ever came their way.
Blind young fools, they've tasted death for it.
But the true person of Odysseus?
He lost his home, he died far from Akhaia."

The old nurse sighed:
"How queer, the way you talk!
Here he is, large as life, by his own fire,
and you deny he ever will get home!
80 Child, you always were mistrustful!
But there is one sure mark that I can tell you:
that scar left by the boar's tusk long ago.
I recognized it when I bathed his feet
and would have told you, but he stopped my mouth,
forbade me, in his craftiness.
Come down,
I stake my life on it, he's here!
Let me die in agony if I lie!"

Penélopê said:
90 "Nurse dear, though you have your wits about you,
still it is hard not to be taken in
by the immortals. Let us join my son, though,
and see the dead and that strange one who killed them."

She turned then to descend the stair, her heart
in tumult. Had she better keep her distance
and question him, her husband? Should she run
up to him, take his hands, kiss him now?
Crossing the door sill she sat down at once
in firelight, against the nearest wall,
100 across the room from the lord Odysseus.
There
leaning against a pillar, sat the man
and never lifted up his eyes, but only waited
for what his wife would say when she had seen him.
And she, for a long time, sat deathly still
in wonderment—for sometimes as she gazed
she found him—yes, clearly—like her husband,
but sometimes blood and rags were all she saw.
Telémakhos' voice came to her ears:

110   "Mother,
cruel mother, do you feel nothing,
drawing yourself apart this way from Father?
Will you not sit with him and talk and question him?
What other woman could remain so cold?
Who shuns her lord, and he come back to her
from wars and wandering, after twenty years?
Your heart is hard as flint and never changes!"

Penélopê answered:
                    "I am stunned, child.
120   I cannot speak to him. I cannot question him.
I cannot keep my eyes upon his face.
If really he is Odysseus, truly home,
beyond all doubt we two shall know each other
better than you or anyone. There are
secret signs we know, we two."

                              A smile
came now to the lips of the patient hero, Odysseus,
who turned to Telémakhos and said:
"Peace: let your mother test me at her leisure.
130   Before long she will see and know me best.
These tatters, dirt—all that I'm caked with now—
make her look hard at me and doubt me still.
As to this massacre, we must see the end.
Whoever kills one citizen, you know,
and has no force of armed men at his back,
had better take himself abroad by night
and leave his kin. Well, we cut down the flower of Ithaka,
the mainstay of the town. Consider that."

Telémakhos replied respectfully:
140   "Dear Father,
enough that you yourself study the danger,
foresighted in combat as you are,
they say you have no rival.
                    We three stand
ready to follow you and fight. I say
for what our strength avails, we have the courage."

And the great tactician, Odysseus, answered:
                                    "Good.

Here is our best maneuver, as I see it:
150 bathe, you three, and put fresh clothing on,
order the women to adorn themselves,
and let our admirable harper choose a tune
for dancing, some lighthearted air, and strum it.
Anyone going by, or any neighbor,
will think it is a wedding feast he hears.
These deaths must not be cried about the town
till we can slip away to our own woods. We'll see
what weapon, then, Zeus puts into our hands."

They listened attentively, and did his bidding,
160 bathed and dressed afresh; and all the maids
adorned themselves. Then Phêmios the harper
took his polished shell and plucked the strings,
moving the company to desire
for singing, for the sway and beat of dancing,
until they made the manor hall resound
with gaiety of men and grace of women.
Anyone passing on the road would say:
"Married at last, I see — the queen so many courted.
Sly, cattish wife! She would not keep — not she! —
170 the lord's estate until he came."

                    So travellers'
thoughts might run — but no one guessed the truth.
Greathearted Odysseus, home at last,
was being bathed now by Eurýnomê
and rubbed with golden oil, and clothed again
in a fresh tunic and a cloak. Athena
lent him beauty, head to foot. She made him
taller, and massive, too, with crisping hair
in curls like petals of wild hyacinth
180 but all red-golden. Think of gold infused
on silver by a craftsman, whose fine art
Hephaistos taught him, or Athena: one
whose work moves to delight: just so she lavished
beauty over Odysseus' head and shoulders.
He sat then in the same chair by the pillar,
facing his silent wife, and said:
                    "Strange woman,
the immortals of Olympos made you hard,
harder than any. Who else in the world

190   would keep aloof as you do from her husband
        if he returned to her from years of trouble,
        cast on his own land in the twentieth year?

        Nurse, make up a bed for me to sleep on.
        Her heart is iron in her breast."

                                        Penélopê
        spoke to Odysseus now. She said:
                                        "Strange man,
        if man you are . . . This is no pride on my part
        nor scorn for you — not even wonder, merely.
200   I know so well how you — how he — appeared
        boarding the ship for Troy. But all the same . . .

        Make up his bed for him, Eurýkleia.
        Place it outside the bedchamber my lord
        built with his own hands. Pile the big bed
        with fleeces, rugs, and sheets of purest linen."

        With this she tried him to the breaking point,
        and he turned on her in a flash raging:
        "Woman, by heaven you've stung me now!
        Who dared to move my bed?
210   No builder had the skill for that — unless
        a god came down to turn the trick. No mortal
        in his best days could budge it with a crowbar.
        There is our pact and pledge, our secret sign,
        built into that bed — my handiwork
        and no one else's!

                        An old trunk of olive
        grew like a pillar on the building plot,
        and I laid out our bedroom round that tree,
        lined up the stone walls, built the walls and roof,
220   gave it a doorway and smooth-fitting doors.
        Then I lopped off the silvery leaves and branches,
        hewed and shaped that stump from the roots up
        into a bedpost, drilled it, let it serve
        as model for the rest. I planed them all,
        inlaid them all with silver, gold and ivory,
        and stretched a bed between — a pliant web
        of oxhide thongs dyed crimson.

There's our sign!
I know no more. Could someone else's hand
230 have sawn that trunk and dragged the frame away?"

Their secret! as she heard it told, her knees
grew tremulous and weak, her heart failed her.
With eyes brimming tears she ran to him,
throwing her arms around his neck, and kissed him,
murmuring:
            "Do not rage at me, Odysseus!
No one ever matched your caution! Think
what difficulty the gods gave: they denied us
life together in our prime and flowering years,
240 kept us from crossing into age together.
Forgive me, don't be angry. I could not
welcome you with love on sight! I armed myself
long ago against the frauds of men,
impostors who might come — and all those many
whose underhanded ways bring evil on!
Helen of Argos, daughter of Zeus and Leda,
would she have joined the stranger,[163] lain with him,
if she had known her destiny? known the Akhaians
in arms would bring her back to her own country?
250 Surely a goddess moved her to adultery,
her blood unchilled by war and evil coming,
the years, the desolation; ours, too.
But here and now, what sign could be so clear
as this of our own bed?
No other man has ever laid eyes on it —
only my own slave, Aktoris, that my father
sent with me as a gift — she kept our door.
You make my stiff heart know that I am yours."

Now from his breast into his eyes the ache
260 of longing mounted, and he wept at last,
his dear wife, clear and faithful, in his arms,
longed for
            as the sunwarmed earth is longed for by a swimmer
spent in rough water where his ship went down
under Poseidon's blows, gale winds and tons of sea.

---

[163] **the stranger:** Paris was the guest of Helen and Meneláos.

Few men can keep alive through a big surf
to crawl, clotted with brine, on kindly beaches
in joy, in joy, knowing the abyss behind:
and so she too rejoiced, her gaze upon her husband,
270   her white arms round him pressed as though forever.
The rose Dawn might have found them weeping still
had not grey-eyed Athena slowed the night
when night was most profound, and held the Dawn
under the Ocean of the East. That glossy team,
Firebright and Daybright, the Dawn's horses
that draw her heavenward for men—Athena
stayed their harnessing.

                    Then said Odysseus:
"My dear, we have not won through to the end.
280   One trial—I do not know how long—is left for me
to see fulfilled. Teirêsias' ghost forewarned me
the night I stood upon the shore of Death, asking
about my friends' homecoming and my own.

But now the hour grows late, it is bed time,
rest will be sweet for us; let us lie down."

To this Penélopê replied:
                    "That bed,
that rest is yours whenever desire moves you,
now the kind powers have brought you home at last.
290   But as your thought has dwelt upon it, tell me:
what is the trial you face? I must know soon;
what does it matter if I learn tonight?"

The teller of many stories said:
                    "My strange one,
must you again, and even now,
urge me to talk? Here is a plodding tale;
no charm in it, no relish in the telling.
Teirêsias told me I must take an oar
and trudge the mainland, going from town to town,
300   until I discover men who have never known
the salt blue sea, nor flavor of salt meat—
strangers to painted prows, to watercraft
and oars like wings, dipping across the water.
The moment of revelation he foretold
was this, for you may share the prophecy:

some traveller falling in with me will say:
'A winnowing fan, that on your shoulder, sir?'
There I must plant my oar, on the very spot,
with burnt offerings to Poseidon of the Waters:
310 a ram, a bull, a great buck boar. Thereafter
when I come home again, I am to slay
full hekatombs to the gods who own broad heaven,
one by one.
          Then death will drift upon me
from seaward, mild as air, mild as your hand,
in my well-tended weariness of age,
contented folk around me on our island.
He said all this must come."

          Penélopê said:
320 "If by the gods' grace age at least is kind,
we have that promise—trials will end in peace."

So he confided in her, and she answered.
Meanwhile Eurýnomê and the nurse together
laid soft coverlets on the master's bed,
working in haste by torchlight. Eurýkleia
retired to her quarters for the night,
and then Eurýnomê, as maid-in-waiting,
lighted her lord and lady to their chamber
with bright brands.

330   She vanished.
                    So they came
into that bed so steadfast, loved of old,
opening glad arms to one another.
Telémakhos by now had hushed the dancing,
hushed the women. In the darkened hall
he and the cowherd and the swineherd slept.

The royal pair mingled in love again
and afterward lay revelling in stories:
hers of the siege her beauty stood at home
340 from arrogant suitors, crowding on her sight,
and how they fed their courtship on his cattle,
oxen and fat sheep, and drank up rivers
of wine out of the vats.
                    Odysseus told
of what hard blows he had dealt out to others

and of what blows he had taken — all that story.
She could not close her eyes till all was told.

His raid on the Kikonês, first of all,
then how he visited the Lotos Eaters,
350 and what the Kyklops did, and how those shipmates,
pitilessly devoured, were avenged.
Then of his touching Aiolos's isle
and how that king refitted him for sailing
to Ithaka; all vain: gales blew him back
groaning over the fishcold sea. Then how
he reached the Laistrygonians' distant bay
and how they smashed his ships and his companions.
Kirkê, then: of her deceits and magic,
then of his voyage to the wide underworld
360 of dark, the house of Death, and questioning
Teirêsias, Theban spirit.
                Dead companions,
many, he saw there, and his mother, too.
Of this he told his wife, and told how later
he heard the choir of maddening Seirênês,
coasted the Wandering Rocks, Kharybdis' pool
and the fiend Skylla who takes toll of men.
Then how his shipmates killed Lord Hêlios' cattle
and how Zeus thundering in towering heaven
370 split their fast ship with his fuming bolt,
so all hands perished.
            He alone survived,
cast away on Kalypso's isle, Ogýgia.
He told, then, how that nymph detained him there
in her smooth caves, craving him for her husband,
and how in her devoted lust she swore
he should not die nor grow old, all his days,
but he held out against her.
             Last of all
380 what sea-toil brought him to the Phaiákians;
their welcome; how they took him to their hearts
and gave him passage to his own dear island
with gifts of garments, gold and bronze . . .
                  Remembering,
he drowsed over the story's end. Sweet sleep
relaxed his limbs and his care-burdened breast.

Other affairs were in Athena's keeping.
Waiting until Odysseus had his pleasure

of love and sleep, the grey-eyed one bestirred
390 the fresh Dawn from her bed of paling Ocean
to bring up daylight to her golden chair,
and from his fleecy bed Odysseus
arose. He said to Penélopê:
                              "My lady,
what ordeals have we not endured! Here, waiting
you had your grief, while my return dragged out—
my hard adventures, pitting myself against
the gods' will, and Zeus, who pinned me down
far from home. But now our life resumes:
400 we've come together to our longed-for bed.
Take care of what is left me in our house;
as to the flocks that pack of wolves laid waste
they'll be replenished: scores I'll get on raids
and other scores our island friends will give me
till all the folds are full again.
                              This day
I'm off up country to the orchards. I must see
my noble father, for he missed me sorely.
And here is my command for you—a strict one,
410 though you may need none, clever as you are.
Word will get about as the sun goes higher
of how I killed those lads. Go to your rooms
on the upper floor, and take your women. Stay there
with never a glance outside or a word to anyone."
Fitting cuirass and swordbelt to his shoulders,
he woke his herdsmen, woke Telémakhos,
ordering all in arms. They dressed quickly,
and all in war gear sallied from the gate,
led by Odysseus.
                              Now it was broad day
420 but these three men Athena hid in darkness,
going before them swiftly from the town.

BOOK 24
WARRIORS, FAREWELL

Meanwhile the suitors' ghosts were called away
by Hermês of Kyllênê,[164] bearing the golden wand
with which he charms the eyes of men or wakens
whom he wills.

---

[164] **Kyllênê:** The mountain birthplace of Hermês in Arcadia.

He waved them on, all squeaking
as bats will in a cavern's underworld,
all flitting, flitting criss-cross in the dark
if one falls and the rock-hung chain is broken.
So with faint cries the shades trailed after Hermês,
10   pure Deliverer.

He led them down dank ways,
over grey Ocean tides, the Snowy Rock,
past shores of Dream and narrows of the sunset,
in swift flight to where the Dead inhabit
wastes of asphodel at the world's end.

Crossing the plain they met Akhilleus' ghost,
Patróklos and Antílokhos, then Aias,
noblest of Danaans after Akhilleus
in strength and beauty. Here the newly dead
20   drifted together, whispering. Then came
the soul of Agamémnon, son of Atreus,
in black pain forever, surrounded by men-at-arms
who perished with him in Aigísthos' hall.

Akhilleus greeted him:
            "My lord Atreidês,
we held that Zeus who loves the play of lightning
would give you length of glory, you were king
over so great a host of soldiery
before Troy, where we suffered, we Akhaians.
30   But in the morning of your life
you met that doom that no man born avoids.
It should have found you in your day of victory,
marshal of the army, in Troy country;
then all Akhaia would have heaped your tomb
and saved your honor for your son. Instead
piteous death awaited you at home."

And Atreus' son replied:
            "Fortunate hero,
son of Pêleus, godlike and glorious,
40   at Troy you died, across the sea from Argos,
and round you Trojan and Akhaian peers
fought for your corpse and died. A dustcloud wrought
by a whirlwind hid the greatness of you slain,
minding no more the mastery of horses.
All that day we might have toiled in battle
had not a storm from Zeus broken it off.

We carried you out of the field of war
down to the ships and bathed your comely body
with warm water and scented oil. We laid you
50 upon your long bed, and our officers
wept hot tears like rain and cropped their hair.
Then hearing of it in the sea, your mother, Thetis,
came with nereids of the grey wave crying
unearthly lamentation over the water,
and trembling gripped the Akhaians to the bone.
They would have boarded ship that night and fled
except for one man's wisdom — venerable
Nestor, proven counselor in the past.
He stood and spoke to allay their fear: 'Hold fast,
60 sons of the Akhaians, lads of Argos.
His mother it must be, with nymphs her sisters,
come from the sea to mourn her son in death.'

Veteran hearts at this contained their dread
while at your side the daughters of the ancient
seagod wailed and wrapped ambrosial shrouding
around you.
       Then we heard the Muses sing
a threnody[165] in nine immortal voices.
No Argive there but wept, such keening[166] rose
70 from that one Muse who led the song.
       Now seven
days and ten, seven nights and ten, we mourned you,
we mortal men, with nymphs who know no death,
before we gave you to the flame, slaughtering
longhorned steers and fat sheep on your pyre.

Dressed by the nereids and embalmed with honey,
honey and unguent in the seething blaze,
you turned to ash. And past the pyre Akhaia's
captains paraded in review, in arms,
80 clattering chariot teams and infantry.
Like a forest fire the flame roared on, and burned
your flesh away. Next day at dawn, Akhilleus,
we picked your pale bones from the char to keep
in wine and oil. A golden amphora
your mother gave for this — Hephaistos' work,
a gift from Dionysos.[167] In that vase,

---

[165] **a threnody:** A dirge or lamentation.   [166] **keening:** A wailing for the dead.   [167] **Dionysos:** God of wine and ecstasy.

Akhilleus, hero, lie your pale bones mixed
with mild Patróklos' bones, who died before you,
and nearby lie the bones of Antílokhos,
90   the one you cared for most of all companions
after Patróklos.
              We of the Old Army,
we who were spearmen, heaped a tomb for these
upon a foreland over Hellê's waters,[168]
to be a mark against the sky for voyagers
in this generation and those to come.
Your mother sought from the gods magnificent trophies
and set them down midfield for our champions. Often
at funeral games after the death of kings
100   when you yourself contended, you've seen athletes
cinch their belts when trophies went on view.
But these things would have made you stare—the treasures
Thetis on her silver-slippered feet
brought to your games—for the gods held you dear.
You perished, but your name will never die.
It lives to keep all men in mind of honor
forever, Akhilleus.
                  As for myself, what joy
is this, to have brought off the war? Foul death
110   Zeus held in store for me at my coming home;
Aigísthos and my vixen cut me down."

While they conversed, the Wayfinder° came near,   Hermês
leading the shades of suitors overthrown
by Lord Odysseus. The two souls of heroes
advanced together, scrutinizing these.
Then Agamémnon recognized Amphímedon,
son of Meláneus—friends of his on Ithaka—
and called out to him:
                  "Amphimedon
120   what ruin brought you into this undergloom?
All in a body, picked men, and so young?
One could not better choose the kingdom's pride.
Were you at sea, aboard ship, and Poseidon
blew up a dire wind and foundering waves,
or cattle-raiding, were you, on the mainland,
or in a fight for some stronghold, or women,

---

[168] **Hellê's waters:** The Hellespont, which is the strait separating Asia Minor from Europe, just north of Troy; the modern Dardanelles.

when the foe hit you to your mortal hurt?
Tell me, answer my question. Guest and friend
I say I am of yours — or do you not remember
130   I visited your family there? I came
with Prince Meneláos, urging Odysseus
to join us in the great sea raid on Troy.
One solid month we beat our way, breasting
south sea and west, resolved to bring him round,
the wily raider of cities."

                 The new shade said:
"O glory of commanders, Agamémnon,
all that you bring to mind I remember well.
As for the sudden manner of our death
140   I'll tell you of it clearly, first to last.
After Odysseus had been gone for years
we were all suitors of his queen. She never
quite refused, nor went through with a marriage,
hating it, ever bent on our defeat.
Here is one of her tricks: she placed her loom,
her big loom, out for weaving in her hall,
and the fine warp of some vast fabric on it.
We were attending her, and she said to us:
'Young men, my suitors, now my lord is dead,
150   let me finish my weaving before I marry,
or else my thread will have been spun in vain.
This is a shroud I weave for Lord Laërtês
when cold Death comes to lay him on his bier.
The country wives would hold me in dishonor
if he, with all his fortune, lay unshrouded.'
We had men's hearts; she touched them; we agreed.
So every day she wove on the great loom —
but every night by torchlight she unwove it,
and so for three years she deceived the Akhaians.
160   But when the seasons brought the fourth around,
as long months waned, and the slow days were spent,
one of her maids, who knew the secret, told us.
We found her unraveling the splendid shroud,
and then she had to finish, willy nilly —
finish, and show the big loom woven tight
from beam to beam with cloth. She washed the shrouding
clean as sun or moonlight.
                Then, heaven knows
from what quarter of the world, fatality
170   brought in Odysseus to the swineherd's wood

far up the island. There his son went too
when the black ship put him ashore from Pylos.
The two together planned our death-trap. Down
they came to the famous town—Telémakhos
long in advance: we had to wait for Odysseus.
The swineherd led him to the manor later
in rags like a foul beggar, old and broken,
propped on a stick. These tatters that he wore
hid him so well that none of us could know him
180   when he turned up, not even the older men.
We jeered at him, took potshots at him, cursed him.
Daylight and evening in his own great hall
he bore it, patient as a stone. That night
the mind of Zeus beyond the stormcloud stirred him
with Telémakhos at hand to shift his arms
from mégaron to storage room and lock it.
Then he assigned his wife her part: next day
she brought his bow and iron axeheads out
to make a contest. Contest there was none;
190   that move doomed us to slaughter. Not a man
could bend the stiff bow to his will or string it,
until it reached Odysseus. We shouted,
'Keep the royal bow from the beggar's hands
no matter how he begs!' Only Telémakhos
would not be denied.

        So the great soldier
took his bow and bent it for the bowstring
effortlessly. He drilled the axeheads clean,
sprang, and decanted arrows on the door sill,
200   glared, and drew again. This time he killed
Antínoös.

        There facing us he crouched
and shot his bolts of groaning at us, brought us
down like sheep. Then some god, his familiar,[169]
went into action with him round the hall,
after us in a massacre. Men lay groaning,
mortally wounded, and the floor smoked with blood.

That was the way our death came, Agamémnon.
Now in Odysseus' hall untended still
210   our bodies lie, unknown to friends or kinsmen

---

[169] **his familiar:** An attendant spirit.

who should have laid us out and washed our wounds
free of the clotted blood, and mourned our passing.
So much is due the dead."

                    But Agamémnon's
tall shade when he heard this cried aloud:
"O fortunate Odysseus, master mariner
and soldier, blessed son of old Laërtês!
The girl you brought home made a valiant wife!
True to her husband's honor and her own,
220 Penélopê, Ikários' faithful daughter!
The very gods themselves will sing her story
for men on earth—mistress of her own heart,
Penélopê!
Tyndáreus' daughter waited, too—how differently!
Klytaimnéstra, the adulteress,
waited to stab her lord and king. That song
will be forever hateful. A bad name
she gave to womankind, even the best."

These were the things they said to one another
230 under the rim of earth where Death is lord.

Leaving the town, Odysseus and his men
that morning reached Laërtês' garden lands,
long since won by his toil from wilderness—
his homestead, and the row of huts around it
where fieldhands rested, ate and slept. Indoors
he had an old slave woman, a Sikel, keeping
house for him in his secluded age.

Odysseus here took leave of his companions.
"Go make yourselves at home inside," he said.
240 "Roast the best porker and prepare a meal.
I'll go to try my father. Will he know me?
Can he imagine it, after twenty years?"

He handed spear and shield to the two herdsmen,
and in they went, Telémakhos too. Alone
Odysseus walked the orchard rows and vines.
He found no trace of Dólios and his sons
nor the other slaves—all being gone that day
to clear a distant field, and drag the stones
for a boundary wall.
250   But on a well-banked plot

Odysseus found his father in solitude
spading the earth around a young fruit tree.

He wore a tunic, patched and soiled, and leggings—
oxhide patches, bound below his knees
against the brambles; gauntlets on his hands
and on his head a goatskin cowl of sorrow.
This was the figure Prince Odysseus found—
wasted by years, racked, bowed under grief.
The son paused by a tall pear tree and wept,
260   then inwardly debated: should he run
forward and kiss his father, and pour out
his tale of war, adventure, and return,
or should he first interrogate him, test him?
Better that way, he thought—
first draw him out with sharp words, trouble him.
His mind made up, he walked ahead. Laërtês
went on digging, head down, by the sapling,
stamping the spade in. At his elbow then
his son spoke out:
270   "Old man, the orchard keeper
you work for is no townsman. A good eye
for growing things he has; there's not a nurseling,
fig tree, vine stock, olive tree or pear tree
or garden bed uncared for on this farm.
But I might add—don't take offense—your own
appearance could be tidier. Old age
yes—but why the squalor, and rags to boot?
It would not be for sloth, now, that your master
leaves you in this condition; neither at all
280   because there's any baseness in your self.
No, by your features, by the frame you have,
a man might call you kingly,
one who should bathe warm, sup well, and rest easy
in age's privilege. But tell me:
who are your masters? whose fruit trees are these
you tend here? Tell me if it's true this island
is Ithaka, as that fellow I fell in with
told me on the road just now? He had
a peg loose, that one: couldn't say a word
290   or listen when I asked about my friend,
my Ithakan friend. I asked if he were alive
or gone long since into the underworld.
I can describe him if you care to hear it:
I entertained the man in my own land

when he turned up there on a journey; never
had I a guest more welcome in my house.
He claimed his stock was Ithakan: Laërtês
Arkeísiadês, he said his father was.
I took him home, treated him well, grew fond of him—
300 though we had many guests—and gave him
gifts in keeping with his quality: seven
bars of measured gold, a silver winebowl
filigreed with flowers, twelve light cloaks,
twelve rugs, robes and tunics—not to mention
his own choice of women trained in service,
the four well-favored ones he wished to take."

His father's eyes had filled with tears. He said:
"You've come to that man's island, right enough,
but dangerous men and fools hold power now.
310 You gave your gifts in vain. If you could find him
here in Ithaka alive, he'd make
return of gifts and hospitality,
as custom is, when someone has been generous.
But tell me accurately—how many years
have now gone by since that man was your guest?
your guest, my son—if he indeed existed—
born to ill fortune as he was. Ah, far
from those who loved him, far from his native land,
in some sea-dingle° fish have picked his bones,   valley
320 or else he made the vultures and wild beasts
a trove ashore! His mother at his bier
never bewailed him, nor did I, his father,
nor did his admirable wife, Penélopê,
who should have closed her husband's eyes in death
and cried aloud upon him as he lay.
So much is due the dead.
                            But speak out, tell me further:
who are you, of what city and family?
where have you moored the ship that brought you here,
330 where is your admirable crew? Are you a peddler
put ashore by the foreign ship you came on?"

Again Odysseus had a fable ready.
"Yes," he said, "I can tell you all those things.
I come from Rover's Passage where my home is,
and I'm King Allwoes' only son. My name
is Quarrelman.
              Heaven's power in the westwind

drove me this way from Sikania,° Sicily
off my course. My ship lies in a barren
340 cove beyond the town there. As for Odysseus,
now is the fifth year since he put to sea
and left my homeland—bound for death, you say.
Yet landbirds flying from starboard crossed his bow—
a lucky augury. So we parted joyously,
in hope of friendly days and gifts to come."

A cloud of pain had fallen on Laërtês.
Scooping up handfuls of the sunburnt dust
he sifted it over his grey head, and groaned,
and the groan went to the son's heart. A twinge
350 prickling up through his nostrils warned Odysseus
he could not watch this any longer.
He leaped and threw his arms around his father,
kissed him, and said:
                        "Oh, Father, I am he!
Twenty years gone, and here I've come again
to my own land!
                        Hold back your tears! No grieving!
I bring good news—though still we cannot rest.
I killed the suitors to the last man!
360 Outrage and injury have been avenged!"

Laërtês turned and found his voice to murmur:
"If you are Odysseus, my son, come back,
give me some proof, a sign to make me sure."

His son replied:
                        "The scar then, first of all.
Look, here the wild boar's flashing tusk
wounded me on Parnassos; do you see it?
You and my mother made me go, that time,
to visit Lord Autólykos, her father,
370 for gifts he promised years before on Ithaka.
Again—more proof—let's say the trees you gave me
on this revetted[170] plot of orchard once.
I was a small boy at your heels, wheedling
amid the young trees, while you named each one.
You gave me thirteen pear, ten apple trees,

---

[170] **revetted:** Protected by a wall or embankment.

and forty fig trees. Fifty rows of vines
were promised too, each one to bear in turn.
Bunches of every hue would hang there ripening,
weighed down by the god of summer days."

380 The old man's knees failed him, his heart grew faint,
recalling all that Odysseus calmly told.
He clutched his son. Odysseus held him swooning
until he got his breath back and his spirit
and spoke again:
          "Zeus, Father! Gods above! —
you still hold pure Olympos, if the suitors
paid for their crimes indeed, and paid in blood!
But now the fear is in me that all Ithaka
will be upon us. They'll send messengers
390 to stir up every city of the islands."

Odysseus the great tactician answered:
"Courage, and leave the worrying to me.
We'll turn back to your homestead by the orchard.
I sent the cowherd, swineherd, and Telémakhos
ahead to make our noonday meal."

                 Conversing
in this vein they went home, the two together,
into the stone farmhouse. There Telémakhos
and the two herdsmen were already carving
400 roast young pork, and mixing amber wine.
During these preparations the Sikel woman
bathed Laërtês and anointed him,
and dressed him in a new cloak. Then Athena,
standing by, filled out his limbs again,
gave girth and stature to the old field captain
fresh from the bathing place. His son looked on
in wonder at the godlike bloom upon him,
and called out happily:
          "Oh, Father,
410 surely one of the gods who are young forever
has made you magnificent before my eyes!"

Clearheaded Laërtês faced him, saying:
"By Father Zeus, Athena and Apollo,
I wish I could be now as once I was,
commander of Kephallenians, when I took

the walled town, Nérikos,[171] on the promontory!
Would god I had been young again last night
with armor on me, standing in our hall
to fight the suitors at your side! How many
420   knees I could have crumpled, to your joy!"

While son and father spoke, cowherd and swineherd
attended, waiting, for the meal was ready.
Soon they were all seated, and their hands
picked up the meat and bread.

                                    But now old Dólios
appeared in the bright doorway with his sons,
work-stained from the field. Laërtês' housekeeper,
who reared the boys and tended Dólios
in his bent age, had gone to fetch them in.
430   When it came over them who the stranger was
they halted in astonishment. Odysseus
hit an easy tone with them. Said he:
"Sit down and help yourselves. Shake off your wonder.
Here we've been waiting for you all this time,
and our mouths watering for good roast pig!"

But Dólios came forward, arms outstretched,
and kissed Odysseus' hand at the wrist bone,
crying out:
                    "Dear master, you returned!
440   You came to us again! How we had missed you!
We thought you lost. The gods themselves have brought you!
Welcome, welcome; health and blessings on you!
And tell me, now, just one thing more: Penélopê,
does she know yet that you are on the island?
or should we send a messenger?"

Odysseus gruffly said,
                                "Old man, she knows.
Is it for you to think of her?"

                                    So Dólios
450   quietly took a smooth bench at the table
and in their turn his sons welcomed Odysseus,
kissing his hands; then each went to his chair

---

[171] **Kephallenians . . . Nérikos:** A town on the west coast of Greece whose exact location is unknown; the Kephallenians are Odysseus's subjects on the mainland.

beside his father. Thus our friends
were occupied in Laërtês' house at noon.

Meanwhile to the four quarters of the town
the news ran: bloody death had caught the suitors;
and men and women in a murmuring crowd
gathered before Odysseus' hall. They gave
burial to the piteous dead, or bore
460 the bodies of young men from other islands
down to the port, thence to be ferried home.
Then all the men went grieving to assembly
and being seated, rank by rank, grew still,
as old Eupeithês rose to address them. Pain
lay in him like a brand for Antínoös,
the first man that Odysseus brought down,
and tears flowed for his son as he began:
"Heroic feats that fellow did for us
Akhaians, friends! Good spearmen by the shipload
470 he led to war and lost—lost ships and men,
and once ashore again killed these, who were
the islands' pride.
                    Up with you! After him!—
before he can take flight to Pylos town
or hide at Elis, under Epeian law!
We'd be disgraced forever! Mocked for generations
if we cannot avenge our sons' blood, and our brothers'!
Life would turn to ashes—at least for me;
rather be dead and join the dead!
480   I say
we ought to follow now, or they'll gain time
and make the crossing."

                    His appeal, his tears,
moved all the gentry listening there;
but now they saw the crier and the minstrel
come from Odysseus' hall, where they had slept.
The two men stood before the curious crowd,
and Medôn[172] said:
                    "Now hear me, men of Ithaka.
490 When these hard deeds were done by Lord Odysseus
the immortal gods were not far off. I saw
with my own eyes someone divine who fought
beside him, in the shape and dress of Mentor;

---

[172] **Medôn:** A herald forced to serve the suitors but faithful to Odysseus.

it was a god who shone before Odysseus,
a god who swept the suitors down the hall
dying in droves."

             At this pale fear assailed them,
and next they heard again the old forecaster,
Halithérsês Mastóridês. Alone
500 he saw the field of time, past and to come.
In his anxiety for them he said:
"Ithakans, now listen to what I say.
Friends, by your own fault these deaths came to pass.
You would not heed me nor the captain, Mentor;
would not put down the riot of your sons.
Heroic feats they did! — all wantonly
raiding a great man's flocks, dishonoring
his queen, because they thought he'd come no more.
Let matters rest; do as I urge; no chase,
510 or he who wants a bloody end will find it."

The greater number stood up shouting "Aye!"
But many held fast, sitting all together
in no mind to agree with him. Eupeithês
had won them to his side. They ran for arms,
clapped on their bronze, and mustered
under Eupeithês at the town gate
for his mad foray.
                   Vengeance would be his,
he thought, for his son's murder; but that day
520 held bloody death for him and no return.

At this point, querying Zeus, Athena said:
"O Father of us all and king of kings,
enlighten me. What is your secret will?
War and battle, worse and more of it,
or can you not impose a pact on both?"

The summoner of cloud replied:
                         "My child,
why this formality of inquiry?
Did you not plan that action by yourself—
530 see to it that Odysseus, on his homecoming,
should have their blood?
                        Conclude it as you will.
There is one proper way, if I may say so:
Odysseus' honor being satisfied,
let him be king by a sworn pact forever,

and we, for our part, will blot out the memory
of sons and brothers slain. As in the old time
let men of Ithaka henceforth be friends;
prosperity enough, and peace attend them."

540   Athena needed no command, but down
in one spring she descended from Olympos
just as the company of Odysseus finished
wheat crust and honeyed wine, and heard him say:
"Go out, someone, and see if they are coming."

One of the boys went to the door as ordered
and saw the townsmen in the lane. He turned
swiftly to Odysseus.
             "Here they come,"
he said, "best arm ourselves, and quickly."

550   All up at once, the men took helm and shield—
four fighting men, counting Odysseus,
with Dólios' half dozen sons. Laërtês
armed as well, and so did Dólios—
greybeards, they could be fighters in a pinch.
Fitting their plated helmets on their heads
they sallied out, Odysseus in the lead.

Now from the air Athena, Zeus's daughter,
appeared in Mentor's guise, with Mentor's voice,
making Odysseus' heart grow light. He said
560   to put cheer in his son:
                "Telémakhos,
you are going into battle against pikemen
where hearts of men are tried. I count on you
to bring no shame upon your forefathers.
In fighting power we have excelled this lot
in every generation."

            Said his son:
"If you are curious, Father, watch and see
the stuff that's in me. No more talk of shame."

570   And old Laërtês cried aloud:
"Ah, what a day for me, dear gods!
to see my son and grandson vie in courage!"

Athena halted near him, and her eyes
shone like the sea. She said:

"Arkeísiadês,
dearest of all my old brothers-in-arms,
invoke the grey-eyed one and Zeus her father,
heft your spear and make your throw."

Power flowed into him from Pallas Athena,
580   whom he invoked as Zeus's virgin child,
and he let fly his heavy spear.
It struck
Eupeithês on the cheek plate of his helmet,
and undeflected the bronze head punched through.
He toppled, and his armor clanged upon him.
Odysseus and his son now furiously
closed, laying on with broadswords, hand to hand,
and pikes: they would have cut the enemy down
to the last man, leaving not one survivor,
590   had not Athena raised a shout
that stopped all fighters in their tracks.

"Now hold!"
she cried, "Break off this bitter skirmish;
end your bloodshed, Ithakans, and make peace."

Their faces paled with dread before Athena,
and swords dropped from their hands unnerved, to lie
strewing the ground, at the great voice of the goddess.
Those from the town turned fleeing for their lives.
But with a cry to freeze their hearts
600   and ruffling like an eagle on the pounce,
the lord Odysseus reared himself to follow—
at which the son of Kronos dropped a thunderbolt
smoking at his daughter's feet.

Athena
cast a grey glance at her friend and said:
"Son of Laërtês and the gods of old,
Odysseus, master of land ways and sea ways,
command yourself. Call off this battle now,
or Zeus who views the wide world may be angry."

610   He yielded to her, and his heart was glad.
Both parties later swore to terms of peace
set by their arbiter, Athena, daughter
of Zeus who bears the stormcloud as a shield—
though still she kept the form and voice of Mentor.

Heroes
and Adventure

A culture celebrates a hero because in some fashion he or she is exemplary: intelligence, vision, physical prowess, courage. The earliest heroes tend to be culture-bringers—individuals who teach the tribe or society about hunting or food plants, about medicine and healing, about ritual and magic. Literature provides portraits of heroes and kings who contribute to the betterment of society through what might be called public works: slaying the dragons of chaos, harnessing wild rivers, eliminating floods, capturing outlaws, and building temples and palaces. Such achievements were often attributed to godlike individuals who combine the roles of hero and king. The Greek Prometheus stole fire from Zeus and gave it to humans. The Mexican Quetzalcoatl stole maize from Food Mountain and taught humans art, architecture, and the sacred calendar. The Chinese Fu Hsi taught people how to use nets for fishing; he also invented the primary symbols of the *I Jing (I Ching),* a book used for divination.

With the development of urban civilization and warfare, the heroes became kings and warriors—men who achieved prowess on the battlefield and garnered wealth and power through their military exploits. Their histories depict individuals who have overcome obstacles and met the trials of manhood with courage, strength, and ingenuity. These are the heroes of epics, figures like Gilgamesh, Rama, Achilles, and Beowulf.

People in the West often trace the idea of the hero back to the portraits of noblemen and warriors in Homer's epics (eighth century B.C.E.), **The Iliad** and **The Odyssey**, models based on an even earlier age of chivalry. In *The Iliad,* Achilles is portrayed as the

p. 537, 185

ultimate superhuman figure known for his superior physical prowess, courage, and fighting skills. The driving purpose of his life is to achieve glory, fame, and honor. Symbolizing excellence in the Trojan War, Achilles was honored with marble memorials and celebrated in song and drama. Military prowess, however, while providing the cornerstone of city-states or empires, does not of itself lead to the sustained development of a civil society, which ultimately is dependent on responsible citizenship, not the energies and ideals of the warrior.

p. 545

A subtle transformation takes place, however, when a reputation for intelligence or cleverness replaces the heavily muscled giant, when David defeats Goliath on the battlefield or when Odysseus outperforms Ajax in the Trojan War. In the Hebrew Scriptures **First Book of Samuel**, David is pictured as an innocent youth, using his shepherd skills to defeat the barbarian Goliath. But there is an additional characteristic that distinguishes David from traditional Greek or Roman heroes: David does not fight for personal fame or honor, but to glorify his God. The Hebrew hero gains favor with God by a righteous life, by virtue and fidelity. David fights Goliath knowing that the God of Israel is on his side; victory is characterized as much by faith as it is by physical prowess.

p. 549

The advent of narrative literature in India dates from the time of the two great epics the *Rāmāyana* and the *Mahabharata*. Like Homer's *Iliad* and *Odyssey,* both the *Rāmāyana* and the *Mahabharata* contain stories, myths, and legends handed down from an earlier, oral tradition of philosophical poems and ballads, hymns and prayers, fables and tales. These legends and tales concern an earlier era of history, dating back to the time between 1500 and 1000 B.C.E., when Aryan invaders established centers of power in the Punjab region of India in their advance eastward. At that time, the conquerors were divided among themselves over the distribution of their newly acquired territories, and both the *Rāmāyana* and the *Mahabharata* center on stories of heroic figures involved in struggles to regain patrimonial kingdoms unjustly denied to them. The *Rāmāyana,* said to be the "first poem," concerns the adventures of the exiled prince Rama, from the kingdom of Kosala, and his beloved Sita.

The most popular human hero in Greece to have earned immortality with his exploits and to have become a god was Heracles, clearly the working-class hero of his time. It was probably in

**Greek Warrior,
fifth century** B.C.E.
*Vase detail of an
armed warrior in a
classic hero pose.
(Erich Lessing/
Art Resource, NY)*

retrospect that special heroes in the ancient world were said to have come from mixed parentage—one human parent and the other a deity. It was a practice the Greeks might have inherited from Mesopotamia, whose great hero Gilgamesh was born of a goddess mother. Apollodorus describes a few of Heracles' labors that earned him fame and deification in his ***Bibliotheca***. The legends of Heracles' adventures in the netherworld especially enhanced his reputation.

p. 556

Today the word *hero* is applied to someone who models extraordinary valor or courage, often during war or other national crisis. Physical courage characterizes the heroes of the world wars in the twentieth century. The twentieth century, however, was also notable for its spiritual heroes, people like Mother Teresa of Calcutta, Nelson Mandela of South Africa, Mahatma Gandhi of India, and Martin Luther King Jr. of the United States. The great heroes in the aftermath of the attack on the World Trade Center in New York City on September 11, 2001, were the firefighters and policemen who gave their lives to save others, and Mayor Giuliani, who was an inspirational leader during the crisis.

■ PRONUNCIATION

Agastya: uh-GUS-tyuh
Ayodhyā: uh-YOH-dyah
Brahmā: BRAH-hmuh
Hanumān: HUH-noo-mahn
Kusha (Kuśa): KOO-shuh
Lakshmana (Lakṣmaṇa): LUKSH-muh-nuh
Laṅkā: LAHNG-kuh
Rāma: RAH-muh
Rāmāyaṇa: ruh-MAH-yuh-nuh
Rāvaṇa: RAH-vuh-nuh
Sita (Sītā): SEE-tah
Vālmīki: VAHL-mih-kee
vānara: VAH-nuh-ruh
Vishnu (Viṣṇu): VISH-noo

❧ HOMER

GREECE, EIGHTH CENTURY B.C.E.

The Iliad focuses on the exploits of Achilles during a brief period toward the end of the Trojan War. For Homer, the fortunes of this war are measured by individual encounters rather than group victories. In the intensity of war, individual decisions can mean life or death, and a single encounter can bring fame or infamy. Warriors such as Hector, Achilles, and Aias live in an elevated sphere where the demands of sacrifice and bravery seem to dwarf humdrum, ordinary peacetime.

It is possible to sympathize with Achilles' anger at Agamemnon in Book 1 for taking away the woman that Achilles had received as booty and to appreciate his reasons for withdrawing from the battle. But Achilles' stubbornness about returning to fight is excessive and causes his close friend Patroclus to risk his life. Patroclus's ensuing death forces Achilles to acknowledge the consequences of his choices. In the background is his mother's warning that he was fated for either a quiet, long life at home in Phthia or a short, glorious life in the Trojan war. The first excerpt included here from Book 18, "Achilles Returns to Battle," describes the moment when Achilles, prompted by the messenger Iris, decides to fight again; she calls him son of Peleus, Achilles' father. Achilles' head is crowned with a golden cloud of fire, and when he announces his return with three tremendous cries, panic runs through the Trojan warriors, causing twelve fighters to be trampled by their own chariots. Achilles is larger than life. The second excerpt from Book 18, "The Immortal Shield," describes the making of Achilles' shield by Hephaestus in response to a request by Achilles' mother, Thetis.

Achilles Killing the Amazon Queen, 540–530 B.C.E. *A Greek amphora, or wine jar, detailing a scene from the Trojan War. (Courtesy of the British Museum)*

◠ The Iliad

Translated by Robert Fagles

FROM BOOK 18
[ACHILLES RETURNS TO BATTLE]

"To arms—son of Peleus! Most terrifying man alive!
200   Defend Patroclus! It's all for him, this merciless battle
pitched before the ships. They're mauling each other now,
Achaeans struggling to save the corpse from harm,
Trojans charging to haul it back to windy Troy.
Flashing Hector's far in the lead, wild to drag it off,
furious to lop the head from its soft, tender neck
and stake it high on the city's palisade.
                                                                    Up with you—
no more lying low! Writhe with shame at the thought
Patroclus may be sport for the dogs of Troy!
Yours, the shame will be yours
210   if your comrade's corpse goes down to the dead defiled!"

But the swift runner replied, "Immortal Iris—
what god has sped you here to tell me this?"

Quick as the wind the rushing Iris answered,
"Hera winged me on, the illustrious wife of Zeus.
But the son of Cronus throned on high knows nothing,
nor does any other immortal housed on Olympus
shrouded deep in snow."
                          Achilles broke in quickly—
"How can I go to war? The Trojans have my gear.
And my dear mother told me I must not arm for battle,
220   not till I see her coming back with my own eyes—
she vowed to bring me burnished arms from the god of fire.
I know of no other armor. Whose gear could I wear?
None but Telamonian Ajax' giant shield.
But he's at the front, I'm sure, engaging Trojans,
slashing his spear to save Patroclus' body."

Quick as the wind the goddess had a plan:
"We know—we too—they hold your famous armor.
Still, just as you are, go out to the broad trench
and show yourself to the Trojans. Struck with fear
230   at the sight of you, they might hold off from attack
and Achaea's fighting sons get second wind,
exhausted as they are . . .
Breathing room in war is all too brief."

And Iris racing the wind went veering off
as Achilles, Zeus's favorite fighter, rose up now
and over his powerful shoulder Pallas slung the shield,[1]
the tremendous storm-shield with all its tassels flaring—
and crowning his head the goddess swept a golden cloud
and from it she lit a fire to blaze across the field.
240   As smoke goes towering up the sky from out a town
cut off on a distant island under siege . . .
enemies battling round it, defenders all day long
trading desperate blows from their own city walls
but soon as the sun goes down the signal fires flash,
rows of beacons blazing into the air to alert their neighbors—
if only they'll come in ships to save them from disaster—
so now from Achilles' head the blaze shot up the sky.
He strode from the rampart, took his stand at the trench

---

[1] **shield:** The famous aegis with the image of Medusa on it is on Athena's shield.

but he would not mix with the milling Argive ranks.
250 He stood in awe of his mother's strict command.
So there he rose and loosed an enormous cry
and off in the distance Pallas shrieked out too
and drove unearthly panic through the Trojans.
Piercing loud as the trumpet's battle cry that blasts
from murderous raiding armies ringed around some city—
so piercing now the cry that broke from Aeacides.[2]
And Trojans hearing the brazen voice of Aeacides,
all their spirits quaked—even sleek-maned horses,
sensing death in the wind, slewed their chariots round
260 and charioteers were struck dumb when they saw that fire,
relentless, terrible, burst from proud-hearted Achilles' head,
blazing as fiery-eyed Athena fueled the flames. Three times
the brilliant Achilles gave his great war cry over the trench,
three times the Trojans and famous allies whirled in panic—
and twelve of their finest fighters died then and there,
crushed by chariots, impaled on their own spears.
And now the exultant Argives seized the chance
to drag Patroclus' body quickly out of range
and laid him on a litter . . .
270 Standing round him, loving comrades mourned,
and the swift runner Achilles joined them, grieving,
weeping warm tears when he saw his steadfast comrade
lying dead on the bier, mauled by tearing bronze,
the man he sent to war with team and chariot
but never welcomed home again alive.

[THE IMMORTAL SHIELD]

540   And the famous crippled Smith replied, "Courage!
Anguish for all that armor—sweep it from your mind.
If only I could hide him away from pain and death,
that day his grim destiny comes to take Achilles,
as surely as glorious armor shall be his, armor
that any man in the world of men will marvel at
through all the years to come—whoever sees its splendor."

     With that he left her there and made for his bellows,
turning them on the fire, commanding, "Work—to work!"
And the bellows, all twenty, blew on the crucibles,
550 breathing with all degrees of shooting, fiery heat

---

[2] **Aeacides:** Sons or descendants of Aeacus, the father of Peleus.

as the god hurried on — a blast for the heavy work,
a quick breath for the light, all precisely gauged
to the god of fire's wish and the pace of the work in hand.
Bronze he flung in the blaze, tough, durable bronze
and tin and priceless gold and silver, and then,
planting the huge anvil upon its block, he gripped
his mighty hammer in one hand, the other gripped his tongs.

    And first Hephaestus makes a great and massive shield,
blazoning well-wrought emblems all across its surface,
560 raising a rim around it, glittering, triple-ply
with a silver shield-strap run from edge to edge
and five layers of metal to build the shield itself,
and across its vast expanse with all his craft and cunning
the god creates a world of gorgeous immortal work.

    There he made the earth and there the sky and the sea
and the inexhaustible blazing sun and the moon rounding full
and there the constellations, all that crown the heavens,
the Pleiades and the Hyades, Orion in all his power too
and the Great Bear[3] that mankind also calls the Wagon:
570 she wheels on her axis always fixed, watching the Hunter,
and she alone is denied a plunge in the Ocean's baths.

    And he forged on the shield two noble cities filled
with mortal men. With weddings and wedding feasts in one
and under glowing torches they brought forth the brides
from the women's chambers, marching through the streets
while choir on choir the wedding song rose high
and the young men came dancing, whirling round in rings
and among them flutes and harps kept up their stirring call —
women rushed to the doors and each stood moved with wonder.
580 And the people massed, streaming into the marketplace
where a quarrel had broken out and two men struggled
over the blood-price for a kinsman just murdered.
One declaimed in public, vowing payment in full —
the other spurned him, he would not take a thing —
so both men pressed for a judge to cut the knot.
The crowd cheered on both, they took both sides,
but heralds held them back as the city elders sat
on polished stone benches, forming the sacred circle,
grasping in hand the staffs of clear-voiced heralds,
590 and each leapt to his feet to plead the case in turn.

---

[3] **Great Bear:** The Great Bear (or Ursa Major) is the Big Dipper, which never descends below the horizon.

Two bars of solid gold shone on the ground before them,
a prize for the judge who'd speak the straightest verdict.

    But circling the other city camped a divided army
gleaming in battle-gear, and two plans split their ranks:
to plunder the city or share the riches with its people,
hoards the handsome citadel stored within its depths.
But the people were not surrendering, not at all.
They armed for a raid, hoping to break the siege—
loving wives and innocent children standing guard
600 on the ramparts, flanked by elders bent with age
as men marched out to war. Ares and Pallas led them,
both burnished gold, gold the attire they donned, and great,
magnificent in their armor—gods for all the world,
looming up in their brilliance, towering over troops.
And once they reached the perfect spot for attack,
a watering place where all the herds collected,
there they crouched, wrapped in glowing bronze.
Detached from the ranks, two scouts took up their posts,
the eyes of the army waiting to spot a convoy,
610 the enemy's flocks and crook-horned cattle coming . . .
Come they did, quickly, two shepherds behind them,
playing their hearts out on their pipes—treachery
never crossed their minds. But the soldiers saw them,
rushed them, cut off at a stroke the herds of oxen
and sleek sheep-flocks glistening silver-gray
and killed the herdsmen too. Now the besiegers,
soon as they heard the uproar burst from the cattle
as they debated, huddled in council, mounted at once
behind their racing teams, rode hard to the rescue,
620 arrived at once, and lining up for assault
both armies battled it out along the river banks—
they raked each other with hurtling bronze-tipped spears.
And Strife and Havoc plunged in the fight, and violent Death—
now seizing a man alive with fresh wounds, now one unhurt,
now hauling a dead man through the slaughter by the heels,
the cloak on her back stained red with human blood.
So they clashed and fought like living, breathing men
grappling each other's corpses, dragging off the dead.

    And he forged a fallow field, broad rich plowland
630 tilled for the third time, and across it crews of plowmen
wheeled their teams, driving them up and back and soon
as they'd reach the end-strip, moving into the turn,
a man would run up quickly
and hand them a cup of honeyed, mellow wine

as the crews would turn back down along the furrows,
pressing again to reach the end of the deep fallow field
and the earth churned black behind them, like earth churning,
solid gold as it was—that was the wonder of Hephaestus' work.

    And he forged a king's estate where harvesters labored,
640 reaping the ripe grain, swinging their whetted scythes.
Some stalks fell in line with the reapers, row on row,
and others the sheaf-binders girded round with ropes,
three binders standing over the sheaves, behind them
boys gathering up the cut swaths, filling their arms,
supplying grain to the binders, endless bundles.
And there in the midst the king,
scepter in hand at the head of the reaping-rows,
stood tall in silence, rejoicing in his heart.
And off to the side, beneath a spreading oak,
650 the heralds were setting out the harvest feast,
they were dressing a great ox they had slaughtered,
while attendant women poured out barley, generous,
glistening handfuls strewn for the reapers' midday meal.

    And he forged a thriving vineyard loaded with clusters,
bunches of lustrous grapes in gold, ripening deep purple
and climbing vines shot up on silver vine-poles.
And round it he cut a ditch in dark blue enamel
and round the ditch he staked a fence in tin.
And one lone footpath led toward the vineyard
660 and down it the pickers ran
whenever they went to strip the grapes at vintage—
girls and boys, their hearts leaping in innocence,
bearing away the sweet ripe fruit in wicker baskets.
And there among them a young boy plucked his lyre,
so clear it could break the heart with longing,
and what he sang was a dirge for the dying year,
lovely . . . his fine voice rising and falling low
as the rest followed, all together, frisking, singing,
shouting, their dancing footsteps beating out the time.

670   And he forged on the shield a herd of longhorn cattle,
working the bulls in beaten gold and tin, lowing loud
and rumbling out of the farmyard dung to pasture
along a rippling stream, along the swaying reeds.
And the golden drovers kept the herd in line,
four in all, with nine dogs at their heels,
their paws flickering quickly—a savage roar!—

a crashing attack — and a pair of ramping lions
had seized a bull from the cattle's front ranks —
he bellowed out as they dragged him off in agony.
680　Packs of dogs and the young herdsmen rushed to help
but the lions ripping open the hide of the huge bull
were gulping down the guts and the black pooling blood
while the herdsmen yelled the fast pack on — no use.
The hounds shrank from sinking teeth in the lions,
they balked, hunching close, barking, cringing away.

　　And the famous crippled Smith forged a meadow
deep in a shaded glen for shimmering flocks to graze,
with shepherds' steadings, well-roofed huts and sheepfolds.

　　And the crippled Smith brought all his art to bear
690　on a dancing circle, broad as the circle Daedalus
once laid out on Cnossos' spacious fields
for Ariadne[4] the girl with lustrous hair.
Here young boys and girls, beauties courted
with costly gifts of oxen, danced and danced,
linking their arms, gripping each other's wrists.
And the girls wore robes of linen light and flowing,
the boys wore finespun tunics rubbed with a gloss of oil,
the girls were crowned with a bloom of fresh garlands,
the boys swung golden daggers hung on silver belts.
700　And now they would run in rings on their skilled feet,
nimbly, quick as a crouching potter spins his wheel,
palming it smoothly, giving it practice twirls
to see it run, and now they would run in rows,
in rows crisscrossing rows — rapturous dancing.
A breathless crowd stood round them struck with joy
and through them a pair of tumblers dashed and sprang,
whirling in leaping handsprings, leading on the dance.

　　And he forged the Ocean River's mighty power girdling
round the outmost rim of the welded indestructible shield.

710　　And once the god had made that great and massive shield
he made Achilles a breastplate brighter than gleaming fire,
he made him a sturdy helmet to fit the fighter's temples,

---

[4] **Ariadne:** Ariadne, the daughter of King Minos, who had hired Daedalus to construct his great palace and a labyrinth at Cnossos (Knossos) on Crete.

beautiful, burnished work, and raised its golden crest
and made him greaves[5] of flexing, pliant tin.
                                        Now,
when the famous crippled Smith had finished off
that grand array of armor, lifting it in his arms
he laid it all at the feet of Achilles' mother Thetis —
and down she flashed like a hawk from snowy Mount Olympus
720 bearing the brilliant gear, the god of fire's gift.

---

[5] greaves: Armor for legs.

ꙮ HEBREW SCRIPTURES
NEAR EAST, C. 900 — C. 100 B.C.E.

Originally single books in Hebrew, the two books of Samuel and the two books of Kings describe the transition of the Hebrew people from a tribal culture to a unified monarchy over a period of some fifty years (C. 1030–C. 975). The books of Samuel are named after the prophet Samuel who combined the roles of priest, soothsayer, anointed of God, and political leader. Scholars believe that the two books are derived from at least two sources, one of which was a contemporary of David in the middle of the tenth century B.C.E., who records events as an eyewitness. He, perhaps, should be regarded as the "the father of history." A second source was in the ninth century. The narrative was then edited over a period of 400 years until a final version was produced C. 550 B.C.E.

At the core of the two books of Samuel are the rather candid biographies of Samuel, Saul, and David. These detailed portraits show individuals striving for righteousness, but who are nevertheless beset with human flaws. Samuel anoints Saul as the first king of Israel, but Saul's career is reminiscent of a Greek tragedy; despite his victories over Israel's enemies — including the perennial Philistines — he is plagued by fits of depression. The excerpt below depicts Saul's decline and David's ascendence, first as a gifted, young musician, called upon to ease Saul's psychological states; later he will triumph over the giant Goliath.

☙ First Book of Samuel

King James version

DAVID AND GOLIATH

16

... But the spirit of the Lord departed from Saul, and an evil spirit from the Lord troubled him. And Saul's servants said unto him, "Behold now, an evil spirit from God troubleth thee. Let our lord now command thy servants, which are before thee, to seek out a man, who is a cunning player on an harp: and it shall come to pass when the evil spirit from God is upon thee, that he shall play with his hand, and thou shalt be well." And Saul said unto his servants, "Provide me now a man that can play well, and bring him to me." Then answered one of the servants, and said, "Behold, I have seen a son of Jesse the Bethlehemite, that is cunning in playing, and a mighty valiant man, and a man of war, and prudent in matters, and a comely person, and the Lord is with him."

Wherefore Saul sent messengers unto Jesse, and said, "Send me David thy son, which is with the sheep." And Jesse took an ass laden with bread, and a bottle of wine, and a kid, and sent them by David his son unto Saul. And David came to Saul, and stood before him: and he loved him greatly, and he became his armour-bearer. And Saul sent to Jesse, saying, "Let David, I pray thee, stand before me: for he hath found favour in my sight." And it came to pass, when the evil spirit from God was upon Saul, that David took an harp, and played with his hand: so Saul was refreshed, and was well, and the evil spirit departed from him.

17

Now the Philistines gathered together their armies to battle, and were gathered together at Shochoh, which belongeth to Judah[1] and pitched between Shochoh and Azekah, in Ephes-dammim. And Saul and the men of Israel were gathered together, and pitched by the valley of Elah, and set the battle in array against the Philistines. And the Philistines stood on a mountain on the one side, and Israel stood on a mountain on the other side: and there was a valley between them.

And there went out a champion out of the camp of the Philistines, named Goliath, of Gath: whose height was six cubits and a span. And he had an helmet of brass upon his head, and he was armed with a coat of mail: and the weight of the coat was five thousand shekels[2] of brass. And he had greaves[3] of brass upon his legs, and a target of brass between his shoulders. And the staff of his spear was like a weaver's beam,[4] and his spear's head weighed six hundred shekels of iron: and one

---

[1] **Judah:** According to tradition, Canaan was divided among the twelve tribes that had exited from Egypt. Judah was given a rather large parcel in the south, bordered by the Philistines on the west and the Dead Sea on the east.

[2] **shekels:** Equivalent to about half an ounce; the coat of mail weighed about 150 lbs.

[3] **greaves:** Armor for the legs.

[4] **beam:** One of the two large rollers used in a loom.

bearing a shield went before him. And he stood and cried unto the armies of Israel, and said unto them, "Why are ye come out to set your battle in array? am not I a Philistine, and you servants to Saul? choose you a man for you, and let him come down to me. If he be able to fight with me, and to kill me, then will we be your servants: but if I prevail against him, and kill him, then shall ye be our servants, and serve us." And the Philistine said, "I defy the armies of Israel this day; give me a man, that we may fight together." When Saul and all Israel heard those words of the Philistine, they were dismayed, and greatly afraid.

Now David[5] was the son of that Ephrathite of Bethlehem-Judah whose name was Jesse, and he had eight sons: and the man went among men for an old man in the days of Saul. And the three eldest sons of Jesse went, and followed Saul to the battle: and the names of his three sons that went to the battle were Eliab, the firstborn, and next unto him Abinadab, and the third, Shammah. And David was the youngest: and the three eldest followed Saul. But David went and returned from Saul to feed his father's sheep at Bethlehem. And the Philistine drew near, morning and evening, and presented himself forty days. And Jesse said unto David his son, "Take now for thy brethren an ephah[6] of this parched corn, and these ten loaves, and run to the camp to thy brethren. And carry these ten cheeses unto the captain of their thousand, and look how thy brethren fare, and take their pledge." Now Saul, and they, and all the men of Israel were in the valley of Elah, fighting with the Philistines.

And David rose up early in the morning, and left the sheep with a keeper, and took, and went, as Jesse had commanded him; and he came to the trench, as the host was going forth to the fight, and shouted for the battle. For Israel and the Philistines had put the battle in array, army against army. And David left his carriage in the hand of the keeper of the carriage, and ran into the army, and came and saluted his brethren. And as he talked with them, behold, there came up the champion (the Philistine of Gath, Goliath by name) out of the armies of the Philistines, and spake according to the same words: and David heard them. And all the men of Israel, when they saw the man, fled from him, and were sore afraid. And the men of Israel said, "Have ye seen this man that is come up? Surely to defy Israel is he come up: and it shall be, that the man who killeth him, the king will enrich him with great riches, and will give him his daughter, and make his father's house free in Israel." And David spake to the men that stood by him, saying, "What shall be done to the man that killeth this Philistine, and taketh away the reproach from Israel? for who is this uncircumcised Philistine, that he should defy the armies of the living God?" And the people answered him after this manner, saying, "So shall it be done to the man that killeth him."

And Eliab his eldest brother heard when he spake unto the men, and Eliab's anger was kindled against David, and he said, "Why camest thou down hither? and with whom hast thou left those few sheep in the wilderness? I know thy pride, and

---

[5] **David:** This next section, which seems to introduce David for the first time, conflicts with the beginning of this account in chapter 16, and is an indication of multiple narrators or editors.

[6] **ephah:** From one third to a whole bushel.

the naughtiness of thine heart; for thou art come down that thou mightest see the battle." And David said, "What have I now done? Is there not a cause?" And he turned from him toward another, and spake after the same manner: and the people answered him again after the former manner. And when the words were heard which David spake, they rehearsed them before Saul: and he sent for him.

And David said to Saul, "Let no man's heart fail because of him: thy servant will go and fight with this Philistine." And Saul said to David, "Thou art not able to go against this Philistine, to fight with him: for thou art but a youth, and he a man of war from his youth." And David said unto Saul, "Thy servant kept his father's sheep, and there came a lion, and a bear, and took a lamb out of the flock: and I went after him, and smote him, and delivered it out of his mouth: and when he arose against me, I caught him by his beard, and smote him, and slew him. Thy servant slew both the lion and the bear: and this uncircumcised Philistine shall be as one of them, seeing he hath defied the armies of the living God." David said moreover, "The Lord that delivered me out of the paw of the lion, and out of the paw of the bear, he will deliver me out of the hand of this Philistine." And Saul said unto David, "Go, and the Lord be with thee."

And Saul armed David with his armour, and he put an helmet of brass upon his head, also he armed him with a coat of mail. And David girded his sword upon his armour, and he assayed to go, for he had not proved[7] it: and David said unto Saul, "I cannot go with these: for I have not proved them." And David put them off him. And he took his staff in his hand, and chose him five smooth stones out of the brook, and put them in a shepherd's bag which he had, even in a scrip[8]; and his sling was in his hand: and he drew near to the Philistine. And the Philistine came on and drew near unto David, and the man that bare the shield went before him. And when the Philistine looked about, and saw David, he disdained him: for he was but a youth, and ruddy, and of a fair countenance. And the Philistine said unto David, "Am I a dog, that thou comest to me with staves?" And the Philistine cursed David by his gods. And the Philistine said to David, "Come to me, and I will give thy flesh unto the fowls of the air, and to the beasts of the field." Then said David to the Philistine, "Thou comest to me with a sword, and with a spear, and with a shield: but I come to thee in the name of the Lord of hosts, the God of the armies of Israel, whom thou hast defied. This day will the Lord deliver thee into mine hand, and I will smite thee, and take thine head from thee, and I will give the carcasses of the host of the Philistines this day unto the fowls of the air, and to the wild beasts of the earth, that all the earth may know that there is a God in Israel. And all this assembly shall know that the Lord saveth not with sword and spear (for the battle is the Lord's), and he will give you into our hands."

And it came to pass when the Philistine arose, and came, and drew nigh to meet David, that David hasted, and ran toward the army to meet the Philistine. And David put his hand in his bag, and took thence a stone, and slang it, and smote the

---

[7] **proved:** The Revised Standard Version has "used to" here; i.e., the shepherd boy was not "used to" armor.

[8] **scrip:** Bag or satchel.

Philistine in his forehead, that the stone sunk into his forehead, and he fell upon his face to the earth. So David prevailed over the Philistine with a sling and with a stone, and smote the Philistine, and slew him; but there was no sword in the hand of David. Therefore David ran and stood upon the Philistine, and took his sword, and drew it out of the sheath thereof, and slew him, and cut off his head therewith. And when the Philistines saw their champion was dead, they fled. And the men of Israel and of Judah arose, and shouted, and pursued the Philistines, until thou come to the valley, and to the gates of Ekron: and the wounded of the Philistines fell down by the way to Shaaraim, even unto Gath, and unto Ekron. And the children of Israel returned from chasing after the Philistines, and they spoiled[9] their tents. And David took the head of the Philistine, and brought it to Jerusalem, but he put his armour in his tent.

And when Saul saw David go forth against the Philistine, he said unto Abner the captain of the host, "Abner, whose son is this youth?" And Abner said, "As thy soul liveth, O king, I cannot tell." And the king said, "Inquire thou whose son the stripling is." And as David returned from the slaughter of the Philistine, Abner took him, and brought him before Saul, with the head of the Philistine in his hand. And Saul said to him, "Whose son art thou, thou young man?" And David answered, "I am the son of thy servant Jesse, the Bethlehemite."

18

And it came to pass when he had made an end of speaking unto Saul, that the soul of Jonathan was knit with the soul of David, and Jonathan loved him as his own soul. And Saul took him that day, and would let him go no more home to his father's house. Then Jonathan and David made a covenant, because he loved him as his own soul. And Jonathan stripped himself of the robe that was upon him, and gave it to David, and his garments, even to his sword, and to his bow, and to his girdle.

And David went out whithersoever Saul sent him, and behaved himself wisely: and Saul set him over the men of war, and he was accepted in the sight of all the people, and also in the sight of Saul's servants. And it came to pass as they came, when David was returned from the slaughter of the Philistine, that the women came out of all cities of Israel, singing and dancing, to meet king Saul, with tabrets, with joy, and with instruments of music. And the women answered one another as they played, and said, "Saul hath slain his thousands, and David his ten thousands." And Saul was very wroth, and the saying displeased him, and he said, "They have ascribed unto David ten thousands, and to me they have ascribed but thousands: and what can he have more but the kingdom?" And Saul eyed David from that day and forward.

And it came to pass on the morrow, that the evil spirit from God came upon Saul, and he prophesied in the midst of the house: and David played with his hand, as at other times: and there was a javelin in Saul's hand. And Saul cast the javelin; for he said, "I will smite David even to the wall with it": and David avoided out of his presence twice.

---

[9] **spoiled:** Plundered.

And Saul was afraid of David, because the Lord was with him, and was departed from Saul. Therefore Saul removed him from him, and made him his captain over a thousand, and he went out and came in before the people. And David behaved himself wisely in all his ways; and the Lord was with him. Wherefore when Saul saw that he behaved himself very wisely, he was afraid of him. But all Israel and Judah loved David, because he went out and came in before them.

And Saul said to David, "Behold, my elder daughter Merab, her will I give thee to wife: only be thou valiant for me, and fight the Lord's battles": for Saul said, "Let not mine hand be upon him, but let the hand of the Philistines be upon him." And David said unto Saul, "Who am I? and what is my life, or my father's family in Israel, that I should be son in law to the king?" But it came to pass at the time when Merab Saul's daughter should have been given to David, that she was given unto Adriel the Meholathite to wife. And Michal Saul's daughter loved David: and they told Saul, and the thing pleased him. And Saul said, "I will give him her, that she may be a snare to him, and that the hand of the Philistines may be against him." Wherefore Saul said to David, "Thou shalt this day be my son in law, in the one of the twain."

And Saul commanded his servants, saying, "Commune with David secretly, and say, 'Behold, the king hath delight in thee, and all his servants love thee: now therefore be the king's son in law.'" And Saul's servants spake those words in the ears of David. And David said, "Seemeth it to you a light thing to be a king's son in law, seeing that I am a poor man, and lightly esteemed?" And the servants of Saul told him, saying, "On this manner spake David." And Saul said, "Thus shall ye say to David, 'The king desireth not any dowry, but an hundred foreskins of the Philistines, to be avenged of the king's enemies.'" But Saul thought to make David fall by the hand of the Philistines. And when his servants told David these words, it pleased David well to be the king's son in law: and the days were not expired. Wherefore David arose and went, he and his men, and slew of the Philistines two hundred men; and David brought their foreskins, and they gave them in full tale to the king, that he might be the king's son in law: and Saul gave him Michal his daughter to wife.

And Saul saw and knew that the Lord was with David, and that Michal Saul's daughter loved him. And Saul was yet the more afraid of David; and Saul became David's enemy continually. Then the princes of the Philistines went forth: and it came to pass after they went forth, that David behaved himself more wisely than all the servants of Saul, so that his name was much set by.

❧ THE RĀMĀYANA

INDIA, C. 550 B.C.E.–C. 400 C.E.

The *Rāmāyana* (Rama's Way), is the most influential and popular work in India and Southeast Asia, and its legendary author, **Vālmīki**, is known as India's "first poet" or *adivaki*. The tragic and romantic story of Prince **Rāma** and his wife **Sita** has been retold in many versions and languages throughout the region. As in the case of Homer's epics, the *Rāmāyana*

ruh-MAH-yuh-nuh
VAHL-mih-kee

RAH-muh
SEE-tah

and the *Mahabharata* have served as a rich lode of lore to be mined by later writers of Indian and Southeast Asian drama, poetry, fiction, dance, and—most recently—television and film. Unlike the Homeric epics, however, in India the *Rāmāyana* and *Mahabharata* are both considered sacred texts, providing religious and moral guidance for Hindus even today. The myths and legends of the Indian epics constitute fundamental elements of a cultural and spiritual tradition that is very much alive today throughout Southeast Asia.

The dating of the *Rāmāyana* is uncertain. The story that forms the core of *Rāmāyana* appeared sometime in the sixth century B.C.E. By that time the Aryans who had migrated into the northwestern region of India were beginning to give up their tribal organization and to form kingdoms that eventually led to the Maurya (c. 321–200 B.C.E.) and Gupta (c. 320–550 C.E.) empires. *Rāmāyana* is attributed to a legendary author named Vālmīki and to a fourth-century Sanskrit version of the poem. Most important, the *Rāmāyana* has come to play a significant role in Hindu religion; its protagonist, Prince Rāma, came to be worshipped as an incarnation of the god **Vishnu** (the Preserver). By the fifteenth century, the divinity of Rāma was well established, and the devotion to Rāma remains an important aspect of Hindu culture today. The so-called "Ram-Lilla," the return of Rāma to **Ayodhyā**, remains an important festival throughout India and parts of Southeast Asia.

The *Rāmāyana* consists of seven books or *kandas* totaling 24,000 verses, about one-fourth the length of the *Mahabharata*. The core story of the *Rāmāyana* revolves around a dispute over the rightful succession to the throne. It also contains elements of the fantastic and marvelous, descriptive accounts of heroic feats and war, and moving descriptions of longing, love, and tragic separation between the lovers Rāma and Sita.

VISH-noo

uh-YOH-dyah

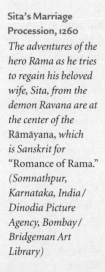

Sita's Marriage Procession, 1260
The adventures of the hero Rāma as he tries to regain his beloved wife, Sita, from the demon Ravana are at the center of the Rāmāyana, *which is Sanskrit for* "Romance of Rama." *(Somnathpur, Karnataka, India / Dinodia Picture Agency, Bombay / Bridgeman Art Library)*

The early books of the *Rāmāyana* describe Rāma's birth, his trials in the forest, and his marriage to Sita. In Book 3, the ten-headed demon **Rāvana** kidnaps Sita and takes her away to his island fortress at **Lanka**, threatening her chastity. In Book 5, the monkey general **Hanumān** leaps across the waters dividing the mainland from Lanka and attempts to bring Sita back alone. She, however, refuses to be touched by any man other than Rāma, not even her rescuer. In the following selection from Book 6, "Yuddha Kanda" (War), Rāma kills Rāvana in order to bring Sita home.

RAH-vuh-nuh
LAHNG-kuh
HUH-noo-mahn

After defeating Rāvana, Rāma returns to his home city of Ayodhyā where he rules in peace and happiness for several years, until he learns that his people have begun questioning his wife's virtue. Setting his duties as king above those as husband, as we learn in Book 7, the *Uttara Kanda* (*Last*), Rāma banishes his wife, not to hear from her again until their two sons, Lava and **Kusa**, show up one day at Ayodhyā and tell the story of Rāma they have learned from the sage Vālmīki. Shortly thereafter, Sita commits herself to the earth rather than return home to Rāma, who follows her in death after dividing his kingdom between their two sons.

KOO-shuh

Rāma unflaggingly follows in the path of *dharma,* his sacred duty. Similarly, his wife Sita exemplifies right action for married women, so that she and Rāma are the ideal couple representing the perfect marriage. Like Pénelopê in Homer's *The Odyssey,* Sita shows that she is devoted to her husband and she succeeds in preserving her chastity. Both Rāma and Sita endure great suffering as they give up their individual desires for the greater good of following their principles. With their moral integrity and heroic self-control, Rāma and Sita represent the embodiment of *dharma*—law—on earth.

FROM BOOK 6

ೞ Yuddha Kanda: The Great War

Translated by Swami Venkatesananda

YUDDHA 21–(22)

On a grass mat with his arm alone as his pillow, Rāma reclined, vowing to propitiate the god of the ocean and thus to secure his help to cross over to Lankā. The arm that had gifted thousands of cows, the arm that had been adorned by unguents and ornaments, the arm that Sītā had used as her pillow, the arm whose strength inspired fear in the enemy-hearts—that arm was the sole support for the head of Rāma, the ascetic, as he lay down on the sea-shore praying to the god of the ocean to show his grace. Rāma resolved: "I should now cross this ocean; or I shall dry up the ocean."

He lay there for three days and nights, without any sign of the ocean-god's pleasure. Rāma was seized with impatience and anger. He said to Lakṣmaṇa:[1] "Here is an

---

[1] **Lakṣmaṇa:** Rāma has three brothers, Lakṣmaṇa, Shatrugha, and Bharata; each is invested with a portion of the god Vishnu, the preserver, who has taken human form in order to defeat the ten-headed demon Rāvaṇa.

example, O Lakṣmaṇa, of how the wicked misinterpret the noble man's virtue: they think it is his weakness! The world respects only the man who is loud and noisy, vain and aggressive! Neither fame nor victory is won by a peaceful approach, O Lakṣmaṇa. See what I do now. Bring my weapon and bring the missiles. I shall dry up the ocean so that the vānaras[2] may walk to Laṅkā."[3]

Rāma got hold of his formidable weapon and took a few terrible missiles and discharged them at the ocean. These caused such a violent commotion that they whipped tidal waves of huge proportions. The creatures of the ocean, the huge snakes and other deep-sea creatures were disturbed and distressed. Mountainous waves rose in the sea. There was a terrifying roar from the ocean. Even Lakṣmaṇa was frightened.

Rāma looked at the ocean and said in great anger: "I shall dry up the entire ocean! Utterly deprived of your essence, O ocean, only a sand-bed will remain." He took the most powerful missile endowed with the powers of the Creator himself and hurled it at the ocean. The effect of this was unimaginable and beyond description. Mountains began to shake. There was an earthquake. There was dense darkness everywhere. The course of the sun, the moon and the planets was disturbed. The sky was illumined as if by the sudden appearance of thousands of meteors. Accompanied by deafening thunderclaps, the sky shone with lightning. Gale-force winds swept the surface of the earth and the ocean. Even the peaks of mountains were dislodged.

Living beings everywhere cried in agony. The waters of the ocean were stirred up so suddenly and with such force that it appeared as though the ocean would overstep its bounds and submerge the land.

YUDDHA 22–23

The deity presiding over the ocean then rose from the ocean and meekly approached Rāma. To Rāma who was standing burning with anger, his weapon ready to discharge the most deadly missile, the Ocean said:

"Rāma, everything in nature is governed by the immutable law which alone determines the inherent characteristic of every element in nature. In accordance with that law, it is natural for the ocean to be unfathomable and impassable. Yet, I shall suggest a way out, and I shall indicate the path by which the vānaras will be able to go over to Laṅkā."

Rāma asked the Ocean: "Against whom shall I direct this unfailing missile which has been readied for the purpose of drying the ocean?" And the Ocean pointed to the well-known Drumakulya inhabited by sinners: directed to this spot, Rāma's missile dried up the ocean there, and, in order to compensate for this action, Rāma blessed that piece of land: "You will be fertile and you will be full of fruit-bearing trees."

---

[2] **vānaras:** The monkeys (or apes) ruled by the monkey-king Sugriva in the forest kingdom of Kiskindha; their military leader, Hanuman, will become one of Rāma's greatest allies.

[3] **Laṅkā:** The capital of the island kingdom where Rāvaṇa, the king of the raksasas or demons, has his magnificent, fortified palace.

The Ocean said: "Rāma, here is Nala who is the son of the great Viśvakarma[4] (the architect of all). Let him construct a bridge across these waters, for he is as good as his father. I shall gladly support that bridge."

Nala at once voluntarily offered: "What the Ocean has said is indeed true. I shall construct the bridge across these waters: and I am as proficient as my father. Actually, the Ocean owes a debt of gratitude to Rāma, for a great service was rendered by Rāma's ancestors to the Ocean. Yet, it was not gratitude that inspired the Ocean to give way; fear did it! The ungrateful man in this world recognises only punishment, not love or affection."

At Rāma's command, thousands of vānaras got ready for the mighty undertaking. They cut down logs of wood; they rolled away huge rocks and stones. They threw all these into the ocean which was greatly agitated by this. Some of the vānaras held a plumbline so that the rocks could be placed in a straight line. With the help of the vānaras of immeasurable strength and mighty deeds, Nala put up the bridge across the ocean, using logs of wood, rocks and stones. The eight hundred mile long bridge took five days to build. Celestial beings (devas or beings of light) and Gandharvas (celestial musicians) watched this marvellous feat.

As soon as the bridge was completed, Vibhīṣana[5] stood guard at the southern (Laṅkā) end, to prevent sabotage by the enemy. Sugrīva[6] then said to Rāma: "Let Hanumān[7] take you and let Aṅgada take Lakṣmaṇa, to Laṅkā." They were ready to depart. [. . .]

[After crossing over the causeway, the vānara and the rakṣasas engage in fierce fighting. They have been joined by Vibhīṣana, Rāvaṇa's brother, who recognizes Rāma's virtue and who will become king of Laṅkā when Rāvaṇa is defeated. Now Rāma and Rāvaṇa face off against each other.]

Yuddha 109, 110, 111

When Rāma and Rāvaṇa began to fight, their armies stood stupefied, watching them! Rāma was determined to win; Rāvaṇa was sure he would die: knowing this, they fought with all their might. Rāvaṇa attacked the standard on Rāma's car; and Rāma similarly shot the standard on Rāvaṇa's car. While Rāvaṇa's standard fell; Rāma's did not. Rāvaṇa next aimed at the "horses" (engines) of Rāma's car: even though he attacked them with all his might, they remained unaffected.

Both of them discharged thousands of missiles: these illumined the skies and created a new heaven, as it were! They were accurate in their aim and their missiles unfailingly hit the target. With unflagging zeal they fought each other, without the least trace of fatigue. What one did the other did in retaliation.

---

[4] **Viśvakarma:** As a creator deity, he has various roles, but is primarily associated with the process of creation. Nala is a monkey prince.

[5] **Vibhīṣana:** A brother of Rāvaṇa, who is noble and virtuous, and becomes Rāma's ally.

[6] **Sugrīva:** An ally.

[7] **Hanumān:** An exceedingly popular monkey god who possesses superhuman abilities and is worshipped throughout India for his healing powers.

Rāvaṇa shot at Mātali[8] who remained unaffected by it. Then Rāvaṇa sent a shower of maces and mallets at Rāma. Their very sound agitated the oceans and tormented the aquatic creatures. The celestials and the holy brāhmaṇas witnessing the scene prayed: "May auspiciousness attend to all the living beings, and may the worlds endure forever. May Rāma conquer Rāvaṇa." Astounded at the way in which Rāma and Rāvaṇa fought with each other, the sages said to one another: "Sky is like sky, ocean is like ocean; the fight between Rāma and Rāvaṇa is like Rāma and Rāvaṇa—incomparable."

Taking up a powerful missile, Rāma correctly aimed at the head of Rāvaṇa; it fell. But another head appeared in its place. Every time Rāma cut off Rāvaṇa's head, another appeared! Rāma was puzzled. Mātali, Rāma's driver, said to Rāma: "Why do you fight like an ordinary warrior, O Rāma? Use the Brahmā-missile; the hour of the demon's death is at hand."

Rāma remembered the Brahmā-missile which the sage Agastya had given him. It had the power of the wind-god for its 'feathers'; the power of fire and sun at its head; the whole space was its body; and it had the weight of a mountain. It shone like the sun or the fire of nemesis. As Rāma took it in his hands, the earth shook and all living beings were terrified. Infallible in its destructive power, this ultimate weapon of destruction shattered the chest of Rāvaṇa, and entered deep into the earth.

Rāvaṇa fell dead. And the surviving demons fled, pursued by the vānaras. The vānaras shouted in great jubilation. The air resounded with the drums of the celestials. The gods praised Rāma. The earth became steady, the wind blew softly and the sun was resplendent as before. Rāma was surrounded by mighty heroes and gods who were all joyously felicitating him on the victory.

---

[8] Mātali: The charioteer of Indra, king of the gods; Indra has sent Mātali to pilot Rāma's chariot.

ꙮ APOLLODORUS
GREECE, FL. SECOND CENTURY B.C.E.

Very little is known about Apollodorus's life, which is usually dated the second century B.C.E., sometimes later. By reputation Apollodorus was an Athenian grammarian; he is known to have written a prose treatise on Greek deities called *On the Gods*. *Bibliotheca (The Library)* is attributed to Apollodorus, but the book's true authorship is unknown. *Bibliotheca*, which contains the story of Heracles' twelve labors, is a compendium of Greek mythology and history; in the words of translator Sir James G. Frazer, it is a "history of the world as it was conceived by the Greeks."

Heracles, whose name means the "glory of Hera," began his life under the shadow of the goddess Hera's wrath, since her husband, Zeus,

Heracles and Greek Heroes, 475–450 B.C.E. *Detail from a red-figure vase showing clothed and semiclothed Greek heroes striking various heroic poses. (Heracles is in the middle of the top row.) (Musée du Louvre, Paris / Peter Willi, Bridgeman Art Library)*

had fathered Heracles with a mortal, Alcmene. Wearing a lion skin and swinging a club, Heracles was a hero of the people who battled with humans and monsters. Though with so much brute strength he did make mistakes and accidentally kill people, he was nevertheless the first mortal who achieved divinity through suffering and hard work. He represented hope for the ordinary man, who placed the following charm over his threshold:

> The son of Zeus, the Conqueror dwells here,
> Heracles. Let no evil thing come near.

The following *Bibliotheca* excerpts detail four of the twelve (or ten) labors assigned to Heracles by the Delphic Oracle after Heracles, in a fit of madness, kills his own children. In the first, he is to conquer the Nemean lion with brute strength. In the second, he will need cleverness for besting the Lernaean hydra. In another of Heracles' labors he is to travel to the edge of the world and steal golden apples from the Hesperides, an ultimate prize akin to acquiring the knowledge held by immortals. The fourth labor described here, actually Heracles' last, involves fetching the

The Pythian priestess then first called him Heracles, for hitherto he was called Alcides. And she told him to dwell in Tiryns, serving Eurystheus for twelve years and to perform the ten labours imposed on him, and so, she said, when the tasks were accomplished, he would be immortal.

– Apollodorus, historian

hound Cerberus from the underworld; this story belongs to a general type known as the "harrowing of hell," in which a hero descends into the underworld in order to steal, plunder, learn something, or rescue someone, feats carried out by such ancient heroes as Theseus, Orpheus, and Aeneas. It is said that Jesus, too, harrowed hell when, according to the Gospel of Nicodemus, he rescues the souls of the righteous from the underworld. After Heracles returns Cerberus to Hades, he has completed his labors and earns immortality, as predicted by the Delphic Oracle.

FROM

Bibliotheca

Translated by Rhoda A. Hendricks

[THE LABORS OF HERACLES]

It fell to the lot of Heracles that he was driven to madness because of the jealousy of Hera, and he threw his own children and Iphicles'[1] two children into the fire. As a result, he punished himself by exile and went to Delphi to ask of the god where he ought to live. Pythia,[2] the priestess of Apollo, then called him Heracles for the first time[3] and told him to go to Tiryns and live in servitude to Eurystheus for twelve years and to carry out the ten labors[4] he would set for him. She said, also, that when he had performed these labors he would become immortal.

When he had heard the oracle, Heracles went to Tiryns and carried out the tasks as Eurystheus ordered him to do. First Eurystheus commanded him to bring back the hide of the Nemean Lion, an animal that could not be wounded and was an offspring of Typhon.[5] When Heracles arrived at Nemea and found the lion, he first shot at him with his bow, but when he realized the creature was invulnerable, he chased after him with his club raised on high.

When the lion fled into a cave with two entrances, Heracles blocked up one of the mouths and went in after the lion through the other. Then, throwing his arms around the animal's neck, he strangled the lion to death and then carried it off on his shoulders. Heracles offered a sacrifice of thanksgiving to Zeus and took the lion to Mycenae. Eurystheus was so filled with terror at Heracles' manly strength that he forbade him to come into the city in the future and ordered him to show the prizes of his labors from outside the walls.

---

[1] **Iphicles:** The twin brother of Heracles.

[2] **Pythia:** Delphi's former name was Pytho, probably named after the monster Python, which was killed by Apollo. Apollo's priestess at Delphi was called the Pythia.

[3] **first time:** Heracles had been called Alcides, after his grandfather Alcaeus.

[4] **labors:** There is disagreement about whether there were ten or twelve labors assigned to Heracles.

[5] **Typhon:** An ancient monster with a hundred burning heads.

For his second labor Eurystheus ordered Heracles to kill the Hydra of Lerna, which lived in the swamp of Lerna and went out into the countryside killing cattle and laying waste to the land. The Hydra had an enormous body and nine heads, one of which was immortal. Heracles went to Lerna in a chariot driven by Iolaus and found the Hydra on the brow of a hill next to the springs of Amymone, where it had its den. Shooting at it with flaming arrows, Heracles drove the creature out, and then, when it came close, he grabbed it and held it tight. But the Hydra wrapped itself around his foot, and he was not able to get free by striking off its heads with his club, for as soon as one head was cut off two grew in its place.

In addition, a huge crab came to the aid of the Hydra and kept biting his foot. He, therefore, killed the crab and called to Iolaus to help him. Iolaus set fire to a part of the woods nearby and, by burning the stumps of the heads with firebrands, kept them from growing out again. Then Heracles cut off the immortal head, and, when he had buried it in the ground, he put a heavy rock over it. Then he split open the body of the Hydra and dipped his arrows in its poison.

Eurystheus, however, said that this labor should not be counted as one of the ten, for he had not overcome the Hydra alone, but with Iolaus' help . . . .

After Heracles had spent eight years and one month in the performance of these labors, since he did not count that of the cattle of Augeas[6] or of the Hydra as acceptable labors, Eurystheus ordered him, as his eleventh labor, to bring the Golden Apples of the Hesperides back to him.

The Golden Apples were not in Libya as some say, but near Atlas in the land of the Hyperboreans,[7] and Earth had presented them to Zeus when he was wed to Hera. They were guarded by an immortal dragon, the offspring of Typhon and Echidna, which had a hundred heads and many different voices. The Hesperides—Aegle, Erytheia, Hespere, and Arethusa—also guarded the Golden Apples.

As he was traveling through Illyria and arrived at the river Eridanus, he came upon the nymphs, the daughters of Zeus and Themis[8] who showed him where Nereus[9] was. Heracles then seized Nereus while he was asleep, and, when Nereus transformed himself into all sorts of shapes, Heracles bound him up and would not let him go until Nereus told him where the apples and the Hesperides were to be found.

As soon as he got the information, Heracles started out across Libya, where the ruler was Poseidon's son Antaeus, who was in the habit of doing away with strangers by compelling them to wrestle. When Heracles was forced to wrestle with him, he

---

[6] **Augeas:** Heracles cleaned Augeas' stables, which had never been cleaned, by diverting two rivers through the stables washing out the manure.

[7] **Hyperboreans:** Unlike other storytellers, Apollodorus places the gardens of the Hesperides in the far west, not the far north. The Hesperides, the garden of the gods situated beside Mount Atlas, was guarded by a huge serpent.

[8] **Themis:** An ancient mother-goddess and also the Titaness wife of Zeus; she was the mother of the three Horae (Hours) and the three Fates.

[9] **Nereus:** Son of Oceanus and Gaia.

picked Antaeus up and killed him by holding him in the air and breaking his body—for when Antaeus was touching the earth he had the power to grow in strength, and for this reason some people said he was Earth's son.

When Heracles had traveled across Libya to the sea beyond, he crossed over to the continent opposite, and on the Caucasus he brought down with his arrow the eagle, the offspring of Echidna and Typhon, that was eating out Prometheus'[10] liver. Then he set Prometheus free and turned Chiron[11] over to Zeus to die—even though he was not mortal—in place of Prometheus.

When Heracles reached the land of the Hyperboreans and came to the place where Atlas was, because Prometheus had instructed him not to go after the apples himself but to hold up the heavens for Atlas and send him for the apples, Heracles followed this course and took up Atlas' burden. When Atlas got possession of three of the apples of the Hesperides, he went back to Heracles. Because he did not want to hold up the sky, Atlas said he would take the apples to Eurystheus himself, and he instructed Heracles to keep on supporting the heavens himself. Heracles then assured him he would, but, by using a trick, he transferred the vault of the heavens to Atlas again. For, as Prometheus had proposed he should do, he urged Atlas to take up the sky so that he could put a pad across his shoulders. When Atlas heard this, he put the apples on the ground and relieved Heracles of the vault of the heavens.

And so, when he had gathered up the apples, Heracles started on his way. Some people, however, say Heracles did not receive the apples from Atlas, but that he killed the serpent that guarded the apples and picked them himself. When he returned to him, Heracles gave the apples to Eurystheus. Eurystheus, however, presented them to Heracles, but Athena took them from him and carried them back again, for it was against divine law for them to be set down anywhere.

The twelfth labor Eurystheus set for him was to bring Cerberus from Hades. Cerberus had three dog-heads, a dragon's tail, and on his back he had the heads of all kinds of snakes.

When Heracles reached Taenarum in Laconia, where the entrance that leads down to Hades is located, he made the descent through it. And when the spirits of the dead saw him, they all fled from him except for Meleager and Medusa[12] the Gorgon. Then he drew his sword on the Gorgon, as though she were living, but he was informed by Hermes[13] that she was only an empty shade.

Then when he drew near the gates of Hades he found Theseus and also Pirithous[14] the one who had sought Persephone in marriage and was for this reason

---

[10] **Prometheus:** Imprisoned by Zeus for giving the gift of fire—or actually stealing it—to humanity.

[11] **Chiron:** Chiron, or Cheiron, was extremely wise and learned; unfortunately he was accidentally wounded by one of Heracles's poisoned arrows. The pain was so great he wished to die, even though he was an immortal. Prometheus agreed to take on Chiron's immortality so that he could happily die.

[12] **Medusa:** The Gorgons are three frightful sisters with snakes for hair; their glance turns men to stone.

[13] **Hermes:** A messenger god, he conducted the souls of the dead to Hades.

[14] **Theseus and Pirithous:** The two friends, Theseus and Pirithous, descended into the underworld so that Pirithous could ask Persephone, Queen of Hades, to be his bride. Hades, Persephone's husband, seated Heracles and Pirithous on stone chairs where they were stuck.

bound there. When they saw Heracles, they reached out to him with their hands as though they expected to be raised up from the dead by his strength. And Heracles did, in truth, take Theseus' hand and raised him from the dead, but when he wanted to raise Pirithous he gave up, because the land shook with an earthquake.

When Heracles asked Pluto[15] for Cerberus, Pluto told him to take him, if he could overpower him without the help of his weapons. Heracles found Cerberus at the gates of Acheron[16] and he threw his arms around his neck and did not loosen his strangle hold until the dog was subdued, even though he was bitten by the dragon in the dog's tail. Then he took the dog off with him and ascended to earth again at Troezen.[17] And when Heracles had shown him to Eurystheus, he took Cerberus back again to Hades.

---

[15] **Pluto:** The name of the king of Hades.

[16] **Acheron:** One of the five rivers of the underworld.

[17] **Troezen:** An ancient city in the Peloponnesus where Theseus was born.

www For links to more information about Sappho and a quiz on her poetry, see bedfordstmartins .com/worldlit compact.

Sappho, the female poet of sixth-century B.C.E. Greece upon whose work many poets of both sexes in ancient Greece and Rome modeled their own, was honored in ancient times as the foremost writer of the Greek lyric. Even though very little of her work remains, that reputation holds. Lyric poetry like Sappho's offers an invaluable glimpse into private emotions and everyday experience seldom seen in Greek epic and drama. Whereas epic writers and tragedians kept a certain distance from their subjects, the personal voice is central to the Greek LYRIC. Sappho recorded life in ancient Greece from a woman's point of view, writing in the first person about romantic love and lust, about celebrations and partings, about jealousy, betrayal, friendship, loss, death, and survival.

An Obscure Life.   Although a great body of legend and conjecture surrounds Sappho, little is known for certain about her. She was born to a well-to-do family sometime in the late seventh century B.C.E. on the Aegean island of Lesbos, off the coast of present-day Turkey, probably at Mytelene. Her mother was named **Cleis**; Sappho probably had two or three brothers. She is said to have been a small and dark-complected woman. Socrates called her beautiful, but others said he must have been thinking about her poetry, not her person. An anonymous commentator wrote that she was "like a nightingale with ill-shapen wings enfolding a tiny body." By a merchant husband or consort named Cercolis, Sappho apparently gave birth to a fair-haired daughter whom she named Cleis, after her mother; she addresses her child tenderly in a number of poems.

KLEE-is

The popular image of Sappho as a woman born before her time, a lonely poet dwelling with a few sympathetic female companions on a remote island outpost of Greek civilization is not corroborated by historical data. During Sappho's lifetime the Greek settlements on the Dodecanese Islands were lively trading centers, ports where people from Asia Minor, the eastern Mediterranean, and the Middle East freely met with Westerners from Greece, Italy, and the western Mediterranean. On these cosmopolitan islands there were enclaves of art and learning that valued women highly. Sixth-century Lesbos was probably a far better place for independent and creative women to live than "Golden Age" fifth-century Athens. By all evidence, Sappho for most of her life lived and wrote within an emotionally close community of women friends and companions. The exact nature of that community is uncertain; the _moisopolon domos,_ or "house of the muses," Sappho refers to may have been anything ranging from an informal association of women friends to a quite formal religious and educational order devoted to **Aphrodite**, the Greek goddess of love, with Sappho as head priestess in charge of both religious rites and the training of young novices. There is a tradition that Sappho died a suicide, throwing herself off a cliff into the sea when her love for a ferryman named Phaon was not returned, but this sounds a lot like folklore. In one

af-roh-DIGH-tee,
AF-ruh-digh-tee

fragment of her work, possibly a poem written on her deathbed, Sappho reminds her daughter that grief is not becoming to a poet's household.

Censorship.   Sappho is counted among a number of great writers whose works have been deliberately and successfully banned. Except for one complete poem and four stanzas of another, all that has been recovered of Sappho's writings are scattered lines and partial stanzas. Sappho's work disappeared not only because of the general neglect of ancient manuscripts during the Middle Ages but also because of specific acts of censorship. Owing to the lesbian themes of some of her poetry (the word *lesbian* derives from Sappho's Lesbos) and perhaps because she was an honored female writer who depicted women as lively, intelligent, and goddess-worshipping, Sappho incurred the all-out animosity of the Christian Church patriarchy during the Middle Ages, more so than any Greek or Roman male writer did. Her poems were twice singled out for destruction by church authorities: In the fourth century the Bishop of Constantinople decreed that her work should be destroyed, and in the eleventh century Pope Gregory VII ordered manuscripts of her poems to be thrown into public bonfires in Rome and Constantinople. Fragments of her work survive only because lines of her poetry were quoted by other poets, by praiseful critics such as Longinus,[1] and by Greek grammarians who wished to cite examples of the Aeolic dialect in which she wrote. In addition, bits and pieces of Sappho's work were found by nineteenth-century Egyptologists who discovered that strips of papyrus torn from manuscripts of her poems had been used to stuff the mouths of mummified crocodiles. It is a measure of the astonishing personal intensity and music of her voice that even fragments of her verse have had the power to move readers deeply, century after century, leaving them longing to possess more of the nine books of odes, elegies, wedding songs, and hymns Sappho is said to have written.

Female Author,
75 c.e.
A late Roman portrait of a female author previously thought to be Sappho, with stylus and tablet. (Erich Lessing / Art Resource, NY)

Celebrant of the Ordinary.   Sappho was able to express in few words what passion and jealousy and lust and tenderness feel like, both physically and spiritually. In some instances these emotions so transcend the poet's gender, time, and circumstances that certain of Sappho's love poems have been translated or adapted again and again, assigned to male and female speakers alike, as in the poem beginning, "He is more than a hero," in which Sappho evokes the physiological sensations of lovesickness. She is also the first Western woman writer of lyrical and intimate accounts of experience that is particularly female — a woman's loss of virginity; a young woman's fear and anticipation of marriage when it is the only way open to her; the way women talk among themselves when they are at ease; the volatile friendships and rivalries among women poets; and often the mixture of pain and joy involved with relationships. Sappho's poetry celebrates not only the formal rites of Aphrodite but also the day-to-day rituals that mark continuities between generations of

The tenth Muse.

– Plato,
describing Sappho

---

[1] **Longinus** (first century c.e.): Obscure author of one of the most influential works of classical literary criticism, the treatise *On the Sublime*, which discusses style in literature.

women, as when the poet dresses her daughter's fair hair and remembers what her own mother used to tell her about fashions in headbands.

■ **FURTHER RESEARCH**

Barnstone, Willis. *Sappho: Lyrics in the Original Greek with Translations.* 1965.
Bowra, C. M. *Greek Lyric Poetry.* 1961.
DuBois, Page. *Sappho Is Burning.* 1995.
Foley, Helene P. *Reflections on Women in Antiquity.* 1981.
Greene, Ellen. *Reading Sappho: Contemporary Approaches.* 1996.
Raynor, Diane. *Sappho's Lyre; Archaic Lyric and Women Poets of Ancient Greece.* 1991.
Snyder, Jane M. *Lesbian Desire in the Lyrics of Sappho.* 1997.

■ **PRONUNCIATION**

Aphrodite: af-roh-DIGH-tee, AF-ruh-digh-tee
Cleis: KLEE-is

℘ Prayer to my lady of Paphos

Translated by Mary Barnard

Prayer to my lady of Paphos[1]

Dapple-throned Aphrodite,
eternal daughter of God,
snare-knitter! Don't, I beg you,

cow my heart with grief! Come,
as once when you heard my far-
off cry and, listening, stepped

from your father's house to your
gold car, to yoke the pair whose
beautiful thick-feathered wings[2]

10

oaring down mid-air from heaven
carried you to light swiftly
on dark earth; then, blissful one,

smiling your immortal smile
you asked, What ailed me now that
made me call you again? What

---

[1] **lady of Paphos:** In one account of her birth, Aphrodite was born from sea foam and was washed ashore on the island of Cyprus, near the city of Paphos.

[2] **wings:** The pretty sparrows that pulled Aphrodite's chariot.

was it that my distracted
heart most wanted? "Whom has
Persuasion to bring round now

20 to your love? Who, Sappho, is
unfair to you? For, let her
run, she will soon run after;

if she won't accept gifts, she
will one day give them; and if
she won't love you—she soon will

love, although unwillingly. . . ."
If ever—come now! Relieve
this intolerable pain!

30 What my heart most hopes will
happen, make happen; you yourself join forces on my side!

Don't ask me what to wear

Translated by Mary Barnard

Don't ask me what to wear

I have no embroidered
headband from Sardis to
give you, Cleis, such as
I wore
        and my mother
always said that in her
day a purple ribbon
looped in the hair was thought
to be high style indeed

but we were dark:
                        a girl
10 whose hair is yellower than
torchlight should wear no
headdress but fresh flowers

∾ Lament for a Maidenhead

Translated by Mary Barnard

FIRST VOICE:
    Like a quince-apple
    ripening on a top
    branch in a tree top

    not once noticed by
    harvesters or if
    not unnoticed, not reached

SECOND VOICE:
    Like a hyacinth in
    the mountains, trampled
    by shepherds until
10   only a purple stain
    remains on the ground

∾ He is more than a hero

Translated by Mary Barnard

He is more than a hero

He is a god in my eyes—
the man who is allowed
to sit beside you—he

who listens intimately
to the sweet murmur of
your voice, the enticing

laughter that makes my own
heart beat fast. If I meet
10   you suddenly, I can't

speak—my tongue is broken;
a thin flame runs under
my skin; seeing nothing,

hearing only my own ears
drumming, I drip with sweat;
trembling shakes my body

and I turn paler than
dry grass. At such times
death isn't far from me

∾ To an army wife in Sardis

Translated by Mary Barnard

To an army wife, in Sardis:

Some say a cavalry corps,
some infantry, some, again,
will maintain that the swift oars

of our fleet are the finest
sight on dark earth; but I say
that whatever one loves, is.

This is easily proved: did
not Helen[1]—she who had scanned
the flower of the world's manhood—

choose as first among men one
who laid Troy's honor in ruin?
warped to his will, forgetting

love due her own blood, her own
child, she wandered far with him.
So Anactoria, although you

being far away forget us,
the dear sound of your footstep
and light glancing in your eyes

10

---

[1] **Helen:** Helen of Troy, although married to Menaleus, chose Paris as her lover; their flight from the Greek mainland to Troy in Asia Minor is the romantic cause of the Trojan War.

20   would move me more than glitter
of Lydian[2] horse or armored
tread of mainland infantry

---

[2] **Lydian:** An ancient kingdom in Asia Minor.

❧ You know the place: then

Translated by Mary Barnard

You know the place: then

Leave Crete and come to us
waiting where the grove is
pleasantest, by precincts

sacred to you; incense
smokes on the altar, cold
streams murmur through the

apple branches, a young
rose thicket shades the ground
10   and quivering leaves pour

down deep sleep; in meadows
where horses have grown sleek
among spring flowers, dill

scents the air. Queen! Cyprian![1]
Fill our gold cups with love
stirred into clear nectar

❧ I have had not one word from her

Translated by Mary Barnard

I have had not one word from her

Frankly I wish I were dead.
When she left, she wept

---

[1] **Queen! Cyprian!:** The poem is addressed to Aphrodite; see note 1 on page 562.

a great deal; she said to
me, "This parting must be
endured, Sappho. I go unwillingly."

I said, "Go, and be happy
but remember (you know
well) whom you leave shackled by love

10 "If you forget me, think
of our gifts to Aphrodite
and all the loveliness that we shared

"all the violet tiaras,
braided rosebuds, dill and
crocus twined around your young neck

"myrrh poured on your head
and on soft mats girls with
all that they most wished for beside them

20 "while no voices chanted
choruses without ours,
no woodlot bloomed in spring without song . . ."

⟡ CONFUCIUS (KONGFUZI)
CHINA, 551–479 B.C.E.

The life story of Confucius[1] has been obscured by layers of legend that
have accrued around his name. It is known that he was born in 551 B.C.E.
in the feudal province of Lu, in eastern China north of the Yangtze River,
probably to a family of the lower aristocracy, although legend has it that
he sprang from more humble origins. Orphaned at an early age, Kongfuzi, or Master Kung (Latinized to "Confucius"), became a philosopher-
teacher after intensive study of the traditional Five Classics,[2] a collection
of poems, lore, and documents rooted in the ancient history of China. As
The Analects report him to have said, "At fifteen I wanted to learn. At
thirty I had a foundation. At forty, a certitude. At fifty, knew the orders of

www For links to
more information
about Confucius,
see bedfordstmartins
.com/worldlit
compact.

---

[1] **Confucius:** The Chinese name for Confucius is Kongfuzi, but the Latinized version, Confucius, is so
ingrained in the tradition of Chinese studies that it is the preferred name—at least for the time being.
[2] **the Five Classics:** The Five Classics, memorized by educated Chinese for some two thousand years, include
the *Book of Songs*, the *Book of Historical Documents*, the *Book of Changes* (the *I Ching*), the *Spring and Autumn
Annals*, and the *Records of Ritual*.

Portrait of Confucius

As the preeminent Chinese philosopher, teacher, and political theorist, Confucius has influenced Eastern and Western political and religious thought for more than two millennia. (Bettmann / CORBIS)

shur-JING

YOW

All Chinese philosophy is essentially the study of how men can best be helped to live together in harmony and good order.

– ARTHUR WALEY, historian and translator, 1949

heaven. At sixty, was ready to listen to them. At seventy, could follow my own heart's desire without overstepping the law" (II.4). Apparently, Confucius began teaching before he knew certitude, for he began teaching just before his mother's death, when he was twenty-three. After a three-year period of grieving, he resumed his teaching and traveled from court to court as a wandering sage trying to teach the way of "Right Government" and "Right Living."

Political Instability. Confucius lived during the political decline of the Zhou dynasty (c. 770–c. 221 B.C.E.), an age of great importance to Chinese culture. It was a time of unprecedented social and technological change during which the arts and letters flourished despite the lack of a strong central government. The power of feudal lords had come to overshadow that of the kings descended from the Zhou invaders, who had overthrown the ancient Shang dynasty.[3] Once the center of political power, these traditional leaders had been reduced to nominal roles as spiritual leaders. Most important for Confucianism, it was a time of instability when the feudal system that had held China intact began to break down; with a weakened central power, rivalries arose among the competing provincial lords. In the last years of his life, Confucius traveled to the courts of these once subordinate lords, unsuccessfully trying to convince them to accept his ways and to convert them into philosopher-kings, an ideal he held in common with Plato. Thus the practical piety, filial obligation, and respect for tradition that Confucius taught arose in part from his intention to preserve the failing integrity of Chinese society. Confucius returned home at the age of sixty-nine and devoted himself to writing. Books attributed to him include the *Book of Songs* (**Shi jing**) and the *Book of Writings (Shu jing)*. He died in 479 B.C.E. an apparent failure; he had not become the valued advisor to a great prince who might have restored the legendary Golden Age of **Yao** (third millennium B.C.E.).

The Analects. The Analects is a compilation of the sayings or teachings of Confucius gathered by his students, which according to tradition numbered some three thousand. Although there is no certain date for their composition, it is thought that the teachings were written down several hundred years after Confucius's death. At some point the writings were organized into their present edition of twenty books. The sayings and anecdotes, which together do not possess the coherence of philosophical essays, seem to answer particular questions or situations. Their terse, truncated style is reminiscent of the verses in the Book of Proverbs in the Hebrew Scriptures.

The selections from *The Analects* here give a fair sample of the basic tenets of Confucius's thought: its focus on the matters of this world; its celebration of the family as the central pillar of political and social life; and its emphasis on practicing a "middle way" that leads to moral propriety and social responsibility. Confucius did not consider himself the originator

---

[3] Shang dynasty (c. 1600–c. 1028 B.C.E.): An early feudal period in Chinese history.

of his ideas, as he clearly states in Book VII: "I have transmitted what was taught to me without making up anything of my own. I have been faithful to and loved the Ancients." At the center of Confucianism, indeed of most Chinese thought, is the idea of the dao, or Way, which in *The Analects* means the virtuous life, the Way of Heaven. For Confucius, following the Way takes effort, a conscious striving for betterment and, above all, instruction. The dao in Daoism is the direct opposite, however; effort as well as ego must be laid aside in Daoism in order to move quietly and harmoniously in the eternal flow of life. Confucius's main teaching was that people should set aside self-interest for the good of others—their immediate family, their province, and their state.

The power that sustains relationships is benevolence, or *jen* (also spelled *ren*); the Chinese ideogram for *jen* is a combination of a sign meaning "human" and the sign for "two"—a respectful relationship based on human feeling, or benevolence. Right conduct at home, achieved through observing ritual and basing action in moral principle, leads ultimately to a balanced individual, family, and state.

■ **FURTHER RESEARCH**

Background
Ames, R. T. *Thinking Through Confucius*. 1987.
Creel, H. G. *Confucius: The Man and the Myth*. 1951.
Fingarette, Herbert. *Confucius: The Sacred as Secular*. 1972.
Wu-chi, Liu. *An Introduction to Chinese Literature*. 1966.

Editions with Commentary
Dawson, Raymond, trans. *Confucius: The Analects*. 1993.
Lau, D. C., trans. *Confucius: The Analects*. 1979.
Waley, Arthur, trans. *The Analects of Confucius*. 1958.

■ **PRONUNCIATION**

Jan Ch'iu: jahn-CHYOO, jahn-CHOO
P'êng: BUNG
Shi jing: shur-JING
Tsêng: DZUNG
Tzu-kung: dzuh-GOHNG
Tzu-hsia: dzuh-SHAH
Tzu-yu: dzuh-YOO
Yao: YOW
Zhou: JOH

According to Confucianism, the daily task of dealing with social affairs in human relations is not something alien to the sage. Carrying on this task is the very essence of the development of the perfection of his personality. He performs it not only as a citizen of society, but also as a "citizen of the universe," *t'ien min,* as Mencius called it.

– YU-LAN FUNG, philosopher, 1948

I have read the books of Confucius with attention, I have made extracts from them; I found that they spoke only the purest morality. . . . He appeals only to virtue, he preaches no miracles, there is nothing in them of religious allegory.

– VOLTAIRE

FROM

∽ The Analects[1]

Translated by Arthur Waley

[ON CONFUCIUS THE MAN]

Book VII

4   In his leisure hours the Master's manner was very free-and-easy, and his expression alert and cheerful.

15   The 'Duke of Shê'[2] asked Tzu-lu about Master K'ung (Confucius). Tzu-lu did not reply. The Master said, Why did you not say 'This is the character of the man: so intent upon enlightening the eager that he forgets his hunger, and so happy in doing so, that he forgets the bitterness of his lot and does not realize that old age is at hand.[3] That is what he is.'

26   The Master fished with a line but not with a net; when fowling he did not aim at a roosting bird.

31   When in the Master's presence anyone sang a song that he liked, he did not join in at once, but asked for it to be repeated and then joined in.

37   The Master's manner was affable yet firm, commanding but not harsh, polite but easy.

Book X

7, 8   When preparing himself for sacrifice he must wear the Bright Robe,[4] and it must be of linen. He must change his food and also the place where he commonly sits. But there is no objection to his rice being of the finest quality, nor to his meat being finely minced. Rice affected by the weather or turned he must not eat, nor fish that is not sound, nor meat that is high. He must not eat anything discoloured or that smells bad. He must not eat what is overcooked nor what is undercooked, nor anything that is out of season. He must not eat what has been crookedly cut, nor any dish that lacks its proper seasoning. The meat that he eats must at the very most not be enough to make his breath smell of meat rather than of rice. As regards wine, no limit is laid down; but he must not be disorderly. He may not drink wine bought at a

---

[1] **The Analects:** Ordinarily, *The Analects* are published in their original sequence. The chapters of selected books have been rearranged here, however, according to the basic themes of Confucianism, to aid readers' understanding. Arthur Waley's original footnotes have been edited for length and style.

[2] **The 'Duke of Shê':** An adventurer, known originally as Shên Chu-liang; first mentioned in 523 B.C.E. and still alive in 475. The title 'Duke of Shê' was one which he had invented for himself.

[3] **old age . . . hand:** According to the traditional chronology Confucius was sixty-two at the time this was said.

[4] **the Bright Robe:** *Ming I*, the 'spirit robe' used during the period of purification.

shop or eat dried meat from the market. He need not refrain from such articles of food as have ginger sprinkled over them; but he must not eat much of such dishes.[5]

After a sacrifice in the ducal palace, the flesh must not be kept overnight. No sacrificial flesh may be kept beyond the third day. If it is kept beyond the third day, it may no longer be eaten. While it is being eaten, there must be no conversation, nor any word spoken while lying down after the repast. Any article of food, whether coarse rice, vegetables, broth or melon, that has been used as an offering must be handled with due solemnity.

12   When the stables were burnt down, on returning from Court, he said, Was anyone hurt? He did not ask about the horses.

[ON EDUCATION]

Book II

15   The Master said, 'He who learns but does not think, is lost.' He who thinks but does not learn is in great danger.[6]

17   The Master said, Yu,[7] shall I teach you what knowledge is? When you know a thing, to recognize that you know it, and when you do not know a thing, to recognize that you do not know it. That is knowledge.[8]

Book VII

1, 2   The Master said, I have 'transmitted what was taught to me without making up anything of my own.' I have been faithful to and loved the Ancients. In these respects, I make bold to think, not even our old P'êng[9] can have excelled me. The Master said, I have listened in silence and noted what was said, I have never grown tired of learning nor wearied of teaching others what I have learnt.

Book XIII

9   When the Master was going to Wei, Jan Ch'iu drove him. The Master said, What a dense population! Jan Ch'iu said, When the people have multiplied, what next should be done for them? The Master said, Enrich them. Jan Ch'iu said, When one has enriched them, what next should be done for them? The Master said, Instruct them.

---

[5] **When preparing . . . dishes:** All the above refers to periods of preparation for sacrifice.

[6] **'He who . . . danger:** I imagine that the first clause is a proverbial saying, and that Confucius meets it with the second clause. The proverb says: 'To learn without thinking is fatal.' Confucius says: To think but not to learn (i.e., study the Way of the ancients) is equally dangerous.

[7] **Yu:** Familiar name of the disciple Tzu-lu.

[8] **That is knowledge:** That knowledge consists in knowing that one does not know is a frequent theme in early Chinese texts.

[9] **our old P'êng:** It is the special business of old men to transmit traditions.

Book XV

35 The Master said, When it comes to Goodness one need not avoid competing with one's teacher.

[ON FILIAL PIETY]

Book II

5 Mêng I Tzu asked about the treatment of parents. The Master said, Never disobey! When Fan Ch'ih[10] was driving his carriage for him, the Master said, Mêng asked me about the treatment of parents and I said, Never disobey! Fan Ch'ih said, In what sense did you mean it? The Master said, While they are alive, serve them according to ritual. When they die, bury them according to ritual and sacrifice to them according to ritual.[11]

7 Tzu-yu[12] asked about the treatment of parents. The Master said, 'Filial sons' nowadays are people who see to it that their parents get enough to eat. But even dogs and horses are cared for to that extent. If there is no feeling of respect, wherein lies the difference?

8 Tzu-hsia asked about the treatment of parents. The Master said, It is the demeanour that is difficult. Filial piety does not consist merely in young people undertaking the hard work, when anything has to be done, or serving their elders first with wine and food. It is something much more than that.

Book IV

18 The Master said, In serving his father and mother a man may gently remonstrate with them. But if he sees that he has failed to change their opinion, he should resume an attitude of deference and not thwart them; may feel discouraged, but not resentful.

Book XIII

18 The 'Duke' of Shê addressed Master K'ung saying, In my country there was a man called Upright Kung.[13] His father appropriated a sheep, and Kung bore witness against him. Master K'ung said, In my country the upright men are of quite another sort. A father will screen his son, and a son his father—which incidentally does involve a sort of uprightness.

---

[10] **Fan Ch'ih:** A disciple.

[11] **Never . . . ritual:** Evidently by 'disobey' Confucius meant 'disobey the rituals.' The reply was intended to puzzle the enquirer and make him think. Here and elsewhere 'sacrifice' means offerings in general and not only animal sacrifice.

[12] **Tzu-yu:** A disciple.

[13] **Upright Kung:** A legendary paragon of honesty.

Book XVII

21 Tsai Yü asked about the three years' mourning,[14] and said he thought a year would be quite long enough: 'If gentlemen suspend their practice of the rites[15] for three years, the rites will certainly decay; if for three years they make no music, music will certainly be destroyed.'[16] (In a year) the old crops have already vanished, the new crops have come up, the whirling drills have made new fire.[17] Surely a year would be enough?

The Master said, Would you then (after a year) feel at ease in eating good rice and wearing silk brocades? Tsai Yü said, Quite at ease. (The Master said) If you would really feel at ease, then do so. But when a true gentleman is in mourning, if he eats dainties, he does not relish them, if he hears music, it does not please him, if he sits in his ordinary seat, he is not comfortable. That is why he abstains from these things. But if you would really feel at ease, there is no need for you to abstain.

When Tsai Yü had gone out, the Master said, How inhuman Yü is! Only when a child is three years old does it leave its parents' arms. The three years' mourning is the universal mourning everywhere under Heaven.[18] And Yü—was he not the darling of his father and mother for three years?

[ON RITUAL AND MUSIC]

Book III

3 The Master said, A man who is not Good, what can he have to do with ritual? A man who is not Good, what can he have to do with music?

4 Lin Fang asked for some main principles in connexion with ritual. The Master said, A very big question. In ritual at large it is a safe rule always to be too sparing rather than too lavish; and in the particular case of mourning-rites, they should be dictated by grief rather than by fear.

Book VIII

2 The Master said, Courtesy not bounded by the prescriptions of ritual becomes tiresome. Caution not bounded by the prescriptions of ritual becomes timidity, daring becomes turbulence, inflexibility becomes harshness.

8 The Master said, Let a man be first incited by the *Songs,* then given a firm footing by the study of ritual, and finally perfected by music.

---

[14] **three years' mourning:** For parents. Three years is often interpreted as meaning 'into the third year,' i.e., twenty-five months.

[15] **practice . . . rites:** The mourning for parents entailed complete suspension of all ordinary activities.

[16] **'If gentlemen . . . destroyed':** A traditional saying.

[17] **new fire:** The ritualists describe four 'fire-changing' rites, one for each season, the new fire being in each case kindled on the wood of a tree appropriate to the season.

[18] **three years' . . . Heaven:** The whole object of this paragraph is to claim Confucius as a supporter of the three years' mourning. This custom was certainly far from being 'universal,' and was probably not ancient.

[On Religion]

Book III

11   Someone asked for an explanation of the Ancestral Sacrifice. The Master said, I do not know. Anyone who knew the explanation could deal with all things under Heaven as easily as I lay this here; and he laid his finger upon the palm of his hand.

Book V

12   Tzu-kung said, Our Master's views concerning culture[19] and the outward insignia of goodness, we are permitted to hear; but about Man's nature[20] and the ways of Heaven[21] he will not tell us anything at all.

Book VII

20   The Master never talked of prodigies, feats of strength, disorders[22] or spirits.

34   When the Master was very ill, Tzu-lu asked leave to perform the Rite of Expiation. The Master said, Is there such a thing?[23] Tzu-lu answered saying, There is. In one of the Dirges it says, 'We performed rites of expiation for you, calling upon the sky-spirits above and the earth-spirits below.' The Master said, My expiation began long ago![24]

Book XI

11   Tzu-lu asked how one should serve ghosts and spirits. The Master said, Till you have learnt to serve men, how can you serve ghosts? Tzu-lu then ventured upon a question about the dead. The Master said, Till you know about the living, how are you to know about the dead?[25]

[On Morality in Government]

Book I

5   The Master said, A country of a thousand war-chariots cannot be administered unless the ruler attends strictly to business, punctually observes his promises, is

---

[19] **culture:** *Chang* ('insignia') means literally 'emblems' (usually representations of birds, beasts, or plants) figuring on banners or dresses to show the rank of the owner. Hence metaphorically, the outward manifestations of an inner virtue.

[20] **Man's nature:** As it is before it has been embellished with 'culture.'

[21] **the ways of Heaven:** T'ien Tao. The Tao taught by Confucius only concerned human behaviour ('the ways of man'); he did not expound a corresponding Heavenly Tao, governing the conduct of unseen powers and divinities.

[22] **disorders:** Disorders of nature; such as snow in summer, owls hooting by day, or the like.

[23] **Is there . . . thing?:** That is, is there any ancient authority for such a rite?

[24] **My expiation . . . ago!:** What justifies me in the eyes of Heaven is the life I have led. There is no need for any rite now.

[25] **to know . . . dead:** For example, whether they are conscious, which was a much debated problem.

economical in expenditure, shows affection towards his subjects in general, and uses the labour of the peasantry only at the proper times of year.[26]

Book II

3   The Master said, Govern the people by regulations, keep order among them by chastisements, and they will flee from you, and lose all self-respect. Govern them by moral force, keep order among them by ritual and they will keep their self-respect and come to you of their own accord.

Book XII

11   Duke Ching of Ch'i[27] asked Master K'ung about government. Master K'ung replied saying, Let the prince be a prince, the minister a minister, the father a father and the son a son. The Duke said, How true! For indeed when the prince is not a prince, the minister not a minister, the father not a father, the son not a son, one may have a dish of millet in front of one and yet not know if one will live to eat it.[28]

Book XIII

6   The Master said, If the ruler himself is upright, all will go well even though he does not give orders. But if he himself is not upright, even though he gives orders, they will not be obeyed.

---

[26] **uses the labour . . . year:** That is, not when they ought to be working in the fields.

[27] **Duke Ching of Ch'i:** Died 490 b.c.e. The last of a long line of powerful and successful dukes.

[28] **one may have . . . eat it:** Figure of speech denoting utter insecurity.

❧ AESCHYLUS
GREECE, C. 525–456 B.C.E.

Aeschylus is the earliest and, in company with his younger contemporaries Sophocles and Euripides,[1] one of the greatest tragedians of fifth-century Athens. Of the more than seventy plays Aeschylus is known to have written, only seven have survived. Nonetheless, these plays were influential in establishing the principles of Greek drama. By introducing a second actor to the Greek stage, Aeschylus moved dialogue to the forefront of drama, giving it a dynamic form approaching that found in modern theater. Above all, like Sophocles, Aeschylus placed before his audiences the life of Athens at a time of that city's transition, exploiting the elements of conflict and crisis that characterize drama to explore the

ES-kuh-lus

---

[1] **Sophocles and Euripides:** Sophocles (496–406 b.c.e.) and Euripides (c. 480–406 b.c.e.), Greek playwrights noted for their tragedies.

www For links to
more information
about Aeschylus,
see bedfordstmartins
.com/worldlit
compact.

competing and often contradictory social, political, and religious forces
at play in his fifth-century city.

Soldier and Playwright.   The son of a wealthy aristocrat who lived at
Eleusis, a town near Athens, Aeschylus was born around 525 B.C.E. From
his epitaph it is known that he fought in the celebrated battle at
Marathon (490 B.C.E.), where Athenian forces roundly defeated the Persians, and it is likely that he also fought in the battles against the Persians
at Salamis and Plataea (480–479 B.C.E.). In the annual drama competitions held during the Festivals of Dionysus,[2] Aeschylus won his first prize
in 484, with his plays taking first place thirteen times after that. In 472, his
play *The Persians*, financed by the then twenty-year-old Pericles[3] (c. 495–
429 B.C.E.) serving as the production's *choregus*, or sponsor, won first
prize and fixed Aeschylus's reputation as far as Sicily, where Hieron, the
ruler of Syracuse, invited him to produce his play. After spending some
time in Sicily, Aeschylus returned to Athens, where he continued to enter
his dramas in competitions, losing to Sophocles in 468, winning first
prize in 467 with a series of plays, including *Seven Against Thebes*, and
again in 458 with the trilogy *The **Oresteia***. Two years later in Gela, Sicily,
Aeschylus died; his four-line epitaph, possibly composed by Aeschylus
himself, subordinates his powerful role as one of the chief dramatists of
his age to his participation in the battle of Marathon:

aw-ruh-STIGH-uh

> Beneath this monument lies the son of Euphorion, Aeschylus
> The Athenian, who died among the rich wheatfields of Gela;
> Of his valor in battle the sacred plains of Marathon may tell
> And too the long-haired Persian who well remembers his worth.

Athens: A City in Flux.   Aeschylus came of age during the twilight of
the ancient tribal ways that had guided social and political affairs in
Greece when it was primarily organized around decentralized rural clans,
whose character and experiences were reflected in the myths they had
handed down from before the eighth century. The *polis*, or city-state, that
had been developing since the seventh century demanded a new system
of law, however, a new code that would accommodate the concentration
of individuals in a city, the exchange of goods and ideas, and a class system distinct from that of the old aristocracy; the *POLIS* also demanded a
reworking of the older myths and legends that no longer mirrored but
still influenced daily life.

---

[2] **Festivals of Dionysus:** Starting at about 530 B.C.E., Athenians held annual spring festivals in honor of Dionysus, the god of wine. During these festivals, playwrights competed for prizes for the best tragedy and the best
comedy. Tragedians presented three related dramas followed by a satyr, often a bawdy play serving to lighten
the mood.

[3] **Pericles** (c. 495–429 B.C.E.): Athenian nobleman and statesman who became one of Athens' greatest leaders in
461 B.C.E. Under Pericles, whose rule lasted until 429 B.C.E., Athens broadened its democratic policies at home
and expanded its empire abroad. The arts, including philosophy and drama, flourished in the Age of Pericles.

Mask of Agamemnon, sixteenth century B.C.E. *This golden mask of Agamemnon is thought to be a portrait of the legendary (and possibly historic) king of Mycenae. Agamemnon is the central character of the first play in Aeschylus's* Oresteia *trilogy. (Bettmann/ CORBIS)*

After years of civil strife under leaders who unsuccessfully tried to serve the different classes of citizens in Athens, the constitutional reformer Cleisthenes (fl. 510 B.C.E.) gained power and restructured Athens' political system. Taking hold when Aeschylus was a young man, these reforms marked a major step toward democracy, enabling more citizens to participate in the political process. Most significant perhaps for *The Oresteia*, Cleisthenes had created ten artificial tribes drawn from geographically separate districts known as demes; each tribe contained members from the upper, middle, and lower classes. The effect was to extend citizenship to a great number of men; women were not citizens and did not participate in the political process, even under the democratic policies in the Age of Pericles. The creation of these artificial tribes accentuated the distinction between kinship ties and civic allegiances dramatized in the plays of Aeschylus and Sophocles.

eh-ree-AH-puh-gus

yoo-MEN-ih-deez

Under Cleisthenes, all free men had full rights and could participate in political decision making by casting votes in the general Assembly. The Council of 500, the main legislative body of Athens, ruled over the Assembly; above the Council were the ARCHONS, men drawn from among the wealthiest citizens, and a body of former archons known as the **Areopagus**. Dating back to the seventh century when it emerged as an advisory council to the top leadership of Athens, the Areopagus initially functioned as a court for high crimes like homicide and exercised broad authority over government policy. By Aeschylus's time, the powers of the Areopagus had been partially reduced, though it still regulated the appointment of officials and heard cases on homicide and some religious offenses. In 462 and 461, about four years before the first production of *The Oresteia*, controversy over the power of the Areopagus flared up when a group of reformers, including Pericles and the unlucky Ephialtes, assassinated for his role in the affair, severely limited the authority of the Areopagus by extending the powers of the Council of 500 and broadening its membership, effectively solidifying the democratic system in Athens. In *The **Eumenides***, the final play of *The Oresteia* trilogy, Aeschylus takes up the issue of these reforms and provides a founding myth for the Areopagus as the guardian of justice perpetually seated "on Ares' Hill." Rather than the aristocratic council attacked by Pericles and Ephialtes, Aeschylus's Areopagus appears to be a court of citizens, suggesting that Aeschylus supported the reforms.

The Plays.   In addition to the three plays of *The Oresteia*—*Agamemnon, The Libation Bearers (The Choephori)*, and *The Eumenides*—four other plays by Aeschylus have survived: *The Persians, Seven Against Thebes, The Suppliants*, and *Prometheus Bound. The Persians*, first produced in 472 B.C.E., is a topical historical play—the only one from this period in Greece—that celebrates the Athenian victory over the Persians at Salamis six years earlier. *Seven Against Thebes* and *The Suppliants*, both produced in the 460s, and *Prometheus Bound*, whose date is uncertain, draw from traditional myths and legends and from the works of Hesiod and Homer. Like Sophocles after him, Aeschylus refashioned the familiar stories of gods and heroes to dramatize both the disjunction and the union of the values and institutions of the older religious system and those of the new *polis* as well as to probe the age-old question of human suffering in a universe presided over by divine forces. *Prometheus Bound*, for example, takes up the myth of its title character, the Titan who stole "fire"—the source of all arts and sciences—from the gods and gave it to man; *The Suppliants* takes up the story of the Danaids, the descendants of Io, an Argive princess transformed into a cow and driven on extensive wanderings by a jealous Hera because Zeus had fallen in love with her. *Seven Against Thebes*, like Sophocles's *Oedipus Rex* and *Antigone*, draws on the story of the curse on the house of Laius that was visited upon Laius's son Oedipus and his family. In all his plays Aeschylus reexamines the philosophical and moral core of myths and legends and asks to what degree individuals are responsible for their actions, and under what conditions, if any, they may challenge divine, legal, and political authority.

The uniqueness of Aeschylean drama seems to reside in this: it is expressed almost entirely in the immemorially old mythic-poetic idiom in which Aeschylus . . . had been raised; and yet it is heavily . . . engaged with the Athenian transition to a new world, a world that in many senses is still ours.

– JOHN HERINGTON, critic, 1986

The Oresteia.   *The Oresteia,* first performed at the Festival of Dionysus in 458 B.C.E., is composed of three plays: *Agamemnon,* the story of Clytemnestra's murder of her husband, King Agamemnon, upon his return home from the Trojan War; *The Libation Bearers,* the story of Orestes' murder of his mother, Clytemnestra, to avenge his father's death; and *The Eumenides,* the story of Orestes' trial for matricide, held in the court of the Areopagus at Athens, to which he has fled. This trilogy dramatizes a society's transition from a tribal form of justice that enforced an ironclad prohibition of blood crimes against immediate kin to a civic system of justice that recognized mitigating factors in homicide cases — even those involving immediate family. In the course of the three plays, the Furies (the Erinyes), serpent-haired female monsters charged with avenging blood crimes against kin, serve as the ministers of the archaic law, while the gods Apollo and Athene represent the new law — one based on trial and persuasion. Despite its emphasis on the contrast between vengeance and justice, *The Oresteia* actually transcends its ostensible theme and may be seen as a work heralding the birth of enlightened civilization out of chaos and darkness.

Agamemnon.   The trilogy opens with *Agamemnon,* a powerful, ritualistic drama that recounts the murder of King Agamemnon of Argos when he returns home triumphant from the Trojan War. Agamemnon returns with Cassandra, the daughter of the Trojan King Priam and Queen Hecuba, and a seer cursed with never being understood. Before Agamemnon's arrival, the monologue of the watchman and the exchange between **Clytemnestra** and the chorus establish a mood of foreboding, intimating the impending murder of the returning king at the hands of his wife and her accomplice and consort, Aegisthus, the king's nephew. The chorus also reminds the audience, as Cassandra's frantic prophecies also do later in the play, of horrors past afflicted on the descendants of Tantalus and Atreus.

kligh-tum-NES-truh

Indeed, the murder of Agamemnon is linked to a bloody cycle of revenge unleashed on the descendants of the House of Atreus in the city of Argos going back several generations, to Tantalus, the great-grandfather of Agamemnon. To test the perceptiveness of the gods who had invited him to a banquet, Tantalus murdered his son Pelops and fed his body to them in a stew; the gods, discovering the trick at once, restored Pelops to life and condemned Tantalus to Hades, where he was eternally tempted to slake his thirst and satisfy his hunger from a pool and a bough of fruit that receded whenever he tried to reach them. Sent back to earth, Pelops eventually betrayed Myrtilus, his conspirator, in a scheme to win Hippodameia as his bride; before dying, Myrtilus cursed Pelops and his descendants, including both of his sons — Thyestes, the father of Aegisthus, and Atreus, the father of Menelaus and Agamemnon. Thyestes and Atreus became bitter enemies, and Atreus eventually repeated Tantalus's horrible crime, secretly murdering his brother's sons and serving them to Thyestes in a stew. Thyestes then cursed Atreus. **Aegisthus**, a later son of Thyestes, by the time of Agamemnon's return to Argos has joined as a consort and conspirator with Clytemnestra, who wants to

ee-JIS-thus

ih-fuh-juh-NIGH-uh,
ih-fuh-juh-NEE-uh

murder her husband to avenge the death of her daughter, **Iphigenia**. (Advised by the seer Calchas, Agamemnon sacrificed his daughter to the goddess Artemis in order to raise the winds to launch the Greek fleet against Troy.)

Having brooded for seven years on the murder of her daughter and enlisted an equally bitter Aegisthus into her service, Clytemnestra has prepared a cold homecoming for her husband. In a spectacular scene, Clytemnestra, with jealousy over Cassandra adding to her rage, lays out a lavish welcome fit only for the gods. As she goads and taunts the reluctant Agamemnon to step down on the blood-red ceremonial carpet, her words of welcome reek with irony and cloak threats of imminent violence.

By the end of the play, Aegisthus and Clytemnestra appear before the horrified chorus, the citizens of the city, and celebrate what they call the justice of their actions. They also make clear that they will rule over Argos with a heavy hand, threatening to subject its citizens to arbitrary discipline. Under the tribal code of retributive justice, Clytemnestra's murder of her husband is justified because he is guilty of a blood-crime against their daughter. As the repeated pattern of crimes and curses makes clear, however, there can be no end to vengeance, and the chorus remains unconvinced of the righteousness of Clytemnestra and Aegisthus's deed and fears for its own civil liberties.

oh-RES-teez

The Libation Bearers. Although not included in this anthology, this play is an important part of *The Oresteia*. In *The Libation Bearers,* Agamemnon's son **Orestes** returns to Argos to avenge his father's murder, but to do so not only must he kill his cousin Aegisthus, but he must also commit the worst crime of all—matricide. By acting out the tribal code of retribution, he becomes part of an endless cycle of revenge. Orestes, who was abetted in his plot by his surviving sister, Electra, is now plagued by the Furies. Following the advice of Apollo, who urged him to kill his mother, he flees from Argos to the Temple of Apollo at Delphi.

How many of us . . . were taught that *The Oresteia* is about the establishment of justice for Western civilization, rather than that it is a great act of mythopoeia [mythmaking] in which politics are sexualized and where the idea of justice becomes defined as "masculine."

– ADRIENNE MUNICH, critic, 1985

The Eumenides. The Temple of Apollo at Delphi is where the beleaguered Orestes is found at the beginning of the trilogy's final play, *The Eumenides.* The Furies, who visit their tortures with special intensity upon those who commit matricide, surround Orestes, who is polluted by his crime. Apollo, who has guided Orestes all along, sends him to Athens where he will be judged in a court of law presided over by none other than the guardian of the city herself, the goddess Athene. Meanwhile the Furies have already begun to make their case against Orestes, justifying their role as agents of a divine justice that takes precedence over that of the younger gods like Apollo who in the Furies' view and undermine the strict code of *lex talionis,* or retributive justice.

As *The Eumenides* proceeds, Athene, a female deity not of woman born, must shift the balance in favor of Orestes before a divided jury of Athenian citizens. As a result of Athene's intervention and vote, Clytemnestra's murder of Agamemnon, justified under the old law, is now condemned; Orestes' murder of his mother, on the other hand, is justified, in part because it is determined that the father's seed alone forms the blood of the offspring. Athene persuades the fearsome Furies to give up their role as avengers of blood crimes and assume the new title and role of Eumenides, or givers of blessings. The new civic order rests on a strict patriarchy whose values are supported by Athene's domestication of the Furies. The play concludes with a final procession of the chorus and the players singing a tribute to Athens and to "all-seeing Zeus," who in *Agamemnon* was described as a just god who ordered the world according to one principle: "Man must suffer to be wise."

■ **FURTHER RESEARCH**

Goldhill, Simon. *Aeschylus: The Oresteia.* 1992.
Herington, John. *Aeschylus.* 1986.
Hogan, James. *A Commentary on the Complete Greek Tragedies: Aeschylus.* 1987.
McCall, Marsh H., ed. *Aeschylus: A Collection of Critical Essays.* 1972.
Munich, Adrienne. "Notorious Signs, Feminist Criticism, and Literary Tradition." In Gayle Green and Coppelia Kahn, eds., *Making a Difference: Feminist Literary Criticism.* 1985.
Podlecki, Anthony J. *The Political Background of Aeschylean Tragedy.* 1966.
Rocco, Christopher. "Democracy and Discipline in Aeschylus's *Oresteia.*" In *Tragedy and Enlightenment: Athenian Political Thought and the Dilemmas of Modernity.* 1997.
Zeitlin, Froma. "The Dynamics of Misogyny." In *Playing the Other: Gender and Society in Classical Greek Literature.* 1996.

■ **PRONUNCIATION**

Aegisthus: ee-JIS-thus
Aeschylus: ES-kuh-lus
Areopagus: eh-ree-AH-puh-gus
Clytemnestra: kligh-tum-NES-truh
Eumenides: yoo-MEN-ih-deez
Iphigenia: ih-fuh-juh-NIGH-uh, ih-fuh-juh-NEE-uh
Oresteia: aw-ruh-STIGH-uh, oh-ruh-STIGH-uh
Orestes: oh-RES-teez, uh-RES-teez

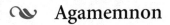 **Agamemnon**

Translated by Robert Fagles

CHARACTERS

WATCHMAN
CLYTAEMNESTRA
HERALD
AGAMEMNON
CASSANDRA
AEGISTHUS
CHORUS, THE OLD MEN OF ARGOS
    AND THEIR LEADER

Attendants of Clytaemnestra and of Agamemnon, bodyguard of Aegisthus

TIME AND SCENE: *A night in the tenth and final autumn of the Trojan war. The house of Atreus in Argos. Before it, an altar stands unlit; a watchman on the high roofs fights to stay awake.*

WATCHMAN:

> Dear gods, set me free from all the pain,
> the long watch I keep, one whole year awake . . .
> propped on my arms, crouched on the roofs of Atreus[1]
> like a dog.
>   I know the stars by heart,
> the armies of the night, and there in the lead
> the ones that bring us snow or the crops of summer,
> bring us all we have—
> our great blazing kings of the sky,
> I know them, when they rise and when they fall . . .

10
> and now I watch for the light, the signal-fire
> breaking out of Troy, shouting Troy is taken.
> So she commands, full of her high hopes.
> That woman—she manoeuvres like a man.
>
> And when I keep to my bed, soaked in dew,
> and the thoughts go groping through the night
> and the good dreams that used to guard my sleep . . .
> not here, it's the old comrade, terror, at my neck.
> I mustn't sleep, no—

[*Shaking himself awake.*]
>   Look alive, sentry.
> And I try to pick out tunes, I hum a little,

20
> a good cure for sleep, and the tears start,
> I cry for the hard times come to the house,
> no longer run like the great place of old.
>
> Oh for a blessed end to all our pain,
> some godsend burning through the dark—

[*Light appears slowly in the east; he struggles to his feet and scans it.*]
>   I salute you!
> You dawn of the darkness, you turn night to day—
> I see the light at last.
> They'll be dancing in the streets of Argos
> thanks to you, thanks to this new stroke of—
>   Aieeeeee!

---

[1] **Atreus:** In Homer, Atreus, the father of Agamemnon and Menelaus, was the king of Mycenae. Aeschylus shifts the location from Mycenae to Argos, in part to reflect recent historical events: in 463 B.C.E. Argos had overtaken Mycenae, after which, in 461, Argos joined Athens in an alliance against Sparta. Orestes' oath in *The Eumenides* vowing that no Argive king will ever rise up against Athens celebrates the alliance of these two cities. [Unless otherwise indicated, the notes are the editors'.]

There's your signal clear and true, my queen!
30   Rise up from bed—hurry, lift a cry of triumph
through the house, praise the gods for the beacon,
if they've taken Troy . . .
                    But there it burns,
fire all the way. I'm for the morning dances.
Master's luck is mine. A throw of the torch
has brought us triple-sixes—we have won!
My move now—

[*Beginning to dance, then breaking off, lost in thought.*]
                    Just bring him home. My king,
I'll take your loving hand in mine and then . . .
the rest is silence. The ox is on my tongue.
Aye, but the house and these old stones,
40   give them a voice and what a tale they'd tell.
And so would I, gladly . . .
I speak to those who know; to those who don't
my mind's a blank. I never say a word.

[*He climbs down from the roof and disappears into the palace through a side entrance.
A* CHORUS, *the old men of Argos who have not learned the news of victory, enters and
marches round the altar.*]
CHORUS:
Ten years gone, ten to the day
our great avenger went for Priam—
    Menelaus and lord Agamemnon,[2]
two kings with the power of Zeus,
the twin throne, twin sceptre,
Atreus' sturdy yoke of sons
50   launched Greece in a thousand ships,
armadas cutting loose from the land,
armies massed for the cause, the rescue—

[*From within the palace* CLYTAEMNESTRA *raises a cry of triumph.*]
the heart within them screamed for all-out war!
Like vultures robbed of their young,
    the agony sends them frenzied,
soaring high from the nest, round and
round they wheel, they row their wings,
stroke upon churning thrashing stroke,

---

[2] **Menelaus and lord Agamemnon:** In the following lines, the chorus alludes to the events of the Trojan War. The Trojan prince, Paris, abducted Menelaus's wife, Helen, precipitating a retaliative war led by the Greek (Argive) commanders Menelaus and his brother Agamemnon, against Troy, which was ruled by King Priam. Helen was Clytaemnestra's half sister.

but all the labour, the bed of pain,
60   the young are lost forever.
Yet someone hears on high—Apollo,
Pan or Zeus[3]—the piercing wail
these guests of heaven raise,
and drives at the outlaws, late
but true to revenge, a stabbing Fury![4]

[CLYTAEMNESTRA *appears at the doors and pauses with her entourage.*]
So towering Zeus the god of guests[5]
drives Atreus' sons at Paris,
all for a woman manned by many
the generations wrestle, knees
70   grinding the dust, the manhood drains,
the spear snaps in the first blood rites
      that marry Greece and Troy.
And now it goes as it goes
and where it ends is Fate.
And neither by singeing flesh
nor tipping cups of wine
nor shedding burning tears can you
enchant away the rigid Fury.

[CLYTAEMNESTRA *lights the altar-fires.*]
We are the old, dishonoured ones,
80   the broken husks of men.
Even then they cast us off,
the rescue mission left us here
to prop a child's strength upon a stick.
What if the new sap rises in his chest?
He has no soldiery in him,
      no more than we,
and we are aged past ageing,
gloss of the leaf shrivelled,
three legs at a time we falter on.
90   Old men are children once again,
      a dream that sways and wavers
into the hard light of day.
                  But you,
daughter of Leda, queen Clytaemnestra,

---

[3] **Apollo, Pan or Zeus:** Apollo, the god of prophecy; Pan, the god of nature; Zeus, the god of the sky and justice.

[4] **Fury:** The Furies are serpent-headed female creatures who avenge blood crimes against kin; their role becomes increasingly important throughout the trilogy.

[5] **Zeus . . . guests:** Zeus, the chief of the Olympian gods, was said to uphold the code of hospitality, which Paris violated by running off with Helen, the wife of his host King Menalaus of Sparta.

what now, what news, what message
drives you through the citadel
   burning victims? Look,
the city gods, the gods of Olympus,
gods of the earth and public markets—
all the altars blazing with your gifts!
100   Argos blazes! Torches
race the sunrise up her skies—
drugged by the lulling holy oils,
   unadulterated,
run from the dark vaults of kings.
   Tell us the news!
What you can, what is right—
Heal us, soothe our fears![6]
Now the darkness comes to the fore,
now the hope glows through your victims,
110 beating back this raw, relentless anguish
   gnawing at the heart.

[CLYTAEMNESTRA *ignores them and pursues her rituals; they assemble for the opening chorus.*]
   O but I still have power to sound the god's command at the roads
that launched the kings. The gods breathe power through my song,
   my fighting strength, Persuasion grows with the years—
I sing how the flight of fury hurled the twin command,
     one will that hurled young Greece
and winged the spear of vengeance straight for Troy!
The kings of birds to kings of the beaking prows, one black,
   one with a blaze of silver
120   skimmed the palace spearhand right
     and swooping lower, all could see,
      plunged their claws in a hare, a mother
bursting with unborn young—the babies spilling,
quick spurts of blood—cut off the race just dashing into life![7]
Cry, cry for death, but good win out in glory in the end.
But the loyal seer[8] of the armies studied Atreus' sons,
two sons with warring hearts—he saw two eagle-kings
   devour the hare and spoke the things to come,
'Years pass, and the long hunt nets the city of Priam,
130   the flocks beyond the walls,

---

[6] **fears:** Past evil (the killing of Iphigenia) makes them apprehensive of the future.

[7] **life:** The portent alludes to the destruction of Troy, but it also refers to the sacrifice of Iphigenia, who dies before the fulfillment of marriage.

[8] **seer:** Calchas was with the army from the beginning of *The Iliad* and foresees hardship for the Greeks and Agamemnon.

a kingdom's life and soul—Fate stamps them out.
Just let no curse of the gods lour on us first,
  shatter our giant armour
   forged to strangle Troy. I see
    pure Artemis bristle in pity—
     yes, the flying hounds of the Father
   slaughter for armies . . . their own victim . . a woman
trembling young, all born to die—She loathes the eagles' feast!'[9]
Cry, cry for death, but good win out in glory in the end.

140   'Artemis, lovely Artemis, so kind
to the ravening lion's tender, helpless cubs,
the suckling young of beasts that stalk the wilds—
   bring this sign for all its fortune,
    all its brutal torment home to birth!
I beg you, Healing Apollo, soothe her before
her crosswinds hold us down and moor the ships too long,
pressing us on to another victim . . .
   nothing sacred, no
    no feast to be eaten
150   the architect of vengeance

[*Turning to the palace.*]
    growing strong in the house
   with no fear of the husband
here she waits
the terror raging back and back in the future
  the stealth, the law of the hearth, the mother—
    Memory womb of Fury child-avenging Fury!'
So as the eagles wheeled at the crossroads,
Calchas clashed out the great good blessings mixed with doom
 for the halls of kings, and singing with our fate
160 we cry, cry for death, but good win out in glory in the end.

    Zeus, great nameless all in all,
    if that name will gain his favour,
     I will call him Zeus.
    I have no words to do him justice,
     weighing all in the balance,
     all I have is Zeus, Zeus—
   lift this weight, this torment from my spirit,
     cast it once for all.

---

[9] **feast:** As the virgin goddess of the hunt and guardian of childbirth and of wildlife, Artemis was angered by the slaughter of the pregnant animals by the eagles, who represent the two kings who will similarly destroy the Trojans. Although Artemis is offended here, ironically Agamemnon's sacrifice of Iphigenia will be made in Artemis' name.

He who was so mighty once,
storming for the wars of heaven,
he has had his day.
And then his son who came to power
met his match in the third fall
and he is gone. Zeus, Zeus—
raise your cries and sing him Zeus the Victor![10]
You will reach the truth:

Zeus has led us on to know,
the Helmsman lays it down as law
that we must suffer, suffer into truth.
We cannot sleep, and drop by drop at the heart
the pain of pain remembered comes again,
and we resist, but ripeness comes as well.
From the gods enthroned on the awesome rowing-bench
there comes a violent love.

So it was that day the king,
the steersman at the helm of Greece,
would never blame a word the prophet said—
swept away by the wrenching winds of fortune
he conspired! Weatherbound we could not sail,
our stores exhausted, fighting strength hard-pressed,
and the squadrons rode in the shallows off Chalkis[11]
where the riptide crashes, drags,

and winds from the north pinned down our hulls at Aulis,
port of anguish . . . head winds starving,
sheets and the cables snapped
and the men's minds strayed,
the pride, the bloom of Greece
was raked as time ground on,
ground down, and then the cure for the storm
and it was harsher—Calchas cried,
'My captains, Artemis must have blood!'—
so harsh the sons of Atreus
dashed their sceptres on the rocks,
could not hold back the tears,

---

[10] **Zeus the Victor!:** These lines describe the succession rebellions of younger gods against their fathers: the youngest of the gods, the Olympian Zeus, overthrew his father, Cronos, just as Cronos had overthrown Ouranos, the first and oldest of the gods. For Aeschylus, the sequence demonstrates a gradual move from violent and arbitrary justice to rule by law and order.

[11] **Chalkis:** The city of Chalkis on the island of Euboea lies across the straits of Euripos from the port city of Aulis, where the Greeks have been stalled by unfavorable winds.

and I still can hear the older warlord saying,
'Obey, obey, or a heavy doom will crush me!—
Oh but doom *will* crush me
    once I rend my child,
      the glory of my house—
210   a father's hands are stained,
blood of a young girl streaks the altar.
Pain both ways and what is worse?
Desert the fleets, fail the alliance?
   No, but stop the winds with a virgin's blood,
     feed their lust, their fury?—feed their fury!—
   Law is law!—
         Let all go well.'

And once he slipped his neck in the strap of Fate,[12]
his spirit veering black, impure, unholy,
once he turned he stopped at nothing,
220   seized with the frenzy
        blinding driving to outrage—
wretched frenzy, cause of all our grief!
Yes, he had the heart
   to sacrifice his daughter,
  to bless the war that avenged a woman's loss,
    a bridal rite that sped the men-of-war.
'My father, father!'—she might pray to the winds;
no innocence moves her judges mad for war.
Her father called his henchmen on,
230   on with a prayer,
        'Hoist her over the altar
like a yearling[13] give it all your strength!
She's fainting—lift her,
   sweep her robes around her,
   but slip this strap in her gentle curving lips . . .
     here, gag her hard, a sound will curse the house'—

and the bridle chokes her voice . . . her saffron robes
pouring over the sand
          her glance like arrows showering
wounding every murderer through with pity
240   clear as a picture, live,

---

[12] **strap of Fate:** This phrase points to the conflict in this passage between free will or choice and necessity as a universal force.

[13] **yearling:** A yearling goat was sacrificed to Artemis for victory.

she strains to call their names . . .
I remember often the days with father's guests
when over the feast her voice unbroken,
   pure as the hymn her loving father
bearing third libations[14] sang to Saving Zeus—
transfixed with joy, Atreus' offspring
      throbbing out their love.

What comes next? I cannot see it, cannot say.
The strong techniques of Calchas do their work.
250   But Justice turns the balance scales,
   sees that we suffer
and we suffer and we learn.
And we will know the future when it comes.
Greet it too early, weep too soon.
   It all comes clear in the light of day.
Let all go well today, well as she could want,

[*Turning to* CLYTAEMNESTRA.]
   our midnight watch, our lone defender,
      single-minded queen.

LEADER:
                              We've come,
Clytaemnestra. We respect your power.
260   Right it is to honour the warlord's woman
once he leaves the throne.
                              But why these fires?
Good news, or more good hopes? We're loyal,
we want to hear, but never blame your silence.

CLYTAEMNESTRA:
Let the new day shine—as the proverb says—
glorious from the womb of Mother Night.

[*Lost in prayer, then turning to the* CHORUS.]
You will hear a joy beyond your hopes.
Priam's citadel—the Greeks have taken Troy!

LEADER:
No, what do you mean? I can't believe it.

CLYTAEMNESTRA:
Troy is ours. Is that clear enough?

LEADER:
                              The joy of it,
270   stealing over me, calling up my tears—

---

[14] **third libations:** The first libation was offered to the Olympians, the second to the spirits of the dead, and the third to Zeus, the Savior. [Translator's note.]

CLYTAEMNESTRA:
>   Yes, your eyes expose your loyal hearts.

LEADER:
>   And you have proof?

CLYTAEMNESTRA:
>   I do,
>   I must. Unless the god is lying.

LEADER:
>   That,
>   or a phantom spirit sends you into raptures.

CLYTAEMNESTRA:
>   No one takes me in with visions — senseless dreams.

LEADER:
>   Or giddy rumour, you haven't indulged yourself —

CLYTAEMNESTRA:
>   You treat me like a child, you mock me?

LEADER:
>   Then when did they storm the city?

CLYTAEMNESTRA:
>   Last night, I say, the mother of this morning.

LEADER:
280 And who on earth could run the news so fast?

CLYTAEMNESTRA:
>   The god of fire — rushing fire from Ida![15]
>   And beacon to beacon rushed it on to me,
>   my couriers riding home the torch.
>   From Troy
>   to the bare rock of Lemnos, Hermes' Spur,
>   and the Escort winged the great light west
>   to the Saving Father's face, Mount Athos hurled it
>   third in the chain and leaping Ocean's back
>   the blaze went dancing on to ecstasy — pitch-pine
>   streaming gold like a new-born sun — and brought
290 the word in flame to Mount Makistos' brow.
>   No time to waste, straining, fighting sleep,
>   that lookout heaved a torch glowing over
>   the murderous straits of Euripos to reach

---

[15] **Ida:** This passage describes the chain of beacon fires reaching from Ida, the mountains near Troy, and reaching across the Aegean island of Lemnos, to Mount Athos (the "Saving Father's face" in line 286) in Northern Greece, southward to Mount Makistos, Mount Messapion, Mount Kithairon, Mount Aegiplanctus, and Mount Arachneus to the watch at Argos. The geography throughout this passage is associated with violence and danger, heightening the foreboding at the beginning of the play: Euripus' channel, for example, which divides the Greek mainland from Euboea, suggests Aulis, where Agamemnon sacrificed Iphigenia; Arachneus, which means "Spider Mountain," foreshadows the web Clytaemnestra is spinning for Agamemnon.

Messapion's watchmen craning for the signal.
Fire for word of fire! tense with the heather
withered gray, they stack it, set it ablaze—
the hot force of the beacon never flags,
it springs the Plain of Asôpos, rears
like a harvest moon to hit Kithairon's crest
300   and drives new men to drive the fire on.
That relay pants for the far-flung torch,
they swell its strength outstripping my commands
and the light inflames the marsh, the Gorgon's Eye,[16]
it strikes the peak where the wild goats range—
my laws, my fire whips that camp!
They spare nothing, eager to build its heat,
and a huge beard of flame overcomes the headland
beetling down the Saronic Gulf, and flaring south
it brings the dawn to the Black Widow's face[17]—
310   the watch that looms above your heads—and now
the true son[18] of the burning flanks of Ida
crashes on the roofs of Atreus' sons!
And I ordained it all.
Torch to torch, running for their lives,
one long succession racing home my fire.

                               One,
first in the laps and last, wins out in triumph.
There you have my proof, *my* burning sign, I tell you—
the power my lord passed on from Troy to me!

LEADER:

We'll thank the gods, my lady—first this story,
320   let me lose myself in the wonder of it all!
Tell it start to finish, tell us all.

CLYTAEMNESTRA:

The city's ours—in our hands this very day!
I can hear the cries in crossfire rock the walls.
Pour oil and wine in the same bowl,
what have you, friendship? A struggle to the end.
So with the victors and the victims—outcries,
you can hear them clashing like their fates.

They are kneeling by the bodies of the dead,
embracing men and brothers, infants over

---

[16] **Gorgon's Eye:** The marsh has been variously identified, but each site reflects Clytaemnestra's imaginative power over geography. [Translator's note.]

[17] **Black Widow's face:** Spider Mountain (Mount Arachnaion).

[18] **the true son:** This passage links Agamemnon to his father's crimes.

330 the aged loins that gave them life, and sobbing,
as the yoke constricts their last free breath,
for every dear one lost.
                                        And the others,
there, plunging breakneck through the night —
the labour of battle sets them down, ravenous,
to breakfast on the last remains of Troy.
Not by rank but chance, by the lots they draw,
they lodge in the houses captured by the spear,
settling in so soon, released from the open sky,
the frost and dew. Lucky men, off guard at last,
340 they sleep away their first good night in years.
If only they are revering the city's gods,
the shrines of the gods who love the conquered land,
no plunderer will be plundered in return.
Just let no lust, no mad desire seize the armies
to ravish what they must not touch —
overwhelmed by all they've won!
                                        The run for home
and safety waits, the swerve at the post,
the final lap of the gruelling two-lap race.
And even if the men come back with no offence
350 to the gods, the avenging dead may never rest —
Oh let no new disaster strike! And here
you have it, what a woman has to say.
Let the best win out, clear to see.
A small desire but all that I could want.

LEADER:
Spoken like a man, my lady, loyal,
full of self-command. I've heard your sign
and now your vision.

[*Reaching towards her as she turns and re-enters the palace.*]
                                        Now to praise the gods.
The joy is worth the labour.

CHORUS:
O Zeus my king and Night, dear Night,
360 queen of the house who covers us with glories,
you slung your net on the towers of Troy,
neither young nor strong could leap
the giant dredge net of slavery,
        all-embracing ruin.
I adore you, iron Zeus of the guests
and your revenge — you drew your longbow
year by year to a taut full draw

till one bolt, not falling short
or arching over the stars,
    could split the mark of Paris![19]

370

The sky stroke of god! — it is all Troy's to tell,
but even I can trace it to its cause:
god does as god decrees.
    And still some say
that heaven would never stoop to punish men
who trample the lovely grace of things
untouchable. How wrong they are!
    A curse burns bright on crime —
        full-blown, the father's crimes will blossom,
          burst into the son's.

380

Let there be less suffering . . .
give us the sense to live on what we need.

        Bastions of wealth
        are no defence for the man
        who treads the grand altar of Justice
          down and out of sight.

Persuasion, maddening child of Ruin
overpowers him — Ruin plans it all.
And the wound will smoulder on,

390

   there is no cure,
a terrible brilliance kindles on the night.
He is bad bronze scraped on a touchstone:
put to the test, the man goes black.
    Like the boy who chases
      a bird on the wing, brands his city,
        brings it down and prays,
but the gods are deaf
to the one who turns to crime, they tear him down.

        So Paris learned:

400

        he came to Atreus' house
        and shamed the tables spread for guests,
          he stole away the queen.

And she left her land *chaos,* clanging shields,
companions tramping, bronze prows, men in bronze,

---

[19] **Paris:** While the chorus speaks explicitly of Paris here, most of what is said may also apply to Agamemnon and those in the House of Atreus whose crimes are visited upon their children.

and she came to Troy with a dowry, death,
strode through the gates
     defiant in every stride,
as prophets of the house looked on and wept,
'Oh the halls and the lords of war,
410   the bed and the fresh prints of love.
I *see* him, unavenging, unavenged,
the stun of his desolation is so clear—
     he longs for the one who lies across the sea
until her phantom seems to sway the house.

         Her curving images,
         her beauty hurts her lord,
         the eyes starve and the touch
           of love is gone,

'and radiant dreams are passing in the night,
420   the memories throb with sorrow, joy with pain . . .
     it is pain to dream and see desires
slip through the arms,
         a vision lost for ever
winging down the moving drifts of sleep.'
So he grieves at the royal hearth
     yet others' grief is worse, far worse.
All through Greece for those who flocked to war
they are holding back the anguish now,
     you can feel it rising now in every house;
430   I tell you there is much to tear the heart.

         They knew the men they sent,
         but now in place of men
         ashes and urns come back
           to every hearth.

War, War, the great gold-broker of corpses
holds the balance of the battle on his spear!
Home from the pyres he sends them,
     home from Troy to the loved ones,
heavy with tears, the urns brimmed full,
440   the heroes return in gold-dust,
dear, light ash for men; and they weep,
they praise them, 'He had skill in the swordplay,'
     'He went down so tall in the onslaught,'
'All for another's woman.' So they mutter
in secret and the rancour steals
towards our staunch defenders, Atreus' sons.

And there they ring the walls, the young,
the lithe, the handsome hold the graves
they won in Troy; the enemy earth
450   rides over those who conquered.

The people's voice is heavy with hatred,
now the curses of the people must be paid,
and now I wait, I listen . . .
    there — there is something breathing
under the night's shroud. God takes aim
    at the ones who murder many;
the swarthy Furies stalk the man
gone rich beyond all rights — with a twist
    of fortune grind him down, dissolve him
460   into the blurring dead — there is no help.
The reach for power can recoil,
the bolt of god can strike you at a glance.

Make me rich with no man's envy,
neither a raider of cities, no,
nor slave come face to face with life
    overpowered by another.

[*Speaking singly.*]
— Fire comes and the news is good,
    it races through the streets
but is it true? Who knows?
470   Or just another lie from heaven?

— Show us the man so childish, wonderstruck,
    he's fired up with the first torch,
then when the message shifts
he's sick at heart.

            — Just like a woman
to fill with thanks before the truth is clear.

— So gullible. Their stories spread like wildfire,
    they fly fast and die faster;
rumours voiced by women come to nothing.

LEADER:
Soon we'll know her fires for what they are,
480   her relay race of torches hand-to-hand —
know if they're real or just a dream,
the hope of a morning here to take our senses.
I see a herald running from the beach

and a victor's spray of olive shades his eyes
and the dust he kicks, twin to the mud of Troy,
shows he has a voice — no kindling timber
on the cliffs, no signal-fires for him.
He can shout the news and give us joy,
or else . . . please, not that.
                              Bring it on,
490   good fuel to build the first good fires.
And if anyone calls down the worst on Argos
let him reap the rotten harvest of his mind.

[*The* HERALD *rushes in and kneels on the ground.*]
HERALD:
Good Greek earth, the soil of my fathers!
Ten years out, and a morning brings me back.
All hopes snapped but one — I'm home at last.
Never dreamed I'd die in Greece, assigned
the narrow plot I love the best.
                              And now
I salute the land, the light of the sun,
our high lord Zeus and the king of Pytho[20] —
500   no more arrows, master, raining on our heads!
At Scamander's banks we took our share,
your longbow brought us down like plague.
Now come, deliver us, heal us — lord Apollo!
Gods of the market, here, take my salute.
And you, my Hermes, Escort,
loving Herald, the herald's shield and prayer! —
And the shining dead of the land who launched the armies,
warm us home . . . we're all the spear has left.
You halls of the kings, you roofs I cherish,
510   sacred seats — you gods[21] that catch the sun,
if your glances ever shone on him in the old days,
greet him well — so many years are lost.
He comes, he brings us light in the darkness,
free for every comrade, Agamemnon lord of men.

Give him the royal welcome he deserves!
He hoisted the pickaxe of Zeus who brings revenge,
he dug Troy down, he worked her soil down,
the shrines of her gods and the high altars, gone! —

---

[20] **king of Pytho:** Pytho is the ancient name for Delphi; the king of Pytho is a reference to the Pythian Apollo.

[21] **gods:** The statues of Zeus, Apollo, and Hermes stand on the eastern facade of the palace.

and the seed of her wide earth he ground to bits.
520   That's the yoke he claps on Troy. The king,
the son of Atreus comes. The man is blest,
the one man alive to merit such rewards.

Neither Paris nor Troy, partners to the end,
can say their work outweighs their wages now.
Convicted of rapine, stripped of all his spoils,
and his father's house and the land that gave it life —
he's scythed them to the roots. The sons of Priam
pay the price twice over.

LEADER:
                     Welcome home
from the wars, herald, long live your joy.

HERALD:
                             Our joy —
530   now I could die gladly. Say the word, dear gods.

LEADER:
    Longing for your country left you raw?

HERALD:
    The tears fill my eyes, for joy.

LEADER:
                  You too,
down with the sweet disease that kills a man
with kindness . . .

HERALD:
              Go on, I don't see what you —

LEADER:
                       Love
for the ones who love you — that's what took you.

HERALD:
                     You mean
the land and the armies hungered for each other?

LEADER:
    There were times I thought I'd faint with longing.

HERALD:
    So anxious for the armies, why?

LEADER:
               For years now,
only my silence kept me free from harm.

HERALD:
                 What,
with the kings gone did someone threaten you?

LEADER:
540   So much . . .

now as you say, it would be good to die.
HERALD:
True, we *have* done well.
Think back in the years and what have you?
A few runs of luck, a lot that's bad.
Who but a god can go through life unmarked?
A long, hard pull we had, if I would tell it all.
The iron rations, penned in the gangways
hock by jowl like sheep. Whatever miseries
break a man, our quota, every sun-starved day.

550 Then on the beaches it was worse. Dug in
under the enemy ramparts—deadly going.
Out of the sky, out of the marshy flats
the dews soaked us, turned the ruts we fought from
into gullies, made our gear, our scalps
crawl with lice.
                        And talk of the cold,
the sleet to freeze the gulls, and the big snows
come avalanching down from Ida. Oh but the heat,
the sea and the windless noons, the swells asleep,
dropped to a dead calm . . .

560 But why weep now?
It's over for us, over for them.
The dead can rest and never rise again;
no need to call their muster. We're alive,
do we have to go on raking up old wounds?
Good-bye to all that. Glad I am to say it.

For us, the remains of the Greek contingents,
the good wins out, no pain can tip the scales,
not now. So shout this boast to the bright sun—
fitting it is—wing it over the seas and rolling earth:

570 'Once when an Argive expedition captured Troy
they hauled these spoils back to the gods of Greece,
they bolted them high across the temple doors,
the glory of the past!'
                        And hearing that,
men will applaud our city and our chiefs,
and Zeus will have the hero's share of fame—
he did the work.
                        That's all I have to say.

LEADER:

> I'm convinced, glad that I was wrong.
> Never too old to learn; it keeps me young.

[CLYTAEMNESTRA *enters with her women.*]

> First the house and the queen, it's their affair,
> but I can taste the riches.

CLYTAEMNESTRA:

580
>   I cried out long ago!—
> for joy, when the first herald came burning
> through the night and told the city's fall.
> And there were some who smiled and said,
> 'A few fires persuade you Troy's in ashes.
> Women, women, elated over nothing.'
>
> You made me seem deranged.
> For all that I sacrificed—a woman's way,
> you'll say—station to station on the walls
> we lifted cries of triumph that resounded

590
> in the temples of the gods. We lulled and blessed
> the fires with myrrh and they consumed our victims.

[*Turning to the* HERALD.]

> But enough. Why prolong the story?
> From the king himself I'll gather all I need.
> Now for the best way to welcome home
> my lord, my good lord . . .
>   No time to lose!
> What dawn can feast a woman's eyes like this?
> I can see the light, the husband plucked from war
> by the Saving God and open wide the gates.
>
> Tell him that, and have him come with speed,

600
> the people's darling—how they long for him.
> And for his wife,
> may he return and find her true at hall,
> just as the day he left her, faithful to the last.[22]
> A watchdog gentle to him alone,

[*Glancing towards the palace.*]

>   savage
> to those who cross his path. I have not changed.
> The strains of time can never break our seal.

----

[22] **last:** In this passage, Clytaemnestra uses a mixture of irony, sarcasm, and lies.

In love with a new lord, in ill repute I am
as practised as I am in dyeing bronze.

That is my boast, teeming with the truth.
610   I am proud, a woman of my nobility—
I'd hurl it from the roofs!

[*She turns sharply, enters the palace.*]
LEADER:
    She speaks well, but it takes no seer to know
    she only says what's right.

[*The* HERALD *attempts to leave; the leader takes him by the arm.*]
                                    Wait, one thing.
    Menelaus, is he home too, safe with the men?
    The power of the land—dear king.
HERALD:
    I doubt that lies will help my friends,
    in the lean months to come.
LEADER:
    Help us somehow, tell the truth as well.
    But when the two conflict it's hard to hide—
    out with it.
HERALD:
620   He's lost, gone from the fleets!
    He and his ship, it's true.
LEADER:
                                    After you watched him
    pull away from Troy? Or did some storm
    attack you all and tear him off the line?
HERALD:
                                            There,
    like a marksman, the whole disaster cut to a word.
LEADER:
    How do the escorts give him out—dead or alive?
HERALD:
    No clear report. No one knows . . .
    only the wheeling sun that heats the earth to life.
LEADER:
    But then the storm—how did it reach the ships?
    How did it end? Were the angry gods on hand?
HERALD:
630   This blessed day, ruin it with *them*?
    Better to keep their trophies far apart.

    When a runner comes, his face in tears,
    saddled with what his city dreaded most,

the armies routed, two wounds in one,
one to the city, one to hearth and home . . .
our best men, droves of them, victims
herded from every house by the two-barb whip
that Ares likes to crack,
                         that charioteer
who packs destruction shaft by shaft,
640   careering on with his brace of bloody mares—
When he comes in, I tell you, dragging that much pain,
wail your battle-hymn to the Furies, and high time!
But when he brings salvation home to a city
singing out her heart—
how can I mix the good with so much bad
and blurt out this?—
                          'Storms swept the Greeks,
and not without the anger of the gods!'

Those enemies for ages, fire and water,²³
sealed a pact and showed it to the world—
they crushed our wretched squadrons.
650   Night looming,
breakers lunging in for the kill
and the black gales come brawling out of the north—
ships ramming, prow into hooking prow, gored
by the rush-and-buck of hurricane pounding rain
by the cloudburst—
                        ships stampeding into the darkness,
lashed and spun by the savage shepherd's hand!

But when the sun comes up to light the skies
I see the Aegean heaving into a great bloom
of corpses . . . Greeks, the pick of a generation
660   scattered through the wrecks and broken spars.

But not us, not our ship, our hull untouched.
Someone stole us away or begged us off.
No mortal—a god, death grip on the tiller,
or lady luck herself, perched on the helm,
she pulled us through, she saved us. Aye,
we'll never battle the heavy surf at anchor,
never shipwreck up some rocky coast.

But once we cleared that sea-hell, not even
trusting luck in the cold light of day,

---

²³ **fire and water:** Lightning and the sea.

670   we battened on our troubles, they were fresh—
       the armada punished, bludgeoned into nothing.
       And now if one of them still has the breath
       he's saying *we* are lost. Why not?
       We say the same of him. Well,
       here's to the best.
                          And Menelaus?
       Look to it, he's come back, and yet . . .
       if a shaft of the sun can track him down,
       alive, and his eyes full of the old fire—
       thanks to the strategies of Zeus, Zeus
680   would never tear the house out by the roots—
       then there's hope our man will make it home.

       You've heard it all. Now you have the truth.

[*Rushing out.*]
CHORUS:
       Who—what power named the name that drove your fate?—
       what hidden brain could divine your future,
       steer that word to the mark,
       to the bride of spears,
          the whirlpool churning armies,
                 Oh for all the world a Helen!
       Hell at the prows, hell at the gates
690   hell on the men-of-war,
       from her lair's sheer veils she drifted
          launched by the giant western wind,
             and the long tall waves of men in armour,
       huntsmen trailing the oar-blades' dying spoor
       slipped into her moorings,
          Simois' mouth[24] that chokes with foliage,
                    bayed for bloody strife,
       for Troy's Blood Wedding Day—she drives her word,
       her burning will to the birth, the Fury
700   late but true to the cause,
       to the tables shamed
          and Zeus who guards the hearth[25]—
             the Fury makes the Trojans pay!
       Shouting their hymns, hymns for the bride
       hymns for the kinsmen doomed

---

[24] **Simois' mouth:** Simois is a river in Troy.

[25] **hearth:** Zeus was the guardian of hospitality.

to the wedding march of Fate.
    Troy changed her tune in her late age,
      and I think I hear the dirges mourning
'Paris, born and groomed for the bed of Fate!'
710   They mourn with their life breath,
    they sing their last, the sons of Priam
        born for bloody slaughter.

    So a man once reared
a lion cub[26] at hall, snatched
from the breast, still craving milk
    in the first flush of life.
A captivating pet for the young,
and the old men adored it, pampered it
    in their arms, day in, day out,
720   like an infant just born.
Its eyes on fire, little beggar,
fawning for its belly, slave to food.

    But it came of age
and the parent strain broke out
and it paid its breeders back.
    Grateful it was, it went
through the flock to prepare a feast,
an illicit orgy — the house swam with blood,
    none could resist that agony —
730   massacre vast and raw!
From god there came a priest of ruin,
adopted by the house to lend it warmth.
And the first sensation Helen brought to Troy . . .
call it a spirit
    shimmer of winds dying
        glory light as gold
      shaft of the eyes dissolving, open bloom
    that wounds the heart with love.
But veering wild in mid-flight
740   she whirled her wedding on to a stabbing end,
slashed at the sons of Priam — hearthmate, friend to the death,
    sped by Zeus who speeds the guest,
a bride of tears, a Fury.

---

[26] **lion cub**: A symbol of Helen as first seen by Paris and the Trojans.

There's an ancient saying[27] old as man himself:
men's prosperity
    never will die childless,
        once full-grown it breeds.
    Sprung from the great good fortune in the race
   comes bloom on bloom of pain—
750   insatiable wealth! But not I,
I alone say this. Only the reckless act
can breed impiety, multiplying crime on crime,
    while the house kept straight and just
is blessed with radiant children.

      But ancient Violence longs to breed,
        new Violence comes
    when its fatal hour comes, the demon comes
    to take her toll—no war, no force, no prayer
    can hinder the midnight Fury stamped
760   with parent Fury moving through the house.

      But Justice shines in sooty hovels,
        loves the decent life.
    From proud halls crusted with gilt by filthy hands
    she turns her eyes to find the pure in spirit—
   spurning the wealth stamped counterfeit with praise,
    she steers all things towards their destined end.

[AGAMEMNON *enters in his chariot, his plunder borne before him by his entourage; behind him,* *half hidden, stands* CASSANDRA. *The old men press towards him.*]
Come, my king, the scourge of Troy,
   the true son of Atreus—
How to salute you, how to praise you
770   neither too high nor low, but hit
the note of praise that suits the hour?
So many prize some brave display,
they prefer some flaunt of honour
   once they break the bounds.
When a man fails they share his grief,
but the pain can never cut them to the quick.
When a man succeeds they share his glory,
torturing their faces into smiles.
But the good shepherd knows his flock.

---

[27] **ancient saying:** In the following lines the chorus, with some equivocation, questions the prevailing view of the time that excessive prosperity inevitably leads to calamity. Evil action and vice, they suggest, not good fortune, leads to grief, and justice and honesty reward even those who are poor.

780   When the eyes seem to brim with love
          and it is only unction, fawning,
       he will know, better than we can know.
       That day you marshalled the armies
       all for Helen — no hiding it now —
       I drew you in my mind in black;
       you seemed a menace at the helm,
          sending men to the grave
       to bring her home, that hell on earth.
       But now from the depths of trust and love
790   I say Well fought, well won —
          the end is worth the labour!
       Search, my king, and learn at last
       who stayed at home and kept their faith
          and who betrayed the city.

AGAMEMNON:
                                   First,
       with justice I salute my Argos and my gods,
       my accomplices who brought me home and won
       my rights from Priam's Troy — the just gods.
       No need to hear our pleas. Once for all
       they consigned their lots[28] to the urn of blood,
800   they pitched on death for men, annihilation
       for the city. Hope's hand, hovering
       over the urn of mercy, left it empty.
       Look for the smoke — it is the city's seamark,
       building even now.
                          The storms of ruin live!
       Her last dying breath, rising up from the ashes
       sends us gales of incense rich in gold.

       For that we must thank the gods with a sacrifice
       our sons will long remember. For their mad outrage
       of a queen we raped their city — we were right.
810   The beast of Argos, foals of the wild mare,[29]
       thousands massed in armour rose on the night
       the Pleiades went down, and crashing through
       their walls our bloody lion lapped its fill,

---

[28] **lots:** In the Athenian courts, citizen jurors cast their votes into one of two urns — one for acquittal, one for conviction.

[29] **wild mare:** Agamemnon refers here to the so-called Trojan horse, a hollowed-out wooden horse by means of which the Greeks secretly entered Troy.

gorging on the blood of kings.

Our thanks to the gods,

long drawn out, but it is just the prelude.

[CLYTAEMNESTRA *approaches with her women; they are carrying dark red tapestries.*
AGAMEMNON *turns to the leader.*]

And your concern, old man, is on my mind.
I hear you and agree, I will support you.
How rare, men with the character to praise
a friend's success without a trace of envy,
820   poison to the heart—it deals a double blow.
Your own losses weigh you down but then,
look at your neighbour's fortune and you weep.
Well I know. I understand society,
the flattering mirror of the proud.

My comrades . . .

they're shadows, I tell you, ghosts of men
who swore they'd die for me. Only Odysseus:
I dragged that man to the wars but once in harness
he was a trace-horse[30] he gave his all for me.
Dead or alive, no matter, I can praise him.

830   And now this cause involving men and gods.
We must summon the city for a trial,
found a national tribunal. Whatever's healthy,
shore it up with law and help it flourish.
Wherever something calls for drastic cures
we make our noblest effort: amputate or wield
the healing iron, burn the cancer at the roots.

Now I go to my father's house—
I give the gods my right hand, my first salute.
The ones who sent me forth have brought me home.

[*He starts down from the chariot, looks at* CLYTAEMNESTRA, *stops, and offers up a prayer.*]
840   Victory, you have sped my way before,
now speed me to the last.

[CLYTAEMNESTRA *turns from the king to the* CHORUS.]
CLYTAEMNESTRA:

Old nobility of Argos

gathered here, I am not ashamed to tell you
how I love the man. I am older,

---

[30] **trace-horse:** Stronger and better fed than the yoked horses at the centre of the team, the trace-horse was depended on for effort in a crisis, as when the chariot would swerve round the post. [Translator's note.]

and the fear dies away . . . I am human.
Nothing I say was learned from others.
This is my life, my ordeal, long as the siege
he laid at Troy and more demanding.
        First,
when a woman sits at home and the man is gone,
the loneliness is terrible,
850 unconscionable . . .
and the rumours spread and fester,
a runner comes with something dreadful,
close on his heels the next and his news worse,
and they shout it out and the whole house can hear;
and wounds—if he took one wound for each report
to penetrate these walls, he's gashed like a dragnet,
more, if he had only died . . .
for each death that swelled his record, he could boast
like a triple-bodied Geryon[31] risen from the grave,
860 'Three shrouds I dug from the earth, one for every body
that went down!'
      The rumours broke like fever,
broke and then rose higher. There were times
they cut me down and eased my throat from the noose.
I wavered between the living and the dead.

[*Turning to* AGAMEMNON.]
         And so
our child is gone, not standing by our side,
the bond of our dearest pledges, mine and yours;
by all rights our child should be here . . .
Orestes. You seem startled.
You needn't be. Our loyal brother-in-arms
870 will take good care of him, Strophios the Phocian.[32]
He warned from the start we court two griefs in one.
You risk all on the wars—and what if the people
rise up howling for the king, and anarchy
should dash our plans?
     Men, it is their nature,
trampling on the fighter once he's down.
Our child is gone. That is my self-defence

---

[31] **Geryon:** Descended from the terrifying Gorgon Medusa, Geryon was a man with three heads (or three bodies), who was king of Erytheia in what is now Cadiz; he was slain by Hercules.

[32] **Strophios the Phocian:** The King of Phocis and ally of Agamemnon, Strophius was the father of Pylades, who helps Orestes when he returns to Argos to slay his father's killers. Clytaemnestra has sent Orestes to Phocis, a region near Delphi, to keep him out of the way.

and it is true.
                    For me, the tears that welled
like springs are dry. I have no tears to spare.
I'd watch till late at night, my eyes still burn,
880   I sobbed by the torch I lit for you alone.

[*Glancing towards the palace.*]
     I never let it die . . . but in my dreams
the high thin wail of a gnat would rouse me,
piercing like a trumpet — I could see you
suffer more than all
the hours that slept with me could ever bear.

I endured it all. And now, free of grief,
I would salute that man the watchdog of the fold,
the mainroyal, saving stay of the vessel,
rooted oak that thrusts the roof sky-high,
890   the father's one true heir.
Land at dawn to the shipwrecked past all hope,
light of the morning burning off the night of storm,
the cold clear spring to the parched horseman —
O the ecstasy, to flee the yoke of Fate!
It is right to use the titles he deserves.
Let envy keep her distance. We have suffered
long enough.

[*Reaching towards* AGAMEMNON.]
                    Come to me now, my dearest,
down from the car of war, but never set the foot
that stamped out Troy on earth again, my great one.

900   Women, why delay? You have your orders.
Pave his way with tapestries.

[*They begin to spread the crimson tapestries between the king and the palace doors.*]
                    Quickly.
Let the red stream flow and bear him home
to the home he never hoped to see — Justice,
lead him in!
                    Leave all the rest to me.
The spirit within me never yields to sleep.
We will set things right, with the god's help.
We will do whatever Fate requires.

AGAMEMNON:
                              There
is Leda's daughter, the keeper of my house.

And the speech to suit my absence, much too long.
910 But the praise that does us justice,
let it come from others, then we prize it.
                                        This—
you treat me like a woman. Grovelling, gaping up at me—
what am I, some barbarian peacocking out of Asia?
Never cross my path with robes and draw the lightning.
Never—only the gods deserve the pomps of honour[33]
and the stiff brocades of fame. To walk on them . . .
I am human, and it makes my pulses stir
with dread.
                    Give me the tributes of a man
and not a god, a little earth to walk on,
920 not this gorgeous work.
There is no need to sound my reputation.
I have a sense of right and wrong, what's more—
heaven's proudest gift. Call no man blest
until he ends his life in peace, fulfilled.
If I can live by what I say, I have no fear.

CLYTAEMNESTRA:
One thing more. Be true to your ideals and tell me—

AGAMEMNON:
True to my ideals? Once I violate them I am lost.

CLYTAEMNESTRA:
Would you have sworn this act to god in a time of terror?

AGAMEMNON:
Yes, if a prophet called for a last, drastic rite.

CLYTAEMNESTRA:
930 But Priam—can you see him if he had your success?

AGAMEMNON:
Striding on the tapestries of god, I see him now.

CLYTAEMNESTRA:
And *you* fear the reproach of common men?

AGAMEMNON:
The voice of the people—aye, they have enormous power.

CLYTAEMNESTRA:
Perhaps, but where's the glory without a little gall?

AGAMEMNON:
And where's the woman in all this lust for glory?

CLYTAEMNESTRA:
But the great victor—it becomes him to give way.

---

[33] **pomps of honour:** Agamemnon fears that stepping down onto these rich tapestries dyed blood-red would be an act of excessive insolence, overreaching the bounds of propriety.

AGAMEMNON:

Victory in this . . . war of ours, it means so much to you?

CLYTAEMNESTRA:

O give way! The power is yours if you surrender,
all of your own free will, to me!

AGAMEMNON:

Enough.

940   If you are so determined—

[*Turning to the women, pointing to his boots.*]

Let someone help me off with these at least.
Old slaves, they've stood me well.

Hurry,
and while I tread his splendours dyed red[34] in the sea
may no god watch and strike me down with envy
from on high. I feel such shame—
to tread the life of the house, a kingdom's worth
of silver in the weaving.

[*He steps down from the chariot to the tapestries and reveals* CASSANDRA, *dressed in the sacred regalia, the fillets, robes, and sceptre of Apollo.*]

Done is done.
Escort this stranger[35] in, be gentle.
Conquer with compassion. Then the gods
950   shine down upon you, gently. No one chooses
the yoke of slavery, not of one's free will—
and she least of all. The gift of the armies,
flower and pride of all the wealth we won,
she follows me from Troy.

And now,
since you have brought me down with your insistence,
just this once I enter my father's house,
trampling royal crimson as I go.

[*He takes his first steps and pauses.*]

CLYTAEMNESTRA:

There is the sea
and who will drain it dry? Precious as silver,
inexhaustible, ever-new, it breeds the more we reap it—
960   tides on tides of crimson dye our robes blood-red.

---

[34] **dyed red:** The dye was from certain mollusks and shellfish, hence the connection to the sea. The dye, sometimes called "Tyrian purple," was dark crimson or purple and associated with royalty.

[35] **stranger:** Cassandra, the captive prophetess and daughter of King Priam of Troy; she was granted the gift of prophecy from Apollo, but when she spurned his amorous advances he vowed that her prophecies would never be understood or believed.

Our lives are based on wealth, my king,
the gods have seen to that.
Destitution, our house has never heard the word.
I would have sworn to tread on legacies of robes,
at one command from an oracle, deplete the house—
suffer the worst to bring that dear life back!

[*Encouraged,* AGAMEMNON *strides to the entrance.*]
When the root lives on, the new leaves come back,
spreading a dense shroud of shade across the house
to thwart the Dog Star's fury.[36] So you return
970   to the father's hearth, you bring us warmth in winter
like the sun—
            And you are Zeus when Zeus
tramples the bitter virgin grape[37] for new wine
and the welcome chill steals through the halls, at last
the master moves among the shadows of his house, fulfilled.

[AGAMEMNON *goes over the threshold; the women gather up the tapestries while* CLYTAEMNES-
TRA *prays.*]
Zeus, Zeus, master of all fulfilment, now fulfil our prayers—
speed our rites to their fulfilment once for all!

[*She enters the palace, the doors close, the old men huddle in terror.*]
CHORUS:
Why, why does it rock me, never stops,
this terror beating down my heart,
    this seer that sees it all—
980   it beats its wings, uncalled unpaid
thrust on the lungs
the mercenary song beats on and on
singing a prophet's strain—
    and I can't throw it off
like dreams that make no sense,
and the strength drains
that filled the mind with trust,
and the years drift by and the driven sand
    has buried the mooring lines
990   that churned when the armoured squadrons cut for Troy . . .
and now I believe it, I can prove he's home,
    my own clear eyes for witness—
                  Agamemnon!

---

[36] **Dog Star's fury:** As the Dog Star, Sirius is the brightest star in the constellation The Greater Dog, Canis Major.

[37] **bitter virgin grape:** A reference to the blood of Iphigeneia.

Still it's chanting, beating deep so deep in the heart
this dirge of the Furies, oh dear god,
not fit for the lyre, its own master
        it kills our spirit
kills our hopes
and it's real, true, no fantasy—
        stark terror whirls the brain
1000   and the end is coming
                Justice comes to birth—
I pray my fears prove false and fall
and die and never come to birth!
Even exultant health, well we know,
        exceeds its limits[38] comes so near disease
it can breach the wall between them.

Even a man's fate, held true on course,
        in a blinding flash rams some hidden reef;
but if caution only casts the pick of the cargo—
1010   one well-balanced cast—
the house will not go down, not outright;
labouring under its wealth of grief
the ship of state rides on.

Yes, and the great green bounty of god,
sown in the furrows year by year and reaped each fall
can end the plague of famine.

But a man's life-blood
        is dark and mortal.
Once it wets the earth
1020   what song can sing it back?
Not even the master-healer[39]
    who brought the dead to life—
Zeus stopped the man before he did more harm.

Oh, if only the gods had never forged
the chain that curbs our excess,
        one man's fate curbing the next man's fate,
my heart would outrace my song, I'd pour out all I feel—
                but no, I choke with anguish,
                mutter through the nights.

---

[38] **limits:** According to the doctrine of the Golden Mean, the ancient Greeks believed that excess and deficiency should be avoided, even in matters of health. [Translator's note.]

[39] **master-healer:** Asclepius, the legendary physician, who was struck down by Zeus when he resurrected a dead man back to life.

1030   Never to ravel out a hope in time
       and the brain is swarming, burning—

[CLYTAEMNESTRA *emerges from the palace and goes to* CASSANDRA, *impassive in the chariot.*]
CLYTAEMNESTRA:
       Won't you come inside? I mean you, Cassandra.
       Zeus in all his mercy wants you to share
       some victory libations with the house.
       The slaves are flocking. Come, lead them
       up to the altar of the god who guards
       our dearest treasures.[40]
                     Down from the chariot,
       this is no time for pride. Why even Heracles,[41]
       they say, was sold into bondage long ago,
1040   he had to endure the bitter bread of slaves.
       But if the yoke descends on you, be grateful
       for a master born and reared in ancient wealth.
       Those who reap a harvest past their hopes
       are merciless to their slaves.
                   From us
       you will receive what custom says is right.

[CASSANDRA *remains impassive.*]
LEADER:
       It's *you* she is speaking to, it's all too clear.
       You're caught in the nets of doom—obey
       if you can obey, unless you cannot bear to.
CLYTAEMNESTRA:
       Unless she's like a swallow, possessed
1050   of her own barbaric song, strange, dark.
       I speak directly as I can—she must obey.
LEADER:
       Go with her. Make the best of it, she's right.
       Step down from the seat, obey her.
CLYTAEMNESTRA:
                     Do it *now*—
       I have no time to spend outside. Already
       the victims crowd the hearth, the Navelstone,
       to bless this day of joy I never hoped to see!—
       our victims waiting for the fire and the knife,
       and you,
       if you want to taste our mystic rites, come now.
       If my words can't reach you—

---

[40] **god . . . treasures:** Apparently a reference to Zeus *Ktêsios,* who protects the house and its possessions. [Translator's note.]

[41] **Heracles:** Hercules, the great hero who once had to serve as a slave to Queen Omphale of Lydia.

[*Turning to the* LEADER.]

1060   Give her a sign,
     one of her exotic handsigns.
LEADER:
                                    I think
     the stranger needs an interpreter, someone clear.
     She's like a wild creature, fresh caught.
CLYTAEMNESTRA:
                                    She's mad,
     her evil genius murmuring in her ears.
     She comes from a *city* fresh caught.
     She must learn to take the cutting bridle[42]
     before she foams her spirit off in blood—
     and that's the last I waste on her contempt!

[*Wheeling, re-entering the palace. The* LEADER *turns to* CASSANDRA, *who remains transfixed.*]
LEADER:
     Not I, I pity her. I will be gentle.
1070   Come, poor thing. Leave the empty chariot—
     Of your own free will try on the yoke of Fate.
CASSANDRA:
     Aieeeeee! Earth—Mother—
                    Curse of the Earth—Apollo Apollo!
LEADER:
     Why cry to Apollo?
     He's not the god to call with sounds of mourning.
CASSANDRA:
     Aieeeeee! Earth—Mother—
                    Rape of the Earth—Apollo Apollo!
LEADER:
     Again, it's a bad omen.
     She cries for the god who wants no part of grief.

[CASSANDRA *steps from the chariot, looks slowly towards the rooftops of the palace.*]
CASSANDRA:
     God of the long road,
                    Apollo *Apollo* my destroyer—
1080   you destroy me once, destroy me twice—
LEADER:
     She's about to sense her own ordeal, I think.
     Slave that she is, the god lives on inside her.
CASSANDRA:
     God of the iron marches,
                    Apollo *Apollo* my destroyer—

---

[42] **cutting bridle:** A sharp-edged bit used in the breaking-in of high-spirited horses. [Translator's note.]

where, where have you led me now? what house—
LEADER:
The house of Atreus and his sons. Really—
don't you know? It's true, see for yourself.
CASSANDRA:
No . . . the house that hates god,
   an echoing womb of guilt, kinsmen
1090   torturing kinsmen, severed heads,
slaughterhouse of heroes, soil streaming blood—
LEADER:
A keen hound, this stranger.
Trailing murder, and murder she will find.
CASSANDRA:
See, my witnesses—
   I trust to them, to the babies
      wailing, skewered on the sword,
their flesh charred, the father gorging on their parts[43]—
LEADER:
We'd heard your fame as a seer,
but no one looks for seers in Argos.
CASSANDRA:
1100   Oh no, what horror, what new plot,
new agony this?—
it's growing, massing, deep in the house,
      a plot, a monstrous—*thing*
         to crush the loved ones, no,
      there is no cure, and rescue's far away and—
LEADER:
I can't read these signs; I knew the first,
the city rings with them.
CASSANDRA:
   You, you godforsaken—you'd do *this*?
The lord of your bed,
1110   you bathe him . . . his body glistens, then—
         how to tell the climax?—
            comes so quickly, see,
      hand over hand shoots out, hauling ropes—
                                          then lunge!
LEADER:
Still lost. Her riddles, her dark words of god—
I'm groping, helpless.

---

[43] **their parts:** Cassandra here alludes to Atreus's murder of Thyestes's sons, from whose corpses he prepared a stew for their father to eat. She may also allude to the murder of Pelops, who was served up in a stew to the gods by his father Tantalus.

CASSANDRA:
No no, look *there*!—

what's that? some net flung out of hell—
No, *she* is the snare,

the bedmate, deathmate, murder's strong right arm!
Let the insatiate discord in the race

1120   rear up and shriek 'Avenge the victim—stone them dead!'[44]

LEADER:

What Fury is this? Why rouse it, lift its wailing
through the house? I hear you and lose hope.

CHORUS:

Drop by drop at the heart, the gold of life ebbs out.
   We are the old soldiers . . . wounds will come
with the crushing sunset of our lives.
   Death is close, and quick.

CASSANDRA:
Look out! *look out*!—

Ai, drag the great bull from the mate!—
a thrash of robes, she traps him—

writhing—
black horn glints, twists—

she gores him through!

1130   And now he buckles, look, the bath swirls red—

There's stealth and murder in the cauldron, do you hear?

LEADER:

I'm no judge, I've little skill with the oracles,
but even I know danger when I hear it.

CHORUS:

What good are the oracles to men? Words, more words,
   and the hurt comes on us, endless words
and a seer's techniques have brought us
   terror and the truth.

CASSANDRA:

The agony—O I am breaking!—Fate's so hard,
   and the pain that floods my voice is mine alone.

1140   Why have you brought me here, tormented as I am?
   Why, unless to die with him, why else?

LEADER AND CHORUS:

Mad with the rapture—god speeds you on
   to the song, the deathsong,

---

[44] **stone them dead:** A death by stoning [ed.]; reserved for the most infamous criminals, since it denoted an expiation of their crime by the entire community. [Translator's note.]

like the nightingale that broods on sorrow,
    mourns her son, her son,[45]
her life inspired with grief for him,
she lilts and shrills, dark bird that lives for night.

CASSANDRA:

The nightingale—O for a song, a fate like hers!
    The gods gave her a life of ease, swathed her in wings,
1150   no tears, no wailing. The knife waits for me.
They'll splay me on the iron's double edge.

LEADER AND CHORUS:

Why?—what god hurls you on, stroke on stroke
    to the long dying fall?
Why the horror clashing through your music,
    terror struck to song?—
why the anguish, the wild dance?
Where do your words of god and grief begin?

CASSANDRA:

Ai, the wedding, wedding of Paris,
death to the loved ones. Oh Scamander,[46]
1160   you nursed my father . . . once at your banks
    I nursed and grew, and now at the banks
of Acheron,[47] the stream that carries sorrow,
it seems I'll chant my prophecies too soon.

LEADER AND CHORUS:

What are you saying? Wait, it's clear,
a child could see the truth, it wounds within,
            like a bloody fang it tears—
    I hear your destiny—breaking sobs,
        cries that stab the ears.

CASSANDRA:

Oh the grief, the grief of the city
1170   ripped to oblivion. Oh the victims,
the flocks my father burned at the wall,
    rich herds in flames . . . no cure for the doom
that took the city after all, and I,
her last ember, I go down with her.

LEADER AND CHORUS:

You cannot stop, your song goes on—
some spirit drops from the heights and treads you down
            and the brutal strain grows—

---

[45] **her son:** Itys, son of Philomela (or in another version, Procne). Philomela was turned into a nightingale after she had inadvertently tricked her husband, Tereus, into eating his son's flesh. [Translator's note.]

[46] **Scamander:** A river at Troy.

[47] **Acheron:** The "river of grief" in Hades.

your death-throes come and come and
                I cannot see the end!

CASSANDRA:

1180   Then off with the veils that hid the fresh young bride—
we will see the truth.
Flare up once more, my oracle! Clear and sharp
as the wind that blows towards the rising sun,
I can feel a deeper swell now, gathering head
to break at last and bring the dawn of grief.
No more riddles. I will teach you.
Come, bear witness, run and hunt with me.
We trail the old barbaric works of slaughter.

These roofs—look up—there is a dancing troupe
1190   that never leaves. And they have their harmony
but it is harsh, their words are harsh, they drink
beyond the limit. Flushed on the blood of men
their spirit grows and none can turn away
their revel breeding in the veins—the Furies!
They cling to the house for life. They sing,
sing of the frenzy that began it all,
strain rising on strain, showering curses
on the man who tramples on his brother's bed.

There. Have I hit the mark or not? Am I a fraud,
1200   a fortune-teller babbling lies from door to door?
Swear how well I know the ancient crimes
that live within this house.

LEADER:
                                    And if I did?
Would an oath bind the wounds and heal us?
But you amaze me. Bred across the sea,
your language strange, and still you sense the truth
as if you had been here.

CASSANDRA:
                                    Apollo the Prophet
introduced me to his gift.

LEADER:
A *god*—and moved with love?

CASSANDRA:
I was ashamed to tell this once,
but now . . .

LEADER:
1210   We spoil ourselves with scruples,
long as things go well.

CASSANDRA:
                                    He came like a wrestler,

magnificent, took me down and breathed his fire
through me and—

LEADER:

You bore him a child?

CASSANDRA:

I yielded,
then at the climax I recoiled—I deceived Apollo!

LEADER:

But the god's skills—they seized you even then?

CASSANDRA:

Even then I told my people all the grief to come.

LEADER:

And Apollo's anger never touched you?—is it possible?

CASSANDRA:

Once I betrayed him I could never be believed.

LEADER:

We believe you. Your visions seem so true.

CASSANDRA:

Aieeeee!—

1220 the pain, the terror! the birth-pang of the seer
who tells the truth—

it whirls me, oh,
the storm comes again, the crashing chords!
Look, you see them nestling at the threshold?
Young, young in the darkness like a dream,
like children really, yes, and their loved ones
brought them down . . .

their hands, they fill their hands
with their own flesh, they are serving it like food,
holding out their entrails . . . now it's clear,
I can see the armfuls of compassion, see the father
reach to taste and—

1230 For so much suffering,
I tell you, someone plots revenge.
A lion[48] who lacks a lion's heart,
he sprawled at home in the royal lair
and set a trap for the lord on his return.
My lord . . . I must wear his yoke, I am his slave.
The lord of the men-of-war, he obliterated Troy—
he is so blind, so lost to that detestable hellhound[49]
who pricks her ears and fawns and her tongue draws out

---

[48] **lion:** Aesthisthus, Clytaemnestra's partner in crime.

[49] **hellhound:** Clytaemnestra is compared to Cerberus, the guardian of Hell or Hades.

her glittering words of welcome—

No, he cannot see

1240   the stroke that Fury's hiding, stealth, and murder.
What outrage—the woman kills the man!

What to call

that . . . monster of Greece, and bring my quarry down?
Viper coiling back and forth?

Some sea-witch?—

Scylla[50] crouched in her rocky nest—nightmare of sailors?
Raging mother of death, storming deathless war against
the ones she loves!

And how she howled in triumph,

boundless outrage. Just as the tide of battle
broke her way, she seems to rejoice that he
is safe at home from war, saved for her.

1250   Believe me if you will. What will it matter
if you won't? It comes when it comes,
and soon you'll see it face to face
and say the seer was all too true.
You will be moved with pity.

LEADER:

Thyestes' feast,

the children's flesh—that I know,
and the fear shudders through me. It's true,
real, no dark signs about it. I hear the rest
but it throws me off the scent.

CASSANDRA:

Agamemnon.

You will see him dead.

LEADER:

Peace, poor girl!

Put those words to sleep.

CASSANDRA:

1260   No use,

the Healer[51] has no hand in this affair.

LEADER:

Not if it's true—but god forbid it is!

CASSANDRA:

You pray, and they close in to kill!

LEADER:

What man prepares this, this dreadful—

---

[50] **Scylla:** A female sea monster with six heads who, along with her companion Charybdis, attacked sailors as they passed through the strait of Messina. (See Homer's *The Odyssey*, Book 12.)

[51] **Healer:** Apollo.

CASSANDRA:
                                        Man?
    You *are* lost, to every word I've said.
LEADER:
                                        Yes —
    I don't see who can bring the evil off.
CASSANDRA:
    And yet I know my Greek, too well.
LEADER:
    So does the Delphic oracle,
    but he's hard to understand.
CASSANDRA:

                                His *fire*! —
1270   sears me, sweeps me again — the torture!
    Apollo Lord of the Light, you burn,
    you blind me —
                        Agony!
                                She is the lioness,
    she rears on her hind legs, she beds with the wolf
    when her lion king goes ranging —
                                        she will kill me —
    Ai, the torture!
                        She is mixing her drugs,
    adding a measure more of hate for me.
    She gloats as she whets the sword for him.
    He brought me home and we will pay in carnage.

    Why mock yourself with these — trappings, the rod,
1280   the god's wreath, his yoke around my throat?
    Before I die I'll tread you —

[*Ripping off her regalia, stamping it into the ground.*]
                        Down, out,
    die die die!
    Now you're down. I've paid you back.
    Look for another victim — I am free at last —
    make her rich in all your curse and doom.

[*Staggering backwards as if wrestling with a spirit tearing at her robes.*]
                        See,
    Apollo himself, his fiery handsi — feel him again,
    he's stripping off my robes, the Seer's robes!
    And after he looked down and saw me mocked,
    even in these, his glories, mortified by friends
1290   I loved, and they hated me, they were so blind
    to their own demise —
                                I went from door to door,

I was wild with the god, I heard them call me
'Beggar! Wretch! Starve for bread in hell!'

And I endured it all, and now he will
extort me as his due. A seer for the Seer.
He brings me here to die like this,
not to serve at my father's altar. No,
the block is waiting. The cleaver steams
with my life blood, the first blood drawn[52]
for the king's last rites.

[*Regaining her composure and moving to the altar.*]

1300   We will die,
but not without some honour from the gods.
There will come another[53] to avenge us,
born to kill his mother, born
his father's champion. A wanderer, a fugitive
driven off his native land, he will come home
to cope the stones of hate that menace all he loves.
The gods have sworn a monumental oath: as his father lies
upon the ground he draws him home with power like a prayer.

Then why so pitiful, why so many tears?
1310   I have seen my city faring as she fared,
and those who took her, judged by the gods,
faring as they fare. I must be brave.
It is my turn to die.

[*Approaching the doors.*]
I address you as the Gates of Death.
I pray it comes with one clear stroke,
no convulsions, the pulses ebbing out
in gentle death. I'll close my eyes and sleep.

LEADER:
So much pain, poor girl, and so much truth,
you've told so much. But if you *see* it coming,
1320   clearly—how can you go to your own death,
like a beast to the altar driven on by god,
and hold your head so high?

CASSANDRA:
                              No escape, my friends,
not now.

---

[52] **first blood drawn**: The *prosphagma*, the blood-offering to the dead which was preliminary to a hero's funeral, or the victim itself. [Translator's note.]

[53] **another**: Orestes, the son of Agamemnon and Clytaemnestra.

LEADER:
But the last hour should be savoured.

CASSANDRA:
My time has come. Little to gain from flight.

LEADER:
You're brave, believe me, full of gallant heart

CASSANDRA:
Only the wretched go with praise like that.

LEADER:
But to go nobly lends a man some grace.

CASSANDRA:
My noble father—you and your noble children.

[*She nears the threshold and recoils, groaning in revulsion.*]

LEADER:
What now? what terror flings you back?
Why? Unless some horror in the brain—

CASSANDRA:
1330
Murder.
The house breathes with murder—bloody shambles!

LEADER:
No, no, only the victims at the hearth.

CASSANDRA:
I know that odour. I smell the open grave.

LEADER:
But the Syrian myrrh,[54] it fills the halls with splendour,
can't you sense it?

CASSANDRA:
Well, I must go in now,
mourning Agamemnon's death and mine.
Enough of life!

[*Approaching the doors again and crying out.*]
Friends—I cried out,
not from fear like a bird fresh caught,
but that you will testify to *how* I died.
1340
When the queen, woman for woman, dies for me,
and a man falls for the man who married grief.
That's all I ask, my friends. A stranger's gift
for one about to die.

LEADER:
Poor creature, you
and the end you see so clearly. I pity you.

---

[54] **Syrian myrrh:** A gum resin used for incense and perfume.

CASSANDRA:
> I'd like a few words more, a kind of dirge,
> it is my own. I pray to the sun,
> the last light I'll see,
> that when the avengers cut the assassins down
> they will avenge me too, a slave who died,
> an easy conquest.

1350
>   Oh men, your destiny.
> When all is well a shadow can overturn it.
> When trouble comes a stroke of the wet sponge,
> and the picture's blotted out. And that,
> I think that breaks the heart.

[*She goes through the doors.*]
CHORUS:
> But the lust for power never dies—
>   men cannot have enough.
> No one will lift a hand to send it
> from his door, to give it warning,
> 'Power, never come again!'

1360
> Take this man: the gods in glory
> gave him Priam's city to plunder,
> brought him home in splendour like a god.
> But now if he must pay for the blood
>   his fathers shed, and die for the deaths
> he brought to pass, and bring more death
> to avenge his dying, show us one
>   who boasts himself born free
> of the raging angel, once he hears—

[*Cries break out within the palace.*]
AGAMEMNON:
>   Aagh!
> Struck deep—the death-blow, deep—
LEADER:
>   Quiet. Cries,
> but who? Someone's stabbed—
AGAMEMNON:

1370
>   Aaagh, again . . .
> second blow—struck home.
LEADER:
>   The work is done,
> you can feel it. The king, and the great cries—
> Close ranks now, find the right way out.

[*But the old men scatter, each speaks singly.*]
CHORUS:
> —I say send out heralds, muster the guard,

they'll save the house.

          —And I say rush in now,
catch them red-handed—butchery running on their blades.

—Right with you, do something—now or never!

—Look at them, beating the drum for insurrection.

                       —Yes,
we're wasting time. They rape the name of caution,
their hands will never sleep.

1380   —Not a plan in sight.
Let men of action do the planning, too.

—I'm helpless. Who can raise the dead with words?

—What, drag out our lives? bow down to the tyrants,
the ruin of the house?

           —Never, better to die
on your feet than live on your knees.

              —Wait,
do we take the cries for signs, prophesy like seers
and give him up for dead?

              —No more suspicions,
not another word till we have proof.

              —Confusion
on all sides—one thing to do. See how it stands
1390   with Agamemnon, once and for all we'll see—

[*He rushes at the doors. They open and reveal a silver cauldron that holds the body of*
AGAMEMNON *shrouded in bloody robes, with the body of* CASSANDRA *to his left and*
CLYTAEMNESTRA *standing to his right, sword in hand. She strides towards the chorus.*]
CLYTAEMNESTRA:
    Words, endless words I've said to serve the moment—
    now it makes me proud to tell the truth.
    How else to prepare a death for deadly men
    who seem to love you? How to rig the nets
    of pain so high no man can overleap them?
    I brooded on this trial, this ancient blood feud
    year by year. At last my hour came.
    Here I stand and here I struck

and here my work is done.
1400   I did it all. I don't deny it, no.
He had no way to flee or fight his destiny—

[*Unwinding the robes from* AGAMEMNON's *body, spreading them before the altar where the old men cluster around them, unified as a chorus once again.*]
our never-ending, all embracing net, I cast it
wide for the royal haul, I coil him round and round
in the wealth, the robes of doom, and then I strike him
once, twice, and at each stroke he cries in agony—
he buckles at the knees and crashes here!
And when he's down I add the third, last blow,
to the Zeus who saves the dead beneath the ground
I send that third blow home in homage like a prayer.

1410   So he goes down, and the life is bursting out of him—
great sprays of blood, and the murderous shower
wounds me, dyes me black and I, I revel
like the Earth when the spring rains come down,
the blessed gifts of god, and the new green spear
splits the sheath and rips to birth in glory!

So it stands, elders of Argos gathered here.
Rejoice if you can rejoice—I glory.
And if I'd pour upon his body the libation
it deserves, what wine could match my words?
1420   It is right and more than right. He flooded
the vessel of our proud house with misery,
with the vintage of the curse and now
he drains the dregs. My lord is home at last.

LEADER:
You appal me, you, your brazen words—
exulting over your fallen king.

CLYTAEMNESTRA:
                              And you,
you try me like some desperate woman.
My heart is steel, well you know. Praise me,
blame me as you choose. It's all one.
Here is Agamemnon, my husband made a corpse
1430   by this right hand—a masterpiece of Justice.
Done is done.

CHORUS:
                    Woman!—what poison[55] cropped from the soil
or strained from the heaving sea, what nursed you,

---

[55] **poison:** Madness was often attributed in antiquity to the eating of some noxious plant or mineral. [Translator's note.]

drove you insane? You brave the curse of Greece.
    You have cut away and flung away and now
the people cast you off to exile,
broken with our hate.

CLYTAEMNESTRA:
                    And now you sentence me? —
you banish *me* from the city, curses breathing
down my neck? But *he* —
name one charge you brought against him then.

1440   He thought no more of it than killing a beast,
and his flocks were rich, teeming in their fleece,
but he sacrificed his own child, our daughter,
the agony I laboured into love
to charm away the savage winds of Thrace.
Didn't the law demand you banish him? —
hunt him from the land for all his guilt?
But now you witness what I've done
and you are ruthless judges.
                   Threaten away!
I'll meet you blow for blow. And if I fall

1450   the throne is yours. If god decrees the reverse,
late as it is, old men, you'll learn your place.

CHORUS:
    Mad with ambition,
          shrilling pride! — some Fury
crazed with the carnage rages through your brain —
    I can see the flecks of blood inflame your eyes!
But vengeance comes — you'll lose your loved ones,
stroke for painful stroke.

CLYTAEMNESTRA:
    Then learn this, too, the power of my oaths.
By the child's Rights I brought to birth,

1460   by Ruin, by Fury — the three gods to whom
I sacrificed this man — I swear my hopes
will never walk the halls of fear so long
as Aegisthus lights the fire on my hearth.
Loyal to me as always, no small shield
to buttress my defiance.
                 Here he lies.
He brutalized me. The darling of all
the golden girls[56] who spread the gates of Troy.
And here his spear-prize . . . what wonders she beheld! —

---

[56] **golden girls:** The plural refers to Chryseis (derived from the word for gold), who was the daughter of Khryse (Chryse), a priest of Apollo. In Homer's *The Iliad* Agamemnon refused to return this girl, whom he had taken as a war captive, to her father and claimed that he would rank her higher than Clytaemnestra.

the seer of Apollo shared my husband's bed,
1470   his faithful mate who knelt at the rowing-benches,
worked by every hand.
                                        They have their rewards.
He as you know. And she, the swan[57] of the gods
who lived to sing her latest, dying song—
his lover lies beside him.
She brings a fresh, voluptuous relish to my bed!

CHORUS:
Oh quickly, let me die—
no bed of labour, no, no wasting illness . . .
bear me off in the sleep that never ends,
                    now that he has fallen,
1480   now that our dearest shield lies battered—
            Woman made him suffer,
                        woman struck him down.

Helen the wild, maddening Helen,
one for the many, the thousand lives
you murdered under Troy. Now you are crowned
with this consummate wreath, the blood
that lives in memory, glistens age to age.
Once in the halls she walked and she was war,
angel of war, angel of agony, lighting men to death.

CLYTAEMNESTRA:
1490   Pray no more for death, broken
as you are. And never turn
    your wrath on her, call her
the scourge of men, the one alone
who destroyed a myriad Greek lives—
Helen the grief that never heals.

CHORUS:
        The *spirit*!—you who tread
the house and the twinborn sons of Tantalus[58]—
you empower the sisters, Fury's twins
            whose power tears the heart!
1500   Perched on the corpse your carrion raven
        glories in her hymn,
                    her screaming hymn of pride.

CLYTAEMNESTRA:
Now you set your judgement straight,
you summon *him*! Three generations
    feed the spirit in the race.

---

[57] **swan**: Apollo's bird who sings when she is about to die.
[58] **sons of Tantalus**: Agamemnon and Menelaus.

Deep in the veins he feeds our bloodlust—
aye, before the old wound dies
it ripens in another flow of blood.

CHORUS:
The great curse of the house, the spirit,
1510　　dead weight wrath—and you can praise it!
Praise the insatiate doom that feeds
relentless on our future and our sons.
Oh all through the will of Zeus,
the cause of all, the one who works it all.
What comes to birth that is not Zeus?
Our lives are pain, what part not come from god?

Oh my king, my captain,
how to salute you, how to mourn you?
What can I say with all my warmth and love?
1520　　Here in the black widow's web you lie,
gasping out your life
in a sacrilegious death, dear god,
reduced to a slave's bed,
my king of men, yoked by stealth and Fate,
by the wife's hand that thrust the two-edged sword.

CLYTAEMNESTRA:
You claim the work is mine, call me
Agamemnon's wife—you are so wrong.
Fleshed in the wife of this dead man,
the spirit lives within me,
1530　　our savage ancient spirit of revenge.
In return for Atreus' brutal feast
he kills his perfect son—for every
murdered child, a crowning sacrifice.

CHORUS:
And *you*, innocent of his murder?
And who could swear to that? and how? . . .
and still an avenger could arise,
bred by the fathers' crimes, and lend a hand.
He wades in the blood of brothers,
stream on mounting stream—black war[59] erupts
1540　　and where he strides revenge will stride,
clots will mass for the young who were devoured.

Oh my king, my captain,
how to salute you, how to mourn you?
What can I say with all my warmth and love?

---

[59] **black war:** Aries, the god of war.

Here in the black widow's web you lie,
gasping out your life
in a sacrilegious death, dear god,
reduced to a slave's bed,
my king of men, yoked by stealth and Fate,
1550   by the wife's hand that thrust the two-edged sword.

CLYTAEMNESTRA:
No slave's death, I think —
no stealthier than the death he dealt
our house and the offspring of our loins,
    Iphigeneia, girl of tears.
Act for act, wound for wound!
Never exult in Hades, swordsman,
here you are repaid. By the sword
you did your work and by the sword you die.

CHORUS:
         The mind reels — where to turn?
1560   All plans dashed, all hope! I cannot think . . .
    the roofs are toppling, I dread the drumbeat thunder
      the heavy rains of blood will crush the house
         the first light rains are over —
       Justice brings new acts of agony, yes,
on new grindstones Fate is grinding sharp the sword of Justice.

Earth, dear Earth,
if only you'd drawn me under
long before I saw him huddled
in the beaten silver bath.
1570   Who will bury him, lift his dirge?

[*Turning* to CLYTAEMNESTRA.]
You, can you dare *this*?
To kill your lord with your own hand
then mourn his soul with tributes, terrible tributes —
do his enormous works a great dishonour.
This god-like man, this hero. Who at the grave
will sing his praises, pour the wine of tears?
Who will labour there with truth of heart?

CLYTAEMNESTRA:
This is no concern of yours.
The hand that bore and cut him down
1580   will hand him down to Mother Earth.
This house will never mourn for him.
    Only our daughter Iphigeneia,
by all rights, will rush to meet him
first at the churning straits,

the ferry[60] over tears—
she'll fling her arms around her father,
pierce him with her love.

CHORUS:
Each charge meets counter-charge.
None can judge between them. Justice.
1590   The plunderer plundered, the killer pays the price.
The truth still holds while Zeus still holds the throne:
the one who acts must suffer—
that is law. Who can tear from the veins
the bad seed, the curse? The race is welded to its ruin.

CLYTAEMNESTRA:
At last you see the future and the truth!
But I will swear a pact with the spirit
born within us. I embrace his works,
cruel as they are but done at last,
    if he will leave our house
1600   in the future, bleed another line
with kinsmen murdering kinsmen.
Whatever he may ask. A few things
are all I need, once I have purged
our fury to destroy each other—
    purged it from our halls.

[AEGISTHUS *has emerged from the palace with his bodyguard and stands triumphant over the body of* AGAMEMNON.]

AEGISTHUS:
O what a brilliant day
it is for vengeance! Now I can say once more
there are gods in heaven avenging men,
blazing down on all the crimes of earth.
Now at last I see this man brought down
1610 in the Furies' tangling robes.[61] It feasts my eyes—
he pays for the plot his father's hand contrived.

Atreus, this man's father, was king of Argos.
My father, Thyestes—let me make this clear—
Atreus' brother challenged him for the crown,
and Atreus drove him out of house and home
then lured him back, and home Thyestes came,
poor man, a suppliant to his own hearth,
to pray that Fate might save him.
    So it did.

---

[60] **ferry:** Charon ferried the dead across the river Styx.

[61] **Furies' tangling robes:** The interweaving of the Furies, who avenge blood crimes, with the justice of the gods.

There was no dying, no staining our native ground
1620   with *his* blood. Thyestes was the guest,
and this man's godless father—

[*Pointing to* AGAMEMNON]

the zeal of the host outstripping a brother's love,
made my father a feast that seemed a feast for gods,
a love feast of his children's flesh.
                                        He cuts
the extremities, feet and delicate hands
into small pieces, scatters them over the dish
and serves it to Thyestes throned on high.
He picks at the flesh he cannot recognize,
the soul of innocence eating the food of ruin—
look,

[*Pointing to the bodies at his feet.*]

1630   that feeds upon the house! And then,
when he sees the monstrous thing he's done, he shrieks,
he reels back head first and vomits up that butchery,
tramples the feast—brings down the curse of Justice:
'Crash to ruin, all the race of Pleisthenes,[62] crash down!'

So you see him, down. And I, the weaver of Justice,
plotted out the kill. Atreus drove us into exile,
my struggling father and I, a babe-in arms,
his last son, but I became a man
and Justice brought me home. I was abroad
1640   but I reached out and seized my man,
link by link I clamped the fatal scheme
together. Now I could die gladly, even I—
now I see this monster in the nets of Justice.

LEADER:

Aegisthus, you revel in pain—you sicken me.
You say you killed the king in cold blood,
single-handed planned his pitiful death?
I say there's no escape. In the hour of judgement,
trust to this, your head will meet the people's
rocks and curses.

AEGISTHUS:

                    You say! you slaves at the oars—
1650   while the master on the benches cracks the whip?
You'll learn, in your late age, how much it hurts
to teach old bones their place. We have techniques—

---

[62] **Pleisthenes:** There is disagreement about this figure: in one version, Pleisthenes is a son of Atreus, who was reared by Thyestes, and killed mistakenly by his father Atreus. In this passage, however, Aeschylus has apparently substituted Pleisthenes for Atreus.

chains and the pangs of hunger,
two effective teachers, excellent healers.
They can even cure old men of pride and gall.
Look—can't you see? The more you kick
against the pricks, the more you suffer.

LEADER:

You, pathetic—
the king had just returned from battle.
1660   You waited out the war and fouled his lair,
you planned my great commander's fall.

AEGISTHUS:

Talk on—
you'll scream for every word, my little Orpheus.[63]
We'll see if the world comes dancing to your song,
your absurd barking—snarl your breath away!
I'll make you dance, I'll bring you all to heel.

LEADER:

You rule Argos? You who schemed his death
but cringed to cut him down with your own hand?

AEGISTHUS:

The treachery was the woman's work, clearly.
I was a marked man, his enemy for ages.
1670   But I will use his riches, stop at nothing
to civilize his people. All but the rebel:
him I'll yoke and break—
no cornfed colt, running free in the traces.
Hunger, ruthless mate of the dark torture-chamber,
trains her eyes upon him till he drops!

LEADER:

Coward, why not kill the man yourself?
Why did the woman, the corruption of Greece
and the gods of Greece, have to bring him down?
Orestes—
If he still sees the light of day,
1680   bring him home, good Fates, home to kill
this pair at last. Our champion in slaughter!

AEGISTHUS:

Bent on insolence? Well, you'll learn, quickly.
At them, men—you have your work at hand!

[*His men draw swords; the old men take up their sticks.*]

LEADER:

At them, fist at the hilt, to the last man—

---

[63] **Orpheus:** The legendary musician and poet from Thrace whose songs charmed all who heard them, including nature and the gods.

AEGISTHUS:

    Fist at the hilt, I'm not afraid to die.

LEADER:

    It's death you want and death you'll have—
    we'll make that word your last.

[CLYTAEMNESTRA *moves between them, restraining* AEGISTHUS.]

CLYTAEMNESTRA:

                    No more, my dearest,
    no more grief. We have too much to reap
    right here, our mighty harvest of despair.
1690   Our lives are based on pain. No bloodshed now.

    Fathers of Argos, turn for home before you act
    and suffer for it. What we did was destiny.
    If we could end the suffering, how we would rejoice.
    The spirit's brutal hoof has struck our heart.
    And that is what a woman has to say.
    Can you accept the truth?

[CLYTAEMNESTRA *turns to leave.*]

AEGISTHUS:

                  But these . . . mouths
    that bloom in filth—spitting insults in my teeth.
    You tempt your fates, you insubordinate dogs—
    to hurl abuse at me, your master!

LEADER:

                    No Greek
1700   worth his salt would grovel at your feet.

AEGISTHUS:

    I—I'll stalk you all your days!

LEADER:

    Not if the spirit brings Orestes home.

AEGISTHUS:

    Exiles feed on hope—well I know.

LEADER:

                   More,
    gorge yourself to bursting—soil justice, while you can.

AEGISTHUS:

    I promise you, you'll pay, old fools—in good time, too!

LEADER:

    Strut on your own dunghill, you cock[64] beside your mate.

CLYTAEMNESTRA:

    Let them howl—they're impotent. You and I have power now.
    We will set the house in order once for all.

[*They enter the palace; the great doors close behind them; the old men disband and wander off.*]

---

[64] **cock:** Like a rooster, one who swaggers or struts.

TEXT IN CONTEXT

∾ SOPHOCLES
GREECE, 496–406 B.C.E.

Sophocles is considered one of the three great Greek tragedians, along with Aeschylus and Euripides. In plays such as *Oedipus the King* and *Antigone,* the noblest of human beings are brought under intense strain as their personal convictions and values come up against the rules of public life and the force of fate. Sophocles' plays question the limits of individual freedom and authority in the face of religious and civic laws, ethical and moral imperatives, and private obligations—the very stuff out of which later playwrights, such as William Shakespeare (1564–1616) in England and Chikamatsu Monzaemon[1] (1653–1724) in Japan, would shape their own great tragedies. Moreover, Sophocles' depiction of what the English poet Matthew Arnold (1822–1888) called the "ebb and flow / Of human misery" evokes sympathy and admiration even in modern audiences moved by the spectacle of dignified suffering conveyed by his plays.

an-TIG-uh-nee

Playwright/Citizen.   Sophocles was born at Colonus, a suburb of Athens, in 496. A general, a priest of Asclepius (god of medicine), and a model citizen, Sophocles served in various civic and administrative posts, participating fully in the rise and decline of his city. The first

WWW   For links to more information about Sophocles, a quiz on *Antigone,* and information about Sophocles' twenty-first-century relevance, see bedfordstmartins .com/worldlit compact.

---

[1] **Chikamatsu Monzaemon** (1653–1724): Japan's greatest playwright, who wrote about history, domestic life, and *shinju,* or suicide, in such dramas as *The Battles of Coxinga, The Uprooted Pine,* and *The Love Suicides at Amijima.*

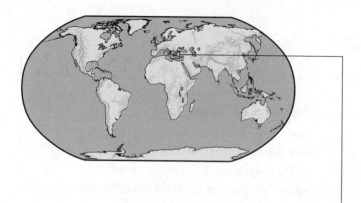

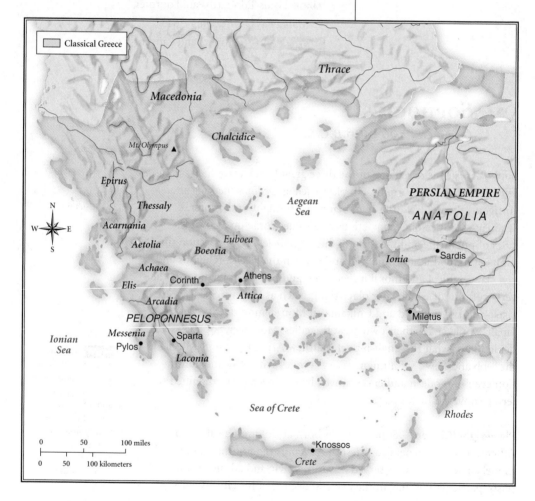

Classical Greece, c. 400 B.C.E.

Although they reached unprecedented cultural heights in art, drama, philosophy, and architecture, the Greeks failed to achieve political unity and harmony. Sophocles' life spanned the years of most of the Persian Wars (500–479 B.C.E.) to just beyond the Peloponnesian War (431–404 B.C.E.). Between the two wars Athens rose to the height of its political and cultural power during the Age of Pericles (461–429 B.C.E.) and declined after the great plague of 429 B.C.E. that killed a third of its population.

notice we have of his public life is his membership in the chorus celebrating the Athenian naval victory over the Persians at Salamis in 480. In 468, Sophocles won his first prize as a playwright, when his *Triptolemus* took first place over a play by Aeschylus at the Great Dionysia. Sophocles was to enjoy twenty-four more such victories in the course of his career, during which he produced more than 120 plays—only seven of which have survived.

Sophocles enjoyed the respect and admiration of his fellow Athenians, not only for his plays but also for his public service and reputation for fairness and affability. His even temper won him the friendship of Herodotus and Aristophanes,[2] among others. Sophocles took charge of the imperial treasury in 443, was elected to be one of the ten *strategoi,* or generals, one of the highest positions of Athenian society, in 440, and served with Pericles in the Samian War.[3] During this time he was involved in forming a "company of the Educated" to promote the discussion and criticism of literature. In later life Sophocles served his state as a diplomat and an ambassador, and was a priest of Halon, a minor god associated with Asclepius whose cult increased following the plague of 429. Sophocles died in 406, less than two years before a starving Athens surrendered to Sparta when the Athenian fleet, once the pride of the Aegean, was defeated at the Battle of the Aegospotami.[4]

The Plays.   In addition to the play included here, the surviving plays of Sophocles are *Ajax, The Women of Trachis, Electra, Philoctetes, Oedipus the King,* and *Oedipus at Colonus.* Drawing on the story of the Trojan War and its aftermath as well as on Greek myth and legend, the plays of Sophocles present archetypal men and women forced to measure their inner strength and principles against the formidable forces of society, history, and fate. Steering a course between the high religious themes of Aeschylus and the topical social criticism of

---

[2] **Herodotus and Aristophanes:** Herodotus (c. 480–c. 425 B.C.E.) was a Greek historian and the author of *The Persian Wars,* considered the first major narrative history in the Western world. Aristophanes (c. 450–c. 386 B.C.E.) was an Athenian dramatist known for satires and comedies; his plays include *The Clouds, Lysistrata,* and *The Frogs.*

[3] **Pericles . . . Samian War:** Pericles (c. 495–429 B.C.E.) was one of the great leaders of Athens under whose reign (461–429 B.C.E.) Athenian society and culture flourished until Athens suffered humiliating defeats in the Peloponnesian War. The Samian War (441–439 B.C.E.) between Athens and Samos was fought to bring the island of Samos, which had broken off from the league of Greek states led by Athens, back into the alliance and back into compliance with Athenian hegemony.

[4] **the Battle of the Aegospotami:** The battle that took place at the mouth of the Aegospotamos, a river flowing into the Hellespont, where Sparta defeated the Athenian fleet in 405 B.C.E., effectively decimating Athenian military power and leading to the defeat of Athens the following year.

Ancient Greece: The Origins of Greek Drama

The creation of tragedy and comedy was one of Greece's major gifts to the West, but the exact origins and evolution of Greek drama, like so many of the brilliant contributions of Greek culture, are unknown. It is safe to assume that the primary antecedent of drama was a chorus of singers and their performances at civic occasions. In the *Poetics,* Aristotle corroborates this idea by maintaining that the origins of tragedy lie in the choral ode or lyric, the dithyramb, which was composed and sung in honor of Dionysus, the god of wine and intoxication. The dithyramb is attributed to the legendary Greek poet Arion, thought to have lived in the seventh century B.C.E. in Corinth. The dithyramb was typically divided into stanzas called strophes, during which the chorus danced in one direction and then reversed itself with the next stanza or antistrophe. It is thought that Arion took a first step toward drama by creating a dialogue between the dithyrambic chorus and its leader. Accompanying the worship of Dionysus was the mask, hung on a wooden column, symbol of the god himself as well as the shifting identities of ecstatic worshippers.

This link to the dithyramb led some scholars to speculate that tragedy had its origins in a ritual dance or play associated with the worship of Dionysus. The fact that "tragedy" or *tragoidia* means "goat song" has not been satisfactorily explained, but it is thought that the chorus in tragedy wore goat-skins. Processionals were held during the Rural Dionysia in December in which participants carried baskets of *phalloi,* used to simulate the fertility of the fields during the autumn sowing of seed. Some think that comedy itself

Theaters of Classical Greece

might have developed out of the revelers who made fun of the sacred phallus. A goat was killed, whose blood not only symbolized the necessary sacrifice for new life, but was part of the reenactment of the Titan's destruction of Dionysus. As the god of spring, Dionysus's death and resurrection symbolized the profound transition in the agricultural cycle from the death of winter to the rebirth of life in the spring. Unfortunately, there are no examples of these ritual texts and the theory itself, however interesting, has been challenged.

A more conservative theory holds that tragedy emerged at the end of the sixth century B.C.E. and was the result of several sources, emanating from the tradition of long oral poems recited at religious festivals. The most important of these festivals for the development of tragedy was the Great Dionysia, held in March and instituted by the tyrant Peisistratus in 534 B.C.E. Peisistratus

Ancient Greece: The Origins of Greek Drama *continued*

brought the cult of Dionysus to Athens from a region north of Eleusis. Thespis, the antecedent of thespian, is regarded as the father of Greek tragedy. It is believed that Thespis was the first actor to appear separate from the chorus on stage; he created speeches for himself, introduced imperson-ation into the dithyrambic dialogue, and initi-ated the prologue. Thespis won recognition in c. 534 B.C.E. with a play about Dionysus, who was played by one actor and a chorus of mor-tals or divine beings in human form. Choe-rilus, Pratinas, and Phrynichus are writers also connected with the early stages of tragedy.

During three consecutive days of the Great Dionysia a contest was held between three dramatists who had been chosen from numerous applicants and were sponsored by wealthy citizens, as required by the state. The sponsors were known as *choregoi,* those who paid the expenses for a chorus at the various lyric or dramatic contests at one of the major festivals in Athens. Each poet provided three tragedies (a trilogy) and a satyr play. The four were known as a tetralogy. Aristotle thought the satyr play, which was performed by a cho-rus of satyrs and dealt in a grotesque manner with mythic subjects, was an early version of

tragedy. The contest was juried by five Athe-nians; the winner received a crown of ivy.

Men played all the parts, both actors and chorus. Masks for both chorus and actors heightened or accentuated character, as did their elevated shoes or boots (*kothornos*). The flute player accompanying the chorus was unmasked. Twelve persons comprised Aeschy-lus's chorus; Sophocles increased the number to fifteen. Aeschylus added a second actor to Thespis's single actor; Sophocles added a third, which became the standard number. For both Thespis and Aeschylus, it was com-mon for the poet to act in his own plays.

Any history of Greek tragedy must also include what is probably the most important ingredient leading to the brilliant flowering of Attic drama, Greek humanism. It is character-ized by the ability of Greek intellectuals and poets to stand back from the drama of human life, to look at its many psychological facets; they were willing to face the conse-quences of excessive confidence or hubris. Greek intellectuals were able to examine and eventually celebrate their passion for human achievement, while acknowledging that fate and the gods set the boundaries for individual ambition.

Euripides, Sophocles' dramas focus on human beings caught between irreconcilable sets of values and confronted with the difficulty of acting consistently according to their principles. Noble in character and bold in action, characters such as Oedipus and Antigone are nonetheless human in their capacity for error and the psychological unawareness that leads them to intense suffering. In *Oedipus Rex,* for example, King Oedipus of Thebes, a model of piety and virtue, pursues an investiga-tion that ultimately reveals he has unwittingly committed unspeakable

crimes—he has killed his father, King Laius, and taken his mother, Jocasta, as his wife. In *Antigone,* the formidable Antigone, princess of Thebes, and Creon, the new king, adamantly refuse to compromise their equally legitimate but opposing positions regarding the burial of Polynices, leading to the downfall of both. Though Sophocles' characters are strongly affected by fate and the will of the gods, the plays

invite one to question to what extent individuals are ultimately responsible for their actions, thus giving voice to the enduring question of
how much human beings are free to determine their life in the face of
forces apparently beyond their control.

The Model Tragedy.   As a playwright, Sophocles was a consummate
craftsman and technical innovator. Aeschylus had already introduced a
second actor into drama; Sophocles increased the number of players to
three, thereby increasing the complexity of the interchanges. Moreover,
Sophocles reduced the number of people in the chorus from fifty to
twelve and introduced painted backdrops to the set. Such changes
allowed for a more subtle and complex development of both plot and
character, perhaps leading in part to Aristotle's tribute to Sophocles'
craftsmanship in *Poetics*,[5] in which *Oedipus the King*, Sophocles' greatest play, serves as the model tragedy. According to Aristotle, a great
tragedy concentrates on a single dramatic conflict, a noble action that
unfolds in the course of a single day. The purpose of the tragedy is to
arouse both pity and terror in the audience in order to effect what he
calls *katharsis,* a purgation of the emotions and a clarification of the
mind that leads to a degree of equanimity, a lightening of the soul. To
arouse pity and fear in the onlooker, a tragedy should depict the fall of
a person of noble character and good fortune who unwittingly commits a grave error (*hamartia*) resulting from a tragic character flaw to
which he or she is blind. It is important that the audience understand
this reversal of fortune to be undeserved, resulting not from vice or
depravity on the part of the hero but rather from some unintentional
miscalculation. For Aristotle, *Oedipus the King* invokes fear because we
identify with Oedipus's lack of self-knowledge and recognize our
inability to fully determine the consequences of our actions; it also
invokes pity, as the audience sympathizes with someone who undeservedly suffers misfortune.

The House of Thebes.   Both *Oedipus the King* and *Antigone* invoke
the story of the curse on the House of Thebes to dramatize the sweeping changes taking place in the fifth century B.C.E. in the political and
cultural life of Athens, especially the move toward democracy, the
decline in the role of religion, and the changing relations between men
and women. The story begins when Laius, the grandson of Cadmus,

> By making [Oedipus]
> criminal in a small
> degree, and miser-
> able in a very great
> one, by investing him
> with some excellent
> qualities, and some
> imperfections, he at
> once inclines us to
> pity and to condemn.
>
> – SAMUEL JOHNSON,
> writer and critic, 1779

---

[5] *Poetics:* One of the earliest works of literary criticism in the West, *Poetics* was compiled from the notes of students who had attended the lectures of the Greek philosopher Aristotle (384–322 B.C.E.).

founder of Thebes, abducts Chrysippus, the beautiful though illegitimate son of Pelops, the king of Pisa, in the Peloponnese. Laius, who had been given refuge at the court of Pelops at the time, thus violates one of the most sacred of relationships—that between a guest and his host. After he is restored to the throne at Thebes, Laius marries Jocasta and eventually learns from the Delphic Oracle that his punishment for having abducted Chrysippus will be to die at the hand of his own son. To prevent the prophecy from being fulfilled, when Jocasta gives birth to a son, Laius hands over the infant, spiked through the ankles to lash its legs together, to shepherds. These men are supposed to leave the baby to die on Mt. Cithaeron. The goodhearted shepherds, however, deliver the boy to the king and queen of Corinth, Polybus and Merope, instead, who give him the name Oedipus, which means "swollen foot," and raise him as their own. While still a young man, Oedipus learns from the Delphic oracle that he will kill his father and marry his mother. In order to escape this prophecy, Oedipus flees his foster parents and, en route to Thebes, encounters his real father and kills him over a quarrel at a crossroads. On the outskirts of Thebes, Oedipus meets the Sphinx who is terrorizing the populace. The Sphinx destroys herself after Oedipus solves her riddle. In gratitude, the city makes Oedipus its ruler and hands over for marriage Jocasta, the widowed queen. And thus Oedipus fulfills the prophecy. Having discovered that he has indeed unwittingly killed his true father and married his mother, Jocasta, who gave him two sons, Eteocles and Polynices, and two daughters, Antigone and Ismene, Oedipus blinds himself and is banished. Jocasta kills herself in despair, and the throne of Thebes descends on Creon, who assumes the role of regent until **Eteocles** and **Polynices** are old enough to take power.

uh-TEE-uh-kleez;
pah-lih-NIGH-seez

The story of Oedipus's banishment is told in *Oedipus at Colonus*, probably Sophocles' last play, written shortly before his death and performed posthumously. *Antigone* begins in the aftermath of the disagreement between Polynices and Eteocles over sharing power at Thebes, though the Chorus from time to time alludes to incidents from the larger legend of the House of Thebes. When Eteocles backs out of an agreement to rule in alternate years, Polynices returns with seven Argive leaders to kill his brother, a story told in Aeschylus's *Seven Against Thebes*. When *Antigone* opens, the two brothers are dead, and their uncle, Creon, has taken over now as king of Thebes. Because he perceives Polynices as a traitor to the *polis*, he refuses him a proper burial. Antigone, while recognizing that Polynices has violated the legal code, insists that a higher and more ancient

code—one that honors blood ties over civic duties—demands that
he be buried.

Antigone.   The dating of Sophocles' plays is an imprecise art. Scholars
believe that *Antigone* dates from the late 440s B.C.E., some years before
the production of *Oedipus the King* in the 430s, even though the events
in *Antigone* follow those in *Oedipus the King. Antigone* has often been
read as a struggle between two antagonistic but clear-cut opposites,
usually the individual and the state. Tied to her brother by the sacred
bonds of kinship, Antigone in this reading subverts the decree of
Creon, who in the interest of civic order must deny her demand that
her offending brother Polynices receive a proper burial. Without a
proper burial, however, a soul cannot cross over the river Styx into the
underworld, so Antigone's concern for Polynices goes beyond a matter
of mere formality or ritual. Her religious responsibility for the destiny
of her brother's soul stands in opposition to the civic law that must
punish enemies of the state.

Antigone represents more than just the individual. She is also a
symbol of a complex set of affiliations to the gods of the underworld
and the household, to the ancient blood code of the family, and to
women, who in fifth-century-B.C.E. Athens did not enjoy the rights of
citizenship granted to men. Creon has his own set of affiliations to the

sky gods, to the new legal code ushered in under the auspices of Athena in Aeschylus's *Eumenides,* and to the patriarchy. *Antigone* thus further dramatizes the transformations taking place in the democratization of Athens, which under Cleisthenes transferred power to districts established by law, not kinship ties.

The tragedy does not rest easily even on these more complex oppositions but rather encourages further scrutiny of Antigone's and Creon's positions. Both Creon and Antigone are right, and both are wrong—Creon, in light of the archaic laws honoring kinship relations; Antigone, in view of the new *POLIS,* which honors civic allegiances. The spectator is left to question seriously the values that each represents. Although Antigone swears to be bound by the blood code associated with the family and with faint traces of a matriarchal lineage, she nonetheless cruelly dismisses **Ismene,** who is both her sister and a woman. Moreover, although Creon declares that he has the interests of the state at heart, he ignores the advice and warnings of his people (embodied by the Chorus), his son Haemon, and the prophet Tiresias. Creon's refusal to bend mirrors Antigone's; her unwillingness to compromise, though supported by the play, thus becomes suspect. Creon's unwillingness to listen to the voice of the people suggests that he is a tyrant, an outmoded political type who contradicts the democratic impetus of the new Athenian state. Yet despite his ultimate fall, his statements about the necessity of relinquishing the ties of blood in the interests of the *polis* were important to the very process of democratization that most Athenians supported.

Further complicating the play is the issue of destiny. As the curse on the House of Thebes unfolds, both Antigone and Creon—and one might add Ismene, Haemon, and even Eurydice—seem to be endowed with freedom of choice and are therefore in some measure the shapers of their own lives. Antigone rejects Ismene's argument, for example, that women should not contend with men, that by nature they must obey the "stronger" sex. Similarly, Tiresias reminds Creon that all human beings will err, but that once they recognize their error they can make amends. It is not certain whether Creon rejects Tiresias's advice, though in the final scene of the play the Chorus seems to suggest that he does. Thus, Sophocles again poses two alternatives: Human destiny is not sealed—human actions and decisions may indeed alter the course of events—or, fate determines the course of human life. Either way may lead to tragic consequences.

is-MEE-nee

■ FURTHER RESEARCH

General Criticism

Knox, Bernard M. W. *The Heroic Temper. Studies in Sophoclean Tragedy.* 1964.
Ringer, Mark. *Electra and the Empty Urn: Metatheater and Role Playing in Sophocles.* 1998.
Scodel, Ruth. *Sophocles.* 1984.
Seale, David. *Vision and Stagecraft in Sophocles.* 1982.
Segal, Charles. *Tragedy and Civilization.* 1981.
Walton, J. Michael. *The Greek Sense of Theatre.* 1985.
Winnington-Ingram, R. P. *Sophocles: An Interpretation.* 1980.
Woodard, Thomas Marion, ed. *Sophocles: A Collection of Critical Essays.* 1966.

Antigone
Goheen, R. F. *The Imagery of Sophocles'* Antigone. 1951.
Griffith, Mark. *Antigone/Sophocles.* 1999.

■ PRONUNCIATION

Antigone: an-TIG-uh-nee
Cadmus (Kadmos): KAD-muhs
Eteocles: uh-TEE-uh-kleez
Eurydice: yoo-RIH-dih-see
Ismene: is-MEE-nee
Jocasta (Iocastê): joh-KAS-tuh, ee-oh-KAS-tee, yoh-KAS-tee
Laius (Laïos): LAY-uhs
Oedipus: ED-uh-pus
Polynices (Polyneices): pah-lih-NIGH-seez
Tiresias (Teiresias): tigh-REE-see-us

ᘒ Antigone

Translated by Robert Fagles

CHARACTERS

ANTIGONE, *daughter of Oedipus and Jocasta*
ISMENE, *sister of Antigone*
A CHORUS *of old Theban citizens and their*
    LEADER
CREON, *king of Thebes, uncle of Antigone*
    and Ismene

A SENTRY
HAEMON, *son of Creon and Eurydice*
TIRESIAS, *a blind prophet*
A MESSENGER
EURYDICE, *wife of Creon*
Guards, attendants, and a boy

TIME AND SCENE: *The royal house of Thebes. It is still night, and the invading armies of Argos have just been driven from the city. Fighting on opposite sides, the sons of Oedipus, Eteocles and Polynices, have killed each other in combat. Their uncle,* CREON, *is now king of Thebes.*

[*Enter* ANTIGONE, *slipping through the central doors of the palace. She motions to her sister,* ISMENE, *who follows her cautiously toward an altar at the center of the stage.*]

ANTIGONE:
    My own flesh and blood—dear sister, dear Ismene,
    how many griefs our father Oedipus[1] handed down!
    Do you know one, I ask you, one grief
    that Zeus will not perfect for the two of us
    while we still live and breathe? There's nothing,
    no pain—our lives are pain—no private shame,
    no public disgrace, nothing I haven't seen
    in your griefs and mine. And now this:
    emergency decree, they say, the Commander
10   has just declared for all of Thebes.
    What, haven't you heard? Don't you see?
    The doom reserved for enemies
    marches on the ones we love the most.

ISMENE:
    Not I, I haven't heard a word, Antigone.
    Nothing of loved ones,
    no joy or pain has come my way, not since
    the two of us were robbed of our two brothers,
    both gone in a day, a double blow—
    not since the armies of Argos vanished,
20   just this very night. I know nothing more,
    whether our luck's improved or ruin's still to come.

ANTIGONE:
    I thought so. That's why I brought you out here,
    past the gates, so you could hear in private.

ISMENE:
    What's the matter? Trouble, clearly . . .
    you sound so dark, so grim.

ANTIGONE:
    Why not? Our own brothers' burial!
    Hasn't Creon graced one with all the rites,
    disgraced the other? Eteocles, they say,
    has been given full military honors,
30   rightly so—Creon's laid him in the earth
    and he goes with glory down among the dead.

---

[1] **Oedipus:** Son of Laïos, king of Thebes, and Jocasta; through a series of events foretold in an oracle, Oedipus unknowingly kills his father, Laius, marries his mother, Jocasta, and replaces his father as king. Learning the truth, as Ismene explains, he blinds himself and goes into exile at Colonus. Jocasta's brother is Creon (Kreon). [All notes are the editors'.]

But the body of Polynices, who died miserably—
why, a city-wide proclamation, rumor has it,
forbids anyone to bury him, even mourn him.
He's to be left unwept, unburied, a lovely treasure
for birds that scan the field and feast to their heart's content.

Such, I hear, is the martial law our good Creon
lays down for you and me—yes, me, I tell you—
and he's coming here to alert the uninformed
in no uncertain terms,
and he won't treat the matter lightly. Whoever
disobeys in the least will die, his doom is sealed:
stoning to death inside the city walls!

There you have it. You'll soon show what you are,
worth your breeding, Ismene, or a coward—
for all your royal blood.

ISMENE:
My poor sister, if things have come to this,
who am I to make or mend them, tell me,
what good am I to you?

ANTIGONE:
                    Decide.
Will you share the labor, share the work?

ISMENE:
What work, what's the risk? What do you mean?

ANTIGONE:
[*Raising her hands.*]
Will you lift up his body with these bare hands
and lower it with me?

ISMENE:
               What? You'd bury him—
when a law forbids the city?

ANTIGONE:
                  Yes!
He is my brother and—deny it as you will—
your brother too.
No one will ever convict me for a traitor.

ISMENE:
So desperate, and Creon has expressly—

ANTIGONE:
                      No,
he has no right to keep me from my own.

ISMENE:
Oh my sister, think—

think how our own father died, hated,[2]
his reputation in ruins, driven on
by the crimes he brought to light himself
to gouge out his eyes with his own hands—
then mother . . . his mother and wife, both in one,
mutilating her life in the twisted noose—
and last, our two brothers dead in a single day,[3]
both shedding their own blood, poor suffering boys,
battling out their common destiny hand-to-hand.

70   Now look at the two of us, left so alone . . .
think what a death we'll die, the worst of all
if we violate the laws and override
the fixed decree of the throne, its power—
we must be sensible. Remember we are women,
we're not born to contend with men. Then too,
we're underlings, ruled by much stronger hands,
so we must submit in this, and things still worse.

I, for one, I'll beg the dead to forgive me—
I'm forced, I have no choice—I must obey
80   the ones who stand in power. Why rush to extremes?
It's madness, madness.

ANTIGONE:
                                              I won't insist,
no, even if you should have a change of heart,
I'd never welcome you in the labor, not with me.
So, do as you like, whatever suits you best—
I will bury him myself.
And even if I die in the act, that death will be a glory.
I will lie with the one I love and loved by him—
an outrage sacred to the gods! I have longer
to please the dead than please the living here:
90   in the kingdom down below I'll lie forever.
Do as you like, dishonor the laws
the gods hold in honor.

ISMENE:
                                              I'd do them no dishonor . . .

---

[2] **our own father . . . hated:** In *Oedipus at Colonus*, which Sophocles wrote after *Antigone*, Oedipus dies a mysterious but honorable death, unlike the one described here. The sisters are with Oedipus, their father, during his banishment from Thebes and witness his suffering and sorrow.

[3] **two brothers . . . day:** As the Chorus alludes to in succeeding lines, Polynices and Eteocles, the sons of Oedipus, fought over rightful rule of Thebes. Exiled by his brother, Polynices assembled an army under the leadership of seven commanders and attacked the city; in the ensuing battle, the brothers ended up killing each other.

but defy the city? I have no strength for that.

ANTIGONE:

You have your excuses. I am on my way,
I'll raise a mound for him, for my dear brother.

ISMENE:

Oh Antigone, you're so rash — I'm so afraid for you!

ANTIGONE:

Don't fear for me. Set your own life in order.

ISMENE:

Then don't, at least, blurt this out to anyone.
Keep it a secret. I'll join you in that, I promise.

ANTIGONE:

100   Dear god, shout it from the rooftops. I'll hate you
all the more for silence — tell the world!

ISMENE:

So fiery — and it ought to chill your heart.

ANTIGONE:

I know I please where I must please the most.

ISMENE:

Yes, if you can, but you're in love with impossibility.

ANTIGONE:

Very well then, once my strength gives out
I will be done at last.

ISMENE:

                                    You're wrong from the start,
you're off on a hopeless quest.

ANTIGONE:

If you say so, you will make me hate you,
and the hatred of the dead, by all rights,
110   will haunt you night and day.
But leave me to my own absurdity, leave me
to suffer this — dreadful thing. I will suffer
nothing as great as death without glory.

[*Exit to the side.*]

ISMENE:

Then go if you must, but rest assured,
wild, irrational as you are, my sister,
you are truly dear to the ones who love you.

[*Withdrawing to the palace.*

Enter a CHORUS, *the old citizens of Thebes, chanting as the sun begins to rise.*]

CHORUS:

Glory! — great beam of the sun, brightest of all
that ever rose on the seven gates of Thebes,
      you burn through night at last!
120   Great eye of the golden day,

mounting the Dirce's banks[4] you throw him back—
the enemy out of Argos, the white shield, the man of bronze—
he's flying headlong now
       the bridle of fate stampeding him with pain!

And he had driven against our borders,
launched by the warring claims of Polynices—
like an eagle screaming, winging havoc
over the land, wings of armor
shielded white as snow,
130   a huge army massing,
crested helmets bristling for assault.

He hovered above our roofs, his vast maw gaping
closing down around our seven gates,
   his spears thirsting for the kill
      but now he's gone, look,
before he could glut his jaws with Theban blood
or the god of fire put our crown of towers to the torch.
He grappled the Dragon[5] none can master—Thebes—
    the clang of our arms like thunder at his back!

140   Zeus hates with a vengeance all bravado,
the mighty boasts of men. He watched them
coming on in a rising flood, the pride
of their golden armor ringing shrill—
and brandishing his lightning
blasted the fighter[6] just at the goal,
rushing to shout his triumph from our walls.

Down from the heights he crashed, pounding down on the earth!
And a moment ago, blazing torch in hand—
    mad for attack, ecstatic
150 he breathed his rage, the storm
   of his fury hurling at our heads!
But now his high hopes have laid him low
and down the enemy ranks the iron god of war

---

[4] **Dirce's banks:** Dirce is a river to the west of Thebes.

[5] **the Dragon:** The people of Thebes were said to have descended from the teeth of a dragon slain by Cadmus, the city's legendary founder.

[6] **the fighter:** Capaneus, the fiercest commander of "the Seven" fighting against Thebes, who boasted that even Zeus could not stop him from toppling the city; as punishment for his vain outburst, Zeus struck him dead with a lightning bolt as he scaled the wall of the fortified city.

deals his rewards, his stunning blows—Ares[7]
rapture of battle, our right arm in the crisis.

Seven captains marshaled at seven gates
seven against their equals, gave
their brazen trophies up to Zeus,
god of the breaking rout of battle,
all but two: those blood brothers,
one father, one mother—matched in rage,
spears matched for the twin conquest—
clashed and won the common prize of death.

But now for Victory! Glorious in the morning,
joy in her eyes to meet our joy
        she is winging down to Thebes,
our fleets of chariots wheeling in her wake—
        Now let us win oblivion from the wars,
thronging the temples of the gods
in singing, dancing choirs through the night!
        Lord Dionysus,[8] god of the dance
        that shakes the land of Thebes, now lead the way!

[*Enter* CREON *from the palace, attended by his guard.*]
        But look, the king of the realm is coming,
        Creon, the new man for the new day,
        whatever the gods are sending now . . .
        what new plan will he launch?
        Why this, this special session?
        Why this sudden call to the old men
        summoned at one command?

CREON:

                                My countrymen,
the ship of state is safe. The gods who rocked her,
after a long, merciless pounding in the storm,
have righted her once more.
                        Out of the whole city
I have called you here alone. Well I know,
first, your undeviating respect
for the throne and royal power of King Laius.
Next, while Oedipus steered the land of Thebes,
and even after he died, your loyalty was unshakable,
you still stood by their children. Now then,

160

170

180

---

[7] **Ares:** The god of war and a protector of Thebes.

[8] **Dionysus:** The god of wine and revels; his mother, Semele, hailed from Thebes.

since the two sons are dead—two blows of fate
190   in the same day, cut down by each other's hands,
both killers, both brothers stained with blood—
as I am next in kin[9] to the dead,
I now possess the throne and all its powers.

Of course you cannot know a man completely,
his character, his principles, sense of judgment,
not till he's shown his colors, ruling the people,
making laws. Experience, there's the test.
As I see it, whoever assumes the task,
the awesome task of setting the city's course,
200   and refuses to adopt the soundest policies
but fearing someone, keeps his lips locked tight,
he's utterly worthless. So I rate him now,
I always have. And whoever places a friend
above the good of his own country, he is nothing:
I have no use for him. Zeus my witness,
Zeus who sees all things, always—
I could never stand by silent, watching destruction
march against our city, putting safety to rout,
nor could I ever make that man a friend of mine
210   who menaces our country. Remember this:
our country *is* our safety.
Only while she voyages true on course
can we establish friendships, truer than blood itself.
Such are my standards. They make our city great.

Closely akin to them I have proclaimed,
just now, the following decree to our people
concerning the two sons of Oedipus.
Eteocles, who died fighting for Thebes,
excelling all in arms: he shall be buried,
220   crowned with a hero's honors, the cups we pour[10]
to soak the earth and reach the famous dead.

But as for his blood brother, Polynices,
who returned from exile, home to his father-city
and the gods of his race, consumed with one desire—
to burn them roof to roots—who thirsted to drink

---

[9] **I am . . . kin:** Creon was a first cousin of Laïos, the king of Thebes whom Oedipus murdered, and he is the brother of Jocasta, the mother of Eteocles and Polynices.

[10] **the cups we pour:** Libations, the ritual offering of liquids to the dead. (See also line 479.)

his kinsmen's blood and sell the rest to slavery:
that man—a proclamation has forbidden the city
to dignify him with burial, mourn him at all.
No, he must be left unburied, his corpse
230   carrion for the birds and dogs to tear,
an obscenity for the citizens to behold!

These are my principles. Never at my hands
will the traitor be honored above the patriot.
But whoever proves his loyalty to the state—
I'll prize that man in death as well as life.
LEADER:
   If this is your pleasure, Creon, treating
our city's enemy and our friend this way . . .
The power is yours, I suppose, to enforce it
with the laws, both for the dead and all of us,
the living.
CREON:
               Follow my orders closely then,
240   be on your guard.
LEADER:
                 We're too old.
Lay that burden on younger shoulders.
CREON:
                         No, no,
I don't mean the body—I've posted guards already.
LEADER:
What commands for us then? What other service?
CREON:
See that you never side with those who break my orders.
LEADER:
Never. Only a fool could be in love with death.
CREON:
Death is the price—you're right. But all too often
the mere hope of money has ruined many men.

[*A* SENTRY *enters from the side.*]
SENTRY:
                    My lord,
I can't say I'm winded from running, or set out
250   with any spring in my legs either—no sir,
I was lost in thought, and it made me stop, often,
dead in my tracks, wheeling, turning back,
and all the time a voice inside me muttering,
"Idiot, why? You're going straight to your death."

Then muttering, "Stopped again, poor fool?
If somebody gets the news to Creon first,
what's to save your neck?"
                              And so,
mulling it over, on I trudged, dragging my feet,
you can make a short road take forever . . .
260   but at last, look, common sense won out,
I'm here, and I'm all yours,
and even though I come empty-handed
I'll tell my story just the same, because
I've come with a good grip on one hope,
what will come will come, whatever fate—

CREON:
Come to the point!
What's wrong—why so afraid?

SENTRY:
First, myself, I've got to tell you,
I didn't do it, didn't see who did—
270   Be fair, don't take it out on me.

CREON:
You're playing it safe, soldier,
barricading yourself from any trouble.
It's obvious, you've something strange to tell.

SENTRY:
Dangerous too, and danger makes you delay
for all you're worth.

CREON:
Out with it—then dismiss!

SENTRY:
All right, here it comes. The body—
someone's just buried it, then run off . . .
sprinkled some dry dust on the flesh,
given it proper rites.

CREON:
280   What?
What man alive would dare—

SENTRY:
                              I've no idea, I swear it.
There was no mark of a spade, no pickaxe there,
no earth turned up, the ground packed hard and dry,
unbroken, no tracks, no wheelruts, nothing,
the workman left no trace. Just at sunup
the first watch of the day points it out—
it was a wonder! We were stunned . . .
a terrific burden too, for all of us, listen:

290   you can't see the corpse, not that it's buried,
really, just a light cover of road-dust on it,
as if someone meant to lay the dead to rest
and keep from getting cursed.
Not a sign in sight that dogs or wild beasts
had worried the body, even torn the skin.

But what came next! Rough talk flew thick and fast,
guard grilling guard—we'd have come to blows
at last, nothing to stop it; each man for himself
and each the culprit, no one caught red-handed,
all of us pleading ignorance, dodging the charges,
300   ready to take up red-hot iron in our fists,
go through fire, swear oaths to the gods—
"I didn't do it, I had no hand in it either,
not in the plotting, not the work itself!"

Finally, after all this wrangling came to nothing,
one man spoke out and made us stare at the ground,
hanging our heads in fear. No way to counter him,
no way to take his advice and come through
safe and sound. Here's what he said:
"Look, we've got to report the facts to Creon,
310   we can't keep this hidden." Well, that won out,
and the lot fell to me, condemned me,
unlucky as ever, I got the prize. So here I am,
against my will and yours too, well I know—
no one wants the man who brings bad news.

LEADER:
                                         My king,
ever since he began I've been debating in my mind,
could this possibly be the work of the gods?

CREON:
                                     Stop—
before you make me choke with anger—the gods!
You, you're senile, must you be insane?
You say—why it's intolerable—say the gods
320   could have the slightest concern for that corpse?
Tell me, was it for meritorious service
they proceeded to bury him, prized him so? The hero
who came to burn their temples ringed with pillars,
their golden treasures—scorch their hallowed earth
and fling their laws to the winds.
Exactly when did you last see the gods
celebrating traitors? Inconceivable!

No, from the first there were certain citizens
who could hardly stand the spirit of my regime,
330   grumbling against me in the dark, heads together,
tossing wildly, never keeping their necks beneath
the yoke, loyally submitting to their king.
These are the instigators, I'm convinced —
they've perverted my own guard, bribed them
to do their work.

            Money! Nothing worse
in our lives, so current, rampant, so corrupting.
Money — you demolish cities, root men from their homes,
you train and twist good minds and set them on
to the most atrocious schemes. No limit,
340   you make them adept at every kind of outrage,
every godless crime — money!

                  Everyone —
the whole crew bribed to commit this crime,
they've made one thing sure at least:
sooner or later they will pay the price.

[*Wheeling on the* SENTRY.]
                  You —
I swear to Zeus as I still believe in Zeus,
if you don't find the man who buried that corpse,
the very man, and produce him before my eyes,
simple death won't be enough for you,
not till we string you up alive
350   and wring the immorality out of you.
Then you can steal the rest of your days,
better informed about where to make a killing.
You'll have learned, at last, it doesn't pay
to itch for rewards from every hand that beckons.
Filthy profits wreck most men, you'll see —
they'll never save your life.

SENTRY:
                Please,
may I say a word or two, or just turn and go?

CREON:
Can't you tell? Everything you say offends me.

SENTRY:
Where does it hurt you, in the ears or in the heart?

CREON:
360   And who are you to pinpoint my displeasure?

SENTRY:
The culprit grates on your feelings,
I just annoy your ears.

CREON:
                        Still talking?
    You talk too much! A born nuisance—
SENTRY:
                                Maybe so,
    but I never did this thing, so help me!
CREON:
                                    Yes you did—
    what's more, you squandered your life for silver!
SENTRY:
    Oh it's terrible when the one who does the judging
    judges things all wrong.
CREON:
                        Well now,
    you just be clever about your judgments—
    if you fail to produce the criminals for me,
370   you'll swear your dirty money brought you pain.

[*Turning sharply, reentering the palace.*]
SENTRY:
    I hope he's found. Best thing by far.
    But caught or not, that's in the lap of fortune:
    I'll never come back, you've seen the last of me.
    I'm saved, even now, and I never thought,
    I never hoped—
    dear gods, I owe you all my thanks!
                                        [*Rushing out.*]
CHORUS:
                        Numberless wonders
    terrible wonders walk the world but none the match for man—
    that great wonder crossing the heaving gray sea,
            driven on by the blasts of winter
380   on through breakers crashing left and right,
            holds his steady course
    and the oldest of the gods he wears away—
    the Earth, the immortal, the inexhaustible—
    as his plows go back and forth, year in, year out
            with the breed of stallions turning up the furrows.

    And the blithe, lightheaded race of birds he snares,
    the tribes of savage beasts, the life that swarms the depths—
            with one fling of his nets
    woven and coiled tight, he takes them all,
390   man the skilled, the brilliant!
    He conquers all, taming with his techniques
    the prey that roams the cliffs and wild lairs,

training the stallion, clamping the yoke across
    his shaggy neck, and the tireless mountain bull.
And speech and thought, quick as the wind
and the mood and mind for law that rules the city—
    all these he has taught himself
and shelter from the arrows of the frost
when there's rough lodging under the cold clear sky
400   and the shafts of lashing rain—
        ready, resourceful man!
          Never without resources
never an impasse as he marches on the future—
only Death, from Death alone he will find no rescue
but from desperate plagues he has plotted his escapes.

Man the master, ingenious past all measure
past all dreams, the skills within his grasp—
    he forges on, now to destruction
now again to greatness. When he weaves in
410   the laws of the land, and the justice of the gods
that binds his oaths together
        he and his city rise high—
          but the city casts out
that man who weds himself to inhumanity
thanks to reckless daring. Never share my hearth
never think my thoughts, whoever does such things.

[*Enter* ANTIGONE *from the side, accompanied by the* SENTRY.]
        Here is a dark sign from the gods—
        what to make of this? I know her,
        how can I deny it? That young girl's Antigone!
420   Wretched, child of a wretched father,
        Oedipus. Look, is it possible?
        They bring you in like a prisoner—
        why? did you break the king's laws?
        Did they take you in some act of mad defiance?
SENTRY:
    She's the one, she did it single-handed—
    we caught her burying the body. Where's Creon?

[*Enter* CREON *from the palace.*]
LEADER:
    Back again, just in time when you need him.
CREON:
    In time for what? What is it?
SENTRY:
               My king,

there's nothing you can swear you'll never do—
430   second thoughts make liars of us all.
I could have sworn I wouldn't hurry back
(what with your threats, the buffeting I just took),
but a stroke of luck beyond our wildest hopes,
what a joy, there's nothing like it. So,
back I've come, breaking my oath, who cares?
I'm bringing in our prisoner—this young girl—
we took her giving the dead the last rites.
But no casting lots this time; this is *my* luck,
my prize, no one else's.
                            Now, my lord,
440   here she is. Take her, question her,
cross-examine her to your heart's content.
But set me free, it's only right—
I'm rid of this dreadful business once for all.

CREON:
Prisoner! Her? You took her—where, doing what?

SENTRY:
Burying the man. That's the whole story.

CREON:
                                    What?
You mean what you say, you're telling me the truth?

SENTRY:
She's the one. With my own eyes I saw her
bury the body, just what you've forbidden.
There. Is that plain and clear?

CREON:
450   What did you see? Did you catch her in the act?

SENTRY:
Here's what happened. We went back to our post,
those threats of yours breathing down our necks—
we brushed the corpse clean of the dust that covered it,
stripped it bare . . . it was slimy, going soft,
and we took to high ground, backs to the wind
so the stink of him couldn't hit us;
jostling, baiting each other to keep awake,
shouting back and forth—no napping on the job,
not this time. And so the hours dragged by
460   until the sun stood dead above our heads,
a huge white ball in the noon sky, beating,
blazing down, and then it happened—
suddenly, a whirlwind!
Twisting a great dust-storm up from the earth,
a black plague of the heavens, filling the plain,

ripping the leaves off every tree in sight,
choking the air and sky. We squinted hard
and took our whipping from the gods.

And after the storm passed—it seemed endless—
470   there, we saw the girl!
And she cried out a sharp, piercing cry,
like a bird come back to an empty nest,
peering into its bed, and all the babies gone . . .
Just so, when she sees the corpse bare
she bursts into a long, shattering wail
and calls down withering curses on the heads
of all who did the work. And she scoops up dry dust,
handfuls, quickly, and lifting a fine bronze urn,
lifting it high and pouring, she crowns the dead
with three full libations.
480   Soon as we saw
we rushed her, closed on the kill like hunters,
and she, she didn't flinch. We interrogated her,
charging her with offenses past and present—
she stood up to it all, denied nothing. I tell you,
it made me ache and laugh in the same breath.
It's pure joy to escape the worst yourself,
it hurts a man to bring down his friends.
But all that, I'm afraid, means less to me
than my own skin. That's the way I'm made.

CREON:

[*Wheeling on* ANTIGONE.]
                                                              You,
490   with your eyes fixed on the ground—speak up.
Do you deny you did this, yes or no?

ANTIGONE:

I did it. I don't deny a thing.

CREON:

[*To the* SENTRY.]
You, get out, wherever you please—
you're clear of a very heavy charge.

[*He leaves;* CREON *turns back to* ANTIGONE.]
You, tell me briefly, no long speeches—
were you aware a decree had forbidden this?

ANTIGONE:

Well aware. How could I avoid it? It was public.

CREON:

And still you had the gall to break this law?

ANTIGONE:
  Of course I did. It wasn't Zeus, not in the least,
500 who made this proclamation — not to me.
  Nor did that Justice, dwelling with the gods
  beneath the earth, ordain such laws for men.
  Nor did I think your edict had such force
  that you, a mere mortal, could override the gods,
  the great unwritten, unshakable traditions.
  They are alive, not just today or yesterday:
  they live forever, from the first of time,
  and no one knows when they first saw the light.

  These laws — I was not about to break them,
510 not out of fear of some man's wounded pride,
  and face the retribution of the gods.
  Die I must, I've known it all my life —
  how could I keep from knowing? — even without
  your death-sentence ringing in my ears.
  And if I am to die before my time
  I consider that a gain. Who on earth,
  alive in the midst of so much grief as I,
  could fail to find his death a rich reward?
  So for me, at least, to meet this doom of yours
520 is precious little pain. But if I had allowed
  my own mother's son to rot, an unburied corpse —
  that would have been an agony! This is nothing.
  And if my present actions strike you as foolish,
  let's just say I've been accused of folly
  by a fool.

LEADER:
          Like father like daughter,
  passionate, wild . . .
  she hasn't learned to bend before adversity.

CREON:
  No? Believe me, the stiffest stubborn wills
  fall the hardest; the toughest iron,
530 tempered strong in the white-hot fire,
  you'll see it crack and shatter first of all.
  And I've known spirited horses you can break
  with a light bit — proud, rebellious horses.
  There's no room for pride, not in a slave,
  not with the lord and master standing by.

  This girl was an old hand at insolence
  when she overrode the edicts we made public.

But once she'd done it — the insolence,
twice over — to glory in it, laughing,
540   mocking us to our face with what she'd done.
I am not the man, not now: she is the man
if this victory goes to her and she goes free.

Never! Sister's child or closer in blood
than all my family clustered at my altar
worshiping Guardian Zeus — she'll never escape,
she and her blood sister, the most barbaric death.
Yes, I accuse her sister of an equal part
in scheming this, this burial.

[*To his attendants.*]
                                    Bring her here!
I just saw her inside, hysterical, gone to pieces.
550   It never fails: the mind convicts itself
in advance, when scoundrels are up to no good,
plotting in the dark. Oh but I hate it more
when a traitor, caught red-handed,
tries to glorify his crimes.

ANTIGONE:
Creon, what more do you want
than my arrest and execution?

CREON:
Nothing. Then I have it all.

ANTIGONE:
Then why delay? Your moralizing repels me,
every word you say — pray god it always will.
So naturally all I say repels you too.
560   Enough.
Give me glory! What greater glory could I win
than to give my own brother decent burial?
These citizens here would all agree,

[*To the* CHORUS.]
they'd praise me too
if their lips weren't locked in fear.

[*Pointing to* CREON.]
Lucky tyrants — the perquisites of power!
Ruthless power to do and say whatever pleases *them*.

CREON:
You alone, of all the people in Thebes,
see things that way.

ANTIGONE:
They see it just that way
570   but defer to you and keep their tongues in leash.

CREON:
> And you, aren't you ashamed to differ so from them?
> So disloyal!

ANTIGONE:
>   Not ashamed for a moment,
> not to honor my brother, my own flesh and blood.

CREON:
> Wasn't Eteocles a brother too—cut down, facing him?

ANTIGONE:
> Brother, yes, by the same mother, the same father.

CREON:
> Then how can you render his enemy such honors,
> such impieties in his eyes?

ANTIGONE:
> He'll never testify to that,
> Eteocles dead and buried.

CREON:
>   He will—
580 if you honor the traitor just as much as him.

ANTIGONE:
> But it was his brother, not some slave that died—

CREON:
> Ravaging our country!—
> but Eteocles died fighting in our behalf.

ANTIGONE:
> No matter—Death longs for the same rites for all.

CREON:
> Never the same for the patriot and the traitor.

ANTIGONE:
> Who, Creon, who on earth can say the ones below
> don't find this pure and uncorrupt?

CREON:
> Never. Once an enemy, never a friend,
> not even after death.

ANTIGONE:
590 I was born to join in love, not hate—
> that is my nature.

CREON:
>   Go down below and love,
> if love you must—love the dead! While I'm alive,
> no woman is going to lord it over me.

[*Enter* ISMENE *from the palace, under guard.*]

CHORUS:
>   Look,
> Ismene's coming, weeping a sister's tears,

loving sister, under a cloud . . .
her face is flushed, her cheeks streaming.
Sorrow puts her lovely radiance in the dark.

CREON:

You—
in my own house, you viper, slinking undetected,
sucking my life-blood! I never knew
600   I was breeding twin disasters, the two of you
rising up against my throne. Come, tell me,
will you confess your part in the crime or not?
Answer me. Swear to me.

ISMENE:

I did it, yes—
if only she consents—I share the guilt,
the consequences too.

ANTIGONE:

No,
Justice will never suffer that—not you,
you were unwilling. I never brought you in.

ISMENE:

But now you face such dangers . . . I'm not ashamed
to sail through trouble with you,
make your troubles mine.

ANTIGONE:

610   Who did the work?
Let the dead and the god of death bear witness!
I have no love for a friend who loves in words alone.

ISMENE:

Oh no, my sister, don't reject me, please,
let me die beside you, consecrating
the dead together.

ANTIGONE:

Never share my dying,
don't lay claim to what you never touched.
My death will be enough.

ISMENE:

What do I care for life, cut off from you?

ANTIGONE:

Ask Creon. Your concern is all for him.

ISMENE:

Why abuse me so? It doesn't help you now.

ANTIGONE:

620   You're right—
if I mock you, I get no pleasure from it,
only pain.

ISMENE:
                    Tell me, dear one,
what can I do to help you, even now?

ANTIGONE:
Save yourself. I don't grudge you your survival.

ISMENE:
Oh no, no, denied my portion in your death?

ANTIGONE:
You chose to live, I chose to die.

ISMENE:
                        Not, at least,
without every kind of caution I could voice.

ANTIGONE:
Your wisdom appealed to one world—mine, another.

ISMENE:
But look, we're both guilty, both condemned to death.

ANTIGONE:
630   Courage! Live your life. I gave myself to death,
long ago, so I might serve the dead.

CREON:
They're both mad, I tell you, the two of them.
One's just shown it, the other's been that way
since she was born.

ISMENE:
                  True, my king,
the sense we were born with cannot last forever . . .
commit cruelty on a person long enough
and the mind begins to go.

CREON:
               Yours did,
when you chose to commit your crimes with her.

ISMENE:
How can I live alone, without her?

CREON:
                   Her?
640   Don't even mention her—she no longer exists.

ISMENE:
What? You'd kill your own son's bride?

CREON:
                  Absolutely:
there are other fields for him to plow.

ISMENE:
               Perhaps,
but never as true, as close a bond as theirs.

CREON:
>A worthless woman for my son? It repels me.

ISMENE:
>Dearest Haemon, your father wrongs you so!

CREON:
>Enough, enough—you and your talk of marriage!

ISMENE:
>Creon—you're really going to rob your son of Antigone?

CREON:
>Death will do it for me—break their marriage off.

LEADER:
>So, it's settled then? Antigone must die?

CREON:
650
>Settled, yes—we both know that.

>[*To the guards.*]

>Stop wasting time. Take them in.
>From now on they'll act like women.
>Tie them up, no more running loose;
>even the bravest will cut and run,
>once they see Death coming for their lives.

>[*The guards escort* ANTIGONE *and* ISMENE *into the palace.* CREON *remains while the old citizens form their* CHORUS.]

CHORUS:
>Blest, they are the truly blest who all their lives
>have never tasted devastation. For others, once
>the gods have rocked a house to its foundations
>   the ruin will never cease, cresting on and on

660
>from one generation on throughout the race—
>like a great mounting tide
>driven on by savage northern gales,
>   surging over the dead black depths
>roiling up from the bottom dark heaves of sand
>and the headlands, taking the storm's onslaught full-force,
>roar, and the low moaning
>   echoes on and on
>   and now
>as in ancient times I see the sorrows of the house,
>the living heirs of the old ancestral kings,
>piling on the sorrows of the dead

670
>   and one generation cannot free the next—
>some god will bring them crashing down,
>the race finds no release.
>And now the light, the hope
>   springing up from the late last root

in the house of Oedipus, that hope's cut down in turn
by the long, bloody knife swung by the gods of death
by a senseless word
                    by fury at the heart.
                                        Zeus,
yours is the power, Zeus, what man on earth
can override it, who can hold it back?
680   Power that neither Sleep, the all-ensnaring
            no, nor the tireless months of heaven
can ever overmaster—young through all time,
mighty lord of power, you hold fast
            the dazzling crystal mansions of Olympus.
And throughout the future, late and soon
as through the past, your law prevails:
no towering form of greatness
            enters into the lives of mortals
                                        free and clear of ruin.
                                                    True,
690   our dreams, our high hopes voyaging far and wide
bring sheer delight to many, to many others
            delusion, blithe, mindless lusts
and the fraud steals on one slowly . . . unaware
till he trips and puts his foot into the fire.
            He was a wise old man who coined
the famous saying: "Sooner or later
foul is fair, fair is foul
to the man the gods will ruin"—
            He goes his way for a moment only
700   free of blinding ruin.

[*Enter* HAEMON *from the palace.*]
                    Here's Haemon now, the last of all your sons.[11]
                    Does he come in tears for his bride,
                    his doomed bride, Antigone—
                    bitter at being cheated of their marriage?

CREON:
We'll soon know, better than seers could tell us.

[*Turning to* HAEMON.]
            Son, you've heard the final verdict on your bride?
            Are you coming now, raving against your father?
            Or do you love me, no matter what I do?

---

[11] **Haemon . . . sons:** Haemon was the youngest son of Creon and Eurydice; their first son was Megareus. (See note 34.)

HAEMON:

Father, I'm your *son* . . . you in your wisdom

710   set my bearings for me—I obey you.

No marriage could ever mean more to me than you,

whatever good direction you may offer.

CREON:

Fine, Haemon.

That's how you ought to feel within your heart,

subordinate to your father's will in every way.

That's what a man prays for: to produce good sons—

households full of them, dutiful and attentive,

so they can pay his enemy back with interest

and match the respect their father shows his friend.

But the man who rears a brood of useless children,

720   what has he brought into the world, I ask you?

Nothing but trouble for himself, and mockery

from his enemies laughing in his face.

Oh Haemon,

never lose your sense of judgment over a woman.

The warmth, the rush of pleasure, it all goes cold

in your arms, I warn you . . . a worthless woman

in your house, a misery in your bed.

What wound cuts deeper than a loved one

turned against you? Spit her out,

like a mortal enemy—let the girl go.

730   Let her find a husband down among the dead.

Imagine it: I caught her in naked rebellion,

the traitor, the only one in the whole city.

I'm not about to prove myself a liar,

not to my people, no, I'm going to kill her!

That's right—so let her cry for mercy, sing her hymns

to Zeus who defends all bonds of kindred blood.

Why, if I bring up my own kin to be rebels,

think what I'd suffer from the world at large.

Show me the man who rules his household well:

740   I'll show you someone fit to rule the state.

That good man, my son,

I have every confidence he and he alone

can give commands and take them too. Staunch

in the storm of spears he'll stand his ground,

a loyal, unflinching comrade at your side.

But whoever steps out of line, violates the laws

or presumes to hand out orders to his superiors,

he'll win no praise from me. But that man

the city places in authority, his orders

750   must be obeyed, large and small,
      right and wrong.
                          Anarchy—
      show me a greater crime in all the earth!
      She, she destroys cities, rips up houses,
      breaks the ranks of spearmen into headlong rout.
      But the ones who last it out, the great mass of them
      owe their lives to discipline. Therefore
      we must defend the men who live by law,
      never let some woman triumph over us.
      Better to fall from power, if fall we must,
760   at the hands of a man—never be rated
      inferior to a woman, never.

LEADER:
                          To us,
      unless old age has robbed us of our wits,
      you seem to say what you have to say with sense.

HAEMON:
      Father, only the gods endow a man with reason,
      the finest of all their gifts, a treasure.
      Far be it from me—I haven't the skill,
      and certainly no desire, to tell you when,
      if ever, you make a slip in speech . . . though
      someone else might have a good suggestion.

770   Of course it's not for you,
      in the normal run of things, to watch
      whatever men say or do, or find to criticize.
      The man in the street, you know, dreads your glance,
      he'd never say anything displeasing to your face.
      But it's for me to catch the murmurs in the dark,
      the way the city mourns for this young girl.
      "No woman," they say, "ever deserved death less,
      and such a brutal death for such a glorious action.
      She, with her own dear brother lying in his blood—
780   she couldn't bear to leave him dead, unburied,
      food for the wild dogs or wheeling vultures.
      Death? She deserves a glowing crown of gold!"
      So they say, and the rumor spreads in secret,
      darkly . . .
                          I rejoice in your success, father—
      nothing more precious to me in the world.
      What medal of honor brighter to his children
      than a father's growing glory? Or a child's
      to his proud father? Now don't, please,
      be quite so single-minded, self-involved,

790   or assume the world is wrong and you are right.
      Whoever thinks that he alone possesses intelligence,
      the gift of eloquence, he and no one else,
      and character too . . . such men, I tell you,
      spread them open—you will find them empty.
                                                    No,
      it's no disgrace for a man, even a wise man,
      to learn many things and not to be too rigid.
      You've seen trees by a raging winter torrent,
      how many sway with the flood and salvage every twig,
      but not the stubborn—they're ripped out, roots and all
800   Bend or break. The same when a man is sailing:
      haul your sheets too taut, never give an inch,
      you'll capsize, and go the rest of the voyage
      keel up and the rowing-benches under.

      Oh give way. Relax your anger—change!
      I'm young, I know, but let me offer this:
      it would be best by far, I admit,
      if a man were born infallible, right by nature.
      If not—and things don't often go that way,
      it's best to learn from those with good advice.

LEADER:
810   You'd do well, my lord, if he's speaking to the point,
      to learn from him,

[*Turning to* HAEMON.]
                          and you, my boy, from him.
      You both are talking sense.
CREON:
                          So,
      men our age, we're to be lectured, are we?—
      schooled by a boy his age?
HAEMON:
      Only in what is right. But if I seem young,
      look less to my years and more to what I do.
CREON:
      Do? Is admiring rebels an achievement?
HAEMON:
      I'd never suggest that you admire treason.
CREON:
                                          Oh?—
      isn't that just the sickness that's attacked her?
HAEMON:
820   The whole city of Thebes denies it, to a man.

CREON:
>   And is Thebes about to tell me how to rule?

HAEMON:
>   Now, you see? Who's talking like a child?

CREON:
>   Am I to rule this land for others—or myself?

HAEMON:
>   It's no city at all, owned by one man alone.

CREON:
>   What? The city *is* the king—that's the law!

HAEMON:
>   What a splendid king you'd make of a desert island—
>   you and you alone.

CREON:

[*To the* CHORUS.]
>   This boy, I do believe,
>   is fighting on her side, the woman's side.

HAEMON:
>   If you are a woman, yes—
840   my concern is all for you.

CREON:
>   Why, you degenerate—bandying accusations,
>   threatening me with justice, your own father!

HAEMON:
>   I see my father offending justice—wrong.

CREON:
>   Wrong?
>   To protect my royal rights?

HAEMON:
>   Protect your rights?
>   When you trample down the honors of the gods?

CREON:
>   You, you soul of corruption, rotten through—
>   woman's accomplice!

HAEMON:
>   That may be,
>   but you'll never find me accomplice to a criminal.

CREON:
>   That's what *she* is,
840   and every word you say is a blatant appeal for her—

HAEMON:
>   And you, and me, and the gods beneath the earth.

CREON:
>   You will never marry her, not while she's alive.

HAEMON:

Then she'll die . . . but her death will kill another.

CREON:

What, brazen threats? You go too far!

HAEMON:

What threat?

Combating your empty, mindless judgments with a word?

CREON:

You'll suffer for your sermons, you and your empty wisdom!

HAEMON:

If you weren't my father, I'd say you were insane.

CREON:

Don't flatter me with Father—you woman's slave!

HAEMON:

You really expect to fling abuse at me
and not receive the same?

CREON:

850   Is that so!
Now, by heaven, I promise you, you'll pay—
taunting, insulting me! Bring her out,
that hateful—she'll die now, here,
in front of his eyes, beside her groom!

HAEMON:

No, no, she will never die beside me—
don't delude yourself. And you will never
see me, never set eyes on my face again.
Rage your heart out, rage with friends
who can stand the sight of you.

[*Rushing out.*]

LEADER:

860   Gone, my king, in a burst of anger.
A temper young as his . . . hurt him once,
he may do something violent.

CREON:

Let him do—
dream up something desperate, past all human limit!
Good riddance. Rest assured,
he'll never save those two young girls from death.

LEADER:

Both of them, you really intend to kill them both?

CREON:

No, not her, the one whose hands are clean—
you're quite right.

LEADER:

But Antigone—

what sort of death do you have in mind for her?

CREON:

870 I'll take her down some wild, desolate path
never trod by men, and wall her up alive
in a rocky vault, and set out short rations,
just a gesture of piety
to keep the entire city free of defilement.[12]
There let her pray to the one god she worships:
Death[13]—who knows?—may just reprieve her from death.
Or she may learn at last, better late than never,
what a waste of breath it is to worship Death.

[*Exit to the palace.*]

CHORUS:

Love, never conquered in battle
880 Love the plunderer laying waste the rich!
Love standing the night-watch
guarding a girl's soft cheek,
you range the seas, the shepherds' steadings off in the wilds—
not even the deathless gods can flee your onset,
nothing human born for a day—
whoever feels your grip is driven mad.
Love!—
you wrench the minds of the righteous into outrage,
swerve them to their ruin—you have ignited this,
this kindred strife, father and son at war
890 and Love alone the victor—
warm glance of the bride triumphant, burning with desire!
Throned in power, side-by-side with the mighty laws!
Irresistible Aphrodite,[14] never conquered—
Love, you mock us for your sport.

[ANTIGONE *is brought from the palace under guard.*]

But now, even I'd rebel against the king,
I'd break all bounds when I see this—
I fill with tears, can't hold them back,
not any more . . . I see Antigone make her way
to the bridal vault where all are laid to rest.

ANTIGONE:

900 Look at me, men of my fatherland,
setting out on the last road

---

[12] **defilement:** In line 43, Antigone noted that the punishment for disobedience was death by stoning. Creon may hope here not only to save the citizens from participating in Antigone's death but to free his own hands from shedding the blood of kin as well.

[13] **god . . . Death:** The god Hades, king of the underworld.

[14] **Aphrodite:** The goddess of love.

looking into the last light of day
the last I'll ever see . . .
the god of death who puts us all to bed
takes me down to the banks of Acheron[15] alive—
     denied my part in the wedding-songs,
no wedding-song in the dusk has crowned my marriage—
I go to wed the lord of the dark waters.

CHORUS:
          Not crowned with glory, crowned with a dirge,
910   you leave for the deep pit of the dead.
          No withering illness laid you low,
          no strokes of the sword—a law to yourself,
          alone, no mortal like you, ever, you go down
          to the halls of Death alive and breathing.

ANTIGONE:
But think of Niobe[16]—well I know her story—
     think what a living death she died,
Tantalus' daughter, stranger queen from the east:
there on the mountain heights, growing stone
binding as ivy, slowly walled her round
920 and the rains will never cease, the legends say
the snows will never leave her . . .
     wasting away, under her brows the tears
showering down her breasting ridge and slopes—
a rocky death like hers puts me to sleep.

CHORUS:
          But she was a god, born of gods,
          and we are only mortals born to die.
          And yet, of course, it's a great thing
          for a dying girl to hear, just hear
          she shares a destiny equal to the gods,
          during life and later, once she's dead.

ANTIGONE:
                                        O you mock me!
930
Why, in the name of all my fathers' gods
why can't you wait till I am gone—
     must you abuse me to my face?
O my city, all your fine rich sons!

---

[15] **Acheron:** A river of sorrow in the underworld.

[16] **Niobe:** The daughter of the Titan Tantalus, Niobe was a Phrygian princess who married Amphion, an early king of Thebes. Niobe earned the wrath of the goddess Leto by boasting that Leto's two children—Apollo and Artemis—did not compare with Niobe's own fourteen children. To avenge the insult, Leto had Apollo and Artemis murder all of Niobe's children, and Niobe was turned into a weeping rock, shedding perpetual tears.

And you, you springs of the Dirce,
holy grove of Thebes where the chariots gather,
          you at least, you'll bear me witness, look,
unmourned by friends and forced by such crude laws
I go to my rockbound prison, strange new tomb—
940   always a stranger, O dear god,
I have no home on earth and none below,
          not with the living, not with the breathless dead.

CHORUS:
          You went too far, the last limits of daring—
          smashing against the high throne of Justice!
               Your life's in ruins, child—I wonder . . .
          do you pay for your father's terrible ordeal?

ANTIGONE:
There—at last you've touched it, the worst pain
the worst anguish! Raking up the grief for father
          three times over, for all the doom
950   that's struck us down, the brilliant house of Laius.
O mother, your marriage-bed
the coiling horrors, the coupling there—
          you with your own son, my father—doomstruck mother!
Such, such were my parents, and I their wretched child.
I go to them now, cursed, unwed, to share their home—
          I am a stranger! O dear brother, doomed
in your marriage[17]—your marriage murders mine,
          your dying drags me down to death alive!

[*Enter* CREON.]

CHORUS:
Reverence asks some reverence in return—
960   but attacks on power never go unchecked,
          not by the man who holds the reins of power.
Your own blind will, your passion has destroyed you.

ANTIGONE:
No one to weep for me, my friends,
no wedding-song—they take me away
in all my pain . . . the road lies open, waiting.
Never again, the law forbids me to see
the sacred eye of day. I am agony!
No tears for the destiny that's mine,
no loved one mourns my death.

---

[17] **your marriage:** Polynices married the daughter of Adrastus, the king of Argos, in order to ensure Argive military support in the war against Thebes.

CREON:

                                     Can't you see?
970   If a man could wail his own dirge *before* he dies,
        he'd never finish.

[*To the guards.*]
                            Take her away, quickly!
        Wall her up in the tomb, you have your orders.
        Abandon her there, alone, and let her choose—
        death or a buried life with a good roof for shelter.
        As for myself, my hands are clean. This young girl—
        dead or alive, she will be stripped of her rights,
        her stranger's rights, here in the world above.

ANTIGONE:
        O tomb, my bridal-bed—my house, my prison
        cut in the hollow rock, my everlasting watch!
980   I'll soon be there, soon embrace my own,
        the great growing family of our dead
        Persephone[18] has received among her ghosts.
                                                    I,
        the last of them all, the most reviled by far,
        go down before my destined time's run out.
        But still I go, cherishing one good hope:
        my arrival may be dear to father,
        dear to you, my mother,
        dear to you, my loving brother, Eteocles—
        When you died I washed you with my hands,
990   I dressed you all, I poured the cups
        across your tombs. But now, Polynices,
        because I laid your body out as well,
        this, this is my reward. Nevertheless
        I honored you—the decent will admit it—
        well and wisely too.
                            Never, I tell you,
        if I had been the mother of children
        or if my husband died, exposed and rotting—
        I'd never have taken this ordeal upon myself,
        never defied our people's will. What law,
1000   you ask, do I satisfy with what I say?
        A husband dead, there might have been another.
        A child by another too, if I had lost the first.
        But mother and father both lost in the halls of Death,

---

[18] **Persephone:** Queen of the underworld.

no brother could ever spring to light again.
For this law alone I held you first in honor.
For this, Creon, the king, judges me a criminal
guilty of dreadful outrage, my dear brother!
And now he leads me off, a captive in his hands,
with no part in the bridal-song, the bridal-bed,
1010   denied all joy of marriage, raising children —
deserted so by loved ones, struck by fate,
I descend alive to the caverns of the dead.

What law of the mighty gods have I transgressed?
Why look to the heavens any more, tormented as I am?
Whom to call, what comrades now? Just think,
my reverence only brands me for irreverence!
Very well: if this is the pleasure of the gods,
once I suffer I will know that I was wrong.
But if these men are wrong, let them suffer
1020   nothing worse than they mete out to me —
these masters of injustice!

LEADER:
Still the same rough winds, the wild passion
raging through the girl.

CREON:
[*To the guards.*]
                        Take her away.
You're wasting time — you'll pay for it too.

ANTIGONE:
Oh god, the voice of death. It's come, it's here.

CREON:
True. Not a word of hope — your doom is sealed.

ANTIGONE:
Land of Thebes, city of all my fathers —
O you gods, the first gods of the race![19]
They drag me away, now, no more delay.
1030   Look on me, you noble sons of Thebes —
the last of a great line of kings,
I alone, see what I suffer now
at the hands of what breed of men —
all for reverence, my reverence for the gods!

[*She leaves under guard: the* CHORUS *gathers.*]

---

[19] **Land . . . race:** The house of Thebes charted its lineage to the gods Aphrodite and Ares, whose daughter Harmonia married Cadmus, the legendary founder of Thebes.

CHORUS:

Danaë,[20] Danaë—
even she endured a fate like yours,
　　in all her lovely strength she traded
the light of day for the bolted brazen vault—
buried within her tomb, her bridal-chamber,
1040　wed to the yoke and broken.
　　　　But she was of glorious birth
　　　　my child, my child
and treasured the seed of Zeus within her womb,
the cloudburst streaming gold!
　　　　The power of fate is a wonder,
　　　　dark, terrible wonder—
　　　　neither wealth nor armies
　　　　towered walls nor ships
　　　　black hulls lashed by the salt
1050　　can save us from that force.

The yoke tamed him too
　　young Lycurgus[21] flaming in anger
king of Edonia, all for his mad taunts
Dionysus clamped him down, encased
in the chain-mail of rock
　　and there his rage
　　　　his terrible flowering rage burst—
sobbing, dying away . . . at last that madman
came to know his god—
1060　　　　the power he mocked, the power
　　　　he hunted in all his frenzy
　　　　trying to stamp out
　　　　the women strong with the god—
　　　　the torch, the raving sacred cries—
　　　　enraging the Muses who adore the flute.

And far north where the Black Rocks
　　cut the sea in half
and murderous straits
split the coast of Thrace
1070　　a forbidding city stands

---

[20] **Danaë:** The daughter of Acrisius, an Argive king; because it was foretold that he would die at the hand of Danaë's son, Acrisius ordered Danaë to be shut up in a tower. Here Zeus comes to her in the form of a shower of golden rain, after which she gives birth to Perseus, who eventually kills Acrisius.

[21] **Lycurgus:** King of Thrace (or Edonia), who was imprisoned by the god Dionysus for trying to thwart the spread of the Dionysian sect.

where once, hard by the walls
the savage Ares thrilled to watch
a king's new queen, a Fury rearing in rage
    against his two royal sons—
        her bloody hands, her dagger-shuttle
stabbing out their eyes—cursed, blinding wounds—
their eyes blind sockets screaming for revenge!²²

They wailed in agony, cries echoing cries
    the princes doomed at birth . . .
and their mother doomed to chains,
walled off in a tomb of stone—
    but she traced her own birth back
to a proud Athenian line and the high gods
and off in caverns half the world away,
born of the wild North Wind
    she sprang on her father's gales,
        racing stallions up the leaping cliffs—
child of the heavens. But even on her the Fates
the gray everlasting Fates rode hard
my child, my child.

[*Enter* TIRESIAS, *the blind prophet, led by a boy.*]
TIRESIAS:
              Lords of Thebes,
I and the boy have come together,
hand in hand. Two see with the eyes of one . . .
so the blind must go, with a guide to lead the way.
CREON:
What is it, old Tiresias? What news now?
TIRESIAS:
I will teach you. And you obey the seer.
CREON:
                   I will,
I've never wavered from your advice before.
TIRESIAS:
And so you kept the city straight on course.
CREON:
I owe you a great deal, I swear to that.
TIRESIAS:
Then reflect, my son: you are poised,
once more, on the razor-edge of fate.

1080

1090

1100

---

²² **And far north . . . revenge:** Lines 1066 to 1077 refer to the story of Phineas, a king of Thrace who supposedly divorced and imprisoned Cleopatra, daughter of Boreas (the north wind) and Athenian princess Orithyea. Phineas's new wife, Eidothea, blinded Cleopatra's two sons as Ares, the god of war, looked on.

CREON:
     What is it? I shudder to hear you.
TIRESIAS:
                              You will learn
     when you listen to the warnings of my craft.
     As I sat on the ancient seat of augury,
     in the sanctuary where every bird I know
     will hover at my hands—suddenly I heard it,
     a strange voice in the wingbeats, unintelligible,
     barbaric, a mad scream! Talons flashing, ripping,
     they were killing each other—that much I knew—
     the murderous fury whirring in those wings
     made that much clear!
1110   I was afraid,
     I turned quickly, tested the burnt-sacrifice,
     ignited the altar at all points—but no fire,
     the god in the fire never blazed.
     Not from those offerings . . . over the embers
     slid a heavy ooze from the long thighbones,
     smoking, sputtering out, and the bladder
     puffed and burst—spraying gall into the air—
     and the fat wrapping the bones slithered off
     and left them glistening white. No fire!
1120 The rites failed that might have blazed the future
     with a sign. So I learned from the boy here:
     he is my guide, as I am guide to others.
                              And it's you—
     your high resolve that sets this plague on Thebes.
     The public altars and sacred hearths are fouled,
     one and all, by the birds and dogs with carrion
     torn from the corpse, the doomstruck son of Oedipus!
     And so the gods are deaf to our prayers, they spurn
     the offerings in our hands, the flame of holy flesh.
     No birds cry out an omen clear and true—
1130 they're gorged with the murdered victim's blood and fat.
     Take these things to heart, my son, I warn you.
     All men make mistakes, it is only human.
     But once the wrong is done, a man
     can turn his back on folly, misfortune too,
     if he tries to make amends, however low he's fallen,
     and stops his bullnecked ways. Stubbornness
     brands you for stupidity—pride is a crime.
     No, yield to the dead!
     Never stab the fighter when he's down.
1140 Where's the glory, killing the dead twice over?

I mean you well. I give you sound advice.
It's best to learn from a good adviser
when he speaks for your own good:
it's pure gain.

CREON:
                    Old man—all of you! So,
you shoot your arrows at my head like archers at the target—
I even have *him* loosed on me, this fortune-teller.
Oh his ilk has tried to sell me short
and ship me off for years. Well,
drive your bargains, traffic—much as you like—
1150   in the gold of India, silver-gold of Sardis.[23]
You'll never bury that body in the grave,
not even if Zeus's eagles rip the corpse
and wing their rotten pickings off to the throne of god!
Never, not even in fear of such defilement
will I tolerate his burial, that traitor.
Well I know, we can't defile the gods—
no mortal has the power.
                    No,
reverend old Tiresias, all men fall,
it's only human, but the wisest fall obscenely
1160   when they glorify obscene advice with rhetoric—
all for their own gain.

TIRESIAS:
Oh god, is there a man alive
who knows, who actually believes . . .

CREON:
                                        What now?
What earth-shattering truth are you about to utter?

TIRESIAS:
. . . just how much a sense of judgment, wisdom
is the greatest gift we have?

CREON:
                            Just as much, I'd say,
as a twisted mind is the worst affliction going.

TIRESIAS:
You are the one who's sick, Creon, sick to death.

CREON:
I am in no mood to trade insults with a seer.

TIRESIAS:
You have already, calling my prophecies a lie.

---

[23] **Sardis:** A place in Asia Minor near the site where electrum, a mixture of silver and gold, was found.

CREON:

1170   Why not?
You and the whole breed of seers are mad for money!

TIRESIAS:
And the whole race of tyrants lusts to rake it in.

CREON:
This slander of yours—
are you aware you're speaking to the king?

TIRESIAS:
Well aware. Who helped you save the city?

CREON:
                                                                You—
you have your skills, old seer, but you lust for injustice!

TIRESIAS:
You will drive me to utter the dreadful secret in my heart.

CREON:
Spit it out! Just don't speak it out for profit.

TIRESIAS:
Profit? No, not a bit of profit, not for you.

CREON:
1180   Know full well, you'll never buy off my resolve.

TIRESIAS:
Then know this too, learn this by heart!
The chariot of the sun will not race through
so many circuits more, before you have surrendered
one born of your own loins, your own flesh and blood,
a corpse for corpses given in return, since you have thrust
to the world below a child sprung for the world above,
ruthlessly lodged a living soul within the grave—
then you've robbed the gods below the earth,
keeping a dead body here in the bright air,
1190   unburied, unsung, unhallowed by the rites.

You, you have no business with the dead,
nor do the gods above—this is violence
you have forced upon the heavens.
And so the avengers, the dark destroyers late
but true to the mark, now lie in wait for you,
the Furies[24] sent by the gods and the god of death
to strike you down with the pains that you perfected!

---

[24] **Furies:** Female spirits who avenge crimes against blood kin, such as patricide or matricide.

There. Reflect on that, tell me I've been bribed.
The day comes soon, no long test of time, not now,
1200   that wakes the wails for men and women in your halls.
Great hatred rises against you—
cities in tumult, all whose mutilated sons
the dogs have graced with burial, or the wild beasts
or a wheeling crow that wings the ungodly stench of carrion
back to each city, each warrior's hearth and home.

These arrows for your heart! Since you've raked me
I loose them like an archer in my anger,
arrows deadly true. You'll never escape
their burning, searing force.

[*Motioning to his escort.*]
1210   Come, boy, take me home.
So he can vent his rage on younger men,
and learn to keep a gentler tongue in his head
and better sense than what he carries now.

[*Exit to the side.*]

LEADER:
The old man's gone, my king—
terrible prophecies. Well I know,
since the hair on this old head went gray,
he's never lied to Thebes.

CREON:
I know it myself—I'm shaken, torn.
It's a dreadful thing to yield . . . but resist now?
1220   Lay my pride bare to the blows of ruin?
That's dreadful too.

LEADER:
But good advice,
Creon, take it now, you must.

CREON:
What should I do? Tell me . . . I'll obey.

LEADER:
Go! Free the girl from the rocky vault
and raise a mound for the body you exposed.

CREON:
That's your advice? You think I should give in?

LEADER:
Yes, my king, quickly. Disasters sent by the gods
cut short our follies in a flash.

CREON:
Oh it's hard,

giving up the heart's desire . . . but I will do it—
1230   no more fighting a losing battle with necessity.

LEADER:

Do it now, go, don't leave it to others.

CREON:

Now—I'm on my way! Come, each of you,
take up axes, make for the high ground,
over there, quickly! I and my better judgment
have come round to this—I shackled her,
I'll set her free myself. I am afraid . . .
it's best to keep the established laws
to the very day we die.

[*Rushing out, followed by his entourage. The* CHORUS *clusters around the altar.*]

CHORUS:

God of a hundred names!
                    Great Dionysus—
1240   Son and glory of Semele![25] Pride of Thebes—
Child of Zeus whose thunder rocks the clouds—
Lord of the famous lands of evening—
King of the Mysteries!
                    King of Eleusis,[26] Demeter's plain
her breasting hills that welcome in the world—
Great Dionysus!
                    Bacchus, living in Thebes
the mother-city of all your frenzied women[27]—
                                        Bacchus
        living along the Ismenus'[28] rippling waters
standing over the field sown with the Dragon's teeth!

You—we have seen you through the flaring smoky fires,
1250   your torches blazing over the twin peaks
where nymphs of the hallowed cave climb onward
                    fired with you, your sacred rage—
we have seen you at Castalia's running spring[29]

---

[25] **Semele:** The mother of Bacchus (Dionysus) who died when Zeus visited her in the form of a thunderbolt; her as-yet-unborn child lived.

[26] **Eleusis:** On the coast of Attica, Eleusis was the site of mystery rites for Persephone, goddess of the underworld, and her mother, Demeter, goddess of grain and harvest.

[27] **frenzied women:** The Bacchae, or female worshippers of Bacchus (Dionysus).

[28] **Ismenus:** A river at Thebes.

[29] **Castalia's running spring:** A spring and pool on Mt. Parnassus, the waters of which were said to bring poetic inspiration.

and down from the heights of Nysa[30] crowned with ivy
the greening shore rioting vines and grapes
   down you come in your storm of wild women
    ecstatic, mystic cries—
         Dionysus—
down to watch and ward the roads of Thebes!
First of all cities, Thebes you honor first

1260 you and your mother, bride of the lightning—
come, Dionysus! now your people lie
in the iron grip of plague,
come in your racing, healing stride
   down Parnassus'[31] slopes
or across the moaning straits.
      Lord of the dancing—
dance, dance the constellations breathing fire!
Great master of the voices of the night!
Child of Zeus, God's offspring, come, come forth!
Lord, king, dance with your nymphs, swirling, raving

1270 arm-in-arm in frenzy through the night
   they dance you, Iacchus°—   Dionysus
      Dance, Dionysus
giver of all good things!

[*Enter a* MESSENGER *from the side.*]

MESSENGER:
       Neighbors,
friends of the house of Cadmus and the kings,
there's not a thing in this mortal life of ours
I'd praise or blame as settled once for all.
Fortune lifts and Fortune fells the lucky
and unlucky every day. No prophet on earth
can tell a man his fate. Take Creon:
there was a man to rouse your envy once,

1280 as I see it. He saved the realm from enemies,
taking power, he alone, the lord of the fatherland,
he set us true on course—he flourished like a tree
with the noble line of sons he bred and reared . . .
and now it's lost, all gone.
      Believe me,
when a man has squandered his true joys,
he's good as dead, I tell you, a living corpse.

---

[30] **Nysa:** A mountain sacred to Dionysus.

[31] **Parnassus:** A mountain near Delphi whose two peaks were sacred to Apollo and Dionysus; the Corcyian Cave, located on the mountain, was sacred to Pan and the woodland nymphs.

Pile up riches in your house, as much as you like—
live like a king with a huge show of pomp,
but if real delight is missing from the lot,
1290   I wouldn't give you a wisp of smoke for it,
not compared with joy.

LEADER:

What now?
What new grief do you bring the house of kings?

MESSENGER:

Dead, dead—and the living are guilty of their death!

LEADER:

Who's the murderer? Who is dead? Tell us.

MESSENGER:

Haemon's gone, his blood spilled by the very hand—

LEADER:

His father's or his own?

MESSENGER:

His own . . .
raging mad with his father for the death—

LEADER:

Oh great seer,
you saw it all, you brought your word to birth!

MESSENGER:

Those are the facts. Deal with them as you will.

[*As he turns to go,* EURYDICE *enters from the palace.*]

LEADER:

1300   Look, Eurydice. Poor woman, Creon's wife,
so close at hand. By chance perhaps,
unless she's heard the news about her son.

EURYDICE:

My countrymen,
all of you—I caught the sound of your words
as I was leaving to do my part,
to appeal to queen Athena[32] with my prayers.
I was just loosing the bolts, opening the doors,
when a voice filled with sorrow, family sorrow,
struck my ears, and I fell back, terrified,
into the women's arms—everything went black.
1310   Tell me the news, again, whatever it is . . .
sorrow and I are hardly strangers.
I can bear the worst.

---

[32] **Athena (Athene):** Goddess of war, wisdom, and arts and crafts.

MESSENGER:

I—dear lady,

I'll speak as an eye-witness. I was there.
And I won't pass over one word of the truth.
Why should I try to soothe you with a story,
only to prove a liar in a moment?
Truth is always best.

So,

I escorted your lord, I guided him
to the edge of the plain where the body lay,

1320 Polynices, torn by the dogs and still unmourned.
And saying a prayer to Hecate of the Crossroads,
Pluto[33] too, to hold their anger and be kind,
we washed the dead in a bath of holy water
and plucking some fresh branches, gathering . . .
what was left of him, we burned them all together
and raised a high mound of native earth, and then
we turned and made for that rocky vault of hers,
the hollow, empty bed of the bride of Death.

And far off, one of us heard a voice,

1330 a long wail rising, echoing
out of that unhallowed wedding-chamber,
he ran to alert the master and Creon pressed on,
closer—the strange, inscrutable cry came sharper,
throbbing around him now, and he let loose
a cry of his own, enough to wrench the heart,
"Oh god, am I the prophet now? going down
the darkest road I've ever gone? My son—
it's *his* dear voice, he greets me! Go, men,
closer, quickly! Go through the gap,

1340 the rocks are dragged back—
right to the tomb's very mouth—and look,
see if it's Haemon's voice I think I hear,
or the gods have robbed me of my senses."

The king was shattered. We took his orders,
went and searched, and there in the deepest,
dark recesses of the tomb we found her . . .
hanged by the neck in a fine linen noose,
strangled in her veils—and the boy,

---

[33] **Hecate . . . Pluto:** Hecate, the queen of the underworld, is associated with night and burial; in her guise as Trivia, she is associated with crossroads. Pluto is another name for Hades, god of the underworld.

his arms flung around her waist,
1350   clinging to her, wailing for his bride,
dead and down below, for his father's crimes
and the bed of his marriage blighted by misfortune.
When Creon saw him, he gave a deep sob,
he ran in, shouting, crying out to him,
"Oh my child—what have you done? what seized you,
what insanity? what disaster drove you mad?
Come out, my son! I beg you on my knees!"
But the boy gave him a wild burning glance,
spat in his face, not a word in reply,
1360   he drew his sword—his father rushed out,
running as Haemon lunged and missed!—
and then, doomed, desperate with himself,
suddenly leaning his full weight on the blade,
he buried it in his body, halfway to the hilt.
And still in his senses, pouring his arms around her,
he embraced the girl and breathing hard,
released a quick rush of blood,
bright red on her cheek glistening white.
And there he lies, body enfolding body . . .
1370   he has won his bride at last, poor boy,
not here but in the houses of the dead.

Creon shows the world that of all the ills
afflicting men the worst is lack of judgment.

[EURYDICE *turns and reenters the palace.*]
LEADER:
What do you make of that? The lady's gone,
without a word, good or bad.
MESSENGER:
                              I'm alarmed too
but here's my hope—faced with her son's death
she finds it unbecoming to mourn in public.
Inside, under her roof, she'll set her women
to the task and wail the sorrow of the house.
1380   She's too discreet. She won't do something rash.
LEADER:
I'm not so sure. To me, at least,
a long heavy silence promises danger,
just as much as a lot of empty outcries.
MESSENGER:
We'll see if she's holding something back,
hiding some passion in her heart.

I'm going in. You may be right—who knows?
Even too much silence has its dangers.

[*Exit to the palace. Enter* CREON *from the side, escorted by attendants carrying* HAEMON's *body on a bier.*]

LEADER:

The king himself! Coming toward us,
look, holding the boy's head in his hands.
1390   Clear, damning proof, if it's right to say so—
proof of his own madness, no one else's,
        no, his own blind wrongs.

CREON:

                            Ohhh,
so senseless, so insane . . . my crimes,
my stubborn, deadly—
Look at us, the killer, the killed,
father and son, the same blood—the misery!
My plans, my mad fanatic heart,
my son, cut off so young!
Ai, dead, lost to the world,
not through your stupidity, no, my own.

LEADER:

1400   Too late,
too late, you see what justice means.

CREON:

                        Oh I've learned
through blood and tears! Then, it was then,
when the god came down and struck me—a great weight
shattering, driving me down that wild savage path,
ruining, trampling down my joy. Oh the agony,
        the heartbreaking agonies of our lives.

[*Enter the* MESSENGER *from the palace.*]

MESSENGER:

                        Master,
what a hoard of grief you have, and you'll have more.
The grief that lies to hand you've brought yourself—

[*Pointing to* HAEMON's *body.*]

the rest, in the house, you'll see it all too soon.

CREON:

What now? What's worse than this?

MESSENGER:

                        The queen is dead.
1410   The mother of this dead boy . . . mother to the end—
poor thing, her wounds are fresh.

CREON:

No, no,
harbor of Death, so choked, so hard to cleanse!—
why me? why are you killing me?
Herald of pain, more words, more grief?
I died once, you kill me again and again!
What's the report, boy . . . some news for me?
My wife dead? O dear god!
Slaughter heaped on slaughter?

[*The doors open; the body of* EURYDICE *is brought out on her bier.*]
MESSENGER:

See for yourself:
now they bring her body from the palace.

CREON:

1420

Oh, no,
another, a second loss to break the heart.
What next, what fate still waits for me?
I just held my son in my arms and now,
look, a new corpse rising before my eyes—
wretched, helpless mother—O my son!

MESSENGER:

She stabbed herself at the altar,
then her eyes went dark, after she'd raised
a cry for the noble fate of Megareus,[34] the hero
killed in the first assault, then for Haemon,
1430   then with her dying breath she called down
torments on your head—you killed her sons.

CREON:

Oh the dread,
I shudder with dread! Why not kill me too?—
run me through with a good sharp sword?
Oh god, the misery, anguish—
I, I'm churning with it, going under.

MESSENGER:

Yes, and the dead, the woman lying there,
piles the guilt of all their deaths on you.

CREON:

How did she end her life, what bloody stroke?

MESSENGER:

She drove home to the heart with her own hand,
1440   once she learned her son was dead . . . that agony.

---

[34] **Megareus:** Haemon's brother; Megareus committed suicide in order to fulfill a prophecy and save Thebes from destruction.

CREON:

> And the guilt is all mine—
> can never be fixed on another man,
> no escape for me. I killed you,
> I, god help me, I admit it all!

[*To his attendants.*]

> Take me away, quickly, out of sight.
> I don't even exist—I'm no one. Nothing.

LEADER:

> Good advice, if there's any good in suffering.
> Quickest is best when troubles block the way.

CREON:

[*Kneeling in prayer.*]

> Come, let it come!—that best of fates for me

1450

> that brings the final day, best fate of all.
> Oh quickly, now—
> so I never have to see another sunrise.

LEADER:

> That will come when it comes;
> we must deal with all that lies before us.
> The future rests with the ones who tend the future.

CREON:

> That prayer—I poured my heart into that prayer!

LEADER:

> No more prayers now. For mortal men
> there is no escape from the doom we must endure.

CREON:

> Take me away, I beg you, out of sight.

1460

> A rash, indiscriminate fool!
> I murdered you, my son, against my will—
> you too, my wife . . .
>   Wailing wreck of a man,
> whom to look to? where to lean for support?

[*Desperately turning from* HAEMON *to* EURYDICE *on their biers.*]

> Whatever I touch goes wrong—once more
> a crushing fate's come down upon my head!

[*The* MESSENGER *and attendants lead* CREON *into the palace.*]

CHORUS:

> Wisdom is by far the greatest part of joy,
> and reverence toward the gods must be safeguarded.
> The mighty words of the proud are paid in full
> with mighty blows of fate, and at long last

1470

> those blows will teach us wisdom.

[*The old citizens exit to the side.*]

Rulers and Citizens

War and peace were two of the most important themes of ancient literature. The dramatic conflict between opposing armies and ideals held a special interest for early poets and writers. The model for all Western epic poets is the Greek Homer, whose extended poems about the Trojan War and its aftermath exposed the ironies and tragedies of warfare; while war elevated certain heroes to greatness, it also revealed pettiness and betrayal. In war there was no clear-cut right side and wrong side; even the gods in Homer were divided in their sympathies between Greek and Trojan. After Homer, Greek writers were faced with the enormous transition of warfare to peace. With the return of heroes from Troy to their respective city-states, the challenge was to transform the warrior-king, like Agamemnon, into a leader who acquires self-knowledge and rules the populace with justice and fairness. The complexities of this transformation from warrior to ruler and citizen were explored by the great playwrights of fifth-century Greece in such plays as **Aeschylus'** *Agamemnon,* **Sophocles'** *The Oedipus Cycle,* Euripides' *Bacchae,* and Aristophanes' *Lysistrata.*

p. 575,
p. 635

The transition to responsible citizen was only partially successful during the Golden Age of Athens under Pericles. By the fifth century B.C.E. in Athens, the city-state (or *polis*) became the arena for a secular or civil religion, in which the responsibilities of citizenship had a "sacred" importance superior to the priesthood with its ceremonial duties. As **Pericles' Funeral Oration,** as recorded by Thucydides indicates, the real heroes were now the citizens who sacrificed their lives for Athens during the first year of the

p. 701

**Bust of Pericles,
495–429** B.C.E.
*The citizen-hero of
Athenian democracy.
(The Art Archive,
JFB)*

Peloponnesian War, and were thus honored for defending
democratic ideals, tolerance, and individualism—representing
thereby the "School of Hellas."

When Athens fell to Sparta at the end of the Peloponnesian War
in 404 B.C.E., the citizen-hero was replaced by the figure whose
heroism was marked by the inner, spiritual qualities of self-discipline
and a simple lifestyle rather than overt or public action. Out of this
major cultural transformation came the famous schools of Greek
philosophy: the Platonists, Cynics, and Stoics. The ultimate citizen of
Athens, ironically, was itinerant philosopher Socrates, the supreme
example of the philosopher-hero who was sentenced to death for
his honesty and outspokenness. His trial and death further tarnished
Athens' already declining reputation for democracy and tolerance. In
Apology, the most famous record of the seventy-year old Socrates's
defiant defense against the charges of impiety and corruption of
Athens' youth, Plato depicts Socrates as a hero with exceptional
mental and spiritual qualities, like leadership and extreme goodness.

p. 720

Head of a Jain
Tirthankara, third to
fourth century B.C.E.
*Jains believe in the
cyclical nature of the
universe, which has
no beginning, end, or
creator. A tirthankara
is a Jain saint.
(Ashmolean
Museum, Oxford,
UK / Bridgeman Art
Library)*

p. 708

p. 709

Diogenes Laertius, a third-century C.E. Greek biographer who, in his
Lives of Eminent Philosophers, depicts Socrates as the ideal Greek
philosopher as this idea must have been understood at the time.
Diogenes' details about Socrates' physique and home life tend to
humanize the great teacher.

During the first millennium B.C.E. in China and India there were
extended discussions about the nature of rulership that went far
beyond the use of force and "might makes right." The goal of several
thinkers in India and China was to eliminate war and create a state
of perpetual peace in which citizens would live in harmony. The Jain
religion of India, which shares certain attitudes with Buddhism,
was founded by Mahavira, a contemporary of the Buddha. Jainism
developed the most radical doctrine of *ahimsa* (literally,
"nonharming"), which was extended to every living thing. As
vegetarians, Jains must not kill or hurt any being. The selection

from **Uttaradhyayana Sutra** is a parable that provides a comparison between the traditional roles of a warrior-king and a monk. p. 697

The history of China from the sixth to the third century B.C.E. was filled with feuding kingdoms and the rise and fall of petty chieftains. But this period also gave rise to the Golden Age of Philosophy. A very small book, the **Dao De Jing (Tao Te Ching)** attributed to Laozi (Lao Tzu) gave rise to Daoism (Taoism). p. 699 Although Daoism provides an optimistic philosophy suited to individual practice, a number of the poems in the *Dao De Jing* deal with the principles of rulership. Poem number 30 conforms to the Daoist precepts that war is futile and wasteful, and that everyone, including the king, should adapt to the essential spiritual harmony of nature, and follow the Dao, a philosophy which usually leads to the withdrawal from political life rather than its reformation. Confucianism, on the other hand, provides a great deal of practical advice for the ruler, as well as for other members of the social hierarchy. Mencius (fourth century B.C.E.) was a disciple of Confucius who attempted to spread Confucianism as he traveled through petty Chinese states advising rulers about proper conduct. Mencius's principles located the seat of rulership in the essential goodness of human nature. In the selection from **Mengzi (Mencius)**, a ruler is directed to an awareness of compassion p. 706 as a directive for rule.

Like China during the period preceding national unity and empire, Rome went through a long period of civil wars. Rome settled down, however, under the expansion and consolidation of power under Augustus—a title which in 27 B.C.E. the Senate conferred on Octavian, whose rule as the first Roman Emperor continued until 14 C.E. The period of relative peace and prosperity extended until 235 C.E., and has thus been called the *Pax Romana, Pax Augusta,* or Augustan Age (27 B.C.E.–235 C.E.). It was the task of Roman historians like Polybius, Livy and **Suetonius** not only to describe p. 712 actual events associated with the building of empire but also to articulate the intangibles of the formation and maintenance of empire, that meeting ground of powerful individuals, governments and destiny. These historical accounts promoted a vision of sociopolitical stability, the restoration of morality, and celebration of service. Although Suetonius had a tendency to mix gossip with facts, his portrait in **The Lives of the Twelve Caesars** of Julius Caesar p. 713

as a divine being reveals some of the extraordinary qualities of this dictator, who ruled Rome from 49 to 44 B.C.E. As Suetonius makes clear, Julius Caesar had a genius for leadership that far exceeded his military prowess.

■ PRONUNCIATION

Dao De Jing: dow-duh-JING, tow-tay-CHING
Diogenes: digh-AH-juh-neez
Jainism: JIGHN-iz-um
Laozi (Lao Tzu): low-DZUH
Mencius: MEN-shee-us
Pericles: PEH-ruh-kleez
Suetonius: soo-ih-TOH-nee-us
Thucydides: thoo-SIH-duh-deez

～ JAINISM
INDIA, SIXTH CENTURY B.C.E.–FIRST CENTURY C.E.

The religion of Jainism was founded by Mahavira, a saint who established a religious community based on the extreme asceticism of Jain doctrines in the sixth century B.C.E. Although similar to Hinduism in many of its teachings, Jainism arose—like Buddhism—as a protest against the over-ritualized practices of Hinduism at the time. At present there are approximately two million Jains in the world.

The ultimate goal of Jainism is to escape the endless cycle of reincarnation imposed on every living thing, including humans. The core doctrine is *ahimsa*, Sanskrit for "nonharming"—practicing no harm in thought, word, or deed toward any living being. At one time extreme measures were taken, such as wearing cloth over the mouth so as not to kill any flying insects when inhaling. In one Jain legend, two merchants were fined their entire fortunes for killing fleas. Since it is impossible not to do some harm to living things during normal human activity, it was the practice of Jain saints to fast until they died in order to minimize their time of inflicting injury. This excerpt from the Jain text Uttaradhyayana Sutra is about the semilegendary king of Mithila, Nami, in northeastern India who severs his ties to the world to become a monk. Ordinarily, in the Jain and Buddhist traditions, such a choice brings relief to the participant; nevertheless the ascetic role of the monk is seen as a continuous struggle, equal in courage and commitment to the role of king.

**Carving from
the Vimala Sha
Temple, 1032**
*The Jain temple at
Vimala Sha is
dedicated to
Rishabhanatha, a
Jain tirthankara,
or saint. (Mount Abu,
Rajasthan, India /
Dinodia Picture
Agency, Bombay,
India / Bridgeman
Art Library)*

FROM

✎ Uttaradhyayana Sutra

Translated by A. L. Basham

TWO WAYS OF LIFE: KING AND MONK

With the fair ladies of his harem King Nami enjoyed pleasures like those of heaven,
And then he saw the light and gave up pleasure. . . .
In Mithilā, when the royal sage Nami left the world
And took to the life of a monk, there was a great uproar.
To the royal sage came the god Indra,[1] disguised as a brāhman,

---

[1] **Indra:** As king of the gods, the most important sky-deity in early Hinduism.

And spoke these words:
"There is fire and storm, your palace is burning!
Good sir, why don't you take care of your harem?"
Nami replied:
10 "Happy we dwell, happy we live, who call nothing whatever our own.
Though Mithilā burn, nothing of mine is burned!
When a monk has left his children and wives, and has given up worldly actions,
Nothing is pleasant to him, nothing unpleasant.
There is much that is good for the sage, the houseless monk
Set free from all ties, who knows himself to be alone."
Indra said:
"Build a wall, with gates and turrets,
And a moat and siege-engines;[2] then you will be a true warrior."
Nami replied:
20 "With faith as his city, hardship and self-control the bolt of the gate,
Patience its strong wall, impregnable in three ways.[3]
With effort as his bow, circumspection in walking its string,
And endurance as its tip, with truth he should bend his bow,
And pierce with the arrow of penance the mail of his enemy, karma.[4]
Thus the sage will conquer in battle, and be free [from samsāra]!"[5]
Indra said:
"By punishing thieves and burglars, pickpockets and robbers,
Keep the city in safety; then you will be a true warrior."
Nami replied:
30 "Often men punish unjustly,
And the guiltless are put in prison, the guilty set free."
Indra said:
"Bring under your yoke, O lord of men, those kings
Who do not bow before you; then you will be a true warrior."
Nami replied:
"Though a man conquer a thousand thousand brave foes in battle,
If he conquers only himself, this is his greatest conquest.
Battle with yourself! Of what use is fighting others?
He who conquers himself by himself will win happiness." . . .

---

[2] **siege-engines:** Such as large catapults for storming fortress walls.

[3] **impregnable . . . three ways:** The three defenses are self-control in thought, word, and deed.

[4] **karma:** The moral cycle of cause and effect in one's life: All actions have consequences, if not in this life, then in the next.

[5] **samsāra:** The cycle of one life after another that results from an attachment to the world of one's senses.

40   Throwing off his disguise, and taking his real shape,
     Indra bowed before him and praised him with sweet words:
          "Well done! You have conquered anger!
          Well done! You have vanquished pride!
          Well done! You have banished delusion!
          Well done! You have put down craving!
          Hurrah for your firmness!
          Hurrah for your gentleness!
          Hurrah for your perfect forbearance!
          Hurrah for your perfect freedom! . . ."
50   Thus act the enlightened, the learned, the discerning.
     They turn their backs on pleasure, like Nami the royal sage.

✺ LAOZI (LAO TZU)
CHINA, C. SIXTH–THIRD CENTURY B.C.E.

As the traditional founder of the ancient spiritual path called Daoism, Laozi (Lao Tzu) proposed a radically different use of force and goals of governing than militarism. Laozi is credited with the series of eighty-one poems known as the Dao De Jing (Tao Te Ching), which promote following the overall direction of life, or following the dao. Rather than seeking control over others through the use of force, Daoism pursues harmonies that might coalesce around a ruler and promote the good life for his or her subjects. Laozi understood that "the use of arms for conquest" inevitably led to a constant need to control one's subjects, since force tends to call forth force in return; subjugation creates rebellion. The last line of Poem 30 stresses the danger of going against the flow of life, the dao.

For more from the Dao De Jing, see page 777.

FROM

✺ Dao De Jing (Tao Te Ching)

Translated by Witter Bynner

30: ONE WHO WOULD GUIDE A LEADER OF MEN

One who would guide a leader of men in the uses of life
Will warn him against the use of arms for conquest.
Weapons often turn upon the wielder,
An army's harvest is a waste of thorns,

Conscription of a multitude of men
Drains the next year dry.
A good general, daring to march, dares also to halt,
Will never press his triumph beyond need.
What he must do he does but not for glory,
10   What he must do he does but not for show,
What he must do he does but not for self;
He has done it because it had to be done,
Not from a hot head.
Let life ripen and then fall,
Force is not the way at all:
Deny the way° of life and you are dead.   dao

⤫ THUCYDIDES
GREECE, C. 460–C. 399 B.C.E.

Along with Herodotus (c. 480–c. 425 B.C.E.), Thucydides is the great historian of classical Greece, one of the two "Fathers of History." His *History
of the Peloponnesian War* describes Athens at the high point of its democratic golden age and traces its decline as the sustained conflict with
Sparta and its allies weakened Athenian alliances and undermined its
democratic ideals. It is a strictly chronological account of the wars between the Athenian empire and Sparta and its allies between 431 and
404 B.C.E. Thucydides did not finish his history, however, for it breaks off
abruptly in 411, more than six years before the end of the war.

Legend has it that this sudden conclusion resulted from Thucydides'
death by assassination, but in truth little is known of Thucydides' life
beyond what he alludes to in his history. He did command the Athenian naval forces at the Battle of Amphipolis in 424, and as a result of
the defeat he suffered there was banished from Athens for twenty years.
During this period in exile, presumably, he had time to write his history
of the war. Writing about the events of his own time, he seems to have
kept careful notes of things as they happened, and, even though he lacked
the news accounts and tape recorders of the contemporary historian, he
re-created speeches and debates from memory and from oral sources,
which he included verbatim in his record. As an exile, he was also in the
unusual position of having access to sources from both sides of the conflict, so he was able to achieve an extraordinary degree of objectivity.
Because he was writing before the end of the war, without the prejudice
of hindsight, Thucydides produced a dramatic and objective narrative of

the events and controversies of the period, with insightful portraits of the statesmen and generals as well as analyses of the psychological, economic, and moral forces at work.

The passage that follows, Pericles's famous Funeral Oration commemorating the Athenian dead after the first year of the war (430 B.C.E.), illustrates Thucydides's dramatic method. Even though he had to reconstruct it, he presents the speech in Pericles's own words. The speech itself is much more than a funeral oration. Pericles uses the occasion to celebrate Athens and its democratic ideals, for which he is remembered as the great champion during the Age of Pericles (461–429 B.C.E.). His defense of majority rule, political equality, the recognition of merit, tolerance, and individualism have made this speech a classic statement of democratic values.

FROM

❧ The Peloponnesian War

Translated by Benjamin Jowett

[PERICLES' FUNERAL ORATION]

In the same winter the Athenians gave a funeral at the public cost to those who had first fallen in this war. It was a custom of their ancestors, and the manner of it is as follows. Three days before the ceremony, the bones of the dead are laid out in a tent which has been erected; and their friends bring to their relatives such offerings as they please. In the funeral procession cypress coffins are borne on wagons, one for each tribe, the bones of the deceased being placed in the coffin of their tribe. Among these is carried one empty bier decked for the missing, that is, for those whose bodies could not be recovered. Any citizen or stranger who pleases joins in the procession: and the female relatives are there to wail at the burial. The dead are laid in the public sepulchre in the most beautiful suburb of the city, in which those who fall in war are always buried—with the exception of those slain at Marathon, who for their singular and extraordinary valour were interred on the spot where they fell. After the bodies have been laid in the earth, a man chosen by the state, of approved wisdom and eminent reputation, pronounces over them an appropriate panegyric, after which all retire. Such is the manner of the burying; and throughout the whole of the war, whenever the occasion arose, the established custom was observed. Meanwhile these were the first that had fallen, and Pericles, son of Xanthippus, was chosen to pronounce their eulogium. When the proper time arrived, he advanced from the sepulchre to an elevated platform in order to be heard by as many of the crowd as possible, and spoke as follows:

"Most of my predecessors in this place have commended him who made this speech part of the law, telling us that it is well that it should be delivered at the burial of those who fall in battle. For myself, I should have thought that the worth which had displayed itself in deeds would be sufficiently rewarded by honours also shown by deeds, such as you now see in this funeral prepared at the people's cost. And I could have wished that the reputations of many brave men were not to be imperilled in the mouth of a single individual, to stand or fall according as he spoke well or ill. For it is hard to speak properly upon a subject where it is even difficult to convince your hearers that you are speaking the truth. On the one hand, the friend who is familiar with every fact of the story may think that some point has not been set forth with that fullness which he wishes and knows it to deserve; on the other, he who is a stranger to the matter may be led by envy to suspect exaggeration if he hears anything above his own nature. For men can endure to hear others praised only so long as they can severally persuade themselves of their own ability to equal the actions recounted: when this point is passed, envy comes in and with it incredulity. However, since our ancestors have stamped this custom with their approval, it becomes my duty to obey the law and to try to satisfy your several wishes and opinions as best I may.

"I shall begin with our ancestors: it is both just and proper that they should have the honour of the first mention on an occasion like the present. They dwelt in the country without break in the succession from generation to generation, and handed it down free to the present time by their valour. And if our more remote ancestors deserve praise, much more do our own fathers, who added to their inheritance the empire which we now possess, and spared no pains to be able to leave their acquisitions to us of the present generation. Lastly, there are few parts of our dominions that have not been augmented by those of us here, who are still more or less in the vigour of life; and the mother country has been furnished by us with everything that can enable her to depend on her own resources whether for war or for peace. That part of our history which tells of the military achievements which gave us our several possessions, or of the ready valour with which either we or our fathers stemmed the tide of Hellenic or foreign aggression, is a theme too familiar to my hearers for me to dilate on, and I shall therefore pass it by. But by what road we reached our position, under what form of government our greatness grew, out of what national habits it sprang—these are subjects which I may pursue before I proceed to my panegyric upon these men; for I think them to be themes upon which on the present occasion a speaker may properly dwell, and to which the whole assemblage, whether citizens or foreigners, may listen with advantage.

"Our constitution does not copy the laws of neighbouring states; we are rather a pattern to others than imitators ourselves. Its administration favours the many instead of the few; this is why it is called a democracy. If we look to the laws, they afford equal justice to all in their private differences; if to social standing, advancement in public life falls to reputation for capacity, class considerations not being allowed to interfere with merit; nor again does poverty bar the way: if a man is able to serve the state, he is not hindered by the obscurity of his condition. The freedom which we enjoy in our government extends also to our ordinary life. There, far from exercising a jealous surveillance over each other, we do not feel called upon to be angry with our neighbour for doing what he likes, or even to indulge in those injurious looks which cannot fail to be offensive, although they inflict no positive penalty.

But all this ease in our private relations does not make us lawless as citizens. Against this fear is our chief safeguard, teaching us to obey the magistrates and the laws, particularly such as regard the protection of the injured, whether they are actually on the statute book, or belong to that code which, although unwritten, yet cannot be broken without acknowledged disgrace.

"Further, we provide plenty of means for the mind to refresh itself from business. We celebrate games and sacrifices all the year round, and the elegance of our private establishments forms a daily source of pleasure and helps to banish our cares; and the magnitude of our city draws the produce of the world into our harbour, so that to the Athenian the fruits of other countries are as familiar a luxury as those of his own.

"If we turn to our military policy, there also we differ from our antagonists. We throw open our city to the world, and never by alien acts exclude foreigners from any opportunity of learning or observing, although the eyes of an enemy may occasionally profit by our liberality; we trust less in system and policy than in the native spirit of our citizens; and in education, where our rivals from their very cradles by a painful discipline seek after manliness, at Athens we live exactly as we please, and yet are just as ready to encounter every legitimate danger. In proof of this it may be noticed that the Lacedæmonians[1] do not invade our country alone, but bring with them all their confederates, while we Athenians advance unsupported into the territory of a neighbour, and fighting upon a foreign soil usually vanquish with ease men who are defending their homes. Our united force was never yet encountered by any enemy, because we have at once to attend to our marine and to despatch our citizens by land upon a hundred different services; thus wherever they engage with some such fraction of our strength, a success against a detachment is magnified into a victory over the nation, and a defeat into a reverse suffered at the hands of our entire people. And yet if with habits not of labour but of ease, and courage not of art but of nature, we are still willing to encounter danger, we have the double advantage of escaping the experience of hardships in anticipation and of facing them in the hour of need as fearlessly as those who are never free from them.

"Nor are these the only points in which our city is worthy of admiration. We cultivate refinement without extravagance and knowledge without effeminacy; wealth we employ more for use than for show, and place the real disgrace of poverty not in owning to the fact but in declining the struggle against it. Our public men have, besides politics, their private affairs to attend to, and our ordinary citizens, though occupied with the pursuits of industry, are still fair judges of public matters; for, unlike any other nation, regarding him who takes no part in these duties not as unambitious but as useless, we Athenians are able to judge at all events if we cannot originate, and instead of looking on discussion as a stumbling-block in the way of action, we think it an indispensable preliminary to any wise action at all. Again, in our enterprises we present the singular spectacle of daring and deliberation, each carried to its highest point, and both united in the same persons, although usually

---

[1] **Lacedæmonians:** The Spartans.

decision is the fruit of ignorance, hesitation of reflection. But the palm of courage will surely be adjudged most justly to those who best know the difference between hardship and pleasure and yet are never tempted to shrink from danger. In generosity we are equally singular, acquiring our friends by conferring, not by receiving, favours. Yet, of course, the doer of the favour is the firmer friend of the two, in order by continued kindness to keep the recipient in his debt, while the debtor feels less keenly from the very consciousness that the return he makes will be a payment, not a free gift. And it is only the Athenians who, fearless of consequences, confer their benefits not from calculations of expediency, but in the confidence of liberality.

"In short, I say that as a city we are the school of Hellas;[2] and I doubt if the world can produce a man, who where he has only himself to depend upon, is equal to so many emergencies, and graced by so happy a versatility as the Athenian. And that this is no mere boast thrown out for the occasion, but plain matter of fact, the power of the state acquired by these habits proves. For Athens alone of her contemporaries is found when tested to be greater than her reputation, and alone gives no occasion to her assailants to blush at the antagonist by whom they have been worsted, or to her subjects to question her title by merit to rule. Rather, the admiration of the present and succeeding ages will be ours, since we have not left our power without witness, but have shown it by mighty proofs; and far from needing a Homer for our panegyrist, or other of his craft whose verses might charm for the moment only for the impression which they gave to melt at the touch of fact, we have forced every sea and land to be the highway of our daring, and everywhere, whether for evil or for good, have left imperishable monuments behind us. Such is the Athens for which these men, in the assertion of their resolve not to lose her, nobly fought and died; and well may every one of their survivors be ready to suffer in her cause.

"Indeed if I have dwelt at some length upon the character of our country, it has been to show that our stake in the struggle is not the same as theirs who have no such blessings to lose, and also that the panegyric of the men over whom I am now speaking might be by definite proofs established. That panegyric is now in a great measure complete; for the Athens that I have celebrated is only what the heroism of these and their like have made her, men whose fame, unlike that of most Hellenes, will be found to be only commensurate with their deserts. And if a test of worth be wanted, it is to be found in their closing scene, and this not only in the cases in which it set the final seal upon their merit, but also in those in which it gave the first intimation of their having any. For there is justice in the claim that steadfastness in his country's battles should be as a cloak to cover a man's other imperfections; for the good action has blotted out the bad, and his merit as a citizen more than outweighed his demerits as an individual. But none of these allowed either wealth with its prospect of future enjoyment to unnerve his spirit, or poverty with its hope of a day of freedom and riches to tempt him to shrink from danger. No, holding that vengeance upon their enemies was more to be desired than any personal blessings,

---

[2] **as a city . . . school of Hellas:** A much-quoted phrase indicating that Athens is the model for the rest of Greece and the world.

and reckoning this to be the most glorious of hazards, they joyfully determined to accept the risk, to make sure of their vengeance and to let their wishes wait; and while committing to hope the uncertainty of final success, in the business before them they thought fit to act boldly and trust in themselves. Thus choosing to die resisting, rather than to live submitting, they fled only from dishonour, but met danger face to face, and after one brief moment, while at the summit of their fortune, escaped, not from their fear, but from their glory.

"So died these men as became Athenians. You, their survivors, must determine to have as unaltering a resolution in the field, though you may pray that it may have a happier issue. And not contented with ideas derived only from words of the advantages which are bound up with the defence of your country, though these would furnish a valuable text to a speaker even before an audience so alive to them as the present, you must yourselves realize the power of Athens, and feed your eyes upon her from day to day, till love of her fills your hearts; and then when all her greatness shall break upon you, you must reflect that it was by courage, sense of duty, and a keen feeling of honour in action that men were enabled to win all this, and that no personal failure in an enterprise could make them consent to deprive their country of their valour, but they laid it at her feet as the most glorious contribution that they could offer. For this offering of their lives made in common by them all they each of them individually received that renown which never grows old, and for a sepulchre, not so much that in which their bones have been deposited, but that noblest of shrines wherein their glory is laid up to be eternally remembered upon every occasion on which deed or story shall call for its commemoration. For heroes have the whole earth for their tomb; and in lands far from their own, where the column with its epitaph declares it, there is enshrined in every breast a record unwritten with no tablet to preserve it, except that of the heart. These take as your model, and judging happiness to be the fruit of freedom and freedom of valour, never decline the dangers of war. For it is not the miserable that would most justly be unsparing of their lives; these have nothing to hope for: it is rather they to whom continued life may bring reverses as yet unknown, and to whom a fall, if it came, would be most tremendous in its consequences. And surely, to a man of spirit, the degradation of cowardice must be immeasurably more grievous than the unfelt death which strikes him in the midst of his strength and patriotism!

"Comfort, therefore, not condolence, is what I have to offer to the parents of the dead who may be here. Numberless are the chances to which, as they know, the life of man is subject; but fortunate indeed are they who draw for their lot a death so glorious as that which has caused your mourning, and to whom life has been so exactly measured as to terminate in the happiness in which it has been passed. Still I know that this is a hard saying, especially when those are in question of whom you will constantly be reminded by seeing in the homes of others blessings of which once you also boasted: for grief is felt not so much for the want of what we have never known, as for the loss of that to which we have been long accustomed. Yet you who are still of an age to beget children must bear up in the hope of having others in their stead; not only will they help you to forget those whom you have lost, but will be to the state at once a reinforcement and a security; for never can a fair or just policy be expected of the citizen who does not, like his fellows, bring to the decision the interests and apprehensions of a father. And those of you who have passed your prime must congratulate yourselves with the thought that the best part of your life was fortunate, and that the brief span that remains will be cheered by the fame of the departed. For it is only the love of honour that never grows old; and honour it is, not gain, as some would have it, that rejoices the heart of age and helplessness.

"Turning to the sons or brothers of the dead, I see an arduous struggle before you. When a man is gone, all are wont to praise him, and should your merit be ever so transcendent, you will still find it difficult not merely to overtake, but even to approach their renown. The living have envy to contend with, while those who are no longer in our path are honoured with a goodwill into which rivalry does not enter. On the other hand, if I must say anything on the subject of female excellence to those of you who will now be in widowhood, it will be all comprised in this brief exhortation. Great will be your glory in not falling short of your natural character; and greatest will be hers who is least talked of among the men whether for good or for bad.

"My task is now finished. I have performed it to the best of my ability, and in words, at least, the requirements of the law are now satisfied. If deeds be in question, those who are here interred have received part of their honours already, and for the rest, their children will be brought up till manhood at the public expense: the state thus offers a valuable prize as the garland of victory in this race of valour, for the reward both of those who have fallen and their survivors. And where the rewards for merit are greatest, there are found the best citizens.

"And now that you have brought to a close your lamentations for your relatives, you may depart."

∾ MENGZI (MENCIUS)
CHINA, C. 371–C. 288 B.C.E.

Very little is known about Mencius's life other than that he was a Chinese philosopher devoted to interpreting and teaching the wisdom tradition of Confucius (Kongfuzi). Mencius expanded on the philosophy of Confucius and contributed to its pervasive influence by adding to it a very optimistic view of human nature. At the center of Mencius's teachings was a belief that human beings were naturally good, known as *jên*. The cornerstone of goodness is compassion, a state in which a person cannot bear that another should suffer. According to Mencius, a person is responsible for showing benevolence toward others, a principle he extends to political policy and the idea of "compassionate government."

In this excerpt from his writings, Mencius says that motivation for ethical action comes from within; he argues that human sensitivity to the suffering of others should lead to a life of benevolence, duty, and wisdom. In contrast, other ethical systems locate the motivation for good behavior outside of the self, in the form of rewards and punishments.

FROM

∾ # Mencius

Translated by D. C. Lau

[COMPASSION]

6.   Mencius said, "No man is devoid of a heart sensitive to the suffering of others. Such a sensitive heart was possessed by the Former Kings and this manifested itself in compassionate government. With such a sensitive heart behind compassionate government, it was as easy to rule the Empire as rolling it on your palm.

"My reason for saying that no man is devoid of a heart sensitive to the suffering of others is this. Suppose a man were, all of a sudden, to see a young child on the verge of falling into a well. He would certainly be moved to compassion, not because he wanted to get in the good graces of the parents, nor because he wished to win the praise of his fellow villagers or friends, nor yet because he disliked the cry of the child. From this it can be seen that whoever is devoid of the heart of compassion is not human, whoever is devoid of the heart of shame is not human, whoever is devoid of the heart of courtesy and modesty is not human, and whoever is devoid of

Tomb of Confucius, 551–479 B.C.E. *The Chinese philosopher Confucius had many followers, but perhaps the most well known was Mencius. With his emphasis on the natural goodness of human nature, or jên, Mencius helped extend and popularize traditional Confucianism. (Private Collection/ Bridgeman Art Library)*

the heart of right and wrong is not human. The heart of compassion is the germ of benevolence; the heart of shame, of dutifulness; the heart of courtesy and modesty, of observance of the rites; the heart of right and wrong, of wisdom. Man has these four germs[1] just as he has four limbs. For a man possessing these four germs to deny his own potentialities is for him to cripple himself; for him to deny the potentialities of his prince is for him to cripple his prince. If a man is able to develop all these four germs that he possesses, it will be like a fire starting up or a spring coming through. When these are fully developed, he can take under this protection the whole realm within the Four Seas, but if he fails to develop them, he will not be able even to serve his parents."

7.   Mencius said, "Is the maker of arrows really more unfeeling than the maker of armour? He is afraid lest he should fail to harm people, whereas the maker of armour is afraid lest he should fail to protect them. The case is similar with the sorcerer-doctor and the coffin-maker. For this reason one cannot be too careful in the choice of one's calling.

   "Confucius said, 'The best neighbourhood is where benevolence is to be found. Not to live in such a neighbourhood when one has the choice cannot by any means be considered wise.' Benevolence is the high honour bestowed by Heaven and the peaceful abode of man. Not to be benevolent when nothing stands in the way is to show a lack of wisdom. A man neither benevolent nor wise, devoid of courtesy and dutifulness, is a slave. A slave ashamed of serving is like a maker of bows ashamed of making bows, or a maker of arrows ashamed of making arrows. If one is ashamed, there is no better remedy than to practice benevolence. Benevolence is like archery: an archer makes sure his stance is correct before letting fly the arrow, and if he fails to hit the mark, he does not hold it against his victor. He simply seeks the cause within himself."

---

[1] **four germs:** Natural capabilities.

ᘉ DIOGENES LAERTIUS
GREECE, FL. THIRD CENTURY C.E.

Diogenes Laertius was a Greek biographer and historian whose *Lives of Eminent Philosophers* is a work in ten volumes that discusses the lives and teachings of Greek philosophers, from Thales in the seventh century B.C.E. to Epicurus in the third century B.C.E. In the case of Socrates, Diogenes Laertius, in a series of anecdotes, bits of narrative, and random teachings, provides the kind of information that later generations would find relevant and interesting about the great philosopher. Plato and Xenophon (c. 431–c. 354 B.C.E.), both disciples of Socrates, also wrote about Socrates, but as a philosopher, describing and defending his ideas about morality and politics (see pages 715–747). Diogenes Laertius captures Socrates in informal moments of ordinary conversation, and supplies homey details about Socrates' regard for his body and his need for exercise. He also includes Socrates' dealings with his first wife, Xanthippe, which are especially interesting.

FROM

∾ Lives of Eminent Philosophers

Translated by R. D. Hicks

[SOCRATES]

Demetrius of Byzantium relates that Crito removed [Socrates] from his workshop and educated him, being struck by his beauty of soul; that he discussed moral questions in the workshops and the market-place, being convinced that the study of nature is no concern of ours; and that he claimed that his inquiries embraced

Whatso'er is good or evil in an house[1];

that frequently, owing to his vehemence in argument, men set upon him with their fists or tore his hair out; and that for the most part he was despised and laughed at, yet bore all his ill-usage patiently. [. . .] when [. . .] some one expressed surprise at his taking it so quietly, Socrates rejoined, "Should I have taken the law of a donkey, supposing that he had kicked me?" Thus far Demetrius.

Unlike most philosophers, he had no need to travel, except when required to go on an expedition. The rest of his life he stayed at home and engaged all the more keenly in argument with anyone who would converse with him, his aim being not to alter his opinion but to get at the truth. They relate that Euripides gave him the treatise of Heraclitus and asked his opinion upon it, and that his reply was, "The part I understand is excellent, and so too is, I dare say, the part I do not understand; but it needs a Delian[2] diver to get to the bottom of it."

He took care to exercise his body and kept in good condition. At all events he served on the expedition to Amphipolis; and when in the battle of Delium Xenophon had fallen from his horse, he stepped in and saved his life. For in the general flight of the Athenians he personally retired at his ease, quietly turning round from time to time and ready to defend himself in case he were attacked. Again, he

---

[1] **Whatso'er is . . . house:** See *The Odyssey*, Book 4.

[2] **Delian:** From the island of Delos.

served at Potidaea, whither he had gone by sea, as land communications were interrupted by the war; and while there he is said to have remained a whole night without changing his position, and to have won the prize of valour. [. . .]

His strength of will and attachment to the democracy are evident from his refusal to yield to Critias and his colleagues when they ordered him to bring the wealthy Leon of Salamis[3] before them for execution, and further from the fact that he alone voted for the acquittal of the ten generals;[4] and again from the facts that when he had the opportunity to escape from the prison he declined to do so, and that he rebuked his friends for weeping over his fate, and addressed to them his most memorable discourses in the prison.

He was a man of great independence and dignity of character. Pamphila in the seventh book of her *Commentaries* tells how Alcibiades once offered him a large site on which to build a house; but he replied, "Suppose, then, I wanted shoes and you offered me a whole hide to make a pair with, would it not be ridiculous in me to take it?" Often when he looked at the multitude of wares exposed for sale, he would say to himself, "How many things I can do without!" And he would continually recite the lines:

> The purple robe and silver's shine
> More fits an actor's need than mine.[5]

. . .

Aristotle says that he married two wives: his first wife was Xanthippe, by whom he had a son, Lamprocles; his second wife was Myrto, the daughter of Aristides the Just, whom he took without a dowry. By her he had Sophroniscus and Menexenus. [. . .]

He could afford to despise those who scoffed at him. He prided himself on his plain living, and never asked a fee from anyone. He used to say that he most enjoyed the food which was least in need of condiment, and the drink which made him feel the least hankering for some other drink; and that he was nearest to the gods in that he had the fewest wants. [. . .]

Moreover, in his old age he learnt to play the lyre, declaring that he saw no absurdity in learning a new accomplishment. As Xenophon relates in the *Symposium*, it was his regular habit to dance, thinking that such exercise helped to keep the body in good condition. He used to say that his supernatural sign warned him beforehand of the future; that to make a good start was no trifling advantage, but a trifle turned the scale; and that he knew nothing except just the fact of his ignorance.

---

[3] **Leon of Salamis:** In 404 B.C.E., Athens was led by a group called the Thirty, led by Critias and Charmides, who began to terrorize citizens. Socrates was one of five citizens ordered to produce Leon of Salamis, a resident alien who was executed.

[4] **the acquittal . . . generals:** In a battle against the Peloponnesians in 406 B.C.E., a number of generals were accused of criminal negligence. Socrates voted against their conviction.

[5] **The purple . . . mine:** Probably these lines are falsely quoted, since they appear to be by the dramatist Philemon, who wrote them after Socrates' death.

He said that, when people paid a high price for fruit which had ripened early, they must despair of seeing the fruit ripen at the proper season. And, being once asked in what consisted the virtue of a young man, he said, "In doing nothing to excess." He held that geometry should be studied to the point at which a man is able to measure the land which he acquires or parts with. [. . .]

He had invited some rich men and, when Xanthippe said she felt ashamed of the dinner, "Never mind," said he, "for if they are reasonable they will put up with it, and if they are good for nothing, we shall not trouble ourselves about them." He would say that the rest of the world lived to eat, while he himself ate to live. [. . .]

When Xanthippe first scolded him and then drenched him with water, his rejoinder was, "Did I not say that Xanthippe's thunder would end in rain?" When Alcibiades declared that the scolding of Xanthippe was intolerable, "Nay, I have got used to it," said he, "as to the continued rattle of a windlass. And you do not mind the cackle of geese." "No," replied Alcibiades, "but they furnish me with eggs and goslings." "And Xanthippe," said Socrates, "is the mother of my children." When she tore his coat off his back in the market-place and his acquaintances advised him to hit back, "Yes, by Zeus," said he, "in order that while we are sparring each of you may join in with 'Go it, Socrates!' 'Well done, Xanthippe!'" He said he lived with a shrew, as horsemen are fond of spirited horses, "but just as, when they have mastered these, they can easily cope with the rest, so I in the society of Xanthippe shall learn to adapt myself to the rest of the world."

These and the like were his words and deeds, to which the Pythian priestess bore testimony when she gave Chaerephon the famous response:

Of all men living Socrates most wise.

. . .

The affidavit in the case,[6] which is still preserved, says Favorinus, in the *Metroön*, ran as follows: "This indictment and affidavit is sworn by Meletus, the son of Meletus of Pitthos, against Socrates, the son of Sophroniscus of Alopece: Socrates is guilty of refusing to recognize the gods recognized by the state, and of introducing other new divinities. He is also guilty of corrupting the youth. The penalty demanded is death." The philosopher then, after Lysias had written a defence for him, read it through and said: "A fine speech, Lysias; it is not, however, suitable to me." For it was plainly more forensic than philosophical. Lysias said, "If it is a fine speech, how can it fail to suit you?" "Well," he replied, "would not fine raiment and fine shoes be just as unsuitable to me?"

Justus of Tiberias in his book entitled *The Wreath* says that in the course of the trial Plato mounted the platform and began: "Though I am the youngest, men of Athens, of all who ever rose to address you"—whereupon the judges shouted out, "Get down! Get down!" When therefore he was condemned by 281 votes more than those given for acquittal, and when the judges were assessing what he should suffer

---

[6] **the case:** The trial of Socrates.

or what fine he should pay, he proposed to pay 25 drachmae. Eubulides indeed says he offered 100. When this caused an uproar among the judges, he said, "Considering my services, I assess the penalty at maintenance in the Prytaneum at the public expense."

Sentence of death was passed, with an accession of eighty fresh votes. He was put in prison, and a few days afterwards drank the hemlock, after much noble discourse which Plato records in the *Phaedo*. [...]

So he was taken from among men; and not long afterwards the Athenians felt such remorse that they shut up the training grounds and gymnasia. They banished the other accusers but put Meletus to death; they honoured Socrates with a bronze statue, the work of Lysippus, which they placed in the hall of processions. [...]

℘ SUETONIUS
ROME, C. 75–140 C.E.

Suetonius's *The Lives of the Twelve Caesars* covers the Roman rulers from Julius Caesar to Domitian. As secretary to the emperor Hadrian, who ruled Rome from 117 to 138 C.E., Suetonius had access to official records and was privy to the conversations of important people. Although Suetonius seems to get personally involved with his material and therefore is

Bust of Julius Caesar
One of the most interesting and prominent of the Roman emperors, Julius Caesar ruled Rome for only five years before he was assassinated by a group of nobles in the Senate. He was known not only as a great conqueror but as an able administrator as well. (Alinari / Art Resource, NY)

not always objective, his collection of facts and anecdotes about the personal lives of the emperors is unique. Suetonius's treatment of Julius Caesar, who ruled Rome for only five years, 49–44 B.C.E., contributes to the conclusion that the emperor was a most unusual ruler whose talent for running an empire went far beyond military conquest and might. In addition to correcting the official calendar, Julius Caesar was committed to public projects that would enhance the beauty and power of Rome, as recounted in this excerpt.

FROM

❧ The Lives of the Twelve Caesars

Translated by Alexander Thomson

JULIUS CAESAR

His thoughts were now fully employed from day to day on variety of great projects for the embellishment and improvement of the city, as well as for guarding and extending the bounds of the empire. In the first place, he meditated the construction of a temple to Mars, which should exceed in grandeur every thing of that kind in the world. For this purpose, he intended to fill up the lake on which he had entertained the people with the spectacle of a sea-fight. He also projected a most spacious theater adjacent to the Tarpeian mount; and also proposed to reduce the civil law to a reasonable compass, and out of that immense and undigested mass of statutes to extract the best and most necessary parts into a few books; to make as large a collection as possible of works in the Greek and Latin languages, for the public use; the province of providing and putting them in proper order being assigned to Marcus Varro. He intended likewise to drain the Pomptine marshes, to cut a channel for the discharge of the waters of the lake Fucinus, to form a road from the Adriatic through the ridge of the Apennine to the Tiber; to make a cut through the isthmus of Corinth, to reduce the Dacians, who had over-run Pontus and Thrace, within their proper limits, and then to make war upon the Parthians, through the Lesser Armenia, but not to risk a general engagement with them, until he had made some trial of their prowess in war. But in the midst of all his undertakings and projects, he was carried off by death; before I speak of which, it may not be improper to give an account of his person, dress, and manners, together with what relates to his pursuits, both civil and military.

It is said that he was tall, of a fair complexion, round limbed, rather full faced, with eyes black and piercing; and that he enjoyed excellent health, except toward the close of his life, when he was subject to sudden fainting-fits, and disturbance in his sleep. He was likewise twice seized with the falling sickness while engaged in active service. He was so nice in the care of his person, that he not only kept the hair of his head closely cut and had his face smoothly shaved, but even caused the hair on other parts of the body to be plucked out by the roots, a practice for which some persons rallied him. His baldness gave him much uneasiness, having often found himself upon that account exposed to the jibes of his enemies. He therefore used to bring forward the hair from the crown of his head; and of all the honors conferred upon him by the senate and people, there was none which he either accepted or used with greater pleasure, than the right of wearing constantly a laurel crown. It is said that he was particular in his dress. For he used the Latus Clavus[1] with fringes about the wrists, and always had it girded about him, but rather loosely. This circumstance gave origin to the expression of Sulla, who often advised the nobles to beware of "the ill-girt boy." [. . .]

He was perfect in the use of arms, an accomplished rider, and able to endure fatigue beyond all belief. On a march, he used to go at the head of his troops, sometimes on horseback, but oftener on foot, with his head bare in all kinds of weather. He would travel post in a light carriage without baggage, at the rate of a hundred miles a day; and if he was stopped by floods in the rivers, he swam across, or floated on skins inflated with wind, so that he often anticipated intelligence of his movements.

In his expeditions, it is difficult to say whether his caution or his daring was most conspicuous. He never marched his army by roads which were exposed to ambuscades, without having previously examined the nature of the ground by his scouts. Nor did he cross over to Britain, before he had carefully examined, in person, the navigation, the harbors, and the most convenient point of landing in the island. When intelligence was brought to him of the siege of his camp in Germany, he made his way to his troops, through the enemy's stations, in a Gaulish dress. He crossed the sea from Brundisium to Dyrrachium, in the winter, through the midst of the enemy's fleets; and the troops, under orders to join him, being slow in their movements, notwithstanding repeated messages to hurry them, but to no purpose, he at last went privately, and alone, aboard a small vessel in the night time, with his head muffled up; nor did he make himself known, or suffer the master to put about, although the wind blew strong against them, until they were ready to sink.

---

[1] **Latus Clavus:** A broad stripe of purple worn on tunics by Senators.

∾ PLATO
GREECE, C. 427–347 B.C.E.

Of the three great philosophers of classical Greece—Socrates, Plato, and Aristotle—only Plato's and Aristotle's teachings, theories, and thoughts were written down. Socrates, a great teacher, didn't publish, so all that is known of his philosophy comes from others, especially from the writings of Plato, one of his students. For Plato, Socrates was a philosopher-hero who pursued truth through questioning, saw self-understanding as the beginning of knowledge, and had the integrity to live his philosophic principles. Following the maxim, "the unexamined life is not worth living," Socrates made his life his most important work. By living and dying for his beliefs, Socrates epitomized some of the most deeply held ideals of his culture, ideals that remain central to the Western tradition. Plato's *Dialogues,* most of which feature Socrates as the central figure, are an extended tribute to Plato's mentor and hero.

www For links to more information about Plato and a quiz on his *Apology,* see bedford stmartins.com/ worldlitcompact.

The Historical Socrates.   Born about 470 B.C.E., Socrates' seventy years spanned a period of profound transformation in Athens. His early life was spent in the Golden Age of classical Athenian culture, the Age of Pericles.[1] Although not much is known about this period in Socrates' life, he seems to have come from a prosperous family, one that was able at least to indulge his interest in learning and philosophical speculation. During these years, he also may have studied the origin and nature of the universe, the traditional subject of philosophical speculation in ancient Greece. But by the beginning of the Peloponnesian War in 431, he began to focus on the study of conduct.

A "street teacher" known for his grotesque appearance—short and stout, with prominent eyes and a snub nose—and for such eccentricities as going barefoot year round, Socrates was sometimes linked with the SOPHISTS, freelance teachers who taught expedient and fashionable ideas to their pupils for a fee. In *Apology,* in which Plato writes in the first person as Socrates, Socrates is anxious to distinguish himself from these popular teachers. He has no art to teach, he claims, nor any rhetorical cleverness to model for his followers. He is just a gadfly asking plain questions and seeking plain answers. If he is the wisest man in Athens, as the Delphic Oracle stated, it is only because he knows that he does not know anything. His approach, perceived as naive arrogance, often annoys those he questions, especially when their conventional beliefs are challenged or held up to mockery. When Socrates questioned what justice or piety or wisdom was, he often arrived at answers different from those that had been previously generally accepted.

---

[1] **Age of Pericles:** The Golden Age of Athens in the fifth century B.C.E. when Pericles (c. 495–429 B.C.E.) was the city's leader. During this period, Athenian democracy reached its height, the Parthenon was constructed, and drama and music flourished.

Socrates
Philosophizing,
150 B.C.E.
*Detail from the
Roman Sarcophagus
(limestone burial
structure) of the
Muses. (The Art
Archive / Musée
du Louvre, Paris /
Dagli Orti)*

I . . . am a sort of
gadfly, given to the
state by God; and the
state is a great and
noble steed who is
tardy in his motions
owing to his very
size, and requires to
be stirred into life.

– SOCRATES,
in *Apology*

Socrates' middle years coincided with the Peloponnesian War (431–404 B.C.E.), the struggle, led by Athens on one side and Sparta on the other, among the city-states of the Greek peninsula. Although Athens had some important victories along the way, Sparta was the eventual winner. The resultant political turmoil in Athens led to the fall of Athenian democracy and the emergence of oligarchic rule. In this tense political atmosphere, Socrates' inquiries into justice, loyalty, and piety were often viewed as unpatriotic or sacrilegious, even though he professed a belief in the gods and had served in the Athenian army and fought heroically in battle. Although Socrates tried to avoid political involvement, the years just before his death in 399 were especially troubled and he was unable to protect himself completely from the controversies of the times. Politics probably played a part in his final condemnation.

Socrates has often been compared to Jesus. Both were charismatic teachers who attracted followers. Both challenged the political and social institutions of their time and place, and were models of the moral and committed life. Both became martyrs for their ideals, choosing to die rather than compromise the principles by which they lived. They differed most significantly, perhaps, in those ideals: Jesus taught love, compassion, and salvation; Socrates taught self-knowledge, critical thinking, and good citizenship. Their teachings form two of the central threads in the tapestry of Western civilization.

Plato's Socrates.   Just as Jesus is largely known through the biographies written of him in the four gospels of the New Testament, Socrates is known through Plato's *Dialogues*. Plato, one of Socrates' students, considered his teacher "of all the men of his time whom I have known . . . the wisest and justest, and best," and made him the hero of nearly all of his philosophic works. From a well-to-do and aristocratic family, Plato knew Socrates only at the end of the elder teacher's life. In *Apology* and **Phaedo**, Plato presents Socrates' trial and execution, events that he witnessed himself as a young man. Disillusioned by Socrates' death, Plato left Athens and traveled abroad for several years. When he returned about fourteen years later, he took up Socrates' mantle as a teacher and founded the Academy, a school that flourished in Athens until 529 C.E., when it was closed by the Byzantine emperor Justinian. Plato taught "in the groves of Academe," the gardens at the school where he met with his students, for the remainder of his long life, writing down the dialogues for which he is known and revered. When he was eighty, after attending the wedding of one of his students, Plato retired to a corner to rest and died peacefully in his sleep.

Plato's philosophic works are literary in character, "dialogues" in which the participants articulate different perspectives on the issues under discussion. The hero of nearly all of Plato's philosophic discussions is Socrates, who is seen employing a question-and-answer technique now known as "the Socratic method." He tests big ideas by analyzing assumptions and seeking clear definitions. When he asks in the *Euthyphro*, for example, "What is piety?", Euthyphro answers that piety "is that which is dear to the gods, and impiety is that which is not dear to them." Socrates then continues his questioning, getting Euthyphro to admit that because the gods disagree among themselves, there are contradictions in his definition. Moreover, he asserts, to define piety as "what is dear to the gods" does not identify what it is that makes something dear. By the end of their conversation Socrates has poked holes in Euthyphro's reasoning and challenged any conventional, untested belief in the gods. Although Socrates purges the definition of *piety* of its indefensible claims, he does not come up with a workable alternative. His approach to knowledge, his questioning, made room for not knowing, for acknowledging ignorance.

Apology.   *Apology*, perhaps the most famous of Plato's writings, depicts mostly in summary Socrates' defense against charges of corrupting the youth of Athens and introducing new divinities. Socrates' three accusers,

The unexamined life is not worth living.
   – SOCRATES,
   in *Apology*

FEE-doh

MEL-ih-tus; AN-uh-tus

Meletus, Anytus, and Lycon, have made their case against him, and as *Apology* begins, Socrates is stating his response. He must convince a jury of 501 citizens to vote for his acquittal.

Socrates responds directly to the current charges by recounting his quest to understand the meaning of the Delphic Oracle's[2] assertion that he, a man who only knows that he knows nothing, is the wisest man in Athens. He describes how those he has questioned—politicians, poets, and artisans—proved to have no greater knowledge than he did, even though they had professed to be able to answer questions that Socrates could not. Finally, he realized that his wisdom was that he *knew* he did not know, and he set out to show others that they were not as wise as they thought they were. His accusers were angry with him, he suggests, because they did not like having their ignorance revealed.

Defiant and uncompromising, Socrates refuses to give the court an excuse for dismissing or reducing the charges against him. He reaffirms his commitment to questioning and to teaching his fundamental truths that "virtue is knowledge" and that "the unexamined life is not worth living." He will not abandon his god-given role as a gadfly sent to sting the citizens of Athens to virtuous living, and he will make no deals in exchange for his life. If he is allowed to live, he will continue to urge his fellow citizens to "know themselves."

Some argue that Socrates takes an elitist stance, unwilling to make compromises that are necessary in a democratic society, thus bringing on himself a just punishment. The democrats in power in Athens in 399 B.C.E. considered Socrates dangerous. Some of the most prominent of Socrates' disciples—Alcibiades, Critias, Plato, and Xenophon,[3] for example—were members of the antidemocratic faction. Socrates' belief that government should be led by trained experts, his questioning, and his refusal to negotiate with the court threatened the party in power. Although at the time the government considered his execution justified, history has adopted Plato's view that Socrates' death was unjust, the martyrdom of a principled and courageous man. In *Phaedo*, Plato reflects on Socrates' execution, praising his hero's courageous integrity in facing death and his piety for dying for his convictions.

KRIGH-toh

The Allegory of the Cave.   The critical side to the Socratic method is most apparent in Plato's early dialogues, works like *Euthyphro* and **Crito**, in which Socrates the gadfly challenges the views of those he questions. In the great dialogues of Plato's middle period, such as *Symposium* or *The Republic*, a different Socrates seems to appear. He continues questioning, but he also has an agenda. It is impossible to know whether the historical

---

[2] **Delphic Oracle:** A shrine to the god Apollo at Delphi, near the foot of Mt. Parnassus. The priestess at the site delivered oracular messages, like the one through which Socrates learned that he was the wisest of men.

[3] **Alcibiades . . . Xenophon:** Alcibiades (c. 450–404 B.C.E.), an Athenian general and political leader; Critias (c. 460–403 B.C.E.), an aristocratic relative of Plato who was one of the thirty tyrants imposed on Athens by the Spartans; Xenophon (c. 430–c. 355 B.C.E.), an Athenian historian banished to Sparta who wrote about Socrates in several of his works.

Socrates held the views on politics, law, aesthetics, theology, psychology, education, and other topics that Plato discusses in later works or if using Socrates' voice had become more of a literary device for the philosophy. Classicist Edith Hamilton asserts that Plato "cannot be separated from Socrates. Almost all that Plato wrote professes to be a report of what Socrates said . . . and it is impossible to decide just what part belongs to each." In any case, the historical Socrates becomes less important in Plato's later works, disappearing altogether in some.

The parable "Allegory of the Cave," from *The Republic*, gives mythological expression to one of Plato's central concepts, the doctrine of Ideas or Forms. In it, Socrates distinguishes four kinds of knowledge, two that are possible within the underground den, or cave, and two that are possible only outside it. In the cave, chained men can see only shadows of objects cast on the wall before them, for the objects casting the shadows are behind them. Were they unchained, they could also see the particular objects themselves that made the shadows, but, still inside the cave, they would not be aware of the larger world outside. They might know the shadows of a chair or a dog and, if unchained, might know the particular chair or dog casting the shadows, but they would not understand the general *idea* of a chair or a dog, which can only be comprehended in the daylight outside of the cave. An IDEALIST, Plato believed that these general Ideas or Forms existed independently of any particular embodiment of them. The highest ideas, symbolized in the parable by the sun, the concepts of the Good, the True, and the Beautiful informed all lesser realities. Thus the parable presents a hierarchical scheme of reality with four distinct levels. Only someone who grasped all four levels could fully comprehend the truth. Such men Plato called "philosopher-kings." Everyone else was caught to some extent in illusion. The light of the sun becomes equivalent to enlightenment itself, the rational perception of truth.

> All European philosophy is but a footnote to Plato.
>
> – ALFRED NORTH WHITEHEAD, philosopher

■ **FURTHER RESEARCH**

Brickhouse, Thomas C. *Socrates on Trial*. 1989.
Gooch, Paul W. *Reflections on Jesus and Socrates: Word and Silence*. 1996.
Gutherie, W. K. C. *The Greek Philosophers: From Thales to Aristotle*. 1950, 1975.
Levin, Richard L., and John Bremer. *The Question of Socrates*. 1961.
Phillopson, Coleman. *The Trial of Socrates*. 1928.
Reeve, C. D. C. *Socrates in the Apology: An Essay on Plato's Apology of Socrates*. 1989.
Richmond, William K. *Socrates and the Western World*. 1954.
Stone, I. F. *The Trial of Socrates*. 1988.
Versényi, Laszlo. *Socratic Humanism*. 1963, 1979.

■ **PRONUNCIATION**

Adeimantus: ad-ee-MAN-tus
Aeacus: EE-uh-kus
Aeantodorus: ee-an-tuh-DOH-rus
Amphipolis: am-FIP-uh-lis
Anytus: AN-uh-tus
Arginusae: ar-jih-NOO-see
Asclepius: us-KLEE-pee-us

Cebes: SEE-beez
Ceos: SEE-ahs
Cephisus: see-FIGH-sus
Chaerephon: KLEH-ruh-fahn
Clazomenian: kluh-ZAH-muh-NEE-un
Crito: KRIGH-toh
Critobulus: krigh-toh-BYOO-lus
Demodocus: duh-MAH-duh-kus
Echecrates: ih-KEK-ruh-teez
Epigenes: eh-PIJ-ih-neez
Evenus: ih-VEE-nus
Gorgias: GORE-jus, GORE-jee-us
Leontium: lee-AHN-shum, lee-AHN-tee-um
Meletus: MEL-ih-tus
Musaeus: myoo-ZEE-us, myoo-ZAY-us
Nicostratus: nigh-KAH-struh-tus
Palamedes: pal-uh-MEE-deez
Phaedo: FEE-doh, FAY-doh
Potidaea: pah-tih-DEE-uh
Prytanes: PRIT-uh-neez
Rhadamanthus: rad-uh-MAN-thus
Simmias: SIM-ee-us
Theages: THEE-uh-jeez
Theozdotides: thee-uz-DOH-tih-deez
Triptolemus: trip-TAH-lih-mus

⤫ Apology

Translated by Benjamin Jowett

How you, O Athenians, have been affected by my accusers, I cannot tell; but I know that they almost made me forget who I was — so persuasively did they speak; and yet they have hardly uttered a word of truth. But of the many falsehoods told by them, there was one which quite amazed me; — I mean when they said that you should be upon your guard and not allow yourselves to be deceived by the force of my eloquence. To say this, when they were certain to be detected as soon as I opened my lips and proved myself to be anything but a great speaker, did indeed appear to me most shameless — unless by the force of eloquence they mean the force of truth; for if such is their meaning, I admit that I am eloquent. But in how different a way from theirs! Well, as I was saying, they have scarcely spoken the truth at all; but from me you shall hear the whole truth: not, however, delivered after their manner in a set oration duly ornamented with words and phrases. No, by heaven! but I shall use the words and arguments which occur to me at the moment; for I am confident in the justice of my cause: at my time of life I ought not to be appearing before you, O men of Athens, in the character of a juvenile orator — let no one expect it of me. And I must beg of you to grant me a favour: — If I defend myself in my accustomed manner, and you hear me using the words which I have been in the habit of using in the agora[1] at the tables of the money-changers, or anywhere else, I would ask you not to be surprised, and not to interrupt me on this account. For I am more than seventy years of age, and appearing now for the first time in a court of law, I am quite a stranger to the language of the place; and therefore I would have you regard me as if I were really a stranger, whom you would excuse if he spoke in his native tongue, and after the fashion of his country:—Am I making an unfair request of you? Never mind the manner, which may or may not be good; but think only of the truth of my words, and give heed to that: let the speaker speak truly and the judge decide justly.

And first, I have to reply to the older charges and to my first accusers, and then I will go on to the later ones. For of old I have had many accusers, who have accused me falsely to you during many years; and I am more afraid of them than of Anytus and his associates, who are dangerous, too, in their own way. But far more dangerous are the others, who began when you were children, and took possession of your minds with their falsehoods, telling of one Socrates, a wise man, who speculated about the heaven above and searched into the earth beneath, and made the worse appear the better cause.[2] The disseminators of this tale are the accusers whom I dread; for their hearers are apt to fancy that such enquirers do not believe in the existence of the gods. And they are many, and their charges against me are of ancient date, and they were made by them in the days when you were more impressible than you are now—in childhood, or it may have been in youth—and the cause when heard went by default, for there was none to answer. And hardest of all, I do not know and cannot tell the names of my accusers; unless in the chance case of a Comic poet.[3] All who from envy and malice have persuaded you—some of them having first convinced themselves—all this class of men are most difficult to deal with; for I cannot have them up here, and cross-examine them, and therefore I must simply fight with shadows in my own defence, and argue when there is no one who answers. I will ask you then to assume with me, as I was saying, that my opponents are of two kinds; one recent, the other ancient: and I hope that you will see the propriety of my answering the latter first, for these accusations you heard long before the others, and much oftener.

Well, then, I must make my defence, and endeavor to clear away in a short time, a slander which has lasted a long time. May I succeed, if to succeed be for my good and yours, or likely to avail me in my cause! The task is not an easy one; I quite understand the nature of it. And so leaving the event with God, in obedience to the law I will now make my defence.

---

[1] **agora:** The marketplace.

[2] **speculated . . . cause:** Socrates is here answering older charges brought against him, specifically that he was a materialist who speculated about the physical world and that he was one of the Sophists who taught expeditious modes of argument rather than truth.

[3] **Comic poet:** Aristophanes, in *The Clouds,* satirized Socrates as a charlatan who promulgated extravagant theories about the physical world.

I will begin at the beginning, and ask what is the accusation which has given rise to the slander of me, and in fact has encouraged Meletus to prefer this charge against me. Well, what do the slanderers say? They shall be my prosecutors, and I will sum up their words in an affidavit: 'Socrates is an evil-doer, and a curious person, who searches into things under the earth and in heaven, and he makes the worse appear the better cause; and he teaches the aforesaid doctrines to others.' Such is the nature of the accusation: it is just what you have yourselves seen in the comedy of Aristophanes, who has introduced a man whom he calls Socrates, going about and saying that he walks in air, and talking a deal of nonsense concerning matters of which I do not pretend to know either much or little—not that I mean to speak disparagingly of any one who is a student of natural philosophy. I should be very sorry if Meletus could bring so grave a charge against me. But the simple truth is, O Athenians, that I have nothing to do with physical speculations. Very many of those here present are witnesses to the truth of this, and to them I appeal. Speak then, you who have heard me, and tell your neighbours whether any of you have ever known me hold forth in few words or in many upon such matters. . . . You hear their answer. And from what they say of this part of the charge you will be able to judge of the truth of the rest.

As little foundation is there for the report that I am a teacher, and take money; this accusation has no more truth in it than the other. Although, if a man were really able to instruct mankind, to receive money for giving instruction would, in my opinion, be an honour to him. There is Gorgias of Leontium, and Prodicus of Ceos, and Hippias of Elis,[4] who go the round of the cities, and are able to persuade the young men to leave their own citizens by whom they might be taught for nothing, and come to them whom they not only pay, but are thankful if they may be allowed to pay them. There is at this time a Parian[5] philosopher residing in Athens, of whom I have heard; and I came to hear of him in this way:—I came across a man who has spent a world of money on the Sophists, Callias, the son of Hipponicus, and knowing that he had sons, I asked him: 'Callias,' I said, 'if your two sons were foals or calves, there would be no difficulty in finding some one to put over them; we should hire a trainer of horses, or a farmer probably, who would improve and perfect them in their own proper virtue and excellence; but as they are human beings, whom are you thinking of placing over them? Is there any one who understands human and political virtue? You must have thought about the matter, for you have sons; is there any one?' 'There is,' he said. 'Who is he?' said I; 'and of what country? and what does he charge?' 'Evenus the Parian,' he replied; 'he is the man, and his charge is five minae.' Happy is Evenus, I said to myself; if he really has this wisdom, and teaches at such a moderate charge. Had I the same, I should have been very proud and conceited; but the truth is that I have no knowledge of the kind.

I dare say, Athenians, that some one among you will reply, 'Yes, Socrates, but what is the origin of these accusations which are brought against you; there must have been something strange which you have been doing? All these rumours and

---

[4] **Gorgias . . . of Elis:** Famous Sophists who taught rhetoric and logic.   [5] **Parian:** From Paros, an island in the Aegean.

this talk about you would never have arisen if you had been like other men: tell us, then, what is the cause of them, for we should be sorry to judge hastily of you.' Now I regard this as a fair challenge, and I will endeavour to explain to you the reason why I am called wise and have such an evil fame. Please to attend then. And although some of you may think that I am joking, I declare that I will tell you the entire truth. Men of Athens, this reputation of mine has come of a certain sort of wisdom which I possess. If you ask me what kind of wisdom, I reply, wisdom such as may perhaps be attained by man, for to that extent I am inclined to believe that I am wise; whereas the persons of whom I was speaking have a superhuman wisdom, which I may fail to describe, because I have it not myself; and he who says that I have, speaks falsely, and is taking away my character. And here, O men of Athens, I must beg you not to interrupt me, even if I seem to say something extravagant. For the word which I will speak is not mine. I will refer you to a witness who is worthy of credit; that witness shall be the God of Delphi[6] — he will tell you about my wisdom, if I have any, and of what sort it is. You must have known Chaerephon; he was early a friend of mine, and also a friend of yours, for he shared in the recent exile of the people,[7] and returned with you. Well, Chaerephon, as you know, was very impetuous in all his doings, and he went to Delphi and boldly asked the oracle to tell him whether — as I was saying, I must beg you not to interrupt — he asked the oracle to tell him whether any one was wiser than I was, and the Pythian prophetess answered, that there was no man wiser. Chaerephon is dead himself; but his brother, who is in court, will confirm the truth of what I am saying.

Why do I mention this? Because I am going to explain to you why I have such an evil name. When I heard the answer, I said to myself, What can the god mean? and what is the interpretation of his riddle? for I know that I have no wisdom, small or great. What then can he mean when he says that I am the wisest of men? And yet he is a god, and cannot lie; that would be against his nature. After long consideration, I thought of a method of trying the question. I reflected that if I could only find a man wiser than myself, then I might go to the god with a refutation in my hand. I should say to him, 'Here is a man who is wiser than I am; but you said that I was the wisest.' Accordingly I went to one who had the reputation of wisdom, and observed him — his name I need not mention; he was a politician whom I selected for examination — and the result was as follows: When I began to talk with him, I could not help thinking that he was not really wise, although he was thought wise by many, and still wiser by himself; and thereupon I tried to explain to him that he thought himself wise, but was not really wise; and the consequence was that he hated me, and his enmity was shared by several who were present and heard me. So I left him, saying to myself, as I went away: Well, although I do not suppose that either of us knows

---

[6] **God of Delphi:** The Oracle of Apollo at Delphi.

[7] **exile of the people:** After the defeat of Athens by Sparta in 404 B.C.E., the democratic leaders of Athens had gone into exile, driven out of the city by the Thirty Tyrants who ruled briefly until democracy was reestablished in 403 B.C.E.

anything really beautiful and good, I am better off than he is,—for he knows nothing, and thinks that he knows; I neither know nor think that I know. In this latter particular, then, I seem to have slightly the advantage of him. Then I went to another who had still higher pretensions to wisdom, and my conclusion was exactly the same. Whereupon I made another enemy of him, and of many others besides him.

Then I went to one man after another, being not unconscious of the enmity which I provoked, and I lamented and feared this: But necessity was laid upon me,—the word of God, I thought, ought to be considered first. And I said to myself, Go I must to all who appear to know, and find out the meaning of the oracle. And I swear to you, Athenians, by the dog I swear!—for I must tell you the truth—the result of my mission was just this: I found that the men most in repute were all but the most foolish; and that others less esteemed were really wiser and better. I will tell you the tale of my wanderings and of the 'Herculean' labours, as I may call them, which I endured only to find at last the oracle irrefutable. After the politicians, I went to the poets; tragic, dithyrambic, and all sorts. And there, I said to myself, you will be instantly detected; now you will find out that you are more ignorant than they are. Accordingly, I took them some of the most elaborate passages in their own writings, and asked what was the meaning of them—thinking that they would teach me something. Will you believe me? I am almost ashamed to confess the truth, but I must say that there is hardly a person present who would not have talked better about their poetry than they did themselves. Then I knew that not by wisdom do poets write poetry, but by a sort of genius and inspiration; they are like diviners or soothsayers who also say many fine things, but do not understand the meaning of them. The poets appeared to me to be much in the same case; and I further observed that upon the strength of their poetry they believed themselves to be the wisest of men in other things in which they were not wise. So I departed, conceiving myself to be superior to them for the same reason that I was superior to the politicians.

At last I went to the artisans, for I was conscious that I knew nothing at all, as I may say, and I was sure that they knew many fine things; and here I was not mistaken, for they did know many things of which I was ignorant, and in this they certainly were wiser than I was. But I observed that even the good artisans fell into the same error as the poets;—because they were good workmen they thought that they also knew all sorts of high matters, and this defect in them overshadowed their wisdom; and therefore I asked myself on behalf of the oracle, whether I would like to be as I was, neither having their knowledge nor their ignorance, or like them in both; and I made answer to myself and to the oracle that I was better off as I was.

This inquisition has led to my having many enemies of the worst and most dangerous kind, and has given occasion also to many calumnies. And I am called wise, for my hearers always imagine that I myself possess the wisdom which I find wanting in others: but the truth is, O men of Athens, that God only is wise; and by his answer he intends to show that the wisdom of men is worth little or nothing; he is not speaking of Socrates, he is only using my name by way of illustration, as if he said, He, O men, is the wisest, who, like Socrates, knows that his wisdom is in truth worth nothing. And so I go about the world, obedient to the god, and search and make enquiry into the wisdom of any one, whether citizen or stranger, who appears to be wise; and if he is not wise, then in vindication of the oracle I show him that he is not wise; and my occupation quite absorbs me, and I have no time to give either to any public matter of interest or to any concern of my own, but I am in utter poverty by reason of my devotion to the god.

There is another thing: — young men of the richer classes, who have not much to do, come about me of their own accord; they like to hear the pretenders examined, and they often imitate me, and proceed to examine others; there are plenty of persons, as they quickly discover, who think that they know something, but really know little or nothing; and then those who are examined by them instead of being angry with themselves are angry with me: This confounded Socrates, they say; this villainous misleader of youth! — and then if somebody asks them, Why, what evil does he practice or teach? they do not know, and cannot tell; but in order that they may not appear to be at a loss, they repeat the ready-made charges which are used against all philosophers about teaching things up in the clouds and under the earth, and having no gods, and making the worse appear the better cause; for they do not like to confess that their pretence of knowledge has been detected — which is the truth; and as they are numerous and ambitious and energetic, and are drawn up in battle array and have persuasive tongues, they have filled your ears with their loud and inveterate calumnies. And this is the reason why my three accusers, Meletus and Anytus and Lycon, have set upon me; Meletus, who has a quarrel with me on behalf of the poets; Anytus, on behalf of the craftsmen and politicians; Lycon, on behalf of the rhetoricians: and as I said at the beginning, I cannot expect to get rid of such a mass of calumny all in a moment. And this, O men of Athens, is the truth and the whole truth; I have concealed nothing, I have dissembled nothing. And yet, I know that my plainness of speech makes them hate me, and what is their hatred but a proof that I am speaking the truth? — Hence has arisen the prejudice against me; and this is the reason of it, as you will find out either in this or in any future enquiry.

I have said enough in my defence against the first class of my accusers; I turn to the second class. They are headed by Meletus, that good man and true lover of his country, as he calls himself. Against these, too, I must try to make a defence: — Let their affidavit be read: it contains something of this kind: It says that Socrates is a doer of evil, who corrupts the youth; and who does not believe in the gods of the state, but has other new divinities of his own. Such is the charge; and now let us examine the particular counts. He says that I am a doer of evil, and corrupt the youth; but I say, O men of Athens, that Meletus is a doer of evil, in that he pretends to be in earnest when he is only in jest, and is so eager to bring men to trial from a pretended zeal and interest about matters in which he really never had the smallest interest. And the truth of this I will endeavour to prove to you.

Come hither, Meletus, and let me ask a question of you. You think a great deal about the improvement of youth?

Yes, I do.

Tell the judges, then, who is their improver; for you must know, as you have taken the pains to discover their corrupter, and are citing and accusing me before them. Speak, then, and tell the judges who their improver is. — Observe, Meletus, that you are silent, and have nothing to say. But is not this rather disgraceful, and a very considerable proof of what I was saying, that you have no interest in the matter? Speak up, friend, and tell us who their improver is.

The laws.

But that, my good sir, is not my meaning. I want to know who the person is, who, in the first place, knows the laws.

The judges, Socrates, who are present in court.

What, do you mean to say, Meletus, that they are able to instruct and improve youth?

Certainly they are.

What, all of them, or some only and not others?

All of them.

By the goddess Here,[8] that is good news! There are plenty of improvers, then. And what do you say of the audience,—do they improve them?

Yes, they do.

And the senators?

Yes, the senators improve them.

But perhaps the members of the assembly corrupt them?—or do they too improve them?

They improve them.

Then every Athenian improves and elevates them; all with the exception of myself; and I alone am their corrupter? Is that what you affirm?

That is what I stoutly affirm.

I am very unfortunate if you are right. But suppose I ask you a question: How about horses? Does one man do them harm and all the world good? Is not the exact opposite the truth? One man is able to do them good, or at least not many;—the trainer of horses, that is to say, does them good, and others who have to do with them rather injure them? Is not that true, Meletus, of horses, or any other animals? Most assuredly it is; whether you and Anytus say yes or no. Happy indeed would be the condition of youth if they had one corrupter only, and all the rest of the world were their improvers. But you, Meletus, have sufficiently shown that you never had a thought about the young: your carelessness is seen in your not caring about the very things which you bring against me.

And now, Meletus, I will ask you another question—by Zeus I will: Which is better, to live among bad citizens, or among good ones? Answer, friend, I say; the question is one which may be easily answered. Do not the good do their neighbours good, and the bad do them evil?

Certainly.

And is there any one who would rather be injured than benefited by those who live with him? Answer, my good friend, the law requires you to answer—does any one like to be injured?

Certainly not.

---

[8] **Here:** Hera, the queen of the gods.

And when you accuse me of corrupting and deteriorating the youth, do you allege that I corrupt them intentionally or unintentionally?

Intentionally, I say.

But you have just admitted that the good do their neighbours good, and evil do them evil. Now, is that a truth which your superior wisdom has recognized thus early in life, and am I, at my age, in such darkness and ignorance as not to know that if a man with whom I have to live is corrupted by me, I am very likely to be harmed by him; and yet I corrupt him, and intentionally, too—so you say, although neither I nor any other human being is ever likely to be convinced by you. But either I do not corrupt them, or I corrupt them unintentionally; and on either view of the case you lie. If my offence is unintentional, the law has no cognizance of unintentional offences: you ought to have taken me privately, and warned and admonished me; for if I had been better advised, I should have left off doing what I only did unintentionally—no doubt I should; but you would have nothing to say to me and refused to teach me. And now you bring me up in this court, which is not a place of instruction, but of punishment.

It will be very clear to you, Athenians, as I was saying, that Meletus has no care at all, great or small, about the matter. But still I should like to know, Meletus, in what I am affirmed to corrupt the young. I suppose you mean, as I infer from your indictment, that I teach them not to acknowledge the gods which the state acknowledges, but some other new divinities or spiritual agencies in their stead. These are the lessons by which I corrupt the youth, as you say.

Yes, that I say emphatically.

Then, by the gods, Meletus, of whom we are speaking, tell me and the court, in somewhat plainer terms, what you mean! for I do not as yet understand whether you affirm that I teach other men to acknowledge some gods, and therefore that I do believe in gods, and am not an entire atheist—this you do not lay to my charge,— but only you say that they are not the same gods which the city recognizes—the charge is that they are different gods. Or, do you mean that I am an atheist simply, and a teacher of atheism?

I mean the latter—that you are a complete atheist.

What an extraordinary statement! Why do you think so, Meletus? Do you mean that I do not believe in the godhead of the sun or moon, like other men?

I assure you, judges, that he does not: for he says that the sun is stone, and the moon earth.[9]

Friend Meletus, you think that you are accusing Anaxagoras:[10] and you have but a bad opinion of the judges, if you fancy them illiterate to such a degree as not to know that these doctrines are found in the books of Anaxagoras the Clazomenian, which are full of them. And so, forsooth, the youth are said to be taught them by

---

[9] **sun . . . earth:** These are the older charges, that Socrates taught atheistic doctrines that challenged the worship of Apollo, god of the sun, and Artemis, goddess of the moon.

[10] **Anaxagoras:** A fifth-century-B.C.E. materialist philosopher from Clazomenae.

Socrates, when there are not unfrequently exhibitions of them at the theatre (price of admission one drachma at the most); and they might pay their money, and laugh at Socrates if he pretends to father these extraordinary views. And so, Meletus, you really think that I do not believe in any god?

I swear by Zeus that you believe absolutely in none at all.

Nobody will believe you, Meletus, and I am pretty sure that you do not believe yourself. I cannot help thinking, men of Athens, that Meletus is reckless and impudent, and that he has written this indictment in a spirit of mere wantonness and youthful bravado. Has he not compounded a riddle, thinking to try me? He said to himself: — I shall see whether the wise Socrates will discover my facetious contradiction, or whether I shall be able to deceive him and the rest of them. For he certainly does appear to me to contradict himself in the indictment as much as if he said that Socrates is guilty of not believing in the gods, and yet of believing in them — but this is not like a person who is in earnest.

I should like you, O men of Athens, to join me in examining what I conceive to be his inconsistency; and do you, Meletus, answer. And I must remind the audience of my request that they would not make a disturbance if I speak in my accustomed manner:

Did ever man, Meletus, believe in the existence of human things, and not of human beings? . . . I wish, men of Athens, that he would answer, and not be always trying to get up an interruption. Did ever any man believe in horsemanship, and not in horses? or in flute-playing, and not in flute-players? No, my friend; I will answer to you and to the court, as you refuse to answer for yourself. There is no man who ever did. But now please to answer the next question: Can a man believe in spiritual and divine agencies, and not in spirits or demigods?

He cannot.

How lucky I am to have extracted that answer, by the assistance of the court! But then you swear in the indictment that I teach and believe in divine or spiritual agencies (new or old, no matter for that); at any rate, I believe in spiritual agencies, — so you say and swear in the affidavit; and yet if I believe in divine beings, how can I help believing in spirits or demigods; — must I not? To be sure I must; and therefore I may assume that your silence gives consent. Now what are spirits or demigods? Are they not either gods or the sons of gods?

Certainly they are.

But this is what I call the facetious riddle invented by you: the demigods or spirits are gods, and you say first that I do not believe in gods, and then again that I do believe in gods; that is, if I believe in demigods. For if the demigods are the illegitimate sons of gods, whether by the nymphs or by any other mothers, of whom they are said to be the sons — what human being will ever believe that there are no gods if they are the sons of gods? You might as well affirm the existence of mules and deny that of horses and asses. Such nonsense, Meletus, could only have been intended by you to make trial of me. You have put this into the indictment because you had nothing real of which to accuse me. But no one who has a particle of understanding will ever be convinced by you that the same men can believe in divine and superhuman things, and yet not believe that there are gods and demigods and heroes.

I have said enough in answer to the charge of Meletus: any elaborate defence is unnecessary; but I know only too well how many are the enmities which I have incurred, and this is what will be my destruction if I am destroyed;—not Meletus, nor yet Anytus, but the envy and detraction of the world, which has been the death of many good men, and will probably be the death of many more; there is no danger of my being the last of them.

Some one will say: And are you not ashamed, Socrates, of a course of life which is likely to bring you to an untimely end? To him I may fairly answer: There you are mistaken: a man who is good for anything ought not to calculate the chance of living or dying; he ought only to consider whether in doing anything he is doing right or wrong—acting the part of a good man or of a bad. Whereas, upon your view, the heroes who fell at Troy were not good for much, and the son of Thetis[11] above all, who altogether despised danger in comparison with disgrace; and when he was so eager to slay Hector, his goddess mother said to him, that if he avenged his companion Patroclus, and slew Hector, he would die himself—'Fate,' she said, in these or the like words, 'waits for you next after Hector;' he, receiving this warning, utterly despised danger and death, and instead of fearing them, feared rather to live in dishonour, and not to avenge his friend. 'Let me die forthwith,' he replies, 'and be avenged of my enemy, rather than abide here by the beaked ships, a laughing-stock and a burden of the earth.' Had Achilles any thought of death and danger? For wherever a man's place is, whether the place which he has chosen or that in which he has been placed by a commander, there he ought to remain in hour of danger; he should not think of death or of anything but of disgrace. And this, O men of Athens, is a true saying.

Strange, indeed, would be my conduct, O men of Athens, if I who, when I was ordered by the generals whom you chose to command me at Potidaea and Amphipolis and Delium,[12] remained where they placed me, like any other man, facing death—if now, when, as I conceive and imagine, God orders me to fulfil the philosopher's mission of searching into myself and other men, I were to desert my post through fear of death, or any other fear; that would indeed be strange, and I might justly be arraigned in court for denying the existence of the gods, if I disobeyed the oracle because I was afraid of death, fancying that I was wise when I was not wise. For the fear of death is indeed the pretence of wisdom, and not real wisdom, being a pretence of knowing the unknown; and no one knows whether death, which men in their fear apprehend to be the greatest evil, may not be the greatest good. Is not this ignorance of a disgraceful sort, the ignorance which is the conceit that man knows what he does not know? And in this respect only I believe myself to differ from men in general, and may perhaps claim to be wiser than they are:—that whereas I know but little of the world below, I do not suppose that I know: but I do know that injustice and disobedience to a better, whether God or man, is evil and dishonourable, and I will never fear or avoid a possible good rather than a certain evil. And therefore

---

[11] **son of Thetis:** Achilles; the scene described here is in Book 28 of *The Iliad.*

[12] **Potidaea . . . Delium:** The sites of three battles in which Socrates fought as a soldier.

if you let me go now, and are not convinced by Anytus, who said that since I had been prosecuted I must be put to death (or if not that I ought never to have been prosecuted at all); and that if I escape now, your sons will all be utterly ruined by listening to my words—if you say to me, Socrates, this time we will not mind Anytus, and you shall be let off, but upon one condition, that you are not to enquire and speculate in this way any more, and that if you are caught doing so again you shall die:—if this was the condition on which you let me go, I should reply: Men of Athens, I honour and love you; but I shall obey God rather than you, and while I have life and strength I shall never cease from the practice and teaching of philosophy, exhorting any one whom I meet and saying to him after my manner: You, my friend,—a citizen of the great and mighty and wise city of Athens,—are you not ashamed of heaping up the greatest amount of money and honour and reputation, and caring so little about wisdom and truth and the greatest improvement of the soul, which you never regard or heed at all? And if the person with whom I am arguing, says: Yes, but I do care; then I do not leave him or let him go at once; but I proceed to interrogate and examine and cross-examine him, and if I think that he has no virtue in him, but only says that he has, I reproach him with undervaluing the greater, and overvaluing the less. And I shall repeat the same words to every one whom I meet, young and old, citizen and alien, but especially to the citizens, inasmuch as they are my brethren. For know that this is the command of God; and I believe that no greater good has ever happened in the state than my service to the God. For I do nothing but go around persuading you all, old and young alike, not to take thought for your persons or your properties, but first and chiefly to care about the greatest improvement of the soul. I tell you that virtue is not given by money, but that from virtue comes money and every other good of man, public as well as private. This is my teaching, and if this is the doctrine which corrupts the youth, I am a mischievous person. But if any one says that this is not my teaching, he is speaking an untruth. Wherefore, O men of Athens, I say to you, do as Anytus bids or not as Anytus bids, and either acquit me or not; but whichever you do, understand that I shall never alter my ways, not even if I have to die many times.

Men of Athens, do not interrupt, but hear me; there was an understanding between us that you should hear me to the end: I have something more to say, at which you may be inclined to cry out; but I believe that to hear me will be good for you, and therefore I beg that you will not cry out. I would have you know, that if you kill such an one as I am, you will injure yourselves more than you will injure me. Nothing will injure me, not Meletus nor yet Anytus—they cannot, for a bad man is not permitted to injure a better than himself. I do not deny that Anytus may, perhaps, kill him, or drive him into exile, or deprive him of civil rights; and he may imagine, and others may imagine, that he is inflicting a great injury upon him: but there I do not agree. For the evil of doing as he is doing—the evil of unjustly taking away the life of another—is greater far.

And now, Athenians, I am not going to argue for my own sake, as you may think, but for yours, that you may not sin against the God by condemning me, who am his gift to you. For if you kill me you will not easily find a successor to me, who, if I may use such a ludicrous figure of speech, am a sort of gadfly, given to the state by God;

and the state is a great and noble steed who is tardy in his motions owing to his very size, and requires to be stirred into life. I am that gadfly which God has attached to the state, and all day long and in all places am always fastening upon you, arousing and persuading and reproaching you. You will not easily find another like me, and therefore I would advise you to spare me. I dare say that you may feel out of temper (like a person who is suddenly awakened from sleep), and you think that you might easily strike me dead as Anytus advises, and then you would sleep on for the remainder of your lives, unless God in his care of you sent you another gadfly. When I say that I am given to you by God, the proof of my mission is this: — if I had been like other men, I should not have neglected all my own concerns or patiently seen the neglect of them during all these years, and have been doing yours, coming to you individually like a father or elder brother, exhorting you to regard virtue; such conduct, I say, would be unlike human nature. If I had gained anything, or if my exhortations had been paid, there would have been some sense in my doing so; but now, as you will perceive, not even the impudence of my accusers dares to say that I have ever exacted or sought pay of any one; of that they have no witness. And I have a sufficient witness to the truth of what I say — my poverty.

Some one may wonder why I go about in private giving advice and busying myself with the concerns of others, but do not venture to come forward in public and advise the state. I will tell you why. You have heard me speak at sundry times and in divers places of an oracle or sign which comes to me, and is the divinity which Meletus ridicules in the indictment. This sign, which is a kind of voice, first began to come to me when I was a child; it always forbids but never commands me to do anything which I am going to do. This is what deters me from being a politician. And rightly, as I think. For I am certain, O men of Athens, that if I had engaged in politics, I should have perished long ago, and done no good either to you or to myself. And do not be offended at my telling you the truth: for the truth is, that no man who goes to war with you or any other multitude, honestly striving against the many lawless and unrighteous deeds which are done in a state, will save his life; he who will fight for the right, if he would live even for a brief space, must have a private station and not a public one.

I can give you convincing evidence of what I say, not words only, but what you value far more — actions. Let me relate to you a passage of my own life which will prove to you that I should never have yielded to injustice from any fear of death, and that 'as I should have refused to yield' I must have died at once. I will tell you a tale of the courts, not very interesting perhaps, but nevertheless true. The only office of state which I ever held, O men of Athens, was that of senator:[13] the tribe Antiochis, which is my tribe, had the presidency at the trial of the generals who had not taken

[13] **office . . . senator:** The Athenian Assembly was composed of 500 members, 50 from each of ten tribes. Each tribe led the Assembly for one-tenth of the year, during which time of leadership its members were known as Prytanes. Socrates, from the tribe of Antiochis, was serving as Prytane following the naval battle of Arginusae in 406 B.C.E., when several Athenian naval commanders were accused of neglecting the dead. Socrates refused to participate in the trial, held in the Assembly, which he deemed to be unjust.

up the bodies of the slain after the battle of Arginusae; and you proposed to try them in a body, contrary to law, as you all thought afterwards; but at the time I was the only one of the Prytanes who was opposed to the illegality, and I gave my vote against you; and when the orators threatened to impeach and arrest me, and you called and shouted, I made up my mind that I would run the risk, having law and justice with me, rather than take part in your injustice because I feared imprisonment and death. This happened in the days of the democracy.[14] But when the oligarchy of the Thirty was in power, they sent for me and four others into the rotunda,[15] and bade us bring Leon the Salaminian from Salamis,[16] as they wanted to put him to death. This was a specimen of the sort of commands which they were always giving with the view of implicating as many as possible in their crimes; and then I showed, not in word only but in deed, that, if I may be allowed to use such an expression, I cared not a straw for death, and that my great and only care was lest I should do an unrighteous or unholy thing. For the strong arm of that oppressive power did not frighten me into doing wrong; and when we came out of the rotunda the other four went to Salamis and fetched Leon, but I went quietly home. For which I might have lost my life, had not the power of the Thirty shortly afterwards come to an end. And many will witness to my words.

Now do you really imagine that I could have survived all these years, if I had led a public life, supposing that like a good man I had always maintained the right and had made justice, as I ought, the first thing? No indeed, men of Athens, neither I nor any other man. But I have been always the same in all my actions, public as well as private, and never have I yielded any base compliance to those who are slanderously termed my disciples, or to any other. Not that I have any regular disciples. But if any one likes to come and hear me while I am pursuing my mission, whether he be young or old, he is not excluded. Nor do I converse only with those who pay; but any one, whether he be rich or poor, may ask and answer me and listen to my words; and whether he turns out to be a bad man or a good one, neither result can be justly imputed to me; for I never taught or professed to teach him anything. And if any one says that he has ever learned or heard anything from me in private which all the world has not heard, let me tell you that he is lying.

But I shall be asked, Why do people delight in continually conversing with you? I have told you already, Athenians, the whole truth about this matter: they like to hear the cross-examination of the pretenders to wisdom; there is amusement in it. Now this duty of cross-examining other men has been imposed upon me by God; and has been signified to me by oracles, visions, and in every way in which the will of divine power has ever intimated to any one. This is true, O Athenians; or, if not true, would be soon refuted. If I am or have been corrupting the youth, those of them who are now grown up and become sensible that I gave them bad advice in the days of

---

[14] **the trial . . . democracy:** Socrates is giving two examples of his opposition to the government, one democratic and one the oligarchy of the Thirty Tyrants who ruled after Athens fell to Sparta.

[15] **rotunda:** The circular building where the Prytanes met.

[16] **Salamis:** An island off the coast near Athens, where Leon fled to escape prosecution.

their youth should come forward as accusers, and take their revenge; or if they do not like to come themselves, some of their relatives, fathers, brothers, or other kinsmen, should say what evil their families have suffered at my hands. Now is their time. Many of them I see in the court. There is Crito, who is of the same age and of the same deme[17] with myself, and there is Critobulus his son, whom I also see. Then again there is Lysanias of Sphettus, who is the father of Aeschines—he is present; and also there is Antiphon of Cephisus, who is the father of Epigenes; and there are the brothers of several who have associated with me. There is Nicostratus the son of Theosdotides, and the brother of Theodotus (now Theodotus himself is dead, and therefore he, at any rate, will not seek to stop him); and there is Paralus the son of Demodocus, who had a brother Theages; and Adeimantus the son of Ariston, whose brother Plato[18] is present; and Aeantodorus, who is the brother of Apollodorus, whom I also see. I might mention a great many others, some of whom Meletus should have produced as witnesses in the course of his speech; and let him still produce them, if he has forgotten—I will make way for him. And let him say, if he has any testimony of the sort which he can produce. Nay, Athenians, the very opposite is the truth. For all these are ready to witness on behalf of the corrupter, of the injurer of their kindred, as Meletus and Anytus call me; not the corrupted youth only—there might have been a motive for that—but their uncorrupted elder relatives. Why should they too support me with their testimony? Why, indeed, except for the sake of truth and justice, and because they know that I am speaking the truth, and that Meletus is a liar.

Well, Athenians, this and the like of this is all the defence which I have to offer. Yet a word more. Perhaps there may be some one who is offended at me, when he calls to mind how he himself on a similar, or even a less serious occasion, prayed and entreated the judges with many tears, and how he produced his children in court, which was a moving spectacle, together with a host of relations and friends; whereas I, who am probably in danger of my life, will do none of these things. The contrast may occur to his mind, and he may be set against me, and vote in anger because he is displeased at me on this account. Now if there be such a person among you,—mind, I do not say that there is,—to him I may fairly reply: My friend, I am a man, and like other men, a creature of flesh and blood, and not 'of wood or stone,' as Homer says,[19] and I have a family, yes, and sons, O Athenians, three in number, one almost a man, and two others who are still young; and yet I will not bring any of them hither in order to petition you for an acquittal. And why not? Not from any self-assertion or want of respect for you. Whether I am or am not afraid of death is another question, of which I will not now speak. But, having regard to public opinion, I feel that such conduct would be discreditable to myself, and to you, and to the whole state. One who has reached my years, and who has a name for wisdom, ought not to demean

---

[17] **deme:** Precinct.

[18] **Plato:** The author of *Apology.*

[19] **'of wood . . .' as Homer says:** In Book 19 of *The Odyssey,* Penélopê addresses these words to her husband, Odysseus, who is disguised as a beggar.

himself. Whether this opinion of me be deserved or not, at any rate the world has decided that Socrates is in some way superior to other men. And if those among you who are said to be superior in wisdom and courage, and any other virtue, demean themselves in this way, how shameful is their conduct! I have seen men of reputation, when they have been condemned, behaving in the strangest manner: they seemed to fancy that they were going to suffer something dreadful if they died, and that they could be immortal if you only allowed them to live; and I think that such are a dishonour to the state, and that any stranger coming in would have said of them that the most eminent men of Athens, to whom the Athenians themselves give honour and command, are no better than women. And I say that these things ought not to be done by those of us who have a reputation; and if they are done, you ought not to permit them; you ought rather to show that you are far more disposed to condemn the man who gets up a doleful scene and makes the city ridiculous, than him who holds his peace.

But, setting aside the question of public opinion, there seems to be something wrong in asking a favour of a judge, and thus procuring an acquittal, instead of informing him and convincing him. For his duty is, not to make a present of justice, but to give judgment; and he has sworn that he will judge according to the laws, and not according to his own good pleasure; and we ought not to encourage you, nor should you allow yourself to be encouraged, in this habit of perjury — there can be no piety in that. Do not then require me to do what I consider dishonourable and impious and wrong, especially now, when I am being tried for impiety on the indictment of Meletus. For if, O men of Athens, by force of persuasion and entreaty I could overpower your oaths, then I should be teaching you to believe that there are no gods, and in defending should simply convict myself of the charge of not believing in them. But that is not so — far otherwise. For I do believe that there are gods, and in a sense higher than that which any of my accusers believe in them. And to you and to God I commit my cause, to be determined by you as is best for you and me.[20]

There are many reasons why I am not grieved, O men of Athens, at the vote of condemnation. I expected it, and am only surprised that the votes are so nearly equal; for I had thought that the majority against me would have been far larger; but now, had thirty votes gone over to the other side, I should have been acquitted. And I may say, I think, that I have escaped Meletus. I may say more; for without the assistance of Anytus and Lycon, any one may see that he would not have had a fifth part of the votes,[21] as the law requires, in which case he would have incurred a fine of a thousand drachmae.

---

[20] The jurors cast their votes, 280 for conviction and 220 against. Next the jury must determine the sentence. Meletus demands death. Socrates is given an opportunity to propose a lighter sentence.

[21] **fifth part of the votes:** A minimum vote of one-fifth of the Assembly, or 100 votes, was required to justify conducting a trial. By dividing the 280 votes among his three accusers, Socrates arrives at a figure that suggests his accusers have not met the minimum required.

And so he proposes death as the penalty. And what shall I propose on my part, O men of Athens? Clearly that which is my due. And what is my due? What return shall be made to the man who has never had the wit to be idle during his whole life; but has been careless of what the many care for — wealth, and family interests, and military offices, and speaking in the assembly, and magistracies, and plots, and parties. Reflecting that I was really too honest a man to be a politician and live, I did not go where I could do no good to you or to myself; but where I could do the greatest good privately to every one of you, thither I went, and sought to persuade every man among you that he must look to himself, and seek virtue and wisdom before he looks to his private interests, and look to the state before he looks to the interests of the state; and that this should be the order which he observes in all his actions. What shall be done to such an one? Doubtless some good thing, O men of Athens, if he has his reward; and the good should be of a kind suitable to him. What would be a reward suitable to a poor man who is your benefactor, and who desires leisure that he may instruct you? There can be no reward so fitting as maintenance in the Prytaneum,[22] O men of Athens, a reward which he deserves far more than the citizen who has won the prize at Olympia in the horse or chariot race, whether the chariots were drawn by two horses or by many. For I am in want, and he has enough; and he only gives you the appearance of happiness, and I give you the reality. And if I am to estimate the penalty fairly, I should say that maintenance in the Prytaneum is the just return.

Perhaps you think that I am braving you in what I am saying now, as in what I said before about the tears and prayers. But this is not so. I speak rather because I am convinced that I never intentionally wronged any one, although I cannot convince you — the time has been too short; if there were a law at Athens, as there is in other cities, that a capital cause should not be decided in one day, then I believe that I should have convinced you. But I cannot in a moment refute great slander; and, as I am convinced that I never wronged another, I will assuredly not wrong myself. I will not say of myself that I deserve any evil, or propose any penalty. Why should I? Because I am afraid of the penalty of death which Meletus proposes? When I do not know whether death is a good or an evil, why should I propose a penalty which would certainly be an evil? Shall I say imprisonment? And why should I live in prison, and be the slave of the magistrates of the year — of the Eleven?[23] Or shall the penalty be a fine, and imprisonment until the fine is paid? There is the same objection. I should have to lie in prison, for money I have none, and cannot pay. And if I say exile (and this may possibly be the penalty which you will affix), I must indeed be blinded by the love of life, if I am so irrational as to expect that when you, who are my own citizens, cannot endure my discourses and words, and have found them so grievous and odious that you will have no more of them, others are likely to endure me. No indeed, men of Athens, that is not very likely. And what a life should I lead, at

---

[22] **Prytaneum:** The place where the Prytanes honored the benefactors of Athens.   [23] **the Eleven:** The committee in charge of prisons and public executions.

my age, wandering from city to city, ever changing my place of exile, and always being driven out! For I am quite sure that wherever I go, there, as here, the young men will flock to me; and if I drive them away, their elders will drive me out at their request; and if I let them come, their fathers and friends will drive me out for their sakes.

Some one will say: Yes, Socrates, but cannot you hold your tongue, and then you may go into a foreign city, and no one will interfere with you? Now I have great difficulty in making you understand my answer to this. For if I tell you that to do as you say would be a disobedience to the God, and therefore that I cannot hold my tongue, you will not believe that I am serious; and if I say again that daily to discourse about virtue, and of those other things about which you hear me examining myself and others, is the greatest good of man, and that the unexamined life is not worth living, you are still less likely to believe me. Yet I say what is true, although a thing of which it is hard for me to persuade you. Also, I have never been accustomed to think that I deserve to suffer any harm. Had I money I might have estimated the offence at what I was able to pay, and not have been much the worse. But I have none, and therefore I must ask you to proportion the fine to my means. Well, perhaps I could afford a mina, and therefore I propose that penalty: Plato, Crito, Critobulus, and Apollodorus, my friends here, bid me say thirty minae, and they will be the sureties. Let thirty minae be the penalty; for which sum they will be ample security to you.[24]

Not much time will be gained, O Athenians, in return for the evil name which you will get from the detractors of the city, who will say that you killed Socrates, a wise man; for they will call me wise, even although I am not wise, when they want to reproach you. If you had waited a little while, your desire would have been fulfilled in the course of nature. For I am far advanced in years, as you may perceive, and not far from death. I am speaking now not to all of you, but only to those who have condemned me to death. And I have another thing to say to them: You think that I was convicted because I had no words of the sort which would have procured my acquittal—I mean, if I had thought fit to leave nothing undone or unsaid. Not so; the deficiency which led to my conviction was not of words—certainly not. But I had not the boldness or impudence or inclination to address you as you would have liked me to do, weeping and wailing and lamenting, and saying and doing many things which you have been accustomed to hear from others, and which, as I maintain, are unworthy of me. I thought at the time that I ought not to do anything common or mean when in danger: nor do I now repent of the style of my defence; I would rather die having spoken after my manner, than speak in your manner and live. For neither in war nor yet at law ought I or any man to use every way of escaping death. Often in battle there can be no doubt that if a man will throw away his arms, and fall on his knees before his pursuers, he may escape death; and in other dangers there are other ways of escaping death, if a man is willing to say and do anything. The difficulty, my friends, is not to avoid death, but to avoid unrighteousness; for that runs faster than death. I am old and move slowly, and the slower runner has overtaken me, and my

---

[24]The jury now casts another split vote on the sentence, ruling for the death penalty.

accusers are keen and quick, and the faster runner, who is unrighteousness, has over-taken them. And now I depart hence condemned by you to suffer the penalty of death, — they too go their ways condemned by the truth to suffer the penalty of villainy and wrong; and I must abide by my award — let them abide by theirs. I suppose that these things may be regarded as fated, — and I think that they are well.

And now, O men who have condemned me, I would fain prophesy to you; for I am about to die, and in the hour of death men are gifted with prophetic power. And I prophesy to you who are my murderers, that immediately after my departure punishment far heavier than you have inflicted on me will surely await you. Me you have killed because you wanted to escape the accuser, and not to give an account of your lives. But that will not be as you suppose: far otherwise. For I say that there will be more accusers of you than there are now; accusers whom hitherto I have restrained: and as they are younger they will be more inconsiderate with you, and you will be more offended at them. If you think that by killing men you can prevent some one from censuring your evil lives, you are mistaken; that is not a way of escape which is either possible or honourable; the easiest and the noblest way is not to be disabling others, but to be improving yourselves. This is the prophecy which I utter before my departure to the judges who have condemned me.

Friends, who would have acquitted me, I would like also to talk with you about the thing which has come to pass, while the magistrates are busy, and before I go to the place at which I must die. Stay then a little, for we may as well talk with one another while there is time. You are my friends, and I should like to show you the meaning of this event which has happened to me. O my judges — for you I may truly call judges — I should like to tell you of a wonderful circumstance. Hitherto the divine faculty of which the internal oracle is the source has constantly been in the habit of opposing me even about trifles, if I was going to make a slip or error in any matter; and now as you see there has come upon me that which may be thought, and is generally believed to be, the last and worst evil. But the oracle made no sign of opposition, either when I was leaving my house in the morning, or when I was on my way to the court, or while I was speaking, at anything which I was going to say; and yet I have often been stopped in the middle of a speech, but now in nothing I either said or did touching the matter in hand has the oracle opposed me. What do I take to be the explanation of this silence? I will tell you. It is an intimation that what has happened to me is a good, and that those of us who think that death is an evil are in error. For the customary sign would surely have opposed me had I been going to evil and not to good.

Let us reflect in another way, and we shall see that there is great reason to hope that death is a good; for one of two things — either death is a state of nothingness and utter unconsciousness, or, as men say, there is a change and migration of the soul from this world to another. Now if you suppose that there is no consciousness, but a sleep like the sleep of him who is undisturbed even by dreams, death will be an unspeakable gain. For if a person were to select the night in which his sleep was undisturbed even by dreams, and were to compare with this the other days and nights of his life, and then were to tell us how many days and nights he had passed in the course of his life better and more pleasantly than this one, I think that any man, I will not say a private man, but even the great king will not find many such days or nights, when compared with the others. Now if death be of such a nature, I say that to die is gain; for eternity is then only a single night. But if death is the journey to another place, and there, as men say, all the dead abide, what good, O my friends and judges, can be greater than this? If indeed when the pilgrim arrives in the world below, he is delivered from the professors of justice in this world, and finds the true judges who are said to give judgment there, Minos and Rhadamanthus and Aeacus and Triptolemus,[25] and other sons of God who were righteous in their own life, that pilgrimage will be worth making. What would not a man give if he might converse with Orpheus and Musaeus and Hesiod[26] and Homer? Nay, if this be true, let me die again and again. I myself, too, shall have a wonderful interest in there meeting and conversing with Palamedes, and Ajax the son of Telamon, and any other ancient hero who has suffered death through an unjust judgment; and there will be no small pleasure, as I think, in comparing my own sufferings with theirs. Above all, I shall then be able to continue my search into true and false knowledge; as in this world, so also in the next and I shall find out who is wise, and who pretends to be wise, and is not. What would not a man give, O judges, to be able to examine the leader of the great Trojan expedition; or Odysseus or Sisyphus,[27] or numberless others, men and women too! What infinite delight would there be in conversing with them and asking them questions! In another world they do not put a man to death for asking questions: assuredly not. For besides being happier than we are, they will be immortal, if what is said is true.

Wherefore, O judges, be of good cheer about death, and know of a certainty, that no evil can happen to a good man, either in life or after death. He and his are not neglected by the gods; nor has my own approaching end happened by mere chance. But I see clearly that the time had arrived when it was better for me to die and be released from trouble; wherefore the oracle gave no sign. For which reason, also, I am not angry with my condemners, or with my accusers; they have done me no harm, although they did not mean to do me any good; and for this I may gently blame them.

Still I have a favour to ask of them. When my sons are grown up, I would ask you, O my friends, to punish them; and I would have you trouble them, as I have troubled you, if they seem to care about riches, or anything more than about virtue; or if they pretend to be something when they are really nothing,—then reprove them, as I have reproved you, for not caring about that for which they ought to care, and thinking that they are something when they are really nothing. And if you do this, both I and my sons will have received justice at your hands.

The hour of departure has arrived, and we go our ways—I to die, and you to live. Which is better God only knows.

---

[25] **Minos . . . Triptolemus:** The four judges of the dead.

[26] **Orpheus . . . Hesiod:** Orpheus and Musaeus were legendary poets; Hesiod was a Greek poet of the eighth century B.C.E.

[27] **Odysseus or Sisyphus:** Both Odysseus and Sisyphus were noted for their cunning.

FROM

∾ Phaedo

Translated by Benjamin Jowett

PERSONS OF THE DIALOGUE:

PHAEDO, *who is the narrator of the Dialogue*   SIMMIAS
    to Echecrates of Phlius   CEBES
SOCRATES   CRITO
APOLLODORUS   ATTENDANT OF THE PRISON

SCENE: *The Prison of Socrates; Place of the Narration: Phlius*

[In this excerpt from the final pages of the *Phaedo,* Plato describes the execution of Socrates. The narrator, Phaedo, and several other friends of Socrates listen to the philosopher prove the immortality of the soul. The excerpt begins as Socrates concludes by describing the virtuous person's hopes for an afterlife.–ED.]

. . . A man of sense ought not to say, nor will I be very confident, that the description which I have given of the soul and her mansions is exactly true. But I do say that, inasmuch as the soul is shown to be immortal, he may venture to think, not improperly or unworthily, that something of the kind is true. The venture is a glorious one, and he ought to comfort himself with words like these, which is the reason why I lengthen out the tale. Wherefore, I say, let a man be of good cheer about his soul, who having cast away the pleasures and ornaments of the body as alien to him and working harm rather than good, has sought after the pleasures of knowledge; and has arrayed the soul, not in some foreign attire, but in her own proper jewels, temperance, and justice, and courage, and nobility, and truth—in these adorned she is ready to go on her journey to the world below, when her hour comes. You, Simmias and Cebes, and all other men, will depart at some time or other. Me already, as a tragic poet would say, the voice of fate calls. Soon I must drink the poison; and I think that I had better repair to the bath first, in order that the women may not have the trouble of washing my body after I am dead.

When he had done speaking, Crito said: And have you any commands for us, Socrates—anything to say about your children, or any other matter in which we can serve you?

Nothing particular, Crito, he replied: only, as I have always told you, take care of yourselves; that is a service which you may be ever rendering to me and mine and to all of us, whether you promise to do so or not. But if you have no thought for yourselves, and care not to walk according to the rule which I have prescribed for you, not now for the first time, however much you may profess or promise at the moment, it will be of no avail.

We will do our best, said Crito: And in what way shall we bury you?

In any way that you like; but you must get hold of me, and take care that I do not run away from you. Then he turned to us, and added with a smile:—I cannot make Crito believe that I am the same Socrates who has been talking and conducting the argument; he fancies that I am the other Socrates whom he will soon see, a dead body—and he asks, How shall he bury me? And though I have spoken many words in the endeavour to show that when I have drunk the poison I shall leave you and go to the joys of the blessed,—these words of mine, with which I was comforting you and myself, have had, as I perceive, no effect upon Crito. And therefore I want you to be surety for me to him now, as at the trial he was surety to the judges for me: but let the promise be of another sort; for he was surety for me to the judges that I would remain, and you must be my surety to him that I shall not remain, but go away and depart; and then he will suffer less at my death, and not be grieved when he sees my body being burned or buried. I would not have him sorrow at my hard lot, or say at the burial, Thus we lay out Socrates, or, Thus we follow him to the grave or bury him; for false words are not only evil in themselves, but they infect the soul with evil. Be of good cheer then, my dear Crito, and say that you are burying my body only, and do with that whatever is usual, and what you think best.

When he had spoken these words, he arose and went into a chamber to bathe; Crito followed him and told us to wait. So we remained behind, talking and thinking of the subject of discourse, and also of the greatness of our sorrow; he was like a father of whom we were being bereaved, and we were about to pass the rest of our lives as orphans. When he had taken the bath his children were brought to him— (he had two young sons and an elder one); and the women of his family also came, and he talked to them and gave them a few directions in the presence of Crito; then he dismissed them and returned to us.

Now the hour of sunset was near, for a good deal of time had passed while he was within. When he came out, he sat down with us again after his bath, but not much was said. Soon the jailer, who was the servant of the Eleven, entered and stood by him, saying:—To you, Socrates, whom I know to be the noblest and gentlest and best of all who ever came to this place, I will not impute the angry feelings of other men, who rage and swear at me, when, in obedience to the authorities, I bid them drink the poison—indeed, I am sure that you will not be angry with me; for others, as you are aware, and not I, are to blame. And so fare you well, and try to bear lightly what must needs be—you know my errand. Then bursting into tears he turned away and went out.

Socrates looked at him and said: I return your good wishes, and will do as you bid. Then turning to us, he said, How charming the man is: since I have been in prison he has always been coming to see me, and at times he would talk to me, and was as good to me as could be, and now see how generously he sorrows on my account. We must do as he says, Crito; and therefore let the cup be brought, if the poison is prepared: if not, let the attendant prepare some.

Yet, said Crito, the sun is still upon the hilltops, and I know that many a one has taken the draught late, and after the announcement has been made to him, he has eaten and drunk, and enjoyed the society of his beloved; do not hurry—there is time enough.

Socrates said: Yes, Crito, and they of whom you speak are right in so acting, for they think that they will be gainers by the delay; but I am right in not following their example, for I do not think that I should gain anything by drinking the poison a little later; I should only be ridiculous in my own eyes for sparing and saving a life which is already forfeit. Please then to do as I say, and not to refuse me.

Crito made a sign to the servant, who was standing by; and he went out, and having been absent for some time, returned with the jailer carrying the cup of poison. Socrates said: You, my good friend, who are experienced in these matters, shall give me directions how I am to proceed. The man answered: You have only to walk about until your legs are heavy, and then to lie down, and the poison will act. At the same time he handed the cup to Socrates, who in the easiest and gentlest manner, without the least fear or change of colour or feature, looking at the man with all his eyes, Echecrates, as his manner was, took the cup and said: What do you say about making a libation out of this cup to any god? May I, or not? The man answered: We only prepare, Socrates, just so much as we deem enough. I understand, he said: but I may and I must ask the gods to prosper my journey from this to the other world— even so—and so be it according to my prayer. Then raising the cup to his lips, quite readily and cheerfully he drank off the poison. And hitherto most of us had been able to control our sorrow; but now when we saw him drinking, and saw too that he had finished the draught, we could no longer forbear, and in spite of myself my own tears were flowing fast; so that I covered my face and wept, not for him, but at the thought of my own calamity in having to part from such a friend. Nor was I the first; for Crito, when he found himself unable to restrain his tears, had got up, and I followed; and at that moment, Apollodorus, who had been weeping all the time, broke out in a loud and passionate cry which made cowards of us all. Socrates alone retained his calmness: What is this strange outcry? he said. I sent away the women mainly in order that they might not misbehave in this way, for I have been told that a man should die in peace. Be quiet then, and have patience. When we heard his words we were ashamed, and refrained our tears; and he walked about until, as he said, his legs began to fail, and then he lay on his back, according to the directions, and the man who gave him the poison now and then looked at his feet and legs; and after a while he pressed his foot hard, and asked him if he could feel; and he said, No; and then his leg, and so upwards and upwards, and showed us that he was cold and stiff. And he felt them himself, and said: When the poison reaches the heart, that will be the end. He was beginning to grow cold about the groin, when he uncovered his face, for he had covered himself up, and said—they were his last words—he said: Crito, I owe a cock to Asclepius; will you remember to pay the debt? The debt shall be paid, said Crito; is there anything else? There was no answer to this question; but in a minute or two a movement was heard, and the attendants uncovered him; his eyes were set, and Crito closed his eyes and mouth.

Such was the end, Echecrates, of our friend; concerning whom I may truly say, that of all the men of his time whom I have known, he was the wisest and justest and best.

FROM

∾ The Republic

Translated by Benjamin Jowett

[THE ALLEGORY OF THE CAVE]

SPEAKERS IN THE DIALOGUE:

SOCRATES   GLAUCON

And now, I said, let me show in a figure how far our nature is enlightened or unenlightened: — Behold! human beings living in an underground den, which has a mouth open towards the light and reaching all along the den; here they have been from their childhood, and have their legs and necks chained so that they cannot move, and can only see before them, being prevented by the chains from turning round their heads. Above and behind them a fire is blazing at a distance, and between the fire and the prisoners there is a raised way; and you will see, if you look, a low wall built along the way, like the screen which marionette players have in front of them, over which they show the puppets.

I see.

And do you see, I said, men passing along the wall carrying all sorts of vessels, and statues and figures of animals made of wood and stone and various materials, which appear over the wall? Some of them are talking, others silent.

You have shown me a strange image, and they are strange prisoners.

Like ourselves, I replied; and they see only their own shadows, or the shadows of one another, which the fire throws on the opposite wall of the cave?

True, he said; how could they see anything but the shadows if they were never allowed to move their heads?

And of the objects which are being carried in like manner they would only see the shadows?

Yes, he said.

And if they were able to converse with one another, would they not suppose that they were naming what was actually before them?

Very true.

And suppose further that the prison had an echo which came from the other side, would they not be sure to fancy when one of the passers-by spoke that the voice which they heard came from the passing shadow?

No question, he replied.

To them, I said, the truth would be literally nothing but the shadows of the images.

That is certain.

And now look again, and see what will naturally follow if the prisoners are released and disabused of their error. At first, when any of them is liberated and compelled suddenly to stand up and turn his neck round and walk and look towards the light, he will suffer sharp pains; the glare will distress him, and he will be unable to see the realities of which in his former state he had seen the shadows; and then conceive some one saying to him, that what he saw before was an illusion, but that now, when he is approaching nearer to being and his eye is turned towards more real existence, he has a clearer vision — what will be his reply? And you may further imagine that his instructor is pointing to the objects as they pass and requiring him to name them — will he not be perplexed? Will he not fancy that the shadows which he formerly saw are truer than the objects which are now shown to him?

Far truer.

And if he is compelled to look straight at the light, will he not have a pain in his eyes which will make him turn away to take refuge in the objects of vision which he can see, and which he will conceive to be in reality clearer than the things which are now being shown to him?

True, he said.

And suppose once more, that he is reluctantly dragged up a steep and rugged ascent, and held fast until he is forced into the presence of the sun himself, is he not likely to be pained and irritated? When he approaches the light his eyes will be dazzled, and he will not be able to see anything at all of what are now called realities.

Not all in a moment, he said.

He will require to grow accustomed to the sight of the upper world. And first he will see the shadows best, next the reflections of men and other objects in the water, and then the objects themselves; then he will gaze upon the light of the moon and the stars and the spangled heaven; and he will see the sky and the stars by night better than the sun or the light of the sun by day?

Certainly.

Last of all he will be able to see the sun, and not mere reflections of him in the water, but he will see him in his own proper place, and not in another; and he will contemplate him as he is.

Certainly.

He will then proceed to argue that this is he who gives the season and the years, and is the guardian of all that is in the visible world, and in a certain way the cause of all things which he and his fellows have been accustomed to behold?

Clearly, he said, he would first see the sun and then reason about him.

And when he remembered his old habitation, and the wisdom of the den and his fellow-prisoners, do you not suppose that he would felicitate himself on the change, and pity them?

Certainly, he would.

And if they were in the habit of conferring honours among themselves on those who were quickest to observe the passing shadows and to remark which of them went before, and which followed after, and which were together; and who were therefore best able to draw conclusions as to the future, do you think that he would care for such honours and glories, or envy the possessors of them? Would he not say with Homer,

> Better to be the poor servant of a poor master,

and to endure anything, rather than think as they do and live after their manner?

Yes, he said, I think that he would rather suffer anything than entertain these false notions and live in this miserable manner.

Imagine once more, I said, such an one coming suddenly out of the sun to be replaced in his old situation; would he not be certain to have his eyes full of darkness?

To be sure, he said.

And if there were a contest, and he had to compete in measuring the shadows with the prisoners who had never moved out of the den, while his sight was still weak, and before his eyes had become steady (and the time which would be needed to acquire this new habit of sight might be very considerable), would he not be ridiculous? Men would say of him that up he went and down he came without his eyes; and that it was better not even to think of ascending; and if any one tried to loose another and lead him up to the light, let them only catch the offender, and they would put him to death.

No question, he said.

This entire allegory, I said, you may now append, dear Glaucon, to the previous argument; the prison-house is the world of sight, the light of the fire is the sun, and you will not misapprehend me if you interpret the journey upwards to be the ascent of the soul into the intellectual world according to my poor belief, which, at your desire, I have expressed — whether rightly or wrongly God knows. But, whether true or false, my opinion is that in the world of knowledge the idea of good appears last of all, and is seen only with an effort; and, when seen, is also inferred to be the universal author of all things beautiful and right, parent of light and of the lord of light in this visible world, and the immediate source of reason and truth in the intellectual; and that this is the power upon which he who would act rationally either in public or private life must have his eye fixed.

I agree, he said, as far as I am able to understand you.

Moreover, I said, you must not wonder that those who attain to this beatific vision are unwilling to descend to human affairs; for their souls are ever hastening into the upper world where they desire to dwell; which desire of theirs is very natural, if our allegory may be trusted.

Yes, very natural.

And is there anything surprising in one who passes from divine contemplations to the evil state of man, misbehaving himself in a ridiculous manner; if, while his eyes are blinking and before he has become accustomed to the surrounding darkness, he is compelled to fight in courts of law, or in other places, about the images or the shadows of images of justice, and is endeavouring to meet the conceptions of those who have never yet seen absolute justice?

Anything but surprising, he replied.

Any one who has common sense will remember that the bewilderments of the eyes are of two kinds, and arise from two causes, either from coming out of the light or from going into the light, which is true of the mind's eye, quite as much as of the bodily eye; and he who remembers this when he sees any one whose vision is perplexed and weak, will not be too ready to laugh; he will first ask whether that soul of man has come out of the brighter life, and is unable to see because unaccustomed to the dark, or having turned from darkness to the day is dazzled by excess of light. And he will count the one happy in his condition and state of being, and he will pity the other; or, if he have a mind to laugh at the soul which comes from below into the light, there will be more reason in this than in the laugh which greets him who returns from above out of the light into the den.

That, he said, is a very just distinction.

But then, if I am right, certain professors of education must be wrong when they say that they can put a knowledge into the soul which was not there before, like sight into blind eyes.

They undoubtedly say this, he replied.

Whereas, our argument shows that the power and capacity of learning exists in the soul already; and that just as the eye was unable to turn from darkness to light without the whole body, so too the instrument of knowledge can only by the movement of the whole soul be turned from the world of becoming into that of being, and learn by degrees to endure the sight of being, and of the brightest and best of being, or in other words, of the good.

Very true.

And must there not be some art which will effect conversion in the easiest and quickest manner; not implanting the faculty of sight, for that exists already, but has been turned in the wrong direction, and is looking away from the truth?

Yes, he said, such an art may be presumed.

And whereas the other so-called virtues of the soul seem to be akin to bodily qualities, for even when they are not originally innate they can be implanted later by habit and exercise, the virtue of wisdom more than anything else contains a divine element which always remains, and by this conversion is rendered useful and profitable; or, on the other hand, hurtful and useless. Did you never observe the narrow intelligence flashing from the keen eye of a clever rogue — how eager he is, how clearly his paltry soul sees the way to his end; he is the reverse of blind, but his keen eye-sight is forced into the service of evil, and he is mischievous in proportion to his cleverness?

Very true, he said.

But what if there had been a circumcision of such natures in the days of their youth; and they had been severed from those sensual pleasures, such as eating and drinking, which, like leaden weights, were attached to them at their birth, and which drag them down and turn the vision of their souls upon the things that are below — if, I say, they had been released from these impediments and turned in the opposite direction, the very same faculty in them would have seen the truth as keenly as they see what their eyes are turned to now.

Very likely.

Yes, I said; and there is another thing which is likely, or rather a necessary inference from what has preceded, that neither the uneducated and uninformed of the truth, nor yet those who never make an end of their education, will be able ministers of State; not the former, because they have no single aim of duty which is the rule of all their actions, private as well as public; nor the latter, because they will not act at all except upon compulsion, fancying that they are already dwelling apart in the islands of the blest.

Very true, he replied.

Then, I said, the business of us who are the founders of the State will be to compel the best minds to attain that knowledge which we have already shown to be the greatest of all—they must continue to ascend until they arrive at the good; but when they have ascended and seen enough we must not allow them to do as they do now.

What do you mean?

I mean that they remain in the upper world: but this must not be allowed; they must be made to descend again among the prisoners in the den, and partake of their labours and honours, whether they are worth having or not.

But is not this unjust? he said; ought we to give them a worse life, when they might have a better?

You have again forgotten, my friend, I said, the intention of the legislator, who did not aim at making any one class in the State happy above the rest; the happiness was to be in the whole State, and he held the citizens together by persuasion and necessity, making them benefactors of the State, and therefore benefactors of one another; to this end he created them, not to please themselves, but to be his instruments in binding up the State.

True, he said, I had forgotten.

Observe, Glaucon, that there will be no injustice in compelling our philosophers to have a care and providence of others; we shall explain to them that in other States, men of their class are not obliged to share in the toils of politics: and this is reasonable, for they grow up at their own sweet will, and the government would rather not have them. Being self-taught, they cannot be expected to show any gratitude for a culture which they have never received. But we have brought you into the world to be rulers of the hive, kings of yourselves and of the other citizens, and have educated you far better and more perfectly than they have been educated, and you are better able to share in the double duty. Wherefore each of you, when his turn comes, must go down to the general underground abode, and get the habit of seeing in the dark. When you have acquired the habit, you will see ten thousand times better than the inhabitants of the den, and you will know what the several images are, and what they represent, because you have seen the beautiful and just and good in their truth. And thus our State which is also yours will be a reality, and not a dream only, and will be administered in a spirit unlike that of other States, in which men fight with one another about shadows only and are distracted in the struggle for power, which in their eyes is a great good. Whereas the truth is that the State in which the rulers are most reluctant to govern is always the best and most quietly governed, and the State in which they are most eager, the worst.

Quite true, he replied.

And will our pupils, when they hear this, refuse to take their turn at the toils of State, when they are allowed to spend the greater part of their time with one another in the heavenly light?

Impossible, he answered; for they are just men, and the commands which we impose upon them are just; there can be no doubt that every one of them will take office as a stern necessity, and not after the fashion of our present rulers of State.

Yes, my friend, I said; and there lies the point. You must contrive for your future rulers another and a better life than that of a ruler, and then you may have a well-ordered State; for only in the State which offers this, will they rule who are truly rich, not in silver and gold, but in virtue and wisdom, which are the true blessings of life. Whereas if they go to the administration of public affairs, poor and hungering after their own private advantage, thinking that hence they are to snatch the chief good, order there can never be; for they will be fighting about office, and the civil and domestic broils which thus arise will be the ruin of the rulers themselves and of the whole State.

Most true, he replied.

And the only life which looks down upon the life of political ambition is that of true philosophy. Do you know of any other?

Indeed, I do not, he said. . . .

℘ ARISTOTLE
GREECE, 384–322 B.C.E.

Plato and Aristotle built on a tradition of rational inquiry that began in the sixth century B.C.E. in Greece when individuals attempted to *understand* the world and not merely to *explain* it through myth or religion. The key assumption for this intellectual pursuit was that the world was essentially rational and knowable, that human reason could grasp its workings. Aristotle's genius consisted of his developing the tools of analysis — in particular, logic and taxonomy[1] — which made the inquiry into the nature of social and material reality both possible and rewarding. Aristotle's works, about four hundred in number, covered nearly all the known fields of knowledge of his time: from astronomy and mathematics to physics, biology, ethics, politics, and literature. There is no doubt that Aristotle laid the foundation for the development of modern science and is therefore a recognizable influence on the modern world.

A Life of Study and Teaching.   Aristotle was born the son of a physician in the north of Greece, in the town of Stagira in Macedonia. When he was seventeen, Aristotle studied at Plato's Academy in Athens, remaining there twenty years until Plato's death in 347 B.C.E. For the next several years Aristotle traveled about and in 342 B.C.E. became the tutor

www For links to more information about Aristotle and a quiz on *Poetics,* see bedford stmartins.com/ worldlitcompact.

---

[1] **logic and taxonomy:** Logic is a system of reasoning in which statements lead to sound conclusions. Taxonomy is the science of classification and labeling. Aristotle believed in a grand hierarchy of being in which every thing and every idea had its place.

Bust of Aristotle
Though considered one of the founders of modern science, Aristotle's contributions were not limited to the realm of science but extended to the fields of literature, philosophy, and art as well. (Erich Lessing/ Art Resource, NY)

of young Alexander of Macedon,[2] returning to Athens to found the Lyceum, a school of philosophy, in 335. Known also as the Peripatetic School because the students walked about on the grounds while Aristotle taught, this school was the first research institution in Greece devoted to science, literature, and philosophy. After Alexander's death in 323, anti-Macedonian feelings in Athens led Aristotle to retire on Macedonia's Chalcidian peninsula, where he died a year later, in 322 B.C.E.

It was typical of Aristotle's gentle, generous thoughtfulness that in his will he provided for all his relatives and dependents—including his slaves. He thanked his wife, Herpyllis, for her goodness and provided a dowry for her. He asked, however, that his bones be placed in the grave of his first wife, Pythias, the adoptive daughter or niece of his close friend Hermias; Aristotle had rescued Pythias from robbers.

Poetics.   Aristotle's *Poetics*, which describes the general nature of Greek literature in the form of somewhat condensed lecture notes, is probably his most popular work among students of literature today. Aristotle was fortunate enough to have a substantial body of classical literature on which to base his analysis, resulting in principles that became, for many Western writers and critics, the measure of a well-made piece of literature. The essential mechanism of the Aristotelian analysis of literature is the separation of a whole subject into its constituent parts and the formation of suitable definitions. *Poetics* begins by distinguishing between various kinds of literature and then describing their basic principles and aims. After a general discussion of Greek poetry, Aristotle moves to epic and tragedy. In contrast to Plato, who questioned the moral impact of art, Aristotle discusses the positive influence of literature on human beings, especially the healthy effect of catharsis, the purgation of the emotions. The following excerpts are taken from the sections dealing with tragedy, which according to Aristotle consists of six parts: plot, character, diction, thought, spectacle, and melody. The soul of tragedy is plot or action.

Aristotle's influence on Western culture has been immense, although at first it took a rather circuitous route. Of the few philosophical works by Aristotle published in his lifetime, only brief fragments remain. Aristotle's lectures on scientific matters, however, recorded by his students and lost from the time of his death until the first century B.C.E., were published in Rome and preserved by Byzantine scholars for several hundred years until they were passed on to great Islamic scholars like Avicenna (980–1037) in Persia and Averroës (1126–1198) in Spain and Morocco, renowned for their studies in medicine and philosophy. Aristotle's treatises were then passed back to Europe where they influenced that continent's revival of learning in the twelfth and thirteenth centuries.

---

[2] **Alexander of Macedon:** Alexander the Great (356–323 B.C.E.) became king of Macedon after the death of his father. Considered the most brilliant general of the ancient, Western world, Alexander extended his empire while spreading the culture of ancient Greece through Egypt, Palestine, Persia, and northern India before he tragically died in Babylon in 323 B.C.E.

Thomas Aquinas (c. 1225–1274) used Aristotelian philosophy to construct the theoretical basis of Medieval Christianity by reconciling the Greek texts of Aristotle with the doctrines of Christianity. Dante, the fourteenth-century Italian poet and creator of *The Divine Comedy,* borrowed from Aristotle's hierarchical thinking and called him "the Master of those who know." After the rise of modern science, Aristotle's importance declined, but the example of his intellect and the compelling nature of his methodology have continued to inspire thinkers to the present day. We might not all be Platonists or Aristotelians,[3] as British Romantic Samuel Taylor Coleridge maintained in the early nineteenth century, but it is still common for modern intellectuals to seek refuge in the basic tenets of the humanism fostered by these men.

> Although his debt to Plato is visible throughout his work, Aristotle rejected his master's forms for a thoroughgoing empiricism: the world of experience is what one needs to understand, and therefore that is what one starts with — all experience, for he had an intellectual energy and curiosity that have never been surpassed and rarely been approached.
> – M. I. FINLEY, historian, 1964

■ **FURTHER RESEARCH**

Background and Criticism

Hardison Jr., O. B. *Aristotle's Poetics.* 1968.

Irwin, Terence. *Aristotle's First Principles.* 1989.

Jaeger, Werner. *Paideia: The Ideals of Greek Culture.* 1939–44.

Olson, Elder, ed. *Aristotle's Poetics and English Literature: A Collection of Critical Essays.* 1965.

Zeller, Eduard. *Outlines of the History of Greek Philosophy.* 1955.

---

[3] **Platonists or Aristotelians:** Coleridge (1772–1834) was referring to two of the major directions of modern Western thought, which seem to originate with Plato and Aristotle: a concern with the spiritual world, the inner world of feelings and beliefs, and a desire to describe and understand the external phenomenal world.

FROM

 Poetics

Translated by T. S. Dorsch

[ON TRAGEDY]

Tragedy, then, is a representation of an action that is worth serious attention, complete in itself, and of some amplitude; in language enriched by a variety of artistic devices appropriate to the several parts of the play; presented in the form of action, not narration; by means of pity and fear bringing about the purgation of such emotions. By language that is enriched I refer to language possessing rhythm, and music or song; and by artistic devices appropriate to the several parts I mean that some are produced by the medium of verse alone, and others again with the help of song.

Now since the representation is carried out by men performing the actions, it follows, in the first place, that spectacle is an essential part of tragedy, and secondly that there must be song and diction, these being the medium of representation. By diction I mean here the arrangement of the verses; song is a term whose sense is obvious to everyone.

In tragedy it is action that is imitated, and this action is brought about by agents who necessarily display certain distinctive qualities both of character and of thought, according to which we also define the nature of the actions. Thought and character are, then, the two natural causes of actions, and it is on them that all men depend for success or failure. The representation of the action is the plot of the tragedy; for the ordered arrangement of the incidents is what I mean by plot. Character, on the other hand, is that which enables us to define the nature of the participants, and thought comes out in what they say when they are proving a point or expressing an opinion.

Necessarily, then, every tragedy has six constituents, which will determine its quality. They are plot, character, diction, thought, spectacle, and song. Of these, two represent the media in which the action is represented, one involves the manner of representation, and three are connected with the objects of the representation; beyond them nothing further is required. These, it may be said, are the dramatic elements that have been used by practically all playwrights; for all plays alike possess spectacle, character, plot, diction, song, and thought.

Of these elements the most important is the plot, the ordering of the incidents; for tragedy is a representation, not of men, but of action and life, of happiness and unhappiness — and happiness and unhappiness are bound up with action. The purpose of living is an end which is a kind of activity, not a quality; it is their characters, indeed, that make men what they are, but it is by reason of their actions that they are happy or the reverse. Tragedies are not performed, therefore, in order to represent character, although character is involved for the sake of the action. Thus the incidents and the plot are the end aimed at in tragedy, and as always, the end is everything. Furthermore, there could not be a tragedy without action, but there could be without character; indeed the tragedies of most of our recent playwrights fail to present character, and the same might be said of many playwrights of other periods. . . . Again, if someone writes a series of speeches expressive of character, and well composed as far as thought and diction are concerned, he will still not achieve the proper effect of tragedy; this will be done much better by a tragedy which is less successful in its use of these elements, but which has a plot giving an ordered combination of incidents. Another point to note is that the two most important means by which tragedy plays on our feelings, that is, "reversals" and "recognitions", are both constituents of the plot. A further proof is that beginners can achieve accuracy in diction and the portrayal of character before they can construct a plot out of the incidents, and this could be said of almost all the earliest dramatic poets.

The plot, then, is the first essential of tragedy, its life-blood, so to speak, and character takes the second place. It is much the same in painting; for if an artist were to daub his canvas with the most beautiful colours laid on at random, he would not give the same pleasure as he would by drawing a recognizable portrait in black and white. Tragedy is the representation of an action, and it is chiefly on account of the action that it is also a representation of persons.

The third property of tragedy is thought. This is the ability to say what is possible and appropriate in any given circumstances; it is what, in the speeches in the play, is related to the arts of politics and rhetoric. The older dramatic poets made their characters talk like statesmen, whereas those of today make them talk like rhetoricians. Character is that which reveals personal choice, the kinds of thing a man chooses or rejects when that is not obvious. Thus there is no revelation of character in speeches in which the speaker shows no preferences or aversions whatever. Thought, on the other hand, is present in speeches where something is being shown to be true or untrue, or where some general opinion is being expressed.

Fourth comes the diction of the speeches. By diction I mean, as I have already explained, the expressive use of words, and this has the same force in verse and in prose.

Of the remaining elements, the music is the most important of the pleasurable additions to the play. Spectacle, or stage-effect, is an attraction, of course, but it has the least to do with the playwright's craft or with the art of poetry. For the power of tragedy is independent both of performance and of actors, and besides, the production of spectacular effects is more the province of the property-man than of the playwright.

Now that these definitions have been established, I must go on to discuss the arrangement of the incidents, for this is of the first importance in tragedy. I have already laid down that tragedy is the representation of an action that is complete and whole and of a certain amplitude—for a thing may be whole and yet lack amplitude. Now a whole is that which has a beginning, a middle, and an end. A beginning is that which does not necessarily come after something else, although something else exists or comes about after it. An end, on the contrary, is that which naturally follows something else either as a necessary or as a usual consequence, and is not itself followed by anything. A middle is that which follows something else, and is itself followed by something. Thus well-constructed plots must neither begin nor end in a haphazard way, but must conform to the pattern I have been describing.

Furthermore, whatever is beautiful, whether it be a living creature or an object made up of various parts, must necessarily not only have its parts properly ordered, but also be of an appropriate size, for beauty is bound up with size and order. A minutely small creature, therefore, would not be beautiful, for it would take almost no time to see it and our perception of it would be blurred; nor would an extremely large one, for it could not be taken in all at once, and its unity and wholeness would be lost to the view of the beholder—if, for example, there were a creature a thousand miles long.

Now in just the same way as living creatures and organisms compounded of many parts must be of a reasonable size, so that they can be easily taken in by the eye, so too plots must be of a reasonable length, so that they may be easily held in the memory. The limits in length to be observed, in as far as they concern performance on the stage, have nothing to do with dramatic art; for if a hundred tragedies had to be performed in the dramatic contests, they would be regulated in length by the water-clock, as indeed it is said they were at one time.[1] With regard to the limit set by the nature of the action, the longer the story is the more beautiful it will be, provided that it is quite clear. To give a simple definition, a length which, as a matter either of probability or of necessity, allows of a change from misery to happiness or from happiness to misery is the proper limit of length to be observed.

A plot does not possess unity, as some people suppose, merely because it is about one man. Many things, countless things indeed, may happen to one man, and some of them will not contribute to any kind of unity; and similarly he may carry out many actions from which no single unified action will emerge. It seems, therefore, that all those poets have been on the wrong track who have written a *Heracleid*, or a *Theseid*,[2] or some other poem of this kind, in the belief that, Heracles being a single person, his story must necessarily possess unity. Homer, exceptional in this as in all other respects, seems, whether by art or by instinct, to have been well aware of what was required. In writing his *Odyssey* he did not put in everything that happened to Odysseus, that he was wounded on Mount Parnassus, for example, or that he feigned madness at the time of the call to arms,[3] for it was not a matter of necessity or probability that either of these incidents should have led to the other; on the contrary, he constructed the *Odyssey* round a single action of the kind I have spoken of, and he did this with the *Iliad* too. Thus, just as in the other imitative arts each individual representation is the representation of a single object, so too the plot of a play, being the representation of an action, must present it as a unified whole; and its various incidents must be so arranged that if any one of them is differently placed or taken away the effect of wholeness will be seriously disrupted. For if the presence or absence of something makes no apparent difference, it is no real part of the whole.

---

[1] There is no evidence elsewhere that this was ever done, and it seems an improbable proceeding. [Translator's note.]

[2] *Heracleid . . . Theseid*: Long narrative poems about the adventures of Heracles and Theseus.

[3] **call to arms:** Action that happened prior to the beginning of *The Iliad*.

❧ BUDDHIST TEXTS
INDIA, FOURTH CENTURY B.C.E.–FIRST CENTURY C.E.

Two great religions were born in India in the sixth century B.C.E., Buddhism and Jainism. **BUDDHISM**, founded by Siddhartha Gautama, the Buddha (563–483 B.C.E.), and **JAINISM**,[1] started by Mahavira (C. 539–468 B.C.E.), arose during a time of great ferment and change in the northeastern provinces of Bihar and Uttar Pradesh. Rival princes and clans in northern India were warring at a time when old tribal structures were breaking down. Simultaneously, urban centers were developing along with a growing middle class. Conditions were ripe for a rebellion against **HINDUISM**, the entrenched religious system of the priestly caste, the **BRAHMINS**,[2] which was becoming more and more rigid in terms of social caste, religious ritual, and the hierarchy of privilege. The gap between rich and poor, literate and illiterate, widened. A sense of hopelessness and dissatisfaction spread among ordinary people.

Both Jainism and Buddhism came into being as part of a heretic tradition of sages who challenged the **VEDIC** tradition behind Hinduism, offering alternatives to urban merchants by shifting the dialogue from social class to personal conduct. Both Buddhism and Jainism promoted a new ethic of compassion—noninjury to all living things—and salvation from *SAMSARA*, the endless round of death and birth, through understanding the basic truths of the universe. In effect they taught that knowledge, the disciplined practice of meditation and learning, and the path of austerity could lead directly to *MOKSHA*, or identification with the universal spirit or world soul; this approach bypassed the role of the priests—an old story in world religion.

Buddhism has had an enormous influence on art, architecture, literature, and institutions for some two millennia. The image of the Buddha as a spiritual being, especially, continues to attract admirers, followers, and imitators. The texts that follow describe both the Buddha's life and his early teachings. A famous biography of the Buddha, written by Ashvaghosha, a Buddhist poet of the first century C.E., covers the major events of the holy man's life. The Buddha's "Sermon at Benares" contains the basic truths of his path to salvation. Another selection deals with the proper mental attitude required for following his recommendations. The Buddha's last instructions before he died reduced his teachings to very simple but extremely difficult to follow lessons. The Buddha was a

> [Buddha] was undoubtedly one of the greatest rationalists of all time, resembling in this respect no one as much as Socrates. Every problem that came his way was automatically subjected to the cold, analytical glare of his intellect. . . . The remarkable fact, however, was the way this objective, critical component of his character was balanced by a Franciscan tenderness so strong as to have caused his message to be subtitled "a religion of infinite compassion."
>
> – HUSTON SMITH, philosopher, 1958

---

[1] **Buddhism . . . Jainism:** Buddhism spread throughout the world and has grown to about 400 million followers. Jainism, derived from the word *Jina*, meaning "conqueror," advocates overcoming all human passions and practicing *ahimsa*, or noninjury to all living creatures. There are between one and two million Jains in India.

[2] **Brahmins:** Members of the priestly class in the caste system of India; the other three original classes were *Kshatriya* (warriors and administrators), *Vaishya* (merchants, farmers, producers), and *Shudra* (laborers).

Hindu Divinities Pay Homage to Buddha, second century B.C.E.
With the founding of Buddhism in the fifth century B.C.E., a new world religion was born. In this relief, Hindu gods venerate Buddha, represented as the enthroned wheel of law. (Victoria and Albert Museum, London / Art Resource, NY)

www For a quiz on Buddhist texts, see bedfordstmartins .com/worldlit compact.

unique blend of head and heart, whose rational approach to problem-solving resembled that of the Greek philosopher Socrates.[3]

Beginning Life as a Prince. Typically the biographies of great religious prophets are written only after they die, when fame and spiritual fervor become intertwined with their historical legacy. As with nearly all founders of world religions in the ancient world—Moses, Zoroaster,

---

[3] **Socrates** (469–399 B.C.E.): A philosopher of ancient Greece, Socrates examined common knowledge with a step-by-step questioning of accepted truths. See p. 715.

Jesus, Laozi, and Mohammed—the Buddha's life story has become a confusing mix of myth, folklore, beliefs, and history. The earliest written accounts of Buddha's life are dated about 200 years after his death.

Siddhartha Gautama was born in 563 B.C.E. at Lumbini, near the town of Kapilavatthu in the Himalayan foothills of southern Nepal, about a hundred miles north of Varanasi (Benares). His father was King or Rajah **Shuddhodana** of the **Sakya** Clan, of the *Kshatriya*, or warrior, caste. Later in life Siddhartha would be called, among several other names, Sakyamuni, meaning "the sage of the Sakyas." Siddhartha's mother was Maya, described by Ashvaghosha in the excerpt presented here as pure and immaculate. According to legend, Siddhartha was born miraculously: He descended from the Tushita heaven,[4] entered the womb of his mother, Maya, as a wondrous white elephant, and was born painlessly from her side. He came forth "Like the sun bursting from a cloud in the morning . . . with his rays which dispelled the darkness."

shoo-DOH-duh-nuh;
SAH-kyuh;
KSHUH-tree-yuh

The Four Signs.   A wise man told Siddhartha's father that his son would be either a king or a wandering holy man. His father wanted Siddhartha to be a king, so he raised his son in great physical comfort, shielding him from human suffering and any other unpleasant reality. Siddhartha eventually married Yashodhara, and together they had a son, Rahula. One day, however, at age twenty-nine, the prince desired to go outside the palace gates. There he met four men who changed his life: an old man, a sick man, a dead man, and an ascetic—a man who had renounced the world. This series of encounters, known as the "Four Signs," represented a time of awakening for Siddhartha, who had known only the sensuous pleasures provided by his father. He learned about the reality of suffering and death, and realized that he would not be young and beautiful forever. He left the luxurious life of the palace, and his wife and child, and ventured into the world to find answers to questions raised by his awareness of mortality.

The Path of Asceticism.   Following the path taken by the ascetic, or holy man, Siddhartha tried sitting for long periods of time in yoga postures meditating. Dissatisfied, he turned to fasting and disciplining his body. After coming close to death, he took food and seated himself beneath a fig tree (a *ficus religiosa*) at Bodhgaya, sixty miles south of Patna and one of the four holy places of Buddhism. It was here that he made his famous pronouncement: "I will not rise from this position on the earth until I have obtained my utmost aim."

Enlightenment.   He sat under the "Bodhi tree" (*bodhi* is Sanskrit for "enlightenment") for forty-nine days. According to legend the original tree was destroyed by the Bengali king Shashanka in the seventh century. An offshoot of the tree still exists today beside the Mahabodhi Temple in Bodhgaya, the most important pilgrimage site for Buddhists from

---

[4]**Tushita heaven:** The heaven of all the buddhas who are awaiting rebirth on earth.

Siddhartha Goes to School, second–fourth century

The Buddha began life as a privileged member of the Indian aristocracy. Here he is shown in relief being escorted to school by various servants and retainers. Siddhartha's early years were extremely sheltered, as his father tried to protect him from the harsh realities of the world. (Victoria and Albert Museum, London / Art Resource, NY)

[Buddhism] has the honorable distinction of being the most tolerant, in theory and history, of the world-faiths.

– E. ROYSTON PIKE, theologian, 1958

around the world. After being attacked by Mara, the Buddhist demon, who tempted him with sexuality and threats of physical harm, Siddhartha learned about the condition of all beings, the causes of birth and rebirth. He recalled his own previous existences, patterns of cause and effect. He understood what caused human pain and how to alleviate it. When the next morning came, the BODHISATTVA — someone en route to buddhahood who assists others — at age thirty-five was enlightened. He had attained perfect illumination. Just as Jesus of Nazareth became the Christ — meaning the "anointed one" — so Siddhartha Gautama became the Buddha — the "awakened one." There are ten titles that the Buddha used for himself and other buddhas, one of which is TATHAGATA, Sanskrit for "he who has arrived at the truth."

The Wandering Teacher and Preacher. Instead of entering NIRVANA[5] immediately, Buddha decided to remain on earth to teach others his new

---

[5] Nirvana: From *nirva*, meaning "to blow," thus an extinguishing of the individual flame of life. In both Hinduism and Buddhism, Nirvana represents a release from the endless transmigration of the soul. In Hinduism, Nirvana is a reunion with Brahma; Buddhism sees Nirvana as a state of blissful nonbeing.

understanding of human suffering and thus lead them to salvation.[6] He preached his first sermon on the fundamentals of what became Buddhism north of Varanasi at Sarnath, in a deer park at Isipatana, to five ascetics who became his first disciples. There he proclaimed the Middle Way, or Path, a road between the extremes of sensuous indulgence and senseless mortification. Although Buddhism takes various forms in various countries, all varieties preserve the same basic doctrines, which are psychological rather than theological. The Four Noble Truths are: Suffering and pain exist (old age, sickness, death, etc.); pain and suffering is caused by our attachments or desires; one can become freed from suffering; and freedom can be gained by following the Eightfold Path. The Eightfold Path is a practical, day-by-day plan for self-improvement: Right Belief,[7] Right Resolve, Right Speech, Right Behavior, Right Occupation, Right Effort, Right Mindfulness, and Right Concentration. The core teachings also include an injunction against killing, forgiveness of enemies, the importance of motive in ethics, and tolerance.

The Buddha then spent forty-five years wandering and teaching, spending time in monasteries donated by wealthy followers to his SANGHA, or communities of monks. He had indeed become the wandering holy man, not a king, the two possible destinies divined as possibilities for him in his childhood. After a last message to his followers to work out their salvation with diligence, Buddha died in the arms of his beloved disciple Ananda at the age of eighty. He was cremated, and his ashes were distributed amongst eight shrines, or *stupas*.

Buddhism Spreads throughout Asia. The Buddha's teachings spread throughout India, and for a millennium they were favored among the ruling classes. One of Buddhism's high points occurred during the reign of the emperor Ashoka (c. 273–c. 232 B.C.E.), the third ruler of the Maurya dynasty (c. 322–c. 185 B.C.E.), which had unified India for the first time. Ashoka converted to Buddhism, erected monasteries, and sent missionaries to Syria, Egypt, and Greece. With its prosperity and the flourishing of art, Ashoka's reign was considered a golden age in ancient India. After hundreds of years, Buddhism gradually died out in India, however, especially after the Muslim invasion in the twelfth century. In the meantime it had spread into Sri Lanka, Burma, and Indonesia in the form of Hinayana or Theravada[8] (School of the Elders) and into China, Japan, Korea, Nepal, and Tibet in the form of Mahayana[9] (Great Career or Great

> Gautama the Buddha seems to have combined in high degree two qualities that are rarely found together and each of which is rarely exemplified in high degree. On the one hand he was a man of rich and responsive human sympathy, of unfailing patience, strength, gentleness, and good will . . . On the other hand, he was a thinker, of unexcelled philosophic power. . . . Buddhism is the only one of the great religions of the world that is consciously and frankly based on a systematic rational analysis of the problem of life, and of the way to its solution.
>
> – E. A. BURTT, philosopher, 1955

---

[6] **salvation:** The *bodhisattva* remains on earth to lead others to salvation.

[7] **Right Belief:** The Sanskrit word for *right* is *samma*, which can mean both right as opposed to wrong and right as in completed or perfected.

[8] **Hinayana or Theravada:** Basic to this branch of Buddhism is a concern with becoming enlightened personally. The principal guide is one's mind or understanding, not ritual or prayer. Buddha is a saint and teacher.

[9] **Mahayana:** This branch of Buddhism is more social in nature, concerned not only with saving the self but also with reaching out to others. The principal guide is one's heart or compassion as strengthened by complex ritual and prayer. Buddha is the savior.

Vehicle). Through time Buddhism has proved to be unimpeded by cultural lines, diverse environments, and changing world conditions.

The enduring influence of Buddhism has extended to some 400 million Buddhists worldwide. Some consider it to be a form of meditation or yoga, and Buddhist meditation centers have sprung up in all parts of the world. Some value Buddhism's ethical system and relate it to ecology. Still others view it as a cosmology, a way of viewing the world. Although originally it was antiauthoritarian, antiritualistic, and nontheistic, some followers nevertheless view Buddhist doctrine as a form of authority, practice Buddhist ritual, and believe the Buddha to be a savior.

Buddhist Texts.   Ashvaghosha (c. 100 C.E.), one of the great Buddhist poets, wrote two long poems, three plays, and various hymns. Tradition suggests that he lived his life in the court of King Kanishka I (first century C.E.) in northern India. One of Ashvaghosha's long Sanskrit poems is *The Life of Buddha (Buddhacarita)*. **Ashvaghosha** employs rich metaphors and imagery in this work to create a divine or supernatural context for Gautama's journey to enlightenment.

ush-vuh-GOH-shuh

The early Buddhists apparently distinguished themselves from the Brahmins and Brahmanic Sanskrit by speaking Pali, a colloquial Indian dialect derived from Sanskrit. Buddhist teachings and commentaries, passed down orally for several hundred years, were written down in Pali by Buddhists in south India and Ceylon in the first century B.C.E. and collected in the Pali Canon. The second division *(Pitaka)* of the Pali Canon, called *The Dhamma* ("Doctrine"), is a collection of sermons and discourses, including commentaries by the Buddha's disciples.

"The Sermon at Benares: The Four Noble Truths" comes from a collection of shorter discourses in the Pali Canon called *Samyutta Nikaya*, or *Connected Group*. According to tradition, the Buddha's first sermon was given north of Varanasi in Sarnath to five ascetics who had earlier abandoned him when he gave up self-mortification and starvation. The Buddha redirects the attention of the five listeners from physical practices to questions of consciousness or understanding. "Right Mindfulness" from the *Majjhima Nikaya*, or *Medium Group*, shorter discourses in the Pali canon, deals with the transience of all life. It is a good example of the Buddha's teaching techniques. Though it comes seventh in the Noble Eightfold Path, it is the basis for all the previous stages since it involves the extension of awareness into every thought and deed. The material devoted to the last days and the death of the Buddha, "The Last Instructions of the Buddha," comes from *Discourse of the Great Passing-away (Mahaparinibbana Sutta),* which is collected in the *Digha Nikaya,* or the *Long Group,* long discourses on the Pali Canon. This extended document describes the last years of the Buddha's life, his return to the hills where he was born, and his last meal in which poisonous mushrooms were accidentally included. His final instructions came after he briefly recovered from illness. Ananda, which means "absolute joy," was one of the ten great disciples of the Buddha. Because of Ananda, the Buddha consented to founding an order of nuns.

■ **FURTHER RESEARCH**

The Buddha
Foucher, C. A. *The Life of the Buddha*. 1963.
Johnston, E. H., trans. *Aśvaghoṣa's Buddhacarita or Acts of the Buddha*. 1978.
Khosla, Sarla. *Asvaghosa and His Times*. 1986.
Oldenberg, Hermann. *Buddha: His Life, His Doctrine, His Order*. 1971.
Thomas, Edward Joseph. *The Life of Buddha as Legend and History*. 1952.

Buddhism
Conze, Edward. *Buddhist Scriptures*. 1959.
De Bary, William Theodore, ed. *The Buddhist Tradition in India, China, and Japan*.
    1969.
Gombrich, Richard. *Theravada Buddhism*. 1988.
Ishikawa, Jun. *The Bodhisattva*. 1990.
Kalupahana, David J. *Buddhist Thought and Ritual*. 1991.
Ray, Reginald A. *Buddhist Saints in India: A Study in Buddhist Values and Orientations*.
    1994.
Sadakata, Akira. *Buddhist Cosmology: Philosophy and Origins*. 1997.
Santiago, J. R. *Sacred Symbols of Buddhism*. 1991.
Tsomo, Karma Lekshe, ed. *Buddhist Women Across Cultures*. 1999.

■ **PRONUNCIATION**

Ashvaghosha (Asvagosha): ush-vuh-GOH-shuh
Dīgha Nikāya: DEE-guh nih-KAH-yuh
Kshatriya: KSHUH-tree-yuh
Mahāparinibbāna Sutta: muh-huh-pah-rih-nee-BAH-nuh SOO-tuh
Majjhima Nikāya: MUH-jih-muh nih-KAH-yuh
Sakya: SAH-kyuh, SHAH-kyuh
Samyutta Nikāya: sum-YOO-tuh nih-KAH-yuh
Shuddhodana (Suddhodana): shoo-DOH-duh-nuh

༄ **ASHVAGHOSHA**
INDIA, C. 100 C.E.

FROM

༄ **The Life of Buddha**

Translated by E. B. Cowell

[BIRTH AND CHILDHOOD]

There was a city, the dwelling-place of the great saint Kapila, having its sides surrounded by the beauty of a lofty broad table-land as by a line of clouds, and itself,
with its high-soaring palaces, immersed in the sky. [. . .]

A king, by name Suddhodana, of the kindred of the sun, anointed to stand at the head of earth's monarchs,—ruling over the city, adorned it, as a bee-inmate a full-blown lotus.

The very best of kings with his train ever near him,—intent on liberality yet devoid of pride; a sovereign, yet with an ever equal eye thrown on all,—of gentle nature and yet with wide-reaching majesty. [. . .]

He, the monarch of the Sâkyas,[1] of native pre-eminence, but whose actual pre-eminence was brought about by his numberless councillors of exalted wisdom, shone forth all the more gloriously, like the moon amidst the stars shining with a light like its own.

To him there was a queen, named Mâyâ, as if free from all deceit (mâyâ)—an effulgence proceeding from his effulgence, like the splendour of the sun when it is free from all the influence of darkness,—a chief queen in the united assembly of all queens.

Like a mother to her subjects, intent on their welfare,—devoted to all worthy of reverence like devotion itself,—shining on her lord's family like the goddess of prosperity,—she was the most eminent of goddesses to the whole world. [. . .]

Then falling from the host of beings in the Tushita heaven,[2] and illumining the three worlds, the most excellent of Bodhisattvas suddenly entered at a thought into her womb, like the Nâga-king[3] entering the cave of Nandâ.

Assuming the form of a huge elephant white like Himâlaya, armed with six tusks, with his face perfumed with flowing ichor, he entered the womb of the queen of king Suddhodana, to destroy the evils of the world. [. . .]

Then one day by the king's permission the queen, having a great longing in her mind, went with the inmates of the gynaeceum into the garden Lumbinî.

As the queen supported herself by a bough which hung laden with a weight of flowers, the Bodhisattva suddenly came forth, cleaving open her womb.

At that time the constellation Pushya was auspicious, and from the side of the queen, who was purified by her vow, her son was born for the welfare of the world, without pain and without illness.

Like the sun bursting from a cloud in the morning,—so he too, when he was born from his mother's womb, made the world bright like gold, bursting forth with his rays which dispelled the darkness. [. . .]

Having thus in due time issued from the womb, he shone as if he had come down from heaven, he who had not been born in the natural way,—he who was

---

A note on the translation: Seventeen cantos, or books, of the original *The Life of Buddha* by Ashvaghosha remain. Significant happenings in the Buddha's life—his miraculous birth, The Four Signs, his search for answers among the ascetics, sitting underneath the Bodhi tree, and the moment of enlightenment—are recounted in this prose translation of the poetic text.

All notes are the editors'. The excerpts are designated by ellipses.

---

[1] **Sâkyas:** The Sakya clan of the *Kshatriya,* or warrior, caste; later in his life the Buddha was referred to as Sakya-muni, meaning "the sage of the Sakyas."

[2] **Tushita heaven:** A special heavenly abode for buddhas awaiting incarnation.

[3] **Nâga-king:** King of the serpents or dragons.

born full of wisdom, not foolish,—as if his mind had been purified by countless aeons of contemplation.

With glory, fortitude, and beauty he shone like the young sun descended upon the earth; when he was gazed at, though of such surpassing brightness, he attracted all eyes like the moon. [. . .]

[THE PROPHECY OF A WANDERING SAGE]

Then having learned by signs and through the power of his penances this birth of him who was to destroy all birth, the great seer Asita[4] in his thirst for the excellent Law came to the palace of the Sâkya king.

Him shining with the glory of sacred knowledge and ascetic observances, the king's own priest,—himself a special student among the students of sacred knowledge,—introduced into the royal palace with all due reverence and respect.

He entered into the precincts of the king's gynaeceum, which was all astir with the joy arisen from the birth of the young prince,—grave from his consciousness of power, his pre-eminence in asceticism, and the weight of old age.

Then the king, having duly honoured the sage, who was seated in his seat, with water for the feet and an arghya offering,[5] invited him (to speak) with all ceremonies of respect [. . .]

The sage, being thus invited by the king, filled with intense feeling as was due, uttered his deep and solemn words, having his large eyes opened wide with wonder: [. . .]

'But hear now the motive for my coming and rejoice thereat; a heavenly voice has been heard by me in the heavenly path, that thy son has been born for the sake of supreme knowledge. [. . .]

'Having forsaken his kingdom, indifferent to all worldly objects, and having attained the highest truth by strenuous efforts, he will shine forth as a sun of knowledge to destroy the darkness of illusion in the world.

'He will deliver by the boat of knowledge the distressed world, borne helplessly along, from the ocean of misery which throws up sickness as its foam, tossing with the waves of old age, and rushing with the dreadful onflow of earth. [. . .]

Having heard these words, the king with his queen and his friends abandoned sorrow and rejoiced; thinking, 'such is this son of mine,' he considered that his excellence was his own.

But he let his heart be influenced by the thought, 'he will travel by the noble path,'—he was not in truth averse to religion, yet still he saw alarm at the prospect of losing his child. [. . .]

When he had passed the period of childhood and reached that of middle youth, the young prince learned in a few days the various sciences suitable to his race, which generally took many years to master.

---

[4] **Asita:** Asita is a wandering sage who predicts that the son of Suddhodana "will shine forth as a sun of knowledge to destroy the darkness of illusion in the world." King Suddhodana, who is growing old, wants his son to succeed him.

[5] **arghya offering:** An offering to a divinity involving the use of flowers, sandalwood paste, grass, and rice.

But having heard before from the great seer Asita his destined future which was to embrace transcendental happiness, the anxious care of the king of the present Sâkya race turned the prince to sensual pleasures.

Then he sought for him from a family of unblemished moral excellence a bride possessed of beauty, modesty, and gentle bearing, of wide-spread glory, Yasodharâ by name, having a name well worthy of her, a very goddess of good fortune. [. . .]

In course of time to the fair-bosomed Yasodharâ,—who was truly glorious in accordance with her name,—there was born from the son of Suddhodana a son named Râhula, with a face like the enemy of Râhu.[6]

Then the king who from regard to the welfare of his race had longed for a son and been exceedingly delighted [at his coming],—as he had rejoiced at the birth of his son, so did he now rejoice at the birth of his grandson. [. . .]

[AWAKENING TO AGE, DISEASE, AND DEATH]

On a certain day he heard of the forests carpeted with tender grass, with their trees resounding with the kokilas, adorned with lotus-ponds, and which had been all bound up in the cold season.

Having heard of the delightful appearance of the city groves beloved by the women, he resolved to go out of doors, like an elephant long shut up in a house.

The king, having learned the character of the wish thus expressed by his son, ordered a pleasure-party to be prepared, worthy of his own affection and his son's beauty and youth.

He prohibited the encounter of any afflicted common person in the highroad; 'heaven forbid that the prince with his tender nature should even imagine himself to be distressed.'

Then having removed out of the way with the greatest gentleness all those who had mutilated limbs or maimed senses, the decrepit and the sick and all squalid beggars, they made the highway assume its perfect beauty. [. . .]

But then the gods, dwelling in pure abodes, having beheld that city thus rejoicing like heaven itself, created an old man to walk along on purpose to stir the heart of the king's son.

The prince having beheld him thus overcome with decrepitude and different in form from other men, with his gaze intently fixed on him, thus addressed his driver with simple confidence:

'Who is this man that has come here, O charioteer, with white hair and his hand resting on a staff, his eyes hidden beneath his brows, his limbs bent down and hanging loose,—is this a change produced in him or his natural state or an accident?'

Thus addressed, the charioteer revealed to the king's son the secret that should have been kept so carefully, thinking no harm in his simplicity, for those same gods had bewildered his mind:

'That is old age by which he is broken down,—the ravisher of beauty, the ruin of vigour, the cause of sorrow, the destruction of delights, the bane of memories, the enemy of the senses.

---

[6] **Râhu:** A demon who causes eclipses by seizing the sun and the moon.

'He too once drank milk in his childhood, and in course of time he learned to grope on the ground; having step by step become a vigorous youth, he has step by step in the same way reached old age.'

Being thus addressed, the prince, starting a little, spoke these words to the charioteer, 'What! will this evil come to me also?' and to him again spoke the charioteer:

'It will come without doubt by the force of time through multitude of years even to my long-lived lord; all the world knows thus that old age will destroy their comeliness and they are content to have it so.' [. . .]

Drawing a long sigh and shaking his head, and fixing his eyes on that decrepit old man, and looking round on that exultant multitude he then uttered these distressed words:

'Old age thus strikes down all alike, our memory, comeliness, and valour; and yet the world is not disturbed, even when it sees such a fate visibly impending.

'Since such is our condition, O charioteer, turn back the horses,—go quickly home; how can I rejoice in the pleasure-garden, when the thoughts arising from old age overpower me?'

Then the charioteer at the command of the king's son turned the chariot back, and the prince lost in thought entered even that royal palace as if it were empty.

But when he found no happiness even there, as he continually kept reflecting, 'old age, old age,' then once more, with the permission of the king, he went out with the same arrangement as before.

Then the same deities created another man with his body all afflicted by disease; and on seeing him the son of Suddhodana addressed the charioteer, having his gaze fixed on the man:

'Yonder man with a swollen belly, his whole frame shaking as he pants, his arms and shoulders hanging loose, his body all pale and thin, uttering plaintively the word "mother," when he embraces a stranger,—who, pray, is this?'

Then his charioteer answered, 'Gentle Sir, it is a very great affliction called sickness, that has grown up, caused by the inflammation of the (three) humours, which has made even this strong man no longer master of himself.'

Then the prince again addressed him, looking upon the man compassionately, 'Is this evil peculiar to him or are all beings alike threatened by sickness?'

Then the charioteer answered, 'O prince, this evil is common to all; thus pressed round by diseases men run to pleasure, though racked with pain.'

Having heard this account, his mind deeply distressed, he trembled like the moon reflected in the waves of water; and full of sorrow he uttered these words in a low voice:

'Even while they see all this calamity of diseases mankind can yet feel tranquillity; alas for the scattered intelligence of men who can smile when still not free from the terrors of disease!

'Let the chariot, O charioteer, be turned back from going outside, let it return straight to the king's palace; having heard this alarm of disease, my mind shrinks into itself, repelled from pleasures.' [. . .]

Then the royal road being specially adorned and guarded, the king once more made the prince go out, having ordered the charioteer and chariot to proceed in a contrary direction (to the previous one).

But as the king's son was thus going on his way, the very same deities created a dead man, and only the charioteer and the prince, and none else, beheld him as he was carried dead along the road.

Then spoke the prince to the charioteer, 'Who is this borne by four men, followed by mournful companions, who is bewailed, adorned but no longer breathing?'

Then the driver,—having his mind overpowered by the gods who possess pure minds and pure dwellings,—himself knowing the truth, uttered to his lord this truth also which was not to be told:

'This is some poor man who, bereft of his intellect, senses, vital airs and qualities, lying asleep and unconscious, like mere wood or straw, is abandoned alike by friends and enemies after they have carefully swathed and guarded him.'

Having heard these words of the charioteer he was somewhat startled and said to him, 'Is this an accident peculiar to him alone, or is such the end of all living creatures?'

Then the charioteer replied to him, 'This is the final end of all living creatures; be it a mean man, a man of middle state, or a noble, destruction is fixed to all in this world.'

Then the king's son, sedate though he was, as soon as he heard of death, immediately sank down overwhelmed, and pressing the end of the chariot-pole with his shoulder spoke with a loud voice,

'Is this end appointed to all creatures, and yet the world throws off all fear and is infatuated! Hard indeed, I think, must the hearts of men be, who can be self-composed in such a road.

'Therefore, O charioteer, turn back our chariot, this is no time or place for a pleasure-excursion; how can a rational being, who knows what destruction is, stay heedless here, in the hour of calamity?' [. . .]

[THE PATH OF ASCETICISM]

Then one day accompanied by some worthy sons of his father's ministers, friends full of varied converse,—with a desire to see the glades of the forest and longing for peace, he went out with the king's permission.

Having mounted his good horse Kamthaka, decked with bells and bridle-bit of new gold, with beautiful golden harness and the chowrie waving, he went forth like the moon mounted on a comet.

Lured by love of the wood and longing for the beauties of the ground, he went to a spot near at hand on the forest-outskirts; and there he saw a piece of land being ploughed, with the path of the plough broken like waves on the water. [. . .]

There he sat down on the ground covered with leaves, and with its young grass bright like lapis lazuli; and, meditating on the origin and destruction of the world, he laid hold of the path that leads to firmness of mind.

Having attained to firmness of mind, and being forthwith set free from all sorrows such as the desire of worldly objects and the rest, he attained the first stage of contemplation, unaffected by sin, calm, and 'argumentative.' [. . .]

Thus did this pure passionless meditation grow within the great-souled one; and unobserved by the other men, there crept up a man in a beggar's dress.

The king's son asked him a question,—he said to him, 'Tell me, who art thou?' and the other replied, 'Oh bull of men, I, being terrified at birth and death, have become an ascetic for the sake of liberation.

'Desiring liberation in a world subject to destruction, I seek that happy inde-structible abode,—isolated from mankind, with my thoughts unlike those of others, and with my sinful passions turned away from all objects of sense.

'Dwelling anywhere, at the root of a tree, or in an uninhabited house, a mountain or a forest,—I wander without a family and without hope, a beggar ready for any fare, seeking only the highest good.'

When he had thus spoken, while the prince was looking on, he suddenly flew up to the sky; it was a heavenly inhabitant who, knowing that the prince's thoughts were other than what his outward form promised, had come to him for the sake of rous-ing his recollection.

When the other was gone like a bird to heaven, the foremost of men was rejoiced and astonished; and having comprehended the meaning of the term dharma,[7] he set his mind on the manner of the accomplishment of deliverance. [. . .]

Then the prince whose form was like the peak of a golden mountain,—whose eye, voice, and arm resembled a bull, a cloud, and an elephant,—whose counte-nance and prowess were like the moon and a lion,—having a longing aroused for something imperishable,—went into his palace.

Then stepping like a lion he went towards the king who was attended by his numerous counsellors, like Sanatkumâra in heaven waiting on Indra resplendent in the assembly of the Maruts.

Prostrating himself, with folded hands, he addressed him, 'Grant me graciously thy permission, O lord of men,—I wish to become a wandering mendicant for the sake of liberation, since separation is appointed for me.'

Having heard his words, the king shook like a tree struck by an elephant, and having seized his folded hands which were like a lotus, he thus addressed him in a voice choked with tears:

'O my son, keep back this thought, it is not the time for thee to betake thyself to dharma; they say that the practice of religion is full of evils in the first period of life when the mind is still fickle. [. . .]

'As separation is inevitable to the world, but not for Dharma, this separation is preferable; will not death sever me helplessly, my objects unattained and myself unsatisfied?'

The monarch, having heard this resolve of his son longing for liberation, and having again exclaimed, 'He shall not go,' set guards round him and the highest pleasures.

---

[7] **dharma:** The ideal order; the way things should be.

Then having been duly instructed by the counsellors, with all respect and affection, according to the sâstras, and being thus forbidden with tears by his father, the prince, sorrowing, entered into his palace. [. . .]

[THE SEARCH FOR ANSWERS]

Having awakened his horse's attendant, the swift Khamdaka, he thus addressed him: 'Bring me quickly my horse Kamthaka, I wish to-day to go hence to attain immortality.

'Since such is the firm content which to-day is produced in my heart, and since my determination is settled in calm resolve, and since even in loneliness I seem to possess a guide, — verily the end which I desire is now before me. [. . .]

The city-roads which were closed with heavy gates and bars, and which could be with difficulty opened even by elephants, flew open of their own accord without noise, as the prince went through.

Firm in his resolve and leaving behind without hesitation his father who turned ever towards him, and his young son, his affectionate people and his unparalleled magnificence, he then went forth out of his father's city.

Then he with his eyes long and like a full-blown lotus, looking back on the city, uttered a sound like a lion, 'Till I have seen the further shore of birth and death I will never again enter the city called after Kapila.' [. . .]

Then Yasodharâ fell upon the ground, like the ruddy goose parted from her mate, and in utter bewilderment she slowly lamented, with her voice repeatedly stopped by sobs:

'If he wishes to practise a religious life after abandoning me his lawful wife widowed, — where is his religion, who wishes to follow penance without his lawful wife to share it with him? [. . .]

'Even if I am unworthy to look on my husband's face with its long eyes and bright smile, still is this poor Râhula never to roll about in his father's lap?

'Alas! the mind of that wise hero is terribly stern, — gentle as his beauty seems, it is pitilessly cruel, — who can desert of his own accord such an infant son with his inarticulate talk, one who would charm even an enemy. [. . .]

For six years, vainly trying to attain merit, [Siddhartha] practised self-mortification, performing many rules of abstinence, hard for a man to carry out.

At the hours for eating, he, longing to cross the world whose farther shore is so difficult to reach, broke his vow with single jujube fruits, sesame seeds, and rice.

But the emaciation which was produced in his body by that asceticism, became positive fatness through the splendour which invested him. [. . .]

Then the seer, having his body evidently emaciated to no purpose in a cruel self-mortification, — dreading continued existence, thus reflected in his longing to become a Buddha:

'This is not the way to passionlessness, nor to perfect knowledge, nor to liberation; that was certainly the true way which I found at the root of the Gambu tree.[8]

---

[8] **Gambu tree:** A rose apple tree *(Eugenia jambos)* belonging to the myrtle family; it is an ornamental tree.

'But that cannot be attained by one who has lost his strength,'—so resuming his care for his body, he next pondered thus, how best to increase his bodily vigour: [. . .]

'True meditation is produced in him whose mind is self-possessed and at rest,—to him whose thoughts are engaged in meditation the exercise of perfect contemplation begins at once.

'By contemplation are obtained those conditions through which is eventually gained that supreme calm, undecaying, immortal state, which is so hard to be reached.'

Having thus resolved, 'this means is based upon eating food,' the wise seer of unbounded wisdom, having made up his mind to accept the continuance of life, [. . .]

Now at that time Nandabalâ, the daughter of the leader of the herdsmen, impelled by the gods, with a sudden joy risen in her heart, had just come near,

Her arm gay with a white shell, and wearing a dark blue woollen cloth, like the river Yamunâ, with its dark blue water and its wreath of foam.

She, having her joy increased by her faith, with her lotus-like eyes opened wide, bowed down before him and persuaded him to take some milk.

By partaking that food having made her obtain the full reward of her birth, he himself became capable of gaining the highest knowledge, all his six senses being now satisfied, [. . .]

Accompanied only by his own resolve, having fixed his mind on the attainment of perfect knowledge, he went to the root of an Asvattha tree,[9] where the surface of the ground was covered with young grass.

Then Kâla,[10] the best of serpents, whose majesty was like the lord of elephants, having been awakened by the unparalleled sound of his feet, uttered this praise of the great sage, being sure that he was on the point of attaining perfect knowledge: [. . .]

'Inasmuch as lines of birds fluttering in the sky offer thee reverential salutation, O lotus-eyed one, and inasmuch as gentle breezes blow in the sky, thou shalt certainly to-day become the Buddha.' [. . .]

Then he sat down on his hams in a posture, immovably firm and with his limbs gathered into a mass like a sleeping serpent's hood, exclaiming, 'I will not rise from this position on the earth until I have obtained my utmost aim.'

Then the dwellers in heaven burst into unequalled joy; the herds of beasts and the birds uttered no cry; the trees moved by the wind made no sound, when the holy one took his seat firm in his resolve.

[ENLIGHTENMENT]

When the great sage, sprung from a line of royal sages, sat down there with his soul fully resolved to obtain the highest knowledge, the whole world rejoiced; but Mâra,[11] the enemy of the good law, was afraid. [. . .]

---

[9] **Asvattha tree:** A fig tree, which has come to be known as the Bo tree (from *Bodhi,* enlightenment).

[10] **Kâla:** Naga king.

[11] **Mâra:** A Hindu demon who brings temptations and threats to the Buddha.

Then Mâra called to mind his own army, wishing to work the overthrow of the Sâkya saint; and his followers swarmed round, wearing different forms and carrying arrows, trees, darts, clubs, and swords in their hands;

Having the faces of boars, fishes, horses, asses, and camels, of tigers, bears, lions, and elephants,—one-eyed, many-faced, three-headed,—with protuberant bellies and speckled bellies;

Blended with goats, with knees swollen like pots, armed with tusks and with claws, carrying headless trunks in their hands, and assuming many forms, with half-mutilated faces, and with monstrous mouths;

Copper-red, covered with red spots, bearing clubs in their hands, with yellow or smoke-coloured hair, with wreaths dangling down, with long pendulous ears like elephants, clothed in leather or wearing no clothes at all; [. . .]

But the great sage having beheld that army of Mâra thus engaged in an attack on the knower of the Law, remained untroubled and suffered no perturbation, like a lion seated in the midst of oxen.

But a woman named Meghakâlî, bearing a skull in her hand, in order to infatuate the mind of the sage, flitted about unsettled and stayed not in one spot, like the mind of the fickle student over the sacred texts.

Another, fixing a kindling eye, wished to burn him with the fire of his glance like a poisonous serpent; but he saw the sage and lo! he was not there, like the votary of pleasure when true happiness is pointed out to him. [. . .]

[ACQUIRING KNOWLEDGE]

Then, having conquered the hosts of Mâra by his firmness and calmness, he the great master of meditation set himself to mediate, longing to know the supreme end.

And having attained the highest mastery in all kinds of meditation, he remembered in the first watch the continuous series of all his former births.

'In such a place I was so and so by name, and from thence I passed and came hither,' thus he remembered his thousands of births, experiencing each as it were over again.

And having remembered each birth and each death in all those various transmigrations, the compassionate one then felt compassion for all living beings. [. . .]

When the second watch came, he, possessed of unequalled energy, received a pre-eminent divine sight, he the highest of all sight-gifted beings.

Then by that divine perfectly pure sight he beheld the whole world as in a spotless mirror.

As he saw the various transmigrations and rebirths of the various beings with their several lower or higher merits from their actions, compassion grew up more within him. [. . .]

FROM

∾ Samyutta Nikaya

Translated by A. L. Basham

The Sermon at Benares: The Four Noble Truths

Thus I have heard. Once the Lord was at Vārānasī,[1] at the deer park called Isipatana. There he addressed the five monks:

There are two ends not to be served by a wanderer. What are these two? The pursuit of desires and of the pleasure which springs from desire, which is base, common, leading to rebirth, ignoble, and unprofitable; and the pursuit of pain and hardship, which is grievous, ignoble, and unprofitable. The Middle Way of the Tathāgata avoids both these ends. It is enlightened, it brings clear vision, it makes for wisdom, and leads to peace, insight, enlightenment, and Nirvāna. What is the Middle Way? . . . It is the Noble Eightfold Path—Right Views, Right Resolve, Right Speech, Right Conduct, Right Livelihood, Right Effort, Right Mindfulness,[2] and Right Concentration. This is the Middle Way. . . .

And this is the Noble Truth of Sorrow. Birth is sorrow, age is sorrow, disease is sorrow, death is sorrow; contact with the unpleasant is sorrow, separation from the pleasant is sorrow, every wish unfulfilled is sorrow—in short all the five components of individuality[3] are sorrow.

And this is the Noble Truth of the Arising of Sorrow. It arises from craving, which leads to rebirth, which brings delight and passion, and seeks pleasure now here, now there—the craving for sensual pleasure, the craving for continued life, the craving for power.

And this is the Noble Truth of the Stopping of Sorrow. It is the complete stopping of that craving, so that no passion remains, leaving it, being emancipated from it, being released from it, giving no place to it.

And this is the Noble Truth of the Way which Leads to the Stopping of Sorrow. It is the Noble Eightfold Path—Right Views, Right Resolve, Right Speech, Right Conduct, Right Livelihood, Right Effort, Right Mindfulness, and Right Concentration.

---

[1] **Vārānasī**: The ancient name of Benares, also spelled Banaras.

[2] **Right Mindfulness**: Becoming fully conscious of one's thoughts and deeds.

[3] **five components of individuality**: Forms, sensations, perceptions, psychic dispositions, and consciousness.

FROM

∾ Majjhima Nikaya

Translated by A. L. Basham

RIGHT MINDFULNESS

The Lord was staying at Sāvatthī at the monastery of Anāthapindaka in the Grove of Jeta. One morning he dressed, took his robe and bowl, and went into Sāvatthī for alms, with the Reverend Rāhula[1] following close behind him. As they walked the Lord, . . . without looking round, spoke to him thus:

"All material forms, past, present, or future, within or without, gross or subtle, base or fine, far or near, all should be viewed with full understanding—with the thought 'This is not mine, this is not I, this is not my soul.'"

"Only material forms, Lord?"

"No, not only material forms, Rāhula, but also sensation, perception, the psychic constructions, and consciousness."[2]

"Who would go to the village to collect alms today, when he has been exhorted by the Lord himself?" said Rāhula. And he turned back and sat cross-legged, with body erect, collected in thought.

Then the Venerable Sāriputta,[3] seeing him thus, said to him: "Develop concentration on inhalation and exhalation, for when this is developed and increased it is very productive and helpful."

Towards evening Rāhula rose and went to the Lord, and asked him how he could develop concentration on inhalation and exhalation. And the Lord said:

"Rāhula, whatever is hard and solid in an individual, such as hair, nails, teeth, skin, flesh, and so on, is called the personal element of earth. The personal element of water is composed of bile, phlegm, pus, blood, sweat, and so on. The personal element of fire is that which warms and consumes or burns up, and produces metabolism of food and drink in digestion. The personal element of air is the wind in the body which moves upwards or downwards, the winds in the abdomen and stomach, winds which move from member to member, and the inhalation and exhalation of the breath. And finally the personal element of space comprises the orifices of ears and nose, the door of the mouth, and the channels whereby food and drink enter, remain in, and pass out of the body. These five personal elements, together with the five external elements, make up the total of the five universal elements. They should all be regarded objectively, with right understanding, thinking 'This is not mine, this is not me, this is not my soul.' With this understanding attitude a man turns from the five elements and his mind takes no delight in them.

---

[1] **Rāhula:** The Buddha's son, who entered the *sangha,* or community of monks, at age seven. He is considered one of the ten great disciples of the Buddha.

[2] **not only . . . consciousness:** That is, the five components of individuality.

[3] **Sāriputta:** A chief disciple.

"Develop a state of mind like the earth, Rāhula. For on the earth men throw clean and unclean things, dung and urine, spittle, pus and blood, and the earth is not troubled or repelled or disgusted. And as you grow like the earth no contacts with pleasant or unpleasant will lay hold of your mind or stick to it.

"Similarly you should develop a state of mind like water, for men throw all manner of clean and unclean things into water and it is not troubled or repelled or disgusted. And similarly with fire, which burns all things, clean and unclean, and with air, which blows upon them all, and with space, which is nowhere established.

"Develop the state of mind of friendliness, Rāhula, for, as you do so, ill-will will grow less; and of compassion, for thus vexation will grow less; and of joy, for thus aversion will grow less; and of equanimity,[4] for thus repugnance will grow less.

"Develop the state of mind of consciousness of the corruption of the body, for thus passion will grow less; and of the consciousness of the fleeting nature of all things, for thus the pride of selfhood will grow less.

"Develop the state of mind of ordering the breath, . . . in which the monk goes to the forest, or to the root of a tree or to an empty house, and sits cross-legged with body erect, collected in thought. Fully mindful he inhales and exhales. When he inhales or exhales a long breath he knows precisely that he is doing so, and similarly when inhaling or exhaling a short breath. While inhaling or exhaling he trains himself to be conscious of the whole of his body, . . . to be fully conscious of the components of his mind, . . . to realize the impermanence of all things, . . . or to dwell on passionlessness . . . or renunciation. Thus the state of ordered breathing, when developed and increased, is very productive and helpful. And when the mind is thus developed a man breathes his last breath in full consciousness, and not unconsciously."

---

[4]**friendliness . . . equanimity:** The four cardinal virtues of Buddhism are friendliness, compassion, joy, and equanimity.

FROM

ꙮ Mahaparinibbana Sutta

Translated by A. L. Basham

The Last Instructions of the Buddha

Soon after this the Lord began to recover, and when he was quite free from sickness he came out of his lodging and sat in its shadow on a seat spread out for him. The Venerable Ānanda went up to him, paid his respects, sat down to one side, and spoke to the Lord thus:

"I have seen the Lord in health, and I have seen the Lord in sickness; and when I saw that the Lord was sick my body became as weak as a creeper, my sight dimmed, and all my faculties weakened. But yet I was a little comforted by the thought that the Lord would not pass away until he had left his instructions concerning the Order."

"What, Ānanda! Does the Order expect that of me? I have taught the truth without making any distinction between exoteric and esoteric doctrines; for . . . with the Tathāgata there is no such thing as the closed fist of the teacher who keeps some things back. If anyone thinks 'It is I who will lead the Order,' or 'The Order depends on me,' he is the one who should lay down instructions concerning the Order. But the Tathāgata has no such thought, so why should he leave instructions? I am old now, Ānanda, and full of years; my journey nears its end, and I have reached my sum of days, for I am nearly eighty years old. Just as a worn out cart can only be kept going if it is tied up with thongs, so the body of the Tathāgata can only be kept going by bandaging it. Only when the Tathāgata no longer attends to any outward object, when all separate sensation stops and he is deep in inner concentration, is his body at ease.

"So, Ānanda, you must be your own lamps, be your own refuges. Take refuge in nothing outside yourselves. Hold firm to the truth as a lamp and a refuge, and do not look for refuge to anything besides yourselves. A monk becomes his own lamp and refuge by continually looking on his body, feelings, perceptions, moods, and ideas in such a manner that he conquers the cravings and depressions of ordinary men and is always strenuous, self-possessed, and collected in mind. Whoever among my monks does this, either now or when I am dead, if he is anxious to learn, will reach the summit."

"All composite things must pass away. Strive onward vigilantly."[1]

---

[1] **"All composite . . . vigilantly"**: The Buddha's last words are sometimes translated as, "Work out your salvation with diligence."

ॐ Laozi (Lao Tzu)

China, c. Sixth Century–Third Century b.c.e.

dow-duh-JING;
tow-tay-CHING

low-DZUH

The collection of poems called the **Dao De Jing** (**Tao Te Ching**) is one of the most popular literary and religious classics in the world; in numbers of translations it is exceeded only by the Bible and the Bhagavad Gita. There are more than a hundred different translations of the Dao De Jing in English alone. It is almost impossible to date this text, just as it is difficult to pinpoint the origins of Daoism (Taoism), the influential religion associated with the Dao De Jing. Furthermore, **Laozi** (Lao Tzu), the legendary author of the Dao De Jing and founder of Daoism, remains a mystery. According to one legend, Laozi was an older contemporary of Confucius (551–479 b.c.e.). They each created very different schools of thought to address the social and political upheaval of the Warring States Period (c. 403–221 b.c.e.), a time when feudalism was decaying, the

Votive Offering of Laozi and Two Attendants, 587

The Chinese philosopher Laozi (Lao Tzu) is pictured in this small carved limestone votive stele, used to hold candles at shrines. 24 × 15 × 11.5 cm. (Special Chinese and Japanese Fund. Courtesy of the Museum of Fine Arts, Boston. Reproduced with permission. © 2000 Museum of Fine Arts, Boston. All rights reserved.)

commoner was emerging, and divisive wars among individual states were prevalent throughout China.

The ideas of Confucius and Laozi are almost totally opposite. Confucius's teachings are generally accessible; he emphasizes observing a hierarchy of loyalties, living deliberately according to prescribed ethical standards, and transforming society through political action. Laozi is more mysterious; he believes in individual, subjective truth, inaction, and a life lived in harmony with the DAO (the Way). Confucius was a

WWW For links to more information about Laozi see bedfordstmartins .com/worldlit compact.

pragmatist; he sought to impose order on the prevailing sociopolitical chaos through a system of guidelines and rules. Laozi, following in the tradition of **QUIETISM**,[1] was a mystic who thought that war was futile and that individuals should withdraw from conflict in order to develop inner resources.

Daoism.   Some scholars believe that Daoism arose in the fifth century B.C.E. as a response to the dominance of Confucian philosophy and politics in China and out of a desire to return to an earlier period of Chinese history when life was simpler and people lived close to nature. The history of Daoism becomes further complicated in the second century C.E. when a split occurred between philosophical Daoism, which is personal, contemplative, and nonsectarian, and religious Daoism, which is cultic and which uses divination and alchemy in an attempt to achieve immortality. The sampling of writings from the Dao De Jing presented here belong to philosophical Daoism, which is brought into focus by Witter Bynner: "Laotzu's quietism is nothing but the fundamental sense commonly inherent in mankind, a common-sense so profound in its simplicity that it has come to be called mysticism. . . . While most of us, as we use life, try to open the universe to ourselves, Laotzu opens himself to the universe."

The Mysterious Old Master.   No details are known with certainty about Laozi's life. Nothing is known about his parents, his childhood, or his education. There is no agreement about when he lived. One legend states that he was immaculately conceived and another that he was born already an old man with white hair and a beard. It was thought that for most of his existence he lived a secluded life as an ordinary bookkeeper of the imperial archives in the province of Honan. The most famous incident of his life occurs near the end of it. Sima Qian, in *Historical Records* (first century B.C.E.), summarizes his career:

> Lao Tzu practiced the Way and its Virtue. He learned to do his work in self-effacement and anonymity. For a long time he lived in Chou, and when he saw that it was breaking up, he left [riding a water buffalo]. At the frontier, the official Yin Hsi said: "Since, sir, you are retiring, I urge you to write me a book." So Lao Tzu wrote a book in two parts, explaining the Way and its Virtue in something over five thousand words. Then he went away. No one knows where he died.

The "book in two parts" is the Dao De Jing, which originally was called simply Laozi. Since the name Laozi means "the old philosopher" or "the old master," it is possible that Laozi was a generic name used for several poets who contributed to the Daoist collection.

Reading the Dao De Jing.   The exact dates for this text, like the dates for Laozi, are unknown. The text, which makes no reference to historical

---

[1] **Quietism:** Scholars use this term to characterize thinkers in the fourth century B.C.E. who advocated withdrawal from the turbulence of society and concentration on inner peace and harmony.

persons or events, was once thought to have originated as early as 500 B.C.E., but recently scholars have dated it in the fourth or third century B.C.E. The earliest known manuscript of the work comes from the Tang dynasty, about a thousand years later. It was probably in the fourth or third century B.C.E. that the text was edited to 5,000 characters divided into eighty-one verses. One of the difficulties of the poems in the Dao De Jing is that they do not provide explanations or definitions. The Dao De Jing begins with what seems to be a series of conclusions about the dao, a word and a concept for which we have no English equivalent.

The Chinese written character for dao is a combination of two characters, one for "head" and the other for "going." Together they have been translated as the "conscious path," "the way," "the flow," and even "God." The second word in the collection's title, *de*, means "virtue" and the third, *Jing*, means "classic" or "text." Altogether the title is something like *The Classic of the Way and Its Virtue*, or simply *The Way of Life*. The first two lines of the first poem in the book have been translated here as "Existence is beyond the power of words / To define." A literal translation would be, "Dao can dao not eternal Dao," or "Way can speak-about not eternal Way." Other translations include:

The Way that can be described is not the eternal Way.

The Flow that can be followed is not the real Flow.

God (the great everlasting infinite First Cause from whom all things in heaven and earth proceed) can neither be defined nor named.

There are ways but the Way is uncharted.

The complexity of Daoism's central tenet is not a deliberate attempt to mystify and confuse the reader, but a recognition of the nature of consciousness and the human tendency to reduce reality to words and definitions in order to conceptualize and categorize it. Language is a distinctly human construct that can only approximate or point to the ultimate, ineffable reality.

Laozi's first poem concludes with, "From wonder into wonder / Existence opens." This kind of writing is akin to proverbs and aphorisms, kernels of truth meant for meditation and contemplation. Pithy sayings were used in the wisdom tradition of the Middle East and are characteristic of the way that Jesus speaks in the New Testament. Although the truths of Daoism are stated simply, their meaning tends to be personal and subjective; the statements are not necessarily meant to be easily understood the first time one hears or reads them. Most of Laozi's poems demand repeated readings; furthermore, their meaning changes as one's circumstances change or as one grows older and gains more experience. Explaining Laozi's poems to others can be difficult.

One way to approach the idea of the dao is to imagine that life is an interrelated system, that all the parts fit together harmoniously, and that this whole system is moving through time, simply flowing along like a vast river, just about the way it should be, with overall purpose and meaning.

> If there is one book in the whole of Oriental literature which should be read above all others, it is, in my opinion, Laotzu's *Book of Tao* . . . It is one of the profoundest books in world philosophy . . . profound and clear, mystic and practical.
> – LIN YUTANG, philosopher, 1955

This flow might be called "the natural way"; Laozi advises: "Tao in the world is like a river flowing home to the sea." The Daoists thought of water as a close analogy for the dao. Water has tremendous power to support objects and carry them along, and with a strong current one learns not to thrash about or to try to go upstream but to swim with the flow, adjusting one's movements to those of the current. The only thing a person must do to be happy is to go along with this grand movement or flow, to let the flow in and out. The Chinese character for a swimmer means "one who knows the nature of water." The ancient Chinese described the two poles of this natural rhythm, the ebb and flow, as *yin* and *yang: Yin* is associated with darkness and enclosure, withdrawal and winter; *yang* is associated with light and openness, expansiveness and summer. At times *yin* is linked to the feminine and *yang* to the masculine, but in fact neither is strictly tied to gender or sex. *Yin* and *yang* are simply metaphors for describing a changing, reciprocal flow from one side to another, just as day flows from light to dark and back again, and the seasons flow from life to death to life again. *Yin* and *yang* are not irreconcilable opposites in the Christian sense of *good* and *evil.* Daoism recognizes a necessity of embracing both poles of the rhythm, both the light and the dark, both the external and the internal. It is essentially a question of merging with this rhythm that is at the heart of the universe, as if life were a dance.

If the Way is simple, why then does there appear to be such disharmony and unhappiness in life? The early Daoist philosophers suggested that people get into trouble when they actively try to control their lives by making arbitrary choices and dominating their surroundings instead of going with the flow. Because human consciousness perceives only a small portion, a fragment of the whole, people do not see how everything is connected and meaningful. People attempt to make adjustments in the world system without understanding it. When one steps outside of the natural flow of nature and attempts to manipulate and construct a better system, one introduces conflicting systems of values and, ultimately, confusion and disorder. The ancient Daoists prized the state of *wu wei*, which literally means "inaction," a way of doing without egotistical effort or motives of gain.

Instead of modeling their lives after symbols of strength and hierarchy—the warrior, the mountain, the spear, the blacksmith, the king— the founders of Daoism valued supple images that illustrate participating or assimilating: water, infants, females, valleys, dancing, swimming. In Witter Bynner's translation,

> Man, born tender and yielding,
> Stiffens and hardens in death.
> All living growth is pliant,
> Until death transfixes it. (#76)

■ **FURTHER RESEARCH**

Background
Gaer, Joseph. *What the Great Religions Believe.* 1963.
Smith, Huston. *The Religions of Man.* 1958.

Laozi
Chan, Wing-tsit, ed. *The Way of Lao Tzu.* 1963.
Chen, Ellen M. *The Tao Te Ching: A New Translation with Commentary.* 1989.
Henricks, Robert G. *Te-tao Ching: Translated from the Ma-wang-tui Texts.* 1993.
Mair, Victor H. *Tao Te Ching: An Entirely New Translation Based on the Recently Discovered Ma-Wang-Tui Manuscripts.* 1990.

■ PRONUNCIATION

Dao De Jing: dow-duh-JING
Laozi: low-DZUH
Tao Te Ching: tow-tay-CHING
Zhuangzi: jwahng-DZUH

⌘ Dao De Jing (Tao Te Ching)

Translated by Witter Bynner

ONE

Existence is beyond the power of words
To define:
Terms may be used
But are none of them absolute.
In the beginning of heaven and earth there were no words,
Words came out of the womb of matter;
And whether a man dispassionately
Sees to the core of life
Or passionately
Sees the surface,
The core and the surface
Are essentially the same,
Words making them seem different
Only to express appearance.
If name be needed, wonder names them both:
From wonder into wonder
Existence opens.

FIFTEEN

Long ago the land was ruled with a wisdom
Too fine, too deep, to be fully understood
And, since it was beyond men's full understanding,
Only some of it has come down to us, as in these sayings:
'Alert as a winter-farer on an icy stream,'

'Wary as a man in ambush,'
'Considerate as a welcome guest,'
'Selfless as melting ice,'
'Green as an uncut tree,'
10 'Open as a valley,'
And this one also, 'Roiled as a torrent.'
Why roiled as a torrent?
Because when a man is in turmoil how shall he find peace
Save by staying patient till the stream clears?
How can a man's life keep its course
If he will not let it flow?
Those who flow as life flows know
They need no other force:
They feel no wear, they feel no tear,
20 They need no mending, no repair.

Sixteen

Be utterly humble
And you shall hold to the foundation of peace.
Be at one with all these living things which, having arisen and flourished,
Return to the quiet whence they came,
Like a healthy growth of vegetation
Falling back upon the root.
Acceptance of this return to the root has been called 'quietism,'
Acceptance of quietism has been condemned as 'fatalism.'
But fatalism is acceptance of destiny
10 And to accept destiny is to face life with open eyes,
Whereas not to accept destiny is to face death blindfold.
He who is open-eyed is open-minded,
He who is open-minded is open-hearted,
He who is open-hearted is kingly,
He who is kingly is godly,
He who is godly is useful,
He who is useful is infinite,
He who is infinite is immune,
He who is immune is immortal.

Nineteen

Rid of formalized wisdom and learning
People would be a hundredfold happier,
Rid of conventionalized duty and honor
People would find their families dear,
Rid of legalized profiteering

People would have no thieves to fear.
These methods of life have failed, all three,
Here is the way, it seems to me:
Set people free,
As deep in their hearts they would like to be,
From private greeds
And wanton needs.

Twenty

Leave off fine learning! End the nuisance
Of saying yes to this and perhaps to that,
Distinctions with how little difference!
Categorical this, categorical that,
What slightest use are they!
If one man leads, another must follow,
How silly that is and how false!
Yet conventional men lead an easy life
With all their days feast-days,
A constant spring visit to the Tall Tower,
While I am a simpleton, a do-nothing,
Not big enough yet to raise a hand,
Not grown enough to smile,
A homeless, worthless waif.
Men of the world have a surplus of goods,
While I am left out, owning nothing.
What a booby I must be
Not to know my way round,
What a fool!
The average man is so crisp and so confident
That I ought to be miserable
Going on and on like the sea,
Drifting nowhere.
All these people are making their mark in the world,
While I, pig-headed, awkward,
Different from the rest,
Am only a glorious infant still nursing at the breast.

Twenty-eight

'One who has a man's wings
And a woman's also
Is in himself a womb of the world'
And, being a womb of the world,
Continuously, endlessly,

Gives birth;
One who, preferring light,
Prefers darkness also
Is in himself an image of the world
10   And, being an image of the world,
Is continuously, endlessly
The dwelling of creation;
One who is highest of men
And humblest also
Is in himself a valley of the world,
And, being a valley of the world,
Continuously, endlessly
Conducts the one source
From which vessels may be usefully filled;
20   Servants of the state are such vessels,
To be filled from undiminishing supply.

Twenty-nine

Those who would take over the earth
And shape it to their will
Never, I notice, succeed.
The earth is like a vessel so sacred
That at the mere approach of the profane
It is marred
And when they reach out their fingers it is gone.
For a time in the world some force themselves ahead
And some are left behind,
10   For a time in the world some make a great noise
And some are held silent,
For a time in the world some are puffed fat
And some are kept hungry,
For a time in the world some push aboard
And some are tipped out:
At no time in the world will a man who is sane
Over-reach himself,
Over-spend himself,
Over-rate himself.

Thirty-six

He who feels punctured
Must once have been a bubble,
He who feels unarmed
Must have carried arms,

He who feels belittled
Must have been consequential,
He who feels deprived
Must have had privilege,
Whereas a man with insight
10   Knows that to keep under is to endure.
What happens to a fish pulled out of a pond?
Or to an implement of state pulled out of a scabbard?
Unseen, they survive.

FORTY-TWO

Life, when it came to be,
Bore one, then two, then three
Elements of things;
And thus the three began
—Heaven and earth and man—
To balance happenings:
Cool night behind, warm day ahead,
For the living, for the dead.
Though a commoner be loth to say
10   That he is only common clay,
Kings and princes often state
How humbly they are leading,
Because in true succeeding
High and low correlate.
It is an ancient thought,
Which many men have taught,
That he who over-reaches
And tries to live by force
Shall die thereby of course,
20   And is what my own heart teaches.

FORTY-THREE

As the soft yield of water cleaves obstinate stone,
So to yield with life solves the insoluble:
To yield, I have learned, is to come back again.
But this unworded lesson,
This easy example,
Is lost upon men.

FORTY-SEVEN

There is no need to run outside
For better seeing,

Nor to peer from a window. Rather abide
At the center of your being;
For the more you leave it, the less you learn.
Search your heart and see
If he is wise who takes each turn:
The way to do is to be.

Seventy-four

Death is no threat to people
Who are not afraid to die;
But even if these offenders feared death all day,
Who should be rash enough
To act as executioner?
Nature is executioner.
When man usurps the place,
A carpenter's apprentice takes the place of the master:
And 'an apprentice hacking with the master's axe
10   May slice his own hand.'

Eighty-one

Real words are not vain,
Vain words not real;
And since those who argue prove nothing
A sensible man does not argue.
A sensible man is wiser than he knows,
While a fool knows more than is wise.
Therefore a sensible man does not devise resources:
The greater his use to others
The greater their use to him,
10   The more he yields to others
The more they yield to him.
The way of life cleaves without cutting:
Which, without need to say,
Should be man's way.

~ ZHUANGZI (CHUANG TZU)
CHINA, C. 369–286 B.C.E.

jwahng-DZUH

Like Laozi (Lao Tzu), the legendary founder of Daoism and author of the Dao De Jing, **Zhuangzi** addressed the turbulent times in China, the Warring States Period (403–221 B.C.E.), characterized by social and political upheaval. There were at least two basic approaches to conflict during this era, political reform and withdrawal into personal development. Confucius (551–479 B.C.E.), Mo Tzu (470–391 B.C.E.), and the so-called Legalists were thinkers who sought concrete social and political reforms that would bring about stability and peace. As a major interpreter of Daoism, Zhuangzi's attention was not on society as a whole but on the reformation of the individual through conforming to the Dao—the invisible, unifying flow that is reality. In a word, Zhuangzi's answer, as Burton Watson explains, was freedom.

Little Is Known about Zhuangzi's Life. Sima Qian (c. 145–85 B.C.E.) writes in his *Historical Records* that Zhuangzi (Chuang Tzu) was a native of Meng, in what is now Honan province. He was married, served as an official in the lacquer garden, and was a contemporary of King Hui of Liang (370–319 B.C.E.). He was certainly acquainted with the Daoism of Laozi and was a constant critic of Confucianism. His attitude toward government officials and high-paying positions is illustrated in the piece called "The Job Offer," in which he tells representatives of the king who have offered him an important position in the realm that he would rather be a tortoise dragging his tail in the mud than be "wrapped and boxed" by the king. His writings constitute a rather small book, some 100,000 words, mostly in the forms of fables, anecdotes, parables, and aphorisms that editors divided into thirty-three sections.

Merging with the Dao. Zhuangzi's ideas about the dao are similar to Laozi's, but Zhuangzi's emphasis is more psychological in the sense that the goal of his writings seems to be to free his readers from all the mental baggage that keeps them from merging with the grand scheme of nature (or Nature). By changing individual consciousness, Zhuangzi expects to change individual lives. He tells the story of a man who visits Laozi seeking help in his life. When Laozi asks the man why he brought a crowd of people along with him, the man turns around and sees no one behind him. The implication was that people carry negative experiences with them: old ideas, childhood training, bad advice, stereotypes, prejudice, guilt, shame—almost as if they were literally accompanied by parents, teachers, priests, and rulers forming a long procession behind them. It is this psychological burden that must be left behind in order to be free.

Zhuangzi's Writings. In order to entice readers into a freer state, Zhuangzi uses humor, illogical perceptions, debates, and incisive metaphors. Zhuangzi's swimmer explains that he is able to stay afloat in rough

The analogy most often used by Taoists to describe the "actionless activity" of *wu-wei* is water; as it follows the line of least resistance down a dry river bed, it pushes and recedes, it effortlessly penetrates every crack and crevice. When it meets resistance it merely rushes by, giving way and then filling up around hardness.

– RAYMOND
VAN OVER,
psychologist, 1973

waters because of his nature, not because of some special technique. An entirely different analogy is provided by the butcher who does not hack at the ox carcass but finds "the spaces between the joints" for cutting up the ox and preserving the edge on his knives. As in the story of the swimmer, the butcher's technique has a literal meaning, but it also symbolizes how one might live, with least effort and with self-care rather than by exerting a lot of energy fighting with tough, unyielding elements. In addition to the swimmer and the butcher, Zhuangzi's heroes are the woodcutter, the Yüan-ch'u bird, even the gamecock. In "The Wasted Gourd" and "The Ailanthus Tree," the focus is on imagination and intelligence, and the fact that, as the old saying goes, a person might not see the forest for the trees. Lacking imagination, individuals are involved in the incidentals and never envision the larger picture, the image of the One into which all particulars merge. Imagination is also the issue when Hui Tzu questions Zhuangzi about his intuition about the activities of fish in "What Fish Enjoy." In "Happiness," Zhuangzi stresses the importance of inaction; "I take inaction to be true happiness," he says. The Chinese word for inaction is *wu-wei*, which does not mean *no* action and withdrawal from life but rather refers to a lack of striving. As Burton Watson explains, inaction is ". . . a course of action that is not founded upon any purposeful motives of gain or striving. In such a state, all human actions become as spontaneous and mindless as those of the natural world." Daoist philosophy meets a critical test with the death of Zhuangzi's wife; when one might expect only grief and protestations about fate, Zhuangzi responds with both honesty and clarity. "The Death of Lao Tan" contains similar insights, as does "Transformations," in which men experience the physical changes brought on by growing old. Both aging and death are part of the grand scheme of Nature. An individual can choose to fight against the continuous transformation of all living things or can learn to adjust and, finally, to accept change. After Zhuangzi's wife died, the philosopher's attitude ultimately changed from grief to a celebration of his and his wife's participation in the larger pattern of the dao.

■ FURTHER RESEARCH

Background
Graham, A. C. *Disputers of the Tao: Philosophical Argument in Ancient China.* 1989.
Waley, Arthur. *Three Ways of Thought in Ancient China.* 1939.

Criticism
Giles, Herbert. *Chuang Tzu: Taoist Philosopher and Chinese Mystic.* 1961.
Wu, Kuang-ming. *The Butterfly as Companion: Meditations on the First Three Chapters of the Chuang Tzu.* 1990.

FROM

∾ Chuang Tzu: Basic Writings

Translated by Burton Watson

[THE WASTED GOURD]

Hui Tzu[1] said to Chuang Tzu, "The king of Wei gave me some seeds of a huge gourd. I planted them, and when they grew up, the fruit was big enough to hold five piculs.[2] I tried using it for a water container, but it was so heavy I couldn't lift it. I split it in half to make dippers, but they were so large and unwieldy that I couldn't dip them into anything. It's not that the gourds weren't fantastically big—but I decided they were no use and so I smashed them to pieces."

Chuang Tzu said, "You certainly are dense when it comes to using big things! In Sung there was a man who was skilled at making a salve to prevent chapped hands, and generation after generation his family made a living by bleaching silk in water. A traveler heard about the salve and offered to buy the prescription for a hundred measures of gold. The man called everyone to a family council. 'For generations we've been bleaching silk and we've never made more than a few measures of gold,' he said. 'Now, if we sell our secret, we can make a hundred measures in one morning. Let's let him have it!' The traveler got the salve and introduced it to the king of Wu, who was having trouble with the state of Yüeh. The king put the man in charge of his troops, and that winter they fought a naval battle with the men of Yüeh and gave them a bad beating. A portion of the conquered territory was awarded to the man as a fief. The salve had the power to prevent chapped hands in either case;[3] but one man used it to get a fief, while the other one never got beyond silk bleaching—because they used it in different ways. Now you had a gourd big enough to hold five piculs. Why didn't you think of making it into a great tub so you could go floating around the rivers and lakes, instead of worrying because it was too big and unwieldy to dip into things! Obviously you still have a lot of underbrush in your head!"

[THE AILANTHUS TREE]

Hui Tzu said to Chuang Tzu, "I have a big tree named ailanthus. Its trunk is too gnarled and bumpy to apply a measuring line to, its branches too bent and twisty to match up to a compass or square. You could stand it by the road and no carpenter would look at it twice. Your words, too, are big and useless, and so everyone alike spurns them!"

Chuang Tzu said, "Maybe you've never seen a wildcat or a weasel. It crouches down and hides, watching for something to come along. It leaps and races east and west, not hesitating to go high or low—until it falls into the trap and dies in the net.

---

[1] **Hui Tzu:** Stands for logical reasoning rather than imagination.

[2] **piculs:** A unit of weight used in Asia; one picul equals about 132 lbs.

[3] **case:** Preventing chapped hands allows for handling weapons.

Then again there's the yak, big as a cloud covering the sky. It certainly knows how to be big, though it doesn't know how to catch rats. Now you have this big tree and you're distressed because it's useless. Why don't you plant it in Not-Even-Anything Village, or the field of Broad-and-Boundless, relax and do nothing by its side, or lie down for a free and easy sleep under it? Axes will never shorten its life, nothing can ever harm it. If there's no use for it, how can it come to grief or pain?"

[WALKING TWO ROADS]

What is acceptable we call acceptable; what is unacceptable we call unacceptable. A road is made by people walking on it; things are so because they are called so. What makes them so? Making them so makes them so. What makes them not so? Making them not so makes them not so. Things all must have that which is so; things all must have that which is acceptable. There is nothing that is not so, nothing that is not acceptable.

For this reason, whether you point to a little stalk or a great pillar, a leper or the beautiful Hsi-shih, things ribald and shady or things grotesque and strange, the Way makes them all into one. Their dividedness is their completeness; their completeness is their impairment. No thing is either complete or impaired, but all are made into one again. Only the man of far-reaching vision knows how to make them into one. So he has no use [for categories], but relegates all to the constant. The constant is the useful; the useful is the passable; the passable is the successful; and with success, all is accomplished. He relies upon this alone, relies upon it and does not know he is doing so. This is called the Way.

But to wear out your brain trying to make things into one without realizing that they are all the same—this is called "three in the morning." What do I mean by "three in the morning"? When the monkey trainer was handing out acorns, he said, "You get three in the morning and four at night." This made all the monkeys furious. "Well, then," he said, "you get four in the morning and three at night." The monkeys were all delighted. There was no change in the reality behind the words, and yet the monkeys responded with joy and anger. Let them, if they want to. So the sage harmonizes with both right and wrong and rests in Heaven the Equalizer. This is called walking two roads.

[PENUMBRA AND SHADOW]

Penumbra said to Shadow, "A little while ago you were walking and now you're standing still; a little while ago you were sitting and now you're standing up. Why this lack of independent action?"

Shadow said, "Do I have to wait for something before I can be like this? Does what I wait for also have to wait for something before it can be like this? Am I waiting for the scales of a snake or the wings of a cicada? How do I know why it is so? How do I know why it isn't so?"[4]

---

[4] **so**: That is, to ordinary men the shadow appears to depend upon something else for its movement, just as the snake depends on its scales (according to Chinese belief) and the cicada on its wings. But do such causal views of action really have any meaning? (Translator's note.)

[The Dream and the Butterfly]

Once Chuang Chou[5] dreamt he was a butterfly, a butterfly flitting and fluttering around, happy with himself and doing as he pleased. He didn't know he was Chuang Chou. Suddenly he woke up and there he was, solid and unmistakable Chuang Chou. But he didn't know if he was Chuang Chou who had dreamt he was a butterfly, or a butterfly dreaming he was Chuang Chou. Between Chuang Chou and a butterfly there must be *some* distinction! This is called the Transformation of Things.

[Cutting Up the Ox]

Cook Ting was cutting up an ox for Lord Wen-hui. At every touch of his hand, every heave of his shoulder, every move of his feet, every thrust of his knee—zip! zoop! He slithered the knife along with a zing, and all was in perfect rhythm, as though he were performing the dance of the Mulberry Grove or keeping time to Ching-shou music.

"Ah, this is marvelous!" said Lord Wen-hui. "Imagine skill reaching such heights!"

Cook Ting laid down his knife and replied, "What I care about is the Way, which goes beyond skill. When I first began cutting up oxen, all I could see was the ox itself. After three years I no longer saw the whole ox. And now—now I go at it by spirit and don't look with my eyes. Perception and understanding have come to a stop and spirit moves where it wants. I go along with the natural makeup, strike in the big hollows, guide the knife through the big openings, and follow things as they are. So I never touch the smallest ligament or tendon, much less a main joint.

"A good cook changes his knife once a year—because he cuts. A mediocre cook changes his knife once a month—because he hacks. I've had this knife of mine for nineteen years and I've cut up thousands of oxen with it, and yet the blade is as good as though it had just come from the grindstone. There are spaces between the joints, and the blade of the knife has really no thickness. If you insert what has no thickness into such spaces, then there's plenty of room—more than enough for the blade to play about in. That's why after nineteen years the blade of my knife is still as good as when it first came from the grindstone.

"However, whenever I come to a complicated place, I size up the difficulties, tell myself to watch out and be careful, keep my eyes on what I'm doing, work very slowly, and move the knife with the greatest subtlety, until—flop! the whole thing comes apart like a clod of earth crumbling to the ground. I stand there holding the knife and look all around me, completely satisfied and reluctant to move on, and then I wipe off the knife and put it away."

"Excellent!" said Lord Wen-hui. "I have heard the words of Cook Ting and learned how to care for life!"

---

[5] **Chuang Chou:** Another name for Zhuangzi (Chuang Tzu).

[The Death of Lao Tan]

When Lao Tan[6] died, Ch'in Shih went to mourn for him; but after giving three cries, he left the room.

"Weren't you a friend of the Master?" asked Lao Tan's disciples.

"Yes."

"And you think it's all right to mourn him this way?"

"Yes," said Ch'in Shih. "At first I took him for a real man, but now I know he wasn't. A little while ago, when I went in to mourn, I found old men weeping for him as though they were weeping for a son, and young men weeping for him as though they were weeping for a mother. To have gathered a group like *that,* he must have done something to make them talk about him, though he didn't ask them to talk, or make them weep for him, though he didn't ask them to weep. This is to hide from Heaven, turn your back on the true state of affairs, and forget what you were born with. In the old days, this was called the crime of hiding from Heaven. Your master happened to come because it was his time, and he happened to leave because things follow along. If you are content with the time and willing to follow along, then grief and joy have no way to enter in. In the old days, this was called being freed from the bonds of God.

"Though the grease burns out of the torch, the fire passes on, and no one knows where it ends."[7]

[Transformations]

Master Ssu, Master Yü, Master Li, and Master Lai were all four talking together. "Who can look upon inaction as his head, on life as his back, and on death as his rump?" they said. "Who knows that life and death, existence and annihilation, are all a single body? I will be his friend!"

The four men looked at each other and smiled. There was no disagreement in their hearts and so the four of them became friends.

All at once Master Yü fell ill. Master Ssu went to ask how he was. "Amazing!" said Master Yü. "The Creator is making me all crookedy like this! My back sticks up like a hunchback and my vital organs are on top of me. My chin is hidden in my navel, my shoulders are up above my head, and my pigtail points at the sky. It must be some dislocation of the yin and yang!"

Yet he seemed calm at heart and unconcerned. Dragging himself haltingly to the well, he looked at his reflection and said, "My, my! So the Creator is making me all crookedy like this!"

"Do you resent it?" asked Master Ssu.

---

[6] **Lao Tan:** Laozi (Lao Tzu, fourth to third century B.C.E.), reputed author of the Dao De Jing.

[7] **ends:** A possible interpretation: Though the fuel is consumed in this particular torch, the fire of knowledge is passed on.

"Why no, what would I resent? If the process continues, perhaps in time he'll transform my left arm into a rooster. In that case I'll keep watch on the night. Or perhaps in time he'll transform my right arm into a crossbow pellet and I'll shoot down an owl for roasting. Or perhaps in time he'll transform my buttocks into cartwheels. Then, with my spirit for a horse, I'll climb up and go for a ride. What need will I ever have for a carriage again?

"I received life because the time had come; I will lose it because the order of things passes on. Be content with this time and dwell in this order and then neither sorrow nor joy can touch you. In ancient times this was called the 'freeing of the bound.' There are those who cannot free themselves, because they are bound by things. But nothing can ever win against Heaven—that's the way it's always been. What would I have to resent?"

Suddenly Master Lai grew ill. Gasping and wheezing, he lay at the point of death. His wife and children gathered round in a circle and began to cry. Master Li, who had come to ask how he was, said, "Shoo! Get back! Don't disturb the process of change!"

Then he leaned against the doorway and talked to Master Lai. "How marvelous the Creator is! What is he going to make out of you next? Where is he going to send you? Will he make you into a rat's liver? Will he make you into a bug's arm?"

Master Lai said, "A child, obeying his father and mother, goes wherever he is told, east or west, south or north. And the yin and yang—how much more are they to a man than father or mother! Now that they have brought me to the verge of death, if I should refuse to obey them, how perverse I would be! What fault is it of theirs? The Great Clod burdens me with form, labors me with life, eases me in old age, and rests me in death. So if I think well of my life, for the same reason I must think well of my death. When a skilled smith is casting metal, if the metal should leap up and say, 'I insist upon being made into a Mo-yeh!'[8] he would surely regard it as very inauspicious metal indeed. Now, having had the audacity to take on human form once, if I should say, 'I don't want to be anything but a man! Nothing but a man!', the Creator would surely regard me as a most inauspicious sort of person. So now I think of heaven and earth as a great furnace, and the Creator as a skilled smith. Where could he send me that would not be all right? I will go off to sleep peacefully, and then with a start I will wake up."

[THE JOB OFFER]

Once, when Chuang Tzu was fishing in the P'u River, the king of Ch'u sent two officials to go and announce to him: "I would like to trouble you with the administration of my realm."

Chuang Tzu held on to the fishing pole and, without turning his head, said, "I have heard that there is a sacred tortoise in Ch'u that has been dead for three

---

[8] **Mo-yeh:** A famous sword of King Ho-lü of Wu (r. 514–496 B.C.E.).

thousand years. The king keeps it wrapped in cloth and boxed, and stores it in the ancestral temple. Now would this tortoise rather be dead and have its bones left behind and honored? Or would it rather be alive and dragging its tail in the mud?"

"It would rather be alive and dragging its tail in the mud," said the two officials.

Chuang Tzu said, "Go away! I'll drag my tail in the mud!"

[Yuan-Chu Bird]

When Hui Tzu was prime minister of Liang, Chuang Tzu set off to visit him. Someone said to Hui Tzu, "Chuang Tzu is coming because he wants to replace you as prime minister!" With this Hui Tzu was filled with alarm and searched all over the state for three days and three nights trying to find Chuang Tzu. Chuang Tzu then came to see him and said, "In the south there is a bird called the Yüan-ch'u—I wonder if you've ever heard of it? The Yüan-ch'u rises up from the South Sea and flies to the North Sea, and it will rest on nothing but the Wu-t'ung tree, eat nothing but the fruit of the Lien, and drink only from springs of sweet water. Once there was an owl who had gotten hold of a half-rotten old rat, and as the Yüan-ch'u passed by, it raised its head, looked up at the Yüan-ch'u, and said, 'Shoo!' Now that you have this Liang state of yours, are you trying to shoo me?"

[What Fish Enjoy]

Chuang Tzu and Hui Tzu were strolling along the dam of the Hao River when Chuang Tzu said, "See how the minnows come out and dart around where they please! That's what fish really enjoy!"

Hui Tzu said, "You're not a fish—how do you know what fish enjoy?"

Chuang Tzu said, "You're not I, so how do you know I don't know what fish enjoy?"

Hui Tzu said, "I'm not you, so I certainly don't know what you know. On the other hand, you're certainly not a fish—so that still proves you don't know what fish enjoy!"

Chuang Tzu said, "Let's go back to your original question, please. You asked me *how* I know what fish enjoy—so you already knew I knew it when you asked the question. I know it by standing here beside the Hao."

[Happiness]

Is there such a thing as supreme happiness in the world or isn't there? Is there some way to keep yourself alive or isn't there? What to do, what to rely on, what to avoid, what to stick by, what to follow, what to leave alone, what to find happiness in, what to hate?

This is what the world honors: wealth, eminence, long life, a good name. This is what the world finds happiness in: a life of ease, rich food, fine clothes, beautiful sights, sweet sounds. This is what it looks down on: poverty, meanness, early death, a bad name. This is what it finds bitter: a life that knows no rest, a mouth that gets no rich food, no fine clothes for the body, no beautiful sights for the eye, no sweet sounds for the ear.

People who can't get these things fret a great deal and are afraid—this is a stupid way to treat the body. People who are rich wear themselves out rushing around on business, piling up more wealth than they could ever use—this is a superficial way to treat the body. People who are eminent spend night and day scheming and wondering if they are doing right—this is a shoddy way to treat the body. Man lives his life in company with worry, and if he lives a long while, till he's dull and doddering, then he has spent that much time worrying instead of dying, a bitter lot indeed! This is a callous way to treat the body.

Men of ardor[9] are regarded by the world as good, but their goodness doesn't succeed in keeping them alive. So I don't know whether their goodness is really good or not. Perhaps I think it's good—but not good enough to save their lives. Perhaps I think it's no good—but still good enough to save the lives of others. So I say, if your loyal advice isn't heeded, give way and do not wrangle. Tzu-hsü wrangled and lost his body. But if he hadn't wrangled, he wouldn't have made a name. Is there really such a thing as goodness or isn't there?

What ordinary people do and what they find happiness in—I don't know whether such happiness is in the end really happiness or not. I look at what ordinary people find happiness in, what they all make a mad dash for, racing around as though they couldn't stop—they all say they're happy with it. I'm not happy with it and I'm not unhappy with it. In the end is there really happiness or isn't there?

I take inaction to be true happiness, but ordinary people think it is a bitter thing. I say: the highest happiness has no happiness, the highest praise has no praise. The world can't decide what is right and what is wrong. And yet inaction can decide this. The highest happiness, keeping alive—only inaction gets you close to this!

Let me try putting it this way. The inaction of Heaven is its purity, the inaction of earth is its peace. So the two inactions combine and all things are transformed and brought to birth. Wonderfully, mysteriously, there is no place they come out of. Mysteriously, wonderfully, they have no sign. Each thing minds its business and all grow up out of inaction. So I say, Heaven and earth do nothing and there is nothing that is not done. Among men, who can get hold of this inaction?

[DEATH OF CHUANG TZU'S WIFE]

Chuang Tzu's wife died. When Hui Tzu went to convey his condolences, he found Chuang Tzu sitting with his legs sprawled out, pounding on a tub and singing. "You lived with her, she brought up your children and grew old," said Hui Tzu. "It should be enough simply not to weep at her death. But pounding on a tub and singing—this is going too far, isn't it?"

---

[9] **Men of ardor:** Men who are willing to sacrifice their lives in order to preserve their honor or save the lives of others.

Chuang Tzu said, "You're wrong. When she first died, do you think I didn't grieve like anyone else? But I looked back to her beginning and the time before she was born. Not only the time before she was born, but the time before she had a body. Not only the time before she had a body, but the time before she had a spirit. In the midst of the jumble of wonder and mystery a change took place and she had a spirit. Another change and she had a body. Another change and she was born. Now there's been another change and she's dead. It's just like the progression of the four seasons, spring, summer, fall, winter.

"Now she's going to lie down peacefully in a vast room. If I were to follow after her bawling and sobbing, it would show that I don't understand anything about fate. So I stopped."

[GAMECOCKS]

Chi Hsing-tzu was training gamecocks for the king. After ten days the king asked if they were ready.

"Not yet. They're too haughty and rely on their nerve."

Another ten days and the king asked again.

"Not yet. They still respond to noises and movements."

Another ten days and the king asked again.

"Not yet. They still look around fiercely and are full of spirit."

Another ten days and the king asked again.

"They're close enough. Another cock can crow and they show no sign of change. Look at them from a distance and you'd think they were made of wood. Their virtue is complete. Other cocks won't dare face up to them, but will turn and run."

[THE SWIMMER]

Confucius was seeing the sights at Lü-liang, where the water falls from a height of thirty fathoms and races and boils along for forty li, so swift that no fish or other water creature can swim in it. He saw a man dive into the water and, supposing that the man was in some kind of trouble and intended to end his life, he ordered his disciples to line up on the bank and pull the man out. But after the man had gone a couple of hundred paces, he came out of the water and began strolling along the base of the embankment, his hair streaming down, singing a song. Confucius ran after him and said, "At first I thought you were a ghost, but now I see you're a man. May I ask if you have some special way of staying afloat in the water?"

"I have no way. I began with what I was used to, grew up with my nature, and let things come to completion with fate. I go under with the swirls and come out with the eddies, following along the way the water goes and never thinking about myself. That's how I can stay afloat."

Confucius said, "What do you mean by saying that you began with what you were used to, grew up with your nature, and let things come to completion with fate?"

"I was born on the dry land and felt safe on the dry land—that was what I was used to. I grew up with the water and felt safe in the water—that was my nature. I don't know why I do what I do—that's fate."

[Woodworker]

Woodworker Ch'ing carved a piece of wood and made a bell stand, and when it was finished, everyone who saw it marveled, for it seemed to be the work of gods or spirits. When the marquis of Lu saw it, he asked, "What art is it you have?"

Ch'ing replied, "I am only a craftsman—how would I have any art? There is one thing, however. When I am going to make a bell stand, I never let it wear out my energy. I always fast in order to still my mind. When I have fasted for three days, I no longer have any thought of congratulations or rewards, of titles or stipends. When I have fasted for five days, I no longer have any thought of praise or blame, of skill or clumsiness. And when I have fasted for seven days, I am so still that I forget I have four limbs and a form and body. By that time, the ruler and his court no longer exist for me. My skill is concentrated and all outside distractions fade away. After that, I go into the mountain forest and examine the Heavenly nature of the trees. If I find one of superlative form, and I can see a bell stand there, I put my hand to the job of carving; if not, I let it go. This way I am simply matching up 'Heaven' with 'Heaven.'[10] That's probably the reason that people wonder if the results were not made by spirits."

---

[10] **matching . . . 'Heaven' with 'Heaven':** Matching his innate nature with the nature of the tree.

∾ CATULLUS
ROME, C. 84–C. 54 B.C.E.

The voice of the Roman lyric poet Catullus speaks directly across some two thousand years in startlingly colloquial language, his tone ranging from leering to loving, from scornful sarcasm to warm affection to bitter grief. From the first century B.C.E. he reports on daily life among his friends, the rich and fast-living younger set in Rome. While he gossips wickedly about bathhouse scandals, back-alley doings, and bisexual politics in the capital, telling who is incestuous or adulterous, there are private and tender moments, too, as when he thanks friends who have stood by him; chronicles his aching love affair with Lesbia, the older woman whose flamboyance both enchants him and breaks his heart; and stands over the lonely grave of his beloved elder brother, who has died in the remote province of Bithynia. Like Sappho,[1] the predecessor he revered and imitated, Catullus is a poet whose love poetry has inspired almost every succeeding generation of poets in the west to translate him anew.

www For links to more information about Catullus and a quiz on his poetry, see bedford stmartins.com/ worldlitcompact.

---

[1] **Sappho** (early sixth century B.C.E.): Greek lyric poet from the island of Lesbos; her love lyrics, some of which Catullus translated into Latin, have been widely influential (see p. 560).

Lovers, first century
In this erotic scene from a fresco in the ancient city of Pompeii, Italy, two lovers coyly approach each other. (Erich Lessing/Art Resource, NY)

From Verona to Rome.   Like Sappho, Catullus grew up far from the intellectual center of the culture he lived in. He was born about 84 B.C.E. in Verona, a city in the northern Italian province of Cisalpine Gaul. The second son of a prosperous contractor for the Roman legions, Gaius Valerius, Catullus was taken in by the circle gathered around the brilliant teacher, poet, and Hellenist Valerius Cato, one of the leaders of the *Neoteri*, or New Poets, who emphasized the craft of poetry. In one of his own poems Catullus claims that he began to write when he was about sixteen. Brilliant, handsome, witty, and with a keen appetite for experience, at some point Catullus made his way to Rome and from that time on regarded it as his home. There he found companions among both the intellectuals and the most avid pleasure-seekers; if the great statesman and orator Marcus Tullius Cicero (106–43 B.C.E.) was his friend, so were the full array of Gelliuses, Quintiuses, and Balbuses who lust, drink, and carouse in his poems. One person whom he and his friends seem to have regarded with mild dislike was Julius Caesar (102–44 B.C.E.) himself, seemingly on the grounds of personality rather than politics: "Caesar? What Caesar?" Catullus jokes in one fragment.

Lesbia.   Clodia Metelli, whom Catullus addresses in his poems as Lesbia in tribute to Sappho, was the wife of Metellus Celer, the governor of Cisalpine Gaul. It is very likely that she came into Catullus's life while he was still living in Verona. She was more than five years older than Catullus, and already notorious for her commanding air, her charm, her caprices, and her sexual appetites; when her husband died in 59 B.C.E., rumors circulated that she had poisoned him to clear the way for an incestuous affair with her brother. Cicero wrote a polemic against her when one of his favorite pupils was accused of trying to poison her. Cicero, who believed Roman women should be quiet, stately matrons, must have been galled to no end by the outspoken Metelli, who lived only a few houses away from him and enjoyed staging riotous salons for politicians opposed to him. The very qualities in Metelli that so irked Cicero made Catullus fall helplessly in love with her. Their affair is chronicled in about forty poems that trace their relationship from its playful, ecstatic beginning through betrayal, jealousy, recriminations, reconciliations, and, finally, contempt. Yet with all the heartbreak, it seems that Catullus does not wish to have forgone meeting and loving Clodia/Lesbia; she is the great experience of his life.

Bithynia and Mortality.   In the year 57, very likely at about the time that Catullus's love affair was ending, he received word that his much-loved elder brother had died while on a diplomatic mission in Bithynia, in what is now Turkey. Catullus arranged for a political appointment and traveled to Bithynia in the entourage of the magistrate Caius Memmius Gemellus. At some time during his tour of duty, Catullus visited his brother's grave, an occasion commemorated movingly in one of his finest poems, 101, famous for its salutation to the dead, *Ave atque vale* ("Hail and farewell," here translated as "Goodbye, goodbye"). This death, perhaps linked in his mind with the death of his relationship with Lesbia, affected Catullus deeply. He had always lived at a riotous pace, as though he sensed death were close and he needed to cram in quickly all the experience he could. His brother's death seems to have confirmed what he had guessed about mortality. He writes in another poem addressed to his brother, "You have darkened my mind."

Catullus remained in Bithynia for about a year, and then, homesick, he returned to his family villa on the shores of Lake Garda. He visited Rome one last time, where he may have resumed his affair with Lesbia. Soon after, though exactly when or how is not known, Catullus died. He was about thirty years old.

The Poetry.   As a young poet Catullus belonged to the bright group of Roman writers known as the Neoterics. While a few of their names are known, Catullus's is the only body of work that has survived. The Neoterics were impatient with the ponderous high-mindedness and patriotic and mythological themes that characterized a good deal of Roman literature.

Formally innovative, intellectually and emotionally sophisticated, Catullus and his colleagues created a poetics of the subjective, the ironic, the erotic. To their contemporaries, who referred to them in Latin as "the new poets" *(Poetae novi)* and in Greek as "the modernists" *(hoi neoteroi)*, it must have seemed as though these writers, known today as the neoterics, had come out of nowhere, for they were almost without precedent in Roman literature.

– CHARLES MARTIN, critic, 1992

They were far more taken by the racy, breezy Roman comedy that mocked pretentiousness and celebrated in colloquial language the everyday life of gossipy servants, lovesick young folk, feasting, and drinking. Such a shift from the high seriousness of earlier Roman poetry effected a revolution in poetics and in sensibility. Contemporary critic Charles Martin characterizes this new poetry as groundbreaking: "Formally innovative, intellectually and emotionally sophisticated, Catullus and his colleagues created a poetics of the subjective, the ironic, the erotic. To their contemporaries, who referred to them in Latin as 'the new poets' (*Poetae novi*) and in Greek as 'the modernists' *(hoi neoteroi),* it must have seemed as though these writers, known today as the neoterics, had come out of nowhere, for they were almost without precedent in Roman literature."

Catullus turned his poems away from epic themes and looked to the sophisticated urban life that teemed before his eyes for his subject. Candor, wit, intimacy, and an astonishing range characterize Catullus's work. That range is discernible even in the brief selection presented here. Lightly, lovingly, in poem 2 Catullus describes his beloved sensuously playing with her tame sparrow—teasing it, cuddling it, feeding it; he says he wishes he might be her, able for a while to forget the pains of love, but it is clear that it is the petted sparrow he envies as well. And in poem 3, when the sparrow dies, his elegy for it begins in the mock-heroic tone of one making a great fuss over a trivial thing, but the poem deepens within a few lines into a genuine rage against the mortality that in the end will devour all lovely things, whether they are trivial or of great importance. Lesbia and her sparrow alike will one day be "lost in darkness / . . . a sad place / from which no one returns." Extravagantly, in poem 5, in the exuberance of first love, he and his sweetheart defy death with their wealth of infinitely multiplied embraces. Finally, in poem 101 the poet stands stricken beside a lonely grave in a far country, death offerings in his hands, surrounded by a vast silence. It may in fact have been Catullus's keen intuition of death's constant presence that enabled him to write poems that spill over with all the beauty and decadence of Roman life.

In his day, Catullus sang and read aloud his poetry before privileged audiences eager to hear him scandalize their friends and acquaintances. Some of his poems may have been collected into a book, but the poems that have survived were found in a copyist's manuscript. Around 1300 C.E. a rolled-up manuscript of Catullus's poems was found in a jar; the manuscript, containing 115 poems ranging from two hundred to nearly four hundred lines of verse, was copied by hand at least three times and then disappeared. While many editors rearrange the poems to reflect what is supposed to be the rise and fall of Catullus's relationship with Metelli, Catullus's poems are printed here in the order in which they appear in the manuscripts.

■ **FURTHER RESEARCH**
Havelock, E. A. *The Lyric Genius of Catullus.* 1964.
Martin, Charles. *Catullus.* 1992.
Quinn, Kenneth. *Catullus: An Interpretation.* 1973.
Wiseman, T. P. *Catullus and His World: A Reappraisal.* 1985.

2: Sparrow, O, sweet sparrow

Translated by Horace Gregory

Sparrow, O, sweet sparrow,
love of my lady love,
she who's always nursing
you between her breasts and
feeding you her finger-tips;
she, that radiant lady,
delicious in her play with you,
for a while forgetting
all the deeper wounds of love . . .
I envy her. This pastime
would raise my heart from darkness.

3: Dress now in sorrow, O all

Translated by Horace Gregory

Dress now in sorrow, O all
your shades of Venus,[1]
and your little cupids weep.

My girl has lost her darling sparrow;
he is dead, her precious toy
that she loved more than her two eyes,
O, honeyed sparrow following her
as a girl follows her mother,
never to leave her breast, but tripping
now here, now there, and always singing
his sweet falsetto
song to her alone.

Now he is gone; poor creature,
lost in darkness,
to a sad place
from which no one returns.

_____

[1] **Venus:** Roman goddess of love (Aphrodite in Greek mythology).

O ravenous hell!
My evil hatred rises against your power,
you that devour
20   all things beautiful;
and now this pitiful, broken sparrow,
who is the cause of my girl's grief,
making her eyes weary and red with sorrow.

✑ 5: Come, Lesbia, let us live and love

Translated by Horace Gregory

Come, Lesbia, let us live and love,
nor give a damn what sour old men say.
The sun that sets may rise again
but when our light has sunk into the earth,
it is gone forever.
        Give me a thousand kisses,
then a hundred, another thousand,
another hundred
        and in one breath
still kiss another thousand,
another hundred.
        O then with lips and bodies joined
many deep thousands;
10   confuse
their number,
        so that poor fools and cuckolds (envious
even now) shall never
learn our wealth and curse us
with their
evil eyes.

✑ 8: Poor damned Catullus,
here's no time for nonsense

Translated by Horace Gregory

Poor damned Catullus, here's no time for nonsense,
open your eyes, O idiot, innocent boy, look at what has happened:
once there were sunlit days when you followed after

where ever a girl would go, she loved with greater
love than any woman knew.
Then you took your pleasure
and the girl was not unwilling. Those were the bright days, gone;
now she's no longer yielding; you must be, poor idiot,
more like a man! not running after
10 her your mind all tears; stand firm, insensitive.
Say with a smile, voice steady, "Good-bye, my girl," Catullus
strong and manly no longer follows you, nor comes when you are calling
him at night and you shall need him.
You whore! Where's your man to cling to, who will praise your beauty,
where's the man that you love and who will call you his,
and when you fall to kissing, whose lips will you devour?
But always, your Catullus will be as firm as rock is.

◌ 51: He is changed to a god he who looks on her

Translated by Horace Gregory

He is changed to a god he who looks on her,
godlike he shines when he's seated beside her,
immortal joy to gaze and hear the fall of
    her sweet laughter.

All of my senses are lost and confounded;
Lesbia rises before me and trembling
I sink into earth and swift dissolution
    seizes my body.

Limbs are pierced with fire and the heavy tongue fails,
10 ears resound with noise of distant storms shaking
this earth, eyes gaze on stars that fall forever
    into deep midnight.

This languid madness destroys you Catullus,
long day and night shall be desolate, broken,
as long ago ancient kings and rich cities
    fell into ruin.

∾ 76: If man can find rich consolation . . .

Translated by Horace Gregory

If man can find rich consolation, remembering his good deeds and all he has done,
if he remembers his loyalty to others, nor abuses his religion by heartless betrayal
of friends to the anger of powerful gods,
then, my Catullus, the long years before you shall not sink in darkness with all
      hope gone,
wandering, dismayed, through the ruins of love.
All the devotion that man gives to man, you have given, Catullus,
your heart and your brain flowed into a love that was desolate, wasted, nor can
      it return.
But why, why do you crucify love and yourself through the years?
Take what the gods have to offer and standing serene, rise forth as a rock against
      darkening skies;
10 and yet you do nothing but grieve, sunken deep in your sorrow, Catullus,
for it is hard, hard to throw aside years lived in poisonous love that has tainted
      your brain
and must end.
If this seems impossible now, you must rise
to salvation. O gods of pity and mercy, descend and witness my sorrow, if ever
you have looked upon man in his hour of death, see me now in despair.
Tear this loathsome disease from my brain. Look, a subtle corruption has entered
      my bones,
no longer shall happiness flow through my veins like a river. No longer I pray
that she love me again, that her body be chaste, mine forever.
Cleanse my soul of this sickness of love, give me power to rise, resurrected, to thrust
      love aside,
20 I have given my heart to the gods, O hear me, omnipotent heaven,
and ease me of love and its pain.

∾ 85: I hate and love

Translated by Horace Gregory

I hate and love.
    And if you ask me why,
I have no answer, but I discern,
can feel, my senses rooted in eternal torture.

∽ 101: Dear brother, I have come these many miles

Translated by Horace Gregory

Dear brother, I have come these many miles, through strange lands to this
    Eastern Continent
to see your grave, a poor sad monument of what you were, O brother.
And I have come too late; you cannot hear me; alone now I must speak
to these few ashes that were once your body and expect no answer.
I shall perform an ancient ritual over your remains, weeping,
(this plate of lentils for dead men to feast upon, wet with my tears)
O brother, here's my greeting: here's my hand forever welcoming you
and I forever saying: good-bye, good-bye.

TEXT IN CONTEXT

 VIRGIL
ROME, 70–19 B.C.E.

pp. 537, 185

uh-NEE-us
DIGH-doh

Virgil achieved fame in his lifetime as the poet of *The Eclogues,* ten pastoral poems about the lives of shepherds, and *The Georgics,* a patriotic poem about methods of farming and the dignity of country life. His works, including his greatest work, *The Aeneid,* a twelve-book epic left unfinished at his death, exerted a profound influence on later European literature and culture. Like Homer's **Iliad** and **Odyssey** and the great Sanskrit epic *Mahabharata, The Aeneid* has inspired generations of subsequent writers and artists, providing them with a rich mine of heroic themes and tragic scenes—**Aeneas** leaving Troy, carrying his father on his shoulders and holding his son by the hand; **Dido** sacrificing herself on a blazing pyre as Aeneas sails away from Carthage; the death of Turnus. Virgil's *Eclogues* and *Georgics* elevated and invigorated the genres of pastoral and didactic poetry, leading to countless imitations produced from his time to the present day. Most significant, his *Aeneid* was a powerful reassessment of the cost of singleminded heroic enterprise. While this story of the founding of Rome by descendants of the conquered city of Troy recalls the Greek epics of Homer, it goes beyond them to stress the theme of *pietas,* public virtue or duty, which Virgil thought lay at the core of Roman civilization and which he saw as attainable only through great suffering and loss.

WWW For links to more information about Virgil, a quiz on *The Aeneid,* and information about the twenty-first century relevance of Virgil, see bedford stmartins.com/ worldlitcompact.

The Poet from Mantua.   Publius Vergilius Maro was born in 70 B.C.E. in or near Mantua, a city in Cisalpine Gaul, a northern province of Italy, where his family owned land in the country. Virgil was educated at nearby Cremona and Milan before moving to Rome for a short time.

A shy and retiring figure, Virgil was never actively engaged in politics, though he circulated among some of the most important and influential people of his time, eventually winning the notice of Octavian[1] himself. However, as we see clearly in *The Aeneid,* Virgil, who had grown up during a time of civil strife, celebrated in his poetry the consolidation of Roman rule. Virgil witnessed the bloody rivalry between Pompey (106–48 B.C.E.) and Julius Caesar (102–44 B.C.E.), the rioting of mobs in Rome, the assassination of Caesar, and the divisive war between Octavian (63 B.C.E.–14 C.E.) and his rival for control over the Roman Empire, Marc Antony (83 B.C.E.–30 C.E.).[2] When Octavian's forces defeated those of Antony and Cleopatra in the battle of Actium (31 B.C.E.), which led to the suicides of the famous couple, Virgil, like most Romans, welcomed the new possibilities for peace under the capable rule of Octavian, soon to be named Augustus Caesar. During the period of civil war, Virgil had already begun to devote himself to the main business of his life: writing poetry of a national character. Having spent most of his life writing poetry while living on his family's property near Mantua, Virgil died at the coastal town of Brundisium on 21 September 19 B.C.E. Although he had asked his friends to destroy the unfinished *Aeneid,* Octavian himself ordered that the manuscript be saved and entrusted it to Varius Rufus, a poet and playwright who saw it through to publication.

The Eclogues and The Georgics.   Between 42 and 37 B.C.E., Virgil wrote *The Eclogues,* also known as *The Bucolics.* Modeled on the pastoral poetry of Theocritus, a Greek Alexandrian poet from the third century B.C.E., *The Eclogues* depicts the idyllic lives of shepherds against an ominous backdrop of rural dispossession and loss. Taking the form of dialogues, poetic contests, and elegiac complaints, these poems celebrate the virtues of an idealized rustic life filled with love, music, and poetry, while at the same time alluding to real events and people in Virgil's time when lands in his own region of Italy were being confiscated from their original owners and handed over as rewards to the military heroes from the wars against Julius Caesar. Virgil's own lands were

> But the word *pietas* with Virgil has much wider associations of meaning: it implies an attitude towards the individual, towards the family, towards the region, and towards the imperial destiny of Rome. And finally Aeneas is "pious" also in his respect towards the gods, and in his punctilious observance of rites and offerings. It is an attitude towards all these things, and therefore implies a unity and an order among them: it is in fact an attitude towards life.
>
> – T. S. Eliot, poet, 1943

---

[1] **Octavian:** Caius (also Gaius) Octavius (63 B.C.E.–14 C.E.), who became Augustus Caesar. After the death of Julius Caesar, Augustus's great uncle, Octavian formed the Second Triumvirate with Marc Antony and Lepidus. Octavian's defeat of his rivals, including Antony and Cleopatra, helped to stabilize Rome and led to the Senate's appointing him emperor and giving him the honorific title "Augustus." During his era, Roman art, culture, and society flourished.

[2] **Pompey . . . Julius Caesar . . . Marc Antony:** Three Roman generals and statesmen who became rivals for power. In 60 B.C.E., Pompey, Cneius Pompeius Magnus (106–48 B.C.E.), and Julius Caesar (102–44 B.C.E.) joined Marcus Licinius Crassus to form the First Triumvirate. Caesar became dictator and consul in 46 B.C.E. but was assassinated by jealous lieutenants just two years later, on March 15, 44 B.C.E. After the assassination, Antony joined Caesar's great-nephew Octavian (later Augustus Caesar) and Lepidus to form the Second Triumvirate.

Model of Ancient Rome
In its ancient heyday, Rome was a remarkably modern city with restaurants, cafés, public baths, theaters, and apartments and houses with indoor plumbing, heat, and running water. (The Art Archive / Museo della Civiltà Romana, Rome / Dagli Orti)

expropriated and eventually returned to him, presumably due to the influence of several important people he names in the poems. The celebrated *Fourth Eclogue,* which predicts the coming of a new age of peace and justice signaled by the birth of a divinely gifted child, was thought by later Christian interpreters to have heralded the coming of Christ.

As someone who had grown up in the country, Virgil was well aware of the importance of the rural countryside, not only as a scene for poetic idylls but also as a place of labor and production. From about 36 to 29 B.C.E., he worked on *The Georgics,* a didactic poem in four books that has often been described as a handbook for farmers and offers a vision of the importance of agriculture and the quiet nobility of country life. While its poems focus minutely on horticulture, animal husbandry, and beekeeping, they also celebrate, without sentimentality, human labor in general, including the arts of war, statesmanship, and poetry.

The Aeneid.   Virgil began writing *The Aeneid* in about 19 B.C.E. *The Aeneid* announced a new advance in the long tradition of epic poetry. Virgil looked to Homer's *Iliad* and *Odyssey* for his epic poem that commemorates even as it invents and embellishes the mythic and historical origins of Rome. Written in dactylic hexameters like his previous two works, Virgil's twelve-book *Aeneid* consists of nearly ten thousand lines in the original Latin.

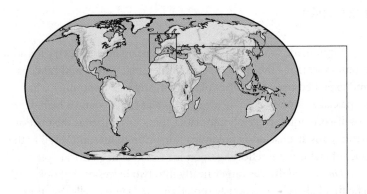

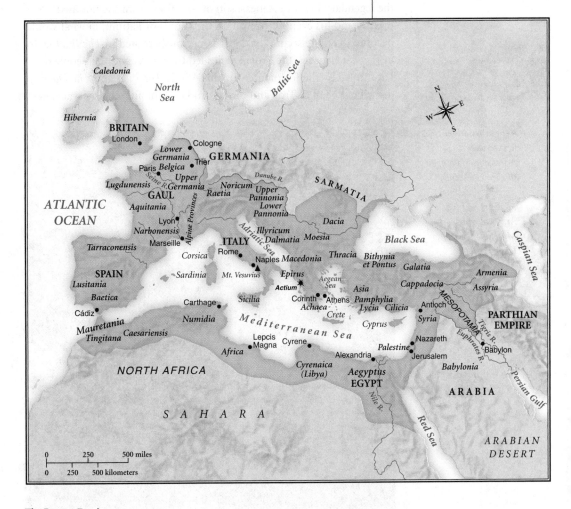

The Roman Empire, 117 C.E.

For close to one hundred fifty years, Rome steadily expanded its borders. In 30 B.C.E. Octavian (the future emperor Augustus) captured Egypt following the suicides of Mark Antony and Cleopatra. Imperial conquest reached its height in 114–117 C.E., when Emperor Trajan seized southern Mesopotamia, the farthest east Rome had yet extended.

Virgil made innovations in the epic devices of oral poetry found in Homer's works — the epithets, epic similes, repetitions, and catalogs — and exploited the possibilities of written language to produce what some call a "literary epic" — a work of great subtlety and a high degree of self-conscious artistry. Some critics think of Homer as the poet of nature, unselfconsciously holding a mirror up to life, and Virgil as the poet of civilization, reflecting upon his world with a critical eye.

The Aeneid divides rather neatly into two halves of six books each: The first half, self-consciously rooted in *The Odyssey,* tells the story of the legendary flight of Aeneas, son of Anchises, from the doomed city of Troy and his eventual arrival on the shores of Latium, in what would become Italy; the second half, self-consciously rooted in *The Iliad,* tells of the war between the Trojan exiles led by Aeneas and the people of Latium led by the formidable Turnus. While *The Iliad* and *The Odyssey* describe the fall of Troy and the return home of an Achaean war hero,

**Aeneas Wounded,
first century**
*A fresco from Pompeii
illustrates a scene
from Virgil's Aeneid.
(The Art Archive /
Archaeological
Museum, Naples /
Dagli Orti)*

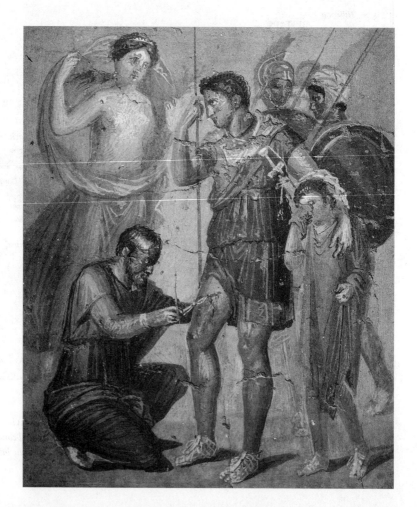

Ancient Rome: Augustus Caesar and the Golden Age

From the first century B.C.E. onward, intellectuals throughout the Greco-Roman world commonly believed that the cosmos operated in long cycles of time, that an era or age inevitably came to an end so that a new period of history might begin. The Greek writer Hesiod (c. 800 B.C.E.) wrote about the degeneration of time from a golden age to a silver, bronze, and, finally, an iron age. In *Politicus* (fourth century B.C.E.), Plato explains how the earth will change directions at the end of a final age and turn in the opposite direction, causing cataclysms at first and then a regeneration of all life and the advent of a new ruler.

Romans viewed Romulus's founding of Rome (c. 753 B.C.E.) and his sighting of twelve birds as omens indicating that Rome would endure twelve centuries. Seven centuries later with the reign of Augustus, they dared to hope that they could pass from one age to another, from the Iron Age to a new Golden Age, without a cosmic catastrophe, or *ekpyrosis,* "destruction by fire."

On the tenth anniversary of Augustus's regime, he inaugurated the Secular Games, a three-day festival meant to purify Rome from past pollution and represent a transition to a world renewed, a messianic Golden Age. With the death of Lepidus in 12 B.C.E., Augustus became Rome's Chief Priest *(pontifex maximus).* Officially, he could not become a god until he died, but in 2 B.C.E. he became "Father of the Fatherland" *(pater patriae),* a title that supported his claim that he was the son of the deified Julius Caesar, the *divi filius.*

In *The Aeneid,* Virgil, the poet laureate of Rome, unveils Rome's destiny and predicts that Rome will regenerate itself indefinitely through Julius's line and under the glorious reign of Augustus. Ruler worship spread throughout the empire, with temples dedicated to Rome and tributes to Augustus as Savior, Benefactor, and the

Augustus, 27 B.C.E.–14 C.E. *The Roman Empire enjoyed a period of relative peace and stability under the long reign of Augustus (a religious title meaning "revered") Caesar (63 B.C.E.–14 C.E.). (The Art Archive / Musée du Louvre, Paris / Dagli Orti)*

God Epiphanes (Manifest). Especially in the eastern provinces, Augustus's gradual deification became a binding political force.

After Augustus's death in 14 C.E., a special priesthood was established to care for his cult.

Odysseus, *The Aeneid* describes the journey of Aeneas away from the fallen city of Troy and the founding of new cities—Alba Longa, the first capital of the Latins, and Rome, founded many generations later by Romulus, a descendant of Aeneas. In linking the founding of Rome to the fall of Troy, Virgil was working a prevailing myth that the Romans were descended from the Trojans into his national epic. Furthermore, he links Aeneas to Octavian, who was named Augustus Caesar in 27 B.C.E., about two years after Virgil began writing *The Aeneid*. Virgil had already lavished praise on Octavian in *The Georgics,* which in several digressions tracks Octavian's rise to power and praises him as the champion of Roman unity and peace. Combining the martial prowess of Achilles with the keen intelligence and foresight of Odysseus, Virgil's Aeneas exhibits the strengths of a warrior-statesman like Octavian, a powerful general and an astute politician.

Book 1 describes the wrath of Juno, who took sides with the Achaeans during the war against Troy. In her anger, Juno sends a storm to batter Aeneas's ships and the hero finds refuge on the shores of Carthage, Dido's home. In Books 2 and 3, Aeneas, now a guest of the widow Dido, tells of the fall of Troy, his flight from the city, and his hazardous journey across the seas. In these books Aeneas also describes how he has learned of his destiny to play a role in the founding of a new city. Book 4 focuses on the love between Dido and Aeneas and its tragic consequences; this book also addresses the struggle between duty and desire that both Dido and Aeneas experience. Book 6 recounts Aeneas's descent into the underworld, where he, like Odysseus, meets people from his past, including Dido and Anchises. Intensifying the conflict between duty and desire, these two meetings in particular heighten Aeneas's intense personal suffering as well as his awareness of great public good. Books 7 through 12 tell of the battles between Aeneas and Turnus over Latium, or Italy.

When Aeneas meets Anchises, the ghost of his father shows him a long line of Roman heroes as yet unborn, from Sylvius, founder of Alba Longa, and Romulus, founder of Rome, to Augustus Caesar. Moreover, Anchises tells him that the principal art of the Romans is the rule of nations and the business of peace. With this vision firmly planted in his mind and his ambition and commitment to his destiny restored, Aeneas returns to his ships to renew his fateful voyage.

Through the character of Aeneas, Virgil explores one of the principal Roman virtues, *pietas,* which comprises the concepts of piety, public virtue, and duty. Aeneas must set aside all that is dear to him in the world—including the great passion of his life, his love for Dido, queen of Carthage—in order to follow the single purpose of the founding of Lavinium, the ancient site and first city of Roman civilization.

■ FURTHER RESEARCH

Anderson, W. S. *The Art of the* Aeneid. 1969.
Bloom, Harold, ed. *Modern Critical Interpretations of the Aeneid.* 1987.
Camps, W. A. *An Introduction to Virgil's* Aeneid. 1969.
Grandsen, K. W. *Virgil, the Aeneid.* 1990.
Griffin, Jasper. *Virgil.* 1986.
Horsfall, Nicholas, ed. *A Companion to the Study of Virgil.* 2000.
Johnson, W. R. *Darkness Visible: A Study of Virgil's* Aeneid. 1976.
Lyne, R. O. A. M. *Further Voices in Virgil's* Aeneid. 1987.
Otis, Brooks. *Virgil: A Study in Civilized Poetry.* 1963, 1985.

■ PRONUNCIATION

Aeneas: uh-NEE-us
Anchises: ang-KIGH-zeez, -seez
Andromache: an-DRAH-muh-kee
Danaans: duh-NAY-unz
Deiphobus: dee-IF-oh-bus, -uh-bus
Dido: DIGH-doh
Dionysus: digh-uh-NIGH-sus
Hecate: HEK-uh-tee
Peneleus: pih-NEE-lee-us
Pirithous: pih-RITH-oos
Sychaeus: sih-KEE-us

 ↶ # The Aeneid

Translated by Frank O. Copley

FROM BOOK 1
[ARRIVING IN CARTHAGE]

My song is arms and a man,[1] the first of Troy
to come to Italy and Lavinian shores,[2]
a fated fugitive, harried on land and sea
by heaven's huge might and Juno's endless hate,[3]
pommeled by wars, till he could found the City

---

[1] **a man:** Aeneas, the son of Anchises, king of Dardania, and Venus, the goddess of love; Aeneas was a member of the royal house of Troy. Anchises' uncle was Laomedon, a king of Troy, and the Dardanians were allies of the Trojans in the war against the Greeks.

[2] **Lavinian shores:** Refers to Lavinium, a city just south of Rome named after the daughter of King Latinus, Lavinia, who marries Aeneas after he arrives in Latium, the southwestern coastal plain of Italy settled by the exiled Trojans.

[3] **Juno's . . . hate:** Known as Hera in Greek mythology, Juno is the queen of the gods and the wife of Jove. Because the Trojan prince Paris praised Venus's (Aphrodite's) beauty above hers, Juno bitterly resented the Trojans and aided their enemies.

and bring his gods to Latium, whence the race
of Latins, our Alban[4] sires, and towering Rome.

Muse, tell me the causes: how was godhead wronged,
how injured the queen of heaven that she must force
10 through many a fall of fate and many a toil
that great, good man: can heaven hold such ill will?

A city once stood, a colony of Tyre,
Carthage,[5] across from Italy and far
from Tiber's mouth,[6] rich and agog for war,
a spot that Juno loved more than all worlds,
more even than Samos:[7] here stood her arms and here
her chariot; throne of mankind it was to be
if Fate allowed; this was her cherished aim.
But men would spring of Trojan blood, she'd heard,
20 and some day lay her Carthage in the dust —
a race of world-wide kings, whose pride was war
and death for Libya: so ran the thread of Fate.

This she feared, remembering, too, that war
when first she fought for her dear Greece at Troy.
Still she recalled the anger and the pain
that sent her there: deep in her heart lay stored
the judgment of Paris,[8] the insult to her beauty,
a hated people, a Ganymede[9] raped to heaven.
Her anger flared; she drove all over the deep
30 the Trojan few that Achilles and Greece had spared,
and kept them far from Latium; year on year
they wandered, dogged by Fate, across the seas.
Such matter it was to found our Roman race. [. . .]

---

[4] **Alban:** Refers to Alba Longa, the city founded by Aeneas's son Ascanius and the home of Romulus, the legendary founder of Rome.

[5] **Tyre, Carthage:** Tyre, a city on the coast of Syria (Lebanon), was home to the Phoenicians; Carthage, settled by Phoenician colonists, is a city on the northern coast of Africa near today's Tunis. Carthage was a traditional enemy of Rome against whom Rome fought a succession of three wars known as the Punic Wars (264–241, 218–201, and 149–146 B.C.E.). Carthage is associated in Virgil's epic with Libya and the Libyan people, natives of the land in which Dido and her Phoenicians have settled.

[6] **Tiber's mouth:** The Tiber, or Tiberus, is a river that flows through Rome; it was at the mouth of the Tiber that the Trojan exiles landed when they arrived in Latium.

[7] **Samos:** An Aegean island known for its worship of Juno (Hera).

[8] **judgment of Paris:** Paris was the son of King Priam of Troy; when Paris judged Juno's beauty to be inferior to that of Aphrodite (Venus), the insulted Juno turned her wrath against the Trojans. Paris's judgment had been influenced by Aphrodite's promise that she would grant him the love of the beautiful Helen, the wife of King Menelaus of Sparta. Paris's abduction of Helen precipitated the Trojan War.

[9] **Ganymede:** A Trojan youth whose beauty won the favor of Jupiter (Zeus), who appointed him to be the cupbearer to the gods, a position held by Juno's daughter Hebe.

[In the section omitted here from the text, the goddess Juno, who is hostile to Aeneas and the Trojans, persuades Aeolus, the god of the winds, to visit a storm upon Aeneas's fleet. Seeing the devastation that ensues, Neptune, the god of the sea, calms the waters, but not before many ships have been wrecked. With seven surviving ships, Aeneas puts in at a harbor on the coast of Libya, the land of the great city of Carthage, ruled by Dido. As Aeneas and his crew rest and ponder their fate, his mother, the goddess Venus, appeals on his behalf to Jove, who assures Venus that her son will prevail in his quest to sail to Italy and found a great city and nation. As the text picks up the story again, Jove has just sent the messenger Mercury to ensure that the people of Carthage, the Tyrians, will give Aeneas a friendly welcome and Aeneas ventures forth.]

Faithful Aeneas lay thinking all night long,
determined, soon as daylight came, to search
this unfamiliar land: Where had the wind
brought him? Who lived here? man? (he saw no homes)
or beast? He must find out and tell his men!

310 In a wooded cave beneath an overhang
he hid his ships where they were screened by trees
above and behind. Then with one friend, Achates,[10]
he went forth, clasping in each hand a spear.
Out in the woods his mother came to meet him.
She seemed a girl; her face and garb were those
of a Spartan maid or Thracian Harpalyce[11]
whipping her horses to outrun Hebrus' current.
Over her shoulder a bow hung ready to hand;
her hair lay loose and scattered by the wind,

320 her flowing gown belted to bare her knee.
She hailed the men: "Tell me, sirs, have you seen
one of my sisters wandering down this way?
She'd have a quiver and spotted lynx-hide cape;
perhaps she was hot on the trail of a foam-flecked boar."

So Venus; and Venus' son replied to her:
"None of your sisters have I seen or heard,
O — what shall I call you? That's no mortal face,
that voice no girl's. You are a goddess, sure!
Sister of Phoebus?[12] One of the Nymphs' descent?

330 Blessed be your name, whatever it is! But help us!
What land is this? On what coasts of the world
have we been tossed? Tell us, for we are lost.
Vast waves and winds have sent us hapless here.
We'll offer prayer and rich blood-sacrifice!"

---

[10] **Achates:** Achates, as will become evident, is Aeneas's most "faithful friend."

[11] **Thracian Harpalyce:** Harpalyce was a legendary huntress and warrior princess from Thrace, a region in the northwest of Greece. What is crucial here is that Venus appears to her son in disguise, one of the many sources of sadness for the hero. Hebrus, in the next line, is one of the chief rivers of Thrace.

[12] **Sister of Phoebus:** Phoebus Apollo, the brother of Venus (Aphrodite); the epithet means "bright" or "shining."

Then Venus: "I am not worthy of such honor.
We girls of Tyre by custom bear the bow
and lace the scarlet boot high on the leg.
This land is Punic; of Tyre, our city and name;
around us are Libyans, people untamed by war.
340 Our queen is Dido; she left the city of Tyre
to escape her brother—a long and tortured tale
of cruel deception. Hear while I tell it briefly.
Her husband, Sychaeus, held the richest lands
in all Phoenicia; he was the man she loved,
her first, to whom her father gave her, a bride,
a virgin. But her brother, the king of Tyre,
Pygmalion,[13] had no peer in monstrous crime.
The two men quarreled; blind for love of wealth
Pygmalion murdered Sychaeus at the altar,
350 catching him off his guard; his sister's love
left him unmoved. He kept the deed long hidden
and cheated the heartsick girl with empty hopes.
But as she slept, her husband's unlaid ghost
came to her, showing a face all strange and pale.
He told of the murder, bared his wounded breast,
and brought the whole foul story to the light.
'Hurry! Run! Leave your fatherland!' he urged,
'and for your help, look, here a treasure buried—
silver and gold, more than you ever knew!'
360 His words led Dido to prepare for flight.
She brought together those who loathed the tyrant
or feared him. Ships, it happened, stood complete;
they seized them, put the treasure aboard. To sea
went greedy Pygmalion's gold. A woman led them!
They came to the place where you shall see the walls
huge rising and the towers of Carthage-town.
Here they bought land—'as much as one bull's hide
enclosed'—for this is the place called 'The Purse.'
But who are you? From what coasts have you come?
370 Where are you going?" Aeneas at these words
heaved a deep sigh and drew speech from his heart:
"My lady, if I began with first-beginnings,
and you were free to hear our tale of toil,
day would lie locked in heaven before the end!
We are from ancient Troy—if to your ears has come
the name of Troy?—We'd traveled many a sea
when storms by sheer chance drove us to Libyan shores.

---

[13] **Pygmalion:** Pygmalion, Dido's brother, was a king of Tyre. (He is not the Pygmalion, king of Cyprus, who fashions his ideal image of a woman into a statue that is given life by Venus, as told in Ovid's *Metamorphoses*.)

I am Aeneas the good; the gods I saved
ride in my ships. My name is known in heaven.
380 My goal is Italy, land of my fathers' line.
With twice ten ships I put to sea from Troy
to follow the path my goddess-mother showed me;
just seven, battered by wind and wave, remain.
I walk these Libyan wastes a helpless stranger
exiled by East and West." Venus could bear
no more, but spoke to end his sad account:

"Whoever you are, the love of heaven saved you
and brought you living to this Tyrian land.
Go now, and make your way to Dido's court.
390 Your men are safe, and changing winds have blown
your ships to safety. This I can tell you now,
unless I was taught to read the birds all wrong.
See there: twelve swans flying in joyful ranks;
Jove's eagle, swooping down from open sky
frightened and scattered them; now with lines new-formed
they've settled to earth or hover over the land.
As they in safety flapped their whistling wings
or soared in a flock to wreathe the sky with song,
just so your ships and men have come to port
400 or under full sail have reached the harbor's mouth.
Go now, and let this pathway guide your steps."

She turned to leave; a glow of light shone out
behind her head; her hair sent forth perfume
ambrosial; she let her train fall full-length down,
and walked in majesty divine! He knew
his mother, and as she hastened off he cried,
"What? Your son? Again so heartless to mock him—
you, too—with empty shows? Why was your hand
not laid in mine? Why could we not speak true?"
410 With this reproach he turned toward Dido's town.
But Venus walled the two in lightless air
and clothed them all about in heavy mist
so none could see them and no man had power
to hold them back or question why they came.
Then she flew off to Paphos, and with smiles
came home again, where incense wreathes her shrine
and hundred altars sweet with fresh-plucked blooms.

The two men meanwhile hurried down the path
and soon were climbing the highest hill that hangs
420 over the town and looks down on its walls.

Aeneas was awed: so vast, where once was camp-ground!
The wonder of gates, and avenues paved, and crowds!
Working like mad, those Tyrians; some at walls,
some toiled at forts, surveying, or hauling stone;
some marked out homesites and drew boundary lines.
They had their laws, their courts, their councilmen.
Here they were dredging a harbor; there they laid
a theater's undercroft, and cut tall columns
out of a quarry cliff to adorn the stage.
430   Like bees in June out in the blooming fields
busy beneath the sun, some teasing out
the new young workers, others pressing down
clear honey or making nectar burst the cells,
still others taking the loads brought in, while others
police the hive and drive off lazy drones:
the work hums on; the combs are sweet with thyme.
"O blessed by Fate! Your walls are building now!"
Aeneas said, as he watched the ramparts rise.
Walled in the cloud (a miracle!), he walked
440   among the workmen, and no one saw him come.

In mid-town was a pleasant, shady park,
marking the spot where Tyrians, tempest-tossed,
had dug to find, as Juno had foretold,
a horse's head — a sign that they should be
great soldiers and good farmers down the years.
Here Dido of Sidon built a temple to Juno
a huge vault filled with wealth and holiness.
Above its steps the doorway was of bronze,
the beams bronze-nailed, the doors and hinges brazen.
450   Here in the park Aeneas saw a sight
that eased his fears and made him first dare hope
for safety, and take heart for all his troubles.
As he searched over the temple, stone by stone,
awaiting the queen, and wondering how this town
had come to be, amazed at the workmen's zeal
and skill, he saw, scene after scene, the war
at Troy, battles now famed through all the world:
the Atrides, Priam, and, savage to both, Achilles.[14]
His tears welled up. "What place, Achates, now,"

---

[14] **Atrides . . . Achilles:** The Atrides (Atreides) are the brothers Menelaus and Agamemnon who joined forces against the Trojans after the Trojan prince Paris abducted Menelaus's wife, Helen. Achilles, the principal hero of the Achaeans, is "savage to both [sides]" because he holds a grudge against Agamemnon, leader of the Achaean forces.

460 he said, "what land does not know all we suffered?
See: Priam! Here too the brave have their reward!
The world has tears; man's lot does touch the heart.
Put off your fears: our story will save us yet!"
Aeneas spoke, and let this empty show
nourish his grief and flood his face with tears.
He saw how men had fought the fight for Troy:
here Greeks retreating, here Trojans pressing hard,
here their allies, here plumed Achilles' car.
Nearby were Rhesus'[15] snowy-canvassed tents—
470 (he knew them and wept!) his men, just fallen to sleep,
betrayed and butchered by bloody Diomede;
gone, too, his fiery team before they knew
the taste of Trojan feed or Xanthus' waters.
And here was Troilus,[16] running, his weapons lost
(poor boy! he was no man to meet Achilles!),
his horses pulled him clinging to his car,
still gripping the reins; his head and shoulders dragged
over the ground; his spear wrote in the dust.
And here the women of Troy in sad parade
480 were bringing the robe to cruel Athena's temple
with humble prayer, beating their breasts in grief:
with stony eyes the goddess stared them down.
And there Achilles peddled the lifeless corpse
of Hector, dragged three times around Troy-walls.
Aeneas could not hold back a cry of pain
to see the car, the ransom, his dead friend,
and Priam stretching out defenseless hands.
He saw himself, surrounded by great Greeks,
and Memnon the Moor,[17] with his Arabian troops.
490 And leading her crescent-shielded Amazons
Penthesilea[18] fought madly amid the host.
One breast lay bare above the sword-belt clasp—
a warrior-maiden who dared to fight with men.

As Aeneas of Troy stood marveling at these sights,
unable to speak or turn his eyes away,
into the temple came Dido the beautiful,
the queen, with all her bodyguard around her.

---

[15] **Rhesus:** A Thracian king allied with the Trojans; it was said that if Rhesus's horses would taste "Trojan feed"
or drink from the waters of the river Xanthus, Troy would not fall. As described here, Diomede and Odysseus
drag the horses away before they can do so.   [16] **Troilus:** One of King Priam's sons who was killed by Achilles.
[17] **Memnon the Moor:** An Ethiopian king allied with the Trojans.   [18] **Penthesilea:** The queen of the Amazons
who supported the Trojans in the war; she was killed by Achilles.

As by Eurotas or on the height of Cynthus[19]
Diana leads her dancing mountain-maids,
500 a thousand ringed about her; there she goes
quiver on back, head-high above them all
(no word betrays her mother's heartfelt joy)—
just so was Dido, and just so her joy
to see her people working, building, planning.
She entered the temple; under its central dome
she took her place enthroned, walled by armed men.
There she sat judging, framing laws, assigning
work to her men by fair shares or by lot,
when all at once a crowd came rushing in.
510 Aeneas saw they had Sergestus, Antheus,
Cloanthus, and others whom the storm at sea
had scattered and carried away to distant shores.
Aeneas was speechless; Achates was struck hard
by joy and fear at once: they were afire
to greet their friends—but still, what did this mean?
Pretending calm, clothed in their cloud, they watched.
What had these men endured? Where were their ships?
Why were they here? Each ship had sent her man
to beg for mercy. Pleading, the group moved on.

520 Once they had entered and gained the right to speak,
Ilioneus, the oldest, pled in peace:
"My lady, Jove has let you found your city
and bring both right and rule to savage tribes.
We're Trojans, helpless, blasted by wind and wave.
We beg you: do us no wrong, nor burn our ships.
Spare a good people! Be merciful! Hear our plea!
We have not come in arms to scorch the earth
of Libya, to plunder your homes and load our ships.
The vanquished have no heart for such presumption.
530 There is a place called 'Westland'[20] by the Greeks,
an ancient country, powerful, warlike, rich;
the Oenotri[21] settled it; now, we hear, their sons
are calling it 'Italy' for their founder's name.[22]
This was our goal.
But all of a sudden waves and rain and wind
drove us on unseen banks; squalls from the south

---

[19] Eurotas . . . Cynthus: Eurotas is a river running near Sparta where Diana (Artemis in Greek mythology), the goddess of the hunt and guardian of animals and birth, was worshiped. Cynthus is a mountain in Delos, where Diana was born.   [20] 'Westland': Hesperia, the land of Evening or the West Land, was what the Greeks called Italy, which lay to their west.   [21] the Oenotri: The original inhabitants of southern Italy.   [22] their founder's name: Italus, the legendary father of Italy.

scattered our ships. Some sank; some hung on reefs
uncharted. We few swam here to your shores.
What kind of people are you? Civilized?
540   What laws are these? We have been kept from shore,
forbidden to land, and met with shows of force.
If men and mortal arms arouse your scorn,
be sure the gods take note of right and wrong.
Aeneas was our chief; he had no peer
in justice, goodness, and the arts of war.
If fate has saved him, if he lives and breathes,
and has not fallen to rest in heartless dark,
we have no fears. However great your kindness,
you'll not regret it. In Sicily, we have towns
550   and arms, for Acestes[23] boasts his Trojan blood.
We're badly damaged: let us beach our craft,
shape timbers in your woods, and strip out oars;
then if we find our friends and chief, we'll sail
for Italy, Latium — Italy with a will!
But if it's finished, if our well-loved lord
is lost at sea, and hope of Iulus[24] gone,
then let us cross to Sicily, whence we came.
Acestes will take us; he shall be our king."
Thus spoke Ilioneus; with one great shout
560   the sons of Troy assented.

Then with a gracious nod, Queen Dido answered:
"Put fear from your hearts, Trojans; dismiss your cares.
Our lot is hard, our kingdom new; for this
our laws are stern, our whole land under guard.
Who knows not Troy, knows not Aeneas' people,
those brave fighters, and that great holocaust?
We Punic folk are not so dull of heart;
the sun starts not his course so far from Tyre.
You're bound for the Westland, Saturn's wide domain?
570   or Sicily, and Acestes for your king?
I'll help you, keep you safe, and send you on.
Or will you settle here and share my realm?
The city I build is yours: pull up your ships.
Trojan, Tyrian, all shall be one to me.
If only that same storm had forced your chief,

---

[23] **Acestes:** A king of Sicily whose mother was from Troy; he offered the Trojans refuge in his lands on their journey.   [24] **Iulus:** Also called Ascanius, Iulus is the son of Aeneas and Creusa. He represents the hope of the future in that he succeeds his father as the ruler of Lavinium, the first city established by the Trojans in Latium, and also founds Alba Longa. In Iulus, Virgil establishes the origin of the Julian emperors of Rome, including Julius Caesar and Augustus.

Aeneas, here too! I'll send out men to search
the shores and all the ends of Libyan land:
he may be safe, but in some backwood lost."

Her words set hearts a-beating in Achates
580   the brave and Lord Aeneas; they longed to burst
their cloud. Achates first was moved to speak:
"My lord, what thought arises in your heart?
Here we are safe; our ships and men are found.
One only is missing, but far at sea we saw
him drowned. The rest is as your mother told us."
Scarce had he spoken when their veiling cloud
burst all at once and turned to clearest air.
There stood Aeneas, splendid in bright light,
grand as a god, for Venus breathed on him
590   to give him strength and vigor, the glow of youth,
and made his eyes shine out with power and joy —
like ivory carved to beauty, like some work
of silver or Parian marble[25] chased with gold.
His presence and his words burst on the queen
and all her men: "You want me? Here I am,
Aeneas the Trojan, saved from Libyan seas.
You pitied, you only, the terrible toil of Troy.
We few that Greece had left on land and sea
have suffered every blow, lost everything,
600   yet you would share your city, your home, with us!
My lady, how can we thank you, we and all
the sons of Troy, now scattered across the earth?
Oh, if the gods note goodness, if there are
such things as justice and hearts that know the right,
you shall be richly blessed. What happy year
bore you? What noble parents got you so?
While rivers run to sea, while shadows cross
the curving hills and fires feed the stars,
your name will live in honor and in praise
610   wherever the world may call me." With these words
he turned to greet Ilioneus, Serestus,
and the others, Gyas the brave, and brave Cloanthus.

Dido of Tyre, struck speechless at the sight
and at the man's misfortune, spoke at last:
"What happened, my lord? What ill luck dogged you here?
What dangers forced you onto rock and reef?

---

[25] **Parian marble:** A kind of marble noted for its particular beauty and found on the island of Paros.

Are you Aeneas of Troy, Anchises' son?
Whom Venus in Phrygia bore by Simois' wave?
Yes! I remember! Teucer[26] came to Tyre
620 driven from Salamis, searching for new realms:
'Would Belus help?' (Belus — my father — was then
reducing fertile Cyprus to his power.)
And since that time I've known the tale of Troy,
the city, your name, and all the Argive kings.
Teucer, who fought the Teucri, praised them high,
and loved to claim descent from Teucrian stock.[27]
Enter my home! My welcome to you all!
My fate, like yours, has harried me through great toil
and trouble, at last to place me in this land.
630 By evil schooled, I know what mercy means."

With that she led Aeneas to her palace
and called for prayers of thanks to all the gods.
Nor did she forget his men: down to the beach
she sent off twenty steers, a hundred hogs
(fat tuskers all), a hundred lambs and ewes,
and wine, god's gift of joy.
In the great hall splendor to ease a king
was set out, and a banquet was prepared;
the cloths were royal red, embroidered fine;
640 on tables massive plate, and golden cups
chased with historic scenes, the long, long line
of deeds heroic since the race began.

Aeneas, whose father-heart could not rest easy,
dispatched Achates to the ships, to tell
Ascanius[28] the news and bring him back;
his every thought was for the son he loved.
"We need gifts, too," he said. "Bring what we saved
when Ilium[29] fell — that coat all worked in gold,
the scarf bordered with yellow acanthus leaves

---

[26] **Teucer:** The half brother of Telamon Ajax, Teucer was a Greek warrior who was banished from his home because he did not bring Ajax back with him from the Trojan War; in his exile he founded Salamis on the island of Cyprus. He was the first to bring Dido news of the Trojan War. (Not to be confused with Teucer, the founder of Troy; see note 27.)

[27] **Teucrian stock:** Dido is here playing on names, for the legendary founder of Troy was also named Teucer, whose descendants, the Trojans, were sometimes called "Teucri." Dido is speaking directly of Teucer, the Greek warrior. (See note 26.)

[28] **Ascanius:** Also called Iulus; Aeneas's son by Creusa. (See note 24.)   [29] **Ilium:** Another name for Troy.

650 that Argive Helen[30] wore, brought from Mycenae
     when she set sail for Troy and wedded bliss
     unlawful—they were her mother Leda's[31] gifts;
     yes, and the staff Ilione used to bear—
     oldest of Priam's daughters—and her chain
     of beads, her golden coronet, thick with gems."
     Achates ran to the ships to speed compliance. . . .

[At the banquet, Venus awakens love in Dido by sending Cupid disguised as Ascanius. Dido embraces the boy, which initiates her love for Aeneas. Dido urges Aeneas to tell the story of the fall of Troy and his years of wandering.]

BOOK 2
[THE FALL OF TROY]

All talking stopped; all faces turned to watch.
Aeneas looked out on the hall and then began:
"What? Know that sorrow again, my lady? What words
can tell how royal Troy, the throne of tears,
fell to the Greeks? I saw that tragedy
and in it played great part. Who'd tell that tale—
Myrmidon, Thracian, or cruel Ulysses'[32] man—
and keep from tears? Now dewy night is fading
from heaven; the setting stars warn men to sleep.
10 But if you want so much to learn our fate,
to hear in a word how Troy travailed and died,
though memory makes me shrink and shudder with grief,
I'll try.
        "Broken by war, forced back by fate,
the Argive kings watched year on year slip by,
then built with help of Pallas'[33] holy hand
a horse tall as a mountain, ribbed with pine—
'For a safe trip home,' they said. (The lie spread fast.)
They threw dice for a crew and slipped them in,
locking them deep inside that lightless cave
20 to fill the monster's womb with men-at-arms.

---

[30] **Argive Helen:** Helen, the wife of the Argive leader King Menelaus of Sparta. In return for Paris's favorable judgment in a beauty contest between herself, Juno (Hera), and Athena, Venus (Aphrodite) offers Helen as a bribe to the Trojan prince Paris. Paris soon after wins Helen's love and takes her from Sparta to Troy, setting off the Trojan War.   [31] **Leda:** The wife of the exiled king of Sparta, Tyndareüs, who lived in Aetolia. From a sexual union with Jove (Zeus), who transformed her into a swan for the purpose, Leda bore Helen, who was hatched from an egg.   [32] **Myrmidon . . . Ulysses:** Ulysses is the Roman name for Odysseus, the son of Laertes, king of Ithaca; one of the greatest of the Greek heroes, known for his cunning and quick-wittedness, Odysseus is the hero of Homer's *Odyssey*. The Myrmidons were the warriors led by Achilles.   [33] **Pallas:** Pallas Athena, the goddess of wisdom; known as Minerva in Roman mythology.

"Offshore lies Tenedos,[34] famed and storied island,
rich and a power while Priam's throne held firm,
now only a bay where keels ride rough to anchor;
thus far they sailed, to hide by moldering piers.
We thought them gone with the wind and homeward bound.
All Troy shook off her shackled years of pain,
threw open the gates, ran out in joy to see
the empty Dorian[35] camp, the vacant shore:
here tented the Thracians, here the cruel Achilles;
30 here lay the fleet, here ranged the ranks of war.
Some stopped to stare at Pallas' deadly gift,
amazed at a horse so huge. Up spoke Thymoetes:
'Inside the walls with it! Station it in our fort!'
(Treason? Or just the turn of fate for Troy?)
But Capys and all our wiser heads bade throw
this Grecian trick and generosity suspect
into the sea, or bring up fire and burn it,
or pierce it and see what hollow wombs might hide.
Divided, bewildered, the people turned here, turned there.

40 "Laocoon[36] strode to the front. (With a crowd of priests
he'd run in fury and haste from Castle Hill.)
He shouted, 'You fools! You wretched, raving fools!
You think the enemy gone? Who left this 'gift'?
Greeks? And you trust it? This is our 'friend,' Ulysses?
That wooden thing holds Argives locked inside,
or else it's an engine built to attack our walls,
to spy on our homes and fall from above on us all.
There's treachery here. A horse? Don't trust it, Trojans!
Whatever it is, I fear Greeks even with gifts.'

50 "So speaking he heaved and hurled his heavy spear
against the creature's flank and vaulted paunch;
the shaft stood trembling; from that wounded womb
came a sound of moaning cavernous and hollow.

---

[34] **Tenedos:** An island in the Aegean, near the coast of the Troad, the region around Troy, where the Greeks sailed to deceive the Trojans into thinking they had given up the battle. They returned, as described here, to wreak havoc on the city of Troy, which had been penetrated by the so-called Trojan Horse, in which an advance team of Greek warriors hid and slipped into the city unbeknownst to the Trojans.   [35] **Dorian:** Greek; the Dorians were a major branch of the early Greek people who moved into northern Greece from Thessaly, eventually moving south to occupy the Peloponnese.   [36] **Laocoon:** A Trojan priest and follower of Neptune. When Laocoon warned the Trojans not to accept the wooden horse offered by the Greeks at Troy, he and his two sons were killed by giant sea-snakes. Thinking Laocoon had insulted the gods by refusing the gift, the Trojans brought the horse inside the city walls, enabling the Greek warriors hidden inside the horse to penetrate their defenses.

And had Fate and our hearts not been perverse,
we would have bloodied that Argive hiding-hole,
and Troy and Priam's towers would still be standing.

    "Up came a man, hands bound behind his back,
dragged on by shepherds shouting, 'Where's the king?
We're Trojan; this stranger met us and surrendered!'
60 (He'd plotted and planned it so, to open Troy
to the Greeks—sure of himself—prepared both ways:
to turn his trick, or keep his day with death.)
From all sides, eager to see, our Trojan men
came rushing to ring the captive round with taunts.
Now hear how Greeks can lie; from this one crime
learn of them all!
We watched him. There he stood, unarmed and frightened,
looking from face to hostile Phrygian face:
'O gods!' he cried, 'what land will take me in?
70 What sea? What's left for one like me? What's left?
I have no place among the Greeks, and now
the Trojans call for my blood to slake their hate.'
His pitiful cry softened our hearts and dulled
our every impulse. What was his name? we asked.
What did he want? How dared he trust to capture?
At last he laid his fear aside and spoke:

    "'I'll tell it all, my lord, yes, all, and tell
it true,' he said. 'I'm Greek. Be that confessed
first off. If Fortune molded Sinon luckless,
80 she shall not mold him foul and a liar, too.[37]
Has anyone told you—has word reached your ears
of Belus' son, Palamedes?[38] Fame has called him
"the great." He hated war; for this, the Greeks
slandered, harried, and hounded the saintly man
down to his death. Now that he's gone, they mourn him.
I was his cousin. My father, a humble man,
sent me, no more than a boy, to be his aide.
While he stood king among the kings, full-fledged,
full-powered, I held my small lieutenancy
90 with honor; but Ulysses' craft and hate

---

[37] **Sinon . . . liar, too:** A Greek master of deceit whose supposed kinship with Palamedes, the warrior who advised Agamemnon to abandon the war against Troy and was executed after Ulysses (Odysseus) brought false charges against him, is strategically designed to win over the Trojans, as is his bluff soldier's speech.   [38] **Belus' son, Palamedes:** Palamedes' father, Belus, as a Greek, is not King Belus of Tyre who is Dido's father.

(you know them!) sent him from this world of men.
That crushed me. I lived in darkness and in sorrow,
privately cursing my cousin's unjust fate.
Then like a fool I talked and swore revenge
if ever my luck should bring me home to Argos.
My silly boasting won me harsh ill will.
That was my downfall; from that hour Ulysses
brought charge after frightening charge, and spread dark hints
among the people, determined to see me dead.
100   He knew no rest until with Calchas'[39] help—
but this is waste! Why tell unwelcome tales?
Why wait? If "Greek" means but one thing to you,
and the name is enough, exact the penalty now!
Ulysses would cheer, Agamemnon pay you well!'

"Then how we burned to question and inquire,
unschooled in crime so vile and Argive craft.
He trembled but talked on, with feigned concern:

"'Many times the Greeks had longed to abandon Troy
and run away home from the weary years of war;
110   and oh, that they had! Many times a blustery sea
blocked them, and storm winds frighted their departure.
And worst: when the wooden fabric stood complete—
that horse—all heaven flashed and roared and rained.
Worried, we sent Eurypylus off to seek
Apollo's will; and the word he brought was grim:
"With blood of a virgin slain[40] you won the winds
when you set sail, you Greeks, for Trojan shores;
with blood you'll buy return: an Argive soul's
the price to pay." When this word reached the ranks
120   men's hearts went numb; an icy tremor ran
down through their bones: whom had Apollo claimed?
Riot was near when the Ithacan° drew Calchas   Ulysses
into our midst. "Speak, priest," he said, "and tell
God's will." (Men prophesied that murder plot
was aimed at me. They watched but said no word.)
Ten days he held his tongue, guarding against
one word that might send some man to his death.
At last Ulysses' bluster brought him round
to speak, as planned, and mark me for the altar.

---

[39]**Calchas:** A Greek seer and priest serving with the Greek forces during the Trojan War.   [40]**Eurypylus . . .
virgin slain:** Iphigenia, the daughter of Agamemnon and Clytemnestra, was sacrificed in order to win favorable
winds from the gods and launch the Greek fleet against Troy. Eurypylus was a Greek commander.

130 No one protested; indignation died,
     now that one wretch was scape for all their fears.

     The dreadful day drew near; the rites were readied—
     salt meal and sacred ribbons for my head.
     I ran from death—yes, ran. I broke my bonds
     by dark of night; in muddy marsh and reeds
     I lay and waited, praying that they would sail.
     Now I've no hope to see the hills of home,
     my little sons, the father that I love—
     the Greeks may well assess on them the price
140 of my escape—their deaths acquit my sin.
     And so, sir, by God's name and power and truth,
     by all the honor that still lives unstained
     in mortal man, have mercy on my pain;
     have mercy on a heart unjustly used!"

     "His tears won him a pardon and our pity.
     Priam at once commanded him relieved
     of shackle and chain, then spoke as to a friend:
     'Whoever you are, you've lost your Greeks: forget them!
     Be one of us! Now speak out, tell the truth:
150 Why the huge horse? Who moved to place it here?
     What is it? An act of worship? A siege machine?'
     Sinon had learned his lines; with Argive art
     he sloughed his irons and raised his hands to heaven:
     'O fires eternal, O power beyond blaspheme,
     be witness,' he cried; 'O altar and unblessed blade
     that I escaped, O ribbons I wore to die:
     I solemnly renounce my Argive oaths
     and curse the Greeks. No law, no loyalty
     bids me beware of telling all I know.
160 And if I keep Troy free, then keep your word
     and promise—if I speak truth and give full measure.
     The Greeks went off to war with hope and trust
     based full and forever on Pallas' help; then crime
     and crime's inventor—Diomede and Ulysses—
     sinfully wrested from her hallowed shrine
     Pallas the Less.[41] They killed the temple guards,
     pulled down her idol, and with hands all blood

---

[41] **Pallas the Less:** The Palladium, a small statue of Minerva (Pallas Athena) that was said to guarantee the safety of Troy so long as it remained in place at Minerva's shrine. Ulysses and Diomede stole the Palladium and desecrated the goddess's shrine, so angering her that she wreaked revenge on the Greek forces she had thitherto supported.

dared touch the virgin goddess' holy bands.
Thereafter nothing was certain. Argive hopes
170   faltered, their strength was gone, their goddess angry.
No room for doubt! Tritonia[42] gave clear sign:
scarce was her image based in camp, when fire
flashed from her staring eyes and salty sweat
ran over her limbs, and thrice (wonder to tell!)
she leaped up, shield in hand, and shook her spear.
"Run!" Calchas warned them. "Take to the seas at once!"—
Never could Argive power cut Troy down
till they went home to learn God's will, and brought
his blessing anew in curved keels over the sea.
180   And home they've gone, riding the wind to Greece.
They'll win God's favor again, recross the water,
and land here unforeseen—so spoke the prophet.
This horse is payment for their heinous crime:
for godhead wronged, for Pallas the Less defiled.
And Calchas bid them build it massive, tall,
beam upon beam, to tower toward the sky—
too wide for the gates, too huge to pass the walls
and by some ancient covenant save your people.
For if your hand should harm Minerva's gift
190   then death (on Calchas' head may that doom fall!)
would come to Priam's Trojans and his power.
But if by your hand it climbed within your city
then Asia would some day march on Grecian walls,
and in that war our grandsons groan and die.'

"Strategy, perjury vile! Sinon by craft
won our belief; tricks and counterfeit tears
took captive men whom Diomede, Achilles,
ten years, and a thousand ships had never tamed!

"Here something worse and far more frightful rose
200   to meet us and trouble our unsuspecting hearts.
Laocoon, chosen by lot as Neptune's priest,
was killing a great bull at his sacred shrine,
when out from Tenedos, over the quiet floods
(I shudder to tell it) two snakes, coil on huge coil
breasting the sea, came slithering toward the shore.
Their necks rose high in the troughs, their blood-red manes
crested the waves; their other parts behind
slid through the water, twin bodies winding vast.

---

[42]**Tritonia:** An epithet for Minerva (Athena) associating her with Lake Tritonis in Libya, her birthplace.

The salt sea gurgled and foamed. Now they reached land.
210 Hot were their eyes, bloodshot and flecked with flame;
through hissing lips their tongues flicked in, flicked out.
Bloodless we fled the sight; they never wavered
but went for Laocoon; first his two young sons —
poor little boys! — they hugged in their twin coils
wrapping them round and tearing at leg and arm.
Laocoon leaped to the rescue, sword in hand;
the great snakes seized him, wrapped him round and round,
two scaly coils at his waist, two at his throat.
Above his head, their heads and necks rose high.
220 With his hands he tried to pry the loops apart,
while blood and venom soaked his sacred bands.
He screamed to make high heaven shudder — screamed
like a bloodied bull run roaring from the altar
to shake free of his neck an ill-aimed ax.
But those twin snakes slipped off toward Castle Hill
and escaped. They made for cruel Tritonia's shrine
and hid at her feet behind her circled shield.

"We stood and shook while into every heart
fresh terror crept. 'He sinned and paid fair price,'
230 we said. 'Laocoon stabbed a sacred thing;
sin rode the spear he hurled against that flank.
Bring the horse home,' we cried, 'and let us pray,
pray to our lady of might.'
We cut through walls and flung our ramparts down.
All stripped for the work; under the horse's feet
we slipped rollers, and from its neck we rove
hempen halyards. Up rode the death machine,
big with armed men, while boys and virgin girls
sang hymns and joyed to lay hand to the lines.
240 Into mid-city the menacing mass rolled on.
O homeland, god-land, Troy! O Dardan walls
famed for your soldier sons! Four times it balked
at the sill, four times its belly rang with arms,
but we pushed on, forgetful, blind, and mad,
to set the luckless monster in our fort.
Even then Cassandra[43] cried, 'Death! Men will die!'
but Apollo had bid the Trojans never heed her.
In festive mood (poor souls! this day would be
our last!), we banked our hallowed shrines with flowers.

---

[43] **Cassandra:** A prophetess and daughter of King Priam and Queen Hecuba of Troy; because she offended Apollo by spurning his advances, he put a curse on her that her prophecies would never be believed.

250 "The vault of heaven turned; night rushed from Ocean
enfolding in vast darkness earth and sky
and Myrmidon guile; on the walls our sentries lay
scattered, wordless, weary, sound asleep.
Now came the Argive ships in battle line
from Tenedos under a silent, friendly moon,
heading for well-known shores. A torch flamed out
from the royal ship. Sinon, by unkind fates
preserved, slipped softly back the bolts of pine
and freed the Greeks from the womb. The opened horse
260 released them; glad from that wooden cave they poured.
Thessander, Sthenelus — lords — and dire Ulysses
let down a rope and slid, then Acamas, Thoas,
Machaon, next Neoptolemus, son of Achilles,
Menelaus, and he who laid the plot, Epeus.
They fell on a city buried in sleep and wine,
murdered the watch, threw open the gate, let in
their friends — a column of schemers, hand in hand.

"It was the hour when gentle sleep first comes,
welcome, by God's grace, welcome to weary men.
270 I dreamed, and there before my eyes stood Hector,
sorrowed and sad, his face a flood of tears.
He seemed as when the chariot dragged him: bruised,
bloody, dusty, thongs through his swollen feet.
O God! How he looked! How changed from that great man,
the Hector who wore Achilles' armor home,
who hurled into Argive ships our Trojan fire.
His beard all dirt, his hair was stiff with blood;
he wore each wound he'd earned before our walls —
our fathers' walls. I dreamed that I wept, too,
280 and hailed the man and let my grief pour out:
'O light of Troy! Dardania's[44] hope unfailing!
What held you, Hector? Where have you been? How long
we waited! Your people — so many of them are dead;
our men, our city have borne so many trials!
We are weary! We see you — but what is wrong? Your face
is clouded dark: Why? Why do I see these wounds?'
He said no word, nor heeded my vain questions,
but with a groan drawn deep from a burdened heart,
'Run, goddess-born,' he cried; 'run from these flames!
290 Greece owns our walls; the towers of Troy are tumbling!

---

[44] **Dardania:** Another name for Troy, so called after King Dardanus, the legendary founder of the city.

To country and king all debts are paid; my hand
had saved them, if any hand had power to save.
Her holy things, her gods, Troy trusts to you.
Take them to share your fate; find walls for them:
wander the wide sea over, then build them great.'
He spoke, and in my hands laid mighty Vesta,
her ribbons, and—from her inmost shrine—her fire.[45]

"And now from the walls came screams and cries and groans.
Louder and louder, although my father's house
300   was set far off, apart, well screened by trees,
came the noise of battle, the terrible clash of arms.
I shook off sleep, and to the highest peak
of the roof I climbed, and stopped and strained to hear:
as when a flame by wild winds driven falls
on a grain field, or a mountain stream in flood
sweeps farms, sweeps crops away and plowman's toil,
and topples trees; high on his cliff the shepherd,
hearing the thunderous noise, sits blank with fear.
Then all—the word of honor, the Argive lie—
310   came clear. Deiphobus'[46] palace crashed and fell
in a holocaust roof-high; Ucalegon's next
caught fire; the straits reflected back the flames.
I heard men shouting, heard the trumpet-call.
Like a fool I seized my sword—what sense had swords?
But I was ablaze to round up men for war
and with them rush to the fort; a senseless wrath
propelled me: 'Glory!' I thought. 'To die in battle!'

"But here came Panthus escaping from Greek spears—
Panthus, priest of Apollo on Castle Hill—
320   arms full of holy things and beaten gods,
trailed by his grandson, panicking toward the gates.
'Panthus, how do we stand? What have we gained?'
He cut me off and answered with a groan:
'Dardania's end, her scapeless hour has come.
Trojan and Troy, we've had our day, our power,
our glory. A heartless Jove has handed all
to the Greeks. Our city is ashes! Greece is lord!
Tall stands the horse inside our fort, and births
her soldiers. Sinon, prancing his glory-dance,

---

[45] **Vesta . . . fire:** The ghost of Hector appears before Aeneas and bids him to take the household gods, the Penates, and flee the city. Vesta is the goddess of the hearth and fire who holds an eternal flame.   [46] **Deiphobus:** One of the sons of King Priam of Troy. Ucalegon in the next line is also a Trojan.

330 sets fire on fire. Through gates flung wide, they come,
those myriads—all who marched from great Mycenae.[47]
Posts have been set, spear locked with spear, to block
our streets; they stand, a line of shining steel,
blades ready for blood. Our first-line watch can scarce
form battle rank; they fight without command.'

"The words of Panthus and God's holy will
sent me toward flames and fighting, where Mars[48] roared
his challenge, and battle cries rose up to heaven.
Friends joined me: Rhipeus and that champion,
340 Epytus, guided by moonlight; Hypanis, Dymas
fell in at my side, and young Coroebus, too,
the son of Mygdon, just now come to Troy,
fired with foolish passion for Cassandra
(accepted, he fought for Priam and his people—
unlucky youth, who would not heed the word
of his prophetic princess!).
I watched them boldly form a battle group,
then spoke to them: 'Good men, brave hearts—but brave
for nothing! If you feel you must fight on
350 and dare to the end, you see how fortune stands.
They've gone from every temple, every shrine,
the gods who blessed our power. You seek to save
a city in flames. But on to war! We'll die!
Sole hope of the vanquished is their hopelessness!'
This fired their mad young hearts afresh. Like wolves
hot for a kill at murky midnight, blind,
driven by horrid belly-lust—their cubs
are waiting with blood-parched throats—through hostile arms
we rushed to death undoubted, held our way
360 through mid-town; night swung sable wings around us.
That night of ruin, night of death—who'd tell
its story or match our sorrows with his tears?
An ancient city, queen of the ages, fell;
the dead men lay by thousands in her streets,
in home and palace, at the hallowed gates
of gods. Nor only Trojans paid their lives;
sometimes courage returned to beaten hearts,
and Danaan victors died. Here grief heartrending,
terror, and death over all in countless forms.

---

[47] **Mycenae:** Agamemnon's home city in Greece.   [48] **Mars:** The Roman god of war and agriculture; Ares in Greek mythology.

370 "Androgeos first approached us, at the head
of a crowd of Greeks; mistakenly he thought
us comrades in arms and spoke to us as friends:
'Hurry, men! You are late! What held you back
so long? The rest have ripped and stripped and fired
Troy. Have you just now left the tall-sparred ships?'
He broke off then (our answers seemed not made
for trust) and sensed he'd fallen amid his foes.
He stopped, clapped hand to mouth, and stumbled back.
As one who, feeling his way through brambles, steps
380 on a sudden snake, jumps and shudders and runs
from head held high to strike, and hood spread wide—
just so Androgeos saw and jumped and fled.
Shield lapped to shield, we charged and hemmed them in.
On unknown ground, they panicked; one by one
we killed them. Fortune blessed our first assault.
Our luck now made Coroebus' heart beat high;
'Look! Fortune,' he said, 'has shown us how to win!
Success lies where she points the way: let's follow!
Let's take their shields and wear the Greek device
390 ourselves. Deceit or daring, who'd ask a foe?
Arms are here for the taking.' He spoke, and seized
Androgeos' plumed helmet and his shield
with its proud device, and buckled on his sword.
Rhipeus, Dymas and all their company
laughed as they took the spoil to arm themselves.
Under false signs we mingled with the Greeks
and many a battle joined while night was blind,
and sent to Orcus[49] many a man of Greece.
Still others scattered and ran for trusted ship
400 and shore, while others in shame and terror climbed
the horse again, to cower in its vast belly.

"'Man, trust not the gods except with their consent!'
Here, dragged by her long, long hair, came Priam's daughter,[50]
holy and virgin, torn from Minerva's[51] shrine;
in vain toward heaven she turned her burning eyes—
eyes, for her soft, young hands were bound with chains.
This sight Coroebus could not bear; his heart
went wild; he rushed against their ranks to die.
Behind him we charged in a body, sword by sword.

---

[49] **Orcus:** The Roman underworld, or land of the dead.   [50] **Priam's daughter:** Cassandra, the prophetess.
[51] **Minerva:** The Roman name for Pallas Athena, goddess of wisdom. (See notes 33 and 41.)

410 And now—disaster! Down from the temple's top
came Trojan spears to spill our wretched blood:
our arms and plumes had wrongly marked us Greeks.
Then—for we'd seized the girl—the Argives roared
with fury, formed ranks and charged: Ajax the chief,[52]
the twin Atridae, the whole Thessalian host;
as when sometimes the winds whirl till they burst
then crash head-on: Westerly, South, and East
rich with his Orient steeds; the woodlands wail
and Nereus[53] stirs his deeps to foam and fury.
420 And those whom darkness and our stratagem
had put to flight pell-mell down every street
now showed themselves; they first detected shields
and swords not ours, and caught our foreign speech.
Sheer numbers crushed us; first Coroebus fell
by hand of Peneleus at Minerva's altar;
and Rhipeus died, the justest man that lived
in Troy, unwavering servant of the right
(yet heaven forsook him); Hypanis died, and Dymas
transfixed by friends; not all your piety,
430 Panthus, could save you, nor Apollo's bands.
Ashes of Troy! Last flame of all I loved!
Bear witness that at your death I never shrank
from sword or sorrow, and had Fate so decreed
I had earned a death at Grecian hands! We ran,
Iphitus, Pelias, and I—one old and tired,
the other limping from Ulysses' wound—
straight toward the sound of war by Priam's palace.

"Here was huge battle to make all other strife
and death through all the city seem like nothing.
440 Here Mars ran wild, and Argives rushed the walls;
we saw them march the 'tortoise' toward the gates.[54]
Up went the ladders next to the very doors;
men climbed the rungs; their left hands held their shields,
bulwark to blows; their right hands seized the roof.
Our Trojans on their side ripped loose and flung
whole towers and rooftrees; seeing the end had come,

---

[52] **Ajax the chief:** Ajax the lesser, son of Oileus, who was punished by the gods for desecrating Minerva's shrine and kidnapping and raping Cassandra; the Atridae of the next line are Agamemnon and Menelaus.

[53] **Nereus:** A sea-god whose fifty daughters with the sea-goddess Doris were known as the Nereids.

[54] **march the 'tortoise' . . . gates:** Refers to the Romans' practice of holding shields over their heads when attacking fortified walls.

as death approached they made these weapons serve.
Gilt beams, the glory that roofed their sires of old,
they tumbled down, while others bared their blades
450   and stood to the doors, a barricade of men.
Our strength came back; we ran toward Priam's walls
to help our friends and give the vanquished valor.

"There was a secret hall and door, a passage
between the royal mansions—a gate that none
would notice; often, while our throne held firm,
Andromache[55]—poor thing!—had walked this way
taking her son to grandsire or to uncle.
Here I slipped in and climbed to the roof; there stood
our Trojans, hurling spear on useless spear.
460   On a steep gable stood a tower, the peak
of the palace, where we were wont to keep the watch
over Troy and Grecian fleet and Argive camp.
We hacked at this where tower and rooftop joined—
the fabric's weakest spot—and tore it loose
from its base and pushed it over; down it went
to crack and shatter and scatter its fragments far
over Argive troops. But more marched up, though stones
and weapons of every kind rained down.

"At the very door of the palace Pyrrhus[56] pranced
470   with a flourish and brazen flash of spear and blade—
like a snake on foul herbs fed, come from his hole
all puffed from a long, cold winter under the soil.
Stripping his skin he turns out sleek and young
and ripples his liquid coils; he lofts his head
up toward the sun and flicks his three-forked tongue.
Periphas and Achilles' charioteer,
the squire Automedon, all the Scyrians,[57] too,
charged the palace and tossed fire toward the roof.
Pyrrhus was leader; he seized a double ax,
480   chopped through the threshold and ripped out post and hinge,
fittings and all, then hacked at oaken beam
and panel to make a huge hole gaping wide.
There stood the house revealed, there stood its halls,
the home of Priam, of a long line of kings;

---

[55] **Andromache:** Hector's wife and the mother of his son, Astyanax.   [56] **Pyrrhus:** Also known as Neoptolomus, the son of Achilles.   [57] **Scyrians:** Fighters from the island of Scyros, where Pyrrhus was born.

there at his doorway stood his bodyguard.
Inside the house rose cries and screams of terror
commingled, while the caverned inmost vaults
shrieked with the women; the outcry struck the stars.
Mothers in fright ran madly round the halls,
490 threw arms about the columns and kissed them close.
On pressed Pyrrhus, strong as his father; nor bolts
nor guards could hold him back. Crash! came the ram;
down fell the door; down tumbled post and hinge.
Force paved a way; in burst the Greeks to slaughter
the guard and fill the palace, wall to wall.
Not so from a broken dam a stream bursts forth
that foams and swirls and sweeps the dikes away;
its crest runs raging over field and plain
to bear off beast and barn. I saw blood drive
500 men mad: Achilles' son, the twin Atridae;
I saw Hecuba[58] her hundred daughters: Priam
fouling with blood the altar flame he'd blessed.
His fifty rooms, rich hope of a line of sons—
pillars of Orient gold, girt proud with spoils—
all fell. Where fire failed, the Argive ruled.

"Perhaps you wish to know how Priam died.
There lay his city—lost, there lay the ruin
that was his palace, there at his hearth, a foe.
The old king threw his armor, long unused,
510 on his shaking shoulders—useless gesture!—bound
his sword at his waist, and rushed to fight and die.
Within the close, beneath heaven's naked pole,
stood a high altar; nearby an old bay tree
leaned toward it and wrapped the household gods in shade.
Here Hecuba and her daughters vainly fled
headlong (like doves before the black rain cloud)
and tight in a ring sat suppliant round the gods.
Then she saw Priam dressed in his young man's arms
and said, 'What dreadful madness, my poor lord,
520 led you to wear those weapons? Where will you charge?
This is no hour for help like yours, no time
for such defense—no, even were Hector here.
Come, stand by me; this altar shall shield us all,

---

[58] **Hecuba:** The queen of Troy, wife of Priam, and mother of Hector.

or you will die with us.' So saying, she placed
the old man at her side on holy ground.

"Here now, escaped from Pyrrhus' blade, Polites,
a son of Priam, dashed through enemy lines,
ran down the cloisters and round the empty halls,
wounded. Enraged at having missed his aim,
530 Pyrrhus pursued him, caught him, and stabbed him down.
He crawled on, till before his parents' eyes
he fell, and with his blood coughed out his life.
Then Priam, though death already gripped him round,
could not hold back or check his angry words:
'You murderer!' he cried. 'You foul blasphemer!
If heaven has righteous gods to mark such acts,
oh, may they thank you well and pay the price
you've earned, who made me watch my own son die,
and with his death befouled a father's eyes.
540 Achilles—you lie, to say you are his son!—
never treated me so! I came a suppliant,
an enemy, yet he honored me and gave me
Hector's corpse to bury and sent me home.'
With that, the old king hurled his harmless spear
to touch and clang against the shield; it stopped
and dangled useless from the brazen boss.
Then Pyrrhus: 'Be my enemy! Tell your tale
to my father! Remember: call me barbarous
and name me "Neoptolemus, son unworthy"!
550 Now die!' He dragged him to the altar, faint
and slipping in the blood his son had shed.
His left hand gripped the old man's hair; his right
drew out a sword and sank it in his side.
So Priam died. His final, fated glance
fell on a Troy in ashes, on the ruins
of Pergama°—sometime proud imperial power,   Troy
'of Asia, king.' On the strand his vast frame lies,
head torn from shoulders, a corpse without a name.

"For the first time then, a savage fear closed round me.
560 I froze. My own dear father's form rose up
as I watched the old king through that horrid wound
gasp out his life. Creusa—alone!—rose up:
my house—in ruins! My son, Iulus—where?
I turned about: What forces still remained?
Not a man! Heartsick and beaten, they had leaped
to the street or thrown themselves into the flames.

"I alone survived—but no! By Vesta's[59] shrine,
lurking wordless, in a dark corner hiding—
Helen! I saw her lighted by the flames
570　as I searched the ruins, looking everywhere.
She feared the fury of a vanquished Troy,
Greek vengeance, a deserted husband's wrath.
A fiendish curse alike to friend and foe,
hated, she'd sought asylum at the altar.
Flame burst in my heart as anger cried, 'Revenge,
for a country lost! Penalty, for her crimes!
Shall she, unscathed, see Sparta? Shall she march
in royal triumph through Mycenae's streets?
She, see her husband, her father's house, her children,
580　trailed by the women of Troy, her Orient slaves?
Yet death by the sword for Priam? Troy in flames?
A shore so often drenched in Trojan blood?
Never! Although men win no fame or glory
for woman punished (such victory earns no praise),
still to have stamped out sin, and made it pay
due price, is good; good, too, to fill the heart
with vengeful flame and vindicate the dead.'
Such the wild thoughts that swept my heart along
when—never before so clear for eye to see—
590　a vision shone through darkness, pure and bright:
my loving mother, goddess confessed, her form
and stature as in heaven. She seized my hand
and held me hard; her sweet lips spoke to me:
'My son, what pain has roused such unchecked wrath?
Are you mad, or have you lost all thought of me?
What? Not look first where your old father waits,
Anchises? See if yet Creusa lives,
your wife? Your son, Ascanius? All around them
Greeks walk their lines at will; but for my care,
600　flames or an enemy blade had borne them off.
No blame to Helen of Sparta's hated face;
no, nor to Paris: gods, the pitiless gods,
threw down the might and golden towers of Troy.
Look, for I'll rip it all away—the cloud
that blocks and blunts your mortal sight, hung dank
and dark around you; you must never fear
a mother's precept or disobey her word.

---

[59]**Vesta:** Roman goddess of the hearth and guardian of the family and community (Hestia in Greek mythology).

Here where you see the masonry all tumbled,
stone upon stone, where dust and smoke boil up,
610   Neptune is rocking our walls, and with his trident
knocking their base-blocks loose; our homes and halls
he'll pull to the ground. There, at the Scaean gates,[60]
Juno in blood-lust waves her columns on
from the ships with her drawn sword.
Look back! On Castle Hill Tritonia sits
in a cloud of flame, flashing her Gorgon head.[61]
Our father himself gives comfort, power, and strength
to the Greeks — yes, hurls the gods against our arms.
Hurry, my son! Take flight! Call this work done!
620   I am always with you, to guide you safely home!'
She spoke, and hid herself in night's black shades.
There rose up faces full of death and hate
for Troy — a ghastly glory of gods.

"Then came collapse, I saw all Ilium fall
in flames — saw Neptune's Troy come crashing down.
As when on mountain top an ancient ash
is hacked by the steel; blow after blow falls
as farmers vie at the felling. The old tree leans,
her foliage shakes, she bows her stricken crown,
630   till bit by bit her wounds win out. She groans
her last and falls and strews the ridge with wreckage.

"Divine grace led me down through flame and foe
with ease; swords made away and flames fell back.

"Soon as I stepped inside my father's house
and ancient home, I sought him out and begged
he'd let me carry him off to the high hills.
He answered, No: his Troy was lost, and life
in exile not for him. 'You young in years
and blood,' said he, 'who yet own strength and sinew,
640   do you take thought for flight.
If heaven had wished me further years of life
they'd saved my home for me. Enough that once
I lived to see my city fall and die.

---

[60]**Scaean gates:** One of the main gates at Troy, outside of which in *The Iliad* the battle between Achilles and Hector took place.

[61]**Gorgon head:** The head of Medusa, a hideous monster with snakes for hair whose visage would turn people to stone; after the hero Perseus decapitated Medusa, he gave the head to Minerva who attached it to her shield.

Just let me lie here; say farewell and leave me.
I'll find death by myself. The foe will say
"Too bad!" and strip my corpse. A grave's well lost.
I've lived unloved of heaven,[62] useless, old,
for years, since Jove, the father of gods and men,
touched and scorched me with lightning's fiery breath.'

650 "He spoke and stood his ground, unmoved, unmoving.
But we burst out in tears — my wife Creusa,
Ascanius, our whole house — 'He must not ruin
us all, or hasten the death that threatens us.'
He would not change, or leave his chosen spot.
I turned to my arms with bitter prayer to die.
What plans could be; what fortune granted now?
'You think, sir, I could take one step and leave
you here? Monstrous! This, from a father's lips?
If by God's law our city must be destroyed,
660 and you are resolved to cap the death of Troy
with death of you and yours, that door stands wide:
Pyrrhus is coming bathed in Priam's blood —
son before father, father by altar slain.
For this you haled me, mother, through steel and flame,
that I might see the enemy in my house,
and you, Ascanius, and Creusa too,
heaped in one bloody sacrificial pile?
Arms, men! To arms! We're lost! Our last day calls us!
Back to the Greeks! I'll see the fight renewed
670 once more. We shall not all die unavenged!'

"I buckled my sword again and strapped my shield
to my left arm with care, then moved outside.
But there at the door my wife fell at my feet
and kissed them, and held Iulus out to me:
'You go to die? Take us, too — anywhere!
But if experience gives you faith in arms,
guard first your home. Abandon us? Your son,
your father, me — once called your wife? To whom?'

"While thus she pled and filled the house with sobs —
680 wonder to tell! — a miracle occurred.
There in our arms, before his parents' eyes,

---

[62] **unloved of heaven:** Jove (Zeus) crippled Anchises with a lightning bolt because Anchises broke his promise
to keep secret that his son, Aeneas, was Venus's child.

Iulus' little cap, right at its peak,
seemed to shed light. A harmless flame licked down
to touch his hair and play about his brow.
In panic terror we slapped at his burning hair
and tried to quench the holy flame with water.
But Father Anchises smiled, and raising eyes
toward heaven, spread out his hands, and spoke in prayer:
'Almighty Jove, if any prayer can bend you,
690   look down and for our merit grant just this:
a sign, father! Confirm this omen for us!'

"Scarce had he spoken when with sudden crash
came thunder on the left; down the dark sky
a meteor fell in a burst of sparks and flame.
We watched it glide high over roof and hall
—so bright!—then bury itself in Ida's woods,[63]
its path marked clear. Behind it, furrow and line
shed light and left a smoking reek of sulphur.
My father now was certain; he turned toward heaven,
700   hailed godhead, and adored the holy star:
'No hesitation now! Lead on! I'll follow,
gods of my fathers! Oh, save my house and line!
Yours was that sign; your will embraces Troy.
I yield, my son; I'll gladly share your way.'

"Just then through our walls we heard a louder noise
of fire and closer rolled the holocaust.
'Come then, dear father, and climb upon my back.
Ride on my shoulders; the load will not be heavy.
Whatever may happen, we'll share a single risk,
710   a single rescue. Iulus, little son,
walk by me! Wife, stay back, but trace my steps!
And all you others, listen to my words!
Outside the city is a hill and shrine
of Ceres,[64] long unused; nearby, a cypress,
gnarled, and for years held sacred by our fathers.
Each go your way; we'll meet at that one spot.
You, father, carry our holies and household gods.
Fresh come from all the fighting, blood, and death,
I dare not touch them till in running stream

---

[63] **Ida's woods:** Ida was a mountain in Phrygia, in the vicinity of Troy.   [64] **Ceres:** Roman goddess of grain and the harvest; Demeter in Greek mythology. She appears here in her capacity as Ceres the Bereft, who mourns the loss of her daughter Proserpina (Persephone).

720 I wash myself.'
With that I spread across my neck and shoulders
a cloak, and over that a lion's skin,
and lifted my burden; little Iulus seized
my right hand, following two steps to my one;
behind us, my wife. We moved through pitch-black plazas,
and I was afraid, though minutes before no spear
nor prowling Greek patrol had worried me.
I started at every breeze; at every sound
I stiffened, fearful alike for father and son.
730 And now I was near the gate, and clear, I thought,
of the streets, when all at once I caught the sound
of many marching feet. My father peered
through the night, and cried out, 'Hurry, son; they're coming.
I see their shields alight and the flash of blades.'
I panicked then, as some strange, unkind power
left me confused and mindless. Hurrying down
byways, I'd left familiar streets behind,
when Creusa — she was gone! Did cruel death take her?
Or had she lost her way? Or stopped to rest?
740 We've never known, nor ever seen her since.
I had not turned around nor marked her lost
until we reached the hill and ancient shrine
of Ceres. Here as we called the roll we found
her missing. Son nor husband — none had seen her.
Half mad, I railed at everyone, god and man:
What had I seen in captured town more cruel?
My son, my father, the household gods of Troy,
I left to my men, deep hidden in the hills.
I turned back to the city, armed again,
750 determined to take my chances, to go back
through all of Troy, and risk my life once more.
First to the walls and that half-hidden gate
where I'd gone out, I turned, and traced my steps
back through the night, my eyes' own light my guide;
no sound relieved the prickling sense of fear.
Then on to my house: Had she — had she perhaps
gone there? All doors were down, Greeks everywhere.
My house was wrapped in flames; wind-whipped they licked
at the roof, then raced in triumph toward the sky.
760 I ran to Priam's palace and the fort:
there on the empty porch of Juno's temple
a squad of sentries with Phoenix and Ulysses
were guarding the spoils. Here all the wealth of Troy,
ripped from her burning temples — holy tables,

wine bowls of solid gold, and captured vestments —
were heaped. Mothers and children, a long, long line,
terrified, stood nearby.
I even dared to shout. I filled the night
and dark streets with my sobbing cries: 'Creusa!'
770 No answer! 'Creusa!' I called, again, again.
I was pressing my search from house to endless house
when a luckless ghost, Creusa's very shade,
rose to my sight — her likeness, taller than life.
My hair stood up in terror; my voice stuck fast.
But then she spoke and banished all my fears:
'Why such indulgence of a pointless pain,
dear husband? Nothing but by the will of God
has happened. You were not meant to take Creusa
with you; so rules the lord of tall Olympus.
780 Go into exile; furrow the empty sea
to a western land of men and fertile fields
where Tiber pours his gentle Tuscan stream.[65]
There is your birthright: wealth, a throne, a queen.
You loved Creusa; but brush away your tears.
I'll catch no sight of Thessaly's haughty halls —
not I! — nor humbly serve the dames of Greece,
I, child of Dardanus, wife of Venus' son.
No; the mother of gods detains me here.
Farewell, and always love the son we share.'
790 With that, for all my tears, for all I hoped
to say, she turned to emptiness and air.
Three times I tried to fold her in my arms,
three times for nothing! The ghost-thing fled my grasp,
light as a breeze, most like the wings of sleep.
The night was gone when I rejoined my friends.

"And here I stood in wonder at the crowd
of people newly come — mothers and men,
children, huddled for exile — poor, lost souls.
They'd brought what they could save; they'd brought their courage;
800 they'd follow the course I set, no matter where.
And now the dawn star rose from Ida's heights
to bring the day. Greek guards were everywhere,
at every gate. We knew no help could come.
Bearing my father, I started toward the hills."

---

[65] **Tuscan stream:** The Tiber is a river in Italy that runs through Rome and was the site of Etruscan settlements, hence the "Tuscan stream."

[Aeneas describes his travels in Book 3. From Delos they travel to Crete and then along the coast of Greece, where they find Helenus, Priam's son, who tells Aeneas how to reach Italy. Warned by Helenus not to land on the southeast coast of Italy, the Trojans sail to Sicily, where Anchises dies.]

BOOK 4
[AENEAS AND DIDO]

Now Dido had felt the heavy slash of care,
the wound that grows in the vein, the lightless flame.
Aeneas' great courage, the glory of his people,
coursed through her mind; fast in her heart lay fixed
his face, his words. She knew no rest or peace.
The next day's lamp of sun was lighting earth,
and Dawn had cleared the sky of dew and dark,
when she, sick soul, spoke to her loving sister:
"Anna! My dreams! They leave me tense with fear!
10 What strange outsider has come here to our home?
How proud his bearing! How brave his heart and hand!
I believe—not lightly—he is a child of gods.
Fear proves the soul debased; but he, though battered
by Fate, tells how he fought war after war.
Had I not fixed it firm within my heart
never to yield myself to marriage bond
since that first love left me cheated by death,
did I not sicken at thought of bed and torch,[66]
to this one sin, this once, I might succumb.
20 No, Anna, I'll speak: Since poor Sychaeus died,
since brother[67] drenched my house with husband's blood,
Aeneas alone has moved my heart and shaken
resolve. I mark the trace of long-dead flame.
But, oh, may the earth gape wide and deep for me,
or the father almighty blast me down to death,
to the paling ghosts of hell and the pit of night,
before I play honor false or break her laws.
The man who first knew union with me stole
my heart; let him keep and guard it in the tomb."
30 She spoke; the well of her tears filled and ran over.

---

[66] **bed and torch:** Used in wedding rituals, the torch was a symbol of marriage. Dido is associated with fire and flames throughout Book 4, from her first marriage with Sychaeus to her false marriage with Aeneas, her rage against Aeneas, and finally her suicide on a burning pyre.   [67] **brother:** Pygmalion of Tyre, who killed Dido's husband Sychaeus in order to have his riches; Book 1, lines 69–97 tell the story of Dido's escape from Tyre.

Then Anna: "Your sister loves you more than life:
why squander youth on endless, lonely grief
with no sweet sons, without the gifts of love?
You think mere ashes, ghosts in the grave, will care?
So be it! You've mourned; you've turned all suitors down
in Libya, and Tyre before. You've scorned Iarbas
and all the chiefs that Africa, proud and rich,
parades: why battle a love that you've found good?
Have you forgotten whose lands you've settled here?
40 This side, Gaetulians (race untamed by war),
savage Numidians, and a barrier sea;
that side, the desert, thirst, the wild nomads
of Barca.[68] Why tell of wars that rise in Tyre
or how your brother threatens?
I'm sure the gods have blessed the Trojans' course,
and Juno favored the wind that blew their ships.
Oh, what a city you'll see, what kingdoms rise,
with such a man! Allied with Trojan arms
Carthage will raise her glory to the sky.
50 Pray for the gods' forgiveness; give them gifts.
Be kind to our guest; weave tissues of delay:
'Winter — the sea is wild — the rains have come —
your ships are damaged — you cannot read the skies.'"

Such talk inflamed her heart with uncurbed love,
gave hope to doubt, and let restraint go free.
First they went to altar and shrine to beg
God's peace; they made due rite of sacrifice:
sheep to Ceres, to Phoebus, to Father Bacchus,
and most to Juno, lady of marriage bonds.
60 Dido the beautiful lifted a cup of wine
and poured it between the horns of a pure white cow,
or danced where the gods watch over blood-rich altars.
Each day began with victims; she slit their throats,
and hung over living vitals to read the signs.
But priests are fools! What help from shrine and prayer
for her madness? Flames devoured her soft heart's-flesh;
the wound in her breast was wordless, but alive.
Fevered and ill-starred, Dido wandered wild
through all the town, like a doe trailing an arrow
70 that she, heedless in Cretan forest, caught

---

[68] **wild nomads of Barca:** The Gaetulians, Numidians, and Barcaeans were the peoples of North Africa near Carthage.

from a shepherd who shot but never knew his bolt
had flown to the mark; she ranges field and grove
of Dicte;[69] the shaft of death clings to her flank.
Now Dido escorted Aeneas from wall to wall,
showed him her Tyrian wealth, her city all built—
she'd start to speak, but in mid-word fall mute.
Again, at wane of day, she'd fill her hall
and ask to hear once more of Troy's travail,
and hang once more, madly, upon each word.
80 Then when they'd parted and the shadowed moon
had paled, and fading stars warned men to sleep,
in the empty hall she'd lie where he had lain,
hearing him, seeing him—gone, and she alone;
or hold Ascanius close, caught by his father's
likeness, in hope of eluding a sinful love.
Her towers grew no taller; her army ceased
maneuvers and worked no more to strengthen port
and bastion for war: work hung half-done, walls stood
huge but unsteady; bare scaffolds met the sky.

90 As soon as Jove's dear wife knew Dido gripped
by the plague and grown too mad to heed report,
she, daughter of Saturn,[70] spoke harsh words to Venus:
"What glorious praise, what rich return you've gained,
you and your son; such might, such fabled power,
now that by godhead twain one woman's conquered!
I'm not deceived: you feared my city, and me,
and hence held Carthage and her halls suspect.
Is there no limit? Why this vast rivalry?
Why not make peace for good, and carry through
100 the match you planned? You've gained your heart's desire:
Dido has drawn love's flame deep as her bones.
Why not join hands, join peoples, share the rule
between us? Let Dido serve her Trojan prince
and lay her dower—her Tyrians—in your hand."

Venus knew Juno spoke with veiled intent
to turn Italian power aside to Carthage.
Thus she replied: "To that, who but the mad
could object? Who'd choose to go to war with you?
If only success may crown our stratagem!

---

[69] **Dicte:** A mountain in Crete.   [70] **Saturn:** The father of the gods Jove, Juno, Pluto, and Neptune was said to have settled in Italy after Jove ousted him from power; Saturnia is another name used for Juno.

110   But I'm not sure of fate: would Jove allow
      a single city for people of Tyre and Troy?
      Approve such mingled blood, such rule conjoint?
      You are his wife: seek out his will. You may.
      You lead, I'll follow." To her then Juno spoke:
      "That shall be my concern. How best to meet
      the need of the moment, hear, while I briefly tell.
      A hunt is planned. Aeneas, and Dido with him,
      are off to the woods soon as tomorrow's sun
      rises and with his ray reveals the world.
120   They'll see the clouds turn black with hail and rain;
      then as their beaters rush to encircle a dell,
      I'll pour down floods and shake all heaven with thunder.
      Their men will scatter in darkness and disappear.
      Your prince of Troy and Dido both will come
      to a cave. I'll be there, too. With your consent,
      I'll join them in marriage and name her 'lawful wife.'
      Their wedding this shall be." No adverse word
      spoke Venus, but nodded. Such tactics made her smile.

      Meanwhile the Dawn arose and left the sea.
130   Out from the gates at sunrise young men ran
      with nets and snares and broad-tipped hunting spears;
      out galloped Moors with packs of keen-nosed hounds.
      The queen was late; beside her hall the lords
      of Carthage waited; there stood her horse, in gold
      and purple caparison, nervous, champing the bit.
      At last she came, surrounded by her vast guard,
      wrapped in a scarlet cloak broidered with lace.
      Gold was her quiver; gold held her plaited hair;
      a brooch of gold fastened her purple gown.
140   In marched a Trojan group, Iulus too,
      smiling and eager. Then, towering over all,
      Aeneas joined them and brought their ranks together.
      Like Apollo, leaving Lycia and streams of Xanthus,
      in winter, to visit Delos, his mother's home!
      He starts the dancing; gathering round his shrine,
      islanders, mountaineers, painted plainsmen sing,
      while he climbs Cynthus.[71] He braids his flowing hair
      and holds it in place with laurel and crown of gold;
      his arrows clang at his back. So fresh, alive,
150   was Aeneas, so matchless the glory of his face.

---

[71] **Cynthus:** A mountain in Delos, said to be the birthplace of Apollo and Diana.

They rode to the hills, to the wayless woods and marches.
Look! Down from a rocky ridge leaped mountain goats
to race downhill; on this side, where the plains
lay open, a line of antelopes flashed past
away from the hillsides, trailing a swirl of dust.
Ascanius—boy on a lively pony—loped
up hill, down dale, with a laugh past these, past those.
Such nerveless beasts! He wished a foam-flecked boar
might come his way, or a lion charge from the hills.

160   Now thunder roared and rumbled across the sky;
soon came black clouds, the hailstorm, and the rain.
The Tyrian people and men of Troy broke ranks,
and with them Venus' grandson° ran for shelter—   Ascanius
anywhere! Rivers in spate rushed down the slopes.
The prince of Troy and Dido both had come
to a cave. The bride's attendants, Earth and Juno,
gave signal: lightning and empyrean flamed
in witness; high in the hills Nymphs made their moan.
That was the day, the first of death and first

170   of evil. Repute, appearance, nothing moved
the queen; she laid no plan to hide her love,
but called it marriage, with this word veiled her shame.

At once Rumor went out through Libya's towns—
Rumor, than whom no evil thing is faster:
speed is her life; each step augments her strength.
Small, a shiver, at first, she soon rears high.
She walks aground; her head hides in the clouds.
Men say that Earth, in fury at the gods,
bore this last child, a sister to the Giants.

180   She is swift of foot and nimble on the wing,
a horror, misshapen, huge. Beneath each feather
there lies a sleepless eye (wonder to tell!),
and a tongue, and speaking lips, and ears erect.
By night she flies far over the shadowed world
gibbering; sleep never comes to rest her eyes.
By day she sits at watch high on a roof
or lofty tower, and terrifies great cities,
as much a vessel of slander as crier of truth.
This time she filled men's minds with varied gossip,

190   chuckling and chanting alike both false and true:
Aeneas had come, born of the blood of Troy;
Dido had deemed him worthy mate and man.
Now they were warming the winter with rich exchange,

forgetful of thrones, ensnared by shameful lust.
Such tales foul Rumor spread upon men's lips,
then turned her course straight off to King Iarbas,
heaped fire into his heart and raked his wrath.

Iarbas, son of a Nymph by Hammon[72] raped,
had raised in his broad realms a hundred shrines
200   to Jove, a hundred altars and vigil fires
with priests at endless prayer; the blood of beasts
fattened the soil, the doors were decked with flowers.
Maddened at heart, enflamed by bitter rumor
he stood at the altar amid the powers of heaven,
raised hands in suppliance, and prayed aloud:

"Almighty Jove, to whom the Moorish kind
on purple couches serve rich food and wine,
do you see this? Or are we fools to fear
your lightning bolt? Are cloud and fire blind,
210   that frighten our hearts, mere noise devoid of strength?
This woman, this immigrant in my bounds, who paid
to build her little town, to whom I granted
tidewater land on terms, rejects my hand
but takes my lord Aeneas to her throne.
And now that Paris and his half-male crew,
with perfumed hair and Persian caps chin-tied,
keeps what he stole, while I bring gifts to shrines —
your shrines — and worship empty shams of glory."

As with hand on altar he made this prayer
220   the almighty heard; his eye turned toward the palace,
toward two in love forgetting their better fame.
He spoke to Mercury then with this command:
"Go, son, summon the Zephyrs[73] and take flight.
Our prince of Troy dawdles in Carthage now
and takes no thought for cities assigned by fate.
Fly with the wind, bring him my word, and speak:
'Such not the man his lovely mother promised,
nor such twice saved by her from Argive arms,
but one to rule a country big with power —
230   Italy, land of the war cry — to pass on

---

[72] **Hammon:** Jove; King Iarbas, Dido's chief Libyan suitor, claims to be descended from Hammon, or Ammon, a Libyan-Egyptian deity who came to be associated with Jove.   [73] **Zephyrs:** The winds; the Zephyr is the warm, west wind.

the blood of Teucer, and bring worlds under law.'
If none of these great glories fires his heart
and for his own renown he'll spend no toil,
does he begrudge his son a fortress Rome?
What plans, what hopes hold him on foreign soil,
blind to Ausonia and Lavinia's land?[74]
'Sail on!' That is all. Bring him this word from me."

He ended. Mercury moved to carry out
the father's command. First he put on his sandals
240 golden, winged, that bear him swift as the wind
high over land and high above the sea,
then took his wand. With this he calls the ghosts
pale out of Orcus,[75] or sends them sorrowing down,
grants sleep, withdraws it, unseals the eyes of death.
With it he drives the winds and sails the clouds.
Now flying he saw the cap and rugged flanks
of Atlas, whose granite shoulders prop the sky—
Atlas: his pine-clad head, forever crowned
with clouds, is buffeted by wind and rain.
250 A glacier clothes his back, and cascades course
down over his face; his beard bristles with ice.
Here Mercury hovering on both wings alike
stopped, then plummeted headlong toward the sea
just like a gull that, round the beaches, round
fish-haunted reefs, skims low across the waves.
So between earth and sky he flew along
toward Libya's sandy shore, cleaving the wind
eastward from Atlas—Mercury, son of Maia.
Soon as his winged feet touched settlement ground,
260 he saw Aeneas footing down forts and raising
new homes. The sword he wore was yellow-starred
with jasper, a cape of glowing Tyrian scarlet
hung from his shoulders—gifts the wealthy queen
had given, and broidered the cloth with thread of gold.
Up stepped the god: "Aeneas! In Carthage now
do you lay foundations and plan a handsome town
for a wife? *Your* throne, *your* state—are they forgotten?
From shining Olympus *he* has sent me down—

---

[74] **Ausonia . . . Lavinia's land:** Italy; Lavinia, whom Aeneas will later marry, is the daughter of Latinus, king of Latium. Ausonia is another name for Italy.   [75] **Orcus:** The land of the dead, or the underworld.

the king of gods, whose nod makes heaven roll.
270 He bade me fly with the wind to bring his word:
what plans, what hopes hold you at leisure here?
If nothing of promised glory moves your heart,
and for your own renown you'll spend no toil,
what of your son? He's growing! Your heir, Iulus:
what of his hopes? A kingdom — Italy — Rome:
these are his due!" With this, the Cyllenian god[76]
left mortal sight, nor waited for reply;
beyond the eye he vanished into air.

Aeneas was frightened out of speech and mind;
280 his hair stood up in terror, his voice stuck fast.
He burned to go, to flee this pleasant land;
God's word, God's great commands had struck him hard.
But what should he do? How dare he tell the queen?
She was mad for love: how could he start his plea?
His mind turned quickly here, turned quickly there,
darting in different ways all round about.
As he weighed the matter this seemed the better course:
he called Sergestus, Mnestheus, Serestus the brave:
"Not a word! Prepare to sail! Call out our people!
290 To battle stations, all: coin some excuse
for these new orders." Meanwhile, let gentle Dido
know nothing, suspect no rupture of their love:
he now would test approaches, seek the time
and kindest way to tell her. Quickly all
in joy at his command obeyed his orders.

But still the queen (who can deceive a lover?)
foretold the scheme, caught contemplated moves,
feared even where all was safe. Then Rumor came
to report the fleet outfitted and ready to sail.
300 Her passion burst control; savage, aflame,
she raced through town, as, at an elevation,
the Thyiad who feels the spur of Bacchic hymns
and dances, and hears Cithaeron shout by night.[77]
At last she addressed Aeneas; her words burst forth:

"You lied! You thought you could conceal a wrong
so vast, and leave my land without one word?

---

[76] **the Cyllenian god:** Mercury (Hermes) is so called because Mt. Cyllene, in Arcadia, was home to his mother, the nymph Maia, as well as his own birthplace.   [77] **the Thyiad . . . night:** Virgil compares Dido here to a Bacchante (Thyiad), a female devotee of Bacchus driven into an ecstatic, uncontrollable passion.

Our love, your right hand given in pledge that day,
a Dido to suffer and die — are these no check?
What? Fit out your fleet beneath a winter sun,
310 and hurry across the sea while north winds howl,
hard-hearted man? Were it no foreign land,
no unknown home you sought, but Troy still stood,
would you send ships through storms like these to Troy?
You run from *me*? In tears, I seize your hand
(what other solace have I left myself?)
and beg you recall our marriage, our wedding day:
if I have served you well, if you have found
delight in me, have mercy! My house is crumbling!
If prayer can still be heard, change, change your heart!
320 You made the Libyan tribes, the Nomad kings,
yes, my own Tyrians, hate me; lost for you
were honor and good repute, my only path
to glory. Cast off, fit only to die, who'll have me,
you whom I entertained — no more say, 'married.'
What now? Wait till Pygmalion levels my walls,
or the Moor Iarbas drags me off in chains?
If only before your flight I had conceived
your child, if only a baby Aeneas played
here in my court, whose face might mirror yours,
330 I'd feel less like one taken and discarded."
She finished. Aeneas, strengthened by Jove's words,
gazed steadily at her and suppressed his pain.
At last he briefly replied, "Speak! List them all —
your favors and courtesies! There is not one
I won't confess. I'll think of you with joy
long as I think at all, and live, and breathe.
But now to the point. I did not mean (believe me!)
to slip away by stealth, nor ever feigned
the wedding torch, or made such league with you.
340 If fate had let me govern my own life
and heal my troubles in the way I willed,
I would be living in Troy with what remained
of my people; Priam's halls would still be standing;
and we, though beaten, had built our walls anew.
But Apollo Grynean[78] sent me to Italy;
'Find Italy! Win her!' declared the oracles.
My love, my home, lie there. You are of Tyre,

---

[78] **Apollo Grynean:** So called after Gryneum, a city in Asia Minor with a major shrine to Apollo.

yet Libyan Carthage holds you, hall and wall:
why take it ill that Trojans look for homes
350   in Italy? Strange lands we too may seek.
Whenever dewy night enshrouds the world
and fiery stars arise, Anchises' ghost,
murky and fearful, warns me in my dreams.
Ascanius, well-loved son: see how I wrong him,
cheating him of Hesperian land and throne!
Now comes a messenger from Jove himself
(I swear it!); he sped through air to bring command.
In the clear light of day I saw that god;
he entered these walls; my ears drank in his words.
360   Cease to enflame my heart and yours with plaints:
not by my choice I go to Italy."

Even as he spoke she turned her face away.
Glancing now here, now there, she viewed the man
from head to foot, wordless. Then speech flared out:
"No goddess your mother, no Dardanus sired your kind,
you liar! No! Caucasus[79] got you on those cliffs
of jagged granite, and tigers suckled you there!
Dissemble? Why? To await some greater wrong?
I wept; he made no sound, nor turned an eye.
370   I loved him; where were his tears, his sympathy?
What else shall I say? Juno, lady and queen,
Jove, son of Saturn, can be unmoved no longer.
Good faith is folly! I saved him, castaway
and helpless, I made him partner to my power.
He'd lost his ships, his men; I rescued them.
My madness flames like fire: 'Apollo' now,
'the oracles' now; now 'sent by Jove himself
a messenger comes through air with dread commands.'
This is the gods' life work! Such cares disturb
380   their peace! You're free; I'll not refute your claims.
Go! Find your Italian throne by wind and wave!
Midway, I trust, if God has power, you'll drink
requital on a reef and scream for Dido!
There'll be no Dido, but a funeral flame
will follow, and when death sunders soul from flesh
my shade will haunt you till my price is paid.
I'll know! Report will reach my ghost in hell!"

---

[79] **Caucasus:** Dido here personifies the Caucasus Mountains, the site of the torture of Prometheus near the Caspian Sea, to characterize the origin of Aeneas's cruelty.

She broke off in mid-speech and, sickened, fled
the light of day—ran from his sight, from him,
390 while he stood trembling, groping, conning a flood
of words. She fainted. Her people raised her up
and bore her to her room and to her bed.

Aeneas the good, though longing to ease her pain
with words of comfort and turn aside her care
(his groans came deep, for love had racked his heart),
obeyed God's orders and sought his fleet again.
Then truly his men fell to; the shore was filled
with hauling of ships. Out swam fresh-painted keels;
men loaded oars still green, and from the woods
400 brought spars half-hewn in haste.
       "Move out!" they heard. "All hands!" "Look lively, now!"
(As when the ants, mindful of winter, attack
a heap of grain and carry it home across
the fields: black goes the column; they bear their prize
down narrow grassy lanes. Some push big kernels
with heave of shoulders; some close the line of march
and hurry stragglers. The path is a froth of toil.)
Dido! What did you feel to see all this?
What cries did you utter when from tower's top
410 you saw the shore all seething, saw the sea
churned up before your eyes, and heard the shouts!
Shameless love, where do you not drive men's hearts?
Again she went and wept and begged, for try
she must; her pride must bend the knee to love,
lest for failing to move she die in vain.

"Anna, you see them rushing round the shore:
the crews are mustered; the canvas calls the breeze;
the men have cheered as garlands dressed the spar.
Could I have known such sorrow was to come,
420 I could have borne it; but now in tears I beg
one favor, Anna, of you: that faithless man
was always with you, told you his secret thoughts;
you knew, as no one else, his gentler moods.
Go, bring to our heartless guest this humble plea:
I joined no Greeks; I took no oath at Aulis[80]
of death to Trojans, I sent no ships to Troy,

---

[80] **Aulis:** The port in Boeotia from which the Greeks set sail for Troy after having sacrificed Iphigenia, Agamemnon's daughter, to stir up favorable winds.

I never harried his father Anchises' ghost.
Why will he lock his ears against my words?
Why haste? Let a broken heart win one last grace:
430   Await a safer passage and favoring winds!
I'll not ask now for the wedlock he betrayed,
or that he resign his darling Latin throne;
I beg for time, an hour of rest from madness,
till fortune teach me how to lose and grieve.
This favor the last your sister asks: be kind!
I'll pay my debt with death to make full measure."[81]

Such was her plea; such sorrows her grieving sister
reported, reported again. But nothing moved him;
no tears nor words could teach his heart to hear.
440   (Fate blocked the way; God closed his ears to pity.)
Like an oak tree, ancient, toughened by the years,
blasted by Alpine winds this way and that
contesting to uproot it; the North Wind howls,
the trunk is shaken, foliage strews the ground.
The tree holds hard; its crown lifts up toward heaven
far as its root grows down toward Tartarus.[82]
Just so Aeneas, by pleas this side and that
assaulted, felt in his heart the thrust of care.
His mind stood firm; tears came, but came in vain.[83]

450   Then Dido, luckless, by fortune terrified,
invited death: to view heaven's vault was pain.
To strengthen her resolve to leave the light,
she saw, when she offered her gifts and censed the altars
(dreadful to tell!), the holy water turn black
and the wine pour down in horrid clots of gore.
She told none, not even Anna, what she'd seen.
Besides, in her house there stood a marble shrine
to her former husband, which she kept sacrosanct,
festooned with white wool bands and feast-day flowers:
460   from it she thought she heard her husband's voice
calling her, calling, when darkness gripped the world.
And on her roof a lonesome owl sang songs
of death; its mournful cry trailed off in sobs.

---

[81] **I'll pay . . . full measure:** The last line here is deliberately ambiguous: It could anticipate Dido's suicide or revenge on Aeneas.   [82] **Tartarus:** The lowest region of the underworld where punishments are meted out to sinners.   [83] **tears . . . in vain:** An ambiguous line. Whose tears are these? Some readers, including St. Augustine, have seen them as the concealed tears of the stoic Aeneas.

Then warnings of seers long dead came crowding back
to fill her with fright. She dreamed herself gone mad,
with Aeneas in wild pursuit; then left alone
to travel, forever friendless, a long, long road,
seeking her Tyrians in an empty world,
like maddened Pentheus[84] seeing the rank of Furies,

470 seeing twin suns and a double Thebes displayed;
or like Orestes racing across the stage
to escape a mother armed with torch and serpent—
and at Agamemnon's door the Dirae[85] wait.

Filled with madness and prisoner of her pain,
she determined to die; and now, with how and when
planned in her mind, she addressed her tearful sister
(concealing intent behind a cloudless brow):
"Anna, I've found a way—applaud your sister!—
that will bring him back, or free me from my love.

480 Near to the ocean's edge and setting sun
lies African land's-end, where giant Atlas
bears on his back the spinning star-tricked wheel.
I've found a religious of that place—a Moor;
she served the Hesperides' temple, fed the snake,
and guarded the holy branches on the tree;
with honey and poppy she made the elixir of sleep.
She swears she can release what hearts she will
with spells, and freight still other hearts with care,
can stop the rivers and reverse the stars,

490 and raise the dead by night: you'll see the earth
groan at her feet and trees climb down the hills.
Sister, I tell you, by your life, by all
that's holy, I take to witchcraft against my will.
Slip into our inner courtyard and build there
a pyre; pile on it the arms that perjured man
hung in my house—take all he left, the bed
of marriage that brought me sorrow. I must destroy
his every devilish trace: so says my Moor."
This much, then silence, and her face turned pale.

500 Yet Anna did not suspect that these strange rites

---

[84] **maddened Pentheus:** A king of Thebes who aroused the wrath of Bacchus by opposing his rites; Bacchus took revenge by driving Pentheus mad and having him murdered by his own mother and other Bacchantes in an ecstatic frenzy. The Furies were not part of the earlier myth or of Euripides' play *The Bacchae,* which tells the story of Pentheus.   [85] **Dirae:** After killing his mother, Clytemnestra, to avenge the death of his father, Agamemnon, Orestes was pursued by the Furies (the Dirae), female creatures who punish those who commit blood-crimes against their kin.

were cover for death; her mind conceived no thought
so mad. Than when Sychaeus died: she feared
no worse, and did as asked.

In the inner court beneath the open sky
the pyre stood huge with pitch pine and with oak.
The queen hung garlands and wreathed the place with boughs
of death; atop, she laid his sword, his garments—
yes, and his image: she knew what she would do.
Ringed by altars the Moor let down her hair,
510 intoned the gods three hundred, Chaos, and Hell,
the Hecates three, Diana the triform virgin.[86]
She sprinkled water labeled "from Avernus,"[87]
selected hairy leaves by moonlight reaped
with brazen sickle (their milky juice turns black),
pulled out the membrane torn from a newborn foal
and snatched from its mother's mouth.
Dido stepped to an altar, blessed her hands,
took meal, slipped off one shoe, unlatched her gown,
then, ready to die, begged gods and stars prophetic
520 to hear her prayer to any power just
and mindful, that cares for lovers wrongly matched.

It was night; all over the world the weary flesh
found peace in sleep; forests and savage seas
rested; in middle course the stars rolled on.
No sound from field, from herd, from painted birds
that swarm the liquid lakes or love the thorn
and thicket: they slept in silence of the night,
healing the heart of care, forgetting pain.
But never the broken-hearted, luckless queen
530 slipped off to sleep or took the night to eyes
and heart. Her torment doubled; desire rose
raging; she ebbed and flowed on waves of wrath.
At last she paused and pondered inner thoughts:
"What shall I do? I'm scorned! Shall I turn and try
my earlier suitors, and beg a Nomad's bed?
I have disdained their hand, how many times?
Well, then, to the Trojan fleet? Hurry to catch

---

[86] **Chaos . . . virgin:** Dido calls up all those associated with the underworld: Chaos, Hell, the Hecates (here meaning the three Furies), and Diana, in her role as the goddess of sorcery and the moon.   [87] **"from Avernus":** Avernus is the lake and wood near Cumae in southern Italy where the entrance to the underworld was said to be; it is from here that Aeneas, in Book 6, begins his descent into the land of the dead.

their final word? Because they prized my help
and remember that musty favor with gratitude?
540 Granted the will, who'd let an unloved woman
tread his proud deck? You fool! You still don't know,
don't see, how the sons of Laomedon can lie?
Well—? Trail his jeering crews, a lovesick girl?
Or board ship with my Tyrians, rank on rank,
around me—men whom just now I saved from Sidon:
bid them make sail and put to sea once more?
No! Die as you've earned! Take steel and end your pains!
You, Anna, hurt by my tears, you topped my folly
with wrongful acts; you tossed me to our foe!
550 I had not the will to pass my life unwed,
unstained, like some wild creature, untouched by guilt.
I did not keep my oath to dead Sychaeus."
Such were the sorrows that broke forth from her breast.

Aeneas knew he would go; on his tall ship,
his preparations made, he took his rest.
In his dreams a godly form appeared again,
just as before, and seemed to warn once more
(in all like Mercury, in voice, complexion,
in the flaxen hair and graceful limbs of youth):
560 "Goddess-born, can you sleep at such an hour,
and fail to see the dangers that surround you—
madman!—nor hear the favoring West Wind blow?
Dido devises malice and foul crime
(she knows she'll die) and roils her anger's waves.
Run! Leave in haste, while haste's within your power.
Soon you will see the ocean churned by ships,
the shore ablaze with savage torch and flames,
if Dawn shall touch you tarrying in this land.
Hurry, now! Ever a various, changeful thing
570 is woman." He spoke and mingled with black night.

This apparition terrified Aeneas.
He tore himself from sleep and harried his men
to haste: "Look lively, there, and man the thwarts!
Off buntlines! Quick! A god from heaven's height
again has bid us speed away and cut
our anchor-lines. We come, O sacred presence,
whoever you are! Again we obey your word.
Be with us in peace! Bless us! Show helpful stars
in heaven!" He spoke, and ripped his flashing sword
580 from sheath, and with the bared blade slashed the lines.

Like ardor held them all. They seized, they ran,
they emptied the beach; their vessels hid the sea.
Men heaved, churned up the foam, and swept the blue.

And now Aurora brought the dawn's new light
to earth, and left Tithonus'[88] golden couch.
Dido was watching, and with the first pale gleam
she saw the fleet, yards squared and outward bound,
and marked the emptiness of shore and pier.
Three times and four she beat her lovely breast
590 and tore her golden hair: "What? Shall he go,"
she said, "and mock my power—that foreigner!
There'll be no general muster? No pursuit?
Will no one hurry to launch my ships? Quick, men,
bring torches, hand out arms, lean on your oars!
What's this? Where am I? What madness warps my mind?
Fool! Has your sacrilege just struck you now?
It should have, the day you offered a throne! Such honor!
And he, they say, brings with him his fathers' gods;
his shoulders carried Anchises, tired and old!
600 Why couldn't I hack his flesh, tear it, and strew
the sea with it? Slaughter his people and his son—
serve up Ascanius at his father's table?
But battle had been uncertain? Grant it so,
why fear, when I meant to die? I'd have thrown fire
and filled their camp with flame: father and son
and people had burned to death to make my pyre.
O Sun, who with your flame light all men's works;
you, Juno, who know my troubles and read them true;
Hecate, hailed at night by town and crossroad;
610 Dirae, gods of a Dido soon to die,
receive my prayer; turn sanction meet and right
upon these wrongs; hear me! If touch he must
on promised port and land—that man accursed!—
and so Jove's laws demand, this end is fixed.
But let brave people harass him with war.
Driven from home, torn from Iulus' arms,
let him beg for help, and see his people die
disgraced. Make him surrender under terms
unjust, and know no happy years of rule,

---

[88] **Tithonus:** The beloved companion of Aurora, goddess of the dawn; Aurora won eternal life for Tithonus but forgot to ask also for eternal youth, so Tithonus grew weak and feebleminded. In some versions of the story, he was shut away from his former lover. Virgil's imagery suggests a more positive outcome.

620 but die untimely, untombed, in miles of sand.
This is my final prayer, poured with my blood.
And you, my Tyrians, hate his race, his kind,
all and always. On my remains bestow
this office: no love, no peace between our peoples!
And from my grave let some avenger rise
to harry the Trojan settlers with fire and sword—
now, some day, whenever we have the power.
Shore against shore, I pray, wave against sea,
sword against sword, fight, father and son, forever!"[89]

630 So said she, and turned her thoughts this way and that,
seeking how soonest to end an unloved life.
To Barce then she spoke—Sychaeus' nurse
(her own lay buried in the fatherland):
"Dear nurse, bring Anna, my sister, here to me.
Tell her to hurry and wash in a running stream,
then bring the victims and holy things I showed her.
Come, both, with sacred ribbons in your hair
I wish to do my office to Stygian Jove[90]
(all duly prepared) to put an end to care
640 and lay that Trojan soul on funeral flames."

This much. In joy, the old nurse hobbled off.
Savage design drove Dido mad with fright.
Her eyes were wild and bloodshot; on her cheek
flush faded to pallor in terror of death so near.
She rushed to the inner court; madly she climbed
up the tall pyre and drew that Trojan sword,
gift that was never meant for such a use.
She saw his Trojan garment and their bed
well-known; then after a moment's tearful thought
650 lay down on the couch and spoke these final words:
"Here, trophies that I loved, while God allowed!
Oh, take my life and free me from my sorrow.
I've lived, and run the course that fate assigned;
in glory my shade now goes beneath the earth.

---

[89] **no love . . . forever:** Dido's curse anticipates the historical conflict between Carthage and Rome, most pointedly during the Punic Wars of 264–241, 218–201, and 149–146 B.C.E. The "avenger" may refer to the great general Hannibal (247–c. 182 B.C.E.) who invaded Italy by crossing over the Alps using elephants to carry equipment and supplies. After many successful victories against the Romans, Hannibal eventually was forced to withdraw his forces from Italy.   [90] **Stygian Jove:** Pluto (Hades in Greek mythology), the ruler of the underworld, associated with the key river of hell, the Styx.

I built a splendid city and saw it walled,
avenged my husband, and made my brother pay—
blessed beyond measure, if only Dardan craft
had never touched upon these shores of mine."
She kissed the couch. "I'll die without revenge,
660   but die, and pass to darkness undismayed.
From shipboard let the heartless Trojan see
my flames! My death ride with him as he sails!"

While she yet spoke, her people saw her fall
crumpled upon the sword, the blade all frothed
with blood, her hands spattered. A scream rose high
in the hall; the city was stricken; Rumor ran wild.
Houses were filled with sobs and lamentations,
with keening of women: the din rose to the skies—
as if an enemy had burst in, and all
670   Carthage or ancient Tyre were falling, while flames
rolled to the roofs, through homes of gods and men.
Anna, half-dead with fear, came running fast:
her fingers tore her face; she beat her breast.
She pushed through the crowd, calling her sister's name:
"Dido, was this what it meant? You lied? to *me*?
Was this the purpose of pyre, altar, and flame?
You left me! What shall I say? You died, but scorned
to take me? You might have let me share your death:
one hour, one stroke of pain had served for two.
680   These hands helped build—this voice of mine helped call
our gods—oh, cruel!—that I must fail you now!
You've killed yourself and me, your people, the lords
of Sidon, and your own city! Oh, let me wash
your wounds, and if some faltering breath remains,
let my lips take it!" With that, she climbed the pyre
and cradled her dying sister in her arms,
cried as she used her dress to stop the blood.
Dido would open her heavy eyes again,
but failed. The gash hissed in her wounded breast.
690   Three times she raised herself up on one arm,
three times fell back, then with an errant eye
sought light in heaven, and moaned that she had found it.

Then Juno in pity for her lingering pain
and laggard death, sent Iris down from heaven
to free her struggling soul from limbs entwined.
(For not at her earned and fated hour she died,

but in a flash of fury, before her days:
Proserpina[91] had not yet cut the lock
from her head, nor sentenced her to life below.)
700   But Iris flew down, dewy and golden-winged,
trailing against the sun a thousand colors.
She stopped over Dido's head: "This sacred lock
I carry to Dis,[92] and from the flesh I free you."
With that she cut the wisp; at once all warmth
dispersed, and life retreated to the winds.

BOOK 6
[AENEAS VISITS THE UNDERWORLD]

[In Book 5, Aeneas, ignorant of Dido's death, sails to Sicily, where to commemorate his father's
death he holds athletic games. In a succession of contests he demonstrates his fairness and concern
for all his company, especially through the dispensing of gifts. Meanwhile, on the beaches, the Trojan women are beguiled by the goddess Iris into burning their men's ships so they may sail
no more. Aeneas puts out the fires and decides to leave the dissenters behind in Sicily. Aeneas
and his men finally sail for Italy, assured of safe passage by the gods, except for the helmsman
Palinurus, who falls overboard and is lost at sea. Now, in Book 6, Aeneas prepares to descend to the
Underworld.]

He spoke, and wept, and gave the ships free rein
until they raised Euboean Cumae's[93] coasts.
Seaward the bows were swung; the anchor's tooth
grounded the ships, their curving quarterdecks
curtained the strand. The young men dashed like flame
to Hesperian shores. Part sought the seeds of fire
hidden in veins of flint, part raided forests,
the wild beasts' homes, found brooks, and marked them out.
But Aeneas the good looked for Apollo's hill
10   and castle, and near it the awesome cave where hid
the Sibyl, the terrifier, whose heart and mind
the Delian seer filled with prophetic speech.
They came to Trivia's[94] grove and golden halls.

---

[91] **Proserpina:** The queen of the underworld, wife of Dis, or Pluto, the god of the underworld, to whom Proserpina offers a lock of hair from persons about to die. Since Dido has unexpectedly committed suicide, Proserpina must send Iris, the goddess of the rainbow and a messenger of the gods, to obtain a lock of Dido's hair.
[92] **Dis:** Another name for the underworld; also a name for the god of the underworld.   [93] **Euboean Cumae:**
Cumae, the Italian town that was home to the Sibyl, priestess of Apollo, the "Delian seer" of line 12. Cumae is
called Euboean here after the people from the city of Chalcis on the island of Euboea who colonized Cumae.
[94] **Trivia:** An epithet of Hecate, the patroness of sorcery and a goddess of the underworld, so named for her
association with crossroads.

Men say that Daedalus,[95] fleeing Minos' power,
dared put his trust in air and widespread wings.
He sailed unwonted ways toward Arctic cold,
and settled lightly, at last, on Cumae's heights.
Safe landed, he made thank-offering first to Phoebus—
the wings he'd used—and built an awesome shrine:
20 on one door, Androgeos'[96] death; the penalty, next,
paid by a sorrowing Athens every year:
seven of her sons; the urn and lots were shown.
On the other side, the isle of Crete rose high;
here a bull's cruel and furtive act of love
with Minos' daughter, their twoform hybrid child,
the Minotaur, monument to love profaned.
Next came that winding, wearying, hopeless house;
but Daedalus pitied a princess lost for love[97]
and solved the riddle and puzzle of those halls,
30 with thread to guide blind feet. You, Icarus, too,
had shared in the masterpiece, had grief allowed.
Twice Daedalus tried to carve your fate in gold,
twice fell a father's hands.
                They had perused
each last detail, had not Achates joined them,
and with him the seer of Phoebus and Trivia,
Deiphobë,[98] Glaucus' daughter. She hailed Aeneas:
"The hour allows no time for seeing sights!
Far better from virgin herd to slaughter bullocks
seven, and seven sheep, and make due prayer."
40 So speaking (the men at once performed the rites
as ordered), she called the Trojans to her shrine.

From Cumae's cliff was hewn a monstrous cave,
with hundred gaping mouths and hundred doors,
whence poured out hundred words, the Sibyl's answers.
As they entered, the priestess cried, "Now hear your dooms!

---

[95]**Daedalus:** The architect of the Labyrinth on Crete. Daedalus was exiled to Crete after murdering his nephew, whose skill rivaled his own. He built the labyrinth to harbor the Minotaur, a creature half human and half bull fathered on King Minos's wife, Pasiphae, by a bull. To end the annual sacrifice of his fellow Athenians to the Minotaur, the hero Theseus killed the monster with the help of Ariadne, Minos's daughter. Daedalus was then imprisoned in the labyrinth for helping Ariadne and Theseus but escaped with his son, Icarus, by fashioning wings for them and flying away. Icarus perished after approaching too close to the sun; Daedalus flew on to Cumae and constructed the temple with the carvings described here. [96]**Androgeos:** The son of King Minos of Crete, whose murder by the Athenians led to the sacrifice of seven young men and seven virgins each year to the Minotaur. (See note 95.) [97]**princess lost for love:** Ariadne. (See note 95.) [98]**Deiphobë:** The Cumaean Sibyl.

'Tis the hour! Behold my god!" And as she spoke
there at the door her face and color changed,
her hair fell in a tangle; she choked, she gasped,
her heart swelled wild and savage; she seemed to grow
50   and utter inhuman sounds, as on her breathed
the power of God. "Trojan," she cried, "you lag?
Aeneas, you lag at prayers? No other power
can blast agape these temple doors." She spoke
no further word. Through hardened Trojan hearts
ran shock and chill; Aeneas was roused to pray:
"Phoebus, help ever-present in Troy's dark days,
who guided the Dardan shaft and hand of Paris
against Achilles,[99] through countless seas that block
vast lands you led me, and to frontier tribes
60   Massylian—tracts that border on the Syrtes.[100]
At last we've reached elusive Italy's coasts:
so far, no farther, let Troy's fate pursue us.
You too may lawfully show us mercy now,
you heavenly powers who hated Troy and all
our Dardan glory. And you, most holy seer,
who know the future, grant (the power I ask
is not unsanctioned) that for Trojan gods,
errant and battered, I find a Latin home.
To Phoebus and Trivia then I'll build a shrine
70   of marble, and name a day 'The Feast of Phoebus.'
You too shall find a temple in my realm;
there I will place your lots and arcane dooms
proclaimed to my people, and men shall be ordained,
lady, to serve you.[101] Write no more on leaves,
lest wanton winds make nonsense of your songs:
let your lips speak!" He said no further word.

Not yet possessed by Phoebus, the weird fay danced
wild in the cave, if she might shake the god
free of her heart, he harassed all the more
80   her lips, her savage soul, suppressing, molding.
And now the temple's hundred mouths gaped wide

---

[99] **who guided . . . Achilles:** As god of archery, Apollo guided Paris's spear toward Achilles' heel, the only vulnerable spot on his body.   [100] **Massylian . . . Syrtes:** The Massylians were a North African tribe; the Syrtes were dangerous shoals off the northern coast of Africa, near Tripoli and Tunis.   [101] **You too . . . serve you:** Aeneas's promise to build the Sibyl a holy shrine alludes to the collection of Sibylline books containing prophetic oracles that were housed in a succession of Roman temples built over time by several rulers.

of themselves; the Sibyl's answer rode the air:
"My son, you have passed all perils of the sea,
but ashore still worse await. To Latium's land
the sons of Troy shall come (this care dismiss),
but coming shall find no joy. War, terror, war,
I see, and Tiber foaming red with blood.
You'll face a Simois, Xanthus, Greeks encamped;
in Latium now a new Achilles lives,
90 he, too, a goddess' son.[102] Troy's burden, Juno,
will never leave you; humble, in need, you'll plead
with every Italian tribe and town for help.
Cause of disaster again a foreign bride,
a match with a woman not of Troy.[103]
Still, never retreat! Gain boldness from disaster!
Where chance allows, march on! Salvation's path
(where least you'd think) a Greek town will reveal."[104]

In words like these the Sibyl from her shrine
sang riddles of terror and bellowed in her cave,
100 wrapping the truth in darkness; such the rein
and spur Apollo gave her maddened heart.
Soon as her lips, deranged and wild, found rest,
Aeneas began "Lady, no face of peril
will strike me strange or rise up unforetold;
I've seized and pondered all things in advance.
One favor! Men say the infernal king has here
his gate; here hell's dark, swampy rivers rise:
allow me to see my well-loved father's face;
show me the way, spread wide the holy doors.
110 Through flames and thousand flying spears I saved him
on these shoulders, with enemies all around.
He shared the route through all those seas with me
and bore the threats of ocean and of sky,
more than the old and ill have strength to bear.
Still more: he used to plead that I seek out
your door in humble access. Lady, have mercy
on father and son! All power is yours; not idly

---

[102] **a goddess' son:** The prophecy compares the war to come in Latium, where the Trojan exiles will land at the mouth of the Tiber River, to the Trojan War; Simois and Xanthus are rivers at Troy. The new Achilles is Turnus, the Rutulian leader who will oppose Aeneas.   [103] **a woman not of Troy:** In keeping with the comparison of the war in Latium to the Trojan War (see note 102), here Virgil compares Lavinia, Aeneas's future wife, to Helen of Troy.   [104] **a Greek town will reveal:** The town is Pallanteum, a colony founded on the Tiber River, at the site of Rome, by the Arcadian Evander. Evander's son, Pallas, will fight with Aeneas against Turnus, who kills Pallas in Book 10.

did Hecate[105] lay Avernus to your charge:
Orpheus could hale a wife's poor ghost from hell
120   by power of music and his Thracian lyre,
and Pollux, saving his twin by altern death,
could pass and repass that road. Why tell of Theseus
or Hercules?[106] I too am of Jove's line."

So he petitioned, with hand on altar laid.
The Sibyl replied: "O child of blood divine,
Anchises' son, descent to hell is easy:
all night, all day black Pluto's[107] door stands wide.
To recall the step, escape to air and sky—
this, this is task and toil! Some few—those loved
130   of Jove, those heavenward rapt by valor's flame,
the sons of God—have done it. Between, all's forest
wrapped round with black Cocytus'[108] coiling streams.
But if you have at heart such love and lust
twice to cross over Styx, hell's darkness twice
to behold, and this mad project gives you joy,
hear what is first to do. A dark tree hides
a bough whose pliant withes and leaves are gold,
to hell's queen sacred. Curtained by a grove
it lies locked in a shadowy, lightless vale.
140   But none may pass beneath this covering earth
till he has plucked the tree's gold-sprouted branch.
This must be brought to Pluto's lovely queen[109]
as offering due. (Break one, a second grows
like it, with leaves and stems of purest gold.)
Search then the treetops; when you find it, pray
and pluck. The branch will come away with ease
if you are elect of Fate. If not, no force
of yours will break it, no cold steel hack it free.

---

[105] **Hecate:** The patroness of sorcery and a goddess of the underworld; Hecate governs over Avernus, the lake and wood near Cumae where the entrance to the underworld was said to be.   [106] **Orpheus . . . Hercules:** Aeneas recites the names of heroes who have been allowed to enter the underworld and return. By means of his enchanting music, Orpheus entered Hades and persuaded Proserpina (Persephone) to allow him to bring his dead wife, Eurydice, back to the land of the living so long as he did not turn back to look at her on their ascent; he did, and she vanished from him. Pollux and his brother Castor, the Dioscuri, were allowed to alternate days between the underworld and the land of the living. The Athenian hero Theseus was trapped in Hades when he tried to help Pirithous abduct Proserpina, the queen of Hades. Theseus was rescued when Hercules, performing one of his labors, came to the underworld to steal the guardian of the gate, the three-headed dog Cerberus.
[107] **Pluto:** The god of the underworld; known as Hades in Greek mythology.   [108] **Cocytus:** The wailing river; one of the rivers of hell.   [109] **Pluto's lovely queen:** Proserpina, the queen of Hell; also known as Persephone in Greek mythology.

Lastly: a friend lies now a lifeless corpse
150 (you did not know!); his death stains all your fleet
while you hang at my door to ask advice.
Now bring him home and lay him in the tomb.
Over black beasts; be this your first atonement.
Then shall you see the grove of Styx, those realms
where the living never tread." She spoke no more.

Aeneas, with saddened face and downcast eye,
stepped from the cave, revolving in his heart
events beyond men's sight. Beside him walked
Achates the loyal, step by troubled step.
160 They spoke of many things, conjecturing much
what friend had died, whose body they must bury.
But high on the beach as they came in they found
Misenus, untimely taken off by death—
Misenus, son of Aeolus, best of all
at sounding the reveille or call to arms.
He had been Hector's man; by Hector's side
he'd marched to glory with trumpet and with spear.
But once Achilles had stripped his chief of life,
he'd joined Aeneas' corps, for he was brave
170 and a fighter, and would obey no lesser man.
But now with a conch he'd blared across the waves—
the fool!—and dared the gods contest his tunes.
Triton accepted and, if the tale be true,
caught him on foaming reefs and drowned him there.[110]
Now, circling round, the company mourned his death,
Aeneas leading. Then, with tears, they turned
to the Sibyl's orders. Quickly they built a mound
and altar, and piled on logs to reach the sky.
They went to a wood, the wild beasts' mountain lair:
180 down came the pine, the oak rang to the ax,
the beech and holm were hewn and split to rail
and billet; great elms came rolling from the hills.

In this work, too, Aeneas took the lead,
urged on his men, and shared their tools and toil.
And yet discouragement circled through his heart
as he viewed the wood—so vast! He fell to prayer:
"Now be the golden bough revealed to us,

---

[110]**Triton . . . drowned him there:** Misenus, the Trojan trumpeter and the son of Aeolus, god of the winds, challenged Triton, a sea-god famous for blowing the conch shell, to a trumpeting contest; for his arrogance Misenus was drowned in the sea. Triton was the son of Neptune (Poseidon), the chief sea-god of the Romans.

here in this endless wood! For all was true
that the seer has prophesied of poor Misenus."
190 Scarce had he spoken when before his face
a pair of doves came flying down the sky
and settled on the turf. Aeneas knew
his mother's birds, and said a joyful prayer:
"If path there be, lead me! Direct your flight
into the woods, where on the rich soil falls
the shade of the tree of wealth. Resolve my fears,
mother in heaven!" With that, he checked his pace
to see what signs they'd give, which way they'd go.
They stopped to feed, then flew on just so far
200 as could be seen by those who followed them.
Then as they reached Avernus'[111] stinking throat,
they rose with a swoop and sailed through brighter air
to perch on the tree they loved, a pair at home;
but—strange!—through the branches came a flash of gold!
As in the winter's cold the mistletoe
grows leafy and green (no child of its parent tree)
and with its yellow fruit loops treetrunks round,
so in the darkness of the oak shone leaves
of gold, thin foil that tinkled in the breeze.
210 Aeneas seized the branch; it clung; he wrenched
it free and brought it to the Sibyl's home.

Meanwhile down on the shore the Trojans mourned
Misenus in thankless office for the dead.
They built his pyre with pitch pine and split oak,
like one great torch, and then with dull dark leaves
they screened its sides. In front they set the cypress,
the death tree; shining armor graced the top.
Some set bronze pots of water over flame
to boil, then washed the body and embalmed it.
220 They wailed the dead, then laid him on the bier,
and covered him with the purple robe he'd known
and loved. They lifted high his heavy bed—
sad office—and in our fathers' way applied
the torch with face averted. Up went the pyre:
incense, food, and oil and wine commingled.
When cinders crumbled and the flames died down,
they quenched the dust and thirsty ash with wine.

---

[111] **Avernus:** This lake, the entrance to the underworld, was given its name, which means "birdless," because the vapors rising from it would kill any bird that flew over it; hence Venus's birds swerve upon their approach to the lake.

Corynaeus gathered the bones in a brazen urn;
he bore pure water three times round his friends,
230 sprinkling them with hyssop of fertile olive,
to wash them clean, then said the last farewell.
Aeneas the good piled high a mounded tomb
(placing upon it the man's arms, oar, and trumpet)
beneath the crag that men now call, for him,
"Mount Misenus," to keep his name forever.

This done, they turned to do the Sibyl's bidding.
There was a cave, deep, huge, and gaping wide,
rocky, guarded by night-black pools and woods;
above it hardly a bird could wing its way
240 safely, such were the vapors that poured forth
from that black throat, and rose toward heaven's vault
(and hence the Greeks have named it "Birdless Cavern").[112]
Here the Sibyl began by bringing oxen
four, black-hided. She sluiced their heads with wine;
between their horns she snipped the tips of bristles
to lay as first fruits on her altar fires,
then called on Hecate, power of heaven and hell.
Acolytes plunged their knives and caught the blood
hot in their salvers. Aeneas killed a lamb,
250 black-fleeced, for the mother of Furies and her sister,
and for the queen of hell,[113] a barren cow.
He built night-altars to the Stygian king
and laid bull's vitals whole upon the flames,
drenching the sizzling meats with olive oil.
Just before sunrise and the dawn's first light,
the earth beneath them bawled, the wooded hills
opened, and in the shadows she-wolves howled.
"Here comes our lady![114] Fall back, unhallowed souls!"
the seer cried. "Out of the grove! Out! Out with you!
260 Aeneas, start down the road! Unsheathe your sword!
Now you need courage and now a steadfast heart!"
With one mad shriek she entered the cavern's mouth;
she led, he followed, step for fearless step.

O gods who rule all souls! O silent shades!
Phlegethon,[115] Chaos, regions of voiceless night!

---

[112] **"Birdless Cavern":** Refers to Avernus, or Aornos in Greek mythology. (See note 111.) [113] **mother of Furies . . . hell:** The mother of the Furies was Nox, or Night (Nyx), and her sister was Earth (Ge or Gaea). The queen of Hell was Proserpina (Persephone). [114] **our lady:** Hecate, who often appears accompanied by hell-hounds, here described as she-wolves. (See note 105.) [115] **Phlegethon:** A river of fire in the underworld.

Grant me apocalypse! Grant me right and power
to show things buried deep in earth and darkness!

They walked obscure through night's dark loneliness
past Pluto's empty halls and vacant thrones:
270 as one might walk through wood beneath a moon
malign and blotched, when Jove has hidden heaven
in shadow, and black night robs the world of color.
Right at the entrance, where hell's throat begins,
Sorrow, Vengeance, and Care have pitched their tents;
there live Diseases pale, and grim Old Age,
Fear, evil-counseling Hunger, shameful Want—
shapes terrible to see—and Death and Toil,
and Death's blood brother, Sleep, and Pleasures vile
even in thought. War, dealer of death, stands watch,
280 and Furies chambered in steel, while mad Sedition
leers through her bedlam braids of snakes and blood.

Midst all, an elm spreads wide her ancient boughs,
opaque and huge; men say this is the home
of Foolish Dreams: they cling beneath each leaf.
And there are wild beasts, monsters of mixed breed;
Centaurs and two-formed Scyllas haunt the doors,
Briareus hundred-handed, savage Hydra
horribly hissing, Chimaera armed with flame,
Gorgons, Harpies, the ghost of bodies three.[116]
290 In sudden terror Aeneas drew his sword
and showed the charging creatures his bare blade;
and had his guide, who knew, not warned that these
were lives unsubstanced, flitting empty shapes,
he had attacked and wasted blows on shadows.

Here leads the road toward hell and Acheron,
that mud-dark stream, wide, swirling, sucking down,
sinking and rising to belch Cocytus'[117] sands.
A frightful ferryman keeps the river-watch,
Charon,[118] a ragged horror, whose thick white beard
300 lies matted upon his chin. His eyes are flames,

---

[116] **Centaurs . . . three:** A catalog of mythical monsters who guard the entrance of hell: Centaurs are half man, half horse; Scyllas are creatures with six heads; Briareus is a giant with fifty heads and one hundred hands; Hydra is a gigantic nine-headed serpent; Chimaera is a dragonlike creature who is part lion, part goat, and part snake; Gorgons are snake-haired female monsters who turn men to stone with their gaze; Harpies are bird-like monsters who carry souls to Hell; and the three-bodied Geryon is the son of the Gorgon Medusa.
[117] **Cocytus:** Like the Acheron, a river of the underworld. [118] **Charon:** The ferryman in Hell.

and knotted rags hang filthy from his frame.
He poles his craft himself, he tends its sail,
and in its rusty hull he freights the dead—
old, but a god's old age is raw and green.
Toward him the whole crowd rushed to the river bank—
mothers and husbands, those that had lived the lives
of bold, brave fighters, boys, unmarried girls,
young men cremated before a father's face—
as many as forest leaves that flutter down
310 at the first autumn frost, or as the birds
that flock to earth from sea when winter's cold
drives them across the deep to sunny lands.
They stood there begging to be first to cross,
their hands outstretched in love of the other shore.
The glowering boatman took now these, now those,
but drove back others and blocked them from the strand.
Aeneas, amazed and by the tumult moved,
said, "Tell me, why this gathering at the river?
What do the souls want? Why do some fall back
320 from shore, while others cross the lead-gray stream?"
Briefly the aged priestess spoke to him:
"Son of Anchises, prince of blood divine,
you see dark, deep Cocytus and swampy Styx,
names not even the gods dare take in vain.
The boatman: Charon; his passengers: the entombed.
Those others are all unburied, a hapless host;
they may not pass the shore, the hoarse, wild waters,
until their bones have found a home and rest.
A hundred years they flutter round this beach;
330 then finally they may approach the longed-for stream."
The son of Anchises checked his pace and stopped,
puzzled and grieved at death's inequities.
He saw, embittered for lack of funeral rites,
Orontes, the Lycian admiral, and Leucaspis.
These two, sailing the wind-swept seas from Troy,
were lost when a Norther sank them, ship and crew.

Then toward them came the helmsman, Palinurus
(plotting his course from Libya by the stars
he'd slipped from his quarterdeck far out at sea);
340 Aeneas scarce recognized his face, so dark
and bitter. He spoke: "Palinurus, what god did this?
Who stole you from us and drowned you in mid-sea?
Tell me! I've never known Apollo lie

till this one message that betrayed my trust.
He said you'd be unharmed afloat, and come
to Italy. Is this then his word, his promise?"
Palinurus answered: "Apollo told no lie,
my lord Aeneas. I was not drowned at sea.
In a sudden lurch, the helm was cast adrift,
350 with me fast to it, for it was in my charge.
Overside I carried it. By all storms I swear
that for myself I feared not half so much
as that your ship, with helm and helmsman lost
overboard, might founder in the rising seas.
Three winter nights I drifted endless miles
of wind-torn water; when the fourth dawn came
from crest of a wave I raised the Italian coast.
I floated ashore by inches, made it safe,
and was clawing my way, slowed by dripping clothes,
360 uphill across sharp rocks, when tribesmen killed me.
(They did not know me, but thought I was fair game.)
And now I lie awash in wind and surf.
And so, by the sky, the light, the air we love,
by Anchises, by all you hope for young Iulus,
rescue me from this misery. Find the bay
of Velia[119] and — for you can! — toss earth upon me.
Or, if your goddess mother show some way
(for not without the nod of heaven, I'm sure,
you sail the boundless pools and streams of hell),
370 give me a hand to cross the waves with you,
that here at last I find my peace, and rest."
Such was his plea, and this the seer's reply:
"Palinurus, whence this blasphemous desire?
Shall you, unburied, look on Styx, the stream
of stern requital — you, pass this beach unbidden?
Think not to change the law of God by prayer.
But hear! Note well! Be solaced, injured soul!
A nearby people, frightened by signs from heaven
all up and down their land, will bury your bones,
380 raise you a mound, do office for the dead,
and name that spot 'Palinurus' for all time."
These words resolved his care; for a time he ceased
to grieve, in joy that earth should bear his name.

---

[119] **the bay of Velia:** A bay to the south of Naples, near what is called Point Palinuro, after Aeneas's drowned helmsman.

They resumed their journey then and neared the stream.
But when the boatman saw them from the Styx
moving through voiceless trees on toward the shore,
he started up and challenged them, and shouted:
"You with the sword, who trespass toward my river,
halt! What are you doing here? Stop where you are!
390 This is the vale of Shades, Dreams, Night, and Sleep.
By law, no flesh may ride the boat of hell.
Alcides? Theseus? Pirithous?[120] 'Twas no joy
to me to see them come and cross my swamp—
'Son of the gods'? 'Unconquered heroes'? Hah!
That first one snapped hell's watchdog to a leash
and dragged him whimpering from the royal door;
the others tried to kidnap Pluto's bride."
To him the Amphrysian seer[121] gave brief reply:
"Here are no schemes like those (cease your concern),
400 nor does that sword mean war. Your ghostly guard
may bark forever to frighten bloodless ghosts,
your queen keep undefiled her uncle's house.
Aeneas of Troy, the good, the great in arms,
has come to the shadowy pit to find his father.
If goodness and greatness leave you unconcerned,
this bough" (she showed it, hidden in her gown)
"you'll know." His hostile, puffed-up fury died,
and with it, debate. He stood amazed and humbled
to see the wand of fate so long unseen;
410 he swung his dead-blue craft stern-on to shore.
The other souls who sat along the thwarts
he herded out and cleared the decks, then called
Aeneas aboard. With groans at his weight, the scow
took water at every ragged, gaping seam.
Slowly it ferried them, seer and man; still whole
it dropped them in foul muck and dry, grey reeds.

At once the world burst round them with wild barking,
for Cerberus[122] crouched there, huge beside his cave.
But when the seer observed his snake-ruff rise,
420 she tossed him sleeping drugs tucked in a ball
of crumbs and honey. He stretched three greedy throats

---

[120]**Alcides . . . Pirithous:** All mortals who passed through the gates of Hell while still alive; Alcides is another name for Hercules. (See note 106.)   [121]**Amphrysian seer:** The Cumaean Sibyl, priestess of Apollo. Virgil here makes an obscure allusion to Apollo, who had once spent a year in the service of King Admetus in Thessaly, where the river Amphyrsia was located.   [122]**Cerberus:** The three-headed dog who guards the gates of Hell.

and wildly gulped; his weird dog's-body crumpled
and sprawled from wall to wall across his cave.
Quickly Aeneas passed the sleeping guard,
and hurried away from the waters of no return.

Now they heard voices, sobs, a strange vast noise
of ghostly babies crying: just at the door
of life they'd lost their share; pulled from the breast
they'd sunk in darkness down to bitter death.
430 Next, those whom perjured witness sent to die.
(Due process, here, and justice fix their homes:
Minos[123] is judge; he draws the lots and holds
assize of the dead, to hear defense and charge.)
Next came the gloom-filled strip of suicides.
Sinless, they'd tossed their own dear lives away
for loathing of the light. Now, just to see
the sky, they'd gladly work for beggar's bread.
The law says no; the grim and loveless stream
prisons them: Styx enfolds them nine times round.

440 Nearby, the plains ran wide in all directions;
these were the Fields of Mourning—such their name.
Here dwell Love's lepers: wasted, ulcered cruel,
they slink down private paths, and hide in thickets
of myrtle; even death brings them no cure.
Aeneas saw Phaedra, Procris, Eriphylë
(tearfully showing the gash her son had made),
Evadne, Pasiphaë, Laodamia too,
all in a group, and Caeneus[124] (once a boy,
but now by fate returned to woman's shape).
450 There too among tall trees walked Punic Dido,
faltering, for her wound still bled. Soon as
the lord of Troy came near and saw her darkly,
midst shadows—as one sees the young new moon

---

[123] **Minos:** Former king of Crete who became judge over the dead after he was killed.   [124] **Phaedra . . . Caeneus:** Women who died from causes related to love and jealousy. Phaedra, wife of the Athenian king Theseus, committed suicide after falling in love with her stepson Hippolotus; Procris, wife of the Phocian Cephalus, was killed by her husband, who mistook her for prey as she spied on him while he was hunting; Eriphylë, wife of Amphiaraüs, was bribed to send her husband off to certain death and was then killed by her own son; Evadne, wife of Capaneus, gave her life on her husband's funeral pyre; Pasiphaë, wife of King Minos, gave birth to the Minotaur and suffered jealousy over her husband's amours, casting a spell on him so that he would infect his lovers with a fatal poison; Laodamia, wife of Protesilaüs, who died at Troy, voluntarily accompanied her husband to the underworld. Caeneus was Caenis, the daughter of King Elatus from Thessaly; when she was raped by Neptune, who afterwards granted her a wish, she asked to be turned into a man so that she would never suffer such a fate again.

(or thinks he saw it) rising through the clouds—
he dropped a tear and spoke with gentle love:
"Poor Dido! Then the news I heard was true,
that with a sword you'd made an end of life?
Your death—was I its cause? By heaven and gods
I swear, by every oath that hell can muster,
460   unwillingly, Lady, I parted from your shore.
The law of God—the law that sends me now
through darkness, bramble, rot, and night profound—
imperious, drove me; nor could I have dreamed
that in my leaving I would hurt you so.
Wait! Let me see you! Do not shrink from me!
Why run? Fate will not let us speak again."
He talked; she watched him, but with eyes of hate
and scorn, for all his soothing words and tears,
then looked away, her gaze fixed on the ground.
470   He tried to plead; her face remained unchanged
as if she were carved of granite or of flint.
At last she drew erect and turned unsmiling
back to the shadowed grove where her first love,
Sychaeus, gave her comfort in his arms.
Aeneas, hard-struck by unkind fate, still watched her
and pitied and wept until she disappeared.

The Sibyl led him farther. Soon they reached
Plain's-End, preserve where meet the great in arms.
Here Tydeus ran up, Parthenopaeus, too,
480   and Adrastus[125] (poor, pale ghost!)—famed soldiers, all;
here, much bewailed on earth, the sons of Troy
fallen in war. Aeneas wept to see
that long parade: Glaucus, Thersilochus, Medon
(Antenor's sons), Polyboetes, priest of Ceres,
Idaeus, armed and gripping his chariot pole.
The souls thronged round him, pressing left and right.
Nor was one look enough; they tried to stop him,
to walk with him and learn why he had come.
But the Argive chiefs, Agamemnon's fighting men,
490   soon as they saw Aeneas and caught the flash
of arms, panicked. Some turned their backs and ran,

---

[125] **Tydeus . . . Adrastus:** Three of the famous Argive warriors known as the Seven against Thebes. They aided
Polyneices in his attempt to wrest power from his brother, Eteocles, who had violated their pact, formed after
their father the former king Oedipus was banished, to share the rule of Thebes.

as once they ran to the ships; some gibbered and squeaked:
a jaw slack-fallen was all their battle cry.

Here too he saw Deiphobus, Priam's son,
his body one bloody wound, his lips hacked off—
his lips and both his hands; his ears were torn
from his head, his nose was lopped—unkindest cut.
He hardly knew him, for he cowered and tried
to hide his gashes. Aeneas addressed him gently:
500 "Deiphobus! Captain! Prince of Teucer's line!
Who felt impelled to such bloodthirsty blows?
Who thought himself so free? On that last night,
I heard, you killed Greeks till you fell exhausted
to die on your dead all helter-skelter piled.
On Cape Rhoeteum I raised your cenotaph—
I took that time—and thrice invoked your ghost.
Your name and armor mark the spot; I found
no trace of you to bury before I sailed."
Deiphobus answered: "You left no work undone;
510 you paid me every due the dead may ask.
Fate and that murdering she-devil from Sparta[126]
gave me these wounds: these are her souvenirs.
That final night: you know how gay we were,
such fools! You must remember all too well.
Even as that deadly horse came bounding up
Troy's hill, its belly big with men-at-arms,
she led our women in the fire dance round,
'to honor God.' She held the biggest torch
and from a high point signaled to the Greeks.
520 I'd come home tired, worried, dead for rest,
to my ill-starred bedroom; there I lay in sleep
so sweet, so deep—most like the peace of death.
My noble wife now stripped my house of weapons;
from under my pillow she even slipped my sword.
She called Menelaus in, threw wide my door—
thinking this lovely gift would please her darling
and make him forget old tales and ugly talk.
In short, the two burst in (he had a friend
to abet his crime, Ulysses): God give the Greeks
530 as much, if I may justly ask revenge!

---

[126] **she-devil from Sparta:** Helen, the wife of Menelaus who was abducted by the Trojan prince Paris, leading to the Trojan War; after Paris's death, the Trojans gave Helen to Deiphobus, who was eventually killed by Menelaus.

But you're alive! Come, tell me now: What chance
has brought you? Did you lose your course at sea?
Did God command? Tell, by what blow of fate
you've come to this grim, sunless, fogbound place?"

As they talked, Aurora with her rosy team
had passed the mid-point of her course in heaven,
and the time allowed might all have been so spent,
had not the Sibyl uttered admonition:
"Night's coming, Aeneas; we're wasting time on tears.
540 The road splits here and leads in two directions.
The right fork stretches beneath the wall of Dis
to Elysium: this is our route. Left runs the road
to Tartarus,[127] where the vile atone their crimes."
Deiphobus then: "Don't chide me, reverend lady!
I'm going—back to my company, back to night.
Go, glory of Troy! Have better luck than I!"
With that last word he turned and walked away.

Aeneas looked quickly round. To the left, he saw
a cliff; at its base, broad battlements triple-walled.
550 A river of swirling flame flowed all around—
Phlegethon, rolling a rubble of grinding rocks.
A gate rose huge, by granite columns flanked;
no mortal power—not even gods at war—
had strength to force it. Its tower of steel stood tall,
and at its gate, Tisiphone,[128] bloody-garbed,
kept sleepless watch eternal, night and day.
From here came forth wild screams, the savage whistle
of whips, the hiss of irons, the rattle of chains.
Aeneas stopped short. He listened and turned pale:
560 "What shapes of sin are here? Speak, Sibyl! What pains
pursue them? The noise is deafening to my ears!"
Then spoke the holy seer: "Great prince of Troy,
no guiltless man may pass the door of sin.
When Hecate laid Avernus to my charge
she showed me the place, and how God punishes.
This kingdom of torment Rhadamanthus[129] rules;

---

[127] **Elysium . . . Tartarus:** Elysium is the region of the underworld where the righteous and virtuous lead a pleasant existence; Tartarus is the part of Hell in which the Titans are confined and where sinners are meted out harsh punishments.   [128] **Tisiphone:** One of the Furies, female creatures who punish those who commit blood-crimes against their kin.   [129] **Rhadamanthus:** The brother of King Minos of Crete and, like him, a judge in hell.

he hears and chastens fraud; all must confess
their sins committed on earth and tucked away
for atonement (death seemed pleasantly remote).
570 At the word 'Guilty!' Tisiphone lifts her lash
and leaps to snap it; her left hand holds out snakes
poised to strike; she summons her savage sisters.[130]
Then only the hellish gates are opened wide
on shrieking hinges. You see what kind of guard
sits at the entry? What shape patrols the door?
Inside is the Hydra's post; her fifty mouths
gape still more black and monstrous. Then the pit
opens toward darkness downward twice as far
as eye looks up toward heaven and Olympus.
580 Down at the bottom the ancient sons of Earth,
the Titans, wallow where the lightning hurled them.
I saw the sons of Aloeus, giant twins,
who attacked high heaven and tried to tear it down
barehanded, and pull Jove from his royal throne—
saw Salmoneus in torment of the damned
for mocking the flame and thunderbolt of Jove.
Driving a four-horse team and shaking a torch
he'd marched in pride through Greece and down the streets
of Elis, demanding honors due a god,
590 the fool: he'd made a lightning bolt of brass
and fashioned his horses' hooves to drum like thunder.
But the father almighty massed his clouds and whirled
his bolt—no pitch pine and no smoky flame
of torch; a fireball rode the pretender down.
Tityus,[131] too, the child of Earth all-mother,
was there to see: his body filled a field
nine acres broad; with curving beak, a vulture
fed on his deathless liver (fertile food
for pain), probing his vitals, making his ribs
600 her home; his flesh, reborn, could never rest.
Why tell of the Lapiths, Pirithous, and Ixion,[132]
. . .

---

[130] **savage sisters:** Alecto and Megaera, sister Furies who also inflict punishment on the sinners here. (See note 128.)   [131] **Tityus:** Virgil has been describing the key sinners of Tartarus: the Titans, the race of giants who fought against the Olympian Jove in his successful war against the god Saturn (Cronos, in Greek). They are the giants Otus and Ephialtes, the sons of Aloeus, who fought against the Olympian gods; Simoneus, who wrongly imitated Jove's power by creating false lightning; and Tityus, who attempted to rape the goddess Latona (Leto in Greek).   [132] **Lapiths . . . Ixion:** Ixion, the king of the Lapiths, a notoriously violent people from Thessaly, was the father of Pirithous. Father and son were punished for similar crimes—the first for having attempted to rape Juno, the second for attempting to kidnap Proserpina.

over whom a black flint, ever about to fall,
hangs menacing. Brightly shines the wedding couch,
deep-cushioned, gilded; royal is the feast
he sees laid out. But there she lies, the worst
of the Furies, and will not let him touch the food:
she jumps to her feet, lifts up her torch, and snarls.

"They too come here who, living, loathed a brother,
drove out a father, or tricked a poor man's trust;
610 who, finding wealth, sat lonely brooding on it
with never a share for a neighbor (legion, they!);
and those for adultery killed, and those who raised
rebellion, heedless of oath and service due;
here they are jailed and wait their dooms. Don't ask
what doom, what shape, what lot entraps them there.
Some roll great boulders; some, spread-eagled, hang
on whirling wheels. One sits, forever sits:
Theseus the luckless; one—poor, wretched Phlegyas[133]—
repeats in the gloom his warning to all men:
620 'Hear this: learn justice; never scorn the gods!'
Here is the man who for a tyrant's gold
enslaved his country; here, the peddler of laws;
here, one who raped his child and called it marriage:
all monsters of insolence, monsters in success.
Had I a hundred tongues, a hundred mouths,
and chords of steel, I could not tell the forms
of all their crimes, nor list the penalties."

When Phoebus' aged seer had thus concluded,
"Come now," she said. "Move on! Complete your task!
630 Let's hurry! I see the walls forged on the hearths
of the Cyclops. There's the arch and there the gate,
where we must place our gift, as we were ordered."
Then, walking together over a lightless road,
they covered the mid-space and approached the door.
Aeneas stood close and with fresh water sprinkled
his body, then set the bough against the door.

Thus with their liturgy to the goddess ended,
they came to the place of joy, the pleasant lawns,
the groves of the lucky, and the blessed homes.[134]

---

[133] **Theseus . . . Phlegyas:** With the help of Pirithous, Theseus tried unsuccessfully to kidnap Proserpina; Phlegyas set fire to the temple of Apollo at Delphi. [134] **place of joy . . . homes:** Aeneas and the Sibyl reach Elysium, the place of eternal happiness and home to Anchises; the "priest of Thrace" in line 645 is Orpheus.

640 These lands are clothed in larger air and light
the color of life; they see their sun, their stars.
Here, figures were training on the grassy grounds,
some playing games, some wrestling in the ring,
and some were treading the dance and singing songs.
There stood, in his poet's gown, the priest of Thrace,
playing his instrument of seven strings
(he plucked with fingers now, and now with plectrum).
Here, Teucer's ancient line, his splendid sons,
greathearted heroes, born in happier days:
650 Ilus, Assaracus, Dardanus,[135] founder of Troy.
Aeneas was startled: there lay cars and arms
at rest, spears stacked, and horses running free
grazing the field. The joy the living knew
in arms and car, their love of grooming horses
to sleekness, followed them beyond the grave.
Aeneas saw others about him on the grass,
feasting and singing cheerful songs of praise.
Above them hung sweet bays, and from a hill
Eridanus[136] tumbled his waters through the grove.

660 Here were the band who for their country bled,
here priests who in the world led saintly lives,
prophets of truth, who spoke as God would speak,
those whose discoveries made a better world,
those who by doing good earned men's remembrance.
Each one wore snow-white bands about his head.
The Sibyl addressed them as they gathered round,
Musaeus[137] first (the crowd surrounded him
and watched him towering shoulder-high above them):
"Tell us, O blessed souls, tell, best of bards,
670 where we may find Anchises? To see him
we came and crossed the floods of Erebus."
Then from the great man came this brief reply:
"None has a place assigned. We live in groves;
our beds are the riverbanks and fields made fresh
by springs. But if you wish so much to find him,
climb up this hill; I'll set you on your way."
He walked ahead, and from the hilltop showed them
the garden land. They left the summit then.

---

[135] **Ilus . . . Dardanus:** Ilus, the father of Laomedon, and his brother Assaracus were early kings of Troy; Dardanus, son of Jove (Zeus) and Electra, was the legendary founder of Troy.   [136] **Eridanus:** A river sometimes identified in legend as the source of the Italian river Po.   [137] **Musaeus:** Legendary poet of Thrace.

Deep in a grassy valley stood the souls
680   mustered for life on earth. With eye alert
Anchises surveyed them, checking off the roll
of all his cherished line: his sons, their sons,
their luck, their destinies, their works and ways.
But when, across the fields, he saw Aeneas
coming, he stretched out both his hands for joy;
tears washed his cheeks; words tumbled from his lips:
"You've come at last! Your father waited long
for love to conquer hardship! Oh, my son!
Do I see your face? And may we talk once more?
690   I knew it would happen! In my heart I knew!
I reckoned the hours with care and told them right.
Over what lands, what endless seas you traveled,
harried by countless dangers, and now you've come!
In Libya, disaster was close: I feared for you."
Aeneas replied: "Father, your tear-stained face,
so often in my mind, compelled me here.
Our fleet is in Tuscan waters! Give me your hand,
let me embrace you, father: don't slip away!"
So speaking, he let the tears course down his face.
700   Three times he tried to fold him in his arms;
three times an empty shade escaped his grasp,
light as the air, most like the wings of sleep.

Just then, far down a slope, Aeneas saw
a grove apart, with foliage thick and rustling:
this was the haven of peace, where Lethe[138] flowed:
about it flitted the nations of mankind
like bees in a meadow on a summer's day
(they stop at bright-hued blooms and cluster close
around white lilies; their humming fills the field).
710   At the sight Aeneas was puzzled and stopped short:
"What did this mean? What river," he asked, "was that?
Who were those people that swarmed about its banks?"
Then Lord Anchises: "Those are souls whose fate
binds them to flesh once more. At Lethe's wave
they drink and forget past years of care and fear.
I've longed to show them to you and tell their names —
the line of my children, the number of my heirs —
that you may rejoice with me for Italy found."

---

[138] **Lethe:** The river of forgetfulness in the underworld, through which all reborn souls must pass on their way
to the upper world.

"What, father? Must I think men's souls rise up
720 from here to the air, and to the sluggish flesh
return? Poor fools! Whence this mad lust for life?"
"I'll, speak at once, dear son, and ease your mind,"
Anchises answered, and told the order of things.

"To begin: the heavens, the earth, the watery wastes,
the lucent globe of moon, the sun, the stars,
exist through inward spirit. Their total mass
by mind is permeated: hence their motion.
From mind and spirit comes life—of man, of beast,
of bird, of monsters under the foam-flecked seas.
730 Life is from heaven—a seed of fire that glows
bright, so far as flesh cannot repress it,
or earthly, death-bound bodies dull its glow.
From flesh come fear, desire, pain, and joy:
its pitch-dark prison blinds us to the light.
And even on that last day when life departs,
not all our evil, all the body's foul
corruption leaves us: deep ingrained, in ways
past comprehension, much has hardened fast.
Our souls, then, suffer pain, and pay the price
740 for wrongs done years before: some, like a cloak
laid off, hang to the winds; some lose their stains
by flood and swirl, or cautery of fire.
We suffer, each, our ghostly selves, then pass—
some few—to gain Elysium's fields of joy.
The years go by; Time makes his cycle just,
our hardened filth is sloughed; intelligence
pure, as of heaven, is left, and breath, and fire.
After a thousand circling years, God calls
these souls to Lethe in a long parade
750 to gain forgetfulness, then view the sky
once more, and wish to put on flesh again."

Anchises spoke no more, and led his son
and the Sibyl, too, deep into the rustling throng,
then up on a mound where they could see the files
approaching and watch the faces as they passed.

"Now you shall see the glory that awaits
the children of Troy and their Italian sons—
all souls of splendor, who shall bear our name.
Hear their story, and learn your destiny.
760 That young man—see him, leaning on his staff?—

by lot will be the first to rise to light
and air with blood of Italy in his veins.
His name is Alban, 'Silvius,'[139] your last child,
born in your old age to your wife, Lavinia,
bred in the forest, king and sire of kings;
through him our line shall rule in Alba Longa.
Next him is Procas, pride of the race of Troy,
and Capys and Numitor and — named after you —
Aeneas Silvius, famed alike for valor
770 and goodness — if ever he gain the Alban throne.
What fine young men! Look at the strength they show!
See how they wear the oak-leaf civil crown!
They'll found Fidenae, Gabii, Nomentum,
and build Collatia's castle on the hills,
Bola, Cora, Pometii, and Castrum.[140]
(Great names they'll be; now they are land unnamed.)

"There's Romulus, son of Mars; with Numitor[141]
he'll take his stand (through Ilia, his mother,
he's of our blood): see, on his head, twin plumes,
780 sign of a father's favor, mark divine.
With him Rome will begin her march to glory,
to world-wide rule, to spirit that rivals heaven.
She'll throw one wall around her seven hills;
she shall be rich in sons, like that great mother
who, mural-crowned, rides through the Eastern world,
god-bearer triumphant; a hundred sons of sons,
all gods, a heavenly host, are in her arms.
But look, now! Look! Here comes your family,
your Roman children: Caesar and all the sons
790 of Iulus who'll come beneath the vault of heaven.
Here is the man you've heard so often promised:
Augustus, son of godhead.[142] He'll rebuild

---

[139] 'Silvius': In lines 756 through 776 Anchises gives Aeneas a vision of the genealogy linking Troy to Rome, from Silvius, the early ruler of Alba Longa and Aeneas's son by the Latium princess Lavinia, to the legendary founder of Rome, Romulus (see notes 21 and 22). Procas, Capys, Numitor, and Aeneas Silvius were all kings of Alba Longa.   [140] Fidenae . . . Castrum: Towns near Rome.   [141] Romulus . . . Numitor: Anchises here gives Aeneas a vision of the glory of Rome from the founding of Rome by Romulus to the age of Augustus Caesar. Romulus and Remus were the twin sons of the Roman god of war, Mars, and Ilia (in some versions, Rea Silvia), whose uncle, Amulius, hoping to secure his power over the throne at Alba Longa, had the boys exposed in the Tiber. Raised in the woods by a she-wolf and a woodpecker, animals sacred to Mars, the boys eventually joined forces with their exiled grandfather, Numitor, the deposed king of Alba Longa, and won back the city. Eventually, after the death of Remus resulting from a quarrel, Romulus went on to found Rome. Numitor had been restored to power by his legendary grandsons.   [142] son of godhead: Augustus, the grand-nephew and later the adopted son and heir of Julius Caesar, who had been deified upon his death.

a golden age in Latium, land where once
Saturn was king. Past India, past the Moor
he'll spread his rule to zones beyond the stars,
beyond the ecliptic, where Adas carries heaven,
and bears on his back the spinning, star-tricked wheel.
Against Augustus' advent, even now
God's oracles have panicked Eastern steppes
800   and roiled the outlets of the seven-twinned Nile.
Not even Hercules crossed so much land
to shoot the bronze-hoofed hind, or bring back peace
to Erymanthan groves, or frighten Lerna;
nor Bacchus, when he drove his tiger team,
with vines for reins, in glory down from Nysa.[143]
(And still we hesitate to fight and win,
or fear to make our stand in Italy?)

"But who is that? He wears the olive crown
and carries hallows. White hair and beard—I know him:
810   that king whose code gave Rome a base of law.[144]
He'll come from little Cures, poor-man's land,
but rise to royal heights. Succeeding him,
Tullus will shatter our peace and lead to war
a people soft, unused to battle line
and glory. Ancus next—a boastful man,
too much enamored of the people's whims.
And there the Tarquins—see?—and their avenger,
Brutus[145] the proud, who'll give us back our power.
He first will rule as consul, first will take
820   the axes; when his sons rise in revolt,
in liberty's name he'll see them put to death
(unhappy father, however the tale be told!)
bested by love of country and lust for praise.

"See—back there!—Decius, Drusus, and Torquatus
the savage headsman, Camillus[146] with his standards,

---

[143] **Erymanthan groves . . . Nysa:** Hercules' labors took him to Cerynaia (where he killed the Cerynaian hind), Erymantha, and Lerna, all sites in Greece; Nysa, the birthplace of Bacchus, has been located, depending on the tradition, in Ethiopia, Libya, India, and Thrace. With these allusions Virgil elaborates on the extent of the Roman Empire.   [144] **that king . . . law:** Numa Pompilias, from the Sabine city of Cures, was the second king of Rome; his reign was marked by law and peace. Tullus (Tullus Hostilius) and Ancus (Ancus Marcius), described in the following lines, were the second and third kings of Rome.   [145] **Brutus:** Brutus (not the betrayer of Julius Caesar) avenged the rape of Lucretia by Sextus, son of the Roman king Tarquinus Superbus (Tarquin the Proud), expelling the king and establishing the first Roman republic in 509 B.C.E.   [146] **Decius . . . Camillus:** Roman heroes from the fourth and third centuries B.C.E.; Drusus was head of the family whose line led to Livia, the second wife of Augustus.

and, just this way, two souls in armor bright,[147]
full of good will while night entombs them here;
but oh, if they see the light, what wars, what strife
they'll set afoot, what battle lines and death:
830 from Gaul and the Alps the father-in-law will march
against the son with Eastern legions massed.
(Children, never grow hardened to wars like those;
against your homeland raise no hostile hand!
Oh, take the lead, show mercy, child of heaven,
throw down that sword, son of my blood!)

"That man[148] will slaughter Greeks and conquer Corinth,
then ride in triumph up high Capitol Hill;
this one[149] will pull Agamemnon's Argos down,
and a king who boasts the blood of brave Achilles—
840 vengeance for Troy and Pallas' fane defiled!
Who'd pass by Cato[150] or Cossus without a word?
Who the Gracchi, or those twin thunderbolts,
the Scipios, bane of Libya? Who Fabricius,
whose need spelled might, or Regulus, sower of seed?
The Fabii rush me, yet he'll be their greatest
'who lone by laggard tactics saves our state.'
Others will forge the bronze to softer breath,
no doubt, and bring the sculptured stone to life,
show greater eloquence, and with their rule
850 map out the skies and tell the rising stars:
you, Roman, remember: Govern! Rule the world!
These are your arts! Make peace man's way of life;
spare the humble but strike the braggart down."
So Lord Anchises; then to their wonder, added:
"See, there: Marcellus, splendid in the spoils

---

[147] **two souls . . . bright:** Julius Caesar and his rival, General Pompey; they fought against each other during the civil war (49–45 B.C.E.).   [148] **That man:** Mummius, a Roman general who conquered Corinth in 167 B.C.E. [149] **this one:** Aemilius Paulus, who defeated the Macedonian king Perseus, who claimed to have blood ties to Achilles, in 168 B.C.E.   [150] **Cato:** Anchises names several figures from Rome's history: Cato, the great Roman orator from the second century B.C.E.; Cossus, a general who vanquished the Etruscan king Tolumnius in 437 B.C.E.; the Gracchi, two brothers who lost their lives while fighting for constitutional reform in the second century B.C.E.; the two Scipios, Publius Cornelius and Publius Scipio Aemilianus, who fought against Carthage in the second and third Punic Wars, respectively; Fabricius, a Roman general who fought against Macedonia in the third century B.C.E.; the Fabii, a powerful family whose numbers include Quintus Fabius Maximus, the "Delayer," whose strategic delaying tactics helped defeat Hannibal in the second Punic War; and finally Marcellus, a Roman general who defeated the Gauls in 222 B.C.E. and fought against Hannibal in the second Punic War. Anchises also alludes to the curse of Dido (end of Book 4), which calls for endless conflict between Carthage and Rome.

of war, in victory tall above his troops.
In the great conflict, he'll set Rome aright
once more, bring down rebellious Gaul and Carthage,
and a third time offer captured arms to Mars."

860   Beside him, Aeneas saw, there walked a man[151]
handsome and young, with armor shining bright,
but brow not joyful, face and eyes downcast.
"Who, father, walks there at Marcellus' side?
His son? Some other of his glorious line?
See how his friends press close! There's greatness there,
yet shadows black as night hang round his head."

Anchises answered as tears rose in his eyes:
"Seek not to know your people's vastest grief!
The world will see him—only that, for Fate
870   will grant no more. The gods had deemed
our power too great, if we had kept this gift.
Mars' people, in his field, beside his city—
how they will grieve! What mourners you will see,
Tiber, as you glide past that new-raised mound![152]
No child of Trojan blood will raise such hopes
among his Latin sires, nor rouse such pride
of offspring in the land of Romulus.
Ah, loyalty, ancient honor, hand unbeaten
in battle! If he'd gone out to fight, no man
880   had dared to face him, whether he went on foot
or spurred a foaming horse against the foe.
Poor boy! If you should break the bars of fate,
you'll be Marcellus. Bring lilies! Fill my hands!
I'll scatter scarlet blooms: so much, at least,
I'll give a grandson's ghost, and do my office,
though vain." Thus over all that place they walked,
through broad and airy fields, and saw the sights.
After Anchises had shown his son each thing
and fired his heart with love of fame to come,
890   then he recounted wars that must be waged,
told of the Rutuli, of Latium's city,
and how he'd bear, or how escape, each blow.

---

[151] **a man:** Marcellus the Younger, the nephew and son-in-law of Augustus Caesar. Destined to succeed Augustus, the young man died when he was only nineteen, hence Anchises' comment in line 869.   [152] **that new-raised mound:** The Campus Martius, or Field of Mars, where Marcellus's tomb was located.

Twin are the gates of sleep; men say that one
is of horn, a ready exit for real shades;
the other is white, of flawless ivory:
this way the dead send false dreams to the world.
Anchises' tale was told. Taking his son
and the Sibyl, he sent them through the ivory gate.
Aeneas made for the ships and joined his friends.
900 Then straight upshore he sailed to Port Caieta.
Out went the anchors; the fleet lay stern to shore.

From Book 8
[Aeneas Views the History of Rome]

[Leaving the Sibyl, Aeneas sails along the coast of Italy until he arrives at the mouth of the Tiber, the land of Latium, ruled by King Latinus. Recognizing that Aeneas could be a rival for Latinus's daughter Lavinia, Turnus, king of the Rutulians, provokes a war against the Trojans. Aeneas is advised to seek help from the Etruscans, who agree to an alliance with the Trojans. As the war shifts to Aeneas's favor, Turnus seeks out Aeneas for a single combat. Prior to this encounter, Aeneas's mother Venus brings him a special armor designed by Vulcan; Rome's future is prophetically carved on the shield.]

But Venus, fair-white among the clouds of heaven,
came with her gifts. In a secluded valley
far from the icy stream she found her son;
she approached him and addressed him with these words:
"Here are my promised gifts, by Vulcan's art
perfected. Challenge the proud Laurentines[153] now,
or savage Turnus, dear son, and have no fear."
So spoke Cytherea,[154] and sought her son's embrace.
On a nearby oak she propped the shining arms,
10 gift of a goddess; they filled his heart brimful
with honor and joy. His eye caressed each piece;
in wonder he touched them, turned them, held them up—
the helmet horror-plumed and bright as flame,
the sword doom-dealing, the corselet of bronze mail
with sanguine gleam, as when some great gray cloud,
catching the sun, glows red and rayed with fire;
the greaves, too, smooth to the touch, all gold and silver,
the spear, the shield—its fabric who could tell?
There stood Italian history, Roman triumphs
20 portrayed by the fire god (for he knew the prophets
and what would be), there all the future line

---

[153] **Laurentines:** Laurentum is the capital city of Latium.   [154] **Cytherea:** Another name for Venus or Aphrodite; she was born near the island Cythera, which became a famous center for Venus worship.

of Ascanius,[155] and their yearly tale of wars.
There in the verdant cave of Mars was shown
the pregnant she-wolf; at her proffered teats
the twin lads[156] tugged and played and sucked the breast
without a tremor. She turned her smooth neck round
and nuzzled each one, shaping them with her tongue.
Rome came next, and the Sabines[157] rudely raped
there as they sat and watched the great spring games:
30   war flared then 'twixt the sons of Romulus
and Tatius[158] the old, king of the stern Curetes.
Later, these same two kings laid quarrels by;
armed, they stood at the altar of Jove, and raised
their patens; a slaughtered pig confirmed the peace.
Nearby was Mettus[159] torn apart by teams
lashed to lungeing (he should have kept his word!) —
the scene showed Tullus[160] dragging that liar's guts
off through the woods; the trees were flecked with blood.
There cried Porsenna,[161] "Take back your exiled Tarquin!"
40   as he laid the city under heavy siege:
the Romans, in liberty's name, ran for their swords.
He looked like fury and threat personified,
because Horatius[162] dared to break the bridge
and Cloelia[163] burst her bonds and swam the stream.
Atop the Tarpeian Rock stood Manlius[164]
by the temple, and held the lofty Capitoline;
and there was the house of Romulus, freshly thatched.
Here were the gates, in gold; a silver goose
with wings outspread, hissed that the Gauls were coming.
50   The Gauls crept through the brush and gained the fort
protected by the darkness — gift of night.
Gold was their hair, and they were clothed in gold.
Their cloaks were gaily striped; on their white necks
lay golden cords. Each held two heavy pikes

---

[155] **Ascanius:** The son of Aeneas and his Trojan wife Creusa.   [156] **twin lads:** Romulus and Remus, suckled by a she-wolf, twin founders of Rome.   [157] **Sabines:** The first group to fight the Romans, because their women had been stolen at an athletic contest, the famed "Rape of the Sabine Women."   [158] **Tatius:** King of the Sabines, whose home was the town Cures (cf. Curetes) in the Sabine district.   [159] **Mettus:** A king of the Albans, who was judged guilty of breaking his loyalty oath to the Romans; he was torn apart by two chariots.   [160] **Tullus:** Tullus Hostilius, king of the Romans, gave the order for Mettus's punishment.   [161] **Porsenna:** King of Etruria; he wanted Rome to take back the tyrant Tarquin, who had been expelled from Rome.   [162] **Horatius:** Horatius Cocles defended the bridge across the Tiber against the Etruscans, until the Romans had the opportunity to destroy it.   [163] **Cloelia:** A Roman prisoner held by the Etruscans, who managed to escape and swim across the Tiber.   [164] **Manlius:** In 390 B.C.E., Manlius saved Rome from the Gauls when he was awakened by honking geese and thus successfully defended the citadel; Tarpeian Rock is a name used for the citadel that stood on Capitoline Hill.

that glittered; long oval shields were their protection.
And there the Salii danced, and nude Luperci;[165]
there were the woolen caps, and the shields that fell
from heaven; in solemn pomp the matrons pure
rode to their prayers. Down near the base was shown
60 the home of the dead and hell's high entrance hall,
the torments of the damned, and Catiline[166]
hung from a cliff and shuddering at the Furies;
the saints apart, with Cato[167] as their judge.
Midst all, the ocean flowed, a band of waves
all golden and yet blue, with hoary foam;
round it, in shining silver, dolphins swam
sweeping the seas and cutting through the waves.
The center showed the battle of Actium —[168]
the bronze-clad ships attacking in a line,
70 Leucata[169] seething, and billows bright with gold.
Augustus led the Italians into battle
with Senate and people, with gods both small and great.
He stood in the sternsheets. Flame poured from his brows
exultant; above him dawned his father's star.
Elsewhere, Agrippa,[170] blessed by gods and winds,
swooped down with his fleet; that proud ensign of war,
the naval crown, shone bright upon his brow.
There Antony,[171] like some savage, gaudy sheik,
hero of Araby and the Sea of Pearls,
80 led Egypt, the lords of the East, and Bactria;[172]
behind him (God forfend!) his Gypsy Queen.
The fleets advanced full speed; then oars aback
in a welter of foam, while spiked rams ripped the wave.
Then — out to sea! As were the Isles of Greece
torn loose and floating, or Alp attacking Alp,
so huge, so tall, were the battling men-o'-war.
Men lobbed the fireball; iron spear-points fell
like rain; fresh bloodshed reddened Neptune's realm.
Her majesty rang her gong for battle stations,

---

[165] **Salii . . . Luperci:** Salii were priests of Mars who danced carrying sacred shields from heaven. Luperci were priests of a fertility cult who celebrated rites wearing only wolf skins.   [166] **Catiline:** A Roman aristocrat whose attempted coup in 63 B.C.E. was foiled by Cicero; Catiline was executed.   [167] **Cato:** A contemporary of Cicero, Cato was a noble republican who stood against Julius Caesar.   [168] **Actium:** The place in northwestern Greece where Augustus defeated the armies of Antony and Cleopatra in 31 B.C.E.   [169] **Leucata:** A promontory on the island of Leucas in northwestern Greece.   [170] **Agrippa:** In charge of Augustus's navy.   [171] **Antony:** A friend of Julius Caesar, rival of Augustus, and famed lover of Cleopatra.   [172] **Bactria:** The region between the Caspian Sea and northwestern India.

90   not yet aware of twin asps at her back.
         Weird gods, fantastic shapes, the dog Anubis,[173]
         stood in phalanx against Minerva, Neptune,
         and Venus. Mars raged up and down the lines,
         chiseled in steel; the Dirae[174] hung in heaven,
         and Discord in torn gown strode grinning by,
         trailed by Bellona[175] with her blood-stained lash.
         Apollo of Actium watched and bent his bow
         above the scene: Egyptians, Indians all,
         Sabaeans, and every Arab fled in terror.
100   Her Majesty herself prayed for a wind,
         made sail, cast off the sheets, and let them run.
         Amid the carnage Vulcan had carved her pale
         with impending death, riding the wind and wave.
         And there, to the south, the Nile, grief-stricken, great,
         offering haven, waving the conquered home
         to hiding spots in his blue creeks and bays.
         But Caesar, riding through Rome in triple triumph,
         promised immortal gifts to Italy's gods:
         three hundred major shrines in all the city.
110   The streets were loud with cheers and joyful noise.
         Women filled every temple with hymn and prayer,
         and slaughtered oxen strewed the altar grounds.
         Caesar, sitting by Phoebus'[176] marble threshold,
         canvassed the gifts a world by that proud door
         had laid. Long files of captive peoples passed,
         in speech outlandish, as in dress and arms.
         Here were Numidians, Berbers in burnoose,
         Levantines, bowmen from the steppes, all carved
         by Vulcan; there Euphrates (gentled now),
120   men of land's end: Walloons,[177] the horned Rhine,
         proud Cossacks, Araxes[178] grumbling at his bridge.

         Such were the scenes on Vulcan's shield: Aeneas
         saw only art, not history, and in joy
         shouldered the fame and fortune of his sons.

---

[173] **Anubis:** The Egyptian god of embalming, usually portrayed as a jackal; to Romans, a symbol of the exotic or outlandish.   [174] **Dirae:** The Latin name for the Furies.   [175] **Bellona:** The Roman goddess of war.   [176] **Phoebus:** Another name for Apollo, god of the sun and civilization.   [177] **Walloons:** A tribe in Belgium.   [178] **Araxes:** An Armenian river bridged by Augustus.

From Book 12
[Aeneas Defeats Turnus]

[For a time the battle raged between the Latins and the Trojans without either side gaining a decided advantage. Aeneas killed the tyrant Mezentius and Turnus dispatched Pallas, son of King Evander. Truces were broken. King Latinus urged the Latins to make peace with the Trojans so that the Trojans might settle in Italy and build their city. The maiden warrior Camilla was killed by a javelin thrown by an Etruscan. Gradually the Trojans seemed to be gaining the advantage over the Latins. After they began to attack the city, Turnus decided to seek out Aeneas in single combat, to risk death for honor, even though his followers tried to dissuade him. Aeneas wore the armor fashioned by the god Vulcan; Turnus's sword broke against this armor.]

In a panic, Turnus ran, seeking escape;
circling wildly, he weaved to left and right.
All round, the tight-packed Trojans hemmed him in;
here a morass, and there high walls, confined him.

Aeneas, too, pursued him, though his knees,
slowed by the arrow,[179] sometimes refused the race;
he kept close on the frightened hero's heels.
As when a hound has cornered a stag hemmed in
by a river, or trapped by fear of scarlet flags:
10 he runs at the frightened animal, barks and snarls.
The stag, wary of traps and riverbanks
runs off, runs back, a thousand ways; the hound
sticks to him, jaws agape—he has him; almost
he has him! His jaws snap shut—on empty air.
Then comes a torrent of barking; bank and pool
re-echo, and heaven's vault rings with the noise.
So Turnus ran, and running called his men,
each one by name, demanding the sword he knew.
Aeneas warned them—Instant death to any
20 who dared approach!—and held them terrified
with threats to level their city despite his wound.
Five times they circled left and five times right,
running, attacking; this was no foolish game
for prizes: Turnus' lifeblood was at stake.

So happened, a bitter olive here had stood
sacred to Faunus,[180] for sailors a place of prayer
(saved from the sea, they'd nailed thank offerings there
for Laurentine Pan, and hung their promised clothes).

---

[179] **arrow:** Aeneas was wounded earlier by an arrow from an unknown attacker.   [180] **Faunus:** Father of Latinus, king of Latium; after his death he became the god of the woods and fields, eventually merging with the god Pan.

The Trojans, with never a thought if it were holy,
30 had taken it out to clear the field for fighting.
Here, when Aeneas had thrown his spear, it stopped,
and here stood fast, prisoned by tough tree roots.
He leaned against it and tried to wrestle the point
free: a weapon might serve to catch the man
where running had failed. Turnus, in panic, prayed:
"Faunus, have mercy! Beloved Earth, hold fast
that spear, if I have ever done you honor
and Trojans have fought over and defiled you."
The prayer was not in vain: God heard his cry.
40 Aeneas hung back, battling the stubborn stump,
but all his effort could not break the clench
of oak-hard wood. And while he leaned and heaved,
Juturna, guised once more as charioteer,
ran out to her brother and handed him his sword.
Venus, in outrage at such shamelessness,
strode in and from the root's grip wrenched the spear.
Both men, with arms regained, took heart again;
one sure of his sword, one boldened by his lance,
they squared off for the battle, breathing hard.

50 To Juno (from a golden cloud she watched
the fight) now spoke the lord of high Olympus:
"When will it end, dear wife? What's left to do?
You know Aeneas is godhead; you confess
him heaven-bound and destined for the stars.
What aim, what hope, in cold mist still enfolds you?
You thought it right that man should wound a god?
That Turnus (Juturna's hand was yours!) recover
the sword he lost and, conquered, gain new strength?
Cease now: it's time! I beg you, bear with me!
60 No more unspoken anguish! No more floods
of bitter care course toward me from your lips!
The end has come. You had fair leave to trouble
the Trojans by land and sea, to rouse foul war,
to blacken a house, turn wedding song to dirge—
all further, I forbid." So Jove proclaimed;
then Saturn's daughter humbly smiled and spoke:

"My lord, it was because I knew your will
that, spite of myself, I left the world and Turnus.
Else you would never see me alone in heaven
70 bear foul and fair; I'd stand flame-wrapped in line
of battle, and wave the Trojans on to fight.

I urged Juturna (yes, I!) to help her brother,
and dare still bolder things to save his life,
but never to throw the spear or draw the bow:
I swear by the wells of Styx,[181] that hear no prayers—
the single oath that binds the heavenly gods.
Now I yield and withdraw; I hate this war.
One favor I beg (no law of fate forbids it!)
for Latium, for the honor of your people:
80   when they make peace and bless the marriage bonds
(so be it!) and join in justice and in law,
the Latins must not change their ancient name
to 'Trojans,' or turn citizens of Troy;
bid no man change his language or his dress.
Always a Latium! Forever, her Alban kings!
Italian hearts make mighty the sons of Rome!
Troy died: let 'Troy' and 'Trojan' rest in peace."

The great creator smiled and answered her:
"You *are* Jove's sister, Saturn's second child,
90   such floods of fury surge within your heart!
But come! Your wrath is needless: softly, now!
I grant your wish and gladly yield to you.
Italians shall keep their fathers' ways and speech,
yes, and their name; except in blood commingled,
Trojans shall sink from sight. I'll teach our Latins
new rite of worship; one tongue shall serve for all.
From Italy's mingled blood one folk shall rise,
surpassing god and man in righteousness,
no nation more devout in prayer to you."
100 Juno assented; in joy, she changed design
and left her cloud, departing from the sky.

This done, the father turned to other thought:
how sever Juturna from her brother's service?
Men tell of twin death-dealers, called the Dirae—
daughters of Night—they and their hellish sister,
Megaera,[182] born in a storm, all three at once,
winged like the wind and girdled with coiling snakes.
Near to the throne of Jove, the king of wrath,
they show themselves, and whet men's fevered fears,
110 whenever the monarch marshals ghastly death

---

[181] Styx: The main river in the Underworld or Hades.   [182] Megaera: Known for jealousy, Megaera was one of the Furies, also known as Erinys or Dirae.

by plague or war, and makes the guilty tremble.
One of these two Jove sent swift down from heaven
to be an omen athwart Juturna's path.
She flew off, spiraling swiftly toward the earth.
Like an arrow sent from a bowstring through the clouds
(the Parthian arms it with wild, bitter poison—
or Cretan, perhaps—and shoots the cureless shaft):
it whistles through the murk, and none observes it:
so sped the daughter of Night down toward the earth.
120 She sighted the Trojan lines, the ranks of Turnus,
then changed at once into the tiny bird
that sometimes perches by night atop the tombs
or lonely towers and sings her bad-luck song—
so formed, the fiend flew at the face of Turnus—
flew in, flew back—and drummed against his shield.
A strange torpor and fright unstrung his limbs;
his hair stood up in fright; his voice stuck fast.

From far, Juturna knew those whistling wings—
the Dira! She let her hair fall loose and tore it,
130 scratched foul weals on her face, and beat her breast:
"How, Turnus, can your sister help you now?
What's left of my resolve? What arts of mine
could save your life? Can I block off this fiend?
I'll leave the battlefield. Fright not the frightened,
you birds of hell! I know those wing beats well:
they sound like death! I know who sent you, too:
great, generous Jove—pay for my maidenhood?
Why did he give me endless life, and steal
my right to die? I'd end my sorrows now,
140 and walk at my brother's side down through the dark.
Immortal—*I?* What joy can life afford me
without you, brother? Somewhere, let Earth gape wide
and deep: let a goddess join the ghosts in hell!"
She covered her head then with her grey-green gown
and, sobbing, sank her godhead in the stream.

And now Aèneas pressed in; he flashed his spear
(huge as a tree) and spoke with savage heart:
"Why this delay? Why, Turnus, do you hang back?
We're running no race; we'll fight now, hand to hand.
150 Change form as you will! Marshal all your powers
of courage and skill; pray for wings to ascend
the stars, or hide in the dungeons of the earth!"
Turnus, proudly: "I fear no fiery words,

soldier! I fear the gods and Jove estranged."
Saying no more, he searched and found a stone,
a huge old boulder, lying on the field,
placed there to settle the boundary of two farms.
That stone twelve chosen men could scarcely lift,
sinewed as are the sons of Earth today;
160   he strained, and raised, and whirled it at his foe,
rising full height and running to make his cast.
But running, moving, he did not know himself—
raising his arms and throwing that monstrous stone:
his knees trembled; his blood ran freezing cold.
The very boulder, spinning through empty space,
failed of the distance and did not strike its blow.
Just as in dreams, when weariness and sleep
press night on our eyes, we seem to try to run
eagerly, vainly, and in mid-trial we fail
170   and fall—our tongue is useless, every muscle
forgets its force; no word, no sound, will come;
so Turnus: no matter how bravely he attacked,
the Dira denied success. His heart was filled
with wavering thoughts: he saw his men, his city—
he halted in fear—he shook at death's approach—
no way to escape—no power to press attack—
his chariot gone—no sister holding the reins.

He wavered; Aeneas flashed the fatal spear,
sighting, gauging his chance, then with full force
180   made the long throw. Rocks hurled from siege machine
whine never so loud, nor from the lightning leaps
such crackling. Like the black tornado sped
the lance freighted with death; finding the gap
'twixt corselet and the shield's last sevenfold orb,
it shrieked its way through Turnus' thigh. He fell,
that huge man, crumpling as his knees gave way.
The Rutuli rose with a groan; the hills around
moaned in answer; tall trees sent back their cry.
Turnus spoke, with the suppliant's outstretched hand
190   and humble glance: "I earned it. I have no plea.
Take what you've won. If a poor father's pain
can touch you, hear me: You had a sire, Anchises—
as old as mine: have mercy on white-haired Daunus.
Return me—or if you will, my lifeless corpse—
to my home. You've won; all Italy saw me beaten
and on my knees; Lavinia is your wife.
Press your ill will no further." Aeneas checked

a savage blow; his eye wavered, he halted;
his hesitation had grown with every word.
200 Just then at shoulder-peak he saw the baldric,
proclaimed by clasp and shining studs the belt
of Pallas, the lad whom Turnus fought and killed:
he wore it — spoils of the fallen, an ill-starred prize.
Aeneas, seeing the trophy, felt fierce pangs
revive; a flame of fury and dreadful rage
flared up; "Shall you escape, dressed in the spoils
of those I loved? No! Pallas wounds you here;
he spills your blood as price and expiation!"
So saying, with savage thrust he sank the blade
210 in Turnus' heart: his limbs fell cold in death;
his life, with a curse and a moan, fled down to hell.

Death and the Underworld

Death is the final mystery, providing the ultimate challenge for all religions. What sacred story unlocks the mystery of the end and alleviates human fears? In a cave at La Ferrassie in southern France, a 60 thousand year old burial site for a Neanderthal family was discovered. Tools and animal bones were buried with the bodies, which lay in sleeping postures. Five of the six were buried in an east-west position. It would appear that Neanderthal man thought of death in relationship to sleep, and possibly believed in some kind of afterlife where tools and food would be appreciated. For millennia humans have been haunted by the idea that death is not simply an end to life on earth, but is a passage into another world. In an early literary example, Homer's Odysseus visits the Underworld, which is a place of darkness and grief; in Book Four of *The Odyssey,* however, the Elysian Field is mentioned, a pleasurable place for dead heroes.

p. 809 By the time of the Roman Virgil's epic, ***The Aeneid*** (c. 19 B.C.E.), the twin vision of the Greek underworld has been extended; it is not only a place of reward and punishment, but, freed from the restrictions of the physical body, it is a place of prophecy.

Co-existent with the fears that surrounded the mysteries of birth, puberty, and death in the ancient world was the postulation of the supernatural, a trans-human or sacred agency that interacted both positively and negatively with the mundane and human. The supernatural became an explanation for the unknown, as well as a metaphor for relieving the fears caused by the unknown. In the urban civilizations along the Tigris and Euphrates Rivers in the third millennium B.C.E., primitive notions about birth and death, abundance and scarcity, were elaborated into complex myths and ritualized into annual ceremonies. If it was intolerable that some form of human life should not continue beyond the grave, the earliest versions of that afterlife in Mesopotamia are certainly distasteful; the dead exist in darkness, feathered like birds, with only dust and clay to eat. The story of the goddess Inanna takes place within this cultural tradition; she not only makes the journey to the underworld or kingdom of death, but returns. *The Descent of Inanna* (p. 899) is the type of journey undertaken by several mythological deities or heroes: Persephone, Attis, Orpheus, Osiris, and Jesus are among the many figures from Mediterranean and Middle Eastern literature who make such a descent and return. In part, such descents into darkness and reemergence into light reflect the agricultural cycle: spring flowering, summer fruition, harvest, the apparent death of winter dormancy, and the renewal of spring.

The selections from *The Upanishads* (p. 955) presented in this section state in a direct, condensed fashion that human beings live in an orderly and just universe that is sustained by what the Hindus call *dharma*. As the basis of human morality—as regulated in the caste system—and cosmic lawfulness, *dharma* is the foundation for the law of karma, whereby good acts—mental or physical—bear good fruit and evil acts produce evil fruit. Unlike the concept of law presented in the Hebrew Scriptures, justice administered according to a written set of laws sanctioned by God, the universal law of karma plays itself out irrespective of a human agency. Moreover, karmic cause and effect can carry over from previous lifetimes and have consequences for one's next reincarnation.

One tradition of the hero in ancient Greece probably predates Homer's warrior-heroes and is reflected in the root of the Greek word *heros,* which means "to watch over, protect." The oldest name for the hero in Greece was *daimon*—or in Latin, *daemon*—believed to mean a guardian spirit that existed halfway between the gods and humans, not unlike the Christian belief in guardian angels. Early Greeks, like the ancient Egyptians and Chinese, associated heroes with a cult of the dead, in which the dead heroes were thought to reside in their tombs and watch over the living, bestowing blessings on the living from the grave. In one form or another, religions of the dead, along with ancestor worship, are thought to be the oldest religions in the world—if not the origin of religion itself. A prayer from **Aeschylus's** play **The Libation Bearers** shows the tomb or grave

Inanna's journey seems to mirror the need of a culture for a ritual that would reconnect it with its psychic roots—the underworld. Her descent . . . drama-tizes an initiation into a feared dimen-sion that was con-ceived as *geographically* remote from the "upper" light world of every-day life and practical concerns.

— ANNE BARING and
JULES CASHFORD,
historians, 1991

p. 909

Scene from The Book of the Dead, 1240 B.C.E. *Egyptians spent much of their lives preparing for their death and for life in the afterworld—a happy and positive place. Here, in a scene from The Book of the Dead, the deceased appear before the god Osiris, the supreme judge. (The Art Archive/Egyptian Museum Cairo/Dagli Orti)*

According as one acts, according as one conducts himself, so does he become. The doer of good becomes good. The doer of evil becomes evil.

— BRIHAD-ARANYAKA UPANISHAD

p. 910

as a threshold between two worlds, the place where contact can be made with the spirits of the dead.

A desirable version of the afterlife came from the Egyptians; at first only the pharaoh enjoyed the pleasures of heaven, but over time immortal life for both rulers and commoners became as elaborate and enjoyable as mortal life, depending on the judgment of Osiris and the truth test for the individual soul. Life after death began to mirror life on earth. The Greek historian Herodotus said that the Egyptians were the first to hold the doctrine that the soul of humans is immortal and that at death the soul re-enters a series of animal bodies until after several thousand years it again reenters a new-born human. The Egyptian idea of reincarnation influenced contemporary Greek thinkers. Plato certainly made repeated use of reincarnation or the transmigration of souls. In Book 10 of **The Republic** Plato does go into some detail about how the next incarnation is chosen by the soul residing in a kind of limbo.

Mystery religions, which were very popular in Classical Greece and Rome, provided instructions about immortality to the initiate. Each of the mystery cults looked to a founding hero who had provided secret rites and a vision of a happy reception in the world beyond the grave. One of the most influential of these cults was Orphism, based on the life and death of the Greek hero Orpheus. The Roman poet Ovid in "Orpheus and Eurydice" from ***Metamorphoses*** tells the story of Orpheus's journey into the underworld and his return.

p. 918

It is at the mysterious margin of two worlds, this world and the next, that the great archetypal figures of mythology seek to reconcile the deepest layers of the human spirit with the transcendent powers of the cosmos. For many writers and thinkers in the ancient world, it was inconceivable that somehow the human journey did not continue beyond the grave. The nature of this transition became a dominant feature of the advent of the most popular mystery religion in the West — Christianity.

■ PRONUNCIATION

Aeschylus: ES-kuh-lus
Dumuzi: doo-moo-ZEE
Ereshkigal: eh-RESH-kee-gawl
Eurydice: yoo-RID-uh-see
Orpheus: ORE-fee-us
shugurra: shoo-GOO-rah
Upanishads: oo-PUN-ih-shudz, oo-PAHN-ih-shahdz

❧ THE DESCENT OF INANNA
ANCIENT SUMER, C. 2000 B.C.E.

The excerpt from *The Descent of Inanna* is the oldest text in this anthology. It was set down by scribes in cuneiform on clay tablets early in the second millennium B.C.E. The repetition and the formulaic phrasing in the text suggest that previous oral versions of it must have existed and that the stories of the goddess Inanna may easily go back to 3500 B.C.E. if not earlier. Inanna played an essential role in ancient Sumer, a kingdom of cities that flourished in the third millennium B.C.E. on the irrigated plains along the Tigris and Euphrates Rivers in what is now southern Iraq, between Baghdad and the Persian Gulf. So highly regarded was Sumer's culture that even after the Babylonian conquest of the region c. 1800 B.C.E., when Semitic Akkadian became the area's common tongue, Sumerian remained the learned language of writers and scholars, just as classical Greek, Latin, and Sanskrit were employed long after they ceased to be everyday spoken languages. Sumerian myths were also integrated

The Goddess Inanna,
2000 B.C.E.

*Before patriarchal
societies became
dominant during the
second millennium
B.C.E., the ancient
Sumerians
worshipped a host of
goddesses, the most
important among
them the great
goddess Inanna. Here
she is seen in relief
with her traditional
wings and with
horned animals at her
feet. (Z. Radovan,
Jerusalem)*

Inanna's descent is a
shamanic journey, a
venturing into the
void, the unknown,
into the dark womb
of the inner Earth for
the wisdom it holds.
In this symbolic
death, she hangs on
a peg, a rotting
corpse, but gains
essential insight and
experience into the
full cycle of existence.

— ELINOR GADON,
scholar, 1989

into the new culture, though adjusted, for example, by substituting Babylonian names.

Stories of Inanna—Queen of Heaven and Earth, Goddess of Love and Beauty, she of the Morning and Evening Star—have been pieced together from thousands of clay fragments excavated from various sites in Iraq and later translated by Samuel Noah Kramer and other scholars. In the earliest parts of these stories, Inanna is an adolescent goddess laying claim to her powers; later, a young fertility goddess discovering her allure and sexuality. *The Descent of Inanna*, one section of the entire goddess's story, recounts a journey to the underworld or kingdom of death; it may in part describe an actual ritual wherein priestesses staged Inanna's descent, death, and return, thereby ensuring another season of fertility in the fields as well as in the homes of Sumer. The lines of repeated text at the beginning of this story suggest that it was originally recited, perhaps chanted, during annual reenactments. The consequences of Inanna's death are told in a later Akkadian version of the story

(c. 1250 B.C.E.), "The Descent of Ishtar," in which winter is described as an absence of fertility.

Inanna's passage is divided into three parts: She first descends into the underworld and dies; she is then revived and ascends to the upper world; finally, a substitute, **Dumuzi,** is found and takes Inanna's place in the region of death. The conclusion of *The Descent of Inanna* suggests an actual shift in the ritual and an accommodation to the agricultural cycle. As in other fertility stories, the goddess will now symbolize the eternal, immutable Mother Nature, while Dumuzi, symbolizing plant life and the annual agricultural cycle that takes place within the context of Nature herself, will make the annual journey to the underworld, where he will remain for half the year — the winter period. When Dumuzi ascends, the new shoots and buds and leaves come with him, and spring returns to the land, a mythic pattern seen again in the Christian Easter celebration. This pattern provides roles for a profound ritual drama, since a priestess or queen can play the role of Inanna and a king or priest the role of Dumuzi, whereby human fertility is thus linked to the fertility of the earth.

The importance of *The Descent of Inanna* lies not only with its antiquity and its influence on literature in the region, but also in its revelation of a unique time in history when the rulers and subjects of Sumer paid reverence to a goddess, whose rituals determined not only the cycle of agriculture but the sexual potency of the king, whose annual consummating marriage with a goddess priestess ensure the fertility of the land and legitimized the king's rule. In the Akkadian version, the goddess's name is Ishtar, her love is Tammuz, and the dark sister of the underworld is still **Ereshkigal.**

> doo-moo-ZEE
>
> Inanna's journey to the underworld has brought a new world order to Sumer. By giving Dumuzi eternal life half the year, Inanna changes the cosmic pattern. Love, which parallels the normal course of the human life cycle — budding, blooming, and dying — is henceforth guaranteed, by being linked to the seasons, an annual renewal.
>
> — DIANE WOLKSTEIN, critic, 1983
>
> eh-RESH-kee-gawl

FROM

The Descent of Inanna

Translated by Diane Wolkstein and Samuel Noah Kramer

From the Great Above she opened her ear to the Great Below.
From the Great Above the goddess opened her ear to the Great Below.
From the Great Above Inanna opened her ear to the Great Below.

My Lady abandoned heaven and earth to descend to the underworld.
Inanna abandoned heaven and earth to descend to the underworld.
She abandoned her office of holy priestess to descend to the underworld.

A note on the translation: This translation is a reworking of Samuel Noah Kramer's rendering by noted folklorist and storyteller Diane Wolkstein. In the interests of readability, the translators have chosen not to indicate gaps or uncertainties in the text. All notes are the editors'.

In Uruk[1] she abandoned her temple to descend to the underworld.
In Badtibira she abandoned her temple to descend to the underworld.
In Zabalam she abandoned her temple to descend to the underworld.
10   In Adab she abandoned her temple to descend to the underworld.
In Nippur she abandoned her temple to descend to the underworld.
In Kish she abandoned her temple to descend to the underworld.
In Akkad she abandoned her temple to descend to the underworld.
She gathered together the seven *me*.
She took them into her hands.
With the *me* in her possession, she prepared herself:

She placed the *shugurra*, the crown of the steppe, on her head.
She arranged the dark locks of hair across her forehead.
She tied the small lapis beads around her neck,
20   Let the double strand of beads fall to her breast,
And wrapped the royal robe around her body.
She daubed her eyes with ointment called "Let him come, Let him come,"
Bound the breastplate called "Come, man, come!" around her chest,
Slipped the gold ring over her wrist,
And took the lapis measuring rod and line in her hand.

Inanna set out for the underworld.
Ninshubur, her faithful servant, went with her.
Inanna spoke to her, saying:
      "Ninshubur, my constant support,
30   My *sukkal* who gives me wise advice,
      My warrior who fights by my side,
      I am descending to the *kur,* to the underworld.
      If I do not return,
      Set up a lament for me by the ruins.
      Beat the drum for me in the assembly places.
      Circle the houses of the gods.
      Tear at your eyes, at your mouth, at your thighs.
      Dress yourself in a single garment like a beggar.
      Go to Nippur, to the temple of Enlil.[2]
40   When you enter his holy shrine, cry out:
      'O Father Enlil, do not let your daughter

---

[1] **Uruk:** Inanna's seven sacred cities and temples are listed here; Uruk is her major city, her primary residence. Seven appears several times in the text as a sacred number. Some speculate that the number came to be considered sacred because it was the number of visible bodies — the sun, the moon, and the five planets; others suggest it could be related to the menstrual cycle, since a twenty-eight-day month is divisible by seven. The number seven reappears in the Hebrew creation story. [2] **Enlil:** A god of unknown attributes; perhaps the god of wind and air. His symbol is a horned crown on a shrine.

Be put to death in the underworld.
Do not let your bright silver
Be covered with the dust of the underworld.
Do not let your precious lapis
Be broken into stone for the stoneworker.
Do not let your fragrant boxwood
Be cut into wood for the woodworker.
Do not let the holy priestess of heaven
50   Be put to death in the underworld.'

If Enlil will not help you,
Go to Ur, to the temple of Nanna.
Weep before Father Nanna.
If Nanna will not help you,
Go to Eridu, to the temple of Enki.[3]
Weep before Father Enki.
Father Enki, the God of Wisdom, knows the food of life,
He knows the water of life;
He knows the secrets.
60   Surely he will not let me die."

Inanna continued on her way to the underworld.
Then she stopped and said:
        "Go now, Ninshubur—
        Do not forget the words I have commanded you."

When Inanna arrived at the outer gates of the underworld,
She knocked loudly.
She cried out in a fierce voice:
        "Open the door, gatekeeper!
        Open the door, Neti!
70   I alone would enter!"

Neti, the chief gatekeeper of the *kur*, asked:
        "Who are you?"

She answered:
        "I am Inanna, Queen of Heaven,
        On my way to the East."

---

[3] **Eridu . . . Enki:** Eridu was an ancient city on the shore of the Persian Gulf; Enki is the god of water and wisdom.

Neti said:
    "If you are truly Inanna, Queen of Heaven,
    On your way to the East,
    Why has your heart led you on the road
80   From which no traveler returns?"

Inanna answered:
    "Because . . . of my older sister, Ereshkigal,
    Her husband, Gugalanna, the Bull of Heaven, has died.
    I have come to witness the funeral rites.
    Let the beer of his funeral rites be poured into the cup.
    Let it be done."

Neti spoke:
    "Stay here, Inanna, I will speak to my queen.
    I will give her your message."

90 Neti, the chief gatekeeper of the *kur,*
    Entered the palace of Ereshkigal,[4] the Queen of the Underworld, and said:
    "My queen, a maid
    As tall as heaven,
    As wide as the earth,
    As strong as the foundations of the city wall,
    Waits outside the palace gates.

    She has gathered together the seven *me.*
    She has taken them into her hands.
    With the *me* in her possession, she has prepared herself:

100   On her head she wears the *shugurra,* the crown of the steppe.
    Across her forehead her dark locks of hair are carefully arranged.
    Around her neck she wears the small lapis beads.
    At her breast she wears the double strand of beads.
    Her body is wrapped with the royal robe.
    Her eyes are daubed with the ointment called 'Let him come, let him come.'
    Around her chest she wears the breastplate called 'Come, man, come!'
    On her wrist she wears the gold ring.
    In her hand she carries the lapis measuring rod and line."

---

[4] **Ereshkigal:** Although here Ereshkigal is Inanna's sister, it is probable that in different contexts they were treated as two sides of the same deity, the goddess of life and death, light and dark. In the Sumerian myth, Ereshkigal is portrayed as spiteful and unfulfilled.

When Ereshkigal heard this,
110 She slapped her thigh and bit her lip.
She took the matter into her heart and dwelt on it.
Then she spoke:
>"Come, Neti, my chief gatekeeper of the *kur,*
>Heed my words:
>Bolt the seven gates of the underworld.
>Then, one by one, open each gate a crack.
>Let Inanna enter.
>As she enters, remove her royal garments.[5]
>Let the holy priestess of heaven enter bowed low."

120 Neti heeded the words of his queen.
He bolted the seven gates of the underworld.
Then he opened the outer gate.
He said to the maid:
>"Come, Inanna, enter."

When she entered the first gate,
From her head, the *shugurra,* the crown of the steppe, was removed.

Inanna asked:
>"What is this?"

She was told:
130 >"Quiet, Inanna, the ways of the underworld are perfect.
>They may not be questioned."

When she entered the second gate,
From her neck the small lapis beads were removed.

Inanna asked:
>"What is this?"

She was told:
>"Quiet, Inanna, the ways of the underworld are perfect.
>They may not be questioned." [. . .]

[Inanna's strand of beads, breastplate, gold ring, and lapis measuring rod were taken from her at gates three to six, respectively.]

---

[5] **remove . . . garments:** The symbols of power and prestige in the world above have no value in the underworld; Inanna will be naked when she confronts death.

When she entered the seventh gate,
140 From her body the royal robe was removed.

Inanna asked:
    "What is this?"

She was told:
    "Quiet, Inanna, the ways of the underworld are perfect.
    They may not be questioned."

Naked and bowed low, Inanna entered the throne room.
Ereshkigal rose from her throne.
Inanna started toward the throne.
The Anunna,[6] the judges of the underworld, surrounded her.
150 They passed judgment against her.

Then Ereshkigal fastened on Inanna the eye of death.
She spoke against her the word of wrath.
She uttered against her the cry of guilt.

She struck her.

Inanna was turned into a corpse,
A piece of rotting meat,
And was hung from a hook on the wall.

When, after three days and three nights,[7] Inanna had not returned,
Ninshubur set up a lament for her by the ruins.
160 She beat the drum for her in the assembly places.
She circled the houses of the gods.
She tore at her eyes; she tore at her mouth; she tore at her thighs.
She dressed herself in a single garment like a beggar.

[Ninshubur seeks help from Enlil and Nanna (the moon god), both of whom refuse.]

Ninshubur went to Eridu and the temple of Enki.
When she entered the holy shrine,

---

[6] Anunna: Also called the Anunnaki, these are the deities of the underworld, seven in number.

[7] three days and three nights: A period of time found throughout the literature of the ancient Near East: In Hebrew scriptures, Jonah is in a whale's belly for three days and nights, and in the New Testament Jesus is in the tomb for the same amount of time. The origin of this three-day period may have been the three days in the lunar cycle when the moon disappears from view, since the moon was a favored symbol of death and rebirth in the ancient world.

She cried out:
> "O Father Enki, do not let your daughter
> Be put to death in the underworld.
> Do not let your bright silver
170 > Be covered with the dust of the underworld.
> Do not let your precious lapis
> Be broken into stone for the stoneworker.
> Do not let your fragrant boxwood
> Be cut into wood for the woodworker.
> Do not let the holy priestess of heaven
> Be put to death in the underworld."

Father Enki said:
> "What has happened?
> What has my daughter done?
180 > Inanna! Queen of All the Lands! Holy Priestess of Heaven!
> What has happened?
> I am troubled. I am grieved."

[In the next stanzas, Father Enki sends two androgynous creatures into the realm of the dead to rescue Inanna, but the underworld judges, the Anunna, demand that a replacement be found for Inanna. Several figures are suggested, including Inanna's sons. Finally Inanna decides that Dumuzi is the one. He runs away and hides, but a fly knows his whereabouts and bargains with Inanna.]

Then a fly appeared.[8]
The holy fly circled the air above Inanna's head and spoke:
> "If I tell you where Dumuzi is,
> What will you give me?"

Inanna said:
> "If you tell me,
> I will let you frequent the beer-houses and taverns.
190 > I will let you dwell among the talk of the wise ones.
> I will let you dwell among the songs of the minstrels."

The fly spoke:
> "Lift your eyes to the edges of the steppe,
> Lift your eyes to Arali.
> There you will find Geshtinanna's brother,
> There you will find the shepherd Dumuzi."

---

[8] **a fly appeared:** The messengers sent to the underworld to rescue Inanna took the form of flies; it is not known if this fly is related to them.

Inanna and Geshtinanna went to the edges of the steppe.
They found Dumuzi weeping.
Inanna took Dumuzi by the hand and said:
200   "You will go to the underworld
Half the year.
Your sister, since she has asked,
Will go the other half.
On the day you are called,
That day you will be taken.
On the day Geshtinanna is called,
That day you will be set free."

Inanna placed Dumuzi in the hands of the eternal.

Holy Ereshkigal! Great is your renown!
210   *Holy Ereshkigal! I sing your praises!*

❧ THE UPANISHADS
INDIA, NINTH CENTURY B.C.E.

> The excerpts from the Brihad-Aranyaka and Chandogya Upanishads describe the cause-and-effect dynamic of a just universe: In both Buddhism and Hinduism, karma means that good thoughts or acts are rewarded with good consequences; bad results in bad. The word *karma* is used both for an individual's actions and the consequences of those actions as well as for the principle of cause and effect in the universe, a pattern which confirms *dharma,* the abiding order of the cosmos. The coupling of reincarnation with karma means that the consequences of actions in a previous life can be experienced in the present. For example, a murderer in one life can be punished in the next. Likewise, a doer of good deeds in one life can be rewarded in the next. Karma, like the Christian teachings about heaven and hell, transcends the legal system of any particular political or social entity and reaffirms larger principles that are integral to the workings of the universe. You might not be caught by the local police, but you will suffer the fruits of your acts, either in this lifetime or in the next. Another way to state this is: What goes around, comes around.

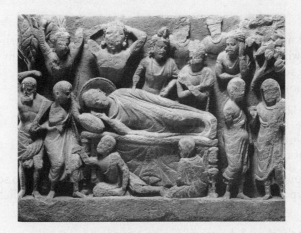

The Maha-pari-nirvana, second to third centuries B.C.E. Maha-pari-nirvana is Buddha's physical passing from this world into a state beyond nirvana, that is, separating from the cycle of rebirths and merging with the absolute. Buddhist belief revolves around the concept of karma: Whatever one is now is a direct result of one's previous actions and determines what one will be. (Courtesy of the British Museum)

FROM

Brihad-Aranyaka Upanishad and Chandogya Upanishad

Translated by Robert Ernest Hume

[KARMA AND REINCARNATION]

According as one acts, according as one conducts himself, so does he become. The doer of good becomes good. The doer of evil becomes evil. One becomes virtuous by virtuous action, bad by bad action.

But people say: "A person is made [not of acts, but] of desires only." [In reply to this I say:] As is his desire, such is his resolve; as is his resolve, such the action he performs; what action *(karma)* he performs, that he procures for himself.

On this point there is this verse: —

Where one's mind is attached — the inner self
Goes thereto with action, being attached to it alone.

Obtaining the end of his action,
Whatever he does in this world,
He comes again from that world
To this world of action.

— So the man who desires.

The Soul of the Released

Now the man who does not desire.—He who is without desire, who is freed from desire, whose desire is satisfied, whose desire is the Soul—his breaths do not depart. Being very Brahma, he goes to Brahman.[1]

On this point there is this verse:—

When are liberated all
The desires that lodge in one's heart,
Then a mortal becomes immortal!
Therein he reaches Brahman!

As the slough of a snake lies on an ant-hill, dead, cast off, even so lies this body. But this incorporeal, immortal Life *(prāṇa)* is Brahman indeed, is light indeed. [. . .]

Accordingly, those who are of pleasant conduct here—the prospect is, indeed, that they will enter a pleasant womb, either the womb of a Brahman, or the womb of a Kshatriya,[2] or the womb of a Vaiśya.[3] But those who are of stinking conduct here—the prospect is, indeed, that they will enter a stinking womb, either the womb of a dog, or the womb of a swine, or the womb of an outcast *(caṇḍāla).*

---

[1] Brahman: The eternal, unnamable Absolute.   [2] Kshatriya: The warrior or administrator caste.   [3] Vaiśya: The merchant or farmer caste.

✎ AESCHYLUS
GREECE, C. 525–456 B.C.E.

I myself pour these lustral waters to the dead, / and speak, and call upon my father.

— ELECTRA, in *The Libation Bearers*

The second play in Aeschylus's classic trilogy, *The Oresteia*, explores the role of the spirit world in human affairs. After a long absence fighting in the Trojan War, Agamemnon, the king, returns to Argos and is killed by his wife, Clytemnestra, in collusion with her lover, Aegisthus. According to popular tradition, the dead Agamemnon then resided in his tomb. In the prayer excerpted here, Electra, Agamemnon's daughter, invokes the power of Agamemnon to curse her mother and Aegisthus and to bring blessings on her and her brother, Orestes. Electra believes that her mother has gotten away with murder and is clinging to a throne that is rightfully hers or her brother's. This passage is a fine illustration of the Greek belief that heroes could influence affairs from the other side of mortality. For more on Aeschylus, please see page 575.

FROM

❦ The Libation Bearers

Translated by Richmond Lattimore

[PRAYER TO THE DEAD]

ELECTRA:

Almighty herald of the world above, the world
below: Hermes, lord of the dead, help me; announce
my prayers to the charmed spirits underground, who watch
over my father's house, that they may hear. Tell Earth
herself, who brings all things to birth, who gives them strength,
then gathers their big yield into herself at last.
I myself pour these lustral waters to the dead,
and speak, and call upon my father: Pity me;
pity your own Orestes. How shall we be lords
10 in our house? We have been sold, and go as wanderers
because our mother bought herself, for us, a man,
Aegisthus, he who helped her hand to cut you down.
Now I am what a slave is, and Orestes lives
outcast from his great properties, while they go proud
in the high style and luxury of what you worked
to win. By some good fortune let Orestes come
back home. Such is my prayer, my father. Hear me; hear.
And for myself, grant that I be more temperate
of heart than my mother; that I act with purer hand.

20 Such are my prayers for us; but for our enemies,
father, I pray that your avenger come, and they
who killed you shall be killed in turn, as they deserve.
Between my prayer for good and prayer for good I set
this prayer for evil; and I speak it against Them.
For us, bring blessings up into the world. Let Earth
and conquering Justice,[1] and all gods beside, give aid.

Such are my prayers; and over them I pour these drink
offerings. Yours the strain now, yours to make them flower
with mourning song, and incantation for the dead.

---

[1] **Justice**: Dice or Dike, goddess of justice.

PLATO

GREECE, 427–347 B.C.E.

The Republic, from Plato's middle period, deals with the important issues of justice and injustice; the education of rulers, women, and children; the nature of a philosopher, types of government, and the nature of poetry. At the end of *The Republic,* Plato returns to a discussion of justice; "The Myth of Er" is used to illustrate that the reward for a life of justice comes in the afterlife. After Er returns to life after having been killed on the battlefield, he describes how souls are judged and either rewarded or punished. Socrates, who was Plato's teacher for seven or eight years, is the principle speaker in "The Myth of Er."

Included in Plato's treatment of the soul before birth and after death are several basic ingredients that are common to other Platonic dialogues, such as *Gorgias, Phaedo,* and *Phaedrus:* the immortality of the soul; the reincarnation of the soul in a series of rebirths; the after death judgement that results in punishment for the unjust and happiness for the just; the hope for an ultimate deliverance for the soul after the purification cycle of several rebirths. The ultimate source for these ideas is unknown, although they were certainly known throughout the Middle East and the Asian sub-continent, and were shared by the Orphic Mysteries, a rather secret religion focused on living a righteous life and the transmigration of souls after death. Plato appears to have added a third group to the two groups of the just and the unjust: the sinners who are judged to be incurable, who are assigned permanently to Tartarus as a warning to others.

For more information about Plato's life and thought, see p. 715.

For more information about Plato's life and thought, see p. 715.

FROM

The Republic

Translated by F. M. Cornford

[THE MYTH OF ER]

My story will not be like Odysseus' tale to Alcinous;[1] but its hero was a valiant man, Er, the son of Armenius, a native of Pamphylia, who was killed in battle. When the dead were taken up for burial ten days later, his body alone was found undecayed.

---

[1] My story . . . Alcinous: Odysseus' recital of his adventures to Alcinous, King of Phaeacia, fills four books of *The Odyssey,* including Odysseus' voyage to the realm of the dead, which Plato would reject as a misleading picture of the afterlife. It became proverbial for a long story. [All notes are the translator's.]

They carried him home, and two days afterwards were going to bury him, when he came to life again as he lay on the funeral pyre. He then told what he had seen in the other world.

He said that, when the soul had left his body, he journeyed with many others until they came to a marvellous place, where there were two openings side by side in the earth, and opposite them two others in the sky above. Between them sat Judges,[2] who, after each sentence given, bade the just take the way to the right upwards through the sky, first binding on them in front tokens signifying the judgement passed upon them. The unjust were commanded to take the downward road to the left, and these bore evidence of all their deeds fastened on their backs. When Er himself drew near, they told him that he was to carry tidings of the other world to mankind, and he must now listen and observe all that went on in that place. Accordingly he saw the souls which had been judged departing by one of the openings in the sky and one of those in the earth; while at the other two openings souls were coming up out of the earth travel-stained and dusty, or down from the sky clean and bright. Each company, as if they had come on a long journey, seemed glad to turn aside into the Meadow, where they encamped like pilgrims at a festival. Greetings passed between acquaintances, and as either party questioned the other of what had befallen them, some wept as they sorrowfully recounted all that they had seen and suffered on their journey under the earth, which had lasted a thousand years;[3] while others spoke of the joys of heaven and sights of inconceivable beauty. There was much, Glaucon, that would take too long to tell; but the sum, he said, was this. For every wrong done to any man sinners had in due course paid the penalty ten times over, that is to say, once in each hundred years, such being the span of human life, in order that the punishment for every offence might be tenfold. Thus, all who have been guilty of bringing many to death or slavery by betraying their country or their comrades in arms, or have taken part in any other iniquity, suffer tenfold torments for each crime; while deeds of kindness and a just and sinless life are rewarded in the same measure. Concerning infants who die at birth or live but a short time he had more to say, not worthy of mention.[4]

The wages earned by honouring the gods and parents, or by dishonouring them and by doing murder, were even greater. He was standing by when one spirit asked another, "Where is Ardiaeus the Great?" This Ardiaeus had been despot in some city of Pamphylia just a thousand years before, and, among many other wicked deeds, he was said to have killed his old father and his elder brother. The answer was: "He has not come back hither, nor will he ever come. This was one of the terrible sights we saw. When our sufferings were ended and we were near the mouth, ready to pass

---

[2] **Judges:** In the myth of the Judgement of the Dead in the *Gorgias,* 523 E, Minos, Rhadamanthys, and Aeacus give judgement 'in the Meadow at the parting of the two ways, one to the Islands of the Blest, the other to Tartarus.'

[3] **a thousand years:** This figure, probably taken from some Orphic or Pythagorean source, is repeated by Virgil, *Aeneid,* vi. 748.

[4] **Concerning . . . mention:** This suggests that a limbo for infants was a feature of the Orphic apocalypse. It appears in *Aeneid* vi. 426 ff.

upwards, suddenly we saw Ardiaeus and others with him. Most of them were despots, but there were some private persons who had been great sinners. They thought that at last they were going to mount upwards, but the mouth would not admit them; it bellowed whenever one whose wickedness was incurable or who had not paid the penalty in full tried to go up.[5] Then certain fierce and fiery-looking men, who stood by and knew what the sound meant, seized some and carried them away; but Ardiaeus and others they bound hand and foot and neck and flinging them down flayed them. They dragged them along the wayside, carding their flesh like wool with thorns and telling all who passed by why this was done to them and that they were being taken to be cast into Tartarus. We had gone through many terrors of every sort, but none so great as the fear each man felt lest the sound should come as he went up; and when it was not heard, his joy was great." Such were the judgements and penalties, and the blessings received were in corresponding measure.

Now when each company had spent seven days in the Meadow, on the eighth they had to rise up and journey on. And on the fourth day afterwards they came to a place whence they could see a straight shaft of light, like a pillar, stretching from above throughout heaven and earth, more like the rainbow than anything else, but brighter and purer. To this they came after a day's journey, and there, at the middle of the light, they saw stretching from heaven the extremities of its chains; for this light binds the heavens, holding together all the revolving firmament, like the under-girths of a ship of war.[6]

And from the extremities stretched the Spindle of Necessity, by means of which all the circles revolve. The shaft of the Spindle and the hook were of adamant, and the whorl partly of adamant and partly of other substances. The whorl was of this fashion. In shape it was like an ordinary whorl; but from Er's account we must imagine it as a large whorl with the inside completely scooped out, and within it a second smaller whorl, and a third and a fourth and four more, fitting into one another like a nest of bowls. For there were in all eight whorls, set one within another, with their rims showing above as circles and making up the continuous surface of a single whorl round the shaft, which pierces right through the centre of the eighth. The circle forming the rim of the first and outermost whorl (Fixed Stars) is the broadest;[7] next in breadth is the sixth (Venus); then the fourth (Mars); then the eighth (Moon);

---

[5] They thought . . . up: So in Virgil, *Georgic* iv. 493, a roar is heard when Orpheus, returning from Hades with Eurydice, looks back, and Eurydice vanishes.

[6] undergirths . . . war: Undergirths were ropes or braces used, either as fixtures or as temporary expedients, to strengthen a ship's hull. Acts xxvii. 17: 'they used helps, undergirding the ship.' It is disputed whether the bond holding the universe together is simply the straight axial shaft or a circular band of light, suggested by the Milky Way, girdling the heaven of Fixed Stars.

[7] The circle . . . broadest: The breadth of the rims is most simply explained as standing for the supposed distances of the orbits from each other. Thus the breadth of the outermost rim would be the distance between the Fixed Stars and Saturn. The names of the planets are given in the *Epinomis*, which was either Plato's latest work or composed by an immediate pupil: Aphrodite (Venus), Hermes (Mercury), Ares (Mars), Zeus (Jupiter), Kronos (Saturn). It is there implied that the Greeks took these names from the Syrians, substituting for Syrian gods the Greek gods identified with them.

then the seventh (Sun); then the fifth (Mercury); then the third (Jupiter); and the second (Saturn) is narrowest of all. The rim of the largest whorl (Fixed Stars) was spangled; the seventh (Sun) brightest; the eighth (Moon) coloured by the reflected light of the seventh; the second and fifth (Saturn, Mercury) like each other and yellower; the third (Jupiter) whitest; the fourth (Mars) somewhat ruddy; the sixth (Venus) second in whiteness. The Spindle revolved as a whole with one motion; but, within the whole as it turned, the seven inner circles revolved slowly in the opposite direction; and of these the eighth (Moon) moved most swiftly; second in speed and all moving together, the seventh, sixth, and fifth (Sun, Venus, Mercury); next in speed moved the fourth (Mars) with what appeared to them to be a counter-revolution;[8] next the third (Jupiter), and slowest of all the second (Saturn).

The Spindle turned on the knees of Necessity. Upon each of its circles stood a Siren, who was carried round with its movement, uttering a single sound on one note, so that all the eight made up the concords of a single scale.[9] Round about, at equal distances, were seated, each on a throne, the three daughters of Necessity, the Fates, robed in white with garlands on their heads, Lachesis, Clotho, and Atropos, chanting to the Sirens' music, Lachesis of things past, Clotho of the present, and Atropos of things to come. And from time to time Clotho lays her right hand on the outer rim of the Spindle and helps to turn it, while Atropos turns the inner circles likewise with her left, and Lachesis with either hand takes hold of inner and outer alternately.

The souls, as soon as they came, were required to go before Lachesis. An Interpreter first marshalled them in order; and then, having taken from the lap of Lachesis a number of lots and samples of lives, he mounted on a high platform and said:

"The word of Lachesis, maiden daughter of Necessity. Souls of a day, here shall begin a new round of earthly life, to end in death. No guardian spirit will cast lots for you,[10] but you shall choose your own destiny. Let him to whom the first lot falls choose first a life to which he will be bound of necessity. But Virtue owns no master:

---

[8] **counter-revolution:** I understand this motion to be a self-motion of the three outer planets, Mars, Jupiter, Saturn, slowing down the 'contrary motion' shared by all the planets, so that these three fall farther and farther behind the Sun-Venus-Mercury group and *appear* to be moving in the opposite sense with a 'counter-revolution,' though really moving more slowly in the same sense.

[9] **Upon each . . . scale:** Aristotle, *de caelo* ii. 9: 'It seems to some thinkers [Pythagoreans] that bodies so great must inevitably produce a sound by their movement: even bodies on the earth do so . . . and as for the sun and the moon, and the stars, so many in number and enormous in size, all moving at a tremendous speed, it is incredible that they should fail to produce a noise of surpassing loudness. Taking this as their hypothesis, and also that the speeds of the stars, judged by their distances, are in the ratios of the musical consonances, they affirm that the sound of the stars as they revolve is concordant. To meet the difficulty that none of us is aware of this sound, they account for it by saying that the sound is with us right from birth and has thus no contrasting silence to show it up; for voice and silence are perceived by contrast with each other, and so all mankind is undergoing an experience like that of a coppersmith, who becomes by long habit indifferent to the din around him' (trans. W. K. C. Guthrie). Aristotle refutes this theory.

[10] **No guardian . . . you:** The idea that the *daemon* (guardian spirit, genius, personified destiny) has an individual allotted to it as its portion appears in Plato's *Phaedo* (myth) 107 D.

as a man honours or dishonours her, so shall he have more of her or less. The blame is his who chooses; Heaven is blameless."[11]

With these words the Interpreter scattered the lots among them all. Each took up the lot which fell at his feet and showed what number he had drawn; only Er himself was forbidden to take one. Then the Interpreter laid on the ground before them the sample lives, many more than the persons there. They were of every sort: lives of all living creatures, as well as of all conditions of men. Among them were lives of despots, some continuing in power to the end, others ruined in mid course and ending in poverty, exile, or beggary. There were lives of men renowned for beauty of form and for strength and prowess, or for distinguished birth and ancestry; also lives of unknown men; and of women likewise. All these qualities were variously combined with one another and with wealth or poverty, health or sickness, or intermediate conditions; but in none of these lives was there anything to determine the condition of the soul, because the soul must needs change its character according as it chooses one life or another.

Here, it seems, my dear Glaucon, a man's whole fortunes are at stake. On this account each one of us should lay aside all other learning, to study only how he may discover one who can give him the knowledge enabling him to distinguish the good life from the evil, and always and everywhere to choose the best within his reach, taking into account all these qualities we have mentioned and how, separately or in combination, they affect the goodness of life. Thus he will seek to understand what is the effect, for good or evil, of beauty combined with wealth or with poverty and with this or that condition of the soul, or of any combination of high or low birth, public or private station, strength or weakness, quickness of wit or slowness, and any other qualities of mind, native or acquired; until, as the outcome of all these calculations, he is able to choose between the worse and the better life with reference to the constitution of the soul, calling a life worse or better according as it leads to the soul becoming more unjust or more just. All else he will leave out of account; for, as we have seen, this is the supreme choice for a man, both while he lives and after death. Accordingly, when he goes into the house of death he should hold this faith like adamant, that there too he may not be dazzled by wealth and such-like evils, or fling himself into the life of a despot or other evil-doer, to work irremediable harm and suffer yet worse things himself, but may know how to choose always the middle course that avoids both extremes, not only in this life, so far as he may, but in every future existence; for there lies the greatest happiness for man.

To return to the report of the messenger from the other world. The Interpreter then said: "Even for the last comer, if he choose with discretion, there is left in store a life with which, if he will live strenuously, he may be content and not unhappy. Let not the first be heedless in his choice, nor the last be disheartened."

---

[11] **Heaven is blameless:** These last words 'became a kind of rallying-cry among the champions of the freedom of the will in the early Christian era' (Adam). They are inscribed on a bust of Plato of the first century B.C. found at Tibur.

After these words, he who had drawn the first lot at once seized upon the most absolute despotism he could find. In his thoughtless greed he was not careful to examine the life he chose at every point, and he did not see the many evils it contained and that he was fated to devour his own children; but when he had time to look more closely, he began to beat his breast and bewail his choice, forgetting the warning proclaimed by the Interpreter; for he laid the blame on fortune, the decrees of the gods, anything rather than himself. He was one of those who had come down from heaven, having spent his former life in a well-ordered commonwealth and become virtuous from habit without pursuing wisdom. It might indeed be said that not the least part of those who were caught in this way were of the company which had come from heaven, because they were not disciplined by suffering; whereas most of those who had come up out of the earth, having suffered themselves and seen others suffer, were not hasty in making their choice. For this reason, and also because of the chance of the lot, most of the souls changed from a good life to an evil, or from an evil life to a good. Yet, if upon every return to earthly life a man seeks wisdom with his whole heart, and if the lot so fall that he is not among the last to choose, then this report gives good hope that he will not only be happy here, but will journey to the other world and back again hither, not by the rough road underground, but by the smooth path through the heavens.

It was indeed, said Er, a sight worth seeing, how the souls severally chose their lives—a sight to move pity and laughter and astonishment; for the choice was mostly governed by the habits of their former life. He saw one soul choosing the life of a swan; this had once been the soul of Orpheus, which so hated all womankind because of his death at their hands that it would not consent to be born of woman.[12] And he saw the soul of Thamyras[13] take the life of a nightingale, and a swan choose to be changed into a man, and other musical creatures do the same. The soul which drew the twentieth lot took a lion's life; this had been Ajax, the son of Telamon, who shrank from being born as a man, remembering the judgement concerning the arms of Achilles.[14] After him came the soul of Agamemnon,[15] who also hated mankind because of his sufferings and took in exchange the life of an eagle. Atalanta's[16] soul drew a lot about half-way through. She took the life of an athlete, which she could not pass over when she saw the great honours he would win. After her he saw the soul of Epeius,[17] son of Panopeus, passing into the form of a craftswoman; and far

---

[12] **He saw . . . woman:** Orpheus was torn in pieces by the Maenads, the women-worshippers of Dionysus.

[13] **Thamyras:** Another singer, who was deprived of sight and of the gift of song for challenging the Muses to a contest.

[14] **Achilles:** After Achilles' death a contest between Ajax and Odysseus for his arms ended in the defeat and suicide of Ajax. The first mention is in *The Odyssey* xi. 543, where the soul of Ajax, summoned from Hades, will not speak to Odysseus.

[15] **Agamemnon:** The conqueror of Troy, murdered by his wife Clytemnestra on his return home.

[16] **Atalanta:** Atalanta's suitors had to race with her for her hand and were killed if defeated. Milanion won by dropping three golden apples given him by Aphrodite, which Atalanta paused to pick up.

[17] **Epeius:** Maker of the wooden horse in which the Greek chieftains entered Troy.

off, among the last, the buffoon Thersites' soul clothing itself in the body of an ape. It so happened that the last choice of all fell to the soul of Odysseus, whose ambition was so abated by memory of his former labours that he went about for a long time looking for a life of quiet obscurity. When at last he found it lying somewhere neglected by all the rest, he chose it gladly, saying that he would have done the same if his lot had come first. Other souls in like manner passed from beasts into men and into one another, the unjust changing into the wild creatures, the just into the tame, in every sort of combination.

Now when all the souls had chosen their lives, they went in the order of their lots to Lachesis; and she gave each into the charge of the guardian genius he had chosen, to escort him through life and fulfil his choice. The genius led the soul first to Clotho, under her hand as it turned the whirling Spindle, thus ratifying the portion which the man had chosen when his lot was cast. And, after touching her, he led it next to the spinning of Atropos, thus making the thread of destiny irreversible. Thence, without looking back, he passed under the throne of Necessity. And when he and all the rest had passed beyond the throne, they journeyed together to the Plain of Lethe through terrible stifling heat; for the plain is bare of trees and of all plants that grow on the earth. When evening came, they encamped beside the River of Unmindfulness, whose water no vessel can hold. All are required to drink a certain measure of this water, and some have not the wisdom to save them from drinking more. Every man as he drinks forgets everything. When they had fallen asleep, at midnight there was thunder and an earthquake, and in a moment they were carried up, this way and that, to their birth, like shooting stars. Er himself was not allowed to drink of the water. How and by what means he came back to the body he knew not; but suddenly he opened his eyes and found himself lying on the funeral pyre at dawn.

And so, Glaucon, the tale was saved from perishing; and if we will listen, it may save us, and all will be well when we cross the river of Lethe. Also we shall not defile our souls; but, if you will believe with me that the soul is immortal and able to endure all good and ill, we shall keep always to the upward way and in all things pursue justice with the help of wisdom. Then we shall be at peace with Heaven and with ourselves, both during our sojourn here and when, like victors in the Games collecting gifts from their friends, we receive the prize of justice; and so, not here only, but in the journey of a thousand years of which I have told you, we shall fare well.

ॐ OVID
ROME, 43 B.C.E.—17 C.E.

"The Story of Orpheus and Eurydice" is found in Ovid's *Metamorphoses*, which was begun around the year 1 C.E., and completed around 8 C.E. The *Metamorphoses* is a large collection of stories about gods, goddesses, heroes, and heroines, which are loosely linked by the theme of physical transformation. Several episodes of transformation occur in the story of Orpheus, who was the greatest musician in ancient Greece; his music charmed not only humans and beasts, but trees and rocks. The first part of his story concerns his marriage to Eurydice, who was bitten by a snake and died. Orpheus, inconsolable at her death, went down to Hades to get her back. The underworld deities, captivated by Orpheus's music, agreed to release her on one condition: Orpheus must walk ahead of Eurydice and not look back while they were in Hades. Orpheus failed the condition and Eurydice remained in Hades. Orpheus wandered the countryside lamenting his loss.

The power of Orpheus's music enchanted birds, animals, and trees, but his spurning of women finally led to his death, which is described in Book 11 of the *Metamorphoses*. Maenads, the female followers of the orgiastic rites of Dionysus, came upon Orpheus, and remembering how he treated women, hurled rocks at his head. But the music of his lyre charmed the stones and they fell harmless at his side. The Maenads then yelled so dreadfully and loudly that the noise of his playing was drowned out, and the stones struck him from all sides. Mortally wounded he fell. In a frenzy, the women tore him apart and scattered his limbs over the fields. Such was the power, however, of his singing, that his head, floating down the River Hebrus, continued to cry for Eurydice and the shore answered back. His head finally came ashore on the isle of Lesbos, where there was an oracular shrine of Orpheus.

Although Orpheus failed in his mission to bring Eurydice back to earth, it was believed that his journey to the underworld and back provided him with the vision that formed the basis of the Orphic Mysteries, which were popular from about the sixth century B.C.E. into the early Christian era. Mystery religions were attractive because they focused on savior figures, secret initiations, and promises of immortality. The core of Orphism was the belief that a moral, ascetic life will lead to an escape from the bondage of the body to rewards in the afterlife. The ultimate goal was to eventually transcend the cycles of reincarnation and to reside in some kind of perpetual divine state. These beliefs are akin to those of Buddhism.

The power of music to bewitch or entrance listeners, even those residing in the underworld, seems to be rooted in the Pythagorean view that music expressed the essential structure of reality. Pythagoras, a sixth century B.C.E. Greek philosopher and mathematician, believed that the same mathematical laws that describe the rhythm and sounds of music also explain the workings of the cosmos. Music has transformative power which is powerfully illustrated by Orpheus's ability to move both animate and inanimate objects.

FROM

∾ Metamorphoses

Translated by Rolfe Humphries

BOOK 10
[THE STORY OF ORPHEUS AND EURYDICE]

So Hymen left there, clad in saffron robe,
Through the great reach of air, and took his way
To the Ciconian country, where the voice
Of Orpheus called him, all in vain.[1] He came there,
True, but brought with him no auspicious words,
No joyful faces, lucky omens. The torch
Sputtered and filled the eyes with smoke; when swung,
It would not blaze: bad as the omens were,
The end was worse, for as the bride went walking
10 Across the lawn, attended by her naiads,
A serpent bit her ankle, and she was gone.
Orpheus mourned her to the upper world,
And then, lest he should leave the shades untried,
Dared to descend to Styx, passing the portal
Men call Taenarian.[2] Through the phantom dwellers,
The buried ghosts, he passed, came to the king
Of that sad realm, and to Persephone,
His consort, and he swept the strings, and chanted:
"Gods of the world below the world, to whom
20 All of us mortals come, if I may speak
Without deceit, the simple truth is this:
I came here, not to see dark Tartarus,[3]
Nor yet to bind the triple-throated monster[4]
Medusa's offspring, rough with snakes. I came
For my wife's sake, whose growing years were taken
By a snake's venom. I wanted to be able
To bear this; I have tried to. Love has conquered.
This god is famous in the world above,
But here, I do not know. I think he may be
30 Or is it all a lie, that ancient story

---

[1] So Hymen . . . vain: Hymen, god of marriage, has just left Greece and arrived in Ciconia, a territory in Thrace. [2] Taenarian: Taenarum, a cape on the southern Peloponnesus, thought to be an entrance to Hades, the underworld. [3] Tartarus: The farthest region in Hades, where the rebellious Titans were imprisoned. [4] triple-throated monster: Cerberus, the three-headed dog that guarded the entrance to Hades. Hercules once bound Cerberus and carried him to the upper world.

Of an old ravishment,[5] and how he brought
The two of you together? By these places
All full of fear, by this immense confusion,
By this vast kingdom's silences, I beg you,
Weave over Eurydice's life, run through too soon.
To you we all, people and things, belong,
Sooner or later, to this single dwelling
All of us come, to our last home; you hold
Longest dominion over humankind.
40 She will come back again, to be your subject,
After the ripeness of her years; I am asking
A loan and not a gift. If fate denies us
This privilege for my wife, one thing is certain:
I do not want to go back either; triumph
In the death of two."
                    And with his words, the music
Made the pale phantoms weep: Ixion's wheel
Was still, Tityos' vultures left the liver,
Tantalus tried no more to reach for the water,
And Belus' daughters rested from their urns,
50 And Sisyphus[6] climbed on his rock to listen.
That was the first time ever in all the world
The Furies[7] wept. Neither the king nor consort
Had harshness to refuse him, and they called her,
Eurydice. She was there, limping a little
From her late wound, with the new shades of Hell.
And Orpheus received her, but one term
Was set: he must not, till he passed Avernus,[8]
Turn back his gaze, or the gift would be in vain.

They climbed the upward path, through absolute silence,
60 Up the steep murk, clouded in pitchy darkness,
They were near the margin, near the upper land,
When he, afraid that she might falter, eager to see her,
Looked back in love, and she was gone, in a moment.

---

[5] **an old ravishment:** Ovid alludes to the story of Pluto's abduction of Proserpina told in Book 5.

[6] **Ixion . . . Sisyphus:** These are all sinners facing eternal tortures. Ixion was chained to a fiery wheel that turned endlessly; Tityos suffered the pain of vultures constantly feeding on his liver; Tantalus stood chin deep in water that receded whenever he tried to drink it, while above him fruit dangled just out of reach; Belus's daughters had to carry water in pitchers punctured with holes; and Sisyphus continually pushed a huge boulder to the top of a hill only to see it roll back down.

[7] **Furies:** Female spirits who avenged crimes against blood kin, especially against fathers and mothers; sometimes thought to inflict the tortures in Hades.

[8] **Avernus:** A poisonous lake and a wood near the entrance to the underworld.

Was it he, or she, reaching out arms and trying
To hold or to be held, and clasping nothing
But empty air? Dying the second time,
She had no reproach to bring against her husband,
What was there to complain of? One thing, only:
He loved her. He could hardly hear her calling
Farewell! when she was gone.

70   The double death
Stunned Orpheus, like the man who turned to stone
At sight of Cerberus, or the couple of rock,
Olenos and Lethaea,[9] hearts so joined
One shared the other's guilt, and Ida's mountain,
Where rivers run, still holds them, both together.
In vain the prayers of Orpheus and his longing
To cross the river once more; the boatman Charon
Drove him away. For seven days he sat there
Beside the bank, in filthy garments, and tasting

80 No food whatever. Trouble, grief, and tears
Were all his sustenance. At last, complaining
The gods of Hell were cruel, he wandered on
To Rhodope and Haemus,[10] swept by the north winds,
Where, for three years, he lived without a woman
Either because marriage had meant misfortune
Or he had made a promise. But many women
Wanted this poet for their own, and many
Grieved over their rejection. His love was given
To young boys only, and he told the Thracians

90 That was the better way: *enjoy that springtime,*
Take those first flowers!
                        There was a hill, and on it
A wide-extending plain, all green, but lacking
The darker green of shade, and when the singer
Came there and ran his fingers over the strings,
The shade came there to listen. The oak-tree came,
And many poplars, and the gentle lindens,
The beech, the virgin laurel, and the hazel
Easily broken, the ash men use for spears,
The shining silver-fir, the ilex bending

100 Under its acorns, the friendly sycamore,
The changing-colored maple, and the willows

---

[9] the couple . . . Lethaea: When Olenos, Lethaea's husband, offered to take on her punishment for offending the gods by bragging of her beauty, both were turned to stone.

[10] Rhodope and Haemus: Mountains in Thrace.

That love the river-waters, and the lotus
Favoring pools, and the green boxwood came,
Slim tamarisks, and myrtle, and viburnum
With dark-blue berries, and the pliant ivy,
The tendrilled grape, the elms, all dressed with vines,
The rowan-trees, the pitch-pines, and the arbute
With the red fruit, the palm, the victor's triumph,
The bare-trunked pine with spreading leafy crest,
110   Dear to the mother of the gods since Attis[11]
Put off his human form, took on that likeness,
And the cone-shaped cypress joined them, now a tree,
But once a boy, loved by the god Apollo
Master of lyre and bow-string, both together. [. . .]

---

[11] **Attis:** A youth associated with the Phrygian mother goddess Cybele; in a fit of madness inspired by the jealous goddess, he castrated himself and was transformed into a pine tree.

TEXT IN CONTEXT

∾ BHAGAVAD GITA

INDIA, C. FIRST CENTURY B.C.E.—FIRST CENTURY C.E.

WWW   For a quiz
on the Bhagavad
Gita, see bedford
stmartins.com/
worldlitcompact.

Tucked into the Bhishma Parva, Book 6 of the *Mahabharata,* appears one of India's most important and influential sacred texts, the Bhagavad Gita. Added to the *Mahabharata* sometime between the first century B.C.E. and the first century C.E., this seven-hundred-verse poem of eighteen chapters or "teachings" has been called "a compendium of the whole Vedic doctrine" of earlier sacred texts such as the Vedas and the Upanishads,[1] and it is often treated as an independent text. Indeed, the Gita, or Song of God as it is often called, is well known throughout the world as an important guide to moral and spiritual action. American writer and naturalist Henry David Thoreau (1817–1862) and Indian spiritual leader Mohandas (Mahatma) Gandhi (1869–1948) were among the work's admirers.

The Bhagavad Gita attempted to weave together the various philosophical strands of the Vedas and the Upanishads, which had been unraveling for centuries, as well as accommodate some of the ideas of the two relatively new religions of Buddhism and Jainism. Just as Greek thinkers and writers of the fifth century B.C.E. aimed to square the mythology and customs of a tribal society with the philosophical needs of a new social formation, the city-state, the Gita sought to synthesize the older teachings of the Vedic tradition with the new demands of the changing Indian society. One of the most influential aspects of the newer religions was the idea of AHIMSA, or nonviolence, by means of

---

[1] **Vedas and Upanishads:** The Vedas, dating from c. 1000 B.C.E., are a group of the earliest sacred texts, written in Sanskrit, from India; they contain hymns and ritual lore considered to be revelation (*sruti*). The Upanishads, dating from the ninth century B.C.E., are sacred texts that are a mystical development of and commentary on the earlier Vedic texts. See pp. 157 and 906.

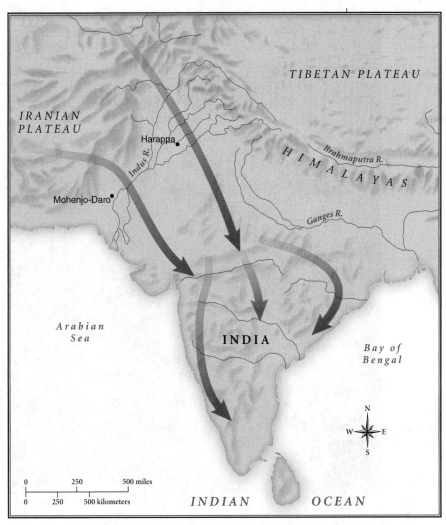

Aryan Migration into India, c. 1500–c. 700 B.C.E.
Two early Indian cities, Harappa and Mohenjo-Daro, located along the Indus River, underwent first a gradual decay and then sudden destruction around 1500 B.C.E. Although archaeologists still search for explanations for these civilizations' demise, they do know it was hastened by the arrival of the Aryans from Central Asia. After 1000 B.C.E., the Aryans continued to migrate into India, mixing with and replacing indigenous peoples. The warrior culture of the Aryans was eventually depicted in the militaristic values and grand battles of the Indian epic the Mahabharata.

which individuals from any class could achieve spiritual liberation. This concept was a problem for the warrior class, the *KSHATRIYA* (Kṣatria), of course, who according to the Vedas fulfilled the duties of their caste by engaging in war. This clash of values provides the basic conflict of the Bhagavad Gita, as the **Pandava** hero Arjuna weighs whether or not it is just to wage war against his kinsmen, the Kauravas.

PAHN-duh-vuh

**Temple of Vishnu,
500**

*A principal Hindu
deity, Vishnu (the
four-armed figure at
left), in the guise of
Krishna, serves as
Arjuna's charioteer
and counselor in the
Bhagavad Gita.
(Borromeo / Art
Resource, NY)*

AR-joo-nuh;
KRISH-nuh; VISH-noo
KOO-roo

The Bhagavad Gita takes the form of an extended dialogue
between **Arjuna** and **Krishna**, the incarnation of the deity **Vishnu**, just
before the war between the cousins begins. Arjuna, who has lost his
heart for battle, surveys the field of **Kuru** with his charioteer, Krishna.
Looking out in "strange pity" at his cousins and uncles, his former
mentors and friends, Arjuna anticipates imminent carnage and is filled
with doubt about the wisdom of engaging in war. Krishna counsels him
about his spiritual and moral obligation to engage in combat and pros-
ecute the war according to the sacred duty of the warrior class into
which he was born. At the same time Krishna teaches Arjuna that in
order to free himself from worldly attachment, Arjuna must perform

his duties without desire for reward and with the understanding that all action should be undertaken as a form of devotion to Vishnu, whose cosmic plan comprehends all that we do. Action taken out of duty, without desire for reward, with devotion to Krishna, and with consciousness of the divinity of all things leads to the ultimate goal of *MOKSHA,* release from *SAMSARA,* or the cycle of death and rebirth.

Arjuna's dilemma stems in part from a desire to renounce the world and a belief that violent action will keep his spirit tied to the material world. The solution to Arjuna's problem is given in stages throughout the dialogue, which in Book 11 culminates in a marvelous revelation of Krishna's divinity. The key teaching is that Arjuna must fulfill his duties as a warrior but with total disregard for the immediate or future consequences. First, he must recognize that the human spirit that acts is not separate from the universal and immortal spirit, Brahman. Once Arjuna realizes that the human soul is in fact a portion of the universal soul that is constantly interacting with the world, Krishna points out that renouncing worldly action goes against the divine scheme of things. To act according to the *DHARMA* (sacred duty) of one's class, then, is to act in accordance with *Dharma* understood as divine law. In other words, in acting out their duties, human beings participate in the divine plan. Thus, Arjuna learns that action is necessary, but that action must be undertaken with discipline and understanding.

Given the immortality of the soul, actions have consequences in the spiritual realm, which is timeless, as well as in the world of historical time. The law of *KARMA,* already articulated in the Upanishads, states that all individuals are locked into a chain of consequences that determines one's status in a future life and that may free one from *samsara.* According to the Gita, one way to liberate the soul from the cycle of death and rebirth is by means of *KARMA-YOGA,* the path of disciplined action. In the Gita, the greatest happiness comes from action performed with detachment from gain and in strict accordance with one's station in life. Any longing for results, or confusion of roles, as Krishna advises Arjuna, subverts the moral and spiritual order. "Your own duty done imperfectly / is better than another man's done well," the teacher tells the warrior. Thus, from Krishna, Arjuna learns that when the warrior or any other class member gives himself up to *dharma* without desire, though his actions have consequences in historical time, they will in fact further the progress of his soul toward *moksha,* a release to a oneness with the supreme spirit, or Brahman, and an escape from the cycle of rebirth. Moreover, what makes possible such liberation, Arjuna learns, is not only the actions one performs but also one's moral and philosophical relation to and understanding of those actions. In other words, it is

[The *Bhagavad-Gita*] is the focal point around which all later Hinduism was to revolve, and so all-embracing is its appeal that it has commanded not only the allegiance of the orthodox but also that of modern and modernist Hindus, and not least of [whom was] Mahatma Gandhi himself. It is the sacred fount from which the popular cults of rapt devotion to God (whether it be Vishnu or Siva) naturally flow.

– R. C. ZAEHNER, critic, 1962

not just what one does—so long as individuals abide by their sacred duty—it is also how one thinks about what one does that matters.

The First Teaching sets the scene of Arjuna's state of mind, his dejection. Excerpts from the Second, Third, and Sixth Teachings follow the exchange between Arjuna and Krishna. Responding to Arjuna's questions, Krishna, the incarnation of the preserver-god Vishnu, gradually imparts the meaning of sacred duty and right action while slowly revealing his own divinity. This revelation culminates in the Eleventh Teaching when Arjuna receives a spectacular vision of Krishna's boundless being in all its fullness and light. In the Eighteenth Teaching, Krishna summarizes the basic ideas for Arjuna: Arjuna must fulfill the warrior role he was born with, but ultimate reality lies with transcending one's individual life and unifying the infinite spirit.

A number of the teachings in the Gita are attractive, even for a Western consciousness: for example, one should perform an action without regard for rewards; one's pure intentions can justify impure actions; and the events of history occur within the larger context of a transcendent reality. Nevertheless, the lessons of the Gita are difficult, even paradoxical. Since Arjuna was born into the warrior caste he must absolutely fulfill his calling. Krishna tells Arjuna that with a tranquil mind he is to kill his relatives and teachers since they all are immortal souls and death is unimportant. Warfare is allowable if performed with detachment. The hero is to be both a warrior and a saint at the same time, practicing both a yoga of understanding and a yoga of action.

■ **FURTHER RESEARCH**

Literary History/Background
Dimock, Edward C. Jr., et al. *The Literatures of India: An Introduction.* 1974.
Flood, Gavin. *An Introduction to Hinduism.* 1996.
Zaehner, R. C. *Hinduism.* 1962, 1966.

Criticism
Minor, Robert. *Modern Interpreters of the Bhagavadgita.* 1986.
Sharpe, Eric. *The Universal Gita: Western Images of the Bhagavad Gita.* 1985.

Translations
Johnson, W. J. *The Bhagavad Gita.* 1994.
Mascaró, Juan. *The Bhagavad Gita.* 1962.
Prabhavananda, Swami, and Christopher Isherwood. *The Song of God: Bhagavad-Gita.* 1944.
Miller, Barbara Stoler. *The Bhagavad Gita: Krishna's Counsel in Time of War.* 1986.

■ **PRONUNCIATION**

Arjuna: AR-joo-nuh
Bhagavad Gita: bah-guh-vahd-GEE-tuh, buh-guh-vud-GEE-tuh
Bhima: BEE-muh

Ancient India: Cycles of Time

The concept of time in Indian literature is very different from time as it was depicted in ancient Mesopotamia, Egypt, and Israel. In those earlier cultures, a mythic or primordial time precedes history and is the occasion for the creation of a mythic cosmology. This is always followed by a transitional period when myth and legend merge with history—a linear or progressive concept of time—and are blended into the culture. Time in Indian myth is a larger beast; it consists of immense, nearly innumerable cycles of years and eons—probably the longest cycles of time ever conceived by any religion. In Indian thought, the world is presently in the last of four epochs, or *Yugas,* the Kali Yuga. According to some calculations, it began Friday, February 18, 3102 B.C.E. and will last 432,000 years. A different expert says that the Kali Yuga will last 10,800,000 years.

The three previous Yugas—the *Krita,* the *Treta,* and the *Dvapara*—are spoken of in the present tense since they repeat endlessly. They represent a process of decline, ages during which life grows worse. In the Krita Yuga, the golden age associated with fullness, men and women are virtuous and all social classes act according to ideals. It lasts 1,728,000 years. In the Treta Yuga virtue diminishes slightly (by one quarter); the four castes begin to decay, and duties are not spontaneous but have to be learned. It lasts 1,296,000 years. In the Dvapara Yuga there is a dangerous balance between darkness and light, good and evil. People grow mean and greedy. It lasts 864,000 years. The Kali Yuga, the present age, is the dark age. Each age ends with darkness, but in the Kali Yuga, darkness deepens. A complete cycle of four Yugas is called *Maha Yuga,* or the Great Yuga, after which is *Pralaya,* meaning "dissolution." A single day of Brahma, the god of creation, or a single *kalpa,* equals 1,000 *Mahayugas* (4,320,000,000

Woman Making Offering to Brahma, 1720. The Hindu creator god Brahma is shown in this Indian miniature with four faces, symbolizing the four Yugas (epochs), the four Vedas (sacred writings), and the four varnas (castes or social classes). (The Art Archive / Marco Polo Gallery Paris / Dagli Orti)

human years); after one *kalpa,* everything is dissolved. After one hundred years of Brahma days and nights, which constitute the gods' existence, all spheres of being and existence sink into the primordial Substance, a condition that remains for a Brahma century, after which the creation-destruction cycle begins anew.

In the context of these great cycles, individual human existence is inconsequential; there is really no need to promote change or reform, to rid society of inequities or oppression. Life's goal is contained in the idea of *dharma,* doing one's sacred duty, which is the core teaching of the Bhagavad Gita. It is within the context of endless time that individual duty fulfills the spirit of Brahman.

927

Bhishma: BEESH-muh
Brahma: BRAH-hmuh
Dhritarashtra: drih-tuh-RAH-shtruh
Drishtadyumna: drish-tuh-DYOOM-nuh
Drona: DROH-nuh
Drupada: DROO-puh-duh
Duryodhana: door-YOH-duh-nuh
Karna: KAR-nuh
Kauravas: KOW-ruh-vuhz
Krishna: KRISH-nuh
Kripa: KRIH-puh
Pandava: PAHN-duh-vuh
Pandu: PAHN-doo
Prajapati: pruh-JAH-puh-tee
Sanjaya: SUN-juh-yuh
Satyaki: SAH-tyuh-kee
Virata: vih-RAH-tuh
Vishnu: VISH-noo
Yudhishthira: yoo-DISH-tih-ruh

FROM

∾ Bhagavad Gita

Translated by Barbara Stoler Miller

THE FIRST TEACHING: ARJUNA'S DEJECTION

DHRITARASHTRA:[1]
> Sanjaya, tell me what my sons
> and the sons of Pandu[2] did when they met,
> wanting to battle on the field of Kuru,[3]
1 > on the field of sacred duty?

SANJAYA:[4]
> Your son Duryodhana,[5] the king,
> seeing the Pandava forces arrayed,
> approached his teacher Drona[6]
2 > and spoke in command.

---

[1] **Dhritarashtra:** The son of Vyasa and Ambika (Kansalya), now the blind king at Hastinapurna and the father of the one hundred brothers known as the Kauravas.

[2] **Pandu:** The son of Vyasa and Ambalika and the father of the five brothers known as the Pandavas.

[3] **field of Kuru:** Kurukshetra, the field where the eighteen-day battle between the Pandavas and the Kauravas is fought.

[4] **Sanjaya:** Dhritarashtra's advisor and the narrator of the Bhagavad Gita.

[5] **Duryodhana:** The eldest of the Kaurava brothers; his jealousy of the great success of the Pandavas has led to the war.

[6] **Drona:** Mentor in the martial arts to the Kauravas and the Pandavas.

"My teacher, see
the great Pandava army arrayed
by Drupada's son,[7]

3　　your pupil, intent on revenge.

Here are heroes, mighty archers
equal to Bhima and Arjuna[8] in warfare,
Yuyudhana, Virata, and Drupada,[9]

4　　your sworn foe on his great chariot.

Here too are Dhrishtaketu, Cekitana,
and the brave king of Benares;
Purujit, Kuntibhoja,

5　　and the manly king of the Shibis.

Yudhamanyu is bold,
and Uttamaujas is brave;
the sons of Subhadra and Draupadi

6　　all command great chariots.

Now, honored priest, mark
the superb men on our side
as I tell you the names

7　　of my army's leaders.

They are you and Bhishma,[10]
Karna[11] and Kripa,[12] a victor in battles,
your own son Ashvatthama,

8　　Vikarna, and the son of Somadatta.

Many other heroes also risk
their lives for my sake,

---

[7] **Drupada's son:** Dhrishtadyumna, the commander of the Pandavas and brother of Draupadi, the wife of the five Pandavas.

[8] **Bhima and Arjuna:** Nominally, the second and third sons of Pandu; they are actually the sons of Pandu's wife Kunti and the gods Vayu (the wind god) and Indra (the chief of the gods), respectively. Yudhishthira, the first-born son of Pandu, is actually the son of Kunti and Dharma (the god of sacred duty and law).

[9] **Yuyudhana . . . Drupada:** These names and those in verse five catalog the chief allies of the Pandavas.

[10] **Bhishma:** The son of King Santanu and Ganga; as the great-uncle of both Duryodhana and Arjuna, he tried to avert war through negotiations but found on the side of the Kauravas.

[11] **Karna:** The first son of Kunti by the sun-god Surya; born before Kunti married Pandu, Karna was abandoned by his mother and raised by a charioteer. Though a half brother of the Pandavas, Karna fights for the Kauravas out of loyalty to his friend Duryodhana.

[12] **Kripa:** Drona's brother-in-law; the list that follows, similar to lists in the Homeric epics, catalogs the chief allies of the Kauravas.

9
bearing varied weapons
and skilled in the ways of war.

10
Guarded by Bhishma, the strength
of our army is without limit;
but the strength of their army,
guarded by Bhima, is limited.

11
In all the movements of battle,
you and your men,
stationed according to plan,
must guard Bhishma well!"

12
Bhishma, fiery elder of the Kurus,
roared his lion's roar
and blew his conch horn,
exciting Duryodhana's delight.

13
Conches and kettledrums,
cymbals, tabors, and trumpets
were sounded at once
and the din of tumult arose.

14
Standing on their great chariot
yoked with white stallions,
Krishna and Arjuna, Pandu's son,
sounded their divine conches.

15
Krishna blew Pancajanya, won from a demon;
Arjuna blew Devadatta, a gift of the gods;
fierce wolf-bellied Bhima blew Paundra,
his great conch of the east.

16
Yudhishthira,[13] Kunti's son, the king,
blew Anantavijaya, conch of boundless victory;
his twin brothers Nakula and Sahadeva[14]
blew conches resonant and jewel toned.

The king of Benares, a superb archer,
and Shikhandin on his great chariot,

---

[13] **Yudhishthira:** See note 8.

[14] **Nakula and Sahadeva:** Nominally, the twin sons of Pandu by his wife, Madri; actually fathered by the Asvins (physicians of heaven), they are the fourth and fifth Pandava brothers. (See also note 8.)

17
Drishtadyumna, Virata, and indomitable Satyaki,[15]
all blew their conches.

18
Drupada, with his five grandsons,
and Subhadra's strong-armed son,[16]
each in his turn blew
their conches, O King.

19
The noise tore the hearts
of Dhritarashtra's sons,
and tumult echoed
through heaven and earth.

20
Arjuna, his war flag a rampant monkey,
saw Dhritarashtra's sons assembled
as weapons were ready to clash,
and he lifted his bow.

21
He told his charioteer:[17]
"Krishna,
halt my chariot
between the armies!

22
Far enough for me to see
these men who lust for war,
ready to fight with me
in the strain of battle.

23
I see men gathered here,
eager to fight,
bent on serving the folly
of Dhritarashtra's son."

24
When Arjuna had spoken,
Krishna halted
their splendid chariot
between the armies.

---

[15] **Drishtadyumna . . . Satyaki:** Drishtadyumna is the son of King Drupada and the brother of Draupadi, the wife of the five Pandavas. Virata is the king of the Matsyas and Satyaki is a kinsman of Krishna. All are fighting for the Pandavas.

[16] **Subhadra's strong-armed son:** Abhimanyu, son of Arjuna and his wife, Subhadra, Krishna's sister.

[17] **his charioteer:** Krishna, the incarnation of the preserver-god Vishnu, is Arjuna's spiritual guide and charioteer.

Facing Bhishma and Drona
and all the great kings,
he said, "Arjuna, see
25   the Kuru men assembled here!"

Arjuna saw them standing there:
fathers, grandfathers, teachers,
uncles, brothers, sons,
26   grandsons, and friends.

He surveyed his elders
and companions in both armies,
all his kinsmen
27   assembled together.

Dejected, filled with strange pity,
he said this:
    "Krishna, I see my kinsmen
28   gathered here, wanting war.

    My limbs sink,
    my mouth is parched,
    my body trembles,
29   the hair bristles on my flesh.

    The magic bow[18] slips
    from my hand, my skin burns,
    I cannot stand still,
30   my mind reels.

    I see omens of chaos,
    Krishna; I see no good
    in killing my kinsmen
31   in battle.

    Krishna, I seek no victory,
    or kingship or pleasures.
    What use to us are kingship,
32   delights, or life itself?

    We sought kingship, delights,
    and pleasures for the sake of those
    assembled to abandon their lives
33   and fortunes in battle.

---

[18] **The magic bow:** Gandiva, a weapon Arjuna won from Agni, the god of fire.

They are teachers, fathers, sons,
and grandfathers, uncles, grandsons,
fathers and brothers of wives,
34   and other men of our family.

I do not want to kill them
even if I am killed, Krishna;
not for kingship of all three worlds,
35   much less for the earth!

What joy is there for us, Krishna,
in killing Dhritarashtra's sons?
Evil will haunt us if we kill them,
36   though their bows are drawn to kill.

Honor forbids us to kill
our cousins, Dhritarashtra's sons;
how can we know happiness
37   if we kill our own kinsmen?

The greed that distorts their reason
blinds them to the sin they commit
in ruining the family, blinds them
38   to the crime of betraying friends.

How can we ignore the wisdom
of turning from this evil
when we see the sin
39   of family destruction, Krishna?

When the family is ruined,
the timeless laws of family duty
perish; and when duty is lost,
40   chaos overwhelms the family.

In overwhelming chaos, Krishna,
women of the family are corrupted;
and when women are corrupted,
41   disorder is born in society.[19]

This discord drags the violators
and the family itself to hell;

---

[19] **disorder . . . society:** That is, the social order of the castes—Brahmin, *Kshatriya* (warrior), *Vaishya* (merchant and farmer), and *Shudra* (laborer and servant)—will be overthrown.

42
for ancestors fall when rites
of offering rice and water lapse.

43
The sins of men who violate
the family create disorder in society
that undermines the constant laws
of caste and family duty.

44
Krishna, we have heard
that a place in hell
is reserved for men
who undermine family duties.

45
I lament the great sin
we commit when our greed
for kingship and pleasures
drives us to kill our kinsmen.

46
If Dhritarashtra's armed sons
kill me in battle when I am unarmed
and offer no resistance,
it will be my reward."

47
Saying this in the time of war,
Arjuna slumped into the chariot
and laid down his bow and arrows,
his mind tormented by grief.

FROM

THE SECOND TEACHING:
PHILOSOPHY AND SPIRITUAL DISCIPLINE

SANJAYA:
1
Arjuna sat dejected,
filled with pity,
his sad eyes blurred by tears.
Krishna gave him counsel. [. . .]
LORD KRISHNA:
11
You grieve for those beyond grief,
and you speak words of insight;
but learned men do not grieve
for the dead or the living.

Never have I not existed,
nor you, nor these kings;

and never in the future
12   shall we cease to exist.

Just as the embodied self
enters childhood, youth, and old age,
so does it enter another body;
13   this does not confound a steadfast man.

Contacts with matter make us feel
heat and cold, pleasure and pain.
Arjuna, you must learn to endure
14   fleeting things—they come and go!

When these cannot torment a man,
when suffering and joy are equal
for him and he has courage,
15   he is fit for immortality.

Nothing of nonbeing comes to be,
nor does being cease to exist;
the boundary between these two
16   is seen by men who see reality.

Indestructible is the presence[20]
that pervades all this;
no one can destroy
17   this unchanging reality.

Our bodies are known to end,
but the embodied self is enduring,
indestructible, and immeasurable;
18   therefore, Arjuna, fight the battle!

He who thinks this self a killer
and he who thinks it killed,
both fail to understand;
19   it does not kill, nor is it killed.

It is not born,
it does not die;
having been,
it will never not be;

---

[20] **the presence:** Krishna means Brahman, the universal spirit that permeates all creation. What Arjuna perceives as mutable and limited is in fact part of the unchanging and infinite soul.

unborn, enduring,
constant, and primordial,
it is not killed
20   when the body is killed.

Arjuna, when a man knows the self
to be indestructible, enduring, unborn,
unchanging, how does he kill
21   or cause anyone to kill?

As a man discards
worn-out clothes
to put on new
and different ones,
so the embodied self
discards
its worn-out bodies
22   to take on other new ones.

Weapons do not cut it,
fire does not burn it,
waters do not wet it,
23   wind does not wither it.

It cannot be cut or burned;
it cannot be wet or withered;
it is enduring, all-pervasive,
24   fixed, immovable, and timeless.

It is called unmanifest,
inconceivable, and immutable;
since you know that to be so,
25   you should not grieve!

If you think of its birth
and death as ever-recurring,
then too, Great Warrior,
26   you have no cause to grieve!

Death is certain for anyone born,
and birth is certain for the dead;
since the cycle is inevitable,
27   you have no cause to grieve!

Creatures are unmanifest in origin,
manifest in the midst of life,

and unmanifest again in the end.
28   Since this is so, why do you lament?

Rarely someone
sees it,
rarely another
speaks it,
rarely anyone
hears it—
even hearing it,
29   no one really knows it.

The self embodied in the body
of every being is indestructible;
you have no cause to grieve
30   for all these creatures, Arjuna!

Look to your own duty;
do not tremble before it;
nothing is better for a warrior
31   than a battle of sacred duty.[21]

The doors of heaven open
for warriors who rejoice
to have a battle like this
32   thrust on them by chance.

If you fail to wage this war
of sacred duty,
you will abandon your own duty
33   and fame only to gain evil.

People will tell
of your undying shame,
and for a man of honor
34   shame is worse than death.

The great chariot warriors will think
you deserted in fear of battle;
you will be despised
35   by those who held you in esteem.

Your enemies will slander you,
scorning your skill

---

[21] **sacred duty:** That is, *dharma;* in Arjuna's case, the responsibilities of the *Kshatriya* class.

36   in so many unspeakable ways—
could any suffering be worse?

37   If you are killed, you win heaven;
if you triumph, you enjoy the earth;
therefore, Arjuna, stand up
and resolve to fight the battle!

38   Impartial to joy and suffering,
gain and loss, victory and defeat,
arm yourself for the battle,
lest you fall into evil.

39   Understanding is defined in terms of philosophy;
now hear it in spiritual discipline.
Armed with this understanding, Arjuna,
you will escape the bondage of action.[22] [. . .]

47   Be intent on action,
not on the fruits of action;
avoid attraction to the fruits
and attachment to inaction!

48   Perform actions, firm in discipline,
relinquishing attachment;
be impartial to failure and success—
this equanimity is called discipline.

49   Arjuna, action is far inferior
to the discipline of understanding;[23]
so seek refuge in understanding—pitiful
are men drawn by fruits of action.

50   Disciplined by understanding,
one abandons both good and evil deeds;
so arm yourself for discipline—
discipline is skill in actions.

Wise men disciplined by understanding
relinquish the fruit born of action;

---

[22] **the bondage of action:** That is, the cycle of death and rebirth in the world of embodied action; to escape the cycle of rebirth *(samsara)* is to attain *moksha*, spiritual liberation and oneness with Brahman.

[23] **discipline of understanding:** Disciplined understanding means something like pure consciousness or intuition as opposed to instrumental or practical reason, which acts on objects in the world.

freed from these bonds of rebirth,

51   they reach a place beyond decay.

When your understanding passes beyond
the swamp of delusion,
you will be indifferent to all

52   that is heard in sacred lore.[24]

When your understanding turns
from sacred lore to stand fixed,
immovable in contemplation,

53   then you will reach discipline.

ARJUNA:

Krishna, what defines a man
deep in contemplation whose insight
and thought are sure? How would he speak?

54   How would he sit? How would he move?

LORD KRISHNA:

When he gives up desires in his mind,
is content with the self within himself,[25]
then he is said to be a man

55   whose insight is sure, Arjuna.

When suffering does not disturb his mind,
when his craving for pleasures has vanished,
when attraction, fear, and anger are gone,

56   he is called a sage whose thought is sure.

When he shows no preference
in fortune or misfortune
and neither exults nor hates,

57   his insight is sure.

When, like a tortoise retracting
its limbs, he withdraws his senses
completely from sensuous objects,

58   his insight is sure.

---

[24] **sacred lore:** That is, the Vedas and Upanishads, according to which strict observance of ritual sacrifice alone leads to *moksha*. Krishna guides Arjuna to understand that the Brahminic recitation of scriptures does not stem from or lead to understanding and hence does not lead to liberation.

[25] **the self within himself:** According to Samkhya theory, within each person lies the immortal, universal self (*purusha*); this pure self is distinct from the "I" or consciousness. When embodied in the realm of matter, the self loses sight of its immortal soul. Through disciplined understanding, the self can know its true nature.

Sensuous objects fade
when the embodied self abstains from food;
the taste lingers, but it too fades
59   in the vision of higher truth.

Even when a man of wisdom
tries to control them, Arjuna,
the bewildering senses
60   attack his mind with violence.

Controlling them all,
with discipline he should focus on me;
when his senses are under control,
61   his insight is sure.

Brooding about sensuous objects
makes attachment to them grow;
from attachment desire arises,
62   from desire anger is born.

From anger comes confusion;
from confusion memory lapses;
from broken memory understanding is lost;
63   from loss of understanding, he is ruined.

But a man of inner strength
whose senses experience objects
without attraction and hatred,
64   in self-control, finds serenity. [. . .]

FROM

THE THIRD TEACHING: DISCIPLINE OF ACTION

ARJUNA:
If you think understanding
is more powerful than action,
why, Krishna, do you urge me
1   to this horrific act?

You confuse my understanding
with a maze of words;
speak one certain truth
2   so I may achieve what is good.
LORD KRISHNA:
Earlier I taught the twofold
basis of good in this world—

for philosophers, disciplined knowledge;
3   for men of discipline, action.

A man cannot escape the force
of action by abstaining from actions;
he does not attain success
4   just by renunciation.

No one exists for even an instant
without performing action;
however unwilling, every being is forced
5   to act by the qualities of nature.[26]

When his senses are controlled
but he keeps recalling
sense objects with his mind,
6   he is a self-deluded hypocrite.

When he controls his senses
with his mind and engages in the discipline
of action with his faculties of action,
7   detachment sets him apart.

Perform necessary action;
it is more powerful than inaction;
without action you even fail
8   to sustain your own body.

Action imprisons the world
unless it is done as sacrifice;
freed from attachment, Arjuna,
9   perform action as sacrifice!

When creating living beings and sacrifice,
Prajapati,[27] the primordial creator, said:
    "By sacrifice will you procreate!
10   Let it be your wish-granting cow!

    Foster the gods with this,
    and may they foster you;

---

[26] **the qualities of nature:** The principles of nature *(praktri)* derive from the three *gunas* (qualities or strands); they are *sattva,* the quality of pure light; *rajas,* the quality of passion or energy; and *tamas,* the quality of iner- tia. The first quality frees the self from its bondage to matter; the second forces it to act in the world; the third binds it in ignorance.

[27] **Prajapati:** As the "lord of creatures," Prajapati is the guardian of living beings.

by enriching one another,

11   you will achieve a higher good.

Enriched by sacrifice, the gods
will give you the delights you desire;
he is a thief who enjoys their gifts

12   without giving to them in return."

Good men eating the remnants
of sacrifice are free of any guilt,
but evil men who cook for themselves

13   eat the food of sin.

Creatures depend on food,
food comes from rain,
rain depends on sacrifice,

14   and sacrifice comes from action.

Action comes from the spirit of prayer,
whose source is OM,[28] sound of the imperishable;
so the pervading infinite spirit

15   is ever present in rites of sacrifice.

He who fails to keep turning
the wheel here set in motion
wastes his life in sin,

16   addicted to the senses, Arjuna.

But when a man finds delight
within himself and feels inner joy
and pure contentment in himself,

17   there is nothing more to be done.

He has no stake here
in deeds done or undone,
nor does his purpose

18   depend on other creatures.

Always perform with detachment
any action you must do;

---

[28] OM: The sacred sound or mantra, associated in the *Upanishads* with *brahman*, the universal spirit that
underlies the cosmos.

performing action with detachment,
19   one achieves supreme good. [. . .]

ARJUNA:
Krishna, what makes a person
commit evil
against his own will,
36   as if compelled by force?

LORD KRISHNA:
It is desire and anger, arising
from nature's quality of passion;
know it here as the enemy,
37   voracious and very evil!

As fire is obscured by smoke
and a mirror by dirt,
as an embryo is veiled by its caul,
38   so is knowledge obscured by this.

Knowledge is obscured
by the wise man's eternal enemy,
which takes form as desire,
39   an insatiable fire, Arjuna.

The senses, mind, and understanding
are said to harbor desire;
with these desire obscures knowledge
40   and confounds the embodied self.

Therefore, first restrain
your senses, Arjuna,
then kill this evil
41   that ruins knowledge and judgment.

Men say that the senses are superior
to their objects, the mind superior to the senses,
understanding superior to the mind;
42   higher than understanding is the self.

Knowing the self beyond understanding,
sustain the self with the self.
Great Warrior, kill the enemy
43   menacing you in the form of desire!

FROM

THE SIXTH TEACHING: THE MAN OF DISCIPLINE

[LORD KRISHNA]:

A man of discipline[29] should always
discipline himself, remain in seclusion,
isolated, his thought and self well controlled,
10   without possessions or hope.

He should fix for himself
a firm seat in a pure place,
neither too high nor too low,
11   covered in cloth, deerskin, or grass.

He should focus his mind and restrain
the activity of his thought and senses;
sitting on that seat, he should practice
12   discipline for the purification of the self.

He should keep his body, head,
and neck aligned, immobile, steady;
he should gaze at the tip of his nose
13   and not let his glance wander.

The self tranquil, his fear dispelled,
firm in his vow of celibacy, his mind restrained,
let him sit with discipline,
14   his thought fixed on me, intent on me.

Disciplining himself,
his mind controlled,
a man of discipline finds peace,
15   the pure calm that exists in me.

Gluttons have no discipline,
nor the man who starves himself,
nor he who sleeps excessively
16   or suffers wakefulness.

When a man disciplines his diet
and diversions, his physical actions,
his sleeping and waking,
17   discipline destroys his sorrow.

---

[29] **man of discipline:** Discipline is *yoga,* from the Sanskrit for "yoking" or binding; the man of discipline is known as a *yogi.* Through certain disciplined action, knowledge, and devotion individuals may align themselves more perfectly to the divine purpose of Krishna.

When his controlled thought
rests within the self alone,
without craving objects of desire,
18   he is said to be disciplined.

"He does not waver, like a lamp sheltered
from the wind" is the simile recalled
for a man of discipline, restrained in thought
19   and practicing self-discipline.

When his thought ceases,
checked by the exercise of discipline,
he is content within the self,
20   seeing the self through himself.

Absolute joy beyond the senses
can only be grasped by understanding;
when one knows it, he abides there
21   and never wanders from this reality.

Obtaining it, he thinks
there is no greater gain;
abiding there, he is unmoved,
22   even by deep suffering.

Since he knows that discipline
means unbinding the bonds of suffering,
he should practice discipline resolutely,
23   without despair dulling his reason.

He should entirely relinquish
desires aroused by willful intent;
he should entirely control
24   his senses with his mind.

He should gradually become tranquil,
firmly controlling his understanding;
focusing his mind on the self,
25   he should think nothing.

Wherever his faltering mind
unsteadily wanders,
he should restrain it
26   and bring it under self-control.

When his mind is tranquil, perfect joy
comes to the man of discipline;

his passion is calmed, he is without sin,
27   being one with the infinite spirit.

Constantly disciplining himself,
free from sin, the man of discipline
easily achieves perfect joy
28   in harmony with the infinite spirit.

Arming himself with discipline,
seeing everything with an equal eye,
he sees the self in all creatures
29   and all creatures in the self.

He who sees me everywhere
and sees everything in me
will not be lost to me,
30   and I will not be lost to him.

I exist in all creatures,
so the disciplined man devoted to me
grasps the oneness of life;
31   wherever he is, he is in me.

When he sees identity in everything,
whether joy or suffering,
through analogy with the self,
32   he is deemed a man of pure discipline. [. . .]

FROM

THE ELEVENTH TEACHING:
THE VISION OF KRISHNA'S TOTALITY

ARJUNA:
To favor me you revealed
the deepest mystery of the self,
and by your words
1   my delusion is dispelled.

I heard from you in detail
how creatures come to be and die,
Krishna, and about the self
2   in its immutable greatness.

Just as you have described
yourself, I wish to see your form

in all its majesty,
3   Krishna, Supreme among Men.

If you think I can see it,
reveal to me
your immutable self,
4   Krishna, Lord of Discipline.

LORD KRISHNA:
Arjuna, see my forms
in hundreds and thousands;
diverse, divine,
5   of many colors and shapes.

See the sun gods, gods of light,
howling storm gods, twin gods of dawn,
and gods of wind, Arjuna,
6   wondrous forms not seen before.

Arjuna, see all the universe,
animate and inanimate,
and whatever else you wish to see;
7   all stands here as one in my body.

But you cannot see me
with your own eye;
I will give you a divine eye to see
8   the majesty of my discipline.

SANJAYA:
O King, saying this, Krishna,
the great lord of discipline,
revealed to Arjuna
9   the true majesty of his form.

It was a multiform, wondrous vision,
with countless mouths and eyes
and celestial ornaments,
10   brandishing many divine weapons.

Everywhere was boundless divinity
containing all astonishing things,
wearing divine garlands and garments,
11   anointed with divine perfume.

If the light of a thousand suns
were to rise in the sky at once,
it would be like the light
12   of that great spirit.

Arjuna saw all the universe
in its many ways and parts,
standing as one in the body
13   of the god of gods. [...]
[ARJUNA]:
I bow to you,
I prostrate my body,
I beg you to be gracious,
Worshipful Lord—
as a father to a son,
a friend to a friend,
a lover to a beloved,
44   O God, bear with me.

I am thrilled,
and yet my mind
trembles with fear
at seeing
what has not been seen before.
Show me, God, the form I know—
be gracious, Lord of Gods,
45   Shelter of the World.

I want to see you
as before,
with your crown and mace,
and the discus in your hand.
O Thousand-Armed God,
assume the four-armed form[30]
embodied
46   in your totality.
LORD KRISHNA:
To grace you, Arjuna,
I revealed
through self-discipline
my higher form,
which no one but you
has ever beheld—
brilliant, total,
47   boundless, primal.

---

[30] **the four-armed form:** Having seen a vision of divinity in its totality, Arjuna asks Krishna to return to his form as Vishnu, a four-armed god.

Not through sacred lore
or sacrificial ritual
or study or charity,
not by rites
or by terrible penances
can I be seen in this form
in the world of men
48   by anyone but you, Great Hero.

Do not tremble
or suffer confusion
from seeing
my horrific form;
your fear dispelled,
your mind full of love,
see my form again
49   as it was.

SANJAYA:
Saying this to Arjuna,
Krishna once more
revealed
his intimate form;
resuming his gentle body,
the great spirit
let the terrified hero
50   regain his breath.

ARJUNA:
Seeing your gentle human form,
Krishna, I recover
my own nature,
51   and my reason is restored.

LORD KRISHNA:
This form you have seen
is rarely revealed;
the gods are constantly craving
52   for a vision of this form.

Not through sacred lore,
penances, charity, or sacrificial rites
can I be seen in the form
53   that you saw me.

By devotion alone
can I, as I really am,
be known and seen
54   and entered into, Arjuna.

Acting only for me, intent on me,
   free from attachment,
   hostile to no creature, Arjuna,
55   a man of devotion comes to me.

FROM

THE EIGHTEENTH TEACHING:
THE WONDROUS DIALOGUE CONCLUDES

[...]
Better to do one's own duty imperfectly
   than to do another man's well;
   doing action intrinsic to his being,
   a man avoids guilt.

Arjuna, a man should not relinquish
   action he is born to, even if it is flawed;
   all undertakings are marred by a flaw,
   as fire is obscured by smoke.

His understanding everywhere detached,
10   the self mastered, longing gone,
   one finds through renunciation
   the supreme success beyond action.

Understand in summary from me
   how when he achieves success
   one attains the infinite spirit,
   the highest state of knowledge.

Armed with his purified understanding,
   subduing the self with resolve,
   relinquishing sensuous objects,
20   avoiding attraction and hatred;

Observing solitude, barely eating,
   restraining speech, body, and mind;
   practicing discipline in meditation,
   cultivating dispassion;

Freeing himself from individuality, force,
   pride, desire, anger, acquisitiveness;
   unpossessive, tranquil,
   he is at one with the infinite spirit.

Being at one with the infinite spirit,
serene in himself, he does not grieve or crave;
impartial toward all creatures,
he achieves supreme devotion to me.

Through devotion he discerns me,
just who and how vast I really am;
and knowing me in reality,
he enters into my presence.

Always performing all actions,
taking refuge in me,
he attains through my grace
the eternal place beyond change.

Through reason, renounce all works
in me, focus on me;
relying on the discipline of understanding,
always keep me in your thought.

If I am in your thought, by my grace
you will transcend all dangers;
but if you are deafened
by individuality, you will be lost.

Your resolve is futile
if a sense of individuality
makes you think, "I shall not fight" —
nature will compel you to.

You are bound by your own action,
intrinsic to your being, Arjuna;
even against your will you must do
what delusion now makes you refuse.

Arjuna, the lord resides
in the heart of all creatures,
making them reel magically,
as if a machine moved them.

With your whole being, Arjuna,
take refuge in him alone —
from his grace you will attain
the eternal place that is peace.
[...]

The Good Life

In contemporary times, the good life has been associated with material things like money, houses, and cars; it also has been linked to success and power. When religions speak of the good life, however, they tend to stress spiritual attributes like peace of mind, hope, love, and compassion. All religions and ancient philosophies address what it means to live the good life and what one's chief aim in life should be. Some look to external, physical rewards, others to an inner state of being associated with the spirit or the soul. Some prophets spoke of eternal reward or punishment and how each was precipitated by one's beliefs and actions in this life. The sacred Indian text the p. 922 **Bhagavad Gita** teaches that the ultimate reward for doing one's duty is transcending ordinary, mortal life and unifying with Brahman. In contrast, the traditional view of the good life in the wisdom tradition of the ancient Near East focused on the benefits of a life of hard work and good fortune, like riches, a long life, a faithful wife, and children who would care for their parents in old age. The root definition of *prosperity* includes both the notion of wealth and the idea of destiny or fate; this double meaning also applies to the word *fortune.* Ancient peoples clearly recognized that individuals were not entirely in control of their lives, that, in fact, there were larger forces at work influencing one's existence, no matter how clever or diligent the individual.

p. 955 The selection from the *Katha Upanishad* represents the ancient wisdom tradition of India. In Western terminology, the underlying teaching of the Upanishads—a collection of spiritual essays—is that the good life is first and primarily a rapprochement with God, but not God in the sense of a father figure residing somewhere in

**Playing Cithara,
first century**
*For some cultures and
religions the good life
meant material
comforts but for
others spiritual needs
were more important.
From this fresco,
painted at the height
of the Roman Empire,
one might assume
that the good life
for these women
consisted of a certain
earthy pleasure in
relaxing, and in
listening to and
playing music.
(The Art Archive/
Archaeological
Museum, Naples/
Dagli Orti (A))*

p. 957

the heavens. In the Upanishads, God is the underlying spiritual condition—the "god-ness"—of all creation; individuals connect with this God, Brahman, through the personal discovery of their own divine nature, deep within the self.

In *The Persian Wars,* the Greek historian Herodotus offers another view of the good life, one based on external measures. He describes an incident involving a wise man named Solon, Athens' ruler in the sixth century B.C.E. Solon adopted the traditional position on the good life by linking it with prosperity: "health, freedom from trouble, fine children, and good looks." But he acknowledged that destiny can reverse a person's good fortune at any time and concluded that life's happiness could be measured only in retrospect, at the time of death.

A third concept of the good life comes from ancient China and the teachings of Confucius in the sixth century B.C.E. Confucius developed an ethics of duty that wove together all classes and members of society. For Confucius the good life was synonymous with conforming to an ethical code, like being a good citizen, obeying laws, holding a job, and providing for one's family and the common good. The focus was not one's state of mind or the accumulation of wealth but rather how one performed one's role in the essential relationships of family, public life, and governance.

Various teachers and prophets—Eastern *and* Western—have shifted attention away from social values and material goods to individual spiritual consciousness and a simple, unadorned life—in Buddhist terms, an ethic of nonattachment to external realities. Greek philosophers in the fourth century B.C.E. attempted to separate "the good life" from politics, economics, and the wiles of fortune when the democratic *POLIS* in Athens collapsed after being defeated by Sparta in the Peloponnesian War in 404 B.C.E. Greek philosophers advocated turning inward; individuals must determine for themselves the best system for leading the good life.

Aristotle, the great classifier in Greek philosophy, used a rational system for determining the end or goal of morality or goodness. He argued that one must determine the ultimate purpose or highest good for a human being, that which distinguishes humans from other creatures. The next step involves establishing criteria for evaluating whether a human is indeed exercising this purpose in his or her life. For Aristotle, the highest good was the exercise of reason; the question then becomes how one then uses reason to lead a virtuous life. Moral virtue consists in developing a rational attitude in all spheres of one's life, which ultimately means seeking the mean between extremes—living a life of moderation.

p. 966

Two other influential moral philosophies arose in Greece from the rather desperate social situation: EPICURIANISM and STOICISM. Epicurus concludes in **"Letter to a Friend"** that the measure of the good life is the experience of pleasure and the avoidance of pain. This principle has often been misinterpreted as the self-indulgent pursuit of pleasure at any cost, an attitude more properly labeled "hedonism." Such pleasure-seeking can result in extremely painful consequences. In contrast, Epicurus promoted a simple life, conquering one's desires through self-discipline and creating community through friendship; by avoiding pain and fear, a person would gain the lasting pleasures, what Epicurus called the "sweetness of life."

Zeno developed the philosophy of Stoicism toward the end of the fourth century B.C.E. It received its name from the *stoa*, or colonnade, in Athens under which Zeno taught. The foundation of Zeno's thought was the belief that there is an overall rational purpose to life that is revealed in nature, or Nature. A person's task, therefore, is to assess one's own life and then discover how to conform to Nature. With an emphasis on duty and the overall purpose of the cosmos, Stoicism was the most adaptable of Greek philosophies to the Roman world. Cicero, the eminent orator and statesman, was one of the Romans who espoused Stoicism; **Marcus Aurelius**—Roman emperor and Stoic philosopher—weighed the attractions of wealth and power against individual conscience. His ***Meditations*** is a kind of spiritual diary in which he explores the dimensions of the virtuous life and the purpose of reality.

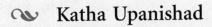

❧ THE UPANISHADS
INDIA, NINTH CENTURY–FIRST CENTURY B.C.E.

Similar to the hierarchy of faculties in Plato's philosophy, which stretches from the physical to the mental, the selection from the Katha Upanishad proposes a hierarchy from bodily senses to Atman. In Hinduism, Atman is the eternal, imperishable essence within each individual. It is roughly equivalent to the concept of the "soul" in Christianity, but it is identical to Brahman on the cosmic level, which represents absolute consciousness. Atman is therefore somewhat closer to the idea of "godness" within. In the first line of the excerpt, it is clear that Atman is the divine passenger, the "Lord" of the chariot, but not its driver. The goal of life is not to repress or control the desires or appetites of the body, the "wild horses" so to speak, but to become "one" with them, to bring them into harmony with the higher faculties. Only "right understanding," complete integration of the various aspects of the human being, can lead to escaping the endless cycle of reincarnation.

FROM

❧ Katha Upanishad

Translated by Juan Mascaró

[DRIVING THE CHARIOT]

Know the Atman as Lord of a chariot; and the body as the chariot itself. Know that reason is the charioteer; and the mind indeed is the reins.

The horses, they say, are the senses; and their paths are the objects of sense. When the soul becomes one with the mind and the senses he is called "one who has joys and sorrows."

He who has not right understanding and whose mind is never steady is not the ruler of his life, like a bad driver with wild horses.

But he who has right understanding and whose mind is ever steady[1] is the ruler of his life, like a good driver with well-trained horses.

He who has not right understanding, is careless and never pure, reaches not the End of the journey; but wanders on from death to death.

But he who has understanding, is careful and ever pure, reaches the End of the journey, from which he never returns.

The man whose chariot is driven by reason, who watches and holds the reins of his mind, reaches the End of the journey,[2] the supreme everlasting Spirit.

Beyond the senses are their objects, and beyond the objects is the mind. Beyond the mind is pure reason, and beyond reason is the Spirit in man.

Beyond the Spirit in man is the Spirit of the universe, and beyond is Purusha,[3] the Spirit Supreme. Nothing is beyond Purusha: He is the End of the path.

The light of the Atman, the Spirit, is invisible, concealed in all beings. It is seen by the seers of the subtle, when their vision is keen and is clear.

The wise should surrender speech in mind, mind in the knowing self, the knowing self in the Spirit of the universe, and the Spirit of the universe in the Spirit of peace.

Awake, arise! Strive for the Highest, and be in the Light! Sages say the path is narrow and difficult to tread, narrow as the edge of a razor.

The Atman is beyond sound and form, without touch and taste and perfume. It is eternal, unchangeable, and without beginning or end: indeed above reasoning. When consciousness of the Atman manifests itself, man becomes free from the jaws of death.

The wise who can learn and can teach this ancient story of Nachiketas, taught by Yama, the god of death, finds glory in the world of Brahman.

He who, filled with devotion, recites this supreme mystery at the gathering of Brahmins, or at the ceremony of the Sradha[4] for the departed, prepares for Eternity, he prepares in truth for Eternity.

---

[1] steady: One's ordinary "mind" tends to jump around, from this to that; steadiness of mind can be achieved through meditation and the various yoga practices.

[2] the End of the journey: The ultimate goal of life is *nirvana:* the extinction of the individual and the ultimate merging with Brahman.

[3] Purusha: The cosmic being out of which the cosmos was created; it is not clear how Purusha is essentially different from Brahman, the ultimate, imperishable being.

[4] the Sradha: The faithful; those who believe and trust.

HERODOTUS
GREECE, C. 480–C. 425 B.C.E.

The Greek historian Herodotus is famous for including personal anecdotes in his writings. In this piece he describes the meeting in 594 B.C.E.
between Solon, the father of Athenian democracy, and Croesus, the king
of Lydia. After instituting democratic reforms in Athens, Solon traveled
to various foreign countries while Athens attempted to conduct itself
according to his new program. Since Solon was reputedly a wise man—
indeed, one of the ancient sages—Croesus, after showing Solon his
wealth, asked the sage to name the happiest man he had ever met. Solon's
reply echoes the wisdom tradition of the ancient Near East, namely that
the good life is measured by earthly abundance: a faithful wife, healthy
and abundant children to care for you in old age, material wealth, and
longevity. But, Solon cautions, these "blessings," finally, cannot be as-
sessed until someone has actually died, since Destiny can intervene at any
moment to destroy a person's reputation and belongings. Croesus, therefore, was not Solon's first choice since Croesus was still alive and subject
to the unknowable designs of Fate.

> He who unites the
> greatest number of
> advantages, and
> retaining them to the
> day of his death, then
> dies peaceably, that
> man alone, sire, is,
> in my judgment,
> entitled to bear the
> name of "happy."
> – HERODOTUS

FROM

The Persian Wars

Translated by George Rawlinson

[SOLON ON HAPPINESS]

When all these conquests had been added to the Lydian empire, and the prosperity
of Sardis was now at its height, there came thither, one after another, all the sages of
Greece living at the time, and among them Solon, the Athenian. He was on his travels, having left Athens to be absent ten years, under the pretense of wishing to see the
world, but really to avoid being forced to repeal any of the laws which, at the request
of the Athenians, he had made for them. Without his sanction the Athenians could
not repeal them, as they had bound themselves under a heavy curse to be governed
for ten years by the laws which should be imposed on them by Solon.

On this account, as well as to see the world, Solon set out upon his travels, in the
course of which he went to Egypt to the court of Amasis, and also came on a visit to
Croesus at Sardis. Croesus received him as his guest, and lodged him in the royal
palace. On the third or fourth day after, he bade his servants conduct Solon over his
treasuries, and show him all their greatness and magnificence. When he had seen
them all, and, so far as time allowed, inspected them, Croesus addressed this question
to him. "Stranger of Athens, we have heard much of thy wisdom and of thy travels

957

through many lands, from love of knowledge and a wish to see the world. I am curious therefore to inquire of thee, whom, of all the men that thou hast seen, thou deemest the most happy?" This he asked because he thought himself the happiest of mortals: but Solon answered him without flattery, according to his true sentiments, "Tellus of Athens, sire." Full of astonishment at what he heard, Croesus demanded sharply, "And wherefore dost thou deem Tellus happiest?" To which the other replied, "First, because his country was flourishing in his days, and he himself had sons both beautiful and good, and he lived to see children born to each of them, and these children all grew up; and further because, after a life spent in what our people look upon as comfort, his end was surpassingly glorious. In a battle between the Athenians and their neighbors near Eleusis,[1] he came to the assistance of his countrymen, routed the foe, and died upon the field most gallantly. The Athenians gave him a public funeral on the spot where he fell, and paid him the highest honors."

Thus did Solon admonish Croesus by the example of Tellus, enumerating the manifold particulars of his happiness. When he had ended, Croesus inquired a second time, who after Tellus seemed to him the happiest, expecting that at any rate, he would be given the second place. "Cleobis and Bito," Solon answered; "they were of Argive race; their fortune was enough for their wants, and they were besides endowed with so much bodily strength that they had both gained prizes at the Games. Also this tale is told of them: — There was a great festival in honor of the goddess Hera at Argos, to which their mother must needs be taken in a car.[2] Now the oxen did not come home from the field in time: so the youths, fearful of being too late, put the yoke on their own necks, and themselves drew the car in which their mother rode. Five and forty furlongs[3] did they draw her, and stopped before the temple. This deed of theirs was witnessed by the whole assembly of worshipers, and then their life closed in the best possible way. Herein, too, God showed forth most evidently, how much better a thing for man death is than life. For the Argive men, who stood around the car, extolled the vast strength of the youths; and the Argive women extolled the mother who was blessed with such a pair of sons; and the mother herself, overjoyed at the deed and at the praises it had won, standing straight before the image, besought the goddess to bestow on Cleobis and Bito, the sons who had so mightily honored her, the highest blessing to which mortals can attain. Her prayer ended, they offered sacrifice and partook of the holy banquet, after which the two youths fell asleep in the temple. They never woke more, but so passed from the earth. The Argives, looking on them as among the best of men, caused statues of them to be made, which they gave to the shrine at Delphi."

When Solon had thus assigned these youths the second place, Croesus broke in angrily, "What, stranger of Athens, is my happiness, then, so utterly set at nought by thee, that thou dost not even put me on a level with private men?"

---

[1] **Eleusis:** A small town some fifteen miles northwest of Athens; home of the Eleusinian Mysteries, the most famous mysteries of the ancient Mediterranean world, which used the story of Demeter and Persephone as the pathway to happiness in the afterlife.

[2] **car:** Chariot.

[3] **furlongs:** A furlong is one-eighth of a mile, or 220 yards.

"Oh! Croesus," replied the other, "thou askedst a question concerning the condition of man, of one who knows that the power above us is full of jealousy, and fond of troubling our lot. A long life gives one to witness much, and experience much oneself, that one would not choose. Seventy years I regard as the limit of the life of man. In these seventy years are contained, without reckoning intercalary[4] months, twenty-five thousand and two hundred days. Add an intercalary month to every other year, that the seasons may come round at the right time, and there will be, besides the seventy years, thirty-five such months, making an addition of one thousand and fifty days. The whole number of the days contained in the seventy years will thus be twenty-six thousand two hundred and fifty, whereof not one but will produce events unlike the rest. Hence man is wholly accident. For thyself, oh! Croesus, I see that thou art wonderfully rich, and art the lord of many nations; but with respect to that whereon thou questionest me, I have no answer to give, until I hear that thou hast closed thy life happily. For assuredly he who possesses great store of riches is no nearer happiness than he who has what suffices for his daily needs, unless it so hap that luck attend upon him, and so he continue in the enjoyment of all his good things to the end of life. For many of the wealthiest men have been unfavored of fortune, and many whose means were moderate have had excellent luck. Men of the former class excel those of the latter but in two respects; these last excel the former in many. The wealthy man is better able to content his desires, and to bear up against a sudden buffet of calamity. The other has less ability to withstand these evils (from which, however, his good luck keeps him clear), but he enjoys all these following blessings: he is whole of limb, a stranger to disease, free from misfortune, happy in his children, and comely to look upon. If, in addition to all this, he end his life well, he is of a truth the man of whom thou art in search, the man who may rightly be termed happy. Call him, however, until he die, not happy but fortunate. Scarcely, indeed, can any man unite all these advantages: as there is no country which contains within it all that it needs, but each, while it possesses some things, lacks others, and the best country is that which contains the most; so no single human being is complete in every respect—something is always lacking. He who unites the greatest number of advantages, and retaining them to the day of his death, then dies peaceably, that man alone, sire, is, in my judgment, entitled to bear the name of 'happy.' But in every matter it behoves[5] us to mark well the end: for oftentimes God gives men a gleam of happiness, and then plunges them into ruin."

Such was the speech which Solon addressed to Croesus, a speech which brought him neither largess[6] nor honor. The king saw him depart with much indifference, since he thought that a man must be an arrant fool who made no account of present good, but bade men always wait and mark the end.

---

[4] **intercalary:** *Intercalary* refers to periods of time added to the regular calendar to equal one solar year. A solar year takes 365 days, five hours, forty-eight minutes, and forty-six seconds, or one revolution of the earth around the sun.

[5] **behoves:** To be necessary.

[6] **largess:** A generous gift.

✺ CONFUCIUS
CHINA, C. 551–C. 479 B.C.E.

Confucius's body of sayings, *The Analects,* so instrumental in shaping Chinese society for more than 2,000 years, are primarily concerned with morality: how to act in society. Like the Buddha in India, Confucius did not seem concerned with explaining the nature of god or the workings of the cosmos. In the following selection of sayings grouped under the subject of "Goodness," Confucius downplays the importance of characteristics like cleverness and pretension, traits that might distinguish an individual from a crowd, and recommends qualities that edify family life and, consequently, help one to fit into all groups beyond the family. The hierarchy of dutiful relationships within the family provides the model, according to Confucianism, on which society itself might be structured.

In this Arthur Waley translation, the Chinese word *xiao,* whose Chinese written character is made up of the symbol for "old" over the symbol for "the child," implying a younger person paying respect and honor to his or her elders, is rendered as *filial piety.* Similar to the connotation of *piety* in the West, where the word is linked to religious practices, *xiao* was originally associated with the prayers and offerings of ancestor worship. Only later was *xiao* connected with living parents; nevertheless, it would seem that some of the religious overtones of ancestor worship were transferred to attitudes toward parents.

The continuous focus in these Confucius sayings is on pleasing other people. The final imperative is a version of the "golden rule," which shows up some five centuries later in the teachings of Jesus of Nazareth (Matthew 7:12; Luke 6:31): Treat others as you would have them treat you. (For more information about Confucius, see p. 000.)

FROM

✺ The Analects

Translated by Arthur Waley

[ON GOODNESS]

Book I

3   The Master said, 'Clever talk and a pretentious manner' are seldom found in the Good.

4   Master Tsêng[1] said, Every day I examine myself on these three points: in acting on behalf of others, have I always been loyal to their interests? In intercourse with my

---

[1] **Master Tsêng:** A disciple of Confucius who was important to the early development of Confucianism.

friends, have I always been true to my word? Have I failed to repeat the precepts that have been handed down to me?

6   The Master said, A young man's duty is to behave well to his parents at home and to his elders abroad, to be cautious in giving promises and punctual in keeping them, to have kindly feelings towards everyone, but seek the intimacy of the Good. If, when all that is done, he has any energy to spare, then let him study the polite arts.[2]

Book IV

3, 4 Of the adage 'Only a Good Man knows how to like people, knows how to dislike them,' the Master said, He whose heart is in the smallest degree set upon Goodness will dislike no one.

6   The Master said, I for my part have never yet seen one who really cared for Goodness, nor one who really abhorred wickedness. One who really cared for Goodness would never let any other consideration come first. One who abhorred wickedness would be so constantly doing Good that wickedness would never have a chance to get at him. Has anyone ever managed to do Good with his whole might even as long as the space of a single day? I think not. Yet I for my part have never seen anyone give up such an attempt because he had not the *strength* to go on. It may well have happened, but I for my part have never seen it.[3]

Book XII

3   Ssu-ma Niu asked about Goodness. The Master said, The Good (*jên*) man is chary (*jên*) of speech. Ssu-ma Niu said, So that is what is meant by Goodness — to be chary of speech? The Master said, Seeing that the doing of it is so difficult, how can one be otherwise than chary of talking about it?[4]

---

[2] **the polite arts:** To recite texts, and to practice archery and manners.

[3] **because he had . . . seen it:** It is the will not the way that is wanting. (Translator's note.)

[4] **The Good . . . about it?:** He first puns on *jên,* "chary," and *jên,* "goodness"; and then in his second reply answers as though his first reply had meant "Goodness is a thing one ought to be chary of talking about." The implication is that the questioner had not yet reached a stage at which the mysteries of *jên* could be revealed to him. (Translator's note.)

∾ ARISTOTLE
GREECE, 384–322 B.C.E.

> With his analysis of the nature of goodness, Aristotle wanted to deter-
> mine what is the essential nature of a human being, and then he wanted
> to provide criteria for valuation: that is, the means for assessing the best
> use of that human capacity to achieve a desirable end. For example, the
> essential nature of a pruning hook is to clip branches and vines; a good
> pruning hook (valuation) cuts easily and well; a bad one breaks or cuts
> poorly. A human's distinctive virtue is the ability to reason, and there are
> two ways to exercise reason: (1) contemplation, knowing for the sake of
> knowing, and (2) deliberation, knowing for the sake of doing or acting.
> Excellence in contemplative reason is found in developing one's ability to
> reason through the study of philosophy, history, science, and literature.
> Excellence in deliberative reason is measured by one's actions; that is,
> moral virtue is determined by one's ability to adopt a rational attitude in
> all spheres of life. Whether it is a question of curbing one's appetites or
> impulses, controlling anger, or renouncing desires for possessions or
> fame, the guiding principle is seeking the mean between extremes. Virtue
> consists in moderation in all things. (For more discussion of Aristotle, see
> page 000.)

FROM

∾ The Nicomachean Ethics

Translated by Philip Wheelwright

[THE DOCTRINE OF THE MEAN]

Differentia of moral virtue: doctrine of the mean

The virtue, or excellence, of anything must be acknowledged to have a twofold
effect on the thing to which it belongs: it renders the thing itself good, and causes it
to perform its function well. The excellence of the eye, for instance, makes both the
eye and its work good, for it is by the excellence of the eye that we see well. Likewise
the proper excellence of horse at once makes a particular horse what he should be,
and also makes him good at running and at carrying his rider and at facing the
enemy. Hence, if this is universally true, the virtue or proper excellence of man will
be just that formed disposition which both makes him good and enables him to perform his function well. We have already indicated how this is accomplished; but we
may clarify the matter by examining wherein the nature of virtue consists.

Of everything that is both continuous and divisible it is possible to take a
greater, a less, or an equal amount; and this may be true either objectively with

respect to the thing in question or else relatively to ourselves. By equal I denote that which is a mean between excess and deficiency. By the objective mean I denote that which is equidistant from both extremes, and this will always be the same for everybody. By the mean that is relative to ourselves I denote that which is neither too much nor too little, and this is not one and the same for everybody. For instance, if ten is many and two is few, then six is the mean considered in terms of the object; for it exceeds and is exceeded by the same amount, and is therefore the mean of an arithmetical proportion. But the mean considered relatively to ourselves cannot be determined so simply: if ten pounds of food is too much for a certain man to eat and two pounds is too little, it does not follow that the trainer will prescribe six pounds, for this may be too much or too little for the man in question—too little for Milo the wrestler, too much for the novice at athletics. This is equally true of running and wrestling.

So it is that an expert in any field avoids excess and deficiency, and seeks and chooses the mean—that is, not the objective mean, but the mean relatively to himself. If, then, every sort of skill perfects its work in this way, by observing the mean and bringing its work up to this standard (which is the reason why people say of a good work of art that nothing could be either taken from it or added to it, implying that excellence is destroyed by excess or deficiency but is preserved by adherence to the mean; and good artists, we say, observe this standard in their work), and if furthermore virtue, like nature, is more exact and better than any art, it follows that virtue will have the property of aiming at the mean. I am speaking, of course, of moral virtue, for it is moral virtue that has to do with feelings and actions, and it is in respect of these that excess, deficiency, and moderation are possible. That is to say, we can feel fear, confidence, desire, anger, pity, and in general pleasure and pain, either too much or too little, and in either case not well; but to feel them at the right times, with reference to the right objects, toward the right people, with the right motive, and in the right manner, is to strike the mean, and therein to follow the best course—a mark of virtue. And in the same way our outward acts admit of excess, deficiency, and the proper mean. Now virtue has to do with feelings and also with outward acts; in both of these excess and deficiency are regarded as faults and are blamed, while a moderate amount is both praised and regarded as right—palpable signs of virtue. Virtue, then, is a kind of moderation, in that it aims at the mean. This conclusion is further confirmed by the fact that while there are numerous ways in which we can go wrong (for evil, according to the Pythagorean[1] figure of speech, belongs to the class of the unlimited, good to that of the limited), there is only one way of going right. That is why the one is easy, the other hard—easy to miss the mark, but hard to hit it. And this offers further evidence that excess and deficiency are characteristic of vice while hitting the mean is characteristic of virtue: "for good is simple, badness manifold."

---

[1] **Pythagorean:** Pythagoras (sixth century B.C.E.), a brilliant mathematician and philosopher, founded a spiritual order centered on the transmigration of souls.

We may conclude, then, that virtue is an habitual disposition with respect to choice, the characteristic quality of which is moderation judged relatively to ourselves according to a determinate principle, *i.e.*, according to such a principle as a man of insight would use. The quality of moderation belongs to virtue in a double sense: as falling between two vices, the one of which consists in excess, the other in deficiency; and also in the sense that while these vices respectively fall short of and exceed the proper standard both of feelings and of actions, virtue both finds and chooses the mean. Hence, in respect of its essence and according to the definition of its basic nature, virtue is a state of moderation; but regarded in its relation to what is best and right it is an extreme.

Accordingly it is not every action nor every feeling to which the principle of the mean is applicable. There are some whose very names imply badness: *e.g.*, malevolence, shamelessness, envy, and among actions, adultery, theft, and murder. These and everything else like them are condemned as being bad in themselves and not merely when in excess or deficiency. To do right in performing them is therefore impossible; their performance is always wrong. Rightness or wrongness in any of them (*e.g.*, in adultery) does not depend on the rightness or wrongness of person and occasion and manner, but on the bare fact of doing it at all. It would be absurd to distinguish moderation, excess, and deficiency in action that is unjust or cowardly or profligate; for we should then have moderation of excess and deficiency, excess of excess, and deficiency of deficiency. The truth of the matter is that just as there can be no excess and deficiency of temperance and courage (for the proper mean is, in its own way, an extreme), so these opposite kinds of conduct likewise do not admit of moderation, excess, and deficiency: they are always wrong, no matter how they are done.

Difficulty of attaining the mean

We have now sufficiently shown that moral virtue consists in observance of a mean, and in what sense this is so: in the sense, namely, of holding a middle position between two vices, one of which involves excess and the other deficiency, and also in the sense of being the kind of a disposition which aims at the middle point both in feelings and in actions. This being the case, it is a hard thing to be good, for it is hard to locate the mean in particular instances; just as to locate the mean point (*i.e.*, the center) of a circle is not a thing that everybody can do, but only the man of science. So, too, anyone can get angry—that is easy—or spend money or give it away; but to do all this to the right person, to the right extent, at the right time, with the right motive, and in the right manner, is not a thing that everyone can do, and is not easy; and that is why good conduct is at once rare and praiseworthy and noble.

Accordingly, whoever aims at the mean should first of all strive to avoid that extreme which is more opposed to it, as in Calypso's advice to "keep the ship well clear of that foaming surf."[2] For of the two extremes one will be more of an evil, the

---

[2] "Keep . . . surf": Advice given by Circe (Kirkê), not Calypso (Kalypso), to Odysseus to minimize loss of men: steer your boat closer to the monster Scylla (Skylla) than the whirlpool Charybdis (Kharybdis). (Homer's *The Odyssey*, Book 12)

other less; therefore, as it is hard to hit the exact mean, we ought to choose the lesser of the two evils and sail, as the saying goes, in the second best way, and this is accomplished most successfully in the manner stated. But we must bear in mind as well the errors to which we personally are prone. These will be different for different individuals, and each may discover them in his own case by noting the occasions on which he feels pleasure or pain. Having discovered them, let him bend himself in the opposite direction; for by steering wide of error we shall strike a middle course, as warped timber is straightened by bending it backwards. Especially and in all cases we must guard against pleasure and what is pleasant, because we cannot estimate it impartially. Hence we ought to feel toward pleasure as the elders of the people felt toward Helen, and on every occasion repeat their saying;[3] for if we dismiss pleasure thus we are less likely to go wrong.

---

[3] saying: "A goddess the woman is to look at. Ah, but still, still, even so, being all that she is, let her go in the ships and take her scourge from us and from our children." (Homer's *The Iliad,* Book 3, lines 132–136)

ᕈ EPICURUS
GREECE, C. 341–270 B.C.E.

Epicurus was born on the island of Samos and taught in Asia Minor before going to Athens in 306 b.c.e., where his followers gave him the Garden — his home and his school, equivalent in some respects to Plato's Academy and Aristotle's Lyceum. Residing in the Garden, Epicurus taught his philosophy and created a religious community of **Epicureans**, which included slaves and women as well as philosophers. They lived a simple, healthy life, avoiding both meat and wine, with the goal of "securing the health of the body and tranquillity of the soul."

eh-pih-KYOO-ree-uns

Epicurus's mature teachings about enduring hardship and travail and his search for the possibilities of happiness in a troubled world apparently resulted from a childhood filled with poverty, suffering, and poor health. The key idea in Epicurus's teachings is that the basis of all knowledge is sensation; the mind is responsible for interpreting sensations and choosing actions that cause sensations of pleasure as opposed to those that cause pain to both the mind and the body. This means that an individual must learn to assess the consequences of actions, since a short-term pleasure might cause long-term pain. It is also necessary to differentiate between lasting and temporal pleasures, and between mental and bodily pleasures in order to make sensible choices. In his "Letter to a Friend," Epicurus does not advocate pursuing pleasures of the body that might be fleeting and that might result, finally, in pain. Rather he

Greek Bathing and Hunting Scene

Epicurean philosophy promoted not only the soundness of the mind but also the soundness and health of the physical body. (The Art Archive/ Bibliothèque des Arts Decoratifs, Paris/ Dagli Orti (A))

yoo-digh-MOH-nee-uh

counsels one to seek the condition denoted by the Greek words *ataraxia*, meaning "serenity," and **eudaemonia**, meaning "happiness" or "well-being." As opposed to the "pleasure of prodigals and sensualists," lasting pleasures are spiritual or psychological.

✺ Letter to a Friend

Translated by Philip Wheelwright

We must consider that of desires some are natural, others empty; that of the natural some are necessary, others not; and that of the necessary some are necessary for happiness, others for bodily comfort, and others for life itself. A right understanding of these facts enables us to direct all choice and avoidance toward securing the health of the body and tranquillity of the soul; this being the final aim of a blessed life. For the aim of all actions is to avoid pain and fear; and when this is once secured for us the tempest of the soul is entirely quelled, since the living animal no longer needs to wander as though in search of something he lacks, hunting for that by which he can fulfill some need of soul or body. We feel a need of pleasure only when we grieve over its absence; when we stop grieving we are in need of pleasure no longer. Pleasure, then, is the beginning and end of the blessed life. For we recognize it as a good which is both primary and kindred to us. From pleasure we begin every act of choice and avoidance; and to pleasure we return again, using the feeling as the standard by which to judge every good.

Now since pleasure is the good that is primary and most natural to us, for that very reason we do not seize all pleasures indiscriminately; on the contrary we often pass over many pleasures, when greater discomfort accrues to us as a result of them.

Similarly we not infrequently judge pains better than pleasures, when the long endurance of a pain yields us a greater pleasure in the end. Thus every pleasure because of its natural kinship to us is good, yet not every pleasure is to be chosen; just as every pain also is an evil, yet that does not mean that all pains are necessarily to be shunned. It is by a scale of comparison and by the consideration of advantages and disadvantages that we must form our judgment on these matters. On particular occasions we may have reason to treat the good as bad, and the bad as good.

Independence of circumstance we regard as a great good: not because we wish to dispense altogether with external advantages, but in order that, if our possessions are few, we may be content with what we have, sincerely believing that those enjoy luxury most who depend on it least, and that natural wants are easily satisfied if we are willing to forego superfluities. Plain fare yields as much pleasure as a luxurious table, provided the pain of real want is removed; bread and water can give exquisite delight to hungry and thirsty lips. To form the habit of a simple and modest diet, therefore, is the way to health: it enables us to perform the needful employments of life without shrinking, it puts us in better condition to enjoy luxuries when they are offered, and it renders us fearless of fortune.

Accordingly, when we argue that pleasure is the end and aim of life, we do not mean the pleasure of prodigals and sensualists, as some of our ignorant or prejudiced critics persist in mistaking us. We mean the pleasure of being free from pain of body and anxiety of mind. It is not a continual round of drunken debauches and lecherous delights, nor the enjoyment of fish and other delicacies of a wealthy table, which produce a pleasant life; but sober reasoning, searching out the motives of choice and avoidance, and escaping the bondage of opinion, to which the greatest disturbances of spirit are due.

The first step and the greatest good is prudence—a more precious thing than philosophy even, for all the other virtues are sprung from it. By prudence we learn that we can live pleasurably only if we live prudently, honorably, and justly, while contrariwise to live prudently, honorably, and justly guarantees a life that is pleasurable as well. The virtues are by nature bound up with a pleasant life, and a pleasant life is inseparable from them in turn.

Is there any better and wiser man than he who holds reverent beliefs about the gods, is altogether free from the fear of death, and has serenely contemplated the basic tendencies *(telê)* of natural law? Such a man understands that the limit of good things is easy to attain, and that evils are slight either in duration or in intensity. He laughs at Destiny, which so many accept as all-powerful. Some things, he observes, occur of necessity, others by chance, and still others through our own agency. Necessity is irresponsible, chance is inconstant, but our own actions are free, and it is to them that praise and blame are properly attached. It would be better even to believe the myths about the gods than to submit to the Destiny which the natural philosophers teach. For the old superstitions at least offer some faint hope of placating the gods by worship, but the Necessity of the scientific philosophers is absolutely unyielding. As to chance, the wise man does not deify it as most men do; for if it were divine it would not be without order. Nor will he accept the view that it is a universal cause even though of a wavering kind; for he believes that what chance bestows is not the good and evil that determine a man's blessedness in life, but the starting-points from which each person can arrive at great good or great evil. He esteems the misfortune of the wise above the prosperity of a fool; holding it better that well chosen courses of action should fail than that ill chosen ones should succeed by mere chance.

Meditate on these and like precepts day and night, both privately and with some companion who is of kindred disposition. Thereby shall you never suffer disturbance, waking or asleep, but shall live like a god among men. For a man who lives constantly among immortal blessings is surely more than mortal.

❧ MARCUS AURELIUS
ROME, 121–180 C.E.

> The nobleman Marcus Aurelius was the emperor of Rome for the last two decades of his life, from 161 to 180 C.E. During that time he led his troops into battle against Germanic tribes in northern Europe. The twelve books of his *Meditations* are a kind of spiritual diary addressed to himself about his private, personal existence; they never mention his

Marcus Aurelius,
121–180

The Roman emperor Marcus Aurelius was a great general whose Meditations *reveal a philosophic and introspective nature unusual in such a powerful ruler. (The Art Archive/Museo Capitolino, Rome/ Dagli Orti (A))*

powerful role as emperor. Marcus Aurelius has been praised for saintliness, a devotion to conscience, and selflessness.

In this excerpt from Book XII of *Meditations,* Marcus Aurelius explains a basic tenet of Stoicism: that Nature or the gods have designed a just universe and an appropriate role for each individual to play. Although people cannot control the external world and the uncertainties of Fortune or Destiny, they can control their attitudes, the courage or cowardice with which they face life's challenges. Stoicism did not sweeten its position by promising that virtue would be rewarded in the afterlife; the virtuous life was its own reward. The metaphor of the theater is commonly used in conjunction with Stoicism: everyone is given a part to play in the great cosmic drama. Although the overall plot of the play is vaguely discernable, the particulars of everyday life and the time of the end are unknown. Each individual must act out his or her part in the best way possible, irrespective of life's hardships and ultimate outcome. Another metaphor that is sometimes used is a hand of playing cards: Everyone is dealt a hand of cards, which represents all those qualities, mind and body with which one is born—tall or short, bright or slow, beautiful or plain. What counts in life are not the cards we are dealt—these can't be changed—but how one plays out his or her individual hand. The "good life" results from conforming to one's designated role: guidance is provided by one's *daemon*—one's inner voice or spirit.

FROM

❧ Meditations

Translated by George Long

To Himself

1.   All those things at which you wish to arrive by a circuitous road you can have now, if you do not refuse them to yourself. And this means, if you will take no notice of all the past, and trust the future to providence, and direct the present only conformably to piety and justice. Conformably to piety, that you may be content with the lot which is assigned to you, for nature designed it for you and you for it. Conformably to justice, that you may always speak the truth freely and without disguise, and do the things which are agreeable to law and according to the worth of each. And let neither another man's wickedness hinder you, nor opinion nor voice, nor yet the sensations of the poor flesh which has grown about you; for the passive part will look to this. If then, whatever the time may be when you shall be near to your departure, neglecting everything else you shall respect only your ruling faculty and the divinity within you, and if you shall be afraid not because you must some time cease to live, but if you shall fear never to have begun to live

according to nature—then you will be a man worthy of the universe which has produced you, and you will cease to be a stranger in your native land, and to wonder at things which happen daily as if they were something unexpected, and to be dependent on this or that. [. . .]

3.   The things are three of which you are composed—a little body, a little breath, intelligence. Of these the first two are yours, so far as it is your duty to take care of them; but the third alone is properly yours. Therefore if you shall separate from yourself, that is, from your understanding, whatever others do or say, and whatever you have done or said yourself, and whatever future things trouble you because they may happen, and whatever in the body which envelops you or in the breath which is by nature associated with the body and attached to you independent of your will, and whatever the external circumfluent vortex whirls round, so that the intellectual power exempt from the things of fate can live pure and free by itself, doing what is just and accepting what happens and saying the truth: if you will separate, I say, from this ruling faculty the things which are attached to it by the impressions of sense, and the things of time to come and of time that is past, and will make yourself like Empedocles' sphere,[1]

All round, and in its joyous rest reposing;

and if you shall strive to live only what is really your life, that is, the present—then you will be able to pass that portion of life which remains for you up to the time of your death, free from perturbations, nobly, and obedient to your own daemon.[2] [. . .]

5.   How can it be that the gods after having arranged all things well and benevolently for mankind, have overlooked this alone, that some men and very good men, and men who, as we may say, have had most communion with the divinity, and through pious acts and religious observances have been most intimate with the divinity, when they have once died should never exist again, but should be completely extinguished?

But if this is so, be assured that if it ought to have been otherwise, the gods would have done it. For if it were just, it would also be possible; and if it were according to nature, nature would have had it so. But because it is not so, if in fact it is not so, be convinced that it ought not to have been so. You see even of yourself that in this inquiry you are disputing with the deity; and we should not thus dispute with the gods, unless they were most excellent and most just; but if this is so, they would not have allowed anything in the ordering of the universe to be neglected unjustly and irrationally. [. . .]

---

[1] **Empedocles' sphere:** Empedocles (fifth century B.C.E.) was a Greek philosopher and scientist who conceived of a spherical universe.

[2] **daemon:** The divine guardian spirit within that provides guidance.

36. Man, you have been a citizen in this great world state: what difference does it make to you whether for five years or three? for that which is conformable to the laws is just for all. Where is the hardship then, if no tyrant nor yet an unjust judge sends you away from the state, but nature who brought you into it? the same as if a praetor[3] who has employed an actor dismisses him from the stage. "But I have not finished the five acts, but only three of them." You say well, but in life the three acts are the whole drama; for what shall be a complete drama is determined by him who was once the cause of its composition, and now of its dissolution: but you are the cause of neither. Depart then satisfied, for he also who releases you is satisfied.

---

[3] **praetor:** A ranking magistrate in ancient Rome.

Camel Caravan, fourteenth century *This detail from a fourteenth-century Catalan atlas shows a group of Westerners en route to Cathay (the name by which north China was known at the time) crossing the Ural Mountains of central Russia. The Medieval Period was a time of increasing exploration and travel between the East and West. (Bridgeman Art Library)*

The Medieval and Early Modern World

100 C.E. - 1650

*I*t is customary for European and American historians to distinguish between a medieval and an early modern world, based on political and social history, technology, the growth of trade and commerce, and the progress of whole civilizations. These terms have a European basis, since the word "medieval" (from *medium aevum,* Latin for "middle period") has long served to distinguish the European Middle Ages from the Renaissance. Normally the European Middle Ages are said to have come to an end in the fifteenth century; the Early Modern Period follows. Part Two will address the Medieval Period (100–1450) and Early Modern Period (1450–1650), extending this distinction to other parts of the world as well.

THE MEDIEVAL PERIOD: 100–1450

The term medieval itself means something different for each civilization to which it is applied. In India, the highest civilization in the first through fourteenth centuries existed in the northern capitals during the Gupta dynasty (c. 320–c. 550). During this time, Indian literature was recorded in the court language, Sanskrit, except in the resistant Tamil culture to the south. The medieval period in China

COMPARATIVE TIMELINE FOR THE MEDIEVAL AND EARLY MODERN WORLD

Date	History and Politics	Literature	Science, Culture, and Technology
C.E. **1–500**			c. 30 Death of Jesus
			47 Paul begins preaching.
		65–70 Gospel of Mark	
		85–90 Gospel of Matthew	
		130 Gospel of John	
	220 End of Han dynasty in China		3rd century Sanskrit becomes literary language of India
	265–420 Chin dynasty in (China)		
	313 Emperor Constantine grants Christians protection.		c. 300 Widespread use of paper in China
	c. 320–c. 353 Reign of Chandragupta I in India; Gupta dynasty established.		
	c. 330 Capital of Roman Empire moves to Constantinople	4th century *The Apocalypse of Paul*	c. 350 Buddhism flourishes in China
	c. 376–c. 415 Reign of Chandragupta II in India	c. 376–c. 415 Kalidasa, *Shakuntala and the Ring of Recollection*	365–427 Tao Qian (Tao Ch'ien), Chinese poet
	395 Permanent division of Eastern and Western Roman Empire	c. 400 St. Augustine, *The Confessions*	c. 405 St. Jerome, *Latin Vulgate Bible*
	410 Visigoths sack Rome		
	420–588 China split into Northern and Southern dynasties		425 University of Constantinople founded

began with the collapse of the Han dynasty in 220 and ended with the fall of China to Mongol invaders in the thirteenth century. Within this period the Tang dynasty, which lasted from the seventh to the ninth century, marked the highest point of Chinese civilization. Japan came under extensive Chinese influence in the eighth century but soon built its own national culture through a process of absorption and synthesis. The height of the Japanese achievement during this time occurred during the Heian period (794–1185), followed by a revival during the late Kamakura and early Muromachi periods (fourteenth and fifteenth centuries). The European Middle Ages specifically refers to the period from the late Roman era to the Renaissance, which began in Italy in the thirteenth century and spread north through Europe in the fourteenth and fifteenth centuries. The Islamic world originated with Muhammad in Arabia in the seventh century; its leaders dominated Near Eastern, Middle Eastern, North African, Spanish, and northern Indian politics for hundreds of years. Its greatest periods of cultural vitality were 750–950 during the Abbasid dynasty in Baghdad and the tenth and eleventh centuries during the late Umayyad dynasty in Cordova.

Date	History and Politics	Literature	Science, Culture, and Technology
	480–500 Hun invasions of India	c. 523 Boethius, *The Consolation of Philosophy*	c. 450 Buddhist monastery and university founded in Nalanda
501–700			537 Hagia Sophia Cathedral built in Constantinople.
	550 End of Gupta dynasty in India		552 Buddhism introduced in Japan
	c. 570 Birth of Muhammad		570 Invention of the abacus
	581–617 Sui dynasty reunifies China		583 Ancient city of Chang'an restored by Sui dynasty
	590–604 Pope Gregory the Great; conversion missions in Europe.		590–604 Pope Gregory the Great standardizes plainchants for church services (Gregorian chant)
	618–907 Tang dynasty revival of the arts and culture in China		596–664 Xuangzang, Chinese Buddhist monk
	622 Muhammad flees Mecca to Medina.		622 Founding of Islam
	623 Muslim conquest of Arabia begins.		
	632 Death of Muhammad		

The Expansion of Cultures.   At different times during the Medieval Period, the major civilizations of the world built capital cities of great wealth and influence, including the twin capitals of Ujayyini and Taamralipti in India, Chang'an in China, Heian (Kyoto) in Japan, Constantinople in Asia Minor, Baghdad in ancient Persia, and Cordova in Andalusia (Spain). Trade routes connecting Europe, the Near East, the Middle East, and the Far East were developed, resulting in an exchange of cultures as well as goods. For instance, a collection of popular stories commonly known as *The Thousand and One Nights* was disseminated along the trade routes in the thirteenth and fourteenth centuries, reflecting the cultures of several regions.

The spread of world religions provided some of the original impetus for the expansion of medieval cultures. Classical Buddhism traveled from India to China by the third century and Japan by the sixth century. Christianity was adopted by the late Roman Empire in the fourth century, established an Eastern stronghold in Constantinople in the fourth and fifth centuries, and spread across Europe from the fifth to eighth centuries. The religion of Islam, born in the spiritual and political turmoil of Arabia in the seventh century, was spread by conquest in a

Date	History and Politics	Literature	Science, Culture, and Technology
501–700 (cont.)	633–656 Islamic conquests to East, West, and South	c. 653 Composition of the Qur'an	
	661 Founding of Umayyad dynasty; capital moved from Medina to Damascus		
		fl. 680–700 Kakinomoto Hitomaro, Japanese poet	691 Completion of the Dome of the Rock in Jerusalem
		699–761 Wang Wei, Chinese poet	c. 700 Invention of gunpowder in China
701–900	710 First permanent capital established at Nara in Japan; beginning of Nara period.	701–762 Li Bai, Chinese poet	
	711 Muslim conquest of Andalusia (Spain)		712 *A Record of Ancient Matters*
	712–756 Reign of Tang Xuanzong in China	712–770 Du Fu, Chinese poet	
	714–741 Charles Martel rules Franks.		720 *Chronicles of Japan*
	732 Battle of Tours; farthest extension of Islamic conquests in Europe		
	750 Founding of Abbasid dynasty in Baghdad	750 Ibn Ishaq, *Life of Muhammad*	750 Construction of the city of Baghdad
	755 Revolt of An Lu-shan weakens Tang rule in China	759 *Man'yoshu* anthology	762 New Eastern capital of Islam established in Baghdad

hundred years across the Middle East, North Africa, and the southern fringe of Europe. When Japan came under Chinese influence in the eighth century, the new Japanese culture and the religion of Shinto borrowed heavily from the Chinese while retaining specific native features.

However they developed, the fortunes of medieval civilizations changed rapidly through contact with other religious, political, and cultural forces. This can easily be seen from the vantage point of medieval Europe. Despite its adoption of Christianity, the Roman Empire fell into decline, with Germanic troops increasingly filling the ranks of the Roman legions until finally the entire civilization crumbled. Remnants of the empire survived for several hundred years (fourth to sixth centuries) with foreign invaders holding rival claims to authority. Christianity itself splintered in two: the western church stayed in Rome, spreading the Gospel in Europe through conversion missions, while the Eastern church established itself in Constantinople as part of the Byzantine empire. The Christian crusaders who attempted to dislodge the Muslims from the Holy Land in the twelfth and thirteenth centuries were eventually driven back, succeeding only in regaining Spain for Christian Europe from the eleventh to the fifteenth centuries.

Date	History and Politics		Literature		Science, Culture, and Technology	
701–900 (cont.)	756	Separate Umayyad caliphate in Andalusia				
	780	Charlemagne crowned Holy Roman Emperor	772–846	Bo Juyi, Chinese poet	768–814	Carolingian cultural revival in Europe under Charlemagne
	786–809	Rule of Harun al-Rashid in Baghdad	8th–10th century	*Beowulf* composed	783	Paper made in Baghdad
	794	Japanese capital moves to Heian (Kyoto); beginning of Heian period	9th century	*The Book of Muhammad's Ladder*	c. 800–c. 850	Consolidation of system of Japanese writing
					c. 830	Invention of algebra by Al-Khwarizm, Arab mathematician
	843	Carolingian Empire divided; development of feudalism				
	885	Tang rulers desert Chang'an			c. 900	Muslims introduce cotton and silk industry in Andalusia
901–1100	907	End of Tang dynasty in China; period of local rule	c. 905	*Kokinshu* anthology		
	912–961	Rule of Abd-al-Rahman III in Andalusia			912–961	Construction of Cordova, with its university library

Meanwhile, in the thirteenth century, both Eastern Europe and the remaining Muslim territories were threatened by an onslaught of Mongols from China, but the invaders fell short in their drive for conquest, after which their strength rapidly diminished. Western and Middle Eastern trade relations with Asia, begun well before the Mongol invasion, continued. Although the Black Death decimated the world's population by as much as a third in the mid fourteenth century, the expansion and development of the world's cultures continued.

"The World" in the Medieval Period.   Despite whatever knowledge they had acquired through historic migration, accidental discoveries, and organized expeditions, educated Europeans, people from the Near and Far East, and North Africans of the Medieval Period had no comprehensive understanding of the true dimensions of the world and the make-up of its inhabitants. (Icelanders had sailed west to the edges of Newfoundland in the fourteenth century, but their attempts at colonization along the coastline failed.) Even some of the known areas of the world, such as sub-Saharan Africa and northern Russia, were so isolated by weather and forbidding geographical features that they were hardly visited by

Date	History and Politics	Literature	Science, Culture, and Technology
901–1100 (cont.)	960–1279 Sung dynasty reunifies China	late 10th century *Beowulf* written in Anglo-Saxon 994–1064 Ibn Hazm, poet and philosopher	980–1037 Ibn Sina (Avicenna), Islamic philosopher
	c. 1000 Leif Ericson visits North America	c. 1000 Murasaki Shikibu, *The Tale of Genji* Sei Shonagon, *The Pillow Book*	
	1002 Dissolution of caliphate of Cordova	c. 1004–1070 Ibn Zaydun, poet	
	1013 Cordova sacked by Berbers.		
	c. 1055 Occupation of Baghdad by Seljuk Turks		
	1066 Norman conquest of England	c. 1070–1141 Judah Ha-Levi, poet 1071–1127 Guillaume IX, Duke of Aquitaine, poet	
	1085 Fall of Toledo to Christians; Spanish reconquest begins.		c. 1080 Bayeux tapestry depicts Norman conquest.
	1095 Pope Urban II preaches the First Crusade.		
	1099 Christian sack of Jerusalem	c. 1100 *The Song of Roland*	

outsiders. The *mappai mundi* or world maps of the period, frequently painted on hide or inscribed on vellum, convey both the era's curiosity about the world and its limited geographical knowledge.

Within the known medieval world of Europe, North Africa, the Near East, and the Far East, travel and military expeditions provided considerable knowledge of faraway lands and to some extent facilitated the sharing of cultures. The animosity between Muslim and Christian societies did not preclude their maintaining trade relations, with the result that cultural contact existed between the Middle East and Europe as well as between the Middle East and the rest of the Near East as early as the eighth century. The Vikings of Scandinavia traveled across Russia to the Middle East in the same period. The two highly developed societies of China and India engaged in commerce with each other early in the Middle Period. Themes of "The Orient" existed everywhere by the end of the period, when India and China were well connected to the Near East and Europe by trade. Still, in the Medieval Period one half of the world knew only itself; its encounter with the other half awaited the European oceanic voyages of exploration of the fifteenth and sixteenth centuries.

Date	History and Politics	Literature	Science, Culture, and Technology
1101–1200			12th century Courtly love literature of southern France spreads throughout Europe.
	1127 Invasion of north China; Sung dynasty retreats to the south	fl. 1129–1150 Marcabru, poet	1122–1204 Eleanor of Aquitaine, patroness of the arts
			1126–1198 Ibn Rushd (Averroes), Islamic philosopher
			1135–1204 Moses Maimonides, Jewish philosopher
	1171–1193 Rule of Saladin	c. 1160 Marie de France, *The Lay of Chevrefoil*	1160–1223 Ibn al-Athir, Muslim historian
		Poetry of the Countess of Dia	
	1180–1185 Gempei Wars; end of Heian dynasty in Japan		1174 Andreas Capellanus, *The Art of Courtly Love*
	1187 Saladin expels Crusaders from Jerusalem		
	1193 Islamic Turks capture Delhi, rule north India		1195 Construction of Chartres Cathedral
	c. 1200 Rise of Mali empire in Africa	c. 1200 Farid ud-Din Attar, *The Conference of the Birds*	c. 1200 Universities of Paris and Oxford founded

India: The Gupta Dynasty.   When the Macedonian ruler Alexander the Great ventured near the Indian borderlands in 330 B.C.E., his soldiers were turned back by a warlord, Chandragupta, who proceeded to establish the Mauryan dynasty in northern India in 323 B.C.E. A later Mauryan ruler, Ashoka the Great (r. 273–232 B.C.E.), renounced warfare and dispatched Buddhist missionaries as far as Syria, Egypt, and Macedonia to promote the cause of understanding. But the Mauryan dynasty fell into decline after Ashoka's death and ended with the murder of its last king in 184 B.C.E.

The Gupta dynasty began in the former territory of the Mauryan dynasty in northeastern India in the early fourth century C.E. Chandragupta I (r. 320–353), taking his name from the first Mauryan ruler, established the Gupta kingdom. His son Samudragupta (r. 353–376) led an expedition south, enhancing his claim as ruler of India. Samudragupta's son, Chandragupta II (r. 376–415), the greatest of the Gupta kings, extended the kingdom across the entire north and established a strong central authority. He created an effective administrative bureaucracy and initiated important public works projects. Trade routes passed through the two capital cities, Ujjayini to the west and the seaport city of Tamralipti to the east, providing access

Date	History and Politics	Literature	Science, Culture, and Technology
1101–1200 (cont.)			c. 1200 Works of Aristotle translated into Latin
1201–1300	1204 Christians sack Constantinople		
	1212 Battle of Las Navas de Talosa; decisive battle of the Reconquest of Spain		1209 Francis of Assisi founds Franciscan Order
	1215 Chingis Khan invades China.		
	1236 Cordova falls to Christians.		
	1258 Mongols conquer Baghdad.		
	1274–1275 Marco Polo visits China		1273 Thomas Aquinas, *Summa Theologica*
	1291 Fall of Acre; end of Crusade states in Asia Minor		
	1300 Ottoman dynasty founded in Middle East		c. 1300 Giotto paints *Histories of St. Francis* in Basilica of Assisi.
1301–1400	1305 Inauguration of Pope Clement V; Papacy removed from Rome to Avignon	early 14th century Dante, *The Divine Comedy*	
	1325 Aztec capital of Tenochtitlan established in Mexico		
	1348–1350 Black Death kills one-third of Europe's population		

to Rome and the Mediterranean in one direction and China and Southeast Asia in the other. Caravans and pilgrimages increased between India and China, enabling Buddhism to spread rapidly from India to the rest of Asia. The increasingly wealthy Gupta capitals became rich depositories of culture and the arts.

The Guptas ruled with unaccustomed liberality. They allowed local kings to keep their titles so long as they declared obedience to the empire. But this feudal form of military organization did not hold up against the invasion of the Huns from northern China during the fifth century. In 480 the Huns overran northern India, in 500 western India as well. Under their pressure the Gupta dynasty collapsed in 550. For six hundred years following the end of the Guptas, India remained decentralized. Small kingdoms often reflected no more than the local economy and tribal history of their regions.

Gupta Literary Culture.   Sanskrit was the basis of Gupta literary culture. The language provided the means for academic studies, not only in grammar and linguistics but also in philosophy, law, religion, the humanities, and scientific and mathematical writing. The major literary works at the time of the Guptas were

Date	History and Politics	Literature	Science, Culture, and Technology
1301–1400 (cont.)	1378 Great Schism; competing papacies in Avignon and Rome	1377 Ibn Khaldun, *Il Muqaddimah* 1386 Chaucer, *Canterbury Tales*	
1401–1500	15th century Height of Aztec and Inca empires		1403 Movable type first used for printing in Korea
	1417 Council of Constance brings end to Great Schism; papacy returned to Rome.		
	1434 Cosimo de'Medici takes control of Florence		1434 Lateen sail adapted for ocean travel; enables Portuguese exploration of West African coast.
	1451–1481 Mehmet II rules Ottoman empire		c. 1445–1450 Gutenberg develops process for printing using movable type in Germany
	1453 Fall of Constantinople to Ottoman Turks; end of Byzantine empire End of Hundred Years' War in Europe		

courtly epics (poetic adaptations of heroic epics); dramas written in mixed prose and poetry; short lyrics governed by strict rules of rhetoric and grammar; and longer poems, primarily devoted to instruction and satire.

The most important Gupta author was Kalidasa (fl. 376–415), a poet, playwright, and the elder statesman of Indian literature. In his masterwork, the drama *Shakuntala and the Ring of Recollection* (p. 1100), Kalidasa draws from a tale in the ancient epic *Mahabharata*, working in the elaborate tradition of Sanskrit drama with its emphasis on emotional development achieved through a series of interlocking scenes. While the plot of *Shakuntala*—the testing of the constancy of love between a king and his young bride and the king's recognition of a child as his own—is relatively uncomplicated, the separation of King Dusyanta and Shakuntala during the play provides emotional intensity, and scenes of estrangement, danger, and hardship add suspense to the drama. Nature figures deeply in the outcome, on both a realistic and symbolic level. The play is not "romantic" in the western sense, but focuses on the conflict within each character between emotional attachment and obligation to social norms. The commonplace comparison of Kalidasa to Shakespeare is based on the relationship each master

Date	History and Politics	Literature	Science, Culture, and Technology
1401–1500 (cont.)	1454 Treaty of Lodi; temporary balance of power among city-states of Italy		1455–1456 First book produced with movable metal type (Gutenberg Bible)
			1456 Joan of Arc burned at the stake in Rouen, France
	1474 King Ferdinand V and Queen Isabella I begin rule of Spain		
	1478 Spanish Inquisition established		
	1482 Portuguese establish trading post at Elmina in the Gulf of Guinea.		c. 1482–1486 Botticelli, *The Birth of Venus*
	1487–1488 Bartholomeu Dias rounds Cape of Good Hope	1486 Pico della Mirandola, *On the Dignity of Man*	1485 Botticelli, *La Primavera*
	1492 Columbus arrives in America.	1492 Columbus, *Diario*	
	Muslims and Jews expelled from Spain		
	1494 Treaty of Tordesillas; Brazil controlled by Portugal, the rest of the Americas by Spain		
	France invades Italy.		
	1497 John Cabot lands on Newfoundland.		

playwright established with his audience, creating several levels of recognition and understanding, and the ability each had to draw on a wide range of emotions and treat matters of immediate concern to his society.

China after the Han Dynasty.   China's medieval period came during the thousand years between the collapse of the Han dynasty in 220 C.E. and the Mongol invasions of the thirteenth century. Between 317 and 589, an invading force of nomads in north China slowly reconstituted themselves into a stable society. In south China, a new culture grew up around migrations into the Yangtze River valley. Later, the Sui dynasty (581–617), the Tang dynasty (618–907), and the northern and southern Sung dynasties (960–1279) reunited the vast regions of China. In this thousand-year period China passed through four broad stages: disorientation brought about by the barbarian invasion, the recovery of its social institutions, a time of high culture, and a process of consolidation and preservation.

The rise of the Sui dynasty in 581 put an end to the rule of separate nomadic dynasties in the north. The Sui dynasty's unification of China brought the southern Yangtze culture into the national mainstream, opened up the seacoasts for

Date	History and Politics	Literature	Science, Culture, and Technology
1401–1500 (cont.)	1497–1499 Vasco de Gama opens European sea route to Indian Ocean.		
1501–1550	1502–1520 Reign of Moctezuma II, emperor of Aztecs	1503–1542 Sir Thomas Wyatt	1503 Leonardo da Vinci, *Mona Lisa*
	1505 Portuguese capture Mombasa on East African coast.		1504 Michelangelo, *David*
			1508–1512 Michelangelo paints ceiling of Sistine Chapel
	1510 Spanish take Tripoli in northern Africa		1509–1510 Raphael, *The School of Athens*
	1513 Portuguese arrive in Canton in China	1513 Machiavelli, *The Prince*	1513–1521 Pope Leo X becomes leading patron of the arts
		1516 More, *Utopia*	
	1517 Luther's Ninety-Five Theses launch the Protestant Reformation.		
	1518 First shipment of slaves leaves Africa for Americas	1519 Cortés, Letters from Mexico	
	1519 Charles I of Spain becomes Holy Roman Emperor Charles V		
	1521 Cortés destroys Aztec capital Tenochtitlan	1521 Luther, Speech at the Diet of Worms	

northern trade, and brought about a massive public works program. But after floods, riots, and an unpopular war led to a rebellion against the Sui dynasty, the Tang dynasty was formed in 618.

The Tang Dynasty.   The Tang dynasty began well. Aristocratic families of north China headed the government, commanded the imperial guards and palace troops of the army, and helped create a well-organized bureaucracy composed of scholars and clerks. The new rulers instituted governmental reforms and built up the military, which opposed Turkish armies to the west and safeguarded the northern border. They intensified horse breeding to produce the one animal that was indispensable for military use and private enjoyment, a fact confirmed in many art works of the period. They also completed an effective system of canals, originally intended to speed communications, but later instrumental in transporting rice from the south.

The ancient city of Chang'an, restored by the Sui dynasty in 583, became the western capital of the Tang dynasty in the early seventh century. Conceived as a vast cosmopolitan center, it was a meeting place for traders, merchants, soldiers,

Date	History and Politics	Literature	Science, Culture, and Technology
1501–1550 (cont.)	1521 Martin Luther excommunicated from Catholic Church		
	1522 Magellan's sailors complete circumnavigation of the world		
	1527 Sack of Rome by army of Charles V	c. 1527–c. 1562 de Las Casas, *History of the Indies*	
	1529 Hapsburg armies defeat Turks at Vienna		
	1531–1536 Pizarro conquers the Inca		
	1534 Anglican church splits from Catholic Church; dissolution of Catholic monasteries in England		1534 Ignatius of Loyola founds the Jesuit Order (Society of Jesus)
	1539 Hernando de Soto arrives in Florida		1536 John Calvin, *Institutes of the Christian Religion*
	1542 Portuguese merchants reach Japan		1543 Copernicus, *On the Revolution of the Celestial Spheres*
			Andreas Vesalius, *On the Fabric of the Human Body*
	1545 Council of Trent; Catholic Counter Reformation		
	1549 Jesuit priest Francis Xavier arrives in Japan		

artists, entertainers, religious pilgrims, courtiers, and the government bureaucracy. Along with Baghdad, Chang'an was one of the great cities of the world in the eighth and ninth centuries. Built in a rectangle composed of outer walls six miles from east to west and five miles from north to south, the city contained fourteen avenues north to south and eleven east to west. The imperial city located at the north end was protected by double walls; adjacent to it was the palace, famed for its works of art and cultural performances. The population of the walled city of Chang'an in the eighth century was approximately a million, with as many people living outside the city walls.

The first weakening of Tang rule occurred during a military rebellion of 755, in which a northern general, An Lushan, marched south from Peking in defiance of the ruler Tang Xuanzong (r. 712–756) to occupy Chang'an. His entrance into the city was unopposed. Although the rebel armies were defeated in 757, the shock of the rebellion dealt a blow to Tang authority and eventually led to the weakening of the aristocracy, the formation of mercenary armies, the ceding of public lands to the wealthy, the closure of borders, and a sharp decline in foreign trade. The Tang dynasty eventually dissolved under the weight of expenses required to

Date	History and Politics	Literature	Science, Culture, and Technology
1551–1600	1555 Peace of Augsburg legitimates Lutheranism; gives German states of Holy Roman Empire the right to determine their religion		1555–1556 Mercury amalgamation process for mining silver introduced in Mexico
	1556 Akbar becomes emperor of Mughal empire		1557 Giovanni Pierluigi da Palestrina, *Pope Marcellus* Mass
	Philip II takes throne in Spain		
	1558 Queen Elizabeth I of England takes the throne		1559 Pope Paul IV establishes Index of Forbidden Books
	1561 Jesuit priests arrive in East Africa		
	1562–1598 Civil war in France between Huguenots and Catholics		1562 Teresa of Avila founds Carmelite convent
	1571 Spain defeats Turkish fleet at Lepanto		
	1576 Mughals take control of Benghal		1577–1579 El Greco completes paintings for Santo Domingo church in Toledo, Spain
	1580 Jesuits arrive in the court of Akbar	1580 Montaigne, *Of Cannibals*	

support its numerous military regions and the condition of its mercenary army, which fell into a state of disorder in the ninth century.

Chinese Culture in the Early Period.   Cultural development in the Early Period (fourth to sixth centuries) was distinctly uneven. The dynasties of north China showed little interest in the arts—they fixed on their need for stability and self-defense. But the local courts of south China, especially among the new Yangtze family dynasties, took a radical turn. Instead of following Confucianism, the philosophy of the Chinese classical period, the southern artists, writers, and performers focused on the values of spontaneity and artistic sensibility, as well as the separation of the artist from the concerns of everyday society. The writing of literary criticism, lyric poetry, and landscape painting occupied these artists during the fourth century. About this time Buddhism also began to contribute significantly to Chinese cultural life. The new religion was accepted in the north as a partial antidote to the grim militaristic society that existed there. In the south, Buddhism and Daoism were equally embraced, due to the reverence for nature common to both religions. This stance was reflected in early landscape painting and classical poetry.

A great innovator in Chinese poetry, Tao Qian (Tao Ch'ien), was born in southeastern China in 365. He witnessed the flight of aristocratic families of the

Date	History and Politics	Literature	Science, Culture, and Technology
1551–1600 (cont.)		c. 1580 Codex Florentino, The Conquest of Mexico	
	1581 Morocco begins southern expansion		
	1588 English navy defeats Spanish Armada		
	1597 First persecution of Christians in Japan		1595 Johannes Kepler, *The Cosmographic Mystery*
	1598 Edict of Nantes makes Catholicism official religion of France; Huguenots tolerated		
	1600 English East India Company founded		
1601–1650	1602 Dutch East India Company founded		
	1603 Tokugawa Ieyasu founds Tokugawa empire in Japan; Tokugawa period begins		1604 Tung-lin Academy founded for Confucian studies
	1605 Death of Akbar; replaced by son Jahangir	1605 Cervantes, *Don Quixote*	1607 Claudio Monteverdi, *Orfeo*

north to the Yangtze valley, and lived to see the breakup of the Eastern Jin (Chin) dynasty in 420. A Daoist, he withdrew from civilization to live in the deep forests near Poyang Lake, and thus he helped create the popular image of the poet as a recluse. Resigning from a minor government post at the age of forty, he retired to the countryside in 406, living the rest of his days, he tells us, "unconcerned with success or failure." Both the substance of his poetry and his way of life became objects of emulation of the later Tang poets. Tao Qian died in 427.

The Culture of the Tang Dynasty.   During the Tang dynasty, Buddhism became a highly visible Chinese export. Scholarly Buddhist monks and pious Chinese laymen served as important cultural models whenever religious pilgrims traveled to India or the West. The Buddhist monk Xuangzang (596–664) helped to establish this pattern. He toured India, the Near East, and the Middle East, taking extensive notes on his journeys. He also translated Chinese literature into Sanskrit and Indian literature into Chinese.

The first half of the eighth century marked the greatest period of Tang culture. The capitol at Chang'an was a brilliant center of civilization. Although Confucianism still dominated the civil service, the well-established Buddhist monasteries recruited many followers, and the Chinese artistic leaning toward self-expression continued to develop in painting and poetry. It is no surprise,

Date	History and Politics	Literature	Science, Culture, and Technology
1601–1650 (cont.)	1612 Tokugawa evicts missionaries from Japan	1611 First performance of Shakespeare's *The Tempest*	1610 Galileo, *Sidereus Nuncius (Starry Messenger)*
	1618 Thirty Years' War begins		c. 1615 Rubens, *Venus at the Mirror*
	1626 French establish colonies on west coast of Africa	1623 Shakespeare, *The Tempest* published	1622–1625 Bernini, *Apollo and Daphne*
	1627 Death of Jahangir; replaced by Shah Jahan		1632 Rembrandt, *The Anatomy Lesson of Dr. Nicolaes Tulp*
			Galileo, *Dialogue Concerning the Two Chief World Systems*
			1633 Galileo stands trial for heresy
	1640 Exclusion policies in effect in Japan		
	1642–1648 Civil Wars in England		
	1644 Ming dynasty ends in China; Qing dynasty begins		
	1648 Peace of Westphalia ends Thirty Years' War		1647–1652 Bernini, *The Ecstasy of St. Theresa*

Palace Scene, fourth to sixth century
Sometimes called the golden age of Hindu history, the Gupta dynasty was noted for its culture and cosmopolitanism. In this palace scene depicted on an exterior fresco in Madhya Pradesh, various castes and ethnic groups are shown. (SEF/Art Resource, NY)

therefore, that the Tang poets, following the writings of Tao Qian (365–427), demonstrated an attitude of independence, developed an ethical justification for living apart from society, and cultivated an interest in nature poetry in particular.

Three of the four great poets of the Tang dynasty (p. 1163) — Wang Wei (c. 699–761), Li Bai (Li Po) (701–762), and Du Fu (Tu Fu) (712–770) — lived during

Two Horsemen, seventh century C.E.
During the Tang dynasty, horse breeding for both military and private purposes was strongly encouraged. (Wallpainting. Dun Huang. Giraudon / Art Resource, NY)

the reign of Tang Xuanzong (r. 712–756), who possessed, among other qualities, a sincere affection for the arts. Though these poets were not afraid of controversy and sometimes reflected on the ills of society, their major claim to greatness lay in their personal expression, with its depth of feeling, style, clarity, and originality. The later Tang poet Bo Juyi (Po Chü-i) (772–846) expressed a more critical view of his society in a time of shrinking prosperity. All of the Tang poets were influenced in one way or another by the Chinese religions—native Confucianism and Daoism, imported Buddhism—though in general the detachment, irony, and spirit of contemplation found in their poems puts them closest to the Buddhist tradition. Wang Wei was a devoted Buddhist, preferring his home in the mountains to the city life of Chang'an. Li Bai, with his unpredictable nature and his love of spontaneity, is considered a Daoist. Du Fu, the most orderly of the Tang poets, seems closer to Confucianism. Bo Juyi is what we might think of as a social poet; in the next generation his trenchant manner endeared the Japanese to his work.

Japan: Birth of a Culture.   Relations between Japanese tribal people and the late Han dynasty in China are recorded in Chinese as early as the first century C.E.

Anecdotal knowledge of the Japanese dates from the third century, when Chinese visitors recorded purchases of pottery, silk and woolens, and bronze objects. No history appears in Japan itself until *A Record of Ancient Matters,* written in Chinese characters in 712. In the centuries between these dates, settlers arrived from the Asian mainland and islands to the south, devoting themselves to the cultivation of rice in the lowlands. This style of life, agricultural yet close to the wildness of nature, must have influenced the early settlers to emphasize such matters as natural beauty, the simplicity of their living arrangements, the impermanence of life, and the virtue of working for the good of the majority. Already struggling to sustain themselves on the island, the Japanese settlers sought out their mainland neighbor China for the knowledge necessary to manage their resources. In the seventh and eighth centuries, merchants of the Tang dynasty of China traded freely with Japan, influencing not only Japan's social institutions but also its philosophy, religion, culture, and art. Nevertheless, from the beginning the differences between China and Japan were greater than the similarities. As soon as they achieved a measure of economic independence in the eighth century, the Japanese sought out the roots of their own national culture. As much as any nation in the world, Japan learned to rely on its own capacities and created itself anew in the process.

One of the most important examples of the Japanese genius for independence through synthesis came in religion. Buddhism was introduced into Japan from Korea in the sixth century. It reinforced Japanese fatalism about life and death, especially through the doctrine of reincarnation. Confucianism, introduced from China largely in the eighth century, reinforced Japanese concern with ethical behavior, including the sacredness of family ties. Shinto, the original Japanese religion, focused on nature worship. It helps account for the scrupulous attention Japanese poetry pays to the seasons and the lives of plants and animals. Shinto also emphasized spontaneity of the emotions, a strong feature of Japanese poetry and drama. Eventually Shinto, Buddhism, and Confucianism adjusted to each other's presence: hardly ever do characters in Japanese literature suffer conflict between religions, because the beliefs amalgamate into one.

The Nara Period: The First Japanese Civilization.   After a century of increasingly sharp struggles among warring family clans, the Japanese constructed their first permanent capital at Nara in 710. The building of the capital graphically reflected Japanese borrowing of Chinese architecture: Nara was a scaled-down version of the Chinese capital at Chang'an. The court adopted a Chinese-style legal code and bureaucracy, as well as installing Chinese Buddhism as the state religion. At the same time, the rulers of the Nara period supported the arts and

Early Japan, 600–800

By about 600, realizing their economy was not self-sufficient, Japanese merchants and traders set out from the island of Kyushu to trade with China. During the seventh and eighth centuries, Chinese culture heavily influenced Japanese social institutions, philosophy, religion, and art. The first permanent Japanese capital was established at Nara in 710; it was followed by Heian (modern-day Kyoto), built in 794.

literary culture, hoping to increase their popularity. They commissioned the *Record of Ancient Matters* (712) to preserve Japanese myths and legends and show continuity from the past to the present. The *Record* was followed by another historical collection, the *Chronicles of Japan* (720), some of which predates the *Record* by decades. The most significant literary work of the Nara period was the *Man'yoshu* anthology (759), including poets of ancient times and the revered late seventh century poet Kakinomoto Hitomaro (fl. 680–700).

   The *Record of Ancient Matters* illustrates how Japan acquired its original system of writing from China. Borrowing Chinese written characters, the Japanese treated them in two distinct ways. Some were used as phonograms, producing a monosyllable according to the Chinese sound of the character. Other characters were used as ideograms, conveying the original idea but not the sound from the Chinese. Since Japanese words are polysyllabic, the use of Chinese characters as monosyllables in a chain to produce the sound of a Japanese word became unmanageable. On the other hand, it was difficult to use Chinese ideograms to signify Japanese words with no connection to the Chinese sound. It was most difficult of all to know which system of representation, phonograms or ideograms, was being employed at a given moment. Despite these problems, most writing of the Nara period (710–784) was done in the dual system of Chinese characters. After this system was abandoned in the next century, many early writings became unintelligible to the later Japanese audience.

The Heian Dynasty.   In 794, the capital was moved from Nara under the direction of the Fujiwara family, the new power behind the throne. The new capital, Heian (modern Kyoto), strategically located with mountains on three sides and rivers on two sides, was another copy on a diminished scale of the Chinese capital of Chang'an. The Heian dynasty lasted continuously for four hundred years and witnessed the creation of great works of literature, many of them based on the activities of its own splendid court society. These included the *Kokinshu* poetry anthology (c. 905), the *Tale of Genji* by Lady Murasaki (c. 1000), and *The Pillow Book* by Sei Shonagon (c. 1000).

The Heian period came to a bitter end with the Gempei Wars of 1180–1185, during which one of the great families of Japan, the Heike, was entirely wiped out while the other, the Genji, gradually ceded authority to the military shogunate, the precursors of *samurai* society. In the upheaval that followed the Gempei Wars, Japanese ideas went through violent reshaping. Following the crumbling of the aristocracy, there arose the concept of *mappo*, "the Last Days of Buddha's Law" or the end of the world. It held that individual salvation would be impossible because people could no longer comprehend or practice the teachings of Buddha. A little later came the doctrine of Pure Land Buddhism, which held that souls could be translated to the Pure Land to the west by simply calling the name of Amida Buddha. While the two doctrines were in conflict, the first representing the fears of the collapsing aristocracy and the second the ambitions of the wealthy peasantry, both gripped the public imagination. They began to appear in popular forms in a newly created literature that focused on the tragedies of the past and the uncertainties of the future. In effect, the death of the aristocracy had led to a new audience for literature and a new direction for them to take. These impulses are evident in *The Tale of the Heike* (1371), the great literary epic of the Gempei

Wars written nearly two hundred years later. The *Noh* drama of the fifteenth century captured the same impulses in a ritualistic, expressionistic stage setting.

Literature for the Ages.   The power of medieval Japanese literature rests in its sense of the sorrowful or tragic and its desire for an end of chaos and a restoration of harmony. Linked to the traditional Japanese passion for survival, this literature bypasses the apparent superficiality of court life to show real individuals struggling with defeat and despair and learning how to overcome them. The rich variety of Japanese writing—narrative poetry, lyric poetry, prose romances, diaries and memoirs, historical tragedies, and drama—points to a love of literary forms and a passion for cultural survival.

The *Man'yoshu,* the wide-ranging poetic anthology produced in the eighth century, reflected early Japanese interest in the poetic tradition. The collection contains both long and short poems, *choka* and *tanka,* and an entire section of loosely constructed oral literature, testifying to some of this work's antiquity. Other poetry provides unique information about the dynasties and rulers of the seventh century. Chief among the poets is Kakinomoto Hitomaro (p. 1309), who wrote in the last two decades of the seventh century. His combination of public and private poetry, exemplified in his use of the *choka,* or ode, conveys the rich emotional qualities that have made him Japan's favorite poet in later times.

The *Kokinshu* anthology (c. 905), the largest single collection of Japanese poetry, exerted an important influence on Heian culture. For several hundred years, members of the court memorized the five-line *tanka* lyrics of the *Kokinshu* in order to repeat them on appropriate occasions. Some *Kokinshu* poets achieved lasting reputations; these included Ono no Komachi (p. 1314), who later became a legendary figure, pictured as either a beautiful young courtesan or a frightening hag suffering unspeakably for her sins.

The Heian court at the beginning of the eleventh century showed tremendous dedication to manners and proper conduct. The ladies-in-waiting of the noble families were designated as the keepers of the court's fashions, but they were also subject to spiteful gossip and the temptations of court intrigues. Two of the most famous of these women served the court at about the same time, though they were at odds with one another. Sei Shonagon (966–1017), author of *The Pillow Book* (p. 1317), a witty collection of reminiscences about the court, drew the caustic criticism of Lady Murasaki Shikibu (978–1030), author of *The Tale of Genji* (p. 1281), a prose romance often called the first novel in world literature.

The Near East: The Christian Enterprise.   At the end of the Ancient World, the Eastern Mediterranean region bore witness to rapidly changing political and religious developments. A new wave of religious feeling came with the rise of Christianity in the Near East. Until the end of the third century, the Christian church competed for attention with popular rivals, the "mystery religions" of Dionysius in Greece, Isis in Egypt, and Mithras in Persia. The ecumenical tendency of Christianity—its desire to expand its circle of believers—and the ethical core it inherited from Judaism became keys to its success with the general population.

The support for Christianity increased as Roman civil authority waned. In 313, Emperor Constantine granted the Christians protection. Around 330, he built an eastern imperial capital in Constantinople, on the ruins of the old Greek city of Byzantium at the southern edge of the Black Sea leading to the Mediterranean. The division of the seat of the Roman Empire into Western and Eastern capitals was mirrored in the creation of the eastern church at Constantinople. The resplendent new capital, with its special emphasis on Greek civilization, became the new center of Christian learning. For centuries, Constantinople was the showpiece of Christian culture, benefiting from its rich trading connections throughout the Far East. Its glory endured until the twelfth and thirteenth centuries, when it was humiliated and finally occupied by the Crusaders.

Although Christianity's alliance with the Western and Eastern capitals of the Roman Empire secured its political position for a time, intellectually the Christians needed to meld the Greco-Roman and Judeo-Christian traditions together. The most advanced Christian writers had been educated in Greek and Roman rhetoric, literature, and philosophy. In the fourth century, three great fathers of the early church who were later canonized as saints—St. Ambrose (c. 340–397), St. Jerome (340–420), and St. Augustine (354–430)—secured the intellectual position of Christianity in the Roman Empire while reconciling classical learning with the Christian faith. St. Ambrose, Bishop of Milan, stoutly defended Christian doctrine, opposing even the emperor when it was necessary to protect the sanctity of the Church. St. Jerome directed the copying of the Greek and Roman classics and produced the first great translation of the Bible from Hebrew and Greek into Latin—the Latin Vulgate Edition. St. Augustine, Bishop of Hippo in North Africa, addressed his most important spiritual writings, *The Confessions* (c. 400) (p. 1047) and *The City of God* (426) to the needs of his time. Although by the time of Augustine's death Hippo lay under siege and the western Roman Empire was being torn apart, Christianity prevailed. It became the dominant religious and cultural force of the region and was well positioned to deal with Rome's successors.

The Christian Cultural Legacy.   The story of Jesus, his life, teachings, crucifixion, and resurrection, as told in the Four Gospels of Matthew, Mark, Luke, and John in the New Testament (p. 1021), is the foundation of Christian worship. In addition, certain medieval Christian practices influenced Western society. Among these, four deserve mention. First is the practice of scriptural interpretation conducted by the early church fathers. Second is the Christian acceptance of Greek and Latin classics for the Christian audience. Third is the practice of charity and tolerance taught by Jesus and exemplified in his life. Fourth is the emphasis placed on the City of God, a world that awaits the believer after the fall of the city of man.

Following the teachings of St. Jerome and St. Augustine, Christians read Hebrew Scriptures, which they called the Old Testament, as a sign of future events that would take place after the coming of Christianity. Thus the story of the prophet Moses was compared to the later story of the coming of Christ. The story of Moses was provided with a *historical* and a *symbolic* interpretation. In its historical aspect, Moses' rescue of the nation of Israel by crossing the Red Sea was said to anticipate Christ's redemption of humanity. In its symbolic aspect, the spiritual life of every Christian was supposed to be linked with the history of the world, so personal salvation followed the deliverance of the children of Israel and the redemption brought about by Jesus. The poet Dante (p. 000) uses symbolic interpretation in writing *The Divine Comedy* (early fourteenth century) when he envisions the progression of the individual soul to heaven as an aspect of God's purpose.

The Christian fathers generally deemed the Greek and Roman classics as acceptable literature, though the process of acceptance was not always simple. Both St. Jerome and St. Augustine agonized over the sinfulness they detected in their own love of the classics. Nevertheless, the church's tolerance prepared the way for the study of classical learning by later Christian scholars. The fact that Jews, Christians, and Muslims all loved literature and wished to preserve worldly knowledge ensured the further development of that knowledge in Europe, North Africa, and the Middle East through the Medieval Period.

Because Jesus had shown love and respect to common people, especially the poor, medieval Christians felt that they should practice humility and service to others. This intention, while not always put into action, encouraged such practices as evangelism, pilgrimage, education, and charity, and inspired devout Christians to work for the betterment of society. The virtues of humility and service were often referred to in medieval times, from sermons to the works of such humanistic authors as Geoffrey Chaucer (p. 000), the poet of *The Canterbury Tales* in the late fourteenth century.

Christian millennial piety, the belief in the coming end of the world and the prospect of immediate salvation, played a role in the Christian enterprise throughout the period. As the year one thousand C.E. approached, some

Christians practiced extreme acts of worship, thinking that the end was near. Also throughout the Medieval Period, the doctrine contained in Jesus' saying "My kingdom is not of this world" flavored Christian practices and attitudes, from the zeal of the first Crusaders to the spiritual practices of those who withdrew from the world and lived a cloistered existence.

While noting these features of Christian belief in the Middle Period, it is necessary to state that some medieval Christians acted in a violent and domineering fashion in contrast to their professed intentions. The Crusades of the twelfth and thirteenth centuries, aimed at capturing the Holy Land from the Muslims, brought untold suffering to Muslims, Jews, and Christians alike. While it can be argued that the Crusades were a response to Muslim holy wars of the seventh and eighth centuries, documents from the period suggest that the Christian attacks were often motivated by greed and regional politics, resulting in horrific acts of cruelty and theft.

The Rise of Islam.   Enormous social and religious ferment came to Arabia in the seventh century. In the city of Mecca, the merchants of the Quraysh tribe paid minimal attention to religious observance while selling their wares for profit. Muhammad (c. 570–632), an orphan born of a poor clan in Mecca, grew up to become a camel driver and eventually a member of the business community. But greater things lay in store. At about age forty, the future prophet of the religion of Islam began receiving visions from the angel Gabriel. Calling existing religious practices into question, Muhammad upset the ways of the Quraysh. He became both a successful preacher and a hunted man. Fleeing Mecca in 622, Muhammad took his followers to the city of Medina, founded the religion of Islam, and began to fight the Unbelievers, that is, the tribes of Arabia including the Quraysh of Mecca. When he died in 632, Muhammad's Muslim followers already ruled most of Arabia.

The astounding vitality of Islam as a religious faith rested largely on its universal claims. Borrowing from both Hebrew Scriptures and the New Testament, it honored the prophets of the past from Moses to Jesus Christ, while denying the divinity of Jesus or any man, including Muhammad himself. Muhammad was the Messenger, completing the work of the Jewish and Christian prophets and delivering the Word of God, which his followers transcribed verbatim in the Muslim holy book, the Qur'an (Koran). Muhammad and his followers saw the Unbelievers as their principal threat. Their JIHAD, or struggle, against them first took the form of public argument but eventually turned to warfare, reaching beyond Arabia's borders and spreading to the farthest corners of the medieval world.

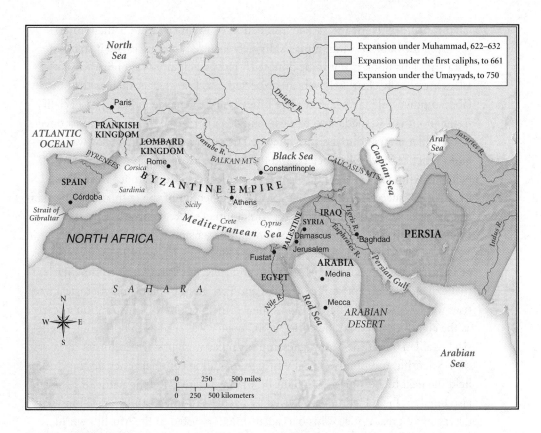

Expansion of Islam to 750

Beginning with Muhammad's campaigns, Islamic armies, in little more than a century, conquered a vast region made up of diverse peoples, cultures, climates, and living conditions. The force uniting these territories was the religion of Islam, which gathered all believers into one community, the umwah.

Islam became a **THEOCRACY**—a state grounded in a religious belief. While it maintained respect for the **PEOPLE OF THE BOOK**—Jews and Christians, whose religious traditions provided the basis for Islam itself—it pursued the destruction of the infidel for a hundred years after the death of Muhammad. Then—as abruptly as it had begun—the period of conquest ceased, and the new rulers of Islam were left with the task of administering a huge territory, consisting of the Near East and portions of Asia Minor, Egypt and North Africa, Spain and southern Italy. A new Eastern capital was established in Baghdad in 750, while a different caliphate, or ruling dynasty, governed in the west, in the Andalusian (Spanish) capital of Cordova. The latter site remained a center of Muslim civilization until the end of the tenth century.

Islamic Cultural Heritage.   The foundation of Islamic culture is the Qur'an (p. 1052), the book of Muhammad's divinely inspired utterances. As it states in Sura 2:1, "This Book is not to be doubted." The principal moral obligations of Islam are equally clear: believers are expected to acknowledge Allah as the one God; to pray while facing Mecca five times a day; to engage in fasting, especially in the month of Ramadan; to make a religious pilgrimage to Mecca at least once in their lifetimes; and to assist the needy. The observance of public law was a religious practice in Muslim society, and the Muslim "church" was a community of believers with no priests, only selected prayer leaders. Muhammad was followed by a CALIPH or "successor," a man known to be a defender of the faith and a guardian of the faithful. The exact formula for Muhammad's succession was unstated at the time of his death, leading to controversy and dissension in later days.

The Qur'an was considered the greatest literary work as well as the holy book of Islam. Its variety, comprehensiveness, and style were praised in commentaries that expanded on its meaning. Arabian and Persian grammars and rhetorical treatises were written with the Qur'an as their principle source of inspiration as early as the eighth century. Besides the Qur'an, poetry was seen as the preeminent classical Arabian literature. Many rules and formulas were prescribed for its composition. Scientific and philosophical writings, including commentaries on the Qur'an, held the next highest place. Humanistic writings were given the name of *adab* and also highly valued. Fiction was viewed as a vehicle of untruthful storytelling, not deserving of great notice. This bias against fiction lasted in the Muslim world until modern times.

The greatest achievement of the early Islamic authors is *The Life of Muhammad* (p. 1082) by Ibn Ishaq (704–767). This lengthy and complicated book, written a little over a hundred years after the Prophet's death, uses as its source material a collection of oral narratives, letters, legal documents, poetry written for special occasions, and battle accounts. For stories passed down for several generations, Ibn Ishaq lists every transmitter of the tale, even commenting on the reliability of the source from time to time by his use of words like "alleges." He does not produce a "master narrative" that gives the appearance of certainty, a common literary device in the West. Instead he leaves the final verification of the information he provides to the reader. This scrupulous method of presentation makes the material almost unreadable at times, but also prepares the way for what came after Ibn Ishaq: detailed biographies of other famous men, accounts of the deeds of the less famous, and—still in the Middle Period—autobiographies.

The Ebb and Flow of Dynasties.   The first four caliphs after the death of Muhammad (632–661) were called *rashidun* or "rightly guided," based on the fact that all four had either been friends or in one case a relative of the Prophet. Men from different families did not constitute a dynasty, and for the time being the seat of Islam remained in Medina. But later, with the conquest of more and more territory, the once intimate nature of the relationships around Muhammad, as well as the unquestioned importance of Arabia as the center of the Islamic world, lost immediacy and strength.

The first caliph, the Prophet's close associate Abu Bakr, argued that the Islamic state should remain a single community. True to his word, he unified the rest of Arabia during his short reign (632–634). Under Caliph Umar ibn al-Khattab (634–644), the Arabs burst into Iraq, Syria, and Egypt, winning a decisive battle against the Persians in 637. Under Uthman ibn Affan (644–656), they extended their territory across North Africa into Libya, and further north and east through Asia Minor. But Uthman was assassinated, in an attack that was shocking and repugnant to most Muslims. He was succeeded by Muhammad Ali, Muhammad's closest surviving relative and an original contender for succession after Muhammad's death. Muhammad Ali ruled under constant threat. Even his favorite wife Aisha accused him of failing to pursue the assassins of Uthman and eventually helped lead the campaign against him. After five contentious years, Muhammad Ali was murdered in 661. Mu'awiyah, the prince of Syria, succeeded him. The capital was moved from Medina to Damascus.

The Umayyad dynasty was formed with Mu'awiyah at its head in 661. In the next hundred years, the Umayyads transformed the conquered territories into a single unified Muslim state. Damascus became a glorious capital, adorned in jeweled and perfumed splendor. The Umayyads completed building the Dome of the Rock in Jerusalem in 691, Islam's claim on the Holy City. Arabic replaced Persian as the language of the court in Damascus, bolstering the claim of continuity of Arab culture despite the relocation of the capital to Syria. And in 711, the Muslims expanded their territory once again with the conquest of Andalusia, today called Spain. The Muslim incursion into Europe was halted at Tours in southern France in 732, when the Frankish leader Charles Martel defeated the Muslim army. Abandoning any further advances in Europe, the Muslims returned to Andalusia.

Two major groups challenged the Umayyad dynasty in the middle of the eighth century: the SHI'ITE followers of the ill-starred Muhammad Ali, whom they viewed as a martyr after his murder in 661, and a large group of non-Arab Muslims, including Persians who had been passed over for advancement by the Umayyads. An uneasy alliance of these two groups drove the Umayyads from Damascus in 750, and the Abbasid dynasty was installed. However, the Umayyad dynasty in Andalusia survived an overthrow attempt and survived for over two hundred years.

The Abbasid Dynasty.   The new rulers of the Abbasid dynasty chose between their supporters once they took office. Rejecting the sectarian Shi'ites, the Abbasids favored the Persians, noted for their sophistication and bureaucratic skills. The Abbasid caliph Al-Mansur built a new capital city at Baghdad, at the western edge of the old Persian Empire. The splendor of the Abbasid court, decorated in Persian fashion, complemented the brilliance of Baghdad itself as the center of a commercial network that soon spread beyond the distant borders of Islam to the ends of the known earth: China, Scandinavia, and Africa.

The greatest prosperity of the Abbasids came during the rule of Harun al-Rashid (r. 786–809). Harun, a contemporary of Charlemagne (r. 780–814), once dazzled the Frankish leader with the gift of an elephant. Harun's flamboyant reputation is probably responsible for his depiction as the tyrannical caliph in *The Thousand and One Nights,* the famous Arabic story collection completed in the thirteenth and fourteenth centuries. In actuality, he was celebrated for his endowment of scholarship and the arts. In Baghdad and across the Islamic world, he produced the greatest meeting ground for philosophers, mathematicians, scientists, legal scholars, poets, and artists in the Middle Period. He also established an efficient bureaucracy modeled after that of the Persian Empire, drained the swamps, and enhanced public works. Harun was not, however, a particularly enlightened ruler by modern political standards. His society depended heavily on slave trade with sub-Saharan Africa, and he reduced women to a lower status than provided for in the Qur'an.

The Abbasid dynasty eventually declined, partly from lack of a commercial infrastructure. Over vast stretches of land where transportation was limited to camel caravans or sailing ships, communications were nearly impossible and tax collection was extraordinarily difficult. Local chieftains who built up sizeable armies for their own protection eventually broke off from Baghdad. Finally the Abbasids capitulated: Persians took over the rule of Baghdad in all but name after 950, and the city was occupied in 1055 by the Seljuk Turks, who used it to stage a bloody invasion of Byzantium. Although Islam recovered from most of the devastation of the Crusades during the twelfth century, Baghdad never regained its former glory. It was conquered again by the Mongols in 1258—the date usually cited as the end of the Abbasid dynasty. In truth, the Abassids had ruled effectively from 750 to about 950.

The Andalusian Experience.   Andalusia was occupied by the Muslims in 711, and its Umayyad rulers escaped a purge attempt by the Abbasids in 750. In 756 Abdul Raman al-Amawi became Umayyad caliph of Andalusia; his dynasty lasted more than two hundred years. By the tenth century, Cordova was the leading city of

Chess Players, 1282

After its founding in the seventh century, Islamic religion and culture spread throughout Europe, Africa, and the Near East, encompassing and embracing many geographies, cultures, and peoples. This miniature showing two chess players is from an Andalusian illuminated manuscript. (El Escoriàl / Giraudon / The Art Resource)

Andalusia, with a population of a half million. Its jewel-encrusted palace and administrative capital of az-Zahra were built in the time of Abd-al-Rahman III (r. 912–961), at the height of Cordova's prestige. For a time, the University of Cordova and its library were the largest in Europe; the university was home to thousands of students and the library contained four hundred thousand manuscripts. Significantly, religious tolerance existed among Jews, Christians, and Muslims in this period. Still, Muslim culture prevailed.

Although conditions gradually worsened for the Muslims in Andalusia as Christians from the north continued to recover territory, the progress of the Reconquest, as the Christian Spaniards called it, was very slow. Though the caliphate of Cordova was dissolved in 1002, and the city was sacked by Berbers in 1013, it recovered and remained Muslim for more than two hundred years. Toledo fell to the Christians in 1085, and the province of Aragon joined Catalonia on the Christian side in 1140. In 1212 the Pope declared a crusade against the

Muslims in Spain and a decisive battle was fought at Las Navas de Talosa outside of Toledo the same year. Cordova finally fell in 1236. In 1492, the year Columbus sailed for America, the Muslims along with the remaining Jews were formally expelled from Spain; those not actually expelled were expected to convert to Christianity. Many remaining Christianized Muslims, called "Moriscos," were either slaughtered or expelled under the reign of King Phillip III between 1609 and 1614.

Forms of Expression of Islamic Culture.   Although Baghdad lost its political autonomy in the middle of the tenth century and the northern cities of Andalusia fell under attack from Spanish Christians late in the eleventh century, Islamic culture persisted in both locations. In Cordova and other centers of Andalusian culture, humanistic writing known as *adab*—literature on a variety of subjects, highlighting the sensibilities of the writer—flourished. Love songs were performed in the brilliant courts; musicology was studied across cultures, and Hebrew and vernacular Spanish elements flavored the Arabic poetry of the period. Prominent among the eleventh century writers from Cordova was Ibn Hazm (994–1064), a philosopher, essayist, and poet. Others representing the richness and diversity of Andalusian poetry included Ibn Zaydun (c. 1004–1070) and a Jewish writer, the poet and philosopher Judah ha-Levi (c. 1070–1141).

The Arab love of learning created the conditions for important breakthroughs in knowledge. All the fields of study covered in the Qur'an—astronomy, mathematics, philosophy, history, medicine, law, art, and literature—received support in the capitals of Baghdad and Cordova. The Islamic philosophers Ibn Sina (Avicenna) (980–1037) and Ibn Rushd (Averroes) (1126–1198) and the Jewish philosopher Moses Maimonides (1135–1204) all sought to reconcile religion and philosophy, while re-investigating the writings of the ancient Greek philosophers Plato and Aristotle. They were largely responsible for the translation of ancient Greek writings into Arabic, from which they were later translated into Latin. The European philosopher St. Thomas Aquinas (1225–1274), credited in the West for reconciling the Greek and Christian philosophies, depended in large part on the translations and commentaries of twelfth century Arabic philosophers. History and biography also figured heavily in the writings of the Arabs of this period. Muslim historians of the Crusades, such as Imad al-Din (1125–1201), Baha ad-Din (1145–1234) and Ibn al-Athir (1160–1233) wrote general histories and biographies of such figures as Saladin (1137–1193), the Turkish sultan and leader of the Third Crusade.

Sufism, the mystical branch of Islamic belief, came to prominence in the ninth century. Its roots lie in the Qur'an, especially in Muhammad's visions of the angel

Gabriel and his ascension through the heavens in a mystical dream. According to Sufi belief, the soul may enjoy direct union with God through mystical practices. Sufism produced great literature, perhaps owing to its struggle to express the ineffable in the written language and thus find divinity in the material world. The poet Farid ud-Din Attar (c. 1141–c. 1221) wrote the entertaining *The Conference of the Birds* (p. 1397), a long poem of religious instruction. The point of the story rests on a pun. A hoopoe (similar to a hornbill) calls the birds together to go on pilgrimage to seek their god, the Simorgh. When they reach their destination, thirty birds are left. The name for "thirty birds" in Persian is *si morgh*, which is also the name of the god they seek. So their god is no longer distinguishable from themselves: they have become one with the divine.

Europe: From Epic to Romance and Beyond.   The concept of the European Middle Ages was first formulated during the Italian Renaissance, when scholars wished to identify the period between the classical age of Greece and Rome and their own era. This medieval age can be broken down in four parts: the first period consists of Roman influence, the creation of Germanic tribal identity, and the rise of kingdoms (100–800 C.E.); the second period extends from the development of the system of feudalism to the beginning of the Crusades (800–1100); the third period includes the Crusades and the consolidation of major European institutions (1100–1300); and the fourth period marks the transition from the medieval to the early modern world (1300–1450). The key development of the European Middle Ages was the political, economic, and social formation of Europe and its interaction with the Near East, the Middle East, the Far East, North Africa, and Asia.

Broadly speaking, the literary production of the Medieval Period follows these historical divisions and the events that define them. The earliest literature reflects the Latin culture of the church and the recording of the heroic literature of the continent, such as the Anglo-Saxon epic poem *Beowulf* (p. 1184). The literature of the next period reflects the courts of the feudal period, up to the time of the *Song of Roland.* The literature of the third period reflects the Crusades, the growth of the courts and the new enthusiasm for romances and the love poetry of the south of France. The literature of the fourth period reflects a broader and more cosmopolitan outlook, nourished in the cities and towns; there is greater access to the Greek and Latin classics, and education is provided in schools and universities. Sophisticated writers like Dante, Boccaccio, and Chaucer borrowed stories of many lands and cultures—from religious and secular sources alike—and women appeared as significant voices in European writing for the first time.

From Rome to the Germanic States.   Roman military rule never included adequate economic planning for the development of conquered territories, so as Rome's authority expanded its economy stagnated. Cities declined due to the lack of trade necessary to support them. Finally the army weakened, especially in the Germanic regions, so that increasingly the Roman legions in the north were actually composed of Franks and other Germans. Slowly the Germanic tribes gathered strength and overcame the Roman defenders. Life was uniformly hard and cruel in the northern warrior societies, but a new system of ethics, justice, and social organization was slowly taking shape, combining ancient tribal customs with borrowed Roman practices. By the beginning of the sixth century, the new possessors of the land had reached a degree of stability. They included the Ostrogoths in what became Italy, the Visigoths in what became southern France and Spain, the Franks and other Germanic tribes in what became northern France and Germany, and the Anglo Saxons in what had been Roman and Celtic Britain.

At the end of the sixth century, Pope Gregory the Great (r. 590–604) sent Benedictine monks and other members of the clergy to convert tribal chieftains,

The Auzon Casket, eighth century c.e.
This early casket, named after the French town in which it was found in the nineteenth century, is remarkable for its depictions of scenes from Roman, Jewish, Christian, and Germanic traditions. It is thought to have been built in Northumbria (England) sometime during the first half of the eighth century. On the left of the visible panel is a scene from Germanic legend and on the right is the Adoration of the Magi. (British Museum)

from central Europe west to the British Isles. The rudimentary Latin culture of the missionaries consisted of the Bible, a brief liturgical handbook, the Benedictine Rule for establishing monasteries, and Gregory's treatise on pastoral care. The missionaries often made their case for conversion within the framework of the native culture of Germanic society. The British historian Bede (d. 735) reports that after speaking to a priest, a pagan counselor tried to persuade his king to convert to Christianity by using traditional Anglo-Saxon eloquence. He spoke as follows:

> A sparrow flies swiftly in one door of the hall, and out through another. While he is inside, he is safe from the winter storms; but after a few moments of comfort, he vanishes from sight into the wintry world from which he came. Even so, man appears on earth for a little while; but of what went before this life or of what follows, we know nothing. Therefore, if this new teaching has brought any more certain knowledge, it seems only right that we should follow it.

The conversion missions were quite successful. The literature of the period contains many sermons, poems, and passages from the Bible translated into the Germanic languages with the same penchant for dramatic effect.

The Kingdom of the Franks.   Ironically, the development of European consciousness awaited pressure from outside the region. When the prophet Muhammad took up arms and swept through Arabia in the early seventh century, he set in motion a process that would propel the Islamic faithful through Syria, Persia, and Egypt into North Africa and across the Mediterranean to the Iberian peninsula (now Spain and Portugal). It fell to the Carolingian Franks to repel the Islamic warriors at Tours in southern France in 732. The Carolingians were named after Charles Martel, who ruled them from 714 to 741. Though they were impoverished and lived far to the north, the Carolingians managed to overcome the Muslims. But the honor of uniting the Franks would be reserved for Charles Martel's grandson, Charlemagne (768–814). Under his authority, Frankish holdings were extended to what became Italy, Bavaria, Austria, and northern Germany. A minor battle against the Basques in the Pyrenees in 778 that caused the death of one of Charlemagne's lords led to the composition of the great epic of feudal society, *The Song of Roland* (p. 1328).

Charlemagne was crowned Holy Roman Emperor by Pope Leo III in his northern capitol at Aix-la-Chapelle on Christmas Day in 800. Whether or not we believe he was taken by surprise by the Pope's appearance at his coronation, his crowning served the interests of both Rome and the Carolingians. It marked the restoration of the Roman Empire, the formal joining of Church and State, the

The Coronation of Charlemagne, fourteenth century

Pope Leo's coronation of the Frankish king Charlemagne as emperor in 800 C.E. marked the restoration of the Roman Empire, the formal joining of Church and State, the consecration of Europe as an idea, and the start of a cultural revival through which learning and the arts would receive recognition. This event is depicted here in the fourteenth-century illuminated French manuscript, The Chronicles of France. *(The Art Archive/Bibliothèque Municipale, Castres/Dagli Orti)*

consecration of Europe as an idea, and the start of a cultural revival through which learning and the arts received recognition. The moment of glory, however, was brief. After the death of Charlemagne, the grandiose conception of an empire stretching from the North Sea to the Mediterranean faltered due to the economic underdevelopment of the entire region, the persistence of local cultures with their own languages and customs, and the fragmentation brought about by Viking raids from the north. In the events that followed, England fell to the Norman Invasion of 1066, in which French troops seized the throne and significantly changed the British language, culture, and society.

Feudalism and the Crusades.   In the ninth and tenth centuries, as the Carolingian enterprise slackened, a feudal system developed in Europe, enabling baronial estates to defend themselves against foreign raids and to cope with the harshness of economic circumstances. Each estate included its own lord and a landed class of knights who pledged, along with their lesser vassals and serfs, to defend him against his enemies. Ties of obedience were created and a feudal society grew out of this vertical system of loyalties. The worldview based on these ties was necessarily limited. No wonder then that the typical literature of the day emphasized rigidly determined knightly virtues, conceived as service to the lord and faith in God, to be maintained even in the harshest conditions. But European feudal society as a whole, especially in the Frankish kingdoms, had already started to implode at the beginning of the First Crusade in 1095. While feudal society depended on the division of Europe into small political entities, the Crusades anticipated the expansion of Christendom, including the reorganization of Europe on a military basis.

Viewed on the surface, the beginning of the Crusades seemed almost accidental. In Asia Minor, Muslim Turks harassed Christian pilgrims traveling to Jerusalem, and Emperor Alexius I of Constantinople sought western aid to curb the attacks. Following a sermon by Pope Urban II, the First Crusade was launched by the Franks and their allies in 1095. Once begun, the Crusades assumed a life of their own. The Christian capture of Jerusalem from the Muslims in 1099 precipitated one of the worst massacres in medieval history. Eyewitnesses reported that for days the streets of the city ran with Muslim and Jewish blood.

The motives of the First Crusade were as much economic as religious or political. While invading Asia Minor, the Crusaders sought a trade route to the Far East. The fixed order of feudal society came to an end. A new society was forming with a different economic base and different cultural values. Trade and commerce developed in the coastal towns and cities and across the continent. In landlocked areas, farmers and serfs flocked to town centers, which clamored for independence from surrounding baronial estates. As the towns grew into cities, schools were established under the administration of the large churches and the new cathedrals. Education changed from the hard regimen of the Benedictines, who taught grammar, rhetoric, and logic according to monastic usage, to the classical models favored by the teachers of the new schools. Secular writings were reintroduced and readings were liberalized.

Though the Crusades persisted in the twelfth and thirteenth centuries, the battles took place far from European soil. At the same time, the mobilization of Europe created a broader consciousness. The motive for warfare changed from the feudal obligation to defend the local lord to the commitment to serve God and country in foreign lands. The Crusades were often viewed by young knights as an opportunity to display their courage and noble breeding. Thus the military class of knights changed from a hardscrabble army to an honorable assembly with a holy cause. On European soil tournaments took the place of battles, and the aristocracy was preoccupied with maintaining estates and providing hospitality and entertainment. Castles and manors were no longer the narrow, fortified spaces they had been in the tenth century, but richer, more commodious quarters. Tastes changed and a new audience emerged at court. The new literature idealized the knighthood that the courts were beginning to create.

Chivalry and the Development of Romance.   Ideals of chivalry, some of them imported from the East as a result of the First Crusade, came to dominate the knightly code of ethics in Europe. Proper behavior was considered an important attribute of true knighthood. The great romances of the twelfth century by the French writer Chretien de Troyes and the German Wolfram von Eschenbach stressed the necessity to display "courtesy" or good breeding. Women served as educators of the men in good behavior, while the theories of courtly love in the South of France insisted that the only true love was the secret devotion of a knight for his aristocratic lady. Such a knight was twice subjugated by his love — the lady was above him in social class and favored by gender — or so the story went. The audience for this material was a mixed courtly society of knights and ladies, along with their retainers and wealthy followers from the towns.

A legendary figure hovered over Anglo-Norman and French court life in this period, helping give birth to courtly romance. Eleanor, Duchess of Aquitaine (1122–1204), was the granddaughter of the first troubadour poet in the southern French province. The child bride of Louis VII, King of France, in 1137, she joined her husband on the Second Crusade in 1147. In 1152, tiring of the confining life of the French monarchy in Paris, she divorced Louis to marry Henry Plantagenet, Duke of Normandy, later Henry II of England (1154–1189). Eleanor reigned as

Queen of England until 1168, when she returned to Poitiers in the south of France. There she revitalized the troubadour song tradition her grandfather had initiated in the courts of southern France. She brought with her the English stories of King Arthur, immortalized in Geoffrey of Monmouth's legendary *History of the Kings of Britain* (1136). King Arthur lived in a supernatural realm populated by the fairies, magicians, and fantasy knights of Celtic legend. In this atmosphere laden with the miraculous, knights were easily separated from their feudal ties to experience new adventures.

The New Spirituality and the Decline of the Papacy.   In the twelfth and early thirteenth centuries, the Catholic Church developed spiritually and artistically. Saint Bernard of Clairvaux (1090–1153), a Cistercian monk who preached the call to the Second Crusade, led a reform movement inside the church that emphasized the mystical association of the believer with God. Following in the spirit of Bernard's entreaties, two new religious orders arose at the beginning of the thirteenth century. The Dominicans emphasized their preaching mission while the Franciscans were known for the simplicity and piety attributed to their founder, St. Francis of Assisi (1182–1226). The story of St. Francis' spiritual sufferings and his concern for the poor gained a huge popular following after his death. He became a major subject of the Italian painter Giotto (1267–1337), whose *Histories of St. Francis* decorate the lower panels of the nave in the Basilica of Assisi.

In the later thirteenth century, the new European monarchies, built around strong nation-states like England and France, began to clamor for control of the Church. The year 1305 marked the beginning of decline in papal authority. Under attack from various heads of state, Pope Clement V removed the Papacy from Rome to Avignon in the South of France, where it remained until 1378. The era of popular Franciscan spirituality, and the later decline of the Papacy, framed the opposite ends of the Roman Catholic experience in the thirteenth century. While the piety of the common people helped to create a spiritual revival, the corruption of church officials led to the humiliation of the church by the princes of Europe. Both the spiritual and worldly aspects of religious life concerned the Italian poet Dante Alighieri (1265–1321), a Florentine exile who wrote *The Divine Comedy* early in the fourteenth century. Dante's visionary poem, *The Inferno* (p. 000), describes a spiritual dream in which the poet visits hell, purgatory, and heaven. Many great lords, recent Popes, and prominent citizens of Florence were consigned by Dante to hell, providing the poet with extensive opportunity for moral satire.

End of an Era.   The medieval world of the late thirteenth and early fourteenth centuries saw great turmoil and change. The expansion of trade through the

Mediterranean in the thirteenth century gave the economy of Europe a boost. Italian cities in particular reflected economic improvement, brought about by increased trade with the Near East. Prosperity spread to the North in the later fourteenth century, but so did a number of new problems. The decline of the Papacy strengthened the hand of developing governments in the new nations of England, France, and Spain. Later in the fifteenth century, these states developed strong monarchies that dominated European political life for centuries to come. The increase in secular authority also helped create a new mental climate in which the state, city, and individual became the dominant moral and cultural forces, while the ideals of the church and the feudal and courtly societies fell away.

Amid the chaos of the fourteenth century, increasingly secularized writers enjoyed a new position. The English author Geoffrey Chaucer (1340–1400) was trained in the schools of London. Chaucer was a man of the middle class — in his *Canterbury Tales* (p. 000) he expressed faith in trade and progress. His father was a wine merchant and he became clerk of the works for the English royal household. Such new writers were individuals, less commonly attached to religious orders or wealthy patrons, but working in greater part out of personal motivation. They were still Christian, but their Christianity no longer dictated all the terms of human behavior. Above all, they possessed a new perspective on the passing of a millennium — a thousand years during which the City of God held precedence over the City of Man.

THE EARLY MODERN WORLD: 1450–1650

The Early Modern Period continued, in a general way, in the direction of the last century of the Medieval Period. This included the expansion of networks of trade and commerce; the growth of towns and cities, often based around seaports; the consolidation of monarchies and empires; and most importantly the secularization of political, social, and cultural life. In the Early Modern Period, however, the path of world development shifted further westward to Europe, and finally across the Atlantic Ocean to the exploration and colonization of the Americas.

Catastrophe and Emergence.   The new period came in the aftermath of several historical upheavals of the late Medieval Period. The devastating Mongol invasions of the thirteenth century ended in the collapse of the Mongol empire and its piecemeal withdrawal from the West and Near East at century's end. This was followed by the founding of the Ottoman dynasty in Turkey and its rapid growth throughout the fourteenth century. Another catastrophic event, microbiological rather than political, was the worldwide pandemic of the Black Death (1348–1350), killing a third to half the population in some places. Historians are still studying the remarkable resurgence of the European economy in the century to follow this devastating occurrence. After the weakening of the Roman Catholic Church at the end of the thirteenth century and the departure of the Popes to Avignon on the French border in 1305, the Avignon Papacy continued until 1378, only to be replaced by the Great Schism, which divided the Church into competing papacies at Avignon and Rome (1378–1417) and further degraded its resources. Finally, the fall of Constantinople to the Ottoman Turks (1453) rekindled the old conflict between Christianity and Islam, now more a matter of global warfare over trade than a Holy War over religious differences.

Other significant world events leading up to the Early Modern Period included the rise of the independent states of West Africa, especially the Mali Empire, in the thirteenth century, and the building of the Aztec capital of Tenochtitlan in Mexico in 1325. Both these powerful civilizations, based on agricultural economies, extensive trade, and technological development, later faced deadly assaults at the hands of Europeans. The economic development of West Africa in the thirteenth and fourteenth centuries could not protect the region from the incursions of militarily superior Portuguese slave traders in the fifteenth century. The brilliant capital of the Aztecs in Mexico fell in 1521 to the Spanish conquistador Cortés, who destroyed the city and scattered its inhabitants in his quest to replace one world with another.

While the transition from the Medieval to the Early Modern World was a global phenomenon, it is nowhere so clearly seen as in the cultural development of Europe, beginning in Italy. The religious epic *The Divine Comedy*, the crowning achievement of the exiled Florentine poet Dante Alighieri (1265–1321), is generally regarded as the last great creation of medieval culture. A generation later, the poetry and prose of two notable Italian authors, Francesco Petrarch (1304–1374) and Giovanni Boccaccio (1313–1375), already represented the rising secular consciousness of the new period. Eventually the Italian cultural movement, grounded in the study of the Greek and Latin classics with a new emphasis on the role of the individual writer and artist, would fashion itself as the RENAISSANCE. Parallel developments took place in the secular thought of England and northern Europe in the late fourteenth, fifteenth, and early sixteenth centuries, augmented by technological advances including the large-scale use of the printing press. Alongside these events, which took the name of HUMANISM, new currents of religious reform, beginning with attacks on the corruption of the Catholic Church and soon extending to questions of doctrine, resulted in the founding of the Protestant religions to rival Catholicism. The PROTESTANT REFORMATION dates from 1517, the year Martin Luther nailed his Ninety-Five Theses against the selling of indulgences by the Roman Catholic Church on the church door at Wittenberg, Germany.

Technology, Navigation, and Trade.   The Early Modern Period introduced fresh employment of material resources, many of which had originated in other regions of the world. The widespread use of gunpowder in artillery and musketry changed warfare on both land and sea. The increased production of paper in Italy and elsewhere contributed to a rise in literacy. The use of movable metal type in printing greatly increased the availability of books and newsletters, hence the circulation of ideas, advancing the cause of the European humanist movement as well as the Protestant Reformation soon to follow. Again, the focal point of these developments in the fifteenth and sixteenth century was Europe. If we search for a reason why so much activity was initiated there, it would boil down to the concentration of sufficient resources—money and materials—to bring the new energies into being.

Perhaps the greatest practical development of the Early Modern Period was oceanic navigation. To be sure, exploration by sea had met with remarkable success centuries and even millennia before. The Phoenicians had circumnavigated Africa around 500 B.C.E.; the Norsemen had colonized Greenland and reached Newfoundland around 1000 C.E.; and Chinese sailors had opened trade routes to the East Indies, Calcutta, and the Strait of Ormuz in the early fifteenth century. But sustained progress in navigation, exploration, settlement, and trade awaited the development of strong capitalist economies to bring together the necessary components from a variety of sources. These included the deployment of navigational equipment such as the astrolabe and the compass; the lateen or fore-and-aft triangular sail; the centerline rudder operated from inside a ship; and the long ships of the Mediterranean suitable for sailing in ocean waters. Final success came in the European voyages of discovery and conquest at the end of the fifteenth century.

The sixteenth century saw further development of the slave trade in West Africa and the establishment of European colonies and spheres of influence around the world. The resultant exploitation of slave labor and expropriation of raw materials forever changed the shape of the world economy. Led by Spain and Portugal, the European nations opened direct lines of trade with Africa, India, and China, sometimes occupying territory in those regions while colonizing the Americas, which they began to call the New World. As a result of the European expansion, other cultures suffered. Merchants, traders, and sailors from the Middle East, India, and China lost control of the exchange of goods from the east coast of Africa to Calicutt (Calcutta), Malacca, and the port towns along the Indian Ocean to the Portuguese, who sailed south and east around the southern tip of Africa. After the Spaniards, led by the Italian sailor Christopher Columbus (1451–1506) and the conquistadors of the early fifteenth century, made landfall in the Americas by sailing west across the Atlantic, tales of the discovery of a New World full of gold and silver spurred the acquisitive desires of Europe so that other nations followed. Finally, the three-year westward voyage of Magellan (1519–1522) accomplished what Columbus had originally sought; a journey around the world, opening up the spice trade of the Far East by sea.

The expansion in trade that accompanied the voyages reshaped the banking practices of Europe, often yielding extensions of credit in the hope of creating vigorous new economies. The new wealth promoted the growth of cities and city-states and the emergence of a new social class of merchants and traders in Italy, Portugal, Spain, and eventually the Netherlands and England. It encouraged the patronage of artists and writers and the development of more lavish monuments to culture. But trading communities also prospered elsewhere, in the major centers of India, China, Africa, and the Ottoman Empire. Two cities of continuing importance were Timbuktu in West Africa, already established in the twelfth century on the land route to the Mediterranean, and Istanbul (formerly Constantinople), the new seat of the Ottoman Empire on the Eastern end of the Mediterranean.

The Ottomans remained traditional Islamic foes of European Christians—but they were also commercial rivals of the new European enterprises. In the latter part of the fifteenth century, Ottoman Turks under Sultan Mehmet II challenged Italy, venturing within the precincts of Venice in 1477 and nearly taking Rome in 1481, falling back only upon the death of their leader. For another two hundred years Ottoman armies would threaten the centers of European commerce and trade, marching to the gates of Vienna as late as 1683. But though the Turks kept the memories of Holy War alive, this was no replay of the Crusades. For their part, the Europeans were unable to muster a unified Christian army. They were, in the words of one writer, on the cusp of a revolution of a different sort—one in which scientific discovery and material progress had come about at the expense of religion. Ironically, the main force the Europeans could bring against the Turks was the power of the printed word. From the 1450s, broadsheets circulating throughout southern Europe warned against the threat of Turkish invasion, the "present terror of the world." Stirred by these warnings, targeted city-states such as the Italian ports responded to the Turkish armies while the whole of Christendom acting together could not.

The Fortunes of Europe.   During the fifteenth and sixteenth centuries Italy was divided into independent city-states, supposedly modeled on the communities of ancient Greece, though they were actually controlled by local princes supported by banking interests. Rome was the home of the Vatican, which dominated its politics; Venice was overseen by a small clique of powerful merchants; Florence and

Milan answered to the Medici and Sforza families respectively. When the Treaty of Lodi established a temporary balance of power among the city-states of Italy in 1454, many of them amassed great wealth from trade, banking, and commerce. Strategically located within sailing distance of Constantinople and the Islamic ports of the eastern Mediterranean, the cities of Florence, Genoa, Pisa, and Rome especially prospered. But stability under the Treaty of Lodi was short-lived; new political rivalries among the cities and the territorial assaults of France and Spain kept Italy in turmoil in the late fifteenth and early sixteenth centuries. Eventually, Emperor Charles V (r. 1519–1558) imposed peace across the Italian peninsula. In this environment, Niccolo Machiavelli (1469–1527) tried to articulate the rules of the new, complex political realities in his treatise *The Prince* (p. 000), dedicated to Cosimo de Medici of Florence in 1513.

In the last quarter of the fifteenth century, Spain united as a Catholic nation under the joint rule of King Ferdinand V (r. 1474–1516) and Queen Isabella I (r. 1474–1504). At home, the pair worked to unify the Iberian peninsula, working through the Spanish Inquisition to arrest and expel Jews and Muslims whom they charged had posed as Christian converts but secretly continued to practice their own faiths. At sea, they financed missions of exploration beginning with that of Columbus. After Ferdinand's death, the crown passed to his grandson Charles I, soon to become Holy Roman Emperor Charles V in 1519. Under Charles, Spain entered its golden age, enriched by wealth from the Americas. Upon Charles' death, his son Phillip II (r. 1556–1598) vowed to spread Catholicism throughout his holdings, put down Protestantism and subdue the Ottoman Turks. Phillip defeated the Turkish fleet at Lepanto in 1571, but lost his armada in a decisive battle with the English in 1588. From that point on, the power of Spain declined and that of England increased.

England under King Henry VII (r. 1485–1509) focused on building royal authority at home and promoting exploration and trade abroad. Eager to compete with his Spanish and Portuguese neighbors, Henry commissioned John Cabot (c. 1450–c. 1499) to find a northwest passage to the Indies. Cabot completed two voyages to the coast of North America, establishing England's later claim to the Atlantic seaboard. Henry's successor, Henry VIII (r. 1508–47), acting largely for personal and political reasons, took the extraordinary measure of cutting the nation's ties to the Catholic Church and declaring himself the head of the Church of England. Despite later conflicts with France, Spain, and the Holy Roman Empire, England managed to partially isolate itself from Europe in the sixteenth and seventeenth centuries. Queen Elizabeth I (r. 1558–1603) consolidated the political gains of the previous hundred years. The defeat of the Spanish armada in 1588 and the further empowerment of the Anglican Church gave the

Henry Bone, *Queen Elizabeth I*, 1755–1834

This is a miniature copy in enamel of the famous Ditchley portrait of Queen Elizabeth painted in 1572 by Marcus Gheerhaerts. The Tudor monarch under whose reign the English Renaissance reached its peak is shown standing on a map of England. (National Trust / Art Resource, NY)

English an unparalleled opportunity to cultivate the arts and culture. Accordingly, some of Shakespeare's greatest plays, including *King Lear, Henry IV Part I,* and *The Tempest,* allude to England's position as a great power, the issues of dynastic succession, and the ethical and moral responsibilities of rulers to their subjects.

The Renaissance and Its Culture.   Later historians would proclaim the existence of the European Renaissance, a time of rebirth and revival as the name implies, beginning in Italy late in the thirteenth century and moving northward and westward through Europe by the sixteenth century. Economically speaking, the Renaissance was a time of growth and expansion following the decimation of the population after the Black Death of 1348. The major cities of Venice, Milan, and Naples, along with Paris and London, grew rapidly in the late fourteenth, fifteenth, and sixteenth centuries. Agricultural improvements and the cultivation of crops kept pace with the growing population. The reclaiming of land from the sea in the north and the enclosure of lands elsewhere helped increase agricultural production and provided pastureland for domestic livestock, particularly wool-bearing sheep. Mining and metallurgy became major industries due to improvement in machinery, and cloth manufacture contributed to the development of merchant labor. As trade strengthened and wealth moved northward, the development of Antwerp, the leading port of the Netherlands, demonstrated the far extension of the Renaissance by the late fifteen hundreds.

The revival of economic and political energies in Italy contributed to the development of courts in the major cities. Unlike medieval courts, the courts of the Italian princes included bankers, traders, and merchants as well as noblemen, soldiers, and entertainers. The women of these courts were better educated and more involved in their operation than medieval women could have been. The practice of law and business was cultivated as a regular part of court activities. Family dynasties grew up around the major cities—the Borgias of Rome and its environs, the Medicis of Florence, and others. Patronage of the arts, on a grander scale than was possible in medieval times, was considered essential to the maintenance of court society.

The culture that was being created in the new courts was heavily secular. As the political power of Italy gravitated from the Papacy in Rome to the larger courts, culture was redefined according to the tastes of the princes. The revival of the classical culture of Greece and Rome was based on this renewal of the arts in the prosperous city-states of Italy. Architecture, statuary, painting, science, music, and literature all benefited from the patronage of the wealthy princes. At the same time, the revival of the classics owed a great deal to the Islamic spirit of learning that had developed under the Abbasid dynasty in Baghdad in the tenth century, along with other medieval centers of culture including Constantinople. From these and other locations and their libraries, Greek, Latin, Hebrew, and Arabic documents were preserved, copied, and translated, eventually finding their way to Renaissance Italy.

While recognizing its debt to the earlier centers of learning, it is also true that Italian Renaissance culture differed significantly from that of the Medieval Period. Among the writers, Francesco Petrarch (1307–1374) was recognized as an early humanist, one of the important founders of the Renaissance. A scholar who translated classical manuscripts, he also expressed himself as an individual in poetry and prose. He was awarded a prize as the first modern Poet Laureate in Naples in 1341. Giovanni Pico Della Mirandola (1463–1494) advanced the notion of Renaissance self-awareness in his oration *On the Dignity of Man* (p. 000), written under the patronage of Lorenzo de' Medici (1449–1492). He pictured man at the center of the universe, the measure of all things. Nicolo Machiavelli (1469–1527) in his political treatise *The Prince* drew on his experience as a diplomat and secretary of the ruling council of Florence to write a realistic account of politics as it was practiced in the Italy of his time. While his observations put him at an opposite pole from Pico Della Mirandola's idealism, he too describes a human-centered universe, only in darker terms.

The northern humanists of the early sixteenth century also depended on the Greek and Latin tradition of the classics; they concentrated to a greater extent than the Italians on subjecting both the secular and religious institutions of the present to critical study based on their readings of the classical literature of the past. The foundational works of Desderius Erasmus (1466–1536) and the young Thomas More (1478–1535) suggest a carefully calculated open-mindedness in approaching the institutions of Europe. Farther removed from the center of power of the Catholic Church than the Italians, the northern humanists shared a certain degree of skepticism about religious practices with the early dissident clergy of the north, including Martin Luther (1483–1546). Soon, however, Erasmus separated himself from Protestant influence, preferring to focus on the story of Christ as a work of philosophy centering on Christian love and ethical behavior, while More vigorously opposed Protestants, some of whom he ordered executed as heretics during his tenure as head of state under King Henry VIII of England. (Ironically, More himself was later beheaded by the same king for refusing to acknowledge him as the head of the Church of England.)

The Christian Religion and the Moral Order.　The long-standing battle between the Catholic Church and its challengers came to a head in the sixteenth century. Weakened spiritually by the Avignon exile (1305–1378) and the Great Schism that resulted in two rival papal authorities (1378–1417), the church tried to recover both its doctrinal and temporal authority in the fifteenth century. But the reconstituted Roman Popes could not reverse the corruption of the church as a whole. A broad movement of frustrated and disappointed Catholics began to oppose what they called papal usurpation, the illegitimacy of the modern Papacy.

Martin Luther had dedicated himself to the service of God during a thunderstorm while a young law student in 1505. After a troubled period spent in a monastery, he seized upon several doctrines that he first found by reading St. Paul: the idea of salvation by faith alone, the doctrine of the priesthood of all believers, and the belief in the absolute authority of the Bible (which suggests the authority of the individual reader as its interpreter). His beliefs taken together represented a challenge to Catholic Orthodoxy, as the church was quick to recognize. After a trial in Rome, he was excommunicated in 1521. The Protestant religion grew through the work of Luther and others, notably John Calvin (1509–1564), in the decades that followed.

The Catholic Church soon launched what was popularly called the Counter-Reformation, in an attempt to clarify doctrine, end abuses, and re-establish its leadership in the Christian community. The Council of Trent (1545–1564) reaffirmed basic Catholic doctrine concerning salvation by faith and good works while pursuing many reforms in practice and structure. It revitalized the Carmelite Order under the Spanish nun Teresa of Avila (1515–1582) and founded the Jesuit Order under Ignatius Loyola (1491–1556). It also hardened the punishments for heretics. The Spanish Inquisition, first established in 1478, was reconstituted, and the Index of Forbidden Books was established in 1559.

Changing relations between the church and society also were reflected in the role the church played during the voyages of discovery and conquest in the New World. The encounter between European soldiers and the indigenous populations of the Americas was frequently a bloody and oppressive affair, sometimes leading to tensions between church and Crown. At times the Spanish priesthood and even the king attempted to restrain the absolute power of the conquistadors. At other times, the instrumentalities of the church, including the Office of the Inquisition transported from Europe, were complicit in the imprisonment, enslavement, and destruction of the native populations. The strained and sometimes brutal relations between the self-designated "discoverers" and the "discovered," with the clergy positioned somewhere in between, would impact the next five hundred years in the multicultural New World.

The Voyages of Discovery and a New Consciousness.   The discovery of the New World, for soon it would receive that name, challenged Europe and its neighbors

TIME AND PLACE

Renaissance Europe: Johannes Gutenberg and the Printing Press

The Renaissance would not have spread as widely and as quickly as it did without the advent of new methods of printing, developed in about 1450 by Johannes Gutenberg (c. 1397–1468) of Mainz. Woodblock printing — the art of carving a text on a wooden block, inking it, and transferring the ink to a new surface — had been invented in China in the seventh century during the Tang dynasty (618–907 C.E.), and by the eleventh century the Chinese had developed a movable type made from clay. Block printing, along with papermaking, had spread from China through Central Asia into Europe by the twelfth century. What was unique to Gutenberg was his method of casting movable metal type, which enabled the printer to rearrange and reuse the letters that made up a given piece of writing. Gutenberg then adapted a wine press so that the type could be arranged on an inked metal plate, then pressed down onto blank sheets of paper.

The Gutenberg press made it possible for printers to quickly produce inexpensive texts in a wide variety of forms. Everything from Bibles to love poems, books of travelers' tales to scientific treatises, political and religious pamphlets to playing cards could now be given mass distribution. Within fifty years of Gutenberg's first book, the Bible, produced in 1455, more than nine million books had been printed on European printing presses alone.

The flood of books was so "troublesome" that in 1559 Pope Paul IV published the *Index Librorum Prohibitorum,* a list of forbidden books, among which were many of the pamphlets and books of the Protestant reformers. Gutenberg's printing press effected a revolution in the production and dissemination of information equivalent to or greater than the development of the personal computer and the Internet in our own time.

Gutenberg Printing Press, 1468. A replica of the printing press designed by Johannes Gutenberg, the German inventor of the method of printing from movable type, is on display at the Gutenberg Museum in Mainz. (The Art Archive / Musée Gutenberg Mayence / Dagli Orti)

www For more information about the culture and context of the Medieval and Early Modern Periods, see bedfordstmartins.com/worldlitcompact.

nearly as much as the arrival of the first Europeans impacted the indigenous population of the Americas—though not so tragically or fatally. The story of the arrival of Columbus and those who followed him, written down in their records of discovery, conquest, and expropriation, gives us an invaluable picture of our ancestors from both sides of the ocean. The Europeans brought a set of unquestioned attitudes that could invite the scrutiny of later generations only because they were recorded so openly and guilelessly. The story of the assault on Mesoamerica by Christopher Columbus, Hernan Cortes, and those to follow them is surely one of the most unconsciously revealing in human history. The tragedy of the encounter speaks for itself. The indigenous population has been estimated at twenty million at the time of first European contact. The population of Tenochtitlan, the Aztec capital of what is now Mexico, was perhaps three hundred thousand—greater than that of the largest European cities of its day. These people were conquered by several hundred Spaniards, through a combination of military strategy, deception, ignorance, bad counsel, and coincidence. Once undertaken, the mass destruction of Mesoamerica through physical attack, appropriation of food, destruction of resources, and the onslaught of disease took on a terrible life of its own. The subsequent voices of humanitarian protest, such as that of the Spanish gentleman Bartolome de las Casas, came too late to turn the tide.

Some writers were so close to the inception of these events that they remained more connected to the perspective of the pre-Columbian world than the post-Columbian. Sir Thomas More created a fictional island off the coast of Brazil based on his fictional account of the adventures of one of the discoverer Amerigo Vespucci's sailors in 1516. The island of More's *Utopia* (p. 000) is a place of European fantasy, spiced with satirical additions of his own making. His story allows us some insight into the European mind of his day, but little into the reality of the new world before him.

By the time of the European writers Montaigne (1533–1592), Cervantes (1547–1616), and Shakespeare (1564–1616)—a hundred years and more after first contact—the greatest authors of the period had developed a world outlook of a totally different stripe than would have been possible a century before. Though they wrote on vastly different subjects, in different forms—Montaigne the essayist, Cervantes the novelist, and Shakespeare the dramatist—they are similar, and similarly modern, in their capacity for introspection and critical judgment. In the works selected here, Montaigne's "Of Cannibals" (p. 000), Cervantes' *Don Quixote* (p. 000), and Shakespeare's *The Tempest* (p. 000), all three artists only allude to the century of discovery and plunder that preceded them, but all reflect a new consciousness, a new way of examining stories and the beliefs that support them to produce conclusions. Products of an age of human aspiration, an age of discovery and power, they reflect both an overwhelming curiosity and a new awareness of the world, including the loss of innocence that must have occurred throughout the very process of discovery. For what they discover is that the attainment of power always leads to questions of truth, honor, and responsibility, questions that may prove impossible to answer.

In this sense—the experience of coming of age in a world with no easy answers—European literature at the end of the sixteenth and the beginning of the seventeenth century is modern indeed.

⌘ THE NEW TESTAMENT
NEAR EAST, FIRST CENTURY–SECOND CENTURY C.E.

A collection of documents from the early Christian community written in the first two centuries after Jesus' death, the New Testament brings together the Hebraic and Hellenic strands of Western culture. The New Testament, which centers on the life and teachings of a Jewish prophet, was written in Greek. Its message was meant to replace the law and covenant between Moses, the Jewish people, and God. Instead of a religion restricted to God's chosen people, the Jews, the new covenant was put forth as a bond with all humankind, and Christianity proclaimed itself a world religion. The twenty-seven books of the New Testament were written in less than a century, beginning about 50 C.E. with Paul's early letters.

Christian Evangelism.   Shortly before his death in about 29 C.E.,[1] Jesus instructed his followers to "go into all the world and preach the gospel," and the books of the New Testament reflect various aspects of that mission. From its beginnings as a sect in Jerusalem after Jesus' death, Christianity soon spread throughout the Mediterranean. Saint Stephen, the first Christian martyr, who was killed about 34 C.E., prophesied the destruction of the Temple in Jerusalem and prompted a persecution of the Christians in Jerusalem by zealous Jews. Those fleeing this persecution scattered and established churches in other places, especially at Antioch, in Asia Minor, a center of early Christian evangelism. In these new religious centers, Gentile, or non-Jewish, converts soon outnumbered the

[1] **29 C.E.:** Jesus was thirty-three at the time of his death. The calendar that divided "B.C." (before Christ) and "A.D." (after Christ) was developed by the sixth-century monk Dionysius Exiguus, who was several years off in determining the date of Jesus' birth. Jesus was actually born sometime between 6 and 4 B.C.E.

Jewish members of the sect, and early Christians concentrated on extending their message beyond the Jewish community in Palestine. Paul's letters, the earliest writings of the New Testament, recount the apostle's missionary activities in the fifth decade of the first century as he established and encouraged new churches in the areas surrounding Palestine. The gospels and the other later books of the New Testament met the growing need in these early churches for historical, ethical, and theological documents explaining a movement that was spreading far beyond its place of origin. Written in Greek, the international language of the day, the New Testament exported the Christian message from Palestine to the whole Mediterranean world.

The Gospels.   Shorter and less varied than the Hebrew Scriptures, the New Testament is made up of four major kinds of writing: biography, history, letters, and apocalyptic vision. The first four books, the Gospels of Matthew, Mark, Luke, and John, tell the life of Jesus from different perspectives. Writing decades after the death of Jesus, the gospel writers were not simply biographers; first and foremost they were evangelists who told the life of Jesus to win converts to Christianity from communities of

Samaritan Woman at the Well

The earliest Christians were persecuted by the Romans for their faith. This wall fresco was found in the catacombs beneath the streets of Rome, where Christians had secret meeting places and tombs. Here, Christ, pictured in Roman garb, approaches a Samaritan woman, a story told in the Gospel of St. John. It was not until the fourth century that Christianity was established as the official religion of the Roman Empire, guaranteeing its survival. (Scala / Art Resource, NY)

Greek, Roman, and Jewish readers. Their narratives, which emphasize the supernatural and mythic elements of Jesus' life, were based largely on oral stories that circulated in the Christian community and differ at times in their facts, such as who was responsible for Jesus' death.

The Gospel of Mark, generally believed to be the first of the gospels, written around 65 or 70 C.E., is the shortest and most matter-of-fact of the four. Although he may have been an eyewitness to some of the events he describes, Mark probably based most of his gospel on oral stories about Jesus. His plain and vigorous style matches the simple, unembellished story that he tells. Because many of the episodes and teachings in Mark's biography reappear in the Gospels of Matthew and Luke, scholars believe that these two later accounts—written between 80 and 95 C.E.—were based on Mark's work. Since they tell essentially the same story and work from a common outline or synopsis of Jesus' life, these three gospels are often referred to as the **Synoptic Gospels**. By comparing the three and noting their differences and similarities, scholars have been able to date their composition and establish the authorship and intent of each. As Matthew is significantly concerned with placing Jesus in a Jewish context, his gospel is sometimes called the Jewish gospel. He traces Jesus' genealogy back to King David, presents him as the Messiah, and often relates his teachings to those of the Hebrew Scriptures. Luke, a physician who addresses his work to a Gentile, largely Greek, audience, presents Jesus as a human and heroic figure.

Written much later, about 130 C.E., the Gospel of John, whose author is unknown but who is not the John of the Book of Revelation, is less interested in biography than are its three predecessors. Instead, this gospel, sometimes called the "spiritual gospel," develops a theological and

> He [the translator] will find one English book and one only, where, as in the *Iliad* itself, perfect plainness of speech is allied with perfect nobleness; and that book is the Bible.
>
> – Matthew Arnold, *Critic*, 1861

Head of Christ, third century C.E.

Christ's life and teachings were written down in the New Testament and disseminated by his faithful followers, becoming the foundation for a new world religion. This early stone inlay depicting the head of Christ already shows him with a halo, a beard, and a gentle demeanor. (© Scala / Art Resource, NY)

symbolic interpretation of Jesus' life and message and is addressed to an audience of Christians who sought to understand the meaning of Jesus' life and message.

Paul's Letters and the Early Church.   Although they do not appear first in the New Testament as it is ordered today, Paul's letters were probably the first written, composed in the decade between 50 and 60 C.E. Paul began his life as Saul of Tarsus—a city in Cilicia in what is now Turkey—the son of parents who were Pharisees, strict followers of Jewish laws. Saul became an enforcer of those laws and a persecutor of the followers of "the way," the new Christians. But, according to tradition, as he was traveling on the road from Jerusalem to Damascus, he was blinded by a light from heaven and was converted to Christianity. Under his Christian name, Paul became the most important of the apostles. His missionary work moved the center of Christianity from Jerusalem to Antioch, in Asia Minor, and his message combined the ethical dimension of Judaism with elements from Greek and Oriental MYSTERY RELIGIONS.[2] His letters, written before the Gospels and addressed to a Gentile rather than a Jewish audience, take up practical matters having to do with church organization, ethical and moral issues, and points of theology and belief. They develop the doctrine of the early Christian church.

The instruction contained in Corinthians, Paul's letter to the citizens of Corinth, includes some of his most enduring writing. Since he was dispensing moral and ethical advice as well as spiritual doctrine, he took care to address the most pressing concerns of his audience. His advice concerning marriage and the relationship between man and wife includes an interesting passage on whether a woman should cover her head when going about her prayers. In another famous passage he compares the body of Christian believers to the human body (in its inseparability) and to the body of the church (united under God). Finally, his brief "sermon on love" in Corinthians 13 is justly famous, both for its doctrine and the language of the King James translation. The word "charity" in the King James is the translation of the Latin word for love, *caritas*. The sentence near the end of our selection, beginning "For now we see through a glass, darkly," suggests the spiritual state of the world as a reflected image, and contrasts this with the state of pure perception in Heaven.

"The Great Code."   The New Testament tells the story of Jesus and places it in historical and prophetic contexts. From a Christian point of view, the New Testament fulfills the Old Testament, so that many Christian readings of the Bible find foreshadowings, or "types," of Christ in the

---

[2] **Greek and Oriental mystery religions:** Underground sects that provided an emotional and ritual alternative to the formal practices of the established religions of ancient Greece and Rome. The secret rites of some of these cults derived from the Near Eastern worship of such deities as Cybele, Isis, and Mithras. The mystery cults offered a balm for persecution and suffering by promising a messiah, and immortality.

ancient Hebrew patriarchs. In this manner, Adam and Joseph and Moses are completed by Jesus; he becomes the "antitype" who fulfills their historical roles and gives ultimate meaning to their stories. As the "second Adam," Jesus redeems Adam's original sin, for the fallen condition of man in the Hebrew Scriptures is resolved by Jesus' sacrifice. Such "typological" readings see the Bible as much more than a loosely connected collection of songs, histories, myths, and stories by many different writers from many different epochs. They reveal a story uniting all of human history, past, present, and future. Whatever one's beliefs, one cannot deny the significance of the Bible in Western culture. It is not only a fund of stories, an anthology of literature, and a handbook of ethics. It is for the West, as Northrop Frye has called it, "the great code," the cosmic diagram of promise and fulfillment through which Westerners plot their history and tell the stories of their lives.

The King James Version.   The King James Version of the New Testament, commissioned at the behest of James I of England in 1611 and recognized for centuries as the standard English translation, is so ingrained in our language and literature that it defines Biblical language for the English-speaking reader. Its richness and variety, in fact, helped make Elizabethan English the great model for the spoken language for centuries to come. However, the King James Version has sometimes been criticized for diverging too far from the literal sense of the original, and it may seem antiquated to some. The reader may wish to consult more recent translations as well, notably the New English Bible and New Revised Standard Version, listed under "Further Research" below.

■ **FURTHER RESEARCH**

Modern Translations
The New English Bible. 1970.
The New Revised Standard Version. 1989.

Commentary
Alter, Robert, and Frank Kermode. *The Literary Guide to the Bible.* 1987.
Beardslee, W. A. *Literary Criticism of the New Testament.* 1970.
Enslin, Morton Scott. *Christian Beginnings.* 1956.
Frye, Northrop. *The Great Code: The Bible and Literature.* 1981.
———. *Words with Power: Being a Second Study of 'The Bible and Literature.'* 1990.
Gabel, John B., and Charles B. Wheeler. *The Bible as Literature: An Introduction.* 1990.
Kee, Howard Clark, Franklin W. Young, and Karlfried Froehlich. *Understanding the New Testament.* 1973.
Pritchard, John Paul. *A Literary Approach to the New Testament.* 1972.

∾ Luke 1–3

[The Birth, Youth, and Baptism of Jesus]

Chapter 1   And . . . the angel Gabriel was sent from God unto a city of Galilee, named Nazareth, to a virgin espoused to a man whose name was Joseph, of the house of David; and the virgin's name was Mary. And the angel came in unto her, and said, "Hail, thou that art highly favoured, the Lord is with thee: blessed art thou among women." And when she saw him, she was troubled at his saying, and cast in her mind what manner of salutation this should be. And the angel said unto her, "Fear not, Mary: for thou hast found favour with God. And, behold, thou shalt conceive in thy womb, and bring forth a son, and shalt call his name JESUS.[1] He shall be great, and shall be called the Son of the Highest: and the Lord God shall give unto him the throne of his father David: and he shall reign over the house of Jacob for ever; and of his kingdom there shall be no end." Then said Mary unto the angel, "How shall this be, seeing I know not a man?" And the angel answered and said unto her, "The Holy Ghost shall come upon thee, and the power of the Highest shall overshadow thee: therefore also that holy thing which shall be born of thee shall be called the Son of God. And, behold, thy cousin Elisabeth, she hath also conceived a son in her old age: and this is the sixth month with her, who was called barren. For with God nothing shall be impossible." And Mary said, "Behold the handmaid of the Lord; be it unto me according to thy word." And the angel departed from her.

And Mary arose in those days, and went into the hill country with haste, into a city of Juda; and entered into the house of Zacharias, and saluted Elisabeth. And it came to pass, that, when Elisabeth heard the salutation of Mary, the babe leaped in her womb; and Elisabeth was filled with the Holy Ghost; and she spake out with a loud voice, and said, "Blessed art thou among women, and blessed is the fruit of thy womb. And whence is this to me, that the mother of my Lord should come to me? For, lo, as soon as the voice of thy salutation sounded in mine ears, the babe leaped in my womb for joy. And blessed is she that believed: for there shall be a performance of those things which were told her from the Lord."

Chapter 2   And it came to pass in those days, that there went out a decree from Cæsar Augustus, that all the world[2] should be taxed. . . . And all went to be taxed, every one into his own city. And Joseph also went up from Galilee, out of the city of Nazareth, into Judæa, unto the city of David, which is called Bethlehem; . . . to be taxed with Mary his espoused wife, being great with child. And so it was, that, while they were there, the days were accomplished that she should be delivered. And she

---

[1] **JESUS:** The name Jesus, the Greek form of the Hebrew Yeshua or Joshua, means "he shall serve."
[2] **world:** That is, the Roman Empire.

brought forth her firstborn son, and wrapped him in swaddling clothes, and laid him in a manger; because there was no room for them in the inn.

And there were in the same country shepherds abiding in the field, keeping watch over their flock by night. And, lo, the angel of the Lord came upon them, and the glory of the Lord shone round about them: and they were sore afraid. And the angel said unto them, "Fear not: for, behold, I bring you good tidings of great joy, which shall be to all people. For unto you is born this day in the city of David a Saviour, which is Christ the Lord. And this shall be a sign unto you; Ye shall find the babe wrapped in swaddling clothes, lying in a manger." And suddenly there was with the angel a multitude of the heavenly host praising God, and saying,

> "Glory to God in the highest,
> And on earth peace,
> Good will toward men."

And it came to pass, as the angels were gone away from them into heaven, the shepherds said one to another, "Let us now go even unto Bethlehem, and see this thing which is come to pass, which the Lord hath made known unto us." And they came with haste, and found Mary, and Joseph, and the babe lying in a manger. And when they had seen it, they made known abroad the saying which was told them concerning this child. And all they that heard it wondered at those things which were told them by the shepherds. But Mary kept all these things, and pondered them in her heart. And the shepherds returned, glorifying and praising God for all the things that they had heard and seen, as it was told unto them.

And when eight days were accomplished for the circumcising of the child, his name was called JESUS, which was so named of the angel before he was conceived in the womb.

And the child grew, and waxed strong in spirit, filled with wisdom: and the grace of God was upon him.

Now his parents went to Jerusalem every year at the feast of the passover. And when he was twelve years old, they went up to Jerusalem after the custom of the feast. And when they had fulfilled the days, as they returned, the child Jesus tarried behind in Jerusalem; and Joseph and his mother knew not of it. But they, supposing him to have been in the company, went a day's journey; and they sought him among their kinsfolk and acquaintance. And when they found him not, they turned back again to Jerusalem, seeking him. And it came to pass, that after three days they found him in the temple, sitting in the midst of the doctors,[3] both hearing them, and asking them questions. And all that heard him were astonished at his understanding and answers. And when they saw him, they were amazed: and his mother said unto him, "Son, why hast thou thus dealt with us? behold, thy father and I have sought thee sorrowing." And he said unto them, "How is that ye sought me? wist ye not that I must be about my Father's business?" And they understood not the saying which

---

[3] **doctors:** Rabbis, teachers.

he spake unto them. And he went down with them, and came to Nazareth, and was subject unto them: but his mother kept all these sayings in her heart.

And Jesus increased in wisdom and stature, and in favour with God and man.

Chapter 3   Now in the fifteenth year of the reign of Tiberius Cæsar, Pontius Pilate being governor of Judæa, and Herod being tetrarch of Galilee, . . . the word of God came unto John the son of Zacharias in the wilderness. And he came into all the country about Jordan, preaching the baptism of repentance for the remission of sins; as it is written in the book of the words of Esaias the prophet, saying,

> "The voice of one crying in the wilderness,
> 'Prepare ye the way of the Lord,
> Make his paths straight.
> Every valley shall be filled,
> And every mountain and hill shall be brought low;
> And the crooked shall be made straight,
> And the rough ways shall be made smooth;
> And all flesh shall see the salvation of God.'"

Then said he to the multitude that came forth to be baptized of him, "O generation of vipers, who hath warned you to flee from the wrath to come? Bring forth therefore fruits worthy of repentance, and begin not to say within yourselves, 'We have Abraham to our father': for I say unto you, that God is able of these stones to raise up children unto Abraham. And now also the axe is laid unto the root of the trees: every tree therefore which bringeth not forth good fruit is hewn down, and cast into the fire." And the people asked him, saying, "What shall we do then?" He answereth and saith unto them, "He that hath two coats, let him impart to him that hath none; and he that hath meat, let him do likewise." Then came also publicans to be baptized, and said unto him, "Master, what shall we do?" And he said unto them, "Exact no more than that which is appointed you." And the soldiers likewise demanded of him, saying, "And what shall we do?" And he said unto them, "Do violence to no man, neither accuse any falsely; and be content with your wages."

And as the people were in expectation, and all men mused in their hearts of John, whether he were the Christ, or not; John answered, saying unto them all, "I indeed baptize you with water; but one mightier than I cometh, the latchet of whose shoes I am not worthy to unloose: he shall baptize you with the Holy Ghost and with fire: whose fan is in his hand, and he will throughly purge his floor, and will gather the wheat into his garner; but the chaff he will burn with fire unquenchable."

And many other things in his exhortation preached he unto the people. But Herod the tetrarch, . . . shut up John in prison.

Now when all the people were baptized, it came to pass, that Jesus also being baptized, and praying, the heaven was opened, and the Holy Ghost descended in a bodily shape like a dove upon him, and a voice came from heaven, which said, "Thou art my beloved Son; in thee I am well pleased."

FROM

ᴄᴡ Matthew 5–7

[THE TEACHINGS OF JESUS:
THE SERMON ON THE MOUNT]

Chapter 5   And seeing the multitudes, he went up into a mountain: and when he was set, his disciples came unto him: and he opened his mouth, and taught them, saying,

"Blessed are the poor in spirit: for theirs is the kingdom of heaven.

"Blessed are they that mourn: for they shall be comforted.

"Blessed are the meek: for they shall inherit the earth.

"Blessed are they which do hunger and thirst after righteousness: for they shall be filled.

"Blessed are the merciful: for they shall obtain mercy.

"Blessed are the pure in heart: for they shall see God.

"Blessed are the peacemakers: for they shall be called the children of God.

"Blessed are they which are persecuted for righteousness' sake: for theirs is the kingdom of heaven. Blessed are ye, when men shall revile you, and persecute you, and shall say all manner of evil against you falsely, for my sake. Rejoice, and be exceeding glad: for great is your reward in heaven: for so persecuted they the prophets which were before you.

"Ye are the salt of the earth: but if the salt have lost his savour, wherewith shall it be salted? It is thenceforth good for nothing, but to be cast out, and to be trodden under foot of men. Ye are the light of the world. A city that is set on an hill cannot be hid. Neither do men light a candle, and put it under a bushel, but on a candlestick; and it giveth light unto all that are in the house. Let your light so shine before men, that they may see your good works, and glorify your Father which is in heaven.

"Think not that I am come to destroy the law, or the prophets: I am not come to destroy, but to fulfil. For verily I say unto you, Till heaven and earth pass, one jot or one tittle shall in no wise pass from the law, till all be fulfilled. Whosoever therefore shall break one of these least commandments, and shall teach men so, he shall be called the least in the kingdom of heaven: but whosoever shall do and teach them, the same shall be called great in the kingdom of heaven. For I say unto you, that except your righteousness shall exceed the righteousness of the scribes and Pharisees,[1] ye shall in no case enter into the kingdom of heaven.

"Ye have heard that it was said by them of old time, 'Thou shalt not kill; and whosoever shall kill shall be in danger of the judgment': but I say unto you, that whosoever is angry with his brother without a cause shall be in danger of the

---

[1] **scribes and Pharisees:** Scribes, official interpreters of the Hebrew scriptures; Pharisees, a Jewish sect that insisted on strict observance of the Mosaic law.

judgment: and whosoever shall say to his brother, 'Raca,' shall be in danger of the council: but whosoever shall say, 'Thou fool,' shall be in danger of hell fire. Therefore if thou bring thy gift to the altar, and there rememberest that thy brother hath aught against thee; leave there thy gift before the altar, and go thy way; first be reconciled to thy brother, and then come and offer thy gift.

"Ye have heard that it was said by them of old time, 'Thou shalt not commit adultery': but I say unto you, that whosoever looketh on a woman to lust after her hath committed adultery with her already in his heart. And if thy right eye offend thee, pluck it out, and cast it from thee: for it is profitable for thee that one of thy members should perish, and not that thy whole body should be cast into hell. And if thy right hand offend thee, cut it off, and cast it from thee: for it is profitable for thee that one of thy members should perish, and not that thy whole body should be cast into hell. It hath been said, 'Whosoever shall put away his wife, let him give her a writing of divorcement': but I say unto you, that whosoever shall put away his wife, saving for the cause of fornication, causeth her to commit adultery: and whosoever shall marry her that is divorced committeth adultery.

"Again, ye have heard that it hath been said by them of old time, 'Thou shalt not forswear thyself, but shalt perform unto the Lord thine oaths': but I say unto you, Swear not at all; neither by heaven; for it is God's throne: nor by the earth; for it is his footstool: neither by Jerusalem; for it is the city of the great King. Neither shalt thou swear by thy head, because thou canst not make one hair white or black. But let your communication be, 'Yea, yea'; 'Nay, nay': for whatsoever is more than these cometh of evil.

"Ye have heard that it hath been said, 'An eye for an eye, and a tooth for a tooth': but I say unto you, that ye resist not evil: but whosoever shall smite thee on thy right cheek, turn to him the other also. And if any man will sue thee at the law, and take away thy coat, let him have thy cloke also. And whosoever shall compel thee to go a mile, go with him twain. Give to him that asketh thee, and from him that would borrow of thee turn not thou away.

"Ye have heard that it hath been said, 'Thou shalt love thy neighbour, and hate thine enemy'. But I say unto you, Love your enemies, bless them that curse you, do good to them that hate you, and pray for them which despitefully use you, and persecute you; that ye may be the children of your Father which is in heaven: for he maketh his sun to rise on the evil and on the good, and sendeth rain on the just and on the unjust. For if ye love them which love you, what reward have ye? do not even the publicans[2] the same? And if ye salute your brethren only, what do ye more than others? do not even the publicans so? Be ye therefore perfect, even as your Father which is in heaven is perfect."

Chapter 6   "Take heed that ye do not your alms before men, to be seen of them: otherwise ye have no reward of your Father which is in heaven.

"Therefore when thou doest thine alms, do not sound a trumpet before thee, as the hypocrites do in the synagogues and in the streets, that they may have glory of

---

[2] **publicans:** Tax collectors.

men. Verily I say unto you, They have their reward. But when thou doest alms, let not thy left hand know what thy right hand doeth: that thine alms may be in secret: and thy Father which seeth in secret himself shall reward thee openly.

"And when thou prayest, thou shalt not be as the hypocrites are: for they love to pray standing in the synagogues and in the corners of the streets, that they may be seen of men. Verily I say unto you, They have their reward. But thou, when thou prayest, enter into thy closet, and when thou hast shut thy door, pray to thy Father which is in secret; and thy Father which seeth in secret shall reward thee openly. But when ye pray, use not vain repetitions, as the heathen do: for they think that they shall be heard for their much speaking. Be not ye therefore like unto them: for your Father knoweth what things ye have need of, before ye ask him. After this manner therefore pray ye: 'Our Father which art in heaven, Hallowed be thy name. Thy kingdom come. Thy will be done in earth, as it is in heaven. Give us this day our daily bread. And forgive us our debts, as we forgive our debtors. And lead us not into temptation, but deliver us from evil: For thine is the kingdom, and the power, and the glory, for ever. Amen.' For if ye forgive men their trespasses, your heavenly Father will also forgive you: but if ye forgive men not their trespasses, neither will your Father forgive your trespasses.

"Moreover when ye fast, be not, as the hypocrites, of a sad countenance: for they disfigure their faces, that they may appear unto men to fast. Verily I say unto you, They have their reward. But thou, when thou fastest, anoint thine head, and wash thy face; that thou appear not unto men to fast, but unto thy Father which is in secret: and thy Father, which seeth in secret, shall reward thee openly.

"Lay not up for yourselves treasures upon earth, where moth and rust doth corrupt, and where thieves break through and steal: but lay up for yourselves treasures in heaven, where neither moth nor rust cloth corrupt, and where thieves do not break through nor steal: for where your treasure is, there will your heart be also. The light of the body is the eye: if therefore thine eye be single, thy whole body shall be full of light. But if thine eye be evil, thy whole body shall be full of darkness. If therefore the light that is in thee be darkness, how great is that darkness! No man can serve two masters: for either he will hate the one, and love the other; or else he will hold to the one, and despise the other. Ye cannot serve God and mammon.[3] Therefore I say unto you, Take no thought for your life, what ye shall eat, or what ye shall drink; nor yet for your body, what ye shall put on. Is not the life more than meat, and the body than raiment? Behold the fowls of the air: for they sow not, neither do they reap, nor gather into barns; yet your heavenly Father feedeth them. Are ye not much better then they? Which of you by taking thought can add one cubit unto his stature? And why take ye thought for raiment? Consider the lilies of the field, how they grow; they toil not, neither do they spin: and yet I say unto you, that even Solomon in all his glory was not arrayed like one of these. Wherefore, if God so clothe the grass of the field, which to day is, and to morrow is cast into the oven, shall he not much more clothe you, O ye of little faith? Therefore take no thought, saying, 'What shall

---

[3] **mammon:** Wealth; money.

we eat?' or, 'What shall we drink?' or, 'Wherewithal shall we be clothed?' (for after all these things do the Gentiles seek:) for your heavenly Father knoweth that ye have need of all these things. But seek ye first the kingdom of God, and his righteousness; and all these things shall be added unto you. Take therefore no thought for the morrow: for the morrow shall take thought for the things of itself. Sufficient unto the day is the evil thereof."

Chapter 7   "Judge not, that ye be not judged. For with what judgment ye judge, ye shall be judged: and with what measure ye mete, it shall be measured to you again. And why beholdest thou the mote[4] that is in thy brother's eye, but considerest not the beam that is in thine own eye? Or how wilt thou say to thy brother, 'Let me pull out the mote out of thine eye'; and, behold, a beam is in thine own eye? Thou hypocrite, first cast out the beam out of thine own eye; and then shalt thou see clearly to cast out the mote out of thy brother's eye.

"Give not that which is holy unto the dogs, neither cast ye your pearls before swine, lest they trample them under their feet, and turn again and rend you.

"Ask, and it shall be given you; seek, and ye shall find; knock, and it shall be opened unto you: for every one that asketh receiveth; and he that seeketh findeth; and to him that knocketh it shall be opened. Or what man is there of you, whom if his son ask bread, will he give him a stone? Or if he ask a fish, will he give him a serpent? If ye then, being evil, know how to give good gifts unto your children, how much more shall your Father which is in heaven give good things to them that ask him? Therefore all things whatsoever ye would that men should do to you, do ye even so to them: for this is the law and the prophets.

"Enter ye in at the strait gate: for wide is the gate, and broad is the way, that leadeth to destruction, and many there be which go in thereat: because strait is the gate, and narrow is the way, which leadeth unto life, and few there be that find it.

"Beware of false prophets, which come to you in sheep's clothing, but inwardly they are ravening wolves. Ye shall know them by their fruits. Do men gather grapes of thorns, or figs of thistles? Even so every good tree bringeth forth good fruit; but a corrupt tree bringeth forth evil fruit. A good tree cannot bring forth evil fruit, neither can a corrupt tree bring forth good fruit. Every tree that bringeth not forth good fruit is hewn down, and cast into the fire. Wherefore by their fruits ye shall know them. Not every one that saith unto me, 'Lord, Lord,' shall enter into the kingdom of heaven; but he that doeth the will of my Father which is in heaven. Many will say to me in that day, 'Lord, Lord, have we not prophesied in thy name? and in thy name have cast out devils? and in thy name done many wonderful works?' And then will I profess unto them, I never knew you: depart from me, ye that work iniquity. Therefore whosoever heareth these sayings of mine, and doeth them, I will liken him unto a wise man, which built his house upon a rock: and the rain descended, and the floods came, and the winds blew, and beat upon that house; and it fell not: for it was founded upon a rock. And every one that heareth these sayings of mine, and doeth them not, shall be likened unto a foolish man, which built his house upon the sand:

---

[4] **mote:** Speck.

and the rain descended, and the floods came, and the winds blew, and beat upon that house; and it fell: and great was the fall of it."

And it came to pass, when Jesus had ended these sayings, the people were astonished at his doctrine: for he taught them as one having authority, and not as the scribes.

ॐ Matthew 13

[THE TEACHINGS OF JESUS: PARABLES]

Chapter 13   The same day went Jesus out of the house, and sat by the sea side. And great multitudes were gathered together unto him, so that he went into a ship, and sat; and the whole multitude stood on the shore. And he spake many things unto them in parables, saying, "Behold, a sower went forth to sow; and when he sowed, some seeds fell by the way side, and the fowls came and devoured them up: some fell upon stony places, where they had not much earth: and forthwith they sprung up, because they had no deepness of earth: and when the sun was up, they were scorched; and because they had no root, they withered away. And some fell among thorns; and the thorns sprung up, and choked them: but others fell into good ground, and brought forth fruit, some an hundredfold, some sixtyfold, some thirtyfold. Who hath ears to hear, let him hear."

And the disciples came, and said unto him, "Why speakest thou unto them in parables?" He answered and said unto them, "Because it is given unto you to know the mysteries of the kingdom of heaven, but to them it is not given. For whosoever hath, to him shall be given, and he shall have more abundance: but whosoever hath not, from him shall be taken away even that he hath. Therefore speak I to them in parables: because they seeing see not; and hearing they hear not, neither do they understand. And in them is fulfilled the prophecy of Esaias,[1] which saith,

'By hearing ye shall hear, and shall not understand;
And seeing ye shall see, and shall not perceive:
For this people's heart is waxed gross,
And their ears are dull of hearing,
And their eyes they have closed;
Lest at any time they should see with their eyes,
And hear with their ears,
And should understand with their heart,
And should be converted,
And I should heal them.'

---

[1] **Esaias:** Isaiah 5:9–10.

But blessed are your eyes, for they see: and your ears, for they hear. For verily I say unto you, that many prophets and righteous men have desired to see those things which ye see, and have not seen them; and to hear those things which ye hear, and have not heard them. Hear ye therefore the parable of the sower. When any one heareth the word of the kingdom, and understandeth it not, then cometh the wicked one, and catcheth away that which was sown in his heart. This is he which received seed by the way side. But he that received the seed into stony places, the same is he that heareth the word, and anon with joy receiveth it; yet hath he not root in himself, but dureth for a while: for when tribulation or persecution ariseth because of the word, by and by he is offended. He also that received seed among the thorns is he that heareth the word; and the care of this world, and the deceitfulness of riches, choke the word, and he becometh unfruitful. But he that received seed into the good ground is he that heareth the word, and understandeth it; which also beareth fruit, and bringeth forth, some an hundredfold, some sixty, some thirty."

FROM

∽ Luke 22–24

[THE BETRAYAL, TRIAL, CRUCIFIXION, AND RESURRECTION OF JESUS]

Chapter 22   Now the feast of unleavened bread drew nigh, which is called the Passover. And the chief priests and scribes sought how they might kill him; for they feared the people.

Then entered Satan into Judas surnamed Iscariot, being of the number of the twelve. And he went his way, and communed with the chief priests and captains, how he might betray him unto them. And they were glad, and covenanted to give him money. And he promised, and sought opportunity to betray him unto them in the absence of the multitude.

Then came the day of unleavened bread, when the passover must be killed. And he sent Peter and John, saying, "Go and prepare us the passover, that we may eat." And they said unto him, "Where wilt thou that we prepare?" And he said unto them, "Behold, when ye are entered into the city, there shall a man meet you; bearing a pitcher of water; follow him into the house where he entereth in. And ye shall say unto the goodman of the house, 'The Master saith unto thee, Where is the guestchamber, where I shall eat the passover with my disciples?' And he shall shew you a large upper room furnished: there make ready." And they went, and found as he had said unto them: and they made ready the passover.

And when the hour was come, he sat down, and the twelve apostles with him. And he said unto them, "With desire I have desired to eat this passover with you before I suffer: for I say unto you, I will not any more eat thereof, until it be fulfilled in the kingdom of God." And he took the cup, and gave thanks, and said, "Take this, and divide it among yourselves: for I say unto you, I will not drink of the fruit of the vine, until the kingdom of God shall come." And he took bread, and gave thanks, and brake it, and gave unto them, saying, "This is my body which is given for you: this do in remembrance of me." Likewise also the cup after supper, saying, "This cup is the new testament in my blood, which is shed for you. But, behold, the hand of him that betrayeth me is with me on the table. And truly the Son of man goeth, as it was determined: but woe unto that man by whom he is betrayed!" And they began to enquire among themselves, which of them it was that should do this thing.

And there was also a strife among them, which of them should be accounted the greatest. And he said unto them, "The kings of the Gentiles exercise lordship over them; and they that exercise authority upon them are called benefactors. But ye shall not be so: but he that is greatest among you, let him be as the younger; and he that is chief, as he that doth serve. For whether is greater, he that sitteth at meat, or he that serveth? is not he that sitteth at meat? but I am among you as he that serveth. Ye are they which have continued with me in my temptations. And I appoint unto you a kingdom, as my Father hath appointed unto me; that ye may eat and drink at my table in my kingdom, and sit on thrones judging the twelve tribes of Israel." And the Lord said, "Simon, Simon, behold, Satan hath desired to have you, that he may sift you as wheat: but I have prayed for thee, that thy faith fail not: and when thou art converted, strengthen thy brethren." And he said unto him, "Lord, I am ready to go with thee, both into prison, and to death." And he said, "I tell thee, Peter, the cock shall not crow this day, before that thou shalt thrice deny that thou knowest me." . . .

And he came out, and went, as he was wont, to the mount of Olives; and his disciples also followed him. And when he was at the place, he said unto them, "Pray that ye enter not into temptation." And he was withdrawn from them about a stone's cast, and kneeled down, and prayed, saying, "Father, if thou be willing, remove this cup from me: nevertheless not my will, but thine, be done." And there appeared an angel unto him from heaven, strengthening him. And being in an agony he prayed more earnestly: and his sweat was as it were great drops of blood falling down to the ground. And when he rose up from prayer, and was come to his disciples, he found them sleeping for sorrow, and said unto them, "Why sleep ye? rise and pray, lest ye enter into temptation."

And while he yet spake, behold a multitude, and he that was called Judas, one of the twelve, went before them, and drew near unto Jesus to kiss him. But Jesus said unto him, "Judas, betrayest thou the Son of man with a kiss?" When they which were about him saw what would follow, they said unto him, "Lord, shall we smite with the sword?" And one of them smote the servant of the high priest, and cut off his right ear. And Jesus answered and said, "Suffer ye thus far." And he touched his ear, and healed him. Then Jesus said unto the chief priests, and captains of the temple, and the elders, which were come to him, "Be ye come out, as against a thief, with swords and staves? When I was daily with you in the temple, ye stretched forth no hands against me: but this is your hour, and the power of darkness."

Then took they him, and led him, and brought him into the high priest's house. And Peter followed afar off. And when they had kindled a fire in the midst of the hall, and were set down together, Peter sat down among them. But a certain maid beheld him as he sat by the fire, and earnestly looked upon him, and said, "This man was also with him." And he denied him, saying, "Woman, I know him not." And after a little while another saw him, and said, "Thou art also of them." And Peter said, "Man, I am not." And about the space of one hour after another confidently affirmed, saying, "Of a truth this fellow also was with him: for he is a Galilæan." And Peter said, "Man, I know not what thou sayest." And immediately, while he yet spake, the cock crew. And the Lord turned, and looked upon Peter. And Peter remembered the word of the Lord, how he had said unto him, "Before the cock crow, thou shalt deny me thrice." And Peter went out, and wept bitterly.

And the men that held Jesus mocked him, and smote him. And when they had blindfolded him, they struck him on the face, and asked him, saying, "Prophesy, who is it that smote thee?" And many other things blasphemously spake they against him.

And as soon as it was day, the elders of the people and the chief priests and the scribes came together, and led him into their council, saying, "Art thou the Christ? tell us." And he said unto them, "If I tell you, ye will not believe: and if I also ask you, ye will not answer me, nor let me go. Hereafter shall the Son of man sit on the right hand of the power of God." Then said they all, "Art thou then the Son of God?" And he said unto them, "Ye say that I am." And they said, "What need we any further witness? for we ourselves have heard of his own mouth."

Chapter 23 And the whole multitude of them arose, and led him unto Pilate. And they began to accuse him, saying, "We found this fellow perverting the nation, and forbidding to give tribute to Cæsar, saying that he himself is Christ a King." And Pilate asked him, saying, "Art thou the King of the Jews?" And he answered him and said, "Thou sayest it." Then said Pilate to the chief priests and to the people, "I find no fault in this man." And they were the more fierce, saying, "He stirreth up the people, teaching throughout all Jewry, beginning from Galilee to this place." When Pilate heard of Galilee, he asked whether the man were a Galilæan. And as soon as he knew that he belonged unto Herod's jurisdiction, he sent him to Herod, who himself also was at Jerusalem at that time.

And when Herod saw Jesus, he was exceeding glad: for he was desirous to see him of a long season, because he had heard many things of him; and he hoped to have seen some miracle done by him. Then he questioned with him in many words; but he answered him nothing. And the chief priests and scribes stood and vehemently accused him. And Herod with his men of war set him at nought, and mocked him, and arrayed him in a gorgeous robe, and sent him again to Pilate. And the same day Pilate and Herod were made friends together: for before they were at enmity between themselves.

And Pilate, when he had called together the chief priests and the rulers and the people, said unto them, "Ye have brought this man unto me, as one that perverteth the people: and, behold, I, having examined him before you, have found no fault in this man touching those things whereof ye accuse him: no, nor yet Herod: for I sent you to him; and, lo, nothing worthy of death is done unto him. I will therefore chastise him, and release him." (For of necessity he must release one unto them at the feast.) And they cried out all at once, saying, "Away with this man, and release unto us Barabbas": (who for a certain sedition made in the city, and for murder, was cast into prison.) Pilate therefore, willing to release Jesus, spake again to them. But they cried, saying, "Crucify him, crucify him." And he said unto them the third time, "Why, what evil hath he done? I have found no cause of death in him: I will therefore chastise him, and let him go." And they were instant with loud voices, requiring that he might be crucified. And the voices of them and of the chief priests prevailed. And Pilate gave sentence that it should be as they required. And he released unto them him that for sedition and murder was cast into prison, whom they had desired; but he delivered Jesus to their will.

And as they led him away, they laid hold upon one Simon, a Cyrenian,[1] coming out of the country, and on him they laid the cross, that he might bear it after Jesus.

And there followed him a great company of people, and of women, which also bewailed and lamented him. But Jesus turning unto them said, "Daughters of Jerusalem, weep not for me, but weep for yourselves, and for your children. For, behold, the days are coming, in the which they shall say, 'Blessed are the barren, and the wombs that never bare, and the paps which never gave suck.' Then shall they begin to say to the mountains, 'Fall on us'; and to the hills, 'Cover us.' For if they do these things in a green tree, what shall be done in the dry?"

And there were also two other, malefactors, led with him to be put to death.

And when they were come to the place, which is called Calvary, there they crucified him, and the malefactors, one on the right hand, and the other on the left. Then said Jesus, "Father, forgive them; for they know not what they do." And they parted his raiment, and cast lots. And the people stood beholding. And the rulers also with them derided him, saying, "He saved others; let him save himself, if he be Christ, the chosen of God." And the soldiers also mocked him, coming to him, and offering him vinegar, and saying, "If thou be the king of the Jews, save thyself." And a superscription also was written over him in letters of Greek, and Latin, and Hebrew, THIS IS THE KING OF THE JEWS.

And one of the malefactors which were hanged railed on him, saying, "If thou be Christ, save thyself and us." But the other answering rebuked him, saying, "Dost not thou fear God, seeing thou art in the same condemnation? And we indeed justly; for we receive the due reward of our deeds: but this man hath done nothing amiss." And he said unto Jesus, "Lord, remember me when thou comest into thy kingdom." And Jesus said unto him, "Verily I say unto thee, To day shalt thou be with me in paradise."

And it was about the sixth hour, and there was a darkness over all the earth until the ninth hour. And the sun was darkened, and the veil of the temple was rent in the midst. And when Jesus had cried with a loud voice, he said, "Father, into thy hands I commend my spirit": and having said thus, he gave up the ghost. Now when the centurion saw what was done, he glorified God, saying, "Certainly this was a righteous man." And all the people that came together to that sight, beholding the

---

[1] **Cyrenian:** A North African.

things which were done, smote their breasts, and returned. And all his acquaintance, and the women that followed him from Galilee, stood afar off, beholding these things.

And, behold, there was a man named Joseph, a counsellor;[2] and he was a good man, and a just: (the same had not consented to the counsel and deed of them;) he was of Arimathæa, a city of the Jews: who also himself waited for the kingdom of God. This man went unto Pilate, and begged the body of Jesus. And he took it down, and wrapped it in linen, and laid it in a sepulchre that was hewn in stone, wherein never man before was laid. And that day was the preparation, and the sabbath drew on. And the women also, which came with him from Galilee, followed after, and beheld the sepulchre, and how his body was laid. And they returned, and prepared spices and ointments; and rested the sabbath day according to the commandment.

Chapter 24   Now upon the first day of the week, very early in the morning, they came unto the sepulchre, bringing the spices which they had prepared, and certain others with them. And they found the stone rolled away from the sepulchre. And they entered in, and found not the body of the Lord Jesus. And it came to pass, as they were much perplexed thereabout, behold, two men stood by them in shining garments: and as they were afraid, and bowed down their faces to the earth, they said unto them, "Why seek ye the living among the dead? He is not here, but is risen: remember how he spake unto you when he was yet in Galilee, saying, 'The Son of man must be delivered into the hands of sinful men, and be crucified, and the third day rise again.'" And they remembered his words, and returned from the sepulchre, and told all these things unto the eleven, and to all the rest. It was Mary Magdalene, and Joanna, and Mary the mother of James, and other women that were with them, which told these things unto the apostles. And their words seemed to them as idle tales, and they believed them not. Then arose Peter, and ran unto the sepulchre; and stooping down, he beheld the linen clothes laid by themselves, and departed, wondering in himself at that which was come to pass.

And, behold, two of them went that same day to a village called Emmaus, which was from Jerusalem about threescore furlongs.[3] And they talked together of all these things which had happened. And it came to pass, that, while they communed together and reasoned, Jesus himself drew near, and went with them. But their eyes were holden that they should not know him. And he said unto them, "What manner of communications are these that ye have one to another, as ye walk, and are sad?" And the one of them, whose name was Cleopas, answering said unto him, "Art thou only a stranger in Jerusalem, and hast not known the things which are come to pass there in these days?" And he said unto them, "What things?" And they said unto him, "Concerning Jesus of Nazareth, which was a prophet mighty in deed and word before God and all the people: and how the chief priests and our rulers delivered

---

[2] **counsellor:** A member of the Sanhedrin, the Jewish high court.

[3] **threescore furlongs:** About seven miles.

him to be condemned to death, and have crucified him. But we trusted that it had been he which should have redeemed Israel: and beside all this, to day is the third day since these things were done. Yea, and certain women also of our company made us astonished, which were early at the sepulchre; and when they found not his body, they came, saying, that they had also seen a vision of angels, which said that he was alive. And certain of them which were with us went to the sepulchre, and found it even so as the women had said: but him they saw not." Then he said unto them, "O fools, and slow of heart to believe all that the prophets have spoken: ought not Christ to have suffered these things, and to enter into his glory?" And beginning at Moses and all the prophets, he expounded unto them in all the scriptures the things concerning himself. And they drew nigh unto the village, whither they went: and he made as though he would have gone further. But they constrained him, saying, "Abide with us: for it is toward evening, and the day is far spent." And he went in to tarry with them. And it came to pass, as he sat at meat with them, he took bread, and blessed it, and brake, and gave to them. And their eyes were opened, and they knew him; and he vanished out of their sight. And they said one to another, "Did not our heart burn within us, while he talked with us by the way, and while he opened to us the scriptures?" And they rose up the same hour, and returned to Jerusalem, and found the eleven gathered together, and them that were with them, saying, "The Lord is risen indeed, and hath appeared to Simon." And they told what things were done in the way, and how he was known of them in breaking of bread.

And as they thus spake, Jesus himself stood in the midst of them, and saith unto them, "Peace be unto you." But they were terrified and affrighted, and supposed that they had seen a spirit. And he said unto them, "Why are ye troubled? and why do thoughts arise in your hearts? Behold my hands and my feet, that it is I myself: handle me, and see; for a spirit hath not flesh and bones, as ye see me have." And when he had thus spoken, he shewed them his hands and his feet. And while they yet believed not for joy, and wondered, he said unto them, "Have ye here any meat?" And they gave him a piece of a broiled fish, and of an honeycomb. And he took it, and did eat before them.

And he said unto them, "These are the words which I spake unto you, while I was yet with you, that all things must be fulfilled, which were written in the law of Moses, and in the prophets, and in the psalms, concerning me." Then opened he their understanding, that they might understand the scriptures, and said unto them, "Thus it is written, and thus it behoved Christ to suffer, and to rise from the dead the third day: and that repentance and remission of sins should be preached in his name among all nations, beginning at Jerusalem. And ye are witnesses of these things. And, behold, I send the promise of my Father upon you: but tarry ye in the city of Jerusalem, until ye be endued with power from on high."

And he led them out as far as to Bethany, and he lifted up his hands, and blessed them. And it came to pass, while he blessed them, he was parted from them, and carried up into heaven. And they worshipped him, and returned to Jerusalem with great joy: and were continually in the temple, praising and blessing God. Amen.

FROM

∾ First Corinthians 11–13

[PAUL: ON THE CHRISTIAN LIFE]

Chapter 11   Be ye followers of me, even as I also am of Christ. Now I praise you, brethren, that ye remember me in all things, and keep the ordinances, as I delivered them to you. But I would have you know, that the head of every man is Christ; and the head of the woman is the man; and the head of Christ is God. Every man praying or prophesying, having his head covered, dishonoureth his head. But every woman that prayeth or prophesieth with her head uncovered dishonoureth her head: for that is even all one as if she were shaven. For if the woman be not covered, let her also be shorn: but if it be a shame for a woman to be shorn or shaven, let her be covered. For a man indeed ought not to cover his head, forasmuch as he is the image and glory of God: but the woman is the glory of the man. For the man is not of the woman; but the woman of the man. Neither was the man created for the woman; but the woman for the man. For this cause ought the woman to have power[1] on her head because of the angels. Nevertheless neither is the man without[2] the woman, neither the woman without the man, in the Lord. For as the woman is of the man, even so is the man also by the woman; but all things of God. Judge in yourselves: is it comely that a woman pray unto God uncovered? Doth not even nature itself teach you, that, if a man have long hair, it is a shame unto him? But if a woman have long hair, it is a glory to her: for her hair is given her for a covering. But if any man seem to be contentious, we have no such custom, neither the churches of God. . . .

Chapter 12   Now concerning spiritual gifts, brethren, I would not have you ignorant. Ye know that ye were Gentiles, carried away unto these dumb idols, even as ye were led. Wherefore I give you to understand, that no man speaking by the Spirit of God calleth Jesus accursed: and that no man can say that Jesus is the Lord, but by the Holy Ghost.

Now there are diversities of gifts, but the same Spirit. And there are differences of administrations, but the same Lord. And there are diversities of operations, but it is the same God which worketh all in all. But the manifestation of the Spirit is given to every man to profit withal. For to one is given by the Spirit the word of wisdom; to another the word of knowledge by the same Spirit; to another faith by the same Spirit; to another the gifts of healing by the same Spirit; to another the working of miracles; to another prophecy; to another discerning of spirits; to another divers kinds of tongues; to another the interpretation of tongues: but all these worketh that one and the selfsame Spirit, dividing to every man severally as he will.

For as the body is one, and hath many members, and all the members of that one body, being many, are one body: so also is Christ. For by one Spirit are we all

---

[1] **power:** A symbol of authority.

[2] **without:** Independent of.

baptized into one body, whether we be Jews or Gentiles, whether we be bond or free; and have been all made to drink into one Spirit. For the body is not one member, but many. If the foot shall say, "Because I am not the hand, I am not of the body"; is it therefore not of the body? And if the ear shall say, "Because I am not the eye, I am not of the body"; is it therefore not of the body? If the whole body were an eye, where were the hearing? If the whole were hearing, where were the smelling? But now hath God set the members every one of them in the body, as it hath pleased him. And if they were all one member, where were the body? But now are they many members, yet but one body. And the eye cannot say unto the hand, "I have no need of thee": nor again the head to the feet, "I have no need of you." Nay, much more those members of the body, which seem to be more feeble, are necessary: and those members of the body, which we think to be less honourable, upon these we bestow more abundant honour; and our uncomely parts have more abundant comeliness. For our comely parts have no need: but God hath tempered the body together, having given more abundant honour to that part which lacked: that there should be no schism in the body; but that the members should have the same care one for another. And whether one member suffer, all the members suffer with it; or one member be honoured, all the members rejoice with it. Now ye are the body of Christ, and members in particular. And God hath set some in the church, first apostles, secondarily prophets, thirdly teachers, after that miracles, then gifts of healings, helps, governments, diversities of tongues. Are all apostles? are all prophets? are all teachers? are all workers of miracles? Have all the gifts of healing? do all speak with tongues? do all interpret? But covet[3] earnestly the best gifts: and yet shew I unto you a more excellent way.

Chapter 13   Though I speak with the tongues of men and of angels, and have not charity, I am become as sounding brass, or a tinkling cymbal.[4] And though I have the gift of prophecy, and understand all mysteries, and all knowledge; and though I have all faith, so that I could remove mountains, and have not charity, I am nothing. And though I bestow all my goods to feed the poor, and though I give my body to be burned, and have not charity, it profiteth me nothing. Charity suffereth long, and is kind; charity envieth not; charity vaunteth not itself, is not puffed up, doth not behave itself unseemly, seeketh not her own, is not easily provoked, thinketh no evil; rejoiceth not in iniquity, but rejoiceth in the truth; beareth all things, believeth all things, hopeth all things, endureth all things. Charity never faileth: but whether there be prophecies, they shall fail; whether there be tongues, they shall cease; whether there be knowledge, it shall vanish away. For we know in part, and we prophesy in part. But when that which is perfect is come, then that which is in part shall be done away. When I was a child, I spake as a child, I understood as a child, I thought as a child: but when I became a man, I put away childish things. For now we see through a glass,[5] darkly; but then face to face: now I know in part; but then shall I know even as also I am known. And now abideth faith, hope, charity, these three; but the greatest of these is charity.

---

[3] **covet:** Strive for.

[4] **brass . . . cymbal:** The gong and the cymbal were instruments used in pagan worship.

[5] **glass:** Mirror.

ST. AUGUSTINE

B. NORTH AFRICA, 354–430

www For links to more information about St. Augustine, and the twenty-first-century relevance of St. Augustine, see bedfordstmartins .com/worldlit compact.

Of the three great doctors of the Latin church in the first millennium of Christianity, the most celebrated is St. Augustine. St. Ambrose (340–397), bishop of Milan, increased the followers of the Christian faith by his ministry and established the church as a strong voice in the secular world; St. Jerome (340–420), a great scholar, translated the Scriptures from their original Hebrew and Greek, creating the Latin Vulgate Bible, the crucial spiritual resource of the European Middle Ages. However, it was Augustine, Bishop of Hippo (an ancient city in present-day Algeria), who more than any other won the hearts and minds of his contemporaries to Christianity. His *Confessions* (c. 400) and *The City of God* (413–26) are considered his greatest writing achievements; he also wrote a number of theological works that helped establish the basis of Christian doctrine. Today St. Augustine is reckoned as the most important early Christian philosopher, rivaled only by St. Thomas Aquinas (1225–1274)[1] in the thirteenth century.

tuh-GAS-tee

Augustine's Life. Born in **Tagaste**, North Africa, in 354, Aurelius Augustinus was the son of a pagan town councilor and a Christian mother. He was probably descended from the dark-skinned Europeanized North African people later known as Berbers. By the time of Augustine's birth, Christianity had established itself as the official religion of the Roman Empire. This did not necessarily mean, however, that a young man of promising abilities would become a Christian. Despite the pleadings of his mother, Monica, Augustine was never baptized in his youth. Educated for a public career like his father, he excelled in his early studies during a licentious period in Carthage (present-day Tunis, in North Africa). For the next nine years, while he taught rhetoric, Augustine followed the doctrine of **MANICHEANISM**, which saw good and evil as the operative forces in the universe. He studied other philosophical systems as well, coming under the influence of **NEOPLATONISM**, which emphasized the soul's striving for perfection in an imperfect world. In 384, Augustine began to accept Christian teachings. Through his reading of the Epistles of St. Paul, he embraced the doctrine of God's grace, which he found necessary to bring about religious conversion. In 387, at the age of thirty-two, he was baptized a Christian by his chief spiritual advisor, Bishop Ambrose of Milan.

After the death of his mother the following year, Augustine entered monastic society, rising in the Catholic hierarchy to become bishop of Hippo in his native North Africa in 396. He spent the rest of his life

---

[1] **St. Thomas Aquinas** (1225–1274): Italian scholastic theologian who, as a follower of Aristotle, reformed Catholic philosophy when he created a complete philosophical system in his *Summa Theologica*, completed in 1273.

ministering to his diocese and writing works of theology and moral philosophy. In his later years, the Roman Empire rapidly disintegrated; Rome was sacked by **Alaric** and the Visigoths in 410, and Hippo itself lay under siege by the VANDALS, a Germanic people, at the time of Augustine's death in 430. Augustine's bones were transported twice in subsequent centuries to protect them from desecration: from Hippo, which was again under attack by the Vandals, to the island of Sardinia in 497; and from Sardinia, under Saracen attack, to Italy in 722.

AL-uh-rik

His Principal Writings. *The Confessions* is the first truly autobiographical work written in the West. Its honesty, passion, and personal relevance have guaranteed it a secure place in the Western literary canon. Augustine's struggle to embrace Christianity is one of the great stories in the history of Europe, and his conversion, the dramatic climax of the book, became the model for all such subsequent accounts. This work also provides unparalleled insight into the life of a favored young man growing up during the last days of the Roman Empire. *The City of God,* written near the end of Augustine's life, celebrates the superiority of the heavenly City of God at a time when Rome was failing. Augustine's other writings take up the issues he had wrestled with as a convert, such as the makeup of the Holy Trinity, the nature of evil, the authority of the priesthood, the relationship between free will and determinism, and the doctrine of grace and its role in salvation. A notable feature of all his work is its

Baptism Scene, third century C.E. *After his conversion and baptism at the age of thirty-two, St. Augustine became one of the fathers of the Latin church, helping to establish the very basis of Christian doctrine. (Erich Lessing / Art Resource, NY)*

practical utility in the service of the spirit: Augustine writes to state beliefs, solve problems, and influence other human beings. In doing so he often forges a close personal bond with the reader.

The Pattern of *The Confessions*.   *The Confessions* covers the period from Augustine's childhood to his struggles over his faith in adulthood to his conversion to Christianity. The autobiographical portion of the work ends with the death of his mother, Monica, in 388, when Augustine was thirty-three. The text's three concluding chapters explain and extol Christian doctrine, with the last being a scriptural interpretation of Genesis. In Catholic terms, the work is a *confession* by nature of its threefold emphasis on admission of sin, declaration of faith, and praise of God. First, Augustine confesses the sins of his childhood, his sins of the flesh beginning in adolescence, his misguided faith as a young man, and the sin of pride that held him back from fully accepting Christianity. Second, through the story of his conversion, Augustine acknowledges his faith in God. And in the closing chapters of the work, Augustine praises God by expounding doctrine on such matters as memory, time and eternity, form and matter, and Creation.

Consciousness of Sin.   The early chapters of *The Confessions* reveal Augustine's extreme consciousness of sin. For instance, he states that as a child he loved classical romances too much: "I wept over the dead **Dido**, 'who sought her end by the sword.' I forsook you [God], and I followed after your lowest creatures" (Book I, ch. 13).[2] He writes that at the age of sixteen "the madness of lust . . . took me completely under its scepter, and I clutched it with both hands" (Book II, ch. 2). About the same time, he and his companions slipped into a walled garden and stole pears from a neighbor's tree. "Those pears I gathered solely that I might steal," he writes, "for if I put any of that fruit in my mouth, my sin was its seasoning" (Book II, ch. 6). The details of his wrongdoings—some of them palpable, some that might have been the product of a guilty conscience—are everywhere, with Augustine's own interpretations of them never far behind. Not surprisingly, St. Augustine was one of the major exponents of the doctrine of original sin in the early church.[3]

From Doubt to Conversion.   In his twenties, the self-described young sensualist rose in the intellectual world of Carthage, where he conducted his studies. At first, he writes, he found the Holy Scriptures "unworthy of

DIGH-doh

---

[2] **"I wept . . . lowest creatures":** This refers to Dido the queen of Carthage, whose suicide is depicted in Book IV of Virgil's *Aeneid*. Dido is one of God's "lowest creatures" because she is a pagan and a suicide as well as the creation of a work of fiction.

[3] **doctrine . . . church:** Augustine believed that all human beings inherit Original Sin caused by the Fall of Adam and Eve, and that only divine grace can restore them to freely seek their salvation. This grace is a gift of God, not the result of human action.

comparison with the nobility of Cicero's writings" (Book III, ch. 5), and a bishop whom his mother sent to speak to him found him unripe for religious instruction. But after traveling to Rome and then to Milan, where he met Bishop Ambrose, he became a CATECHUMEN in the Catholic faith. Step by step, his reading of the PLATONISTS led him to consider the Epistles of Paul in the New Testament. Now, with the combination of his reading and his exposure to Christian doctrine, Augustine moved toward conversion.

The most famous passage in *The Confessions* begins in Augustine's backyard in Milan. There, in a small garden attached to his house, he finds himself driven by "the tumult in my breast" (Book VIII, ch. 8). Excoriating himself for his sins, uncertain of where to turn with his faith, he finds himself interrupted by a new sound:

> And lo, I heard from a nearby house, a voice like that of a boy or a girl, I know not which, chanting and repeating over and over, "Take up and read, take up and read." (Book VIII, ch. 12)

Opening his book of the Epistles of Paul, Augustine read the first passage he saw:

> Not in rioting and drunkenness, not in chambering and impurities, not in strife and envying; but put you on the Lord Jesus Christ, and make not provision for the flesh in its concupiscences. (*Romans* 13:13–14. Cited in *The Confessions* Book VIII, ch. 12)

His conversion followed. The holy text and the living Augustine had been joined. Clearly he hoped that his own story would serve others, leading them to the Bible so that it might act upon them as it had upon him.

Keys to Interpretation.   Crucial to Augustine's work is his scriptural interpretation. The core of *The Confessions*—its dual status as the first true autobiography in the Western tradition and the first lengthy description of the journey of the Christian soul toward God—is dependent on this mode of understanding, which holds that the Old Testament prefigures the New Testament; that is, what is promised under the Old Law is fulfilled in the New Law of Christ. For example, Exodus, the story of the deliverance of the Jewish people from slavery, is fulfilled eternally in the redemption of mankind by Christ. Similarly, Augustine wants to be understood not only as himself but also as a representative of all mankind seeking fulfillment in salvation.

The reader of St. Augustine will also notice the rhetorical energy of *The Confessions.* Even in translation, the work echoes the cadences and rhythms of Augustine's original, which exploits the rich verbal effects of late classical Latin. Trained in the art of rhetoric, or persuasive communication, Augustine embraced literary style as a means of promoting Christian doctrine. Often the energy of his prose comes from a melodic questioning:

> Who will bring to my mind the sins of my infancy? For in your sight no man is clean of sin, not even the infant who has lived but a day upon earth. Who will bring this to my mind? (Book I, ch. 7)

Augustine (354–430) is the single most important of the Latin church fathers. His works range widely over an enormous number of subjects. In them he puts his own personal stamp on Christian theology, on church-state relations, on the classical tradition, and on Rome as a historical phenomenon. . . . He is the only Latin church father with a truly philosophical mind, who enjoys thinking as an activity in its own right.

– MARCIA L. COLISH, Scholar, 1997

At other times, Augustine endows his arguments with repetitions of imagery, sounds, and sense, much as a poet would or as might be heard today in an excellent sermon:

> Therefore, I defiled the very source of friendship by the filth of concupiscence, and its clear waters I befouled with the lust of hell. Yet foul and vicious as I was, with overflowing vanity, I took pride in being refined and cultured. (Book III, ch. 1)

The Historical Legacy. In the centuries following St. Augustine's death, Western Europe as it is known today slowly rose out of the ashes of the ruined Roman Empire. When it did, it could claim a Christian culture based on classical foundations. Along with his contemporaries St. Ambrose and St. Jerome, St. Augustine helped establish that foundation. Augustine's special vision offered a reading of Christian theology that, following the Pauline Letters, saw individual, historical man traveling on a spiritual pilgrimage toward God and salvation. This theme of HOMO VIATOR, or man as a traveler through life, is taken up in one way or another by writer after writer throughout the European Middle Ages and beyond. It is most notable of all in Dante's *The Divine Comedy,* finished in 1321.

■ **FURTHER RESEARCH**

Translations
Pine-Coffin, R. S., trans. *St. Augustine: Confessions.* 1961.
Ryan, John K., trans. *The Confessions of St. Augustine.* 1960.

Biography and Criticism
Brown, Peter. *Augustine of Hippo.* 1967.
O'Donnell, James J. *Augustine.* 1985.
Smith, Warren Thomas. *Augustine, His Life and Thought.* 1980.

Background and Interpretation
Auerbach, Erich. *Scenes from the Drama of European Literature.* 1959.
Clark, Gillian. *Augustine: The Confessions.* 1993.
Gilson, Etienne. *The Christian Philosophy of St. Augustine.* 1960.
Ladner, Gerhard. *The Idea of Reform.* 1959.

■ **PRONUNCIATION**

Alaric: AL-uh-rik
Dido: DIGH-doh
homo viator: HOH-moh vee-AH-tore, vee-AY-tur
Tagaste: tuh-GAS-tee

∾ The Confessions

Translated by John K. Ryan

FROM BOOK VIII
THE GRACE OF FAITH

Chapter 5

Thus by the burdens of this world I was sweetly weighed down, just as a man often is in sleep. Thoughts wherein I meditated upon you were like the efforts of those who want to arouse themselves but, still overcome by deep drowsiness, sink back again. Just as no man would want to sleep forever, and it is the sane judgment of all men that it is better to be awake, yet a man often defers to shake off sleep when a heavy languor pervades all his members, and although the time to get up has come, he yields to it with pleasure even although it now irks him. In like manner, I was sure that it was better for me to give myself up to your love than to give in to my own desires. However, although the one way appealed to me and was gaining mastery, the other still afforded me pleasure and kept me victim. I had no answer to give to you when you said to me, "Rise, you who sleep, and arise from the dead, and Christ will enlighten you."[1] When on all sides you showed me that your words were true, and I was overcome by your truth, I had no answer whatsoever to make, but only those slow and drowsy words, "Right away. Yes, right away." "Let me be for a little while." But, "Right away—right away" was never right now, and "Let me be for a little while" stretched out for a long time.

In vain was I delighted with your law according to the inward man, when another law in my members fought against the law of my mind, and led me captive in the law of sin which was in my members.[2] For the law of sin is force of habit, whereby the mind is dragged along and held fast, even against its will, but still deservedly so, since it was by its will that it had slipped into the habit. Unhappy man

---

A note on the translation: Throughout the European Middle Ages, *The Confessions* was a popular work. The first modern English translation was by W. H. D. Rouse for the Loeb Classical Library in 1912. The text is still useful for anyone who wants to compare Augustine's Latin with a facing page English translation. Our translation is an authorized Catholic version by John K. Ryan (1959); all notes are the translator's unless otherwise indicated. Ryan's edition is footnoted with references to the Catholic Douay Bible, following the arrangement of Biblical texts to be found there (for instance, the Psalms are numbered somewhat differently from standard Protestant versions).

---

[1] **"Rise . . . you":** Eph. 5:14.

[2] **In vain . . . members:** Cf. Rom. 7:22, 23.

that I was! Who would deliver me from the body of this death, unless your grace through Jesus Christ our Lord?[3]

Chapter 8: In the Garden

Then, during that great struggle in my inner house, which I had violently raised up against my own soul in our chamber,[4] in my heart, troubled both in mind and in countenance, I turn upon Alypius[5] and cry out to him: "What is the trouble with us? What is this? What did you hear? The unlearned rise up and take heaven by storm,[6] and we with all our erudition but empty of heart, see how we wallow in flesh and blood! Are we ashamed to follow, because they have gone on ahead of us? Is it no shame to us not even to follow them?" I said some such words, and my anguish of mind tore me from him, while astounded he looked at me and kept silent. I did not speak in my usual way. My brow, cheeks, eyes, color, and tone of voice spoke of my state of mind more than the words that I uttered.

Attached to our lodging there was a little garden; we had the use of it, as of the whole house, for our host, the owner of the house, did not live in it. The tumult within my breast hurried me out into it, where no one would stop the raging combat that I had entered into against myself, until it would come to such an end as you knew of, but as I knew not. I suffered from a madness that was to bring health, and I was in a death agony that was to bring life: for I knew what a thing of evil I was, but I did not know the good that I would be after but a little while. I rushed, then, into the garden, and Alypius followed in my steps. Even when he was present I was not less alone—and how could he desert me when I was reduced to such a state? We sat down as far as we could from the house. Suffering from a most fearful wound, I quaked in spirit, angered by a most turbulent anger, because I did not enter into your will and into a covenant with you,[7] my God. For all my bones cried out[8] to me to enter into that covenant, and by their praises they lifted me up to the skies. Not by ships, or in chariots, or on foot do we enter therein; we need not go even so far as I had gone from the house to the place where we were sitting. For not only to go, but even to go in thither was naught else but the will to go, to will firmly and finally, and not to turn and toss, now here, now there, a struggling, half-maimed will, with one part rising upwards and another falling down.

Finally, in the shifting tides of my indecision, I made many bodily movements, such as men sometimes will to make but cannot, whether because they lack certain members or because those members are bound with chains, weakened by illness, or hindered in one way or another. If I tore my hair, and beat my forehead, if I locked

---

[3] **Who would . . . Lord?:** Cf. Rom. 7:24, 25.

[4] **which I . . . chamber:** Cf. Isa. 26:20; Matt. 6:6.

[5] **Alypius:** His Friend Alypius is also seeking Christian conversion.

[6] **The unlearned . . . storm:** Cf. Matt. 11:12.

[7] **because I . . . with you:** Cf. Ezech. 16:8.

[8] **For all . . . cried out:** Cf. Ps. 34:10.

my fingers together and clasped my knees, I did so because I willed it. But I could have willed this and yet not done it, if the motive power of my limbs had not made its response. Therefore I did many things in which to will was not the same as the ability to act. Yet I did not do that which I wanted to do with an incomparably greater desire, and could have done as soon as I willed to act, for immediately, when I made that act of will, I would have willed with efficacy. In such an act the power to act and the will itself are the same, and the very act of willing is actually to do the deed. Yet it was not done: it was easier for the body to obey the soul's most feeble command, so that its members were moved at pleasure, than for the soul to obey itself and to accomplish its own high will wholly within the will.

Chapter 11: The Voice of Continence

Thus I was sick and tormented, and I upbraided myself much more bitterly than ever before. I twisted and turned in my chain, until it might be completely broken, although now I was scarcely held by it, but still held by it I was. Within the hidden depths of my soul, O Lord, you urged me on. By an austere mercy you redoubled the scourges[9] of fear and shame, lest I should give in again, and lest that thin little remaining strand should not be broken through but should grow strong again and bind me yet more firmly.

Within myself I said: "Behold, let it be done now, now let it be done," and by those words I was already moving on to a decision. By then I had almost made it, and yet I did not make it. Still, I did not slip back into my former ways, but close by I stood my ground and regained my breath. Again I tried, and I was but a little away from my goal, just a little away from it, and I all but reached it and laid hold of it. Yet I was not quite there, and I did not reach it, and I did not catch hold of it. I still hesitated to die to death and to live to life, for the ingrown worse had more power over me than the untried better. The nearer came that moment in time when I was to become something different, the greater terror did it strike into me. Yet it did not strike me back, nor did it turn me away, but it held me in suspense.

My lovers of old, trifles of trifles and vanities of vanities,[10] held me back. They plucked at my fleshy garment, and they whispered softly: "Do you cast us off?" and "From that moment we shall no more be with you forever and ever!" and again, "From that moment no longer will this thing and that be allowed to you, forever and ever!" What did they suggest by what I have called "this thing and that," what, O my God, did they suggest? May your mercy turn away all that from your servant's soul! What filth did they suggest! What deeds of shame! But now by far less than half did I hear them. For now it was not as if they were openly contradicting me, face to face, but as if they were muttering behind my back, and as if they were furtively picking at me as I left them, to make me look back again. Yet they did delay me, for I hesitated to tear myself away, and shake myself free of them, and leap over to that place where

---

[9] **redoubled the scourges:** Cf. *Aeneid*, v, 457.

[10] **My lovers . . . vanities:** Cf. Eccles. 1:2.

I was called to be. For an overpowering habit kept saying to me, "Do you think that you can live without them?"

But now it asked this in a very feeble voice. For from that way in which I had set my face and where I trembled to pass, there appeared to me the chaste dignity of continence, serene and joyous, but in no wanton fashion, virtuously alluring, so that I would come to her and hesitate no longer. To lift me up and embrace me, she stretched forth her holy hands, filled with varied kinds of good examples. Many were the boys and girls, there too a host of youths, men and women of every age, grave widows and aged virgins, and in all these continence herself was in no wise barren but a fruitful mother[11] of children, of joys born of you, O Lord, her spouse.

She smiled upon me with an enheartening mockery, as if to say: "Cannot you do what these youths and these maidens do? Or can these youths and these maidens do this of themselves, and not rather in the Lord their God? The Lord their God gave me to them. Why do you stand on yourself, and thus stand not at all? Cast yourself on him. Have no fear. He will not draw back and let you fall. Cast yourself trustfully on him: he will receive you and he will heal you." I felt great shame, for I still heard the murmurings of those trifles, and still I delayed and hung there in suspense. Again she smiled, as if to say: "Turn deaf ears to those unclean members of yours upon the earth, so that they may be mortified. They tell you of delights, but not as does the law of the Lord your God."[12] This debate within my heart was solely of myself against myself. But Alypius, standing close by my side, silently awaited the outcome of my strange emotion.

Chapter 12: The Voice as of a Child

But when deep reflection had dredged out of the secret recesses of my soul all my misery and heaped it up in full view of my heart, there arose a mighty storm, bringing with it a mighty downpour of tears. That I might pour it all forth with its own proper sounds, I arose from Alypius's side — to be alone seemed more proper to this ordeal of weeping — and went farther apart, so that not even his presence would be a hindrance to me. Such was I at that moment, and he sensed it, for I suppose that I had said something in which the sound of my voice already appeared to be choked with weeping. So I had arisen, while he, in deep wonder, remained there where we were sitting. I flung myself down, how I do not know, under a certain fig tree, and gave free rein to my tears.[13] The floods burst from my eyes, an acceptable sacrifice to you.[14] Not indeed in these very words but to this effect I spoke many things to you: "And you, O Lord, how long?[15] How long, O Lord, will you be angry forever?[16]

---

[11] **fruitful mother:** Cf. Ps. 112:9.

[12] **"Turn deaf . . . your God":** Cf. Ps. 118:85.

[13] **I flung . . . tears:** Cf. *Aeneid*, vii, 499.

[14] **The floods . . . to you:** Cf. Ps. 50:19.

[15] **"And you . . . long":** Ps. 6:4.

[16] **How long . . . forever?:** Ps. 78:5.

Remember not our past iniquities."[17] For I felt that I was held by them, and I gasped forth these mournful words, "How long, how long? Tomorrow and tomorrow? Why not now? Why not in this very hour an end to my uncleanness?"

Such words I spoke, and with most bitter contrition I wept within my heart. And lo, I heard from a nearby house, a voice like that of a boy or a girl, I know not which, chanting and repeating over and over, "Take up and read. Take up and read."[18] Instantly, with altered countenance, I began to think most intently whether children made use of any such chant in some kind of game, but I could not recall hearing it anywhere. I checked the flow of my tears and got up, for I interpreted this solely as a command given to me by God to open the book and read the first chapter I should come upon. For I had heard how Anthony had been admonished by a reading from the Gospel at which he chanced to be present, as if the words read were addressed to him: "Go, sell what you have, and give to the poor, and you shall have treasure in heaven, and come, follow me,"[19] and that by such a portent he was immediately converted to you.

So I hurried back to the spot where Alypius was sitting, for I had put there the volume of the apostle when I got up and left him. I snatched it up, opened it, and read in silence the chapter on which my eyes first fell: "Not in rioting and drunkenness, not in chambering and impurities, not in strife and envying; but put you on the Lord Jesus Christ, and make not provision for the flesh in its concupiscences."[20] No further wished I to read, nor was there need to do so. Instantly, in truth, at the end of this sentence, as if before a peaceful light streaming into my heart, all the dark shadows of doubt fled away.

Then, having inserted my finger, or with some other mark, I closed the book, and, with a countenance now calm, I told it all to Alypius. What had taken place in him, which I did not know about, he then made known to me. He asked to see what I had read: I showed it to him, and he looked also at what came after what I had read for I did not know what followed. It was this that followed: "Now him that is weak in the faith take unto you,"[21] which he applied to himself and disclosed to me. By this admonition he was strengthened, and by a good resolution and purpose, which were entirely in keeping with his character, wherein both for a long time and for the better he had greatly differed from me, he joined me without any painful hesitation.

Thereupon we went in to my mother; we told her the story, and she rejoiced. We related just how it happened. She was filled with exultation and triumph, and she blessed you, "who are able to do above that which we ask or think."[22] She saw that

---

[17] **Remember . . . iniquities:** Ps. 78:8.

[18] **"Take up and read."** In Latin, "Tolle lege, tolle lege." This famous passage came to symbolize Christian conversion in the Middle Ages. [Ed.]

[19] **"Go . . . follow me":** Matt. 19:21.

[20] **"Not in . . . concupiscences":** Rom. 13:13, 14.

[21] **"Now him . . . unto you":** Rom. 14:1.

[22] **"who are . . . or think":** Cf. Eph. 3:20.

through me you had given her far more than she had long begged for by her piteous tears and groans. For you had converted me to yourself, so that I would seek neither wife nor ambition in this world, for I would stand on that rule of faith where, so many years before, you had showed me to her. You turned her mourning into a joy[23] far richer than that she had desired, far dearer and purer than that she had sought in grandchildren born of my flesh.[24]

---

[23] You turned . . . a joy: Cf. Ps. 29:12.

[24] she had sought . . . flesh: Monica had made efforts to arrange a lawful marriage for her son. Cf. *Confessions*, Book VI, ch. 13.

∾ THE QUR'AN (THE KORAN)
ARABIA, 651–652

iz-LAHM

koo-RAHN

AH-luh

The Qur'an, or Koran, which means "reading" or "recital," is the sacred text of the nation of believers called **Islam**, the third major religion to originate in the Middle East after Judaism and Christianity. For believers in Islam, or Muslims, the **Qur'an** is not considered a book of prophecy but is the Word of God, **Allah**, delivered in the Arabic language between the years 610–632 C.E. to the prophet Muhammad; it completes the earlier prophecies of the great prophets of the Hebrew Scriptures and the New Testament, including Abraham, Moses, David, and Jesus. Muslims believe that the earthly Qur'an is a copy of the divine Qur'an that, inscribed in gold on tablets of marble in heaven, exists for eternity and is in all aspects—religious, moral, historical—the only true guide to the conduct of life. All important tasks begun by believing Muslims are undertaken "in the name of God, the Compassionate, the Merciful." The monotheism of the Qur'an and its ascription to Muhammad as its divine Messenger are contained in the first two lines of the prayer, "There is no god but Allah, and Muhammad is his prophet." Strictly speaking, the Qur'an cannot be translated; versions in other languages may be used for the purposes of teaching and conversion, but the true Word of God is in Arabic alone. Far from limiting the spread of the Qur'an and Islam—whose followers number over one billion—this belief has served as a powerful protector of the Arabic language throughout the world.

The political and cultural impact of the religion of Islam and its holy book can hardly be overstated. A language, a religion, and a culture were carried abroad together during the expansion of Muslim territory in the seventh and early eighth centuries. By the time of the death of Muhammad in 632 C.E., Islam, which means "submitting oneself to God," was already well established throughout Arabia. For another century Muhammad's followers initiated a period of ***jihad***,[1] or holy war, during which they moved out of the Arabian peninsula, conquering Syria, Persia, Armenia, Egypt, and eventually North Africa, Spain, and a large part of Asia Minor. The Muslim expansion under the **Umayyad** dynasty[2] reached Constantinople in 718 and southern France in 732, one hundred years after Muhammad's death. Muslim culture took hold in the conquered territories, coming to full flower under the **Abbasid** dynasty,[3] located in Baghdad, between 750 and 950. Except in times of *JIHAD*, other peoples were tolerated in the Muslim world, and this relative openness made possible great intellectual advances in philosophy, the arts, and science. Even to this day, Islam's inclusiveness has had much to do with its widespread acceptance: Its believers come from many races in all parts of the world.

jih-HAHD

oo-MIGH-yad

uh-BAS-id

The Prophet Muhammad.   Muhammad was born about 570 C.E. in the trading town of Mecca near the west coast of Arabia to a poor clan, the Hashim, of the Quraysh tribe. Orphaned as a child, he worked as a young man for his uncle Abu-Talib as a camel driver on caravans. About 595 he married **Khadijah**, a rich widow who tested him by having him lead her trading caravan to Syria before proposing marriage to him. Muhammad's marriage prospered, and together he and his wife had four daughters whom they were able to marry to substantial men in the community. While Muhammad was busy attaining a position of prominence himself and brooding over the fate of Mecca, he had a vision of the angel Gabriel who said to him:

kah-DEE-jah

> Recite in the name of your Lord who created — created man from
>   clots of blood.
> Recite! Your Lord is the Most Bountiful One, who by the pen
>   taught man what he did not know.

This was the first fragment of the Qur'an. (It is now the opening of Sura 96.) After an interval of two to three years, Muhammad's visions began again, sometimes in dreams and sometimes in daytime reveries. Over a period of twenty-two years the entire Qur'an was transmitted to him in this way. As far as is known, Muhammad was illiterate. But he recited the

---

[1] *jihad:* In its sense of "holy war," *jihad* first referred to the struggle of the people of Medina, Muhammad's followers, against the "unbelievers" of Mecca. When Muslim armies moved out of Arabia across North Africa and Spain and followed the trade routes through Asia Minor in the seventh and eighth centuries, a permanent state of war was believed to exist between Islam and nations of unbelievers beyond its borders. Jews and Christians, "People of the Book," were generally exempted from jihad.

[2] **Umayyad dynasty:** Formed from a distant branch of Muhammad's family in 661. Under this dynasty the capital was moved to Damascus, in Syria. The dynasty's limited claim to ancestry, its poor administrative record, and a series of political crises led to its overthrow in Damascus in 749. A caliphate of the Umayyad dynasty survived in Andalusia (Spain) until 1031.

[3] **Abbasid dynasty:** This dynasty, established in 750, proclaimed an end to "secular Arab" rule and moved the capital to Baghdad, in Iraq. Deeply influenced by its neighbor Persia, the Abbasid regime enjoyed its "golden age" late in the eighth century.

received verses to his followers, who memorized them, and eventually the verses were recorded by scribes—according to legend, on anything they could find, including parchment, leather, palm leaves, even camel bones.

Muhammad began preaching in Mecca about 613, three years after receiving the first of his visions. Like other prophets throughout history, he preached at a time of frustration and social unrest, and he called for a renewal of faith; at the same time, he introduced new religious beliefs and practices. The chief topics of his early preaching included God's goodness and power, the necessity to meet God for judgment, the proper response to God of gratitude and worship, the need to exhibit generosity, and his own vocation as God's prophet. Soon Muhammad encountered opposition from some of the rich merchants in Mecca having to do with several aspects of his preaching. To these wealthy businessmen, Muhammad's insistence on generosity toward the poor suggested a condemnation of excessive wealth. Moreover, Muhammad's avowal that he was the Prophet of God made the merchants think he was trying to seize political control of Mecca. Finally, Muhammad recanted the so-called satanic verses that favored the worship of certain idols, saying they had been received in a false vision sent by the devil. After considering the issue further, Muhammad opposed the worship of any images whatever and denounced polytheism. As the Qur'an states, "There is no god but God." It is likely that the local merchants supported the shrines around Mecca because of their proximity to the centers of trade and commerce from which they benefited, and for this reason they opposed Muhammad's condemnation of idol worship.

The Hegira.   Under pressure from the Meccan merchants, Muhammad's followers began to migrate, first to Abyssinia around 615 and later to Medina in 622. The reasons for the twofold migration are still debated, but it is known that Muhammad's clan, the Hashim, came under political pressure in Mecca in 616, and both Muhammad's uncle and protector, Abu-Talib, and Muhammad's wife, Khadijah, died in 619. Facing hostility at home, Muhammad began to negotiate with emissaries from Medina, another coastal city in western Arabia, and in September 622 fled Mecca in the middle of the night, arriving in Medina with his supporters. This emigration, called the **Hegira** in Latin (or ***hijrah*** in Arabic), established Muhammad as a dignitary in Medina. He became the city's chief arbiter of disputes, and soon the city became a community of believers, or *UMWAH*, under Muhammad's spiritual leadership.

In the remaining decade of his life, Muhammad subdued opposition in Medina, confronted and defeated his old opponents in Mecca, and became virtual ruler of western Arabia. The continuing conflict between the Byzantine empire and Persia to the north and east enhanced the position of the new Arabian Muslims, since they represented a religiously based community of impressive numbers and relative stability. In March 632, Muhammad led a holy pilgrimage, or *HAJJ*, to Mecca, a "pilgrimage of farewell" in his case, that has since become common practice for every Muslim, who is expected to make the journey at least once in his or her lifetime. Muhammad died in Medina on June 8, 632.

hih-JIGH-ruh; HIJ-ruh

oom-WAH

HAHJ

Abbasid Qur'an, ninth century
The Qur'an, Islam's holy book, recounts the Word of God as told to Muhammad, the Prophet and divine Messenger. The holy Qur'an informs the daily life and culture of all its followers. It is the central text of one of the great world religions whose millions of adherents inhabit countries all over the world. (Detail: The Art Archive / Turkish and Islamic Art Museum, Istanbul / Dagli Orti)

The Text of the Qur'an.   In 651–652 C.E., under the CALIPH **Othman**, Muhammad's secretary **Zaid Ibn Thabit** collected the prophet's recitations and edited them into 114 suras, or chapters, creating the Qur'an in Arabic. Each of the 114 suras is titled with a word, such as "Women" or "Jonah," suggesting its contents. The suras vary in length from nearly three hundred verses to a few words; although the shortest suras were often the earliest, all suras now are arranged in descending order, from the longest to the shortest, in the Qur'an. Partly because of this arrangement, the Qur'an as a whole is not connected by a narrative thread, and indeed its longer suras jump from subject to subject. The style of the suras varies considerably as well. Some of the short suras have the power of a brief sermon, including moral exhortations to lead a good life, while the long chapters detail prescriptions for the improvement of the society of the believers and are often legalistic in tone.

   The fact that the Qur'an is considered holy, a direct message from God, makes it comparable to the Torah — the Books of Genesis, Exodus, Leviticus, Numbers, and Deuteronomy in the **Hebrew Scriptures**. Muhammad is rarely named in the Qur'an; he is usually called **al-Rasul**, or "Messenger." Although the influence of the Qur'an on later Arabic literature has been tremendous, Muhammad rejected attempts to see himself as a gifted poet or storyteller. In fact, for many centuries Muslims regarded serious literature as limited to works touching on philosophy,

KAY-lif AHTH-mun
ZIDE IB-un THAH-bit

p. 78
ahl-rah-SOOL

ethics, morals, or spiritual concerns; storytelling was generally dismissed as unworthy. Poetry, which was held in high esteem before the Qur'an, continued to flourish after Muhammad's death.

The Book for Believers: The Story of the Cow.   From the start the Qur'an states its purpose clearly. The Word of God is intended for believers, so that they may follow the right path. As **Sura** 2: The Cow says, "This Book is not to be doubted. It is a guide for the righteous." Sura 2 begins by distinguishing believers from unbelievers; in the story Moses brings his followers a command from God to sacrifice a cow. They are at first incredulous. Muhammad compares this incredulity to the reluctance of "People of the Book" — Christians and Jews — to believe in his prophecy, clinging instead to what they already know. The figure of Abraham is used to explain the presence of the *KAʿBAH*, the sacred House of the Black Stone, in Mecca, following the injunction: "Make the place where Abraham stood a place of worship."[4] Thus Sura 2 emphasizes the continuity of prophecy that began with Abraham and has its completion in Muhammad. Also in Sura 2, the nature of righteousness is defined:

> Righteousness does not consist in whether you face towards the East or the West. The Righteous man is he who believes in God and the Last Day, in the angels and the Book and the prophets; who, though he loves it dearly, gives away his wealth to kinsfolk, to orphans, to the destitute, to the traveler in need and to beggars, and for the redemption of captives; who attends to his prayers and renders the alms levy; who is true to his promises and steadfast in adversity and in times of war. Such are the true believers; such are the God-fearing. (2:176)

Men and Women.   To modern-day Western readers, the ancient religious texts of the Middle East, especially the Hebrew Scriptures and the Qur'an, treat women harshly, subordinating them to their husbands and calling for punishment for such offenses as disloyalty and infidelity. One frequently cited passage in Sura 4 of the Qur'an leaves little doubt as to this position.

> Men have authority over women because God has made the one superior to the other, and because they spend their wealth to maintain them. Good women are obedient. They guard their unseen parts because God has guarded them. As for those from whom you fear disobedience, admonish them, forsake them in beds apart, and beat them. Then if they obey you, take no further action against them. Surely God is high, supreme. (4:34)

On the other hand, the Qur'an contains passages demonstrating respect for women within the limits of their assigned roles. The beginning

---

SOO-rah

KAH-buh

[4] **the Kaʿbah . . . worship:** This is the destination of holy pilgrimage *(hajj)* for Muslims, the site of prayer where they pay reverence to the Black Stone. The Stone is kept in the *Kaʿbah*, a cubical house in the center of Mecca.

The Near East: The Dome of the Rock (687–698 C.E.)

The Dome of the Rock was built during the rule of Caliph Abd al-Malik a little more than half a century after the death of Muhammad. It marks the spot where, according to the Qur'an, the Prophet ascended into the heavens in a spiritual dream or journey. The Dome also symbolizes the Islamic conception of the relationship between the Jewish, Christian, and Muslim faiths. It is raised over the rock on which Abraham is believed to have prepared his son Isaac as a sacrifice to Jehovah, the same ground on which the Temple of Solomon was later twice built and twice destroyed. The Dome is also situated near the Church of the Holy Sepulchre, the place where Christ is believed to have been crucified, and several of the Dome's principal architectural features strive to imitate or surpass those of that Christian monument. The architectural style of the Dome of the

The Dome of the Rock. *A contemporary view of Jerusalem with the Dome of the Rock in the distance. (The Art Archive / Dagli Orti)*

Rock came from its Muslim builders, with its beautifully colored inner pillars encircling the Rock; the octagonal outer wall, once done in mosaics but later replaced by sea-blue porcelain; and the Dome itself, a wooden curved cupola about seventy-five feet in diameter covered in gold.

The Jewish heritage of the site begins with the story of Abraham and Isaac and continues with the construction of Solomon's Temple, erected over the Rock itself on a level plateau in about 950 B.C.E. Constantly falling under attack after the death of Solomon, the temple finally was destroyed by the Babylonian warrior Nebuchadnezzar in 587 B.C.E. Languishing in captivity until 539, the remaining peoples of Judah returned to Jerusalem and rebuilt the Temple beginning in 520. The area was conquered again by Alexander the Great in the fourth century B.C.E. and faced further invasion and desecration until the time of the Roman emperors. Rebuilt by King Herod in 20 B.C.E. in an effort to win the admiration of the Jews, the Temple was finally destroyed by the Roman general Titus in 70 C.E. All that was left of the Second Temple of Solomon was a portion of the western edifice now known as the Wailing Wall, a site of Jewish prayer and mourning.

Early in the seventh century C.E., Bedouin tribes from Arabia led an explosive wave of conquest prompted by the teachings of the Prophet Muhammad and the faith of Islam. Five years after Muhammad's death in 632, Muslim soldiers were encamped outside the gates of Jerusalem. Muhammad's own injunction that a new temple be built over the ruins of the old was followed to the letter, resulting in the Dome of the Rock, the greatest monument to the Muslim faith. Today this monument stands as a commemoration both of Muhammad's ascent into heaven and his followers' determination to prevail in the Holy Land.

of Sura 4: Women, for example, reminds believers of the common origin of all humanity, and pledges to honor motherhood in particular.

> You people! Have fear of your Lord, who created you from a single soul. From that soul he created its spouse, and through them He bestrewed the earth with countless men and women.
> Fear God, in whose name you plead with one another, and honor the Mothers who bore you. God is ever watching you. (4:1–2)

The Qur'an also prescribes Islamic laws governing inheritance, including provisions for women, children, orphans, the disabled, and even slaves. While these laws still discriminate against women, who could inherit only half the sum that a similarly situated male would inherit, they insist on compassion and respect for surviving families, the poor, and those otherwise unable to support themselves. It should be remembered that the enactment of strict laws against such offenses as the taking of the widow of a deceased male relative by his brother — a common practice of the day — represented a gain for women of the time, grounding the treatment of women in a context of respect for human rights, no matter how limited it might seem according to a modern perspective.

The Story of the Table. In Sura 5: The Table, the angel Gabriel addresses Jews and Christians ("People of the Book"), chastising them for falling away from their covenant with God. Then he addresses the Apostle Muhammad, explaining that the Jewish Torah and the Christian Gospels are precursors to the "Book with the truth" (the Qur'an). He also addresses the People of the Book, in an interesting passage, concerning the question of religious tolerance.

> We have ordained a law and assigned a path for each of you. Had God pleased, He could have made of you one community: but it is His wish to prove you by that which He has bestowed upon you. Vie with each other in good works, for to God shall you all return and He will resolve your differences for you. (5:49)

While conceding nothing to what are regarded as the false beliefs of the Jews and Christians, this passage clarifies why Muslims are encouraged to tolerate these faiths, in the hope that their practitioners will adopt Islam voluntarily.

In particular, this chapter militates against the Christian belief in the divinity of Jesus. At the end of the chapter, the following story is told: The disciples request of Jesus that the Lord send them down a table of food from heaven. In reply, God sends down the table, but also tests Jesus, asking him whether he ever has said to mankind, "Worship me and my mother as gods besides God." Jesus denies this, saying that he has only said "Serve God, my Lord and your Lord." God then declares that the righteous will be saved, and is praised as all-powerful.

Visions of Heaven and Hell. The linked sections, Sura 55: The Merciful and Sura 56: That Which Is Coming, describe the joy of creation, man's choice between heaven and hell, and the two states of existence after death. Some of the lyricism and the sensual imagery in the descriptions of the gardens of the saved recall Psalms or even The Song of Solomon from the Hebrew Scriptures. These short suras are among the most inspired—and the most controversial—in the Qur'an.

The Concluding Suras.   Several of the concluding suras are fine examples of the richness and range of the shorter pieces. Sura 93: Daylight is an admonition to treat the lowly of this world with care and respect. Sura 96: Clots of Blood is believed to be Muhammad's first vision, when he is called upon to recite the messages he receives. Sura 109: The Unbelievers seems to be a charm to keep the godless away. Sura 110: Help foresees a day when "God's help and victory come, and you see men embrace God's faith in multitudes." Characteristically, it advises humility. Sura 112: Oneness is often seen as a summary of the spiritual message of the Qur'an.

The Abiding Qur'an.   After centuries of conflict among Jews, Christians, and Muslims, the Qur'an is still one of the least understood books in the West. While it is based on many of the prophecies found in the Hebrew Scriptures and the New Testament, it differs markedly from Judaism and especially Christianity in some major tenets. It recognizes neither original sin nor the divinity of Jesus. Muhammad himself is only human, while the message he receives is divine. God is all-powerful, and human conduct is subjected to close scrutiny. Moral behavior is carefully prescribed, especially with regard to what would be called ethics and property rights today. Prayer rituals and religious pilgrimages are a part of the prescribed way of life. Little consideration is given to the individual, because God's ways are beyond man's comprehension or ability to predict, so man need not arrive at an understanding of God. There is no priesthood in Islam, but a community of believers guided by an imam, a man who sets the time and leads the chanting for prayer.

The idea of *jihad,* which ordinarily means "struggle," vigilance over one's own moral and spiritual behavior, has also the broader meaning of holy warfare. Holy wars against the unbeliever certainly have existed in Islamic history, most notably in its first hundred years. Muslim conduct, however, generally has been restrained by a strict code of ethics that is full of prohibitions against aggressive behavior. Muslims are not supposed to strike the first blow and are forbidden to exact unequal punishment or vengeance. The same orthodoxy that insists on moral absolutism helps to maintain the Islamic code of justice in law and political conduct, which considers the nature of the enemy. Tolerance is a prominent feature of Islamic thought, extending particularly to the "People of the Book," Jews and Christians, whom Muslims usually have regarded as capable of redemption rather than enemies to be mistreated. From a scholarly perspective, one sees in the sufferings of the twentieth and twenty-first centuries how linked Islamic civilization is to Judaism and Christianity and how the fate of all three societies is inextricably connected.

One of the most dramatic of these [first] conversions was that of Umar ibn al-Khattab, who was devoted to the old paganism, passionately opposed to Muhammad's message, and determined to wipe out the new sect. But he was also an expert in Arabian poetry, and the first time he heard the words of the Qur'an he was overcome by their extraordinary eloquence. As he said, the language broke through all his reservations about its message: "When I heard the Qur'an my heart was softened and I wept, and Islam entered me."

– KAREN ARMSTRONG, Historian, 2000

■ **FURTHER RESEARCH**

Translations

Abdel Haleem, M. A. S. *The Qur'an, A New Translation*. 2004.
'Ali, Ahmed. *Al-Qur'an, A Contemporary Translation*. 1987.
Arberry, A. J. *The Koran Interpreted*. 1955.
Asad, Muhammad. *The Message of the Koran*. 1980.

Reference Works

McAuliffe, Jane Dommen, ed. *Encyclopedia of the Qur'an*. 2001.
Watt, W. Montgomery. *Companion to the Qur'an*. 1967.

Studies and Interpretations

Abdel Haleem, M. A. *Understanding the Qur'an: Themes and Style*. 2001.
Abu Hamdiyyah, Mohammad. *The Qur'an: An Introduction*. 2000.
Bell, Richard, and W. Montgomery Watt. *Introduction to the Koran*. 1970.
Boullata, I. J. *Literary Structures of Religious Meaning in the Qur'an*. 2000.
Cleary, Thomas. *The Essential Koran: The Heart of Islam*. 1993.
Cook, Michael. *The Koran: A Very Short Introduction*. 2000.
Hawting, G. R., and Abdul-Kader A. Shareef (eds.). *Approaches to the Qur'an*. 1993.
Nelson, K. L. *The Art of Reciting the Koran*. 1985.
Rahman, Fazlur. *Major Themes of the Qur'an*. 1980.
Rippin, Andrew (ed.). *The Qur'an: Formative Interpretation*. 1999.
——. *The Qur'an and Its Interpretive Tradition*. 2001.
Robinson, Neal. *Discovering the Qur'an*. 1996.
Sells, Michael. *Approaching the Qur'an: The Early Revelations*. 1999.
Sherif, Faruq. *A Guide to the Contents of the Qur'an*. 1995.
Walud, Amina. *Qur'an and Woman: Rereading the Sacred Text from a Woman's Perspective*. 1999.

■ **PRONUNCIATION**

Abbasid: uh-BAS-id, AB-uh-sid
Allah: AH-luh, AH-lah
al-Rasul: ahl-rah-SOOL
caliph Othman: KAY-lif AHTH-mun, ooth-MAHN
hajj: HAHJ
hijrah: HIJ-ruh
Hegira: hih-JIGH-ruh, HEJ-uh-ruh
jihad: jih-HAHD
Ka'bah: KAH-buh, KAH-uh-buh
Khadijah: kah-DEE-juh
Qur'an: koo-RAHN, koh-RAHN
sura: SOO-rah
umwah: oom-WAH
Umayyad: oo-MIGH-yad
Zaid Ibn Thabit: ZIDE IB-un THAH-bit

༄ The Koran

Translated by N. J. Dawood

SURA 1: THE EXORDIUM

1:1

In the name of God
the compassionate
the merciful

Praise be to God, Lord of the Universe,
The Compassionate, the Merciful,
Sovereign of the Day of Judgement!
You alone we worship, and to You alone
we turn for help.
Guide us to the straight path,

1:7

The path of those whom You have favoured,
Not of those who have incurred Your wrath,
Nor of those who have gone astray.

FROM

SURA 2: THE COW

In the Name of God, the Compassionate, the Merciful

2:1 *Alif lām mīm.* This Book is not to be doubted. It is a guide for the righteous, who believe in the unseen and are steadfast in prayer; who give in alms[1] from what We gave them; who believe in what has been revealed to you[2] and what was revealed before you, and have absolute faith in the life to come. These are rightly guided by their Lord; these shall surely triumph.

As for the unbelievers, it is the same whether or not you forewarn them; they will not have faith. God has set a seal upon their hearts and ears; their sight is dimmed and grievous punishment awaits them.

There are some who declare: 'We believe in God and the Last Day,' yet they are no true believers. They seek to deceive God and those who believe in Him: but they 2:10 deceive none save themselves, though they may not perceive it. There is a sickness in

---

A note on the translation: Our translation by N. J. Dawood, first published in 1956 and revised until 1990, captures in idiomatic English the difficult prose of the *Qur'an*. We continue to use this translation despite several excellent competitors. Ahmed 'Ali's *The Qur'an, A Contemporary Translation* (1987) is an impressive verse translation with some controversial readings. Abdel Haleem's *The Qur'an, A New Translation* (2004) is the most current prose version. We have supplemented the Dawood version with readings from recent translators in some of the footnotes that follow.

---

[1] **give in alms:** Or, "give to the cause."   [2] **you:** Muhammad.

their hearts which God has aggravated: they shall be sternly punished for the lies they tell.

When they are told: 'You shall not do evil in the land,' they reply: 'Surely we are doing only what is good.' But it is they who are the evil-doers, though they may not perceive it.

And when they are told: 'Believe as others believe,' they reply: 'Are we to believe as fools believe?' It is they who are the fools, if they but knew it!

When they meet the faithful, they declare: 'We, too, are believers.' But when alone with their devils they say to them: 'We follow none but you: we were only mocking.' God will mock them and keep them long in sin, ever straying from the right path.

Such are those that barter guidance for error: they profit nothing, nor are they
2:17 on the right path. They are like one who kindled a fire, but as soon as it lit up all
2:18 around him God put it out and left him in darkness: they do not see. Deaf, dumb, and blind, they will never return to the right path.

Or like those who, beneath a dark storm-cloud charged with thunder and lightning, thrust their fingers into their ears at the sound of every thunder-clap for fear of death (God thus encompasses the unbelievers). The lightning almost snatches away their sight: whenever it flashes upon them they walk on, but as soon as it darkens they stand still. Indeed, if God pleased, He could take away their hearing and their sight: God has power over all things.

You people! Serve your Lord, who has created you and those who have gone before you, so that you may guard yourselves against evil; who has made the earth a bed for you and the sky a dome, and has sent down water from the sky to bring forth fruits for your sustenance. Do not knowingly set up other gods beside God.

2:23 If you doubt what We have revealed to Our servant, produce one chapter comparable to it. Call upon your idols to assist you, if what you say be true. But if you fail (as you are sure to fail), then guard yourselves against the Fire whose fuel is men and stones, prepared for the unbelievers.

Proclaim good tidings to those who have faith and do good works. They shall dwell in gardens watered by running streams: whenever they are given fruit to eat they will say: 'This is what we used to eat before,' for they shall be given the like. Wedded to chaste spouses, they shall abide therein for ever.

God does not disdain to make comparison with a gnat or with a larger creature. The faithful know that it is the truth from their Lord, but the unbelievers ask: 'What could God mean by this comparison?'

By such comparisons God confounds many and enlightens many. But He con-
2:27 founds none except the evil-doers, who break His covenant after accepting it, and put asunder what He has bidden to be united, and perpetrate corruption in the land. These will surely be the losers. [. . .]

2:67 When Moses said to his people: 'God commands you to sacrifice a cow,' they replied: 'Are you trifling with us?'

'God forbid that I should be so foolish!' he rejoined.

'Call on your Lord,' they said, 'to make known to us what kind of cow she shall be.'

He replied: 'Your Lord says: "Let her be neither an old cow nor a young heifer, but in between." Do, therefore, as you are bidden.'

'Call on your Lord,' they said, 'to make known to us what her colour shall be.'

He replied: 'Your Lord says: "Let the cow be yellow, a rich yellow, pleasing to those that see it."'

2:70   'Call on your Lord,' they said, 'to make known to us the exact type of cow she shall be; for to us cows look all alike. If God wills we shall be rightly guided.'

Moses replied: 'Your Lord says: "Let her be a healthy cow, not worn out with ploughing the earth or watering the field; a cow free from any blemish."'

'Now you have told us all,' they answered. And they slaughtered a cow, after they had nearly declined to do so. [. . .]

2:122   Children of Israel, remember the favour I have bestowed upon you, and that I exalted you above the nations. Guard yourselves against a day on which no soul shall stand for another: when no ransom shall be accepted from it, no intercession avail it, no help be given it.

When his Lord put Abraham to the proof by enjoining on him certain commandments and Abraham fulfilled them, He said: 'I have appointed you a leader of mankind.'

'And what of my descendants?' asked Abraham.

'My covenant,' said He, 'does not apply to the evil-doers.'

We made the House³ a resort and a sanctuary for mankind, saying: 'Make the place where Abraham stood a house of worship.' We enjoined Abraham and Ishmael to cleanse Our House for those who walk round it, who meditate in it, and who kneel and prostrate themselves.

'Lord,' said Abraham, 'make this a secure land and bestow plenty upon its people, those of them that believe in God and the Last Day.'

'As for those that do not,' He answered, 'I shall let them live awhile, and then shall drag them to the scourge of the Fire: an evil fate.'

2:127   Abraham and Ishmael built the House and dedicated it, saying: 'Accept this from us, Lord. You are the One that hears all and knows all. Lord, make us submissive to You; make of our descendants a community that will submit to You. Teach us our rites of worship and turn to us with mercy; You are the Forgiving One, the Merciful. Lord, send forth to them an apostle of their own who shall declare to them Your revelations, and shall instruct them in the Book and in wisdom, and shall purify them of sin. You are the Mighty, the Wise One.'

Who but a foolish man would renounce the faith of Abraham? We chose him
2:131   in this world, and in the world to come he shall abide among the righteous. When his Lord said to him: 'Submit,' he answered: 'I have submitted to the Lord of the Universe.'

2:132   Abraham enjoined the faith on his children, and so did Jacob, saying: 'My children, God has chosen for you the true faith. Do not depart this life except in full submission.'

---

³ **the House:** The Ka'bah in Mecca.

Were you present when death came to Jacob? He said to his children: 'What will you worship when I am gone?' They replied: 'We will worship your God and the God of your forefathers Abraham and Ishmael and Isaac: the One God. To Him we will submit.'

That community has passed away. Theirs is what they did and yours what you have done. You shall not be questioned about their actions.

They say: 'Accept the Jewish or the Christian faith and you shall be rightly guided.' Say: 'By no means! We believe in the faith of Abraham, the upright one. He was no idolater.'

2:136   Say: 'We believe in God and that which has been revealed to us; in what was revealed to Abraham, Ishmael, Isaac, Jacob, and the tribes; to Moses and Jesus and the other prophets by their Lord. We make no distinction among any of them, and to Him we submit.'

If they accept your faith, they shall be rightly guided; if they reject it, they shall surely be in schism. Against them God is your all-sufficient defender. He hears all and knows all.

We take on God's own dye. And who has a better dye than God's? Him will we worship.

Say: 'Would you dispute with us about God, who is our Lord and your Lord? We shall both be judged by our works. To Him alone we are devoted.

'Do you claim that Abraham, Ishmael, Isaac, Jacob, and the tribes, were all Jews or Christians?' Say: 'Who knows better, you or God? Who is more wicked than the man who hides a testimony he has received from God? God is never heedless of what you do.'

2:141   That community has passed away. Theirs is what they did and yours what you have done. You shall not be questioned about their actions. [. . .]

2:176   Righteousness does not consist in whether you face towards the East or the West. The righteous man is he who believes in God and the Last Day, in the angels and the Book and the prophets; who, though he loves it dearly, gives away his wealth to kinsfolk, to orphans, to the destitute, to the traveller in need and to beggars, and for the redemption of captives; who attends to his prayers and renders the alms levy; who is true to his promises and steadfast in trial and adversity and in times of war. Such are the true believers; such are the God-fearing.

2:178   Believers, retaliation is decreed for you in bloodshed: a free man for a free man, a slave for a slave, and a female for a female. He who is pardoned by his aggrieved brother shall be prosecuted according to usage and shall pay him a liberal fine. This is a merciful dispensation from your Lord. He that transgresses thereafter shall be sternly punished.

Men of understanding! In retaliation you have a safeguard for your lives; perchance you will guard yourselves against evil.

It is decreed that when death approaches, those of you that leave property shall bequeath it equitably to parents and kindred. This is a duty incumbent on the righteous. He that alters a will after hearing it shall be accountable for his crime. God hears all and knows all.

2:182 He that suspects an error or an injustice on the part of a testator and brings about a settlement among the parties incurs no guilt. God is forgiving and merciful.

2:183 Believers, fasting is decreed for you as it was decreed for those before you; perchance you will guard yourselves against evil. Fast a certain number of days, but if any one among you is ill or on a journey, let him fast a similar number of days later; and for those that cannot endure it there is a penance ordained: the feeding of a poor man. He that does good of his own accord shall be well rewarded; but to fast is better for you, if you but knew it.

In the month of Ramaḍān the Koran was revealed, a book of guidance for mankind with proofs of guidance distinguishing right from wrong.[4] Therefore whoever of you is present in that month let him fast. But he who is ill or on a journey shall fast a similar number of days later on.

God desires your well-being, not your discomfort. He desires you to fast the whole month so that you may magnify God and render thanks to Him for giving you His guidance.

2:186 If My servants question you about Me, tell them that I am near. I answer the prayer of the suppliant when he calls to Me; therefore let them answer My call and put their trust in Me, that they may be rightly guided.

It is now lawful for you to lie with your wives on the night of the fast; they are a comfort to you as you are to them. God knew that you were deceiving yourselves. He has relented towards you and pardoned you. Therefore you may now lie with them and seek what God has ordained for you. Eat and drink until you can tell a white thread from a black one in the light of the coming dawn. Then resume the fast till nightfall and do not approach them, but stay at your prayers in the mosques.

These are the bounds set by God: do not approach them. Thus He makes known His revelations to mankind that they may guard themselves against evil.

2:188 Do not devour one another's property by unjust means, nor bribe the judges with it in order that you may wrongfully and knowingly usurp the possessions of other men.

2:189 They question you about the phases of the moon. Say: 'They are seasons fixed for mankind and for the pilgrimage.'

Righteousness does not consist in entering your dwellings from the back.[5] The righteous man is he that fears God. Enter your dwellings by their doors and fear God, so that you may prosper.

Fight for the sake of God those that fight against you, but do not attack them first.[6] God does not love aggressors.

Slay them wherever you find them.[7] Drive them out of the places from which they drove you. Idolatry is more grievous than bloodshed. But do not fight them

---

[4] **with proofs . . . wrong:** Alternatively: "with proofs of guidance and salvation."

[5] **entering . . . back:** A custom of pagan Arabs returning from pilgrimage.

[6] **Fight . . . them first:** Literally, "Do not overstep the limits," whether by attacking first or fighting excessively.

[7] **Slay them . . . find them:** This and the following phrases consider what believers should do if attacked within the holy grounds of Mecca.

within the precincts of the Holy Mosque unless they attack you there; if they attack you put them to the sword. Thus shall the unbelievers be rewarded: but if they mend their ways, know that God is forgiving and merciful.

2:193   Fight against them until idolatry is no more and God's religion reigns supreme. But if they desist, fight none except the evil-doers.

A sacred month for a sacred month: sacred things too are subject to retaliation. If anyone attacks you, attack him as he attacked you. Have fear of God, and know that God is with the righteous.

Give generously for the cause of God and do not with your own hands cast yourselves into destruction. Be charitable; God loves the charitable.

2:196   Make the pilgrimage and visit the Sacred House for His sake. If you cannot, send such offerings as you can afford and do not shave your heads until the offerings have reached their destination. But if any of you is ill or suffers from an ailment of the head, he must do penance either by fasting or by almsgiving or by offering a sacrifice.

If in peacetime anyone among you combines the visit with the pilgrimage, he must offer such gifts as he can afford; but if he lacks the means let him fast three days during the pilgrimage and seven when he has returned; that is, ten days in all. That is incumbent on him whose family are not present at the Holy Mosque. Have fear of God: know that God is stern in retribution.

2:197   Make the pilgrimage in the appointed months. He that intends to perform it in those months must abstain from sexual intercourse, obscene language, and acrimonious disputes while on pilgrimage. God is aware of whatever good you do. Provide well for yourselves: the best provision is piety. Fear Me, then, you that are endowed with understanding.

It shall be no offence for you to seek the bounty of your Lord. When you come running from 'Arafāt[8] remember God as you approach the sacred monument. Remember Him that gave you guidance when you were in error. Then go out from the place whence the pilgrims will go out and implore the forgiveness of God. God is forgiving and merciful. And when you have fulfilled your sacred duties, remember God as you remember your forefathers or with deeper reverence.

There are some who say: 'Lord, give us abundance in this world.' These shall
2:201   have no share in the world to come. But there are others who say: 'Lord, give us what is good both in this world and in the world to come, and keep us from the torment of the Fire.' These shall have a share, according to what they did. Swift is God's reckoning.

Give glory to God on the appointed days. He that departs on the second day incurs no sin, nor does he who stays on longer, if he truly fears God. Have fear of God, then, and know that you shall all be gathered before Him.

There are some whose views on this life please you: they even call on God to vouch for that which is in their hearts; whereas in fact they are the deadliest of your

---

[8] 'Arafāt: A location near Mecca.

2:205 opponents. No sooner do they leave you than they hasten to do evil in the land, destroying crops and cattle. God does not love evil.

2:206 When they are told: 'Have fear of God,' vanity carries them off to sin. Sufficient for them shall be Hell, an evil resting-place.

But there are others who would give away their lives in order to find favour with God. God is compassionate to His servants.

Believers, submit all of you to God and do not walk in Satan's footsteps; he is your inveterate foe. If you lapse after the veritable signs that have been shown to you, know that God is mighty and wise.

Are they waiting for God to come down to them in the shadow of a cloud, with all the angels? Their fate will have been settled then. To God shall all things return.

Ask the Israelites how many conspicuous signs We gave them. He that tampers with the gift of God after it is bestowed on him shall find that God is stern in retribution.

For the unbelievers the life of this world is decked with all manner of temptations. They scoff at the faithful, but those that fear God shall be above them on the Day of Resurrection. God gives unstintingly to whom He will.

2:213 Mankind were once but one community. Then God sent forth prophets to give them good news and to warn them, and with these He sent down the Book with the Truth, that it might serve as arbiter in the disputes of men. (None disputed it save those to whom it was given, and that was through envy of one another, after veritable signs had been vouchsafed them.) So God guided by His will those who believed in the truth which had been disputed. God guides whom He will to a straight path.

Did you suppose that you would go to Paradise untouched by the suffering which was endured by those before you? Affliction and adversity befell them; and so shaken were they that each apostle, and those who shared his faith, cried out: 'When will God's help come?' God's help is ever near.

2:215 They will ask you about almsgiving. Say: 'Whatever you bestow in charity must go to parents and to kinsfolk, to the orphans and to the destitute and to the traveller in need. God is aware of whatever good you do.'

2:216 Fighting is obligatory for you, much as you dislike it. But you may hate a thing although it is good for you, and love a thing although it is bad for you. God knows, but you know not.

They ask you about the sacred month. Say: 'To fight in this month is a grave offence; but to debar others from the path of God, to deny Him, and to expel His worshippers from the Holy Mosque, is far more grave in His sight. Idolatry is more grievous than bloodshed.'

They will not cease to fight against you until they force you to renounce your faith—if they are able. But whoever of you recants and dies an unbeliever, his works shall come to nothing in this world and in the world to come. Such men shall be the tenants of the Fire, wherein they shall abide for ever.

Those that have embraced the Faith, and those that have fled their land and fought for the cause of God, may hope for God's mercy. God is forgiving and merciful. [. . .]

FROM

SURA 4: WOMEN

In the Name of God, the Compassionate, the Merciful

4:1   YOU PEOPLE! Have fear of your Lord, who created you from a single soul. From that soul He created its spouse, and through them He bestrewed the earth with countless men and women.

Fear God, in whose name you plead with one another, and honour the mothers who bore you. God is ever watching you.

Give orphans the property which belongs to them. Do not exchange their valuables for worthless things or cheat them of their possessions; for this would surely be a grievous sin. If you fear that you cannot treat orphans[9] with fairness, then you may marry other women who seem good to you: two, three, or four of them. But if you fear that you cannot maintain equality among them, marry one only or any slave-girls you may own. This will make it easier for you to avoid injustice.

Give women their dowry as a free gift; but if they choose to make over to you a part of it, you may regard it as lawfully yours.

4:5   Do not give the feeble-minded the property with which God has entrusted you for their support; but maintain and clothe them with its proceeds, and speak kind words to them.

4:6   Put orphans to the test until they reach a marriageable age. If you find them capable of sound judgement, hand over to them their property, and do not deprive them of it by squandering it before they come of age.

Let not the rich guardian touch the property of his orphan ward; and let him who is poor use no more than a fair portion of it for his own advantage.

When you hand over to them their property, call in some witnesses; sufficient is God's accounting of your actions.

Men shall have a share in what their parents and kinsmen leave; and women shall have a share in what their parents and kinsmen leave: whether it be little or much, they shall be legally entitled to a share.

If relatives, orphans, or needy men are present at the division of an inheritance, give them, too, a share of it, and speak kind words to them.

Let those who are solicitous about the welfare of their young children after their own death take care not to wrong orphans. Let them fear God and speak for justice.

4:10   Those that devour the property of orphans unjustly, swallow fire into their bellies; they shall burn in a mighty conflagration.

God has thus enjoined you concerning your children:

A male shall inherit twice as much as a female. If there be more than two girls, they shall have two-thirds of the inheritance; but if there be one only, she shall inherit the half. Parents shall inherit a sixth each, if the deceased have a child; but if he leave no child and his parents be his heirs, his mother shall have a third. If he have brothers, his mother shall have a sixth after payment of any legacy he may have bequeathed or any debt he may have owed.

---

[9] **orphans:** Orphan girls.

You may wonder whether your parents or your children are more beneficial to you. But this is the law of God; surely God is all-knowing and wise.

4:12   You shall inherit the half of your wives' estate if they die childless. If they leave children, a quarter of their estate shall be yours after payment of any legacy they may have bequeathed or any debt they may have owed.

Your wives shall inherit one quarter of your estate if you die childless. If you leave children, they shall inherit one-eighth, after payment of any legacy you may have bequeathed or any debt you may have owed.

If a man or a woman leave neither children nor parents and have a brother or a sister, they shall each inherit one-sixth. If there be more, they shall equally share the third of the estate, after payment of any legacy he may have bequeathed or any debt he may have owed, without prejudice to the rights of the heirs. That is a commandment from God. God is all-knowing, and gracious.

4:13   Such are the bounds set by God. He that obeys God and His apostle shall dwell for ever in gardens watered by running streams. That is the supreme triumph. But he that defies God and His apostle and transgresses His bounds, shall be cast into a Fire wherein he will abide for ever. Shameful punishment awaits him.

If any of your women commit a lewd act, call in four witnesses from among yourselves against them; if they testify to their guilt confine them to their houses till death overtakes them or till God finds another way for them.[10]

4:16   If two men among you commit a lewd act, punish them both. If they repent and mend their ways, let them be. God is forgiving and merciful.

God forgives those who commit evil in ignorance and then quickly turn to Him in penitence. God will pardon them. God is all-knowing and wise. But He will not forgive those who do evil and, when death comes to them, say: 'Now we repent!' Nor those who die unbelievers: for them We have prepared a woeful scourge.

4:19   Believers, it is unlawful for you to inherit the women of your deceased kinsmen against their will, or to bar them from re-marrying, in order that you may force them to give up a part of what you have given them, unless they be guilty of a proven lewd act. Treat them with kindness; for even if you dislike them, it may well be that you dislike a thing which God has meant for your own abundant good.

4:20   If you wish to replace one wife with another, do not take from her the dowry you have given her even if it be a talent of gold. That would be improper and grossly unjust; for how can you take it back when you have lain with each other and entered into a firm contract?

You shall not marry the women whom your fathers married: all previous such marriages excepted. That was an evil practice, indecent and abominable.

Forbidden to you are your mothers, your daughters, your sisters, your paternal and maternal aunts, the daughters of your brothers and sisters, your foster-mothers, your foster-sisters, the mothers of your wives, your step-daughters who are in your charge, born of the wives with whom you have lain (it is no offence for you to marry your step-daughters if you have not consummated your marriage with their

---

[10] **till God . . . for them:** Commonly divorce, before which time women must remain in the household for a three month period.

mothers), and the wives of your own begotten sons. You are also forbidden to take in marriage two sisters at one and the same time: all previous such marriages excepted.

4:24   Surely God is forgiving and merciful. Also married women, except those whom you own as slaves. Such is the decree of God. All women other than these are lawful for you, provided you court them with your wealth in modest conduct, not in fornication. Give them their dowry for the enjoyment you have had of them as a duty; but it shall be no offence for you to make any other agreement among yourselves after you have fulfilled your duty. Surely God is all-knowing and wise.

4:25   If any one of you cannot afford to marry a free believing woman, let him marry a slave-girl who is a believer (God best knows your faith: you are born one of another). Marry them with the permission of their masters and give them their dowry in all justice, provided they are honourable and chaste and have not entertained other men. If after marriage they commit adultery, they shall suffer half the penalty inflicted upon free adulteresses. Such is the law for those of you who fear to commit sin: but if you abstain, it will be better for you. God is forgiving and merciful.

4:26   God desires to make this known to you and to guide you along the paths of those who have gone before you, and to turn to you with mercy. God is all-knowing and wise.

God wishes to forgive you, but those who follow their own appetites wish to see you stray grievously into error. God wishes to lighten your burdens, for man was created weak.

Believers, do not consume your wealth among yourselves in vanity, but rather trade with it by mutual consent.

Do not kill yourselves.[11] God is merciful to you, but he that does that through wickedness and injustice shall be burned in fire. That is easy enough for God.

If you avoid the enormities you are forbidden, We shall pardon your misdeeds and usher you in with all honour. Do not covet the favours by which God has exalted some among you above others. Men shall be rewarded according to their deeds, and women shall be rewarded according to their deeds. Rather implore God to bestow on you His gifts. Surely God has knowledge of all things.

To every parent and kinsman We have appointed heirs who will inherit from them. As for those with whom you have entered into agreements, let them, too, have their share. Surely God bears witness to all things.

4:34   Men have authority over women because God has made the one superior to the other, and because they spend their wealth to maintain them. Good women are obedient. They guard their unseen parts because God has guarded them. As for those from whom you fear disobedience, admonish them, forsake them in beds apart, and beat them. Then if they obey you, take no further action against them. Surely God is high, supreme.

If you fear a breach between a man and his wife, appoint an arbiter from his people and another from hers. If they wish to be reconciled, God will bring them together again. Surely God is all-knowing and wise. [. . .]

---

[11] **Do not kill yourselves:** That is, "Do not kill each other."

FROM

Sura 5: The Table

In the Name of God, the Compassionate, the Merciful

5:15 [. . .] People of the Book! Our apostle has come to reveal to you much of what you have hidden of the Scriptures, and to forgive you much. A light has come to you from God and a glorious Book, with which God will guide to the paths of peace those that seek to please Him; He will lead them by His will from darkness to the light; He will guide them to a straight path.

Unbelievers are those who declare: 'God is the Messiah, the son of Mary.' Say: 'Who could prevent God, if He so willed, from destroying the Messiah, the son of Mary, his mother, and all the people of the earth? God has sovereignty over the heavens and the earth and all that lies between them. He creates what He will; and God has power over all things.'

5:18 The Jews and the Christians say: 'We are the children of God and His loved ones.' Say: 'Why then does He punish you for your sins? Surely you are mortals of His own creation. He forgives whom He will and punishes whom He pleases. God has sovereignty over the heavens and the earth and all that lies between them. All shall return to Him.'

5:19 People of the Book! Our apostle has come to you with revelations after an interval which saw no apostles, lest you say: 'No one has come to give us good news or to warn us.' Now someone has come to give you good news and to warn you. God has power over all things. [. . .]

5:35 Believers, have fear of God and seek the right path to Him. Fight valiantly for His cause, so that you may triumph.

As for the unbelievers, if they offered all that the earth contains and as much besides to redeem themselves from the torment of the Day of Resurrection, it shall not be accepted from them. Woeful punishment awaits them.

They will strive to get out of the Fire, but get out of it they shall not. Lasting punishment awaits them. [. . .]

5:40 Did you not know that God has sovereignty over the heavens and the earth? He punishes whom He will and forgives whom He pleases. God has power over all things.

5:41 Apostle, do not grieve for those who plunge headlong into unbelief; those who say with their tongues: 'We believe,' but have no faith in their hearts, and those Jews who listen to lies and listen to others who have not come to you. They tamper with words out of their context and say: 'If this be given you, accept it; if not, then beware!'

You cannot help a man if God intends to try him. Those whose hearts God does not intend to purify shall be held up to shame in this world, and in the world to come grievous punishment awaits them.

They listen to falsehoods and practise what is unlawful. If they come to you, give them your judgement or avoid them. If you avoid them, they can in no way harm you; but if you do act as their judge, judge them with fairness. God loves those that deal justly.

But how will they come to you for judgement when they already have the Torah which enshrines God's own judgement? Soon after, they will turn their backs: they are no true believers.

5:44   We have revealed the Torah, in which there is guidance and light. By it the prophets who submitted to God judged the Jews, and so did the rabbis and the divines, according to God's Book which had been committed to their keeping and to which they themselves were witnesses.

Have no fear of man; fear Me, and do not sell My revelations for a paltry sum. Unbelievers are those who do not judge according to God's revelations.

We decreed for them a life for a life, an eye for an eye, a nose for a nose, an ear for an ear, a tooth for a tooth, and a wound for a wound. But if a man charitably forbears from retaliation, his remission shall atone for him. Transgressors are those that do not judge according to God's revelations.

After them We sent forth Jesus son of Mary, confirming the Torah already revealed, and gave him the Gospel, in which there is guidance and light, corroborating what was revealed before it in the Torah: a guide and an admonition to the
5:47   righteous. Therefore let those who follow the Gospel judge according to what God has revealed therein. Evil-doers are those that do not judge according to God's revelations.

5:48   And to you We have revealed the Book with the truth. It confirms the Scriptures which came before it and stands as a guardian over them. Therefore give judgement among men according to God's revelations, and do not yield to their whims or swerve from the truth made known to you.

We have ordained a law and assigned a path for each of you. Had God pleased, He could have made of you one community: but it is His wish to prove you by that which He has bestowed upon you. Vie with each other in good works, for to God shall you all return and He will resolve your differences for you. [. . .]

5:65   If the People of the Book accept the true faith and keep from evil, We will pardon them their sins and admit them to the gardens of delight. If they observe the Torah and the Gospel and what has been revealed to them from their Lord, they shall enjoy abundance from above and from beneath.

There are some among them who are righteous men; but there are many among them who do nothing but evil.

Apostle, proclaim what has been revealed to you from your Lord; if you do not, you will surely fail to convey His message. God will protect you from all men. God does not guide the unbelievers.

Say: 'People of the Book, you will attain nothing until you observe the Torah and the Gospel and that which has been revealed to you from your Lord.' [. . .]

5:75   The Messiah, the son of Mary, was no more than an apostle: other apostles passed away before him. His mother was a saintly woman. They both ate earthly food.

See how We make plain to them Our revelations. See how they ignore the truth.

Say: 'Will you serve instead of God that which can neither harm nor help you? God is He who hears all and knows all.'

Say: 'People of the Book! Do not transgress the bounds of truth in your religion. Do not yield to the desires of those who have erred before; who have led many astray and have themselves strayed from the even path.' [. . .]

One day God will gather all the apostles and ask them: 'How were you received?' 5:110 They will reply: 'We have no knowledge. You alone know what is hidden.' God will say: 'Jesus son of Mary, remember the favour I bestowed on you and on your mother: how I strengthened you with the Holy Spirit, so that you preached to men in your cradle and in the prime of manhood; how I instructed you in the Book and in wisdom, in the Torah and in the Gospel; how by My leave you fashioned from clay the likeness of a bird and breathed into it so that, by My leave, it became a living bird; how, by My leave, you healed the blind man and the leper, and by My leave restored the dead to life; how I protected you from the Israelites when you had come to them with clear signs: when those of them who disbelieved declared: "This is but plain sorcery"; how, when I enjoined the disciples to believe in Me and in My apostle, they replied: "We believe; bear witness that we submit."'

'Jesus son of Mary,' said the disciples, 'can your Lord send down to us from heaven a table spread with food?'

He replied: 'Have fear of God, if you are true believers.'

5:113   'We wish to eat of it,' they said, 'so that we may reassure our hearts and know that what you said to us is true, and that we may be witnesses of it.'

5:114   'Lord,' said Jesus son of Mary, 'send down to us from heaven a table spread with food, that it may mark a feast for the first of us and the last of us: a sign from You. Give us our sustenance; You are the best provider.'

God replied: 'I am sending one to you. But whoever of you disbelieves hereafter shall be punished as no man will ever be punished.'

Then God will say: 'Jesus son of Mary, did you ever say to mankind: "Worship me and my mother as gods besides God?"'

'Glory be to You,' he will answer, 'I could never have claimed what I have no right to. If I had ever said so, You would have surely known it. You know what is in my mind, but I know not what is in Yours. You alone know what is hidden. I told them only what You bade me. I said: "Serve God, my Lord and your Lord." I 5:117 watched over them while living in their midst, and ever since You took me to Yourself, You have been watching them. You are the witness of all things. If You punish them, they surely are Your servants; and if You forgive them, surely You are mighty and wise.'

God will say: 'This is the day when their truthfulness will benefit the truthful. They shall for ever dwell in gardens watered by running streams. God is pleased with them, and they are pleased with Him. That is the supreme triumph.'

5:120   God has sovereignty over the heavens and the earth and all that they contain. He has power over all things.

SURA 55: THE MERCIFUL

In the Name of God, the Compassionate, the Merciful

IT IS the Merciful who has taught the Koran.

55:1   He created man and taught him articulate speech. The sun and the moon pursue their ordered course. The plants and the trees bow down in adoration.

He raised the heaven on high and set the balance of all things, that you might not transgress that balance. Give just weight and full measure.

He laid the earth for His creatures, with all its fruits and blossom-bearing palm, chaff-covered grain and scented herbs. Which of your Lord's blessings would you[12] deny?

He created man from potter's clay, and the jinn from smokeless fire. Which of your Lord's blessings would you deny?

The Lord of the two easts[13] is He, and the Lord of the two wests. Which of your Lord's blessings would you deny?

55:19   He has let loose the two oceans:[14] they meet one another. Yet between them
55:20   stands a barrier which they cannot overrun. Which of your Lord's blessings would you deny?

Pearls and corals come from both. Which of your Lord's blessings would you deny?

His are the ships that sail like mountains upon the ocean. Which of your Lord's blessings would you deny?

All that lives on earth is doomed to die. But the face of your Lord will abide for ever, in all its majesty and glory. Which of your Lord's blessings would you deny?

All who dwell in heaven and earth entreat Him. Each day some mighty task engages Him. Which of your Lord's blessings would you deny?

Mankind and jinn, We shall surely find the time to judge you! Which of your Lord's blessings would you deny?

Mankind and jinn, if you have power to penetrate the confines of heaven and earth, then penetrate them! But this you shall not do except with Our own authority. Which of your Lord's blessings would you deny?

55:35   Flames of fire shall be lashed at you, and molten brass. There shall be none to help you. Which of your Lord's blessings would you deny?

When the sky splits asunder, and reddens like a rose or stainèd leather (which of your Lord's blessings would you deny?), on that day neither man nor jinnee will be asked about his sins. Which of your Lord's blessings would you deny?

The wrongdoers will be known by their looks; they shall be seized by their forelocks and their feet. Which of your Lord's blessings would you deny?

---

[12] **you:** This is a plural form of *you*, addressed to humanity and the *jinn*, sometimes mischievous spirits who cohabit with man. See the next verse.

[13] **the two easts:** The points at which the sun rises in summer and in winter.

[14] **the two oceans:** Salt water and fresh water.

That is the Hell which the sinners deny. They shall wander between fire and water fiercely seething. Which of your Lord's blessings would you deny?

But for those that fear the majesty of their Lord there are two gardens (which of your Lord's blessings would you deny?) planted with shady trees. Which of your Lord's blessings would you deny?

55:51   Each is watered by a flowing spring. Which of your Lord's blessings would you deny?

55:52   Each bears every kind of fruit in pairs. Which of your Lord's blessings would you deny?

They shall recline on couches lined with thick brocade, and within reach will hang the fruits of both gardens. Which of your Lord's blessings would you deny?

Therein are bashful virgins whom neither man nor jinnee will have touched before. Which of your Lord's blessings would you deny?

Virgins as fair as corals and rubies. Which of your Lord's blessings would you deny?

Shall the reward of goodness be anything but good? Which of your Lord's blessings would you deny?

And beside these there shall be two other gardens (which of your Lord's blessings would you deny?) of darkest green. Which of your Lord's blessings would you deny?

55:66   A gushing fountain shall flow in each. Which of your Lord's blessings would you deny?

Each planted with fruit-trees, the palm and the pomegranate. Which of your Lord's blessings would you deny?

In each there shall be virgins chaste and fair. Which of your Lord's blessings would you deny?

Dark-eyed virgins, sheltered in their tents (which of your Lord's blessings would you deny?), whom neither man nor jinnee will have touched before. Which of your Lord's blessings would you deny?

They shall recline on green cushions and fine carpets. Which of your Lord's blessings would you deny?

55:78   Blessed be the name of your Lord, the Lord of majesty and glory!

SURA 56: THAT WHICH IS COMING

In the Name of God, the Compassionate, the Merciful

WHEN THAT which is coming comes—and no soul shall then deny its coming—
56:1   some shall be abased and others exalted.

When the earth shakes and quivers, and the mountains crumble away and scat-
56:6   ter abroad into fine dust, you shall be divided into three multitudes: those on the right (blessed shall be those on the right); those on the left (damned shall be those on the left); and those to the fore (foremost shall be those). Such are they that shall be brought near to their Lord in the gardens of delight: a whole multitude from the men of old, but only a few from the latter generations.

They shall recline on jewelled couches face to face, and there shall wait on them immortal youths with bowls and ewers and a cup of purest wine (that will neither pain their heads nor take away their reason); with fruits of their own choice and flesh of fowls that they relish. And theirs shall be the dark-eyed houris, chaste as virgin pearls: a guerdon for their deeds.

There they shall hear no idle talk, no sinful speech, but only the greeting, 'Peace! Peace!'

56:27   Those on the right hand—happy shall be those on the right hand! They shall recline on couches raised on high in the shade of thornless sidrs and clusters of talh;[15] amidst gushing waters and abundant fruits, unforbidden, never-ending.

We created the houris and made them virgins, loving companions for those on the right hand: a multitude from the men of old, and a multitude from the latter generations.

As for those on the left hand (wretched shall be those on the left hand!) they shall dwell amidst scorching winds and seething water: in the shade of pitch-black smoke, neither cool nor refreshing. For they have lived in comfort and persisted in the heinous sin,[16] saying: 'When we are once dead and turned to dust and bones, shall we be raised to life? And our forefathers, too?'

Say: 'Those of old, and those of the present age, shall be brought together on an appointed day. As for you sinners who deny the truth, you shall eat the fruit of the Zaqqūm tree and fill your bellies with it. You shall drink scalding water: yet you shall

56:55   drink it as the thirsty camel drinks.'

56:56   Such shall be their fare on the Day of Reckoning.

We created you: will you not believe then in Our power?

Behold the semen you discharge: did you create it, or We?

It was We that ordained death among you. Nothing can hinder Us from replacing you by others like yourselves or transforming you into beings you know nothing of.

You surely know of the First Creation. Why, then, do you not reflect? Consider the seeds you grow. Is it you that give them growth, or We? If We pleased, We could turn your harvest into chaff, so that, filled with wonder, you would exclaim: 'We are laden with debts! Surely we have been robbed!'

Consider the water which you drink. Was it you that poured it from the cloud, or We? If We pleased, We could turn it bitter. Why, then, do you not give thanks?

Observe the fire which you light. Is it you that create its wood, or We? A reminder for man We made it, and for the traveller a comfort.

56:74   Praise, then, the name of your Lord, the Supreme One.

I swear by the shelter of the stars (a mighty oath, if you but knew it) that this is a glorious Koran, safeguarded in a book which none may touch except the purified; a revelation from the Lord of the Universe.

Would you scorn a scripture such as this, and earn your daily bread denying it?

When under your very eyes a man's soul is about to leave him (We are nearer to him than you, although you cannot see Us), why do you not restore it, if you will not be judged hereafter? Answer this, if what you say be true!

---

[15] **talh:** Acacia trees.   [16] **the heinous sin:** Idolatry.

Thus, if he is favoured, his lot will be repose and plenty, and a garden of delight. If he is one of those on the right hand, he will be greeted with, 'Peace be with you!' by those on the right hand.

But if he is an erring disbeliever, his welcome will be scalding water, and he will burn in Hell.

56:96   This is surely the indubitable truth. Praise, then, the name of your Lord, the Supreme One.

SURA 93: DAYLIGHT

In the Name of God, the Compassionate, the Merciful

93:1   BY THE light of day, and by the dark of night, your Lord has not forsaken you,[17] nor does He abhor you.

The life to come holds a richer prize for you than this present life. You shall be gratified with what your Lord will give you.

93:6   Did He not find you an orphan and give you shelter?

Did He not find you in error and guide you?

Did He not find you poor and enrich you?

93:11   Therefore do not wrong the orphan, nor chide away the beggar. But proclaim the goodness of your Lord.

SURA 96: CLOTS OF BLOOD

In the Name of God, the Compassionate, the Merciful

96:1   RECITE IN the name of your Lord who created — created man from clots of blood.

Recite! Your Lord is the Most Bountiful One, who by the pen taught man what he did not know.

Indeed, man transgresses in thinking himself his own master: for to your Lord all things return.

Observe the man who rebukes Our servant when he prays. Think: does he follow the right guidance or enjoin true piety?

96:13   Think: if he denies the Truth and pays no heed, does he not realize that God observes all?

No. Let him desist, or We will drag him by the forelock, his lying, sinful forelock. Then let him call his helpmates. We will call the guards of Hell.

96:19   No, never obey him! Prostrate yourself and come nearer.

SURA 109: THE UNBELIEVERS

In the Name of God, the Compassionate, the Merciful

109:1   SAY: 'UNBELIEVERS, I do not worship what you worship, nor do you worship what I worship. I shall never worship what you worship, nor will you ever worship what I

109:6   worship. You have your own religion, and I have mine.'

---

[17] **you:** Muhammad.

SURA 110: HELP

In the Name of God, the Compassionate, the Merciful

110:1 WHEN GOD's help and victory come, and you see men embrace God's faith in multi-
110:3 tudes, give glory to your Lord and seek His pardon. He is ever disposed to mercy.

SURA 112: ONENESS

In the Name of God, the Compassionate, the Merciful

112:1 SAY: 'GOD is One, the Eternal God. He begot none, nor was He begotten. None is
112:4 equal to Him.'

☙ MUHAMMAD IBN ISHAQ
ARABIA, 704–767

see-RAHT
ahn-nah-BEE
IB-un is-HAHK

*The Life of Muhammad (**Sirat an-Nabi**),* the most complete biography of Muhammad, was compiled by **Muhammad Ibn Ishaq**, the grandson of a freed slave, in the eighth century about one hundred years after the Prophet's death. This collection of stories and oral legends, poetry, and accounts of Muhammad's raids provides the life story of Muhammad only alluded to in the Qur'an, where he is the Messenger rather than the subject of the story. While *The Life of Muhammad* is comparable in some respects to the Gospels of the New Testament, it differs in that it is understood by Muslims to be a secular work, not to be equated with the Qur'an. Its importance, however, should not be underestimated. The life story of Muhammad—the supreme political leader and founder of the nation of Islam as well as its Messenger of God—demanded a unique kind of representation for the Muslims of the eighth century, intent as they were on continuing the Prophet's work by spreading their faith throughout the world.

Literary Form and Content.   To these Muslims the literary status of the biography of Muhammad was highly important. Although other first-hand accounts of the life of the Prophet had been assembled (**Wahb ibn Munabbih**, an ambitious historian, had collected stories of Muhammad before Ibn Ishaq began to write), *The Life* was viewed as *the* work of its kind, helping to establish an entire literary genre, the *SIRA,* or exemplary life story. *The Life* consists of a number of literary forms, the most important of which is the *HADITH,* the report of a saying of Muhammad on a particular subject. Imbedded in the text are also examples of a form of poetry called *MARATHI* (originally meaning "dirge"), verse written on an important occasion. The text also contains a written legal agreement

WAH-hub IB-un
moo-NAH-bee

SEE-rah

hah-DEETH

muh-RAH-thee

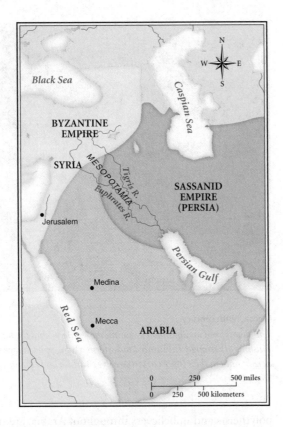

Arabia in
Muhammad's
Lifetime
*In the last decade of
his life, Muhammad
gained control of vir-
tually all of western
Arabia. After
Muhammad's death
in 632, the Prophet's
followers took Islam
into Persian and
Byzantine territories.*

concerning the scope of Muhammad's authority over the people of Medina. Finally, in order to relate the events of Muhammad's embattled
later life, *The Life* relies on MAGHAZI, legendary accounts of "the raids of   muh-GAH-zee
the Prophet." While the use of the edifying story, the celebratory ode, or
the battle narrative does not begin with *The Life of Muhammad*, by bringing together such different forms in a single literary work Ibn Ishaq and
his followers founded a brilliant Islamic method of writing.

The Life begins with the tale of Muhammad's miraculous birth, reminiscent of the story of the birth of Jesus in the Gospels. Accounts of the
infancy of Muhammad were taken from legends, for the most part; only
his status as a poor orphan is actually mentioned in the Qur'an. The stories of his later childhood and maturity, including his marriage to the
wealthy merchant **Khadijah**, all suggest his future vocation as a prophet.   kah-DEE-juh
Particularly noteworthy is the work's concentration on Muhammad's
personal qualities, including his deep seriousness at all times and his
forceful nature, as well as on his efforts to decide matters of great importance to his people. His traits would later be imitated by the faithful. The
events of Muhammad's subsequent life, including the revelations of the
angel Gabriel in the desert, Muhammad's vocation as a preacher in
Mecca, his founding of a community of believers, their flight to Medina
and eventual triumphant return to Mecca, and the wars against the

Mecca, ninth century

This detail from an illuminated Qur'an shows Mecca and the tomb of Muhammad. All Muslims are strongly encouraged to perform a hajj, *a pilgrimage to the holy site of Mecca, at least once in their life. (The Art Archive/Turkish and Islamic Art Museum, Istanbul/ Dagli Orti)*

www   For links to more information about Ibn Ishaq and a quiz on *The Life of Muhammad,* see bedfordstmartins .com/worldlit compact.

polytheists and unbelievers throughout Arabia, are treated in the rest of the narrative. Many details of Muhammad's adult life, such as his struggles against the merchant lords of Mecca and his meetings with the citizens of Medina, were passed down orally through personal accounts and family histories. The battle stories, or *maghazi,* from his later years were already being collected by a new class of historians in his lifetime, creating a new genre.

This short outline only begins to suggest the drama of Muhammad's life, his inner turmoil before his resolution to become the Prophet of God, followed by the fulfillment of his promise in the destiny of Islam. In *The Life,* despite his fierce devotion to Islam, Muhammad never loses his humanity, experiencing doubt in the midst of revelation and exercising compassionate judgment in his victories over the chiefs of Mecca. Although his life is held by others to be exemplary, he often protests that he should not be the subject of religious veneration, for he is only

ah-BOO BAH-kur

human, a prophet chosen by God, while God is without bounds. As **Abu Bakr** says to the mourners after his death, "O men, if anyone worships Muhammad, Muhammad is dead; if anyone worships God, God is alive, immortal."

The Reading of the Text.   In *The Life of Muhammad,* Ibn Ishaq takes considerable care to indicate the source of each story about Muhammad.

His frequent use of the *isnad*, or attribution, sometimes frustrates one's desire to "get on with the story." But historical necessities dictated this practice. The need to cite sources came from the presence of many false stories about Muhammad, circulated by friends and enemies alike. Often Ibn Ishaq includes more than one version of a story, and sometimes he quotes sources believed to be unfriendly to Muhammad; by doing this he wishes to provide his contemporaries with a narrative they can submit to common sense, judging it according to the credibility of the individuals who knew Muhammad and reported things about him.

While *The Life* deliberately leaves final judgment to the reader, its melange of forms creates a variety of effects: wonder, entertainment, instruction, and moral edification. Ibn Ishaq modestly directs the reader through the maze of detail. Hoary old legends are often prefaced with the cautionary "It is alleged," and some stories end with the intentionally equivocal "God knows best."

is-NAHD

The Beginnings of Islamic Scholarship. By the time Muhammad Ibn Ishaq compiled the biography of the Prophet three generations after the death of Muhammad, others had begun to undertake the same effort. Ibn Ishaq's work shows a thoroughness in tracking down stories and in bringing together materials from different literary genres that helped make his work superior to the rest. According to the English translator Alfred Guillaume, "No book known to the Arabs or to us can compare in comprehensiveness, arrangement, or systematic treatment." Even so, the version of *The Life of Muhammad* that has come down to us is the result of further editing by **Ibn Hisham** (d. c. 835–840). Scholars believe Ibn Hisham's version contains most of Ibn Ishaq's original volume, in part because stories unfavorable to Muhammad have survived the editing process when one might believe they would have been the first to go.

IB-un hih-SHAHM

During and after the composition of *The Life of Muhammad*, many works were written to explain Islam and its traditions. These included commentaries on the Qur'an as well as scholarly treatments of history, jurisprudence, political philosophy, natural philosophy, and theology. Thus was laid the foundation for Islamic culture in the centuries to come. The decisive role of later Islamic translators in preserving the classics of Greek and Latin, especially the works of Plato and Aristotle, further illustrates a love of documentation suggested early on in Ibn Ishaq's treatment of the story of Muhammad.

■ **FURTHER RESEARCH**

Translation
Guillaume, A. (trans. and ed.) *The Life of Muhammad: A Translation of Ishaq's Sirat Rasul Allah*. 1955.

Biographies
Armstrong, Karen. *Muhammad: A Biography of the Prophet*. 1992.
Gabrieli, Francesco. *Muhammad and the Conquests of Islam*. 1968.
Nasr, Sayyid Hossein. *Muhammad: Man of Allah*. 1982.
Rodinson, Maxime. *Muhammad*. 1980.

History and Criticism

Allen, Roger. *An Introduction to Arabic Literature.* 2000.

Lichtenstadter, Ilse. *Introduction to Classical Arabic Literature.* 1974.

Menocal, Maria Rosa. *The Arabic Role in Medieval Literary History.* 1990.

Reynolds, Dwight F. *Interpreting the Self: Autobiography in the Arabic Literary Tradition.* 2001.

■ PRONUNCIATION

Abu Bakr (Abū Bakr): ah-BOO BAH-kur
Abu Talib (Abū Ṭālib): ah-BOO TAH-lib
Hadith: hah-DEETH
Ibn Hisham: IB-un hih-SHAHM
Ibn Ishaq: IB-un is-HAHK
isnad: is-NAHD
Khadija (Khadīja): kah-DEE-juh
maghazi: muh-GAH-zee
marathi: muh-RAH-thee
sira: SEE-rah
Sirat-an-Nabi: see-RAHT ahn-nah-BEE
Wahb ibn Munabbih: WAH-hub IB-un moo-NAH-bee

FROM

∾ The Life of Muhammad

Translated by Alfred Guillaume

THE BIRTH OF THE APOSTLE AND HIS SUCKLING

The apostle was born on Monday, 12th Rabīʿuʾl-awwal, in the year of the elephant. [. . .]

Ḥalīma the apostle's foster-mother used to say that she went forth from her country with her husband and little son whom she was nursing, among the women of her tribe, in search of other babies to nurse. This was a year of famine when they were destitute. She was riding a dusky she-donkey of hers and an old she-camel which did not yield a drop of milk. They could not sleep the whole night because of the weeping of her hungry child. She had no milk to give him, nor could their she-

---

A note on the translation. In this anthology's excerpts from the translation by Alfred Guillaume, the subtitles given to sections of the work have been retained, some of the attributions introducing the stories have been cut, and the stories have been edited for length. Most of the notes, including references to the Qurʾan, are derived from the Guillaume edition; one passage requiring further explanation has been marked "Editor's Note."

camel provide a morning draught, but we were hoping for rain and relief. 'I rode upon my donkey which had kept back the other riders through its weakness and emaciation so that it was a nuisance to them. When we reached Mecca, we looked out for foster children, and the apostle of God was offered to every one of us, and each woman refused him when she was told he was an orphan, because we hoped to get payment from the child's father. We said, "An orphan! and what will his mother and grandfather do?" and so we spurned him because of that. Every woman who came with me got a suckling except me, and when we decided to depart I said to my husband: "By God, I do not like the idea of returning with my friends without a suckling; I will go and take that orphan." He replied, "Do as you please; perhaps God will bless us on his account." So I went and took him for the sole reason that I could not find anyone else. I took him back to my baggage, and as soon as I put him in my bosom, my breasts overflowed with milk which he drank until he was satisfied, as also did his foster-brother. Then both of them slept, whereas before this we could not sleep with him. My husband got up and went to the old she-camel and lo, her udders were full; he milked it and he and I drank of her milk until we were completely satisfied, and we passed a happy night. In the morning my husband said: "Do you know, Ḥalīma, you have taken a blessed creature?" I said, "By God, I hope so." . . .

We ceased not to recognize this bounty as coming from God for a period of two years, when I weaned him. He was growing up as none of the other children grew and by the time he was two he was a well-made child. We brought him to his mother, though we were most anxious to keep him with us because of the blessing which he brought us. I said to her: "I should like you to leave my little boy with me until he becomes a big boy, for I am afraid on his account of the pest[1] in Mecca." We persisted until she sent him back with us.

Some months after our return he and his brother were with our lambs behind the tents when his brother came running and said to us, "Two men clothed in white have seized that Qurayshī brother of mine and thrown him down and opened up his belly, and are stirring it up." We ran towards him and found him standing up with a livid face. We took hold of him and asked him what was the matter. He said, "Two men in white raiment came and threw me down and opened up my belly and searched therein for I know not what." So we took him back to our tent. [. . .]

Thaur b. Yazīd [. . .] told me that some of the apostle's companions asked him to tell them about himself. He said: 'I am what Abraham my father prayed for and the good news of Jesus. When my mother was carrying me she saw a light proceeding from her which showed her the castles of Syria. I was suckled among the B. Saʿd b. Bakr, and while I was with a brother of mine behind our tents shepherding the lambs, two men in white raiment came to me with a gold basin full of snow. Then they seized me and opened up my belly, extracted my heart and split it; then they extracted a black drop from it and threw it away; then they washed my heart and my

---

[1] **pest:** Plague.

belly with that snow until they had thoroughly cleaned them. Then one said to the other, weigh him against ten of his people; they did so and I outweighed them. Then they weighed me against a hundred and then a thousand, and I outweighed them. He said, "Leave him alone, for by God, if you weighed him against all his people he would outweigh them."' [. . .]

The Apostle of God Marries Khadīja

Khadīja was a merchant woman of dignity and wealth. She used to hire men to carry merchandise outside the country on a profit-sharing basis, for Quraysh were a people given to commerce. Now when she heard about the prophet's truthfulness, trustworthiness, and honourable character, she sent for him and proposed that he should take her goods to Syria and trade with them, while she would pay him more than she paid others. He was to take a lad of hers called Maysara. The apostle of God accepted the proposal, and the two set forth until they came to Syria.

The apostle stopped in the shade of a tree near a monk's cell, when the monk came up to Maysara and asked who the man was who was resting beneath the tree. He told him that he was of Quraysh, the people who held the sanctuary; and the monk exclaimed: 'None but a prophet ever sat beneath this tree.'

Then the prophet sold the goods he had brought and bought what he wanted to buy and began the return journey to Mecca. The story goes that at the height of noon when the heat was intense as he rode his beast, Maysara saw two angels shading the apostle from the sun's rays. When he brought Khadīja her property she sold it and it amounted to double or thereabouts. Maysara for his part told her about the two angels who shaded him and of the monk's words. Now Khadīja was a determined, noble, and intelligent woman possessing the properties with which God willed to honour her. So when Maysara told her these things she sent to the apostle of God and — so the story goes — said: 'O son of my uncle I like you because of our relationship and your high reputation among your people, your trustworthiness and good character and truthfulness.' Then she proposed marriage. Now Khadīja at that time was the best born woman in Quraysh, of the greatest dignity and, too, the richest. All her people were eager to get possession of her wealth if it were possible. [. . .]

The apostle of God told his uncles of Khadīja's proposal, and his uncle Ḥamza b. 'Abdu'l-Muṭṭalib went with him to Khuwaylid b. Asad and asked for her hand and he married her.

She was the mother of all the apostle's children except Ibrāhīm, namely al-Qāsim (whereby he was known as Abu'l-Qāsim); al-Ṭāhir, al-Ṭayyib,[2] Zaynab, Ruqayya, Umm Kulthūm, and Fāṭima.

Al-Qāsim, al-Ṭayyib, and al-Ṭāhir died in paganism. All his daughters lived into Islam, embraced it, and migrated with him to Medina. [. . .]

---

[2] **al-Ṭāhir, al-Ṭayyib:** Two epithets (The Pure, The Good) applied to one son, 'Abdullah. Of Khadīja's six children by Muhammad, the two sons died and the four daughters lived.

THE PROPHET'S MISSION

When Muhammad the apostle of God reached the age of forty God sent him in compassion to mankind, 'as an evangelist to all men'.[3] . . .

Al-Zuhrī related [. . .] that when Allah desired to honour Muhammad and have mercy on His servants by means of him, the first sign of prophethood vouchsafed to the apostle was true visions, resembling the brightness of daybreak, which were shown to him in his sleep. And Allah, she said, made him love solitude so that he liked nothing better than to be alone.

'Abdu'l-Malik [. . .] the Thaqafite who had a retentive memory related to me from a certain scholar that the apostle at the time when Allah willed to bestow His grace upon him and endow him with prophethood would go forth for his affair and journey far afield until he reached the glens of Mecca and the beds of its valleys where no house was in sight; and not a stone or tree that he passed by but would say, 'Peace unto thee, O apostle of Allah.' And the apostle would turn to his right and left and look behind him and he would see naught but trees and stones. Thus he stayed seeing and hearing so long as it pleased Allah that he should stay. Then Gabriel came to him with the gift of God's grace whilst he was on Ḥirā' in the month of Ramaḍān. [. . .]

When it was the night on which God honoured him with his mission and showed mercy on His servants thereby, Gabriel brought him the command of God. 'He came to me,' said the apostle of God, 'while I was asleep, with a coverlet of brocade whereon was some writing, and said, "Read!" I said, "What shall I read?" He pressed me with it so tightly that I thought it was death; then he let me go and said, "Read!" I said, "What shall I read?" He pressed me with it again so that I thought it was death; then he let me go and said "Read!" I said, "What shall I read?" He pressed me with it the third time so that I thought it was death and said "Read!" I said, "What then shall I read?"—and this I said only to deliver myself from him, lest he should do the same to me again. He said:

> "Read in the name of thy Lord who created,
> Who created man of blood coagulated.
> Read! Thy Lord is the most beneficent,
> Who taught by the pen,
> Taught that which they knew not unto men."[4]

So I read it, and he departed from me. And I awoke from my sleep, and it was as though these words were written on my heart. Now none of God's creatures was more hateful to me than an (ecstatic) poet or a man possessed: I could not even look at them. I thought, Woe is me poet or possessed—Never shall Quraysh say this of me! I will go to the top of the mountain and throw myself down that I may kill myself and gain rest. So I went forth to do so and then when I was midway on the mountain, I heard a voice from heaven saying, "O Muhammad! thou art the apostle

---

[3] 'as an evangelist to all men': Sura 34.27.

[4] 'Read in . . . not unto men': Sura 96.1–5.

of God and I am Gabriel." I raised my head towards heaven to see who was speaking, and lo, Gabriel in the form of a man with feet astride the horizon, saying, "O Muhammad! thou art the apostle of God and I am Gabriel." I stood gazing at him, moving neither forward nor backward; then I began to turn my face away from him, but towards whatever region of the sky I looked, I saw him as before. And I continued standing there, neither advancing nor turning back, until Khadīja sent her messengers in search of me and they gained the high ground above Mecca and returned to her while I was standing in the same place; then he parted from me and I from him, returning to my family. And I came to Khadīja and sat by her thigh and drew close to her. She said, "O Abū'l-Qāsim,[5] where hast thou been? By God, I sent my messengers in search of thee, and they reached the high ground above Mecca and returned to me." I said to her, "Woe is me poet or possessed." She said, "I take refuge in God from that O Abū'l-Qāsim. God would not treat you thus since he knows your truthfulness, your great trustworthiness, your fine character, and your kindness. This cannot be, my dear. Perhaps you did see something." "Yes, I did," I said. Then I told her of what I had seen; and she said, "Rejoice, O son of my uncle, and be of good heart. Verily, by Him in whose hand is Khadīja's soul, I have hope that thou wilt be the prophet of this people." ' [. . .]

The Apostle's Public Preaching
and the Response

People began to accept Islam, both men and women, in large numbers until the fame of it was spread throughout Mecca, and it began to be talked about. Then God commanded His apostle to declare the truth of what he had received and to make known His commands to men and to call them to Him. Three years elapsed from the time that the apostle concealed his state until God commanded him to publish his religion, according to information which has reached me. Then God said, 'Proclaim what you have been ordered and turn aside from the polytheists.'[6] And again, 'Warn thy family, thy nearest relations, and lower thy wing[7] to the followers who follow thee.' And 'Say, I am the one who warns plainly'.[8] [. . .]

When the apostle's companions prayed they went to the glens so that their people could not see them praying, and while Saʿd b. Abū Waqqāṣ was with a number of the prophet's companions in one of the glens of Mecca, a band of polytheists came upon them while they were praying and rudely interrupted them. They blamed them for what they were doing until they came to blows, and it was on that occasion that Saʿd smote a polytheist with the jawbone of a camel and wounded him. This was the first blood to be shed in Islam.

When the apostle openly displayed Islam as God ordered him his people did not withdraw or turn against him, so far as I have heard, until he spoke disparagingly of their gods. When he did that they took great offence and resolved unanimously to treat him as an enemy, except those whom God had protected by Islam from such

---

[5] Abū'l-Qāsim: Muhammad's name of honor.

[6] 'Proclaim . . . polytheists': Sura 15.94.   [7] lower thy wing: Deal gently with. Sura 26.214.   [8] 'Say, I am . . . plainly': Sura 15.8, 9.

evil, but they were a despised minority. Abū Ṭālib his uncle treated the apostle kindly and protected him, the latter continuing to obey God's commands, nothing turning him back. When Quraysh saw that he would not yield to them and withdrew from them and insulted their gods and that his uncle treated him kindly and stood up in his defence and would not give him up to them, some of their leading men went to Abū Ṭālib. [. . .] They said, 'O Abū Ṭālib, your nephew has cursed our gods, insulted our religion, mocked our way of life[9] and accused our forefathers of error; either you must stop him or you must let us get at him, for you yourself are in the same position as we are in opposition to him and we will rid you of him.' He gave them a conciliatory reply and a soft answer and they went away.

The apostle continued on his way, publishing God's religion and calling men thereto. In consequence his relations with Quraysh deteriorated and men withdrew from him in enmity. They were always talking about him and inciting one another against him. Then they went to Abū Ṭālib a second time and said, 'You have a high and lofty position among us, and we have asked you to put a stop to your nephew's activities but you have not done so. By God, we cannot endure that our fathers should be reviled, our customs mocked and our gods insulted. Until you rid us of him we will fight the pair of you until one side perishes,' or words to that effect. Thus saying, they went off. Abū Ṭālib was deeply distressed at the breach with his people and their enmity but he could not desert the apostle and give him up to them.

Yaʿqūb [. . .] told me that he was told that after hearing these words from the Quraysh Abū Ṭālib sent for his nephew and told him what his people had said. 'Spare me and yourself,' he said. 'Do not put on me a burden greater than I can bear.' The apostle thought that his uncle had the idea of abandoning and betraying him, and that he was going to lose his help and support. He answered, 'O my uncle, by God, if they put the sun in my right hand and the moon in my left on condition that I abandoned this course, until God has made it victorious, or I perish therein, I would not abandon it.' Then the apostle broke into tears, and got up. As he turned away his uncle called him and said, 'Come back, my nephew,' and when he came back, he said, 'Go and say what you please, for by God I will never give you up on any account.'

When the Quraysh perceived that Abū Ṭālib had refused to give up the apostle, and that he was resolved to part company with them, they went to him with ʿUmāra b. al-Walīd b. al-Mughīra and said, according to my information, 'O Abū Ṭālib, this is ʿUmāra, the strongest and most handsome young man among Quraysh, so take him and you will have the benefit of his intelligence and support; adopt him as a son and give up to us this nephew of yours, who has opposed your religion and the religion of your fathers, severed the unity of your people, and mocked our way of life, so that we may kill him. This will be man for man.' He answered, 'By God, this is an evil thing that you would put upon me, would you give me your son that I should feed him for you, and should I give you my son that you should kill him? By God, this shall never be.' Al-Muṭʿim b. ʿAdīy said, 'Your people have treated you fairly and have taken pains to avoid what you dislike. I do not think that you are willing to accept anything from

---

[9] **our way of life:** *Aḥlam*, the civilization of the pre-Islamic Arabs.

them.' Abū Ṭālib replied, 'They have not treated me fairly, by God, but you have agreed to betray me and help the people against me, so do what you like,' or words to that effect. So the situation worsened, the quarrel became heated and people were sharply divided, and openly showed their animosity to their opponents. . . .

Then the Quraysh incited people against the companions of the apostle who had become Muslims. Every tribe fell upon the Muslims among them, beating them and seducing them from their religion. God protected His apostle from them through his uncle, who, when he saw what Quraysh were doing, called upon B. Hāshim and B. al-Muṭṭalib to stand with him in protecting the apostle. This they agreed to do, with the exception of Abū Lahab, the accursed enemy of God. [. . .]

The Night Journey and the Ascent to Heaven

Ziyād b. ʿAbdullāh al-Bakkāʾī [. . .] told me the following: Then the apostle was carried by night from the mosque at Mecca to the Masjid al-Aqṣā, which is the temple of Aelia, when Islam had spread in Mecca among the Quraysh and all the tribes.

The following account reached me from ʿAbdullāh b. Masʿūd and Abū Saʿīd al-Khudrī, and ʿĀʾisha the prophet's wife, and Muʿāwiya b. Abū Sufyān, and al-Hasan b. Abūʾl-Ḥasan al-Baṣrī, and Ibn Shihāb al-Zuhrī and Qatāda and other traditionists, and Umm Hāniʾ d. of Abū Ṭālib. It is pieced together in the story that follows, each one contributing something of what he was told about what happened when he was taken on the night journey. The matter of the place[10] of the journey and what is said about it is a searching test and a matter of God's power and authority wherein is a lesson for the intelligent; and guidance and mercy and strengthening to those who believe. It was certainly an act of God by which He took him by night in what way He pleased[11] to show him His signs which He willed him to see so that he witnessed His mighty sovereignty and power by which He does what He wills to do.

According to what I have heard ʿAbdullāh b. Masʿūd used to say: Burāq, the animal whose every stride carried it as far as its eye could reach on which the prophets before him used to ride was brought to the apostle and he was mounted on it. His companion (Gabriel) went with him to see the wonders between heaven and earth, until he came to Jerusalem's temple. There he found Abraham the friend of God, Moses, and Jesus assembled with a company of the prophets, and he prayed with them. Then he was brought three vessels containing milk, wine, and water respectively. The apostle said: 'I heard a voice saying when these were offered to me: If he takes the water he will be drowned and his people also; if he takes the wine he will go astray and his people also; and if he takes the milk he will be rightly guided and his people also. So I took the vessel containing milk and drank it. Gabriel said to me, You have been rightly guided and so will your people be, Muhammad.'

I was told that al-Ḥasan said that the apostle said: 'While I was sleeping in the Ḥijr Gabriel came and stirred me with his foot. I sat up but saw nothing and lay

---

[10] the place: or *(masra)* "time."

[11] in what way He pleased: This leaves open the question of whether it was an actual physical journey or a nocturnal vision.

down again. He came a second time and stirred me with his foot. I sat up but saw nothing and lay down again. He came to me the third time and stirred me with his foot. I sat up and he took hold of my arm and I stood beside him and he brought me out to the door of the mosque and there was a white animal, half mule, half donkey, with wings on its sides with which it propelled its feet, putting down each forefoot at the limit of its sight and he mounted me on it. Then he went out with me keeping close to me. [. . .]

In his story al-Ḥasan said: 'The apostle and Gabriel went their way until they arrived at the temple at Jerusalem. There he found Abraham, Moses, and Jesus among a company of the prophets. The apostle acted as their imam in prayer. Then he was brought two vessels, one containing wine and the other milk. The apostle took the milk and drank it, leaving the wine. Gabriel said: "You have been rightly guided to the way of nature[12] and so will your people be, Muhammad. Wine is forbidden you." Then the apostle returned to Mecca and in the morning he told Quraysh what had happened. Most of them said, "By God, this is a plain absurdity! A caravan takes a month to go to Syria and a month to return and can Muhammad do the return journey in one night?" Many Muslims gave up their faith; some went to Abū Bakr and said, "What do you think of your friend now, Abū Bakr? He alleges that he went to Jerusalem last night and prayed there and came back to Mecca." He replied that they were lying about the apostle; but they said that he was in the mosque at that very moment telling the people about it. Abū Bakr said, "If he says so then it is true. And what is so surprising in that? He tells me that communications from God from heaven to earth come to him in an hour of a day or night and I believe him, and that is more extraordinary than that at which you boggle!" He then went to the apostle and asked him if these reports were true, and when he said they were, he asked him to describe Jerusalem to him.' [. . .]

One of Abū Bakr's family told me that 'Ā'isha the prophet's wife used to say: 'The apostle's body remained where it was but God removed his spirit by night.' [. . .]

I have heard that the apostle used to say, 'My eyes sleep while my heart is awake.' Only God knows how revelation came and he saw what he saw. But whether he was asleep or awake, it was all true and actually happened. [. . .]

THE ASCENT TO HEAVEN

One whom I have no reason to doubt told me on the authority of Abū Saʿīd al-Khudrī: I heard the apostle say, 'After the completion of my business in Jerusalem a ladder was brought to me finer than any I have ever seen. It was that to which the dying man looks when death approaches. My companion mounted it with me until we came to one of the gates of heaven called the Gate of the Watchers. An angel called Ismāʿīl was in charge of it, and under his command were twelve thousand angels each of them having twelve thousand angels under his command.' As he told

---

[12] **the way of nature:** Or, "the true primeval religion."

this story the apostle used to say, 'and none knows the armies of God but He.'[13] When Gabriel brought me in, Ismāʿīl asked who I was, and when he was told that I was Muhammad he asked if I had been given a mission,[14] and on being assured of this he wished me well.

A traditionist who had got it from one who had heard it from the apostle told me that the latter said: 'All the angels who met me when I entered the lowest heaven smiled in welcome and wished me well except one who said the same things but did not smile or show that joyful expression which the others had. And when I asked Gabriel the reason he told me that if he had ever smiled on anyone before or would smile on anyone hereafter he would have smiled on me; but he does not smile because he is Mālik, the Keeper of Hell. I said to Gabriel, he holding the position with regard to God which he has described to you "obeyed there, trustworthy,"[15] "Will you not order him to show me hell?" And he said, "Certainly! O Mālik, show Muhammad Hell." Thereupon he removed its covering and the flames blazed high into the air until I thought that they would consume everything. So I asked Gabriel to order him to send them back to their place which he did. I can only compare the effect of their withdrawal to the falling of a shadow, until when the flames retreated whence they had come, Mālik placed their cover on them.'

In his tradition Abū Saʿīd al-Khudrī said that the apostle said: 'When I entered the lowest heaven I saw a man sitting there with the spirits of men passing before him. To one he would speak well and rejoice in him saying: "A good spirit from a good body" and of another he would say "Faugh!" and frown, saying: "An evil spirit from an evil body." In answer to my question Gabriel told me that this was our father Adam reviewing the spirits of his offspring; the spirit of a believer excited his pleasure, and the spirit of an infidel excited his disgust so that he said the words just quoted.

'Then I saw men with lips like camels; in their hands were pieces of fire like stones which they used to thrust into their mouths and they would come out of their posteriors. I was told that these were those who sinfully devoured the wealth of orphans.

'Then I saw men in the way of the family of Pharaoh,[16] with such bellies as I have never seen; there were passing over them as it were camels maddened by thirst when they were cast into hell, treading them down, they being unable to move out of the way. These were the usurers.

'Then I saw men with good fat meat before them side by side with lean stinking meat, eating of the latter and leaving the former. These are those who forsake the women which God has permitted and go after those he has forbidden.

'Then I saw women hanging by their breasts. These were those who had fathered bastards on their husbands.'

---

[13] 'and none knows . . . but He': Sura 74.34.

[14] given a mission: Or perhaps simply "sent for."

[15] 'obeyed there, trustworthy': Sura 81.21.

[16] 'in the way of . . . Pharaoh': Cf. Sura 40.49, "Cast the family of Pharaoh into the worst of all punishments."

Ja'far b. 'Amr told me from al-Qāsim b. Muhammad that the apostle said: 'Great is God's anger against a woman who brings a bastard into her family. He deprives the true sons of their portion and learns the secrets of the *harim.*'

To continue the tradition of Sa'īd al-Khudrī: 'Then I was taken up to the second heaven and there were the two maternal cousins Jesus, Son of Mary, and John, son of Zakariah. Then to the third heaven and there was a man whose face was as the moon at the full. This was my brother Joseph, son of Jacob. Then to the fourth heaven and there was a man called Idrīs. "And we have exalted him to a lofty place."[17] Then to the fifth heaven and there was a man with white hair and a long beard, never have I seen a more handsome man than he. This was the beloved among his people Aaron son of 'Imrān. Then to the sixth heaven, and there was a dark man with a hooked nose like the Shanū'a. This was my brother Moses, son of 'Imrān. Then to the seventh heaven and there was a man sitting on a throne at the gate of the immortal mansion.[18] Every day seventy thousand angels went in not to come back until the resurrection day. Never have I seen a man more like myself. This was my father Abraham. Then he took me into Paradise and there I saw a damsel with dark red lips and I asked her to whom she belonged, for she pleased me much when I saw her, and she told me "Zayd b. Hāritha." The apostle gave Zayd the good news about her.'

From a tradition of 'Abdullah b. Mas'ūd from the prophet there has reached me the following: When Gabriel took him up to each of the heavens and asked permission to enter he had to say whom he had brought and whether he had received a mission and they would say 'God grant him life, brother and friend!' until they reached the seventh heaven and his Lord. There the duty of fifty prayers a day was laid upon him.

The apostle said: 'On my return I passed by Moses and what a fine friend of yours he was! He asked me how many prayers had been laid upon me and when I told him fifty he said, "Prayer is a weighty matter and your people are weak, so go back to your Lord and ask him to reduce the number for you and your community." I did so and He took off ten. Again I passed by Moses and he said the same again; and so it went on until only five prayers for the whole day and night were left. Moses again gave me the same advice. I replied that I had been back to my Lord and asked him to reduce the number until I was ashamed, and I would not do it again. He of you who performs them in faith and trust will have the reward of fifty prayers.' [. . .]

THE APOSTLE RECEIVES THE ORDER TO FIGHT

The apostle had not been given permission to fight or allowed to shed blood before the second 'Aqaba. He had simply been ordered to call men to God and to endure insult and forgive the ignorant. The Quraysh had persecuted his followers, seducing some from their religion, and exiling others from their country. They had to choose whether to give up their religion, be maltreated at home, or to flee the country, some to Abyssinia, others to Medina.

---

[17] 'And we have . . . place': Sura 19.58.

[18] the immortal mansion: In view of what follows this would seem to mean Paradise itself.

When Quraysh became insolent towards God and rejected His gracious purpose, accused His prophet of lying, and ill treated and exiled those who served Him and proclaimed His unity, believed in His prophet, and held fast to His religion, He gave permission to His apostle to fight and to protect himself against those who wronged them and treated them badly.

The first verse which was sent down on this subject from what I have heard from 'Urwa b. al-Zubayr and other learned persons was: 'Permission is given to those who fight because they have been wronged. God is well able to help them, — those who have been driven out of their houses without right only because they said God is our Lord. Had not God used some men to keep back others, cloisters and churches and oratories and mosques wherein the name of God is constantly mentioned would have been destroyed. Assuredly God will help those who help Him. God is Almighty. Those who if we make them strong in the land will establish prayer, pay the poor-tax, enjoin kindness, and forbid iniquity. To God belongs the end of matters.[19] The meaning is: 'I have allowed them to fight only because they have been unjustly treated while their sole offence against men has been that they worship God. When they are in the ascendant they will establish prayer, pay the poor-tax, enjoin kindness, and forbid iniquity, i.e. the prophet and his companions all of them.' Then God sent down to him: 'Fight them so that there be no more seduction,'[20] i.e. until no believer is seduced from his religion. 'And the religion is God's,' i.e.[,] Until God alone is worshipped.

When God had given permission to fight and this clan of the Anṣār had pledged their support to him in Islam and to help him and his followers, and the Muslims who had taken refuge with them, the apostle commanded his companions, the emigrants of his people and those Muslims who were with him in Mecca, to emigrate to Medina and to link up with their brethren the Anṣār. 'God will make for you brethren and houses in which you may be safe.' So they went out in companies, and the apostle stayed in Mecca waiting for his Lord's permission to leave Mecca and migrate to Medina. [. . .]

The Apostle's Illness in the House of 'Āʾisha

['Āʾisha, the prophet's wife, said:] 'The apostle went out walking between two men of his family, one of whom was al-Fadl b. al-cAbbas. His head was bound in a cloth and his feet were dragging as he came to my house. [. . .]

Then the apostle's illness worsened and he suffered much pain. He said, 'Pour seven skins of water from different wells over me so that I may go out to the men and instruct them.' We made him sit down in a tub belonging to Ḥafṣa d. 'Umar and we poured water over him until he cried, 'Enough, enough!'

---

[19] 'To God . . . matters': Sura 22.40–42.

[20] 'Fight them . . . seduction': Sura 2.198.

Al-Zuhrī said that Ayyūb b. Bashīr told him that the apostle went out with his head bound up and sat in the pulpit. The first thing he uttered was a prayer over the men of Uḥud asking God's forgiveness for them and praying for them a long time; then he said, 'God has given one of his servants the choice between this world and that which is with God and he has chosen the latter.' Abū Bakr perceived that he meant himself and he wept, saying, 'Nay, we and our children will be your ransom.' He replied, 'Gently, Abū Bakr,' adding, 'See to these doors that open on to the mosque and shut them except one from Abū Bakr's house, for I know no one who is a better friend to me than he.' [. . .]

Al-Zuhrī said, Ḥamza b. 'Abdullah b. 'Umar told me that 'Ā'isha said: 'When the prophet became seriously ill he ordered the people to tell Abū Bakr to superintend the prayers.[21] 'Ā'isha told him that Abū Bakr was a delicate man with a weak voice who wept much when he read the Quran. He repeated his order nevertheless, and I repeated my objection. He said, "You are like Joseph's companions; tell him to preside at prayers." My only reason for saying what I did was that I wanted Abū Bakr to be spared this task, because I knew that people would never like a man who occupied the apostle's place, and would blame him for every misfortune that occurred, and I wanted Abū Bakr to be spared this.' [. . .]

Al-Zuhrī said that Anas b. Mālik told him that on the Monday on which God took His apostle he went out to the people as they were praying the morning prayer. The curtain was lifted and the door opened and out came the apostle and stood at 'Ā'isha's door. The Muslims were almost seduced from their prayers for joy at seeing him, and he motioned to them that they should continue their prayers. The apostle smiled with joy when he marked their mien in prayer, and I never saw him with a nobler expression than he had that day. Then he went back and the people went away thinking that the apostle had recovered from his illness. Abū Bakr returned to his wife in al-Sunḥ. . . .

Abū Bakr b. 'Abdullah b. Abū Mulayka told me that when the Monday came the apostle went out to morning prayer with his head wrapped up while Abū Bakr was leading the prayers. When the apostle went out the people's attention wavered, and Abū Bakr knew that the people would not behave thus unless the apostle had come, so he withdrew from his place; but the apostle pushed him in the back, saying, 'Lead the men in prayer,' and the apostle sat at his side praying in a sitting posture on the right of Abū Bakr. When he had ended prayer he turned to the men and spoke to them with a loud voice which could be heard outside the mosque: 'O men, the fire is kindled, and rebellions come like the darkness of the night. By God, you can lay nothing to my charge. I allow only what the Quran allows and forbid only what the Quran forbids.' . . .

Ya'qūb b. 'Utba from al-Zuhrī from 'Urwa from 'Ā'isha said: The apostle came back to me from the mosque that day and lay in my bosom. A man of Abū Bakr's family came in to me with a toothpick in his hand and the apostle looked at it in

---

[21] **to superintend the prayers:** As this office was a sign of leadership, A'isha assumed that Muhammad wished Abū Bakr to succeed him. [Editors' note]

such a way that I knew he wanted it, and when I asked him if he wanted me to give it him he said Yes; so I took it and chewed it for him to soften it and gave it to him. He rubbed his teeth with it more energetically than I had ever seen him rub before; then he laid it down. I found him heavy in my bosom and as I looked into his face, lo his eyes were fixed and he was saying, 'Nay, the most Exalted Companion is of paradise.' I said, 'You were given the choice and you have chosen, by Him Who sent you with the truth!' And so the apostle was taken. . . .

Al-Zuhrī said, and Saʿīd b. al-Musayyib from Abū Hurayra told me: When the apostle was dead ʿUmar got up and said: 'Some of the disaffected will allege that the apostle is dead, but by God he is not dead: he has gone to his Lord as Moses b. ʿImrān went and was hidden from his people for forty days, returning to them after it was said that he had died. By God, the apostle will return as Moses returned and will cut off the hands and feet of men who allege that the apostle is dead.' When Abū Bakr heard what was happening he came to the door of the mosque as ʿUmar was speaking to the people. He paid no attention but went in to ʿĀʾisha's house to the apostle, who was lying covered by a mantle of Yamanī cloth. He went and uncovered his face and kissed him, saying, 'You are dearer than my father and mother. You have tasted the death which God had decreed: a second death will never overtake you.' Then he replaced the mantle on the apostle's face and went out. ʿUmar was still speaking and he said, 'Gently, ʿUmar, be quiet.' But ʿUmar refused and went on talking, and when Abū Bakr saw that he would not be silent he went forward to the people who, when they heard his words, came to him and left ʿUmar. Giving thanks and praise to God he said: 'O men, if anyone worships Muhammad, Muhammad is dead: if anyone worships God, God is alive, immortal.' Then he recited this verse: 'Muhammad is nothing but an apostle. Apostles have passed away before him. Can it be that if he were to die or be killed you would turn back on your heels? He who turns back does no harm to God and God will reward the grateful.'[22] By God, it was as though the people did not know that this verse had come down until Abū Bakr recited it that day. The people took it from him and it was (constantly) in their mouths. ʿUmar said, 'By God, when I heard Abū Bakr recite these words I was dumbfounded so that my legs would not bear me and I fell to the ground; knowing that the apostle was indeed dead.'

---

[22] 'Muhammad is . . . the grateful': Sura 3.138.

❧ KALIDASA
INDIA, C. FOURTH CENTURY

When *Shakuntala (**Abhijñanasakuntala**)* was first translated into English by William Jones in 1789, the play caused a sensation in Europe, especially in Germany where Goethe said it made a "transcendental impression" on him, and in a poetic tribute counseled readers: "If you want to designate both the heaven and earth by a common name / I refer you to the *Sákuntalā*. . . ." Goethe's excitement came from his having discovered a work that in every way fulfilled what he would later define as "world literature," a work that speaks across centuries and transcends the particularities of its cultural origins. Kalidasa's masterwork is also the finest example of Sanskrit drama from classical India, a literature similar in its mythic subject matter and its origins in ancient ritual to Greek drama.

An Obscure Life.   Little is known about Kalidasa beyond the fact that he is named as the author in the prologues of three surviving plays. Even the time when he lived is a matter of speculation, with scholars suggesting dates that range over several centuries. Hints in the plays and circumstantial historical evidence have led most commentators to locate him during the reign of the third Gupta ruler, **Chandragupta** II (376–415), at the height of India's classical golden age.

According to a popular legend, Kalidasa was orphaned as an infant, raised in illiteracy by an oxcart driver, married by fraud to a princess who cast him out when she discovered his ignorance, and ultimately given the power of poetry by the goddess Kali. From this mythic biography the playwright and poet earned the name Kalidasa, meaning "the slave of Kali." His plays, however, would indicate that he was a highly educated and well-traveled man, not an ignorant peasant. His descriptions of court life suggest that he was probably a court poet and perhaps an emissary for the king. His references to Ujjayini, one of the great cities of Gupta India, indicate that he probably lived there as a member of the intelligentsia. And his descriptions of nature reveal him to have been a close observer of the natural world especially drawn to the mountains of north India. He holds a position of utmost prominence in Indian literature, similar to that of Homer, Dante, or Shakespeare in the West.

Seven works have been attributed to Kalidasa: two volumes of poetry, two epics, and three plays. The earliest was probably the poem *The Gathering of the Seasons (Raghuramsam)*, which describes nature at different times of the year and compares the beauty of nature to the beauty of a woman; nature and the woman ultimately become one. The long lyric poem *The Cloud Messenger (Meghadutam)* tells of a love message transmitted from central India to the Himalayas by a cloud. The two epics *Raghu's Dynasty (Raghuvamsam)* and *The Birth of Kumara (Kumarasambhavam)* treat mythological subjects. Kalidasa is most remembered for his plays, *Malavika and Agnimitra (Malavikagnimitram)*, *Urvasi Won*

uh-bij-NYAH-nuh
shuh-KOON-tuh-luh

shuh-KOON-tuh-luh

chun-druh-GOOP-tuh

www   For links to more information about Kalidasa and a quiz on *Shakuntala*, see bedfordstmartins .com/worldlit compact.

Lovers, 475–510 C.E.
Shakuntala,
Kalidasa's epic play,
is essentially a love
story, the romantic
tale of the courtship,
secret marriage,
separation, and
reunion of King
Dushyanta and the
semidivine
Shakuntala. (Lovers.
Wallpainting. Scala/
Art Resources, NY)

This fusion of esthetic
and spiritual, of
sensual and religious
values is perhaps
unknown, in equal
measure, in any other
country. Kalidasa is
the best exponent of
this singularly Indian
approach to life. His
imagination dwells
on love which seems
at first to be of the
earth, but which
leads imperceptibly
into heavenly vistas.
What appears as
gross sensuality is
soon transformed
into domestic felicity,
which culminates in
divine ecstasy.
– K. KRISHNAMOORTHY,
critic, 1972

nah-tyuh-SHAHS-truh
p. 749

by Valor (*Vikramorvasiyam*), and his masterwork, *Shakuntala and the Ring of Recollection*. All three plays develop essentially the same story, that of a king separated from his beloved but ultimately reunited with her, a masterplot of Sanskrit drama.

Sanskrit Drama. Sanskrit was the literary language of classical India. Codified and formalized in the fourth century B.C.E., it became, like classical Arabic or church Latin, a formal written language distinct from the spoken language in everyday use. While such languages may be appropriate for epic poems and religious ritual, they do not work well in drama, especially with characters whose speech is meant to sound like that of real people. Kalidasa and other early Sanskrit dramatists solved this problem by using two languages. Kings, gods, and other important male characters spoke in Sanskrit verse. Women and men of lower castes, including the **BRAHMIN** buffoon, spoke in vernacular languages, and often in prose.

Like Greek drama in the West, Sanskrit drama probably has its roots in religious ritual. The prayers that begin and end the action are one indication of this heritage, as is the underlying theme in all the plays that compares the human order under a king to the divine order ruled by Indra, the ruling deity in the Hindu **PANTHEON** of gods. Also like Greek drama, Sanskrit drama has its book of theory, the The *Treatise on Drama* (**Natyashastra**), comparable to **The Poetics** of Aristotle. The date and authorship of *The Treatise* are still in dispute. Like *The Poetics, The Treatise* analyzes the elements of drama, discussing literary components like character and plot as well as such theatrical concerns as costume, gesture, movement, and the physical layout of theaters. Theatrical elements, especially gesture and dance, play a more important role in Indian drama than similar elements (called "spectacle" by Aristotle) do in the drama of the West.

Aristotle's focus on tragedy in *The Poetics* elevated that genre to preeminence in the West. *The Treatise* concentrates on the NATAKA, or heroic romance, the genre to which *Shakuntala* and Kalidasa's other plays belong. To achieve its goal of "pleasurable instruction," the *nataka* tells a well-known story, often from one of the heroic epics. Its central character is a mythic figure, a warrior-king with divine elements in his ancestry. Unlike the Greek tragic heroes, whose flaws bring suffering and usually death, the Sanskrit hero-kings are idealized types and the dramatic action is heroic and comic rather than tragic. In Sanskrit drama, plot, character, and language combine with music, dance, gesture, and other theatricalities to create an emotional mood, or RASA, shared by author, actors, and members of the audience. Indian dramatic theory identifies eight *rasas* (aesthetic emotions) that can focus a drama: the erotic, the heroic, the disquieting, the furious, the comic, the marvellous, the horrible, and the pathetic. Only two are appropriate to the *nataka* form, the erotic and the heroic. Instead of a CATHARSIS of pity and fear, the Indian heroic romance seeks to induce a mood of harmony and peace, as the love story embodying the erotic *rasa* and the kingship story embodying the heroic *rasa* are resolved together and harmoniously in the end. The effect of the play, then, is to affirm the connection between the divine and the human realms as the central characters fulfill the roles they have been born to play in the cosmic order.

Shakuntala.   Kalidasa faithfully follows these dramatic conventions in *Shakuntala*. The hero and heroine are both semidivine figures. King **Dushyanta** is descended from the great King **Puru** and can trace his ancestry back to the lunar dynasty of Indian legend. Early in the play he establishes that Shakuntala is not the daughter of a Brahmin sage from a caste beneath his own warrior caste but is also of semidivine ancestry, the daughter of a royal sage and a celestial nymph. Dushyanta has all the attributes of a perfect ruler: He is generous, intelligent, a great hunter, a fine painter, a protector of his people, and the warrior called by Indra to battle the gods' enemies. Shakuntala embodies the virtues her culture admires in women, modesty and submissiveness, but also displays a significant measure of self-respect and energy, actively seeking celestial refuge, for instance, for herself and her child after the king's rejection. The other conventional role in the drama is that of the Buffoon, the king's companion **Madhavya**, who is much like one of Shakespeare's fools, speaking plain truth to the king. The action of *Shakuntala* follows the story of Dushyanta and Shakuntala, their courtship and secret marriage, and their separation as the king returns to court to take up his royal duties. Their reunion, which affirms the marriage and establishes the harmony of the ruler pair, also reveals the heir to Dushyanta, his son, Bharata, destined to become the great ruler of India and the subject of the epic poem *Mahabharata*.

> Kalidasa understood in the fifth century what Europe did not learn until the nineteenth, and even now comprehends only imperfectly: that the world was not made for man, that man reaches his full stature only as he realises the dignity and worth of life that is not human.
>
> – ARTHUR W. RYDER, critic, 1912

doosh-YAHN-tuh; POO-roo

MAH-duv-yuh

uh-nuh-SOO-yuh
pree-yum-VAH-duh

The *Mahabharata* was the source for Kalidasa's play, a familiar story that he elaborated and refined. The original story had only three characters, the king, Shakuntala, and Kanva. Kalidasa gave richness and depth to these central figures by adding minor characters such as Shakuntala's two attendants, the members of the King's entourage, and, later in the play, the fisherman and the policemen. He also added Durvasas's curse and the ring, devices that give probability to the action and absolve the king from responsibility for his forgetfulness. Instead of appearing as a ruthless Don Juan, the king, when he resists the physical attractions of Shakuntala because he believes she is another man's wife, shows himself a restrained man and a devoted ruler.

Kalidasa's distinctive contribution to the story is most evident in the poetry of the play and in his evocation of character and setting. Although Shakuntala and Dushyanta are idealized stock characters, they are given depth and complexity by their companions. **Anasuya**'s seriousness and **Priyamvada**'s playful teasing reveal contrasting sides of Shakuntala's character, while Madhavya and the king's other attendants similarly add dimension to the sovereign's character. The settings are especially significant, even though Sanskrit plays were, like Shakespeare's, performed on a bare stage. The poetry of the opening acts evokes the natural green world where Shakuntala is identified with the deer and the jasmine flowers and the king with the bee that disrupts Shakuntala's repose. This setting is more than just scenic; it is a sacred grove, an earthly paradise where hunting ceases and animals and humans live together in a peaceable kingdom. Shakuntala, whose name alludes to the shakunta birds who nurtured and protected her as an infant before she was adopted by the sage Kanva, is a child of nature. In this sacred and sensual setting, the passions of the king and the maiden are aroused, culminating in the inevitable natural marriage at the end of Act III.

When the king is recalled to the city, his conflict between duty *(DHARMA)* and sensual desire *(KAMA)*, the main theme of the *nataka* genre, is brought into focus. Dushyanta prolongs his stay in the sacred grove by claiming he has a duty to protect the place and by sending Madhavya in his place to respond to the summons. When he does return to his duties, the demands of kingship absorb all of his attention and erase memories of the forest and of his marriage, an amnesia made dramatically believable by **Durvasas'** spell. The royal city, with its palace intrigues and official duties, is Dushyanta's milieu. It is also home to a barren marriage. When Shakuntala arrives she is out of place, for she signifies nature. So unnatural is the city that the mango flowers in the palace's pleasure garden "bloom without spreading pollen," symbolic of the barrenness of the king's urban marriage. In this setting the king is unable to recognize Shakuntala, and he drives her away. Remorseful after the ring restores his memory, he cancels the festival of spring.

door-VAH-sus

Resolution is achieved in a *DEUS EX MACHINA* ending. After Dushyanta serves as a warrior for the god Indra, he is reunited with Shakuntala in a celestial garden recalling the sacred grove of the play's opening scenes. This transcendental reunion resolves the conflict between duty and desire and amends the earlier barrenness of Dushyanta's reign as he recognizes his and Shankutala's son, Bharata, who is destined to become India's founding monarch.

■ **FURTHER RESEARCH**

Lal, P. *Great Sanskrit Plays.* 1964.
Ragan, Chandra, ed. and trans. *Kalidasa: The Loom of Time.* 1989. A long introduction and translations of several of Kalidasa's works.
Stoler Miller, Barbara, ed. and trans. *Theater of Memory: The Plays of Kalidasa.* 1984. Includes essays on Kalidasa, Sanskrit dramatic theory, and the Sanskrit theater as well as translations of the plays.
Wells, Henry W. *The Classical Drama of India.* 1963.

■ **PRONUNCIATION**

Abhijñanasakuntala: uh-bij-NYAH-nuh shuh-KOON-tuh-luh, uh-bid-YAH-nuh
Anasūyā: uh-nuh-SOO-yuh
Aparājitā: uh-puh-RAH-jih-tuh
Ayodhyā: uh-YOH-dyuh
Bharatavarsa: bah-ruh-tuh-VAR-shuh
Chandragupta: chun-druh-GOOP-tuh, chahn-druh-
Caturikā: chuh-TOO-rih-kah
Dhanamitra: duh-nuh-MIT-ruh
Durvāsas: door-VAH-sus
Duṣyanta: doosh-YAHN-tuh
Haṁsapadikā: hawng-suh-PAH-dih-kuh
Hastināpura: hus-tih-NAH-poo-ruh
Jayanta: JIGH-yun-tuh
Karabhaka: kuh-ruh-BAH-kuh
Māḍhavya: MAH-duv-yuh
Madhukarikā: muh-doo-KAH-rih-kuh
Mārīca: muh-REE-chuh
Marīci: muh-REE-chee
Mitrāvasu: mih-TRAH-vuh-soo
moksha: MOKE-shuh
Natyashastra: nah-tyuh-SHAHS-truh
Parabhṛtikā: puh-ruh-BUR-tih-kuh
Priyaṁvadā: pree-yum-VAH-duh
Puru: POO-roo
Raivataka: righ-VAH-tuh-kuh
Śakuntalā: shuh-KOON-tuh-luh
śamī: SHUH-mee, SHAH-mee
Sānumatī: sah-NOO-muh-tee
Śāradvata: shuh-RUD-vuh-tuh
Śārṅgarava: sharng-guh-RUH-vuh
Sarvadamana: sar-vuh-DAH-muh-nuh
śirīṣa: shih-REE-shuh
Somarāta: soh-muh-RAH-tuh
Somatīrtha: soh-muh-TEER-tuh
sṛṅgāra: shurng-GAH-ruh
Sūcaka: SOO-chuh-kuh

If you would enjoy the flowers of early years / and the fruits of age advanced, / If you want to have something that charms, / something that is enchanting, / If you want to designate both the heaven / and earth by a common name, / I refer you to the Sákuntala and thus express these all.

– JOHANN WOLFGANG VON GOETHE

svabhāvokti: svuh-buh-VOKE-tee, swuh-
svarga: SVAR-guh
svayaṃvara: svuh-YUM-vuh-ruh, swuh-
Taralikā: tuh-RAH-lih-kuh
Triśaṅku: tree-SHAHNG-koo
Triṣṭubh: TRISH-toob
Vasumatī: vuh-soo-MUH-tee, -MAH-tee
Vātāyana: vah-TAH-yuh-nuh
Vetravatī: vay-truh-VUH-tee, -VAH-tee
vidūṣaka: vih-DOO-shuh-kuh
Viṣṇu: VISH-noo
Viśvāmitra: vish-vuh-MIT-ruh
Yakṣī: YUK-shee, YAHK-

☙ Śakuntalā and the Ring of Recollection

Translated by Barbara Stoler Miller

CHARACTERS

Players in the prologue:
DIRECTOR, *Director of the players and manager of the theater.*
ACTRESS, *The lead actress.*

Principal roles:
KING, *Duṣyanta, the hero; ruler of Hastināpura; a royal sage of the lunar dynasty of Puru.*
ŚAKUNTALĀ, *The heroine; daughter of the royal sage Viśvāmitra and the celestial nymph Menakā; adoptive daughter of the ascetic Kaṇva.*
BUFFOON, *Māḍhavya, the king's comical brahman companion.*

Members of Kaṇva's hermitage:
ANASŪYĀ *and* PRIYAMVADĀ, *Two young female ascetics; friends of Śakuntalā.*
KAṆVA, *Foster father of Śakuntalā and master of the hermitage; a sage belonging to the lineage of the divine creator Marīci, and thus related to Mārīca.*
GAUTAMĪ, *The senior female ascetic.*
ŚĀRṄGARAVA *and* ŚĀRADVATA, *Kaṇva's disciples.*
Various inhabitants of the hermitage: a monk with his two pupils, two boy ascetics (named Gautama and Nārada), a young disciple of Kaṇva, a trio of female ascetics.

Members of the king's forest retinue:
CHARIOTEER, *Driver of the king's chariot.*
GUARD, *Raivataka, guardian of the entrance to the king's quarters.*

A note on the translation: Ever since William Jones first introduced this work to the West with his English translation in 1789, it has intrigued Western readers and translators. Translators of Kalidasa's work are sometimes awed by its antiquity and its serious themes, casting it into almost scriptural language. Barbara Stoler Miller's translation nicely captures the many different voices in Kalidasa's play. We have retained her use of diacritical marks such as the Ś in Śakuntala that indicates an English *sh* sound. The pronunciation guide includes a rendering that indicates an unmarked sounding of the words.

GENERAL, *Commander of the king's army.*
KARABHAKA, *Royal messenger.*
Various attendants, including Greco-Bactrian bow-bearers.

Members of the king's palace retinue:
CHAMBERLAIN, *Vātāyana, chief officer of the king's household.*
PRIEST, *Somarāta, the king's religious preceptor and household priest.*
DOORKEEPER, *Vetravatī, the female attendant who ushers in visitors and presents messages.*
PARABHṚTIKĀ *and* MADHUKARIKĀ, *Two maids assigned to the king's garden.*
CATURIKĀ, *A maidservant.*

City dwellers:
MAGISTRATE, *The king's low-caste brother-in-law; chief of the city's policemen.*
POLICEMEN, *Sūcaka and Jānuka.*
FISHERMAN, *An outcaste.*

Celestials:
MĀRĪCA, *A divine sage; master of the celestial hermitage in which Śakuntalā gives birth to her son; father of Indra, king of the gods, whose armies Duṣyanta leads.*
ADITI, *Wife of Mārīca.*
MĀTALI, *Indra's charioteer.*
SĀNUMATĪ, *A nymph; friend of Śakuntalā's mother Menakā.*
Various members of Mārīca's hermitage: two female ascetics, Mārīca's disciple Gālava.
BOY, *Sarvadamana, son of Śakuntalā and Duṣyanta; later known as Bharata.*

Offstage voices:
VOICES OFFSTAGE, *From the backstage area or dressing room; behind the curtain, out of view of the audience. The voice belongs to various players before they enter the stage, such as the monk, Śakuntalā's friends, the buffoon, Mātali; also to figures who never enter the stage, such as the angry sage Durvāsas, the two bards who chant royal panegyrics* (vaitālikau).
VOICE IN THE AIR, *A voice chanting in the air from somewhere offstage: the bodiless voice of Speech quoted in Sanskrit by Priyaṁvadā; the voice of a cuckoo who represents the trees of the forest blessing Śakuntalā in Sanskrit; the voice of Haṁsapadikā singing a Prakrit love song.*

The setting of the play shifts from the forest hermitage (Acts I–IV) to the palace (Acts V–VI) to the celestial hermitage (Act VII). The season is early summer when the play begins and spring during the sixth act; the passage of time is otherwise indicated by the birth and boyhood of Śakuntalā's son.

ACT I

The water that was first created,
the sacrifice-bearing fire, the priest,
the time-setting sun and moon,
audible space that fills the universe,
what men call nature, the source of all seeds,
the air that living creatures breathe—
through his eight embodied forms,
may Lord Śiva come to bless you![1]

---

[1] **The water . . . to bless you:** This benedictory verse, or *nandi,* is one of the traditional rituals recited before the performance of a Sanskrit play. It is addressed to Śiva, or Shiva, the patron god of creation and the drama who is manifest in the eight forms listed in the verse: water, fire, the priest, Sun, Moon, space, earth, and air.

Prologue

DIRECTOR: [*Looking backstage.*] If you are in costume now, madam, please come on
stage!

ACTRESS: I'm here, sir.

DIRECTOR: Our audience is learned. We shall play Kālidāsa's new drama called
Śakuntalā and the Ring of Recollection. Let the players take their parts to heart!

ACTRESS: With you directing, sir, nothing will be lost.

DIRECTOR: Madam, the truth is:

> I find no performance perfect
> until the critics are pleased;
> the better trained we are
> the more we doubt ourselves.

ACTRESS: So true . . . now tell me what to do first!

DIRECTOR: What captures an audience better than a song?
Sing about the new summer season and its pleasures:

> To plunge in fresh waters
> swept by scented forest winds
> and dream in soft shadows
> of the day's ripened charms.

ACTRESS: [*Singing.*]

> Sensuous women
> in summer love
> weave
> flower earrings
> from fragile petals
> of mimosa
> while wild bees
> kiss them gently.

DIRECTOR: Well sung, madam! Your melody enchants the audience. The silent theater is like a painting. What drama should we play to please it?

ACTRESS: But didn't you just direct us to perform a new play called *Śakuntalā and the
Ring of Recollection*?

DIRECTOR: Madam, I'm conscious again! For a moment I forgot.

> The mood of your song's melody
> carried me off by force,
> just as the swift dark antelope
> enchanted King Duṣyanta.

[*They both exit; the prologue ends. Then the* KING *enters with his* CHARIOTEER, *in a chariot, a
bow and arrow in his hand, hunting an antelope.*]

CHARIOTEER: [*Watching the* KING *and the antelope.*]

> I see this black buck move
> as you draw your bow
> and I see the wild bowman Śiva,
> hunting the dark antelope.[2]

KING: Driver, this antelope has drawn us far into the forest. There he is again:

50
> The graceful turn of his neck
> as he glances back at our speeding car,
> the haunches folded into his chest
> in fear of my speeding arrow,
> the open mouth dropping
> half-chewed grass on our path—
> watch how he leaps, bounding on air,
> barely touching the earth.

[*He shows surprise.*]
    Why is it so hard to keep him in sight?

CHARIOTEER: Sir, the ground was rough. I tightened the reins to slow the chariot and the buck raced ahead. Now that the path is smooth, he won't be hard to catch.

60 KING: Slacken the reins!

CHARIOTEER: As you command, sir. [*He mimes the speeding chariot.*] Look!

> Their legs extend as I slacken the reins,
> plumes and manes set in the wind, ears angle back;
> our horses outrun their own clouds of dust,
> straining to match the antelope's speed.

KING: These horses would outrace the steeds of the sun.[3]

> What is small suddenly looms large,
> split forms seem to reunite,
> bent shapes straighten before my eyes—
70
> from the chariot's speed
> nothing ever stays distant or near.

CHARIOTEER: The antelope is an easy target now. [*He mimes the fixing of an arrow.*]

VOICE OFFSTAGE: Stop! Stop, king! This antelope belongs to our hermitage! Don't kill him!

CHARIOTEER: [*Listening and watching.*] Sir, two ascetics are protecting the black buck from your arrow's deadly aim.

KING: [*Showing confusion.*] Rein in the horses!

CHARIOTEER: It is done!

---

[2] **I see . . . the dark antelope:** Here, the Charioteer compares the king as a hunter with the god Śiva, who pursued the creator-god Prajapati who had taken the form of an antelope.

[3] **steeds of the sun:** Horses that pull the chariot of the sun-god.

[*He mimes the chariot's halt. Then a* MONK *enters with* TWO PUPILS, *his hand raised.*]

MONK: King, this antelope belongs to our hermitage.

80   Withdraw your well-aimed arrow! Your weapon should rescue victims, not destroy the innocent!

KING: I withdraw it. [*He does as he says.*]

MONK: An act worthy of the Puru dynasty's shining light!

> Your birth honors
> the dynasty of the moon!
> May you beget a son
> to turn the wheel of your empire!

THE TWO PUPILS: [*Raising their arms.*] May you beget a son to turn the wheel of your empire!

90   KING: [*Bowing.*] I welcome your blessing.

MONK: King, we were going to gather firewood. From here you can see the hermitage of our master Kaṇva on the bank of the Mālinī river. If your work permits, enter and accept our hospitality.

> When you see the peaceful rites of devoted ascetics,
> you will know how well your scarred arm protects us.

KING: Is the master of the community there now?

MONK: He went to Somatīrtha, the holy shrine of the moon, and put his daughter Śakuntalā in charge of receiving guests.

> Some evil threatens her, it seems.

100 KING: Then I shall see her. She will know my devotion and commend me to the great sage.

MONK: We shall leave you now.

[*He exits with his pupils.*]

KING: Driver, urge the horses on! The sight of this holy hermitage will purify us.

CHARIOTEER: As you command, sir. [*He mimes the chariot's speed.*]

KING: [*Looking around.*] Without being told one can see that this is a grove where ascetics live.

CHARIOTEER: How?

KING: Don't you see —

> Wild rice grains under trees
> where parrots nest in hollow trunks,
> stones stained by the dark oil
> of crushed iṅgudī nuts,
> trusting deer who hear human voices
> yet don't break their gait,
> and paths from ponds streaked
> by water from wet bark cloth.

110

CHARIOTEER: It is perfect.

KING: [*Having gone a little inside.*] We should not disturb the grove! Stop the chariot and let me get down!

120   CHARIOTEER: I'm holding the reins. You can dismount now, sir.

KING: [*Dismounting.*] One should not enter an ascetics' grove in hunting gear. Take these! [*He gives up his ornaments and his bow.*] Driver, rub down the horses while I pay my respects to the residents of the hermitage!

CHARIOTEER: Yes, sir!

[*He exits.*]

KING: This gateway marks the sacred ground. I will enter. [*He enters, indicating he feels an omen.*]

> The hermitage is a tranquil place,
> yet my arm is quivering . . .
> do I feel a false omen of love
> or does fate have doors everywhere?

130   VOICE OFFSTAGE: This way, friends!

KING: [*Straining to listen.*] I think I hear voices to the right of the grove. I'll find out.

[*Walking around and looking.*]

Young female ascetics with watering pots cradled on their hips are coming to water the saplings. [*He mimes it in precise detail.*] This view of them is sweet.

> These forest women have beauty
> rarely seen inside royal palaces —
> the wild forest vines far surpass
> creepers in my pleasure garden.

I'll hide in the shadows and wait.

[*ŚAKUNTALĀ and her two friends enter, acting as described.*]

ŚAKUNTALĀ: This way, friends!

140   ANASŪYĀ: I think Father Kaṇva cares more about the trees in the hermitage than he cares about you. You're as delicate as a jasmine, yet he orders you to water the trees.

ŚAKUNTALĀ: Anasūyā, it's more than Father Kaṇva's order. I feel a sister's love for them. [*She mimes the watering of trees.*]

KING: [*To himself.*] Is this Kaṇva's daughter? The sage does show poor judgment in imposing the rules of the hermitage on her.

> The sage who hopes to subdue
> her sensuous body by penances
> is trying to cut firewood
150 > with a blade of blue-lotus leaf.

Let it be! I can watch her closely from here in the trees. [*He does so.*]

ŚAKUNTALĀ: Anasūyā, I can't breathe! Our friend Priyaṁvadā tied my bark dress too tightly! Loosen it a bit!

ANASŪYĀ: As you say. [*She loosens it.*]

PRIYAṀVADĀ: [*Laughing.*] Blame your youth for swelling your breasts. Why blame me?

KING: This bark dress fits her body badly, but it ornaments her beauty . . .

A tangle of duckweed adorns a lotus,
a dark spot heightens the moon's glow,
160   the bark dress increases her charm—
beauty finds its ornaments anywhere.

ŚAKUNTALĀ: [*Looking in front of her.*] The new branches on this mimosa tree are like fingers moving in the wind, calling to me. I must go to it! [*Saying this, she walks around.*]

PRIYAṀVADĀ: Wait, Śakuntalā! Stay there a minute! When you stand by this mimosa tree, it seems to be guarding a creeper.

ŚAKUNTALĀ: That's why your name means "Sweet-talk."

KING: "Sweet-talk" yes, but Priyaṁvadā speaks the truth about Śakuntalā:

Her lips are fresh red buds,
her arms are tendrils,
170   impatient youth is poised
to blossom in her limbs.

ANASŪYĀ: Śakuntalā, this is the jasmine creeper who chose the mango tree in marriage, the one you named "Forestlight." Have you forgotten her?

ŚAKUNTALĀ: I would be forgetting myself? [*She approaches the creeper and examines it.*] The creeper and the tree are twined together in perfect harmony. Forestlight has just flowered and the new mango shoots are made for her pleasure.

PRIYAṀVADĀ: [*Smiling.*] Anasūyā, don't you know why Śakuntalā looks so lovingly at Forestlight?

ANASŪYĀ: I can't guess.

180 PRIYAṀVADĀ: The marriage of Forestlight to her tree makes her long to have a husband too.

ŚAKUNTALĀ: You're just speaking your own secret wish. [*Saying this, she pours water from the jar.*]

KING: Could her social class be different from her father's?[4] There's no doubt!

She was born to be a warrior's bride,
for my noble heart desires her—
when good men face doubt,
inner feelings are truth's only measure.

Still, I must learn everything about her.

ŚAKUNTALĀ: [*Flustered.*] The splashing water has alarmed a bee. He is flying from the
190   jasmine to my face. [*She dances to show the bee's attack.*]

KING: [*Looking longingly.*]

Bee, you touch the quivering
corners of her frightened eyes,
you hover softly near

---

[4] **her social class . . . father's:** The Hindu caste system forbade marrying outside one's class. Kaṇva's daughter, a Brahmin, would not have been eligible to marry a king of the warrior caste.

to whisper secrets in her ear;
a hand brushes you away,
but you drink her lips' treasure—
while the truth we seek defeats us,
you are truly blessed.

ŚAKUNTALĀ: This dreadful bee won't stop. I must escape. [*She steps to one side, glanc-*
200   *ing about.*] Oh! He's pursuing me. . . . Save me! Please save me! This mad bee is
chasing me!

BOTH FRIENDS: [*Laughing.*] How can we save you? Call King Duṣyanta. The grove is
under his protection.

KING: Here's my chance. Have no fear . . . [*With this half-spoken, he stops and speaks
to himself.*] Then she will know that I am the king. . . . Still, I shall speak.

ŚAKUNTALĀ: [*Stopping after a few steps.*] Why is he still following me?

KING: [*Approaching quickly.*]

While a Puru king rules the earth
to punish evildoers,
who dares to molest
210   these innocent young ascetics?

[*Seeing the KING, all act flustered.*]

ANASŪYĀ: Sir, there's no real danger. Our friend was frightened when a bee attacked
her. [*She points to ŚAKUNTALĀ.*]

KING: [*Approaching ŚAKUNTALĀ.*] Does your ascetic practice go well? [*ŚAKUNTALĀ
stands speechless.*]

ANASŪYĀ: It does now that we have a special guest. Śakuntalā, go to our hut and
bring the ripe fruits. We'll use this water to bathe his feet.

KING: Your kind speech is hospitality enough.

PRIYAṀVADĀ: Please sit in the cool shadows of this shade tree and rest, sir.

KING: You must also be tired from your work.

ANASŪYĀ: Śakuntalā, we should respect our guest. Let's sit down. [*All sit.*]

220   ŚAKUNTALĀ: [*To herself.*] When I see him, why do I feel an emotion that the forest
seems to forbid?

KING: [*Looking at each of the girls.*] Youth and beauty complement your friendship.

PRIYAṀVADĀ: [*In a stage whisper.*] Anasūyā, who is he? He's so polite, fine looking,
and pleasing to hear. He has the marks of royalty.

ANASŪYĀ: I'm curious too, friend. I'll just ask him. [*Aloud.*] Sir, your kind speech
inspires trust. What family of royal sages do you adorn? What country mourns
your absence? Why does a man of refinement subject himself to the discomfort
of visiting an ascetics' grove?

ŚAKUNTALĀ: [*To herself.*] Heart, don't faint! Anasūyā speaks your thoughts.

230   KING: [*To himself.*] Should I reveal myself now or conceal who I am? I'll say it this
way: [*Aloud.*] Lady, I have been appointed by the Puru king as the officer in
charge of religious matters. I have come to this sacred forest to assure that your
holy rites proceed unhindered.

ANASŪYĀ: Our religious life has a guardian now.

[ŚAKUNTALĀ *mimes the embarrassment of erotic emotion.*]

BOTH FRIENDS: [*Observing the behavior of* ŚAKUNTALĀ *and the* KING; *in a stage whisper.*] Śakuntalā, if only your father were here now!

ŚAKUNTALĀ: [*Angrily.*] What if he were?

BOTH FRIENDS: He would honor this distinguished guest with what he values most in life.

ŚAKUNTALĀ: Quiet! Such words hint at your hearts' conspiracy. I won't listen.

240   KING: Ladies, I want to ask about your friend.

BOTH FRIENDS: Your request honors us, sir.

KING: Sage Kaṇva has always been celibate, but you call your friend his daughter. How can this be?

ANASŪYĀ: Please listen, sir. There was a powerful royal sage[5] of the Kauśika clan . . .

KING: I am listening.

ANASŪYĀ: He begot our friend, but Kaṇva is her father because he cared for her when she was abandoned.

KING: "Abandoned"? The word makes me curious. I want to hear her story from the beginning.

250   ANASŪYĀ: Please listen, sir. Once when this great sage was practicing terrible austerities on the bank of the Gautamī river, he became so powerful that the jealous gods sent a nymph named Menakā to break his self-control.

KING: The gods dread men who meditate.

ANASŪYĀ: When springtime came to the forest with all its charm, the sage saw her intoxicating beauty . . .

KING: I understand what happened then. She is the nymph's daughter.

ANASŪYĀ: Yes.

KING: It had to be!

No mortal woman could give birth to such beauty—
260   lightning does not flash out of the earth.

[ŚAKUNTALĀ *stands with her face bowed. The* KING *continues speaking to himself.*]
My desire is not hopeless. Yet, when I hear her friends teasing her about a bridegroom, a new fear divides my heart.

PRIYAṀVADĀ: [*Smiling, looking at* ŚAKUNTALĀ, *then turning to the* KING.] Sir, you seem to want to say more.

[ŚAKUNTALĀ *makes a threatening gesture with her finger.*]
KING: You judge correctly. In my eagerness to learn more about your pious lives, I have another question.

PRIYAṀVADĀ: Don't hesitate! Ascetics can be questioned frankly.

KING: I want to know this about your friend:

Will she keep the vow of hermit life
270   only until she marries . . .

---

[5] **royal sage:** Viśvāmitra, born into the warrior caste, attained the spiritual powers of a Brahmin sage.

or will she always exchange
loving looks with deer in the forest?

PRIYAṀVADĀ: Sir, even in her religious life, she is subject to her father, but he does intend to give her to a suitable husband.

KING: [*To himself.*] His wish is not hard to fulfill.

Heart, indulge your desire —
now that doubt is dispelled,
the fire you feared to touch
is a jewel in your hands.

280 ŚAKUNTALĀ: [*Showing anger.*] Anasūyā, I'm leaving!

ANASŪYĀ: Why?

ŚAKUNTALĀ: I'm going to tell Mother Gautamī that Priyaṁvada is talking nonsense.

ANASŪYĀ: Friend, it's wrong to neglect a distinguished guest and leave as you like.

[*ŚAKUNTALĀ starts to go without answering.*]

KING: [*Wanting to seize her, but holding back, he speaks to himself.*] A lover dare not act on his impulsive thoughts!

I wanted to follow the sage's daughter,
but decorum abruptly pulled me back;
I set out and returned again
without moving my feet from this spot.

290 PRIYAṀVADĀ: [*Stopping ŚAKUNTALĀ.*] It's wrong of you to go!

ŚAKUNTALĀ: [*Bending her brow into a frown.*] Give me a reason why!

PRIYAṀVADĀ: You promised to water two trees for me. Come here and pay your debt before you go! [*She stops her by force.*]

KING: But she seems exhausted from watering the trees:

Her shoulders droop, her palms
are red from the watering pot —
even now, breathless sighs
make her breasts shake;
beads of sweat on her face
300 wilt the flower at her ear;
her hand holds back
disheveled locks of hair.

Here, I'll pay her debt!

[*He offers his ring. Both friends recite the syllables of the name on the seal and stare at each other.*]
Don't mistake me for what I am not! This is a gift from the king to identify me as his royal official.

PRIYAṀVADĀ: Then the ring should never leave your finger. Your word has already paid her debt. [*She laughs a little.*] Śakuntalā, you are freed by this kind man . . . or perhaps by the king. Go now!

ŚAKUNTALĀ: [*To herself.*] If I am able to . . . [*Aloud.*] Who are you to keep me or
310   release me?

KING: [*Watching* ŚAKUNTALĀ.] Can she feel toward me what I feel toward her? Or is
my desire fulfilled?

> She won't respond directly to my words,
> but she listens when I speak;
> she won't turn to look at me,
> but her eyes can't rest anywhere else.

VOICE OFFSTAGE: Ascetics, be prepared to protect the creatures of our forest grove!
King Duṣyanta is hunting nearby!

> Dust raised by his horses' hooves
320   > falls like a cloud of locusts swarming
> at sunset over branches of trees
> where wet bark garments hang.

> In terror of the chariots, an elephant
> charged into the hermitage
> and scattered the herd of black antelope,
> like a demon foe of our penances—
> his tusks garlanded with branches
> from a tree crushed by his weight,
> his feet tangled in vines
330   > that tether him like chains.

[*Hearing this, all the girls are agitated.*]

KING: [*To himself.*] Oh! My palace men are searching for me and wrecking the grove.
I'll have to go back.

BOTH FRIENDS: Sir, we're all upset by this news. Please let us go to our hut.

KING: [*Showing confusion.*] Go, please. We will try to protect the hermitage.

[*They all stand to go.*]

BOTH FRIENDS: Sir, we're ashamed that our bad hospitality is our only excuse to
invite you back.

KING: Not at all. I am honored to have seen you.

[ŚAKUNTALĀ *exits with her two friends, looking back at the* KING, *lingering artfully.*]
I have little desire to return to the city. I'll join my men and have them camp
near the grove. I can't control my feelings for Śakuntalā.

340   > My body turns to go,
> my heart pulls me back,
> like a silk banner
> buffeted by the wind.

[*All exit.*]

ACT II

[*The* BUFFOON *enters, despondent.*]

BUFFOON: [*Sighing.*] My bad luck! I'm tired of playing sidekick to a king who's hooked on hunting. "There's a deer!" "There's a boar!" "There's a tiger!" Even in the summer midday heat we chase from jungle to jungle on paths where trees give barely any shade. We drink stinking water from mountain streams foul with rusty leaves. At odd hours we eat nasty meals of spit-roasted meat. Even at night I can't sleep. My joints ache from galloping on that horse. Then at the crack of dawn, I'm woken rudely by a noise piercing the forest. Those sons of bitches hunt their birds then. The torture doesn't end—now I have sores on top of my bruises. Yesterday, we lagged behind. The king chased a buck into the hermitage. As luck would have it, an ascetic's daughter called Śakuntalā caught his eye. Now he isn't even thinking of going back to the city. This very dawn I found him wide-eyed, mooning about her. What a fate! I must see him after his bath. [*He walks around, looking.*] Here comes my friend now, wearing garlands of wild flowers. Greek women carry his bow in their hands.[6] Good! I'll stand here pretending my arms and legs are broken. Maybe then I'll get some rest.

[*He stands leaning on his staff. The* KING *enters with his retinue, as described.*]

KING: [*To himself.*]

> My beloved will not be easy to win,
> but signs of emotion revealed her heart—
> even when love seems hopeless,
> mutual longing keeps passion alive.

[*He smiles.*] A suitor who measures his beloved's state of mind by his own desire is a fool.

> She threw tender glances
> though her eyes were cast down,
> her heavy hips swayed
> in slow seductive movements,
> she answered in anger
> when her friend said, "Don't go!"
> and I felt it was all for my sake . . .
> but a lover sees in his own way.

BUFFOON: [*Still in the same position.*] Dear friend, since my hands can't move to greet you, I have to salute you with my voice.

KING: How did you cripple your limbs?

BUFFOON: Why do you ask why I cry after throwing dust in my eyes yourself?

---

[6] **Greek women . . . hands:** Probably women from Asia Minor who were employed by the Gupta rulers as bodyguards and bow-bearers.

KING: I don't understand.

BUFFOON: Dear friend, when a straight reed is twisted into a crooked reed, is it by its own power, or is it the river current?

KING: The river current is the cause.

BUFFOON: And so it is with me.

KING: How so?

40   BUFFOON: You neglect the business of being a king and live like a woodsman in this awful camp. Chasing after wild beasts every day jolts my joints and muscles till I can't control my own limbs anymore. I beg you to let me rest for just one day!

KING: [*To himself.*] He says what I also feel. When I remember Kaṇva's daughter, the thought of hunting disgusts me.

> I can't draw my bowstring
> to shoot arrows at deer
> who live with my love
> and teach her tender glances.

BUFFOON: Sir, you have something on your mind. I'm crying in a wilderness.

50   KING: [*Smiling.*] Yes, it is wrong to ignore my friend's plea.

BUFFOON: Live long! [*He starts to go.*]

KING: Dear friend, stay! Hear what I have to say!

BUFFOON: At your command, sir!

KING: When you have rested, I need your help in some work that you will enjoy.

BUFFOON: Is it eating sweets? I'm game!

KING: I shall tell you. Who stands guard?

GUARD: [*Entering.*] At your command, sir!

KING: Raivataka! Summon the general!

[*The* GUARD *exits and reenters with the* GENERAL.]

GUARD: The king is looking this way, waiting to give you his orders. Approach him,
60   sir!

GENERAL: [*Looking at the* KING.] Hunting is said to be a vice, but our king prospers.

> Drawing the bow only hardens his chest,
> he suffers the sun's scorching rays unburned,
> hard muscles mask his body's lean state —
> like a wild elephant, his energy sustains him.

[*He approaches the* KING.] Victory, my lord! We've already tracked some wild beasts. Why the delay?

KING: Mādhavya's[7] censure of hunting has dampened my spirit.

GENERAL: [*In a stage whisper, to the* BUFFOON.] Friend, you stick to your opposition!
70   I'll try to restore our king's good sense. [*Aloud.*] This fool is talking nonsense. Here is the king as proof:

---

[7] **Mādhavya:** The Buffoon.

> A hunter's belly is taut and lean,
> his slender body craves exertion;
> he penetrates the spirit of creatures
> overcome by fear and rage;
> his bowmanship is proved
> by arrows striking a moving target—
> hunting is falsely called a vice.
> What sport can rival it?

80 BUFFOON: [*Angrily.*] The king has come to his senses. If you keep chasing from forest to forest, you'll fall into the jaws of an old bear hungry for a human nose . . .

KING: My noble general, we are near a hermitage; your words cannot please me now.

> Let horned buffaloes plunge into muddy pools!
> Let herds of deer huddle in the shade to eat grass!
> Let fearless wild boars crush fragrant swamp grass!
> Let my bowstring lie slack and my bow at rest!

GENERAL: Whatever gives the king pleasure.

KING: Withdraw the men who are in the forest now and forbid my soldiers to disturb the grove!

90
> Ascetics devoted to peace
> possess a fiery hidden power,
> like smooth crystal sunstones
> that reflect the sun's scorching rays.

GENERAL: Whatever you command, sir!

BUFFOON: Your arguments for keeping up the hunt fall on deaf ears!

[*The* GENERAL *exits.*]

KING: [*Looking at his* RETINUE.] You women, take away my hunting gear! Raivataka, don't neglect your duty!

RETINUE: As the king commands!

[*They exit.*]

BUFFOON: Sir, now that the flies are cleared out, sit on a stone bench under this shady
100   canopy. Then I'll find a comfortable seat too.

KING: Go ahead!

BUFFOON: You first, sir!

[*Both walk about, then sit down.*]

KING: Māḍhavya, you haven't really used your eyes because you haven't seen true beauty.

BUFFOON: But you're right in front of me, sir!

KING: Everyone is partial to what he knows well, but I'm speaking about Śakuntalā, the jewel of the hermitage.

BUFFOON: [*To himself.*] I won't give him a chance! [*Aloud.*] Dear friend, it seems that you're pursuing an ascetic's daughter.

110 KING: Friend, the heart of a Puru king wouldn't crave a forbidden fruit . . .

The sage's child is a nymph's daughter,
rescued by him after she was abandoned,
like a fragile jasmine blossom
broken and caught on a sunflower pod.

BUFFOON: [*Laughing.*] You're like the man who loses his taste for dates and prefers
sour tamarind! How can you abandon the gorgeous gems of your palace?
KING: You speak this way because you haven't seen her.
BUFFOON: She must be delectable if you're so enticed!
KING: Friend, what is the use of all this talk?

120   The divine creator imagined perfection
and shaped her ideal form in his mind—
when I recall the beauty his power wrought,
she shines like a gemstone among my jewels.

BUFFOON: So she's the reason you reject the other beauties!
KING: She stays in my mind:

A flower no one has smelled,
a bud no fingers have plucked,
an uncut jewel, honey untasted,
unbroken fruit of holy deeds—
130   I don't know who is destined
to enjoy her flawless beauty.

BUFFOON: Then you should rescue her quickly! Don't let her fall into the arms of
some ascetic who greases his head with iṅgudī oil!
KING: She is someone else's ward and her guardian is away.
BUFFOON: What kind of passion did her eyes betray?
KING: Ascetics are timid by nature:

Her eyes were cast down in my presence,
but she found an excuse to smile—
modesty barely contained the love
140   she could neither reveal nor conceal.

BUFFOON: Did you expect her to climb into your lap when she'd barely seen you?
KING: When we parted her feelings for me showed despite her modesty.

"A blade of kuśa grass
pricked my foot,"
the girl said for no reason
after walking a few steps away;
then she pretended to free
her bark dress from branches
where it was not caught
150   and shyly glanced at me.

BUFFOON: Stock up on food for a long trip! I can see you've turned that ascetics'
grove into a pleasure garden.

KING: Friend, some of the ascetics recognize me. What excuse can we find to return
to the hermitage?

BUFFOON: What excuse? Aren't you the king? Collect a sixth of their wild rice as
tax!

KING: Fool! These ascetics pay tribute that pleases me more than mounds of jewels.

> Tribute that kings collect
> from members of society decays,
160 but the share of austerity
> that ascetics give lasts forever.

VOICE OFFSTAGE: Good, we have succeeded!

KING: [*Listening.*] These are the steady, calm voices of ascetics.

GUARD: [*Entering.*] Victory, sir! Two boy ascetics are waiting near the gate.

KING: Let them enter without delay!

GUARD: I'll show them in. [*He exits; reenters with the boys.*] Here you are!

FIRST BOY: His majestic body inspires trust. It is natural when a king is virtually
a sage.

> His palace is a hermitage
170 with its infinite pleasures,
> the discipline of protecting men
> imposes austerities every day—
> pairs of celestial bards praise
> his perfect self-control,
> adding the royal word "king"
> to "sage," his sacred title.

SECOND BOY: Gautama, is this Duṣyanta, the friend of Indra?[8]

FIRST BOY: Of course!

SECOND BOY:

> It is no surprise that this arm of iron
180 rules the whole earth bounded by dark seas—
> when demons harass the gods, victory's hope
> rests on his bow and Indra's thunderbolt.

BOTH BOYS: [*Coming near.*] Victory to you, king!

KING: [*Rising from his seat.*] I salute you both!

BOTH BOYS: To your success, sir! [*They offer fruits.*]

KING: [*Accepting their offering.*] I am ready to listen.

---

[8] **Indra:** Lord of heaven, ruler of the gods, the god of thunder and rain, and the sustainer of the universe; comparable to Zeus in the Greek pantheon.

BOTH BOYS: The ascetics know that you are camped nearby and send a petition
to you.

KING: What do they request?

190 BOTH BOYS: Demons are taking advantage of Sage Kaṇva's absence to harass us. You
must come with your charioteer to protect the hermitage for a few days!

KING: I am honored to oblige.

BUFFOON: [*In a stage whisper.*] Your wish is fulfilled!

KING: [*Smiling.*] Raivataka, call my charioteer! Tell him to bring the chariot and
my bow!

GUARD: As the king commands!   [*He exits.*]

BOTH BOYS: [*Showing delight.*]

> Following your ancestral duties
> suits your noble form —
> the Puru kings are ordained
200 > to dispel their subjects' fear.

KING: [*Bowing.*] You two return! I shall follow.

BOTH BOYS: Be victorious!   [*They exit.*]

KING: Māḍhavya, are you curious to see Śakuntalā?

BUFFOON: At first there was a flood, but now with this news of demons, not a drop
is left.

KING: Don't be afraid! Won't you be with me?

BUFFOON: Then I'll be safe from any demon . . .

GUARD: [*Entering.*] The chariot is ready to take you to victory . . . but Karabhaka has
just come from the city with a message from the queen.

210 KING: Did my mother send him?

GUARD: She did.

KING: Have him enter then.

GUARD: Yes. [*He exits; reenters with* KARABHAKA.] Here is the king. Approach!

KARABHAKA: Victory, sir! Victory! The queen has ordered a ceremony four days from
now to mark the end of her fast. Your Majesty will surely give us the honor of his
presence.

KING: The ascetics' business keeps me here and my mother's command calls me
there. I must find a way to avoid neglecting either!

BUFFOON: Hang yourself between them the way Triśaṅku hung between heaven and
220 earth.[9]

KING: I'm really confused . . .

> My mind is split in two
> by these conflicting duties,
> like a river current split
> by boulders in its course.

---

[9] **the way Triśaṅku . . . heaven and earth:** A mythic king who ends up suspended between heaven and earth
as a result of a struggle between Viśvāmitra and the gods.

[*Thinking.*] Friend, my mother has treated you like a son. You must go back and report that I've set my heart on fulfilling my duty to the ascetics. You fulfill my filial duty to the queen.

BUFFOON: You don't really think I'm afraid of demons?

230   KING: [*Smiling.*] My brave brahman, how could you be?

BUFFOON: Then I can travel like the king's younger brother.

KING: We really should not disturb the grove! Take my whole entourage with you!

BUFFOON: Now I've turned into the crown prince!

KING: [*To himself.*] This fellow is absent-minded. At any time he may tell the palace women about my passion. I'll tell him this: [*Taking the BUFFOON by the hand, he speaks aloud.*] Dear friend, I'm going to the hermitage out of reverence for the sages. I really feel no desire for the young ascetic Śakuntalā.

> What do I share with a rustic girl
> reared among fawns, unskilled in love?
240   Don't mistake what I muttered
> in jest for the real truth, friend!

[*All exit.*]

ACT III

[*A disciple of* KAṆVA *enters, carrying kuśa grass for a sacrificial rite.*]

DISCIPLE: King Duṣyanta is certainly powerful. Since he entered the hermitage, our rites have not been hindered.

> Why talk of fixing arrows?
> The mere twang of his bowstring
> clears away menacing demons
> as if his bow roared with death.

I'll gather some more grass for the priests to spread on the sacrificial altar. [*Walking around and looking, he calls aloud.*] Priyaṁvadā, for whom are you bringing the ointment of fragrant lotus root fibers and leaves? [*Listening.*] What

10   are you saying? Śakuntalā is suffering from heat exhaustion? They're for rubbing on her body? Priyaṁvadā, take care of her! She is the breath of Father Kaṇva's life. I'll give Gautamī this water from the sacrifice to use for soothing her.

[*He exits; the interlude ends. Then the* KING *enters, suffering from love, deep in thought, sighing.*]

KING:

> I know the power ascetics have
> and the rules that bind her,
> but I cannot abandon my heart
> now that she has taken it.

[*Showing the pain of love.*] Love, why do you and the moon both contrive to deceive lovers by first gaining our trust?

Arrows of flowers and cool moon rays
20   are both deadly for men like me—
the moon shoots fire through icy rays
and you hurl thunderbolts of flowers.

[*Walking around.*] Now that the rites are concluded and the priests have dismissed me, where can I rest from the weariness of this work? [*Sighing.*] There is no refuge but the sight of my love. I must find her. [*Looking up at the sun.*] Śakuntalā usually spends the heat of the day with her friends in a bower of vines on the Mālinī riverbank. I shall go there. [*Walking around, miming the touch of breeze.*] This place is enchanted by the wind.

A breeze fragrant with lotus pollen
30   and moist from the Mālinī waves
can be held in soothing embrace
by my love-scorched arms.

[*Walking around and looking.*]

I see fresh footprints
on white sand in the clearing,
deeply pressed at the heel
by the sway of full hips.

I'll just look through the branches. [*Walking around, looking, he becomes joyous.*] My eyes have found bliss! The girl I desire is lying on a stone couch strewn with flowers, attended by her two friends. I'll eavesdrop as they confide in one
40   another. [*He stands watching.* ŚAKUNTALĀ *appears as described, with her two friends.*]

BOTH FRIENDS: [*Fanning her affectionately.*] Śakuntalā, does the breeze from this lotus leaf please you?

ŚAKUNTALĀ: Are you fanning me?

[*The friends trade looks, miming dismay.*]

KING: [*Deliberating.*] Śakuntalā seems to be in great physical pain. Is it the heat or is it what is in my own heart? [*Miming ardent desire.*] My doubts are unfounded!

Her breasts are smeared with lotus balm,
her lotus-fiber bracelet hangs limp,
her beautiful body glows in pain—
love burns young women like summer heat
50   but its guilt makes them more charming.

PRIYAMVADĀ: [*In a stage whisper.*] Anasūyā, Śakuntalā has been pining since she first saw the king. Could he be the cause of her sickness?

ANASŪYĀ: She must be suffering from lovesickness. I'll ask her . . . [*Aloud.*] Friend, I have something to ask you. Your pain seems so deep . . .

ŚAKUNTALĀ: [*Raising herself halfway.*] What do you want to say?

ANASŪYĀ: Śakuntalā, though we don't know what it is to be in love, your condition reminds us of lovers we have heard about in stories. Can you tell us the
cause of your pain? Unless we understand your illness, we can't begin to find
a cure.

60 KING: Anasūyā expresses my own thoughts.

ŚAKUNTALĀ: Even though I want to, suddenly I can't make myself tell you.

PRIYAṀVADĀ: Śakuntalā, my friend Anasūyā means well. Don't you see how sick you
are? Your limbs are wasting away. Only the shadow of your beauty remains . . .

KING: What Priyaṁvadā says is true:

> Her cheeks are deeply sunken,
> her breasts' full shape is gone,
> her waist is thin, her shoulders bent,
> and the color has left her skin—
> tormented by love,
70 > she is sad but beautiful to see,
> like a jasmine creeper
> when hot wind shrivels its leaves.

ŚAKUNTALĀ: Friends, who else can I tell? May I burden you?

BOTH FRIENDS: We insist! Sharing sorrow with loving friends makes it bearable.

KING:

> Friends who share her joy and sorrow
> discover the love concealed in her heart—
> though she looked back longingly at me,
> now I am afraid to hear her response.

ŚAKUNTALĀ: Friend, since my eyes first saw the guardian of the hermits' retreat, I've
80 felt such strong desire for him!

KING: I have heard what I want to hear.

> My tormentor, the god of love,
> has soothed my fever himself,
> like the heat of late summer
> allayed by early rain clouds.

ŚAKUNTALĀ: If you two think it's right, then help me to win the king's pity. Otherwise, you'll soon pour sesame oil and water[10] on my corpse . . .

KING: Her words destroy my doubt.

PRIYAṀVADĀ: [*In a stage whisper.*] She's so dangerously in love that there's no time to
90 lose. Since her heart is set on the ornament of the Puru dynasty, we should
rejoice that she desires him.

ANASŪYĀ: What you say is true.

---

[10] **sesame oil and water:** Used in traditional Hindu funeral rites.

PRIYAṀVADĀ: [*Aloud.*] Friend, by good fortune your desire is in harmony with nature. A great river can only descend to the ocean. A jasmine creeper can only twine around a mango tree.

KING: Why is this surprising when the twin stars of spring serve the crescent moon?

ANASŪYĀ: What means do we have to fulfill our friend's desire secretly and quickly?

PRIYAṀVADĀ: "Secretly" demands some effort. "Quickly" is easy.

ANASŪYĀ: How so?

100 PRIYAṀVADĀ: The king was charmed by her loving look; he seems thin these days from sleepless nights.

KING: It's true . . .

> This golden armlet
> slips to my wrist
> without touching the scars
> my bowstring has made;
> its gemstones are faded
> by tears of secret pain
> that every night wets my arm
> 110   where I bury my face.

PRIYAṀVADĀ: [*Thinking.*] Compose a love letter and I'll hide it in a flower. I'll deliver it to his hand on the pretext of bringing an offering to the deity.

ANASŪYĀ: This subtle plan pleases me. What does Śakuntalā say?

ŚAKUNTALĀ: I'll try my friend's plan.

PRIYAṀVADĀ: Then compose a poem to declare your love!

ŚAKUNTALĀ: I'm thinking, but my heart trembles with fear that he'll reject me.

KING: [*Delighted.*]

> The man you fear will reject you
> waits longing to love you, timid girl—
> a suitor may lose or be lucky,
> 120   but the goddess always wins.

BOTH FRIENDS: Why do you belittle your own virtues? Who would cover his body with a piece of cloth to keep off cool autumn moonlight?

ŚAKUNTALĀ: [*Smiling.*] I'm trying to follow your advice. [*She sits thinking.*]

KING: As I gaze at her, my eyes forget to blink.

> She arches an eyebrow,
> struggling to compose the verse—
> the down rises on her cheek,
> showing the passion she feels.

ŚAKUNTALĀ: I've thought of a verse, but I have nothing to write it on.

130 PRIYAṀVADĀ: Engrave the letters with your nail on this lotus leaf! It's as delicate as a parrot's breast.

ŚAKUNTALĀ: [*Miming what* PRIYAṀVADĀ *described.*] Listen and tell me this makes sense!

BOTH FRIENDS: We're both paying attention.

ŚAKUNTALĀ: [*Singing.*]

> I don't know
> your heart,
> but day and night
> for wanting you,
> love violently
> tortures
> my limbs,
> cruel man.

KING: [*Suddenly revealing himself.*]

> Love torments you, slender girl,
> but he completely consumes me —
> daylight spares the lotus pond
> while it destroys the moon.

BOTH FRIENDS: [*Looking, rising with delight.*] Welcome to the swift success of love's desire!

[*ŚAKUNTALĀ tries to rise.*]

KING: Don't exert yourself!

> Limbs lying among crushed petals
> like fragile lotus stalks
> are too weakened by pain
> to perform ceremonious acts.

ANASŪYĀ: Then let the king sit on this stone bench!

[*The KING sits; ŚAKUNTALĀ rises in embarrassment.*]

PRIYAṀVADĀ: The passion of two young lovers is clear. My affection for our friend makes me speak out again now.

KING: Noble lady, don't hesitate! It is painful to keep silent when one must speak.

PRIYAṀVADĀ: We're told that it is the king's duty to ease the pain of his suffering subjects.

KING: My duty, exactly!

PRIYAṀVADĀ: Since she first saw you, our dear friend has been reduced to this sad condition. You must protect her and save her life.

KING: Noble lady, our affection is shared and I am honored by all you say.

ŚAKUNTALĀ: [*Looking at PRIYAṀVADĀ.*] Why are you keeping the king here? He must be anxious to return to his palace.

KING:

> If you think that my lost heart
> could love anyone but you,
> a fatal blow strikes a man
> already wounded by love's arrows!

170 ANASŪYĀ: We've heard that kings have many loves. Will our dear friend become a sorrow to her family after you've spent time with her?

KING: Noble lady, enough of this!

> Despite my many wives,
> on two the royal line rests—
> sea-bound earth
> and your friend.

BOTH FRIENDS: You reassure us.

PRIYAṀVADĀ: [*Casting a glance.*] Anasūyā, this fawn is looking for its mother. Let's take it to her!

[*They both begin to leave.*]

180 ŚAKUNTALĀ: Come back! Don't leave me unprotected!

BOTH FRIENDS: The protector of the earth is at your side.

ŚAKUNTALĀ: Why have they gone?

KING: Don't be alarmed! I am your servant.

> Shall I set moist winds in motion
> with lotus-leaf fans to cool your pain,
> or rest your soft red lotus feet
> on my lap to stroke them, my love

ŚAKUNTALĀ: I cannot sin against those I respect!

[*Standing as if she wants to leave.*]

KING: Beautiful Śakuntalā, the day is still hot.

190
> Why should your frail limbs
> leave this couch of flowers
> shielded by lotus leaves
> to wander in the heat?

[*Saying this, he forces her to turn around.*]

ŚAKUNTALĀ: Puru king, control yourself! Though I'm burning with love, how can I give myself to you?

KING: Don't fear your elders! The father of your family knows the law. When he finds out, he will not blame you.

> The daughters of royal sages often marry
> in secret[11] and then their fathers bless them.

200 ŚAKUNTALĀ: Release me! I must ask my friends' advice!

KING: Yes, I shall release you.

---

[11] **marry in secret:** The king invokes the *gandharva* form of marriage, a secret union by mutual consent that is permitted for the warrior caste under Hindu law. By the beginning of Act IV, this secret marriage is assumed to have taken place.

ŚAKUNTALĀ: When?

KING:

> Only let my thirsting mouth
> gently drink from your lips,
> the way a bee sips nectar
> from a fragile virgin blossom.

[*Saying this, he tries to raise her face.* ŚAKUNTALĀ *evades him with a dance.*]

VOICE OFFSTAGE: Red goose,[12] bid farewell to your gander! Night has arrived!

ŚAKUNTALĀ: [*Flustered.*] Puru king, Mother Gautamī is surely coming to ask about my health. Hide behind this tree!

210 KING: Yes.

[*He conceals himself and waits. Then* GAUTAMĪ *enters with a vessel in her hand, accompanied by* ŚAKUNTALĀ'*s two friends.*]

BOTH FRIENDS: This way, Mother Gautamī!

GAUTAMĪ: [*Approaching* ŚAKUNTALĀ.] Child, does the fever in your limbs burn less?

ŚAKUNTALĀ: Madam, I do feel better.

GAUTAMĪ: Kuśa grass and water will soothe your body. [*She sprinkles* ŚAKUNTALĀ'*s head.*] Child, the day is ended. Come, let's go back to our hut! [*She starts to go.*]

ŚAKUNTALĀ: [*To herself.*] My heart, even when your desire was within reach, you were bound by fear. Now you'll suffer the torment of separation and regret. [*Stopping after a few steps, she speaks aloud.*] Bower of creepers, refuge from my torment, I say goodbye until our joy can be renewed . . . [*Sorrowfully,* ŚAKUN-TALĀ *exits with the other women.*]

220 KING: [*Coming out of hiding.*] Fulfillment of desire is fraught with obstacles.

> Why didn't I kiss her face
> as it bent near my shoulder,
> her fingers shielding lips
> that stammered lovely warning?

Should I go now? Or shall I stay here in this bower of creepers that my love enjoyed and then left?

> I see the flowers her body pressed
> on this bench of stone,
> the letter her nails inscribed
230 > on the faded lotus leaf,
> the lotus-fiber bracelet
> that slipped from her wrist —
> my eyes are prisoners
> in this empty house of reeds.

---

[12] **Red goose:** Also known as the sheldrake, this bird and her mate were said to be inseparable by day but doomed to be parted every night.

VOICE IN THE AIR: King!

> When the evening rituals begin,
> shadows of flesh-eating demons swarm
> like amber clouds of twilight,
> raising terror at the altar of fire.

240   KING: I am coming.

> [*He exits.*]

ACT IV

[*The two friends enter, miming the gathering of flowers.*]

ANASŪYĀ: Priyaṁvadā, I'm delighted that Śakuntalā chose a suitable husband for herself, but I still feel anxious.

PRIYAṀVADĀ: Why?

ANASŪYĀ: When the king finished the sacrifice, the sages thanked him and he left. Now that he has returned to his palace women in the city, will he remember us here?

PRIYAṀVADĀ: Have faith! He's so handsome, he can't be evil. But I don't know what Father Kaṇva will think when he hears about what happened.

ANASŪYĀ: I predict that he'll give his approval.

10   PRIYAṀVADĀ: Why?

ANASŪYĀ: He's always planned to give his daughter to a worthy husband. If fate accomplished it so quickly, Father Kaṇva won't object.

PRIYAṀVADĀ: [*Looking at the basket of flowers.*] We've gathered enough flowers for the offering ceremony.

ANASŪYĀ: Shouldn't we worship the goddess who guards Śakuntalā?

PRIYAṀVADĀ: I have just begun. [*She begins the rite.*]

VOICE OFFSTAGE: I am here!

ANASŪYĀ: [*Listening.*] Friend, a guest is announcing himself.

PRIYAṀVADĀ: Śakuntalā is in her hut nearby, but her heart is far away.

20   ANASŪYĀ: You're right! Enough of these flowers!

[*They begin to leave.*]

VOICE OFFSTAGE: So . . . you slight a guest . . .

> Since you blindly ignore
> a great sage like me,
> the lover you worship
> with mindless devotion
> will not remember you,
> even when awakened —
> like a drunkard who forgets
> a story he just composed!

30   PRIYAṀVADĀ: Oh! What a terrible turn of events! Śakuntalā's distraction has offended someone she should have greeted. [*Looking ahead.*] Not just an ordinary

person, but the angry sage Durvāsas himself cursed her and went away in a frenzy of quivering, mad gestures. What else but fire has such power to burn?

ANASŪYĀ: Go! Bow at his feet and make him return while I prepare the water for washing his feet!

PRIYAṀVADĀ: As you say.   [*She exits.*]

ANASŪYĀ: [*After a few steps, she mimes stumbling.*] Oh! The basket of flowers fell from my hand when I stumbled in my haste to go. [*She mimes the gathering of flowers.*]

PRIYAṀVADĀ: [*Entering.*] He's so terribly cruel! No one could pacify him! But I was
40   able to soften him a little.

ANASŪYĀ: Even that is a great feat with him! Tell me more!

PRIYAṀVADĀ: When he refused to return, I begged him to forgive a daughter's first offense, since she didn't understand the power of his austerity.

ANASŪYĀ: Then? Then?

PRIYAṀVADĀ: He refused to change his word, but he promised that when the king sees the ring of recollection, the curse will end. Then he vanished.

ANASŪYĀ: Now we can breathe again. When he left, the king himself gave her the ring engraved with his name. Śakuntalā will have her own means of ending the curse.

PRIYAṀVADĀ: Come friend! We should finish the holy rite we're performing for her.

[*The two walk around, looking.*]

50   Anasūyā, look! With her face resting on her hand, our dear friend looks like a picture. She is thinking about her husband's leaving, with no thought for herself, much less for a guest.

ANASŪYĀ: Priyaṁvadā, we two must keep all this a secret between us. Our friend is fragile by nature; she needs our protection.

PRIYAṀVADĀ: Who would sprinkle a jasmine with scalding water?

[*They both exit; the interlude ends. Then a* DISCIPLE *of* KAṆVA *enters, just awakened from sleep.*]

DISCIPLE: Father Kaṇva has just returned from his pilgrimage and wants to know the exact time. I'll go into a clearing to see what remains of the night. [*Walking around and looking.*] It is dawn.

The moon sets over the western mountain
60   as the sun rises in dawn's red trail—
rising and setting, these two bright powers
portend the rise and fall of men.

When the moon disappears, night lotuses
are but dull souvenirs of its beauty—
when her lover disappears, the sorrow
is too painful for a frail girl to bear.

ANASŪYĀ: [*Throwing aside the curtain and entering.*] Even a person withdrawn from worldly life knows that the king has treated Śakuntalā badly.

DISCIPLE: I'll inform Father Kaṇva that it's time for the fire oblation. [*He exits.*]

70 ANASŪYĀ: Even when I'm awake, I'm useless. My hands and feet don't do their work. Love must be pleased to have made our innocent friend put her trust in a liar . . . but perhaps it was the cure of Durvāsas that changed him . . . otherwise, how could the king have made such promises and not sent even a message by now? Maybe we should send the ring to remind him. Which of these ascetics who practice austerities can we ask? Father Kaṇva has just returned from his pilgrimage. Since we feel that our friend was also at fault, we haven't told him that Śakuntalā is married to Duṣyanta and is pregnant. The problem is serious. What should we do?

PRIYAṀVADĀ: [*Entering, with delight.*] Friend, hurry! We're to celebrate the festival of
80 Śakuntalā's departure for her husband's house.

ANASŪYĀ: What's happened, friend?

PRIYAṀVADĀ: Listen! I went to ask Śakuntalā how she had slept. Father Kaṇva embraced her and though her face was bowed in shame, he blessed her: "Though his eyes were filled with smoke, the priest's oblation luckily fell on the fire. My child, I shall not mourn for you . . . like knowledge given to a good student I shall send you to your husband today with an escort of sages."

ANASŪYĀ: Who told Father Kaṇva what happened?

PRIYAṀVADĀ: A bodiless voice was chanting when he entered the fire sanctuary. [*Quoting in Sanskrit.*]

> Priest, know that your daughter
> 90 carries Duṣyanta's potent seed
> for the good of the earth—
> like fire in mimosa wood.

ANASŪYĀ: I'm joyful, friend. But I know that Śakuntalā must leave us today and sorrow shadows my happiness.

PRIYAṀVADĀ: Friend, we must chase away sorrow and make this hermit girl happy!

ANASŪYĀ: Friend, I've made a garland of mimosa flowers. It's in the coconut-shell box hanging on a branch of the mango tree. Get it for me! Meanwhile I'll prepare the special ointments of deer musk, sacred earth, and blades of dūrvā grass.

100 PRIYAṀVADĀ: Here it is!

[ANASŪYĀ *exits;* PRIYAṀVADĀ *gracefully mimes taking down the box.*]

VOICE OFFSTAGE: Gautamī! Śārṅgarava and some others have been appointed to escort Śakuntalā.

PRIYAṀVADĀ: [*Listening.*] Hurry! Hurry! The sages are being called to go to Hastināpura.

ANASŪYĀ: [*Reentering with pots of ointments in her hands.*] Come, friend! Let's go!

PRIYAṀVADĀ: [*Looking around.*] Śakuntalā stands at sunrise with freshly washed hair while the female ascetics bless her with handfuls of wild rice and auspicious words of farewell. Let's go to her together.

[*The two approach as* ŚAKUNTALĀ *enters with* GAUTAMĪ *and other female ascetics, and strikes a posture as described. One after another, the female ascetics address her.*]

FIRST FEMALE ASCETIC: Child, win the title "Chief Queen" as a sign of your hus-
110   band's high esteem!
SECOND FEMALE ASCETIC: Child, be a mother to heroes!
THIRD FEMALE ASCETIC: Child, be honored by your husband!
BOTH FRIENDS: This happy moment is no time for tears, friend.

[*Wiping away her tears, they calm her with dance gestures.*]
PRIYAṀVADĀ: Your beauty deserves jewels, not these humble things we've gathered
    in the hermitage.

[*Two boy ascetics enter with offerings in their hands.*]
BOTH BOYS: Here is an ornament for you!

[*Everyone looks amazed.*]
GAUTAMĪ: Nārada, my child, where did this come from?
FIRST BOY: From Father Kaṇva's power.
GAUTAMĪ: Was it his mind's magic?
120   SECOND BOY: Not at all! Listen! You ordered us to bring flowers from the forest trees
    for Śakuntalā.

> One tree produced this white silk cloth,
> another poured resinous lac to redden her feet—
> the tree nymphs produced jewels in hands
> that stretched from branches like young shoots.

PRIYAṀVADĀ: [*Watching* ŚAKUNTALĀ.] This is a sign that royal fortune will come to
    you in your husband's house.

[ŚAKUNTALĀ *mimes modesty.*]
FIRST BOY: Gautama, come quickly! Father Kaṇva is back from bathing. We'll tell
    him how the trees honor her.
130   SECOND BOY: As you say.

                                                [*The two exit.*]
BOTH FRIENDS: We've never worn them ourselves, but we'll put these jewels on your
    limbs the way they look in pictures.
ŚAKUNTALĀ: I trust your skill.

[*Both friends mime ornamenting her. Then* KAṆVA *enters, fresh from his bath.*]
KAṆVA:

> My heart is touched with sadness
> since Śakuntalā must go today,
> my throat is choked with sobs,
> my eyes are dulled by worry—
> if a disciplined ascetic
> suffers so deeply from love,
140   > how do fathers bear the pain
> of each daughter's parting?

[*He walks around.*]
BOTH FRIENDS: Śakuntalā, your jewels are in place; now put on the pair of silken cloths.

[*Standing, ŚAKUNTALĀ wraps them.*]
GAUTAMĪ: Child, your father has come. His eyes filled with tears of joy embrace you. Greet him reverently!
ŚAKUNTALĀ: [*Modestly.*] Father, I welcome you.
KAṆVA: Child,

> May your husband honor you
> the way Yayāti honored Śarmiṣṭhā.
> As she bore her son Puru,[13]
150　　may you bear an imperial prince.

GAUTAMĪ: Sir, this is a blessing, not just a prayer.
KAṆVA: Child, walk around the sacrificial fires!

[*All walk around;* KAṆVA *intoning a prayer in Vedic meter.*]

> Perfectly placed around the main altar,
> fed with fuel, strewn with holy grass,
> destroying sin by incense from oblations,
> may these sacred fires purify you!

　　You must leave now! [*Looking around.*] Where are Śārṅgarava and the others?
DISCIPLE: [*Entering.*] Here we are, sir!
KAṆVA: You show your sister the way!
160　ŚĀRṄGARAVA: Come this way!

[*They walk around.*]
KAṆVA: Listen, you trees that grow in our grove!

> Until you were well watered
> she could not bear to drink;
> she loved you too much
> to pluck your flowers for her hair;
> the first time your buds bloomed,
> she blossomed with joy—
> may you all bless Śakuntalā
> as she leaves for her husband's house.

[*Miming that he hears a cuckoo's cry.*]

170

> The trees of her forest family
> have blessed Śakuntalā—
> the cuckoo's melodious song
> announces their response.

---

[13] Yayāti . . . Śarmiṣṭhā . . . Puru: Yayāti and Śarmiṣṭhā are the parents of Puru, the king whose service to others characterized the rulers of the Paurava dynasty. Duṣyanta is descended from Puru and is one of the Paurava rulers.

VOICE IN THE AIR:

> May lakes colored by lotuses mark her path!
> May trees shade her from the sun's burning rays!
> May the dust be as soft as lotus pollen!
> May fragrant breezes cool her way!

[*All listen astonished.*]

GAUTAMĪ: Child, the divinities of our grove love you like your family and bless you. We bow to you all!

180 ŚAKUNTALĀ: [*Bowing and walking around; speaking in a stage whisper.*] Priyaṁvadā, though I long to see my husband, my feet move with sorrow as I start to leave the hermitage.

PRIYAṀVADĀ: You are not the only one who grieves. The whole hermitage feels this way as your departure from our grove draws near.

> Grazing deer
> drop grass,
> peacocks
> stop dancing,
> vines loose
190   pale leaves
> falling
> like tears.

ŚAKUNTALĀ: [*Remembering.*] Father, before I leave, I must see my sister, the vine Forestlight.

KAṆVA: I know that you feel a sister's love for her. She's right here.

ŚAKUNTALĀ: Forestlight, though you love your mango tree, turn to embrace me with your tendril arms! After today, I'll be so far away . . .

KAṆVA:

> Your merits won you the husband
> I always hoped you would have
200   and your jasmine has her mango tree—
> my worries for you both are over.

Start your journey here!

ŚAKUNTALĀ: [*Facing her two friends.*] I entrust her care to you.

BOTH FRIENDS: But who will care for us? [*They wipe away their tears.*]

KAṆVA: Anasūyā, enough crying! You should be giving Śakuntalā courage!

[*All walk around.*]

ŚAKUNTALĀ: Father, when the pregnant doe who grazes near my hut gives birth, please send someone to give me the good news.

KAṆVA: I shall not forget.

ŚAKUNTALĀ: [*Miming the interrupting of her gait.*] Who is clinging to my skirt?

[*She turns around.*]

210 KAṆVA: Child,

The buck whose mouth you healed with oil
when it was pierced by a blade of kuśa grass
and whom you fed with grains of rice—
your adopted son will not leave the path.

ŚAKUNTALĀ: Child, don't follow when I'm abandoning those I love! I raised you
when you were orphaned soon after your birth, but now I'm deserting you too.
Father will look after you. Go back! [*Weeping, she starts to go.*]
KAṆVA: Be strong!

220
Hold back the tears that blind
your long-lashed eyes—
you will stumble if you cannot see
the uneven ground on the path.

ŚĀRṄGARAVA: Sir, the scriptures prescribe that loved ones be escorted only to the
water's edge. We are at the shore of the lake. Give us your message and return!
ŚAKUNTALĀ: We shall rest in the shade of this fig tree.

[*All walk around and stop;* KAṆVA *speaks to himself.*]
KAṆVA: What would be the right message to send to King Duṣyanta? [*He ponders.*]
ŚAKUNTALĀ: [*In a stage whisper.*] Look! The wild goose cries in anguish when her
mate is hidden by lotus leaves. What I'm suffering is much worse.
ANASŪYĀ: Friend, don't speak this way!

230
This goose spends
every long night
in sorrow
without her mate,
but hope lets her
survive
the deep pain
of loneliness.

KAṆVA: Śārṅgarava, speak my words to the king after you present Śakuntalā!
ŚĀRṄGARAVA: As you command, sir!
KAṆVA:

240
Considering our discipline,
the nobility of your birth
and that she fell in love with you
before her kinsmen could act,
acknowledge her with equal rank
among your wives—
what more is destined for her,
the bride's family will not ask.

ŚĀRṄGARAVA: I grasp your message.

KAṆVA: Child, now I must instruct you. We forest hermits know something about
250   worldly matters.

ŚĀRṄGARAVA: Nothing is beyond the scope of wise men.

KAṆVA: When you enter your husband's family:

> Obey your elders, be a friend to the other wives!
> If your husband seems harsh, don't be impatient!
> Be fair to your servants, humble in your happiness!
> Women who act this way become noble wives;
> sullen girls only bring their families disgrace.

But what does Gautamī think?

GAUTAMĪ: This is good advice for wives, child. Take it all to heart!

260   KAṆVA: Child, embrace me and your friends!

ŚAKUNTALĀ: Father, why must Priyaṁvadā and my other friends turn back here?

KAṆVA: They will also be given in marriage. It is not proper for them to go there now.
    Gautamī will go with you.

ŚAKUNTALĀ: [*Embracing her father.*] How can I go on living in a strange place, torn
    from my father's side, like a vine torn from the side of a sandalwood tree grow-
    ing on a mountain slope?

KAṆVA: Child, why are you so frightened?

> When you are your husband's honored wife,
> absorbed in royal duties and in your son,
270 > born like the sun to the eastern dawn,
> the sorrow of separation will fade.

[ŚAKUNTALĀ *falls at her father's feet.*]
    Let my hopes for you be fulfilled!

ŚAKUNTALĀ: [*Approaching her two friends.*] You two must embrace me together!

BOTH FRIENDS: [*Embracing her.*] Friend, if the king seems slow to recognize you,
    show him the ring engraved with his name!

ŚAKUNTALĀ: Your suspicions make me tremble!

BOTH FRIENDS: Don't be afraid! It's our love that fears evil.

ŚĀRṄGARAVA: The sun is high in the afternoon sky. Hurry, please!

ŚAKUNTALĀ: [*Facing the sanctuary.*] Father, will I ever see the grove again?

KAṆVA:

280
> When you have lived for many years
> as a queen equal to the earth
> and raised Duṣyanta's son
> to be a matchless warrior,
> your husband will entrust him
> with the burdens of the kingdom
> and will return with you
> to the calm of this hermitage.

GAUTAMĪ: Child, the time for our departure has passed. Let your father turn back! It would be better, sir, if you turn back yourself. She'll keep talking this way forever.

290 KAṆVA: Child, my ascetic practice has been interrupted.

ŚAKUNTALĀ: My father's body is already tortured by ascetic practices. He must not grieve too much for me!

KAṆVA: [Sighing.]

> When I see the grains of rice
> sprout from offerings you made
> at the door of your hut,
> how shall I calm my sorrow!

[ŚAKUNTALĀ exits with her escort.]

BOTH FRIENDS: [Watching ŚAKUNTALĀ.] Śakuntalā is hidden by forest trees now.

KAṆVA: Anasūyā, your companion is following her duty. Restrain yourself and return with me!

300 BOTH FRIENDS: Father, the ascetics' grove seems empty without Śakuntalā. How can we enter?

KAṆVA: The strength of your love makes it seem so. [Walking around in meditation.] Good! Now that Śakuntalā is on her way to her husband's family, I feel calm.

> A daughter belongs to another man—
> by sending her to her husband today,
> I feel the satisfaction
> one has on repaying a loan.

[All exit.]

ACT V

[The KING and the BUFFOON enter; both sit down.]

BUFFOON: Pay attention to the music room, friend, and you'll hear the notes of a song strung into a delicious melody . . . the lady Haṃsapadikā is practicing her singing.

KING: Be quiet so I can hear her!

VOICE IN THE AIR: [Singing.]

> Craving sweet
> new nectar,
> you kissed
> a mango bud once—
> how could you
> 10   forget her, bee,
> to bury your joy
> in a lotus

KING: The melody of the song is passionate.

BUFFOON: But did you get the meaning of the words?

KING: I once made love to her. Now she reproaches me for loving Queen Vasumatī. Friend Māḍhavya, tell Haṃsapadikā that her words rebuke me soundly.

BUFFOON: As you command! [*He rises.*] But if that woman grabs my hair tuft, it will be like a heavenly nymph grabbing some ascetic . . . there go my hopes of liberation![14]

20   KING: Go! Use your courtly charm to console her.

BUFFOON: What a fate!

[*He exits.*]

KING: [*To himself.*] Why did hearing the song's words fill me with such strong desire? I'm not parted from anyone I love . . .

> Seeing rare beauty,
> hearing lovely sounds,
> even a happy man
> becomes strangely uneasy . . .
> perhaps he remembers,
> without knowing why,
30 > loves of another life
> buried deep in his being.

[*He stands bewildered. Then the* KING'S CHAMBERLAIN *enters.*]

CHAMBERLAIN: At my age, look at me!

> Since I took this ceremonial bamboo staff
> as my badge of office in the king's chambers
> many years have passed; now I use it
> as a crutch to support my faltering steps.

A king cannot neglect his duty. He has just risen from his seat of justice and though I am loath to keep him longer, Sage Kaṇva's pupils have just arrived. Authority to rule the world leaves no time for rest.

40 > The sun's steeds were yoked before time began,
> the fragrant wind blows night and day,
> the cosmic serpent always bears earth's weight,[15]
> and a king who levies taxes has his duty.

Therefore, I must perform my office. [*Walking around and looking.*]

> Weary from ruling them like children,
> he seeks solitude far from his subjects,
> like an elephant bull who seeks cool shade
> after gathering his herd at midday.

[*Approaching.*] Victory to you, king! Some ascetics who dwell in the forest at the
50   foothills of the Himālayas have come. They have women with them and bring a message from Sage Kaṇva. Listen, king, and judge!

---

[14] **if that woman . . . liberation:** The Buffoon is comparing his chances of being released from the grip of the courtesan to the ascetic's hopes for liberation from *samsara,* the wheel of rebirth.

[15] **cosmic serpent . . . earth's weight:** In Hindu mythology the earth rests on the cosmic serpent Sesa.

KING: [*Respectfully.*] Are they Sage Kaṇva's messengers?

CHAMBERLAIN: They are.

KING: Inform the teacher Somarāta that he should welcome the ascetics with the prescribed rites and then bring them to me himself. I'll wait in a place suitable for greeting them.

CHAMBERLAIN: As the king commands.   [*He exits.*]

KING: [*Rising.*] Vetravatī, lead the way to the fire sanctuary.

DOORKEEPER: Come this way, king!

60 KING: [*Walking around, showing fatigue.*] Every other creature is happy when the object of his desire is won, but for kings success contains a core of suffering.

> High office only leads to greater greed;
> just perfecting its rewards is wearisome —
> a kingdom is more trouble than it's worth,
> like a royal umbrella one holds alone.

TWO BARDS OFFSTAGE: Victory to you, king!

FIRST BARD:

> You sacrifice your pleasures every day
> to labor for your subjects —
> as a tree endures burning heat
70 > to give shade from the summer sun.

SECOND BARD:

> You punish villains with your rod of justice,
> you reconcile disputes, you grant protection —
> most relatives are loyal only in hope of gain,
> but you treat all your subjects like kinsmen.

KING: My weary mind is revived. [*He walks around.*]

DOORKEEPER: The terrace of the fire sanctuary is freshly washed and the cow is waiting to give milk for the oblation. Let the king ascend!

KING: Vetravatī, why has Father Kaṇva sent these sages to me?

> Does something hinder their ascetic life?
80 > Or threaten creatures in the sacred forest?
> Or do my sins stunt the flowering vines?
> My mind is filled with conflicting doubts.

DOORKEEPER: I would guess that these sages rejoice in your virtuous conduct and come to honor you.

[*The ascetics enter;* ŚAKUNTALĀ *is in front with* GAUTAMĪ; *the* CHAMBERLAIN *and the* KING's PRIEST *are in front of her.*]

CHAMBERLAIN: Come this way, sirs!

ŚĀRṄGARAVA: Śāradvata, my friend:

> I know that this renowned king is righteous
> and none of the social classes follows evil ways,

but my mind is so accustomed to seclusion
90   that the palace feels like a house in flames.

ŚĀRADVATA: I've felt the same way ever since we entered the city.

As if I were freshly bathed, seeing a filthy man,
pure while he's defiled, awake while he's asleep,
as if I were a free man watching a prisoner,
I watch this city mired in pleasures.

ŚAKUNTALĀ: [*Indicating she feels an omen.*] Why is my right eye twitching?
GAUTAMĪ: Child, your husband's family gods turn bad fortune into blessings! [*They walk around.*]
PRIEST: [*Indicating the* KING.] Ascetics, the guardian of sacred order has left the seat of justice and awaits you now. Behold him!
100 ŚĀRṄGARAVA: Great priest, he seems praiseworthy, but we expect no less.

Boughs bend, heavy with ripened fruit,
clouds descend with fresh rain,
noble men are gracious with wealth—
this is the nature of bountiful things.

DOORKEEPER: King, their faces look calm. I'm sure that the sages have confidence in what they're doing.
KING: [*Seeing* ŚAKUNTALĀ.]

Who is she? Carefully veiled
to barely reveal her body's beauty,
surrounded by the ascetics
110   like a bud among withered leaves.

DOORKEEPER: King, I feel curious and puzzled too. Surely her form deserves closer inspection.
KING: Let her be! One should not stare at another man's wife!
ŚAKUNTALĀ: [*Placing her hand on her chest, she speaks to herself.*] My heart, why are you quivering? Be quiet while I learn my noble husband's feelings.
PRIEST: [*Going forward.*] These ascetics have been honored with due ceremony. They have a message from their teacher. The king should hear them!
KING: I am paying attention.
SAGES: [*Raising their hands in a gesture of greeting.*] May you be victorious, king!
120 KING: I salute you all!
SAGES: May your desires be fulfilled!
KING: Do the sages perform austerities unhampered?
SAGES:

Who would dare obstruct the rites
of holy men whom you protect—
how can darkness descend
when the sun's rays shine?

KING: My title "king" is more meaningful now. Is the world blessed by Father Kaṇva's health?

SAGES: Saints control their own health. He asks about your welfare and sends this
130   message . . .

KING: What does he command?

ŚĀRṄGARAVA: At the time you secretly met and married my daughter, affection made me pardon you both.

> We remember you to be a prince of honor;
> Śakuntalā is virtue incarnate —
> the creator cannot be condemned
> for mating the perfect bride and groom.

And now that she is pregnant, receive her and perform your sacred duty together.

GAUTAMĪ: Sir, I have something to say, though I wasn't appointed to speak:

140
> She ignored her elders
> and you failed to ask her kinsmen —
> since you acted on your own,
> what can I say to you now?

ŚAKUNTALĀ: What does my noble husband say?

KING: What has been proposed?

ŚAKUNTALĀ: [*To herself.*] The proposal is as clear as fire.

ŚĀRṄGARAVA: What's this? Your Majesty certainly knows the ways of the world!

> People suspect a married woman who stays
> with her kinsmen, even if she is chaste —
150
> a young wife should live with her husband,
> no matter how he despises her.

KING: Did I ever marry you?

ŚAKUNTALĀ: [*Visibly dejected, speaking to herself.*] Now your fears are real, my heart!

ŚĀRṄGARAVA:

> Does one turn away from duty in contempt
> because his own actions repulse him?

KING: Why ask this insulting question?

ŚĀRṄGARAVA:

> Such transformations take shape
> when men are drunk with power.

KING: This censure is clearly directed at me.

160 GAUTAMĪ: Child, this is no time to be modest. I'll remove your veil. Then your husband will recognize you.

[*She does so.*]

KING: [*Staring at* ŚAKUNTALĀ.]

Must I judge whether I ever married
the flawless beauty they offer me now?
I cannot love her or leave her, like a bee
near a jasmine filled with frost at dawn.

[*He shows hesitation.*]

DOORKEEPER: Our king has a strong sense of justice. Who else would hesitate when
beauty like this is handed to him?

ŚĀRṄGARAVA: King, why do you remain silent?

KING: Ascetics, even though I'm searching my mind, I don't remember marrying this
lady. How can I accept a woman who is visibly pregnant when I doubt that I am
the cause?

ŚAKUNTALĀ: [*In a stage whisper.*] My lord casts doubt on our marriage. Why were my
hopes so high?

ŚĀRṄGARAVA: It can't be!

Are you going to insult the sage
who pardons the girl you seduced
and bids you keep his stolen wealth,
treating a thief like you with honor?

ŚĀRADVATA: Śārṅgarava, stop now! Śakuntalā, we have delivered our message and the
king has responded. He must be shown some proof.

ŚAKUNTALĀ: [*In a stage whisper.*] When passion can turn to this, what's the use of
reminding him? But, it's up to me to prove my honor now. [*Aloud.*] My noble
husband . . . [*She breaks off when this is half-spoken.*] Since our marriage is in
doubt, this is no way to address him. Puru king, you do wrong to reject a simple-
hearted person with such words after you deceived her in the hermitage.

KING: [*Covering his ears.*] Stop this shameful talk!

Are you trying to stain my name
and drag me to ruin—
like a river eroding her own banks,
soiling water and uprooting trees?

ŚAKUNTALĀ: Very well! If it's really true that fear of taking another man's wife turns
you away, then this ring will revive your memory and remove your doubt.

KING: An excellent idea!

ŚAKUNTALĀ: [*Touching the place where the ring had been.*] I'm lost! The ring is gone
from my finger. [*She looks despairingly at* GAUTAMĪ.]

GAUTAMĪ: The ring must have fallen off while you were bathing in the holy waters at
the shrine of the goddess near Indra's grove.

KING: [*Smiling.*] And so they say the female sex is cunning.

ŚAKUNTALĀ: Fate has shown its power. Yet, I will tell you something else.

KING: I am still obliged to listen.

ŚAKUNTALĀ: One day, in a jasmine bower, you held a lotus-leaf cup full of water in
your hand.

KING: We hear you.

ŚAKUNTALĀ: At that moment the buck I treated as my son approached. You coaxed it with the water, saying that it should drink first. But he didn't trust you and wouldn't drink from your hand. When I took the water, his trust returned. Then you jested, "Every creature trusts what its senses know. You both belong to the forest."

KING: Thus do women further their own ends by attracting eager men with the honey of false words.

GAUTAMĪ: Great king, you are wrong to speak this way. This child raised in an ascetics' grove doesn't know deceit.

KING: Old woman,

> When naive female beasts show cunning,
> what can we expect of women who reason?
> Don't cuckoos let other birds nurture
> their eggs and teach the chicks to fly?

ŚAKUNTALĀ: [*Angrily.*] Evil man! You see everything distorted by your own ignoble heart. Who would want to imitate you now, hiding behind your show of justice, like a well overgrown with weeds?

KING: [*To himself.*] Her anger does not seem feigned; it makes me doubt myself.

> When the absence of love's memory
> made me deny a secret affair with her,
> this fire-eyed beauty bent her angry brows
> and seemed to break the bow of love.

[*Aloud.*] Lady, Duṣyanta's conduct is renowned, so what you say is groundless.

ŚAKUNTALĀ: All right! I may be a self-willed wanton woman! But it was faith in the Puru dynasty that brought me into the power of a man with honey in his words and poison in his heart. [*She covers her face at the end of the speech and weeps.*]

ŚĀRṄGARAVA: A willful act unchecked always causes pain.

> One should be cautious
> in forming a secret union—
> unless a lover's heart is clear,
> affection turns to poison.

KING: But sir, why do you demean me with such warnings? Do you trust the lady?

ŚĀRṄGARAVA: [*Scornfully.*] You have learned everything backwards.

> If you suspect the word of one
> whose nature knows no guile,
> then you can only trust
> people who practice deception.

KING: I presume you speak the truth. Let us assume so. But what could I gain by deceiving this woman?

ŚĀRṄGARAVA: Ruin.

KING: Ruin? A Puru king has no reason to want his own ruin!

ŚĀRADVATA: Śārṅgarava, this talk is pointless. We have delivered our master's message and should return.

> Since you married her, abandon her or take her—
> absolute is the power a husband has over his wife.

GAUTAMĪ: You go ahead.

[*They start to go.*]

250 ŚAKUNTALĀ: What? Am I deceived by this cruel man and then abandoned by you?
[*She tries to follow them.*]

GAUTAMĪ: [*Stopping.*] Śārṅgarava my son, Śakuntalā is following us, crying pitifully. What will my child do now that her husband has refused her?

ŚĀRṄGARAVA: [*Turning back angrily.*] Bold woman, do you still insist on having your way?

[ŚAKUNTALĀ *trembles in fear.*]

> If you are what the king says you are,
> you don't belong in Father Kaṇva's family—
> if you know that your marriage vow is pure,
> you can bear slavery in your husband's house.

Stay! We must go on!

260 KING: Ascetic, why do you disappoint the lady too?

> The moon only makes lotuses open,
> the sun's light awakens lilies—
> a king's discipline forbids him
> to touch another man's wife.

ŚĀRṄGARAVA: If you forget a past affair because of some present attachment, why do you fear injustice now?

KING: [*To the* PRIEST.] Sir I ask you to weigh the alternatives:

> Since it's unclear whether I'm deluded
> or she is speaking falsely—
270 > should I risk abandoning a wife
> or being tainted by another man's?

PRIEST: [*Deliberating.*] I recommend this . . .

KING: Instruct me! I'll do as you say.

PRIEST: Then let the lady stay in our house until her child is born. If you ask why: the wise men predict that your first son will be born with the marks of a king who turns the wheel of empire. If the child of the sage's daughter bears the marks, congratulate her and welcome her into your palace chambers. Otherwise, send her back to her father.

KING: Whatever the elders desire.

280   PRIEST: Child, follow me!

ŚAKUNTALĀ: Mother earth, open to receive me!

[*Weeping,* ŚAKUNTALĀ *exits with the* PRIEST *and the hermits. The* KING, *his memory lost through the curse, thinks about her.*]

VOICE OFFSTAGE: Amazing! Amazing!

KING: [*Listening.*] What could this be?

PRIEST: [*Reentering, amazed.*] King, something marvelous has occurred!

KING: What?

PRIEST: When Kaṇva's pupils had departed,

> The girl threw up her arms and wept,
> lamenting her misfortune . . . then . . .

KING: Then what?

PRIEST:

290
> Near the nymph's shrine a ray of light
> in the shape of a woman carried her away.

[*All mime amazement.*]

KING: We've already settled the matter. Why discuss it further?

PRIEST: [*Observing the* KING.] May you be victorious!

[*He exits.*]

KING: Vetravatī, I am bewildered. Lead the way to my chamber!

DOORKEEPER: Come this way, my lord! [*She walks forward.*]

KING:

> I cannot remember marrying
> the sage's abandoned daughter,
> but the pain my heart feels
> makes me suspect that I did.

[*All exit.*]

ACT VI

[*The* KING's *wife's brother, who is city* MAGISTRATE, *enters with two policemen leading a* MAN *whose hands are tied behind his back.*]

BOTH POLICEMEN: [*Beating the* MAN.] Speak, thief? Where'd you steal this handsome ring with the king's name engraved in the jewel?

MAN: [*Showing fear.*] Peace, sirs! I wouldn't do a thing like that.

FIRST POLICEMAN: Don't tell us the king thought you were some famous priest and gave it to you as a gift!

MAN: Listen, I'm a humble fisherman who lives near Indra's grove.

SECOND POLICEMAN: Thief, did we ask you about your caste?

MAGISTRATE: Sūcaka, let him tell it all in order! Don't interrupt him!

BOTH POLICEMEN: Whatever you command, chief!

10   MAN: I feed my family by catching fish with nets and hooks.

MAGISTRATE: [*Mocking.*] What a pure profession![16]

MAN:

> The work I do
> may be vile
> but I won't deny
> my birthright—
> a priest
> doing his holy rites
> pities the animals
> he kills.

20 MAGISTRATE: Go on!

MAN: One day as I was cutting up a red carp, I saw the shining stone of this ring in its belly. When I tried to sell it, you grabbed me. Kill me or let me go! That's how I got it!

MAGISTRATE: Jānuka, I'm sure this ugly butcher's a fisherman by his stinking smell. We must investigate how he got the ring. We'll go straight to the palace.

BOTH POLICEMEN: Okay. Go in front, you pickpocket!

[*All walk around.*]

MAGISTRATE: Sūcaka, guard this villain at the palace gate! I'll report to the king how we found the ring, get his orders, and come back.

BOTH POLICEMEN: Chief, good luck with the king!

[*The* MAGISTRATE *exits.*]

30 FIRST POLICEMAN: Jānuka, my hands are itching to tie on his execution garland.[17] [*He points to the* MAN.]

MAN: You shouldn't think about killing a man for no reason.

SECOND POLICEMAN: [*Looking.*] I see our chief coming with a letter in his hand. It's probably an order from the king. You'll be thrown to the vultures or you'll see the face of death's dog[18] again . . .

MAGISTRATE: [*Entering.*] Sūcaka, release this fisherman! I'll tell you how he got the ring.

FIRST POLICEMAN: Whatever you say, chief!

SECOND POLICEMAN: The villain entered the house of death and came out again. [*He unties the prisoner.*]

MAN: [*Bowing to the* MAGISTRATE.] Master, how will I make my living now?

40 MAGISTRATE: The king sends you a sum equal to the ring. [*He gives the money to the* MAN.]

MAN: [*Bowing as he grabs it.*] The king honors me.

---

[16] **a pure profession:** A sarcastic comment about fishing, a profession that requires the killing of animals.

[17] **execution garland:** Condemned prisoners were dressed in sacrificial robes and garlands at the time of execution.

[18] **death's dog:** In Hindu mythology, the path of death is guarded by two four-eyed dogs.

FIRST POLICEMAN: This fellow's certainly honored. He was lowered from the execution stake and raised up on a royal elephant's back.

SECOND POLICEMAN: Chief, the reward tells me this ring was special to the king.

MAGISTRATE: I don't think the king valued the stone, but when he caught sight of the
ring, he suddenly seemed to remember someone he loved, and he became
deeply disturbed.

FIRST POLICEMAN: You served him well, chief!

SECOND POLICEMAN: I think you better served this king of fish. [*Looking at the fisherman with jealousy.*]

50 MAN: My lords, half of this is yours for your good will.

FIRST POLICEMAN: It's only fair!

MAGISTRATE: Fisherman, now that you are my greatest and dearest friend, we should
pledge our love over kadamba-blossom wine. Let's go to the wine shop!

[*They all exit together; the interlude ends. Then a nymph named* SĀNUMATĪ *enters by the
skyway.*]

SĀNUMATĪ: Now that I've performed my assigned duties at the nymph's shrine, I'll
slip away to spy on King Duṣyanta while the worshipers are bathing. My friendship with Menakā makes me feel a bond with Śakuntalā. Besides, Menakā asked
me to help her daughter. [*Looking around.*] Why don't I see preparations for the
spring festival in the king's palace? I can learn everything by using my mental
powers, but I must respect my friend's request. So be it! I'll make myself invis-
60   ible and spy on these two girls who are guarding the pleasure garden.

[SĀNUMATĪ *mimes descending and stands waiting. Then a* MAID *servant named Parabhṛtikā,
"Little Cuckoo," enters, looking at a mango bud. A* SECOND MAID, *named Madhukarikā, "Little
Bee," is following her.*]

FIRST MAID:

> Your pale green stem
> tinged with pink
> is a true sign
> that spring has come —
> I see you,
> mango-blossom bud,
> and I pray
> for a season of joy.

SECOND MAID: What are you muttering to yourself?

70 FIRST MAID: A cuckoo goes mad when she sees a mango bud.

SECOND MAID: [*Joyfully rushing over.*] Has the sweet month of spring come?

FIRST MAID: Now's the time to sing your songs of love.

SECOND MAID: Hold me while I pluck a mango bud and worship the god of love.

FIRST MAID: Only if you'll give me half the fruit of your worship.

SECOND MAID: That goes without saying . . . our bodies may be separate, but our
lives are one . . . [*Leaning on her friend, she stands and plucks a mango bud.*] The

mango flower is still closed, but this broken stem is fragrant. [*She makes the dove gesture with her hands.*]

> Mango blossom bud,
> I offer you to Love
> 80   as he lifts
> his bow of passion.
> Be the first
> of his flower arrows
> aimed at lonely girls
> with lovers far away!

[*She throws the mango bud.*]

MAGISTRATE: [*Angrily throwing aside the curtain and entering.*] Not now, stupid girl! When the king has banned the festival of spring, how dare you pluck a mango bud!

BOTH MAIDS: [*Frightened.*] Please forgive us, sir. We don't know what you mean.

90   CHAMBERLAIN: Did you not hear that even the spring trees and the nesting birds obey the king's order?

> The mango flowers bloom without spreading pollen,
> the red amaranth buds, but will not bloom,
> cries of cuckoo cocks freeze though frost is past,
> and out of fear, Love holds his arrow half-drawn.

BOTH MAIDS: There is no doubt about the king's great power!

FIRST MAID: Sir, several days ago we were sent to wait on the queen by Mitrāvasu, the king's brother-in-law. We were assigned to guard the pleasure garden. Since we're newcomers, we've heard no news.

100   CHAMBERLAIN: Let it be! But don't do it again!

BOTH MAIDS: Sir, we're curious. May we ask why the spring festival was banned?

SĀNUMATĪ: Mortals are fond of festivals. The reason must be serious.

CHAMBERLAIN: It is public knowledge. Why should I not tell them? Has the scandal of Śakuntalā's rejection not reached your ears?

BOTH MAIDS: We only heard from the king's brother-in-law that the ring was found.

CHAMBERLAIN: [*To himself.*] There is little more to tell. [*Aloud.*] When he saw the ring, the king remembered that he had married Śakuntalā in secret and had rejected her in his delusion. Since then the king has been tortured by remorse.

> Despising what he once enjoyed,
> 110   he shuns his ministers every day
> and spends long sleepless nights
> tossing at the edge of his bed —
> when courtesy demands that
> he converse with palace women,
> he stumbles over their names,
> and then retreats in shame.

SĀNUMATĪ: This news delights me.

CHAMBERLAIN: The festival is banned because of the king's melancholy.

BOTH MAIDS: It's only right.

120   VOICE OFFSTAGE: This way, sir!

CHAMBERLAIN: [*Listening.*] The king is coming. Go about your business!

BOTH MAIDS: As you say.

[*Both maids exit. Then the* KING *enters, costumed to show his grief, accompanied by the* BUFFOON *and the* DOORKEEPER.]

CHAMBERLAIN: [*Observing the* KING.] Extraordinary beauty is appealing under all conditions. Even in his lovesick state, the king is wonderful to see.

> Rejecting his regal jewels,
> he wears one golden bangle
> above his left wrist;
> his lips are pale with sighs,
> his eyes wan from brooding at night—
130 > like a gemstone ground in polishing,
> the fiery beauty of his body
> makes his wasted form seem strong.

SĀNUMATĪ: [*Seeing the* KING.] I see why Śakuntalā pines for him though he rejected and disgraced her.

KING: [*Walking around slowly, deep in thought.*]

> This cursed heart slept
> when my love came to wake it,
> and now it stays awake
> to suffer the pain of remorse.

SĀNUMATĪ: The girl shares his fate.

140   BUFFOON: [*In a stage whisper.*] He's having another attack of his Śakuntalā disease. I doubt if there's any cure for that.

CHAMBERLAIN: [*Approaching.*] Victory to the king! I have inspected the grounds of the pleasure garden. Let the king visit his favorite spots and divert himself.

KING: Vetravatī, deliver a message to my noble minister Piśuna: "After being awake all night, we cannot sit on the seat of justice today. Set in writing what your judgment tells you the citizens require and send it to us!"

DOORKEEPER: Whatever you command!   [*She exits.*]

KING: Vātāyana, attend to the rest of your business!

CHAMBERLAIN: As the king commands!   [*He exits.*]

150   BUFFOON: You've cleared out the flies. Now you can rest in some pretty spot. The garden is pleasant now in this break between morning cold and noonday heat.

KING: Dear friend, the saying "Misfortunes rush through any crack" is absolutely right:

> Barely freed by the dark force
> that made me forget Kaṇva's daughter,

my mind is threatened by an arrow
of mango buds fixed on Love's bow.

BUFFOON: Wait, I'll destroy the love god's arrow with my wooden stick. [*Raising his staff, he tries to strike a mango bud.*]

KING: [*Smiling.*] Let it be! I see the majesty of brahman bravery. Friend, where may I sit to divert my eyes with vines that remind me of my love?

BUFFOON: Didn't you tell your maid Caturikā, "I'll pass the time in the jasmine bower. Bring me the drawing board on which I painted a picture of Śakuntalā with my own hand!"

KING: Such a place may soothe my heart. Show me the way!

BUFFOON: Come this way!

[*Both walk around; the nymph* SĀNUMATĪ *follows.*]
The marble seat and flower offerings in this jasmine bower are certainly trying to make us feel welcome. Come in and sit down!

[*Both enter the bower and sit.*]
SĀNUMATĪ: I'll hide behind these creepers to see the picture he's drawn of my friend. Then I'll report how great her husband's passion is.

[*She does as she says and stands waiting.*]
KING: Friend, now I remember everything. I told you about my first meeting with Śakuntalā. You weren't with me when I rejected her, but why didn't you say anything about her before? Did you suffer a loss of memory too?

BUFFOON: I didn't forget. You did tell me all about it once, but then you said, "It's all a joke without any truth." My wit is like a lump of clay, so I took you at your word . . . or it could be that fate is powerful . . .

SĀNUMATĪ: It is!

KING: Friend, help me!

BUFFOON: What's this? It doesn't become you! Noblemen never take grief to heart. Even in storms, mountains don't tremble.

KING: Dear friend, I'm defenseless when I remember the pain of my love's bewilderment when I rejected her.

When I cast her away, she followed her kinsmen,
but Kaṇva's disciple harshly shouted, "Stay!"
The tearful look my cruelty provoked
burns me like an arrow tipped with poison.

SĀNUMATĪ: The way he rehearses his actions makes me delight in his pain.

BUFFOON: Sir, I guess that the lady was carried off by some celestial creature or other.

KING: Who else would dare to touch a woman who worshiped her husband? I was told that Menakā is her mother. My heart suspects that her mother's companions carried her off.

SĀNUMATĪ: His delusion puzzled me, but not his reawakening.

BUFFOON: If that's the case, you'll meet her again in good time.

KING: How?

BUFFOON: No mother or father can bear to see a daughter parted from her husband.

KING:

> Was it dream or illusion or mental confusion,
> or the last meager fruit of my former good deeds?
> It is gone now, and my heart's desires are
> like riverbanks crumbling of their own weight.

BUFFOON: Stop this! Isn't the ring evidence that an unexpected meeting is destined
to take place?

KING: [*Looking at the ring.*] I only pity it for falling from such a place.

> Ring, your punishment is proof
> that your face is as flawed as mine—
> you were placed in her lovely fingers,
> glowing with crimson nails, and you fell.

SĀNUMATĪ: The real pity would have been if it had fallen into some other hand.

BUFFOON: What prompted you to put the signet ring on her hand?

SĀNUMATĪ: I'm curious too.

KING: I did it when I left for the city. My love broke into tears and asked, "How long
will it be before my noble husband sends news to me?"

BUFFOON: Then? What then?

KING: Then I placed the ring on her finger with this promise:

> One by one, day after day,
> count each syllable of my name!
> At the end, a messenger will come
> to bring you to my palace.

But in my cruel delusion, I never kept my word.

SĀNUMATĪ: Fate broke their charming agreement!

BUFFOON: How did it get into the belly of the carp the fisherman was cutting up?

KING: While she was worshiping at the shrine of Indra's wife, it fell from her hand
into the Gaṅgā.[19]

BUFFOON: It's obvious now!

SĀNUMATĪ: And the king, doubtful of his marriage to Śakuntalā, a female ascetic, was
afraid to commit an act of injustice. But why should such passionate love need a
ring to be remembered?

KING: I must reproach the ring for what it's done.

BUFFOON: [*To himself.*] He's gone the way of all madmen . . .

KING:

> Why did you leave her delicate finger
> and sink into the deep river?

---

[19] the Gaṅgā: The river Ganges.

230   of course . . .

> A mindless ring can't recognize virtue,
> but why did I reject my love?

BUFFOON: [*To himself again.*] Why am I consumed by a craving for food?
KING: Oh ring! Have pity on a man whose hate is tormented because he abandoned his love without cause! Let him see her again!

[*Throwing the curtain aside, the maid* CATURIKĀ *enters, with the drawing board in her hand.*]
CATURIKĀ: Here's the picture you painted of the lady. [*She shows the drawing board.*]
BUFFOON: Dear friend, how well you've painted your feelings in this sweet scene. My eyes almost stumble over the hollows and hills.
SĀNUMATĪ: What skill the king has! I feel as if my friend were before me.
KING:

240
> The picture's imperfections are not hers,
> but this drawing does hint at her beauty.

SĀNUMATĪ: Such words reveal that suffering has increased his modesty as much as his love.
BUFFOON: Sir, I see three ladies now and they're all lovely to look at. Which is your Śakuntalā?
SĀNUMATĪ: Only a dim-witted fool like this wouldn't know such beauty!
KING: You guess which one!
BUFFOON: I guess Śakuntalā is the one you've drawn with flowers falling from her loosened locks of hair, with drops of sweat on her face, with her arms hanging
250   limp and tired as she stands at the side of a mango tree whose tender shoots are gleaming with the fresh water she poured. The other two are her friends.
KING: You are clever! Look at these signs of my passion!

> Smudges from my sweating fingers
> stain the edges of the picture
> and a tear fallen from my cheek
> has raised a wrinkle in the paint.

Caturikā, the scenery is only half-drawn. Go and bring my paints!
CATURIKĀ: Noble Mādhavya, hold the drawing board until I come back!
KING: I'll hold it myself.   [*He takes it, the maid exits.*]

260
> I rejected my love when she came to me,
> and how I worship her in a painted image—
> having passed by a river full of water,
> I'm longing now for an empty mirage.

BUFFOON: [*To himself.*] He's too far gone for a river now! He's looking for a mirage!
     [*Aloud.*] Sir, what else do you plan to draw here?
SĀNUMATĪ: He'll want to draw every place my friend loved.

KING:

> I'll draw the river Mālinī
> flowing through Himālaya's foothills
> where pairs of wild geese nest in the sand
270   and deer recline on both riverbanks,
> where a doe is rubbing her left eye
> on the horn of a black buck antelope
> under a tree whose branches
> have bark dresses hanging to dry.

BUFFOON: [*To himself.*] Next he'll fill the drawing board with mobs of ascetics wearing long grassy beards.

KING: Dear friend, I've forgotten to draw an ornament that Śakuntalā wore.

BUFFOON: What is it?

SĀNUMATĪ: It will suit her forest life and her tender beauty.

KING:

280   I haven't drawn the mimosa flower on her ear,
> its filaments resting on her cheek,
> or the necklace of tender lotus stalks,
> lying on her breasts like autumn moonbeams.

BUFFOON: But why does the lady cover her face with her red lotus-bud fingertips and
stand trembling in fear? [*Looking closely.*] That son-of-a-bee who steals nectar
from flowers is attacking her face.

KING: Drive the impudent rogue away!

BUFFOON: You have the power to punish criminals. You drive him off!

KING: All right! Bee, favored guest of the flowering vines, why do you frustrate your-
290   self by flying here?

> A female bee waits on a flower,
> thirsting for your love—
> she refuses to drink
> the sweet nectar without you.

SĀNUMATĪ: How gallantly he's driving him away!

BUFFOON: When you try to drive it away, this creature becomes vicious.

KING: Why don't you stop when I command you?

> Bee, if you touch the lips of my love
> that lure you like a young tree's virgin buds,
300   lips I gently kissed in festivals of love,
> I'll hold you captive in a lotus flower cage.

BUFFOON: Why isn't he afraid of your harsh punishment? [*Laughing, he speaks to
himself.*] He's gone crazy and I'll be the same if I go on talking like this. [*Aloud.*]
But sir, it's just a picture!

KING: A picture? How can that be?

SĀNUMATĪ: When I couldn't tell whether it was painted, how could he realize he was looking at a picture?

KING: Dear friend, are you envious of me?

> My heart's affection made me feel
> the joy of seeing her—
> but you reminded me again
> that my love is only a picture.

[*He wipes away a tear.*]

SĀNUMATĪ: The effects of her absence make him quarrelsome.

KING: Dear friend, why do I suffer this endless pain?

> Sleepless nights prevent our meeting in dreams;
> her image in a picture is ruined by my tears.

SĀNUMATĪ: You have clearly atoned for the suffering your rejection caused Śakuntalā.

CATURIKĀ: [*Entering.*] Victory my lord! I found the paint box and started back right away . . . but I met Queen Vasumatī with her maid Taralikā on the path and she grabbed the box from my hand, saying, "I'll bring it to the noble lord myself!"

BUFFOON: You were lucky to get away!

CATURIKĀ: The queen's shawl got caught on a tree. While Taralikā was freeing it, I made my escape.

KING: Dear friend, the queen's pride can quickly turn to anger. Save this picture!

BUFFOON: You should say, "Save yourself!" [*Taking the picture, he stands up.*] If you escape the woman's deadly poison, then send word to me in the Palace of the Clouds.　　　　　　　　　　　　　　　　　　　　　　[*He exits hastily.*]

SĀNUMATĪ: Even though another woman has taken his heart and he feels indifferent to the queen, he treats her with respect.

DOORKEEPER: [*Entering with a letter in her hand.*] Victory, king!

KING: Vetravatī, did you meet the queen on the way?

DOORKEEPER: I did, but when she saw the letter in my hand, she turned back.

KING: She knows that this is official and would not interrupt my work.

DOORKEEPER: King, the minister requests that you examine the contents of this letter. He said that the enormous job of reckoning the revenue in this one citizen's case had taken all his time.

KING: Show me the letter! [*The girl hands it to him and he reads barely aloud.*] What is this? "A wealthy merchant sea captain named Dhanamitra has been lost in a shipwreck and the laws say that since the brave man was childless, his accumulated wealth all goes to the king." It's terrible to be childless! A man of such wealth probably had several wives. We must find out if any one of his wives is pregnant!

DOORKEEPER: King, it's said that one of his wives, the daughter of a merchant of Ayodhyā, has performed the rite to ensure the birth of a son.[20]

---

[20] **the rite . . . a son:** A rite (*pumsavana*) performed in the third month of pregnancy.

KING: The child in her womb surely deserves his parental wealth. Go! Report this to
my minister!

DOORKEEPER: As the king commands! [*She starts to go.*]

KING: Come here a moment!

DOORKEEPER: I am here.

350 KING: Is it his offspring or not?

> When his subjects lose a kinsman,
> Duṣyanta will preserve the estates—
> unless there is some crime.
> Let this be proclaimed.

DOORKEEPER: It shall be proclaimed loudly. [*She exits; reenters.*] The king's order will
be as welcome as rain in the right season.

KING: [*Sighing long and deeply.*] Families without offspring whose lines of succession
are cut off lose their wealth to strangers when the last male heir dies. When I die,
this will happen to the wealth of the Puru dynasty.

360 DOORKEEPER: Heaven forbid such a fate!

KING: I curse myself for despising the treasure I was offered.

SĀNUMATĪ: He surely has my friend in mind when he blames himself.

KING:

> I abandoned my lawful wife, the holy ground
> where I myself planted my family's glory,
> like earth sown with seed at the right time,
> ready to bear rich fruit in season.

SĀNUMATĪ: But your family's line will not be broken.

CATURIKĀ: [*In a stage whisper.*] The king is upset by the story of the merchant. Go
and bring noble Mādhavya from the Palace of the Clouds to console him!

370 DOORKEEPER: A good idea!

[*She exits.*]

KING: Duṣyanta's ancestors are imperiled.

> Our fathers drink the yearly libation
> mixed with my childless tears,
> knowing that there is no other son
> to offer the sacred funeral waters.

[*He falls into a faint.*]

CATURIKĀ: [*Looking at the bewildered* KING.] Calm yourself, my lord!

SĀNUMATĪ: Though a light shines, his separation from Śakuntalā keeps him in a state
of dark depression. I could make him happy now, but I've heard Indra's consort
consoling Śakuntalā with the news that the gods are hungry for their share of

380 the ancestral oblations and will soon conspire to have her husband welcome his
lawful wife. I'll have to wait for the auspicious time, but meanwhile I'll cheer my
friend by reporting his condition.

[*She exits, flying into the air.*]

VOICE OFFSTAGE: Help! Brahman-murder!

KING: [*Regaining consciousness, listening.*] Is it Mādhavya's cry of pain? Who's there?

DOORKEEPER: King, your friend is in danger. Help him!

KING: Who dares to threaten him?

DOORKEEPER: Some invisible spirit seized him and dragged him to the roof of the Palace of the Clouds.

KING: [*Getting up.*] Not this! Even my house is haunted by spirits.

390   When I don't even recognize
the blunders I commit every day,
how can I keep track
of where my subjects stray?

VOICE OFFSTAGE: Dear friend! Help! Help!

KING: [*Breaking into a run.*] Friend, don't be afraid! I'm coming!

VOICE OFFSTAGE: [*Repeating the call for help.*] Why shouldn't I be afraid? Someone is trying to split my neck in three, like a stalk of sugar cane.

KING: [*Casting a glance.*] Quickly, my bow!

BOW-BEARER: [*Entering with a bow in hand.*] Here are your bow and quiver.

[*The* KING *takes his bow and arrows.*]

VOICE OFFSTAGE:

400   I'll kill you as a tiger kills struggling prey!
I'll drink fresh blood from your tender neck!
Take refuge now in the bow Duṣyanta lifts
to calm the fears of the oppressed!

KING: [*Angrily.*] How dare you abuse my name? Stop, carrion-eater! Or you will not live! [*He strings his bow.*] Vetravatī, lead the way to the stairs!

DOORKEEPER: This way, king.

[*All move forward in haste.*]

KING: [*Searching around.*] There is no one here!

VOICE OFFSTAGE: Help! Help! I see you. Don't you see me? I'm like a mouse caught by a cat! My life is hopeless!

410   KING: Don't count on your powers of invisibility! My magical arrows will find you. I aim this arrow:

It will strike its doomed target
and spare the brahman it must save —
a wild goose can extract the milk
and leave the water untouched.

[*He aims the arrow. Then Indra's charioteer* MĀTALI *enters, having released the* BUFFOON.]

MĀTALI: King!

Indra sets demons as your targets;
draw your bow against them!

Send friends gracious glances
420   rather than deadly arrows!

KING: [*Withdrawing his arrow.*] Mātali, welcome to great Indra's charioteer!

BUFFOON: [*Entering.*] He tried to slaughter me like a sacrificial beast and this king is greeting him with honors!

MĀTALI: [*Smiling.*] Your Majesty, hear why Indra has sent me to you!

KING: I am all attention.

MĀTALI: There is an army of demons descended from one-hundred-headed Kāla-nemi, known to be invincible . . .

KING: I have already heard it from Nārada, the gods' messenger.

MĀTALI:

He is invulnerable to your friend Indra,
430   so you are appointed to lead the charge—
the moon dispels the darkness of night
since the sun cannot drive it out.

Take your weapon, mount Indra's chariot, and prepare for victory!

KING: Indra favors me with this honor. But why did you attack Mādhavya?

MĀTALI: I'll tell you! From the signs of anguish Your Majesty showed, I knew that you were despondent. I attacked him to arouse your anger.

A fire blazes when fuel is added;
a cobra provoked raises its hood—
men can regain lost courage
440   if their emotions are aroused.

KING: [*In a stage whisper.*] Dear friend, I cannot disobey a command from the lord of heaven. Inform my minister Piśuna of this and tell him this for me:

Concentrate your mind on guarding my subjects!
My bow is strung to accomplish other work.

BUFFOON: Whatever you command!

[*He exits.*]

MĀTALI: Mount the chariot, Your Majesty!

[*The* KING *mimes mounting the chariot; all exit.*]

ACT VII

[*The* KING *enters with* MĀTALI *by the skyway, mounted on a chariot.*]

KING: Mātali, though I carried out his command, I feel unworthy of the honors Indra gave me.

MĀTALI: [*Smiling.*] Your Majesty, neither of you seems satisfied.

You belittle the aid you gave Indra
in face of the honors he conferred,
and he, amazed by your heroic acts,
deems his hospitality too slight.

KING: No, not so! When I was taking leave, he honored me beyond my heart's desire and shared his throne with me in the presence of the gods:

> Indra gave me a garland of coral flowers
> tinged with sandalpowder from his chest,
> while he smiled at his son Jayanta,
> who stood there barely hiding his envy.

MĀTALI: Don't you deserve whatever you want from Indra?

> Indra's heaven of pleasures has twice
> been saved by rooting out thorny demons—
> your smooth-jointed arrows have now done
> what Viṣṇu once did with his lion claws.[21]

KING: Here too Indra's might deserves the praise.

> When servants succeed in great tasks,
> they act in hope of their master's praise—
> would dawn scatter the darkness
> if he were not the sun's own charioteer?

MĀTALI: This attitude suits you well! [*He moves a little distance.*] Look over there, Your Majesty! See how your own glorious fame has reached the vault of heaven!

> Celestial artists are drawing your exploits
> on leaves of the wish-granting creeper[22]
> with colors of the nymphs' cosmetic paints,
> and bards are moved to sing of you in ballads.

KING: Mātali, in my desire to do battle with the demons, I did not notice the path we took to heaven as we climbed through the sky yesterday. Which course of the winds are we traveling?

MĀTALI:

> They call this path of the wind Parivaha—
> freed from darkness by Viṣṇu's second stride,
> it bears the Gaṅgā's three celestial streams
> and turns stars in orbit, dividing their rays.

KING: Mātali, this is why my soul, my senses, and my heart feel calm. [*He looks at the chariot wheels.*] We've descended to the level of the clouds.

MĀTALI: How do you know?

---

[21] **what Viṣṇu . . . lion claws:** Appearing as Narsimha, half man and half lion, Vishnu killed the demon Hiranyakashyap who was threatening to destroy the world.

[22] **the wish-granting creeper:** The *kalpalata* vine or kalpa tree symbolizes prosperity and is supposed to fulfill all wishes and desires.

KING:

40
    Crested cuckoos fly between the spokes,
    lightning flashes glint off the horses' coats,
    and a fine mist wets your chariot's wheels—
    all signs that we go over rain-filled clouds.

MĀTALI: In a moment you'll be back in your own domain, Your Majesty.

KING: [*Looking down.*] Our speeding chariot makes the mortal world appear fantastic. Look!

    Mountain peaks emerge as the earth descends,
    branches spread up from a sea of leaves,
    fine lines become great rivers to behold—
50   the world seems to hurtle toward me.

MĀTALI: You observe well! [*He looks with great reverence.*] The beauty of earth is sublime.

KING: Mātali, what mountain do I see stretching into the eastern and western seas, rippled with streams of liquid gold, like a gateway of twilight clouds?

MĀTALI: Your Majesty, it is called the "Golden Peak," the mountain of the demigods, a place where austerities are practiced to perfection.

    Mārīca, the descendant of Brahmā,
    a father of both demons and gods,
    lives the life of an ascetic here
60   in the company of Aditi, his wife.

KING: One must not ignore good fortune! I shall perform the rite of circumambulating the sage.

MĀTALI: An excellent idea!

[*The two mime descending.*]
KING: [*Smiling.*]

    The chariot wheels make no sound,
    they raise no clouds of dust,
    they touch the ground unhindered—
    nothing marks the chariot's descent.

MĀTALI: It is because of the extraordinary power that you and Indra both possess.

KING: Mātali, where is Mārīca's hermitage?

MĀTALI: [*Pointing with his hand.*]

70
    Where the sage stands staring at the sun,
    as immobile as the trunk of a tree,
    his body half-buried in an ant hill,
    with a snake skin on his chest,
    his throat pricked by a necklace
    of withered thorny vines,

wearing a coil of long matted hair
filled with nests of śakunta birds.

KING: I do homage to the sage for his severe austerity.

MĀTALI: [*Pulling hard on the chariot reins.*] Great king, let us enter Mārīca's her-
80　　mitage, where Aditi nurtures the celestial coral trees.

KING: This tranquil place surpasses heaven. I feel as if I'm bathing in a lake of nectar.

MĀTALI: [*Stopping the chariot.*] Dismount, Your Majesty!

KING: [*Dismounting.*] Mātali, what about you?

MĀTALI: I have stopped the chariot. I'll dismount too. [*He does so.*] This way, Your
Majesty! [*He walks around.*] You can see the grounds of the ascetics' grove ahead.

KING: I am amazed!

> In this forest of wish-fulfilling trees
> ascetics live on only the air they breathe
> and perform their ritual ablutions
90　　in water colored by golden lotus pollen.
> They sit in trance on jeweled marble slabs
> and stay chaste among celestial nymphs,
> practicing austerities in the place
> that others seek to win by penances.

MĀTALI: Great men always aspire to rare heights! [*He walks around, calling aloud.*] O
venerable Śākalya, what is the sage Mārīca doing now? What do you say? In
response to Aditi's question about the duties of a devoted wife, he is talking in a
gathering of great sages' wives.

KING: [*Listening.*] We must wait our turn.

100　MĀTALI: [*Looking at the* KING.] Your Majesty, rest at the foot of this aśoka tree. Meanwhile, I'll look for a chance to announce you to Indra's father.

KING: As you advise . . . [*He stops.*]

MĀTALI: Your Majesty, I'll attend to this.　　　　　　　　　　　　　　　[*He exits.*]

KING: [*Indicating he feels an omen.*]

> I have no hope for my desire.
> Why does my arm throb in vain?
> Once good fortune is lost,
> it becomes constant pain.

VOICE OFFSTAGE: Don't be so wild! Why is his nature so stubborn?

KING: [*Listening.*] Unruly conduct is out of place here. Whom are they reprimand-
110　　ing? [*Looking toward the sound, surprised.*] Who is this child, guarded by two
female ascetics? A boy who acts more like a man.

> He has dragged this lion cub
> from its mother's half-full teat
> to play with it, and with his hand
> he violently tugs its mane.

[*The* BOY *enters as described, with two female ascetics.*]

BOY: Open your mouth, lion! I want to count your teeth!

FIRST ASCETIC: Nasty boy, why do you torture creatures we love like our children? You're getting too headstrong! The sages gave you the right name when they called you "Sarvadamana, Tamer-of-everything."

120 KING: Why is my heart drawn to this child, as if he were my own flesh? I don't have a son. That is why I feel tender toward him . . .

SECOND ASCETIC: The lioness will maul you if you don't let go of her cub!

BOY: [*Smiling.*] Oh, I'm scared to death! [*Pouting.*]

KING:

> This child appears to be
> the seed of hidden glory,
> like a spark of fire
> awaiting fuel to burn.

FIRST ASCETIC: Child, let go of the lion cub and I'll give you another toy!

BOY: Where is it? Give it to me! [*He reaches out his hand.*]

130 KING: Why does he bear the mark of a king who turns the wheel of empire?

> A hand with fine webs connecting the fingers
> opens as he reaches for the object greedily,
> like a single lotus with faint inner petals
> spread open in the red glow of early dawn.

SECOND ASCETIC: Suvratā, you can't stop him with words! The sage Mārkaṇḍeya's son left a brightly painted clay bird in my hut. Get it for him!

FIRST ASCETIC: I will!   [*She exits.*]

BOY: But until it comes I'll play with this cub.

KING: I am attracted to this pampered boy . . .

140
> Lucky are fathers whose laps give refuge
> to the muddy limbs of adoring little sons
> when childish smiles show budding teeth
> and jumbled sounds make charming words.

SECOND ASCETIC: Well, he ignores me. [*She looks back.*] Is one of the sage's sons here? [*Looking at the* KING.] Sir, please come here! Make him loosen his grip and let go of the lion cub! He's tormenting it in his cruel child's play.

KING: [*Approaching the* BOY, *smiling.*] Stop! You're a great sage's son!

> When self-control is your duty by birth,
> why do you violate the sanctuary laws
150 > and ruin the animals' peaceful life,
> like a young black snake in a sandal tree?

SECOND ASCETIC: Sir, he's not a sage's son.

KING: His actions and his looks confirm it. I based my false assumption on his presence in this place. [*He does what she asked; responding to the* BOY's *touch, he speaks to himself.*]

> Even my limbs feel delighted
> from the touch of a stranger's son —
> the father at whose side he grew
> must feel pure joy in his heart.

SECOND ASCETIC: [*Examining them both.*] It's amazing! Amazing!

160 KING: What is it, madam?

SECOND ASCETIC: This boy looks surprisingly like you. He doesn't even know you, and he's acting naturally.

KING: [*Fondling the child.*] If he's not the son of an ascetic, what lineage does he belong to?

SECOND ASCETIC: The family of Puru.

KING: [*To himself.*] What? His ancestry is the same as mine . . . so this lady thinks he resembles me. The family vow of Puru's descendants is to spend their last days in the forest.

> As world protectors they first choose
170 > palaces filled with sensuous pleasures,
> but later, their homes are under trees
> and one wife shares the ascetic vows.

[*Aloud.*] But mortals cannot enter this realm on their own.

SECOND ASCETIC: You're right, sir. His mother is a nymph's child. She gave birth to him here in the hermitage of Mārīca.

KING: [*In a stage whisper.*] Here is a second ground for hope! [*Aloud.*] What famed royal sage claims her as his wife?

SECOND ASCETIC: Who would even think of speaking the name of a man who rejected his lawful wife?

180 KING: [*To himself.*] Perhaps this story points to me. What if I ask the name of the boy's mother? No, it is wrong to ask about another man's wife.

FIRST ASCETIC: [*Returning with a clay bird in her hand.*] Look, Sarvadamana, a śakunta! Look! Isn't it lovely?

BOY: Where's my mother?

BOTH ASCETICS: He's tricked by the similarity of names.[23] He wants his mother.

SECOND ASCETIC: Child, she told you to look at the lovely clay śakunta bird.

KING: [*To himself.*] What? Is his mother's name Śakuntalā? But names can be the same. Even a name is a mirage . . . a false hope to herald despair.

BOY: I like this bird! [*He picks up the toy.*]

190 FIRST ASCETIC: [*Looking frantically.*] Oh, I don't see the amulet-box on his wrist!

KING: Don't be alarmed! It broke off while he was tussling with the lion cub. [*He goes to pick it up.*]

BOTH ASCETICS: Don't touch it! Oh, he's already picked it up! [*With their hands on their chests, they stare at each other in amazement.*]

KING: Why did you warn me against it?

---

[23] **the similarity of names:** The boy confuses the word *śakunta* (bird) with *Śakuntalā* (woman of birds).

FIRST ASCETIC: It contains the magical herb called Aparājitā,[24] honored sir. Mārīca gave it to him at his birth ceremony. He said that if it fell to the ground no one but his parents or himself could pick it up.

KING: And if someone else does pick it up?

FIRST ASCETIC: Then it turns into a snake and strikes.

KING: Have you two seen it so transformed?

200   BOTH ASCETICS: Many times.

KING: [*To himself, joyfully.*] Why not rejoice in the fulfillment of my heart's desire? [*He embraces the child.*]

SECOND ASCETIC: Suvratā, come, let's tell Śakuntalā that her penances are over.

[*Both ascetics exit.*]

BOY: Let me go! I want my mother!

KING: Son, you will greet your mother with me.

BOY: My father is Duṣyanta, not you!

KING: This contradiction confirms the truth.

[ŚAKUNTALĀ *enters, wearing the single braid of a woman in mourning.*]

ŚAKUNTALĀ: Even though Sarvadamana's amulet kept its natural form instead of changing into a snake, I can't hope that my destiny will be fulfilled. But maybe what my friend Sānumatī reports is right.

210   KING: [*Looking at* ŚAKUNTALĀ.] It is Śakuntalā!

> Wearing dusty gray garments,
> her face gaunt from penances,
> her bare braid[25] hanging down —
> she bears with perfect virtue
> the trial of long separation
> my cruelty forced on her.

ŚAKUNTALĀ: [*Seeing the* KING *pale with suffering.*] He doesn't resemble my noble husband. Whose touch defiles my son when the amulet is protecting him?

BOY: [*Going to his mother.*] Mother, who is this stranger who calls me "son"?

220   KING: My dear, I see that you recognize me now. Even my cruelty to you is transformed by your grace.

ŚAKUNTALĀ: [*To herself.*] Heart, be consoled! My cruel fate has finally taken pity on me. It is my noble husband!

KING:

> Memory chanced to break my dark delusion
> and you stand before me in beauty,
> like the moon's wife Rohiṇī
> as she rejoins her lord after an eclipse.

---

[24] **Aparājitā:** An herb whose name means invincible.

[25] **bare braid:** A sign that a woman is separated from her lover.

ŚAKUNTALĀ: Victory to my noble husband! Vic . . . [*She stops when the word is half-spoken, her throat choked with tears.*]

KING: Beautiful Śakuntalā,

230
    Even choked by your tears,
    the word "victory" is my triumph
    on your bare pouting lips,
    pale-red flowers of your face.

BOY: Mother, who is he?

ŚAKUNTALĀ: Child, ask the powers of fate!

KING: [*Falling at* ŚAKUNTALĀ'*s feet.*]

    May the pain of my rejection
    vanish from your heart;
    delusion clouded my weak mind
    and darkness obscured good fortune—
240
    a blind man tears off a garland,
    fearing the bite of a snake.

ŚAKUNTALĀ: Noble husband, rise! Some crime I had committed in a former life surely came to fruit and made my kind husband indifferent to me.

[*The* KING *rises.*]
    But how did my noble husband come to remember this woman who was doomed to pain?

KING: I shall tell you after I have removed the last barb of sorrow.

    In my delusion I once ignored
    a teardrop burning your lip—
    let me dry the tear on your lash
250
    to end the pain of remorse!

[*He does so.*]

ŚAKUNTALĀ: [*Seeing the signet ring.*] My noble husband, this is the ring!

KING: I regained my memory when the ring was recovered.

ŚAKUNTALĀ: When it was lost, I tried in vain to convince my noble husband who I was.

KING: Let the vine take back this flower as a sign of her union with spring.

ŚAKUNTALĀ: I don't trust it. Let my noble husband wear it!

[MĀTALI *enters.*]

MĀTALI: Good fortune! This meeting with your lawful wife and the sight of your son's face are reasons to rejoice.

KING: The sweet fruit of my desire! Mātali, didn't Indra know about all this?

260 MĀTALI: What is unknown to the gods? Come Your Majesty! The sage Mārīca grants you an audience.

KING: Śakuntalā, hold our son's hand! We shall go to see Mārīca together.

ŚAKUNTALĀ: I feel shy about appearing before my elders in my husband's company.

KING: But it is customary at a joyous time like this. Come! Come!

[*They all walk around. Then* MĀRĪCA *enters with* ADITI; *they sit.*]

MĀRĪCA: [*Looking at the* KING.]

> Aditi, this is king Duṣyanta,
> who leads Indra's armies in battle;
> his bow lets your son's thunderbolt
> lie ready with its tip unblunted.

ADITI: He bears himself with dignity.

270 MĀTALI: Your Majesty, the parents of the gods look at you with affection reserved for a son. Approach them!

KING: Mātali, the sages so describe this pair.

> Source of the sun's twelve potent forms,
> parents of Indra, who rules the triple world,
> birthplace of Viṣṇu's primordial form,
> sired by Brahmā's sons, Marīci and Dakṣa.

MĀTALI: Correct!

KING: [*Bowing.*] Indra's servant, Duṣyanta, bows to you both.

MĀRĪCA: My son, live long and protect the earth!

280 ADITI: My son, be an invincible warrior!

ŚAKUNTALĀ: I worship at your feet with my son.

MĀRĪCA:

> Child, with a husband like Indra
> and a son like his son Jayanta,
> you need no other blessing.
> Be like Indra's wife Paulomī!

ADITI: Child, may your husband honor you and may your child live long to give both families joy! Be seated!

[*All sit near* MĀRĪCA.]

MĀRĪCA: [*Pointing to each one.*]

> By the turn of fortune,
> virtuous Śakuntalā, her noble son,
290 > and the king are reunited —
> faith and wealth with order.

KING: Sir, first came the success of my hopes, then the sight of you. Your kindness is unparalleled.

> First flowers appear, then fruits,
> first clouds rise, then rain falls,

        but here the chain of events is reversed —
        first came success, then your blessing.

MĀTALI: This is the way the creator gods give blessings.

KING: Sir, I married your charge by secret marriage rites. When her relatives brought
300   her to me after some time, my memory failed and I sinned against the sage
    Kaṇva, your kinsman. When I saw the ring, I remembered that I had married his
    daughter. This is all so strange!

        Like one who doubts the existence
        of an elephant who walks in front of him
        but feels convinced by seeing footprints,
        my mind has taken strange turns.

MĀRĪCA: My son, you need not take the blame. Even your delusion has another
    cause. Listen!

KING: I am attentive.

310 MĀRĪCA: When Menakā took her bewildered daughter from the steps of the nymph's
    shrine and brought her to my wife, I knew through meditation that you had
    rejected this girl as your lawful wife because of Durvāsas' curse, and that the
    curse would end when you saw the ring.

KING: [*Sighing.*] So I am freed of blame.

ŚAKUNTALĀ: [*To herself.*] And I am happy to learn that I wasn't rejected by my hus-
    band without cause. But I don't remember being cursed. Maybe the empty heart
    of love's separation made me deaf to the curse . . . my friends did warn me to
    show the ring to my husband . . .

MĀRĪCA: My child, I have told you the truth. Don't be angry with your husband!

320   You were rejected when the curse
        that clouded memory made him cruel,
        but now darkness is lifted
        and your power is restored —
        a shadow has no shape
        in a badly tarnished mirror,
        but when the surface is clean
        it can easily be seen.

KING: Sir, here is the glory of my family! [*He takes the child by the hand.*]

MĀRĪCA: Know that he is destined to turn the wheel of your empire!

330   His chariot will smoothly cross
        the ocean's rough waves
        and as a mighty warrior
        he will conquer the seven continents.
        Here he is called Sarvadamana,
        Tamer-of-everything;

> later when his burden is the world,
> men will call him Bharata, Sustainer.[26]

KING: Since you performed his birth ceremonies, we can hope for all this.

ADITI: Sir, let Kaṇva be told that his daughter's hopes have been fulfilled. Menakā, who loves her daughter, is here in attendance.

ŚAKUNTALĀ: [*To herself.*] The lady expresses my own desire.

MĀRĪCA: He knows everything already through the power of his austerity.

KING: This is why the sage was not angry at me.

MĀRĪCA: Still, I want to hear his response to this joyful reunion. Who is there?

DISCIPLE: [*Entering.*] Sir, it is I.

MĀRĪCA: Gālava, fly through the sky and report the joyous reunion to Kaṇva in my own words: "The curse is ended. Śakuntalā and her son are embraced by Duṣyanta now that his memory is restored."

DISCIPLE: As you command, sir!   [*He exits.*]

MĀRĪCA: My son, mount your friend Indra's chariot with your wife and son and return to your royal capital!

KING: As you command, sir!

MĀRĪCA: My son, what other joy can I give you?

KING: There is no greater joy, but if you will:

> May the king serve nature's good!
> May priests honor the goddess of speech!
> And may Śiva's dazzling power
> destroy my cycle of rebirths![27]

[*All exit.*]

---

[26] **Bharata, Sustainer:** According to Indian mythical geography, the earth consists of seven islands surrounded by seven seas. The legendary Bharata, celebrated for his dharmic rule, was called the Sustainer. He created an empire of such great extent that all of India came to be called Bharata, or Bharatavarśa.

[27] **May the king . . . rebirths:** The traditional ending of all Sanskrit plays; in this verse the king calls for the blessings of the gods on himself and the universal order.

Poets of the Tang Dynasty

The Tang dynasty (618–907) is known as the golden age of Chinese classical poetry. It was a time of great fruition in Chinese culture brought about in part by the opening of China to outside cultural influences in dance, music, and architecture from central Asia, the steppe region, India, Persia, and Tibet as well as the Islamic world. The capital city of Chang'an (Ch'ang-an), with a population of nearly two million people, was one of the greatest cities in the world and boasted a rich cosmopolitanism. Located on the Wei River in Jingji (Shenshi) Province, Chang'an was a locus of trade from central Asia and a city bustling with merchants, travelers, and intellectuals representing various countries. Moreover, the Tang, particularly in the seventh century, was an era when Chinese rulers such as Xuanzong (Hsuan Tsung; 712–756) not only patronized poetry but were often distinguished poets themselves. Indeed, in Tang-dynasty China writing poetry was a pastime and means of entertainment for all educated people. Merchants and officials wrote poems in transacting their business; friends and lovers used poems to make their feelings known to each other; and Buddhist and Daoist monks wrote poems as part of their spiritual practices. Even popular courtesans were known for their songs as well as their charms.

Among the hundreds of conventional and imitative poets of the Tang dynasty, **Wang Wei** (c. 699–761), **Li Bai** (Li Po; 701–762), **Du Fu** (Tu Fu; 712–770), and **Bo Juyi** (Po Chü-i; 772–846) are standouts for their depth of feeling, stylistic innovation, clarity of expression, and originality. The work of these four poets has attained the status of world literature and spawned a legion of admirers, imitators, and translators that continues to grow in China and throughout the world today.

> The difference between T'ang poetry and the *Book of Poetry* is the difference between a carefully arranged flower twig in a vase, where every angle and curve is carefully studied, and the luxuriant growth of a wild garden.
>
> – LIN YU-TANG, critic, 1942

wahng-WAY; lee-BIGH

doo-FOO; boh-joo-EE

THE TANG DYNASTY AND ITS POETS

The Tang dynasty began after the murder of Yangdi (Yang Ti), the last of the Sui emperors, in 618, when the general Li Yuan succeeded him. Nine years later, the emperor Tang Taizong (T'ang T'ai-tsung; r. 626–49) took over the throne and proved to be a highly effective leader, securing and expanding China's borders, revising its system of laws, and bringing peace and prosperity to the land. Taizong and his successors, including his son Gaozong (Kao Tsung; r. 635–684), presided over a flourishing in the arts, particularly in sculpture and poetry. They strengthened the *CHIN-SHI* system[1] of civil service examinations in order to bring diverse talent from the population into the bureaucracy, and they founded a major center of learning, the Imperial Academy, in the increasingly cosmopolitan capital city. In 690 Gaozong's wife Wu Zetian (Wu Tse-t'ien; r. 684–705) proclaimed herself emperor. Under Empress Wu the writing of poetry became a required part of the new *chin-shi,* the gateway to all government positions. Spurred by the competitive atmosphere of these examinations, many students, scholars, and officials matched wits and talent in poetry contests.

Court Ladies, tenth century
Ladies of the court receive instructions in adornment in what is thought to be a Tang dynasty painted scroll. (British Museum)

---

[1] *chin-shi* **system:** First begun in the Sui dynasty (581–618 C.E.) under Yang Jian and formalized during the Tang era, the *chin-shi* system of civil service examinations brought bright and talented men from all over China into the government bureaucracy.

Female Musician, 619–906

Poetry and music permeated every aspect of Tang-dynasty society. In the booming capital city of Chang'an (Ch'ang-an), courtesans were as well versed in the musical arts as they were in other forms of artistic expression. (Werner Forman/Art Resource, NY)

After Wu's reign, Tang Xuanzong (r. 712–756), a poet and patron of the arts, presided for many years over a prosperous Chinese culture and society. It was under his reign that Wang Wei, Li Bai, and Du Fu wrote what many consider China's greatest poetry. But Xuanzong was eventually brought down, in part because of his relationship with the beautiful but scheming concubine Yang Guifei (Yang Kuei-fei; 719–756). Under the influence of Yang Guifei, the Turkish-born general An Lushan, whom Yang Guifei adopted as a son, led the An Lushan Rebellion of 755, seizing the eastern capital of Luoyang and declaring himself emperor. An Lushan was killed by his own men, and the rebellion was eventually put down. For her role in the intrigue, Yang Guifei was executed, and her story—that of a beautiful concubine who brings down an empire—became a favorite narrative of Chinese and Japanese writers, including Du Fu and Bo Juyi. After the rebellion, the central authority of the Tang emperor at Chang'an was weakened. Increased rivalry among landed families as well as peasant revolts and incursions along the borders further eroded the empire until it finally fell in 907. Du Fu and Bo Juyi record the decline of the Tang, an ending they observed with some bitterness and regret.

THE RISE OF BUDDHISM

In the early years of the Tang, Buddhism, which had been growing in China since the second century C.E., became increasingly influential, and Buddhist monasteries became important centers of learning and culture. Although a challenge to native Confucianism, a religious philosophy stressing duty to family and state, Buddhism often found common ground with Daoism (Taoism). Many Tang poets, some of whom were monks, were drawn to Buddhism's otherworldliness, its doctrine of the insubstantiality of worldly things, and its emphasis on enlightenment and salvation by means of disciplined practice and grace. None of the poets whose work is presented here, however, can be tied strictly to a particular sect or religious philosophy, though certain tendencies can be seen in their work. Wang Wei and Bo Juyi, for example, are most heavily influenced by Buddhism; Du Fu, by Confucianism; and Li Bai, by Daoism.

TANG POETRY AND POETICS

In Chinese, the word for poetry in general, *SHI*, means the natural expression or outward manifestation of intense feeling. In the words of "The Canon of Shun" in the *Book of History*,[2] "Poetry expresses in words the intent of the heart." In this context, expression of feeling transcends the private emotions of the writer, for when expressed in its purest form the "intent of the heart" corresponds to the dao,[3] or the underlying principle of nature that encompasses all being. For the poets of early China, the signs or patterns *(wen)* of calligraphic writing were reproductions of natural patterns such as the veins in leaves, the markings of birds, or the shapes of stones, themselves a revelation of the deeper, universal design of the dao. To write poetry, then, was to come to recognize the dao in oneself as it corresponded to the dao in nature and in the cosmos. The Han dynasty poet Lu Ji (261–303 C.E.) characterizes this process when he writes that the poet "traps heaven and earth / In the cage of form."

---

[2] *Book of History:* (*Xu Kin, Shu King,* or *Shang-shu*) An ancient collection of documents on history and politics written in prose and dating back to the early years of the Zhou dynasty (c. 1027–256 B.C.E.), if not before. It was one of the earliest works of history and a foundation for Confucian ideas.

[3] **the dao:** Translated as "the Way," *dao* (*Tao*) refers to the basic principle of order that underlies the cosmos in Daoist thought; it is said to be the origin of all things as well as the path to peace and salvation. For Laozi (Lao Tzu), the dao is unknowable and cannot be spoken; hence, it can only be intuited.

Tang-era poets drew from and made innovations to a variety of past poetic forms. The earliest forms of Chinese lyric poetry, *shi,* are found in the *Classic of Poetry (Shi jing),* a collection of court poems, folk songs, and ritual hymns dating to the eleventh century B.C.E. and compiled sometime in the seventh century B.C.E. These poems, of varying length, generally were written in four-character (four-syllable) lines whose every other line rhymed. During the Han dynasty (206 B.C.E.–220 C.E.), poets developed from this basic four-character line the five- to seven-syllable verse form known as *GUSHI* ("old style verse"), which in turn became the basis for later developments, including the *LUSHI* ("regulated verse"), a form originating in the Tang era. As perfected by the Tang poets, the *lushi* is a highly structured form of poetry consisting of eight lines of five or seven syllables and emphasizing aesthetic balance and order.

The *lushi,* however, was not the only form for the poets featured in the selections that follow. Wang Wei, Li Bai, Du Fu, and Bo Juyi wrote in a variety of poetic forms, including the *YUEFU,* or folk ballads, which evolved into literary ballads written in quatrains of five-character lines; and the *FU,* or "rhapsody," with lines of various metrical lengths. Li Bai, with his penchant for strong drink and his wild nature, preferred the freedom of the *yuefu* to the strict regimen of the *lushi,* a form more suited to the Confucian Du Fu. Li Bai, however, wrote *lushi* and *gushi* as well as *yuefu.* The *yuefu* form was also adapted by the Tang poets to criticize society and its politics. This "new ballad" or "new *yuefu*" was perfected by the second generation poet Bo Juyi, who used it to criticize the abuses he witnessed after the An Lushan Rebellion. Both Li Bai and Bo Juyi also experimented with the *ci (tz'u),* a lyrical form with varied line lengths modeled on songs introduced from central Asia. Until Li Bai and Bo Juyi, *ci* had been thought of as a low form of poetry.

A NOTE ON TRANSLATION

Selecting translations always vexes editors, but the difficulty of selection becomes particularly acute when it comes to poems translated into English from non-European languages such as Sanskrit, Chinese, or Japanese, whose sound structures, grammatical features, and systems of writing depart drastically from Western languages. Unlike English, the Chinese poetic language is paratactic. That is, in Chinese the relationships between words are not fixed by articles,

> Savor his poetry, and there is a painting in each poem; look carefully at his paintings, and each one contains a poem.
> – SU DONGPO, writer, eleventh century, on Wang Wei

linking words, and indicators of tense, agency, and number to the extent that they are in English. On the subject of translating Chinese, Yip Wai-lim gives the example of *sung-feng,* a common poetic phrase that literally means "pine-wind." Should the English translator render the phrase as "wind in the pine," "the wind in the pines," "the wind blowing through the pine trees," or "pine wind"? Transla-tors of even the shortest Chinese poem face endless decisions like this one as well as others that are more complex.

■ FURTHER RESEARCH

Anthologies and Commentary

Cooper, Arthur. *Li Po and Tu Fu.* 1973.

Hamill, Sam. *Crossing the Yellow River: Three Hundred Poems from the Chinese.* 2000.

Liu, Wu-chi, and Irving Yucheng Lo. *Sunflower Splendor: Three Thousand Years of Chinese Poetry.* 1975.

Owen, Stephen. *The Great Age of Chinese Poetry: The High Tang.* 1981.

Red Pine. *Poems of the Masters.* 2003.

Single Authors

Hawkes, David. *A Little Primer of Tu Fu.* 1967.

Hinton, David. *Selected Poems of Li Po.* 1996.

——. *Selected Poems of Po-Chu-i.* 1999.

——. *Selected Poems of Tu Fu.* 1989.

——. *Selected Poems of Wang Wei.* 2006.

Wagner, Marsha. *Wang Wei.* 1981.

Waley, Arthur. *The Life and Times of Po Chu-i.* 1949.

——. *The Poetry and Career of Li Po.* 1950.

Watson, Burton. *Po-Chu-i: Selected Poems.* 2000.

Yu, Pauline. *The Poetry of Wang Wei.* 1980.

Background/History

Chen, Kenneth. *The Chinese Transformation of Buddhism.* 1973.

Cheng, Francois. *Chinese Poetic Writing.* 1982.

Hightower, James, and Florence Chia-Ying Yeh. *Studies in Chinese Poetry.* 1988.

Liu, James. *The Art of Chinese Poetry.* 1962.

Owen, Stephen. *Traditional Chinese Poetry and Poetics: An Omen of the World.* 1985.

Yip, Wai-lim. *Chinese Poetry: Major Modes and Genres.* 1976.

Yu, Pauline. *The Reading of Imagery in the Chinese Poetic Tradition.* 1987.

■ PRONUNCIATION

Bo Juyi (Po Chü-i): boh-joo-EE
Du Fu (Tu Fu): doo-FOO
Li Bai (Li Po): lee-BIGH (lee POH)
Wang Wei: wahng-WAY

❧ WANG WEI

B. CHINA, C. 699–761

Wang Wei was born into an aristocratic family living in what is now the Province of Shanxi (Shansi). A gifted youth of great accomplishment in poetry, painting, and music, Wang Wei, when he was about sixteen, moved to the capital city of Chang'an (Ch'ang-an) where he was well received in the court. In 723 he passed the *chin-shi* civil service examination and began a career as a mid level official, serving as Assistant Secretary of Music in Chang'an before being transferred to the provinces after a minor infraction caused him to lose favor. After taking on the role of the poet in exile, a persona that Du Fu and Li Bai would also adopt, Wang Wei returned to city life briefly before purchasing an estate on the Wang River in the mountains south of Chang'an. Here Wang Wei began to cultivate in his poetry and painting the deep appreciation for and sensitivity to landscape and nature for which he is celebrated. Though he would return to the active life of Chang'an in 734 after the death of his wife, his estate on the Wang River served as a retreat for the poet for the rest of his life.

During his government service, Wang Wei was sent on diplomatic missions to various regions of China. When the An Lushan Rebellion took place in 755, Wang Wei was taken by the rebels, imprisoned, and eventually forced to work for them. After the rebellion was quashed by imperial forces, Wang Wei was at first accused of collaboration with the rebels. But the intervention of his brother and two poems displaying his loyalty to Emperor Xuanzong that he had written while with the rebels saved Wang Wei from execution. Restored to favor in the court, Wang Wei was appointed Right Assistant Director of the Council of State in 759, two years before he died.

Group of Musicians, 618–906 C.E.

Music was an integral part of Tang-dynasty culture. Wang Wei was an accomplished musician as well as an outstanding poet. (Earthenware. Israel Museum)

Wang Wei possessed little desire for worldly success. As he grew older, he preferred the quiet serenity of his home in the mountains to the noise of the bustling capital, the clear light of the moon to the flickering lanterns of the palace. The Buddhist character of his poetry has been aptly described by Pauline Yu who observes that it lies not in doctrinal statements but in attitude: "His contemplative, dispassionate observations of the sensory world affirm its beauty at the same time as they call its ultimate reality into question, by emphasizing its vagueness, relativity, and 'emptiness.'" A poet with a highly visual sensibility, Wang Wei is famous for his depiction of landscape, which he blends with a consciousness of the illusory nature of worldly things. Moving between the concrete and the abstract, between the perceiving subject and the object, Wang Wei disturbs the fixed landscape with an awareness of mutability and the relativity of sensuous experience. The empty mountains, endless spaces, and mists without resting places of his poetry suggest the transience of human experience in contrast to the constant movement and cycles of seasonal change in nature. Thus, Wang Wei's mountains and rivers are often elusive, intimating a purer world just beyond what can be grasped by the five senses.

✎ Hermitage at Chung-nan Mountain

Translated by Sam Hamill

Growing older, I grow into the Tao:[1]
now I make my home in southern mountains,

and go there on a whim to wander alone.
But even in all this splendor, things remain empty.[2]

I climb to the headwaters
where clouds rise up from emptiness.

If I chance to meet another hermit in the woods,
we talk and laugh and never even think of home.

---

[1] **Tao:** "The Way," or dao, here referring to the path toward enlightenment accessed through Buddhist practices and teachings.

[2] **But . . . things remain empty:** This line suggests the transcendence of material distinctions and differences through an intuition of the underlying unity of all things.

✂ Crossing the Yellow River

Translated by Sam Hamill

A little boat on the great river
whose waves reach the end of the sky—

suddenly a great city, ten thousand
houses dividing sky from wave.

Between the towns there are
hemp and mulberry trees in the wilds.

Look back on the old country:
wide waters; clouds; and rising mist.

✂ Li Bai
b. *China, 701–762*

Li Bai (Li Po) ranks with Du Fu as one of the greatest poets of the celebrated golden Tang era in China. Known in Japan as the great master Rihaku, Li Bai exerted a profound influence on Chinese and Japanese literature, and through the translations of Ezra Pound and Arthur Waley, on to American poets of the Beat generation. Because of his deep feeling for nature, his brash disregard for convention, and his love of the common people, Li Bai has also been compared to European Romantic poets such as Goethe and Wordsworth. As in the work of those poets, a melancholy strain of loss and regret tempers even Li Bai's most celebratory poems, and scenes of conviviality and union with nature are often revisited as memories only.

The Itinerant Poet.   Li Bai was born, probably in Chinese Turkestan west of Kansu, in 701, just before the end of the reign of Empress Wu. He seems to have spent his childhood in Sichuan, where he studied the Confucian classics and practiced swordsmanship, poetry, and other gentlemanly arts. In his mid-twenties he left home to travel throughout northern and central China, taking advantage of the improved roads and bridges and greater assurance of safety made possible by the Tang dynasty. Li Bai's penchant for traveling continued throughout his life; his numerous poems thanking friends for their hospitality and the number of places mentioned in his poetry testify to his love of being on the road. Sometimes called the Old Wine Genius, Li Bai lost the first of his four wives because he spent too much time with a group of fellow poets who came to be called the Six Idlers of the Bamboo Valley.

Li Bai, 1510–1551

The celebrated poet Li Bai (Li Po) is shown here in a garden with friends and admirers in a sixteenth-century Chinese painting. (The Art Archive / Private Collection, Paris / Dagli Orti)

In his extensive travels, Li Bai had occasion to meet and befriend many important people, among them the Daoist priests Wu Yun and Hou Jizhang (Ho Chi-chang)—from whom Li Bai received the name "Banished Immortal"—as well as the emperor himself, Xuanzong, who granted Li Bai patronage and appointed him to the prestigious Han Lin Academy. In the service of Xuanzong, Li Bai was commissioned to write various commemorative poems, tributes, and even edicts, all in verse. In the short time he was in the service of the court (742–44), Li Bai amplified his reputation for drunkenness, giving rise to numerous stories about his life. Du Fu, who wrote a number of poems praising and jesting with his friendly rival, names Li Bai among "Eight Immortals of the Wine Cup," in which he quips, "Does his Majesty know that his humble servant is a drunken angel?"

When in 755 the revolt of An Lushan forced the emperor to flee the capital, Li Bai, who was in the service of one of the emperor's sons, was arrested and sentenced to death. His life was spared by the minister of war, and Li Bai was banished to southwestern China. Eventually an amnesty enabled him to return to the region of the lower Yangtze, where he died in 762. Legend has it that Li Bai drowned in a drunken stupor, falling off a boat as he tried to embrace the moon reflected in the water, but it may well be that he died of pneumonia or another natural cause.

Although he studied Daoism, Li Bai celebrated—often with a pensive, melancholy sense of regret and longing—wine, romance, love, and friendship in his work. With its author's high-spirited rebellion against poetic and social conventions and his emphasis on worldly indulgence, Li Bai's poetry stood in direct opposition to the rigid hierarchy of the Confucian tradition in China. The boastful, reckless, and iconoclastic quality of his poetry has made Li Bai one of China's best-known poets and earned for him from time to time the disfavor of state-commissioned *literati*—Confucianist and Communist—interested in enforcing conformity.

∾ Going to Visit Tai-T'ien Mountain's Master[1] of the Way without Finding Him

Translated by David Hinton

A dog barks among the sounds of water.
Dew stains peach blossoms. In forests,

I sight a few deer, then at the creek,
hear nothing of midday temple bells.

Wild bamboo parts blue haze. A stream
hangs in flight beneath emerald peaks.

No one knows where you've gone. Still,
for rest, I've found two or three pines.

---

[1] **Tai-t'ien Mountain's Master:** Sacred to Daoists, this mountain is where the legendary Liu Chen (Liu Ch'en) was said to have met with divine maidens.

∾ Drinking Alone beneath the Moon

Translated by David Hinton

1

Among the blossoms, a single jar of wine.
No one else here, I ladle it out myself.

Raising my cup, I toast the bright moon,
and facing my shadow makes friends three,

though moon has never understood wine,
and shadow only trails along behind me.

Kindred a moment with moon and shadow,
I've found a joy that must infuse spring:

10   I sing, and moon rocks back and forth;
I dance, and shadow tumbles into pieces.

Sober, we're together and happy. Drunk,
we scatter away into our own directions:

intimates forever, we'll wander carefree
and meet again in Star River[1] distances.

2

Surely, if heaven didn't love wine,
there would be no Wine Star in heaven,

and if earth didn't love wine, surely
there would be no Wine Spring on earth.

Heaven and earth have always loved wine,
20   so how could loving wine shame heaven?

I hear clear wine called enlightenment,
and they say murky wine is like wisdom:

once you drink enlightenment and wisdom,
why go searching for gods and immortals?

Three cups and I've plumbed the great Way,[2]
a jarful and I've merged with occurrence

appearing of itself. Wine's view is lived:
you can't preach doctrine to the sober.

3

It's April in Ch'ang-an, these thousand
30   blossoms making a brocade of daylight.

Who can bear spring's lonely sorrows, who
face it without wine? It's the only way.

---

[1] **Star River:** The Milky Way. It was thought that the great rivers of China formed a cyclic pattern: flowing east into the sea, then mounting to the sky to become the Star River, then returning to earth in the west at the rivers' source.

[2] **the great Way:** The dao (Tao).

Success or failure, life long or short:
our fate's given by Changemaker at birth.

But a single cup evens out life and death,
our ten thousand concerns unfathomed,

and once I'm drunk, all heaven and earth
vanish, leaving me suddenly alone in bed,

forgetting that person I am even exists.
40   Of all our joys, this must be the deepest.

Sent to My Two Little Children in the East of Lu[1]

Translated by Burton Watson

Wu land mulberry leaves grow green,
already Wu silkworms have slept three times.
I left my family in the east of Lu;
who sows our fields there on the dark side of Mt. Kuei?[2]
Spring chores too long untended,
river journeys that leave me dazed—
south winds blow my homing heart;
it soars and comes to rest before the wine tower.
East of the tower a peach tree grows,
10   branches and leaves brushed with blue mist,
a tree I planted myself,
parted from it these three years.
The peach now is tall as the tower
and still my journey knows no return.
P'ing-yang, my darling girl,
picks blossoms, leaning by the peach,
picks blossoms and does not see me;
her tears flow like a welling fountain.
The little boy, named Po-ch'in,
20   is shoulder high to his elder sister;
side by side they walk beneath the peach—

---

[1] **Lu:** Lu is the ancient name for Shandong (Shantung) Province, where Li Bai left his family while traveling in the south, which he refers to here as Wu, the name of an ancient kingdom in southeast China.

[2] **Mt. Kuei:** Mt. Gui, a mountain in Shandong.

who will pat them with loving hands?
I lose myself in thoughts of them;
day by day care burns out my heart.
On this piece of cut silk I'll write my far-away thoughts
and send them floating down the river Wen-yang.[3]

---

[3] **Wen-yang:** A river in Shandong.

∾ DU FU
B. CHINA, 712–770

Though he was relatively neglected in his own day, subsequent generations of Chinese readers came to consider the Confucian poet Du Fu (Tu
Fu) China's greatest poet. A versatile and innovative master of all the
forms of poetry practiced in the High Tang era, Du Fu also displayed in
his poetry an unprecedented concern for the personal and social consequences of historical change. Du Fu's poetry engages both the historical
and personal events in his life to such a high degree that he is often called
a poet-historian. Unlike the poetry of Wang Wei, whose meditative
descriptions of nature give one a feeling of timelessness, Du Fu's work
records with sadness and compassion the harsh realities of everyday life,
the suffering of the poor, and, in his later poetry, the decline of the Tang
dynasty after the An Lushan Rebellion of 755. He also criticizes those who
fail to live up to the Confucian standards of duty and piety, particularly
targeting the corrupt officials of Emperor Xuanzong's court. Du Fu's own
life was marked by disappointment and failure, and in his poetry the
boundary between public and private experience often blurs.

Du Fu was born in 712 to a family of midlevel scholar-officials. His
mother was the great-granddaughter of the former emperor Taizong,
and his grandfather was Du Shenyan, an important court poet in the previous generation. Though he showed promise as a youth, Du Fu twice
failed the *chin-shi* examinations (in 735 and 747), and despite his family's
connections was unable to obtain special appointment to a government
position. He spent much of his life traveling throughout China, cultivating his art as a poet, working on his painting and musical skills, and relying on the generosity of distant family members and other patrons for
support and patronage. In 744 or 745 the as-yet unacknowledged Du Fu
met the already-famous Li Bai, inaugurating one of literary history's
most celebrated friendships. The disciplined and humble Confucian Du
Fu may seem an unlikely friend for the irreverent and reckless Daoist Li
Bai, who teased Du Fu for laboring too hard and suffering too much over
his poetry. Despite their different sensibilities, or perhaps because of
them, the two poets developed a strong friendship and each devoted several poems to the other.

Du Fu, eighteenth century

A late portrait of an older and contemplative Du Fu (Tu Fu). (The Art Archive / British Library)

Du Fu was offered a government post in 755, the year of the An Lushan Rebellion. Though he was not in Chang'an when it was seized, he was cut off from the court party fleeing to the west and like Wang Wei was soon captured and held by the rebels. Escaping his captors, Du Fu joined Xuanzong's court in exile at Sichuan and returned with them to Chang'an when it was recaptured in 757. Though the post he had so long tried to secure now seemed within his grasp, he managed to offend the court and was exiled to Huazhou where he held a minor post. Unhappy with his job, Du Fu left it behind and took to traveling again. He spent two years in Chengdu, the capital of Sichuan province, where he held the title of assistant deputy in the Ministry of Works and served as a military advisor. Despite the instability in his life, Du Fu was particularly productive in his later years when he was again dependent on the good grace of patrons. In fact, the poems of his later years are imbued with an intensity and a sense of peace and dignity, signifying that Du Fu was able to rise above his misfortune. These poems also show Du Fu continuing to experiment with new poetic forms. When his patron at Chengdu died, Du Fu undertook several voyages down the Yangtze River toward the lakes region in central China. Weakened by illness, Du Fu died in 770, most likely while on the Yangtze.

Du Fu's Confucian sensibilities are evident in his poetry, noted for its technical perfection. He was drawn to the technical challenges posed by the *lushi*, or regulated verse, of which form he is still considered the undisputed master. In the formal perfection of his style, he manages to present his personal suffering in an objective light, tying it to the larger events taking place in China and blurring the distinction between his personal plight and the collective misfortune of the Chinese people in a time of great difficulty.

∾ To Li Po° on a Winter Day   Li Bai

Translated by Sam Hamill

Alone in my secluded hut,
I think of you all day, Li Po.

Whenever I read of friendship,
I remember your friendly poems.

Harsh winds tatter your old clothes
as you search for the wine of endless life.

Unable to go with you, I remember only
that old hermitage we'd hoped to make a home.

∾ P'eng-Ya Song

Translated by David Hinton

I remember long ago slipping away
in precarious depths of night. The moon
bright on Po-shui Mountain, I eluded
rebel armies and fled with my family

far north by foot on P'eng-ya Road.[1]
By then, most people we met had lost all
shame. Scattered bird cries haunted
valleys. No one returned the way we came.

My silly, starved girl bit me and screamed.
Afraid tigers and wolves might hear,
I cradled her close, holding her mouth,
but she squirmed loose, crying louder still.

Looking after us gallantly, my little boy
searched out sour-plum feasts. Of ten days,
half were all thunder and rain—mud
and more mud to drag ourselves through.

We didn't plan for rain. Clothes ever
colder, the road slippery, an insufferable
day's travel often took us but a few short
miles by nightfall. Wild fruit replaced

what little food we had carried with us.
Low branches became our home. We left dew-
splashed rocks each morning, and passed
nights at the smoke-scored edge of heaven.

We had stopped at T'ung-chia Marsh,
planning to cross Lu-tu Pass, when you
took us in, Sun Tsai, old friend, your
kindness towering like billowing clouds.

Dusk already become night, you hung lanterns
out and swung door after door wide open.
You soothed our feet with warm water
and cut paper charms to summon our souls,

then called your wife and children in, their
eyes filling with tears for us. My chicks

10

20

30

---

[1] **I remember . . . P'eng-ya Road:** This poem records the arduous 140-mile journey along the P'eng-ya Road from Fengxian, where Du Fu (Tu Fu) had moved his family, to Fuzhou, where he hoped to secure their safety from the An Lushan Rebellion.

soon drifted away in sleep, but you brought
them back, offering choice dishes of food.

You and I, you promised, will be forever
bound together like two dear brothers.
And before long, you emptied our rooms,
40   leaving us to joy and peace and rest.

In these times overrun with such calamity,
how many hearts are so open and generous?
A year of months since we parted, and still
those Mongols spin their grand catastrophes.

How long before I've grown feathers and wings
and settled beside you at the end of flight?

❧ Restless Night

Translated by Burton Watson

The cool of bamboo invades my room;
moonlight from the fields fills the corners of the court;
dew gathers till it falls in drops;
a scattering of stars, now there, now gone.
A firefly threading the darkness makes its own light;
birds at rest on the water call to each other;
all these lie within the shadow of the sword—
Powerless I grieve as the clear night passes.

❧ Flying from Trouble

Translated by Florence Ayscough

At fifty a white-headed old man,
South, North, I fly from troubles of the State.

Coarse cloth wound round dried bones.
Walk back, forth; alas am still not warm.

❧ Bo Juyi
B. CHINA, 772–846

Like Du Fu, Bo Juyi (Po Chü-i) wrote many poems criticizing government inefficiency and corruption and sympathizing with the suffering of the people. Whereas Du Fu (Tu Fu) was a master of *lushi,* or regulated verse, Bo Juyi is known for his innovations in the *yuefu,* the ballad form he adapted to write poems of social criticism. Also in contrast to Du Fu whose poetic talent went largely unnoticed in his lifetime, Bo Juyi enjoyed tremendous popularity while alive. He once said that when he walked the nearly four thousand leagues from Chang'an to Jiangxi he found his poems everywhere, posted at village schools, monasteries, and inns, but that he regretted that his best work was neglected in favor of what he thought of as literary trifles. His popularity, which extended to Japan, was in large part due to the simplicity of his style. According to legend, after composing his poems Bo Juyi would read them to a peasant woman and revise any lines that she could not understand. Bo Juyi's popularity may also be attributed to the topical and romantic themes of some of his poems, such as those found in his most famous work, *The Song of Unending Sorrow,* about the tragic love between Emperor Xuanzong and his villainous concubine Yang Guifei. Many of his poems focus on gardening, eating, keeping pets, drinking wine, and making money — everyday matters that broadened the parameters of what was considered appropriate subject matter for poetry.

The son of a poor scholar-official at Xinzheng in Henan (Honan) Province, Bo Juyi was born in 772. His early years, like those of many young men born in similar circumstances, were spent studying for the *chin-shi* civil service examinations, which he passed in 800. Three years later, having passed an advanced examination, he began a career as a government official in Chang'an, eventually gaining an appointment to Han-Lin Academy in 807. Bo Juyi was married in 808 and began his important friendship with Yuan Zhen (779–831), the author of *The Story of Ying-ying.* Here, too, he got himself into trouble by writing poems critical of the government; he was stripped of his rank and sent into exile as a marshal to Jiujiang (Xunyang) in 815. In exile, Bo Juyi began to study Chan Buddhism with monks at local temples on Mount Lu, where he eventually built a retreat celebrated in his poetry. After three years in Jiujiang, Bo Juyi was transferred to Zhongzhou in Sichuan Province, and in 819 he returned to Chang'an. Eventually he served as the governor of Hangzhou (822–24), the governor of Suzhou (825–26), the senior librarian of the Imperial Library at Chang'an (827), and the governor of Henan Province at Luoyang (829–31), the eastern capital. During this time Bo Juyi kept up his study of Buddhism and continued writing poetry. In 832 he finally settled in at the Xiangshan Monastery on the river Yi south of Luoyang, where he lived until his death in 846.

Despite his later practice of Chan Buddhism, Bo Juyi early on held a Confucian notion that poetry should serve as an agent of moral improvement. While Bo Juyi's poems of social criticism, the "new *yuefu*" or "new ballads," received a great deal of attention in his own time (and have continued to), he also wrote lyric poems, *lushi* and *kushi,* of great intensity, clarity, and simplicity. Recent critics have seen in his lyric poetry an expression of his Chan Buddhism, whose practitioners seek to dissolve the ego so that the mind is emptied of all attachments and the true reality of things may appear in its profound simplicity and transparency. Bo Juyi's poems are always intensely personal, even as they embrace the objective world and the tumultuous society in which he lived.

～ Watching the Reapers

Translated by Arthur Waley

Tillers of the earth have few idle months:
In the fifth month[1] their toil is double-fold.
A south wind visits the fields at night;
Suddenly the ridges are covered with yellow corn.
Wives and daughters shoulder baskets of rice,
Youths and boys carry flasks of wine,
In a long train, to feed the workers in the field —
The strong reapers toiling on the southern hill,
Whose feet are burned by the hot earth they tread,
10   Whose backs are scorched by the flames of the shining sky
Tired they toil, caring nothing for the heat,
Grudging the shortness of the long summer day.
A poor woman with a young child at her side
Follows behind, to glean the unwanted grain.
In her right hand she holds the fallen ears,
On her left arm a broken basket hangs.
Listening to what they said as they worked together
I heard something that made me very sad:
They lost in grain-tax[2] the whole of their own crop;
20   What they glean here is all they will have to eat.

And I to-day — in virtue of what desert
Have I never once tended field or tree?

---

[1] **the fifth month:** The middle of summer

[2] **grain-tax:** Excessive taxation to finance the extravagances of Xuanzong's court and military adventures placed a heavy burden on the peasants and eventually led to peasant revolts.

My government-pay is three hundred "stones";
At the year's end I have still grain in hand.
Thinking of this, secretly I grew ashamed
And all day the thought lingered in my head.

Madly Singing in the Mountains

Translated by Arthur Waley

There is no one among men that has not a special failing;
And my failing consists in writing verses.
I have broken away from the thousand ties of life;
But this infirmity still remains behind.
Each time that I look at a fine landscape,
Each time that I meet a loved friend,
I raise my voice and recite a stanza of poetry
And marvel as though a God had crossed my path.
Ever since the day I was banished to Hsün-yang
Half my time I have lived among the hills.
And often, when I have finished a new poem,
Alone I climb the road to the Eastern Rock.
I lean my body on the banks of white Stone;
I pull down with my hands a green cassia branch.
My mad singing startles the valleys and hills;
The apes and birds all come to peep.
Fearing to become a laughing-stock to the world,
I choose a place that is unfrequented by men.

∾ BEOWULF

ENGLAND, EIGHTH CENTURY–TENTH CENTURY

BAY-oh-woolf

While *Beowulf* is renowned as one of the world's great poems, it also holds many mysteries. Despite the efforts of generations of scholars, its date, place of composition, and status as a literary work are still subject to discussion. The two major events in the only existing version of the poem — the youthful **Beowulf**'s encounters with the monsters Grendel and his mother, and the elder Beowulf's final battle with the dragon — were drawn from ancient Scandinavian and Germanic mythology. The poem's historical allusions refer us to northern Europe in the fifth and sixth centuries. The idea of the *comitatus* — the association of warriors that provides the major bonding element in society — is Germanic from the same or a later period. Eventually, the story traveled to England, where the surviving portion of the poem, originally composed orally, was written down in Anglo-Saxon near the end of the tenth century. The "Christian coloring" of the poem, along with frequent references to the antiquity of its pagan setting, probably was added after the poem reached England.

Epic Origins.　Thematically, *Beowulf* belongs to an ancient epic tradition found in a number of early societies. Like the Sumerian hero Gilgamesh and the Greek Achilles in Homer's *The Iliad*, Beowulf is stronger and wiser than other men, though he remains mortal. The poem emphasizes the importance of the hero as the protector of his people, while insisting that no man is secure before fate or knows what awaits him after death. In its two surviving sections it appears to contrast the strength of the young warrior to his vulnerability fifty years later; his own death anticipates the end of the warrior society to which he belongs. For this reason, the first part of *Beowulf* is usually taken to be an epic celebration, while the last part is considered a literary elegy, commemorating both its hero and the culture he represents. Its closest surviving analogues are Scandinavian and Germanic epics of the early medieval period such as the *Volsungasaga* and the *Nibelungenlied*. The same tradition is reflected in German composer Richard Wagner's nineteenth-century opera cycle, *The Ring of the Nibelungs*.

The Old Norse prose epic *Volsungasaga*, drawn from Germanic and Scandinavian legends of the fifth to eighth century, was probably composed during the Age of the Vikings (800–1070), though it survives only in a manuscript of the thirteenth century. The *Nibelungenlied*, a South German courtly epic composed at the beginning of the thirteenth century, invokes the same cycle of heroic stories. Both these works contain the Final Battle, the tale of the destruction of the gods, which occurs at the end of the heroic era. Other works in the Germanic tradition, nearly contemporary to *Beowulf*, consist of fragmentary battle descriptions composed in alliterative poetry. These include the Old German *Hildebrandslied* and the Anglo-Saxon *Fight at Finnsburh*. The story behind the *Fight at Finnsburh* is repeated in *Beowulf* itself.

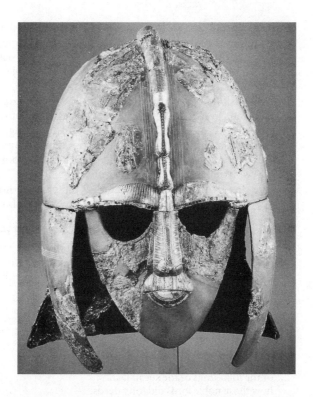

Anglo-Saxon Helmet, seventh century
This magnificent helmet is one of only four Anglo-Saxon helmets in existence. The eyebrows are thin strands of silver wire and garnet, and each ends in a gilt boar's head. Between the eyebrows, two gilded dragons' heads lie nose to nose, with the upper one's body running in a low crest over the crown of the helmet. The helmet was recovered from the site of the ship burial at Sutton Hoo in 1939. (British Museum)

The Christian impulse represented in *Beowulf* established itself in England after the migration of Germanic tribes in the fifth and sixth centuries. The church historian the Venerable Bede (673–735) writes in his *Ecclesiastical History of the English People* (731) about the English monk Caedmon, who composed Anglo-Saxon Christian poetry in the latter half of the seventh century. Sermons and other Christian documents in Anglo-Saxon also attest to the translation of Christian doctrine from Latin sources to the vernacular English of the time. The linguistic state of the Beowulf story when it first arrived in England remains uncertain. It was probably translated into Anglo-Saxon from linguistically related Scandinavian or Germanic sources soon after its arrival.

Oral Formulaic Poetry and the Language of *Beowulf*.   The proof of the Scandinavian and Germanic origins of *Beowulf* lies in its language and verse form. The immediate sources of the Anglo-Saxon manuscript of the poem cannot be dated precisely, but it comes from a period when scribes attached to English courts and monasteries were encouraged to record the poetry and prose of the vernacular language. *Beowulf* is composed in the traditional poetic meter described as *oral-formulaic poetry* (referring to its manner of composition) or *alliterative poetry* (referring to its formal poetic features).

Oral-formulaic poetry consists of poetry either chanted or spoken, perhaps to the accompaniment of a harp or another instrument, using a

> The general structure of the poem . . . is essentially a balance, an opposition of ends and beginnings. In its simplest terms it is a contrasted description of two moments in a great life, rising and setting; an elaboration of the ancient and intensely moving contrast between youth and age, first achievement and final death. . . .
>
> –J. R. R. TOLKIEN, scholar and editor, 1936

number of stock phrases or formulas in order to enhance the poet's opportunities for expression while enabling him to remember long stories. The formulas often consist of metaphorical descriptions: for instance, a ruler may be called a "shepherd of his people," a "ring-giver," or a "shield" in time of war. His wife, who assists the king by offering hospitality to visitors, is described as a "peace weaver" or "cup bearer" as well as the queen. Even elements of nature are assigned stock epithets: for instance, the ocean may be called a "whale-road." In Anglo-Saxon poetry there are many parallel names for the things most commonly described. These commonly used synonyms help to create a large poetic vocabulary, called a "word-hoard" in Anglo-Saxon.

The standard form of versification is alliterative four-stress poetry. Each poetic line is made up of four feet, two to a half-line, with a pause halfway through the line. Alliteration, the repetition of a single sound at the beginning of words, often occurs in two or three of the four stressed words in the line, at least one of which is found in each half-line, and it is usually governed by the first letter of the first stressed word in the second half-line. Thus we have the opening lines of *Beowulf*, with the alliterative syllables in italics:

> Hwaet! We *Gar-Dena*   in *gear-dagum*
> *Theod*-cyninga,   *thrym* gefrunon,
> Hu tha *aethelingas*   *ellen* fremedon!

> Listen! We have heard of the glory in bygone days
> of the folk-kings of the spear-Danes,
> how those noble lords did lofty deeds.

While irregularities in the verse form are frequent, the combination of four-stress lines and alliterative language dominates the poem. English verse translations, though they contain a more modern vocabulary than is found in Anglo-Saxon, usually mimic some of the features found in the old language.

Effects of the Poetry.   *Beowulf* is a narrative poem with the action moving ahead step by step. This simple style is called PARATAXIS, from a Greek word that means "putting one foot in front of the other." The narrative of *Beowulf* becomes more complicated, however, whenever the writer embellishes the main story by having his characters introduce another, earlier story for comparison or contrast. The secondary narratives are sometimes no more than anecdotes or historical references taking up a few lines, but other times they are lengthy self-contained stories with a detailed relationship to the main story. Scholars originally called these stories within the story *digressions;* increasingly, however, they are seen to be integral parts of the primary narrative, parallel reflections on the events described in the story.

A special case of the embellishment of the main story comes when the poet steps out of the time frame of the narrative to reveal more recent history—material later than the events described in the poem, but known to himself and his audience—which reflects on the main story. Often this reflection is ironic; it undercuts or calls into question something about the action of the poem. For example, King Hrothgar of the Geats erects a great hall in which he favors his followers by distributing gifts among them. In the middle of the description of this magnificent hall, the poet mentions a future event, known to the audience, when the hall will be destroyed by fire due to a feud within the ruling family.

> The hall towered,
> high and horn-gabled—it awaited hostile fires,
> the surges of war. The time was not yet near
> that the sword-hate of sworn in-laws
> should arise after ruthless violence.

Another kind of irony exists in the form of understatement. For example, after Beowulf is killed by the dragon near the end of the poem, his loyal young retainer **Wiglaf** chastises his companions who have run away from the dragon-fight. He remarks to them with mock politeness, "Too few supporters thronged around our prince in his great peril." Then he adds more bluntly that these companions will have neither a share of the dragon's treasure nor the benefits of Beowulf's kingdom that they previously enjoyed. He ends his speech in a fury: "Death is better for any earl than a life of dishonor!" The statement taken as a whole amounts to a kind of prophecy: Wiglaf, Beowulf's only loyal supporter during the fight, is shown by the poet to predict the future.

WEE-lahf,
WIG-lahf

The Flow of the Epic. In the beginning of the poem, the young lord Beowulf of the Geats travels across the sea to **Heorot** hall, ruled by King **Hrothgar** in the land of the Danes. Heorot is in crisis: it has sustained bloody raids by **Grendel**, a monster who has been devouring its warriors. Beowulf and his men are warmly greeted by the lords of Heorot, with the exception of **Unferth**, a Danish champion who insults him by belittling his physical prowess and courage. After getting the better of Unferth in a verbal contest, Beowulf retires for the night with his men in the great hall. When all fall asleep, Grendel arrives in the darkness and feasts on one of Beowulf's men. Beowulf grapples with the monster, tearing off his arm at the shoulder. Mortally wounded, Grendel flees. In the morning, Beowulf follows his bloody trail back to the swampy pool where he has sunk and died. Heorot hall celebrates Beowulf's feat with a feast, and his deed is memorialized in song. But after they all retire, a second monster invades the hall and kills **Aeschere**, the chief advisor of King Hrothgar. At daybreak Beowulf tracks this monster back to the same pool and dives underwater. In an underwater chamber Beowulf discovers the body of Grendel, the first monster, and kills Grendel's mother, who had attacked the hall to avenge the death of her son. Thus he purges the evil from Heorot at last. After another celebration at Hrothgar's court, Beowulf returns to the kingdom of the Geats where he shares the gifts he has received with his own king, **Hygelac**. He is given a great hall and land of his own, and the first part ends.

HEH-oh-rote
HROHTH-gar
GREN-dul

UN-furth

ASH-hay-ruh

HIH-yuh-lak

So far the poem has told the deeds of the energetic young hero that are rewarded by celebrations and gifts. Beowulf is justly praised by the endangered court of Heorot. When the monsters are slain, society is the winner; good triumphs over evil, and peace and order are restored.

Peoples and Places in *Beowulf*

The history and legends depicted in Beowulf *took place in a northern Europe peopled by warring tribes, particularly the Danes, Swedes, and Geats. Heorot is the presumed location of Hrothgar's hall, around which most of the action is centered in the first part of the story.*

Epic into Elegy.   A different world is depicted in the second part of the poem. It begins with a brief account of the fortunes of the Geats over the next fifty years, the period of Beowulf's reign. Then it turns to the story of a dragon and his hoard of ancient treasure, abandoned by a royal house centuries before. The dragon, disturbed by the theft of a cup from his treasure-hoard by a fugitive from Beowulf's court, burns down the Geatish stronghold. Beowulf pursues the dragon, taking with him eleven retainers and the man who stole the flagon. In the dragon-fight, Beowulf's sword and his other defenses fail him. Seeing this, his retainers flee, except for the youthful Wiglaf who tells Beowulf to take heart and joins the battle. Finally the dragon bites Beowulf fatally on the neck. Wiglaf strikes it a mortal blow and Beowulf disembowels it. Feeling the dragon's poison take effect, Beowulf commands Wiglaf to bring the treasure for him to see. He orders his burial in a barrow overlooking the sea, gives Wiglaf his collar, ring, and helmet, and names him the last successor of his royal line. The Geats prepare Beowulf for cremation and the treasure for burial. Wiglaf delivers the eulogy. It is fitting, the poet concludes, to mourn such a great king.

The episode of the dragon-fight shows the Geats in dissolution. The recovery of the treasure is essentially meaningless, since it is buried again at the end of the poem. There can be no celebration in the great hall—it has been destroyed by the dragon—and Beowulf's followers have deserted him in his hour of need. Wiglaf inherits the throne for the moment but will have no successor. The circle of society confirmed by the giving of gifts and the telling of stories of past heroes will soon be broken. Earlier in the poem, foreshadowing its tragic conclusion, a famous speech sometimes called "the song of the last survivor" mourns the passing of all the heroic societies.

> "Hold now, o thou earth, for heroes cannot,
> the wealth of men—Lo, from you long ago
> those good ones first obtained it. Death in war
> and awful deadly harm have swept away
> all my people who have passed from life,
> and left the joyful hall. Now I have none
> to bear the sword or burnish the bright cup,
> the precious vessel—all that host has fled."

Past, Present, Future.   The Anglo-Saxon audience of *Beowulf* had the advantage of historical perspective in viewing this narrative. As the poem states, the great lords of the past have gone from the earth, with their treasures scattered, destroyed, or expended. There remain only echoes of the old society, such as the ideal of the *comitatus,* the men who banded together in the interest of protection and stability. Some would say it was important to preserve the memories of the past because they inspired those still living to rise to noble actions. Although the monsters and the dragon are only symbols of the past, they also remind the audience that other enemies have survived, threatening them whenever their vigilance decreases.

Interpretations of the meaning of *Beowulf* have varied greatly over the last two hundred years. In the nineteenth century the poem was viewed as an antiquity, a way of directly reading the age of heroes, and the Christian element was largely ignored as an irrelevant addition. For a time in the twentieth century, especially during World War II in England, the poem was treated as a fable of the heroism necessary to preserve civilization. Recent critics tend to view the poem as a reflection of the values and interests of late Anglo-Saxon society, written down sometime after the demise of the Germanic society it dramatizes. But the poem also raises questions about the epic poet and his audience, including whatever drives one to construct a heroic past out of legends and stories in the first place. An analogy for Americans might be our fascination with the history of our western frontier, which, insofar as it actually existed, effectively vanished by the beginning of the twentieth century. What did

> Here at the end of this poem there is only the structure men make, a frail shell around their solidarity, fated to have only a brief space of time before the final burning. It is a boundary situation. . . . The Geats' riding [around the burial mound] and their speaking of the words of praise draw the audience into the poet's circle of human solidarity. We too can see and honor, always against the terrible darkness, Beowulf's qualities: strength, mercy, gentleness, and above all an unquenchable passion for glory.
>
> – EDWARD B. IRVING JR., critic, 1989

Beowulf mean in its own time? Who preserved it, and why? This and related questions invite further speculation.

If, as scholars now suggest, the manuscript was completed at the end of the tenth century, it existed in its final written form for less than a century before the Battle of Hastings in 1066, in which the Norman French conquered the Anglo-Saxons and established a new society in England. Those who recalled the legends of their ancestors in *Beowulf* rapidly faded from the scene, overwhelmed by the Norman arrival and the subsequent reshaping of English language and culture. So *Beowulf*, a work that celebrated antiquity, became irrelevant to the newly created Anglo-Norman society and vanished from memory for centuries to come.

■ FURTHER RESEARCH

Editions and Translations
Chickering, Howell D. *Beowulf: A Dual-Language Edition. Translated with Introduction and Commentary.* 1977.
Mitchell, Bruce, and Fred C. Robinson. *Beowulf: An Edition.* 1998.

Translations with Selected Criticism
Donoghue, Daniel, ed. *Beowulf: Verse Translation, Authoritative Text, Contexts, Criticism.* Translation by Seamus Heaney. 2002.
Howe, Nicholas, ed. *Beowulf: Prose Translation, Backgrounds and Contexts, Criticism.* Translation by E. Talbot Donaldson. 2002.

Anthologies of Literary Criticism
Baker, Peter S., ed. *Beowulf: Basic Readings.* 1995.
Bjork, Robert E., and John D. Niles, eds. *A Beowulf Handbook.* 1997.
Chase, Colin, ed. *The Dating of Beowulf.* 1981.
Fulk, R. D., ed. *Interpretations of Beowulf.* 1991.

Works of Literary Criticism
Bonjour, A. *The Digressions in Beowulf.* 1950.
Evans, A. C. *The Sutton Hoo Ship Burial.* 1986.
Hill, John. *The Cultural World in Beowulf.* 1995.
Irving, Edward B. *Rereading Beowulf.* 1989.
Niles, John D. *Beowulf: The Poem and Its Tradition.* 1983.
Stanley, E. G. *In the Foreground: Beowulf.* 1994.

■ PRONUNCIATION

Anglo-Saxon pronunciation is basically consistent. All consonants and vowels are pronounced, and long vowels sound as they did before the time of Shakespeare: *ah, ei, ee, oh, oo.* The short *a* sounds roughly equivalent to the short *o* in *hop.* A short final *e* is pronounced unaccented, as *uh.* Diphthongs are pronounced as a single syllable, with the first vowel predominating: *Healfdene,* for example, sounds like HAY-ulf-day-nuh. While most consonants are pronounced as in modern English, there are some exceptions: *sc* is pronounced like modern *sh* (scip, ship); *cg* like modern *dg* (ecg, edge); *h* after a vowel like German *ch* (ich, ach); *c* before *i* or *e* like *ch* in child (cild, child); *c* after *i, e* like soft *ch* (micel, much); *g* before *i* or *e* like *y* in yet (giefu, gift); *g* after *i, e* like *y* in yet (hefig, heavy); and the special symbols þ (thorn) and ð (eth) which interchangeably produce the "th" sound.

In Anglo-Saxon versification, the first syllable of a word is generally stressed, as in BAY-oh-woolf (*Beowulf*). Pronunciation guides for the most important Anglo-Saxon names in the text are given on page 1192.

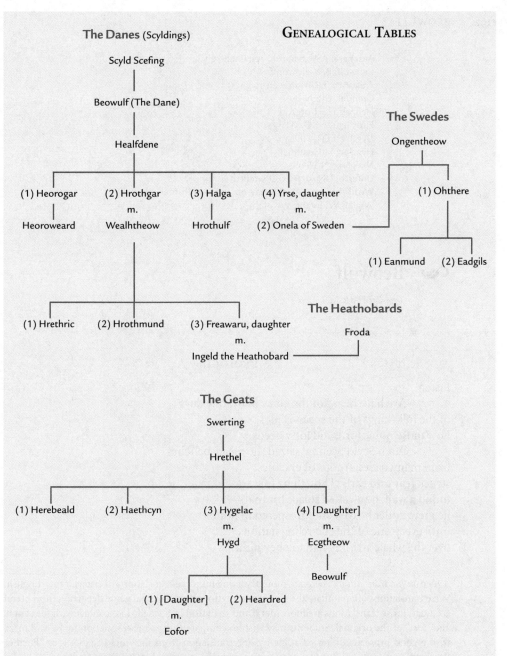

The Danes (Scyldings)

Scyld Scefing

Beowulf (The Dane)

Healfdene

(1) Heorogar   (2) Hrothgar   (3) Halga   (4) Yrse, daughter

Heoroweard   m.   Hrothulf   m.
   Wealhtheow   (2) Onela of Sweden

(1) Hrethric   (2) Hrothmund   (3) Freawaru, daughter

m.

Ingeld the Heathobard

The Swedes

Ongentheow

(1) Ohthere

(1) Eanmund   (2) Eadgils

The Heathobards

Froda

The Geats

Swerting

Hrethel

(1) Herebeald   (2) Haethcyn   (3) Hygelac   (4) [Daughter]

m.   m.

Hygd   Ecgtheow

Beowulf

(1) [Daughter]   (2) Heardred

m.

Eofor

Variants on names of tribes

Danes: Bright-Danes, East-Danes, Half-Danes, Ingwines, North-Danes, Ring-Danes, South-Danes, Spear-Danes, West-Danes. Also, Scyldings: Battle-Scyldings, Honor-Scyldings, Victory-Scyldings.

Geats: Sea-Geats, War-Geats, Weders (Weather-Geats). See Waegmundings, below.

Swedes: Scylfings.

Merovingians: includes the Franks and the Hetware.

Waegmundings: Family branch of the Geats. Includes Beowulf, Ecgtheow, Wiglaf.

Aeschere: ASH-hay-ruh, ASH-heh-ruh
Beowulf: BAY-oh-woolf
Freawaru: FRAY-ah-wah-roo
Grendel: GREN-dul
Heorot: HEH-oh-rote
Hrothgar: HROHTH-gar
Hygd: HEED, HEE-yid
Hygelac: HIH-yuh-lak
Naegling: NAY-ling
Unferth: UN-furth, OON-fehrth
Wealhtheow: WAY-ahl-thay-oh, WEH-ahlh-theh-oh
Wiglaf: WEE-lahf, WIG-lahf

 # Beowulf

Translated by R. M. Liuzza

PROLOGUE

Listen!
    We have heard of the glory in bygone days
of the folk-kings of the spear-Danes,
how those noble lords did lofty deeds.
    Often Scyld Scefing[1] seized the mead-benches
from many tribes, troops of enemies,
struck fear into earls. Though he first was
found a waif, he awaited solace for that—
he grew under heaven and prospered in honor
until every one of the encircling nations
10 over the whale's-riding had to obey him,

A note on the translation: There are more than one hundred translations of *Beowulf* into English. Verse translations often imitate the sound and rhythm of the original while departing from literal accuracy. Prose translations are more literal and analytical but usually lose contact with the syntax and "feel" of the original. Students may wish to compare this poetic translation by R. M. Liuzza with a good prose rendition or a line-by-line translation from the Anglo Saxon. (See "Further Research.")

    The *Beowulf* manuscript is divided into forty-three sections not counting the prologue, which tells of Scyld Scefing's miraculous arrival, life, death, and funeral. The present translation follows these section divisions. Brief notes on the "digressions" are included when necessary. Some footnotes rely in whole or in part on the translator's notes; notes substantially supplied by the editors of this anthology are marked [Ed.].

---

[1] **Scyld Scefing:** "Shield, Son of Sheaf." The legendary founder of the Danish royal house whose story introduces the poem. [Ed.]

grant him tribute. That was a good king!
A boy was later born to him,
young in the courts, whom God sent
as a solace to the people—He saw their need,
the dire distress they had endured, lordless,
for such a long time. The Lord of Life,
Wielder of Glory, gave him worldly honor;
Beowulf,[2] the son of Scyld, was renowned,
his fame spread wide in Scandinavian lands.
20 Thus should a young man bring about good
with pious gifts from his father's possessions,
so that later in life loyal comrades
will stand beside him when war comes,
the people will support him—with praiseworthy deeds
a man will prosper among any people.
      Scyld passed away at his appointed hour,
the mighty lord went into the Lord's keeping;
they bore him down to the brimming sea,
his dear comrades, as he himself had commanded
30 while the friend of the Scyldings wielded speech—
that dear land-ruler had long held power.
In the harbor stood a ring-prowed ship,
icy, outbound, a nobleman's vessel;
there they laid down their dear lord,
dispenser of rings, in the bosom of the ship,
glorious, by the mast. There were many treasures
loaded there, adornments from distant lands;
I have never heard of a more lovely ship
bedecked with battle-weapons and war-gear,
40 blades and byrnies;[3] in its bosom lay
many treasures, which were to travel
far with him into the keeping of the flood.
With no fewer gifts did they furnish him there,
the wealth of nations, than those did who
at his beginning first sent him forth
alone over the waves while still a small child.[4]
Then they set a golden ensign
high over his head, and let the waves have him,
gave him to the Deep with grieving spirits,
50 mournful in mind. Men do not know

---

[2] **Beowulf:** This Beowulf, son of Scyld Scefing, should not be confused with the young hero of the poem, a Geat who supports the Danes in their need. [Ed.]

[3] **byrnies:** A coat of ring-mail (light armor).

[4] **while still a small child:** Scyld's sumptuous burial is ironically contrasted to his discovery as an infant sent adrift on the sea with no belongings. [Ed.]

how to say truly—not trusted counselors,
nor heroes under the heavens—who received that cargo.

I

Then Beowulf Scylding, beloved king,
was famous in the strongholds of his folk
for a long while—his father having passed away,
a lord from earth—until after him arose
the great Healfdene, who held the glorious Scyldings
all his life, ancient and fierce in battle.
Four children, all counted up,
60 were born to that bold leader of hosts:
Heorogar, Hrothgar, and Halga the Good,
I heard that . . . was Onela's queen,[5]
dear bedfellow of the Battle-Scylfing.
Then success in war was given to Hrothgar,
honor in battle, so that his beloved kinsmen
eagerly served him, until the young soldiers grew
into a mighty troop of men. It came to his mind
that he should order a hall-building,
have men make a great mead-house
70 which the sons of men should remember forever,
and there inside he would share everything
with young and old that God had given him,
except for the common land and the lives of men.
Then the work, as I've heard, was widely proclaimed
to many nations throughout this middle-earth,
to come adorn the folk-stead. It came to pass
swiftly among men, and it was soon ready,
the greatest of halls; he gave it the name "Heorot",[6]
he who ruled widely with his words.
80 He remembered his boast; he gave out rings,
treasure at table. The hall towered
high and horn-gabled—it awaited hostile fires,
the surges of war; the time was not yet near
that the sword-hate of sworn in-laws
should arise after ruthless violence.[7]
A bold demon who waited in darkness

---

[5] **Onela's queen:** The Swedish king Onela appears later in the story, causing much distress to Beowulf's nation.

[6] **"Heorot":** Literally "hart," a male deer.

[7] **after ruthless violence:** The poet tells us that Hrothgar's palace will be destroyed during the course of a later feud among his kinsmen. [Ed.]

wretchedly suffered all the while,
for every day he heard the joyful din
loud in the hall, with the harp's sound,
90 the clear song of the scop.[8] He said
who was able to tell of the origin of men
that the Almighty created the earth,
a bright and shining plain, by seas embraced,
and set, triumphantly, the sun and moon
to light their beams for those who dwell on land,
adorned the distant corners of the world
with leaves and branches, and made life also,
all manner of creatures that live and move.
— Thus this lordly people lived in joy,
100 blessedly, until one began
to work his foul crimes — a fiend from hell.
This grim spirit was called Grendel,
mighty stalker of the marches, who held
the moors and fens; this miserable man
lived for a time in the land of giants,
after the Creator had condemned him
among Cain's race — when he killed Abel[9]
the eternal Lord avenged that death.
No joy in that feud — the Maker forced him
110 far from mankind for his foul crime.
From thence arose all misbegotten things,
trolls and elves and the living dead,
and also the giants who strove against God
for a long while — He gave them their reward for that.

II

When night descended he went to seek out
the high house, to see how the Ring-Danes
had bedded down after their beer-drinking.
He found therein a troop of nobles
asleep after the feast; they knew no sorrow
120 or human misery. The unholy creature,
grim and ravenous, was ready at once,

---

[8] **song of the scop:** A scop is a poet-singer. This is the first of several scenes of poetic entertainment in the poem.

[9] **he killed Abel:** The notion that monsters were descended from Cain was a medieval commonplace. See Genesis 4: 1–16 (p. 88). [Ed.]

ruthless and cruel, and took from their rest
thirty thanes;[10] thence he went
rejoicing in his booty, back to his home,
to seek out his abode with his fill of slaughter.
When in the dim twilight just before dawn
Grendel's warfare was made known to men,
then lamentation was lifted up after the feasting,
a great morning-sound. Unhappy sat
130   the mighty lord, long-good nobleman,
suffered greatly, grieved for his thanes,
once they beheld that hostile one's tracks,
the accursed spirit; that strife was too strong,
loathsome and long.
                             It was not longer
than the next night until he committed
a greater murder, mourned not at all
for his feuds and sins — he was too fixed in them.
Then it was easy to find a thane
who sought his rest elsewhere, farther away,
140   a bed in the outbuildings, when was pointed out —
truly announced with clear tokens —
that hall-thane's hate; he kept himself afterwards
farther and safer, who escaped the fiend.
So he ruled, and strove against right,
one against all, until empty stood
the best of houses. And so for a great while —
for twelve long winters the lord of the Scyldings
suffered his grief, every sort of woe,
great sorrow, for to the sons of men
150   it became known, and carried abroad
in sad tales, that Grendel strove
long with Hrothgar, bore his hatred,
sins and feuds, for many seasons,
perpetual conflict; he wanted no peace
with any man of the Danish army,
nor ceased his deadly hatred, nor settled with money,
nor did any of the counselors need to expect
bright compensation from the killer's hands,[11]

---

[10] **thirty thanes:** A "thane" is a retainer, one of the troop of companions surrounding a heroic king in Germanic literature.

[11] **killer's hands:** Germanic and Anglo-Saxon law allowed that a murderer could make peace with the family of his victim by paying compensation, or *wergild*. In a poetic understatement, we are told that Grendel will not pay the *wergild* to mitigate his crimes.

for the great ravager relentlessly stalked,
160 a dark death-shadow, lurked and struck
old and young alike, in perpetual night
held the misty moors. Men do not know
whither such whispering demons wander about.
        Thus the foe of mankind, fearsome and solitary,
often committed his many crimes,
cruel humiliations; he occupied Heorot,
the jewel-adorned hall, in the dark nights —
he saw no need to salute the throne,
he scorned the treasures; he did not know their love.
170 That was deep misery to the lord of the Danes,
a breaking of spirit. Many a strong man sat
in secret counsel, considered advice,
what would be best for the brave at heart
to save themselves from the sudden attacks.
At times they offered honor to idols
at pagan temples, prayed aloud
that the soul-slayer might offer assistance
in the country's distress.[12] Such was their custom,
the hope of heathens — they remembered hell
180 in their minds, they did not know the Maker,
the Judge of deeds, they did not know the Lord God,
or even how to praise the heavenly Protector,
Wielder of glory. Woe unto him
who must thrust his soul through wicked force
in the fire's embrace, expect no comfort,
no way to change at all! It shall be well for him
who can seek the Lord after his deathday
and find security in the Father's embrace.

III

With the sorrows of that time the son of Healfdene
190 seethed constantly; nor could the wise hero
turn aside his woe — too great was the strife,
long and loathsome, which befell that nation,
violent, grim, cruel, greatest of night-evils.
        Then from his home the thane of Hygelac,[13]

---

[12] **soul-slayer . . . in the country's distress:** The Danes, who are still pagans, pray to the devil for deliverance. [Ed.]

[13] **thane of Hygelac:** Beowulf, nephew of Hygelac and the hero of the poem. He announces himself by name considerably later (l. 343). [Ed.]

a good man among the Geats, heard of Grendel's deeds —
he was of mankind the strongest of might
in those days of this life,
noble and mighty. He commanded to be made
a good wave-crosser, said that that war-king
200 he would seek out over the swan's-riding,
the renowned prince, when he was in need of men.
Wise men did not dissuade him at all
from that journey, though he was dear to them;
they encouraged his bold spirit, inspected the omens.
From the Geatish nation that good man
had chosen the boldest champions, the best
he could find; one of fifteen,
he sought the sea-wood. A wise sailor
showed the way to the edge of the shore.
210 The time came — the craft was on the waves,
moored under the cliffs. Eager men
climbed on the prow — the currents eddied,
sea against sand — the soldiers bore
into the bosom of the ship their bright gear,
fine polished armor; the men pushed off
on their wished-for journey in that wooden vessel.
Over the billowing waves, urged by the wind,
the foamy-necked floater flew like a bird,
until in due time on the second day
220 the curved-prowed vessel had come so far
that the seafarers sighted land,
shining shore-cliffs, steep mountains,
wide headlands — then the waves were crossed,
the journey at an end. Thence up quickly
the people of the Weders[14] climbed onto the plain,
moored their ship, shook out their mail-shirts,
their battle-garments; they thanked God
that the sea-paths had been smooth for them.
    When from the wall the Scyldings' watchman,
230 whose duty it was to watch the sea-cliffs,
saw them bear down the gangplank bright shields,
ready battle-gear, he was bursting with curiosity
in his mind to know who these men were.

---

[14] **Weders:** An alternative name for the Geats. For other alternative names see the list provided on page 1191.

This thane of Hrothgar rode his horse
down to the shore, and shook mightily
his strong spear, and spoke a challenge:
"What are you, warriors in armor, wearing
coats of mail, who have come thus sailing
over the sea-road in a tall ship,
240   hither over the waves? Long have I been
the coast-warden, and kept sea-watch
so that no enemies with fleets and armies
should ever attack the land of the Danes.
Never more openly have there ever come
shield-bearers here, nor have you heard
any word of leave from our warriors
or consent of kinsmen. I have never seen
a greater earl on earth than that one among you,
a man in war-gear; that is no mere courtier,
250   honored only in weapons—unless his looks belie him,
his noble appearance! Now I must know
your lineage, lest you go hence
as false spies, travel further
into Danish territory. Now, you sea-travelers
from a far-off land, listen to my
simple thought—the sooner the better,
you must make clear from whence you have come."

IV

    The eldest one answered him,
leader of the troop, unlocked his word-hoard:
260   "We are men of the Geatish nation
and Hygelac's hearth-companions.
My father was well-known among men,
a noble commander named Ecgtheow;
he saw many winters before he passed away,
ancient, from the court; nearly everyone
throughout the world remembers him well.
With a friendly heart have we come
seeking your lord, the son of Healfdene,
guardian of his people; be of good counsel to us!
270   We have a great mission to that famous man,
ruler of the Danes; nor should any of it be
hidden, I think. You know, if things are
as we have truly heard tell,
that among the Scyldings some sort of enemy,
hidden evildoer, in the dark nights

manifests his terrible and mysterious violence,
shame and slaughter. With a generous spirit
I can counsel Hrothgar, advise him how,
wise old king, he may overcome this fiend—
280 if a change should ever come for him,
a remedy for the evil of his afflictions,
and his seething cares turn cooler;
or forever afterwards a time of anguish
he shall suffer, his sad necessity, while there stands
in its high place the best of houses."
              The watchman spoke, as he sat on his horse,
a fearless officer: "A sharp shield-warrior
must be a judge of both things,
words and deeds, if he would think well.
290 I understand that to the Scylding lord
you are a friendly force. Go forth, and bear
weapons and armor—I shall guide your way;
and I will command my young companions
to guard honorably against all enemies
your ship, newly-tarred, upon the sand,
to watch it until the curved-necked wood
bears hence across the ocean-streams
a beloved man to the borders of the Weders—
and such of these good men as will be granted
300 that they survive the storm of battle."
They set off—their vessel stood still,
the roomy ship rested in its riggings,
fast at anchor. Boar-figures shone[15]
over gold-plated cheek-guards,
gleaming, fire-hardened; they guarded the lives
of the grim battle-minded. The men hastened,
marched together, until they could make out
the timbered hall, splendid and gold-adorned—
the most famous building among men
310 under the heavens—where the high king waited;
its light shone over many lands.
Their brave guide showed them the bright court
of the mighty ones, so that they might go
straight to it; that fine soldier
wheeled his horse and spoke these words:

---

[15] **Boar-figures shone:** The boar was a sacred animal in Germanic mythology; archaeologists have unearthed several Anglo-Saxon helmets with boar images on them.

"Time for me to go. The almighty Father
guard you in his grace,
safe in your journeys! I must to the sea,
and hold my watch against hostile hordes."

V

320   The road was stone-paved, the path led
the men together. Their mail coats shone
hard, hand-linked, bright rings of iron
rang out on their gear, when right to the hall
they went trooping in their terrible armor.
Sea-weary, they set their broad shields,
wondrously-hard boards, against the building's wall;
they sat on a bench—their byrnies rang out,
their soldiers' war-gear; their spears stood,
the gear of the seamen all together,
330 a gray forest of ash. That iron troop
was worthy of its weapons.
                              Then a proud warrior
asked those soldiers about their ancestry:
"From whence do you carry those covered shields,
gray coats of mail and grim helmets,
this troop of spears? I am herald and servant
to Hrothgar; never have I seen
so many foreign men so fearless and bold.
For your pride, I expect, not for exile,
and for greatness of heart you have sought out Hrothgar."
340 The courageous one answered him,
proud prince of the Weders, spoke words
hardy in his helmet: "We are Hygelac's
board-companions—Beowulf is my name.
I wish to explain my errand
to the son of Healfdene, famous prince,
your lord, if he will allow us,
in his goodness, to greet him."
Wulfgar spoke—a prince of the Wendels,
his noble character was known to many,
350 his valor and wisdom: "I will convey
to the friend of the Danes, lord of the Scyldings,
giver of rings, what you have requested,
tell the famous prince of your travels,
and then quickly announce to you the answer
which that good man sees fit to give me."
                              He hastily returned to where Hrothgar sat

old and gray-haired, with his band of earls;
he boldly went, stood by the shoulder
of the Danish king—he knew the noble custom.
360 Wulfgar spoke to his friend and lord:
"There have arrived here over the sea's expanse,
come from afar, men of the Geats;
the oldest among them, the fighting men
call Beowulf. They have requested
that they, my lord, might be allowed
to exchange words with you—do not refuse them
your reply, gracious Hrothgar!
In their war-trappings they seem worthy
of noble esteem; notable indeed is that chief
370 who has shown these soldiers the way hither."

VI

Hrothgar spoke, protector of the Scyldings:
"I knew him when he was nothing but a boy—
his old father was called Ecgtheow,
to whom Hrethel the Geat gave in marriage
his only daughter; now his daring son
has come here, sought a loyal friend.
Seafarers, in truth, have said to me,
those who brought to the Geats gifts and money
as thanks, that he has thirty
380 men's strength, strong in battle,
in his handgrip. Holy God
in His grace has guided him to us,
to the West-Danes, as I would hope,
against Grendel's terror. To this good man
I shall offer treasures for his true daring.
Be hasty now, bid them enter
to see this troop of kinsmen all assembled;
and tell them in your words that they are welcome
to the Danish people."
390   He announced from within:
"My conquering lord commands me to tell you,
ruler of the East-Danes, that he knows your ancestry,
and you are to him, hardy spirits,
welcome hither from across the rolling waves.
Now you may go in your war-gear
under your helmets to see Hrothgar,
but let your battle-shields and deadly spears
await here the result of your words."

      The mighty one arose, and many a man with him,

400 powerful thanes; a few waited there,

guarded their battle-dress as the bold man bid them.

They hastened together as the man led them,

under Heorot's roof; [the warrior went]

hardy in his helmet, until he stood on the hearth.

Beowulf spoke—his byrnie gleamed on him,

war-net sewn by the skill of a smith—:

"Be well, Hrothgar! I am Hygelac's kinsman

and young retainer; in my youth I have done

many a glorious deed. This business with Grendel

410 was made known to me on my native soil;

seafarers say that this building stands,

most excellent of halls, idle and useless

to every man, after evening's light

is hidden under heaven's gleaming dome.

Then my own people advised me,

the best warriors and the wisest men,

that I should, lord Hrothgar, seek you out,

because they knew the might of my strength;

they themselves had seen me, bloodstained from battle,

420 come from the fight, when I captured five,

slew a tribe of giants, and on the salt waves

fought sea-monsters by night, survived that tight spot,

avenged the Weders' affliction—they asked for trouble!—

and crushed those grim foes; and now with Grendel,

that monstrous beast, I shall by myself have

a word or two with that giant. From you now I wish,

ruler of the Bright-Danes, to request,

protector of the Scyldings, a single favor,

that you not refuse me, having come this far,

430 protector of warriors, noble friend to his people,—

that I might alone, o my own band of earls

and this hardy troop, cleanse Heorot.

I have also heard that this evil beast

in his wildness does not care for weapons,

so I too will scorn—so that Hygelac,

my liege-lord, may be glad of me—

to bear a sword or a broad shield,

a yellow battle-board, but with my grip

I shall grapple with the fiend and fight for life,

440 foe against foe. Let him put his faith

in the Lord's judgment, whom death takes!

I expect that he will, if he is allowed to win,

eat unafraid the folk of the Geats

in that war-hall, as he has often done,
the host of the Hrethmen. You'll have no need
to cover my head—he will have done so,
gory, bloodstained, if death bears me away;
he will take his kill, think to taste me,
will dine alone without remorse,
450 stain his lair in the moor; no need to linger
in sorrow over disposing of my body!
Send on to Hygelac, if battle should take me,
the best battledress, which my breast wears,
finest of garments; it is Hrethel's heirloom,
the work of Weland.[16] *Wyrd*[17] always goes as it must!"

VII

       Hrothgar spoke, protector of the Scyldings:
"For past favors, my friend Beowulf,
and for old deeds, you have sought us out.
Your father struck up the greatest of feuds,
460 when he killed Heatholaf by his own hand
among the Wylfings. When the Weder tribe
would not harbor him for fear of war,
thence he sought the South-Dane people
over the billowing seas, the Honor-Scyldings;
then I first ruled the Danish folk
and held in my youth this grand kingdom,
city of treasure and heroes—then Heorogar
was dead, my older brother unliving,
Healfdene's firstborn—he was better than I!
470 Later I settled that feud with fee-money;
I sent to the Wylfings over the crest of the waves
ancient treasures; he swore oaths to me.[18]
It is a sorrow to my very soul to say
to any man what Grendel has done to me—
humiliated Heorot with his hateful thoughts,

---

[16]**the work of Weland:** The legendary blacksmith of the Norse gods. The antiquity of weapons and armor added to their value.

[17]*Wyrd:* The Anglo-Saxon word for "fate"; it is sometimes partly personified, though not as much as the Roman goddess Fortuna, or Fortune.

[18]**he swore oaths to me:** Hrothgar recalls the time Beowulf's father Ecgtheow paid him compensation for a man he had killed. Ecgtheow swore an oath of loyalty to Hrothgar and the Danes as a result. Hrothgar publicly interprets the arrival of Beowulf, Ecgtheow's son, as a repayment of the oath. [Ed.]

his sudden attacks. My hall-troop,
my warriors, are decimated; *wyrd* has swept them away
into Grendel's terror. God might easily
put an end to the deeds of this mad enemy!
480 Often men have boasted, drunk with beer,
officers over their cups of ale,
that they would abide in the beerhall
Grendel's attack with a rush of sword-terror.
Then in the morning this meadhall,
lordly dwelling, was drenched with blood,
when daylight gleamed, the benches gory,
the hall spattered and befouled; I had fewer
dear warriors when death took them away.
Now sit down at my feast, drink mead in my hall,
490 men's reward of victory, as your mood urges."
          Then a bench was cleared in the beerhall
for the men of the Geats all together;
the strong-minded men went to sit down,
proud in their strength. A thane did his service,
bore in his hands the gold-bright ale-cup,
poured the clear sweet drink. The scop sang
brightly in Heorot—there was the joy of heroes,
no small gathering of Danes and Geats.

VIII

          Unferth[19] spoke, son of Ecglaf,
500 who sat at the feet of the Scylding lord,
unbound his battle-runes—Beowulf's journey,
that brave seafarer, sorely vexed him,
for he did not wish that any other man
on this middle-earth should care for glory
under the heavens, more than he himself:
"Are you the Beowulf who strove with Breca
in a swimming contest on the open sea,
where in your pride you tried the waves
and for a foolish boast risked your life
510 in the deep water? No man, whether
friend or foe, could dissuade you two

---

[19] **Unferth:** Unferth holds influence in Hrothgar's court; he is twice referred to as a spokesman or orator. His taunting of Beowulf is a form of testing found in other epic tales. Perhaps significantly, his name means either "un-peace" or "unreason." [Ed.]

from that sad venture, when you swam in the sea;
there you seized in your arms the ocean-streams,
measured the sea-ways, flailed your hands
and glided over the waves — the water roiled,
wintry surges. In the keeping of the water
you toiled for seven nights, and he outswam you,
and had more strength. Then in the morning
the swells bore him to the Heathoream shore;
520 from thence he sought his own sweet land,
beloved by his people, the land of the Brondings,
the fair fortress, where he had his folk,
his castle and treasure. He truly fulfilled,
the son of Beanstan, his boast against you.
So I expect a worse outcome from you —
though you may have survived the storm of battle,
some grim combats — if for Grendel you dare
to lie in wait the whole night long."
       Beowulf spoke, son of Ecgtheow:
530 "What a great deal, Unferth my friend,
drunk with beer, you have said about Breca,
told his adventures! I will tell the truth —
I had greater strength on the sea,
more ordeals on the waves than any other man.
When we were just boys we two agreed
and boasted — we were both still
in our youth — that out on the great ocean
we would risk our lives, and we did just that.
We had bare swords, when we swam in the sea,
540 hard in our hands; we thought to protect
ourselves from whales. Not for anything
could he swim far from me on the sea-waves,
more swiftly on the water, nor would I go from him.
We two were together on the sea
for five nights, until the flood drove us apart,
surging waves, coldest of weathers,
darkening night, and a northern wind,
knife-sharp, pushed against us. The seas were choppy;
the fishes of the sea were stirred up by it.
550 There my coat of armor offered help,
hard, hand-locked, against those hostile ones,
my woven battle-dress lay on my breast
adorned with gold. Down to the ocean floor
a grisly foe dragged me, gripped me fast
in his grim grasp, yet it was given to me
to stab that monster with the point of my sword,

my war-blade; the storm of battle took away
that mighty sea-beast, through my own hand.

IX

Time and again those terrible enemies
560 sorely threatened me. I served them well
with my dear sword, as they deserved.
They got no joy from their gluttony,
those wicked maneaters, when they tasted me,
sat down to their feast on the ocean floor —
but in the morning, wounded by my blade,
they were washed ashore by the ocean waves,
dazed by sword-blows, and since that day
they never hindered the passage of any
sea-voyager. Light shone from the east,
570 God's bright beacon; the waves grew calm,
so that I could see the sea-cliffs,
the windswept capes. *Wyrd* often spares
an undoomed man, when his courage endures!
And so it came about that I was able to kill
nine of these sea-monsters. I have never heard
of a harder night-battle under heaven's vault,
nor a more wretched man on the water's stream;
yet I escaped alive from the clutches of my enemies,
weary from my journey. Then the sea washed me up,
580 the currents of the flood, in the land of the Finns,
the welling waters. I have never heard a word
about any such contest concerning you,
such sword-panic. In the play of battle
Breca has never — nor you either —
done a deed so bold and daring
with his decorated blade — I would never boast of it! —
though you became your brothers' killer,
your next of kin; for that you needs must suffer
punishment in hell, no matter how clever you are.
590 I will say it truly, son of Ecglaf,
that never would Grendel have worked such terror,
that gruesome beast, against your lord,
or shames in Heorot, if your courage and spirit
were as fierce as you yourself fancy they are;
but he has found that he need fear no feud,
no storm of swords from the Victory-Scyldings,
no resistance at all from your nation;
he takes his toll, spares no one

in the Danish nation, but indulges himself,
600 hacks and butchers and expects no battle
from the Spear-Danes. But I will show him
soon enough the strength and courage
of the Geats in war. Afterwards, let him who will
go bravely to mead, when the morning light
of a new day, the sun clothed in glory
shines from the south on the sons of men!"
　　　　Then the giver of treasure was greatly pleased,
gray-haired and battle-bold; the Bright-Danes' chief
had faith in his helper; that shepherd of his folk
610 recognized Beowulf's firm resolution.
There was man's laughter, lovely sounds
and winsome words. Wealhtheow went forth,
Hrothgar's queen, mindful of customs;
adorned with gold, she greeted the men in the hall,
then that courteous wife offered the full cup
first to the guardian of the East-Danes' kingdom,
bid him be merry at his beer-drinking,
beloved by his people; with pleasure he received
the feast and cup, victorious king.
620 The lady of the Helmings then went about
to young and old, gave each his portion
of the precious cup, until the moment came
when the ring-adorned queen, of excellent heart,
bore the mead-cup to Beowulf;
she greeted the Geatish prince, thanked God
with wise words that her wish had come to pass,
that she could rely on any earl for relief
from those crimes. He took the cup,
the fierce warrior, from Wealhtheow,
630 and then eager for battle he made his announcement.
Beowulf spoke, son of Ecgtheow:
"I resolved when I set out over the waves,
sat down in my ship with my troop of soldiers,
that I would entirely fulfill the wishes
of your people, or fall slain,
fast in the grip of my foe. I shall perform
a deed of manly courage, or in this meadhall
I will await the end of my days!"
These words well pleased that woman,
640 the boasting of the Geat; she went, the gold-adorned
and courteous folk-queen, to sit beside her lord.
　　　　Then, as before, there in that hall were
strong words spoken, the people happy,

the sounds of a victorious nation, until shortly
the son of Healfdene wished to seek
his evening rest; he knew that the wretched beast
had been planning to do battle in the high building
from the time they could first see the sunrise
until night fell darkening over all,
650 and creatures of shadow came creeping about
pale under the clouds. The company arose.
One warrior greeted another there,
Hrothgar to Beowulf, and wished him luck,
gave him control of the wine-hall in these words:
"I have never entrusted to any man,
ever since I could hold and hoist a shield,
the great hall of the Danes—except to you now.
Have it and hold it, protect this best of houses,
be mindful of glory, show your mighty valor,
660 watch for your enemies! You will have all you desire,
if you emerge from this brave undertaking alive."

X

Then Hrothgar and his troop of heroes,
protector of the Scyldings, departed from the hall;
the war-chief wished to seek Wealhtheow,
his queen's bedchamber. The glorious king
had set against Grendel a hall-guardian
—as men had heard said—who did special service
for the king of the Danes, kept a giant-watch.
Surely the Geatish prince greatly trusted
670 his mighty strength, the Maker's favor,
when he took off his iron byrnie,
undid his helmet, and gave his decorated iron,
best of swords, to his servant
and bid him hold his battle-gear.
The good man, Beowulf the Geat,
spoke a few boasting words before he lay down:
"I consider myself no poorer in strength
and battle-deeds than Grendel does himself;
and so I will not kill him with a sword,
680 put an end to his life, though I easily might;
he knows no arts of war, no way to strike back,
hack at my shield-boss, though he be brave
in his wicked deeds; but tonight we two will
forego our swords, if he dare to seek out
a war without weapons—and then let the wise Lord

grant the judgment of glory, the holy God,
to whichever hand seems proper to Him."
         He lay down, battle-brave; the bolster took
the earl's cheek, and around him many
690 a bold seafarer sank to his hall-rest.
None of them thought that he should thence
ever again seek his own dear homeland,
his tribe or the town in which he was raised,
for they had heard it said that savage death
had swept away far too many of the Danish folk
in that wine-hall. But the Lord gave them
a web of victory, the people of the Weders,
comfort and support, so that they completely,
through one man's craft, overcame their enemy,
700 by his own might. It is a well-known truth
that mighty God has ruled mankind
always and forever.
           In the dark night he came
creeping, the shadow-goer. The bowmen slept
who were to hold that horned hall—
all but one. It was well-known to men
that the demon foe could not drag them under
the dark shadows if the Maker did not wish it;
but he, wakeful, keeping watch for his enemy,
awaited, enraged, the outcome of battle.

XI

710 Then from the moor, in a blanket of mist,
Grendel came stalking—he bore God's anger;
the evil marauder meant to ensnare
some of human-kind in that high hall.
Under the clouds he came until he clearly knew
he was near the wine-hall, men's golden house,
finely adorned. It was not the first time
he had sought out the home of Hrothgar,
but never in his life, early or late,
did he find harder luck or a hardier hall-thane.
720 To the hall came that warrior on his journey,
bereft of joys. The door burst open,
fast in its forged bands, when his fingers touched it;
bloody-minded, swollen with rage, he swung open
the hall's mouth, and immediately afterwards
the fiend strode across the paved floor,
went angrily; in his eyes stood

a light not fair, glowing like fire.
He saw in the hall many a soldier,
a peaceful troop sleeping all together,
730 a large company of thanes—and he laughed inside;
he meant to divide, before day came,
this loathsome creature, the life of each
man from his body, when there befell him
the hope of a feast. But it was not his fate
to taste any more of the race of mankind
after that night. The kinsman of Hygelac,
mighty one, beheld how that maneater
planned to proceed with his sudden assault.
Not that the monster meant to delay—
740 he seized at once at his first pass
a sleeping man, slit him open suddenly,
bit into his joints, drank the blood from his veins,
gobbled his flesh in gobbets, and soon
had completely devoured that dead man,
feet and fingertips. He stepped further,
and took in his hands the strong-hearted
man in his bed; the monster reached out
towards him with his hands—he quickly grabbed him
with evil intent, and sat up against his arm.
750 As soon as that shepherd of sins discovered
that he had never met on middle-earth,
in any region of the world, another man
with a greater handgrip, in his heart he was
afraid for his life, but none the sooner could he flee.
His mind was eager to escape to the darkness,
seek out a host of devils—his habit there
was nothing like he had ever met before.
The good kinsman of Hygelac remembered then
his evening speech, and stood upright
760 and seized him fast. His fingers burst;
the giant turned outward, the earl stepped inward.
The notorious one meant—if he might—
to turn away further and flee, away
to his lair in the fen; he knew his fingers
were held in a hostile grip. That was an unhappy journey
that the harm-doer took to Heorot!
The great hall resounded; to the Danes it seemed,
the city's inhabitants, and every brave earl,
like a wild ale-sharing. Both were angry,
770 fierce house-wardens—the hall echoed.
It was a great wonder that the wine-hall

withstood their fighting and did not fall to the ground,
that fair building—but it was fastened
inside and out with iron bands,
forged with skill. From the floor there flew
many a mead-bench, as men have told me,
gold-adorned, where those grim foes fought.
The Scylding elders had never expected
that any man, by any ordinary means,
780 could break it apart, beautiful, bone-adorned,
or destroy it with guile, unless the embrace of fire
might swallow it in flames. The noise swelled
new and stark—among the North-Danes was
horrible terror, in each of them
who heard through the wall the wailing cry—
God's adversary shrieked a grisly song
of horror, defeated, the captive of Hell
bewailed his pain. He pinned him fast,
he who among men was the strongest of might
790 in those days of this life.

XII

That protector of earls would not for anything
let that murderous visitor escape alive—
he did not consider his days on earth
of any use at all. Many an earl
in Beowulf's troop drew his old blade,
longed to protect the life of his liege-lord,
the famous captain, however they could.
But they did not know as they entered the fight,
those stern-minded men of battle,
800 and thought to strike from all sides
and seek his soul, that no sword,
not the best iron anywhere in the world,
could even touch that evil sinner,
for he had worked a curse on weapons,
every sort of blade. His separation from the world
in those days of this life
would have to be miserable, and that alien spirit
would travel far into the keeping of fiends.
Then he discovered, who had done before
810 so much harm to the race of mankind,
so many crimes—he was marked by God—
that his body could bear it no longer,
but the courageous kinsman of Hygelac

had him in hand—hateful to each
was the life of the other. The loathsome creature felt
great bodily pain; a gaping wound opened
in his shoulder-joint, his sinews sprang apart,
his joints burst asunder. Beowulf was given
glory in battle—Grendel was forced
820   to flee, mortally wounded, into the fen-slopes,
seek a sorry abode; he knew quite surely
that the end of his life had arrived,
the sum of his days. The will of the Danes
was entirely fulfilled in that bloody onslaught!
He who had come from afar had cleansed,
wise and stout-hearted, the hall of Hrothgar,
warded off attack. He rejoiced in his night-work,
his great courage. That man of the Geats
had fulfilled his boast to the East-Danes,
830   and entirely remedied all their distress,
the insidious sorrows they had suffered
and had to endure from sad necessity,
no small affliction. It was a clear sign,
when the battle-brave one laid down the hand,
arm and shoulder—there all together
was Grendel's claw—under the curved roof.

XIII

Then in the morning was many a warrior,
as I have heard, around that gift-hall,
leaders of the folk came from far and near
840   throughout the wide land to see that wonder,
the loathsome one's tracks. His parting from life
hardly seemed sad to any man
who examined the trail of that inglorious one,
how he went on his weary way,
defeated by force, to a pool of sea-monsters,
doomed, put to flight, and left a fatal trail.
The water was welling with blood there—
the terrible swirling waves, all mingled together
with hot gore, heaved with the blood of battle,
850   concealed that doomed one when, deprived of joys,
he lay down his life in his lair in the fen,
his heathen soul—and hell took him.
Then the old retainers returned from there,
and many a youth on the joyful journey,
bravely rode their horses back from the mere,

men on their steeds. There they celebrated
Beowulf's glory: it was often said
that south or north, between the two seas,
across the wide world, there was none
860   better under the sky's expanse
among shield-warriors, nor more worthy to rule—
though they found no fault with their own friendly lord,
gracious Hrothgar, but said he was a good king.
At times the proud warriors let their horses prance,
their fallow mares fare in a contest,
wherever the footpaths seemed fair to them,
the way tried and true. At times the king's thane,
full of grand stories, mindful of songs,
who remembered much, a great many
870   of the old tales, found other words
truly bound together; he began again
to recite with skill the adventure of Beowulf
adeptly tell an apt tale,
and weave his words.[20] He said nearly all
that he had heard said of Sigemund's[21]
stirring deeds, many strange things,
the Volsung's strife, his distant voyages
obscure, unknown to all the sons of men,
his feuds and crimes—except for Fitela,
880   when of such things he wished to speak to him,
uncle to nephew—for always they were,
in every combat, companions at need;
a great many of the race of giants
they slaughtered with their swords. For Sigemund
no small fame grew after his final day,
after that hardened soldier, prince's son,
had killed a dragon, keeper of a hoard;
alone, he dared to go under gray stones,
a bold deed—nor was Fitela by his side;
890   yet so it befell him that his sword pierced

---

[20] **the king's thane . . . weave his words:** These interesting lines describe Hrothgar's scop improvising an account of Beowulf's deed, drawing on a repertoire of heroic formulae with which he and the audience are already familiar. [Ed.]

[21] **Sigemund:** Beowulf is praised by being compared to Sigemund, the legendary monster-slayer of Germanic epic, then contrasted to Heremod, a former king of the Danes who descended into tyranny. The story of Sigemund's slaying of the dragon (ll. 875–900) may foreshadow the dragon fight in the second part of *Beowulf*. The story of Heremod (ll. 901–915) describes a king who falls into dissolution and betrays his own people. [Ed.]

the wondrous serpent, stood fixed in the wall,
the manly iron; the dragon met his death.
That fierce creature had gone forth in courage
so that he could possess that store of rings
and use them at his will; the son of Wæls
loaded his sea-boat, bore the bright treasure
to the ship's hold. The serpent melted in its own heat.

      He was the most famous of exiles, far and wide,
among all people, protector of warriors,
900 for his noble deeds—he had prospered for them—
since the struggles of Heremod had ceased,
his might and valor. Among the Eotens
he was betrayed into his enemies' hands,
quickly dispatched. The surging of cares
had crippled him too long; he became a deadly burden
to his own people, to all noblemen;
for many a wise man had mourned
in earlier times over his headstrong ways
who had looked to him for relief from affliction,
910 hoped that that prince's son would prosper,
receive his father's rank, rule his people,
hoard and fortress, a kingdom of heroes,
the Scylding homeland. The kinsman of Hygelac
became to all of the race of mankind
a more pleasant friend; sin possessed him.

      Sometimes, competing, the fallow paths
they measured on horseback. When morning's light
raced on and hastened away, many a retainer,
stout-hearted, went to see the high hall
920 to see the strange wonder; the king himself,
guard of the treasure-hoard, strode glorious
from the woman's chambers with a great entourage,
a chosen retinue, and his royal queen with him
measured the meadhall-path with a troop of maidens.

XIV

      Hrothgar spoke—he went to the hall,
stood on the steps, beheld the steep roof
plated with gold, and Grendel's hand:
"For this sight let us swiftly offer thanks
to the Almighty! Much have I endured
930 of dire grief from Grendel, but God may always
work, Shepherd of glory, wonder upon wonder.
It was not long ago that I did not expect

ever in my life to experience relief
from any of my woes, when, stained with blood,
this best of houses stood dripping, gory,
a widespread woe to all wise men
who did not expect that they might ever
defend the people's fortress from its foes,
devils and demons. Now a retainer has done
940   the very deed, through the might of God,
which we all could not contrive to do
with all our cleverness. Lo, that woman could say,
whosoever has borne such a son
into the race of men, if she still lives,
that the God of Old was good to her
in childbearing. Now I will cherish you,
Beowulf, best of men, like a son
in my heart; hold well henceforth
your new kinship. You shall have no lack
950   of the worldly goods which I can bestow.
Often have I offered rewards for less,
honored with gifts a humbler man,
weaker in battle. Now by yourself
you have done such deeds that your fame will endure
always and forever—may the Almighty
reward you with good, as He has already done!"
        Beowulf spoke, son of Ecgtheow:
"Freely and gladly have we fought this fight,
done this deed of courage, daringly faced
960   this unknown power. I would much prefer
that you might have seen the foe himself
decked in his finery, fallen and exhausted!
With a hard grip I hoped to bind him
quickly and keenly on the killing floor,
so that for my handgrasp he would have to
lie squirming for life, unless he might slip away;
I could not—the Creator did not wish it—
hinder his going, no matter how hard I held
that deadly enemy; too overwhelming was
970   that fiend's flight. Yet he forfeited his hand,
his arm and shoulder, to save his life,
to guard his tracks—though he got thereby,
pathetic creature, little comfort;
the loathsome destroyer will live no longer,
rotten with sin, but pain has seized him,
grabbed him tightly in its fierce grip,
its baleful bonds—and there he shall abide,

guilty of his crimes, the greater judgment,
how the shining Maker wishes to sentence him."
980 　　　Then the son of Ecglaf[22] was more silent
in boasting words about his battle-works
after the noblemen, through the earl's skill,
looked on the hand over the high roof,
the enemy's fingers; at the end of each nail
was a sharp tip, most like steel,
heathen talons, the terrible spikes
of that awful warrior; each of them agreed
that not even the hardest of ancient and honorable
irons could touch him, or injure at all
990 the bloody battle-paw of that baleful creature.

XV

　　　Then it was quickly commanded that Heorot
be adorned by hands inside; many there,
men and women, prepared that wine-hall,
the guest-house. Gold-dyed tapestries
shone on the walls, many wonderful sights
to any man who might look on them.
That shining building was nearly shattered
inside, entirely, fast in its iron bands,
its hinges sprung; the roof alone survived
1000 unharmed, when that horrible creature,
stained with foul deeds, turned in his flight,
despairing of life. Death is not an easy
thing to escape—try it who will—
but compelled by necessity all must come
to that place set aside for soul-bearers,
children of men, dwellers on earth,
where the body, fast on its bed of death,
sleeps after the feast.
　　　　　Then was the set time
that the son of Healfdene went to the hall;
1010 the king himself wished to share in the feast.
I have never heard of a greater host
who bore themselves better before their treasure-giver.
Those men in their glory moved to their benches,

---

[22] **son of Ecglaf:** Unferth.

rejoiced in the feast; fairly those kinsmen
took many a full mead-cup,
stouthearted in the high hall,
Hrothgar and Hrothulf. Heorot within was
filled with friends — no false treacheries
did the people of the Scyldings plot at that time.[23]

1020 He gave to Beowulf the blade of Healfdene,
a golden war-standard as a reward for victory,
the bright banner, a helmet and byrnie,
a great treasure-sword — many saw them
borne before that man. Beowulf received
the full cup in the hall, he felt no shame
at that gift-giving before his bowmen;
never have I heard tell of four treasures
given more graciously, gold-adorned,
from one man to another on the ale-benches.

1030 On the crown of the helmet as a head-protector
a ridge, wound with wire, stood without,
so that the file-sharp swords might not terribly
harm him, shower-hard, when shield-fighters
had to go against hostile forces.
The protector of earls ordered eight horses
with ornamented bridles led into the building,
in under the eaves; on one sat
a saddle, skillfully tooled, set with gemstones;
that was the warseat of the high-king

1040 when the son of Healfdene sought to perform
his swordplay — the widely-known warrior
never failed at the front, when the slain fell about him.
And the lord of the Ingwines gave ownership
of both of them to Beowulf,
the horses and weapons, bid him use them well.
So manfully did the mighty prince,
hoard-guard of warriors, reward the storm of battle
with steeds and treasures that none who will speak
the truth rightfully could ever reproach them.

---

[23] **no false treacheries . . . at that time:** This refers to later dissension among the Danes, culminating in the usurpation of the royal throne by Hrothgar's nephew Hrothulf. [Ed.]

XVI

1050   Then the lord of earls, to each of those
on the meadbenches who had made with Beowulf
a sea-journey, gave jeweled treasures,
antique heirlooms, and then ordered
that gold be paid for the man whom Grendel
had wickedly slain — he would have done more,
if wise God and one man's courage
had not prevented that fate. The Maker ruled all
of the race of mankind, as He still does.
Therefore understanding is always best,
1060 spiritual foresight — he must face much,
both love and hate, who long here
endures this world in these days of strife.
      Noise and music mingled together
before the leader of Healfdene's forces,
the harp was touched, tales often told,
when Hrothgar's scop was set to recite
among the mead-tables his hall-entertainment
about the sons of Finn, surprised in ambush,
when the hero of the Half-Danes, Hnæf the Scylding
1070 had to fall in a Frisian slaughter.[24]
      Hildeburh, indeed, had no need to praise
the good faith of the Jutes. Guiltless, she was
deprived of her dear ones in that shieldplay,
her sons and brothers — sent forth to their fate,
dispatched by spears; she was a sad lady!
Not without cause did she mourn fate's decrees,
the daughter of Hoc, after daybreak came
and she could see the slaughter of her kin
under the very skies where once she held

---

[24] **Frisian slaughter:** Part of this story (ll. 1068–1158) is found in a fragment of another Anglo-Saxon poem, *The Fight at Finnsburh.* It involves a conflict between a warrior's duty to avenge the slaying of his leader and his duty to obey a sworn oath. Finn, king of Frisia, marries a Danish princess, Hildeburh, in an effort to make peace between the Frisians and Danes. But when Hildeburh's brother Hnaef and his Danish followers visit her at Finnsburh they are attacked by a dissident band of Frisians (called the Jutes here). Hnaef is killed in the fighting, as well as Finn's son by Hildeburh. With both sides severely reduced, the warrior Hengest assumes leadership of the Danes. A truce is declared, extending protection to the surviving Danish guests of the Frisians under the condition that no one speak of the fight again. After two Frisians, Guthlaf and Oslaf, foolishly lament the tragedy, violating the oath of silence, Hengest and his Danish companions seize the opportunity to avenge the death of Hnaef, killing Finn, stealing his treasure, and carrying Hildeburh back to her Danish people. [Ed.]

1080 the greatest worldly joys. War took away
all of the thanes of Finn, except a few,
so that he could not continue at all
a fight with Hengest on the battlefield,
nor could that woeful remnant drive away
the prince's thane—so they offered them terms:
they would clear out another hall for them,
a house and high-seat, of which they should have
half the control with the sons of the Jutes,
and Folcwalda's son, with feasting and gifts,
1090 should honor the Danes each and every day,
gladden the troops of Hengest with gold rings
and ancient treasures, ornamented gold,
just as often as he would encourage
the hosts of the Frisians in the beerhall.
They swore their pledges then on either side,
a firm compact of peace. With unfeigned zeal
Finn swore his oaths to Hengest, pledged that he,
with the consent of his counselors, would
support with honor those sad survivors,
1100 and that none should break their pact in word or deed,
nor through malice should ever make mention,
though they should serve their ring-giver's slayer,
without a lord, as they were led by need—
and if, provoking, any Frisian spoke
reminding them of all their murderous hate,
then with the sword's edge they should settle it.
        The oath was made ready, and ancient gold
was brought from the hoard; the Battle-Scyldings'
best fighting-man was ready for the fire.
1110 It was easy to see upon that pyre
the bloodstained battle-shirt, the gilded swine,
iron-hard boar-images, the noblemen
with fatal wounds—so many felled by war!
Then Hildeburh commanded at Hnæf's pyre
that her own son be consigned to the flames
to be burnt, flesh and bone, placed on the pyre
at his uncle's shoulder; the lady sang
a sad lament. The warrior ascended;
to the clouds coiled the mighty funeral fire,
1120 and roared before their mound; their heads melted,
their gashes burst open and spurted blood,
the deadly body-bites. The flame devoured,
most greedy spirit, those whom war destroyed
of both peoples—their glory departed.

XVII

The warriors left to seek their native lands,
bereft of friends, to behold Frisia,
their homes and high fortresses. Hengest still
stayed there with Finn that slaughter-stained winter,
unwilling, desolate. He dreamt of home,
1130 though on the frozen sea he could not steer
his ring-prowed ship — the ocean raged with storms,
strove with the wind, and winter locked the waves
in icy bonds, until there came another
year to the courtyard — as it yet does,
always observing its seasons and times,
bright glorious weather. Gone was the winter,
and fair the bosom of earth; the exile burned
to take leave of that court, yet more he thought
of stern vengeance than of sea-voyages,
1140 how he might arrange a hostile meeting,
remind the Jutish sons of his iron sword.
So he did not refuse the world's custom
when the son of Hunlaf placed a glinting sword,
the best of battle-flames, upon his lap;
its edge was not unknown among the Jutes.
And so, in turn, to the bold-minded Finn
befell cruel sword-evil in his own home,
when Guthlaf and Oslaf spoke of their grief,
the fierce attack after their sea voyage,
1150 and cursed their wretched lot — the restless heart
could not restrain itself. The hall was stained
with the lifeblood of foes, and Finn was slain,
the king among his host; the queen was seized.
The Scylding bowmen carried to their ships
all the house property of that earth-king,
whatever they could find in Finn's homestead,
brooches and bright gems. On their sea journey
they bore that noble queen back to the Danes
and led her to her people.
                                    The lay was sung,
1160 the entertainer's song. Glad sounds rose again,
the bench-noise glittered, cupbearers gave
wine from wondrous vessels. Wealhtheow came forth
in her golden crown to where the good two
sat, nephew and uncle; their peace was still whole then,
each true to the other. Likewise Unferth, spokesman,
sat at the foot of the Scylding lord; everyone trusted his spirit,

that he had great courage, though to his kinsmen he had
not been merciful in sword-play. Then the lady of the Scyldings spoke:
    "Take this cup, my noble courteous lord,
1170   giver of treasure! Be truly joyful,
gold-friend of men, and speak to the Geats
in mild words, as a man should do!
Be gracious to the Geats, mindful of the gifts
which you now have from near and far.
I have been told that you would take this warrior
for your son. Heorot is cleansed,
the bright ring-hall — use your many rewards
while you can, and leave to your kinsmen
the folk and kingdom, when you must go forth
1180   to face the Maker's decree. I know that my own
dear gracious Hrothulf will hold in honors
these youths, if you should give up the world
before him, friend of the Scyldings;
I expect that he would wish to repay
both our sons kindly, if he recalls all
the pleasures and honors that we have shown him,
in our kindness, since he was a child."
She turned to the bench where her boys sat,
Hrethric and Hrothmund, and the hero's son,
1190   all the youths together; the good man,
Beowulf the Geat, sat between the brothers.

XVIII

    The flagon was borne to him, a friendly greeting
conveyed with words, and wound gold
offered with good will, two armlets,
garments and rings, and the greatest neck-collar
ever heard of anywhere on earth.
Under heaven I have not heard tell of a better
hoard-treasure of heroes, since Hama carried off
to the bright city the Brosinga necklace,
1200   the gem and its treasures; he fled the treachery
of Eormanric,[25] chose eternal counsel.

---

[25] **Hama . . . fled the treachery of Eormanric:** The legendary Brosinga necklace was associated with the Norse goddess Freya. A certain Hama is accused of stealing it from Eormanric, king of the Ostrogoths (d. 375), into whose care it has fallen. "Eternal counsel" may refer to Hama's retreat into a monastery.

Hygelac the Geat on his last journey
had that neck-ring, nephew of Swerting,
when under the banner he defended his booty,
the spoils of slaughter. Fate struck him down
when in his pride he went looking for woe,
a feud with the Frisians.[26] He wore that finery,
those precious stones, over the cup of the sea,
that powerful lord, and collapsed under his shield.

1210 Into Frankish hands came the life of that king,
his breast-garments, and the great collar too;
a lesser warrior looted the corpses
mown down in battle; Geatish men
held that killing field.
                                    The hall swallowed the noise.
Wealhtheow stood before the company and spoke:
"Beowulf, beloved warrior, wear this neck-ring
in good health, and enjoy this war-garment,
treasure of a people, and prosper well,
be bold and clever, and to these boys be

1220 mild in counsel—I will remember you for that.
You have made it so that men will praise you
far and near, forever and ever,
as wide as the seas, home of the winds,
surround the shores of earth. Be while you live
blessed, o nobleman! I wish you well
with these bright treasures. Be to my sons
kind in your deeds, keeping them in joys!
Here each earl is true to the other,
mild in his heart, loyal to his liege-lord,

1230 the thanes united, the nation alert,
the troop, having drunk at my table, will do as I bid."
                                    She went to her seat. The best of feasts it was—
the men drank wine, and did not know *wyrd*,
the cruel fate which would come to pass
for many an earl once evening came,
and Hrothgar departed to his own dwelling,

---

[26]**feud with the Frisians**: The Brosinga necklace, a gift of Wealhtheow to Beowulf, soon will pass from Beowulf's hands to Hygd, wife of his lord, the Geatish King Hygelac. Hygelac in turn will wear the necklace on his final adventure, an ill-fated raid against the Frisians. After the raid, he is caught among the rear guard of his returning army by the Frankish leader Theudebert, in a battle in which Beowulf plays a heroic part. Hygelac dies along with most of his followers and the Franks recover their stolen treasure, while Beowulf escapes. [Ed.]

the mighty one to his rest. Countless men
guarded that hall, as they often had before.
They cleared away bench-planks, spread cushions
1240 and bedding on the floor. One of those beer-drinkers
lay down to his rest fated, ripe for death.
They set at their heads their round battle-shields,
bright boards; there on the bench was
easily seen over the noblemen
the high battle-helmet, the ringed byrnie,
the mighty wooden spear. It was their custom
to be always ready, armed for battle,
at home or in the field, every one of them,
on whatever occasion their overlord
1250 had need of them; that was a good troop.

XIX

      They sank into sleep—one paid sorely
for his evening rest, as had often happened
when Grendel guarded that gold-hall,
committed his wrongs until he came to his end,
died for his sins. It was clearly seen,
obvious to all men, that an avenger still
lived on after that enemy for a long time
after that grim battle—Grendel's mother,
monster-woman, remembered her misery,
1260 she who dwelt in those dreadful waters,
the cold streams, ever since Cain
killed with his blade his only brother,
his father's kin; he fled bloodstained,
marked for murder, left the joys of men,
dwelled in the wasteland. From him awoke
many a fateful spirit—Grendel among them,
hateful accursed foe, who found at Heorot
a wakeful warrior waiting for battle.
There the great beast began to seize him,
1270 but he remembered his mighty strength,
the ample gifts which God had given him,
and trusted the Almighty for mercy,
favor and support; thus he overcame the fiend,
subdued the hellish spirit. He went away wretched,
deprived of joy, to find his place of death,
mankind's foe. But his mother still
greedy, grim-minded, wanted to go

on her sorrowful journey to avenge her son's death.
　　　　She reached Heorot, where the Ring-Danes
1280 slept throughout the building; sudden turnabout
came to men, when Grendel's mother
broke into the hall. The horror was less
by as much as a maiden's strength,
a woman's warfare, is less than an armed man's
when a bloodstained blade, its edges strong,
hammer-forged sword, slices through
the boar-image on a helmet opposite.
Then in the hall was the hard edge drawn,
swords over seats, many a broad shield
1290 raised in hands — none remembered his helmet
or broad mail-shirt when that terror seized them.
She came in haste and meant to hurry out,
save her life, when she was surprised there,
but she had quickly seized, fast in her clutches,
one nobleman when she went to the fens.
He was the dearest of heroes to Hrothgar
among his comrades between the two seas,
mighty shield-warrior, whom she snatched from his rest,
a glorious thane. Beowulf was not there,
1300 but another place had been appointed
for the famous Geat after the treasure-giving.
Heorot was in an uproar — she took the famous hand,
covered in gore; care was renewed,
come again to the dwellings. That was no good exchange,
that those on both sides should have to bargain
with the lives of friends.
　　　　　　　　Then the wise old king,
gray-bearded warrior, was grieved at heart
when he learned that he no longer lived —
the dearest of men, his chief thane, was dead.
1310 Quickly Beowulf was fetched to the chambers,
victory-blessed man. Just before dawn
that noble champion came with his companions,
went with his men to where the old king waited
wondering whether the Almighty would ever
work a change after his tidings of woe.
Across the floor walked the worthy warrior
with his small troop — the hall-wood resounded —
and with his words he addressed the wise one,
lord of the Ingwines, asked him whether
1320 the night had been agreeable, after his urgent summons.

XX

Hrothgar spoke, protector of the Scyldings:
"Ask not of joys! Sorrow is renewed
for the Danish people. Æschere is dead,
elder brother of Yrmenlaf,
my confidant and my counselor
my shoulder-companion in every conflict
when we defended our heads when the footsoldiers clashed
and struck boar-helmets. As a nobleman should be,
always excellent, so Æschere was!

1330 In Heorot he was slain by the hand
of a restless death-spirit; I do not know
where that ghoul went, gloating with its carcass,
rejoicing in its feast. She avenged that feud
in which you killed Grendel yesterday evening
in your violent way with a crushing vice-grip,
for he had diminished and destroyed my people
for far too long. He fell in battle,
it cost him his life, and now has come another
mighty evil marauder who means to avenge

1340 her kin, and too far has carried out her revenge,
as it may seem to many a thane
whose spirit groans for his treasure-giver,
a hard heart's distress — now that hand lies dead
which was wont to give you all good things.
        I have heard countrymen and hall-counselors
among my people report this:
they have seen two such creatures,
great march-stalkers holding the moors,
alien spirits. The second of them,

1350 as far as they could discern most clearly,
had the shape of a woman; the other, misshapen,
marched the exile's path in the form of a man,
except that he was larger than any other;
in bygone days he was called 'Grendel'
by the local folk. They knew no father,
whether before him had been begotten
any more mysterious spirits. That murky land
they hold, wolf-haunted slopes, windy headlands,
awful fenpaths, where the upland torrents

1360 plunge downward under the dark crags,
the flood underground. It is not far hence
— measured in miles — that the mere stands;
over it hangs a grove hoar-frosted,

a firm-rooted wood looming over the water.
Every night one can see there an awesome wonder,
fire on the water. There lives none so wise
or bold that he can fathom its abyss.
Though the heath-stepper beset by hounds,
the strong-horned hart, might seek the forest,
1370 pursued from afar, he will sooner lose
his life on the shore than save his head
and go in the lake — it is no good place!
The clashing waves climb up from there
dark to the clouds, when the wind drives
the violent storms, until the sky itself droops,
the heavens groan. Now once again all help
depends on you alone. You do not yet know
this fearful place, where you might find
the sinful creature — seek it if you dare!
1380 I will reward you with ancient riches
for that feud, as I did before,
with twisted gold, if you return alive."

XXI

Beowulf spoke, son of Ecgtheow:
"Sorrow not, wise one! It is always better
to avenge one's friend than to mourn overmuch.
Each of us shall abide the end
of this world's life; let him who can
bring about fame before death — that is best
for the unliving man after he is gone.
1390 Arise, kingdom's guard, let us quickly go
and inspect the path of Grendel's kin.
I promise you this: he will find no protection —
not in the belly of the earth nor the bottom of the sea,
nor the mountain groves — let him go where he will!
For today, you must endure patiently
all your woes, as I expect you will."
The old man leapt up, thanked the Lord,
the mighty God, for that man's speech.
    Then for Hrothgar a horse was bridled
1400 with plaited mane. The wise prince
rode in full array; footsoldiers marched
with shields at the ready. The tracks were seen
far and wide on the forest paths,
a trail through the woods, where she went forth
over the murky moor, bore the young man's

lifeless body, the best of all those
who had held watch over Hrothgar's home.
The son of nobles crossed over
the steep stone cliffs, the constricted climb,
1410 a narrow solitary path, a course unknown,
the towering headlands, home of sea-monsters.
He went before with just a few
wise men to see the way,
until suddenly he saw mountain-trees,
stunted and leaning over gray stone,
a joyless wood; the water went under
turbid and dreary. To all the Danes,
the men of the Scyldings, many a thane,
it was a sore pain at heart to suffer,
1420 a grief to every earl, when on the seacliff
they came upon the head of Æschere.
The flood boiled with blood — the folk gazed on —
and hot gore. At times a horn sang
its eager war-song. The footsoldiers sat down.
They saw in the water many kinds of serpents,
strange sea-creatures testing the currents,
and on the sloping shores lay such monsters
as often attend in early morning
a sorrowful journey on the sail-road,
1430 dragons and wild beasts. They rushed away
bitter, enraged; they heard the bright noise,
the sound of the battle-horn. A Geatish bowman
cut short the life of one of those swimmers
with a bow and arrow, so that in his body stood
the hard war-shaft; he was a slower swimmer
on the waves, when death took him away.
At once in the water he was assailed
with the barbed hooks of boar-pikes,
violently attacked and dragged ashore,
1440 the strange wave-roamer; the men inspected
this grisly visitor.
                Beowulf geared up
in his warrior's clothing, cared not for his life.
The broad war-shirt, woven by hand,
cunningly made, had to test the mere —
it knew well how to protect his bone-house
so that a battle-grip might not hurt his breast
nor an angry malicious clutch touch his life.
The shining helmet protected his head,
set to stir up the sea's depths,

1450 seek that troubled water, decorated with treasure,
       encircled with a splendid band, as a weapon-smith
       in days of old had crafted it with wonders,
       set boar-images, so that afterwards
       no blade or battle-sword might ever bite it.
       Not the smallest of powerful supports was that
       which Hrothgar's spokesman lent him at need;
       that hilted sword was named Hrunting,
       unique among ancient treasures—
       its edge was iron, etched with poison-stripes,
1460 hardened with the blood of war; it had never failed
       any man who grasped it in his hands in battle,
       who dared to undertake a dreadful journey
       into the very home of the foe—it was not the first time
       that it had to perform a work of high courage.
       Truly, the son of Ecglaf, crafty in strength,
       did not remember what he had said before,
       drunk with wine, when he lent that weapon
       to a better swordsman; he himself did not dare
       to risk his life under the rushing waves,
1470 perform a lordly act; for that he lost honor,
       his fame for courage. Not so with the other,
       when he had geared himself up for battle.

XXII

        Beowulf spoke, son of Ecgtheow:
       "Consider now, famous kinsman of Healfdene,
       wise prince, now that I am eager to depart,
       gold-friend to men, what we spoke of before:
       if ever in your service I should
       lose my life, that you would always be
       in a father's place to me when I have passed away.
1480 Be a protector to my band of men,
       my boon-companions, if battle should take me,
       and send on to Hygelac, beloved Hrothgar,
       the gifts of treasure which you have given me.
       The lord of the Geats will understand by that gold,
       the son of Hrethel will see by that treasure,
       that I found a ring-giver who was good
       in ancient customs, and while I could, enjoyed it.
       And let Unferth have that ancient heirloom,
       that well-known man have my wave-patterned sword,
1490 hard-edged, splendid; with Hrunting I shall
       win honor and fame, or death will take me!"

After these words the Weder-Geat man
hastened boldly, by no means wished to
stay for an answer; the surging sea received
the brave soldier. It was the space of a day
before he could perceive the bottom.
Right away she who held that expanse of water,
bloodthirsty and fierce, for a hundred half-years,
grim and greedy, perceived that some man
1500 was exploring from above that alien land.
She snatched at him, seized the warrior
in her savage clutches, but none the sooner
injured his sound body—the ring-mail encircled him,
so that she could not pierce that war-dress,
the locked coat of mail, with her hostile claws.
Then that she-wolf of the sea swam to the bottom,
and bore the prince of rings into her abode,
so that he might not—no matter how strong—
wield his weapons, but so many wonders
1510 set upon him in the water, many a sea-beast
with battle-tusks tearing at his war-shirt,
monsters pursuing him.
                  Then the earl perceived
that he was in some sort of battle-hall
where no water could harm him in any way,
and, for the hall's roof, he could not be reached
by the flood's sudden rush—he saw a fire-light,
a glowing blaze shining brightly.
Then the worthy man saw that water-witch,
a great mere-wife; he gave a mighty blow
1520 with his battle-sword—he did not temper that stroke—
so that the ring-etched blade rang out on her head
a greedy battle-song. The guest discovered then
that the battle-flame would not bite,
or wound her fatally—but the edge failed
the man in his need; it had endured many
hand-to-hand meetings, often sheared through helmets,
fated war-garments. It was the first time
that the fame of that precious treasure had fallen.
           Again he was stalwart, not slow of zeal,
1530 mindful of glory, that kinsman of Hygelac—
the angry challenger threw away that etched blade,
wrapped and ornamented, so that it lay on the earth,
strong, steel-edged. He trusted his strength,
the might of his handgrip—as a man should do
if by his warfare he thinks to win

long-lasting praise: he cares nothing for his life.
The man of the War-Geats grabbed by the shoulder
Grendel's mother—he had no regret for that feud;
battle-hardened, enraged, he swung her around,
1540 his deadly foe, so she fell to the ground.
Quickly she gave him requital for that
with a grim grasp, and grappled him to her—
weary, he stumbled, strongest of warriors,
of foot-soldiers, and took a fall.
She set upon her hall-guest and drew her knife,
broad, bright-edged; she would avenge her boy,
her only offspring. On his shoulders lay
the linked corselet; it defended his life,
prevented the entrance of point and blade.
1550 There the son of Ecgtheow would have ended his life
under the wide ground, the Geatish champion,
had not his armored shirt offered him help,
the hard battle-net, and holy God
brought about war-victory—the wise Lord,
Ruler of the heavens, decided it rightly,
easily, once he stood up again.

XXIII

He saw among the armor a victorious blade,
ancient giant-sword strong in its edges,
an honor in battle; it was the best of weapons,
1560 except that it was greater than any other man
might even bear into the play of battle,
good, adorned, the work of giants.
The Scyldings' champion seized its linked hilt,
fierce and ferocious, drew the ring-marked sword
despairing of his life, struck in fury
so that it caught her hard in the neck,
broke her bone-rings; the blade cut through
the doomed flesh—she fell to the floor,
the sword was bloody, the soldier rejoiced.
1570 The flames gleamed, a light glowed within
even as from heaven clearly shines
the firmament's candle. He looked around the chamber,
passed by the wall, hefted the weapon
hard by its hilt, that thane of Hygelac,
angry and resolute—nor was the edge useless
to that warrior, but he quickly wished
to pay back Grendel for the many battle-storms

which he had wrought on the West-Danes
much more often than on one occasion,
1580 when Hrothgar's hall-companions
he slew in their beds, devoured sleeping
fifteen men of the Danish folk,
and made off with as many more,
a loathsome booty. He paid him back for that,
the fierce champion, for on a couch he saw
Grendel lying lifeless,
battle-weary from the wound he received
in the combat at Heorot. His corpse burst open
when he was dealt a blow after death,
1590 a hard sword-stroke, and his head chopped off.
       Soon the wise men saw it,
those who kept watch on the water with Hrothgar —
all turbid were the waves, and troubled,
the sea stained with blood. The graybearded
elders spoke together about the good one,
said they did not expect that nobleman
would return, triumphant, to seek
the mighty prince; to many it seemed
that the sea-wolf had destroyed him.
1600 The ninth hour came; the noble Scyldings
abandoned the headland, and home went
the gold-friend of men. The guests sat[27]
sick at heart, and stared into the mere;
they wished, but did not hope, that they would
see their lord himself.
             Then the sword began,
that blade, to waste away into battle-icicles
from the war-blood; it was a great wonder
that it melted entirely, just like ice
when the Father loosens the frost's fetters,
1610 unwraps the water's bonds — He wields power
over times and seasons; that is the true Maker.
The man of the Geats took no more precious treasures
from that place — though he saw many there —
than the head, and the hilt as well,
bright with gems; the blade had melted,
the ornamented sword burned up; so hot was the blood

---

[27] **The guests sat:** The Geats who had come to Heorot with Beowulf.

of the poisonous alien spirit who died in there.
Soon he was swimming who had survived in battle
the downfall of his enemies, dove up through the water;
1620 the sea-currents were entirely cleansed,
the spacious regions, when that alien spirit
gave up life-days and this loaned world.
      The defender of seafarers came to land,
swam stout-hearted; he rejoiced in his sea-booty,
the great burden which he brought with him.
That splendid troop of thanes went towards him,
thanked God, rejoiced in their prince,
that they might see him safe and sound.
Then from that bold man helmet and byrnie
1630 were quickly unstrapped. Under the clouds
the mere stewed, stained with gore.
They went forth, followed the trail,
rejoicing in their hearts; they marched along the road,
the familiar path; proud as kings
they carried the head from the sea-cliff
with great trouble, even for two pairs
of stout-hearted men; four of them had to
bear, with some strain, on a battle-pole
Grendel's head to the gold-hall,
1640 until presently fourteen proud
and battle-hardy Geats came to the hall,
warriors marching; the lord of those men,
mighty in the throng, trod the meadhall-plain.
Then the ruler of thanes entered there,
daring in actions, honored in fame,
battle-brave hero, to greet Hrothgar.
Then, where men were drinking, they dragged by its hair
Grendel's head across the hall-floor,
a grisly spectacle for the men and the queen.
1650 Everyone stared at that amazing sight.

XXIV

      Beowulf spoke, son of Ecgtheow:
"Look! son of Healfdene, prince of the Scyldings,
we have brought you gladly these gifts from the sea
which you gaze on here, a token of glory.
Not easily did I escape with my life
that undersea battle, did my brave deed
with difficulty—indeed, the battle would have been
over at once, if God had not guarded me.

Nor could I achieve anything at that battle
1660   with Hrunting, though that weapon is good;
but the Ruler of Men granted to me
that I might see on the wall a gigantic old sword,
hanging glittering—He has always guided
the friendless one—so I drew that weapon.
In that conflict, when I had the chance, I slew
the shepherds of that house. Then that battle-sword
burned up with its ornaments, as the blood shot out,
hottest battle-sweat. I have brought the hilt
back from the enemy; I avenged the old deeds,
1670   the slaughter of Danes, as seemed only right.
Now you have my word that you may in Heorot
sleep without care with your company of men,
and every thane, young and old,
in your nation; you need fear nothing,
prince of the Scyldings, from that side,
no deadly manslaughters, as you did before."
       Then the golden hilt was placed in the hand
of the gray-haired war-chief, wise old leader,
that old work of giants; it came to the keeping
1680   of the Danish lord after the fall of demons,
a work of wonder-smiths; and when that evil-hearted man,
God's adversary, gave up the world,
guilty of murders—and his mother too—
it passed to the possession of the best
of world-kings between the two seas,
of all those that dealt out treasures in Danish lands.
       Hrothgar spoke—he studied the hilt
of the old heirloom, where was written[28] the origin
of ancient strife, when the flood slew,
1690   rushing seas, the race of giants—
they suffered awfully. That was a people alien
to the eternal Lord; a last reward
the Ruler gave them through the raging waters.
Also, on the sword-guard of bright gold
was rightly marked in rune-letters,
set down and said for whom that sword,
best of irons, had first been made,

---

[28] **Hrothgar spoke . . . where was written:** The hilt of the sword belonging to the monsters depicts the story of the flood, written or carved in runic letters of the old Germanic alphabet and surrounded by a serpentine pattern of twisted lines. Hrothgar interprets the runes, which have magical and symbolic qualities. [Ed.]

with scrollery and serpentine patterns. Then spoke
the wise son of Healfdene—all fell silent:
1700   "One may, indeed, say, if he acts in truth
and right for the people, remembers all,
old guardian of his homeland, that this earl was
born a better man! My friend Beowulf,
your glory is exalted throughout the world,
over every people; you hold it all with patient care,
and temper strength with wisdom. To you I shall fulfill
our friendship, as we have said. You shall become a comfort
everlasting to your own people,
and a help to heroes.
                        Not so was Heremod[29]
1710 to the sons of Ecgwala, the Honor-Scyldings;
he grew not for their delight, but for their destruction
and the murder of Danish men.
Enraged, he cut down his table-companions,
comrades-in-arms, until he turned away alone
from the pleasures of men, that famous prince;
though mighty God exalted him in the joys
of strength and force, advanced him far
over all men, yet in his heart he nursed
a blood-ravenous breast-hoard. No rings did he give
1720 to the Danes for their honor; he endured, joyless,
to suffer the pains of that strife,
a long-lasting harm to his people. Learn from him,
understand virtue! For your sake I have told this,
in the wisdom of my winters.
                        It is a wonder to say
how mighty God in His great spirit
allots wisdom, land and lordship
to mankind; He has control of everything.
At times He permits the thoughts of a man
in a mighty race to move in delights,
1730 gives him to hold in his homeland
the sweet joys of earth, a stronghold of men,
grants him such power over his portion of the world,
a great kingdom, that he himself cannot
imagine an end to it, in his folly.
He dwells in plenty; in no way plague him

---

[29] **Not so was Heremod:** Hrothgar recalls Heremod, the figure of the failed king who betrays his people, the Danes. See lines 901–915. [Ed.]

illness or old age, nor do evil thoughts
darken his spirit, nor any strife
or sword-hate shows itself, but all the world
turns to his will; he knows nothing worse.

XXV

1740   At last his portion of pride within him
grows and flourishes, while the guardian sleeps,
the soul's shepherd — that sleep is too sound,
bound with cares, the slayer too close
who, sinful and wicked, shoots from his bow.
Then he is struck in his heart, under his helmet
with a bitter dart — he knows no defense —
the strange, dark demands of evil spirits;
What he has long held seems too little,
angry and greedy, he gives no golden rings
1750 for vaunting boasts, and his final destiny
he neglects and forgets, since God, Ruler of glories,
has given him a portion of honors.
In the end it finally comes about
that the loaned life-dwelling starts to decay
and falls, fated to die; another follows him
who doles out his riches without regret,
the earl's ancient treasure; he heeds no terror.
Defend yourself from wickedness, dear Beowulf,
best of men, and choose the better,
1760 eternal counsel; care not for pride,
great champion! The glory of your might
is but a little while; soon it will be
that sickness or the sword will shatter your strength,
of the grip of fire, or the surging flood,
or the cut of a sword, or the flight of a spear,
or terrible old age — or the light of your eyes
will fail and flicker out; in one fell swoop
death, o warrior, will overwhelm you.
        Thus, a hundred half-years I held the Ring-Danes
1770 under the skies, and kept them safe from war
from many tribes throughout this middle-earth,
from spears and swords, so that I considered none
under the expanse of heaven my enemy.
Look! Turnabout came in my own homeland,
grief after gladness, when Grendel became
my invader, ancient adversary;
for that persecution I bore perpetually

the greatest heart-cares. Thanks be to the Creator,
eternal Lord, that I have lived long enough
1780 to see that head, stained with blood,
with my own eyes, after all this strife!
Go to your seat, enjoy the feast,
honored in battle; between us shall be shared
a great many treasures, when morning comes."
      Glad-hearted, the Geat went at once
to take his seat, as the wise one told him.
Then again as before, a feast was prepared
for the brave ones who occupied the hall
on this new occasion. The dark helm of night
1790 overshadowed the troop. The soldiers arose;
the gray-haired ruler was ready for bed,
the aged Scylding. Immeasurably well
did rest please the Geat, proud shield-warrior;
at once a chamberlain led him forth,
weary from his adventure, come from afar,
he who attended to all the needs
of that thane, for courtesy, as in those days
all battle-voyagers used to have.
      The great-hearted one rested; the hall towered
1800 vaulted and gold-adorned; the guest slept within
until the black raven, blithe-hearted, announced
the joy of heaven.[30] Then light came hurrying
[bright over shadows;] the soldiers hastened,
the noblemen were eager to travel
back to their people; the bold-spirited visitor
wished to seek his far-off ship.
      The hardy one ordered Hrunting to be borne
to the son of Ecglaf, bid him take his sword,
lordly iron; he thanked him for the loan,
1810 and said that he regarded it as a good war-friend,
skillful in battle, and the sword's edges
he did not disparage; he was a noble man.
And when the warriors were eager for their way,
equipped in their war-gear, the nobleman went,
the Danes' honor, to the high seat where the other was:
the hero, brave in battle, saluted Hrothgar.

---

[30] **the black raven . . . joy of heaven:** A bird usually linked with war and death, the raven is rarely seen as a harbinger of joy. Here the poet uses the image ironically: the raven announces a dawn free of slaughter.

XXVI

Beowulf spoke, son of Ecgtheow:
"Now we seafarers, come from afar,
wish to say that we desire
1820 to seek Hygelac. Here we were honorably
entertained with delights; you have treated us well.
If ever on earth I can do any thing
to earn more of your affection,
than the battle-deeds I have done already,
ruler of men, I will be ready at once.
If ever I hear over the sea's expanse
that your neighbors threaten you with terror
as your enemies used to do,
I will bring you a thousand thanes,
1830 heroes to help you. I have faith in Hygelac—
the lord of the Geats, though he be young,
shepherd of his people, will support me
with words and deeds, that I might honor you well
and bring to your side a forest of spears,
the support of my might, whenever you need men.
If ever Hrethric decides, son of a prince,
to come to the Geatish court, he will find
many friends there; far-off lands
are better sought by one who is himself good."
1840   Hrothgar spoke in answer to him:
"The wise Lord has sent those words
into your heart; I have never heard
a shrewder speech from such a young man.
You are strong in might, and sound in mind,
prudent in speech! I expect it is likely
that if it should ever happen that the spear
or the horrors of war take Hrethel's son,
or sickness or sword strike the shepherd of his people,
your lord, and you still live,
1850 that the sea-Geats could not select
a better choice anywhere for king,
hoard-guard of heroes, if you will hold
the realm of your kinsmen. Your character pleases me
better and better, beloved Beowulf.
You have brought it about that between our peoples,
the Geatish nation and the spear-Danes,
there shall be peace, and strife shall rest,
the malicious deeds that they endured before,
as long as I shall rule this wide realm,

1860 and treasures together; many shall greet
     another with gifts across the gannet's bath;
     the ring-necked ship shall bring over the sea
     tribute and tokens of love. I know these nations
     will be made fast against friend and foe,
     blameless in everything, in the old way."
             The protector of heroes, kinsman of Healfdene,
     gave him twelve great treasures in the hall;
     bid him seek his own dear people in safety
     with those gifts, and quickly come again.
1870 Then the good king, of noble kin, kissed
     that best of thanes and embraced his neck,
     the Scylding prince; tears were shed
     by that gray-haired man. He was of two minds —
     but in his old wisdom knew it was more likely
     that never again would they see one another,
     brave in their meeting-place. The man was so dear to him
     that he could not hold back the flood in his breast,
     but in his heart, fast in the bonds of his thought,
     a deep-felt longing for the dear man
1880 burned in his blood. Beowulf from thence,
     gold-proud warrior, trod the grassy lawn,
     exulting in treasure; the sea-goer awaited
     its lord and owner, where it rode at anchor.
     As they were going, the gift of Hrothgar
     was often praised; that king was peerless,
     blameless in everything, until old age took from him
     — it has injured so many — the joy of his strength.

XXVII

             Those men of high courage then came to the sea,
     that troop of young retainers, bore their ring-mail,
1890 locked shirts of armor. The coast-guard observed
     the return of those earls, as he had once before;
     he did not greet those guests with insults
     on the clifftop, but he rode towards them,
     said that the warriors in their shining armor
     would be welcome in their ships to the people of the Weders.
     The sea-curved prow, the ring-necked ship,
     as it lay on the sand was laden with war-gear,
     with horses and treasures; the mast towered high
     over Hrothgar's hoard-gifts.
1900 To the ship's guardian he gave a sword,
     bound with gold, so that on the mead-benches

he was afterwards more honored by that heirloom,
that old treasure. Onward they went, the ship
sliced through deep water, gave up the Danish coast.
The sail by the mast was rigged fast with ropes,
a great sea-cloth; the timbers creaked,
the wind over the sea did not hinder at all
the wave-floater on its way; the sea-goer sped on,
floated foamy-necked, forth upon the waves,
1910   the bound prow over the briny streams,
until they could make out the cliffs of Geatland,
familiar capes; the keel drove forward
thrust by the wind, and came to rest on land.
Right away the harbor-guard was ready at the shore,
who for a long time had gazed far
over the currents, eager for the beloved men;
he moored the broad-beamed ship on the beach
fast with anchor-ropes, lest the force of the waves
should drive away the handsome wooden vessel.
1920   He bade that the nobleman's wealth be borne ashore,
armor and plated gold; they had not far to go
to seek their dispenser of treasure,
Hygelac son of Hrethel, where he dwelt at home
with his companions, near the sea-wall.
          The building was splendid, the king quite bold,
high in his hall, Hygd very young,
wise, well-mannered, though few winters
had the daughter of Hæreth passed within
the palace walls—yet not poor for that,
1930   nor stingy of gifts to the Geatish people,
of great treasures. She considered Thryth's pride,[31]
famous folk-queen, and her terrible crimes;
no man so bold among her own retainers
dared to approach her, except as her prince,
or dared to look into her eyes by day;
for he knew that deadly bonds, braided by hand,
were waiting for him—first the hand-grip,
and quickly after a blade appointed,
so that a patterned sword had to settle things,
1940   proclaim the execution. That is no queenly custom
for a lady to perform—no matter how lovely—

---

[31] **Thryth's pride:** After introducing Hygd, the young and virtuous bride of Hygelac, the poet considers the story of Thryth, who is said to have changed her malevolent character after her marriage to Offa I, king of the Angles, in the late fourth century. [Ed.]

that a peace-weaver should deprive of life
a friendly man after a pretended affront.
The kinsman of Hemming put a halt to that:
then ale-drinkers told another tale,
said she caused less calamity to the people,
less malicious evil, after she was
given gold-adorned to the young champion,
fair to that nobleman, when to Offa's floor
1950 she sought a journey over the fallow sea
at her father's wish, where she afterwards
on the throne, famous for good things,
used well her life while she had it,
held high love with that chief of heroes,
of all mankind, as men have told me,
the best between the two seas,
of all the races of men; therefore Offa,
in gifts and battle, spear-bold man,
was widely honored, and held in wisdom
1960 his own homeland. From him arose Eomer
as a help to heroes, kinsman of Hemming,
grandson of Garmund, skilled in violence.

XXVIII

The hardy man with his hand-picked troop
went across the sand, trod the sea-plain,
the wide shore. The world's candle shone,
hastening from the south. They had survived their journey,
went boldly to where they knew
the protector of earls, slayer of Ongentheow,[32]
good young battle-king, gave out rings
1970 in his fortress. To Hygelac
the arrival of Beowulf was quickly reported,
that to the enclosures his battle-companion,
protector of warriors, came walking alive
back to his court, safe from his battle-play.
Quickly, as the powerful one commanded,
the hall was cleared out inside for the foot-guests.
He sat down with him, who had survived the fight,

---

[32] **slayer of Ongentheow:** This distinction is given to Hygelac, though several of his followers actually killed the Swedish king. The entire story of the enmity between the Swedes and the Geats is taken up again after the death of Beowulf, ll. 2922–2998. [Ed.]

kinsmen together, after he greeted
his friend and liege-lord with a formal speech,
1980 with courteous words and cups of mead.
The daughter of Hæreth passed through the hall,
cared for the people, bore the cup
to the hand of the hero. Hygelac began
to question his companion courteously
in the high hall—curiosity pressed him
to know how the sea-Geats' adventures were:
          "How did you fare, beloved Beowulf,
in your journey, when you suddenly resolved
to seek a far-off strife over the salt sea,
1990 a battle in Heorot? Did you better at all
the well-known woe of Hrothgar,
the famous prince? For that I seethed
with heart-care and distress, mistrusted the adventure
of my beloved man; long I implored
that you not seek that slaughter-spirit at all,
let the south-Danes themselves make
war against Grendel. I say thanks to God
that I might see you again safe and sound."
          Beowulf spoke, son of Ecgtheow:
2000 "It is no mystery to many men,
my lord Hygelac—the great meeting,
what a time of great struggle Grendel and I
had in that place where he made so many
sorrows for the victory-Scyldings,
life-long misery—I avenged them all,
so that none of Grendel's tribe needs to boast
anywhere on earth of that uproar at dawn,
whoever lives longest of that loathsome kind,
enveloped in foul evil. First I came there
2010 to the ring-hall to greet Hrothgar;
quickly the famous kinsman of Healfdene,
once he knew of my intentions,
assigned me a seat with his own sons.
That troop was in delight; never in my life
have I seen among hall-sitters, under heaven's vault,
a more joyous feast. At times the famous queen,
bond of peace to nations, passed through the hall,
urged on her young sons; often she gave
twisted rings before she took her seat.
2020 At times before the hall-thanes the daughter of Hrothgar
bore the ale-cup to the earls in the back—
Freawaru, I heard the men in the hall

call her, when the studded treasure-cup
was passed among them. She is promised,
young, gold-adorned, to the gracious son of Froda;[33]
the ruler of the Scyldings has arranged this,
the kingdom's shepherd, and approves the counsel
that he should settle his share of feud and slaughter
with this young woman. But seldom anywhere
2030 after the death of a prince does the deadly spear rest
for even a brief while, though the bride be good!
      It may, perhaps, displease the Heathobards' prince,
and every retainer among his tribe,
when across the floor, following that woman, goes
a noble son of the Danes, received with honors;
on him glitters an ancestral heirloom,
hard, ring-adorned, once a Heathobard treasure
as long as they were able to wield their weapons.

XXIX

And then in that deadly shield-play they undid
2040 their beloved comrades and their own lives.
Then an old spear-bearer speaks over his beer,[34]
who sees that ring-hilt and remembers all
the spear-deaths of men — his spirit is grim —
begins, sad-minded, to test the mettle
of a young thane with his innermost thoughts,
to awaken war, and says these words:
      "Can you, my friend, recognize that sword,
which your father bore into battle
in his final adventure beneath the helmet,
2050 that dear iron, when the Danes struck him,
ruled the field of slaughter after the rout of heroes,
when Withergyld fell — those valiant Scyldings?
Now here some son or other of his slayer
walks across this floor, struts in his finery,

---

[33] **son of Froda:** Froda and his son Ingeld were Heathobards, a people in a long-standing feud with the Danes. After Froda is killed, Hrothgar attempts to secure peace by marrying his daughter Freawaru to Ingeld. Eventually Hrothgar and his kinsmen destroy Ingeld's army when he attacks them while visiting Heorot. Beowulf correctly predicts the failure of the alliance scheme, ll. 2029–2068. [Ed.]

[34] **speaks over his beer:** Beowulf imagines a Heathobard veteran visiting the Danish palace, seeing a Danish youth bear the sword of a slain Heathobard ancestor, and inciting the son of the dead Heathobard to take revenge. [Ed.]

brags of the murder and bears that treasure
which ought, by right, to belong to you."
   He urges and reminds him on every occasion
with cruel words, until the time comes
that Freawaru's thane, for his father's deeds,
2060 sleeps, bloodstained from the bite of a sword,
forfeits his life; from there the other
escapes alive, for he knows the land well.
Then on both sides the sworn oaths of earls
will be broken, once bitter violent hate
wells up in Ingeld, and his wife-love
grows cooler after his surging cares.
Thus I expect that the Heathobards' part
in the Danish alliance is not without deceit,
nor their friendship fast.
      I will speak further
2070 concerning Grendel, so that you might certainly know,
giver of treasure, how it turned out,
the heroic wrestling-match. When heaven's gem
slipped under the ground, the angry spirit came,
horrible, evening-grim, sought us out
where, unharmed, we guarded the hall.
The attack came first against Hondscio[35] there,
deadly to that doomed man—he fell first,
a girded champion; Grendel was
that famous young retainer's devourer,
2080 gobbled up the body of that beloved man.
None the sooner did that slayer, blood in his teeth,
mindful of misery, mean to leave
that gold-hall empty-handed,
but in his mighty strength he tested me,
grabbed with a ready hand. A glove hung
huge, grotesque, fast with cunning clasps;
it was all embroidered with evil skill,
with the devil's craft and dragons' skins.
Inside there, though I was innocent,
2090 that proud evil-doer wanted to put me,
one of many; but it was not to be,
once I angrily stood upright.

---

[35] **Hondscio:** Beowulf's companion, slain by Grendel.

XXX

It is too long to tell how I handed back payment
to the people's enemy for all his evils—
there, my prince, I did honor to your people
with my actions. He escaped away,
enjoyed his life a little while longer;
yet behind him, guarding his path, was his right
hand in Heorot, and wretched, he went hence,
2100 sad at heart, and sank to the sea-floor.
       For that bloody onslaught the friend of the Scyldings
repaid me greatly with plated gold,
many treasures, when morning came,
and we had gathered together to the feast again.
There was song and joy; the aged Scylding,
widely learned, told of far-off times;
at times the brave warrior touched the song-wood,
delight of the harp, at times made lays
both true and sad, at times strange stories
2110 he recounted rightly. That great-hearted king,
gray-bearded old warrior wrapped in his years,
at times began to speak of his youth again,
his battle-strength; his heart surged within him
when, old in winters, he remembered so much.
And so there inside we took our ease
all day long, until night descended
again upon men. There, quickly ready
with revenge for her griefs, Grendel's mother
journeyed sorrowful; death took her son,
2120 the war-hate of the Weders. That monstrous woman
avenged her son, killed a soldier
boldly at once—there the life of Æschere,
wise old counselor, came to its end.
And when morning came the men of the Danes
were not able to burn his body, death-weary,
with flames, nor place him on a funeral pyre,
beloved man; she bore away his corpse
in her evil embrace under the upland streams.
That, to Hrothgar, was the most wrenching distress
2130 of all those that had befallen that folk-leader.
Then the prince—by your life—implored me,
his mind wracked, that in the roaring waves
I should do a noble deed, put my life in danger,
perform glorious things—he promised me reward.
In the waves I found, as is widely known,

a grim, horrible guardian of the abyss.
There for a while, we fought hand-to-hand;
the sea foamed with blood, and I severed the head
of Grendel's mother with a mighty sword
2140   in that [battle-]hall; I barely managed
to get away with my life—I wasn't doomed yet—
and the protector of earls once again gave me
many treasures, that kinsman of Healfdene.

XXXI

    So that nation's king followed good customs;
in no wise have I lost those rewards,
the prize for my strength, but the son of Healfdene
offered me treasures at my own choice,
which I wish to bring to you, o war-king,
to show good will. Still all my joys
2150   are fixed on you alone; I have few
close kinsmen, my Hygelac, except for you."
    He ordered to be borne in the boar standard,
the helmet towering in battle, the gray byrnie,
the decorated sword, and told this story:
"Hrothgar gave me this battle-gear,
wise prince, and commanded particularly
that first I should tell you the story of his gift—
he said that Heorogar the king first had it,
lord of the Scyldings, for a long while;
2160   none the sooner would he give to his own son,
the valiant Heoroward—loyal though he was—
that breast-armor. Use all well!"
Then, as I've heard, four swift horses,
fallow as apples, well-matched, followed
that war-gear; he gave him as a gift
the horses and harness—as kinsman should behave,
never knitting a net of malice for another
with secret plots, preparing death
for his hand-picked comrades. Hygelac's nephew
2170   was loyal to him, hardy in the fight,
and each man to the other mindful of benefits.—
I heard that he gave the necklace to Hygd,
the wondrous ornamented treasure which Wealhtheow
                                      had given him,
to that lord's daughter, along with three horses
graceful and saddle-bright; her breast was adorned
the more graciously after that ring-giving.

So the son of Ecgtheow showed himself brave,
renowned for battles and noble deeds,
pursued honor, by no means slew, drunken,
2180 his hearth-companions; he had no savage heart,
but the great gift which God had given him,
the greatest might of all mankind, he held,
brave in battle. He had been long despised,
as the sons of the Geats considered him no good,
nor did the lord of the Weders wish to bestow
many good things upon him on the meadbenches,
for they assumed that he was slothful,
a cowardly nobleman.[36] Reversal came
to the glorious man for all his griefs.
2190 The protector of earls, battle-proud king,
ordered the heirloom of Hrethel brought in,
adorned with gold; among the Geats there was
no finer treasure in the form of a sword.
He laid the sword in Beowulf's lap,
and gave him seven thousand hides of land,[37]
a hall and a princely throne. Both of them held
inherited land in that nation, a home
and native rights, but the wider rule
was reserved to the one who was higher in rank.
2200 Then it came to pass[38] amid the crash of battle
in later days, after Hygelac lay dead,
and for Heardred the swords of battle held
deadly slaughter under the shield-wall,
when the Battle-Scylfings sought him out,
those hardy soldiers, and savagely struck down
the nephew of Hereric in his victorious nation—
then came the broad kingdom
into Beowulf's hands; he held it well
for fifty winters—he was then a wise king,
2210 old guardian of his homeland—until
in the dark nights a dragon began his reign,

---

[36] **he had been . . . cowardly nobleman:** This allusion to Beowulf's sluggish youth seems at odds with the hero's own account, but it is a common motif concerning young heroes of folklore, including two Old Norse sagas related to *Beowulf.* [Ed.]

[37] **seven thousand hides of land:** The unit of land known as a "hide" originally meant the land necessary to support one family. Beowulf's estate must have been very extensive.

[38] **Then it came to pass:** In this transition intended to cover fifty years, the events leading to Beowulf's rule are drastically truncated and may be a late addition. For a fuller account of Hygelac's death, his son Heardred's murder, and Beowulf's succession to the throne, see ll. 2354–2390. [Ed.]

who guarded his hoard in the high heaths
and the steep stone barrows; the path below
lay unknown to men. Some sort of man
went inside there, found his way to
the heathen hoard—his hand . . .
inlaid with jewels.[39] He got no profit there,
though he had been trapped in his sleep
by a thief's trickery: the whole nation knew,
2220   and all the people around them, that he was enraged.

XXXII

Not for his own sake did he who sorely harmed him
break into that worm-hoard, or by his own will,
but in sad desperation some sort of slave
of a warrior's son fled the savage lash,
the servitude of a house, and slipped in there,
a man beset by sins. Soon he gazed around
and felt the terror from that evil spirit;
yet . . .
  . . . made . . .
2230   . . . when the terror seized him
he snatched a jeweled cup.
    There were many such
antique riches in that earth-hall,
for in ancient days an unknown man
had thought to hide them carefully there,
the rich legacy of a noble race,
precious treasures. In earlier times
death had seized them all, and he who still survived
alone from that nation's army lingered there,
a mournful sentry, expected the same,
2240   that he might enjoy those ancient treasures
for just a little while. A waiting barrow
stood in an open field near the ocean waves,
new on the cape, safe with crafty narrow entrances;
he bore within the noble wealth,
the plated gold, that guardian of rings,
a share worthy of a hoard, and spoke few words:

---

[39] **his hand . . . inlaid with jewels:** The manuscript is damaged here and some text is unreadable. This much is clear: a thief takes a cup from the dragon's treasure-hoard. The thief does not profit from this, though the dragon sleeps through the theft. Although more lines are damaged and the reading is conjectural, the story is elaborated in ll. 2221–2231. [Ed.]

"Hold now, o thou earth, for heroes cannot,
the wealth of men—Lo, from you long ago
those good ones first obtained it! Death in war,
2250 and awful deadly harm have swept away
all of my people who have passed from life,
and left the joyful hall. Now have I none
to bear the sword or burnish the bright cup,
the precious vessel—all that host has fled.
Now must the hardened helm of hammered gold
be stripped of all its trim; the stewards sleep
who should have tended to this battle-mask.
So too this warrior's coat, which waited once
the bite of iron over the crack of boards,
2260 molders like its owner. The coat of mail
cannot travel widely with the war-chief,
beside the heroes. Harp-joy have I none,
no happy song; nor does the well-schooled hawk
soar high throughout the hall, nor the swift horse
stamp in the courtyards. Savage butchery
has sent forth many of the race of men!"

So, grieving, he mourned his sorrow,
alone after all. Unhappy sped
both days and nights, until the flood of death
2270 broke upon his heart. An old beast of the dawn
found that shining horde standing open—
he who, burning, seeks the barrows,
a fierce and naked dragon, who flies by night
in a pillar of fire; people on earth
fear him greatly. It is his nature to find
a hoard in the earth, where, ancient and proud,
he guards heathen gold, though it does him no good.

Three hundred winters that threat to the people
held in the ground his great treasury,
2280 wondrously powerful, until one man
made him boil with fury; he bore to his liege-lord
the plated cup, begged for peace
from his lord. Then the hoard was looted,
the hoard of rings fewer, a favor was granted
the forlorn man; for the first time
his lord looked on that ancient work of men.

When the dragon stirred, strife was renewed;
he slithered along the stones, stark-hearted he found
his enemy's footprint—he had stepped too far
2290 in his stealthy skill, too close to the serpent's head.
Thus can an undoomed man easily survive

wrack and ruin, if he holds to the Ruler's
grace and protection! The hoard-guardian
searched along the ground, greedy to find
the man who had sorely harmed him while he slept;
hot, half-mad, he kept circling his cave
all around the outside, but no one was there
in that wilderness to welcome his warfare
and the business of battle. Soon he returned to his barrow,
2300 sought his treasure; he soon discovered
that some man had disturbed his gold,
his great wealth. The hoard-guardian waited
impatiently until evening came;
the barrow's shepherd was swollen with rage,
the loathsome foe would repay with fire
his precious drinking-cup. Then day was departed
to the delight of that worm; he did not linger
on the barrow wall, but took off burning
in a burst of flames. The beginning was terror
2310 to the people on land, and to their ring-giving lord
the ending soon would be sore indeed.

XXXIII

Then that strange visitor began to spew flames
and burn the bright courts; his burning gleams
struck horror in men. That hostile flier
would leave nothing alive.
The worm's warfare was widely seen,
his ferocious hostility, near and far,
how the destroyer hated and harmed
the Geatish people, then hastened to his hoard,
2320 his dark and hidden hall, before the break of day.
He had surrounded the people of that region with fire,
flames and cinders; he took shelter in his barrow,
his walls and warfare — but that trust failed him.
To Beowulf the news was quickly brought
of that horror — that his own home,
best of buildings, had burned in waves of fire,
the gift-throne of the Geats. To the good man that was
painful in spirit, greatest of sorrows;
the wise one believed he had bitterly offended
2330 the Ruler of all, the eternal Lord,
against the old law; his breast within groaned
with dark thoughts — that was not his custom.
The fire-dragon had found the stronghold of that folk,

that fortress, and had razed it with flames
entirely and from without; for that the war-king,
prince of the Weders, devised revenge.
Then the lord of men bade them make,
protector of warriors, a wondrous war-shield,
all covered with iron; he understood well
2340 that wood from the forest would not help him,
linden against flames. The long-good nobleman
had to endure the end of his loaned days,
this world's life—and so did the worm,
though he had held for so long his hoarded wealth.
    Then that prince of rings scorned to seek out
the far-flung flier with his full force of men,
a large army; he did not dread that attack,
nor did he worry much about the dragon's warfare,
his strength or valor, because he had survived
2350 many battles, barely escaping alive
in the crash of war, after he had cleansed,
triumphant hero, the hall of Hrothgar,
and at battle crushed Grendel and his kin,
that loathsome race.
        It was not the least
of hand-to-hand combats when Hygelac was slain,
when the king of the Geats, in the chaos of battle,
the lord of his people, in the land of the Frisians,
the son of Hrethel, died sword-drunk,
beaten by blades. Beowulf escaped from there
2360 through his own strength, took a long swim;
he had in his arms the battle-armor
of thirty men, when he climbed to the cliffs.
By no means did the Hetware[40] need to exult
in that fight, when they marched on foot to him,
bore their linden shields; few came back
from that brave soldier to seek their homes.
The son of Ecgtheow crossed the vast sea,
wretched, solitary, returned to his people,
where Hygd offered him the hoard and kingdom,
2370 rings and royal throne; she did not trust
that her son could hold the ancestral seat
against foreign hosts, now that Hygelac was dead.
But despite their misery, by no means

---

[40] **Hetware:** A Frankish tribe evidently on the side of the Frisians.

could they prevail upon that prince at all
that he should become lord over Heardred,
or choose to rule the kingdom.
Yet he upheld him in the folk with friendly counsel,
good will and honors, until he was older,
and ruled the Weder-Geats.
                    Wretched exiles,
2380   the sons of Ohthere, sought him out across the seas;[41]
they had rebelled against the Scylfings' ruler,
the best of all the sea-kings
who dispensed treasure in the Swedish lands,
a famous king. That cost him his life:
for his hospitality he took a mortal hurt
with the stroke of a sword, that son of Hygelac;
and the son of Ongentheow afterwards went
to seek out his home, once Heardred lay dead,
and let Beowulf hold the high throne
2390   and rule the Geats—that was a good king.

XXXIV

In later days he did not forget[42]
that prince's fall, and befriended Eadgils
the wretched exile; across the open sea
he gave support to the son of Ohthere
with warriors and weapons. He wreaked his revenge
with cold sad journeys, and took the king's life.
        And so the son of Ecgtheow had survived
every struggle, every terrible onslaught,
with brave deeds, until that one day
2400   when he had to take his stand against the serpent.
Grim and enraged, the lord of the Geats
took a dozen men to seek out the dragon;
he had found out by then how the feud arose,
the baleful violence; the precious vessel
had come to him through the thief's hands.

---

[41] **the sons . . . across the seas:** Eanmund and Eadgils, sons of the former Swedish king Ohthere, rebelled against his brother the successor king Onela, and fled to the court of the Geats. The Geatish king Heardred, son of Hygelac, offered them protection, but King Onela of Sweden followed them and murdered Heardred. This paved the way for Beowulf's succession as King of the Geats. [Ed.]

[42] **he did not forget:** Beowulf, whose revenge for the death of his lord Heardred takes an indirect form—he supports Eadgil's return to Sweden, where Eadgil kills Onela.

He was the thirteenth man among that troop,
who had brought about the beginning of that strife,
a sad-minded captive—wretched and despised
he led the way to that plain. He went against his will
2410 to where he alone knew the earth-hall stood,
an underground cave near the crashing waves,
the surging sea; inside it was full
of gems and metal bands. A monstrous guardian,
eager for combat, kept his gold treasures
ancient under the ground; getting them
was no easy bargain for any man.
      The battle-hardened king sat down on the cape,
then wished good health to his hearth-companions,
the gold-friend of the Geats. His heart was grieving,
2420 restless and ripe for death—the doom was immeasurably near
that was coming to meet that old man,
seek his soul's treasure, split asunder
his life and his body; not for long was
the spirit of that noble king enclosed in its flesh.
      Beowulf spoke, the son of Ecgtheow:[43]
"In my youth I survived many storms of battle,
times of strife—I still remember them all.
I was seven years old when the prince of treasures,
friend to his people, took me from my father;[44]
2430 Hrethel the king held me and kept me,
gave me gems and feasts, remembered our kinship.
I was no more hated to him while he lived
—a man in his stronghold—than any of his sons,
Herebeald and Hæthcyn and my own Hygelac.
For the eldest, undeservedly,
a death-bed was made by the deeds of a kinsman,
after Hæthcyn with his horn bow
struck down his own dear lord with an arrow—
he missed his mark and murdered his kinsman,
2440 one brother to the other with a bloody shaft.
That was a fight beyond settling, a sinful crime,
shattering the heart; yet it had to be

---

[43] **Beowulf spoke, the son of Ecgtheow:** Beowulf's account of his life runs from ll. 2426–2509. [Ed.]

[44] **took me from my father:** It was a frequent practice among Germanic peoples for youths to be sent to another household away from their parents to be trained as warriors. In Beowulf's case, he was sent to the royal household of his uncle, King Hrethel. [Ed.]

that a nobleman lost his life unavenged.
      So it is sad for an old man
to live to see his young son
ride on the gallows[45] — then let him recount a story,
a sorry song, when his son hangs
of comfort only to the ravens, and he cannot,
though old and wise, offer him any help.
2450 Each and every morning calls to mind
his son's passing away; he will not care
to wait for any other heir or offspring
in his fortress, when the first one has
tasted evil deeds and fell death.
He looks sorrowfully on his son's dwelling,
the deserted wine-hall, the windswept home,
bereft of joy — the riders sleep,
heroes in their graves; there is no harp-music,
no laughter in the court, as there had been long before.

XXXV

2460 He takes to his couch and keens a lament
all alone for his lost one; all too vast to him
seem the fields and townships.
         So the protector of the Weders
bore surging in his breast heartfelt sorrows
for Herebeald. He could not in any way
make amends for the feud with his murderer,
but neither could he hate that warrior
for his hostile deeds, though he was not dear to him.
Then with the sorrow which befell him too sorely,
he gave up man's joys, chose God's light;
2470 he left to his children his land and strongholds
    — as a blessed man does — when he departed this life.
      Then there was strife between Swedes and Geats,[46]
a quarrel in common across the wide water,
hard hostility after Hrethel died,

---

[45] **ride on the gallows:** When Hrethel's son Haethcyn accidentally killed his elder brother Herebeald, there was no way for the father to avenge the son's death, either by payment or retribution. The image of the young son on the gallows may refer to the Germanic practice of ritually hanging the body of a man who did not die in battle. If this interpretation is correct, the "old man" is Hrethel himself.

[46] **strife between Swedes and Geats:** This refers to a time a generation before the conflicts of Heardred, Eanmund and Eadgils; the Swedish-Geat feud is longstanding.

until the sons of Ongentheow
were bold and warlike, wanted no peace
over the sea, but around the Hill of Sorrows
they carried out a terrible and devious campaign.
My friends and kinsmen got revenge for those
2480 feuds and evils — as it is said —
although one of them paid for it with his own life,
a hard bargain; that battle was fatal
for Hæthcyn, king of the Geats.
Then, I've heard, the next morning, one kinsman
avenged the other with the sword's edge,
when Ongentheow attacked Eofor;
his battle-helm slipped, the old Scylfing
staggered, corpse-pale; Eofor's hand recalled
his fill of feuds, and did not withhold the fatal blow.[47]
2490   I have paid in battle for the precious treasures
he gave me, as was granted to me,
with a gleaming sword; he gave me land,
a joyous home. He had no need
to have to go seeking among the Gifthas
or the Spear-Danes or the Swedes
for a worse warrior, or buy one with his wealth;
always on foot I would go before him,
alone in the front line — and all my life
I will wage war, while this sword endures,
2500 which before and since has served me well,
since I slew Dæghrefn, champion of the Hugas,
with my bare hands in front of the whole army.
He could not carry off to the Frisian king
that battle-armor and that breast-adornment,
but there in the field the standard-bearer fell,
a nobleman in his strength; no blade was his slayer,
but my warlike grip broke his beating heart,
cracked his bone-house. Now the blade's edge,
hand and hard sword, shall fight for the hoard."
2510   Beowulf spoke, said boasting words
for the very last time: "I have survived
many battles in my youth; I will yet

---

[47] **did not withhold the fatal blow:** At the battle of Ravenswood, Hygelac was avenged for the death of his brother Haethcyn by his follower Eofor's killing of the Swedish king Ongentheow. The battle is described in ll. 2922–2999. [Ed.]

seek out, an old folk-guardian, a feud
and do a glorious deed, if only that evildoer
will come out to me from his earth-hall."
Then for the last time he saluted
each of the soldiers, his own dear comrades,
brave in their helmets: "I would not bear a sword
or weapon to this serpent, if I knew any other way
2520 I could grapple with this great beast
after my boast, as I once did with Grendel;
but I expect the heat of battle-flames there,
steam and venom; therefore shield and byrnie
will I have on me. From the hoard's warden
I will not flee a single foot, but for us
it shall be at the wall as *wyrd* decrees,
the Ruler of every man. My mind is firm—
I will forego boasting against this flying foe.
Wait on the barrow, protected in your byrnies,
2530 men in war-gear, to see which of the two of us
after the bloody onslaught can better
bear his wounds. It is not your way,
nor proper for any man except me alone,
that he should match his strength against this monster,
do heroic deeds. With daring I shall
get that gold—or grim death
and fatal battle will bear away your lord!"
　　　Then that brave challenger stood up by his shield,
stern under his helmet, bore his battle-shirt
2540 under the stone-cliffs, trusted the strength
of a single man—such is not the coward's way.
He saw then by the wall—he who had survived
a great many conflicts, good in manly virtues,
the crash of battles when footsoldiers clashed—
stone arches standing, and a stream
shooting forth from the barrow; its surge
was hot with deadly flames, and near the hoard
he could not survive for very long
unburnt, for the dragon's flaming breath.
2550 Enraged, the ruler of the Weder-Geats
let a word burst forth from his breast,
shouted starkly; the sound entered
and resounded battle-clear under the gray stone.
Hate was stirred up—the hoard-warden recognized
the voice of a man; there was no more time
to sue for peace. First there issued
the steam of that great creature out of the stone,

hot battle-sweat; the earth bellowed.
The warrior in the barrow turned his shield-board
2560 against the grisly stranger, lord of the Geats,
when the writhing beast's heart was roused
to seek combat. The good war-king
had drawn his sword, its edges undulled,
an ancient heirloom; each of the two
hostile ones was horrified by the other.
He stood stouthearted behind his steep shield,
that friend and commander, when the worm coiled itself
swiftly together—he waited in his war-gear.
Then coiled, burning, slithering he came,
2570 rushing to his fate. The shield defended well
the life and limb of the famous lord
for less time than he might have liked;
there on that day for the first time
he faced the outcome, and *wyrd* did not
grant victory in battle. The lord of the Geats
raised his hand, struck that mottled horror
with his ancient sword, so that that edge failed
bright against the bony scales, bit less strongly
that the king of that nation needed it to do,
2580 hard-pressed in battle. Then the barrow-warden
was more savage after that battle-stroke,
and spit out gruesome fire; wide sprang
the battle-flames. The gold-friend of the Geats
did not boast of his glorious victories; his bare sword
failed at need, as it should never have done,
that ancient good iron. It was no easy journey
for the famous son of Ecgtheow to agree
to give up his ground in that place;
he was forced, against his will, to find
2590 a place of rest elsewhere—just as every one of us
must give up these loaned days.
                                It was not long
until those two great creatures came together again.
The hoard-guard took heart, his breast swelled with breath
once again; he suffered anguish,
trapped by flames, he who had once ruled his folk.
His comrades, hand-chosen, sons of noblemen,
did not take their stand in a troop around him,
with warlike valor—they fled to the woods
and saved their lives. The spirit rose up in sorrow
2600 in the heart of one of them; nothing can overrule
kinship at all, in one who thinks well.

XXXVI

He was called Wiglaf, Weohstan's son,
a worthy shield-warrior, a prince of the Scylfings,[48]
kinsman of Ælfhere. He saw his liege-lord
suffer heat under his war-helmet;
he recalled the honors he had received from him,
the wealthy homestead of the Waegmundings,
every folk-right that his father had possessed;
he could not hold back—his hand seized
2610   the pale linden shield, and he drew his old sword.
It was known among men as the heirloom of Eanmund,
son of Ohthere; that friendless exile
was slain in battle with the edge of a sword
by Weohstan, who brought to his kinsman
the burnished helmet, the ringed byrnie
the old giant-work sword; Onela gave to him
the war-equipment of his young kinsman,
the shining armor—he never spoke of a feud,
though he had slain his brother's son.
2620   He kept that war-gear for a great many years,
the blade and byrnie, until his boy could
perform brave deeds like his father before him;
he gave him among the Geats that battle-gear,
every piece of it, when, old, he departed this life
and went forth. That was the first time
that the young warrior had to weather
the storm of battle beside his noble lord.
His courage did not melt, nor did his kinsman's legacy
weaken in war; the worm discovered that,
2630   when they began to meet together.
　　　　Wiglaf spoke, said to his companions
many true words—he was mournful at heart—
"I remember the time that we took mead together,
when we made promises to our prince
in the beer-hall—he gave us these rings—
that we would pay him back for this battle-gear,
these helmets and hard swords, if such a need
as this ever befell him. For this he chose us from the army
for this adventure by his own will,

---

[48] **a prince of the Scylfings:** Wiglaf's nationality is in question: he is both a Swede and a Waegmunding. His tribal allegiance to Beowulf is more important than his mixed nationality. [Ed.]

2640 thought us worthy of glory, and gave me these treasures—
for this he considered us good spear-warriors,
proud helmet-wearers, even though our prince,
shepherd of his people, intended to perform
this act of courage all alone,
because he has gained the most glory among men,
reckless heroic deeds. Now the day has come
that our noble lord has need of the support
of good warriors; let us go to it,
help our warlord, despite the heat,
2650 grim fire-terror. God knows for my part
that I would much prefer that the flames should enfold
my body alongside my gold-giving lord.
It seems wrong to me that we should bear shields
back to our land, unless we first might
finish off this foe, defend the life
of the prince of the Weders. I know full well
that he does not deserve to suffer
this torment all alone among the Geatish troop,
or fall in the struggle; now sword and helmet,
2660 byrnie and battle-dress, shall be ours together!"
      He hurried through the deadly fumes, bore his helmet
to the aid of his lord, spoke little:
"Dear Beowulf, do all well,
as in your youth you said you would,
that you would never let in your whole life
your fame decline; now firm in deeds,
single-minded nobleman, with all your strength
you must protect your life—I will support you."
After these words the worm came angrily,
2670 terrible vicious creature, a second time,
scorched with surging flames, seeking out his enemies,
the hated men. The hot flames rolled in waves,
burned the shield to its rim; the byrnie was not
of any use to the young soldier,
but he showed his courage under his kinsman's shield,
the young warrior, when his own was
charred to cinders. Still the battle-king
remembered his glory, and with his mighty strength
swung his warblade with savage force,
2680 so that it stuck in the skull. Nægling shattered—
the sword of Beowulf weakened at battle,
ancient and gray. It was not granted to him
that iron-edged weapons might ever
help him in battle; his hand was too strong,

he who, I am told, overtaxed every blade
with his mighty blows, when he bore to battle
a wound-hardened weapon — it was no help to him at all.
      Then that threat to the people for a third time,
fierce fire-dragon, remembering his feud,
2690 rushed on the brave man, hot and bloodthirsty,
when he saw the chance, seized him by the neck
in his bitter jaws; he was bloodied
by his mortal wounds — blood gushed in waves.

XXXVII

Then, I have heard, in his king's hour of need
the earl beside him showed his bravery,
the noble skill which was his nature.
He did not heed that head when he helped his kinsman;
that brave man's hand was burned, so that
he struck that savage foe a little lower down,
2700 the soldier in armor, so that his sword plunged in
bejeweled and bloody, so that the fire began
to subside afterwards. The king himself
still had his wits, drew the war-dagger,
bitter and battle-sharp, that he wore in his byrnie;
the protector of the Weders carved through the worm's midsection.
They felled their foe — their force took his life —
and they both together had brought him down,
the two noble kinsmen; a thane at need,
as a man should be! But that, for the prince, was
2710 his last work of victory, by his own will,
of worldly adventures.
               When the wound
which the earth-dragon had worked on him
began to burn and swell, he soon realized
that in his breast, with an evil force,
a poison welled; then the nobleman went,
still wise in thought, so that he sat
on a seat by the wall. On that work of giants he gazed,
saw how stone arches and sturdy pillars
held up the inside of that ancient earth-hall.
2720 Then with his hands the thane, immeasurably good,
bathed with water his beloved lord,
the great prince, spattered with gore,
sated with battle, and unstrapped his helmet.
Beowulf spoke — despite his wound,
that deadly cut; he knew clearly

that his allotted life had run out,
and his joys in the earth; all gone
was his portion of days, death immeasurably near:
      "Now I should wish to give my war-gear
2730 to my son, if there had been such,
flesh of my flesh, if fate had granted me
any heir. I held this people
fifty winters; there was no folk-king,
not any of the neighboring tribes,
who dared to face me with hostile forces
or threaten fear. The decrees of fate
I awaited on earth, held well what was mine,
I sought no intrigues, nor swore many
false or wrongful oaths. For all that I may
2740 have joy, though sick with mortal wounds,
because the Ruler of men need not reproach me
with the murder of kinsmen, when my life
quits my body. Now go quickly
to look at the hoard under the hoary stone,
dear Wiglaf, now that the worm lies dead,
sleeps with his wounds, stripped of his treasure.
Hurry, so I might witness that ancient wealth,
those golden goods, might eagerly gaze on
the bright precious gems, and I might more gently,
2750 for that great wealth, give up my
life and lordship, which I have held so long."

XXXVIII

      Then swiftly, I have heard, the son of Weohstan
after these words obeyed his lord,
sick with wounds, wore his ring-net,
the woven battle-shirt, under the barrow's roof.
As he went by the seat he saw there, triumphant,
the brave young warrior, many bright jewels,
glittering gold scattered on the ground,
wonders on the walls, and the lair of that worm,
2760 the old dawn-flier—flagons standing,
ancient serving-vessels without a steward,
their trappings all moldered; there was many a helmet
old and rusty, a number of arm-bands
with twisted ornaments.—Treasure may easily,
gold in the ground, give the slip
to any one of us: let him hide it who will!—
Likewise he saw an ensign, all golden,

hanging high over the hoard, greatest hand-work,
linked together with skill; light gleamed from it
2770 so that he could see the cave's floor,
survey those strange artifacts. There was no sign
of the serpent there—a sword had finished him off.
Then the hoard in that barrow, as I've heard, was looted,
ancient work of giants, by one man alone;
he piled in his arms cups and plates,
whatever he wanted; he took the ensign too,
brightest of beacons. His aged lord's blade
—its edge was iron—had earlier harmed
the one who was protector of those treasures
2780 for such a long time, who bore his fiery terror
flaming before the hoard, seething fiercely
in the darkest night, until he died a bloody death.
      The messenger rushed out, eager to return,
burdened with treasures; he was burning to know
whether, stout-hearted, he would find still alive
the prince of the Weders, weakened by wounds,
in the place where he had left him on that plain.
Then with the treasures he found the famous prince,
his own lord, his life at an end,
2790 all bloody; he began once more
to sprinkle water on him, until the point of a word
escaped from his breast.
      Old, full of grief, he looked on the gold:
      "For all these treasures, I offer thanks
with these words to the eternal Lord,
King of Glory, for what I gaze upon here,
that I was able to acquire such wealth
for my people before my death-day.
Now that I have sold my old lifespan
2800 for this hoard of treasures, they will attend
to the needs of the people; I can stay no longer.
The brave in battle will bid a tomb be built
shining over my pyre on the cliffs by the sea;
it will be as a monument to my people
and tower high on Whale's Head,
so that seafarers afterwards shall call it
'Beowulf's Barrow', when their broad ships
drive from afar over the darkness of the flood."
      The boldminded nobleman took from his neck
2810 a golden circlet, and gave it to the thane,
the young spear-carrier, and the gold-covered helmet,
ring and byrnie, bid him use them well:

"You are the last survivor of our lineage,
the Waegmundings; fate has swept away
all of my kinsmen, earls in their courage,
to their final destiny; I must follow them."
That was the last word of the old warrior,
his final thought before he chose the fire,
the hot surging flames—from his breast flew
2820 his soul to seek the judgment of the righteous.

XXXIX

             Then it came to pass with piercing sorrow
that the young warrior had to watch
his most precious lord fare so pitifully,
his life at an end. Likewise his slayer lay dead,
the awesome earth-dragon deprived of his life,
overcome by force. The coiled serpent
could no longer rule his hoard of rings—
edges of iron did away with him,
the hard, battle-scarred shards of the smithy,
2830 so that the wide-flier, stilled by his wounds,
toppled to the ground near his treasure-house.
No more soaring about in the skies
at midnight, preening in his precious treasures,
showing his face—he fell to earth
through that war-commander's handiwork.
Indeed, few men on earth, no matter how strong,
could succeed at that, as I have heard tell,
though he were daring in every deed,
could rush against the reek of that venomous foe,
2840 or rifle through that ring-hall with his hands,
if he should find a waking warden
waiting in that barrow. Beowulf's share
of that royal treasure was repaid by his death—
each of them had journeyed to the end
of this loaned life.
                         It was not long before
the men late for battle left the woods,
ten of those weak traitors all together
who had not dared to hoist their spears
when their lord of men needed them most;
2850 now shamefaced, they carried their shields
and battledress to where the old man lay dead,
to stare at Wiglaf. He sat exhausted,
a foot-soldier at his lord's shoulder,

tried to rouse him with water—but it was no use.
He could not, no matter how much he wanted,
keep the life in the body of his captain,
nor change any bit of the Ruler's decree;
the judgment of God would guide the deeds
of every man, as it still does today.
2860 Then it was easy to get a grim answer
from that youth to those who gave up courage.
Wiglaf spoke, son of Weohstan,
looked, sad-hearted, on those unloved:
           "He can say—o yes—who would speak the truth
that the liege-lord who gave you those gifts of treasures,
the military gear that you stand in there,
when on the ale-benches he often handed out
helmets and byrnies to the hall-sitters,
a lord to his followers, whatever he could find
2870 finest anywhere, far or near—
that all that battle-dress he absolutely
and entirely threw away, when war beset him.
Our nation's king had no need to boast
of his comrades-in-arms! But the Ruler of victories
allowed that he, alone with his blade,
might avenge himself when he needed your valor.
Only a little life-protection could I offer
him in battle, but began nevertheless
to support my kinsman beyond my own strength;
2880 ever the worse was the deadly enemy
when I struck with my sword, a fire less severe
surging from his head. Too few supporters
thronged around our prince in his great peril.
Now the getting of treasure, the giving of swords,
and all the happy joys of your homeland,
shall end for your race; empty-handed
will go every man among your tribe,
deprived of his land-rights, when noblemen learn
far and wide of your flight,
2890 your inglorious deed. Death is better
for any earl than a life of dishonor!"

XL

He bade that the battle-work be announced to the camp
up by the cliff's edge, where that troop of earls,
shield-bearers, sat sad-minded
all the long morning, expecting either

the final day of their dear lord
or his homecoming. He who rode up to the cape
was not at all silent with his new tidings,
but he spoke truly in the hearing of all:
2900   "Now is the joy-giver of the Geatish people,
the lord of the Weders, laid on his deathbed,
holding a place of slaughter by the serpent's deeds;
beside him lies his life-enemy,
sick with knife-slashes; he could not with his sword
make in the monstrous beast
any kind of wound. Wiglaf sits,
Weohstan's offspring, over Beowulf,
one earl over the other, now dead;
he holds with desperate heart the watch
over friend and foe.
2910   Now this folk may expect
a time of trouble, when this is manifest
to the Franks and Frisians, and the fall of our king
becomes widespread news. The strife was begun
hard with the Hugas, after Hygelac came
travelling with his ships to the shores of Frisia,
where the Hetware attacked him in war,
advanced with valor and a vaster force,
so that the warrior in his byrnie had to bow down,
and fell amid the infantry; not at all did that lord
2920 give treasure to his troops. Ever after that
the Merovingians have not shown mercy to us.
      Nor do I expect any peace or truce
from the Swedish nation, but it has been well-known
that Ongentheow ended the life
of Haethcyn, son of Hrethel, in Ravenswood,
when in their arrogant pride the Geatish people
first sought out the Battle-Scylfings.[49]
Immediately the ancient father of Ohthere,
old and terrifying, returned the attack—
2930 the old warrior cut down the sea-captain,
rescued his wife, bereft of her gold,
Onela's mother and Ohthere's;
and then hunted down his deadly enemies
until they escaped, with some difficulty,

---

[49] **the Geatish people . . . Battle-Scylfings:** In his speech, the messenger describes the bitter hostility of the Swedes after the battle of Ravenswood, repeating the history of Swedish and Geatish battles in greater detail. It is part of his ceremonial task to give warning about the future. [Ed.]

bereft of their lord, into Ravenswood.
With his standing army he besieged those sword-leavings,
weary, wounded; he kept threatening woe
to that wretched troop the whole night through—
in the morning, he said, with the edge of his sword
2940 he would gut them, and leave some on the gallows-tree
as sport for birds. But for those sad-hearted men
solace came along with the sunrise,
after they heard Hygelac's horn and trumpet
sounding the charge, when the good man came
following the trail of that people's troop.

XLI

The bloody swath of the Swedes and Geats,
the slaughter of men, was easily seen,
how the folk had stirred up feud between them.
That good man then departed, old, desperate,
2950 with a small band of kinsmen, sought his stronghold,
the earl Ongentheow turned farther away;
he had heard of proud Hygelac's prowess in battle,
his war-skill; he did not trust the resistance
he might muster against the seafarers' might
to defend from the wave-borne warriors his treasure,
his women and children; he ran away from there,
old, into his fortress. Then the pursuit was offered
to the Swedish people, the standard of Hygelac
overran the place of refuge,
2960 after the Hrethlings thronged the enclosure.
There with the edge of a sword was Ongentheow,
old graybeard, brought to bay,
so that the king of that nation had to yield
to Eofor's will. Angrily he struck;
Wulf the son of Wonred lashed at him with his weapon,
so that with his blow the blood sprang in streams
from under his hair. Yet the ancient Scylfing
was undaunted, and dealt back quickly
a worse exchange for that savage stroke,
2970 once the ruler of that people turned around.
The ready son of Wonred could not
give a stroke in return to the old soldier,
for he had cut through the helmet right on his head
so that he collapsed, covered in blood,
fell to the ground—he was not yet fated to die,
but he recovered, though the cut hurt him.

The hardy thane of Hygelac then let
his broad blade, as his brother lay there,
his ancient giant-made sword, shatter that gigantic helmet
2980　over the shield-wall; then the king stumbled,
shepherd of his people, mortally stricken.
　　　　There were many there who bandaged his kinsman,
quickly raised him up, when a way was clear for them,
so that they had control of that killing field.
Then one warrior plundered another,
took from Ongentheow the iron byrnie,
his hard hilted sword and his helmet too,
and carried the old man's armor to Hygelac.
He took that war-gear and promised him gifts
2990　among his people—and he kept that promise;
the king of the Geats repaid that carnage,
the offspring of Hrethel, when he made it home,
gave to Eofor and Wulf extravagant treasures,
gave them each lands and locked rings,
worth a hundred thousand. Not a man in this world could
reproach those rewards, since they had won them
　　　　　　　　　　with their deeds;
and to Eofor he gave his only daughter,
the pride of his home, as a pledge of his friendship.
　　　　That is the feud and the fierce enmity,
3000　savage hatred among men, that I expect now,
when the Swedish people seek us out
after they have learned that our lord
has perished, who had once protected
his hoard and kingdom against all hostility,
after the fall of heroes, the valiant Scyldings,
worked for the people's good, and what is more,
performed noble deeds. Now we must hurry
and look upon our people's king,
and go with him who gave us rings
3010　on the way to the pyre. No small part
of the hoard shall burn with that brave man,
but countless gold treasures, grimly purchased,
and rings, here at last with his own life
paid for; then the flames shall devour,
the fire enfold—let no warrior wear
treasures for remembrance, nor no fair maiden
have a ring-ornament around her neck,
but sad in mind, stripped of gold, she must
walk a foreign path, not once but often,
3020　now that leader of our troop has laid aside laughter,

his mirth and joy. Thus many a cold morning
shall the spear be grasped in frozen fingers,
hefted by hands, nor shall the sound of the harp
rouse the warriors, but the dark raven,
greedy for carrion, shall speak a great deal,
ask the eagle how he fared at his feast
when he plundered corpses with the wolf."[50]

        Thus that brave speaker was speaking
a most unlovely truth; he did not lie much
3030 in words or facts. The troop of warriors arose;
they went, unhappy, to the Cape of Eagles,
with welling tears to look at that wonder.
There on the sand they found the soulless body
of the one who gave them rings in earlier times
laid out to rest; the last day
had come for the good man, when the war-king,
prince of the Weders, died a wondrous death.
But first they saw an even stranger creature,
a loathsome serpent lying on the plain
3040 directly across from him; grim with his colors
the fire-dragon was, and scorched with his flames.
He was fifty feet long, lying there
stretched out; once he had joy in the air
in the dark night, and then down he would go
to seek his den, but now he was fast in death;
he had come to the end of his cave-dwelling.
Cups and vessels stood beside him,
plates lay there and precious swords,
eaten through with rust, as if in the bosom of the earth
3050 they had lain for a thousand winters;
all that inheritance was deeply enchanted,
the gold of the ancients was gripped in a spell
so that no man in the world would be able to touch
that ring-hall, unless God himself,
the true King of Victories, Protector of men,
granted to whomever He wished to open the hoard,
to whatever person seemed proper to Him.

---

[50] **when he . . . the wolf:** The eagle, wolf, and raven, the "beasts of battle," are a recurring motif in Anglo-Saxon poetry.

XLII

Then it was plain that the journey did not profit
the one who had wrongfully hidden under a wall
3060 that great treasure. The guardian had slain
that one and few others, then that feud was
swiftly avenged. It is a wonder to say
where a valiant earl should meet the end
of his span of life, when he may no longer
dwell in the meadhall, a man with his kinsmen.
So it was with Beowulf, when he sought the barrow's guardian
and a hostile fight; even he did not know
how his parting from life should come to pass,
since until doomsday mighty princes had deeply
3070 pronounced, when they placed it there,
that the man who plundered that place would be
harried by hostile demons, fast in hellish bonds,
grievously tortured, guilty of sins,
unless the Owner's grace had earlier
more readily favored the one eager for gold.
Wiglaf spoke, son of Weohstan:
"Often many earls must suffer misery
through the will of one man, as we have now seen.
We could not persuade our dear prince,
3080 shepherd of a kingdom, with any counsel,
that he should not greet that gold-guardian,
let him lie there where he long had been,
inhabit the dwellings until the end of the world:
he held to his high destiny. The hoard is opened,
grimly gotten; that fate was too great
which impelled the king of our people thither.
I was in there, and looked over it all,
the hall's ornaments, when a way was open to me;
by no means gently was a journey allowed
3090 in under that earth-wall. In eager haste I seized
in my hands a great mighty burden
of hoard-treasure, and bore it out hither
to my king. He was still conscious then,
thoughtful and alert; he spoke of many things,
an old man in his sorrow, and ordered that I greet you;
he asked that you build a great high barrow
for your prince's deeds, in the place of his pyre,
mighty and glorious, since he was of men
the most worthy warrior throughout the wide world,
3100 while he could enjoy the wealth of a hall.

Let us now make haste for one more time
to see and seek out that store of cunning gems,
the wonder under the wall; I will direct you
so that you can inspect them up close,
abundant rings and broad gold. Let the bier be ready,
quickly prepared, when we come out,
then let us bear our beloved lord,
that dear man, to where he must long
rest in the keeping of the Ruler."
3110   Then the son of Weohstan, brave battle-warrior,
let it be made known to many heroes
and householders, that they should bring from afar
the wood for the pyre to that good one,
the leader of his folk: "Now the flames must devour,
the black blaze rise over the ruler of warriors,
who often awaited the showers of iron
when the storm of arrows hurled from bow-strings
shot over the wall, the shafts did their duty
swift on feather-wings, sent on the arrow-heads."
3120   Lo, then the wise son of Weohstan
summoned from that host some of the best
of the king's thanes, seven altogether;
he went, one of eight, under that evil roof;
one of the brave warriors bore in his hands
a flaming torch, and went before them.
It was not chosen by lots who should loot that hoard,
once the men saw it sitting in the hall,
every part of it unprotected,
lying there wasting; there was little lament
3130 that they should have to hurry out with
the precious treasures. They also pushed the dragon,
the worm over the cliff-wall, let the waves take him,
the flood embrace the guard of that finery;
then the twisted gold, an uncountable treasure,
was loaded in a wagon, and the noble one was carried,
the Gray-haired warrior, to the Cape of Whales.

XLIII

The people of the Geats then prepared for him
a splendid pyre upon the earth,
hung with battle-shields and helmets
3140 and bright byrnies, as he had bidden;
there in the middle they laid the mighty prince,
the heroes lamenting their dear lord.

Then the warriors kindled there on the cliff
the greatest of funeral pyres; dark over the flames
the woodsmoke rose, the roaring fire
mingled with weeping—the wind lay still—
until it had broken that bone-house
hot at the heart. With heavy spirits
they mourned their despair, the death of their lord;
3150 and a sorrowful song sang the Geatish woman,
with hair bound up, for Beowulf the king,
with sad cares, earnestly said
that she dreaded the hard days ahead,
the times of slaughter, the host's terror,
harm and captivity. Heaven swallowed the smoke.
            Then the Weder people wrought for him
a barrow on the headland; it was high and broad,
visible from afar to sea-voyagers,
and in ten days they built the beacon
3160 of that battle-brave one; the ashes of the flames
they enclosed with a wall, as worthily
as the most clever of men could devise it.
In the barrow they placed rings and bright jewels,
all the trappings that those reckless men
had seized from the hoard before,
let the earth hold the treasures of earls,
gold in the ground, where it yet remains,
just as useless to men as it was before.
Then round the mound rode the battle-brave men,
3170 offspring of noblemen, twelve in all,
they wished to voice their cares and mourn their king,
utter sad songs and speak of that man;
they praised his lordship and his proud deeds
judged well his prowess. As it is proper
that one should praise his lord with words,
should love him in his heart when the fatal hour comes,
when he must from his body be led forth,
so the men of the Geats lamented
the fall of their prince, those hearth-companions;
3180 they said that he was of all the kings of the world
the mildest of men and the most gentle,
the kindest to his folk and the most eager for fame.

TEXT IN CONTEXT

∿ MURASAKI SHIKIBU (LADY MURASAKI)
B. JAPAN, C. 973–C. 1030

GEN-jee

The Tale of Genji (*Genji Monogatari*) (c. 1022), often considered Japan's greatest classic and a masterpiece of prose fiction, has been called the world's first psychological novel, remarkable for its subtle and dramatic evocation of character as well as its complex and elegant style. All Japanese recognize Genji, much as English readers know King Arthur or Indian readers are familiar with Prince Rama.[1] Indeed, throughout the nearly one thousand years since *The Tale of Genji* first appeared, literary echoes and images of Lady Murasaki and the shining prince Genji have appeared in later novels and poems as well as on screen paintings and porcelains. Moreover, the story of **Genji** has been retold in countless forms, from *Nō* plays and the Japanese puppet theater known as Bunraku to short stories and film. As *Genji*'s earliest translator into English noted, even European readers may recognize Lady Murasaki from the familiar motif in Japanese art of a woman seated at a writing desk, pen in hand, with the moon reflected on a lake in the background.

Early Life and Education.   Murasaki Shikibu is a double nickname, derived from her father's title "Shikibu" and the name of her novel's main female character Murasaki. Murasaki Shikibu was destined for a life at court, for her father, Fujiwara no Tametoki, was a minor court

---

[1] **Prince Rama:** The hero of the great Indian epic the *Ramayana*, composed and revised from about 550 B.C.E. to 400 C.E.

official and a member of a branch of the ruling Fujiwara clan. She was
born around 973 in the capital city of Heian (now Kyoto). Like that
of many European women before the nineteenth century, Murasaki's
education focused on abilities thought to increase a woman's value
in men's eyes, skills such as fine handwriting, the rote memorization
of classical poetry, and playing the *koto* and *biwa*, both stringed
instruments. Like some of her European counterparts, Lady Murasaki
managed to acquire a broader education, in part by eavesdropping
on her brother's Chinese lessons. By her own account she excelled at
Chinese, more so than her brother, but propriety led her to conceal
her proficiency. Because Japanese women ordinarily did not receive

www For links to
more information
about Lady Murasaki,
see bedfordstmartins
.com/worldlit
compact.

**Lady Murasaki,
seventeenth or
eighteenth century**
*The famous author
of the classic* Tale of
Genji *is shown here
quietly reading. (The
Art Archive/Private
Collection, Paris/
Dagli Orti)*

Heian Japan: The Heian Court

The Heian period (794–1185) began with the removal of the imperial family from the court at Nara to resettle at Heian (now Kyoto). The new period was dominated by the powerful Fujiwara family, living in the royal court in the capital along with their ladies in waiting and other courtiers. While court intrigues were not uncommon, the era was one of peace, prosperity, and isolation, characterized by a dedication to the refinement of manners and a flourishing of the arts. The "cloud dwellers" of the imperial court lived in virtual seclusion even from members of the lower aristocracy, cultivating *miyabi*, an aesthetic sensibility that permeated the speech, dress, and deportment of the courtiers, who transformed the business of governance into the "rule of taste," a subtle display of indirection and suggestion.

The conduct of affairs in the court is documented in the *nikki* or diaries of writers including Lady Murasaki and Sei Shonagon, and the nuanced behavior of the courtiers is romanticized in the *monogatari* or works of fiction, best represented by *The Tale of Genji* by Lady Murasaki. Sei Shonagon, in the chapter

Court ladies and their maids, twelfth century   *Ladies of the Heian court are shown in this detail from the Tale of Genji Scroll. (The Art Archive/Laurie Platt Winfrey)*

"The Sliding Screen in Back of the Hall" from *The Pillow Book*, describes a day with the emperor, who asks all the ladies in waiting to

training in writing Chinese characters—the official literary language, excellence in which earned men distinction and rank—women wrote in Japanese characters called KANA, which expressed the language as it was spoken. Writing in *kana*, Lady Murasaki incorporated two literary genres characteristic of the Heian period. One was the *nikki* or prose diary, a collection of thoughts and poetry written by a woman emphasizing her personal reflections. The "diary" was usually written over gaps of time and referred to remembered moments from the past, but it was always written as if responding to the present. The poetry it quoted, whether original or the work of another writer, was composed in the WAKA form, a short, highly sophisticated lyric that furnished a

TIME AND PLACE

Heian Japan: The Heian Court *continued*

write down the first ancient poem that they recall. The etiquette of the court suggests that the ladies should alter one of the lines in the five-line *waka* to include praise of the emperor himself. Further exercises include supplying the ending of a *waka* selected at random from the massive anthology of Japanese poetry, the *Kokinshu*, after the beginning lines are read. The emperor tells the ladies in waiting exemplary stories of great feats of memory by those who came before them in the "old days." Though revered by the court as a font of wisdom, the emperor himself is very young—fourteen years old.

As in so much court life, the emphasis in romantic affairs—especially in *The Tale of Genji*—was not the aggressiveness of sexual conquest but a sensibility that stemmed from what the Japanese called *mono no aware,* a delicate but profound feeling for, and sensitivity to, things in the world. Lady Murasaki's novel masterfully evokes this complex feeling, even in the midst of the untimely deaths or tragic circumstances that frame the melancholy of Genji's romantic life. At the same time, as Sei

Shonagon suggests through the more realistic medium of the *nikki* or diary, the services expected of the ladies in waiting for men of the court were not always so etherealized. Sorrow, disappointment, a sense of loss, and the undesired sacrifice of privacy were common results. Sometimes even the practice of heightened sensitivity to life was exhausting. Shonagon speaks at one point of withdrawing from the court for a needed rest.

For most of their writing, however, both Lady Murasaki and Sei Shonagon uphold the values of the court. Shonagon often speaks of being inspired by the simplest gesture of the emperor or his child bride, and fiercely upholds the decorum of the court's daily rituals. Lady Murasaki, if anything, is more socially conservative than Shonagon: she speaks of her as "someone who makes such an effort to distinguish herself from others" that she will "fall in people's esteem." The modernity of the court, consisting in large part in its ethic of refinement, could also prove to be a limit: behind it, one senses the isolation and fragility of its sensibility.

kind of "fact" on which the rest of the text could be grounded. The other popular genre was the MONOGATARI, a "tale" or "telling of things"—a fictional account that also incorporated *waka* as a kind of poetic distillation of the ideas expressed in the story.

When she was in her early twenties, Lady Murasaki experienced two tragedies: the death of her older sister, with whom she was close, and the death of her husband of only two years, Fujiwara Nobutaka. After briefly joining her father, who had accepted a governorship in the northern province of Echizen, Lady Murasaki returned with her only child to Heian, where she began writing *The Tale of Genji*. At the capital she served as attendant to Empress Akiko Shoshi, whose residence at

the imperial palace gave the writer firsthand experience of the complex
rivalries and the sometimes comic, sometimes tragic, consequences of
her mistress's naivete and strict standards of moral conduct. Critics
have noted many parallels between Murasaki's recorded accounts of her
years with Shoshi in *Murasaki Shikibu Nikki* (*Lady Murasaki's Diary*)
and the incidents that occur in *The Tale of Genji*. With Shoshi, Lady
Murasaki was able to put her extraordinary knowledge of Chinese to
good use, for the princess wanted to learn the language, forbidden to
women under Confucian tenets that relegated women to a low level of
the intellectual hierarchy.

Although the court, including the emperor, apparently admired
The Tale of Genji, Lady Murasaki noted in her diary that after hearing
some passages of her tale the emperor announced that "this lady has
been reading the *Annals of Japan*," giving rise to rumors that she prided
herself on her learning and earning her the nickname, "Dame Annals."
Little is known of Lady Murasaki's life after 1010, the year her *Diary*
ends. *The Tale of Genji* was completed by 1022, and Lady Murasaki
participated in ceremonies at the birth of the Emperor Go-Ryozen
in 1025. It is thought that she died around 1030.

The Tale of Genji.   This work is a poetic study of the psychology of
longing and love among elite members of the court in medieval Japan;
it is also an extended meditation on the passing of time, the mutability
of life, and the inevitability of disappointment and death. Tragic in
tone and plot, the novel views the lives of its characters from a Buddhist perspective, which holds that one's fate in the present is tied to
actions performed in the past. In its insistence on the fleeting, even illusory nature of human existence, as well as the impurity or disorder of
human relationships, the novel suggests that happiness must be found
elsewhere, in the Pure Land beyond the cycle of death and rebirth,
which one attains through right practices and through the grace of
Buddha. Yet *The Tale of Genji* contains some of the most moving and
sensitive depictions of nature in all of world literature, its characters'
moods associated with such intricate details of the natural world as the
subtle fragrance of a particular flower or a perfumed robe, the array of
colors in the sky at sunset, the slant of moonlight in a passageway on a
cold night, or the sound of raindrops gently troubling the surface of a
pool. Murasaki, like many Japanese artists, pays great attention to the
seasons, reflecting the natural cycle of change as well as the impermanence of things.

The fifty-four chapters of *The Tale of Genji* consist of a series of
overlapping episodes centered primarily on the romantic adventures of
the eponymous hero, Genji, the "shining one," the son of the emperor

and his wife, Kiritsubo, an aristocratic woman of low rank. Covering a period of seventy-five years and involving hundreds of characters, the story of Genji's quest divides into two main parts, beginning with his birth and continuing to his death at the age of fifty-two; these are followed by a story that begins nine years after Genji's death and focuses on the lives of Niou, Genji's grandson, and Kaoru, Genji's nominal son, really the son of his wife, Nyosan, known as the Third Princess, and her lover, Kashiwagi.

Genji in Love.   Recent scholarship identifies three major parts to *Genji*. The first, chapters 1 through 33, recounts Genji's complicated succession of marriages and romances up to age thirty-nine. The precocious and charmingly handsome son of the emperor, the "shining" Genji is kept in subordinate positions at court because of a prophecy warning that disaster would befall the state should he take the throne. Genji enjoys great popularity within aristocratic circles, and his beauty and elegance draw many women to him, including his father's new consort, Lady Fujitsubo, a woman who resembles his mother, who died when Genji was only three. After his marriage to Aoi, with whom he has a son named Yugiri, Genji finds himself more attracted to Lady Fujitsubo than to his new wife. In the meantime, Genji enters into romantic affairs with several other women, including the lower-class Evening Faces (**Yugao**) and the proud and jealous Lady **Rokujo**. Even as Genji pursues these various love interests, his passion for Fujitsubo remains strong, and eventually Fujitsubo bears Genji a son, who is thought to be the emperor's. After the emperor's death, the remorseful and guilt-ridden Fujitsubo renounces court life and takes vows as a Buddhist nun, a direction that other of Genji's lovers will take as well: Of the ten major female characters with whom Genji becomes involved, five become nuns, two die at a young age, and three manage to go on with their lives. Thus, *The Tale of Genji* presents the reader with its protagonist's many love affairs, all tinged with transgression and sadness, romantic impossibility, and unhappy consequences.

After the birth of his son by Fujitsubo, Genji eventually becomes involved with other women, including Oborozukiyo, Murasaki (Fujitsubo's niece whom he marries as a second wife), and the Lady of Akashi. His affair with Oborozukiyo, the sister of his mother's former rival Kokiden, leads to his being exiled from the court for eight years, during which time he meets the Lady of Akashi with whom he has a daughter. After Genji's return to court, his son by Fujitsubo succeeds to the throne as Emperor Reizei, under whom Genji serves as a minister. When Reizei learns that Genji is really his father, he is inspired by filial piety to give him the throne. Genji dissuades his son from abdicating

yoo-GOW
ROH-koo-joh

The Tale of Genji
does not dwell on
[Genji's] iniquitous
and immoral acts,
but rather recites
over and over again
his awareness of the
sorrow of existence,
and represents him
as a good man
who combines in
himself all good
things in men.

– MOTOORI
NORINAGA,
eighteenth century,
poet and scholar

and receives royal favors. Now prospering, Genji builds the Rokujo Palace, where he is joined by, among others, the Lady of Akashi and his favorite love, Murasaki, who receives the most prestigious quarters. Now in his mid-thirties, Genji finally seems to have found peace, though he now falls in love anew with Tamakazura.

Although Genji's many romances and marriages may bring to mind the European Don Juan, we must remember that polygamy was an accepted, even essential, practice among the aristocracy in Lady Murasaki's time. A wealthy nobleman with only one or two wives might be subject to reproach from his peers or thought to be antisocial or indelicate for not having more. It was common for aristocratic men to have a primary wife and two or three secondary wives. While early marriages, such as Genji's to the Princess Aoi, often were arranged for political purposes, later marriages by mutual consent were for love. Moreover, as seen in **The Pillow Book** by Lady Murasaki's plain-spoken contemporary Sei Shonagon (c. 966–1017), amorous affairs at court were commonplace, despite the era's Confucianist restrictions. Thus, having many lovers was not frowned on for men, though as seen in *Genji* and *The Pillow Book* this tacit acceptance did not prevent sometimes extreme jealousy and rivalry among both men and women.

p. 1317

Disappointment and Death.   The second major part of the novel begins with chapter 34, New Herbs: Part 1. At forty years old, Genji agrees somewhat reluctantly to marry Nyosan, the Third Princess, the daughter of retired emperor Suzaku. Genji's fortunes take a turn for the worse from then on, and the mood of the novel as a whole becomes progressively more somber. Murasaki, for whom he has developed an even greater affection and respect, takes ill following her jealousy over Genji's new wife. Taking advantage of Genji's preoccupation with the failing Murasaki, Kashiwagi, the son of Genji's friend **To no Chujo**, seduces the Third Princess, who eventually gives birth to a son, Kaoru. Kaoru, the hero of the third part of the novel, generally is thought to be Genji's. While Genji, mindful of his own past adulterous affair with Lady Fujitsubo, remains resigned to the news, Kashiwagi dies from shame, and the Third Princess renounces the world to become a nun; shortly after, Murasaki dies. Finally, the grief-stricken Genji also renounces the world, disposes of his property, and goes away to die.

toh-noh-CHOO-joh

The final twelve chapters focus on the life of Kaoru, whose story begins eight years after Genji's death, which is never described. Though Kaoru's adventures in some ways mirror Genji's own, this illegitimate son lacks the taste, refinement, and chivalry of his supposed father.

Some critics see this third section as a sign that Lady Murasaki had come to believe that her society was in decline, that the era of fine taste and cultivation embodied in Genji, "the shining one," was a thing of the past. Thus, the great novel ends on a note of nostalgic resignation, added to the feelings of sadness and regret already invoked throughout the story.

As Earl Miner has suggested, Genji's heroism derives from his "artistic command of life." Genji does not engage in martial competition, nor does he act in accordance with any doctrine of chivalry. That kind of hero would arise in the next generation of Japanese literature, in works such as *The Tale of the Heike,* composed in 1371.[2]

While only a reading of the complete novel allows one to appreciate fully its richness and complexity, the episodic structure of *The Tale of Genji* enables the reader to appreciate its poetic style and the complexity of its characters even in a single chapter. "Evening Faces" captures the subtlety of Genji's romantic dealings, the intensity of his passion, and the hapless fate of some of his heroines. It characterizes too the tone of sadness and regret that ensues when misfortune befalls one of Genji's ill-fated lovers.

Evening Faces.   In "Evening Faces" Genji embarks on a romantic but tragic affair with one of the women described in an earlier chapter—the lover of his best friend and brother-in-law To no Chujo. The seventeen-year-old prince, accompanied by his faithful servant Koremitsu, goes to see his old nurse. While visiting the dying woman, Genji is attracted to a beautiful visitor in the neighbor's house. He calls this woman Evening Faces, or Yugao, after the white flowers of the yugao; like them, she is "hapless" but beautiful, out of place in the shabby surroundings of the neighborhood. Genji and Yugao meet over his gift of a suggestive poem written on a scented fan, capturing the spirit of elaborate indirection on which Lady Murasaki's culture prided itself. Although the mysterious young woman ranks far beneath Genji socially, the amorous prince determines to win her affection. But shortly after he consummates this brief affair, the vengeful spirit of Lady Rokujo, a jilted lover, haunts the pair and appears as a ghost to take the life of his new love.

Even in this early chapter Genji begins to grasp the transience and fragility of life and reflects on the promise of a life beyond, an afterlife

---

[2] **Heike . . . 1371:** One of the great heroic tales of early Japan, *The Tale of the Heike* chronicles the rise and fall of the Taira family in the twelfth century and the war with the Minamoto clan, also known as the Genji, fought between 1180 and 1185 C.E.

among "the highest summits of the Pure Land." The latter sentiment is an allusion to the Tendai Buddhism that permeates the religious dimensions of the novel, recognizing that all things of this world are fleeting and that human beings are caught up in a cycle of death and reincarnation from which they can only hope to escape eventually to a land of purity and bliss.

In the rest of the story, Genji concerns himself more with the fate of others and less with his own romantic instincts, which so often lead to disaster for the women he encounters. He grows in understanding and forbearance while coming to recognize his human limitations. Eventually fate and the passage of time rob him of his vital force, and he passes from the scene without further mention. In a like manner, the tone of the entire tale darkens, possibilities vanish, and somber expression of the impermanence of life takes over. Lady Murasaki herself appears to deepen her perspective in the course of her great work, accommodating to the generational tragedy she describes along with an increased awareness of the mutability of the world, which seemed so bright and shining once but later becomes the site of uncertainty and illusion.

■ **FURTHER RESEARCH**

Biography
Bowring, Richard. *Murasaki Shikibu: Her Diary and Poetic Memoirs.* 1982.

Background/History
Kato, Shuichi. *A History of Japanese Literature: From the* Man'yoshu *to Modern Times.* 1997.
Keene, Donald. *Seeds in the Heart: Japanese Literature from the Earliest Times to the Late Sixteenth Century.* 1993, 1999.
Morris, Ivan. *The World of the Shining Prince.* 1964. Reprint, 1994.

Criticism
Bowring, Richard. *The Tale of Genji.* 1988.
Field, Norma. *The Splendor of Longing in* The Tale of Genji. 1987.
Miner, Earl. "The Heroine: Identity, Recurrence, Destiny." In *Ukifune: Love in* The Tale of Genji, ed. by Andrew Pekarik. 1982.
Shirane, Haruo. *The Bridge of Dreams: A Poetics of* The Tale of Genji. 1987.

■ **PRONUNCIATION**

To no Chujo: toh-noh-CHOO-joh
Genji: GEN-jee
Kiyomizu: kee-yoh-MEE-zoo
Koremitsu: koh-reh-MIT-soo
Nijo: NEE-joh
Rokujo: ROH-koo-joh
Ukon: OO-kone
Yugao: yoo-GOW

FROM

∾ The Tale of Genji

Translated by Edward G. Seidensticker

CHAPTER 4

Evening Faces

On his way from court to pay one of his calls at Rokujō,[1] Genji stopped to inquire after his old nurse, Koremitsu's mother, at her house in Gojō.[2] Gravely ill, she had become a nun. The carriage entrance was closed. He sent for Koremitsu and while he was waiting looked up and down the dirty, cluttered street. Beside the nurse's house was a new fence of plaited cypress. The four or five narrow shutters above had been raised, and new blinds, white and clean, hung in the apertures. He caught outlines of pretty foreheads beyond. He would have judged, as they moved about, that they belonged to rather tall women. What sort of women might they be? His carriage was simple and unadorned and he had no outrunners. Quite certain that he would not be recognized, he leaned out for a closer look. The hanging gate, of something like trelliswork, was propped on a pole, and he could see that the house was tiny and flimsy. He felt a little sorry for the occupants of such a place—and then asked himself who in this world had more than a temporary shelter.[3] A hut, a jeweled pavilion, they were the same. A pleasantly green vine was climbing a board wall. The white flowers, he thought, had a rather self-satisfied look about them.

"'I needs must ask the lady far off yonder,'"[4] he said, as if to himself.

An attendant came up, bowing deeply. "The white flowers far off yonder are known as 'evening faces,'"[5] he said. "A very human sort of name—and what a shabby place they have picked to bloom in."

It was as the man said. The neighborhood was a poor one, chiefly of small houses. Some were leaning precariously, and there were "evening faces" at the sagging eaves.

"A hapless sort of flower. Pick one off for me, would you?"

The man went inside the raised gate and broke off a flower. A pretty little girl in long, unlined yellow trousers of raw silk came out through a sliding door that

---

[1] **Rokujō:** Genji is on his way to meet Lady Rokujo, who is highly jealous of Genji's other lovers. Rokujō is the site where Genji builds a fabulous mansion.

[2] **Gojō:** A town southwest of Osaka.

[3] **who . . . a temporary shelter:** An allusion to a poem from the *Kokinshu* (987): "Where in all this world shall I call home? / A temporary shelter is my home."

[4] **'I needs . . . far off yonder':** An allusion to a poem from the *Kokinshu* (1007): "I needs must ask the lady far off yonder / What flower it is off there that blooms so white."

[5] **evening faces:** The Japanese name for this flowering gourd is *yugao*.

Prince Genji, twelfth century

Written during the height of the Heian dynasty (784–1185), The Tale of Genji is one of the most famous works of Japanese literature, and its author, Lady Murasaki, one of its most celebrated artists. The epic life and loves of Prince Genji and his family as told by Murasaki have inspired countless plays, poems, short stories, and films. (CORBIS)

seemed too good for the surroundings. Beckoning to the man, she handed him a heavily scented white fan.

"Put it on this. It isn't much of a fan, but then it isn't much of a flower either."

Koremitsu, coming out of the gate, passed it on to Genji.

"They lost the key, and I have had to keep you waiting. You aren't likely to be recognized in such a neighborhood, but it's not a very nice neighborhood to keep you waiting in."

Genji's carriage was pulled in and he dismounted. Besides Koremitsu, a son and a daughter, the former an eminent cleric, and the daughter's husband, the governor of Mikawa, were in attendance upon the old woman. They thanked him profusely for his visit.

The old woman got up to receive him. "I did not at all mind leaving the world, except for the thought that I would no longer be able to see you as I am seeing you now. My vows seem to have given me a new lease on life, and this visit makes me certain that I shall receive the radiance of Lord Amitābha[6] with a serene and tranquil heart." And she collapsed in tears.

Genji was near tears himself. "It has worried me enormously that you should be taking so long to recover, and I was very sad to learn that you have withdrawn from the world. You must live a long life and see the career I make for myself. I am sure that if you do you will be reborn upon the highest summits of the Pure Land. I am told that it is important to rid oneself of the smallest regret for this world."

Fond of the child she has reared, a nurse tends to look upon him as a paragon even if he is a half-wit. How much prouder was the old woman, who somehow gained stature, who thought of herself as eminent in her own right for having been permitted to serve him. The tears flowed on.

Her children were ashamed for her. They exchanged glances. It would not do to have these contortions taken as signs of a lingering affection for the world.

Genji was deeply touched. "The people who were fond of me left me when I was very young. Others have come along, it is true, to take care of me, but you are the only one I am really attached to. In recent years there have been restrictions upon my movements, and I have not been able to look in upon you morning and evening as I would have wished, or indeed to have a good visit with you. Yet I become very depressed when the days go by and I do not see you. 'Would that there were on this earth no final partings.'"[7] He spoke with great solemnity, and the scent of his sleeve, as he brushed away a tear, quite flooded the room.

Yes, thought the children, who had been silently reproaching their mother for her want of control, the fates had been kind to her. They too were now in tears.

Genji left orders that prayers and services be resumed. As he went out he asked for a torch, and in its light examined the fan on which the "evening face" had rested. It was permeated with a lady's perfume, elegant and alluring. On it was a poem in a disguised cursive hand that suggested breeding and taste. He was interested.

> "I think I need not ask whose face it is,
> So bright, this evening face, in the shining dew."

"Who is living in the house to the west?" he asked Koremitsu. "Have you perhaps had occasion to inquire?"

At it again, thought Koremitsu. He spoke somewhat tartly. "I must confess that these last few days I have been too busy with my mother to think about her neighbors."

"You are annoyed with me. But this fan has the appearance of something it might be interesting to look into. Make inquiries, if you will, please, of someone who knows the neighborhood."

---

[6] **Lord Amitābha:** The Buddha of Infinite Life and Light described in the Amitabha Sutra, who, taking compassion on the suffering of sentient beings in the world, vowed to create a Pure Land where through his grace the faithful would find refuge.

[7] **'Would that . . . no final partings':** An allusion to a poem by Ariwara no Narihira in the *Kokinshu* (901): "Would that my mother might live a thousand years. / Would there were on this earth no final partings."

Koremitsu went in to ask his mother's steward, and emerged with the information that the house belonged to a certain honorary vice-governor. "The husband is away in the country, and the wife seems to be a young woman of taste. Her sisters are out in service here and there. They often come visiting. I suspect the fellow is too poorly placed to know the details."

His poetess would be one of the sisters, thought Genji. A rather practiced and forward young person, and, were he to meet her, perhaps vulgar as well—but the easy familiarity of the poem had not been at all unpleasant, not something to be pushed away in disdain. His amative propensities, it will be seen, were having their way once more.

Carefully disguising his hand, he jotted down a reply on a piece of notepaper and sent it in by the attendant who had earlier been of service.

> "Come a bit nearer, please. Then might you know
> Whose was the evening face so dim in the twilight."

Thinking it a familiar profile, the lady had not lost the opportunity to surprise him with a letter, and when time passed and there was no answer she was left feeling somewhat embarrassed and disconsolate. Now came a poem by special messenger. Her women became quite giddy as they turned their minds to the problem of replying. Rather bored with it all, the messenger returned empty-handed. Genji made a quiet departure, lighted by very few torches. The shutters next door had been lowered. There was something sad about the light, dimmer than fireflies, that came through the cracks.

At the Rokujō house, the trees and the plantings had a quiet dignity. The lady herself was strangely cold and withdrawn. Thoughts of the "evening faces" quite left him. He overslept, and the sun was rising when he took his leave. He presented such a fine figure in the morning light that the women of the place understood well enough why he should be so universally admired. On his way he again passed those shutters, as he had no doubt done many times before. Because of that small incident he now looked at the house carefully, wondering who might be within.

"My mother is not doing at all well, and I have been with her," said Koremitsu some days later. And, coming nearer: "Because you seemed so interested, I called someone who knows about the house next door and had him questioned. His story was not completely clear. He said that in the Fifth Month or so someone came very quietly to live in the house, but that not even the domestics had been told who she might be. I have looked through the fence from time to time myself and had glimpses through blinds of several young women. Something about their dress suggests that they are in the service of someone of higher rank. Yesterday, when the evening light was coming directly through, I saw the lady herself writing a letter. She is very beautiful. She seemed lost in thought, and the women around her were weeping."

Genji had suspected something of the sort. He must find out more.

Koremitsu's view was that while Genji was undeniably someone the whole world took seriously, his youth and the fact that women found him attractive meant that to refrain from these little affairs would be less than human. It was not realistic to hold that certain people were beyond temptation.

"Looking for a chance to do a bit of exploring, I found a small pretext for writing to her. She answered immediately, in a good, practiced hand. Some of her women do not seem at all beneath contempt."

"Explore very thoroughly, if you will. I will not be satisfied until you do."

The house was what the guardsman would have described as the lowest of the low, but Genji was interested. What hidden charms might he not come upon!

He had thought the coldness of the governor's wife, the lady of "the locust shell," quite unique. Yet if she had proved amenable to his persuasions the affair would no doubt have been dropped as a sad mistake after that one encounter. As matters were, the resentment and the distinct possibility of final defeat never left his mind. The discussion that rainy night would seem to have made him curious about the several ranks. There had been a time when such a lady would not have been worth his notice. Yes, it had been broadening, that discussion! He had not found the willing and available one, the governor of Iyo's daughter, entirely uninteresting, but the thought that the stepmother must have been listening coolly to the interview was excruciating. He must await some sign of her real intentions.

The governor of Iyo returned to the city. He came immediately to Genji's mansion. Somewhat sunburned, his travel robes rumpled from the sea voyage, he was a rather heavy and displeasing sort of person. He was of good lineage, however, and, though aging, he still had good manners. As they spoke of his province, Genji wanted to ask the full count of those hot springs,[8] but he was somewhat confused to find memories chasing one another through his head. How foolish that he should be so uncomfortable before the honest old man! He remembered the guardsman's warning that such affairs are unwise, and he felt sorry for the governor. Though he resented the wife's coldness, he could see that from the husband's point of view it was admirable. He was upset to learn that the governor meant to find a suitable husband for his daughter and take his wife to the provinces. He consulted the lady's young brother upon the possibility of another meeting. It would have been difficult even with the lady's cooperation, however, and she was of the view that to receive a gentleman so far above her would be extremely unwise.

Yet she did not want him to forget her entirely. Her answers to his notes on this and that occasion were pleasant enough, and contained casual little touches that made him pause in admiration. He resented her chilliness, but she interested him. As for the stepdaughter, he was certain that she would receive him hospitably enough however formidable a husband she might acquire. Reports upon her arrangements disturbed him not at all.

Autumn came. He was kept busy and unhappy by affairs of his own making, and he visited Sanjō infrequently. There was resentment.

As for the affair at Rokujō, he had overcome the lady's resistance and had his way, and, alas, he had cooled toward her. People thought it worthy of comment that his passions should seem so much more governable than before he had made her his. She was subject to fits of despondency, more intense on sleepless nights when

---

[8] **hot springs:** The province of Iyo was known for its hot springs.

she awaited him in vain. She feared that if rumors were to spread the gossips would make much of the difference in their ages.

On a morning of heavy mists, insistently roused by the lady, who was determined that he be on his way, Genji emerged yawning and sighing and looking very sleepy. Chūjō, one of her women, raised a shutter and pulled a curtain aside as if urging her lady to come forward and see him off. The lady lifted her head from her pillow. He was an incomparably handsome figure as he paused to admire the profusion of flowers below the veranda. Chūjō followed him down a gallery. In an aster robe that matched the season pleasantly and a gossamer train worn with clean elegance, she was a pretty, graceful woman. Glancing back, he asked her to sit with him for a time at the corner railing. The ceremonious precision of the seated figure and the hair flowing over her robes were very fine.

He took her hand.

> "Though loath to be taxed with seeking fresher blooms,
> I feel impelled to pluck this morning glory."

"Why should it be?"

She answered with practiced alacrity, making it seem that she was speaking not for herself but for her lady:

> "In haste to plunge into the morning mists,
> You seem to have no heart for the blossoms here."

A pretty little page boy, especially decked out for the occasion, it would seem, walked out among the flowers. His trousers wet with dew, he broke off a morning glory for Genji. He made a picture that called out to be painted.

Even persons to whom Genji was nothing were drawn to him. No doubt even rough mountain men wanted to pause for a time in the shade of the flowering tree, and those who had basked even briefly in his radiance had thoughts, each in accordance with his rank, of a daughter who might be taken into his service, a not ill-formed sister who might perform some humble service for him. One need not be surprised, then, that people with a measure of sensibility among those who had on some occasion received a little poem from him or been treated to some little kindness found him much on their minds. No doubt it distressed them not to be always with him.

I had forgotten: Koremitsu gave a good account of the fence peeping to which he had been assigned. "I am unable to identify her. She seems determined to hide herself from the world. In their boredom her women and girls go out to the long gallery at the street, the one with the shutters, and watch for carriages. Sometimes the lady who seems to be their mistress comes quietly out to join them. I've not had a good look at her, but she seems very pretty indeed. One day a carriage with outrunners went by. The little girls shouted to a person named Ukon that she must come in a hurry. The captain[9] was going by, they said. An older woman came out and

---

[9]**The captain:** Tō no Chūjō, the head of the Fujiwara clan and Genji's brother-in-law, is a friend and rival whose actions in the novel both parallel and contrast with Genji's; in this case, he is a former lover of Evening Faces.

motioned to them to be quiet. How did they know? she asked, coming out toward the gallery. The passage from the main house is by a sort of makeshift bridge. She was hurrying and her skirt caught on something, and she stumbled and almost fell off. 'The sort of thing the god of Katsuragi[10] might do,' she said, and seems to have lost interest in sightseeing. They told her that the man in the carriage was wearing casual court dress and that he had a retinue. They mentioned several names, and all of them were undeniably Lord Tō no Chūjō's guards and pages."

"I wish you had made positive identification." Might she be the lady of whom Tō no Chūjō had spoken so regretfully that rainy night?

Koremitsu went on, smiling at this open curiosity. "I have as a matter of fact made the proper overtures and learned all about the place. I come and go as if I did not know that they are not all equals. They think they are hiding the truth and try to insist that there is no one there but themselves when one of the little girls makes a slip."

"Let me have a peep for myself when I call on your mother."

Even if she was only in temporary lodgings, the woman would seem to be of the lower class for which his friend had indicated such contempt that rainy evening. Yet something might come of it all. Determined not to go against his master's wishes in the smallest detail and himself driven by very considerable excitement, Koremitsu searched diligently for a chance to let Genji into the house. But the details are tiresome, and I shall not go into them.

Genji did not know who the lady was and he did not want her to know who he was. In very shabby disguise, he set out to visit her on foot. He must be taking her very seriously, thought Koremitsu, who offered his horse and himself went on foot.

"Though I do not think that our gentleman will look very good with tramps for servants."

To make quite certain that the expedition remained secret, Genji took with him only the man who had been his intermediary in the matter of the "evening faces" and a page whom no one was likely to recognize. Lest he be found out even so, he did not stop to see his nurse.

The lady had his messengers followed to see how he made his way home and tried by every means to learn where he lived; but her efforts came to nothing. For all his secretiveness, Genji had grown fond of her and felt that he must go on seeing her. They were of such different ranks, he tried to tell himself, and it was altogether too frivolous. Yet his visits were frequent. In affairs of this sort, which can muddle the senses of the most serious and honest of men, he had always kept himself under tight control and avoided any occasion for censure. Now, to a most astonishing degree, he would be asking himself as he returned in the morning from a visit how he could wait through the day for the next. And then he would rebuke himself. It was madness, it was not an affair he should let disturb him. She was of an extraordinarily gentle and quiet nature. Though there was a certain vagueness about her, and indeed an almost childlike quality, it was clear that she knew something about men. She did

---

[10] **the god of Katsuragi:** This god was so ugly that he would come out only at night to work on a bridge he had been ordered to build.

not appear to be of very good family. What was there about her, he asked himself over and over again, that so drew him to her?

He took great pains to hide his rank and always wore travel dress, and he did not allow her to see his face. He came late at night when everyone was asleep. She was frightened, as if he were an apparition from an old story. She did not need to see his face to know that he was a fine gentleman. But who might he be? Her suspicions turned to Koremitsu. It was that young gallant, surely, who had brought the strange visitor. But Koremitsu pursued his own little affairs unremittingly, careful to feign indifference to and ignorance of this other affair. What could it all mean? The lady was lost in unfamiliar speculations.

Genji had his own worries. If, having lowered his guard with an appearance of complete unreserve, she were to slip away and hide, where would he seek her? This seemed to be but a temporary residence, and he could not be sure when she would choose to change it, and for what other. He hoped that he might reconcile himself to what must be and forget the affair as just another dalliance; but he was not confident.

On days when, to avoid attracting notice, he refrained from visiting her, his fretfulness came near anguish. Suppose he were to move her in secret to Nijō. If troublesome rumors were to arise, well, he could say that they had been fated from the start. He wondered what bond in a former life might have produced an infatuation such as he had not known before.

"Let's have a good talk," he said to her, "where we can be quite at our ease."

"It's all so strange. What you say is reasonable enough, but what you do is so strange. And rather frightening."

Yes, she might well be frightened. Something childlike in her fright brought a smile to his lips. "Which of us is the mischievous fox spirit?[11] I wonder. Just be quiet and give yourself up to its persuasions."

Won over by his gentle warmth, she was indeed inclined to let him have his way. She seemed such a pliant little creature, likely to submit absolutely to the most outrageous demands. He thought again of Tō no Chūjō's "wild carnation," of the equable nature his friend had described that rainy night. Fearing that it would be useless, he did not try very hard to question her. She did not seem likely to indulge in dramatics and suddenly run off and hide herself, and so the fault must have been Tō no Chūjō's. Genji himself would not be guilty of such negligence—though it did occur to him that a bit of infidelity might make her more interesting.

The bright full moon of the Eighth Month came flooding in through chinks in the roof. It was not the sort of dwelling he was used to, and he was fascinated. Toward dawn he was awakened by plebeian voices in the shabby houses down the street.

"Freezing, that's what it is, freezing. There's not much business this year, and when you can't get out into the country you feel like giving up. Do you hear me, neighbor?"

---

[11] **fox spirit:** Foxes disguised as humans were said to seduce or otherwise harass unsuspecting people. [Editors' note.]

He could make out every word. It embarrassed the woman that, so near at hand, there should be this clamor of preparation as people set forth on their sad little enterprises. Had she been one of the stylish ladies of the world, she would have wanted to shrivel up and disappear. She was a placid sort, however, and she seemed to take nothing, painful or embarrassing or unpleasant, too seriously. Her manner elegant and yet girlish, she did not seem to know what the rather awful clamor up and down the street might mean. He much preferred this easygoing bewilderment to a show of consternation, a face scarlet with embarrassment. As if at his very pillow, there came the booming of a foot pestle, more fearsome than the stamping of the thunder god, genuinely earsplitting. He did not know what device the sound came from, but he did know that it was enough to awaken the dead. From this direction and that there came the faint thump of fulling hammers against coarse cloth; and mingled with it—these were sounds to call forth the deepest emotions—were the calls of geese flying overhead. He slid a door open and they looked out. They had been lying near the veranda. There were tasteful clumps of black bamboo just outside and the dew shone as in more familiar places. Autumn insects sang busily, as if only inches from an ear used to wall crickets at considerable distances. It was all very clamorous, and also rather wonderful. Countless details could be overlooked in the singleness of his affection for the girl. She was pretty and fragile in a soft, modest cloak of lavender and a lined white robe. She had no single feature that struck him as especially beautiful, and yet, slender and fragile, she seemed so delicately beautiful that he was almost afraid to hear her voice. He might have wished her to be a little more assertive, but he wanted only to be near her, and yet nearer.

"Let's go off somewhere and enjoy the rest of the night. This is too much."

"But how is that possible?" She spoke very quietly. "You keep taking me by surprise."

There was a newly confiding response to his offer of his services as guardian in this world and the next. She was a strange little thing. He found it hard to believe that she had had much experience of men. He no longer cared what people might think. He asked Ukon to summon his man, who got the carriage ready. The women of the house, though uneasy, sensed the depth of his feelings and were inclined to put their trust in him.

Dawn approached. No cocks were crowing. There was only the voice of an old man making deep obeisance to a Buddha, in preparation, it would seem, for a pilgrimage to Mitake.[12] He seemed to be prostrating himself repeatedly and with much difficulty. All very sad. In a life itself like the morning dew, what could he desire so earnestly?

"Praise to the Messiah to come," intoned the voice.

"Listen," said Genji. "He is thinking of another world."

> "This pious one shall lead us on our way
> As we plight our troth for all the lives to come."

---

[12] **Mitake:** A shrine south of Nara in the Yoshino Mountains.

The vow exchanged by the Chinese emperor and Yang Kuei-fei[13] seemed to bode ill, and so he preferred to invoke Lord Maitreya, the Buddha of the Future; but such promises are rash.

> "So heavy the burden I bring with me from the past,
> I doubt that I should make these vows for the future."

It was a reply that suggested doubts about his "lives to come."

The moon was low over the western hills. She was reluctant to go with him. As he sought to persuade her, the moon suddenly disappeared behind clouds in a lovely dawn sky. Always in a hurry to be off before daylight exposed him, he lifted her easily into his carriage and took her to a nearby villa. Ukon was with them. Waiting for the caretaker to be summoned, Genji looked up at the rotting gate and the ferns that trailed thickly down over it. The groves beyond were still dark, and the mist and the dews were heavy. Genji's sleeve was soaking, for he had raised the blinds of the carriage.

"This is a novel adventure, and I must say that it seems like a lot of trouble.

> "And did it confuse them too, the men of old,
> This road through the dawn, for me so new and strange?

"How does it seem to you?" She turned shyly away.

> "And is the moon, unsure of the hills it approaches,
> Foredoomed to lose its way in the empty skies?"

"I am afraid."

She did seem frightened, and bewildered. She was so used to all those swarms of people, he thought with a smile.

The carriage was brought in and its traces propped against the veranda while a room was made ready in the west wing. Much excited, Ukon was thinking about earlier adventures. The furious energy with which the caretaker saw to preparations made her suspect who Genji was. It was almost daylight when they alighted from the carriage. The room was clean and pleasant, for all the haste with which it had been readied.

"There are unfortunately no women here to wait upon His Lordship." The man, who addressed him through Ukon, was a lesser steward who had served in the Sanjō mansion of Genji's father-in-law. "Shall I send for someone?"

"The last thing I want. I came here because I wanted to be in complete solitude, away from all possible visitors. You are not to tell a soul."

The man put together a hurried breakfast, but he was, as he had said, without serving women to help him.

Genji told the girl that he meant to show her a love as dependable as "the patient river of the loons."[14] He could do little else in these strange lodgings.

---

[13] **Yang Kuei-fei:** The concubine of a Chinese emperor noted for her extraordinary beauty; their love affair, like that of the Trojan prince Paris and Helen, led to the downfall of an empire as well as to Yang Kuei-fei's execution.

[14] **"the patient . . . loons":** An allusion to a poem in the *Man'yoshu* (4458): "The patient river of the patient loons / Will not run dry. My love will outlast it."

The sun was high when he arose. He opened the shutters. All through the badly neglected grounds not a person was to be seen. The groves were rank and overgrown. The flowers and grasses in the foreground were a drab monotone, an autumn moor. The pond was choked with weeds, and all in all it was a forbidding place. An outbuilding seemed to be fitted with rooms for the caretaker, but it was some distance away.

"It is a forbidding place," said Genji. "But I am sure that whatever devils emerge will pass me by."

He was still in disguise. She thought it unkind of him to be so secretive, and he had to agree that their relationship had gone beyond such furtiveness.

"Because of one chance meeting by the wayside
The flower now opens in the evening dew.

"And how does it look to you?"

"The face seemed quite to shine in the evening dew,
But I was dazzled by the evening light."

Her eyes turned away. She spoke in a whisper.

To him it may have seemed an interesting poem.

As a matter of fact, she found him handsomer than her poem suggested, indeed frighteningly handsome, given the setting.

"I hid my name from you because I thought it altogether too unkind of you to be keeping your name from me. Do please tell me now. This silence makes me feel that something awful might be coming."

"Call me the fisherman's daughter."[15] Still hiding her name, she was like a little child.

"I see. I brought it all on myself? A case of *warekara*?"[16]

And so, sometimes affectionately, sometimes reproachfully, they talked the hours away.

Koremitsu had found them out and brought provisions. Feeling a little guilty about the way he had treated Ukon, he did not come near. He thought it amusing that Genji should thus be wandering the streets, and concluded that the girl must provide sufficient cause. And he could have had her himself, had he not been so generous.

Genji and the girl looked out at an evening sky of the utmost calm. Because she found the darkness in the recesses of the house frightening, he raised the blinds at the veranda and they lay side by side. As they gazed at each other in the gathering dusk, it all seemed very strange to her, unbelievably strange. Memories of past wrongs quite left her. She was more at ease with him now, and he thought her charming.

---

[15] **"Call me the fisherman's daughter":** An allusion to a classic poem: "A fisherman's daughter, I spend my life by the waves, / The waves that tell us nothing. I have no home."

[16] *warekara:* Genji's phrase contains an allusion to a classic poem from the *Kokinshu:* "The grass the fishermen take, the *warekara:* / 'I did it myself.' I shall weep but I shall not hate you."

Beside him all through the day, starting up in fright at each little noise, she seemed delightfully childlike. He lowered the shutters early and had lights brought.

"You seem comfortable enough with me, and yet you raise difficulties."

At court everyone would be frantic. Where would the search be directed? He thought what a strange love it was, and he thought of the turmoil the Rokujō lady was certain to be in. She had every right to be resentful, and yet her jealous ways were not pleasant. It was that sad lady to whom his thoughts first turned. Here was the girl beside him, so simple and undemanding; and the other was so impossibly forceful in her demands. How he wished he might in some measure have his freedom.

It was past midnight. He had been asleep for a time when an exceedingly beautiful woman appeared by his pillow.

"You do not even think of visiting me, when you are so much on my mind. Instead you go running off with someone who has nothing to recommend her, and raise a great stir over her. It is cruel, intolerable." She seemed about to shake the girl from her sleep. He awoke, feeling as if he were in the power of some malign being. The light had gone out. In great alarm, he pulled his sword to his pillow and awakened Ukon. She too seemed frightened.

"Go out to the gallery and wake the guard. Have him bring a light."

"It's much too dark."

He forced a smile. "You're behaving like a child."

He clapped his hands and a hollow echo answered. No one seemed to hear. The girl was trembling violently. She was bathed in sweat and as if in a trance, quite bereft of her senses.

"She is such a timid little thing," said Ukon, "frightened when there is nothing at all to be frightened of. This must be dreadful for her."

Yes, poor thing, thought Genji. She did seem so fragile, and she had spent the whole day gazing up at the sky.

"I'll go get someone. What a frightful echo. You stay here with her." He pulled Ukon to the girl's side.

The lights in the west gallery had gone out. There was a gentle wind. He had few people with him, and they were asleep. They were three in number: a young man who was one of his intimates and who was the son of the steward here, a court page, and the man who had been his intermediary in the matter of the "evening faces." He called out. Someone answered and came up to him.

"Bring a light. Wake the other, and shout and twang your bowstrings. What do you mean, going to sleep in a deserted house? I believe Lord Koremitsu was here."

"He was. But he said he had no orders and would come again at dawn."

An elite guardsman, the man was very adept at bow twanging. He went off with a shouting as of a fire watch. At court, thought Genji, the courtiers on night duty would have announced themselves, and the guard would be changing. It was not so very late.

He felt his way back inside. The girl was as before, and Ukon lay face down at her side.

"What is this? You're a fool to let yourself be so frightened. Are you worried about the fox spirits that come out and play tricks in deserted houses? But you needn't worry. They won't come near me." He pulled her to her knees.

"I'm not feeling at all well. That's why I was lying down. My poor lady must be terrified."

"She is indeed. And I can't think why."

He reached for the girl. She was not breathing. He lifted her and she was limp in his arms. There was no sign of life. She had seemed as defenseless as a child, and no doubt some evil power had taken possession of her. He could think of nothing to do. A man came with a torch. Ukon was not prepared to move, and Genji himself pulled up curtain frames to hide the girl.

"Bring the light closer."

It was a most unusual order. Not ordinarily permitted at Genji's side, the man hesitated to cross the threshold.

"Come, come, bring it here! There is a time and place for ceremony."

In the torchlight he had a fleeting glimpse of a figure by the girl's pillow. It was the woman in his dream. It faded away like an apparition in an old romance. In all the fright and horror, his confused thoughts centered upon the girl. There was no room for thoughts of himself.

He knelt over her and called out to her, but she was cold and had stopped breathing. It was too horrible. He had no confidant to whom he could turn for advice. It was the clergy one thought of first on such occasions. He had been so brave and confident, but he was young, and this was too much for him. He clung to the lifeless body.

"Come back, my dear, my dear. Don't do this awful thing to me." But she was cold and no longer seemed human.

The first paralyzing terror had left Ukon. Now she was writhing and wailing. Genji remembered a devil a certain minister had encountered in the Grand Hall.[17]

"She can't possibly be dead." He found the strength to speak sharply. "All this noise in the middle of the night—you must try to be a little quieter." But it had been too sudden.

He turned again to the torchbearer. "There is someone here who seems to have had a very strange seizure. Tell your friend to find out where Lord Koremitsu is spending the night and have him come immediately. If the holy man is still at his mother's house, give him word, very quietly, that he is to come too. His mother and the people with her are not to hear. She does not approve of this sort of adventure."

He spoke calmly enough, but his mind was in a turmoil. Added to grief at the loss of the girl was horror, quite beyond describing, at this desolate place. It would be past midnight. The wind was higher and whistled more dolefully in the pines. There came a strange, hollow call of a bird. Might it be an owl? All was silence, terrifying solitude. He should not have chosen such a place—but it was too late now. Trembling violently, Ukon clung to him. He held her in his arms, wondering if she might be about to follow her lady. He was the only rational one present, and he could think of nothing to do. The flickering light wandered here and there. The upper parts of the screens behind them were in darkness, the lower parts fitfully in the light. There was a persistent creaking, as of someone coming up behind them. If only

---

[17] **a devil . . . in the Grand Hall:** The *Okagami* tells how Fujiwara Tadahira met a devil in the Shishinden. It withdrew when informed that he was on the emperor's business.

Koremitsu would come. But Koremitsu was a nocturnal wanderer without a fixed abode, and the man had to search for him in numerous places. The wait for dawn was like the passage of a thousand nights. Finally he heard a distant crowing. What legacy from a former life could have brought him to this mortal peril? He was being punished for a guilty love, his fault and no one else's, and his story would be remembered in infamy through all the ages to come. There were no secrets, strive though one might to have them. Soon everyone would know, from his royal father down, and the lowest court pages would be talking; and he would gain immortality as the model of the complete fool.

Finally Lord Koremitsu came. He was the perfect servant who did not go against his master's wishes in anything at any time; and Genji was angry that on this night of all nights he should have been away, and slow in answering the summons. Calling him inside even so, he could not immediately find the strength to say what must be said. Ukon burst into tears, the full horror of it all coming back to her at the sight of Koremitsu. Genji too lost control of himself. The only sane and rational one present, he had held Ukon in his arms, but now he gave himself up to his grief.

"Something very strange has happened," he said after a time. "Strange— 'unbelievable' would not be too strong a word. I wanted a priest—one does when these things happen—and asked your reverend brother to come."

"He went back up the mountain yesterday. Yes, it is very strange indeed. Had there been anything wrong with her?"

"Nothing."

He was so handsome in his grief that Koremitsu wanted to weep. An older man who has had everything happen to him and knows what to expect can be depended upon in a crisis; but they were both young, and neither had anything to suggest.

Koremitsu finally spoke. "We must not let the caretaker know. He may be dependable enough himself, but he is sure to have relatives who will talk. We must get away from this place."

"You aren't suggesting that we could find a place where we would be less likely to be seen?"

"No, I suppose not. And the women at her house will scream and wail when they hear about it, and they live in a crowded neighborhood, and all the mob around will hear, and that will be that. But mountain temples are used to this sort of thing. There would not be much danger of attracting attention." He reflected on the problem for a time. "There is a woman I used to know. She has gone into a nunnery up in the eastern hills. She is very old, my father's nurse, as a matter of fact. The district seems to be rather heavily populated, but the nunnery is off by itself."

It was not yet full daylight. Koremitsu had the carriage brought up. Since Genji seemed incapable of the task, he wrapped the body in a covering and lifted it into the carriage. It was very tiny and very pretty, and not at all repellent. The wrapping was loose and the hair streamed forth, as if to darken the world before Genji's eyes.

He wanted to see the last rites through to the end, but Koremitsu would not hear of it. "Take my horse and go back to Nijō, now while the streets are still quiet."

He helped Ukon into the carriage and himself proceeded on foot, the skirts of his robe hitched up. It was a strange, bedraggled sort of funeral procession, he thought, but in the face of such anguish he was prepared to risk his life. Barely conscious, Genji made his way back to Nijō.

"Where have you been?" asked the women. "You are not looking at all well."

He did not answer. Alone in his room, he pressed a hand to his heart. Why had he not gone with the others? What would she think if she were to come back to life? She would think that he had abandoned her. Self-reproach filled his heart to breaking. He had a headache and feared he had a fever. Might he too be dying? The sun was high and still he did not emerge. Thinking it all very strange, the women pressed breakfast upon him. He could not eat. A messenger reported that the emperor had been troubled by his failure to appear the day before.

His brothers-in-law came calling.

"Come in, please, just for a moment." He received only Tō no Chūjō and kept a blind between them. "My old nurse fell seriously ill and took her vows in the Fifth Month or so. Perhaps because of them, she seemed to recover. But recently she had a relapse. Someone came to ask if I would not call on her at least once more. I thought I really must go and see an old and dear servant who was on her deathbed, and so I went. One of her servants was ailing, and quite suddenly, before he had time to leave, he died. Out of deference to me they waited until night to take the body away. All this I learned later. It would be very improper of me to go to court with all these festivities coming up,[18] I thought, and so I stayed away. I have had a headache since early this morning—perhaps I have caught cold. I must apologize."

"I see. I shall so inform your father. He sent out a search party during the concert last night, and really seemed very upset." Tō no Chūjō turned to go, and abruptly turned back. "Come now. What sort of brush did you really have? I don't believe a word of it."

Genji was startled, but managed a show of nonchalance. "You needn't go into the details. Just say that I suffered an unexpected defilement. Very unexpected, really."

Despite his cool manner, he was not up to facing people. He asked a younger brother-in-law to explain in detail his reasons for not going to court. He got off a note to Sanjō with a similar explanation.

Koremitsu came in the evening. Having announced that he had suffered a defilement, Genji had callers remain outside, and there were few people in the house. He received Koremitsu immediately.

"Are you sure she is dead?" He pressed a sleeve to his eyes.

Koremitsu too was in tears. "Yes, I fear she is most certainly dead. I could not stay shut up in a temple indefinitely, and so I have made arrangements with a venerable priest whom I happen to know rather well. Tomorrow is a good day for funerals."

"And the other woman?"

"She has seemed on the point of death herself. She does not want to be left behind by her lady. I was afraid this morning that she might throw herself over a cliff. She wanted to tell the people at Gojō, but I persuaded her to let us have a little more time."

"I am feeling rather awful myself and almost fear the worst."

---

[18] **festivities coming up:** There were many Shinto rites during the Ninth Month.

"Come, now. There is nothing to be done and no point in torturing yourself. You must tell yourself that what must be must be. I shall let absolutely no one know, and I am personally taking care of everything."

"Yes, to be sure. Everything is fated. So I tell myself. But it is terrible to think that I have sent a lady to her death. You are not to tell your sister, and you must be very sure that your mother does not hear. I would not survive the scolding I would get from her."

"And the priests too: I have told them a plausible story." Koremitsu exuded confidence.

The women had caught a hint of what was going on and were more puzzled than ever. He had said that he had suffered a defilement, and he was staying away from court; but why these muffled lamentations?

Genji gave instructions for the funeral. "You must make sure that nothing goes wrong."

"Of course. No great ceremony seems called for."

Koremitsu turned to leave.

"I know you won't approve," said Genji, a fresh wave of grief sweeping over him, "but I will regret it forever if I don't see her again. I'll go on horseback."

"Very well, if you must." In fact Koremitsu thought the proposal very ill advised. "Go immediately and be back while it is still early."

Genji set out in the travel robes he had kept ready for his recent amorous excursions. He was in the bleakest despair. He was on a strange mission and the terrors of the night before made him consider turning back. Grief urged him on. If he did not see her once more, when, in another world, might he hope to see her as she had been? He had with him only Koremitsu and the attendant of that first encounter. The road seemed a long one.

The moon came out, two nights past full. They reached the river. In the dim torchlight, the darkness off towards Mount Toribe was ominous and forbidding; but Genji was too dazed with grief to be frightened. And so they reached the temple.

It was a harsh, unfriendly region at best. The board hut and chapel where the nun pursued her austerities were lonely beyond description. The light at the altar came dimly through cracks. Inside the hut a woman was weeping. In the outer chamber two or three priests were conversing and invoking the holy name in low voices. Vespers seemed to have ended in several temples nearby. Everything was quiet. There were lights and there seemed to be clusters of people in the direction of Kiyomizu. The grand tones in which the worthy monk, the son of the nun, was reading a sutra brought on what Genji thought must be the full flood tide of his tears.

He went inside. The light was turned away from the corpse. Ukon lay behind a screen. It must be very terrible for her, thought Genji. The girl's face was unchanged and very pretty.

"Won't you let me hear your voice again?" He took her hand. "What was it that made me give you all my love, for so short a time, and then made you leave me to this misery?" He was weeping uncontrollably.

The priests did not know who he was. They sensed something remarkable, however, and felt their eyes mist over.

"Come with me to Nijō," he said to Ukon.

"We have been together since I was very young. I never left her side, not for a single moment. Where am I to go now? I will have to tell the others what has happened. As if this weren't enough, I will have to put up with their accusations." She was sobbing. "I want to go with her."

"That is only natural. But it is the way of the world. Parting is always sad. Our lives must end, early or late. Try to put your trust in me." He comforted her with the usual homilies, but presently his real feelings came out. "Put your trust in me—when I fear I have not long to live myself." He did not after all seem likely to be much help.

"It will soon be light," said Koremitsu. "We must be on our way."

Looking back and looking back again, his heart near breaking, Genji went out. The way was heavy with dew and the morning mists were thick. He scarcely knew where he was. The girl was exactly as she had been that night. They had exchanged robes and she had on a red singlet of his. What might it have been in other lives that had brought them together? He managed only with great difficulty to stay in his saddle. Koremitsu was at the reins. As they came to the river Genji fell from his horse and was unable to remount.

"So I am to die by the wayside? I doubt that I can go on."

Koremitsu was in a panic. He should not have permitted this expedition, however strong Genji's wishes. Dipping his hands in the river, he turned and made supplication to Kiyomizu. Genji somehow pulled himself together. Silently invoking the holy name, he was seen back to Nijō.

The women were much upset by these untimely wanderings. "Very bad, very bad. He has been so restless lately. And why should he have gone out again when he was not feeling well?"

Now genuinely ill, he took to his bed. Two or three days passed and he was visibly thinner. The emperor heard of the illness and was much alarmed. Continuous prayers were ordered in this shrine and that temple. The varied rites, Shinto and Confucian and Buddhist, were beyond counting. Genji's good looks had been such as to arouse forebodings. All through the court it was feared that he would not live much longer. Despite his illness, he summoned Ukon to Nijō and assigned her rooms near his own. Koremitsu composed himself sufficiently to be of service to her, for he could see that she had no one else to turn to. Choosing times when he was feeling better, Genji would summon her for a talk, and she soon was accustomed to life at Nijō. Dressed in deep mourning, she was a somewhat stern and forbidding young woman, but not without her good points.

"It lasted such a very little while. I fear that I will be taken too. It must be dreadful for you, losing your only support. I had thought that as long as I lived I would see to all your needs, and it seems sad and ironical that I should be on the point of following her." He spoke softly and there were tears in his eyes. For Ukon the old grief had been hard enough to bear, and now she feared that a new grief might be added to it.

All through the Nijō mansion there was a sense of helplessness. Emissaries from court were thicker than raindrops. Not wanting to worry his father, Genji fought to control himself. His father-in-law was extremely solicitous and came to Nijō every day. Perhaps because of all the prayers and rites the crisis passed—it had lasted some twenty days—and left no ill effects. Genji's full recovery coincided with the final cleansing of the defilement. With the unhappiness he had caused his father much on his mind, he set off for his apartments at court. For a time he felt out of things, as if he had come back to a strange new world.

By the end of the Ninth Month he was his old self once more. He had lost weight, but emaciation only made him handsomer. He spent a great deal of time gazing into space, and sometimes he would weep aloud. He must be in the clutches of some malign spirit, thought the women. It was all most peculiar.

He would summon Ukon on quiet evenings. "I don't understand it at all. Why did she so insist on keeping her name from me? Even if she *was* a fisherman's daughter it was cruel of her to be so uncommunicative. It was as if she did not know how much I loved her."

"There was no reason for keeping it secret. But why should she tell you about her insignificant self? Your attitude seemed so strange from the beginning. She used to say that she hardly knew whether she was waking or dreaming. Your refusal to identify yourself, you know, helped her guess who you were. It hurt her that you should belittle her by keeping your name from her."

"An unfortunate contest of wills. I did not want anything to stand between us; but I must always be worrying about what people will say. I must refrain from things my father and all the rest of them might take me to task for. I am not permitted the smallest indiscretion. Everything is exaggerated so. The little incident of the 'evening faces' affected me strangely and I went to very great trouble to see her. There must have been a bond between us. A love doomed from the start to be fleeting—why should it have taken such complete possession of me and made me find her so precious? You must tell me everything. What point is there in keeping secrets now? I mean to make offerings every week, and I want to know in whose name I am making them."

"Yes, of course—why have secrets now? It is only that I do not want to slight what she made so much of. Her parents are dead. Her father was a guards captain. She was his special pet, but his career did not go well and his life came to an early and disappointing end. She somehow got to know Lord Tō no Chūjō—it was when he was still a lieutenant. He was very attentive for three years or so, and then about last autumn there was a rather awful threat from his father-in-law's house. She was ridiculously timid and it frightened her beyond all reason. She ran off and hid herself at her nurse's in the western part of the city. It was a wretched little hovel of a place. She wanted to go off into the hills, but the direction she had in mind has been taboo since New Year's. So she moved to the odd place where she was so upset to have you find her. She was more reserved and withdrawn than most people, and I fear that her unwillingness to show her emotions may have seemed cold."

So it was true. Affection and pity welled up yet more strongly.

"He once told me of a lost child. Was there such a one?"

"Yes, a very pretty little girl, born two years ago last spring."

"Where is she? Bring her to me without letting anyone know. It would be such a comfort. I should tell my friend Tō no Chūjō, I suppose, but why invite criticism? I doubt that anyone could reprove me for taking in the child. You must think up a way to get around the nurse."

"It would make me very happy if you were to take the child. I would hate to have her left where she is. She is there because we had no competent nurses in the house where you found us."

The evening sky was serenely beautiful. The flowers below the veranda were withered, the songs of the insects were dying too, and autumn tints were coming over the maples. Looking out upon the scene, which might have been a painting, Ukon thought what a lovely asylum she had found herself. She wanted to avert her eyes at the thought of the house of the "evening faces." A pigeon called, somewhat discordantly, from a bamboo thicket. Remembering how the same call had frightened the girl in that deserted villa, Genji could see the little figure as if an apparition were there before him.

"How old was she? She seemed so delicate, because she was not long for this world, I suppose."

"Nineteen, perhaps? My mother, who was her nurse, died and left me behind. Her father took a fancy to me, and so we grew up together, and I never once left her side. I wonder how I can go on without her. I am almost sorry that we were so close. She seemed so weak, but I can see now that she was a source of strength."

"The weak ones do have a power over us. The clear, forceful ones I can do without. I am weak and indecisive by nature myself, and a woman who is quiet and withdrawn and follows the wishes of a man even to the point of letting herself be used has much the greater appeal. A man can shape and mold her as he wishes, and becomes fonder of her all the while."

"She was exactly what you would have wished, sir." Ukon was in tears. "That thought makes the loss seem greater."

The sky had clouded over and a chilly wind had come up. Gazing off into the distance, Genji said softly:

> "One sees the clouds as smoke that rose from the pyre,
> And suddenly the evening sky seems nearer."

Ukon was unable to answer. If only her lady were here! For Genji even the memory of those fulling blocks was sweet.

"In the Eighth Month, the Ninth Month, the nights are long,"[19] he whispered, and lay down.

The young page, brother of the lady of the locust shell, came to Nijō from time to time, but Genji no longer sent messages for his sister. She was sorry that he seemed angry with her and sorry to hear of his illness. The prospect of accompanying her husband to his distant province was a dreary one. She sent off a note to see whether Genji had forgotten her.

"They tell me you have not been well.

> "Time goes by, you ask not why I ask not.
> Think if you will how lonely a life is mine.

---

[19] **"In the Eighth . . . nights are long":** Genji quotes from "The Fulling Blocks at Night" by the Tang-dynasty Chinese poet Bo Juyi.

"I might make reference to Masuda Pond."[20]

This was a surprise; and indeed he had not forgotten her. The uncertain hand in which he set down his reply had its own beauty.

"Who, I wonder, lives the more aimless life.

> "Hollow though it was, the shell of the locust
> Gave me strength to face a gloomy world.

"But only precariously."

So he still remembered "the shell of the locust." She was sad and at the same time amused. It was good that they could correspond without rancor. She wished no further intimacy, and she did not want him to despise her.

As for the other, her stepdaughter, Genji heard that she had married a guards lieutenant. He thought it a strange marriage and he felt a certain pity for the lieutenant. Curious to know something of her feelings, he sent a note by his young messenger.

"Did you know that thoughts of you had brought me to the point of expiring?

> "I bound them loosely, the reeds beneath the eaves,[21]
> And reprove them now for having come undone."

He attached it to a long reed.

The boy was to deliver it in secret, he said. But he thought that the lieutenant would be forgiving if he were to see it, for he would guess who the sender was. One may detect here a note of self-satisfaction.

Her husband was away. She was confused, but delighted that he should have remembered her. She sent off in reply a poem the only excuse for which was the alacrity with which it was composed:

> "The wind brings words, all softly, to the reed,
> And the under leaves are nipped again by the frost."

It might have been cleverer and in better taste not to have disguised the clumsy handwriting. He thought of the face he had seen by lamplight. He could forget neither of them, the governor's wife, seated so primly before him, or the younger woman, chattering on so contentedly, without the smallest suggestion of reserve. The stirrings of a susceptible heart suggested that he still had important lessons to learn.

Quietly, forty-ninth-day services[22] were held for the dead lady in the Lotus Hall on Mount Hiei. There was careful attention to all the details, the priestly robes and the scrolls and the altar decorations. Koremitsu's older brother was a priest of considerable renown, and his conduct of the services was beyond reproach. Genji summoned a doctor of letters with whom he was friendly and who was his tutor in

---

[20] **Masuda Pond:** An allusion to the following lines from the *Shūishū:* "Long the roots of the Masuda water shield, / Longer still the aimless, sleepless nights."

[21] **"reeds . . . eaves":** "Reeds beneath the eaves," *Nokiba no ogi,* is the girl's name.

[22] **forty-ninth-day services:** According to Buddhist tradition, a dead spirit exists in a sort of limbo for forty-nine days before being reincarnated.

Chinese poetry and asked him to prepare a final version of the memorial petition. Genji had prepared a draft. In moving language he committed the one he had loved and lost, though he did not mention her name, to the mercy of Amitābha.

"It is perfect, just as it is. Not a word needs to be changed." Noting the tears that refused to be held back, the doctor wondered who might be the subject of these prayers. That Genji should not reveal the name, and that he should be in such open grief—someone, no doubt, who had brought a very large bounty of grace from earlier lives.

Genji attached a poem to a pair of lady's trousers which were among his secret offerings:

> "I weep and weep as today I tie this cord.
> It will be untied in an unknown world to come."

He invoked the holy name with great feeling. Her spirit had wandered uncertainly these last weeks. Today it would set off down one of the ways of the future.

His heart raced each time he saw Tō no Chūjō. He longed to tell his friend that "the wild carnation" was alive and well; but there was no point in calling forth reproaches.

In the house of the "evening faces," the women were at a loss to know what had happened to their lady. They had no way of inquiring. And Ukon too had disappeared. They whispered among themselves that they had been right about that gentleman, and they hinted at their suspicions to Koremitsu. He feigned complete ignorance, however, and continued to pursue his little affairs. For the poor women it was all like a nightmare. Perhaps the wanton son of some governor, fearing Tō no Chūjō, had spirited her off to the country? The owner of the house was her nurse's daughter. She was one of three children and related to Ukon. She could only long for her lady and lament that Ukon had not chosen to enlighten them. Ukon for her part was loath to raise a stir, and Genji did not want gossip at this late date. Ukon could not even inquire after the child. And so the days went by bringing no light on the terrible mystery.

Genji longed for a glimpse of the dead girl, if only in a dream. On the day after the services he did have a fleeting dream of the woman who had appeared that fatal night. He concluded, and the thought filled him with horror, that he had attracted the attention of an evil spirit haunting the neglected villa.

Early in the Tenth Month the governor of Iyo left for his post, taking the lady of the locust shell with him. Genji chose his farewell presents with great care. For the lady there were numerous fans,[23] and combs of beautiful workmanship, and pieces of cloth (she could see that he had had them dyed specially) for the wayside gods. He also returned her robe, "the shell of the locust."

> "A keepsake till we meet again, I had hoped,
> And see, my tears have rotted the sleeves away."

---

[23] **numerous fans:** Because the sound of the Japanese word for "fan," *ogi*, bodes well for a reunion, fans were often given as farewell presents.

There were other things too, but it would be tedious to describe them. His messenger returned empty-handed. It was through her brother that she answered his poem.

> "Autumn comes, the wings of the locust are shed.
> A summer robe returns, and I weep aloud."

She had remarkable singleness of purpose, whatever else she might have. It was the first day of winter. There were chilly showers, as if to mark the occasion, and the skies were dark. He spent the day lost in thought.

> "The one has gone, to the other I say farewell.
> They go their unknown ways. The end of autumn."

I had hoped, out of deference to him, to conceal these difficult matters; but I have been accused of romancing, of pretending that because he was the son of an emperor he had no faults. Now perhaps, I shall be accused of having revealed too much.

Courts and Codes of Rule

The courtly societies of the Japanese Nara and Heian periods (710–1185) and the European courts of a somewhat later time (particularly 1095–1250) passed through parallel stages of development, and in both cases the narrative and lyric poetry favored by the courts reflected their changing cultures. In both Japan and Europe the traditional poetry of the early period gave way to poetry based more on proper decorum and suggestions of romance conducted at court.

Long before Lady Murasaki wrote **The Tale of Genji**, a national literary culture had developed in Japan as the country was separating itself from Chinese influences. In the first collection of Japanese poetry, the *Man'yoshu* anthology (eighth century), traditional literature and folkways of early Japan were recovered and set alongside the poetry of later court writers such as **Kakinomoto Hitomaro** (fl. 680–700). In Europe, the Frankish leader Charlemagne (r. 789–814) and the English King Alfred the Great (r. 871–899) each set about recovering ancient texts, from Latin and the Germanic languages, respectively. The Anglo-Saxon text of *Beowulf* was copied and preserved in an English monastery around 1000. Later, in the north of France on the eve of the First Crusade (ca. 1095), *The Song of Roland* was composed from earlier versions.

These periods of cultural recovery reflected a time of transition in both societies. Formerly, political control had centered in local strongholds, land was owned by the feudal lords, and crops were planted and harvested by the peasants loyal to their masters. Around the time of the cultural revivals, however, economic and social control passed to the ruling dynasties of great lords, trade increased due to better transportation and communication, and government

p. 1281

kah-kee-noh-MOH-toh
hee-toh-MAH-roh

**Model of the Six
Heian Period Poets,
c. 1850**
*This model by a
nineteenth-century
Japanese artist depicts
the* Rokkasen, *the six
best-known* waka
*poets, including Ono
no Kamachi and
Ariwara no Narihira.
(Seattle Art Museum.
Partial and promised
gift of the Robert B.
and Honey Dootson
Collection. 91.152.
Photo: Paul Macapia)*

koh-KIN-shoo

became more centralized. The centers of power were shifting to the
capital cities.

Courts and the Forms of Literature.   The highest period of culture
and refinement in Japanese and European court life came after the
consolidation of the courts. In Japan, the Heian court (794–1185)
sponsored the publication of Japan's second literary collection, the
Kokinshu anthology, c. 905. The *Kokinshu* honored the work of
certain *Man'yoshu* poets such as Kakinomoto Hitomaro, but concentrated on the major poets of the middle of the ninth century
who reflected the increasingly sophisticated, understated, and even
artificial sentiment of refined courtly society. The principal poetic
form of this anthology was the WAKA, a five-line poem of 31 syllables.
The book itself became a collection of short poems to be memorized. Indeed, knowledge of the thousand *waka* in the *Kokinshu* and
the ability to compose original poetry in the same style were marks
of distinction for the courtiers and ladies in waiting of the Heian
court, as author Sei Shonagon tells us. Hearing a court official recite
waka from memory, she says, "Deeply impressed, I wished that all
this might indeed continue for a thousand years."
    Similarly, in Europe the poems and songs of the troubadours
(courtly entertainers) and the stories of courtly romance that arose in
the courts of southern France, especially Provence, reflected a new
era of social refinement in the middle of the eleventh century. As
historian Norman Cantor suggests, the word "court" itself expanded
in meaning.

> The term *court,* whose meaning heretofore was almost exclusively
> legal and governmental, began to take on the additional
> connotation of an aristocratic social center, and "courtly" became a

synonym for "refined" and "sophisticated." . . . All these elements
have been used to explain the sentimental ideals that are found in
the troubadour lyrics of southern France in the late eleventh and
first half of the twelfth centuries.

The comparison of European and Japanese courtly societies rests
in large part on their parallel economic and social development, as
well as their ideas of what made their cultures important in the first
place. The strong Japanese drive to establish a separate national
identity was largely responsible for the publication of the *Man'yoshu*
anthology. The idea of European unity depended upon the self-
identification of the region as a collection of independent though
culturally related states. Of special importance to the preservation of
both Japanese and European culture was the role of writing—in
Japan the use of crude paper, in Europe the predominance of the
scriptorium, or monastic center for the copying and preserving of
texts.

Men and Women.   The new courts stressed the need to regulate
the social practices of the lower aristocracy and their retainers,
from propertied knights all the way to servants. Men were no
longer viewed merely as warriors and tillers of the soil, but as self-
conscious individuals who were candidates for education, to be
taught manners and etiquette by the rulers at court or their wives
and consorts. The role of women was also enlarged: they became
the new teachers, converting the men to observe proper behavior.
At the same time, the special status of women was recognized, and
men's relationships with women were made subject to restraint and
formal codes of conduct. (The working out of these relationships
differed in the two societies, largely due to the impact of different
religious beliefs and social customs.) As they were being sought
out by the men of court, women of the aristocracy were better educated than in the past, and they began to play a role in the creation
of courtly literature as well as being the subjects of love interest in
men's poetry. In Japan, women became the leading writers of the
courts. In Europe, individual women were recognized as the intellectual and creative peers of men, while a much larger group of
women helped form the audiences of the new courtly romances
and popular songs. Even where the literature was not written *by*
the women of the court, it was often written *for* them.
   Much can be learned about the role of the courts as conveyors of
culture by reading the manuals addressed to correct behavior and the

creation of proper literature. What is not readily apparent from these sources can be acquired by reading the actual literature — both fiction and nonfiction — created during this period. Two fundamental aspects of the new courtly literature are noteworthy: its codification of social practices on the one hand, and the feminization of its literary themes on the other.

The Codes of Rule.   We can see the importance of developing rules for courtly conduct in a variety of sources. The *Kokinshu* anthology (c. 905) begins with a preface by one of its editors, Ki no Tsurayuki, in which he declared that great poetry is timeless, an eternal way of finding meaning and beauty in the world. "Those who know poetry and who understand the heart of things will look up to the old and admire the new as they look up to the moon in the broad sky." Tsurayuki insisted that great poetry requires discipline as to theme, treatment, and formal considerations, and he criticizes even the most recognized poets of past and present for falling short in these areas. As already has been pointed out, the Heian court writer Sei Shonagon was quick to see that poetry and good manners were really the same thing. In her perceptive and often satirical accounts in **The Pillow Book**, she equated displays of poor taste in human

p. 1317

Alram von Gresten with his lady,
c. 1310–1340
Alram von Gresten was a German Minnesinger *of noble background who composed in the courtly love tradition of the Middle Ages. He is depicted in the Manesse Codex, a collection of the love lyrics of the period. (akg-images)*

interactions and poetry. In fact, in the Heian court the two often went hand in hand. The lover leaving his consort's dwelling before dawn should write her a poem celebrating their night together while walking home in the morning dew. The poem should be delivered immediately by a courier, to avoid the needless agony of waiting. Shonagon's descriptions provide us a useful background for understanding the characters in Lady Murasaki's *The Tale of Genji*.

One of the most intriguing documents of the courtly society in the south of France is *The Art of Courtly Love* (literally, *The Art of Honest Loving*) by Andreas Capellanus (fl. 1170–1186), the monk attached to the court of Marie of Champagne in Poitiers. Borrowing from Ovid's classical Latin work *The Art of Love*, possibly Ibn Hazm's Arabic treatise on love *The Dove's Necklace*, the literary records of disputations at the courts of the period, and Ovid's later volume *The Cure for Love*, Capellanus offered rules for love, portrayed dialogues between lovers of different social classes, and summarized "cases" of love, possibly argued out as a form of entertainment in Marie's court, before adding a "rejection of love" (consisting of citations from Ovid and the Bible on the evils of carnal love) in his concluding chapter. Perhaps it is not surprising that the work is full of contradictions. At one point Capellanus prescribes a chaste notion of love, so that both innocent participants are ennobled by their shared attachment to one another. A moment later he is saying the only true love is discovered in the act of adultery. His beginning definition of love seems to be that of a disease: "a certain inborn suffering derived from the sight of and excessive meditation upon the beauty of the opposite sex, which causes each one to wish above all things the embraces of the other and by common desire to carry out all of love's precepts in the other's embrace." But at the end he advises his student lover to retain his chastity at all costs. We are back to Paul's description of love as "charity, set forth in heaven."

The Feminization of the Literature. Perhaps the most striking aspect of the treatment of love in medieval Japanese and European courts is the appearance of the feminine voice. The Japanese writers of the Heian courts included the novelist Lady Murasaki, the diarist Sei Shonagon, and the poet **Ono no Kamachi**.

OH-noh noh-koh-MAH-chee

A leading author of short romances in European literature of the twelfth century was the Anglo Norman poet Marie de France, apparently educated in France and writing her many of her works in a courtly society in west England. In both worlds, the presence of a woman's hand is unmistakable in the writing. While Murasaki and

Shonagon differed in their approaches, their subject was the same—the Heian court from the perspective of a particular observer. Ono no Komachi, notorious for her poems of sexual longing and blighted passion, projected tremendous strength from her five-line *waka*. Marie de France, working with traditional stories from French romances, viewed the outcomes of her plots from an ironic, detached perspective.

The nature of the courtly audience was another aspect of the feminization of the literature. The love affairs of knights and ladies in the court, part of both Japanese and European literature of the time, could not possibly have been undertaken in the light of day without drastic consequences. In the European cycles, Tristan and Iseult, Lancelot and Guinevere, and the illicit loves they represented were the creations of fiction, portrayed in much the same way that a modern soap opera portrays adultery—as a transgression in which the lovers constantly face the danger of discovery and retribution, yet

p. 1325

somehow remain untouched by the circumstances. In **"The Lay of Chevrefoil,"** the story told by Marie de France of a meeting in the woods between Iseult and her lover-knight, the encounter is provocative, charming, and educational at the same time. Although the deception of the king, Iseult's husband, is at the heart of the story, even the lords at court must have found this sublimated tale of romantic love suitable for performance before their mixed audience—and the women loved it.

■ **FURTHER RESEARCH**

Editions (by subject)

Carter, Steven D., ed. *Traditional Japanese Poetry: An Anthology.* 1991.

Levy, Ian Hideo, trans. *The Ten Thousand Leaves: A Translation of the Man'yoshu.* vol. 1, 1981.

Cranston, Edwin A., trans. *A Waka Anthology. Volume One: The Gem-Glistening Cup.* 1993.

McCullough, Helen Craig, ed. *Kokin Wakashu: The First Imperial Anthology of Japanese Poetry.* 1985.

Rodd, Laura Rasplica, and Mary Catherine Henkenius, trans. *Kokinshu: A Collection of Poems Ancient and Modern.* 1984.

Morris, Ivan, trans. *The Pillow Book of Sei Shonagon.* 2 vols. 1967.

Burgess, Glyn S., and Keith Busby. *The Lais of Marie de France.* 1986.

Hanning, Robert, and Joan Ferrante. *The Lais of Marie de France.* 1978.

Literary Criticism

Brower, Robert H., and Earl Miner. *Japanese Court Poetry.* 1961.

McCullough, Helen Craig. *Brocade by Night: Kokin Wakashu and the Court Style in Japanese Classical Poetry.* 1984.

Morris, Ivan. *The World of the Shining Prince: Court Life in Ancient Japan.* 1967.

Ferrante, Joan. *The Glory of Her Sex: Women's Roles in the Composition of Medieval Texts.* 1997.

Kay, Sarah. "Courts, Clerks, and Courtly Love." In Roberta L. Krueger, ed. *The Cambridge Companion to Medieval Romance.* 2000.

■ PRONUNCIATION

Japanese
Genji: GEN-ji
Fujiwara no Korechika: foo-jee-WAH-rah-noh koh-reh-CHEE-kah
hanka: HAHN-kah
Heian: HAY-un
Kakinomoto Hitomaro: kah-kee-noh-MOH-toh hee-toh-MAH-roh
Ki no Tsurayuki: KEE noh-tsoo-rah-YOO-kee
Kokinshu: koh-KIN-shoo
Man'yoshu: mahn-YOH-shoo
Nara: NAH-rah
Ono no Komachi: OH-noh noh-koh-MAH-chee
Sei Shonagon: SAY shoh-NAH-gon
Teishi (Empress Sadako): TAY-shee, sah-DAH-koh
Temmu: TEM-oo
waka: WAH-kah

French
Breton: breh-TAWNG, BRET-un
Chevrefoil: shev-ruh-FOIL
Iseult: ee-SOOLT
lai: LAY

∾ KAKINOMOTO HITOMARO
JAPAN, FL. 680–700

Much of what is known about Kakinomoto Hitomaro, the poet responsible for some of the most esteemed Japanese verse, comes from the texts of his poems in the *Man'yoshu.* Though a courtier of low rank, he was undoubtedly a favorite of the court and greatly admired by the other poets. His first published poem was an elegy for the son of Emperor Temmu, written in 689. His personal love poems were dedicated to at least two different wives. According to legend he died in the western province of Iwami around the age of fifty. Equally known for his earlier court compositions and his later personal poetry, he was called "the saint of poetry."

Were it not for changes in the practice of eulogizing the royal family of Japan, Hitomaro's early poetry and the direction of early Japanese poetry as a whole might have developed differently. During the reign of

Emperor Temmu (673–686), the style of poetry practiced at the Nara court changed. Extolled during his reign, Temmu was hailed extravagantly at the time of his death; elegies written to honor him include the formulation "our Lord, a very god." Three years later, Emperor Temmu's son, the crown prince Kusakabe, died before he could ascend to the throne. Hitomaro was commissioned to write an elegy for the prince, and following its success he became the leading court poet of his day. For a time, this ceremonial poetry took center stage, while his more personal poetry had to wait.

The conventions of emotional expression that Hitomaro developed during his attachment to the court can be seen in his later personal poetry as well. As he grew older he expressed a sad and mournful view of existence in his work. His greatest poetry was never far from descriptions of death and its capacity to undo the human bond of love. His most memorable works lament a parting from his wife and the death of a later wife. In the poem of parting (not included here) Hitomaro stirs the reader's sensual imagination with an image of his young wife, "who swayed to my side in sleep like sleek seaweed," while at the same time presenting her as a passing reality. The same imagery appears in his first poem on the death of his later wife, when a messenger comes to tell him "that my girl, / who swayed to me in sleep / like seaweed of the offing, / was gone. . . ." In the battle between life and death, death conquers, and the sensuous world is destroyed. As the second poem on his wife's death observes most bitterly, "My wife, whom I thought was of this world, is ash."

FROM

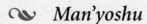 *Man'yoshu*

Translated by Ian Hideo Levy

On the Death of His Wife: I

On the Karu Road
is the village of my wife,
and I desired to meet her intimately,
but if I went there too much
the eyes of others would cluster around us,
and if I went there too often
others would find us out.
And so I hoped
that later we would meet
like tangling vines,

10

trusted that we would
as I would trust a great ship,
and hid my love:
faint as jewel's light,
a pool walled in by cliffs.

Then came the messenger,
　　his letter tied
　　to a jewelled catalpa twig,
to tell me,
20　　　　in a voice
　　　like the sound
　　　of a catalpa bow,
that my girl,
who had swayed to me in sleep
like seaweed of the offing,
was gone
like the coursing sun
gliding into dusk,
like the radiant moon
30　secluding itself behind the clouds,
gone like the scarlet leaves of autumn.

I did not know what to say,
　　　　　　what to do,
but simply could not listen
and so, perhaps to solace
a single thousandth
　　　of my thousand-folded longing,
I stood at the Karu market
where often she had gone,
40　and listened,
but could not even hear
the voices of the birds
that cry on Unebi Mountain,
　　where the maidens
　　　　　wear strands of jewels,
and of the ones who passed me
on that road,
　　straight as a jade spear,
not one resembled her.
50　I could do nothing
but call my wife's name
and wave my sleeves.

Envoys

Too dense the yellowed leaves
on the autumn mountain:
my wife is lost
and I do not know the path
to find her by.

With the falling away
of the yellowed leaves,
I see the messenger
with his jewelled catalpa staff,
and I recall the days I met her.

On the Death of His Wife: II

She was my wife,
to whom my thoughts gathered
thick as the spring leaves,
like the myriad branches budding
on the zelkova tree
on the embankment (a short step
from her gate),
that we would bring
and look at together
while she was of this world.
She was my wife,
on whom I depended,
but now, unable to break
the course of this world,
she shrouds herself from me
in heavenly white raiments
on a withered, sun-simmered plain,
and rises away in the morning
like a bird,
and conceals herself
like the setting sun.

Each time our infant,
the memento she left,
cries out in hunger,
I, though a man,
having nothing to give it,
hug it to my breast.
Inside the wedding house
where the pillows we slept on

lie pushed together,
I live through the days
desolate and lonely
and sigh through the nights.
Lament as I may,
I know nothing I can do.
Long for her as I may,
I have no way to meet her.
100   And so when someone said,
"The wife you long for
dwells on Hagai Mountain,
            of the great bird,"
I struggled up here,
kicking the rocks apart,
but it did no good:
my wife, whom I thought
was of this world,
is ash.

Envoys

110   The autumn moon crosses the heavens
as it did when I watched last year,
but my wife, who watched with me—
the drift of the year has taken her.

Leaving my wife on Hikide Mountain
by the Fusuma Road,
I think of the path she has taken,
and I am hardly alive.

I come home
and gaze inside:
120   facing outward
on the haunted floor,
my wife's boxwood pillow.

∾ ONO NO KOMACHI

JAPAN, FL. 850

The *Kokinshu,* or *Collection of Ancient and Modern Times,* consisted of twenty volumes and more than a thousand poems. In the 150 years since the appearance of the earlier *Man'yoshu* collection, much had changed. While the *Kokinshu* honored the work of *Man'yoshu* poet Kakinomoto Hitomaro (fl. 680–700) and included some ancient Japanese poetry collected from court archives, it concentrated on the works of the major Japanese poets of the middle of the ninth century, including the celebrated Ariwara no Narihira (825–880) and Ono no Komachi, as well as the works of the anthology's principal compiler Ki no Tsurayuki (862–946) and his contemporaries. The *Kokinshu,* though much more sophisticated than the *Man'yoshu,* registering the effects of more than a hundred years of predominantly Chinese influence, still attempted to restore Japanese national culture to greatness. In this it was quite successful. Often cited in later works, with its poetry becoming habitual to the thinking of educated Japanese, it opened the way for the brilliant advances in Japanese literature during the next century of the Heian period (794–1185).

The principal editor of the new anthology and the author of its Japanese preface, Ki no Tsurayuki (862–946) took up his literary task at about the age of forty. His Japanese preface, which expresses a love of lived experience and beautiful display—common to all later Japanese culture, not only literature—has been called the first work on aesthetics, or the theory of beauty, in Japanese literature. The best poetry in the collection is noteworthy for its connection to everyday life, its personal touches, and its thematic unity, none of which were distinguishing characteristics of the formal, allusive, and indirect Chinese poetry of the day. Tracing the origin of poetry back to "when heaven and earth first appeared," the Japanese preface states that poetry portrays the beauty that can be found in the everyday events of human life:

> The seeds of Japanese poetry lie in the human heart and grow into leaves of ten thousand words. Many things happen to the people of this world, and all that they think and feel is given expression in the description of things they see and hear. When we hear the warbling of the mountain thrush in the blossoms or the voice of the frog in the water, we know every living being has its song.

One of the most famous authors in the collection, though not the most frequently represented, is Ono no Komachi (fl. 850). The *Kokinshu* contains eighteen of her poems. She was legendary throughout Japan for her physical beauty, her reputation for passionate relationships, her anger at mistreatment and rejection, her emotional and intellectual complexity, and her capacity for expressing vulnerability in defeat. In the *Kokinshu* her poems speak to every aspect of passion: sleeplessness, yearning, missed words of love, pursuit, abandonment, despair. A final poem, curiously placed among some supposedly humorous works at the end of the collection, pronounces: "my blazing passion / wakens me   my pounding heart / shoots flame   then turns to cinders" (1030).

Despite her fame, Ono no Komachi was attacked by Ki no Tsurayuki in his Japanese preface:

> Ono no Komachi is a modern Princess Sotori [a libertine]. She is full of sentiment but weak. Her poetry is like a noble lady who is suffering from a sickness, but the weakness is natural to a woman's poetry.

Popular legends concerning Komachi after her death also drew a harsh moral. In a famous play by the *Nō* dramatist Zeami Motokiyo (1364–1443) she is depicted as a frightening old hag, despised by passers-by. History, however, has treated her with considerably more respect. Later generations of scholars have admired her poems' combination of emotional richness and pure skill. One critic has remarked, "What is especially individual about Komachi is that her strongest passions seem to bring forth her most complex techniques."

FROM

∾ *Kokinshu*

Translated by Laurel Rasplica Rodd with Mary Catherine Henkenius

552: IN LOVE-TORMENTED SLEEP I SAW HIM

in love-tormented
sleep I saw him beside me—
    had I known my love's
visit was but a dream   I
should never have awakened

553: SINCE THAT BRIEF SLEEP WHEN FIRST I SAW

since that brief sleep when
first I saw the one I love
    it is those fleeting
dreams   ephemera of the
night   on which I now rely

554: WHEN MY YEARNING GROWS UNENDURABLE

when my yearning grows
unendurable   all through
    the jet-black hours of
night   I sleep with my robes turned
inside out   awaiting him

938:   I HAVE SUNK TO THE BOTTOM

*When Funya no Yasuhide was appointed Secretary of Mikawa, he wrote,
"Won't you come for a tour of the provinces?" and Komachi replied with
this poem.*

I have sunk to the
bottom   and like the rootless
shifting water weeds
should the currents summon me
I too would drift away

1030:   NO MOON LIGHTS THE NIGHT

no moon lights the night
nor can I meet my lover
my blazing passion
wakens me   my pounding heart
shoots flame   then turns to cinders

SEI SHONAGON
B. JAPAN, C. 966–1017

The *Makura no Soshi*, known in English as *The Pillow Book,* brims with
vignettes, stories, essays, and lists concerning court life in imperial Japan
at the turn of the tenth century. Its author, Sei Shonagon, is usually
counted among the greatest Japanese prose stylists. Her flights of lyricism, merciless descriptions, and compilations of "lists" of things to
praise or condemn made her work popular as soon as it appeared; her
candid and often revealing account of her career as a lady-in-waiting for
Teishi (Empress Sadako) helps one understand this rich and sophisticated period of Japanese history. Often compared to Lady Murasaki's *The
Tale of Genji*, written at about the same time, *The Pillow Book* treats the
real lives of men and women at court while *Genji* transforms their stories
into a highly stylized work of fiction. Both works are classics in their way,
each a reflection of the other's world.

Sei Shonagon's origins and her subsequent fate are partially obscured.
Her father, Kiyohara no Motosuke (908–990), was a recognized poet and
scholar as well as a minor public official. Sei Shonagon's real name is a
mystery; *sei* is an alternate pronunciation of the first character of her
family surname, Kiyohara, and *shonagon* means "minor counselor," a
name commonly applied to those who served at court or to their dependents. Shonagon served Empress Sadako (976–1000), the first consort of
Emperor Ichijo (980–1011), as a lady-in-waiting from 993 to 1000, when

the young empress died following the birth of her second child. The end of Shonagon's life is unrecorded, though certain stories, possibly driven by jealousy, suggest that she died in poverty.

We know that Sei Shonagon had enemies. An attractive, energetic, and formidable woman whom men constantly attended, she was distinguished by her ingenuity, her sharp wit, and (some would say) her arrogance and snobbery. Lady Murasaki, who completed her masterpiece, *The Tale of Genji*, in about 1010, was particularly competitive with Shonagon, both as a writer and as a lady-in-waiting for a rival empress. Lady Murasaki wrote of Shonagon with crushing sarcasm:

> [She] has the most extraordinary air of self-satisfaction. Yet, if we stop to examine those Chinese writings of hers that she so presumptuously scatters about the place, we find that they are full of imperfections. Someone who makes such an effort to be different from others is bound to fall in people's esteem, and I can only think that her future will be a hard one. She is a gifted woman, to be sure. Yet, if one gives free rein to one's emotions even under the most inappropriate circumstances, if one has to sample each interesting thing that comes along, people are bound to regard one as frivolous. And how can things turn out well for such a woman?

Scattered throughout *The Pillow Book* are accounts of the court, including Sei Shonagon's wonderment upon her first arrival, punctuated by her sharp observation of customas ("In Spring It Is the Dawn," "Especially Delightful Is the First Day"). In "The Sliding Screen in the Back of the Hall" Shonagon participates in her first poetry competition, for which she is expected to know the entire *Kokinshu*, the tenth-century Japanese anthology of more than a thousand poems. Here she is a beginner at court, painfully shy and trying to measure up to the standards expected of her.

> As a writer she is incomparably the best poet of her time, a fact which is apparent only in her prose and not at all in the conventional *uta* [lyrics] for which she is also famous. Passages such as that about the stormy lake or the few lines about crossing a moonlit river show a beauty of phrasing that Murasaki, a much more deliberate writer, certainly never surpassed.
>
> – ARTHUR WALEY, translator, 1928

FROM

∾ The Pillow Book

Translated by Ivan Morris

IN SPRING IT IS THE DAWN

In spring it is the dawn that is most beautiful. As the light creeps over the hills, their outlines are dyed a faint red and wisps of purplish cloud trail over them.

In summer the nights. Not only when the moon shines, but on dark nights too, as the fireflies flit to and fro, and even when it rains, how beautiful it is!

In autumn the evenings, when the glittering sun sinks close to the edge of the hills and the crows fly back to their nests in threes and fours and twos; more charming still is a file of wild geese, like specks in the distant sky. When the sun has set, one's heart is moved by the sound of the wind and the hum of the insects.

In winter the early mornings. It is beautiful indeed when snow has fallen during the night, but splendid too when the ground is white with frost; or even when there is no snow or frost, but it is simply very cold and the attendants hurry from room to room stirring up the fires and bringing charcoal, how well this fits the season's mood! But as noon approaches and the cold wears off, no one bothers to keep the braziers alight, and soon nothing remains but piles of white ashes.

Especially Delightful Is the First Day

Especially delightful is the first day of the First Month,[1] when the mists so often shroud the sky. Everyone pays great attention to his appearance and dresses with the utmost care. What a pleasure it is to see them all offer their congratulations to the Emperor and celebrate their own new year![2]

I also enjoy the seventh day, when people pluck the young herbs that have sprouted fresh and green beneath the snow. It is amusing to see their excitement when they find such plants growing near the Palace, by no means a spot where one might expect them.

This is the day when members of the nobility who live outside the Palace arrive in their magnificently decorated carriages to admire the blue horses.[3] As the carriages are drawn over the ground-beam of the Central Gate, there is always a tremendous bump, and the heads of the women passengers are knocked together; the combs fall out of their hair, and may be smashed to pieces if the owners are not careful. I enjoy the way everyone laughs when this happens.

I remember one occasion when I visited the Palace to see the procession of blue horses. Several senior courtiers were standing outside the guard-house of the Left Division; they had borrowed bows from the escorts, and, with much laughter, were twanging them to make the blue horses prance. Looking through one of the gates of the Palace enclosure, I could dimly make out a garden fence, near which a number of ladies, several of them from the Office of Grounds, went to and fro. What lucky women, I thought, who could walk about the Nine-Fold Enclosure[4] as though they had lived there all their lives! Just then the escorts passed close to my carriage — remarkably close, in fact, considering the vastness of the Palace grounds — and I could actually see the texture of their faces. Some of them were not properly powdered; here and there their skin showed through unpleasantly like the dark patches of earth in a garden where the snow has begun to melt. When the horses in the

---

[1] **the First Month:** In the Japanese lunar calendar, the moon is full on the fifteenth day of each month. The calendar is ahead of the Western calendar by about seventeen to forty-five days: on average, about a month.

[2] **new year:** New Year's Day is the time to pay respects to one's superiors and celebrate the passage of a year, corresponding in some ways to a Western birthday.

[3] **blue horses:** At the Festival of the Blue Horses, twenty-one horses, originally steel-gray, were paraded before the emperor to mark the beginning of an auspicious new year.

[4] **the Nine-Fold Enclosure:** A figure of speech denoting the enormous walled-in grounds of the Imperial Palace, a city in itself.

procession reared wildly, I shrank into the back of my carriage and could no longer see what was happening.

On the eighth day there is great excitement in the Palace as people hurry to express their gratitude, and the clatter of carriages is louder than ever—all very fascinating.

The fifteenth day is the festival of the full-moon gruel, when a bowl of gruel is presented to His Majesty. On this day all the women of the house carry gruel-sticks, which they hide carefully from each other. It is most amusing to see them walking about, as they await an opportunity to hit their companions. Each one is careful not to be struck herself and is constantly looking over her shoulder to make sure that no one is stealing up on her. Yet the precautions are useless, for before long one of the women manages to score a hit. She is extremely pleased with herself and laughs merrily. Everyone finds this delightful—except, of course, the victim, who looks very put out.[5] [. . .]

Sometimes when the women are hitting each other the men also join in the fun. The strange thing is that, when a woman is hit by one of the men, she often gets angry and bursts into tears; then she will upbraid the man and say the most awful things about him—most amusing. Even in the Palace, where the atmosphere is usually so solemn, everything is in confusion on this day, and no one stands on ceremony.

It is fascinating to see what happens during the period of appointments. However snowy and icy it may be, candidates of the Fourth and Fifth Ranks come to the Palace with their official requests. Those who are still young and merry seem full of confidence. For the candidates who are old and white-haired things do not go so smoothly. Such men have to apply for help from people with influence at Court; some of them even visit ladies-in-waiting in their quarters and go to great lengths in pointing out their own merits. If young women happen to be present, they are greatly amused. As soon as the candidates have left, they mimic and deride them—something that the old men cannot possibly suspect as they scurry from one part of the Palace to another, begging everyone, 'Please present my petition favourably to the Emperor' and 'Pray inform Her Majesty about me.' It is not so bad if they finally succeed, but it really is rather pathetic when all their efforts prove in vain.

THE SLIDING SCREEN IN THE BACK OF THE HALL

The sliding screen in the back of the hall in the north-east corner of Seiryō Palace[6] is decorated with paintings of the stormy sea and of the terrifying creatures with long arms and long legs that live there. When the doors of the Empress's room were open,

---

[5] **The fifteenth day . . . very put out:** Concerning the ceremony of the gruel at the first full moon, it was believed that if a woman was struck in the flanks with a gruel-stick she would produce a male child. It became a custom for the women to run about the house hitting each other playfully with these sticks.

[6] **The sliding screen . . . of Seiryō Palace:** Seiryō Palace was the emperor's residence in the Imperial Palace. The sliding screen, with its terrifying Chinese figures, protected the emperor and empress from evil spirits when they met privately.

we could always see this screen. One day we were sitting in the room, laughing at the paintings and remarking how unpleasant they were. By the balustrade of the veranda stood a large celadon vase, full of magnificent cherry branches; some of them were as much as five foot long, and their blossoms overflowed to the very foot of the railing. Towards noon the Major Counsellor, Fujiwara no Korechika,[7] arrived. He was dressed in a cherry-coloured Court cloak, sufficiently worn to have lost its stiffness, a white under-robe, and loose trousers of dark purple; from beneath the cloak shone the pattern of another robe of dark red damask. Since His Majesty was present, Korechika knelt on the narrow wooden platform before the door and reported to him on official matters.

A group of ladies-in-waiting was seated behind the bamboo blinds. Their cherry-coloured Chinese jackets hung loosely over their shoulders with the collars pulled back; they wore robes of wistaria, golden yellow, and other colours, many of which showed beneath the blind covering the half-shutter. Presently the noise of the attendants' feet told us that dinner was about to be served in the Daytime Chamber, and we heard cries of 'Make way. Make way.'

The bright, serene day delighted me. When the Chamberlains had brought all the dishes into the Chamber, they came to announce that dinner was ready, and His Majesty left by the middle door. After accompanying the Emperor, Korechika returned to his previous place on the veranda beside the cherry blossoms. The Empress pushed aside her curtain of state and came forward as far as the threshold. We were overwhelmed by the whole delightful scene. It was then that Korechika slowly intoned the words of the old poem,

> The days and the months flow by,
> But Mount Mimoro lasts forever.[8]

Deeply impressed, I wished that all this might indeed continue for a thousand years.

As soon as the ladies serving in the Daytime Chamber had called for the gentlemen-in-waiting to remove the trays, His Majesty returned to the Empress's room. Then he told me to rub some ink on the inkstone. Dazzled, I felt that I should never be able to take my eyes off his radiant countenance. Next he folded a piece of white paper. 'I should like each of you,' he said, 'to copy down on this paper the first ancient poem that comes into your head.'

'How am I going to manage this?' I asked Korechika, who was still out on the veranda.

'Write your poem quickly,' he said, 'and show it to His Majesty. We men must not interfere in this.' Ordering an attendant to take the Emperor's inkstone to each of the women in the room, he told us to make haste. 'Write down any poem you happen to remember,' he said. 'The Naniwazu[9] or whatever else you can think of.'

---

[7] **Fujiwara no Korechika:** The brother of Empress Teishi (Sadako) who was exiled in 966 because he was the principal rival of Fujiwara no Michinaga, the most powerful political figure in Japan after this date.

[8] **The days . . . lasts forever:** Wishing his sister prosperity, Korechika quotes from a poem from the *Man'yoshu*.

[9] **The Naniwazu:** A famous poem from the *Kokinshu*, supposedly the first poem composed by an emperor.

For some reason I was overcome with timidity; I flushed and had no idea what to do. Some of the other women managed to put down poems about the spring, the blossoms, and such suitable subjects; then they handed me the paper and said, 'Now it's your turn.' Picking up the brush, I wrote the poem that goes,

> The years have passed
> And age has come my way.
> Yet I need only look at this fair flower
> For all my cares to melt away.

I altered the third line, however, to read, 'Yet I need only look upon my lord.'[10]

When he had finished reading, the Emperor said, 'I asked you to write these poems because I wanted to find out how quick you really were.

'A few years ago,' he continued, 'Emperor Enyū ordered all his courtiers to write poems in a notebook. Some excused themselves on the grounds that their handwriting was poor; but the Emperor insisted, saying that he did not care in the slightest about their handwriting or even whether their poems were suitable for the season. So they all had to swallow their embarrassment and produce something for the occasion. Among them was His Excellency, our present Chancellor,[11] who was then Middle Captain of the Third Rank. He wrote down the old poem,

> Like the sea that beats
> Upon the shores of Izumo
> As the tide sweeps in,
> Deeper it grows and deeper —
> The love I bear for you.

But he changed the last line to read, "The love I bear my lord!", and the Emperor was full of praise.'

When I heard His Majesty tell this story, I was so overcome that I felt myself perspiring. It occurred to me that no younger woman would have been able to use my poem[12] and I felt very lucky. This sort of test can be a terrible ordeal: it often happens that people who usually write fluently are so overawed that they actually make mistakes in their characters.

Next the Empress placed a notebook of *Kokin Shū* poems before her and started reading out the first three lines of each one, asking us to supply the remainder. Among them were several famous poems that we had in our minds day and night; yet for some strange reason we were often unable to fill in the missing lines. Lady Saishō, for example, could manage only ten, which hardly qualified her as knowing her *Kokin Shū*. Some of the other women, even less successful, could remember only about half-a-dozen poems. They would have done better to tell the Empress quite

---

[10] **'Yet I need only look upon my lord':** Shonagon has altered this poem, from the *Kokinshu,* to praise Emperor Ichijo.

[11] **our present Chancellor:** Fujiwara no Michitaka (see note 7). The origin of this poem is unknown.

[12] **no younger woman . . . my poem:** Shonagon's choice of this poem, referring to herself in the line "And age has come my way," is appropriate. At the time she is thirty, while the empress and emperor are twenty and sixteen, respectively.

simply that they had forgotten the lines; instead they came out with great lamentations like 'Oh dear, how could we have done so badly in answering the questions that Your Majesty was pleased to put to us?' — all of which I found rather absurd.

When no one could complete a particular poem, the Empress continued reading to the end. This produced further wails from the women: 'Oh, we all knew that one! How could we be so stupid?'

'Those of you,' said the Empress, 'who had taken the trouble to copy out the *Kokin Shū* several times would have been able to complete every single poem I have read. In the reign of Emperor Murakami there was a woman at Court known as the Imperial Lady of Senyō Palace. She was the daughter of the Minister of the Left who lived in the Smaller Palace of the First Ward, and of course you have all heard of her. When she was still a young girl, her father gave her this advice: "First you must study penmanship. Next you must learn to play the seven-string zither better than anyone else. And also you must memorize all the poems in the twenty volumes of the *Kokin Shū*."

'Emperor Murakami,' continued Her Majesty, 'had heard this story and remembered it years later when the girl had grown up and become an Imperial Concubine. Once, on a day of abstinence,[13] he came into her room, hiding a notebook of *Kokin Shū* poems in the folds of his robe. He surprised her by seating himself behind a curtain of state; then, opening the book, he asked, "Tell me the verse written by such-and-such a poet, in such-and-such a year and on such-and-such an occasion." The lady understood what was afoot and that it was all in fun, yet the possibility of making a mistake or forgetting one of the poems must have worried her greatly. Before beginning the test, the Emperor had summoned a couple of ladies-in-waiting who were particularly adept in poetry and told them to mark each incorrect reply by a *go* stone.[14] What a splendid scene it must have been! You know, I really envy anyone who attended that Emperor even as a lady-in-waiting.

'Well,' Her Majesty went on, 'he then began questioning her. She answered without any hesitation, just giving a few words or phrases to show that she knew each poem. And never once did she make a mistake. After a time the Emperor began to resent the lady's flawless memory and decided to stop as soon as he detected any error or vagueness in her replies. Yet, after he had gone through ten books of the *Kokin Shū*, he had still not caught her out. At this stage he declared that it would be useless to continue. Marking where he had left off, he went to bed. What a triumph for the lady!

'He slept for some time. On waking, he decided that he must have a final verdict and that if he waited until the following day to examine her on the other ten volumes, she might use the time to refresh her memory. So he would have to settle the matter that very night. Ordering his attendants to bring up the bedroom lamp, he resumed his questions. By the time he had finished all twenty volumes, the night was well advanced; and still the lady had not made a mistake.

---

[13] **day of abstinence:** An inauspicious day when it was important to stay inside and abstain from all pleasurable activities.

[14] **a *go* stone:** A small black or white stone marker used in a Chinese boardgame.

'During all this time His Excellency, the lady's father, was in a state of great agitation. As soon as he was informed that the Emperor was testing his daughter, he sent his attendants to various temples to arrange for special recitations of the Scriptures. Then he turned in the direction of the Imperial Palace and spent a long time in prayer. Such enthusiasm for poetry is really rather moving.'

The Emperor, who had been listening to the whole story, was much impressed. 'How can he possibly have read so many poems?' he remarked when Her Majesty had finished. 'I doubt whether I could get through three or four volumes. But of course things have changed. In the old days even people of humble station had a taste for the arts and were interested in elegant pastimes. Such a story would hardly be possible nowadays, would it?'

The ladies in attendance on Her Majesty and the Emperor's own ladies-in-waiting who had been admitted into Her Majesty's presence began chatting eagerly, and as I listened I felt that my cares had really 'melted away.'

∾ MARIE DE FRANCE
B. FRANCE, FL. 1170–1180

Marie de France wrote in Norman French in the second half of the twelfth century. She was best loved for twelve original short verse romances known as **Breton lais.** Her contemporary, Denis Piramus, rather quaintly referred to her as "Lady Marie, who wrote in rhyme and composed the verses of **lais** which are not at all true. And so is she much praised because of it and the rhyme loved everywhere; for all love it greatly and hold it dear—counts, barons, and knights." In recent times she has been called by her translators Robert Hanning and Joan Ferrante "perhaps the greatest woman author of the Middle Ages, and certainly the creator of the finest medieval short fiction before Boccaccio and Chaucer."

breh-TAWNG

LAY

Since several of Marie de France's works came from English sources and the surviving manuscripts were found in England, it is believed that she was a member of the Anglo-Norman or Angevin aristocracy who lived part of her life in England. Whoever she was, Marie de France displayed a remarkable literary background for a woman of her era. Living in the midst of a literary revival to which she herself was a major contributor, Marie developed a unique form of storytelling that treated courtly love themes with great poetic economy and clarity of language. Her *Breton lais* were far briefer than other romances, composed in rhymed octasyllabic couplets that required great compression of meaning. The poems are marked by "signatures," often the titles of the works, that utilize romantic symbols such as the nightingale, the swan, or in the case of the "The Lay of Chevrefoil," the honeysuckle; frequently these signatures symbolize the meaning at the poem's core.

Mirror of Love,
1320–30
Romantic, courtly
scenes are beautifully
carved onto the back
of this French ivory
mirror. (Giraudon/
Art Resource)

www For links to
more information
about Marie de
France and a quiz
on "The Lay of
Chevrefoil" ("The
Honeysuckle"), see
bedfordstmartins
.com/worldlit
compact.

shev-ruh-FOIL

ee-SOOLT

Marie did not take a single position on the subject of love. She showed respect for her sources, understanding each artist to be bound by the conventions of his or her "matter." Yet she often added a sense of mystery in her writing as well. "The Lay of Chevrefoil" presents love in its simplest yet most elusive aspect as that which exists and therefore cannot be questioned, a power that makes us both greater and less than ourselves. In the sweep of passion, danger or even death may result from an unguarded moment; but sometimes luck is on the side of the lovers after all. This open-ended definition of love provides the storyteller with a grand array of possibilities, as Marie undoubtedly knew well.

In "The Lay of **Chevrefoil**," Marie alludes to the familiar legend of Tristan and Iseult,[1] including the king's anger, the envy of the court, and the necessity that the lovers meet in secret. In the *lai*, the love of Tristan and Iseult is expressed in the image of the honeysuckle and the hazel tree, two plants that require each other in order to survive. In material rife with the makings of melodrama, Marie uses this one reference to suggest the true nature of the lovers' attraction. Their encounter is made possible not so much by craft or guile as by the lovers' perfect, intuitive understanding of each other's thoughts. **Iseult** is not even named in "The Lay of Chevrefoil": Calling her only "the queen," Marie emphasizes both the impossibility and the fragile truth of Iseult and Tristan's love.

Marie's *lai* centers on a happy moment the lovers share in a forest in Cornwall despite the odds against them. About the outcome of their

---

[1] **legend of Tristan and Iseult:** The French author Joseph Bedier (1864–1938) distilled the many versions of this story into a simplified core story, which was translated into English as *The Romance of Tristan and Iseult* in 1945. His edition is a useful introduction to the subject.

meeting the poet is discreet, saying the pair "took great joy in each other," hastening to add, "He spoke to her as much as he desired, / she told him whatever she liked." Iseult promises Tristan that she will plead for his right to return to King Mark's court, then leaves him. Tristan returns to Wales, where he writes down this *lai* in order, he says, to "remember the words" describing his adventure.

∽ The Lay of Chevrefoil (The Honeysuckle)

Translated by Robert Hanning and Joan Ferrante

I should like very much
to tell you the truth
about the *lai* men call *Chevrefoil*—
why it was composed and where it came from.
Many have told and recited it to me
and I have found it in writing,
about Tristan and the queen
and their love that was so true,
that brought them much suffering
10   and caused them to die the same day.
King Mark was annoyed,
angry at his nephew Tristan;
he exiled Tristan from his land
because of the queen whom he loved.
Tristan returned to his own country,
South Wales, where he was born,
he stayed a whole year;
he couldn't come back.
Afterward he began to expose himself
20   to death and destruction.
Don't be surprised at this:
for one who loves very faithfully
is sad and troubled
when he cannot satisfy his desires.
Tristan was sad and worried,
so he set out from his land.
He traveled straight to Cornwall,
where the queen lived,
and entered the forest all alone—
30   he didn't want anyone to see him;
he came out only in the evening

when it was time to find shelter.
He took lodging that night,
with peasants, poor people.
He asked them for news
of the king—what he was doing.
They told him they had heard
that the barons had been summoned by ban.
They were to come to Tintagel
40   where the king wanted to hold his court;
at Pentecost they would all be there,
there'd be much joy and pleasure,
and the queen would be there too.
Tristan heard and was very happy;
she would not be able to go there
without his seeing her pass.
The day the king set out,
Tristan also came to the woods
by the road he knew
50   their assembly must take.
He cut a hazel tree in half,
then he squared it.
When he had prepared the wood,
he wrote his name on it with his knife.
If the queen noticed it—
and she should be on the watch for it,
for it had happened before
and she had noticed it then—
she'd know when she saw it,
60   that the piece of wood had come from her love.
This was the message of the writing
that he had sent to her:[1]
he had been there a long time,
had waited and remained
to find out and to discover
how he could see her,
for he could not live without her.
With the two of them it was just
as it is with the honeysuckle
70   that attaches itself to the hazel tree:
when it has wound and attached
and worked itself around the trunk,

---

[1] **This was the message . . . sent to her:** It is unclear whether the message is written on the wood (perhaps Tristan's name or something in code) or not. Another editor, Glyn S. Burgess, translates the original, "This was all he wrote, because he had sent her word that he had been there a long time. . . ."

the two can survive together;
but if someone tries to separate them,
the hazel dies quickly
and the honeysuckle with it.
"Sweet love, so it is with us:
You cannot live without me, nor I without you."
The queen rode along;
80   she looked at the hillside
and saw the piece of wood; she knew what it was,
she recognized all the letters.
The knights who were accompanying her,
who were riding with her,
she ordered to stop:
she wanted to dismount and rest.
They obeyed her command.
She went far away from her people
and called her girl
90   Brenguein, who was loyal to her.
She went a short distance from the road;
and in the woods she found him
whom she loved more than any living thing.
They took great joy in each other.
He spoke to her as much as he desired,
she told him whatever she liked.
Then she assured him
that he would be reconciled with the king—
for it weighed on him
100   that he had sent Tristan away;
he'd done it because of the accusation.
Then she departed, she left her love,
but when it came to the separation,
they began to weep.
Tristan went to Wales,
to wait until his uncle sent for him.
For the joy that he'd felt
from his love when he saw her,
by means of the stick he inscribed
110   as the queen had instructed,
and in order to remember the words,
Tristan, who played the harp well,
composed a new *lai* about it.
I shall name it briefly:
in English they call it *Goat's Leaf*
the French call it *Chevrefoil*.
I have given you the truth
about the *lai* that I have told here.

TEXT IN CONTEXT

THE SONG OF ROLAND
FRANCE, LATE ELEVENTH CENTURY

shawn-SAWNG
duh-ZHEST

WWW   For a quiz
on *The Song of Roland,*
see bedford
stmartins.com/
worldlitcompact.

When performed before a French audience at the end of the eleventh century, *The Song of Roland* must have constituted entertainment of the highest order. This heroic epic, a ***chanson de geste*** or "tale of deeds," depicted the tragic death of Count Roland, a courageous battle leader of the army of Charlemagne, King of the Franks, in an ambush in the Pyrenees of northern Spain over three centuries before at the hands of the Muslim enemy, the Saracens. To its contemporary audience it signified more than a historical poem; it was a patriotic celebration of the Franks at the dawn of the First Crusade.[1] It established the legendary Roland as the perfect Christian knight within the social and moral framework of his era. Thus Frankish patriotism was served as the Crusaders themselves swept across the Holy Land toward Jerusalem. Eventually, of course, the spirit of *The Song of Roland* would fade. The Crusades would run their course, and the European courtly literature that replaced the *chanson de geste* would express a different view of culture and society, centered more on the refinement and mystery of romance than on war and patriotism.

---

[1] **at the dawn of the First Crusade:** Pope Urban preached the First Crusade in 1095. Chroniclers state that crusaders riding off to battle sang verses of *The Song of Roland* as they went.

Sculpture of Roland, thirteenth century
As the exemplary Christian warrior, Roland became part of the symbolic imagery used in the Gothic cathedrals of Europe. This statue is found in a sculpture group on the South Porch of Chartres Cathedral. (© Sonia Halliday)

The Story of Roland.   Scraps of information remain about the historical Roland. In Einhard's *Life of Charlemagne*,[2] written about 830, an account of the king's campaign in Spain relates that the Basques of the northern Pyrenees, not the Muslim Saracens, ambushed the rear guard of Charlemagne's army, "forced them down into the valley beneath, joined battle with them and killed them to the last man." In this battle several members of the Frankish nobility died, including "Roland, Lord of the Breton Marches." The date was August 15, 778.

In reality, Charlemagne had entered Spain at the request of a Saracen, Sulaiman Al-Arabi, governor of Barcelona and Gerona, to

---

[2] **Einhard's *Life of Charlemagne:*** Einhard served Charlemagne at his court in Aix-la-Chapelle from 791 until the king's death in 814. His was the only contemporary biography of the Frankish king.

Medieval Europe: Chartres Cathedral of Notre Dame

The Gothic cathedrals of Europe were created during a time of tremendous social and cultural ferment. In the twelfth century these great edifices, with their spacious interiors, towering vaulted roofs, brilliant high windows, massive columns supported by buttresses, and tall single or double spires were first erected in France, then in Germany and England. Perhaps the most beautiful and the longest standing without major alteration is the Chartres Cathedral in the province of Orleans in northern France. The original church was destroyed by fire in 1134. Construction of the cathedral, with its two magnificent towers, royal portal, and rose window, was halted by a second fire in 1194. From then on, the job of building this massive sanctuary continued unabated through the thirteenth century, with the nave, transept, and choir having all been completed by 1220.

The character of a medieval European cathedral was determined by its use of the symbolic imagery of the Christian faith and by the particular imagination and competence of its master builder—in how he exploited the possibilities of stone and glass; in his choice of the weight and height of the structure's ceilings, walls, and towers; in his design of the buttresses that supported the outer walls. Christian imagery was depicted in stained-glass windows, in sculptures adorning the inner walls as well as the outer edifice, and in the cruciform design, or the cross shape, of the cathedral itself. The enormity of Chartres can be partially comprehended in the height of its spires (350 and 375 feet) and in the area and height of its windows. By 1260, 22,000 square feet of glass had been installed in 186 windows of approximately half the height of the cathedral's walls. The beautiful glass windows, including many originals; the massive grouped sculptures along the outer ledges of the

cathedral; the majestic height of the nave, or central section, as seen from within the church; and the structure's grand yet graceful flying buttresses remain today. Entire books have been written and films created to interpret the design and meaning of this great cathedral.

In cathedrals throughout Europe, Roland was a subject of veneration. At Chartres two magnificent works honor him. A thirteenth-century sculpture in the south portal doorway shows the tall young knight as the Christian champion, bearing Charlemagne's standard in his right hand while steadying his shield with the fleur-de-lys of France by his left arm (see p. 1329). The other piece, a luminous thirteenth-century stained glass window in the north section of the ambulatory, depicts scenes near the end of the battle of Roncevaux: one shows Roland blowing his horn and attempting to break his sword, with Charlemagne moving vainly to save the rear guard from destruction (see p. 1333).

Chartres Cathedral. *The great Gothic cathedral of Notre Dame de Chartres in Chartres, France. (The Art Archive / Dagli Orti)*

fight another Saracen, the **Emir** Abd al Rahman of Cordova. Al-Arabi had promised the cooperation of other leaders in the region and offered to submit to Frankish authority if the armed intervention were successful. The political complications of the actual story were suppressed in the epic poem to make Charlemagne's struggle a simpler one of good against evil—good represented by the Frankish Christian army and evil represented by the Saracens as a whole.

In the poetic epic, Roland is accompanied by his friends, including Oliver, Archbishop **Turpin**, and others, while he is hounded and betrayed by his enemy, his uncle **Ganelon**. Archbishop Turpin, a historical figure, reportedly was nowhere near the battle in question; the other characters are known to us only through the poem itself, though they may have been included in an older cycle of stories already familiar to French audiences.

The plot of *The Song of Roland* is simple. Due to the connivance of Ganelon with the enemy, the rear guard of Charlemagne's army under the leadership of the young Count Roland is separated from the main force and attacked by the Saracens. Roland, too proud to call for help, refuses to sound the battle-horn (Olifant) until the situation is hopeless and his forces are about to be massacred. Finally Charlemagne, hearing the belated note of the horn, counterattacks, too late to save his army. He drives the foe from the field, buries Roland and his company of knights, then captures, arraigns, and executes Ganelon and other traitors within his own ranks. The poet, apparently uninterested in creating suspense, repeatedly reminds the listener of the outcome of the story as the action unfolds.

A Christian Feudal Epic. *The Song of Roland* elevates, with its stately repetitious stanzas, the figure of Roland as the exemplary Christian knight, emphasizing his courage, steadfastness, faith in God, and role as defender of both the crown and the Catholic Church. But Roland is also subordinated to the larger context; he is the model Christian warrior just as Charlemagne is the model Christian king. The reciprocal ties joining Roland and Charlemagne are part of the hierarchical structure of loyalties common throughout feudal society in the European Middle Ages. All the Frankish vassal knights including Roland are bound to Charlemagne, while he is bound to protect them on one hand and is himself the vassal of God on the other. For this reason, the epic does not end with the death of Roland; the rest of the poem confirms the restoration of the authority of both Charlemagne and militant Christianity.

eh-MEER

toor-PANG
gah-nuh-LAWNG

We shall never know what it was that turned the obscure disaster which befell the rear guard of Charlemagne's army on 15 August 778, when Roland count of Brittany was killed, into one of the most memorable incidents in Christian epic. No doubt, like many other military disasters, it was relieved by some signal act of heroism of which "history" has left no record. But the story lived.

–R. W. SOUTHERN, scholar, 1953

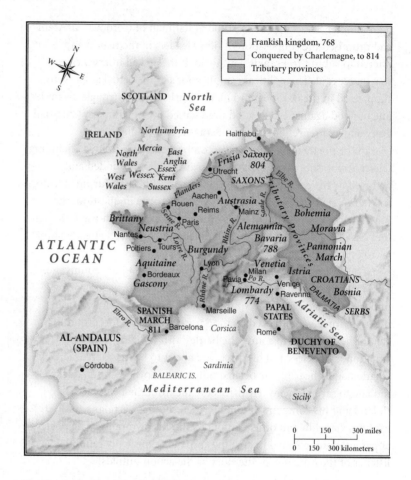

The Carolingian Empire under Charlemagne, 768–814
The conquests of Charlemagne temporarily united almost all of Western Europe. Although this empire was divided into three parts by the Treaty of Verdun in 843, it was substantially reunited as the Holy Roman Empire in the twelfth century.

In the moral and ethical framework of the knightly epic, every character stands for specific virtues and may also exhibit specific faults. Roland is strong but rash; his uninstructed courage does not contain an equal measure of wisdom. Oliver, his friend, though lacking Roland's strength, is the wiser of the two: in an important passage in the poem, he angrily upbraids Roland for not calling for help sooner than he does. Turpin is the model of the fighting priest, bloodily dispatching Muslims with his sword with the name of God on his lips. Ganelon, meanwhile, is the archvillain, led by jealousy, false pride, and a desire for revenge to betray not only Roland but the entire Frankish kingdom.

Art or Propaganda?   *The Song of Roland* is organized in *laisses*, or stanzas, composed of a varied number of ten-syllable lines, elements of which may be repeated in subsequent stanzas. While the action moves briskly with this device of incremental repetition, prominent features of the characters and specific scenes are often viewed from several different angles in succeeding stanzas, referred to as *laisses similaires*. By use of this device, the poetic language is concentrated in a manner unique among major works of Western literature. Due to the multi-dimensional treatment there is often a pictorial quality to the descriptions of leading characters, as if they had just stepped down from a stained-glass window or emerged from an illuminated manuscript. For instance, the portrait of Charlemagne, though dignified,

LES

LES see-mee-LEHR

Roland fighting the Saracen King Marsilion, thirteenth century
This stained glass panel is part of the Charlemagne Window, which recounts the story of Roland, in the north section of the ambulatory at Chartres Cathedral. (© Sonia Halliday)

economical, and conventional, includes stylistic idiosyncrasies such as his habit of stroking or pulling his beard. And there is particular artistry in the economical rendering of emotional states, such as the description of Ganelon's anger in council or the encounter between Roland and Oliver over sounding the horn. The gestures of the characters are often larger than life, most tellingly in the case of Roland, who literally blows his brains out while sounding the Olifant. The work's realism is pointed, with descriptions of the killing, maiming, and gore on the battlefield perhaps unparalleled in epic poetry; it also extends to the dignified scene of the burial of Roland and his peers by the grieving king. The most familiar rhetorical feature of the poem is the way it contrasts two qualities within a single line, as when the poet states "Pagans are wrong, the Christian cause is right" (laisse 79) or "Roland's a hero, and Oliver is wise" (laisse 87).

The blunt partisanship of the poem disturbs some readers, especially in light of the more objective treatment of Christian invaders by Muslim historians during the Crusades. *The Song of Roland,* of course, is a dramatic poem, probably declaimed orally, not a work of history according to the modern understanding of the term. Even so, it is hard to find another instance before modern times in which political and religious fervor produced a more one-dimensional figure than the Christian Crusader of this period. Thus *The Song of Roland* is a striking example of the fusion of art and propaganda, a powerful work in which subjective political emotion overwhelms objective distance.

The Love of War.   The only love expressed in *The Song of Roland* seems to be that of the warrior for warfare and for his fellow warriors. The love that Roland and his company express for one another completely overshadows the forgettable presence of Roland's fiancée, who dies late in the poem after collapsing in Charlemagne's arms at the news of Roland's death. Even the Muslims receive their due as warriors; though portrayed as crueler than the Christians and owing their allegiance to the devil, they are praised more often than not in the poem's descriptions of battle. This love of war in *The Song of Roland* is nowhere else so evident in Western literature except in **The Iliad**, a work with which *Roland* invites comparison.

P. 537

■ **FURTHER RESEARCH**

Translations with Commentary
Brault, Gerard J., ed. *The Song of Roland: An Analytical Edition.* 2 vols. 1978.
Burgess, Glyn S., trans. *The Song of Roland.* 1990.

Goldin, Frederick, trans. *The Song of Roland*. 1978.
Terry, Patricia, trans. *The Song of Roland*. Second edition, 1992.
Owen, D. D. R., trans. *The Song of Roland: The Oxford Text*. 1972.

History and Criticism
Cook, Robert Francis. *The Sense of the Song of Roland*. 1987.
Jones, George Fenwick. *The Ethos of the Song of Roland*. 1963.
Kibler, William W., and Leslie Zarker Morgan, eds. *Approaches to Teaching the Song of Roland*. 2006.
Le Gentil, Pierre. *The Song of Roland*. Translated by Frances F. Beer. 1969.
Lejeune, Rita, and Jacques Stiennon. *The Legend of Roland in the Middle Ages*. Translated by Christine Trollope. 1971.
Owen, D. D. R. *The Legend of Roland: A Pageant of the Middle Ages*. 1973.
Vance, Eugene. *Reading the Song of Roland*. 1970.

Roland and Medieval Culture
Auerbach, Erich. *Mimesis*. 1953. 83–107.
Southern, R. W. *The Making of the Middle Ages*. 1953. 241–246.

Related Literature
Thorpe, Lewis, trans. *Einhard and Notker the Stammerer: Two Lives of Charlemagne*. 1969.

■ PRONUNCIATION

Aix (la Chapelle): EKS (lah-shah-PEL)
Aude: ODE
Baligant: bal-ee-GAWNG
Blancandrin: blawng-kawng-DRANG
chanson de geste: shawn-SAWNG duh-ZHEST
Chanson de Roland: shawn-SAWNG duh-roh-LAWNG
Durendal: doo-rawn-DAHL
ecclesia militans: ih-KLEE-zhee-uh MIH-lih-tanz, eh-KLAY-zee-uh
    MIH-lih-tahnz
Emir: eh-MEER
Ganelon: gah-nuh-LAWNG
laisse: LES
laisses similaires: LES see-mee-LEHR
Mahum: mah-OOM
Marsile: mar-SEEL
Montjole: mung-ZWHAW
Naimon: neh-MAWNG
Roncevaux: rawngs-VO
Turpin: toor-PANG

ᘛ The Song of Roland

Translated by Patricia Terry

1

The mighty Charles,   our Emperor and King,
Seven long years   has been at war in Spain;
That lofty land   lies conquered to the sea.
No fortress now   is standing in his way,
No walls, no towns   remain for him to break,
Except for Saragossa,   high on its hill,
Ruled by Marsile,   who has no love for God;
He serves Apollo,   and to Mohammed[1] prays—
But he will come,   and soon, to evil days! AOI[2]

2

In Saragossa,   the pagan King, Marsile,
Walks through an orchard,   in the shadow of the trees.
The King reclines   on a blue marble bench;
His host assembles,   some twenty thousand men.
He speaks these words   to all his dukes and counts:
"Now hear, my lords,   what evils weigh us down!
For Charles has come,   the ruler of sweet France,[3]
To seize our lands,   and bring us to our knees.
I have no army   to fight against his own;
10 No men of mine   will drive him to defeat—
Give me your counsel,   as you are true and wise,

A note on the translation: The earliest known manuscript of *The Song of Roland* is the so-called Oxford version, written in old French between 1125 and 1150 and derived from a text composed between 1095 and 1100. A number of other partial versions from later dates also exist. The edited version presented in this anthology concentrates on the events leading up to the fatal battle between Roland and the Saracens; it ends with Roland's death and burial, leaving out the story of Charlemagne's revenge against the Saracens and the execution of Ganelon. Most of the footnotes to the poem are derived from the translator's notes; those supplied by the editors of this volume are marked [Ed.].

---

[1] **Apollo . . . Mohammed:** Two of the three gods of the Saracens mentioned in the poem. Since the Saracens are Muslims, they would regard Apollo as pagan and strenuously oppose his worship. The third god mentioned elsewhere, Tervagant, is of uncertain origin. [Ed.]

[2] AOI: This mark at the end of various stanzas throughout the poem is of unknown origin and purpose. [Ed.]

[3] **sweet France:** In the poem, even the Saracens speak of *dulce France.*

Save me from death,   and from this bitter shame."
Mute are the pagans,   except for one alone:
Blancandrin speaks,   whose castle is Val-Fonde.

3

Among the pagans   Blancandrin was wise,
A trusted vassal,   a brave and loyal knight,
Clever enough   to think of good advice.
He tells the King,   "You need not be afraid.
Send word to Charles,   the arrogant, the proud,
That you in friendship   salute him as your lord.
Offer him gifts: bears and lions and dogs,
And seven hundred camels,   a thousand hawks,
Four hundred mule-loads   of silver and of gold,
10 And fifty carts   to form a wagon-train.
He'll have enough   to pay his hired men.
He has campaigned   so long here in this land,
He won't refuse   to go back home to Aix.[4]
Say you will meet him   in France, on Michael's Day,
To be converted,   adopt the Christian law,
And do him homage   in friendship and good will.
If hostages are needed,   say you will send
Ten, even twenty,   to witness your good faith:
We'll have to yield   the sons our wives have borne—
20 It's certain death,   but I will send my own.
Better that they   should sacrifice their heads
Than that we lose   our honor and our pride,
And live as beggars   with all our rights denied!" AOI

4

Said Blancandrin,   "I swear by my right hand,
And by this beard   that ripples on my chest,
You'll see the French   disband their troops and go,
The Franks will soon   be on their way to France.
And when each one   has found his home again,
Charles, in the chapel   that he has built in Aix,
Will give a feast   in honor of the saint,
On Michael's Day,   when we'll have sworn to come—
But of our coming   the French will see no sign.

---

[4] **Aix:** Aix la Chapelle, Charlemagne's capital in the north of France.

10 The King is proud,   and cruel is his heart;
He'll have the heads   of all our men cut off.
But better far   that they should lose their heads
Than that we lose   this shining land, fair Spain,
And be condemned   to hardship and disgrace."
The pagans say,   "That may well be the case!"

5

The King declared   the council at an end.
He summoned forth   Clarin of Balaguer,
Estramariz,   and Eudropin his peer,
Long-bearded Guarlan,   and with him Priamon,
And Machiner,   his uncle Maheu,
And Joüner,   Malbien d'Oltremer,
And Blancandrin,   to be his embassy;
These ten he chose   from his most evil men.
"Barons, my lords,   you'll go to Charlemagne;
10 He is in Cordres,[5]   holding the town besieged.
The olive branch   you'll carry in your hands,
A sign of peace   and your humility.
If you are clever,   if you persuade the King,
Much gold and silver   shall be your thanks from me,
Fiefdoms and land,   as much as you desire."
The pagans say,   "That's all that we require." AOI

8

The Emperor Charles   is joyful, jubilant:
The lofty walls   of Cordres are torn down,
His catapults   have laid its towers low;
His knights rejoice,   for great is their reward—
Silver and gold,   and costly gear for war.
In all the city   no pagan now remains
Who isn't dead   or one of the true Faith.
In a great orchard,   Charlemagne sits in state.
With him are Roland,   and Oliver, his friend;
10 A Duke called Samson,   and fiery Anseïs,
Geoffroy of Anjou,   flag-bearer for the King;
The two companions   Gerin and Gerier.
And with these barons   is no small group of men,

---

[5] **Cordres:** Possibly Cordova, but then that city would be in northern Spain. The poet's notions of geography are vague at best.

For fifteen thousand   came with them from sweet France.
The knights are seated   on carpets of white silk;
The older men,   or clever, pass the time
Playing backgammon,   or else they sit at chess;
The nimble youths   prefer to fence with swords.
Beneath a pine,   beside a briar-rose,
20 A throne is placed—   it's made of purest gold.
There sits the King,   the ruler of sweet France;
White is his beard,   and silver streaks his hair,
Handsome his form,   his bearing very proud:
No stranger needs   to have him pointed out.
The Saracens dismount   and come on foot
To greet the King,   as friendly envoys would.

9

Then Blancandrin   begins to make his speech.
He says to Charles,   "May God grant you His grace,
That glorious Lord   to whom all men must pray!
We've come to you   at King Marsile's command;
He's learned about the law   that saves men's souls,
And of his wealth   he wants to offer you
Lions and bears,   and hunting dogs on chains,
And seven hundred camels,   a thousand hawks,
Silver and gold   four hundred mules will bear,
10 And fifty carts   to form a wagon-train.
These will be loaded   with silver coins and gold,
Enough for you   to well reward your men.
You have campaigned   so long here in this land,
It must be time   to go back home to Aix;
My lord Marsile   says he will follow you."
The Emperor Charles   holds both hands up toward God;
He bows his head,   and gives himself to thought. AOI

10

The Emperor Charles   sits with his head bent low.
He was not known   for answering in haste:
Always he liked   to take his time to speak.
When he looked up,   his face was stern and proud.
Thus he replies: "You've spoken well indeed.
But King Marsile   has been no friend of mine;
Of what you say,   although your words are fair,
How shall I know   how much I can believe?"
"Take hostages,"   the Saracen replies,

10 "Ten or fifteen   or twenty you shall have;
Though he risks death,   I'll send a son of mine,
And there will be   some even nobler men.
When, in your palace   at Aix, you hold the feast
That celebrates   Saint Michael of the Sea,[6]
My lord Marsile   declares that he will come,
And, in those baths   which were God's gift to you,
He will be baptized,   adopt the Christian faith."
Then answers Charles,   "It still is not too late."[7] AOI

12

Beneath a pine   the Emperor takes his place,
And calls his barons   to say what they would do.
Duke Ogier,   Archbishop Turpin came,
Richard the Old,   his nephew called Henri,
From Gascony   the brave Count Acelin,
Thibaut of Reims,   his cousin Count Milon,
And there were both   Gerin and Gerier—
Count Roland came,   together with these two,
And Oliver,   so noble and so brave;
10 The Franks of France,   more than a thousand men.
Ganelon came   by whom they were betrayed.
And then began   the talks that evil swayed. AOI

14

The King has brought   his discourse to an end.
And now Count Roland   has risen to his feet;
He speaks his mind   against the Saracens,
Saying to Charles,   "No good comes of Marsile!
It's seven years   since first we came to Spain;
For you I've conquered   Noples and Commibles,
I took Val-Terre   and all the land of Pine,
And Balaguer,   Tudela, Sedilie.
There King Marsile   displayed his treachery:
10 Of his vile pagans   he sent to you fifteen;
Each in his hand   held high the olive branch,
And when they spoke,   we heard this very speech.
You let your Franks   decide what should be done;

---

[6] **Saint Michael of the Sea:** The sanctuary of Mont St. Michel, accessible only at low tide, is named after the saint.

[7] **"It still is not too late":** *Uncore purrat guarir,* "He may yet be saved." [Ed.]

The plan they chose   was foolishness indeed:
You sent two Counts   as envoys to the King,
Basant was one,   the other was Basile—
They left their heads   on a hill near Haltilies!
Finish the fight   the way it was begun:
To Saragossa   lead on your gathered host,
20 Besiege the city,   at any cost, remain;
Avenge those men   so villainously slain!" AOI

15

The Emperor Charles   has kept his head bowed down;
He strokes his beard,   arranges his moustache,
And to his nephew   says neither yes nor no.
The French are silent,   except for Ganelon;
He stands up straight   and comes before the King,
With wrathful pride   begins his argument,
Saying to Charles: "Believe no underling,
Not me, not Roland,   who speaks against your good!
When King Marsile   sends messengers to say
10 He'll place his hands in yours,   and be your man,
He'll do you homage   for all the lands of Spain,
And he'll observe   our holy Christian law—
Whoever urges you   to scorn this peace
Does not care, Sire,   what kind of death we die.
A man too proud   will recklessly advise;
Let's heed no fools,   and keep to what is wise!" AOI

20

"My valiant knights,"   says Charles the Emperor,
"Choose for me now   the nobleman of France
Who is to take   my message to Marsile."
"I name," says Roland,   "Stepfather Ganelon."
The Franks reply,   "He'd do it very well;
We could not make   a wiser choice than this."
Count Ganelon   half choking in his rage,
Pulls from his neck   the splendid marten furs,
Over a tunic   made of the finest silk.
10 Steel-grey his eyes   and very proud his face,
His carriage noble,   his chest is large around;
He looks so handsome,   his peers all turn and stare.
He says, "You fool,   rash are your words, and wild.
Everyone knows   I'm stepfather to you,
Yet you name me   the envoy of Marsile!

If God should grant   that I come home again,
I won't forget—   be sure I'll find a way
To pay you back,   as long as you're alive!"
"I hear," says Roland,   "your foolishness and pride.
20   Everyone knows   I answer threats with scorn;
A man of wisdom   this embassy requires—
I'll take your place,   if the King so desires." AOI

21

Ganelon says,   "You shall not take my place!
You're not my man,   nor am I your liege-lord.
King Charles commands me   to serve him in this way:
In Saragossa   I'll talk to King Marsile.
But something else,   some kind of prank I'll play,
Fit to relieve   my fury at this wrong."
Roland replies   with laughter loud and long. AOI

22

Count Ganelon,   when he hears Roland laugh,
Suffers such pain   he nearly splits with rage,
And he comes close   to falling in a faint.
He says to Roland,   "I have no love for you,
For you have swayed   this council to your will!
My rightful King,   you see me here at hand,
Ready to do   whatever you command." AOI

26

"Sire," says the Count,   "now grant me leave to go;
Since go I must,   I care not for delay."
The King replies,   "In Jesu's name and mine!"
Then Charles' right hand   absolves the Count from sin;
The staff and letter   are both given to him.

28

Ganelon rides   under tall olive trees;
Now he has met   the envoys from Marsile.
Blancandrin waits   to ride with the French knight.
Both of them talk   with great diplomacy.
Says Blancandrin,   "I marvel at your King—
For he has conquered   the whole of Italy,
And then to England   he crossed the salty sea

So that the Saxons   would pay Saint Peter's fee.
And what of Spain   will Charlemagne require?"
10   The Count replies,   "That's hidden in his mind.
A greater King   no man will ever find." AOI

29

Says Blancandrin,   "The Franks are noble men;
But they do wrong,   those warlike dukes and counts
When by the counsel   they give to Charlemagne
They wear him out,   and others suffer too."
Ganelon says,   "Of this I could accuse
Only Count Roland—   who'll pay for it some day.
Not long ago,   when Charles sat at his ease,
His nephew came   dressed in his battle gear—
He'd gone for plunder   somewhere near Carcasonne.
10   In Roland's hand   an apple shone, bright red;
He told his uncle,   'Accept it, my fair lord!
I bring you here   the crowns of all the kings.'
But his great pride   will lead him on too far,
For every day   we see him risk his life.
If he were killed,   there'd be an end to strife." AOI

30

Says Blancandrin,   "Evil is Roland's heart.
He'd have the world   surrender to his will,
Proclaim his right   to every land on earth!
But by whose help   can he attempt so much?"
"The Franks of France!   He so commands their love,
They'll never fail him,   they're with him to a man.
He gives them gifts   of silver and much gold,
War-horses, mules,   brocades and costly arms;
The King himself   won't cross him in the least:
10   By Roland's sword   he'll rule to the far East!" AOI

31

So Ganelon   and Blancandrin ride on
Until they've made   a solemn pact: they vow
That they will seek   to have Count Roland slain.
They go their way,   and then dismount at last
In Saragossa   where a tall yew tree stands.
Under a pine   a throne has been set up,
Draped in brocade   of Alexandrian silk.

There sits the King,   the ruler of all Spain;
Around him wait   his twenty thousand men.
10 Not one of them   lets fall a single word;
They're all intent   on what they hope to hear
From those two men   who even now appear.

32

Now Blancandrin   has come before Marsile,
And by the fist   he holds Count Ganelon.
He speaks these words: "Mohammed keep you safe,
Apollo too,   whose Law we all obey!
We have delivered   your message to King Charles;
When he had heard us,   he raised his hands on high
To praise his God,   but gave us no reply.
Now he has sent you   one of his noble lords,
A Count of France,   a man of power and wealth.
10 From him you'll learn   if there is hope for peace."
Marsile replies,   "We'll hear him; let him speak."

33

Count Ganelon   has taken careful thought,
Now he begins   in well-considered words,
Subtly contrived—   the Count knows how to talk.
He tells Marsile: "May God grant you His grace,
That glorious Lord   to whom all men must pray!
Now by the will   of Charlemagne the King,
You must accept   the holy Christian law,
And half of Spain   he'll let you hold in fief.
Should you refuse   agreement to these terms,
10 You'll find yourself   a captive and in chains,
Taken by force   to answer Charles at Aix.
There you'll be judged,   and you will be condemned
To die a death   of infamy and shame."
At that Marsile   in fear and fury raised
A throwing spear—   its feathering was gold;
He would have struck,   but that his men took hold. AOI

38

Into an orchard   the pagan King retired,
And with him went   the wisest of his men.
Blancandrin came   whose heavy beard was grey,
And Jurfaret,   Marsile's own son and heir,

And the Caliph,   his uncle and good friend.
Says Blancandrin,   "Summon the Frenchman here—
I have his word   that he will serve our cause."
Marsile replies,   "Then bring him to me now."
Blancandrin takes   the Count by the right hand,
10 Walks through the orchard,   and leads him to Marsile.
They plot the treason   that cunning will conceal. AOI

43

"Fair Ganelon,"   then says the pagan King,
"You'll see no soldiers   better at war than mine,
And I can summon   four hundred thousand knights.
Can I not fight   King Charles and all his Franks?"
"If you should try it,"   Count Ganelon replies,
"I tell you this,   you'd massacre your men.
Forget that folly,   and hear what I advise:
To Charlemagne   send such a royal gift
As to amaze   and gratify the French.
10 Send twenty men   as hostages for you,
And then the King   will go home to sweet France.
Behind his army   the rear-guard will remain,
And with them Roland,   the nephew of the King,
And Oliver,   so worthy and so brave.
And there they die—   if you'll do as I say.
King Charles will see   the downfall of his pride;
He'll have no wish   to carry on the fight." AOI

44

Answers Marsile,   "My fair lord Ganelon,
Tell me the way   Count Roland can be killed."
Ganelon says,   "Here is the plan I've made:
The King will cross   the mountain pass at Cize,
With a strong guard   remaining far behind.
He'll leave his nephew,   Count Roland, in the rear,
Oliver too,   in whom he has such faith,
With them a host   of twenty thousand Franks.
Then of your pagans,   a hundred thousand men
10 Must be sent out   to launch the first attack.
You'll see the Frenchmen   wounded and overcome—
Not that I say   your men won't suffer too.
If you attack   a second time that way,
You can be sure   that Roland won't escape.
Once you have done   this brave and knightly deed,
All your life long   from warfare you'll be freed."

45

"With that same blow   that struck Count Roland down,
You would cut off   the Emperor's right arm;
His mighty host   you'd scatter and destroy,
Nor would he find   so great a force again.
All of his Empire   would be restored to peace."
Marsile fell on his neck;   with joy he swore
That Ganelon   should loot his treasure-store. AOI

46

Then says Marsile,   "Why talk more . . .
There's no good counsel   unless . . .
Give me your oath   that Roland is to die."
"Just as you like!"   Count Ganelon replies.
He swore by relics   he carried in his sword,
And so forever   turned from his rightful lord. AOI

52

King Marsile places   his arm around the Count,
Saying to him,   "Valiant you are, and wise.
But as you keep   your God's most holy law,
I charge you never   to turn your heart from me!
Of all I own   I'll give you a good part:
Ten mules are loaded   with fine Arabian gold,
And every year   you'll have as much again.
Give Charles the keys   to this broad city's walls,
Tell him its treasures   will henceforth be his own,
10 And then have Roland   appointed to the guard.
If I can find him   crossing some narrow pass,
There I'll attack   and fight him to the death."
Ganelon says,   "Then let us speed the day."
He mounts his horse,   and quickly rides away. AOI

54

The Emperor Charles   rose early on that day.
Now, having prayed   at matins and a mass,
He goes outside   and stands on the green grass.
Roland is with him,   the noble Oliver,
Naimon the Duke,   and many others too.
Ganelon comes,   treacherous and forsworn.
All of his cunning   he puts into his speech,

Saying to Charles,   "I greet you in God's name!
Here are the keys   to King Marsile's fair town;
10 From Saragossa,   treasures beyond all price,
And twenty nobles,   hostages—guard them well!
But King Marsile   has asked me to explain
Why you won't see   his uncle, the Caliph:
Before my eyes   four hundred thousand men
All armed in mail,   some with their helmets closed,
Swords at their belts,   the hilts inlaid with gold,
Sailed with that lord   out to the open sea.
They fled because   they hated Christian law
Which they refused   to honor and to keep.
20 They sailed away,   but had not gone four leagues
When they were caught   in such a frightful storm
They all were drowned.   So perished the Caliph.
Were he alive,   he'd be here with me now.
As for Marsile,   my lord, you can be sure
That well before   a single month has passed,
He'll follow you   when you return to France.
There he'll accept   the Faith that you uphold,
Both of his hands   he'll place between your own,
And do you homage   for all his lands in Spain."
30 Then said the King,   "For this may God be thanked!
You have done well,   and great shall be your prize."
Among the hosts,   a thousand trumpets sound;
The French break camp,   they load each mule and horse,
And toward sweet France   they gladly set their course. AOI

55

King Charles the Great   has conquered all of Spain,[8]
Captured its forts,   its cities laid to waste;
His war, he says,   has now come to its end.
The Emperor rides   once more toward his sweet France.
From Roland's spearhead   the flag of battle flies;
When, from a hilltop,   it waves against the sky,
The French make camp   throughout the countryside.
Pagans are riding   through valleys deep and dark.
They wear their hauberks,   tunics of double chain,
10 Their helmets laced;   bright swords hang at their sides,
Shields at their necks,   a pennon on each lance.
Where trees grow thick   high on a hill they wait,

---

[8] **has conquered all of Spain:** Returning to Charlemagne, the poet picks up the opening lines of his story.

Four hundred thousand   watching for day's first light.
Alas! If only   the French could see that sight! AOI

56

The day is over,   the night grows calm and still.
The Emperor Charles   goes to his bed and sleeps.
In dream he rides   through the great pass at Cize;
Clasped in his hands   he holds an ashwood spear:
Count Ganelon   wrenches it from his grasp,
And brandishes the spear   with such fierce strength,
He sends wood splinters   flying against the sky.
King Charles sleeps on,   not opening his eyes.

57

After that dream   another vision came:
He was in France,   in his chapel at Aix.
A vicious bear   was biting his right arm.
Out of the forest   he sees a leopard run,
And he himself   it cruelly attacks.
From his great hall   a swift hound gallops out
And comes to Charles,   running with leaps and bounds,
Seizes the bear,   biting its right ear off,
Then in its fury   attacks the leopard too.
10 The Frenchmen watch   the mighty battle rage,
But they don't know   which side will win the fight.
King Charles sleeps on,   and does not wake all night. AOI

58

Darkness of night   gives way to shining dawn.
Throughout the host,   clarion trumpets sound.
Proud, on his horse,   the Emperor appears.
"Barons, my lords,"   says Charlemagne the King,
"Narrow and dark   will be this mountain pass —
Who shall remain   to guard us from the rear?"
Ganelon says,   "Choose Roland, my stepson.
You have no baron   as valorous as he."
Fiercely the King   looks at the one who spoke.
10 And says to him: "Vile demon that you are![9]

---

[9] **Vile demon that you are:** An attempt has been made to take this remark literally — that Charlemagne believes Ganelon has made a pact with the devil, or is the devil incarnate, and chooses to "relive Abraham's agony" by not opposing Ganelon at this point. See Brault, *An Analytical Edition*, vol. 1 p. 199.

You are insane,   possessed by deadly rage!
And in the vanguard —   who'll have the leader's place?"
Ganelon says,   "Count Ogier the Dane.
None would do better;   everyone knows his fame."

59

Count Roland heard   what Ganelon proposed,
And then he answered   with knightly courtesy:
"Noble stepfather,   now I must hold you dear,
For you have named me   commander of this guard.
The King of France   won't lose by my neglect
War-horse or palfrey,   that I can promise you;
He shall not lose   a single riding-mule,
Saddle-horse, pack-horse —   none shall give up its life
Until our swords,   take payment for that prize."
10 Ganelon says,   "I know you tell no lies." AOI

61

"My rightful lord,"   says Roland to the King,
"Give me the bow   you're holding in your hand;
I promise you   that no man here will say
I let it fall,   like Ganelon that day
The envoy's staff   dropped out of his right hand."
The Emperor Charles   sits with his head bowed low,
Pulls his moustache,   and srokes his long white beard,
While in his eyes   unwilling tears appear.

63

The Emperor Charles   calls Roland to come forth.
"My noble nephew,   this is what I intend:
Half of my army   shall stay behind with you.
Accept their service,   and then you will be safe."
Count Roland answers,   "Never will I agree.
May God destroy me,   if I so shame my race!
Just twenty thousand   shall serve me, valiant Franks.
You'll cross the mountains,   safely in France arrive —
And fear no man   as long as I'm alive!"

64

Roland has mounted   the horse he rides to war. AOI
There comes to join him   his friend Count Oliver,

And Gerin comes,   the brave Count Gerier,
And Oton comes,   with him Count Berenger,
And Astor comes,   and fiery Anseïs,
And old Gérard,   the Count of Roussillon,
The powerful and wealthy   Duke Gaïfier.
Says the Archbishop,   "My head on it, I'll go!"
"And I am with you,"   answers Count Gautier,
10   "I'm Roland's vassal—   my help is his by right."
Then they select   the twenty thousand knights. AOI

67

All the Twelve Peers   have stayed behind in Spain;
They guard the pass   with twenty thousand Franks,
Courageous men   who do not fear to die.
And now King Charles   is riding home again;
He drapes his cloak   to hide his grieving face.
Duke Naimon rides   next to the Emperor;
He says to Charles,   "What weighs your spirits down?"
The King replies,   "Who asks me that does wrong.
I can't keep silent   the sorrow that I feel,
10   For Ganelon   will be the doom of France.
Last night an angel   sent me a warning dream:
I held a spear—   he broke it from my grasp,
That Count who named   my nephew to the guard.
And I left Roland   among that pagan race—
God! If I lose him,   no one can take his place." AOI

68

Charlemagne weeps;   he can't hold back his tears.
They grieve for him,   his hundred thousand Franks,
And for Count Roland   are suddenly afraid.
A traitor's lies   left him to die in Spain—
Rich gifts the pagan   bestowed on Ganelon:
Silver and gold,   brocades and silken cloaks,
Camels and lions,   fine horses, riding mules.
Now King Marsile   summons the lords of Spain,
His counts and viscounts,   his chieftains and his dukes,
10   His high emirs,   and all their warrior sons:
Four hundred thousand   assemble in three days.
In Saragossa   the drums begin to sound;
They place Mohammed   high on the citadel—
No pagan fails   to worship him and pray.
And then they ride   with all their might and main

Searching the land,   through valleys, over hills,
Until they see   the battle-flags of France.
The Twelve Companions   are waiting with the guard;
When they are challenged,   the fighting will be hard.

79

The pagans wear   Saracen coats of mail,
Most of them furnished   with triple-layered chain.
From Saragossa   come the good helms they lace;
They gird on swords   whose steel comes from Vienne.
Their shields are strong;   Valencia made their spears;
Their battle flags   are crimson, blue and white.
All mules and palfreys   must now be left behind.
Each mounts his war-horse;   in close-knit ranks they ride.
Fair is the day,   the sun shines bright and clear,
10 Weapons and armor   glitter with fiery light,
A thousand trumpets   command more splendor still.
That great shrill clamor   reaches the Frenchmen's camp.
Oliver says,   "Companion, it would seem
That we will have   some Saracens to fight."
Roland replies,   "God grant that you be right!
Here we will stand,   defending our great King.
This is the service   a vassal owes his lord:
To suffer hardships,   endure great heat and cold,
And in a battle   to lose both hair and hide.
20 Now every Frank   prepare to strike great blows—
Let's hear no songs   that mock us to our shame!
Pagans are wrong,   the Christian cause is right.
A bad example   I'll be in no man's sight." AOI

80

Count Oliver   has climbed up on a hill.
From there he searches   the valley to his right,
And sees that host   of pagan Saracens.
Then he calls out   to Roland, his sworn friend:
"Coming from Spain   I see the fiery glow
Of shining hauberks,   the blazing steel of helms.
For our brave Franks   this means great toil and pain.
And that foul traitor,   false-hearted Ganelon,
Knew this—that's why   he named us to the guard."
10 Count Roland answers,   "Stop, Oliver, be still!
Of my stepfather   I'll let no man speak ill."

83

Oliver says,   "The pagan might is great—
It seems to me,   our Franks are very few!
Roland, my friend,   it's time to sound your horn;
King Charles will hear,   and bring his army back."
Roland replies,   "You must think I've gone mad!
In all sweet France   I'd forfeit my good name!
No! I will strike   great blows with Durendal,
Crimson the blade   up to the hilt of gold.
To those foul pagans   I promise bitter woe—
10 They all are doomed   to die at Roncevaux!" AOI

84

"Roland, my friend,   let the Oliphant sound!"[10]
King Charles will hear it,   his host will all turn back,
His valiant barons   will help us in this fight."
Roland replies,   "Almighty God forbid
That I bring shame   upon my family,
And cause sweet France   to fall into disgrace!
I'll strike that horde   with my good Durendal;
My sword is ready,   girded here at my side,
And soon you'll see   its keen blade dripping blood.
10 The Saracens   will curse the evil day
They challenged us,   for we will make them pay." AOI

86

Oliver says,   "Never would you be blamed;
I've seen the pagans,   the Saracens of Spain.
They fill the valleys,   cover the mountain peaks;
On every hill,   and every wide-spread plain,
Vast hosts assemble   from that alien race;
Our company   numbers but very few."
Roland replies,   "The better, then, we'll fight!
The saints and angels,   almighty God forbid
That I betray   the glory of sweet France!
10 Better to die   than learn to live with shame—
Charles loves us more   as our keen swords win fame."

---

[10] let the Oliphant sound!: Roland's famous horn, made of ivory. Translations vary as to whether it is a common or proper noun, a word for horn or the name of the horn itself. [Ed.]

87

Roland's a hero,   and Oliver is wise;[11]
Both are so brave   men marvel at their deeds.
When they mount chargers,   take up their swords and shields,
Not death itself   could drive them from the field.
They are good men;   their words are fierce and proud.
With wrathful speed   the pagans ride to war.
Oliver says,   "Roland, you see them now.
They're very close,   the King too far away.
You were too proud   to sound the Oliphant:
10 If Charles were with us,   we would not come to grief.
Just look up there!   Close to the Aspre Pass,
The rear-guard stands,   grieving for what must come.
To fight this battle   means not to fight again."
Roland replies,   "Don't speak so foolishly!
Cursed be the heart   that cowers in the breast!
We'll hold our ground;   if they will meet us here,
Our foes will find us   ready with sword and spear." AOI

89

Archbishop Turpin   comes forward then to speak.
He spurs his horse   and gallops up a hill,
Summons the Franks,   and preaches in these words:
"My noble lords,   Charlemagne left us here,
And may our deaths   do honor to the King!
Now you must help   defend our holy Faith!
War is upon us—   I need not tell you that—
Before your eyes   you see the Saracens.
Confess your sins,   ask God to pardon you;
10 I'll grant you absolution   to save your souls.
If you should die,   that will be martyrdom,
And you'll have places   in highest Paradise."
The French dismount;   they kneel upon the ground.
Then the Archbishop,   blessing them in God's name,
Told them, for penance,   to strike when battle came.

---

[11] **Roland's a . . . is wise:** *Rollant est proz e Oliver est sage.* The usual English translation is "Roland is strong [brave, good] and Oliver is wise," with the implication that the two virtues are opposed. Terry points out that in Old French *proz* also means the capacity for giving good counsel and concludes, "The wisdom of heroes is different from, but at least equal to, the voice of reason." [Ed.]

91

At Roncevaux[12]   Count Roland passes by,
Riding his charger,   swift-running Veillantif.
He's armed for battle,   splendid in shining mail.
As he parades,   he brandishes his lance,
Turning the point   straight up against the sky,
And from the spearhead   a banner flies, pure white,
With long gold fringes   that beat against his hands.
Radiant, fair to see,   he laughs for joy.
Now close behind him   comes Oliver, his friend,
10 With all the Frenchmen   cheering their mighty lord.
Fiercely his eyes   confront the Saracens;
Respectfully, fondly   he gazes at the Franks,
Speaking these gallant words   to cheer their hearts:
"Barons, my lords,   softly now, keep the pace!
Here come the pagans   looking for martyrdom.
We'll have such plunder   before the day is out,
As no French king   has ever won before!"
And at this moment   the armies join in war. AOI

92

Oliver says,   "I have no heart for words.
You were too proud   to sound the Oliphant:
No help at all   you'll have from Charlemagne.
It's not his fault—   he doesn't know our plight,
Nor will the men   here with us be to blame.
But now, ride on,   to fight as you know how.
Barons, my lords,   in battle hold your ground!
And in God's name,   I charge you, be resolved
To strike great blows   for those you have to take.
10 Let's not forget   the war-cry of King Charles!"
He says these words,   and all the Franks cry out;
No one who heard   that mighty shout, "Montjoie!"[13]
Would soon forget   the valor of these men.
And then, how fiercely,   God! they begin to ride,
Spurring their horses   to give their utmost speed,
They race to strike—   what else is there to do?
The Saracens stand firm;   they won't retreat.
Pagans and Christians,   behold! in battle meet.

---

[12] **At Roncevaux:** *as porz d'Espaigne*—the pass, the "gates of Spain."

[13] **"Montjoie!":** Charlemagne's sword, supposedly made from the holy lance that wounded Jesus on the cross. [Ed.]

93

King Marsile's nephew,   Aelroth is his name,
First of the pagans,   rides out before the host,
Taunting our Franks   with loud malicious words:
"Today, foul Frenchmen,   you'll break a lance with us;
You stand here now   abandoned and betrayed!
The King was mad   to leave you at the pass:
This day sweet France   will see its pride cast down.
The Emperor Charles   will lose his good right arm!"
Count Roland hears him,   God! with what pain and rage!
10 He spurs his horse   to run with all its might,
Levels his lance,   strikes Aelroth such a blow
His shield is shattered,   the hauberk split in two,
The pagan's bones   crack open in his chest,
His broken spine   sticks out behind his back
So that the spear   drives out his very soul.
Under the thrust   the body starts to fall,
And Roland hurls him   a spear's length from his horse;
He falls down dead,   his neck broken in two.
But still Count Roland   gives him these parting words:
20 "Foul infidel,   King Charles is not a fool,
Nor was he ever   unfaithful to his trust.
Wisely he chose   that we should guard the pass;
Sweet France will lose   no glory here today
Strike on, you Franks!   First blood will win the fight!
Their cause is evil,   and we are in the right." AOI

104

Now wondrous battle   rages throughout the field.
Roland fights on,   not caring to keep safe,
Strikes with his spear   until the shaft is gone—
And fifteen blows   it gave before it broke.
Then from its scabbard   he draws great Durendal,
Spurs on and charges   Chernuble of Muneigre,
Slashing his helmet   where the bright rubies gleam,
Slices his hood   and downward through his hair,
Between the eyes   he cuts his face in two,
10 Through the bright hauberk,   of tightly-woven mail,
And all his body   down to the groin is split.
Then through the saddle   adorned with threads of gold,
The sword drives deep   into the pagan's horse,
Cleaving the spine   where there's a joint or no—
Both man and beast   fall dead in thick green grass.

Then Roland says,   "Foul serf, you've found your doom.
See how Mohammed   protects you in the fray!
No man so vile   will win this fight today."

110

Now fierce and grim   the battle rages on.
Oliver, Roland—   how valiantly they fight!
Turpin delivers   more than a thousand blows;
Among the Peers   none dreams of holding back,
And all together,   the Franks, as one man, strike.
By hundreds, thousands,   the pagans fall and die;
There's no way out   except for those who flee:
Each one who stays   is living his last day.
But others die—   the best among the Franks—
10 They'll never see   their families again,
Or Charlemagne   who waits beyond the pass.
A fearful storm   that very day strikes France;
Through rushing winds   long peals of thunder roar,
And heavy rains,   enormous hailstones fall,
Great bolts of lightning   are striking everywhere.
Now the whole earth   is trembling dreadfully
From Saint Michel   all the way down to Sens,
From Besançon   to Wissant on the sea;
There is no stronghold   without a shattered wall.
20 At noontime shadows   darken the light of day;
The only brightness   comes when the black sky cracks,
And no man sees it   who isn't terrified.
Many declare,   "The world is at an end—
The Day of Wrath   has come upon us now!"
But they know nothing,   and they believe a lie.
The heavens grieve   that Roland is to die.

112

Now King Marsile   through a deep valley rides
With the great host   he summoned to his aid:
Twenty battalions   march with the Saracen.
Their helmets gleam   with gold and precious stones,
Bright are their shields,   their hauberks saffron-gold.
With seven hundred trumpets   sounding the charge,
Their coming echoes   for many miles around.
Then Roland says,   "Oliver, brother, friend,
Foul Ganelon   has sent us to our deaths;
10 But his betrayal   can never be concealed,
And we can leave   our vengence to King Charles.

We'll have a battle   to try our utmost strength,
Fiercer than any   the world has seen before.
I'll strike them down   with Durendal, my sword,
And you, companion,   strike with your own Halteclere.
We've carried them   through so many far lands,
So many battles   we've won thanks to these blades!
No evil songs   to mock them shall be made." AOI

113

The Franks can see   that hosts of Saracens
All through the field   advance on every side.
They cry out often   to Roland, Oliver,
The Twelve French Peers,   to come to their defense.
Archbishop Turpin   counsels them in this way:
"Barons, my lords,   surrender not to fear,
But in God's name,   I pray you, hold your ground,
That no man mock you   in a malicious song—
Better to die   with honor on this field!
10 Very soon now   we'll meet our promised end;
We cannot hope   to live beyond today.
But this I tell you   is true without a doubt:
For you stand open   the gates of Paradise;
You'll take your places   beside the Innocents."
Hearing these words,   the Frenchmen all rejoice;
"Montjoie!" they cry,   as with a single voice. AOI

128

Count Roland sees   the slaughter of the Franks.
He says these words   to Oliver his friend:
"Noble companion,   how does it look to you?
So many Franks   lie dead upon the field—
Well could we weep   for that fair land, sweet France,
Which will not see   these valiant lords again.
Oh! Charles, my friend,   if only you were here!
Oliver, brother,   how can we call him back?
Is there no way   for us to send him word?"
10 Oliver answers,   "No, I do not know how.
Better to die   than lose our honor now." AOI

129

Then Roland says,   "I'll sound the Oliphant.
King Charles will hear it   on the high mountain pass;
I promise you,   the Franks will all turn back."

Oliver answers,   "Then you would bring disgrace
And such dishonor   on your whole family
The shame of it   would last them all their lives.
Three times I asked,   and you would not agree;
You still can do it,   but not with my consent.
To sound the horn   denies your valor now.
10 And both your arms   are red with blood of foes!"
The Count replies,   "I've struck some pretty blows." AOI

130

Then Roland says,   "This is a heavy fight.
I'll blow my horn,   and Charlemagne will hear."
Oliver says,   "Then you'll disgrace your name.
Each time I asked you,   companion, you refused.
If Charles were with us,   we would not come to grief.
No one can say   our Franks have been to blame.
I promise you—   I swear it by my beard—
If I should live   to see my sister's face,
You'll never lie   in Aude's sweet embrace!" AOI

131

Then says the Count,   "You're angry at me. Why?"
Oliver answers,   "Roland, you are to blame.
Allied with reason,   courage is not unwise;
Men of good sense   do more for us than fools.
You were reckless,   and so these Franks have died.
Never again   will we serve Charlemagne.
Had you believed me,   my lord would be here now,
We would have fought   and beat the Saracens,
Marsile would be   our prisoner, or dead.
10 We are the victims   of your great prowess now!
We won't be there,   alas! to help King Charles,
A man whose peer   will not be seen on earth.
And you will die,   leaving sweet France to shame.
Brothers-in-arms   we've been until this day;
Now we have only   a last farewell to say." AOI

132

Archbishop Turpin,   hearing the angry words,
Urges his horse   with spurs made of pure gold,
And riding up,   reproaches both of them:
"Roland, my lord,   and you, Lord Oliver,

End your dispute,   I pray you, in God's name.
It's too late now   to blow the horn for help,
But just the same,   that's what you'd better do.
If the King comes,   at least we'll be avenged—
Why should the Spaniards   go home safe to rejoice?
10 And then the Franks   will ride back to this place;
They'll find us dead,   our bodies hacked by swords,
Put us in coffins   carried on horses' backs,
And they will weep   for pity and for grief.
We will be buried   with honor in a church,
And not be eaten   by wolves and pigs and dogs."
Then Roland answers: "Your words are true, my lord."

133

Count Roland presses   the horn against his mouth;
He grasps it hard,   and sounds a mighty blast.
High are the hills,   that great voice reaches far—
They hear it echo   full thirty leagues around.
Charlemagne hears,   and so do all his men.
The Emperor says,   "Our Franks are in a fight!"
Count Ganelon   returns a swift reply:
"Except from you,   I'd take that for a lie!" AOI

134

And now Count Roland,   in anguish and in pain,
With all his strength   sounds the great horn again.
A fountain of bright blood   leaps from his mouth;
His brain is bursting   against his forehead's bone.
That mighty voice   cries out a second time;
Charlemagne hears it,   high on the mountain pass,
Duke Naimon listens,   and so do all the Franks.
Then says the King,   "That is Count Roland's horn!
He'd never sound it,   except for an attack."
10 Ganelon says,   "What battle can there be?
You have grown old,   your hair is streaked with white;
The words you speak   could well befit a child.
You ought to know   how great is Roland's pride—
The wonder is   God suffers it so long.
He captured Noples,   and not by your command,
And then flushed out   the Saracens inside;
He fought them all,   Roland, your loyal man,
And then took water   and washed the field of blood,
Hoping that you   would not detect the fight.

20 Just for a rabbit   he'll blow his horn all day!
He's only boasting   how he'll outdo his peers.
No one on earth   would meet him in the field!
Ride on, I tell you!   What are we waiting for?
We've far to go   to see our lands once more." AOI

135

Blood is flowing   over Count Roland's mouth;
His brain has broken   right through his forehead's bone.
He sounds the horn   in anguish and in pain.
Charlemagne hears,   and so do all the Franks.
Then says the King,   "How long that horn resounds!"
Duke Naimon answers,   "Great valor swells the sound!
Roland is fighting: he must have been betrayed—
And by that man   who tells you to hang back.
Take up your arms,   let your war-cry ring out!
10 Your household needs you,   now speed to its defense.
You've heard enough   how Roland's horn laments!"

136

The Emperor Charles   orders his horns to sound.
The French dismount,   prepare themselves for war.
They put on hauberks,   helmets and golden swords;
Their shields are good,   heavy their spears and strong,
Their battle-flags   are crimson, blue and white.
Riding their chargers,   the barons of the host
Spur on and gallop   back through the mountain pass.
Each to the other   pronounces this same vow:
"When we get there,   if Roland's still alive,
10 We'll fight beside him,   striking hard blows and straight."
What does it matter?   Their help will come too late.

140

Count Roland looks at   the mountains and the hills
Where all around him   the Franks are lying dead;
He weeps for them,   as a true knight would do.
"Barons, my lords,   may God forgive your sins,
And grant your souls   a place in Paradise;
On holy flowers   may you forever rest!
I've never seen   vassals better than you;
You followed me   so loyally and long,
For Charlemagne   we've won such mighty lands!

10 The King's own household,   alas! brings him to woe.
And that fair country   where it is sweet to live
Today laid waste   and cruelly bereaved!
Barons of France,   because of me you die;
I can't protect you,   I cannot keep you safe:
Look now to God   who never told a lie.
Oliver, brother,   faithful I'll be to you;
I'll die of grief,   if not by pagan spears.
My lord, companion,   there's still work for us here!"

142

A man who knows   all captives will be slain
In such a battle   fights to the end of strength;
And so the Franks   like lions face their foes.
Behold Marsile: as a true knight would do,
He sits the horse   that he has named Gaignon,
Pricks with sharp spurs,   and rides against Bevon,
The lord of Beaune   and also of Dijon.
He breaks his shield,   the hauberk splits in two—
With that one blow   he fells the Frenchman dead.
10 Then Marsile kills   Ivoire and Ivon too,
And with them dies   Gérard of Roussillon.
Seeing that, Roland,   who isn't far away,
Says to the pagan,   "God smite you with His curse!
To you I owe   these good companions slain—
Nor shall we part   before that debt is paid!
Now is the time   to teach you my sword's name."
With that he charges   as a true knight would do;
The Count's keen sword   cuts off Marsile's right hand.
Then Jurfaleu   surrenders his blond head—
20 He was a Prince,   the son of King Marsile.
The pagans cry,   "Mohammed help us now!
Gods of our country,   give us revenge on Charles,
For he has sent   such felons here to fight
That death itself   can't drive them from the field."
They tell each other,   "Let's get away from here!"
A hundred thousand   run from the French attack;
Whoever calls,   they won't be coming back.

145

And when the pagans   see how few Franks are left,
They take much pride   and comfort from the fact,
Telling each other,   "King Charles is in the wrong."

Then the Caliph,   astride a sorrel horse,
Pricks with gold spurs   and gallops from behind
To land his spear   deep in Oliver's back.
The gleaming hauberk   shatters and splits away,
The spear goes through   and opens up his chest.
Says the Caliph,   "You've taken a hard blow!
10 Charlemagne left you   to wait here for your doom.
Let him not glory   in what he's done to Spain—
Your death alone   avenges all our slain."

147

Oliver knows   he has a fatal wound.
He longs for vengeance—   he'll never have enough.
In the melee   he fights on valiantly,
He cuts through spears,   the pagans' studded shields,
And feet and fists   and saddle-trees and spines.
Whoever watched him   cut pagans limb from limb,
Bodies piled up   around him on the ground,
Would know that once   he'd seen a noble lord.
The Count remembers   the war-cry of King Charles,
10 And loud and clear   his voice rings out, "Montjoie!"
He calls to Roland,   summons his friend and peer,
"My lord, companion,   come fight beside me now!
We'll part in sorrow   before the sun goes down." AOI

148

Roland is there;   he sees Oliver's face,
The skin is ashen,   so pallid it looks grey,
And from his wounds   bright blood is spurting out;
Its heavy drops   flow down him to the ground.
"O God!" says Roland,   "I don't know what to do.
Was such great valor   destined to be cut down!
My noble friend,   you'll have no peer on earth.
Alas, sweet France!   Now you have fallen low,
Bereft of vassals,   so many valiant men;
10 The Emperor Charles   will sorely feel the lack."
With these words Roland   faints on his horse's back. AOI

149

Here is Count Roland   unconscious on his horse;
Oliver, wounded   and very close to death,

Has bled so much   that both his eyes are dimmed:
Now far or near   he can't see well enough
To give a name   to any man alive.
When he encounters   Count Roland in the field,
Oliver strikes him,   cleaving his golden helm
Brilliant with jewels—   the nose-piece cracks in two—
And yet the blade   does not touch face or head.
10 Roland's eyes open,   and looking at his friend,
Softly and gently   he asks him only this:
"My lord, companion,   it's Roland—did you know?
I've always loved you;   did you intend that blow?
You gave no challenge   before you charged at me."
Oliver says,   "I recognize your voice,
But I can't see you—   God keep you in His sight!
I struck at you!   I pray you, pardon me."
Roland replies,   "I am not hurt at all;
I do forgive you,   here and in front of God."
20 When he had spoken,   each leaned down toward his friend.
So, with great love,   they parted in the end.

150

Oliver suffers   the agonies of death;
He feels his eyes   turn back into his head,
He cannot hear,   he cannot see at all.
Now he dismounts,   and lying on the ground,
Aloud he asks   forgiveness for his sins;
He clasps his hands,   and holds them toward the sky,
Praying that God   will grant him Paradise,
And give His blessing   to Charles and to sweet France,
And to Count Roland   above all other men.
10 Then his heart fails him,   his shining helmet bows.
All of his body   sinks down against the ground;
The Count is dead—   no longer did he stay.
Lord Roland weeps,   lamenting bitterly;
Many have grieved,   but no man more than he.

156

Roland delivers   many a skillful blow,
But now his body   is fevered, drenched with sweat,
His head is throbbing;   he is in dreadful pain,
His temples broken   from sounding his great horn.
Longing to know   if Charles is on his way,

Weakly, once more,   he blows the Oliphant.
King Charles stands still,   listening to that call;
"My lords," he says,   "now we have come to woe!
My nephew Roland   takes leave of us this day—
His horn's voice tells me   he won't be long alive.
Who wants to be there   had better speed his horse.
Let every trumpet   the host commands resound!"
And sixty thousand   rang from the lofty peaks
Down through the valleys,   echoing loud and clear.
The pagans, listening,   think it no empty boast—
They say, "Here come   King Charles and all his host." AOI

160

The pagans say,   "Ours were unlucky stars!
Would that this evil day   had never dawned!
We've lost our Peers,   our lords have all been slain,
The valiant Charles   is coming back again.
Now we can hear   the trumpets of his host,
The mighty clamor   when the Franks shout 'Montjoie!'
And this Count Roland   is hideously fierce—
He can't be conquered   by men of flesh and blood.
Let's cast our lances   and then leave him alone."
The Saracens   throw many javelins,
Lances and darts,   and feathered throwing spears.
Count Roland's shield   is broken and pierced through,
His hauberk's mail   is cracked and split apart,
And still his body   has not been touched at all.
But Veillantif   has suffered thirty wounds;
Beneath Count Roland   he falls dead to the ground.
Then all the pagans   yield to their fear and flee;
And Roland stands,   dismounted, on the field. AOI

161

The pagans flee,   furious and enraged,
Trying their best   to get away in Spain.
Count Roland lacks the means   to chase them now,
For he has lost   his war-horse Veillantif;
Against his will   he has to go on foot.
He went to give   Archbishop Turpin help,
Unlaced his helmet,   removed it from his head,
And then took off   the hauberk of light mail;
The under-tunic   he cut into long strips
With which he stanched   the largest of his wounds.

Then, lifting Turpin,   carried him in his arms
To soft green grass,   and gently laid him down.
In a low voice   Roland made this request:
"My noble lord,   I pray you, give me leave,
For our companions,   the men we held so dear,
Must not be left   abandoned now in death.
I want to go   and seek out every one,
Carry them here,   and place them at your feet."
Said the Archbishop,   "I grant it willingly.
20 The field belongs,   thank God, to you and me."

162

Alone, Count Roland   walks through the battlefield,
Searching the valleys,   searching the mountain heights.
Gerin he found,   and Gerier his friend,
He found Aton   and then Count Berenger,
Proud Anseïs he found,   and then Samson,
Gérard the Old,   the Count of Roussillon.
He took these barons,   and carried every one
Back to the place   where the Archbishop was,
And then he put them   in ranks at Turpin's knees.
10 Seeing them, Turpin   cannot restrain his tears;
Raising his hand,   he blesses all the dead.
And then he says,   "You've come to grief, my lords!
May God in His glory   receive your souls,
Among bright flowers   set you in Paradise!
Now I must die,   in anguish and in pain;
Never again   will I see Charlemagne."

163

Roland goes back   to search the field once more,
And his companion   he finds there, Oliver.
Lifting him in his arms,   he holds him close,
Brings him to Turpin   as quickly as he can,
Beside the others   places him on a shield;
Turpin absolves him,   signing him with the cross,
And then they yield   to pity and to grief.
Count Roland says,   "Brother-in-arms, fair friend,
You were the son   of Renier, the Duke
10 Who held the land   where Runers valley lies.
For breaking lances,   for shattering thick shields,
Bringing the proud   to terror and defeat,
Giving the worthy   protection and advice,

Crushing vile pagans,   who cannot see the light,
In all the world   there is no better knight."

164

When Roland sees   that all his peers are dead,
And Oliver   whom he so dearly loved,
He feels such sorrow   that he begins to weep;
Drained of all color,   his face turns ashen pale,
His grief is more   than any man could bear,
He falls down, fainting   whether he will or no.
Says the Archbishop,   "Baron, you've come to woe."

168

Now Roland knows   that death is very near.
His ears give way,   he feels his brains gush out.
He prays that God   will summon all his peers;
Then, for himself,   he prays to Gabriel.
Taking the horn,   to keep it from all shame,
With Durendal   clasped in his other hand,
He goes on, farther   than a good cross-bow shot,
West into Spain,   crossing a fallow field.
Up on a hilltop,   under two lofty trees,
10 Four marble blocks   are standing on the grass.
But when he comes there,   Count Roland faints once more,
He falls down backward;   now he is at death's door.

169

High are the hills   and very tall the trees,
The four great blocks   of polished marble shine;
On the green grass   the Count is lying still.
A Saracen   watches with steady eyes:
This man feigned death,   hiding among the slain;
His face and body   he had besmeared with blood.
Now he stands up   and dashes forward fast—
He's handsome, strong   and very valiant too,
But he won't live   to profit from his pride;
10 He falls on Roland,   wanting to have his arms,
And says these words: "Charles' nephew lost the fight!
When I go home,   his sword shall be my prize."
But as he pulls it,   Roland comes back to life.

170

Count Roland feels   the pagan take his sword,
And opening his eyes,   he says just this:
"You look to me   like no one on our side!"
Raising the horn   he'd wanted to keep safe,
He strikes the helmet   shining with gold and jewels,
Shatters the steel,   smashes the skull and bones;
He puts both eyes   out of the pagan's head,
And sends his body   crashing against the ground.
And then he asks him,   "How did you get so brave,
10 Dog, to attack me   with or without just cause?
Whoever heard this   would say you were insane!
But I have cracked   the Oliphant's broad bell;
Its gold and crystals   were shattered as it fell."

171

Now Roland feels   that he is going blind.
The Count stands upright,   using what strength remains;
All of the color   has vanished from his face.
In front of him   there is a dark grey stone.
He strikes ten blows   in bitterness and grief;
The steel blade grates   but will not break or dent.
Then Roland cries,   "O Holy Mary, help!
O Durendal,   alas for your fair fame!
My life is over,   you won't be in my care.
10 We've won such battles   together in the field,
So many lands   we've conquered, you and I,
For Charles to rule   whose beard is silver-grey.
No man must have you   who fights and runs away!
You have been long   in a good vassal's hands;
You'll have no equal   in all of holy France."

172

Count Roland strikes   the hard sardonyx stone;
The steel blade grates   but will not chip or break.
When Roland sees   he can't destroy his sword,
Then, to himself,   grieving, he speaks its praise:
"O Durendal,   how fair you are, and bright!
Against the sunlight   your keen steel gleams and flames!
Charles was that time   in Moriane's Vales
When, by God's will,   an angel from the sky

Said to bestow you   upon a chieftain Count:
10 The noble King   girded you at my side.
With you I won him   Anjou and Brittany,
Conquered Poitou   and after that all Maine,
With you I won him   that free land, Normandy,
Conquered Provence,   and then all Aquitaine,
And Lombardy,   Romagna after that.
With you I won him   Bavaria, Flanders,
Bulgaria   and all of Poland too;
Constantinople   paid homage to King Charles,
In Saxony   he does as he desires.
20 With you I conquered   the Irish and the Scots,
And England too   the King holds as his own.
So many countries   we've won him, many lands
Ruled by King Charles   whose flowing beard is white.
For your sake now   I suffer grief and pain —
Better to die   than leave you here in Spain.
Almighty Father,   keep sweet France from that shame!"

174

Count Roland feels   the very grip of death
Which from his head   is reaching for his heart.
He hurries then   to go beneath a pine;
In the green grass   he lies down on his face,
Placing beneath him   the sword and Oliphant;
He turns his head   to look toward pagan Spain.
He does these things   in order to be sure
King Charles will say,   and with him all the Franks,
The noble Count   conquered until he died.
10 He makes confession,   for all his sins laments,
Offers his glove   to God in penitence. AOI

176

And now Count Roland,   lying beneath a pine,
Has turned his face   to look toward pagan Spain;
And he begins   remembering these things:
The many lands   his valor won the King,
Sweet France, his home,   the men of his own line,
And Charlemagne   who raised him in his house —
The memories   make him shed tears and sigh.
But not forgetting   how close he is to death,
He prays that God   forgive him all his sins:
10 "O my true Father,   O Thou who never lied,

Thou who delivered   Lazarus from the grave,
Who rescued Daniel   out of the lions' den,
Keep now my soul   from every peril safe,
Forgive the sins   that I have done in life."
Roland's right glove   he offers now to God.
Saint Gabriel comes   and takes it from his hand.
His head sinks down   to rest upon his arm;
Hands clasped in prayer,   Roland has met his end.
God sends from heaven   the angel Cherubin,
20 Holy Saint Michael   who saves us from the sea,
And with these two   the angel Gabriel flies.
Count Roland's soul   they bring to Paradise.

204

King Charlemagne   returns to Roncevaux.
He sees the dead;   his eyes are filled with tears.
He tells the Franks,   "My lords, walk slowly on;
I'll go before you   into the battlefield—
I know I'll find   my nephew's body there.
One time at Aix   during a solemn feast,
My valiant knights   were making boastful vows
To fight great battles   and do heroic deeds.
I heard my nephew   say he could promise this:
10 If he must die   fighting in some strange land,
We'd find his body   beyond his men and peers,
His head still turned   to face the enemy;
He'd end his life   in valor, conquering."
A greater distance   than flies a stick well thrown,
He goes ahead,   then climbs a hill alone.

205

The Emperor, seeking   the place where Roland fell,
Crosses a meadow   covered with plants whose flowers
Are all stained crimson   with the life-blood of France.
He feels such sorrow   he cannot help but weep.
And now he finds,   close to the two great trees,
Three blocks of stone   where Durendal cut deep;
On the green grass   he sees his nephew, dead.
It is no wonder   he's overwhelmed with woe.
The King dismounts   and runs across the field.
10 He takes Count Roland   and holds him in his arms,
Falls with him, fainting,   his grief so racks his heart.

213

Then Charles has Roland   made ready for the grave,
And Oliver,   Archbishop Turpin too,
Their chests cut open   while he himself looks on,
The three men's hearts   withdrawn and wrapped in silk,
And in a coffin   of pure white marble placed.
When that is done,   the bodies of the lords
Are taken up   and washed with spice and wine;
Around each baron   they place a deerskin shroud.
Charlemagne orders   Thibault and Geboin,
10 Milon the Count   and the Marquis Oton
To lead the carts   in which they were conveyed,
All covered over   with palls of silk brocade. AOI

214

The Emperor Charles   is anxious to depart,
But pagan outposts   rise up along his way.
Then from the closest,   two messengers arrive;
For Baligant,   they summon Charles to war:
"This is no time,   proud King, to go away!
The great Emir   is riding on your heels
With all the hosts   he led across the sea.
We'll know today   what courage you command!" AOI
At that King Charles,   his hand upon his beard,
10 Thinks once again   of all that he has lost.
With fiery pride   he gazes at his men,
Then in a voice   mighty and clear he cries,
"Barons of France,   take up your arms and ride!"

The Crusades: War and Faith in the Middle Ages

The Song of Roland, composed at the end of the eleventh century, coincided with the beginning of the First Crusade in 1096. At that time, Christian knights from across Europe joined together — ostensibly to come to the aid of Constantinople, but actually to recover Jerusalem from the Muslims and occupy the Holy Land. This "holy war" — as formulated according to Christian doctrine in the tenth and eleventh centuries — was often portrayed as a belated response to the Muslim conquest of the Middle East nearly four hundred years before. But since Christians and Muslims had found ways to live peaceably together in the interim, especially in Muslim Spain, the Christian Crusades satisfied new political ambitions as much as they reflected longstanding political and religious differences. The Crusades helped the Papacy assert itself against not only Muslims but also quarreling factions inside European religious and secular society. They helped European kings consolidate their authority and set the goals for European expansion until the voyages to the New World in the sixteenth century, and they provided the unattached knights of Europe with opportunities for acquiring wealth through plunder, taking pressure off their lords to distribute land among them. Finally, the Crusades strengthened the hand of the Roman Catholic Church against their ancient rival, the Byzantine emperor. But by re-opening the "holy war" with the Muslims, the First Crusade also left Muslims with a bitter determination to repel further Western expansion. The documents of the Crusades contrast the Christian and Muslim viewpoints.

p. 1336

Battle between Christians and Muslims, thirteenth century
The beginning of the First Crusade in 1096 inaugurated a new period of conflict between two great world religions for more than two centuries and had lasting repercussions for both sides. The Crusades marked Western Christendom's attempted expansion outside of Europe. Wherever the Christian and Muslim armies collided, it brought about a period of intense cultural interaction. (The Art Archive / Biblioteca Nazionale Marciana, Venice/Dagli Orti)

MUSLIMS, CHRISTIANS, AND THE BYZANTINE EMPIRE

In the last ten years of his life, from 622 to 632, Muhammad assumed political as well as civil and religious authority over much of Arabia. Muhammad addressed his enemies in Mecca and elsewhere in Arabia first by a series of raids and later by territorial conquest. In these battles he followed the words of the Qur'an.

> Fight for the sake of God those that fight against you, but do not attack them first. God does not love aggressors.

> Slay them wherever you find them. Drive them out of the places from which they drove you. Idolatry is more grievous than bloodshed. . . .
>
> Fight against them until idolatry is no more and God's religion remains supreme. But if they desist, fight none except the evil-doers.

(SURA 2: *THE COW*. 191–193)

His Muslim followers undertook a massive *JIHAD*, or "struggle," following his death, breaking out of the Arabian peninsula in every direction. To the north and east they conquered Syria, Armenia, and Persia; they penetrated Asia Minor, where they unsuccessfully besieged Constantinople, the seat of the Byzantine empire, in 718. To the west they conquered Egypt, crossed North Africa, and reached the Straits of Gibraltar, leading to the Iberian Peninsula. Their first contact with the Christian armies of Europe came in 711 after they crossed the Straits of Gibraltar into what is now Spain. Continuing across the Pyrenees mountains into southern France, they were finally stopped by the Merovingian Franks under Charles Martel[1] — the grandfather of Charlemagne — near **Poitiers** in 732, and retreated to safety back across the Pyrenees. These events marked the limit of Muslim expansion in the eighth century, resulting in a reconfiguration of the map of what is now identified as Europe, North Africa, the Middle East, and Asia Minor. The Frankish kingdom, soon to become the seat of Western Christendom, held what is now most of France and Germany; Islam occupied Spain, North Africa, Arabia, most of the Middle East and the trade routes to India; the Byzantine empire, which had lost North Africa, Egypt, Syria, and Palestine to the Muslim invasion, continued to occupy Asia Minor and part of what is now eastern Europe. Italy was contested among the Lombards, Norman Franks, and Byzantine armies.

The Muslims of the eighth century soon consolidated their power, attained great wealth, and became the most advanced society in the world, with their influence reaching as far as Russia, Scandinavia,

jee-HAHD

pwah-TYAY

---

[1]**Merovingian Franks . . . Charles Martel:** The Merovingian dynasty of Frankish kings lasted from 481 to 751. Charles Martel, mayor of the Merovingian territory of Austrasia from 714 to 741, was the first ruler in the Carolingian family line, which succeeded the Merovingians to power in 751. Charlemagne, the grandson of Charles Martel, ruled as king of the Franks from 768 to 814.

and the Far East. The authority of Islam, previously the domain of the **Umayyad** dynasty (661–750), was firmly established in the new capital of Baghdad with the victory of the **Abbasid** dynasty (750–1258), which survived a number of wars among Muslims until its gradual dissolution after the eleventh century. For their part, the Christians won major victories in the First Crusade (1096–99), conquering Nicaea, Antioch, and finally Jerusalem, but soon after the Crusade ended they began losing conquered territory again. They failed to regain this territory in the Second Crusade (1147–48), and lost Jerusalem itself to the Muslim leader **Saladin**[2] in 1187. In the Third Crusade (1189–1193), the Christians failed to regain Jerusalem, and while the Fourth Crusade (1201–1204) resulted in the conquest of Constantinople, temporarily dismembering the Byzantine empire, it failed again to overcome the Muslims. Islam soon recovered its strength in Syria and Egypt and began to force the Christians out of the Middle East early in the thirteenth century. Repeated Christian attempts to recapture Jerusalem also failed; the Crusaders lost their last bridgehead in the region with the fall of **Acre**, a Syrian port, in 1291.

DOCUMENTS OF THE FIRST CRUSADE

The First Crusade was preached by Pope Urban II (1088–99) before assembled church officials and members of the French aristocracy in Clermont, France, on November 27, 1095. The Council of Clermont had been assembled to address problems within the Catholic Church, including the breakdown of order throughout its realms. Turning at last from church reform, Pope Urban introduced "another affair that concerns you and God. Hastening to the way, you must help your brothers living in the Orient, who need your aid for which they have already cried out many times."

The immediate reason for this undertaking was a plea for assistance from the Byzantine emperor **Alexius Comnenus** (r. 1081–1118), whose armies had been diminished by the Seljuk Turks, a Muslim people, in Asia Minor. Pope Urban called for vengeance on the Turks for atrocities committed against Christian pilgrims traveling to Jerusalem, and he prayed for the expulsion of Muslims from

---

Margin notes:
oo-MAH-yad
uh-BAS-id
SAH-lah-din
AY-kur
p. 1379
uh-LEK-see-us
kahm-NEE-nus

---

[2] **Saladin:** Saladin (1137–1193) held power in Egypt from 1171 until his death, first subjugating Syria and then retaking Jerusalem in 1187. He was highly praised by his supporters and enemies alike for his military skill, enlightened governance, and honesty.

Council of Clermont, 1337

This miniature from a French illuminated manuscript shows the arrival of Pope Urban II in Clermont, France, where he preached before the assembled knights, lords, and church leaders, calling on them to take up arms against the Muslim occupiers of the Holy Land. (Giraudon / Art Resource, NY)

Jerusalem. He concluded his call with this promise: "Undertake this journey for the remission of your sins, with the assurance of the imperishable glory of the kingdom of Heaven." Thus the Christian sponsorship of the Crusades combined a call for possession of the Holy Land with a promise of salvation for fallen soldiers.

The Crusaders, largely made up of Franks from northern and southern France, Normandy, and Norman Sicily, made their way by the end of 1096 to Constantinople, where Emperor Alexius had begun to have misgivings about calling on Frankish assistance, fearing that his allies might become his occupiers. As the desire of the Crusaders to conquer the line of Muslim cities on the way to Jerusalem became evident, Alexius withdrew his own armies, but the Frankish army swept south anyway, destroying Antioch in Syria before marching on to Jerusalem. Accounts of the sack of Jerusalem depict the massacre of Muslims within the city walls as well as the incineration of the Jews who had sought refuge in their ancient synagogue. An excerpt from the anonymous ***History of the First Crusade***, written by an unidentified Frankish Crusader, mixes respect for the military prowess of

The massacre at Jerusalem profoundly impressed all the world. No one can say how many victims it involved; but it emptied Jerusalem of its Moslem and Jewish inhabitants. Many even of the Christians were horrified by what had been done; and amongst the Moslems, who had been ready hitherto to accept the Franks as another factor in the tangled politics of the time, there was henceforward a clear determination that the Franks must be driven out. It was this bloodthirsty proof of Christian fanaticism that recreated the fanaticism of Islam.

– STEVEN RUNCIMAN,
The First Crusade,
1980

p. 1381

Muslim Troops Leaving a Fortress, twelfth century
The Crusades from a Muslim perspective, from an Egyptian manuscript fragment. (The Art Archive / British Museum)

the enemy with approval of the massacre of the inhabitants of Jerusalem. It unapologetically describes Christian atrocities, including the robbing of the graves of the Turkish dead at Antioch and the sacking of the cities of Marra and Jerusalem. Nothing, not even cannibalism, escapes the notice of the chronicler.

The same battles were also described by Muslim historians of the twelfth and thirteenth centuries, writing from the accounts of direct participants as they were passed down through the oral tradition. They generally concentrated not only on the tragedy of the Muslim defeat in the First Crusade but also on the mistakes in strategy and tactics that contributed to the disaster. One of the best of these historians, **Ibn al-Athir** (1160–1233), wrote an encyclopedic work called *The Collection of Histories* in which he took special notice of the Crusades. He focused on the campaigns of Saladin, the ruler of Egypt and leader of the Muslim forces who recaptured Jerusalem from the Christians in 1186. The account of the behavior of Saladin in Jerusalem after the capture of the city, while not innocent of bloodshed, stands in significant contrast to the story of the Christian conquest of Jerusalem eighty-eight years before.

IB-un ahl-ah-THEER

■ **FURTHER RESEARCH**

History

Hamilton, Bernard. *The Crusades.* 1998.

Holt, P. M. *The Age of the Crusades. The Near East from the Eleventh Century to 1517.* 1986.

Maalouf, Amin. *The Crusades through Arab Eyes.* 1984.

Riley-Smith, Jonathan. *The Crusades: A Short History.* 1987.

Runciman, Stephen. *A History of the Crusades.* 3 vols. 1951–54.

Source Materials

Gabrieli, F., ed. *Arab Historians of the Crusades.* Trans. E. J. Costello. 1969.

Hallam, E., ed. *Chronicles of the Crusades.* 1989.

Peters, Edward, ed. *The First Crusade: The Chronicle of Fulcher of Chartres and Other Source Materials.* 1971.

■ **PRONUNCIATION**

Abbasid: uh-BAS-id, AB-uh-sid

Acre: AH-kur, AY-kur

Alexius Comnenus: uh-LEK-see-us kahm-NEE-nus

Ibn al-Athir: IB-un ahl-ah-THEER

jihad: jee-HAHD

Poitiers: pwah-TYAY

Saladin: SAH-lah-din, SAL-uh-din

Umayyad: oo-MAY-yad

❧ ROBERT THE MONK
B. FRANCE, FL. 1095

Numerous chronicles recorded Pope Urban's call for the First Crusade at the Council of Clermont in 1095, including Robert the Monk's account in his *History of the Crusade to Jerusalem.* Urban's speech, praised as a masterpiece of its kind, benefited from the strategic arrangement of its parts: an invocation to the Franks; a report of Turkish attacks on Christian settlements in the Holy Land; a call to arms; a response to anticipated objections based on safety and personal comfort; a call for unity among the Crusaders themselves; a reminder of the plight of Jerusalem; a response to the rallying cry of the assembled listeners; an injunction that the old and sick should be exempted from service; and an admonition to return from this "pilgrimage" in humility and a spirit of sacrifice.

Pope Urban had political as well as religious reasons for launching this Crusade. His call to arms came after the Council of Clermont had deliberated for days on the reform of the Catholic Church and its role in establishing order and peace throughout Europe. The formation of a volunteer army of knights to support the claims of the Catholic Church abroad would set a strong precedent for the future. It also has been suggested that Pope Urban might have wished to establish a Christian foothold in the Middle East and Asia Minor, with the eventual goal of the conquest of Constantinople, the seat of the Byzantine empire and Eastern Christianity, as well as Jerusalem.

Map of Jerusalem, 1099

This schematic map is from the Chronicles of the Crusades, *by Robert the Monk, French abbot of St. Remy who was present at the conquest of Jerusalem in 1099. (Dagli Orti/ Corbis)*

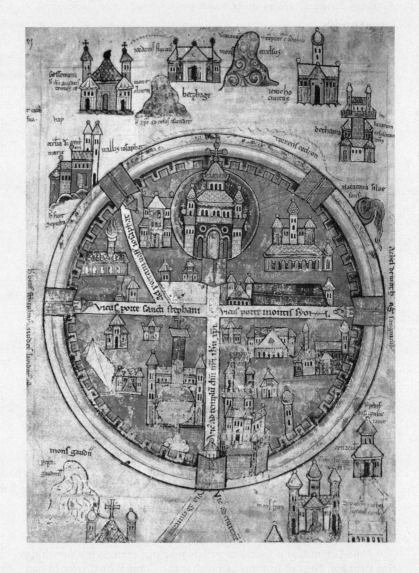

ꝏ Pope Urban II's Call to the First Crusade

Translated by Frederic Austin Ogg

In the year of our Lord's Incarnation one thousand and ninety-five, a great council was convened within the bounds of Gaul, in Auvergne, in the city which is called Clermont. Over this Pope Urban II presided, with the Roman bishops and cardinals. This council was a famous one on account of the concourse of both French and German bishops, and of princes as well. Having arranged the matters relating to the Church, the lord Pope went forth into a certain spacious plain, for no building was large enough to hold all the people. The Pope then, with sweet and persuasive eloquence, addressed those present in words something like the following, saying:

"Oh, race of Franks, race beyond the mountains,[1] race beloved and chosen by God (as is clear from many of your works), set apart from all other nations by the situation of your country, as well as by your Catholic faith and the honor you render to the holy Church: to you our discourse is addressed, and for you our exhortations are intended. We wish you to know what a serious matter has led us to your country, for it is the imminent peril threatening you and all the faithful that has brought us hither.

"From the confines of Jerusalem and from the city of Constantinople a grievous report has gone forth and has been brought repeatedly to our ears; namely, that a race from the kingdom of the Persians, an accursed race, a race wholly alienated from God, 'a generation that set not their heart aright, and whose spirit was not steadfast with God,'[2] has violently invaded the lands of those Christians and has depopulated them by pillage and fire. They have led away a part of the captives into their own country, and a part they have killed by cruel tortures. They have either destroyed the churches of God or appropriated them for the rites of their own religion. They destroy the altars, after having defiled them with their uncleanness. . . . The kingdom of the Greeks[3] is now dismembered by them and has been deprived of territory so vast in extent that it could not be traversed in two months' time.

"On whom, therefore, rests the labor of avenging these wrongs and of recovering this territory, if not upon you—you, upon whom, above all other nations, God has conferred remarkable glory in arms, great courage, bodily activity, and strength to humble the heads of those who resist you? Let the deeds of your ancestors encourage you and incite your minds to manly achievements—the glory and greatness of King Charlemagne and of his son Louis,[4] and of your other monarchs, who have destroyed the kingdoms of the Turks and have extended the sway of the holy Church

---

[1] **beyond the mountains:** The Alps.

[2] **'a generation . . . with God':** Psalms 78:8.

[3] **The kingdom of the Greeks:** The Byzantine empire.

[4] **Charlemagne and of his son Louis:** Charlemagne was king of the Franks from 771 to 814; Louis the Pious succeeded him as king of the Franks from 814 to 840.

over lands previously pagan. Let the holy sepulcher of our Lord and Saviour, which is possessed by the unclean nations especially arouse you, and the holy places which are now treated with ignominy and irreverently polluted with the filth of the unclean. Oh most valiant soldiers and descendants of invincible ancestors, do not degenerate, but recall the valor of your ancestors.

"But if you are hindered by love of children, parents, or wife, remember what the Lord says in the Gospel, 'He that loveth father or mother more than me is not worthy of me.'[5] 'Every one that hath forsaken houses, or brethren, or sisters, or father, or mother, or wife, or children, or lands, for my name's sake, shall receive an hundred-fold, and shall inherit everlasting life.'[6] Let none of your possessions restrain you, nor anxiety for your family affairs. For this land which you inhabit, shut in on all sides by the seas and surrounded by the mountain peaks, is too narrow for your large population; nor does it abound in wealth; and it furnishes scarcely food enough for its cultivators. Hence it is that you murder and devour one another, that you wage war, and that very many among you perish in civil strife.

"Let hatred, therefore, depart from among you; let your quarrels end; let wars cease; and let all dissensions and controversies slumber. Enter upon the road of the Holy Sepulcher; wrest that land from the wicked race, and subject it to yourselves. That land which, as the Scripture says, 'floweth with milk and honey'[7] was given by God into the power of the children of Israel. Jerusalem center of the earth; the land is fruitful above all others, like another paradise of delights. This spot the Redeemer of mankind has made illustrious by His advent, has beautified by His sojourn, has consecrated by His passion, has redeemed by His death, has glorified by His burial.

"This royal city, however, situated at the center of the earth, is now held captive by the enemies of Christ and is subjected, by those who do not know God, to the worship of the heathen. She seeks, therefore, and desires to be liberated, and ceases not to implore you to come to her aid. From you especially she asks succor, because, as we have already said, God has conferred upon you, above all other nations, great glory in arms. Accordingly, undertake this journey eagerly for the remission of your sins, with the assurance of the reward of imperishable glory in the kingdom of heaven."

When Pope Urban had skillfully said these and very many similar things, he so centered in one purpose the desires of all who were present that all cried out, "It is the will of God! It is the will of God!" When the venerable Roman pontiff heard that, with eyes uplifted to heaven, he gave thanks to God and, commanding silence with his hand, said:

"Most beloved brethren, today is manifest in you what the Lord says in the Gospel, 'Where two or three are gathered together in my name, there am I in the midst of them.'[8] For unless God had been present in your spirits, all of you would

---

[5] 'He that loveth . . . not worthy of me': Matthew 10:37.

[6] 'Every one that hath . . . everlasting life': Matthew 19:29.

[7] 'floweth . . . honey': Numbers 13:27.

[8] 'Where two . . . in the midst of them': Matthew 18:20.

not have uttered the same cry; since, although the cry issued from numerous mouths, yet the origin of the cry was one. Therefore I say to you that God, who implanted this in your breasts, has drawn it forth from you. Let that, then, be your war cry in battle, because it is given to you by God. When an armed attack is made upon the enemy, let this one cry be raised by all the soldiers of God: 'It is the will of God! It is the will of God!'

"And we neither command nor advise that the old or feeble, or those incapable of bearing arms, undertake this journey. Nor ought women to set out at all without their husbands, or brothers, or legal guardians. For such are more of a hindrance than aid, mor, more of a burden than an advantage. Let the rich aid the needy; and according to their wealth let them take with them experienced soldiers. The priests and other clerks,[9] whether secular or regular, are not to go without the consent of their bishop; for this journey would profit them nothing if they went without permission. Also, it is not fitting that laymen should enter upon the pilgrimage without the blessing of their priests.

"Whoever, therefore, shall decide upon this holy pilgrimage, and shall make his vow to God to that effect, and shall offer himself to Him for sacrifice, as a living victim, holy and acceptable to God, shall wear the sign of the cross of the Lord on his forehead or on his breast. When he shall return from his journey, having fulfilled his vow, let him place the cross on his back between his shoulders. Thus shall ye, indeed, by this twofold action, fulfill the precept of the Lord, as He commands in the Gospel, 'He that taketh not his cross, and followeth after me, is not worthy of me.'"[10]

∾ HISTORY OF THE FIRST CRUSADE
FRANCE, EARLY TWELFTH CENTURY

The anonymous French *History of the First Crusade* was one of the earliest such chronicles; later annals would follow the two-hundred-year progress of the Christian fighters in the Holy Land. The narrator of the *History* speaks directly from within the action, giving a firsthand account of an attack by the Seljuk Turks as he begins. The reaction of the Crusaders to this massed attack reveals one of the motives for their undertaking:

> There was among us a quiet exchange of words, praising God and taking Counsel and saying: "Be unanimous in every way in the faith of Christ and the victory of the holy cross, for today, if it pleases God, you will all become rich. . . ."

As the narrative resumes, the Christians have their enemies on the run. When the writer praises the Turkish warriors, he does so in terms similar

---

[9] **other clerks:** Members of the clergy.
[10] **'He that taketh . . . worthy of me':** Luke 14:27

Crusader,
twelfth century
*Detail of a Crusader
on the move from
a Syrian fresco
illustrating a battle
between the Knights
Templar (a religious
military order
founded during the
Crusades) and the
Muslims. (The Art
Archive / Templar
Chapel, Cressac /
Dagli Orti)*

to those in *The Song of Roland:* They are great fighters, but as unbelievers they do not enjoy the favor of God.

As the story turns to the sieges of Antioch, Marra, and Jerusalem, the writer describes at length the deeds of the Franks, which include violating mosques, plundering corpses, engaging in cannibalism, and breaking sacred oaths, resulting in the murder or enslavement of the civilian population. Apparently, the author assumed his readers' sympathy with the Christian cause.

FROM

∾ History of the First Crusade

Translated by James B. Ross

THE FIRST CONTACT OF CRUSADERS AND TURKS

Impressions of the People and the Country in Anatolia

The first day of our departure from the city [Constantinople], we reached a bridge and we stayed there two days. The third day our men rose before dawn and, since it was still night, they did not see well enough to hold to the same route, and they divided into two corps which were separated by two days' march. In the first group were Bohemond, Robert of Normandy, the prudent Tancred and many others; in the second were the count of St. Giles, Duke Godfrey, the bishop of Puy, Hugh the Great, the count of Flanders and many others.

The third day [July 1, 1097], the [Seljuk] Turks violently burst upon Bohemond and his companions. At once the Turks began to shriek, scream, and cry out in high voices, repeating some diabolical sound in their own language. The wise Bohemond, seeing the innumerable Turks at a distance, shrieking and crying out in demoniac voices, at once ordered all the knights to dismount and the tents to be pitched quickly. Before the tents were pitched, he said to all the soldiers: "Lords, and valiant soldiers of Christ, here we are confronted on all sides by a difficult battle. Let all the knights advance bravely and let the foot soldiers quickly and carefully pitch the tents."

When all this was done, the Turks had already surrounded us on all sides, fighting, throwing javelins and shooting arrows marvellously far and wide. And we, although we did not know how to resist them nor to endure the weight of so great an enemy, nevertheless we met that encounter with united spirit. And our women on that day were a great help to us, in bearing drinking water to our fighters and perhaps also in always comforting those fighting and defending. The wise Bohemond sent word forthwith to the others, that is, to the count of St. Giles, to Duke Godfrey, Hugh the Great, the bishop of Puy and all the other knights of Christ, to hasten and come quickly to the battle, saying, "If today they wish to fight, let them come bravely." . . .

Our men wondered greatly whence could have sprung such a great multitude of Turks, Arabs, Saracens, and others too numerous to count, for almost all the mountains and hills and valleys and all the plains, both within and without, were covered entirely by that excommunicated race. There was among us a quiet exchange of words, praising God and taking counsel and saying: "Be unanimous in every way in the faith of Christ and the victory of the holy cross, for today, if it pleases God, you will all become rich." . . .

On the approach of our knights, the Turks, Arabs, Saracens, Angulans [unidentifiable], and all the barbarous peoples fled quickly through the passes of the mountains and the plains. The number of the Turks, Persians, Paulicians, Saracens, Angulans, and other pagans was three hundred and sixty thousand, without counting the Arabs, whose number no one knows except God alone. They fled extremely quickly to their tents but were not allowed to remain there long. Again they resumed their flight and we pursued them, killing them during one whole day; and we took much booty, gold, silver, horses, asses, camels, sheep, cows, and many other things which we do not know. If the Lord had not been with us in this battle, if He had not quickly sent us the other division, none of ours would have escaped, because from the third hour up to the ninth hour the battle continued. But God all-powerful, pious and merciful, who did not permit His knights to perish nor to fall into the hands of the enemy, sent aid to us rapidly. But two of our knights died there honourably . . . and other knights and foot soldiers whose names I do not know, found death there.

Who will ever be wise or learned enough to describe the prudence, the military skill, and the fortitude of the Turks? They thought to terrorize the race of the Franks by the threats of their arrows, as they have terrorized the Arabs, Saracens and Armenians, Syrians and Greeks. But, if it pleases God, they will never prevail over such a great people as ours. In truth they say they are of the race of the Franks and that no man, except the Franks and themselves, ought rightly to be called a knight. Let me speak the truth which no one will dare to contest; certainly, if they had always been firm in the faith of Christ and holy Christianity, if they had been willing to confess one Lord in three persons, and the Son of God born of a virgin, who suffered, rose from the dead, ascended into heaven in the sight of His disciples and sent the consolation of the Holy Spirit, and if they had believed in right mind and faith that He reigns in heaven and on earth, no one could have been found more powerful or courageous or gifted in war; and nevertheless, by the grace of God, they were conquered by our men. This battle took place on the first of July. . . .

And we kept going on [July–August, 1097], pursuing the most iniquitous Turks who fled each day before us. . . . And we pursued them through deserts and a land without water or inhabitants from which we scarcely escaped and got out alive. Hunger and thirst pressed us on all sides, and there was almost nothing for us to eat, except the thorns which we pulled and rubbed between our hands; on such food we lived miserably. In that place there died most of our horses, so that many of our knights became foot soldiers; and from lack of horses, cattle took the place of war steeds and in this extreme necessity goats, sheep, and dogs were used by us for carrying.

Then we began to enter an excellent region, full of nourishment for the body, of delights and all kinds of good things, and soon we approached Iconium. The inhabitants of this country [probably Armenians] persuaded and warned us to carry with us skins full of water, because for the journey one day thence there is a great dearth of water. We did so until we came to a certain river and there we camped for two days. . . .

We . . . penetrated into a diabolic mountain [in the Antitaurus], so high and so narrow that no one dared to go before another on the path which lay open on the mountain; there the horses plunged down and one packhorse dragged over another. On all sides the knights were in despair; they beat their breasts in sorrow and sadness, wondering what to do with themselves and their arms. They sold their shields and their best coats of mail with helmets for only three or five pennies or for anything at all; those who failed to sell them, threw them away for nothing and proceeded. . . .

Finally [October, 1097] our knights reached the valley in which is situated the royal city of Antioch, which is the capital of all Syria and which the Lord Jesus Christ gave to St. Peter, prince of the apostles, in order that he might recall it to the cult of the holy faith, he who lives and reigns with God the Father in the unity of the Holy Spirit, God through all the ages. Amen. . . .

At the Siege of Antioch

The next day [March 7, 1098], at dawn, some Turks went forth from the city and collected all the fetid corpses of the Turkish dead which they could find on the bank of the river and buried them at the mosque beyond the bridge, before the gate of the city. With the bodies they buried cloaks, bezants [gold coins], pieces of gold, bows, arrows, and many other objects which we cannot name. Our men, hearing that the Turks had buried their dead, all prepared themselves and hastened to the diabolic edifice. They ordered the tombs to be dug up and broken, and dragged from the burial places. They threw all the corpses into a certain ditch and carried the severed heads to our tents so that the number of them should be known exactly. . . . At this sight the Turks mourned exceedingly and were sad unto death for on that day they did nothing in their sorrow except weep and utter cries. . . .

The Taking of Marra

The Saracens, seeing that our men had sapped the wall, were struck with terror and fled within the city. All this took place on Saturday at the hour of vespers, at sunset, December 11th [1098]. Bohemond sent word by an interpreter to the Saracen chiefs that they with their wives and children and other belongings should take refuge in a palace which is above the gate and he himself would protect them from sentence of death.

Then all our men entered the city and whatever of value they found in the houses or hiding places each one took for his own. When day came, wherever they found anyone of the enemy, either man or woman, they killed him. No corner of the city was empty of Saracen corpses, and no one could go through the streets of the city without stepping on these corpses. At length Bohemond seized those whom he had ordered to go to the palace and took from them everything they had, gold, silver, and other ornaments; some he had killed, others he ordered to be led to Antioch to be sold.

Now the stay of the Franks in this city was one month and four days, during which the bishop of Orange died. There were some of our men who did not find there what they needed, both because of the long stay and the pressure of hunger, for outside the city they could find nothing to take. They sawed open the bodies of the dead because in their bellies they found bezants hidden; others cut the flesh in strips and cooked them for eating. . . .

The Sack of Jerusalem

Entering the city [July 15, 1099], our pilgrims pursued and killed Saracens up to the Temple of Solomon, in which they had assembled and where they gave battle to us furiously for the whole day so that their blood flowed throughout the whole temple. Finally, having overcome the pagans, our knights seized a great number of men and women, and they killed whom they wished and whom they wished they let live. . . . Soon the Crusaders ran throughout the city, seizing gold, silver, horses, mules, and houses full of all kinds of goods.

Then rejoicing and weeping from extreme joy our men went to worship at the sepulchre of our Saviour Jesus and thus fulfilled their pledge to Him. . . .

Then, our knights decided in council that each one should give alms with prayers so that God should elect whom He wished to reign over the others and rule the city. They also ordered that all the Saracen dead should be thrown out of the city because of the extreme stench, for the city was almost full of their cadavers. The live Saracens dragged the dead out before the gates and made piles of them, like houses. No one has ever heard of or seen such a slaughter of pagan peoples since pyres were made of them like boundary marks, and no one except God knows their number.

✦ IBN AL-ATHIR

MESOPOTAMIA, 1160–1233

Ibn al-Athir was a Mesopotamian historian who wrote an encyclopedic compendium of knowledge titled *The Collection of Histories,* covering the period from legendary times to 1231. He treated the period after 1000 C.E. with great authority and originality. His chief virtues as a historian lay in his independence of mind and ability to organize materials for study; his only fault was an occasional tendency to treat his sources and historical chronology a little lightly in the interest of telling the story. Though he lived a century after the First Crusade, he studied the Muslim defeats at Antioch, Marra, and Jerusalem carefully, seeking the internal causes of the Muslim catastrophe while never sparing the cruelties of the Frankish invaders. His report on the actions of the great sultan of Egypt, Saladin, based on first-hand observation, was perhaps the more impressive because, as the supporter of the earlier ruler Nur ad-Din, he was critical of Saladin's earlier role in uniting the Muslims of Egypt and Syria. In his account of Saladin's victory over the Christian army at the battle of Hittīn and his subsequent siege of Jerusalem, Ibn al-Athir followed the reports of earlier annalists but wrote in a clear, objective style that helped solidify his reputation. He depicted Saladin as a brilliant field commander who dealt harshly but fairly with his enemies and whose conquest of Jerusalem proved virtually bloodless compared to the Christian massacre of the Muslim and Jewish occupants of the city nearly ninety years before.

Richard I and Saladin, 1340

This fourteenth-century illuminated manuscript shows the Crusader King Richard I in deadly combat with his archenemy, Saladin, the most powerful and respected Muslim warrior-king. Though they met many times on the field of battle, both men held a grudging respect for the other's leadership. (The Art Archive / British Museum)

FROM

∾ The Collection of Histories

Translated by Francesco Gabrieli. Translated from the Italian by E. J. Costello.

THE BATTLE OF HITTĪN

While the reunited Franks were on their way to Saffuriyya, Saladin called a council of his amīrs. Most of them advised him not to fight, but to weaken the enemy by repeated skirmishes and raids. Others however advised him to pillage the Frankish territories, and to give battle to any Frankish army that might appear in their path, "Because in the East people are cursing us, saying that we no longer fight the infidels but have begun to fight Muslims instead. So we must do something to justify ourselves and silence our critics." But Saladin said: "My feeling is that we should confront all the enemy's forces with all the forces of Islām; for events do not turn out according to man's will and we do not know how long a life is left to us, so it is foolish to dissipate this concentration of troops without striking a tremendous blow in the Holy War." So on Thursday, 2 July 1187, the fifth day after we encamped at Uqhuwana, he struck camp and moved off up the hill outside Tiberias, leaving the city behind him. When he drew near to the Franks, however, there was no one to be seen, for they had not yet left their tents. So he went back down the hill with his army. At night he positioned troops where they would prevent the enemy from giving battle and then attacked Tiberias with a small force, breached the wall and took the city by storm during the night. The inhabitants fled for refuge to the citadel, where the Countess and her children were, and defended themselves there while the lower town was sacked and burned.

When the Franks learned that Saladin had attacked Tiberias and taken it and everything in it, burning the houses and anything they could not remove, they met to take counsel. Some advised the King to meet the Muslims in battle and chase them out of Tiberias, but the Count intervened to say: "Tiberias belongs to me and my wife. There is no question that Saladin is master there now and that only the citadel remains, where my wife is immured. For my part, if he takes the citadel, my wife and all my possessions there and then goes away I shall be happy enough. By God, I have observed the armies of Islām over the course of the years and I have never seen one equal to Saladin's army here in numbers or in fighting power. If he takes Tiberias he will not be able to stay there, and when he has left it and gone away we will retake it; for if he chooses to stay there he will be unable to keep his army together, for they will not put up for long with being kept away from their homes and families. He will be forced to evacuate the city, and we will free our prisoners." But Prince Arnāt of al-Karak replied: "You have tried hard to make us afraid of the Muslims. Clearly you take their side and your sympathies are with them, otherwise you would not have spoken in this way. As for the size of their army, a large load of fuel will be good for the fires of Hell. . . ." "I am one of you," said the Count, "and if you advance then I shall advance with you, and if you retreat I shall retreat. You will see what will happen." The generals decided to advance and give battle to the

Muslims, so they left the place where they had been encamped until now and advanced on the Muslim army. When Saladin received the news he ordered his army to withdraw from its position near Tiberias; his only reason for besieging Tiberias was to make the Franks abandon their position and offer battle. The Muslims went down to the water (of the lake). The weather was blazingly hot and the Franks, who were suffering greatly from thirst, were prevented by the Muslims from reaching the water. They had drained all the local cisterns, but could not turn back for fear of the Muslims. So they passed that night tormented with thirst. The Muslims for their part had lost their first fear of the enemy and were in high spirits, and spent the night inciting one another to battle. They could smell victory in the air, and the more they saw of the unexpectedly low morale of the Franks the more aggressive and daring they became; throughout the night the cries *Allāh akbar* (God is great) and "there is no God but Allāh" rose up to heaven. Meanwhile the Sultan was deploying the vanguard of archers and distributing the arrows.

On Saturday 24 rabī‘ II / 4 July 1187 Saladin and the Muslims mounted their horses and advanced on the Franks. They too were mounted, and the two armies came to blows. The Franks were suffering badly from thirst, and had lost confidence. The battle raged furiously, both sides putting up a tenacious resistance. The Muslim archers sent up clouds of arrows like thick swarms of locusts, killing many of the Frankish horses. The Franks, surrounding themselves with their infantry, tried to fight their way toward Tiberias in the hope of reaching water, but Saladin realized their objective and forestalled them by planting himself and his army in the way. He himself rode up and down the Muslim lines encouraging and restraining his troops where necessary. The whole army obeyed his commands and respected his prohibitions. One of his young mamlūks led a terrifying charge on the Franks and performed prodigious feats of valour until he was overwhelmed by numbers and killed, when all the Muslims charged the enemy lines and almost broke through, slaying many Franks in the process. The Count saw that the situation was desperate and realized that he could not withstand the Muslim army, so by agreement with his companions he charged the lines before him. The commander of that section of the Muslim army was Taqi ad-Din ‘Umar, Saladin's nephew. When he saw that the Franks charging his lines were desperate and that they were going to try to break through, he sent orders for a passage to be made for them through the ranks.

One of the volunteers had set fire to the dry grass that covered the ground; it took fire and the wind carried the heat and smoke down on to the enemy. They had to endure thirst, the summer's heat, the blazing fire and smoke and the fury of battle. When the Count fled the Franks lost heart and were on the verge of surrender, but seeing that the only way to save their lives was to defy death they made a series of charges that almost dislodged the Muslims from their position in spite of their numbers, had not the grace of God been with them. As each wave of attackers fell back they left their dead behind them; their numbers diminished rapidly, while the Muslims were all around them like a circle about its diameter. The surviving Franks made for a hill near Hittīn, where they hoped to pitch their tents and defend themselves. They were vigorously attacked from all sides and prevented from pitching more than one tent, that of the King. The Muslims captured their great cross, called the "True Cross", in which they say is a piece of the wood upon which, according to them, the Messiah was crucified. This was one of the heaviest blows that could be inflicted on them and made their death and destruction certain. Large numbers of their cavalry and infantry were killed or captured. The King stayed on the hillside with five hundred of the most gallant and famous knights.

I was told that al-Malik al-Afdal, Saladin's son, said: "I was at my father Saladin's side during that battle, the first that I saw with my own eyes. The Frankish King had retreated to the hill with his band, and from there he led a furious charge against the Muslims facing him, forcing them back upon my father. I saw that he was alarmed and distraught, and he tugged at his beard as he went forward crying: 'Away with the Devil's lie!' The Muslims turned to counter-attack and drove the Franks back up the hill. When I saw the Franks retreating before the Muslim onslaught I cried out for joy: 'We have conquered them!' But they returned to the charge with undiminished ardour and drove our army back toward my father. His response was the same as before, and the Muslims counter-attacked and drove the Franks back to the hill. Again I cried: 'We have beaten them!' but my father turned to me and said: 'Be quiet; we shall not have beaten them until that tent falls!' As he spoke the tent fell, and the Sultan dismounted and prostrated himself in thanks to God, weeping for joy." This was how the tent fell: the Franks had been suffering terribly from thirst during that charge, which they hoped would win them a way out of their distress, but the way of escape was blocked. They dismounted and sat down on the ground and the Muslims fell upon them, pulled down the King's tent and captured every one of them, including the King, his brother, and Prince Arnāt of Karak, Islām's most hated enemy. They also took the ruler of Jubáil, the son of Humphrey (of Toron), the Grand Master of the Templars, one of the Franks' greatest dignitaries, and a band of Templars and Hospitallers. The number of dead and captured was so large that those who saw the slain could not believe that anyone could have been taken alive, and those who saw the prisoners could not believe that any had been killed. From the time of their first assault on Palestine in 491 / 1098 until now the Franks had never suffered such a defeat.

When all the prisoners had been taken Saladin went to his tent and sent for the King of the Franks and Prince Arnāt of Karak. He had the King seated beside him and as he was half-dead with thirst gave him iced water to drink. The King drank, and handed the rest to the Prince, who also drank. Saladin said: "This godless man did not have my permission to drink, and will not save his life that way." He turned on the Prince, casting his crimes in his teeth and enumerating his sins. Then he rose and with his own hand cut off the man's head. "Twice," he said, "I have sworn to kill that man when I had him in my power: once when he tried to attack Mecca and Medina, and again when he broke the truce to capture the caravan." When he was dead and had been dragged out of the tent the King began to tremble, but Saladin calmed and reassured him. As for the ruler of Tripoli, when he escaped from the battle, as we have described, he went to Tyre and from there made his way to Tripoli. He was there only a few days before he died of rage and fury at the disaster that had befallen the Franks in particular, and all Christendom in general.

When Saladin had brought about the downfall of the Franks he stayed at the site of the battle for the rest of the day, and on the Sunday returned to the siege of

Tiberias. The Countess sent to request safe-conducts for herself and her children, companions and possessions, and he granted her this. She left the citadel with all her train, and Saladin kept his word to her and let her escape unmolested. At the Sultan's command the King and a few of the most distinguished prisoners were sent to Damascus, while the Templars and Hospitallers were rounded up to be killed. The Sultan realized that those who had taken them prisoner were not going to hand them over, for they hoped to obtain ransoms for them, and so he offered fifty Egyptian *dinar* for each prisoner in these two categories. Immediately he got two hundred prisoners, who were decapitated at his command. He had these particular men killed because they were the fiercest of all the Frankish warriors, and in this way he rid the Muslim people of them. He sent orders to his commander in Damascus to kill all those found in his territory, whoever they belonged to, and this was done.

A year later I crossed the battlefield, and saw the land all covered with their bones, which could be seen even from a distance, lying in heaps or scattered around. These were what was left after all the rest had been carried away by storms or by the wild beasts of these hills and valleys. . . .

JERUSALEM RECONQUERED

When Saladin had completed his conquest of Ascalon and the surrounding regions he sent for the Egyptian fleet and a large detachment of troops under Husām ad-Din Lu'lu' al-Hajib, a man well known for his courage, energy and initiative. This force set out by sea, intercepting Frankish communications; every Frankish vessel they sighted they attacked, and captured every galley. When they arrived and Saladin could rely on their support, he marched from Ascalon to Jerusalem. The venerable Patriarch, who carried greater authority than the King himself, was there and so was Baliān ibn Barzān, ruler of ar-Ramla, who was almost equal in rank to the King. The knights who had survived Hittīn had also concentrated there. The inhabitants of that region, Ascalon and elsewhere had also gathered in Jerusalem, so there was a great concourse of people there, each one of whom would choose death rather than see the Muslims in power in their city; the sacrifice of life, possessions and sons was for them a part of their duty to defend the city. During that interval they fortified it by every means to hand, and then all mounted the walls, resolved to defend them with all their might, and showed determination to fight to the limit of their ability in the defence of Jerusalem. They mounted catapults to ward off attempts to approach the city and besiege it.

During Saladin's advance one of the amīrs went ahead with his band of men without taking any precautions to defend himself; a troop of Franks who had left Jerusalem on reconnaissance came face to face with him and in a battle killed him and some of his men, which caused great grief and sorrow to the Muslims. Half-way through rajab / September 1187 they besieged Jerusalem. As they approached they saw on the walls a terrifying crowd of men and heard an uproar of voices coming from the inhabitants behind the walls that led them to infer the number of people who must be assembled there. For five days the Sultan rode round the city to decide on the best point for the attack, for the city was more strongly defended than ever before. The only point at which to attack was on the north side, near the Bab 'Amuda and the Church of Zion. So on 20 rajab Saladin moved his army to the north side, and on the same evening began to mount his siege-engines. Next morning they were all ready and began their battery of the walls, from which the Franks replied with other machines that they had constructed there. Then began the fiercest struggle imaginable; each side looked on the fight as an absolute religious obligation. There was no need for a superior authority to drive them on: they restrained the enemy without restraint, and drove them off without being driven back. Every morning the Frankish cavalry made sorties to fight and provoke the enemy to battle; several of both sides fell in these encounters. Among the Muslim martyrs was the amīr 'Izz ad-Din Isa ibn Malik, one of the leading amīrs and the son of the ruler of Ja'bar. Every day he had led the attack himself, and at his death passed to God's great mercy; a man dear to Muslims both great and small, whose death brought grief and sorrow to many. They charged like one man, dislodged the Franks from their positions and drove them back into the city. When the Muslims reached the moat they crossed it, came up under the walls and began to breach them, protected by their archers and by continuous artillery fire which kept the walls clear of Franks and enabled the Muslims to make a breach and fill it with the usual materials.

When the Franks saw how violently the Muslims were attacking, how continuous and effective was the fire from the ballistas and how busily the sappers were breaching the walls, meeting no resistance, they grew desperate, and their leaders assembled to take counsel. They decided to ask for safe-conduct out of the city and to hand Jerusalem over to Saladin. They sent a deputation of their lords and nobles to ask for terms, but when they spoke of it to Saladin he refused to grant their request. "We shall deal with you," he said, "just as you dealt with the population of Jerusalem when you took it in 492 / 1099, with murder and enslavement and other such savageries!" The messengers returned empty-handed. Then Baliān ibn Barzān asked for safe-conduct for himself so that he might appear before Saladin to discuss developments. Consent was given, and he presented himself and once again began asking for a general amnesty in return for surrender. The Sultan still refused his requests and entreaties to show mercy. Finally, despairing of this approach, Baliān said: "Know, O Sultan, that there are very many of us in this city, God alone knows how many. At the moment we are fighting half-heartedly in the hope of saving our lives, hoping to be spared by you as you have spared others; this is because of our horror of death and our love of life. But if we see that death is inevitable, then by God we shall kill our children and our wives, burn our possessions, so as not to leave you with a *dinar* or a *drachma* or a single man or woman to enslave. When this is done, we shall pull down the Sanctuary of the Rock and the Masjid al-Aqsa and the other sacred places, slaughtering the Muslim prisoners we hold—5,000 of them— and killing every horse and animal we possess. Then we shall come out to fight you like men fighting for their lives, when each man, before he falls dead, kills his equals; we shall die with honour, or win a noble victory!" Then Saladin took counsel with his advisers, all of whom were in favour of his granting the assurances requested by the Franks, without forcing them to take extreme measures whose outcome could not be foreseen. "Let us consider them as being already our prisoners," they said, "and allow them to ransom themselves on terms agreed between us." The Sultan agreed to give the Franks assurances of safety on the understanding that each man, rich and poor alike, should pay ten *dinar,* children of both sexes two *dinar* and women five *dinar.* All who paid this sum within forty days should go free, and those who had not paid at the end of the time should be enslaved. Balian ibn Barzān offered 30,000 *dinar* as ransom for the poor, which was accepted, and the city surrendered on Friday 2 October 1187, a memorable day on which the Muslim flags were hoisted over the walls of Jerusalem.

The Grand Patriarch of the Franks left the city with the treasures from the Dome of the Rock, the Masjid al-Aqsa, the Church of the Resurrection and others, God alone knows the amount of the treasure; he also took an equal quantity of money. Saladin made no difficulties, and when he was advised to sequestrate the whole lot for Islām, replied that he would not go back on his word. He took only the ten *dinar* from him, and let him go, heavily escorted, to Tyre.

At the top of the cupola of the Dome of the Rock there was a great gilded cross. When the Muslims entered the city on the Friday, some of them climbed to the top of the cupola to take down the cross. When they reached the top a great cry went up from the city and from outside the walls, the Muslims crying the *Allāh akbar* in their joy, the Franks groaning in consternation and grief. So loud and piercing was the cry that the earth shook.

Once the city was taken and the infidels had left, Saladin ordered that the shrines should be restored to their original state. The Templars had built their living-quarters against al-Aqsa, with storerooms and latrines and other necessary offices, taking up part of the area of al-Aqsa. This was all restored to its former state. The Sultan ordered that the Dome of the Rock should be cleansed of all pollution, and this was done. On the following Friday, 4 sha'bān / 9 October, the Muslims celebrated the communal Friday prayers there. Among them was the Sultan, who also prayed at the Mosque of the Rock with Muhyi ad-Din ibn az-Zaki, qadi of Damascus, as imām and preacher. Then Saladin appointed a qadi and an (ordinary) imām for the five canonic prayers, and ordered that a pulpit should be built for him. He was told that Nur ad-Din had once had one made in Aleppo, which he had commanded the workmen to embellish and construct to the best of their ability, saying: "We have made this to set up in Jerusalem." The carpenters had taken so many years to make it that it had no rival in the whole of Islām. Saladin had it brought from Aleppo and set up in Jerusalem, more than twenty years after it was made. This was one of the noble deeds of Nur ad-Din and one of his good works, God have mercy on him!

After the Friday prayer Saladin gave orders for the restoration of al-Aqsa, giving every encouragement to its embellishment and having it faced with stone and fine mosaics. Marble of an unrivalled quality was brought, and golden tesserae from Constantinople and other necessary materials that had been kept in store for years, and the work of restoration was begun. To hide the pictures that covered the walls, the Franks had set slabs of marble over the Rock, concealing it from sight, and Saladin had them removed. It had been covered with the marble because the priests had sold a good part of it to the Franks who came from abroad on pilgrimages and bought pieces for their weight in gold in the hope of benefiting by its health-giving influences. Each of them, on his return home with a piece of this stone, would build a church for it and enclose it in the altar. One of the Frankish Kings of Jerusalem, afraid that it would all disappear, had it covered with a slab of marble to preserve it. When it was uncovered Saladin had some beautiful Qur'āns brought to the mosque, and magnificent copies of the sections of the Holy Book for use in worship. He established reciters of the Qur'ān there, heaping them with bountiful endowments. So Islām was restored there in full freshness and beauty. This noble act of conquest was achieved, after "Umar ibn al-Khattāb—God have mercy on him!—by no one but Saladin, and that is a sufficient title to glory and honour."

The Frankish population of Jerusalem who had not departed began to sell at very low prices all their possessions, treasures and whatever they could not carry with them. The merchants from the army and the non-Frankish Christians in Jerusalem bought their goods from them. The latter had asked Saladin's permission to remain in their homes if they paid the tax, and he had granted them this, so they stayed and bought up Frankish property. What they could not sell, beds and boxes and casks, the Franks left behind; even superb columns of marble and slabs of marble and mosaics in large quantities. Thus they departed.

✺ Farid ud-Din Attar

B. Iran, c. 1145–c. 1221

fah-REED

oo-DEEN ah-TAR

www For a quiz on
*The Conference of the
Birds,* see bedford
stmartins.com/
worldlitcompact.

The dates of **Farud ud-Din Attar's** birth and death are uncertain. He was born in the city of Neishapour in what is now northeastern Iran—also the home of the famous Persian poet Omar Khayyam (died c. 1123), author of *The Rubaiyat*—sometime around 1145. His name Attar, from the Persian word for perfume, identifies him as a perfumer, pharmacist, and medical practitioner, a profession he inherited from his father. Educated in medicine, Arabic, and theosophy at an Islamic school in Mashhad, he started work in his father's pharmacy before taking off several years to travel throughout the Middle East—to Egypt, Syria, Arabia, Turkestan, and India as well as important cities in Persia. Such travels were common at the time, particularly for Muslims on a spiritual quest and for poets who, like the troubadours of the West, went off in search of poetic inspiration.

One legend has it that Attar wrote 114 literary works, a number equal to the number of suras in the Qur'an (Koran), but the true number was probably fewer. Today he is remembered largely for two works, *Memorials of the Saints (Tadhkirat al-Auliya),* a collection of anecdotes about the lives of Islamic saints, and *The Conference of the Birds.* How Attar became a believer in **Sufism** is unknown. One story claims that he was accused of heresy, a danger for a believer in Sufism, which challenged the role of the established religious authorities. Even his death remains a mystery. One account reports that he died at the hands of the Mongols who invaded northern Persia in 1229 and were said to have massacred all 1.7 million **Neishapour** inhabitants. But Attar probably died earlier than the time of the invasion. In either case, his career marks the end of a great age of poetry in Persia. His younger follower, Rumi, would survive to write Persian poetry only by escaping to Turkey and eventually to Asia Minor.

nee-shah-POOR

Sufism.   Like mystics in all regions, the Sufis sought a direct, unmediated experience of the divine and pursued meditation and other spiritual disciplines as ways of achieving purification and approaching God. Some Sufi sects, which practice a form of dance as a spiritual discipline, are referred to as "whirling dervishes." *Sufi,* from the Arabic word for a wearer of wool, originally identified the mystical practitioners by the coarse cloth used in their clothing, similar to the hair shirts worn by some Western mystics who disciplined the body to free the spirit. Sufi doctrine asserts that God alone exists, extending the Islamic notion that there is no absolute reality except for God. This belief does not lead to **pantheism,** which asserts that everything is divine, but rather to **monism,** to the one truth that God alone is. This doctrine, along with their rejection of institutional mediators between humans and God, often brought Sufis dangerously close to heresy in the eyes of established Islamic clergy. **Mansur al-Hallaj**, for example, a tenth-century Sufi, after experiencing the unity of all things, was executed in Baghdad in 922 for asserting "I am the truth,"

mahn-SOOR

ahl-hah-LEJ

Phoenix Tile, 1270–80 C.E.
In Attar's spiritual allegory The Conference of the Birds, *a group of birds led by a hoopoe (similar to a hornbill) take a journey toward enlightenment. (British Museum / All rights reserved.)*

or "I am God." Attar considered al-Hallaj, who appeared to him in a dream, one of his important teachers.

The goal of Sufi practice is the extinction of the ego and the total identification of the believer with the divine, a state the Sufis describe as love. The process of arriving at this unified consciousness, the Way (*tariqah*), has clearly defined stages: repentance, avoidance of doubt, abstinence, poverty, perseverance, trust in God, and contentment. These spiritual states, which may overlap and do not necessarily occur in any particular order, make up the stages of the spiritual journey undertaken by the believer. They are also the beliefs on which Attar's poetry is based.

The Conference of the Birds.   Attar's famous poem translates the doctrines and disciplines of Sufism into popular **ALLEGORY**, a narrative in which the characters, settings, and episodes are meant to stand for another order of persons, places, and events. In the poem's allegorical

> Attar, along with Chaucer and Dante, was a great genius of community and how that involves the path toward enlightenment.
>
> – COLEMAN BARKS, translator

FRAME NARRATIVE, a story that frames another story, a hoopoe—a bird similar to the hornbill found in Europe, Africa, and Asia—calls a conference of birds to organize an expedition of all birds to seek their god, the Simorgh. At first the birds are enthusiastic, but when they consider the difficulty of the journey they manufacture excuses for why they are unable to go. The nightingale, for example, says he must remain behind to sing for the lovers who listen for his song, and the duck claims that he will be unable to stay clean while traveling. The hoopoe, who represents a spiritual teacher or Sufi master, answers each bird's excuses with a brief theological challenge and a story, parable, or fable to illustrate his point. After challenging all the birds' excuses, the hoopoe responds to their questions about the journey, its difficulties, with similar tales and fables. Finally, before setting out, the hoopoe describes each of the seven valleys of the Way that the birds will pass through on their journey: the quest, love, insight into mystery, detachment, unity, bewilderment, and nothingness. He illustrates each of these spiritual challenges with stories.

The actual journey takes up only a few pages of the poem. Only thirty birds arrive at the final destination. When they meet their god, the Simorgh, whose name means thirty *(si)* birds *(morgh)*, they allegorically fulfill the purpose of their quest. The Simorgh is themselves; the birds have become one with the divine.

Since there are no words to describe the mystical experience or the spiritual stages leading to it, the poet must speak in metaphors. Just as the birds' journey stands for the process of spiritual discipline and growth in the poem, so carnal love represents unity with the divine, sleep suggests spiritual contemplation, and intoxication stands for religious ecstasy. A number of the hoopoe's stories seem to transgress the strictures of Islam which, for example, forbids drinking and illicit sexuality. In "The Story of the Princess Who Loved a Slave," the hoopoe addresses spiritual bewilderment through a forbidden relationship across class lines, the couple's sexual fulfillment symbolizing spiritual ecstasy and understanding. Such dangerous stories may have been meant to challenge readers to abandon conventional dogmas and give fresh consideration to their spiritual condition.

The hoopoe's commentary frames all his stories, so their theological purpose is not forgotten. Perhaps the poet hoped the reader might also experience the unity of the divine and the human, since finally it was believed that there is no distinction between worldly and spiritual love.

■ FURTHER RESEARCH

Translations
Darbandi, Afkham, and Dick Davis. *The Conference of the Birds.* 1984.
Nott, C. S. *The Conference of the Birds.* 1971.

Commentary and Background
Fadiman, James, and Robert Frager, eds. *Essential Sufism.* 1997.
Morris, James Winston. "Reading *The Conference of the Birds.*" In *Approaches to the Asian Classics,* edited by William Theodore de Bary and Irene Bloom. 1990.
Yarshater, E. *Persian Literature.* 1987.

■ PRONUNCIATION

Azra'el: AZ-ray-el
Bismillah: bis-MIL-uh
Farid ud-Din Attar: fah-REED oo-DEEN ah-TAR, AT-ur
Mansur al-Hallaj: mahn-SOOR ahl-hah-LEJ
Neishapour: nee-shah-POOR

FROM

ꙮ The Conference of the Birds

Translated by Afkham Darbandi and Dick Davis

The Birds Assemble and the Hoopoe Tells Them of the Simorgh

The world's birds gathered for their conference
And said: 'Our constitution makes no sense.
All nations in the world require a king;
How is it we alone have no such thing?
Only a kingdom can be justly run;
We need a king and must inquire for one.'

They argued how to set about their quest.
The hoopoe fluttered forward; on his breast
There shone the symbol of the Spirit's Way
10   And on his head Truth's crown, a feathered spray.
Discerning, righteous and intelligent,
He spoke: 'My purposes are heaven-sent;
I keep God's secrets, mundane and divine,
In proof of which behold the holy sign
Bismillah[1] etched for ever on my beak.
No one can share the grief with which I seek
Our longed-for Lord, and quickened by my haste
My wits find water in the trackless waste.
I come as Solomon's close friend and claim

A note on the translation: The following selections from *The Conference of the Birds* are taken from the first English translation of the complete poem, that by Afkham Darbandi and Dick Davis published in 1984. This translation in rhymed couplets captures the character of Attar's *mathnavi* verse form, which rhymes the two halves of each line. Notes are the editors' unless otherwise indicated.

[1] *Bismillah:* "In the name of God": the opening words of the Qur'an. [Translator's note.]

20 The matchless wisdom of that mighty name
   (He never asked for those who quit his court,
   But when I left him once alone he sought
   With anxious vigilance for my return—
   Measure my worth by this great king's concern!).
   I bore his letters—back again I flew—
   Whatever secrets he divined I knew;
   A prophet loved me; God has trusted me;
   What other bird has won such dignity?
   For years I travelled over many lands,
30 Past oceans, mountains, valleys, desert sands,
   And when the Deluge rose I flew around
   The world itself and never glimpsed dry ground;
   With Solomon I set out to explore
   The limits of the earth from shore to shore.
   I know our king—but how can I alone
   Endure the journey to His distant throne?
   Join me, and when at last we end our quest
   Our king will greet you as His honoured guest.
   How long will you persist in blasphemy?
40 Escape your self-hood's vicious tyranny—
   Whoever can evade the Self transcends
   This world and as a lover he ascends.
   Set free your soul; impatient of delay,
   Step out along our sovereign's royal Way:
   We have a king; beyond Kaf's[2] mountain peak
   The Simorgh lives, the sovereign whom you seek,
   And He is always near to us, though we
   Live far from His transcendent majesty.
   A hundred thousand veils of dark and light
50 Withdraw His presence from our mortal sight,
   And in both worlds no being shares the throne
   That marks the Simorgh's power and His alone—
   He reigns in undisturbed omnipotence,
   Bathed in the light of His magnificence—
   No mind, no intellect can penetrate
   The mystery of His unending state:
   How many countless hundred thousands pray
   For patience and true knowledge of the Way
   That leads to Him whom reason cannot claim,
60 Nor mortal purity describe or name;

_____

[2] **Kaf:** A city in northwestern Saudi Arabia.

There soul and mind bewildered miss the mark
And, faced by Him, like dazzled eyes, are dark—
No sage could understand His perfect grace,
Nor seer discern the beauty of His face.
His creatures strive to find a path to Him,
Deluded by each new, deceitful whim,
But fancy cannot work as she would wish;
You cannot weigh the moon like so much fish!
How many search for Him whose heads are sent
70 Like polo-balls in some great tournament
From side to giddy side—how many cries,
How many countless groans assail the skies!
Do not imagine that the Way is short;
Vast seas and deserts lie before His court.
Consider carefully before you start;
The journey asks of you a lion's heart.
The road is long, the sea is deep—one flies
First buffeted by joy and then by sighs;
If you desire this quest, give up your soul
80 And make our sovereign's court your only goal.
First wash your hands of life if you would say:
"I am a pilgrim of our sovereign's Way";
Renounce your soul for love; He you pursue
Will sacrifice His inmost soul for you. [. . .]

The Parrot's Excuse

The pretty parrot was the next to speak,
Clothed all in green, with sugar in her beak,
And round her neck a circle of pure gold.
Even the falcon cannot boast so bold
A loveliness—earth's variegated green
Is but the image of her father's sheen,
And when she talks the fascinating sound
Seems sweet as costly sugar finely ground;
She trilled: "I have been caged by heartless men,
10 But my desire is to be free again;
If I could reassert my liberty
I'd find the stream of immortality
Guarded by Khezr[3]—his cloak is green like mine,
And this shared colour is an open sign

---

[3] **Khezr:** An enigmatic prophet mentioned in the Qur'an.

I am his equal or equivalent.
Only the stream Khezr watches could content
My thirsting soul — I have no wish to seek
This Simorgh's throne of which you love to speak.

THE HOOPOE ANSWERS HER

The hoopoe said: "You are a cringing slave —
This is not noble, generous or brave,
To think your being has no other end
Than finding water and a loyal friend.
Think well — what is it that you hope to gain?
Your coat is beautiful, but where's your brain?
Act as a lover and renounce your soul;
With love's defiance seek the lover's goal.

AN OSTENTATIOUS BIRD

Another bird declared: 'My happiness
Comes from the splendid things which I possess:
My palace walls inlaid with gold excite
Astonishment in all who see the sight.
They are a world of joy to me — how could
I wrench my heart from this surpassing good?
There I am king; all bow to my commands —
Shall I court ruin in the desert sands?
Shall I give up this realm, and live without
10   My certain glory in a world of doubt?
What rational mind would give up paradise
For wanderings filled with pain and sacrifice?'

THE HOOPOE ANSWERS HIM

The hoopoe said: 'Ungrateful wretch! Are you
A dog that you should need a kennel too?
This world's a kennel's filthy murk at best;
Your palace is a kennel with the rest.
If it seems paradise, at your last breath
You'll know it is your dungeon after death.
There'd be no harm in palaces like yours,
Did not the thought of death beat at our doors.

A KING WHO BUILT A SPLENDID PALACE

A king who loved his own magnificence
Once built a palace and spared no expense.
When this celestial building had been raised,
The gorgeous carpets and its splendour dazed
The crowd that pressed around—a servant flung
Trays heaped with money to the scrabbling throng.
The king now summoned all his wisest friends
And said: "What do I lack? Who recommends
Improvements to my court?" "We must agree,"
10 They said, "no man could now or ever see,
In all the earth, a palace built like this."
An old ascetic spoke. "One thing's amiss,"
He said; "there's one particular you lack.
This noble structure has a nasty crack
(Though if it weren't for that it would suffice
To be the heavenly court of paradise)."
The king replied: "What crack? Where is it? Where?
If you've come here for trouble, then take care!"
The man said: "Lord, it is the truth I tell—
20 And through that crack will enter Azra'el.[4]
It may be you can block it, but if not,
Then throne and palace are not worth a jot!
Your palace now seems like some heavenly prize,
But death will make it ugly to your eyes;
Nothing remains for ever and you know—
Although you live here now—that this is so.
Don't pride yourself on things that cannot last;
Don't gallop your high-stepping horse so fast.
If one like me is left to indicate
30 Your faults to you, I pity your sad fate."

THE SPIDER

You've seen an active spider work—he seems
To spend his life in self-communing dreams;
In fact the web he spins is evidence
That he's endowed with some far-sighted sense.
He drapes a corner with his cunning snare
And waits until a fly's entangled there,

---

[4] **Azra'el:** The angel of death. [Translators' note.]

Then dashes out and sucks the meagre blood
Of his bewildered, buzzing, dying food.
He'll dry the carcass then, and live off it
10 For days, consuming bit by tasty bit—
Until the owner of the house one day
Will reach up casually to knock away
The cunning spider's home—and with her broom
She clears both fly and spider from the room.

Such is the world, and one who feeds there is
A fly trapped by that spider's subtleties;
If all the world is yours, it will pass by
As swiftly as the blinking of an eye;
And though you boast of kings and patronage,
20 You are a child, an actor on a stage.
Don't seek for wealth unless you are a fool;
A herd of cows is all that you can rule!
Whoever lives for banners, drums and glory
Is dead; the dervish understands this story
And calls it windy noise—winds vainly flap
The banners, hollowly the brave drums tap.
Don't gallop on the horse of vanity;
Don't pride yourself on your nobility.
They skin the leopard for his splendid pelt;
30 They'll flay you too before your nose has smelt
A whiff of danger. When your life's made plain,
Which will be better, death or chastening pain?
You cannot hold your head up then—obey!
How long must you persist in childish play?
Either give up your wealth or lay aside
The rash pretensions of your crazy pride.
Your palace and your gardens! They're your gaol,
The dungeon where your ruined soul will wail.
Forsake this dusty pride, know what it's worth;
40 Give up your restless pacing of the earth.
To see the Way, look with the eyes of thought;
Set out on it and glimpse the heavenly court—
And when you reach that souls' asylum, then
Its glory will blot out the world of men.

THE RESTLESS FOOL AND THE DERVISH

A fool dashed onward at a reckless pace
Till in the desert he came face to face
With one who wore the ragged dervish cloak,

And asked: "What is your work?" The dervish spoke:
"Poor shallow wretch, can you not see I faint
With this strict pressure of the world's constraint?"
"Constraint? That can't be right," the man replied;
"The empty desert stretches far and wide."
The dervish said: "If there is no strict Way,
10 How has it led you to me here today?"

A myriad promises beguile your mind,
But flames of greed are all that you can find.
What are such flames? Tread down the world's desire,
And like a lion shun this raging fire.
Accomplish this, and you will find your heart;
There waits your palace, pure in every part.
Fire blocks the path, the goal is long delayed—
Your heart's a captive and your soul's afraid,
But in the midst of such an enterprise
20 You will escape this universe of lies.
When worldly pleasures cloy, prepare to die—
The world gives neither name nor truth, pass by!
The more you see of it the less you see,
How often must I warn you to break free?

A Bird Asks How Long the Journey Is, and the Hoopoe Describes the Seven Valleys of the Way

Another bird said: "Hoopoe, you can find
The way from here, but we are almost blind—
The path seems full of terrors and despair.
Dear Hoopoe, how much further till we're there?"

"Before we reach our goal," the hoopoe said,
"The journey's seven valleys lie ahead;
How far this is the world has never learned,
For no one who has gone there has returned—
Impatient bird, who would retrace this trail?
10 There is no messenger to tell the tale,
And they are lost to our concerns below—
How can men tell you what they do not know?
The first stage is the Valley of the Quest;
Then Love's wide valley is our second test;
The third is Insight into Mystery,
The fourth Detachment and Serenity—
The fifth is Unity; the sixth is Awe,
A deep Bewilderment unknown before,

20   The seventh Poverty and Nothingness—
     And there you are suspended, motionless,
     Till you are drawn—the impulse is not yours—
     A drop absorbed in seas that have no shores.

THE VALLEY OF BEWILDERMENT

     Next comes the Valley of Bewilderment,
     A place of pain and gnawing discontent—
     Each second you will sigh, and every breath
     Will be a sword to make you long for death;
     Blinded by grief, you will not recognize
     The days and nights that pass before your eyes.
     Blood drips from every hair and writes "Alas"
     Beside the highway where the pilgrims pass;
     In ice you fry, in fire you freeze—the Way
10   Is lost, with indecisive steps you stray—
     The Unity you knew has gone; your soul
     Is scattered and knows nothing of the Whole.
     If someone asks: "What is your present state;
     Is drunkenness or sober sense your fate,
     And do you flourish now or fade away?"
     The pilgrim will confess: "I cannot say;
     I have no certain knowledge any more;
     I doubt my doubt, doubt itself is unsure;
     I love, but who is it for whom I sigh?
20   Not Moslem, yet not heathen; who am I?
     My heart is empty, yet with love is full;
     My own love is to me incredible."

THE STORY OF THE PRINCESS WHO LOVED A SLAVE

     A great king had a daughter whose fair face
     Was like the full moon in its radiant grace,
     She seemed a Joseph,[5] and her dimpled chin
     The well that lovely youth was hidden in—
     Her face was like a paradise; her hair
     Reduced a hundred hearts to love's despair;
     Her eyebrows were two bows bent back to shoot
     The arrows of love's passionate dispute;

---

[5] **Joseph:** The story of Joseph, the favorite son of Jacob, recounted in both the Qur'an and the Hebrew Scriptures, is frequently alluded to in *The Conference of the Birds*. Since Joseph was said to be of unsurpassed beauty, he is frequently compared to heroes and heroines as the standard for beauty.

The pointed lashes of her humid eyes
10 Were thorns strewn in the pathway of the wise;
The beauty of this sun deceived the train
Of stars attendant on the moon's pale reign;
The rubies of her mouth were like a spell
To fascinate the angel Gabriel—
Beside her smile, her sweet, reviving breath,
The waters of eternal life seemed death;
Whoever saw her chin was lost and fell
Lamenting into love's unfathomed well;
And those she glanced at sank without a sound—
20 What rope could reach the depths in which they drowned?
It happened that a handsome slave was brought
To join the retinue that served at court,
A slave, but what a slave! Compared with him
The sun and moon looked overcast and dim.
He was uniquely beautiful—and when
He left the palace, women, children, men
Would crowd into the streets and market-place,
A hundred thousand wild to see his face.
One day the princess, by some fateful chance,
30 Caught sight of this surpassing elegance,
And as she glimpsed his face she felt her heart,
Her intellect, her self-control depart—
Now reason fled and love usurped its reign;
Her sweet soul trembled in love's bitter pain.
For days she meditated, struggled, strove,
But bowed at last before the force of love
And gave herself to longing, to the fire
Of passionate, insatiable desire.

Attendant on the daughter of the king
40 Were ten musicians, slave girls who could sing
Like nightingales—whose captivating charms
Would rival David's[6] when he sang the psalms.
The princess set aside her noble name
And whispered to these girls her secret shame
(When love has first appeared who can expect
The frenzied lover to be circumspect?),
Then said: "If I am honest with this slave

---

[6] **David** (c. 1012–c. 972 B.C.E.): King of the ancient Hebrews whose story is told in both the Hebrew Scriptures and the Qur'an. Traditionally regarded as the author of many of the Psalms.

And tell my love, who knows how he'll behave?
My honour's lost if he should once discover
50   His princess wishes that she were his lover!
But if I can't make my affection plain
I'll die, I'll waste away in secret pain;
I've read a hundred books on chastity
And still I burn — what good are they to me?
No, I must have him; this seductive youth
Must sleep with me and never know the truth —
If I can secretly achieve my goal
Love's bliss will satisfy my thirsting soul."
Her girls said: "Don't despair; tonight we'll bring
60   Your lover here and he won't know a thing."
One of them went to him — she simpered, smiled,
And O! how easily he was beguiled;
He took the drugged wine she'd prepared — he drank,
Then swooned — unconscious in her arms he sank,
And in that instant all her work was done;
He slept until the setting of the sun.
Night came and all was quiet as the grave;
Now, stealthily, the maidens brought this slave,
Wrapped in a blanket, to their mistress' bed
70   And laid him down with jewels about his head.
Midnight: he opened his dazed, lovely eyes
And stared about him with a mute surprise —
The bed was massy gold; the chamber seemed
An earthly paradise that he had dreamed;
Two candles made of ambergris burnt there
And with their fainting fragrance filled the air;
The slave girls made such music that his soul
Seemed beckoned onward to some distant goal;
Wine passed from hand to hand; the candles' light
80   Flared like a sun to drive away the night.
But all the joys of this celestial place
Could not compare with her bewitching face,
At which he stared as if struck senseless, dumb,
Lost both to this world and the world to come —
His heart acknowledged love's supremacy;
His soul submitted to love's ecstasy;
His eyes were fixed on hers, while to his ears
The girls' song seemed the music of the spheres;
He smelt the burning candles' ambergris;
90   His mouth burnt with the wine, then with her kiss;
He could not look away, he could not speak,
But tears of eloquence coursed down his cheek —

And she too wept, so that each kiss was graced
With salty sweetness mingled in one taste,
Or he would push aside her stubborn hair
And on her lovely eyes in wonder stare.
Thus, in each other's arms, they passed the night
Until, worn out by sensual delight,
By passion, by the vigil they had kept,
100 As dawn's cool breeze awoke, the young man slept.

Then, as he slept, they carried him once more
And laid him gently on his own hard floor.
He woke, he slowly knew himself again—
Astonishment, regret, grief's aching pain
Swept over him (though what could grief achieve?
The scene had fled and it was vain to grieve).
He bared his body, ripped his tattered shirt,
Tore out his hair, besmeared his head with dirt—
And when his friends asked what assailed his heart,
110 He cried: "How can I say? Where could I start?
No dreamer, no, no seer could ever see
What I saw in that drunken ecstasy;
No one in all the world has ever known
The bliss vouchsafed to me, to me alone—
I cannot tell you what I saw; I saw
A stranger sight than any seen before."
They said: "Try to remember what you've done,
And of a hundred joys describe just one."
He answered: "Was it me who saw that face?
120 Or did some other stand there in my place?
I neither saw nor heard a thing, and yet
I saw and heard what no man could forget."
A fool suggested: "It's some dream you had;
Some sleepy fantasy has sent you mad."
He asked: "Was it a dream, or was it true?
Was I drunk or sober? I wish I knew—
The world has never known a state like this,
This paradox beyond analysis,
Which haunts my soul with what I cannot find,
130 Which makes me speechless speak and seeing blind.
I saw perfection's image, beauty's queen,
A vision that no man has ever seen
(What is the sun before that face?—God knows
It is a mote, a speck that comes and goes!).
But did I see her? What more can I say?
Between this 'yes' and 'no' I've lost my way!"

The Grieving Mother and the Sufi

Beside her daughter's grave a mother grieved.
A sufi said: "This woman has perceived
The nature of her loss; her heart knows why
She comes to mourn, for whom she has to cry—
She grieves, but knowledge makes her fortunate:
Consider now the sufi's wretched state!
What daily, nightly vigils I must keep
And never know for whom it is I weep;
I mourn in lonely darkness, unaware
10 Whose absence is the cause of my despair.
Since she knows what has caused her agony,
She is a thousand times more blest than me—
I have no notion of what makes me weep,
What prompts the painful vigils I must keep.
My heart is lost, and here I cannot find
That rope by which men live, the rational mind—
The key to thought is lost; to reach this far
Means to despair of who and what you are.
And yet it is to see within the soul—
20 And at a stroke—the meaning of the Whole."

The Man Who Had Lost His Key

A sufi heard a cry: "I've lost my key;
If it's been found, please give it back to me—
My door's locked fast; I wish to God I knew
How I could get back in. What can I do?"
The sufi said: "And why should you complain?
You know where this door is; if you remain
Outside it—even if it is shut fast—
Someone no doubt will open it at last.
You make this fuss for nothing; how much more
10 Should I complain, who've lost both key and door!"
But if this sufi presses on, he'll find
The closed or open door which haunts his mind.
Men cannot understand the sufis' state,
That deep Bewilderment which is their fate.
To those who ask: "What can I do?" reply:
"Bid all that you have done till now goodbye!"
Once in the Valley of Bewilderment
The pilgrim suffers endless discontent,
Crying: "How long must I endure delay,
20 Uncertainty? When shall I see the Way?

When shall I know? O, when?" But knowledge here
Is turned again to indecisive fear;
Complaints become a grateful eulogy
And blasphemy is faith, faith blasphemy.

THE BIRDS DISCOVER THE SIMORGH

The thirty birds read through the fateful page
And there discovered, stage by detailed stage,
Their lives, their actions, set out one by one —
All that their souls had ever been or done:
And this was bad enough, but as they read
They understood that it was they who'd led
The lovely Joseph into slavery —
Who had deprived him of his liberty
Deep in a well, then ignorantly sold
10   Their captive to a passing chief for gold.[7]
(Can you not see that at each breath you sell
The Joseph you imprisoned in that well,
That he will be the king to whom you must
Naked and hungry bow down in the dust?)
The chastened spirits of these birds became
Like crumbled powder, and they shrank with shame.
Then, as by shame their spirits were refined
Of all the world's weight, they began to find
A new life flow towards them from that bright
20   Celestial and ever-living Light —
Their souls rose free of all they'd been before;
The past and all its actions were no more.
Their life came from that close, insistent sun
And in its vivid rays they shone as one.
There in the Simorgh's[8] radiant face they saw
Themselves, the Simorgh of the world — with awe
They gazed, and dared at last to comprehend
They were the Simorgh and the journey's end.
They see the Simorgh — at themselves they stare,
30   And see a second Simorgh standing there;
They look at both and see the two are one,
That this is that, that this, the goal is won.

---

[7] **led the lovely Joseph . . . for gold:** Joseph's brothers, jealous of their father's favoritism, cast Joseph into a
well and sold him into slavery.

[8] **the Simorgh:** The meaning of this crucial moment depends on a pun: *si* means "thirty," *morgh* means
"bird(s)." . . . It was probably this pun which suggested the idea of the poem to Attar. [Translators' note.]

They ask (but inwardly; they make no sound)
The meaning of these mysteries that confound
Their puzzled ignorance—how is it true
That 'we' is not distinguished here from 'you'?
And silently their shining Lord replies:
'I am a mirror set before your eyes,
And all who come before my splendour see
40 Themselves, their own unique reality;
You came as thirty birds and therefore saw
These selfsame thirty birds, not less nor more;
If you had come as forty, fifty—here
An answering forty, fifty, would appear;
Though you have struggled, wandered, travelled far,
It is yourselves you see and what you are.'
(Who sees the Lord? It is himself each sees;
What ant's sight could discern the Pleiades?
What anvil could be lifted by an ant?
50 Or could a fly subdue an elephant?)
'How much you thought you knew and saw; but you
Now know that all you trusted was untrue.
Though you traversed the Valleys' depths and fought
With all the dangers that the journey brought,
The journey was in Me, the deeds were Mine—
You slept secure in Being's inmost shrine.
And since you came as thirty birds, you see
These thirty birds when you discover Me,
The Simorgh, Truth's last flawless jewel, the light
60 In which you will be lost to mortal sight,
Dispersed to nothingness until once more
You find in Me the selves you were before.'
Then, as they listened to the Simorgh's words,
A trembling dissolution filled the birds—
The substance of their being was undone,
And they were lost like shade before the sun;
Neither the pilgrims nor their guide remained.
The Simorgh ceased to speak, and silence reigned.

Andalusian and European Love Lyrics

The creation of the most renowned love lyrics of the European Middle Ages depended on three principal factors: the rich Arabic culture in the Andalusian (Spanish) courts in the eleventh century; the development of the neighboring courts in the south of France in the twelfth and early thirteenth centuries; and the spread of the idea of refined love to other European countries. One important feature of this literary movement was the veneration of women; along with it came the sublimation of sexual longing expressed in the poetry. At the same time, themes of knights in combat, so popular at the beginning of the Crusades, gave way to a more idealized form of chivalry, emphasizing the practice of knightly manners and fidelity to the rules of love at court. Eventually the figure of the knight itself gave way to that of the courtier as poet.

ANDALUSIAN ORIGINS

Following their expansion through Asia Minor, North Africa, and Spain in the eighth century, the conquering Muslims soon developed a more open, tolerant society, declaring that the Christians and Jews living under their authority were PEOPLE OF THE BOOK (Hebrew Scriptures and the New Testament) and protecting them within the Islamic state. This protection proved important in Andalusia, under whose CALIPHATE (the leading religious and political office) Muslims, Christians, and Jews enjoyed mutual commerce and communication. In this way, the population shared a common culture deferential to Islam, and developed a vernacular language composed of Spanish, Hebrew, and Arabic elements called *MOZARABIC.*

moh-ZEH-ruh-bik

Andalusia inherited the rich Islamic culture of the Middle East, famous for its architecture, philosophy, literature, music, and courtly society. Borrowing from the ancient Arabic poetic tradition that included the lengthy and complex *QASIDAHS* or odes, Andalusian writers had a sophisticated base on which to create their work. The new poetry, with its apparent spontaneity dictated in part by traditional rules of composition, reflected the cultivation of the courtly society. While the language usually employed for this poetry was Arabic, Jewish writers also adapted Hebrew poetry to fit the new style. Gradually Andalusian poetry adopted vernacular forms of expression from the Mozarabic language, broadening its popular appeal.

kuh-SEE-duhs

ARABIC, JEWISH, AND MOZARABIC POETRY

The cosmopolitan culture of Andalusia reached its height in Cordova in the tenth and eleventh centuries. During this time the *GHAZAL* or love poem developed from the opening lines of the classical *qasidah;* originally distinguished by nostalgia, the *ghazal* became increasingly direct and sensual. Love was either celebrated as a source of exuberant joy or regarded as an unhealthy obsession. Eventually two more poetic forms grew out of the *ghazal*. One, the MUWASHSHAH, contained five or six identically rhymed strophes followed by a short concluding stanza called a KHARJA, expressing direct emotion, usually in Mozarabic. The second form, the ZAJAL, consisted of elaborately rhymed strophes or stanzas in Mozarabic, without the *kharja* ending. The development of these types of love poetry made Andalusian poetry both more accessible and more immediate in tone.

GAZ-ul

moo-WAH-shah
KAR-juh
zah-JAHL

Several trends were at work in Andalusian poetry at this time. **Ibn Hazm**, a young poet and scholar from Cordova, wrote *The Dove's Necklace*, a treatise on love including many of his own poems, in 1022. His poetry and other Arabic and Jewish poetry of his day expressed the ideal of refinement in love, deriving largely from the influence of the Greek philosopher Plato. Other Arabic love poetry

IB-un HAH-zum,
HAZ-um, p. 1419

◀ **Lovers, 1344**
While the earliest courtly love poetry had its roots in Muslim Spain, its European counterpart lasted well into the fourteenth century, as this late manuscript illumination of a gentleman paying court to a lady attests. (The Art Archive / Science Academy, Lisbon / Dagli Orti)

IB-un zigh-DOON

p. 1429

JOO-duh hah-LAY-vee

p. 1431

proh-vawn-SAHL

of Ibn Hazm's time was less restrained. In the eleventh century the Muslim court of Cordova saw an exchange of poetry between the famous courtier **Ibn Zaydun** and his lover Wallada, the daughter of the last of the caliphs in her family line. Zaydun's meditative *ghazal,* **"Written from al-Zahrā,"** expresses the melancholy typical of earlier Arabic odes.

In the early twelfth century a number of Jewish poets, including **Judah ha-Levi** (Yehuda Ha Levi), wrote poems in Hebrew employing the Arabic style. His love poems also recall the lush imagery of The Song of Solomon from Hebrew Scriptures. The poem **"The Apple"** combines Arabic and Hebrew sentiment, describing the captivity of the male lover in terms of courtly love and the physical attributes of his beloved in the language of the Scriptures.

DEVELOPMENTS IN THE SOUTH OF FRANCE

In part because of a booming agricultural economy and an increase in trade generated by the Crusades, rich courts developed in the south of France, especially in Provence and Languedoc, in the latter half of the eleventh century. The region was distinguished by its unique language, **Provençal**, and its cultural refinement. Especially famous was the love poetry composed by professional artists at court called troubadours, who sometimes accompanied themselves on a musical instrument but more often were accompanied by a musician called a *joglar.*

There was a strong historical reason for the patronage of poetry by these courts. Changes in property laws allowed women to inherit estates, and several women, notably Eleanor of Aquitaine and her daughter, Marie of Champagne, established reputations not only as new members of the landed nobility but as patrons of the arts. They particularly encouraged the composition of songs of love. They may have been responsible for introducing ideas of jurisprudence into the love poems designed for courtly entertainment. Knights and other court followers were taught to plead a case for their love, and Eleanor and her daughter even passed down "verdicts" on the love pleadings in the court of Poitiers, one of the leading cities in southern France.

The Provençal poetry is often associated with the treatise *The Art of Courtly Love,* written by the twelfth century priest Andreas

Troubadour, thirteenth century

A troubadour plays musical court to two princesses and their attendants. (The Art Archive / Real Biblioteca de lo Escorial / Dagli Orti)

Capellanus at the court in Poitiers. In it, Capellanus examines the phenomenon of *fin'amor*, or refined love, as it was practiced in the lavish courts of his day. This doctrine of love, which later scholars would term courtly love, lay behind much of the poetry being written in the region in the twelfth century. The kind of love discussed by Capellanus includes the sublimation of sexual desire; the worship of the aristocratic lady of one's choosing; and obedience to the rules of secrecy and discretion. Some of this work was probably seen as entertainment, designed to flatter and delight the lord and lady of the household. But the doctrine of *fin'amor* also may have been intended to educate all men and women of rank in courtly society in the etiquette properly attached to love.

fin-ah-MORE

PROVENÇAL POETRY

gee-YOME

p. 1432

The first recorded Provençal troubadour, **Guillaume IX**, duke of Aquitaine, composed love poems in two different styles, bawdy and refined. Eventually his zesty tales of sexual exploits, replete with double meanings and vulgar humor, gave way to more sophisticated poems of *fin'amor*. Guillaume's patronage encouraged other poets to follow in his footsteps, and also may have influenced their choice of themes. A suitably cautious approach to love can be found in

mar-kuh-BROO

p. 1436

Marcabru's "By the fountain in the orchard." Here, a knight attempting to catch a lady's attention defers to her despondency over the absence of her lover, who is off on Crusade. Seeing her innocence reflected in her failure to understand his flirtation, the knight wisely retreats.

One consequence of the poetry of *fin'amor* was the elevation of women to a position of near-adoration. In medieval society this represented a considerable advance for the women at court, surrounded as they were by a hitherto unruly and unmannerly knighthood. And yet the women still were spoken for, rather than speaking for themselves. Gradually, however, women of high birth developed a poetic idiom of their own. As had happened in the Arabic courts of Spain, some European women became poets and performers. In

p. 1437

her poem "Of things I'd rather keep in silence," the **Countess of Dia** addresses her complaint to her lover in a voice both candid and authoritative.

THE FATE OF THE LYRIC TRADITION

In both Andalusia and the south of France, the courtly poets suffered a cruel fate in the thirteenth century. In Andalusia, the Spanish Reconquest was virtually assured by the Christian victory over Muslim forces at Las Navas de Tolosa, between Toledo and Cordova, in 1212. Cordova fell in 1236, and the activity of the remaining Andalusian courts was significantly curtailed. Meanwhile, in 1209 Pope Innocent III preached the Albigensian Crusade, directed against the rulers of the south of France who had tolerated the presence of **Catharist** heretics in their region. Soon the southern courts and their cultures were all but destroyed and the Provençal language was officially replaced by French. Whatever was left of the old culture was quashed in the middle of the thirteenth century by

KATH-ur-ist

the heresy hunters of the Catholic Inquisition, who followed the Crusaders into the region.

FROM COURTLY LOVE TO RENAISSANCE SONNET

Gradually the love songs of the troubadours and the doctrine of fin'amor spread across Europe, influencing the poets of Christian Spain and Portugal, northern France, Germany, and Italy. Wherever they went, they were influenced by the courtly and literary environment of the host country. But in another hundred years, a more profound change began to occur in Italy—a change in sensibility that would affect all the arts, from sculpture and painting to poetry and music. This was the phenomenon of Renaissance humanism, emphasizing the enriched expression of individual personality.

p. 1439

The earliest model of the Renaissance poet was **Francesco Petrarch** (1307–1374), whose celebrated sonnets to Laura invested the European lyric with a personal intensity and depth of feeling rarely achieved by either the troubadours of Provence or his immediate Italian predecessors. Petrarch's crafted poems, reflecting the unresolved tension between physical desire and love, were further influenced by the resurgence of classical studies in the Humanist tradition. Widely translated in all the vernacular languages of Europe, Petrarch's work had such influence that later writers of lyrics found it difficult to avoid being seen as his imitators.

The sonnet, a fourteen-line poem with a fixed ordering of stanzas and a consistent rhyme scheme throughout, was more narrowly structured than the ordinary Provençal or European courtly love lyric. It required considerable compression of material, and the ordering of the stanzas often resulted in inner tensions of logic and emotion within a single poem. For the Italian sonnets of Petrarch, the rhyme scheme was not as challenging as it would prove to be in other languages, because Italian is a Romance language with a large rhyming vocabulary. The eight-line, six-line stanza division of the Italian sonnet allowed Petrarch to either expand upon or challenge his original idea in the second and final stanza.

Like the earlier courtly love poetry, the sonnet form spread throughout Europe. The practice of the sonnet became an enduring phenomenon, with perhaps its greatest period of popularity coming in the sixteenth century in Italy, Spain, France, and England.

p. 1444
p. 1445

The British nobleman **Sir Thomas Wyatt** (1503–1542) achieved fame by skillfully translating Petrarchan sonnets into English and writing his own sonnets in imitation of them. Several generations later, the London playwright **William Shakespeare** (1564–1616) published his sonnets near the end of his lifetime. While Wyatt's refashioning of Petrarch reveals at once both his indebtedness and innovation concerning the work of the master, Shakespeare's ambivalent attitude towards both the subject matter and form of the sonnet is one of the pleasures of his work.

Petrarchan poetry employed certain conventional motifs, or thematic elements, including paradoxes (opposite qualities placed in close connection), conceits (extended, often unexpected metaphors), and lengthy descriptions of imagined thoughts of the beloved, which could run from favorable response to cold indifference. There were also multiple comparisons of the beloved's physical features to images drawn from nature or other sources. What first seemed original in Petrarch's poetry grew stale through repetition (for instance, the lady's cheeks compared to a rose), so that eventually Shakespeare challenged this kind of imagery with his Sonnet 130, which begins by categorically stating "My mistress' eyes are nothing like the sun."

■ **FURTHER RESEARCH**

Anthologies and Collections
Franzen, Cola. *Poems of Arab Andalusia.* 1989.
Goldin, Frederick. *Lyrics of the Troubadours and Trouveres.* 1963.
O'Donoghue, Bernard. *The Courtly Love Tradition.* 1982.
Press, Alan R. *Anthology of Troubadour Lyric Poetry.* 1971.

Criticism and History
Bergin, Thomas. *Petrarch.* 1970.
Bogin, Meg. *The Women Troubadours.* 1980.
Lewis, C. S. *The Allegory of Love: A Study in Medieval Tradition.* 1936.
Minta, Stephen. *Petrarch and Petrarchism: The English and French Traditions.* 1980.
Vendler, Helen. *The Art of Shakespeare's Sonnets.* 1997.
Waller, Marguerite R. *Petrarch's Poetics and Literary History.* 1980.

■ **PRONUNCIATION**

Cathars, Catharist: KATH-urz, KATH-ur-ist
Cordova: KORE-duh-vuh
fin'amor: fin-ah-MORE
ghazal: GAZ-ul
Guillaume: gee-YOME
Ibn Hazm: IB-un HAH-zum, HAZ-um
Ibn Zaydun: IB-un zigh-DOON

joglar: joh-GLAR
Judah ha-Levi: JOO-duh hah-LAY-vee
kharja: KAR-juh
Marcabru: mar-kuh-BROO
Mozarabic: moh-ZEH-ruh-bik
muwashshah: moo-WAH-shah
Provençal: proh-vawn-SAHL
Provence: proh-VAWNS, proh-VAWNGS
qasidah: kuh-SEE-duh
Toledo: toh-LAY-doh
trobairitz: troh-bigh-RITS
troubadour: troo-bah-DOHR
vers: VEHRS
zajal: zah-JAHL

∾ IBN HAZM
B. ANDALUSIA (SPAIN), 994–1064

Ibn Hazm, an Islamic philosopher known for his encyclopedic treatment of the religions of the West and Asia Minor, endured many hardships as a young man. The sack of his native Cordova by Berber tribesmen in 1012, the death of his father later the same year, and the death of his first love in 1013 led to his decision to dedicate himself to serious studies as a moral and spiritual response to an unstable world. He accepted a request less than a decade later to write a treatise on love, stating that those who have grieved excessively should perform an apparently light task in order to strengthen the soul for hard work ahead. He completed the treatise in 1022, before reaching thirty.

The Dove's Necklace.   The treatise entitled *Tawq al-hamamah,* or *The Dove's Necklace,* consisted of thirty chapters "about love and lovers." A remarkable example of Arabic *adab,* or sophisticated writing—what Europeans call *belles lettres*—this frank treatment of love made up partly of the author's own reflections, including his poetry, was attacked by Muslim authorities for "encouraging evil"—language from the Qur'an. Nevertheless, it enjoyed immense popular success in Andalusia and was translated many times over during the European Middle Ages.

The chief source of Ibn Hazm's philosophy of love is in the writings of Plato, especially *The Symposium.* The importance of love for Ibn Hazm lies in spiritual attainment, though he recognizes physical attraction. Like Plato and most Arabic writers of his own day, Ibn Hazm takes into account homosexual as well as heterosexual love. He distances himself from Christian teaching on one hand and Ovid's *The Art of Love,* with its emphasis on sexual conquest, on the other. At the same time, he does include a "moral" ending to his work—a chapter on continence—somewhat similar to the retractions found in other writers on love, including Ovid and Andreas Capellanus.

The Dove's Necklace devotes ten chapters to the origins of love; twelve to the circumstances in which love is found; six to the catastrophes to

Reconciliation, thirteenth century

Very few illustrated manuscripts survive from the Andalusian (Muslim) period in Spanish history. This illustration is from a romance that tells the story of a young merchant who falls in love with a handmaiden (personal servant). In this scene the merchant supplicates the handmaiden's mistress, pleading for her help in winning the heart of his beloved. (From the "Hadith Bayad wa Riyad" manuscript, folio 26v.
© *Biblioteca Apostolica Vaticana)*

which love is subject; and two to the evils of passion and the superiority of continence (which means sexual restraint rather than complete abstinence). Ibn Hazm concludes his work by listing the calamities he has endured in his brief lifetime and stating his hope that his good behavior in the world will justify his having written on the subject of love. The excerpt presented here includes material taken primarily from the work's first section, on the origins of love, which addresses the signs of love, falling in love through a description of the beloved, love at first sight, love after a long familiarity, and love because of a single personal quality. The final excerpt comes from a later chapter on the unity of love. These selections exclude Ibn Hazm's poetic interludes and concentrate on the prose writing.

Ibn Hazm also achieved a reputation as a poet. In his poetry, too, he stresses the spiritual aspect of love, an emphasis common among the Muslim upper classes of his time. Thus he borrows from an existing tradition when he writes about love's secrecy, its hidden signs, and its power and authority. In the poem "My Beloved Comes," his seemingly original comparison of the rainbow to the peacock's tail is an example of metaphor long practiced in the refined poetic tradition.

FROM

ꙮ The Dove's Necklace

Translated by A. J. Arberry

Love has certain signs which the intelligent man quickly detects and the shrewd man readily recognizes. Of these the first is the brooding gaze: the eye is the wide gateway of the soul, the scrutinizer of its secrets, conveying its most private thoughts and giving expression to its deepest-hid feelings. You will see the lover gazing at the beloved unblinkingly; his eyes follow the loved one's every movement, withdrawing as he withdraws, inclining as he inclines, just as the chameleon's stare shifts with the shifting of the sun.

The lover will direct his conversation to the beloved even when he purports, however earnestly, to address another: the affection is apparent to anyone with eyes to see. When the loved one speaks, the lover listens with rapt attention to his every word; he marvels at everything the beloved says, however extraordinary and absurd his observations may be; he believes him implicitly even when he is clearly lying, agrees with him though he is obviously in the wrong, testifies on his behalf for all that he may be unjust, follows after him however he may proceed and whatever line of argument he may adopt. The lover hurries to the spot where the beloved is at the moment, endeavours to sit as near to him as possible, sidles up close to him, lays aside all occupations that might oblige him to leave his company, makes light of any matter, however weighty, that would demand his parting from him, is very slow to move when he takes his leave of him.

Other signs of love are that sudden confusion and excitement betrayed by the lover when he unexpectedly sees the one he loves coming upon him unawares, that agitation which overmasters him on beholding someone who resembles his beloved or on hearing his name suddenly pronounced. A man in love will give prodigally, to the limit of his capacity, in a way that formerly he would have refused; as if he were the one receiving the donation, he the one whose happiness is the object in view; all this in order that he may show off his good points, and make himself desirable. How often has the miser opened his purse-strings, the scowler relaxed his frown, the coward leapt heroically into the fray, the clod suddenly become sharp-witted, the boor turned into the perfect gentleman, the stinker transformed into the elegant dandy, the sloucher smartened up, the decrepit recaptured his lost youth, the godly gone wild, the self-respecting kicked over the traces — and all because of love!

All these signs are to be observed even before the fire of love is properly kindled, ere its conflagration truly bursts forth, its blaze waxes fierce, its flames leap up. But when the fire really takes a hold and is firmly established, then you will see the secret whispering, the unconcealed turning away from all present but the beloved.

Other outward signs and tokens of love are the following, which are apparent to all having eyes in their heads: abundant and exceeding cheerfulness at finding oneself with the beloved in a narrow space, and a corresponding depression on being together in a wide expanse; to engage in a playful tug of war for anything the one or the other lays hold of; much clandestine winking; leaning sideways and supporting oneself against the object of one's affection; endeavouring to touch his hand and whatever part of his body one can reach, while engaged in conversation; and drinking the remainder of what the beloved has left in his cup, seeking out the very spot against which his lips were pressed.

There are also contrary signs that occur according to casual provocations and accidental incitements and a variety of motivating causes and stimulating thoughts. Opposites are of course likes, in reality; when things reach the limit of contrariety, and stand at the furthest bounds of divergency, they come to resemble one another. This is decreed by God's omnipotent power, in a manner that baffles entirely the human imagination. Thus, when ice is pressed a long time in the hand, it finally produces the same effect as fire. We find that extreme joy and extreme sorrow kill equally; excessive and violent laughter sends the tears coursing from the eyes. It is a very common phenomenon in the world about us. Similarly with lovers: when they love each other with an equal ardour and their mutual affection is intensely strong, they will turn against one another without any valid reason, each purposely contradicting the other in whatever he may say; they quarrel violently over the smallest things, each picking up every word that the other lets fall and wilfully misinterpreting it. All these devices are aimed at testing and proving what each is seeking in the other.

Now the difference between this sham, and real aversion and contrariness born of deep-seated hatred and inveterate contention, is that lovers are very quickly reconciled after their disputes. You will see a pair of lovers seeming to have reached the extreme limit of contrariety, to the point that you would reckon not to be mended even in the instance of a person of most tranquil spirit and wholly exempt from rancour, save after a long interval, and wholly irreparable in the case of a quarrelsome man; yet in next to no time you will observe them to have become the best of friends once more; silenced are those mutual reproaches, vanished that disharmony; forthwith they are laughing again and playfully sporting together. The same scene may be enacted several times at a single session. When you see a pair of lovers behaving in such a fashion, let no doubt enter your mind, no uncertainty invade your thoughts; you may be sure without hesitation, and convinced as by an unshakable certainty, that there lies between them a deep and hidden secret—the secret of true love. Take this then for a sure test, a universally valid experiment: it is the product only of an equal partnership in love and a true concord of hearts. I myself have observed it frequently.

Another sign is when you find the lover almost entreating to hear the loved one's name pronounced, taking an extreme delight in speaking about him, so that the subject is a positive obsession with him; nothing so much rejoices him, and he is not in the least restrained by the fear that someone listening may realize what he is about, and someone present will understand his true motives. Love for a thing renders you blind and deaf. If the lover could so contrive that in the place where he happens to be there should be no talk of anything but his beloved, he would never leave that spot for any other in the whole world.

It can happen that a man sincerely affected by love will start to eat his meal with an excellent appetite; yet the instant the recollection of his loved one is excited, the food sticks in his throat and chokes his gullet. It is the same if he is drinking or talking—he begins to converse with you gaily enough, then all at once he is invaded by a chance thought of his dear one. You will notice the change in his manner of speaking, the instantaneous failure of his conversational powers; the sure signs are his long silences, the way he stares at the ground, his extreme taciturnity. One moment he is all smiles, lightly gesticulating; the next he has become completely boxed up, sluggish, distrait, rigid, too weary to utter a single word, irritated by the most innocent question.

Love's signs also include a fondness for solitude and a pleasure in being alone, as well as a wasting of the body not accompanied by any fever or ache preventing free activity and liberty of movement. The walk is also an unerring indication and never-deceiving sign of an inward lassitude of spirit. Sleeplessness too is a common affliction of lovers; the poets have described this condition frequently, relating how they watch the stars, and giving an account of the night's interminable length.

Another sign of love is that you will see the lover loving his beloved's kith and kin and the intimate ones of his household, to such an extent that they are nearer and dearer to him than his own folk, himself, and all his familiar friends.

Weeping is a well-known sign of love, except that men differ very greatly from one another in this particular. Some are ready weepers; their tear-ducts are always overflowing, and their eyes respond immediately to their emotions, the tears rolling down at a moment's notice. Others are dry-eyed and barren of tears; to this category I myself belong. This is the result of my habit of eating frankincense to abate the palpitation from which I have suffered since childhood. I will be afflicted by some shocking blow, and at once feel my heart to be splitting and breaking into fragments; I have a choking sensation in my heart more bitter than colocynth, that prevents me from getting my words out properly, and sometimes well nigh suffocates me. My eyes therefore respond to my feelings but rarely, and then my tears are exceedingly sparse.

You will see the lover, when unsure of the constancy of his loved one's feelings for him, perpetually on his guard in a way that he never troubled to be before; he polishes his language, he refines his gestures and his glances, particularly if he has the misfortune and mischance to be in love with one given to making unjust accusations, or of a quarrelsome disposition.

Another sign of love is the way the lover pays attention to the beloved; remembering everything that falls from his lips; searching out all the news about him, so that nothing small or great that happens to him may escape his knowledge; in short, following closely his every movement. Upon my life, sometimes you will see a complete dolt under these circumstances become most keen, a careless fellow turn exceedingly quick-witted.

One of the strangest origins of passion is when a man falls in love through merely hearing the description of the other party, without ever having set eyes on the beloved. In such a case he will progress through all the accustomed stages of love; there will be the sending to and fro of messengers, the exchange of letters, the anxiety, the deep emotion, the sleeplessness; and all this without actual sight of the object of affection. Stories, descriptions of beautiful qualities, and the reporting of news about the fair one have a manifest effect on the soul; to hear a girl's voice singing behind a wall may well move the heart to love, and preoccupy the mind.

All this has occurred to more than one man. In my opinion, however, such a love is a tumbledown building without any foundations. If a man's thoughts are absorbed by passionate regard for one whom he has never seen, the inevitable result is that whenever he is alone with his own reflections, he will represent to himself a purely imaginary picture of the person whose identity he keeps constantly before his mind; no other being than this takes shape in his fantasy; he is completely carried away by his imagination, and visualizes and dreams of her only. Then if some day he actually sees the object of his fanciful passion, either his love is confirmed or it is wholly nullified. Both these alternatives have actually happened and been known.

This kind of romance usually takes place between veiled ladies of guarded palaces and aristocratic households, and their male kinsfolk; the love of women is more stable in these cases than that of men, because women are weak creatures and their natures swiftly respond to this sort of attraction, which easily masters them completely.

Often it happens that love fastens itself to the heart as the result of a single glance. This variety of love is divided into two classes. The first class is the contrary of what we have just been describing, in that a man will fall head over heels in love with a mere form, without knowing who that person may be, what her name is, or where she lives. This sort of thing happens frequently enough.

The second class is the contrary of what we shall be describing in the chapter next following, if God wills. This is for a man to form an attachment at first sight with a young lady whose name, place of abode and origin are known to him. The difference here is the speed or tardiness with which the affair passes off. When a man falls in love at first sight, and forms a sudden attachment as the result of a fleeting glance, that proves him to be little steadfast, and proclaims that he will as suddenly forget his romantic adventure; it testifies to his fickleness and inconstancy. So it is with all things; the quicker they grow, the quicker they decay; while on the other hand slow produced is slow consumed.

Some men there are whose love becomes true only after long converse, much contemplation, and extended familiarity. Such a one is likely to persist and to be steadfast in his affection, untouched by the passage of time; what enters with difficulty goes not out easily. That is my own way in these matters, and it is confirmed by Holy Tradition. For God, as we are informed by our teachers, when He commanded the Spirit to enter Adam's body, that was like an earthen vessel—and the Spirit was afraid, and sorely distressed—said to it, "Enter in unwillingly, and come forth again unwillingly!"

I have myself seen a man of this description who, whenever he sensed within himself the beginnings of a passionate attachment, or conceived a penchant for some form whose beauty he admired, at once employed the device of shunning that person and giving up all association with him, lest his feelings become more intense and the affair get beyond his control, and he find himself completely stampeded. This proves how closely love cleaves to such people's hearts, and once it lays hold of them never looses its grip.

I indeed marvel profoundly at all those who pretend to fall in love at first sight; I cannot easily prevail upon myself to believe their claims, and prefer to consider such love as merely a kind of lust. As for thinking that that sort of attachment can really possess the inmost heart and penetrate the veil of the soul's recess, that I cannot under any circumstances credit. Love has never truly gripped my bowels, save after a long lapse of time and constant companionship with the person concerned, sharing with him all that while my every occupation, be it earnest or frivolous. So I am alike in consolation and in passion; I have never in my life forgotten any romance, and my nostalgia for every former attachment is such that I well nigh choke when I drink and suffocate when I eat. The man who is not so constituted quickly finds complete relief and is at rest again; I have never wearied of anything once I have known it, and neither have I hastened to feel at home with it on first acquaintance. Similarly, I have never longed for a change for change's sake, in any of the things that I have possessed; I am speaking here not only of friends and comrades, but also of all the other things a man uses—clothes, riding-beast, food, and so on.

Life holds no joy for me, and I do nothing but hang my head and feel utterly cast down, ever since I first tasted the bitterness of being separated from those I love. It is an anguish that constantly revisits me, an agony of grief that ceases not for a moment to assail me. My remembrance of past happiness has abated for me every joy that I may look for in the future. I am a dead man, though counted among the living, slain by sorrow and buried by sadness, entombed while yet a dweller on the face of this mortal earth. God be praised, whatever be the circumstances that befall us; there is indeed no other God but He!

As for what transpires at first blush as a result of certain accidental circumstances—physical admiration, and visual enchantment which does not go beyond mere external forms—and this is the very secret and meaning of carnal desire; when carnal desire moreover becomes so overflowing that it surpasses these bounds, and when such an overflow coincides with a spiritual union in which the natural instincts share equally with the soul, the resulting phenomenon is called passionate love. Herein lies the root of the error which misleads a man into asserting that he loves two persons, or is passionately enamoured of two entirely different individuals. All this is to be explained as springing out of carnal desire, as we have just described; it is called love only metaphorically, and not in the true meaning of the term. As for the true lover, his yearning of the soul is so excessive as to divert him from all his religious and mundane occupations; how then should he have room to busy himself with a second love affair?

Know now—may God exalt you!—that love exercises an effective authority, a decisive sovereignty over the soul; its commands cannot be opposed; its ordinances may not be flouted; its rule is not to be transgressed; it demands unwavering obedience, and against its dominion there is no appeal. Love untwists the firmest plaits and looses the tightest strands; it dissolves that which is most solid, undoes that which is most firm; it penetrates the deepest recesses of the heart, and makes lawful things most strictly forbidden.

I have known many men whose discrimination was beyond suspicion, men not to be feared deficient in knowledge, or wanting in taste, or lacking in discernment, who nevertheless described their loved ones as possessing certain qualities not by any means admired by the general run of mankind or approved according to the accepted canons of beauty. Yet those qualities had become an obsession with them, the sole object of their passion, and the very last word (as they thought) in elegance. Thereafter their loved ones vanished, either into oblivion, or by separation, or jilting, or through some other accident to which love is always liable; but those men never lost their admiration for the curious qualities which provoked their approval of them, neither did they ever afterwards cease to prefer these above other attributes that are in reality superior to them.

Let me add a personal touch. In my youth I loved a slave-girl who happened to be a blonde; from that time I have never admired brunettes, not though their dark tresses set off a face as resplendent as the sun, or the very image of beauty itself. I find this taste to have become a part of my whole make-up and constitution since those early days; my soul will not suffer me to acquire any other, or to love any type but that. This very same thing happened to my father also (God be pleased with him!), and he remained faithful to his first preference until the term of his earthly life was done.

Were it not that this world below is a transitory abode of trial and trouble, and paradise a home where virtue receives its reward, secure from all annoyances, I would have said that union with the beloved is that pure happiness which is without alloy, and gladness unsullied by sorrow the perfect realization of hopes and the complete fulfillment of one's dreams.

I have tested all manner of pleasures, and known every variety of joy; and I have found that neither intimacy with princes, nor wealth acquired, nor finding after lacking, nor returning after long absence, nor security after fear, and repose in a safe refuge—none of these things so powerfully affects the soul as union with the beloved, especially if it come after long denial and continual banishment. For then the flame of passion waxes exceeding hot, and the furnace of yearning blazes up, and the fire of eager hope rages ever more fiercely.

The fresh springing of herbs after the rains, the glitter of flowers when the night clouds have rolled away in the hushed hour between dawn and sunrise, the plashing of waters as they run through the stalks of golden blossoms, the exquisite beauty of white castles encompassed by verdant meadows—not lovelier is any of these than union with the well-beloved, whose character is virtuous, and laudable her disposition, whose attributes are evenly matched in perfect beauty. Truly that is a miracle of wonder surpassing the tongues of the eloquent, and far beyond the range of the most cunning speech to describe: the mind reels before it, and the intellect stands abashed.

❧ My Beloved Comes

Translated by Cola Franzen

You came to me just before
the Christians rang their bells.
The half-moon was rising
looking like an old man's eyebrow
or a delicate instep.

And although it was still night,
when you came, a rainbow
gleamed on the horizon,
showing as many colors
as a peacock's tail.

IBN ZAYDUN

B. ANDALUSIA (SPAIN), 1004–1070

Ibn Zaydun, the Andalusian master of the themes of passion and longing, was already a famous court poet before he fell in love with Wallada, the daughter of the last Umayyad caliph of Cordova. The story of their ill-fated love affair later became a staple of literary legends in the Arab world. It seems that Wallada emerged better off from this relationship than Ibn Zaydun. While his greatest poetry recalls their love affair with deepest melancholy, she insults him in some of her later work in picturesque language:

> For all his virtue Ibn Zaydun loves rods inside trousers.
> If he spotted a penis up a palm-tree, he'd turn into a whole flock
> of birds.

At times, however, the writing of the two is so similar in passionate intensity that scholars have argued over who actually wrote the verses in question.

Ibn Zaydun was born in 1004 to an aristocratic family claiming descent from the Quraysh, the tribe of Muhammad in Arabia. After the fall of the Umayyads in Cordova in 1031, Ibn Zaydun became closely connected with the new Jahwarid dynasty, and was almost immediately appointed ambassador to the neighboring Andalusian kingdoms. He lost favor with the Jahwarid king, Abu l'Hazm, a decade later and was imprisoned briefly before escaping and finally being reinstated to his ambassadorial duties. In later life he served as ambassador for the Abbasid government in Seville, eventually helping them to conquer his native Cordova. He died in Seville in 1070.

Ibn Zaydun is most famous for three poems: The "Poem in N," a fiery fifty-two verse *qasidah* that expresses his longing for Wallada; a *ghazal* called "Written from al-Zahrā'," set in a beautiful garden outside Cordova; and a prison letter he entitled "The Serious Epistle," begging his sovereign Abu l'Hazm for his release. In "Written from al-Zahrā'," included here, Ibn Zaydun recalls the past when he and Wallada met in the place he now returns to. This traditional love poem describes the poet's journey to a place of sanctuary and his recovery of feeling through the restoration of his memories.

Written from al-Zahrā'

Translated by Cola Franzen

From al-Zahrā'[1]
I remember you with passion.
The horizon is clear,
the earth's face serene.

The breeze grows faint
with the coming of dawn.
It seems to pity me
and lingers, full of tenderness.

The meandering waterway
with its silvery waters
shows a sparkling smile.
It resembles a necklace
unclasped and thrown aside.

A day like those delicious ones
now gone by
when seizing the dream of destiny
we were thieves of pleasure.

Today, alone,
I distract myself with flowers
that attract my eyes like magnets.
The wind roughhouses with them
bending them over.

The blossoms are eyes.
They see my sleeplessness
and weep for me;
their iridescent tears overflow
staining the calyx.[2]

In the bright sun
red buds light up the rose bushes
making the morning
brighter still.

---

[1] **al-Zahrā':** A legendary palace outside of Cordova whose gardens were noted for their opulence and splendor.

[2] **calyx:** The external part of a flower, of a cuplike shape.

Fragrant breaths come from the pome
of the waterlilies,
sleepyheads with eyes
half-opened by dawn.

Everything stirs up the memory
of my passion for you
still intact in my chest
although my chest might seem
40   too narrow to contain it.

If, as I so desire,
we two could again be made one,
that day would be the noblest
of all days.

Would God grant calm to my heart
if it could cease to remember you
and refrain from flying
to your side
on wings trembling with desire?

50   If this passing breeze
would consent to carry me along,
it would put down at your feet
a man worn out by grief.

Oh, my most precious jewel,
the most sublime,
the one preferred by my soul,
as if lovers dealt in jewels!

In times gone by
we demanded of each other
60   payments of pure love
and were happy as colts
running free in a pasture.

But now I am the only one
who can boast of being loyal.
You left me
and I stay here,
still sad, still loving you.

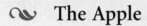

JUDAH HA-LEVI
B. ANDALUSIA (SPAIN), 1075–1141

Judah ha-Levi was born in Tudela in northern Andalusia, near the frontier with Christian Spain, in 1075. While still a youth, he journeyed to Granada where he was befriended by the poet Moses Ibn Ezra. After Granada was attacked in 1090, he moved to Castille, leaving there when the Jews fell under persecution in 1109. He wrote brilliant secular poetry until about 1125, when he began to reconsider his vocation. Already considered the greatest Andalusian Jewish poet and cultural authority, he became disenchanted, both with his writing of secular literature and his participation in the Andalusian Jewish community. Finally he decided to travel to Jerusalem, a decision that became the source of some of his most important writing though it also posed personal difficulties for him. Cut off from his own community in Andalusia, he reestablished himself for a time in Egypt. Although he may have died there in 1141 without having completed his pilgrimage to the Holy Land, a legend relates that he was killed by a Muslim as he approached the gates of Jerusalem.

Like many other Jewish poets, Judah ha-Levi wrote poems in Hebrew though he borrowed many of the conventions of Arabic poetry. Advances in Islamic scholarship actually increased interest in Scriptural studies and the use of Hebrew among the Jews. Ha-Levi's early love songs sometimes incorporated images from The Song of Solomon while using Arabic figures of speech and subject matter. "The Apple," a short lyric poem, is an inspired fusion of Arabic and Hebrew culture.

The Apple

Translated by David Goldstein

You have captured me with your charm, my lady;
You have enslaved me brutally in your prison.
From the very day that we had to part
I have found no likeness to your beauty.
I console myself with a rosy apple,
Whose scent is like the myrrh of your nose and your lips,
Its shape like your breast, and its colour
Like the hue which is seen on your cheeks.

❧ GUILLAUME IX, DUKE OF AQUITAINE
B. PROVENCE (FRANCE), 1071–1127

Guillaume IX, duke of Aquitaine, was known for his deeds as well as his songs. The lord of an immense domain and leader of the disastrous Crusade of 1101, he was a notorious womanizer and a constant source of irritation for the church. He is important to the courtly love tradition for two reasons: He is often spoken of as the first troubadour poet, and—perhaps because of his rank—his poems, twelve in all, were carefully preserved. As he grew older, his songs changed from bawdy backroom ballads to attacks on the clergy to showpieces of courtly and religious devotion.

The artistic relationship of Guillaume to the poets of preceding and succeeding generations is somewhat obscure. His relatively sophisticated subject matter, rhyme schemes, and style could not have developed in a vacuum. The earlier poetry that he knew was constructed from the ruins of the Latin tradition and whatever poetry existed in the Romance languages, and through contact with the culture of the courts of Andalusia. Guillaume influenced the generation that followed him by supporting other troubadours wherever he held court. At Poitiers there appears to have been a poetic line of succession: Guillaume IX was followed by the troubadours Cercamon (fl. 1137–1153) and Marcabru (fl. 1129–1150). More significant than this, perhaps, is the fact that Guillaume practiced "high" and "low" poetry, both of which would have a future with his successors.

VEHR

The song "My companions, I am going to make a *vers* that is refined" is the raucous account of a man with two female lovers, whom he compares to "good and noble horses." His problem is that they will not abide by the arrangement. The women live in two castles within his domain; although one woman is married to another man, the poet boasts that he has first rights to her. The poem is characterized by its chauvinistic point of view and its conspicuous bad taste. For instance, the poet deliberately names the two women, exposing their identities and destroying whatever may be left of their reputations.

A world apart from this poem is the one that begins "Now when we see the meadows once again," one of the early defining texts of the doctrine of courtly love, addressed to a mixed audience of lords and ladies. Here Guillaume practices and preaches the art of refinement. He rebukes himself for having wanted love so much that he has frequently lost it, and he acknowledges that he will never gain love without first obeying its laws. This time he is careful to conceal the identity of his beloved.

My companions, I am going to make a *vers* that is refined

Translated by Frederick Goldin

My companions,[1] I am going to make a *vers* that is refined,
and it will have more foolishness than sense,
and it will all be mixed with love and joy and youth.

Whoever does not understand it, take him for a peasant,
whoever does not learn it deep in his heart.
It is hard for a man to part from love that he finds to his desire.

I have two good and noble horses for my saddle,
they are good, adroit in combat, full of spirit,
but I cannot keep them both, one can't stand the other.

---

[1] **My companions:** By addressing the poem to his male friends, Guillaume helps to establish its unmannerly type, despite his disclaimer that it is "refined."

10   If I could tame them as I wish,
I would not want to put my equipment anywhere else,
for I'd be better mounted then than any man alive.

One of them was the fastest of the mountain horses,
but for a long time now it has been so fierce and shy,
so touchy, so wild, it fights off the currycomb.

The other was nurtured down there around Confolens,
and you never saw a prettier one, I know.
I won't get rid of that one, not for gold or silver.

I gave it to its master as a grazing colt;
20   but I reserved the right
that for every year he had it, I got it for more than a hundred.

You knights, counsel me in this predicament,
no choice ever caused me more embarrassment:
I can't decide which one to keep, Na Agnes or Na Arsen.[2]

Of Gimel I have the castle and the fief,
and with Niol I show myself proud to everyone,
for both are sworn to me and bound by oath.

---

[2]**Na Agnes . . . Arsen:** *Na* is the shortened form of *domina*, an address to a lady.

❧ Now when we see the meadows once again

Translated by Frederick Goldin

Now when we see the meadows once again
in flower and the orchards turning green,
streams and fountains running clear,
the breezes and the winds,
it is right that each man celebrate the joy
that makes him rejoice.

Now I must not say anything but good of Love.
Why do I get not one bit of it?
Maybe I wasn't meant for more.

10   And yet how freely
it gives great joy to any man who upholds
its rules.

This is the way it has always been with me:
I never had the joy of what I loved,
and I never will, as I never did.
For I am aware,
I do many things and my heart says,
"It is all nothing."

And so I know less than anyone what pleasure is,
20   because I want what I cannot have.
And yet, one wise saying tells me
the certain truth:
"When the heart is good, its power is good,
if a man knows patience."

Surely no one can ever be Love's
perfect man unless he gives it homage in humility
and is obliging to strangers
and acquaintances,
and to all the people of that realm
30   obedient.

A man who wants to be a lover
must meet many people with obedience,
and must know how to do
the things that fit in court,
and must keep, in court, from speaking
like a vulgar man.

Concerning this *vers* I tell you a man is all the more noble
as he understands it, and he gets more praise;
and all the strophes are built exactly
40   on the same meter,
and the melody, which I myself am happy about,
is fine and good.

Let my *vers,* since I myself do not,
appear before her,
Mon Esteve, and let it be the witness
for my praise.

MARCABRU
PROVENCE (FRANCE), FL. 1129–1150

Marcabru, who although he was low-born enjoyed the patronage of the court of Poitiers, could not have differed more from Guillaume IX in his approach. His poems attack other troubadours and advocates of courtly love as hypocritical and depraved, caught up in the vices of the world, while he defends what he calls true love, the love of friendship. Although Marcabru depicts himself as a flawed person who cannot live up to his own ideals, one suspects him of trying to have his argument both ways: Only he, it seems, is honest enough to confess his faults. And is not "the love of friendship" courtly love restored to its original principles of devotion and mutual trust?

The poem "By the fountain in the orchard" maintains a high moral tone despite the narrator's confession of inappropriate desires. In the poem, Marcabru depicts a knight pursuing a lady who is grieving for her lover off fighting in the Crusades. The knight is finally chastened and educated by the lady's fidelity to her absent lover. The portrayal of true love as a virtue is all the more forceful for remaining unstated.

By the fountain in the orchard

Translated by Frederick Goldin

By the fountain in the orchard,
where the grass is green down to the sandy banks,
in the shade of a planted tree,
in a pleasant setting of white flowers
and the ancient song of the new season,
I found her alone, without a companion,
this girl who does not want my company.

She was a young girl, and beautiful,
the daughter of a castle lord.
And just as I reckoned the birds
must be filling her with joy, and the green things,
in this sweet new time,
and she would gladly hear my little speech,
suddenly her whole manner changed.

Her eyes welled up beside the fountain,
and she sighed from the depths of her heart,

10

"Jesus," she said, "King of the world,
because of You my grief increases,
I am undone by your humiliation,[1]
20   for the best men of this whole world
are going off to serve you, that is your pleasure.

"With you departs my so
handsome, gentle, valiant, noble friend;
here, with me, nothing of him remains but the great distress,
the frequent desiring, and the tears.
Ai! damn King Louis,
he gave the orders and the sermons,
and grief invaded my heart."

When I heard how she was losing heart,
30   I came up to her beside the clear stream.
"Beautiful one," I said, "with too much weeping
your face grows pale, the color fades;
you have no reason to despair, now,
for He who makes the woods burst into leaf
has the power to give you joy in great abundance."

"Lord," she said, "I do believe
that God may pity me
in the next world, time without end,
like many other sinners,
40   but here He wrests from me the one thing
that made my joy increase. Nothing matters now,
for he has gone so far away."

---

[1] **your humiliation:** God was humiliated, the lady says, by the failure of the Second Crusade, led by King Louis VII of France in 1147.

❧ COUNTESS OF DIA
PROVENCE (FRANCE), FL. 1160

The first and probably the best of the *trobairitz,* or women poets, the Countess of Dia combined in unique fashion the common song and the courtly lyric. She shares with her female counterparts a demand for personal respect, physical and emotional satisfaction, and above all plain speaking in matters of love. She treats the conventions of courtly love with skepticism: She scrutinizes the behavior of a lover to see whether it matches the standards he has supposedly adopted. Above all, she affirms her own need for satisfaction in her relationships.

The poem beginning "Of things I'd rather keep in silence I must sing," in which the poet gives a messenger instructions on what to say to a lover who has spurned her, stays within the conventions of courtly love; the poet reminds her lover of their past relationship and demands that he respond to her with more courtesy in the future, warning him also against the excessive pride that may be his undoing.

❧ Of things I'd rather keep in silence I must sing

Translated by Magda Bogin

Of things I'd rather keep in silence I must sing:
so bitter do I feel toward him
whom I love more than anything.
With him my mercy and fine manners are in vain,
my beauty, virtue and intelligence.
For I've been tricked and cheated
as if I were completely loathesome.

There's one thing, though, that brings me recompense:
I've never wronged you under any circumstance,
10   and I love you more than Seguin loved Valensa.
At least in love I have my victory,
since I surpass the worthiest of men.
With me you always act so cold,
but with everyone else you're so charming.

I have good reason to lament
when I feel your heart turn adamant
toward me, friend: it's not right another love
take you away from me, no matter what she says.
Remember how it was with us in the beginning
20   of our love! May God not bring to pass
that I should be the one to bring it to an end.

The great renown that in your heart resides
and your great worth disquiet me,
for there's no woman near or far

who wouldn't fall for you if love were on her mind.
But you, my friend, should have the acumen
to tell which one stands out above the rest.
And don't forget the stanzas we exchanged.

My worth and noble birth should have some weight,
my beauty and especially my noble thoughts;
so I send you, there on your estate,
this song as messenger and delegate.
I want to know, my handsome noble friend,
why I deserve so savage and so cruel a fate.
I can't tell whether it's pride or malice you intend.

But above all, messenger, make him comprehend
that too much pride has undone many men.

30

∾ FRANCESCO PETRARCH
B. ITALY, 1304–1374

Although only forty years separate Francesco Petrarch from his country-
man Dante Alighieri, Petrarch is often described as the first Renaissance
man, partly because of the breadth of his interests and his curiosity about
the world. He possessed even more talents than Dante: a poet in both his
native Italian and in Latin; a classical scholar who edited manuscripts of
Cicero and Livy and wrote the biographies of Roman heroes; an advisor
to the Doge of Venice and the Holy Roman Emperor; a traveler who knew
the Rhineland, the Low Country of the Netherlands, and most of France
and Italy; a landscape gardener, a fisherman, a lute player, and a climber
of mountains. He saw, like Dante, the corruption of the Catholic Church,
but he looked beyond Christian doctrine in addressing how to live
morally. A humanist by instinct, he granted this world its value and never
scorned the pleasures and beauty it offered. He also paid self-conscious
attention to the drama of his own personal life as a lover, scholar, and
man of letters.

Like Dante, Petrarch's parents were exiled from Florence in 1301
following factional disputes in the city. Petrarch was born in 1304 in a
Tuscan village and moved frequently, both as a child and an adult. He
spent a peaceful adolescence near Avignon, was sent to Montpellier to
study law, but devoted most of his study to the Latin classics. After six
years at the University of Bologna, he squandered his small inheritance
and took orders as a chaplain from 1330 to 1348. He claimed to have
met the apparently unattainable woman he called Laura in a church in
Avignon in 1327; we know nothing about her life and death except that his

**Andrea del
Castagno,** *Petrarch,*
Fifteenth Century
*The humanist
scholar-poet
Francesco Petrarch is
shown here with a
book under his arm.
(Scala / Art Resource,
NY)*

DOMINVS FRANCISCHVS PETRARCHA

lifelong collection of 366 Italian lyrics dedicated to her memory, the *Can-zoniere,* was collected and published the year of his death.

Petrarch was not the first to write the sonnet and certainly not the first to make an unattainable woman the central image of a body of poems, but he showed how supple the sonnet form could be and how richly suited Italian was to romantic poetry in the hands of a master. The *Canzoniere* are difficult to translate into English with anything resem-bling the sound of Petrarch's sinuous Italian, though the reader can sometimes discover the uniquely private and passionate voice of the poet, his pride, boldness, complexity, and sensual awareness. Petrarch refuses to moralize or pass judgment; instead he recreates for us with power and tenderness the contradictions of the physical and moral world he knew.

FROM

ꙮ # Canzoniere

Translated by Patricia Clark Smith

1: OH YOU, WHO IN THESE SCATTERED RHYMES MAY FIND

Oh you, who in these scattered rhymes may find
echoes of sighs that I once fed my heart
when I was young, when I was still in part
this man you see, that boy now left behind;

if you yourself have had one turn to writhe
in love's extremes of harsh delight, soft pain,
balanced between false hope, sweet love-in-vain,
I pray you'll read and pity and forgive.

There's talk of me on every street in town,
10 and I know why; although I feel that shame,
shame's not the deepest reason why I weep,

nor even penitence, but that stark dawn
of understanding how it's all a dream,
all that we love, all that we ache to keep.

3: IT WAS THE VERY DAY THE SUN'S OWN LIGHT

It was the very day the sun's own light
grew dim to mark the passion of Our Lord

when I myself succumbed without a word,
struck down, my lady, simply by your sight.[1]

That one day least auspicious for romance
I walked unwary through the people's sorrow,
through grieving streets, all open to the blow
Love dealt amid that universal penance.

Love found its way to my heart through my eyes;
10 now my tears pool and gather, overflow
outward through those same gates where I was breached.

But you, my love, were never so surprised,
and I ask whether it is fair, or no,
Love laid me low, and left you so untouched?

---

[1] **It was the . . . your sight:** The day Petrarch first saw Laura was April 6, 1327, then supposed to be the exact anniversary of the crucifixion, as opposed to the movable feast of Good Friday. He also tells us Laura died of plague on that same date in 1348.

90: SOMETIMES SHE'D COMB HER YELLOW BRAIDS OUT LOOSE

Sometimes she'd comb her yellow braids out loose
for winds to tease and tangle in bright air,
and all that light caught in her eyes, her hair.
Most things have faded now. But once I used

to see her gauging me with thoughtful eyes:
with pity true or false, it's all the same.
My soul dry kindling, waiting for her flame,
and could I help it I was set ablaze?

I tell you, she was like a goddess walking,
10 a pulsing sun to keep a man from cold,
radiant, gold, that spirit danced abroad;

when she spoke, I divined the angels talking.
You say she's just a woman growing old?
Her bow's gone slack, her arrow's in my side.

292: THOSE EYES I RAVED ABOUT IN ARDENT RHYME

Those eyes I raved about in ardent rhyme,
the arms, the hands, the feet, the loving face
that split my soul in two, and made me pass
my life apart from all the common throng,

the tumbled mane of uncut gold that shone,
that angel smile whose flash made me surmise
the very earth had turned to Paradise,
have come to dust: no life, no sense. Undone.

And I live on, in sorrow and self-scorn
10 here where the light I steered by gleams no more
for my dismasted ship, wracked by the storm.

Let there be no more love songs! The dear spring
of my accustomed art has been drained dry,
my lyre itself dissolved in so much weeping.

333: GO FORTH, MY ELEGIES, TO THAT HARD STONE

Go forth, my elegies, to that hard stone
beneath whose weight my dearest treasure lies.
Call her, and she may answer from the skies,
but here lies only rotting flesh and bone.

Tell her how I grow weary of my life,
of navigating through this dark expanse;
only these scattered pages save my sense,
these stepping-stones to lead me out of grief.

I'll go on telling how she lived and died,
10 and how she's living now, beyond all death,
so that the world may better learn her grace

and love her. Let her linger by my side
at my death, which grows nearer as I breathe,
to beckon me toward her transcendent peace.

❧ SIR THOMAS WYATT
B. ENGLAND, 1503–1542

One of the leading English Renaissance poets, Sir Thomas Wyatt the Elder, was born at Allington Castle in Kent and eventually studied at St. John's College at Cambridge. After graduation he served as a diplomat in the court of Henry VIII of England, where he cultivated the life of a Renaissance courtier and gentleman. In addition to composing his own poetry, he translated and imitated the great Italian poets, especially Petrarch, and he was the first to introduce the sonnet form into English verse. His reworking of Petrarch's Song 157, "Whoso List to Hunt," equals or excels the original. Wyatt refashions some elements of Petrarch's poem to conform to the rather dangerous life of the English court. In this version, the "hind," or deer, most likely refers to Anne Boleyn, a young lady of the court under the watchful eye of Henry VIII and therefore off-limits to any lowly courtiers.

❧ Whoso List to Hunt

Whoso list° to hunt, I know where is an hind,   wishes
    But as for me, alas, I may no more;
    The vain travail hath wearied me so sore,
    I am of them that furthest come behind.
Yet may I by no means my wearied mind
    Draw from the deer, but as she fleeth afore
    Fainting I follow; I leave off therefore,
    Since in a net I seek to hold the wind.
Who list her hunt, I put him out of doubt,
10   As well as I, may spend his time in vain.
    And graven with diamonds in letters plain,
There is written her fair neck round about,
    "*Noli me tangere*,[1] for Caesar's I am,
    And wild for to hold, though I seem tame."

---

[1] **"*Noli me tangere*, . . . tame":** "Touch me not." Caesar's deer were said to be fitted with collars so inscribed, to keep them safe from poachers.

❧ WILLIAM SHAKESPEARE
B. *ENGLAND, 1564–1616*

Although best known for his plays, Shakespeare was also a master of the longer narrative poem and the lyric, and he was celebrated in his own time as a great poet. Shakespeare privately circulated a collection of his sonnets for many years, finally publishing them in 1609. Some of the poems are highly mysterious in their references, and they have given rise to much speculation about the person or persons to whom they are addressed and about Shakespeare's sexuality. Although one might read them as philosophical poems, many of the sonnets are simply personal poetry written to note particular occasions.

Sonnet 18, "Shall I compare thee to a summer's day," is one of the great love poems of the English Renaissance. The poem abandons the anticipated cataloging of the lover's body for an elaboration on the theme of love's transcendence, enabled by the verse itself. Sonnet 116 also praises the power of love to confer a kind of permanence. Another poem with tortuous logic, Sonnet 129, "Th' expense of spirit in a waste of shame," focuses on the torments of passion, fierce expectation beforehand and bitter woe afterward. The word *expense* suggests multiple meanings, including sexual expenditure but also revenge or physical violence. Sonnet 130, "My mistress' eyes are nothing like the sun," is a spoof of the Petrarchan sonnet, with its habit of praising the parts of a lady in a poetic catalog; Shakespeare calls for more honest expression.

For more information about Shakespeare, see page 1812.

❧ Sonnet 18

Shall I compare thee to a summer's day?
Thou art more lovely and more temperate:
Rough winds do shake the darling buds of May,
And summer's lease hath all too short a date:
Sometime too hot the eye of heaven shines,
And often is his gold complexion dimm'd;
And every fair from fair° sometime declines,   *beauty*
By chance or nature's changing course untrimm'd;°   *unadorned*
But thy eternal summer shall not fade,
10 Nor lose possession of that fair thou owest;°   *own, have*
Nor shall Death brag thou wander'st in his shade,
When in eternal lines to time thou grow'st:
    So long as men can breathe, or eyes can see,
    So long lives this, and this gives life to thee.

❧ Sonnet 116

Let me not to the marriage of true minds
Admit impediments.   Love is not love
Which alters when it alteration finds,
Or bends with the remover to remove:
O, no! it is an ever-fixed mark,
That looks on tempests and is never shaken;
It is the star to every wandering bark,°   ship
Whose worth's unknown, although his height be taken.°   measured
Love's not Time's fool, though rosy lips and cheeks
10 Within his bending sickle's compass come;
Love alters not with his brief hours and weeks,
But bears it out even to the edge of doom.
    If this be error and upon me proved,
    I never writ, nor no man ever loved.

❧ Sonnet 129

Th' expense of spirit in a waste of shame
Is lust in action;[1] and till action, lust
Is perjured, murderous, bloody, full of blame,
Savage, extreme, rude, cruel, not to trust;
Enjoyed no sooner but despiséd straight:
Past reason hunted; and no sooner had,
Past reason hated, as a swallowed bait,
On purpose laid to make the taker mad:
Mad in pursuit, and in possession so;
10 Had, having, and in quest to have, extreme;
A bliss in proof,[2] and proved, a very woe;
Before, a joy proposed; behind, a dream.
All this the world well knows; yet none knows well
To shun the heaven that leads men to this hell.

---

[1] **Th' expense . . . action:** The first one and one-half lines might be paraphrased, "Lust, when acted upon, expels the spirit (life, soul, vital force) in a waste (a desert, as well as a squandering) of shame."

[2] **bliss in proof:** Blissful at the moment it is experienced.

∾ Sonnet 130

My mistress' eyes are nothing like the sun;
Coral is far more red than her lips' red;
If snow be white, why then her breasts are dun;
If hairs be wires, black wires grow on her head.
I have seen roses damasked, red and white,
But no such roses see I in her cheeks;
And in some perfumes is there more delight
Than in the breath that from my mistress reeks.
I love to hear her speak, yet well I know
That music hath a far more pleasing sound;
I grant I never saw a goddess go;
My mistress, when she walks, treads on the ground.
And yet, by heaven, I think my love as rare
As any she belied with false compare.

TEXT IN CONTEXT

Dante Alighieri, The Inferno   1460

TIME AND PLACE: Medieval Italy: The City of Florence   1450

IMAGE: Dante and Virgil   1453

CHART: Dante's Hell   1461

IN THE WORLD: Dante and the Medieval World Picture   1620

∾ DANTE ALIGHIERI
B. *ITALY, 1265–1321*

DAHN-tay
ah-lih-GYEH-ree

Certain writers have come to represent the age in which they wrote, from whence their influence has carried into the modern world: Homer and Confucius from ancient times, Shakespeare from the Elizabethan Age in England, Voltaire from the Enlightenment in Europe, and **Dante Alighieri** in the European Middle Period. In fact, Dante included himself among the six greatest writers of all time in Canto IV of *Inferno*, the first part of his literary masterpiece, the *Divine Comedy*, which like a GOTHIC cathedral embodies the elaborate construct of Christianity in the Middle Period.

At the outset it appears as if the *Divine Comedy* is solely a religious text reflecting the worldview of medieval Christianity: Dante's pilgrim travels the spiritual universe, from the underworld of Hell to the outer reaches of Heaven, a realm systematized into a single worldview and set of values by the medieval Roman Catholic Church. With Satan at the center of the earth and God on the outer circumference of the universe, the good or evil of an individual could be measured by his or her proximity to one or the other in the afterlife. Dante's pilgrimage has also been read as an allegorical journey of the soul or spiritual descent into darkness and subsequent ascension through knowledge, repentance, and a beatific vision. What gives depth as well as breadth to Dante's epic is the knowledge and history layered into the work, reflecting the diversity of learning in the thirteenth and fourteenth centuries: philosophy, theology, poetry—including works by Muslim poets and scholars[1]—, and

---

[1] **Muslim . . . scholars:** See "In the World: Dante and the Medieval World Picture," p. 1620.

Florentine, European, and papal politics. The term *architecture* is often applied to the "towering edifice" that Dante, one of the most learned men of the European Middle Ages, constructed out of words in his *Divine Comedy*, a truly timeless work of art as interesting and profound today as it was in the fourteenth century.

Transforming Beatrice.   Very little is known about Dante's early life in Florence or about his parents, although his father probably accrued some wealth as a money changer; his mother died when he was young. Nothing is known about Dante's formal education, but his scholarly and literary writings suggest that he studied the standard classical and medieval works of literature, rhetoric, and theology. Because of his evident talents he was entertained in the leading families of Florence. He married Gemma Donati in about 1285 with whom he had at least three children, one of whom, Pietro, became an important commentator on the *Comedy*.

Undoubtedly the most important event of Dante's early life was his encounter with **Beatrice** Portinari. Nothing is known for certain about Beatrice, and some have questioned her very existence. Tradition, however, has it that Dante first saw her when they were both nine years old, that he fell in love with her at first sight, and, although he saw her only a few times and they married others, she had a tremendous impact on his life. Beatrice died in 1290, at twenty-five. It was perhaps her death at such an early age that allowed Dante to idealize her, to transform her into a spiritual symbol of inspiration for the sake of his writings and his own growth as a person. Influenced by the courtly love lyrics of the troubadours of twelfth-century France, especially their tendency to spiritualize what would otherwise be seen as purely physical attraction, Dante began his apprenticeship as a writer by composing prose and poetry celebrating Beatrice. By 1294 he had written thirty-one poems with prose commentary focusing on his devotion to her, published in a collection titled *The New Life* (*La Vita Nuova*). In this work Beatrice, whose name means "she who blesses," is already a transcendent figure, capable of transformative power. Later she plays an even more important role in the *Divine Comedy*, becoming not only a divine intercessor for the protagonist but also his spiritual guide to Paradise.

Political Affairs.   As a young man Dante became actively involved in the political affairs of Florence, which, with some eighty thousand inhabitants, was a city second only to Paris in size in Europe. When looking at Dante's time, local politics should be seen as part of the

BEE-uh-tris

www   For links to more information about Dante, a quiz on the *Inferno*, and information about the twenty-first-century relevance of Dante, see bedford stmartins.com/worldlitcompact.

Medieval Italy: The City of Florence

A common interpretation of the Italian Renaissance suggests that the new era of the Florentine republic, beginning in the thirteenth century, marked the rise of the individual and the birth of a new concept of liberty: social, economic, and cultural. The creative spirit of later Florentines — from Dante to Michelangelo — was said to derive from this atmosphere of political freedom. In actuality, the creation of the Florentine republic, a city-state with its own governmental structure, never produced such an unequivocally free society. Florence of the thirteenth century had come into being after centuries of vulnerability to flooding, invasions, and other external threats. As the city became more secure internal conflict grew, creating political factions within it. What held Florentine society together was a more conservative force: family wealth and influence, civil and economic bonds of mutual protection, and a ritualized code of behavior that united the citizens against external and internal enemies.

For the middle classes, the cohesive force in Florentine society might be thought of as the desire to survive at all costs in uncertain times where the political favor of the powerful was necessary though hard to guarantee. Less is known about the lives of poorer Florentines, for although scrupulous records help us to understand the functioning of the whole society, the neighborhoods of the poorer Florentines were architecturally fragile and left few remains. The real wealth of medieval Florence, however, could be seen in its religious, public, and private monuments: the great cathedral, the Duomo, built in the fourteenth century; the huge monastic churches, Santa Croce (Franciscan) and Santa Maria Novella (Dominican), situated at opposite ends of the city; the open market, still in use until the end of the nineteenth

The city of Florence *The view of Florence from across the Arno River. The cathedral, the Duomo Santa Maria del Fiore, is to the left. (The Art Archive/Travelsite/Colasanti)*

century; the Uffizi palace, now a world-famous art museum; and the other great public buildings, beginning with the Palazzo Vecchio, standing on the city square, the Piazza della Signoria. The great bridge across the Arno, Ponte Vecchio, decorated with shops along the walkway, is the only such remnant of the Middle Ages, the other bridges having been dynamited by the Nazis during their retreat from Italy in World War II. Other surviving buildings include the palaces of the richest families of the city, including the Donati Tower and the Medici Palace.

The spirit of the embattled city is perhaps best embodied in the sense of drama and ritual that it provides. Florentine history is filled with the great scenes enacted in the Piazza della Signoria, including the processions of cardinals and civic leaders alike, the public pageants and saint's days, and the public execution of those whose ambition overwhelmed their sense of restraint. This same pageantry that Dante recalls in his *Inferno*, a place seen to contain a disproportionately large number of the citizens of Florence, may be a mark not so much of the freedom of a city as its iron-willed resistance against misfortune.

larger struggle between the church and secular powers, between the princes of the Roman Catholic Church and the princes of the Holy Roman Empire. Internal wars and divisiveness were tearing Florence and Italy apart in the thirteenth century, and, as a city official, diplomat, and essayist, Dante was passionately involved with the fate of both. In Florence, the **Guelphs**, who supported the Papacy, and the **Ghibellines**, who supported the Holy Roman Empire, were engaged in a civil war. On the side of the Guelphs, Dante probably participated in two decisive battles in 1289, Campaldinoa and the taking of Caprona, in which the Ghibellines were finally vanquished. The Guelphs then split over the issue of papal influence in Florence. Dante was a member of the White Guelphs, who sought to preserve an independent republic. Dante became one of six guild representatives who governed the city and, when the pope encroached on Florentine politics with threats of excommunication and confiscation of possessions, Dante and two others were sent on a mission to Rome in 1301 to query the pope about whether he intended to actively support the Blacks. Dante hoped that a secular leader of sufficient stature, such as the head of the Holy Roman Empire, might unify Italy and thereby bring peace to Florence.

Dante never returned to Florence. In a *coup d'état,* the Blacks gained power and moved to eliminate the leaders of the Whites. When Dante chose not to return to Florence to face charges, he was sentenced to two years of exile and a large fine. This penalty was subsequently extended to permanent exile with the threat of being burned alive should he return to the city.

Life in Exile.   As an exiled Florentine, Dante wandered from town to town in Italy, finding temporary lodgings with a variety of patrons. In poignant lines from the early part of Canto XVII in *Paradiso,* Dante describes the painful experience of exile, how he will leave behind everything that he loves most dearly. He will suffer from going up and down another man's stairs. But worst of all will be the ungrateful and wicked company who are angry and vindictive towards Dante.

He had already written several treatises connected to his studies. *The Banquet* (*Il Convivio*) was an extension of *The New Life,* plus an explanation of Dante's literary views. *On the Illustrious Vernacular* (*De vulgari eloquentia*), written in Latin during the same period, defends the use of Italian in serious literature and supports the role of the Italian writer in contemporary society. Later, the *Comedy* itself was written in vernacular Italian, intended for a broad audience and the promotion of cultural identity. A pamphlet written sometime between 1308 and 1317, *De Monarchia,* placed hope for healing Italy's afflictions and

GWELFS
GIB-uh-leens

[. . .] A turn to a religious view of man and his fate . . . meant freeing [Dante] as a poet to represent the human with a subtle, many-sided realism that had no parallel in his time, and has not been surpassed since. . . . He can, for the first, fill his poem with many spirits and many voices besides his own, and with all the sights and sounds and smells of God's world.

– FRANCIS FERGUSSON, critic, 1966

divisiveness in a clear separation of the powers of the church and state and the investiture of two powerful leaders, a secular emperor and a sacred pope. Crowned in 1308, the new emperor Henry VII began to unite Italy, giving possibility to Dante's vision; Florence, however, rebuffed him, and the emperor died suddenly in 1313.

All the learning and the living that underlay Dante's early writings became part of the complex fabric of the *Comedy*, to which Dante devoted himself from 1312 until his death in 1321. The first two parts of the *Comedy*, the *Inferno* and the *Purgatorio*, were immediately recognized as great works of literature. With the work Dante hoped to gain an honorable return to his beloved Florence, but that did not happen. After finishing the last cantos of *Paradiso*, Dante died in Ravenna of malaria at the age of fifty-six and was buried there; Florence is still trying to procure his bones. Dante's great work was first called the *Divine Comedy* (*Divina Commedia*) by a Venetian publisher in 1555.

The *Divine Comedy*. The *Divine Comedy* is not an EPIC in the conventional sense, but if by *epic* one means a lengthy and elevated poem that deals with serious issues in a vast or cosmic setting, then Dante's extended narrative certainly qualifies. His heroes are not Homer's or Virgil's warriors of the battlefield. They are warriors of the spirit, redefining the arena of adventure for the Middle Ages and beyond.

Dante called his monumental work the *Commedia*, a COMEDY, because it had a happy ending. The story is essentially that of a pilgrimage by a person named Dante through the three spiritual realms of the Catholic world—Hell, Purgatory, and Heaven—during the Easter season. Because of the importance of the Trinity in medieval Catholic theology, the number three plays a key role in Dante's elaborate literary design. Each of the major divisions of the work points to a person of the Trinity and contains thirty-three cantos: the *Inferno*, identified with God the Father and judgment, includes one additional canto as a general introduction; the acts of the Son involving salvation are connected to *Purgatorio*; and the sustaining grace of the Holy Spirit is linked to *Paradiso*. Both *Purgatorio* and *Paradiso* contain thirty-three cantos, bringing the total number of cantos of all three works to one hundred, a perfect number.

The overall geography of Dante's world in the *Comedy* follows generally the cosmic system devised by Ptolemy, the Alexandrian astronomer of the second century. The heavens with their planets revolve around the earth. The geographical center of the earth's surface is Jerusalem; at the eastern edge is the Ganges River and at the western edge of the Mediterranean is the Straits of Gibraltar. Directly opposite from Jerusalem is the mountain of Purgatory. In the center of the earth, at a point farthest from the warmth of God's love in the Heavens, is Hell, where Satan is frozen in ice. All the rivers of Hell, symbolizing the tears of human suffering, flow toward the center in order to torment its residents.

The *Inferno* begins on the evening of Maundy Thursday, or Holy Thursday, with Dante lost in a wood. At dawn on Good Friday, he meets the poet Virgil, who serves as his guide through Hell, a funnel-shaped region extending from the earth's surface to the center of the earth, a depression formed when Lucifer plunged from Heaven into the earth. Nine separate descending circles are divided into three major divisions; those associated with the mildest of sins are located at the top and those with the worst at the bottom. *Inferno* ends on Easter morning, as Dante and Virgil arrive in Purgatory, a mountain on an island in the sea at the opposite end of the earth from Lucifer's fall.

From the beginning of *Purgatorio*, there is a joyful, hopeful tone totally different from the despair of the *Inferno*. Dante the pilgrim,

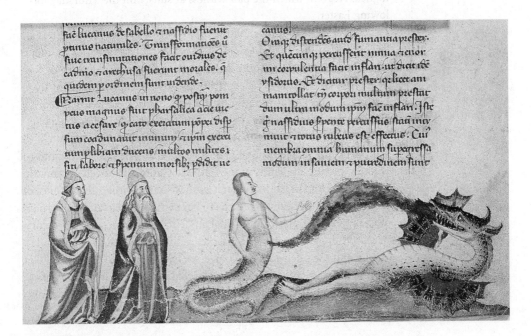

Dante and Virgil, fourteenth century
This illustration from the Inferno *shows Dante and Virgil encountering a dragon and a sea monster. (Giraudon/Art Resource, NY)*

having learned about avoiding sin in Hell, now learns of the virtues of being purged of the seven deadly sins on the seven terraces in the middle of Purgatory. In Canto XXVII the poets cross through a wall of fire, a symbol of transformation, into Earthly Paradise. Virgil, having reached a place where he "can discern nothing further," gives a farewell speech. His job as guide comes to an end because Purgatory is as far as reason can carry the individual pilgrim, and Virgil is a virtuous pagan lacking belief in God, with only his reason to guide him. Dante then learns about the Earthly Paradise and experiences the freedom of action associated with being purged of sin. Finally, the epitome of beauty and virtue, the veiled Beatrice, becomes Dante's next guide. She scolds Dante for lapsing into material desires, which is perhaps a confession by the poet of his own waywardness. After Dante has been bathed in the river Lethe, washing away all memory of sin, he is allowed to look at Beatrice without her veil and is blinded by the vision. His virtues are strengthened by drinking from the waters of the Eunoe; he is now ready to experience the celestial Paradise. Beatrice leads Dante through the three regions of this realm: the seven planets of ancient astronomy, the circles of fixed stars, and the Empyrean, or highest Heaven, which the pair witness at sunset on the Thursday following Easter.

As the third and final volume of the *Divine Comedy*, *Paradiso* is a celebration of the starry heavens of an earth-centered cosmos as understood by medieval astronomy. As Dante and Beatrice ascend from planet to planet, various redeemed souls provide explanations for the heavenly bodies. Appropriate Christian doctrines are also discussed. The seven planets plus the circle of fixed stars and the *primum mobile*[2] equal (again) the number nine; the Empyrean, or Heaven, is tenth, a symbol of unity and the totality of the universe. The last three cantos of *Paradiso* picture the saints of the Catholic Church arranged in a mystic white rose with God at its center. Canto XXXII identifies the thrones of the most blessed; Beatrice returns to her eternal throne and St. Bernard of Clairvaux becomes Dante's final guide to a climactic, beatific vision. Bernard's prayers on behalf of Dante lead to a final vision of the Holy Trinity and the oneness of the universe. This culminating vision of God represents a difficult task for the poet: to describe that which by definition transcends words—the ineffable. Dante's answer is to focus on

---

[2]*primum mobile:* In the Ptolemaic universe, this is the outermost sphere with the earth as its center, causing all the heavenly bodies to revolve with it.

the effect of the vision on its human witness rather than on the vision itself. The result of Dante's artistry is the experience of merging with the divine, the final and ultimate goal of the medieval pilgrim.

Inferno.   Because sin is always more interesting than goodness, and because Dante's depictions of sin's punishments are so insightful and imaginative, the *Inferno* has been the most popular volume of the trilogy for modern readers. Canto I begins with the statement that the pilgrim Dante, at thirty-five years of age, has lost his way and found himself in a "dark wood"—a different kind of beginning from those in Homer's epics or Virgil's *Aeneid*, in which a grand theme is explicitly announced. A very visual poet, Dante begins with what seems to be an ordinary situation in accordance with the manner of his narrator, who is a simplified, at times more naive, version of himself. Dante's style, however, becomes more elevated as his pilgrim advances—literally, climbs—to Purgatory and then Paradise. On the literal level, the poem follows the dramatic adventures of this Dante as he journeys through three realms, encountering various sinners and saints from both the ancient world and contemporary Italy, learning from their lives, and progressing from confusion to spiritual illumination.

The first lines of the *Inferno*, however, hint at another layer of meaning, symbolic or allegorical. The pilgrim is at an age when questions traditionally arise about one's spiritual condition; the "dark wood" mirrors the inner confusion and fear people may experience when they reach midlife. When Dante sees the sunrise and decides to climb the Mount of Joy, where he confronts three animals, it is clear that Dante the poet is deliberately entering into a symbolic realm.

The three animals that rebuff Dante appear to represent the three major kinds of sins—incontinence (or lack of restraint), violence, and fraud—and correspond to the three divisions of Hell. Enter Virgil, who explains that he has been sent to guide Dante through a descent into Hell and an ascent to Purgatory, where he will be replaced by Beatrice. Virgil stands for reason and conscience as well as the best ideals of the Roman Empire. As a great poet, Virgil was a hero to Dante. Virgil sought to unify the Roman Empire with his epic the *Aeneid*, as Dante's poem would do for all of Italy, not just Florence. In addition, Virgil had written the *Fourth Eclogue*, which seemed to many Christians to have predicted the advent of a child messiah and, in Book IV of the *Aeneid*, he had described a descent into Hades, making him an appropriate guide for Dante. As Virgil tells him, Dante is to go on this journey to gain knowledge. Virgil engages in dialogue with Dante, answering his questions and probing his understanding.

KAHN-truh-PAH-soh

In Canto III, the two poets pass through the Gate of Hell and view for the first time a ***contrapasso***, or symbolic retribution. In Dante's Hell, more picturesque and altogether different from most other literary depictions of Hell, where general horrors engulf an entire group of sinners, individual punishments are fashioned for different sins. Dante's view of accountability was consistent with medieval theology, which held that individuals had free will and therefore chose sin. Thus they could be assigned punishments as individuals, regardless of their family or social situations. For example, because opportunists and the cowardly took no moral stand in life for either good or evil, they are adrift in Hell. Corrupt public officials who accepted bribes are boiled in pitch because, like bribes that cling to the sinner, pitch is sticky. And fortune-tellers and diviners who predicted the future during their time on earth now can look only backwards, as their heads have been turned around.

The first circle of Hell, found in Canto IV, is for virtuous pagans. Modern readers might sympathize with the likes of the great poets of antiquity, Homer, Horace, Ovid, and Lucan, but the medieval Christian view was clear on this point: Jesus alone was the gateway to Heaven. Thus the noble and virtuous pagans were held here at the threshold of Hell. Souls guilty of carnal sin are found in Canto V. Those who are led by their desires are blown about by the winds of desire. Dante's method of depicting sinners is to present appropriate examples who would be known to his readers and to develop more complete portraits of just a few of them. He does not analyze the sin abstractly, but rather he vividly shows how people following their desires and yielding to temptation can drift into damnation, as is the case with the most famous couple in the *Divine Comedy*, the young lovers **Paolo** and **Francesca**. Despite their condemnation, their story is told with great sensitivity and sympathy.

POW-loh
frahn-CHES-kah

The first of several political prophecies about Florence is uttered in Canto VI by the glutton **Ciacco** the Hog, who is buried in swill. In subsequent cantos, Dante forthrightly locates his political enemies in various circles of Hell. In Cantos X and XI, the circle reserved for heretics serves as a mezzanine between the upper Hell, for sins of incontinence, and the lower Hell, for violence and fraud. After witnessing the instigators of war boiling in blood, Dante enters the memorable Wood of the Suicides in Canto XIII, where the Violent Against Themselves are punished and their souls are denied human form. Even though the church considered suicide a sin, **Piero della Vigne**'s narrative elicits sympathy. In Canto XV, Brunetto Latini, Dante's teacher and mentor, is also treated with delicacy

CHAH-koh

pee-EHR-oh
deh-lah-VEEN-yay

and respect, despite the fact that his sin of homosexuality is acknowledged and punished with a burning rain. This canto is a reminder to the reader that Hell is filled with humans who might not have appeared evil but who nevertheless committed sins. In certain cases, however, Dante seems to be torn between the justice of a particular punishment and sympathy for the vagaries of human nature; after all, most human beings are a mixture of noble sentiments and carnal weaknesses.

At the end of Canto XVII, Virgil and Dante descend into the third and lowest area of Hell—for premeditated fraud—on the back of Geryon, a marvelous monster with the face of a man and a serpent's body. The eighth circle of Hell called the Malebolge (evil ditches) is divided into ten trenches, or **Bolgia**, peopled with different kinds of sinners associated with fraud. The Simoniacs are set upside down in holes and their feet are on fire. Dante locates Ulysses (Odysseus), whom Homer describes in the *Odyssey* as quick-witted and clever, in Bolgia Eight (Canto XXVI), the place for evil counselors. Italians traced their ancestry back to the Trojans, and Odysseus was the architect of the ruse of the wooden horse, which led to the destruction of Troy in the Trojan War. Hidden in a great flame, a proud Ulysses recounts his exploration of the Western ocean. His death by shipwreck on Purgatory Mountain is a symbolic statement that courage and intelligence alone cannot save man.

The climax of the *Inferno* occurs in the last three cantos, when the poets reach the ninth circle of Hell. Here the sinners are so far from the warmth of God's love that they are frozen in a lake of ice, symbolic of the condition of their hearts. One of the lasting images of this section is Ugolino gnawing on the skull of **Ruggieri** in Canto XXXIII, in which **Ugolino** tells their story of betrayal and infamy. The great pathos associated with the starvation of children makes this episode one of the most memorable in the entire poem. In the final canto and at the utter bottom of Hell is the master of evil himself, Satan, with great flapping wings and a treacherous threesome in his mouths: Judas Iscariot, Brutus, and Cassius. (For modern readers, Brutus and Cassius, two of the Roman assassins of Julius Caesar, may not meet the same standard of evil as the betrayer of Jesus, and the portrait of Satan may not inspire such fear.)

Dante was a dramatist, a genius who created an imaginary world through which the attentive reader might journey. The encyclopedic, intimidating mountain of saints and sinners, virtues and deadly sins, bits of geography, elaborate political maneuvers from Florence and the Holy Roman Empire—all of which might have a literal as well as other

BOLE-jee-uh

roo-JEH-ree
oo-goh-LEE-no

Dante is an exiled, aggressive, self-righteous, salvation-bent intellectual, humbled only to rise assured and ardent, zealously prophetic, politically messianic, indignant, nervous, muscular, theatrical, energetic—he is at once our brother and our engenderer.

– ALLEN MANDELBAUM, translator, 1980

layers of meaning—fit into Dante's own highly architectural vision of God's plan for the world. The almost immediate fame of the *Comedy* is testified to by several line-by-line commentaries by contemporaries of Dante, as if his work did indeed hold the key to salvation. Today there are hundreds of such line-by-line commentaries.

■ FURTHER RESEARCH

Translations
Hollander, Robert, and Jean Hollander, trans. *Inferno*. 2000.
Mandelbaum, Allen, trans. *Inferno*. 1980.
Sinclair, John D., trans. *The Divine Comedy. I: Inferno*. 1961.
Singleton, Charles S., trans. *The Divine Comedy*. 1970.

Bibliography, Biography, and Background
Golino, Carlo. *Dante Alighieri*. 1979.
Lansing, Richard, ed. *The Dante Encyclopedia*. 2000.
Lewis, R. W. B. *Dante*. 2001.
Morgan, Alison. *Dante and the Medieval Other World*. 1990.
Sterns, Monroe. *Dante: Poet of Love*. 1965.

Commentary and Criticism
Auerbach, Erich. *Dante: Poet of the Secular World*. 1961.
Fergusson, Francis. *Dante*. 1966.
Fowlie, Wallace. *A Reading of Dante's "Inferno."* 1981.
Freccero, John, ed. *Dante: A Collection of Critical Essays*. 1965.
———. *Dante: The Poetics of Conversion*. 1986.
Jacoff, Rachel, ed. *The Cambridge Companion to Dante*. 1993.
Santayanna, George. *Three Philosophical Poets*. 1927.
Sayers, Dorothy. *Further Papers on Dante*. 1957.
———. *Introductory Papers on Dante*. 1954.

■ PRONUNCIATION

Accorso: ah-KORE-soh
Acheron: AK-uh-rahn
Acre: AH-kruh, AY-kur
Aldobrandi: ahl-doh-BRAHN-dee
Amidei: ah-mee-DAY-ee
Amphiaraus: am-fee-uh-RAY-us
Anaxagoras: an-ak-SAG-oh-rus
Anchises: ang-KIGH-seez
Antaeus: an-TEE-us
Arachne: uh-RAK-nee
Argenti, Filippo: ar-JEN-tee, fih-LEE-poh, fih-LIP-oh
Arles: ARL
Athamas: ATH-uh-mus
Averroës: uh-VEH-roh-eez
Avicenna: av-ih-SEN-uh
Azzolino: ah-tsoh-LEE-noh
Bacchiglione: bah-kee-LYOH-nee, -lee-OH-nee
Beatrice: BEE-uh-tris, bay-ah-TREE-chay

Bolgia: BOLE-jee-uh
Boniface VIII: BAH-nih-fus
Borsiere, Guglielmo: bore-SYAY-ray, goo-LYEL-moh, bore-see-AY-ray,
    goo-lee-EL-moh
Buondelmonte: bwone-del-MONE-tay
Cacus: KAY-kus
Caina: kah-EE-nuh
Capaneus: KAP-uh-noos
Casalodi: kah-sah-LOH-dee
Cassius: KASH-us
Ceperano: chay-peh-RAH-noh
Cerberus: SUR-bur-us
Charon: KAHR-ahn
Chiron: KIGH-rahn
Ciacco: CHAH-koh
Cocytus: koh-SIGH-tus
contrapasso: KAHN-truh-PAH-soh
Dante Alighieri: DAHN-tay ah-lih-GYEH-ree
Deianira: dee-uh-NIGH-ruh
Diogenes: digh-AH-jih-neez
Dioscorides: digh-us-KORE-ih-deez
Divina Commedia: dih-VEE-nuh kah-MED-ee-uh
Erinyes: eh-RIN-ee-eez
Euryalus: yoo-RIGH-uh-lus
Farinata degli Uberti: fah-ree-NAH-tah DEH-lyee oo-BEHR-tee
Fiesole: fyeh-SOH-lay, fee-eh-SOH-lay
Francesca: frahn-CHES-kah
Garisenda: gah-rih-SEN-duh
Geryon: JEE-ree-ahn, GEH-ree-ahn
Ghibellines: GIB-uh-leens
Gualdrada: gwahl-DRAH-dah
Guelphs: GWELFS
Guerra, Guido: GWEH-ruh, GWEE-doh
Guido of Montefeltro: GWEE-doh, mone-tay-FEL-troh
Hypsipyle: hip-SIP-uh-lee
Judecca: joo-DEK-uh
Maccabees: MAK-uh-beez
Malebolge: mal-uh-BOWL-jay
Malebranche: mahl-uh-BRANK-eh
Maremma: muh-REM-uh
Montaperti: mawn-tah-PEHR-tee
Obizzo of Esti: oh-BIT-soh, ES-tee
Paolo: POW-loh
Penthesilea: pen-thu-sih-LEE-uh
Phlegethon: FLEG-uh-thon
Phlegyas: FLEG-ee-us
Piero della Vigne: pee-EHR-oh deh-lah-VEEN-yay
Pistoia: pis-TOH-yah
Priscian: PRISH-un
Ptolomea: tahl-oh-MEE-uh
Quarnero: kwar-NAY-roh
Rinier da Corneto: reen-YEHR dah-kohr-NAY-toh
Rinier Pazzo: reen-YEHR PAHT-soh

Romagna: roh-MAHN-yah
Ruggieri: roo-JEH-ree
Rusticucci, Jacopo: roo-stih-KOO-chee, JAH-koh-poh
Scipio: SKIP-ee-oh, SIP-ee-oh
Semiramis: seh-MEE-ruh-mis
Ser Brunetto Latini: sehr broo-NET-oh lah-TEE-nee
Sychaeus: sih-KEE-us
Strophades: STRAH-fuh-deez
Tagliacozzo: tahl-yah-KAWT-soh
Tityus: TIT-ee-us
Ubaldini: oo-bahl-DEE-nee
Ugolino: oo-goh-LEE-no

ᘐ Inferno

Translated by Robert Pinsky

CANTO I

[*The Dark Wood: the Three Beasts; Virgil.* Near dawn on the morning of Good Friday, 1300 C.E., at the age of thirty-five, Dante awakes to find himself in a dark forest. As he begins to climb a hill, he meets three beasts that symbolize aspects of sinfulness: a leopard, a lion, and a wolf. As Dante despairs of continuing on he meets Virgil, poet of ancient Rome, who offers to guide him through Hell and Purgatory. He is told that another will lead him to Heaven.]

Midway on our life's journey,[1] I found myself
   In dark woods, the right road lost. To tell
   About those woods is hard—so tangled and rough

And savage that thinking of it now, I feel
   The old fear stirring: death is hardly more bitter.
   And yet, to treat the good I found there as well

A note on translation: Italian offers many possibilities for rhyme. In English, however, *terza rima* is nearly impossible to duplicate with hard or "perfect" rhymes (*air* with *care*). The Robert Pinsky translation stays close to the language, phrasing, and meaning of the Italian text in readable, contemporary English, while using partial or "approximate" rhymes (*air* with *war*). The canto summaries (in brackets) have been added by the editors. The notes used in this selection are the editors'. They have been intentionally kept to a minimum and do not represent all possible meanings or explanations.

---

[1] **life's journey:** Dante was thirty-five at the time, 1300 C.E. This is a reference to Psalm 90:10: "The days of our years are three score years and ten." Also see Isaiah 38:10, "In the midst of my days I shall go to the gates of Hell."

DANTE'S HELL

Cantos I-II	*The Dark Wood*	
Canto III		Neutrals

River Acheron

Canto IV	**Circle 1: Limbo**
Canto V	**Circle 2: Lust**
Canto VI	**Circle 3: Gluttony**
Canto VII	**Circle 4: Avarice and Prodigality**
	Circle 5: Anger and Sullenness
Canto VIII	*River Styx* (of mud)

Canto IX	*Gate of Dis*
Canto X	**Circle 6: Heresy**

Canto XI	**Circle 7: Violence**
Canto XII	*River Phlegethon* (of blood)
	1. against others: murderers and plunderers
Canto XIII	2. against self: suicides and squanderers
Canto XIV	3. against God:
	blasphemers
Canto XV-XVI	sodomites
Canto XVII	usurers

The Malebolge

Canto XVIII	**Circle 8: Fraud**
	1. panderers and seducers
	2. flatterers
Canto XIX	3. simoniacs
Canto XX	4. diviners
Canto XXI-XXII	5. grafters
Canto XXIII	6. hypocrites
Canto XXIV-XXV	7. thieves
Canto XXVI-XXVII	8. false counselors
Canto XXVIII	9. sowers of scandal and schism
Canto XXIX-XXX	10. falsifiers and counterfeiters

Canto XXXI	*Descent to Cocytus, the Frozen Floor of Hell*
	Circle 9: Treachery
Canto XXXII	1. *Caina* (against relatives)
	2. *Antenora* (against homeland or party)
Canto XXXIII	3. *Ptolomea* (against guests)
Canto XXXIV	4. *Judecca* (against benefactors)
	Satan

I'll tell what I saw, though how I came to enter
   I cannot well say, being so full of sleep
   Whatever moment it was I began to blunder

10 Off the true path. But when I came to stop
   Below a hill that marked one end of the valley
   That had pierced my heart with terror, I looked up

Toward the crest and saw its shoulders already
   Mantled in rays of that bright planet that shows
   The road to everyone, whatever our journey.

Then I could feel the terror begin to ease
   That churned in my heart's lake all through the night.
   As one still panting, ashore from dangerous seas,

Looks back at the deep he has escaped, my thought
20 Returned, still fleeing, to regard that grim defile
   That never left any alive who stayed in it.

After I had rested my weary body awhile
   I started again across the wilderness,
   My left foot always lower on the hill,

And suddenly—a leopard,[2] near the place
   The way grew steep: lithe, spotted, quick of foot.
   Blocking the path, she stayed before my face

And more than once she made me turn about
   To go back down. It was early morning still,
30 The fair sun rising with the stars attending it

As when Divine Love set those beautiful
   Lights into motion at creation's dawn,[3]
   And the time of day and season combined to fill

My heart with hope of that beast with festive skin—
   But not so much that the next sight wasn't fearful:
   A lion came at me, his head high as he ran,

---

[2] **leopard:** Jeremiah 5:6: "Wherefore a lion out of the forest shall slay them, a wolf of the evening shall spoil them a leopard shall watch over their cities."

[3] **dawn:** In Christian mythology, the stars were supposed to have been set in motion during creation in the spring of the year, the same date as the crucifixion. This is the morning of Good Friday.

Roaring with hunger so the air appeared to tremble.
  Then, a grim she-wolf—whose leanness seemed to compress
  All the world's cravings, that had made miserable

40 Such multitudes; she put such heaviness
  Into my spirit, I lost hope of the crest.
  Like someone eager to win, who tested by loss

Surrenders to gloom and weeps, so did that beast
  Make me feel, as harrying toward me at a lope
  She forced me back toward where the sun is lost.

While I was ruining myself back down to the deep,
  Someone appeared—one who seemed nearly to fade
  As though from long silence. I cried to his human shape

In that great wasteland: "Living man or shade,
50   Have pity and help me, whichever you may be!"
  "No living man, though once I was," he replied.

"My parents both were Mantuans from Lombardy,
  And I was born *sub Julio*,[4] the latter end.
  I lived in good Augustus's Rome, in the day

Of the false gods who lied. A poet, I hymned
  Anchises' noble son,[5] who came from Troy
  When superb Ilium[6] in its pride was burned.

But you—why go back down to such misery?
  Why not ascend the delightful mountain, source
60   And principle that causes every joy?"

"Then are you Virgil? Are you the font that pours
  So overwhelming a river of human speech?"
  I answered, shamefaced. "The glory and light are yours,

That poets follow—may the love that made me search
  Your book in patient study avail me, Master!
  You are my guide and author, whose verses teach

---

[4] *sub Julio*: "Under Julius Caesar"; Virgil was born in 70 B.C.E.

[5] **Anchises' noble son:** Aeneas, the hero of Virgil's *The Aeneid*.

[6] **Ilium:** Troy or the citadel of Troy.

The graceful style whose model has done me honor.
See this beast driving me backward—help me resist,
For she makes all my veins and pulses shudder."

70 "A different path from this one would be best
For you to find your way from this feral place,"
He answered, seeing how I wept. "This beast,

The cause of your complaint, lets no one pass
Her way—but harries all to death. Her nature
Is so malign and vicious she cannot appease

Her voracity, for feeding makes her hungrier.
Many are the beasts she mates: there will be more,
Until the Hound comes[7] who will give this creature

A painful death. Not nourished by earthly fare,
80 He will be fed by wisdom, goodness and love.
Born between Feltro and Feltro,[8] he shall restore

Low Italy, as Nisus fought to achieve.
And Turnus, Euryalus, Camilla[9] the maiden—
All dead from wounds in war. He will remove

This lean wolf, hunting her through every region
Till he has thrust her back to Hell's abyss
Where Envy first dispatched her on her mission.

Therefore I judge it best that you should choose
To follow me, and I will be your guide
90 Away from here and through an eternal place:

To hear the cries of despair, and to behold
Ancient tormented spirits as they lament
In chorus the second death[10] they must abide.

---

[7]**Until the Hound comes:** A prophecy by Dante, possibly referring to his patron Can Grande della Scala, the Lord of Verona, and Dante's benefactor during his exile from Florence, or to Henry VIII of Luxemberg, the Holy Roman Emperor.

[8]**Feltro and Feltro:** Often translated Feltro and Feltro referring to Verona, which is in between the towns of Feltro and Montefeltro.

[9]**Nisus . . . Camilla:** Four characters in *The Aeneid* who die in Aeneas's conquest of Italy.

[10]**second death:** The second death is suffering of the damned in Hell.

Then you shall see those souls who are content
   To dwell in fire[11] because they hope some day
   To join the blessed: toward whom, if your ascent

Continues, your guide will be one worthier than I—
   When I must leave you, you will be with her.
   For the Emperor who governs from on high

100 Wills I not enter His city, where none may appear
   Who lived like me in rebellion to His law.
   His empire is everything and everywhere,

But that is His kingdom, His city, His seat of awe.
   Happy is the soul He chooses for that place!"
   I: "Poet, please—by the God you did not know—

Help me escape this evil that I face,
   And worse. Lead me to witness what you have said,
   Saint Peter's gate,[12] and the multitude of woes—"

Then he set out, and I followed where he led.

CANTO II

[*Preparing for the Descent: the Three Women of Heaven.* When Dante voices his fears about the journey, Virgil scolds him, relating that he was sent by Beatrice, Dante's beloved on earth, who was concerned about his salvation. Beatrice in turn was sent by Saint Lucia, who was asked by the Virgin Mary herself to attend to Dante. Assured of such support, Dante agrees to continue.]

Day was departing, and the darkening air
   Called all earth's creatures to their evening quiet
   While I alone was preparing as though for war

To struggle with my journey and with the spirit
   Of pity, which flawless memory will redraw:
   O Muses, O genius of art, O memory whose merit

---

[11] **dwell in fire:** The burning in Purgatory.

[12] **Saint Peter's gate:** The gate of penitence into Purgatory.

Has inscribed inwardly those things I saw—
   Help me fulfill the perfection of your nature.
   I commenced: "Poet, take my measure now:

10 Appraise my powers before you trust me to venture
   Through that deep passage where you would be my guide.
   You write of the journey Silvius's father

Made to immortal realms[13] although he stayed
   A mortal witness, in his corruptible body.
   That the Opponent of all evil bestowed

Such favor on him befits him, chosen for glory
   By highest heaven to be the father of Rome
   And of Rome's empire—later established Holy,

Seat of great Peter's heir. You say he came
20 To that immortal world, and things he learned
   There led to the papal mantle[14]—and triumph for him.

Later, the Chosen Vessel° too went and returned,   St. Paul
   Carrying confirmation of that faith
   Which opens the way with salvation at its end.

But I—what cause, whose favor, could send me forth
   On such a voyage? I am no Aeneas or Paul:
   Not I nor others think me of such worth,

And therefore I have my fears of playing the fool
   To embark on such a venture. You are wise:
30 You know my meaning better than I can tell."

And then, like one who unchooses his own choice
   And thinking again undoes what he has started,
   So I became: a nullifying unease

Overcame my soul on that dark slope and voided
   The undertaking I had so quickly embraced.
   "If I understand," the generous shade retorted,

---

[13] **immortal realms:** A reference to Aeneas's visit to the underworld (*The Aeneid*, VI).

[14] **papal mantle:** The founding of Rome led to the first pope, Saint Peter.

"Cowardice grips your spirit—which can twist
  A man away from the noblest enterprise
  As a trick of vision startles a shying beast.

40 To ease your burden of fear, I will disclose
  Why I came here, and what I heard that compelled
  Me first to feel compassion for you: it was

A lady's voice that called me where I dwelled
  In Limbo[15]—a lady so blessed and fairly featured
  I prayed her to command me. Her eyes out-jeweled

The stars in splendor. 'O generous Mantuan spirit,'
  She began in a soft voice of angelic sound,
  'Whose fame lives still, that the world will still inherit

As long as the world itself shall live: my friend—
50 No friend of Fortune—has found his way impeded
  On the barren slope, and fear has turned him round.

I fear he may be already lost, unaided:
  So far astray, I've come from Heaven too late.
  Go now, with your fair speech and what is needed

To save him; offer the help you have to give
  Before he is lost, and I will be consoled.
  I am Beatrice, come from where I crave

To be again, who ask this. As love has willed,
  So have I spoken. And when I return
60 Before my Lord, He will hear your praises told.'

Then she was silent; and I in turn began,
  'O Lady of goodness, through whom alone mankind
  Exceeds what the sky's least circle can contain

Within its compass:[16] so sweet is your command
  Had I already obeyed, it would feel too late.
  But tell me how you so fearlessly descend

---

[15] **Limbo:** The place where the virtuous pagans and unbaptized children are forever suspended between punishment and bliss.

[16] **compass:** A reference to the cycle of the moon.

To such a center—from that encompassing state
　　You long to see again?' 'You yearn for the answer
　　Deeply,' she said, 'so I will tell in short

70　How I can come to Limbo, yet feel no terror:
　　Fear befits things with power for injury,
　　Not things that lack such power. God the Creator

Has by His mercy made me such that I
　　Cannot feel what you suffer: none of this fire
　　Assails me. In Heaven a Lady[17] feels such pity

For this impediment where I send you, severe
　　Judgment is broken by her grace on high.
　　To Lucy[18] she said: "Your faithful follower

Needs you: I commend him to you." Lucy, the foe
80　Of every cruelty, found me where I sat
　　With Rachel[19] of old, and urged me: "Beatrice, true

Glory of God, can you not come to the aid
　　Of one who had such love for you he rose
　　Above the common crowd? Do you not heed

The pity of his cries? And do your eyes
　　Not see death near him, in a flood the ocean
　　Itself can boast no power to surpass?"

Never on earth was anyone spurred to motion
　　So quickly, to seize advantage or fly from danger,
90　As at these words I hurried here from Heaven—

Trusting your eloquence, whose gift brings honor
　　Both to yourself and to all those who listen.'
　　Having said this, she turned toward me the splendor

Of her eyes lucent with tears—which made me hasten
　　To save you, even more eagerly than before:
　　And so I rescued you on the fair mountain

---

[17] **a Lady:** Virgin Mary.

[18] **Lucy:** St. Lucy of Syracuse (third century), a martyr.

[19] **Rachel:** Rachel was mother of Joseph and Benjamin in the Hebrew Scriptures (Genesis 29–35).

Where the beast blocked the short way up. Therefore,
    What is this? Why, why should you hold back?
    Why be a coward rather than bolder, freer—

100 Since in the court of Heaven for your sake
    Three blessed ladies[20] watch, and words of mine
    Have promised a good as great as you might seek?"

As flowers bent and shrunken by night at dawn
    Unfold and straighten on their stems, to wake
    Brightened by sunlight, so I grew strong again—

Good courage coursing through my heart, I spoke
    Like one set free: "How full of true compassion
    Was she who helped me, how courteous and quick

Were you to follow her bidding—and your narration
110 Has restored my spirit. Now, on: for I feel eager
    To go with you, and cleave to my first intention.

From now, we two will share one will together:
    You are my teacher, my master, and my guide."
    So I spoke, and when he moved I followed after

And entered on that deep and savage road.

Canto III

[*Gate of Hell and Vestibule: the Uncommitted and Indifferent. River Acheron: Charon.* Dante and Virgil come to the gate of hell. The inscription over the entrance terrifies Dante, but Virgil leads him inside to a vestibule at the edge of hell itself. They hear the groans of those who have led uncommitted lives, choosing neither good nor evil during their time on earth. They pass the soul of Pope Celestine V and approach a group waiting to be ferried across the river Acheron by Charon the boatman. At first Charon refuses to transport Dante, since he is a living soul and the boat is intended for the dead, but Virgil appeases him. Dante faints; he awakes on the other shore.]

THROUGH ME YOU ENTER INTO THE CITY OF WOES,
    THROUGH ME YOU ENTER INTO ETERNAL PAIN,
    THROUGH ME YOU ENTER THE POPULATION OF LOSS.

---

[20] **Three blessed ladies:** Mary, Lucy, and Beatrice.

JUSTICE MOVED MY HIGH MAKER, IN POWER DIVINE,
WISDOM SUPREME, LOVE PRIMAL. NO THINGS WERE
BEFORE ME NOT ETERNAL[21]; ETERNAL I REMAIN.

ABANDON ALL HOPE, YOU WHO ENTER HERE.
These words I saw inscribed in some dark color
Over a portal. "Master," I said, "make clear

10 Their meaning, which I find too hard to gather."
Then he, as one who understands: "All fear
Must be left here, and cowardice die. Together,

We have arrived where I have told you: here
You will behold the wretched souls who've lost
The good of intellect."[22] Then, with good cheer

In his expression to encourage me, he placed
His hand on mine: so, trusting to my guide,
I followed him among things undisclosed.

The sighs, groans and laments at first were so loud,
20 Resounding through starless air, I began to weep:
Strange languages, horrible screams, words imbued

With rage or despair, cries as of troubled sleep
Or of a tortured shrillness—they rose in a coil
Of tumult, along with noises like the slap

Of beating hands, all fused in a ceaseless flail
That churns and frenzies that dark and timeless air
Like sand in a whirlwind. And I, my head in a swirl

Of error, cried: "Master, what is this I hear?
What people are these, whom pain has overcome?"
30 He: "This is the sorrowful state of souls unsure,

Whose lives earned neither honor nor bad fame.
And they are mingled with angels of that base sort
Who, neither rebellious to God nor faithful to Him,

---

[21] ETERNAL: Primal matter, the heavens and divinities like angels.
[22] **good of intellect:** Knowledge of God.

Chose neither side, but kept themselves apart —
    Now Heaven expels them, not to mar its splendor,
    And Hell rejects them, lest the wicked of heart

Take glory over them."[23] And then I: "Master,
    What agony is it, that makes them keen their grief
    With so much force?" He: "I will make brief answer:

40 They have no hope of death, but a blind life
    So abject, they envy any other fate.
    To all memory of them, the world is deaf.

Mercy and justice disdain them. Let us not
    Speak of them: look and pass on." I looked again:
    A whirling banner sped at such a rate

It seemed it might never stop; behind it a train
    Of souls, so long that I would not have thought
    Death had undone so many. When more than one

I recognized had passed, I beheld the shade
50   Of him who made the Great Refusal,[24] impelled
    By cowardice: so at once I understood

Beyond all doubt that this was the dreary guild
    Repellent both to God and His enemies —
    Hapless ones never alive, their bare skin galled

By wasps and flies, blood trickling down the face,
    Mingling with tears for harvest underfoot
    By writhing maggots. Then, when I turned my eyes

Farther along our course, I could make out
    People upon the shore of some great river.
60   "Master," I said, "it seems by this dim light

That all of these are eager to cross over —
    Can you tell me by what law, and who they are?"
    He answered, "Those are things you will discover

---

[23] **glory over them:** Those who choose neither good nor evil. In the words of Revelation (3:16) "art lukewarm."

[24] **Great Refusal:** Probably a reference to Pope Celestine V, who at the age of eighty, was elected pope in 1294 and resigned five months later.

When we have paused at Acheron's dismal shore."[25]
   I walked on with my head down after that,
   Fearful I had displeased him, and spoke no more.

Then, at the river—an old man in a boat:
   White-haired, as he drew closer shouting at us,
   "Woe to you, wicked souls! Give up the thought

70 Of Heaven! I come to ferry you across
   Into eternal dark on the opposite side,
   Into fire and ice! And you there—leave this place,

You living soul, stand clear of these who are dead!"
   And then, when he saw that I did not obey:
   "By other ports, in a lighter boat," he said,

"You will be brought to shore by another way."
   My master spoke then, "Charon,[26] do not rage:
   Thus is it willed where everything may be

Simply if it is willed. Therefore, oblige,
80   And ask no more." That silenced the grizzled jaws
   Of the gray ferryman of the livid marsh,

Who had red wheels of flame about his eyes.
   But at his words the forlorn and naked souls
   Were changing color, cursing the human race,

God and their parents. Teeth chattering in their skulls,
   They called curses on the seed, the place, the hour
   Of their own begetting and their birth. With wails

And tears they gathered on the evil shore
   That waits for all who don't fear God. There demon
90   Charon beckons them, with his eyes of fire;

Crowded in a herd, they obey if he should summon,
   And he strikes at any laggards with his oar.
   As leaves in quick succession sail down in autumn

---

[25] **Acheron's dismal shore:** Acheron is the river of death in Greek mythology.

[26] **Charon:** The boatman in Greek mythology who ferried souls across the river Styx to Hades.

Until the bough beholds its entire store
    Fallen to the earth, so Adam's evil seed
    Swoop from the bank when each is called, as sure

As a trained falcon, to cross to the other side
    Of the dark water; and before one throng can land
    On the far shore, on this side new souls crowd.

100   "My son," said the gentle master, "here are joined
    The souls of all who die in the wrath of God,
    From every country, all of them eager to find

Their way across the water—for the goad
    Of Divine Justice spurs them so, their fear
    Is transmuted to desire. Souls who are good

Never pass this way; therefore, if you hear
    Charon complaining at your presence, consider
    What that means." Then, the earth of that grim shore

Began to shake: so violently, I shudder
110   And sweat recalling it now. A wind burst up
    From the tear-soaked ground to erupt red light and batter

My senses—and so I fell, as though seized by sleep.

Canto IV

[First Circle, Limbo: the Unbaptized; the Virtuous Pagans. After Dante awakes they descend into the First Circle of Hell, Limbo, where they hear wailing from the inhabitants. These are the sinless souls who died unbaptized or were born before Christ; their punishment is not physical but mental, knowing they can never be saved. In a special region, Dante and Virgil talk with the four great classical poets Homer, Horace, Ovid, and Lucan. Dante is recognized along with Virgil as completing a company of six. Dante then sees a number of legendary figures from Greece and Rome; the group includes the Moorish philosopher Avicenna and scholar Averroës. Virgil conveys Dante to the next stage of their journey.]

Breaking the deep sleep that filled my head,
    A heavy clap of thunder startled me up
    As though by force; with rested eyes I stood

Peering to find where I was—in truth, the lip
    Above the chasm of pain, which holds the din
    Of infinite grief: a gulf so dark and deep

And murky that though I gazed intently down
   Into the canyon, I could see nothing below.
   "Now we descend into the sightless zone,"

10   The poet began, dead pale now: "I will go
   Ahead, you second." I answered, seeing his pallor,
   "How can I venture here if even you,

Who have encouraged me every time I falter,
   Turn white with fear?" And he: "It is the pain
   People here suffer that paints my face this color

Of pity, which you mistake for fear. Now on:
   Our long road urges us forward." And he entered
   The abyss's first engirdling circle, and down

He had me enter it too. Here we encountered
20   No laments that we could hear—except for sighs
   That trembled the timeless air: they emanated

From the shadowy sadnesses, not agonies,
   Of multitudes of children and women and men.
   He said, "And don't you ask, what spirits are these?

Before you go on, I tell you: they did not sin;
   If they have merit, it can't suffice without
   Baptism, portal to the faith you maintain.

Some lived before the Christian faith, so that
   They did not worship God aright—and I
30   Am one of these. Through this, no other fault,

We are lost, afflicted only this one way:
   That having no hope, we live in longing." I heard
   These words with heartfelt grief that seized on me

Knowing how many worthy souls endured
   Suspension in that Limbo.[27] "Dear sir, my master,"
   I began, wanting to be reassured

---

[27] **Suspension in that Limbo:** The virtuous pagans, living before Jesus's time, could not have known him and therefore could not have been saved.

In the faith that conquers every error, "Did ever
    Anyone go forth from here—by his own good
    Or perhaps another's—to join the blessed, after?"

40 He understood my covert meaning, and said,
    "I was new to this condition, when I beheld
    A Mighty One who descended here, arrayed

With a crown of victory.[28] And He re-called
    Back from this place the shade of our first parent,°   Adam
    And his son Abel, and other shades who dwelled

In Limbo. Noah, and Moses the obedient
    Giver of laws, went with Him, and Abraham
    The patriarch. King David and Israel went,

And Israel's sire and children, and Rachel for whom
50   He labored so long, and many others—and His
    Coming here made them blessed, and rescued them.

Know this: no human soul was saved, till these."
    We did not stop our traveling while he spoke,
    But kept on passing through the woods—not trees,

But a wood of thronging spirits; nor did we make
    Much distance from the place where I had slept,
    When I saw a fire that overcame a bleak

Hemisphere of darkness. Well before we stopped
    To address them, I could see people there and sense
60   They were honorable folk. "O Master apt

In science and art, who honor both, what wins
    These shades distinction? Who are they who command
    A place so separate from the other ones?"

And he: "Their honored names, which still resound
    In your life above, have earned them Heaven's grace,
    Advancing them here." Meanwhile a voice intoned:

---

[28] **crown of victory:** A victory over Hell, referring to the belief that Jesus descended into Hell—after the crucifixion and before the resurrection—and rescued certain heroes of Hebrew Scriptures. The event is called the Harrowing of Hell (see Gospel of Nicodemus).

"Hail the great Poet, whose shade had left this place
　　And now returns!" After the voice fell still,
　　I saw four great shades making their way to us,

70　Their aspect neither sad nor joyful. "Note well,"
　　My master began, "the one who carries a sword
　　And strides before the others, as fits his role

Among these giants: he is Homer,[29] their lord
　　The sovereign poet; the satirist follows him —
　　Horace, with Lucan last, and Ovid[30] third:

That lone voice just now hailed me by a name
　　Each of them shares with me; in such accord
　　They honor me well." And so I saw, all come

Together there, the splendid school of the lord
80　Of highest song who like an eagle soars high
　　Above the others. After they had shared a word

Among themselves, they turned and greeted me
　　With cordial gestures, at which my master smiled;
　　And far more honor: that fair company

Then made me one among them — so as we traveled
　　Onward toward the light I made a sixth
　　Amid such store of wisdom. Thus we strolled,

Speaking of matters I will not give breath,
　　Silence as fitting now as speech was there.
90　At length, a noble castle blocked our path,

Encircled seven times by a barrier
　　Of lofty walls, and defended round about
　　By a handsome stream we strode across: it bore

Our weight like solid ground; and after that
　　I passed through seven gateways with the sages.
　　We came to a fresh green meadow,[31] where we met

---

[29] **Homer:** Homer (eighteenth century B.C.E.) was the epic poet of war in *The Iliad*.

[30] **Horace . . . Ovid:** Roman poets: Horace (65–8 B.C.E.), Ovid (43 B.C.E.–17 C.E.), and Lucan (39–65 C.E.)

[31] **green meadow:** The setting is reminiscent of the Elysian fields in Greek mythology, but the symbolism of the castle is disputed. Seven is an important number in medieval symbolism; perhaps the castle is a citadel of learning surrounded by the seven liberal arts (grammar, rhetoric, logic, arithmetic, geometry, music, and astronomy).

A group of people. With grave, deliberate gazes
  And manners of great authority, they spoke
  Sparingly and in gentle, courtly voices.

100 We drew aside to a place where we could look
  From a spacious well-lit height and view them all:
  On that enameled green I saw—and take

Glory within me for having seen them, still—
  The spirits of the great: I saw Electra
  With many companions, among whom I knew well

Which shades were those of Aeneas and of Hector,
  And Caesar[32]—who wore his armor, falcon-eyed.
  I saw Camilla, and Penthesilea beside her;

I saw King Latinus on the other side,
110 And sitting by him his daughter Lavinia.[33]
  I saw that Brutus from whom Tarquin fled,

I saw Lucretia, Julia, Marcia, Cornelia;
  And sitting at a distance separately
  I saw lone Saladin[34] of Arabia.

I raised my eyes a little, and there was he
  Who is acknowledged Master° of those who know,   Aristotle
  Sitting in a philosophic family

Who look to him and do him honor. I saw
  Nearest him, in front, Plato and Socrates.
120 I saw Democritus, who strove to show

That the world is chance; Zeno, Empedocles,
  Anaxagoras, Thales, Heraclitus,
  Diogenes.[35] The collector of qualities

---

[32] **Electra . . . Caesar:** Like Julius Caesar (d. 44 B.C.E.), these are prominent figures in Roman legend and history: Electra, mother of Dardanus, the founder of Troy; Hector, a Trojan hero; Aeneas, the hero of *The Aeneid*.

[33] **Camilla . . . Lavinia:** Lavinia is Aeneas's wife. Camilla is a warrior in *The Aeneid*; Penthesilea is a Trojan who fought the Greeks; Latinus is king of Latium (in Italy).

[34] **Brutus . . . Saladin:** Brutus (not the Brutus involved with assassinating Julius Caesar, but an earlier Roman who defeated Tarquin) founded the Roman Republic, and was its first Consul. The four women were models of Roman virtue. Saladin (d. 1193), sultan of Egypt and Syria, was famed for his victories in the Third Crusade, including the recapture of Jerusalem.

[35] **Democritus . . . Diogenes:** Famous Greek philosophers from the seventh to fourth centuries B.C.E.

Of things, Dioscorides. And Orpheus,
  Cicero, Linus, Seneca[36] the moralist,
  Euclid the geometer, Ptolemy, Hippocrates,

Galen, Avicenna, Averroës[37] who discussed
  The Philosopher in his great commentary—
  I saw so many I cannot tally the list;

130 For my demanding theme so pulls my story,
  To multiply the telling would be too little
  For the multitude of fact that filled my journey.

The company of six divide and dwindle
  To two; my wise guide leads me from that quiet
  Another way—again I see air tremble,

And come to a part that has no light inside it.

Canto V

[*Second Circle. Minos. The Carnal—Cleopatra, Dido, Helen, Paris, Paolo and Francesca.*   Since
Hell is an inverted cone, the circumference of each succeeding circle is smaller than the previous
one. The Second Circle is filled with carnal sinners and presided over by Minos, the ancient judge
of the underworld. Minos attempts unsuccessfully to impede Dante. Virgil shows Dante the shades
of those buffeted by the storms of lust and punished for their sins. Among them are Cleopatra,
Helen of Troy, and Achilles. Dante singles out the soul of Francesca da Rimini, who relates her
tragic love affair with her brother-in-law Paolo. She blames the reading of a love story for their
downfall. Dante faints.]

So I descended from first to second circle—
  Which girdles a smaller space and greater pain,
  Which spurs more lamentation. Minos[38] the dreadful

---

[36] **Dioscorides . . . Seneca:** Seneca was a Roman playwright and philosopher (d. 65 C.E.); Dioscorides (first
century C.E.), a Greek physician; Orpheus and Linus, mythical poets; Cicero (d. 43 B.C.E.), a Roman orator.

[37] **Euclid . . . Averroës:** Euclid (fourth century B.C.E.), was a Greek mathematician; Ptolemy (second century
C.E.), an Alexandrian astronomer who devised the "Ptolemaic universe," in which the earth is a fixed center
around which the heavenly bodies circle—a concept believed in by Dante. Hippocrates and Galen were Greek
physicians (fourth and second centuries B.C.E.), Avicenna (d. 1037) was an Arab physician whose writings on
medicine, science, and philosophy influenced Europeans for several hundred years; and Averroës (d. 1298) was
an Islamic scholar from north Africa and Spain, whose commentary on Aristotle was respected by Dante.

[38] **Minos:** In classical mythology, the judge of the underworld.

Snarls at the gate. He examines each one's sin,
  Judging and disposing as he curls his tail:
  That is, when an ill-begotten soul comes down,

It comes before him, and confesses all;
  Minos, great connoisseur of sin, discerns
  For every spirit its proper place in Hell,

10 And wraps himself in his tail with as many turns
  As levels down that shade will have to dwell.
  A crowd is always waiting: here each one learns

His judgment and is assigned a place in Hell.
  They tell; they hear—and down they all are cast.
  "You, who have come to sorrow's hospice, think well,"

Said Minos, who at the sight of me had paused
  To interrupt his solemn task mid-deed:
  "Beware how you come in and whom you trust,

Don't be deceived because the gate is wide."
20 My leader answered, "Must you too scold this way?
  His destined path is not for you to impede:

Thus is it willed where every thing may be
  Because it has been willed. So ask no more."
  And now I can hear the notes of agony

In sad crescendo beginning to reach my ear;
  Now I am where the noise of lamentation
  Comes at me in blasts of sorrow. I am where

All light is mute, with a bellowing like the ocean
  Turbulent in a storm of warring winds,
30 The hurricane of Hell in perpetual motion

Sweeping the ravaged spirits as it rends,
  Twists, and torments them. Driven as if to land,
  They reach the ruin: groaning, tears, laments,

And cursing of the power of Heaven. I learned
  They suffer here who sinned in carnal things—
  Their reason mastered by desire, suborned.

As winter starlings riding on their wings
   Form crowded flocks, so spirits dip and veer
   Foundering in the wind's rough buffetings,

40 Upward or downward, driven here and there
   With never ease from pain nor hope of rest.
   As chanting cranes will form a line in air,

So I saw souls come uttering cries—wind-tossed,
   And lofted by the storm. "Master," I cried,
   "Who are these people, by black air oppressed?"

"First among these you wish to know," he said,
   "Was empress of many tongues—she so embraced
   Lechery that she decreed it justified

Legally, to evade the scandal of her lust:
50   She is that Semiramis[39] of whom we read,
   Successor and wife of Ninus, she possessed

The lands the Sultan rules. Next, she who died
   By her own hand for love, and broke her vow
   To Sychaeus's ashes.[40] After her comes lewd

And wanton Cleopatra. See Helen,[41] too,
   Who caused a cycle of many evil years;
   And great Achilles,[42] the hero whom love slew

In his last battle. Paris and Tristan[43] are here—"
   He pointed out by name a thousand souls
60   Whom love had parted from our life, or more.

When I had heard my teacher tell the rolls
   Of knights and ladies of antiquity,
   Pity overwhelmed me. Half-lost in its coils,

---

[39] **Semiramis:** Semiramis was the legendary Queen of Assyria; her capital Babylon is here confused with Babylon of Egypt which was ruled by the Sultan.

[40] **Sychaeus's ashes:** The widow is Dido who broke faith with the memory of her husband Sichaeus by having an affair with Aeneas.

[41] **Cleopatra . . . Helen:** Queen of Egypt, mistress of Julius Caesar and Marc Antony. She committed suicide after Antony's death, in 30 B.C.E. Helen's love affair with Paris was supposedly the cause of the Trojan war.

[42] **Achilles:** In medieval versions of the Trojan war, including of Statius, Paris kills Achilles because of Achilles's love for the Trojan Polyxena.

[43] **Tristan:** The lover of Iseult in the medieval romance *Tristan and Iseult*.

"Poet," I told him, "I would willingly
   Speak with those two[44] who move along together,
   And seem so light upon the wind." And he:

"When they drift closer—then entreat them hither,
   In the name of love that leads them: they will respond."
   Soon their course shifted, and the merciless weather

70 Battered them toward us. I called against the wind,
   "O wearied souls! If Another does not forbid,
   Come speak with us." As doves whom desire has summoned,

With raised wings steady against the current, glide
   Guided by will to the sweetness of their nest,
   So leaving the flock where Dido was, the two sped

Through the malignant air till they had crossed
   To where we stood—so strong was the compulsion
   Of my loving call. They spoke across the blast:

"O living soul, who with courtesy and compassion
80   Voyage through black air visiting us who stained
   The world with blood: if heaven's King bore affection

For such as we are, suffering in this wind,
   Then we would pray to Him to grant you peace
   For pitying us in this, our evil end.

Now we will speak and hear as you may please
   To speak and hear, while the wind, for our discourse,
   Is still. My birthplace is a city[45] that lies

Where the Po finds peace with all its followers.
   Love, which in gentle hearts is quickly born,
90   Seized him for my fair body—which, in a fierce

Manner that still torments my soul, was torn
   Untimely away from me. Love, which absolves
   None who are loved from loving, made my heart burn

---

[44] **those two:** Paolo and Francesca of Rimini.

[45] **city:** Ravenna, in northern Italy, the home of Francesca.

With joy so strong that as you see it cleaves
    Still to him, here. Love gave us both one death.
    Caina awaits the one[46] who took our lives."

These words were borne across from them to us.
    When I had heard those afflicted souls, I lowered
    My head, and held it so till I heard the voice

100   Of the poet ask, "What are you thinking?" I answered,
    "Alas—that sweet conceptions and passion so deep
    Should bring them here!" Then, looking up toward

The lovers: "Francesca, your suffering makes me weep
    For sorrow and pity—but tell me, in the hours
    Of sweetest sighing, how and in what shape

Or manner did Love first show you those desires
    So hemmed by doubt?" And she to me: "No sadness
    Is greater than in misery to rehearse

Memories of joy, as your teacher well can witness.
110   But if you have so great a craving to measure
    Our love's first root, I'll tell it, with the fitness

Of one who weeps and tells. One day, for pleasure,
    We read of Lancelot,[47] by love constrained:
    Alone, suspecting nothing, at our leisure.

Sometimes at what we read our glances joined,
    Looking from the book each to the other's eyes,
    And then the color in our faces drained.

But one particular moment alone it was
    Defeated us: *the longed-for smile*, it said,
120   *Was kissed by that most noble lover*: at this,

This one, who now will never leave my side,
    Kissed my mouth, trembling. A Galeotto,[48] that book!
    And so was he who wrote it; that day we read

---

[46]**Caina . . . one:** Francesca's husband and Paolo's brother, Gianciotto Malatesta. Caina is the circle of Cain, the deepest circle of Hell in Canto XXXII.

[47]**Lancelot:** The lover of King Arthur's wife Guinevere.

[48]**Galeotto:** Galeotto, which means "pander," was the intermediary between Guinevere and Lancelot.

No further." All the while the one shade spoke,
    The other at her side was weeping; my pity
    Overwhelmed me and I felt myself go slack:

Swooning as in death, I fell like a dying body.

Canto VI

[*Third Circle. Cerberus. The Gluttons—Ciacco.*   The Third Circle contains the gluttons, who lie under a constant rain while a dog-like demon, Cerberus, torments them. Virgil quiets Cerberus by throwing dirt into his three gullets. A soul from Florence nicknamed Ciacco ("the pig") recognizes Dante and explains why he is in Hell. At the end of the Canto, Virgil and Dante find Plutus blocking their way.]

Upon my mind's return from swooning shut
    At hearing the piteous tale of those two kin,
    Which confounded me with sadness at their plight,

I see new torments and tormented ones again
    Wherever I step or look. I am in the third
    Circle, a realm of cold and heavy rain—

A dark, accursed torrent eternally poured
    With changeless measure and nature. Enormous hail
    And tainted water mixed with snow are showered

10 Steadily through the shadowy air of Hell;
    The soil they drench gives off a putrid odor.
    Three-headed Cerberus,[49] monstrous and cruel,

Barks doglike at the souls immersed here, louder
    For his triple throat. His eyes are red, his beard
    Grease-black, he has the belly of a meat-feeder

And talons on his hands: he claws the horde
    Of spirits, he flays and quarters them in the rain.
    The wretches, howling like dogs where they are mired

And pelted, squirm about again and again,
20   Turning to make each side a shield for the other.
    Seeing us, Cerberus made his three mouths yawn

---

[49] **Cerberus:** Guardian of Hades in Greek mythology.

To show the fangs — his reptile body aquiver
In all its members. My leader, reaching out
To fill both fists with as much as he could gather,

Threw gobbets of earth down each voracious throat.
Just as a barking dog grows suddenly still
The moment he begins to gnaw his meat,

Struggling and straining to devour it all,
So the foul faces of Cerberus became —
30   Who thundered so loudly at the souls in Hell

They wished that they were deaf. We two had come
Over the shades subdued by the heavy rain —
Treading upon their emptinesses, which seem

Like real bodies. All lay on the ground but one,
Who sat up, seeing us pass. "You who are led
Through this Hell — recognize me if you can:

You who were made before I was unmade."
And I to him: "The anguish you endure
Perhaps effaces whatever memory I had,

40   Making it seem I have not seen you before;
But tell me who you are, assigned so sad
A station as punishment — if any is more

Agony, none is so repellent." He said:
"Your city, so full of envy that the sack
Spills over, held me once when I enjoyed

The bright life up above. The name I took
Among you citizens was Ciacco;[50] the sin
Of gluttony brought me here. You see me soak

To ruin in battering rain — but not alone,
50   For all of these around me share the same
Penalty for the same transgression as mine."

Then he fell silent, but I answered him,
"Ciacco, I feel your misery; its weight
Bids me to weep. But what of things to come? —

---

[50] **Ciacco:** A Florentine whose name means "hog."

Tell if you can the divided city's fate,
  And of the citizens: is any one just?
  And tell me why such schism threatens it."

He answered, "After long argument they must
  Descend to bloodshed, and the rustic bloc[51]
60   With much offense will expel the other first.

Then, through the power of one who while we speak
  Is temporizing, that party too will fall
  Within three years, the ousted coming back

With head held high; and long will they prevail
  Despite the others' cries of shame and despair
  Under their burdens. Only two men[52] of all

Are truly just—whose words the rest ignore,
  For the triple sparks of envy, greed, and pride
  Ignite their hearts." "I'd have you tell me more,"

70 I pleaded, once his grievous words were said,
  "Farinata, Mosca, Tegghiaio, men of good reason,
  Jacopo Rusticucci, Arrigo[53]: the good

Was their hearts' purpose in life, so tell what portion
  Their souls inherit now. I long to know
  If they feel Heaven's sweetness, or Infernal poison."

He said, "Their souls are among the blackest in Hell,
  With different faults that weigh them to the pit.
  If you descend that far you may see them all—

But pray you: when you return to earth's sweet light,
80   Recall my memory there to the human world.
  Now, I respond and speak no more." With that,

His eyes went crooked and squinted, his head rolled;
  He regarded me a moment, then bent his head
  And fell back down with the others, blind and quelled.

---

[51] **rustic bloc:** A reference to the White Guelphs, who drove the "others" (the Black Guelphs) out of Florence—but the Black Guelphs aided by Pope Boniface ultimately triumphed.

[52] **two men:** The identity of the "two men" is unknown.

[53] **Farinata . . . Arrigo:** Recent Florentines. Except for Arrigo, who does not appear again, the others are mentioned in Cantos X, XVI, and XXVIII.

"He will not wake again," my master said,
    "Until the angel's conclusive trumpet sounds
    And the hostile Power comes—and the waiting dead

Wake to go searching for their unhappy tombs:
    And resume again the form and flesh they had,
90   And hear that which eternally resounds."

So with slow steps we traversed that place of mud
    Through rain and shades commingled, once or twice
    Speaking of the future life: and so I said,

"Master, these torments—tell me, will they increase
    After the Judgment,[54] or lessen, or merely endure,
    Burning as much as now?" He said, "In this,

Go back to your science,[55] which teaches that the more
    A creature is perfect, the more it perceives the good—
    And likewise, pain. The accursèd people here

100   Can never come to true perfection; instead,
    They can expect to come closer then than now."
    Traveling the course of the encircling road,

And speaking more than I repeat, we two
    Continued our way, until the circuit came
    To where the path descends—and there we saw

Plutus,[56] the great Enemy, and confronted him.

---

[54] **the Judgment:** The Last Judgment by Christ when the dead will be joined again to their bodies.

[55] **your science:** Aristotle's teaching.

[56] **Plutus:** The classical god of wealth, who is possibly combined here with Pluto, the king of Hades.

CANTO VII

[*Fourth Circle: The Avaricious and the Prodigal. Plutus; Fortune. Fifth Circle: The Wrathful and Sullen.*   Plutus, the ancient god of wealth, guards the avaricious and prodigal in Circle Four. After silencing him, Virgil and Dante encounter two groups of sinners who push great weights around in circles. They meet, exchange insults, and continue on, repeating their futile journey. Virgil explains that wealth is distributed among the living by a special divinity known as Fortune. At a little after midnight of Good Friday, the poets arrive at Circle Five and confront a swamp of souls mired in slime. After a detour they arrive at the foot of a tower.]

"*Pape Satàn, pape Satàn, aleppe!*"[57]
    Plutus began in a guttural, clucking voice.
    The courteous sage who knew all reassured me:

"Don't let fear harm you; whatever power he has
    Cannot prevent us climbing down this rock."
    Then, turning back toward that swollen face,

He answered — "Silence, accursèd wolf! Attack
    Your own insides with your devouring rage:
    Bound for the pit, this is no causeless trek.

10 It is willed above, where Michael wreaked revenge
    On pride's rebellion."[58] Just as sails swollen with wind
    As soon as the mast is snapped collapse and plunge,

That savage beast fell shrinking to the ground.
    So we descended to the fourth defile
    To experience more of that despondent land

That sacks up all the universe's ill.
    Justice of God! Who is it that heaps together
    So much peculiar torture and travail?

How is it that we choose to sin and wither?
20 Like waves above Charybdis,[59] each crashing apart
    Against the one it rushes to meet, here gather

---

[57] "*Pape Satàn . . . aleppe!*": Apparently a threat to, or perhaps an invocation of, Satan, but its meaning is conjectural.

[58] **pride's rebellion:** A reference to the rebel angels in Heaven, who were cast out by Michael and his angels.

[59] **Charybdis:** The whirlpool in the Italian Straits of Messina made famous in Homer's *The Odyssey*.

People who hurry forward till they must meet
    And dance their round. Here I saw more souls
    Than elsewhere, spreading far to the left and right:

Each pushes a weight against his chest, and howls
    At his opponent each time that they clash:
    "Why do you squander?" and "Why do you hoard?" Each wheels

To roll his weight back round again: they rush
    Toward the circle's opposite point, collide
30   Painfully once more, and curse each other afresh;

And after that refrain each one must head
    Through his half-circle again, to his next joust.
    My own heart pained by those collisions, I said:

"Who are these, Master? — and are the shades who contest
    Here on our left all clergy, with tonsured head?"
    He answered: "Every one of the shades here massed

In the first life had a mind so squinty-eyed
    That in his spending he heeded no proportion —
    A fact they bark out plainly when they collide

40 At the circle's facing points, that mark division
    Between opposite faults. Those bare of head
    Were clerics, cardinals, popes, in whom the passion

Of avarice has wrought excess." I said,
    "Among these, Master, I'm sure I'll recognize
    Some who were thus polluted." He replied,

"The thought you hold is vain: just as the ways
    That made these souls so foul were undiscerning,
    So they are dim to discernment in this place.

Here they will keep eternally returning
50   To the two butting places: from the grave
    These will arise fists closed; and those, pates shining.

Wrongness in how to give and how to have
    Took the fair world from them and brought them this,
    Their ugly brawl, which words need not retrieve.

Now you can see, my son, how ludicrous
    And brief are all the goods in Fortune's ken,
    Which humankind contend for: you see from this

How all the gold there is beneath the moon,
    Or that there ever was, could not relieve
60   One of these weary souls." I: "Master, say then

What is this Fortune you mention, that it should have
    The world's goods in its grip?" He: "Foolish creatures,
    How great an ignorance plagues you. May you receive

My teaching: He who made all of Heaven's features
    In His transcendent wisdom gave them guides[60]
    So each part shines on all the others, all nature's

Illumination apportioned. So too, for goods
    Of worldly splendor He assigned a guide
    And minister—she, when time seems proper, spreads

70 Those vanities from race to race, this blood
    Then that, beyond prevention of human wit.
    Thus one clan languishes for another's good

According to how her judgment may dictate—
    Which is invisible, like a snake in grass.
    Your wisdom cannot resist her; in her might

Fortune,[61] like any other god, foresees,
    Judges, and rules her appointed realm. No truces
    Can stop her turning. Necessity decrees

That she be swift, and so men change their places
80   In rapid permutation. She is cursed
    Too often by those who ought to sing her praises,

Wrongfully blamed and defamed. But she is blest,
    And does not hear it; happy among the choir
    Of other primal creatures, she too is placed

---

[60] **guides:** Angelic orders that serve as guides in all areas of life.

[61] **Fortune:** Dame Fortune, thought to be an instrument of God.

In bliss, rejoicing as she turns her sphere.
   Now we descend to greater wretchedness:
   Already every star that was rising higher

When I set out[62] is sinking, and long delays
   Have been forbidden us." We traveled across
90   To the circle's farther edge, above the place

Where a foaming spring spills over into a fosse.
   The water was purple-black; we followed its current
   Down a strange passage. This dismal watercourse

Descends the grayish slopes until its torrent
   Discharges into the marsh whose name is Styx.[63]
   Gazing intently, I saw there were people warrened

Within that bog, all naked and muddy—with looks
   Of fury, striking each other: with a hand
   But also with their heads, chests, feet, and backs,

100 Teeth tearing piecemeal. My kindly master explained:
   "These are the souls whom anger overcame,
   My son; know also, that under the water are found

Others, whose sighing makes these bubbles come
   That pock the surface everywhere you look.
   Lodged in the slime they say: 'Once we were grim

And sullen in the sweet air above, that took
   A further gladness from the play of sun;
   Inside us, we bore acedia's° dismal smoke.   bitterness

We have this black mire now to be sullen in.'
110   This canticle they gargle from the craw,
   Unable to speak whole words." We traveled on

Through a great arc of swamp between that slough
   And the dry bank—all the while with eyes
   Turned toward those who swallow the muck below;

And then at length we came to a tower's base.

---

[62] **When I set out:** After midnight of Good Friday, it is now early Saturday morning.

[63] **Styx:** Another of the five rivers in the classical Hades.

Canto VIII

[*Fifth Circle (continued): The Wrathful and Sullen. Phlegyas; Filippo Argenti.* Continuing the account of Circle Five, Dante inquires about the meaning of certain signal lights; just then a boat approaches steered by Phlegyas, the guardian of this circle. After Virgil silences Phlegyas, the two poets get into the boat. While crossing the swamp the soul of Filippo Argenti rises out of the muck and Dante reacts angrily towards him, risking the very sin punished in this circle; but Virgil praises Dante. The boat leaves them near the entrance to the city of Dis, guarded by devils who threaten to prevent Dante from entering the city, gateway to the lower region of Hell. Virgil alone cannot prevail against them, but he assures Dante that assistance is on the way.]

Continuing, I tell how for some time
    Before we reached the lofty tower's base[64]
    Our eyes were following two points of flame

Visible at the top; and answering these
    Another returned the signal, so far away
    The eye could barely catch it. I turned to face

My sea of knowledge and said, "O Master, say:
    What does this beacon mean? And the other fire —
    What answer does it signal? And who are they

10 Who set it there?" He said: "It should be clear:
    Over these fetid waves, you can perceive
    What is expected — if this atmosphere

Of marsh fumes doesn't hide it." Bow never drove
    Arrow through air so quickly as then came
    Skimming across the water a little skiff

Guided by a single boatman at the helm:
    "Now, evil soul," he cried out, "you are caught!"
    "Phlegyas, Phlegyas[65] — you roar in vain this time,"

My lord responded. "You'll have us in your boat
20   Only as long as it takes to cross the fen."
    Like one convinced that he has been the butt

Of gross deception, and bursting to complain,
    Phlegyas held his wrath. We boarded the boat,
    My leader first — it bobbed without a sign

---

[64] **lofty tower's base:** The tower that guards the entrance to lower Hell.

[65] **Phlegyas:** In his anger at Apollo for seducing his daughter, Phlegyas set fire to one of Apollo's temples.

Of being laden until it carried my weight.
   As soon as we embarked, the ancient prow
   Turned swiftly from shore; it made a deeper cut

Into the water than it was wont to do
   With others. In the dead channel one rose abeam
30   Coated with mud, and addressed me: "Who are you,

To come here before your time?" And I to him:
   "Although I come, I do not come to remain—"
   Then added, "Who are you, who have become

So brutally foul?" "You see me: I am one
   Who weeps," he answered. And I to him, "In weeping
   And sorrow remain, cursed soul—for I have seen

Through all that filth: I know you!" He started gripping
   With both hands at the boat. My master stood
   And thrust him back off, saying, "Back to safekeeping

40 Among the other dogs." And then my guide
   Embraced my neck and kissed me on the face
   And said, "Indignant soul, blessed indeed

Is she who bore you. Arrogant in his vice
   Was that one when he lived. No goodness whatever
   Adorning his memory, his shade is furious.

In the world above, how many a self-deceiver
   Now counting himself a mighty king will sprawl
   Swinelike amid the mire when life is over,

Leaving behind a name that men revile."
50   And I said, "Master, truly I should like
   To see that spirit pickled in this swill,

Before we've made our way across the lake."
   And he to me: "Before we see the shore,
   You will be satisfied, for what you seek

Is fitting." After a little, I saw him endure
   Fierce mangling by the people of the mud—
   A sight I give God thanks and praises for:

"Come get Filippo Argenti!"[66] they all cried,
    And crazed with rage the Florentine spirit bit
60   At his own body. Let no more be said

Of him, but that we left him still beset;
    New cries of lamentation reached my ear,
    And I leaned forward to peer intently out.

My kindly master said, "A city draws near
    Whose name is Dis,[67] of solemn citizenry
    And mighty garrison." I: "Already clear

Are mosques—I see them there within the valley,
    Baked red as though just taken from the fire."
    And he, "It is fire blazing eternally

70 Inside of them that makes them so appear
    Within this nether Hell." We had progressed
    Into the deep-dug moats that circle near

The walls of that bleak city, which seemed cast
    Of solid iron; we journeyed on, to complete
    An immense circuit before we reached at last

A place where the boatman shouted, "Now get out!
    Here is the entrance." Above the gates I saw
    More than a thousand[68] of those whom Heaven had spat

Like rain, all raging: "Who is this, who'd go
80   Without death through the kingdom of the dead?"
    And my wise master made a sign, to show

That he desired to speak with them aside.
    And then they tempered their great disdain a bit,
    Answering: "You, by yourself, may come inside;

---

[66] **Filippo Argenti:** A wealthy, Florentine contemporary of Dante.

[67] **Dis:** In the Roman mythology used by Dante, Dis refers both to Pluto the master of hell, or hell itself. Here Dante uses the name to mean Satan and his fortified city in lower Hell.

[68] **thousand:** The rebel angels (Revelation 12:9).

But let that other depart, who dares set foot
    Within this kingdom. Let him retrace alone
    His foolish way — try if he can! — and let

You remain here, who have guided such a one
    Over terrain so dark." You judge, O reader,
90   If I did not lose heart, or believe then,

Hearing that cursèd voice, that I would never
    Return from there. "O my dear guide," I said,
    "Who has restored my confidence seven times over,

And drawn me out of peril — stay at my side,
    Do not desert me now like this, undone.
    If we can go no farther, let us instead

Retrace our steps together." That nobleman
    Who led me there then told me, "Do not fear:
    None can deprive us of the passage One

100 Has willed for us to have. Wait for me here
    And feed your spirit hope and comfort: remember,
    I won't abandon you in this nether sphere."

So he goes away and leaves me, the gentle father,
    While I remain in doubt, with yes and no
    Vying in my head. What they discussed together

Or what my guide proposed, I do not know,
    For they were out of hearing. Before much time,
    The demons scrambled back, where we would go —

And then I saw our adversaries slam
110   The portals of the entrance in the face
    Of my master, who remained outside and came

Back to me walking slowly, with downcast eyes.
    His brow devoid of confidence, he said,
    "Who has denied me this abode of sighs?"

And then he said to me, "Don't be dismayed
    By my vexation: I will conquer this crew,
    However they contrive to block our road.

This insolence of theirs is nothing new;
　　At a less secret gate they've shown it before,
120　　One still unbolted and open,[69] as you know:

You read the deadly inscription that it bore.
　　Already on this side of it—down the steep pass,
　　Passing the circles without an escort—be sure

Someone is coming to open the city to us."

Canto IX

[*Fifth and Sixth Circles: The Arch-Heretics. Dis: The Furies; the Gorgon Medusa.* Virgil assures Dante that he knows the way through Hell, since he has visited once before. Three Furies on the tower of Dis attempt to use the power of Medusa to turn Dante into stone. Virgil saves Dante by covering his eyes. An angelic messenger arrives and opens the gate of Dis with his wand. Virgil and Dante pass through the gate and enter Lower Hell and the sixth circle, where they are confronted with the torments of heretics in an area like a vast cemetery.]

The outward color cowardice painted me
　　When I beheld my leader turning back
　　Repressed his own new pallor more hurriedly.

He paused with an attentive air, but like
　　One listening, not watching—for the eye
　　Saw little in air so dark and fog so thick.

"We have to win this battle," he started to say,
　　"Or else . . . and she,[70] who offered so much aid—
　　Late though it seems to be, and still on the way."

10　I could see plainly how he strove to hide
　　His sentence's beginning with its close,
　　In different words from those he would have said—

Scaring me none the less, each broken phrase
　　Leading me to a meaning perhaps much worse
　　Than any it held. "Does anyone whose place

---

[69] **unbolted and open:** In the legend of the Harrowing of Hell, Jesus burst through the gates and bolts resisting his entry.

[70] **she:** By Beatrice.

Is the first circle, where the only curse
    Is having no hope, ever come down so far
    As this grim hollow?" I asked him. "Such a course,"

He said, "is rare among us, though once before
20   I have been down here—beckoned as a shade
    By wicked Erichtho,[71] the conjuror

Who used to summon spirits of the dead
    Back to their bodies. My own flesh was but still
    A little while denuded of my shade,

The time she made me enter within this wall
    To draw a spirit from the circle of Judas[72]—
    Which is the lowest and darkest place of all,

And farthest from the heaven whose dome encloses
    Everything in creation. I know the way:
30   Be sure of that. This quagmire which produces

So strong a stench surrounds the city of woe
    We cannot enter now except with wrath."
    And he said more that I don't remember now—

My eyes were on the tower we stood beneath,
    For at its glowing top three hellish Furies[73]
    Suddenly appeared: like women, but with a wreath

Of bright green hydras girdled about their bodies,
    Bloodstained, with squirming vipers in a crown
    Fringing their savage temples. "The fierce Erinyes,"

40   He said, who knew those handmaids of the queen[74]
    Of eternal sorrows: "Megaera on the left;
    Alecto howls on the right; and in between,

Tisiphone." Each one was clawing her breast,
    And each was beating herself—and screamed so loud
    I pressed against him, flinching at the blast.

---

[71] **Erichtho:** A Greek sorceress; the story of Virgil's descent may have been invented by Dante or was the product of medieval legends.

[72] **circle of Judas:** Judecca, named after Judas, who betrayed Jesus, is the lowest part of Hell.

[73] **Furies:** Three avenging, female spirits from Greek mythology, also called the Erinyes.

[74] **the queen:** Proserpine, wife of Pluto and Queen of Hell—same as the Greek Persephone.

"O let Medusa[75] come," the Furies bayed
    As they looked down, "to make him stone! We grieve
    Not avenging the assault of Theseus!"[76] He said,

"Turn your back; close your eyes: should Gorgon arrive
50   And show herself, then if you looked at her—
    There would be no returning back above."

He turned me around himself, and to make sure,
    Not trusting mine alone he covered my face
    With his hands too. O you whose mind is clear:

Understand well the lesson that underlies
    The veil of these strange verses I have written.
    Across the turbid waves now came the noise

Of a fearsome crash, by which both shores were shaken:
    A sound like that of a wind that gathers force
60   From waves of heat in violent collision

And batters the forest, and on its unchecked course
    Shatters the branches and tears them to the ground
    And sweeps them off in dustclouds, with scornful roars,

And the wild beasts and shepherds flee at the sound.
    Taking his hands from my eyes, he said, "Now look:
    There where the very harshest fumes abound,

Across the ancient scum." As frogs are quick
    To vanish through water and hunch on bottom sand
    As soon as they see their enemy the snake,

70 So I saw more than a thousand souls of the ruined
    Flee before one° who strode across the Styx   *an angel*
    Dry-shod as though on land. With his left hand

He cleared the polluted air before his face
    And only in that annoyance did he seem tired.
    I knew assuredly he was sent to us

---

[75] **Medusa:** One of the Gorgons from Greek mythology; her appearance turned men to stone.

[76] **Theseus:** A legendary king of Athens who attempted to rescue Persephone (Proserpine) from Hades. He gained fame by killing the Minotaur on Crete.

From Heaven, and I turned my head to regard
  The master—who signaled that I should be mute
  And bow before him. Ah, to me he appeared

So full of high disdain! He went to the gate
80 And opened it by means of a little wand,
  And there was no resistance. "O race cast out

From Heaven, exiles despised there," he intoned
  From that grim threshold, "Why this insolence?
  Why do you kick against that Will whose end

Cannot be thwarted, and whose punishments
  Many times over have increased your pain?
  What use to butt at what the fates dispense?

Remember, your Cerberus's throat and chin,[77]
  For just this reason, still are stripped of fur."
90 Then he turned back on the filthy path again,

Not speaking a word to us, but with the air
  Of one whom other matters must concern
  Than those who stand before him. And so, secure

After those holy words, we in our turn
  Stepped forward toward the city and through the gate,
  Entering without dispute. Anxious to learn

What their condition was who populate
  A fortress so guarded, I cast my eye around
  As soon as I was in—and saw a great

100 Plain filled with woe and torment. As on the land
  At Arles where the river Rhône grows more subdued,
  Or at Pola[78] where the Quarnero sets a bound

For Italy, bathing her borders, on every side
  The ground is made uneven by the tombs—
  So it was here: but these were of a mode

---

[77] **throat and chin:** An allusion to Hercules dragging Cerberus from Hades with a chain.

[78] **Arles . . . Pola:** Arles in Provence and Pola in Istri, both located near water, were ancient cemeteries.

More bitter, for among the graves were flames
    That made the sepulchers glow with fiercer heat
    Than a smith could need. Among these catacombs

The lids were raised, with sounds of woe so great
110   Those within surely suffered horrible pain.
    "Master," I said, "who are these people that are shut

Ensepulchered within these coffers of stone,
    Making their sounds of anguish from inside?"
    He answered, "Here, arch-heretics lie—and groan

Along with all the converts that they made,
    The followers of every sect, with like
    Entombed with like. A greater multitude

Crowds into these graves than you may think they take.
    Some sepulchers grow hotter, and some less."
120   He turned to the right, and we continued to walk

Between the anguish and the high parapets.

Canto X

[*Sixth Circle (continued): The Heretics—Epicurus, Farinata degli Uberti, Cavalcante dei Cavalcanti.* On the path between the city wall and the tombs, Dante and Virgil are confronted by the Ghibelline leader Farinata degli Uberti. They discuss Florentine politics and are interrupted by the soul of Cavalcante de' Cavalcanti, who inquires about his son Guido, once Dante's best friend. The father interprets Dante's reply to mean that his son is dead and falls back in the tomb. Farinata prophesies about Dante's banishment from Florence. The poets continue on the path.]

And now, along the narrow pathway that ran
    Between those tortures and the city wall,
    I followed my master. "O matchless power," I began,

"Who lead me through evil's circles at your will,
    Speak to me with the answers that I crave
    About these souls and the sepulchers they fill:

Might they be seen? The cover of each grave
    Is lifted open, and no one is on guard."
    "When they return from Jehoshaphat[79] above,"

---

[79]**Jehoshaphat:** According to Hebrew Scriptures, the last judgment will take place in the Valley of Jehoshaphat near Jerusalem (Joel 3:2, 12).

10   He answered, "bearing the bodies that they had,
        All shall be closed. Here Epicurus[80] lies
        With all his followers, who call the soul dead

When the flesh dies. The question that you raise
        Will soon be answered now that we are inside—
        And so will the secret wish you don't express."

I said, "Dear guide, believe me: I do not hide
        My heart from you, except through my intention
        To speak but little, the way that you have said

Earlier I ought to be disposed." "O Tuscan!—
20   Who travel alive through this, the city of fire,
        While speaking in so courteous a fashion—

If it should please you, stop a moment here.
        Your way of speaking shows that you were born
        In the same noble fatherland: there where

I possibly have wrought excessive harm."
        This sound erupted from a coffer of stone—
        I drew back toward my guide in my alarm.

"What are you doing?" he said. "Go back again!
        And see where Farinata[81] has sat up straight;
30   From the waist up, you may behold the man."

Already my eyes were on his: he sat upright,
        And seemed by how he bore his chest and brow
        To have great scorn for Hell. My leader set

Firm hands upon me at once, and made me go
        Forward between the rows of sepulchers,
        Saying: "Choose fitting words," as we wended through.

At his tomb's foot, I felt his proud gaze pierce
        Mine for a moment; and then as if in disdain
        He spoke and asked me, "Who were your ancestors?"

---

[80] **Epicurus:** A Greek philosopher (341–270 B.C.E.) famous for his doctrine of pleasure and his denial of immortality.

[81] **Farinata:** Farinata degli Uberti, head of the Florentine Ghibellines when they twice expelled Guelphs from Florence.

40 Eager to comply with that, I made all plain,
      Concealing nothing: whereupon he raised
      His brows a little. Then he said, "These men

Were enemies to me; they fiercely opposed
      Me and my forebears and my party—so, twice,
      I scattered them." "If ousted and abused,"

I answered, "they returned to claim their place
      From every quarter: yours have not learned that art
      Of return so well."[82] Then suddenly the face

Of a shade appeared beside him, showing the part
50   From the chin up—I think through having risen
      Erect on his knees: his gaze began to dart

Anxiously round me, as though in expectation
      Of someone with me. But when that hope was gone
      He wept: "If you can journey through this blind prison

By virtue of high genius—where is my son,
      And why is he not with you?" And my rejoinder:
      "My own strength has not brought me, but that of one°   Beatrice

Who guides me through here, and is waiting yonder—
      Toward one your Guido perhaps had scorned." I well
60   Deduced his name[83] from his words and from his manner

Of punishment, and thus could answer in full.
      Suddenly straightening up, the shade cried out,
      "What?—did I hear you say he 'had'? Oh tell:

Is he not still alive? Does the sweet light
      Not strike his eyes?" Perceiving my delay
      In giving any answer, he fell back flat,

Face upward, appearing no more. But not so he,
      The great soul at whose beckoning I had paused;
      He did not change his features in any way,

---

[82] **If ousted . . . so well:** While the Guelphs, who were of Dante's party, were able to return to Florence from exile, the Ghibellines became permanent exiles.

[83] **his name:** Cavalcante, a leading Guelph; his son Guido, a friend and rival poet to Dante, married Farinata's daughter and died of malaria in exile.

70 Nor bend his neck or waist. "The point you raised—"
      He resumed where interrupted: "My kin not good
      At learning that art—I feel more agonized

By that accursèd fact than by this bed.
      But when the Lady's face who rules this place
      Has kindled fewer than fifty times,"[84] he said,

"Then you will know how heavy that art weighs.[85]
      Now tell me (may you regain the sweet world's vantage),
      Why is that people so fierce in its decrees

Toward my kin?" I answered, "It was the carnage
80   And devastation that dyed the Arbia red
      Which made the prayers in our temple[86] savage."

Shaking his head, "I was not alone," he sighed.
      "And surely I would not have chosen to join
      The others without some cause, but where all agreed

To level Florence[87]—there, I was alone:
      One, who defended her before them all."
      "Ah, pray you (so may your seed find peace again)

Unravel a knot that makes my reason fail,"
      I said. "If I hear rightly, you seem to foresee
90   What time will bring, and yet you seem to deal

Differently with the present." He answered me:
      "Like someone with faulty vision, we can behold
      Remote things well, for so much light does He

Who rules supreme still grant us; but we are foiled
      When things draw near us, and our intelligence
      Is useless when they are present. So of your world

---

[84] **fifty times:** The lady is Proserpina, goddess of the moon; fifty months later in 1304, an attempt to restore exiles to Florence—including Dante—failed.

[85] **weighs:** Here Farinata predicts Dante's exile.

[86] **temple:** Probably the Church of St. John; the Arbia is a stream near Montaperti, a mound, where the Ghibellines defeated the Guelphs in 1260.

[87] **To level Florence:** At Montaperti the Ghibellines proposed the destruction of Florence.

In its present state, we have no evidence
    Or knowledge, except if others bring us word:
    Thus you can understand that with no sense

100 Left to us, all our knowledge will be dead
    From that Moment when the future's door is shut."[88]
    Then, moved by compunction for my fault, I said:

"Will you now tell the one who fell back flat
    His son is truly still among the living?
    Tell him what caused my silence: that my thought

Had wandered into that error which your resolving
    Just wiped away." And now I heard my guide
    Calling me back; so, hurriedly contriving

To learn, I begged the shade to say if he could
110 Who lay there with him, and I heard him answer:
    "I lie with over a thousand of the dead;

The second Frederick is among the number,
    And the Cardinal;[89] of others I will not speak."
    With that he hid himself. I walked back over

To the ancient poet, with my thoughts at work
    Mulling the words that bore such menace to me.
    My guide set out, and as we walked he spoke:

"Why is it you're disturbed?" I told him why;
    "Preserve in memory what you have heard
120 Against yourself," the sage advised. "And I pray

You, listen" — he raised a finger at the word.
    "When you confront her° radiance, whose eyes can see   Beatrice's
    Everything in their fair clarity, be assured

Then you shall learn what your life's journey will be."
    He turned to the left; and leaving the city wall
    Behind our backs we continued on our way

---

[88] **future's door is shut:** Time itself ends on Judgment Day.

[89] **The second Frederick . . . Cardinal:** Cardinal Ottaviano degli Ubaldini from a leading Ghibelline family; Frederick II, Holy Roman Emperor from 1215–1250; known for his materialism, he denied immortality of the soul.

Toward the center which was now our goal,
    Following a path that strikes the valley floor:
    And from that valley rose an odor so foul

130 The stench repelled us even high up there.

Canto XI

[*Sixth Circle (continued): The Arrangement of Hell.* Standing on the edge of the Sixth Circle, Dante and Virgil look down upon the Seventh. While they accustom themselves to the stench below, Virgil explains the arrangement of Hell and the last three circles: Circle Seven is reserved for sins of violence; Circle Eight contains sins of fraud; Circle Nine is for sins of treachery. Virgil explains why usurers are linked to blasphemers and sodomites.]

Up on the topmost rim of a deep-cut bank
    Formed by a circle of massive, fissured rock,
    We stood above a pen more cruel. The stink

Thrown up from the abyss had grown so thick
    Its excess drove us to shelter in the space
    Behind a great tomb's lid. It bore a plaque

Inscribed: "I hold Pope Anastasius,
    Drawn by Photinus from the proper path."[90]
    "We must put off descending farther than this,"

10 My master said, "until this rotten breath
    Has become familiar to our sense of smell."
    "Discover some matter to fill the lost time with,

Pray you," I answered, "so we may use it well."
    "I am so minded," he said, and then: "My son,
    Within these rocks three lesser circles fall,

Each one below another, like those you have seen,
    And all of them are packed with accursèd souls;
    In order that hereafter the sight alone

May be sufficient, you will hear what rules
20   Determine how and why they are constrained.
    The end of every wickedness that feels

---

[90] **"I hold . . . the proper path"**: Pope Anastasius (fifth century) was thought to have been persuaded by the theologian Photinus to deny the divinity of Jesus.

Heaven's hatred is injustice—and each end
    Of this kind, whether by force or fraud, afflicts
    Some other person. But since fraud is found

In humankind as its peculiar vice,
    It angers God more: so the fraudulent
    Are lower, and suffer more unhappiness.

The whole first circle is for the violent;
    But, because violence involves a deed
30   Against three persons, its apportionment

And fabrication are in three rings: to God,
    To one's self, or one's neighbor, all violence
    Is done—to them, or to their things instead,

As I'll explain. By violence, death and wounds
    Of grievous kinds are inflicted on one's neighbor;
    And on his property—arson, ruinous offense,

Extortion. So the first ring is the harbor
    Of torment for the homicides and those
    Who strike out wrongfully: despoiler, robber,

40 And plunderer, in various companies.
    One may lay violent hands on his own being,
    Or what belongs to himself, and all of these

Repent in vain within the second ring:
    He who deprives himself of your world sins thus;
    Or gambles; or dissipates whatever thing

He has of worth; or weeps when he should rejoice.
    Violence against the Deity, too, exists:
    To deny and blaspheme Him in the heart does this,

As does despising Nature and her gifts;
50   Therefore the smallest ring imprints its mark
    On Sodom and Cahors[91] and him who speaks

---

[91] **Sodom and Cahors:** Cahors in France was identified with the sin of usury (charging interest on loans); Sodom was identified with sodomy.

Contemptuously of God with all his heart.
　　Fraud, which bites every conscience, a man may play
　　Either on one who trusts him, or one who does not.

The latter of the two is seen to destroy
　　Only those bonds of love that nature makes:
　　So in the second circle hypocrisy,

Flatterers, sorcery, larceny, simoniacs,
　　With pimps, barrators, and such filth have their nest.
60　But the other kind of fraud not only forsakes

The love that nature makes, but the special trust
　　That further, added love creates: therefore
　　At the universe's core, inside the least

Circle, the seat of Dis, every betrayer
　　Eternally is consumed." "Master, you state
　　All of this lucidly, and you make clear

Just what it is that distinguishes this pit
　　And those it holds. But what of those condemned
　　To languish in the thick marsh, that other set

70　Beaten by rain, those driven by the wind,
　　And those who collide and clash with angry tongues:
　　How is it that all these are not confined

In the red city to suffer, if their wrongs
　　Have brought God's anger on them? And if not,
　　Then why are they in such a plight?" "What brings

Your thoughts to wander so from the proper route?
　　Where has your mind been gazing? Don't you recall
　　A passage in your *Ethics*,[92] the words that treat

Three dispositions counter to Heaven's will:
80　Incontinence, malice, insane brutality?
　　And how incontinence is less distasteful

To God, and earns less blame? Think carefully
　　About this doctrine, consider who they are
　　Whose punishment is above, outside: you'll see

---

[92] *Ethics:* Aristotle's *Nicomachean Ethics.*

Clearly why they are apart from the wicked here,
  And why His vengeance smites them with less wrath."
  "O sun, that makes all troubled vision clear,

You give solutions I am so contented with
  That asking, no less than knowing, pleases me.
90   But please," I said, "could we retrace our path

Back to the place where you said usury
  Offends celestial Goodness, and solve that knot?"
  He said, "For the comprehending, philosophy

Serves in more places than one to demonstrate
  How Nature takes her own course from the design
  Of the Divine Intelligence, and Its art.

Study your *Physics*[93] well, and you'll be shown
  In not too many pages that your art's good
  Is to follow Nature insofar as it can,

100 As a pupil emulates his master; God
  Has as it were a grandchild[94] in your art.
  By these two, man should thrive and gain his bread—

If you remember Genesis—from the start.
  But since the usurer takes a different way,
  He contemns Nature both in her own sort

And in her follower as well, while he
  Chooses to invest his hope another place.
  But now come follow me: it pleases me

To go now; for above us in the skies
110   The Fish are quivering at the horizon's edge,
  And the whole Wagon lies over Caurus[95]—and this,

Farther ahead, is where we descend the ridge."

---

[93] *Physics:* Aristotle's *Physics.*

[94] **a grandchild:** Nature is God's "art." If the poet's art follows nature, then it becomes God's grandchild.

[95] **The Fish . . . Caurus:** the Wagon is the constellation of the Great Bear; Caurus is the northwest wind in classical mythology; the Fish (Pisces) is just appearing on the horizon. In other words, the stars indicate it is 4:00 a.m. of Holy Saturday.

CANTO XII

[*Seventh Circle, Ring One: the Violent against Neighbors—Alexander the Great, Attila the Hun. The Minotaur; Chiron.*   Making their way through fallen rocks, Dante and Virgil encounter the Minotaur, guardian of the circle of the violent. Virgil causes the Minotaur to rage and they quickly bypass him and enter round one of Circle Seven, composed of sinners who have committed violence against their neighbors. These souls are boiled in a river of blood and tortured by centaurs shooting arrows. Virgil asks Chiron, the leader of the centaurs, to provide them with a guide across the river. Chiron chooses Nessus, who points out some of those condemned to this circle: Alexander the Great, Attila the Hun, and several Florentines.]

The alp-like place we came for our descent
    Down the steep bank was one no eye would seek,
    Because of what was there. This side of Trent,

There is a place a landslide fell and struck
    The Adige's flank:[96] because of unstable ground
    Or earthquake, rocks once tumbled from the peak

And formed a passage where people can descend.
    Such was the footing we had down that ravine—
    And at the broken chasm's edge we found

10 The infamy of Crete, conceived within
    The false cow's shell.[97] When he saw us come his way
    He bit himself in rage like one insane.

My master called, "Perhaps you think you see
    The Duke of Athens[98]—the one who dealt you death
    Up in the world. Beast, take yourself away:

This is no man your sister[99] taught; in truth,
    He has come here to witness your punishment."
    As a bull breaks loose in the deathblow's aftermath,

And plunges back and forth, but though unspent
20   Cannot go forward, so did the Minotaur act.
    My wary guide cried, "Run to the descent—

---

[96] **Adige's flank:** The flank of a mountain on the Adige River near Trent in northern Italy.

[97] **false cow's shell:** Pasiphae, wife of King Minos of Crete, hid in a false cow and mated with a bull; the Minotaur with the head of a bull and the body of a man was the fruit of that passion.

[98] **Duke of Athens:** Theseus who sailed to Crete and killed the Minotaur in the labyrinth.

[99] **your sister:** Ariadne, daughter of Pasiphae, who taught Theseus the secret of the labyrinth.

Go quickly, while he's raging." So we picked
    Our way down over a rubble of scattered stone
    That shifted under me often as I walked,

With the new weight. While I was climbing down
    I thought to myself; and soon my master said,
    "You may be thinking about this ruined terrain

Guarded by the feral rage that I defied
    And quelled just now. Know then: that other time
30   I journeyed here, this rock had not yet slid.

It must have been a little before He came
    To Dis, if I have reckoned rightly, to take
    The great spoil of the upper circle[100] with Him—

When the deep, fetid valley began to shake
    Everywhere, so that I thought the universe
    Felt love: the force that has brought chaos back

Many times over, say some philosophers.[101]
    And at that moment this ancient rock, both here
    And elsewhere, tumbled to where it now appears.

40 But keep your eyes below us, for coming near
    Is the river of blood—in which boils everyone
    Whose violence hurt others." O blind desire

Of covetousness, O anger gone insane—
    That goad us on through life, which is so brief,
    To steep in eternal woe when life is done.

I saw a broad moat bending in a curve
    Encircling the plain, just as my guide had said:
    Between the moat and the bottom of the cliff

Centaurs[102] who were armed with bows and arrows sped
50   In file, as on a hunt they might be found
    When they were in the world. When we appeared

---

[100] **upper circle:** The Harrowing of Hell and the earthquake accompanying the crucifixion of Jesus.

[101] **philosophers:** Some Greek philosophers, such as Empedocles (fifth century B.C.E.), taught that the world is balanced between love and hate; if one predominates over the other chaos results.

[102] **Centaurs:** Mythological creatures that are half-man and half-horse.

They halted, and three came forward from the band
    With bows and shafts they chose, held ready to aim.
    One hailed us from a distance: "You who descend

The hillside, for what torment have you come?
    Tell us from there—if not, I draw my bow!"
    "We will make answer to Chiron,"[103] my guide told him,

"Who is beside you; you always brought yourself woe
    Because your will was hasty." He nudged me and said,
60   "That one is Nessus: he who met death through

Fair Deianira,[104] and by himself satisfied
    Vengeance for himself. The middle one whose gaze
    Is directed at his breast, with lowered head,

Is the great Chiron, tutor of Achilles.
    The other is Pholus,[105] full of rage. They circle
    The moat by thousands; if any soul should rise

Out of the blood more than its guilt makes lawful,
    They pierce it with their arrows." As we came close,
    Chiron drew an arrow's notch back through the tangle

70 Of beard along his jaw to clear a space
    For his large mouth, and to the others he said:
    "Have you observed how that one's steps displace

Objects his body touches? Feet of the dead
    Are not accustomed to behave like that."
    And my good leader, who by this time stood

Quite near the Centaur's chest, just opposite
    The place where Chiron's two natures joined, replied:
    "He is indeed alive, and in that state,

Alone; it falls to me to be his guide
80   Through the dark valley. It is necessity,
    And not his pleasure, that puts him on this road.

---

[103] **Chiron:** A wise centaur, teacher of heroes such as Achilles.

[104] **Deianira:** Nessus fell in love with Deianira, Hercules's wife; Hercules shot Nessus with a poisoned arrow, and, while dying, contaminated a robe that killed Hercules when he put it on.

[105] **Pholus:** A centaur who died from one of Hercules's poisoned arrows.

From singing alleluia one came to me
   To give me this strange mission; he is no thief,
   Nor I a spirit given to larceny.

But by the Power that lets me walk a path
   So savage, give us a member of your pack
   To come along as companion to us both

And show us where the ford is—and on his back
   Carry this one who, not a spirit, cannot
90   Fly through the air." Then Chiron turned and spoke,

Bending his torso toward Nessus on his right,
   "Go back and guide them, then; and turn away
   The challenge of any other troops you meet."

Now with a trusty escort, we made our way
   Along the boiling crimson—those boiled inside
   Shrieking beside us. On some it came so high

It covered their eyebrows. The mighty centaur said,
   "These are the tyrants given to blood and plunder.
   Here they lament the merciless harm they did:

100 Here's Alexander, and he who held Sicily under
   For many a sad year, fierce Dionysius;[106]
   That black hair there is Azzolino's; and yonder,

That other fairer head is Obizzo[107] of Esti's:
   In the world above, the man his stepson slew."
   I turned toward the poet, whose answer was,

"Let him be first guide, I your second, now."
   A little farther on, the centaur stopped
   At a crowd seeming to rise from the boiling flow

Up to the throat. He showed us one who kept
110   Off to one side. "Within the bosom of God
   He stabbed another's heart, and it has dripped

---

[106] **Alexander . . . Dionysius:** Alexander the Great of Macedon (356–323 B.C.E.) and Dionysius of Syracuse in Sicily (fourth century B.C.E.), both treated here as tyrants.

[107] **Azzolino's . . . Obizzo:** Obizzo and Azzolino were two tyrannical rulers in northern Italy in the thirteenth century.

Blood ever since upon the Thames,"[108] he said.
    I saw some others whose head and even chest
    Came up above the stream, and in that crowd

Were many I recognized. The blood decreased,
    Sinking by more and more until it cooked
    Only the feet, and that is where we crossed.

"To here, you have seen the boiling stream contract,"
    He said. "From here, its bed grows deeper again
120   Till it completes its circle, to reconnect

With where God's justice makes the tyrants groan:
    It goads Attila, a scourge on earth, and Pyrrhus,
    And Sextus;[109] there also are eternally drawn

The tears, unlocked by boiling, milked from the eyes
    Of Rinier Pazzo and Rinier da Corneto[110]—men
    Who brought such warfare to the public ways."

Then he turned back, and crossed the ford again.

Canto XIII

[*Seventh Circle, Ring Two: the Violent against Themselves. The Wood of Suicides—Piero della Vigne. The Squanderers (Violent against their Property)—Arcolano (Lano) da Squarcia, Jacopo da Santo Andrea.* In the second round of Circle Seven, Virgil and Dante enter the wood of suicides. This wild forest is infested by Harpies eating the leaves of trees that encase the souls of the suicides. Dante speaks at length with one of them, Piero della Vigne, a famous statesman and scholar. Piero explains the circumstances of his suicide and his later transformation into a bush. The poets also encounter the shades of Lano da Squarcia and Jacopo da Santo Andrea, chased by greyhounds. Another soul in a bush complains about the situation in Florence.]

Nessus had not yet reached the other side
    When we moved forward into woods unmarked
    By any path. The leaves not green, earth-hued;

---

[108] **Thames:** In order to avenge the death of his father, Guy de Montfort of England in 1272 stabbed his cousin Prince Henry in a church in Viterbo, Italy during a church service. The victim's heart was thought to be in a casket in Westminster Abbey.

[109] **Atilla . . . Sextus:** Attila the Hun, the "Scourge of God," invaded Italy in the fifth century; Pyrrhus, the third century B.C.E. king who fought against Rome, or Sextus, the son of Achilles who killed Priam, ruler of Troy; Sextus was a first-century Roman Pirate.

[110] **Rinier . . . Corneto:** Both Riniers were thirteenth century robbers.

The boughs not smooth, knotted and crooked-forked;
    No fruit, but poisoned thorns. Of the wild beasts
    Near Cecina and Corneto,[111] that hate fields worked

By men with plough and harrow, none infests
    Thickets that are as rough or dense as this.
    Here the repellent Harpies[112] make their nests,

10 Who drove the Trojans from the Strophades
    With dire announcements of the coming woe.
    They have broad wings, a human neck and face,

Clawed feet, and swollen, feathered bellies; they caw
    Their lamentations in the eerie trees.
    Here the good master began, "Before you go

Farther, be aware that now you are in this,
    The second ring—and so you shall be until
    The horrible sand. Look well, for here one sees

Things which in words would be incredible."
20   On every side, I heard wailing voices grieve,
    Yet I could not see anyone there to wail,

And so I stopped, bewildered. I believe
    My guide believed that in my belief the voices
    I heard from somewhere in among the grove

Came somehow from people who were in hiding places—
    And therefore the master said, "If you remove
    A little branch from any one of these pieces

Of foliage around us, the thoughts you have
    Will also be broken off." I reached my hand
30   A little in front of me and twisted off

One shoot of a mighty thornbush—and it moaned,
    "Why do you break me?" Then after it had grown
    Darker with blood, it began again and mourned,

---

[111] **near Cecina and Corneto:** The district between the river Cecina and the town of Corneto.

[112] **Harpies:** Harpies were birds with women's faces and bird bodies that drove Aeneas from the Strophades Islands in the Ionian Sea.

"Why have you torn me? Have you no pity, then?
   Once we were men, now we are stumps of wood:
   Your hand should show some mercy, though we had been

The souls of serpents." As flames spurt at one side
   Of a green log oozing sap at the other end,
   Hissing with escaping air, so that branch flowed

40 With words and blood together — at which my hand
   Released the tip, and I stood like one in dread.
   "Had he been able to credit or comprehend

Before, O wounded spirit," my sage replied,
   "What he had witnessed only in my verses,[113]
   His hand would never have performed this deed

Against you. But the fact belief refuses
   Compelled me, though it grieves me, thus to prompt him.
   But tell him who you are, so that his praises

May make amends by freshening your fame
50   When he returns again to the world above,
   As he is permitted." And the broken stem:

"Your words have so much sweetness they contrive
   To draw me out of silence: I am enticed
   To talk a little while, may it not prove

Burdensome to you. I am he who possessed
   Both keys to Frederick's heart — and I turned either,
   Unlocking and locking with so soft a twist

I kept his secrets from almost any other.
   To this, my glorious office, I stayed so true
60   I lost both sleep and life.[114] The harlot that never

Takes its whore's eyes from Caesar's retinue —
   The common fatal Vice of courts° — inflamed   envy
   All minds against me; and they, inflamed so,

---

[113] **in my verses:** In Virgil's *The Aeneid*.

[114] **both sleep and life:** Piero della Vigne, chief advisor to the Emperor Frederick II, was accused of treason, blinded, and imprisoned; he committed suicide in 1249. He held "both keys": that is, mercy and judgment.

So inflamed Augustus° that the honors I claimed   Frederick
    In gladness were converted into pain.
    My mind, in its disdainful temper, assumed

Dying would be a way to escape disdain,
    Making me treat my juster self unjustly.
    And by this tree's strange roots, I swear again:

70 I never betrayed my lord, who was so worthy
    Of honor. If you return to the world above,
    Either of you, please comfort my memory

Still prostrate from the blow that Envy gave."
    The poet waited a moment, then said to me,
    "Since he is silent, don't waste the time you have,

But speak, and ask him what you wish." And I:
    "You question him, and ask what you discern
    Would satisfy me; I cannot because of pity

That fills my heart." Therefore my guide began,
80   "For this man freely to do the thing you say,
    Imprisoned spirit, tell him if you can

And if it pleases you, in just what way
    The soul is bound in knots like these; give word
    Also, if any soul could be set free

From members such as these." It puffed air hard,
    And soon that exhalation became a voice.
    "You shall be answered briefly then," it uttered;

"When the fierce soul has quit the fleshly case
    It tore itself from, Minos sends it down
90   To the seventh depth. It falls to this wooded place—

No chosen spot, but where fortune flings it in—
    And there it sprouts like a grain of spelt, to shoot
    Up as a sapling, then a wild plant: and then

The Harpies, feeding on the foliage, create
    Pain, and an outlet for the pain as well.
    We too shall come like the rest, each one to get

His cast-off body—but not for us to dwell
    Within again, for justice must forbid
    Having what one has robbed oneself of; still,

100   Here we shall drag them, and through the mournful wood
    Our bodies will be hung: with every one
    Fixed on the thornbush of its wounding shade."

We both were still attentive when it was done,
    Thinking it might have more to say to us—
    When an uproar surprised us, just as when

A hunter mindful of wild boar and the chase
    Suddenly hears the beasts and crashing brush.
    There on our left came two at a desperate pace,

Naked, torn, so hard pressed they seemed to crash
110   Headlong through every tangle the wood contained.
    The one in front cried, "Come now, come in a rush,

O death!" The other shouted, falling behind,
    "Your legs were not so nimble when you ran
    At the jousting of the Toppo,[115] Lano my friend!"

And then, perhaps because his breath began
    To fail him, he stopped and hunched against a bush
    As if to make himself and its branches one.

Behind them, eager as greyhounds off the leash,
    Black bitches filled the woods, avid and quick.
120   They set their teeth on the one who stopped to crouch,

And tore his limbs apart; and then they took
    The wretched members away. Then my escort
    Led me by one hand to the bush—which spoke,

Grieving in vain through places where it was hurt
    And bled: "Jacopo da Santo Andrea," it cried,
    "What did you gain by shielding in me? What part

---

[115] **At the jousting of the Toppo:** The two souls are spendthrift, thirteenth-century nobles, Giacomo of Padua and Lano of Siena; the latter was killed at the river Toppo in 1288.

Had I in your sinful life?" My master said,
  When he was standing above it, "And who were you,
  Who through so many wounds exhale this blood

130 Mixed with sad words?" It answered, "O souls—you two
  Who arrive to see this shameful havoc crush
  My leaves and tear them from me—gather them now,

And bring them to the foot of this wretched bush.
  In life I was of the city that chose to leave
  Mars, her first patron, and take the Baptist:[116] for which

The art of Mars will always make her grieve.
  And if his semblance did not in part remain
  Still at the Arno, she would not survive—

And later, when they pitched the city again
140   Over the ashes left by Attila,[117] those
  Striving to refound it would have worked in vain.

And I—I made my own house be my gallows."

CANTO XIV

[Seventh Circle, Ring Three (First Zone): the Violent against God, Nature, and Art—the Blasphemers—Capaneus.   Round three of Circle Seven contains the violent against God or Nature. They dwell on a desert of hot sand: the blasphemers are lying supine, the usurers are sitting, and the sodomites are running, while a rain of fire falls on all of them. The poets view the shade of Capaneus, who sinned against God. After coming to a place where the river Phlegethon overflows, Virgil explains how a magnificent statue on the island of Crete is the source of the four rivers of the underworld, or Hell: the Styx, Acheron, Phlegethon, and Cocytus.]

Compelled by the love I bear my native place,
  I gathered the scattered sprays and gave them again
  To him who was already faint of voice.

From there we proceeded to the boundary line
  At which the third and second rings divide:
  And there a dreadful form of justice is seen.

---

[116] **the Baptist:** According to legend, Mars plagued Florence with wars when he was replaced as city patron by John the Baptist, and was only partially appeased when his statue was preserved on a bridge—the Ponte Vecchio—over the Arno.

[117] **Attila:** A mistaken notion that Florence was destroyed by Attila the Hun.

To make these new things clear: we two now stood
   On a plain whose bed rejects all plants — bare, flat,
   Garlanded all around by the woeful wood

10 Just as the wood is by the sorrowful moat.
   And here we stayed our steps at the very edge.
   The ground was dry deep sand, resembling that

Which Cato[118] trod. O vengeance of God, how much
   Should you be feared by all of those who read
   What my eyes saw! It was a great assemblage

Of naked souls in herds, all of whom mourned
   Most miserably and seemed to be subject
   To different laws. Some lay upon the ground,

Supine; some sat hunched up; while others walked
20   Restlessly about. It seemed that those who moved
   Were the more numerous, those who lay abject

In torment, fewest — but it was they who grieved
   With tongues most loosened by pain. All over the sand
   Distended flakes of fire drifted from aloft

Slowly as mountain snow without a wind.
   As when Alexander in India's hottest region
   Saw flames fall on his army, intact to the ground,

And had his soldiers tramp the accumulation
   To extinguish them before the fire could spread,[119]
30   Eternal fire descended in such profusion

Sand kindled like tinder under flint, and made
   The pain redouble — with their dancing hands
   Not resting even for a moment they pawed

Themselves now here, now there, and beat the brands
   Of fresh fire off. "O Master," I began,
   "Who vanquish all except the stubborn fiends

---

[118] **Cato:** Roman general (first century B.C.E.) in north Africa, fighting against Caesar in the Civil War.

[119] **before the fire could spread:** A medieval legend concerning Alexander the Great's conquest of India.

That opposed us at the gate: who is that one,[120]
    The great one seeming to pay no heed to the fire,
    Who lies disdainful and scowling, so that the rain

40 Seems not to ripen him?" He appeared to hear
    Me ask about him, and shouted, "What I was
    Alive, I am in death! Though Jove may wear

His smith[121] out, from whom anger made him seize
    The sharpened bolt that smote me my last day;
    And though he wears out every smith he has

At Mongibello's black forge;[122] and though he cry,
    'Help, help, good Vulcan!' just the way he did
    Amid the battle of Phlegra,[123] and hurl at me

With all his might—he still will not have had
50   The pleasure of his vengeance." Then my guide
    Spoke with more force than I had heard, and said,

"O Capaneus, that this unquenched pride
    Remains in you just punishes you the more:
    No torment but this raging of yours could goad

With agony enough to match your ire."
    Then gentler, to me: "He was one of seven kings
    Who besieged Thebes, and bore—seems still to bear—

Disdain for God. But as I said, his revilings
    Earn his breast fitting badges. Now follow my steps:
60   Tread, not the scorching sand, but a path that clings

Close to the wood." In silence we reached a place
    Where gushing from the woods a small stream poured
    So red that it still makes me shudder. As issues

---

[120] **that one:** In Greek legend, Capaneus is one of the seven kings who besieged Thebes; he boasted that he would burn the city even if Zeus opposed it, and he was killed by a thunderbolt for his presumption.

[121] **smith:** Vulcan; the Greek Hephaestus.

[122] **Mongibello . . . forge:** Mongibello is a name for Mt. Etna, the interior of which served as Vulcan's forge.

[123] **battle of Phlegra:** At Phlegra, Jove defeated the Giants (Titans).

That stream from Bulicame[124] that is shared
   Among the prostitutes, so this brook flowed
   Down and across the sand. It was stone-floored;

Stone lined both banks and the margins on each side;
   And I could see that this would be our route.
   "In all that I have shown you," my master said,

70 "Since first we entered through that open gate
   Whose threshold no one ever is denied,
   Nothing your eyes have seen is so worth note

As this present stream which quenches in its flood
   All of the flames above it." So word for word
   My master spoke, and I asked him for the food

To fill the appetite these words inspired.
   He answered, "In the middle of the sea
   Lies a waste land called Crete, a realm whose lord[125]

Governed the world in its age of purity.
80   The mountain Ida is there, which once was glad
   With foliage and waters, and now must lie

Deserted, like some worn thing by time decayed.
   Long ago Rhea chose it for her child
   As his safe cradle; and since they had to hide,

Made all there shout whenever her infant wailed.[126]
   Within the mountain stands an immense Old Man,
   Who turns his back toward Damietta,[127] to hold

His gaze on Rome as on his mirror: of fine
   Gold is his head, pure silver his arms and breast;
90   Down to the fork is brass, and from there down

---

[124] **Bulicame:** A sulphurous spring near Viterbo, whose water fed the houses of prostitution.

[125] **lord:** The god Saturn was said to have ruled Crete during the golden age.

[126] **Long ago . . . wailed:** Saturn swallowed his own children to prevent one of his sons from overthrowing him; Rhea preserved Jupiter by substituting a stone for him (which Saturn swallowed) and hiding the baby Jupiter in a cave on Mt. Ida. Mountain spirits hid his crying by clashing their swords and shields.

[127] **Within the mountain . . . Damietta:** A city in Egypt. With the different metals (see lines 88–93), the old man seems to represent the ages of humanity, which have degenerated from gold to iron and clay.

The choicest iron comprises all the rest
    But the right foot, of clay baked hard as brick:
    On it, more weight than on the left is pressed.

Every part but the gold head bears a crack,
    A fissure dripping tears that collect and force
    Their passage down the cavern from rock to rock

Into this valley's depth, where as a source
    They form the Acheron, Styx, and Phlegethon.[128]
    Then their way down is by this narrow course

100 Until, where all descending has been done,
    They form Cocytus[129] — and about that pool
    I shall say nothing, for you will see it soon."

And I to him: "But if this stream does fall
    Thus from our world, then why does it appear
    At only this border?" And he: "As you know well,

The place is round; although you have come far,
    Toward the pit by left turns always down,
    You haven't completed all the circle: therefore,

If anything new appears that we haven't seen,
110   It should not bring amazement to your face."
    And I said, "Where are Lethe[130] and Phlegethon?

For you are silent regarding one of these,
    And say the rain of tears creates the other."
    He: "All your questions please me; but in one case

The boiling of this red water should give the answer.
    Lethe you shall see, but out of this abyss:
    There where, repented guilt removed, souls gather

To cleanse themselves." Then, "Now it is time for us
    To leave the wood. The margins are not afire,
120   And make a pathway — over them, come close

Behind me: every flame is extinguished here."

---

[128] **Acheron, Styx, and Phlegethon:** Rivers of the classical underworld.

[129] **Cocytus:** The lowest part of Hell.

[130] **Lethe:** The river of forgetfulness; Dante places it on the summit of Purgatory, as a passage into Paradise.

CANTO XV

[Seventh Circle, Ring Three (Second Zone): the Violent against God, Nature, and Art—the Sodomites—Brunetto Latini. Walking along the riverbank, the poets meet a group of souls including one of Dante's favorite teachers, Brunetto Latini, who follows them. Despite the fact that Brunetto is punished as a sodomite, Dante shows him great respect. Brunetto prophesies about Dante's quarrel with the Florentines and then describes some of his companions.]

Now the firm margin bears us, under the vapor
 Rising from the stream to form a shade and fend
 The fire off, sheltering both banks and water.

As Flemings between Wissant and Bruges,[131] to defend
 Against the tide that rushes in on them,
 Construct a bulwark to drive the sea from land;

And Paduans on the Brenta[132] do, to stem
 The water and protect their castle and town
 Before Carentana feels the heat—in the same

10 Manner those banks were made, except the one
 Who built them did not make them as high or thick,
 Whoever he was. And I could not have seen

The wood that lay behind us, had I looked back,
 When we encountered another troop of souls
 Who looked at us the way that men will look

At one another at dusk, when daylight fails
 Under a new moon: knitting their brows at us
 The way old tailors do when threading needles.

While I was being examined by them thus,
20 One recognized me, and took me by the hem,
 Crying, "Why what a marvel!" I fixed my eyes

On his scorched face as he reached out his arm,
 And the baked features I saw did not forestall
 My knowing him—I reached back down to him,

---

[131] **Wissant and Bruges:** Two cities that mark the ends of the dike for Dante.

[132] **Brenta:** A river flowing through Padua fed by the melting snows from the mountains of Carentana in Austria.

My hand toward his face, and answered his call:
 "Are you here, Ser Brunetto?"[133] He replied,
 "My son, may it not displease you, if awhile

Brunetto Latini turns back to walk instead
 With you a little, and lets the train go on."
30 "I beg it of you with all my heart," I said—

"And should you prefer that you and I sit down,
 If it pleases him with whom I go, I will."
 He said, "If any of this flock, O son,

Stops even for an instant, he must lie still
 A hundred years, not brushing off the fire
 That strikes him. Go, then: I'll follow at your heel,

And then rejoin my band who walk in a choir
 Lamenting their eternal woes." Afraid
 To step down to his level from where we were,

40 I bent my head, as in reverence. He said,
 "What destiny or fortune makes you come
 Before your final day; and who is this guide?"

"In the bright life above," I answered him,
 "I came into a valley and lost my way,
 Before my age had reached its ripening time—

I turned my back on the place but yesterday.
 He appeared to me at dawn, when I had turned
 To go back down, and this path is the way

By which he leads me home." Then he returned:
50 "If you keep navigating by your star
 You'll find a glorious port, if I discerned

Well in the fair life. Had my years been more,
 So I could witness how heaven has been kind
 To you, I would have wished your work good cheer.

---

[133] **Ser Brunetto:** Brunetto Latini (c. 1210–1294), active in Guelph politics, and the author of *Treasure*, about civil duty, and *Little Treasure*, a verse poem about an allegorical journey. Dante addresses Brunetto with the polite form *voi* ("you"), showing respect: *voi* is used only in the *Inferno* for Brunetto Latini and Farinata in Canto X. "Ser," short for *messer*, is an honorific title used for a notary.

But that ungrateful, malignant folk who descend
   From those brought down from Fiesole[134] long ago,
   And who still smack of mountains and rocky ground,

Will make themselves, for good things that you do,
   Your enemies—and there is reason in that:
60   Among the bitter sorb-trees, it seems undue

When the sweet fig[135] in season comes to fruit.
   The world's old saying is that they are blind:
   A people greedy, envious, proud—see fit

To cleanse their habits from yourself. You'll find
   Your fortune holds such honor as will induce
   One party and the other to contend

In hunger to consume you—then the grass
   Will be well kept at a distance from the goat.
   Let the Fiesolan beasts go find their mess

70 By feeding on themselves, and spare the shoot
   (If any still should grow on their heap of dung)
   In which the sacred seed is living yet

Of Romans who remained when Florence went wrong,
   Becoming a nest for the malevolent."
   "Could I have everything for which I long,

You would not still endure this banishment
   Away from human nature," I replied.
   "Your image—dear, fatherly, benevolent—

Being fixed inside my memory, has imbued
80   My heart: when in the fair world, hour by hour
   You taught me, patiently, it was you who showed

The way man makes himself eternal; therefore,
   The gratitude I feel toward you makes fit
   That while I live, I should declare it here.

---

[134] **Fiesole:** According to tradition, Florence was founded by a mixture of Romans and Fiesolans after Caesar destroyed the hill-town of Fiesole, where stone was quarried for Florence.

[135] **sorb-trees . . . fig:** The fig refers to Dante, the sorb is a kind of sour apple.

And what you tell me of my future, I write—
   And keep it with another text as well,
   Till both are glossed by a lady° of good wit   Beatrice

And knowledge, if I reach her. This much still
   I say: so long as conscience is not betrayed,
90   I am prepared for Fortune to do her will.

My ears find nothing strange in what you have said:
   As Fortune pleases let her wheel be turned,
   And as he must let the peasant turn his spade."

When he heard these words my master's head inclined
   Toward the right, and looking at me he said,
   "He who has listened well will understand."

And none the less I continued as I had
   In speech with Ser Brunetto—would he tell
   Which among his companions had enjoyed

100 Most eminence and fame in life? "It is well,"
   He answered, "for me to say the names of some
   But nothing of the rest. To name them all

Would demand speaking more words than we have time—
   All clerics and men of letters, all renowned,
   And in the world all stained by this one crime.°   sodomy

Priscian trudges in that unhappy band,
   As does Francesco d'Accorso.[136] And if you crave
   To see such scurf, among them you can find

One[137] whom the Servant of Servants asked to leave
110   The Arno for Bacchiglione; and there
   He left his body, distended in its nerve

And muscle. And now, although I would say more,
   My speech and walking with you must be brief:
   On the sand, I see new smoke rise, where appear

---

[136] **Priscian . . . d'Accorso:** A thirteenth-century Ghibelline lawyer and law professor who taught at Oxford and Bologna; Priscian was a sixth century grammarian.

[137] **One:** Andrea de'Mozzi, bishop of Florence (1287–1295), was transferred because of his scandalous life to Vicenza on the Bacchiglione by Pope Boniface VIII, the "Servant of Servants."

New souls, with whom I must not be. I live
  In my *Tesoro*—your judgment being won
  For it, I ask no more." And he went off,

Seeming to me like one of those who run
  Competing for the green cloth in the races
120 Upon Verona's field[138]—and of them, like one

Who gains the victory, not one who loses.

Canto XVI

[*Seventh Circle, Ring Three (Second Zone continued): the Violent against God, Nature and Art—the Sodomites.* Dante and Virgil continue along the riverbank, approaching a large waterfall that plunges over a cliff into the Eighth Circle. Dante discusses news of home with three Florentines, Guido Guerra, Tegghiaio Aldobrandi, and Jacopo Rusticucci. Virgil urges Dante to be courteous to these Florentines. Dante tells them Florence has degenerated. As the poets near the waterfall, Virgil asks for the cord tied around Dante's waist and throws it into the abyss. Up rises a sea monster.]

I was already where we heard the noise
  Of water winding downward as it spilled
  To the next circle with a sound like bees,

When three shades bolted from a troop that filed
  Under the rain of torment. Running toward us,
  They cried: "Stop here, O you who are appareled

Like one in our own degenerate city's dress."
  Ah me!—what wounds both old and new I saw
  Where flames had burned their limbs: the same distress

10 Pains me again when I recall it now.
  My teacher heeded their cries, then faced me to say,
  "Now wait a little: to these three, one should show

Courtesy. Were it not for the fire let fly
  By the nature of this place, I'd say such haste
  Befits you more than them." We stopped; the three[139]

---

[138] **Verona's field:** It was traditional to hold a foot-race on the first Sunday in Lent, in which the runners were naked; the winner received a piece of green cloth and the loser a rooster.

[139] **the three:** The three Guelph leaders from Florence form a circle and are compared to wrestlers.

Resumed their old lament—and when they had raced
    Up to us, linked their bodies in a wheel.
    As champions, naked and oiled, before the thrust

And parry begin, will eye their grip and circle
20   Seeking advantage, so each directed his face
    Toward me, turning his neck against the pull

Of the ever-moving feet. "If our sandy place
    Of squalor and charred features scorched of hair,"
    One of them said, "lead you to show to us,

And what we ask, contempt—may our fame inspire
    You to inform us who you are who pass
    Through Hell with living footsteps. This man here,

Whose tracks you see me trample, though he goes
    Naked and peeled was of a rank more high
30   Than you suppose: his noble grandmother was

The good Gualdrada; his own name used to be
    Guido Guerra,[140] and in his life he attained
    Much with his counsel and his sword. And he

Who treads the sand behind my feet is named
    Tegghiaio Aldobrandi,[141] a man whose voice
    The world should more have prized. And I, condemned

With them, am Jacopo Rusticucci,[142] whose fierce
    Wife more than anything brought me wretchedness."
    Could I be shielded from the fire, at this

40 I would have thrown myself down into the fosse
    Among them—and so my teacher would permit,
    I think; but knowing how that fiery place

Would burn and bake me, fear drained the appetite
    My good will gave me to embrace them. I said,
    "No: it was not contempt but sorrow I felt

---

[140] **Guido Guerra:** A political leader in Florence; Gualdrada, his grandmother, was famous for her beauty.

[141] **Tegghiaio Aldobrandi:** Like Guido Guerra, Aldobrandi advised Florence not to invade Siena in 1260 when the Florentines were defeated at Montaperti.

[142] **Jacopo Rusticucci:** A political activist who blames his wife for his sodomy.

At your condition—inscribed so deep inside
   It will not leave me soon—when this my lord
   Spoke words to me which I knew prophesied

Such men as you were coming. I always heard
50   (Since I am of your city), and have told over
   Lovingly, your names and actions, both revered.

I leave the bitter gall behind, and aspire
   Toward the sweet fruits promised by my guide,
   But first I must go downward to the core."

"As your soul long may guide your limbs," he said,
   "With your fame shining after you: so tell
   If courtesy and valor still abide

Within our city, where they used to dwell.
   Or are they gone from it entirely now—
60   By Guglielmo Borsiere,[143] who came to Hell

Only a short time past, whom you see go
   Among our legion, we have heard things said
   That cause us much affliction." "Newcomers to you,

O Florence, and sudden profits, have led to pride
   And excess that you already mourn!" I spoke
   With face uplifted; the three, who understood,

Then looked at one another with the look
   Of men who hear the truth. "If times occur,"
   They all replied, "when it again will take

70 So little effort to answer another's desire,
   Count yourself happy speaking as you wish.
   Therefore, if you escape from this dark sphere

To see the beauty of the stars, and relish
   The pleasure then of saying, 'I was there'—
   Speak word of us to others." Then in a rush

---

[143] **Guglielmo Borsiere:** A Florentine pursemaker (*borsiere*, Italian for pursemaker) and man of peace.

They broke their wheel, and as they fled, the blur
    Of legs resembled wings; it took less time
    Than saying "Amen" for them to disappear.

And then my master left, I after him;
80   And we had traveled but a little distance
    Before the sound of falling water came

From so near we could scarcely hear our voices.
    As the river[144] which is first to carve its course
    East down the Apennines from Viso's sources—

Called Acquacheta up high, before it pours
    To its low bed at Forlì—clears the spine
    Above San Benedetto dell'Alpe and roars

In a single cataract that might have been
    A thousand; just so, down a precipitous bank,
90   Dark water drummed so loudly it would pain

Our ears before much longer. I had a hank
    Of cord[145] wrapped round me—with it I had planned
    To take the leopard with the painted flank;

I loosed it from me at my master's command
    And passed it to him, knotted and coiled up.
    Turning to the right he flung it from his hand

Some distance off the edge and down the slope,
    Into the depth of the abyss. I thought,
    "Some strangeness surely will answer from the deep

100 The strange signal the master just set out,
    And follows so attentively with his eye"—
    One must take care with those who have the wit

Not only to observe the action, but see
    The thought as well! For, "Soon now will arise
    The thing I look for: soon," he said to me,

---

[144] **the river:** Montone River.

[145] **cord:** The meaning of this "cord" is uncertain; some suggest it is the cord worn by Franciscans and that Dante may have been connected to them thereby.

"What your mind dreams will be before your eyes."
    A man should close his lips, if he's able to,
    When faced by truth that has the face of lies,

But here I cannot be silent; reader, I vow
110   By my *Commedia*'s lines — so may they not fail
    Of lasting favor — that as I was peering through

That murky air, a shape swam up to instill
    Amazement in the firmest heart: a thing
    Rising the way a man who dives to pull

His anchor free from shoals it is caught among,
    Or something else hidden in the sea, with feet
    Drawn in beneath him, surges — surfacing

Back from the deep with both arms held up straight.

CANTO XVII

[*Seventh Circle, Ring Three (Third Zone): the Violent against God, Nature, and Art — the Usurers. Geryon.* The monster Geryon, symbol of fraud, comes ashore. While Virgil arranges passage to the next circle of Hell, Dante approaches a group of usurers disputing among themselves. Identified by the coats of arms on their empty purses, the usurers include members of the Gianfigliazzi family from Florence and the Scrovegni family from Padua, among others. Pausing briefly to speak to the Paduan Scrovegni, Dante returns to Virgil. The anxious Dante and a reassuring Virgil climb onto Geryon's back and descend into the next circle.]

"Behold the beast that has the pointed tail,
    That crosses mountains, leaves walls and weapons broken,
    And makes the stench of which the world is full!"

So did my leader address me, then paused to beckon
    Him ashore near where the causeway came to an end.
    And fraud's foul emblem came closer, till he had taken

His head and chest from the deep to rest on land
    Before us, not drawing his tail up onto the bank.
    His face was a just man's face, outwardly kind,

10 And he was like a serpent all down his trunk.
    He had two paws, both hairy to the armpits;
    His back and breast and both sides down to the shank

Were painted with designs of knots and circlets.
    No Tartar or Turk has ever woven a cloth
    More colored in field and figure, nor were the nets

Arachne loomed.[146] The way beached boats are both
    On land and partly in water, or the way
    The beaver squats[147] to battle fish to the death

In the deep-drinking Germans' land — so lay
20   That worst of beasts upon the edge of stone
    That bounds the sand. His tail was quivery

And restless in the void where it hung down
    Squirming its venomed fork with an upward twist,
    Armed like a scorpion. "Now we must incline

Our path a little — as far as the evil beast
    That crouches over there," my master said.
    So we descended on the right, and paced

Ten steps along the edge to keep well wide
    Of sand and flames. Coming to where he was,
30   I saw on the sand just on from where we stood

Some people sitting near the open space.
    The master said, "To experience this ring
    Fully, go forward: learn what their state is,

But let your conversation not be long.
    Till you return, I'll parley with this beast,
    So we may borrow his shoulders." I went along

The seventh circle's margin alone, and passed
    To where those doleful people sat. Their woes
    Burst from their eyes, their hands were doing their best

40 To shield them from the torments, shifting place
    From here to there — one moment from falling flames,
    The next, the burning ground: just like the ways

---

[146] **Arachne loomed:** Arachne challenged Minerva (Athena) to a weaving contest; she lost and was changed into a spider.

[147] **squats:** Beavers were thought to catch fish by dangling their tails in the water.

Of dogs in summer when they scratch, sometimes
  With paw and others with muzzle, they behaved
  As though fleas or flies or gadflies bit their limbs.

When I grew closer to the people grieved
  By the flames falling on them, I did not find
  Any I recognized, but I perceived

Each had a purse hung round his neck — adorned
50   With certain colors and a certain device,
  Which each of them with hungry eyes consumed.

Looking among them, I saw a yellow purse
  That bore a lion in azure. Looking farther,
  I saw another, blood-red, that showed a goose

Depicted in a color whiter than butter.
  Then one of them — whose wallet,[148] which was white,
  Displayed a pregnant sow portrayed in azure —

Said to me: "What are you doing in this pit?
  Be off with you! And since you are living, know
60   My neighbor Vitaliano[149] will come to sit

Here on my left. These Florentines din me so
  Because I am a Paduan; often they cry,
  'Bring on the sovereign knight whose sack will show

Three goats!' "[150] With that, he twisted his mouth awry
  In a perverse grimace, and like an ox
  Licking its nose, thrust out his tongue at me.

Then, fearing that a longer stay might vex
  Him who had cautioned that the time I spent
  With them be brief, I left those worn-out souls —

70 And found my leader already on our mount,
  Seated upon that savage creature's back.
  He said, "Be bold and strong; for now the descent

---

[148] **wallet:** The various coats of arms on the purses of Italian usurers.

[149] **Vitaliano:** From Padua, but otherwise unknown.

[150] **'Bring on . . . goats':** Biamonte, a prominent Florentine money-lender.

Must be by such a stairway. The place you take
    Should be in front, so I can come between
    To protect you from the tail." Like those who shake,

Feeling the quartan fever coming on—
    Their nails already blue, so that they shiver
    At the mere sight of shade—such I was then;

But shame rebuked me, which makes a servant braver
80   In a good master's presence. I took my seat
    Upon those ugly shoulders. I did endeavor

(But my voice would not come the way I thought)
    To say, "Be sure you hold me tight!" But he,
    Who'd rescued me from other dangers, put

His two strong arms around me to steady me
    As soon as I had mounted up, commanding,
    "Geryon,[151] move ahead—but carefully:

Keep your arcs wide; go slowly when descending;
    Be mindful of this new burden that you bear."
90   As a boat moves back and back, to leave its landing,

So slowly did Geryon withdraw from shore.
    Then when he felt himself quite free, he turned
    And brought his tail to where his foreparts were,

And stretching it out he moved it so it churned
    The way a swimming eel does; and his paws
    Gathered the air toward him. When Phaëthon[152] spurned

The reins, so that the sky as one still sees
    Was scorched, I doubt that there was greater fear
    (Nor when pathetic Icarus[153] felt his thighs

100 Unfeathering from the melting wax, to hear
    His father crying, "You are falling now!")
    Than mine, perceiving I was in sheer air—

---

[151] **Geryon:** A winged, three-headed monster killed by Hercules.

[152] **Phaëthon:** Phaëthon borrowed the chariot of the sun from his father Apollo and lost control of it, scorching the earth and the heavens, creating the Milky Way.

[153] **Icarus:** The son of Daedalus, who attached wings to his son with wax; when Icarus flew too near the sun the wax melted and he fell into the sea.

Surrounded by it, and realizing I saw
    Nothing at all around me but the beast.
    Onward he swam with motion more and more slow

As he wheeled round descending; but that I guessed
    Only by feeling the wind against my face
    And from below. On our right the sound increased

From the whirlpool roaring horribly under us.
110   I stretched my head out forward, looking down—
    Growing more frightened even than I was,

Because as we descended I heard the din
    Of lamentations and I could see the fire.
    And so I shook, the more tightly holding on.

And I saw then—I had not seen it before—
    That he was wheeling and making his descent,
    For the great torments now were drawing near

On every side. As a falcon being sent
    Stays on the wing seeing no lure or bird
120   A long while, making the falconer lament,

"Ah me, you are sinking now!"—and comes down tired,
    With many wheelings, where it swiftly set out,
    And alights peeved and sullen, far from its lord:

So Geryon circled and landed at the foot
    Of the jagged rock; and once unburdening
    His shoulders of our bodies, he did not wait,

But vanished like an arrow from the string.

Canto **XVIII**

[*Eighth Circle (Malebolge), Bolgia One: the Panders and Seducers. Bolgia Two: the Flatterers—Jason and Thaïs.* They land at the edge of Circle Eight and the Malebolge, which consists of ten concentric circles or "evil pouches." Each bolgia contains sinners being punished for a kind of fraud. The pimps and the seducers form two lines in the first ditch; moving in opposite directions, they are whipped by devils. Dante speaks with Venedico Caccianemico from Bologna, who in turn points out other Bolognesi. Crossing a bridge, they observe the flatterers in the second ditch. Among others they see the legendary Jason and Thaïs.]

There is a place called Malebolge[154] in Hell,
    Constructed wholly of iron-colored stones,
    Including the circumferential wall.

Right in the center of this malign field yawns
    A wide deep pit;[55] concerning its design
    I shall say more in time. A belt remains

Between the base of that high wall of stone
    And the central pit, a circular band divided
    In ten concentric valleys, as in a plan

10 Where guardian moats successively are graded
    Around a castle's walls. In such a place
    A series of small bridges would be provided,

Out from the fortress threshold and across
    To the last bank: just so from the rock wall's foot
    Ran spokewise ridges, crossing over each fosse

And its embankment, extending to the pit
    That gathers them and cuts them off. This place
    Was where we found ourselves when we alit

From Geryon's back; the poet, leading us,
20   Held to the left, and I came on behind.
    To my right side I saw new tortures, new woes,

And new tormentors, with whom the first ditch teemed.
    Down at its bottom were naked sinners. The crowd
    Massed on our side of the center paced the ground

---

[154] **Malebolge:** Italian for "evil pouches."
[155] **pit:** The ninth and last circle of Hell (see Cantos XXI–XXXIV).

Headed toward us, while those on the other side
  Walked facing as we did, but with a greater pace:
  As when the Romans, because of the multitude

Gathered for the Jubilee, had pilgrims cross
  The bridge with one side kept for all those bound
30 Toward St. Peter's, facing the Castle, while those

Headed toward the Mount[156] were all assigned
  The other side. Along the dismal rock
  In both directions, I saw demons — horned

And carrying large scourges; and they struck
  Savagely from behind. Ah, at the first blow
  How terribly they forced them to be quick

Lifting their heels! None waited to undergo
  The second or the third. As I walked on,
  One of the wretches looking from below

40 Met my eyes: instantly I said, "I have seen
  This fellow before," and paused to make him out;
  And my kind leader gave me leave to turn

A short way back. That tortured spirit thought
  To hide himself by lowering his face,
  But that did little good, and I cried out:

"You, looking at the ground there — surely if those
  Features you wear are not false, you are named
  Venedico Caccianemico.[157] Say what it is

That brings you sauces of such a pungent kind."
50 And he to me: "I tell it unwillingly;
  But your plain speech compels me, bringing to mind

Memories of the former world. It was I
  Who brought Ghisolabella to do the will
  Of the Marchese, however it may be

---

[156] **Gathered for the Jubilee . . . Mount:** The Jubilee of the Church was instituted by Boniface VIII in 1300; one end of the bridge from the city to St. Peter's points to the Castle of St. Angelo; the other end points to Mount Giordano.

[157] **Venedico Caccianemico:** From a leading family of Bologna; he betrayed his sister Ghisolabella to the Marquis of Esti.

That the obscene history is told. But still,
    I am not the only Bolognese here,
    Crying in torment—in truth, the place is so full

That there are fewer tongues alive up there
    Between Savena and Reno, being taught
60   How to say *sipa*;[158] and if what you desire

Is evidence to confirm it—just give some thought
    To our avaricious nature." And as he spoke,
    A demon came and lashed him, crying out,

"Get moving, pimp! This is no place to look
    For women to sell!" Rejoining my escort,
    I came with him to where a ridge of rock

Jutted from the bank; we climbed it without much effort,
    And turning right along its craggy bridge
    Left that eternal circling. We reached the part

70 Where a space yawning underneath the ridge
    Gives passage to the scourged, and there he said,
    "Stop: let the sight of this other great assemblage

Of ill-begotten souls impress you; they strode
    The way we did, so you could not see their faces."
    From the old bridge we looked down at the crowd

Filing toward us, also driven by lashes.
    The kind guide said, without my questioning,
    "See where that great one sheds, as he advances,

No tears for pain—how much the look of a king
80   He still keeps! He is Jason, who took the ram
    Of Colchis[159] by courage and canny reckoning.

He passed the isle of Lemnos after the time
    When its bold, pitiless women killed every male;
    His deceitful gifts and fair words overcame

---

[158] **Savena . . . *sipa*:** Savena and Reno are two rivers bordering Bologna; *sipa* is Bolognese for "yes."

[159] **Jason . . . Colchis:** Leader of the Argonauts's voyage to steal the Golden Fleece; he seduced and abandoned Hypsipyle, Princess of Lemnos, after saving her father from Lemnos's women; he seduced Medea, Princess of Colchis, and then abandoned her.

The young Hypsipyle there, who'd had the skill
    To deceive the rest. He left her great with child,
    Forlorn; and such guilt brings him torment in Hell,

Avenging Medea as well. With him are sealed
    All those who cheat such ways: let this suffice
90   For the first valley, and knowledge of those held

Between its jaws." We had now reached the place
    At which the narrow pathway cuts across
    The second bank, the shoulder of which supplies

The abutment for another arch's base.
    Now we could hear the sounds of people's screams
    From the next fosse's pocket, and the noise

Made by their puffing snouts and by their palms
    As they struck themselves. The banks were caked with mold
    That clings there, formed by an exhalation that steams

100 From down below, offensive to behold
    And to inhale. The bottom is so far down
    That we could nowhere see it until we scaled

The ridge's high point at the arch's crown.
    When we had reached it, I saw deep down in the fosse
    People immersed in filth that seemed to drain

From human privies. Searching it with my eyes
    I saw one there whose head was so befouled
    With shit, you couldn't tell which one he was —

Layman or cleric. Looking at me, he howled,
110   "And why are you so greedy to look at me
    When all of these are just as filthy?" I called:

"Because, if memory serves me properly,
    I saw you once when your hair was dry, before —
    I know you are Alessio Interminei

Of Lucca,[160] which is why I eye you more
    Than all the rest." And he then, beating his head:
    "Down here is where my flatteries, that store

---

[160] **Alessio Interminei Of Lucca:** From a prominent family in Lucca, little is known about him.

With which my tongue seemed never to be cloyed,
    Have sunk me." Then my leader gave me advice:
120   "Extend your gaze a little farther ahead,

So that your eyes may fully observe the face
    Of that disheveled strumpet who in the mire
    Scratches her body, as she stands or squats,

With shit-rimmed fingers—she is Thaïs, the whore
    Who, asked, '*And is my favor with you great?*'
    Replied, '*Enormous,*' to her paramour[161]—

And let our sight be satisfied with that."

Canto XIX

[*Eighth Circle, Bolgia Three: the Simonists—Pope Nicholas III.* The third bolgia contains the souls of the simonists, those who trafficked in sacred objects and relics. They are stuck upside down in holes with only the burning soles of their feet protruding. The poets descend to speak with Pope Nicholas III, who is kicking wildly; he mistakes Dante for Pope Boniface VIII, who because of his sins will follow him here. Nicholas describes his sins and those of Boniface and his successor Clement V. Dante declaims against the damage that corrupt popes do to the Church. Having inverted their calling, they are punished by inversion. Virgil is pleased with Dante's remarks and carries him to the top of the next bridge.]

O Simon Magus,[162] and O you wretched crowd
    Of those who follow him and prostitute
    In your rapacity the things of God

Which should be brides of righteousness, to get
    Silver and gold—it is time the trumpet sounded
    For you: the third pouch is where you are put.

Now we were at the next tomb, having ascended
    To where the ridge hangs over the fosse's middle.
    O Supreme Wisdom, your mighty art is extended

10   Through Heaven, on earth, and in the world of evil,
    And with what justice is your Power assigned!
    I saw that the livid stone which lined the channel,

---

[161] **Who . . . paramour:** This scene describes an incident in a play by the Roman playwright Terence (c. 186–c. 159 B.C.E.).

[162] **Simon Magus:** In the Bible, Simon Magus offered to buy spiritual powers from the Apostles (Acts 8:9–24). The selling of any spiritual good, like a Church position, is known as simony.

Both walls and floor, was full of holes, all round
    And of an equal size. They seemed to me
    Not any wider or smaller than those designed

For the baptizings in my fair San Giovanni[163] —
    One of which many years ago I broke,
    To save one drowning there: and let this be

My seal to clear the matter. From each hole stuck
20   A sinner's feet and legs: the rest of him,
    From the calf up, inside. They twitched and shook

Because the soles of both feet were aflame —
    So violently, it seemed their joints could burst
    Rope or snap withes. As flames on oil will skim

Across the surface, so here the quick fire coursed
    From heel to toe. "Master," I asked, "tell me,
    Who is that one who seems to squirm the worst

And to be sucked by the reddest flames?" And he:
    "If you desire for me to carry you there,
30   By that bank[164] sloping down more gradually,

Then you can speak with him directly and hear
    From him about himself and his misdeeds."
    And I: "I like what pleases you. You are

My lord, you know I follow where your will leads —
    You also know the things I leave unsaid."
    Then we came onto the fourth dike; where its sides

Slope down we descended to our left, and stood
    Upon its narrow, perforated floor,
    My master not releasing me from his side

40 Until he reached the hole of that sufferer
    Whose legs thrashed out such sorrow. I began,
    "O miserable soul, whoever you are,

---

[163] **San Giovanni:** The Baptistery of Florence had several fonts; Dante was apparently baptized in one of them, although the drowning incident has not been explained.

[164] **bank:** The Malebolge slants toward the center, so that the inner edge of a ditch has an easier slope than the outer edge.

Planted here like a fence post upside down:[165]
  Speak, if you can." I stood as does the friar
  Who has confessed a vile assassin — head down,

And tied in place — who calls him back to defer
  Death for a little while; and then he cried,
  "Boniface, are you already standing there —

Already standing there? The writing lied
50   By several years! Are you so soon replete
  With all that getting, for which you weren't afraid

To take the beautiful Lady by deceit,
  And then to do her outrage?"[166] I became
  Like those who, feeling laughed at, hesitate,

Not comprehending what's been said to them
  And helpless to reply. Then Virgil said,
  "Answer him quickly: say you are not him,

Not who he thinks." I spoke as I was bid,
  At which the shade squirmed hard with both his feet;
60   Then, sighing and in a mournful voice, replied,

"What do you ask me, then? If you were brought
  Down from the bank to discover who I am,
  Then know that I was vested with the great

Mantle of power; a son who truly came
  Out of the she-bear,[167] I longed so much to advance
  The cubs that filling my purse was my great aim —

And here I have pursed myself, to my expense.
  Beneath my head are souls who preceded me
  In simony, mashed flat and squeezed through dense

70 Layers of fissured rock. I too shall lie
  Pushed down in turn when that other one has come:
  My abrupt question assumed that you were he.

---

[165] **upside down:** Assassins were buried alive with their heads downward.

[166] **the beautiful Lady . . . her outrage:** The speaker, Pope Nicholas III (1277–80) in 1300 had been in Hell for twenty years; with his foreknowledge, he mistakes Dante for Bonifice VIII, who did not die until 1303.

[167] **son . . . she-bear:** Nicholas was an Orsini, whose crest was a she-bear.

But already longer is the span of time
   I have been cooking my feet while planted reversed
   Than he, feet scarlet, will be planted the same:

For then a lawless shepherd[168] of the west
   Will follow him, of uglier deeds, well chosen
   For covering him and me when both are pressed

Under his skull. He'll be a second Jason,[169]
80   And as the first, so Maccabees recounts,
   Was treated softly by his monarch, this one

Will get soft treatment from the King of France."
   In my reply, I don't know if I erred
   With too much boldness in my vehemence:

"Pray tell me: how much treasure did our Lord
   Ask of Saint Peter before He put the keys
   Into his keeping? Surely He required

Nothing but 'Follow me.' Neither did those
   With Peter, or Peter himself, take silver or gold
90   From Matthias,[170] who was chosen for that place

Lost by the guilty soul. Stay where you're held,
   For these are your deservèd punishments—
   Guard well the ill-earned gains that made you bold

In opposing Charles.[171] Except that reverence
   For the great keys you held in the happy life
   Forbids, my speech would be still more intense:

For avarice like yours distributes grief,
   Afflicting the world by trampling on the good
   And raising the wicked. Shepherds like yourself

---

[168] **lawless shepherd:** Pope Clement V (1305–1314); he received support from King Philip of France because he agreed to move the papacy from Rome to Avignon, France.

[169] **second Jason:** Jason became the High Priest of the Jews by bribing the king with silver (2 Maccabees 4:7).

[170] **Matthias:** Matthias was picked to replace Judas among the apostles (Acts 1:15–26).

[171] **Charles:** Nicholas was supposed to have been bribed to join a conspiracy against Charles of Anjou (1226–1285), King of Sicily.

100 The Evangelist intended, when he said
> That she who sits upon the waters was seen
> By him in fornication with kings. She had

> Seven heads from birth, and from ten horns had drawn
> Her strength—so long as virtue pleased her spouse.[172]
> You made a god of gold and silver: wherein

> Is it you differ from the idolatrous—
> Save that you worship a hundred, they but one?
> Ah Constantine! What measure of wickedness

> Stems from that mother—not your conversion, I mean:
110 Rather the dowry that the first rich Father
> Accepted from you!"[173] And while I sang this strain,

> Whether he felt the bite of conscience, or anger,
> He kicked out hard with both his feet; indeed,
> I think my guide approved, with a look of pleasure

> Listening to the sound of true words said.
> And then he lifted me in his arms again,
> My weight full on his chest; and when he had,

> He climbed the same path he had taken down;
> Nor did he tire while holding me embraced
120 But carried me to the summit of the span

> From the fourth dike to the fifth, then gently released
> His burden—gently because the passage was hard,
> So steep and rocky that goats might be hard pressed;

> And there before me another valley appeared.

---

[172] **She had . . . spouse:** The imagery of the whore from the Book of Revelation (17:1–3) is applied to the Papacy: the "spouse" (the bridegroom) is the Pope, the "seven heads" are the sacraments, the "ten horns" are the commandments.

[173] **the dowry . . . from you:** Based on a forgery called the Donation of Constantine, it was believed in Dante's time that the Roman Emperor Constantine, when he removed his government to Byzantium (fourth century), had endowed the Roman Church under Pope Sylvester I (the "first rich Father") with temporal power in the West.

Canto XX

[*Eighth Circle, Bolgia Four: the Diviners and Magicians—Amphiaraus, Tiresias.*   From the bridge above the fourth ditch, the poets view the souls of soothsayers, diviners and magicians; their heads are twisted around on their bodies, giving them the appearance of walking backwards. When Dante shows pity for their punishment Virgil scolds him and names some of the sinners, both from antiquity and modern times: Amphiaraus, Tiresias, Aruns, Eurypylus, Michael Scot, Guido Bonatti, and Asdente. Virgil mentions the prophetess Manto and explains the founding of Mantua.]

The new pains of Hell that I saw next demand
    New lines for this Canto XX of the first Canzon,
    Which is of those submerged in the underground.

Readying myself at the cliff's brink, I looked down
    Into the canyon my master had revealed
    And saw that it was watered by tears of pain:

All through the circular valley I beheld
    A host of people coming, weeping but mute.
    They walked at a solemn pace that would be called

10 Liturgical here above. But as my sight
    Moved down their bodies, I sensed a strange distortion
    That made the angle of chin and chest not right—

The head was twisted backwards: some cruel torsion
    Forced face toward kidneys, and the people strode
    Backwards, because deprived of forward vision.

Perhaps some time a palsy has wrung the head
    Of a man straight back like these, or a terrible stroke—
    But I've never seen one do so, and doubt it could.

Reader (God grant you benefit of this book)
20   Try to imagine, yourself, how I could have kept
    Tears of my own from falling for the sake

Of our human image so grotesquely reshaped,
    Contorted so the eyes' tears fell to wet
    The buttocks at the cleft. Truly I wept,

Leaning on an outcrop of that rocky site,
    And my master spoke to me: "Do you suppose
    You are above with the other fools even yet?

Here, pity lives when it is dead to these.[174]
    Who could be more impious than one who'd dare
30   To sorrow at the judgment God decrees?

Raise your head—raise it and see one walking near
    For whom the earth split open before the eyes
    Of all the Thebans. 'Why are you leaving the war,

Amphiaraus,'[175] the others shouted, 'what place
    Are you rushing to?' as he plunged down the crevice
    To Minos, who seizes all. See Amphiaraus

Making his shoulders his breast; because his purpose
    Was seeing too far ahead, he looks behind
    And stumbles backwards. And here is Tiresias[176]—

40   The seer who changed from male to female, unmanned
    Through all his body until the day he struck
    A second time with his staff at serpents entwined

And resumed his manly plumage. He with his back
    Shoved nose to the other's front is called Aruns.[177]
    Living on the slopes the Carrarese work

From villages below, he had clear vistas:
    From his cave among white marble he could scan
    The stars, or gaze at waves below in the distance.

And she, whose loose hair covers her breasts unseen
50   On the side away from you, where other hair grows,
    Was Manto[178]—who searched through many lands, and then

---

[174] **Here, pity . . . to these:** This line suggests that there should be no sympathy or pity for the damned; the next two lines state that God's judgment is to be trusted. The reader should be aware of the irony here: the damned are Dante's creation.

[175] **Amphiaraus:** A Greek priest who hid himself in the battle, Seven against Thebes, and was swallowed up by the earth.

[176] **Tiresias:** The famous oracle from Thebes. He was once transformed into a woman when he saw two snakes coupling; seven years later he was made a man again when he saw the same scene.

[177] **Aruns:** An Etruscan soothsayer who predicted Caesar's victory in the Civil War.

[178] **Manto:** Daughter of Tiresias, the Theban soothsayer.

Settled in the place where I was born. Of this,
   Hear me awhile: her father dead, and Bacchus's
   City° enslaved, she for a long time chose   Thebes

To roam the world. Where a wall of mountains rises
   To form fair Italy's border above Tirolo
   Lies Lake Benaco,[179] fed by a thousand sources:

Garda and Val Camonica and Pennino[180]
   Are watered by streams that settle in that lake.
60   The island amid it the pastors of Trentino,

Brescia, or Verona might bless,[181] if they should take
   A way that leads there. At the shore's low place,
   Peschiera's splendid fortress towers make

Their challenge to the Brescians and Bergamese.
   There, all the cascades Benaco cannot contain
   Within its bosom join in one river that flows

Through rich green pasture. As soon as it starts to run,
   The water, Benaco no more, is Mincio instead,
   And joining the Po at Govèrnolo, it soon

70 Spreads to a marsh — in summer, sometimes fetid.
   There Manto the savage virgin saw in mid-fen
   A stretch of dry land, untilled, uninhabited:

And there she stayed and lived, where she could shun
   All humans to ply her arts in a place she shared
   Only with servants. And when her life was gone

And her soul descended, there its shell was interred.
   Afterward, families scattered about that country
   Gathered where marsh on all sides made a ward

Against attackers. And when they built their city
80   Over her bones, with no lots or divination
   They named it Mantua. Before fool Casalodi

---

[179] **Lake Benaco:** The present Lake Garda.

[180] **Garda . . . Pennino:** Two towns and a valley (Val Camonica) below the lake.

[181] **The island . . . might bless:** A chapel on the island was under the joint jurisdiction of three bishops.

Was deceived by Pinamonte,[182] its population
    Was larger. So let no other history,
    I charge you, belie my city's true inception."

I: "Master, your speech inspires such certainty
    And confidence that any contradiction
    Of what you say would be dead coals to me.

But speak again of these souls in sad procession:
    Are any passing below us worthy of note?
90   For my mind keeps turning back in that direction."

Then he: "That one, whose beard has spread in a mat
    That covers his brown shoulders, was augur when Greece
    Was short of males. He divined the time to cut

The first ship's cable at Aulis, along with Calchas.
    His name, as my tragedy° sings—you who know it   *The Aeneid*
    Entirely know the passage—is Eurypylus.[183]

That other with skinny flanks is Michael Scot,[184]
    Who truly knew the game of magic fraud.
    See Guido Bonatti; and Asdente[185]—too late,

100 He wishes he'd stuck to leather and cobbler's thread,
    Repenting here his celebrated predictions.
    And this wretched crowd of women all chose to trade

Loom, spindle and thimble for the telling of fortunes,
    Potions, wax images, incantation and charm.
    But come: already, Cain-in-the-moon positions

Both hemispheres with his pale blue thorns, his term
    Closes in the waves below Seville[186]—the round moon
    That, deep in the wood last night, brought you no harm."

Even while he spoke the words, we were moving on.

---

[182] **Pinamonte:** A Ghibelline who persuaded Count Casalodi, a Guelph, to exile the nobles of Mantua; Pinamonte then seized Casalodi's power in 1272.

[183] **Calchas . . . Eurypylus:** The Greeks used two oracles, Calchas and Eurypylus, to determine when they should set sail for Troy and the Trojan War.

[184] **Michael Scot:** A thirteenth-century Scotch scholar, who spent time in Frederick II's court in Italy.

[185] **Bonatti . . . Asdente:** Asdente, a shoemaker from Parma, was noted for soothsaying; Bonatti was the private astrologer to Guido of Montefeltro (Canto XXVII).

[186] **But come . . . Seville:** In Christian folklore Cain was placed in the moon after murdering Abel; Cain with his thorns is like the man in the moon, which is setting on the Western horizon beyond Spain. It is early Saturday morning in Jerusalem.

CANTO XXI

[*Eighth Circle, Bolgia Five: the Barrators—Malacoda.*   From the bridge over the fifth ditch Dante can view the souls of those guilty of graft; they are boiled in pitch. Suddenly a devil runs in carrying a new sinner and hurls him into the pitch. Devils poke at him with prongs. Virgil descends to negotiate passage with the devils, who appoint their leader Malacoda to speak for them. Virgil calls to Dante to come out from behind the rocks where he had been cowering. All the bridges to the next bolgia are broken; Dante would prefer that they go alone, but Malacoda names a squad of devils to accompany the poets and Virgil agrees to this plan.]

And so we went from bridge to bridge, and spoke
    Of things which my *Commedia* does not mean
    To sing. We reached the summit, stopping to look

At the next fissure of Malebolge, the vain
    Lamenting that was next—and what I beheld
    Was an astounding darkness. As is done

In winter, when the sticky pitch is boiled
    In the Venetian Arsenal[187] to caulk
    Their unsound vessels while no ship can be sailed,

10 And so instead one uses the time to make
    His ship anew, another one repairs
    Much-voyaged ribs, and some with hammers strike

The prow, and some the stern; and this one makes oars
    While that one might twist rope, another patch
    The jib and mainsail—so, not by any fires

But by some art of Heaven, a heavy pitch
    Was boiling there below, which overglued
    The banks on every side. I saw that much,

But could see nothing in it but the flood
20   Of bubbles the boiling raised, and the whole mass
    Swelling and settling. While I stared down, my guide,

Crying, "Watch out!—watch out!" pulled me across
    Toward him from where I stood. I turned my head
    Like someone eager to find out what it is

---

[187] **Venetian Arsenal:** The Venetian arsenal, one of the largest in Europe, was a shipyard where weapons were also made and stored.

He must avoid, who finding himself dismayed
    By sudden fear, while he is turning back
    Does not delay his flight: what I beheld

Hurrying from behind us up the rock
    Was a black demon. Ah, in his looks a brute,
30   How fierce he seemed in action — running the track

With his wings held outspread, and light of foot:
    Over one high sharp shoulder he had thrown
    A sinner, carrying both haunches' weight

On the one side, with one hand holding on
    To both the ankles. Reaching our bridge, he spoke:
    "O Malebranche,[188] here is another one

Of Santa Zita's elders![189] While I go back
    To bring more from his homeland, thrust him below.
    His city gives us an abundant stock:

40 Every citizen there except Bonturo[190]
    Practices barratry; and given cash
    They can contrive a *yes* from any *no.*"

He hurled the sinner down, then turned to rush
    Back down the rocky crag; and no mastiff
    Was ever more impatient to shake the leash

And run his fastest after a fleeing thief.
    The sinner sank below, only to rise
    Rump up — but demons under the bridge's shelf

Cried, "Here's no place to show your Sacred Face![191]
50   You're not out in the Serchio[192] for a swim!
    If you don't want to feel our hooks — like this! —

Then stay beneath the pitch." They struck at him
    With over a hundred hooks, and said, "You'll need
    To dance in secret here — so grab what scam

---

[188] **Malebranche:** Italian for "evil-claws," the name for devils.

[189] **Santa Zita's elders:** Elders from Lucca, here named from Lucca's patron saint who died in 1275.

[190] **Bonturo:** A notorious swindler in Lucca, still living in 1300.

[191] **Sacred Face:** Ancient Byzantine crucifix in the Cathedral of Lucca.

[192] **Serchio:** River near Lucca.

You're able to, in darkness." Then they did
   Just as cooks have their scullions do to steep
   The meat well into the cauldron—with a prod

From their forks keeping it from floating up.
   My good guide said, "So it will not be seen
60   That you are here, find some jagged outcrop

And crouch behind it to give yourself a screen.
   No matter what offenses they offer me,
   Do not be frightened: I know how things are done

Here—once before I was in such a fray."[193]
   And then he passed beyond the bridge's head,
   And coming to the sixth bank suddenly

He needed to keep a steady front. They bayed
   And rushed at him with all the rage and uproar
   Of dogs that charge some wretched vagabond

70 Who suddenly is forced to plead; they tore
   From under the bridge and raised their forks at him;
   But he cried, "Not so savage!—before you dare

To touch me with your forks, choose one to come
   Forward to hear me out, and then decide
   Whether to hook me." They all cried out one name:

"Let Malacoda[194] go!" So the others stood
   While one strode forward to him, sneering, "What
   Good will it do him?" So my master said,

"Do you, O Malacoda, think I could get
80   Through all of your defenses safely as this
   Except by Heaven's will and happy fate?

Now let us pass—for Heaven also decrees
   That I should show another this savage road."
   The demon's pride fell so much he let loose

---

[193] **Here . . . fray:** In Canto VIII, Virgil and Dante had trouble with fallen angels trying to enter Dis.
[194] **Malacoda:** Italian for "evil-tail."

His hook, which fell down at his feet, and said:
   "Now no one strike him." To me, my leader called,
   "Now you may come back safely to my side,

You who crouch squatting behind the splintered shield
   Of stone, upon the bridge." At this I stirred
90   And quickly joined him—and the devils milled

Toward us, pressing forward, so that I feared
   They might not keep the pact. So I once saw
   The soldiers frightened when they removed their guard

Out of Caprona[195] by treaty—as they withdrew
   Passing among so many enemies.
   I kept as close by my guide as I could go,

And all the while I did not take my eyes
   Away from their expressions . . . which were not good!
   They lowered their hooks, but I heard one give voice:

100   "Should I just touch him on the rump?" Replied
   The others, "Yes—go on and give him a cut."
   But the demon who was talking with my guide

Turned around instantly on hearing that,
   Saying, "Hold—hold, Scarmiglione!" To us
   He said, "You can't go farther by this route,

Because along this ridge the sixth arch lies
   All shattered at the bottom. But if you still
   Wish to go forward, a ridge not far from this

Does have a place where you can cross at will.
110   It was yesterday, five hours later than now,
   That the twelve hundred and sixty-sixth year fell

Since the road here was ruined.[196] I'm sending a crew
   Out of my company in that direction
   To see if sinners are taking the air. You go

---

[195] **Caprona:** A castle near Pisa, which was seized by Florentine and Luccan troops in 1298.

[196] **It was yesterday . . . ruined:** Dante dated the earthquake at the Crucifixion at Good Friday noon 34 C.E., 1266 years before 1300. It is presently 7 a.m. of Holy Saturday.

With them, for they'll not harm you in any fashion.
    Come, Alichino and Calcabrina," he cried,
    "And you, Cagnazzo; and to be the captain

Of all ten, Barbariccia. And in the squad,
    Take Libicocco and Draghignazzo too,
120   And Ciriatto with his tusky head,

And also Graffiacane and Farfarello,
    And crazy Rubicante.[197] Search all around
    The pools of boiling tar. And see these two

Get safely over to where the dens are spanned
    By the next ridge, whose arc is undestroyed."
    "O me! O master, what do I see," I groaned;

"We need no escort if you know the road —
    And as for me, I want none. If you are cautious,
    As is your custom, then how can you avoid

130 Seeing them grind their teeth and with ferocious
    Brows threaten to do us harm?" And he returned,
    "I tell you, have no fear: it is the wretches

Who boil here that they menace — so let them grind
    As fiercely as they like, and scowl their worst."
    And then the company of devils turned,

Wheeling along the left-hand bank. But first
    Each signaled their leader with the same grimace:
    Baring their teeth, through which the tongue was pressed;

And the leader made a trumpet of his ass.

---

[197] **Alichino . . . Rubicante:** Insulting names for demons; Graffiacane, for example, means "dog-scratcher."

Canto XXII

[*Eighth Circle, Bolgia Five (continued): the Grafters—Fra Gomita and Michel Zanche.* As they walk along the bolgia, Dante sees how the sinners are tormented. One of the sinners from Navarre is encouraged by Virgil to tell his story. After the sinner tells about Fra Gomita and Michel Zanche, he tries to escape from the devils by diving into the pitch. The devils quarrel among themselves and two of them fall into the ditch. Virgil and Dante move on.]

I have seen horsemen moving camp before,
   And when they muster, and when an assault begins,
   And beating a retreat when they retire;

I have seen coursers, too, O Aretines,[198]
   Over your lands, and raiders setting out,
   And openings of jousts and tourneys—with signs

By bell and trumpet and drum, and signals set
   On castles by native and foreign signalry:
   But I never saw so strange a flageolet

10 Send foot or horsemen forth, nor ship at sea
   Guided by land or star! We journeyed now
   With the ten demons. Ah, savage company—

But as the saying has it, one must go
   With boozers in the tavern and saints in church.
   Intent upon the pitch, I tried to know

All that I could of the nature of this pouch
   And those who burn in it. Like dolphins who warn
   Sailors[199] to save their vessels, when they arch

Their backs above the water, so we could discern
20   From time to time a sinner show his back
   To alleviate his pain, and then return

To hiding quicker than a lightning stroke.
   And as at water's edge or in a ditch
   Frogs lie, concealing their feet and all their bulk

---

[198] **Aretines:** The Aretines, from Arezzo, were defeated by Florence in 1289.

[199] **Like dophins . . . Sailors:** The belief that dolphins warned ships about an approaching storm.

With snouts above the surface: at the approach
   Of Barbariccia, sinners who lay just so,
   Concealing themselves on every side, would twitch

And pull back under the boiling. I saw—and now
   My heart still shudders as I tell it—one stay,
30   Just as it happens that while one jumps below

Another frog might linger where they lay:
   And Graffiacane, who was nearest, hooked
   Him by his pitch-thick hair, so it looked to me

As if he had caught an otter. (I could connect
   Each of them with his name, for I had noted
   Carefully who they were when they were picked,

And also what they called each other.) They shouted,
   "O Rubicante, grip him between your claws
   And flay him." "Master—this wretch who's so ill-fated

40   And fallen into the hands of enemies:
   I pray you, find out who he is," I said.
   Going to his side at once, he asked what place

He came from. "I was born," replied the shade,
   "In the kingdom of Navarre.[200] My mother sent
   Me to become the servant of a lord,

For she had borne me to a rascal bent
   On destroying both himself and all he had.
   Being admitted to the establishment

Of good King Thibaut's household,[201] I employed
50   Myself at barratry—which is the path
   I pay for in this boiling." So he said;

Then Ciriatto, the demon from whose mouth
   Two boar-like tusks protruded, made him feel
   How one of them could rip. The mouse in truth

---

[200] **I was born . . . Navarre:** His identity is unknown; Navarre is the Basque territory in Spain.
[201] **King Thibaut's household:** Thibaut II of Navarre (1253–1270).

Had come among some vicious cats; and still
 Barbariccia locked him in a tight embrace,
 Saying, "Stand back, while I enfork him well,"

But to my master: "Ask him what you please—
 If there is more you'd like to learn from him
60 Before he's butchered by another of us."

So my guide asked, "Among the sinners who swim
 Under the pitch, are any others you know
 Italian?" He said, "I parted with one who came

From there, just now. Would I were still below
 Hidden with him, for then I'd need not dread
 Their hooks and talons." Then cried Libicocco,

"We have endured too much!" With that he clawed
 His grapple into the other's arm, and tearing
 Ripped out a muscle. Draghignazzo also made

70 As if he meant to give his legs a goring,
 At which their captain wheeled against them all.
 When they were somewhat quiet, without deferring

His questions my leader asked the sinner, who still
 Was staring at his wound: "Who was it you said
 You parted from when you did yourself such ill

By coming ashore?" "Fra Gomita,"[202] he replied,
 "He of Gallura, vessel of every deceit,
 Who kept the enemies that his master had

So cunningly in hand, they praised him for it.
80 He took their cash and sent them on their way
 Smoothly, as he recounts. And he was great

In other enterprises, equally:
 No petty barrator but a lordly one.
 Don Michel Zanche of Logodoro[203] and he

---

[202] **Fra Gomita:** A friar who was Judge of Gallura, a division of Sardinia; he was hanged for selling prisoners their freedom.

[203] **Don Michel Zanche of Logodoro:** Zanche was a governor of Logodoro, a division of Sardinia.

Keep company together; when they go on
　　About Sardinia, their tongues don't tire.
　　But O me—look at how that other demon

Is grinding his teeth! Though I would tell you more
　　I fear he's getting ready to scratch my itch."
90　　To Farfarello, whose eyes rolled eager for gore,

Their marshal turned and shouted his reproach:
　　"Get back, vile bird!" The sinner: "If you would hear
　　Tuscans or Lombards, there are some I can fetch—

But let the Malebranche stand back there
　　So those who come will not fear their revenge,
　　And I will make some seven souls appear

For the lone one that I am—and I won't change
　　My place from where I sit, but summon them
　　By whistling, as we do when we can emerge."

100　Cagnazzo raised his muzzle at this claim;
　　Shaking his head from side to side, he said,
　　"Just listen to this cunning trick—his aim

Is to jump back below." And he, who had
　　A great supply of wiles at his command,
　　Replied, "It's true that I am cunning indeed

At contriving greater sorrows for the band
　　I dwell with." Then Alichino held himself in
　　No longer, and opposed the others: "My friend,"

He said, "if you dare plunge back in again,
110　　I'll not come merely galloping after you
　　But beating my wings above the pitch. The screen

Formed by the bank will hide us when we go
　　Down from this ridge: we'll see if you, alone,
　　Are a match for all of us."[204] O reader, hear now

Of a new sport: led by the very one
　　Who first opposed it, all now turned their eyes
　　To the other shore. Timing exactly when,

---

[204] **we'll see . . . us:** They are attempting to cross the inner side of the dike.

Feet firm against the ground, the Navarrese
    Suddenly leaped and instantly broke free
120   Out of their custody. Each demon, at this,

Felt stung by his misdoing—especially he
    Who caused the blunder. So crying out, "You're caught!"
    He flew away in pursuit, but futilely:

Wings could not gain on terror; down out of sight
    The sinner dove, and the demon swooped back up,
    Raising his breast—no different in his flight

Than when the wild duck makes a sudden escape
    By diving just as the falcon plummets close,
    Then veers back up, vexed at his thwarted grip.

130 Then Calcabrina, who was furious
    The trick had worked, went flying after the pair,
    Eager to see the sinner evade the chase

So there could be a fight. When the barrator
    Had disappeared, the demon turned his claws
    Upon his comrade and grappled him in midair

Above the fosse. But his opponent was
    A full-grown hawk equipped with claws to respond
    Truly and well; and as they fought, the brace

Fell into the middle of the boiling pond.
140   The heat unclenched them at once; but though released
    They could not rise, because their wings were gummed

And clotted. Barbariccia, like the rest
    Lamenting, hastily dispatched a squad
    Of four who flew across to the bank we faced,

Each with a fork; hurrying from either side
    They descended to their posts with hooks extended
    To the mired pair, already baked inside

Their crusts; and we two left them thus confounded.

CANTO XXIII

[*Eighth Circle, Bolgia Five (continued): the Grafters. Bolgia Six: the Hypocrites—Catalano and Loderingo; Caiaphas.*   As they walk along, Dante looks behind him, sees they are being pursued by the devils, and is reminded of Aesop's fable about the frog and the mouse. Virgil and Dante slide down the rock of the ditch, eluding the devils. In the sixth ditch are the hypocrites, who wear brilliant gowns made of lead. One of the shades, Fra Catalano, describes himself and another friar, Loderingo. On the ground are Caiaphas and others of the Jewish Council; they are being crucified. After seeking passage out of this bolgia, Virgil realizes he had been tricked by the devils of the fifth bolgia.]

Silent, alone, sans escort, with one behind
    And one before, as Friars Minor use,
    We journeyed. The present fracas turned my mind

To Aesop's fable of the frog and mouse:[205]
    Now and *this moment* are not more similar
    Than did the tale resemble the newer case,

If one is conscientious to compare
    Their ends and their beginnings. Then, as one thought
    Springs from the one before it, this now bore

10 Another which redoubled my terror: that—
    Having been fooled because of us, with wounds
    And mockery to make them the more irate,

With anger added to their malice—the fiends,
    More fiercely than a dog attacks a hare,
    Would soon come after us. I felt the ends

Of my hair bristling already from the fear.
    Intent on what was behind us on the road,
    "Master," I said, "unless you can obscure

Both you and me from sight, and soon, I dread
20   The Malebranche, already after us—
    And I imagine them so clearly, indeed

---

[205] **fable of the frog and mouse:** A fable wrongly ascribed to Aesop (sixth century B.C.E.?) about a frog that gives a ride across a stream to a mouse, tries to drown the mouse, but is seized by a kite (hawklike bird) while the mouse goes free.

I hear them now." "Were I of lead-backed glass,°   mirror
    I would not take your outward countenance in
    Quicker than I do your inward one in this,"

He said; "This moment, your thoughts entered mine—
    In aspect and in action so alike
    I have made both their counsels into one:

If the right bank is sloped so as to make
    A way to reach the next fosse, then we can
30   Escape the chase we both imagine." He spoke

With barely time to tell me of his plan
    Before I saw them coming—wings spread wide,
    Eager to seize us, not far and closing in.

My leader took me up at once, and did
    As would a mother awakened by a noise
    Who sees the flames around her, and takes her child,

Concerned for him more than herself, and flies
    Not staying even to put on a shift:
    Supine he gave himself to the rocky place

40 Where the hard bank slopes downward to the cleft,
    Forming one side of the adjacent pouch.
    No water coursing a sluice was ever as swift

To turn a landmill's wheel on its approach
    Toward the vanes, as my master when he passed
    On down that bank that slanted to the ditch,

Hurtling along with me upon his breast
    Not like his mere companion, but like his child.
    Just as his feet hit bottom, on the crest

Above us they appeared—but now they held
50   Nothing to fear, for that high Providence
    That made them keepers of the fifth ditch willed

That they should have no power to leave its bounds.
    Down at the bottom, we discovered a set
    Of painted people, who slowly trod their rounds

Weeping, with looks of weariness and defeat.
    Their cloaks, cowls covering the eyes and face,
    Resembled those of Cluny's[206] monks in cut.

These cloaks were gilded on the side that shows
    So that the eye was dazzled—but all of lead
60   On the inside: so heavy, compared to these

The capes inflicted by Frederick were made
    Of woven straw.[207] O heavy mantle to bear
    Through eternity! As ever, we pursued

Our course by turning to the left, and bore
    Along with them, intent on how they moaned.
    But they came slowly, burdened as they were—

So that with every step we took we found
    Our company was new. I asked my guide,
    "Pray find some person here, by looking round

70 As we walk on, whom I know by name or deed."
    And one among them caught the Tuscan speech:
    "Stay your quick steps through this dark air," he cried

As we came past him. "Perhaps what you beseech
    You can obtain from me." At which my guide
    Turned back to me, with: "Wait: let him approach

And then proceed at his pace." So I stayed,
    And saw two coming who by their faces appeared
    In a great haste of mind to reach my side

Although their burden held them in retard,
80   As did the crowding. When they came up together
    They looked at me askance without a word

For some good while. Then, turning toward each other
    They said, "This one appears to be alive,
    Judging by how his throat moves; but if, rather,

---

[206] **Cluny's:** Cluny was a large monastery in France; in Dante's day the monks were known for their luxurious wear.

[207] **woven straw:** A story attributed to Frederick II (Canto X) that he had traitors wrapped in lead coats which were then melted on them.

These two are dead, what privilege can they have,
    To go unencumbered by the heavy stole?"
    And then to me, "O Tuscan, you who arrive

At the sad hypocrites' assembly: pray tell—
    Not scorning to so address us—who you are."
90   "At the great town," I said, "on the beautiful

Waters of Arno, I was born, and there
    I grew up, and the body I wear now
    I have always had—but who are you, who bear

Upon your cheeks these distillates of woe?
    What is your punishment that glitters so bright?"
    "The orange cloaks are lead," said one of the two,

"So thick, that we their scales creak at the weight.
    We both were Jovial Friars,[208] and Bolognese:
    As for names, I was Catalano, and that

100 Was Loderingo,[209] and we were your city's choice—
    The way they usually choose one man—
    To keep the peace: and what we were still shows

In the Gardingo district." Then I began:
    "O Friars, your evil—" but that was all I said,
    For as I spoke my eye was caught by one

Upon the ground, where he was crucified
    By three stakes. When he saw me there he squirmed
    All over, and puffing in his beard, he sighed;

Fra Catalano, observing this, explained:
110   "The one[210] impaled there you are looking at
    Is he who counseled the Pharisees to bend

[208]**Jovial Friars:** Knights of the Blessed Virgin Mary, a military order founded in 1261, to protect the weak; known for their easy life.

[209]**Catalano . . . Loderingo:** Two men who helped found the Friars were appointed joint Governors to Florence in 1266; they were charged with corruption. The quarter of Florence called the Gardingo was destroyed by a civil war caused by the Friars.

[210]**The one:** Caiaphas, the high priest under Pontius Pilate, advised that Jesus be crucified (John 11:49–50).

The expedient way, by letting one man be put
  To torture for the people. You see him stretch
  Naked across the path to feel the weight

Of everyone who passes; and in this ditch,
  Trussed the same way, are racked his father-in-law
  And others of that council[211] which was such

A seed of evil for the Jews." I saw
  Virgil, who had been marveling over the man
120 Doomed to be stretched out vilely crosswise so

In the eternal exile. He spoke words then,
  Directed to the friar: "Be it allowed,
  And if it pleases you, could you explain

What passage there may be on the right-hand side
  By which we two can journey away from here,
  Without requiring those black angels' aid

To come and take us from this valley floor?"
  And he replied, "Nearer than you may hope
  Is a rock ridge that starts from the circular

130 Great wall surrounding us, and spans the top
  Of all the savage valleys except for this—
  Where it is broken and fallen down the slope

Rather than arching over: and at that place,
  You can mount up by climbing the debris
  Of rock along the slopes of the crevasse

And piled up at the bottom." Silently
  My leader stood a moment bowing his head,
  Then, "He who hooks the sinners, back that way,

Supplied a bad account of this," he said.
140 The friar: "In Bologna the saying goes,
  As I have heard, that the Devil is endowed

With many vices—among them, that he lies
  And is the father of lies, I have also heard."
  And then my guide moved onward, setting the pace

---

[211] **father-in-law . . . council:** Annas, "father-in-law" to Caiaphas, along with the Jewish Sanhedrin.

With mighty strides, and with his features stirred
    To some disturbance by his anger yet;
    And leaving those burdened souls I too went forward,

Following in the tracks of his dear feet.

Canto XXIV

[*Eighth Circle, Bolgia Six: the Hypocrites (continued). Bolgia Seven: the Thieves—Vanni Fucci.*
The poets climb with difficulty out of the ditch of hypocrisy and reach the seventh bridge. They see
sinners tormented by swarms of snakes. One soul, Vanni Fucci of Pistoia, repeatedly burns into
ashes and is reintegrated like the legendary Phoenix. Dante recognizes him as a former political
enemy. Fucci predicts events leading to the defeat of the Florentine Whites.]

In that part of the young year[212] when the sun
    Goes under Aquarius to rinse his beams,
    And the long nights already begin to wane

Toward half the day, and when the hoarfrost mimes
    The image of her white sister upon the ground—
    But only a while, because her pen, it seems,

Is not sharp long—a peasant who has found
    That he is running short of fodder might rise
    And go outside and see the fields have turned

10 To white, and slap his thigh, and back in the house
    Pace grumbling here and there like some poor wretch
    Who can't see what to do; and then he goes

Back out, and finds hope back within his reach,
    Seeing in how little time the world outside
    Has changed its face, and takes his crook to fetch

His sheep to pasture. I felt this way, dismayed
    By my master's stormy brow; and quickly as this,
    The hurt had found its plaster. For when we stood

Before the ruined bridge, my leader's face
20   Turned to me with a sweet expression, the same
    As I had first beheld at the mountain's base.

---

[212] **the young year:** About January 20th.

He opened his arms, after he took some time
    To consult himself and study the ruin well,
    And taking hold of me began the climb.

As one who works and reckons all the while
    Seems always to have provided in advance,
    So, lifting me up one great boulder's wall,

He kept his eye on another eminence,
    Saying, "Next, grapple that one—but make sure
30   That it will bear you, first." That path of stones

Would not provide a road for those who wore
    Lead mantles, for we—he weightless, I helped up—
    Could barely make our way from spur to spur.

Had it not been that on that bank the slope
    Was shorter than on the other, I do not know
    How he'd have fared, but I'd have had to stop

And would have been defeated; but it was true
    In each valley that the contour of the land
    Made one side higher and the other low,

40 Because of the way all Malebolge inclined
    Downward toward the mouth of the lowest pit.
    At length we reached the place at which we found

The last stone broken off, and there I sat
    As soon as I was up—so out of breath
    Were my spent lungs I felt that I could get

No farther than I was. "To cast off sloth
    Now well behooves you," said my master then:
    "For resting upon soft down, or underneath

The blanket's cloth, is not how fame is won—
50   Without which, one spends life to leave behind
    As vestige of himself on earth the sign

Smoke leaves on air, or foam on water. So stand
    And overcome your panting—with the soul,
    Which wins all battles if it does not despond

Under its heavy body's weight. And still
    A longer ladder remains for us to climb;[213]
    To leave these shades behind does not fulfill

All that's required. If you understand me, come:
    Act now, to profit yourself." I got to my feet,
60   Showing more breath than I felt, and said to him,

"Go on, for I am strong and resolute."
    And so, ascending the ridge, we took our way:
    It was quite rugged, narrow and difficult,

Far steeper than the last. To seem to be
    Not too fatigued, I was talking while I trudged,
    When a voice arose—one ill equipped to say

Actual words—from the new fosse we had reached.
    I don't know what it said, though I was now
    At the high point of the bridge which overarched

70 The ditch there, but whoever spoke from below
    Seemed to be moving. I turned quick eyes to peer
    Down into the dark, but the bottom didn't show—

Wherefore I said, "Master, pray lead from here
    To the next belt, and let us descend the wall:
    Just as I cannot decipher the things I hear,

So too I look but make out nothing at all
    From where we are." "I'll give no other response,"
    He said, "but do it, for fitting petitions call

For deeds, not words." Where the bridge's end adjoins
80   The eighth bank, we descended, and then that pouch
    Showed itself to me: I saw in its confines

Serpents—a frightening swarm, of weird kinds such
    As to remember now still chills my blood.
    Let Libya boast no more of her sands so rich

---

[213] **A longer ladder . . . climb:** The distance from the earth's center to the summit of Purgatory.

In reptiles, for though they spawn the chelydrid,
 Cenchres with amphisbaena, the jaculi
 And phareae,[214] she never, though one include

All Ethiopia and the lands that lie
 On the Red Sea, has shown a pestilence
90 So numerous or of such malignancy.

Amid this horde, cruel, grim and dense,
 People were running, naked and terrified,
 Without a hope of hiding or a chance

At heliotrope[215] for safety. Their hands were tied
 Behind their backs — with snakes, that thrust between
 Where the legs meet, entwining tail and head

Into a knot in front. And look! — at one
 Near us a serpent darted, and transfixed
 Him at the point where neck and shoulders join.

100 No *o* or *i* could be made with strokes[216] as fast
 As he took fire and burned and withered away,
 Sinking; and when his ashes came to rest

Ruined on the ground, the dust spontaneously
 Resumed its former shape. Just so expires
 The Phoenix in its flames, great sages[217] agree,

To be born again every five hundred years;
 During its life, it feeds on neither grain
 Nor herb but amomum and incense's tears,

And at its end the sheet it's shrouded in
110 Is essence of nard and myrrh. As one who falls
 And knows not how — if a demon pulled him down,

Or another blockage human life entails —
 And when he rises stares about confused
 By the great anguish that he knows he feels,

---

[214] **chelydrid . . . phareae:** Venomous snakes mentioned by the Roman poet Lucan (39–65 C.E.).

[215] **heliotrope:** Heliotrope, or bloodstone, was thought to cure snake bite, and also to make its wearer invisible.

[216] **No *o* or *i* . . . strokes:** That is, letters that can be made with a single stroke.

[217] **great sages:** The phoenix story about a bird that dies and is reborn out of its own ashes is told by Ovid and Lucan among others; medieval writers linked the phoenix to Jesus.

And looking, sighs; so was that sinner dazed
    When he stood up again. Oh, power of God!
    How severe its vengeance is, to have imposed

Showers of such blows. My leader asked the shade
    To tell us who he was. "The time is brief
120   Since I rained down from Tuscany," he replied,

"Into this gullet. It was a bestial life,
    Not human, that pleased me best, mule that I was.
    I am Vanni Fucci,[218] beast—and aptly enough,

Pistoia was my den." And, "Master, please
    Bid him not slip away, but ask what sin
    It was," I said, "that thrust him to this place,

For in his time I have known him as a man
    Of blood and rage." The sinner, who had heard,
    Without dissembling turned mind and face—which shone

130 The color of shame—to me; then he declared,
    "That you have caught me here amid this grief
    Causes me suffering worse than I endured

When I was taken from the other life.
    I cannot refuse your question: I must be
    Thrust this far down because I was a thief

Who took adornments from the sacristy—
    For which another, falsely, was condemned.[219]
    But, lest you delight too much in what you see

If ever you escape from this dark ground:
140   Open your ears to what I now pronounce,
    And listen. First, Pistoia strips her land

---

[218] **Vanni Fucci:** Fucci was the illegitimate son ("mule") of a noble from Pistoia, north of Florence, and violent leader of the Black Guelphs.

[219] **Who took . . . condemned:** The sacristy in the Pistoia Cathedral contained treasures, some of which were stolen in 1293. An innocent man was hanged for the theft.

Of Blacks, then Florence changes her citizens
　　And ways.[220] From Val di Magra, Mars draws a great
　　Vapor, and thick clouds muffle its turbulence

Till stormy, bitter, impetuous war breaks out
　　On Campo Piceno—where suddenly, it breaks through
　　And tears the mist and strikes at every White:

And I have told it to bring grief to you."

Canto XXV

[*Eighth Circle, Bolgia Seven (continued): the Thieves.*　After Vanni Fucci makes an obscene gesture toward God, snakes attack him and he flees. He is chased by Cacus, a centaur, who strives to increase his punishment. Virgil and Dante witness the painful and hideous transformations of several Florentine thieves in bolgia seven.]

The thief held up his hands when he was through,
　　And "God," he cried, making the fig[221] with both—
　　"Take these: I aim them squarely up at you!"

The serpents were my friends from that time forth,
　　For then one coiled itself about his neck
　　As if to say, "That's all then, from your mouth,"

And another went around his arms to snake
　　Them tight and cinch itself in front, so tied
　　They couldn't budge enough to gesture. Alack,

10　Pistoia,[222] Pistoia!—Why haven't you decreed
　　Your own incineration, so that you dwell
　　On earth no more, since you surpass your seed

In evildoing? In all the circles of Hell
　　I saw no spirit so arrogant to God,
　　Not even him[223] who fell from the Theban wall.

---

[220] **Florence . . . ways:** The division of the Guelphs into Blacks and Whites spread from Pistoia to Florence; in Pistoia the Blacks were expelled by the Whites, but in Florence the dominance of the Blacks in 1302 led to Dante's exile.

[221] **fig:** An obscene gesture.

[222] **Pistoia:** Pistoia was founded by Cataline, a conspirator against the Roman Republic in the first century B.C.E.

[223] **him:** Capaneus (Canto XIV).

Speaking no more then, Vanni Fucci fled,
    And next I saw a centaur full of rage:
    "Where is he? Where is the bitter one?" he cried

As he charged up. I think more snakes than lodge
20   In Maremma's swamp were riding on his croup,
    Swarming along his back up to the edge

Of our human form. He bore behind his nape,
    Along the shoulders, a dragon with wings spread wide:
    If any blocked the path, it burned them up.

"This centaur's name is Cacus,"[224] my master said,
    "Who underneath the stones of Aventine
    Many a time has made a lake of blood.

He doesn't walk the same road as his clan
    Because by theft and fraud he tried to get
30   The splendid herd that lay near him—a sin

That ended his crooked habits: he died for it.
    When Hercules's club rained onto his head
    Some hundred blows, he lived to feel ten hit."

While he was saying this, the centaur sped
    Beyond us, and three new spirits appeared below;
    They went unnoticed by me or by my guide

Until they shouted to us, "Who are you?"
    At which we ceased our talk and turned to them.
    I did not know them, but as people do

40 When chance disposes, one had some cause to name
    Another—"Where have we left Cianfa?"[225] he said.
    To be sure my leader heard, I signaled him

To stay alert, with a finger that I laid
    From chin to nose. Reader, if you are slow
    To credit what I tell you next, it should

---

[224] **Cacus:** A monster who stole cattle from Hercules and dragged them backwards into his cave. His brothers are the Centaurs (Canto XII).

[225] **Cianfa:** A thief from a noble Florentine family.

Be little wonder, for I who saw it know
   That I myself can hardly acknowledge it:
   While I was staring at the sinners below

A serpent darted forward that had six feet,
50   And facing one of the three it fastened on him
   All over — with the middle feet it got

A grip upon the belly, with each fore-limb
   It clasped an arm; its fangs gripped both his cheeks;
   It spread its hind feet out to do the same

To both his thighs, extending its tail to flex
   Between them upward through to the loins behind.
   No ivy growing in a tree's bark sticks

As firmly as the horrid beast entwined
   Its limbs around the other. Then, as if made
60   Out of hot wax, they clung and made a bond

And mixed their colors; and neither could be construed
   As what it was at first — so, as the track
   Of flame moves over paper, there is a shade

That moves before it that is not yet black,
   And the white dies away. The other two
   Were looking on, and cried, "Ah me, now look

At how you change, Agnello![226] — already you
   Are neither two nor one." Now the two heads
   Had become one; we watched the two shapes grow

70 Into one face, where both were lost. The sides
   Grew two arms, fused from lengths that had been four;
   Thighs, legs, chest, belly merged; and in their steads

Grew members that were never seen before.
   All of the former features were blotted out.
   A perverse shape, with both not what they were,

Yet neither — such, its pace deliberate,
   It moved away. The way a lizard can dash
   Under the dog day's scourge, darting out

---

[226]**Agnello:** Another thief.

Between the hedges so that it seems a flash
80   Of lightning if it spurts across the road,
        So did a fiery little serpent rush

Toward the bellies of the two who stayed;
        Peppercorn black and livid, it struck out,
        Transfixing one in the place where we are fed°   navel

When life begins — then fell before his feet,
        Outstretched. The pierced one gazed at it and stood
        Not speaking, only yawning as if a fit

Of sleep or fever had taken him. He eyed
        The serpent, the serpent him. From this one's wound
90   And that one's mouth smoke violently flowed,

And their smoke met. Let Lucan now attend
        In silence, who has told the wretched fates
        Of Nasidius and Sabellus[227] — till he has learned

What I will let fly next. And Ovid, who writes
        Of Cadmus and Arethusa,[228] let him be still —
        For though he in his poet-craft transmutes

One to a serpent, and makes the other spill
        Transformed into a fountain, I envy him not:
        He never transformed two individual

100   Front-to-front natures so both forms as they met
        Were ready to exchange their substance. The twain
        Reacted mutually: the reptile split

Its tail to make a fork; the wounded one
        Conjoined his feet. The legs and thighs were pressed
        So tight no mark of juncture could be seen;

The split tail took the shape the other lost,
        Its skin grew softer, and the other's hard.
        I saw the arms draw inward to be encased

---

[227] **Nasidius and Sabellus:** Two soldiers in Cato's army (Lucan's *Pharsalia*), bitten by serpents.

[228] **Cadmus and Arethusa:** Pursued by a river-god, the nymph Arethusa asked Artemis to change her into a fountain; Cadmus, founder of Thebes, was changed into a serpent after killing a sacred dragon.

Inside the armpits; the animal's feet appeared
110   To lengthen as the other's arms grew less.
        The hind paws, twisting together like a cord,

Became the member man conceals. From his,
        The wretch had grown two feet. While the smoke veils
        Each one with colors that are new, and grows

Hair here and strips it there, the one shape falls
        And one comes upright. But neither turned aside
        The unholy lights that stared above the muzzles

They each were changing: the one who newly stood
        Drew his in toward his temples, and from the spare
120   Matter from that, ears issued from the head,

Behind smooth cheeks; what didn't course to an ear
        But was retained became the face's nose,
        And fleshed the lips to the thickness they should bear.

He that lay prone propelled his nose and face
        Forward, and shrank his ears back into the head
        As a snail does its horns. The tongue that was

Whole and prepared for speech was split instead —
        And in the other the forked tongue formed one piece:
        And the smoke ceased. The soul that had been made

130   A beast fled down the valley with a hiss;
        The other, speaking now, spat after it,[229]
        Turned his new shoulders on it to address

The third, and said: "I'll have Buoso[230] trot
        On all fours down this road, as I have done!"
        And so I saw that seventh deadweight[231] transmute

And mutate — and may its strangeness excuse my pen,
        If it has tangled things. And though my eyes
        Were somewhat in confusion at the scene,

---

[229] **spat after it:** It was thought that human spit was poisonous to snakes.

[230] **Buoso:** The identity of this Buoso is not known.

[231] **seventh deadweight:** The sinners of this ditch.

My mind somewhat bewildered, yet none of these
140   Could flee to hide himself so secretly
    That I could not distinguish well the face

Of Puccio Sciancato,[232] who of the three
    Companions that we first took notice of,
    Alone was not transformed; the other[233] was he

Whose death, Gaville, you have good cause to grieve.

Canto **XXVI**

[*Eighth Circle, Bolgia Seven (continued): the Thieves. Bolgia Eight: Evil Counselors—Ulysses.* After Dante declaims against the city of Florence, the poets crest the bridge over bolgia eight, where evil counselors are punished; each one is wrapped in a burning flame except for Ulysses and Diomedes, who are tortured in a double flame. Virgil, who had written about Ulysses in *The Aeneid,* inquires how he died. With great dignity Ulysses explains how he and his men sailed past Gibraltar to the vast Atlantic and finally the Southern Hemisphere. Within sight of the mountain of Purgatory, Ulysses drowned in a storm that wrecked his ship.]

Rejoice, O Florence, since you are so great,
    Beating your wings on land and on the sea,
    That in Hell too your name is spread about!

I found among those there for their thievery
    Five of your citizens, which carries shame
    For me—and you gain no high honor thereby.

But if we dream the truth near morning time,
    Then you will feel, before much time has gone,
    What Prato[234] and others crave for you—and come

10 Already, it would not have come too soon.
    And truly, let it, since it must come to pass:
    For it will all the heavier weigh me down,

The older I become. We left the place,
    And on the stairway that the jutting stone
    A little while before had offered us

---

[232] **Puccio Sciancato:** A third thief from a Florentine family.

[233] **the other:** Francesco Cavalcanti, a Florentine living in Gaville, was killed for his oppressions by the towns-people; his family avenged him.

[234] **Prato:** Perhaps a reference to the rebellion of Prato, north of Florence, against Florence.

On our descent, my guide climbed up again
   And drew me up to pursue our lonely course.
   Without the hand the foot could not go on,

Climbing that jagged ridge's rocks and spurs.
20   I sorrowed then, and when I turn my mind
   To what I saw next, sorrow again —and force

My art to make its genius more restrained
   Than is my usual bent, lest it should run
   Where virtue doesn't: so that if any kind

Star or some better thing has made it mine
   I won't myself negate the gift in me.
   As many as the fireflies a peasant has seen

(Resting on a hill that time of year when he
   Who lights the world least hides his face from us,
30   And at the hour when the fly gives way

To the mosquito[235]) all down the valley's face,
   Where perhaps he gathers grapes and tills the ground:
   With flames that numerous was Hell's eighth fosse

Glittering, as I saw when I attained
   A place from which its floor could be made out.
   And as the one avenged by bears divined

That what he saw was Elijah's chariot[236]
   Carried by rearing horses to Heaven's domain—
   For with his eyes he couldn't follow it

40 Except by looking at the flame alone,
   Like a small cloud ascending: so each flame moves
   Along the ditch's gullet with not one

Showing its plunder, though every flame contrives
   To steal away a sinner. I had climbed up
   To balance where the bridge's high point gives

A better view, and if I didn't grip
   A rock I would have fallen from where I stood
   Without a push. Seeing how from the top

---

[235] **at the hour . . . mosquito:** A midsummer evening.
[236] **Elijah's chariot:** Elisha saw Elijah's ascension in a chariot (2 Kings 11:23–4).

I gazed intently down, my master said,
50   "Within the flames are spirits; each one here
    Enfolds himself in what burns him." I replied,

"My Master, to hear you say it makes me sure,
    But I already thought it; already, too,
    I wanted to ask you who is in that fire

Which at its top is so split into two
    It seems to surge from the pyre Eteocles
    Shared with his brother?"[237] He answered, "In it go

Tormented Ulysses and Diomedes[238]
    Enduring vengeance together, as they did wrath;
60   And in their flame they grieve for their device,

The horse that made the doorway through which went forth
    The Romans' noble seed. Within their fire
    Now they lament the guile that even in death

Makes Deidamia mourn Achilles,[239] and there
    They pay the price for the Palladium."
    "Master," I said, "I earnestly implore,

If they can speak within those sparks of flame —
    And pray my prayer be worth a thousand pleas —
    Do not forbid my waiting here for them

70 Until their horned flame makes its way to us;
    You see how yearningly it makes me lean."
    And he to me: "Your prayer is worthy of praise,

And therefore I accept it. But restrain
    Your tongue, leave speech to me — Greeks that they were,
    They might treat words of yours with some disdain."

My master waited as the flame drew near
    For the right place and moment to arrive,
    Then spoke: "O you, who are two within one fire:

---

[237] **Eteocles . . . brother:** Eteocles and his brother Polynices, sons of Oedipus, killed each other.

[238] **Ulysses and Diomedes:** Two Greek leaders in the Trojan War; they stole the sacred image of Pallas Athene, the "Palladium" that protected Troy and they devised the wooden horse, within which Greek warriors hid, that led to Troy's downfall.

[239] **Makes . . . Achilles:** Ulysses and Diomedes persuaded Achilles to leave his lover Deidamia and go to Troy where Achilles died.

If I deserved of you while I was alive—
80   If I deserved anything great or small
         From you when I wrote verse, then do not move;

But rather grant that one of you will tell
         Whither, when lost, he went away to die."
         The greater horn of flame began to flail

And murmur like fire the wind beats, and to ply
         Its tip which, as it vibrated here and there
         Like a tongue in speech, flung out a voice to say:

"When Circe[240] had detained me more than a year
         There near Gaeta,[241] before it had that name
90   Aeneas gave it, and I parted from her,

Not fondness for my son, nor any claim
         Of reverence for my father, nor love I owed
         Penelope,[242] to please her, could overcome

My longing for experience of the world,
         Of human vices and virtue. But I sailed out
         On the deep open seas, accompanied

By that small company that still had not
         Deserted me, in a single ship. One coast
         I saw, and then another, and I got

100   As far as Spain, Morocco, Sardinia, a host
         Of other islands that the sea bathes round.
         My men and I were old and slow when we passed

The narrow outlet where Hercules let stand
         His markers beyond which men were not to sail.
         On my left hand I had left Ceuta[243] behind,

And on the other sailed beyond Seville.
         'O brothers who have reached the west,' I began,
         'Through a hundred thousand perils, surviving all:

---

[240] **Circe:** A goddess and enchantress who turned men into beasts in Homer's *The Odyssey.*

[241] **Gaeta:** Named after Aeneas's nurse (*The Aeneid,* 7).

[242] **Penelope:** The wife of Ulysses.

[243] **narrow outlet . . . Ceuta:** The Pillars of Hercules, located at the Strait of Gibraltar, were thought to be the western edge of the habitable world. Ceuta is a north African city at the Strait.

So little is the vigil we see remain
110   Still for our senses, that you should not choose
To deny it the experience—behind the sun

Leading us onward—of the world which has
No people in it. Consider well your seed:
You were not born to live as a mere brute does,

But for the pursuit of knowledge and the good.'
Then all of my companions grew so keen
To journey, spurred by this little speech I'd made,

I would have found them difficult to restrain.
Turning our stern toward the morning light,
120   We made wings of our oars, in an insane

Flight, always gaining on the left. The night
Showed all the stars, now, of the other pole—
Our own star fallen so low, no sign of it

Rose from the sea. The moon's low face glowed full
Five times since we set course across the deep,
And as many times was quenched invisible,

When dim in the distance we saw a mountaintop:²⁴⁴
It seemed the highest I had ever seen.
We celebrated—but soon began to weep,

130   For from the newfound land a storm had grown,
Rising to strike the forepart of the ship.
It whirled the vessel round, and round again

With all the waters three times, lifting up
The stern the fourth—as pleased an Other°—to press   god
The prow beneath the surface, and did not stop

Until the sea had closed up over us."

---

²⁴⁴ **mountaintop:** Mount Purgatory.

Canto **XXVII**

[*Eighth Circle, Bolgia Eight (continued): the Evil Counselors—Guido of Montefeltro.*   A second
flame approaches, containing the soul of Count Guido of Montefeltro, a famous Ghibelline leader.
After Guido hears news from Dante about the province of Romagna, he tells about his betrayal by
Pope Boniface VIII. Having withdrawn from the world, Guido was persuaded by Boniface to
devise a stratagem by which the Pope's enemies might be defeated. Guido's treacherous plan
landed him in Hell.]

The flame already was quiet and erect again,
　　Done speaking, and, as the gentle poet allowed,
　　Leaving us, when behind it another one

Was drawing near, the confused sound it made
　　Drawing our eyes toward its flickering tip.
　　As the Sicilian bull (which bellowed loud

For the first time when he who gave it shape[245]
　　With his file's art was forced to give it his voice,
　　Justly) would use a victim's cries, sealed up

10　Inside its body, to bellow—so that, though brass,
　　It seemed transfixed with pain when it was heated:
　　So, having at first no passage or egress

From fire, the melancholy words were transmuted
　　Into fire's language. But after the words had found
　　Their passage through the tip, and it vibrated

As the tongue had in trying to form their sound,
　　We heard it say, "O you toward whom I guide
　　My voice, and who a moment ago intoned

In Lombard,[246] 'Now continue on your road,
20　I do not ask you more'—though I may be
　　Late in my coming here, don't be annoyed

To stop and speak; you see that I am free
　　Of annoyance, though I burn. If you just fell
　　Into this viewless world from Italy,

---

[245] **he who gave it shape:** Perillus fashioned for Phalaris, tyrant of Sicily, a brazen bull for roasting victims and
was the first victim.

[246] **Lombard:** Virgil spoke the Lombard dialect.

Sweet land above, from which I carry all
    My guilt, then tell me: is it peace or war
    That occupies the Romagnoles? — I[247] hail

From the hill country between Urbino and where,
    High up the ridge, the Tiber has its source."
30   I was still crouched and intently giving ear

When my guide nudged me, saying, "You may discourse
    With him: he is Italian." Already prepared
    To answer, I said: "That Romagna of yours,

O soul concealed below, is not yet cleared
    And never was — in her tyrants' hearts — of war:
    Though when I left, no war had been declared.

Ravenna[248] still remains as many a year,
    Polenta's eagle brooding above the town
    So its wings cover Cervia. The land that bore

40 The long siege, once, and struck the Frenchmen down
    Into a bloody heap, finds itself now
    Held underneath the Green Paws[249] once again.

Both the old mastiff and new of Verrucchio,
    Who treated Montagna in an evil way,
    Sink their teeth in, the way they always do.

Along the Santerno and the Lamone lie
    Cities the Lionet of the White Lair rules,
    Who changes sides and shifts his loyalty

From summer to winter. And the town that feels
50   The Savio bathe its flank, just as it lies
    Between a plain and mountains,[250] also dwells

Somewhere between tyranny's and freedom's ways.
    And now I pray you — tell us who you are.
    Don't be more grudging than another was

---

[247] **I:** Guido, Count of Montefeltro, head of the Ghibellines in Romagna and a soldier, died in 1298.

[248] **Ravenna:** The major city in Romagna, ruled then, along with Cervia, by the Polenta family.

[249] **Green Paws:** Forlì defeated the French, but then was seized by the Ordelaffi family, whose coat of arms had green claws.

[250] **plain and mountains:** In this passage Dante alludes to cities of Romagna, their rulers, and coats of arms.

In answering you, so may your name endure,
    Proudly in the world above." After the fire
    Roared in its way awhile, it began to stir

Its sharp tip rapidly, first here, then there,
    Then formed this breath: "If I believed I gave
60   My answer to one who'd ever go once more

Back to the world, this tongue of flame would have
    No motion. But since, if what I hear is true,
    None ever returned from this abyss alive,

Not fearing infamy I will answer you.
    I was a man of arms, and after that
    Became a corded friar,[251] hopeful to do

Penance by wearing the rope; indeed that thought
    Might well have been fulfilled, but the High Priest[252]—
    May evil befall him!—led me to commit

70 Again the sins that I had practiced at first:
    And how and why, now listen and I'll disclose.
    My actions, when my form was still encased

In the flesh and bones my mother gave me, were those
    Of the fox, not the lion. I was expert
    In all the stratagems and covert ways,

And practiced them with so much cunning art
    The sound extended to the earth's far end.
    But when I saw that I had reached that part

Of life when we should let our sails descend
80   And coil the ropes—then what had pleased me before
    Now grieved me: penitent and confessed, I joined

An order and—woe to say!—my life as friar
    Would have availed me. The Prince of new Pharisees
    Nearby the Lateran was making war,

---

[251] **corded friar:** A Franciscan.

[252] **High Priest:** Pope Boniface VIII.

And not against the Saracens or Jews,
  His enemies all being Christians:[253] and none
  Had been at Acre's conquest, nor one of those

Who went as merchants to the Sultan's domain;[254]
  And he respected neither the supreme
90 Office and holy orders that were his own,

Nor in me the friar's cord which at one time
  Made those who wore it leaner. As Constantine
  Sought out Sylvester in Soracte, his aim

To have him cure his leprosy[255] — this man
  Came seeking me as one who meant to find
  A doctor to cure the fever he was in,

Of pride. He asked my counsel, and I remained
  Silent, because his words seemed drunk to me.
  And then he spoke again: 'Now understand,

100 Your heart should not respond mistrustfully,
  For I absolve you in advance, henceforth:
  Instruct me, so that I can find a way

To level Palestrina to the earth.
  I have the power to lock and unlock Heaven,
  As you know; for the keys[256] are two, whose worth

Seemed not dear to my predecessor.' Then, driven
  To where the gravity of his argument
  Made silence seem worse counsel, I said: 'Given,

Father, that you are washing me of the taint
110 Of this sin into which I now must fall —
  Large promises with fulfillments that are scant

---

[253] **His enemies . . . Christians:** On Guido's advice, Boniface broke faith with the Colonna who had surrendered to the papal forces and destroyed Palestrina, the Colonna's stronghold.

[254] **Sultan's domain:** Acre, the last stronghold of the Christians in Palestine, surrendered to the Muslims in 1291. An earlier pope forbade commerce with Muslims.

[255] **leprosy:** Prior to his conversion, the Emperor Constantine got leprosy from persecuting Christians; following a dream, he summoned Pope Sylvester from Mount Soracte, was converted and healed.

[256] **keys:** Pope Celestine V, who resigned the papacy after five months, had given up the keys of damnation and absolution.

Will bring your high throne triumph over all.'
    And Francis came for me the moment I died,
    But one of these black cherubim of Hell

Appeared; and, 'Do not carry him off,' it said,
    'Do not deprive me: he must be carried down
    Among my servants, because he counseled fraud,

And I have hovered near his hair since then,
    Until this moment—for no one has absolution
120   Without repenting; nor can one will a sin

And repent at once, because the contradiction
    Precludes it.' How I shuddered—O wretched me!
    'Perhaps you did not think I was a logician,'

He said, and took me, and carried me away
    To Minos, who coiled his tail eight times around
    His scaly back, and gnawed it angrily

And then declared, 'This wicked one is bound
    For the fire of thievery.' So I am lost
    Where you see me wander, in this garment wound,

130 Bitter to myself." And as his discourse ceased
    The grieving flame departed, its horn's sharp point
    Tossing about and twisting as it passed.

We journeyed on, my leader and I, and went
    To the next arch of the ridge: and looking under,
    We saw the fosse where they pay the due amount

Who earned their burden by splitting things asunder.

Canto XXVIII

[*Eighth Circle, Bolgia Nine: the Sowers of Discord and Schism—Muhammad and Ali, Curio, Mosca, Bertran de Born.* The poets pass over the bridge and view the mutilated souls of bolgia nine, the sowers of discord. They encounter a number of souls famous for having caused schisms— political, religious, social—including Muhammad and his son-in-law Ali. They also meet the souls of Pier da Medicina, Caius Curio, Mosca de' Lamberti, and Bertran de Born.]

Who could find words, even in free-running prose,
    For the blood and wounds I saw, in all their horror—
    Telling it over as often as you choose,

It's certain no human tongue could take the measure
    Of those enormities. Our speech and mind,
    Straining to comprehend them, flail, and falter.

If all the Apulians who long ago mourned
    Their lives cut off by Trojans[257] could live once more,
    Assembled to grieve again with all those stained

10 By their own blood in the long Carthaginian war[258]—
    Rings pillaged from their corpses poured by the bushel,
    As Livy[259] writes, who never was known to err—

And they who took their mortal blows in battle
    With Robert Guiscard,[260] and those whose bones were heaped
    At Ceperano, killed in the Puglian betrayal,

And the soldiers massacred in the stratagem shaped
    By old Alardo, who conquered without a weapon
    Near Tagliacozzo[261] when their army was trapped—

And some were showing wounds still hot and open,
20   Others the gashes where severed limbs had been:
    It would be nothing to equal the mutilation

---

[257] **Apulians . . . Trojans:** A reference to losses by the Apulians in the battles with the Trojans under Aeneas. The battles were in southern Italy.

[258] **Carthaginian war:** The Second Punic War between Rome and Carthage (218–201 B.C.E.), in which Hannibal gathered three bushels of rings from dead Romans.

[259] **Livy:** Roman historian (first century C.E.).

[260] **Guiscard:** The Norman war under Guiscard (1015–1085) against Greeks and Saracens.

[261] **Ceperano . . . Tagliacozzo:** The town Ceperano was betrayed by the barons of Apulia; men at Tagliacozzo were defeated by a trick by Alardo, rather than by military might.

I saw in that Ninth Chasm. No barrel staved-in
    And missing its end-piece ever gaped as wide
    As the man I saw split open from his chin

Down to the farting-place, and from the splayed
    Trunk the spilled entrails dangled between his thighs.
    I saw his organs, and the sack that makes the bread

We swallow turn to shit. Seeing my eyes
    Fastened upon him, he pulled open his chest
30   With both hands, saying, "Look how Mohammed[262] claws

And mangles himself, torn open down the breast!
    Look how I tear myself! And Alì[263] goes
    Weeping before me—like me, a schismatic, and cleft:

Split open from the chin along his face
    Up to the forelock. All you see here, when alive,
    Taught scandal and schism, so they are cleavered like this.

A devil waits with a sword back there to carve
    Each of us open afresh each time we've gone
    Our circuit round this road, where while we grieve

40 Our wounds close up before we pass him again—
    But who are you that stand here, perhaps to delay
    Torments pronounced on your own false words to men?"

"Neither has death yet reached him, nor does he stay
    For punishment of guilt," my master replied,
    "But for experience. And for that purpose I,

Who am dead, lead him through Hell as rightful guide,
    From circle to circle. Of this, you can be as sure
    As that I speak to you here at his side."

More than a hundred shades were gathered there
50   Who hearing my master's words had halted, and came
    Along the trench toward me in order to stare,

---

[262] **Mohammed** (570–632): The founder of Islam, was thought by Dante to be a Christian convert and then a schismatic.

[263] **Alì:** Muhammad's son-in-law who assumed the caliphate in 656 and was assassinated in 661; the dispute over his succession to leadership resulted in the division of Islam into the Sunni and Shia sects.

Forgetting their torment in wonder for a time.
   "Tell Fra Dolcino,²⁶⁴ you who may see the sun,
   If he wants not to follow soon to the same

Punishment, he had better store up grain
   Against a winter siege and the snows' duress,
   Or the Novarese will easily bring him down" —

After he had lifted his foot to resume the pace,
   Mohammed spoke these words, and having spoken
60 He stepped away again on his painful course.

Another there, whose face was cruelly broken,
   The throat pierced through, the nose cut off at the brow,
   One ear remaining, stopped and gazed at me, stricken

With recognition as well as wonder. "Ah, you,"
   His bleeding throat spoke, "you here, yet not eternally
   Doomed here by guilt — unless I'm deceived, I knew

Your face when I still walked above in Italy.
   If you return to the sweet plain I knew well
   That slopes toward Marcabò from Vercelli,

70 Remember Pier da Medicina.²⁶⁵ And tell
   Ser Guido and Angiolello, the two best men
   Of Fano: if we have foresight here in Hell

Then by a tyrant's treachery²⁶⁶ they will drown
   Off La Cattolica — bound and thrown in the sea
   From their ships. Neptune has never seen, between

Cyprus and Majorca, whether committed by
   Pirates or Argives, such a crime. The betrayer
   Who sees from one eye only (he holds a city

Found bitter by another who's with me here)
80 Will lure them to set sail for truce-talks: then,
   When he has dealt with them, they'll need no prayer

---

²⁶⁴ **Fra Dolcino:** Head of the Apostolic Brothers, a communal sect, that escaped into the hills near Novara, but they were starved out by Papal forces; some were executed. Dolcino was burned alive with his mistress in 1307.

²⁶⁵ **Pier da Medicina:** Of uncertain identity.

²⁶⁶ **treachery:** It is thought the tyrant Malestino, the one-eyed Lord of Rimini, murdered two leaders of the opposite party in order to gain control of Fano, a town on the Adriatic coast.

For safe winds near Focara—not ever again.”[267]
    Then I to him: “If you’d have me be the bearer
    Of news from you to those above, explain—

What man do you mean, who found a city bitter?”
    Then he grasped one shade near him by the jaw,
    And opened the mouth, and said, “This is the creature,

He does not speak, who once, in exile, knew
    Words to persuade Caesar at the Rubicon—
90   Affirming, to help him thrust his doubt below,

‘Delaying when he’s ready hurts a man.’ ”
    I saw how helpless Curio’s[268] tongue was cut
    To a stub in his throat, whose speech had been so keen.

One with both hands lopped off came forward to shout,
    Stumps raised in the murk to spatter his cheeks with blood,
    “Also remember Mosca!”[269] I too gave out

A slogan urging bloodshed, when I said
    ‘Once done it’s done with’: words which were seeds of pain
    For the Tuscan people.” Then, when he heard me add,

100 “—and death to your family line,” utterly undone
    By sorrow heaped upon his sorrow, the soul
    Went away like one whom grief has made insane.

I stayed to see more, one sight so incredible
    As I should fear to describe, except that conscience,
    Being pure in this, encourages me to tell:

I saw—and writing it now, my brain still envisions—
    A headless trunk that walked, in sad promenade
    Shuffling the dolorous track with its companions,

And the trunk was carrying the severed head,
110   Gripping its hair like a lantern, letting it swing,
    And the head looked up at us: “Oh me!” it cried.

---

[267] **not ever again:** After being invited for a parley, the men were drowned before reaching the coast.

[268] **Curio’s:** Curio, a first-century B.C.E. Roman Tribune, advised Julius Caesar to cross the Rubicon and invade the Roman Republic, which started the Civil War.

[269] **Mosca:** He is blamed for initiating civil strife in Florence; he advised the Amidei family to avenge their daughter, who had been jilted by a Buondelmonte. Buondelmonte was murdered and sixty years later Mosca’s own family were either killed or exiled.

He was himself and his lamp as he strode along,
    Two in one, and one in two—and how it can be,
    Only He knows, who so ordains the thing.

Reaching the bridge, the trunk held the head up high
    So we could hear his words, which were "Look well,
    You who come breathing to view the dead, and say

If there is punishment harder than mine in Hell.
    Carry the word, and know me: Bertran de Born,[270]
120   Who made the father and the son rebel

The one against the other, by the evil turn
    I did the young king, counseling him to ill.
    David and Absalom[271] had nothing worse to learn

From the wickedness contrived by Achitophel.
    Because I parted their union, I carry my brain
    Parted from this, its pitiful stem: Mark well

This retribution that you see is mine."

Canto XXIX

[*Eighth Circle, Bolgia Nine (continued): the Sowers of Discord and Schism—Geri del Bello. Bolgia Ten: the Falsifiers—Griffolino, Capocchio.* The time is shortly after noon on Saturday. Dante is filled with sadness at the sight of so much suffering. When Virgil questions him about this, Dante replies that he had seen a relative of his, Geri del Bello, whose murder has not yet been avenged of members of the family. From the bridge overlooking the last ditch of Malebolge, the poets see bolgia ten, filled with falsifiers. They are divided into four groups: alchemists, impersonators, counterfeiters, and liars, and punished in a variety of painful ways. Griffolino from Arezzo, an alchemist, explains why he was burned at the stake. Capocchio da Siena reinforces Dante's comments about the Sienese.]

That mass of people wounded so curiously
    Had made my eyes so drunk they had a passion
    To stay and weep. But Virgil said to me,

"What are you staring at? Why let your vision
    Linger there down among the disconsolate
    And mutilated shades? You found no reason

---

[270] **Bertran de Born:** Lord of Hautefort in Provence, a twelfth-century noble and poet, advised Prince Henry to revolt against his father Henry II of England.

[271] **David and Absalom:** Achitophel was Absalom's advisor in his rebellion against King David (2 Samuel 15:12; 16:20–17:4).

To delay like this at any other pit.
    Consider, if counting them is what you plan:
    This valley extends along a circular route

10 For twenty-two miles. And already the moon
    Is under our feet:[272] the time we are allowed
    Has now grown short, and more is to be seen

Than you see here." "If you had given heed
    To what my reason is for looking, perhaps
    You would have granted a longer stay," I said.

Meanwhile my guide went on, and in his steps
    I followed while I answered—but told him, too,
    "Inside that hollow, where for a little lapse

Of time I gazed so steadily just now,
20   I think a spirit of my own blood laments
    The guilt that brings so great a cost below."

The master answered, "Let your intelligence
    Distract itself with thoughts of him no more.
    Attend to other things, while he remains

Down where he is, below the bridge—for there
    I saw him with his finger point you out
    And fiercely threaten you. And I could hear

Them call him Geri del Bello.[273] So complete
    Was your preoccupation with the one
30   Who once held Altaforte, you never set

Your eyes in his direction till he was gone."
    And "O my guide," I said, "his violent death,
    For which as yet no vengeance has been done

By any of those he shares dishonor with,
    Is what has made him full of indignation—
    And that is why he continued on his path

---

[272] **under our feet:** The sun, unseen, is overhead; it is about 2 p.m. and only four hours remain for the Hell portion of the journey.

[273] **Geri del Bello:** A cousin of Dante's father; a member of the Sachetti family murdered him after he caused trouble, which led to a feud between the families.

Without addressing me, and with this action
    He makes my pity for him greater yet."
    So we continued in our conversation,

40 Walking the ridge until we reached the spot
    Where the next valley could first be seen below—
    Down to the bottom, had there been more light.

Up above Malebolge's last cloister now
    Where we could see its lay-brothers under us,
    Their strange laments beset me, each an arrow

Whose shaft was barbed with pity—and at this,
    I lifted up my hands and blocked my ears.
    The suffering was such, if one could place

All of the sick who endure disease's course
50   In Val di Chiana's hospital from July
    All through September, and all the sufferers

In Maremma and Sardinia,[274] to lie
    All in one ditch together, so was this place;
    From it a stench, like that which usually

Is given off by festering limbs, arose.
    Keeping as ever to the left, on down
    We came, to the ridge's final bank. The fosse

Grew clearer to my sight, in which the one
    Who serves as minister of the Lord on high,
60   Unerring Justice, lets her punishments rain

Upon the shades whose sin is to falsify;
    She has recorded them upon her scroll.
    I think it could not have been sadder to see

Aegina's whole population fallen ill
    When such corruption crowded through the air
    That, down to the small worms, every animal

---

[274] **Maremma and Sardinia:** The island of Sardinia and the region of Maremma were plagued by malaria.

Succumbed (and afterward, the poets aver
　　As certain, the ancient populace was restored
　　Out of the seed of ants[275]) than to see there,

70　All through that murky valley, how a horde
　　Of shades lay languishing in scattered heaps:
　　One lay upon his belly, another poured

Across his neighbor's shoulders, or perhaps
　　Moved on all fours along the dismal track.
　　In silence, walking with deliberate steps,

We went on, watching and listening to the sick,
　　Who could not raise their bodies. I could see
　　Two who were sitting propped up back to back,

As pan is leaned against pan to warm them dry,
80　Each of them spotted with scabs from head to foot.
　　And I have never seen a stableboy

Who knows that he is making his master wait,
　　Or one unhappy to be still awake,
　　Work with a currycomb at such a rate

As each of these was laboring to rake
　　His nails all over himself—scratching and digging
　　For the great fury of the itch they tried to slake,

Which has no other relief: their nails were snagging
　　Scabs from the skin as a knifeblade might remove
90　Scales from a carp, or as if the knife were dragging

Still larger scales some other fish might have.
　　"O you who with your fingers scrape the mail
　　From your own flesh, and sometimes make them serve

As pincers: say if any of these who dwell
　　Below here with you come from Italy,
　　So may your nails suffice you in this toil

---

[275] **ants:** Depopulated by pestilence, the island of Aegina was repopulated when Jupiter transformed ants into humans.

That you perform throughout eternity—"
    My leader said, addressing one of the two.
    "Both of us are Italians, whom you see

100 Disfigured here," he answered, weeping. "But who
    Are you, who ask us?" My guide said, "I am one
    Who accompanies this living man; we go

Downward from level to level, and I mean
    To show him Hell." Their mutual support
    Was broken at his words; they turned to lean

Closer to me, both trembling and alert,
    With others who overheard what he had said.
    Drawing near me, my good master said, "Now start:

Speak to them as you choose." So I complied,
110   Beginning thus: "So that your memory
    In men's minds in the former world won't fade

But live on under many suns, tell me
    Who you and your people are; your punished state,
    Loathsome and hideous although it be,

Should not discourage you from speaking out."
    "I was of Arezzo," one answered, "and died by fire
    At Albero of Siena's orders, and yet

That which I died for is not what brought me here.
    The truth is that I told him, speaking in jest,
120   That I knew how to lift myself through air,

In flight: he, curious, but not much blessed
    With wit, asked me to train him in that skill;
    I failed to make him Daedalus[276]—which sufficed

For him to have me burned: the sentence fell
    On me from one who held him as a son.
    But alchemy, which I plied in the world so well,

---

[276] **Arezzo . . . Daedalus:** Griffolino of Arezzo told slow-witted Albero that he could fly; when Griffolino failed at flight, Albero, the natural son of the Bishop—the Inquisitor of Siena—had his father burn him as a magician. Daedalus invented wings for human flight (Canto XVII).

Is why I was doomed to this last ditch of ten
    By Minos, who cannot err in his decrees."
    I asked the poet, "Has there ever been

130   Another people as vain as the Sienese?
    Certainly not the French themselves, by far."
    The other leprous one,[277] at hearing this,

Responded, "Some, you'll grant exceptions for:
    Stricca, who knew how to spend in moderation,
    And Niccolò, who was progenitor

Of the costly cult of cloves — a fine tradition
    For the rich garden where such seeds take root.
    And let that company also be an exception

Where Caccia d'Asciano freely spent out
140   His vineyard and his forest, and where the one
    They nicknamed Muddlehead[278] displayed his wit.

But so you know who seconds you in this vein
    Against the Sienese, come sharpen your gaze
    In my direction, where you may well discern

The answer given to you by my face:
    I am Capocchio's shade — the counterfeiter
    Of metals by alchemy; if I trust my eyes,

You recall how good I was at aping nature."

---

[277] **leprous one:** Capocchio was burned for alchemy in Siena in 1293.

[278] **Stricca . . . Muddlehead:** The men named here were members of the notorious Spendthrift Club in Siena (see Lano in Canto XIII); Muddlehead is the nickname for Abbagliato, one of the members.

Canto XXX

[*Eighth Circle, Bolgia Ten (continued): the Falsifiers—Gianni Schicchi and Myrrha; Master Adam; Potiphar's Wife; Sinon the Greek.*   Two legendary examples of insanity are described: the hallucinatory Athamas and the hysterical Hecuba. Then two insane spirits, Capocchio and Myrrha, rush in. After listening to Master Adam with his swollen belly, Dante inquires about two other tortured souls: one is the Greek Sinon and the other is Potiphar's wife, Joseph's accuser. An exchange of insults between Sinon and Master Adam provides some details about their stories. Virgil chides Dante for listening so intently to the exchange, but grants him forgiveness.]

Once, in the time when Juno was furious
    With the Theban blood because of Semele[279]—
    As more than once she showed them—Athamas

Grew so insane that, seeing his wife walk by
    Carrying their children one on either hand,
    He cried: "Come, let us spread the nets and try

To take the lioness with the cubs she spawned,
    As they pass by!" And reaching out to strike
    With pitiless claws, he took the one they named

10   Learchus, and whirled him, and dashed him on a rock;
    She drowned herself and the other child she held.
    And when Fortune brought down the Trojans, who took

Risks proudly once, all-daring—their kingdom quelled
    And blotted out entirely with their king—
    Hecuba, wretched, a captive, after they killed

Polyxena with her there witnessing,
    Saw her Polydorus washed ashore: the weight
    Of sorrow drove her mad,[280] her soul so wrung

She began barking like a dog. And yet,
20   No fury of Thebes or Troy was ever seen
    So cruel—not any rending of beasts, and not

Tearing of human limbs—as I saw shown
    By two pale, naked shades who now ran up
    Biting, the way a pig does loosed from the pen.

---

[279] **Semele:** The daughter of King Cadmus of Thebes and loved by Jupiter, whose wife Juno took revenge on the Theban household by driving Athamas insane. Athamas was the husband of Ino, Semele's sister.

[280] **drove her mad:** Hecuba's family was destroyed when the Greeks conquered Troy: she was enslaved; her husband Priam was killed; her daughter Polyxena was sacrificed; her son Polydorus was murdered by Polymnestor.

One charged Capocchio and bit his nape,
    And sank his tusks in deep, and dragged him along
    On the hard bottom, letting his belly scrape.

The spirit from Arezzo,[281] shivering
    Where he was left, told me, "That monstrousness
30   Is Gianni Schicchi;[282] he runs rabid among

The others here, and graces them like this."
    "Oh," I responded, "so may that other one
    Not fix its teeth on you, disclose to us

What shade it is—before it bolts again."
    He answered, "That one is the ancient soul
    Of Myrrha[283] the infamous, whose love was drawn

Toward her father beyond what's honorable.
    She engaged in sin with him by falsifying
    Herself as someone else; and Schicchi as well,

40 Who runs off yonder, counterfeited: when trying
    To acquire the finest lady of the herd,
    He pretended he was Buoso Donati dying

And willed himself a legacy, each word
    In proper form."[284] When both of the raging pair
    On whom I kept my eyes had disappeared,

I turned to see the ill-born others there:
    One would be shaped exactly like a lute
    Had he been cut off at the groin, from where

A man is forked. The heavy dropsical state,
50   Which makes the body's members so ill sorted
    With undigested humors the face seems not

---

[281] **spirit from Arezzo:** Griffolino (Canto XXIX).

[282] **Gianni Schicchi:** For the story of this mimic, see lines 39–44 and note 284 below.

[283] **Myrrha:** Daughter of the King of Cyprus who disguised herself as another woman in order to sleep with her father.

[284] **and Schicchi . . . proper form:** When Buoso Donati died, the mimic Schicchi conspired with Buoso's nephew and imitated the dead man in his bed; he dictated a new will to a lawyer, giving himself a mare called "the lady of the stud."

To answer to the swollen belly, had parted
 His lips—the way the hectic being spurred
 By thirst curls one lip up, the other distorted

Toward the chin. He said, "You who have fared
 To this unhappy world, and yet arrive
 Unpunished—I know not why—think, and regard

The misery of Master Adam.[285] Alive,
 I had in abundance all I wanted; now,
60 Alas! one drop of water is what I crave.

The rivulets that down to the Arno flow
 From the green hills of Casentino,[286] and make
 Their channels cool and spongy as they go,

Are constantly before me—nor do they lack
 Effect: their image parches me far worse
 Than the face-wasting blight with which I'm sick.

The unbending Justice that wracks me thus makes use,
 Fittingly, of the same place where I sinned,
 To speed my sighs the quicker on their course:

70 There is Romena, where I falsely coined
 The currency that bears the Baptist's face,
 For which, on earth, I left my body burned—

But if I could behold, here in this place,
 The miserable soul of Guido, or that
 Of Alessandro, or set my eyes on his

Who is their brother, I would not trade the sight
 For Fonte Branda![287] One is already inside—
 If the raging shades who course the circle about

Have spoken truly. But since my limbs are tied,
80 What use is that to me? Were I still light
 Enough to move even one inch ahead

---

[285] **Master Adam:** Served the Counts of Romena (see line 77) by counterfeiting coins with the figure of John the Baptist on them, for which he was burned in 1281.

[286] **Casentino:** Romena is a town in Casentino, a region on the upper Arno.

[287] **Fonte Branda:** A spring near Siena, or possibly a fountain in Romena.

Every hundred years, I would have set out
    Upon the road already, trying to find
    Him in this mutilated people—despite

The circuit being eleven miles around
    And at least half a mile across its track.
    It's because of them that I am in this kind

Of family: they persuaded me to make
    Those florins that contained three carats of dross."
90   I asked him, "Who are that pair of wretches who smoke

As wet hands do in winter, lying close
    Next to your body on the right-hand side?"
    "I found them here—they have not changed their place—

When I first fell like rain to this steep grade,
    And I believe that neither will turn over
    For all eternity. This false one[288] made

Her accusation defaming Joseph; the other
    Is the false Sinon,[289] Trojan Greek," he responded.
    "They reek so badly because of raging fever."

100 One of the pair—perhaps because offended
    By such dark naming—made a fist and struck
    Him on his rigid belly, which resounded

Just like a drum. And Master Adam paid back
    That blow by striking his neighbor in the face
    With an arm that was just as hard, and spoke:

"Though I am kept from moving by the mass
    Of my too-heavy limbs, you can be sure
    I have an arm kept free for such a case."

The other answered, "When you went to the fire
110   Your arm was not so ready[290]—though indeed
    For counterfeiting, it was ready, and more."

---

[288] **This false one:** Potiphar's wife (Genesis 39:6–20) infamously accused Joseph of trying to seduce her after he refused to sleep with her.

[289] **Sinon:** Sinon fooled the Trojans by pretending that he was a deserter from the Greeks; he persuaded the Trojans to bring into Troy the wooden horse containing Greek warriors as a compensation for the stolen Palladium, the sacred statue of Athena.

[290] **not so ready:** Master Adam was tied up.

"Here you speak truth," the dropsied one replied.
  "However, at Troy, when truth was their demand,
  Your witness was not so true." "I falsified

In speech: you made false coinage," Sinon returned,
  "And I am in this place for a single sin—
  And you, for more than any other fiend."

"You perjurer, remember the horse again,"
  The one who had the swollen paunch came back,
120   "And may the fact torment you: your role is known

By the whole world." "And torment," answered the Greek,
  "To you—from thirst's tongue-cracking agonies,
  And the foul waters that swell your belly to make

It rise up like a hedgerow blocking your eyes."
  And then the counterfeiter answered, "Thus
  Disease, as usual, spreads your gaping jaws;

For if I suffer thirst or feel distress
  Engorged with humors, you burn, your head aches hard—
  And you would lick Narcissus's looking glass[291]

130 Without delaying for too many a word
  Of invitation, if you only could."
  I listened to them intently—then I heard

My master: "Stare a little longer," he said,
  "And I will quarrel with you!" When I heard him
  Speaking to me in anger as he had,

I turned to him with such a feeling of shame
  That it still circles through my memory.
  As one who dreams he is harmed may in the dream

Wish that it were a dream—and therefore he
140   Longs for the thing that is, as if it were not:
  So I, unable to speak, was yearning to say

Something to excuse myself—and by doing that
  I did excuse myself, at the same time
  As I was failing to do it in my thought.

---

[291] **Narcissus's looking glass:** Narcissus fell in love with his own image reflected in the water of a spring.

"A greater fault would be cleansed by lesser shame
    Than yours a moment ago," the master said.
    "So let your sadness be disburdened: come—

Do not forget I am always at your side,
    Should fortune bring you again to where you hear
150   People who are arguing as those two did:

Wanting to hear them is a low desire."

Canto XXXI

[*Passage to Cocytus. The Giants—Nimrod, Ephialtes, Antaeus.*   The poets cross the bank separating Circles Eight and Nine. Dante hears a horn and sees two high towers in the distance. Virgil explains the towers are actually giants who guard the central pit of Hell; their lower halves are buried in the ground. The first is Nimrod, who built the Tower of Babel; the second is the rebel Ephialtes. The poets arrive at the giant Antaeus, whom Virgil persuades to transport them. Antaeus cradles Dante and Virgil in his hand and lowers them to the bottom of the pit, Cocytus, the ninth and final Circle of Hell.]

One and the same tongue made me feel its sting,
    Tinting one cheek and the other, then supplied
    Balm: so I've heard Achilles' lance[292] could bring

(The one his father gave him) first harm, then good.
    We turned our backs upon that valley of woes
    And climbed its girdling bank to the other side,

Crossing in silence. Here it was something less
    Than night and less than day, so that my vision
    Reached only a little way ahead of us;

10 But I could hear a horn blast—its concussion
    So loud it would make a thunderclap seem faint;
    And the sound guided my eyes in its direction

Back to one place, where all my attention went.
    After the dolorous rout, when Charlemagne
    Had lost his holy army and Roland sent

The signal from his horn,[293] it must have been
    Less terrible a sound. Before my head
    Was turned that way for long, I saw a line

---

[292] **Achilles' lance:** Peleus, the father of Achilles, had a spear that could heal the wound it caused.

[293] **signal from his horn:** In *The Song of Roland* about the crusade against the Saracens in Spain, Roland blows his horn to tell Charlemagne that his command in the rear has been defeated. See page 1336.

Of what seemed lofty towers. Then I said,
20   "Master, what city is this?" "Because you peer
        Into the dark from far off," he replied,

"Your imagination goes astray. Once there,
        You will see plainly how distance can deceive
        The senses — so spur yourself a little more."

And then he took me by the hand, with love,
        Saying, "Before we go much farther along,
        Learn now, in order that the fact may prove

Less strange: these are not towers but a ring
        Of giants — each one standing in the pit
30   Up to the navel." As mist is vanishing,

Little by little vision starts picking out
        Shapes that were hidden in the misty air:
        Just so, as I began to penetrate

Into that thick and murky atmosphere,
        Fear gathered in me as my error fled —
        For, as on Montereggione's wall[294] appear

Towers that crown its circle, here, arrayed
        All round the bank encompassing the pit
        With half their bulk like towers above it, stood

40   Horrible giants, whom Jove still rumbles at
        With menace when he thunders.[295] I descried
        The face of one already, and the set

Of his great chest and shoulders, and a wide
        Stretch of his belly above the abyss's walls,
        And the arms along his sides. (Nature indeed,

When she abandoned making these animals,
        Did well to keep such instruments from Mars;
        Though she does not repent of making whales

---

[294] **Montereggione's wall:** A castle built to protect Siena from Florence.

[295] **Jove . . . thunders:** In classical mythology, the Titans attacked Olympus, home of the gods, and were overthrown by Jove (Zeus).

Or elephants, a person who subtly inquires
50   Into her ways will find her both discreet
    And just, in her decision: if one confers

The power of the mind, along with that
    Of immense strength, upon an evil will
    Then people will have no defense from it.)

To me his face appeared as long and full
    As the bronze pinecone[296] of St. Peter's at Rome,
    With all his other bones proportional,

So that the bank, which was an apron for him
    Down from his middle, showed above it such height
60   Three men of Friesland[297] could not boast to come

Up to his hair. Extending down from the spot
    Where one would buckle a mantle I could see
    Thirty spans[298] of him. The fierce mouth started to shout,

"Raphèl maì amècche zabì almi"[299] —
    Sweeter psalms would not fit it — and then my guide
    Addressed him: "Soul, in your stupidity

Keep to your horn, and when you have the need
    Use that to vent your rage or other passion;
    Search at your neck the strap where it is tied,

70 And try to see it, O spirit in confusion,
    Aslant your own great chest." Having said that,
    He told me, "This is Nimrod:[300] his accusation

He himself makes; for through his evil thought
    There is no common language the world can use:
    Leave him alone then, rather than speak for naught —

---

[296] **bronze pinecone:** In Dante's day, a bronze pinecone about eight-feet high was in front of St. Peter's Cathedral, now in the Vatican.

[297] **men of Friesland:** Inhabitants of present-day Netherlands, famous for their extraordinary height.

[298] **Thirty spans:** About fifteen feet.

[299] *Raphèl . . . almi*: Nonsense sounds.

[300] **Nimrod:** A giant who designed the Tower of Babel in Hebrew mythology, the cause of multiple languages; as a hunter, he carries a horn (Genesis 10:8–10, 11:1–9).

For every language is to him as his
    Is to all others: no one fathoms it."
    So, turning left, we quit that giant's place,

And at the distance of a crossbow's shot
80   Another, fiercer and greater, is what we found:
    What master could have fettered him like that

I do not know, but his right arm was chained
    Behind him and the other arm before,
    Clasped by a chain that also held him bound

From the neck down, so that it was wound as far
    As the fifth coil on the part of him that showed.
    "This proud one had a wish to test his power

Against supreme Jove: this is how he is paid,"
    My guide said. "Ephialtes[301] is his name;
90   And when the giants made the gods afraid

Awesome endeavors were put forth by him.
    He cannot move these arms he strove with once."
    I said, "If it's possible for me to come

To where my eyes might have experience
    Of immense Briareus,[302] I wish I could."
    "Antaeus,[303] whom you'll see some distance hence,

Can speak, and is unchained as well," he said;
    "He will convey us to sin's profoundest abyss.
    The one you wish to see is farther ahead,

100 And he is bound and fashioned as this one is,
    Though somewhat more ferocious in his look."
    No tower was ever shaken by the throes

Of a great earthquake as Ephialtes shook
    Himself at hearing this. As never before
    I was afraid of dying, and wouldn't lack

---

[301] **Ephialtes:** The giants Ephialtes and his brother tried to reach Olympus by piling Mt. Pelion on top of Mt. Ossa.

[302] **Briareus:** A Titan with a hundred arms and fifty heads.

[303] **Antaeus:** A Titan who did not participate in the war against the gods; he was known for eating lions. He kept his strength through contact with the earth; Hercules defeated him in a wrestling match by lifting him off the ground.

A cause of death beyond that very fear,
  Had I not seen his fetters. Then we went on
  And reached Antaeus—who rose five ells or more,

Not reckoning his head, above the stone.
110   "O you, who—in that fateful valley that made
  Scipio inheritor of glory when

Hannibal along with all his followers fled
  Showing his back[304]—once garnered as your prey
  A thousand lions: you through whom, it is said

By some, your brothers might have carried the day
  In their high war, if you had been there then
  Among the sons of earth in battle: pray,

Now set us down below—do not disdain
  To do so—where Cocytus is locked in cold.
120   Do not compel us to seek some other one

Like Typhon or Tityus.[305] This man can yield
  The thing that's longed for here; therefore bend down
  And do not curl your lip. He can rebuild

Your fame on earth—he lives, and living on
  Longer is his expectation, if grace does not
  Summon him to itself untimely soon."

So spoke my master; and the giant stretched out
  In haste those hands whose grip clasped Hercules,
  And took my leader. Virgil, when he felt that,

130   Said to me, "Now come here, that I may seize
  Good hold of you," and of himself and me
  He made one bundle. As seems to one who sees

The leaning tower at Garisenda,[306] when he
  Is under the leaning side, and when a cloud
  Is passing over going the other way

---

[304] **Scipio . . . back:** Scipio saved the Roman Republic in 202 B.C.E. when he defeated Hannibal's army in a valley in Tunisia.

[305] **Typhon or Tityus:** Two giants who were cast into Tartarus for offending Jove.

[306] **Garisenda:** A leaning tower in Bologna that appears to fall when a cloud passes over it moving in the opposite direction to the lean.

From how the tower inclines, so in my dread
    Antaeus seemed to me as I watched him lean—
    That moment, I would have wished for another road!

But having stooped he set us gently upon
140   That bottom Lucifer is swallowed in
    Along with Judas;[307] nor did he stay bent down,

But like a ship's mast raised himself again.

Canto **XXXII**

[*Ninth Circle, Ring One (Caina): Traitors against Kin—Camiscion de' Pazzi. Ring Two (Antenora): Traitors against Country and Party—Bocca degli Abati.* In order to describe this dismal region, Dante invokes the Muses. The poets walk across the frozen lake of Caina, the first division of the Ninth Circle, which contains traitors to their kindred trapped in the ice. One of them, Camiscion de' Pazzi, identifies the Alberti brothers, Mordred, Focaccia, Sassol Mascheroni, and Carlino de' Pazzi. The poets move into Antenora, the second division of this circle, where traitors to party and country are punished. Dante kicks and curses one of the spirits, Bocca degli Abati, who contributed to the defeat of the Florentine Guelphs at Monaperti. Abati mentions other sinners: Tesauro de' Beccheria, Gianni de' Soldanieri, Ganelon, and Tebaldello de Zambrasi. The poets see a sinner gnawing on the head of another. Dante offers to tell the sinner's story if his cause is just.]

If I had harsh and grating rhymes, to befit
    That melancholy hole which is the place
    All the other rocks converge and thrust their weight,

Then I could more completely press the juice
    From my conception. But since I lack such lines,
    I feel afraid as I come to speak of this:

It is not jokingly that one begins
    To describe the bottom of the universe—
    Not a task suited for a tongue that whines

10 *Mamma* and *Dadda.* May the muses[308] help my verse
    As when they helped Amphion wall Thebes, so that
    Word not diverge from fact as it takes its course.

O horde, beyond all others ill-begot,
    Who dwell in that place so hard to speak about:
    Better for you to be born a sheep or goat!

---

[307] **Lucifer . . . Judas:** Inhabitants of Cocytus.

[308] **muses:** The muses assisted the musician Amphion charm the mountain-rocks for building the walls of Thebes.

When we were deep in the darkness of the pit
    Beneath the giant's feet, much farther down,
    And I still gazed back up the high wall of it:

"Watch how you step," I heard a voice intone,
20   "Be careful that you do not set your feet
    On the weary, wretched brothers' heads." Whereon

I turned, and saw before me and underfoot
    A lake that ice made less like water than glass;
    In Austria, never has the Danube set

So thick a veil above its current as this,
    Nor, under its cold sky, has the far-off Don:
    Had Mount Tambernic fallen to strike that ice,

Or Pietrapana,[309] it would not even then
    Creak, even at its edge. As the frog lies
30   Snout above water to croak in the season when

The peasant woman often has reveries
    Of gleaning, spirits—livid to where the cheeks
    Turn color with shame—were locked inside the ice,

Teeth chattering the note a stork's beak makes.
    Each held his face turned down; they testified
    Cold by their mouths, and misery by the looks

Their eyes bore. After a time while I surveyed
    The scene around me, I glanced down at my feet,
    And saw two shades there packed in head to head

40 So tightly that their hair was interknit.
    "O you whose breasts are pressed together," I said,
    "Who are you?" They bent back their necks at that,

And having raised their faces to me, they shed
    Tears, welling now from eyes already moist
    To flow down over their lips, where the frost glued

Each to the other, ever more tightly fused:
    Iron clamps never held beam to beam so fast—
    And like two goats, each butted the one he faced

---

[309] **Mount Tambernic . . . Pietrapana:** Tambernic may be a mountain in the Alps; Mt. Pietrapana is in Tuscany.

In a helpless rage. Another, who had lost
50   Both ears to frost, spoke with his face still down:
      "Why stare at us so long? If you insist

On knowing who these two are, the valley wherein
      Bisenzio's stream begins its long descent
      Once was their father Albert's and their own.[310]

They issued from one body, and if you went
      All over Caina[311] you could not find a shade
      Worthier to be frozen in punishment:

Not him whose breast and shadow the impaling blade
      In Arthur's hand[312] pierced with one stroke; nor him
60   They called Focaccia;[313] nor this other whose head

So blocks me I can see no farther: his name,
      Sassol Mascheroni,[314] is one you recognize
      If you are Tuscan. And — so you need not claim

Any more speech of me — my own name was
      Camiscion de' Pazzi[315] and this is where I await
      Carlino's[316] coming to make my sin seem less."

I saw a thousand faces after that,
      All purple as a dog's lips from the frost:
      I still shiver, and always will, at the sight

70   Of a frozen pond. All through the time we progressed
      Toward the core where all gravity convenes,
      I quaked in that eternal chill; and next —

---

[310] **the valley . . . their own:** Upon the death Count Albert degli Alberti, c. 1280, his two sons fought over their inheritance and killed each other.

[311] **Caina:** The outermost subdivision of Cocytus, named for Cain, slayer of his brother Abel, where traitors to their relatives are punished.

[312] **Arthur's hand:** King Arthur lanced his nephew Mordred with such force that daylight was seen through the body.

[313] **Focaccia:** A noble from Pistoia who murdered his uncle.

[314] **Sassol Mascheroni:** A Florentine who murdered his nephew.

[315] **Camiscion de' Pazzi:** An unknown Florentine who murdered a relative.

[316] **Carlino's:** He betrayed a castle belonging to the Florentine Whites in 1302; by comparison, his guilt will absolve Camiscion.

I don't know whether by will or fate or chance—
    Walking among the heads I struck my foot
    Hard in the face of one, with violence

That set him weeping as he shouted out,
    "Why trample me? And if you have not come
    To add more vengeance for Montaperti's defeat,[317]

Then why do you molest me?" I turned from him;
80   "Master," I said, "I pray you: wait for me here
    While I resolve a doubt concerning his name;

Then you shall hurry me on as you desire."
    My leader stopped, and I addressed the shade
    Who was still cursing as bitterly as before:

"And who are you who reviles another?" I said.
    "Nay, who are you," he answered, "who thus contrive
    To go through Antenora[318] striking the head

And cheeks of others—which even were you alive
    Would be too much." "Alive is what I am,"
90   I told him, "and if fame is what you crave,

Then you might value having me note your name
    Among the others." He answered, "What I desire
    Is quite the opposite—get you gone, and come

To trouble me no more, inept as you are,
    Not knowing how to flatter at this great depth."
    Then I reached out and seized him by the hair

And shook his scruff. "Now name yourself forthwith—
    Or not a hair will remain," I threatened him.
    He answered, "Though you pluck me bald in your wrath,

100 I will not tell you nor show you who I am,
    Not if you fall a thousand times on my pate."
    Already I had twisted round my palm

---

[317] **Montaperti's defeat:** At the battle of Montaperti in 1260, Bocca degli Abati who was supposedly fighting for the Guelphs against the Ghibellines, betrayed them by cutting off the hand of the Guelph standard-bearer causing confusion among the horse soldiers.

[318] **Antenora:** The second division of Cocytus for traitors to country, named for Antenor, the Trojan, who betrayed his city to the Greeks.

A length of hair, and pulled some clumps right out,
    And he was barking, with his eyes held down,
    When a new voice called: "Bocca, what is it—

What ails you? Are you so weary of the tune
    Your jaws create that now you are barking, too?
    What devil is at you?" "Now," said I, "I am done:

I have no further need to speak with you,
110   Accursed traitor, for now, to your disgrace,
    I will report about you what is true."

"Then go away," he answered, "tell what you choose—
    But don't be silent, if you do get out,
    About that one so quick just now to use

His tongue. Here he laments the silver he got
    From Frenchmen's hands. 'I saw him,' you can declare,
    'The man of Duera,[319] down where the sinners are put

To cool.' And if they ask who else was there,
    The man of Beccheria[320] is at your side,
120   Whose gullet was slit by Florence. Also here,

A little farther along your way, reside
    Gianni de' Soldanieri[321] with Ganelon
    And Tebaldello[322] who opened Faenza wide

While it was asleep." We had left him, moving on,
    When I saw two shades frozen in a single hole—
    Packed so close, one head hooded the other one;

The way the starving devour their bread, the soul
    Above had clenched the other with his teeth
    Where the brain meets the nape. And at the skull

---

[319] **man of Duera:** Buoso of Duera, a Ghibelline, betrayed the ruler of Naples in 1265 by accepting a bribe from French invaders giving them free passsage.

[320] **man of Beccheria:** A Papal representative in Florence who was executed in 1258 for treason: plotting with the exiled Ghibellines.

[321] **Gianni de' Soldanieri:** A Florentine noble who switched to the Guelphs when the Ghibellines were exiled.

[322] **Ganelon . . . Tebaldello:** Tebaldello of Faenza, east of Florence, betrayed Ghibelline refugees to Guelphs; Ganelon betrayed Roland in *The Song of Roland*.

130 And other parts, as Tydeus berserk with wrath
     Gnawed at the head of Menalippus,[323] he chewed.
     "You, showing such bestial hatred for him beneath,

Whom you devour: tell me your reason," I cried,
     "And, on condition that your grievance is right,
     Knowing both who you are and what wrong deed

This one committed against you, I may yet
     Repay you for whatever you may say,
     Up in the world above—by telling it,

If that with which I speak does not go dry."

Canto XXXIII

[*Ninth Circle, Ring Two (Antenora continued): Count Ugolino. Ring Three: Ptolomea: Traitors against Guests and Hosts—Fra Alberigo, Branca D'Oria.*   The man gnawing on the other's head is Count Ugolino, a Pisan who allied himself with the Guelphs of Florence. Betrayed by Archbishop Ruggieri, Ugolino and his two sons and grandsons were locked in a tower to die of starvation. Moved by the story, Dante issues an invective against Pisa. The poets move on to Ptolomea, the third division, where treachery against guests and hosts is punished. They hear the story of Fra Alberigo, whose soul is in Hell but whose earthly body is occupied by a demon. Dante reacts angrily against the Genoese.]

Pausing in his savage meal, the sinner raised
     His mouth and wiped it clean along the hair
     Left on the head whose back he had laid waste.

Then he began: "You ask me to endure
     Reliving a grief so desperate, the thought
     Torments my heart even as I prepare

To tell it. But if my words are seeds, with fruit
     Of infamy for this traitor that I gnaw,
     I will both speak and weep within your sight.

10 I don't know who you are that come here, or how,
     But you are surely Florentine to my ear.
     I was Count Ugolino,[324] you must know:

---

[323] **Tydeus . . . Menalippus:** In the war against Thebes, Tydeus was mortally wounded by Melanippus, whom he killed; as he lay dying, Tydeus gnawed on Menalippus's head.

[324] **Count Ugolino:** The Guelph governor of Pisa, betrayed by Archbishop Ruggieri, leader of the Ghibellines, in 1289.

This is Archbishop Ruggieri. You will hear
    Why I am such a neighbor to him as this:
    How, through my trust and his devices, I bore

First being taken, then killed, no need to trace;
    But things which you cannot have heard about —
    The manner of my death, how cruel it was —

I shall describe, and you can tell from that
20   If he has wronged me. A slit in the Tower Mew°   prison
    (Called Hunger's Tower after me, where yet

Others will be closed up) had let me view
    Several moons already, when my bad dream
    Came to me, piercing the future's veil right through:

This man appeared as lord of the hunt; he came
    Chasing a wolf and whelps,[325] on that high slope
    That blocks the Pisans' view of Lucca. With him

His lean hounds ran, well trained and eager; his troop —
    Gualandi, Sismondi, Lanfranchi[326] — had been sent
30   To ride in front of him. With no escape,

After a short run, father and sons seemed spent;
    I saw their flanks, that sharp fangs seemed to tear.
    I woke before dawn, hearing the complaint

Of my own children, who were with me there,
    Whimpering in their sleep and asking for bread.
    You grieve already, or truly cruel you are,

As you think of what my heart began to dread —
    And if not now, then when do you shed a tear?
    They were awake now, with the hour when food

40 Was usually brought us drawing near,
    And each one apprehensive from his dream.
    And then I heard them nailing shut the door

---

[325] **wolf and whelps:** Ugolino and his four sons.
[326] **Gualandi . . . Lanfranchi:** Pisan families opposed to Ugolino.

Into that fearful tower—a pounding that came
　　From far below. Hearing that noise, I stared
　　Into my children's faces, not speaking to them.

Inside me I was turned to stone, so hard
　　I could not weep; the children wept. And my
　　Little Anselmo, peering at me, inquired:

'Father, what ails you?' And still I did not cry,
50　　Nor did I answer, all that day and night
　　Until the next sun dawned. When one small ray

Found its way into our prison, and I made out
　　In their four faces the image of my own,
　　I bit my hands for grief; when they saw that,

They thought I did it from my hunger's pain,
　　And suddenly rose. 'Father: our pain,' they said,
　　'Will lessen if you eat us—you are the one

Who clothed us in this wretched flesh: we plead
　　For you to be the one who strips it away.'
60　　I calmed myself to grieve them less. We stayed

Silent through that and then the following day.
　　O you hard earth, why didn't you open then?
　　When we had reached the fourth day, Gaddo lay

Stretched at my feet where he had fallen down:
　　'Father, why don't you help me?' he said, and died.
　　And surely as you see me, so one by one

I watched the others fall till all were dead,
　　Between the fifth day and the sixth. And I,
　　Already going blind, groped over my brood—

70　Calling to them, though I had watched them die,
　　For two long days. And then the hunger had more
　　Power than even sorrow had over me."

When he had finished, with a sideways stare
　　He gripped the skull again in his teeth, which ground
　　Strong as a dog's against the bone he tore.

Ah, Pisa! You shame the peoples of the fair land
    Where *sì*° is spoken: slow as your neighbors are   yes
    To punish you, may Gorgona shift its ground,

And Capraia,[327] till those islands make a bar
80   To dam the Arno, and drown your populace —
    Every soul in you! Though Ugolino bore

The fame of having betrayed your fortresses,
    Still it was wrong in you to so torment
    His helpless children. You Thebes[328] of latter days,

Their youthful ages made them innocent! —
    Uguccione, Brigata, and the two
    My song has named already. On we went,

To where frost roughly swathes a people who,
    Instead of downward, turn their faces up.
90   There, weeping keeps them from weeping — for as they do,

Grief finds a barrier where the eyes would weep
    But forced back inward, adds to their agonies:
    A crystal visor of prior tears fills the cup

Below the eyebrow with a knot of ice.
    And though, as when a callus has grown numb,
    The cold had sucked all feeling from my face

I sensed a wind, and wondered from where it came:
    "Master, who moves this? Is it not the case
    All vapors are extinguished[329] in this realm?"

100 "Soon," he responded, "you will reach a place
    Where your own eyes — beholding what source this blast
    Is poured by from above — will answer this."

---

[327] **Gorgona . . . Capraia:** Two islands in the mouth of the Arno, in view of Pisa.

[328] **Thebes:** Ancient Thebes was known for its crimes against family.

[329] **All vapors are extinguished:** Since it was believed that the heat of the sun caused winds; Dante wonders how he feels wind in this place.

And then one wretch encased in the frozen crust
　　Cried out to us, "O souls so cruel that here,
　　Of all the stations, you're assigned the last —

Lift the hard veils away from my face, I implore,
　　So that before the weeping freezes again
　　I can release a little of this despair

And misery that swell my heart." Whereon
110　　I said, "If you would have me help you, disclose
　　To me who you are: if I don't help you then,

May I be sent to the bottom of the ice."
　　He answered, "I am Fra Alberigo,[330] the man
　　Of fruit from the evil garden; in this place

I get my payment, date for fig." "Oh then,"
　　I said to him, "you are already dead?"
　　"I do not know what state my body is in,

Nor how it fares in the world above," he said.
　　"For Ptolomea's[331] privilege is this:
120　　Down to this place a soul is often conveyed

Before it is sent forth by Atropos.[332]
　　So that you may more willingly scrape the cowl
　　Of tears made hard as glass that coats my face,

Know that as soon as a soul commits betrayal
　　The way I did, a devil displaces it
　　And governs inside the body until its toll

Of years elapses. Meanwhile, down to this vat
　　The soul falls headlong — so it could be true
　　That this shade, wintering here behind me, yet

---

[330] **Fra Alberigo:** A Jovial Friar (Canto XXIII), who in order to get revenge for an injury, invited his brother and son to a banquet. They were assassinated when the Alberigo said, "Bring the fruit." Since a date is worth more than a fig, to get dates for figs meant getting more than one bargained for.

[331] **Ptolomea's:** The third division of Cocytus is for treachery to guests, named for Ptolemy, who murdered his father-in-law Simon Maccabeaus and two of his sons at a banquet.

[332] **Atropos:** One of the four Fates; Atropos determines the time of death.

130 Appears above on earth too: you must know,
       If you were sent down only a short time past.
       He is Ser Branca d'Oria;[333] it's years ago

He first arrived here to be thus encased."
       "Now you deceive me, for I am one who knows
       That Branca d'Oria is not deceased:

He eats and drinks and sleeps and puts on clothes,"
       I told him. And he answered, "In the ditch
       Ruled by the Malebranche above, that seethes

And bubbles with the lake of clinging pitch,
140   The shade of Michel Zanche had not arrived
       When this, his killer, had a devil encroach

His body (as did his kinsman, when they contrived
       Together to perform their treachery)
       And take his place in it. Now, as I craved,

Reach out your hand and open my eyes for me."
       I did not open them — for to be rude
       To such a one as him was courtesy.

Ah Genoese! — to every accustomed good,
       Strangers; with every corruption, amply crowned:
150   Why hasn't the world expunged you as it should?

For with Romagna's worst spirit I have found
       One of you — already, for deeds he was guilty of,
       Bathed in Cocytus: in soul now underground

Who in body still appears alive, above.

---

[333] **Ser Branca d'Oria:** A Ghibelline from Genoa who murdered his father-in-law Michel Zanche (Canto XXII) at a banquet around 1290.

Canto **XXXIV**

[*Ninth Circle, Ring Four (Judecca): Traitors against Masters and Benefactors. The Center: Satan.*
The poets move to Judecca, named after Judas Iscariot, where traitors to benefactors are deposited.
Dante notices a giant figure that proves to be Satan, King of Hell, immersed in ice to his chest.
Satan has three faces in different colors, six weeping eyes, and three bloody mouths that hold
Judas, Brutus, and Cassius. His three pairs of beating wings move the icy winds through Cocytus.
At six p.m. Saturday evening, Virgil decides they must leave. They climb down Satan's body until
they arrive at the center of the earth, where they see Satan's leg protruding from the ground; Satan
is upside down. After Virgil explains this inverted geography, the poets climb out of Hell, emerging
at dawn in the Southern Hemisphere beside Mount Purgatory.]

"And now, *Vexilla regis prodeunt*
　　Inferni[334] — therefore, look," my master said
　　As we continued on the long descent,

"And see if you can make him out, ahead."
　　As though, in the exhalation of heavy mist
　　Or while night darkened our hemisphere, one spied

A mill — blades turning in the wind, half-lost
　　Off in the distance — some structure of that kind
　　I seemed to make out now. But at a gust

10　Of wind, there being no other shelter at hand,
　　　I drew behind my leader's back again.
　　　By now (and putting it in verse I find

Fear in myself still) I had journeyed down
　　To where the shades were covered wholly by ice,
　　Showing like straw in glass — some lying prone,

And some erect, some with the head toward us,
　　And others with the bottoms of the feet;
　　Another like a bow, bent feet to face.

When we had traveled forward to the spot
20　　From which it pleased my master to have me see
　　　That creature whose beauty once had been so great,[335]

---

[334] ***Vexilla . . . Inferni:*** "The banners of the King of Hell advance"; in the original version, this phrase is a parody of a sixth-century Latin hymn used during Holy Week.

[335] **creature . . . had been so great:** Lucifer, from the Latin for "light-bearer," was the brightest of the angels before the rebellion in Heaven. Dante also calls him Satan, Dis, and Beelzebub.

He made me stop, and moved from in front of me.
    "Look: here is Dis," he said, "and here is the place
    Where you must arm yourself with the quality

Of fortitude." How chilled and faint I was
    On hearing that, you must not ask me, reader —
    I do not write it; words would not suffice:

I neither died, nor kept alive — consider
    With your own wits what I, alike denuded
30   Of death and life, became as I heard my leader.

The emperor of the realm of grief protruded
    From mid-breast up above the surrounding ice.
    A giant's height, and mine, would have provided

Closer comparison than would the size
    Of his arm and a giant. Envision the whole
    That is proportionate to parts like these.

If he was truly once as beautiful
    As he is ugly now, and raised his brows
    Against his Maker — then all sorrow may well

40 Come out of him. How great a marvel it was
    For me to see three faces on his head:
    In front there was a red one; joined to this,

Each over the midpoint of a shoulder, he had
    Two others — all three joining at the crown.
    That on the right appeared to be a shade

Of whitish yellow; the third had such a mien
    As those who come from where the Nile descends.[336]
    Two wings spread forth from under each face's chin,

Strong, and befitting such a bird, immense —
50   I have never seen at sea so broad a sail —
    Unfeathered, batlike, and issuing three winds

---

[336] **As those . . . Nile descends:** Ethiopians. The three faces parody the Trinity, but symbolism of the three colors is unclear: they might represent races of humanity or qualities such as hatred, ignorance, and impotence.

That went forth as he beat them, to freeze the whole
    Realm of Cocytus that surrounded him.
    He wept with all six eyes, and the tears fell

Over his three chins mingled with bloody foam.
    The teeth of each mouth held a sinner, kept
    As by a flax rake: thus he held three of them

In agony. For the one the front mouth gripped,
    The teeth were as nothing to the claws, which sliced
60   And tore the skin until his back was stripped.

"That soul," my master said, "who suffers most,
    Is Judas Iscariot:[337] head locked inside,
    He flails his legs. Of the other two, who twist

With their heads down, the black mouth holds the shade
    Of Brutus: writhing, but not a word will he scream;
    Cassius[338] is the sinewy one on the other side.

But night is rising again, and it is time
    That we depart, for we have seen the whole."
    As he requested, I put my arms round him,

70 And waiting until the wings were opened full
    He took advantage of the time and place
    And grasped the shaggy flank, and gripping still,

From tuft to tuft descended through the mass
    Of matted hair and crusts of ice. And then,
    When we had reached the pivot of the thighs,

Just where the haunch is at its thickest, with strain
    And effort my master brought around his head
    To where he'd had his legs: and from there on

He grappled the hair as someone climbing would—
80   So I supposed we were heading back to Hell.
    "Cling tight, for it is stairs like these," he sighed

---

[337] **Judas Iscariot:** The disciple who in the Gospels is said to have betrayed Jesus.

[338] **Cassius:** Along with Brutus and others, the assassins of Julius Caesar in 44 B.C.E.; Dante regarded Caesar as the founder of an empire, so his betrayers rivaled Judas's betrayal of Jesus.

Like one who is exhausted, "which we must scale
　　To part from so much evil." Then he came up
　　Through a split stone, and placed me on its sill,

And climbed up toward me with his cautious step.
　　I raised my eyes, expecting I would see
　　Lucifer as I left him — and saw his shape

Inverted, with his legs held upward. May they
　　Who are too dull to see what point I had passed[339]
90　　Judge whether it perplexed me. "Come — the way

Is long, the road remaining to be crossed
　　Is hard: rise to your feet," the master said,
　　"The sun is at mid-tierce."[340] We had come to rest

In nothing like a palace hall; instead
　　A kind of natural dungeon enveloped us,
　　With barely any light, the floor ill made.

"Before I free myself from the abyss,
　　My master," I said when I was on my feet,
　　"Speak, and dispel my error: where is the ice?

100　And how can he be fixed head-down like that?
　　And in so short a time, how can it be
　　Possible for the sun to make its transit

From evening to morning?" He answered me,
　　"You imagine you are still on the other side,
　　Across the center of the earth, where I

Grappled the hair on the evil serpent's hide
　　Who pierces the world. And all through my descent,
　　You were on that side; when I turned my head

And legs about, you passed the central point
110　To which is drawn, from every side, all weight.
　　Now you are on the opposite continent

---

[339] **point I had passed:** They pass the center of the earth, from the Northern to the Southern Hemisphere.

[340] **mid-tierce:** A name given to the religious divisions of the day after sunrise; "middle tierce" is about 7:30 a.m.

Beneath the opposite hemisphere[341] to that
    Which canopies the great dry land therein:
    Under the zenith of that one is the site

Whereon the Man was slain who without sin
    Was born and lived; your feet this minute press
    Upon a little sphere whose rounded skin

Forms the Judecca's other, outward face.
    Here it is morning when it is evening there;
120   The one whose hair was like a ladder for us

Is still positioned as he was before.
    On this side he fell down from Heaven; the earth,
    Which till then stood out here, impelled by fear

Veiled itself in the sea and issued forth
    In our own hemisphere. And possibly,
    What now appears on this side fled its berth

And rushing upward left a cavity:[342]
    This hollow where we stand." There is below,
    As far from Beelzebub as one can be

130 Within his tomb, a place one cannot know
    By sight, but by the sound a little runnel
    Makes as it wends the hollow rock its flow

Has worn, descending through its winding channel:
    To get back up to the shining world from there
    My guide and I went into that hidden tunnel;

---

[341] **hemisphere:** They are under the Southern Hemisphere, opposite to the Northern Hemisphere, at the center of which is Jerusalem (Ezekiel 5:5).

[342] **cavity:** To escape from Satan falling from Heaven, land of the Southern Hemisphere went to the Northern Hemisphere; the ocean filled the hole left by the land. The interior of earth, also wishing to avoid Satan, moved upwards forming Mount Purgatory thereby creating a "cavity."

And following its path, we took no care
    To rest, but climbed: he first, then I — so far,
    Through a round aperture I saw appear

Some of the beautiful things that Heaven bears,
140 Where we came forth, and once more saw the stars.[343]

---

[343] **stars:** The *Purgatorio* and the *Paradiso* also end with "stars," which are emblems of God's universe for the believer.

Dante and the Medieval World Picture

p. 1460

The Dante scholar Karl Vossler believed that the worldview of a certain time created the background for great literature, but he also held that the genius of a single author might be said to summarize an entire worldview. Thus his introduction to *Medieval Culture: An Introduction to Dante and His Times* (1929) states, "Dante sums up so many sides of his own age, and the study of his background carries us over so wide a field, that a work such as this may very well serve as a gateway to the study of medieval culture in all its manifold activities." The texts in this section provide background for Dante's *Divine Comedy*—the **Inferno** in particular—and may enlighten us further regarding medieval culture as a whole.

Recent scholarship suggests that in addition to drawing inspiration from Greek and Roman classics and European literature, Dante was also influenced by apocalyptic and visionary literature outside the main body of European culture. Journeys to the underworld, voyages of discovery, and encounters with the dead are a staple of world literature from the earliest times to the present. Vossler acknowledged the existence of medieval Irish, Scandinavian, and Arabic works of this nature but did not believe they could have influenced Dante. Some other works, such as the fourth century Latin *Visio Pauli* (Vision of St. Paul or Apocalypse of Paul), had only indirect influence on Dante, according to Vossler. Later studies, however, suggest Dante was acquainted with more literature than was thought possible in Vossler's time, including the tale of Muhammad's Night Journey, alluded to in the Qur'an and circulated in medieval versions that go under the general heading **The Book of Muhammad's Ladder**.

p. 1642

p. 1626

Domenico di
Michelino, *The Divine
Comedy Illuminating
Florence*, 1465
*Dante is shown
holding a copy of the
Divine Comedy and
surrounded by images
of Hell, Purgatory,
and Paradise. This
fresco is in the dome
of the cathedral of
Santa Maria del Fiore
in Florence, itself
depicted in the
painting on the right.
(The Art Archive /
Duomo Florence /
Dagli Orti)*

TWO LATIN SOURCES: VISION AND CONSOLATION

Whether or not it directly influenced the *Divine Comedy,* the *Visio
Pauli* or **Apocalypse of Paul** set an early standard for Christian
vision literature. This apocryphal work was attributed to St. Paul,
following his Biblical description of being caught up into Paradise
in 2 *Corinthians* 12:2, 4.

> I know a man in Christ who fourteen years ago was caught up to
> the third heaven — whether in the body or out of the body I do not
> know. . . . And he heard things that cannot be told, which man
> may not utter.

The original work was written in Greek in the fourth century, translated into Latin, Coptic, Syriac and Ethiopic, and later, by way of
Old French, passed into almost every European vernacular language. Although deemed inauthentic as Scripture by the Catholic
Church, it was popular for centuries, and its vivid descriptions of
hell were used frequently in sermons. The version in this anthology
was written in Latin in the fifth or sixth century. Of interest to

Boethius visited by Philosophy in prison, twelfth century
This English illumination shows Boethius visited by Philosophy as he awaits execution. (The Art Archive / Bodian Library Oxford / The Bodian Library)

p. 1633

readers of Dante's *The Inferno* are certain features unique to this visionary text: a description of the judgment of souls at their deaths, and of the different types of clergy whose sins are specifically condemned.

An acknowledged source of Dante's great poem was ***The Consolation of Philosophy*** by the early Christian philosopher and translator Boethius (480–526), who had the good and bad fortune to live during the long reign of the Ostrogothic Roman Emperor Theodoric (r. 476–526). Boethius was useful to Theodoric because of his knowledge of Greek and his suitability as a diplomatic ambassador to Constantinople. Later, however, Theodoric suspected Boethius of disloyalty and imprisoned and executed him without trial in the last year of his reign. Though Boethius made important contributions to medieval learning by his translations of Aristotle, Porphyry and other philosophers, he gained lasting fame from his own book, *The Consolation*, consisting of his imaginary dialog with the allegorical figure of Lady Philosophy concerning his imprisonment by Theodoric. Boethius' topic, the unfair sufferings of the just, was suited to its contemporary audience, especially after his own execution. In Dante's homage to Boethius, he is given a seat in heaven: he appears among the Christian philosophers in *Paradiso X.* Dante wrote elsewhere that he began to read Boethius' *Consolation* while still a young man, shortly after the death of his beloved Beatrice.

Muhammad's Ladder of Vision.   A more controversial possible influence on Dante is *The Book of Muhammad's Ladder,* the story of Muhammad's Night Journey. This journey is first mentioned in the Qur'an, in chapter 17, book 1:

> Glory be to Him who made His servant go by night from the Sacred Temple [Mecca] to the Farther Temple [Jerusalem, the throne of God].

This bare text held the kernel of a great story—Muhammad's spiritual vision—that was elaborated upon by various *hadith,* or sayings, many of which were collected in the *Life of Muhammad* composed by Ibn Ishaq in the eighth century. A more comprehensive version, the Arabic *Book of Muhammad's Ladder,* was completed perhaps a century later by an anonymous author who combined traditional sayings and Qur'anic commentaries with bits and pieces of Muslim, Jewish, and Christian accounts of fabulous journeys, ascent narratives, tales of the underworld, and popular legends. During the twelfth century, when Peter the Venerable struggled to make Islamic literature known to a Christian audience, if only in order to refute it, *The Book of Muhammad's Ladder* was translated into Castilian. In the thirteenth century it was translated into Latin and Old French by order of Alfonso X, King of Castile. Our text, the Old French version, states its aim clearly:

> . . . so that people may learn about Muhammad's life and knowledge, and so that after they have heard and become acquainted with the errors and unbelievable things that he recounts in this book, the legitimate Christian religion and truth which is in Christ will thus be more fitting and pleasing to embrace and keep to for all those who are good Christians.

It is difficult to state with certainty that *The Book of Muhammad's Ladder* was a direct source for the *Divine Comedy.* But considering the popularity of this story in Dante's century, it is hard to imagine he did not know it; and despite his embrace of Christian theology, it is clear that he knew the writings of the Islamic philosopher Avicenna (980–1037), who wrote his own version of Muhammad's night journey. Finally, while no one today would accuse Dante of sympathy for Sufism, the mystical branch of Islamic faith, he could hardly have avoided encountering the Sufi-influenced writings of Avicenna on visionary experience.

BROADENING THE SCOPE

Dante's familiarity with medieval vision literature, whether *The Apocalypse of Paul,* Boethius's *Consolation of Philosophy,* or the apocryphal *Book of Muhammad's Ladder,* can hardly be doubted. Details from *The Apocalypse of Paul* strongly suggest that he was influenced by it; Boethius' influence in *The Consolation of Philosophy* has already been suggested. In the case of Muhammad's Night Journey, Dante may well have sought to make his *Divine Comedy* a response to the claims of Islam, and thus played off the Muslim story to suit his own purposes. In any case, descriptions of journeys to the underworld predate either Christianity or Islam: they go back to the Sumerian story of Innana, Homer's description in the Greek *Odyssey,* and Virgil's imitation of the same journey in the Roman *Aeneid.* This literary device, frequently used in works of broader narrative dimensions, becomes the whole vehicle of the *Divine Comedy.*

■ **FURTHER RESEARCH**

Translations and Commentary
Elliott, J. K., ed. and trans. *The Apocryphal New Testament.* 1993.
Green, Richard, trans. *Boethius: Consolation of Philosophy.* 1962.
Hyatte, Reginald, ed. and trans. *The Prophet of Islam in Old French.* 1997.

Background and History
Colish, Marcia L. *Medieval Foundations of the Western Intellectual Tradition, 400–1400.* 1998.
Curtius, Ernst R. *European Literature and the Latin Middle Ages.* Translated from German by Willard R. Trask. 1953.
Gardiner, Eileen. *Medieval Visions of Heaven and Hell.* 1993.
——— . *Visions of Heaven and Hell before Dante.* 1989.
Heath, Peter. *Allegory and Philosophy in Avicenna (Ibn Sina).* 1992.
Menocal, Maria Rosa. *The Arabic Role in Medieval Literary History.* 2nd edition, 2004.
Patch, H. R. *The Tradition of Boethius: A Study of His Importance in Medieval Culture.* 1935.
Vossler, Karl. *Medieval Culture: An Introduction to Dante and His Times.* 2 vols. Translated from German by William C. Lawton. 1929.

THE APOCALYPSE OF PAUL
GREECE, FOURTH CENTURY

Although it is an Apocryphal text—a work deemed inauthentic and denied a place in the New Testament—the Greek *Apocalypse of Paul*, completed in the fourth century, was influential in conveying the Christian picture of heaven and hell to European believers in the Middle Ages. Dante's *Inferno* may derive some of its representation of the punishments meted out to sinners in hell from this popular work. Dante cites Paul's journey to hell in the *Inferno* 2:22–24 with a telling comment:

> Later, the Chosen Vessel [Paul] too went there and returned,
>> Carrying confirmation of that faith
>> Which opens the way with salvation at its end.

Many versions of the Vision of Paul were produced—first in Greek, then in Latin, Coptic, and Syriac. The Latin versions of the fifth and sixth centuries were the best organized, though they remained lengthy and diffuse. Shorter versions were produced eventually, probably for the convenience of preachers eager to depict the torments of hell to their congregations. The English version of the work was abridged again in the nineteenth century by Victorian translators in order to delete some of those same graphic descriptions. The version reprinted here is a restored contemporary translation of the Latin narrative.

The story begins with the supposed discovery of the document itself in a box buried under Paul's house in Tarsus in 388 C.E. In the story, Paul is transported to heaven. He sees the created world below him and encounters the good and bad angels, one of whom, a guardian angel, shows him hell. After this, the Archangel Michael shows him heaven before returning him to earth.

In the vision of hell, the sinners are described by their sins but are also associated with their professions: they include members of the clergy. They are all spectacularly punished, whether tortured by implements, stoned, forced to gnaw their own bodies, consumed by fire, swallowed by worms and dragons, or thrown into holes. St. Paul himself does not experience any physical torment and finally intercedes, along with the other angels, to request that God grant one day without torment for the sinners. The request is granted and Paul proceeds to meet the Archangel for the journey to heaven.

FROM

❧ The Apocalypse of Paul

Translated by J. K. Elliott

The angel answered and said to me, "Do you understand why you go hence?" And I said, "Yes, sir." And he said to me, "Come and follow me, and I will show you the souls of the godless and sinners, that you may know what manner of place it is." And I went with the angel, and he carried me towards the setting of the sun, and I saw the beginning of heaven founded on a great river of water, and I asked, "What is this river of water?" And he said to me, "This is the ocean which surrounds all the earth." And when I was at the outer limit of the ocean I looked, and there was no light in that place, but darkness and sorrow and sadness; and I sighed.

And I saw there a river boiling with fire, and in it a multitude of men and women immersed up to the knees, and other men up to the navel, others even up to the lips, others up to the hair. And I asked the angel and said, "Sir, who are those in the fiery river?" And the angel answered and said to me, "They are neither hot nor cold, because they were found neither in the number of the just nor in the number of the godless. For those spent the time of their life on earth passing some days in prayer, but others in sins and fornications, until their death." And I asked him and said, "Who are these, sir, immersed up to their knees in fire?" He answered and said to me, "These are they who when they have gone out of church occupy themselves with idle disputes. Those who are immersed up to the navel are those who, when they have taken the body and blood of Christ, go and fornicate and do not cease from their sins till they die. Those who are immersed up to the lips are those who slander each other when they assemble in the church of God; those up to the eyebrows are those who nod to each other and plot spite against their neighbour."

And I saw to the north a place of various and diverse punishments full of men and women, and a river of fire ran down into it. I observed and I saw very deep pits and in them several souls together, and the depth of that place was about three thousand cubits, and I saw them groaning and weeping and saying, "Have pity on us, O Lord!" and no one had pity on them. And I asked the angel and said, "Who are these, sir?" And the angel answered and said to me, "These are they who did not hope in the Lord, that they would be able to have him as their helper." And I asked and said, "Sir, if these souls remain for thirty or forty generations thus one upon another, I believe the pits would not hold them unless they were dug deeper." And he said to me, "The Abyss has no measure, for beneath it there stretches down below that which is below it; and so it is that if perchance anyone should take a stone and throw it into a very deep well after many hours it would reach the bottom, such is the abyss. For when the souls are thrown in there, they hardly reach the bottom in fifty years."

When I heard this, I wept and groaned over the human race. The angel answered and said to me, "Why do you weep? Are you more merciful than God? For though God is good, he knows that there are punishments, and he patiently bears with the human race, allowing each one to do his own will in the time in which he dwells on the earth."

I observed the fiery river and saw there a man being tortured by Tartaruchian angels having in their hands an iron instrument with three hooks with which they pierced the bowels of that old man; and I asked the angel and said, "Sir, who is that old man on whom such torments are imposed?" And the angel answered and said to me, "He whom you see was a presbyter who did not perform his ministry well: when he had been eating and drinking and committing fornication he offered the host to the Lord at his holy altar."

And I saw not far away another old man led on by evil angels running with speed, and they pushed him into the fire up to his knees, and they struck him with stones and wounded his face like a storm, and did not allow him to say, "Have pity on me!" And I asked the angel, and he said to me, "He whom you see was a bishop and did not perform his episcopate well, who indeed accepted the great name but did not enter into the witness of him who gave him the name all his life, seeing that he did not give just judgement and did not pity widows and orphans, but now he receives retribution according to his iniquity and his works."

And I saw another man in the fiery river up to his knees. His hands were stretched out and bloody, and worms proceeded from his mouth and nostrils, and he was groaning and weeping, and crying he said, "Have pity on me! For I am hurt more than the rest who are in this punishment." And I asked, "Sir, who is this?" And he said to me, "This man whom you see was a deacon who devoured the oblations and committed fornication and did not do right in the sight of God; for this cause he unceasingly pays this penalty."

And I looked closely and saw alongside of him another man, whom they delivered up with haste and cast into the fiery river, and he was in it up to the knees; and the angel who was set over the punishments came with a great fiery razor, and with it he cut the lips of that man and the tongue likewise. And sighing, I lamented and asked, "Who is that, sir?" And he said to me, "He whom you see was a reader and read to the people, but he himself did not keep the precepts of God; now he also pays the proper penalty."

And I saw another multitude of pits in the same place, and in the midst of it a river full with a multitude of men and women, and worms consumed them. But I lamented, and sighing asked the angel and said, "Sir, who are these?" And he said to me, "These are those who exacted interest on interest and trusted in their riches and did not hope in God that he was their helper."

And after that I looked and saw another place, very narrow, and it was like a wall, and fire round about it. And I saw inside men and women gnawing their tongues, and I asked, "Sir, who are these?" And he said to me, "These are they who in church disparage the Word of God, not attending to it, but as it were making naught of God and his angels; for that reason they now likewise pay the proper penalty."

And I observed and saw another pool in the pit and its appearance was like blood, and I asked and said, "Sir, what is this place?" And he said to me, "Into that pit stream all the punishments." And I saw men and women immersed up to the lips, and I asked, "Sir, who are these?" And he said to me, "These are the magicians who prepared for men and women evil magic arts and did not cease till they died."

And again I saw men and women with very black faces in a pit of fire, and I sighed and lamented and asked, "Sir, who are these?" And he said to me, "These are fornicators and adulterers who committed adultery, having wives of their own; like-wise also the women committed adultery, having husbands of their own; therefore they unceasingly suffer penalties."

And I saw there girls in black raiment, and four terrifying angels having in their hands burning chains, and they put them on the necks of the girls and led them into darkness; and I, again weeping, asked the angel, "Who are these, sir?" And he said to me, "These are they who, when they were virgins, defiled their virginity unknown to their parents; for which cause they unceasingly pay the proper penalties."

And again I observed there men and women with hands cut and their feet placed naked in a place of ice and snow, and worms devoured them. Seeing them I lamented and asked, "Sir, who are these?" And he said to me, "These are they who harmed orphans and widows and the poor, and did not hope in the Lord, for which cause they unceasingly pay the proper penalties."

And I observed and saw others hanging over a channel of water, and their tongues were very dry, and many fruits were placed in their sight, and they were not permitted to take of them, and I asked, "Sir, who are these?" And he said to me, "These are they who broke their fast before the appointed hour; for this cause they unceasingly pay these penalties."

And I saw other men and women hanging by their eyebrows and their hair, and a fiery river drew them, and I said, "Who are these, sir?" And he said to me, "These are they who join themselves not to their own husbands and wives but to whores, and therefore they unceasingly pay the proper penalties."

And I saw other men and women covered with dust, and their countenance was like blood, and they were in a pit of pitch and sulphur running in a fiery river, and I asked, "Sir, who are these?" And he said to me, "These are they who committed the iniquity of Sodom and Gomorrah, the male with the male, for which reason they unceasingly pay the penalties."

And I observed and saw men and women clothed in bright garments, but with their eyes blind, and they were placed in a pit, and I asked, "Sir, who are these?" And he said to me, "These are heathen who gave alms, and knew not the Lord God, for which reason they unceasingly pay the proper penalties." And I observed and saw other men and women on a pillar of fire, and beasts were tearing them in pieces, and they were not allowed to say, "Lord have pity on us!" And I saw the angel of torments putting heavy punishments on them and saying, "Acknowledge the Son of God; for this was prophesied to you when the divine Scriptures were read to you, and you did not attend; for which cause God's judgement is just, because your actions have apprehended you and led you into these punishments." But I sighed and wept, and I asked and said, "Who are these men and women who are strangled in the fire and pay their penalties?" And he answered me, "These are women who defiled the image of God by bringing forth infants out of the womb, and these are the men who lay with them. And their infants addressed the Lord God and the angels who were set over the punishments, saying, 'Avenge us of our parents, for they defiled the image of God, having the name of God but not observing his precepts; they gave us for food to dogs and to be trodden on by swine; others they threw into the river.' But the infants were handed over to the angels of Tartarus who were set over the punishments, that they might lead them to a spacious place of mercy; but their fathers and mothers were tortured in a perpetual punishment."

And after that I saw men and women clothed with rags full of pitch and fiery sulphur, and dragons were coiled about their necks and shoulders and feet, and angels with fiery horns restrained them and smote them, and closed their nostrils, saying to them, "Why did you not know the time in which it was right to repent and serve God, and did not do it?" And I asked, "Sir, who are these?" And he said to me, "These are they who seemed to renounce the world, putting on our garb, but the impediments of the world made them wretched, so that they did not maintain a single Agape, and they did not pity widows and orphans; they did not receive the stranger and the pilgrim, nor did they offer an oblation and they did not show mercy to their neighbour. Moreover not even on one day did their prayer ascend pure to the Lord God, but many impediments of the world detained them, and they were not able to do right in the sight of God, and the angels enclosed them in the place of punishments. And those who were in punishments saw them and said to them, 'We indeed neglected God when we lived in the world and you also did likewise; when we were in the world we indeed knew that we were sinners, but of you it was said, "These are just and servants of God." Now we know that in vain you were called by the name of the Lord, for which cause you pay the penalties.'"

And sighing I wept and said, "Woe unto men, woe unto sinners! Why were they born?" And the angel answered and said to me, "Why do you lament? Are you more merciful than the Lord God who is blessed forever, who established judgement and sent forth every man to choose good and evil in his own will and do what pleases him?" Then I lamented again very greatly, and he said to me, "Do you lament when as yet you have not seen greater punishments? Follow me and you shall see seven times greater than these."

And he carried me to the north and placed me above a well, and I found it sealed with seven seals; and the angel who was with me said to the angel of that place, "Open the mouth of the well that Paul, the well-beloved of God, may see, for authority is given him that he may see all the torments of hell." And the angel said to me, "Stand far off that you may be able to bear the stench of this place." When the well was opened, immediately there arose from it a disagreeable and evil stench, which surpasses all punishments; and I looked into the well, and I saw fiery masses glowing on all sides and anguish, and the mouth of the well was narrow so as to admit one man only. And the angel answered and said to me, "If any man has been put into this well of the abyss and it has been sealed over him, no remembrance of him shall ever be made in the sight of the Father and his Son and the holy angels." And I said, "Who are these, sir, who are put into this well?" And he said to me, "They are those who do not confess that Christ has come in the flesh and that the Virgin Mary brought him forth, and those who say that the bread and cup of the Eucharist of blessing are not the body and blood of Christ."

And I looked from the north to the west and I saw there the worm that never rests, and in that place there was gnashing of teeth; and the worms were one cubit long, and had two heads, and there I saw men and women in the cold gnashing their teeth. And I asked and said, "Sir, who are these in this place?" And he said to me, "These are they who say that Christ did not rise from the dead and that this flesh will not rise again." And I asked and said, "Sir, is there no fire nor heat in this place?" And he said to me, "In this place there is nothing else but cold and snow." And again he said to me, "Even if the sun should rise upon them, they do not become warm on account of the excessive coldness of that place and the snow."

But hearing these things I stretched out my hands and wept, and sighing again I said, "It were better for us if we had not been born, all of us who are sinners."

But when those who were in that place saw me weeping with the angel, they cried out and wept saying, "Lord God have mercy upon us!" And after these things I saw the heavens open, and Michael the archangel descending from heaven, and with him was the whole army of angels, and they came to those who were placed in punishment, and seeing him, again weeping, they cried out and said, "Have pity on us! Michael the archangel, have pity on us and on the human race for because of your prayers the earth continues. We now see the judgement and acknowledge the Son of God! It was impossible for us before these things to pray for this, before we entered into this place; for we heard that there was a judgement before we went out of the world, but impediments and the life of the world did not allow us to repent." And Michael answered and said, "Hear Michael speaking! I am he who stands in the sight of God every hour. As the Lord lives, in whose sight I stand, I do not stop one day or one night praying incessantly for the human race, and I indeed pray for those who are on the earth; but they do not cease committing iniquity and fornications, and they do not do any good while they are placed on earth; and you have consumed in vanity the time in which you ought to have repented. But I have always prayed thus, and I now beseech that God may send dew and send forth rains upon the earth, and now I continue to pray until the earth produce its fruits, and I say that if anyone has done but a little good I will strive for him, protecting him till he escapes the judgement of punishments. Where are your prayers? Where are your penances? You have lost your time contemptibly. But now weep, and I will weep with you and the angels who are with me with the well-beloved Paul, if by chance the merciful God will have pity and give you refreshment." But hearing these words they cried out and wept greatly, and all said with one voice, "Have pity on us, Son of God!" And I, Paul, sighed and said, "O Lord God! Have pity on your creation, have pity on the sons of men, have pity on your own image."

And I looked and saw the heaven move like a tree shaken by the wind. Suddenly, they threw themselves on their faces before the throne. And I saw twenty-four elders and the four beasts adoring God, and I saw an altar and veil and throne, and all were rejoicing; and the smoke of a good odour rose near the altar of the throne of God, and I heard the voice of one saying, "For what reason do our angels and ministers intercede?" And they cried out, saying, "We intercede seeing your many kindnesses to the human race." And after these things I saw the Son of God descending from heaven, and a diadem was on his head. And seeing him, all those who were placed in punishment exclaimed with one voice saying, "Have pity, Son of the High God! It is you who have granted rest for all in the heavens and on earth, and on us likewise have mercy, for since we have seen you we have refreshment." And a voice went out from the Son of God through all the punishments, saying, "And what work have you done that you demand refreshment from me? My blood was poured out for your sakes, and even so you did not repent; for your sakes I wore the crown of thorns on my head; for you I received buffets on my cheeks, and you did not repent. I asked for water when hanging on the cross, and they gave me vinegar mixed with gall, with a spear they opened my right side, for my name's sake they slew my prophets and just men, and in all these things I gave you the chance for repentance and you would not. Now, however, for the sake of Michael the archangel of my covenant and the angels who are with him, and because of Paul the well-beloved, whom I would not grieve, for the sake of your brethren who are in the world and offer oblations, and for the sake of your sons, because my commandments are in them, and more for the sake of my own kindness, on the day on which I rose from the dead, I give to you all who are in punishment a night and a day of refreshment forever." And they all cried out and said, "We bless you, Son of God, that you have given us a night and a day of respite. For a refreshment of one day is better for us than all the time of our life which we were on earth, and if we had plainly known that this place was intended for those who sin, we would have worked no other work, we would have done no business, and we would have done no iniquity: what need had we to be born in the world? For here our pride is captured which ascended from our mouth against our neighbour; our plagues and excessive anguish and the tears and the worms which are under us, these are much worse for us than the pains which we have left behind us." When they had said this, the evil angels of torment were angered with them, saying, "How long do you lament and sigh? For you had no mercy. For this is the judgement of God who had no mercy. But you received this great grace of a day and a night's refreshment on the Lord's Day for the sake of Paul the well-beloved of God who descended to you."

And after that the angel said to me, "Have you seen all these things?" And I said, "Yes, sir." And he said to me, "Follow me, and I will lead you into Paradise, that the just who are there may see you, for lo, they hope to see you, and they are ready to come to meet you in joy and gladness!" . . .

❧ BOETHIUS
B. ROME, 480–526

Boethius was born to a distinguished Roman family and educated in the Greek and Roman classics. He translated into Latin the Greek philosopher Porphyry's *Introduction to the Categories of Aristotle* as well as Aristotle's collected writings on logic that make up the *Organon*. He wrote a commentary on a work of Cicero and short works of his own on logic. In addition, he wrote on several subjects contained in the medieval *quadrivium*: arithmetic, geometry, music, astronomy, and several works on theology. Had he lived longer or devoted himself completely to his studies, he would undoubtedly have been the principal philosopher of the early Middle Ages.

Following the advice of Socrates that philosophers should act as public servants, Boethius became a Consul of Rome in 510. He served

Fortune turning her wheel, fifteenth century
Fortune displays her wheel, on which people prosper only to fall. This illumination comes from Jean de Meun's translation of The Consolation of Philosophy. *(The Art Archive / Bibliotèque Municipale Rouan / Dagli Orti)*

under Theodoric, King of the Ostrogoths, who had conquered the Western Empire between 489 and 493. For the most part a temperate leader, Theodoric preserved the Roman Senate and the consular system while keeping the final authority of government in his hands. It is uncertain exactly how Boethius eventually came under suspicion of treason—perhaps his advocacy of the independence of the Senate, or perhaps his desire to reestablish close ties between the Western and Eastern Empire; but it is worth noting another accusation, that of sacrilege, which appeared to be based on his practice of philosophy. Thus his life's trajectory followed that of Socrates; he too was a philosopher who chose to live in a political environment that harbored hostility toward intellectuals, and suffered the consequences.

The Consolation of Philosophy, written as Boethius awaited execution, is a serene work of moral philosophy, teaching patience and acceptance of one's fate in a world caught up in the pursuit of fame and fortune. True happiness, according to this philosophy, resides in the pursuit of reason, as well as self-mastery and devotion to God. Borrowing from many traditions, including Neoplatonism, Christian theology, and stoicism, *The Consolation* captured its readers through its synthesis of prior beliefs and its familiar, seemingly personal form of presentation.

The first chapter of *The Consolation* finds Boethius bemoaning his fate in the dungeon when he is visited by Lady Philosophy. At first he refuses her efforts to console him, spilling out a litany of grievances in the hope that she will support his cause. While she recognizes the injustice done to him, she sees his misfortune in a larger context, and by the end of the chapter begins to direct his attention outside his own predicament. The early part of the narrative is framed by the narrative poems of Boethius; they spell out his quarrel with his evil fortune. The tone shifts after his long prayer for deliverance in Poem 5, especially with the intervention of Lady Philosophy in Poems 6 and 7 near the end of the chapter.

   Dante refers several times to the influence of Boethius' *Consolation of Philosophy* on his intellectual and spiritual growth, and he appears to borrow some of the description of the central characters in narrating the conversations in the *Divine Comedy*. The figure of troubled mankind is present in Dante the pilgrim, traveling through Hell with Virgil as his guide; the figure of Philosophy is present first in Virgil in Hell, later in Beatrice as she accompanies Dante through Purgatory and Heaven in the hope of saving his soul. While there are many sources of the *Divine Comedy*, surely Boethius' little book is one.

FROM

∾ The Consolation of Philosophy

Translated by Richard Green

Book I

POEM 1

I who once wrote songs with keen delight am now by sorrow driven to take up melancholy measures. Wounded Muses tell me what I must write, and elegiac verses bathe my face with real tears. Not even terror could drive from me these faithful companions of my long journey. Poetry, which was once the glory of my happy and flourishing youth, is still my comfort in this misery of my old age.

   Old age has come too soon with its evils, and sorrow has commanded me to enter the age which is hers. My hair is prematurely gray, and slack skin shakes on my exhausted body. Death, happy to men when she does not intrude in the sweet years, but comes when often called in sorrow, turns a deaf ear to the wretched and cruelly refuses to close weeping eyes.

   The sad hour that has nearly drowned me came just at the time that faithless Fortune favored me with her worthless gifts. Now that she has clouded her deceitful face, my accursed life seems to go on endlessly. My friends, why did you so often think me happy? Any man who has fallen never stood securely.

PROSE 1

Lady Philosophy appears to him and
drives away the Muses of poetry.

While I silently pondered these things, and decided to write down my wretched complaint, there appeared standing above me a woman of majestic countenance whose flashing eyes seemed wise beyond the ordinary wisdom of men. Her color was bright, suggesting boundless vigor, and yet she seemed so old that she could not be thought of as belonging to our age. Her height seemed to vary: sometimes she seemed of ordinary human stature, then again her head seemed to touch the top of the heavens. And when she raised herself to her full height she penetrated heaven itself, beyond the vision of human eyes. Her clothing was made of the most delicate threads, and by the most exquisite workmanship; it had—as she afterwards told me— been woven by her own hands into an everlasting fabric. Her clothes had been darkened in color somewhat by neglect and the passage of time, as happens to pictures exposed to smoke. . . . This robe had been torn, however, by the hands of violent men, who had ripped away what they could. In her right hand, the woman held certain books; in her left hand, a scepter.

When she saw the Muses of poetry standing beside my bed and consoling me with their words, she was momentarily upset and glared at them with burning eyes. "Who let these whores from the theater come to the bedside of this sick man?" she said. "They cannot offer medicine for his sorrows; they will nourish him only with their sweet poison. They kill the fruitful harvest of reason with the sterile thorns of the passions; they do not liberate the minds of men from disease, but merely accustom them to it. I would find it easier to bear if your flattery had, as it usually does, seduced some ordinary dull-witted man; in that case, it would have been no concern of mine. But this man has been educated in the philosophical schools of the Eleatics and the Academy.[1] Get out, you Sirens; your sweetness leads to death. Leave him to be cured and made strong by my Muses."

And so the defeated Muses, shamefaced and with downcast eyes, went sadly away. My sight was so dimmed by tears that I could not tell who this woman of imperious authority might be, and I lay there astonished, my eyes staring at the earth, silently waiting to see what she would do. She came nearer and sat at the foot of my bed. When she noticed my grief-stricken, downcast face, she reproved my anxiety with this song.

POEM 2

"Alas! how this mind is dulled, drowned in the overwhelming depths. It wanders in outer darkness, deprived of its natural light. Sick anxiety, inflated by worldly winds, swells his thoughts to bursting.

---

[1] **Eleatics and the Academy:** The Eleatics represent a school of Greek philosophy at Elia in Italy. The Academy is the traditional name for Plato's school of philosophy.

"Once this man was free beneath the open heaven, and he used to run along heavenly paths. He saw the splendor of the red sun, the heaven of the cold moon. And any star that pursued its vagrant paths, returning through various spheres, this master understood by his computations.

"Beyond all this, he sought the causes of things: why the sighing winds vex the seawaves; what spirit turns the stable world; and why the sun rises out of the red east to fall beneath the western ocean. He sought to know what tempers the gentle hours of spring and makes them adorn the earth with rosy flowers; what causes fertile autumn to flow with bursting grapes in a good year.

"This man used to explore and reveal Nature's secret causes. Now he lies here, bound down by heavy chains, the light of his mind gone out; his head is bowed down and he is forced to stare at the dull earth.

PROSE 2

*Seeing his desperate condition, Philosophy speaks
more gently and promises to cure him.*

"But," she said, "it is time for medicine rather than complaint." Fixing me with her eyes, she said: "Are you not he who once was nourished by my milk and brought up on my food; who emerged from weakness to the strength of a virile soul? I gave you weapons that would have protected you with invincible power, if you had not thrown them away. Don't you recognize me? Why don't you speak? Is it shame or astonishment that makes you silent? I'd rather it were shame, but I see that you are overcome by shock." When she saw that I was not only silent but struck dumb, she gently laid her hand on my breast and said: "There is no danger. You are suffering merely from lethargy, the common illness of deceived minds. You have forgotten yourself a little, but you will quickly be yourself again when you recognize me. To bring you to your senses, I shall quickly wipe the dark cloud of mortal things from your eyes." Then, she dried my tear-filled eyes with a fold of her robe.

POEM 3

Then, when the night was over, darkness left me and my eyes regained their former strength; just as when the stars are covered by swift Corus, and the sky is darkened by storm clouds, the sun hides and the stars do not shine; night comes down to envelop the earth. But if Boreas, blowing from his Thracian cave, beats and lays open the hiding day, then Phoebus shines forth, glittering with sudden light, and strikes our astonished eyes with his rays.[2]

---

[2] **just as . . . his rays:** Corus, the north-west wind; Boreas, the north wind. Thrace, part of modern Turkey, was regarded by the ancients as an extreme northern place. Phoebus is the sun.

PROSE 3

Boethius recognizes Lady Philosophy.
She promises to help him as she has always helped
those who love and serve her.

In a similar way, I too was able to see the heavens again when the clouds of my sorrow were swept away; I recovered my judgment and recognized the face of my physician. When I looked at her closely, I saw that she was Philosophy, my nurse, in whose house I had lived from my youth. "Mistress of all virtues," I said, "why have you come, leaving the arc of heaven, to this lonely desert of our exile? Are you a prisoner, too, charged as I am with false accusations?"

She answered, "How could I desert my child, and not share with you the burden of sorrow you carry, a burden caused by hatred of my name? Philosophy has never thought it right to leave the innocent man alone on his journey. Should I fear to face my accusers, as though their enmity were something new? Do you suppose that this is the first time wisdom has been attacked and endangered by wicked men? We fought against such rashness and folly long ago, even before the time of our disciple Plato. And in Plato's own time, his master Socrates, with my help, merited the victory of an unjust death.[3] Afterwards, the inept schools of Epicureans, Stoics, and others, each seeking its own interests, tried to steal the inheritance of Socrates and to possess me (in spite of my protests and struggles), as though I were the spoils of their quarreling. They tore this robe which I had woven with my own hands and, having ripped off some little pieces of it, went away supposing that they possessed me wholly.[4] Then, when traces of my garments were seen on some of them, they were rashly thought to be my friends, and they were therefore condemned by the error of the profane mob. . . .

POEM 4

"The serene man who has ordered his life stands above menacing fate and unflinchingly faces good and bad fortune. This virtuous man can hold up his head unconquered. The threatening and raging ocean storms which churn the waves cannot shake him; nor can the bursting furnace of Vesuvius, aimlessly throwing out its smoky fire; nor the fiery bolts of lightning which can topple the highest towers. Why then are we wretched, frightened by fierce tyrants who rage without the power to harm us? He who hopes for nothing and fears nothing can disarm the fury of these impotent men; but he who is burdened by fears and desires is not master of himself. He throws away his shield and retreats; he fastens the chain by which he will be drawn.

---

[3] **his master Socrates . . . unjust death:** Socrates was accused of corrupting youth and ridiculing the gods. In 309 B.C., the Athenian state condemned him to death (by drinking poison).

[4] **They tore . . . me wholly:** Philosophy's robe is the figure of the unity of true philosophy; this unity was, in Boethius' opinion, shattered by such limited philosophies as Epicureanism, based on the principle of pleasure, and Stoicism, based on the principle that whatever happens must be accepted without grief or joy.

PROSE 4

Boethius gives an account of his public career and especially of the causes of his present misery.

"Do you understand what I have told you," Philosophy asked; "have my words impressed you at all, or are you 'like the ass which cannot hear the lyre'? Why are you crying? Speak out, don't hide what troubles you. If you want a doctor's help, you must uncover your wound."

I pulled myself together and answered: "Do I have to explain; isn't the misery of my misfortune evident enough? I should think this place alone would make you pity me. Compare this prison with my library at home which you chose as your own and in which you often discussed with me the knowledge of human and divine things. Did I look like this? Was I dressed this way when I studied nature's mysteries with you, when you mapped the courses of the stars for me with your geometer's rod, when you formed my moral standards and my whole view of life according to the norm of the heavenly order? Are these miseries the rewards your servants should expect? You yourself proposed the course I have followed when you made Plato say that civil governments would be good if wise men were appointed rulers, or if those appointed to rule would study wisdom. Further, you decreed in the words of the same philosopher that government of the commonwealth ought to be in the hands of wise men; that if it should be left to unscrupulous and wicked men, they would bring about the ruin of the good.

"On this authority, I decided to apply to public administration the principles I had learned privately from you. You, and God who gave you to the minds of wise men, know that I became a magistrate only because of the unanimous wish of all good men. For these reasons I have become involved in grave and hopeless trouble with dishonest men; and, as always happens to the administrator of independent conscience, I have had to be willing to make powerful enemies in the interest of safeguarding justice. . . .

[Boethius follows with a description of his political struggles.]

"It seems to me that I can see wicked men everywhere celebrating my fall with great pleasure, and all the criminally depraved concocting new false charges. I see good men terrorized into helplessness by my danger, and evil men encouraged to risk any crime with impunity and able to get away with it by bribery. The innocent are deprived not only of their safety, but even of any defense. Now hear my appeal.

POEM 5

Boethius concludes with a prayer.

"Creator of the star-filled universe, seated upon your eternal throne You move the heavens in their swift orbits. You hold the stars in their assigned paths, so that sometimes the shining moon is full in the light of her brother sun and hides the lesser stars; sometimes, nearer the sun she wanes and loses her glory. You ordain that Hesperus, after rising at nightfall to drive the cold stars before him, should change his role and, as Lucifer, grow pale before the rising sun.[5]

---

[5] **You ordain that . . . rising sun:** Evening Star (Hesperus) and Morning Star (Lucifer) both signify the planet Venus. Literally the poet says that Hesperus changes his customary reins (i.e., his chariot) to become Lucifer.

"When the cold of winter makes the trees bare, You shorten the day to a briefer span; but when warm summer comes, You make the night hours go swiftly. Your power governs the changing year: in spring, Zephyrus renews the delicate leaves[6] that Boreas, the wind of winter, had destroyed; and Sirius burns the high corn in autumn that Arcturus had seen in seed.[7]

"Nothing escapes Your ancient law; nothing can avoid the work of its proper station. You govern all things, each according to its destined purpose. Human acts alone, O Ruler of All, You refuse to restrain within just bounds. Why should uncertain Fortune control our lives?

"Harsh punishment, deserved by the criminal, afflicts the innocent. Immoral scoundrels now occupy positions of power and unjustly trample the rights of good men. Virtue, which ought to shine forth, is covered up and hides in darkness, while good men must suffer for the crimes of the wicked. Perjury and deceit are not held blameworthy as long as they are covered by the color of lies. When these scoundrels choose to use their power they can intimidate even powerful kings, because the masses fear them.

"O God, whoever you are who joins all things in perfect harmony, look down upon this miserable earth! We men are no small part of Your great work, yet we wallow here in the stormy sea of fortune. Ruler of all things, calm the roiling waves and, as You rule the immense heavens, rule also the earth in stable concord."

PROSE 5

Philosophy suggests that the source of the prisoner's trouble is within himself and begins to reassure him.

While I poured out my long sad story, Philosophy looked on amiably, quite undismayed by my complaints. Then she said: "When I first saw you downcast and crying, I knew you were in misery and exile. But without your story I would not have known how desperate your exile is. You have not been driven out of your homeland; you have willfully wandered away. Or, if you prefer to think that you have been driven into exile, you yourself have done the driving, since no one else could do it. For if you can remember your true country you know that it is not, as Athens once was, ruled by many persons; rather 'it has one ruler and one king,' who rejoices in the presence of citizens, not in their expulsion. To be governed by his power and subject to his laws is the greatest liberty. Surely you know the oldest law of your true city, that the citizen who has chosen to establish his home there has a sacred right not to be driven away. The man who lives within the walls of that city need not fear banishment; but if he loses his desire to live there, he loses also the assurance of safety. And so, I am not so much disturbed by this prison as by your attitude. I do not need your library with its glass walls and ivory decoration, but I do need my place in your mind. For there I have placed not books but that which gives value to books, the ideas which are found in my writings.

---

[6]**Zephyrus . . . leaves:** Zephyrus, the west wind, was said to produce fruits and flowers by his breath.

[7]**Sirius . . . in seed:** Sirius, the dog-star, supposedly supplied great heat to cause crops to ripen. Arcturus was the brightest star in the constellation Boötes.

"What you have said about your merits in the commonwealth is true; your many services deserve even more than you claim. And what you have said about the truth or falsity of the accusations against you is well known to everyone. You were right to speak sparingly of the crimes and deceit of your enemies; such things are better talked about by the man in the street who hears about them. You have sharply protested the injustice done you by the Senate; and you have expressed sorrow for the accusations against me and the weakening of my place in the public esteem. Finally, you protested against Fortune in sorrow and anger, and complained that rewards are not distributed equally on the grounds of merit. At the end of your bitter poem, you expressed the hope that the same peace which rules the heavens might also rule the earth. But because you are so upset by sorrow and anger, and so blown about by the tumult of your feelings, you are not now in the right frame of mind to take strong medicine. For the time being, then, I shall use more gentle treatment, so that your hardened and excited condition may be softened by gentle handling and thus prepared for more potent remedies.

POEM 6

"The fool who plants his seed in the hard ground when summer burns with the sun's heat must feed on acorns in the fall, because his hope of harvest is in vain. Do not look for violets in purple meadows when fields are blasted by winter winds. And do not cut your vine branches in the spring if you want to enjoy the grapes, for Bacchus brings his fruit in autumn.

"God assigns to every season its proper office; and He does not permit the condition He has set to be altered. Every violent effort to upset His established order will fail in the end.

PROSE 6

Philosophy begins to remind Boethius of certain
basic truths which will place his misfortunes
in proper perspective.

"First," Philosophy said, "will you let me test your present attitude with a few questions, so that I can decide on a way to cure you?"

"Ask whatever you like," I replied, "and I will try to answer."

"Do you think," she began, "that this world is subject to random chance, or do you believe that it is governed by some rational principle?"

"I cannot suppose that its regular operation can be the result of mere chance; indeed, I know that God the Creator governs his work, and the day will never come when I can be shaken from the truth of this judgment."

"That is true," Philosophy answered, "and you said as much in your poem a while ago when you deplored the fact that only men were outside God's care. You did not doubt that all other things were ruled by reason. Strange, isn't it, that one who has so healthy an attitude should be so sick with despair. We must search further, because obviously something is missing. Tell me, since you have no doubt that the world is ruled by God, do you know *how* it is governed?"

"I don't quite get the point of your question, so I am unable to answer."

"You see, I was right in thinking that you had some weakness, like a breach in the wall of a fort, through which the sickness of anxiety found its way into your soul.

"But tell me, do you remember what the end, or goal, of all things is—the goal toward which all nature is directed?"

"I heard it once," I answered, "but grief has dulled my memory."

"Well, do you know where all things come from?"

I answered that I knew all things came from God.

"How then," she went on, "is it possible that you can know the origin of all things and still be ignorant of their purpose? But this is the usual result of anxiety; it can change a man, but it cannot break him and cannot destroy him.

"I want you to answer this, too: do you remember that you are a man?"

"How could I forget that," I answered.

"Well then, what is a man? Can you give me a definition?"

"Do you mean that I am a rational animal, and mortal? I know that, and I admit that I am such a creature."

"Do you know nothing else about what you are?"

"No, nothing."

"Now, I know another cause of your sickness, and the most important: you have forgotten what you are. And so I am fully aware of the reason for your sickness and the remedy for it too. You are confused because you have forgotten what you are, and, therefore, you are upset because you are in exile and stripped of all your possessions. Because you are ignorant of the purpose of things, you think that stupid and evil men are powerful and happy. And, because you have forgotten how the world is governed, you suppose that these changes of your fortune came about without purpose. Such notions are enough to cause not only sickness but death. But be grateful to the Giver of health that nature has not entirely forsaken you. For you have the best medicine for your health in your grasp of the truth about the way the world is governed. You believe that the world is not subject to the accidents of chance, but to divine reason. Therefore, you have nothing to fear. From this tiny spark, the living fire can be rekindled. But the time has not yet come for stronger remedies. It is the nature of men's minds that when they throw away the truth they embrace false ideas, and from these comes the cloud of anxiety which obscures their vision of truth. I shall try to dispel this cloud by gentle treatment, so that when the darkness of deceptive feeling is removed you may recognize the splendor of true light.

POEM 7

"Stars hidden by black clouds send down no light. If the wild south wind churns up the sea, the waves which once were clear as glass, as clear as the bright days, seem muddy and filthy to the beholder. The flowing stream, tumbling down from the high mountain, is often blocked by the stone broken off from the rocky cliff.

"So it is with you. If you want to see the truth in clear light, and follow the right road, you must cast off all joy and fear. Fly from hope and sorrow. When these things rule, the mind is clouded and bound to the earth."

The Book of Muhammad's Ladder

Spain, twelfth century

The popular version of Mohammad's ascent to heaven, generally referred to as *The Book of the Ladder*, was compiled from a variety of sources, chiefly *hadith* or tales of the life of Muhammad derived from the narrative of the Qur'an and probably completed in Arabic in the ninth century. It was translated into Castilian in the twelfth century and Latin and Old French in the thirteenth century. There is considerable speculation whether Dante knew the work; at the least, he was probably aware of the existence of a Latin version attributed to Bonaventura da Siena around 1264. How to interpret textual similarities between *The Book of the Ladder* and the *Divine Comedy* is still a matter of controversy.

The Book of the Ladder emphasizes the literal details of the Prophet's vision and the ensuing description of heaven and hell. In this regard the work falls into the genre of Apocalypse, for which there is considerable precedent. Christians of the period would have been familiar with the Apocalypse of St. John, as well as the Apocalypse of Paul. Like these works, *The Book of the Ladder* describes the recording of the narrative directly from the testimony of the visionary. In *The Book of the Ladder*, Muhammad entrusts the story to his close followers Abu Bakr and Ibn Abbas to write it down, demanding that they ask questions in order to verify their report.

Many of the physical details of hell resemble those in Christian accounts of vision. Details of location, the devils, the punishments, and the tools of punishment are similar, as are descriptions of the locations of specific sinners and their punishments. But there are also significant differences in *The Book of the Ladder* from Christian accounts. Divergences from Christian doctrine, such as Muhammad's direct contact with God in heaven, his intercession on behalf of his own followers, the death of the angels, and the love of God for Muhammad's followers leading to the reservation of a special place for them in heaven might have struck the Christian audience as doctrinal errors of the first magnitude. On the other hand, some of the same features, such as a successful plea for intercession, are also present in the Apocalypse of Paul.

The motivation behind the European translations of *The Book of the Ladder* for Christian consumption was to expose the "fallacies" of Islamic belief. The result, however, is harder to determine. Whether Dante might have been influenced to write the *Divine Comedy* as a "counter text" to *The Book of the Ladder*, as has been argued, would have depended on his own and his audience's reaction to the Islamic material. An alternative explanation is that any borrowing from *The Book of the Ladder* merely reflects the medieval practice of indiscriminately quoting from other works whether one agreed with them or not. At very least, *The Book of the Ladder* should be recognized as an important work in the Islamic tradition that became available for consumption in Europe prior to the writing of the *Divine Comedy*.

FROM

The Book of Muhammad's Ladder

Translated by Reginald Hyatte

CHAPTER TEN

After Gabriel and I, Muhammad, left the aforesaid angels, we went further. As we were proceeding, I looked and saw an extraordinarily large angel who was sitting on a throne, and he held between his hands a very great pillar by means of which he would destroy heaven and earth were he to strike it with a single blow. When Gabriel saw this pillar, he immediately began to weep. Then I said to him: "Gabriel, why are you weeping?" He answered me: "Muhammad, do you know who that angel is?" And I told him: "No, as Our Lord God is aware." Thereupon Gabriel said to me: "Know, Muhammad, that this angel is the guardian of hell." When I heard this, I went towards him and greeted him, and he did not respond to me at all. Gabriel said to him: "How is it that you do not answer the best man who was ever sent forth?" The angel asked him: "Who is he then?" Gabriel answered him: "He is Muhammad, the great Messenger of Our Lord." The angel said: "Has he already been sent?" And Gabriel replied: "Yes." Forthwith the angel came to me and greeted me, and he told me that those of my people who go to hell will suffer less hardship than all the others.

CHAPTER ELEVEN

When the guardian of hell told me, Muhammad, what you heard concerning my people, I looked at his face and saw that he had a very sad expression, and I asked him why he was so downcast. He answered me by saying: "Know, Muhammad, that I grieve very much on account of people who disobey Our Lord, which they would not do if they willed, and for this reason I am sad." "Indeed," I said, "you speak truly. But I pray you to tell me one thing about which I shall ask you." And he said to me: "Gladly." "Do tell me then how hell is constituted and, also, the angels who are there, and what sort of life they lead." Immediately he began to speak thus: "Muhammad, know that when hell was first formed, Our Lord God kindled a fire on top of it for seventy thousand years so that it became completely red. And next He had another fire burn on top of it for the same length of time until it became entirely white. Afterwards He kindled yet a third fire on top of it for another seventy thousand years so that it became completely black and incomparably dark. And this fire burns [forever] from its own substance with a wondrous intensity, but it does not emit any flame at all. Regarding the angels present there about whom you ask, know that Our Lord created them wholly of fire, and they are sustained by fire; and if for a single hour they were to leave the flame, they would die straightway and could not live without it, exactly as fish could not without water. Furthermore, He created them mute and deaf, and He placed in their hearts more hardness and cruelty than could be told, so that they know how to do nothing except torment and harass sinners.

Therefore God made them deaf and mute so they would hear neither the sinners' voices nor the cries that they make when they torture them. He made them so cruel that if by chance they saw the sinners showing any sign of humility, they would have no pity or concern at all for them or their humility. Apart from the affliction of hell fire that the sinners suffer, they have another very cruel punishment, for the angels present there torment them with enormous iron clubs and hammer them very hard because of the great cruelty that is in them, just as Our Lord says in the Koran: 'We placed Our strong and harsh and cruel angels in hell so that they might do Our bidding, and they obey Us in all that We order them to do.'[1] After the guardian related all these things to me, most terrified both I and Gabriel left him, and we proceeded until we arrived at the first heaven, and this is the heaven of the moon. . . .

Chapter Seventy-Two

When Gabriel finished relating the aforesaid matters to me, Muhammad, Prophet and Messenger of God, just as I recounted them to you, I entreated him most gently to tell me what the pains of hell are like and in what manner they are dispensed in conformity with the transgressions that sinners have committed. He answered me that he would most gladly do so. Thereupon he began to tell me the following: "Know, Muhammad, that Our Lord God ordained and established the first gate of hell named *Gihenne* in order to give it to those who worship idols and believe in images, just as He relates in the Koran when He says: 'You who worship idols of wood and metal, you will become dry logs in hell and material to fuel the fire.'[2] The second named *Lada* is prepared for those who believe in the true religion of God and then abandon it. The third named *Halhatina* is prepared for those who amass wealth by wrongful means and the peoples called Gog and Magog, for there they will be burned and tormented harshly; the fourth named *Halzair*, for those who play dice or some other sort of game, because they get angry and utter words which they ought not against Our Lord; the fifth called *Çakar*, for those who do not say the prayers that they ought [and do not give] alms [from their possessions] to the poor; the sixth named *Halgahym*, for those who are unwilling to believe what the prophets and messengers of Our Lord say, rather they deny what they say and dispute their words, just as Our Lord Himself says in the Koran: 'You who do not believe my prophets and messengers, the fire of Halgahym will be yours and will fall to your lot.'[3] The seventh called *Halkehuya* is prepared for those who deceive and cheat people in regard to weights and measures. All the remainder of hell is divided into seven parts, of which six are prepared for those who give Our Lord God a partner and say that some other is equal to Him and for those, too, who are unwilling to endure hardship or inconvenience for Our Lord and prefer to do what they wish rather than have His grace. And all the above cited sorts of people are erased from the book of life forevermore."

---

[1] 'We placed . . . them to do': *Sura* 66.6.

[2] 'You who . . . the fire': *Sura* 21.98.

[3] 'You who . . . to your lot': *Sura* 48.13.

CHAPTER SEVENTY-THREE

After the matters which you heard above, Gabriel related to me further that on Judgment Day, Our Lord God will have brought before Him a beast so very big that it is impossible to imagine. Seventy thousand ranks of angels will lead the beast, and each of the ranks will be as large as all the sky and the whole earth. These angels will prepare in hell four pillars, of which each will be as long as the distance that could be covered in seventy [thousand] years, and its width will be half of that. The pillars will be set up in the four corners of hell, and the aforesaid beast will be attached there in order to torment sinners, as you will hear later. This beast has thirty thousand mouths, and in each mouth, thirty thousand teeth, and each of them is thirty thousand times sharper than the sharpest sword that could be found in the whole world. In each of its lips is a very large iron ring and an enormous chain, too, and in each chain are seventy thousand iron links, and at each of the links is an angel who holds it. These angels are so large and strong that each of them could swallow the whole world without ever noticing it. What shall I tell you about the beast's appearance? Know that it is so awfully hideous and horrible to behold that if it were at one end of the world and a man at the opposite end were to see it, it is so frightening that he would of necessity lose consciousness and memory because of this. When the angels lead the beast before Our Lord, they will say to it: "Behold God Who made you, and obey Him in what He will order you [to do]." When the beast hears this, it will be more frightened and dispirited than anyone knows save Our Lord God. Immediately it will say to the angels: "I entreat you to tell me why Our Lord asked for me and if He has made any other thing stronger than me in order to torment me." Thereupon the angels will answer it and will swear by God's power that they know nothing about this. Then the beast will begin to tremble all over and strike one leg against another and rattle its teeth together very violently owing to the fear it has of God. When it is brought into the presence of Our Lord, it will kneel before Him and will say to Him: "Dear Lord God, You Who are powerful above all things, I entreat You to tell me if You have made any other thing meant to torment me." Our Lord will answer it and will swear by His power and majesty that He has made no other thing meant to torment it: "[Rather, I created you for the purpose of tormenting] others and in order to avenge Myself on My enemies and destroy those who did not believe in Me and took from Me My unity and divided Me into several parts." Then the beast will say to Him in reply: "Lord, I entreat You to allow me to bow before You on account of this favor that You have granted me." And Our Lord will permit it. Straightway it will lower its head and will kneel before Him and will say to Him: "Glory to You, Lord God Who are lofty and powerful above all things." After speaking, it will sigh. I, Muhammad, swear by God Who had me see these things in such a short time that it will sigh so very loudly that if men in the world were to hear but a single one of its sighs, they all would perforce die of fright. Then Our Lord will order it to go into hell. Without delay it will begin to walk, and it will send forth so large a flame through its mouth that it will be seen throughout the world. And it will emit such a very great quantity of smoke through its nostrils as to make the air so exceedingly dark that people will not be able to see one another, save those illuminated by

Our Lord's grace. The said angels [will walk] on the right and the left of this beast and will lead it into hell.

Chapter Seventy-Four

When Gabriel told me about the said beast and angels in the manner I related to you, I was so greatly frightened that my heart began to quake in my breast. But despite all this, I did not fail to entreat Gabriel most gently to tell me whether everyone assembled on Judgment Day will see this beast or only God and His angels will. He answered me by saying that all the people will see it and will be extremely terrified of it; consequently, they will shudder so very severely that it will seem to each as if his heart is going to stop in his breast and all his limbs, to separate from one another because of the intense trembling. Furthermore, they will lose consciousness and memory owing to fear of the beast as well as their sins which they will recall. Then Our Lord will order to be brought before Him a pair of scales, of which the middle shaft is as long as the distance from the east all the way to the west. Each of the two scales is so very large that it would cover the whole world. One of these scales consists of brightness and the other, darkness, and the one of brightness is on the right side of Our Lord, and the one of darkness, on the left. Good deeds will be put into the scale of brightness, and wrongs, into the one consisting of darkness. And a man will have two buckets just like those in which water is carried, and each will be as large as the greatest distance that the eyes can take in. [And into one of the buckets he will put his good deeds, and into the other, the sins that he committed.] When he arrives at the balance, he will empty the bucket with his good acts into the scale of brightness and the other bucket into the scale of darkness, and he will place himself between the two scales. [If] the sins weigh more than the good acts, he will go towards the side of darkness, and if the good deeds weigh more than the sins, he will go towards the side of brightness. "I tell you furthermore, Muhammad, that God will do so much for you that if there is someone, of whatever religion he may be, who has committed every sin of which he is capable and has done no good at all, and if he can manage to possess a written note saying *Le halla hilalla Muhagmet raçur halla*, which means 'There is no other god besides God, and Muhammad is His Messenger,' and he puts it into the scale of brightness, this note will weigh much more than all his sins in the other scale. Afterwards his sins recorded in the universal register will all be obliterated at once so that they will no longer appear, nor will Our Lord ever recall them." . . .

Chapter Seventy-Nine

After Gabriel finished his account concerning the aforesaid matters, I, Muhammad, Prophet and Messenger of God, looked and saw that the sinners endured different sorts of torment in hell, whereupon I felt such great sorrow in my heart that I began to perspire all over owing to the profound anguish it caused me. For I saw that some had their lips cut off with large scissors of glowing fire, and then I asked Gabriel who they were. He told me that they had spread talk in order to put people at odds, and others with their tongues cut out had borne false witness.[4] Then I saw others hanging by their genitalia from fiery hooks, and they had committed adultery in this world. Afterwards I saw so many women that it was amazing, and they all were hanging by the middle of their genitalia from large chunks of wood, and these blocks were suspended from chains of fire that burned more wondrously than could be described. I asked Gabriel who these women were, and he told me that they were profligate women who had not desisted from committing acts of debauchery and fornication. Moreover, subsequently I saw many men who had most comely persons and appeared very well dressed, and I recognized that they were rich men from among my people, and they were all burning in the fire. I asked Gabriel why these men were burning, for I indeed know that they used to give many alms to the poor. Gabriel answered me that even though they had given alms, they had been quite prideful, and they had done much wrong to the common people. And in this manner I saw all the sinners, who were tormented in conformity with their individual sins. Then I entreated Gabriel to take me away from the place where we were, for I felt such great pity and grief in seeing this that I could in no way endure it. Thereupon he said to me: "Muhammad, what do you think of the very numerous and momentous things that Our Lord has revealed to you through His compassion?" I answered him: "Indeed, no human heart could conceive of the honor or the good that Our Lord God has bestowed upon me, inasmuch as He has had me see His power and His glory and has revealed to me the possessions and honors prepared for good people and the punishments and torments to be administered to sinners." Subsequently Gabriel said to me: "Muhammad, have you thoroughly committed to memory all that you saw?" I answered him. "Yes." "Then go," said he, "and just as you saw all these things, tell and reveal them to your people so that they may know them and keep to the straight path of the faith and may consider and mind how to enter paradise and preserve themselves from hell."

---

[4] **He told . . . false witness:** *Sura* 24.22–23.

❧ GEOFFREY CHAUCER
B. ENGLAND, C. 1340–1400

For giving readers a vivid, lively, and delightful panorama of life in medieval England, no writer has exceeded Geoffrey Chaucer, one of the great English poets. Drawing on his wide reading in English, French, and Italian literature as well as his experience as a statesman, Chaucer crafted his most important work, *The Canterbury Tales*, which he left unfinished at his death. Like Boccaccio's *Decameron* and the Arabic *Thousand and One Nights*, *The Canterbury Tales* is a collection of tales told within an overarching frame story. From ribald and bawdy to pious and chaste, this succession of stories told by a group of English pilgrims on their way from London to Canterbury displays the variety of human character. In the individual portraits of each traveler—from the noble Knight to the base Miller, the lanky Clerk to the robust Franklin, the delicate Prioress to the earthy Wife of Bath—Chaucer creates unique and complex characters with all their vices and virtues as well as a picture of fourteenth-century England and its moral, social, philosophical, and spiritual concerns.

Chaucer and His Times.   Chaucer was born in the commercial center of London about 1340, into a family of French descent who had made their fortune in trade. The poet's father was a wine merchant and connected to the royal family's entourage. Chaucer's education is uncertain but most of it probably came at court. He entered the service of King Edward III in 1357, served in his army in France, and was captured at Rheims in 1358. He was eventually ransomed by the king and returned to England, but not before he had established excellent literary connections with the French writers of his day. In 1367 he traveled as a diplomatic emissary to Europe and is thought to have met Petrarch in Italy in 1372. He became immersed in Italian literature as well, including Dante's *Divine Comedy*, Petrarch's poetry, and possibly the works of Giovanni Boccaccio (1313–1375).

Chaucer's fortunes rose and fell with the political changes in England in the late fourteenth century. After falling out of favor as a supporter of Richard II in 1386, he recovered his influence several years later, and in 1389 was named Clerk of the Works, responsible for the properties of the Crown including those at Westminster and the Tower of London. Despite further setbacks, he lived comfortably until his death in 1400. He was buried in the "poet's corner" in Westminster Abbey, one of the king's properties that he had himself administered.

Chaucer's Poetry.   Chaucer cultivated his literary interests while performing the duties of the various public offices he held. His diplomatic missions helped to broaden the scope of his poetry, influenced as it was by Latin, French, and Italian literature. Chaucer's early poems adopt familiar motifs from continental models, though even early on Chaucer demonstrated a genius for innovation. *The Book of the Duchess* is an

www For links to more information about Chaucer, a quiz on "The Wife of Bath's Tale," and a discussion of the twenty-first-century relevance of Chaucer, see bedfordstmartins .com/worldlit compact.

The Wife of Bath, 1400–1410

The Ellesmere manuscript of The Canterbury Tales, *from which this illustration is taken, is thought to be Chaucer's most complete text, copied shortly after his death. In it, each pilgrim is shown astride a horse in the margin near where his or her tale begins. (Art Resource, NY)*

elegy, written on the occasion of the death of John of Gaunt's first wife, Blanche, Duchess of Lancaster, in 1369. The poem takes the form of a dream, suggested by the narrator's reading of "A romaunce." *The House of Fame* (c. 1374–1386), a second and unfinished long poem, uses the dream convention for comic purposes; it is a vision of love in which a series of parties petition the goddess Fame, whose blessing will confer upon them a good name. Birds play an important role in *The Parliament of Fowls,* written sometime between 1375 and 1385. The poem invokes the popular tradition that birds choose their mates on St. Valentine's Day. Such bird fables are found not only in medieval and Latin literature but in Islamic literature as well; the most famous of such Islamic tales is **Conference of the Birds** by Farid ud-Din Attar.

p. 1397

Chaucer's greatest love poem, *Troilus and Criseyde* (c. 1385), tells the story of the romance between Troilus, a hero from the Trojan War, and Cressida, who does not appear in classical literature but derives from medieval stories. Boccaccio's *Il Filostrato* was Chaucer's most immediate source for the love story, which tells how Troilus engages the services of the older matchmaker Pandarus to win the love of Cressida. The work is noteworthy for pushing the theme of courtly love close to full-blown tragedy.

The Canterbury Tales. Chaucer's greatest poem, *The Canterbury Tales*, began in 1386 and was left unfinished at his death. Though incomplete, this delightful set of tales consists of a prologue and twenty-four stories in more than 170,000 lines of verse, which begins as a socially diverse group of travelers set out on a pilgrimage to Canterbury, "the hooly blesful martir for to seke." Every year groups of pilgrims made the journey from London to Canterbury, to the shrine of Saint Thomas à Becket, the former archbishop of Canterbury who was murdered in the cathedral in 1170. To entertain one another along the way, Harry Bailly, the host of the journey and the proprietor of the Tabard Inn, where the journey begins, proposes that each of the twenty-nine pilgrims tell four stories, two on the way to Canterbury and two on the return. Chaucer's actual intention was most likely to complete only the stories on the way to the shrine, in itself a prodigious task. Whatever the author's plan, Chaucer produced a compendium of remarkably varied tales in a number of literary genres that brings to life the social, philosophical, and religious world of fourteenth-century England.

Through the combined perspectives of the General Prologue, each teller's prologue, and the tales each tells, a multifaceted portrait of each character emerges. Although some characters—such as the Knight, the Parson, and the Nun's Priest—display values consistent with their occupations and thus command respect, others—such as the Pardoner, the Summoner, and the Friar—vacillate between their professed values and their real actions and intentions. The Monk, for example, loves to hunt, and the Friar is overly fond of riches; worst of all is the Pardoner, an outright hypocrite. The "portrait gallery of pilgrims," as the General Prologue is sometimes called, is actually a picture of English society in all its diversity.

The Wife of Bath: Prologue. Many readers see the Wife of Bath, with her worldly ways, self-assured contentiousness, and resolute independence, as the most colorful, vital, and engaging character in *The Canterbury Tales*. In her prologue, she single-handedly takes up the offensive against the doctrine of celibacy and those who would appeal to church doctrine to legitimate their abuse of, and contempt for, women. The Wife of Bath's prologue argues that women deserve to be respected and declares their independence from male tyranny. This argument is enhanced by the Wife's vital and earthy celebration of love and sexuality. She proudly

> I read Chaucer still with as much pleasure as any of our poets. He is a master of manners and of description and the first tale-teller in the true enlivened, natural way.
>
> – ALEXANDER POPE, poet, eighteenth century

boasts that "Housbondes at chirche dore I have had fyve," and that she is ruled by both Venus and Mars:

> For certes, I am al Venerien
> In feelynge, and myn herte is marcien.
> Venus me yaf my lust, my likerousnesse,
> And mars yaf me my sturdy hardynesse.

Her boldness and tenacity derive in part from her experience of the world, which she claims provides a more powerful authority on which to base judgment than do books, with their false doctrines and wrong-headed assumptions about women. As she puts it: "Experience, though noon auctoritee / Were in this world, is right ynogh for me / To speke of wo that is in marriage."

The Wife of Bath: Tale.   The Wife's tale is one of a series sometimes called the "marriage group" that show marriage in a variety of forms. The story the Wife tells takes the form of a popular romance about a handsome knight and a loathsome lady. The knight, who commits rape, will be pardoned for his act if he can discover what it is that women most desire. The loathsome lady promises to tell him provided that he marry her. What the knight learns is that women above all want "sovereynetee / As wel over hir housbond as hir love / And for to been in maistrie hym above"; that is, sovereignty over their husbands and lovers, and to be above them in mastery. When the knight finally submits to love the old woman, she transforms into a beautiful young woman and the story ends well for both parties.

Chaucer's Language.   Although the language of Chaucer's day may be recognizable to the modern reader as English, changes in sound, meaning, spelling, and grammar between the fourteenth and seventeenth centuries render Chaucer's English difficult today without careful study. The final "e" sounds in the original text, for example, though gradually phased out of the spoken language in Chaucer's time, were still pronounced to capture rhyme and meter. Initial consonants such as the "k" in "knight" also are pronounced, and the "gh" in "knight" or "drought" is pronounced as "ch," as in the German *nach*. Most other consonant sounds in Chaucer's English are similar to modern English, but long vowel sounds are not. As a general rule, these long vowels sound as they do in Spanish, French, and German today.

The following example, the opening of the General Prologue, should be compared with Theodore Morrison's translation beginning on page 000. Unfortunately, even the best translations cannot fully capture the delightful rhythm and melody of Chaucer's verse:

> Whan that Aprill with his shoures soote
> The droghte of March hath perced to the roote,
> And bathed every veyne in swich licour
> Of which vertu engendred is the flour;
> Whan Zephirus eek with his sweete breeth

Inspired hath in every holt and heeth
The tendre croppes, and the yonge sonne
Hath in the Ram his halve cours yronne,
And smale fowele maken melodye,
That slepen al the nyght with open yë
(So priketh hem nature in hir corages),—
Thanne longen folk to goon on pilgrimages,
And palmeres for to seken straunge strondes,
To ferne halwes, kowthe in sondry londes;
And specially from every shires ende
Of Engelond to Caunterbury they wende,
The hooly blisful martir for to seke,
That ham hath holpen whan that they were seeke.

■ **FURTHER RESEARCH**

Editions
Benson, Larry D. *The Riverside Chaucer.* 3d ed. 1987.

Biography
Howard, Donald R. *Chaucer: His Life, His Works, His World.* 1987.
Pearsall, Derek. *The Life of Geoffrey Chaucer: A Critical Biography.* 1992.

Criticism
Benson, C. David. *Chaucer's Drama of Style: Poetic Variety and Contrast in* The Canterbury Tales. 1986.
Burrow, J. A. *Ricardian Poetry.* 1971.
Crane, Susan. *Gender and Romance in Chaucer's* Canterbury Tales. 1994.
Howard, Donald R. *The Idea of* The Canterbury Tales. 1976.
Patterson, Lee. *Chaucer and the Subject of History.* 1991.
Pearsall, Derek A. *The Canterbury Tales.* 1985.
Ruggiers, Paul G. *The Art of the Canterbury Tales.* 1965.
_____. *Editing Chaucer: The Great Tradition.* 1984.
Weatherbee, Winthrop. *Geoffrey Chaucer:* The Canterbury Tales. 1989.

❧ The Canterbury Tales

Translated by Theodore Morrison

FROM

GENERAL PROLOGUE

As soon as April pierces to the root
The drought of March, and bathes each bud and shoot
Through every vein of sap with gentle showers
From whose engendering liquor spring the flowers;

When zephyrs have breathed softly all about
Inspiring every wood and field to sprout,
And in the zodiac the youthful sun
His journey halfway through the Ram has run;[1]
When little birds are busy with their song
10 Who sleep with open eyes the whole night long
Life stirs their hearts and tingles in them so,
Then off as pilgrims people long to go,
And palmers° to set out for distant strands   pilgrims
And foreign shrines renowned in many lands.
And specially in England people ride
To Canterbury[2] from every countryside
To visit there the blessed martyred saint
Who gave them strength when they were sick and faint.
        In Southwark at the Tabard one spring day
20 It happened, as I stopped there on my way,
Myself a pilgrim with a heart devout
Ready for Canterbury to set out,
At night came all of twenty-nine assorted
Travelers, and to that same inn resorted,
Who by a turn of fortune chanced to fall
In fellowship together, and they were all
Pilgrims who had it in their minds to ride
Toward Canterbury. The stable doors were wide,
The rooms were large, and we enjoyed the best,
30 And shortly, when the sun had gone to rest,
I had so talked with each that presently
I was a member of their company
And promised to rise early the next day
To start, as I shall show, upon our way.
        But none the less, while I have time and space,
Before this tale has gone a further pace,
I should in reason tell you the condition
Of each of them, his rank and his position,
And also what array they all were in;
40 And so then, with a knight I will begin.
        A Knight was with us, and an excellent man,
Who from the earliest moment he began
To follow his career loved chivalry,
Truth, openhandedness, and courtesy.
He was a stout man in the king's campaigns

---

[1] **the youthful sun . . . Ram has run:** The sun is in Aries, the Ram, from mid March to early April.

[2] **Canterbury:** A city sixty miles southeast of London; site of Canterbury Cathedral, the shrine of St. Thomas à Becket ("the blessed martyred saint"), who was murdered there in 1170.

And in that cause had gripped his horse's reins
In Christian lands and pagan through the earth,
None farther, and always honored for his worth.
He was on hand at Alexandria's fall.
50 He had often sat in precedence to all
The nations at the banquet board in Prussia.
He had fought in Lithuania and in Russia,
No Christian knight more often; he had been
In Moorish Africa at Benmarin,
At the siege of Algeciras in Granada,
And sailed in many a glorious armada
In the Mediterranean, and fought as well
At Ayas and Attalia when they fell
In Armenia and on Asia Minor's coast.
60 Of fifteen deadly battles he could boast,
And in Algeria, at Tremessen,
Fought for the faith and killed three separate men
In single combat. He had done good work
Joining against another pagan Turk
With the king of Palathia. And he was wise,
Despite his prowess, honored in men's eyes,
Meek as a girl and gentle in his ways.
He had never spoken ignobly all his days
To any man by even a rude inflection.
70 He was a knight in all things to perfection.
He rode a good horse, but his gear was plain,
For he had lately served on a campaign.
His tunic was still spattered by the rust
Left by his coat of mail, for he had just
Returned and set out on his pilgrimage.
   His son was with him, a young Squire, in age
Some twenty years as near as I could guess.
His hair curled as if taken from a press.
He was a lover and would become a knight.
80 In stature he was of a moderate height
But powerful and wonderfully quick.
He had been in Flanders, riding in the thick
Of forays in Artois and Picardy,
And bore up well for one so young as he,
Still hoping by his exploits in such places
To stand the better in his lady's graces.
He wore embroidered flowers, red and white,
And blazed like a spring meadow to the sight.
He sang or played his flute the livelong day.
90 He was as lusty as the month of May.

His coat was short, its sleeves were long and wide.
He sat his horse well, and knew how to ride,
And how to make a song and use his lance,
And he could write and draw well, too, and dance.
So hot his love that when the moon rose pale
He got no more sleep than a nightingale.
He was modest, and helped whomever he was able,
And carved as his father's squire at the table.
     But one more servant had the Knight beside,
100 Choosing thus simply for the time to ride:
A Yeoman, in a coat and hood of green.
His peacock-feathered arrows, bright and keen,
He carried under his belt in tidy fashion.
For well-kept gear he had a yeoman's passion.
No draggled feather might his arrows show,
And in his hand he held a mighty bow.
He kept his hair close-cropped, his face was brown.
He knew the lore of woodcraft up and down.
His arm was guarded from the bowstring's whip
110 By a bracer, gaily trimmed. He had at hip
A sword and buckler, and at his other side
A dagger whose fine mounting was his pride,
Sharp-pointed as a spear. His horn he bore
In a sling of green, and on his chest he wore
A silver image of St. Christopher,
His patron, since he was a forester.
     There was also a Nun, a Prioress,
Whose smile was gentle and full of guilelessness.
"By St. Loy!" was the worst oath she would say.
120 She sang mass well, in a becoming way,
Intoning through her nose the words divine,
And she was known as Madame Eglantine.
She spoke good French, as taught at Stratford-Bow,[3]
For the Parisian French she did not know.
She was schooled to eat so primly and so well
That from her lips no morsel ever fell.
She wet her fingers lightly in the dish
Of sauce, for courtesy was her first wish.
With every bite she did her skillful best
130 To see that no drop fell upon her breast.
She always wiped her upper lip so clean
That in her cup was never to be seen

---

[3] **Stratford-Bow:** A convent in Middlesex, near London.

A hint of grease when she had drunk her share.
She reached out for her meat with comely air.
She was a great delight, and always tried
To imitate court ways, and had her pride,
Both amiable and gracious in her dealings.
As for her charity and tender feelings,
She melted at whatever was piteous.
140 She would weep if she but came upon a mouse
Caught in a trap, if it were dead or bleeding.
Some little dogs that she took pleasure feeding
On roasted meat or milk or good wheat bread
She had, but how she wept to find one dead
Or yelping from a blow that made it smart,
And all was sympathy and loving heart.
Neat was her wimple in its every plait,
Her nose well formed, her eyes as gray as slate.
Her mouth was very small and soft and red.
150 She had so wide a brow I think her head
Was nearly a span broad, for certainly
She was not undergrown, as all could see.
She wore her cloak with dignity and charm,
And had her rosary about her arm,
The small beads coral and the larger green,
And from them hung a brooch of golden sheen,
On it a large A and a crown above;
Beneath, "All things are subject unto love."
    A Priest accompanied her toward Canterbury,
160 And an attendant Nun, her secretary.
    There was a Monk, and nowhere was his peer,
A hunter, and a roving overseer.
He was a manly man, and fully able
To be an abbot. He kept a hunting stable,
And when he rode the neighborhood could hear
His bridle jingling in the wind as clear
And loud as if it were a chapel bell.
Wherever he was master of a cell
The principles of good St. Benedict,
170 For being a little old and somewhat strict,
Were honored in the breach, as past their prime.
He lived by the fashion of a newer time.
He would have swapped that text for a plucked hen
Which says that hunters are not holy men,
Or a monk outside his discipline and rule
Is too much like a fish outside his pool;
That is to say, a monk outside his cloister.

But such a text he deemed not worth an oyster.
I told him his opinion made me glad.
180 Why should he study always and go mad,
Mewed in his cell with only a book for neighbor?
Or why, as Augustine commanded, labor
And sweat his hands? How shall the world be served?
To Augustine be all such toil reserved!
And so he hunted, as was only right.
He had greyhounds as swift as birds in flight.
His taste was all for tracking down the hare,
And what his sport might cost he did not care.
His sleeves I noticed, where they met his hand,
190 Trimmed with gray fur, the finest in the land.
His hood was fastened with a curious pin
Made of wrought gold and clasped beneath his chin,
A love knot at the tip. His head might pass,
Bald as it was, for a lump of shining glass,
And his face was glistening as if anointed.
Fat as a lord he was, and well appointed.
His eyes were large, and rolled inside his head
As if they gleamed from a furnace of hot lead.
His boots were supple, his horse superbly kept.
200 He was a prelate to dream of while you slept.
He was not pale nor peaked like a ghost.
He relished a plump swan as his favorite roast.
He rode a palfrey brown as a ripe berry.
    A Friar was with us, a gay dog and a merry,
Who begged his district with a jolly air.
No friar in all four orders[4] could compare
With him for gallantry; his tongue was wooing.
Many a girl was married by his doing,
And at his own cost it was often done.
210 He was a pillar, and a noble one,
To his whole order. In his neighborhood
Rich franklins[5] knew him well, who served good food,
And worthy women welcomed him to town;
For the license that his order handed down,
He said himself, conferred on him possession
Of more than a curate's power of confession.
Sweetly the list of frailties he heard,
Assigning penance with a pleasant word.

---

[4] **all four orders:** The monastic orders: Franciscan, Dominican, Carmelite, and Augustinian.
[5] **Rich franklins:** Landowners or country gentlemen who were not noblemen.

He was an easy man for absolution
220 Where he looked forward to a contribution,
For if to a poor order a man has given
It signifies that he has been well shriven,
And if a sinner let his purse be dented
The Friar would stake his oath he had repented.
For many men become so hard of heart
They cannot weep, though conscience makes them smart.
Instead of tears and prayers, then, let the sinner
Supply the poor friars with the price of dinner.
For pretty women he had more than shrift.
230 His cape was stuffed with many a little gift,
As knives and pins and suchlike. He could sing
A merry note, and pluck a tender string,
And had no rival at all in balladry.
His neck was whiter than a fleur-de-lis°   lily
And yet he could have knocked a strong man down.
He knew the taverns well in every town.
The barmaids and innkeepers pleased his mind
Better than beggars and lepers and their kind.
In his position it was unbecoming
240 Among the wretched lepers to go slumming.
It mocks all decency, it sews no stitch
To deal with such riffraff; but with the rich,
With sellers of victuals, that's another thing.
Wherever he saw some hope of profiting,
None so polite, so humble. He was good,
The champion beggar of his brotherhood.
Should a woman have no shoes against the snow,
So pleasant was his *"In principio"*[6]
He would have her widow's mite before he went.
250 He took in far more than he paid in rent
For his right of begging within certain bounds.
None of his brethren trespassed on his grounds!
He loved as freely as a half-grown whelp.
On arbitration-days[7] he gave great help,
For his cloak was never shiny nor threadbare
Like a poor cloistered scholar's. He had an air
As if he were a doctor or a pope.
It took stout wool to make his semicope[8]

---

[6] **"In principio":** "In the beginning"—the opening phrase of the Gospel of St. John; the friar uses Latin ostentatiously to puff up his authority.   [7] **arbitration-days:** Special days for settling disputes.   [8] **semicope:** A cape or jacket.

That plumped out like a bell for portliness.
260 He lisped a little in his rakishness
To make his English sweeter on his tongue,
And twanging his harp to end some song he'd sung
His eyes would twinkle in his head as bright
As the stars twinkle on a frosty night.
Hubert this gallant Friar was by name.
     Among the rest a Merchant also came.
He wore a forked beard and a beaver hat
From Flanders. High up in the saddle he sat,
In figured cloth, his boots clasped handsomely,
270 Delivering his opinions pompously,
Always on how his gains might be increased.
At all costs he desired the sea policed
From Middleburg in Holland to Orwell.
He knew the exchange rates, and the time to sell
French currency, and there was never yet
A man who could have told he was in debt
So grave he seemed and hid so well his feelings
With all his shrewd engagements and close dealings.
You'd find no better man at any turn;
280 But what his name was I could never learn.
     There was an Oxford Student too, it chanced,
Already in his logic well advanced.
He rode a mount as skinny as a rake,
And he was hardly fat. For learning's sake
He let himself look hollow and sober enough.
He wore an outer coat of threadbare stuff,
For he had no benefice for his enjoyment
And was too unworldly for some lay employment.
He much preferred to have beside his bed
290 His twenty volumes bound in black or red
All packed with Aristotle from end to middle
Than a sumptuous wardrobe or a merry fiddle.
For though he knew what learning had to offer
There was little coin to jingle in his coffer.
Whatever he got by touching up a friend
On books and learning he would promptly spend
And busily pray for the soul of anybody
Who furnished him the wherewithal for study.
His scholarship was what he truly heeded.
300 He never spoke a word more than was needed,
And that was said with dignity and force,
And quick and brief. He was of grave discourse,
Giving new weight to virtue by his speech,

And gladly would he learn and gladly teach.
    There was a Lawyer, cunning and discreet,
Who had often been to St. Paul's porch to meet
His clients. He was a Sergeant of the Law,
A man deserving to be held in awe,
Or so he seemed, his manner was so wise.
310 He had often served as Justice of Assize
By the king's appointment, with a broad commission,
For his knowledge and his eminent position.
He had many a handsome gift by way of fee.
There was no buyer of land as shrewd as he.
All ownership to him became fee simple.[9]
His titles were never faulty by a pimple.
None was so busy as he with case and cause,
And yet he seemed much busier than he was.
In all cases and decisions he was schooled
320 That were of record since King William[10] ruled.
No one could pick a loophole or a flaw
In any lease or contract he might draw.
Each statute on the books he knew by rote.
He traveled in a plain, silk-belted coat.
    A Franklin traveled in his company.
Whiter could never daisy petal be
Than was his beard. His ruddy face gave sign
He liked his morning sop of toast in wine.
He lived in comfort, as he would assure us,
330 For he was a true son of Epicurus[11]
Who held the opinion that the only measure
Of perfect happiness was simply pleasure.
Such hospitality did he provide,
He was St. Julian[12] to his countryside
His bread and ale were always up to scratch.
He had a cellar none on earth could match.
There was no lack of pasties in his house,
Both fish and flesh, and that so plenteous
That where he lived it snowed of meat and drink.
340 With every dish of which a man can think,
After the various seasons of the year,
He changed his diet for his better cheer.

---

[9] **fee simple:** Ownership without legal restrictions.

[10] **King William:** William the Conqueror (ruled 1066–1087 C.E.).

[11] **Epicurus** (341–270 B.C.E.): Greek philosopher taught that refined pleasure was the greatest good.

[12] **St. Julian:** Patron saint of hospitality.

He had coops of partridges as fat as cream,
He had a fishpond stocked with pike and bream.
Woe to his cook for an unready pot
Or a sauce that wasn't seasoned and spiced hot!
A table in his hall stood on display
Prepared and covered through the livelong day.
He presided at court sessions for his bounty
350　And sat in Parliament often for his county.
A well-wrought dagger and a purse of silk
Hung at his belt, as white as morning milk.
He had been a sheriff and county auditor.
On earth was no such rich proprietor!

. . .

　　　　With us came also an astute Physician.
400　There was none like him for a disquisition
On the art of medicine or surgery,
For he was grounded in astrology.
He kept his patient long in observation,
Choosing the proper hour for application
Of charms and images by intuition
Of magic, and the planets' best position.
For he was one who understood the laws
That rule the humors, and could tell the cause
That brought on every human malady,
410　Whether of hot or cold, or moist or dry.
He was a perfect medico, for sure.
The cause once known, he would prescribe the cure,
For he had his druggists ready at a motion
To provide the sick man with some pill or potion—
A game of mutual aid, with each one winning.
Their partnership was hardly just beginning!
He was well versed in his authorities,
Old Aesculapius, Dioscorides,
Rufus, and old Hippocrates, and Galen,
420　Haly, and Rhazes, and Serapion,
Averroës, Bernard, Johannes Damascenus,
Avicenna, Gilbert, Gaddesden, Constantinus.[13]
He urged a moderate fare on principle,
But rich in nourishment, digestible;
Of nothing in excess would he admit.
He gave but little heed to Holy Writ.

---

[13] **Aesculapius . . . Constantinus:** Ancient and medieval medical authorities from Greece, Arabia, and England.

His clothes were lined with taffeta; their hue
Was all of blood red and of Persian blue,
Yet he was far from careless of expense.
430 He saved his fees from times of pestilence,
For gold is a cordial, as physicians hold,
And so he had a special love for gold.
　　A worthy woman there was from near the city
Of Bath, but somewhat deaf, and more's the pity.
For weaving she possessed so great a bent
She outdid the people of Ypres and of Ghent.[14]
No other woman dreamed of such a thing
As to precede her at the offering,
Or if any did, she fell in such a wrath
440 She dried up all the charity in Bath.
She wore fine kerchiefs of old-fashioned air,
And on a Sunday morning, I could swear,
She had ten pounds of linen on her head.
Her stockings were of finest scarlet-red,
Laced tightly, and her shoes were soft and new.
Bold was her face, and fair, and red in hue.
She had been an excellent woman all her life.
Five men in turn had taken her to wife,
Omitting other youthful company—
450 But let that pass for now! Over the sea
She had traveled freely; many a distant stream
She crossed, and visited Jerusalem
Three times. She had been at Rome and at Boulogne,
At the shrine of Compostella, and at Cologne.[15]
She had wandered by the way through many a scene.
Her teeth were set with little gaps between.
Easily on her ambling horse she sat.
She was well wimpled, and she wore a hat
As wide in circuit as a shield or targe.[16]
460 A skirt swathed up her hips, and they were large.
Upon her feet she wore sharp-roweled spurs.
She was a good fellow; a ready tongue was hers.
All remedies of love she knew by name,
For she had all the tricks of that old game.
　　There was a good man of the priest's vocation,
A poor town Parson of true consecration,
But he was rich in holy thought and work.

---

[14]**Ypres . . . Ghent:** Cities in Flanders renowned for their textiles.

[15]**Compostella . . . Cologne:** Shrines famous during the Middle Ages.

[16]**targe:** A small shield.

Learned he was, in the truest sense a clerk
Who meant Christ's gospel faithfully to preach
470 And truly his parishioners to teach.
He was a kind man, full of industry,
Many times tested by adversity
And always patient. If tithes[17] were in arrears,
He was loth to threaten any man with fears
Of excommunication; past a doubt
He would rather spread his offering about
To his poor flock, or spend his property.
To him a little meant sufficiency.
Wide was his parish, with houses far asunder,
480 But he would not be kept by rain or thunder,
If any had suffered a sickness or a blow,
From visiting the farthest, high or low,
Plodding his way on foot, his staff in hand.
He was a model his flock could understand,
For first he did and afterward he taught.
That precept from the Gospel he had caught,
And he added as a metaphor thereto,
"If the gold rusts, what will the iron do?"
For if a priest is foul, in whom we trust,
490 No wonder a layman shows a little rust.
A priest should take to heart the shameful scene
Of shepherds filthy while the sheep are clean.
By his own purity a priest should give
The example to his sheep, how they should live.
He did not rent his benefice[18] for hire,
Leaving his flock to flounder in the mire,
And run to London, happiest of goals,
To sing paid masses in St. Paul's for souls,
Or as chaplain from some rich guild take his keep,
500 But dwelt at home and guarded well his sheep
So that no wolf should make his flock miscarry.
He was a shepherd, and not a mercenary.
And though himself a man of strict vocation
He was not harsh to weak souls in temptation,
Not overbearing nor haughty in his speech,
But wise and kind in all he tried to teach.
By good example and just words to turn
Sinners to heaven was his whole concern.
But should a man in truth prove obstinate,

---

[17] **tithes:** Regular offerings to the church.

[18] **benefice:** His appointment as pastor.

510 Whoever he was, of rich or mean estate,
The Parson would give him a snub to meet the case.
I doubt there was a priest in any place
His better. He did not stand on dignity
Nor affect in conscience too much nicety,
But Christ's and his disciples' word he sought
To teach, and first he followed what he taught.
       There was a Plowman with him on the road,
His brother, who had forked up many a load
Of good manure. A hearty worker he,
520 Living in peace and perfect charity.
Whether his fortune made him smart or smile,
He loved God with his whole heart all the while
And his neighbor as himself. He would undertake,
For every luckless poor man, for the sake
Of Christ to thresh and ditch and dig by the hour
And with no wage, if it was in his power.
His tithes on goods and earnings he paid fair.
He wore a coarse, rough coat and rode a mare.
       There also were a Manciple, a Miller,
530 A Reeve, a Summoner, and a Pardoner,
And I — this makes our company complete.
       As tough a yokel as you care to meet
The Miller was. His big-beefed arms and thighs
Took many a ram put up as wrestling prize.
He was a thick, squat-shouldered lump of sins.
No door but he could heave it off its pins
Or break it running at it with his head.
His beard was broader than a shovel, and red
As a fat sow or fox. A wart stood clear
540 Atop his nose, and red as a pig's ear
A tuft of bristles on it. Black and wide
His nostrils were. He carried at his side
A sword and buckler. His mouth would open out
Like a great furnace, and he would sing and shout
His ballads and jokes of harlotries and crimes.
He could steal corn and charge for it three times,
And yet was honest enough, as millers come,
For a miller, as they say, has a golden thumb.
In white coat and blue hood this lusty clown,
550 Blowing his bagpipes, brought us out of town.
       The Manciple was of a lawyers' college,
And other buyers might have used his knowledge
How to be shrewd provisioners, for whether
He bought on cash or credit, altogether

He managed that the end should be the same:
He came out more than even with the game.
Now isn't it an instance of God's grace
How a man of little knowledge can keep pace
In wit with a whole school of learned men?
560   He had masters to the number of three times ten
Who knew each twist of equity and tort;
A dozen in that very Inn of Court
Were worthy to be steward of the estate
To any of England's lords, however great,
And keep him to his income well confined
And free from debt, unless he lost his mind
Or let him scrimp, if he were mean in bounty;
They could have given help to a whole county
In any sort of case that might befall;
570   And yet this Manciple could cheat them all!
        The Reeve was a slender, fiery-tempered man.
He shaved as closely as a razor can.
His hair was cropped about his ears, and shorn
Above his forehead as a priest's is worn.
His legs were very long and very lean.
No calf on his lank spindles could be seen.
But he knew how to keep a barn or bin,
He could play the game with auditors and win.
He knew well how to judge by drought and rain
580   The harvest of his seed and of his grain.
His master's cattle, swine, and poultry flock,
Horses and sheep and dairy, all his stock,
Were altogether in this Reeve's control.
And by agreement, he had given the sole
Accounting since his lord reached twenty years.
No man could ever catch him in arrears.
There wasn't a bailiff, shepherd, or farmer working
But the Reeve knew all his tricks of cheating and shirking.
He would not let him draw an easy breath.
590   They feared him as they feared the very death.
He lived in a good house on an open space,
Well shaded by green trees, a pleasant place.
He was shrewder in acquisition than his lord.
With private riches he was amply stored.
He had learned a good trade young by work and will.
He was a carpenter of first-rate skill.
On a fine mount, a stallion, dappled gray,
Whose name was Scot, he rode along the way.
He wore a long blue coat hitched up and tied

600 As if it were a friar's, and at his side
    A sword with rusty blade was hanging down.
    He came from Norfolk, from nearby the town
    That men call Bawdswell. As we rode the while,
    The Reeve kept always hindmost in our file.
       A Summoner in our company had his place.
    Red as the fiery cherubim his face.
    He was pocked and pimpled, and his eyes were narrow.
    He was lecherous and hot as a cock sparrow.
    His brows were scabby and black, and thin his beard.
610 His was a face that little children feared.
    Brimstone or litharge bought in any quarter,
    Quicksilver, ceruse, borax, oil of tartar,
    No salve nor ointment that will cleanse or bite
    Could cure him of his blotches, livid white,
    Or the nobs and nubbins sitting on his cheeks.
    He loved his garlic, his onions, and his leeks.
    He loved to drink the strong wine down blood-red.
    Then would he bellow as if he had lost his head,
    And when he had drunk enough to parch his drouth,
620 Nothing but Latin issued from his mouth.
    He had smattered up a few terms, two or three,
    That he had gathered out of some decree—
    No wonder; he heard law Latin all the day,
    And everyone knows a parrot or a jay
    Can cry out "Wat" or "Poll" as well as the pope;
    But give him a strange term, he began to grope.
    His little store of learning was paid out,
    So *"Questio quod juris"*[19] he would shout.
    He was a goodhearted bastard and a kind one.
630 If there were better, it was hard to find one.
    He would let a good fellow, for a quart of wine,
    The whole year round enjoy his concubine
    Scot-free from summons, hearing, fine, or bail,
    And on the sly he too could flush a quail.
    If he liked a scoundrel, no matter for church law.
    He would teach him that he need not stand in awe
    If the archdeacon threatened with his curse—
    That is, unless his soul was in his purse,
    For in his purse he would be punished well.
640 "The purse," he said, "is the archdeacon's hell."
    Of course I know he lied in what he said.
    There is nothing a guilty man should so much dread

---

[19] ***"Questio quod juris"***: "The question is, what law?," i.e., what law applies?

As the curse that damns his soul, when, without fail,
The church can save him, or send him off to jail.
He had the young men and girls in his control
Throughout the diocese; he knew the soul
Of youth, and heard their every last design.
A garland big enough to be the sign
Above an alehouse balanced on his head,
650   And he made a shield of a great round loaf of bread.
          There was a Pardoner of Rouncivalle[20]
With him, of the blessed Mary's hospital,
But now come straight from Rome (or so said he).
Loudly he sang, "Come hither, love, to me,"
While the Summoner's counterbass trolled out profound—
No trumpet blew with half so vast a sound.
This Pardoner had hair as yellow as wax,
But it hung as smoothly as a hank of flax.
His locks trailed down in bunches from his head,
660   And he let the ends about his shoulders spread,
But in thin clusters, lying one by one.
Of hood, for rakishness, he would have none,
For in his wallet he kept it safely stowed.
He traveled, as he thought, in the latest mode,
Disheveled. Save for his cap, his head was bare,
And in his eyes he glittered like a hare.
A Veronica[21] was stitched upon his cap,
His wallet lay before him in his lap
Brimful of pardons from the very seat
670   In Rome. He had a voice like a goat's bleat.
He was beardless and would never have a beard.
His cheek was always smooth as if just sheared.
I think he was a gelding or a mare;
But in his trade, from Berwick down to Ware,
No pardoner could beat him in the race,
For in his wallet he had a pillow case
Which he represented as Our Lady's veil;
He said he had a piece of the very sail
St. Peter, when he fished in Galilee
680   Before Christ caught him, used upon the sea.
He had a latten[22] cross embossed with stones
And in a glass he carried some pig's bones,
And with these holy relics, when he found

---

[20]**Rouncivalle:** A religious house and hospital outside of London.   [21]**A Veronica:** A copy of the veil of St. Veronica, said to have imprinted the image of Christ's face when Veronica used it to wipe Jesus' face on his way to the Crucifixion.   [22]**latten:** A metal alloy.

Some village parson grubbing his poor ground,
He would get more money in a single day
Than in two months would come the parson's way.
Thus with his flattery and his trumped-up stock
He made dupes of the parson and his flock.
But though his conscience was a little plastic
690 He was in church a noble ecclesiastic.
Well could he read the Scripture or saint's story,
But best of all he sang the offertory,
For he understood that when this song was sung,
Then he must preach, and sharpen up his tongue
To rake in cash, as well he knew the art,
And so he sang out gaily, with full heart.
     Now I have set down briefly, as it was,
Our rank, our dress, our number, and the cause
That made our sundry fellowship begin
700 In Southwark, at this hospitable inn
Known as the Tabard, not far from the Bell.
But what we did that night I ought to tell,
And after that our journey, stage by stage,
And the whole story of our pilgrimage.
But first, in justice, do not look askance
I plead, nor lay it to my ignorance
If in this matter I should use plain speech
And tell you just the words and style of each
Reporting all their language faithfully.
710 For it must be known to you as well as me
That whoever tells a story after a man
Must follow him as closely as he can.
If he takes the tale in charge, he must be true
To every word, unless he would find new
Or else invent a thing or falsify.
Better some breadth of language than a lie!
He may not spare the truth to save his brother.
He might as well use one word as another.
In Holy Writ Christ spoke in a broad sense,
720 And surely his word is without offense.
Plato, if his are pages you can read,
Says let the word be cousin to the deed.
So I petition your indulgence for it
If I have cut the cloth just as men wore it,
Here in this tale, and shown its very weave.
My wits are none too sharp, you must believe.
     Our Host gave each of us a cheerful greeting
And promptly of our supper had us eating.
The victuals that he served us were his best.

730   The wine was potent, and we drank with zest.
    Our Host cut such a figure, all in all,
    He might have been a marshal in a hall.
    He was a big man, and his eyes bulged wide,
    No sturdier citizen lived in all Cheapside.[23]
    Lacking no trace of manhood, bold in speech,
    Prudent, and well versed in what life can teach,
    And with all this he was a jovial man.
    And so when supper ended he began
    To jolly us, when all our debts were clear.
740   "Welcome," he said. "I have not seen this year
    So merry a company in this tavern as now,
    And I would give you pleasure if I knew how.
    And just this very minute a plan has crossed
    My mind that might amuse you at no cost.
        "You go to Canterbury — may the Lord
    Speed you, and may the martyred saint reward
    Your journey! And to while the time away
    You mean to talk and pass the time of day,
    For you would be as cheerful all alone
750   As riding on your journey dumb as stone.
    Therefore, if you'll abide by what I say,
    Tomorrow, when you ride off on your way,
    Now, by my father's soul, and he is dead,
    If you don't enjoy yourselves, cut off my head!
    Hold up your hands, if you accept my speech."
        Our counsel did not take us long to reach.
    We bade him give his orders at his will.
    "Well, sirs," he said, "then do not take it ill,
    But hear me in good part, and for your sport,
760   Each one of you, to make our journey short,
    Shall tell two stories, as we ride, I mean,
    Toward Canterbury; and coming home again
    Shall tell two other tales he may have heard
    Of happenings that some time have occurred.
    And the one of you whose stories please us most,
    Here in this tavern, sitting by this post
    Shall sup at our expense while we make merry
    When we come riding home from Canterbury.
    And to cheer you still the more, I too will ride
770   With you at my own cost, and be your guide.
    And if anyone my judgment shall gainsay
    He must pay for all we spend along the way.

---

[23] **Cheapside:** A commercial street in London.

If you agree, no need to stand and reason
Tell me, and I'll be stirring in good season."
    This thing was granted, and we swore our pledge
To take his judgment on our pilgrimage,
His verdict on our tales, and his advice.
He was to plan a supper at a price
Agreed upon; and so we all assented
780 To this command, and we were well contented.
The wine was fetched; we drank, and went to rest.
    Next morning, when the dawn was in the east,
Up sprang our Host, who acted as our cock,
And gathered us together in a flock,
And off we rode, till presently our pace
Had brought us to St. Thomas' watering place.
And there our host began to check his horse.
"Good sirs," he said, "you know your promise, of course.
Shall I remind you what it was about?
790 If evensong and matins don't fall out,
We'll soon find who shall tell us the first tale.
But as I hope to drink my wine and ale,
Whoever won't accept what I decide
Pays everything we spend along the ride.
Draw lots, before we're farther from the Inn.
Whoever draws the shortest shall begin.
Sir Knight," said he, "my master, choose your straw.
Come here, my lady Prioress, and draw,
And you, Sir Scholar, don't look thoughtful, man!
800 Pitch in now, everyone!" So all began
To draw the lots, and as the luck would fall
The draw went to the Knight, which pleased us all.
And when this excellent man saw how it stood,
Ready to keep his promise, he said, "Good!
Since it appears that I must start the game,
Why then, the draw is welcome, in God's name.
Now let's ride on, and listen, what I say."
And with that word we rode forth on our way,
And he, with his courteous manner and good cheer,
810 Began to tell his tale, as you shall hear.
. . .

PROLOGUE TO THE WIFE OF BATH'S TALE

"Experience, though all authority
Was lacking in the world, confers on me
The right to speak of marriage, and unfold
Its woes. For, lords, since I was twelve years old

—Thanks to eternal God in heaven alive—
I have married at church door no less than five
Husbands, provided that I can have been
So often wed, and all were worthy men.
But I was told, indeed, and not long since,
10   That Christ went to a wedding only once
At Cana, in the land of Galilee.
By this example he instructed me
To wed once only—that's what I have heard!
Again, consider now what a sharp word,
Beside a well, Jesus, both God and man,
Spoke in reproving the Samaritan:
'Thou hast had five husbands'—this for a certainty
He said to her—and the man that now hath thee
Is not thy husband.' True, he spoke this way,
20   But what he meant is more than I can say
Except that I would ask why the fifth man
Was not a husband to the Samaritan?
To just how many could she be a wife?
I have never heard this number all my life
Determined up to now. For round and round
Scholars may gloze, interpret, and expound,
But plainly, this I know without a lie,
God told us to increase and multiply.
That noble text I can well understand.
30   My husband—this too I have well in hand—
Should leave both father and mother and cleave to me.
Number God never mentioned, bigamy,
No, nor even octogamy; why do men
Talk of it as a sin and scandal, then?
     "Think of that monarch, wise King Solomon.[24]
It strikes me that *he* had more wives than one!
To be refreshed, God willing, would please me
If I got it half as many times as he!
What a gift he had, a gift of God's own giving,
40   For all his wives! There isn't a man now living
Who has the like. By all that I make out
This king had many a merry first-night bout
With each, he was so thoroughly alive.
Blessed be God that I have married five,
And always, for the money in his chest
And for his nether purse, I picked the best.
In divers schools ripe scholarship is made,

---

[24] **King Solomon:** Solomon had 700 wives and 300 concubines (1 Kings 2:3).

And various practice in all kinds of trade
Makes perfect workmen, as the world can see.
50 Five husbands have had turns at schooling me.
Welcome the sixth, whenever I am faced
With yet another. I don't mean to be chaste
At all costs. When a spouse of mine is gone,
Some other Christian man shall take me on,
For then, says the Apostle,[25] I'll be free
To wed, in God's name, where it pleases me.
To marry is no sin, as we can learn
From him; better to marry than to burn,
He says. Why should I care what obloquy
60 Men heap on Lamech[26] and his bigamy?
Abraham was, by all that I can tell,
A holy man; so Jacob was as well,
And each of them took more than two as brides,
And many another holy man besides.
Where, may I ask, in any period,
Can you show in plain words that Almighty God
Forbade us marriage? Point it out to me!
Or where did he command virginity?
The Apostle, when he speaks of maidenhood,
70 Lays down no law. This I have understood
As well as you, milords, for it is plain.
Men may advise a woman to abstain
From marriage, but mere counsels aren't commands.
He left it to our judgment, where it stands.
Had God enjoined us all to maidenhood
Then marriage would have been condemned for good.
But truth is, if no seed were ever sown,
In what soil could virginity be grown?
Paul did not dare command a thing at best
80 On which his Master left us no behest.
     "But now the prize goes to virginity.
Seize it whoever can, and let us see
What manner of man shall run best in the race!
But not all men receive this form of grace
Except where God bestows it by his will.
The Apostle was a maid, I know; but still,
Although he wished all men were such as he,

---

[25] **the Apostle:** St. Paul, who recommends in 1 Corinthians 7:8–9 that celibacy is preferable to marriage, marriage to promiscuity.

[26] **Lamech:** A man with two wives (Genesis 4:19–24).

It was only *counsel* toward virginity.
To be a wife he gave me his permission,
90   And so it is no blot on my condition
Nor slander of bigamy upon my state
If when my husband dies I take a mate.
A man does virtuously, St. Paul has said,
To touch no woman—meaning in his bed.
For fire and fat are dangerous friends at best.
You know what this example should suggest.
Here is the nub: he held virginity
Superior to wedded frailty,
And frailty I call it unless man
100 And woman both are chaste for their whole span.
        "I am not jealous if maidenhood outweighs
My marriages; I grant it all the praise.
It pleases them, these virgins, flesh and soul
To be immaculate. I won't extol
My own condition. In a lord's household
You know that every vessel can't be gold.
Some are of wood, and serve their master still.
God calls us variously to do his will.
Each has his proper gift, of all who live,
110 Some this, some that, as it pleases God to give.
        "To be virgin is a high and perfect course,
And continence is holy. But the source
Of all perfection, Jesus, never bade
Each one of us to go sell all he had
And give it to the poor; he did not say
That all should follow him in this one way.
He spoke to those who would live perfectly,
And by your leave, lords, that is not for me!
The flower of my best years I find it suits
120 To spend on the acts of marriage and its fruits.
        "Tell me this also: why at our creation
Were organs given us for generation,
And for what profit were we creatures made?
Believe me, not for nothing! Ply his trade
Of twisting texts who will, and let him urge
That they were only given us to purge
Our urine; say without them we should fail
To tell a female rightly from a male
And that's their only object—say you so?
130 It won't work, as experience will show.
Without offense to scholars, I say this,
They were given us for both these purposes,

That we may both be cleansed, I mean, and eased
Through intercourse, where God is not displeased.
Why else in books is this opinion met,
That every man should pay his wife his debt?
Tell me with what a man should hope to pay
Unless he put his instrument in play?
They were supplied us, then, for our purgation,
140 But they were also meant for generation.
     "But none the less I do not mean to say
That all those who are furnished in this way
Are bound to go and practice intercourse.
The world would then grant chastity no force.
Christ was a maid, yet he was formed a man,
And many a saint, too, since the world began,
And yet they lived in perfect chastity.
I am not spiteful toward virginity.
Let virgins be white bread of pure wheat-seed.
150 Barley we wives are called, and yet I read
In Mark, and tell the tale in truth he can,
That Christ with barley bread cheered many a man.[27]
In the state that God assigned to each of us
I'll persevere. I'm not fastidious.
In wifehood I will use my instrument
As freely by my Maker it was lent.
If I hold back with it, God give me sorrow!
My husband shall enjoy it night and morrow
When it pleases him to come and pay his debt.
160 But a husband, and I've not been thwarted yet,
Shall always be my debtor and my slave.
From tribulation he shall never save
His flesh, not for as long as I'm his wife!
I have the power, during all my life,
Over his very body, and not he.
For so the Apostle has instructed me,
Who bade men love their wives for better or worse.
It pleases me from end to end, that verse!"
     The Pardoner, before she could go on,
170 Jumped up and cried, "By God and by St. John,
Upon this topic you preach nobly, Dame!
I was about to wed, but now, for shame,
Why should my body pay a price so dear?

---

[27] **That Christ . . . a man:** The miracle of feeding some five thousand people with five loaves and two fishes (Mark 8:1–21; John 6:9).

I'd rather not be married all this year!"
     "Hold on," she said. "I haven't yet begun.
You'll drink a keg of this before I'm done,
I promise you, and it won't taste like ale!
And after I have told you my whole tale
Of marriage, with its fund of tribulation—
180 And I'm the expert of my generation,
For I myself, I mean, have been the whip—
You can decide then if you want a sip
Out of the barrel that I mean to broach.
Before you come too close in your approach,
Think twice. I have examples, more than ten!
'The man who won't be warned by other men,
To other men a warning he shall be.'
These are the words we find in Ptolemy.
You can read them right there in his *Almagest*."[28]
190   "Now, Madame, if you're willing, I suggest,"
Answered the Pardoner, "as you began,
Continue with your tale, and spare no man.
Teach us your practice—we young men need a guide."
     "Gladly, if it will please you," she replied.
"But first I ask you, if I speak my mind,
That all this company may be well inclined,
And will not take offense at what I say.
I only mean it, after all, in play.
     "Now, sirs, I will get onward with my tale.
200 If ever I hope to drink good wine or ale,
I'm speaking truth: the husbands I have had,
Three of them have been good, and two were bad.
The three were kindly men, and rich, and old.
But they were hardly able to uphold
The statute which had made them fast to me.
You know well what I mean by this, I see!
So help me God, I can't help laughing yet
When I think of how at night I made them sweat,
And I thought nothing of it, on my word!
210 Their land and wealth they had by then conferred
On me, and so I safely could neglect
Tending their love or showing them respect.
So well they loved me that by God above
I hardly set a value on their love.
A woman who is wise is never done

---

[28] **Almagest:** This aphorism appears not in the *Almagest* but in a collection of Ptolemy's writings.

Busily winning love when she has none,
But since I had them wholly in my hand
And they had given me their wealth and land,
Why task myself to spoil them or to please
220 Unless for my own profit and my ease?
I set them working so that many a night
They sang a dirge, so grievous was their plight!
They never got the bacon, well I know,
Offered as prize to couples at Dunmow²⁹
Who live a year in peace without repentance!
So well I ruled them, by my law and sentence,
They were glad to bring me fine things from the fair
And happy when I spoke with a mild air,
For God knows I could chide outrageously.
230   "Now judge if I could do it properly!
You wives who understand and who are wise,
This is the way to throw dust in their eyes.
There isn't on the earth so bold a man
He can swear false or lie as a woman can.
I do not urge this course in every case,
Just when a prudent wife is caught off base;
Then she should swear the parrot's mad who tattled
Her indiscretions, and when she's once embattled
Should call her maid as witness, by collusion.
240 But listen, how I threw them in confusion:
    "'Sir dotard, this is how you live?' I'd say.
'How can my neighbor's wife be dressed so gay?
She carries off the honors everywhere.
I sit at home. I've nothing fit to wear.
What were you doing at my neighbor's house?
Is she so handsome? Are you so amorous?
What do you whisper to our maid? God bless me,
Give up your jokes, old lecher. They depress me.
When I have a harmless friend myself, you balk
250 And scold me like a devil if I walk
For innocent amusement to his house.
You drink and come home reeling like a souse
And sit down on your bench, worse luck, and preach.
Taking a wife who's poor — this is the speech
That you regale me with — costs grievously,
And if she's rich and of good family,
It is a constant torment, you decide,

---

²⁹**the bacon . . . at Dunmow:** A town in southeastern England that awarded such a prize to couples who had
no quarrels or doubts about marriage for a year after their wedding.

To suffer her ill humor and her pride.
And if she's fair, you scoundrel, you destroy her
260 By saying that every lecher will enjoy her;
For chastity at best has frail protections
If a woman is assailed from all directions.
    "'Some want us for our wealth, so you declare,
Some for our figure, some think we are fair,
Some want a woman who can dance or sing,
Some want kindness, and some philandering,
Some look for hands and arms well turned and small.
Thus, by your tale, the devil may take us all!
Men cannot keep a castle or redoubt
270 Longer, you tell me, than it can hold out.
Or if a woman's plain, you say that she
Is one who covets each man she may see,
For at him like a spaniel she will fly
Until she finds some man that she can buy.
Down to the lake goes never a goose so gray
But it will have a mate, I've heard you say.
It's hard to fasten — this too I've been told —
A thing that no man willingly will hold.
Wise men, you tell me as you go to bed,
280 And those who hope for heaven should never wed.
I hope wild lightning and a thunderstroke
Will break your wizened neck! You say that smoke
And falling timbers and a railing wife
Drive a man from his house. Lord bless my life!
What ails an old man, so to make him chide?
We cover our vices till the knot is tied,
We wives, you say, and then we trot them out.
Here's a fit proverb for a doddering lout!
An ox or ass, you say, a hound or horse,
290 These we examine as a matter of course.
Basins and also bowls, before we buy them,
Spoons, spools, and such utensils, first we try them,
And so with pots and clothes, beyond denial;
But of their wives men never make a trial
Until they are married. After that, you say,
Old fool, we put our vices on display.
    "'I am in a pique if you forget your duty
And fail, you tell me, to praise me for my beauty,
Or unless you are always doting on my face
300 And calling me "fair dame" in every place,
Or unless you give a feast on my birthday
To keep me in good spirits, fresh and gay,

Or unless all proper courtesies are paid
To my nurse and also to my chambermaid,
And my father's kin with all their family ties—
You say so, you old barrelful of lies!
    "'Yet just because he has a head of hair
Like shining gold, and squires me everywhere,
You have a false suspicion in your heart
310 Of Jenkin, our apprentice. For my part
I wouldn't have him if you died tomorrow!
But tell me this, or go and live in sorrow:
That chest of yours, why do you hide the keys
Away from me? It's my wealth, if you please,
As much as yours. Will you make a fool of me,
The mistress of our house? You shall not be
Lord of my body and my wealth at once!
No, by St. James himself, you must renounce
One or the other, if it drives you mad!
320 Does it help to spy on me? You would be glad
To lock me up, I think, inside your chest.
"Enjoy yourself, and go where you think best,"
You ought to say; "I won't hear tales of malice.
I know you for a faithful wife, Dame Alice."
A woman loves no man who keeps close charge
Of where she goes. We want to be at large.
Blessed above all other men was he,
The wise astrologer, Don Ptolemy,
Who has this proverb in his *Almagest:*
330 "Of all wise men his wisdom is the best
Who does not care who has the world in hand."
Now by this proverb you should understand,
Since you have plenty, it isn't yours to care
Or fret how richly other people fare,
For by your leave, old dotard, you for one
Can have all you can take when day is done.
The man's a niggard to the point of scandal
Who will not lend his lamp to light a candle;
His lamp won't lose although the candle gain.
340 If you have enough, you ought not to complain.
    "'You say, too, if we make ourselves look smart,
Put on expensive clothes and dress the part,
We lay our virtue open to disgrace.
And then you try to reinforce your case
By saying these words in the Apostle's name:
"In chaste apparel, with modesty and shame,
So shall you women clothe yourselves," said he,

"And not in rich coiffure or jewelry,
Pearls or the like, or gold, or costly wear."[30]

350 Now both your text and rubric, I declare,
I will not follow as I would a gnat!
   "'You told me once that I was like a cat,
For singe her skin and she will stay at home,
But if her skin is smooth, the cat will roam.
No dawn but finds her on the neighbors calling
To show her skin, and go off caterwauling.
If I am looking smart, you mean to say,
I'm off to put my finery on display.
   "'What do you gain, old fool, by setting spies?

360 Though you beg Argus[31] with his hundred eyes
To be my bodyguard, for all his skill
He'll keep me only by my own free will.
I know enough to blind him, as I live!
   "'There are three things, you also say, that give
Vexation to this world both south and north,
And you add that no one can endure the fourth.
Of these catastrophes a hateful wife—
You precious wretch, may Christ cut short your life!—
Is always reckoned, as you say, for one.

370 Is this your whole stock of comparison,
And why in all your parables of contempt
Can a luckless helpmate never be exempt?
You also liken woman's love to hell,
To barren land where water will not dwell.
I've heard you call it an unruly fire;
The more it burns, the hotter its desire
To burn up everything that burned will be.
You say that just as worms destroy a tree
A wife destroys her spouse, as they have found

380 Who get themselves in holy wedlock bound.'
   "By these devices, lords, as you perceive,
I got my three old husbands to believe
That in their cups they said things of this sort,
And all of it was false; but for support
Jenkin bore witness, and my niece did too.
These innocents, Lord, what I put them through!
God's precious pains! And they had no recourse,
For I could bite and whinny like a horse.

---

[30] "In chaste apparel . . . costly wear": Timothy 2:9.

[31] **Argus:** In Greek mythology, a giant with a hundred eyes; the goddess Hera had him spy on her husband, Zeus, who had amorous designs on the beautiful Io.

Though in the wrong, I kept them well annoyed,
390   Or oftentimes I would have been destroyed!
First to the mill is first to grind his grain.
I was always the first one to complain,
And so our peace was made; they gladly bid
For terms to settle things they never did!
    "For wenching I would scold them out of hand
When they were hardly well enough to stand.
But this would tickle a man; it would restore him
To think I had so great a fondness for him!
I'd vow when darkness came and out I stepped,
400   It was to see the girls with whom he slept.
Under this pretext I had plenty of mirth!
Such wit as this is given us at our birth.
Lies, tears, and needlework the Lord will give
In kindness to us women while we live.
And thus in one point I can take just pride:
In the end I showed myself the stronger side.
By sleight or strength I kept them in restraint,
And chiefly by continual complaint.
In bed they met their grief in fullest measure.
410   There I would scold; I would not do their pleasure.
Bed was a place where I would not abide
If I felt my husband's arm across my side
Till he agreed to square accounts and pay,
And after that I'd let him have his way.
To every man, therefore, I tell this tale:
Win where you're able, all is up for sale.
No falcon by an empty hand is lured.
For victory their cravings I endured
And even feigned a show of appetite.
420   And yet in old meat I have no delight;
It made me always rail at them and chide them,
For though the pope himself sat down beside them
I would not give them peace at their own board.
No, on my honor, I paid them word for word.
Almighty God so help me, if right now
I had to make my last will, I can vow
For every word they said to me, we're quits.
For I so handled the contest by my wits
That they gave up, and took it for the best,
430   Or otherwise we should have had no rest.
Like a mad lion let my husband glare,
In the end he got the worst of the affair.
    "Then I would say, 'My dear, you ought to keep

In mind how gentle Wilkin looks, our sheep.
Come here, my husband, let me kiss your cheek!
You should be patient, too; you should be meek.
Of Job and of his patience when you prate
Your conscience ought to show a cleaner slate.
He should be patient who so well can preach.
440 If not, then it will fall on me to teach
The beauty of a peaceful wedded life.
For one of us must give in, man or wife,
And since men are more reasonable creatures
Than women are, it follows that *your* features
Ought to exhibit patience. Why do you groan?
You want my body yours, and yours alone?
Why, take it all! Welcome to every bit!
But curse you, Peter, unless you cherish it!
Were I inclined to peddle my *belle chose,*[32]
450 I could go about dressed freshly as a rose.
But I will keep it for your own sweet tooth.
It's your fault if we fight. By God, that's truth!'
        "This was the way I talked when I had need.
But now to my fourth husband I'll proceed.
        "This fourth I married was a roisterer.
He had a mistress, and my passions were,
Although I say it, strong; and altogether
I was young and stubborn, pert in every feather.
If anyone took up his harp to play,
460 How I could dance! I sang as merry a lay
As any nightingale when of sweet wine
I had drunk my draft. Metellius, the foul swine,
Who beat his spouse until he took her life
For drinking wine, had I only been his wife,
He'd never have frightened me away from drinking!
But after a drink, Venus gets in my thinking,
For just as true as cold engenders hail
A thirsty mouth goes with a thirsty tail.
Drinking destroys a woman's last defense
470 As lechers well know by experience.
        "But, Lord Christ, when it all comes back to me,
Remembering my youth and jollity,
It tickles me to the roots. It does me good
Down to this very day that while I could
I took my world, my time, and had my fling.

---

[32] *belle chose:* "Beautiful thing" in French.

But age, alas, that poisons everything
Has robbed me of my beauty and my pith.
Well, let it go! Good-by! The devil with
What cannot last! There's only this to tell:
480 The flour is gone, I've only chaff to sell.
Yet I'll contrive to keep a merry cheek!
But now of my fourth husband I will speak.
    "My heart was, I can tell you, full of spite
That in another he should find delight.
I paid him for this debt; I made it good.
I furnished him a cross of the same wood,
By God and by St. Joce—in no foul fashion,
Not with my flesh; but I put on such passion
And rendered him so jealous, I'll engage
490 I made him fry in his own grease for rage!
On earth, God knows, I was his purgatory;
I only hope his soul is now in glory.
God knows it was a sad song that he sung
When the shoe pinched him; sorely was he wrung!
Only he knew, and God, the devious system
By which outrageously I used to twist him.
He died when I came home from Jerusalem.
He is buried near the chancel, under the beam
That holds the cross. His tomb is less ornate
500 Than the sepulcher where Darius[33] lies in state
And which the paintings of Appelles graced
With subtle work. It would have been a waste
To bury him lavishly. Farewell! God save
His soul and give him rest! He's in his grave.
    "And now of my fifth husband let me tell.
God never let his soul go down to hell
Though he of all five was my scourge and flail!
I feel it on my ribs, right down the scale,
And ever shall until my dying day.
510 And yet he was so full of life and gay
In bed, and could so melt me and cajole me
When on my back he had a mind to roll me,
What matter if on every bone he'd beaten me!
He'd have my love, so quickly he could sweeten me.
I loved him best, in fact; for as you see,
His love was a more arduous prize for me.
We women, if I'm not to tell a lie,

---

[33] **Darius:** Legendary king of Persia (c. 521–486 B.C.E.), notorious for his wealth.

Are quaint in this regard. Put in our eye
A thing we cannot easily obtain,
520   All day we'll cry about it and complain.
Forbid a thing, we want it bitterly,
But urge it on us, then we turn and flee.
We are chary of what we hope that men will buy.
A throng at market makes the prices high;
Men set no value on cheap merchandise,
A truth all women know if they are wise.
        "My fifth, may God forgive his every sin,
I took for love, not money. He had been
An Oxford student once, but in our town
530   Was boarding with my good friend, Alison.
She knew each secret that I had to give
More than our parish priest did, as I live!
I told her my full mind, I shared it all.
For if my husband pissed against a wall
Or did a thing that might have cost his life,
To her, and to another neighbor's wife,
And to my niece, a girl whom I loved well,
His every thought I wouldn't blush to tell.
And often enough I told them, be it said.
540   God knows I made his face turn hot and red
For secrets he confided to his shame.
He knew he only had himself to blame.
        "And so it happened once that during Lent,
As I often did, to Alison's I went,
For I have loved my life long to be gay
And to walk out in April or in May
To hear the talk and seek a favorite haunt.
Jenkin the student, Alice, my confidante,
And I myself into the country went.
550   My husband was in London all that Lent.
I had the greater liberty to see
And to be seen by jolly company.
How could I tell beforehand in what place
Luck might be waiting with a stroke of grace?
And so I went to every merrymaking.
No pilgrimage was past my undertaking.
I was at festivals, and marriages,
Processions, preachings, and at miracle plays,
And in my scarlet clothes I made a sight.
560   Upon that costume neither moth nor mite
Nor any worm with ravening hunger fell.

And why, you ask? It was kept in use too well.
    "Now for what happened. In the fields we walked,
The three of us, and gallantly we talked,
The student and I, until I told him he,
If I became a widow, should marry me.
For I can say, and not with empty pride,
I have never failed for marriage to provide
Or other things as well. Let mice be meek;
570 A mouse's heart I hold not worth a leek.
He has one hole to scurry to, just one,
And if that fails him, he is quite undone.
    "I let this student think he had bewitched me.
(My mother with this piece of guile enriched me!)
All night I dreamed of him—this too I said;
He was killing me as I lay flat in bed;
My very bed in fact was full of blood;
But still I hoped it would result in good,
For blood betokens gold, as I have heard.
580 It was a fiction, dream and every word,
But I was following my mother's lore
In all this matter, as in many more.
    "Sirs—let me see; what did I mean to say?
Aha! By God, I have it! When he lay,
My fourth, of whom I've spoken, on his bier,
I wept of course; I showed but little cheer,
As wives must do, since custom has its place,
And with my kerchief covered up my face.
But since I had provided for a mate,
590 I did not cry for long, I'll freely state.
And so to church my husband on the morrow
Was borne away by neighbors in their sorrow.
Jenkin, the student, was among the crowd,
And when I saw him walk, so help me God,
Behind the bier, I thought he had a pair
Of legs and feet so cleanly turned and fair
I put my heart completely in his hold.
He was in fact some twenty winters old
And I was forty, to confess the truth;
600 But all my life I've still had a colt's tooth.
My teeth were spaced apart; that was the seal
St. Venus printed, and became me well.
So help me God, I was a lusty one,
Pretty and young and rich, and full of fun.
And truly, as my husbands have all said,

I was the best thing there could be in bed.
For I belong to Venus in my feelings,
Though I bring the heart of Mars to all my dealings.
From Venus come my lust and appetite,
610 From Mars I get my courage and my might,
Born under Taurus, while Mars stood therein.
Alas, alas, that ever love was sin!
I yielded to my every inclination
Through the predominance of my constellation;
This made me so I never could withhold
My chamber of Venus, if the truth be told,
From a good fellow; yet upon my face
Mars left his mark, and in another place.
For never, so may Christ grant me intercession,
620 Have I yet loved a fellow with discretion,
But always I have followed appetite,
Let him be long or short or dark or light.
I never cared, as long as he liked me,
What his rank was or how poor he might be.
      "What should I say, but when the month ran out,
This jolly student, always much about,
This Jenkin married me in solemn state.
To him I gave land, titles, the whole slate
Of goods that had been given me before;
630 But my repentance afterward was sore!
He wouldn't endure the pleasures I held dear.
By God, he gave me a lick once on the ear,
When from a book of his I tore a leaf,
So hard that from the blow my ear grew deaf.
I was stubborn as a lioness with young,
And by the truth I had a rattling tongue,
And I would visit, as I'd done before,
No matter what forbidding oath he swore.
Against this habit he would sit and preach me
640 Sermons enough, and he would try to teach me
Old Roman stories, how for his whole life
The man Sulpicius Gallus left his wife
Only because he saw her look one day
Bareheaded down the street from his doorway.
      "Another Roman he told me of by name
Who, since his wife was at a summer's game
Without his knowledge, thereupon forsook
The woman. In his Bible he would look
And find that proverb of the Ecclesiast
650 Where he enjoins and makes the stricture fast
That men forbid their wives to rove about.

Then he would quote me this, you needn't doubt:
'Build a foundation over sands or shallows,
Or gallop a blind horse across the fallows,
Let a wife traipse to shrines that some saint hallows,
And you are fit to swing upon the gallows.'
Talk as he would, I didn't care two haws
For his proverbs or his venerable saws.
Set right by him I never meant to be.
660 I hate the man who tells my faults to me,
And more of us than I do, by your pleasure.
This made him mad with me beyond all measure.
Under his yoke in no case would I go.

    "Now, by St. Thomas, I will let you know
Why from that book of his I tore a leaf,
For which I got the blow that made me deaf.

    "He had a book, *Valerius,* he called it,
And *Theophrastus,*[34] and he always hauled it
From where it lay to read both day and night
670 And laughed hard at it, such was his delight.
There was another scholar, too, at Rome
A cardinal, whose name was St. Jerome;
He wrote a book against Jovinian.
In the same book also were Tertullian,
Chrysippus, Trotula, Abbess Héloise
Who lived near Paris; it contained all these,
Bound in a single volume, and many a one
Besides; the Parables of Solomon
And Ovid's *Art of Love.*[35] On such vacation
680 As he could snatch from worldly occupation
He dredged this book for tales of wicked wives.
He knew more stories of their wretched lives
Than are told about good women in the Bible.
No scholar ever lived who did not libel
Women, believe me; to speak well of wives
Is quite beyond them, unless it be in lives
Of holy saints; no woman else will do.
Who was it painted the lion,[36] tell me who?

---

[34] *Valerius . . . Theophrastus:* Walter Map's *Letter of Valerius Concerning Not Marrying* and Theophrastus's *Book Concerning Marriage* are two misogynist treatises in Jenkin's library.

[35] **St. Jerome . . . Art of Love:** St. Jerome's *Reply to Jovinian* accused women of licentiousness; Tertullian wrote treatises on modesty; Chrysippus is a misogynist mentioned in Jerome. Trotula was a female doctor, and Héloïse (Eloise) is the infamous lover of Abelard. Ovid's *Art of Love* and the Parables of Solomon are two other scandalous texts.

[36] **Who . . . the lion:** Aesop tells of a lion who, when shown a picture of a man killing a lion, remarks that lions would draw a picture of the reverse.

By God, if women had only written stories
690 Like wits and scholars in their oratories,
They would have pinned on men more wickedness
Than the whole breed of Adam can redress.
Venus's children clash with Mercury's;
The two work evermore by contraries.
Knowledge and wisdom are of Mercury's giving,
Venus loves revelry and riotous living,
And with these clashing dispositions gifted
Each of them sinks when the other is uplifted.
Thus Mercury falls, God knows, in desolation
700 In the sign of Pisces, Venus's exaltation,
And Venus falls when Mercury is raised.
Thus by a scholar no woman can be praised.
The scholar, when he's old and cannot do
The work of Venus more than his old shoe,
Then sits he down, and in his dotage fond
Writes that no woman keeps her marriage bond!
    "But now for the story that I undertook—
To tell how I was beaten for a book.
    "Jenkin, one night, who never seemed to tire
710 Of reading in his book, sat by the fire
And first he read of Eve, whose wickedness
Delivered all mankind to wretchedness
For which in his own person Christ was slain
Who with his heart's blood bought us all again.
'By this,' he said, 'expressly you may find
That woman was the loss of all mankind.'
    "He read me next how Samson lost his hair.
Sleeping, his mistress clipped it off for fair;
Through this betrayal he lost both his eyes.
720 He read me then—and I'm not telling lies—
How Deianeira, wife of Hercules,
Caused him to set himself on fire. With these
He did not overlook the sad to-do
Of Socrates with *his* wives—he had two.
Xantippe emptied the pisspot on his head.
This good man sat as patient as if dead.
He wiped his scalp; he did not dare complain
Except to say 'With thunder must come rain.'
    "Pasiphaë,[37] who was the queen of Crete,

---

[37] **Pasiphaë:** Wife of Minos, king of Crete; angered at Minos, Poseidon caused Pasiphaë to fall in love with a bull, after which she gave birth to the Minotaur, part human and part beast.

730 For wickedness he thought her story sweet.
    Ugh! That's enough, it was a grisly thing,
    About her lust and filthy hankering!
    And Clytemnestra[38] in her lechery
    Who took her husband's life feloniously,
    He grew devout in reading of her treason.
    And then he told me also for what reason
    Unhappy Amphiaraus[39] lost his life.
    My husband had the story of *his* wife,
    Eriphyle, who for a clasp of gold
740 Went to his Grecian enemies and told
    The secret of her husband's hiding place,
    For which at Thebes he met an evil grace.
    Livia and Lucilia,[40] he went through
    Their tale as well, they killed their husbands, too.
    One killed for love, the other killed for hate.
    At evening Livia, when the hour was late,
    Poisoned her husband, for she was his foe.
    Lucilia doted on her husband so
    That in her lust, hoping to make him think
750 Ever of her, she gave him a love-drink
    Of such a sort he died before the morrow.
    And so at all turns husbands come to sorrow!
        "He told me then how one Latumius,
    Complaining to a friend named Arrius,
    Told him that in his garden grew a tree
    On which his wives had hanged themselves, all three,
    Merely for spite against their partnership.
    'Brother,' said Arrius, 'let me have a slip
    From this miraculous tree, for, begging pardon,
760 I want to go and plant it in my garden.'
        "Then about wives in recent times he read,
    How some had murdered husbands lying abed
    And all night long had let a paramour
    Enjoy them with the corpse flat on the floor;
    Or driven a nail into a husband's brain
    While he was sleeping, and thus he had been slain;
    And some had given them poison in their drink.

---

[38] **Clytemnestra:** Clytemnestra killed her husband, King Agamemnon, on his return from the Trojan War.

[39] **Unhappy Amphiaraus:** Knowing that only her brother Adrastus would survive the war against Thebes, Eriphyle, the wife of Argive warrior Amphiaraus, forced him to go into that battle.

[40] **Livia and Lucilia:** Notorious Roman women who killed their husbands; Lucilia's husband was the poet Lucretius.

He told more harm than anyone can think,
And seasoned his wretched stories with proverbs
770 Outnumbering all the blades of grass and herbs
On earth. 'Better a dragon for a mate,
Better,' he said, 'on a lion's whims to wait
Than on a wife whose way it is to chide.
Better,' he said, 'high in the loft to bide
Than with a railing wife down in the house.
They always, they are so contrarious,
Hate what their husbands like,' so he would say.
'A woman,' he said, 'throws all her shame away
When she takes off her smock.' And on he'd go:
780 'A pretty woman, unless she's chaste also,
Is like a gold ring stuck in a sow's nose.'
Who could imagine, who would half suppose
The gall my heart drank, raging at each drop?
    "And when I saw that he would never stop
Reading all night from his accursed book,
Suddenly, in the midst of it, I took
Three leaves and tore them out in a great pique,
And with my fist I caught him on the cheek
So hard he tumbled backward in the fire.
790 And up he jumped, he was as mad for ire
As a mad lion, and caught me on the head
With such a blow I fell down as if dead.
And seeing me on the floor, how still I lay,
He was aghast, and would have fled away,
Till I came to at length, and gave a cry.
'Have you killed me for my lands? Before I die,
False thief,' I said, 'I'll give you a last kiss!'
    "He came to me and knelt down close at this,
And said, 'So help me God, dear Alison,
800 I'll never strike you. For this thing I have done
You are to blame. Forgive me, I implore.'
So then I hit him on the cheek once more
And said, 'Thus far I am avenged, you thief.
I cannot speak. Now I shall die for grief.'
But finally, with much care and ado,
We reconciled our differences, we two.
He let me have the bridle in my hand
For management of both our house and land.
To curb his tongue he also undertook,
810 And on the spot I made him burn his book.
And when I had secured in full degree
By right of triumph the whole sovereignty,

And he had said, 'My dear, my own true wife,
Do as you will as long as you have life;
Preserve your honor and keep my estate,'
From that day on we had settled our debate.
I was as kind, God help me, day and dark
As any wife from India to Denmark,
And also true, and so he was to me.
820 I pray the Lord who sits in majesty
To bless his soul for Christ's own mercy dear.
And now I'll tell my tale, if you will hear."
     "Dame," laughed the Friar, "as I hope for bliss,
It was a long preamble to a tale, all this!"
     "God's arms!" the Summoner said, "it is a sin,
Good people, how friars are always butting in!
A fly and a friar will fall in every dish
And every question, whatever people wish.
What do you know, with your talk about 'preambling'?
830 Amble or trot or keep still or go scrambling,
You interrupt our pleasure."
                              "You think so,
Sir Summoner?" said the Friar. "Before I go,
I'll give the people here a chance or two
For a laugh at summoners, I promise you."
     "Curse on your face," the Summoner said, "curse me,
If I don't tell some stories, two or three,
On friars, before I get to Sittingborne,[41]
With which I'll twist your heart and make it mourn,
840 For you have lost your temper, I can see."
     "Be quiet," cried our Host, "immediately,"
And ordered, "Let the woman tell her tale.
You act like people who've got drunk on ale.
Do, Madame, tell us. That is the best measure."
     "All ready, sir," she answered "at your pleasure,
With the license of this worthy Friar here."
     "Madame, tell on," he said. "You have my ear."

THE WIFE OF BATH'S TALE

In the old days when King Arthur ruled the nation,
Whom Welshmen speak of with such veneration,
This realm we live in was a fairy land.
The fairy queen danced with her jolly band
On the green meadows where they held dominion.

---

[41] **Sittingborne:** A town forty miles north of London.

This was, as I have read, the old opinion;
I speak of many hundred years ago.
But no one sees an elf now, as you know,
For in our time the charity and prayers
10   And all the begging of these holy friars
Who swarm through every nook and every stream
Thicker than motes of dust in a sunbeam,
Blessing our chambers, kitchens, halls, and bowers,
Our cities, towns, and castles, our high towers,
Our villages, our stables, barns, and dairies,
They keep us all from seeing any fairies,
For where you might have come upon an elf
There now you find the holy friar himself
Working his district on industrious legs
20   And saying his devotions while he begs.
Women are safe now under every tree.
No incubus is there unless it's he,
And all they have to fear from him is shame.

    It chanced that Arthur had a knight who came
Lustily riding home one day from hawking,
And in his path he saw a maiden walking
Before him, stark alone, right in his course.
This young knight took her maidenhead by force,
A crime at which the outcry was so keen
30   It would have cost his neck, but that the queen,
With other ladies, begged the king so long
That Arthur spared his life, for right or wrong,
And gave him to the queen, at her own will,
According to her choice, to save or kill.

    She thanked the king, and later told this knight,
Choosing her time, "You are still in such a plight
Your very life has no security.
I grant your life, if you can answer me
This question: what is the thing that most of all
40   Women desire? Think, or your neck will fall
Under the ax! If you cannot let me know
Immediately, I give you leave to go
A twelvemonth and a day, no more, in quest
Of such an answer as will meet the test.
But you must pledge your honor to return
And yield your body, whatever you may learn."

    The knight sighed; he was rueful beyond measure.
But what! He could not follow his own pleasure.
He chose at last upon his way to ride
50   And with such answer as God might provide

To come back when the year was at the close.
And so he takes his leave, and off he goes.
    He seeks out every house and every place
Where he has any hope, by luck or grace,
Of learning what thing women covet most.
But it seemed he could not light on any coast
Where on this point two people would agree,
For some said wealth and some said jollity,
Some said position, some said sport in bed
60 And often to be widowed, often wed.
Some said that to a woman's heart what mattered
Above all else was to be pleased and flattered.
That shaft, to tell the truth, was a close hit.
Men win us best by flattery, I admit,
And by attention. Some say our greatest ease
Is to be free and do just as we please,
And not to have our faults thrown in our eyes,
But always to be praised for being wise.
And true enough, there's not one of us all
70 Who will not kick if you rub us on a gall.
Whatever vices we may have within,
We won't be taxed with any fault or sin.
    Some say that women are delighted well
If it is thought that they will never tell
A secret they are trusted with, or scandal.
But that tale isn't worth an old rake handle!
We women, for a fact, can never hold
A secret. Will you hear a story told?
Then witness Midas! For it can be read
80 In Ovid that he had upon his head
Two ass's ears that he kept out of sight
Beneath his long hair with such skill and sleight
That no one else besides his wife could guess.
He loved her well, and trusted her no less.
He begged her not to make his blemish known,
But keep her knowledge to herself alone.
She swore that never, though to save her skin,
Would she be guilty of so mean a sin,
And yet it seemed to her she nearly died
90 Keeping a secret locked so long inside.
It swelled about her heart so hard and deep
She was afraid some word was bound to leap
Out of her mouth, and since there was no man
She dared to tell, down to a swamp she ran—
Her heart, until she got there, all agog—

And like a bittern booming in the bog
She put her mouth close to the watery ground:
"Water, do not betray me with your sound!
I speak to you, and you alone," she said.
100 "Two ass's ears grow on my husband's head!
And now my heart is whole, now it is out.
I'd burst if I held it longer, past all doubt."
Safely, you see, awhile you may confide
In us, but it will out; we cannot hide
A secret. Look in Ovid if you care
To learn what followed; the whole tale is there.
     This knight, when he perceived he could not find
What women covet most, was low in mind;
But the day had come when homeward he must ride,
110 And as he crossed a wooded countryside
Some four and twenty ladies there by chance
He saw, all circling in a woodland dance,
And toward this dance he eagerly drew near
In hope of any counsel he might hear.
But the truth was, he had not reached the place
When dance and all, they vanished into space.
No living soul remained there to be seen
Save an old woman sitting on the green,
As ugly a witch as fancy could devise.
120 As he approached her she began to rise
And said, "Sir knight, here runs no thoroughfare.
What are you seeking with such anxious air?
Tell me! The better may your fortune be.
We old folk know a lot of things," said she.
     "Good mother," said the knight, "my life's to pay,
That's all too certain, if I cannot say
What women covet most. If you could tell
That secret to me, I'd requite you well."
     "Give me your hand," she answered. "Swear me true
130 That whatsoever I next ask of you,
You'll do it if it lies within your might
And I'll enlighten you before the night."
     "Granted, upon my honor," he replied.
     "Then I dare boast, and with no empty pride,
Your life is safe," she told him. "Let me die
If the queen herself won't say the same as I.
Let's learn if the haughtiest of all who wear
A net or coverchief upon their hair
Will be so forward as to answer 'no'
140 To what I'll teach you. No more; let us go."

With that she whispered something in his ear,
And told him to be glad and have no fear.
　　When they had reached the court, the knight declared
That he had kept his day, and was prepared
To give his answer, standing for his life.
Many the wise widow, many the wife,
Many the maid who rallied to the scene,
And at the head as justice sat the queen.
Then silence was enjoined; the knight was told
150　In open court to say what women hold
Precious above all else. He did not stand
Dumb like a beast, but spoke up at command
And plainly offered them his answering word
In manly voice, so that the whole court heard.
　　"My liege and lady, most of all," said he,
"Women desire to have the sovereignty
And sit in rule and government above
Their husbands, and to have their way in love.
That is what most you want. Spare me or kill
160　As you may like; I stand here by your will."
　　No widow, wife, or maid gave any token
Of contradicting what the knight had spoken.
He should not die; he should be spared instead;
He was worthy of his life, the whole court said.
　　The old woman whom the knight met on the green
Sprang up at this. "My sovereign lady queen,
Before your court has risen, do me right!
It was I who taught this answer to the knight,
For which he pledged his honor in my hand,
170　Solemnly, that the first thing I demand,
He would do it, if it lay within his might.
Before the court I ask you, then, sir knight,
To take me," said the woman, "as your wife,
For well you know that I have saved your life.
Deny me, on your honor, if you can."
　　"Alas," replied this miserable man,
"That was my promise, it must be confessed.
For the love of God, though, choose a new request!
Take all my wealth, and let my body be."
180　　"If that's your tune, then curse both you and me,"
She said "Though I am ugly, old, and poor,
I'll have, for all the metal and the ore
That under earth is hidden or lies above,
Nothing, except to be your wife and love."
　　"My love? No, my damnation, if you can!

Alas," he said, "that any of my clan
Should be so miserably misallied!"
    All to no good; force overruled his pride,
And in the end he is constrained to wed,
190 And marries his old wife and goes to bed.
    Now some will charge me with an oversight
In failing to describe the day's delight,
The merriment, the food, the dress at least.
But I reply, there was no joy nor feast;
There was only sorrow and sharp misery.
He married her in private, secretly,
And all day after, such was his distress,
Hid like an owl from his wife's ugliness.
    Great was the woe this knight had in his head
200 When in due time they both were brought to bed.
He shuddered, tossed, and turned, and all the while
His old wife lay and waited with a smile.
    "Is every knight so backward with a spouse?
Is it," she said, "a law in Arthur's house?
I am your love, your own, your wedded wife,
I am the woman who has saved your life.
I have never done you anything but right.
Why do you treat me this way the first night?
You must be mad, the way that you behave!
210 Tell me my fault, and as God's love can save,
I will amend it, truly, if I can."
    "Amend it?" answered this unhappy man.
"It can never be amended, truth to tell.
You are so loathsome and so old as well,
And your low birth besides is such a cross
It is no wonder that I turn and toss.
God take my woeful spirit from my breast!"
    "Is this," she said, "the cause of your unrest?"
    "No wonder!" said the knight. "It truly is."
220   "Now sir," she said, "I could amend all this
Within three days, if it should please me to,
And if you deal with me as you should do.
    "But since you speak of that nobility
That comes from ancient wealth and pedigree,
As if *that* constituted gentlemen,
I hold such arrogance not worth a hen!
The man whose virtue is pre-eminent,
In public and alone, always intent
On doing every generous act he can,
230 Take him—he is the greatest gentleman!

Christ wills that we should claim nobility
From him, not from old wealth or family.
Our elders left us all that they were worth
And through their wealth and blood we claim high birth,
But never, since it was beyond their giving,
Could they bequeath to us their virtuous living;
Although it first conferred on them the name
Of gentlemen, they could not leave that claim!
    "Dante the Florentine on this was wise:

240 'Frail is the branch on which man's virtues rise' —
Thus runs his rhyme — 'God's goodness wills that we
Should claim from him alone nobility.'[42]
Thus from our elders we can only claim
Such temporal things as men may hurt and maim.
    "It is clear enough that true nobility
Is not bequeathed along with property,
For many a lord's son does a deed of shame
And yet, God knows, enjoys his noble name.
But though descended from a noble house

250 And elders who were wise and virtuous,
If he will not follow his elders, who are dead,
But leads, himself, a shameful life instead,
He is not noble, be he duke or earl.
It is the churlish deed that makes the churl.
And therefore, my dear husband, I conclude
That though my ancestors were rough and rude,
Yet may Almighty God confer on me
The grace to live, as I hope, virtuously.
Call me of noble blood when I begin

260 To live in virtue and to cast out sin.
    "As for my poverty, at which you grieve,
Almighty God in whom we all believe
In willful poverty chose to lead his life,
And surely every man and maid and wife
Can understand that Jesus, heaven's king,
Would never choose a low or vicious thing.
A poor and cheerful life is nobly led;
So Seneca and others have well said.
The man so poor he doesn't have a stitch,

270 If he thinks himself repaid, I count him rich.
He that is covetous, he is the poor man,
Pining to have the things he never can.

---

[42] **'God's goodness . . . nobility':** *Purgatorio,* Canto VII.

It is of cheerful mind, true poverty.
Juvenal[43] says about it happily:
'The poor man as he goes along his way
And passes thieves is free to sing and play.'
Poverty is a good we loathe, a great
Reliever of our busy worldly state,
A great amender also of our minds
280 As he that patiently will bear it finds.
And poverty, for all it seems distressed,
Is a possession no one will contest.
Poverty, too, by bringing a man low,
Helps him the better both God and self to know.
Poverty is a glass where we can see
Which are our true friends, as it seems to me.
So, sir, I do not wrong you on this score;
Reproach me with my poverty no more.
      "Now, sir, you tax me with my age; but, sir,
290 You gentlemen of breeding all aver
That men should not despise old age, but rather
Grant an old man respect, and call him 'father.'
      "If I am old and ugly, as you have said,
You have less fear of being cuckolded,
For ugliness and age, as all agree,
Are notable guardians of chastity.
But since I know in what you take delight,
I'll gratify your worldly appetite.
      "Choose now, which of two courses you will try:
300 To have me old and ugly till I die
But evermore your true and humble wife,
Never displeasing you in all my life,
Or will you have me rather young and fair
And take your chances on who may repair
Either to your house on account of me
Or to some other place, it well may be.
Now make your choice, whichever you prefer."
      The knight took thought, and sighed, and said to her
At last, "My love and lady, my dear wife,
310 In your wise government I put my life.
Choose for yourself which course will best agree
With pleasure and honor, both for you and me.
I do not care, choose either of the two;
I am content, whatever pleases you."

---

[43]**Juvenal:** Roman satiric poet (c. 60–140 C.E.); see *Satires* X (Book 1) for the quote.

"Then have I won from you the sovereignty,
Since I may choose and rule at will?" said she.
     He answered, "That is best, I think, dear wife."
     "Kiss me," she said. "Now we are done with strife,
For on my word, I will be both to you,
320 That is to say, fair, yes, and faithful too.
May I die mad unless I am as true
As ever wife was since the world was new.
Unless I am as lovely to be seen
By morning as an empress or a queen
Or any lady between east and west,
Do with my life or death as you think best.
Lift up the curtain, see what you may see."
     And when the knight saw what had come to be
And knew her as she was, so young, so fair,
330 His joy was such that it was past compare.
He took her in his arms and gave her kisses
A thousand times on end; he bathed in blisses.
And she obeyed him also in full measure
In everything that tended to his pleasure.
     And so they lived in full joy to the end.
And now to all us women may Christ send
Submissive husbands, full of youth in bed,
And grace to outlive all the men we wed.
And I pray Jesus to cut short the lives
340 Of those who won't be governed by their wives;
And old, ill-tempered niggards who hate expense,
God promptly bring them down with pestilence!

TEXT IN CONTEXT

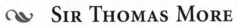 SIR THOMAS MORE
B. ENGLAND, 1478–1535

The early life of Sir Thomas More marked him for a future of uncommon privilege and authority, but no one could have predicted the many parts he would play in an astonishing intellectual, religious, social, and political drama, not to mention the precipitous rise and fatal fall of his personal fortunes. Born in London, the son of a judge, he became a page in the house of the Archbishop of Canterbury at twelve, studied law at Oxford and practiced it at the Inns of Court, entering Parliament in 1504 at the age of 26. Soon his home attracted the leading intellectual lights of England and northern Europe, and he engaged in a variety of projects, including writing history, religion, and poetry, and translating works from Latin. As one of the members of the philosophical school of HUMANISM, he was a close friend of Desiderius Erasmus of Rotterdam (1466–1536), who wrote his most famous work, *In Praise of Folly* (1509), while staying in More's house in London. The young More joined Erasmus and his cohorts in a radical interrogation of Christianity as well as a critique of the operations of the modern state. In later years, however, More's path would diverge significantly from the skeptical practices of humanism.

Like Erasmus, the young More adopted the persona of an ironist and satirist, holding conventional wisdom up to scrutiny and demanding that life be lived with intellectual curiosity, critical study, and above all independence of spirit. In 1506 the two authors collaborated on a Latin translation of the Greek playwright Lucian, whose satirical style would influence their own celebrated works, particularly Erasmus' *In Praise of Folly* and More's *Utopia* (1516). But despite the interest both

Hans Holbein the Younger, Portrait of Sir Thomas More *Holbein's famous portrait was painted in 1527 when Sir Thomas More was in the service of Henry VIII, the English Tudor king. One critic has called it "a straightforward but rather impersonal likeness, in which [More's] robes of state and the Tudor rose on his gold livery collar tell us as much, or as little, about him as his detached gaze."* (© The Frick Collection, New York)

men shared in the classical literature of Greece and Rome, Erasmus' religious interest influenced More to a greater degree in the long run. This influence was manifested in the desire they shared to address the weaknesses of contemporary spiritual life by recalling the roots of Christian belief.

In More's early masterpiece, *Utopia,* the citizens are a people guided by natural law rather than religious doctrine, reflecting the humanist critique he had undertaken. But—and this is the critical point—More himself remained a relentless defender of the Catholic faith all his life, choosing to address the weaknesses of the Church from within. While Erasmus maintained contact with the rebellious young priest **Martin Luther**, who was excommunicated from the Catholic p. 1754 Church in 1521 and founded his own Protestant religion in the decade that followed, More's support of Catholicism intensified to the extent that he carried his convictions to the political stage in England, becoming the great enemy of Protestantism after his appointment as Lord Chancellor by King Henry VIII in 1529.

Knowledge and Power.   More might have lived out his days as a Latin classicist and a philosophical and religious writer of the first magnitude. In his early life he displayed no attraction to the exercise of authority for its own sake. His unfinished *History of Richard III,* written for the most part before the publication of *Utopia,* exposed King Richard's abuse of power on the throne of England and later served as a model for Shakespeare's famous play. More hardly could have realized how prophetic his historical study would turn out to be when he entered into the service of King Henry VIII in 1517. At first, there appeared to be a meeting of minds between King and commoner. Henry spent long hours discussing matters of learning and politics with his new counselor, obviously benefiting from the sessions. After King Henry sent More on a diplomatic mission to Emperor Charles V, he knighted More in 1521, made him Speaker of the House of Commons in 1523, and then Lord Chancellor, second in power only to the king himself, in 1529.

During his association with Henry VIII, More was increasingly caught up in defense of the Catholic Church against the Protestant movement. In particular, he helped Henry VIII write *Defense of the Seven Sacraments,* a treatise against Martin Luther. For this, Pope Leo X bestowed the title Defender of the Faith on Henry in 1521. Next, More responded to Martin Luther's attack on Henry VIII with another pamphlet. Then he turned his attention to the followers of William Tyndale, whose Protestant translation of the Bible was published in 1525. His growing fury at the reformers was not restricted to written polemics or legal warnings. After his appointment as Lord Chancellor, he had six of Tyndale's supporters burnt at the stake and saw to it that others were imprisoned.

But More's own service under King Henry VIII would come to a bitter end. As he grew older he became not only more certain in his Christian faith, but more skeptical of the natural decency of mankind and more aware of the moral tragedies brought about by human folly, including that of his royal master. He was unable to stop Henry VIII's passion for wars, his impulsive and lust-driven marriages, and his brutal termination of relationships with women unable to bear him a male heir. Finally, after Henry VIII became estranged from Pope Clement VII, who refused to grant him an annulment to his marriage with Catherine of Aragon, More refused to swear an oath of allegiance to the maddened King. For this, he was imprisoned in the Tower of London in 1534 and beheaded in 1535. (Outspoken to the end, he asked the executioner to spare his beard, because *it,* at least, had never committed treason.) His severed head was mounted over London Bridge as a sign to others who might rebel against the King's authority. His last work, the *Dialogue of Comfort Against Tribulation,* which he wrote in anticipation of his execution while imprisoned in the Tower, is reminiscent of Boethius's, **Consolation of Philosophy**, written before his own execution by his lord, the Emperor Theodoric, a millennium before.

p. 1633

Utopia, **the Work.**   *Utopia* is divided into two parts, or "books" as they are called. Book One describes a meeting between More, his friend Peter Giles of Antwerp, and the fictional character Raphael Hythloday, supposedly a sailor who has accompanied the discoverer Amerigo Vespucci on his last three voyages to the New World. The name of this clever but somewhat addled character has significance: Raphael suggests the welcoming archangel from the Apocryphal Book of Tobias, while Hythloday appears to be derived from Greek *huthlos,* "nonsense," and *daien,* "peddlar." For most of Book One, More and Giles listen to Hythloday offering his views on a number of matters, ending with his praise of the inhabitants of the island of Utopia, who he says own property in common and "are so well governed with so few laws." In Book Two, having been asked to do so, Hythloday describes Utopia, its people and customs, in a more or less orderly fashion. At the end of Book Two, after Hythloday describes the island's attitude towards religion, More the author responds to this long, circumstantial, and sometimes argumentative account.

The work was completed the year before Martin Luther wrote his Ninety-Five Theses and nailed them to his church's door in Wittenberg, Germany. More was still at the stage of gentlemanly argument concerning church reform when he wrote *Utopia,* but it is generally conceded that his view of the fictional society he describes is strict, rigorous, and at times judgmental. His satire cuts two ways. The reasonable practices of the people of Utopia are set against the moral confusion and decay of modern-day Europe, while their lack of adherence to Christianity is treated as soulless and dangerous.

More made some effort to maintain that this was a true account he engaged in, later printing a series of letters supposedly exchanged among his humanist friends, including Peter Giles, discussing the encounter with Hythloday as if it had occurred and debating the merits of Utopia as if it were a real place. This effort to achieve the appearance of truth is obviously rhetorical, having antecedents in the work of Greek and Roman writers. It was also an effort to maintain public interest in the book, an effort that by and large succeeded.

The More of *Utopia*.   Scholars have deliberated over the apparent hardening of purpose in the life of Thomas More. It is certainly true

Thomas More's Island of Utopia, engraving, 1518
This illustration appeared in one of the first editions of Utopia. *Its creator was*
Ambrosius Holbein, brother of the more famous Hans Holbein the Younger.
(The Art Archive)

that the younger More was remarkable for his spontaneity, curiosity,
and spirit of innovation. He was also very much a creature of his time.
Like Erasmus, he embraced the printing press as a vehicle of reform
as well as a means of self-promotion. He also saw it as an instrument
for the recovery of lost knowledge. The study of the Bible, the enjoyment of the Latin classics, engagement in philosophical dispute and

Early Modern Europe: The World According to Thomas More

Thomas More wrote *Utopia* in 1516, several decades after the European voyages of discovery began. The only discovery narrative we are certain More read was *The First Four Voyages of Amerigo Vespucci,* published in Lisbon in 1504. In the first voyage, described by Vespucci in a letter to Piero Soderini, passages such as the following may have caught More's eye as he was constructing *Utopia,* both for what was said and the way in which it was presented.

> [The natives] live and are contented with what nature gives them. The wealth that we enjoy in this our Europe and elsewhere, such as gold, jewels, pearls, and other riches, they hold as nothing: and although they have them in their own hands, they do not labor to obtain them, nor do they value them.

Because *Utopia* itself is resonant in irony and contradiction, it seems fitting that of all the voyage narratives circulated at the time, Vespucci's account was thought to be least reliable. Vespucci was a shadowy figure, a self-publicist who wrote in poor Italian, described improbable events, and told salacious stories about native women. Perhaps More intended some of Vespucci's unreliable character to rub off on his erratic fictional narrator, Hythloday, as well.

Subsequent accounts of voyages to imagined lands dot the Early Modern Period. While not as rhetorically sophisticated as More's *Utopia,* they share the quality of being "about" something more than the spectacle described. Significant among them is the *The New Atlantis* (1627) by the prominent philosopher and lawyer Francis Bacon (1561–1626). A traveler journeys to the fictional land of Bensalem, where he is told of the history of its founder, its acquaintance with Christianity, and its emphasis on scientific experiments. Unlike Utopia, Bensalem is a world in which scientific knowledge is encouraged and of great use to its citizens. This fable may be in part a tract advocating the creation of a scientific academy in Britain. But it also justifies the pursuit of knowledge as the pursuit of higher standing in the world—of power, even of empire.

Any work meriting comparison to More's strangely speculative, at times playful, account has to deal with some of the mental operations of *Utopia:* the use of the narrative itself as part of the process of discovery, the contrast of the discovered world and the European world of expectations, the lessons to be derived from the discovery, and the element of satire—both against the civilized European world and the discovered world. Taking these matters into account, *Utopia's* most compelling descendants are Shakespeare's *The Tempest* (p. 1818) and Swift's *Gulliver's Travels* (see Volume 2).

controversy—all these activities received an enormous boost from the early printed books of his day. At the same time, More studied the contemporary writings of the first navigators of the ocean, their discoveries of strange lands and their half-truthful, half-fantastic accounts of the human beings, animals, and natural features they found there. His *Utopia* borrows from the old—Plato's *Republic* and other classical speculations on the state of the ideal society—while it also includes the new—the stories of "lost" worlds encountered by the new discoverers.

Perhaps the greatest debt More shows to classical learning comes from Lucian (c. 125 C.E.–180 C.E.), the Greek rhetorician and satirist whose dialogues More and Erasmus had studied closely. The kind of dialogue that takes place in *Utopia* is not Platonic, arriving at conclusions foreseen by the philosopher who dominates the discussion; instead it is Ciceronian, entertaining several views without producing a result upon which the participants can agree. There is still, however, room for satirical attacks on existing practices and moral pronouncements about human behavior. Certain arguments are undertaken so vigorously that one may assume agreement on the part of the writer. A second important element in More's *Utopia,* having to do with its status as fiction, also shows dependency on Lucian's satire. The most popular work of Lucian was *A True Story,* which contrary to its name is a fictional account of a trip to the moon. In effect, More created a new genre, the utopian novel, with a little help from his classical guides.

In one sense, More's fabulous island is modeled after England. The landscape bears similar markers, down to the name of the capital city, Amaurot ("Darkling City")—foggy perhaps, like London. But More derives the word "utopia" itself from the Greek words *eu topos,* "good place," and *ou topos,* "nowhere." His attitude toward religion in the book may appear to be similarly enigmatic. The natives of Utopia embrace no organized religion, only a common belief in God. Both their faith and their social organization suggests the primitive communism of early Christian societies, in which property was shared in common, though this is something More never insists upon. But while it appears that the citizens of Utopia are at least as moral as believing Christians in the world, it also seems they are missing something spiritually. Perhaps most confusing is the fact that the supposed narrator of the story, Hythloday, the one purely fictional character in the work, is not completely reliable. His bias towards the perfection of this orderly state is not fully endorsed by the author or his friends, despite the carefully developed fiction that Hythloday is a real person known to the company of humanists surrounding More himself. What, then, is the meaning of the work as a whole?

To its many readers, *Utopia* has been many things: a popular and often imitated literary satire, a serious political proposal for a reformed society, or a somber reflection on human character and its limitations. A more personal approach to the controversy about the nature of his book involves consideration of the predispositions of More's thinking. How much continuity exists between the young philosopher and the mature Catholic moralist? Is the book an incitement to consider the ordering of society from a new perspective or a commentary on the inability of society to exist in an unregulated state of freedom? Perhaps some continuity can be found in this: More was always a careful and disciplined thinker, even when he used satire as his preferred form of expression. He expected the reader to be able to arrive at answers through a similar reasoning process. It is that process that gives a semblance of truth to More's cleverest work of fiction.

■ **FURTHER RESEARCH**

Translations
Adams, Robert M. *Utopia: A Revised Translation, Backgrounds, Criticism*. 1992.
Miller, Clarence. *Utopia*. 2001.

Biography
Ackroyd, Peter. *The Life of Thomas More*. 1998.
Guy, John. *Thomas More*. 2000.
Marius, Richard. *Thomas More: a Biography*. 1984.

History and Criticism
Baker-Smith, Dominic. *More's Utopia*. 1991.
Greenblatt, Stephen. *Renaissance Self-Fashioning*. 1980.
Hexter, J. H. *The Vision of Politics on the Eve of the Reformation*. 1973.
Logan, George. *The Meaning of More's Utopia*. 1983.
Nelson, William, ed. *Twentieth Century Interpretations of Utopia*. 1968.
Sylvester, R. S., and G. Marc'hadour, eds. *Essential Articles for the Study of Thomas More*. 1977.

FROM

 # Utopia

Translated by Clarence H. Miller

ON THE BEST FORM OF A COMMONWEALTH

AND

ON THE NEW ISLAND OF UTOPIA

a Truly Precious Book
No Less Profitable than Delightful
by
the Most Distinguished and Learned Gentleman
Thomas More
Citizen and Undersheriff
of the Illustrious City of London

BOOK 2

THE DISCOURSE OF RAPHAEL HYTHLODAY
ON THE BEST FORM OF A COMMONWEALTH

The island of the Utopians is two hundred miles across in the middle, where it is widest, and throughout most of the island it is not much narrower, but toward both ends it narrows a bit. These ends, curling around into a circle with a circumference of five hundred miles, make the whole island look like a new moon. The sea flows in between the horns through a strait about eleven miles wide and then spreads out into a huge empty space protected from the wind on all sides, like an enormous, smooth, unruffled lake; thus almost the whole inner coast serves as a harbor and allows ships to go from shore to shore in all directions, much to the advantage of the people. The jaws of the strait are dangerous, on one side because of shallows, on the other because of rocks. In just about the middle of the channel, one rock stands out, visible and hence harmless; they have built and garrisoned a tower on it. The other rocks are hidden and treacherous. The channels are known only to the Utopians themselves, and hence it hardly ever happens that a foreigner enters the bay without a Utopian pilot. Indeed they themselves find it hard to enter it safely, except that they set their course by means of some signals on the shore. By moving these to different locations, they can easily lure an enemy fleet to shipwreck, no matter how large it is.

On the outside coast there are not a few ports. But everywhere the landing places are so well defended, either naturally or artificially, that a few troops can keep a huge army from coming ashore. According to report, however (and the appearance of the place bears it out), their land was once not surrounded by the ocean. But Utopus, who conquered the island and named it after himself (for before that time it had been called Abraxa) and who brought its crude and rustic mob to a level of culture and humanity beyond almost all other mortals, after he won the victory at his first assault, had a channel cut fifteen miles wide at the point where the land adjoined the continent, and thus caused the sea to flow all around the land. And since he set not only the inhabitants to this task but also employed his own soldiers (to keep the inhabitants from thinking the work was imposed on them as a humiliation), the labor was shared by a great multitude of workers and was finished in an incredibly short time, so that the neighboring peoples (who at first ridiculed the project as silly) were overwhelmed with wonder and fear.

The island has fifty-four cities,[1] all of them large and splendid and having exactly the same language, customs, institutions, and laws. They have the same layout and they look the same, insofar as the terrain allows. Those which are closest to each other are separated by twenty-four miles. None is so isolated that it is more than a day's journey on foot from another city. Every year each city sends three old and experienced citizens to Amaurot[2] to discuss problems common to the whole

---

[1] **fifty-four cities:** England had fifty-three counties, not counting the royal city of London. Evidently More equated the city-states of Utopia with these counties.

[2] **Amaurot:** The capital city. Many details of the physical description of Amaurot are comparable to that of London: its location on a hill, its situation on a tidal river, the presence of a smaller stream, and so on.

island. For that city, which is located at the navel of the land, so to speak, and hence is most convenient as a meeting place for the delegates from everywhere, is the capital and chief city.

The land is so well distributed that no city has less than twelve miles of ground on all sides, though it may have much more in some directions, namely where the cities are furthest apart from one another. None of them is driven by any desire to extend its boundaries. Indeed, whatever land they have, they consider themselves its tenant-farmers, not its landlords. In the countryside, throughout the fields, they have conveniently located houses, each provided with farming tools. They are inhabited by the citizens, who take turns going out to live there. No country household has fewer than forty men and women, besides the two slaves bound to the land; it is presided over by a master and mistress who are sober and mature. Every thirty households are ruled by one phylarch.[3] Every year twenty from each household return to the city, having fulfilled their two-year stint in the country. They are replaced by twenty substitutes from the city, who are to be trained by those who have already been there a year and hence are more skilled in farmwork; the substitutes themselves will train another group the following year, for if everyone were new and equally ignorant of farming, the crops would suffer from lack of skill. Although this system of exchanging farmers is customary, to keep anyone from being forced to live this hard life for a long time, nevertheless many who have a natural bent for agricultural pursuits apply for and are allowed additional years.

They farm the land, raise cattle, cut wood, and convey it to the cities by the most convenient route, whether by sea or by land. They raise a huge number of chickens, and they have a marvelous method of doing it. The hens do not sit on the eggs. For the Utopians themselves tend a great number of eggs, keeping them alive and hatching them them in constant warmth. As soon as the chicks emerge from the shell, they recognize and follow human beings around as if they were their mothers.

They raise very few horses and none but high-spirited ones, which serve no other purpose than the training of young people in horsemanship. For ploughing and hauling they use oxen; they grant that they are inferior to horses in short sprints, but they consider them superior over the long haul and less subject to diseases; moreover, they require less effort and expense to maintain, and when they have served out their term, they can be used for food.

Grain they use only for bread. For they drink either wine made from grapes or cider made from apples or pears or else plain water, which they often boil with honey or licorice, of which they have plenty. Although they know (and they know it very well) how much produce is needed by a city and its surrounding population, they plant far more grain and raise far more cattle than they need for their own use, giving the surplus to their neighbors. All the supplies that are necessary but not available in the country they get from the city, giving nothing in exchange; the city magistrates provide them the goods with no bargaining. For every month many of them gather there on the feast day. On the day of harvesting, the phylarchs of the

---

[3] **phylarch:** From a Greek compound, *phylon* + *arche*, meaning "tribal leader."

farmers inform the city magistrates how many citizens should be sent out; since they arrive at precisely the right time, such a large crowd of workers gets the harvest almost completely done in one day if they have good weather.

THEIR CITIES, ESPECIALLY AMAUROT

If you know one of their cities, you know them all, so similar are they in all respects (so far as the terrain allows). And so I will describe one of them (it doesn't much matter which one). But why choose any one except Amaurot? For it is the most notable and takes precedence over the others because the senate meets there; and no other is better known to me, since I lived there for five whole years.

Amaurot, then, is situated on the gentle slope of a mountain; its shape is almost square. Beginning almost at the crest of the hill, it stretches two miles down to the river Anyder;[4] its width is slightly greater along the river than it is at the hilltop. The source of the Anyder is eighty miles above Amaurot, a small spring which is amplified by tributaries, two of them sizeable, until, when it reaches the city itself, it is five hundred yards wide. Then for sixty miles it flows on, getting wider and finally flowing into the ocean. In the space between the city and the coast, and also for some miles above the city, the tide flows and ebbs for six whole hours in a swift current. Seawater flows in to a point thirty miles upstream, filling the whole channel of the Anyder and driving the river water upstream. It also makes the water salty somewhat higher up; from there the river gradually grows fresh and it is pure when it flows by the city. And at ebb tide it flows pure and fresh nearly all the way to the mouth of the river.

The city is connected to the opposite bank of the river by a bridge made not of pilings and planks but of beautifully arched stonework; it is placed at a point furthest from the sea so that ships can sail unobstructed along that whole side of the city. They also have another stream, not large but very gentle and pleasant, which gushes from a spring on the same mountain where the city is located; it flows down through the middle of the city into the Anyder. The Amaurotians have fortified the head and spring of this stream, which is located a little outside the city, surrounding it with walls that link it to the city, so that if an enemy ever attacks them, the water cannot be diverted or contaminated. From this stream the water is channeled in tile conduits to the various districts in the lower parts of the city. Where the terrain makes this impossible, rainwater collected in large cisterns serves the same purpose.

The city is surrounded by a high, thick wall with many towers and bastions. On three sides the wall is surrounded by a moat that is dry but wide and deep and blocked by thorn hedges; on the fourth side the river itself serves as a moat. The streets are laid out to facilitate traffic and to offer protection from the wind. The buildings are by no means ugly; the houses extend in a continuous row along the whole block, facing the row on the other side of the street; the housefronts along each block are separated by a street twenty feet wide. Behind the houses, a large

---

[4] **Anyder:** From Greek, meaning "waterless." Perhaps referring to its tidal nature (i.e. the Thames also flows into the sea).

garden, as long on each side as the block itself, is hemmed in on all sides by the backs of the rowhouses.

There is no house which does not have a door opening on the street and a back-door into the garden. The double doors, which open easily with a push of the hand and close again automatically, allow anyone to come in — so there is nothing private anywhere. For every ten years they exchange the houses themselves by drawing lots. The Utopians place great stock by these gardens; in them they grow vines, fruit trees, herbs, and flowers, all so bright and well tended that I have never seen anything more flourishing and elegant. In gardening they are motivated not only by their own pleasure but also by competition among the various blocks to see which has the best garden. And certainly you will not easily find any feature of the whole city that is of greater use to the citizens or gives them more pleasure. For that reason the founder of the city seems to have devoted more attention to these gardens than he did to any-thing else.

For they say that in the very beginning Utopus himself laid out the whole plan of the city. But he left it to succeeding ages to complete the adornment and landscaping that could not be completed during one lifetime. Thus in their annals, which have been diligently and scrupulously kept up since the island was captured 1,760 years ago, it is recorded that at first their dwellings were humble, mere huts and shacks, built of wood gathered at random, the walls plastered with mud. The roofs came to a point and were thatched with straw. But now all houses have a handsome appearance and are built three stories high. The outer sections of the walls are made of fieldstone, quarried rock, or brick, and the space between is filled up with gravel and cement. The roofs are flat and are coated with a sort of plaster which is not expensive but is formulated so as to be fireproof and more weather-resistant than lead. They com-monly use glass (which is very plentiful there) to keep out the wind; sometimes they also use thin linen, soaked in clear oil or treated with resin — a method which has two advantages: it lets in more light and keeps out more drafts. . . .

OCCUPATIONS

Farming is the one occupation in which all of them are skilled, men and women alike. They are all trained in it from childhood on, partly by instruction in the class-room, partly by being taken out to play at it, as it were, in the fields near the city, not merely looking on but doing the work themselves for bodily exercise.

Besides farming (which, as I said, is common to all of them) everyone is taught some trade of his own. The ordinary ones are working with wool or linen or labor-ing as a stone mason, blacksmith, or carpenter. No other trade there employs any number worth mentioning. As for their clothing — which is uniform throughout the island for all age groups and varies only to indicate sex or marital status, and which is not unappealing to the eye, allows freedom of movement, and is adapted to either heat or cold — as for their clothing, I say, each household makes its own.

Everybody learns one or the other of these trades, including women as well as men. But women, as the weaker sex, engage in lighter crafts, mostly working with wool or linen. The other trades, which require more strength, are relegated to the men. Generally children take up their father's trade, for most are naturally inclined to it. But if anyone is drawn to another occupation, he is transferred by adoption into another household where he can work at the trade he wants to pursue. The move is supervised not only by his father but also by the magistrates, to make sure the master of his adoptive household is respectable and responsible. Actually, if someone has mastered one trade and wants to learn another besides, he gets permission to do so by the same procedure. When he has mastered both, he practices whichever he wants to, unless the city has a greater need for the other.

The chief and practically the only function of the syphogrants[5] is to take care and see to it that no one lounges around in idleness but rather that everyone practices his trade diligently, but not working from early morning till late at night, exhausted by constant labor like a beast of burden. For such grievous labor is fit only for slaves, and yet almost everywhere it is the way workmen live, except in Utopia. Dividing the day and night into twenty-four equal hours, they devote only six to work, three before noon, when they go to lunch. After lunch they take two hours of rest in the afternoon, then three more given over to work, after which they have dinner. Counting the first hour after noon as ending at one o'clock, it is eight o'clock when they go to bed. Sleep takes up eight hours.

The intervals between work, meals, and sleep they are allowed to spend however they like, provided that the time they have free from work is not wasted in debauchery and idleness but spent well in some other pursuit, according to their preference. Many devote these intervals to intellectual activities. For every day they have regular lectures in the hours before dawn; attendance is required only from those who have been specially chosen to devote themselves to learning. But a great number of men, and also women, from all orders of society flock to hear these lectures, some one sort, some another, as each is naturally inclined. But if someone wishes to spend this same time practicing his trade (as do many whose temperaments are not suited to any abstract discipline), they are quite free to do so; indeed they are also praised for doing so, since their labor contributes to the common good.

After dinner they devote one hour to recreation, during the summer in the gardens, during the winter in the common rooms where they have their meals. There they either play music or entertain themselves with conversation. They do not so much as know about dice and other such pointless and pernicious games, but they do play two games not unlike chess. In one of them numbers fight against each other, one taking over the other; in the other game virtues are lined up in a battlefront against the vices. This game shows very cleverly both how the vices fight among themselves but join forces against the virtues, and also which vices are opposed to which virtues, what forces they bring to bear openly, what instruments they use to attack indirectly, what defenses the virtues use to fend off the forces of the vices, how they evade their assaults, and finally by what methods one side or the other wins the victory.

But at this point, it is necessary to examine the matter in more detail to avoid making a mistake. If only six hours are devoted to work, you might think that there

---

[5] **syphogrants:** From a Greek compound, apparently meaning "wise old man."

would necessarily be some shortage of supplies. But that is so far from being true that six hours is not only enough to produce abundantly all the necessities and comforts of life but is even more than enough. This you, too, will understand if you consider what a large part of the population in other countries live their lives in idleness. First, almost all the women do, and they make up almost half the population. Or in places where the women work, the men take their place and lie around snoring. Add to that the huge idle crowd of priests and religious, as they are called. Throw in all the rich, especially the landlords of estates who are commonly called gentlemen and nobles. Include with them their retainers, that rank cesspool of worthless swashbucklers. Add, finally, the strong and sturdy beggars who feign some disease as a pretext for their idleness. You will certainly find that it takes far fewer than you thought to produce everything that mortals use.

Now consider how few of these workers are occupied in necessary trades, since, where money is the measure of everything, many completely futile and superfluous crafts must be practiced just to support over-indulgence and wanton luxury. Now if that same crowd who are presently working were divided up among the few trades needed to produce the few commodities that nature requires, the resulting abundance of goods would drive prices down so low that craftsmen could not make a living. But if all those who work away at pointless tasks and, together with them, that whole crowd of lazy, languid idlers (any single one of whom consumes twice as much as any of the workers who produce the goods), if they all were put to work—and useful work at that—you can easily see how little time would be enough and more than enough time to produce all the goods required for human needs and conveniences—and pleasures, too, as long as they are true and natural ones.

And this very point is confirmed by the experience of the Utopians. For there, in the whole city and the surrounding territory, out of all the men and women who are old enough and strong enough to work, barely five hundred are exempted from work. Among them the syphogrants, who are legally relieved from work, nevertheless do not exempt themselves; they work so as to motivate others to work by giving a good example. The same immunity is enjoyed by those to whom the people give total leisure to pursue various branches of learning, but only after the priests have recommended them and the syphogrants have chosen them by a secret ballot. If any of them disappoints the hopes they had in him, he is put back to work; and on the other hand, it happens, not infrequently, that an artisan, devoting his free time to intellectual pursuits, works so diligently and makes such progress that he is exempted from working at his trade and promoted to the scholarly class. From this order of scholars are chosen ambassadors, priests, tranibors, and finally the ruler himself, who was called Barzanes in their ancient language, but is named Ademus[6] in the modern tongue. The remaining group, which is neither idle nor devoted to useless trades, is so large that it is easy to imagine how many goods they produce in so few hours.

---

[6] **Barzanes . . . Ademus:** Barzanes, "Son of Zeus," and Ademus, "without a people," both from Greek. The use of the second term may suggest that the ruler of a people is separated from them by the fact of rule; this appears to be a more "modern" perception than that implied by "Son of Zeus."

Apart from what I have just said, they have it easier because in most of the necessary trades they do not need to expend as much labor as in other nations. First of all, building or repairing structures everywhere else requires the continuous effort of so many workers for the simple reason that what a father has built his worthless heir allows to fall gradually into disrepair. Thus what could have been maintained with a minimum of effort has to be totally rebuilt, at great expense, by the next heir. Moreover, it often happens that a house that cost someone enormous sums to build seems contemptible to someone of more fastidious taste; after a short time it falls into ruin through neglect and the owner builds another house somewhere else, at no less expense. But among the Utopians, from the time when everything was settled and the commonwealth was established, it very rarely happens that a new site is chosen on which to build houses; and they not only repair damage quickly when it happens but they take preventive measures against it. The result is that their buildings last a very long time and require very little work, and sometimes construction workers have so little to do that they are set to shaping timbers or squaring and fitting stones at home, so that if they ever need to build anything, it can be constructed more quickly.

Now as for their clothing, notice how little labor it requires. First of all, at work they wear informal garments made of leather or skins which last for seven years. When they go out in public they put on cloaks which cover these rough clothes; throughout the island they are all of the same color, that of the natural wool. Thus they not only get along with much less woolen cloth than anywhere else, but it also costs much less. But linen is easier to work and hence they use more of it; they are concerned only about the whiteness of linen and the neatness of wool, for they place no value on fineness of weave. The result is that in other places four or five woolen cloaks and the same number of silk shirts are not enough for one person, and if he is a bit fastidious, not even ten will do, but there everybody is content with one, which generally lasts for two years. Naturally there is no reason why he should want any more, for if he got them he would have no more protection against the cold, and his clothing would not look the least bit more fashionable.

Therefore, since everyone is employed in a useful trade and the trades themselves require less labor, the result is a great abundance of everything, so that sometimes they bring out an enormous number of people to repair the public roads, if any have deteriorated. It happens very often, when there is no occasion even for that kind of work, that they publicly decree a shorter workday. For the magistrates do not compel anyone to engage in superfluous labor against his will, since the structure of the commonwealth is primarily designed to relieve all the citizens from as much bodily labor as possible, so that they can devote their time to the freedom and cultivation of the mind. For that, they think, constitutes a happy life.

SOCIAL RELATIONS

Now is the time, I think, to explain how they treat each other, how they interact with one another, and what system they have for distributing goods.

And so, while the city is made up of households, the households themselves consist mostly of blood relatives. Girls, when they grow up and marry, move into the dwellings of their husbands. But sons and, after them, grandsons remain in the household and are subject to the oldest parent, unless his mind is failing because of old age; in that case he is replaced by the next oldest. But to keep the city from being either over- or underpopulated, they see to it that no household (and each city, apart from its territory, has six thousand of them) has fewer than ten or more than sixteen adults. For it is not possible to set a limit for children. This limit is easily maintained by transferring persons from households with too many people to those with too few. But if it should happen that the whole city grows too large, they use the excess to supply underpopulated cities. But if it should happen that throughout the island the whole mass of the population should swell inordinately, they sign up citizens from each city and send them as colonists to live under their own laws on the nearest part of the continent, wherever the natives have a lot of land left over and uncultivated; they adopt any natives who choose to live with them. Assenting willingly to the same style of life and the same customs, the natives are easily assimilated, and that to the advantage of both groups. For by means of their institutions the Utopians make the land easily support both peoples, whereas before it provided a meager and skimpy living for only one. The natives who refuse to live under their laws are driven out of the territory the Utopians have marked off for their use; if they resist, the Utopians make war against them. For they think it is quite just to wage war against someone who has land which he himself does not use, leaving it fallow and unproductive, but denying its possession and use to someone else who has a right, by the law of nature, to be maintained by it.[7] If any of their cities is ever accidentally so reduced in population that they cannot replenish it from other parts of the island and still keep the full quota in those cities (which they say has only happened twice in their whole history because of a virulent plague), then they resupply it with citizens immigrating from a colony. For they would rather allow the colonies to disappear than let any of the cities on the island shrink in size.

But, to return to the citizens' way of life, the oldest man, as I said, presides over a household. Wives serve their husbands and children their parents, and generally the younger serve the older. Each city is divided into four equal districts. In the middle of each district is a marketplace for all sorts of commodities. The products of each household are taken to designated houses there and each kind of goods is separately stored in a warehouse. From them each head of household goes to get whatever he and his household need, and he takes away whatever he wants, paying no money and giving absolutely nothing in exchange for it. For why should he be denied anything, since there is plenty of everything and no one need fear that anyone would want to ask for more than he needs? For why should anyone be suspected of asking for too much if he is certain he will never lack for anything? Certainly fear of want makes all kinds of animals greedy and rapacious, but only mankind is made so by pride, which makes them consider their own glory enhanced if they excel others in displaying superfluous possessions; in the Utopian scheme of things there is no place at all for such a vice.

---

[7] **For they think . . . maintained by it:** The process of "giving" land to the natives and then taking it back if they don't exploit it by farming anticipates some colonial attitudes in the modern world. More may have shared this bias with his Utopians.

Adjoining the marketplaces I mentioned are food markets, to which vegetables, fruit, and bread are brought, and also fish and edible birds and beasts are conveyed from designated places outside the city where there is a stream to wash away refuse and offal. From here they bring the cattle which have been slaughtered and cleaned by the hands of bondsmen. For they do not allow their own citizens to become accustomed to butchering animals; they think that to do so gradually eliminates compassion, the finest feeling of human nature. They do not allow anything filthy or foul to be brought into the city, for air tainted by such rottenness might engender disease.

Furthermore, each block has spacious halls located at equal intervals, each known by its own name. The syphogrants look after them, and to each of them are assigned thirty families (namely fifteen on either side) who eat their meals there. Stewards from each hall gather in the market at a designated hour and get food according to the number of mouths they have to feed.

But their first priority is the sick, who are cared for in public hospitals. They have four of them on the outskirts of the city, a little outside the walls; they are as capacious as four little towns so that no matter how many people are sick they do not need to be crowded uncomfortably together, and so that those who have contagious diseases that can be transferred from one person to another can be kept at a distance from the main body of the patients. These hospitals are so equipped and provided with everything that promotes health, the care provided in them is so gentle and solicitous, the doctors who are in constant attendance are so skilled that, although no one is sent there against his will, there is still almost no one in the whole city who would not rather be lodged there than at home when he is in failing health.

After the stewards of the hospitals have received the food prescribed by the physicians, the best of what is left is divided equitably among the halls, according to the number fed by each one, except that they pay special attention to the ruler, the high priest, and the tranibors, and also to ambassadors and all foreigners (if there are any, for they are few and far between); but when there are any, designated residences are furnished and prepared for them. At the times fixed for lunch and dinner, the whole syphograncy, alerted by the blast of a bronze trumpet, convenes in these halls, except for those who are bedridden in the hospitals or at home. Nevertheless, no one is forbidden to take home food from the marketplace once the halls have been supplied with their quotas, for they know that no one would lightly choose to do so; though no one is prohibited from eating at home, still no one does it willingly, for it is not considered proper and it would be foolish to go to the trouble of preparing an inferior meal at home when a splendid and sumptuous one is ready and waiting in a hall nearby.

In this hall slaves perform all the chores which are somewhat heavy or dirty. But the women are solely responsible for preparing and cooking the food and making arrangements for the whole meal, each household taking its turn. They sit at three tables or more, according to the number of diners. The men sit with their backs to the wall, the women on the outside, so that if they should suddenly feel ill, as happens, sometimes, when they are pregnant, they can get up and go out to the nurses without disturbing the seating arrangement.

The nurses are seated separately with the nursing infants in a little room assigned to them; it never lacks a fire and clean water and also cradles so that when they want they can either lay them down or take off their swaddling clothes and let them refresh themselves by playing freely. Every mother nurses her own child unless death or disease prevents it. When that happens, the wives of the syphogrants immediately find a nurse, and that is not hard to do. For those who can are more than willing because everyone praises their compassion and the infant who is brought up this way takes the nurse as its natural mother.

Children who are under five sit in the nurses' den. Other minors, among whom they include members of both sexes who are not yet old enough to marry, either serve the diners, or, if they are too young and not strong enough for that, stand by— and that in absolute silence. Both groups eat what is handed to them by those seated at table, nor is any other time set aside for them to eat.

The syphogrant and his wife sit at the head table, which is the place of honor and overlooks the whole assembly, since it is placed crosswise in the highest part of the chamber. Next to them sit two of the oldest persons, for they sit in groups of four at all the tables. But if a church is located in that syphograncy, the priest and his wife sit with the syphogrant so as to preside. On both sides of them sit younger people, and then older people again, and so on throughout the whole hall. And so people sit with their coevals, and yet they are mixed in with a different age group. They say that this arrangement was adopted so that the dignity of the elders and the respect due them would keep the young people from indulging in improper language or behavior, since nothing can be done or said at table which would escape the notice of the persons sitting nearby on all sides.

The dishes of food are not served to the highest places and then downward to the others, but rather the choicest pieces are served first to the old people (whose places are marked) and then equitable shares are served to the rest. But some of the delicacies which are not in sufficient supply to be distributed to the whole hall are given by the old people, as they see fit, to those sitting near them. Thus respect for the elders is maintained and yet everyone has the same advantage from it.

Lunch and dinner always begin with some reading that concerns morals, but it is brief lest it be tedious. Taking off from this, the elders begin the discussion, but not in a gloomy and sour fashion. And they do not take up the whole meal with long disquisitions. No, they would much rather listen to the young people, and they even deliberately challenge them so as to learn about the temperament and intelligence of each of them as revealed in the free give and take of tabletalk.

Lunches are quite brief, dinners more ample because the one is followed by work and the other by rest and sleep during the night, which they think contribute more to good digestion. They never dine without music and after dinner they never lack for tasty desserts. They light incense and sprinkle perfumes and spare no effort to cheer up the diners. For they tend to incline to the position that no kind of pleasure ought to be forbidden as long as no harm comes of it.

This is the way they live in the city. But in the country, since they live far apart, they all eat in their own homes. No household has any shortage of food, since, after all, everything eaten by the city-dwellers comes from the farmers. . . .

[KNOWLEDGE AND MORAL PHILOSOPHY]

They learn the various branches of knowledge in their own language, which has no lack of vocabulary, is not unpleasant to the ear, and is not surpassed by any other in the expression of thought. It has spread throughout most of that part of the world, though everywhere else it is corrupted in various ways.

Of all the philosophers whose names are so famous in this known part of the world, they had not so much as heard of any before our arrival, and yet in music, dialectic, arithmetic, and geometry, they have made almost the same discoveries as our own ancient writers did. But though they measure up to our ancient writers in almost all respects, they are not up to the discoveries of modern dialecticians.[8] . . . But they are very expert in the orbits of stars and the movement of heavenly bodies. In fact, they have devised instruments of various designs which enable them to understand very accurately the movements and positions of the sun and moon and also the other stars which are visible in their hemisphere. But as for the conjunctions and oppositions of the planets and the whole fraud of divination by the stars, they have never so much as dreamed of it. By means of signs that they have perceived from long observation they predict rainstorms, winds, and other changes in the weather. But concerning the causes of those phenomena, and concerning tides and the saltiness of the ocean, and in general concerning the origin and nature of the heavens and the world, they agree on some points with our own ancient philosophers, and on others, just as the ancients disagreed with one another, they also differ from all the ancients and propose new theories, and yet they do not entirely agree among themselves.

In that area of philosophy which deals with ethics, they discuss the same issues as we do. They inquire about the goods of the mind and body and external goods, and whether the designation "good" applies to all of these or only to the gifts of the mind. They discuss virtue and pleasure, but the primary and principal controversy is about what they think human happiness consists in, whether one thing or many. On this point they seem over-inclined to the position which claims that all or the most important part of human happiness consists of pleasure. And what is even more surprising, they claim support for this self-indulgent view even from religion, which is sober and strict and, indeed, almost gloomy and stern. For they never analyze happiness unless they combine some religious principles with the rational analysis of philosophy, since they think that without such principles reason by itself is too weak and deficient to investigate true happiness.

These principles are of this sort: that the soul is immortal, and by the beneficence of God is born for happiness; that our virtues and good deeds will be rewarded after this life, and our crimes have punishments prepared for them. Though these are religious principles, the Utopians still think that reason leads them to believe and grant them; if they are eliminated, the Utopians have no hesitation in affirming that

---

[8] **But though . . . dialectitians:** A practical people, the Utopians have mastered the European quadrivium (music, arithmetic, geometry, and astronomy). Dialectic (logic), one-third of the trivium, is only mentioned slightingly. Grammar and rhetoric are left out. The implicit disinterest in the liberal arts, including the practice of law, is worth noting.

no one could be so stupid as not to feel that he ought to pursue his own pleasure by hook or crook. He would only be concerned not to sacrifice a greater pleasure for a lesser one and not to pursue one that would be requited by pain. For they think it would be truly insane to pursue virtue, which is harsh and difficult, and not only to banish the pleasures of life but even to seek out pain of your own accord, and to expect to get nothing out of it (for how can you get anything out of it if you get nothing after death, since you have spent your whole life here without pleasure, that is, wretchedly?). But as it is, they think happiness consists not in every sort of pleasure but in pleasure that is good and honorable, for they believe that our nature is drawn to pleasure as the highest good by virtue itself, whereas the opposite faction attributes happiness to virtue alone.

And then they define virtue as living according to nature; to that end, they say, we were created by God. We follow the guidance of nature when we obey reason in choosing and avoiding things. Furthermore, reason above all inspires mortals to love and revere the majesty of God, to whom we owe our very existence and our capacity to be happy. Secondly, reason admonishes and encourages us to lead lives with as little anxiety and as much joy as possible and, beyond that, to exert ourselves in helping all others achieve the same end because of our natural fellowship. For not even the gloomiest and sternest advocate of virtue, who despises pleasure so much that he would impose toil, vigils, and mortifications on you, would refrain from enjoining you to do as much as you can to alleviate the poverty and distress of others, and he would think it praiseworthy and humane for one human being to rescue and comfort another, since the very essence of humanity (and no virtue is more proper to human beings) is to relieve the distress of others, eliminate sadness from their lives, and restore them to a joyful life, that is, to pleasure. Why should nature not impel us to do the same for ourselves? For either a joyful life, that is, a life of pleasure, is wrong and in that case we should not only not help anyone to achieve it but rather we should do all we can to make everyone avoid it as harmful and deadly, or if you are not only allowed but even required to obtain it for others, why not do so first of all for yourself? You should be no less well-disposed to yourself than to others. For when nature prompts you to be good to others, she does not require you to turn around and be cruel and merciless to yourself. Nature herself, they say, prescribes as the aim of all our actions a joyful life, that is, pleasure, and they define virtue as following the prescriptions of nature.[9] But when nature invites mortals to help each other to lead cheerful lives (and she is certainly right to do so, since no one is so far above the rank of human beings that nature should care for him alone, whereas in fact she is equally concerned about all those whom she groups together as belonging to the same species), she also, of course, forbids you time after time to seek your own advantages in ways that create disadvantages for others.

---

[9] **Nature . . . prescriptions of nature:** The concept of "following nature" owes something to several philosophies, Stoicism and Epicureanism. Even Seneca, a Stoic, remarks that mistreating the body is "disgusting." The more agreeable philosophy here would be a kind of Epicureanism, emphasizing the enjoyment of life but avoiding the stigma of decadence to which it is often attached.

Therefore they think that not only private agreements must be kept but also public laws which have either been promulgated by a good ruler or which a people not oppressed by a tyrant or deceived by some trick have laid down by common consent to govern the distribution of vital commodities, that is, the means to pleasure. As long as these laws are not broken, to look out for your own good is prudent; to promote the public good is pious. But to deprive someone else of pleasure to promote your own is wrong; on the other hand, to deprive yourself of something to give it to someone else is a work of humanity and kindness and it always brings you more good than it takes away. For it is counterbalanced by gifts given in return, and also your consciousness of having done a good deed and the thought of the love and good will of those you have benefited will give you mental pleasure that outweighs any loss of bodily comfort. Finally, as religion makes clear to true believers, God will repay the loss of brief and paltry pleasures with enormous and never-ending joy. Following this line of reasoning and having considered the matter long and hard, they think that all our actions, including also our virtuous deeds, are directed toward pleasure as our happiness and final end.

They define pleasure as any motion or state of the mind or body which produces delight in accord with the guidance of nature. Not without reason do they add that the impulse must be in accord with nature. For just as not only our senses but also our reason pursues whatever is pleasurable by nature, that is, pleasures not achieved through wrongdoing, or acquired with the loss of a greater pleasure, or followed by hardship, so too they hold that all those unnatural pleasures which mortals agree to call delightful by the emptiest of fictions (as if it were in their power to change the thing by changing the name) are so far from contributing to happiness that they actually hinder it because, once they have taken over the mind, they occupy it totally and leave no room for true and genuine pleasures. For a great many things are not pleasurable by their very nature and are, in fact, for the most part bitter, but through the perverse enticement of evil desires they are not only thought to be the greatest pleasures but are even included among the primary reasons for living.

Among those who pursue false pleasures they include those whom I mentioned before who think that the finer the gown they wear the better they are. On this one point they are wrong twice over. They are no less deceived in thinking the gown is better than in imagining they themselves are. For if you consider the usefulness of a garment, why is wool woven with fine thread better than wool woven with coarser thread? But they think they excel in fact, not merely in their illusions. They ruffle their feathers; they believe that they are more valuable because of their clothes. And on that basis, honors they would not have dared hope for in cheaper clothes they demand as rightly due to their elegant gown, and they are outraged if someone passes them by without due deference.

And then isn't it equally stupid to be much taken with empty and worthless honors? For what natural pleasure is there in someone's baring his head to you or bending his knee? Will that relieve the pain in your own knee or cure the delirium in your head? It is amazing how some are caught up in this imaginary, specious pleasure: delightfully insane, they flatter themselves and take pride in their imagined nobility simply because they happen to be descended from a long series of ancestors who are considered to be rich, above all rich landlords (for nowadays there is no other source of nobility except wealth), and yet they think they are not a whit the less noble even if their ancestors have left them no wealth or they themselves have squandered it.

With these they group the persons I mentioned before who are enthralled by gems and precious stones and almost think they have been deified if they ever get a fine specimen, especially if it is the sort most highly valued in their own times; for not all sorts are highly regarded by all persons and at all times. But they do not buy such a stone unless it is removed from its gold setting and exposed, and even then not unless the seller swears and guarantees that it is a genuine jewel and a true gemstone; so afraid are they that their eyes may be deceived by a counterfeit substituted for a real stone. For why should your eyes be any less delighted by a counterfeit since they cannot distinguish it from a real one? To you each of them should have equal value, no less so, by heaven, than they would to a blind man.

What about people who keep superfluous wealth under lock and key, taking delight not in using the amassed treasure but merely in contemplating it? Do they feel any real delight or rather are they not deluded by a false pleasure? How about those who are subject to a different vice and hide away their gold, intending not only never to use it but perhaps never even to see it any more; in their anxiety not to lose it, they lose it. For surely it is lost if it is buried in the ground so as to be of no use to you and perhaps not to any other mortal. But still, when the treasure is hidden away, you feel carefree and happy. If a thief took it away and you died ten years later without knowing of the theft, in all those years that you lived after the money was stolen, what difference did it make to you whether it was removed or remained safe? In either case its usefulness to you was the same.

To these categories of absurd enjoyment they add gambling (a sort of madness they know of only through hearsay, not experience) and also hunting and falconry. For what pleasure can there be, they say, in throwing dice on a gaming table? Even if there were any pleasure in it, you have done it so often that mere repetition should have made you sick of it. How can it be delightful to hear the barking and howling of dogs? — isn't that a disgusting noise? Why do hunters feel more pleasure when a dog chases a hare than when a dog chases a dog? For in either case the action is the same, that is, running, if that is what pleases you. Or if you are attracted by the hope of carnage and the expectation of seeing the slaughter with your own eyes, you ought instead to be moved to compassion when you see a little hare torn to pieces by a dog, a weak creature tormented by a stronger one, a timid creature fleeing from a ferocious beast, a harmless creature from a cruel hound. And so the Utopians have assigned the whole business of hunting to the butchers, whose trade (as I said before) is conducted entirely by slaves, considering it beneath the dignity of free men. They consider it the lowest function of the trade. The other activities of butchers are more useful and honorable, since they contribute much more and destroy animals only out of necessity, whereas the hunter seeks nothing but pleasure from the slaughter and butchering of some poor little creature. Even in beasts themselves, according to the Utopians, such an eagerness to view carnage springs from a cruel disposition, or else the continual indulgence in such brutal pleasure finally degenerates into cruelty.

Though the herd of mortals consider such pursuits as these and others like them (for there is no end to them) to be pleasures, the Utopians firmly hold that they have nothing to do with pleasure, since there is no natural sweetness in them. Though they ordinarily produce sensual joy (which seems to be the function of pleasure), the Utopians are unwilling to change their minds. The reason they seem pleasant is not the nature of the things themselves but the perverse habits of their devotees, whose vicious attitudes cause them to embrace what is bitter as sweet, just as the defective tastebuds of pregnant women make them think that pitch and tallow are sweeter than honey. And yet no one's judgment, if it is vitiated by disease or habit, can change the nature of pleasure, or of anything else for that matter.

True pleasures they divide into various classes, assigning some to the mind, others to the body. To the mind they attribute understanding and the sweetness which springs from the contemplation of the truth. To these they add the pleasure of looking back on a lifetime of good deeds and the sure hope of happiness to come.

They divide bodily pleasure into two kinds: one is the sweetness which pervades the senses, either when the supplies our natural heat has used up are replenished (as they are by food and drink) or else when the excessive elements overburdening our bodies are discharged. This happens when we purge our intestines of excrement, or go about generating children or when the itching in some part of the body is alleviated by rubbing or scratching. But sometimes pleasure results not from the replenishment sought by our bodily members nor from relieving them of excess but from some secret but remarkable power which tickles, excites, and attracts our senses to itself, such as the pleasure arising from music.

They claim that there is another kind of bodily pleasure which consists in the balanced and quiet condition of the body, that is, when a person's health is not disturbed by any disease. Such health, as long as it is not interrupted by any pain, is delightful in itself, even though it is not affected by any external pleasure. Though it is less obvious and affects the senses less grossly than the insistent desire for food and drink, nevertheless many Utopians hold it to be the greatest pleasure of all. Almost all of them believe that it is a great pleasure and the foundation and basis, as it were, of all the others, since it is the only one which keeps our lives peaceful and desirable; and, if you take it away, there is no room left for any pleasure at all. For the mere absence of pain without health they regard as insensibility, certainly not as pleasure.

They have long since rejected the position of those who think that stable and undisturbed health should not be considered to be a pleasure because, they say, its presence can be felt only through some external stimulus (for they, too, have debated this question intensely). But now they are in almost complete agreement with the opposite position, that health is actually essential to pleasure. For according to them, disease brings pain, which is unalterably opposed to pleasure, in the same way as disease is opposed to health. Why not conclude, in turn, that there is pleasure in undisturbed health? On this point they do not think it makes any difference whether the disease is a pain or the pain comes from the disease; in either case the effect is the same. Thus, if health itself is a pleasure or if it necessarily brings pleasure with it as fire brings heat, the result in either case is that, wherever health is, stable pleasure cannot be lacking.

Moreover, when we eat, they say, what happens is that health, which has begun to fail, now has food as its ally in the battle against hunger. As it gradually becomes stronger, the very progress toward its ordinary vigor brings with it the pleasure of being reinvigorated. And so if health finds joy in the struggle, will it not rejoice when the victory is won? But when it has at last happily recovered its former strength, which was the sole object of the whole struggle, will it immediately become insensible and fail to recognize and embrace its own good? The idea that health is not perceived they consider to be very far from the truth. For when we are awake, who does not perceive that he is healthy—except someone who is not? Who can be so constricted by dullness and lethargy that he does not admit that health is delightful and enjoyable? And what is enjoyment but another name for pleasure?

Above all they embrace the pleasures of the mind, which they consider the first and foremost of all pleasures. They think that mental pleasure springs primarily from the practice of the virtues and the consciousness of a good life. Of the pleasures supplied by the body they give the first place to health. As for the pleasure of eating and drink and whatever else falls under a similar category of delight, they think they should be sought, but only for the sake of health, for such activities are not enjoyable in themselves but only insofar as they counter the unnoticed encroachments of ill health. And therefore a wise man, they say, should ward off disease rather than seek medicine for it and avoid pain rather than seek relief from it; just so it would be better not to have any need for such pleasure than to be relieved by it.

If anyone thinks that this kind of pleasure makes him happy, he must also confess that his life would be the happiest of all if it could be spent in perpetual hunger, thirst, and itching, followed by eating, drinking, scratching, and rubbing—and who can fail to see that such a life would be not only foul but also miserable? Certainly these are the lowliest of all pleasures, since they are the least unadulterated and never occur except in conjunction with the pain contrary to them. Thus the pleasure of eating is coupled with hunger, and not in equal proportions, for the pain is both longer and more intense. For it begins before the pleasure and never departs until the pleasure also ceases. Therefore they do not place much stock in such pleasures, except insofar as necessity demands them. But they also rejoice in them and gratefully acknowledge the kindness of Mother Nature, who uses the sweetest pleasures to entice her offspring to do what they must always be doing out of necessity. How irksome our lives would be if the daily ailments of hunger and thirst had to be warded off by drugs and bitter medications like the other diseases which afflict us less often?

They gladly cherish beauty, strength, agility as special and enjoyable gifts of nature. Certainly the pleasures which are mediated by our ears, eyes, and noses and which nature assigned as proper and peculiar to the human race (for no other kind of creature admires the design and beauty of the world, or is moved by the beauty of fragrances except to distinguish kinds of food, or recognizes the harmonious or discordant intervals in sounds), these pleasures, I say, they cultivate as adding a certain enjoyable spice to their lives. In all of them, however, they impose the limitation that a lesser should not impede a greater pleasure or that a pleasure should not cause pain at some later time—and they think this will necessarily happen if the pleasure is dishonorable.

They think it is certainly quite mad for someone to despise a beautiful figure, to deplete his strength, to turn agility into torpor, to wear out his body with fasting, to ruin his health, and to scorn the other favors bestowed by nature, unless he neglects his own good so as to work more avidly for the the good of others or the public welfare, and in return for his effort he expects greater pleasure from God. Otherwise to inflict pain on oneself without doing anyone any good—simply to gain the empty shadow of virtue or to be able to bear with less distress adversities that may never come—this they consider to be insane and the mark of a mind that is both cruel to itself and ungrateful to nature, rejecting her benefits and not deigning to be beholden to her.

This is their view of virtue and pleasure; and in the absence of religious inspiration from heaven revealing something holier, they think human reason can discover no truer doctrine. I do not have time now to examine whether or not their teaching is correct, nor is it necessary, since I undertook to present their principles, not to defend them. But whatever validity their precepts may have, I am fully persuaded that nowhere will you find a more extraordinary people or a happier commonwealth. . . .

[CONCLUSION]

I have described to you as accurately as I can the plan of their commonwealth, which I certainly consider to be not only the best but also the only kind worthy of the name. For elsewhere they always talk about the public good but they are concerned with their own private welfare; here, where there is no private property, everyone works seriously for the public good. And for good reason in both places, for elsewhere is there anyone who does not know that unless he looks out for his own personal interest he will die of hunger, no matter how flourishing the commonwealth may be; therefore necessity causes him to think he should watch out for his own good, not that of others, that is, of the people. On the other hand, here, where everything belongs to everyone, no one doubts that (as long as care is taken that the public storehouses are full) nothing whatever will be lacking to anyone for his own use. For the distribution of goods is not niggardly; no one is a pauper or a beggar there, and though no one has anything, all are rich.

For what greater wealth can there be than to be completely spared any anxiety and to live with a joyful and tranquil frame of mind, with no worries about making a living, not vexed by a wife's complaints and demands, not fearing a son will end up in poverty, not concerned about a daughter's dowry, but secure about the livelihood and happiness of himself and his own, his wife, children, grandchildren, great-grandchildren, great-great-grandchildren, and however long a line of descendants noblemen presume they will have. Indeed those who worked before but are now disabled are no less provided for than those who are still working.

At this point I wish that someone would venture to compare with this equity the justice to be found in other nations, where I'll be damned if I can find any trace whatever of justice or equity. For what sort of justice is it for some nobleman or goldsmith or moneylender or, in short, any of the others who either do nothing at all or something that is not very necessary for the commonwealth, to live luxuriously and splendidly in complete idleness or doing some superfluous task? And at the same time a laborer, a teamster, a blacksmith or farmer works so long and so hard that a beast of burden could hardly sustain it, performing tasks so necessary that without them no commonwealth could survive at all for even a single year, and yet they earn such a meager living and lead such miserable lives that beasts of burden seem to be better off, since they do not have to work so incessantly, their fodder is not much worse (and to them it tastes better), and in the meantime they are not afraid of what will happen to them. These workers are driven to toil without profit or gain in the present; they are crushed by the thought that they will be poverty-stricken in their old age, for their daily wages are not enough for that very day, much less can they accumulate any surplus which might be put aside every day to provide for their old age.

Is a commonwealth not unjust and ungrateful if it lavishes so many benefits on noblemen, as they are called, and goldsmiths, and the rest of that crew who are either idle or else merely flatterers and providers of empty pleasures, but makes no proper provision for farmers, colliers, laborers, teamsters, and blacksmiths, without whom there would be no commonwealth at all; unmindful of their sleepless labors and forgetting their many and great contributions, it first uses up the labors of their flourishing years, and then, when they are worn down by old age and diseases, it is totally ungrateful and rewards them with a miserable death. And how about this: every day the rich scrape away something from the wages of the poor, not only by private chicanery but also by public laws. Before, it seemed unjust that those who deserve the most from the commonwealth should receive the least, but now, by promulgating a law, they have transmuted this perversion into justice. From my observation and experience of all the flourishing nations everywhere, what is taking place, so help me God, is nothing but a conspiracy of the rich, as it were, who look out for themselves under the pretext of serving the commonwealth. They think up and devise all ways and means, first of keeping (and having no fear of losing) what they have heaped up through underhanded deals, and then of taking advantage of the poor by buying their labor and toil as cheaply as possible. Once the rich have decreed in the name of the public (including the poor) that these schemes must be observed, then they become laws.

But after these depraved creatures, in their insatiable greed, have divided among themselves all the goods which would have sufficed for everyone, they are still very far from the happiness of the Utopian commonwealth; there, once the use of money was abolished, and together with it all greed for it, what a mass of troubles was cut away, what a crop of crimes was pulled up by the roots! Is there anyone who does not know that fraud, theft, plunder, strife, turmoil, contention, rebellion, murder, treason, poisoning, crimes which are constantly punished but never held in check, would die away if money were eliminated? And also that at the very instant when money disappeared, so would fear, anxiety, worries, toil, and sleepless nights? Indeed, poverty itself, which seems to be merely the lack of money, would itself immediately fade away if money were everywhere totally abolished.

To make this clearer, imagine some barren year of bad harvests when many thousands of people die of hunger. I maintain it is clear that at the end of this famine, if you examined the barns of the rich, you would find so much grain that if it had been divided among those swept away by starvation and disease, no one would have noticed any effect at all of the failure of weather and soil. It would have been easy to provide food if that blessed money, that invention very clearly designed to open the way to what we need to live, were not the only barrier to keep us from it. I have no doubt that the rich also understand this and are not unaware how much better it would be to lack no necessities than to abound in so many superfluities, to be relieved of so many troubles than to be hemmed in by such great wealth. And in fact I have no doubt that everyone's concern for his own well-being or the authority of our savior Christ (who is so wise that he cannot be unaware of what is best and so good that he would never advise what he knew was not the best) would long since have easily drawn the whole world to adopt the laws of this commonwealth, if it were not held back by one and only one monster, the prince and parent of all plagues, pride.

Pride measures prosperity not by her own advantages but by the disadvantages of others. She would not even wish to be a goddess unless there were some wretches left whom she could order about and lord it over, whose misery would make her happiness seem all the more extraordinary, whose poverty can be tormented and exacerbated by a display of her wealth. This infernal serpent, pervading the human heart, keeps men from reforming their lives, holding them back like a suckfish.

Since pride is too firmly fixed in the minds of men to be easily plucked out, I am glad that this form of commonwealth, which I would gladly see adopted by everyone, is at least enjoyed by the Utopians; they have followed ethical principles which enabled them to lay the foundations of a commonwealth that is not only most happy but also, so far as human prescience can foresee, likely to last forever. For now that they have eradicated factional strife and ambition at home, along with the other vices, there is no danger that they can be disturbed by domestic discord, which has been the sole reason for the downfall of many prosperous and splendidly fortified cities. But as long as their domestic tranquility and wholesome social structure is preserved, the envy of all the surrounding princes cannot shock or unsettle their dominion, though in the past they have often unsuccessfully tried to do so.

When Raphael had ended his tale, there occurred to me quite a few institutions established by the customs and laws of that nation which seemed to me quite absurd, not only in their way of waging war, their religious beliefs and practices, and other institutions as well, but also (and above all) in the very point which is the principal foundation of their whole social structure, namely their common life and subsistence with no exchange of money. That one fact entirely undermines all nobility, magnificence, splendor, and majesty, which are (in the popular view) the true adornments and ornaments of a commonwealth.[10] Nevertheless, I knew that his talk had worn him out, and I was not sure whether he could endure to listen to an

---

[10] **That one fact . . . commonwealth:** More appears to defend the exchange of money, and by implication the holding of private property, at the end of Hythloday's monologue. The author's tone here is difficult to determine.

opinion contrary to his own—especially since I remembered that he had reproached some persons precisely because they thought they would not be considered wise unless they could find some way of picking apart the ideas of others—and so, having praised their regimen and his own exposition, I took his hand and led him in to dinner, though first I said we would have another time to consider these matters more thoroughly and to confer more fully. I only wish this would happen someday!

Meanwhile, just as I can hardly agree with all the points he made (even though he is a person of unquestionable learning and wide experience of human affairs), so too I readily confess that in the Utopian commonwealth are very many features which in our societies I would wish rather than expect to see.

THE END OF THE SECOND BOOK

The End of the Afternoon Discourse
of Raphael Hythloday
about the Laws and Institutions
of the Little-known Island of Utopia
Recorded by the Most Illustrious
and Learned Gentleman
Master Thomas More
Citizen and Undersheriff of London

Varieties of Humanism

p. 1705

Many elements of Sir Thomas More's *Utopia* reflect the practices of the philosophical school of HUMANISM, a cultural and intellectual impulse that flourished during the European Renaissance. Characterized by a revival of interest in the classics, an individualistic and critical spirit, and a shift from religious to secular concerns, humanism began in Italy and spread throughout Europe during the Early Modern Period, helping to mark the transition from the medieval to the modern Western world. The Italian Renaissance, beginning in the fourteenth century, coincided with a period of cultural, economic, and social development in the Italian city-states, preeminently Florence. In succeeding centuries, parallel developments in northern Europe followed a new concentration of wealth and culture to northern European cities, contributing to a new era of artistic and intellectual achievement. As the Renaissance spread throughout Europe, so did the humanism of the Early Modern Period, in conscious reaction to the medieval world that had come before. Challenging the Christian domination of literature, art, and scholarship, humanism sought to restore the classics, the love of learning for its own sake, the enjoyment of literature as a source of cultivation and entertainment, and the use of secular subject matter in art. Developing at different times and in different places, Renaissance humanism took on many forms.

> From Petrarch to More, Renaissance humanism flexibly served whomever it seemed politically expedient to follow .... Renaissance humanism continues to exercise a powerful influence upon the modern humanities, yet ... humanism is not the idealized celebration of humaneness that it often claimed to be, but has a hard core of pragmatism.
> – JERRY BROTTON, scholar, 2006

THE HUMANIST PRELUDE: ARABIC SCHOLARSHIP OF THE LATER MIDDLE AGES

Scholars of the European Renaissance have increasingly come to recognize the shaping role of Arabic learning and culture in the late Middle Period. The works of Avicenna and Averroes offered new interpretations of the Greek philosophers that compelled serious writers of their day to return to the ancient sources. Arabic historians and travelers, as well as philosophers, began to attract European interest between the twelfth and fourteenth centuries, although the effect of their writing was not always immediate due to slowness of translation. The case of Ibn Khaldun (1332–1406), author of *Il Muqaddimah* or *Introduction to History,* is noteworthy in this respect. His direct impact on European political theory cannot be proven, because his work remained untranslated for centuries; but his objective analysis of political history probably influenced writers in the West through intermediaries. Since the nineteenth century, when his work became generally available, he has been called "the father of sociology." His writing is thus often compared to that of Niccolò Machiavelli (1469–1527), particularly in his parallel use of Aristotle's *Politics* as a source.

p. 1732

HUMANIST WRITERS OF THE ITALIAN RENAISSANCE

Among the first Europeans to capture the new spirit of humanism and to ardently pursue the Latin classics was the Florentine poet and scholar **Francesco Petrarch** (1304–1374). Along with his protégé Giovanni Boccaccio (1313–1375), Petrarch led the movement to

p. 1439

Giambattista Zelotti, Portrait of Niccolò Machiavelli, sixteenth century *Machiavelli transformed political writing and is sometimes thought to be the founder of modern political science. (© Alinari / Art Resource)*

NICOLAVS MACHIAVELLVS. HISTORIAR SCRIPTOR.

Portrait of Pico della Mirandola, sixteenth century
Giovanni Pico della Mirandola believed in the virtually unlimited intellectual potential of human beings. (© Scala / Art Resource)

revive classical Latin, in his prose as well as many of his poems. A later Florentine, Giovanni Pico della Mirandola (1463–1494), a follower of the Latin scholar Marsilio Ficino (1433–1499), attempted to reconcile Greek, Christian, Hebrew, and Islamic ideas. His essay ***On the Dignity of Man*** is a celebration of the genius of the cultures of the past brought together in a vision of human potential. Niccolò Machiavelli, a humanist scholar seeking the favor of the powerful Medici family in Florence, attempted to draw lessons from the Greco-Roman past and apply them to contemporary civil and political situations. While his famous work ***The Prince*** (1513) has been blamed for its ruthless political realism and seems cruelly "modern" to many, his study of history has humanist roots.

p. 1740

p. 1745

MARTIN LUTHER: ANTI-HUMANIST

As Renaissance humanism spread to northern Europe, it continued to take on different forms. Sir Thomas More borrowed from Desiderius Erasmus of Rotterdam (1469–1536) and other northern humanists, particularly in the area of Bible study. The Protestant leader Martin Luther (1483–1546) shared some of the humanists' interest in critiquing Christianity based on close study of the text of the Bible, as his historic **"Speech at the Diet of Worms"** confirms. Proclaiming himself and other readers as fit judges of Scripture, Luther opposed the hierarchy of the Catholic Church with its centuries of interpretation of the Bible. But his opposition did not stop at the Church; he finally grew more and more contemptuous of the humanists as well. In his tract *The Enslaved Will,* Luther attacked Erasmus of Rotterdam by arguing that the longstanding Biblical disputes among the Fathers of the Church should be submitted only to the understanding of the general reader, not to professional classicists like Erasmus. The difference, he argued, lay in taking over the project of interpretation rather than choosing a new master; in this sense, Luther was a true revolutionary, though he opposed political rebellion as such. Of peasant origins himself, schooled in the Bible rather than the classics, and supported chiefly by the availability of the printing press, Luther argued for the right to make a new beginning. His fierce independence marked him as a man of his time, while his reinvention of the personal relationship

p. 1755

Martin Luther preaching to the faithful, 1561
In this detail from the altarpiece at Torslunde Kirke, a church in Denmark, the Protestant leader Martin Luther preaches to the faithful, some of whom are receiving the wine of communion. (*The Art Archive / Nationalmuseet Copenhagen Denmark / Dagli Orti*)

to God and Christ marked him as a Protestant to his followers, a heretic in the eyes of the Catholic Church, and an innovator rather than an inheritor of the classical tradition.

Where Erasmus stayed with the middle ground, reading and interpreting the Bible based on its original texts while conducting his entire effort with the discipline of the scholar, both More and Luther deviated from this course, More to the side of Catholic orthodoxy and Luther to the side of Protestant rebellion. The great irony of the age can be seen in this final division in the practice of humanism. Erasmus, a true humanist, never lost his appreciation of either More or Luther, but he understood the risk each took in serving a higher truth that transcended logic and discipline alike.

∾ IBN KHALDUN
B. TUNISIA, 1332–1406

Born into an aristocratic family in Tunis in 1332, Abd-al-Rhman Ibn Khaldun received an extraordinary education in the QUR'AN (KORAN), the HADITH, law, and Arabic poetry and language at the hands of tutors and scholars. In his early twenties he left Tunis for Fez, where he began his long political career. A talented and gifted scholar, thinker, and observer of human affairs, Ibn Khaldun had a turbulent career, working under several different rulers in Spain and in Northern Africa, until about 1375 when he was forced to take refuge in a village in Oran, Algeria. There he began his *Universal History,* which many readers celebrate as the first great work of historical writing in world literature. In 1377 he completed the work's famous introduction, known as *The Muqaddimah.* In 1383, Ibn Khaldun set out to make his *HAJJ,* the Muslim's required pilgrimage to Mecca, but was detained in Cairo by the Egyptian ruler al-Malik az-Zahir Barquq, who was drawn to the writer's considerable abilities as an administrator and legal adviser. Ibn Khaldun spent the rest of his life in Cairo, where he became professor of law at Qamhiyah College and was appointed to various offices, including a prestigious judgeship.

The Muqaddimah, sometimes translated as "Introduction" or "Prolegomena," is one of the first books to reflect critically on the sociological, geographical, cultural, and even psychological factors that play into the making of history. For this reason Ibn Khaldun is sometimes called the

Sultan, Fourteenth
Century
*This miniature from
an illuminated
manuscript shows a
sultan dispensing
justice. (Giraudon /
Art Resource, NY)*

"father of sociology." The selections included here draw from Chapter 3 of his great treatise, where Ibn Khaldun discusses the origins of dynasties and royal authority, the various ways in which such authority may be eroded, and the relations between the ruler and his ministers and subjects. Like Machiavelli in *The Prince,* Ibn Khaldun is concerned to show the mechanisms by which a ruler maintains and loses his authority, and he supports his analysis with historical examples. For Ibn Khaldun, however, the consequences of a breakdown of authority are not just the loss of power but the breakdown of civilization itself.

༞ Il Muqaddimah

Translated by Franz Rosenthal

FROM

CHAPTER 3

On dynasties, royal authority, and the caliphate

21   THE TRUE CHARACTER AND DIFFERENT KINDS OF ROYAL AUTHORITY

Royal authority is an institution that is natural to mankind. We have explained before that human beings cannot live and exist except through social organization and co-operation for the purpose of obtaining their food and other necessities of life. When they have organized, necessity requires that they deal with each other and satisfy their needs. Each one will stretch out his hand for whatever he needs and (try simply to) take it, since injustice and aggressiveness are in the animal nature. The others, in turn, will try to prevent him from taking it, motivated by wrathfulness and spite and the strong human reaction when one's own property is menaced. This causes dissension, which leads to hostilities, and hostilities lead to trouble and bloodshed and loss of life, which lead to the destruction of the species. Now, (the human species) is one of the things the Creator has especially (enjoined us) to preserve.

People, thus, cannot persist in a state of anarchy and without a ruler who keeps them apart. Therefore, they need a person to restrain them. He is their ruler. As is required by human nature, he must be a forceful ruler, one who exercises authority. In this connection, group feeling is absolutely necessary, for as we have stated before, aggressive and defensive enterprises can succeed only with the help of group feeling. As one can see, royal authority of this kind is a noble institution, toward which all claims are directed, and one that needs to be defended. Nothing of the sort can materialize except with the help of group feelings, as has been mentioned before.

Group feelings differ. Each group feeling exercises its own authority and superiority over the people and family adhering to it. Not every group feeling has royal authority. Royal authority, in reality, belongs only to those who dominate subjects, collect taxes, send out (military) expeditions, protect the frontier regions, and have no one over them who is stronger than they. This is generally accepted as the real meaning of royal authority.

There are people whose group feeling falls short of accomplishing (one or another of these things which constitute) part of (real royal authority), such as protecting the frontier regions, or collecting taxes, or sending out (military) expeditions. Such royal authority is defective and not royal authority in the real meaning of the term.

Then, there are people whose group feeling is not strong enough to gain control over all the other group feelings or to stop everyone, so that there exists an authority superior to theirs. Their royal authority is also defective, and not royal authority in the real meaning of the term. It is exercised, for instance, by provincial amirs and regional chieftains who are all under one dynasty. This situation is often found in far-flung dynasties. I mean that there are rulers of provincial and remote regions who rule their own people but also obey the central power of the dynasty.

22   EXAGGERATED HARSHNESS IS HARMFUL TO ROYAL AUTHORITY AND IN MOST CASES CAUSES ITS DESTRUCTION

The interest subjects have in their ruler is not interest in his person and body, for example, in his good figure, handsome face, large frame, wide knowledge, good handwriting, or acute mind. Their interest in him lies in his relation to them. Royal and governmental authority is something relative, a relationship between ruler and subjects. Government becomes a reality when (a ruler) rules over subjects and handles their affairs. A ruler is he who has subjects, and subjects are persons who have a ruler. The quality accruing to the ruler from the fact of his correlative relation with his subjects is called "rulership." That is, he rules them, and if such rulership and its concomitants are of good quality, the purpose of government is most perfectly achieved. If such rulership is good and beneficial, it will serve the interests of the subjects. If it is bad and unfair, it will be harmful to them and cause their destruction.

Good rulership is equivalent to mildness. If the ruler uses force and is ready to mete out punishment and eager to expose the faults of people and to count their sins, (his subjects) become fearful and depressed and seek to protect themselves against him through lies, ruses, and deceit. This becomes a character trait of theirs. Their mind and character become corrupted. They often abandon (the ruler) on the battlefield and (fail to support his) defensive enterprises. The decay of (sincere) intentions causes the decay of (military) protection. The subjects often conspire to kill the ruler. Thus, the dynasty decays, and the fence (that protects it) lies in ruin. If the ruler continues to keep a forceful grip on his subjects, group feeling will be destroyed. If the ruler is mild and overlooks the bad sides of his subjects, they will trust him and take refuge with him. They love him heartily and are willing to die for him in battle against his enemies. Everything is then in order in the state.

The concomitants of good rulership are kindness to, and protection of, one's subjects. The true meaning of royal authority is realized when the ruler defends his subjects. To be kind and beneficent toward them is part of being mild to them and showing an interest in the way they live. These things are important for the ruler in gaining the love of his subjects.

An alert and very shrewd person rarely has the habit of mildness. Mildness is usually found in careless and unconcerned persons. The least (of the many drawbacks) of alertness (in a ruler) is that he imposes tasks upon his subjects that are beyond their ability, because he is aware of things they do not perceive and, through his genius, foresees the outcome of things at the start. (The ruler's excessive demands) may lead to his subjects' ruin. Muhammad[1] said: "Follow the pace of the weakest among you."

---

[1] **Muhammad** (c. 570–632): the prophet and founder of Islam to whom Allah dictated the sacred scriptures of the Qur'an.

Muhammad therefore made it a condition that the ruler should not be too shrewd. For this quality is accompanied by tyrannical and bad rulership and by a tendency to make the people do things that it is not in their nature to do.

The conclusion is that it is a drawback in a political leader to be (too) clever and shrewd. Cleverness and shrewdness imply that a person thinks too much, just as stupidity implies that he is too rigid. In the case of all human qualities, the extremes are reprehensible, and the middle road is praiseworthy. This is, for instance, the case with generosity in relation to waste and stinginess, or with bravery in relation to foolhardiness and cowardice. And so it is with all the other human qualities. For this reason, the very clever person is said to have the qualities of a devil. He is called a "satan," or "a would-be satan," and the like. [. . .]

38   COMMERCIAL ACTIVITY ON THE PART OF THE RULER IS HARMFUL TO HIS SUBJECTS AND RUINOUS TO THE TAX REVENUE

A dynasty may find itself in financial straits, as we have mentioned before, on account of the number of (its luxurious) habits and on account of its expenditure and the insufficiency of the tax revenue to pay for its needs. It may require more money and higher revenues. Then, it sometimes imposes customs duties on the commercial activities of its subjects. Sometimes, it increases the kinds of customs duties, if (customs duties as such) had been introduced before. Sometimes, it applies torture to its officials and tax collectors and sucks their bones dry. (This happens) when officials and tax collectors are observed to have appropriated a good deal of tax money, which their accounts do not show.

Sometimes, the ruler himself may engage in commerce and agriculture, from desire to increase his revenues. He sees that merchants and farmers make (large) profits and have plenty of property and that their gains correspond to the capital they invest. Therefore, he starts to acquire livestock and fields in order to cultivate them for profit, purchase goods, and expose himself to fluctuations of the market. He thinks that this will improve his revenues and increase his profits.

However this is a great error. It causes harm to the subjects in many ways. First, farmers and merchants will find it difficult to buy livestock and merchandise and to procure cheaply the things that belong to (farming and commerce). The subjects have all the same or approximately the same amount of wealth. Competition between them already exhausts, or comes close to exhausting, their financial resources. Now, when the ruler, who has so much more money than they, competes with them, scarcely a single one of them will any longer be able to obtain the things he wants, and everybody will become worried and unhappy.

Furthermore, the ruler can appropriate much of (the agricultural produce and the available merchandise), if it occurs to him. (He can do this) by force or by buying things up at the cheapest possible price. Further, there may be no one who would dare to bid against him. Thus, he will be able to force the seller to lower his price. Further, when agricultural products such as corn, silk, honey, and sugar, etc., or goods of any kind, become available, the ruler cannot wait for a favourable market and a boom, because he has to take care of government needs. Therefore, he forces the merchants or farmers who deal in these particular products to buy from him. He will be satisfied only with the highest prices and more. (The merchants and farmers, on the other hand), will exhaust their liquid capital in such transactions. The merchandise they thus acquire will remain useless on their hands. They themselves will no longer be able to trade, which is what enables them to earn something and make their living. Often, they need money. Then, they have to sell the goods (that they were forced to buy from the ruler), at the lowest prices, during a slump in the market. Often, the merchant or farmer has to do the same thing over again. He thus exhausts his capital and has to go out of business.

This becomes an oft-repeated process. The trouble and financial difficulties and the loss of profit that it causes the subjects take away from them all incentives to effort, thus ruining the fiscal (structure). Most of the revenue from taxes comes from farmers and merchants, especially once customs duties have been introduced and the tax revenue has been augmented by means of them. Thus, when the farmer gives up agriculture and the merchant goes out of business, the revenue from taxes vanishes altogether or becomes dangerously low.

Were the ruler to compare the revenue from taxes with the small profits (he reaps from trading himself), he would find the latter negligible in comparison with the former. Even if (his trading) were profitable, it would still deprive him of a good deal of his revenue from taxes, so far as commerce is concerned. It is unlikely that customs duties would be levied on (the ruler's commercial activities). If, however, the same deals were made by others, the customs duties would be included in the tax total.

Furthermore (the trading of the ruler) may cause the destruction of civilization and hence the disintegration of the dynasty. When the subjects can no longer make their capital larger through agriculture and commerce, it will decrease and disappear as the result of expenditure. This will ruin their situation.

The Persians made no one king except members of the royal house. Further, they chose him from among those who possessed virtue, religion, education, liberality, bravery, and nobility. Then, they stipulated in addition that he should be just. Also, he was not to take a farm, as this would harm his neighbours. He was not to engage in trade, as this would of necessity raise the prices of all goods. And he was not to use slaves as servants, since they would not give good and beneficial advice.

It should be known that the finances of a ruler can be increased, and his financial resources improved, only through the revenue from taxes. This can be improved only through the equitable treatment of people with property and regard for them, so that their hopes rise, and they have the incentive to start making their capital bear fruit and grow. This, in turn, increases the ruler's revenues in taxes.

Amirs and other men in power in a country who engage in commerce and agriculture, reach a point where they undertake to buy agricultural products and goods from their owners who come to them, at prices fixed by themselves as they see fit. Then, they resell these things to the subjects under their control, at the proper times, at prices fixed by themselves. This is even more dangerous, harmful, and ruinous for the subjects than the aforementioned (procedure). The ruler is often influenced to choose such a (course) by those sorts of people—I mean, merchants and farmers—who bring him into contact with the profession in which they have been reared.

They work with him, but for their own profit, to garner quickly as much money as they may wish, especially through profits reaped from doing business without having to pay taxes and customs duties. Exemption from taxes and customs duties is more likely than anything else to cause one's capital to grow, and it brings quick profits. These people do not understand how much damage is caused the ruler by each decrease in the revenue from taxes. The ruler, therefore, must guard against such persons, and not pay any attention to suggestions that are harmful to his revenues and his rule. [. . .]

41   INJUSTICE BRINGS ABOUT THE RUIN OF CIVILIZATION

Attacks on people's property remove the incentive to acquire and gain property. People, then, become of the opinion that the purpose and ultimate destiny of (acquiring property) is to have it taken away from them. The extent and degree to which property rights are infringed upon determines the extent and degree to which the efforts of the subjects to acquire property slacken. When attacks on (property) are extensive and general, affecting all means of making a livelihood, business inactivity, too, becomes general. If the attacks upon property are but light, the stoppage of gainful activity is correspondingly slight. Civilization and its well-being as well as business prosperity depend on productivity and people's efforts in all directions in their own interest and profit. When people no longer do business in order to make a living, and when they cease all gainful activity, the business of civilization slumps, and everything decays. People scatter everywhere in search of sustenance, to places outside the jurisdiction of their present government. The population of the particular region becomes sparse. The settlements there become empty. The cities lie in ruins. The disintegration causes the disintegration of the status of dynasty and ruler, because (their peculiar status) constitutes the form of civilization and the form necessarily decays when its matter (in this case, civilization) decays.

One may compare here the story that al-Mas'ûdî[2] tells in connection with the history of the Persians. In the days of King Bahrâm b. Bahrâm, the Môbedhân, the chief religious dignitary among the Persians, expressed to the King his disapproval of the latter's injustice and indifference to the consequences that his injustice must bring upon the dynasty. He did this through a parable, which he placed in the mouth of an owl. The King, hearing an owl's cry, asked the Môbedhân whether he understood what it was saying. He replied: "A male owl wanted to marry a female owl. The female owl, as a condition prior to consent, asked the male owl for the gift of twenty villages ruined in the days of Bahrâm, that she might hoot in them. (The male owl) accepted her condition and said to her: 'If the King continues to rule, I shall give you a thousand ruined villages. This is of all wishes the easiest to fulfil.'"

The King was stirred out of his negligence by that story. He had a private (talk) with the Môbedhân and asked him what he had in mind. He replied: "O King, the might of royal authority materializes only through the religious law, obedience

---

[2] **al Mas'ûdî:** Hassan ibn Ali al-Mas'ûdî (c. 890–957) Muslim historian, geographer, and traveler, whose historical reflection and critical analysis anticipates the work of Ibn Khaldun. King Bahram (Varhran) was a third-century ruler of the Sassanian empire that stretched over what is now Iran and Iraq.

toward God, and compliance with His commands and prohibitions. The religious law persists only through royal authority. Mighty royal authority is achieved only through men. Men persist only with the help of property. The only way to property is through cultivation. The only way to cultivation is through justice. Justice is a balance set up among mankind. The Lord set it up and appointed an overseer of it, and that is the ruler. You, O King, went after the farms and took them away from their owners and cultivators. They are the people who pay the land tax and from whom one gets money. You gave their farms as fiefs to your entourage and servants and to sluggards. They did not cultivate them and did not heed the consequences. (They did not look for the things) that would be good for the farms. They were leniently treated with regard to the land tax (and were not asked to pay it), because they were close to the king. The remaining landowners who did pay the land tax and cultivated their farms had to carry an unjust burden. Therefore, they left their farms and abandoned their settlements. They took refuge in farms that were far away or difficult (of access), and lived on them. Thus, cultivation slackened, and the farms were ruined. There was little money, and soldiers and subjects perished. Neighbouring rulers coveted the Persian realm, because they were aware of the fact that the basic materials that alone maintain the foundation of a realm had been cut off."

When the King heard that, he proceeded to look into (the affairs of) his realm. The farms were taken away from the intimates of the ruler and restored to their owners. They were again treated, as they had formerly been treated. They began again to cultivate (their farms). Those who had been weak gained in strength. The land was cultivated, and the country became prosperous. There was much money for the collectors of the land tax. The army was strengthened. The enemies' sources of (strength) were cut off. The frontier garrisons were manned. The ruler proceeded to take personal charge of his affairs. His days were prosperous, and his realm was well organized.

The lesson this teaches is that injustice ruins civilization, which has as its consequence the complete destruction of the dynasty. In this connection, one should disregard the fact that dynasties (centred) in great cities often infringe upon justice and still are not ruined. It should be known that this is the result of a relationship that exists between such infringements and the situation of the urban population. When a city is large and densely populated and unlimited in the variety of its conditions, the loss it suffers from hostile acts and injustice is small, because such losses take place gradually. Because of the great variety of conditions and the manifold productivity of a particular city, any loss may remain concealed. Its consequences will become visible only after some time. Thus, the dynasty which committed the infringements (of justice) may be replaced before the city is ruined. Another dynasty may make its appearance and restore the city with the help of its wealth. Thus, the (previous) loss which had remained concealed is made up and is scarcely noticed. This, however, happens only rarely. The proven fact is that civilization inevitably suffers losses through injustice and hostile acts, as we have mentioned, and it is the dynasty that suffers consequently.

Injustice should not be understood to imply only the confiscation of money or other property from the owners, without compensation and without cause. It is commonly understood in that way, but it is something more general than that. Whoever takes someone's property, or uses him for forced labour, or presses an unjustified claim against him, or imposes upon him a duty not required by the religious law, does an injustice to that particular person. People who collect unjustified taxes commit an injustice. Those who infringe upon property commit an injustice. Those who take away property commit an injustice. Those who deny people their rights commit an injustice. Those who, in general, take property by force, commit an injustice. It is the dynasty that suffers from all these acts, inasmuch as civilization, which is the substance of the dynasty, is ruined when people have lost all incentive.

This is what Muhammad actually had in mind when he forbade injustice. He meant the resulting destruction and ruin of civilization, which ultimately permits the eradication of the human species. This is what the religious law quite generally and wisely aims at in emphasizing five things as necessary: the preservation of (1) religion, (2) the soul (life), (3) the intellect, (4) progeny, and (5) property.

Since, as we have seen, injustice calls for the eradication of the species by leading to the ruin of civilization, it contains in itself a good reason for being prohibited. Consequently, it is important that it be forbidden.

If injustice were to be committed by every individual, the list of deterring punishments that would then have been given for it (in the religious law) would be as large as that given for the other (crimes) which lead to the destruction of the human species and which everybody is capable of committing, such as adultery, murder, and drunkenness. However, injustice can be committed only by persons who cannot be touched, only by persons who have power and authority. Therefore, injustice has been very much censured, and repeated threats against it have been expressed in the hope that perhaps the persons who are able to commit injustice will find a restraining influence in themselves.

One of the greatest injustices and one contributing most to the destruction of civilization is the unjustified imposition of tasks and the use of the subjects for forced labour. This is so because labour belongs to the things that constitute capital. Gain and sustenance represent the value realized from labour among civilized people. By their efforts and all their labours they (acquire) capital and (make a) profit. They have no other way to make a profit except (through labour). Subjects employed in cultural enterprises gain their livelihood and profit from such activities. Now, if they are obliged to work outside their own field and are used for forced labour unrelated to their (ordinary ways of) making a living, they no longer have any profit and are thus deprived of the price of their labour, which is their capital (asset). They suffer, and a good deal of their livelihood is gone, or even all of it. If this occurs repeatedly, all incentive to cultural enterprise is destroyed, and they cease utterly to make an effort. This leads to the destruction and ruin of civilization.

An injustice even greater and more destructive of civilization and the dynasty is the appropriation of people's property by buying their possessions as cheaply as possible and then reselling the merchandise to them at the highest possible prices by means of forced sales and purchases. Often, people have to accept (high) prices with the privilege of later payment. They console themselves for the loss they suffer with the hope that the market will fluctuate in favour of the merchandise that had been sold to them at such a high price, and that their loss will be cancelled later on. But then, they are required to make payment at once, and they are forced to sell the merchandise at the lowest possible price. The loss involved in the two transactions affects their capital.

This (situation) affects all kinds of merchants, those resident in town and those who import merchandise from elsewhere, the pedlars and shopkeepers who deal in food and fruit, and the craftsmen who deal in the instruments and implements that are in general use. The loss affects all professions and classes quite generally. This goes on from hour to hour. It causes capital funds to dwindle. The only possibility that remains is for the merchants to go out of business, because their capital is gone, as it can no longer be restored by the profits. Merchants who come from elsewhere for the purchase and sale of merchandise are slow to come, because of that situation. Business declines, and the subjects lose their livelihood, which, generally, comes from trading. Therefore, if no (trading) is being done in the markets, they have no livelihood, and the tax revenue of the ruler decreases or deteriorates, since, in the middle (period) of a dynasty and later on, most of the tax revenue comes from customs duties on commerce. This leads to the dissolution of the dynasty and the decay of urban civilization. The disintegration comes about gradually and imperceptibly.

This happens whenever the ways and means of seizing property described above are used. On the other hand, if it is taken outright and if the hostile acts are extended to affect the property, the wives, the lives, the skins, and the honour of people, it will lead to sudden disintegration and decay and the quick destruction of the dynasty. It will result in disturbances leading to complete destruction.

On account of these evil consequences, all such (unfair activities) are prohibited by the religious law. The religious law legalizes the use of cunning in trading, but forbids depriving people of their property illegally. The purpose is to prevent such evil (consequences), which would lead to the destruction of civilization through disturbances or the lack of opportunity to make a living.

It should be known that all these (practices) are caused by the need for more money on the part of dynasty and ruler, because they have become accustomed to luxurious living. Their expenditure increases, and much spending is done. Their ordinary income does not meet (the expenditures). Therefore, the ruler invents new sorts and kinds of taxes, in order to increase the revenues and to be able to balance the budget. But luxury continues to grow, and spending increases on account of it. The need for (appropriating) people's property becomes stronger and stronger. In this way, the authority of the dynasty shrinks until its influence is wiped out and its identity lost and it is defeated by an attacker. [. . .]

Giovanni Pico della Mirandola

B. Italy, 1463–1494

Giovanni Pico, a child prodigy, was the youngest son of the ruler of Mirandola, a principality in northern Italy. At the age of sixteen he began studying at the University of Ferrara, then moved on to those at Padua and Paris. Here he absorbed the Greek and Latin classics, the Hebrew Kabala and Talmud, Arabic philosophy, and Christian theology. Synthesizing these various traditions, the young man planned treatises that would exhibit not only their compatibility but also the basic unity of truth. Like the Arabic philosopher Avicenna and Doctor Faustus in Marlowe's play, Pico took the world's learning as his domain — but there was a price to pay for challenging the establishment. When he was just twenty-three, he published 900 theses as a kind of compendium of philosophical assertions to be debated in Rome by the best intellects of Europe. The Roman Catholic Church, however, under Pope Innocent VIII (r. 1484–92), declared thirteen of the theses to be heretical and prevented the debate from taking place. Pico retired from public view and wrote an *Apology* (1489) to defend his religious ideas. In the end Pico submitted to the authority of the Church, and Pope Alexander VI (r. 1492–1503) removed the ban on his writings shortly before his death.

Pico described himself as an *explorator*, and the depth of his learning led him to value the wisdom of all ages and cultures. He believed that beneath the symbolic surfaces of differing philosophical and religious traditions was a unitary thread binding them together. At the center of this intellectual complex was Pico's belief in the virtually unlimited intellectual potential of human beings. The work in which he argues for that potential is his oration *On the Dignity of Man* (1486), which is excerpted here.

FROM

On the Dignity of Man

Translated by Charles Glenn Wallis

Most venerable fathers, I have read in the records of the Arabians that Abdul the Saracen,[1] on being asked what thing on, so to speak, the world's stage, he viewed as most greatly worthy of wonder, answered that he viewed nothing more wonderful than man. And Mercury's, "a great wonder, Asclepius,[2] is man!" agrees with that

---

[1] **Abdul the Saracen:** Probably Abd Allah, Muhammad's cousin (c. seventh century C.E.).

[2] **Asclepius:** The legendary Greek healer and physician. He is a speaker in Mercury's (Hermes Trismegistus) dialogue. Hermes Trismegistus is a legendary sage associated with arcane teachings of neo-Platonism and the Kabala.

opinion. On thinking over the reason for these sayings, I was not satisfied by the many assertions made by many men concerning the outstandingness of human nature: that man is the messenger between creatures, familiar with the upper and king of the lower; by the sharpsightedness of the senses, by the hunting-power of reason, and by the light of intelligence, the interpreter of nature; the part in between the standstill of eternity and the flow of time; and, as the Persians say, the bond tying the world together, nay, the nuptial bond; and, according to David,[3] "a little lower than the angels." These reasons are great but not the chief ones, that is, they are not reasons for a lawful claim to the highest wonder as to a prerogative. Why should we not wonder more at the angels themselves and at the very blessed heavenly choirs?

Finally, it seemed to me that I understood why man is the animal that is most happy, and is therefore worthy of all wonder; and lastly, what the state is that is allotted to man in the succession of things,[4] and that is capable of arousing envy not only in the brutes but also in the stars and even in minds beyond the world. It is wonderful and beyond belief. For this is the reason why man is rightly said and thought to be a great marvel and the animal really worthy of wonder. Now hear what it is, fathers; and with kindly ears and for the sake of your humanity, give me your close attention:

Now the highest Father, God the master-builder, had, by the laws of His secret wisdom, fabricated this house, this world which we see, a very superb temple of divinity. He had adorned the super-celestial region with minds. He had animated the celestial globes with eternal souls; He had filled with a diverse throng of animals the cast-off and residual parts of the lower world. But, with the work finished, the Artisan desired that there be someone to reckon up the reason of such a big work, to love its beauty, and to wonder at its greatness. Accordingly, now that all things had been completed, as Moses and Timaeus[5] testify, He lastly considered creating man. But there was nothing in the archetypes from which He could mold a new sprout, nor anything in His storehouses which He could bestow as a heritage upon a new son, nor was there an empty judiciary seat where this contemplator of the universe could sit. Everything was filled up; all things had been laid out in the highest, the lowest, and the middle orders. But it did not belong to the paternal power to have failed in the final parturition, as though exhausted by childbearing; it did not belong to wisdom, in a case of necessity, to have been tossed back and forth through want of a plan; it did not belong to the loving-kindness which was going to praise divine liberality in others to be forced to condemn itself. Finally, the best of workmen decided that that to which nothing of its very own could be given should be, in composite fashion, whatsoever had belonged individually to each and every thing. Therefore He took up man, a work of indeterminate form; and, placing him at the midpoint of the world, He spoke to him as follows:

---

[3] **David:** King David, Psalm 8:5.

[4] **the succession of things:** That is, the great chain of being, or hierarchical pattern from God down to the smallest organism.

[5] **Timaeus:** A speaker in one of Plato's dialogues.

"We have given to thee, Adam, no fixed seat, no form of thy very own, no gift peculiarly thine, that thou mayest feel as thine own, have as thine own, possess as thine own the seat, the form, the gifts which thou thyself shalt desire. A limited nature in other creatures is confined within the laws written down by Us. In conformity with thy free judgment, in whose hands I have placed thee, thou art confined by no bounds; and thou wilt fix limits of nature for thyself. I have placed thee at the center of the world, that from there thou mayest more conveniently look around and see whatsoever is in the world. Neither heavenly nor earthly, neither mortal nor immortal have We made thee. Thou, like a judge appointed for being honorable, art the molder and maker of thyself; thou mayest sculpt thyself into whatever shape thou dost prefer. Thou canst grow downward into the lower natures which are brutes. Thou canst again grow upward from thy soul's reason into the higher natures which are divine."

O great liberality of God the Father! O great and wonderful happiness of man! It is given him to have that which he chooses and to be that which he wills. As soon as brutes are born, they bring with them, "from their dam's bag," as Lucilius[6] says, what they are going to possess. Highest spirits have been, either from the beginning or soon after, that which they are going to be throughout everlasting eternity. At man's birth the Father placed in him every sort of seed and sprouts of every kind of life. The seeds that each man cultivates will grow and bear their fruit in him. If he cultivates vegetable seeds, he will become a plant. If the seeds of sensation, he will grow into brute. If rational, he will come out a heavenly animal. If intellectual, he will be an angel, and a son of God. And if he is not contented with the lot of any creature but takes himself up into the center of his own unity, then, made one spirit with God and settled in the solitary darkness of the Father, who is above all things, he will stand ahead of all things. Who does not wonder at this chameleon which we are? Or who at all feels more wonder at anything else whatsoever? It was not unfittingly that Asclepius the Athenian said that man was symbolized by Proteus[7] in the secret rites, by reason of our nature sloughing its skin and transforming itself; hence metamorphoses were popular among the Jews and the Pythagoreans.[8] For the more secret Hebrew theology at one time reshapes holy Enoch[9] into an angel of divinity, whom they call *malach hashechina*, and at other times reshapes other men into other divinities. According to the Pythagoreans, wicked men are deformed into brutes and, if you believe Empedocles,[10] into plants too. And copying them, Maumeth[11]

---

[6] **Lucilius** (second century B.C.E.): A Roman satirical poet.

[7] **Proteus:** Greek god of the sea who eluded his opponents by shape-shifting.

[8] **Pythagoreans:** The followers of the Greek philosopher and mathematician Pythagoras (c. 582–c. 507 B.C.E.). They believed in the transmigration of souls and in the need to follow rituals to prepare for the next life.

[9] **Enoch:** Genesis 5:18–24 describes Enoch, the father of Methusaleh; Hebrews 11:5 suggests that he was taken by God without experiencing death.

[10] **Empedocles** (c. 492–435 B.C.E.): Greek natural philosopher who believed that the basic elements of all substance were earth, air, fire, and water and that change is generated by the cyclic and opposing forces of love and strife.

[11] **Maumeth** (c. 570–632): Muhammad, the great Prophet of Islam to whom Allah dictated the sacred scriptures of the Qur'an.

often had it on his lips that he who draws back from divine law becomes a brute. And his saying so was reasonable: for it is not the rind which makes the plant, but a dull and non-sentient nature; not the hide which makes a beast of burden, but a brutal and sensual soul; not the spherical body which makes the heavens, but right reason; and not a separateness from the body but a spiritual intelligence which makes an angel. For example, if you see a man given over to his belly and crawling upon the ground, it is a bush not a man that you see. If you see anyone blinded by the illusions of his empty and Calypso-like[12] imagination, seized by the desire of scratching, and delivered over to the senses, it is a brute not a man that you see. If you come upon a philosopher winnowing out all things by right reason, he is a heavenly not an earthly animal. If you come upon a pure contemplator, ignorant of the body, banished to the innermost places of the mind, he is not an earthly, not a heavenly animal; he more superbly is a divinity clothed with human flesh.

Who is there that does not wonder at man? And it is not unreasonable that in the Mosaic and Christian holy writ man is sometimes denoted by the name "all flesh" and at other times by that of "every creature"; and man fashions, fabricates, transforms himself into the shape of all flesh, into the character of every creature. Accordingly, where Evantes the Persian tells of the Chaldaean theology, he writes that man is not any inborn image of himself, but many images coming in from the outside: hence that saying of the Chaldaeans:[13] *enosh hu shinuy vekamah tevaoth baal chayim,* that is, man is an animal of diverse, multiform, and destructible nature.

But why all this? In order for us to understand that, after having been born in this state so that we may be what we will to be, then, since we are held in honor, we ought to take particular care that no one may say against us that we do not know that we are made similar to brutes and mindless beasts of burden. But rather, as Asaph the prophet says: "Ye are all gods, and sons of the most high," unless by abusing the very indulgent liberality of the Father, we make the free choice, which he gave to us, harmful to ourselves instead of helpful toward salvation. Let a certain holy ambition invade the mind, so that we may not be content with mean things but may aspire to the highest things and strive with all our forces to attain them: for if we will to, we can. Let us spurn earthly things; let us struggle toward the heavenly. Let us put in last place whatever is of the world; and let us fly beyond the chambers of the world to the chamber nearest the most lofty divinity. There, as the sacred mysteries reveal, the seraphim, cherubim, and thrones[14] occupy the first places. Ignorant of how to yield to them and unable to endure the second places, let us compete with the angels in dignity and glory. When we have willed it, we shall be not at all below them.

---

[12] **Calypso-like:** Pico is perhaps confusing Calypso with Circe from *The Odyssey.*

[13] **Chaldaeans:** An ancient Semitic people who invaded Babylon in the tenth century B.C.E.; Pico uses the term here to mean the priest-astronomers or astrologers associated with ancient Babylonian literature and lore.

[14] **seraphim . . . thrones:** In the medieval Christian hierarchy, seraphim, cherubim, and thrones constitute the highest order of angels.

Niccolò Machiavelli

B. *Italy, 1469–1527*

Niccolò Machiavelli was born into a family struggling to gain the recognition of the Florentine aristocracy. Although his father had a small inheritance and practiced law in Florence, the family never enjoyed a secure fortune. Therefore Machiavelli received a modest education in Latin, grammar, and mathematics from a series of tutors. He commented on his early life, "I was born poor, and I learned to know want before enjoyment." Machiavelli began his career as a civil servant and minor diplomat for the Florentine republic in 1498, following the expulsion of the powerful Medici family from the city in 1494. But when the Medicis returned to power in 1512, they removed Machiavelli from office and dashed any immediate hopes he had of political preferment. Instead, he was imprisoned, tortured, and banished from Florence on suspicion of committing crimes against the state. Once released, he retired to his home in the outskirts of Florence and wrote *The Prince* (1513) — still in hopes, he said, of regaining the trust of the Medici family. He explained his efforts in this way: "If they read this work of mine, they would see that I have not wasted the fifteen years I have spent in the study of politics; and anyone ought to be glad to use a man who has gained a great deal of experience at other people's expense."

In writing *The Prince*, Machiavelli broke with the classical models of political theory because he felt that the realities of the Renaissance had rendered them obsolete. He argued that neither Aristotle's *Politics* nor Plato's *Republic* could account for the corrupt and dangerous politics of the fourteenth-century Italian city-states. Instead, perhaps with one eye on the financial support his work might receive, Machiavelli addressed a thoroughly practical issue: how a ruler could successfully secure and hold power while calling forth the least amount of resistance from the people he ruled. He did not attempt to deal with this question as a matter of morality. While a prince might prefer to treat his subjects with kindness and generosity, the circumstances he was confronting were likely to require harsher measures. Therefore, Machiavelli said, a prince must "learn how to be not good, and to use that ability or not as is required." Insisting that human beings act in the last instance out of self-interest and therefore can never be fully trusted, *The Prince* advises would-be rulers to use deceit, cunning, and force as necessary to achieve their ultimate objective — remaining in power.

Machiavelli's project contained the radical idea of the pure creation of politics from nothing — with no natural law governing political behavior, no clear set of moral or ethical standards, and no criterion for success beyond self-preservation. He is one of the first writers to emphasize *what seems* over *what is* — since the control of appearances will lead to the control of reality. In this sense, the ruler is like the director on a stage for whom there must be willing and well-cued performers available at all times to present the message that is the play. These are some of Machiavelli's concerns as he addresses his thoughts to the reader.

So far as we know, Machiavelli never read *Il Muqaddimah,* or *Intro-duction to History,* written by Ibn Khaldun in 1377. There is no record of the translation of this highly original Arabic work for hundreds of years after its first publication. This is an important issue, because there is both similarity and difference between *Il Muqaddimah* and *The Prince.* The similarity lies in the decision of both writers to view the political world objectively and describe its real workings instead of the way it should work ideally. The difference lies in Ibn Khaldun's insistence that ultimately politics is determined by "group feeling," that is, the consent of the masses to be governed. Machiavelli characteristically gives little agency to the masses and instead views politics as properly governed by the will of the prince.

FROM

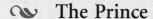 # The Prince

Translated by Allan H. Gilbert

CHAPTER 15

On the Things for Which Men, and Especially Princes, Are Praised or Censured

It now remains to see what should be the methods and conduct of a prince in deal-ing with his subjects and his friends. And because I know that many have written on this topic, I fear that when I too write I shall be thought presumptuous, because, in discussing it, I break away completely from the principles laid down by my predeces-sors. But since it is my purpose to write something useful to an attentive reader, I think it more effective to go back to the practical truth of the subject than to depend on my fancies about it. And many have imagined republics and principalities that never have been seen or known to exist in reality. For there is such a difference between the way men live and the way they ought to live, that anybody who aban-dons what is for what ought to be will learn something that will ruin rather than pre-serve him, because anyone who determines to act in all circumstances the part of a good man must come to ruin among so many who are not good. Hence, if a prince wishes to maintain himself, he must learn how to be not good, and to use that ability or not as is required.

Leaving out of account, then, things about an imaginary prince, and consider-ing things that are true, I say that all men, when they are spoken of, and especially princes, because they are set higher, are marked with some of the qualities that bring them either blame or praise. To wit, one man is thought liberal, another stingy (using a Tuscan word, because *avaricious* in our language is still applied to one who desires to get things through violence, but *stingy* we apply to him who refrains too much from using his own property); one is thought open-handed, another grasping; one cruel, the other compassionate; one is a breaker of faith, the other reliable; one is effeminate and cowardly, the other vigorous and spirited; one is philanthropic, the other egotistic; one is lascivious, the other chaste; one is straight-forward, the other crafty; one hard, the other easy to deal with; one is firm, the other unsettled; one is religious, the other unbelieving; and so on.

And I know that everybody will admit that it would be very praiseworthy for a prince to possess all of the above-mentioned qualities that are considered good. But since he is not able to have them or to observe them completely, because human conditions do not allow him to, it is necessary that he be prudent enough to understand how to avoid getting a bad name because he is given to those vices that will deprive him of his position. He should also, if he can, guard himself from those vices that will not take his place away from him, but if he cannot do it, he can with less anxiety let them go. Moreover, he should not be troubled if he gets a bad name because of vices without which it will be difficult for him to preserve his position. I say this because, if everything is considered, it will be seen that some things seem to be virtuous, but if they are put into practice will be ruinous to him; other things seem to be vices, yet if put into practice will bring the prince security and well-being.

Chapter 16

On Liberality and Parsimony

Beginning, then, with the first of the above-mentioned qualities, I assert that it is good to be thought liberal.[1] Yet liberality, practiced in such a way that you get a reputation for it, is damaging to you, for the following reasons: If you use it wisely and as it ought to be used, it will not become known, and you will not escape being censured for the opposite vice. Hence, if you wish to have men call you liberal, it is necessary not to omit any sort of lavishness. A prince who does this will always be obliged to use up all his property in lavish actions; he will then, if he wishes to keep the name of liberal, be forced to lay heavy taxes on his people and exact money from them, and do everything he can to raise money. This will begin to make his subjects hate him, and as he grows poor he will be little esteemed by anybody. So it comes about that because of this liberality of his, with which he has damaged a large number and been of advantage to but a few, he is affected by every petty annoyance and is in peril from every slight danger. If he recognizes this and wishes to draw back, he quickly gets a bad name for stinginess.

Since, then, a prince cannot without harming himself practice this virtue of liberality to such an extent that it will be recognized, he will, if he is prudent, not care about being called stingy. As time goes on he will be thought more and more liberal, for the people will see that because of his economy his income is enough for him, that he can defend himself from those who make war against him, and that he can enter upon undertakings without burdening his people. Such a prince is in the end liberal to all those from whom he takes nothing, and they are numerous; he is stingy to those to whom he does not give, and they are few. In our times we have seen big

---

[1] **liberal:** Generous.

things done only by those who have been looked on as stingy; the others have utterly failed. Pope Julius II,[2] though he made use of a reputation for liberality to attain the papacy, did not then try to maintain it, because he wished to be able to make war. The present King of France[3] has carried on great wars without laying unusually heavy taxes on his people, merely because his long economy has made provision for heavy expenditures. The present King of Spain,[4] if he had continued liberal, would not have carried on or completed so many undertakings.

Therefore a prince ought to care little about getting called stingy, if as a result he does not have to rob his subjects, is able to defend himself, does not become poor and contemptible, and is not obliged to become grasping. For this vice of stinginess is one of those that enables him to rule. Somebody may say: Caesar,[5] by means of his liberality, became emperor, and many others have come to high positions because they have been liberal and have been thought so. I answer: Either you are already a prince, or you are on the way to become one. In the first case liberality is dangerous; in the second it is very necessary to be thought liberal. Caesar was one of those who wished to attain dominion over Rome. But if, when he had attained it, he had lived for a long time and had not moderated his expenses, he would have destroyed his authority. Somebody may answer: Many who have been thought very liberal have been princes and done great things with their armies. I answer: The prince spends either his own property and that of his subjects or that of others. In the first case he ought to be frugal; in the second he ought to abstain from no sort of liberality. When he marches with his army and lives on plunder, loot, and ransom, a prince controls the property of others. To him liberality is essential, for without it his soldiers would not follow him. You can be a free giver of what does not belong to you or your subjects, as were Cyrus,[6] Caesar, and Alexander, because to spend the money of others does not decrease your reputation but adds to it. It is only the spending of your own money that hurts you.

There is nothing that eats itself up as fast as does liberality, for when you practice it you lose the power to practice it, and become poor and contemptible, or else to escape poverty you become rapacious and therefore are hated. And of all the things against which a prince must guard himself, the first is being an object of contempt and hatred. Liberality leads you to both of these. Hence there is more wisdom in keeping a name for stinginess, which produces a bad reputation without hatred, than in striving for the name of liberal, only to be forced to get the name of rapacious, which brings forth both bad reputation and hatred.

---

[2] **Pope Julius II:** Giuliano della Rovere (1443–1513), reigned as Pope Julius from 1503 to 1513.

[3] **King of France:** Louis XII (1462–1515), king of France from 1498 to 1515.

[4] **King of Spain:** King Ferdinand (1452–1516) jointly ruled Spain with Isabella I from 1474 to 1504, and was also king of Aragon, Sicily, and Naples.

[5] **Caesar:** Julius Caesar (100–44 B.C.E.), powerful member of the First Triumvirate of Rome, was appointed dictator of Rome in 44 B.C.E., the year of his famous assassination on the Ides of March by Marcus Brutus.

[6] **Cyrus:** Cyrus the Great (d. 529 B.C.E.), king of Persia from 559 B.C.E. and ruler of the Persian empire from 550 to 529 B.C.E.

CHAPTER 17

*On Cruelty and Pity, and Whether It Is Better
to Be Loved or to Be Feared, and* Vice Versa

Coming then to the other qualities already mentioned, I say that every prince should wish to be thought compassionate and not cruel; still, he should be careful not to make a bad use of the pity he feels. Cesare Borgia[7] was considered cruel, yet this cruelty of his pacified the Romagna, united it, and changed its condition to that of peace and loyalty. If the matter is well considered, it will be seen that Cesare was much more compassionate than the people of Florence, for in order to escape the name of cruel they allowed Pistoia[8] to be destroyed. Hence a prince ought not to be troubled by the stigma of cruelty, acquired in keeping his subjects united and faithful. By giving a very few examples of cruelty he can be more truly compassionate than those who through too much compassion allow disturbances to continue, from which arise murders or acts of plunder. Lawless acts are injurious to a large group, but the executions ordered by the prince injure a single person. The new prince, above all other princes, cannot possibly avoid the name of cruel, because new states are full of perils. Dido in Vergil puts it thus: "Hard circumstances and the newness of my realm force me to do such things, and to keep watch and ward over all my lands."[9]

All the same, he should be slow in believing and acting, and should make no one afraid of him, his procedure should be so tempered with prudence and humanity that too much confidence does not make him incautious, and too much suspicion does not make him unbearable.

All this gives rise to a question for debate: Is it better to be loved than to be feared, or the reverse? I answer that a prince should wish for both. But because it is difficult to reconcile them, I hold that it is much more secure to be feared than to be loved, if one of them must be given up. The reason for my answer is that one must say of men generally that they are ungrateful, mutable, pretenders and dissemblers, prone to avoid danger, thirsty for gain. So long as you benefit them they are all yours; as I said above, they offer you their blood, their property, their lives, their children, when the need for such things is remote. But when need comes upon you, they turn around. So if a prince has relied wholly on their words, and is lacking in other preparations, he falls. For friendships that are gained with money, and not with greatness and nobility of spirit, are deserved but not possessed, and in the nick of time one cannot avail himself of them. Men hesitate less to injure a man who makes himself loved than to injure one who makes himself feared, for their love is held by a chain of obligation, which, because of men's wickedness, is broken on every occasion for the sake of selfish profit; but their fear is secured by a dread of punishment which never fails you.

---

[7] **Cesare Borgia:** The son of Pope Alexander VI, Borgia (1476–1507) resigned his cardinalship to lead a treacherous campaign to seize power over the cities of Romagna.

[8] **Pistoia:** A city under Florentine rule that was plagued with bloody factional rioting while Florentine authorities looked on without taking definitive action against the rival parties.

[9] **"Hard . . . my lands":** *Aeneid* I, 563–64.

Nevertheless the prince should make himself feared in such a way that, if he does not win love, he escapes hatred. This is possible, for to be feared and not to be hated can easily coexist. In fact it is always possible, if the ruler abstains from the property of his citizens and subjects, and from their women. And if, as sometimes happens, he finds that he must inflict the penalty of death, he should do it when he has proper justification and evident reason. But above all he must refrain from taking property, for men forget the death of a father more quickly than the loss of their patrimony. Further, causes for taking property are never lacking, and he who begins to live on plunder is always finding cause to seize what belongs to others. But on the contrary, reasons for taking life are rarer and fail sooner.

But when a prince is with his army and has a great number of soldiers under his command, then above all he must pay no heed to being called cruel, because if he does not have that name he cannot keep his army united or ready for duty. It should be numbered among the wonderful feats of Hannibal[10] that he led to war in foreign lands a large army, made up of countless types of men, yet never suffered from dissension, either among the soldiers or against the general, in either bad or good fortune. His success resulted from nothing else than his inhuman cruelty, which, when added to his numerous other strong qualities, made him respected and terrible in the sight of his soldiers. Yet without his cruelty his other qualities would not have been adequate. So it seems that those writers have not thought very deeply who on one side admire his accomplishment and on the other condemn the chief cause for it. . . .

Returning, then, to the debate on being loved and feared, I conclude that since men love as they please and fear as the prince pleases, a wise prince will evidently rely on what is in his own power and not on what is in the power of another. As I have said, he need only take pains to avoid hatred.

CHAPTER 18

In What Way Faith Should Be Kept by Princes

Everybody knows how laudable it is in a prince to keep his faith and to be an honest man and not a trickster. Nevertheless, the experience of our times shows that the princes who have done great things are the ones who have taken little account of their promises and who have known how to addle the brains of men with craft. In the end they have conquered those who have put their reliance on good faith.

You must realize, then, that there are two ways to fight. In one kind the laws are used, in the other, force. The first is suitable to man, the second to animals. But because the first often falls short, one has to turn to the second. Hence a prince must know perfectly how to act like a beast and like a man. This truth was covertly taught to princes by ancient authors, who write that Achilles and many other ancient princes were turned over for their up-bringing to Chiron the centaur,[11] that he

---

[10] **Hannibal:** Carthaginian general (247–182 B.C.E.), one of Rome's greatest threats, who led his troops over the Alps from Spain into Italy.

[11] **Chiron the centaur:** Mythical half man, half horse; said to be the tutor of legendary heroes Achilles, Theseus, Jason, and Hercules.

might keep them under his tuition. To have as teacher one who is half beast and half man means nothing else than that a prince needs to know how to use the qualities of both creatures. The one without the other will not last long.

Since, then, it is necessary for a prince to understand how to make good use of the conduct of the animals, he should select among them the fox and the lion, because the lion cannot protect himself from traps, and the fox cannot protect himself from the wolves. So the prince needs to be a fox that he may know how to deal with traps, and a lion that he may frighten the wolves. Those who act like the lion alone do not understand their business. A prudent ruler, therefore, cannot and should not observe faith when such observance is to his disadvantage and the causes that made him give his promise have vanished. If men were all good, this advice would not be good, but since men are wicked and do not keep their promises to you, you likewise do not have to keep yours to them. Lawful reasons to excuse his failure to keep them will never be lacking to a prince. It would be possible to give innumerable modern examples of this and to show many treaties and promises that have been made null and void by the faithlessness of princes. And the prince who has best known how to act as a fox has come out best. But one who has this capacity must understand how to keep it covered, and be a skilful pretender and dissembler. Men are so simple and so subject to present needs that he who deceives in this way will always find those who will let themselves be deceived.

I do not wish to keep still about one of the recent instances. Alexander VI[12] did nothing else than deceive men, and had no other intention; yet he always found a subject to work on. There never was a man more effective in swearing that things were true, and the greater the oaths with which he made a promise, the less he observed it. Nonetheless his deceptions always succeeded to his wish, because he thoroughly understood this aspect of the world.

It is not necessary, then, for a prince really to have all the virtues mentioned above, but it is very necessary to seem to have them. I will even venture to say that they damage a prince who possesses them and always observes them, but if he seems to have them they are useful. I mean that he should seem compassionate, trustworthy, humane, honest, and religious, and actually be so; but yet he should have his mind so trained that, when it is necessary not to practice these virtues, he can change to the opposite, and do it skilfully. It is to be understood that a prince, especially a new prince, cannot observe all the things because of which men are considered good, because he is often obliged, if he wishes to maintain his government, to act contrary to faith, contrary to charity, contrary to humanity, contrary to religion. It is therefore necessary that he have a mind capable of turning in whatever direction the winds of Fortune and the variations of affairs require, and, as I said above, that he should not depart from what is morally right, if he can observe it, but should know how to adopt what is bad, when he is obliged to.

A prince, then, should be very careful that there does not issue from his mouth anything that is not full of the above-mentioned five qualities. To those who see and

---

[12] **Alexander VI:** Cardinal Rodrigo Borgia, pope from 1492 to 1503 and father of Cesare Borgia.

hear him he should seem all compassion, all faith, all honesty, all humanity, all religion. There is nothing more necessary to make a show of possessing than this last quality. For men in general judge more by their eyes than by their hands; everybody is fitted to see, few to understand. Everybody sees what you appear to be; few make out what you really are. And these few do not dare to oppose the opinion of the many, who have the majesty of the state to confirm their view. In the actions of all men, and especially those of princes, where there is no court to which to appeal, people think of the outcome. A prince needs only to conquer and to maintain his position. The means he has used will always be judged honorable and will be praised by everybody, because the crowd is always caught by appearance and by the outcome of events, and the crowd is all there is in the world; there is no place for the few when the many have room enough. A certain prince of the present day,[13] whom it is not good to name, preaches nothing else than peace and faith, and is wholly opposed to both of them, and both of them, if he had observed them, would many times have taken from him either his reputation or his throne.

CHAPTER 19

On Avoiding Contempt and Hatred

But because I have spoken of the more important of the qualities above, I wish to cover the others briefly with this generality. To wit, the prince should give his attention, as is in part explained above, to avoiding the things that make him hateful and contemptible. As long as he escapes them, he will have done his duty, and will find no danger in other injuries to his reputation. Hatred, as I have said, comes upon him chiefly from being rapacious and seizing the property and women of his subjects. He ought to abstain from both of these, for the majority of men live in contentment when they are not deprived of property or honor. Hence the prince has to struggle only with the ambition of the few, which can be restrained in many ways and with ease. Contempt is his portion if he is held to be variable, volatile, effeminate, cowardly, or irresolute. From these a prince should guard himself as from a rock in the sea. He should strive in all his actions to give evident signs of greatness, spirit, gravity, and fortitude. Also in the private affairs of his subjects he should make it understood that his opinion is irrevocable. In short he should keep up such a reputation that nobody thinks of trying to deceive him or outwit him.

The prince who makes people hold that opinion has prestige enough. And if a prince has a high reputation, men hesitate to conspire against him and hesitate to attack him, simply because he is supposed to be of high ability and respected by his subjects. For a prince must needs have two kinds of fear: one within his state, because of his subjects; the other without, because of foreign rulers. From these dangers he defends himself with good weapons and good friends. And if his weapons are good, he will always have good friends. Conditions within the state, too, will always remain settled when those without are settled, if they have not already been

---

[13] **A certain prince . . . day:** Ferdinand II of Spain.

unsettled by some conspiracy. And when things without are in movement, if he has ruled and lived as I have said, and does not fail himself, he will surely repel every attack, as I said Nabis the Spartan[14] did.

But with respect to his subjects, when there is no movement without, he has to fear that they will make a secret conspiracy. From this the prince protects himself adequately if he avoids being hated and despised and keeps the people satisfied with him. The latter necessarily follows the former, as was explained above at length. Indeed one of the most potent remedies the prince can have against conspiracies is not to be hated by the majority of his subjects. The reason for this is that a man who conspires always thinks he will please the people by killing the prince; but when he thinks he will offend them by it, he does not pluck up courage to adopt such a plan, because the difficulties that fall to the portion of conspirators are numerous. Experience shows that there have been many conspiracies and that few have come out well. They fail because the conspirator cannot be alone, and he can get companions only from those who, he thinks, are discontented. But as soon as you have revealed your purpose to a malcontent, you have given him an opportunity to become contented, because he evidently can hope to gain every advantage from his knowledge. Such is his position that, seeing on the one hand certain gain, and on the other gain that is uncertain and full of danger, he must needs be a rare friend, or, at any rate, an obstinate enemy of the prince, if he keeps faith with you. To put the thing briefly, I say that on the part of those who conspire there is nothing but fear, jealousy, and the expectation of punishment, which terrifies them. But on the part of the prince are the majesty of his high office, the laws, the power of his friends and his party that protects him. Evidently when the popular good-will is joined to all these things, it is impossible that anybody can be so foolhardy as to conspire against him. Ordinarily the conspirator must be afraid before the execution of his evil deed, but in this case he also has reason to fear after his transgression, because he will have the people against him and therefore cannot hope for any escape. . . .

I conclude, therefore, that a prince need not pay much attention to conspiracies when the people are well-disposed to him. But when they are unfriendly and hate him, he must fear everything and everybody. Further, well-organized governments and wise princes have striven with all diligence not to make the upper classes feel desperate, and to satisfy the populace and keep them contented. In fact this is one of the most important matters a prince has to deal with.

Among the kingdoms well organized and well governed in our times is France. In this country there are numerous good institutions on which depend the liberty and security of the king. The first of these is the parliament and its authority. He who organized this kingdom[15] set up the parliament because he knew the ambition of the nobles and their arrogance, and judged it necessary that the nobility should have a bit in its mouth to restrain it. On the other hand, he knew the hatred, founded on fear, of the generality of men for the nobles, and intended to secure the position

---

[14] **Nabis the Spartan:** A tyrant of Sparta (r. 207–192 B.C.E.), noted for his cruelty.

[15] **He . . . kingdom:** Possibly Louis IX (1214–1270), who promoted the use of Roman law in France and set up the Parlement de Paris.

of the latter. Yet he did not wish this to be the special concern of the king, because he wished to relieve the king from the hatred he would arouse among the great if he favored the people, and among the people if he favored the nobles. Therefore he set up a third party as judge, to be the one who, without bringing hatred on the king, should restrain the nobles and favor the people. This institution could not be better or more prudent, nor could there be a stronger cause for the security of the king and the realm. From this can be deduced another important idea: To wit, princes should have things that will bring them hatred done by their agents, but should do in person those that will give pleasure. Once more I conclude that a prince should esteem the nobles, but should not make himself hated by the populace.

. . .

Chapter 25

The Power of Fortune in Human Affairs,
and to What Extent She Should Be Relied On

It is not unknown to me that many have been and still are of the opinion that the affairs of this world are so under the direction of Fortune and of God that man's prudence cannot control them; in fact, that man has no resource against them. For this reason many think there is no use in sweating much over such matters, but that one might as well let Chance take control. This opinion has been the more accepted in our times, because of the great changes in the state of the world that have been and now are seen every day, beyond all human surmise. And I myself, when thinking on these things, have now and then in some measure inclined to their view. Nevertheless, because the freedom of the will should not be wholly annulled, I think it may be true that Fortune is arbiter of half of our actions, but that she still leaves the control of the other half, or about that, to us.

I liken her to one of those raging streams that, when they go mad, flood the plains, ruin the trees and the buildings, and take away the fields from one bank and put them down on the other. Everybody flees before them; everybody yields to their onrush without being able to resist anywhere. And though this is their nature, it does not cease to be true that, in calm weather, men can make some provision against them with walls and dykes, so that, when the streams swell, their waters will go off through a canal, or their currents will not be so wild and do so much damage. The same is true of Fortune. She shows her power where there is no wise preparation for resisting her, and turns her fury where she knows that no walls and dykes have been made to hold her in. And if you consider Italy—the place where these variations occur and the cause that has set them in motion—you will see that she is a country without dykes and without any wall of defence. If, like Germany, Spain, and France, she had had a sufficient bulwark of military vigor, this flood would not have made the great changes it has, or would not have come at all.

And this, I think, is all I need to say on opposing oneself to Fortune, in general. But limiting myself more to particulars, I say that a prince may be seen prospering today and falling in ruin tomorrow, though it does not appear that he has changed in his nature or any of his qualities. I believe this comes, in the first place, from the causes that have been discussed at length in preceding chapters. That is, if a prince bases himself entirely on Fortune, he will fall when she varies. I also believe that a ruler will be successful who adapts his mode of procedure to the quality of the times, and likewise that he will be unsuccessful if the times are out of accord with his procedure. Because it may be seen that in things leading to the end each has before him, namely glory and riches, men proceed differently. One acts with caution, another rashly; one with violence, another with skill; one with patience, another with its opposite; yet with these different methods each one attains his end. Still further, two cautious men will be seen, of whom one comes to his goal, the other does not. Likewise you will see two who succeed with two different methods, one of them being cautious and the other rash. These results are caused by nothing else than the nature of the times, which is or is not in harmony with the procedure of men. It also accounts for what I have mentioned, namely, that two persons, working differently, chance to arrive at the same result; and that of two who work in the same way, one attains his end, but the other does not.

On the nature of the times also depends the variability of the best method. If a man conducts himself with caution and patience, times and affairs may come around in such a way that his procedure is good, and he goes on successfully. But if times and circumstances change, he is ruined, because he does not change his method of action. There is no man so prudent as to understand how to fit himself to this condition, either because he is unable to deviate from the course to which nature inclines him, or because, having always prospered by walking in one path, he cannot persuade himself to leave it. So the cautious man, when the time comes to go at a reckless pace, does not know how to do it. Hence he comes to ruin. Yet if he could change his nature with the times and with circumstances, his fortune would not be altered. . . .

I conclude, then, that since Fortune is variable and men are set in their ways, they are successful when they are in harmony with Fortune and unsuccessful when they disagree with her. Yet I am of the opinion that it is better to be rash than over-cautious, because Fortune is a woman and, if you wish to keep her down, you must beat her and pound her. It is evident that she allows herself to be overcome by men who treat her in that way rather than by those who proceed coldly. For that reason, like a woman, she is always the friend of young men, because they are less cautious, and more courageous, and command her with more boldness.

∾ MARTIN LUTHER
B. GERMANY, 1483–1546

Martin Luther's roots were in the Middle Ages. Son of a peasant miner, he grew up in a religious household. Intending to study law at the University of Erfurt, he had a conversion experience in 1505 and instead of Erfurt entered an Augustinian monastery. During his assignment to the new

University of Wittenberg, Luther discovered the foundation of his theology in the biblical book of Romans, written by the apostle Paul, which contains the doctrine that humans are justified by faith alone—not by works, not by priestly mediation, not by sacraments, not by church membership. Faith was the answer, in Luther's belief, to the uncompromising judgments of a terrifying Father-God. He focused on the individual's direct relationship with God, as guided by the authority of God's word in the Bible.

In 1510 on a mission to Rome, Luther was shocked at the secular excesses of the Church hierarchy—the sale of indulgences, the worship of relics, and the proliferation of saints. Initially supported by humanists such as Desiderius Erasmus (1466–1536), Luther began to formulate plans for reforming the Church and curbing its excesses. Luther's ninety-five theses and his defiance of the pope and his Church led inevitably to open confrontations with the Catholic hierarchy. The first hearing on his writings and ideas was held at Augsburg in 1518; Luther refused to recant. When the Church issued a papal bull of condemnation to Luther in 1520, he publicly burned it. Excommunication did not immediately follow because Frederick the Wise (1463–1525) of Saxony, Luther's prince, scheduled a hearing before the 1521 Diet of Worms (the assembly of princes of the Holy Roman Empire), and Charles V (r. 1519–58), its leader.

One can only imagine the drama surrounding this meeting. Luther was asked whether he defended his writings or rejected them—of special concern was a tract, *The Babylonian Captivity of the Church* (1520), in which Luther recommended two rather than seven sacraments and denied the mediating role of the priesthood between laity and God. Surprisingly, Luther asked for time to think, and the hearing was postponed.

Lucas Cranach the Elder, *Martin Luther,* **1529**
This painting of the religious reformer Martin Luther was done by the great German portraitist of the Reformation, Lucas Cranach. (Erich Lessing / Art Resource, NY)

The next day, Luther defended his writings to a crowded hall, giving his famous answers documented in the piece included here. Following the direction of Charles, four out of six electors declared Luther a heretic. Charles returned the next day to affirm his Catholicism and to denounce Luther.

The Diet of Worms failed to heal the breach that continued to widen as Luther's movement gained support from laity as well as princes. Luther married, had children, and spent the rest of his life writing and formulating the direction for the new Lutheran Church. Luther introduced hymn singing and German-language (rather than Latin) church services. He also reformed the liturgy. His greatest literary and religious contribution to the Reformation, however, was his translation of the Bible into vernacular German, making it accessible to ordinary people.

❧ Speech at the Diet of Worms

Translated by Roger A. Hornsby

[HERE I STAND]

"Most serene emperor, most illustrious princes, most clement lords, obedient to the time set for me yesterday evening, I appear before you, beseeching you, by the mercy of God, that your most serene majesty and your most illustrious lordships may deign to listen graciously to this my cause—which is, as I hope, a cause of justice and of truth. If through my inexperience I have either not given the proper titles to some, or have offended in some manner against court customs and etiquette, I beseech you to kindly pardon me, as a man accustomed not to courts but to the cells of monks. I can bear no other witness about myself but that I have taught and written up to this time with simplicity of heart, as I had in view only the glory of God and the sound instruction of Christ's faithful.

"Most serene emperor, most illustrious princes, concerning those questions proposed to me yesterday on behalf of your serene majesty, whether I acknowledged as mine the books enumerated and published in my name and whether I wished to persevere in their defense or to retract them, I have given to the first question my full and complete answer, in which I still persist and shall persist forever. These books are mine and they have been published in my name by me, unless in the meantime, either through the craft or the mistaken wisdom of my emulators, something in them has been changed or wrongly cut out. For plainly I cannot acknowledge anything except what is mine alone and what has been written by me alone, to the exclusion of all interpretations of anyone at all.

"In replying to the second question, I ask that your most serene majesty and your lordships may deign to note that my books are not all of the same kind.

"For there are some in which I have discussed religious faith and morals simply and evangelically, so that even my enemies themselves are compelled to admit that these are useful, harmless, and clearly worthy to be read by Christians. Even the bull, although harsh and cruel, admits that some of my books are inoffensive, and yet allows these also to be condemned with a judgment which is utterly monstrous. Thus, if I should begin to disavow them, I ask you, what would I be doing? Would not I, alone of all men, be condemning the very truth upon which friends and enemies equally agree, striving alone against the harmonious confession of all?

"Another group of my books attacks the papacy and the affairs of the papists as those who both by their doctrines and very wicked examples have laid waste the Christian world with evil that affects the spirit and the body. For no one can deny or conceal this fact, when the experience of all and the complaints of everyone witness that through the decrees of the pope and the doctrines of men the consciences of the faithful have been most miserably entangled, tortured, and torn to pieces. Also, property and possessions, especially in this illustrious nation of Germany, have been devoured by an unbelievable tyranny and are being devoured to this time without letup and by unworthy means. [Yet the papists] by their own decrees (as in dist. 9 and 25; ques. 1 and 2) warn that the papal laws and doctrines which are contrary to the gospel or the opinions of the fathers are to be regarded as erroneous and reprehensible. If, therefore, I should have retracted these writings, I should have done nothing other than to have added strength to this [papal] tyranny and I should have opened not only windows but doors to such great godlessness. It would rage farther and more freely than ever it has dared up to this time. Yes, from the proof of such a revocation on my part, their wholly lawless and unrestrained kingdom of wickedness would become still more intolerable for the already wretched people; and their rule would be further strengthened and established, especially if it should be reported that this evil deed had been done by me by virtue of the authority of your most serene majesty and of the whole Roman Empire. Good God! What a cover for wickedness and tyranny I should have then become.

"I have written a third sort of book against some private and (as they say) distinguished individuals—those, namely, who strive to preserve the Roman tyranny and to destroy the godliness taught by me. Against these I confess I have been more violent than my religion or profession demands. But then, I do not set myself up as a saint; neither am I disputing about my life, but about the teaching of Christ. It is not proper for me to retract these works, because by this retraction it would again happen that tyranny and godlessness would, with my patronage, rule and rage among the people of God more violently than ever before.

"However, because I am a man and not God, I am not able to shield my books with any other protection than that which my Lord Jesus Christ himself offered for his teaching. When questioned before Annas about his teaching and struck by a servant, he said: 'If I have spoken wrongly, bear witness to the wrong' [John 18:19–23]. If the Lord himself who knew that he could not err, did not refuse to hear testimony against his teaching, even from the lowliest servant, how much more ought I, who am the lowest scum and able to do nothing except err, desire and expect that somebody should want to offer testimony against my teaching! Therefore, I ask by the mercy of God, may your most serene majesty, most illustrious lordships, or anyone at all who is able, either high or low, bear witness, expose my errors, overthrowing them by the writings of the prophets and the evangelists. Once I have been taught I shall be quite ready to renounce every error, and I shall be the first to cast my books into the fire.

"From these remarks I think it is clear that I have sufficiently considered and weighed the hazards and dangers, as well as the excitement and dissensions aroused in the world as a result of my teachings, things about which I was gravely and forcefully warned yesterday. To see excitement and dissension arise because of the Word of God is to me clearly the most joyful aspect of all in these matters. For this is the way, the opportunity, and the result of the Word of God, just as He [Christ] said, 'I have not come to bring peace but a sword. For I have come to set a man against his father,' etc. [Matt. 10:34–35]. Therefore, we ought to think how marvelous and terrible is our God in his counsels, lest by chance what is attempted for settling strife grows rather into an intolerable deluge of evils, if we begin by condemning the Word of God. And concern must be shown lest the reign of this most noble youth, Prince Charles (in whom after God is our great hope), become unhappy and inauspicious. I could illustrate this with abundant examples from Scripture—like Pharaoh, the king of Babylon, and the kings of Israel who, when they endeavored to pacify and strengthen their kingdoms by the wisest counsels, most surely destroyed themselves. For it is He who takes the wise in their own craftiness [Job 5:13] and overturns mountains before they know it [Job 9:5]. Therefore we must fear God. I do not say these things because there is a need of either my teachings or my warnings for such leaders as you, but because I must not withhold the allegiance which I owe my Germany. With these words I commend myself to your most serene majesty and to your lordships, humbly asking that I not be allowed through the agitation of my enemies, without cause, to be made hateful to you. I have finished."

When I had finished, the speaker for the emperor said, as if in reproach, that I had not answered the question, that I ought not call into question those things which had been condemned and defined in councils; therefore what was sought from me was not a horned response, but a simple one, whether or not I wished to retract.

Here I answered:

"Since then your serene majesty and your lordships seek a simple answer, I will give it in this manner, neither horned nor toothed: Unless I am convinced by the testimony of the Scriptures or by clear reason (for I do not trust either in the pope or in councils alone, since it is well known that they have often erred and contradicted themselves), I am bound by the Scriptures I have quoted and my conscience is captive to the Word of God. I cannot and I will not retract anything, since it is neither safe nor right to go against conscience.

"I cannot do otherwise, here I stand, may God help me, Amen."

❧ Michel Eyquem de Montaigne
b. France, 1533–1592

Reading **Montaigne**, one is immediately struck by the apparent modernity of his views, especially his skepticism about absolute truth, his questioning of the shifting grounds of identity, his acceptance of the limits of human understanding, and his tolerant recognition of cultural differences. Yet as his biographers and critics have noted, the author of the *Essays* (1580–95), a collection of unpretentious reflections on his own life, is rooted firmly in the material and intellectual experience of the European **Renaissance**. Montaigne's renunciation of human claims to knowledge, power, and authority seems to fly in the face of the great celebrations of those qualities in **Giovanni Pico della Mirandola** and **Niccolò Machiavelli**, but his *Essays* combine the nobleman's graceful poise, the humanist's love of the classics, and the practicality of the public observer. Above all, he shares with his age its desire for self-understanding, characterized most notably in an epithet he had engraved on a medallion: *"Que sais-je?"* — "What do I know?" His *Essays,* composed over the last twenty years of his life in the midst of relentless political turmoil, not only represent Montaigne's attempts to answer that question but also introduce a new literary genre in the West.

Early Love of Latin. When Michel de Montaigne was born on February 28, 1533, his wealthy father brought him up for two years among peasants in order to bond him with people of the lowest class before hiring a German tutor and two attendants to care for his son and to speak to him only in Latin. Montaigne tells us that he was six years old before he understood his native French, and he praises his father for enabling him to acquire a flawless Latin "without the whip and tears" of a grammar school. From age six to twelve Montaigne attended the College de Guyenne in Bordeaux. Once he left school, Montaigne spent a good deal of time in Paris before beginning his career as a lawyer in the high court of Bordeaux. As a magistrate, Montaigne was necessarily involved in the growing conflict between the Catholics and Protestants in France, which eventually amounted to religious civil war. Although he was a Catholic loyalist, Montaigne disagreed with the cruel punishments the government dealt to the Protestant **Huguenots**,[1] and his outrage at these sufferings is echoed in his appeals for tolerance and moderation in the *Essays.*

Marriage and Retirement. In 1565, Montaigne married Françoise de La Chassaigne. Shortly thereafter, his father asked him to translate a Latin

mone-TEN

p. 1740; 1744

www For a quiz on "Of Cannibals" and information about the twenty-first century relevance of Montaigne, see bedfordstmartins .com/worldlit compact.

HYOO-guh-nahts

---

[1] **Huguenots:** French Calvinists, who were members of the Reformed Church, founded about 1555 in France by the Protestant reformer John Calvin. The Huguenots were condemned as heretics and subject to persecution in predominantly Catholic France in the fifteenth and sixteenth centuries.

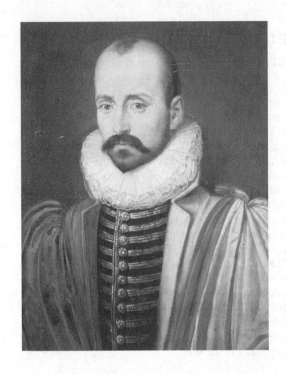

Jean-Baptiste Mauzaisse, *Michel de Montaigne*
This portrait of the French humanist and author Montaigne was painted in the nineteenth century. (The Art Archive / Musée du Château de Versailles / Dagli Orti)

Montaigne resists simple definitions. He is the first essayist, a skeptic, an acute student of himself and of man, a champion of a man-based morality, a vivid and charming stylist, and many other things besides. No one description tells nearly enough, and indeed it is hard to see which one to place at the center.

– DONALD FRAME, critic, 1943

work, *The Book of Creatures, or Natural Theology,* by the fifteenth-century Spanish writer Raymond Sebond. After his father died in 1568, Montaigne inherited the family estate, the Château de Montaigne, about thirty miles from Bordeaux. Two years later, perhaps disappointed with a lack of political preferment, Montaigne retired to his beloved book-lined study in the tower at the château in order to devote his time to reading and writing. It was here that he began his *Essays* in 1572, the first edition of which was published in 1580. He added to his *Essays* until the end of his life, publishing three editions before his death in 1592, after which appeared the complete four-book version we read today.

"Of Cannibals."   "Of Cannibals" (1580) reveals a cautious, but nonetheless genuine, respect for the cultural values and practices of non-European people. Montaigne engages the question of cultural difference evident between the various human communities, especially between the primitive and the civilized. He notices that human perception of other cultures is relative to the perspective of the beholder, and he wonders characteristically whether it is not the so-called civilized peoples who are the true barbarians. Despite his love of classical learning, Montaigne entertains the possibility that native peoples might be able to teach Europeans something about human relationships, politics, and philosophy. Breaking with the view, sometimes linked to Machiavelli, that Greco-Roman history and philosophy should serve up the only models for European states, Montaigne sees possible models for statecraft in the new world. As he says in "Of Cannibals,"

> I am sorry that Lycurgus and Plato[2] did not know [the natives]; for it seems to me that what we actually see in these nations surpasses not only all the pictures in which poets have idealized the golden age and all their inventions in imagining a happy state of man, but also the conceptions and the very desire of philosophy. They could not imagine a naturalness so pure and simple as we see by experience; nor could they believe that our society could be maintained with so little artifice and human solder.

This tolerance, respect for others, and acceptance of the limits of knowledge typify Montaigne's version of Renaissance humanism.

■ FURTHER RESEARCH

Biography
Frame, Donald. *Montaigne: A Biography.* 1965.
Friedrich, Hugo. *Montaigne.* 1991.

Criticism
Bencivenga, Ermanno. *The Discipline of Subjectivity: An Essay on Montaigne.* 1990.
Burke, Peter. *Montaigne.* 1981.
Frame, Donald. *Montaigne's Essais: A Study.* 1969.
Saynce, R. A. *The Essays of Montaigne: A Critical Exploration.* 1972.
Shklar, Judith. *Ordinary Vices.* 1984.
Starobinski, Jean. *Montaigne in Motion.* 1982; trans. Arthur Goldhammer, 1985.
Tetel, Marcel. *Montaigne.* 1990.

■ PRONUNCIATION

Huguenots: HYOO-guh-nahts
Montaigne: mone-TEN

---

[2] **Lycurgus and Plato:** Lycurgus (ninth century B.C.E.), the lawgiver, perhaps mythic, of Sparta; Plato (427?–347 B.C.E.), Greek philosopher and author of *The Republic.* Montaigne associates both Lycurgus and Plato with creating ideal models of society.

FROM

 # Essays

Translated by Donald M. Frame

OF CANNIBALS

When King Pyrrhus[1] passed over into Italy, after he had reconnoitered the formation of the army that the Romans were sending to meet him, he said: "I do not know what barbarians these are" (for so the Greeks called all foreign nations), "but the formation

---

[1] **King Pyrrhus:** King of Epirus (c. 318–272 B.C.E.), who invaded Rome in 280 B.C.E. at a high cost of lives among his soldiers.

of this army that I see is not at all barbarous." The Greeks said as much of the army that Flaminius brought into their country, and so did Philip, seeing from a knoll the order and distribution of the Roman camp, in his kingdom, under Publius Sulpicius Galba.[2] Thus we should beware of clinging to vulgar opinions, and judge things by reason's way, not by popular say.

I had with me for a long time a man who had lived for ten or twelve years in that other world which has been discovered in our century, in the place where Ville-gaignon landed, and which he called Antarctic France.[3] This discovery of a bound-less country seems worthy of consideration. I don't know if I can guarantee that some other such discovery will not be made in the future, so many personages greater than ourselves having been mistaken about this one. I am afraid we have eyes bigger than our stomachs, and more curiosity than capacity. We embrace every-thing, but we clasp only wind.

Plato[4] brings in Solon, telling how he had learned from the priests of the city of Saïs in Egypt that in days of old, before the Flood, there was a great island named Atlantis, right at the mouth of the Strait of Gibraltar, which contained more land than Africa and Asia put together, and that the kings of that country, who not only possessed that island but had stretched out so far on the mainland that they held the breadth of Africa as far as Egypt, and the length of Europe as far as Tuscany, under-took to step over into Asia and subjugate all the nations that border on the Mediter-ranean, as far as the Black Sea; and for this purpose crossed the Spains, Gaul, Italy, as far as Greece, where the Athenians checked them; but that some time after, both the Athenians and themselves and their island were swallowed up by the Flood.

It is quite likely that the extreme devastation of waters made amazing changes in the habitations of the earth, as people maintain that the sea cut off Sicily from Italy—

> 'Tis said an earthquake once asunder tore
> These lands with dreadful havoc, which before
> Formed but one land, one coast
> — VIRGIL[5]

—Cyprus from Syria, the island of Euboea from the mainland of Boeotia; and else-where joined lands that were divided, filling the channels between them with sand and mud:

> A sterile marsh, long fit for rowing, now
> Feeds neighbor towns, and feels the heavy plow.
> — HORACE[6]

---

[2] **Flaminius . . . Galba:** Roman generals who fought against Philip V, king of Macedon (221–179 B.C.E.).

[3] **Antarctic France:** Nicolas Durand de Villegaignon (1510–1571?), a French explorer, landed in Brazil (Antarctic France) in 1555.

[4] **Plato** (427?–347 B.C.E.): Greek philosopher and author of dialogues on various topics, including the *Timaeus*, in which he mentions the myth of Atlantis.

[5] **Virgil:** Publius Vergilius Maro (70–19 B.C.E.), the greatest of the Roman epic poets and author of *The Aeneid*, from which the quote is taken (3:414–15).

[6] **Horace:** Horatius Flaccus (65–8 B.C.E.), Roman lyric poet and author of *Art of Poetry*, from which these lines are taken (65–66).

But there is no great likelihood that that island was the new world which we have just discovered; for it almost touched Spain, and it would be an incredible result of a flood to have forced it away as far as it is, more than twelve hundred leagues; besides, the travels of the moderns have already almost revealed that it is not an island, but a mainland connected with the East Indies on one side, and elsewhere with the lands under the two poles; or, if it is separated from them, it is by so narrow a strait and interval that it does not deserve to be called an island on that account.

It seems that there are movements, some natural, others feverish, in these great bodies, just as in our own. When I consider the inroads that my river, the Dordogne, is making in my lifetime into the right bank in its descent, and that in twenty years it has gained so much ground and stolen away the foundations of several buildings, I clearly see that this is an extraordinary disturbance; for if it had always gone at this rate, or was to do so in the future, the face of the world would be turned topsy-turvy. But rivers are subject to changes: now they overflow in one direction, now in another, now they keep to their course. I am not speaking of the sudden inundations whose causes are manifest. In Médoc,[7] along the seashore, my brother, the sieur d'Arsac, can see an estate of his buried under the sands that the sea spews forth; the tops of some buildings are still visible; his farms and domains have changed into very thin pasturage. The inhabitants say that for some time the sea has been pushing toward them so hard that they have lost four leagues of land. These sands are its harbingers; and we see great dunes of moving sand that march half a league ahead of it and keep conquering land.

The other testimony of antiquity with which some would connect this discovery is in Aristotle,[8] at least if that little book *Of Unheard-of Wonders* is by him. He there relates that certain Carthaginians, after setting out upon the Atlantic Ocean from the Strait of Gibraltar and sailing a long time, at last discovered a great fertile island, all clothed in woods and watered by great deep rivers, far remote from any mainland; and that they, and others since, attracted by the goodness and fertility of the soil, went there with their wives and children, and began to settle there. The lords of Carthage, seeing that their country was gradually becoming depopulated, expressly forbade anyone to go there any more, on pain of death, and drove out these new inhabitants, fearing, it is said, that in course of time they might come to multiply so greatly as to supplant their former masters and ruin their state. This story of Aristotle does not fit our new lands any better than the other.

This man I had was a simple, crude fellow—a character fit to bear true witness; for clever people observe more things and more curiously, but they interpret them; and to lend weight and conviction to their interpretation, they cannot help altering history a little. They never show you things as they are, but bend and disguise them according to the way they have seen them; and to give credence to their judgment and attract you to it, they are prone to add something to their matter, to stretch it out and amplify it. We need a man either very honest, or so simple that he has not the

---

[7] **Médoc:** A region in southwestern France.

[8] **Aristotle** (384–322 B.C.E.): Greek philosopher; he did not write the book mentioned here.

stuff to build up false inventions and give them plausibility; and wedded to no theory. Such was my man; and besides this, he at various times brought sailors and merchants, whom he had known on that trip, to see me. So I content myself with his information, without inquiring what the cosmographers say about it.

We ought to have topographers who would give us an exact account of the places where they have been. But because they have over us the advantage of having seen Palestine, they want to enjoy the privilege of telling us news about all the rest of the world. I would like everyone to write what he knows, and as much as he knows, not only in this, but in all other subjects; for a man may have some special knowledge and experience of the nature of a river or a fountain, who in other matters knows only what everybody knows. However, to circulate this little scrap of knowledge, he will undertake to write the whole of physics. From this vice spring many great abuses.

Now, to return to my subject, I think there is nothing barbarous and savage in that nation, from what I have been told, except that each man calls barbarism whatever is not his own practice; for indeed it seems we have no other test of truth and reason than the example and pattern of the opinions and customs of the country we live in. *There* is always the perfect religion, the perfect government, the perfect and accomplished manners in all things. Those people are wild, just as we call wild the fruits that Nature has produced by herself and in her normal course; whereas really it is those that we have changed artificially and led astray from the common order, that we should rather call wild. The former retain alive and vigorous their genuine, their most useful and natural, virtues and properties, which we have debased in the latter in adapting them to gratify our corrupted taste. And yet for all that, the savor and delicacy of some uncultivated fruits of those countries is quite as excellent, even to our taste, as that of our own. It is not reasonable that art should win the place of honor over our great and powerful mother Nature. We have so overloaded the beauty and richness of her works by our inventions that we have quite smothered her. Yet wherever her purity shines forth, she wonderfully puts to shame our vain and frivolous attempts:

> Ivy comes readier without our care;
> In lonely caves the arbutus grows more fair;
> No art with artless bird song can compare.
> — PROPERTIUS[9]

All our efforts cannot even succeed in reproducing the nest of the tiniest little bird, its contexture, its beauty and convenience; or even the web of the puny spider. All things, says Plato,[10] are produced by nature, by fortune, or by art; the greatest and most beautiful by one or the other of the first two, the least and most imperfect by the last.

---

[9] **Propertius:** Sextus Propertius (c. 50–c. 16 B.C.E.), Roman poet noted for his moving elegiac poems; the quote is from *Elegies* 1:2.10–12.

[10] **Plato:** In the *Laws.*

These nations, then, seem to me barbarous in this sense, that they have been fashioned very little by the human mind, and are still very close to their original naturalness. The laws of nature still rule them, very little corrupted by ours; and they are in such a state of purity that I am sometimes vexed that they were unknown earlier, in the days when there were men able to judge them better than we. I am sorry that Lycurgus[11] and Plato did not know of them; for it seems to me that what we actually see in these nations surpasses not only all the pictures in which poets have idealized the golden age and all their inventions in imagining a happy state of man, but also the conceptions and the very desire of philosophy. They could not imagine a naturalness so pure and simple as we see by experience; nor could they believe that our society could be maintained with so little artifice and human solder. This is a nation, I should say to Plato, in which there is no sort of traffic, no knowledge of letters, no science of numbers, no name for a magistrate or for political superiority, no custom of servitude, no riches or poverty, no contracts, no successions, no partitions, no occupations but leisure ones, no care for any but common kinship, no clothes, no agriculture, no metal, no use of wine or wheat. The very words that signify lying, treachery, dissimulation, avarice, envy, belittling, pardon—unheard of.[12] How far from this perfection would he find the republic that he imagined: *Men fresh sprung from the gods* [Seneca].[13]

> These manners nature first ordained.
> — VIRGIL[14]

For the rest, they live in a country with a very pleasant and temperate climate, so that according to my witnesses it is rare to see a sick man there; and they have assured me that they never saw one palsied, bleary-eyed, toothless, or bent with age. They are settled along the sea and shut in on the land side by great high mountains, with a stretch about a hundred leagues wide in between. They have a great abundance of fish and flesh which bear no resemblance to ours, and they eat them with no other artifice than cooking. The first man who rode a horse there, though he had had dealings with them on several other trips, so horrified them in this posture that they shot him dead with arrows before they could recognize him.

Their buildings are very long, with a capacity of two or three hundred souls; they are covered with the bark of great trees, the strips reaching to the ground at one end and supporting and leaning on one another at the top, in the manner of some of our barns, whose covering hangs down to the ground and acts as a side. They have wood so hard that they cut with it and make of it their swords and grills to cook their food. Their beds are of a cotton weave, hung from the roof like those in our ships, each man having his own; for the wives sleep apart from their husbands.

---

[11] **Lycurgus:** A Spartan lawgiver (perhaps mythic) of the ninth century B.C.E. who wrote about ideal societies.

[12] **This is a nation . . . unheard of:** Shakespeare borrowed from this entire passage in Florio's translation of *The Tempest,* Act II, scene 1, lines 137–58 (see pages 000–00).

[13] **[Seneca]:** Lucius Annaeus Seneca (c. 3 B.C.E.–c. 65 C.E.), Roman statesman and dramatist; the quote is from his *Epistles* 90.

[14] **Virgil:** From his *Georgics,* a poem about agricultural life (Book 2:20).

They get up with the sun, and eat immediately upon rising, to last them through the day; for they take no other meal than that one. Like some other Eastern peoples, of whom Suidas[15] tells us, who drank apart from meals, they do not drink then; but they drink several times a day, and to capacity. Their drink is made of some root, and is of the color of our claret wines. They drink it only lukewarm. This beverage keeps only two or three days; it has a slightly sharp taste, is not at all heady, is good for the stomach, and has a laxative effect upon those who are not used to it; it is a very pleasant drink for anyone who is accustomed to it. In place of bread they use a certain white substance like preserved coriander. I have tried it; it tastes sweet and a little flat.

The whole day is spent in dancing. The younger men go to hunt animals with bows. Some of the women busy themselves meanwhile with warming their drink, which is their chief duty. Some one of the old men, in the morning before they begin to eat, preaches to the whole barnful in common, walking from one end to the other, and repeating one single sentence several times until he has completed the circuit (for the buildings are fully a hundred paces long). He recommends to them only two things: valor against the enemy and love for their wives. And they never fail to point out this obligation, as their refrain, that it is their wives who keep their drink warm and seasoned.

There may be seen in several places, including my own house, specimens of their beds, of their ropes, of their wooden swords and the bracelets with which they cover their wrists in combats, and of the big canes, open at one end, by whose sound they keep time in their dances. They are close shaven all over, and shave themselves much more cleanly than we, with nothing but a wooden or stone razor. They believe that souls are immortal, and that those who have deserved well of the gods are lodged in that part of heaven where the sun rises, and the damned in the west.

They have some sort of priests and prophets, but they rarely appear before the people, having their home in the mountains. On their arrival there is a great feast and solemn assembly of several villages — each barn, as I have described it, makes up a village, and they are about one French league from each other. The prophet speaks to them in public, exhorting them to virtue and their duty; but their whole ethical science contains only these two articles: resoluteness in war and affection for their wives. He prophesies to them things to come and the results they are to expect from their undertakings, and urges them to war or holds them back from it; but this is on the condition that when he fails to prophesy correctly, and if things turn out otherwise than he has predicted, he is cut into a thousand pieces if they catch him, and condemned as a false prophet. For this reason, the prophet who has once been mistaken is never seen again.

Divination is a gift of God; that is why its abuse should be punished as imposture. Among the Scythians,[16] when the soothsayers failed to hit the mark, they were laid, chained hand and foot, on carts full of heather and drawn by oxen, on which they were burned. Those who handle matters subject to the control of human capacity are excusable if they do the best they can. But these others, who come and

---

[15] **Suidas:** A Greek lexicographer from the tenth century C.E.

[16] **Scythians:** Nomadic people noted for barbarity who occupied southeastern Europe until about 300 B.C.E.

trick us with assurances of an extraordinary faculty that is beyond our ken, should they not be punished for not making good their promise, and for the temerity of their imposture?

They have their wars with the nations beyond the mountains, further inland, to which they go quite naked, with no other arms than bows or wooden swords ending in a sharp point, in the manner of the tongues of our boar spears. It is astonishing what firmness they show in their combats, which never end but in slaughter and bloodshed; for as to routs and terror, they know nothing of either.

Each man brings back as his trophy the head of the enemy he has killed, and sets it up at the entrance of his dwelling. After they have treated their prisoners well for a long time with all the hospitality they can think of, each man who has a prisoner calls a great assembly of his acquaintances. He ties a rope to one of the prisoner's arms, by the end of which he holds him, a few steps away, for fear of being hurt, and gives his dearest friend the other arm to hold in the same way; and these two, in the presence of the whole assembly, kill him with their swords. This done, they roast him and eat him in common and send some pieces to their absent friends. This is not, as people think, for nourishment, as of old the Scythians used to do; it is to betoken an extreme revenge. And the proof of this came when they saw the Portuguese, who had joined forces with their adversaries, inflict a different kind of death on them when they took them prisoner, which was to bury them up to the waist, shoot the rest of their body full of arrows, and afterward hang them. They thought that these people from the other world, being men who had sown the knowledge of many vices among their neighbors and were much greater masters than themselves in every sort of wickedness, did not adopt this sort of vengeance without some reason, and that it must be more painful than their own; so they began to give up their old method and follow this one.

I am not sorry that we notice the barbarous horror of such acts, but I am heartily sorry that, judging their faults rightly, we should be so blind to our own. I think there is more barbarity in eating a man alive than in eating him dead; and in tearing by tortures and the rack a body still full of feeling, in roasting a man bit by bit, in having him bitten and mangled by dogs and swine (as we have not only read but seen within fresh memory, not among ancient enemies, but among neighbors and fellow citizens, and what is worse, on the pretext of piety and religion), than in roasting and eating him after he is dead.

Indeed, Chrysippus and Zeno,[17] heads of the Stoic sect, thought there was nothing wrong in using our carcasses for any purpose in case of need, and getting nourishment from them; just as our ancestors, when besieged by Caesar in the city of Alésia, resolved to relieve their famine by eating old men, women, and other people useless for fighting.

> The Gascons once, 'tis said, their life renewed
> By eating of such food.
> — JUVENAL[18]

---

[17] **Chrysippus and Zeno:** Chrysippus (280–206 B.C.E.) and Zeno of Cittium (c. 333–264 B.C.E.), Greek philosophers and founders of Stoicism, a philosophy emphasizing the importance of virtuous action in accordance with nature.

[18] **Juvenal** (fl. second century C.E.): Roman poet known for his harsh satires; the quote is from *Satires* 15:93–94.

And physicians do not fear to use human flesh in all sorts of ways for our health, applying it either inwardly or outwardly. But there never was any opinion so disordered as to excuse treachery, disloyalty, tyranny, and cruelty, which are our ordinary vices.

So we may well call these people barbarians, in respect to the rules of reason, but not in respect to ourselves, who surpass them in every kind of barbarity.

Their warfare is wholly noble and generous, and as excusable and beautiful as this human disease can be; its only basis among them is their rivalry in valor. They are not fighting for the conquest of new lands, for they still enjoy that natural abundance that provides them without toil and trouble with all necessary things in such profusion that they have no wish to enlarge their boundaries. They are still in that happy state of desiring only as much as their natural needs demand; anything beyond that is superfluous to them.

They generally call those of the same age, brothers; those who are younger, children; and the old men are fathers to all the others. These leave to their heirs in common the full possession of their property, without division or any other title at all than just the one that Nature gives to her creatures in bringing them into the world.

If their neighbors cross the mountains to attack them and win a victory, the gain of the victor is glory, and the advantage of having proved the master in valor and virtue; for apart from this they have no use for the goods of the vanquished, and they return to their own country, where they lack neither anything necessary nor that great thing, the knowledge of how to enjoy their condition happily and be content with it. These men of ours do the same in their turn. They demand of their prisoners no other ransom than that they confess and acknowledge their defeat. But there is not one in a whole century who does not choose to die rather than to relax a single bit, by word or look, from the grandeur of an invincible courage; not one who would not rather be killed and eaten than so much as ask not to be. They treat them very freely, so that life may be all the dearer to them, and usually entertain them with threats of their coming death, of the torments they will have to suffer, the preparations that are being made for that purpose, the cutting up of their limbs, and the feast that will be made at their expense. All this is done for the sole purpose of extorting from their lips some weak or base word, or making them want to flee, so as to gain the advantage of having terrified them and broken down their firmness. For indeed, if you take it the right way, it is in this point alone that true victory lies:

> It is no victory
> Unless the vanquished foe admits your mastery.
> – CLAUDIAN[19]

The Hungarians, very bellicose fighters, did not in olden times pursue their advantage beyond putting the enemy at their mercy. For having wrung a confession from him to this effect, they let him go unharmed and unransomed, except, at most, for exacting his promise never again to take up arms against them.

---

[19] **Claudian:** Claudius Claudianus (c. 370–c. 404 C.E.), Roman lyric and epic poet; author of the panegyric poem *Of the Sixth Consulate of Honorius,* from which the quote is taken (ll. 248–49).

We win enough advantages over our enemies that are borrowed advantages, not really our own. It is the quality of a porter, not of valor, to have sturdier arms and legs; agility is a dead and corporeal quality; it is a stroke of luck to make our enemy stumble, or dazzle his eyes by the sunlight; it is a trick of art and technique, which may be found in a worthless coward, to be an able fencer. The worth and value of a man is in his heart and his will; there lies his real honor. Valor is the strength, not of legs and arms, but of heart and soul; it consists not in the worth of our horse or our weapons, but in our own. He who falls obstinate in his courage, *if he has fallen, he fights on his knees* [Seneca]. He who relaxes none of his assurance, no matter how great the danger of imminent death; who, giving up his soul, still looks firmly and scornfully at his enemy—he is beaten not by us, but by fortune; he is killed, not conquered.

The most valiant are sometimes the most unfortunate. Thus there are triumphant defeats that rival victories. Nor did those four sister victories, the fairest that the sun ever set eyes on—Salamis, Plataea, Mycale, and Sicily—ever dare match all their combined glory against the glory of the annihilation of King Leonidas and his men at the pass of Thermopylae.[20]

Who ever hastened with more glorious and ambitious desire to win a battle than Captain Ischolas to lose one? Who ever secured his safety more ingeniously and painstakingly than he did his destruction? He was charged to defend a certain pass in the Peloponnesus against the Arcadians. Finding himself wholly incapable of doing this, in view of the nature of the place and the inequality of the forces, he made up his mind that all who confronted the enemy would necessarily have to remain on the field. On the other hand, deeming it unworthy both of his own virtue and magnanimity and of the Lacedaemonian name to fail in his charge, he took a middle course between these two extremes, in this way. The youngest and fittest of his band he preserved for the defense and service of their country, and sent them home; and with those whose loss was less important, he determined to hold this pass, and by their death to make the enemy buy their entry as dearly as he could. And so it turned out. For he was presently surrounded on all sides by the Arcadians, and after slaughtering a large number of them, he and his men were all put to the sword. Is there a trophy dedicated to victors that would not be more due to these vanquished? The role of true victory is in fighting, not in coming off safely; and the honor of valor consists in combating, not in beating.

To return to our story. These prisoners are so far from giving in, in spite of all that is done to them, that on the contrary, during the two or three months that they are kept, they wear a gay expression; they urge their captors to hurry and put them to the test; they defy them, insult them, reproach them with their cowardice and the number of battles they have lost to the prisoners' own people.

I have a song composed by a prisoner which contains this challenge, that they should all come boldly and gather to dine off him, for they will be eating at the same

---

[20] **Salamis . . . Thermopylae:** Sites of famous Greek victories against the Persians and Carthaginians in the fifth century B.C.E.; Leonidas was the Spartan king who led the famous standoff against the Persians at Thermopylae in 480 B.C.E.

time their own fathers and grandfathers, who have served to feed and nourish his body. "These muscles," he says, "this flesh and these veins are your own, poor fools that you are. You do not recognize that the substance of your ancestors' limbs is still contained in them. Savor them well; you will find in them the taste of your own flesh." An idea that certainly does not smack of barbarity. Those that paint these people dying, and who show the execution, portray the prisoner spitting in the face of his slayers and scowling at them. Indeed, to the last gasp they never stop braving and defying their enemies by word and look. Truly here are real savages by our standards; for either they must be thoroughly so, or we must be; there is an amazing distance between their character and ours.

The men there have several wives, and the higher their reputation for valor the more wives they have. It is a remarkably beautiful thing about their marriages that the same jealousy our wives have to keep us from the affection and kindness of other women, theirs have to win this for them. Being more concerned for their husbands' honor than for anything else, they strive and scheme to have as many companions as they can, since that is a sign of their husbands' valor.

Our wives will cry "Miracle!" but it is no miracle. It is a properly matrimonial virtue, but one of the highest order. In the Bible, Leah, Rachel, Sarah,[21] and Jacob's wives gave their beautiful handmaids to their husbands; and Livia seconded the appetites of Augustus, to her own disadvantage; and Stratonice, the wife of King Deiotarus,[22] not only lent her husband for his use a very beautiful young chambermaid in her service, but carefully brought up her children, and backed them up to succeed to their father's estates.

And lest it be thought that all this is done through a simple and servile bondage to usage and through the pressure of the authority of their ancient customs, without reasoning or judgment, and because their minds are so stupid that they cannot take any other course, I must cite some examples of their capacity. Besides the warlike song I have just quoted, I have another, a love song, which begins in this vein: "Adder, stay; stay, adder, that from the pattern of your coloring my sister may draw the fashion and the workmanship of a rich girdle that I may give to my love; so may your beauty and your pattern be forever preferred to all other serpents." This first couplet is the refrain of the song. Now I am familiar enough with poetry to be a judge of this: not only is there nothing barbarous in this fancy, but it is altogether Anacreontic.[23] Their language, moreover, is a soft language, with an agreeable sound, somewhat like Greek in its endings.

Three of these men, ignorant of the price they will pay some day, in loss of repose and happiness, for gaining knowledge of the corruptions of this side of the ocean; ignorant also of the fact that of this intercourse will come their ruin (which I

---

[21] **Leah, Rachel, Sarah:** See Genesis 30 for the stories of Jacob's wives Leah and Rachel; see Genesis 16 for the story of Abraham's wife Sarah and her handmaid Hagar.

[22] **King Deiotarus:** The story of Livia is told in *Life of Augustus* by the Roman writer Suetonius (c. 69–c. 149); the story of Stratonice and Deiotarus, the Tetrarch of Galatia, is told in *On the Bravery of Women,* by the Roman writer Plutarch (46?–c. 120).

[23] **Anacreontic** (c. 563–c. 478 B.C.E.): Anacreon, Greek poet celebrated for his love poetry.

suppose is already well advanced: poor wretches, to let themselves be tricked by the desire for new things, and to have left the serenity of their own sky to come and see ours!)—three of these men were at Rouen, at the time the late King Charles IX was there. The king talked to them for a long time; they were shown our ways, our splendor, the aspect of a fine city. After that, someone asked their opinion, and wanted to know what they had found most amazing. They mentioned three things, of which I have forgotten the third, and I am very sorry for it; but I still remember two of them. They said that in the first place they thought it very strange that so many grown men, bearded, strong, and armed, who were around the king (it is likely that they were talking about the Swiss of his guard) should submit to obey a child, and that one of them was not chosen to command instead. Second (they have a way in their language of speaking of men as halves of one another), they had noticed that there were among us men full and gorged with all sorts of good things, and that their other halves were beggars at their doors, emaciated with hunger and poverty; and they thought it strange that these needy halves could endure such an injustice, and did not take the others by the throat, or set fire to their houses.

I had a very long talk with one of them; but I had an interpreter who followed my meaning so badly, and who was so hindered by his stupidity in taking in my ideas, that I could get hardly any satisfaction from the man. When I asked him what profit he gained from his superior position among his people (for he was a captain, and our sailors called him king), he told me that it was to march foremost in war. How many men followed him? He pointed to a piece of ground, to signify as many as such a space could hold; it might have been four or five thousand men. Did all his authority expire with the war? He said that this much remained, that when he visited the villages dependent on him, they made paths for him through the underbrush by which he might pass quite comfortably.

All this is not too bad—but what's the use? They don't wear breeches.

❧ MIGUEL DE CERVANTES SAAVEDRA
B. SPAIN, 1547–1616

One of the great works of world literature, characterized by the French literary critic Charles Sainte-Beuve as the "bible of humanity," *Don Quixote* (1605, 1615) has been translated into more languages than any other book except the Bible. The lean and angular protagonist Don Quixote and his rotund companion Sancho Panza have entered the visual iconography of our culture, and we use the adjective *QUIXOTIC* and the phrase *tilting at windmills* to describe impractical idealism of the sort exemplified by the knight of La Mancha. *Don Quixote* is often considered the first Western novel. Its story of a wanderer encountering a series of adventures, its use of a hero and a contrasting foil, its challenge to romantic

kee-HOH-tay

www For links to more information about Cervantes and his twenty-first-century relevance, see bedfordstmartins .com/worldlit compact.

Don Quixote poster
The story of Don Quixote has captured readers' imaginations through the centuries. Here, in an advertisement for a nineteenth-century play based on Cervantes's novel, the title character is shown with his faithful horse against the symbolic windmill. (The Art Archive / Victoria and Albert Museum London / Sally Chappell)

conventions and ideas, and its thematic conflict between illusion and reality have become commonplaces of later novels.

Don Quixote begins as a story that will reveal the absurdity of romantic idealism, but by the end it apparently reverses itself. For as foolish and mistaken as Don Quixote is, he nevertheless wins the love and allegiance of those he meets—and of the reader. The novel may begin with a Machiavellian intent, to make us more aware of the realities of the world, but by the end we are celebrating idealism and imagination, no matter how impractical they are. Thus *Don Quixote* tests the realism and individualism of its time by celebrating an impossible chivalric dream, an idealistic mythology of a golden age inherited from the past and kept alive in an age of iron by an absurd and improbable knight. This unlikely hero does not prove himself like Hernán Cortés by seeking new lands to rule. True to his inner vision, Don Quixote represents the triumph of the ideal that challenges the worldliness and realism informing many of the texts of the period.

A Life of Adventure. The life of Miguel de Cervantes Saavedra reads like an improbable romance played out on the stage of Spain at the height of its GOLDEN AGE.[1] The fourth of seven children of a poor doctor, Cervantes spent his childhood fleeing with his family from his father's

---

[1] **Spain . . . golden age:** The latter part of the sixteenth century and most of the seventeenth century is known as the golden age of Spanish literature, during the period when Spain was also a dominant European power. Besides Cervantes, the great authors of the period were poets Garcilaso de la Vega (c. 1501–1536), Juan Boscán Almogaver (c. 1490–1542), and Luis de Góngora y Argote (1561–1627); novelists Mateo Alemán (1547–c. 1614) and Francisco Gómez de Quevedo y Villegas (1580–1645); dramatists Tirso de Molina (c. 1580–1648), Lope de Vega (1562–1635), and Pedro Calderón de la Barca (1600–1681).

creditors. After a brief formal education in Córdoba and at a Jesuit school in Seville, he was convicted of dueling and fled to Italy to avoid his sentence. In Rome he served the Cardinal Nuncio Acquaviva for a time before enlisting in the Spanish army, then engaged in battling the Turks for control of the Mediterranean. At the Battle of Lepanto in 1571, Cervantes got up from his sick bed to fight heroically. He was decorated for his bravery, but battle wounds left him permanently disabled in his left hand. Nevertheless he went on to participate in campaigns at Tunis, Sardinia, Naples, Sicily, and Genoa before returning to Spain. On the return trip in 1575, his ship was captured by pirates and he and his brother Rodrigo were both sold into slavery in Algiers. During five years in slavery, Cervantes made five unsuccessful escape attempts; his daring so impressed the Dey of Algiers, Hassan Pacha, that his life was spared after each attempt. Finally, in 1580, he was ransomed and returned to Spain.

Penniless, disabled, and desperate, Cervantes turned to the stage to make money, but he was not a successful playwright, even after writing twenty or thirty plays. After he married Catalina Salaza y Vozmediano in 1584, to support his growing family he accepted a civil service job as a commissary collecting food for the Spanish navy. The post of provisioner for the Armada afforded opportunities for creative accounting, and Cervantes spent several stints in jail as a result of disputes with the Treasury Department, which claimed he had illegally appropriated wheat or money for himself.

During his time in jail, as legend has it, Cervantes wrote the first part of *Don Quixote*, which was published in 1605. With this novel he achieved the recognition he had failed to find writing for the theater. In the next decade *Don Quixote* went through ten editions, and it inspired an imitator (writing under the pen name Alonzo Fernandez de Avellaneda) to publish a sequel. This pseudo-Quixote was partly responsible for prompting Cervantes to write his own continuation of the story. *Don Quixote*, Part II, appeared in 1615, not long before he died, coincidentally on the same day as William Shakespeare, April 23, 1616.

An Age of Transition.   At the end of the sixteenth century, when *Don Quixote* was written, the traditional feudal system in Spain was disappearing and being replaced by a modern capitalist system. The small landowners, the *hidalgos*, the class to which Don Quixote belonged, were being forced into poverty and many were driven off the land and into the cities, where they gave up their precarious status as "gentlemen" to enter the mercantile BOURGEOISIE. Caught in this historic change, Don Quixote, at the beginning of the novel, sells some of his land so that he can remain a while longer in the country. He uses some of this money to buy books, CHIVALRIC ROMANCES, which allow him to escape the distressing economic realities of his situation. These popular stories — works like *Amadis of Gaul* (1508), the Lancelot cycle, and others based on them — featured romantic knights and ladies, perilous adventures, mysterious spells, heroic deeds, and miraculous escapes, and were the pulp fiction of the day.

It can be said that all prose fiction is a variation on the theme of *Don Quixote*. . . . The poverty of the Don suggests that the novel is born with the appearance of money, as a social element — money, the great solvent of the solid fabric of the old society, the great generator of illusion. Or, which is to say the same thing, the novel is born in response to snobbery.

– LIONEL TRILLING, "Manners, Morals and the Novel," 1948

Don Quixote. Cervantes uses the conceit of Quixote's addiction to romances as a way to contrast medieval idealism with RENAISSANCE REALISM. The Don has read so many chivalric romances that he has decided to undertake his own knightly quest. In rusty armor and a makeshift helmet, he sets out to aid damsels in distress and to fight for the glory of his imaginary lady Dulcinea. He has been so imbued with the tales of adventure he has read that everything he sees is transformed in the romantic filter of his mind: Windmills become giants, a herd of sheep becomes an attacking army, country inns are castles. Don Quixote does not look like a hero. Tall and gaunt and leaning on his lance, he is physically unprepossessing. He is a comic imitation of a medieval knight, who, in spite of his armor, is not a Renaissance man of power. He is not a prince, nor is he a trickster or magician. When tricks are played in *Don Quixote,* they are usually played on the Don. He is the butt, not the perpetrator. The Duke and Duchess invite him to their castle, for example, so that they can contrive a series of practical jokes to play on him.

Unlike his Renaissance compatriots—whether politicians, scientists, or explorers—Quixote does not seek to master external reality. He is uncomfortable in his time and he does not relish the struggle for power and supremacy. His speech to Sancho in Book I, Chapter 11, describes the lost golden age that embodied the chivalric ideals he pursues. In that time, he tells Sancho, "Fraud, deceit, or malice had not yet mingled with truth and sincerity. Justice held her ground, undisturbed and unassailed by the efforts of favor and interest, that now so much impair, pervert, and beset her. Arbitrary law had not yet established itself in the mind of the judge, for then there was no cause to judge and no one to be judged." His mission as knight-errant is to attack the wickedness of his age of iron and remain true to his vision of a past golden age. The symbol of Quixote's idealism is Dulcinea, the lady for whom he undertakes his knightly quest. Although she turns out to be a figment of his imagination or just a peasant girl, Dulcinea is nonetheless real as an ideal for him to believe in.

His squire, the peasant Sancho Panza, recognizes the common reality in Quixote's adventures, but he is unable to make his master see what he sees. So this unlikely duo—the gaunt and doleful idealist and his rotund and realistic squire—become an anomalous pair of chivalric adventurers in a world of con men, government agents, shrewd innkeepers, and cunning shopkeepers; their adventures degenerate into a series of misunderstandings, miscommunications, slapstick encounters, and practical jokes. On more than one occasion Don Quixote makes things worse by his chivalric interference. Yet through it all he retains his belief in himself, his mistress, and his mission.

Sancho Panza goes on the road for more down-to-earth reasons. As a realist—a person of common sense who knows that windmills are windmills—he has a large stock of folk sayings and proverbs that explain any situation, and he is savvy enough to survive a host of dangerous encounters. He accompanies Quixote to better himself. His dream is the Renaissance dream of power: he wants, like Prospero, to rule an island. Near the end of Part II, his dream comes true, if only as part of an elaborate

> Quixote's exploits are his last hurrah. He has one last chance to make the world as interesting as he dreams it to be.
>
> – TERRY GILLIAM, director, 2003

practical joke. There are wonderful parodic echoes of Machiavelli's advice to the prince in Quixote's advice to Sancho as he goes off to govern Baratario. Sancho is a surprisingly successful governor, especially shrewd when faced with impossible judicial decisions. But just as surprisingly, he gives up his kingdom and returns to serve again as Don Quixote's squire. He learns the limitations of power and leaves his "island" to rejoin Quixote and his ideals.

In the end, Sancho's realism is transformed by the Don's idealism, and *Don Quixote* seems to have reversed its original intent. Instead of being a critique of chivalric idealism, it has become a celebration of Quixote's idealistic madness. Even the practical Sancho is won over to the impossible ideals of his master: he believes in the imaginary Dulcinea and is ready to start out on another journey. Don Quixote, no longer mad, is at last aware that Dulcinea was an illusion, a disillusionment that costs him his life. He and Sancho have changed places, and the final pages of the novel make us aware of the loss when such divine madness is gone from the world.

■ FURTHER RESEARCH

Biography
Byron, William. *Cervantes: A Biography*. 1978.

Commentary
Canavaggio, Jean. *Cervantes*. 1990.
Close, A. J. *Don Quixote*. 1990.
Gilman, Stephen. *The Novel According to Cervantes*. 1989.
Mancing, Howard. *The Chivalric World of Don Quijote: Style, Structure, and Narrative Technique*. 1982.
Nelson, Lowry, ed. *Cervantes: A Collection of Critical Essays*. 1969.
Riley, E. C. *Don Quixote*. 1986.

■ PRONUNCIATION

Quixote: kee-HOH-tay
Rocinante: roh-thee-NAHN-tay, roh-zee-NAN-tee

Don Quixote is the first modern novel, perhaps the most eternal novel ever written, and certainly the fountainhead of European and American fiction: here we have Gogol and Dostoevsky, Dickens and Nabokov, Borges and Bellow, Sterne and Diderot in their genetic nakedness, once more taking to the road with the gentleman and the squire, believing that the world is what we read and discovering that the world reads us.

— CARLOS FUENTES,
2003

FROM

∾ Don Quixote

Translated by Edith Grossman

PART I

Chapter I

WHICH DESCRIBES THE CONDITION AND
PROFESSION OF THE FAMOUS GENTLEMAN
DON QUIXOTE OF LA MANCHA

Somewhere in La Mancha, in a place whose name I do not care to remember, a gentleman lived not long ago, one of those who has a lance and ancient shield on a shelf and keeps a skinny nag and a greyhound for racing. An occasional stew, beef more often than lamb, hash most nights, eggs and abstinence on Saturdays, lentils on Fridays, sometimes squab as a treat on Sundays—these consumed three-fourths of his income.[1] The rest went for a light woolen tunic and velvet breeches and hose of the same material for feast days, while weekdays were honored with dun-colored coarse cloth. He had a housekeeper past forty, a niece not yet twenty, and a man-of-all-work who did everything from saddling the horse to pruning the trees. Our gentleman was approximately fifty years old; his complexion was weathered, his flesh scrawny, his face gaunt, and he was a very early riser and a great lover of the hunt. Some claim that his family name was Quixada, or Quexada, for there is a certain amount of disagreement among the authors who write of this matter, although

---

A note on the translation: Don Quixote is a very large book; its 126 chapters add up to nearly a thousand pages. Our translation, the stylistically faithful version of Edith Grossman, is especially alert to the sophistication of Cervantes, whose remark in his preface to *Don Quixote,* "I only wanted to offer it to you plain and bare," is one of his many subterfuges. This eight-chapter excerpt dealing with the first adventures of the mad knight errant sets the stage for the events to follow. Don Quixote's satirical journey throughout Spain, his numerous dramatic meetings and episodes, and the discussions of many subjects along the way (concerning literature, history, ideals, the imagination, and other matters) combine to constitute what the translator calls "the first—and probably the greatest—modern novel."

In Part I, Chapter VI, the author cites a number of volumes in Don Quixote's library. These are popular romances of the day, which the priest will decide whether to burn as unholy or preserve for whatever reason. The priest's deliberations over each book offer Cervantes the chance to make his own evaluations, serious or satirical, of these works. The seemingly endless catalog of books also allows Cervantes to show Don Quixote's obsession with chivalry; but since the books mentioned really existed, we supply information about them in the notes.

Footnotes are derived from the translator's except where indicated by [Ed.].

---

[1] **a gentleman . . . his income:** Cervantes describes typical aspects of the ordinary life of the rural gentry. The indications of their reduced circumstances include the foods eaten by Don Quixote: beef, for example, was less expensive than lamb.

reliable conjecture seems to indicate that his name was Quexana. But this does not matter very much to our story; in its telling there is absolutely no deviation from the truth.

And so, let it be said that this aforementioned gentleman spent his times of leisure—which meant most of the year—reading books of chivalry with so much devotion and enthusiasm that he forgot almost completely about the hunt and even about the administration of his estate; and in his rash curiosity and folly he went so far as to sell acres of arable land in order to buy books of chivalry to read, and he brought as many of them as he could into his house; and he thought none was as fine as those composed by the worthy Feliciano de Silva,[2] because the clarity of his prose and complexity of his language seemed to him more valuable than pearls, in particular when he read the declarations and missives of love, where he would often find written: *The reason for the unreason to which my reason turns so weakens my reason that with reason I complain of thy beauty.* And also when he read: . . . *the heavens on high divinely heighten thy divinity with the stars and make thee deserving of the deserts thy greatness deserves.*

With these words and phrases the poor gentleman lost his mind, and he spent sleepless nights trying to understand them and extract their meaning, which Aristotle himself, if he came back to life for only that purpose, would not have been able to decipher or understand. Our gentleman was not very happy with the wounds that Don Belianís gave and received, because he imagined that no matter how great the physicians and surgeons who cured him, he would still have his face and entire body covered with scars and marks. But, even so, he praised the author for having concluded his book with the promise of unending adventure, and he often felt the desire to take up his pen and give it the conclusion promised there; and no doubt he would have done so, and even published it, if other greater and more persistent thoughts had not prevented him from doing so. He often had discussions with the village priest—who was a learned man, a graduate of Sigüenza[3]—regarding who had been the greater knight, Palmerín of England or Amadís of Gaul; but Master Nicolás, the village barber, said that none was the equal of the Knight of Phoebus, and if any could be compared to him, it was Don Galaor, the brother of Amadís of Gaul, because he was moderate in everything: a knight who was not affected, not as weepy as his brother, and incomparable in questions of courage.

In short, our gentleman became so caught up in reading that he spent his nights reading from dusk till dawn and his days reading from sunrise to sunset, and so with too little sleep and too much reading his brains dried up, causing him to lose his mind. His fantasy filled with everything he had read in his books, enchantments as well as combats, battles, challenges, wounds, courtings, loves, torments, and other impossible foolishness, and he became so convinced in his imagination of the truth of all the countless grandiloquent and false inventions he read that for him no

---

[2] **Feliciano de Silva:** The author of several novels of chivalry; the phrases cited by Cervantes are typical of the language in these books that drove Don Quixote mad.

[3] **graduate of Sigüenza:** The allusion is ironic: Sigüenza was a minor university whose graduates had the reputation of not being very well educated.

history in the world was truer. He would say that El Cid Ruy Díaz[4] had been a very good knight but could not compare to Amadís, the Knight of the Blazing Sword, who with a single backstroke cut two ferocious and colossal giants in half. He was fonder of Bernardo del Carpio[5] because at Roncesvalles[6] he had killed the enchanted Roland by availing himself of the tactic of Hercules when he crushed Antaeus, the son of Earth, in his arms. He spoke highly of the giant Morgante because, although he belonged to the race of giants, all of them haughty and lacking in courtesy, he alone was amiable and well-behaved. But, more than any of the others, he admired Reinaldos de Montalbán,[7] above all when he saw him emerge from his castle and rob anyone he met, and when he crossed the sea and stole the idol of Mohammed made all of gold, as recounted in his history. He would have traded his housekeeper, and even his niece, for the chance to strike a blow at the traitor Guenelon.[8]

The truth is that when his mind was completely gone, he had the strangest thought any lunatic in the world ever had, which was that it seemed reasonable and necessary to him, both for the sake of his honor and as a service to the nation, to become a knight errant and travel the world with his armor and his horse to seek adventures and engage in everything he had read that knights errant engaged in, righting all manner of wrongs and, by seizing the opportunity and placing himself in danger and ending those wrongs, winning eternal renown and everlasting fame. The poor man imagined himself already wearing the crown, won by the valor of his arm, of the empire of Trebizond at the very least; and so it was that with these exceedingly agreeable thoughts, and carried away by the extraordinary pleasure he took in them, he hastened to put into effect what he so fervently desired. And the first thing he did was to attempt to clean some armor that had belonged to his great-grandfathers and, stained with rust and covered with mildew, had spent many long years stored and forgotten in a corner. He did the best he could to clean and repair it, but he saw that it had a great defect, which was that instead of a full sallet helmet with an attached neckguard, there was only a simple headpiece; but he compensated for this with his industry, and out of pasteboard he fashioned a kind of half-helmet that, when attached to the headpiece, took on the appearance of a full sallet. It is true that in order to test if it was strong and could withstand a blow, he took out his sword and struck it twice, and with the first blow he undid in a moment what it had taken him a week to create; he could not help being disappointed at the ease with

---

[4] **El Cid Ruy Díaz:** A historical figure of the eleventh century who passed into legend and literature. A major Spanish epic poem carries his name.

[5] **Bernardo del Carpio:** A legendary hero, the subject of ballads as well as poems and plays.

[6] **Roncesvalles:** The site in the Pyrenees, called Roncesvaux in French, where Charlemagne's army supposedly fought the Saracens in 778 (actually the rear guard of the army was ambushed by the Basques). The epic poem *The Song of Roland* (p. 1336) includes a fictional account of this battle. Bernardo del Carpio's name was attached to the story at a later time. [Ed.]

[7] **Reinaldos de Montalbán:** A hero of the French chansons de geste (songs of deeds); in some Spanish versions, he takes part in the battle of Roncesvalles.

[8] **Guenelon:** Ganelon in French; the traitor supposedly responsible for the defeat of Charlemagne's army and the death of Roland at Roncesvalles.

which he had hacked it to pieces, and to protect against that danger, he made another one, placing strips of iron on the inside so that he was satisfied with its strength; and not wanting to put it to the test again, he designated and accepted it as an extremely fine sallet.

Then he went to look at his nag, and though its hooves had more cracks than his master's pate and it showed more flaws than Gonnella's horse, that *tantum pellis et ossa fuit,*[9] it seemed to him that Alexander's Bucephalus and El Cid's Babieca were not its equal. He spent four days thinking about the name he would give it; for—as he told himself—it was not seemly that the horse of so famous a knight, and a steed so intrinsically excellent, should not have a worthy name; he was looking for the precise name that would declare what the horse had been before its master became a knight errant and what it was now; for he was determined that if the master was changing his condition, the horse too would change its name to one that would win the fame and recognition its new position and profession deserved; and so, after many names that he shaped and discarded, subtracted from and added to, unmade and remade in his memory and imagination, he finally decided to call the horse *Rocinante,*[10] a name, in his opinion, that was noble, sonorous, and reflective of what it had been when it was a nag, before it was what it was now, which was the foremost nag in all the world.

Having given a name, and one so much to his liking, to his horse, he wanted to give one to himself, and he spent another eight days pondering this, and at last he called himself *Don Quixote,*[11] which is why, as has been noted, the authors of this absolutely true history determined that he undoubtedly must have been named Quixada and not Quexada, as others have claimed. In any event, recalling that the valiant Amadís had not been content with simply calling himself Amadís but had added the name of his kingdom and realm in order to bring it fame, and was known as Amadís of Gaul, he too, like a good knight, wanted to add the name of his birthplace to his own, and he called himself *Don Quixote of La Mancha,*[12] thereby, to his mind, clearly stating his lineage and country and honoring it by making it part of his title.

Having cleaned his armor and made a full helmet out of a simple headpiece, and having given a name to his horse and decided on one for himself, he realized that the only thing left for him to do was to find a lady to love; for the knight errant without a lady-love was a tree without leaves or fruit, a body without a soul. He said to himself:

"If I, because of my evil sins, or my good fortune, meet with a giant somewhere, as ordinarily befalls knights errant, and I unseat him with a single blow, or cut his body in half, or, in short, conquer and defeat him, would it not be good to have someone to whom I could send him so that he might enter and fall to his knees

---

[9] *tantum pellis et ossa fuit:* Pietro Gonnella, the jester at the court of Ferrarra, had a horse famous for being skinny. The Latin translates as "was nothing but skins and bones."

[10] *Rocinante: Rocin* means "nag"; *ante* means "before," both temporally and spatially.

[11] *Quixote:* The section of armor that covers the thigh.

[12] *La Mancha:* La Mancha was not one of the noble medieval kingdoms associated with knighthood.

before my sweet lady, and say in the humble voice of surrender: 'I, lady, am the giant Caraculiambro, lord of the island Malindrania, defeated in single combat by the never sufficiently praised knight Don Quixote of La Mancha, who commanded me to appear before your ladyship, so that your highness might dispose of me as you chose'?"

Oh, how pleased our good knight was when he had made this speech, and even more pleased when he discovered the one he could call his lady! It is believed that in a nearby village there was a very attractive peasant girl with whom he had once been in love, although she, apparently, never knew or noticed. Her name was Aldonza Lorenzo,[13] and he thought it a good idea to call her the lady of his thoughts, and, searching for a name that would not differ significantly from his and would suggest and imply that of a princess and great lady, he decided to call her *Dulcinea of Toboso,*[14] because she came from Toboso, a name, to his mind, that was musical and beautiful and filled with significance, as were all the others he had given to himself and everything pertaining to him.

Chapter II

WHICH TELLS OF THE FIRST SALLY THAT
THE INGENIOUS DON QUIXOTE MADE FROM
HIS NATIVE LAND

And so, having completed these preparations, he did not wish to wait any longer to put his thought into effect, impelled by the great need in the world that he believed was caused by his delay, for there were evils to undo, wrongs to right, injustices to correct, abuses to ameliorate, and offenses to rectify. And one morning before dawn on a hot day in July, without informing a single person of his intentions, and without anyone seeing him, he armed himself with all his armor and mounted Rocinante, wearing his poorly constructed helmet, and he grasped his shield and took up his lance and through the side door of a corral he rode out into the countryside with great joy and delight at seeing how easily he had given a beginning to his virtuous desire. But as soon as he found himself in the countryside he was assailed by a thought so terrible it almost made him abandon the enterprise he had barely begun; he recalled that he had not been dubbed a knight, and according to the law of chivalry, he could not and must not take up arms against any knight; since this was the case, he would have to bear blank arms, like a novice knight without a device on his shield, until he had earned one through his own efforts. These thoughts made him waver in his purpose; but, his madness being stronger than any other faculty, he resolved to have himself dubbed a knight by the first person he met, in imitation of many others who had done the same, as he had read in the books that had brought him to this state. As for his arms being blank and white,[15] he planned to clean them so much that when the dubbing took place they would be whiter than ermine; he

---

[13] **Aldonza Lorenzo:** Aldonza, considered to be a common rustic name, had comic connotations.

[14] *Dulcinea of Toboso:* Her name is based on the word *dulce* ("sweet").

[15] **blank and white:** Pun based on the word *blanco,* which means both "blank" and "white."

immediately grew serene and continued on his way, following only the path his horse wished to take, believing that the virtue of his adventures lay in doing this.

And as our new adventurer traveled along, he talked to himself, saying:

"Who can doubt that in times to come, when the true history of my famous deeds comes to light, the wise man who compiles them, when he begins to recount my first sally so early in the day, will write in this manner: 'No sooner had rubicund Apollo spread over the face of the wide and spacious earth the golden strands of his beauteous hair, no sooner had diminutive and bright-hued birds with dulcet tongues greeted in sweet, mellifluous harmony the advent of rosy dawn, who, forsaking the soft couch of her zealous consort, revealed herself to mortals through the doors and balconies of the Manchegan horizon, than the famous knight Don Quixote of La Mancha, abandoning the downy bed of idleness, mounted his famous steed, Rocinante, and commenced to ride through the ancient and illustrious countryside of Montiel.'"

And it was true that this was where he was riding. And he continued:

"Fortunate the time and blessed the age when my famous deeds will come to light, worthy of being carved in bronze, sculpted in marble, and painted on tablets as a remembrance in the future. O thou, wise enchanter, whoever thou mayest be, whose task it will be to chronicle this wondrous history! I implore thee not to overlook my good Rocinante, my eternal companion on all my travels and peregrinations."

Then he resumed speaking as if he truly were in love:

"O Princess Dulcinea, mistress of this captive heart! Thou hast done me grievous harm in bidding me farewell and reproving me with the harsh affliction of commanding that I not appear before thy sublime beauty. May it please thee, Señora, to recall this thy subject heart, which suffers countless trials for the sake of thy love."

He strung these together with other foolish remarks, all in the manner his books had taught him and imitating their language as much as he could. As a result, his pace was so slow, and the sun rose so quickly and ardently, that it would have melted his brains if he had had any.

He rode almost all that day and nothing worthy of note happened to him, which caused him to despair because he wanted an immediate encounter with someone on whom to test the valor of his mighty arm. Some authors say his first adventure was the one in Puerto Lápice; others claim it was the adventure of the windmills; but according to what I have been able to determine with regard to this matter, and what I have discovered written in the annals of La Mancha, the fact is that he rode all that day, and at dusk he and his horse found themselves exhausted and half-dead with hunger; as he looked all around to see if he could find some castle or a sheepfold with shepherds where he might take shelter and alleviate his great hunger and need, he saw an inn not far from the path he was traveling, and it was as if he had seen a star guiding him not to the portals, but to the inner towers of his salvation. He quickened his pace and reached the inn just as night was falling.

At the door there happened to be two young women, the kind they call ladies of easy virtue, who were on their way to Sevilla with some muledrivers who had decided to stop at the inn that night, and since everything our adventurer thought, saw, or imagined seemed to happen according to what he had read, as soon as he saw the inn it appeared to him to be a castle complete with four towers and spires of gleaming silver, not to mention a drawbridge and deep moat and all the other details depicted on such castles. He rode toward the inn that he thought was a castle, and when he was a short distance away he reined in Rocinante and waited for a dwarf to appear on the parapets to signal with his trumpet that a knight was approaching the castle. But when he saw that there was some delay, and that Rocinante was in a hurry to get to the stable, he rode toward the door of the inn and saw the two profligate wenches standing there, and he thought they were two fair damsels or two gracious ladies taking their ease at the entrance to the castle. At that moment a swineherd who was driving his pigs—no excuses, that's what they're called—out of some mudholes blew his horn, a sound that pigs respond to, and it immediately seemed to Don Quixote to be just what he had desired, which was for a dwarf to signal his arrival; and so with extreme joy he rode up to the inn, and the ladies, seeing a man armed in that fashion, and carrying a lance and shield, became frightened and were about to retreat into the inn, but Don Quixote, inferring their fear from their flight, raised the pasteboard visor, revealing his dry, dusty face, and in a gallant manner and reassuring voice, he said to them:

"Flee not, dear ladies, fear no villainous act from me; for the order of chivalry which I profess does not countenance or permit such deeds to be committed against any person, least of all highborn maidens such as yourselves."

The women looked at him, directing their eyes to his face, hidden by the imitation visor, but when they heard themselves called maidens, something so alien to their profession, they could not control their laughter, which offended Don Quixote and moved him to say:

"Moderation is becoming in beauteous ladies, and laughter for no reason is foolishness; but I do not say this to cause in you a woeful or dolorous disposition, for mine is none other than to serve you."

The language, which the ladies did not understand, and the bizarre appearance of our knight intensified their laughter, and his annoyance increased and he would have gone even further if at that moment the innkeeper had not come out, a man who was very fat and therefore very peaceable, and when he saw that grotesque figure armed with arms as incongruous as his bridle, lance, shield, and corselet, he was ready to join the maidens in their displays of hilarity. But fearing the countless difficulties that might ensue, he decided to speak to him politely, and so he said:

"If, Señor, your grace seeks lodging, except for a bed (because there is none in this inn), a great abundance of everything else will be found here."

Don Quixote, seeing the humility of the steward of the castle-fortress, which is what he thought the innkeeper and the inn were, replied:

"For me, good castellan, anything will do, for

my trappings are my weapons,
and combat is my rest,"[16]

---

[16] **"my trappings . . . my rest":** Lines from a well-known ballad; the innkeeper's response cites the next two lines.

The host believed he had called him castellan because he thought him an upright Castilian, though he was an Andalusian from the Sanlúcar coast,[17] no less a thief than Cacus and as malicious as an apprentice page, and so he responded:

"In that case, your grace's beds must be bare rocks, and your sleep a constant vigil; and this being true, you can surely dismount, certain of finding in this poor hovel more than enough reason and reasons not to sleep in an entire year, let alone a single night."

And having said this, he went to hold the stirrup for Don Quixote, who dismounted with extreme difficulty and travail, like a man who had not broken his fast all day long.

Then he told his host to take great care with his horse, because it was the best mount that walked this earth. The innkeeper looked at the horse and did not think it as good as Don Quixote said, or even half as good; after leading it to the stable, he came back to see what his guest might desire, and the maidens, who by this time had made peace with him, were divesting him of his armor; although they removed his breastplate and backpiece, they never knew how or were able to disconnect the gorget or remove the counterfeit helmet, which was tied on with green cords that would have to be cut because the ladies could not undo the knots; but he absolutely refused to consent to this, and so he spent all night wearing the helmet and was the most comical and curious figure anyone could imagine; as they were disarming him, and since he imagined that those well-worn and much-used women were illustrious ladies and damsels from the castle, he said to them with a good deal of grace and verve:

> Never was a knight
> so well-served by ladies
> as was Don Quixote
> when he first sallied forth:
> fair damsels tended to him;
> princesses cared for his horse,[18]

or Rocinante, for this is the name, noble ladies, of my steed, and Don Quixote of La Mancha is mine; and although I did not wish to disclose my name until the great feats performed in your service and for your benefit would reveal it, perforce the adaptation of this ancient ballad of Lancelot to our present purpose has been the cause of your learning my name before the time was ripe; but the day will come when your highnesses will command, and I shall obey, and the valor of this my arm will betoken the desire I have to serve you."

The women, unaccustomed to hearing such high-flown rhetoric, did not say a word in response; they only asked if he wanted something to eat.

"I would consume any fare," replied Don Quixote, "because, as I understand it, that would be most beneficial now."

---

[17] **Sanlúcar coast:** In Cervantes's time this was known as a gathering place for criminals.

[18] **Never was . . . his horse:** Don Quixote paraphrases a ballad about Sir Lancelot, the famous knight of King Arthur's Round Table.

It happened to be a Friday, and in all the inn there was nothing but a few pieces of a fish that in Castilla is called cod, and in Andalucía codfish, and in other places salt cod, and elsewhere smoked cod. They asked if his grace would like a little smoked cod, for there was no other fish to serve him.

"Since many little cod," replied Don Quixote, "all together make one large one, it does not matter to me if you give me eight *reales* in coins or in a single piece of eight. Moreover, it well might be that these little cod are like veal, which is better than beef, and kid, which is better than goat. But, in any case, bring it soon, for the toil and weight of arms cannot be borne if one does not control the stomach."

They set the table at the door of the inn to take advantage of the cooler air, and the host brought Don Quixote a portion of cod that was badly prepared and cooked even worse, and bread as black and grimy as his armor; but it was a cause for great laughter to see him eat, because, since he was wearing his helmet and holding up the visor with both hands, he could not put anything in his mouth unless someone placed it there for him, and so one of the ladies performed that task. But when it was time to give him something to drink, it was impossible, and would have remained impossible, if the innkeeper had not hollowed out a reed, placing one end in the gentleman's mouth and pouring some wine in the other; and all of this Don Quixote accepted with patience in order not to have the cords of his helmet cut. At this moment a gelder of hogs happened to arrive at the inn, and as he arrived he blew on his reed pipe four or five times, which confirmed for Don Quixote that he was in a famous castle where they were entertaining him with music, and that the cod was trout, the bread soft and white, the prostitutes ladies, the innkeeper the castellan of the castle, and that his decision to sally forth had been a good one. But what troubled him most was not being dubbed a knight, for it seemed to him he could not legitimately engage in any adventure if he did not receive the order of knighthood.

Chapter III

WHICH RECOUNTS THE AMUSING MANNER IN WHICH DON QUIXOTE WAS DUBBED A KNIGHT

And so, troubled by this thought, he hurried through the scant meal served at the inn, and when it was finished, he called to the innkeeper and, after going into the stable with him, he kneeled before him and said:

"Never shall I rise up from this place, valiant knight, until thy courtesy grants me a boon I wish to ask of thee, one that will redound to thy glory and to the benefit of all humankind."

The innkeeper, seeing his guest at his feet and hearing these words, looked at him and was perplexed, not knowing what to do or say; he insisted that he get up, but Don Quixote refused until the innkeeper declared that he would grant the boon asked of him.

"I expected no less of thy great magnificence, my lord," replied Don Quixote. "And so I shall tell thee the boon that I would ask of thee and thy generosity has granted me, and it is that on the morrow thou wilt dub me a knight, and that this night in the chapel of thy castle I shall keep vigil over my armor, and on the morrow, as I have said, what I fervently desire will be accomplished so that I can, as I needs must do, travel the four corners of the earth in search of adventures on behalf of those in need, this being the office of chivalry and of knights errant, for I am one of them and my desire is disposed to such deeds."

The innkeeper, as we have said, was rather sly and already had some inkling of his guest's madness, which was confirmed when he heard him say these words, and in order to have something to laugh about that night, he proposed to humor him, and so he told him that his desire and request were exemplary and his purpose right and proper in knights who were as illustrious as he appeared to be and as his gallant presence demonstrated; and that he himself, in the years of his youth, had dedicated himself to that honorable profession, traveling through many parts of the world in search of adventures, to wit the Percheles in Málaga, the Islas of Riarán, the Compás in Sevilla, the Azoguejo of Segovia, the Olivera of Valencia, the Rondilla in Granada, the coast of Sanlúcar, the Potro in Córdoba, the Ventillas in Toledo,[19] and many other places where he had exercised the light-footedness of his feet and the light-fingeredness of his hands, committing countless wrongs, bedding many widows, undoing a few maidens, deceiving several orphans, and, finally, becoming known in every court and tribunal in almost all of Spain; in recent years, he had retired to this castle, where he lived on his property and that of others, welcoming all knights errant of whatever category and condition simply because of the great fondness he felt for them, so that they might share with him their goods as recompense for his virtuous desires.

He also said that in this castle there was no chapel where Don Quixote could stand vigil over his arms, for it had been demolished in order to rebuild it, but, in urgent cases, he knew that vigils could be kept anywhere, and on this night he could stand vigil in a courtyard of the castle; in the morning, God willing, the necessary ceremonies would be performed, and he would be dubbed a knight, and so much of a knight there could be no greater in all the world.

He asked if he had any money; Don Quixote replied that he did not have a copper *blanca,* because he never had read in the histories of knights errant that any of them ever carried money. To this the innkeeper replied that he was deceived, for if this was not written in the histories, it was because it had not seemed necessary to the authors to write down something as obvious and necessary as carrying money and clean shirts, and if they had not, this was no reason to think the knights did not carry them; it therefore should be taken as true and beyond dispute that all the knights errant who fill so many books to overflowing carried well-provisioned purses for whatever might befall them; by the same token, they carried shirts and a small chest stocked with unguents to cure the wounds they received, for in the fields and clearings where they engaged in combat and were wounded there was not always someone who could heal them, unless they had for a friend some wise enchanter who instantly came to their aid, bringing through the air, on a cloud, a damsel or a dwarf bearing a flask of water of such great power that, by swallowing a single drop, the knights were so completely healed of their injuries and wounds that it was as if no

---

[19] **Percheles in Málaga . . . Ventillas in Toledo:** These were all famous underworld haunts.

harm had befallen them. But in the event such was not the case, the knights of yore deemed it proper for their squires to be provisioned with money and other necessities, such as linen bandages and unguents to heal their wounds; and if it happened that these knights had no squire—which was a rare and uncommon thing—they themselves carried everything in saddlebags so finely made they could barely be seen on the haunches of their horse, as if they were something of greater significance, because, except in cases like these, carrying saddlebags was not well-favored by knights errant; for this reason he advised, for he could still give Don Quixote orders as if he were his godson, since that is what he soon would be, that from now on he not ride forth without money and the provisions he had described, and then he would see how useful and necessary they would be when he least expected it.

Don Quixote promised to do as he advised with great alacrity, and so it was arranged that he would stand vigil over his arms in a large corral to one side of the inn; and Don Quixote gathered all his armor together and placed it on a trough that was next to a well, and, grasping his shield, he took up his lance and with noble countenance began to pace back and forth in front of the trough, and as he began his pacing, night began to fall.

The innkeeper told everyone in the inn about the lunacy of his guest, about his standing vigil over his armor and his expectation that he would be dubbed a knight. They marveled at so strange a form of madness and went to watch him from a distance, and saw that with a serene expression he sometimes paced back and forth; at other times, leaning on his lance, he turned his eyes to his armor and did not turn them away again for a very long time. Night had fallen, but the moon was so bright it could compete with the orb whose light it reflected, and therefore everything the new knight did was seen clearly by everyone. Just then it occurred to one of the muledrivers in the inn to water his pack of mules, and for this it was necessary to move Don Quixote's armor, which was on the trough; our knight, seeing him approach, said in a booming voice:

"O thou, whosoever thou art, rash knight, who cometh to touch the armor of the most valiant knight who e'er girded on a sword! Lookest thou to what thou dost and toucheth it not, if thou wanteth not to leave thy life in payment for thy audacity."

The muleteer cared nothing for these words—and it would have been better for him if he had, because it meant caring for his health and well-being; instead, he picked up the armor by the straps and threw it a good distance away. And seeing this, Don Quixote lifted his eyes to heaven and, turning his thoughts—or so it seemed to him—to his lady Dulcinea, he said:

"Help me, Señora, in this the first affront aimed at this thy servant's bosom; in this my first challenge letteth not thy grace and protection fail me."

And saying these and other similar phrases, and dropping his shield, he raised his lance in both hands and gave the muledriver so heavy a blow on the head that he knocked him to the ground, and the man was so badly battered that if the first blow had been followed by a second, he would have had no need for a physician to care for his wounds. Having done this, Don Quixote picked up his armor and began to pace again with the same tranquility as before. A short while later, unaware of what had happened—for the first muledriver was still in a daze—a second approached, also intending to water his mules, and when he began to remove the armor to allow access to the trough, without saying a word or asking for anyone's favor, Don Quixote again dropped his shield and again raised his lance, and did not shatter it but instead broke the head of the second muledriver into more than three pieces because he cracked his skull in at least four places. When they heard the noise, all the people in the inn hurried over, among them the innkeeper. When he saw this, Don Quixote took up his shield, placed his hand on his sword, and said:

"O beauteous lady, strength and vigor of my submissive heart! This is the moment when thou needs must turn the eyes of thy grandeur toward this thy captive knight, who awaiteth so great an adventure."

And with this he acquired, it seemed to him, so much courage that if all the muledrivers in the world had charged him, he would not have taken one step backward. The wounded men's companions, seeing their friends on the ground, began to hurl stones at Don Quixote from a distance, and he did what he could to deflect them with his shield, not daring to move away from the trough and leave his armor unprotected. The innkeeper shouted at them to stop because he had already told them he was crazy, and that being crazy he would be absolved even if he killed them all. Don Quixote shouted even louder, calling them perfidious traitors and saying that the lord of the castle was a varlet and a discourteous knight for allowing knights errant to be so badly treated, and that if he had already received the order of chivalry, he would enlighten him as to the full extent of his treachery.

"But you, filthy and lowborn rabble, I care nothing for you; throw, approach, come, offend me all you can, for you will soon see how perforce you must pay for your rash insolence."

He said this with so much boldness and so much courage that he instilled a terrible fear in his attackers, and because of this and the persuasive arguments of the innkeeper, they stopped throwing stones at him, and he allowed the wounded men to withdraw and resumed his vigil over his armor with the same serenity and tranquility as before.

The innkeeper did not think very highly of his guest's antics, and he decided to cut matters short and give him the accursed order of chivalry then and there, before another misfortune occurred. And so he approached and begged his pardon for the impudence these lowborn knaves had shown, saying he had known nothing about it but that they had been rightfully punished for their audacity. He said he had already told him there was no chapel in the castle, nor was one necessary for what remained to be done, because according to his understanding of the ceremonies of the order, the entire essence of being dubbed a knight consisted in being struck on the neck and shoulders, and that could be accomplished in the middle of a field, and he had already fulfilled everything with regard to keeping a vigil over his armor, for just two hours of vigil satisfied the requirements, and he had spent more than four. Don Quixote believed everything and said he was prepared to obey him, and that he should conclude matters with as much haste as possible, because if he was attacked again and had already been dubbed a knight, he did not intend to leave a single person alive in the castle except for those the castellan ordered him to spare, which he would do out of respect for him.

Forewarned and fearful, the castellan immediately brought the book in which he kept a record of the feed and straw he supplied to the muledrivers, and with a candle end that a servant boy brought to him, and the two aforementioned damsels, he approached the spot where Don Quixote stood and ordered him to kneel, and reading from his book as if he were murmuring a devout prayer, he raised his hand and struck him on the back of the neck, and after that, with his own sword, he delivered a gallant blow to his shoulders, always murmuring between his teeth as if he were praying. Having done this, he ordered one of the ladies to gird Don Quixote with his sword, and she did so with a good deal of refinement and discretion, and a good deal was needed for them not to burst into laughter at each moment of the ceremony, but the great feats they had seen performed by the new knight kept their laughter in check. As she girded on his sword, the good lady said:

"May God make your grace a very fortunate knight and give you good fortune in your fights."

Don Quixote asked her name, so that he might know from that day forth to whom he was obliged for the benison he had received, for he desired to offer her some part of the honor he would gain by the valor of his arm. She answered very humbly that her name was Tolosa, and that she was the daughter of a cobbler from Toledo who lived near the stalls of the Sancho Bienaya market, and no matter where she might be she would serve him and consider him her master. Don Quixote replied that for the sake of his love, would she have the kindness to henceforth ennoble herself and call herself Doña Tolosa.[20] She promised she would, and the other girl accoutred him with his knightly spurs, and he had almost the same conversation with her as with the one who girded on his sword. He asked her name, and she said she was called Molinera, the miller's girl, and that she was the daughter of an honorable miller from Antequera, and Don Quixote also implored her to ennoble herself and call herself Doña Molinera, offering her more services and good turns.

And so, these never-before-seen ceremonies having been performed at a gallop, in less than an hour Don Quixote found himself a knight, ready to sally forth in search of adventures, and he saddled Rocinante and mounted him, and, embracing his host, he said such strange things to him as he thanked him for the boon of having dubbed him a knight that it is not possible to adequately recount them. The innkeeper, in order to get him out of the inn, replied with words no less rhetorical but much more brief, and without asking him to pay for the cost of his lodging, he allowed him to leave at an early hour.

Chapter IV

**CONCERNING WHAT HAPPENED TO OUR
KNIGHT WHEN HE LEFT THE INN**

It must have been dawn when Don Quixote left the inn so contented, so high-spirited, so jubilant at having been dubbed a knight that his joy almost burst the

---

[20] **Doña Tolosa:** The unwarranted use of the honorific terms *don* and *doña* was often satirized in the literature of the Renaissance.

cinches of his horse. But calling to mind the advice of his host regarding the necessary provisions that he had to carry with him, especially money and shirts, he resolved to return to his house and outfit himself with everything, including a squire, thinking he would take on a neighbor of his, a peasant who was poor and had children but was very well suited to the chivalric occupation of squire. With this thought he guided Rocinante toward his village, and the horse, as if he could see his stall, began to trot with so much eagerness that his feet did not seem to touch the ground.

Don Quixote had not gone very far when it seemed to him that from a dense wood on his right there emerged the sound of feeble cries, like those of a person in pain, and as soon as he heard them he said:

"I give thanks to heaven for the great mercy it has shown in so quickly placing before me opportunities to fulfill what I owe to my profession, allowing me to gather the fruit of my virtuous desires. These cries, no doubt, belong to some gentleman or lady in need who requires my assistance and help."

And, pulling on the reins, he directed Rocinante toward where he thought the cries were coming from. And after he had taken a few steps into the wood, he saw a mare tied to an oak, and tied to another was a boy about fifteen years old, naked from the waist up, and it was he who was crying out, and not without cause, for with a leather strap a robust peasant was whipping him and accompanying each lash with a reprimand and a piece of advice. For he was saying:

"Keep your tongue still and your eyes open."

And the boy replied:

"I won't do it again, Señor; by the Passion of Christ I won't do it again, and I promise I'll be more careful from now on with the flock."

And when Don Quixote saw this, he said in an angry voice:

"Discourteous knight, it is not right for you to do battle with one who cannot defend himself; mount your horse and take up your lance" — for a lance was leaning against the oak where the mare was tied — "and I shall make you understand that what you are doing is the act of a coward."

The peasant, seeing a fully armed figure ready to attack and brandishing a lance in his face, considered himself a dead man, and with gentle words he replied:

"Señor Knight, this boy I'm punishing is one of my servants, and his job is to watch over a flock of sheep I keep in this area, and he's so careless that I lose one every day, and when I punish his carelessness, or villainy, he says I do it out of miserliness because I don't want to pay him his wages, and by God and my immortal soul, he lies."

"You dare to say 'He lies' in my presence, base varlet?" said Don Quixote. "By the sun that shines down on us, I am ready to run you through with this lance. Pay him now without another word; if you do not, by the God who rules us I shall exterminate and annihilate you here and now. Untie him immediately."

The peasant lowered his head and, without responding, he untied his servant, and Don Quixote asked the boy how much his master owed him. He said wages for nine months, at seven *reales* a month. Don Quixote calculated the sum and found that it amounted to seventy-three *reales,*[21] and he told the peasant to take that amount

---

[21]**seventy-three *reales:*** The editor of the Spanish text of *Don Quixote* speculates that the error in arithmetic may be an intentional ironic allusion to Cervantes's three terms of imprisonment for keeping faulty accounts.

from his purse unless he wanted to die on their account. The terrified farmer replied that by the danger in which he found himself and the oath he had sworn—and so far he had sworn to nothing—the total was not so high, because from that amount one had to subtract and take into account three pairs of shoes that he had given his servant and a *real* for the two bloodlettings he had provided for him when he was sick.

"All of that is fine," said Don Quixote, "but the shoes and bloodlettings should compensate for the blows you have given him for no reason, for if he damaged the hide of the shoes you paid for, you have damaged the hide of his body, and if the barber drew blood when he was sick, you have drawn it when he was healthy; therefore, by this token, he owes you nothing."

"The difficulty, Señor Knight, is that I have no money here: let Andrés come with me to my house, and I'll pay him all the *reales* he deserves."

"Me, go back with him?" said the boy. "Not me! No, Señor, don't even think of it; as soon as we're alone he'll skin me alive, just like St. Bartholomew."

"No, he will not," replied Don Quixote. "It is enough for me to command and he will respect me, and if he swears to me by the order of chivalry that he has received, I shall let him go free, and I shall guarantee the payment."

"Señor, your grace, think of what you are saying," said the boy. "For this master of mine is no knight and he's never received any order of chivalry; he's Juan Haldudo the rich man, and he lives in Quintanar."

"That is of no importance," replied Don Quixote. "For there can be knights among Haldudos, especially since each man is the child of his deeds."

"That's true," said Andrés, "but what deeds is this master of mine the son of if he denies me my wages and my sweat and my labor?"

"I don't deny them, Andrés, my brother," answered the farmer. "Be so kind as to come with me, and I swear by all the orders of chivalry in the world that I'll pay you, as I've said, one *real* after another, and they'll be perfumed by my goodwill and pleasure."

"I absolve you from perfumes," said Don Quixote. "Just pay him in *reales,* and that will satisfy me, and be sure you fulfill what you have sworn; if you do not, by that same vow I vow that I shall return to find and punish you, and find you I shall, even if you conceal yourself like a wall lizard. And if you wish to know who commands you to do this, so that you have an even greater obligation to comply, know that I am the valiant Don Quixote of La Mancha, the righter of wrongs and injustices, and now go with God, and do not even think of deviating from what you have promised and sworn, under penalty of the penalty I have indicated to you."

And having said this, he spurred Rocinante and soon left them behind. The farmer followed him with his eyes, and when he saw that he had crossed the wood and disappeared from view, he turned to his servant Andrés and said:

"Come here, my son; I want to pay you what I owe you, as that righter of wrongs has ordered me to do."

"I swear," said Andrés, "that your grace better do the right thing and obey the commands of that good knight, may he live a thousand years; for, as he's a valiant man and a fair judge, heaven be praised, if you don't pay me he'll come back and do what he said!"

"I swear, too," said the farmer, "but because I love you so much, I want to increase the debt so I can increase the payment."

And seizing him by the arm, he tied the boy to the oak tree again and gave him so many lashes that he left him half-dead.

"Now, Señor Andrés," said the farmer, "you can call the righter of wrongs; you'll see how he can't undo this one. Though I don't think it's over yet, because I feel like skinning you alive, just as you feared."

But at last he untied him and gave him permission to go in search of his judge so that he could carry out the sentence. Andrés left in a fairly gloomy frame of mind, swearing he would find the valiant Don Quixote of La Mancha and tell him, point by point, what had happened, and that his master would have to pay a fine and damages. Even so, the boy left weeping and his master stayed behind to laugh.

In this way the valiant Don Quixote righted a wrong, and exceedingly pleased with what had occurred, for it seemed to him that he had given a happy and noble beginning to his chivalric adventures, he was very satisfied with himself as he rode to his village, saying in a quiet voice:

"Well mayest thou call thyself the most fortunate of ladies in the world today, O most beauteous of all the beauteous, Dulcinea of Toboso! For it is thy portion to have as vassal and servant to thy entire will and disposition so valiant and renowned a knight as Don Quixote of La Mancha is and will be, for he, as all men know, received the order of chivalry yesterday and today he has righted the greatest wrong and injustice that iniquity e'er devised and cruelty e'er committed: today he removed the whip from the hand of a merciless enemy who, without reason, did flog that delicate child."

Saying this, he arrived at a road that divided in four, and immediately there came to his imagination the crossroads where knights errant would begin to ponder which of those roads they would follow, and in order to imitate them, he remained motionless for a time, and after having thought very carefully, he loosened the reins and subjected his will to Rocinante's, and the horse pursued his initial intent, which was to head back to his own stall.

And having gone about two miles, Don Quixote saw a great throng of people who, as he subsequently discovered, were merchants from Toledo on their way to Murcia to buy silk. There were six of them, holding sunshades, and four servants on horseback, and three boys on foot leading the mules. No sooner had Don Quixote seen them than he imagined this to be a new adventure; and in order to imitate in every way possible the deeds he had read in his books, this seemed the perfect opportunity for him to perform one that he had in mind. And so, with gallant bearing and great boldness, he set his feet firmly in the stirrups, grasped his lance, brought the shield up to his chest, and, stopping in the middle of the road, he waited until those knights errant, for that is what he deemed and considered them to be, had reached him; and when they had come close enough to see and hear him, Don Quixote raised his voice and, in an imperious manner, he said:

"Halt, all of you, unless all of you confess that in the entire world there is no damsel more beauteous than the empress of La Mancha, the peerless Dulcinea of Toboso."

The merchants stopped when they heard these words and saw the strange appearance of the one who said them, and because of his appearance and words, they soon saw the madness of the man, but they wished to see at their leisure the purpose of the confession he was demanding, and one of them, who was something of a jokester and clever in the extreme, said:

"Señor Knight, we do not know this good lady you have mentioned; show her to us, for if she is as beautiful as you say, we will gladly and freely confess the truth you ask of us."

"If I were to show her to you," replied Don Quixote, "where would the virtue be in your confessing so obvious a truth? The significance lies in not seeing her and believing, confessing, affirming, swearing, and defending that truth; if you do not, you must do battle with me, audacious and arrogant people. And whether you come one by one, as the order of chivalry demands, or all at once, in the vicious manner of those of your ilk, here I am, ready and waiting for you, certain of the rightness of my claim."

"Señor Knight," replied the merchant, "in the name of all these princes, of whom I am one, and in order not to burden our consciences with the confession of something we have never seen or heard, and which, moreover, is so prejudicial to the empresses and queens of Alcarria and Extremadura, I implore your grace to have the goodness to show us a portrait of this lady, even if it is no larger than a grain of wheat; for with a single thread one has the entire skein, and we will be satisfied and certain, and your grace will be recompensed and requited, and although I believe we are so partial to your position that even if her portrait shows us that she is blind in one eye and that blood and brimstone flow from the other, despite all that, to please your grace, we will praise her in everything you might wish."

"Nothing flows from her, vile rabble," replied Don Quixote, burning with rage. "Nothing flows from her, I say, but amber and delicate musk; and she is not blind or humpbacked but as upright as a peak of the Guadarramas. But you will pay for how you have blasphemed against beauty as extraordinary as that of my lady!"

And, having said this, he lowered his lance and charged the man who had spoken, with so much rage and fury that if, to the daring merchant's good fortune, Rocinante had not tripped and fallen on the way, things would have gone badly for him. Rocinante fell, and his master rolled some distance on the ground, and when he tried to get up, he could not: he was too burdened by lance, shield, spurs, helmet, and the weight of his ancient armor. And as he struggled to stand, and failed, he said:

"Flee not, cowards; wretches, attend; for it is no fault of mine but of my mount that I lie here."

One of the muledrivers, who could not have been very well intentioned, heard the poor man on the ground making these insolent statements, and he could not stand by without giving him his response in the ribs. And walking up to him, he took the lance, broke it into pieces, and with one of them he began to beat our knight so furiously that notwithstanding and in spite of his armor, he thrashed Don Quixote as if he were threshing wheat. His masters shouted for him to stop and let him be, but by now the muledriver's blood was up and he did not want to leave the game until he had brought into play the last of his rage, and having recourse to the other pieces of the lance, he shattered them all on the wretched man on the ground, who, despite that storm of blows raining down on him, did not once close his mouth but continued to rail against heaven and earth and these wicked knaves, which is what they seemed to him.

The muledriver tired, and the merchants continued on their way, taking with them stories to tell about the beaten man for the rest of the journey. And he, when he found himself alone, tried again to see if he could stand, but if he could not when he was hale and healthy, how could he when he was beaten almost to a pulp? And still he considered himself fortunate, for it seemed to him that this was the kind of mishap that befell knights errant, and he attributed it all to his horse's misstep, but his body was so bruised and beaten it was not possible for him to stand.

Chapter V

IN WHICH THE ACCOUNT OF OUR KNIGHT'S
MISFORTUNE CONTINUES

Seeing, then, that in fact he could not move, he took refuge in his usual remedy, which was to think about some situation from his books, and his madness made him recall that of Valdovinos and the Marquis of Mantua, when Carloto[22] left him wounded in the highlands, a history known to children, acknowledged by youths, celebrated, and even believed by the old, and, despite all this, no truer than the miracles of Mohammed. This is the tale that seemed to him perfectly suited for the situation in which he found himself, and so, with displays of great emotion, he began to roll about on the ground and to say with faint breath exactly what people say was said by the wounded Knight of the Wood:

> Where art thou, my lady,
> that thou weepest not for my ills?
> Dost not know of them, lady,
> Or art thou truly false?

And in this way he continued reciting the ballad until the lines that say:

> O noble Marquis of Mantua,
> mine uncle and natural lord!

And as luck would have it, when he reached this line, a farmer from his village happened to pass by, a neighbor of his on the way home after taking a load of wheat to the mill; the farmer, seeing a man lying there, approached and asked who he was and what the trouble was that made him complain so pitifully. Don Quixote no doubt thought the farmer was the Marquis of Mantua, his uncle, and so the only answer he gave was to go on with the ballad, recounting his misfortune and the love of the emperor's son for his wife, all of it just as it is told in the ballad.

The farmer was astounded when he heard these absurdities, and after removing the visor, which had been shattered in the beating, he wiped the fallen man's

---

[22] **Marquis of Mantua . . . Carloto:** These characters appear in the well-known ballad that Don Quixote recites.

face, which was covered in dust, and as soon as he had wiped it he recognized him and said:

"Señor Quijana!"—for this must have been his name when he was in his right mind and had not yet changed from a quiet gentleman into a knight errant—"Who has done this to your grace?"

But Don Quixote went on reciting his ballad in response to every question. Seeing this, the good man, as carefully as he could, removed the breastplate and backpiece to see if he was wounded but did not see blood or cuts of any kind. He managed to lift him from the ground and with a good deal of effort put him on his own donkey, because he thought it a steadier mount. He gathered up his arms, even the broken pieces of the lance, and tied them on Rocinante, and leading the horse by the reins and the jackass by the halter, he began to walk toward his village, very dispirited at hearing the nonsense that Don Quixote was saying; Don Quixote was no less dispirited, for he was so beaten and broken that he could barely keep his seat on the burro, and from time to time he would raise his sighs to heaven, which obliged the farmer to ask him again to tell him what was wrong; one cannot help but think that the devil made Don Quixote recall stories suited to the events that had occurred, because at that point, forgetting about Valdovinos, he remembered the Moor Abindarráez, when the governor of Antequera, Rodrigo de Narváez, captured him and brought him back to his domain as his prisoner.[23] So when the farmer asked him again how he felt and what was wrong, he answered with the same words and phrases that the captive scion of the Abencerraje family said to Rodrigo de Narváez, just as he had read them in the history of *Diana,* by Jorge de Montemayor, where they are written, and he did this so deliberately that as the farmer walked along he despaired at hearing such an enormous amount of foolishness; in this way he realized that his neighbor was mad, and he hurried to reach the village in order to rid himself of the impatience Don Quixote provoked in him with his long-winded harangue. When it was concluded, Don Quixote went on to say:

"Your grace should know, Don Rodrigo de Narváez, that this beautiful Jarifa I have mentioned to you is now the lovely Dulcinea of Toboso, for whose sake I have performed, perform now, and shall perform in the future the most famous feats of chivalry the world has seen, sees now, and will ever see."

To this the farmer replied:

"Look, your grace, poor sinner that I am, I'm not Don Rodrigo de Narváez or the Marquis of Mantua, but Pedro Alonso, your neighbor, and your grace isn't Valdovinos or Abindarráez, but an honorable gentleman, Señor Quijana."

"I know who I am," replied Don Quixote, "and I know I can be not only those I have mentioned but the Twelve Peers of France[24] as well, and even all the nine

---

[23] **the Moor . . . his prisoner:** This story is included in Jorge de Montemayor's *Diana* (ca. 1559), the first of the Spanish pastoral novels; it is one of the volumes in Don Quixote's library.

[24] **Twelve Peers of France:** Knights chosen by the king of France and called peers because they were equal in skill and courage. They appear in *The Song of Roland.*

paragons of Fame,[25] for my deeds will surpass all those they performed, together or singly."

Having these exchanges and others like them, they reached the village as night was falling, but the farmer waited until it grew a little darker, so that no one would see what a poor knight the beaten gentleman was. When he thought the right time had come, he entered the village and came to Don Quixote's house, which was in an uproar; the priest and barber, who were great friends of Don Quixote, were there, and in a loud voice his housekeeper was saying to them:

"What does your grace think, Señor Licentiate Pero Pérez"—for this was the priest's name—"of my master's misfortune? Three days and no sign of him, or his horse, or his shield, or his lance, or his armor. Woe is me! Now I know, and it's as true as the death I owe God, that those accursed books of chivalry he's always reading have driven him crazy; and now I remember hearing him say time and time again, when he was talking to himself, that he wanted to become a knight errant and go out in the wide world in search of adventures. Those books should go straight to Satan and Barrabas, for they have ruined the finest mind in all of La Mancha."

His niece said the same and even added:

"You should know, Master Nicolás"—for this was the name of the barber—"that it often happened that my dear uncle would read these cruel books of adventures for two days and nights without stopping, and when he was finished he would toss away the book and pick up his sword and slash at the walls, and when he was very tired he would say that he had killed four giants as big as four towers, and the sweat dripping from him because of his exhaustion he would say was blood from the wounds he had received in battle, and then he would drink a whole pitcher of cold water and become cured and calm again, saying that the water was a precious drink brought to him by Esquife the Wise, a great wizard and a friend of his. But I am to blame for everything because I didn't let your graces know about the foolishness of my dear uncle so that you could help him before it went this far, and burn all these wicked books, and he has many that deserve to be burned, just as if they belonged to heretics."

"That is what I say, too," said the priest, "and by my faith, no later than tomorrow we will have a public proceeding, and they will be condemned to the flames so that they do not give occasion to whoever reads them to do what my good friend must have done."

The farmer and Don Quixote heard all of this, which allowed the farmer to understand finally what his neighbor's sickness was, and so he called out:

"Your graces, open to Señor Valdovinos and to Señor Marquis of Mantua, who is badly wounded, and to Señor the Moor Abindarráez, captive of the valiant Rodrigo de Narváez, governor of Antequera."

At the sound of his voice they all came out, and since some recognized their friend, and others their master and uncle, who had not yet dismounted from the donkey because he could not, they ran to embrace him, and he said:

---

[25]**nine paragons of Fame:** The nine were Joshua, David, Judah Macabee, Hector, Alexander the Great, Julius Caesar, King Arthur, Charlemagne, and Godfrey of Bouillon (a leader of the First Crusade).

"Stop, all of you, for I have been sorely wounded on account of my horse. Take me to my bed and call, if such is possible, Uganda the Wise, that she may heal and tend to my wounds."

"Look, all of you," said the housekeeper, "in what an evil hour my heart knew exactly what was wrong with my master. Your grace can go up and rest easy, because without that gander woman coming here, we'll know how to cure you. And I say that these books of chivalry should be cursed another hundred times for bringing your grace to such a pass!"

They led him to his bed and looked for his wounds but could find none, and he said it was simple bruising because he had taken a great fall with Rocinante, his horse, as they were doing battle with ten of the most enormous and daring giants one could find anywhere in the world.

"Tut, tut!" said the priest. "So there are giants at the ball? By the Cross, I shall burn them before nightfall tomorrow."

They asked Don Quixote a thousand questions, but the only answer he gave was that they should give him something to eat and let him sleep, which was what he cared about most. They did so, and the priest questioned the farmer at length regarding how he had found Don Quixote. He told the priest everything, including the nonsense Don Quixote had said when he found him and brought him home, giving the licentiate an even greater desire to do what he did the next day, which was to call on his friend, the barber Master Nicolás, and go with him to the house of Don Quixote,

Chapter VI

REGARDING THE BEGUILING AND
CAREFUL EXAMINATION CARRIED OUT BY
THE PRIEST AND THE BARBER OF THE LIBRARY
OF OUR INGENIOUS GENTLEMAN

who was still asleep. The priest asked the niece for the keys to the room that contained the books responsible for the harm that had been done, and she gladly gave them to him. All of them went in, including the housekeeper, and they found more than a hundred large volumes, very nicely bound, and many other smaller ones; and as soon as the housekeeper saw them, she hurried out of the room and quickly returned with a basin of holy water and a hyssop and said to the priest:

"Take this, Señor Licentiate, and sprinkle this room, so that no enchanter, of the many in these books, can put a spell on us as punishment for wanting to drive them off the face of the earth."

The licentiate had to laugh at the housekeeper's simplemindedness, and he told the barber to hand him the books one by one so that he could see what they contained, for he might find a few that did not deserve to be punished in the flames.

"No," said the niece, "there's no reason to pardon any of them, because they all have been harmful; we ought to toss them out the windows into the courtyard, and make a pile of them and set them on fire; or better yet, take them to the corral and light the fire there, where the smoke won't bother anybody."

The housekeeper agreed, so great was the desire of the two women to see the death of those innocents; but the priest was not in favor of doing that without even reading the titles first. And the first one that Master Nicolás handed him was *The Four Books of Amadís of Gaul,*[26] and the priest said:

"This one seems to be a mystery, because I have heard that this was the first book of chivalry printed in Spain,[27] and all the rest found their origin and inspiration here, and so it seems to me that as the proponent of the doctrine of so harmful a sect, we should, without any excuses, condemn it to the flames."

"No, Señor," said the barber, "for I've also heard that it is the best of all the books of this kind ever written, and as a unique example of the art, it should be pardoned."

"That's true," said the priest, "and so we'll spare its life for now. Let's see the one next to it."

"It is," said the barber, "the *Exploits of Esplandián,* who was the legitimate son of Amadís of Gaul."

"In truth," said the priest, "the mercy shown the father will not help the son. Take it, Señora Housekeeper, open that window, throw it into the corral, and let it be the beginning of the pile that will fuel the fire we shall set."

The housekeeper was very happy to do as he asked, and the good Esplandián went flying into the corral, waiting with all the patience in the world for the fire that threatened him.

"Next," said the priest.

"This one," said the barber, "is *Amadís of Greece,* and I believe that all these over here come from the line of Amadís."

"Well, let them all go into the corral," said the priest. "For the sake of burning Queen Pintiquiniestra, and the shepherd Darinel and all his eclogues, and the perverse and complicated language of their author, I would burn along with them the father who sired me if he were to appear in the form of a knight errant."

"I'm of the same opinion," said the barber.

"And so am I," added the niece.

"Well, then," said the housekeeper, "hand them over and into the corral with them."

They handed them to her, and there were a good many of them, and she saved herself a trip down the stairs and tossed them all out the window.

"Who's that big fellow?" asked the priest.

"This," replied the barber, "is *Don Olivante of Laura.*"[28]

"The author of that book," said the priest, "was the same one who composed *Garden of Flowers,* and the truth is I can't decide which of the two is more true or, I should say, less false; all I can say is that this one goes to the corral, because it is silly and arrogant."

---

[26] *The Four Books of Amadís of Gaul:* Published in their complete version in 1508, these are the first in a long series of novels of chivalry devoted to the exploits of Amadís, a prototypical knight, and his descendants.

[27] **first book . . . in Spain:** The Catalan novel *Tirant lo Blanc* was published in 1490; Cervantes probably knew the translation into Castillian published in 1511.

[28] *Don Olivante of Laura:* Published by Antonio de Torquemada in 1564.

"This next one is *Felixmarte of Hyrcania*,"[29] said the barber.

"Is Sir Felixmarte there?" the priest responded. "Well, by my faith, into the corral with him quickly, despite his strange birth and resounding adventures, for the harshness and dryness of his style allow no other course of action. Into the corral with him and this other one, Señora Housekeeper."

"With pleasure, Señor," she replied, and with great joy she carried out her orders.

"This one is *The Knight Platir*,"[30] said the barber.

"That's an old book," said the priest, "and I don't find anything in it that would warrant forgiveness. Let it join the others, with no defense."

And that is what happened. Another book was opened and they saw that its title was *The Knight of the Cross*.[31]

"Because of the holy name this book bears one might pardon its stupidity, but as the saying goes, 'The devil can hide behind the cross.' Into the fire."

Picking up another book, the barber said:

"This is *The Mirror of Chivalry*."[32]

"I already know his grace," said the priest. "There you'll find Reinaldos de Montalbán and his friends and companions, greater thieves than Cacus, and the Twelve Peers along with that true historian Turpín, and the truth is I'm inclined to condemn them to no more than perpetual exile, if only because they contain part of the invention of the famous Matteo Boiardo, from which the cloth was woven by the Christian poet Ludovico Ariosto,[33] who, if I find him here, speaking in some language not his own, I will have no respect for him at all; but if he speaks in his own language, I bow down to him."

"Well, I have him in Italian," said the barber, "but I don't understand it."

"There's no reason you should," replied the priest, "and here we would pardon the captain if he had not brought it to Spain and translated it into Castilian, for he took away a good deal of its original value, which is what all who attempt to translate books of poetry into another language will do as well: no matter the care they use and the skill they show, they will never achieve the quality the verses had in their first birth. In fact, I say that this book, and all those you find that deal with the matter of France, should be thrown into a dry well and kept there until we can agree on what should be done with them, except for a *Bernardo del Carpio* that's out there, and another called *Roncesvalles*,[34] for these, on reaching my hands, will pass into the housekeeper's and then into the fire, with no chance of a pardon."

---

[29] *Felixmarte of Hyrcania:* Published by Lenchor Ortega de Ubeda in 1556.

[30] *The Knight Platir:* Published anonymously in 1533: fourth book of a series about Palmerin, another fictional hero.

[31] *The Knight of the Cross:* Published anonymously in two parts, 1521 and 1526.

[32] *The Mirror of Chivalry:* An unfaithful prose translation of Matteo Boiardo's *Orlando inamorato* (*Roland in Love*) published in three parts; attributed to Lopez de Santa Cataline (1533, 1536) and Pedro de Reynosa (1550).

[33] **Ludovico Ariosto:** Cervantes disliked the Spanish translations of Ariosto, including the one by Jeronimo de Urrea (1549) which he refers to in the next paragraph.

[34] *Bernardo del Carpio . . . Roncesvalles:* This refers to two poems, by Agustin Alonso (1585) and Francisco Garrido Vicena (1555) respectively.

All this the barber seconded, and thought it right and proper, for he understood that the priest was so good a Christian and so loved the truth that he would not speak a falsehood for anything in the world. And opening another book, he saw that it was *Palmerín of the Olive,*[35] and with it was another called *Palmerín of England,* and seeing this, the priest said:

"The olive branch should be cut up immediately and burned until there's nothing left but ashes, but the palm branch of England should be kept and preserved as something unique; a chest should be made for it like the one Alexander found among the spoils of Darius and which he designated for preserving the works of the poet Homer. This book, my friend, has authority for two reasons: one, because it is very good in and of itself, and two, because it is well-known that it was composed by a wise and prudent king of Portugal. All the adventures in the castle of Miraguarda are excellent and very artful; the language is courtly and clear, for it takes into account and respects the decorum of the person speaking with a good deal of exactness and understanding. I say, therefore, that unless you are of another mind, Master Nicolás, this one and *Amadís of Gaul* should escape the fire, and all the rest, without further investigation or inquiry, should perish."

"No, my friend," the barber responded, "for the one I have here is the renowned *Don Belianís.*"[36]

"Well, that one," replied the priest, "and its second, third, and fourth parts need a little dose of rhubarb to purge their excess of choler, and it would be necessary to remove everything about the castle of Fame and other, more serious impertinences, and therefore they are given a delayed sentence, and the degree to which they are emended will determine if mercy or justice are shown to them; in the meantime, my friend, keep them in your house, but permit no one to read them."

"It will be my pleasure," replied the barber.

And not wishing to tire himself further with the perusal of books of chivalry, he ordered the housekeeper to take all the large ones to the corral. This was not said to a foolish woman or a deaf one, but to a person who would rather burn the books than weave a piece of cloth, no matter how large or fine it might be, and she seized almost eight at a time and threw them out the window. Because she took so many together, one of them fell at the feet of the barber, who wanted to see which one it was and saw that it said: *History of the Famous Knight Tirant lo Blanc.*[37]

"God help me!" said the priest with a great shout. "Here is Tirant lo Blanc. Let me have it, friend, for I state here and now that in it I have found a wealth of pleasure and a gold mine of amusement. Here is Don Quirieleisón of Montalbán, that valiant knight, and his brother Tomás of Montalbán, and the knight Fonseca, not to mention the battle that the brave Tirant waged against the Alani, and the witticisms of the damsel Placerdemivida, and the loves and lies of the widow Reposada, and the lady Emperatriz, beloved of Hipólito, her squire. I tell you the truth, my friend, when

---

[35] *Palmerín of the Olive:* The first of the Palmerín novels, published in 1511, of uncertain authorship.

[36] *Don Belianís:* Written by Jeronimo Fernandez and published in 1547.

[37] *Tirant lo Blanc:* See note 27 above.

I say that because of its style, this is the best book in the world: in it knights eat, and sleep, and die in their beds, and make a will before they die, and do everything else that all the other books of this sort leave out. For these reasons, since the author who composed this book did not deliberately write foolish things but intended to entertain and satirize, it deserves to be reprinted in an edition that would stay in print for a long time. Take it home and read it, and you'll say that everything I've said about it is true."

"I'll do that," answered the barber. "But what shall we do with these small books that remain?"

"These," said the priest, "are probably not about chivalry; they must be poetry."

And opening one, he saw that it was *Diana*, by Jorge de Montemayor,[38] and he said, believing that all the others were of the same genre:

"These do not deserve to be burned like the rest, because they do not and will not cause the harm that books of chivalry have, for they are books of the understanding and do no injury to anyone."

"Oh, Señor!" said the niece. "Your grace should send them to be burned, just like all the rest, because it's very likely that my dear uncle, having been cured of the chivalric disease, will read these and want to become a shepherd and wander through the woods and meadows singing and playing, and, what would be even worse, become a poet, and that, they say, is an incurable and contagious disease."

"What the girl says is true," said the priest, "and it would be a good idea to remove from the path of our friend this obstacle and danger. And, to begin with Montemayor's *Diana*, I am of the opinion that it should not be burned, but that everything having to do with the wise Felicia and the enchanted water, and almost all the long verses, should be excised, and let it happily keep all the prose and the honor of being the first of such books."

"This next one," said the barber, "is called *Diana the Second, by the Salamancan*, and here's another one with the same name, whose author is Gil Polo."[39]

"The one by the Salamancan," replied the priest, "should join and add to the number of those condemned in the corral, and the one by Gil Polo should be preserved as if it were by Apollo himself; and move on, my friend, and let's hurry; it's growing late."

"This book," said the barber, opening another one, "is *The Ten Books of Fortune in Love*, composed by Antonio de Lofraso, a Sardinian poet."[40]

"By the orders I received," said the priest, "since Apollo was Apollo, and the muses muses, and poets poets, no book as amusing or nonsensical has ever been written, and since, in its way, it is the best and most unusual book of its kind that has seen the light of day, anyone who has not read it can assume that he has never read anything entertaining. Give it to me, friend, for I value finding it more than if I were given a cassock of rich Florentine cloth."

---

[38] *Diana*, by Jorge de Montemayor: See note 23 above.

[39] *Diana the Second* . . . **Gil Polo:** The second version, titled *Diana in Love*, was highly esteemed.

[40] *The Ten Books* . . . **poet:** Published in 1573; elsewhere, Cervantes mocked this book.

He set it aside with great delight, and the barber continued, saying:

"These next ones are *The Shepherd of Iberia, Nymphs of Henares,* and *Deceptions of Jealousy.*"[41]

"Well, there's nothing else to do," said the priest, "but turn them over to the secular arm of the housekeeper; and don't ask me why, for I'd never finish."

"This one is *The Shepherd of Fílida.*"[42]

"He isn't a shepherd," said the priest, "but a very prudent courtier; keep that as if it were a precious jewel."

"This large one here," said the barber, "is called *Treasury of Various Poems.*"[43]

"If there weren't so many," said the priest, "they would be more highly esteemed; this book needs a weeding and clearing out of certain base things contained among all its grandeurs. Keep it, because its author is a friend of mine, and out of respect for other, more heroic and elevated works that he has written."

"This," said the barber, "is *The Songbook*[44] by López Maldonado."

"The author of that book," replied the priest, "is also a great friend of mine, and when he recites his verses they amaze anyone who hears them, and the delicacy of his voice when he sings them is enchanting. He's somewhat long-winded in the eclogues, but you can't have too much of a good thing: keep it with the chosen ones. But what's that book next to it?"

"*La Galatea,*[45] by Miguel de Cervantes," said the barber.

"This Cervantes has been a good friend of mine for many years, and I know that he is better versed in misfortunes than in verses. His book has a certain creativity; it proposes something and concludes nothing. We have to wait for the second part he has promised; perhaps with that addition it will achieve the mercy denied to it now; in the meantime, keep it locked away in your house, my friend."

"Gladly," the barber responded. "And here are three all together: *La Araucana,* by Don Alonso de Ercilla, *La Austríada,* by Juan Rufo, a magistrate of Córdoba, and *El Monserrate,*[46] by Cristóbal de Virués, a Valencian poet."

"All three of them," said the priest, "are the best books written in heroic verse in the Castilian language, and they can compete with the most famous from Italy: keep them as the richest gems of poetry that Spain has."

The priest wearied of seeing more books, and so, without further reflection, he wanted all the rest to be burned; but the barber already had one open, and it was called *The Tears of Angelica.*[47]

---

[41] *The Shepherd of Iberia, Nymphs of Henares,* **and** *Deceptions of Jealousy:* The first, by Bernardo de la Vega, was published in 1591; the second, by Bernardo Gonzalez de Bobadilla, was published in 1587; the third, by Bartolome Lopez de Encino, was published in 1586.

[42] *The Shepherd of Fílida:* Published by Luis Galvez de Montalvo in 1582.

[43] *Treasury of Various Poems:* Published by Pedra de Padilla in 1580.

[44] *The Songbook:* Published by Gabriel Lopez Maldonado and his collaborator, Miguel de Cervantes, in 1586.

[45] *La Galatea:* This pastoral novel was the first work published by Cervantes, in 1585.

[46] *La Araucana . . . La Austríada . . . El Monserrate:* Epic poems of the Spanish renaissance, published in 1569, 1584, and 1588 respectively.

[47] *The Tears of Angelica:* Published by Luis Barahona de Soto in 1586.

MIGUEL DE CERVANTES SAAVEDRA

"I would shed them myself," said the priest when he heard the name, "if I had sent such a book to be burned, because its author was one of the famous poets not only of Spain but of the world, and he had great success translating some fables by Ovid."

Chapter VII

REGARDING THE SECOND SALLY OF OUR GOOD
KNIGHT DON QUIXOTE OF LA MANCHA

At this point, Don Quixote began to shout, saying:

"Here, here, valiant knights; here each must show the might of his valiant arm, for the courtiers are winning the tourney."

Because of their response to this noise and uproar, the examination of the remaining books went no further; and so, it is believed that into the flames, without being seen or heard, went *La Carolea* and *The Lion of Spain,* along with *The Deeds of the Emperor,*[48] composed by Don Luis de Ávila, which no doubt were among the remaining books; perhaps, if the priest had seen them, they would not have suffered so harsh a sentence.

When they reached Don Quixote, he was already out of bed, still shouting and engaging in senseless acts, slashing forehand and backhand with his sword and as awake as if he had never slept. They seized him and forced him back to bed, and after he had calmed down somewhat, he turned to speak to the priest and said:

"In truth, Señor Archbishop Turpín, it is a great discredit to those of us called the Twelve Peers to do nothing more and allow the courtier knights victory in this tourney, when we, the knights who seek adventures, have won glory on the three previous days."

"Be still, my friend," said the priest, "for it is God's will that fortune changes, and that what is lost today is won tomorrow; your grace should tend to your health now, for it seems to me your grace must be fatigued, if not badly wounded."

"Not wounded," said Don Quixote, "but bruised and broken, there is no doubt about that, for the ignoble Don Roland beat me mercilessly with the branch of an oak tree, all on account of envy, because he sees that I alone am his rival in valorous deeds. But my name would not be Reinaldos de Montalbán if, upon rising from this bed, I did not repay him in spite of all his enchantments; for now, bring me something to eat, since I know that is what I need most at present, and leave my revenge to me."

They did as he asked: they gave him food, and he went back to sleep, and they marveled at his madness.

That night, the housekeeper burned and consigned to the flames all the books that were in the corral and in the house, and some must have been in the fire that should have been preserved in perpetual archives; but their destiny, and the sloth of the examiner, did not permit this, and so, as the proverb says, at times the just must pay for sinners.

---

[48] *La Carolea . . . The Lion of Spain . . . The Deeds of the Emperor:* The first two are epic poems by Jeronimo Sempere (1560) and Pedro de la Vecilla Castellanos (1586) respectively; the third work is unknown.

One of the remedies that the priest and the barber devised for their friend's illness was to wall up and seal off the room that held the books, so that when he got up he would not find them—perhaps by removing the cause, they would end the effect—and they would say that an enchanter had taken the books away, along with the room and everything in it; and this is what they did, with great haste. Two days later Don Quixote got out of bed, and the first thing he did was to go to see his books, and since he could not find the library where he had left it, he walked back and forth looking for it. He went up to the place where the door had been, and he felt it with his hands, and his eyes looked all around, and he did not say a word; but after some time had passed, he asked his housekeeper what had become of the library and his books. The housekeeper, who had been well-instructed in how she should respond, said:

"What library and what anything is your grace looking for? There's no more library and no more books in this house, because the devil himself took them away."

"It wasn't a devil," replied the niece, "but an enchanter who came on a cloud one night, after the day your grace left here, and he dismounted from the serpent he was riding and entered the library, and I don't know what he did inside, but after a little while he flew up through the roof and left the house full of smoke; and when we had the presence of mind to see what he had done, we could find no books and no library; the only thing the housekeeper and I remember very clearly is that as the evil old man was leaving, he shouted that because of the secret enmity he felt for the owner of the books and the room, he had done damage in the house, which we would see soon enough. He also said he was called Muñatón the Wise."

"He must have said Frestón,"[49] said Don Quixote.

"I don't know," the housekeeper replied, "if he was called Frestón or Fritón; all I know is that his name ended in *tón*."

"That is true," said Don Quixote. "He is a wise enchanter, a great enemy of mine who bears me a grudge because he knows through his arts and learning that I shall, in time, come to do battle in single combat with a knight whom he favors and whom I am bound to vanquish, and he will not be able to stop it, and for this reason he attempts to cause me all the difficulties he can; but I foresee that he will not be able to contravene or avoid what heaven has ordained."

"Who can doubt it?" said the niece. "But, Señor Uncle, who has involved your grace in those disputes? Wouldn't it be better to stay peacefully in your house and not wander around the world searching for bread made from something better than wheat, never stopping to think that many people go looking for wool and come back shorn?"

"Oh, my dear niece," replied Don Quixote, "how little you understand! Before I am shorn I shall have plucked and removed the beard of any man who imagines he can touch even a single hair of mine."

The two women did not wish to respond any further because they saw that he was becoming enraged.

---

[49] **Frestón:** The enchanter Frestón is the alleged author of *Don Belianis of Greece,* a chivalric novel.

So it was that he spent two very quiet weeks at home, showing no signs of wanting to repeat his initial lunacies, and during this time he had lively conversations with his two friends the priest and the barber, in which he said that what the world needed most were knights errant and that in him errant chivalry would be reborn. The priest at times contradicted him, and at other times he agreed, because if he did not maintain this ruse, he would not have been able to talk to him.

During this time, Don Quixote approached a farmer who was a neighbor of his, a good man—if that title can be given to someone who is poor—but without much in the way of brains. In short, he told him so much, and persuaded and promised him so much, that the poor peasant resolved to go off with him and serve as his squire. Among other things, Don Quixote said that he should prepare to go with him gladly, because it might happen that one day he would have an adventure that would gain him, in the blink of an eye, an ínsula,[50] and he would make him its governor. With these promises and others like them, Sancho Panza,[51] for that was the farmer's name, left his wife and children and agreed to be his neighbor's squire.

Then Don Quixote determined to find some money, and by selling one thing, and pawning another, and undervaluing everything, he managed to put together a reasonable sum. He also acquired a round shield, which he borrowed from a friend, and doing the best he could to repair his broken helmet, he informed his squire of the day and time he planned to start out so that Sancho could supply himself with whatever he thought he would need. He ordered him in particular to bring along saddlebags, and Sancho said he certainly would bring them and also planned to take along a donkey he thought very highly of because he wasn't one for walking any great distance. As for the donkey, Don Quixote had to stop and think about that for a while, wondering if he recalled any knight errant who had with him a squire riding on a donkey, and none came to mind, yet in spite of this he resolved to take Sancho along, intending to obtain a more honorable mount for him at the earliest opportunity by appropriating the horse of the first discourteous knight he happened to meet. He furnished himself with shirts and all the other things he could, following the advice the innkeeper had given him; and when this had been accomplished and completed, without Panza taking leave of his children and wife, or Don Quixote of his housekeeper and niece, they rode out of the village one night, and no one saw them, and they traveled so far that by dawn they were certain they would not be found even if anyone came looking for them.

Sancho Panza rode on his donkey like a patriarch, with his saddlebags, and his wineskin, and a great desire to see himself governor of the ínsula his master had promised him. Don Quixote happened to follow the same direction and route he had followed on his first sally, which was through the countryside of Montiel, and he rode there with less difficulty than he had the last time, because at that hour of the

---

[50] **ínsula:** The Latin word for "island" that appears frequently in novels of chivalry; Cervantes uses it throughout for comic effect.

[51] **Sancho Panza:** *Panza* means "belly" or "paunch."

morning the sun's rays fell obliquely and did not tire them. Then Sancho Panza said to his master:

"Señor Knight Errant, be sure not to forget what your grace promised me about the ínsula; I'll know how to govern it no matter how big it is."

To which Don Quixote replied:

"You must know, friend Sancho Panza, that it was a very common custom of the knights errant of old to make their squires governors of the ínsulas or kingdoms they won, and I have resolved that so amiable a usage will not go unfulfilled on my account; on the contrary, I plan to improve upon it, for they sometimes, and perhaps most times, waited until their squires were old, and after they had had their fill of serving, and enduring difficult days, and nights that were even worse, they would grant them the title of count, or perhaps even marquis, of some valley or province of greater or smaller size; but if you live and I live, it well might be that before six days have passed I shall win a kingdom that has others allied to it, and that would be perfect for my crowning you king of one of them. And do not think this is any great thing; for events and eventualities befall knights in ways never seen or imagined, and I might well be able to give you even more than I have promised."

"If that happens," replied Sancho Panza, "and I became king through one of those miracles your grace has mentioned, then Juana Gutiérrez,[52] my missus, would be queen, and my children would be princes."

"Well, who can doubt it?" Don Quixote responded.

"I doubt it," Sancho Panza replied, "because in my opinion, even if God rained kingdoms down on earth, none of them would sit well on the head of Mari Gutiérrez. You should know, Señor, that she isn't worth two *maravedís* as a queen; she'd do better as a countess, and even then she'd need God's help."

"Leave it to God, Sancho," said Don Quixote, "and He will give what suits her best; but do not lower your desire so much that you will be content with anything less than the title of captain general."

"I won't, Señor," Sancho replied, "especially when I have a master as distinguished as your grace, who will know how to give me everything that's right for me and that I can handle."

Chapter VIII

REGARDING THE GOOD FORTUNE OF THE VALOROUS DON QUIXOTE IN THE FEARFUL AND NEVER IMAGINED ADVENTURE OF THE WINDMILLS, ALONG WITH OTHER EVENTS WORTHY OF JOYFUL REMEMBRANCE

As they were talking, they saw thirty or forty of the windmills found in that countryside, and as soon as Don Quixote caught sight of them, he said to his squire:

"Good fortune is guiding our affairs better than we could have desired, for there you see, friend Sancho Panza, thirty or more enormous giants with whom I intend

---

[52]**Juana Gutiérrez:** Sancho's wife has several other names, including Mari Gutiérrez, Juana Panza, Teresa Cascajo, and Teresa Panza.

to do battle and whose lives I intend to take, and with the spoils we shall begin to grow rich, for this is righteous warfare, and it is a great service to God to remove so evil a breed from the face of the earth."

"What giants?" said Sancho Panza.

"Those you see over there," replied his master, "with the long arms; sometimes they are almost two leagues long."

"Look, your grace," Sancho responded, "those things that appear over there aren't giants but windmills, and what looks like their arms are the sails that are turned by the wind and make the grindstone move."

"It seems clear to me," replied Don Quixote, "that thou art not well-versed in the matter of adventures: these are giants; and if thou art afraid, move aside and start to pray whilst I enter with them in fierce and unequal combat."

And having said this, he spurred his horse, Rocinante, paying no attention to the shouts of his squire, Sancho, who warned him that, beyond any doubt, those things he was about to attack were windmills and not giants. But he was so convinced they were giants that he did not hear the shouts of his squire, Sancho, and could not see, though he was very close, what they really were; instead, he charged and called out:

"Flee not, cowards and base creatures, for it is a single knight who attacks you."

Just then a gust of wind began to blow, and the great sails began to move, and, seeing this, Don Quixote said:

"Even if you move more arms than the giant Briareus,[53] you will answer to me."

And saying this, and commending himself with all his heart to his lady Dulcinea, asking that she come to his aid at this critical moment, and well-protected by his shield, with his lance in its socket, he charged at Rocinante's full gallop and attacked the first mill he came to; and as he thrust his lance into the sail, the wind moved it with so much force that it broke the lance into pieces and picked up the horse and the knight, who then dropped to the ground and were very badly battered. Sancho Panza hurried to help as fast as his donkey could carry him, and when he reached them he discovered that Don Quixote could not move because he had taken so hard a fall with Rocinante.

"God save me!" said Sancho. "Didn't I tell your grace to watch what you were doing, that these were nothing but windmills, and only somebody whose head was full of them wouldn't know that?"

"Be quiet, Sancho my friend," replied Don Quixote. "Matters of war, more than any others, are subject to continual change; moreover, I think, and therefore it is true, that the same Frestón the Wise who stole my room and my books has turned these giants into windmills in order to deprive me of the glory of defeating them: such is the enmity he feels for me; but in the end, his evil arts will not prevail against the power of my virtuous sword."

"God's will be done," replied Sancho Panza.

He helped him to stand, and Don Quixote remounted Rocinante, whose back was almost broken. And, talking about their recent adventure, they continued on the road

---

[53] **Briareus:** A giant in Greek mythology who had fifty heads and a hundred arms.

to Puerto Lápice,[54] because there, said Don Quixote, he could not fail to find many diverse adventures since it was a very heavily trafficked place; but he rode heavyhearted because he did not have his lance; and expressing this to his squire, he said:

"I remember reading that a Spanish knight named Diego Pérez de Vargas, whose sword broke in battle, tore a heavy bough or branch from an oak tree and with it did such great deeds that day, and thrashed so many Moors, that he was called Machuca, the Bruiser, and from that day forward he and his descendants were named Vargas y Machuca. I have told you this because from the first oak that presents itself to me I intend to tear off another branch as good as the one I have in mind, and with it I shall do such great deeds that you will consider yourself fortunate for deserving to see them and for being a witness to things that can hardly be believed."

"It's in God's hands," said Sancho. "I believe everything your grace says, but sit a little straighter, it looks like you're tilting, it must be from the battering you took when you fell."

"That is true," replied Don Quixote, "and if I do not complain about the pain, it is because it is not the custom of knights errant to complain about any wound, even if their innards are spilling out because of it."

"If that's true, I have nothing to say," Sancho responded, "but God knows I'd be happy if your grace complained when something hurt you. As for me, I can say that I'll complain about the smallest pain I have, unless what you said about not complaining also applies to the squires of knights errant."

Don Quixote could not help laughing at his squire's simplemindedness; and so he declared that he could certainly complain however and whenever he wanted, with or without cause, for as yet he had not read anything to the contrary in the order of chivalry. Sancho said that it was time to eat. His master replied that he felt no need of food at the moment, but that Sancho could eat whenever he wished. With this permission, Sancho made himself as comfortable as he could on his donkey, and after taking out of the saddlebags what he had put into them, he rode behind his master at a leisurely pace, eating and, from time to time, tilting back the wineskin with so much gusto that the most self-indulgent tavern-keeper in Málaga might have envied him. And as he rode along in that manner, taking frequent drinks, he did not think about any promises his master had made to him, and he did not consider it work but sheer pleasure to go around seeking adventures, no matter how dangerous they might be.

In short, they spent the night under some trees, and from one of them Don Quixote tore off a dry branch to use as a lance and placed on it the iron head he had taken from the one that had broken. Don Quixote did not sleep at all that night but thought of his lady Dulcinea, in order to conform to what he had read in his books of knights spending many sleepless nights in groves and meadows, turning all their thoughts to memories of their ladies. Sancho Panza did not do the same; since his stomach was full, and not with chicory water, he slept the entire night, and if his master had not called him, the rays of the sun shining in his face and the song of

---

[54] **Puerto Lápice:** An entrance to the mountains of the Sierra Morena between La Mancha and Andalucia.

numerous birds joyfully greeting the arrival of the new day would have done nothing to rouse him. When he woke he made another pass at the wineskin and found it somewhat flatter than it had been the night before, and his heart grieved, for it seemed to him they were not likely to remedy the lack very soon. Don Quixote did not wish to eat breakfast because, as has been stated, he meant to live on sweet memories. They continued on the road to Puerto Lápice, and at about three in the afternoon it came into view.

"Here," said Don Quixote when he saw it, "we can, brother Sancho Panza, plunge our hands all the way up to the elbows into this thing they call adventures. But be advised that even if you see me in the greatest danger in the world, you are not to put a hand to your sword to defend me, unless you see that those who offend me are baseborn rabble, in which case you certainly can help me; but if they are gentlemen, under no circumstances is it licit or permissible for you, under the laws of chivalry, to help me until you are dubbed a knight."

"There's no doubt, Señor," replied Sancho, "that your grace will be strictly obeyed in this; besides, as far as I'm concerned, I'm a peaceful man and an enemy of getting involved in quarrels or disputes. It's certainly true that when it comes to defending my person I won't pay much attention to those laws, since laws both human and divine permit each man to defend himself against anyone who tries to hurt him."

"I agree," Don Quixote responded, "but as for helping me against gentlemen, you have to hold your natural impulses in check."

"Then that's just what I'll do," replied Sancho, "and I'll keep that precept as faithfully as I keep the Sabbath on Sunday."

As they were speaking, there appeared on the road two Benedictine friars mounted on two dromedaries, for the two mules they rode on were surely no smaller than that. They wore their traveling masks and carried sunshades. Behind them came a carriage, accompanied by four or five men on horseback, and two muledrivers on foot. In the carriage, as was learned later, was a Basque lady going to Sevilla, where her husband was preparing to sail for the Indies to take up a very honorable post. The friars were not traveling with her, although their route was the same, but as soon as Don Quixote saw them, he said to his squire:

"Either I am deceived, or this will be the most famous adventure ever seen, because those black shapes you see there must be, and no doubt are, enchanters who have captured some princess in that carriage, and I needs must do everything in my power to right this wrong."

"This will be worse than the windmills," said Sancho. "Look, Señor, those are friars of St. Benedict, and the carriage must belong to some travelers. Look carefully, I tell you, look carefully at what you do, in case the devil is deceiving you."

"I have already told you, Sancho," replied Don Quixote, "that you know very little about the subject of adventures; what I say is true, and now you will see that it is so."

And having said this, he rode forward and stopped in the middle of the road that the friars were traveling, and when they were close enough so that he thought they could hear what he said, he called to them in a loud voice:

"You wicked and monstrous creatures, instantly unhand the noble princesses you hold captive in that carriage, or else prepare to receive a swift death as just punishment for your evil deeds."

The friars pulled on the reins, taken aback as much by Don Quixote's appearance as by his words, and they responded:

"Señor, we are neither wicked nor monstrous, but two religious of St. Benedict who are traveling on our way, and we do not know if there are captive princesses in that carriage or not."

"No soft words with me; I know who you are, perfidious rabble," said Don Quixote.

And without waiting for any further reply, he spurred Rocinante, lowered his lance, and attacked the first friar with so much ferocity and courage that if he had not allowed himself to fall off the mule, the friar would have been thrown to the ground and seriously injured or even killed. The second friar, who saw how his companion was treated, kicked his castle-size mule and began to gallop across the fields, faster than the wind.

Sancho Panza, who saw the man on the ground, quickly got off his donkey, hurried over to the friar, and began to pull off his habit. At this moment, two servants of the friars came over and asked why he was stripping him. Sancho replied that these clothes were legitimately his, the spoils of the battle his master, Don Quixote, had won. The servants had no sense of humor and did not understand anything about spoils or battles, and seeing that Don Quixote had moved away and was talking to the occupants of the carriage, they attacked Sancho and knocked him down, and leaving no hair in his beard unscathed, they kicked him breathless and senseless and left him lying on the ground. The friar, frightened and terrified and with no color in his face, did not wait another moment but got back on his mule, and when he was mounted, he rode off after his companion, who was waiting for him a good distance away, wondering what the outcome of the attack would be; they did not wish to wait to learn how matters would turn out but continued on their way, crossing themselves more than if they had the devil at their backs.

Don Quixote, as has been said, was talking to the lady in the carriage, saying:

"O beauteous lady, thou canst do with thy person as thou wishest, for the arrogance of thy captors here lieth on the ground, vanquished by this my mighty arm; and so that thou mayest not pine to know the name of thy emancipator, know that I am called Don Quixote of La Mancha, knight errant in search of adventures, and captive of the beauteous and peerless Doña Dulcinea of Toboso, and as recompense for the boon thou hast received from me, I desire only that thou turnest toward Toboso, and on my behalf appearest before this lady and sayest unto her what deeds I have done to gain thy liberty."

One of the squires accompanying the carriage was a Basque, who listened to everything that Don Quixote was saying; and seeing that he would not allow the carriage to move forward but said it would have to go to Toboso, the squire approached Don Quixote and, seizing his lance, in bad Castilian and even worse Basque, he said:

"Go on, mister, you go wrong; by God who make me, if don't let carriage go, as I be Basque I kill you."

Don Quixote understood him very well and replied with great serenity:

"If you were a gentleman, as you are not, I would already have punished your foolishness and audacity, unhappy creature."

To which the Basque replied:

"Not gentleman me? As Christian I make vow to God you lie. Throw away lance and pull out sword and soon see which one make horse drink. Basque by land, noble by sea, noble by devil, if say other thing you lie."

"Now you will see,[55] said Agrajes," replied Don Quixote.

And after throwing his lance to the ground, he drew his sword, grasped his shield, and attacked the Basque, determined to take his life. The Basque, who saw him coming at him in this manner, wanted to get off the mule, which, being one of the inferior ones for hire, could not be trusted, but all he could do was draw his sword; it was his good fortune, however, to be next to the carriage, and he seized one of the pillows and used it as a shield, and the two of them went at each other as if they were mortal enemies. The rest of the people tried to make peace between them but could not, because the Basque said in his tangled words that if they did not allow him to finish his fight, he himself would kill his mistress and everyone else who got in his way. The lady in the carriage, stunned and fearful at what she saw, had the coachman drive some distance away, and from there she watched the fierce contest, in the course of which the Basque went over Don Quixote's shield and struck a great blow with his to his shoulder, and if it had not been protected by armor, he would have opened it to the waist. Don Quixote, who felt the pain of that enormous blow, gave a great shout, saying:

"O lady of my soul, Dulcinea, flower of beauty, come to the aid of this thy knight, who, for the sake of thy great virtue, finds himself in grave peril!"

Saying this, and grasping his sword, and protecting himself with his shield, and attacking the Basque were all one, for he was determined to venture everything on the fortune of a single blow.

The Basque, seeing him attack in this fashion, clearly understood the courage in this rash act and resolved to do the same as Don Quixote. And so he waited for him, shielded by his pillow, and unable to turn the mule one way or the other, for the mule, utterly exhausted and not made for such foolishness, could not take another step.

As has been said, Don Quixote was charging the wary Basque with his sword on high, determined to cut him in half, and the Basque, well-protected by his pillow, was waiting for him, his sword also raised, and all the onlookers were filled with fear and suspense regarding the outcome of the great blows they threatened to give to each other, and the lady in the carriage and all her maids were making a thousand vows and offerings to all the images and houses of devotion in Spain so that God would deliver the squire and themselves from the great danger in which they found themselves.

But the difficulty in all this is that at this very point and juncture, the author of the history leaves the battle pending, apologizing because he found nothing else written about the feats of Don Quixote other than what he has already recounted. It is certainly true that the second author[56] of this work did not want to believe that so curious

---

[55] **"Now you will see":** Agrajes, a character in *Amadís of Gaul,* would say these words before doing battle; it became a proverbial expression used at the beginning of a fight.

[56] **the second author:** Cervantes (the narrator), claims in the following chapter to have arranged for the translation of another (fictional) author's book. This device was common in novels of chivalry.

a history would be subjected to the laws of oblivion, or that the great minds of La Mancha possessed so little interest that they did not have in their archives or writing tables a few pages that dealt with this famous knight; and so, with this thought in mind, he did not despair of finding the conclusion to this gentle history, which, with heaven's help, he discovered in the manner that will be revealed in part two.

TEXT IN CONTEXT

William Shakespeare, **The Tempest** **1818**

IMAGE: *Prospero* by Robert Dighton 1813
TIME AND PLACE: Early Modern England:
    The Port of London 1814
IMAGE: Dominic Letts as Caliban 1819
IN THE WORLD: O Brave New World! 1887

WILLIAM SHAKESPEARE
B. ENGLAND, 1564–1616

WWW For links to more information about Shakespeare and a quiz on *The Tempest,* see bedfordstmartins .com/worldlit compact.

In the 1623 Folio, the first collected edition of William Shakespeare's works, fellow poet and critic Ben Jonson (1572–1637) paid tribute to his great contemporary:

> Triumph, my *Britaine,* thou hast one to showe,
>   To whom all scenes of *Europe* homage owe.
> He was not of an age, but for all time!

Jonson's lines do not exaggerate, for from the sixteenth century to the present Shakespeare's tragedies, comedies, histories, and romances throughout the world have been performed on stage, adapted for film, and studied for their dramatic techniques, the complexity of their characters, their history, and their philosophy. From the naive magnanimity of King Lear and the mean vindictiveness of Iago, through the hopeless innocence of Juliet and the sprightly savvy of Beatrice, to the deep self-questioning of Hamlet, Shakespeare's plays evoke a full range of human passions and experiences. The plays allow viewers to see the RENAISSANCE mind in all its complexity, as characters vie for love and power in an atmosphere shot through with a tragic sense that forces beyond human reckoning may at any moment thwart the best of human efforts.

Stratford-on-Avon.   About William Shakespeare's early life little is known, but much has been invented. He was born in Stratford-on-Avon, a market town in Warwickshire, just northwest of London, in April 1564. William's father, John Shakespeare, was a glove maker

and leather worker who through his trade and a fortunate marriage to Mary Arden, heiress of a small estate, rose to become a member of the city council and Bailiff at Stratford. As the son in a respectable family, young William most likely received the standard education in Latin grammar, reading, and writing at the Stratford grammar school. Biographers have speculated that Shakespeare must have enjoyed the bustling life of Stratford, with its renowned local fairs, visiting theater companies, and ample countryside in which a young imaginative boy could exercise his fancy. All we know for certain is that on November 27, 1582, the Bishop of Worcester issued a marriage license to William Shakespeare and Anne Hathaway; the parish records show the birth of a daughter in 1583 and a set of twins, a son and daughter, in 1585. Sometime between 1582 and 1592, Shakespeare began to take part in the theater in London, for which Robert Greene in a letter called the young actor and writer "an upstart Crow," a player so bold as to think he could write plays.

A Man of the Theater.   When London theaters reopened in 1594 after being closed for two years by an outbreak of the plague, Shakespeare was performing with one of the most prominent acting companies,

Early Modern England: The Port of London

At the beginning of the sixteenth century agriculture was the principal industry of England, while cloth trade with Europe made up the principal export. When the English, French, and Dutch undertook voyages of economic and territorial expansion, the whole concept of wealth acquired a more dynamic capitalist character. In the second half of the sixteenth century and the opening decades of the seventeenth the great British joint-stock companies were founded, financing commerce with the Middle East, India, China, and North America. Not only did the new trade create prosperity, it awakened public curiosity about the vastly enlarging known world. *Hakluyt's Principal Navigations, Voyages, and Discoveries of the English Nation,* published in 1589, contained accounts of the great English navigators of the century.

The City of London began a corresponding demographic and physical expansion around 1550. England rapidly changed from a medieval kingdom into an early modern nation-state; London, the center of the nation and the hub of commerce, accommodated the changes. Stunning political developments in the latter half of the century—from the crowning of Queen Elizabeth I in 1558 to the defeat of the Spanish Armada in 1588—consolidated London's position as one of the great cities of the world.

London's location on the Thames River was a source of strength for the English economy. The Thames and its tributaries stretched across half of southern England, with London the great port of entry to the English Channel. The most famous tributary, the Fleet, running along the western

Plan of London, c. 1580   This map was included in the famous atlas Civitates Orbis Terrarum *during Shakespeare's time. (The Art Archive/Eileen Tweedy)*

boundary of London, was also a major site for the disposal of sewage, graphically described in a contemporary poem by Ben Jonson, "On the Famous Voyage." An effective system of sewage control was not developed until after the Great Stink of 1858, during which the members of Parliament had to receive medical attention to continue breathing. Since the Thames also presented other risks to navigation, the Company of Watermen was formed in 1555 to ensure safe travel up and down the river. Eventually a row of city bridges was built, but until 1729 the only one standing was London Bridge, in use since the thirteenth century.

At the City of London the Thames broadened into the Pool of London, wide and deep enough to constitute a major seaport thirty miles from the coast, easily defensible and of great commercial importance. Thus the Thames and the London became dominant symbols of England's power by the time of William Shakespeare.

the Lord Chamberlain's Men, along with the great actors Richard Burbage and William Kemp. Proceeds from his theatrical endeavors and various business transactions proved remarkably profitable for the young actor and writer, and in 1597 Shakespeare purchased New Place, one of the finest houses in Stratford. Two years later Shakespeare joined Burbage and others to found the Globe Theatre, one of the most important playhouses in London, built to the specifications of the actor–proprietors, members of the Chamberlain's Men. After Queen Elizabeth's death in 1603, this troupe, now called the King's Men and fast becoming the preeminent company at Court and in the city, received the sponsorship of James I.

The King's Men.   By this time, Shakespeare was already celebrated as a writer. In 1598, Francis Mere compared Shakespeare favorably to Plautus and Seneca, noting that whereas these writers are known for comedy and tragedy, respectively, "Shakespeare among the English is the most excellent in both kinds for the stage." Among the plays written up to this time are many of the histories, including *Richard III, King John,* and Parts One and Two of *Henry IV; The Comedy of Errors, A Midsummer Night's Dream,* and *The Taming of the Shrew* among other comedies; and *Titus Andronicus* and *Romeo and Juliet* among the tragedies. Between 1598 and 1609, a period of incredible artistic productivity for the poet-dramatist, Shakespeare completed more than fifteen major plays, including *Hamlet, Othello,* and *King Lear* among the tragedies; *As You Like It* and *All's Well That Ends Well* among the comedies; and *Pericles Prince of Tyre,* a romance. The King's Men now had established a stronghold over London theater, having acquired in 1608 Blackfriar's Theatre. Unlike the Globe, Blackfriar's was an enclosed playhouse, which enabled the players to hold winter performances. Around 1610, Shakespeare retired from London to his home at Stratford, where he wrote his final plays — *Cymbeline, The Winter's Tale, The Tempest,* and *Henry VIII* — and died April 23, 1616.

The Plays.   As Ben Jonson's tribute points out, Shakespeare was at home writing both tragedies and comedies, but he was equally adept at writing history plays and what some call romances; most important, however, many of his greatest dramas blur the boundaries among these genres. Like other ELIZABETHAN dramatists, Shakespeare often disregarded the classical "unities" derived from Aristotle's *Poetics,* refusing to limit the action to a single day and to a single place. What distinguishes his plays are their intricacy of plot, brilliant display of language, and presentation of complex characters that, despite their historical particularity, have

Historical arguments claiming that Shakespeare could not have intended Prospero to be seen as unattractive or Caliban as sympathetic are denying to the Renaissance's greatest playwright precisely that complexity of sensibility which is what we have come to value most in Shakespearian drama.

– STEPHEN ORGEL, critic, 1987

fascinated readers throughout the world for four hundred years. Prince Hal from *Henry IV,* Hamlet, and Rosalind from *As You Like It* come to us as visitations from a political and social reality constructed entirely differently from ours; yet they exert a lively, almost palpable presence even to contemporary readers and spectators.

The Tempest.   *The Tempest* was first performed at Court in 1611 and published in what is known as the First Folio of 1623.[1] Its transgressive spirit and deliberate mixing of forms—tragedy, comedy, masque, satire—suggest that *The Tempest* self-consciously addresses the playwright's art and celebrates the artist's power to transcend the social and aesthetic codes and conventions of the time, even as it questions the moral consequences of breaking such boundaries. The play more generally questions the relationship between nature and art, especially as that relationship is negotiated by the playwright, here compared to a magician. Indeed, Prospero becomes a composite figure of the forms of power, assembling in his various guises the prince, the playwright, the magician, and the father, thus blurring the distinctions and highlighting the resemblances among those roles. The comic subplot involving Stephano and Trinculo parodies, as it mirrors, the important questions about the responsibilities of princes, the governance of state, the building of empires, and the treatment (and nature) of the prince's subjects. Although Prospero shapes the events that take place on his island and even exerts dominion over nature, as when he conjures up the storm that sets the plot in motion, he recognizes and accepts the limitations of his legitimate power.

While many of Shakespeare's plays are based on earlier plays or popular legends, *The Tempest* may have its origins in the story of the wreck of a ship, the *Sea Adventurer,* off the coast of Bermuda in 1609. En route to Virginia from Plymouth, the *Sea Adventurer*'s passengers included the new governor of Virginia, Sir Thomas Gates. After being stranded for nine months, the entire group of 150 crew and passengers managed to sail back to Jamestown on two smaller boats that they

> *The Tempest . . .* declares no all-embracing triumph for colonialism. Rather it serves as a limit text in which the characteristic operations of colonialist discourse may be discerned—as an instrument of exploitation, a register of beleaguerment and a site of radical ambivalence.
>
> — PAUL BROWN, critic, 1985

---

[1] **First Folio of 1623:** The First Folio, printed between February 1622 and November 1623, was the first printed collection of Shakespeare's plays. Divided into comedies, histories, and tragedies, the Folio serves as the foundation for all subsequent editions of the plays, except *Pericles,* which was not included. The First Folio was published by Edward Blount and the printers William and Isaac Jaggard, with editorial assistance from the actors and co-owners of Shakespeare's company, the King's Men, particularly Jon Heminge and Henry Condell, who wrote a dedication and preface. The Folio was based on previously printed (quarto) versions of some of the plays and from manuscript fragments, transcripts, and players' prompt-books for the eighteen plays that had not been printed before.

had built. Accounts of these adventures began to appear in 1610, leading to speculation that Shakespeare either had read the accounts or may have been acquainted with one of the authors. What is important, however, is that Shakespeare constructs out of such an adventure a play that engages key questions about the nature of power, politics, art, and humanity.

■ **FURTHER RESEARCH**

Biography
Burgess, Anthony. *Shakespeare.* 1970.
Schoenbaum, S. *William Shakespeare: A Compact Documentary Life.* 1977.

Background
Bradbrook, Muriel. *The Rise of the Common Player.* 1964.
Gurr, Andrew. *The Shakespearean Stage: 1574–1642.* 3rd ed. 1992.
Robinson, Randal. *Unlocking Shakespeare's Language: Help for the Teacher and Student.* 1989.
Taylor, Gary. *Reinventing Shakespeare: A Cultural History from the Restoration to the Present.* 1989.

Criticism
Felperin, Howard. *Shakespearean Romance.* 1972.
Fiedler, Leslie. *The Stranger in Shakespeare.* 1972.
Graff, Gerald, and James Phelan. *William Shakespeare: The Tempest: A Case Study in Critical Controversy.* 2000.
Greenblatt, Stephen J. *Shakespearean Negotiations.* 1988.
_____. *Learning to Curse: Essays in Early Modern Culture.* 1990.
Hillman, Richard. *Shakespearean Subversions: The Trickster and the Play-Text.* 1992.
Hulme, Peter, and William H. Sherman, eds. *The Tempest and Its Travels.* 2000.
Kermode, Frank. *The Tempest.* 1954.
Kernan, Alvin B. *The Playwright as Magician: Shakespeare's Image of the Poet in the English Public Theater.* 1979.
Vaughan, Alden T., and Virginia Mason Vaughan. *Shakespeare's Caliban: A Cultural History.* 1991.

> Shakespeare approximates the remote, and familiarizes the wonderful; the event which he represents will not happen, but if it were possible, its effects would probably be such as he has assigned.
> – SAMUEL JOHNSON,
> *Preface to Shakespeare,* 1765

❧ The Tempest

THE SCENE: *An uninhabited island.*

NAMES OF THE ACTORS

ALONSO, *King of Naples*
SEBASTIAN, *his brother*
PROSPERO, *the right Duke of Milan*
ANTONIO, *his brother, the usurping Duke of Milan*
FERDINAND, *son to the King of Naples*
GONZALO, *an honest old councilor*
ADRIAN *and* FRANCISCO, *lords*
CALIBAN, *a savage and deformed slave*
TRINCULO, *a jester*
STEPHANO, *a drunken butler*

MASTER OF A SHIP
BOATSWAIN
MARINERS
MIRANDA, *daughter to Prospero*
ARIEL, *an airy spirit*
IRIS ⎫
CERES ⎟
JUNO ⎬ [*presented by*] *spirits*
NYMPHS ⎟
REAPERS ⎭
[OTHER SPIRITS ATTENDING ON PROSPERO]

ACT I

Scene 1

On a ship at sea.

A tempestuous noise of thunder and lightning heard. Enter a SHIPMASTER *and a* BOATSWAIN.

MASTER: Boatswain!

BOATSWAIN: Here, master. What cheer?

MASTER: Good,[1] speak to th' mariners! Fall to't yarely,[2] or we run ourselves aground. Bestir, bestir!   *Exit.*

Enter MARINERS.

BOATSWAIN: Heigh, my hearts! Cheerly, cheerly, my hearts! Yare, yare! Take in the topsail! Tend to th' master's whistle! Blow till thou burst thy wind, if room enough![3]

Enter ALONSO, SEBASTIAN, ANTONIO, FERDINAND, GONZALO, *and others.*

ALONSO: Good boatswain, have care. Where's the master? Play the men.[4]

BOATSWAIN: I pray now, keep below.

10   ANTONIO: Where is the master, bos'n?

BOATSWAIN: Do you not hear him? You mar our labor. Keep your cabins; you do assist the storm.

GONZALO: Nay, good, be patient.

BOATSWAIN: When the sea is. Hence! What cares these roarers for the name of king? To cabin! Silence! Trouble us not!

GONZALO: Good, yet remember whom thou hast aboard.

---

[1] **Good:** Good fellow. [All notes in this selection are from editor Robert Langbaum.]   [2] **yarely:** Briskly.
[3] **Blow . . . enough!:** The storm can blow and split itself as long as there is open sea without rocks to maneuver in.   [4] **Play the men:** Act like men.

Dominic Letts as Caliban, 1995
The Royal Shakespeare Company is recognized as today's foremost theater ensemble specializing in the production of Shakespeare's plays. This photo is from the company's 1995 staging of The Tempest *in Stratford-upon-Avon. (Henrietta Butler / ArenaPAL)*

BOATSWAIN: None that I more love than myself. You are a councilor; if you can command these elements to silence and work the peace of the present,[5] we will not hand[6] a rope more. Use your authority. If you cannot, give thanks you have lived

20 so long, and make yourself ready in your cabin for the mischance of the hour, if it so hap. Cheerly, good hearts! Out of our way, I say.   *Exit.*

GONZALO: I have great comfort from this fellow. Methinks he hath no drowning mark upon him; his complexion is perfect gallows.[7] Stand fast, good Fate, to his hanging! Make the rope of his destiny our cable, for our own doth little advantage.[8] If he be not born to be hanged, our case is miserable.

Exit [with the rest].

Enter BOATSWAIN.

BOATSWAIN: Down with the topmast! Yare! Lower, lower! Bring her to try with main course![9] [*A cry within.*] A plague upon this howling! They are louder than the weather or our office.

Enter SEBASTIAN, ANTONIO, *and* GONZALO.

Yet again? What do you here? Shall we give o'er[10] and drown? Have you a mind

30 to sink?

SEBASTIAN: A pox o' your throat, you bawling, blasphemous, incharitable dog!

BOATSWAIN: Work you, then.

---

[5]**work . . . present:** Restore the present to peace (since as a councilor his job is to quell disorder).   [6]**hand:** Handle.   [7]**drowning . . . gallows:** Alluding to the proverb, "He that's born to be hanged need fear no drowning."   [8]**doth . . . advantage:** Gives us little advantage.   [9]**Bring . . . course!:** Heave to, under the mainsail.   [10]**give o'er:** Give up trying to run the ship.

ANTONIO: Hang, cur! Hang, you whoreson, insolent noisemaker! We are less afraid to be drowned than thou art.

GONZALO: I'll warrant him for[11] drowning, though the ship were no stronger than a nutshell and as leaky as an unstanched[12] wench.

BOATSWAIN: Lay her ahold, ahold! Set her two courses![13] Off to the sea again! Lay her off![14]

Enter MARINERS *wet.*

MARINERS:
All lost! To prayers, to prayers! All lost!   [*Exeunt.*]

BOATSWAIN:
40   What, must our mouths be cold?

GONZALO:
The King and Prince at prayers! Let's assist them,
For our case is as theirs.

SEBASTIAN:
                   I am out of patience.

ANTONIO:
We are merely° cheated of our lives by drunkards.   *completely*
This wide-chopped° rascal—would thou mightst lie drowning   *big-mouthed*
The washing of ten tides![15]

GONZALO:
                 He'll be hanged yet,
Though every drop of water swear against it
And gape at wid'st to glut him.

50   [*A confused noise within:*] "Mercy on us!"
"We split, we split!" "Farewell, my wife and children!"
"Farewell, brother!" "We split, we split, we split!"

                                         [*Exit* BOATSWAIN.]

ANTONIO:
Let's all sink wi' th' King.

SEBASTIAN:
                 Let's take leave of him.

                                Exit [*with* ANTONIO].

GONZALO: Now would I give a thousand furlongs of sea for an acre of barren ground—long heath,[16] brown furze, anything. The wills above be done, but I would fain die a dry death.   *Exit.*

---

[11] **warrant him for:** Guarantee him against. [12] **unstanched:** Wide-open. [13] **Set . . . courses!:** The ship is still being blown dangerously to shore, so the boatswain orders that the foresail be set in addition to the mainsail; but the ship still moves toward shore. [14] **off:** Away from the shore. [15] **would . . . tides:** Pirates were hanged on the shore and left there until three tides had washed over them. [16] **heath:** Heather.

Scene 2

The island. In front of PROSPERO's *cell.*

Enter PROSPERO *and* MIRANDA.

MIRANDA:
    If by your art, my dearest father, you have
    Put the wild waters in this roar, allay them.
    The sky, it seems, would pour down stinking pitch
    But that the sea, mounting to th' welkin's cheek,[17]
    Dashes the fire out. O, I have suffered
    With those that I saw suffer! A brave[18] vessel
    (Who had no doubt some noble creature in her)
    Dashed all to pieces! O, the cry did knock
    Against my very heart! Poor souls, they perished!
10   Had I been any god of power, I would
    Have sunk the sea within the earth or ere
    It should the good ship so have swallowed and
    The fraughting[19] souls within her.

PROSPERO:
                    Be collected.
    No more amazement. Tell your piteous heart
    There's no harm done.

MIRANDA:
               O, woe the day!

PROSPERO:
                   No harm.
    I have done nothing but in care of thee,
    Of thee my dear one, thee my daughter, who
    Art ignorant of what thou art, naught knowing
    Of whence I am, nor that I am more better
20   Than Prospero, master of a full poor cell,
    And thy no greater father.[20]

MIRANDA:
              More to know
    Did never meddle° with my thoughts.   *mingle*

PROSPERO:
                   'Tis time
    I should inform thee farther. Lend thy hand
    And pluck my magic garment from me. So.

[*Lays down his robe.*]
    Lie there, my art. Wipe thou thine eyes; have comfort.

---

[17] **welkin's cheek:** Face of the sky.   [18] **brave:** Fine, gallant (the word often has this meaning in the play).
[19] **fraughting:** Forming her freight.   [20] **thy . . . father:** Thy father, no greater than the Prospero just described.

The direful spectacle of the wrack, which touched
The very virtue of compassion in thee,
I have with such provision° in mine art   foresight
So safely ordered that there is no soul—
30   No, not so much perdition° as an hair   loss
Betid° to any creature in the vessel   happened
Which thou heard'st cry, which thou saw'st sink. Sit down;
For thou must now know farther.

MIRANDA:
                                   You have often
Begun to tell me what I am; but stopped
And left me to a bootless inquisition,
Concluding, "Stay; not yet."

PROSPERO:
                                   The hour's now come;
The very minute bids thee ope thine ear.
Obey, and be attentive. Canst thou remember
A time before we came unto this cell?
40   I do not think thou canst, for then thou wast not
Out° three years old.   fully

MIRANDA:
                                   Certainly, sir, I can.

PROSPERO:
By what? By any other house or person?
Of anything the image tell me that
Hath kept with thy remembrance.

MIRANDA:
                                   'Tis far off,
And rather like a dream than an assurance
That my remembrance warrants.[21] Had I not
Four or five women once that tended me?

PROSPERO:
Thou hadst, and more, Miranda. But how is it
That this lives in thy mind? What seest thou else
50   In the dark backward and abysm of time?
If thou rememb'rest aught ere thou cam'st here,
How thou cam'st here thou mayst.

MIRANDA:
                                   But that I do not.

PROSPERO:
Twelve year since, Miranda, twelve year since,
Thy father was the Duke of Milan and
A prince of power.

---

[21] **remembrance warrants:** Memory guarantees.

MIRANDA:

Sir, are not you my father?

PROSPERO:

Thy mother was a piece° of virtue, and   masterpiece
She said thou wast my daughter; and thy father
Was Duke of Milan; and his only heir
And princess, no worse issued.[22]

MIRANDA:

O the heavens!
60   What foul play had we that we came from thence?
Or blessèd was't we did?

PROSPERO:

Both, both, my girl!
By foul play, as thou say'st, were we heaved thence,
But blessedly holp° hither.   helped

MIRANDA:

O, my heart bleeds
To think o' th' teen that I have turned you to,[23]
Which is from my remembrance! Please you, farther.

PROSPERO:

My brother and thy uncle, called Antonio—
I pray thee mark me—that a brother should
Be so perfidious!—he whom next thyself
Of all the world I loved, and to him put
70   The manage of my state,[24] as at that time
Through all the signories[25] it was the first,
And Prospero the prime duke, being so reputed
In dignity, and for the liberal arts
Without a parallel. Those being all my study,
The government I cast upon my brother
And to my state grew stranger, being transported
And rapt in secret studies. Thy false uncle—
Dost thou attend me?

MIRANDA:

Sir, most heedfully.

PROSPERO:

Being once perfected° how to grant suits,   grown skillful
80   How to deny them, who t' advance, and who
To trash for overtopping,[26] new-created

---

[22] **no worse issued:** Of no meaner lineage than he.   [23] **teen . . . to:** Sorrow I have caused you to remember.
[24] **manage . . . state:** Management of my domain.   [25] **signories:** Lordships (of Italy).   [26] **trash for overtopping:** (1) Check the speed of (as of hounds); (2) cut down to size (as of overtall trees) the aspirants for political favor who are growing too bold.

The creatures that were mine, I say—or changed 'em,
Or else new-formed 'em²⁷—having both the key²⁸
Of officer and office, set all hearts i' th' state
To what tune pleased his ear, that now he was
The ivy which had hid my princely trunk
And sucked my verdure out on't. Thou attend'st not?

MIRANDA:
    O, good sir, I do.

PROSPERO:
                I pray thee mark me.
I thus neglecting worldly ends, all dedicated
90   To closeness° and the bettering of my mind—   seclusion
With that which, but by being so retired,
O'erprized all popular rate, in my false brother
Awaked an evil nature,²⁹ and my trust,
Like a good parent,³⁰ did beget of him
A falsehood in its contrary as great
As my trust was, which had indeed no limit,
A confidence sans bound. He being thus lorded—
Not only with what my revenue yielded
But what my power might else exact, like one
100   Who having into truth—by telling of it,³¹
Made such a sinner of his memory
To credit his own lie, he did believe
He was indeed the Duke, out o' th' substitution
And executing th' outward face of royalty
With all prerogative.³² Hence his ambition growing—
Dost thou hear?

MIRANDA:
            Your tale, sir, would cure deafness.

PROSPERO:
    To have no screen between this part he played
And him he played it for, he needs will be

---

²⁷**new-created . . . 'em:** He re-created my following—either exchanging my adherents for his own, or else transforming my adherents into different people.

²⁸**key:** A pun leading to the musical metaphor.

²⁹**With . . . nature:** With that dedication to the mind which, were it not that it kept me from exercising the duties of my office, would surpass in value all ordinary estimate, I awakened evil in my brother's nature.

³⁰**good parent:** Alluding to the proverb cited by Miranda in line 120.

³¹**like . . . it:** Like one who really had these things—by repeatedly saying he had them (*into* = unto).

³²**out . . . prerogative:** As a result of his acting as my substitute and performing the outward functions of royalty with all its prerogatives.

Absolute Milan.[33] Me (poor man) my library
110   Was dukedom large enough. Of temporal royalties
He thinks me now incapable; confederates
(So dry° he was for sway) wi' th' King of Naples   thirsty
To give him annual tribute, do him homage,
Subject his coronet to his crown, and bend
The dukedom, yet unbowed (alas, poor Milan!),
To most ignoble stooping.

MIRANDA:
                          O the heavens!

PROSPERO:
Mark his condition,[34] and th' event;° then tell me   outcome
If this might be a brother.

MIRANDA:
                          I should sin
To think but nobly of my grandmother.
Good wombs have borne bad sons.

PROSPERO:
120   Now the condition.
This King of Naples, being an enemy
To me inveterate, hearkens my brother's suit;
Which was, that he, in lieu o' th' premises[35]
Of homage and I know not how much tribute,
Should presently extirpate me and mine
Out of the dukedom and confer fair Milan,
With all the honors, on my brother. Whereon,
A treacherous army levied, one midnight
Fated to th' purpose, did Antonio open
130   The gates of Milan; and, i' th' dead of darkness,
The ministers° for th' purpose hurried thence   agents
Me and thy crying self.

MIRANDA:
                          Alack, for pity!
I, not rememb'ring how I cried out then,
Will cry it o'er again; it is a hint°   occasion
That wrings mine eyes to 't.

PROSPERO:
                          Hear a little further,
And then I'll bring thee to the present business
Which now's upon's; without the which this story
Were most impertinent.

---

[33] **Absolute Milan:** Duke of Milan in fact.   [34] **condition:** Terms of his pact with Naples.   [35] **in . . . premises:** In return for the guarantees.

MIRANDA:

                              Wherefore did they not

   That hour destroy us?

PROSPERO:

                             Well demanded, wench.

140   My tale provokes that question. Dear, they durst not,

   So dear the love my people bore me; nor set

   A mark so bloody on the business; but,

   With colors fairer, painted their foul ends.

   In few,° they hurried us aboard a bark;   *few words*

   Bore us some leagues to sea, where they prepared

   A rotten carcass of a butt,° not rigged,   *tub*

   Nor tackle, sail, nor mast; the very rats

   Instinctively have quit it. There they hoist us,

   To cry to th' sea that roared to us; to sigh

150   To th' winds, whose pity, sighing back again,

   Did us but loving wrong.

MIRANDA:

                            Alack, what trouble

   Was I then to you!

PROSPERO:

                      O, a cherubin

   Thou wast that did preserve me! Thou didst smile,

   Infusèd with a fortitude from heaven,

   When I have decked[36] the sea with drops full salt,

   Under my burden groaned; which[37] raised in me

   An undergoing stomach,° to bear up   *spirit of endurance*

   Against what should ensue.

MIRANDA:

                      How came we ashore?

PROSPERO:

   By providence divine.

160   Some food we had, and some fresh water, that

   A noble Neapolitan, Gonzalo,

   Out of his charity, who being then appointed

   Master of this design, did give us, with

   Rich garments, linens, stuffs, and necessaries

   Which since have steaded° much. So, of his gentleness,   *been of use*

   Knowing I loved my books, he furnished me

   From mine own library with volumes that

   I prize above my dukedom.

---

[36] **decked:** Covered (wept salt tears into the sea).   [37] **which:** That is, Miranda's smile.

MIRANDA:

Would I might

But ever see that man!

PROSPERO:

Now I arise.

170   Sit still, and hear the last of our sea sorrow.
Here in this island we arrived; and here
Have I, thy schoolmaster, made thee more profit
Than other princess' can,° that have more time   princesses can have
For vainer hours, and tutors not so careful.

MIRANDA:

Heavens thank you for't! And now I pray you, sir—
For still 'tis beating in my mind—your reason
For raising this sea storm?

PROSPERO:

Know thus far forth.

By accident most strange, bountiful Fortune
(Now my dear lady)³⁸ hath mine enemies
180   Brought to this shore; and by my prescience
I find my zenith° doth depend upon   apex of fortune
A most auspicious star, whose influence
If now I court not, but omit,° my fortunes   neglect
Will ever after droop. Here cease more questions.
Thou art inclined to sleep. 'Tis a good dullness,
And give it way. I know thou canst not choose.

[MIRANDA *sleeps.*]

Come away, servant, come! I am ready now.
Approach, my Ariel! Come!

Enter ARIEL.

ARIEL:

All hail, great master! Grave sir, hail! I come
190   To answer thy best pleasure; be't to fly,
To swim, to dive into the fire, to ride
On the curled clouds. To thy strong bidding task°   tax to the utmost
Ariel and all his quality.³⁹

PROSPERO:

Hast thou, spirit,

Performed, to point,° the tempest that I bade thee?   in every detail

ARIEL:

To every article.
I boarded the King's ship. Now on the beak,°   prow
Now in the waist,° the deck,° in every cabin,   amid ships, poop

---

³⁸ (**Now . . . lady**): Formerly my foe, now my patroness.   ³⁹ **quality:** Cohorts (Ariel is leader of a band of spirits).

I flamed amazement.[40] Sometimes I'd divide
And burn in many places; on the topmast,
200   The yards, and boresprit° would I flame distinctly,°   bowsprit, in different places
Then meet and join. Jove's lightnings, the precursors
O' th' dreadful thunderclaps, more momentary
And sight-outrunning were not. The fire and cracks
Of sulfurous roaring the most mighty Neptune
Seem to besiege, and make his bold waves tremble;
Yea, his dread trident shake.

PROSPERO:
                              My brave spirit!
Who was so firm, so constant, that this coil°   uproar
Would not infect his reason?

ARIEL:
                              Not a soul
But felt a fever of the mad and played
210   Some tricks of desperation. All but mariners
Plunged in the foaming brine and quit the vessel,
Then all afire with me. The King's son Ferdinand,
With hair up-staring° (then like reeds, not hair),   standing on end
Was the first man that leapt; cried "Hell is empty,
And all the devils are here!"

PROSPERO:
                              Why, that's my spirit!
But was not this nigh shore?

ARIEL:
                              Close by, my master.

PROSPERO:
But are they, Ariel, safe?

ARIEL:
                              Not a hair perished.
On their sustaining° garments not a blemish,   buoying them up
But fresher than before; and as thou bad'st me,
220   In troops I have dispersed them 'bout the isle.
The King's son have I landed by himself,
Whom I left cooling of the air with sighs
In an odd angle of the isle, and sitting,
His arms in this sad knot.

[*Illustrates with a gesture.*]

PROSPERO:
                              Of the King's ship,
The mariners, say how thou hast disposed,
And all the rest o' th' fleet.

---

[40] **flamed amazement:** Struck terror by appearing as (St. Elmo's) fire.

ARIEL:
>   Safely in harbor
> Is the King's ship; in the deep nook where once
> Thou call'dst me up at midnight to fetch dew
> From the still-vexed Bermoothes,° there she's hid;   Bermudas
230 The mariners all under hatches stowed,
> Who, with a charm joined to their suff'red° labor,   undergone
> I have left asleep. And for the rest o' th' fleet,
> Which I dispersed, they all have met again,
> And are upon the Mediterranean flote°   sea
> Bound sadly home for Naples,
> Supposing that they saw the King's ship wracked
> And his great person perish.

PROSPERO:
>   Ariel, thy charge
> Exactly is performed; but there's more work.
> What is the time o' th' day?

ARIEL:
>   Past the mid season.°   noon

PROSPERO:
240 At least two glasses.° The time 'twixt six and now   two o'clock
> Must by us both be spent most preciously.

ARIEL:
> Is there more toil? Since thou dost give me pains,°   hard tasks
> Let me remember° thee what thou hast promised,   remind
> Which is not yet performed me.

PROSPERO:
>   How now? Moody?
> What is't thou canst demand?

ARIEL:
>   My liberty.

PROSPERO:
> Before the time be out? No more!

ARIEL:
>   I prithee,
> Remember I have done thee worthy service,
> Told thee no lies, made thee no mistakings, served
> Without or grudge or grumblings. Thou did promise
> To bate me[41] a full year.

PROSPERO:
250   Dost thou forget
> From what a torment I did free thee?

---

[41] **bate me:** Reduce my term of service.

ARIEL:

                        No.

PROSPERO:

    Thou dost; and think'st it much to tread the ooze
    Of the salt deep,
    To run upon the sharp wind of the North,
    To do me business in the veins° o' th' earth   streams
    When it is baked° with frost.   caked

ARIEL:

                      I do not, sir.

PROSPERO:

    Thou liest, malignant thing! Hast thou forgot
    The foul witch Sycorax[42] who with age and envy
    Was grown into a hoop? Hast thou forgot her?

ARIEL:

    No, sir.

PROSPERO:

260   Thou hast. Where was she born? Speak! Tell me!

ARIEL:

    Sir, in Argier.°   Algiers

PROSPERO:

                  O, was she so? I must
    Once in a month recount what thou hast been,
    Which thou forget'st. This damned witch Sycorax,
    For mischiefs manifold, and sorceries terrible
    To enter human hearing, from Argier,
    Thou know'st, was banished. For one thing she did
    They would not take her life. Is not this true?

ARIEL:

    Ay, sir.

PROSPERO:

    This blue-eyed[43] hag was hither brought with child
270   And here was left by th' sailors. Thou, my slave,
    As thou report'st thyself, wast then her servant.
    And, for thou wast a spirit too delicate
    To act her earthy and abhorred commands,
    Refusing her grand hests,° she did confine thee,   commands
    By help of her more potent ministers,
    And in her most unmitigable rage,
    Into a cloven pine; within which rift

---

[42] **Sycorax:** Name not found elsewhere; probably derived from Greek *sys*, "sow," and *korax,* which means both "raven"—see line 322—and "hook"—hence perhaps "hoop." [43] **blue-eyed:** Referring to the livid color of the eyelid, a sign of pregnancy.

Imprisoned thou didst painfully remain
A dozen years; within which space she died
280 And left thee there, where thou didst vent thy groans
As fast as millwheels strike. Then was this island
(Save for the son that she did litter here,
A freckled whelp, hagborn) not honored with
A human shape.

ARIEL:
                Yes, Caliban her son.

PROSPERO:
  Dull thing, I say so! He, that Caliban
Whom now I keep in service. Thou best know'st
What torment I did find thee in; thy groans
Did make wolves howl and penetrate the breasts
Of ever-angry bears. It was a torment
290 To lay upon the damned, which Sycorax
Could not again undo. It was mine art,
When I arrived and heard thee, that made gape
The pine, and let thee out.

ARIEL:
                I thank thee, master.

PROSPERO:
  If thou more murmur'st, I will rend an oak
And peg thee in his knotty entrails till
Thou hast howled away twelve winters.

ARIEL:
                  Pardon, master.
I will be correspondent° to command   obedient
And do my spriting gently.[44]

PROSPERO:
              Do so; and after two days
I will discharge thee.

ARIEL:
              That's my noble master!
300 What shall I do? Say what? What shall I do?

PROSPERO:
  Go make thyself like a nymph o' th' sea. Be subject
To no sight but thine and mine, invisible
To every eyeball else.[45] Go take this shape
And hither come in't. Go! Hence with diligence!   *Exit* [ARIEL].

---

[44] **do . . . gently:** Render graciously my services as a spirit.   [45] **invisible . . . else:** Ariel is invisible to everyone in the play except Prospero; Henslowe's *Diary,* an Elizabethan stage account, lists "a robe for to go invisible."

Awake, dear heart, awake! Thou hast slept well.
Awake!

MIRANDA:
          The strangeness of your story put
Heaviness in me.

PROSPERO:
                 Shake it off. Come on.
We'll visit Caliban, my slave, who never
Yields us kind answer.

MIRANDA:
                  'Tis a villain, sir,
I do not love to look on.

PROSPERO:
310   But as 'tis,
We cannot miss° him. He does make our fire,   *do without*
Fetch in our wood, and serves in offices
That profit us. What, ho! Slave! Caliban!
Thou earth, thou! Speak!

CALIBAN [*Within*]:
                    There's wood enough within.

PROSPERO:
Come forth, I say! There's other business for thee.
Come, thou tortoise! When?[46]

Enter ARIEL *like a water nymph.*
Fine apparition! My quaint° Ariel,   *ingenious*
Hark in thine ear.

[*Whispers.*]
ARIEL:
            My lord, it shall be done.   *Exit.*

PROSPERO:
Thou poisonous slave, got by the devil himself
320   Upon thy wicked dam, come forth!

Enter CALIBAN.
CALIBAN:
As wicked dew as e'er my mother brushed
With raven's feather from unwholesome fen
Drop on you both! A southwest blow on ye
And blister you all o'er!

PROSPERO:
For this, be sure, tonight thou shalt have cramps,
Side-stitches that shall pen thy breath up. Urchins[47]

---

[46] **When?:** Expression of impatience.　[47] **Urchins:** Goblins in the shape of hedgehogs.

Shall, for that vast of night that they may work,[48]
All exercise on thee; thou shalt be pinched
As thick as honeycomb, each pinch more stinging
Than bees that made 'em.

CALIBAN:

330   I must eat my dinner.
This island's mine by Sycorax my mother,
Which thou tak'st from me. When thou cam'st first,
Thou strok'st me and made much of me; wouldst give me
Water with berries in't; and teach me how
To name the bigger light, and how the less,
That burn by day and night. And then I loved thee
And showed thee all the qualities o' th' isle,
The fresh springs, brine pits, barren place and fertile.
Cursed be I that did so! All the charms

340 Of Sycorax — toads, beetles, bats, light on you!
For I am all the subjects that you have,
Which first was mine own king; and here you sty me
In this hard rock, whiles you do keep from me
The rest o' th' island.

PROSPERO:

                    Thou most lying slave,
Whom stripes° may move, not kindness! I have used thee   lashes
(Filth as thou art) with humane care, and lodged thee
In mine own cell till thou didst seek to violate
The honor of my child.

CALIBAN:

           O ho, O ho! Would't had been done!

350 Thou didst prevent me; I had peopled else
This isle with Calibans.

MIRANDA:[49]

                    Abhorrèd slave,
Which any print of goodness wilt not take,
Being capable of all ill![50] I pitied thee,
Took pains to make thee speak, taught thee each hour
One thing or other. When thou didst not, savage,
Know thine own meaning, but wouldst gabble like
A thing most brutish, I endowed thy purposes
With words that made them known. But thy vile race,
Though thou didst learn, had that in't which good natures

---

[48] **vast . . . work:** The long, empty stretch of night during which malignant spirits are allowed to be active.
[49] MIRANDA: Many editors transfer this speech to Prospero as inappropriate to Miranda.   [50] **capable . . . ill:** Susceptible only to evil impressions.

360   Could not abide to be with. Therefore wast thou
        Deservedly confined into this rock, who hadst
        Deserved more than a prison.

CALIBAN:
        You taught me language, and my profit on't
        Is, I know how to curse. The red plague rid you
        For learning me your language!

PROSPERO:
                            Hagseed, hence!
        Fetch us in fuel. And be quick, thou'rt best,°   you'd better
        To answer other business. Shrug'st thou, malice?
        If thou neglect'st or dost unwillingly
        What I command, I'll rack thee with old[51] cramps,
370   Fill all thy bones with aches, make thee roar
        That beasts shall tremble at thy din.

CALIBAN:
                            No, pray thee.
        [*Aside*] I must obey. His art is of such pow'r
        It would control my dam's god, Setebos,
        And make a vassal of him.

PROSPERO:
                   So, slave, hence!   *Exit* CALIBAN.

Enter FERDINAND; *and* ARIEL (*invisible*), *playing and singing.*

        Ariel's song.

        Come unto these yellow sands,
            And then take hands.
        Curtsied when you have and kissed
            The wild waves whist,[52]
        Foot it featly° *here and there;*   nimbly
380   *And, sweet sprites, the burden bear.*
            Hark, hark!
                [Burden, dispersedly.]*[53] Bow, wow!*
        The watchdogs bark.
                [Burden, dispersedly.] *Bow, wow!*
        Hark, hark! I hear
        The strain of strutting chanticleer
            Cry cock-a-diddle-dow.

---

[51] **old:** Plenty of (with an additional suggestion, "such as old people have").   [52] **when . . . whist:** When you have, through the harmony of kissing in the dance, kissed the wild waves into silence (?); when you have kissed in the dance, the wild waves being silenced (?).   [53] **[Burden, dispersedly]:** An undersong, coming from all parts of the stage; it imitates the barking of dogs and perhaps in the end the crowing of a cock.

FERDINAND:

Where should this music be? I' th' air or th' earth?
It sounds no more; and sure it waits upon
Some god o' th' island. Sitting on a bank,
390 Weeping again the King my father's wrack,
This music crept by me upon the waters
Allaying both their fury and my passion°   grief
With its sweet air. Thence I have followed it,
Or it hath drawn me rather; but 'tis gone.
No, it begins again.

> *Ariel's song.*
>
> *Full fathom five thy father lies;*
>   *Of his bones are coral made;*
> *Those are pearls that were his eyes;*
> 400   *Nothing of him that doth fade*
> *But doth suffer a sea change*
> *Into something rich and strange.*
> *Sea nymphs hourly ring his knell:*
>   [Burden.] *Ding-dong.*
> *Hark! Now I hear them—ding-dong bell.*

FERDINAND:

The ditty does remember my drowned father.
This is no mortal business, nor no sound
That the earth owes.° I hear it now above me.   owns

PROSPERO:

The fringèd curtains of thine eye advance°   raise
And say what thou seest yond.

MIRANDA:

                    What is't? A spirit?
410 Lord, how it looks about! Believe me, sir,
It carries a brave form. But 'tis a spirit.

PROSPERO:

No, wench; it eats, and sleeps, and hath such senses
As we have, such. This gallant which thou seest
Was in the wrack; and, but he's something stained
With grief (that's beauty's canker), thou mightst call him
A goodly person. He hath lost his fellows
And strays about to find 'em.

MIRANDA:

                    I might call him
A thing divine; for nothing natural
I ever saw so noble.

PROSPERO:

420   [*Aside*] It goes on, I see,

As my soul prompts it. Spirit, fine spirit, I'll free thee
Within two days for this.

FERDINAND:
                                    Most sure, the goddess
On whom these airs attend! Vouchsafe my prayer
May know if you remain[54] upon this island,
And that you will some good instruction give
How I may bear me° here. My prime request,   conduct myself
Which do I last pronounce, is (O you wonder!)
If you be maid or no?

MIRANDA:
                            No wonder, sir,
But certainly a maid.

FERDINAND:
                            My language? Heavens!
430   I am the best of them that speak this speech,
Were I but where 'tis spoken.

PROSPERO:
                            How? The best?
What wert thou if the King of Naples heard thee?

FERDINAND:
A single[55] thing, as I am now, that wonders
To hear thee speak of Naples. He does hear me;
And that he does I weep. Myself am Naples,
Who with mine eyes, never since at ebb, beheld
The King my father wracked.

MIRANDA:
                            Alack, for mercy!

FERDINAND:
Yes, faith, and all his lords, the Duke of Milan
And his brave son[56] being twain.[57]

PROSPERO:
                            [*Aside*] The Duke of Milan
440   And his more braver daughter could control° thee,   refute
If now 'twere fit to do't. At the first sight
They have changed eyes.° Delicate Ariel,   fallen in love
I'll set thee free for this. [*To* FERDINAND] A word, good sir.
I fear you have done yourself some wrong.[58] A word!

MIRANDA:
Why speaks my father so ungently? This
Is the third man that e'er I saw; the first

---

[54]**Vouchsafe . . . remain:** May my prayer induce you to inform me whether you dwell.   [55]**single:** (1) Solitary;
(2) helpless.   [56]**son:** The only time Antonio's son is mentioned.   [57]**twain:** Two (of these lords).   [58]**done . . .
wrong:** Said what is not so.

That e'er I sighed for. Pity move my father
To be inclined my way!

FERDINAND:

O, if a virgin,
And your affection not gone forth, I'll make you
The Queen of Naples.

PROSPERO:

450   Soft, sir! One word more.
[*Aside*] They are both in either's pow'rs. But this swift business
I must uneasy make, lest too light winning
Make the prize light. [*To* FERDINAND] One word more! I charge thee
That thou attend me. Thou dost here usurp
The name thou ow'st not, and hast put thyself
Upon this island as a spy, to win it
From me, the lord on't.

FERDINAND:

No, as I am a man!

MIRANDA:

There's nothing ill can dwell in such a temple.
If the ill spirit have so fair a house,
Good things will strive to dwell with't.

PROSPERO:

460   Follow me.
[*To* MIRANDA] Speak not you for him; he's a traitor. [*To* FERDINAND] Come!
I'll manacle thy neck and feet together;
Sea water shalt thou drink; thy food shall be
The fresh-brook mussels, withered roots, and husks
Wherein the acorn cradled. Follow!

FERDINAND:

No.
I will resist such entertainment till
Mine enemy has more pow'r.

He draws, and is charmed from moving.

MIRANDA:

O dear father,
Make not too rash a trial of him, for
He's gentle and not fearful.[59]

PROSPERO:

What, I say,
470   My foot my tutor?[60] [*To* FERDINAND] Put thy sword up, traitor —
Who mak'st a show but dar'st not strike, thy conscience

---

[59] **gentle . . . fearful:** Of noble birth and no coward.   [60] **My . . . tutor?:** Am I to be instructed by my inferior?

Is so possessed with guilt! Come, from thy ward!°   fighting posture
For I can here disarm thee with this stick°   his wand
And make thy weapon drop.

MIRANDA:

                     Beseech you, father!

PROSPERO:

Hence! Hang not on my garments.

MIRANDA:

                           Sir, have pity.
I'll be his surety.

PROSPERO:

                Silence! One word more
Shall make me chide thee, if not hate thee. What,
An advocate for an impostor? Hush!
Thou think'st there is no more such shapes as he,
480   Having seen but him and Caliban. Foolish wench!
To th' most of men this is a Caliban,
And they to him are angels.

MIRANDA:

               My affections
Are then most humble. I have no ambition
To see a goodlier man.

PROSPERO:

    [*To* FERDINAND] Come on, obey!
Thy nerves° are in their infancy again   sinews
And have no vigor in them.

FERDINAND:

              So they are.
My spirits, as in a dream, are all bound up.
My father's loss, the weakness which I feel,
The wrack of all my friends, nor this man's threats
490   To whom I am subdued, are but light to me,
Might I but through my prison once a day
Behold this maid. All corners else o' th' earth
Let liberty make use of. Space enough
Have I in such a prison.

PROSPERO:

[*Aside*] It works. [*To* FERDINAND] Come on.
[*To* ARIEL] Thou hast done well, fine Ariel! [*To* FERDINAND] Follow me.
[*To* ARIEL] Hark what thou else shalt do me.

MIRANDA:

                   Be of comfort.
My father's of a better nature, sir,
Than he appears by speech. This is unwonted
Which now came from him.

PROSPERO:

                  Thou shalt be as free

500   As mountain winds; but then° exactly do   *until then*

    All points of my command.

ARIEL:

                  To th' syllable.

PROSPERO:

    [*To* FERDINAND] Come, follow. [*To* MIRANDA] Speak not for him.   *Exeunt.*

ACT II

Scene 1

Another part of the island.

Enter ALONSO, SEBASTIAN, ANTONIO, GONZALO, ADRIAN, FRANCISCO, *and others.*

GONZALO:

    Beseech you, sir, be merry. You have cause

    (So have we all) of joy; for our escape

    Is much beyond our loss. Our hint of° woe   *occasion for*

    Is common; every day some sailor's wife,

    The master of some merchant,[61] and the merchant,

    Have just our theme of woe. But for the miracle,

    I mean our preservation, few in millions

    Can speak like us. Then wisely, good sir, weigh

    Our sorrow with our comfort.

ALONSO:

                  Prithee, peace.

10 SEBASTIAN [*Aside to* ANTONIO]: He receives comfort like cold porridge.[62]

ANTONIO [*Aside to* SEBASTIAN]: The visitor[63] will not give him o'er so.[64]

SEBASTIAN:

    Look, he's winding up the watch of his wit;

    by and by it will strike.

GONZALO: Sir—

SEBASTIAN [*Aside to* ANTONIO]: One. Tell.[65]

GONZALO:

    When every grief is entertained, that's[66] offered

    Comes to th' entertainer—

SEBASTIAN: A dollar.

GONZALO: Dolor comes to him, indeed. You have spoken truer than you purposed.

20 SEBASTIAN: You have taken it wiselier[67] than I meant you should.

---

[61] **master . . . merchant:** Captain of some merchant ship. [62] **He . . . porridge:** "He" is Alonso; a pun on "peace," since porridge contained peas. [63] **visitor:** Spiritual comforter. [64] **give . . . so:** Release him so easily. [65] **One. Tell:** He has struck one; keep count. [66] **that's:** That which is. [67] **taken it wiselier:** Understood my pun.

GONZALO: Therefore, my lord—

ANTONIO: Fie, what a spendthrift is he of his tongue!

ALONSO: I prithee, spare.[68]

GONZALO: Well, I have done. But yet—

SEBASTIAN: He will be talking.

ANTONIO: Which, of he or Adrian, for a good wager, first begins to crow?

SEBASTIAN: The old cock.[69]

ANTONIO: The cock'rel.[70]

SEBASTIAN: Done! The wager?

30   ANTONIO: A laughter.[71]

SEBASTIAN: A match!

ADRIAN: Though this island seem to be desert—

ANTONIO: Ha, ha, ha!

SEBASTIAN: So, you're paid.

ADRIAN: Uninhabitable and almost inaccessible—

SEBASTIAN: Yet—

ADRIAN: Yet—

ANTONIO: He could not miss't.

ADRIAN: It must needs be of subtle, tender, and delicate temperance.[72]

40   ANTONIO: Temperance was a delicate wench.

SEBASTIAN: Ay, and a subtle, as he mostly learnedly delivered.

ADRIAN: The air breathes upon us here most sweetly.

SEBASTIAN: As if it had lungs, and rotten ones.

ANTONIO: Or as 'twere perfumed by a fen.

GONZALO: Here is everything advantageous to life.

ANTONIO: True; save means to live.

SEBASTIAN: Of that there's none, or little.

GONZALO: How lush and lusty the grass looks! How green!

ANTONIO: The ground indeed is tawny.

50   SEBASTIAN: With an eye[73] of green in't.

ANTONIO: He misses not much.

SEBASTIAN: No; he doth but mistake the truth totally.

GONZALO: But the rarity of it is—which is indeed almost beyond credit—

SEBASTIAN: As many vouched rarities are.

GONZALO: That our garments, being, as they were, drenched in the sea, hold, notwithstanding, their freshness and glosses, being rather new-dyed than stained with salt water.

ANTONIO: If but one of his pockets could speak, would it not say he lies?[74]

SEBASTIAN: Ay, or very falsely pocket up his report.[75]

---

[68] **spare**: Spare your words.   [69] **old cock**: Gonzalo.   [70] **cock'rel**: Young cock; Adrian.   [71] **A laughter**: The winner will have the laugh on the loser.   [72] **temperance**: Climate (in the next line, a girl's name).   [73] **eye**: Spot (also perhaps Gonzalo's eye).   [74] **pockets . . . lies**: The inside of Gonzalo's pockets are stained.   [75] **or . . . report**: Unless the pocket were, like a false knave, to receive without resentment the imputation that it is unstained.

60 GONZALO: Methinks our garments are now as fresh as when we put them on first in
      Afric, at the marriage of the King's fair daughter Claribel to the King of Tunis.

SEBASTIAN: 'Twas a sweet marriage, and we prosper well in our return.

ADRIAN: Tunis was never graced before with such a paragon to their queen.

GONZALO: Not since widow Dido's time.

ANTONIO: Widow? A pox o' that! How came that "widow" in? Widow Dido!

SEBASTIAN: What if he had said "widower Aeneas"[76] too? Good Lord, how you take it!

ADRIAN: "Widow Dido," said you? You make me study of that. She was of Carthage,
      not of Tunis.

GONZALO: This Tunis, sir, was Carthage.

70 ADRIAN: Carthage?

GONZALO: I assure you, Carthage.

ANTONIO: His word is more than the miraculous harp.[77]

SEBASTIAN: He hath raised the wall and houses too.

ANTONIO: What impossible matter will he make easy next?

SEBASTIAN: I think he will carry this island home in his pocket and give it his son for
      an apple.

ANTONIO: And, sowing the kernels of it in the sea, bring forth more islands.

GONZALO: Ay!

ANTONIO: Why, in good time.[78]

80 GONZALO [*To* ALONSO]: Sir, we were talking that our garments seem now as fresh as
      when we were at Tunis at the marriage of your daughter, who is now Queen.

ANTONIO: And the rarest that e'er came there.

SEBASTIAN: Bate,[79] I beseech you, widow Dido.

ANTONIO: O, widow Dido? Ay, widow Dido!

GONZALO: Is not, sir, my doublet as fresh as the first day I wore it? I mean, in a sort.

ANTONIO: That "sort" was well fished for.

GONZALO: When I wore it at your daughter's marriage.

ALONSO:
      You cram these words into mine ears against
      The stomach of my sense.[80] Would I had never
90   Married my daughter there! For, coming thence,
      My son is lost; and, in my rate,° she too,   opinion
      Who is so far from Italy removed
      I ne'er again shall see her. O thou mine heir
      Of Naples and of Milan, what strange fish
      Hath made his meal on thee?

---

[76] **"widower Aeneas"**: The point of the joke is that Dido was a widow, but one doesn't ordinarily think of
her that way; and the same with Aeneas.   [77] **harp**: Of Amphion, which only raised the *walls* of Thebes;
whereas Gonzalo has rebuilt the whole ancient city of Carthage by identifying it mistakenly with modern
Tunis.   [78] **in good time**: Hearing Gonzalo reaffirm his false statement about Tunis and Carthage, Antonio suggests that Gonzalo will indeed, at the first opportunity, carry this island home in his pocket.   [79] **Bate**: Except.
[80] **against . . . sense**: Though my mind (or feelings) have no appetite for them.

FRANCISCO:

                        Sir, he may live.
I saw him beat the surges under him
And ride upon their backs. He trod the water,
Whose enmity he flung aside, and breasted
100   The surge most swol'n that met him. His bold head
'Bove the contentious waves he kept, and oared
Himself with his good arms in lusty stroke
To th' shore, that o'er his wave-worn basis bowed,[81]
As stooping to relieve him. I not doubt
He came alive to land.

ALONSO:

                      No, no, he's gone.

SEBASTIAN [*To* ALONSO]:

Sir, you may thank yourself for this great loss,
That would not bless our Europe with your daughter,
But rather loose her to an African,
110   Where she, at least, is banished from your eye
Who hath cause to wet the grief on't.

ALONSO:

                      Prithee, peace.

SEBASTIAN:

You were kneeled to and importuned otherwise
By all of us; and the fair soul herself
Weighed, between loathness and obedience, at
Which end o' th' beam should bow.[82] We have lost your son,
I fear, forever. Milan and Naples have
Moe widows in them of this business' making
Than we bring men to comfort them.
120   The fault's your own.

ALONSO:

                So is the dear'st o' th' loss.

GONZALO:

My Lord Sebastian,
The truth you speak doth lack some gentleness,
And time to speak it in. You rub the sore
When you should bring the plaster.

SEBASTIAN:

                      Very well.

ANTONIO:

And most chirurgeonly.°   *like a surgeon*

---

[81] **o'er . . . bowed:** The image is of a guardian cliff on the shore.   [82] **fair . . . bow:** Claribel's unwillingness to marry was outweighed by her obedience to her father.

GONZALO [*To* ALONSO]:
　　It is foul weather in us all, good sir,
　　When you are cloudy.
SEBASTIAN [*Aside to* ANTONIO]:
130　　　　　　　　　　　　　Foul weather?
ANTONIO [*Aside to* SEBASTIAN]:
　　　　　　　　　　　　　　Very foul.
GONZALO:
　　Had I plantation[83] of this isle, my lord—
ANTONIO:
　　He'd sow't with nettle seed.
SEBASTIAN:
　　　　　　　　　　　Or docks, or mallows.
GONZALO:
　　And were the king on't, what would I do?
SEBASTIAN:
　　Scape being drunk for want of wine.
GONZALO:
　　I' th' commonwealth I would by contraries[84]
　　Execute all things. For no kind of traffic°　　　　　　　　　　trade
　　Would I admit; no name of magistrate;
140　　Letters° should not be known; riches, poverty,　　　　　　learning
　　And use of service,° none; contract, succession,°　　servants, inheritance
　　Bourn,° bound of land, tilth,° vineyard, none;　　boundary, agriculture
　　No use of metal, corn, or wine, or oil;
　　No occupation; all men idle, all;
　　And women too, but innocent and pure;
　　No sovereignty.
SEBASTIAN:
　　　　　　　　　　Yet he would be king on't.
ANTONIO:
　　The latter end of his commonwealth forgets the beginning.
GONZALO:
　　All things in common nature should produce
150　　Without sweat or endeavor. Treason, felony,
　　Sword, pike, knife, gun, or need of any engine°　　　　　weapon
　　Would I not have; but nature should bring forth,
　　Of it own kind, all foison,° all abundance,　　　　　　　abundance
　　To feed my innocent people.
SEBASTIAN:
　　No marrying 'mong his subjects?

---

[83] **plantation:** Colonization (Antonio then puns by taking the word in its other sense).　　[84] **by contraries:** In contrast to the usual customs.

ANTONIO:
> None, man, all idle — whores and knaves.

GONZALO:
> I would with such perfection govern, sir,
> T' excel the Golden Age.

SEBASTIAN [*Loudly*]:
> Save his Majesty!

ANTONIO [*Loudly*]:
160 > Long live Gonzalo!

GONZALO:
> And — do you mark me, sir?

ALONSO:
> Prithee, no more. Thou dost talk nothing to me.

GONZALO: I do well believe your Highness; and did it to minister occasion[85] to these gentlemen, who are of such sensible[86] and nimble lungs that they always use to laugh at nothing.

ANTONIO: 'Twas you we laughed at.

GONZALO: Who in this kind of merry fooling am nothing to you; so you may continue, and laugh at nothing still.

ANTONIO: What a blow was there given!

170 SEBASTIAN: And it had not fall'n flatlong.[87]

GONZALO: You are gentlemen of brave mettle; you would lift the moon out of her sphere if she would continue in it five weeks without changing.

Enter ARIEL *(invisible) playing solemn music.*

SEBASTIAN: We would so, and then go a-batfowling.[88]

ANTONIO: Nay, good my lord, be not angry.

GONZALO: No, I warrant you; I will not adventure my discretion so weakly.[89] Will you laugh me asleep? For I am very heavy.

ANTONIO: Go sleep, and hear us.

[*All sleep except* ALONSO, SEBASTIAN, *and* ANTONIO.]

ALONSO:
> What, all so soon asleep? I wish mine eyes
> Would, with themselves, shut up my thoughts. I find
180 > They are inclined to do so.

SEBASTIAN:
> Please you, sir,
> Do not omit the heavy offer of it.
> It seldom visits sorrow; when it doth,
> It is a comforter.

---

[85] **minister occasion:** Afford opportunity.   [86] **sensible:** Sensitive.   [87] **flatlong:** With the flat of the sword.   [88] **We . . . a-batfowling:** We would use the moon for a lantern in order to hunt birds at night by attracting them with a light and beating them down with bats; i.e., in order to gull simpletons like you (?).   [89] **adventure . . . weakly:** Risk my reputation for good sense because of your weak wit.

ANTONIO:

We two, my lord,
Will guard your person while you take your rest,
And watch your safety.

ALONSO:

Thank you. Wondrous heavy.

[ALONSO *sleeps. Exit* ARIEL.]

SEBASTIAN:

What a strange drowsiness possesses them!

ANTONIO:

190   It is the quality o' th' climate.

SEBASTIAN:

Why
Doth it not then our eyelids sink? I find not
Myself disposed to sleep.

ANTONIO:

Nor I: my spirits are nimble.
They fell together all, as by consent.
They dropped as by a thunderstroke. What might,
Worthy Sebastian — O, what might? — No more!
And yet methinks I see it in thy face,
What thou shouldst be. Th' occasion speaks thee, and
200   My strong imagination sees a crown
Dropping upon thy head.

SEBASTIAN:

What? Art thou waking?

ANTONIO:

Do you not hear me speak?

SEBASTIAN:

I do; and surely
It is a sleepy language, and thou speak'st
Out of thy sleep. What is it thou didst say?
This is a strange repose, to be asleep
With eyes wide open; standing, speaking, moving,
And yet so fast asleep.

ANTONIO:

Noble Sebastian,
210   Thou let'st thy fortune sleep — die, rather; wink'st
Whiles thou art waking.

SEBASTIAN:

Thou dost snore distinctly;
There's meaning in thy snores.

ANTONIO:

I am more serious than my custom. You

Must be so too, if heed me; which to do
Trebles thee o'er.[90]

SEBASTIAN:

Well, I am standing water.

ANTONIO:

I'll teach you how to flow.

SEBASTIAN:

220   Do so. To ebb
Hereditary sloth instructs me.

ANTONIO:

O,
If you but knew how you the purpose cherish
Whiles thus you mock it; how, in stripping it,
You more invest it![91] Ebbing men, indeed,
Most often do so near the bottom run
By their own fear or sloth.

SEBASTIAN:

Prithee, say on.
The setting of thine eye and cheek proclaim
230   A matter from thee; and a birth, indeed,
Which throes thee much[92] to yield.

ANTONIO:

Thus, sir:
Although this lord of weak remembrance, this
Who shall be of as little memory
When he is earthed, hath here almost persuaded
(For he's a spirit of persuasion, only
Professes to persuade[93]) the King his son's alive,
'Tis as impossible that he's undrowned
As he that sleeps here swims.

SEBASTIAN:

240   I have no hope
That he's undrowned.

ANTONIO:

O, out of that no hope
What great hope have you! No hope that way is
Another way so high a hope that even
Ambition cannot pierce a wink beyond,
But doubt discovery there.[94] Will you grant with me
That Ferdinand is drowned?

---

[90] **Trebles thee o'er:** Makes thee three times what thou now art.   [91] **You . . . it!:** In stripping the purpose off you, you clothe yourself with it all the more.   [92] **throes thee much:** Causes you much pain.   [93] **only . . . persuade:** His only profession is to persuade.   [94] **Ambition . . . there:** The eye of ambition can reach no farther, but must even doubt the reality of what it discerns thus far.

SEBASTIAN:

He's gone.

ANTONIO:

Then tell me.

250   Who's the next heir of Naples?

SEBASTIAN:

Claribel.

ANTONIO:

She that is Queen of Tunis; she that dwells
Ten leagues beyond man's life;[95] she that from Naples
Can have no note—unless the sun were post;°   messenger
The man i' th' moon's too slow—till newborn chins
Be rough and razorable; she that from whom
We all were sea-swallowed,[96] though some cast[97] again,
And, by that destiny, to perform an act
Whereof what's past is prologue, what to come,
260   In yours and my discharge.

SEBASTIAN:

What stuff is this? How say you?
'Tis true my brother's daughter's Queen of Tunis;
So is she heir of Naples; 'twixt which regions
There is some space.

ANTONIO:

A space whose ev'ry cubit
Seems to cry out "How shall that Claribel
Measure us back to Naples? Keep in Tunis,
And let Sebastian wake!" Say this were death
That now hath seized them, why, they were no worse
270   Than now they are. There be that can rule Naples
As well as he that sleeps; lords that can prate
As amply and unnecessarily
As this Gonzalo; I myself could make
A chough[98] of as deep chat. O, that you bore
The mind that I do! What a sleep were this
For your advancement! Do you understand me?

SEBASTIAN: Methinks I do.

ANTONIO: And how does your content
Tender[99] your own good fortune?

---

[95] **Ten . . . life:** It would take a lifetime to get within ten leagues of the place.   [96] **she . . . sea-swallowed:** She who is separated from Naples by so dangerous a sea that we were ourselves swallowed up by it.   [97] **cast:** Cast upon the shore (with a suggestion of its theatrical meaning, which leads to the next metaphor).   [98] **chough:** Jackdaw (a bird that can be taught to speak a few words).   [99] **Tender:** Regard (i.e., do you like your good fortune).

SEBASTIAN:
280   I remember
You did supplant your brother Prospero.

ANTONIO:
                                                    True.
And look how well my garments sit upon me,
Much feater° than before. My brother's servants   *more becomingly*
Were then my fellows; now they are my men.

SEBASTIAN:
But, for your conscience—

ANTONIO:
Ay, sir, where lies that? If 'twere a kibe,[100]
'Twould put me to my slipper; but I feel not
This deity in my bosom. Twenty consciences
290   That stand 'twixt me and Milan, candied be they
And melt, ere they molest! Here lies your brother,
No better than the earth he lies upon—
If he were that which now he's like, that's dead—
Whom I with this obedient steel (three inches of it)
Can lay to bed forever; whiles you, doing thus,
To the perpetual wink for aye might put
This ancient morsel, this Sir Prudence, who
Should not upbraid our course. For all the rest,
They'll take suggestion as a cat laps milk;
300   They'll tell the clock° to any business that   *say yes*
We say befits the hour.

SEBASTIAN:
                                    Thy case, dear friend,
Shall be my precedent. As thou got'st Milan,
I'll come by Naples. Draw thy sword. One stroke
Shall free thee from the tribute which thou payest,
And I the King shall love thee.

ANTONIO:
                                    Draw together;
And when I rear my hand, do you the like,
To fall it on Gonzalo.

[*They draw.*]
SEBASTIAN:
310   O, but one word!

Enter ARIEL *(invisible) with music and song.*
ARIEL:
My master through his art foresees the danger

---

[100] **kibe**: Chilblain on the heel.

That you, his friend, are in, and sends me forth
(For else his project dies) to keep them living.

Sings in GONZALO'*s ear.*

> *While you here do snoring lie,*
> *Opened-eye conspiracy*
> > *His time doth take.*
> *If of life you keep a care,*
> *Shake off slumber and beware.*
> > *Awake, awake!*

ANTONIO:

320   Then let us both be sudden.

GONZALO [*Wakes*]:

                    Now good angels

    Preserve the King!

[*The others wake.*]

ALONSO:

    Why, how now? Ho, awake! Why are you drawn?
    Wherefore this ghastly looking?

GONZALO:

                    What's the matter?

SEBASTIAN:

    Whiles we stood here securing your repose,
    Even now, we heard a hollow burst of bellowing
    Like bulls, or rather lions. Did't not wake you?
    It struck mine ear most terribly.

ALONSO:

330   I heard nothing.

ANTONIO:

    O, 'twas a din to fright a monster's ear,
    To make an earthquake! Sure it was the roar
    Of a whole herd of lions.

ALONSO:

                    Heard you this, Gonzalo?

GONZALO:

    Upon mine honor, sir, I heard a humming,
    And that a strange one too, which did awake me.
    I shaked you, sir, and cried. As mine eyes opened,
    I saw their weapons drawn. There was a noise,
    That's verily.° 'Tis best we stand upon our guard,   the truth
340   Or that we quit this place. Let's draw our weapons.

ALONSO:

    Lead off this ground, and let's make further search
    For my poor son.

GONZALO:

                     Heavens keep him from these beasts!
For he is, sure, i' th' island.

ALONSO:

                     Lead away.

ARIEL:

    Prospero my lord shall know what I have done.
So, King, go safely on to seek thy son.   *Exeunt.*

Scene 2

Another part of the island.

Enter CALIBAN *with a burden of wood. A noise of thunder heard.*

CALIBAN:

    All the infections that the sun sucks up
    From bogs, fens, flats, on Prosper fall, and make him
    By inchmeal° a disease! His spirits hear me,   *inch by inch*
    And yet I needs must curse. But they'll nor pinch,
    Fright me with urchin shows,° pitch me i' th' mire,   *impish apparitions*
    Nor lead me, like a firebrand,[101] in the dark
    Out of my way, unless he bid 'em. But
    For every trifle are they set upon me;
    Sometime like apes that mow° and chatter at me,   *make faces*
10   And after bite me; then like hedgehogs which
    Lie tumbling in my barefoot way and mount
    Their pricks at my footfall; sometime am I
    All wound with adders, who with cloven tongues
    Do hiss me into madness.

Enter TRINCULO.

                     Lo, now, lo!
    Here comes a spirit of his, and to torment me
    For bringing wood in slowly. I'll fall flat.
    Perchance he will not mind me.

[Lies down.]

TRINCULO: Here's neither bush nor shrub to bear off[102] any weather at all, and
20   another storm brewing; I hear it sing i' th' wind. Yond same black cloud, yond
    huge one, looks like a foul bombard[103] that would shed his liquor. If it should
    thunder as it did before, I know not where to hide my head. Yond same cloud
    cannot choose but fall by pailfuls. What have we here? A man or a fish? Dead or
    alive? A fish! He smells like a fish; a very ancient and fishlike smell, a kind of not
    of the newest Poor John.[104] A strange fish! Were I in England now, as once I was,
    and had but this fish painted,[105] not a holiday fool there but would give a piece of

---

[101] **like a firebrand:** In the form of a will-o'-the-wisp.   [102] **bear off:** Ward off.   [103] **bombard:** Large leather jug.
[104] **Poor John:** Dried hake (a type of fish).   [105] **painted:** As a sign hung outside a booth at a fair.

silver. There would this monster make a man;[106] any strange beast there makes a man. When they will not give a doit[107] to relieve a lame beggar, they will lay out ten to see a dead Indian. Legged like a man! And his fins like arms! Warm, o' my troth! I do now let loose my opinion, hold it no longer. This is no fish, but an islander, that hath lately suffered by a thunderbolt. [*Thunder.*] Alas, the storm is come again! My best way is to creep under his gaberdine; there is no other shelter hereabout. Misery acquaints a man with strange bedfellows. I will here shroud till the dregs of the storm be past.

[*Creeps under* CALIBAN's *garment.*]
Enter STEPHANO *singing, a bottle in his hand.*
STEPHANO:

> *I shall no more to sea, to sea;*
> > *Here shall I die ashore.*

This is a very scurvy tune to sing at a man's funeral. Well, here's my comfort.
[*Drinks.*]

> *The master, the swabber, the boatswain, and I,*
> > *The gunner, and his mate,*
> *Loved Mall, Meg, and Marian, and Margery,*
> > *But none of us cared for Kate.*
> > *For she had a tongue with a tang,*
> > *Would cry to a sailor "Go hang!"*
> *She loved not the savor of tar nor of pitch;*
> *Yet a tailor might scratch her where'er she did itch.*
> > *Then to sea, boys, and let her go hang!*

This is a scurvy tune too; but here's my comfort. *Drinks.*

CALIBAN: Do not torment me! O!

STEPHANO: What's the matter? Have we devils here? Do you put tricks upon 's with savages and men of Inde, ha? I have not scaped drowning to be afeared now of your four legs. For it hath been said, "As proper a man as ever went on four legs cannot make him give ground"; and it shall be said so again, while Stephano breathes at' nostrils.

CALIBAN: The spirit torments me. O!

STEPHANO: This is some monster of the isle, with four legs, who hath got, as I take it, an ague. Where the devil should he learn our language? I will give him some relief, if it be but for that. If I can recover him, and keep him tame, and get to Naples with him, he's a present for any emperor that ever trod on neat's leather.[108]

CALIBAN: Do not torment me, prithee; I'll bring my wood home faster.

STEPHANO: He's in his fit now and does not talk after the wisest. He shall taste of my bottle; if he have never drunk wine afore, it will go near to remove his fit. If I can

---

[106] **make a man:** Pun: make a man's fortune.   [107] **doit:** Smallest coin.   [108] **neat's leather:** Cowhide.

recover him and keep him tame, I will not take too much[109] for him. He shall pay
for him that hath him, and that soundly.

CALIBAN: Thou dost me yet but little hurt. Thou wilt anon; I know it by thy
trembling.[110] Now Prosper works upon thee.

STEPHANO: Come on your ways, open your mouth; here is that which will give
language to you, cat.[111] Open your mouth. This will shake your shaking, I can
tell you, and that soundly. [*Gives* CALIBAN *drink.*] You cannot tell who's your
70   friend. Open your chaps[112] again.

TRINCULO: I should know that voice. It should be—but he is drowned; and these are
devils. O, defend me!

STEPHANO: Four legs and two voices—a most delicate monster! His forward voice
now is to speak well of his friend; his backward voice is to utter foul speeches
and to detract. If all the wine in my bottle will recover him, I will help his ague.
Come! [*Gives drink.*] Amen! I will pour some in thy other mouth.

TRINCULO: Stephano!

STEPHANO: Doth thy other mouth call me? Mercy, mercy! This is a devil, and no
monster. I will leave him; I have no long spoon.[113]

80   TRINCULO: Stephano! If thou beest Stephano, touch me and speak to me; for I am
Trinculo—be not afeared—thy good friend Trinculo.

STEPHANO: If thou beest Trinculo, come forth. I'll pull thee by the lesser legs. If any be
Trinculo's legs, these are they. [*Draws him out from under* CALIBAN's *garment.*] Thou
art very Trinculo indeed! How cam'st thou to be the siege[114] of this mooncalf?[115]
Can he vent Trinculos?

TRINCULO: I took him to be killed with a thunderstroke. But art thou not drowned,
Stephano? I hope now thou art not drowned. Is the storm overblown? I hid me
under the dead mooncalf's gaberdine for fear of the storm. And art thou living,
Stephano? O Stephano, two Neapolitans scaped!

90   STEPHANO: Prithee do not turn me about; my stomach is not constant.

CALIBAN:

[*Aside*] These be fine things, and if they be not sprites.
That's a brave god and bears celestial liquor.
I will kneel to him.

STEPHANO: How didst thou scape? How cam'st thou hither? Swear by this bottle how
thou cam'st hither. I escaped upon a butt of sack which the sailors heaved
o'erboard—by this bottle which I made of the bark of a tree with mine own
hands since I was cast ashore.

CALIBAN: I'll swear upon that bottle to be thy true subject, for the liquor is not
earthly.

STEPHANO: Here! Swear then how thou escap'dst.

100   TRINCULO: Swum ashore, man, like a duck. I can swim like a duck, I'll be sworn.

---

[109] **I . . . much:** Too much will not be enough.   [110] **trembling:** Trinculo is shaking with fear.   [111] **here . . . cat:**
Alluding to the proverb "Liquor will make a cat talk."   [112] **chaps:** Jaws.   [113] **long spoon:** Alluding to the proverb
"He who sups with (i.e., from the same dish as) the devil must have a long spoon."   [114] **siege:** Excrement.
[115] **mooncalf:** Monstrosity.

STEPHANO: Here, kiss the book. [*Gives him drink.*] Though thou canst swim like a duck, thou art made like a goose.

TRINCULO: O Stephano, hast any more of this?

STEPHANO: The whole butt, man. My cellar is in a rock by th' seaside, where my wine is hid. How now, mooncalf? How does thine ague?

CALIBAN: Hast thou not dropped from heaven?

STEPHANO: Out o' th' moon, I do assure thee. I was the Man i' th' Moon when time was.

CALIBAN: I have seen thee in her, and I do adore thee. My mistress showed me thee,
110   and thy dog, and thy bush.[116]

STEPHANO: Come, swear to that; kiss the book. [*Gives him drink.*] I will furnish it anon with new contents. Swear. [CALIBAN *drinks.*]

TRINCULO: By this good light, this is a very shallow monster! I afeard of him? A very weak monster! The Man i' th' Moon? A most poor credulous monster! Well drawn,[117] monster, in good sooth!

CALIBAN: I'll show thee every fertile inch o' th' island; and I will kiss thy foot. I prithee, be my god.

TRINCULO: By this light, a most perfidious and drunken monster! When's god's asleep, he'll rob his bottle.

120 CALIBAN: I'll kiss thy foot. I'll swear myself thy subject.

STEPHANO: Come on then. Down, and swear!

TRINCULO: I shall laugh myself to death at this puppy-headed monster. A most scurvy monster! I could find in my heart to beat him—

STEPHANO: Come, kiss.

TRINCULO: But that the poor monster's in drink. An abominable monster!

CALIBAN:
       I'll show thee the best springs; I'll pluck thee berries;
       I'll fish for thee, and get thee wood enough.
       A plague upon the tyrant that I serve!
       I'll bear him no more sticks, but follow thee,
130   Thou wondrous man.

TRINCULO: A most ridiculous monster, to make a wonder of a poor drunkard!

CALIBAN:
       I prithee let me bring thee where crabs° grow;   crab apples
       And I with my long nails will dig thee pignuts,°   earthnuts
       Show thee a jay's nest, and instruct thee how
       To snare the nimble marmoset. I'll bring thee
       To clust'ring filberts, and sometimes I'll get thee
       Young scamels[118] from the rock. Wilt thou go with me?

---

[116] **My . . . bush:** The Man in the Moon was banished there, according to legend, for gathering brushwood with his dog on Sunday.   [117] **Well drawn:** A good pull at the bottle.   [118] **scamels:** Perhaps a misprint for "seamels" or "seamews," a kind of sea bird.

STEPHANO: I prithee now, lead the way without any more talking. Trinculo, the King and all our company else being drowned, we will inherit here. Here, bear my
140   bottle. Fellow Trinculo, we'll fill him by and by again.

CALIBAN *sings drunkenly.*
CALIBAN: Farewell, master; farewell, farewell!
TRINCULO: A howling monster! A drunken monster!
CALIBAN:

> *No more dams I'll make for fish,*
> *Nor fetch in firing*
> *At requiring,*
> *Nor scrape trenchering,*[119] *nor wash dish.*
> *'Ban, 'Ban, Ca—Caliban*
> *Has a new master. Get a new man!*

Freedom, high day! High day, freedom! Freedom, high day, freedom!
150   STEPHANO: O brave monster! Lead the way.   *Exeunt.*

ACT III

Scene 1

In front of PROSPERO'S *cell.*

Enter FERDINAND, *bearing a log.*
FERDINAND:

There be some sports are painful, and their labor
Delight in them sets off;° some kinds of baseness   cancels
Are nobly undergone, and most poor matters
Point to rich ends. This my mean task
Would be as heavy to me as odious, but
The mistress which I serve quickens what's dead
And makes my labors pleasures. O, she is
Ten times more gentle than her father's crabbed;
And he's composed of harshness. I must remove
10   Some thousands of these logs and pile them up,
Upon a sore injunction. My sweet mistress
Weeps when she sees me work, and says such baseness
Had never like executor. I forget;[120]
But these sweet thoughts do even refresh my labors,
Most busiest when I do it.[121]

---

[119] *trenchering:* Trenchers, wooden plates.   [120] **forget:** Forget my task.   [121] **Most . . . it:** My thoughts are busiest when I am (the Folio's *busie lest* has been variously emended; *it* may refer to "task," line 4, the understood object in line 13).

Enter MIRANDA; *and* PROSPERO *(behind, unseen).*

MIRANDA:

Alas, now pray you,

Work not so hard! I would the lightning had
Burnt up those logs that you are enjoined to pile!
Pray set it down and rest you. When this burns,
'Twill weep for having wearied you. My father

20 Is hard at study; pray now rest yourself;
He's safe for these three hours.

FERDINAND:

O most dear mistress,

The sun will set before I shall discharge
What I must strive to do.

MIRANDA:

If you'll sit down,

I'll bear your logs the while. Pray give me that;
I'll carry it to the pile.

FERDINAND:

No, precious creature,

I had rather crack my sinews, break my back,
Than you should such dishonor undergo
While I sit lazy by.

MIRANDA:

It would become me

As well as it does you; and I should do it

30 With much more ease; for my good will is to it,
And yours it is against.

PROSPERO [*Aside*]:

Poor worm, thou art infected!

This visitation[122] shows it.

MIRANDA:

You look wearily.

FERDINAND:

No, noble mistress, 'tis fresh morning with me
When you are by at night. I do beseech you,
Chiefly that I might set it in my prayers,
What is your name?

MIRANDA:

Miranda. O my father,

I have broke your hest to say so!

FERDINAND:

Admired Miranda![123]

---

[122]**visitation:** (1) Visit; (2) attack of plague (referring to metaphor of "infected").   [123]**Admired Miranda!:** *Admired* means "to be wondered at"; the Latin *Miranda* means "wonderful."

Indeed the top of admiration, worth
What's dearest to the world! Full many a lady
40   I have eyed with best regard, and many a time
Th' harmony of their tongues hath into bondage
Brought my too diligent ear. For several virtues
Have I liked several women; never any
With so full soul but some defect in her
Did quarrel with the noblest grace she owed,
And put it to the foil.° But you, O you,   defeated it
So perfect and so peerless, are created
Of every creature's best.

MIRANDA:
                                    I do not know
One of my sex; no woman's face remember,
50   Save, from my glass, mine own. Nor have I seen
More that I may call men than you, good friend,
And my dear father. How features are abroad
I am skilless of; but, by my modesty
(The jewel in my dower), I would not wish
Any companion in the world but you;
Nor can imagination form a shape,
Besides yourself, to like of. But I prattle
Something too wildly, and my father's precepts
I therein do forget.

FERDINAND:
                                    I am, in my condition,
60   A prince, Miranda; I do think, a king
(I would not so), and would no more endure
This wooden slavery than to suffer
The fleshfly blow my mouth. Hear my soul speak!
The very instant that I saw you, did
My heart fly to your service; there resides,
To make me slave to it; and for your sake
Am I this patient log-man.

MIRANDA:
                                    Do you love me?

FERDINAND:
O heaven, O earth, bear witness to this sound,
And crown what I profess with kind event
70   If I speak true! If hollowly, invert
What best is boded me[124] to mischief! I,

---

[124]**What . . . me:** Whatever good fortune fate has in store for me.

Beyond all limit of what else i' th' world,
Do love, prize, honor you.

MIRANDA:

I am a fool
To weep at what I am glad of.

PROSPERO:

[*Aside*] Fair encounter
Of two most rare affections! Heavens rain grace
On that which breeds between 'em!

FERDINAND:

Wherefore weep you?

MIRANDA:

At mine unworthiness, that dare not offer
What I desire to give, and much less take
What I shall die to want. But this is trifling;[125]
80   And all the more it seeks to hide itself,
The bigger bulk it shows. Hence, bashful cunning,
And prompt me, plain and holy innocence!
I am your wife, if you will marry me;
If not, I'll die your maid. To be your fellow
You may deny me; but I'll be your servant,
Whether you will or no.

FERDINAND:

My mistress, dearest,
And I thus humble ever.

MIRANDA:

My husband then?

FERDINAND:

Ay, with a heart as willing
As bondage e'er of freedom.° Here's my hand.   to win freedom

MIRANDA:

90   And mine, with my heart in't; and now farewell
Till half an hour hence.

FERDINAND:

A thousand thousand!

Exeunt FERDINAND *and* MIRANDA *in different directions.*

PROSPERO:

So glad of this as they I cannot be,
Who are surprised withal; but my rejoicing
At nothing can be more. I'll to my book;
For yet ere suppertime must I perform
Much business appertaining.   *Exit.*

---

[125] **this is trifling:** To speak in riddles like this.

Scene 2

Another part of the island.

Enter CALIBAN, STEPHANO, *and* TRINCULO.

STEPHANO: Tell not me! When the butt is out, we will drink water; not a drop before. Therefore bear up and board 'em![126] Servant monster, drink to me.

TRINCULO: Servant monster? The folly of this island! They say there's but five upon this isle; we are three of them. If th' other two be brained like us, the state totters.

STEPHANO: Drink, servant monster, when I bid thee; thy eyes are almost set in thy head.

TRINCULO: Where should they be set else? He were a brave monster indeed if they were set in his tail.

STEPHANO: My man-monster hath drowned his tongue in sack. For my part, the sea
10   cannot drown me. I swam, ere I could recover the shore, five-and-thirty leagues off and on, by this light. Thou shalt be my lieutenant, monster, or my standard.[127]

TRINCULO: Your lieutenant, if you list;[128] he's no standard.

STEPHANO: We'll not run, Monsieur Monster.

TRINCULO: Nor go[129] neither; but you'll lie like dogs, and yet say nothing neither.

STEPHANO: Mooncalf, speak once in thy life, if thou beest a good mooncalf.

CALIBAN: How does thy honor? Let me lick thy shoe. I'll not serve him; he is not valiant.

TRINCULO: Thou liest, most ignorant monster; I am in case[130] to justle[131] a constable. Why, thou deboshed[132] fish thou, was there ever man a coward that hath drunk
20   so much sack as I today? Wilt thou tell a monstrous lie, being but half a fish and half a monster?

CALIBAN: Lo, how he mocks me! Wilt thou let him, my lord?

TRINCULO: "Lord" quoth he? That a monster should be such a natural![133]

CALIBAN: Lo, lo, again! Bite him to death, I prithee.

STEPHANO: Trinculo, keep a good tongue in your head. If you prove a mutineer— the next tree![134] The poor monster's my subject, and he shall not suffer indignity.

CALIBAN: I thank my noble lord. Wilt thou be pleased to hearken once again to the suit I made to thee?

STEPHANO: Marry,[135] will I. Kneel and repeat it; I will stand, and so shall Trinculo.

Enter ARIEL, *invisible.*

CALIBAN:
30   As I told thee before, I am subject to a tyrant,
    A sorcerer, that by his cunning hath
    Cheated me of the island.

ARIEL:
    Thou liest.

---

[126] **board 'em:** Drink up.   [127] **standard:** Standard-bearer, ensign (pun since Caliban is so drunk he cannot stand).   [128] **if you list:** If it please you (with pun on "list" as pertaining to a ship that leans over to one side).   [129] **go:** Walk.   [130] **case:** Fit condition.   [131] **justle:** Jostle.   [132] **deboshed:** Debauched.   [133] **natural:** Idiot.   [134] **the next tree:** You will be hanged.   [135] **Marry:** An expletive, from "By the Virgin Mary."

CALIBAN:

Thou liest, thou jesting monkey thou!
I would my valiant master would destroy thee.
I do not lie.

STEPHANO: Trinculo, if you trouble him any more in's tale, by this hand, I will supplant some of your teeth.

TRINCULO: Why, I said nothing.

40 STEPHANO: Mum then, and no more. Proceed.

CALIBAN:

I say by sorcery he got this isle;
From me he got it. If thy greatness will
Revenge it on him—for I know thou dar'st,
But this thing[136] dare not—

STEPHANO:

That's most certain.

CALIBAN:

Thou shalt be lord of it, and I'll serve thee.

STEPHANO:

How now shall this be compassed?
Canst thou bring me to the party?

CALIBAN:

Yea, yea, my lord! I'll yield him thee asleep,
50 Where thou mayst knock a nail into his head.

ARIEL:

Thou liest; thou canst not.

CALIBAN:

What a pied[137] ninny's this! Thou scurvy patch!°   clown
I do beseech thy greatness, give him blows
And take his bottle from him. When that's gone,
He shall drink naught but brine, for I'll not show him
Where the quick freshes[138] are.

STEPHANO: Trinculo, run into no further danger! Interrupt the monster one word further and, by this hand, I'll turn my mercy out o' doors and make a stockfish[139] of thee.

60 TRINCULO: Why, what did I? I did nothing. I'll go farther off.

STEPHANO: Didst thou not say he lied?

ARIEL: Thou liest.

STEPHANO: Do I so? Take thou that! [*Strikes* TRINCULO.] As you like this, give me the lie another time.

TRINCULO: I did not give the lie. Out o' your wits, and hearing too? A pox o' your bottle! This can sack and drinking do. A murrain[140] on your monster, and the devil take your fingers!

---

[136]**thing:** That is, Trinculo.   [137]**pied:** Referring to Trinculo's parti-colored jester's costume.   [138]**quick freshes:** Living springs of fresh water.   [139]**stockfish:** Dried cod, softened by beating.   [140]**murrain:** Plague (that infects cattle).

CALIBAN: Ha, ha, ha!

STEPHANO: Now forward with your tale. [*To* TRINCULO] Prithee, stand further off.

CALIBAN:

70   Beat him enough. After a little time
    I'll beat him too.

STEPHANO:

              Stand farther. Come, proceed.

CALIBAN:

    Why, as I told thee, 'tis a custom with him
    I' th' afternoon to sleep. There thou mayst brain him,
    Having first seized his books, or with a log
    Batter his skull, or paunch° him with a stake,   *stab in the belly*
    Or cut his wezand° with thy knife. Remember   *windpipe*
    First to possess his books; for without them
    He's but a sot, as I am, nor hath not

80   One spirit to command. They all do hate him
    As rootedly as I. Burn but his books.
    He has brave utensils° (for so he calls them)   *fine furnishings*
    Which, when he has a house, he'll deck withal.
    And that most deeply to consider is
    The beauty of his daughter. He himself
    Calls her a nonpareil. I never saw a woman
    But only Sycorax my dam and she;
    But she as far surpasseth Sycorax
    As great'st does least.

STEPHANO:

90   Is it so brave a lass?

CALIBAN:

    Ay, lord. She will become thy bed, I warrant,
    And bring thee forth brave brood.

STEPHANO: Monster, I will kill this man. His daughter and I will be King and Queen —
    save our Graces! — and Trinculo and thyself shall be viceroys. Dost thou like the
    plot, Trinculo?

TRINCULO: Excellent.

STEPHANO: Give me thy hand. I am sorry I beat thee; but while thou liv'st, keep a
    good tongue in thy head.

CALIBAN:

    Within this half hour will he be asleep.

100   Wilt thou destroy him then?

STEPHANO:

              Ay, on mine honor.

ARIEL: This will I tell my master.

CALIBAN:

    Thou mak'st me merry; I am full of pleasure.
    Let us be jocund. Will you troll the catch°   *sing the round*
    You taught me but whilere?°   *just now*

STEPHANO: At thy request, monster, I will do reason, any reason.[141] Come on, Trinculo, let us sing. *Sings.*

> *Flout 'em and scout°'em*   jeer at
> *And scout 'em and flout 'em!*
110   *Thought is free.*

CALIBAN: That's not the tune.

ARIEL *plays the tune on a tabor*[142] *and pipe.*

STEPHANO: What is this same?

TRINCULO: This is the tune of our catch, played by the picture of Nobody.[143]

STEPHANO: If thou beest a man, show thyself in thy likeness. If thou beest a devil, take't as thou list.

TRINCULO: O, forgive me my sins!

STEPHANO: He that dies pays all debts. I defy thee. Mercy upon us!

CALIBAN: Art thou afeard?

STEPHANO: No, monster, not I.

CALIBAN:

120   Be not afeard; the isle is full of noises,
     Sounds and sweet airs that give delight and hurt not.
     Sometimes a thousand twangling instruments
     Will hum about mine ears; and sometime voices
     That, if I then had waked after long sleep,
     Will make me sleep again; and then, in dreaming,
     The clouds methought would open and show riches
     Ready to drop upon me, that, when I waked,
     I cried to dream again.

STEPHANO: This will prove a brave kingdom to me, where I shall have my music for

130   nothing.

CALIBAN: When Prospero is destroyed.

STEPHANO: That shall be by and by; I remember the story.

TRINCULO: The sound is going away; let's follow it, and after do our work.

STEPHANO: Lead, monster; we'll follow. I would I could see this taborer; he lays it on.

TRINCULO [*To* CALIBAN]: Wilt come?[144] I'll follow Stephano.   *Exeunt.*

Scene 3

Another part of the island.

Enter ALONSO, SEBASTIAN, ANTONIO, GONZALO, ADRIAN, FRANCISCO, *etc.*

GONZALO:

     By'r Lakin,° I can go no further, sir;   By our Lady

---

[141] **any reason:** Anything within reason.   [142] *tabor:* Small drum worn at the side.   [143] **picture of Nobody:** Alluding to the picture of No-body—a man all head, legs, and arms, but without trunk—on the title page of the anonymous comedy *No-body and Some-body.*   [144] **Wilt come?:** Caliban lingers because the other two are being distracted from his purpose by the music.

My old bones ache. Here's a maze trod indeed
Through forthrights and meanders.[145] By your patience,
I needs must rest me.

ALONSO:

                Old lord, I cannot blame thee,
Who am myself attached° with weariness   *seized*
To th' dulling of my spirits. Sit down and rest.
Even here I will put off my hope, and keep it
No longer for my flatterer. He is drowned
Whom thus we stray to find; and the sea mocks
10   Our frustrate search on land. Well, let him go.

ANTONIO:

[*Aside to* SEBASTIAN] I am right glad that he's so out of hope.
Do not for one repulse forgo the purpose
That you resolved t' effect.

SEBASTIAN:

[*Aside to* ANTONIO]   The next advantage
Will we take throughly.

ANTONIO:

[*Aside to* SEBASTIAN]   Let it be tonight;
For, now they are oppressed with travel, they
Will not nor cannot use such vigilance
As when they are fresh.

SEBASTIAN:

[*Aside to* ANTONIO] I say tonight. No more.

Solemn and strange music; and PROSPERO *on the top*[146] *(invisible). Enter several strange Shapes, bringing in a banquet; and dance about it with gentle actions of salutations; and, inviting the King etc. to eat, they depart.*

ALONSO:

What harmony is this? My good friends, hark!

GONZALO:

Marvelous sweet music!

ALONSO:

20   Give us kind keepers,° heavens! What were these?   *guardian angels*

SEBASTIAN:

A living drollery.° Now I will believe   *puppet show*
That there are unicorns; that in Arabia
There is one tree, the phoenix' throne; one phoenix
At this hour reigning there.

ANTONIO:

                I'll believe both;

---

[145] **forthrights and meanders:** Straight and winding paths.   [146] *top:* Upper stage (or perhaps a playing area above it).

And what does else want credit, come to me,
And I'll be sworn 'tis true. Travelers ne'er did lie,
Though fools at home condemn 'em.

GONZALO:
                                   If in Naples
I should report this now, would they believe me
If I should say I saw such islanders?

30   (For certes these are people of the island)
Who, though they are of monstrous shape, yet note,
Their manners are more gentle, kind, than of
Our human generation you shall find
Many—nay, almost any.

PROSPERO:
                      [Aside] Honest lord,
Thou hast said well; for some of you there present
Are worse than devils.

ALONSO:
                       I cannot too much muse
Such shapes, such gesture, and such sound, expressing
(Although they want the use of tongue) a kind
Of excellent dumb discourse.

PROSPERO:
                [Aside] Praise in departing.[147]

FRANCISCO:
They vanished strangely.

SEBASTIAN:
40   No matter, since
They have left their viands behind; for we have stomachs.
Will't please you taste of what is here?

ALONSO:
                  Not I.

GONZALO:
Faith, sir, you need not fear. When we were boys,
Who would believe that there were mountaineers
Dewlapped[148] like bulls, whose throats had hanging at 'em
Wallets of flesh? Or that there were such men
Whose heads stood in their breasts? Which now we find
Each putter-out of five for one[149] will bring us
Good warrant of.

---

[147] **Praise in departing:** Save your praise for the end.   [148] **Dewlapped:** With skin hanging from the neck (like mountaineers with goiter).   [149] **putter-out . . . one:** Traveler who insures himself by depositing a sum of money to be repaid fivefold if he returns safely.

ALONSO:
                    I will stand to, and feed;
50   Although my last, no matter, since I feel
The best is past. Brother, my lord the Duke,
Stand to, and do as we.

Thunder and lightning. Enter ARIEL, *like a harpy; claps his wings upon the table; and with a*
quaint device the banquet vanishes.

ARIEL:
     You are three men of sin, whom destiny—
That hath to instrument this lower world
And what is in't—the never-surfeited sea
Hath caused to belch up you and on this island,
Where man doth not inhabit, you 'mongst men
Being most unfit to live. I have made you mad;
And even with suchlike valor[150] men hang and drown
Their proper selves.

   [ALONSO, SEBASTIAN, *etc. draw their swords.*]
60   You fools! I and my fellows
Are ministers of Fate. The elements,
Of whom your swords are tempered, may as well
Wound the loud winds, or with bemocked-at stabs
Kill the still-closing[151] waters, as diminish
One dowle° that's in my plume. My fellow ministers
Are like invulnerable. If you could hurt,[152]
Your swords are now too massy for your strengths
And will not be uplifted. But remember
(For that's my business to you) that you three
70   From Milan did supplant good Prospero;
Exposed unto the sea, which hath requit it,[153]
Him and his innocent child; for which foul deed
The pow'rs, delaying, not forgetting, have
Incensed the seas and shores, yea, all the creatures,
Against your peace. Thee of thy son, Alonso,
They have bereft; and do pronounce by me
Ling'ring perdition (worse than any death
Can be at once) shall step by step attend
You and your ways; whose wraths to guard you from,
80   Which here, in this most desolate isle, else falls
Upon your heads, is nothing but heart's sorrow[154]
And a clear life ensuing.

---

[150] **suchlike valor:** The courage that comes of madness.   [151] **still-closing:** Ever closing again (as soon as wounded).   [152] **If . . . hurt:** Even if you could hurt us.   [153] **requit it:** Avenged that crime.   [154] **nothing . . . sorrow:** Only repentance (will protect you from the wrath of these powers).

He vanishes in thunder; then, to soft music, enter the Shapes again, and dance with mocks and mows,[155] *and carrying out the table.*

PROSPERO:
Bravely the figure of this harpy hast thou
Performed, my Ariel; a grace it had, devouring.[156]
Of my instruction hast thou nothing bated
In what thou hadst to say. So, with good life[157]
And observation strange,[158] my meaner ministers[159]
Their several kinds have done.[160] My high charms work,
And these, mine enemies, are all knit up
90   In their distractions. They now are in my pow'r;
And in these fits I leave them, while I visit
Young Ferdinand, whom they suppose is drowned,
And his and mine loved darling.   [*Exit above.*]

GONZALO:
I' th' name of something holy, sir, why stand you
In this strange stare?

ALONSO:
                    O, it is monstrous, monstrous!
Methought the billows spoke and told me of it;
The winds did sing it to me; and the thunder,
That deep and dreadful organ pipe, pronounced
The name of Prosper; it did bass my trespass.[161]
100 Therefore my son i' th' ooze is bedded; and
I'll seek him deeper than e'er plummet sounded
And with him there lie mudded.   *Exit.*

SEBASTIAN:
                    But one fiend at a time,
I'll fight their legions o'er![162]

ANTONIO:
                    I'll be thy second.

                    Exeunt [SEBASTIAN *and* ANTONIO].

GONZALO:
All three of them are desperate; their great guilt,
Like poison given to work a great time after,
Now 'gins to bite the spirits. I do beseech you,
That are of suppler joints, follow them swiftly

---

[155] *mocks and mows:* Mocking gestures and grimaces.   [156] *devouring:* In making the banquet disappear.
[157] *good life:* Good lifelike acting.   [158] *observation strange:* Remarkable attention to my wishes.   [159] **meaner ministers:** Inferior to Ariel.   [160] **Their . . . done:** Have acted the parts their natures suited them for.   [161] **bass my trespass:** Made me understand my trespass by turning it into music for which the thunder provided the bass part.   [162] **their legions o'er:** One after another to the last.

And hinder them from what this ecstasy°   madness
May now provoke them to.

ADRIAN:

              Follow, I pray you.

                            Exeunt omnes.

ACT IV

Scene 1

In front of PROSPERO's *cell.*

Enter PROSPERO, FERDINAND, *and* MIRANDA.

PROSPERO:

    If I have too austerely punished you,
    Your compensation makes amends; for I
    Have given you here a third of mine own life,
    Or that for which I live; who once again
    I tender to thy hand. All thy vexations
    Were but my trials of thy love, and thou
    Hast strangely° stood the test. Here, afore heaven,   wonderfully
    I ratify this my rich gift. O Ferdinand,
    Do not smile at me that I boast her off,[163]
10   For thou shalt find she will outstrip all praise
    And make it halt° behind her.   limp

FERDINAND:

                    I do believe it
    Against an oracle.[164]

PROSPERO:

    Then, as my gift, and thine own acquisition
    Worthily purchased, take my daughter. But
    If thou dost break her virgin-knot before
    All sanctimonious ceremonies may
    With full and holy rite be minist'red,
    No sweet aspersion[165] shall the heavens let fall
    To make this contract grow; but barren hate,
20   Sour-eyed disdain, and discord shall bestrew
    The union of your bed with weeds so loathly
    That you shall hate it both. Therefore take heed,
    As Hymen's lamps shall light you.[166]

---

[163]**boast her off:** Includes perhaps the idea of showing her off. [164]**Against an oracle:** Though an oracle should declare otherwise. [165]**aspersion:** Blessing (like rain on crops). [166]**As . . . you:** As earnestly as you pray that the torch of the god of marriage shall burn without smoke (a good omen for wedded happiness).

FERDINAND:
As I hope

For quiet days, fair issue, and long life,
With such love as 'tis now, the murkiest den,
The most opportune place, the strong'st suggestion
Our worser genius can,[167] shall never melt
Mine honor into lust, to take away
The edge° of that day's celebration   *keen enjoyment*
30   When I shall think or Phoebus' steeds are foundered°   *lamed*
    Or Night kept chained below.[168]

PROSPERO:
Fairly spoke.

Sit then and talk with her; she is thine own.
What, Ariel! My industrious servant, Ariel!

Enter ARIEL.

ARIEL:
What would my potent master? Here I am.

PROSPERO:
Thou and thy meaner fellows your last service
Did worthily perform; and I must use you
In such another trick. Go bring the rabble,[169]
O'er whom I give thee pow'r, here to this place.
Incite them to quick motion; for I must
40   Bestow upon the eyes of this young couple
    Some vanity of[170] mine art. It is my promise,
    And they expect it from me.

ARIEL:
Presently?

PROSPERO:
Ay, with a twink.

ARIEL:
Before you can say "Come" and "Go,"
And breathe twice and cry, "So, so,"
Each one, tripping on his toe,
Will be here with mop and mow.
Do you love me, master? No?

PROSPERO:
Dearly, my delicate Ariel. Do not approach
Till thou dost hear me call.

---

[167] **Our . . . can:** Our evil spirit can offer.   [168] **Or . . . below:** That either day will never end or night will never come.   [169] **rabble:** "Thy meaner fellows."   [170] **vanity of:** Illusion conjured up by.

ARIEL:

50   Well; I conceive.°   understand

                                                               Exit.

PROSPERO:

Look thou be true.[171] Do not give dalliance
Too much the rein; the strongest oaths are straw
To th' fire i' th' blood. Be more abstemious,
Or else good night your vow!

FERDINAND:

                     I warrant you, sir.
The white cold virgin snow upon my heart[172]
Abates the ardor of my liver.[173]

PROSPERO:

                     Well.
Now come, my Ariel; bring a corollary[174]
Rather than want a spirit. Appear, and pertly!
No tongue! All eyes! Be silent. *Soft music.*

Enter IRIS.[175]

IRIS:

60   Ceres, most bounteous lady, thy rich leas
Of wheat, rye, barley, fetches,[176] oats, and peas;
Thy turfy mountains, where live nibbling sheep,
And flat meads thatched with stover,[177] them to keep;
Thy banks with pionèd and twillèd brims,[178]
Which spongy April at thy hest betrims
To make cold nymphs chaste crowns; and thy broom groves,
Whose shadow the dismissèd bachelor loves,
Being lasslorn; thy pole-clipt vineyard;[179]
And thy sea-marge, sterile and rocky-hard,
70   Where thou thyself dost air°—the queen o' th' sky,[180]   take the air
Whose wat'ry arch and messenger am I,
Bids thee leave these, and with her sovereign grace,

JUNO *descends*.[181]

Here on this grass plot, in this very place,
To come and sport; her peacocks fly amain.[182]
Approach, rich Ceres, her to entertain.

---

[171] **Look . . . true:** Prospero appears to have caught the lovers in an embrace.   [172] **The . . . heart:** Her pure white breast on mine (?).   [173] **liver:** Supposed seat of sexual passion.   [174] **corollary:** Surplus (of spirits).   [175] IRIS: Goddess of the rainbow and Juno's messenger.   [176] **fetches:** Vetch (a kind of forage).   [177] **flat . . . stover:** Meadows covered with a kind of grass used for winter fodder.   [178] **banks . . . brims:** Obscure; may refer to the trenched and ridged edges of banks that have been repaired after the erosions of winter.   [179] **pole-clipt vineyard:** Vineyard whose vines grow neatly around (embrace) poles (though possibly the word is "poll-clipped," i.e., pruned).   [180] **queen . . . sky:** Juno.   [181] JUNO *descends:* This direction seems to come too soon, but the machine may have lowered her very slowly.   [182] **amain:** Swiftly (peacocks, sacred to Juno, drew her chariot).

Enter CERES.

CERES:

Hail, many-colored messenger, that ne'er
Dost disobey the wife of Jupiter,
Who, with thy saffron wings, upon my flow'rs
Diffusest honey drops, refreshing show'rs,
80 And with each end of thy blue bow dost crown
My bosky° acres and my unshrubbed down,   shrubbed
Rich scarf to my proud earth. Why hath thy queen
Summoned me hither to this short-grassed green?

IRIS:

A contract of true love to celebrate
And some donation freely to estate°   bestow
On the blessed lovers.

CERES:

          Tell me, heavenly bow,
If Venus or her son, as thou dost know,
Do now attend the Queen? Since they did plot
The means that dusky Dis my daughter got,[183]
90 Her and her blind boy's scandaled company
I have forsworn.

IRIS:

          Of her society
Be not afraid, I met her Deity
Cutting the clouds towards Paphos,[184] and her son
Dove-drawn with her. Here thought they to have done
Some wanton charm upon this man and maid,
Whose vows are, that no bed-right shall be paid
Till Hymen's torch be lighted. But in vain;
Mars's hot minion is returned again;[185]
Her waspish-headed son[186] has broke his arrows,
100 Swears he will shoot no more, but play with sparrows
And be a boy right out.[187]

[JUNO *alights.*]

CERES:

          Highest queen of state,
Great Juno, comes; I know her by her gait.

JUNO:

How does my bounteous sister? Go with me
To bless this twain, that they may prosperous be
And honored in their issue.

---

[183] **Since . . . got:** Alluding to the abduction of Proserpine by Pluto (Dis), god of the underworld. [184] **Paphos:** In Cyprus, center of Venus's cult.   [185] **Mars's . . . again:** Mars's lustful mistress (Venus) is on her way back to Paphos.   [186] **waspish-headed son:** Cupid is irritable and stings with his arrows.   [187] **a boy right out:** An ordinary boy.

They sing.
JUNO:

> Honor, riches, marriage blessing,
> Long continuance, and increasing,
> Hourly joys be still upon you!
> Juno sings her blessings on you.

110 [CERES:] *Earth's increase, foison plenty,*
> *Barns and garners never empty,*
> *Vines with clust'ring bunches growing,*
> *Plants with goodly burden bowing;*
> *Spring come to you at the farthest*
> *In the very end of harvest.*[188]
> *Scarcity and want shall shun you,*
> *Ceres' blessing so is on you.*

FERDINAND:
> This is a most majestic vision, and
> Harmonious charmingly. May I be bold
> To think these spirits?

PROSPERO:
>   Spirits, which by mine art
120 I have from their confines called to enact
> My present fancies.

FERDINAND:
>   Let me live here ever!
> So rare a wond'red[189] father and a wise
> Makes this place Paradise.

JUNO *and* CERES *whisper, and send* IRIS *on employment.*
PROSPERO:
>   Sweet now, silence!
> Juno and Ceres whisper seriously.
> There's something else to do. Hush and be mute,
> Or else our spell is marred.

IRIS:
> You nymphs, called Naiades, of the windring[190] brooks,
> With your sedged crowns and ever-harmless looks,
> Leave your crisp° channels, and on this green land   rippling
130 Answer your summons; Juno does command.
> Come, temperate nymphs, and help to celebrate
> A contract of true love; be not too late.

Enter certain NYMPHS.

---

[188] *Spring . . . harvest:* May there be no winter in your lives.   [189] **wond'red:** Possessed of wonders; i.e., both wonderful and wonder-working, and therefore to be wondered at.   [190] **windring:** Winding and wandering (?).

You sunburned sicklemen, of August weary,
Come hither from the furrow and be merry.
Make holiday; your rye-straw hats put on,
And these fresh nymphs encounter everyone
In country footing.°   dance

Enter certain REAPERS, *properly habited. They join with the* NYMPHS *in a graceful dance; towards the end whereof* PROSPERO *starts suddenly and speaks;*[191] *after which, to a strange, hollow, and confused noise, they heavily*[192] *vanish.*

PROSPERO:
  [*Aside*] I had forgot that foul conspiracy
  Of the beast Caliban and his confederates
140 Against my life. The minute of their plot
  Is almost come. [*To the* SPIRITS] Well done!
  Avoid!° No more!   Begone!

FERDINAND:
  This is strange. Your father's in some passion
  That works him strongly.

MIRANDA:
                              Never till this day
  Saw I him touched with anger so distempered.

PROSPERO:
  You do look, my son, in a movèd sort,°   troubled state
  As if you were dismayed; be cheerful, sir.
  Our revels now are ended. These our actors,
  As I foretold you, were all spirits and
  Are melted into air, into thin air;
150 And, like the baseless fabric of this vision,
  The cloud-capped towers, the gorgeous palaces,
  The solemn temples, the great globe itself,
  Yea, all which it inherit, shall dissolve,
  And, like this insubstantial pageant faded,
  Leave not a rack° behind. We are such stuff   wisp of cloud
  As dreams are made on, and our little life
  Is rounded with a sleep. Sir, I am vexed.
  Bear with my weakness; my old brain is troubled.
  Be not disturbed with my infirmity.
160 If you be pleased, retire into my cell
  And there repose. A turn or two I'll walk
  To still my beating mind.

FERDINAND, MIRANDA:
                              We wish your peace.

                              Exit [FERDINAND *with* MIRANDA].

---

[191] *speaks:* Breaking the spell, which depends on silence.   [192] *heavily:* Reluctantly.

PROSPERO:
　　Come with a thought! I thank thee, Ariel.[193] Come.

Enter ARIEL.

ARIEL:
　　Thy thoughts I cleave to. What's thy pleasure?

PROSPERO:
　　　　　　　　　　　　　　　　　　　　　Spirit,
　　We must prepare to meet with Caliban.

ARIEL:
　　Ay, my commander. When I presented[194] Ceres,
　　I thought to have told thee of it, but I feared
　　Lest I might anger thee.

PROSPERO:

170　　Say again, where didst thou leave these varlets?°　　　　　　　ruffians

ARIEL:
　　I told you, sir, they were red-hot with drinking;
　　So full of valor that they smote the air
　　For breathing in their faces, beat the ground
　　For kissing of their feet; yet always bending
　　Towards their project. Then I beat my tabor;
　　At which like unbacked° colts they pricked their ears,　　　unbroken
　　Advanced° their eyelids, lifted up their noses　　　　　　lifted up
　　As they smelt music. So I charmed their ears
　　That calflike they my lowing followed through

180　　Toothed briers, sharp furzes, pricking goss,° and thorns,　　gorse
　　Which ent'red their frail shins. At last I left them
　　I' th' filthy mantled[195] pool beyond your cell,
　　There dancing up to th' chins, that the foul lake
　　O'erstunk their feet.

PROSPERO:
　　　　　　　　　　　This was well done, my bird.
　　Thy shape invisible retain thou still.
　　The trumpery[196] in my house, go bring it hither
　　For stale° to catch these thieves.　　　　　　　　　　　decoy

ARIEL:
　　　　　　　　　I go, I go.　　　　　　　　　　　　　*Exit.*

PROSPERO:
　　A devil, a born devil, on whose nature
　　Nurture can never stick; on whom my pains,

190　　Humanely taken, all, all lost, quite lost!
　　And as with age his body uglier grows,

---

[193] **thank thee, Ariel:** For the masque (?).　[194] **presented:** Acted the part of (?); introduced (?).　[195] **filthy mantled:** Covered with filthy scum.　[196] **trumpery:** The "glistering apparel" mentioned in the next stage direction.

So his mind cankers. I will plague them all,
Even to roaring. *Enter* ARIEL, *loaden with glistering apparel, etc.*
      Come, hang them on this line.[197]

[PROSPERO *and* ARIEL *remain, invisible.*] *Enter* CALIBAN, STEPHANO, *and* TRINCULO, *all wet.*

CALIBAN:
    Pray you tread softly, that the blind mole may not
    Hear a foot fall. We now are near his cell.

STEPHANO:
    Monster, your fairy, which you say is a harmless fairy,
    has done little better than played the Jack[198] with us.

TRINCULO: Monster, I do smell all horse piss, at which my nose is in great indigna-
200 tion.

STEPHANO: So is mine. Do you hear, monster? If I should take a displeasure against
    you, look you—

TRINCULO: Thou wert but a lost monster.

CALIBAN:
    Good my lord, give me thy favor still.
    Be patient, for the prize I'll bring thee to
    Shall hoodwink[199] this mischance. Therefore speak softly.
    All's hushed as midnight yet.

TRINCULO: Ay, but to lose our bottles in the pool—

STEPHANO: There is not only disgrace and dishonor in that, monster, but an infinite
210 loss.

TRINCULO: That's more to me than my wetting. Yet this is your harmless fairy, monster.

STEPHANO: I will fetch off my bottle, though I be o'er ears[200] for my labor.

CALIBAN:
    Prithee, my king, be quiet. Seest thou here?
    This is the mouth o' th' cell. No noise, and enter.
    Do that good mischief which may make this island
    Thine own forever, and I, thy Caliban,
    For aye thy footlicker.

STEPHANO: Give me thy hand. I do begin to have bloody thoughts.

TRINCULO: O King Stephano! O peer![201] O worthy Stephano, look what a wardrobe
220 here is for thee!

CALIBAN: Let it alone, thou fool! It is but trash.

TRINCULO: O, ho, monster! We know what belongs to a frippery.[202] O King Stephano!

STEPHANO: Put off that gown, Trinculo! By this hand, I'll have that gown!

TRINCULO: Thy Grace shall have it.

---

[197] **line:** Lime tree (linden).   [198] **Jack:** (1) Knave; (2) jack-o'-lantern, will-o'-the-wisp.   [199] **hoodwink:** Put out of sight.   [200] **o'er ears:** Over my ears in water.   [201] **O King . . . peer!:** Alluding to the song "King Stephen was and a worthy peer; / His breeches cost him but a crown," quoted in *Othello* II, iii.   [202] **frippery:** Old-clothes shop; i.e., we are good judges of castoff clothes.

CALIBAN:
> The dropsy drown this fool! What do you mean
> To dote thus on such luggage?[203] Let't alone,
> And do the murder first. If he awake,
> From toe to crown he'll fill our skins with pinches,
> Make us strange stuff.

230 STEPHANO: Be you quiet, monster. Mistress line, is not this my jerkin?[204]
> [*Takes it down.*] Now is the jerkin under the line.[205] Now, jerkin, you are like to lose your hair and prove a bald jerkin.[206]

TRINCULO: Do, do! We steal by line and level,[207] and't like[208] your Grace.

STEPHANO: I thank thee for that jest. Here's a garment for't. Wit shall not go unrewarded while I am king of this country. "Steal by line and level" is an excellent pass of pate.[209] There's another garment for't.

TRINCULO: Monster, come put some lime[210] upon your fingers, and away with the rest.

CALIBAN:
> I will have none on't. We shall lose our time

240
> And all be turned to barnacles,[211] or to apes
> With foreheads villainous low.

STEPHANO: Monster, lay-to your fingers; help to bear this away where my hogshead of wine is, or I'll turn you out of my kingdom. Go to, carry this.

TRINCULO: And this.

STEPHANO: Ay, and this.

A noise of hunters heard. Enter divers SPIRITS *in shape of dogs and hounds, hunting them about;* PROSPERO *and* ARIEL *setting them on.*

PROSPERO: Hey, Mountain, hey!

ARIEL: Silver! There it goes, Silver!

PROSPERO:
> Fury, Fury! There, Tyrant, there! Hark, hark!

[CALIBAN, STEPHANO, *and* TRINCULO *are driven out.*]
> Go, charge my goblins that they grind their joints

250
> With dry convulsions,[212] shorten up their sinews
> With agèd cramps, and more pinch-spotted make them
> Than pard or cat o' mountain.[213]

ARIEL:

> > > Hark, they roar!

---

[203] **luggage:** Useless encumbrances.   [204] **jerkin:** Kind of jacket.   [205] **under the line:** Pun: (1) under the lime tree; (2) under the equator.   [206] **bald jerkin:** Sailors proverbially lost their hair from fevers contracted while crossing the equator.   [207] **line and level:** By plumb line and carpenter's level; i.e., according to rule (with pun on "line").   [208] **and't like:** If it please.   [209] **pass of pate:** Sally of wit.   [210] **lime:** Birdlime (which is sticky; thieves have sticky fingers).   [211] **barnacles:** Kind of geese supposed to have developed from shellfish.   [212] **dry convulsions:** Such as come when the joints are dry from old age.   [213] **pard . . . mountain:** Leopard or catamount.

PROSPERO:
>Let them be hunted soundly. At this hour
>Lies at my mercy all mine enemies.
>Shortly shall all my labors end, and thou
>Shalt have the air at freedom. For a little,
>Follow, and do me service.   *Exeunt.*

ACT V

Scene 1

In front of PROSPERO'S *cell.*

Enter PROSPERO *in his magic robes, and* ARIEL.

PROSPERO:
>Now does my project gather to a head.
>My charms crack not, my spirits obey, and time
>Goes upright with his carriage.[214] How's the day?

ARIEL:
>On the sixth hour, at which time, my lord,
>You said our work should cease.

PROSPERO:
>   I did say so
>When first I raised the tempest. Say, my spirit,
>How fares the King and 's followers?

ARIEL:
>   Confined together
>In the same fashion as you gave in charge,
>Just as you left them—all prisoners, sir,
>In the line grove which weather-fends[215] your cell.
>They cannot budge till your release. The King,
>His brother, and yours abide all three distracted,
>And the remainder mourning over them,
>Brimful of sorrow and dismay; but chiefly
>Him that you termed, sir, the good old Lord Gonzalo.
>His tears runs down his beard like winter's drops
>From eaves of reeds.[216] Your charm so strongly works 'em,
>That if you now beheld them, your affections
>Would become tender.

PROSPERO:
>   Dost thou think so, spirit?

ARIEL:
>Mine would, sir, were I human.

10

---

[214] **time . . . carriage:** Time does not stoop under his burden (because there is so little left to do).   [215] **weather-fends:** Protects from the weather.   [216] **eaves of reeds:** A thatched roof.

PROSPERO:

20   And mine shall.
        Hast thou, which art but air, a touch, a feeling
        Of their afflictions, and shall not myself,
        One of their kind, that relish all as sharply,
        Passion as they, be kindlier moved than thou art?
        Though with their high wrongs I am struck to th' quick,
        Yet with my nobler reason 'gainst my fury
        Do I take part. The rarer action is
        In virtue than in vengeance. They being penitent,
        The sole drift of my purpose doth extend
30   Not a frown further. Go, release them, Ariel.
        My charms I'll break, their senses I'll restore,
        And they shall be themselves.

ARIEL:

                                            I'll fetch them, sir.   *Exit.*

PROSPERO:

        Ye elves of hills, brooks, standing lakes, and groves,
        And ye that on the sands with printless foot
        Do chase the ebbing Neptune, and do fly him°   fly with him
        When he comes back, you demi-puppets that
        By moonshine do the green sour ringlets[217] make,
        Whereof the ewe not bites; and you whose pastime
        Is to make midnight mushrumps,° that rejoice   mushrooms
40   To hear the solemn curfew; by whose aid
        (Weak masters[218] though ye be) I have bedimmed
        The noontide sun, called forth the mutinous winds,
        And 'twixt the green sea and the azured vault
        Set roaring war; to the dread rattling thunder
        Have I given fire and rifted Jove's stout oak
        With his own bolt; the strong-based promontory
        Have I made shake and by the spurs° plucked up   roots
        The pine and cedar; graves at my command
        Have waked their sleepers, oped, and let 'em forth
50   By my so potent art. But this rough magic
        I here abjure; and when I have required
        Some heavenly music (which even now I do)
        To work mine end upon their senses that
        This airy charm is for, I'll break my staff,
        Bury it certain fathoms in the earth,
        And deeper than did ever plummet sound
        I'll drown my book.

---

[217] **ringlets:** "Fairy rings," little circles of rank grass supposed to be formed by the dancing of fairies.

[218] **masters:** That is, masters of supernatural power.

[*Solemn music.*]

Here enters ARIEL *before; then* ALONSO, *with a frantic gesture, attended by* GONZALO; SEBASTIAN *and* ANTONIO *in like manner, attended by* ADRIAN *and* FRANCISCO. *They all enter the circle which* PROSPERO *had made, and there stand charmed; which* PROSPERO *observing, speaks.*

A solemn air, and the best comforter
To an unsettled fancy, cure thy brains,
60   Now useless, boiled within thy skull! There stand,
For you are spell-stopped.
Holy Gonzalo, honorable man,
Mine eyes, ev'n sociable to the show of thine,
Fall fellowly drops.[219] The charm dissolves apace;
And as the morning steals upon the night,
Melting the darkness, so their rising senses
Begin to chase the ignorant fumes that mantle
Their clearer reason. O good Gonzalo,
My true preserver, and a loyal sir
70   To him thou follow'st, I will pay thy graces
Home[220] both in word and deed. Most cruelly
Didst thou, Alonso, use me and my daughter.
Thy brother was a furtherer in the act.
Thou art pinched for't now, Sebastian. Flesh and blood,
You, brother mine, that entertained ambition,
Expelled remorse and nature;° whom, with Sebastian   **natural feeling**
(Whose inward pinches therefore are most strong),
Would here have killed your king, I do forgive thee,
Unnatural though thou art. Their understanding
80   Begins to swell, and the approaching tide
Will shortly fill the reasonable shore,
That now lies foul and muddy. Not one of them
That yet looks on me or would know me. Ariel,
Fetch me the hat and rapier in my cell.
I will discase me,° and myself present   **disrobe**
As I was sometime Milan. Quickly, spirit!
Thou shalt ere long be free.

                                 [*Exit* ARIEL *and returns immediately.*]

ARIEL *sings and helps to attire him.*

      Where the bee sucks, there suck I;
      In a cowslip's bell I lie;
90   *There I couch when owls do cry.*

---

[219] **ev'n . . . drops:** Associating themselves with the (tearful) appearance of your eyes, shed tears in sympathy.
[220] **pay . . . Home:** Repay thy favors thoroughly.

> *On the bat's back I do fly*
> *After summer merrily.*
> *Merrily, merrily shall I live now*
> *Under the blossom that hangs on the bough.*

PROSPERO:

Why, that's my dainty Ariel! I shall miss thee,
But yet thou shalt have freedom; so, so, so.
To the King's ship, invisible as thou art!
There shalt thou find the mariners asleep
Under the hatches. The master and the boatswain
100 Being awake, enforce them to this place,
And presently, I prithee.

ARIEL:

I drink the air before me, and return
Or ere your pulse twice beat.   *Exit.*

GONZALO:

All torment, trouble, wonder, and amazement
Inhabits here. Some heavenly power guide us
Out of this fearful country!

PROSPERO:

                          Behold, sir King,
The wrongèd Duke of Milan, Prospero.
For more assurance that a living prince
Does now speak to thee, I embrace thy body,
110 And to thee and thy company I bid
A hearty welcome.

ALONSO:

                          Whe'r thou be'st he or no,
Or some enchanted trifle° to abuse me,   apparition
As late I have been, I not know. Thy pulse
Beats, as of flesh and blood; and, since I saw thee,
Th' affliction of my mind amends, with which,
I fear, a madness held me. This must crave[221]
(And if this be at all) a most strange story.
Thy dukedom I resign and do entreat
Thou pardon me my wrongs. But how should Prospero
Be living and be here?

PROSPERO:

                          First, noble friend,
120 Let me embrace thine age, whose honor cannot
Be measured or confined.

---

[221] **crave:** Require (to account for it).

GONZALO:
                              Whether this be
Or be not, I'll not swear.

PROSPERO:
                              You do yet taste
Some subtleties²²² o' th' isle, that will not let you
Believe things certain. Welcome, my friends all.
[*Aside to* SEBASTIAN *and* ANTONIO] But you, my brace of lords, were I so
    minded,
I here could pluck his Highness' frown upon you,
And justify° you traitors. At this time   prove
I will tell no tales.

SEBASTIAN:
        [*Aside*] The devil speaks in him.

PROSPERO:
                              No.
130 For you, most wicked sir, whom to call brother
Would even infect my mouth, I do forgive
Thy rankest fault—all of them; and require
My dukedom of thee, which perforce I know
Thou must restore.

ALONSO:
                    If thou beest Prospero,
Give us particulars of thy preservation;
How thou hast met us here, whom three hours since
Were wracked upon this shore; where I have lost
(How sharp the point of this remembrance is!)
My dear son Ferdinand.

PROSPERO:
                      I am woe for't, sir.

ALONSO:
140 Irreparable is the loss, and patience
Says it is past her cure.

PROSPERO:
                      I rather think
You have not sought her help, of whose soft grace
For the like loss I have her sovereign aid
And rest myself content.

ALONSO:
                      You the like loss?

---

²²²**subtleties:** Deceptions (referring to pastries made to look like something else, e.g., castles made out of
sugar).

PROSPERO:

As great to me, as late,[223] and supportable
To make the dear loss, have I means much weaker
Than you may call to comfort you; for I
Have lost my daughter.

ALONSO:

      A daughter?
O heavens, that they were living both in Naples,
150 The King and Queen there! That they were, I wish
Myself were mudded in that oozy bed
Where my son lies. When did you lose your daughter?

PROSPERO:

In this last tempest. I perceive these lords
At this encounter do so much admire°   wonder
That they devour their reason, and scarce think
Their eyes do offices° of truth, their words   perform services
Are natural breath. But, howsoev'r you have
Been justled from your senses, know for certain
That I am Prospero, and that very duke
160 Which was thrust forth of Milan, who most strangely
Upon this shore, where you were wracked, was landed
To be the lord on't. No more yet of this;
For 'tis a chronicle of day by day,
Not a relation for a breakfast, nor
Befitting this first meeting. Welcome, sir;
This cell's my court. Here have I few attendants,
And subjects none abroad.[224] Pray you look in.
My dukedom since you have given me again,
I will requite you with as good a thing,
170 At least bring forth a wonder to content ye
As much as me my dukedom.

Here PROSPERO *discovers*[225] FERDINAND *and* MIRANDA *playing at chess.*

MIRANDA:

Sweet lord, you play me false.

FERDINAND:

        No, my dearest love,
I would not for the world.

MIRANDA:

Yes, for a score of kingdoms you should wrangle,
And I would call it fair play.[226]

---

[223] **As . . . late:** As great to me as your loss, and as recent. [224] **abroad:** On the island. [225] *discovers:* Reveals (by opening a curtain at the back of the stage). [226] **for . . . play:** If we were playing for stakes just short of the world, you would protest as now; but then, the issue being important, I would call it fair play so much do I love you (?).

ALONSO:

                          If this prove
A vision of the island, one dear son
Shall I twice lose.

SEBASTIAN:

                    A most high miracle!

FERDINAND:

Though the seas threaten, they are merciful.
I have cursed them without cause.

[*Kneels.*]

ALONSO:

                         Now all the blessings
180   Of a glad father compass thee about!
Arise, and say how thou cam'st here.

MIRANDA:

                      O, wonder!
How many goodly creatures are there here!
How beauteous mankind is! O brave new world
That has such people in't!

PROSPERO:

                'Tis new to thee.

ALONSO:

What is this maid with whom thou wast at play?
Your eld'st acquaintance cannot be three hours.
Is she the goddess that hath severed us
And brought us thus together?

FERDINAND:

                  Sir, she is mortal;
But by immortal providence she's mine.
190   I chose her when I could not ask my father
For his advice, nor thought I had one. She
Is daughter to this famous Duke of Milan,
Of whom so often I have heard renown
But never saw before; of whom I have
Received a second life; and second father
This lady makes him to me.

ALONSO:

                   I am hers.
But, O, how oddly will it sound that I
Must ask my child forgiveness!

PROSPERO:

                There, sir, stop.
Let us not burden our remembrance with
A heaviness that's gone.

GONZALO:

200   I have inly wept,
        Or should have spoke ere this. Look down, you gods,
        And on this couple drop a blessèd crown!
        For it is you that have chalked forth the way
        Which brought us hither.

ALONSO:

                        I say amen, Gonzalo.

GONZALO:
        Was Milan thrust from Milan that his issue
        Should become kings of Naples? O, rejoice
        Beyond a common joy, and set it down
        With gold on lasting pillars. In one voyage
        Did Claribel her husband find at Tunis,
210   And Ferdinand her brother found a wife
        Where he himself was lost; Prospero his dukedom
        In a poor isle; and all of us ourselves
        When no man was his own.

ALONSO:
        [*To* FERDINAND *and* MIRANDA] Give me your hands.
        Let grief and sorrow still embrace his heart
        That doth not wish you joy.

GONZALO:

                        Be it so! Amen!

Enter ARIEL, *with the* MASTER *and* BOATSWAIN *amazedly following.*
        O, look, sir; look, sir! Here is more of us!
        I prophesied if a gallows were on land,
        This fellow could not drown. Now, blasphemy,
        That swear'st grace o'erboard,[227] not an oath on shore?
220   Hast thou no mouth by land? What is the news?

BOATSWAIN:
        The best news is that we have safely found
        Our king and company; the next, our ship,
        Which, but three glasses since, we gave out split,
        Is tight and yare° and bravely rigged as when   shipshape
        We first put out to sea.

ARIEL:
            [*Aside to* PROSPERO] Sir, all this service
        Have I done since I went.

PROSPERO:
            [*Aside to* ARIEL] My tricksy spirit!

---

[227] **That . . . o'erboard:** That (at sea) swearest enough to cause grace to be withdrawn from the ship.

ALONSO:

　　These are not natural events; they strengthen

　　From strange to stranger. Say, how came you hither?

BOATSWAIN:

　　If I did think, sir, I were well awake,

230　I'd strive to tell you. We were dead of sleep

　　And (how we know not) all clapped under hatches;

　　Where, but even now, with strange and several noises

　　Of roaring, shrieking, howling, jingling chains,

　　And moe diversity of sounds, all horrible,

　　We were awaked; straightway at liberty;

　　Where we, in all our trim, freshly beheld

　　Our royal, good, and gallant ship, our master

　　Cap'ring to eye° her. On a trice, so please you,　　　　　　　*dancing to see*

　　Even in a dream, were we divided from them

　　And were brought moping° hither.　　　　　　　　　　　　　　*in a daze*

ARIEL:

240　　　　　　　　[*Aside to* PROSPERO] Was't well done?

PROSPERO:

　　[*Aside to* ARIEL] Bravely, my diligence. Thou shalt be free.

ALONSO:

　　This is as strange a maze as e'er men trod,

　　And there is in this business more than nature

　　Was ever conduct° of. Some oracle　　　　　　　　　　　　　*conductor*

　　Must rectify our knowledge.

PROSPERO:

　　　　　　　　　　　　　　Sir, my liege,

　　Do not infest your mind with beating on

　　The strangeness of this business. At picked leisure,

　　Which shall be shortly, single I'll resolve you

　　(Which to you shall seem probable) of every

250　These happened accidents;[228] till when, be cheerful

　　And think of each thing well. [*Aside to* ARIEL] Come hither, spirit.

　　Set Caliban and his companions free.

　　Untie the spell. [*Exit* ARIEL.] How fares my gracious sir?

　　There are yet missing of your company

　　Some few odd lads that you remember not.

Enter ARIEL, *driving in* CALIBAN, STEPHANO, *and* TRINCULO, *in their stolen apparel.*

STEPHANO: Every man shift for all the rest, and let no man take care for himself; for

　　all is but fortune. *Coragio,*[229] bully-monster, *coragio!*

260　TRINCULO: If these be true spies which I wear in my head, here's a goodly sight.

---

[228] **single . . . accidents:** I myself will solve the problems (and my story will make sense to you) concerning
each and every incident that has happened.　　[229] ***Coragio:*** Courage (Italian).

CALIBAN:

    O Setebos,[230] there be brave spirits indeed!

    How fine my master is! I am afraid

    He will chastise me.

SEBASTIAN:

              Ha, ha!

    What things are these, my Lord Antonio?

    Will money buy 'em?

ANTONIO:

             Very like. One of them

    Is a plain fish and no doubt marketable.

PROSPERO:

    Mark but the badges[231] of these men, my lords,

    Then say if they be true. This misshapen knave,

    His mother was a witch, and one so strong

270   That could control the moon, make flows and ebbs,

    And deal in her command without her power.[232]

    These three have robbed me, and this demi-devil

    (For he's a bastard one) had plotted with them

    To take my life. Two of these fellows you

    Must know and own; this thing of darkness I

    Acknowledge mine.

CALIBAN:

           I shall be pinched to death.

ALONSO:

    Is not this Stephano, my drunken butler?

SEBASTIAN:

    He is drunk now. Where had he wine?

ALONSO:

    And Trinculo is reeling ripe. Where should they

280   Find this grand liquor that hath gilded 'em?

    How cam'st thou in this pickle?

TRINCULO: I have been in such a pickle, since I saw you last, that I fear me will never out of my bones. I shall not fear flyblowing.[233]

SEBASTIAN: Why, how now, Stephano?

STEPHANO: O, touch me not! I am not Stephano, but a cramp.

PROSPERO: You'd be king o' the isle, sirrah?

STEPHANO: I should have been a sore[234] one then.

290 ALONSO: This is a strange thing as e'er I looked on.

PROSPERO:

    He is as disproportioned in his manners

---

[230] **Setebos:** The god of Caliban's mother.   [231] **badges:** Worn by servants to indicate to whose service they belong; in this case, the stolen clothes are badges of their rascality.   [232] **control . . . power:** Dabble in the moon's realm without the moon's legitimate authority.   [233] **pickle . . . flyblowing:** Pickling preserves meat from flies.   [234] **sore:** (1) Tyrannical; (2) aching.

As in his shape. Go, sirrah, to my cell;
Take with you your companions. As you look
To have my pardon, trim it handsomely.

CALIBAN:
Ay, that I will; and I'll be wise hereafter,
And seek for grace. What a thrice-double ass
Was I to take this drunkard for a god
And worship this dull fool!

PROSPERO:
                                    Go to! Away!

ALONSO:
Hence, and bestow your luggage where you found it.

SEBASTIAN:
300   Or stole it rather.

                                    [*Exeunt* CALIBAN, STEPHANO, *and* TRINCULO.]

PROSPERO:
Sir, I invite your Highness and your train
To my poor cell, where you shall take your rest
For this one night; which, part of it, I'll waste
With such discourse as, I not doubt, shall make it
Go quick away—the story of my life,
And the particular accidents gone by
Since I came to this isle. And in the morn
I'll bring you to your ship, and so to Naples,
Where I have hope to see the nuptial
310   Of these our dear-beloved solemnizèd;
And thence retire me to my Milan, where
Every third thought shall be my grave.

ALONSO:
                                    I long
To hear the story of your life, which must
Take° the ear strangely.   captivate

PROSPERO:
                          I'll deliver° all;   tell
And promise you calm seas, auspicious gales,
And sail so expeditious that shall catch
Your royal fleet far off. [*Aside to* ARIEL] My Ariel, chick,
That is thy charge. Then to the elements
Be free, and fare thou well! [*To the others*] Please you, draw near.

                                    Exeunt omnes.

EPILOGUE

Spoken by PROSPERO.

> Now my charms are all o'erthrown,
> And what strength I have's mine own,
> Which is most faint. Now 'tis true
> I must be here confined by you,
> Or sent to Naples. Let me not,
> Since I have my dukedom got
> And pardoned the deceiver, dwell
> In this bare island by your spell;
> But release me from my bands°   bonds
10 With the help of your good hands.[235]
> Gentle breath° of yours my sails   favorable comment
> Must fill, or else my project fails,
> Which was to please. Now I want°   lack
> Spirits to enforce, art to enchant;
> And my ending is despair
> Unless I be relieved by prayer,°   this petition
> Which pierces so that it assaults
> Mercy itself and frees all faults.
> As you from crimes would pardoned be,
20 Let your indulgence set me free.   *Exit.*

---

[235] *good hands:* Applause to break the spell.

O Brave
New World!

The shock of the first encounters between European colonizers and the indigenous people of the New World was so overwhelming that serious consequences exist to the present day. The European conquest of the New World, prompted by commercial motives and the desire to convert the natives to Christianity, resulted in mass slaughter, epidemics against which native people had no resistance, and slavery: in point of fact, the result constituted genocide. The Europeans' view of the native inhabitants as "savages," along with their methods of engaging in warfare and enforcing authoritarian rule, their use of the natives as slaves, and their insistence on the legal right of occupation to justify this conduct left an ugly heritage which has been all the more difficult to address because it hardly has been confronted until recent times.

Historians have recorded in detail the events of such conquests from a European point of view, and elsewhere in this volume are several literary reflections on the early encounters from a European perspective. The play *The Tempest* by Shakespeare, the essay **"Of Cannibals"** by Montaigne, the fictional *Utopia* by More, and even the comic novel *Don Quixote* by Cervantes fall among them. Only bits and pieces remain of what the indigenous people thought of the forces against them, but those fragments are of great interest. p. 1818
p. 1761
p. 1705
p. 1776

EUROPEAN MOTIVES

The economic motives for exploration and conquest in the Early Modern Period surely should drive any discussion of the goals of the European adventurers. In Spain the last Moorish stronghold fell in 1492, the same year that Christopher Columbus (1451–1506) was

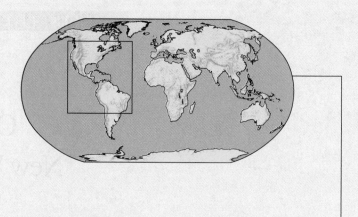

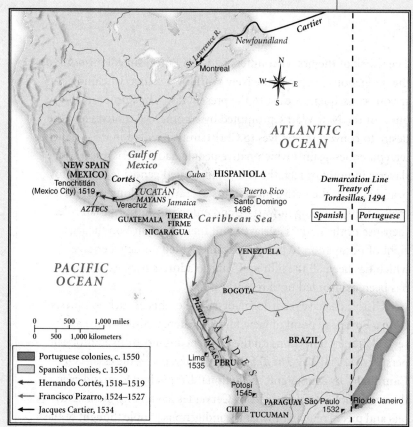

European Colonization of the Americas in the Sixteenth Century

Spanish and Portuguese explorers claimed Central and South America for their respective monarchs, who supported the voyages in part because they desired the precious metals thought to be deposited in these regions. There was relatively little exploration of North America at this time, except for the voyage of Jacques Cartier (1491–1557) down the St. Lawrence River; permanent settlement would come later, in the seventeenth century, primarily by the French and English.

dispatched on his voyage of discovery by King Ferdinand and
Queen Isabella. Also in that year the monarchs signed a decree
expelling Jews and unconverted Muslims from Spain; although
many of their estates already had been confiscated, a considerable
amount of wealth, especially gold, left the country with the involun-
tary exiles. For this and other reasons, including over four centuries
of war with Spanish Muslims, Spain was gold-poor. Therefore
Columbus presented his plan to reach what he thought to be Asian
sources of gold and spice at an opportune time. Legends about vast
stores of gold on islands in the Indies across the Atlantic fed the
fantasies of navigators and royalty alike, stimulating the financing of
expeditions. The fervor of Christian missionary societies to convert
"heathen natives" also helped motivate the European settlement of
the Americas once the continent was "discovered." This conversion
mission became Europe's greatest religious campaign since the
Crusades—and as was true of the Crusades, the prospect of economic gain coincided neatly with the new spiritual ambitions.

THE CAUSE OF COLUMBUS

In many respects, Columbus set a pattern for his successors. His
Diario, or journal, records the voyage of 1492 that would radically
change almost every significant natural and social feature of the
planet: the distribution of its flora and fauna and its genetic pools
and populations as well as its economic, political, and cultural life.
It is fortunate Columbus kept a journal of his voyage, since daily
ship's logs were uncommon until the sixteenth century and
Columbus himself seems not to have kept one on subsequent journeys. In its mixture of dogged detail, shrewd observation, personal
revelation, fantasy, and self-promotion, the *Diario* allows us to peer
through the lens of expectations with which Columbus beheld the
American land and peoples. In fact, the narrative of the *Diario*
helped set the stage for the subsequent story of American colonization. This is what modern scholars mean when they speak of the
Renaissance "construction" of the New World and the people in it.
Europe's expectations of America were set in motion while the
physical place was still being "discovered" by navigators, and these
expectations became a powerful factor in shaping the subsequent
direction of the European occupation.

p. 1894

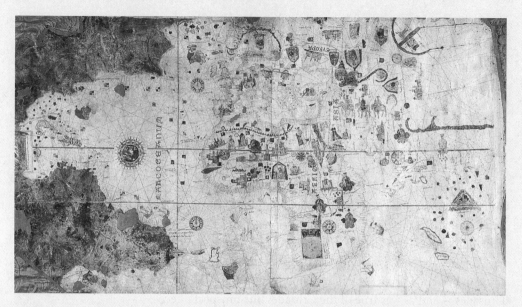

Juan de la Cosa, *Map of the New World,* **1500**
Drawn by Columbus's pilot and cartographer, this is the first European map of the
Caribbean and the coast of the New World. (*Museo Naval, Madrid*)

Even at the beginning there were problems with this picture.
Columbus's harsh and sometimes fatal treatment of natives on his
first expedition, followed by similar policies enacted in the colony he
left behind in Hispaniola (Haiti), captured the attention of a young
man who migrated there to teach the natives Christianity in 1502.
Though he himself later helped suppress a native revolt and was
rewarded with land and property for his actions, Bartolomé de Las
Casas developed such an antipathy to Spanish colonial practices that
he began to agitate for reform. After being ordained a Dominican
priest in 1512, he freed his own slaves and pressed his criticisms upon
the Spanish Crown. Las Casas eventually prevailed, with the result
that the great estates of Spanish slaveholders were broken up in 1542
and slavery itself was legally abolished in the colonies in 1573. His
several volumes of writings on the subject, including *A Brief Account*
p. 1903 *of the Destruction of the Indies* (1542) and ***A History of the Indies***
(c. 1564), are a permanent record of his successful protest.

CORTÉS AND MEXICO: THE SPANISH STORY

The abuses exposed by Las Casas stemmed from the European belief
that the natives of the New World were subhuman and thereby

exempted from treatment as rational souls possessing legal rights. This belief, of course, gave permission to Columbus and the conquerors who followed him to deceive, betray, overwhelm or kill, and send into slavery the indigenous peoples without legal or moral constraints. Hernán Cortés was such a *conquistador,* observing no restraints on his conduct in dealing with what he regarded as a subhuman race. At the same time, Cortés displayed other qualities normally associated with leadership: among them intelligence, close observation of detail, and accurate calculation. Vastly outnumbered by the Aztec people, who themselves constituted a powerful empire capable of great cruelty and absolutism, he won control of the Aztec capital city of Tenochtitlán in 1519 by cunning and guile along with superior Spanish weaponry. In his **Second Letter** to the King of Spain he provides an account of the conquest. Because he felt no necessity to conceal the truth and scrupulously reported events as they had happened, Cortés provided information in copious detail that became highly valuable to later historians.

p. 1907

THE AZTEC STORY

The story of the building of the city of **Tenochtitlán** and the rule of its king **Moctezuma** (Montezuma) is contained in codices written in Nahuatl, the Aztec language, later reproduced in book form. These documents or their copies, available to modern scholars in Mexican and European archives, tell the story of the development of Aztec culture and describe the negotiations between Cortés and Moctezuma and the subsequent battle leading to the Spanish destruction of the city of Tenochtitlán in 1521.

tay-nawch-teet-LAHN

mahk-tuh-ZOO-muh,
mahn-tuh-ZOO-muh

It has frequently been pointed out that the Aztecs themselves had controlled an empire from which they extracted considerable tribute and slaves before the Spanish arrival. Toward the end of their rule, they celebrated frequent, bloody religious sacrifices in Tenochtitlán, employing captured enemies as victims. At the time of the Spanish arrival Tenochtitlán had been in existence nearly two hundred years and the Aztecs had expanded their empire for a hundred years. Stretching from what is now central Mexico south to present-day Guatemala and from the Pacific Ocean to the Gulf of Mexico, it held a population of several million.

Powerful as the Aztecs were, they proved helpless before the Spaniards. One reason may have been traceable to their belief in an

Diego Durán, *Montezuma*, 1579

This illustration from the Dominican friar Diego Durán's History of the Indies of New Spain *(c. 1579–81) shows the great Aztec king Montezuma sending ambassadors to the Spanish conquistadors. Diego Durán (1537–1588) was born in Spain, but spent most of his life in Texcoco and Mexico City. (The Art Archive / Biblioteca Nacional Madrid / Dagli Orti)*

ancient legend concerning a culture hero who was also a ruler, **Quetzalcoatl.** In the legend, Quetzalcoatl had left his people, the Toltecs (an earlier civilization in Mexico), promising to return from the East one day and resume leadership. The force of the myth was such that to some of the Aztecs, the arrival of Cortés seemed the fulfillment of prophecy. Aztec accounts of the Spanish arrival make much of the legend and its importance to the people. Whatever its ultimate effect, it was apparently a factor in the reluctance of Moctezuma to confront Cortés directly. The **Codex Florentino** relates the terrible story of the destruction of Tenochtitlán and the subjection of the Aztecs within the context of this ancient legend.

■ **PRONUNCIATION**

Moctezuma (Montezuma): mahk-tuh-ZOO-muh, mahn-tuh-ZOO-muh
Quetzalcoatl: ketz-ul-ko-AH-tul
Tenochtitlán: tay-nawch-teet-LAHN

ketz-ul-ko-AH-tul

p. 1914

❧ CHRISTOPHER COLUMBUS
B. *ITALY, 1451–1506*

Christopher Columbus, or Cristóbal Colón as he is called in Spanish, the man whose name means "Christ-bearing dove," was born in the republic of Genoa, Italy, the son of a weaver. "At a tender age," as he says, he went to sea for the first time, probably on short voyages along the coastlines. In 1476, when a merchant ship on which he was serving was attacked and sunk off the coast of Portugal, Columbus swam ashore and made his way to Lisbon, the European center of navigational study, where he lived in the Genoese community. Sometime between coming to Lisbon and 1484, when he began his quest to finance an expedition, he became obsessed with the idea that it would be possible to reach the Indies by sailing westward. Contrary to popular myth, Columbus did not set out to prove that the earth was round; by his time, the idea of a spherical earth was widely accepted, and the real difficulty people found with his proposal lay in his estimate of the distance between Europe and the Indies; many thought — rightly so — that Columbus underestimated, and that ships of the time could not carry enough provisions to cross the open ocean presumed to lie between Europe and Asia.

Failing to interest Portugal in his plan, Columbus finally convinced the Spanish monarchs Ferdinand V (1452–1516) and Isabella I (1451–1504) to finance the expedition. The three caravels, the *Pinta,* the *Niña,* and the *Santa Maria,* left Spain on August 3, 1492, heading for the Canary Islands; from there, the trip was remarkably uneventful except for the growing anxiety and surliness of the crew, whom Columbus tried to calm by falsifying the log, telling them each day that they had sailed fewer miles than was actually the case. The ships made landfall on the sunny morning of October 12, 1492, on the island of San Salvador in the Bahamas, where the Taino people, who called the island Guanahani, ran down the beach and swam out to greet the ships.

On this first voyage Columbus explored not only the island where he landed but also the shores of Hispaniola and Cuba, which he believed to be Japan. The *Santa Maria* ran aground off Hispaniola on Christmas Day, and a fort called *La Navidad* was built from its shattered timbers; thirty-nine men stayed behind to run it. The *Pinta* and *Niña* set sail for home with a number of native prisoners, most of whom died on the passage or soon after landing on European soil in the spring of 1493. Christopher Columbus, along with his brothers Bartolomé and Diego, immediately readied a second voyage to establish a colony on Hispaniola. When his seventeen ships arrived in the Lesser Antilles on November 3, 1493, word had obviously traveled around the Caribbean about the prisoners who had been snatched on the earlier expedition; this time, villages stood empty everywhere Columbus and his crew passed. The thirty-nine sailors who had been left behind had been killed by the natives.

Columbus was under a great deal of pressure from the Spanish Crown to produce some kind of wealth from his discoveries. Consequently he loaded his ships with five hundred slaves, three hundred of whom survived the journey to Spain. That, however, was not sufficient payment on his debt. So Columbus instituted a tax system requiring certain amounts of gold from individual natives; anyone who did not pay had his hands cut off. The Taino population was already dwindling due to the barbaric treatment they suffered on plantations and in the mines, and to mass suicides. When Columbus went off to explore Jamaica and the Cuban coastline, some men returned to Spain to entreat the Crown to recall Columbus; the colony was in chaos, and the treatment of the natives was vicious even by the standards of the times.

In March of 1496, Columbus was granted a third expedition, which left for the Caribbean in May of 1498. Determined to reach China, Columbus sailed along the coast of Venezuela, discovering for the first time the mainland of a continent. In a long report to Ferdinand and Isabella, Columbus described the area in terms of the original Paradise, the biblical Eden, shaped like a woman's breast. Back on Hispaniola, conditions were chaotic: Indians were dying and the Spanish, some sick with syphilis, were feuding. In 1500 the Spanish court sent a replacement for Columbus, who was returned to Spain in chains to be tried. He was acquitted, and in 1502 he somehow wrangled a fourth voyage from the court, which turned out to be another failure at finding gold. After returning to Spain in 1504, he lived for two more years, depressed and in poor health.

FROM

∾ Diario

Translated by Robert H. Fuson

THE OUTWARD VOYAGE
3 AUGUST TO 10 OCTOBER 1492

In the Name of Our Lord Jesus Christ

Most Christian, exalted, excellent, and powerful princes, King and Queen of the Spains and of the islands of the sea, our Sovereigns: It was in this year of 1492 that Your Highnesses concluded the war with the Moors who reigned in Europe. On the second day of January, in the great city of Granada, I saw the royal banners of Your Highnesses placed by force of arms on the towers of the Alhambra, which is the fortress of the city. And I saw the Moorish king come to the city gates and kiss the royal hands of Your Highnesses, and those of the Prince, my Lord. Afterwards, in that same month, based on the information that I had given Your Highnesses about the land of India and about a Prince who is called the Great Khan, which in our language means "Kings of Kings," Your Highnesses decided to send me, Christopher Columbus, to the regions of India, to see the Princes there and the peoples and the lands, and to learn of their disposition, and of everything, and the measures which could be taken for their conversion to our Holy Faith. . . .

Therefore, after having banished all the Jews from all your Kingdoms and realms, during this same month of January Your Highnesses ordered me to go with a sufficient fleet to the said regions of India. For that purpose I was granted great favors and ennobled; from then henceforward I might entitle myself *Don* and be High Admiral of the Ocean Sea and Viceroy and perpetual Governor of all the islands and continental land that I might discover and acquire, as well as any other future discoveries in the Ocean Sea. Further, my eldest son shall succeed to the same position, and so on from generation to generation for ever after.

I left Granada on Saturday, the 12th day of the month of May in the same year of 1492 and went to the town of Palos, which is a seaport. There I fitted out three vessels, very suited to such an undertaking. I left the said port well supplied with a large quantity of provisions and with many seamen on the third day of the month of August in the said year, on a Friday, half an hour before sunrise. I set my course for the Canary Islands of Your Highnesses, which are in the Ocean Sea, from there to embark on a voyage that will last until I arrive in the Indies and deliver the letter of Your Highnesses to those Princes, and do all that Your Highnesses have commanded me to do.

To this end I decided to write down everything I might do and see and experience on this voyage, from day to day, and very carefully. Also, Sovereign Princes, besides describing each night what takes place during the day, and during the day the sailings of the night, I propose to make a new chart for navigation, on which I will set down all the sea and lands of the Ocean Sea, in their correct locations and with their correct bearings. Further, I shall compile a book and shall map everything by latitude and longitude. And above all, it is fitting that I forget about sleeping and devote much attention to navigation in order to accomplish this. And these things will be a great task. [. . .]

THE DISCOVERY OF THE BAHAMAS
11 OCTOBER TO 27 OCTOBER 1492

Thursday, 11 October 1492

I sailed to the WSW, and we took more water aboard than at any other time on the voyage. I saw several things that were indications of land. At one time a large flock of sea birds flew overhead, and a green reed was found floating near the ship. The crew of the *Pinta* spotted some of the same reeds and some other plants; they also saw what looked like a small board or plank. A stick was recovered that looks manmade, perhaps carved with an iron tool. Those on the *Niña* saw a little stick covered with barnacles. I am certain that many things were overlooked because of the heavy sea, but even these few made the crew breathe easier; in fact, the men have even become cheerful. I sailed 81 miles from sunset yesterday to sunset today. As is our custom, vespers were said in the late afternoon, and a special thanksgiving was offered to God for giving us renewed hope through the many signs of land He has provided.

After sunset I ordered the pilot to return to my original westerly course, and I urged the crew to be ever-vigilant. I took the added precaution of doubling the number of lookouts, and I reminded the men that the first to sight land would be given a silk doublet as a personal token from me. Further, he would be given an annuity of 10,000 maravedíes from the Sovereigns.

About 10 o'clock at night, while standing on the sterncastle, I thought I saw a light to the west. It looked like a little wax candle bobbing up and down. It had the same appearance as a light or torch belonging to fishermen or travellers who alternately raised and lowered it, or perhaps were going from house to house. I am the first to admit that I was so eager to find land that I did not trust my own senses, so I called for Pedro Gutiérrez, the representative of the King's household, and asked him to watch for the light. After a few moments, he too saw it. I then summoned Rodrigo Sánchez of Segovia, the comptroller of the fleet, and asked him to watch for the light. He saw nothing, nor did any other member of the crew. It was such an uncertain thing that I did not feel it was adequate proof of land.

The moon, in its third quarter, rose in the east shortly before midnight. I estimate that we were making about 9 knots and had gone some 67H miles between the beginning of night and 2 o'clock in the morning. Then, at two hours after midnight, the *Pinta* fired a cannon, my prearranged signal for the sighting of land.

I now believe that the light I saw earlier was a sign from God and that it was truly the first positive indication of land. When we caught up with the *Pinta,* which was always running ahead because she was a swift sailer, I learned that the first man to sight land was Rodrigo de Triana, a seaman from Lepe.

I hauled in all sails but the mainsail and lay-to till daylight. The land is about six miles to the west.

Friday, 12 October 1492
(Log entry for 12 October is combined
with that of 11 October.)

At dawn we saw naked people, and I went ashore in the ship's boat, armed, followed by Martín Alonso Pinzón, captain of the *Pinta,* and his brother, Vincente Yáñez Pinzón, captain of the *Niña.* I unfurled the royal banner and the captains brought the flags which displayed a large green cross with the letters F and Y at the left and right side of the cross. Over each letter was the appropriate crown of that Sovereign.[1] These flags were carried as a standard on all of the ships. After a prayer of thanksgiving I ordered the captains of the *Pinta* and *Niña,* together with Rodrigo de Escobedo (secretary of the fleet), and Rodrigo Sánchez of Segovia (comptroller of the fleet) to bear faith and witness that I was taking possession of this island for the King and Queen. I made all the necessary declarations and had these testimonies carefully written down by the secretary. In addition to those named above, the entire company of the fleet bore witness to this act. To this island I gave the name *San Salvador,* in honor of our Blessed Lord.

---

[1] Over each . . . Sovereign: Ferdinand and Isabella, co-regents of Spain.

No sooner had we concluded the formalities of taking possession of the island than people began to come to the beach, all as naked as their mothers bore them, and the women also, although I did not see more than one very young girl. All those that I saw were young people, none of whom was over 30 years old. They are very well-built people, with handsome bodies and very fine faces, though their appearance is marred somewhat by very broad heads and foreheads, more so than I have ever seen in any other race. Their eyes are large and very pretty, and their skin is the color of Canary Islanders or of sunburned peasants, not at all black, as would be expected because we are on an east–west line with Hierro in the Canaries. These are tall people and their legs, with no exceptions, are quite straight, and none of them has a paunch. They are, in fact, well proportioned. Their hair is not kinky, but straight, and coarse like horsehair. They wear it short over the eyebrows, but they have a long hank in the back that they never cut. Many of the natives paint their faces; others paint their whole bodies; some, only the eyes or nose. Some are painted black, some white, some red; others are of different colors.

The people here called this island *Guanahaní* in their language, and their speech is very fluent, although I do not understand any of it. They are friendly and well-dispositioned people who bear no arms except for small spears, and they have no iron. I showed one my sword, and through ignorance he grabbed it by the blade and cut himself. Their spears are made of wood, to which they attach a fish tooth at one end, or some other sharp thing.

I want the natives to develop a friendly attitude toward us because I know that they are a people who can be made free and converted to our Holy Faith more by love than by force. I therefore gave red caps to some and glass beads to others. They hung the beads around their necks, along with some other things of slight value that I gave them. And they took great pleasure in this and became so friendly that it was a marvel. They traded and gave everything they had with good will, but it seems to me that they have very little and are poor in everything. I warned my men to take nothing from the people without giving something in exchange.

This afternoon the people of San Salvador came swimming to our ships and in boats made from one log. They brought us parrots, balls of cotton thread, spears, and many other things, including a kind of dry leaf [2] that they hold in great esteem. For these things we swapped them little glass beads and hawks' bells.

Many of the men I have seen have scars on their bodies, and when I made signs to them to find out how this happened, they indicated that people from other nearby islands come to San Salvador to capture them; they defend themselves the best they can. I believe that people from the mainland come here to take them as slaves. They ought to make good and skilled servants, for they repeat very quickly whatever we say to them. I think they can easily be made Christians, for they seem to have no religion. If it pleases Our Lord, I will take six of them to Your Highnesses when I depart, in order that they may learn our language.

---

[2] dry leaf: Tobacco.

Saturday, 13 October 1492

After sunrise people from San Salvador again began to come to our ships in boats fashioned in one piece from the trunks of trees. These boats are wonderfully made, considering the country we are in, and every bit as fine as those I have seen in Guinea. They come in all sizes. Some can carry 40 or 50 men; some are so small that only one man rides in it. The men move very swiftly over the water, rowing with a blade that looks like a baker's peel. They do not use oarlocks, but dip the peel in the water and push themselves forward. If a boat capsizes they all begin to swim, and they rock the boat until about half of the water is splashed out. Then they bail out the rest of the water with gourds that they carry for that purpose.

The people brought more balls of spun cotton, spears, and parrots. Other than the parrots, I have seen no beast of any kind on this island.

I have been very attentive and have tried very hard to find out if there is any gold here. I have seen a few natives who wear a little piece of gold hanging from a hole made in the nose. By signs, if I interpret them correctly, I have learned that by going to the south, or rounding the island to the south, I can find a king who possesses a lot of gold and has great containers of it. I have tried to find some natives who will take me to this great king, but none seems inclined to make the journey.

Tomorrow afternoon I intend to go to the SW. The natives have indicated to me that not only is there land to the south and SW, but also to the NW. I shall go to the SW and look for gold and precious stones. Furthermore, if I understand correctly, it is from the NW that strangers come to fight and capture the people here.

The island is fairly large and very flat. It is green, with many trees and several bodies of water. There is a very large lagoon in the middle of the island and there are no mountains. It is a pleasure to gaze upon this place because it is all so green, and the weather is delightful. In fact, since we left the Canaries, God has not failed to provide one perfect day after the other.

I cannot get over the fact of how docile these people are. They have so little to give but will give it all for whatever we give them, if only broken pieces of glass and crockery. One seaman gave three Portuguese *ceitis* (not even worth a penny!) for about 25 pounds of spun cotton. I probably should have forbidden this exchange, but I wanted to take the cotton to Your Highnesses, and it seems to be in abundance. I think the cotton is grown on San Salvador, but I cannot say for sure because I have not been here that long. Also, the gold they wear hanging from their noses comes from here, but in order not to lose time I want to go to see if I can find the island of Japan.

When night came, all of the people went ashore in their boats.

[. . .] All the people I have seen so far resemble each other. They have the same language and customs, except that these on Fernandina seem to be somewhat more domestic and tractable, and more subtle, because I notice that when they bring cotton and other things to the ship they drive a harder bargain than those of the first islands visited. And also, on Fernandina I saw cotton clothes made like short tunics. The people seem better disposed, and the women wear a small piece of cotton in front of their bodies, though it barely covers their private parts. I do not recognize any religion in the people, and I believe that they would turn Christian quickly, for they seem to understand things quite well.

This is a very green, level, and fertile island, and I have no doubt that the people sow and reap grain, and also many other things, year around. I saw many trees quite different from ours. Many of them have branches of different kinds, all on one trunk;[3] one twig is of one kind and another of another, and so different from each other that it is the greatest wonder of the world. How great is the diversity of one kind from the other. For example, one branch has leaves like cane, another like mastic; thus on one tree five or six kinds, and all so different. Nor are these grafted so that one can say that the graft does it, for these trees are right there in the woods, and the people do not take care of them.

Here the fishes are so unlike ours that it is amazing; there are some like dorados, of the brightest colors in the world—blue, yellow, red, multi-colored, colored in a thousand ways; and the colors are so bright that anyone would marvel and take a great delight at seeing them. Also, there are whales. I have seen no land animals of any sort, except parrots and lizards—although a boy told me that he saw a big snake. I have not seen sheep, goats, or any other beasts, but I have only been here a very short time—half a day—yet if there were any, I could not have failed to have seen some. The circumnavigation of this island I shall write about after I have done it. [. . .]

During this time I walked among the trees, which are the most beautiful I have ever seen. I saw as much greenery, in such density, as I would have seen in Andalucia in May. And all of the trees are so different from ours as day is from night, and so are the fruits, the herbage, the rocks, and everything. It is true that some of the trees are like those in Castile, but most of them are very different. There are so many trees of so many different kinds that no one can say what they are, nor compare them to those of Castile.

The people on Fernandina are the same as the others already mentioned: of the same condition, usually nude, of the same stature, and willing to give what they had for whatever we gave them. Some of the ships' boys traded broken glass and bowls to them for spears. The others that had gone for the water told me that they had been in the houses and found them very simple but clean, with beds and furnishings that were like nets[4] of cotton.

The houses look like Moorish tents, very tall, with good chimneys. But I have not seen a village yet with more than 12 or 15 houses. I also learned that the cotton coverings were worn by married women or women over 18 years of age. Young girls go naked. And I saw dogs: mastiffs and pointers. One man was found who had a piece of gold in his nose, about half the size of a *castellano*,[5] and on which my men say they saw letters. I scolded them because they would not exchange or give what

---

[3] **trees . . . trunk:** There is no such tree, but Columbus may have seen a complex community of epiphytes and vines amid the trees.   [4] **nets:** Columbus's first reference to hammocks, although he had almost certainly seen them before on San Salvador.   [5] *castellano:* Half of a gold ducat, worth about $10.

was wanted, for I wished to see what and whose money that was, but they answered me that the man would not barter for it.

Sunday, 21 October 1492

At 10 o'clock in the morning I arrived at *Cabo del Isleo*[6] and anchored, as did the other two ships. After having eaten, I went ashore and found no settlement except one house. I found no one; the inhabitants must have fled in fear, for all their house-wares were left behind. I did not permit my men to touch a thing, and I went with my captains to see the island. If the other islands are very green and beautiful and fertile, this is much more, with great and green groves of trees. There are some large lakes and above and around them is the most wonderful wooded area. The woods and vegetation are as green as in April in Andalucía, and the song of the little birds might make a man wish never to leave here. The flocks of parrots that darken the sun and the large and small birds of so many species are so different from our own that it is a wonder. In addition, there are trees of a thousand kinds, all with fruit according to their kind, and they all give off a marvelous fragrance. I am the saddest man in the world for not knowing what kinds of things these are because I am very sure that they are valuable. I am bringing a sample of everything I can.

While going around one of the lagoons I saw a serpent,[7] which we killed with lances, and I am bringing Your Highnesses the skin. When it saw us, it went into the lagoon, and we followed it in because the water is not very deep. This serpent is about 6 feet long. I think there are many such serpents in these lagoons. The people here eat them and the meat is white and tastes like chicken.

I recognized the aloe[8] here, and tomorrow I am going to have 1,000 pounds of it brought to the ship because they tell me that it is very valuable. Also, while looking for good water, we stumbled onto a settlement about two miles from where we are anchored. When the people sensed our coming, they left their houses and fled, hiding their clothing and other things they had in the woods. I did not allow my men to take anything, not even something the value of one pin. Eventually some of the men came to us, and I gave one of them some hawks' bells and some small glass beads. He left very contented and very happy. And in order that our friendship might grow, and that something be asked of them, I requested water. Later, after I returned to the ship, they came to the beach with their gourds filled and were very delighted to give it to us. I ordered that they be given another string of glass beads, and they said they would return in the morning. I wanted to top off all of the ships' water casks while I had the chance.

If the weather permits, I shall depart this Cabo del Isleo and sail around Isabela until I find the king and see if I can get from him the gold which I hear that he wears.

---

[6] *Cabo del Isleo:* Cape of the Island.   [7] **serpent:** An iguana.   [8] **aloe:** Columbus was probably confusing *Agave americana* (or one of its close relatives) with either *Aloe vera* or *lignum aloe*. The former is grown as an ornamental indoor plant that serves as a readily accessible burn remedy. It is native to the Mediterranean area and was certainly known to Columbus. *Lignum aloe* is mentioned by Marco Polo. It is a fragrant, resinous wood used as incense.

Then I shall sail for another great island which I strongly believe should be Japan, according to the signs made by the San Salvador Indians with me. They call that island *Colba*,[9] where they say there are many great ships and navigators. And from that island I intend to go to another that they call *Bohío*,[10] which is also very large. As to any others that lie in between, I shall see them in passing, and according to what gold or spices I find, I will determine what I must do. But I have already decided to go to the mainland and to the city of Quisay,[11] and give Your Highnesses' letters to the Grand Khan and ask for a reply and return with it.

---

[9] *Colba:* The reference is the first to Cuba, but the name *Cuba* is not used until October 23.

[10] *Bohío:* The Indian name for Hispaniola.

[11] *Quisay:* Quinsay; the modern city of Hangzhou, China.

∾ Bartolomé de Las Casas
b. Spain, 1484–1566

Born in Seville, Spain, Bartolomé de Las Casas was only eighteen years old when he first saw Columbus parading through the streets of Seville with seven Taino slaves, a number of parrots, and other exotic items. His father, Pedro, returning from accompanying Columbus on his second voyage, gave Bartolomé a Taino slave; the youth was later returned to the Indies. Bartolomé went to Hispaniola with his father in 1502 as a teacher to impart Christian doctrine to the natives. He was rewarded for helping subdue native revolts with an *encomienda,* a tract of land with accompanying native workers. He was ordained a Dominican priest in 1512, the first priest ordained in the New World. Shortly thereafter he underwent a shift in attitude; he renounced his encomienda and, deeply troubled by the Europeans' cruel treatment of the natives, gradually became the champion of human rights for them. For the next decades, Las Casas traveled back and forth between Spain and the New World defending the rights of natives and proposing schemes for coexistence with them.

A most unusual event took place when the king of Spain—who was also the Holy Roman Emperor—questioned Spain's policies in America, in part because of Las Casas's criticism. Charles V scheduled a great debate in 1550, held in Valladolid, Spain, about whether natives had souls, and how that would influence colonizing the New World. Las Casas's opponent was Juan Ginés de Sepúlveda (1490?–1573), who argued that the natives' inferior natures warranted the inhumane treatment; they were, in Aristotle's terms, "slaves by nature." Las Casas's arguments that natives were rational beings finally won the day, and the Council of the Indies eventually abolished slavery in the "Ordinances of Discovery and Settlement" of 1573.

Bartolomé de Las Casas, the early Spanish historian and Dominican missionary. (The Art Archive / General Archive of the Indies Seville / Dagli Orti)

Las Casas's most famous writings are *A Brief Account of the Destruction of the Indies* (1542) and the *History of the Indies*. The first selection from the *History of the Indies* shows the ease with which killing could take place; Las Casas was traveling with a friend in Cuba when he observed the slaughter of innocent natives. The second piece concerns a sermon he heard in Hispaniola in which the priest, Fray Antonio de Montesinos, rebuked the Spanish for their inhumanity; it contains the phrase that vibrates through Las Casas's mission: "Are these not men? Do they not have rational souls?" The authorities asked Montesinos, who was one of the first Spaniards to protest the cruel treatment of natives, to recant in his next sermon, but instead he reinforced his argument with more scripture.

FROM

❧ The History of the Indies

Translated by George Sanderlin

[Slaughtering Indians in Cuba]

They arrived at the town of Caonao[1] in the evening. Here they found many people, who had prepared a great deal of food consisting of cassava bread and fish, because they had a large river close by and also were near the sea. In a little square were 2,000 Indians, all squatting because they have this custom, all staring, frightened, at the mares. Nearby was a large *bohio,* or large house, in which were more than 500 other Indians, close-packed and fearful, who did not dare come out.

When some of the domestic Indians the Spaniards were taking with them as servants (who were more than 1,000 souls . . .) wished to enter the large house, the Cuban Indians had chickens ready and said to them: "Take these—do not enter here." For they already knew that the Indians who served the Spaniards were not apt to perform any other deeds than those of their masters.

There was a custom among the Spaniards that one person, appointed by the captain, should be in charge of distributing to each Spaniard the food and other things the Indians gave. And while the captain was thus on his mare and the others mounted on theirs, and the father himself was observing how the bread and fish were distributed, a Spaniard, in whom the devil is thought to have clothed himself, suddenly drew his sword. Then the whole hundred drew theirs and began to rip open the bellies, to cut and kill those lambs—men, women, children, and old folk, all of whom were seated, off guard and frightened, watching the mares and the Spaniards. And within two credos, not a man of all of them there remains alive.

The Spaniards enter the large house nearby, for this was happening at its door, and in the same way, with cuts and stabs, begin to kill as many as they found there, so that a stream of blood was running, as if a great number of cows had perished. Some of the Indians who could make haste climbed up the poles and woodwork of the house to the top, and thus escaped.

The cleric had withdrawn shortly before this massacre to where another small square of the town was formed, near where they had lodged him. This was in a large house where all the Spaniards also had to stay, and here about forty of the Indians who had carried the Spaniards' baggage from the provinces farther back were stretched out on the ground, resting. And five Spaniards chanced to be with the cleric. When these heard the blows of the swords and knew that the Spaniards were killing the Indians—without seeing anything, because there were certain houses between—they put hands to their swords and are about to kill the forty Indians . . . to pay them their commission.

The cleric, moved to wrath, opposes and rebukes them harshly to prevent them, and having some respect for him, they stopped what they were going to do, so the

---

[1] **Caonao:** Village in Cuba.

forty were left alive. The five go to kill where the others were killing. And as the cleric had been detained in hindering the slaying of the forty carriers, when he went he found a heap of dead, which the Spaniards had made among the Indians, which was certainly a horrible sight.

When Narváez, the captain, saw him he said: "How does Your Honor like what these our Spaniards have done?"

Seeing so many cut to pieces before him, and very upset at such a cruel event, the cleric replied: "That I commend you and them to the devil!"

The heedless Narváez remained, still watching the slaughter as it took place, without speaking, acting, or moving any more than if he had been marble. For if he had wished, being on horseback and with a lance in his hands, he could have prevented the Spaniards from killing even ten persons.

Then the cleric leaves him, and goes elsewhere through some groves seeking Spaniards to stop them from killing. For they were passing through the groves looking for someone to kill, sparing neither boy, child, woman, nor old person. And they did more, in that certain Spaniards went to the road to the river, which was nearby. Then all the Indians who had escaped with wounds, stabs, and cuts—all who could flee to throw themselves into the river to save themselves—met with the Spaniards who finished them.

Another outrage occurred which should not be left untold, so that the deeds of our Christians in these regions may be observed. When the cleric entered the large house where I said there were about 500 souls—or whatever the number, which was great—and saw with horror the dead there and those who had escaped above by the poles or woodwork, he said to them:

"No more, no more. Do not be afraid. There will be no more, there will be no more."

With this assurance, believing that it would be thus, an Indian descended, a well-disposed young man of twenty-five or thirty years, weeping. And as the cleric did not rest but went everywhere to stop the killing, the cleric then left the house. And just as the young man came down, a Spaniard who was there drew a cutlass or half sword and gives him a cut through the loins, so that his intestines fall out. [. . .]

The Indian, moaning, takes his intestines in his hands and comes fleeing out of the house. He encounters the cleric [. . .] and the cleric tells him some things about the faith, as much as the time and anguish permitted, explaining to him that if he wished to be baptized he would go to heaven to live with God. The sad one, weeping and showing pain as if he were burning in flames, said yes, and with this the cleric baptized him. He then fell dead on the ground. [. . .]

Of all that has been said, I am a witness. I was present and saw it; and I omit many other particulars in order to shorten the account.

"ARE THESE NOT MEN?"

When Sunday and the hour to preach arrived, . . . Father Fray Antonio de Montesinos ascended the pulpit and took as the text and foundation of his sermon, which he carried written out and signed by the other friars: "I am the voice of one crying in the desert." After he completed his introduction and said something concerning the subject of Advent, he began to emphasize the aridity in the desert of Spanish consciences in this island, and the ignorance in which they lived; also, in what danger of eternal damnation they were, from taking no notice of the grave sins in which, with such apathy, they were immersed and dying.

Then he returns to his text, speaking thus: "I have ascended here to cause you to know those sins, I who am the voice of Christ in the desert of this island. Therefore it is fitting that you listen to this voice, not with careless attention, but with all your heart and senses. For this voice will be the strangest you ever heard, the harshest and hardest, most fearful and most dangerous you ever thought to hear."

This voice cried out for some time, with very combative and terrible words, so that it made their flesh tremble, and they seemed already standing before the divine judgment. Then, in a grand manner, the voice . . . declared what it was, or what that divine inspiration consisted of: "This voice," he said, "declares that you are all in mortal sin, and live and die in it, because of the cruelty and tyranny you practice among these innocent peoples.

"Tell me, by what right or justice do you hold these Indians in such a cruel and horrible servitude? On what authority have you waged such detestable wars against these peoples, who dwelt quietly and peacefully on their own land? Wars in which you have destroyed such infinite numbers of them by homicides and slaughters never before heard of? Why do you keep them so oppressed and exhausted, without giving them enough to eat or curing them of the sicknesses they incur from the excessive labor you give them, and they die, or rather, you kill them, in order to extract and acquire gold every day?

"And what care do you take that they should be instructed in religion, so that they may know their God and creator, may be baptized, may hear Mass, and may keep Sundays and feast days? Are these not men? Do they not have rational souls? Are you not bound to love them as you love yourselves? Don't you understand this? Don't you feel this? Why are you sleeping in such a profound and lethargic slumber? Be assured that in your present state you can no more be saved than the Moors or Turks, who lack the faith of Jesus Christ and do not desire it."

In brief, the voice explained what it had emphasized before in such a way that it left them astonished—many numb as if without feeling, others more hardened than before, some somewhat penitent, but none, as I afterward understood, converted.

When the sermon was concluded, Antonio de Montesinos descended from the pulpit with his head not at all low, for he was not a man who would want to show fear—as he felt none—if he displeased his hearers by doing and saying what seemed fitting to him, according to God. With his companion he goes to his thatch house where, perhaps, they had nothing to eat but cabbage broth without olive oil, as sometimes happened. But after he departed, the church remains full of murmurs so that, as I believe, they scarcely permitted the Mass to be finished. One may indeed suppose that a reading from the *Contempt of the World*[2] was not given at everyone's table that day.

---

[2] *Contempt of the World:* A book about the rigors of a spiritual life written by Diego de Estella (1524–1578), Franciscan friar and mystic, in Spanish and published in 1586. Inspirational works are read during mealtimes for monks. Las Casas's remark is ironical.

After finishing their meal, which must not have been very appetizing, the whole city gathers at the house of the Admiral, Don Diego Columbus . . ., especially the king's officials, the treasurer and auditor, factor and comptroller. They agree to go rebuke and frighten the preacher and the others, if not to punish him as a scandalous man, sower of a new and unheard of doctrine which condemned them all. [. . .]

⌘ HERNÁN CORTÉS
B. SPAIN, 1485–1547

Columbus had opened up and explored the "new" lands of the Americas, but he had not brought riches to the Spanish Crown. When gold fell in short supply during the Middle Ages, legends began to circulate in Spain about cities of gold located somewhere in the west, and conquistadors like Hernán Cortés followed their dreams of discovering a golden paradise. After giving up the study of law, Cortés was encouraged at age nineteen to make his fortune in the Indies. He went to Cuba and, rising up through the ranks, became secretary to Diego Velásquez (1465–1524), the island's governor. He finally got permission at age thirty-three to lead an

Cortés Arriving in the New World, 1519–22
A drawing by an Indian artist of the sixteenth century depicts the Spanish conquistador Hernán Cortés with his sword drawn and flag flying as he approaches a plant-carrying native. (Vatican Museum, Rome)

expedition to the mainland of Mexico to rescue several Spaniards from an earlier expedition and to explore the coastline. Later Velásquez would realize that Cortés had violated the terms of his expedition and was indeed intent on venturing into the interior of Mexico in order to colonize the new territory and become, if possible, its Spanish ruler. At the very least, Cortés sought a major share of the anticipated riches.

Cortés's letters not only provided a record of his encounter with the indigenous peoples of Mexico but also served as political instruments by which he sought to ingratiate himself with King Charles I of Spain, who in November of 1519 became Charles V of the Holy Roman Empire (r. 1519–58). Cortés's first letter was sent in July of 1519 at a time when his forces had a precarious hold over the Aztec capital city of Tenochtitlán. His second letter, parts of which are presented here, describe the initial encounter with the Aztec rulers and the living conditions in the capital. We cannot entirely trust Cortés's description of the momentous meeting between himself and Moctezuma (whom Cortés called Mutezuma) or the transcription of the conversation. The theme of Moctezuma's speech clearly refers to the legendary return of Quetzalcoatl and the feeling that the Aztecs, or Mexica, were somehow immigrants to the region and temporary rulers. Cortés's detailed descriptions of the beautiful city illustrate the rather high standard of living enjoyed by the Aztecs—at least the ruling classes—and raise the question why it was necessary to destroy the city and to eradicate the culture after the Aztecs' defeat. Shortly after Cortés, the Spanish colonists became involved in an extended debate about their treatment of indigenous peoples.

∽ Letters from Mexico

Translated by Anthony Pagden

FROM THE SECOND LETTER

On the following day I left this city and after traveling for half a league came to a causeway which runs through the middle of the lake for two leagues until it reaches the great city of Temixtitan, which is built in the middle of the lake. This causeway is as wide as two lances, and well built, so that eight horsemen can ride abreast. In the two leagues from one end to the other there are three towns, and one of them, which is called Misicalcango, is in the main built on the water, and the other two, which are called Niciaca and Huchilohuchico, are built on the shore, but many of their houses are on the water. The first of these cities has three thousand inhabitants, the second more than six thousand, and the third another four or five thousand, and in all of them there are very good houses and towers, especially the houses of the chiefs and persons of high rank, and the temples or oratories where they keep their idols.

In these cities there is much trading in salt, which they extract from the water of the lake and from the shallow area which is covered by the waters of the lake. They bake it in some way to make cakes, which are sold to the inhabitants and also beyond.

Thus I continued along this causeway, and half a league before the main body of the city of Temixtitan, at the entrance to another causeway which meets this one from the shore, there is a very strong fortification with two towers ringed by a wall four yards wide with merloned battlements all around commanding both causeways. There are only two gates, one for entering and one for leaving. Here as many as a thousand men came out to see and speak with me, important persons from that city, all dressed very richly after their own fashion. When they reached me, each one performed a ceremony which they practice among themselves; each placed his hand on the ground and kissed it. And so I stood there waiting for nearly an hour until everyone had performed his ceremony. Close to the city there is a wooden bridge ten paces wide across a breach in the causeway to allow the water to flow, as it rises and falls. The bridge is also for the defense of the city, because whenever they so wish they can remove some very long broad beams of which this bridge is made. There are many such bridges throughout the city as later Your Majesty will see in the account I give of it.

After we had crossed this bridge, Mutezuma came to greet us and with him some two hundred lords, all barefoot and dressed in a different costume, but also very rich in their way and more so than the others. They came in two columns, pressed very close to the walls of the street, which is very wide and beautiful and so straight that you can see from one end to the other. It is two-thirds of a league long and has on both sides very good and big houses, both dwellings and temples.

Mutezuma came down the middle of this street with two chiefs, one on his right hand and the other on his left. One of these was that great chief who had come on a litter to speak with me, and the other was Mutezuma's brother, chief of the city of Yztapalapa, which I had left that day. And they were all dressed alike except that Mutezuma wore sandals whereas the others went barefoot; and they held his arm on either side. When we met I dismounted and stepped forward to embrace him, but the two lords who were with him stopped me with their hands so that I should not touch him; and they likewise all performed the ceremony of kissing the earth. When this was over Mutezuma requested his brother to remain with me and to take me by the arm while he went a little way ahead with the other; and after he had spoken to me all the others in the two columns came and spoke with me, one after another, and then each returned to his column.

When at last I came to speak to Mutezuma himself I took off a necklace of pearls and cut glass that I was wearing and placed it round his neck; after we had walked a little way up the street a servant of his came with two necklaces, wrapped in a cloth, made from red snails' shells, which they hold in great esteem; and from each necklace hung eight shrimps of refined gold almost a span in length. When they had been brought he turned to me and placed them about my neck, and then continued up the street in the manner already described until we reached a very large and beautiful house which had been very well prepared to accommodate us. There he took me by the hand and led me to a great room facing the courtyard through which we entered. And he bade me sit on a very rich throne, which he had had built for him and then left saying that I should wait for him. After a short while, when all those of my company had been quartered, he returned with many and various treasures of gold and silver and featherwork, and as many as five or six thousand cotton garments, all very rich and woven and embroidered in various ways. And after he had given me these things he sat on another throne which they placed there next to the one on which I was sitting, and addressed me in the following way:

"For a long time we have known from the writings of our ancestors that neither I, nor any of those who dwell in this land, are natives of it, but foreigners who came from very distant parts; and likewise we know that a chieftain, of whom they were all vassals, brought our people to this region. And he returned to his native land and after many years came again, by which time all those who had remained were married to native women and had built villages and raised children. And when he wished to lead them away again they would not go nor even admit him as their chief; and so he departed. And we have always held that those who descended from him would come and conquer this land and take us as their vassals. So because of the place from which you claim to come, namely, from where the sun rises, and the things you tell us of the great lord or king who sent you here, we believe and are certain that he is our natural lord, especially as you say that he has known of us for some time. So be assured that we shall obey you and hold you as our lord in place of that great sovereign of whom you speak; and in this there shall be no offense or betrayal whatsoever. And in all the land that lies in my domain, you may command as you will, for you shall be obeyed; and all that we own is for you to dispose of as you choose. Thus, as you are in your own country and your own house, rest now from the hardships of your journey and the battles which you have fought, for I know full well of all that has happened to you from Puntunchan to here, and I also know how those of Cempoal and Tascalteca have told you much evil of me; believe only what you see with your eyes, for those are my enemies, and some were my vassals, and have rebelled against me at your coming and said those things to gain favor with you. I also know that they have told you the walls of my houses are made of gold, and that the floor mats in my rooms and other things in my household are likewise of gold, and that I was, and claimed to be, a god; and many other things besides. The houses as you see are of stone and lime and clay."

Then he raised his clothes and showed me his body, saying, as he grasped his arms and trunk with his hands, "See that I am of flesh and blood like you and all other men, and I am mortal and substantial. See how they have lied to you? It is true that I have some pieces of gold left to me by my ancestors; anything I might have shall be given to you whenever you ask. Now I shall go to other houses where I live, but here you shall be provided with all that you and your people require, and you shall receive no hurt, for you are in your own land and your own house."[1]

I replied to all he said as I thought most fitting, especially in making him believe that Your Majesty was he whom they were expecting; and with this he took his leave.

---

[1] **"See . . . house"**: Both this speech and the following one seem to be fabricated or enhanced by Cortés, perhaps in order to justify his later conduct.

When he had gone we were very well provided with chickens, bread, fruit and other requisites, especially for the servicing of our quarters. In this manner I spent six days, very well provisioned with all that was needed and visited by many of those chiefs. [. . .]

Thinking of all the ways and means to capture him without causing a disturbance, I remembered what the captain I had left in Vera Cruz had written to me about the events in the city of Almería, and how all that had happened there had been by order of Mutezuma. I left a careful watch on the crossroads and went to Mutezuma's houses, as I had done at other times, and after having joked and exchanged pleasantries with him and after he had given me some gold jewelry and one of his daughters and other chiefs' daughters to some of my company, I told him that I knew of what had happened in the city of Nautecal (or Almería, as we called it), and the Spaniards who had been killed there; and that Qualpopoca excused himself by saying that all had been done by Mutezuma's command, and that as his vassal he could not have done otherwise. [. . .] He immediately sent for certain of his men to whom he gave a small stone figure in the manner of a seal, which he carried fastened to his arm, and he commanded them to go to the city of Almería, which is sixty or seventy leagues from Temixtitan, and to bring Qualpopoca, and to discover who were the others who had been concerned with the death of the Spaniards and to bring them likewise. If they did not come voluntarily, they were to be brought as prisoners, and if they resisted capture, Mutezuma's messengers were to request of certain communities close to the city, which he indicated to them, to send forces to seize them, but on no account to return without them.

These left at once, and after they had gone I thanked Mutezuma for the great care which he had taken in this matter, for it was my responsibility to account to Your Highness for those Spaniards, but asked that he should stay in my quarters until the truth were known and he was shown to be blameless. I begged him not to take this ill, for he was not to be imprisoned but given all his freedom, and I would not impede the service and command of his domains, and he should choose a room in those quarters where I was, whichever he wished. There he would be very much at his ease and would certainly be given no cause for annoyance or discomfort, because as well as those of his service my own men would serve him in all he commanded. In this we spent much time reasoning and discussing, all of which is too lengthy to write down and too tedious and too little pertinent to the issue to give Your Highness an account; so I will say only that at last he said he would agree to go with me. Then he ordered the room where he wished to stay to be prepared, and it was very well prepared. When this was done many chiefs came, and removing their garments they placed them under their arms, and walking barefoot they brought a simple litter, and weeping carried him in it in great silence. Thus we proceeded to my quarters with no disturbance in the city, although there was some agitation which, as soon as Mutezuma knew of it, he ordered to cease; and all was quiet and remained so all the time I held Mutezuma prisoner, for he was very much at his ease and kept all his household — which is very great and wonderful, as I will later relate — with him as before. And I and those of my company satisfied his needs as far as was possible. [. . .]

This great city of Temixtitan[2] is built on the salt lake, and no matter by what road you travel there are two leagues from the main body of the city to the mainland. There are four artificial causeways leading to it, and each is as wide as two cavalry lances. The city itself is as big as Seville or Córdoba. The main streets are very wide and very straight; some of these are on the land, but the rest and all the smaller ones are half on land, half canals where they paddle their canoes. All the streets have openings in places so that the water may pass from one canal to another. Over all these openings, and some of them are very wide, there are bridges made of long and wide beams joined together very firmly and so well made that on some of them ten horsemen may ride abreast.

Seeing that if the inhabitants of this city wished to betray us they were very well equipped for it by the design of the city, for once the bridges had been removed they could starve us to death without our being able to reach the mainland, as soon as I entered the city I made great haste to build four brigantines, and completed them in a very short time. They were such as could carry three hundred men to the land and transport the horses whenever we might need them.

This city has many squares where trading is done and markets are held continuously. There is also one square twice as big as that of Salamanca,[3] with arcades all around, where more than sixty thousand people come each day to buy and sell, and where every kind of merchandise produced in these lands is found; provisions as well as ornaments of gold and silver, lead, brass, copper, tin, stones, shells, bones, and feathers. They also sell lime, hewn and unhewn stone, adobe bricks, tiles, and cut and uncut woods of various kinds. There is a street where they sell game and birds of every species found in this land: chickens, partridges and quails, wild ducks, flycatchers, widgeons, turtledoves, pigeons, cane birds, parrots, eagles and eagle owls, falcons, sparrow hawks and kestrels, and they sell the skins of some of these birds of prey with their feathers, heads and claws. They sell rabbits and hares, and stags and small gelded dogs which they breed for eating.

There are streets of herbalists where all the medicinal herbs and roots found in the land are sold. There are shops like apothecaries', where they sell ready-made medicines as well as liquid ointments and plasters. There are shops like barbers' where they have their hair washed and shaved, and shops where they sell food and drink. There are also men like porters to carry loads. There is much firewood and charcoal, earthenware braziers and mats of various kinds like mattresses for beds, and other, finer ones, for seats and for covering rooms and hallways. There is every sort of vegetable, especially onions, leeks, garlic, common cress and watercress, borage, sorrel, teasels and artichokes; and there are many sorts of fruit, among which are cherries and plums like those in Spain.

They sell honey, wax, and a syrup made from maize canes, which is as sweet and syrupy as that made from the sugar cane. They also make syrup from a plant which in the islands is called *maguey,* which is much better than most syrups, and from this

---

[2] **Temixtitan:** Tenochtitlán.   [3] **Salamanca:** The marketplace in Tlateloco.

plant they also make sugar and wine,[4] which they likewise sell. There are many sorts of spun cotton, in hanks of every color, and it seems like the silk market at Granada, except here there is a much greater quantity. They sell as many colors for painters as may be found in Spain and all of excellent hues. They sell deerskins, with and without the hair, and some are dyed white or in various colors. They sell much earthenware, which for the most part is very good; there are both large and small pitchers, jugs, pots, tiles, and many other sorts of vessel, all of good clay and most of them glazed and painted. They sell maize both as grain and as bread and it is better both in appearance and in taste than any found in the islands or on the mainland. They sell chicken and fish pies, and much fresh and salted fish, as well as raw and cooked fish. They sell hen and goose eggs, and eggs of all the other birds I have mentioned, in great number, and they sell *tortillas* made from eggs.

Finally, besides those things which I have already mentioned, they sell in the market everything else to be found in this land, but they are so many and so varied that because of their great number and because I cannot remember many of them nor do I know what they are called I shall not mention them. Each kind of merchandise is sold in its own street without any mixture whatever; they are very particular in this. Everything is sold by number and size, and until now I have seen nothing sold by weight. There is in this great square a very large building like a courthouse, where ten or twelve persons sit as judges. They preside over all that happens in the markets, and sentence criminals. There are in this square other persons who walk among the people to see what they are selling and the measures they are using; and they have been seen to break some that were false.

There are, in all districts of this great city, many temples or houses for their idols. They are all very beautiful buildings, and in the important ones there are priests of their sect who live there permanently; and, in addition to the houses for the idols, they also have very good lodgings. All these priests dress in black and never comb their hair from the time they enter the priesthood until they leave; and all the sons of the persons of high rank, both the lords and honored citizens also, enter the priesthood and wear the habit from the age of seven or eight years until they are taken away to be married; this occurs more among the first-born sons, who are to inherit, than among the others. They abstain from eating things, and more at some times of the year than at others; and no woman is granted entry nor permitted inside these places of worship.

Amongst these temples there is one, the principal one, whose great size and magnificence no human tongue could describe, for it is so large that within the precincts, which are surrounded by a very high wall, a town of some five hundred inhabitants could easily be built. All round inside this wall there are very elegant quarters with very large rooms and corridors where their priests live. There are as many as forty towers, all of which are so high that in the case of the largest there are

---

[4] *maguey . . . wine: Maguey* is any of several varieties of agave; the wine made from this plant is called pulque.

fifty steps leading up to the main part of it; and the most important of these towers is higher than that of the cathedral of Seville. They are so well constructed in both their stone and woodwork that there can be none better in any place, for all the stonework inside the chapels where they keep their idols is in high relief, with figures and little houses, and the woodwork is likewise of relief and painted with monsters and other figures and designs. All these towers are burial places of chiefs, and the chapels therein are each dedicated to the idol which he venerated.

There are three rooms within this great temple for the principal idols, which are of remarkable size and stature and decorated with many designs and sculptures, both in stone and in wood. Within these rooms are other chapels, and the doors to them are very small. Inside there is no light whatsoever; there only some of the priests may enter, for inside are the sculptured figures of the idols, although, as I have said, there are also many outside.

The most important of these idols, and the ones in whom they have most faith, I had taken from their places and thrown down the steps; and I had those chapels where they were cleaned, for they were full of the blood of sacrifices; and I had images of Our Lady and of other saints put there, which caused Mutezuma and the other natives some sorrow. First they asked me not to do it, for when the communities learnt of it they would rise against me, for they believed that those idols gave them all their worldly goods, and that if they were allowed to be ill treated, they would become angry and give them nothing and take the fruit from the earth leaving the people to die of hunger. I made them understand through the interpreters how deceived they were in placing their trust in those idols which they had made with their hands from unclean things. They must know that there was only one God, Lord of all things, who had created heaven and earth and all else and who made all of us; and He was without beginning or end, and they must adore and worship only Him, not any other creature or thing. And I told them all I knew about this to dissuade them from their idolatry and bring them to the knowledge of God our Saviour. All of them, especially Mutezuma, replied that they had already told me how they were not natives of this land, and that as it was many years since their forefathers had come here, they well knew that they might have erred somewhat in what they believed, for they had left their native land so long ago; and as I had only recently arrived from there, I would better know the things they should believe, and should explain to them and make them understand, for they would do as I said was best. Mutezuma and many of the chieftains of the city were with me until the idols were removed, the chapel cleaned and the images set up, and I urged them not to sacrifice living creatures to the idols, as they were accustomed, for, as well as being most abhorrent to God, Your Sacred Majesty's laws forbade it and ordered that he who kills shall be killed. And from then on they ceased to do it, and in all the time I stayed in that city I did not see a living creature killed or sacrificed.

The figures of the idols in which these people believe are very much larger than the body of a big man. They are made of dough from all the seeds and vegetables which they eat, ground and mixed together, and bound with the blood of human hearts which those priests tear out while still beating. And also after they are made they offer them more hearts and anoint their faces with the blood. Everything has an idol dedicated to it, in the same manner as the pagans who in antiquity honored their gods. So they have an idol whose favor they ask in war and another for agriculture; and likewise for each thing they wish to be done well they have an idol which they honor and serve.

∿ CODEX FLORENTINO
MEXICO, C. 1580

Because of Benardino de Sahagun, a Franciscan friar who arrived in New Spain in 1529, we have an account of the Conquest of Mexico recorded by Aztec witnesses. The *Codex Florentino* is a copy of the *General History of the Things of New Spain,* a twelve-volume compilation that de Sahagun sent to Europe around 1580. This part of the narrative tells the story of how Moctezuma II, the Aztec ruler, received Cortés and his soldiers as they entered the capital city of Tenochtitlán, and what transpired in the aftermath.

The account of the meeting between two powerful rulers from utterly disparate worlds is shocking even today. The Spaniards carried with them the Renaissance notion that individuals could make and shape history. As Christians they lived within a linear concept of time and history, guided by a God whose dominion extended over the earth and heavens; this God granted them a mandate to conquer and exploit pagan lands and their peoples who, in their view, were reduced to a subhuman state by superstition and ignorance. For the Spaniards, Tenochtitlán, glorious as it was, was a steppingstone in a larger scheme of conquest.

For Moctezuma and his followers, however, the encounter was fundamentally a religious or mythological event. Their lives were shaped by the precarious, reciprocal relationship between the human, natural, and divine worlds. Nothing — no tree or bird — was simply itself; everything vibrated within a web of sacred meaning and divine implication. As a result, there was no easy or quick way to untangle the Spaniards from the myth of Quetzalcoatl of omens and signs — plus the exotic physical appearance of the armored and plumed Spaniards — had initially intertwined them.

The lengthy description of the uncontested entry of the Spaniards into the city, their house arrest and humiliation of Moctezuma, their surprise attack on the Aztecs at the feast of Huitzilopochtli, the counterattack by the Aztecs driving the Spaniards from the city, and the return of the Spaniards and their subsequent victory are all derived from Aztec materials. There are numerous discrepancies between this composite version and the letter of Cortés to the King of Spain. One of the deepest matters touched on in the Aztec account is Moctezuma's loss of authority during the Spanish attack; he is repudiated by his own people before dying at the hands of the Spaniards. The Aztec version is also far more tragic than Cortés's account will allow, ending in the utter destruction of the city.

FROM

ꙮ The Conquest of Mexico

Translated by Angel Maria Garibay K. and Lysander Kemp

Edited by Miguel León-Portilla

[Moctezuma II, the Aztec ruler, receives omens and warnings that according to prophecy Quetzalcoatl, ancient king of the Toltecs, is returning to resume his throne. He begins to prepare for the encounter, on the strength of messages from outlying districts that the Spaniards are marching toward the city of Tenochtitlán.]

MOTECUHZOMA INSTRUCTS HIS MESSENGERS

Motecuhzoma then gave orders to Pinotl of Cuetlaxtlan and to other officials. He said to them: "Give out this order: a watch is to be kept along all the shores at Nauhtla, Tuztlan, Mictlancuauhtla,[1] wherever the strangers appear." The officials left at once and gave orders for the watch to be kept.

Motecuhzoma now called his chiefs together: Tlilpotonque, the serpent woman,[2] Cuappiatzin, the chief of the house of arrows,[3] Quetzalaztatzin, the keeper of the chalk,[4] and Hecateupatiltzin, the chief of the refugees from the south. He told them the news that had been brought to him and showed them the objects he had ordered made. He said: "We all admire these blue turquoises, and they must be guarded well. The whole treasure must be guarded well. If anything is lost, your houses will be destroyed and your children killed, even those who are still in the womb."

A note on the translation: The primary sources of *The Conquest of Mexico* are the Nahuatl and Spanish texts of Bernardino de Sahagun's *Historia General de las Cosas de Nueva Espana* (1946), edited by Miguel León-Portilla for *The Broken Spears: The Aztec Account of the Conquest of Mexico* (1992).

---

[1] **Nauhtla . . . Mictlancuauhtla:** Places along the Gulf of Mexico.

[2] **the serpent woman:** The ruler's chief counselor was traditionally given this title; the earth goddess had both masculine and feminine qualities.

[3] **arrows:** The suffix *-tzin* indicates a high rank.

[4] **chalk:** Official in charge of ceremonial colors used by the priests.

The year 13-Rabbit[5] now approached its end. And when it was about to end, they appeared, they were seen again. The report of their coming was brought to Motecuhzoma, who immediately sent out messengers. It was as if he thought the new arrival was our prince Quetzalcoatl.

This is what he felt in his heart: *He has appeared! He has come back! He will come here, to the place of his throne and canopy, for that is what he promised when he departed!*

Motecuhzoma sent five messengers to greet the strangers and to bring them gifts. They were led by the priest in charge of the sanctuary of Yohualichan. The second was from Tepoztlan; the third from Tizatlan; the fourth, from Huehuetlan; and the fifth, from Mictlan the Great.[6] He said to them: "Come forward, my Jaguar Knights, come forward. It is said that our lord has returned to this land. Go to meet him. Go to hear him. Listen well to what he tells you; listen and remember."

MOTECUHZOMA'S DESPAIR

[Moctezuma's envoys are menaced by the Spaniards and sent back home. Next Moctezuma sends magicians and wizards. They see a horrifying vision of the destruction of Tenochtitlán and report the vision back to Moctezuma.]

When the envoys arrived in the city, they told Motecuhzoma what had happened and what they had seen. Motecuhzoma listened to their report and then bowed his head without speaking a word. For a long time he remained thus, with his head bent down. And when he spoke at last, it was only to say: "What help is there now, my friends? Is there a mountain for us to climb? Should we run away? We are Mexicanos: would this bring any glory to the Mexican nation?

"Pity the old men, and the old women, and the innocent little children. How can they save themselves? But there is no help. What can we do? Is there nothing left us?

"We will be judged and punished. And however it may be, and whenever it may be, we can do nothing but wait."

MOTECUHZOMA GOES OUT TO MEET CORTÉS

The Spaniards arrived in Xoloco,[7] near the entrance to Tenochtitlán. That was the end of the march, for they had reached their goal.

Motecuhzoma now arrayed himself in his finery, preparing to go out to meet them. The other great princes also adorned their persons, as did the nobles and their chieftains and knights. They all went out together to meet the strangers.

They brought trays heaped with the finest flowers—the flower that resembles a shield; the flower shaped like a heart; in the center, the flower with the sweetest

---

[5] **year 13-Rabbit:** Years were counted by four names (Reed, Flint, House, or Rabbit) and a number from 1 to 13; thus a cycle of years would run to 52.

[6] **Yohualichan . . . Mictlan the Great:** The first four places are in the Lake Texcoco region; the fifth is Mitla in the Oaxaca region.

[7] **Xoloco:** The region on the south end of Tenochtitlan, next to the bridge, over the canal.

aroma; and the fragrant yellow flower, the most precious of all. They also brought garlands of flowers, and ornaments for the breast, and necklaces of gold, necklaces hung with rich stones, necklaces fashioned in the petatillo style.

Thus Motecuhzoma went out to meet them, there in Huitzillan.[8] He presented many gifts to the Captain and his commanders, those who had come to make war. He showered gifts upon them and hung flowers around their necks; he gave them necklaces of flowers and bands of flowers to adorn their breasts; he set garlands of flowers upon their heads. Then he hung the gold necklaces around their necks and gave them presents of every sort as gifts of welcome.

SPEECHES OF MOTECUHZOMA AND CORTÉS

When Motecuhzoma had given necklaces to each one, Cortés asked him: "Are you Motecuhzoma? Are you the king? Is it true that you are the king Motecuhzoma?"

And the king said: "Yes, I am Motecuhzoma." Then he stood up to welcome Cortés; he came forward, bowed his head low and addressed him in these words: "Our lord, you are weary. The journey has tired you, but now you have arrived on the earth. You have come to your city, Mexico. You have come here to sit on your throne, to sit under its canopy.[9]

"The kings who have gone before, your representatives, guarded it and preserved it for your coming. The kings Itzcoatl, Motecuhzoma the Elder, Axayacatl, Tizoc and Ahuitzol[10] ruled for you in the City of Mexico. The people were protected by their swords and sheltered by their shields.

"Do the kings know the destiny of those they left behind, their posterity? If only they are watching! If only they can see what I see!

"No, it is not a dream. I am not walking in my sleep. I am not seeing you in my dreams. . . . I have seen you at last! I have met you face to face! I was in agony for five days, for ten days, with my eyes fixed on the Region of the Mystery.[11] And now you have come out of the clouds and mists to sit on your throne again.

"This was foretold by the kings who governed your city, and now it has taken place. You have come back to us; you have come down from the sky. Rest now, and take possession of your royal houses. Welcome to your land, my lords!"

When Motecuhzoma had finished, La Malinche translated his address into Spanish so that the Captain could understand it. Cortés replied in his strange and savage tongue, speaking first to La Malinche: "Tell Motecuhzoma that we are his friends. There is nothing to fear. We have wanted to see him for a long time, and now we have seen his face and heard his words. Tell him that we love him well and that our hearts are contented."

---

[8] **Huitzillan:** A region of Tenochtitlán north of Xoloco.   [9] **canopy:** An extraordinary speech in which Motecuhzoma speaks to Cortés as if he were a deity returning to claim his earthly throne.   [10] **Itzcoatl . . . Ahuitzol:** Previous Aztec rulers; Itzcoatl began his rule in 1428 and Motecuhzoma II began to rule in 1502.   [11] **Region of the Mystery:** The heavens, which were divided into thirteen different heavens, the most important of which is Omeyocan, the home of Ometeotl and the source of life.

Then he said to Motecuhzoma: "We have come to your house in Mexico as friends. There is nothing to fear."

La Malinche translated this speech and the Spaniards grasped Motecuhzoma's hands and patted his back to show their affection for him.

THE SPANIARDS TAKE POSSESSION OF THE CITY

When the Spaniards entered the Royal House, they placed Motecuhzoma under guard and kept him under their vigilance. They also placed a guard over Itzcuauhtzin,[12] but the other lords were permitted to depart.

Then the Spaniards fired one of their cannons, and this caused great confusion in the city. The people scattered in every direction; they fled without rhyme or reason; they ran off as if they were being pursued. It was as if they had eaten the mushrooms that confuse the mind, or had seen some dreadful apparition. They were all overcome by terror, as if their hearts had fainted. And when night fell, the panic spread through the city and their fears would not let them sleep.

In the morning the Spaniards told Motecuhzoma what they needed in the way of supplies: tortillas, fried chickens, hens' eggs, pure water, firewood and charcoal. Also: large, clean cooking pots, water jars, pitchers, dishes and other pottery. Motecuhzoma ordered that it be sent to them. The chiefs who received this order were angry with the king and no longer revered or respected him. But they furnished the Spaniards with all the provisions they needed—food, beverages and water, and fodder for the horses.

THE SPANIARDS REVEAL THEIR GREED

When the Spaniards were installed in the palace, they asked Motecuhzoma about the city's resources and reserves and about the warriors' ensigns and shields. They questioned him closely and then demanded gold.

Motecuhzoma guided them to it. They surrounded him and crowded close with their weapons. He walked in the center, while they formed a circle around him.

When they arrived at the treasure house called Teucalco, the riches of gold and feathers were brought out to them: ornaments made of quetzal feathers, richly worked shields, disks of gold, the necklaces of the idols, gold nose plugs, gold greaves and bracelets and crowns.

The Spaniards immediately stripped the feathers from the gold shields and ensigns. They gathered all the gold into a great mound and set fire to everything else, regardless of its value. Then they melted down the gold into ingots. As for the precious green stones, they took only the best of them; the rest were snatched up by the Tlaxcaltecas. The Spaniards searched through the whole treasure house, questioning and quarreling, and seized every object they thought was beautiful.

---

[12] **Itzcuauhtzin:** Ruler of Tlatloloco.

THE SEIZURE OF MOTECUHZOMA'S TREASURES

Next they went to Motecuhzoma's storehouse, in the place called Totocalco [Place of the Palace of the Birds],[13] where his personal treasures were kept. The Spaniards grinned like little beasts and patted each other with delight.

When they entered the hall of treasures, it was as if they had arrived in Paradise. They searched everywhere and coveted everything; they were slaves to their own greed. All of Motecuhzoma's possessions were brought out: fine bracelets, necklaces with large stones, ankle rings with little gold bells, the royal crowns and all the royal finery—everything that belonged to the king and was reserved to him only. They seized these treasures as if they were their own, as if this plunder were merely a stroke of good luck. And when they had taken all the gold, they heaped up everything else in the middle of the patio.

La Malinche called the nobles together. She climbed up to the palace roof and cried: "Mexicanos, come forward! The Spaniards need your help! Bring them food and pure water. They are tired and hungry; they are almost fainting from exhaustion! Why do you not come forward? Are you angry with them?"

The Mexicans were too frightened to approach. They were crushed by terror and would not risk coming forward. They shied away as if the Spaniards were wild beasts, as if the hour were midnight on the blackest night of the year. Yet they did not abandon the Spaniards to hunger and thirst. They brought them whatever they needed, but shook with fear as they did so. They delivered the supplies to the Spaniards with trembling hands, then turned and hurried away.

THE PREPARATIONS FOR THE FIESTA

[The fiesta of Huitzilopochtli, according to Sahagun, "was the most important of their fiestas. It is like our Easter and fell at almost the same time." Cortés left Tenochtitlán twenty days before the fiesta to fight Panfilo de Narvaez who had been sent by Diego Velazques, governor of Cuba, to arrest Cortés. His deputy, Pedro de Alvarado, murdered the Aztec celebrants at the height of the fiesta.]

The Aztecs begged permission of their king to hold the fiesta of Huitzilopochtli. The Spaniards wanted to see this fiesta to learn how it was celebrated. A delegation of the celebrants came to the palace where Motecuhzoma was a prisoner, and when their spokesman asked his permission, he granted it to them.

As soon as the delegation returned, the women began to grind seeds of the chicalote.[14] These women had fasted for a whole year. They ground the seeds in the patio of the temple.

The Spaniards came out of the palace together, dressed in armor and carrying their weapons with them. They stalked among the women and looked at them one by one; they stared into the faces of the women who were grinding seeds. After this

---

[13] **Palace of the Birds:** The zoo attached to the royal palaces.

[14] **chicalote:** Prickly poppy; other texts say they used amaranth seeds.

cold inspection, they went back into the palace. It is said that they planned to kill the celebrants if the men entered the patio.

The Spaniards Attack the Celebrants

At this moment in the fiesta, when the dance was loveliest and when song was linked to song, the Spaniards were seized with an urge to kill the celebrants. They all ran forward, armed as if for battle. They closed the entrances and passageways, all the gates of the patio: the Eagle Gate in the lesser palace, the Gate of the Canestalk and the Gate of the Serpent of Mirrors. They posted guards so that no one could escape, and then rushed into the Sacred Patio to slaughter the celebrants. They came on foot, carrying their swords and their wooden or metal shields.

They ran in among the dancers, forcing their way to the place where the drums were played. They attacked the man who was drumming and cut off his arms. Then they cut off his head, and it rolled across the floor.

They attacked all the celebrants, stabbing them, spearing them, striking them with their swords. They attacked some of them from behind, and these fell instantly to the ground with their entrails hanging out. Others they beheaded: they cut off their heads, or split their heads to pieces.

They struck others in the shoulders, and their arms were torn from their bodies. They wounded some in the thigh and some in the calf. They slashed others in the abdomen, and their entrails all spilled to the ground. Some attempted to run away, but their intestines dragged as they ran; they seemed to tangle their feet in their own entrails. No matter how they tried to save themselves, they could find no escape.

Some attempted to force their way out, but the Spaniards murdered them at the gates. Others climbed the walls, but they could not save themselves. Those who ran into the communal houses were safe there for a while; so were those who lay down among the victims and pretended to be dead. But if they stood up again, the Spaniards saw them and killed them.

The blood of the warriors flowed like water and gathered into pools. The pools widened, and the stench of blood and entrails filled the air. The Spaniards ran into the communal houses to kill those who were hiding. They ran everywhere and searched everywhere; they invaded every room, hunting and killing.

The Aztecs Retaliate

When the news of this massacre was heard outside the Sacred Patio, a great cry went up: "Mexicanos, come running! Bring your spears and shields! The strangers have murdered our warriors!"

This cry was answered with a roar of grief and anger: the people shouted and wailed and beat their palms against their mouths. The captains assembled at once, as if the hour had been determined in advance. They all carried their spears and shields.

Then the battle began. The Aztecs attacked with javelins and arrows, even with the light spears that are used for hunting birds. They hurled their javelins with all their strength, and the cloud of missiles spread out over the Spaniards like a yellow cloak.

The Spaniards immediately took refuge in the palace. They began to shoot at the Mexicans with their iron arrows and to fire their cannons and arquebuses. And they shackled Motecuhzoma in chains.

MOTECUHZOMA'S MESSAGE

At sunset, Itzcuauhtzin climbed onto the roof of the palace and shouted this proclamation: "Mexicanos! Tlatelolcas! Your king, the lord Motecuhzoma, has sent me to speak for him. Mexicanos, hear me, for these are his words to you: 'We must not fight them. We are not their equals in battle. Put down your shields and arrows.'

"He tells you this because it is the aged who will suffer most, and they deserve your pity. The humblest classes will also suffer, and so will the innocent children who still crawl on all fours, who still sleep in their cradles.

"Therefore your king says: 'We are not strong enough to defeat them. Stop fighting, and return to your homes.' Mexicanos, they have put your king in chains; his feet are bound with chains."

When Itzcuauhtzin had finished speaking, there was a great uproar among the people. They shouted insults at him in their fury, and cried: "Who is Motecuhzoma to give us orders? We are no longer his slaves!" They shouted war cries and fired arrows at the rooftop. The Spaniards quickly hid Motecuhzoma and Itzcuauhtzin behind their shields so that the arrows would not find them.

The Mexicans were enraged because the attack on the captains had been so treacherous: their warriors had been killed without the slightest warning. Now they refused to go away or to put down their arms.

THE SPANIARDS ARE BESIEGED

The royal palace was placed under siege. The Mexicans kept a close watch to prevent anyone from stealing in with food for the Spaniards. They also stopped delivering supplies: they brought them absolutely nothing, and waited for them to die of hunger.

After they had trapped the Spaniards in the palace, the Mexicans kept them under attack for seven days, and for twenty-three days they foiled all their attempts to break out. During this time all the causeways were closed off. The Mexicans tore up the bridges, opened great gaps in the pavement and built a whole series of barricades; they did everything they could to make the causeways impassable. They also closed off the roads by building walls and roadblocks; they obstructed all the roads and streets of the city.

THE SPANIARDS ABANDON THE CITY

[Cortés returned to Tenochtitlán to defend against the Aztecs. Both Motecuhzoma and Itzcuauhtzin were killed, but the details of their deaths are unknown. The massacre of the escaping Spaniards has come to be known as "La Noche Triste," the Night of Sorrows.]

At midnight the Spaniards and Tlaxcaltecas came out in closed ranks, the Spaniards going first and the Tlaxcaltecas following. The allies kept very close behind, as if they were crowding up against a wall. The sky was overcast and rain fell all night in the darkness, but it was gentle rain, more like drizzle or a heavy dew.

The Spaniards carried portable wooden bridges to cross the canals. They set them in place, crossed over and raised them again. They were able to pass the first three canals—the Tecpantzinco, the Tzapotlan, and the Atenchicalco—without being seen. But when they reached the fourth, the Mixcoatechialtitlan, their retreat was discovered.

THE MASSACRE AT THE CANAL OF THE TOLTECS

When the Spaniards reached the Canal of the Toltecs, in Tlaltecayohuacan, they hurled themselves headlong into the water, as if they were leaping from a cliff. The Tlaxcaltecas, the allies from Tliliuhquitepec, the Spanish foot soldiers and horsemen, the few women who accompanied the army—all came to the brink and plunged over it.

The canal was soon choked with the bodies of men and horses; they filled the gap in the causeway with their own drowned bodies. Those who followed crossed to the other side by walking on the corpses.

When they reached Petlalco, where there was another canal, they crossed over on their portable bridge without being attacked by the Aztecs. They stopped and rested there for a short while, and began to feel more like men again. Then they marched on to Popotla.

Dawn was breaking as they entered the village. Their hearts were cheered by the brightening light of this new day: they thought the horrors of the retreat by night were all behind them. But suddenly they heard war cries and the Aztecs swarmed through the streets and surrounded them. They had come to capture Tlaxcaltecas for their sacrifices. They also wanted to complete their revenge against the Spaniards.

The Aztecs harried the army all the way to Tlacopan. Chimalpopoca, the son of Motecuhzoma, was killed in the action at Tlilyuhcan by an arrow from the crossbows. Tlaltecatzin, the Tepanec prince, was wounded in the same action and died shortly after. He had served the Spaniards as a guide and advisor, pointing out the best roads and short cuts.

TENOCHTITLÁN AFTER THE DEPARTURE OF CORTÉS

When the Spaniards left Tenochtitlán, the Aztecs thought they had departed for good and would never return. Therefore they repaired and decorated the temple of their god, sweeping it clean and throwing out all the dirt and wreckage.

Then the eighth month arrived, and the Aztecs celebrated it as always.[15] They adorned the impersonators of the gods, all those who played the part of gods in the

---

[15] **the eighth month . . . always:** The eighth month corresponds to June 22–July 11, and the fiesta celebrated Huixtocihuatl, goddess of salt.

ceremonies, decking them with necklaces and turquoise masks and dressing them in the sacred clothing. This clothing was made of quetzal feathers, eagle feathers and yellow parrot feathers. The finery of the gods was in the care of the great princes.

The Plague Ravages the City

While the Spaniards were in Tlaxcala, a great plague[16] broke out here in Tenochtitlán. It began to spread during the thirteenth month and lasted for seventy days, striking everywhere in the city and killing a vast number of our people. Sores erupted on our faces, our breasts, our bellies; we were covered with agonizing sores from head to foot.

The illness was so dreadful that no one could walk or move. The sick were so utterly helpless that they could only lie on their beds like corpses, unable to move their limbs or even their heads. They could not lie face down or roll from one side to the other. If they did move their bodies, they screamed with pain.

A great many died from this plague, and many others died of hunger. They could not get up to search for food, and everyone else was too sick to care for them, so they starved to death in their beds.

Some people came down with a milder form of the disease; they suffered less than the others and made a good recovery. But they could not escape entirely. Their looks were ravaged, for wherever a sore broke out, it gouged an ugly pockmark in the skin. And a few of the survivors were left completely blind.

The Spaniards Launch Their Brigantines

The Spaniards now decided to attack Tenochtitlán and destroy its people. The cannons were mounted in the ships, the sails were raised and the fleet moved out onto the lake. The flagship led the way, flying a great linen standard with Cortés's coat of arms. The soldiers beat their drums and blew their trumpets; they played their flutes and chirimias[17] and whistles.

When the ships approached the Zoquiapan quarter,[18] the common people were terrified at the sight. They gathered their children into the canoes and fled helter-skelter across the lake, moaning with fear and paddling as swiftly as they could. They left all their possessions behind them and abandoned their little farms without looking back.

Our enemies seized all our possessions. They gathered up everything they could find and loaded it into the ships in great bundles. They stole our cloaks and blankets, our battle dress, our tabors and drums, and carried them all away. The Tlatelolcas followed and attacked the Spaniards from their boats but could not save any of the plunder.

---

[16] **plague:** Starting in Veracruz, smallpox ravaged the Mexican population, killing hundreds of thousands of people, perhaps millions. Motecuhzoma's successor Cuitlahua died from smallpox.

[17] **chirimias:** Similar to shepherd's pipes.

[18] **Zoquiapan quarter:** Southwestern Tenochtitlán.

When the Spaniards reached Xoloco, near the entrance to Tenochtitlán, they found that the Indians had built a wall across the road to block their progress. They destroyed it with four shots from the largest cannon. The first shot did little harm, but the second split it and the third opened a great hole. With the fourth shot, the wall lay in ruins on the ground.

Two of the brigantines, both with cannons mounted in their bows, attacked a flotilla of our shielded canoes. The cannons were fired into the thick of the flotilla, wherever the canoes were crowded closest together. Many of our warriors were killed outright; others drowned because they were too crippled by their wounds to swim away. The water was red with the blood of the dead and dying. Those who were hit by the steel arrows were also doomed; they died instantly and sank to the bottom of the lake.

The Sufferings of the Inhabitants

The Spanish blockade caused great anguish in the city. The people were tormented by hunger, and many starved to death. There was no fresh water to drink, only stagnant water and the brine of the lake, and many people died of dysentery.

The only food was lizards, swallows, corncobs and the salt grasses of the lake. The people also ate water lilies and the seeds of the colorin, and chewed on deerhides and pieces of leather. They roasted and seared and scorched whatever they could find and then ate it. They ate the bitterest weeds and even dirt.

Nothing can compare with the horrors of that siege and the agonies of the starving. We were so weakened by hunger that, little by little, the enemy forced us to retreat. Little by little they forced us to the wall.

The Battle in the Market Place

On one occasion, four Spanish cavalrymen entered the market place. They rode through it in a great circle, stabbing and killing many of our warriors and trampling everything under their horses' hooves. This was the first time the Spaniards had entered the market place, and our warriors were taken by surprise. But when the horsemen withdrew, the warriors recovered their wits and ran in pursuit.

It was at this same time that the Spaniards set fire to the temple and burned it to the ground. The flames and smoke leaped high into the air with a terrible roar. The people wept when they saw their temple on fire; they wept and cried out, fearing that afterward it would be plundered.

The battle lasted for many hours and extended to almost every corner of the market place. There was no action along the wall where the vendors sold lime, but the fighting raged among the flower stalls, and the stalls offering snails, and all the passageways between them.

Some of our warriors stationed themselves on the rooftops of the Quecholan district, which is near the entrance to the market place, and from there they hurled stones and fired arrows at the enemy. Others broke holes in the rear walls of all the houses of Quecholan, holes just big enough for a man's body to pass through. When the cavalry attacked and were about to spear our warriors, or trample them, or cut off their retreat, they slipped through the holes and the mounted men could not follow.

THE FINAL OMEN

At nightfall it began to rain, but it was more like a heavy dew than a rain. Suddenly the omen appeared, blazing like a great bonfire in the sky. It wheeled in enormous spirals like a whirlwind and gave off a shower of sparks and red-hot coals, some great and some little. It also made loud noises, rumbling and hissing like a metal tube placed over a fire. It circled the wall nearest the lakeshore and then hovered for a while above Coyonacazco. From there it moved out into the middle of the lake, where it suddenly disappeared. No one cried out when this omen came into view: the people knew what it meant and they watched it in silence.

Nothing whatever occurred on the following day. Our warriors and the Spanish soldiers merely waited in their positions. Cortés kept a constant watch, standing under a many-colored canopy on the roof of the lord Aztautzin's house, which is near Amaxac. His officers stood around him, talking among themselves.

CUAUHTEMOC'S SURRENDER

The Aztec leaders gathered in Tolmayecan to discuss what they should do. Cuauhtemoc and the other nobles tried to determine how much tribute they would have to pay and how best to surrender to the strangers. Then the nobles put Cuauhtemoc into a war canoe, with only three men to accompany him: a captain named Teputztitloloc, a servant named Iaztachimal and a boatman named Cenyautl. When the people saw their chief departing, they wept and cried out: "Our youngest prince is leaving us! He is going to surrender to the Spaniards! He is going to surrender to the 'gods'!"

The Spaniards came out to meet him. They took him by the hand, led him up to the rooftop and brought him into the presence of Cortés. The Captain stared at him for a moment and then patted him on the head. Then he gestured toward a chair and the two leaders sat down side by side.

The Spaniards began to shoot off their cannons, but they were not trying to hit anyone. They merely loaded and fired, and the cannonballs flew over the Indians' heads. Later they put one of the cannons into a boat and took it to the house of Coyohuehuetzin, where they hoisted it to the rooftop.

THE FLIGHT FROM THE CITY

Once again the Spaniards started killing and a great many Indians died. The flight from the city began and with this the war came to an end. The people cried: "We have suffered enough! Let us leave the city! Let us go live on weeds!" Some fled across the lake, others along the causeways, and even then there were many killings. The Spaniards were angry because our warriors still carried their shields and *macanas*.[19]

Those who lived in the center of the city went straight toward Amaxac, to the fork in the road. From there they fled in various directions, some toward Tepeyacac, others toward Xoxohuiltitlan and Nonohualco; but no one went toward Xoloco or Mazatzintamalco. Those who lived in boats or on the wooden rafts anchored in the lake fled by water, as did the inhabitants of Tolmayecan. Some of them waded in water up to their chests and even up to their necks. Others drowned when they reached water above their heads.

The grownups carried their young children on their shoulders. Many of the children were weeping with terror, but a few of them laughed and smiled, thinking it was great sport to be carried like that along the road.

Some of the people who owned canoes departed in the daytime, but the others, the majority, left by night. They almost crashed into each other in their haste as they paddled away from the city.

THE SPANIARDS HUMILIATE THE REFUGEES

The Spanish soldiers were stationed along the roads to search the fleeing inhabitants. They were looking only for gold and paid no attention to jade, turquoise or quetzal feathers. The women carried their gold under their skirts and the men carried it in their mouths or under their loincloths. Some of the women, knowing they would be searched if they looked prosperous, covered their faces with mud and dressed themselves in rags. They put on rags for skirts and rags for blouses; everything they wore was in tatters. But the Spaniards searched all the women without exception: those with light skins, those with dark skins, those with dark bodies.

A few of the men were separated from the others. These men were the bravest and strongest warriors, the warriors with manly hearts. The youths who served them were also told to stand apart. The Spaniards immediately branded them with hot irons, either on the cheek or the lips.

The day on which we laid down our shields and admitted defeat was the day 1-Serpent in the year 3-House. [. . .][20]

---

[19] *macanas:* Flattened clubs.

[20] **3-House:** August 13, 1521.

GLOSSARY OF LITERARY AND CRITICAL TERMS

Accent The emphasis given to a syllable or word, especially in poetry, that stresses a particular word in a line and may be used to define a poetic foot.

Acropolis The most fortified part of a Greek city, located on a hill; the most famous acropolis is in Athens, the site of the Parthenon.

Act A major division in the action of a play. In many full-length plays, acts are further divided into SCENES, which often mark a point in the action when the location changes or when a new character enters.

Adab An Islamic literary genre distinguished by its humanistic concerns on a variety of subjects that highlights the sensibilities and interests of authors and flourished throughout the tenth and eleventh centuries.

Aeneas The hero of Virgil's *Aeneid*, the Trojan Aeneas wanders for years after the Greek destruction of Troy before reaching the shores of Italy, where his descendants would later found the city of Rome.

Age of Pericles The golden age of Athens in the fifth century B.C.E. when Pericles (c. 495–429 B.C.E.) was the head of the Athenian government. During this period, Athenian democracy was at its apex; the Parthenon was constructed and drama and music flourished.

Ahimsa The Buddhist belief that all life is one and sacred, resulting in the principle of nonviolence toward all living things.

Allegory A narrative in which the characters, settings, and episodes stand for something else. Traditionally, most allegories come in the form of stories that correlate to spiritual concepts; examples of these can be found in Dante's *Divine Comedy* (1321). Some later allegories allude to political, historical, and sociological ideas.

Alliteration The repetition of the same consonant sound or sounds in a sequence of words, usually at the beginning of a word or stressed syllable: "*d*escending *d*ew *d*rops"; "*l*uscious *l*emons." Alliteration derives from the sounds, not the spelling of words; for example, "*k*een" and "*c*ar" alliterate, but "*c*ar" and "*c*ite" do not. Used sparingly, alliteration can intensify ideas by emphasizing key words.

Allusion A brief reference, sometimes direct, sometimes indirect, to a person, place, thing, event, or idea in history or literature. Such references could be to a scene in one of Shakespeare's plays, a historic figure, a war, a great love story, a biblical authority, or anything else that might enrich an author's work. Allusions, which function as a kind of shorthand, imply that the writer and the reader share similar knowledge.

Ambiguity Allows for two or more simultaneous interpretations of a word, phrase, action, or situation, all of whose meanings are supported by the work. Deliberate ambiguity can contribute to the effectiveness and richness of a piece of writing; unintentional ambiguity obscures meaning and may confuse readers.

Anagnorisis The discovery or recognition that takes place in a tragedy, resulting in the protagonist's PERIPETEIA, or reversal of fortune.

Anagram A word or phrase made up of the same letters as another word or phrase; *heart* is an anagram of *earth*. Often considered merely an exercise of one's ingenuity, anagrams are sometimes used by writers to conceal proper names, veil messages, or suggest an important connection between words, such as that between *hated* and *death*.

Antagonist The character, force, or collection of forces in fiction or drama that opposes the PROTAGONIST and gives rise to the conflict in the story; an opponent of the protagonist, such as Caliban in Shakespeare's play *The Tempest*.

Anthropocentric Human-centered. A point of view that considers everything in the world or universe in terms of its relation to or value for human beings.

Apostrophe A statement or address made to an implied interlocutor, sometimes a nonhuman figure, or PERSONIFICATION. Apostrophes often provide a speaker with the opportunity to reveal his or her thoughts.

Archetype A universal symbol that evokes deep and sometimes unconscious responses in a reader. In literature, characters, images, and themes that symbolize universal meanings and basic human experiences are considered archetypes. Common literary archetypes include quests, initiations, scapegoats, descents to the underworld, and ascents to heaven.

Archon The chief ruler of Athens during the classical era.

Aryans A people who settled in Iran (Persia) and northern India in prehistoric times. Gradually, they spread through India in the first millennium B.C.E., extending their influence to southern India in the first three centuries C.E. Through their early writings in the Sanskrit language, the VEDAS, they established the basis of Hinduism and Indian culture.

Aside In drama, a speech directed to the audience that supposedly is not audible to the other characters onstage.

Assonance The repetition of vowel sounds in nearby words, as in "asl*ee*p under a tr*ee*" or "*ea*ch *e*vening." When words also share similar endings, as in "asl*eep* in the d*eep*," RHYME occurs. Assonance is an effective means of emphasizing important words.

Autobiography A narrative form of biography in which an author accounts for his or her own life and character to a public audience. As a literary genre, autobiography developed differently in several cultures: the *Confessions* of St. Augustine, written in Latin in the fifth century, served as a model in Europe; Ibn Ishaq's biography of Muhammad, written in Arabic in the eighth century, served as the model for both biographies and autobiographies by later Arabic writers.

Ballad A narrative verse form originally meant to be sung; it generally tells a dramatic tale or a simple story. Ballads are associated with the oral traditions or folklore of common people. The folk ballad stanza usually consists of four lines of alternating tetrameter (four accented syllables) and trimeter (three accented syllables) and follows a rhyme scheme of *abab* or *abcb*.

Ballad stanza A four-line stanza, known as a QUATRAIN, consisting of alternating eight- and six-syllable lines. Usually, only the second and fourth lines rhyme (an *abcb* pattern). Samuel Taylor Coleridge adapted the ballad stanza in *The Rime of the Ancient Mariner* (1798).

Bhakti From the Sanskrit for *devotion*, refers to the popular mystical movement stemming from Hinduism. In contrast to forms of Hinduism that stress knowledge, ritual, and good works, Bhakti cults emphasize that personal salvation may be achieved through the loving devotion and ecstatic surrender of an individual to a chosen deity, such as Shiva, Vishnu, and their consorts, often worshiped as a child, parent, beloved, or master.

Bible A collection of writings sacred to Christianity made up of the Hebrew Scriptures (also known as the Old Testament), containing the history, teachings, and literature of the ancient Hebrews and Jews, and the New Testament, the history, teachings, and literature associated with Jesus of Nazareth and his followers.

Biography A nonfiction literary genre that provides the history of an individual's life, detailing not only the facts of that life but also insights into the individual's personality and character. Biography is distinguished from autobiography in that it is written by someone other than the person who is the subject of the work. Biography became popular as a form beginning in the Renaissance.

Black Death A devastating disease that swept through Europe in the fourteenth century, leaving a trail of death in its wake.

Blank verse Unrhymed IAMBIC PENTAMETER. Blank verse is often considered the form closest to the natural rhythms of English speech and is therefore the most common pattern found in traditional English narrative and dramatic poetry, from Shakespeare to the writers of the early twentieth century.

Blazon A catalog of similes or metaphors drawn from nature wherein the fair parts of the lover's body are compared to what eventually came to be a stock set of images drawn from nature, seen in the Song of Songs, and earlier love poems. Shakespeare's "My mistress's eyes are nothing like the sun" parodies this convention.

Bodhisattva In Buddhism, a person who temporarily puts off nirvana in order to assist others on earth; one who has achieved great moral and spiritual enlightenment and is en route to becoming a Buddha.

Brahman In the UPANISHADS—sacred Hindu texts—Brahman is the ultimate reality, the single unifying essence of the universe that transcends all names and descriptions. A Brahman, or Brahmin, is also a Hindu priest and thus of the highest caste in the traditional Hindu caste system.

Brahmanic period The period in ancient India (c. 1000–600 B.C.E.), in which VEDIC society was dominated by the Brahmins and every aspect of Aryan life was under the control of religious rituals. Both heroic epics of Indian culture, the *Mahabharata* and the *Ramayana*, were originally formulated and told in this period, though transcribed to written form much later, between 400 B.C.E. and 400 C.E.

Brahmin The priestly caste, the highest in the traditional Hindu caste system; a Hindu priest. Also spelled BRAHMAN.

Buddhism A religion founded in India in the sixth century B.C.E. by Siddhartha Gautama, the Buddha. While Buddhism has taken different forms in the many areas of the world to which it has spread, its central tenet is that life is suffering caused by desire. In order to obtain salvation, or nirvana, one must transcend desire through following an eightfold path that includes the practice of right action and right mindfulness.

Cacophony In literature, language that is discordant and difficult to pronounce. Cacophony (from the Greek for "bad sound") may be unintentional, or it may be used for deliberate dramatic effect; also refers to the combination of loud, jarring sounds.

Caesura A pause within a line of poetry that contributes to the line's RHYTHM. A caesura can occur anywhere within a line and need not be indicated by punctuation. In scansion, caesuras are indicated by two vertical lines.

Caliph The chief civil and religious leader of a Muslim state, as a successor of Muhammad.

Caliphate Both the reign or term of a caliph as well as the area over which he rules.

Calvinists A Protestant denomination whose adherents follow the beliefs originally outlined by French Protestant reformer, John Calvin (1509–1564), especially predestination and salvation of the elect through God's grace alone.

Canon The works generally considered by scholars, critics, and teachers to be the most important to read and study and that collectively constitute the masterpieces of literature. Since the 1960s, the traditional English and American literary canons, consisting mostly of works by white male writers, have been expanding to include many female writers and writers of varying ethnic backgrounds. At the same time the world literature canon, as constructed in the West, has been broadened to include many works from non-Western literatures, especially those of Asia and Africa.

Canzoniere Medieval Italian lyric poetry. Masters of the form included Petrarch, Dante, Tasso, and Cavalcanti.

Caste The hereditary class to which a member of Hindu society belongs; stemming from the teachings of the VEDAS, Hindu society observes a strict hierarchy with the Brahmins, or priests, at the top; followed by the KSHA-TRIYAS, or warriors and rulers; and the *Vaisyas*, or farmers, merchants, and artisans; and a fourth class, added later than the others, the *Shudras*, servants. Only members of the first three "twice-born" castes could study the VEDAS and take part in religious rituals. Outside of this system were the outcastes, known as Untouchables.

Catechumen In the early Christian church, an individual officially recognized as a Christian and admitted to religious instruction required for full membership in the church.

Catharsis Meaning "purgation," or the release of the emotions of pity and fear by the audience at the end of a tragedy. In *Poetics,* Aristotle discusses the importance of catharsis. The audience faces the misfortunes of the PROTAGONIST, which elicit pity and compassion. Simultaneously, the audience confronts the protagonist's failure, thus receiving a frightening reminder of human limitations and frailties.

Character, characterization A character is a person presented in a dramatic or narrative work; characterization is the process by which a writer presents a character to the reader.

Chin-Shi Examinations First begun in the Sui dynasty in China (581–618 C.E.) under Yang Jian and formalized during the Tang era, the system of chin-shi examinations brought bright and talented men from all over China into the government bureaucracy.

Chivalric romances Idealized stories from the medieval period that espoused the values of a sophisticated courtly society. These tales centered around the lives of knights who were faithful to God, king, and country and willing to sacrifice themselves for these causes and for the love and protection of women. Chivalric romances were highly moral and fanciful, often pitting knights against dark or supernatural forces.

Choka A Japanese form of an ode associated with Kakinomoto Hitomaro (late seventh century); a long poem often inspired by public occasions but also full of personal sentiment.

Chorus In Greek tragedies, a group of people who serve mainly as commentators on the play's characters and events, adding to the audience's understanding of a play by expressing traditional moral, religious, and social attitudes. Choruses are occasionally used by modern playwrights.

Christianity A world religion founded in Palestine in the first millennium C.E. upon the teachings of Jesus Christ, whose followers believe he is the Messiah prophesied in the Hebrew Scriptures (Old Testament). The central teachings of Christianity are that Jesus of Nazareth was the son of God, that his crucifixion and resurrection from the dead provide atonement for the sins of humanity, and that through faith in Jesus individuals might attain eternal life. Christianity has played a central role in the history of Europe and the Americas.

Chthonic From the Greek *chthonios,* meaning "in the earth," *chthonic* refers to the underworld spirits and deities in ancient religion and mythology.

Cliché An idea or expression that has become tired and trite from overuse.

Colloquial Informal diction that reflects casual, conversational language and often includes slang expressions.

Comedy A work intended to interest, involve, and amuse readers or an audience, in which no terrible disaster occurs and which ends happily for the main characters.

Comic relief A humorous scene or incident that alleviates tension in an otherwise serious work. Often these moments enhance the thematic significance of a story in addition to providing humor.

Comitatus Arrangement whereby young warriors attached themselves to the leader of a group and defended him in return for his economic and legal protection. Also, the bond among warriors attached to such a leader.

Conceit A figure of speech elaborating a surprising parallel between two dissimilar things. It was a favorite poetic device of the Petrarchan sonneteers and the English metaphysical poets of the seventeenth century.

Conflict In a literary work, the struggle between opposing forces. The PROTAGONIST is engaged in a conflict with the antagonist.

Confucianism A religious philosophy that has influenced Chinese and East Asian spirituality and culture for more than two thousand years. Based on the writings of Confucius (Kongfuzi; 551–479 B.C.E.), Confucianism asserts that humans can improve and even perfect themselves through education and moral reform. In its various manifestations, Confucianism has affected the social and political evolution of China and East Asia while providing a spiritual and moral template.

Connotation Implications going beyond the literal meaning of a word that derive from how the word has been commonly used and from ideas or things associated with it. For example, the word *eagle* in the United States connotes ideas of liberty and freedom that have little to do with the term's literal meaning.

Consonance A common type of near-rhyme or half rhyme created when identical consonant sounds are preceded by different vowel sounds: *home, same; worth, breath.*

Convention A characteristic of a literary genre that is understood and accepted by readers and audiences because it has become familiar. For example, the division of a play into acts and scenes is a dramatic convention, as are SOLILOQUIES and ASIDES.

Cosmogony An explanation for the origins of the universe and how the functioning of the heavens is related to the religious, political, and social organization of life on earth. The primary function of creation myths, such as the Hebrew Book of Genesis and the Mesopotamian *Epic of Creation,* is to depict a cosmogonic model of the universe.

Cosmology The metaphysical study of the origin and nature of the universe.

Cosmopolis A large city inhabited by people from many different countries.

Counter-Reformation The period of Catholic revival and reform from the beginning of the pontificate of Pope Pius IV in 1560 to the end of the Thirty Years' War in 1648 in response to the Protestant Reformation. Spearheaded in great part by members of the Society of Jesus (the Jesuits), it was a period in which the Roman Catholic church reaffirmed the veneration of saints and the authority of the pope and initiated many institutional reforms.

Couplet A two-line stanza.

Creation myth A symbolic narrative of the beginning of the world as configured by a particular society or culture. Examples of creation myths range from the Mesopotamian classic *Epic of Creation* to the Book of Genesis in Hebrew Scriptures to the creation myths of the Ancient Mexicans of the Americas.

Crisis The moment in a work of drama or fiction in which the elements of the conflict reach the point of maximum tension. The crisis is not necessarily the emotional crescendo, or climax.

Cultural criticism An approach to literature that focuses on the historical, social, political, and economic contexts of a work. Cultural critics use widely eclectic strategies, such as anthropology, NEW HISTORICISM, psychology, gender studies, and DECONSTRUCTION, to analyze not only literary texts but everything from radio talk shows to comic strips, calendar art, advertising, travel guides, and baseball cards.

Cuneiform The wedge-shaped writing characters that stood for syllables or sounds and not letters in ancient Akkadian, Assyrian, Persian, and Babylonian inscriptions.

Daoism (Taoism) A religion/philosophy based on the Dao De Jing (Tao Te Ching) of Laozi (Lao Tzu) that emphasizes individual freedom, spontaneity, mystical experience, and self-transformation, and is the antithesis of CONFUCIANISM. In pursuit of the dao, or the Way — the eternal creative reality that is the essence of all things — practitioners embrace simplicity and reject learned wisdom. The Daoist tradition has flourished in China and East Asia for more than two thousand years.

Deconstructionism An approach to literature that suggests that literary works do not yield single, fixed meanings because language can never say exactly what one intends it to mean. Deconstructionism seeks to destabilize meaning by examining the gaps in and ambiguities of a text's language. Deconstructionists pay close attention to language in order to discover and describe how a variety of close readings of any given work can be generated.

Denouement French term meaning "unraveling" or "unknotting" used to describe the resolution of a PLOT following the action's climax.

Deus ex machina Latin for "god from the machine," a phrase originally applied to Greek plays, especially those by Euripides, in which resolution of the conflict was achieved by the intervention of a god who was lowered onto the stage mechanically. In its broader use, the phrase is applied to any plot that is resolved by an improbable or fortuitous device from outside the action.

Dharma Cosmic order or law in the Hindu tradition that includes the natural and moral laws that apply to all beings and things.

Dialect A type of informal diction. Dialects are spoken by definable groups of people from a particular geographic region, economic group, or social class. Writers use dialect to express and contrast the education, class, and social and regional backgrounds of their characters.

Dialogue Verbal exchange between CHARACTERS. Dialogue reveals firsthand characters' thoughts, responses, and emotional states.

Diaspora From the Greek for "dispersion," this term was initially applied to the Jews exiled to Babylonia after the destruction of the Temple of Jerusalem in 586 B.C.E. and again forced into exile after the Romans defeated Jerusalem in 70 C.E. The term now refers to other peoples who have been forced from their homelands, such as the Africans uprooted by the slave trade.

Diction A writer's choice of words, phrases, sentence structure, and figurative language, which combine to help create meaning.

Didactic Literature intended to teach or convey instruction, especially of a moral, ethical, or religious nature, such as a didactic essay or poem.

Digressions In epics such as *Beowulf,* these are narratives imbedded in the story to illustrate a point. Digressions frequently remind the audience of events occurring either before or after those treated in the story.

Dionysiac festival In Athens, plays were performed during two major festivals in honor of the god Dionysus: the Lenaea during January and February, and the Great Dionysia in March and April.

Dionysus The god of wine in Greek mythology whose cult originated in Thrace and Phrygia, north and east of the Greek peninsula. Dionysus was often blamed for people's irrational behavior and for chaotic situations. However, many Greeks also believed that Dionysus taught them good farming skills, especially those related to wine production.

Greek tragedy evolved from a ceremony that honored Dionysus, and the theater in Athens was dedicated to him.

Dithyramb Originally a highly passionate, lyrical hymn sung during the rites of Dionysius in Greece, dithyramb now refers to any impassioned sequence of verse or prose, often characterized by irregular or unrestrained rhythms and extravagant imagery.

Divine Comedy Dante Alighieri's fourteenth-century narrative poem that deals with the poet's imaginary journey through hell, purgatory, and paradise.

Drama Derived from the Greek word *dram,* meaning "to do" or "to perform," *drama* may refer to a single play, a group of plays, or to plays in general. Drama is designed to be performed in a theater: Actors take on the roles of CHARACTERS, perform indicated actions, and deliver the script's DIALOGUE.

Dramatic monologue A type of lyric or narrative poem in which a speaker addresses an imagined and distinct audience in such a way as to reveal a dramatic situation and, often unintentionally, some aspect of his or her temperament or personality.

Dravidians A group of dark-skinned peoples of India who were either ancient occupants of the southern peninsula, refugees of earlier tribes pushed down from the north, or late arrivals to India from the Mediterranean seacoast.

Elegiac couplets The conventional strophic form of Latin elegiac love poetry, consisting of one dactylic hexameter line followed by one dactylic pentameter line. A dactylic hexameter line is composed of six feet, each foot comprising one long, or accented, and two short, or unaccented, syllables; the sixth foot may be shortened by one or two syllables; a pentameter line consists of five such feet. The elegiac couplet is also known as a "distich."

Elegy A mournful, contemplative lyric poem often ending in consolation, written to commemorate someone who has died. *Elegy* may also refer to a serious, meditative poem that expresses a speaker's melancholy thoughts.

Elizabethan Of or characteristic of the time when Elizabeth I (1558–1603) was the queen of England. This era was perhaps the most splendid literary period in the history of English literature in that it encompassed the works of Sidney, Spenser, Marlowe, and Shakespeare, among many others, and saw the flourishing of such genres as poetry, especially the SONNET, and was a golden age of drama of all forms.

Elysian Fields In Greek mythology, some fortunate mortals spend their afterlife in the bliss of these Islands of the Blest, rather than in Hades, the underworld.

End-stopped line A line in a poem after which a pause occurs. End-stopped lines reflect normal speech patterns and are often marked by punctuation.

Enjambment In poetry, a line continuing without a pause into the next line for its meaning; also called a run-on line.

Epic A long narrative poem told in a formal, elevated style that focuses on a serious subject and chronicles heroic deeds and events important to a culture or nation. It usually includes a supernatural dimension, like the gods in Homer. Most epics follow established conventions, such as beginning *in medias res* (in the middle of things); employing elaborate comparisons known as epic similes; and identifying characters with repeated epithets, such as "wily Odysseus." Oral or folk epics, recited tales told for many generations before being written down, such as *The Iliad* and *Sunjata,* are sometimes distinguished from literary epics like *The Aeneid* or *Paradise Lost,* whose original creation was the work of a single poet.

Epicureanism The doctrines of Epicurus (341–270 B.C.E.), the Greek philosopher who espoused a life of pleasure and the avoidance of pain; commonly thought of as a license for indulgence, Epicureanism actually stipulates a life of simplicity and morality.

Essay A literary form that is an analytical, interpretive, or critical composition usually shorter and less formal than a dissertation or thesis and more personal in nature. The term was coined in the Renaissance by the master of the form, Montaigne (1533–1592), who chose it to underscore that his writings (from the French word *essai,* literally meaning "trial," or "test") were attempts toward understanding.

Euphony From the Greek for "good sound"; refers to language that is smooth and musically pleasant to the ear.

Exposition A narrative device often used at the beginning of a work to provide necessary background information about characters and their circumstances. Exposition explains such matters as what has gone on before; the relationships between characters; theme; and conflict.

Farce A form of humor based on exaggerated, improbable incongruities. Farce involves rapid shifts in action and emotion as well as slapstick comedy and extravagant dialogue.

Feminist criticism An approach to literature that seeks to correct or supplement a predominantly male-dominated critical perspective with a feminist consciousness. Feminist criticism places literature in a social context and uses a broad range of disciplines, including history, sociology, psychology, and linguistics, to provide interpretations that are sensitive to feminist issues.

Feudalism A system of government that existed with some variations in Europe, China, and Japan in the Middle Period. The feudal system refers to a mode of agricultural production in which peasants worked for landowners, or lords, in return for debt forgiveness, food, and military protection.

Fiction Literature created from the imagination and not presented as fact, though it may be based on a true story or real-life situation. Genres of fiction include the short story, the novella, and the novel.

Figures of speech Ways of using language that deviate from the literal, denotative meanings of words, through comparison, exaggeration, or other verbal devices in order to suggest additional meanings or effects.

Fixed form A poem characterized by a fixed pattern of lines, syllables, or METER. A SONNET is a

fixed form of poetry because it must have fourteen lines.

Flashback A literary or dramatic device that allows a past occurrence to be inserted into the chronological order of a narrative.

Foil A character in a literary work or drama whose behavior or values contrast with those of another character, typically the PROTAGONIST.

Foot A poetic foot is a poem's unit of measurement, defined by an accented syllable and a varying number of unaccented syllables. In English, the iambic foot, an accented syllable followed by an unaccented syllable, is the most common.

Foreshadowing Providing hints of what is to happen in order to build suspense.

Formalism A type of criticism dominant in the early twentieth century that emphasizes the form of an artwork. Two of its prominent schools are Russian formalism, which favors the form of an artwork over its content and argues that it is necessary for literature to defamiliarize the ordinary objects of the world, and American NEW CRITICISM, which treats a work of art as an object and seeks to understand it through close, careful analysis.

Founding myth A story that explains how a particular nation or culture came to be, such as Virgil's *Aeneid,* which describes the founding of Rome. Many epic poems, sometimes called national epics, are founding myths.

Four classes In Hindu tradition, humans are created as one of four classes, or VARNA: in descending order, the BRAHMINS (priests), the KSHATRIYA (warriors), the *Vaisya* (merchants and farmers), and the *Shudra* (laborers and servants).

Framed narration Also called *framed tale.* A story within a story. In Chaucer's *Canterbury Tales,* each pilgrim's story is framed by the story of the pilgrimage itself. This device, used by writers from ancient times to the present, enjoyed particular popularity during the thirteenth, fourteenth, and fifteenth centuries and was most fully developed in *The*

Arabian Nights, a work in which the framing is multilayered.

Free verse Highly irregular poetry, typically, free verse employs varying line patterns and rhythms and does not rhyme.

Freudian criticism A method of literary criticism associated with Freud's theories of psychoanalysis. Early Freudian critics sought to illustrate how literature is shaped by the unconscious desires of the author, but the term now more broadly encompasses many schools of thought that link psychoanalysis to the interpretation of literature.

Gaia From the Greek *Ge* meaning "earth," Gaia or Gaea was an earth goddess, mother of the Titans in Greek mythology.

Gay and lesbian criticism School of literary criticism that focuses on the representation of homosexuality in literature; also interested in how homosexuals read literature and to what extent sexuality and gender is culturally constructed.

Gender criticism Literary school that analyzes how an author's or a reader's sex affects the writing and reading experiences.

Genre A category of artistic works or literary compositions that have a distinctive style or content. Poetry, fiction, and drama are genres. Different genres have dominated at various times and places. Traditional genres include tragedy, comedy, romance, novel, epic, and lyric.

Georgic poetry Poetry dealing with the practical aspects of agriculture and rural affairs as first seen in the work of the Greek poet Nicander of Colophon (second century B.C.E.) and practiced by later poets such as Virgil (70–19 B.C.E.).

Ghazal A form of lyric poetry composed of three to seven couplets, called *sh'ir,* that follow the strict rhyme scheme of *aa ba ca da,* and so on, known as the *qafiyah.* Strict adherence to the form requires the use of the *radif,* a word that is repeated in a pattern dictated by the first couplet, throughout the poem. Literally meaning "dialogue with the beloved," the *ghazal,* as practiced in Arabia, Persia, Turkey, and India beginning around 1200, became the predominant form for love poetry.

Gnostics Members of an ancient sect in the Middle East who believed that hidden knowledge held the key to the universe. Throughout history there have been Gnostics who have formed secret societies with secret scriptures and who have believed they understood the workings of the cosmos.

Golden Age of Arabic science The period of the Abbassid caliphs, between 750 and 945 C.E., particularly the reigns of Harun al-Rashid (786–809) and al-Ma'mun (813–833). Al-Ma'mun founded a scientific academy in Baghdad, collected and had translated many ancient Greek and Indian manuscripts upon which Arab scholars built, and encouraged scholarship of all kinds, resulting in major advances in mathematics, astronomy, medicine, and geography.

Golden Age of Spain The "Siglo de Oro" period from the early sixteenth century to the end of the seventeenth century that is considered the high point of Spain's literary history. The age began with the political unification of Spain around 1500 and extended through 1681, the year in which Pedro Calderon (1600–1681) died. In addition to Calderon, this period saw the flourishing of such writers as Cervantes (1547–1616) and Lope de Vega (1562–1635).

Gothic A style of literature (especially novels) in the late eighteenth and early nineteenth centuries that reacted against the mannered decorum of earlier literature. Gothic novels explore the darker side of human experience; they are often set in the past and in foreign countries, and they employ elements of horror, mystery, and the supernatural.

Greater Dionysia In ancient Greece, dramas were performed at festivals that honored the god Dionysus: the Lenaea during January and February and the Greater Dionysia in March and April. The best tragedies and comedies were awarded prizes by an Athenian jury.

Gupta dynasty The time of the reign of the Gupta emperors (320–550), considered the golden age of classical Indian history. The dynasty, established by Chandragupta I (r. 320–35), disintegrated in the middle of the sixth century. It was during this period that the great poetry of Kalidasa was written.

Hadith Islamic source of religious law and moral guidance. According to tradition, the Hadith were passed down orally to the prophet Muhammad, and today they are critical to the study of the early development of Islam.

Hajj The pilgrimage to Mecca, Saudi Arabia, one of the five pillars of Islam and the duty of every Muslim at least once in his or her lifetime.

Hamartia A tragic flaw or error that in ancient Greek tragedies leads to the hero's reversal of fortune, known as the *peripeteia*.

Hebrew Scriptures A collection of thirty-nine books sacred to Judaism sometimes called the Hebrew Bible, these writings contain the history, teachings, and literature of the ancient Hebrews and Jews; called the Old Testament by Christians.

Hellene The name for a Greek, dating from the inhabitants of ancient Greece, who took their name from Hellen, the son of the legendary Deucalion and Pyrrha.

Hellenism The language, thought, art, customs, and literature characteristic of classical Greece.

Heroic couplet A rhymed, iambic-pentameter stanza of two lines that completes its thought within the two-line form. Alexander Pope (1688–1744), the most accomplished practitioner of the form in English, included this couplet in his *Essay on Criticism:* "True wit is nature to advantage dressed, / What oft was thought, but ne'er so well expressed."

Heroic poetry Narrative verse that is elevated in mood and uses a dignified, dramatic, and formal style to describe the deeds of aristocratic warriors and rulers. Typically, it was transmitted orally over several generations and written down at a later date. Examples of the form include *The Iliad* and *The Odyssey*.

Hexameter couplets The conventional strophic form of Greek and Latin epic poetry consisting of two dactylic hexameter lines; each line is composed of six feet, and each foot comprises one long (accented) and two short (unaccented) syllables. The final foot is known as a catalectic foot, for it is generally shortened by one or two syllables.

Hieroglyphic writing A writing system using picture symbols to represent sounds, words, or images instead of alphabetical letters. It was used by the ancient Egyptians, Mexicans, and others.

Hieros gamos Literally, "sacred marriage"; a fertility ritual in which the god-king or priest-king is united with the goddess or priestess-queen in order to provide a model for the kingdom and establish the king's right to rule.

Hinduism The major religion of India based on the ancient doctrines found in the SANSKRIT texts known as the VEDAS and the UPANISHADS, dating from 1000 B.C.E.

Historical criticism An approach to literature that uses history as a means of understanding a literary work. Such criticism moves beyond both the facts of an author's life and the text itself to examine the social and intellectual contexts in which the author composed the work.

Homeric Hymns At one time attributed to Homer, the *Homeric Hymns* (seventh through sixth centuries B.C.E.) are now believed to have been created by poets from a Homeric school or simply in the style of Homer. Five of the longer hymns contain important stories about gods such as Demeter, DIONYSUS, Apollo, Aphrodite, and Hermes.

Homo viator Latin for "man the traveler," used by Augustine to signify man's pilgrimage through life toward God.

Hoplite The name used to designate the foot soldiers of ancient Greece.

Hubris Exaggerated pride or arrogance; in Greek tragedies, hubris causes fatal errors.

Huguenots French Protestant members of the Reformed Church established in France by

John Calvin in about 1555. Due to religious persecution, many Huguenots fled to other countries in the sixteenth and seventeenth centuries.

Humanism The learning or cultural impulse that flourished during the European Renaissance characterized by a revival of classical letters, an individualistic and critical spirit, and a shift from religious to secular concerns.

Hundred Years' War A series of wars between the English and the French that lasted from 1337 to 1453 in which England lost all of its possessions in France except Calais, also eventually lost in 1565.

Hymn A form of lyric poetry, characterized by solemnity and high religious feeling, intended to be sung in praise of gods or heroic men and women.

Hyperbole A figure of speech; using overstatement or extravagant exaggeration.

Iambic pentameter A poetic line made up of five feet, or iambs, or a ten-syllable line.

Idealism Philosophical Idealism in its various forms holds that objects of perception are in reality mental constructs and not the material objects themselves.

Ideogram A pictorial symbol used in writing that stands for an idea or concept.

Image A verbal representation of a sensory phenomenon — visual, auditory, olfactory, etc. The two types of images are literal and figurative. Literal images are very detailed, almost photographic; figurative images are more abstract and often use symbols.

Imam The leader of prayer in a Muslim mosque; also a title indicating respect for a man of learning.

In medias res Literally, "in the midst of things"; a term used to characterize the beginning of epic poems, which typically start at a crucial point far along in the story. Earlier details are conveyed by means of flashbacks and digressions.

Inquisition A medieval institution established by the Fourth Lateran Council of the Roman Catholic Church, which met in 1215 and was presided over by Pope Innocent III. The Inquisition was formed largely to combat heresy in the aftermath of the Albigensian Crusade in Spain (1209–1229).

Irony A device used in writing and speech to deliberately express ideas so they can be understood in two ways. In drama, irony occurs when a character does not know something that the other characters or the audience knows.

Islam A world religion founded in the seventh century C.E. on the teachings of the prophet Muhammad, whose followers believe that the Qur'an (Koran), the holy book of Islam, contains the revelations of Allah. The Five Pillars of Islam are: to recite the creed, "There is no God but Allah, and Muhammad is his Prophet"; to acknowledge the oneness of Allah in prayer five times each day by reciting the opening verses of the Qur'an; to practice charity and help the needy; to fast in the month of Ramadan; and to make the *hajj*, or pilgrimage to Mecca, at least once in a lifetime if possible. Islam has played a major role in the history of the Middle East and Asia.

Jainism A religion founded in India by Mahavira (d. 468 B.C.E.), a contemporary of the Buddha. In reaction to the rigid and hierarchical structure of traditional Hinduism, Jainism teaches that divinity resides within each individual. Salvation is achieved through the ascetic renunciation of the world and through the practice of AHIMSA, nonviolence toward all living beings.

Jen (Ren) As a basic element of CONFUCIANISM, *jen* means "benevolence" or "love for fellow humans"; Mencius (fourth century B.C.E.) argued that all humans are endowed with *jen*; also spelled *ren*.

Jesuits A Roman Catholic religious order founded in 1540 by Ignatius Loyola (1491–1556) under the title the Society of Jesus as part of the wider Counter-Reformation.

Jewish mysticism Like all forms of mysticism, Jewish mysticism focuses on learning and practices that lead to unity with the creator; its teachings are contained in the Cabala (Kabala, Kabbalah).

Jihad From the Arabic *jahada,* meaning "striving," "struggle," or "exertion," *jihad* denotes a spiritual struggle for perfection and self-control by practicing Muslims, as well as a struggle for the faith conducted peacefully with unbelievers. This term also came to mean a holy war conducted by Muslims against unbelievers or enemies of Islam carried out as a religious duty. After the death of Muhammad in 632, Muslim conquests extended beyond Arabia until early into the next century.

Judgment of Paris In Greek legend, Paris (Alexandros) was selected by the god Zeus to judge which of three goddesses was the most beautiful. He chose Aphrodite, who had bribed him by agreeing to help him seduce Helen, the most beautiful woman in the world. Paris' abduction of Helen and refusal to return her was the cause of the Trojan War.

Ka'ba (ka'bah) The sacred Muslim shrine at Mecca, toward which believers turn when praying.

Kana The portion of the Japanese writing system that represents syllables.

Karma In Hindu and Buddhist philosophy, the totality of a person's actions in any one of the successive states of that person's existence, thought to determine the fate of the next stage. More generally, fate or destiny.

Karma-yoga One of four types of yoga; the practitioner of karma-yoga strives to serve humanity selflessly and without ego, a practice that purifies the heart and prepares the heart and mind for the reception of divine light, or the attainment of knowledge of the self.

Kharja The short, two- or four-line tag ending of an Arabic *muwashshah,* a long, formal beginning to a poem consisting of five or six end-rhymed stanzas. The *Kharja* was often written in Mozarabic, the spoken language of Andalusia (Spain) that included elements of Arabic, Spanish, and Hebrew.

Kshatriya The second highest of the four primary Hindu castes, the military or warrior caste just below the Brahmin class.

Lacunae Spaces where something has been left out; particularly, a gap or missing portion of a text.

Laisses In Medieval poetry, stanzas composed of a variable number of ten-syllable lines; the concluding line of the first stanza is repeated as a refrain at the end of subsequent stanzas.

Lay (Lai) A song or musical interlude; by extension, a poem accompanied by a musical instrument. Marie de France, a popular Anglo-Norman poet of the twelfth century, composed what she called "Breton Lais," short versions of courtly romances suitable for recitation.

Leitmotifs Themes, brief passages, or single words repeated within a work.

Line A sequence of words. In poetry, lines are typically measured by the number of feet they contain.

Lingam The phallic symbol through which Shiva is worshipped in his personification as the creative and reproductive power in the universe.

Literary epic A literary epic—as distinguished from folk epics such as the *Mahabharata* or *The Iliad,* which are made up of somewhat loosely linked episodes and closely follow oral conventions—is written with self-conscious artistry, has a tightly knit organic unity, and is stylistically rooted in a written, literate culture. In actuality, great epics often blur the distinction between the oral or folk epic and the literary epic.

Logos In ancient Greece, philosophers such as Aristotle (384–322 B.C.E.) used *logos* to mean reason or thought as opposed to *pathos* or feeling and emotion. Logos was thought of as the controlling principle of the universe made manifest in speech or rhetoric.

Lushi A highly structured Chinese form of poetry consisting of eight lines of five or seven syllables each. Also referred to as "regulated verse."

Lyric Originally, poetry composed to the accompaniment of a lyre (a stringed musical instrument). By extension, lyric is any poetry that expresses intense personal emotion in a manner suggestive of a song, as opposed to narrative poetry that relates the events of a story. Short poems, often on the subject of love, exist in most of the world's cultures and can fall under the common designation of lyric.

Ma'at An ancient Egyptian word for the idea of "right order" or justice, the basis of both cosmic order and a civil society. *Ma'at* was associated with either the sun-god Re or the creator Ptah.

Maghazi Legendary accounts of "the raids of the Prophet" in Islamic literature, examples of which can be found in Ibn Ishaq's *The Life of Muhammad,* which depicts events of Muhammad's embattled later life.

Mahabharata One of the two great epics of ancient India and the longest poem in world literature, consisting of nearly 100,000 stanzas—more than seven times longer than *The Iliad* and *The Odyssey* combined. Attributed to Vyasa, whose name means the "compiler" or "arranger," the *Mahabharata* was composed between the fifth century B.C.E. and the fourth century C.E.; written in Sanskrit, the epic appeared in its final written form sometime in the fourth century C.E.

Manicheanism A dualistic religion founded by Mani, a Persian philosopher, in the third century C.E. Combining Christian, Buddhist, and Zoroastrian elements, Mani taught that there were two gods, one good and one evil, a school of belief that affected such later church thinkers as Augustine of Hippo, as seen in his *Confessions.*

Manuscript illumination The elaborate illustration of manuscripts (handwritten and handmade books) in the Middle Ages with beautiful images, borders, and letters, embellished with luminous color, especially gold.

Marathi A Sanskritic language of western India spoken by the Marathas, known as the SAMURAI of western India for their defense of Hinduism against the onslaught of the Muslim invaders of India.

Marxist criticism Literary criticism that evolved from Karl Marx's political and economic theories. In the view of Marxist critics, texts must be understood in terms of the social class and the economic and political positions of their characters.

Masque Developed in the Renaissance, masques are highly stylized and structured performances with an often mythological or allegorical plot, combining drama, music, song, and dance in an elaborate display.

Materialism A worldview that explains the nature of reality in terms of physical matter and material conditions rather than by way of ideas, emotions, or the supernatural.

Mathnavi Persian poetic form used for romantic, epic, didactic, and other types of poems whose subjects demand a lengthy treatment; its verse structure is similar to that of the Western heroic couplet, but with two rhyming halves in a single line.

Maurya dynasty The Indian dynasty that existed between 322 and 185 B.C.E. Established by Chandragupta Maurya (r. 322–296 B.C.E.), the dynasty eventually united all of India except for the extreme south under one imperial power. During this period trade flourished, agriculture was regulated, weights and measures were standardized, and money first came into use.

Maya From the Sanskrit for "deception" or "illusion," *maya* is the veil drawn over the ultimate, eternal reality of BRAHMAN and therefore represents the phenomenal world of appearances that humans misinterpret as the only reality.

Me According to Sumerian philosophers, the *me* were the divine laws and rules that governed the universe as well as the cultural elements, like metalworking and the arts, that constituted urban life. In Sumerian mythology, the *me* are the gift of the goddess Inanna to humankind.

Medieval Romances See CHIVALRIC ROMANCES.

Menippian satire Named for its originator, the Greek Cynic philosopher Menippus (first half of the third century B.C.E.), Menippian satire uses a mixture of prose, dialogue, and verse to make ludicrous a whole social class or a broad spectrum of social types. The form is some-times called an "anatomy" because it catalogs the many social and intellectual types who constitute the social group it satirizes.

Metaphor A comparison of two things that does not use the words *like* or *as*. For example, "love is a rose."

Meter The RHYTHM of a poem based on the number of syllables in each line and which syllables are accented. See also FOOT.

Middle Ages A term applied specifically to Europe, dating from the decline of the Roman Empire in the fourth to sixth cen-turies to the revival of learning and the arts in the Early Modern or Renaissance period in the late fourteenth and fifteenth centuries.

Millenarianism A utopian belief that the end of time is imminent, after which there will be a thousand-year era of perfect peace on earth.

Ming dynasty (1368–1644) Founded by Zhu Yuan-zhang, who restored native Chinese rule from the Mongols who had ruled China during the previous Yuan dynasty (1271–1368) established by Kubla Khan. The Ming dynasty saw a flourishing of Chinese culture, the restoration of CONFUCIANISM, and the rise of the arts, including porcelain, architecture, drama, and the novel.

Miyabi A Japanese term denoting a delicate taste for the beautiful—a refined sensibility for subtle nuances of style and form in art, lit-erature, and social conduct.

Moira In Greek mythology, the deity who assigns to every person his or her lot.

Moksha In the Hindu tradition, the *moksha* is the highest goal for all humans; it means the final liberation from all earthly, material exis-tence and complete union with God or the ultimate reality.

Monism A unitary conception of the world in which everything that is—the whole of reality—constitutes an inseparable self-inclusive whole, as opposed to dualism, which sees reality as made up of opposing elements, such as mind and matter, and good and evil.

Monogatari Loosely translated from the Japa-nese as "tale" or the "telling of things,"

monogatari refers to the genre of fiction; as in the case of NIKKI, *monogatari* were written in KANA and often contained poetic passages in the form of WAKA. Lady Murasaki's *The Tale of Genji* is perhaps the greatest example of the *monogatari* in Japanese literature.

Monologue A speech of significant length deliv-ered by one person; in drama, speech in which a CHARACTER talks to himself or herself or reveals personal secrets without addressing another character.

Monotheism The doctrine or belief that there is only one deity or God, such as Allah or Yaweh, as opposed to the polytheistic reli-gions of ancient Greece and Rome that involved the worship of numerous gods.

Mozarabic Pertaining to Spanish Christians and Jews who were permitted to practice their religions during the period of Muslim rule in Andalusia. Also refers to the vernacular lan-guage spoken in Andalusia, a combination of Arabic, Christian, and Hebrew elements.

Mullah (Mulla) A Muslim teacher or inter-preter of Muslim religious law; the more cur-rent usage is as a general title of respect for a learned person.

Muse In ancient Greek mythology, any of the nine daughters of Zeus who presided over the arts; current usage denotes a muse as the spirit that inspires a poet or artist to create.

Muwashshah A conventional Andalusian love poem, usually written in Arabic but occasion-ally in Hebrew, consisting of five or six end-rhymed stanzas followed by a brief "tag" ending called a KHARJA, usually written in MOZARABIC.

Mystery religions Mystery cults were very popular in ancient Greece and Rome for at least one thousand years, beginning around 1000 B.C.E. The details of each cult were kept a secret, but all cults shared a rigorous rite of initiation, a concern about death, and a hope for immortality centered on a deity who had personal knowledge of the afterlife. The most popular Greek versions were the Orphic and Eleusinian mysteries. The mysteries of Isis and Mithra were favored in the Roman world.

Mysticism The belief that communion with God can be achieved intuitively through contemplation and meditation on the divine spirit akin to an act of faith rather than through the intellect.

Mythological criticism A type of literary criticism that focuses on the archetypal stories common to all cultures. Initiated by Carl Jung in the early twentieth century, mythological criticism seeks to reveal how the psychological impulses and patterns lodged deep in human consciousness take the form of ARCHETYPAL stories and are the basis for literature.

Narrative poem A poem that tells a story. Ballads, epics, and romances are typically narrative poems.

Narrator The voice that in fiction describes the PLOT or action of a story. The narrator can speak in the first, second, or third person and, depending on the effect the author wishes to create, can be very visible or almost invisible (an explicit or an implicit narrator); he or she also can be involved in the action or be removed from it. See also POINT OF VIEW and SPEAKER.

Nasib The prelude or introductory stanzas of a QASIDAH, the Arabic lyric form comparable to the ode.

Nataka In Sanskrit drama, the heroic romance with an idealized warrior king as its central figure and a comic story concentrating on heroic and erotic themes.

Necropolis Literally meaning "city of the dead," *necropolis* was the name given to a cemetery in the ancient world.

Neo-Confucianism Refers generally to the philosophical tradition in China and Japan based on the thought of Confucius (Kongfuzi, 551–479 B.C.E.) and his commentators, particularly Mencius (Mengzi, c. 371–c. 288 B.C.E.) and Zhu Xi (Chu Hi, 1130–1200). Neo-Confucianism, which arose during the Sung dynasty (960–1279), asserts that an understanding of things must be based on their underlying principles; in moral and political philosophy, it emphasizes the study of history, loyalty to family and nation, and order.

Neoplatonism Considered the last great Greek philosophy, Neoplatonism was developed by Plotnus (204–270 C.E.), based on his reading of the works of Plato. This school of philosophy espouses a single source from which all forms of existence emanate and with which the soul seeks a mystical union.

New Criticism A type of formalist literary criticism that disregards historical and biographical information to focus on the text. The New Critics perform a close reading of a work and give special attention to technical devices such as irony and ambiguity.

New Historicism A school of literary criticism developed in the 1980s in part as a reaction to NEW CRITICISM and other formalist methods of literary analysis. In contrast to formalism, which focuses strictly on internal relations of form and structure in a text, New Historicism emphasizes the relation of the text to its historical and cultural contexts. New Historicists make a self-conscious attempt to place their own critical practice within the political and historical framework of their own time, and align the language, rhetorical strategies, and other features of the texts they study with those of works not usually considered literary.

New Testament The sacred writings of Christianity, which tell the life of Jesus in the Gospels, the history of the establishment of the early church in Paul's Epistles, and the prophesy of the ultimate fulfillment of Christian history in the Revelation of St. John the Divine. From the Christian perspective, the New Testament fulfills the prophesies of the Hebrew Scriptures, known to Christians as the Old Testament.

Nikki An important genre of Japanese literature, the prose diary, which flourished among women writers in the Heian period; these diaries were written primarily in KANA, the woman's form of writing, which formed the basis of the vernacular literary tradition in Japan, and, like *The Tale of Genji,* contained poetic passages in the form of WAKA.

Nirvana In Buddhism, the state of perfect blessedness achieved by the extinction of individual existence and absorption of the soul into the supreme spirit, or by the extinction of all earthly passions and desires.

Nō The highly elaborate and ritualistic classical theater of Japan, known for its minimalist approach to plot, scenery, and stage effects and the stately performance and Zen-like mastery of its actors; *Nō* means "talent" or "accomplishment."

Novel An extended work of fictional prose narrative. The novel is a modern outgrowth of earlier genres such as the romance. There is considerable debate as to the origins of the novel; some critics trace it to Cervantes' *Don Quixote* (1605), others to Lady Murasaki's *The Tale of Genji* (c. 1022).

Octave A STANZA of eight lines in poetry.

Ode An elevated form of LYRIC generally written on a single theme, using varied metric and rhyme patterns. With the ode, poets working within classical schemes can introduce considerable innovation. There are three major types of odes in English: the Pindaric, or Regular; the Horatian; and the Irregular. The Pindaric ode is structured by three-strophe divisions, modulating between the strophe, antistrophe, and epode, which vary in tone. The Horatian ode uses only one STANZA type; variation is introduced within each stanza. The Irregular ode, sometimes called the English ode, allows wide variety among stanza forms, rhyme schemes, and metrical patterns. Related forms adopted by particular cultures include the Arabic QASI-DAH and the ancient Japanese CHOKA.

Oedipus complex Sigmund Freud's conception of the unconscious male desire to kill one's own father and sleep with one's own mother. The term derives from the Greek myth of Oedipus, who unknowingly murdered his father and married his mother; his self-inflicted punishment was to blind himself. FREUDIAN CRITICS do not take the complex or the story literally, but frequently use the concept to examine in literature the guilt associated with competition with or hostility toward one's father.

Onomatopoeia The quality of a word that sounds like the thing it refers to: for example, the *buzz* of bees.

Open form Also known as *free verse.* A type of poetry that does not follow established conventions of METER, RHYME, and STANZA.

Opera A musical drama in which the dialogue is sung to orchestral accompaniment. As a form, it has its origins in the liturgical drama of the Middle Ages. In sixteenth-century Italy, opera rose to grand musical productions marked by elaborate costuming, scenery, and choreography.

Organic form The concept that the structure of a literary work develops according to an internal logic. The literary work grows and becomes an organic whole that follows the principles of nature, not mechanics. The created work of art is akin to a growing plant that relies on all of its parts working together.

Oxymoron A rhetorical figure of speech in which contradictory terms are combined, such as *jumbo shrimp* and *deafening silence.*

Panegyric An oration or eulogy in praise of some person or achievement. Primarily associated with classical antiquity, panegyrics continued to be written through the Middle Ages and Renaissance, especially in Elizabethan England, the Spanish Golden Age, and in France under Louis XIV.

Pantheism Literally, "God everywhere," the belief that God is immanent throughout the universe—that God is manifest in all things.

Pantheon Generally, all the deities of a particular religion considered collectively; also, a temple dedicated to all the gods; specifically, the temple built in Rome by Agrippa in 27 C.E. and rebuilt by Hadrian in the second century C.E.

Paraphrase To rewrite or say the same thing using different words.

Parataxis Literally, "placing one thing after another." The term refers to linear narrative, often employed in storytelling, consisting of a series of sentences or clauses joined by a coordinator (that happened . . . , then this happened . . .).

Parody A humorous imitation of another, usually serious, work. Parody can be a form of literary criticism that exposes defects in a work, or it can function as an acknowledgement of a work's cultural and literary importance.

Pastoral poetry A poem or a play dealing with the lives of shepherds or rural life in general and usually depicting shepherds as representative of a simple life of innocence and serenity as opposed to the misery and corruption of city or court life. An early example of the form is Virgil's *Eclogues,* which greatly influenced the Renaissance work of such writers as Dante, Petrarch, and Shakespeare.

Patois A regional dialect of a language.

Patrician Originally, the hereditary aristocracy and nobility of ancient Rome. Later the term referred to any person who by birth or special compensation belonged to the nobility. More current usage denotes a person of high birth or a person of refined upbringing and manners.

Pax Romana Literally meaning "Roman peace," this is the long period of comparative peace enforced on states in the Roman Empire between the years 27 B.C.E. and 180 C.E.

People of the Book (Dhimmi) The Muslim name for Jews and Christians, followers of the teachings of the prophets of Hebrew Scriptures and the New Testament. Under normal conditions Islamic authorities granted Jews and Christians religious tolerance.

Peloponnesian War (431–404 B.C.E.) War between the Athenian and Spartan alliance systems that encompassed most of the Greek world. The war set new standards for warfare—Athens used its navy to support the land offensive, for instance—but the new tactics also prolonged the fighting; instead of there being one decisive battle, the war dragged on for three decades. Eventually, Athens was defeated, and Sparta took over the defeated power's overseas empire.

Peripeteia (Peripety) A character's reversal of fortune in the denouement of a plot. In tragedy, it means the hero's destruction, in comedy his or her happy resolution.

Persian Wars A series of wars between a coalition of Greek city-states and the Persian empire fought between 500 and 449 B.C.E.; the Greek victory set the stage for the flourishing of Greek culture.

Persona Literally, persona means "mask." In literature, a persona is a speaker created by a writer to tell a story or to speak in a poem. A persona is not a character in a story or narrative, nor does it necessarily directly reflect the author's personal voice.

Personification A figure of speech in which abstractions or inanimate objects are given human qualities or form.

Petrarchan conceit From *concept* or *conception,* this was an originally novel form of metaphor in which the speaker of a poem compared his or her beloved to something else, such as a doe, a rose, a summer's day, or even a newly discovered land. Originating with the Italian poet Petrarch, the freshness of this device soon wore off and the Petrarchan conceit became a stale convention, revitalized by only the most ingenious poets.

Petrarchan sonnet A fourteen-line lyric poem. The Petrarchan SONNET was the first basic sonnet form. It is divided into an eight-line octet and a six-line sestet, each with a specific but varied pattern of rhymes, for example *ab ba cd ec de.*

Philistines A powerful non-Semitic tribe that in biblical times inhabited the tract of land between Judea and Egypt; in almost perpetual war with the Israelites, they were ultimately conquered by the Romans.

Phonogram A letter, character, or mark used to represent a sound.

Picaresque A novel loosely structured around an episodic succession of adventures of a rogue hero—a *picaro*—who is on an aimless journey. The picaresque tale often provides a sweeping and satiric view of society and its customs. Examples include Petronius's *The Satyricon* and Voltaire's *Candide.*

Pictograph A picture used to represent an idea; hieroglyphics are pictographs.

Pietas In ancient Roman Stoic philosophy, *pietas* is respect for authority.

Platonic Characteristic of the philosophy of Plato, essentially connoting idealistic or visionary outlooks.

Platonic love A pure, spiritual love that is based on intellectual appreciation of the other person and is unmixed with sexual desire.

Platonist One who adheres to the philosophy of Plato, especially the doctrine that holds that things exist only as ideas in the mind rather than as material objects independent of the mind.

Plebeians Members of the ancient Roman lower class or common people, as opposed to PATRICIANS.

Plot The pattern of events told in a narrative or drama. Plot has a causal sequence and a unifying theme, in contrast to story, which is the simple narrative of the action.

Point of view The perspective from which the author, SPEAKER, or NARRATOR presents a story. A point of view might be localized within a CHARACTER, in which case the story is told from a first-person point of view. There is a range of possibilities between first-person point of view and omniscience, wherein a story is told from a perspective unlimited by time, place, or character.

Polis Greek term meaning "city"; designates the Greek city-states, such as Athens and Sparta, that arose in the sixth century B.C.E.

Polytheism The belief in or worship of many gods as opposed to monotheism, which is the doctrine or worship of a single god.

Pragmatism A philosophical approach that evaluates ideas and beliefs in terms of their usefulness and applicability to practical action.

Prologue Text that typically is placed prior to an introduction or that replaces a traditional introduction; often discusses events of importance for the general understanding of the work.

Protagonist A leading figure or the main character in a drama or other literary work.

Protestant Reformation See REFORMATION.

Psychological criticism An approach to literature that draws on psychoanalytic theories, especially those of Sigmund Freud (1856–1939) and Jacques Lacan (1901–1981), to understand more fully a text, its writer, and readers.

Pun A play on words that relies on a word's having more than one meaning or sounding like another word.

Punic Wars The series of wars between Rome and Carthage during the third and second centuries B.C.E.—the first taking place between 264 and 241 B.C.E., the second between 218 and 201, and the third between 149 and 146—which the Romans ultimately won.

Qasidah An Arabic form of lyric poetry, comparable to the ode, originally composed orally and consisting of several dozen to some sixty rhymed couplets, expressing reflection and sentiment while evoking scenes of desert life, romantic memories, and a tone of despair or self-glorification. Later literary versions of the *qasidah* often lost their desert setting but retained their reflective, romantic character.

Quatrain A stanza of four lines in a poem.

Quetzalcoatl The most important god of Mesoamerica, whose name means Plumed Serpent or Precious Twin. As a god, he was instrumental in creating the four previous worlds; as a hero-ruler of Tollan, he assumed the mantle of the priesthood of Quetzalcoatl, fell from grace, and delivered a messianic promise to return home.

Quietism Scholars use this term to characterize Chinese thinkers in the fourth century B.C.E. who advocated withdrawal from the turbulence of society and concentration on inner peace and harmony.

Quixotic Like Don Quixote, or having the characteristics of being romantic in the extreme, absurdly chivalrous, or foolishly idealistic.

Qur'an The sacred writings of Islam revealed by Allah to the prophet Muhammad.

Rahil That part of a QASIDAH's (or ode's) structure in Persian poetry—the "disengagement"—that tells of a solitary journey on horseback or camelback, or more metaphorically, of the separation of the poet from the source of his sorrowful memory.

Rasa Indian dramatic theory identifies eight *rasa*s (aesthetic emotions) that can focus a drama: the erotic, the heroic, the disquieting, the furious, the comic, the marvelous, the horrible, and the pathetic. Only two are appropriate for the NATAKA form, the erotic and the heroic.

Reader-response criticism A critical approach to literature in which the primary focus falls on the reader or the process of reading, not on the author. Reader-response critics believe that a literary work does not possess a fixed idea or meaning; meaning is a function of the perspective of the reader.

Realism Most broadly defined, realism is the attempt to represent the world accurately in literature. As a literary movement, Realism flourished in Russia, France, England, and America in the latter half of the nineteenth century. It emphasized not only accurate representation but the "truth," usually expressed as the consequence of a moral choice. Realist writers deemphasized the shaping power of the imagination and concerned themselves with the experiences of ordinary, middle-class subjects and the dilemmas they faced.

Recognition Based on the Greek concept of tragedy, recognition, or ANAGNORISIS, is the point in a story when the PROTAGONIST discovers the truth about his or her situation. Usually this results in a drastic change in the course of the plot.

Reformation Refers to the Protestant Reformation, this sixteenth-century challenge to the authority of the Catholic Church caused a permanent rift in the Christian world, with those loyal to the pope remaining Catholic and those rejecting papal authority forming new Protestant faiths such as the Anglican, Lutheran, Calvinist, Anabaptist, and Presbyterian. The Reformation originated—and was most successful—in Northern Europe, especially Germany; its notable leaders include Martin Luther and John Calvin.

Renaissance The revival of art, literature, and learning in Europe in the fourteenth, fifteenth, and sixteenth centuries based on classical Greek and Roman sources. The movement began in Italy, spread throughout Europe, and marked the transition from the medieval to the modern Western world.

Renaissance man A term used to describe someone accomplished in many disciplines, especially in both science and the arts, like Leonardo da Vinci and other figures of the European Renaissance.

Resolution The point in the plot of a narrative work or drama that occurs after the climax and generally establishes a new understanding; also known as *falling action.*

Reversal The point in the plot of a story or drama when the fortunes of the PROTAGONIST change unexpectedly; also known as the PERIPITEIA.

Rhyme The repetition of identical or similar-sounding words or syllables, usually accented, in lines of poetry. Rhymes may occur within or at the end of lines.

Rhythm The pattern of stressed and unstressed syllables in prose and especially in poetry that can lend emphasis, reinforce a sound association, or suggest regularity or recurrence. The rhythm of a literary work can affect the emotional response of the reader or listener.

Rishi (Rṣi) Sanskrit for sage or holy man.

Romance A medieval tale based on heroic conduct, adventure, or chivalric love, sometimes in a supernatural setting. Medieval romances were composed in France in the twelfth century, spreading to Germany, Spain, England, and other countries in the next several centuries. Later, in the seventeenth century, the romance form was parodied in Miguel de Cervantes's literary masterpiece, *Don Quixote.*

Romantic hero The PROTAGONIST of a romance, novel, or poem who is shaped by experiences that frequently take the form of combat, love, or adventure. The Romantic hero is judged by his actions more than his thoughts, and he is often on a journey that will affect his moral development.

Ruba'i (plural, Ruba'iyat) Equivalent to the quatrain in Western poetry, a *ruba'i* is a very intricate Persian poetic line structure consisting of four lines of equal length, divided into half lines, with the first, second, and fourth lines rhyming.

Samsara A Hindu term for the cycle of birth, life, death, and rebirth; many Hindu practices are aimed at obtaining release, or MOKSHA, from the otherwise endless repetition of life and death.

Samurai Japanese feudal aristocrat and member of the hereditary warrior class. Denied recognition during the Meiji period (1867–1912).

Sangha The Sanskrit word for a fraternity or association often formed out of spiritual or learning communities.

Sanskrit The classical language of ancient India, in which many of the major Hindu religious and literary texts were written.

Satire A literary or dramatic genre whose works, such as Petronius's *Satyricon* and Jonathan Swift's (1667–1745) *Gulliver's Travels,* ridicule human behavior.

Satyr In classical mythology, a minor woodland deity represented as part man and part goat whose chief characteristics are riotous merriment and lasciviousness.

Scansion A system of poetic analysis that involves dividing lines into feet and examining patterns of stressed and unstressed syllables. Scansion is a mechanical way of breaking down verse in order to understand the regularities and irregularities of its METER.

Scene In drama, a subdivision of an ACT.

Scholasticism The dominant philosophical system of the twelfth to fourteenth centuries in Europe, based on the writings of Aristotle and his commentators, including Avicenna (Ibn Sina) and Averroes (Ibn Rushdi). The great Christian Scholastic philosopher, St. Thomas Aquinas, completed his *Summa Theologica* in 1273.

Script The written version or text of a play or movie that is used by the actors.

Sentimentality Extravagant emotion; T. S. Eliot defined this as "emotion in excess of the facts."

Septuagint A Greek version of the Hebrew Scriptures (Old Testament), so called because the ancient tradition was that it was completed in seventy or seventy-two days by seventy-two Palestinian Jews, for Ptolemy II of Egypt.

Sestet A STANZA of six lines; the last stanza of a Petrarchan SONNET is a sestet.

Setting The time, place, and social environment in a narrative or a drama.

Shastra A treatise for authoritative instruction among the Hindu, especially a treatise explaining the VEDAS.

Shi In China, the term used to designate poetry in general.

Shi'ite One of the two great branches of the Muslim faith. Shi'ites insisted on a strict line of family succession from Muhammad and rejected interpretations of Islam construed after the death of Muhammad. They soon were considered heretical by the majority branch, Sunnite (Sunna) Muslims. Present-day Shi'ites primarily occupy Iran and southern Iraq.

Shintoism The indigenous polytheistic religion of Japan, the beliefs of which stress the worship of nature, ancestors, and ancient heroes, and the divinity of the emperor.

Shiva (Śiva) The Hindu god of destruction and creation and a member of the supreme Hindu trinity of Shiva, Brahma, and Vishnu.

Shogun A military ruler of feudal Japan between 1192 and 1867. The shogunate was an inherited position in the military that operated under the nominal control of the emperor.

Sikhism The beliefs of those who belong to the Hindu religious sect founded in northern India around 1500 C.E., based on a belief in one God and on a rejection of the caste system and idolatry.

Simile A figure of speech, introduced by *like* or *as,* in which two things are compared as equals.

Sira Muslim genre of the exemplary life story. This term, first applied to Ibn Ishaq's *The Life of Muhammad,* was later applied to other narratives of exemplary lives, such as Ibn Shaddad's biography of the great warrior Saladin (d. 1193). Later writers like al-Mu'ayyad al-Shirazi (d. 1077) wrote autobiographies that were also called *sira* as the meaning of the term expanded.

Smirti (Smṛti) One of the two major classifications of Hindu sacred texts. *Smirti,* which means "memory," comprises Hindu texts other than the VEDAS, which are considered SRUTI, or revealed (heard) texts. *Smirti* may be thought of as a secondary category of sacred literature that includes the Sutras, the Puranas, and the Indian epics the *Ramayana* and the *Mahabharata.*

Sociological criticism School of literary criticism that seeks to place a work of art in its social context and define the relationship between the two. Like Marxist critics, sociological critics are oriented toward social class, political ideology, gender roles, and economic conditions in their analyses.

Soliloquy A dramatic speech in which a character speaks his or her inner thoughts aloud before the audience.

Sonnet A fourteen-line lyric poem. The first basic sonnet form is the Italian or Petrarchan sonnet, which is divided into an eight-line octet and a six-line SESTET (see PETRARCHAN SONNET). The English or Shakespearean sonnet is divided into three four-line QUATRAINS followed by a two-line couplet; the quatrains are rhymed *abab cdcd efef* and the couplet is also end-rhymed, *gg.*

Sophists Literally, "wise men." Greek teachers who provided instruction in logic and rhetoric to pupils who could afford their expensive fees. Rhetoric was a new discipline whose study was observed to provide an advantage in politics and in the courts. *Sophist* came to mean one who used argumentation to undermine traditional beliefs.

Speaker The person or PERSONA who speaks in a poem, often a created identity who cannot be equated with the poet.

Spiritual autobiography An autobiography that gives special importance to self-examination, interpretation of Scripture, and belief in predestination. St. Augustine's *Confessions* (c. 400), detailing a life of sin, conversion, and spiritual rebirth, is generally regarded as the archetypal spiritual autobiography.

Sprezzatura An Italian term that has no equivalent in English, *sprezzatura* suggests a quality of perfect composure and nonchalance, the ability to act with studied artifice while giving the appearance of effortless spontaneity.

Sruti One of the two major classifications of Hindu sacred texts. *Sruti,* which means "hearing," is reserved for the primary sacred texts of Hinduism, the VEDAS, including the Smahtas, the Brahmanas, and the Aranyakas, the most important of which is the UPANISHADS.

Stage directions Written directions explaining how actors are to move onstage. See also SCRIPT.

Stanza A poetic verse of two or more lines, sometimes characterized by a common pattern of RHYME and METER.

Stock responses Predictable responses to language and symbols. See also CLICHÉ.

Stoicism A school of thought founded by the Greek philosopher Zeno c. 308 B.C.E. Stoicism advocated the view that virtue is the ultimate goal of life and that the virtuous seek happiness within by overcoming their passions and emotions while remaining independent of the external natural world, which follows immutable laws.

Stress A syllable receiving emphasis in accordance with a metrical pattern.

Style The distinctive manner in which an author writes and thus makes his or her work unique. A style provides a kind of literary signature for the writer.

Subplot A PLOT subordinate to the main plot of a literary work or drama.

Sufism A devotional movement among certain Muslims emphasizing the union of the devotee with God through ritual and ascetic practices, who hold to a kind of PANTHEISM and practice extreme asceticism in their lives.

Suspense The anxious emotion of an audience or reader anticipating the outcome of a story or drama, typically having to do with the fate of the PROTAGONIST or another character with whom a sympathetic attachment has been formed.

Symbol A representative of something by association. Though a symbol is often confused with a metaphor, a metaphor compares two dissimilar things while a symbol associates two things. For example, the *word* "tree" is a symbol for an *actual* tree. Some symbols have values that are accepted by most people. A flag, for instance, is for many a symbol of national pride, just as a cross is widely seen as a symbol of Christianity. Knowledge of a symbol's cultural context is sometimes necessary to understand its meaning; an apple pie is an American symbol of innocence that a Japanese person, for example, would not necessarily recognize.

Syncretism Combining disparate philosophical or religious beliefs, such as the blending of Christianity or Islam with indigenous religions.

Synoptic Gospels The first three gospels of the New Testament, which give a similar account of the life, death, and Resurrection of Jesus.

Syntax The way parts of speech are arranged in a sentence.

TANAK An acronym used to describe three groupings in Hebrew Scriptures: the Torah (Pentateuch, or first five books), the Nebi'im, (the Prophets), and Ketubim (the Writings); also spelled TENACH.

Tanka A Japanese verse form of thirty-one syllables in five unrhymed lines, the first and third having five syllables each, the second, fourth, and fifth having seven. See also WAKA.

Tantrism A minor Hindu tradition written down in scriptures called Tantras. Tantrism holds the supreme deity to be feminine and teaches that spiritual liberation can be won through erotic practices.

Taoism See DAOISM.

Tathagata An epithet for the Buddha that means "thus gone," having attained enlightenment.

Tercets A unit or group of three lines of verse, usually rhymed.

Terza rima A verse form composed of iambic three-line stanzas, with lines of ten or eleven syllables. Terza rima employed most brilliantly in Dante's (1265–1321) *Divine Comedy.*

Tetragrammaton The four consonants of the Hebrew alphabet, YHWH, used to approximate God's secret name; this name and its utterances are believed to contain special powers.

Tezcatlipoca In Aztec mythology, he was the warrior god of the north and the god of sin and misery with an obsidian knife. In Toltec mythology, he was also the brother and/or antithesis of Quetzalcoatl.

Thanatos "Death" in Greek. According to Sigmund Freud, our two primary drives are Eros (love) and Thanatos (death).

Theme A topic of discussion or a point of view embodied in a work of art.

Theocracy Government of the state by God or a god as represented by a person or persons claiming to have divine authority.

Tone A manner of expression in writing that indicates a certain attitude toward the subject or the implied audience.

Tour de force A masterly or brilliant creation, production, or performance; the phrase translates literally from the original French as "feat of strength."

Tragedy A dramatic or literary form originating in Greece that deals with serious human actions and issues. The actions are meant to create feelings of fear and compassion in the spectator that are later released (CATHARSIS). Typically, the main character is of a high stature or rank, so his or her fall is substantial. Even though tragedies are sad, they seem both just and believable. The tragedy raises serious moral and philosophical questions about the meaning of life and fate.

Tragicomedy A drama that combines tragedy and comedy and in which moral values are particularly questioned or ridiculed.

Travel narratives Also known as travel literature, a form of narrative that recounts the incidents that occur and the people and things that the narrator meets and sees while visiting a place with which she or he is typically unfamiliar. Prose and poetic accounts about exploration and adventure in unfamiliar lands and places as well as in more or less familiar locations are considered travel narratives. Examples of the genre include the travels of Marco Polo and the travels of Ibn Battuta.

Triplet In poetry, a group of three rhyming lines of verse.

Trobairitz Female troubadours, both members of the nobility and independent artists. See TROUBADOURS.

Troubadours Lyric poets and composers, sometimes of aristocratic rank but more often artists attached to regional courts, who flourished in the south of France in the twelfth and thirteenth centuries. Their compositions in the Provencal language centered on the subject of love. Their work derived in part from Arabic sources in Andalusia, and their influence spread throughout Europe in the thirteenth and fourteenth centuries.

Umrah Known as the "lesser pilgrimage"; in contrast to the *hajj*, which must be performed in the last month of the Islamic calendar year, *umrah* is a pilgrimage to Mecca that can be undertaken at any time.

Understatement A figure of speech that says less than what is intended. In Anglo-Saxon poetry, a special form of understatement known as the litote is an ironic form of address in which the full importance of something is concealed in order to force the listener to discover it by paying close attention.

Upanishads A body of sacred texts dating from the ninth century B.C.E. that provide a mystical development of and commentary on earlier VEDIC texts.

Urdu An Indo-European language closely related to Hindi. Urdu is the official language of Pakistan and is also spoken in India and Bangladesh.

Utopia In literature, a romance or other work describing an ideal place whose inhabitants live under seemingly perfect conditions. Though the term did not exist until coined by Sir Thomas More in 1516, earlier works such as Plato's *Republic* and Bacon's *New Atlantis* can be termed utopias due to the societies they depict.

Vandals Fierce warriors from near the Russian steppes who invaded Roman Gaul (France) in the fifth century C.E. and advanced through Spain to North Africa. They were notorious for their destruction of cities.

Varna Sanskrit word for "color" used in the sense of "class" to indicate the four classes or castes of Hinduism in India.

Vedas The earliest Indian sacred texts, written in Sanskrit, dating from sometime between 1000 and 500 B.C.E.; they contain hymns and ritual lore considered to be revelation, or SRUTI.

Vedic The Old Indic language of the VEDAS, it was an early form of Sanskrit.

Vernacular fiction Fiction that attempts to capture accurately the typical speech, mannerisms, or dialect of a region. The *Satyricon* of the Roman author Petronius is often considered the first work of vernacular fiction.

Waka Traditional Japanese poetry based on Chinese models that rose to prominence in the Heian Period (794–1195). The *waka* is a short five-line lyric consisting of thirty-one syllables with 5-7-5-7-7 syllables to a line. Writing *waka* was an important activity of the Heian aristocracy as well as their court followers. The poetry anthology *Kokinshu* (c. 905) is the most celebrated collection of *waka*. Now generally called *tanka*, these poems are still written today.

Xiaopin A Chinese form of autobiographical essay that became an important medium in China in the late sixteenth century.

Yahweh A form of the Hebrew name for God in the Hebrew Scriptures.

Yin and yang A pair of opposites derived from a dualistic system of ancient Chinese philosophy; symbolically representing the sun and the moon, *yang* is positive, active, and strong, while *yin* is negative, passive, and weak. All things in the universe are formed from the dynamic interaction of these forces.

Yoni A representation of the vulva, a symbol used in the worship of the goddess Shakti in Hinduism.

Yuefu Chinese folk ballads that, during the Han dynasty, evolved into literary ballads written in quatrains of five-word lines. The ballad typically presented a monologue of dialogue presenting, in dramatic form, some misfortune.

Zajal One of two poetic forms that came to dominate the performance of the GHAZAL, or love poem, which consisted of elaborately rhymed strophes or stanzas in MOZARABIC, without the KHARJA ending.

Zen prominent school of Buddhism that seeks to reveal the essence of the enlightened mind. Zen teaches that everyone has the potential to attain enlightenment but that most are unaware of this potential because they are ignorant. The way to attain enlightenment is through transcending the boundaries of common thought, and the method of study is most frequently the intense, personal instruction of a student by a Zen master.

Zhong Guo The translation of the Chinese characters for "Middle Kingdom," which denotes what today is translated as China.

Ziggurat A temple tower of the ancient Akkadians and Babylonians in the form of a terraced pyramid with each story smaller than the one below it.

Zoroastrianism A dualistic religion founded in ancient Persia by Zoroaster (c. 12th century–7th century B.C.E.). It teaches that two powerful forces—light and darkness, good and evil—are engaged in a struggle that will eventually erupt into a cataclysmic war in which good will prevail, leading to the destruction of the earth.

Zuihitsu Japanese for "following the brush" and translated as "occasional writing" or "essays," *zuihitsu* denotes a genre of Japanese writing mixing poetry and prose that arose primarily among women writers during the Heian Period. Sei Shonagon's *Pillow Book* is an example of *zuihitsu*.

Acknowledgments continued from p. ii

Aeschylus, "Prayer to the Dead" from *The Libation Bearers,* translated by Richmond Lattimore, from *The Complete Greek Tragedies,* Volume I. Copyright 1953 by the University of Chicago. Reprinted with the permission of the University of Chicago Press.

Dante Alighieri, *The Inferno,* translated by Robert Pinsky, from *The Inferno of Dante: A New Verse Translation* by Robert Pinsky. Copyright © 1994 by Robert Pinsky. Reprinted by permission of Farrar, Straus and Giroux, LLC.

Apollodorus, "The Labors of Heracles" from *Bibliotheca,* translated by Rhoda A. Hendricks, from *Classical Gods and Heroes: Myths as Told by the Ancient Authors.* Copyright © 1972 by Rhoda A. Hendricks. Reprinted with permission.

Aristotle, "On Tragedy" (editors' title) from *Poetics,* translated by T. S. Dorsch, from *Classical Literary Criticism.* Copyright © 1965 by T. S. Dorsch. Reprinted with the permission of Penguin Group (UK) Ltd.

Farid Ud-Din Attar, "The Story of Sheikh Sam'an" from *The Conference of the Birds,* translated by Afkham Darbandi and Dick Davis. Copyright © 1984 by Afkham Darbandi and Dick Davis. Reprinted with the permission of Penguin Group (UK) Ltd.

St. Augustine, excerpts from *The Confessions of St. Augustine,* edited by John K. Ryan. Copyright © 1960 by Doubleday, a division of Bantam Doubleday Dell Publishing Group, Inc. Used by permission of Doubleday, a division of Random House, Inc.

A. L. Basham (trans.), "Two Ways of Life: King and Monk" from "Uttaradhyayana"; "Sermon at Benares: The Four Noble Truths" from "Samyutta Nikaya"; "Right Mindfulness" from "Majjhima Nikaya"; and "The Last Instructions of the Buddha" from "Mahaparinibbana Sutra" from *Sources of Indian Tradition,* compiled by William Theodore de Bary et al. Copyright © 1958 by Columbia University Press. Reprinted with the permission of the publisher.

Bo Juyi, "Madly Singing in the Mountains," translated by Arthur Waley, from *170 Chinese Poems* (New York: Alfred A. Knopf, 1919). "Watching the Reapers," translated by Arthur Waley, from *Chinese Poems* (London: Allen & Unwin, 1946). All reprinted with the permission of the Estate of Arthur Waley.

Bartolomé de las Casas, excerpts from *The History of the Indies,* translated by George Sanderlin, from *Bartolomé de las Casas: A Selection of His Writings.* Copyright © 1971 by Alfred A. Knopf, Inc. Used by permission of Alfred A. Knopf, a division of Random House, Inc.

Catullus, poems 2, 3, 5, 8, 51, 76, 85, and 101, translated by Horace Gregory. Copyright © 1956, 1972 by the Estate of Horace Gregory, from his *Poems of Catullus* (W. W. Norton, 1972). Used with permission.

Miguel de Cervantes Saavedra, Part I, Chapters 1–8 from *Don Quixote,* translated by Edith Grossman. Copyright © 2003 by Edith Grossman. Reprinted with the permission of HarperCollins Publishers.

Geoffrey Chaucer, "General Prologue," "Prologue to the Wife of Bath's Tale," and "The Wife of Bath's Tale" from *The Canterbury Tales,* Revised Edition, translated by Theodore Morrison. Copyright 1949, renewed © 1977 by Theodore Morrison. Reprinted with the permission of Viking Penguin, a division of Penguin Group (USA) Inc.

Chuang Tzu (Zhuangzi), "The Wasted Gourd," "The Ailanthus Tree," "Walking Two Roads," "Penumbra and Shadow," "The Dream and the Butterfly," "Cutting Up the Ox," "The Death of Lao Tan," "Transformations," "The Job Offer," "Happiness," "Death of Chuang Tzu's Wife," "Gamecocks," and "Woodworker" from *Chuang Tzu: Basic Writings,* translated by Burton Watson. Copyright © 1964, 1996 by Columbia University Press. Reprinted with the permission of the publisher. "Yuan-Chu Bird," "What Fish Enjoy," and "The Swimmer" (editors' titles) from *The Complete Works of Chuang Tzu,* translated by Burton Watson. Copyright © 1968 by Columbia University Press. Reprinted with the permission of the publisher.

Christopher Columbus, excerpt from *The Log of Christopher Columbus,* translated by Robert H. Fuson (Blue Ridge Summit, Penn.: International Marine/TAB Books, 1992). Copyright © 1987 by Robert H. Fuson. Copyright © 2004 by Amelia F. Fuson. Reprinted with the permission of Amelia F. Fuson.

Confucius (Kongfuzi), "On Confucius the Man," "On Education," "On Goodness," "On Filial Piety," "On Ritual and Music," "On Religion," and "On Morality in Government" from *The Analects of Confucius,* translated by Arthur Waley. Copyright 1938 by George Allen & Unwin, Ltd. Reprinted with the permission of Scribner, an imprint of Simon & Schuster Adult Publishing Group, and the Estate of Arthur Waley.

Hernán Cortés, excerpts from "The Second Letter" from *Letters from Mexico,* translated by Anthony Pagden. Copyright © 1986 by Anthony Pagden. Reprinted with the permission of Yale University Press.

Countess of Dia, "Of things I'd rather keep in silence I must sing" from *The Woman Troubadours,* translated by Magda Bogin (London: Paddington, 1976). Reprinted with the permission of the translator.

Stephanie Dalley (trans.), excerpts from "The Epic of Creation" from *Myths from Mesopotamia.* Copyright ©

© 1989 by Cola Franzen. Reprinted with the permission of City Lights Books.

Kakinomoto Hitomaro, "On the Death of His Wife: I and II," translated by Ian Hideo Levy from *Ten Thousand Leaves: A Translation of the Man'yoshu, Japan's Premier Anthology of Classical Poetry.* Copyright © 1980 by Princeton University Press. Reprinted with permission.

Kalidasa, "Shakuntala and the Ring of Recollection" from *Theater of Memory: The Plays of Kalidasa,* translated by Barbara Stoler Miller. Copyright © 1984 by Barbara Stoler Miller. Reprinted with the permission of Columbia University Press.

The Koran, excerpts from *The Koran,* Fifth Edition, translated by N. J. Dawood. Copyright © 1956, 1959, 1966, 1968, 1974, 1990 by N. J. Dawood. Reprinted with the permission of Penguin Group (UK) Ltd.

Samuel Noah Kramer and Diane Wolkstein (trans.), "The Gates to the Underworld" from "Descent of Inanna" from *Sumerian Mythology: Study of Spiritual and Literary Achievement in the Third Millennium* B.C. Copyright © 1972. Reprinted with the permission of Mildred Kramer and the University of Pennsylvania Press.

Lao Tzu (Laozi), poems 1, 15, 16, 19, 20, 28, 29, 30, 36, 42, 43, 47, 74, and 81 from *Dao De Jing,* translated by Witter Bynner. Reprinted with the permission of the Witter Bynner Foundation for Poetry.

Li Bai, "Going to Visit Tai-T'ien Mountain's Master of the Way Without Finding Him," and "Drinking Alone Beneath the Moon," translated by David Hinton, from *The Selected Poems of Li Po.* Copyright © 1996 by David Hinton. Reprinted with the permission of New Directions Publishing Corp. "Sent to My Two Little Children in the East of Lu" from *The Columbia Book of Chinese Poetry: From Early Times to the Thirteenth Century,* translated by Burton Watson. Copyright © 1984 by Columbia University Press. Reprinted with the permission of the publisher.

R. M. Liuzza (trans.), *Beowulf.* Copyright © 1999 by R. M. Liuzza. Reprinted by permission of Broadview Press.

Martin Luther, "Here I Stand" from *Luther's Works: Career of the Reformer,* Volume 32, translated by Roger A. Hornsby. Copyright © 1958 by Fortress Press. Reprinted with the permission of Augsburg Fortress.

Niccolò Machiavelli, excerpt from "The Prince" from *Machiavelli: The Prince and Other Works,* translated by Allan H. Gilbert (Putney, VT: Hendricks House, Inc. Publishers, 1964). Reprinted with the permission of the publisher.

Marcabru, "By the fountain in the orchard," translated by Frederick Goldin from *The Lyrics of the Troubadour and Trouvères,* translated by Frederick Goldin. Copyright © 1973 by Frederick Goldin. Used by permission of Doubleday, a division of Random House, Inc.

Juan Mascaró (trans.), "Driving the Chariot" from "Katha Upanishad" from *The Upanishads.* Copyright © 1965 by Juan Mascaró. Reprinted with the permission of Penguin Group (UK) Ltd.

Mencius (Mengzi), "Compassion" from *Mencius,* translated by D. C. Lau. Copyright © 1970 by D. C. Lau. Reprinted with the permission of Penguin Group (UK) Ltd.

Michel Eyquem de Montaigne, "Of Cannibals" from *The Complete Essays of Montaigne,* translated by Donald M. Frame. Copyright 1943 by Donald M. Frame, renewed © 1971. Copyright 1948, © 1957, 1958 by the Board of Trustees of the Leland Stanford Junior University. All rights reserved. Used with the permission of Stanford University Press, www.sup.org.

Thomas More, excerpts from Book 2 from *Utopia,* translated by Clarence H. Miller. Copyright © 2001 by Yale University. Reprinted with the permission of Yale University Press.

Murasaki Shikibu, Chapter 4 from *The Tale of Genji,* translated by Edward Seidensticker. Copyright © 1976 by Edward G. Seidensticker. Used by permission of Alfred A. Knopf, a division of Random House, Inc.

Ono no Komachi, 552 ["In love-tormented sleep / I saw him"], 553 ["Since that brief sleep when / first I saw"], 554 ["When my yearning grows / unendurable"], 938 ["I have sunk to the / bottom"], and 1030 ["No moon lights the night"] from *Kokinshu: A Collection of Poems Ancient and Modern,* translated and annotated by Laurel Rasplica Rodd with Mary Catherine Henkenius (Princeton: Princeton University Press, 1984). Reprinted Boston, MA: Cheng & Tsui, 1996. Reprinted with the permission of Laurel Rasplica Rodd.

Ovid, "The Creation" and "The Story of Orpheus and Eurydice" from *Metamorphoses,* translated by Rolfe Humphries. Copyright © 1955 by Rolfe Humphries. Reprinted with the permission of Indiana University Press.

Giovanni Pico della Mirandola, "The Oration on the Dignity of Man," translated by Charles Glenn Wallis (Indianapolis, IN: Bobbs-Merrill/Library of Liberal Arts, 1965). Copyright 1940 by Charles Glenn Wallis. Reprinted with the permission of Eleanor Van Trump Glenn.

Petrarch, *Canzoniere* 1 ["Oh you, who in these scattered rhymes may find"], 3 ["It was the very day the sun's own light"], 90 ["Sometimes she'd comb her yellow braids out loose"], 292 ["Those eyes I raved about in ardent rhyme"], and 333 ["Go forth, my elegies, to that hard stone"], translated by Patricia Clark Smith. Reprinted with the permission of the translator.

Plato, Book 10, "The Myth of Er" from *The Republic,* translated by F. M. Cornford. Reprinted with the permission of Oxford University Press, Ltd.

James B. Ross (trans.), "The First Contact of the Crusaders and the Turks" from *The Portable Medieval Reader,* by James Bruce Ross and Mary Martin McLaughlin. Copyright 1949 by Viking Penguin, Inc., renewed © 1976 by James Bruce Ross and Mary Martin McLaughlin. Reprinted with the permission of Viking Penguin, a division of Penguin Group (USA) Inc.

N. K. Sandars (trans.), *The Epic of Gilgamesh* from *The Epic of Gilgamesh,* Second Revised Edition. Copyright © 1960, 1964, 1972 by N. K. Sandars. Reprinted with the permission of Penguin Group (UK) Ltd.

Sappho selections, from *Sappho: A New Translation,* by Mary Barnard. Copyright © 1958 by the Regents of the University of California, renewed 1986 by Mary Barnard. Reprinted with the permission of the University of California Press.

Sei Shonagon, excerpts from *The Pillow Book of Sei Shonagon,* translated by Ivan Morris. Copyright © 1967 by Ivan Morris. Reprinted with the permission of Columbia University Press.

William Shakespeare, *The Tempest,* edited by Robert Langbaum. Copyright © 1964, 1987 by Robert Langbaum for Introduction, Annotations, and Compilation. Reprinted with the permission of Dutton Signet, a division of Penguin Group (USA) Inc.

William Kelly Simpson (trans.), "Hymn to Aten" from *Literature of Ancient Egypt: An Anthology of Stories, Instructions, and Poetry,* edited by William Kelly Simpson. Copyright © 1972 by Yale University Press. Reprinted with the permission of Yale University Press.

Sophocles, *Antigone* from *Three Theban Plays,* translated by Robert Fagles. Copyright © 1982 by Robert Fagles. Reprinted with the permission of Viking Penguin, a division of Penguin Group (USA) Inc.

Barbara Stoler Miller (trans.), "The First Teaching: Arjuna's Dejection"; excerpt from "The Second Teaching: Philosophy and Spiritual Discipline"; excerpt from "The Third Teaching: Discipline of Action"; excerpt from "The Sixth Teaching: The Man of Discipline"; excerpt from "The Eleventh Teaching: The Vision of Krishna's Totality"; and excerpt from "The Eighteenth Teaching: The Wondrous Dialogue Concludes" from *The Bhagavad Gita: Krishna's Council in Time of War.* Copyright © 1986 by Barbara Stoler Miller. Used by permission of Bantam Books, a division of Random House, Inc.

Valmiki, excerpts from *The Concise Ramayana of Valmiki,* by Swami Venkatesanada, the State University of New York Press © 1988, State University of New York. All rights reserved.

Wang Wei, "Hermitage at Chung-nan Mountain," and "Crossing the Yellow River," translated by Sam Hamill from *Crossing the Yellow River: Three Hundred Poems from the Chinese.* Copyright © 2000 by Sam Hamill. Reprinted with the permission of BOA Editions, Ltd., www.boaeditions.org.

INDEX